# Oxford Textbook of Psychopathology

OXFORD LIBRARY OF PSYCHOLOGY

# Oxford Textbook of Psychopathology

FOURTH EDITION

*Edited by*

Robert F. Krueger and Paul H. Blaney

# OXFORD
UNIVERSITY PRESS

Oxford University Press is a department of the University of Oxford. It furthers the University's objective of excellence in research, scholarship, and education by publishing worldwide. Oxford is a registered trade mark of Oxford University Press in the UK and certain other countries.

Published in the United States of America by Oxford University Press
198 Madison Avenue, New York, NY 10016, United States of America.

© Oxford University Press 2023

All rights reserved. No part of this publication may be reproduced, stored in a retrieval system, or transmitted, in any form or by any means, without the prior permission in writing of Oxford University Press, or as expressly permitted by law, by license, or under terms agreed with the appropriate reproduction rights organization. Inquiries concerning reproduction outside the scope of the above should be sent to the Rights Department, Oxford University Press, at the address above.

You must not circulate this work in any other form
and you must impose this same condition on any acquirer.

Library of Congress Cataloging-in-Publication Data
Names: Krueger, Robert F., editor. | Blaney, Paul H., editor.
Title: Oxford textbook of psychopathology / [edited by] Robert F. Krueger, Paul H. Blaney.
Other titles: Textbook of psychopathology
Description: 4. | New York, NY : Oxford University Press, [2023] |
Includes bibliographical references and index. |
Identifiers: LCCN 2022040700 (print) | LCCN 2022040701 (ebook) |
ISBN 9780197542521 (hardback) | ISBN 9780197542545 (epub)
Subjects: MESH: Mental Disorders | Psychopathology
Classification: LCC RC454 (print) | LCC RC454 (ebook) | NLM WM 140 |
DDC 616.89—dc23/eng/20230124
LC record available at https://lccn.loc.gov/2022040700
LC ebook record available at https://lccn.loc.gov/2022040701

DOI: 10.1093/med-psych/9780197542521.001.0001

Printed by Sheridan Books, Inc., United States of America

# CONTENTS

*Preface* vii
*About the Editors* ix
*Contributors* xi

## Part I • Foundations and Perspectives

1. Classification in Traditional Nosologies 3
   *Jared W. Keeley, Lisa Chung,* and *Christopher Kleva*
2. Historical and Philosophical Considerations in Studying Psychopathology 33
   *Peter Zachar, Konrad Banicki,* and *Awais Aftab*
3. The Hierarchical Taxonomy of Psychopathology 54
   *Christopher C. Conway* and *Grace N. Anderson*
4. The Research Domain Criteria Project: Integrative Translation for Psychopathology 78
   *Bruce N. Cuthbert, Gregory A. Miller, Charles Sanislow,* and *Uma Vaidyanathan*
5. Complex Systems Approaches to Psychopathology 103
   *Laura Bringmann, Marieke Helmich, Markus Eronen,* and *Manuel Voelkle*
6. Developmental Psychopathology 123
   *Dante Cicchetti*

## Part II • Major Clinical Syndromes

7. Generalized Anxiety Disorder, Panic Disorder, Social Anxiety Disorder, and Specific Phobia 147
   *Richard E. Zinbarg, Alexander L. Williams, Amanda M. Kramer,* and *Madison R. Schmidt*
8. Obsessive-Compulsive and Related Disorders 181
   *Jonathan S. Abramowitz*
9. Posttraumatic Stress Disorder and Dissociative Disorders 199
   *Richard J. McNally*
10. Mania and Bipolar Spectrum Disorders 228
    *June Gruber, Victoria Cosgrove, Alyson Dodd, Sunny J. Dutra, Stephen P. Hinshaw, Stevi G. Ibonie, Piyumi Nimna Kahawage, Thomas D. Meyer, Greg Murray, Robin Nusslock, Kasey Stanton, Cynthia M. Villanueva,* and *Eric A. Youngstrom*
11. Depression: Social and Cognitive Aspects 257
    *Rick E. Ingram, Jessica Balderas, Kendall Khonle,* and *Joe Fulton*

12. Diagnosis, Comorbidity, and Psychopathology of Substance-Related Disorders   277
    *Ty Brumback* and *Sandra A. Brown*
13. Substance Use and Substance Use Disorders   296
    *Kenneth J. Sher, W. E. Conlin,* and *R. O. Pihl*
14. Schizophrenia: Presentation, Affect and Cognition, Pathophysiology and Etiology   332
    *Angus MacDonald III* and *Caroline Demro*
15. Social Functioning and Schizophrenia   352
    *Jill M. Hooley* and *Stephanie N. DeCross*
16. Paranoia and Paranoid Beliefs   380
    *Richard P. Bentall*
17. Sexual Dysfunction   404
    *Cindy M. Meston, Bridget K. Freihart,* and *Amelia M. Stanton*
18. Eating Disorders   424
    *Howard Steiger, Linda Booij, Annie St-Hilaire,* and *Lea Thaler*
19. Life-Span and Multicultural Perspectives   450
    *Thomas M. Achenbach*
20. Attention Deficit Hyperactivity Disorder   474
    *Siri Noordermeer* and *Jaap Oosterlaan*
21. Autism Spectrum Disorders   492
    *Fred R. Volkmar* and *Kevin Pelphrey*
22. Functional Somatic Symptoms   510
    *Peter Henningsen, Theo K. Bouman,* and *Constanze Hausteiner-Wiehle*
23. Sleep and Circadian Rhythm Disorders   523
    *Lampros Bisdounis, Simon D. Kyle, Kate E. A. Saunders, Elizabeth A. Hill,* and *Colin A. Espie*
24. Paraphilia, Gender Dysphoria, and Hypersexuality   549
    *James M. Cantor*

**Part III • Personality Disorders**

25. The DSM-5 Level of Personality Functioning Scale   579
    *Johannes Zimmermann, Christopher J. Hopwood,* and *Robert F. Krueger*
26. The DSM-5 Maladaptive Trait Model for Personality Disorders   604
    *Colin D. Freilich, Robert F. Krueger, Kelsey A. Hobbs, Christopher J. Hopwood,* and *Johannes Zimmermann*
27. Narcissistic Personality Disorder and Pathological Narcissism   628
    *Aaron L. Pincus*
28. Borderline Personality Disorder: Contemporary Approaches to Conceptualization and Etiology   650
    *Timothy J. Trull* and *Johanna Hepp*
29. Schizotypy and Schizotypic Psychopathology: Theory, Evidence, and Future Directions   678
    *Mark F. Lenzenweger*
30. Psychopathy and Antisocial Personality Disorder   716
    *Christopher J. Patrick, Laura E. Drislane, Bridget M. Bertoldi,* and *Kelsey L. Lowman*

*Index*   749

# PREFACE

Although this *Textbook* may also serve active professionals by providing them with reviews and updates, it is aimed primarily at graduate students taking an advanced survey course in abnormal psychology and psychopathology. Among texts that might be used in such courses, it has some distinctive aspects. It provides unusually thorough coverage of novel and emerging approaches to studying psychopathology, including a focus on modern approaches to personality disorders. Throughout the volume, the focus is on what is known about psychopathological constructs; while assessment and intervention are sometimes mentioned, they are not covered systematically. Regarding traditional mental disorder categories, we assume that, when studying this volume, the reader has *DSM-5* at hand and that systematic repetition of *DSM-5* criteria here would be an unwarranted redundancy.

Scholars commonly use abbreviations (usually initializations) in place of their common terms. Because it can be hard for a reader to keep track of their meanings, in this *Textbook* brief glossaries of selected abbreviations have been added at the beginning of most chapters. The reader should be alert with respect to the following abbreviations, as they are defined differently in various chapters: AD, AS, ASPD, CD, ED, PD, PE, and SSD.

We have opted to forgo standard citation practice with respect to *DSM* and *ICD* within chapters. The meaning of those abbreviations will likely be obvious to the reader, but, as examples, we here note that *DSM-5* refers to the current edition of the *Diagnostic and Statistical Manual of Mental Disorder*, published in 2013 by the American Psychiatric Association, while *ICD-11* refers to the current version of the *International Classification of Diseases*, effective in 2022 and published in 2019 by the World Health Organization.

As with the prior three editions of this *Textbook*, it is the product of an effort to enlist the best possible array of experts and to charge those individuals with the task of summarizing what future mental health professionals should know. Authors were given considerable latitude; as a result, the reader is exposed to a variety of outlooks and emphases when moving from chapter to chapter. The roster of chapters shows some continuity from prior editions but also important changes and innovations reflecting contemporary developments in the study of psychopathology. Changes reflect recent progress in the field plus (in the case of returning authors) developments in these individuals' thinking.

—Robert F. Krueger
Minneapolis, Minnesota

—Paul H. Blaney
Emory, Virginia

May 2022

# ABOUT THE EDITORS

**Robert F. Krueger, PhD**

Dr. Krueger is Distinguished McKnight University Professor in the Department of Psychology at the University of Minnesota. He completed his undergraduate and graduate work at the University of Wisconsin, Madison, and his clinical internship at Brown University. Professor Krueger's major interests lie at the intersection of research on psychopathology, personality, behavior genetics, health, and aging. He has received several major awards, including the University of Minnesota McKnight Land-Grant Professorship, the American Psychological Association's Award for Early Career Contributions, the Award for Early Career Contributions from the International Society for the Study of Individual Differences, and an American Psychological Foundation Theodore Millon Mid-Career Award. He is a Fellow of the American Psychopathological Association (APPA) and the Association for Psychological Science (APS). He has been named a Clarivate Analytics Highly Cited Researcher, and Research.com ranks him in the top 100 most impactful psychologists in the world. He is also editor of the *Journal of Personality Disorders*.

**Paul H. Blaney, PhD**

Dr. Blaney received his BA degree from Eastern Nazarene College, Quincy, Massachusetts, and his PhD in clinical psychology from the University of Minnesota. He held faculty positions at the University of Texas at Austin, the University of Miami, and Emory & Henry College, from which Dr. Blaney retired at the end of the 2013–2014 academic year. He served on the editorial boards of a number of journals, including the *Journal of Abnormal Psychology* and the *Journal of Personality and Social Psychology*. While at the University of Miami, he was Associate Dean of the College of Arts and Sciences, and, from 2000 to 2005, he was Dean of Faculty of Emory & Henry College.

# CONTRIBUTORS

Jonathan S. Abramowitz
University of North Carolina at Chapel Hill
Chapel Hill, NC, USA

Thomas M. Achenbach
University of Vermont
Burlington, VT, USA

Awais Aftab
Case Western Reserve University
Cleveland, OH, USA

Grace N. Anderson
Fordham University
Bronx, NY, USA

Jessica Balderas
University of Kansas
Lawrence, KS, USA

Konrad Banicki
Jagiellonian University
Kraków, Poland

Richard P. Bentall
University of Sheffield
Sheffield, UK

Bridget M. Bertoldi
Florida State University
Tallahassee, FL, USA

Lampros Bisdounis
University of Oxford
Oxford, UK

Linda Booij
McGill University
Montreal, QC, Canada

Theo K. Bouman
University of Groningen
Groningen, The Netherlands

Laura Bringmann
University of Groningen
Groningen, The Netherlands

Sandra A. Brown
University of California
San Diego, CA, USA

Ty Brumback
Northern Kentucky University
Highland Heights, KY, USA

James M. Cantor
Toronto Sexuality Centre
Toronto, Canada

Lisa Chung
Virginia Commonwealth University
Richmond, VA, USA

Dante Cicchetti
University of Minnesota
Minneapolis, MN, USA

W. E. Conlin
University of Missouri
Columbia, MO, USA

Christopher C. Conway
Fordham University
Bronx, NY, USA

Victoria Cosgrove
Stanford University
Stanford, CA, USA

Bruce N. Cuthbert
National Institute of Mental Health
Bethesda, MD, USA

Stephanie N. DeCross
Harvard University
Cambridge, MA, USA

Caroline Demro
University of Minnesota
Minneapolis, MN, USA

Alyson Dodd
Northumbria University
Newcastle-upon-Tyne, UK

Laura E. Drislane
Sam Houston State University
Huntsville, TX, USA

Sunny J. Dutra
William James College
Boston, MA, USA

Markus Eronen
University of Groningen
Groningen, The Netherlands

Colin A. Espie
University of Oxford
Oxford, UK

Bridget K. Freihart
  University of Texas
  Austin, TX, USA
Colin D. Freilich
  University of Minnesota
  Minneapolis, MN, USA
Joe Fulton
  University of Kansas
  Lawrence, KS, USA
June Gruber
  University of Colorado at Boulder
  Boulder, CO, USA
Constanze Hausteiner-Wiehle
  Berufsgenossenschaftliche
    Unfallklinik Murnau
  Murnau am Staffelsee, Germany
Marieke Helmich
  University of Groningen
  Groningen, The Netherlands
Peter Henningsen
  Technische Universität München
  Munich, Germany
Johanna Hepp
  Heidelberg University
  Mannheim, Germany
Elizabeth A. Hill
  University of Oxford
  Oxford, UK
Stephen P. Hinshaw
  University of California
  Berkeley, CA, USA
Kelsey A. Hobbs
  University of Minnesota
  Minneapolis, MN, USA
Jill M. Hooley
  Harvard University
  Cambridge, MA, USA
Christopher J. Hopwood
  University of Zurich
  Zurich, Switzerland
Stevi G. Ibonie
  University of Colorado
  Boulder, CO, USA
Rick E. Ingram
  University of Kansas
  Lawrence, KS, USA
Piyumi Nimna Kahawage
  Swinburne University of Technology
  Melbourne, Australia
Jared W. Keeley
  Virginia Commonwealth University
  Richmond, VA, USA

Kendall Khonle
  University of Kansas
  Lawrence, KS, USA
Christopher Kleva
  Virginia Commonwealth University
  Richmond, VA, USA
Amanda M. Kramer
  Northwestern University
  Evanston, IL, USA
Robert F. Krueger
  University of Minnesota
  Minneapolis, MN, USA
Simon D. Kyle
  University of Oxford
  Oxford, UK
Mark F. Lenzenweger
  The State University of New York at
    Binghamton
  Binghamton, NY
  and
  Weill Cornell Medical College
  New York, NY, USA
Kelsey L. Lowman
  Florida State University
  Tallahassee, FL, USA
Angus MacDonald III
  University of Minnesota
  Minneapolis, MN, USA
Richard J. McNally
  Harvard University
  Cambridge, MA, USA
Cindy M. Meston
  University of Texas
  Austin, TX, USA
Thomas D. Meyer
  University of Texas
  Houston, TX, USA
Gregory A. Miller
  University of California at Los Angeles
  Los Angeles, CA, USA
Greg Murray
  Swinburne University of Technology
  Melbourne, Australia
Siri Noordermeer
  Vrije Universiteit
  Amsterdam, The Netherlands
Robin Nusslock
  Northwestern University
  Evanston, IL, USA
Jaap Oosterlaan
  Vrije Universiteit
  Amsterdam, The Netherlands
  and

Amsterdam UMC
Amsterdam, The Netherlands

**Christopher J. Patrick**
Florida State University
Tallahassee, FL, USA

**Kevin Pelphrey**
University of Virginia
Charlottesville, VA, USA

**R. O. Pihl**
McGill University
Montreal, QC, Canada

**Aaron L. Pincus**
Pennsylvania State University
University Park, PA, USA

**Charles Sanislow**
Wesleyan University
Middletown, CT, USA

**Kate E. A. Saunders**
University of Oxford
Oxford, UK

**Madison R. Schmidt**
Northwestern University
Evanston, IL, USA

**Kenneth J. Sher**
University of Missouri
Columbia, MO, USA

**Amelia M. Stanton**
University of Texas
Austin, TX, USA

**Kasey Stanton**
University of Wyoming
Laramie, WY, USA

**Howard Steiger**
McGill University
Montreal, QC, Canada

**Annie St-Hilaire**
McGill University
Montreal, QC, Canada

**Lea Thaler**
McGill University
Montreal, QC, Canada

**Timothy J. Trull**
University of Missouri
Columbia, MO, USA

**Uma Vaidyanathan**
Boehringer-Ingelheim
Washington, DC, USA

**Cynthia M. Villanueva**
University of Colorado at Boulder
Boulder, CO, USA

**Manuel Voelkle**
Humboldt-Universität zu Berlin
Berlin, Germany

**Fred R. Volkmar**
Yale University
New Haven, CT, USA

**Alexander L. Williams**
Northwestern University
Evanston, IL, USA

**Eric A. Youngstrom**
University of North Carolina
Chapel Hill, NC, USA

**Peter Zachar**
Auburn University Montgomery
Montgomery, AL, USA

**Johannes Zimmermann**
University of Kassel
Kassel, Germany

**Richard E. Zinbarg**
Northwestern University
Evanston, IL, USA

PART I

# Foundations and Perspectives

CHAPTER

# 1  Classification in Traditional Nosologies

Jared W. Keeley, Lisa Chung, *and* Christopher Kleva

Diagnosis is simple. The clinician meets with the patient and assesses his or her symptoms in an interview. Given the list of symptoms, the clinician then consults the current version of the *DSM* or *ICD* and decides which diagnoses are relevant. However, like most things that appear to be simple, the topic of classification becomes more complicated upon examination. For example, even the name for this topic is more complicated that many readers might think. In popular usage, terms like *diagnosis, classification, taxonomy*, and *nosology* are often treated as if they either are synonyms or, at least, are largely interchangeable. However, to those who study this topic, these four terms have separable meanings.

Diagnostic systems, generally called classifications, are lists of terms for conventionally accepted concepts that are used to describe psychopathology. *Classification*, when the term is used specifically, refers to the activity of forming groups. *Diagnosis*, as this word is used in medicine and the mental health field, is the process by which individuals are assigned to already existing groups. *Taxonomy* is a term usually reserved for the study of how groups are formed. In effect, taxonomy is a meta-level concept that looks at different theoretical ways in which classifications can be organized, studied, and changed. *Nosology* is the specific application of taxonomy (which can apply to chemistry, zoology, or how to best arrange products in the grocery store) in the context of medical sciences.

The classification of mental disorders has a lengthy history. The first description of a specific syndrome is usually ascribed to an Egyptian account of dementia dating to about 3000 BCE. An early classification of mental disorders was found in the Ayurveda, an ancient Indian system of medicine (Menninger et al., 1963). Ancient Greek and Egyptian writings refer to disorders remarkably similar to concepts of hysteria, paranoia, mania, and melancholia. Since then, numerous classifications have emerged, and enthusiasm for classifying mental disorders has waxed and waned. During the last half of the twentieth century, classification was a prominent theme in the study of psychopathology. Following World War II and the foundation of the United Nations, the World Health Organization (WHO) took over responsibility for managing international health classification systems, resulting in the sixth edition of the *International Classification of Diseases and Related Health Conditions* (*ICD*) published in 1948, which including mental disorders for the first time. The release of the *ICD-6* corresponded to the development of the first edition of the *Diagnostic and Statistical Manual of Mental Disorders* (*DSM*) in the United States, first published in 1952, in recognition of a need for a unified system in the United States (Grob, 1991; Houts, 2000). Currently, *DSM* is in its fifth edition and the *ICD* is in its 11th edition.

This productivity has not, however, resolved some of the fundamental problems confronting psychiatric classification. Unresolved issues include the nature of the entities being classified, the definition of what is a mental disorder, the nosological principles for organizing psychiatric classifications,

---

**Abbreviations**
| | |
|---|---|
| AD | autistic disorder |
| AMPD | alternative model of personality disorders |
| ASD | autism spectrum disorder |
| CDD | childhood disintegrative disorder |
| FFM | five factor model |
| LAF | low anxiety fearlessness |
| NOS | not otherwise specified |
| PCL-R | Psychopathy Checklist—Revised |
| RDoC | Research Domain Criteria |
| SCID | Structured clinical interview for *DSM* |

the distinction between normality and pathology, and the validity of many diagnoses. Controversies exist regarding the definition and logical status of some diagnoses and even whether some entities are pathological conditions. For example, heated debates occurred in the 1960s and 1970s over whether homosexuality should be considered a mental disorder. Current debates exist on whether Internet addiction belongs in an official classification. Presently, there is no consensus regarding the taxonomic principles for resolving these controversies (Kamens et al., 2019).

This chapter provides an overview of some issues associated with the classification of psychopathology in traditional nosologies. The next chapter ("Historical and Philosophical Considerations in Studying Psychopathology") will address modern alternatives to the nosological approaches discussed in this chapter. In discussing these issues, the chapter presents an overview of psychiatric classification from a historical perspective so that the reader can understand how these issues have arisen and who have been the central authors involved in discussions of these issues.

**Purpose of Classification**

Classification involves creating and defining the boundaries of concepts (Sartorius, 1990). Through this process, diagnostic entities are defined (Kendell, 1975) and the boundaries of the discipline are ultimately established. The reason that psychiatric classification has had such an impact is that it has defined the field of psychopathology. For example, should Alzheimer's disease, alcoholism, or oppositional behavior in a child be considered mental disorders? Should they instead be considered medical disorders or just problems of everyday living? A classification of mental disorders stipulates the range of problems to which mental health professions lay claim.

Classifications serve several purposes with specific goals. The goals of a good classification scheme include (1) providing a *nomenclature* for practitioners, (2) serving as a basis for organizing and *retrieving information*, (3) *describing* the common patterns of symptom presentation, (4) providing the basis for *prediction*, (5) forming the basis for the *development of theories*, and (6) serving *sociopolitical functions*.

The first major function of a classification is the provision of a standard *nomenclature* that facilitates description and communication. A nomenclature is simply a list of names or terms within a classification system. At its most basic level, a classification of psychopathology allows clinicians to talk to each other about the "things" in their world: the patients and clients who seek the care of mental health professionals. Without a classification system, clinicians would be reduced to talking about clients one after another without any way of grouping these clients into similar types. A classification allows the clinician to have a set of nouns that can be used to provide an overview of the clinician's world when talking to other clinicians, laypeople, insurance companies, or other professionals. Note that this purpose provides a shorthand and does not imply or require any scientific reality to the concepts.

Second, a classification structures *information retrieval*. Information in a science is organized around its major concepts. Knowing a diagnostic concept helps the clinician to retrieve information about such matters as etiology, treatment, and prognosis. A classification shapes the way information is organized thereby influencing all aspects of clinical practice and research. In the current world, in which information is easily retrieved by electronic searches on the Internet, classificatory concepts are useful devices by which professionals, family members, clients, and interested laypeople can obtain information about the prognosis, treatment, and current research related to various mental disorders.

Third, by providing a nomenclature to describe all levels of psychopathology, a classification establishes the *descriptive basis* for a science of psychopathology. Most sciences have their origins in description. Only when phenomena are systematically organized is a science in the position to transform accounts of individual cases into principles and generalizations. Cases that are diagnosed with a particular disorder should be similar in important ways to other cases with that same diagnosis, and these cases should be different in important ways from cases belonging to other diagnoses.

The fourth goal of classification, *prediction*, is the most pragmatic from the perspective of clinicians. What a mental health professional typically wants from a diagnosis is information that is relevant to the most effective treatment and management of his or her patient. A classification that is useful for prediction is a system in which there is strong evidence that patients with different diagnoses respond differentially to a specific treatment or one that informs how to best manage the nature of that person's condition. Classifications are also clinically useful if the categories are associated with different clinical courses even when the disorders are not treated.

Fifth, by providing systematic descriptions of phenomena, a classification establishes the foundations for the *development of theories*. In the natural sciences, especially biology and chemistry, a satisfactory classification was an important precursor for theoretical progress (Hull, 1988). The systematic classification of species by Linnaeus stimulated important questions about the nature of phenomena or processes that accounted for the system—questions that ultimately led to the theory of evolution. For these reasons, classification occupies a central role in research. For example, the National Institute of Mental Health (NIMH) in the United States has instituted a large-scale project designed to identify common pathological mechanisms that could guide informed understanding of mental disorders (termed the Research Domain Criteria [RDoC] project; NIMH, 2012). The RDoC will be discussed at greater length in the next chapter as an alternative to traditional classifications.

Finally, no classification system exists in a vacuum. Rather, a classificatory system exists in a context of groups and individuals that stand to benefit from the classification. For example, a classification of mental disorders can serve the social purpose of identifying a subset of the population that society has deemed need treatment. However, the *sociopolitical functions* of a classification are not always so altruistic. The American Psychiatric Association, through its production of the various editions of the *DSM*, has developed a lucrative printing business that serves as a major funding source for the organization (Frances, 2014). At a more individual level, some authors have argued that the classification of mental disorders serves the objective of maintaining the social power of the majority by marginalizing and stigmatizing those people who fall under the domain of "mental illness" (e.g., Kirk & Kutchins, 1992; Kutchins & Kirk, 1997).

## History of Classification

Although attempts to classify psychopathology date to ancient times, our intent is to provide only a brief overview of major developments, especially those occurring in the past century, as a context for understanding modern classifications. Examining previous classifications shows that many current issues have a long history. For example, writers in the eighteenth century, like many contemporary authorities, believed that the biological sciences had solved the problems of classification and that biological taxonomies could serve as a model for classifying psychopathology. The Edinburgh physician William Cullen, for example, applied Linnaeus's principles for classifying species to illnesses. The result, published in 1769, was a complex structure involving classes, orders, genera, and species of illness (cited by Kendell, 1990). One class was neurosis (Cullen introduced the concept as a general term for mental disorders) that was subdivided into 4 orders, 27 genera, and more than 100 species. Contemporaneous critics, who believed that there were far fewer diagnoses, dismissed Cullen as a "botanical nosologist" (Kendell, 1990). Nonetheless, interest in applying the principles of biological classification to abnormal behavior continues today, as does the debate over the number of diagnoses. "Splitters" seek to divide mental disorders into increasingly narrowly defined categories, whereas "lumpers" maintain that a few broadly defined categories are adequate to represent psychopathology (Havens, 1985). One compromise is to create a hierarchical solution (again, similar to biology) in which there are a relatively small number of higher order groups divided into more specific varieties at lower levels of the hierarchy.

The features used to classify mental disorders varied substantially across eighteenth- and nineteenth-century classifications. Some diagnoses were little more than single symptoms, whereas others were broader descriptions resembling syndromes. Yet other diagnoses were based on speculative, early pre-psychology theories about how the mind worked. As a result, many classifications from the nineteenth century relied heavily on traditional philosophical analyses of the faculties or attempted to organize disorders around poorly articulated views of etiology.

### Kraepelin

With the work of Emil Kraepelin, the structure of modern classification began to take shape. Kraepelin was born in 1856, the same year as Sigmund Freud, an ironic fact considering that they established two very different approaches to conceptualizing psychopathology. Kraepelin was influenced by two traditions (Berrios & Hauser, 1988). The first was the scientific approach to medicine that dominated German medical schools in the late nineteenth century. Many important medical breakthroughs, especially in bacteriology, occurred in Germany during that period. German psychiatrists of the time generally believed that mental disorders were biological and that psychiatry would gradually be replaced by neurology. Kraepelin was also influenced by early work in experimental psychology (Kahn, 1959).

During his medical training, he worked for a year in the laboratory of Wilhelm Wundt (*1832–1920*), one of the first experimental psychologists. In early research, Kraepelin applied Wundt's methods to the study of mental disorders.

Kraepelin's reputation was based on his textbooks of psychiatry. Like most textbook authors, Kraepelin organized his volumes with chapters on each of the major groupings of mental disorders. What has become known as *Kraepelin's classifications* (Menninger et al., 1963) are little more than the table of contents to the nine published editions of his textbooks. In the sixth edition, Kraepelin included two chapters that attracted considerable international attention. One chapter focused on the concept of dementia praecox (now called schizophrenia) which included hebephrenia, catatonia, and paranoia as subtypes—descriptions that remained intact up through *ICD-10* and *DSM-IV* but were removed in the current editions. The other chapter discussed manic-depressive insanity—a revolutionary idea that combined mania and melancholia, two concepts that had been considered separate entities since the writings of Hippocrates. The two diagnoses, dementia praecox and manic-depressive psychosis, established a fundamental distinction between psychotic and mood disorders that forms a linchpin of contemporary classifications.

### The Early Editions of the DSM and ICD

In medicine, the official classification of medical disorders is the *ICD*, published by the WHO. Historically, this classification began at the end of the nineteenth century when a group named the International Statistical Institute commissioned a committee headed by Jacques Bertillon (*1851–1922*) to generate a classification of causes of death. This classification, initially known as *The Bertillon Classification of Causes of Death*, was adopted as an official international classification of medical disorders at a meeting of 26 countries in France in 1900. The name of the classification was slightly modified in the early 1900s to *The International Classification of Causes of Death*. This original version of *ICD* was revised at subsequent conferences held in 1909, 1920, 1929, and 1938 (Reed et al., 2016).

After World War II, the WHO met to generate a sixth revision of this classification. A decision was made at that point to expand the classification beyond causes of death and to include all diseases regardless of whether those diseases led to death or not (i.e., morbidity as well as mortality). The name of the classification was revised accordingly to the *International Statistical Classification of Diseases, Injuries, and Causes of Death, Sixth Revision* (*ICD-6*; World Health Organization, 1948). Because it focused on all diseases, *ICD-6* added a section devoted to mental disorders.

The undertaking and consequent publication of the ICD-6 by the WHO "marked the beginning of a new era in international vital and health statistics" (Reed et al., 2016). The WHO recognized the importance of agreed-upon international rules for mortality and morbidity data. An essential component to ensure success was international cooperation by other countries, recommending that governments establish their own national committees to collect vital and health statistics. The national committees were to communicate with the WHO, which would serve as the central source and governing body for international health statistics.

Shortly after the publication of *ICD-6*, the American Psychiatric Association published its first official classification of mental disorders (*DSM-I*; American Psychiatric Association [APA], 1952). The creation of this classification was justified because there were four different classifications of psychopathology in use in the United States during World War II, a situation that American psychiatry found embarrassing. Thus, the United States created its own nomenclature that blended features of the previous four systems (Grob, 1991).

Generally, other countries in the world were like the United States in that, instead of adopting *ICD-6* as the official system, most decided to use locally created classificatory systems whose diagnostic concepts did not have international acceptance. Only five countries adopted the *ICD-6* classification of mental disorders: Finland, New Zealand, Peru, Thailand, and the United Kingdom. To understand why, the WHO asked British psychiatrist Erwin Stengel to review the classifications of mental disorders used in various countries. Stengel's review (1959) was very important because he carefully documented the widespread differences that existed in terminology from country to country (and even within countries). Stengel concluded that the variation in classifications from one country to another meant there was a failure for these systems to become useful nomenclatures. In addition, Stengel documented how different subsections of these classifications were organized according to quite variable beliefs about the etiologies of the disorders being classified. Stengel suggested that the solution was to develop a classification that simply provided operational definitions of mental disorders without reference to etiology. This suggestion led to the eighth revision of the mental disorders section of *ICD* (World Health Organization, 1968), which was to include a glossary defining the various components of psychopathology to go with the list of diagnoses. Unfortunately, the glossary was not ultimately included. However, at the same time, American psychiatrists did publish a second edition of *DSM* (i.e., *DSM-II*; APA, 1968). *DSM-II*, unlike *ICD-8*, contained short prose definitions of the basic categories in this system; however, the diagnostic terms and structure were otherwise almost identical.

## Criticisms of Classifications Through the 1960s

During the 1950s and 1960s, concern about the reliability of psychiatric diagnoses surfaced. Problems with levels of diagnostic agreement had been noted in the 1930s. Masserman and Carmichael (1938), for example, reported that 40% of diagnoses in a series of patients followed up 1 year later required major revision. Ash (1949) compared the diagnoses of three psychiatrists who jointly interviewed 52 individuals applying to work for the Central Intelligence Agency (CIA). These clinicians agreed on the diagnosis for only 20% of the applicants, and, in 30% of the cases, all three psychiatrists made a different diagnosis. Beck (1962) reviewed a series of reliability studies and reported that the highest level of interclinician agreement was 42% for *DSM-I*. The problem with reliability was further highlighted by the UK/US Diagnostic Project, which found major differences in diagnostic practice between Britain and the United States (Cooper et al., 1972; Kendell et al., 1971). These studies suggested that Americans had an overinclusive concept of schizophrenia and tended to apply the diagnosis to any psychotic patient. British psychiatrists, in contrast, were more specific in the use of schizophrenia as a diagnosis. These differences probably stemmed from both differences in the definition of schizophrenia as well as its application by individual psychiatrists.

Diagnostic unreliability creates major problems for clinical practice and research. For example, the results of studies on patients with schizophrenia as diagnosed in Britain cannot generalize to patients diagnosed as having schizophrenia in the United States if these results are based on different applications of the concept of schizophrenia. However, the problem was not confined to schizophrenia. The reliability studies of the 1960s and 1970s were interpreted as indicating that clinicians had problems achieving high levels of agreement for any area of psychopathology. More modern commentators on this literature have suggested, however, that the criticisms of diagnostic reliability during this era were overstated (Kirk & Kutchins, 1992).

Concurrent with the empirical studies questioning the reliability of psychiatric diagnosis, psychiatry came under considerable attack from the antipsychiatry movement. Much of this criticism focused on the clinical activities of diagnosis and classification. Szasz (1961) went so far as to argue that mental illness was a myth.

By the late 1960s, three major criticisms of psychiatric classification were popular. First, psychiatric diagnosis was widely thought to be unreliable. Second, classification and diagnosis were considered fundamental components of the medical model that was questioned as the basis for understanding mental disorders. This model clashed with other models, particularly those stemming from behavioral and humanistic perspectives that were influential in clinical and counseling psychology. The medical model of illness was viewed as both speculative and as demeaning of patients. Third, widespread concern was expressed, particularly among many sociologists and psychologists, about the labeling and stigmatizing effects of psychiatric diagnoses (Goffman, 1959, 1963; Scheff, 1966, 1975). Labeling theorists tended to view mental illness and other forms of deviant behavior as largely politically defined and reinforced by social factors and agencies. Psychiatric diagnoses were considered to be self-fulfilling prophecies in which patients adopted the behaviors implied by the label. Their arguments were bolstered by philosophers such as Foucault (1988), who condemned psychiatry as little more than an agent of social control.

A demonstration of these issues was contained in a paper published in *Science* by Rosenhan (1973), titled "On Being Sane in Insane Places." In this study, 8 normal persons sought admission to 12 different inpatient psychiatry units. All accurately reported information about themselves except that they gave false names to avoid a mental hospital record, and they reported hearing an auditory hallucination in which a voice said "thud," "empty," or "hollow." In all instances, the pseudo-patients were admitted. Eleven of these admissions were diagnosed as schizophrenia, the other as mania. On discharge, which occurred on average 20 days later, all received the diagnosis of schizophrenia in remission. Rosenhan concluded that mental health professionals were unable to distinguish between sanity and insanity, an observation that was eagerly seized by the antipsychiatry movement. However, the Rosenhan study was not without its critics. Rosenhan's paper resulted in an explosion of responses that challenged his research and claimed that psychiatric diagnosing is a valid and meaningful process. The majority of the criticisms focused on Rosenhan's flawed methodology and his unfounded interpretations that clinicians are unable to distinguish between those who are sane and those who are insane (Farber, 1975; Millon, 1975; Spitzer, 1975; Weiner, 1975).

### The Neo-Kraepelinians

During the 1970s, a small but effective group of researchers emerged in North American psychiatry (Compton & Guze, 1995). These individuals influenced both academic psychiatry and practice. The movement, usually referred to as the *neo-Kraepelinians* (Klerman, 1978), sought to reaffirm psychiatry as a branch of medicine. The neo-Kraepelinians emphasized the importance of diagnosis and classification. The movement was a reaction to the antipsychiatrists and the psychoanalytic dominance of North American psychiatry. Klerman's assumptions of the neo-Kraepelinian positions included emphasizing the medical roots of psychiatry, such that psychiatry provides treatment for people who are sick with mental illness. Klerman further highlighted that the biological aspect of mental illness should be the central focus, and any area of psychopathology that might represent a disease process (e.g., schizophrenia) belonged to psychiatry, whereas other areas could be assigned to ancillary professions such as psychology, social work, and nursing. The neo-Kraepelinians, in the attempt to medicalize psychiatric disorders, emphasized qualitative distinctions between normality and illness, a view criticized by writers such as Szasz, who considered mental disorders to be problems of living that are on a continuum with normal behavior. Furthermore, the position of the neo-Kraepelinians suggested different forms of disorders, which laid the basis for the continued use of a categorical approach to classification.

The neo-Kraepelinians believed that psychiatry should be founded on scientific knowledge. This assumption insisted on a solid empirical foundation to ensure psychiatry as a medical specialty. The neo-Kraepelinians placed additional emphasis on diagnosis and classification by proposing that diagnosis is the basis for treatment decisions and clinical care—a view that contrasted with that of psychoanalysts, who believed that descriptive classification focused on superficial behavioral aspects of patients' lives (Havens, 1981). Klerman stressed the importance the neo-Kraepelinians placed on improving the reliability and validity of diagnoses through the use of statistical techniques.

Reading these propositions more than 50 years later reveals the extent to which the neo-Kraepelinians felt the need to reaffirm the medical and biological aspects of psychiatry. They felt embattled and surrounded by powerful influences that advocated a very different approach. These propositions now seem curiously dated, perhaps indicating the extent to which the neo-Kraepelinian movement was successful in achieving its objectives. In many ways these propositions are now widely accepted within the profession, although most would probably express these positions less vehemently. Klerman's statements also indicated the importance that the neo-Kraepelinians placed on diagnosis and classification. The way to ensure that their views were adopted was to develop a new classification system. The antipsychiatry movement's concerns about labeling and other negative reactions to psychiatric diagnosis provided an important context that spawned *DSM-III* (APA, 1980), but the neo-Kraepelinian movement provided the agenda (Rogler, 1997).

### DSM-III and Its Successors

*DSM-III* was the culmination of the neo-Kraepelinian efforts to reestablish psychiatry as a branch of medicine with diagnosis and classification as fundamental components. The classification took more than 5 years of extensive committee work and consultation to produce.

*DSM-III* differed from *DSM-II* in four major ways. First, *DSM-III* adopted more specific and detailed diagnostic criteria, as compared to *DSM-II*, in order to define the various categories of mental disorders. If a patient met the diagnostic criteria, then the patient was said to belong to the category. Before *DSM-III*, most definitions of specific mental disorders were in prose format and implicitly referred to the "essence" of the disorder. Since the publication of *DSM-III*, the use of diagnostic criteria has reflected a shift to a prototype model whereby a category is defined not by a list of necessary and sufficient conditions but rather by a list of characteristics that any individual member may or may not have. Thus, two individuals may qualify for the same diagnosis even though they have few symptoms in common as long as each of them has enough of the listed symptoms to attain the specified threshold. The more characteristics the individual evidences, the better fit that person is to the category (Cantor et al., 1980). The intent of using these diagnostic criteria was to make the diagnostic process more explicit and clear-cut, thus improving reliability. Second, *DSM-III* proposed a multiaxial system of classification. Thus, instead of assigning one diagnosis per patient, as was typical with *DSM-I* and *DSM-II*, clinicians were expected to categorize the patients along five axes: (I) symptom picture, (II) personality style, (III) medical disorder, (IV) environmental stressors, and (V) role impairment. Third, *DSM-III* substantially reorganized the hierarchical arrangement of mental disorder categories. In *DSM-I* and *DSM-II*, the hierarchical system of organization recognized two fundamental dichotomies: (1) organic versus non-organic disorders and (2) psychotic versus neurotic disorders. *DSM-III* dropped these dichotomies and instead organized mental disorders under 17 major headings based on the phenomenology of the disorder (e.g., "mood disorder" or "psychotic disorder"). Fourth, *DSM-III* was a much larger document than its predecessors. *DSM-I* contained 108 categories and was 130 pages in length. In contrast, *DSM-III* had 256 categories and was 494 pages long.

By almost any standard, *DSM-III* was an astounding success. Financially, it sold very well. As a result of this success, the American Psychiatric Association developed a publication arm of the organization that began to publish a large number of *DSM*-related books and other psychiatric works. Although explicitly an American classification, *DSM-III* quickly became popular in Europe, overshadowing the *ICD-9* (1977), particularly among academics and researchers.

Another way of measuring the success of *DSM-III* is in terms of research. *DSM-III* stimulated a great deal of research, especially regarding the definitions of the categories proposed in this classification. As a result of this research, *DSM-III-R* (APA, 1987) was published with the explicit goal of revising the diagnostic criteria for the categories stemming from new research findings. However, like most committee products, the changes from *DSM-III* to *DSM-III-R* were not limited to diagnostic criteria. A number of new categories were introduced, including a group of diagnoses associated with the general category of "sleep disorders." Additionally, many specific categories were revised (e.g., histrionic personality disorder), dropped (e.g., attention deficit disorder without hyperactivity), or added (e.g., premenstrual syndrome had its name changed and was added to an appendix of *DSM-III-R*).

Because of the revolutionary impact of *DSM-III*, the mental disorders section of *ICD-10* (World Health Organization, 1992) was substantially changed relative to earlier *ICDs*. *ICD-9*, published in 1977, had been very similar to *ICD-8*. Hence, *ICD-10* was published in two versions: a clinical version that contained prose descriptions of categories and a research version that contained diagnostic criteria. However, *ICD-10* did not adopt a multiaxial system.

As work was progressing on *ICD-10*, a decision was made to perform another revision of *DSM-III* that, it was hoped, would make it more similar to *ICD-10*. Indeed, a special "harmonization" committee was established and work on the two manuals proceeded, to some degree, in parallel. The result was *DSM-IV* (APA, 1994). The committee work that went into the creation of *DSM-IV* was extensive. The American Psychiatric Association even sponsored special research projects that attempted to empirically resolve important debates that had arisen around classificatory issues. One example of such a research project was the 1999 *DSM* Research Planning Conference sponsored by the American Psychiatric Association and the NIMH. This conference established the research priorities for future *DSM* editions, which included addressing the continued dissatisfaction with the *DSM* nomenclature (Kupfer et al., 2002).

*DSM-IV* was larger than previous *DSMs* in terms of the sheer size of its publication and the number of categories. Interestingly, different commentators have computed different numbers for the total diagnoses in *DSM-IV*, ranging from just under 300 to just under 400 (cf. Follette & Houts, 1996; Kutchins & Kirk, 1997; Sarbin, 1997; Stone, 1997). Despite the intent of making *DSM-IV* more like *ICD-10*, *DSM-IV* and *ICD-10* are quite different. Of 176 diagnostic categories that shared similar names, there were intentional conceptual differences in 21% (First, 2009). However, there were unintentional nonconceptual differences in 78% of categories; only one disorder—transient tic disorder—was identical between the two systems (First, 2009). The most impactful difference between the two systems was the *DSM-IV* "clinical significance" criterion, which required the presence of distress and/or functional impairment for diagnosis. *ICD-10* did not always consider the presence of distress and/or functional impairment a requirement (Reed et al., 2016). Additionally, the *ICD-10* used diagnostic guidelines rather than criteria, which provided greater flexibility in their interpretation and application than the *DSM-IV* descriptions.

In 2000, the American Psychiatric Association published a text revision of *DSM-IV*, titled *DSM-IV-TR*, which updated the prose sections of the manual but left the diagnostic criteria and number of diagnoses mostly the same. Two exceptions included dropping the clinical significance criterion from the tic disorders and adjusting it to account for nonconsenting victims of paraphilic disorders (First & Pincus, 2002).

The current editions of *DSM* and *ICD* have undergone yet another revision. *DSM-5* was published in May 2013; *ICD-11* was approved in 2019. The co-chairs of *DSM-5* hoped to make *DSM-5* as revolutionary as *DSM-III* had been. The major changes that they instituted with *DSM-5* were to add diagnostic spectra (e.g., the autism spectrum and the schizophrenia spectrum), offer dimensional alternatives or enhancements to categorical diagnosis (e.g., the five dimensions for describing personality disorder in Section III titled "Emerging Measures and Models"), improve the assessment of dysfunction as a result of psychopathology (the adoption of the WHO Disability Assessment Schedule [WHODAS] in place of the Global Assessment of Functioning [GAF], also in Section III), and drop the multiaxial approach to diagnosis that appeared in *DSM-III* and *DSM-IV* (all diagnoses are now in a single section of the manual instead of spread across five axes; APA, 2012a; 2013).

Just as *DSM-III* was partially driven by the attempt to overcome the reliability issues with *DSM-I* and *DSM-II*, one goal of *DSM-5* was to address meta-structure issues that became prominent with *DSM-III-R* and *DSM-IV* (Regier et al., 2012). Specifically, the arrangement of disorders within the manual could be informed by empirical findings rather than based solely on phenomenological similarity or work group arrangement. An example is the dissolution of the childhood disorders grouping of *DSM-IV*, whereby some disorders were placed under a neurodevelopmental heading (e.g., intellectual disability, attention deficit hyperactivity disorder [ADHD], autism spectrum disorder) and others were placed with similar-appearing "adult" disorders (e.g., reactive attachment disorder in the trauma- and stressor-related disorders group).

In its final form, *DSM-5* contained 584 diagnostic categories (compared to 357, by our count, in *DSM-IV*). The size of *DSM-5* also grew to 947 pages from 886 pages in *DSM-IV* while the purchase cost of the manual more than doubled. In contrast, the number of categories with diagnostic criteria was reduced from 201 in *DSM-IV* to 138 in *DSM-5*.

With respect to the development of the *ICD-11*, the WHO focused on enhancing clinical utility and global applicability (Reed, 2010). They were dedicated to addressing the global mental health gap between those who need services and those who receive them, and they sought to develop the *ICD-11* as a mechanism for better identifying individuals with mental health needs. A three-step plan was developed to provide guidance for the structure of the Mental and Behavioral Disorders chapter in the *ICD-11*. The first step involved evaluating the scientific evidence and information regarding the actual use of the ICD in clinical practice, including two major surveys of psychiatrists and psychologists (Evans et al., 2013; Reed et al., 2011). The second step consisted of two field studies that examined how clinicians from around the world conceptualize mental disorders and their relation to one another (Reed et al., 2013; Roberts et al., 2012). These findings were used to inform the structure (or table of contents) of the manual. The third step involved two sets of field studies designed to evaluate the proposed diagnostic guidelines (Keeley et al., 2016). One evaluated how global mental health clinicians apply the guidelines to a set of case vignettes with the intent of identifying confusions or clarifications. The other examined reliability and feasibility in clinical settings. The development process also involved an attempt to synchronize the *ICD-11* and *DSM-5*. It is important to note that any differences between the two systems were intentional. For example, there are distinct differences in regards to sleep disorders and sexual health and gender identity which *ICD-11* justifies as being more consistent with current evidence and clinical practice (Reed et al., 2016).

**Taxonomic Issues**

A number of controversies have arisen around the classification of psychopathology. The purpose of the following list is not to provide a comprehensive overview but simply to list the issues and controversies that are frequently raised about psychiatric classification.

*Classification of Syndromes, Disorders, or Diseases*

The terms "syndrome," "disorder," and "disease" can (erroneously) be used interchangeably to describe mental health conditions. In fact, these three terms refer to explicitly different assumptions about the nature of the category they describe. At the most basic level of description, a person experiences *symptoms* (self-reported issues) and evidences *signs* (observed by others) of a problem. As mentioned before, if mental health professionals were forced to idiosyncratically describe the unique pattern of symptoms and signs for every patient, their work would be hopelessly stymied by trying to account for each patient. However, symptoms and signs often co-occur. When they co-occur with sufficient frequency, that condition is termed a *syndrome*. Note that the concept of a syndrome does not include any assumptions about the cause of the condition or why those symptoms belong together. It is a purely descriptive notion.

A *disorder*, on the other hand, provides an additional level of description beyond that of a syndrome. A disorder is a pattern of symptoms and signs that includes an implied impact on the functioning of the individual. While some causal factors might be understood for a disorder, its etiology is still unclear or multiply determined. In contrast, a *disease* is a condition where the etiology is known, and the path from the causal agent to the symptoms and signs it causes is more or less clear.

By way of example, a condition known as general paresis was the most common single disorder represented in mental asylums in the mid to late 1800s. Initial investigations found that certain individuals exhibited similar symptoms: grandiose delusions and excitable behavior. At that point, the concept would properly be termed a syndrome. After further investigation, it became clear that these individuals followed a similar course. The problem began with excitable, grandiose behavior but progressed to degenerative muscle movements, paralysis, and eventually death. Once the course and outcome were known, general paresis was more properly termed a disorder. Many theories were posited about the cause of the disorder, varying from overindulgence in alcohol to inflammation of the meninges. However, eventually the discovery came that it was tertiary syphilis, having migrated from a genital infection through a long dormant phase to the central nervous system. When general paresis was understood as a syphilitic infection, the concept became a disease (Blashfield & Keeley, 2010).

The history of general paresis is important in classification because it was a mental disorder that was understood as a disease and eradicated with proper treatment (i.e., penicillin). Paresis was a major victory for the science of psychiatry, as the majority of asylum patients could be successfully (and simply) treated and sent home. Many individuals believed that all other mental health conditions (especially schizophrenia) would follow similar developments, eventually being "cured" once the proper cause was known. Unfortunately, no other conditions to date have enjoyed the scientific success of general paresis. Rather, nearly all mental health categories are more properly termed "disorders," in that their cause and therefore treatment are much more ambiguous.

### Classification of Disorders Versus Classification of Individuals

On the surface, this controversy appears to be a somewhat simple-minded issue of terminology. Individual patients are diagnosed with various mental disorders. A classification system contains the names of mental disorders that have been recognized or are officially sanctioned as diagnoses by some governing body. What difference does it make whether a classification system is said to classify disorders or individuals?

Interestingly, however, the authors of *DSM-IV-TR* did think that this distinction made a difference. They adopted an explicit position relative to this issue.

> A common misconception is that a classification of mental disorders classifies people, when actually what are being classified are disorders that people have. For this reason, the text of the *DSM-IV* (as did the text of *DSM-III-R*) avoids the use of expressions such as "a schizophrenic" or "an alcoholic" and instead uses the more accurate, but admittedly more cumbersome, "an individual with Schizophrenia" or "an individual with Alcohol Dependence." (APA, 2000, p. xxxi)

The *DSM-IV-TR* adopted this position to try to avoid the problem of stigma. Mental disorders largely refer to undesirable aspects of the human condition. Most of us do not want to be diagnosed with a mental disorder. To call someone "schizophrenic" is to imply that that individual is a member of a diagnostic category that is immutable, unchanging, and destructive both to that person and to the significant others in that person's life. The contrasting language of "an individual with schizophrenia" implies that the person is not inherently schizophrenic, but that schizophrenia, being a disease of the brain, is something that happens to people without the occurrence of the disease being their fault. By saying that *DSM* is a classification of disorders, the authors were trying to emphasize the value of beneficence so that no or minimal harm was done by assigning psychiatric diagnoses to individual human beings.

On the other hand, as mentioned at the beginning of this chapter, diagnosis is the process of assigning individuals to categories. Individual clinicians are concerned with the process of how best to characterize the individuals they see. The mental disorder groups characterized in a classification would not exist without individuals who instantiated those symptoms. Admittedly, the population of individuals with mental disorders is not permanent, as many mental disorders are time limited (a person initially does not have the disorder, then does, and goes back to not having it). The conditions that define the presence or absence of the disorder state become crucial to understanding if the classification captures individuals, disorders, or both. Thus, the definition of *mental disorder* has profound consequences for what the classification captures.

## Definition of Mental Disorder

The definition of the domain to which a classification of mental disorders applies—that is, all mental disorders—is an important aspect of the classification. The early editions of the *DSM* and *ICD* did not provide any definition of a mental disorder. An attempt to define this concept was provided with *DSM-III* by the head of the task force that created this classification. Robert Spitzer's view about how to define a mental disorder became controversial when he claimed "mental disorders are a subset of medical disorders" (Spitzer et al., 1977, p. 4). Many viewed this statement as an attempt to secure exclusive rights to mental disorder treatment for psychiatry, thereby excluding or marginalizing other disciplines such as psychology and social work. However, a psychologist on the *DSM-III* task force, Millon (1983), stated that this sentiment was never the official perspective of those creating *DSM-III*.

One year later, Spitzer and Endicott (1978) made an explicit attempt to define both mental disorder and medical disorder, with the former being a subset of the latter. It is worth reproducing their definitions *in toto*.

> A medical disorder is a relatively distinct condition resulting from an organismic dysfunction which in its fully developed or extreme form is directly and intrinsically associated with distress, disability, or certain other types of disadvantage. The disadvantage may be of physical, perceptual, sexual, or interpersonal nature. Implicitly there is a call for action on the part of the person who has the condition, the medical or its allied professions, and society.
>
> A mental disorder is a medical disorder whose manifestations are primarily signs or symptoms of a psychological (behavioral) nature, or if physical, can be understood only using psychological concepts. (p. 18)

Wakefield (1993) argued that Spitzer and Endicott's definition of a mental disorder failed on many levels to successfully operationalize the role of dysfunction inherent to mental disorders. Consequently, Wakefield (1992a, 1992b, 1993) provided an alternative definition of mental disorders, in which he placed dysfunction within an evolutionary framework to better distinguish disorders from non-disorders. Wakefield's approach to mental disorders, termed "harmful dysfunction," considered mental disorders as "failures of internal mechanisms to perform naturally selected functions" resulting in impairment (Wakefield, 1999, p. 374). Wakefield appreciated the fact that defining a disorder must incorporate both value-based (the harm element) and scientific-based (the dysfunction element) criteria.

Wakefield and others have argued that both values and science are inherent components to the way in which *DSM-III* and its successors have defined individual mental disorders (see Sadler, 2005). Distress, or harm, is included either by definition (feelings of depression, anxiety, etc.) or through the criterion of clinical significance. *Clinical significance* refers to the judgment made by the clinician that the severity of the dysfunction present in the disorder justifies treatment. Spitzer and Wakefield (1999) justified the inclusion of clinical significance in the *DSM*s as a means of limiting false-positive diagnoses (i.e., individuals who are symptomatic but do not qualify for a full diagnosis of a disorder). Note, however, that clinical significance is not an objectively defined concept but rather requires a subjective decision by a clinician regarding when a set of symptoms warrants clinical attention. For a classification system that has argued its strength is objectivity and freedom from clinical bias, the explicit inclusion of subjectivity in the definition of a mental disorder is a problem.

Wakefield's harmful dysfunction approach has not been without its critics. Lilienfeld and Marino (1995) criticized Wakefield's evolutionary basis of mental disorders, arguing that mental disorders do not have defined properties and are not necessarily evolutionary dysfunctions. To use a medical example, sickle-cell anemia is evolutionarily functional in malaria-prone regions but typically dysfunctional in malaria-free environments. Similar arguments can be made with specific phobias, such as snake phobias, which could be quite functional when an individual human lives near poisonous snakes; however, a snake phobia is of less functional use for the typical person living in a large city in which snakes are uncommon. Other critics (Fulford, 1999; Richters & Cicchetti, 1993; Sadler & Agich, 1995) have provided analyses and substitutes to Wakefield's harmful dysfunction concept. For further discussion on the debate centered on Wakefield's harmful dysfunction approach, we refer the reader to a recent review about how the debate is related to the *DSM-5* (Wakefield, 2016).

As mentioned briefly in the beginning of this chapter, lack of a consensual definition of mental disorders has important consequences. Definitions establish boundaries, in this case the boundary regarding what is and what is not a mental disorder and hence the boundaries of the mental health profession. The current definition posed in *DSM-5* reflects the logic of Wakefield's harmful dysfunction concept but is more lenient regarding the cause of the dysfunction. Furthermore, the *DSM-5* definition included the phrase "clinically significant disturbance," but the definition did not clarify the meaning of this phrase (APA, 2013, p. 20). The WHODAS, in Section III, was included to give clinicians more precision in the measurement of dysfunction.

## Dimensions Versus Categories

Although the term "classification" traditionally applies to a system of classes or categories, a number of contemporary writers have suggested that dimensional approaches to the classification of psychopathology would be preferable (Widiger & Samuel, 2005; Widiger et al., 2005).

The debate about categorical versus dimensional models is an old one. Advocates for each model tended to adopt particular theoretical and statistical approaches. Advocates of a dimensional model were often users of factor analysis, whereby advocates of a categorical model favored cluster analysis. Factor analysis is a multivariate statistical procedure pioneered in the 1930s by L. L. Thurstone (1934) and his colleagues.

The first known application of a dimensional approach to the classification of psychopathology was performed by a priest and psychiatrist named Thomas Moore. Moore (1930) gathered data on individuals with schizophrenia and subjected his descriptive information to a factor analysis. The result was five factors, which, in retrospect, were quite contemporary in their meaning. Using modern terms, these five factors could be named as follows:

1. Positive symptoms of schizophrenia
2. Negative symptoms of schizophrenia
3. Manic symptoms
4. Depressive symptoms
5. Symptoms of cognitive decline (dementia)

Shortly after World War II, Eysenck (1947), a psychologist in Great Britain, became a strong advocate for a dimensional approach to all psychopathology. He argued for three basic dimensions (Eysenck & Eysenck, 1976) that could be used to organize all descriptive information about mental disorders, which he called:

1. Neuroticism
2. Extroversion
3. Psychoticism

He used *neuroticism* to refer to individuals who were anxious or prone to negative feelings versus those who were emotionally calm and steady. *Extroversion* referred to an individual's proneness to be outgoing versus introverted. His description of *psychoticism* included a variety of other constructs, including constraint, impulsivity, sensation-seeking, and even creativity. Eysenck believed that high levels of the personality trait psychoticism made one prone to schizophrenia or other psychotic disorders. These three dimensions have resurfaced in one form or another in many later models, although the same names are sometimes applied to slightly different constructs.

Eysenck was a protégé of Aubrey Lewis, a leading British psychiatrist of his time. Later Lewis and Eysenck split over Eysenck's determined advocacy of a dimensional model. Lewis, a physician, believed that a categorical/disease model of psychopathology was more appropriate. Shortly after this split between Eysenck and Lewis in the late 1950s, a related debate appeared in the British literature about whether depression was best viewed from a dimensional perspective or from a categorical model (Kendell, 1968; see Klein, 2010, for a modern discussion of this issue).

After Eysenck, other dimensional models of psychopathology began to appear. Within child psychopathology, Achenbach (1966, 1995) became a proponent of a dimensional model with two constructs: (1) an internalizing dimension and (2) an externalizing dimension. *Internalizing* referred to children who displayed internally expressed emotional problems, like anxiety or depression, whereas *externalizing* referred to children who acted out through disruptive behavior. More recently, Krueger (1999; Krueger et al., 2005; Forbes et al., 2016) has shown that this two-dimensional approach can be generalized to account for a subset of common *DSM* diagnoses. Additionally, Eaton et al. (2012) replicated the internalizing-externalizing structural model which was found to be applicable to both men and women. Under that context, generalized anxiety disorder, major depressive disorder, and other anxiety disorders loaded onto a common factor, while antisocial personality disorder and substance use disorders loaded onto a second factor. However, that organization left many facets of psychopathology unaccounted for (e.g., bipolar disorders, psychotic disorders). Later work investigated a wider range of disorders and found a more complicated structure, but the dimensions of internalizing and externalizing remained (Conway et al., 2020; Kotov et al., 2017). Studies of this kind formed the basis of the meta-structure of the *DSM-5* and, to a lesser degree, *ICD-11*. Note that these structures are often hierarchical in nature, with higher-order factors corresponding to more general domains and lower-order factors referring to more specific manifestations. Similar to our earlier mention of lumpers and splitters, some advocates prefer description at the broader, higher level while others are more focused on the lower, narrower descriptors.

Another subset of psychopathology that has been a focus of dimensional investigation is the personality disorders. A variety of investigators such as James McKeen Cattell (*1860–1944*), Joy Paul Guilford (*1897–1987*), and Lewis Goldberg (*1932–*) developed dimensional approaches to personality traits in normal human beings. McCrae and Costa (1990) expanded this earlier research into what has become known as the Five-Factor Model (FFM) of personality with five dimensions:

1. Neuroticism
2. Extroversion
3. Agreeableness
4. Openness
5. Conscientiousness

Clark (2007) expressed concern about the application of the FFM to personality disorders because the most commonly used measure of the FFM, known as the NEO-PI-R, was designed to measure normal-range personality. For example, the construct of openness, as measured in normal-range personality, does not seem to be meaningfully related to pathology, but a separate construct—oddity—does capture behaviors of interest like magical or obsessive thinking (Watson et al., 2008). Cicero et al. (2019) investigated how symptoms of schizophrenia and schizotypal traits align with the personality taxonomy, finding that positive symptoms were linked to psychoticism while negative symptoms linked to extraversion. Recent work has compared the domain overlap between common personality measures (Crego et al., 2018) and the large degree of overlap between normal and abnormal personality presentations with respect to psychopathology (Widiger & Crego, 2019).

Many models of normal and disordered personality were considered by the *DSM-5* work group concerned with personality disorders. In the end, the work group developed its own distillation of these models that—when empirically tested—largely resembled the domains of the FFM (Krueger et al., 2012). Through an iterative process, they refined a list of 37 initial personality facets into a best-fitting model that contains 25 facets loading onto five higher-order domains (negative affect, detachment, antagonism, disinhibition, and psychoticism). While the structure resembles the FFM, it was intended to represent the more extreme and/or pathological variants of those traits (Krueger et al., 2012).

The *ICD-11* approach to classifying personality disorder also moved toward a dimensional model, although it looks somewhat different from the *DSM-5* proposal (Tyrer et al., 2015). First, personality disorder is classified along a severity continuum, moving from severe to moderate to mild personality disorder, with an option to indicate a subthreshold personality difficulty that is not severe or impairing enough to warrant a clinical diagnosis. Next, one may indicate the presence or absence of each of five personality trait domains (negative affectivity, dissocial, disinhibition, anankastic, and detachment). Four of those domains overlap substantially with similar personality concepts in the *DSM-5* model (negative affectivity, dissocial, disinhibition, and detachment); however, the *ICD-11* does not include a psychoticism domain. In the *ICD* tradition, schizotypal presentations are conceptualized as a psychotic disorder and not a personality disorder. Instead, the *ICD-11* includes the domain of anankastic features, which is characterized by rigidity, perfectionism, and overregulation of one's own and other's behavior.

Although statistical work on the categorical approach to the classification of psychopathology has not been as extensive, a number of studies have appeared. The most notable of these efforts were Maurice Lorr's use of cluster analysis to study individuals with schizophrenia (Lorr, 1966) and Paul Meehl's development of *taxometrics*—a set of techniques aimed at discerning the latent categorical vs. dimensional status of specific psychopathological constructs (Meehl, 1995; cf. Schmidt et al., 2004). Interestingly, the majority of taxometric studies have supported dimensional structures for mental disorders rather than categorical, although some have favored distinct groups of disordered individuals (Haslam et al., 2012, 2020). An analysis that parallels the logic of factor analysis but is used to identify categories is called *latent class analysis* (for a single indicator variable) or *latent profile analysis* (for multiple indicator variables). In essence, the analysis helps the investigator identify the number of possible groups that exist in a sample of individuals. A relevant example is the debate surrounding whether posttraumatic stress disorder (PTSD) is best represented by a single group—and single diagnosis—differentiated only on severity or multiple groups that differ in symptom type. The *DSM-5* elected to expand the symptoms of PTSD to incorporate a wider range of presentations within a single diagnosis, whereas the *ICD-11* opted to split the diagnosis of PTSD into two: regular PTSD and complex PTSD (Elklit et al., 2013; Wolf et al., 2015).

A new analysis approach termed *factor mixture analysis* (Muthen, 2006; Muthen & Muthen, 2010) creates hybrid dimensional-categorical models, where the taxonicity and dimensionality of a set of measures can be examined simultaneously. This sort of model would represent distinct groups of individuals (taxa) that vary along some latent dimension (i.e., an ordering of the groups). Interestingly, when this sort of hybrid model is employed, some studies find that dimensional structures continue to be favored (Eaton et al., 2011, 2013; Wright et al., 2013), whereas others find taxons meaningfully differentiated by underlying dimensions (Bernstein et al., 2010; Lenzenweger et al., 2008; Picardi et al., 2012).

Most classifications of psychopathology employ categories because they offer certain advantages. In everyday life, categorical concepts are used because they are familiar and easy. Psychiatrists have been trained in a tradition associated with medical and biological classification, and this influence has colored mental health classification. Both biological and medical classificatory systems are categorical; however, in regard to medical classification, certain portions can be viewed as dimensional (e.g., hypertension).

The tendency to think categorically should not be underestimated. Work in anthropology suggests that hierarchically organized categorical systems are the product of universal cognitive mechanisms that have evolved as adaptive ways of managing information (Atran, 1990; Berlin, 1992). In his study of various indigenous cultures, Berlin (1992) found that these societies had hierarchical organizations for the living things they encounter in their environment, and the structure of these "folk taxonomies" tended to be universal—but not concordant with scientific classifications. Evidence from cognitive and developmental psychologists shows that children seem to learn about the natural world through category formation (Hatano & Inagaki, 1994; Hickling & Gelman, 1995; Kalish, 2007; Nguyen, 2008). It is not surprising, therefore, that people, including clinicians, prefer to use concepts that are the products of these cognitive mechanisms that favor categorical concepts (Gelman, 2003; Yoon, 2009).

There are, however, substantial disadvantages to using categories. Categorical diagnoses often result in the loss of some information. Categorical systems also depend on nonarbitrary boundaries or at least on points of rarity between syndromes, as are seen in the valley between the two modes in a bimodal frequency histogram (Kendell, 1975, 1989).

Haslam (2002) outlined a taxonomy of "kinds of kinds," or a model of category types ranging from true categories to true dimensions. The truest form of a category is what various philosophers have termed a "natural kind" (Kripke, 1980; Putnam, 1982). A natural kind represents a group with a unitary etiology that leads to necessary outcomes and a discrete separation from other psychopathologic syndromes. However, true natural kinds are rare or nonexistent in the realm of psychopathology (Zachar, 2000). It could be that certain groups are qualitatively separate from other entities but lack the underlying "essence" of a natural kind, which Haslam termed "discrete kinds." An example would be the qualitative difference between regular and endogenous depression proposed by some (van Loo et al., 2012). Even though depression exists on a severity dimension, these authors would claim that a qualitative shift occurs at a certain threshold, creating a truly different kind. However, categories of mental disorders are not always well demarcated. When a category does not have a clear boundary, Haslam terms it a "fuzzy kind." A fuzzy kind exists when there is a definable group, but the characteristics of that group blend into other groups. Next, there are phenomena, such as hypertension, that can be thought of existing along a dimension (measured by blood pressure), but for which there are functional reasons to categorically scale the dimension (i.e., a cut point above which the person is seen as needing medical intervention). The choice of the cut point may be debatable, but the presence of a cut point serves a pragmatic purpose. These sorts of groups are termed "practical kinds" (Haslam, 2002; Zachar, 2000). The final entry in Haslam's taxonomy consists of true dimensions, or continua of psychological characteristics that do not justify any cut point.

From this discussion, the selection of the type of theoretical concept to use in classification (i.e., dimensions vs. categories) is fundamental to the development of a classification. Jaspers (1963) suggested that different classificatory models might be required for different forms of psychopathology. This idea has merit. Some conditions, especially those traditionally described as organic disorders, are similar to diagnoses in physical medicine. These could probably best be represented using a categorical model in which diagnoses are specified by diagnostic criteria. Other areas of psychopathology, especially the affective disorders and personality disorders, might be better represented using a dimensional framework. However, the distinction between categories and dimensions is a human convenience that we force on the world. A better approach might be to think about how categories *and* dimensions can best be used to describe a given psychopathological phenomenon and how they each might be better for individual purposes, such as clinical diagnosis versus research.

Interestingly, the issue of dimensions versus categories became a focus of significant controversy within *DSM-5*. The Personality and Personality Disorders Work Group for *DSM-5* was orchestrated in hopes of offering an alternative model that would address the shortcomings of the *DSM-IV* (Morey et al., 2015; Zachar et al., 2016). The categorical model led to a significant level of co-occurrences and heterogeneity among personality disorders. It is fairly common for an individual to meet the criteria for multiple personality disorders and for them to present differently than another person diagnosed with the same disorder. In fact, many individuals do not fall neatly into an arranged category, which has led personality disorder-not otherwise specified (PD-NOS) to be the most frequently diagnosed personality disorder. The work group proposed an empirically supported, hybrid model, termed the Alternative Model of Personality Disorders (AMPD), whereby some personality disorder categories would be retained while also including a dimensional model to describe individuals who did not fit neatly into a category (Skodol, 2012). Additionally, the proposed model mirrored the popular FFM of personality by mapping pathological variants of the Big Five personality factors onto personality disorders as well as the lower-order personality facets. The creators of the AMPD conceptualized personality disorders as a result of the interaction of personality functioning impairment and pathological personality traits. Within the work group, there was not unanimous agreement on the best approach involving dimensions and/or categories (Zachar et al., 2016). This hybrid structure was a compromise that could capitalize on the benefits of both categories and dimensions. However, the Board of Trustees of the American Psychiatric Association did not accept the proposal, electing to keep the same 10 categorical personality disorders found in *DSM-IV*. Instead, the work group proposal was published as a separate chapter in Section III of the manual to foster further research, with the hope of adopting those portions of the model that achieve sufficient empirical support.

### Atheoretical Approach to Classification

At the times that *DSM-I* and *DSM-II* were written, the dominant theory in psychiatry was psychoanalysis (Blashfield et al., 2014; Cooper & Blashfield, 2016). However, as the psychoanalytic perspective began to lose favor, a more biological approach began to emerge as the force behind explaining and conceptualizing mental disorders. The committee members of *DSM-III* (headed by Spitzer) were sensitive to this division between the psychoanalytic and biological explanations of mental disorders. Consequently, the determination was made that *DSM-III* would be theory-neutral in order for the classification to be more accessible to all mental health professionals. This approach has been preserved throughout the modern *DSMs* and mirrored in the *ICD* but has sparked a number of criticisms on the failure of specifying a theory to guide the classification system (Castiglioni & Laudisa, 2014; Harkness et al., 2014). Most writers who have thought about the recent classification systems agree that the implicit theoretical model associated with these systems is the biological (medical) approach (Harkness et al., 2014; Sedler, 2016). According to Harkness, Reynolds, and Lilienfeld (2014), the refusal by the authors of these classifications to postulate a theory of psychopathology explicitly hinders scientific progress within the field and removes focus from the evolved adaptive systems which underlie pathology.

Though the authors of *DSM-III* denied having a theory, Sadler (2005) argued that certain values or assumptions are nonetheless embedded in the structure of the *DSM*s and *ICD*s that emerge with their application. Because these six values, as discussed by Sadler, do represent the beginning of a theory of psychopathology, each of them will be discussed next.

The first is the value of *empiricism*, which is the belief that the contents of psychiatric classification are based on scientific research, complete with testable hypotheses and controlled clinical trials. This empirical advancement discourages the exclusive use of expert opinions and clinical judgment when making nosological decisions, as was seen in early editions of the *DSM* and *ICD*.

Second, Sadler discussed how the classification is *hypo-narrative*, a term he coined to describe the manuals' lack of storytelling qualities. Narrativity was especially lost during the transition from *DSM-II* to *DSM-III*, when disorder descriptions became symptom listings. Applying this language to diagnosing an individual loses the richness of the "biographical" explanation of the individual. However, Sadler argued that the role of classifications is not to capture necessarily the life story of each patient but to address the signs and symptoms associated with diagnosis. Hypo-narrativity leads the clinician to focus exclusively on the symptoms of a patient, rather than on the interactions between the symptoms and the relationships, priorities, aspirations, and daily functioning of the patient. It is these interactions that provide the plot line for the patient's story.

A third assumption of modern classifications is *individualism* (La Roche et al., 2015; Poland, 2016). As expressed in the *DSM* definition of mental disorder, psychopathology resides within the individual and is not the manifestation of the interactions of the individual with others or with the social forces around that individual (APA, 2013). The *DSM* and *ICD* have notoriously ignored pathological processes that exist among individuals, like family systems or romantic partners, and a group of researchers have been petitioning to include diagnoses of relational processes for decades (Wambolt et al., 2015). For example, a married couple might be highly dysfunctional even though neither individual qualifies for an individual mental health disorder. Another example of the effect of focusing on individualism as a value can be seen with the removal of gender identity disorder as a mental disorder. Nonbinary, gender fluid, or non-cisgender identities should not be classified as mental disorders because the struggles associated with such identities are induced by society and not something inherent within the individual (Drescher et al., 2012).

Fourth, psychiatric disorders are assumed to have a *natural essence*. In other words, disorders follow a natural order whereby etiologies are multifactorial—including biological, psychological, and sociocultural influences. Sadler stated that this assumption is important to understanding the atheoretical approach of these classifications because they stipulate that multiple theories, not just one all-encompassing explanation, are essential to understanding mental disorders. According to Bueter (2019), the inherent pluralism of this approach allows the classifications to fill a multitude of roles expected of them. Because the classifications—which possess influence and a special power over public perception of mental health due to their required use in many contexts, such as healthcare reimbursement or research funding—are often expected to fit a one-size-fits-all purpose, a pluralistic nature allows them to fit a variety of contexts and has many advantages for describing the breadth of psychopathology. With its tenth edition, the *ICD* attempted to directly address the one-size-fits-all problem by publishing several versions of the classification: one for clinical use, one for research, and one specifically for use in primary care. Regardless, this pluralistic approach impedes monistic beliefs that a single theory (like evolution in biology) could account for the entire landscape, as might be the agenda of biologically oriented researchers (Bueter, 2019).

The fifth value, *pragmatism*, refers to the use of classifications as a means to help individuals with mental disorders. The *DSM* and *ICD* exist for a practical purpose: the desire to improve the condition of individuals who are suffering or impaired. This pragmatism creates a difference from scientific disciplines that are studied for their own sake, like chemistry. The elements in the periodic table may change as new ones are discovered, but those additions do not vary over time as a function of society's demands. Because psychiatric classifications exist to serve a societal function, they can never be objectively separated from that function, meaning that societal values will always play a role in defining mental disorders. As the needs and priorities of a society changes, so will the conditions that are included in these manuals. For example, both *DSM* and *ICD* considered including a disorder intended to capture problematic (or addicted) Internet usage in their latest edition.

Finally, Sadler described the sixth implicit value of psychiatric classifications as *traditionalism*. The diagnostic concepts in the *DSM*s and *ICD*s have a history. The modern classifications have been built on past classifications. Trying to maintain continuity over time is important both for psychiatry and for the other mental health professions. Sadler suggested that the continuity of a classification system results in this system becoming familiar, being valued, and serving as the basis of a long-standing research and clinical infrastructure.

### Organization of Recent Classifications by Work Groups

The process used to formulate and revise the *DSM*s and *ICD*s warrants comment. A lengthy consultation process with panels of experts and the profession at large was used to ensure the face or content validity of diagnoses and widespread acceptance of the resulting system. The consultation process was partly a scientific exercise designed to produce a classification based on the best available evidence and expertise and partly a social-political process designed to ensure the acceptability of the resulting product. Because scientific and political objectives often run counter to each other, compromises were necessary.

With *DSM-III*, a task force handled the process and established advisory committees. These committees were composed of experts whose task was to identify and define diagnostic categories in their areas. Each committee also had a panel of consultants to provide additional advice and information. As the process continued, drafts of *DSM-III* were circulated to the profession for review and comment. Finally, field trials were conducted to evaluate the proposals and identify problems.

Although a similar process was used for *DSM-III-R*, *DSM-IV* went a step further. Work groups were established to address specific diagnostic classes, and each group followed a three-stage process. First, comprehensive literature reviews were conducted so that *DSM-IV* reflected current knowledge. Second, existing data sets were reanalyzed to evaluate diagnostic concepts and provide information on the performance of diagnostic criteria. Third, extensive field trials were conducted to address specific issues.

The *DSM-5* work group process appeared to be fairly different from the work group process of its predecessors. The work groups often had broader agenda, and their assignments were not just to one family of disorders. For example, the anxiety disorder work group of *DSM-5* had responsibility for the categories of separation anxiety disorder, body dysmorphic disorder, social phobia, substance-induced obsessive-compulsive disorder, PTSD, and dissociative amnesia. In addition, from the rationales presented for changes in categories, there appeared to be obvious interaction across the work groups. For example, substance-induced obsessive-compulsive disorder, as mentioned earlier, involved interaction with the work group for substance use disorders. Under the family of schizophrenic disorders, the psychotic disorders work group and the personality disorders work group integrated their efforts.

The *ICD*s have followed a similar organizational structure. However, being an international manual, the selection of individuals also included international politics. The *ICD-10* was criticized for largely being a European product develop by European experts. In response, the *ICD-11* explicitly made attempts to include on every work group individuals from low- and middle-income countries (International Advisory Group, 2011).

There are many laudable features to the process used to revise and develop each edition. Each work group faced a major undertaking that required careful analysis of information as well as consultation with other experts in the field. This division of labor into work groups probably contributed to the acceptance of the resulting classifications. But there were also problems with the process. The initial structure for *DSM-III* was established when the work groups were identified. Each was given a defined area of psychopathology. The separation into committees along major topic areas led to both personal and conceptual conflicts. Psychopathology is not readily divisible into discrete areas. Overlap occurred between various committees, leading to dispute. Once a committee was established with a given mandate, that committee was reluctant to relinquish domains of psychopathology that might have been better classified elsewhere. The superordinate task force was responsible for resolving these disputes and ensuring integration. Inevitably, political processes within and between work groups influenced the solutions adopted. Additionally, who is selected to be a member of the work group is not without its own biases and limitations. Typically, those researchers with the most publications or most notable reputations are selected. To date, it is rare for clinicians to be selected, and never has an individual with the diagnoses in question been included, despite these individuals' perspectives potentially being useful regarding the usability and acceptability of the resulting product (Kamens et al., 2019). The people selected to be on work groups tend to publish together, receive grants together, and otherwise have similar viewpoints, creating an ingroup that perpetuates a group-think process (Blashfield & Reynolds, 2012). Furthermore, the process of discussions among the work group is influenced by nonscientific processes. As noted by Frances and Widiger (2012), two of the developers of *DSM-IV*, experts tend to be very opinionated and assertive in their beliefs, leading to the person with the loudest voice being the most influential.

## Measurement and Methodological Issues

The final section of this chapter addresses more practical concerns about the classification of mental disorders. While it is good to debate the ontological status of the term "mental disorder" and consider the political forces that impact classification schemes, at some point, practical decisions must be made regarding actual patients. Many of these practical concerns embody decisions about measurement, or how one assesses the nature of the condition. We adopt some of the standard terms of psychological measurement theory, including concepts like reliability and validity, to elucidate issues surrounding psychiatric diagnosis.

### Reliability

The reliability of a classification of mental disorders is the degree of diagnostic agreement among users. Reliability is clearly important; diagnoses have little value for communication or prediction if there are high levels of disagreement among clinicians. As Kendell (1975) pointed out, the accuracy of clinical and prognostic decisions based on a diagnosis cannot be greater than the reliability with which the diagnosis is made, and most writers allege that reliability places an upper limit on the validity of a given diagnosis (Spitzer & Fleiss, 1975; Spitzer & Williams, 1980).

A variety of factors influence reliability estimates. For instance, variations in patient characteristics influence clinicians' diagnostic decisions. Farmer and Chapman (2002) found that clinicians were much more consistent in providing a diagnosis of narcissistic personality disorder to men than to women. Some studies have examined the influence of variables such as race, age, and low socioeconomic status on diagnosis (Abreu, 1999; James & Haley, 1995; Littlewood, 1992). Einfeld and Aman (1995) suggest that reliability in *DSM* diagnoses appears to deteriorate markedly as patient IQ scores decrease. Furthermore, it is important to note that reliability estimates based on well-controlled research studies are likely inflated relative to reliability in day-to-day practice in clinical settings.

### HISTORY

As noted earlier in this chapter, reliability became a major focus of empirical criticisms of psychiatric diagnosis during the 1950s and 1960s. Generally, the impression from these studies was that psychiatrists and clinical psychologists, when independently diagnosing the same cases, did not agree on the diagnoses that they were assigning to cases. Interestingly, as the methodology of these studies improved, the estimates of reliability generally appeared more positive than in the early, rather hastily designed studies. One study in this series (Ward et al., 1962) made the additional conclusion that the reason for this relative lack of diagnostic agreement among clinicians (i.e., poor reliability) was that the definitions of the diagnostic categories in *DSM-I* were too vague. Although the methodology of the Ward et al. study had serious limitations (Blashfield, 1984), this conclusion appealed to the field, and the Ward et al. (1962) paper was often cited prior to the publication of *DSM-III*, when diagnostic criteria were used to improve the precision of defining diagnostic categories.

Another source of variability in early research on reliability was the statistical procedure used to provide reliability estimates. In earlier years, this was a serious problem (Zubin, 1967). By the mid-1970s, a statistic named *kappa* became the standard technique for estimating diagnostic reliability. Kappa corrects for chance levels of agreement between raters and thus is an improvement on a simple percentage of agreement. However, a limitation of this statistic is its instability when the base rate of a diagnosis within a sample is less than 5% (Spitznagel & Helzer, 1985).

## ASSESSING RELIABILITY

It is instructive to compare reliability as applied to psychiatric classification with reliability as applied to psychological tests. In test theory, "reliability" refers to the consistency of scores obtained with the same test on different occasions or with different sets of equivalent items (Anastasi, 1982). If a test is reliable, parallel scales constructed from an equivalent pool of items will yield the same measurement values. The extent to which this does not occur indicates the extent to which measurement is influenced by error. Traditionally, the reliability of psychological tests is assessed in three ways: (1) test-retest reliability, (2) alternative forms, and (3) internal consistency. A fourth method directly relevant to the clinical enterprise is interrater reliability, or the consistency of different diagnosticians regarding the same patient.

*Test-Retest Reliability.* The test-retest method assumes that the administration of the same scale at different points in time represents parallel tests. Memory for items is the most common confound with this approach. High test-retest reliability is to be expected only when measuring a variable assumed to be stable; some mental disorders are assumed to follow a relatively stable course (e.g., autism spectrum disorders), but many disorders (e.g., mood disorders) are assumed to fluctuate across time. In a multisite collaborative study of *DSM-IV* disorders, Zanarini et al. (2000) found that test-retest kappa coefficients ranged from 0.35 to 0.78 for a variety of clinical disorders and from 0.39 to 1.00 for personality disorders. However, more recent research has questioned just how consistent personality disorder diagnoses are across time, finding substantial fluctuation across categorical personality disorder types (Hopwood et al., 2013).

*Alternative Forms.* The alternative-form method uses equivalent or parallel measures of the same construct. Ideally, different sources of information should converge on the same conclusions. Hilsenroth, Baity, Mooney, and Meyer (2004) examined three sources of information regarding depressive symptoms: in vivo interviews, videotaped interviews, and chart reviews. Clinicians made reliable ratings of depressive symptoms across in vivo interviews and videotaped interviews, but chart reviews were not consistent with either. Similarly, Samuel and colleagues (2013) examined the convergence of clinician-assigned personality disorder diagnoses, self-report questionnaires, and semi-structured interviews. They found that the convergence of these methods was low, but they equally predicted clients' functioning at a 5-year follow-up, suggesting that the difference in reliability may not have much practical importance. Diagnostic disagreement can occur when clinicians have different kinds and amounts of information on which to base diagnosis. This problem may arise from differences in clinicians' ability to elicit information, the way patients respond to questions, and the availability of information from other sources. Thus, there are important sources of variance that can contribute to unreliability, including differences in clinical skill, patient responsiveness, and diagnostic setting.

*Internal Consistency.* Internal consistency measures (split-half techniques and coefficient alpha) assume each item on a scale is like a miniature scale. Thus, internal consistency estimates the extent to which the items in a scale are homogeneous. In psychological testing, this estimate of reliability is the most common. Morey (1988) examined the internal consistency of diagnostic criteria for personality disorders and found low correlations among criteria used to diagnose the same disorder. Other studies have found higher estimates of internal consistency, but using logistic regression and calculations of sensitivity and specificity have concluded that some criteria for certain personality disorders could be dropped because they do not form a cohesive diagnosis (Farmer & Chapman, 2002). These criticisms (among others) have led to some of the changes proposed in *DSM-5*'s Section III regarding personality disorder diagnosis. However, care should be taken with such conclusions. It is reasonable to posit heterogeneous symptom groupings for which internal consistency estimates are therefore inappropriate means of measurement, just as test-retest estimates are inappropriate for diagnoses expected to change over time.

*Interrater Reliability.* The three forms of reliability just discussed focus on the construct underlying the diagnosis. However, discrepancies can also occur in the application of the diagnosis. Two clinicians, for example, may disagree about what diagnosis is best for the same case. In studies of interrater reliability, two or more clinicians interview each patient either conjointly in a single interview or in separate interviews close together in time. In *DSM-I* and *DSM-II*, consistency among clinicians was low, and the advent of diagnostic criteria in *DSM-III* was supposed to increase reliability. However, claims that reliability has increased seem to be overstated; diagnostic reliability does not seem to be substantially different over time (Vanheule et al., 2014).

The field trials for *DSM-5* utilized a methodology that gave a realistic estimate of how reliable diagnoses for these conditions are under natural clinical conditions versus the stricter standardization present in research protocols (often through structured interviews). As might be expected, test-retest reliabilities were lower, with kappas ranging from 0 to 0.78, with some common diagnoses not faring as well as might be expected (e.g., major depressive disorder = 0.28; Regier et al., 2013). The *ICD-11* field trials used a methodology whereby the raters had access to the exact same information; as a result, reliability estimates were higher (Reed et al., 2018). Furthermore, a meta-analysis of diagnostic methods found that concordance between structured diagnostic interviews and standard clinical evaluations varied widely, with some diagnostic areas having relatively good agreement (e.g., eating disorders kappa = .70) and others relatively poor between the two methods (e.g., affective disorders kappa = .14; Rettew et al., 2009). While structured interviews do typically result in higher reliability estimates, correcting for the interviewers accessing the same information versus conducting separate interviews seems to account for much of the discrepancy in reliability (Chmielewski et al., 2015). Generally, the more training and structure provided in the diagnostic assessment, the higher the reliability coefficients will be; however, one must consider whether the procedure used to obtain a high reliability is feasible for implementation in daily clinical use. With *DSM-III*, obtaining higher reliability was an explicit goal. Now, some have questioned if test-retest reliability should be a goal in and of itself (Kraemer et al., 2012).

## Validity

The main impetus for the development of *DSM-III* was the perceived crisis surrounding diagnostic reliability. Many clinicians purported that a set of criteria could not be valid if it were not first reliable. Although this assumption is not necessarily true (Carey & Gottesman, 1978; Faust & Miner, 1986), the creators of *DSM-III* saw the production of a reliable diagnostic system as their primary task. After establishing reliability, researchers could turn their attention to issues of validity.

"Validity" in common usage refers to the truth-value of a statement. However, it is important to note that using *valid* in that sense does not imply that there is only one valid conclusion for a given set of facts; rather, there are many possible valid conclusions based on one's point of view.

## HISTORY

The concept of validity is often discussed within the context of the classification of psychopathology, but, ironically, like many classificatory concepts themselves, finding a clearly specified, thoughtfully articulated definition of validity has proved elusive. Two major approaches to diagnostic validity have been discussed in the past 50 years. One is a relatively common-sense, medicine-based approach that appeals to psychiatrists. The other, which often is discussed in more abstract, empirical contexts, is the view psychologists have about validity based on their experience with different forms of assessment.

A short paper published by Eli Robins (*1921–1994*) and Samuel Guze (*1923–2000*) of Washington University in 1970 contained the major discussion of validity from the medical perspective. Robins and Guze were leaders of the neo-Kraepelinian group whose views led to *DSM-III*. Robins and Guze discussed validity in the context of five phases of research that would demonstrate that a diagnostic concept represented a disease. These five phases were (1) clinical description (i.e., establishing that the disorder represents a "syndrome" of symptoms that can be empirically shown to co-occur at relatively high rate), (2) laboratory studies (which establish the biological substrate of the disorder), (3) delimitation from other disorders (which would establish that the disorders are relatively, though not perfectly, divided into discrete categories), (4) follow-up studies (which show that the individuals with this disorder have a common course to their symptom patterns), and (5) family studies (which establish the genetic basis of the biological phenomenon associated with the disorder). Robins and Guze believed that their approach to validity stemmed not only from the medical research of Thomas Sydenham (*1624–1689*) but also was consistent with the views of validity adopted by German medical researchers of the late nineteenth century, when the latter resolved the etiologies of many bacterial diseases (e.g., tuberculosis, smallpox, syphilis).

The other approach to the meaning of validity when applied to psychiatric classification has come from the work of psychologists who have drawn on discussions of validity in the context of psychological tests. Joseph Zubin at Columbia University was one of the first to promote the application of a psychological testing view of validity to psychiatric diagnosis. Zubin (1967) stated that the broad concept of validity should be subdivided into four subsidiary concepts: (1) concurrent validity, (2) predictive validity, (3) construct validity, and (4) content validity.

In the past few years, a new development has occurred in the approach to diagnostic validity. This approach is represented by a concept titled *clinical utility*, which, like the views of Robins and Guze, has a pragmatic emphasis. In the words of First et al. (2004), clinical utility "is the extent to which the *DSM* assists clinical decision makers in fulfilling the various clinical functions of a psychiatric classification system" (p. 947). According to First (2010), the clinical functions of a psychiatric classification are (1) assisting clinicians in communicating clinical information; (2) assisting the selection of effective interventions; (3) predicting course, prognosis, and future management needs; and (4) differentiating disorder from non-disorder for the purpose of determining who might benefit from treatment. Verheul (2005) argued that increased clinical utility (especially regarding communication and clinical decision-making) may provide the rationale for shifting from a categorical to dimensional model of personality disorder. Reed (2010) has argued that clinical utility should be the driving force for making classificatory decisions when more convincing scientific information is equivocal or not available.

## ISSUES

The psychiatric approach to validity, embodied by the work of Robins and Guze (1970), is based on the medical concept of disease, which has proved elusive in its own right (Aboraya et al., 2005; Jablensky, 2016). Many, but not all, references to the concept of disease are making assumptions about *essentialism*. According to essentialism, a category is defined by some*thing* (an essence) that causes one to be a member of the category. For example, when syphilis was found to be the cause of general paresis, the essence of the disease category became the presence of syphilis in the central nervous system. Thus, a valid category is one that has an identifiable etiological agent. Schizophrenia is valid to the degree that some*thing* causes one to have schizophrenia.

Essentialism has proved problematic even in the realm of physical diseases (Lemoine, 2013). Even in the most archetypal cases of "disease," for example—a bacterial infection—it is impossible to define the disease category in a way that corresponds to the state of nature and is free of human value assumptions (Smith, 2001). The disease is not the presence of bacteria, as perfectly healthy individuals have the bacteria in their system. Rather, the disease is an interaction effect that emerges from the presence of the bacteria and an immunological weakness, among other factors. In short, diseases have multiple causes in even the simplest of cases; therefore, to define them as having simple, reified essences is inappropriate at best. The essentialist view of validity has proved even less effective in the case of psychiatric conditions, the causes of which are complex and multiply determined (Dekkers & Rikkert, 2006; Zachar, 2000). Alzheimer's disease is another example of this phenomenon. While often termed a genetic disease, there is no singular genetic cause of Alzheimer's, and the presence of a gene known to cause Alzheimer's does not guarantee an individual will contract the disease. Instead, a host of genetic and environmental factors are known to influence the likelihood of contracting Alzheimer's, which is only diagnosed when the associated symptomology (i.e., the interaction of the factors within the individual) is present (Dekkers & Rikkert, 2006). In fact, while defining the terms "disease" and "health" may be of philosophical importance to medicine, concrete definitions are still illusive (Lemoine, 2013).

In contrast, the psychological approach to validity has been based on psychometric test theory. A psychological test is considered valid to the extent to which its items and resultant scores reflect the construct of interest. For instance, the items on a test should represent the entire domain of the construct, which is generally termed *content validity*.

For example, a test of depression should have items that sample all the relevant symptoms and expressions generally considered to be a part of depression. In the same fashion, the diagnostic criteria used to define a mental disorder category should represent the range of behaviors associated with that category.

Second, the test may be considered valid if it meets some predetermined criterion, that is, *criterion validity*. To continue with the example of depression, a test of depression would be criterion valid if it consistently classified people in the same manner as a *DSM-5* diagnosis. The criterion is context-dependent. In one context, one might consider a diagnosis from a structured interview (e.g., the Structured Clinical Interview for *DSM* [SCID]) the "gold standard," whereas in another context, an unstructured interview might be the appropriate criterion.

The third and perhaps most important aspect of validity for psychological tests is *construct validity*—the degree to which the scores on the test measure what they are expected to measure (Cronbach & Meehl, 1955; Smith & Combs, 2010). This definition has several implications. First, raters should respond consistently to items that are meant to tap into the same construct, assuming that the construct is meant to be stable across time and homogenous. In that sense, reliability is an integral part of validity in that a measure's reliability should be consistent with the description of the construct. Second, the items on a test should correlate with each other. In the context of mental disorders, different items, which represent different symptoms, should co-occur (i.e., the construct is a syndrome). The degree to which the items correlate should be consistent with the supposed homogeneity or heterogeneity of the construct. Third, the test score should be related to measures of other constructs in an expected pattern. For example, a test of depression should be negatively correlated with a measure of positive affect. Furthermore, test scores should be related to other measures of the same construct using different measurement methods. This approach is usually evaluated using the classic multitrait-multimethod procedure described by Campbell and Fiske (1959).

A fourth concept of validity—*structural validity*—defines how closely a set of symptoms defined by the literature match how a disorder actually presents in reality (Jacobs & Krueger, 2015). A statistical procedure termed *structural equation modeling* (SEM) allows researchers to evaluate structural validity. SEM is a correlational and regressional technique that models complex interrelationships in a multivariate format and allows one to test a variety of hypotheses regarding a construct (Campbell-Sills & Brown, 2006; Bentler & Savalei, 2010). It involves testing reliability and factor structures of measures as well as the relationships between measures. For example, Neumann, Johansson and Hare (2013) examined the interrelationships between clinical anxiety/fearless ratings (LAF) and the factor structure of the Psychopathy Checklist Revised (PCL-R) in a sample of prisoners. Using SEM, Neumann, Johansson and Hare sought to determine to what degree the PCL-R accounted for LAF factors, which may be part of the psychopathy construct and unaccounted for in the PCL-R model. Consistent with previous research, SEM analysis indicated that the PCL-R superordinate factor set was able to account for all LAF factors without changes to the PCL-R model. Put another way, if LAF factors are a part of the psychopathy construct, they are already accounted for by the PCL-R (Neumann et al., 2013).

Despite developments in psychological testing, substantial theoretical limitations to the psychological test approach to validation exist in the context of mental disorders. The construct validation approach used in psychology assumes that the construct is already well-defined. If the concept of a construct changes, as is inherent in any empirical science, any test purporting to measure that construct must be revalidated. In a strange way, the psychological test approach puts the cart before the horse as the structure of the diagnostic construct must be assumed before it can be investigated.

### Diagnostic Overlap

Another major problem with *DSM* is the degree of diagnostic overlap that occurs throughout the classification. For example, of those in the general population who meet criteria for a disorder, half meet criteria for two or more other mental disorders (Kessler et al., 2005), a phenomenon termed *comorbidity*.

#### HISTORY

In 1984, Boyd and associates published a landmark empirical study that documented a surprisingly high degree of overlap among mental disorders. The sample was taken from a large (nearly 12,000 participants) multisite epidemiological study performed after the publication of *DSM-III*. *DSM-III* included specific exclusionary criteria to prevent the overlap of certain diagnoses. However, Boyd et al. found that if the exclusionary criteria were ignored, instances in which an individual received more than one diagnosis were quite common. For instance, the diagnostic overlap between major depressive disorder and agoraphobia was 15 times what might be expected by chance. Boyd et al. also found that the diagnostic overlap among mental disorders for which no exclusionary criteria were given in *DSM-III* was also quite high (e.g., the co-occurrence of schizophrenia and alcohol abuse/dependence was 10 times greater than expected by chance).

Stimulated by the Boyd et al. (1984) finding, the NIMH sponsored a conference of prominent psychiatrists and psychologists, in the late 1980s, to discuss the implications of this finding, the results of which were later published (Maser & Cloninger, 1990). Later, the NIMH funded a large-scale epidemiological analysis of the occurrence of mental disorders in the United States in two research studies known as the National Comorbidity Survey (Kessler et al., 1994) and the National Comorbidity Survey Replication (Kessler et al., 2005). The results showed that virtually all mental disorders showed a high rate of diagnostic overlap with almost all other mental disorders.

Krueger and Markon (2006) have reviewed the resulting literature on the comorbidity of mental disorders. They noted that this term was rarely used before the mid-1980s when the Boyd et al. study was published, but that, in the next two decades, approximately 8,500 journal articles appeared of relevance to the concept of comorbidity.

**THE MEANING OF COMORBIDITY**

The issue of diagnostic overlap has been termed "comorbidity," although there are those who contend the term is a misnomer (Lilienfeld et al., 1994). Feinstein (1970) introduced the term "comorbidity" in the context of medical epidemiology. Later, Lilienfeld (2003) reported that Feinstein had never intended for the term to refer to all cases of diagnostic overlap, as seems to be its current usage in the literature. In general, one would expect a certain degree of overlap simply by chance. However, when disorders co-occur at greater than chance levels, the overlap begins to have implications for the classification system.

For example, a patient may present with a case of panic disorder and be concurrently depressed. On the other hand, a patient presenting with panic may have a comorbid diagnosis of ADHD. In these cases, it could be that depression and panic are meaningfully correlated; that is, the depression may cause the panic or vice versa, a third variable could cause both, or some alternative complex causal model could account for the relationship. However, when two co-occurring conditions are not meaningfully related but simply overlap by chance, as could be the case with panic and ADHD, that sort of comorbidity is of decidedly less theoretical interest. Given the base rates of disorders in the population, one would expect a certain number of cases to present with overlap just by chance. Hypothetically, if there were a 10% chance of having panic disorder and a 15% chance of having ADHD, one would expect a 1.5% (10% × 15%) chance of having both conditions in the general population. However, epidemiological work on psychiatric disorders has shown that various mental disorders co-occur at a rate in the population much greater than that expected by chance (Boyd et al., 1984; Kessler et al., 1994, 2005).

When disorders co-occur at greater than chance levels, comorbidity begins to have implications for the classification system. As stated before, the authors of *DSM-III* and beyond have assumed that the categories in the classification are relatively discrete. However, if there is significant covariance between these conditions, that assumption of discreteness is untenable. For example, unipolar affective disorders and anxiety disorders co-occur at a very high rate. This finding has led some authors to contend that these disorders are not discrete conditions but varied expressions of a single disorder (Wilamowska et al., 2010). If that is the case, the current diagnostic system is not accurately "carving nature at the joints."

However, there are also artifactual reasons why disorders could co-occur at greater than chance levels. For instance, *Berksonian bias* (Berkson, 1946) states that a person with comorbid disorders has twice the chance of seeking treatment as does a person with a single disorder and so has a greater chance of being included in studies. Similarly, comorbidity rates may be overestimated because of clinical selection bias or because individuals with multiple disorders may be more impaired and thus overrepresented in treatment studies. However, significant rates of comorbidity occur even in community-based samples (e.g., Kessler et al., 2005). Finally, it has been demonstrated that structured interviews generate much higher rates of diagnosis overall, and higher rates of comorbidity specifically, than do unstructured interviews (Verheul & Widiger, 2004; Zimmerman et al., 2005). However, such differences in diagnostic method may not be artifactual because structured interviews ensure that the breadth of psychopathology is assessed, whereas unstructured interviews address only salient points, and legitimate disorders may be overlooked.

Recently, increased attention has been paid to developing statistical models of comorbidity (e.g., Borsboom et al., 2011; Kotov et al., 2017; Krueger & Markon, 2006). Using sophisticated multivariate statistical methods, it is possible to test potential causal models of comorbidity, thereby elucidating the structure of the classification of mental disorders and suggesting changes to the arrangement of the *DSM*. For example, there is increasing support for organizing both childhood and adult disorders along internalizing and externalizing spectra (Kotov et al., 2017; Krueger et al., 2005). Indeed, this approach led the creators of *DSM-5* and *ICD-11* to place internalizing groups of disorders (e.g., anxiety, depressive, and somatic disorders) and externalizing disorders (e.g., impulsive, disruptive conduct, and substance use disorders) sequentially next to each other in the organization of the manual (Krueger et al., 2011; Roberts et al., 2012).

A similar approach has argued that all mental health disorders share a common liability. A common finding in the history of psychopathological research is that a factor analysis of symptoms, disorders, or measurement scales will often result in a single factor—sometimes termed a "*p*-factor"—that seems to account for a substantial amount of the overlap in people's presentations (Caspi et al., 2014). There are multiple possible interpretations of this general factor, including but not limited to the distress felt by people with a mental disorder, a common genetic liability, and common social factors like stigma.

One approach to understanding comorbidity is that groups of disorders, *diagnostic spectra*, are more accurately classified together than as discrete disorders. Criticisms of the structure and organization of previous versions led *DSM-5* and *ICD-11* work groups to reconceptualize many sections of the manual. One area of controversy in the literature regards the distinctions among pervasive developmental disorders (i.e., Kamp-Becker et al., 2010; Klin & Volkmar, 2003). Pervasive developmental disorders have included diagnoses such as autistic disorder (AD), Asperger's disorder (AS), childhood disintegrative disorder (CDD), Rhett's syndrome, and miscellaneous categories. Since AD was first included in *DSM-III-R* (APA, 1987) and AS was first included in *DSM-IV* (APA, 1994), researchers have questioned the uniqueness of these diagnoses. The distinction between AD and AS was popularized by Wing (1981) when she coined the phrase "Asperger's disorder" to discuss symptoms first described by Hans Asperger (1944). Ironically, Wing (2000) later wrote that she did not intend to imply that AS and AD were distinct disorders. Regardless, varying conceptualizations of these diagnoses have been present since Asperger's 1944 description of what is now called Asperger's disorder and Kanner's 1943 description of autism.

Many researchers have since examined AS and AD to garner additional understanding of the etiology, symptoms, and potential differences in presentation between these diagnoses. Although some studies have proclaimed differences between AD and AS (i.e., Ghaziuddan & Gerstein, 1996; Paul et al., 2009; Szatmari et al., 2009), many researchers have concluded that there are no distinguishable or useful differences beyond variations in severity (i.e., Ozonoff et al., 2000; Rogers & Ozonoff, 2005; Szatmari et al., 1989). Subsequently, arguments for the combination of AD and AS into one spectrum diagnosis are prevalent (i.e., Miller & Ozonoff, 2000; Via et al., 2011). The *DSM-5* neurodevelopmental disorders work group created a new autism spectrum disorder (ASD) diagnosis that incorporates all individuals who previously held a pervasive developmental disorder diagnosis. Under this "umbrella" there will be a great deal of individualization in symptom presentation and functioning level. The *DSM-5* work group anticipated these variations and stated that individuals who meet criteria for ASD should additionally be described based on intellectual level and language ability.

The variation present in this example reflects many areas of psychopathological classification. When differences between two disorders are difficult to identify, it is possible that the disorders may actually be variable presentations of the same, broader diagnosis. Other spectra included in *DSM-5* and *ICD-11* include a disruptive behavior spectrum of impulse control disorders, conduct disorder, and oppositional defiant disorder; a spectrum of obsessive-compulsive disorders including things like body dysmorphic disorder and trichotillomania; and a psychotic spectrum including schizophrenia, schizoaffective disorder, delusional disorder, and schizotypal personality disorder. When the meta-structure of these disorders has been examined, externalizing and psychotic dimensions seem to emerge, supporting the notion of grouping these disorders (Wright et al., 2013). The relatedness within each of these potential spectra also represents the dimensionality of mental health disorders in general. Ultimately, the criteria for a clinical diagnosis are met at a cutoff that splits the dimension between normal functioning and each of the graded severities of the respective disorders (Bernstein et al., 2010). The next chapter, on diagnostic alternatives, will go into greater detail about the background, rationale, and research support for large-scale models that attempt to represent this overlap.

## Conclusion

This chapter starts with the sentence "Diagnosis is simple." Approximately 17,000 words and 190 references later, diagnosis does not seem so simple. This chapter has focused on a taxonomic view of modern psychiatric classification. The organization of this chapter, just by itself, was a complex act of classification into topics, history, discussion of controversies, terminology, and reviews of the writings of others. We could have used quite different organizational principles to structure our chapter. For instance, we could have written the chapter with a chronological structure moving from one *ICD* and

*DSM* edition to another. We could have organized the chapter by professions—what psychiatrists have written about classification, what psychologists have said, what philosophers have written, etc. We could have focused on the prominent individuals in the classification literature: Kraepelin, Menninger, Spitzer, Zubin, Lorr, Frances, Robins, etc. We could have emphasized diagnostic concepts that have been controversial and why: dementia praecox, neurosis, homosexuality, premenstrual syndrome, narcissistic personality disorder, masochistic personality disorder, online gaming addiction, etc.

Like most "simple" topics, when thought about carefully, diagnosis becomes complex. Our organization of this chapter represented our view of a controversial but important area of concern regarding how knowledge about psychopathology is organized. It is important for the reader of this chapter to note that the problems and dilemmas enumerated here have no easy resolution, if a resolution is even possible. No "perfect" approach to classification exists. Each attempt has its own flaws and limitations. The task of the mental health field is to determine which classificatory scheme best matches the values and goals of the discipline and would be the most useful for their purpose. But perhaps it is even more important to recognize the limitations of the system because it is all too easy to accept a classification system as "given." We hope this chapter will not only inspire a healthy skepticism regarding the traditional nosological systems but also help the reader to appreciate the necessity and importance of classification within the mental health field.

## Acknowledgments

We would like to thank Danny Burgess, Hannah Morton, and Roger Blashfield for their work on previous versions of this chapter.

## References

Aboraya, A., France, C., Young, J., Curci, K., & Lepage, J. (2005). The validity of psychiatric diagnosis revisited: The clinician's guide to improve the validity of psychiatric diagnosis. *Psychiatry, 2*, 48–55.

Abreu, J. M. (1999). Conscious and nonconscious African-American stereotypes: Impact on first impression and diagnostic ratings by therapist. *Journal of Community and Clinical Psychology, 67*, 387–393.

Achenbach, T. M. (1966). The classification of children's psychiatric symptoms: A factor-analytic study. *Psychological Monographs: General and Applied, 80* (7, whole no. 615).

Achenbach, T. M. (1995). Empirically based assessment and taxonomy: Applications to clinical research. *Psychological Assessment, 7*, 261–274.

American Psychiatric Association (APA). (1952). *Diagnostic and statistical manual of mental disorders* (1st ed.). Washington, DC: Author.

American Psychiatric Association (APA). (1968). *Diagnostic and statistical manual of mental disorders* (2nd ed.). Washington, DC: Author.

American Psychiatric Association (APA). (1980). *Diagnostic and statistical manual of mental disorders* (3rd ed.). Washington, DC: Author.

American Psychiatric Association (APA). (1987). *Diagnostic and statistical manual of mental disorders* (3rd ed., rev.). Washington, DC: Author.

American Psychiatric Association (APA). (1994). *Diagnostic and statistical manual of mental disorders* (4th ed.). Washington, DC: Author.

American Psychiatric Association (APA). (2000). *Diagnostic and statistical manual of mental disorders* (4th ed., text revision). Washington, DC: Author.

American Psychiatric Association (APA). (2012a). Proposed draft revisions to DSM disorders and criteria. http://www.dsm5.org/ProposedRevision/Pages/Default.aspx

American Psychiatric Association (APA). (2012b). Rationale for the proposed changes to the personality disorders classification in DSM-5. http://www.dsm5.org/Documents/Personality%20Disorders/Rationale%20for%20the%20Proposed%20changes%20to%20the%20Personality%20Disorders%20in%20DSM-5%205-1-12.pdf

American Psychiatric Association (APA). (2013). *Diagnostic and statistical manual of mental disorders* (5th ed.). Washington, DC: Author.

Anastasi, A. (1982). *Psychological testing* (5th ed.). New York: Macmillan.

Ash, P. (1949). The reliability of psychiatric diagnoses. *Journal of Abnormal and Social Psychology, 44*, 272–276.

Asperger, H. (1944). Die "autistischen psychopathen" im kindesalter. *Archiv fur Psychiatrie und Nervenkrankheitem, 117*, 76–136. (Reprinted in *Autism and Asperger syndrome*, by U. Frith, Ed., 1991, Cambridge: Cambridge University Press).

Atran, S. (1990). *Cognitive foundations of natural history: Towards an anthropology of science*. Cambridge: Cambridge University Press.

Beck, A. T. (1962). Reliability of psychiatric diagnoses: A critique of systematic studies. *American Journal of Psychiatry, 119*, 210–216.

Bentler, P. M., & Savalei, V. (2010). Analysis of correlation structures: Current status and open problems. *Statistics in the Social Sciences: Current Methodological Developments*, 1–36.

Berkson, J. (1946). Limitations of the application of the four-fold table analysis to hospital data. *Biometrics Bulletin, 2*, 47–53.

Berlin, B. (1992). *Ethnobiological classification: Principles of categorization of plants and animals in traditional societies*. Princeton, NJ: Princeton University Press.

Bernstein, A., Stickle, T. R., Zvolensky, M. J., Taylor, S., Abramowitz, J., & Stewart, S. (2010). Dimensional, categorical or dimensional-categories: Testing the latent structure of anxiety sensitivity among adults using factor-mixture modeling. *Behavior Therapy, 41*, 515–529.

Berrios, G. E., & Hauser, R. (1988). The early development of Kraepelin's ideas on classification: A conceptual history. *Psychological Medicine, 18*, 813–821.

Blashfield, R. K. (1984). *The classification of psychopathology: Neo-Kraepelinian and quantitative approaches*. New York: Plenum Press.

Blashfield, R. K., & Keeley, J. (2010). A short history of a psychiatric diagnostic category that turned out to be a disease. In T. Millon, R. Krueger, & E. Simonsen (Eds.), *Contemporary directions in psychopathology* (pp. 324–336). New York: Guilford.

Blashfield, R. K., Keeley, J. W., Flanagan, E. H., & Miles, S. R. (2014). The cycle of classification: DSM-I through DSM-5. *Annual Review of Clinical Psychology*, 10, 25–51. https://doi-org.proxy.library.vcu.edu/10.1146/annurev-clinpsy-032813-153639

Blashfield, R. K., & Reynolds, S. M. (2012). An invisible college view of the DSM-5 personality disorder classification. *Journal of Personality Disorders*, 26, 821–829.

Borsboom, D., Cramer, A., Schmittmann, V., Epskamp, S., & Waldorp, L. (2011). The small world of psychopathology. *PLoS One*, 6, e27407. doi:10.1371/journal.pone.0027407

Boyd, J. H., Burke, J. D., Gruenberg, E., Holzer, C. E., Rae, D. S., George, L. K., et al. (1984). Exclusion criteria of DSM-III: A study of cooccurrence of hierarchy-free syndromes. *Archives of General Psychiatry*, 41, 983–989.

Bueter, A. (2019). A multi-dimensional pluralist response to the DSM-Controversies. *Perspectives on Science*, 27, 316–343. doi:10.1162/posc_a_00309

Campbell, D. T., & Fiske, D. W. (1959). Convergent and discriminant validation by the multitrait-multimethod matrix. *Psychological Bulletin*, 56, 81–105.

Campbell-Sills, L., & Brown, T. A. (2006). Research considerations: Latent variable approaches to studying the classification and psychopathology of mental disorders. In F. Andrasik (Ed.), *Comprehensive handbook of personality and psychopathology: Vol. 2. Adult psychopathology* (pp. 21–35). Hoboken, NJ: Wiley.

Cantor, N., Smith, E. E., French, R., & Mezzich, J. (1980). Psychiatric diagnosis as prototype categorization. *Journal of Abnormal Psychology*, 89, 181–193.

Carey, G., & Gottesman, I. I. (1978). Reliability and validity in binary ratings. *Archives of General Psychiatry*, 35, 1454–1459.

Caspi, A., Houts, R. M., Belsky, D. W., Goldman-Mellor, S. J., Harrington, H., Israel, S., Meier, M. H., Ramrakha, S., Shalev, I., Poulton, R., & Moffitt, T. E. (2014). The p factor: One general psychopathology factor in the structure of psychiatric disorders? *Clinical Psychological Science*, 2, 119–137. doi:10.1177/2167702613497473

Castiglioni, M., & Laudisa, F. (2014). Toward psychiatry as a "human" science of mind: The case of depressive disorders in DSM-5. *Frontiers in Psychology*, 5, 1517.

Chmielewski, M., Clark, L. A., Bagby, R. M., & Watson, D. (2015). Method matters: Understanding diagnostic reliability in DSM-IV and DSM-5. *Journal of Abnormal Psychology*, 124, 764–769. https://doi.org/10.1037/abn0000069

Cicero, D. C., Jonas, K. G., Li, K., Perlman, G., & Kotov, R. (2019). Common taxonomy of traits and symptoms: Linking schizophrenia symptoms, schizotypy, and normal personality. *Schizophrenia Bulletin*, 45, 1336–1348.

Clark, L. A. (2007). Assessment and diagnosis of personality disorder: Perennial issues and an emerging reconceptualization. *Annual Review of Psychology*, 58, 227–258.

Compton, W. M., & Guze, S. B. (1995). The neo-Kraepelinian revolution in psychiatric diagnosis. *European Archives of Psychiatry and Clinical Neuroscience*, 245, 196–201.

Conway, C. C., Latzman, R. D., & Krueger, R. F. (2020). A meta-structural model of common clinical disorder and personality disorder symptoms. *Journal of Personality Disorders*, 34, 88–106. https://doi.org/10.1521/pedi_2019_33_383

Cooper, R., & Blashfield, R. K. (2016). Re-evaluating DSM-I. *Psychological Medicine*, 46, 449–456.

Cooper, J. E., Kendell, R. E., Gurland, B. J., Sharpe, L., Copeland, J. R. M., & Simon, R. (1972). *Psychiatric diagnosis in New York and London* [Maudsley Monograph No. 20]. London: Oxford University Press.

Crego, C., Oltmanns, J. R., & Widiger, T. A. (2018). FFMPD scales: Comparisons with the FFM, PID-5, and CAT-PD-SF. *Psychological assessment*, 30, 62–73. https://doi.org/10.1037/pas0000495

Cronbach, L. J., & Meehl, P. E. (1955). Construct validity in psychological tests. *Psychological Bulletin*, 52, 281–302.

Dekkers, W., & Rikkert, M. O. (2006). What is a genetic cause? The example of Alzheimer's Disease. *Medicine, Health Care, and Philosophy*, 9, 273–284. doi:10.1007/s11019-006-9005-7

Drescher, J., Cohen-Kettenis, P., & Winter, S. (2012). Minding the body: Situating gender identity diagnoses in the ICD-11. *International Review of Psychiatry*, 24, 568–577.

Eaton, N. R., Krueger, R. F., Markon, K. E., Keyes, K. M., Skodol, A. E., Wall, M., Hasin, D. S., & Grant, B. F. (2013). The structure and predictive validity of the internalizing disorders. *Journal of Abnormal Psychology*, 122, 86–92.

Eaton, N. R., Keyes, K. M., Krueger, R. F., Balsis, S., Skodol, A. E., Markon, K. E., . . . Hasin, D. S. (2012). An invariant dimensional liability model of gender differences in mental disorder prevalence: Evidence from a national sample. *Journal of Abnormal Psychology*, 121, 282–288. http://dx.doi.org.proxy.library.vcu.edu/10.1037/a0024780

Eaton, N. R., Krueger, R. F., South, S. C., Simms, L. J., & Clark, L. A. (2011). Contrasting prototypes and dimensions in the classification of personality pathology: Evidence that dimensions, but not prototypes, are robust. *Psychological Medicine*, 41, 1151–1163.

Einfeld, S. L., & Aman, M. (1995). Issues in the taxonomy of psychopathology of mental retardation. *Journal of Autism and Developmental Disorders*, 25, 143–167.

Elklit, A., Hyland, P., & Shevlin, M. (2013). Evidence of symptom profiles consistent with posttraumatic stress disorder and complex posttraumatic stress disorder in different trauma samples. *European Journal of Psychotraumatology*, 5, 24221. doi:10.3402/ejpt.v5.24221

Evans, S. C., Reed, G. M., Roberts, M. C., Esparza, P., Watts, A. D., Correia, J. M., . . . Saxena, S. (2013). Psychologists' perspectives on the diagnostic classification of mental disorders: Results from the WHO-IUPsyS Global Survey. *International Journal of Psychology*, 48, 177–193.

Eysenck, H. J. (1947). *Dimensions of personality*. London: Routledge & Kegan Paul.

Eysenck, H. J., & Eysenck, S. B. (1976). *Psychoticism as a dimension of personality*. London: Hodder & Stoughton.

Farber, I. E. (1975). Sane and insane: Constructions and misconstructions. *Journal of Abnormal Psychology*, 84, 589–620.

Farmer, R. F., & Chapman, A. L. (2002). Evaluation of DSM-IV personality disorder criteria as assessed by the Structured Clinical Interview for DSM-IV Personality Disorders. *Comprehensive Psychiatry*, 43, 285–300.

Faust, D., & Miner, R. A. (1986). The empiricist and his new clothes: DSM-III in perspective. *American Journal of Psychiatry*, 143, 962–967.

Feinstein, A. R. (1970). The pre-therapeutic classification of comorbidity in chronic disease. *Journal of Chronic Diseases*, 23, 455–468.

First, M. B. (2009). Harmonization of ICD-11 and DSM-V: Opportunities and challenges. *British Journal of Psychiatry, 195*, 382–390.

First, M. B. (2010). Clinical utility in the revision of the Diagnostic and Statistical Manual of Mental Disorders (DSM). *Professional Psychology: Research and Practice, 41*, 465–473. doi:10.1037/a0021511

First, M. B., & Pincus, H. A. (2002). The *DSM-IV Text Revision*: Rationale and potential impact on clinical practice. *Psychiatric Services, 53*, 288–292.

First, M. B., Pincus, H. A., Levine, J. B., Williams, J. B. W., Ustun, B., & Peele, R. (2004). Clinical utility as a criterion for revising psychiatric diagnoses. *American Journal of Psychiatry, 161*, 946–954.

Follette, W. C., & Houts, A. C. (1996). Models of scientific progress and the role of theory in taxonomy development: A case study of the DSM. *Journal of Consulting and Clinical Psychology, 64*, 1120–1132.

Forbes, M., Tackett, J., Markon, K., & Krueger, R. (2016). Beyond comorbidity: Toward a dimensional and hierarchical approach to understanding psychopathology across the life span. *Development and Psychopathology, 28*, 971–986. doi:10.1017/S0954579416000651

Foucault, M. (1988). *Politics, philosophy, and culture*. London: Routledge.

Frances, A. (2014). *Saving normal: An insider's revolt against out-of-control psychiatric diagnosis, DSM-5, big pharma, and the medicalization of ordinary life*. New York: William Morrow.

Frances, A. J., & Widiger, T. (2012). Psychiatric diagnosis: Lessons from the DSM-IV past and cautions for the DSM-5 future. *Annual Review of Clinical Psychology, 8*, 109–130.

Fulford, K. W. M. (1999). Nine variations and a coda on the theme of an evolutionary definition of dysfunction. *Journal of Abnormal Psychology, 108*, 412–420.

Gelman, S. (2003). *The essential child: Origins of essentialism in everyday thought*. New York: Oxford University Press.

Ghaziuddin, M., & Gerstein, L. (1996). Pedantic speaking style differentiates Asperger syndrome from high-functioning autism. *Journal of Autism and Developmental Disorders, 26*(6), 585–595.

Goffman, E. (1959). The moral career of the mental patient. *Psychiatry, 22*, 123–142.

Goffman, E. (1963). *Stigma*. Englewood Cliffs, NJ: Prentice-Hall.

Grob, G. (1991). Origins of *DSM–I*: A study in appearance and reality. *American Journal of Psychiatry, 148*, 421–431.

Harkness, A., Reynolds, S., & Lilienfeld, S. (2014). A review of systems for psychology and psychiatry: Adaptive Systems, Personality Psychopathology Five (PSY-5), and the DSM-5. *Journal of Personality Assessment, 96*, 121–139.

Haslam, N. (2002). Kinds of kinds: A conceptual taxonomy of psychiatric categories. *Philosophy, Psychiatry, and Psychology, 9*, 203–217.

Haslam, N., Holland, E., & Kuppens, P. (2012). Categories versus dimensions in personality and psychopathology: A quantitative review of taxometric research. *Psychological Medicine, 42*, 903–920.

Haslam, N., McGrath, M., Viechtbauer, W., & Kuppens, P. (2020). Dimensions over categories: A meta-analysis of taxometric research. *Psychological Medicine, 50*, 1418–1432. doi:10.1017/S003329172000183X

Hatano, G., & Inagaki, K. (1994). Young children's naïve theory of biology. *Cognition, 50*, 171–188.

Havens, L. (1981). Twentieth-century psychiatry: A view from the sea. *American Journal of Psychiatry, 138*, 1279–1287.

Havens, L. (1985). Historical perspectives on diagnosis in psychiatry. *Comprehensive Psychiatry, 26*, 326–336.

Hickling, A., & Gelman, S. (1995). How does your garden grow? Evidence of an early conception of plants as biological kinds. *Child Development, 66*, 856–876.

Hilsenroth, M. J., Baity, M. R., Mooney, M. A., & Meyer, G. J. (2004). DSM–IV Major Depressive Episode criteria: An evaluation of reliability and validity across three different rating methods. *International Journal of Psychiatry in Clinical Practice, 8*, 3–10.

Hopwood, C. J., Morey, L. C., Donnellan, M. B., Samuel, D. B., Grilo, Carlos, M., . . . Skodol, A. E. (2013). Ten-year rank-order stability of personality traits and disorders in a clinical sample. *Journal of Personality, 81*, 335–344.

Houts, A. (2000). Fifty years of psychiatric nomenclature: Reflections on the 1943 War Department Technical Bulletin, Medical 203. *Journal of Clinical Psychology, 56*, 935–967.

Hull, D. L. (1988). *Science as a process*. Chicago: University of Chicago Press.

International Advisory Group for the Revision of ICD-10 Mental and Behavioural Disorders. (2011). A conceptual framework for the revision of the ICD-10 classification of mental and behavioural disorders. *World Psychiatry, 10*, 86–92.

Jablensky, A. (2016). Psychiatric classifications: Validity and utility. *World Psychiatry, 15*, 26–31. https://doi.org/10.1002/wps.20284

Jacobs, K. L., & Krueger, R. F. (2015). The importance of structural validity. In P. Zachar, D. Stoyanov, M. Aragona, & A. Jablensky (Eds.), *Alternative perspectives on psychiatric validation* (pp. 189–200). New York: Oxford University Press.

James, J. W., & Haley, W. E. (1995). Age and health bias in practicing clinical psychologists. *Psychology and Aging, 10*, 610–616.

Jaspers, K. (1963). *General psychopathology* (J. Hoenig & M. W. Hamilton, Trans.). Manchester, UK: University of Manchester Press.

Kahn, E. (1959). The Emil Kraepelin memorial lecture. In B. Pasamanick (Ed.), *Epidemiology of mental disorders* (pp. 1–38). Washington, DC: AAAS.

Kalish, C. W. (2007). Pragmatic and prescriptive aspects of children's categorization. In C. Kalish, & M. Sabbagh (Eds.), *Conventionality in cognitive development. New directions in child and adolescent development* (pp. 39–52). New York: Wiley.

Kamens, S. R., Cosgrove, L., Peters, S. M., Jones, N., Flanagan, E., Longden, E., Schulz, S., Robbins, B. D., Olsen, S., Miller, R., & Lichtenberg, P. (2019). Standards and guidelines for the development of diagnostic nomenclatures and alternatives in mental health research and practice. *Journal of Humanistic Psychology, 59*, 401–427. doi.org/10.1177/0022167818763862

Kamp-Becker, I., Smidt, J., Ghahreman, M., Heizel-Gutenbrunner, M., Becker, K., & Remschmidt, H. (2010). Categorical and dimensional structure of autism spectrum disorders: The nosologic validity of Asperger syndrome. *Journal of Autism and Developmental Disorders, 40*, 921–929.

Kanner, L. (1943). Autistic disturbances of affective contact. *Nervous Child, 2*(3), 217–250.

Keeley, J. W., Reed, G. M., Roberts, M., Evans, S., Medina-Mora, M. E., Robles, R., Rebello, T., Sharan, P., Gureje, O., First, M. B., Andrews, H. F., Ayuso-Mateos, J. L., Gaebel,

W., Zielasek, J., & Saxena, S. (2016). Developing a science of clinical utility in diagnostic classification systems: Field study strategies for ICD-11 Mental and Behavioural Disorders. *American Psychologist, 71*, 3–16.

Kendell, R. E. (1968). *The classification of depressive illness*. London: Oxford University Press.

Kendell, R. E. (1975). *The role of diagnosis in psychiatry*. Oxford, UK: Blackwell.

Kendell, R. E. (1989). Clinical validity. In L. N. Robins & J. E. Barrett (Eds.), *The validity of psychiatric diagnosis* (pp. 305–321). New York: Raven Press.

Kendell, R. E. (1990). A brief history of psychiatric classification in Britain. In N. Sartorius, A. Jablensky, D. A. Regier, J. D. Burke, Jr., & R. M. A. Hirschfeld (Eds.), *Sources and traditions of psychiatric classification* (pp. 139–151). Toronto, Canada: Hogrefe & Huber.

Kendell, R. E., Cooper, J. E., Gourlay, A. J., Sharpe, L., & Gurland, B. J. (1971). Diagnostic criteria of American and British psychiatrists. *Archives of General Psychiatry, 25*, 123–130.

Kessler, R. C., Chiu, W., Demler, O., & Walters, E. E. (2005). Prevalence, severity, and comorbidity of 12-month *DSM–IV* disorders in the National Comorbidity Survey Replication. *Archives of General Psychiatry, 62*, 617–627.

Kessler, R. C., McGonagle, K. A., Zhao, S., Nelson, C. B., Hughes, M., Eschlman, S., et al. (1994). Lifetime and 12-month prevalence of *DSM–III–R* psychiatric disorders in the United States: Results from the National Comorbidity Survey. *Archives of General Psychiatry, 51*, 8–19.

Kirk, S. A., & Kutchins, H. (1992). *The selling of DSM: The rhetoric of science in psychiatry*. Hawthorne, NY: William deGruyter.

Klein, D. (2010). Chronic depression: Diagnosis and classification. *Current Directions in Psychological Science, 19*, 96–100. doi:10.1177/0963721410366007

Klerman, G. L. (1978). The evolution of a scientific nosology. In J. C. Shershow (Ed.), *Schizophrenia: Science and practice* (pp. 99–121). Cambridge, MA: Harvard University Press.

Klin, A., & Volkmar, F. R. (2003). Asperger syndrome: Diagnosis and external validity. *Child and Adolescent Psychiatric Clinics, 12*, 1–13.

Kotov, R., Krueger, R. F., Watson, D., Achenbach, T. M., Althoff, R. R., Bagby, R. M., . . . Zimmerman, M. (2017). The Hierarchical Taxonomy of Psychopathology (HiTOP): A dimensional alternative to traditional nosologies. *Journal of Abnormal Psychology, 126*, 454–477. http://dx.doi.org/10.1037/abn0000258

Kraemer, H. C., Kupfer, D. J., Clarke, D. E., Narrow, W. E., & Regier, D. A. (2012). DSM-5: How reliable is reliable enough? *American Journal of Psychiatry, 169*, 13–15.

Kripke, S. (1980). *Naming and necessity*. Cambridge, MA: Harvard University Press.

Krueger, R. F. (1999). The structure of common mental disorders. *Archives of General Psychiatry, 56*, 921–926.

Krueger, R. F., Derringer, J., Markon, K. E., Watson, D., & Skodol, A. E. (2012). Initial construction of a maladaptive personality trait model and inventory for DSM-5. *Psychological Medicine, 42*, 1879–1890. doi:10.1017/S0033291711002674

Krueger, R. F., Eaton, N. R., Derringer, J., Markon, K. E., Watson, D., & Skodol, A. E. (2011). Personality in DSM-5: Helping delineate personality disorder content and framing the metastructure. *Journal of Personality Assessment, 93*, 325–331.

Krueger, R. F., & Markon, K. E. (2006). Reinterpreting comorbidity: A model-based approach to understanding and classifying psychopathology. *Annual Review of Clinical Psychology, 2*, 111–133.

Krueger, R. F., Markon, K. E., Patrick, C. J., & Iacono, W. G. (2005). Externalizing psychopathology in adulthood: A dimensional-spectrum conceptualization and its implications for *DSM–V*. *Journal of Abnormal Psychology, 114*, 537–550.

Kupfer, D. J., First, M. B., & Regier, D. E. (2002). *A research agenda for DSM–V*. Washington, DC: American Psychiatric Association.

Kutchins, H., & Kirk, S. A. (1997). *Making us crazy*. New York: Free Press.

La Roche, M. J., Fuentes, M. A., & Hinton, D. (2015). A cultural examination of the DSM-5: Research and clinical implications for cultural minorities. *Professional Psychology: Research and Practice, 46*, 183–189. doi:10.1037/a0039278

Lemoine, M. (2013). Defining disease beyond conceptual analysis: An analysis of conceptual analysis in philosophy of medicine. *Theoretical Medicine and Bioethics, 34*, 309–325. https://doi.org/10.1007/s11017-013-9261-5

Lenzenweger, M. F., Clarkin, J. F., Yeomans, F. E., Kernberg, O. F., & Levy, K. N. (2008). Refining the borderline personality disorder phenotype through finite mixture modeling: Implications for classification. *Journal of Personality Disorders, 22*, 313–331.

Lilienfeld, S. O. (2003). Comorbidity between and within childhood externalizing and internalizing disorders: Reflections and directions. *Journal of Abnormal Child Psychology, 31*, 285–291.

Lilienfeld, S. O., & Marino, L. (1995). Mental disorder as a Roschian concept: A critique of Wakefield's "harmful dysfunction" analysis. *Journal of Abnormal Psychology, 104*, 411–420.

Lilienfeld, S. O., Waldman, I. D., & Israel, A. C. (1994). A critical examination of the use of the term and concept of comorbidity in psychopathology research. *Clinical Psychology: Science and Practice, 1*, 71–83.

Littlewood, R. (1992). Psychiatric diagnosis and racial bias: Empirical and interpretive approaches. *Social Science and Medicine, 34*, 141–149.

Lorr, M. (Ed.). (1966). *Explorations in typing psychotics*. New York: Pergamon Press.

Maser, J. D., & Cloninger, C. R. (Eds.). (1990). *Comorbidity of mood and anxiety disorders*. Washington, DC: American Psychiatric Press.

Masserman, J. H., & Carmichael, H. T. (1938). Diagnosis and prognosis in psychiatry. *Journal of Mental Science, 84*, 893–946.

McCrae, R. R., & Costa, P. T. (1990). *Personality in adulthood*. New York: Guilford.

Meehl, P. E. (1995). Bootstraps taxometrics: Solving the classification problem in psychopathology. *American Psychologist, 50*, 266–275.

Menninger, K., Mayman, M., & Pruyser, P. (1963). *The vital balance*. New York: Viking Press.

Miller, J. N., & Ozonoff, S. (2000). The external validity of Asperger disorder: Lack of evidence from the domain of neuropsychology. *Journal of Abnormal Psychology, 109*, 227–238.

Millon, T. (1975). Reflections on Rosenhan's "On being sane in insane places." *Journal of Abnormal Psychology, 84,* 456–461.

Millon, T. (1983). The *DSM–III*: An insider's perspective. *American Psychologist, 38,* 804–814.

Moore, T. V. (1930). The empirical determination of certain syndromes underlying praecox and manic-depressive psychoses. *American Journal of Psychiatry, 86,* 719–738.

Morey, L. C. (1988). Personality disorders in the *DSM–III* and *DSM–III–R*: Convergence, coverage and internal consistency. *American Journal of Psychiatry, 145,* 573–577.

Morey, L. C., Benson, K. T., Busch, A. J., & Skodol, A. E. (2015). Personality disorders in DSM-5: Emerging research on the alternative model. *Current Psychiatry Reports, 17,* 24. https://doi.org/10.1007/s11920-015-0558-0

Muthen, B. (2006). Should substance use disorders be considered as categorical or dimensional? *Addiction, 101,* 6–16.

Muthen, L. K., & Muthen, B. O. (2010). *Mplus User's Guide.* 6th ed. Los Angeles, CA: Muthen & Muthen.

National Institute of Mental Health. (July, 2012). Research Domain Criteria (RDoC). http://www.nimh.nih.gov/research-funding/rdoc/index.shtml

Neumann, C. S., Johansson, P. T., & Hare, R. D. (2013). The Psychopathy Checklist-Revised (PCL-R), low anxiety, and fearlessness: A structural equation modeling analysis. *Personality Disorders: Theory, Research, and Treatment, 4,* 129–137.

Nguyen, S. P. (2008). Children's evaluative categories and inductive inferences within the domain of food. *Infant & Child Development, 17,* 285–299. https://doi-org.proxy.library.vcu.edu/10.1002/icd.553

Ozonoff, S., South, M., & Miller, J. N. (2000). *DSM-IV*-defined Asperger syndrome: Cognitive, behavioral and early history differentiation from high-functioning autism. *Autism, 4*(1), 29–46.

Paul, R., Orlovski, S. M., Marcinko, H. C., & Volkmar, F. (2009). Conversational behaviors in youth with high-functioning ASD and Asperger syndrome. *Journal of Autism and Developmental Disorders, 39,* 115–125.

Picardi, A., Viroli, C., Tarsitani, L., Miglio, R., de Girolamo, G., Dell'Acqua, G., & Biondi, M. (2012). Heterogeneity and symptom structure of schizophrenia. *Psychiatry Research, 198,* 386–394.

Poland, J. (2016). DSM-5 and Research Concerning Mental Illness. In S. Demazeux & P. Singy (Eds.), *DSM-5 in perspective: Philosophical reflections on the psychiatric Babel.* New York: Springer. doi:10.1007/978-94-017-9765-8

Putnam, D. (1982). Natural kinds and human artifacts. *Mind, 91,* 418–419.

Reed, G. (2010). Toward ICD-11: Improving the clinical utility of WHO's International Classification of Mental Disorders. *Professional Psychology: Research and Practice, 41,* 457–464.

Reed, G. M., Correia, J., Esparza, P., Saxena, S., & Maj, M. (2011). The WPA-WHO global survey of psychiatrists' attitudes towards mental disorders classification. *World Psychiatry, 10,* 118–131.

Reed, G. M., Roberts, M. C., Keeley, J., Hoopell, C., Matsumoto, C., Sharan, P., . . . Medina-Mora, M. E. (2013). Mental health professionals' natural taxonomies of mental disorders: Implications for clinical utility of ICD-11 and DSM-5. *Journal of Clinical Psychology, 69,* 1191–1212.

Reed, G. M., Robles, R., & Domínguez-Martínez, T. (2016). Classification of mental and behavioral disorders. In J. C. Norcross, G. R. VandenBos, & D. K. Freedheim (Eds.), *APA handbook of clinical psychology.* Washington, DC: American Psychological Association.

Reed, G. M., Sharan, P., Rebello, T. J., Keeley, J. W., Elena Medina-Mora, M., Gureje, O., . . . Pike, K. M. (2018). The ICD-11 developmental field study of reliability of diagnoses of high-burden mental disorders: Results among adult patients in mental health settings of 13 countries. *World Psychiatry, 17,* 174–186. https://doi.org/10.1002/wps.20524

Regier, D. A., Kuhl, E. A., Narrow, W. E., & Kupfer, D. J. (2012). Research planning for the future of psychiatric diagnosis. *European Psychiatry, 27,* 553–556.

Regier, D. A., Narrow, W. E., Clarke, D. E., Kraemer, H. C., Kuramoto, S. J., Kuhl, E. A., & Kupfer, D. J. (2013). DSM-5 field trials in the United States and Canada, part II: Test-retest reliability of selected categorical diagnoses. *American Journal of Psychiatry, 170,* 59–70.

Rettew, D. C., Lynch, A. D., Achenbach, T. M., Dumenci, L., & Ivanova, M. Y. (2009). Meta-analyses of agreement between diagnoses made from clinical evaluations and standardized diagnostic interviews. *International Journal of Methods in Psychiatric Research, 18,* 169–184.

Richters, J. E., & Cicchetti, D. (1993). Mark Twain meets *DSM–III–R*: Conduct disorder, development, and the concept of harmful dysfunction. *Development and Psychopathology, 5,* 5–29.

Roberts, M., Medina-Mora, M., Reed, G., Keeley, J., Sharan, P., Johnson, D., Mari, J., Ayuso-Mateos, J., Gureje, O., Xiao, Z., Maruta, T., Khoury, B., Robles, R., & Saxena, S. (2012). A global clinicians' map of mental disorders to improve ICD-11. *International Review of Psychiatry, 24,* 578–590.

Robins, E., & Guze, S. B. (1970). Establishment of diagnostic validity in psychiatric illness: Its application to schizophrenia. *American Journal of Psychiatry, 126,* 983–987.

Rogers, S. J., & Ozonoff, S. (2005). Annotation: What do we know about sensory dysfunction in autism? A critical review of the empirical evidence. *Journal of Child Psychology and Psychiatry, 46*(12), 1255–1268.

Rogler, L. H. (1997). Making sense of historical changes in the Diagnostic and Statistical Manual of Mental Disorders: Five propositions. *Journal of Health and Social Behavior, 38,* 9–20.

Rosenhan, D. (1973). On being sane in insane places. *Science, 114,* 316–322.

Sadler, J. Z. (2005). *Values and psychiatric diagnosis.* New York: Oxford University Press.

Sadler, J. Z., & Agich, G. (1995). Diseases, functions, values, and psychiatric classification. *Philosophy, Psychiatry, and Psychology, 2,* 219–231.

Samuel, D. B., Sanislow, C. A., Hopwood, C. J., Shea, M. T., Skodol, A. E., Morey, L. C., Ansell, E. B., Markowitz, J. C., Zanarini, M. C., & Grilo, C. M. (2013). Convergent and incremental predictive validity of clinician, self-report, and structured interview diagnoses for personality disorders over 5 years. *Journal of Consulting and Clinical Psychology, 81,* 650–659. https://doi.org/10.1037/a0032813

Sarbin, T. R. (1997). On the futility of psychiatric diagnostic manuals (*DSM*s) and the return of personal agency. *Applied and Preventive Psychology, 6,* 233–243.

Sartorius, N. (1990). Classifications in the field of mental health. *World Health Statistics Quarterly, 43,* 269–272.

Scheff, T. J. (1966). *Being mentally ill: A sociological theory.* Chicago: Aldine.

Scheff, T. J. (1975). *Labeling madness.* Englewood Cliffs, NJ: Prentice-Hall.

Schmidt, N. B., Kotov, R., & Joiner, T. E. (2004). *Taxometrics: Towards a new diagnostic scheme for psychopathology*. Washington, DC: American Psychological Association.

Sedler, M. (2016). Medicalization in psychiatry: The medical model, descriptive diagnosis, and lost knowledge. *Medicine, Health Care, and Philosophy, 19*(2), 247–252.

Skodol, A. E. (2012). Personality disorders in DSM-5. *Annual Review of Clinical Psychology, 8*, 317–344. https://doi.org/10.1146/annurev-clinpsy-032511-143131

Smith, K. (2001). A disease by any other name: Musings on the concept of genetic disease. *Medicine, Health Care, and Philosophy, 4*, 19–30.

Smith, G. T., & Combs, J. (2010). Issues of construct validity in psychological diagnoses. In T. Million, R. F. Krueger, & E. Simonsen (Eds.), *Contemporary directions in psychopathology scientific foundations of the DSM-V and ICD-11* (pp. 205–222). New York: Guilford.

Spitzer, R. L. (1975). On pseudoscience in science, logic in remission and psychiatric diagnosis: A critique of Rosenhan's "On being sane in insane places." *Journal of Abnormal Psychology, 84*, 442–452.

Spitzer, R., & Endicott, J. (1978). Medical and mental disorder: Proposed definition and criteria. In R. Spitzer & D. Klein (Eds.), *Critical issues in psychiatric diagnosis* (pp. 15–40). New York: Raven Press.

Spitzer, R. L., & Fleiss, J. L. (1975). A reanalysis of the reliability of psychiatric diagnosis. *British Journal of Psychiatry, 125*, 341–347.

Spitzer, R., Sheehy, M., & Endicott, J. (1977). *DSM–III*: Guiding principles. In V. Rakoff, H. Stancer, & H. Kedward (Eds.), *Psychiatric diagnosis*. New York: Brunner/Mazel.

Spitzer, R., & Wakefield, J. (1999). *DSM–IV* diagnostic criterion for clinical significance: Does it help solve the false positives problem? *American Journal of Psychiatry, 156*, 1856–1864.

Spitzer, R. L., & Williams, J. B. W. (1980). Classification in psychiatry. In H. I. Kaplan, A. M. Freeman, & B. J. Sadock. (Eds.), *Comprehensive textbook of psychiatry III* (pp. 1035– 1072). Baltimore: Williams & Wilkins.

Spitznagel, E. L., & Helzer, J. E. (1985). A proposed solution to the base rate problem in the kappa statistic. *Archives of General Psychiatry, 44*, 1069–1077.

Stengel, E. (1959). Classification of mental disorders. *Bulletin of the World Health Organization, 21*, 601–663.

Stone, M. H. (1997). *Healing the mind: A history of psychiatry from antiquity to the present*. New York: Norton.

Szasz, T. S. (1961). *The myth of mental illness*. New York: Hoeber-Harper.

Szatmari, P., Bartolucci, G., & Bremner, R. (1989). Asperger's syndrome and autism: Comparison of early history and outcome. *Developmental Medicine and Child Neurology, 31*, 709–720.

Szatmari, P., Bryson, S., Duku, E., Vaccarella, L., Zwaigenbaum, L., Bennett, T., & Boyle, M. H. (2009). Similar developmental trajectories in autism and Asperger syndrome: From early childhood to adolescence. *Journal of Child Psychology and Psychiatry, 50*, 1459–1467. doi:10.1111/j.1469-7610.2009.02123.x

Thurstone, L. L. (1934). The vectors of the mind. *Psychological Review, 41*, 1–32.

Tyrer, P., Reed, G. M., & Crawford, M. J. (2015). Classification, assessment, prevalence, and effect of personality disorder. *Lancet, 385*, 717–726.

Vanheule, S., Desmet, M., Meganck, R., Inslegers, R., Willemsen, J., De Schryver, M., & Devisch, I. (2014). Reliability in psychiatric diagnosis with the DSM: Old wine in new barrels. *Psychotherapy and Psychosomatics, 83*, 313–314. https://doi.org/10.1159/000358809

van Loo, H. M., de Jonge, P., Romeijn, J-W., Kessler, R. C., & Schoevers, R. (2012). Data-driven subtypes of major depressive disorder: A systematic review. *BMC Medicine, 10*, 156. doi:10.1186/1741-7015-10-156

Verheul, R. (2005). Clinical utility for dimensional models of personality pathology. *Journal of Personality Disorders, 19*, 283–302.

Verheul, R., & Widiger, T. A. (2004). A metaanalysis of the prevalence and usage of the personality disorder not otherwise specified (PDNOS) diagnosis. *Journal of Personality Disorders, 18*, 309–319.

Via, E., Radua, J., Cardoner, N., Happé, F., & Mataix-Cols, D. (2011). Meta-analysis of gray matter abnormalities in autism spectrum disorder: Should Asperger disorder be subsumed under a broader umbrella of autistic spectrum disorder?. *Journal of General Psychiatry, 68*, 409–418. doi:10.1001/archgenpsychiatry.2011.27.

Wakefield, J. (1992a). The concept of mental disorder: On the boundary between biological facts and social values. *American Psychologist, 47*, 373–388.

Wakefield, J. (1992b). Disorder as harmful dysfunction: A conceptual critique of *DSM–III–R's* definition of mental disorder. *Psychological Review, 99*, 232–247.

Wakefield, J. C. (1993). Limits of operationalization: A critique of Spitzer and Endicott's (1978) proposed operational criteria for mental disorder. *Journal of Abnormal Psychology, 102*, 160–172.

Wakefield, J. C. (1999). Evolutionary versus prototype analyses of the concept of disorder. *Journal of Abnormal Psychology, 108*, 374–399.

Wakefield, J. C. (2016). Diagnostic issues and controversies in DSM-5: Return of the false positives problem. *Annual Review of Clinical Psychology, 12*, 105–132. https://doi.org/10.1146/annurev-clinpsy-032814-112800

Wambolt, M., Kaslow, N., & Reiss, D. (2015). Description of relational processes: Recent changes in DSM-5 and proposals for ICD-11. *Family Process, 54*, 6–16. doi:10.1111/famp.12120

Ward, C. H., Beck, A. T., Mendelson, M., Mock, J. E., & Erbaugh, J. K. (1962). The psychiatric nomenclature. *Archives of General Psychiatry, 8*, 198–205.

Watson, D., Clark, L. A., & Chmielewski, M. (2008). Structures of personality and their relevance to psychopathology: II. Further articulation of a comprehensive unified trait structure. *Journal of Personality, 76*, 1545–1586.

Weiner, B. (1975). "On being sane in insane places": A process (attributional) analysis and critique. *Journal of Abnormal Psychology, 84*, 433–441.

Widiger, T. A., & Crego, C. (2019). The bipolarity of normal and abnormal personality structure: Implications for assessment. *Psychological Assessment, 31*, 420–431. https://doi.org/10.1037/pas0000546

Widiger, T. A., & Samuel, D. B. (2005). Diagnostic categories or dimensions? A question for the *Diagnostic and Statistical Manual of Mental Disorders—Fifth Edition*. *Journal of Abnormal Psychology, 114*, 494–504.

Widiger, T. A., Simonsen, E., Krueger, R., Livesley, W., & Verheul, R. (2005). Personality disorder research agenda for the *DSM–V*. *Journal of Personality Disorders, 19*, 315–338.

Wilamowska, Z. A., Thompson-Hollands, J., Fairholme, C. P., Ellard, K. K., Farchione, T. J., & Barlow, D. H. (2010). Conceptual background, development, and preliminary data from the unified protocol for transdiagnostic treatment of emotional disorders. *Depression and Anxiety, 27*, 882–890.

Wing, L. (1981). Asperger syndrome: A clinical account. *Psychological Medicine, 11*, 115–130.

Wing, L. (2000). Past and future research on Asperger syndrome. In A. Klin & F. Volkmar (Eds.), *Asperger syndrome* (418–432). New York: Guilford.

Wolf, E. J., Miller, M. W., Kilpatrick, D., Resnick, H. S., Badour, C. L., Marx, B. P., Keane, T. M., Rosen, R. C., & Friedman, M. J. (2015). ICD-11 complex PTSD in U.S. national and veteran samples: Prevalence and structural associations with PTSD. *Clinical Psychological Science, 3*, 215–229.

World Health Organization. (1948). *Manual of international statistical classification of diseases, injuries, and causes of death* (6th rev.). Geneva: Author.

World Health Organization. (1968). *Manual of international statistical classification of diseases, injuries, and causes of death* (8th rev.). Geneva: Author.

World Health Organization. (1977). *Manual of international statistical classification of diseases, injuries, and causes of death* (9th rev.). Geneva: Author.

World Health Organization. (1992). *Manual of international statistical classification of diseases, injuries, and causes of death* (10th rev.). Geneva: Author.

Wright, A. G., Krueger, R. F., Hobbs, M. J., Markon, K. E., Eaton, N. R., & Slade, T. (2013). The structure of psychopathology: Toward an expanded quantitative empirical model. *Journal of Abnormal Psychology, 122*, 281–294.

Yoon, C. K. (2009). *Naming nature.* New York: Norton.

Zachar, P. (2000). Psychiatric disorders are not natural kinds. *Philosophy, Psychiatry, and Psychology, 7*, 167–182.

Zachar, P., Krueger, R. F., & Kendler, K. S. (2016). Personality disorder in DSM-5: An oral history. *Psychological Medicine, 46*, 1–10. doi:10.1017/S0033291715001543

Zanarini, M. C., Skodol, A. E., Bender, D., Dolan, R., Sanislow, C., Schaefer, E., et al. (2000). The collaborative longitudinal personality disorders study: II. Reliability of Axis I and Axis II diagnoses. *Journal of Personality Disorders, 14*, 291–299.

Zimmerman, M., Rothschild, L., & Chelminski, I. (2005). The prevalence of DSM–IV personality disorders in psychiatric outpatients. *American Journal of Psychiatry, 162*, 1911–1918.

Zubin, J. (1967). Classification of the behavior disorders. *Annual Review of Psychology, 18*, 373–406.

# CHAPTER 2

# Historical and Philosophical Considerations in Studying Psychopathology

Peter Zachar, Konrad Banicki, *and* Awais Aftab

## Introduction

In this chapter, our account of historical and philosophical considerations in studying psychopathology emphasizes how, across the ages, psychopathologists have grappled with whether a descriptive or hypothetical-conjectural approach best promotes the advancement of knowledge. To explain what we mean by this, let us explore a related but distinct contrast—that between syndromic versus causal/etiological approaches.

The syndromic approach has typically relied on descriptions of surface-level phenomena (i.e., signs and symptoms) and is referred to as "descriptive" for that reason. Because the causes of psychiatric disorders have been poorly understood (and continue to remain so due to the complex nature of these conditions), the causal approach has been dominated by conjectural hypotheses for the most part. The contrast between syndromic and etiological approaches has therefore played out as a contrast between descriptive and conjectural approaches, but this is not always the case. Syndromic approaches can be conjectural (e.g., the syndromic entity of "hysteria" is widely contested), and etiological approaches can be descriptive (e.g., reporting that syphilis is the cause of general paresis).

In fact, whether we consider something a description or a conjecture is a theoretical issue that depends on background assumptions. Consider Galileo Galilei's (*1564–1642*) description of the four moons of Jupiter. What Galileo saw through his telescope were points of light near the planet Jupiter, which he initially considered to be distant stars. He soon realized, however, that the movements of these points of light did not match the movements of the stars. In his model of the galaxy, the stars do not move relative to each other because they are all very far away. Jupiter does move relative to the stars because it is a planet within our solar system and relatively close to us. These four points of light were also moving relative to the stars and remaining within proximity of Jupiter. In Galileo's model of the solar system, as one planet orbiting the Sun—the Earth—has a moon, other planets could have moons as well. Galileo concluded that the four points of light are moons of Jupiter.

Some of Galileo's contemporaries were not persuaded that these points of light could be described as moons—in part because they had doubts about using telescopes to view far distant events. Whether claims about the moons of Jupiter are considered more descriptive or more conjectural depend on various background theories about optics and the organization of the solar system and the galaxy. If you accept these theories, reports of moons orbiting Jupiter will be considered descriptions. The more agreement there is on the background theoretical assumptions, the less disagreement there is on "what" is being described. This suggests that what are considered "descriptive" approaches to psychopathology are approaches where there has been comparative agreement among multiple parties regarding the background assumptions.

One can also look to history to see how the lines have shifted. In the 1950s, the Freudian theory of the Oedipus complex was widely accepted and reporting that a patient has Oedipal conflicts would have been treated as a description. In one version of the Oedipal situation, a young boy has a strong attachment to his mother and may see his father as a rival. According to the Oedipus complex theory, this tension is resolved if the boy forgoes a special relationship with his mother as something unobtainable and identifies with his father. Today, there are still men who desire a seemingly unobtainable relationship and lose interest in it if they ever do obtain it in favor of a new hard-to-obtain relationship, but this is rarely described as an unresolved Oedipal conflict. The Freudian theoretical framework is no longer a taken-for-granted background.

New descriptions can also make previously unnoticed things apparent if their background assumptions are also accepted. For example, in the late 1970s, the conditions of being a Holocaust survivor who isolates himself from interpersonal attachments, a rape victim having flashbacks, and a combat veteran who has panic attacks when exposed to sudden loud sounds were all classified as posttraumatic stress disorder (PTSD) (Scott, 1990; Zachar & McNally, 2017). Once a conjecture that there are chronic, trauma-produced disorders became a background assumption, it became apparent that these different conditions were all variations of the same phenomenon.

Others, however, believe that describing trauma as the cause of "PTSD" symptoms is an implausible conjecture. Instead, they argue that temperaments, personality traits, family history, and previous experiences with psychiatric distress can produce a range of disorders such as depression, addiction, and personality disorders. In their view, these disorders can all be associated with nonspecific symptoms such as feeling estranged from others, diminished interest in pleasure, and sleep problems, which in many cases are incorrectly being described as PTSD and "explained" by a faddish assumption of how the mind deals with trauma (McHugh & Treisman, 2007).

Conjecture, importantly, can take us beyond what is readily apparent—with the goal being that the conjectures of today articulate the descriptions of tomorrow. Throughout the history of psychopathology, however, when conjecture was seen as taking us too far beyond anything apparent in an agreed upon sense, there were calls to limit claims to what are more readily considered to be descriptions. When someone believes a conjecture is too tenuous, they may say "don't speculate, just describe."

In this chapter we will follow a tug of war between description and conjecture from the seventeenth to the early twenty-first century. More recently, some opposition has arisen to the descriptive psychopathology model of the *DSM-III* and its successors—with a renewed focus on discovering the hidden causes of disorders. This raises questions about the nature of causality and the relationship between mind and body, which we will briefly explore. We conclude the chapter by looking at how more descriptive versus more conjectural commitments continue to assert themselves in the study of psychopathology in the contrast between scientific realism and scientific anti-realism.

## A Tug of War Between Description and Conjecture

Our account begins with what historians such as Porter (1987) call the "long eighteenth century," which encompasses developments in the seventeenth century associated with the beginning of modern philosophy and the culmination of the Scientific Revolution. In England, the Scientific Revolution's center of gravity was the Royal Society of London.

Medical knowledge was an important focus of the Royal Society (Porter, 1989). One of the most revered physicians of the day, Thomas Sydenham (*1624–1689*), was never invited to join the Royal Society due to his cantankerous personality. He was, however, close to two Royal Society luminaries, the chemist Robert Boyle (*1627–1691*) and the philosopher John Locke (*1632–1704*). Locke was also a physician, and both he and Boyle joined Sydenham at the bedside of Sydenham's patients (Anstey, 2011; Cunningham, 1989). These three thinkers mutually influenced each other and, as conveyed through the writings of Locke, introduced the philosophy of empiricism.

*Empiricism* is often defined as the view that all knowledge begins with experience and therefore there are no innate ideas, but this definition does not fully capture empiricism in the philosopher's sense. Prior to making claims about the role of experience and observation, the empiricists were skeptical about hypothetical notions such as the Divine Right of Kings and Papal Infallibility. In the seventeenth century, people were killing each other over such notions. By emphasizing the importance of being verified in experience, the empiricists could relegate these conjectures to the domain of an unverifiable "metaphysics."

Empiricism as a philosophy has evolved over the centuries (Quine, 1951; Sellars, 1956; van Fraassen, 2002). This includes abandoning the view that our knowledge of the world is grounded in observation alone. Contemporary empiricism acknowledges that observation occurs in cooperation with background assumptions. Two features, however, are shared by empiricists across the ages, and these features should be kept in mind when we refer to empiricism throughout the rest of the chapter. These are:

a. Experience is partial, so our knowledge about the world is provisional and potentially revisable.
b. Our proclivity for making conjectures can result in the adoption of strong commitments to abstract concepts, such as immortal souls, special life forces, and Oedipal conflicts, that are remote from any consideration of fact.

## From Speculative to Descriptive Medicine (Seventeenth Century)

The Scientific Revolution dismantled the dominance of Aristotelian philosophy in the scholarly community. Its target was not only Aristotle's (384–322 BCE) theories of motion used in astronomy and elsewhere but the speculative Aristotelian essentialism. For Aristotle, the essence (or nature) of a thing is what makes something be what it is. Aristotelians believed that human beings possess a specific intellectual faculty for knowing essences.

In seventeenth-century medicine, the dominant perspective was called the *Galenist tradition*. The Galenists explained health and disease with respect to the theory of the four humors, specifically blood, phlegm, yellow bile, and black bile. According to this theory, having the right balance of humors was the essence of health, imbalance the essence of disease. For instance, excessive black bile was associated with melancholia, excessive blood and yellow bile with mania. Treatments such as bloodletting, purgatives, and emetics aimed at restoring balance.

The theory that diseases are due to humoral imbalances has been rejected by medical science. Furthermore, nothing in modern physiology corresponds to black bile. The notion that these conjectures about the essences of disease were mistaken and therefore not about anything real raises the question about the relation between scientific conjectures and reality in general. We return to this issue in the final section of the chapter.

In contrast to the conjectural approach of the Galenists, Sydenham favored using trial and error to discover which treatments work (Bynum, 1993; Cunningham, 1989). Much of Sydenham's practice involved working with epidemics, such as smallpox. This gave him an opportunity to see large numbers of cases during outbreaks and describe what is called the *natural history of diseases*.[1] In addition to symptom presentation, these natural history descriptions included identifying precipitants and time courses. They also included noting the effects of interventions and experiments.

The Galenist physicians of the day criticized Sydenham for adopting this nontheoretical, practical approach, accusing him of being aligned with the quack doctors who relied on their own experience to treat symptoms rather selecting treatments to counteract theoretically inferred humoral imbalances (Wear, 1989). A common pejorative for these quack doctors was "empirics."

Working closely with Sydenham, Locke (1689/1997) famously introduced a distinction between real essences (hidden natures) and nominal essences (observable features we use to identify kinds) and argued that, for things like diseases, we do not know real essences, only nominal essences. For Locke, natural history descriptions did not eschew causes, only conjectures about ultimate causes and essences. Sydenham, for example, emphasized less speculative proximate causes. This is illustrated in Sydenham's (1682) essay on hysteria, which he believed to be a family of different symptom presentations shared by women and men.

> It would take up too much time to enumerate all the symptoms belonging to hysteric diseases; so much do they vary, and differ from each other.... Nor do they only differ so greatly, but are so irregular likewise, that they cannot be comprehended under any uniform appearance, as is usual in other diseases; but are a kind of disorderly train of symptoms, so that 'tis a difficult task to write the history of this disease. The *Procatarctic* [i.e., predisposing], or *external causes* thereof are either violent motions of the body, or, more frequently some great commotion of mind ... either of anger, grief, terror, or the like passions. (p. 223)

In addition to describing the relevant proximate causes of hysteria, this quote from Sydenham illustrates another important feature of seventeenth-century medicine: its awareness of what Porter (1987) called the *protean* nature of psychiatric

---

[1] As with most thinkers in this period, innovations were gradual and Sydenham held a mix of older and new ideas, including humoral notions.

problems. By "protean" Porter meant that, for any one person, what symptoms he or she experiences can be continually changing and fluid. Melancholia, mania, hysteria, and hypochondriasis could merge into each other as the symptom picture shifted. Complicating the job of the historian, the concepts of the seventeenth century had only passing resemblances to our current concepts. For example, hypochondriasis was the male version of hysteria. Jointly, hysteria and hypochondriasis encompassed many internalizing symptoms: depressions, anxieties, phobias, traumas, and somatic concerns.

## From Immortal Souls and Disturbed Bodies to Disturbed Minds (Eighteenth Century)

The first half of the eighteenth century was not much different than the last half of the seventeenth. In these years, many new descriptions of diseases were articulated, but reliance on conjecture continued unabated in medicine (Ackerknecht, 1982). During this time period there were genuine advances in the natural sciences, but attempts to apply them to medicine, called *iatro-physics* and *iatro-chemistry*, consisted in conjectures about nerve vibrations and intestinal fermentations—shifting from humors to anatomy, but still mostly conjectural.

The eighteenth century also saw the rise of fashionable nervous diseases in works like George Cheyne's (*1672–1743*) monograph of 1733, *The English Malady*, the focus of which was hysteria, hypochondriasis, and melancholia. Cheyne did not work in a mental asylum; rather, he was a society physician or "spa doctor," tending to the affluent (Shorter, 1997). These difficulties became fashionable in part because they were more likely to manifest in those who were prosperous.

We cannot assume that the people living in past centuries shared the same background assumptions about the mind and its disorders that we do. Suzuki (1995) argued that the concept of mind that was dominant during the seventeenth and early eighteenth century was intimately associated with the soul, which was considered to be immortal and therefore not subject to decay and disease. The body, however, as a window to the soul, was not immortal and could become diseased. This meant that mental faculties considered essential to human nature, such as reason and judgment, remained intact but could be indirectly affected by illusory sensory images produced by lower faculties such as imagination and memory which were directly affected by alterations in the body.

For hysterical complaints in women, one popular conjecture was that the womb gave off toxic vapors—indeed suffering from "the vapors" became a common diagnosis. Likewise, melancholic and hypochondriacal men were said to be suffering from "the spleen." Various notions about the gastrointestinal nature of hysteria and hypochondriasis persisted even into the next century. In Charles Dicken's (*1812–1870*) novella *A Christmas Carol*, published in 1843, when Marley's ghost asked Scrooge why he doubted his sense experience, which clearly indicated that Marely was sitting there before him, Scrooge replied,

> Because . . . a little thing affects them. A slight disorder of the stomach makes them cheats. You may be an undigested bit of beef, a blot of mustard, a crumb of cheese, a fragment of an underdone potato. There's more of gravy than of grave about you, whatever you are! (pp. 20–21)

And later, Scrooge says,

> You see this toothpick?" . . . I have but to swallow this, and be for the rest of my days persecuted by a legion of goblins, all of my own creation. Humbug, I tell you! Humbug! (p. 21)

The Enlightenment movement in the eighteenth century was a cultural phenomenon too diverse to be adequately described here. Besides spawning both the American and French Revolutions, the Enlightenment advocated for a thoroughgoing naturalism. By *naturalism*, we mean Enlightenment thinkers began banishing theological and supernatural assumptions from science in a way that would have been shocking to seventeenth-century Christian thinkers such as Boyle and Locke.

During the Enlightenment, references to the soul became optional, even questionable, and an important change occurred in which the mind was no longer co-extensive with an incorruptible soul. The mind became naturalized. After this separation, it became theoretically possible for the mind itself to be directly diseased (i.e., a concept of actual *psychopathology* was introduced). Suzuki (1995) has suggested that in this new psychological model, rather than illusory sensory images being presented to an intact faculty of reason, a directly disturbed faculty of reason actively misperceived intact sensory images.

With this new concept of mental disorder came the potential for specialization. As Porter (1987) argued, throughout eighteenth century, private asylums were established with care varying from poor to quite good and humane. Many physicians used their own homes to supplement their incomes and, over time, came to think of managing mental disorder as their area of expertise. As early as 1758, William Battie's *(1703–1776) Treatise on Madness* argued that hospitals for the insane should be asylums that promote recovery, not warehouses where patients are locked away and chained up. This approach came to be known as "moral treatment," where *moral* treatment primarily in this context meant humane and psychological.

Histories of psychopathology usually describe moral treatment as a revolutionary development introduced in the 1790s at the York Retreat in England and by Phillipe Pinel *(1745–1826)* in Paris. Porter (1987), however, claimed that the York Retreat and Pinel's reforms are better seen as banging the drum about an important change in outlook that had already been occurring for some time. Within the medical profession, this change was likely irreversible when, in 1788, the physicians of King George III of England *(1738–1820)* admitted that they had failed to cure his debilitating mental problems and turned his treatment over to private asylum physicians who specialized in mental disorder.

## The Development of a Descriptive Clinical Science (Nineteenth Century)

In the first part of the nineteenth century, optimism about the therapeutic value of the asylum resulted in new institutions being founded throughout Europe. With the opportunity to observe large numbers of cases, many new descriptions of disorders were articulated. These included descriptions of "partial insanity" conditions such as paranoia and obsessiveness that were not as severe as the cases of mania and dementia treated by the asylum doctors but were more serious than the hysteria and hypochondriasis treated by the spa doctors. By mid-century, the asylums were asked to accommodate more patients than they could handle—especially patients with severe problems. As chronic cases increased, the asylums ceased to be therapeutic environments, and became warehouses.

The growth of asylums occurred at the same time that German and Austrian countries invented what we would recognize as the modern research university. By *modern research university* we mean one that trains graduate students and postdoctoral students to be producers of knowledge. Prior to the Franco-Prussian war which resulted in the unification of Germany in 1871, the German Confederation was made up of more than 40 independent states, many of them with their own flagship university. Professorships were prestigious appointments, and the competition for them was stiff. To even teach as an adjunct (or *privatdocent*), one had to complete a habilitation thesis (i.e., sustained postdoctoral scholarship demonstrating one's ability to make an independent contribution to the knowledge base). Due to this institutional structure, the German research universities became hotbeds of scholarly activity.

Several new departments of psychiatry were created at this time and, after mid-century, began establishing their own clinics—a trend initiated in 1865 by the Berlin psychiatrist Wilhelm Griesinger *(1817–1868)*. After the unification of Germany, the leading research psychiatrist of his day was Theodor Meynert *(1833–1892)* at the University of Vienna (and one of Sigmund Freud's most admired mentors). University psychiatrists such as Meynert viewed asylum patients as incurable and had no interest in clinical practice or promulgating psychological descriptions (Shorter, 1997). They were academics searching for the anatomical causes of diseases. As Meynert wrote,

> The study of human anatomy in its current form has passed from a solely descriptive science to something higher, to a form of knowledge that attempts to explain. (quoted in Shorter, 1997, p. 77)

Asylum doctors opined that the researchers were interested in brain tissues, not people. The academics, an elite group, disparaged the scientific/medical qualifications of the asylum doctors and saw them as standing in the way of progress (Harrington, 2019).

Meynert and his students' search for the pathological anatomy of mental disorders did not succeed. Thus, beginning in 1896, Emile Kraepelin *(1856–1926)* reemphasized natural history descriptions in contrast with what he considered the conjectural brain mythology of the Meynert school. Kraepelin studied with Wilhelm Wundt *(1832–1920)*, who is widely considered the founder of scientific psychology (Engstrom & Kendler, 2015). The reason most of the credit for founding the discipline of psychology is attributed to Wundt is that he started a journal, founded a lab to train doctoral students, and wrote textbooks. Kraepelin argued that Wundt's new experimental psychology was natural science. Psychiatry, Kraepelin believed, was a clinical science—a science of psychopathology. It should draw on the biological sciences but its descriptions should also be consistent with the new science of psychology.

As noted above, during these years, hysteria and hypochondriasis referred to broad collections of depressions, fears, somatic concerns, emotional lability, and so on. In the asylum setting, the category of mania, encompassing delusions, agitations, paranoia, obsessions, and impulsivity, was also broader than it is today. In the 1860s, the private asylum doctor Karl Kahlbaum (*1828–1899*) claimed that these broad categories were merely symptom clusters—transient combinations of symptoms that are nonspecific and cut across different diseases (Kendler & Engstrom, 2017). The goal of psychiatrists, argued Kahlbaum, should be to delineate the natural disease forms in which symptoms manifest.

In this notion of natural disease forms we see conjecture, but conjecture that is grounded in a clinical description, specifically the description of general paresis of the insane. General paresis was the most prevalent mental disorder in late nineteenth-century asylums. Its symptoms included personality changes, mood disturbances, and delusions. Ninety-one years before general paresis was confirmed to be the result of untreated syphilis, it was demarcated as a distinct disease entity using natural history descriptions alone. Epilepsy, tuberculosis, and smallpox were also demarcated by natural history descriptions, not conjectures about causes.

Unlike other university psychiatrists, Kraepelin was not hostile to the asylum doctors, and his career-spanning goal was to describe natural disease entities (Heckers & Kendler, 2020). He also argued that symptoms are nonspecific but can be grouped with respect to shared course, treatment, and outcome. This natural history approach resulted in the famous Kraepelinian dichotomy of dementia praecox (i.e., schizophrenia) featuring a deteriorating course, and manic depressive illness featuring a recurrent course (Kraepelin, 1907).

In Kraepelin's view, natural disease entities continually manifest heterogeneity and lack of specificity at the symptom level, in part due to the randomizing influence of individuals' reactions to distress (i.e., personality) (Hoff, 2003). To accurately identify the disease entities, Kraepelin proposed that clinical description needs to converge with etiology (e.g., head injury or extreme stress) and an underlying pathology (e.g., degenerating nerve cells).

Bentall (2003) called this Kraepelin's "big idea." Kraepelin believed that an accurate descriptive classification would lead the way to etiology and pathology, and vice versa. Each is like one part of the Rosetta Stone, upon which the very same message was written in three different but still mutually translatable languages.

## The Unity of Science Project and the *Methodenstreit*

Kraepelin's notion of a convergence between description, etiology, and pathogenesis expresses another development in nineteenth-century philosophy, called the *unity of science project*. The unity of science project is typically traced back to the *Positivist* movement as elaborated by its founder August Comte (*1798–1857*) in the mid-nineteenth century (Comte, 1856; Kolakowski, 1969).

Comte proposed a hierarchy of scientific disciplines, ordered by decreasing generality and increasing complexity. He began with mathematics at the base of the hierarchy, which deals with quantities only and is thus the most general and least complex of the sciences. Second are disciplines focused on the inorganic world, such as astronomy, physics, and chemistry. Next are all the sciences investigating the living domain, such as biology and ecology. Finally, Comte placed sociology at the top of the hierarchy. Neither psychology nor psychopathology was included in Comte's list. We can speculate that both would have a foot in biology but, from this grounding, also have a hand raising up to grasp sociology.

Kolakowski (1969) called attention to the historical dimension of Comte's hierarchy in which it takes longer for more complex sciences to reach a mature, or "positive" stage of development, especially since they must depend on results achieved by their simpler predecessors. From this perspective, to describe psychiatry, psychology, or psychopathology as immature sciences implies that their subject matter is more complex than the subject matter of more mature sciences.

At roughly the same time that Comte developed his positive philosophy, John Stuart Mill (*1806–1873*) published *A System of Logic* (Mill, 1843/2015). Firmly rooted in the tradition of British empiricism, Mill claimed that any genuinely scientific claim must be based on the content provided by observation, which is extended by the method of induction. With induction, observations of particular events form the basis for inferring general maxims and laws. For instance, one can observe that a copper penny conducts electricity, that a copper coil conducts electricity, and that a copper wire conducts electricity and infer the law-like statement that all copper conducts electricity. Mill considered induction to be a universal method common to all genuine sciences.

According to Mill, the "moral sciences" could also become genuine inductive sciences even though what kinds of laws might explain such complex domains remained hidden. Similar to how moral treatment in the late eighteenth century meant "psychological" treatment, for Mill moral sciences meant "sciences of the mind."

### The European Methodenstreit

As noted above, one of the contributions of the Enlightenment was deemphasizing the importance of an incorruptible soul, thus making the notion of a diseased mind potentially less controversial. This, however, was not a sudden transition. Particularly in Germanic countries, in the early part of the nineteenth century the importance of soul, spirit, and a special life force persisted. In part, this persistence of the spirit was defended by a romanticist movement that resisted the notion of an all-encompassing scientific method that brought everything under its scope. This led to a reaction in the middle part of the century in which the romanticist approach was criticized as too conjectural. A purely physical, natural science approach was promoted in its place.

In the latter part of the nineteenth century, some thinkers came to believe that the natural scientists who rejected romanticist attachments to the notion of spirit had thrown a baby out with the bath water. This led to yet another reaction, known as the *Methodenstreit* (methodological dispute). The goal of the *Methodenstreit* thinkers was not to preserve and defend romanticist notions of spirit and life forces but to justify some autonomy for the human sciences while still attributing to them a genuinely scientific form of rationality. For them, the human sciences included history but also cultural studies and psychology.

One important thinker in this tradition was the historian Wilhelm Dilthey (*1833–1911*) who distinguished between the *Naturwissenschaften* (natural sciences) and *Geisteswissenschaften* (human sciences). These two distinct sciences, he believed, differed in terms of their subject matter, respectively, the physical versus the mental (subjective, lived experience). They also differed in terms of their proper methods, respectively, explanation (*Erklären*) based on causal, deterministic, and law-like connections for the natural sciences versus understanding (*Verstehen*) based on meanings, goals, and values for the human sciences.

We will say more about this latter distinction shortly when we describe the work of Karl Jaspers.

A different approach was taken by Wilhelm Windelband (*1848–1915*) who distinguished between *nomothetic* and the *idiographic* methods which can be used to study the same phenomena. To oversimplify, this distinction is mirrored in the contrast between a research study in which different samples (of persons) are compared to each other and a case study of one person.

In adopting a nomothetic approach, one seeks to discover generalizations that apply to entire classes. For example, one factor that makes people in general more vulnerable to alcoholism is a tendency to discount future rewards such as a promotion at work in favor of short-term rewards such a night of drinking with friends (Petry, 2006). Another general theory of alcoholism is that the brain circuitry that mediates "liking" is different from the circuitry that mediates "wanting." This explains why alcoholics continue to drink, wanting and craving ever more, even when the drink no longer affords them pleasure (Berridge & Robinson, 2016).

In contrast, with an idiographic approach one studies particular entities in time and space. Idiographic accounts can be thought of as descriptions in a natural history sense, but they are also potentially interpretive. An example of an idiographic approach would be a case study of how someone named Walker developed alcoholism. It might include a natural history description of his family history, his history of increasing alcohol use, and the consequences his drinking has for him and his family. More interpretively, it could also assert that the men in the Walker family have been heavy drinkers going back to the 1800s, and our Walker has incorporated this into his identity, believing that drinking is what real Walker men do.

By the latter part of the nineteenth century, as John Stuart Mill foresaw, it had become indisputable that psychology and related disciplines should aspire to the status of sciences, but it was less clear which methodological approach should be adopted. The *Methodenstreit* constituted a background against which the new disciplines of psychology, psychiatry, and psychoanalysis attempted to justify their status as genuine sciences.

With respect to the influence of the *Methodenstreit* on the philosophy of psychopathology, Karl Jaspers (*1883–1969*), through his book *General Psychopathology*, remains a dominant reference, especially in Europe. Let us briefly look at what Japsers had to say.

## Karl Jaspers: Methodological Pluralism for Psychopathology (Twentieth Century)

Jaspers (1968/1997a, 1968/1997b) hoped to integrate a scientific approach to psychiatry with the traditional humanities. Rather than limit psychopathology to one methodological approach alone, he sought to make room for different perspectives (i.e., both the nomothetic and idiographic). Studying things from more than one perspective is called *pluralism*. Jasper's precondition for being pluralistic about methodological perspectives is that the employment of any method should be accompanied by a recognition of its background assumptions, justification, and proper domain.

The framework of methodological pluralism is important for thinking about Jaspers' two most frequently discussed contributions to psychopathology: the application of Dilthey's *Erklären* (explanation) versus *Verstehen* (understanding) distinction and the employment of the sociologist Max Weber's notion of *ideal types* (Hoerl, 2013; Schwartz et al., 1989; Wiggins & Schwartz, 1991).

The *explanation versus understanding* contrast calls attention to different kinds of connections that can manifest in clinical phenomena. The first are causal and ideally law-like connections. One example would be the connection between tangles and plaques in the brain and the manifestation of Alzheimer's type dementia. Jaspers believed that these connections are revealed through an inductive method founded on repeated experience with many cases. What is expressed by such connections is *explanation*.

The second kind of connections are meaningful ones. Understanding meaningful connections depend on "empathy," consisting of a reenactment in one's imagination of the other person's mental life. "We sink ourselves into the psychic situation," as Jaspers (1968/1997a) said, "and understand genetically by empathy how one psychic event emerges from another" (p. 301). For example, returning to the example of Walker, we might understand how his failed business and the meaning of that failure for him, related to his father's business failures many years earlier, are part of the context for his most recent episode of depression. *Understanding* refers to seeing connections that are more individualist than the general connections of law-like causal explanations. For Jaspers, both ways of comprehending clinical phenomena are important.

Jaspers also thought that thinking in terms of *ideal types* could expand and enrich the conceptual repertoire of psychopathology. The ideal-type framework had been originally developed within sociology and was intended to express a kind of blended nomothetic-idiographic perspective, serving as a conceptual vehicle "for the scrutiny and systematic characterization of *individual concrete patterns* which are *significant in their uniqueness.*" (Weber, 1949, p. 100, emphases added).

An ideal type, be it historical, sociological, or psychopathological, is always rooted in observation of a particular phenomenon, which is then made abstract by leaving out some of the details. For Jaspers, the ideal type is different from the average or the general type in a statistical sense (Fulford, Thornton, & Graham, 2006). The ideal type consists of those aspects of a particular phenomenon "that are *the most striking . . . the most unique* or *interesting*" (Ghaemi, 2003, p. 179, emphases added).

To illustrate, if borderline personality disorder (BPD) is thought of as an ideal type, it becomes a tool for thinking about a particular person that calls your attention to features of the case that are important for your goals and purposes. In the *DSM*, borderline personality disorder is a general diagnostic concept, but used as an ideal type it would also be an understanding of how a single person is borderline without reducing that person to the diagnosis. An important feature of the ideal type framework is that even the most optimally chosen ideal type will never exhaust the infinite complexity and richness of the individual phenomenon (i.e., the person).

According to Jaspers, ideal types have a relatively limited application, being relevant for psychiatric disorders that cannot be conceptualized as disease entities or general clinical syndromes. This claim can be best understood in the context of Jasper's notion that psychiatric conditions can be divided into three groups:

1. *Somatic entities*, such as brain tumors and Alzheimer's disease, that display mental symptoms
2. *Psychological and developmental syndromes* covering easily recognizable major psychoses like bipolar disorder and schizophrenia
3. *Psychopathies* (*Psychopatien*), referring more or less to personality disorders and neuroses (i.e., anxiety, depression, somatic concerns, etc.)

Jaspers (1968/1997b) conceived of these three classes as "essentially different from each other" without prospects for a "single unifying and comprehensive viewpoint from which any systematic ordering ... could emerge" (p. 610).

In Jaspers's view, somatic entities did not pose methodological challenges because their etiology and underlying pathology had been identified and they seemed to form classes in which membership is clear. He considered the psychoses to be syndromes that, like general paresis before them, look like disease forms even though etiology and underlying pathology have not been adequately identified. With respect to personality disorders and neuroses, Jaspers thought that it was better not to conceptualize them as disease forms. Indeed, they may be so entwined with a person's individuality that to label them as diseases might even be insulting. Instead, Jaspers recommended employing the framework of ideal types.

### Freud and Psychoanalysis: A Different Reaction to the Methodenstreit

As noted above, thinkers such as Meynert believed that psychiatry should be an explanatory, natural science. Before he decided to take a degree in medicine, Sigmund Freud (*1856–1939*) was a scientist in the physiological lab of Ernst Brucke (*1819–1892*), who was one of the leading antiromantic scientists of the mid-nineteenth century. During his medical training, Freud worked with Meynert. This pedigree was important to Freud, and he always contended that psychoanalysis was one of the natural sciences.

A few years before he introduced psychoanalysis in his famous book the *Interpretation of Dreams* (1900/1953), Freud (1895/1965) wrote a manuscript (published posthumously under the title of *Project for a Scientific Psychology*) in which he proposed a clinical science founded in study of neurology. However, as his actual clinical work evolved into psychoanalysis proper, he employed a more narrative-based, conjectural approach. For Freud and his followers, many of these conjectures became taken-for-granted background assumptions (e.g., the Oedipus complex and repressed unconscious mental processes).

Freud himself failed to acknowledge this transition and continued to describe psychoanalysis as an explanatory, natural science. This led to the criticism that psychoanalysis did not substantiate its claim to being genuine science and instead rested on case studies and unsupported conjectures. The critics included Kraepelin and scholars in both psychology and the philosophy of science (Dalzell, 2018; Gellner, 2008; Popper, 1963). Also a critic, Jaspers claimed that Freud mistook his understanding of meaningful connection in his patients' lives as general casual connections in the nomothetic sense (Kräupl Taylor, 1987).

An important feature of the early history of psychoanalysis was Freud's belief that sexuality from infancy and beyond is the primary source of human motivation. By infantile sexuality, Freud meant pleasure based on the experience of the body in the first few years of life (Sulloway, 1979). For Freud the most important causes of behavior were desires for pleasure that were not accessible to consciousness but operated nevertheless. Freud saw sexuality as a biological phenomenon and believed that by rooting motivation in biology, psychoanalysis could maintain its link with the medical sciences. Throughout his career, he resisted any attempts to deemphasize the importance of sexuality. After Freud died 1939, however, psychoanalysis evolved, especially in Britain and the United States. Two of the most important developments were ego psychology and object relations theory.

*Ego psychology* incorporated a model of healthy personality functioning, placing increased emphasis on conscious adaptation to reality but staying committed to the importance of biologically based drives for human motivation (Blanck & Blanck, 1974; Erikson, 1950; Hartmann, 1958). Psychoanalytic ideas about defense mechanisms such as projection and repression were elaborated on by ego psychologists. Object relations theorists, in contrast, rooted human motivation in the psychological need to establish relationships and emphasized how representations of self and other develop (Fairbairn, 1952; Klein, 1964; Winnicott, 1965). Attachment theory in developmental psychology originated in the object relations tradition (Ainsworth & Bowlby, 1991; Bowlby, 1969).

Despite a shared willingness to extend Freudian ideas, ego psychological and object relation theorists were also keen to trace their ideas back to Freud himself, and the two camps battled over which of them were the more legitimate Freudians (Greenberg & Mitchell, 1983). Partly due to the ego psychological and object relations theorists continued commitments to various Freudian background assumptions, critics continued to evaluate their clinical descriptions as too conjectural.

In the 1950s, psychoanalysis became the dominant force in American psychiatry, with most major university psychiatry departments being led by psychoanalysts and training models being psychoanalytically oriented. Rather than the profession operating under a shared psychoanalytic paradigm, however, theoretical disputes between warring camps continued.

In the next section we will see the beginning of a transition that occurred in US departments of psychiatry in which biologically oriented psychiatrists assumed control of the institutional reins (Harrington, 2019; Luhrmann, 2000). Although the shift in institutional control happened suddenly, it would be a mistake to conclude that the psychoanalysts' influence disappeared.

For example, both borderline and narcissistic disorders as disturbances in the structure of the self were described as part of a détente between ego psychological and object relations theories in the late 1960s and early 1970s (Kernberg, 1969, 1975; Kohut, 1971). Borderline disturbances involve a failure to modulate strong positive and negative views of self and others. Narcissistic disturbances involve modulating negative emotions by adopting a grandiose view of the self.

Borderline and narcissistic disturbances were incorporated into the *DSM-III* in 1980 as specific personality disorders and have been included in each subsequent manual. In general, psychoanalytic perspectives tend to view all kinds of psychopathology (including depression and schizophrenia) as expression of personality. In 2013, the Alternative *DSM-5* Model for Personality Disorders included disturbances in self and interpersonal functioning as one of the essential features of any personality disorder, drawing on research conducted from object relations perspectives (Bender et al., 2011).

Over time, as borderline and narcissist disturbances have become more detached from psychoanalytic conjectures, they are increasingly viewed as descriptively valid (Beck et al., 2004; Linehan, 1993; Millon et al., 2009). They have also been important targets of scientific research, especially borderline disturbances (McGlashan et al., 2005; Pincus & Roche, 2011; Skodol et al., 2005; Zanarini et al., 2003).

**Rethinking Causation in Psychopathology**

Beginning in the early 1970s, a group of psychiatrists at Washington University in St. Louis sought to replace the conjectures of the psychoanalytic model with a more research-oriented and biomedical model. The challenge was that previous iterations of the biomedical approach to psychiatry were mostly conjectural. Led by Eli Robins (*1921–1994*) and Samuel Guze (*1924–2000*), they argued that the reason psychiatry had not made progress in developing a biologically grounded nosology was because its psychoanalytically based descriptions were too conjectural and inadequate to the task. They began, therefore, with redescribing clinical syndromes based on observable signs and self-reported symptoms only, without making inferences about unconscious processes (Feighner et al., 1972; Robins & Guze, 1970).

Just as Kraepelin explicitly emphasized both the symptomatic/descriptive level and the importance of etiology and underlying pathology, Robins and Guze (1970), labeled as *neo-Kraepelinians*, supplemented natural history descriptions with laboratory findings (endophenotypes and biomarkers) and family studies (i.e., genetics) with the hope that they could eventually explain disorders. Like Kraepelin, Robins, and Guze thought that description, etiology, and underlying pathology should ultimately converge.

At about this same time, Robins began working with the psychiatrist Robert Spitzer (*1932–2015*) and the psychologist Jean Endicott (b. 1936) to develop a set of diagnostic criteria for use in research (Spitzer et al., 1978). Spitzer was trained as a psychoanalyst, but his interest lay in developing ratings scales, and he worked closely with Endicott, who was trained in psychometrics (Decker, 2013).

Spitzer is best known for revolutionizing psychiatric diagnosis when, as leader of the *DSM-III* revision, he oversaw the implementation of an operational definition approach to psychopathology which used observable signs and self-reported symptoms as diagnostic criteria. This operational approach, which describes recognizable clinical features and minimizes the need to make theoretical inferences, is often called *descriptive psychopathology*.

Despite an initial alliance with Spitzer, the Washington University psychiatrists thought that Spitzer paid too much attention to making the *DSM-III* useful for practicing clinicians by including diagnoses such as borderline personality disorder (Decker, 2013). In their view, natural history descriptions could identify only 14 valid syndromes, and they believed that cases that could not be classified into one of these 14 categories should be coded as undiagnosed psychiatric illness (Feighner et al., 1972).

The diagnostic criteria and the list of disorders in the *DSM* were revised two more times before the end of the twentieth century (i.e., the *DSM-III-R* and the *DSM-IV*). By the beginning of the twenty-first century, doubts were building over the

*DSM*'s usefulness for promoting the advancement of knowledge.

The historian of psychiatry Berrios (2003) argued that the science of psychopathology is suffering because there is a mismatch between descriptive psychopathology and recent advances in neuroscience, with the descriptive landscape being much the same as it was 100 years ago. There are, he argued, many more potentially relevant symptoms than those contained in the current classification, but the descriptive project has been foreclosed and largely limited to accounts offered in the nineteenth century. He also noted that, despite the age-old importance of natural *history*, the current descriptive landscape is often cross-sectional, considering a single point and time rather than how symptoms develop, waxing and waning, over time.

Indeed, some psychiatrists argue that the *DSM* classifications have become barriers to progress. For example, Hyman (2010) reported that when he was director of the National Institute of Mental Health (NIMH), grant applications for studying the treatment of cognitive symptoms of schizophrenia had a difficult time winning approval because those symptoms were not listed in the *DSM* and had not been given an indication for treatment by the US Food and Drug Administration. Hyman claimed that the *DSM* criteria have been inappropriately reified, by which he means that, rather than seeing diagnostic criteria as provisional indicators of revisable concepts, they are treated like true identifying features of fixed entities.

Likewise, when he was the director of the NIMH, Insel (2013) argued that psychiatry cannot succeed in developing a classification based on biomarkers and cognitive deficits if the symptom-based diagnoses of the *DSM* remain the gold standard. According to Insel, scientists need to study not just how *DSM* symptoms cluster together, but also how genetic, imaging, physiological, and cognitive data cluster with symptoms as well. Insel here was responding to the premature closure of the symptom space on the part of grant reviewers after learning that grant applications for his new research domain criteria (RDoC) initiative had received low scores because they did not use *DSM* symptoms and/or categories (Zachar et al., 2019).

RDoC is a framework that seeks to focus research efforts not on discrete disorders, such as major depression (present vs. absent) but on dimensions of psychological functioning, such as negative emotionality, that span the normal and abnormal (from low to high). One criterion for a dimension to be included in RDoC is that it must have been shown to be implemented in a neural circuit. In fact, Insel specifically stated that mental disorders are biological disorders involving brain circuits. This conjecture, that mental disorders are brain disorders whose causes are to be discovered by neuroscientists, raises interesting philosophical issue about the nature of causation in psychopathology.

## Two Approaches to Causation in Psychopathology

The philosophical literature on causality is extensive and beyond the scope of our chapter. Pernu (2019) helpfully simplified the conceptualization of causality for psychopathology by distinguishing two broad clusters of philosophical views, which we will call production accounts and regularity accounts.

### PRODUCTION ACCOUNTS

Production accounts understand causation in terms of specific physical processes. These processes are continuous, unbroken chains of events connecting cause and effect, in which interactions between cause and effect involve energy transfer. The interaction of billiard balls is a common example of energy transfer. When one ball hits another ball and causes it to move, kinetic energy from the first ball is transferred to the second.

In medicine, production accounts take the form of *mechanistic models*. According to Craver and Darden (2013), mechanisms are "entities and activities with spatial and temporal properties organized to produce, underlie, or maintain a phenomenon" (p. 11). Mechanistic models take a process, decompose it into components, and then describe how those components interact to produce the process.

How an action potential is produced in a neuron is a common example of a mechanistic model. The components include sodium and potassium ions, gated protein channels, and a lipid membrane. These components interact to produce the action potential. This model is also an abstraction that ignores many particular features of neurons. For instance, although blood oxygen levels and membrane turnover are important features of neurons, they can be ignored when our goal is to describe the actional potential (Craver, 2009).

In mechanistic neuroscientific models, the task is to show how different parts of the brain interact to produce or maintain the disorder. For example, if we want to understand how the death of a child caused someone to grieve, with cause involving some kind of energy transfer, the grief reaction has to be decomposed into physical-neural parts that involve a transfer of energy.

**REGULARITY ACCOUNTS**

Regularity accounts are derived from empiricist suspicions of conjectures about things not observed. According to the empiricist philosopher David Hume (*1711–1776*), we observe that causes occur before effects, that causes and effects are conjoined in space and time, and that when the cause occurs, the effect follows (Hume, 1739/2000, 1748/2007). What we observe, says Hume, are regularities or dependencies between events—but we do not observe "causality" in terms of the cause *making* the effect happen.

One example of advocating for the Humean approach to causality in psychology can be seen in the work the behaviorist B. F. Skinner (*1904–1990*). As a commited philosophical empiricist, Skinner was suspicious about causation. He thus claimed that his work on operant conditioning only described the regularities that occur between behaviors and patterns of reinforcement (Skinner, 1953).

A more recent regularity account in the philosophy of science is Woodward's (2003, 2008) interventionist model. According to this view, if you make an intervention on X, and it is reliably followed by a change in Y, then X is the cause of Y. In this account, the reliability of the change often depends on the appropriate background conditions being present. For example, tackling someone to the ground will reliably be followed by a sudden increase in negative emotion if it occurs in the office, but not if it occurs on the football field.

For X to be the cause of Y, there also must be a contrast where an intervention on X changes Y, but, if the intervention had not occurred, and everything else stayed the same, then Y would not have changed. For example, let's say that someone on average needs 4 or more weeks of exposure habituation therapy to achieve long-term reduction of obsessive-compulsive symptoms. In contrast, 1–3 weeks of therapy on average will not lead to long-term reductions of symptom.

If the person had 1 year of therapy, they would experience a reduction of symptoms as well, but it is not the case that, in contrast, less than 1 year of therapy would not lead to a reduction in symptoms. Three months of therapy on average would also lead to a reduction of symptoms. The 1 year of therapy is a cause, but not the kind of cause sought for in the interventionist model. It is too fine-grained and has no noncausal contrast. Although broader (or more coarse-grained), 4 or more weeks of therapy more accurately describes the cause.

This model has several attractive features with respect to the study of psychopathology. For one, it connects causation with the practical issue of interventions, making it relevant for thinking about causality in treatment settings. In fact, the practice of making an intervention and describing the results was an important part of the natural history approach.

Another attractive feature of the interventionist account is that it places no a priori restrictions on which level of analysis can have genuine causal power. If intervening on X reliably leads to a change in Y, then X is a cause of Y.

For instance, in reductionist models, the causal power of psychosocial variables like social status is ultimately explained by how social status is implemented in the brain. The causality is *reduced to* brain activity. In the interventionist account, however, top-down causation can also occur in which manipulation of upper-level psychosocial events can cause changes in lower-level brain events. For example, Raleigh and colleagues (1984) have shown that you can intervene to raise a male monkey's position in a social dominance hierarchy (X) by removing higher status monkeys from the troupe. When a lower ranking monkey gains higher social status, that change in status is reliably followed by a rise in serotonin levels in that monkey's brain (Y). The intervention, however, was on social status so the change in social status was the cause of the change in serotonin levels.

A third attractive feature of the interventionist account is that a relatively coarse-grained event, such as giving an unemployed person a meaningful job, might be a more preferable explanation for something like the remission of a depressive episode than would be theories about fine-grained events such as alterations in the connections between neurons in the person's brain. Although alterations in connections between neurons are reasonable causes of things like the remission of depressive episodes, on the interventionist account, the causal contrast is between giving the person a job versus the person remaining unemployed.

As noted above, if production accounts (mechanistic models) incorporate an energy transfer notion of causation, then they are likely to promote understanding the mind as expressing physical brain functions. One feature of the interventionist model that people find attractive is that it does not push all the causal work down to the level of the brain.

Put side by side, these alternative approaches raise important issues about the nature of the relationship between the mental and the physical. We briefly explore this relationship in the next section.

## Psychopathology and the Mental: Nonreductive Approaches

The realm of psychopathology is complicated by the thorny questions of the relationship between the "mental" and the "physical." Historically, two important solutions have been dualism and reductionism. In *dualism*, mind and brain are considered distinct. Traditionally dualists see mind and brain as separable entities. Others dualists believe that that minds do not exist apart from brains but the *properties* of the mind such as the feeling of distress are mental not physical properties. [2]

*Reductionism* implies that if we knew everything there was to know about the biology of the brain, psychological explanations would be rendered superfluous because any explanation that utilizes psychological constructs could instead be reduced to an explanation that utilizes neurobiological constructs. This has also been termed "greedy reductionism" because the lower level of explanation is seen as capable of "eating up" the higher level of explanation (Dennett, 1995).

On the surface, the RDoC project would seem to be in the reductionist camp given its emphasis on brain circuits, but the story is more complex. RDoC does give priority to psychological constructs whose implementation in the brain has at least been tentatively described, but RDoC is not seeking to replace descriptions of psychological functions with description of brain states (Cuthbert & Kozak, 2013; Miller & Bartholomew, 2020). RDoC seeks to use information from neuroscience to redescribe the psychological functions (or symptoms) that are important in psychopathology and may even identify symptoms not yet recognized.

In this respect, RDoC is potentially consistent with philosophical work in recent decades that has developed accounts that rely on neither dualism nor greedy reductionism. The philosophical term of art is "nonreductionism." To briefly illustrate the nonreductionist notion that mind and brain are not separate entities, but the mind is not fully reducible to the brain, let us look at what philosophers of mind refer to as the *4E framework*.

### The Embodied, Embedded, Enacted, and Extended Mind (4E Perspectives in Psychopathology)

Traditional approaches to cognitive science view cognition in terms of information processing and manipulation of abstract internal representations mediating between sensory input and motor outputs. The 4E framework refers to a family of disparate perspectives that were grouped together beginning around 2006 because of their shared opposition to viewing cognition as something that occurs completely within the confines of the brain (Drayson, 2009; Newen et al., 2018).

Although the 4E framework is primarily about cognitive science, it has also been applied to psychopathology. As in the cognitive sciences, 4E philosophy of psychopathology is best seen as an alliance of perspectives with some shared, overlapping features. Those who advocate for the 4E framework oppose the reduction of mental disorders to brain disorders (de Haan, 2020a; Glackin et al., 2021; Maiese, 2016; Nielsen & Ward, 2018). In their view, mental disorders cannot be localized to specific brain circuits and isolated from an individual's social and cultural context. For example, Fuchs (2018) articulates his perspective as follows:

> [P]sychic processes may not be reduced to the brain or to localized neural activities; they are embodied, inherently intentional, and context related; and they are inseparable from the intersubjective world of shared meanings and interactions. . . . this applies to dysfunctional or disordered mental processes as well. (Fuchs, 2018, p. 253)

This may sound to readers like the return of the *Geisteswissenschaften*, and certainly some of the philosophical perspectives included in the 4E framework are historically rooted in the European human sciences tradition, but the 4E framework also draws on dynamical systems theory, which is historically rooted in mathematics and the natural sciences (Varela et al., 1991). Dynamical systems theory studies how complex systems develop over time and seeks to make complex sciences more mature in Comte's sense.

---

[2] A similar view that the concepts/terms of psychology cannot not be replaced with the concepts of neuroscience is not called property dualism but *nonreductive materialism*. The latter view holds that the experience of distress cannot be fully explained by neuroscience, but it is not a special mental property.

4E's nonreductionist emphasis also calls to mind the biopsychosocial model of psychopathology, which for many years has been an important framework for thinking about psychopathology in both psychiatry and psychology (Bolton & Gillett, 2019; Engel, 1977). Introduced as an extension of the medical model, the biopsychosocial model claims that although diseases and disorders are implemented in biology, in many cases, understanding how they develop, are maintained, and resolved requires taking psychological and sociocultural factors into consideration.

The biopsychosocial model is so ingrained in the study of psychopathology that some features of the 4E framework which are novel for cognitive science are already taken for granted in psychopathology. The 4E framework does, however, articulate some ideas that are left too vague in the biopsychosocial model. More specifically, the 4E framework views the mind as *embodied*, *embedded*, *enacted*, and *extended*. Let us briefly explain each of these notions.

To say the mind is *embodied* emphasizes that mental functioning is entangled with biological functioning and cannot exist apart from it. One way to think about this is to see the entire nervous system as a single organ that inhabits the whole body—all of which is the substrate of the mind.

Lakoff and Johnson (1980) argued that our subjective experience is entwined with our experience of having bodies. For example, we describe happiness as "up" and sadness as "down" (i.e., "I'm feeling *up*" and "My spirits *rose*" vs. "I'm feeling *down*" and "My spirits *sank*"; Lakoff & Johnson, 1980, p. 15). According to the embodiment perspective, many taken-for-granted givens in our mental lives have bodily bases. Human bodies are vertically oriented, and positive and negative emotions alter our posture, so describing the experience of happiness with the physical metaphor being up and sadness with being down makes sense to us. In fact, "depression" is a description of bodily posture. In contrast, were a linguistically competent mammal to have a body oriented horizontally more like that of a dog, perhaps an experience of happiness would be described as being "forward."

To say that the mind is *embedded* stresses that the mind is not isolated from the world but dependent on the physical, social, and cultural environments we inhabit. In psychopathology, embeddedness is seen in the emphasis placed on stress and trauma in the etiology of some disorders. Embeddedness also emphasizes the importance of context. For example, Horwitz and Wakefield (2007) argued that experiencing symptoms of depression in the context of the loss of a loved one indicates normal grief, not a disorder. If, instead, those same symptoms appear out of the blue without any precipitants, they more like indicate a depressive disorder.

The *enactive mind* is best understood in contrast to a model in which the mind reacts to stimuli in reflex-like ways, often due to the triggering of brain circuits (Ellis, 2000). The enactive mind is consistent with William James's (*1842–1910*) notion of the mind as an organ of adaptation that is shaped by the world and actively shapes the world (James, 1890). This can be seen in a process called *circular causality*. In circular causality, changes in the environment can influence the individual in ways that change brain activity. These changes in brain activity can result in changes in the individual's interactions with the environment, which in turn can change the environment (thus completing the circle).

A more specific example of circular causality is the active *gene–environment correlation* (Scarr & McCartney, 1983). People with a vulnerability to alcoholism may actively seek out and shape environments in which drinking occurs. Fellow drinkers jointly create an environment, encouraging each other to drink excessively and excluding nondrinkers from the group. Rather than a genetic inheritance directly causing alcoholism, an inherited disposition leads some people to occupy and actively shape environments that in turn enable heavy drinking. According to the enactive perspective, the explanation of alcoholism should not be limited to the brain and the individual's internal psychological functioning but also include the individual's dynamic interaction with the world.

Psychopathology may also reflect deficient enactivism. De Haan (2020b) and Nielsen (2021) suggest this possibility by writing about psychopathology as inflexible. For instance, one of the best predictors of a depressive episode is experiencing stress in the previous 6 months (Kendler, Karkowski, & Prescott, 1998, 1999). In a depressive disorder though, this depressive reaction can settle into a stable state in which the depression symptoms are locked in and persist long after the stress that precipitated the episode has been resolved. In dynamic systems theory this is called *hysteresis*, referring to a change of state lagging behind changes in causation. It is a failure to adapt to changing conditions.

The *extended mind*, as Hoffman (2016) notes, is a stronger and more novel view for psychopathology. According to this view, parts of the world are parts of the mind: that is, the mind extends out into the world, such that it is not confined to the physical body of the organism and is partly constituted in world. To illustrate, for people with some kinds of brain injuries, their beliefs about how to navigate around their home city may be stored in notebooks, and recall is a process of checking the notebook. In this case, internal processes (such as the intention to visit the museum) and an external resource (transcribed beliefs about where the museum is located) are coupled together to form an integrated cognitive system (Clark & Chalmers, 1998).

Consider, for instance, the process of self-regulating emotion. Some clinicians claim that, for young children, emotional regulation is normally accomplished externally through interactions with parents (Bowlby, 1969). For example, when children are upset, their parents can soothe them. Over time, positive interactions with parents are internalized and become an inner resource. As they mature, children can draw on such internalized resources to regulate emotion on their own (Mahler et al., 1975; Zachar, 2000).

Psychodynamic models of some personality disorders view the internalization process as having been disrupted (Mahler, 1971). For example, part of the pathology of borderline personality disorder is an inability to regulate emotion internally, which manifests as intense and fluctuating positive and negative emotions. For some patients, analogous to the notebooks of patients with brain injury, drawing on external sources of regulation can promote emotional stability. It may also be the case that regulating emotion externally is not in itself a problem; rather, the external resources (relationships) that are available to the person are unreliable (Linehan, 1993; Potter, 2009). Indeed, Bray (2008) suggests that the lack of interpersonal boundaries and concerns about abandonment that are characteristic of patients with borderline personality disorder could be seen as a consequence of other people being an extended part of the borderline mind.

## Conjecture, Scientific Realism, and Scientific Anti-Realism

Throughout this chapter we have explored a tug of war that has occurred between more descriptive and more conjectural approaches to psychopathology. The chapter began with a brief description of the Galenist model of medicine and its reference to things that do not actually exist—such as black bile. We also saw Kraepelin referring to Meynert's neuromythology. This referred, among other things, to a conjecture on Meynert's part that mania is caused by an increased supply of blood in the cortex and depression by a decrease. The extent to which scientific conjectures about things not directly observed refer to something real is the problem of scientific realism and anti-realism. It has been lurking in the background throughout our discussion, and, in this last section, we bring it into the foreground. This section includes some of the more difficult philosophical ideas presented in the chapter.

Over the centuries, there have been many debates about scientific authority within society and culture. These cultural debates include

- Galileo versus the Catholic Church on the Copernican theory
- Evolutionists versus creationists on the origins of species
- The scientific community versus the anti-vaccination movement

According to scientific realism, the proposition *planets in our solar system revolve around the sun* is true no matter what we happen to believe because reality is mind-independent. Successful science describes this mind-independent reality.

Some philosophers assert that because the opponents of the Copernican theory claimed that the Copernican model is useful for making predictions about the movements of planets but is not literally true, they were analogous to contemporary scientific anti-realists (Massimi, 2008). Within the philosophy of science, however, both scientific realists and anti-realists strongly support the authority of Galileo, evolutionists, and vaccine science in the cultural debates. Comparing the debate between scientific realists and anti-realist with the debates about scientific authority is deceptive.

What then is *scientific anti-realism?* More closely associated with the philosophy of empiricism, scientific anti-realism is a doctrine of epistemic fallibilism, especially doubt that one can know with certainty about things that are at least partially beyond their appearances. According to scientific anti-realism, knowledge of such things is dependent on concepts and hence not mind-independent in a way that scientific realism demands. It is a descendant of the more descriptive and anti-conjectural perspective described at the beginning of this chapter.

Throughout history, previously accepted scientific theories such as the sun-centered model of the solar system and the theory that autism is caused by emotionally distant parenting have turned out to be mistaken conjectures. According to *the pessimistic induction*, it is likely that some currently accepted scientific theories will also turn out to be mistaken conjectures as well (Laudan, 1981). Anti-realists are sympathetic to the pessimistic induction.

The disciplines in which scientific realism and anti-realism debates have most thrived are physics, psychology, and psychopathology. For instance, the idea of a hypothetical construct as set forth by MacCorquodale and Meehl (1948) and Cronbach and Meehl (1955) has a scientific realist tone. An example of a hypothetical construct is the personality trait of neuroticism. People who score high on the trait of neuroticism are more likely to experience negative emotions such as anger, fear, and sadness. According to realism about psychological constructs, neuroticism is a hidden attribute of a person that is causally reflected in behavior.

Another example of a hidden cause of behavior is major depressive disorder. According to the scientific realist view, self-reported symptoms such as fatigue and concentration problems are correlated because they reflect an underlying depressive disorder. In developing diagnostic criteria for depression and/or items on a depression scale, psychiatrists and psychologists seek to identify behaviors and self-reports of experiences that are observable indicators of this hidden construct.

There is common ground between by this realist view and the mathematical model used in factor analysis (Borsboom et al., 2003). In factor analysis, the hidden, common causes of the observable indicators are called *latent variables*. When adopting scientific realism, practitioners of factor analysis see the mathematical properties of their technique as having the power to detect hidden realities (latent variables), similar to how astrophysicists see their complex mathematic tools as enabling them to detect hidden realities (i.e., black holes and subatomic particles).

One can also adopt a more anti-realist stance about causally important latent variables "discovered" with factor analysis (van der Maas et al., 2014). In a striking hypothesis, van der Maas et al. (2006) argued that as long as the observable indicators are positively correlated, factor analysis will extract latent variables even if the positive correlations are not the result of hidden, common causes but the result of direct causal connections between the observable indicators themselves. That is to say, rather than level of fatigue and concentration problems being correlated because they are both caused by the same underlying mood disturbance, they may instead have direct causal connections with each other; that is, being fatigued causes concentration problems. In this view, a depressive disorder occurs if depression symptoms enter into causal relationship with each other, and, once established, this *causal network* maintains itself over time even after precipitating causes are no longer operating (i.e., hysteresis, as defined above). For these kind of conditions, latent variables discovered by factor analysis are not real.

Other mathematical models are inherently aligned with a more anti-realist view. One example is principal components analysis (Borsboom et al., 2003). In principal components analysis, the latent variable is a composite constructed out of the observable indicators. For example, the variable of socioeconomic status (SES) is constructed out of correlations between variables such as income, education, and occupation. Variations in income, education, and occupation are not caused by SES: they are parts of SES.

Let's look at what scientific anti-realism would say about the hypothetical personality trait of neuroticism. According to the anti-realist, there is no hidden entity in the mind-brain called neuroticism that causes a person to experience fear, anger, and sadness. Various temperamental, affective, cognitive, and perceptual processes in the context of one's personal history combine to raise the probability of having these negative emotions, but the particular menu of processes that play causal roles for occurrences of these emotions is constantly changing. Behavioral consistency emerges, but it is not caused by a hidden trait called neuroticism any more than a person's income and educational level are caused by his SES.

### A Conditional and Partial Scientific Realism in the Philosophy of Science

Some philosophers of science have adopted a position that is harder to classify as scientific realism or anti-realism (Fine, 1986; Schaffner, 1993; Zachar, 2014). One example of this view is the empiricist philosopher Rudolf Carnap's (1956/1991) distinction between questions internal to a linguistic framework and those external to it.

Let us use the example of schizophrenia. Carnap argued that, internal to a linguistic (or scientific) framework, there are norms for deciding if a hypothetical construct such as schizophrenia can be considered real. These norms are stipulations such as (a) there are disorders of psychopathology, (b) schizophrenia is a psychotic disorder, (c) schizophrenia has a genetic component, and (d) schizophrenia requires 6 or more months of continuous symptoms. For complex sciences such as psychopathology, many different norms have been proposed, and it is hard to keep them all straight or consistent—that is part of their complexity.

According to Carnap, discussions about what norms to accept are practical matters, focused on consequences.[3] For example, those who reject the view that there are disorders of psychopathology often do so because they believe that the concept of psychopathology is harmful, contributing to stigmatization and blaming the person (Chapman, 2019; Johnstone & Boyle, 2018; Rashed, 2019). Those who advocate for the study of psychopathology tend to believe that rejecting the concept of psychopathology would lead to other negative consequences such as the minimizing of suffering (Frances, 2013; Roth & Kroll, 1986).

Carnap said that once there is agreement on various stipulations and methodological and statistical norms, they become background assumptions, and, internal to the agreed-on framework, one can do the research and potentially learn if schizophrenia is real according to the norms one has adopted. For Carnap, however, no one can absolutely decide whether schizophrenia is real external to all possible frameworks whatsoever.

Independently of Carnap, the psychiatrist Kenneth Kendler (1990, 2020) came to similar conclusions. Kendler was involved in the *DSM-III-R* and *DSM-IV* revisions. During the early days of the *DSM-IV* revision he realized that which diagnostic criteria are best will partly be contingent on our concept for that disorder. Consider schizophrenia. Assume that one set of criteria does better at predicting that the disorder runs in families and another set does better at predicting long-term outcome. Each criterion set also demarcates different groups: a broad group that includes paranoid and schizotypal personality types for the first set and a narrow group of early-onset psychosis for the second. Which criterion set is better? Are these different groups subtypes of one disorder or two disorders? Answering such questions, Kendler realized, is not just a matter of doing more and better studies but contingent on prior assumptions about the nature of a valid schizophrenic disorder. For example, if we assume that a real schizophrenic disorder would show improvement with antipsychotic medicine, the second set of criteria would likely be better.

Another version of this view is the *internal realism* of the philosopher Hillary Putnam (1988, 1990). By internal realism Putnam meant that we can describe a situation in different ways by using alternative conceptual frameworks. Once we adopt a framework with its own set of background assumptions, however, within that framework, there are facts that are independent of our preferences, statements that can be objectively true and false, and so on.

For example, if you adopt the *DSM* definition of schizophrenia as your framework and then hypothesize that schizophrenia has a deteriorating course, you can empirically test that hypothesis. In fact, *DSM*-defined schizophrenia does not always have a deteriorating course. The most common outcome is remitting-improving (Morgan et al., 2021). Other common outcomes are persistent symptoms, late decline, and late improvement. Those outcomes are matters of fact, but such facts do not preclude potentially embracing an alternative concept of schizophrenia in which a deteriorating course is the most common outcome and labeling other outcomes as something different from schizophrenia (such as schizophreniform disorder, attenuated psychosis, and so on). As to which of these concepts we should embrace, there are no determinate framework-free answers.

When someone asks if schizophrenia is real, they are typically looking for a settled, absolute answer. It either is or is not real independent of how we happen to think about it. For Carnap and Putnam, making claims about the reality of schizophrenia independent from a set of background concepts that we embrace would require being able to adopt a god's-eye view. For philosophical empiricists, such an absolute view is beyond the reach of human understanding. In fact, agreeing that something is real internal to a framework but not absolutely real independent of our conceptions/assumptions could be considered an anti-realist position—which is why we noted above that these perspectives can be hard to definitively classify as realist or anti-realist.

## Conclusion

Looking back through the history of psychopathology, we have emphasized a long-standing tug of

---

[3] Contemporary empiricists would allow that previous scientific findings can always potentially inform decisions about what norms/concepts to accept.

war between descriptions and conjectures. Although we began this story in the seventeenth century, the contrast likely reaches back into prehistory. Ages ago humans started to notice that some members of their clan experienced declines from previous levels of functioning with respect to adaptive skills that involve perception, cognition, emotion, and behavior, although it is unlikely our ancestors articulated such insights using those specific psychological concepts. Many of them would have noted that these changes were accompanied by increased levels of suffering. Quite likely, they also attended to what Sydenham, as quoted above, called the irregularity of the changes—and how the menu of problems shifted over time.

Given humans' inherent predilection for explaining "why," from the very beginning they surely formulated conjectures about what was happening. Conjectures seen as too speculative or as conflicting would eventually initiate attempts to articulate descriptions that people could agree on. Indeed, once the process commenced, asking what came first, the conjecture or the description, would be a chicken-or-egg problem.

The distinction between what is considered more descriptive versus more conjectural could be seen as part of the conceptual history of psychosis, anxiety, depression, conduct problems, substance abuse, developmental disorders, and so on. One could even potentially distinguish psychodynamic, biological, cognitive-behavioral, and psychometric-quantitative conceptualizations with reference to what they consider descriptions, acceptable conjectures, and unacceptable conjectures.

As we have suggested, the distinction between description and conjecture is fluid. Claims that are in conformity with accepted background assumptions tend to be considered descriptions, whereas claims that extend beyond current assumptions tend to be considered conjectures. As background assumptions are added and removed, what was seen as conjectural can be considered descriptive, and older descriptions start looking like conjectures.

Articulating background assumptions is a challenging task. These assumptions may be so taken for granted that they are not seen as assumptions or as having a theoretical character. One practical reason for attempting to articulate such assumptions is that when they are taken for granted, they may be seen as necessary and inevitable, but when seen as assumptions having a theoretical character, they may gain some contingency. A perception of contingency supports the empiricist belief that our knowledge of psychopathology is provisional and potentially revisable—which we believe is a historically entrenched, philosophical assumption of any scientific approach to the study of psychopathology.

**References**

Ackerknecht, E. H. (1982). *A short history of medicine*. Johns Hopkins University Press.

Ainsworth, M. S., & Bowlby, J. (1991). An ethological approach to personality development. *American Psychologist, 46*(4), 333–341.

Anstey, P. R. (2011). *John Locke and natural philosophy*. Oxford University Press.

Beck, A. T., Freeman, A., & Davis, D. (2004). *Cognitive therapy of personality disorders*, 2nd ed. Guilford.

Bender, D. S., Morey, L. C., & Skodol, A. E. (2011). Toward a model for assessing level of personality functioning in DSM-5, part I: A review of theory and methods. *Journal of Personality Assessment, 93*(4), 332–346.

Bentall, R. P. (2003). *Madness explained: Psychosis and human nature*. Penguin.

Berridge, K. C., & Robinson, T. E. (2016). Liking, wanting, and the incentive-sensitization theory of addiction. *American Psychologist, 71*(8), 670–679.

Berrios, G. E. (2003). The language of psychiatry and its history. In T. Hamanaka & G. E. Berrios (Eds.), *Two millennia of psychaitry in west and east* (pp. 81–91). Gakuju Shoin.

Blanck, G., & Blanck, R. (1974). *Ego psychology: Theory and practice*. Columbia University Press.

Bolton, D., & Gillett, G. (2019). *The biopsychosocial model of health and disease: New philosophical and scientific developments*. Palgrave Pivot.

Borsboom, D. G., Mellenbergh, G. J., & van Heerden, J. (2003). The theoretical status of latent variables. *Psychological Review, 110*(2), 203–219.

Bowlby, J. (1969). *Attachment and loss* (vol. 1). Basic Books.

Bray, A. (2008). The extended mind and borderline personality disorder. *Australasian Psychiatry, 16*(1), 8–12.

Bynum, W. F. (1993). Nosology. In W. F. Bynum & R. Porter (Eds.), *Companion encyclopedia of the history of medicine* (vol. 1, pp. 335–356). Routledge.

Carnap, R. (1956/1991). Empiricism, sematics, and ontology. In R. Boyd, P. Gasper, & J. D. Trout (Eds.), *The philosophy of science* (pp. 85–97). MIT Press.

Chapman, R. (2019). Neurodiversity theory and its discontents: Autism, schizophrenia, and the social model of disability. In S. Tekin & R. Bluhm (Eds.), *The Bloomsbury companion to philosophy of psychiatry* (pp. 371–390). Bloomsbury.

Clark, A., & Chalmers, D. (1998). The extended mind. *Analysis, 58*(1), 7–19.

Comte, A. (1856). *The positive philosophy of Auguste Comte* (H. Martineau, Trans.). Calvin Blanchard.

Craver, C. F. (2009). Mechanisms and natural kinds. *Philosophical Psychology, 22*(5), 575–594.

Craver, C. F., & Darden, L. (2013). *In search of mechanisms: Discoveries across the life sciences*. University of Chicago Press.

Cronbach, L. J., & Meehl, P. E. (1955). Construct validity in psychological tests. *Psychological Bulletin, 52*(4), 281–302.

Cunningham, A. (1989). Thomas Sydenham and 'the good old cause'. In R. French & A. Wear (Eds.), *The medical revolution of the seventeenth century* (pp. 164–190). Cambridge University Press.

Cuthbert, B. N., & Kozak, M. J. (2013). Constructing constructs for psychopathology: The NIMH research domain criteria. *Journal of Abnormal Psychology, 122*(3), 928–937.

de Haan, S. (2020a). An enactive approach to psychiatry. *Philosophy, Psychiatry, & Psychology, 27*(1), 3–25.

de Haan, S. (2020b). *Enactive psychiatry*. Cambridge University Press.

Dalzell, T. G. (2018). *Freud's Schreber between psychiatry and psychoanalysis*. Routledge.

Decker, H. S. (2013). *The making of DSM-III®: A diagnostic manual's conquest of American psychiatry*. Oxford University Press.

Dennett, D. C. (1995). *Darwin's dangerous idea*. Simon & Schuster.

Dickens, C. (1843). *A Christmas carol*. Chapman and Hall.

Drayson, Z. (2009). Embodied cognitive science and its implications for psychopathology. *Philosophy, Psychiatry & Psychology, 16*(4), 329–340.

Ellis, R. D. (2000). Integrating the physiological and the phenomenological dimensions of affect and motivation. In R. D. Ellis & N. Newton (Eds.), *The caldron of consciousness: Motivation, affect and self-organization—An anthology*. (pp. 3–26). John Benjamins Publishing Company.

Engel, G. L. (1977). The need for a new medical model: A challenge for biomedicine. *Science, 196*(4286), 129–136.

Engstrom, E. J., & Kendler, K. S. (2015). Emil Kraepelin: Icon and reality. *American Journal of Psychiatry, 172*, 1190–1196.

Erikson, E. H. (1950). *Childhood and society*. W. W. Norton & Company.

Fairbairn, W. R. (1952). *Psychoanalytic studies of the personality*. Routledge & Kegan Paul.

Feighner, J. P., Robins, E., Guze, S. B., Woodruff, R. A., Winokur, G., & Munoz, R. (1972). Diagnostic criteria for use in psychiatric research. *Archives of General Psychiatry, 26*, 57–63.

Fine, A. (1986). *The shaky game: Einstein, realism, and the quantum theory*. University of Chicago Press.

Frances, A. (2013). The British Psychological Society enters the silly season. *Psychiatric Times*.

Freud, S. (1895/1953). *Project for a scientific psychology: The standard edition of the complete psychological works of Sigmund Freud, Volume I* (J. Strachey, Trans.). Hogarth.

Freud, S. (1900/1965). *The interpretation of dreams* (J. Strachey, Trans.). Avon Books.

Fuchs, T. (2018). *Ecology of the brain: the phenomenology and biology of the embodied mind*. Oxford University Press.

Fulford, K. W. M., Thornton, T., & Graham, G. (2006). *Oxford textbook of philosophy and psychiatry*. Oxford University Press.

Gellner, E. (2008). *The psychoanalytic movement: The cunning of unreason*: John Wiley & Sons.

Ghaemi, N. S. (2003). *The concepts of psychiatry: a pluralistic approach to the mind and mental illness*. Johns Hopkins University Press.

Glackin, S. N., Roberts, T., & Krueger, J. (2021). Out of our heads: Addiction and psychiatric externalism. *Behavioural Brain Research, 398*, 112936.

Greenberg, J. R., & Mitchell, S. A. (1983). *Object relations in psychoanalytic theory*. Harvard University Press.

Harrington, A. (2019). *Mind fixers: Psychiatry's troubled search for the biology of mental illness*. W. W. Norton & Company.

Hartmann, H. (1958). *Ego psychology and the problem of adaptation*. International Universities Press.

Heckers, S., & Kendler, K. S. (2020). The evolution of Kraepelin's nosological principles. *World Psychiatry, 19*(3), 381–388.

Hoerl, C. (2013). Jaspers on explaining and understanding in psychiatry. In G. Stanghellini & T. Fuchs (Eds.), *One century of Karl Jaspers' general psychopathology* (pp. 107–120). Oxford University Press.

Hoff, P. (2003). Emil Kraepelin's concept of clinical psychiatry. In T. Hamanaka & G. E. Berrios (Eds.), *Two millennia of psychiatry in west and east* (pp. 65–79). Gakuju Shoin.

Hoffman, G. A. (2016). Out of our skulls: How the extended mind thesis can extend psychiatry. *Philosophical Psychology, 29*(8), 1160–1174.

Horwitz, A. V., & Wakefield, J. C. (2007). *The loss of sadness: How psychiatry transformed normal sorrow into depressive disorder*. Oxford University Press.

Hume, D. (1739/2000). *A treatise of human nature*. Oxford University Press.

Hume, D. (1748/2007). *An enquiry concerning human understanding*. Oxford University Press.

Hyman, S. E. (2010). The diagnosis of mental disorders: The problem of reification. *Annual Review of Clinical Psychology, 6*, 155–179.

Insel, T. (2013). Directors Blog: Transforming Diagnosis. http://www.nimh.nih.gov/about/director/2013/transforming-diagnosis.shtml

James, W. (1890). *The principles of psychology*. Holt.

Jaspers, K. (1968/1997a). *General psychopathology* (J. Hoenig & M. W. Hamilton, Trans. vol. 1). Johns Hopkins University Press.

Jaspers, K. (1968/1997b). *General psychopathology* (J. Hoenig & M. W. Hamilton, Trans. vol. 2). Johns Hopkins University Press.

Johnstone, L., & Boyle, M. (2018). *The power threat meaning framework*. British Psychological Society.

Kendler, K. S. (1990). Toward a scientific psychiatric nosology. *Archives of General Psychiatry, 47*, 969–973.

Kendler, K. S. (2020). Kendler introduction to chapter 2. In K. S. Kendler & P. Zachar (Eds.), *Toward a philosophical approach to psychiatry* (pp. 30–32). Cambridge Scholars Publishing.

Kendler, K. S., & Engstrom, E. J. (2017). Kahlbaum, Hecker, and Kraepelin and the transition from psychiatric symptom complexes to empirical disease forms. *American Journal of Psychiatry, 174*(2), 102–109.

Kendler, K. S., Karkowski, L. M., & Prescott, C. A. (1998). Stressful life events and major depression: Risk period, long-term contextual threat, and diagnostic specificity. *Journal of Nervous & Mental Disease, 186*(11), 661–669.

Kendler, K. S., Karkowski, L. M., & Prescott, C. A. (1999). Causal relationship between stressful life events and the onset of major depression. *American Journal of Psychiatry, 156*(6), 837–841.

Kernberg, O. F. (1969). Factors in the psychoanalytic treatment of narcissistic personalities. *Bulletin of the Menninger Clinic, 33*, 191–196.

Kernberg, O. F. (1975). *Borderline conditions and pathological narcissism*. Jason Aronson.

Klein, M. (1964). *Contributions to psychoanalysis (1921–1945)*. McGraw-Hill.

Kohut, H. (1971). *The analysis of the self: A systematic psychoanalytic approach to the treatment of narcissistic personality disorders*. International Universities Press.

Kolakowski, L. (1969). *The alienation of reason: A history of positivist thought* (N. Guterman, Trans.). Doubleday.

Kraepelin, E. (1907). *Clinical psychiatry* (A. R. Diendorf, Trans.). Macmillan.

Kräupl Taylor, F. (1987). Psychoanalysis: A philosophical critique. *Psychological Medicine, 17*, 557–560.

Lakoff, G., & Johnson, M. (1980). *Metaphors we live by*. University of Chicago Press.

Laudan, L. (1981). A confutation of convergent realism. *Philosophy of Science, 48*(1), 19–49.

Linehan, M. M. (1993). *Cognitive-behavioral treatment of borderline personality disorder*. Guilford.

Locke, J. (1689/1997). *An essay concerning human understanding*. Penguin Books.

Luhrmann, T. R. (2000). *Of two minds: An anthropologist looks at American psychiatry*. Alfred A. Knopf.

MacCorquodale, K., & Meehl, P. E. (1948). On a distinction between hypothetical constructs and intervening variables. *Psychological Review, 55*(2), 95–107.

Mahler, M. S. (1971). A study of the separation-individuation process and its possible application to borderline phenomena in the psychoanalytic situation. *Psychoanalytic Study of the Child, 26*, 403–424.

Mahler, M. S., Pine, F., & Bergman, A. (1975). *The psychological birth of the human infant*. Basic Books.

Maiese, M. (2016). *Embodies selves and divided minds*. Oxford: Oxford University Press.

Massimi, M. (2008). Why there are no ready-made phenomena: What philosophers of science should learn from Kant. *Royal Institute of Philosophy Supplement, 63*, 1–35.

McGlashan, T. H., Grilo, C. M., Sanislow, C. A., Ralevski, E., Morey, L. C., Gunderson, J. G., . . . Pagano, M. (2005). Two-year prevalence and stability of individual DSM-IV criteria for schizotypal, borderline, avoidant, and obsessive-compulsive personality disorders: Toward a hybrid model of axis II disorders. *American Journal of Psychiatry, 162*(5), 883–889.

McHugh, P. R., & Treisman, G. (2007). PTSD: A problematic diagnostic category. *Journal of Anxiety Disorders, 21*(2), 211–222.

Mill, J. S. (1843/2015). *A system of logic*. Theophania Publishing.

Miller, G. A., & Bartholomew, M. A. (2020). Challenges in the relationship between psychological and biological phenomena in psychopathology. In K. S. Kendler, J. Parnas, & P. Zachar (Eds.), *Levles of analysis in psychopathology: Cross-disciplinary perspectives* (pp. 238–266). Cambridge University Press.

Millon, T., Millon, C., Roger, D., & Grossman, S. (2009). *Millon clinical multiaxial inventory-III (MCMI-III): Manual*. Pearson.

Morgan, C., Dazzan, P., Lappin, J., Heslin, M., Donoghue, K., Fearon, P., . . . Reininghaus, U. (2021). Rethinking the course of psychotic disorders: Modelling long-term symptom trajectories. *Psychological Medicine*, 1–10.

Newen, A., De Bruin, L., & Gallagher, S. (2018). 4E cognition: Historical roots, key concepts, and central issues. In A. Newen, L. De Bruin, & S. Gallagher (Eds.), *The Oxford handbook of 4E cognition* (pp. 3–18). Oxford University Press.

Nielsen, K. (2021). Comparing two enactive perspectives on mental disorder. *Philosophy, Psychiatry, and Psychology, 28*, 197–200.

Nielsen, K., & Ward, T. (2018). Towards a new conceptual framework for psychopathology: Embodiment, enactivism, and embedment. *Theory & Psychology, 28*(6), 800–822.

Pernu, T. K. (2019). Causal explanation in psychiatry. In S. Tekin & R. Bluhm (Eds.), *The Bloomsbury companion to philosophy of psychiatry* (pp. 217–236). Bloomsbury.

Petry, N. (2006). Early onset alcoholism: A separate or unique predictor of delay discounting? Comment on Dom et al (2006). *Addiction, 101*(2), 292–292.

Pincus, A., L., & Roche, M. J. (2011). Narcissistic grandiosity and narcissistic vulnerability. In W. K. Campbell & J. D. Miller (Eds.), *The handbook of narcissism and narcissistic personality disorder* (pp. 31–40). John Wiley & Sons.

Popper, K. (1963). *Conjectures and refutations: The growth of scientific knowledge*. Routledge.

Porter, R. (1987). *Mind-forg'd manacles*. Harvard University Press.

Porter, R. (1989). The early Royal Society and the spread of medical knowledge. In R. French & A. Wear (Eds.), *The medical revolution of the seventeenth century* (pp. 272–293). Cambridge University Press.

Potter, N. N. (2009). *Mapping the edges and the in-between*. Oxford University Press.

Putnam, H. (1988). *Representation and reality*. MIT Press.

Putnam, H. (1990). *Realism with a human face*. Harvard University Press.

Quine, W. V. (1951). Main trends in recent philosophy: Two dogmas of empiricism. *Philosophical Review, 60*, 20–43.

Raleigh, M. J., McGuire, M. T., Brammer, G. L., & Yuwiler, A. (1984). Social and environmental influences on blood serotonin concentrations in monkeys. *Archives of General Psychiatry, 41*(4), 405–410.

Rashed, M. A. (2019). *Madness and the demand for recognition: A philosophical inquiry into identity and mental health activism*. Oxford University Press.

Robins, E., & Guze, S. B. (1970). Establishment of diagnostic validity in psychiatric illness: Its application to schizophrenia. *American Journal of Psychiatry, 126*(7), 983–986.

Roth, M., & Kroll, J. (1986). *The reality of mental illness*. Cambridge University Press.

Scarr, S., & McCartney, K. (1983). How people make their own environments: A theory of genotype→environment effects. *Child Development, 54*(2), 424–435.

Schaffner, K. F. (1993). *Discovery and explanation in biology and medicine*. University of Chicago Press.

Schwartz, M. A., Wiggins, O. P., & Norko, M. A. (1989). Prototypes, ideal types, and personality disorders: The return to classical psychiatry. *Journal of Personality Disorders, 3*(1), 1–9.

Scott, W. J. (1990). PTSD in DSM-III: A case in the politics of diagnosis and disease. *Social Problems, 37*(3), 294–310.

Sellars, W. (1956). Empiricism and the philosophy of mind. In H. Feigl & M. Scriven (Eds.), *Minnesota studies in the philosophy of science* (vol. 1, pp. 253–329). University of Minnesota Press.

Shorter, E. (1997). *A history of psychiatry*. John Wiley & Sons.

Skinner, B. F. (1953). *Science and human behavior*. Macmillan.

Skodol, A. E., Pagano, M. E., Bender, D. S., Shea, M. T., Gunderson, J. G., Yen, S., . . . McGlashan, T. H. (2005). Stability of functional impairment in patients with schizotypal, borderline, avoidant, or obsessive-compulsive personality disorder over two years. *Psychological Medicine, 35*(3), 443–451.

Spitzer, R. L., Endicott, J., & Robins, E. (1978). Research diagnostic criteria. *Archives of General Psychiatry, 35*, 773–782.

Sulloway, F. J. (1979). *Freud, biologist of the mind*. Basic Books.

Suzuki, A. (1995). Dualism and the transformation of psychiatric language in the seventeenth and eighteenth centuries. *History of Science, 33*(4), 417–447.

Sydenham, T. (1682). Hysteric disorders and cure of invererate dejection (J. Swan, Trans.). In R. Hunter & I. Macalpine (Eds.), *Three hundred years of psychiatry (1535–1860)* (pp. 221–224). Oxford University Press.

van der Maas, H. L. J., Dolan, C. V., Grasman, R., P. P. P., M., W. J., Huizenga, H., M., & Raijmakers, M. E. J. (2006). A dynamical model of general intelligence: The positive manifold of intelligence by mutualism. *Psychological Review, 113*, 842–861.

van der Maas, H. L. J., Kan, K.-J., & Borsboom, D. (2014). Intelligence is what the intelligence test measures. Seriously. *Journal of Intelligence, 2*, 12–15.

van Fraassen, B. C. (2002). *The empirical stance.* Yale University Press.

Varela, F. J., Thompson, E., & Rosch, E. (1991). *The embodied mind: Cognitive science and human experience.* MIT Press.

Wear, A. (1989). Medical practice in late seventeenth- and early eighteenth-century England: Continuity and union. In R. French & A. Wear (Eds.), *The medical revolution of the seventeenth century* (pp. 294–320). Cambridge University Press.

Weber, M. (1949). *The methodology of the social sciences* (E. A. Shils & H. A. Finch, Trans.). Free Press.

Wiggins, O. P., & Schwartz, M. A. (1991). Research into personality disorders: The alternatives of dimensions and ideal types. *Journal of Personality Disorders, 5*(1), 69–81.

Winnicott, D. W. (1965). *The maturational process and the facilitating environment.* International Universities Press.

Woodward, J. (2003). *Making things happen: A theory of causal explanation.* Oxford University Press.

Woodward, J. (2008). Cause and explanation in psychiatry: An interventionist perspective. In K. S. Kendler & J. Parnas (Eds.), *Philosophical issues in psychiatry: Explanation, phenomenology, and nosology* (pp. 136–184). Johns Hopkins University Press.

Zachar, P. (2000). Child development and the regulation of affect and cognition in consciousness: A view from object relations theory. In R. D. Ellis & N. Newton (Eds.), *The caldron of consciousness: Motivation, affect and self-organization—An anthology.* (pp. 205–222). John Benjamins.

Zachar, P. (2014). *A metaphysics of psychopathology.* MIT Press.

Zachar, P., & McNally, R. J. (2017). Vagueness, the sorites paradox, and posttraumatic stress disorder. In G. Keil, L. Keuck, & R. Hauswald (Eds.), *Vagueness in psychiatry.* (pp. 169–188). Oxford University Press.

Zachar, P., Regier, D. A., & Kendler, K. S. (2019). The aspirations for a paradigm shift in DSM-5: An oral history. *Journal of Nervous & Mental Disease, 202*(4), 346–352.

Zanarini, M. C., Frankenburg, F. R., Hennen, J., & Silk, K. R. (2003). The longitudinal course of borderline psychopathology: 6-year prospective follow-up of the phenomenology of borderline personality disorder. *American Journal of Psychiatry, 160*(2), 274–283.

# CHAPTER 3

# The Hierarchical Taxonomy of Psychopathology

Christopher C. Conway *and* Grace N. Anderson

It is difficult to overstate how important a valid diagnostic system is to understanding psychopathology. It structures research agendas, clinical visits, and all manner of professional training. It is the lexicon professionals use to communicate with one another and to interface with other entities, such as insurance and legal systems.

Official nomenclatures are under continuous revision. Scholars are always searching for a more accurate map of mental health problems. This evolution is evident in the periodic re-releases of official diagnostic manuals (e.g., *DSM-I, -II, -III, -IV,* and, currently, *-5*). Those updates tend to be conservative, akin to adding a handful of new chemical elements to the periodic table every decade or so. The purpose of this chapter is to describe a qualitatively different approach to diagnosis that accomplishes something more like systematically reshuffling the familiar layout of the periodic table. The new approach is called the *Hierarchical Taxonomy of Psychopathology* (HiTOP), and it differs from prevailing systems in that it was formulated on the basis of findings from systematic research. We argue that it overcomes many of the conceptual problems associated with categorical diagnosis that have frustrated researchers and clinicians. We begin the chapter by reviewing the structure and limitations of categorical taxonomies, and we then describe the origins, format, and implications of empirically based diagnosis.

## Categorical Classification Systems

The *DSM* and *ICD* are the dominant classification systems, also called *nosologies*, in the United States and abroad, respectively. Their history, organization, and utility are described in detail elsewhere in this volume. In this section, we focus on the parts of these systems that motivated investigators to explore alternative classifications. For simplicity, we refer to the particulars of *DSM*, but the same considerations generally apply to *ICD*.

For our purposes, the key thing to know about *DSM* is that it was originally constructed on the basis of expert opinion. Specialists (mostly psychiatrists) met to trade clinical observations and speculate about the mental dysfunctions causing their patients' problems. These sorts of formulations were deduced primarily from clinical experiences rather than systematic research. In other words, expert consensus—or occasionally just the loudest voice in the room—shaped the diagnoses printed in early editions of *DSM* (Spiegel, 2005). Because of the conservative revision process, many of those same constructs persist in *DSM-5* today.

*DSM* portrays mental disorders as categorical entities. Generally, a person is either a member or nonmember of each category, although some finer gradations of pathology are possible for select diagnoses. Patients are sorted into these categories

---

**Abbreviations**
DBT dialectical behavior therapy
fMRI functional magnetic resonance imaging
GWAS genome-wide association study
HiTOP Hierarchical Taxonomy of Psychopathology
MDD major depressive disorder
NESARC National Epidemiologic Survey on Alcohol and Related Conditions
PD personality disorder
PID-5 Personality Inventory for *DSM-5*
SAD social anxiety disorder
SSRI selective serotonin reuptake inhibitors

if they express enough of the diagnostic criteria, which represent our hypotheses about how mental disorders manifest. A cutoff point, separating cases from noncases, is designated for each condition. Patients qualify for *DSM-5* major depressive disorder (MDD), for example, when they satisfy at least five of the nine total diagnostic criteria. Any fewer criteria, regardless of the severity of a patient's depressed mood, and MDD is ruled out.

## Problems with Categories

*DSM*'s categorical structure is the status quo. *DSM* diagnoses have been the basic units of mental health disciplines for many decades. As mentioned, quite a few have been conserved through iterations of *DSM* with little or no modification, despite years of research.

There have been complaints throughout *DSM*'s history regarding the validity of categorical diagnoses and their utility in clinical practice. The list of criticisms, recorded in detail elsewhere (e.g., Widiger & Samuel, 2005), is long and compelling. They became the catalyst for new systems, such as HiTOP, that are more closely based on scientific data collected over the past 40 years or so since the publication of *DSM-III*. We catalog some of the main problems with categorical rubrics here to clarify, by comparison, the benefits of a system that does not assume mental disorders are binary categories.

### *Comorbidity*

If mental disorders are in fact discrete entities, each with a distinctive etiology, pathophysiology, illness course, and so on, then disorders should not overlap substantially. However, large-scale studies document that disorders co-occur at rates well above what would be predicted by chance (e.g., Kessler et al., 2005). Indeed, in the community, a small percentage of the population is responsible for over half of the total number of diagnoses recorded (Caspi et al., 2020). In outpatient care, if a patient is diagnosed with a mental disorder, the odds are better than 50/50 that they will be diagnosed with two or more conditions (Brown et al., 2001). This effect is even more pronounced in inpatient hospital settings.

Comorbidity muddles the design and interpretation of research projects. Imagine an investigator who is studying attentional bias in panic disorder. They hypothesize that people with panic disorder more readily direct attention to danger cues. They recruit a clinical sample and estimate the correlation between panic and this information-processing outcome. After wrapping up the study, they realize there could be a potential confound: almost all panic disorder cases were also diagnosed with agoraphobia, so perhaps the observed correlation between panic and attentional bias was attributable to agoraphobia instead.

A possible solution is to recruit a "pure" sample of panic disorder cases—people diagnosed with panic disorder but no other conditions. This method would certainly minimize the chances of a spurious correlation. The only problem is that this sample is unrepresentative of the population of people with panic disorder. Panic is correlated with diverse other mental health problems, especially agoraphobia, so the observed effect in this "pure" group would be unlikely to generalize to populations of interest.

Clinicians face the same kind of dilemma. In ordinary practice, most patients qualify for multiple categorical diagnoses. Consider a patient who presents with attention deficit hyperactivity disorder, drug use disorder, and antisocial personality disorder (PD). A psychotherapist is confronted with a tough choice: Address the problems simultaneously or treat them sequentially? If simultaneously, what shared phenomenon or process among these conditions should be in the foreground? If sequentially, in what order? There is virtually no empirical guidance for this type of decision.

### *Heterogeneity*

Two patients with the same diagnostic label may look very different from one another. This is called *within-category variability*, and it characterizes most *DSM* conditions. It occurs because (1) a diverse constellation of signs and symptoms can contribute to any diagnosis, and (2) only a subset of symptoms is needed to cross the diagnostic threshold. Recall the case of MDD, where any five of nine symptoms could qualify a patient for the diagnosis. This implies that two patients could share a diagnosis but have only one depressive symptom in common. Investigators have used simple mathematics to quantify this problem, finding close to 1,000 different possible symptom presentations that fit the *DSM-5* MDD criteria (Fried & Nesse, 2015). The situation is worse for posttraumatic stress disorder (PTSD): there are more than 600,000 ways to qualify PTSD (Galatzer-Levy & Bryant, 2013).

In research projects based on categorical diagnoses, it is impossible to tell what disorder components are responsible for a correlation with some outcome variable. *DSM-5* PTSD, for instance, is characterized by several loosely related symptom domains: intrusions (e.g., flashbacks), avoidance (e.g., steering clear of trauma-related places), negative cognitions and moods (e.g., self-blame), and altered arousal and reactivity (e.g., hypervigilance). If a study finds that the PTSD syndrome is correlated with some outcome, it is not obvious which symptom domains are responsible for the observed effect. Conceptualizing PTSD as a categorical entity—collapsing across the subunits—misses the opportunity to explore these nuances.

Diagnostic heterogeneity is problematic in treatment arenas, too. Psychotherapies are typically geared toward categorical diagnoses. There is no guarantee, however, that they target all symptom components equally. If cognitive therapy for PTSD addresses, say, traumatic intrusions and negative cognitions, then people diagnosed with PTSD primarily by virtue of other problems (e.g., avoidance and hyperarousal) would not be expected to benefit substantially from treatment.

### Unreliability

The interpretability of diagnoses depends on some reasonable degree of consistency across raters and time. Disagreement among raters suggests that the constructs mean different things to different people. This type of inconsistency makes it difficult to be sure whether a sample of people with, say, conduct disorder in one clinic or study is really equivalent to a sample of people with conduct disorder in another. Observations of limited consistency across time would contradict assumptions about the temporal stability of most forms of psychopathology (e.g., PDs).

Findings in large-scale studies point to problematic reliability for categorical conditions. In field trials for *DSM-5*, about 40% of the diagnoses studied did not reach acceptable levels of interrater agreement in real-world practice settings (Regier et al., 2013). Longitudinal studies that track patients over time also document instability in diagnostic status over time. For instance, one prospective study of 160 patients diagnosed with borderline PD—an intractable condition, according to received wisdom—discovered that more than 10% of diagnoses remitted within 6 months (Gunderson et al., 2003).

### Fuzzy Boundary with Normality

Breaking a natural continuum into parts throws away information. For example, collapsing ambient temperature into two categories called "hot" and "cold" sacrifices precision. Say the cutpoint is 60°F. Now a 59°F day is considered categorically different from a 61°F day, whereas 61°F and 100°F are considered equivalently hot. The same practical problem occurs when investigators dichotomize a dimension of, say, depression severity into cases versus noncases of MDD.

There is no empirical evidence to justify this practice for mental disorder. To the contrary, quantitative research shows that people differ by degree, not by kind, on virtually all mental health constructs studied so far (Haslam et al., 2020). According to the extensive literature on this topic (Haslam et al., 2020; Krueger et al., 2018, Markon et al., 2011), the best way to summarize how people differ from one another with respect to any mental health condition is to assume a dimension of severity—marked by nearly infinite gradations—rather than mutually exclusive classes.

### Blind Spots in Coverage

There are well over 300 diagnoses codified in *DSM-5*. It is ironic, then, that categorical nosologies are sometimes criticized for poor coverage, meaning they do not adequately capture the range of conditions that clinicians encounter in ordinary practice. A common scenario is that patients will present with symptoms representing an amalgam of features from various "official" disorders. This combination of problems, also called a *syndrome*, creates significant distress and impairment, leading the patient to seek out professional help. Nevertheless, it does not align with the profile of any single *DSM* diagnosis. These cases can fall through the cracks in the healthcare system, failing to qualify for services reserved for people whose complaints fit neatly into a particular diagnostic category. In several mental health domains (e.g., eating disorders, PDs), this has led to "other specified"—called "not otherwise specified" in *DSM-IV*—to be the most common diagnosis (e.g., Verheul, Bartak, & Widiger, 2007).

### Multifinality

In medicine, a diagnosis implies a particular pathogenesis. Each illness can be traced to its own distinct causal mechanisms. This is decidedly not the case for psychopathology. Despite immense resources devoted to discovering *the* cause for various *DSM* diagnoses, none has been established or appear forthcoming. With few exceptions, there is no one-to-one correspondence between a risk factor and any categorical mental health outcome.

Instead, potent risk factors are virtually always related to multiple categorical disorders. This phenomenon has been termed *multifinality* by developmentalists, who observed that adverse events early on in life conferred risk for an array of mental health outcomes (Cicchetti & Rogosch, 1996). It implies that when the architects of official nosologies divided mental health problems into mutually exclusive categories, they did not delineate disorders with meaningfully separate etiologies and correlates.

## A Quantitative Nosology

This report card raises serious questions about the utility of categorical diagnoses for mental health research and practice. No matter how advanced the research technology, how large and representative the sample, how insightful the investigator, the findings built around *DSM* will be, to some extent, difficult to interpret. Perhaps we should not continue to anchor all of the field's knowledge to these suboptimal representations of psychopathology.

Overhauling the diagnostic system would not necessarily mean starting over. Decades of clinical observation and empirical research into the basic features of mental disorder provide a palette to work with. The key proposed change is to bring systematic data analysis, *and not just expert committees*, to the foreground to find out how those building blocks tend to assort into meaningful clinical problems. This quantitative approach moves as far away as possible from the clinical opinion and political processes that have played such a major role in the development of categorical systems (see, e.g., Zachar et al., 2016).

Quantitative nosology's mandate is to summarize mental health problems according to observed patterns of covariation. This means that researchers use quantitative analysis to determine how psychopathology signs and symptoms cluster together. These empirically derived clusters are the constructs (i.e., clinical phenomena) that comprise the new taxonomy.

We can loosely define quantitative analysis as examining correlations among mental health problems. Correlations reflect co-occurrence or clustering. We can identify diagnostic constructs by finding clinical phenomena that tend to cluster together. For instance, if sadness, insomnia, weight loss, and thoughts of dying co-occur, we might posit depression as a common thread through all of these experiences. We can infer constructs—unobservable characteristics (e.g., depression, extraversion, intelligence, humor)—that explain why the building blocks of psychopathology assort in systematic ways.

The principal method of quantitative analysis in this area is called *factor analysis*. To oversimplify, factor analysis establishes continuously distributed, *unobserved* traits (i.e., factors) that explain correlations among a set of *observed* behaviors (for more information, see Brown, 2015). It was formulated at the turn of the twentieth century to test the hypothesis that a general cognitive ability factor accounted for similarity in performance across several more specific cognitive tasks (e.g., working memory, processing speed, vocabulary). The factors are considered *latent* variables, meaning they are not observable; we infer their existence from patterns of correlation among *manifest*, or observable, outcomes. To understand the difference between latent and manifest concepts, consider that a clinician might directly observe tearfulness, tiredness, and weight loss (i.e., manifest phenomena), whereas the hypothesis "this patient is depressed"—where depression is a latent phenomenon—is inferred from those observations.

We will refer to the application of factor analysis and related methods as *structural research*, because they describe the way different components of psychopathology fit together. Structural research has a long history in clinical psychology and psychiatry. Early studies examined the relations among symptoms reported by psychiatric patients in an attempt to discern patterns in their presenting problems (e.g., Moore, 1930). There were similar investigations into the coherence of affective experiences in community and clinical populations that spawned a robust line of work into the composition of anxiety and depression (Mineka et al., 1998), which was perhaps the clearest forerunner of contemporary quantitative nosology.

Structural research caught on most quickly in the developmental psychopathology literature; this field has been conceptualizing mental health problems in terms of empirically derived dimensions for decades. Achenbach's (1966) factor analytic research into youth mental health complaints was the main catalyst. He found that recognizable mental health problems like anxiety, depression, and somatic complaints could be conceptualized as aspects of a broad internalizing dimension and delinquency, conduct problems, and aggression could be conceptualized as aspects of an externalizing dimension (Achenbach et al., 1991).

Subsequent research in adult populations detected similar patterns. Kreuger, Caspi, Moffitt, and Silva (1998) found that internalizing and externalizing factors summarized the interrelations among anxiety and depressive diagnoses, on the one hand, and substance use and antisocial behavior diagnoses, on the other, in a New Zealand community sample. Krueger (1999) then analyzed US epidemiological data and found that the same two dimensions explained comorbidity among *DSM-III-R* diagnoses. This latter study made the case for a more elaborated, hierarchical structure in which the internalizing factor broke apart into two subordinate factors, which he labeled distress and fear. Distress accounted for especially high comorbidity among depression and generalized anxiety disorder (GAD), whereas fear represented the clustering between panic disorder and the phobias.

The investigations by Krueger and colleagues were a turning point for structural research and, more broadly, the quantitative nosology endeavor. They have inspired a tremendous amount of empirical work over the past 20 years. These structural studies formed the evidence base for HiTOP, which we turn to in the next section.

Much of the ensuing research was oriented around comorbidity patterns among categorical diagnoses. Many large-scale datasets from epidemiological and community-based research included a diverse roster of interviewer-rated diagnoses, and this was the perfect environment for making sense of comorbidity. A meta-analysis, now more than 15 years old, of these efforts supported a model of diagnostic correlations that was anchored by factors that closely paralleled the internalizing and externalizing factors that had originally appeared in developmental research (Krueger & Markon, 2006). Moreover, it again raised the possibility that there were discernable subdimensions within the internalizing spectrum; the internalizing factor in this meta-analytic model bifurcated into distress and fear subfactors, mirroring the factor analysis reported by Krueger (1999).

Later studies with even broader diagnostic coverage revealed other factors adjoining the internalizing and externalizing dimensions. Kotov et al. (2011) searched for clusters of diagnoses in a sample of about 3,000 outpatients who completed a comprehensive interview for *DSM-IV* clinical disorder and PD diagnoses. They described three other factors in this dataset: thought disorder (psychosis, mania, and cluster A PDs), somatoform (hypochondriasis, pain disorder, undifferentiated somatoform disorder), and antagonism (cluster B and paranoid PDs).

Results in other samples converged with these new findings (e.g., Forbes et al., 2017; Sellbom, 2017).

We acknowledge that at first glance a research agenda based on *DSM* diagnoses does not seem likely to move us meaningfully beyond diagnostic categories. After all, the whole purpose of a quantitative nosology is to transcend the traditional categorical system. However, this line of research is valuable because it illustrates that structural research can uncover unobserved dimensions that in theory predispose to clinically recognizable mental health problems. These dimensions offer another way to conceptualize mental disorders. Nevertheless, there are certain constraints. *DSM* diagnoses may not be the optimal way to sort symptoms. As mentioned, categorical diagnoses most often reflect a heterogeneous symptom set. This means that structural research based on diagnoses cannot speak to the organization of fine-grained signs, symptoms, and maladaptive personality traits.

Structural research therefore increasingly has bypassed diagnoses to focus on more basic units of psychopathology. Markon's (2010) analysis of more than 100 interviewer-rated symptoms in a British epidemiological study extended the evolving structural model "downward" in the sense of zooming in on the homogeneous components that compose psychological disorders. Factor analysis showed that the symptoms in this study clustered into 20 tight-knit subordinate, or lower-order, dimensions. For instance, hazardous alcohol use, physiological withdrawal, and social role failures secondary to alcohol use cohered into an "alcohol problems" dimension. In turn, Markon (2010) examined how these 20 lower-order dimensions assembled into higher-order factors. This process revealed the familiar internalizing and externalizing factors alongside thought disorder—marked by hallucinations, paranoia, and eccentricity—and pathological introversion—marked by social anxiety, unassertiveness, and dependence.

Other research teams followed Markon's (2010) lead. Symptom-based investigations generated insights into the intermediate factors that function as the connective tissue between manifest symptoms and higher-order factors like internalizing and externalizing. A study by Waszczuk, Kotov, Ruggero, Gamez, and Watson (2017) involving two treatment-seeking samples illustrates this point. They administered an interview measure of *every* symptom of *DSM-IV* anxiety and depressive disorders and found that these manifest variables reflected 31 fairly homogeneous latent factors, such as irritability, dissociation, and anhedonia. These subordinate factors cohered into 8 intermediate factors called syndromes (e.g., vegetative symptoms, cognitive depression, mania); these were subsumed by even broader factors called distress, fear, and obsessive compulsive disorder (OCD)/mania; and surmounting them all was a unifying internalizing factor.

Wazczuk et al.'s (2017) approach demonstrates that clinical phenomena can be organized hierarchically, with several tiers of recognizable constructs arrayed across very high levels of resolution (e.g., trouble eating in front of others) to very low levels (e.g., internalizing). Other research confirmed that this principle extended beyond the internalizing domain (e.g., Kotov et al., 2017).

As quantitative nosologists reviewed this literature, a picture of the higher-order dimensions of psychopathology began to emerge. The internalizing factor was defined by anxiety, depression, and sexual and eating problems; thought disorder by mania and psychotic experiences; detachment by emotional and social disengagement; and somatoform by preoccupation with medically unexplained somatic problems (Krueger et al., 2018). The broad externalizing dimension was differentiated into *disinhibited* externalizing, identified by antisocial behavior and substance misuse, and antagonistic externalizing, marked by antisocial behavior and maladaptive personality traits like narcissism, attention-seeking, and manipulativeness. The evidence base was stronger for some of these dimensions than others, partly because some of them were only evident in research with comprehensive psychopathology assessment. For example, it was clear that antagonistic externalizing and detachment factors were rooted primarily in characteristics normally associated with PD (e.g., Wright & Simms, 2015).

This research program gained more traction as the main structural elements were replicated across diverse contexts. The hierarchical model of psychopathological symptoms and diagnoses appeared fairly uniform across developmental stage, gender, nation, and clinical setting (Krueger et al., 2003). This generalizability supported the hypothesis that these empirically derived groupings of clinical phenomena might have broad utility as diagnostic tools.

## The Hierarchical Taxonomy of Psychopathology

Investigators recognized that this theoretical framework had the potential to improve on categorical diagnostic systems. In 2015, a group of quantitative nosologists founded the HiTOP consortium to synthesize the work that had been done already into a consensus quantitative model of psychopathology, mobilize continued structural research, and explore its applications (Kotov et al., 2017). As an organization open to all sorts of professionals interested in advancing mental disorder diagnosis, it has expanded steadily in recent years.

### The HiTOP Model

One of the consortium's first acts was to integrate the available evidence to sketch a model of the major dimensions of psychopathology (Figure 3.1; reprinted from Conway et al., 2019). The HiTOP model is a proposal; it is a work in progress intended to evolve with new data. Figure 3.1 is a conceptual diagram, as opposed to a representation of results from a single empirical study. It pieces together evidence from independent studies that have surveyed different sections of this landscape.

The diagram's vertical axis represents breadth. Constructs higher up in the figure reflect characteristics that explain the coherence of constructs situated at lower levels. We will start at the base at work our way up. The *symptom components* are tight-knit clusters of symptomatic behaviors. For instance, a tendency to scan the environment for threats and an exaggerated startle response are part of a symptom component called hyperarousal. *Maladaptive personality traits* occupy the same tier of the hierarchy as symptom components. These are homogeneous individual differences discovered in research on the building blocks of PD.

The symptom components and maladaptive traits assort into dimensional *syndromes* at the next level of the hierarchy. For example, we tend to summarize the co-occurrence of sadness, anhedonia, insomnia, fatigue, and suicidality by referring to a depression syndrome. By definition, constructs at this level are more complex than symptom components and maladaptive traits. Note that the term "syndrome" generally denotes a disease category, and, indeed, many of the syndromes listed in Figure 3.1 are named after *DSM* diagnoses. However, here a syndrome is a continuous index of severity of a constellation of homogeneous symptoms and traits. The naming scheme is meant to illustrate the link with *DSM* symptoms; people can see that the familiar categorical constructs are represented, albeit with some reformatting, in the HiTOP framework.

The syndrome concepts presented in Figure 3.1 are provisional pieces of the HiTOP system. To

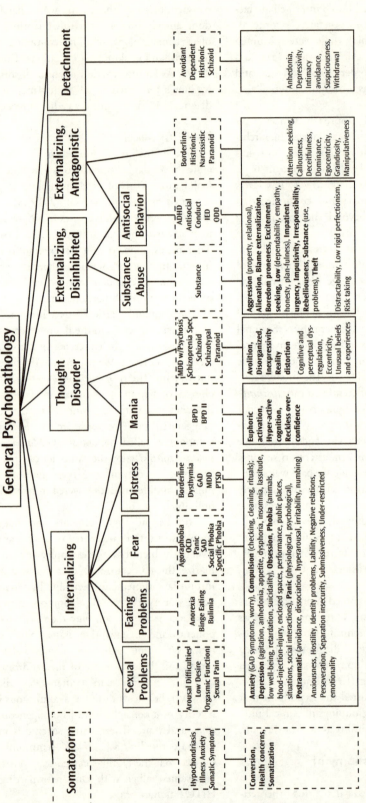

Figure 3.1 Hierarchical Taxonomy of Psychopathology (HiTOP) consortium working model. Constructs higher in the figure are broader and more general, whereas constructs lower in the figure are narrower and more specific. Starting at the top and working down, the levels are: superspectrum (i.e., general psychopathology), spectrum (e.g., internalizing), subfactor (e.g., distress), syndrome (e.g., depression), and symptom components (e.g., anhedonia) and maladaptive traits (e.g., anxiousness). Dashed lines denote provisional elements requiring further study. At the lowest level of the hierarchy, symptom components are listed in the upper half of the box, and maladaptive traits in the lower half; for heuristic purposes, conceptually related signs and symptoms (e.g., Phobia) are indicated in bold, with specific manifestations indicated in parentheses. ADHD, attention-deficit/hyperactivity disorder; BPD, bipolar disorder; GAD, generalized anxiety disorder; HiTOP, Hierarchical Taxonomy of Psychopathology; IED, intermittent explosive disorder; MDD, major depressive disorder; OCD, obsessive-compulsive disorder; ODD, oppositional defiant disorder; SAD, separation anxiety disorder; PD, personality disorder; PTSD, posttraumatic stress disorder.

date, there is limited research on how fine-grain symptom components and maladaptive traits tend to co-occur (cf. Forbes et al., in press; Waszczuk et al., 2017). This is reflected in the fact that symptom components and maladaptive traits are matched to groups of syndromes, rather than particular syndromes, in Figure 3.1. Much more is known about the ways syndromes assemble into subfactors and spectra, in large part because of the availability of large community and epidemiologic studies that involve diagnosis-based assessments.

Features shared across syndromes are represented by *subfactors*. Recall the fear and distress constructs that summarized distinct patterns of internalizing problems. The fear dimension embodies the processes that trigger pronounced defensive reactions (similar to the "fight or flight" response) to real or perceived immediate threats. This sort of psychological and physiological overreaction is evident in panic, for instance, where uncomfortable internal sensations are interpreted as signs of an imminent medical problem like a heart attack. At a similar level of breadth to fear and distress are substance use, antisocial behavior, eating problems, and sexual problem subfactors.

*Spectrum* constructs are at the next level up. These are often the focus of structural research, especially factor analyses of categorical diagnoses (e.g., Krueger & Markon, 2006). As mentioned earlier, there is solid evidence for thought disorder, internalizing, and externalizing—especially the latter two—as dimensions that explain patterns in manifest psychopathology. Based primarily on PD research distinguishing disinhibition and antagonism as separate personality dimensions that underpin fairly different sets of clinical phenomena, the HiTOP model splits externalizing into two spectra: disinhibited and antagonistic (e.g., Krueger et al., 2012).

The somatoform spectrum is provisional. It is clear that *DSM-5* somatic symptom disorder and illness anxiety disorder often co-occur with anxiety disorders and that anxiety is the predominant reaction to somatic issues in these conditions (APA, 2013). Nevertheless, the available structural research suggests that somatoform and internalizing problems are meaningfully distinct (Kotov et al., 2011; Sellbom, 2017). The detachment spectrum has also attracted less attention, although structural analyses of PD data over the past couple decades consistently identify this dimension, which represents avoidance of social and emotional engagement. Traces of detachment are evident in autism, as well as in PDs associated with suspiciousness, aloofness, and withdrawal (e.g., avoidant, schizoid).

Surmounting all the spectra is a *superspectrum* called the general factor of psychopathology (Lahey et al., 2012). It is also known as the *p*-factor due to its conceptual similarity to intelligence's *g*-factor that is theorized to encompass all mental abilities (Caspi et al., 2014). It accounts for the correlations among the six spectra. For example, internalizing and externalizing dimensions often are correlated around .50 (Krueger & Markon, 2006), hinting at a common substrate. There are many theories as to what this general factor might represent, but none has been seriously tested (Caspi & Moffitt, 2018). The leading hypothesis is that it reflects general distress, demoralization, and/or impairment that pervade all types of mental health conditions.

### Implications of a Quantitative Approach

As mentioned, HiTOP involves the same basic units that make up the *DSM*, but it reshuffles them according to how they tend to cluster together empirically. We can think of HiTOP as a diagnostic tool—an alternative to *DSM*—that is distinguished by its emphasis on *hierarchy* and *dimensions*.

#### HIERARCHY

Figure 3.1 clearly reflects HiTOP's hierarchical view of clinical phenomena. From this perspective, there is no single, "optimal" level of resolution for mental health problems. Any condition can be conceptualized at varying levels of resolution. Clark and Watson (2019) provide an example involving insomnia. They start with sleep difficulties reported as "I woke up much earlier than usual." This symptom could be conceptualized as part of a tight-knit symptom cluster representing problems with *terminal insomnia* (i.e., difficulty with early morning awakenings). Alternatively, it could also be considered a reflection of a broader *insomnia* construct, which encompasses trouble sleeping at early, middle, and late points of the sleep cycle. At an even broader level, there is evidence that it is part of a *depression* syndrome that involves sleep, weight, mood, and cognitive problems. Finally, a pattern of early awakenings also can be thought of as an *internalizing* problem; terminal insomnia and other sleep disruptions permeate various expressions of anxiety and depression.

To repeat, there is no optimal level of resolution, or frame of reference, for any mental health problem. One can zoom in as far as possible to consider a manifest symptom in terms of its specific ecology or context. What biological processes regulate difficulty returning to sleep after an unexpected awakening? How can the patient limit sunlight exposure during the early morning hours when they would like to be asleep? Alternately, one can just as easily zoom out and address the more general context in which the symptom is embedded. What biological factors predispose people to internalizing problems? What behavioral treatments are known to alleviate internalizing distress?

The researcher or clinician can choose the level of abstraction that is best suited for their particular objective. If the question concerns a process that mental health problems have in common, they can focus on a higher-order dimension. This is how the HiTOP model copes with comorbidity among categorical diagnoses. Professionals can work directly with the construct(s) hypothesized to reflect psychopathological processes that shape multiple conditions.

On the other hand, if the research or clinical question has to do with a very specific problem, such as anxiety in performance situations (e.g., public speaking), one can bypass categorical diagnoses and zero in on the particular symptom component or trait of interest. This flexibility allows a bit more control over the problem of heterogeneity that is baked into diagnostic categories. Some people with *DSM-5* social anxiety disorder qualify for the diagnosis on the basis of significant performance anxiety, but others struggle primarily with other forms of social interaction anxiety (e.g., difficulty talking to coworkers and authority figures). The syndrome (in *DSM*'s case, a categorical syndrome) collapses across these more specific features. HiTOP allows case conceptualization, diagnosis, research, and treatment to focus on these detailed, lower-order elements if need be.

HiTOP's hierarchical format mirrors other individual difference domains. Cognitive ability and personality are structured in much the same way. We alluded to the general intelligence factor ($g$) that purportedly explains why people who perform well on one IQ "subtest" (e.g., putting blocks together to make a pattern, remembering who wrote "Hamlet," recalling a string of numbers) tend to do well on the others. There is also a range of intermediate abilities, akin to HiTOP spectra and subfactors, such as verbal memory, visuospatial reasoning, and processing speed. Others are narrower still (e.g., vocabulary, matrix reasoning), mirroring symptom components and maladaptive traits.

### DIMENSIONS

Using dimensions, it is much easier to consistently rate people in terms of severity. There is much more room on a dimension to decide that person X has much more of a quality than person Y, but slightly less than person Z. This subtlety is impossible with binary diagnoses. A categorical depression diagnosis does not discriminate between the person who seemingly has never had a gloomy day in their life and the person who for the past 2 years has been actively suicidal, sad, sleeping poorly, and feeling worthless but is missing a fifth criterion that would cross the threshold for an MDD diagnosis.

This extra information in the dimensional system fosters reliability. People's relative position on a psychopathology dimension is stable over brief intervals. Clinicians have better agreement regarding the severity of clinical phenomena (Markon et al., 2011). This is in large part because dimensions avoid the tricky business of deciding whether a patient falls just above or below a categorical threshold. In other words, dimensions largely sidestep the problem of fuzzy boundaries between psychopathology and normality. The dimensional hypothesis embraces that fuzziness; it assumes a continuum of clinical problems that applies to everyone from the most healthy to the most sick. Everyone is "on the spectrum" according to this model.

## Research Utility

HiTOP is a descriptive system—another way of cataloging psychopathology—but it can do more than describe. In this section, we cover how HiTOP dimensions are applied to advance real-world research into the causes and consequences of psychopathology. That is, we examine associations between dimensional psychopathology constructs and variables outside the HiTOP system. These associations reflect the model's *research utility*. Whereas the structural research underpinning Figure 3.1 tells us what HiTOP "is," studies focused on research utility tell us what the model "does."

### Siloed Research Literatures

The misconception that *DSM* diagnoses have distinctive ecosystems (e.g., separate causes) has generated a very decentralized literature. It makes sense, from that perspective, for investigators to study one disorder at a time. As a result, knowledge has accumulated in a piecemeal fashion.

This applies not just to individual research projects but also to entire careers. Today it is still common for investigators to build a research program around one condition (e.g., "I am a borderline PD expert"), and this trend was even stronger in earlier generations. Researchers sometimes even screen out people with other diagnoses from data collection to minimize "noise." Perhaps at the most extreme, training environments can be explicitly structured around a single *DSM* condition, as is the case with some US Veterans Affairs sites that specialize in PTSD.

This norm creates information silos. Each study or each research program tells only part of the story relevant to a particular cause, correlate, or outcome. These often have a much more complex web of associations with psychopathology than we assume. Connecting the dots is rarely easy because there tends to be very little cross-talk among research teams that are working on different diagnoses.

The field is gradually coming to terms with this inefficiency. It helps when high-profile research findings raise awareness of the problem. The most prominent one in recent memory involves molecular genetics. When the human genome was sequenced, many investigators proclaimed that it was only a matter of time until the gene(s) that determined every *DSM* diagnosis were identified. After years of research and millions of funding dollars, it became apparent that there was no gene "for" any single diagnosis (Kendler, 2005). Quite the opposite was true: each disorder was related to many different genes, and relevant genes were linked to many disorders. Genetic effects were crossing diagnostic boundaries. This observation has fundamentally changed the way psychiatric geneticists define the phenotypes they study, and they more rarely target *DSM* diagnoses (Waszczuk et al., 2020).

In sum, huge bodies of information have amassed around *DSM* diagnoses. This makes for a fractured, incomplete picture of how psychopathology relates to important risks and outcomes. This is probably not the optimal way to set up a research agenda. HiTOP provides an outlet by offering an alternative research heuristic that proposes to completely restructure the design and interpretation of empirical studies.

### An Integrative Approach

We introduce this heuristic with an example. Consider a study on psychophysiological responses to a social stressor. The investigator hypothesizes that people diagnosed with social anxiety disorder (SAD) will overreact—in terms of heart rate, sweat, and respiration—to a standard "evaluative" stressor. The research participants, a mix of people with and without SAD, undergo a common test in stress research: they are asked to deliver an impromptu speech in front of a small audience. Electrodes record physiological activity throughout the task.

The study design and conceptual hypothesis (SAD → hyperarousal) seem sound; they are what we are used to finding in journal articles. Consider how they might be reframed from a HiTOP perspective. First, social anxiety is conceived of as a dimension, as opposed to a dichotomy. A dimensional operationalization makes it easier to identify the individual differences in anxiety among the research participants. Second, as illustrated in Figure 3.1, social anxiety can be conceptualized at multiple levels of analysis. It has both coarse and fine components, just as we mentioned that insomnia is reflected in higher- and lower-level constructs in the internalizing domain.

What this means practically is that a researcher can empirically test, *not just assume*, which social anxiety constructs contribute to the outcome. This flexibility is not possible with categorical rubrics, where the syndrome is the preordained level of analysis. This obscures which part(s) of the clinical picture are "driving" the associations with the outcome. A *DSM* diagnosis is therefore a little bit like a black box—a mix of unknowable components—that HiTOP can unpack.

Returning to the example, one can envision a number of different ways that social anxiety—conceptualized hierarchically—relates to physiological arousal in the face of evaluative stress. (1) It might be that a very specific symptom component, such as performance anxiety, predicts hyperarousal. Or (2) hyperarousal could depend primarily on the broader constellation of symptom components that make up the SAD syndrome. Alternately (3) it could be that hyperarousal is a common feature of all fear-related disorders, shared by any condition marked by a very sensitive "fight or flight" response. Finally, (4) the key ingredient might be the general propensity to experience negative affect, represented by the internalizing spectrum. Still other scenarios are possible. The take-home message is that we need not assume categorical syndromes are "where the action is"; we can empirically test out all of the possible pathways.

This methodology can be applied to any substantive research area—neuroscience, personality, social relationships, development, and so on. Indeed, this heuristic has generated new insights into how mental disorders onset, develop, and shape important life outcomes (reviewed in Conway et al., 2019). To give a sense of HiTOP's possible research applications, we selectively review this expanding body of evidence in the remainder of this section. For convenience, we group the literature into four topics: personality, genetics, neurobiology, and social environment. We concentrate on two principal themes that cut across this work. First, thinking hierarchically can change the questions we ask about psychopathology. Instead of hypothesizing about the correlation between one syndrome and one outcome, we can inquire about the levels of analysis (e.g., maladaptive trait, syndrome, spectrum) in a particular psychopathology domain that are most relevant to the outcome.

Second, examining HiTOP's criterion validity tells us a lot about its research utility. If empirically derived psychopathology dimensions relate in expected ways to external variables, then they have predictive and explanatory power. Therefore, the effects observed in these studies indicate how useful the heuristic might be going forward. If all effects are very small, or if syndrome constructs tend to have the most explanatory power, then it might make sense to continue to use (dimensionalized) *DSM* operational definitions of mental disorder to test substantive theories. But if meaningful effects are evident across multiple levels of analysis, then there is some evidence to support this model's utility.

### Personality

Just as is the case with psychopathology within the HiTOP framework, the most influential framework for understanding personality traits is hierarchical. Thus most students learn that personality traits are often characterized in terms of five dimensions—neuroticism, extraversion, conscientiousness, agreeableness, and openness—each of which can be broken down into more specific facets and even smaller "nuances" (Mõttus et al., 2017).

There is more than just architectural resemblance between the domains. Personality is thought to lay the foundation for mental disorder (Clark, 2005). Indeed, this overlap is reflected in the HiTOP model, which rests in part on maladaptive personality traits at the base of the hierarchy. Moreover, several of HiTOP's broader constructs, such as the detachment and antagonistic externalizing spectra, derive almost entirely from research on personality and PD (e.g., Wright & Simms, 2015).

We are beginning to learn about the empirical connections between the two hierarchical domains (Widiger et al., 2019). One early effort involved more than 1,000 middle-age participants in the Minnesota Twin and Family Study who completed diagnostic interviews and personality questionnaires (Krueger et al., 2001). Krueger et al. (2001) used factor analysis to model internalizing as the commonality among anxiety and depressive disorders and externalizing as the commonality among antisocial behavior and substance use disorders. Individual differences on internalizing were significantly correlated with neuroticism (mean $r$ across gender = .25), but not constraint (a near-neighbor of conscientiousness; mean $r$ = .03), which is the ability to keep impulses in check. Externalizing had the opposite pattern of associations (neuroticism $r$ = .02, constraint $r$ = .24). Meanwhile, neither internalizing nor externalizing was linked substantially to extraversion (mean $r$ = −.04).

Among the traits Krueger et al. (2001) examined, neuroticism has perhaps attracted the most research attention. High neuroticism is associated with all manner of physical and mental health problems, especially anxiety and depression (Kotov et al., 2010). Psychologists have designated it as a serious public health problem (Lahey, 2009). More recent personality research has found an even closer correspondence between neuroticism and internalizing than what was reported in the Minnesota Twin and Family Study. In a large cohort of high schoolers enriched for risk of anxiety and depression, Griffith et al. (2010) asked teens to make personality ratings, which included several self- and peer-rated neuroticism scales, and administered standard diagnostic interviews to assess mental disorder. In this study, there was a near-perfect correlation between neuroticism and internalizing ($r$ = .98), whereas neuroticism was much more modestly related to externalizing ($r$ = .29).

Most applied work has involved the HiTOP spectrum-level constructs. To represent lower-level dimensions, factor analysis tends to require a wide variety of manifest symptom or disorder variables, and there are relatively few research projects with that sort of comprehensive psychopathology coverage. One such study involved a thorough diagnostic workup and personality assessment in an epidemiological sample of 6,000 adults who responded to the National Comorbidity Survey (Levin-Aspenson et al., 2019). Analysis of the correlations among diagnoses yielded a four-tiered structural model: the *p*-factor was at the summit, and, at a second level, it bifurcated into internalizing and externalizing. At the third level, internalizing divided into fear and distress, and, at the fourth, a thought disorder factor broke off of distress. The *p*-factor had medium ($r \approx .40$) and small ($r \approx .10$) correlations with neuroticism and extraversion, respectively. By examining effects of lower-level dimensions, the authors were able to determine that the *p*-factor's correlation with neuroticism was driven by internalizing dimensions and that its (inverse) correlation with extraversion was attributable to the fear dimension in particular.

Sellbom and colleagues (2020) extended this approach (i.e., studying broad and specific psychopathology phenotypes in relation to personality) to a wider set of personality domains. They recruited 3,000 adults to respond to 29 self-report measures of psychopathology and one measure of maladaptive personality traits. These maladaptive traits came from a leading dimensional model of PD that includes negative affectivity, detachment, antagonism, disinhibition, and psychoticism. These five broad domains have close ties to the primary dimensions of the Five Factor Model of personality. Factor analysis reduced the psychopathology data to 10 factors, which represented syndromes like depression, panic, and psychosis. The interrelationships of these 10 factors were themselves factor analyzed to produce even broader latent dimensions. The factors representing anxiety and depression symptoms cohered into higher-order distress and fear subfactors, which, in turn, coalesced into an even broader internalizing spectrum. Alongside internalizing were thought disorder (encompassing obsessive-compulsive and psychosis factors) and externalizing (inattention, alcohol, and drug problems) spectra. Finally, all three of these spectrum constructs were modeled as representations of a superordinate *p*-factor.

With the complex model of mental disorder symptoms set, Sellbom et al. (2020) tested the dimensional constructs' associations with personality traits. Nearly all of these effects were about as large as was expected, attesting to the robust, predictable relations between the personality and psychopathology domains. Noteworthy results included strong associations of negative affectivity with internalizing ($r = .84$); psychoticism—a trait capturing eccentricity, unusual beliefs, and perceptual aberrations—with thought disorder ($r = .74$); and disinhibition—an amalgam of impulsivity and irresponsibility, similar to (low) constraint—with externalizing ($r = .75$). Also, negative affectivity ($r = .90$), detachment ($r = .74$), and psychoticism ($r = .78$) were all intimately related to the general factor of psychopathology.

Together, these results demonstrate that many broad psychopathology dimensions have close analogs in the personality literature, consistent with prominent theories of temperament and personality as core factors in the development of mental disorder (Clark, 2005). Future research will focus on the best ways to overlay these two domains in evolving structural models of psychopathology (Widiger et al., 2019).

## Genetics

Findings from the quantitative genetics literature strongly suggest that conditions that tend to cluster together phenotypically also tend to have a shared genetic substrate (Waszczuk et al., 2020). That is, the separable individual difference factors emerging from structural research on phenotypes (e.g., fear, distress, thought disorder) appear to line up with distinct genetic factors. This is evidence that the phenotypic dimensions compiled in HiTOP summarize meaningfully distinct etiological pathways to mental illness (Lahey et al., 2017).

In an investigation of 2,000 Norwegian twins, the genetic correlations (i.e., indices of overlap among genes that predispose to different phenotypes) among 22 clinical disorder and PD diagnoses pointed to four underlying genetic factors, interpretable as internalizing, disinhibited externalizing, antagonistic externalizing, and detachment (Kendler et al., 2011). Several other projects confirm the genetic coherence of individual spectra. For example, in the Minnesota Twin and Family Study ($N \approx 2,000$), antisocial behavior, conduct disorder, and various forms of substance dependence were evaluated in a sample of biological and adoptive families (Hicks et al., 2013). The phenotypic correlations among these antisocial behavior and substance misuse conditions supported a unifying externalizing factor, which turned out to be highly heritable, such that 61% of the individual differences on the factor were attributable to genetic differences among participants.

There is evidence for distinct genetic factors at lower levels of the HiTOP model, too, although the data are more limited. Studies find that more homogeneous clusters of conditions, such as symptom components, have unique genetic causes. However, these sources of variation tend to be smaller than those for higher-order dimensions (e.g., Kendler et al., 2013).

A constraint of quantitative genetic research is that it cannot pinpoint the parts of the genome that confer risk. It is based entirely on differences in relatedness among individuals, not direct measurement of genetic variation. This is where molecular genetic methods come in. As genomic technology grows increasingly easy to use, there has been an explosion of research into the specific genetic sequences that contribute to psychopathology. Genome-wide association studies (GWASs) simultaneously examine thousands of genetic polymorphisms in relation to psychopathology phenotypes.

Despite the promise of new technologies, the yield in terms of credible breakthroughs has been limited. The signal associated with particular variants tends to be fairly weak and inconsistent across studies (Sullivan et al., 2018). Part of the problem appears to be the phenotyping, which has not kept pace with technological advancement on the genetic side of the equation. There is concern that categorical disorders—some of which, as described at the outset, were formulated a century ago on the basis of clinical intuition—might not systematically map onto human genetic differences.

There is growing interest in alternate phenotypic approaches that can advance molecular genetic research in psychopathology. HiTOP is a promising solution. It minimizes the problem of heterogeneous diagnostic categories, which attenuate the connection between genes and psychopathology when a variant is associated with part, but not all, of the diagnostic picture (e.g., cognitive, but not vegetative, components of depression). It also accommodates the significant multifinality—called "pleiotropy" in genetics—evident in the psychiatric genetics literature. GWASs show that the genes implicated in one diagnostic category are typically related to various other conditions; a one-gene-to-many-conditions pattern rather than one-gene-to-one-condition relationship (e.g., Sullivan et al., 2018). This makes it virtually impossible to create a distinctive etiological model for any categorical disorder.

To be more precise, HiTOP addresses the problems of heterogeneity and pleiotropy by explicitly disentangling the broad and specific phenotypes that compose a particular psychopathology domain. With a hierarchical structure, it should be possible to discover what genetic variants confer widespread vulnerability to mental illness (e.g., at the superspectrum or spectrum level), as compared to variants that have a more specific influence at, say, the symptom component level (e.g., Waldman et al., 2020).

A number of large-scale investigations have now published linkages between genetic polymorphisms and broad psychopathology phenotypes, such as the $p$-factor, internalizing, and fear (reviewed in Waszczuk et al., 2020). These studies adopt the same structural research methods that illuminate the HiTOP constructs and use the resulting, continuously distributed factors, as opposed to categories, as targets in gene finding studies. This approach appears to be accelerating the hunt for replicable genetic risk factors, but research in this area is just beginning.

### Neurobiology

Much like specific collections of genes are known to contribute to diverse mental health conditions, the same neural circuitry is implicated in vulnerability to various categorical disorders. Psychiatry has long lamented this state of affairs. The refrain is that "there is no biological test for any mental disorder," at least as portrayed in *DSM*. This desideratum is called a "pathognomonic" marker, a risk factor that has a one-to-one relationship with a disorder. This is a common feature of modern medical diagnoses that has not materialized for psychopathology; it is impossible to discern one category from another on the basis of some neurobiological signature. Multifinality is the rule, not the exception, in this area (Latzman et al., 2020).

Amygdala responsivity in the face of threat is a well-known example. When people are presented with threatening cues in the functional magnetic resonance imaging (fMRI) scanner, limbic regions such as the amygdala come online (Hariri et al., 2003). Amygdala reactivity is stronger for some people than others, though. This variation is related to risk for depression, anxiety, posttraumatic distress, and substance misuse, among other clinical problems (for a meta-analysis, see McTeague et al., 2020). Elevated activity in this region is a *nonspecific* risk marker. This type of multifinality in fact characterizes many other indices of brain structure and function that show up in popular etiological accounts of psychopathology, especially anxiety and depression (Zald & Lahey, 2017).

HiTOP provides neurobiologists with a framework that can help to make sense of these findings. One early study used factor analysis to create a hierarchical model of externalizing problems in a group of almost 2,000 European 14-year-olds recruited through their high schools (Castellanos-Ryan et al., 2014). (This is a massive sample size by the standards of neuroimaging research, which is expensive.) Their model consisted of substance abuse and antisocial behavior subfactors, plus a broader externalizing spectrum. Adolescents performed tasks in the fMRI scanner related to inhibition and reward sensitivity. For example, neural activity was monitored as adolescents anticipated the receipt of a monetary reward. The research team reported that the model's three dimensions were associated with different patterns of task-related neural activity. Whereas the externalizing factor had its strongest connection with activity in the substantia nigra and subthalamic nucleus, individual differences in the antisocial behavior factor were linked with frontal cortex activation.

This result indicates that a hierarchical description of externalizing problems can identify new connections between brain function and externalizing problems. They also found effects for these latent factors on behavioral and subjective report variables assessed during the brain scans. That is, the three psychopathology dimensions were differentially related to self-reported and task-based tendencies to make impulsive decisions and inhibit inappropriate responses (Castellanos-Ryan et al., 2014).

There has been substantial interest in the neural correlates of the $p$-factor. Several teams have found that brain activation patterns during popular neuroimaging tasks, such as when participants complete working memory tasks, show meaningful relationships to $p$ (e.g., Kaczkurkin et al., 2019). Studies have also examined *structural* brain differences as a function of $p$. For example, in one sample of children (ages 6–10), the $p$-factor was inversely associated with gray matter volume in prefrontal regions (Snyder, Hankin et al., 2017). In this same sample, the internalizing factor, but not $p$-factor, was related to gray matter reductions in limbic areas like the amygdala.

## Social Environment

Psychopathology does not occur in a vacuum. The environmental context, and social milieu in particular, are intimately intertwined with the onset, severity, and time course of common mental health problems. Countless presentations, articles, and books have delved into the nature of this complex association. Yet, from a HiTOP perspective, most of this investigation has been incomplete, unnecessarily focused on *DSM* constructs that may not best represent how psychopathology manifests as a function of environmental exposures.

Childhood maltreatment is an especially powerful vulnerability factor; its effects endure long after the abuse or neglect stops. Moreover, it confers risk for virtually every known mental health condition. HiTOP is well-suited to handle this nonspecificity. The framework recognizes all possible pathways from early adversity to psychopathology, ranging from the most general (e.g., impact on the $p$-factor) to the highly specific (e.g., impact on maladaptive personality traits).

Keyes et al. (2012) started a line of inquiry into this topic. They analyzed data from the National Epidemiologic Survey on Alcohol and Related Conditions (NESARC), a general population sample of more than 43,000 US adults who completed face-to-face diagnostic interviews. Keyes et al. (2012) found that various retrospectively reported maltreatment events, such as physical abuse and neglect, were robustly related with the full gamut of *DSM-IV* diagnoses. This result echoed those from many other studies. The advancement was that Keyes et al. discovered that maltreatment was not consistently associated with the parts of diagnoses that were unshared with related conditions. They observed that maltreatment predicted higher standing on the internalizing and externalizing factors, which represented the common elements among their constituent diagnoses, and that effects on individual diagnoses were all mediated through these spectrum-level constructs.

A number of other longitudinal studies corroborated the NESARC result (Caspi et al., 2014; Conway et al., 2018). Another study, which was technically cross-sectional, monitored 2,000 low-income children, half of whom had verified histories of maltreatment (e.g., confirmed by review of health department records) (Vachon et al., 2015). Structural analysis of symptom scales indicated that the various observed mental health problems (e.g., withdrawal, somatic complaints, rule-breaking) could be effectively summarized with the familiar internalizing and externalizing dimensions. As in Keyes et al. (2012), maltreatment was linked to these spectrum-level constructs but not to the unique parts of each of the more homogeneous symptom dimensions.

None of these studies modeled the $p$-factor, but they hinted that stressor effects might transcend the spectra. This would explain why maltreatment seems have fairly uniform effects on all types of mental health problems. Other research on social stressors in adolescence and adulthood has explicitly examined the *p*-factor (e.g., Snyder, Young, & Hankin, 2017). One investigation studied the impact of peer victimization, a strong predictor of academic and social success in adolescence and beyond. The dataset included 3,000 14- and 15-year-olds who reported on victimization experiences (e.g., verbal abuse, relational aggression) and psychological symptoms (Forbes et al., 2020). The authors represented the adolescents' symptom scores with a hierarchical model capped by the *p*-factor. Peer victimization was reliably linked to all psychopathology dimensions in the model; a history of victimization corresponded to about a 1 to 1.5 standard deviation increase in internalizing, externalizing, and *p*. Mediation analyses showed that almost all of victimization's effects on internalizing and externalizing were attributable to its effect on *p*. The authors concluded that victimization confers vulnerability to such a broad range of problems because of its relationship to the *p*-factor.

## Summary

We can take away at least two lessons from the growing literature on HiTOP's research utility. First, the data generally support psychopathology dimensions' criterion validity (i.e., prediction of external variables). Not only do HiTOP constructs systematically relate to other variables *within* the model—as when an internalizing dimension accounts for the pattern of correlations among anxiety, depression, and somatic problems—but they also reliably predict variables *outside* the model, such as individual differences in brain function and personality. This type of information builds confidence in the interpretability and validity of the HiTOP constructs.

Second, HiTOP can unify literatures that until now have been developed in quasi-independent silos. For any given risk factor, enormous bodies of research have sprung up around the many individual diagnostic categories. These data say nothing, though, about whether risk is conveyed at the level of diagnoses (i.e., syndromes) or through higher- or lower-level pathways. HiTOP lifts this constraint. Many of the findings so far indicate that risk factors operate primarily at the level of broader psychopathology dimensions. However, this need not be the case for every risk factor or in every population. The point is that HiTOP allows an empirical test of how risk factors act on psychopathology instead of assuming it occurs at the syndrome level. This flexibility should improve the precision and power of etiological theories of mental disorder.

## Clinical Utility

Categorical diagnoses can be a headache for practitioners. Problems like rampant comorbidity and marked heterogeneity complicate clinical judgments like what primary diagnosis to assign and what treatment is indicated. Surveys of clinicians suggest that more detailed characterization of patients—beyond a binary label—would improve their ability to make valid decisions about diagnosis, prognosis, and treatment (e.g., Maj, 2020). In this section, we describe how HiTOP can foster sound decision making in several aspects of ordinary practice.

### Assessment

#### DIMENSIONAL ASSESSMENT

In a dimensional system like HiTOP, assessment focuses on quantitative indices of severity. This perspective presumes that people differ in mental health as a matter of degree, not as a matter of kind. It implies that every patient can be scored on a psychopathology variable, whereas in traditional evaluations a clinician might "skip out" of a particular domain when a patient does not satisfy one or more cardinal requirements for the *DSM* diagnosis. Even if the assessor is focused on syndromes, these can be measured quantitatively (e.g., as a composite score), as when clinicians disregard "skip-out rules" to evaluate the severity of all disorder symptoms (e.g., Watson et al., 2012).

To be interpretable, dimensional scores require norms. *Norms* are summaries of scale scores drawn from a population of interest. A patient's performance is compared to the norms to figure out where they fall in relation to an appropriate comparison group. If a normative sample of prisoners scores on average a 50 (standard deviation = 5) on a measure of aggression, then when a primary care patient scores 62 on that same measure the physician can be assured that the examinee is highly aggressive. These norms allow more precision, relative to a binary diagnosis, in determining the amount or severity of psychopathological constructs (e.g., Stasik-O'Brien et al., 2019).

Although dimensions convey more information than dichotomies, it could be argued that binary diagnoses, at first glance, lend themselves better to clinical decision-making. So many practical decisions are categorical: whether to treat, what treatment to administer, whether to hospitalize, and so on. Often when patients cross the threshold of a binary diagnosis, these other decisions follow closely on their heels without weighing much extra clinical data. After all, categorical diagnoses in medicine are intended to connote prognosis and treatment, not to mention etiology, pathophysiology, and time course.

When assessing dimensional HiTOP constructs, there are no such obvious thresholds. There has been increasing attention, therefore, to the idea of empirically based cutoffs to guide categorical decisions. For a given dimension, it is possible to determine a range of scores that imply different actions. One can imagine different spans of a continuum that indicate different treatment intensities, such as "none," "watchful waiting," "outpatient care," and "inpatient care." This graded approach is consistent with the logic behind *stepped care* (also called *staged care*) that, in an effort to economically allocate scarce intervention resources, matches patients with the treatment intensity appropriate to their current status (e.g., Davison, 2000).

Dimensional assessment is not an entirely foreign concept. In medicine, characteristics like blood pressure, cholesterol, and weight are all natural continua, but cutoffs have been artificially imposed to help with decision-making. These cutoffs are usually based on empirical findings regarding ranges of the continuum that are associated with morbidity or mortality. For example, the designations "overweight" and "obese" are two successive categories that have been superimposed on a continuum to identify people who might benefit from lifestyle change and/or medical intervention.

In psychology, intelligence is the poster child for dimensional assessment. IQ is a natural gradient, but it is useful for clinical purposes to delimit regions of the continuum that imply a need for services, such as an individualized education plan for school children. A cutoff based on empirical norms is incorporated into the *DSM-5* diagnosis of intellectual disability, such that an IQ score that falls 2 standard deviations below the population mean is necessary (albeit not sufficient) for a diagnosis. This integration of continuous psychometric information with categorical decisions is an instructive model for dimensional assessment based on HiTOP constructs.

## HIERARCHICAL ASSESSMENT

A HiTOP-oriented assessment routine is highly flexible with respect to breadth. It allows clinical description at the various levels of resolution demarcated in Figure 3.1, as opposed to the syndrome-only approach implicit in *DSM*. The assessment protocol can "telescope" or unfold across different HiTOP strata depending on the task at hand.

The desired degree of specificity could depend on a number of factors. Most generally, it depends on the goal of the assessment. If a patient is referred for OCD, the assessor may choose to concentrate on the symptom components and maladaptive traits most strongly associated with this syndrome, such as checking, compulsions, and rituals. If instead the objective is to screen for risk of any mental disorder, the assessor may target broader dimensions like the *p*-factor.

Available assessment time might also constrain the areas of the HiTOP model an evaluator can reasonably cover. When time is short, it may make sense to briefly screen the severity of the six spectra (Ruggero et al., 2019). If more time is allowed, an assessor may choose to probe a larger number of lower-order dimensions. In this same vein, interviewers might take advantage of follow-up visits to drill down into a spectrum that was flagged during an intake evaluation. This more detailed coverage can help to develop a nuanced clinical picture that might be used to guide ongoing treatment or predict salient life outcomes.

The general idea is that scores on narrow symptom dimensions (e.g., insomnia, appetite loss) represent the variation on broader dimensions (e.g., distress) in greater depth (Clark & Watson, 2019). Conversely, broader dimensions summarize the information conveyed by narrower ones at a higher level of abstraction and are, as a result, comparatively heterogeneous. The hierarchical perspective on psychopathology allows assessors to adjust their focus as a function of the clinical setting and purpose of the evaluation.

## CASE ILLUSTRATION

What would HiTOP-informed assessment look like in the clinic? Imagine that a 30-year-old woman is referred to you complaining of depression, worry, and obsessive thoughts about contamination. As mentioned, the first step might be to screen for elevations across the higher-order aspects of the HiTOP model. The Personality Inventory for *DSM-5* (PID-5; Krueger et al., 2012), which has a 25-item brief version, might be a fairly quick way to document clinical problems at the spectrum level. That is, the PID-5 has scales that map on to the internalizing (PID-5 Negative Affectivity), disinhibited externalizing (Disinhibition), antagonistic externalizing (Antagonism), detachment (Detachment), and thought disorder (Psychoticism) spectra.

The next step would be to conduct further assessment of the most pressing problem areas, as identified by comparing the patient's PID-5 scores to normative data (see, e.g., Miller et al., 2022). In our case, the PID-5 profile signaled a spike in internalizing problems and, to a much lesser extent, detachment. Thus, you might choose to next administer the Inventory of Depression and Anxiety Symptoms (IDAS-II; Watson et al., 2012), an empirically derived measure of the general and specific components of the internalizing spectrum. The specific dimensions, mapping on to the symptom component level of the HiTOP model, include traumatic intrusions, insomnia, appetite loss, mania, suicidality, and more. Based on the presenting problems, we would expect elevations on Dysphoria, which is a broad scale that encompasses the general features of emotional disorders, such as depressed mood and worry; Well-being, a specific scale that taps into (the opposite pole of) anhedonia, a common feature in depression; and Cleaning, a specific scale that measures contamination fears and compulsive cleaning behavior.

There are many other measures that capture the higher- and lower-order features of internalizing, detachment, and other domains of the HiTOP framework. Kotov et al. (2017) presented a thorough but nonexhaustive list, and more are cataloged on a website maintained by the HiTOP consortium (https://psychology.unt.edu/hitop). More information on approaching clinical assessment through a HiTOP lens is available from Ruggero et al. (2019). Finally, it is worth mentioning that, as of this writing, an omnibus self-report questionnaire to survey the entirety of the psychopathology landscape, as mapped by the HiTOP consortium so far, is under development but not yet published (Simms et al., 2022). Once this measure is available, it will represent a comprehensive tool for assessing dimensional psychopathology phenotypes. There are plans for interview forms and computerized adaptive tests, which should enable huge savings in administration time, to supplement the questionnaire version.

### Prognosis

Patients are often interested in knowing about the natural course of an illness and the burden that they can expect it to impose over time. Practitioners are interested in monitoring naturalistic and treatment-mediated improvements in psychopathology over time. Categorical diagnoses are not ideally suited for these tasks. They tend to be fairly unstable, and they provide the coarsest possible index of status change (i.e., a binary no vs. yes). In theory, then, dimensions are a superior way to conceptualize clinical change and render prognostic judgments.

A growing evidence base attests to HiTOP's ability to predict clinical outcomes. A consistent finding is that HiTOP spectra show high temporal stability over short and long intervals. In a Dutch general population study, Vollebergh et al. (2001) found impressive continuity in distress, fear, and externalizing factors over a 1-year span (autocorrelation range = .85 to .96). Continuity does not decline much in studies with longer retest intervals (e.g., Krueger et al., 1998). These data suggest that empirically derived dimensions are better reflections, compared to categorical disorders, of the stable individual differences that contribute to mental disorder and shape clinical outcomes.

All mental health systems are concerned with risk of harm to self and others that can accompany psychopathology. There are some data that indicate psychopathology dimensions might be a superior way to forecast risk of suicide than are categorical diagnoses. In the NESARC study, Eaton et al. (2013) found that the distress subfactor was a potent predictor of suicide attempts across a 3-year interval separating assessment waves. Individual differences in distress explained roughly one-third of the variation in suicidality. In contrast, each categorical mental disorder—including some of the usual suspects, such as major depression—in the study explained no more than 1% of outcome variance after adjusting for distress.

Other research in large samples has since reinforced this finding. For example, in a longitudinal study of more than 30,000 children around 10 years old, a *p*-factor reliably predicted suicide attempt history at age 18 (standardized effect = .25), whereas lower-order factors representing inattention, impulsivity, opposition, and anxiety/emotion domains had comparatively small effects (O'Reilly et al., 2020).

Often psychosocial functioning is as much a target of intervention as are mental disorder symptoms. Psychologists are eager to predict breakdowns in normative function that might derail symptom improvement or signal the need for more intensive care. Psychopathology dimensions generally seem to do a better job at predicting such impairment over time. A decade-long study in a large cohort of PD patients showed that quantitative representations of mental disorders were more reliable markers of impairment across various intervals than categorical indices of the same constructs (Morey et al., 2012). Kotov et al. (2016) found that, in a group of 628 first-admission psychosis patients, dimensions in the thought disorder spectrum predicted sizable proportions of variance in social functioning measures (e.g., residential independence) 20 years after their first clinical contact.

## Treatment

Psychologists tend to design treatments that target one *DSM* diagnosis. Again, this makes perfect sense if those diagnoses truly represent natural kinds with distinct underlying psychological malfunctions. In this case, each diagnosis would seem to require its own unique intervention. The best-practice treatment guidelines published by professional bodies reflect this way of thinking (e.g., American Psychiatric Association, 2019; US Department of Veterans Affairs, 2019).

Earlier we reviewed many of the conceptual and practical problems with addressing each categorical disorder as a discrete problem in healthcare settings. But psychology training programs and professional organizations rarely acknowledge these dilemmas, so it is perhaps unsurprising that mental health professionals rarely follow categorically oriented treatment guidelines in ordinary practice. Instead of matching a categorical disorder to its indicated treatment, psychologists are apt to address the most salient patient characteristics, which inevitably cut across *DSM* entities (e.g., anger, worry) (e.g., Rodriguez-Seijas et al., 2017). Indeed, there is some empirical evidence that psychiatrists prescribe medications more as a function of outstanding symptom characteristics (e.g., suicidality, psychomotor retardation) than diagnoses (e.g., MDD) per se (Waszczuk et al., 2017). Thus, practitioners seem to be overriding practice guidelines to focus their energies on clinically recognizable symptom clusters, rather than *DSM* labels.

There is an alternative way to coordinate treatment that is more compatible with the HiTOP approach. Just as an assessment routine can "telescope" to address broader or narrower clinical problems depending on the context, so, too, can treatment expand or contract to address phenomena that transcend *DSM* diagnoses. We spend the remainder of this section describing one such treatment that has gained a strong foothold in the literature over the past decade and has developed hand in hand with the HiTOP framework.

### UNIFIED PROTOCOL FOR THE TRANSDIAGNOSTIC TREATMENT OF EMOTIONAL DISORDERS

The Unified Protocol for the Transdiagnostic Treatment of Emotional Disorders (UP) is a psychological treatment intended to address the full array of emotional disorders (Barlow et al., 2017). The term "emotional disorder" is a bit difficult to pin down, but it refers loosely to mental disorders marked primarily by emotion dysregulation. In the literature this typically means anxiety and depression, but maladaptive reactions to negative emotion are implicated in numerous other *DSM* disorders, ranging from somatic symptom disorder to alcohol use disorder.

The UP targets ineffective reactions to negative emotion that end up prolonging emotional problems. Again, this process is not unique to any *DSM* diagnosis; one could argue it is part and parcel of countless mental health problems (Barlow et al., 2014). Despite reason to believe this is a shared underlying mechanism for an array of emotional disorders, at least 50 separate psychological treatments have been developed and accredited (as evidence-based) for anxiety and depression (Cassiello-Robbins et al., 2020). Virtually all of these are geared toward a single disorder entity.

A comprehensive intervention that goes straight to the source of these different expressions of emotion dysregulation could kill two (or more) birds with one stone. In theory, it would be effective regardless of the exact variety of emotion dysregulation a patient manifests (e.g., illness anxiety, social withdrawal, panic) because the underlying problem is more or less the same. Moreover, its effects might be expected to percolate to any comorbid emotional disorders that are not the primary treatment target. Thus, while a patient's nominal goal for a course of UP might be to overcome obsessions and compulsions, the information and skills they acquire might indirectly resolve co-occurring issues with depression and worry.

The UP is a cognitive-behavioral therapy (CBT), meaning that it concentrates on how people think about (e.g., forecast, interpret) emotions and what they do (e.g., avoid, lash out) in response to them. It differs from traditional CBT protocols, which tend to be tied to a specific disorder (e.g., CBT for panic disorder) in that it tackles defensive reactions to a broad range of emotional experiences. That is, most CBTs limit themselves to the primary emotional processes implicated in a particular *DSM* diagnosis (e.g., sadness and anhedonia in depression). Also, the UP is modular. Its components can be deployed in an order tailor-made to address a particular presenting problem. Paraphrasing Payne et al. (2014), its modules include (1) promoting emotional awareness, (2) cognitive flexibility, (3) alternative ways to cope with emotion, (4) tolerating physical distress, and (5) deliberate exposure to intense emotion. The combination of all this instruction and experience is meant to change a patient's relationship with their emotions. It intends to build greater awareness and flexibility in thinking about emotion and a belief that emotions—even intense ones—can be tolerated without sacrificing current goals.

The UP appears to work. In the largest trial so far, 223 patients with anxiety disorder diagnoses were randomly assigned to undergo either the UP or a single-disorder protocol (SDP) (Barlow et al., 2017). There were four SDPs, one to match each of the primary anxiety disorder categories selected into the study (i.e., panic disorder, GAD, OCD, and SAD), and each was a gold-standard CBT for that condition. (Three of the four SDPs were developed by the same team responsible for the UP.) The point of the trial was to determine whether the UP, which can be applied to all emotional disorders, might be just as effective as the various SDPs, which each target only one emotional disorder. This is known as a *non-inferiority trial*.

Patients in the UP condition were engaged in treatment for 16 weeks, whereas the SDPs lasted 16 to 21 weeks, depending on the primary diagnosis. Evaluators who were blind to patients' treatment assignment rated the severity of anxiety problems at the end of treatment and at a 6-month follow-up appointment. The impact of the UP on clinical severity was almost indistinguishable from that of the SDPs. The Hedges *g* value—a statistic that, much like Cohen's *d*, represents a group difference in terms of standard deviation units—was –0.03 immediately posttreatment and 0.03 6 months later.

Other empirical studies corroborate this result, although none has matched the size and rigor of Barlow et al.'s (2017) investigation. A meta-analysis of 15 trials indicated generally large gains in anxiety, depression, and quality-of-life domains after UP treatment (Sakiris & Berle, 2019). Recent reviews also highlight the UP's "portability," which is one of its main assets. Researchers are applying the UP to treat the full gamut of emotional disorders and neighboring diagnoses (Cassiello-Robbins et al., 2020). Over 70 studies—a mix of case studies, open trials, and randomized trials—report examinations of the UP in the context of insomnia, eating disorders, bipolar disorders, borderline PD, and more. It has even been modified to address conditions that are not formal *DSM* diagnoses, such as nonsuicidal self-injury and minority stress. This reflects an incredible degree of flexibility for a psychological treatment.

To tie this literature back to HiTOP, the lesson is that *DSM* entities need not be the focus of psychological treatment. It is possible, even advantageous, to orient intervention around empirically derived constructs that transcend *DSM* categories. Indeed, this is how recent presentations of the UP have framed it (e.g., Barlow et al., 2020). The UP explicitly targets the common features of emotional disorders, such as maladaptive responses to negative emotion, that are represented by HiTOP's internalizing spectrum. By chipping away at this broad vulnerability, it may end up having an observable effect on *many* emotional problems that belong to the internalizing domain (Figure 3.1).

Some data from Barlow et al.'s (2017) study bear directly on this hypothesis. Sauer-Zavala et al. (2020) analyzed the effect of treatment condition on neuroticism, which, as reviewed earlier, is conceptually and empirically a close match to the internalizing spectrum. The authors found that, although there were no differences in neuroticism at treatment baseline (as would be expected if random assignment went according to plan), patients in the UP condition reported lower neuroticism levels at the posttreatment assessment than those in the SDP condition (a standardized mean difference of 0.32). Thus, the UP, formulated to operate on the shared mechanisms of emotional disorders, seems to have an impact on neuroticism, a broad individual difference factor theorized to set the stage for, and maintain, a variety of emotional problems.

### THE FUTURE OF TRANSDIAGNOSTIC TREATMENTS

The UP might be a template for other treatment protocols that target cross-cutting characteristics like those portrayed in Figure 3.1. Indeed, scholars have speculated that this tactic has utility beyond the internalizing spectrum (Hopwood et al., 2019;

Mullins-Sweatt et al., 2020; Ruggero et al., 2019). Much of the theorizing has concerned ways that treatment could address broad, spectrum-level constructs to achieve far-reaching impacts on clinically recognizable problems (including syndromes), just as the UP seems to have an effect on a variety of categorical anxiety and depressive disorders.

Most of these proposals are just untested recommendations at this point, but they seem to be a worthwhile area for research investment. Plus, there is evidence beyond the UP literature that treatments are able to confer transdiagnostic benefits, putting this enterprise on reasonably strong conceptual footing. The evolution of dialectical behavior therapy (DBT) is a good case in point (Linehan, 1993). Originally developed to treat recurrent suicidality, it was first tested on people with borderline PD. It was perceived to be so effective with complex cases that clinicians successfully applied it to other often-intractable problems, such as eating disorders, substance dependence, and chronic depression (e.g., Lynch, Morse, Mendelson, & Robins, 2003). This wide range of effects hints that DBT may be altering processes at the source of multiple mental disorders, perhaps those reflected in the internalizing and disinhibited externalizing spectra (e.g., Neacsiu et al., 2014).

A similar observation has been made about certain psychiatric medications that exert an influence on multiple diagnostic categories. Selective serotonin reuptake inhibitors (SSRIs) clearly fit the bill. Psychiatrists prescribe SSRIs for any number of conditions, ranging from depression to smoking cessation to sexual dysfunction (Bostic & Rho, 2006). The precise mechanisms of action of SSRIs remain uncertain despite their widespread use. However, there is some evidence that, to the extent that SSRIs work, they intervene on broad characteristics like neuroticism. For example, in a study of patients randomized to take an SSRI called paroxetine or an inert placebo, those in the SSRI condition experienced almost a 7-fold larger drop in neuroticism compared to those taking placebo (Tang et al., 2009).

These case examples (the UP, DBT, and SSRIs) arguably are "proof of concept" for a transdiagnostic approach to mental health treatment. Broad, often modular, treatments that address a cluster of related problems theorized to share common psychopathological processes appear to be feasible and effective. If others like the UP can be developed and empirically vetted, then mental healthcare delivery might become far more efficient and reach more of the people who need it. In principle, they overcome (or at least mitigate) practical barriers surrounding training and dissemination that today limit access to evidence-based care on a broad scale.

## Summary

HiTOP has clinical value in a number of ways. For one thing, dimensional assessment provides a more detailed characterization of patient problems. Even a dimensional representation of *DSM* categories (e.g., a symptom count) is more informative than a binary label. This extra information is hypothesized to translate into a more nuanced clinical picture and more prognostic power.

The hierarchical structure expands the possible targets for intervention beyond syndromes (see the vertical axis of Figure 3.1). Interventions can focus on processes, whether broad or narrow, that transcend traditional disorder boundaries. Regarding broad constructs, there is reason to believe that targeting mechanisms common to many disorders (e.g., cognitive styles, behavioral patterns) can have far-reaching therapeutic benefits. The HiTOP model can guide interventionists to these areas where they can get the most traction.

## Conclusion

The problems with categorical diagnoses are as frustrating as ever, and now there is a viable alternative. HiTOP is based on objective data, enabling a more accurate representation of psychopathology than diagnoses rooted, to some degree, in clinical intuition. Its utility extends far beyond description, though. The model unlocks new research avenues and paves the way for more precise theory. It also promises to streamline clinical services, which could conserve scarce resources and extend mental healthcare to more people who desperately need it. Whereas the structural model is what HiTOP "is," these research and clinical applications represent what HiTOP can "do."

Work on this model is just now shifting into a high gear. The HiTOP consortium was founded in 2015, and a new wave of empirical studies is testing the boundaries of how we can use the model. As the database grows, we will gain a better sense of if, when, and how HiTOP might reasonably supplement, and perhaps supplant, categorical models on a broad scale.

## References

Achenbach, T. M. (1966). The classification of children's psychiatric symptoms: A factor-analytic study. *Psychological Monographs: General and Applied, 80*(7), 1–37. doi:10.1037/h0093906

Achenbach, T. M., Howell, C. T., Quay, H. C., Conners, C. K., & Bates, J. E. (1991). National survey of problems and competencies among four-to sixteen-year-olds: Parents' reports for normative and clinical samples. *Monographs of the Society for Research in Child Development*, 1–131.

American Psychiatric Association (APA). (2019). Clinical practice guidelines. https://www.psychiatry.org/psychiatrists/practice/clinical-practice-guidelines

Barlow, D. H., Farchione, T. J., Bullis, J. R., Gallagher, M. W., Murray-Latin, H., Sauer-Zavala, S., Bentley, K. H., Thompson-Hollands, J., Conklin, L. R., & Boswell, J. F. (2017). The unified protocol for transdiagnostic treatment of emotional disorders compared with diagnosis-specific protocols for anxiety disorders: A randomized clinical trial. *JAMA Psychiatry*, 74(9), 875–884. doi:10.1001/jamapsychiatry.2017.2164

Barlow, D. H., Farchione, T. J., Fairholme, C. P., Ellard, K. K., Boisseau, C. L., Allen, L. B., & May, J. T. E. (2015). *Unified protocol for transdiagnostic treatment of emotional disorders: Therapist guide*. Oxford University Press.

Barlow, D. H., Harris, B. A., Eustis, E. H., & Farchione, T. J. (2020). The unified protocol for transdiagnostic treatment of emotional disorders. *World Psychiatry*, 19(2), 245–246. doi:10.1002/wps.20748

Barlow, D. H., Sauer-Zavala, S., Carl, J. R., Bullis, J. R., & Ellard, K. K. (2014). The nature, diagnosis, and treatment of neuroticism: Back to the future. *Clinical Psychological Science*, 2(3), 344–365.

Bostic, J. Q., & Rho, Y. (2006). Target-symptom psychopharmacology: Between the forest and the trees. *Child and Adolescent Psychiatric Clinics*, 15(1), 289–302. doi:10.1016/j.chc.2005.08.003

Brown, T. A. (2015). *Confirmatory factor analysis for applied research*. Guilford.

Brown, T. A., Campbell, L. A., Lehman, C. L., Grisham, J. R., & Mancill, R. B. (2001). Current and lifetime comorbidity of the DSM-IV anxiety and mood disorders in a large clinical sample. *Journal of Abnormal Psychology*, 110(4), 585–599. doi:10.1037//0021-843x.110.4.585

Caspi, A., Houts, R. M., Ambler, A., Danese, A., Elliott, M. L., Hariri, A., Harrington, H., Hogan, S., Poulton, R., & Ramrakha, S. (2020). Longitudinal assessment of mental health disorders and comorbidities across 4 decades among participants in the Dunedin birth cohort study. *JAMA Network Open*, 3(4), e203221. doi:10.1001/jamanetworkopen.2020.3221

Caspi, A., Houts, R. M., Belsky, D. W., Goldman-Mellor, S. J., Harrington, H., Israel, S., Meier, M. H., Ramrakha, S., Shalev, I., & Poulton, R. (2014). The p factor: One general psychopathology factor in the structure of psychiatric disorders? *Clinical Psychological Science*, 2(2), 119–137. doi:10.1177/2167702613497473

Caspi, A., & Moffitt, T. E. (2018). All for one and one for all: Mental disorders in one dimension. *American Journal of Psychiatry*, 175(9), 831–844. doi:10.1176/appi.ajp.2018.17121383

Cassiello-Robbins, C., Southward, M. W., Tirpak, J. W., & Sauer-Zavala, S. (2020). A systematic review of Unified Protocol applications with adult populations: Facilitating widespread dissemination via adaptability. *Clinical Psychology Review*, 78, 101852. doi:10.1016/j.cpr.2020.101852

Castellanos-Ryan, N., Struve, M., Whelan, R., Banaschewski, T., Barker, G. J., Bokde, A. L., Bromberg, U., Büchel, C., Flor, H., & Fauth-Bühler, M. (2014). Neural and cognitive correlates of the common and specific variance across externalizing problems in young adolescence. *American Journal of Psychiatry*, 171(12), 1310–1319. doi:10.1176/appi.ajp.2014.13111499

Cicchetti, D., & Rogosch, F. A. (1996). Equifinality and multifinality in developmental psychopathology. *Development and Psychopathology*, 8(4), 597–600.

Clark, L. A. (2005). Temperament as a unifying basis for personality and psychopathology. *Journal of Abnormal Psychology*, 114(4), 505–521. doi:10.1037/0021-843X.114.4.505

Clark, L. A., & Watson, D. (2019). Constructing validity: New developments in creating objective measuring instruments. *Psychological Assessment*, 31(12), 1412–1427. doi:10.1037/pas0000626

Conway, C. C., Forbes, M. K., Forbush, K. T., Fried, E. I., Hallquist, M. N., Kotov, R., Mullins-Sweatt, S. N., Shackman, A. J., Skodol, A. E., & South, S. C. (2019). A hierarchical taxonomy of psychopathology can transform mental health research. *Perspectives on Psychological Science*, 14(3), 419–436. doi:10.1177/1745691618810696

Conway, C. C., Raposa, E. B., Hammen, C., & Brennan, P. A. (2018). Transdiagnostic pathways from early social stress to psychopathology: A 20-year prospective study. *Journal of Child Psychology and Psychiatry*, 59(8), 855–862. doi:10.1111/jcpp.12862

Davison, G. C. (2000). Stepped care: doing more with less?. *Journal of Consulting and Clinical Psychology*, 68(4), 580.

Eaton, N. R., Krueger, R. F., Markon, K. E., Keyes, K. M., Skodol, A. E., Wall, M., . . . Grant, B. F. (2013). The structure and predictive validity of the internalizing disorders. *Journal of Abnormal Psychology*, 122(1), 86.

Forbes, M. K., Kotov, R., Ruggero, C. J., Watson, D., Zimmerman, M., & Krueger, R. F. (2017). Delineating the joint hierarchical structure of clinical and personality disorders in an outpatient psychiatric sample. *Comprehensive Psychiatry*, 79, 19–30. doi:10.1016/j.comppsych.2017.04.006

Forbes, M. K., Magson, N. R., & Rapee, R. M. (2020). Evidence that different types of peer victimization have equivalent associations with transdiagnostic psychopathology in adolescence. *Journal of Youth and Adolescence*, 49(3), 590–604. doi:10.1007/s10964-020-01202-4

Forbes, M. K., Sunderland, M., Rapee, R. M., Batterham, P. J., Calear, A. L., . . . Krueger, R. F. (in press). A detailed hierarchical model of psychopathology: From individual symptoms up to the general factor of psychopathology. *Clinical Psychological Science*.

Fried, E. I., & Nesse, R. M. (2015). Depression sum-scores don't add up: Why analyzing specific depression symptoms is essential. *BMC Medicine*, 13(1), 72. doi:10.1186/s12916-015-0325-4

Galatzer-Levy, I. R., & Bryant, R. A. (2013). 636,120 ways to have posttraumatic stress disorder. *Perspectives on Psychological Science*, 8(6), 651–662. doi:10.1177/1745691613504115

Griffith, J. W., Zinbarg, R. E., Craske, M. G., Mineka, S., Rose, R. D., Waters, A. M., & Sutton, J. M. (2010). Neuroticism as a common dimension in the internalizing disorders. *Psychological Medicine*, 40(7), 1125–1136. doi:10.1017/S0033291709991449

Gunderson, J. G., Bender, D., Sanislow, C., Yen, S., Rettew, J. B., Dolan-Sewell, R., Dyck, I., Morey, L. C., McGlashan, T. H., & Shea, M. T. (2003). Plausibility and possible determinants of sudden "remissions" in borderline patients. *Psychiatry: Interpersonal and Biological Processes*, 66(2), 111–119. doi:10.1521/psyc.66.2.111.20614

Hariri, A. R., Mattay, V. S., Tessitore, A., Fera, F., & Weinberger, D. R. (2003). Neocortical modulation of the amygdala response to fearful stimuli. *Biological Psychiatry, 53*(6), 494–501.

Haslam, N., McGrath, M. J., Viechtbauer, W., & Kuppens, P. (2020). Dimensions over categories: A meta-analysis of taxometric research. *Psychological Medicine*, 1–15. doi:10.1017/S003329172000183X

Hicks, B. M., Foster, K. T., Iacono, W. G., & McGue, M. (2013). Genetic and environmental influences on the familial transmission of externalizing disorders in adoptive and twin offspring. *JAMA Psychiatry, 70*(10), 1076–1083. doi:10.1001/jamapsychiatry.2013.258

Hopwood, C. J., Bagby, R. M., Gralnick, T., Ro, E., Ruggero, C., Mullins-Sweatt, S., Kotov, R., Bach, B., Cicero, D. C., & Krueger, R. F. (2019). Integrating psychotherapy with the hierarchical taxonomy of psychopathology (HiTOP). *Journal of Psychotherapy Integration.*

Kaczkurkin, A. N., Moore, T. M., Sotiras, A., Xia, C. H., Shinohara, R. T., & Satterthwaite, T. D. (2019). Approaches to defining common and dissociable neurobiological deficits associated with psychopathology in youth. *Biological Psychiatry.* doi:10.1016/j.biopsych.2019.12.015

Kendler, K. S. (2005). "A gene for . . .": The nature of gene action in psychiatric disorders. *American Journal of Psychiatry, 162*(7), 1243–1252. doi:10.1176/appi.ajp.162.7.1243

Kendler, K. S., Aggen, S. H., Knudsen, G. P., Røysamb, E., Neale, M. C., & Reichborn-Kjennerud, T. (2011). The structure of genetic and environmental risk factors for syndromal and subsyndromal common DSM-IV axis I and all axis II disorders. *American Journal of Psychiatry, 168*(1), 29–39. doi:10.1176/appi.ajp.2010.10030340

Kendler, K. S., Aggen, S. H., & Neale, M. C. (2013). Evidence for multiple genetic factors underlying DSM-IV criteria for major depression. *JAMA Psychiatry, 70*(6), 599–607. doi:10.1001/jamapsychiatry.2013.751

Kendler, K. S., & First, M. B. (2010). Alternative futures for the DSM revision process: Iteration v. paradigm shift. *The British Journal of Psychiatry, 197*(4), 263–265. doi:10.1192/bjp.bp.109.076794

Kessler, R. C., Chiu, W. T., Demler, O., & Walters, E. E. (2005). Prevalence, severity, and comorbidity of 12-month DSM-IV disorders in the national comorbidity survey replication. *Archives of General Psychiatry, 62*(6), 617–627. doi:10.1001/archpsyc.62.6.617

Keyes, K. M., Eaton, N. R., Krueger, R. F., McLaughlin, K. A., Wall, M. M., Grant, B. F., & Hasin, D. S. (2012). Childhood maltreatment and the structure of common psychiatric disorders. *The British Journal of Psychiatry, 200*(2), 107–115. doi:10.1192/bjp.bp.111.093062

Kotov, R., Foti, D., Li, K., Bromet, E. J., Hajcak, G., & Ruggero, C. J. (2016). Validating dimensions of psychosis symptomatology: Neural correlates and 20-year outcomes. *Journal of Abnormal Psychology, 125*(8), 1103.

Kotov, R., Gamez, W., Schmidt, F., & Watson, D. (2010). Linking "big" personality traits to anxiety, depressive, and substance use disorders: A meta-analysis. *Psychological Bulletin, 136*(5), 768–821. doi:10.1037/a0020327

Kotov, R., Krueger, R. F., Watson, D., Achenbach, T. M., Althoff, R. R., Bagby, R. M., Brown, T. A., Carpenter, W. T., Caspi, A., & Clark, L. A. (2017). The hierarchical taxonomy of psychopathology (HiTOP): A dimensional alternative to traditional nosologies. *Journal of Abnormal Psychology, 126*(4), 454–477. doi:10.1037/abn0000258

Kotov, R., Ruggero, C. J., Krueger, R. F., Watson, D., Yuan, Q., & Zimmerman, M. (2011). New dimensions in the quantitative classification of mental illness. *Archives of General Psychiatry, 68*(10), 1003–1011. doi:10.1001/archgenpsychiatry.2011.107

Krueger, R. F. (1999). The structure of common mental disorders. *Archives of General Psychiatry, 56*(10), 921–926. doi:10.1001/archpsyc.56.10.921

Krueger, R. F., Caspi, A., Moffitt, T. E., & Silva, P. A. (1998). The structure and stability of common mental disorders (DSM-III-R): A longitudinal-epidemiological study. *Journal of Abnormal Psychology, 107*(2), 216–227. doi:10.1037//0021-843x.107.2.216

Krueger, R. F., Chentsova-Dutton, Y. E., Markon, K. E., Goldberg, D., & Ormel, J. (2003). A cross-cultural study of the structure of comorbidity among common psychopathological syndromes in the general health care setting. *Journal of Abnormal Psychology, 112*(3), 437–447. doi:10.1037/0021-843x.112.3.437

Krueger, R. F., Derringer, J., Markon, K. E., Watson, D., & Skodol, A. E. (2012). Initial construction of a maladaptive personality trait model and inventory for DSM-5. *Psychological Medicine, 42*(9), 1879–1890. doi:10.1017/S0033291711002674

Krueger, R. F., Kotov, R., Watson, D., Forbes, M. K., Eaton, N. R., Ruggero, C. J., Simms, L. J., Widiger, T. A., Achenbach, T. M., & Bach, B. (2018). Progress in achieving quantitative classification of psychopathology. *World Psychiatry, 17*(3), 282–293. doi:10.1002/wps.20566

Krueger, R. F., & Markon, K. E. (2006). Reinterpreting comorbidity: A model-based approach to understanding and classifying psychopathology. *Annual Review of Clinical Psychology. Psychol., 2,* 111–133. doi:10.1146/annurev.clinpsy.2.022305.095213

Krueger, R. F., McGue, M., & Iacono, W. G. (2001). The higher-order structure of common DSM mental disorders: Internalization, externalization, and their connections to personality. *Personality and Individual Differences, 30*(7), 1245–1259.

Lahey, B. B. (2009). Public health significance of neuroticism. *American Psychologist, 64*(4), 241–256. doi:10.1037/a0015309

Lahey, B. B., Applegate, B., Hakes, J. K., Zald, D. H., Hariri, A. R., & Rathouz, P. J. (2012). Is there a general factor of prevalent psychopathology during adulthood? *Journal of Abnormal Psychology, 121*(4), 971–977. doi:10.1037/a0028355

Lahey, B. B., Krueger, R. F., Rathouz, P. J., Waldman, I. D., & Zald, D. H. (2017). A hierarchical causal taxonomy of psychopathology across the life span. *Psychological Bulletin, 143*(2), 142–186. doi:10.1037/bul0000069

Latzman, R. D., DeYoung, C. G., & HiTop Neurobiology Workgroup. (2020). Using empirically-derived dimensional phenotypes to accelerate clinical neuroscience: The hierarchical taxonomy of psychopathology (HiTOP) framework. *Neuropsychopharmacology, 45*(7), 1083–1085. doi:10.1038/s41386-020-0639-6

Levin-Aspenson, H. F., Khoo, S., & Kotelnikova, Y. (2019). Hierarchical taxonomy of psychopathology across development: Associations with personality. *Journal of Research in Personality, 81,* 72–78.

Linehan, M. M. (1993). *Cognitive behavioural therapy of borderline personality disorder.* Guilford.

Lynch, T. R., Morse, J. Q., Mendelson, T., & Robins, C. J. (2003). Dialectical behavior therapy for depressed older adults: A randomized pilot study. *American Journal of Geriatric Psychiatry, 11*(1), 33–45.

Maj, M. (2020). Beyond diagnosis in psychiatric practice. *Annals of General Psychiatry, 19*(1), 27. doi:10.1186/s12991-020-00279-2

Markon, K. E. (2010). Modeling psychopathology structure: A symptom-level analysis of Axis I and II disorders. *Psychological Medicine, 40*(2), 273–288. doi:10.1017/S0033291709990183

Markon, K. E., Chmielewski, M., & Miller, C. J. (2011). The reliability and validity of discrete and continuous measures of psychopathology: A quantitative review. *Psychological Bulletin, 137*(5), 856–879. doi:10.1037/a0023678

Mattay, V. S., Goldberg, T. E., Fera, F., Hariri, A. R., Tessitore, A., Egan, M. F., Kolachana, B., Callicott, J. H., & Weinberger, D. R. (2003). Catechol o-methyltransferase val158-met genotype and individual variation in the brain response to amphetamine. *Proceedings of the National Academy of Sciences, 100*(10), 6186–6191. doi:10.1073/pnas.0931309100

McTeague, L. M., Rosenberg, B. M., Lopez, J. W., Carreon, D. M., Huemer, J., Jiang, Y., Chick, C. F., Eickhoff, S. B., & Etkin, A. (2020). Identification of common neural circuit disruptions in emotional processing across psychiatric disorders. *American Journal of Psychiatry, 177*(5), 411–421. doi:10.1176/appi.ajp.2019.18111271

Miller, J. D., Bagby, R. M., Hopwood, C. J., Simms, L. J., & Lynam, D. R. (2022). Normative data for PID-5 domains, facets, and personality disorder composites from a representative sample and comparison to community and clinical samples. *Personality Disorders: Theory, Research, and Treatment*.

Mineka, S., Watson, D., & Clark, L. A. (1998). Comorbidity of anxiety and unipolar mood disorders. *Annual Review of Psychology, 49*(1), 377–412. doi:10.1146/annurev.psych.49.1.377

Moore, T. V. (1930). The empirical determination of certain syndromes underlying praecox and manic-depressive psychoses. *The American Journal of Psychiatry, 86*, 719–738. http://dx.doi.org/10.1176/ajp.86.4.719

Morey, L. C., Hopwood, C. J., Markowitz, J. C., Gunderson, J. G., Grilo, C. M., McGlashan, T. H., . . . Skodol, A. E. (2012). Comparison of alternative models for personality disorders, II: 6-, 8-and 10-year follow-up. *Psychological Medicine, 42*(8), 1705–1713.

Mõttus, R., Kandler, C., Bleidorn, W., Riemann, R., & McCrae, R. R. (2017). Personality traits below facets: The consensual validity, longitudinal stability, heritability, and utility of personality nuances. *Journal of Personality and Social Psychology, 112*(3), 474–490. doi:10.1037/pspp0000100

Mullins-Sweatt, S. N., Hopwood, C. J., Chmielewski, M., Meyer, N. A., Min, J., Helle, A. C., & Walgren, M. D. (2020). Treatment of personality pathology through the lens of the hierarchical taxonomy of psychopathology: Developing a research agenda. *Personality and Mental Health, 14*(1), 123–141. doi:10.1002/pmh.1464

Neacsiu, A. D., Eberle, J. W., Kramer, R., Wiesmann, T., & Linehan, M. M. (2014). Dialectical behavior therapy skills for transdiagnostic emotion dysregulation: A pilot randomized controlled trial. *Behaviour Research and Therapy, 59*, 40–51. doi:10.1016/j.brat.2014.05.005

O'Reilly, L. M., Pettersson, E., Quinn, P. D., Klonsky, E. D., Lundström, S., Larsson, H., . . . D'Onofrio, B. M. (2020). The association between general childhood psychopathology and adolescent suicide attempt and self-harm: A prospective, population-based twin study. *Journal of Abnormal Psychology, 129*(4), 364.

Payne, L. A., Ellard, K. K., Farchione, T. J., Fairholme, C. P., & Barlow, D. H. (2014). Emotional disorders: A unified transdiagnostic protocol. In *Clinical handbook of psychological disorders: A step-by-step treatment manual*, 5th ed. (pp. 237–274). Guilford.

Regier, D. A., Narrow, W. E., Clarke, D. E., Kraemer, H. C., Kuramoto, S. J., Kuhl, E. A., & Kupfer, D. J. (2013). DSM-5 field trials in the United States and Canada, part II: Test-retest reliability of selected categorical diagnoses. *American Journal of Psychiatry, 170*(1), 59–70. doi:10.1176/appi.ajp.2012.12070999

Rodriguez-Seijas, C., Eaton, N. R., Stohl, M., Mauro, P. M., & Hasin, D. S. (2017). Mental disorder comorbidity and treatment utilization. *Comprehensive Psychiatry, 79*, 89–97.

Ruggero, C. J., Kotov, R., Hopwood, C. J., First, M., Clark, L. A., Skodol, A. E., . . . Zimmermann, J. (2019). Integrating the Hierarchical Taxonomy of Psychopathology (HiTOP) into clinical practice. *Journal of Consulting and Clinical Psychology, 87*(12), 1069.

Sakiris, N., & Berle, D. (2019). A systematic review and meta-analysis of the unified protocol as a transdiagnostic emotion regulation based intervention. *Clinical Psychology Review*, 101751. doi:10.1016/j.cpr.2019.101751

Sauer-Zavala, S., Fournier, J. C., Steele, S. J., Woods, B. K., Wang, M., Farchione, T. J., & Barlow, D. H. (2020). Does the unified protocol really change neuroticism? Results from a randomized trial. *Psychological Medicine*, 1–10. doi:10.1017/S0033291720000975

Sellbom, M. (2017). Mapping the MMPI–2–RF specific problems scales onto extant psychopathology structures. *Journal of Personality Assessment, 99*(4), 341–350. doi:10.1080/00223891.2016.1206909

Sellbom, M., Carragher, N., Sunderland, M., Calear, A. L., & Batterham, P. J. (2020). The role of maladaptive personality domains across multiple levels of the HiTOP structure. *Personality and Mental Health, 14*(1), 30–50. doi:10.1002/pmh.1461

Simms, L. J., Wright, A. G., Cicero, D., Kotov, R., Mullins-Sweatt, S. N., Sellbom, M., . . . Zimmermann, J. (2022). Development of measures for the Hierarchical Taxonomy of Psychopathology (HiTOP): A collaborative scale development project. *Assessment, 29*(1), 3–16.

Snyder, H. R., Hankin, B. L., Sandman, C. A., Head, K., & Davis, E. P. (2017). Distinct patterns of reduced prefrontal and limbic gray matter volume in childhood general and internalizing psychopathology. *Clinical Psychological Science, 5*(6), 1001–1013.

Snyder, H. R., Young, J. F., & Hankin, B. L. (2017). Strong homotypic continuity in common psychopathology-, internalizing-, and externalizing-specific factors over time in adolescents. *Clinical Psychological Science, 5*(1), 98–110. doi:10.1177/2167702616651076

Spiegel, A. (2005). The dictionary of disorder. *The New Yorker, 3*, 56–63.

Stasik-O'Brien, S. M., Brock, R. L., Chmielewski, M., Naragon-Gainey, K., Koffel, E., McDade-Montez, E., O'Hara, M. W., & Watson, D. (2019). Clinical utility of the inventory of depression and anxiety symptoms (IDAS). *Assessment, 26*(5), 944–960. doi:10.1177/1073191118790036

Sullivan, P. F., Agrawal, A., Bulik, C. M., Andreassen, O. A., Børglum, A. D., Breen, G., Cichon, S., Edenberg, H. J.,

Faraone, S. V., & Gelernter, J. (2018). Psychiatric genomics: An update and an agenda. *American Journal of Psychiatry, 175*(1), 15–27. doi:10.1176/appi.ajp.2017.17030283

Tang, T. Z., DeRubeis, R. J., Hollon, S. D., Amsterdam, J., Shelton, R., & Schalet, B. (2009). Personality change during depression treatment: A placebo-controlled trial. *Archives of General Psychiatry, 66*(12), 1322–1330. doi:10.1001/archgenpsychiatry.2009.166

US Department of Veterans Affairs. (2009, June 03). VA/DoD Clinical Practice Guidelines. https://www.healthquality.va.gov/guidelines/MH/ptsd/

Vachon, D. D., Krueger, R. F., Rogosch, F. A., & Cicchetti, D. (2015). Assessment of the harmful psychiatric and behavioral effects of different forms of child maltreatment. *JAMA Psychiatry, 72*(11), 1135–1142. doi:10.1001/jamapsychiatry.2015.1792

Verheul, R., Bartak, A., & Widiger, T. (2007). Prevalence and construct validity of personality disorder not otherwise specified (PDNOS). *Journal of Personality Disorders, 21*, 359–370.

Vollebergh, W. A., Iedema, J., Bijl, R. V., de Graaf, R., Smit, F., & Ormel, J. (2001). The structure and stability of common mental disorders: the NEMESIS study. *Archives of General Psychiatry, 58*(6), 597–603.

Waldman, I. D., Poore, H. E., Luningham, J. M., & Yang, J. (2020). Testing structural models of psychopathology at the genomic level. *BioRxiv*, 502039.

Waszczuk, M. A., Eaton, N. R., Krueger, R. F., Shackman, A. J., Waldman, I. D., Zald, D. H., Lahey, B. B., Patrick, C. J., Conway, C. C., & Ormel, J. (2020). Redefining phenotypes to advance psychiatric genetics: Implications from hierarchical taxonomy of psychopathology. *Journal of Abnormal Psychology, 129*(2), 143–161. doi:10.1037/abn0000486

Waszczuk, M. A., Kotov, R., Ruggero, C., Gamez, W., & Watson, D. (2017). Hierarchical structure of emotional disorders: From individual symptoms to the spectrum. *Journal of Abnormal Psychology, 126*(5), 613–634. doi:10.1037/abn0000264

Watson, D., O'Hara, M. W., Naragon-Gainey, K., Koffel, E., Chmielewski, M., Kotov, R., . . . Ruggero, C. J. (2012). Development and validation of new anxiety and bipolar symptom scales for an expanded version of the IDAS (the IDAS-II). *Assessment, 19*(4), 399–420.

Widiger, T. A., & Samuel, D. B. (2005). Diagnostic categories or dimensions? A question for the Diagnostic and statistical manual of mental disorders—fifth edition. *Journal of Abnormal Psychology, 114*(4), 494–504. doi:10.1037/0021-843X.114.4.494

Widiger, T. A., Sellbom, M., Chmielewski, M., Clark, L. A., DeYoung, C. G., Kotov, R., Krueger, R. F., Lynam, D. R., Miller, J. D., & Mullins-Sweatt, S. (2019). Personality in a hierarchical model of psychopathology. *Clinical Psychological Science, 7*(1), 77–92.

Wright, A. G., & Simms, L. J. (2015). A metastructural model of mental disorders and pathological personality traits. *Psychological Medicine, 45*(11), 2309–2319. doi:10.1017/S0033291715000252

Zachar, P., Krueger, R. F., & Kendler, K. S. (2016). Personality disorder in DSM-5: An oral history. *Psychological Medicine, 46*(1), 1–10. doi:10.1017/S0033291715001543

Zald, D. H., & Lahey, B. B. (2017). Implications of the hierarchical structure of psychopathology for psychiatric neuroimaging. *Biological Psychiatry: Cognitive Neuroscience and Neuroimaging, 2*(4), 310–317. doi:10.1016/j.bpsc.2017.02.003

# CHAPTER 4

# The Research Domain Criteria Project: Integrative Translation for Psychopathology

Bruce N. Cuthbert, Gregory A. Miller, Charles Sanislow, *and* Uma Vaidyanathan

## Introduction

This is an exciting period in psychopathology. New methodologies such as magnetic resonance imaging (MRI) and computational modeling are maturing rapidly, conceptual ideas about the nature and structure of mental disorders continue to evolve, and the field is exploring new strategies for research in order to improve diagnosis and treatment. At the same time, traditional methods continue to prevail in research and clinical practice. Current approaches to classification and diagnosis follow patterns that are well over a century old, relying almost entirely upon clinical interviews to assess presenting symptoms and signs. The persistent reliance on these practices is striking given marked progress in many areas of science. The situation is understandable given the ingrained status of current diagnostic classes in all spheres of mental disorders. However, debates about these traditional attitudes are increasing as scientific advances permeate the field. This chapter about the Research Domain Criteria (RDoC) is one of several entries in this edition that feature novel ideas for conceptualizing and studying psychopathology. RDoC represents an example of a strategy for *translational research*, which can be defined as the attempt to "seek fundamental knowledge about the nature and behavior of living systems and the application of that knowledge to enhance health, lengthen life, and reduce illness and disability" (Lauer, 2016, p. 1).

The RDoC initiative is distinct from other novel approaches in this volume in three ways. First, the project was initiated by a governmental funding agency, the US National Institute of Mental Health (NIMH, part of the National Institutes of Health [NIH]) in 2009 as a research framework for psychopathology. Second, the RDoC framework is distinguished by the nature of its organization, attempting formally to meld into one schema disparate aspects of measurement classes and influences on mental health. Finally, RDoC is not intended to supplant current diagnostic manuals but rather to provide novel approaches for research. All three of these aspects revolve around a central aim: to promote studies that embody new ways of thinking about and studying psychopathology in terms of disruptions in basic functions, as manifested and analyzed by measurements in multiple response systems. The long-term goal is to provide a literature that will facilitate changes in all aspects of mental health practice—assessment, treatment, and prevention.

Why implement a novel framework for translational research? The rationale is that while morbidity

---

**Abbreviations**
B-SNIP   Bipolar-Schizophrenia Network for Intermediate Phenotypes
ERP      evoked response potential
HiTOP   Hierarchical Taxonomy of Psychopathology
RDC     Research Diagnostic Criteria
RDoC   Research Domain Criteria
RFA     Request for Applications
rsFC    resting-state functional connectivity
SSD     schizophrenia spectrum disorder

and mortality have been reduced markedly for many conditions (e.g., cancer, heart disease) over the past several decades, the severe burden of mental disorders persists unmitigated (Insel, 2009). A strong case can be made that the prevailing diagnostic system is a significant part of the problem, particularly with respect to research and its translation into clinical practice. While it is difficult to change a system so entrenched in health systems, insurance billing, and government policies, a marked shift is necessary for progress to be made.

In this chapter, we discuss the rationale for RDoC, summarize its major elements, consider the philosophy of science issues that permeate it (and our field), and review examples of research designs and results that illustrate the framework for both adult and child/adolescent disorders. Several articles have described in detail the original RDoC development process and the components of the framework (e.g., Kozak & Cuthbert, 2016; Morris et al., 2021; Sanislow et al., 2010); this chapter is dedicated to explicating in more depth the principles and concepts of the initiative.

## Rationale
### Beginnings of Psychiatric Nosology

A brief account of views about mental illness over the past two centuries provides context for why and how RDoC came about (see Kendler, 2020; Miller, 2020; Chapter 2, this volume). The nineteenth century was a time of marked advances in the field of medicine. Physicians continued to follow the age-old practice of describing and diagnosing illnesses in terms of their symptoms, with the assumption that underlying pathologies existed and that their causes would eventually be discovered. These hopes were gradually realized as scientific technologies and investigations progressed toward an understanding of physical etiology. For instance, edema was recognized in ancient civilizations and known as "dropsy" (a contraction of "hydropsy," i.e., *water*) due to its primary symptom as the accumulation of fluid in various parts of the body, but differentiation of the multiple causes of edema only began in the early 1800s, when two English physicians reported distinct cardiac versus renal etiologies.

Early students of mental illness followed a similar approach to diagnosis. Individuals generally came to clinical attention when their condition necessitated admission to insane asylums. Their symptoms, typically psychosis or severe depression, were so extreme that early psychiatrists became known as "alienists" (from *aliéné*, French for "insane"). It is little wonder that these debilitating conditions were regarded unquestionably as diseases that were not only qualitatively different from normal behavior, but from other mental diseases as well.

The care of mentally ill patients gradually improved during the nineteenth century. The patchwork system of private hospitals and religious institutions gave way to government-supported asylums in Europe and the United States, which in turn fostered a growing cadre of psychiatrists with formal training and a systematic approach to diagnosis. Those pioneers grappled with a number of fundamental issues regarding mental illnesses that still resonate today. These included the question as to whether mental disorders are better regarded as diseases of the "mind" (following the tradition of mental states established by Enlightenment philosophers) or diseases of the brain (in line with other areas of contemporary medicine), and, if the latter, whether brain pathophysiology should be regarded as disorders of specific locations or of neural circuits (Stoyanov et al., 2019). Notably, psychiatrists such as Emil Kraepelin and Eugen Bleuler regarded mental disorders as involving both mental and physiological aspects (Bleuler, 1911/1950) and attempted to define and differentiate diseases through careful clinical observations of symptoms, severity, and course of illness. Kraepelin, in particular, saw mental illnesses as "natural disease units" (*natuerliche Krankheitseinheit*; Heckers, 2008) even though he never conclusively decided whether dementia praecox and manic-depressive illness (now schizophrenia and bipolar disorder, respectively) were separate diseases or not. Such viewpoints continue to resonate in modern deliberations, not only about the list of mental disorders but about assumptions (often implicit) regarding the nature of psychopathology.

The failure to establish definitive findings regarding the nature and causes of mental illness (with rare exceptions such as neurosyphilis) resulted in an impasse that was partly responsible for the rise of psychoanalytic psychiatry in the late nineteenth century and its dominance throughout most of the twentieth century, led by such legendary figures as Freud, Jung, and Horney. Initial hopes that psychoanalytic theories could lay the basis for scientific progress were dashed as the various schools of thought failed to develop consensus about the nature of clinical phenomena. Etiological theories and diagnostic practices depended more on the particular school in which therapists were trained than on scientific rigor, resulting in a lack of a coherent set of diagnostic and clinical practices (Lieberman & Ogas, 2015).

In response to the diagnostic quandary, an initial psychodynamic nomenclature issued by the US War Department in 1943 was adapted in the early1950s to generate early versions of the *DSM* that provided lists of specific disorders and brief diagnostic descriptions and criteria (i.e., *DSM-I* in 1952 and *DSM-II* in 1968); however, these largely retained psychodynamic theories not based on scientific data. As a result, the early manuals made little progress to address the issues of interclinician reliability and scientific validity (Spitzer & Fleiss, 1974).

### The Modern Era of Nosology with the DSM: Successes and Problems

Small cadres of research psychiatrists, notably including a group at Washington University in Saint Louis, began working on more systematic descriptions of disorders in hopes of overcoming the reliability and validity problems that were so severe that they threatened psychiatry as a medical discipline (Lieberman & Ogas, 2015). The first widely noted manuscript to address this concern became a foundational document for modern psychiatry, listing five criteria for validating mental disorders: clinical description, laboratory studies (largely aspirational at that time), delimitation from other disorders, course and outcome, and familial incidence (Robins & Guze, 1970). This paper was followed by another landmark article that outlined observational studies of patients to demonstrate for a small number of putative disorders the potential use of descriptive criteria for diagnosis (Feighner et al., 1972).

These seminal papers were formative for the Research Diagnostic Criteria (RDC), intended explicitly to "enable research investigators to apply a consistent set of criteria for the description or selection of samples of subjects with functional psychiatric illnesses" that would "enable investigators to select relatively homogeneous groups of subjects who meet specific diagnostic criteria." (Spitzer et al., 1978, pp. 773 and 774, respectively). The RDC provided an extensive list of disorders, each with detailed diagnostic criteria, but did not attempt to cover all psychiatric phenomena. It was designed to foster research where it seemed ripe for pursuit rather than to serve as a handbook for routine clinical use: "The choice of which diagnostic categories to include in the RDC . . . was based on our judgment of the major problems of current psychiatric research" (Spitzer et al., 1978, p. 775).

The climax of the effort to rescue the problematic diagnostic standards of the *DSM-I* and *DSM-II* manuals ensued shortly thereafter with the publication of the third edition of the *DSM*, adhering closely to the ideas and criteria (and often the exact language) of the RDC. The *DSM-III* was a paradigm shift, fundamental to the development of modern psychiatric nosology and affecting not only clinical practice but also research grant applications, scientific journals, and regulatory agencies such as the US Food and Drug Administration (FDA). Its polythetic diagnostic system (requiring a certain number of symptoms from a longer list; e.g., five of nine symptoms for a major depressive episode) provided quasi-quantitative criteria for making a diagnosis, and its atheoretical stance enabled investigators of all clinical perspectives to employ the manual. (The other prominent diagnostic manual in recent decades is the mental and behavioral section of the *ICD*, the international standard published by the World Health Organization. The *ICD* employs brief descriptions of disorders rather than polythetic criteria, but the listing of disorders is generally quite similar to that of the *DSM*.)

This summary of the history that eventuated in the current diagnostic system is intended to help the reader appreciate two essential points in the *DSM-III* architecture that, for all its influence, had particular reverberations for the future. First, the framers of the *DSM-III*, in no small part due to the welter of competing theories and schools with divergent etiological hypotheses, continued to depend on the nineteenth-century practice of defining disorders by descriptive signs and symptoms (Engstrom & Kendler, 2015; see also Scull, 2021, p. 5: "To attempt to diagnose illness using patient symptoms resembles the approach of the eighteenth, not twenty-first century medicine."). Furthermore, they continued the practice of earlier psychiatrists in assuming that careful clinical descriptions would define specific diseases (earning the sobriquet of "neo-Kraepelinians").

Second, the disorder definitions were developed to promote reliability rather than validity (Hyman, 2010). As explained in the *DSM-III* regarding the pre-release field trials, "Perhaps the most important part of the study was the evaluation of diagnostic reliability" (American Psychiatric Association [APA], 1980, p. 5); and a few pages later, ". . . for most of the categories the diagnostic criteria are based on clinical judgment, and have not yet been fully validated by data about such important correlates as clinical course, outcome, family history, and treatment response" (APA, 1980, p. 8): that is, the *Robins and Guze criteria* (1970). In other words, validity was explicitly deferred in favor of reliability, with the aspirational assumption that the former could eventually be addressed once the latter was sufficiently improved.

Although revisions have occurred periodically (the current version is *DSM-5*, released in 2013), the basic *DSM/ICD* architecture has persisted across the 40-plus years since *DSM-III*'s publication. Despite its pervasive influence, scientific reservations about the system began relatively early (e.g., "the existence of an official taxonomy also has become an unintended straitjacket, as more researchers have limited themselves to the DSM criteria rather than investigating different sets of criteria" (Clark et al., 1995, p. 123). Unfortunately, "the focus on reliability came at a time when the scientific understanding of mental disorders was embryonic and could not yield valid disease definitions" (Hyman, 2010, p. 155). As methodologies in areas such as genetics, psychophysiology (including neuroimaging, large-array evoked response potentials [ERPs], and other techniques), and psychometrically sound behavioral measures have evolved from experimental demonstrations to commonplace methods, the practice of studying disorders defined in the absence of any etiological factors has become increasingly untenable.

## New Directions for Research

The keen awareness of the need to move in new directions is exemplified by a comment from one of the groups considering revisions for the *DSM-5* revision process: "Although a move to an etiologically and pathophysiologically based diagnostic system for psychiatry will be extraordinarily difficult, it is nevertheless essential, based on the increasing belief that many, and perhaps most, of the current symptom clusters of *DSM* will ultimately not map onto distinct disease states" (Charney et al., 2002, p. 34).

Investigators also had suggestions about some of the specific directions that new research should take, as expressed by the well-respected genetics group at Cardiff, Wales.

> [S]tudies would benefit from a focus on specific symptoms as well as cognitive and neurocognitive endophenotypes with the confounding effects of diagnostic practices removed. . . . This work will need to take a developmental perspective since it is likely that the manifestations of these phenotypes will vary with age, and longitudinal studies will certainly be required. Aetiological research . . . should now end its exclusive love affair with DSM and ICD categories. The goal must now be to relate research on aetiology and pathogenesis to specific psychopathological syndromes and phenotypes defined by studies of cognition and neuroimaging. (Owen et al., 2011, p. 174)

As these viewpoints indicate, the problem was not that scientists were unaware of the issues with the diagnostic system, nor lacking in new ideas for conducting research. Rather, a significant impediment concerned the custom that study sections (National Institutes of Health peer review committees convened to evaluate and score grant applications) for mental disorders research traditionally prioritized study designs limited to single *DSM* disorders, typically as compared to healthy controls. This was due in no small part to the fact that the various disorders listed in the *DSM-III* became reified relatively quickly after its release (and persisted in subsequent editions). A former NIMH director noted that "The problematic effects of diagnostic reification were revealed repeatedly in genetic studies, imaging studies, clinical trials, and types of studies where the rigid, operationalized criteria of the DSM-IV defined the goals of the investigation despite the fact that they appeared to be poor mirrors of nature" (Hyman, 2010, p. 158). It is reasonable to infer that such a situation was facilitated by the bequeathed concept of "natural disease units" stemming from the strong Kraepelinian core of the *DSM-III* and its successors; the neo-Kraepelinian view promoted adherence to an essentialist view of disorders (i.e., the notion that there must be some essence that categorically defined and distinguished a disease; Astle & Fletcher-Watson, 2020). It was thereby understandable that study sections would regard the *DSM* diagnostic classes as a high priority for both diagnosis and treatment despite the growing evidence of poor discriminability of such classes.

Another related problem affected the grant review process. Science generally depends on a consensus paradigm for its deliberations to provide a common basis for discussion, a core element at the heart of study section evaluations. Reified *DSM* disorders constituted a hegemonic architecture for consensus in grant reviews (dubbed an "epistemic prison" by Hyman, 2010) that was difficult to transcend. Investigators (as well as the authors of *DSM* editions) were generally aware that disorders as listed in the manuals were heuristic rather than natural kinds, and individual scientists might well have diverse alternative hypotheses, but, in the forum of a review committee, there was little basis for deciding on the merits of alternative research approaches.

NIMH experienced this phenomenon directly with a 2001 funding set-aside (a Request for Applications [RFA]) termed "Modular Phenotyping for Major Mental Disorders," a sort of RDoC prototype. Citing heterogeneity and mechanisms that cut across disorders, the aim of the announcement was to support research that would "dissect currently defined mental disorder syndromes into component symptom clusters or dimensions" and "select a specific symptom cluster or dimension (i.e., an illness module) for intensive analysis." The announcement further called for "hypothesis-driven, experimental methods to discern and map the biobehavioral mechanisms and neurobiological systems that account for disturbed behavior" (NIMH, 2001, p. 3). Although the announcement was well received by the field (as evidenced by an ample number of applications), not one received a fundable score; there was simply insufficient consensus among applicants and reviewers regarding criteria for such aspects as the specific topics of study, the number and types of measures to include, or the kinds of analyses to be employed.

As one might imagine, this issue occurs across many areas of science. For instance, as of this writing, there is spirited debate regarding the longstanding focus on beta-amyloid and tau proteins as primary etiological factors in Alzheimer's disease (Hascup & Hascup, 2020). As one researcher commented,

> Despite billions of dollars spent, there are still no effective pharmacotherapies for Alzheimer's Disease (AD). The problem plaguing AD research may well lie at the level of study design/data collection. Because we depend on a peer-reviewed system for funding, in order to get a fundable grant in AD, we all have to meet pre-conceived criteria for appropriate methodology, which has led us all to essentially propose similar study designs and collect essentially the same data. So not shockingly, we are all finding the same thing. And our evidence based approach for determining treatments is leading to the same path of failed clinical trial studies. . . . When we start studying dementia/AD outside the boundaries of what is presumed to be known about the disease is when we will fully start to characterize it. (Au, 2019, pp. 1–2)

These comments aptly relate to the situation that existed for peer reviews of mental disorder grant applications. The challenge for NIMH was not so much to exhort investigators to devise innovative ideas regarding mental disorders. Rather, the imperative was to devise a set of criteria that are mutually understood by applicants and reviewers and thus could enable study designs and research methodologies that diverge from traditional *DSM* approaches to be peer-reviewed in consistent fashion. In essence, the problem was how to implement an ecosystem for grant review that allows applications from diverse perspectives and areas of psychopathology to be considered on an equal footing and for the best to emerge with strong scores.

In short, the need was to craft a research architecture for diagnostic approaches which transcend symptom-based syndromes by incorporating data that include behavioral/psychological functions, implementing biological systems, developmental trajectories, and environmental effects. Movement in this direction required that these aspects were well established and contributing steadily to cumulative literatures on measurement and classification; however, such literatures could not be created as long as clinical research was conducted solely within the current diagnostic system. This paradox provided the rationale for a new framework for experimental psychopathology research.

## The RDoC Project

The NIMH released a major update of its Strategic Plan in 2008. As part of this plan, two of the four major Strategic Objectives contained language referring to new initiatives that would link behavioral and physiological measures in order study dimensions of functioning related to mental disorders.

The key statement was contained in Strategy 1.4 of the plan: "Develop, for research purposes, new ways of classifying mental disorders based on dimensions of observable behavior and neurobiological measures" (NIMH, 2008). The phrase "new ways of classifying mental disorders" denotes the intent to devise novel criteria for forming groups or dimensions to serve as independent variables in experimental studies (e.g., on the basis of behavioral and/or biological measures rather than traditional disorder categories). (Some observers mistakenly construed the phrase as implying an attempt to propose an alternative to the *DSM-5*, but that was not the purpose). RDoC is formally agnostic regarding *DSM/ICD* categories, based on the stance that any potential changes to *DSM* categories (or its overall architecture) can only be evaluated on the basis of data from various alternative scientific approaches.

The elaboration of this strategy directly addressed the two salient obstacles to research progress summarized above: viz., the reliance on symptoms in defining disorders and the lack of validity in current diagnostic classes.

> [T]he way that mental disorders are defined in the present diagnostic system does not incorporate current information from integrative neuroscience research, and thus is not optimal for making scientific gains through neuroscience approaches.... Many mental disorders may be considered as falling along multiple dimensions (e.g., cognition, mood, social interactions), with traits that exist on a continuum ranging from normal to extreme.... To clarify the underlying causes of mental disorders, it will be necessary to define, measure, and link basic biological and behavioral components of normal and abnormal functioning.... By linking basic biological and behavioral components, it will become possible to construct valid, reliable phenotypes (measurable traits or characteristics) for mental disorders. (NIMH, 2008, p. 10)

The language in the second Strategic Objective specifically acknowledged the importance of developmental and environmental influences. This objective included a directive to "define the developmental trajectories of mental disorders," with a related aim to "Link studies of brain development with behavioral development to understand how brain regions critical for mental disorders are associated with typical and atypical behavioral functioning" (NIMH, 2008, p. 13). The importance of environmental factors was recognized in both objectives, as these interact with developmental trajectories and genetic variation.

These ideas fall under the purview of psychophysiology, a discipline that is central to this undertaking given its long-standing status as a field that focuses (both philosophically and empirically) on the relationships between behavioral/cognitive constructs and physiological phenomena (Miller et al., 2016). An editorial in the initial issue of the field's eponymous journal succinctly expresses the relevance for RDoC: "Psychophysiology provides a method for bringing both physiological and psychological aspects of behavior into a single field of discourse by which truly organismic constructs may be created" (Ax, 1964, p. 1). The principle expressed in that statement is notable in that advances from new technologies such as neuroimaging or computational modeling of behavior fit readily under the aegis of "organismic constructs."

## The RDoC Framework

The RDoC framework represents the organizing principles of the project and includes four major elements (Figure 4.1; see Cuthbert & Insel, 2013, for a concise summary). First, the various "dimensions of observable behavior and neurobiological measures" noted above are grouped in superordinate domains of functioning, such as Cognitive and Social Processes domains, each with multiple dimensions (e.g., dimensions of Attention and Working Memory in the Cognitive Domain). Second, the dimensions can be measured by multiple classes of variables (such as brain activity recordings, behaviors, and self-report instruments), which are referred to in the framework as "Units of Analysis." Third, developmental trajectories as studied across the lifespan have a high priority in examining normative development and the transitions to psychopathology. Fourth, environmental influences of all types, both negative and positive, are critically important factors in studying the etiology of psychopathology. These principles are detailed below. Strategy 1.4 (the defining statement of the new goal) included four specific aims that add further provisos regarding the domains and units of analysis; these are accordingly addressed first, followed by a discussion of the development and environmental factors.

### Aim 1

"Initiate a process for bringing together experts in clinical and basic sciences to jointly identify the fundamental behavioral components that may span multiple disorders (e.g., executive functioning . . .) and that are more amenable to neuroscience approaches" (NIMH, 2008).

A working group of NIMH staff convened in early 2009 to determine the various aspects of the framework and devise a process for generating the set of "fundamental components" that comprise the central core of the RDoC concept. The components are conceived in terms of psychological constructs as used in the traditional sense (e.g., MacCorquodale & Meehl, 1948; Kozak & Miller, 1982) but with a psychophysiological orientation. RDoC constructs are jointly defined by (1) evidence for a basic psychological or behavioral function and (2) evidence for a neural circuit or system that plays a major role in implementing the given function (along with guidance that the

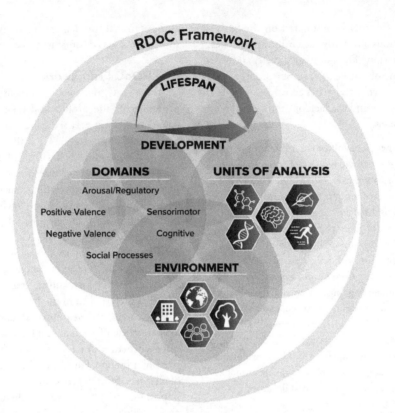

**Figure 4.1** Major elements of the Research Domain Criteria (RDoC) framework. Domains are superordinate groupings that contain the various dimensional RDoC constructs, with each domain containing three to six related constructs. The Units of Analysis depict examples of the various classes of measurement that could be used to study constructs, such as genetics, molecular/cellular recordings, brain circuit activity, self-report instruments, and behavior. Developmental trajectories are viewed from a life span perspective. The Environment represents the wide range of potentially relevant aspects, such as the built environment, cultural factors, neighborhoods, and social factors (often referred to collectively as the *exposome*). Inclusion of the Development and/or Environment elements is encouraged in experimental designs in order to study the effects of the contexts in which domains and constructs are studied. The overlaps among the four circles are intended to connote the importance of studying interactions among the four elements.

construct should have relevance to mental disorders). Basically, RDoC calls for studies that explore various aspects of psychopathology in terms of these constructs, which will in most cases be narrower and more focused than current diagnostic classes and yet will often be transdiagnostic.

At present, the constructs included in RDoC are grouped into six broad domains as determined by the working group: Negative Valence Systems (responses to aversive situations), Positive Valence Systems (responses to appetitive situations), Cognitive Systems, Social Processes, Arousal/Regulatory Systems, and Sensorimotor Systems (NIMH, 2020). The constructs were defined in a series of workshops beginning in 2011 by groups of scientists with specialized expertise in the respective domains (one meeting for each domain; see Kozak & Cuthbert, 2016, for procedural details and the RDoC website for the proceedings, NIMH, 2020).

Starting with a set of candidate constructs based on the working group's literature review and pre-workshop survey responses from the field, the experts evaluated the strength of data for both psychological functions and implementing neural systems. The participants accepted some candidate constructs (often with varying degrees of modification), declined others, and created new constructs in keeping with the guidelines; a definition was written for each approved construct. As an example of the workshop process, the mirror neuron system (initially nominated) was not included because the experts at the workshop reported that it was as yet not clear what the function of the system was, and so it did not meet the criterion for "evidence for a basic psychological or behavioral function." Note that this decision only reflects the stringency of the criteria for vetting constructs that can serve as exemplars of the RDoC framework, rather than signifying that the mirror neuron system is considered unworthy for further studies; in fact, this would suggest continuing the research to understand such a potentially important construct for social interactions.

The constructs that emerged from the workshops were regarded as strong examples of a main principle: to study psychopathology via psychophysiological constructs that are more specific in nature than are broad diagnostic syndromes. Some constructs and domains were given relatively new names to avoid carry-over implications from related terms that could be misleading; for instance, the term "fear" has a long history with many different shades of meaning (and science), so the term "acute threat" was adopted to represent a more specific meaning. (See the workshop proceedings for insight into the various perspectives and considerations that had to be discussed; NIMH, 2020.)

As these points imply, the intention from the beginning was that the set of constructs should not be a fixed grouping. As befits a research framework, constructs were anticipated to undergo continual change on the basis of new data—whether new, revised, merged with others, or deleted. Moreover, the initial constructs were seen as exemplars that could guide investigators in proposing and validating new constructs through research. In this manner, the framework could grow with the progress of psychological science and neuroscience. Changes that have occurred since the project's inception include a revision of constructs in the Positive Valence domain, the addition of the Sensorimotor Systems domain, and ongoing discussions of revisions to Negative Valence constructs.

These alterations highlight one of the most important (and often misunderstood) points to be emphasized: the central purpose of RDoC is not to curate a list of domains and constructs per se (important as they are for actual research). Rather, the core is a set of principles by which the constructs and hypotheses are derived in order to foster research that diverges from studies of traditional disorder categories. Ongoing research progress depends on a flexible framework that can accommodate the pace of scientific advances over time.

## Aim 2

"Integrate the fundamental genetic, neurobiological, behavioral, environmental, and experiential components that comprise these disorders."

One of the major complications in our field concerns the various ways of construing and assessing mental illness. These include various data sources; for example, behavior (in structured behavioral tasks or observations of behavior in various contexts), measurements of brain structure and/or activity, and phenomenology (the patient's reports or other manifestations of his or her subjective experiences). Although opinions differ as to which of these kinds of data are most informative, it may be most fruitful not to choose one to the exclusion of others or even to privilege one over the others. As per the classic "blind men and the elephant" metaphor, what is important is to figure out how these various classes of measurement relate in order to reach a comprehensive understanding. From a scientific perspective, a difficult methodological challenge concerns the frequent modest-to-low relations among various measurement classes in studies of mental disorders or indeed normal behavioral/psychological concepts (Kozak & Miller, 1982; Lang, 2010; Miller & Bartholomew, 2020). This is a long-standing problem in many areas of psychological science, not only in psychopathology (Campbell & Fiske, 1959). In the mental disorders arena, one obvious example is the low correspondence between symptom-based diagnostic classes and biological measures.

It is sometimes assumed that these issues simply reflect measurement error and that improved methodologies will solve the problem, but this premise greatly underestimates the complexity of the various systems involved in functional behavior. As a pioneering group of psychophysiologists noted, "Somatic responses are often discussed and sometimes experimented on because they are thought to be the flesh-and-blood embodiments of certain immaterial realities which psychological analysis seems to discover: psychological concepts such as emotion, anxiety, stress, inner tension, [etc.] . . . . [But] rather than being hopeful of homologies between the somatic responses and psychological concepts built from other materials, we should be surprised by their discovery and rather astonished at the simplicity of the universe" (Davis et al., 1955, p. 1). This is an explicit reason that RDoC constructs are unlikely to be considered as direct equivalents of those stemming from psychological concepts derived mostly from self-reports or common words (e.g., "enjoyment" or "negative affect").

Accordingly, a significant aim of RDoC is to foster studies that examine the complex relations among different classes of measurement (i.e., the units of analysis). Investigators are encouraged (but not required) to include multiple units of analysis in their studies, choosing a subset appropriate to the research question. As one way to assist investigators in understanding and applying RDoC principles to their research, a two-dimensional RDoC matrix was cumulated as the workshops progressed. The rows of the matrix contain the domains and constructs, and the columns denote the units of analysis. The latter currently include genes, molecules, cells, measures of circuit activity (e.g., functional MRI [fMRI] or large-array ERPs), peripheral physiology (e.g., cortisol or heart rate), behavior (e.g., performance on psychological tasks or quantitative assessments of behavior in various contexts), and self-reports (including paper/pencil instruments or quantified interviews) (see Kozak & Cuthbert, 2016, for details). For each cell representing the intersection of a construct and a unit of analysis, workshop participants generated a provisional list of variables reported in the literature as measures of the construct (see the online matrix for further information; NIMH, 2019).

Like domains and constructs, the units of analysis and variable lists are intended as a heuristic set of exemplars for investigators to become familiar with the RDoC organization and principles rather than as an exhaustive and static compendium. It should be noted that the units of analysis pertain to data acquired from individuals, whereas developmental time periods and/or environmental influences represent important contexts that affect individuals; in other words, it is important to study the effects of development and the environment on individuals, as assessed by selected units of analysis.

*Aim 3*

"Determine the full range of variation, for normal to abnormal, among the fundamental components to improve understanding of what is typical versus pathological."

As mentioned earlier, the beginnings of organized psychiatric practice originated with patients who were so impaired that alienists understandably concluded that they were observing a severe disease that was distinct from normality, a position particularly associated with Kraepelin and other early nosologists. Although outside the scope of this chapter, it should be noted that dimensional theories also date back to the beginnings of psychopathology (e.g., Bleuler, 1911/1950) and have been extensively studied since that time (e.g., Clark et al., 1995). However, the neo-Kraepelinian renaissance, starting with the Feighner criteria in 1972 and culminating in the *DSM-III* in 1980, established the contemporary precedent for considering psychiatric disorders as specific disease entities. Well over a century after Kraepelin's time, this assumption—having generalized to almost all other disorders—continues to drive research as well as clinical services: both the *DSM* and *ICD* manuals depend on dichotomous, ill/not ill diagnostic practices.

The continued reliance on binary categories remains one of the most constraining aspects that nineteenth-century psychiatric perspectives bequeathed to contemporary research. Modern medicine matured when scientists were gradually able to discover basic mechanisms and functions and then determine the malfunctions in those systems that eventuated in disorders. To the extent possible, such mechanisms, rather than just their downstream symptoms, became the target of intervention or prevention. These developments were followed by the acquisition of population-level distributions of relevant measurements, and it became feasible to gauge increasing levels of risk (or early pathology) over time with dimensional quantitative measures (such as glucose tolerance for diabetes risk). Furthermore, clinical researchers could establish cut points on dimensional distributions to demarcate different ranges of risk or disorder, which may be revised periodically on the basis of new data (e.g., American Heart Association News, 2018). From this perspective, it is not surprising that attempts to apply continuous biological or behavioral measures to symptom-based dichotomies of mental illness versus health have been unsuccessful (Kapur et al., 2012).

Organizing the framework around fundamental dimensions of behavior, as viewed in terms of population-level distributions, enables RDoC to foster a research perspective aligned with other contemporary areas of health research. RDoC inverts the usual paradigm for conceptualizing psychopathology: Rather than defining illnesses on the basis of presenting signs and symptoms and then searching for a disease-related problem, RDoC treats psychopathology in terms of varying degrees of dysregulation in normal-range functioning, considered from a relatively specific, construct-oriented focus. This approach has important ramifications for translational research in that studies of basic processes (in humans and nonhuman animals) can be applied much more directly to clinically significant issues (Anderzhanova, Kirmeier, & Wotiak, 2017). Moreover, following the course of basic functions across developmental trajectories may provide advantages for research projects that examine risk factors over time or implement prevention strategies employing dimensionally oriented research designs (Zalta & Shankman, 2016).

### Aim 4

"Develop reliable and valid measures of these fundamental components of mental disorders for use in basic studies and in more clinical settings."

Measurement represents a critical component of the RDoC program and particularly for the development of behavioral tasks or self-report instruments specifically conceived in terms of RDoC or similar constructs. Although evidence for a psychological function is a necessary criterion for any RDoC construct, the particular tasks or measures generating that evidence may vary in strength and specificity. For instance, a number of tasks align closely with the cognitive control construct (Braver et al., 2021); on the other hand, tasks across the Social Domain are generally less well-developed and there are fewer, and less well-validated, measures (although progress is under way; e.g., Gur & Gur, 2016; Hawco et al., 2019). This situation is related to the history of various constructs and particularly the progress made in studying relevant neural systems and in developing tasks that were generated for testing theoretical models. For example, brain structures involved with working memory were first identified in the 1930s, and the development of generative models in the early 1970s (Baddeley, 2003) contributed to the localization of relevant neural systems (D'Esposito & Postle, 2015). Developing and clarifying functional constructs from both psychological and neurophysiological perspectives accordingly represents a high priority (a challenge that confronts the field as a whole, not confined to RDoC).

The binary, disease/no-disease legacy of the *DSM/ICD* system represents another issue. Many instruments have been devised to assess either psychopathology (ranging from mild to severe) or normal behavior (e.g., personality and other traits). Such dichotomized distinctions often occur for self-report instruments but can also be a concern for behavioral tasks not designed to accommodate psychometric characteristics observed across the span from high-performing healthy individuals to severely impaired patients (e.g., Chapman & Chapman, 1978). Accordingly, another priority concerns the creation of tasks that span the entire range of functioning both for behavioral tasks and self-report instruments (e.g., a self-report scale for aggression, Krueger et al., 2007).

Priorities for developing behavioral tasks are changing rapidly due to the accelerating pace of computational models for studying behavior–brain relationships (Ferrante et al., 2019; Sanislow et al., 2019), an area whose varied origins crystallized as *computational neuroscience* in a seminal volume in 1990 (Schwartz, 1990). These methods have been increasingly applied to mental disorders, inspired in part by the nascent RDoC framework that called for psychophysiological constructs rather than symptom-based syndromes as the fundamental unit of analysis (Adams et al., 2016). Broadly speaking, there are two main computational approaches relevant to psychopathology (Huys, 2018). The first concerns the use of machine learning tools (also referred to as *data-driven approaches*) to "utilize large data sets and sophisticated mathematical techniques to characterize either the latent organization of the data (i.e., unsupervised learning), or multivariate relationships between specified groups of variables (i.e., supervised learning)" (Ferrante et al., 2018, p. 480). As one example, Kernbach et al. (2018) applied a sophisticated machine-learning algorithm to resting-state brain connectivity data gathered from a large sample of three groups of youth aged 7–21 (attention deficit hyperactivity disorder [ADHD], autism spectrum disorder [ASD], or typically developing), which returned three factors of network connections whose combined effects were related dimensionally to both ADHD and ASD.

The second approach involves the testing of mathematical models of brain–behavior relationships, and it is this aspect that most pertains to task development. The essence of the strategy is to specify models involving multiple parameters relevant to particular tasks and then test how closely sets of specific parameter values match observed data; this enables quantitative tests of the model and revisions as needed to the parameter set. (Often, multiple models are compared to determine which most closely accounts for real-world results.) For instance, a working memory task might involve both behavioral and neurophysiological parameters such as the number of items to store, the extent of decay in memory across time, ERPs, and fMRI (Lemaire & Portrat, 2018). This approach is well-suited for evaluating the kinds of brain–behavior relationships involved with RDoC constructs and has prompted considerable attention regarding both the advantages and the cautions as the field proceeds (Teufel & Fletcher, 2016). A detailed discussion of this growing area is beyond the scope of this chapter (e.g., see Mujica-Parodi & Strey, 2020).

*Development and Environment*

The field of developmental psychopathology has a well-established history, and research on developmental trajectories is a critical area for understanding the processes that occur during transitions from normal-range functioning to dysregulation (Chapter 6, this volume; Rutter & Sroufe, 2000). For some time, child-onset and adult-onset behaviors generally were regarded as mostly distinct. However, developmental psychopathology's emphasis on a life span approach helped move the field toward a continuous perspective on trajectories. Even for disorders that typically have onsets in adulthood, many symptoms of mental disorders are evident by adolescence (Casey et al., 2014). The relationship between the risk for childhood-onset and adult-onset disorders has long been established for mental disorders such as depression and anxiety (Rutter & Sroufe, 2000). Data from genetics and other fields indicate that similar patterns hold for psychotic-spectrum conditions: "There is now a need to focus upon the relationships among the neurodevelopmental syndromes that typically present in childhood and between these and the disorders that typically present in adulthood" (Owen et al., 2011, p. 174).

RDoC aligns with many of the components of developmental psychopathology, such as full-range dimensional aspects and the use of multiple measurement classes. The framework adds such aspects as constructs jointly defined by behavior and biology and an emphasis on functional dimensions rather than symptom-based disorders (Astle & Fletcher-Watson, 2020). While the field has shown considerable interest in RDoC research (e.g., Beauchaine & Hinshaw, 2020; Mittal & Wakschlag, 2017), it is clear that growth trajectories bring additional complexities: functional constructs emerge at varying points across development, their characteristics change over time (Posner & Rothbart, 2000), and the neural systems that implement various functions can shift as the brain develops (Sullivan, 2005). The result has been an ongoing outreach to communicate with the field in various ways to provide more guidance for investigators in elucidating these important developmental aspects (e.g., Garvey et al., 2016; Pacheco et al., 2022; NIMH, 2020). Overall, it is important to bear in mind that the framework is a set of principles intended to enable maximum flexibility in creating research designs that address the investigator's theories and hypotheses. As recently pointed out, "Interpreting the RDoC matrix as a starting point rather than definitive, future research may reveal developmental variations that are not currently captured" (Casey et al., 2014, p. 351).

The influence of the environment (encompassing, for these purposes, all social and physical aspects) is an equally important etiological factor (and also included in Strategic Objective 2). Such influences have often been perceived as situations that begin when babies begin to acquire behavioral repertoires and interact with family members (e.g., attachment, Rutter & Sroufe, 2000). However, research has more recently reported that prenatal effects, such as maternal stress or diet, can result in epigenetic modifications that result in lifelong susceptibility to mental and physical disorders (Bale et al., 2010). Clearly, the number and scope of environmental factors are not only vast, but also depend on the particular stage of the life span being studied. The pervasiveness of environmental effects is daunting yet, at the same time, indicates the need for new measurement and analytic methods (Smith & Pollak, 2021).

In sum, developmental and environmental factors (and their interactions) represent critical components of the RDoC framework. They exert significant effects on the various dimensional constructs described above and, as such, are overarching concepts that are infused throughout all aspects of RDoC.

## Philosophy of Science Fundamentals in RDoC

The nature of the relationship between mind and body is a topic that has occupied philosophers and scientists since the time of Descartes and continues to pose difficult challenges both for conceptualizations of disorder and for practical issues of study design and interpretation. RDoC adopts a novel stance toward this issue in several respects, which are summarized in this section. The mostly implicit perspective of current nosologies serves as a jumping-off point for discussing the various aspects of RDoC's philosophy.

*Mind–Body Considerations*

A number of observers have recently discussed the paradoxical relationship that has developed between the essentialist, categorical approach of the *DSM/ICD* tradition discussed above and the growing expectation (as accentuated by such efforts as the "Decade of the Brain" in the 1990s) that biological explanations of mental illness were nearly within reach and that they would resolve the aforementioned scientific and clinical problems. *DSM* and *ICD* diagnostic criteria are almost exclusively psychological in that they cite self-reports and behavioral symptoms with little or no biological measures, yet those diagnostic categories were used to drive research priorities that were increasingly focused on biological phenomena (Scull, 2021). As *DSM/ICD* criteria are generally remote at best from biological mechanisms, they have proved an unproductive guide to research intended to identify those mechanisms (Kapur et al., 2012).

From a contemporary perspective, such a clinical research strategy was almost certain to be unsuccessful with respect to progress on mental illness. This is due to issues discussed above: first, that diagnostic practice continues to follow a nineteenth-century model in which symptoms and signs are necessary and sufficient to define particular "natural disease units" and, second, that each disease will be associated on a one-to-one basis with a specific pathophysiology. However, these assumptions have been shown to be unworkable due to the nature of mental illness and its characteristically divergent manifestations in expressive language, overt functional behavior, and central and peripheral physiology (Lang, 1968; Miller, 2010; Miller & Bartholomew, 2020; Miller & Keller, 2000).

### Toward Alternative Paradigms to Reconcile Mind and Body

Given that overt impairments in mental illnesses are fundamentally problems of functioning and mental states, the field is increasingly realizing that an approach to accounting for mental disorders that treats them as primarily biological is not likely to succeed (Belluck & Carey, 2013). Miller (2010) provided numerous examples of the widespread adoption of, and faith in, the premise that a focus on biology will suffice and discussed its logical and public policy shortcomings. Conversely, given that biological phenomena instantiate and support psychological phenomena, and given that there is no question that biologically framed interventions can alter psychological function (and vice versa; Miller, 2010; Yee et al., 2015), neglect of biological phenomena (genes, cellular mechanisms, neural systems) in a diagnostic system attending almost exclusively to psychological signs and symptoms also surely has to fail as a path toward discovering the relevant biology. This realization is a major reason for the emphasis on studies that include measures from multiple response systems.

However, it is not sufficient to declare, diplomatically, that we must incorporate all of the possible types of data that are available simply because they exist as aspects of psychopathology. Merely adding social and environmental phenomena does not suffice either. The oft-cited "biopsychosocial model" (Engel, 1977) is not a formal model; it is just a list of three realms of phenomena (biology, psychology in the sense of phenomena about a single person, and social processes), typically handled distinctly and originally proposed simply as a guide for clinicians in interactions with patients. In contrast, a model specifies mechanisms connecting the elements of such a list. We must develop an approach that feasibly connects various domains of observable phenomena and also connects the unobserved and the observed. The RDoC framework is not a specific model per se, but instead calls for formal analyses of relationships between the elements of the RDoC framework (Adams et al., 2016). Crucially, a way is needed to relate the biological and the psychological, not just as enumerated neighbors but as coherently linked features of the research enterprise and of the very concept of mental health and mental illness.

### The Role of Public Data in Psychopathology Research and Theory

From its inception, the RDoC initiative has been especially attentive to philosophy of science issues that are central to conceptualizations of mental health and mental illness. The very term "mental," referring to private events that only an individual can access, challenges the desire of modern Western science to rely as much as possible on public phenomena—events that, in principle, any observer can detect and measure. It is not that science cannot accommodate unobserved events or laws about which one makes inferences from observed events; that is in fact routine in the sciences. MacCorquodale & Meehl (1948) provided guidelines for psychological science to make inferences from one or more public events to hypothetical constructs (Kozak & Miller, 1982): public data are aggregated into intervening variables, and bridge principles "indicate how the processes envisaged by the theory are related to empirical [i.e., observed] phenomena" (Hempel, 1966, p. 72). Hempel (1966, p. 74) went on to explain that "Without bridge principles ... a theory would have no explanatory power [and] would be incapable of test." But there has been no consensus about the constructs to use in understanding mental illness and about the bridge principles to use in making inferences from public data to mental health and mental illness constructs.

It helps to clarify the nature of scientific data by considering how the concept has evolved. In historical perspective, the common modern term "empirical science" is incoherent. A central contribution of the British Empiricist school to modern Western philosophy was an emphasis on distinguishing between public events and an individual's experience of those events (that which is "empirical" in the traditional sense, going back to ancient Greek philosophy). "Empirical" knowledge came to be understood as fundamentally unscientific, even contrary to science, for which only public data are data. But, by the twentieth century, the common meaning of "empirical" had evolved to refer to the portion of one's private experience that is directly driven by the public events one observes. Modern science relies on the assumption that any typical observer will see the water level in a glass rising as the ice melts. Each observer has direct access only to their own perception of that phenomenon, but we assume that any attentive observer will have the same perception.

The role of subjective experience (conscious or unconscious) in modern science thus must be considered carefully (Lang, 1984). What one feels is not scientific, empirical data, in the modern sense of publicly observable phenomena, though for many in our field and most laypeople such feelings are assumed to be what is most important in mental health and mental illness. Early behaviorists sought to leave subjective experience out of science entirely, though this attempt failed along with their larger effort to avoid hypothetical constructs altogether. At present it is widely recognized that we can make inferences about subjective experience from public data (self-report, overt behavior, biological measures), but the question of what role subjective experience should have in studying, understanding, preventing, and treating psychopathology and how to include it in rigorous science is not settled.

*An Integrative Approach*

The 2008 NIMH Strategic Plan that gave birth to the RDoC initiative shifted from a primary reliance on biological reductionism and instead emphasized an integrative approach in which psychological phenomena and biological phenomena have equal status (Kozak & Cuthbert, 2016; Lake et al., 2017). RDoC did not turn away from heavy reliance on biological constructs and observations, but it restored equally heavy reliance on psychological constructs and observations—not those derived from the Freudian tradition, as the pre-1980 *DSMs* did, but those that have emerged in modern psychological science. It consistently champions the inclusion of psychological and biological constructs and observations on an equal footing.

As discussed earlier, the RDoC framework provides guidelines for inclusion of psychophysiological constructs (the rows of the evolving RDoC matrix). The initial selection of those constructs and their ongoing evolution relied primarily on how strong a basis the human and nonhuman animal literatures provide for characterizing the construct and grounding it in available psychological and biological data. The current set of constructs does not attempt to cover all of mental health and mental illness because not everything that is of interest to clinicians and clinical researchers is well studied nor is there good evidence of relevant neural circuits or other biological mechanisms. As a research framework intended to demonstrate how functions defined by brain–behavior relationships can be applied to psychopathology, it has been acknowledged that some clinical phenomena may not (for the foreseeable future, at least) be represented as RDoC constructs.

Some have found the RDoC initiative still too biologically oriented (e.g., Lilienfeld, 2014). While it is true that some presentations of RDoC posed the ideas in reductionistic terms, there was a concomitant emphasis on psychological and behavioral aspects. For example, although an early RDoC paper contained the statement "mental disorders can be addressed as disorders of brain circuits," an ensuing elaboration pointed out the importance of integrative connections between functional behavior and brain: "Examples where clinically relevant models of circuitry-behavior relationships augur future clinical use include fear/extinction, reward, executive function, and impulse control" (Insel et al., 2010, p. 749). Others have cast RDoC as not sufficiently biological (e.g., Ross & Margolis, 2019). Criticisms of RDoC as too biological or too psychological reflect assumptions about the primacy of one or the other that have not been productive, as well as a misreading of RDoC as foregrounding one over the other.

*Causation in Biology–Psychology Relationships*

The degree of biological reductionism implicit and sometimes explicit in psychopathology research in recent decades embodies premises that such reduction is desirable and feasible (Miller, 2010; Miller & Bartholomew, 2020). The notion is often that biology is the level of analysis where the real action is—the point at which the true causes of mental illness lie and where the most effective measures to prevent and treat it should be directed; thus, that reducing psychological constructs to biological constructs and understanding psychological interventions entirely in terms of their biological effects are appropriate steps as a matter of both good science and effective public health.

However, the philosophy of science literature has repeatedly shown those premises to be untenable even in principle across decades of evaluation. As is often the case for relationships among various areas of science, important aspects of psychological science cannot be represented adequately in biological science. For instance, with respect to various levels of psychological and biological mechanisms, "macro findings are indispensable to explanations of phenomena of interest by (a) providing information regarding higher levels of organization in mechanisms, (b) including information not contained within certain micro explanations and (c) providing more general and stable causal explanations relative to micro explanations in certain situations" (Sharp & Miller, 2019, p. 18; see also Miller, 2010, for extended critique, and Miller & Bartholomew, 2020, for suggestions of further reading on this point).

A relatively recent approach in that literature has been developed by a group of philosophers of science known as the "new mechanists," who are developing fundamental changes in the way we understand relationships among different types of phenomena, including causal relationships. For instance, Bechtel (2020) distinguished production mechanisms from control mechanisms. To simplify, one can imagine production mechanisms arranged in linear order: we feed materials into a machine that heats them, blends them, bends them, and produces a new material. In contrast, control mechanisms typically involve both local feedback and a hierarchical relationship among a larger set of control mechanisms. The relationships among them may be what Bechtel called "heterarchical," meaning not just top-down control but a mix of top-down and bottom-up control mechanisms that can even make the "up" and "down" metaphors inadequate. For instance, the control mechanisms by which we maintain blood pressure (and in fact quite different pressures in different arteries) are many and complex in their interrelationships.

Thomas and Sharp (2019) interpreted and extended the new mechanist approach for psychologists and neuroscientists with a proposal for integrating biological and psychological constructs and phenomena. They discussed a strategy for developing a nonreductionist understanding of the ways in which psychological functions are implemented in biological structures. In turn, this strategy draws on a construal of the relationship between biology and psychology developed by earlier philosophers (e.g., Fodor, 1968, 1974). "The biological monism that has dominated American psychiatry for 40 years and more has been unable to solve questions of causation. That should not come as a surprise. There is mounting evidence for the importance of social factors in the genesis of major mental disturbance" (Scull, 2021, p. 4). Those social factors are not readily reducible to biology. Bolton (2013) similarly argued that some aspects of mental illness can be understood in biological terms, while other aspects will be better understood (and treated) using psychological constructs, phenomena, and methods.

The state of the art with respect to causation between biological and psychological events is such that there is not a single instance in which we have worked out the full causal chain. Furthermore, for logical as well as practical reasons, it is not at all apparent that we will ever be able to do so. Claims such as that mental illness is a brain disease, and goals such as the pursuit of the genes or circuits that explain mental illness, are not only untenable but misleading with respect to causation. It is at best premature to view biological mechanisms as "underlying" psychological phenomena or psychological mechanisms "underlying" biological phenomena. We do not know how biology/psychology causation works, and we should not pretend that we do in designing or revising a diagnostic system, developing research funding priorities, or talking with our patients. The hope offered some years ago that casting mental illness as merely physical illness would destigmatize mental illness has proved unsuccessful (Miller, 2010) and has fostered overreliance on pharmaceutical interventions.

## Levels Versus Units of Analysis

A feature of RDoC that is very intentional is its use of the term "units" rather than "levels" of analysis. Woodward (2020) provided a critique of the many ways that the "levels" metaphor has been used. As discussed by Borsboom and Cramer

(2013), Kendler (2012), Miller (2010), and Miller and Bartholomew (2020), the "levels" metaphor carries undesirable baggage.

> Traditionally, researchers tend to think of these levels as being intrinsically ordered, in the sense that genes cause brains and brains cause behaviors. However, in our view it is extremely likely that once researchers start taking the dynamics of symptomatology seriously, they will find feedback loops that cross the borders of traditional thinking. Naturally, genetic differences may predispose to the development of disorders, but persistent symptomatology (e.g., insomnia or loss of appetite) may cause differential gene expression just as well; in turn, such changes may affect a person's brain state and ultimately feed back into the environment [in] extended feedback loops. (Borsboom & Cramer, 2013, pp. 116–117)

Given such an understanding of the relationships among different facets of and mechanisms in mental illness, the implication of some reductive or causal ordering of "levels" is inappropriate, and the reductionism that the "levels of analysis" metaphor encourages is counterproductive. The RDoC initiative chose to characterize the columns of its initial matrix as "units of analysis" rather than "levels of analysis" specifically to avoid implying any causal ordering among those elements. RDoC is explicitly agnostic about what may be optimal ways of thinking about the relationships among them. This is an inherently nonreductionist stance while remaining open to scientific (and philosophical) advances that may point to reductionist or other relationships among them.

## Designing and Conducting RDoC Research

The background discussed above provides a basis for addressing how RDoC principles can be applied for research. The criteria emphasize psychophysiological constructs, dimensional approaches to functions, research designs that integrate multiple units of analysis, and inclusion of developmental aspects and environmental influences. There have been many misperceptions of the framework and how it is to be used, so it may be helpful at the outset to clarify some important aspects.

### Context: Scientific Funding Policies

The unique status of a psychopathology framework generated by a funding agency necessitates some explanation as to why its architecture is designed as it is and how that relates to devising research designs. Although this section may be of particular interest to readers in the United States, the application of RDoC principles concerns all investigators interested in utilizing the matrix for RDoC-oriented studies.

The goal of most grant-funding solicitations emanating from governmental agencies is to encourage applications in a specified scientific area or methodology, minimizing constraints on the "what" or "how" in order to encourage innovative ideas. As the experience with the NIMH "modular phenotyping" RFA showed, some guidance is necessary to communicate the high-level strategic goals for a particular area of research; however, it is always a desideratum for applicants to be as free as possible in choosing the particular research question, specific aims, and methods. Accordingly, while the current RDoC domains and constructs are considered as promising subjects for exploring psychopathology, an equally (or more) important role concerns their status as exemplars that illustrate the principles of dimensional functions for investigators interested in developing other aspects of dysregulated behavior.

There have been at least two kinds of misunderstandings about these policies (see Lake et al., 2017, for discussion of other common misunderstandings of RDoC). First are misapprehensions of NIH funding policies. Grant applications for RFAs can be returned by an Institute if the application is judged to be nonresponsive to the RFA criteria, while almost all other applications submitted by scientists ("investigator-initiated applications" in NIH-speak) are accepted for review in order to promote new ideas. Also, funding decisions are based heavily on scores in peer review, such that reviewers' perspectives play a major role in receiving a grant award (cf. the Alzheimer example mentioned earlier; Au, 2019).

In this context, the early RDoC RFAs (NIMH, 2012) prompted complaints that investigators could not use RDoC for their research because the particular construct that they wished to study was not listed in the matrix. This was not so. Although the RFAs specified that only constructs emerging from the original workshops could be included in research designs (in order to evaluate the grant application/peer review process for the new approach), they also stated that researchers were encouraged to submit ideas for new constructs via the investigator-initiated process. Others objected that NIMH no longer accepted applications focused on *DSM* disorders, which was also not true. The RFAs stated that applications focusing on *DSM* disorders per se would not be accepted given the intent to solicit RDoC-oriented studies. However, *DSM*-based applications have always been accepted through the investigator-initiated process and continue to represent a majority of the clinical research grants at NIMH. At present, as planned from the beginning, RDoC- and *DSM*-oriented grant submissions are all reviewed as investigator-initiated applications. In fact, because of the *DSM* hegemony that had existed in peer review, RDoC has likely provided an example to open the way for other types of non-*DSM* applications to be given equal consideration in study sections.

The second misunderstanding has come about due to the distinction between the aims of funding agencies, as described above, and the practices of academic research for formal theory construction. Some critiques have asserted that RDoC omits various important specifications and hypotheses. For instance, a recent review commented that "RDoC does not explicitly promote theory building or the generation of falsifiable mechanistic explanations" (Haeffel et al., 2021, p. 12). However, developing and testing theories is a task for investigators to propose in grant applications. In contrast, the role of RDoC is to specify a new set of criteria for translational research (i.e., relationships among multiple measures of dimensional constructs relevant to psychopathology); these standards apply to all RDoC-oriented research, whether they involve tests of theories, data-driven studies of new phenotypes, or other aims.

## RDoC-Oriented Constructs and Experimental Designs

We consider in this section some of the considerations involved in devising RDoC-oriented research designs. The focus here is particularly on new or revised constructs, which are at the heart of progress for RDoC's translational goals. In keeping with the emphasis on particular constructs and specific aspects of psychopathology, RDoC studies typically have a narrower purview compared to the broad syndromes represented by *DSM* disorders. This approach facilitates transdiagnostic explorations of specific functions and basic-to-abnormal dimensional studies. For instance, in carrying out a transdiagnostic study of mood and anxiety disorders, the focus might be on reward valuation or reward learning rather than clinical instruments used to diagnose a particular disorder.

The initial set of considerations outlines three aspects regarding RDoC-like constructs in research designs. One issue concerns the appropriate level of granularity for studying new constructs, a common problem in studying brain–behavior relationships (Poeppel & Adolfi, 2020). Broad constructs may be too ambiguous and vague for the RDoC context, as in concepts such as positive affect or internalizing, and may well subsume multiple circuits or functions (Sanislow, 2016). On the other hand, overly detailed constructs (e.g., proposing a construct for each nucleus related to threat in the amygdala) are likely to be too numerous and complex to be useful. Subconstructs were included in several instances where clearly appropriate, such as the RDoC concept of perception (with subconstructs of vision, audition, etc.), which provides examples of appropriately finer granularity.

A second, related consideration concerns the variety of psychological concepts and constructs that are similar, but not identical, to RDoC constructs. For instance, the RDoC construct of Cognitive Control has a substantial history in the literature, but there are many related psychological constructs (e.g., effortful control, self-regulation, and impulse control, to name but a few). While these concepts overlap to varying degrees, there are also multiple distinctions that are further complicated by differing levels of granularity (Nigg, 2017). Adding to the complexity, data suggest that self-report and behavioral measures may not entirely possess the same conceptual factor structures (Enkavi & Poldrack, 2020; Sharma et al., 2013). RDoC aligns with the cognitive neuroscience field in supporting ongoing research that continues to unravel and clarify the nature of concepts that share such knotty relationships and thus welcomes related constructs that are compatible with the RDoC approach.

A third design consideration concerns the examination of complex behavior in an RDoC context. Adaptive behavior requires effective interactions among multiple brain/behavior systems (motivational, perceptual, motoric, etc.), the precise combinations depending on environmental circumstances and the current state of the organism. While it is reasonable to conduct studies of particular functional systems (e.g., RDoC constructs) in relative isolation, ultimately there is a pressing need to examine interactions among systems—both for a fundamental understanding of basic behavior based on human and animal experiments (Anderzhanova et al., 2017) and for the unpacking of complex psychopathological phenomena such as hallucinations (Ford, 2016). Accordingly, studies examining research questions that involve multiple constructs are strongly encouraged (e.g., Cohen et al., 2017; Gibb et al., 2016).

To summarize, the preceding considerations highlight various aspects of the need for a flexible approach to implementing RDoC-oriented research questions. Classifications have been defined as "cognitive structures imposed on data to make them more intelligible and useful for specific human purposes" (Hyman, 2021, p. 24). This comment applies to RDoC constructs (as with traditional psychological constructs) even though they do not comprise a formal system like the *DSM*. They represent well-replicated findings about the current state of the science with respect to various functions; however, there is no claim that RDoC constructs are definitive or "correct" in any way or an exhaustive list of functions. In fact, a major goal is for RDoC constructs to be refined by new data, often resulting in revised perspectives or multiple novel constructs that clarify our knowledge. For instance, the concept of a straightforward brain "reward circuit" was exciting news nearly 70 years ago (Olds & Milner, 1954); since then, science has revealed multiple aspects of mammalian reward systems (Berridge & Kringelbach, 2015)—including unexpected relationships between appetitive and aversive functions in what were traditionally regarded as "reward" circuits (Kutlu et al., 2021).

Accordingly, in considering research questions for an RDoC-oriented application, it is important to create study designs that incorporate RDoC principles rather than utilize a construct from the extant RDoC matrix simply because it is one of the listed entries. The essential point is to consider carefully the posited relationship between the function embodied in the research question and its implementing neural system, and to develop a programmatic line of research that explores the hypothesized relationships and their import for psychopathology.

A different set of ideas for research designs concerns how RDoC constructs are related to *DSM* categories because the latter have been involved in the majority of RDoC-themed studies to date. There are two broad themes in this respect. First, an increasing number of studies examine relations among various measures (e.g., genetics, functioning, neural systems, symptoms) across different disorder classes, such as schizophrenia and bipolar disorder or mood and anxiety disorders, that can contribute to an understanding of the prevalent comorbidity of disorders. The growing realization that such overlaps are common contributed to the inception of the RDoC project, and, in turn, transdiagnostic studies have increased over the past decade since RDoC began (Dalgleish et al., 2020).

Transdiagnostic studies implement a variety of research designs. One approach is to form transdiagnostic groups (i.e., the independent variable) on the basis of particular measures. For example, one ongoing research program explored effects in large samples that included patients with a variety of primary diagnoses from various mood, anxiety, and posttraumatic stress disorders (Lang et al., 2016). In a representative study, psychophysiological measures were recorded while patients imagined short narrative scripts depicting their own personally threatening material (e.g., encountering a large spider, being trapped during a car accident) and other standard scripts describing neutral situations. Patients were grouped into five quintiles (i.e., the independent variable), independent of diagnosis, according to a composite physiological reactivity measure—heart rate response and the startle blink magnitude elicited by an intense noise burst during imagery—calculated by the differences in magnitude between threatening and neutral scenes (both measures typically larger for emotionally evocative scenes). The dependent variables, a composite negative affectivity score (self-report measures of anxiety and depression) and a functional impairment scale, might be expected to be positively related to physiological responsiveness under the usual assumption that higher reactions to threat are associated with greater avoidance and distress. However, the results showed an inverse linear relationship across quintiles: higher reactivity was associated with less negative affectivity and lower functional impairment.

The investigators noted that the proportion of patients with a principal diagnosis of anxious-misery disorders (e.g., generalized anxiety disorders or depression) was progressively larger across the highest to lowest quintile of physiological reactivity; in contrast, the opposite trend occurred for patients with circumscribed fear (e.g., specific phobia or circumscribed social phobia). Still, approximately 30% of the most reactive quintile were patients with anxious-misery disorders, with a similar percentage for patients with circumscribed fear disorders in the least reactive quintile. These data are consistent with prior *DSM*-oriented studies from the same group. For instance, patients with PTSD showed widely varying physiological responsivity to personal anxiogenic images, with high reactivity for single-trauma patients and blunted responsiveness with a multiple or chronic traumatic history (McTeague et al., 2010). Similarly, McTeague et al. (2009)

reported that patients with specific social phobia responded most strongly to their personal fear scenes, while those with generalized social phobia showed attenuated physiological reactivity. Overall, these results indicate that it may be useful to focus on response mechanisms rather than diagnoses in order to consider treatments that could be targeted to the individual patient's particular dysfunction.

Somewhat more common designs involve analyses that group participants into clusters based on combinations of variables, often in data-driven computational analyses. An excellent example of this type is the Bipolar-Schizophrenia Network for Intermediate Phenotypes (B-SNIP) study, which involved two large cohorts—one initial sample and a replication sample, each with more than 700 patients and 200 or more controls—enrolling patients with either schizophrenia, schizoaffective disorder, or bipolar disorder (Clementz et al., 2021). A large number of behavioral and psychophysiological measures were obtained, with principal components analyses used to reduce 44 individual variables into nine factors comprising cognitive and stop-signal tasks, anti-saccade measures, and ERPs related to auditory stimuli. In turn, a cluster analysis of these factors was used to derive three "biotypes" (clusters) from the total patient sample. The *DSM* diagnostic categories were distributed across the three biotypes in both the original and replication samples. Schizophrenia probands were somewhat more numerous in Biotype 1 and bipolar probands more numerous in Biotype 3; however, all three biotypes included at least 20% of each *DSM* category. Two clusters were comprised of participants with very impaired cognitive performance, one cluster with blunted ERP reactivity, and the other with hyperreactive ERPs, while the third cluster scored close to control subjects on both cognitive performance and ERP reactivity. The second sample replicated the initial cohort closely. Importantly, in both studies a number of external validators were differentiated more precisely by the biotypes than by *DSM* diagnoses, including cortical thinning as measured by structural MRI, social functioning, and similar but less marked patterns of response in close relatives (Clementz et al., 2016). Once again, these data suggest that measures combining behavior and psychophysiological responses may provide more distinction in terms of pathological mechanisms and potential treatment targets than traditional disorder classes (Clementz et al., 2021).

A second theme involves explorations of the dimensional aspects of RDoC constructs, whether a severity range within diagnosed patients or the broader normal-to-abnormal spectrum. These often relate to the usual inclusion of *DSM* diagnoses in research designs, but with analyses of a single large sample including both patient and control groups in order to study the dimensionality of various response measures that extend from normal-range to variably abnormal. As one example from a recent RDoC-oriented study, fMRI data were acquired from participants in two groups (schizophrenia spectrum disorder [SSD] and healthy controls) while they observed facial expressions (fearful, happy, etc.) in one session and imitated the expressions in a separate session (Hawco et al., 2019). A cluster analysis of fMRI reactivity scores (defined by the difference in fMRI activation between the "imitate" and "observe" conditions in a canonical "simulation circuit" of frontoparietal areas) was used to divide the sample into three groups of high, medium, and low reactivity. Notably, membership in the three groups was not related to diagnosis, nor to education or clinical ratings in the SSD group. Analyses relating reactivity to a principal component representing social cognition and neurocognitive scores showed that reactivity was inversely related to functional measures in both patients and controls, although functional scores for controls were much higher than that of SSD patients. High reactivity participants showed increased activation not only in the canonical simulation circuit but also in more diffuse patterns that extended to other cortical areas, prompting the inference that these individuals activated a more extensive network to compensate for local deficiencies. In contrast, low-reactivity participants inferentially suppressed activity in task-irrelevant areas to optimize performance.

Data for a replication sample that included euthymic bipolar patients in addition to SSD patients and controls demonstrated the same three patterns across groups (cf. similar distributions of patients across the three clusters in the B-SNIP study; Clementz et al., 2021). The investigators concluded by emphasizing the importance of examining dimensional measures across controls and patients: "participants showed greater similarity to members of their own cluster than to other members of their diagnostic group. This result calls into question the implicit assumption in case-control designs that groups are homogeneous but distinct from each other. Our results are more consistent with the RDoC framework, as we have demonstrated a gradient of neural efficiency to inefficiency mirroring better to poorer cognitive performance, respectively" (Hawco et al., 2019, p. 529). The results also provide another instance of the divergence between different response measures: there was no difference in average neural efficiency during social processing tasks between patients and controls but functional differences in performance were highly significant, highlighting the need to relate dimensional aspects of data across measures to understand the nature of impaired functioning and neural circuit activity.

*Development and Environment in RDoC Designs*

Work that is aligned with RDoC principles in studying developmental processes in youth and their relationship to psychopathology generally exemplifies one of two modes. The first examines cross-sectional similarities and distinctions within and across various disorders. Similar to findings in adult participants, such studies have found far more overlap among various forms of psychopathology with respect to both biology and behavior as compared to results that align with specific disorders. For example, in a transdiagnostic sample of youth diagnosed with various disorders such as bipolar spectrum disorder, ADHD, and disruptive behavior disorders, Bebko et al. (2014) found that, across diagnostic groups, scores on a measure of behavioral and emotional dysregulation were positively associated with left middle prefrontal activity to the "win" condition of a reward paradigm. The authors concluded that "elevated left prefrontal activity may reflect heightened sensitivity to reward-related cues and may be a biomarker of pathophysiologic processes associated with behavioral and emotional dysregulation and heightened reward sensitivity across different diagnoses in youth" (Bebko et al., 2014, p. 78).

As a second example, Kaczkurkin et al. (2020) examined structural brain similarities and differences in a large sample of youth who met criteria for an anxiety/depressive disorder or those with no psychiatric diagnoses. Analyses of structural brain measures in the internalizing sample, using a semi-supervised machine learning tool, returned two transdiagnostic subtypes. Subtype 1 had smaller brain volumes as well as reduced cortical thickness, resting state activity, and white matter integrity; furthermore, cognitive tests were associated with poorer functioning across multiple domains including executive function, social cognition, and episodic memory. Subtype 2, on the other hand, showed intact cognitive functioning, brain structure, and brain function while still demonstrating clinically significant levels of psychopathology. Both of these studies represent the increasing trend toward transdiagnostic analyses in developmental samples (Astle & Fletcher-Watson, 2020).

The second line of studies focuses on examining trajectories of development and inferring what processes potentially go awry in psychopathology. For example, Cropley et al. (2021) used a normative model of brain morphology from structural MRI data to predict symptom ratings for seven independent dimensions from more than 1,000 participants in the Philadelphia Neurodevelopmental Cohort (PNC); they found that deviation of brain-predicted age from true chronological age was associated with psychosis, obsessive compulsive symptoms, and general psychopathology. Older than predicted brain morphology was associated with greater symptom severity along these dimensions, especially in frontal cortical and subcortical nuclei.

The transdiagnostic and developmental trajectory threads are complementary and provide the warp and weft of the tapestry of mental disorders. They depict the normative development of brain structure and function; assess when, how, and where potential deviations occur; and explore how such discrepancies are related to dimensions of clinical phenomena beyond diagnostic categories. Layered on top of this complex picture of development and its trajectories is the crucial factor of environment. Environment, as defined in the RDoC framework, is used in the broadest sense of the word and can include varying factors such as neighborhoods, schools, family, and events that occur to an individual (e.g., traumatic incidents). Every type of environment can also interact with the point in development at which it occurs and influence various aspects of behavior and biology.

For example, in a meta-analysis of 109 studies, McLaughlin and colleagues (2019) examined the impact of exposure to threat or violence in children and found that reductions in amygdala volume, increased amygdala reactivity to threat cues, and greater threat-related activation in the anterior insula were observed across studies. In contrast, children exposed to deprivation showed reduced volume and thickness of the dorsolateral prefrontal cortex and superior parietal cortex. These results suggest that different types of developmental and environmental insults are associated with distinct patterns of altered brain measures. As another example from an ongoing longitudinal study, resting-state functional connectivity (rsFC) measures were acquired from youth who had experienced maltreatment at two points in late adolescence (ages 16 and 19). Maltreatment was associated with increases in rsFC from age 16 to 19 among default mode, dorsal attention, and frontoparietal systems; furthermore, the increases in rsFC mediated the relationship among maltreatment and depressive symptoms at age 19 (Rakesh et al., 2021). Similar to the McLaughlin et al. (2019) results, the investigators noted the importance of attending to the potential differences resulting from different types of maltreatment—a problem that is noted in many studies and has received increasing attention with respect to concepts and methodologies (e.g., Smith & Pollak, 2021).

An individual's temperament and predisposition represent another factor in the Rubik's cube of interactions regarding development and environment. The significance of temperament for both normal-range and disordered behavior of many kinds has been recognized for some time (Clark, 2005). Studies of temperament trajectories that include an RDoC perspective have increasingly highlighted their role for risk across all areas of psychopathology (e.g., Wakschlag et al., 2018), and systematic ideas about integrating temperament and development with the RDoC framework have been proposed (Ostlund et al., 2021).

The few studies reviewed here are representative of the larger literature indicating that development is equally important for disorders traditionally distinguished as "childhood-onset" and "adult-onset" conditions. The gradual onset of aberrant functioning suggests opportunities for early intervention, and many strategies for prevention research in mental disorders have been developed (Arango et al., 2018). However, the current diagnostic system is not well-designed for prevention studies. The use of a symptom-based diagnostic nosology means that psychopathological processes are, by definition, already well-established by the time of diagnosis (Insel, 2009); the binary diagnostic system also hampers the use of dimensional outcome measures. Furthermore, the heterogeneity and comorbidity of disorders, related to issues of multifinality and equifinality (Cicchetti & Rogosch, 1996), make it difficult to decide on the particular intervention or groups to be included in any given trial. As prevention experts have noted, "Risk or protective factors do not seem to be specific for particular mental disorders. . . . Although some interventions could be more specific, . . . public health interventions, whether population-wide or in a high-risk subgroup, might have low specificity and reduce incidence or improve outcomes across disorders" (Arango et al., 2018, p. 596).

The RDoC framework fosters research designs that contribute to mitigating these problems. Studies can be focused on particular constructs (e.g., fearful behavior, self-regulation) that are defined in terms of both psychological and biological aspects, and dimensional approaches enable quantitative dependent variables in both respects. Due to methodological advances in various areas, it is also increasingly possible to identify dimensions of early problems before they are clinically overt (Gur et al., 2014; Wakschlag et al., 2018). Experimental designs to implement RDoC prevention studies of various types have already been delineated in detail (Zalta & Shankman, 2016), notably including a "prevention-mechanism" trial paradigm designed to focus on proximal mechanisms related to RDoC constructs that are free of the constraints and heterogeneity of categorial diagnostic systems (Goldstein & Morris, 2016).

## Conclusion and Future Directions

The RDoC initiative is an experimental psychopathology program that provides a framework for research intended to foster alternative approaches to conceptualizing and studying mental illness. Prefaced by a review outlining the historical trends in psychiatric nosology that eventuated in the need for such a project, this chapter has summarized the major elements of the RDoC framework, important ideas in the philosophy of science that permeate its concepts, and issues and considerations involved in designing RDoC-oriented studies.

Seen in retrospect, psychiatric diagnosis is in many respects a case of history repeating itself, and an understanding of the factors that have contributed to this pattern is important for considering future research. Modern psychiatric nosology had its roots in the nineteenth century, following other areas of medical research in attempting to define diseases on the basis of symptom patterns that were expected over time to reveal underlying pathologies. The inability to establish definitive diagnostic classes due to multiple difficulties of science and philosophy were partly responsible for the rise of psychoanalytic theories that also were unable to reach consensus regarding etiology or diagnosis (Lang, 1984). The imperative to provide a comprehensive diagnostic manual as medicine became more systematized in the mid-twentieth century resulted in a reversion to the use of symptoms and signs for diagnosis ("neo-Kraepelinians"), albeit with more precise criteria; unfortunately, despite caveats in the *DSM-III* manual, its disorders quickly became reified and thus viewed by many as natural disease entities.

The consequence was that the listed disorders rapidly became the sine qua non for various purposes such as research grant applications, journal articles, regulatory approvals, and insurance coverage. Ironically, just as twenty-first-century scientific methodologies (e.g., fMRI, psychometrically sophisticated behavioral tasks) matured sufficiently to resume the paradigms and practices of nineteenth-century medical research—that is, seeking to understand disorders in terms of departures from normal functioning in such aspects as behavioral performance or brain structure and activity—the diagnostic system had become so entrenched as to daunt any efforts at fundamental revisions to scientific and clinical approaches. Furthermore, various disciplines in the mental illness arena differentially focused on psychology, biology, or phenomenology, often to the exclusion of other data sources. Clearly, no one class of information offers the sole answer, and ignoring mind–body challenges hampers efforts at integration.

Given this context, RDoC is necessarily a research program—one intended to provide components that emphasize systematic and long-term change rather than promoting a shift to a prematurely developed compendium of psychopathology or clinical nosology. A key aspect of the RDoC framework is concisely expressed in a recent commentary (as contrasted to categorical approaches): "Clinical description, laboratory studies, and family (now genetic) studies do not converge at all on distinct categories. Rather, modern studies are consistent with psychiatric disorders as heterogeneous quantitative deviations from health" (Hyman, 2021, p. 6). These various "quantitative deviations" are implemented in RDoC as psychophysiological constructs, and multisystem measurement and analysis are encouraged to address directly the knotty problems of mind–body issues and modest covariation among measures that have impeded progress in understanding mental illness. A strong emphasis is placed on the study of constructs and measures within the context of developmental trajectories and their interactions with all manner of environmental effects. Finally, a high priority is given to devising age-appropriate measures that span the range from normal functioning to varying degrees of abnormality.

With respect to the next steps for RDoC, one important direction is to continue the rapidly expanding application of computational analyses, both for more precise definition of model-based constructs and for new clinical phenotypes (e.g., B-SNIP biotypes; Clementz et al., 2021) based on data-driven analyses (Huys, 2018). New technologies also have promise for providing novel information, such as digital measurements that acquire data from mobile devices regarding various aspects of behavior and cognitive processes (Torous et al., 2017) and natural-language analyses that provide RDoC-oriented dimensional phenotypes from electronic health records (McCoy et al., 2018). One important topic, related ultimately to granularity, is the oft-asked question of whether observed similarities across diagnostic groups in transdiagnostic studies are due to the same mechanisms or involve differences at other levels of analysis that would suggest divergent mechanisms. A related topic concerns the differing patterns of abnormality among various types of measurement that are found across distinct groups (e.g., Lang et al., 2016; Hawco et al., 2019). These kinds of challenges reflect the difficult scientific terrain that will be encountered as investigators engage with the complexity of trying to understand normal processes and their relationships to psychopathology.

At the outset, we referred to the current period as an exciting time for psychopathology, and RDoC has been a salient part of the ongoing scientific ferment. It is important to acknowledge that RDoC is one of a number of projects pursuing innovative approaches to diagnosis and clinical practice, including three examples noted here. The Hierarchical Taxonomy of Psychopathology (HiTOP) project includes dimensional and hierarchical components (as does RDoC) (see Chapter 3, this volume). A second research program explores disorders in terms of symptom networks that are causally connected and interact in multiple ways; formal modeling techniques are applied to construct the networks and analyze the complex relationships among the nodes (Borsboom & Cramer, 2013). Finally, clinical staging is a transdiagnostic approach that employs quasi-dimensional measurements to follow the evolution of psychopathology over time, delineating successive illness stages in terms of symptom domains such as psychosis or mood rather than traditional disorders (McGorry & Hickie, 2019).

While these other projects are more oriented toward nosological and clinical use in the relatively proximal future as compared to RDoC, they share a transdiagnostic approach and research flexibility. It augurs well for the future that after so many decades constrained to a single diagnostic paradigm, multiple innovative efforts toward change are simultaneously under way. It can be hoped that all of these projects will share some central concepts while at the same time contributing divergent methodologies and data that continually stimulate progress. To this end, RDoC will continue its role with a perspective on viewing psychopathology in terms of quantitative deviations from normal functioning and the importance of integrative analyses across multiple measures. In the near term, advances in all of these areas are likely to be incremental and largely oriented around current *DSM/ICD* diagnostic classes—whether considered singly or in transdiagnostic cohorts. However, the first steps of a long journey are under way. Those in the early stages of their careers can anticipate many promising opportunities in the coming decades to reduce the burden of suffering from mental disorders through improved understanding, assessment, treatment, and prevention of psychopathology.

## Acknowledgments

The authors report no biomedical financial interests or potential conflicts of interest.

## References

Adams, R. A., Huys, Q. J. M., & Roiser, J. P. (2016). Computational psychiatry: Towards a mathematically informed understanding of mental illness. *Journal of Neurology, Neurosurgery, & Psychiatry, 87*, 53–63.

American Heart Association News. (2018). Hypertension guidelines, one year later: Monitoring the change. American Heart Association. https://www.heart.org/en/news/2018/11/27/hypertension-guidelines-one-year-later-monitoring-the-change

American Psychiatric Association (APA). (1980). *Diagnostic and statistical manual of mental disorders,* 3rd ed. Washington, DC: Author.

Anderzhanova, E., Kirmeier, T., & Wotjak, C. (2017). Animal models in psychiatric research: The RDoC system as a new framework for endophenotype-oriented translational neuroscience. *Neurobiology of Stress, 7,* 47–56.

Arango, C., Díaz-Caneja, C. M., McGorry, P., D., Rapoport, J., Sommer, I. E., Vorstman, J. A., McDaid, D., Marín, O., Serrano-Drozdowskyj, Freedman, R., & Carpenter, W. (2018). Preventive strategies for mental health. *Lancet Psychiatry, 5,* 591–604.

Astle, D. E., & Fletcher-Watson, S. (2020). Beyond the core-deficit hypothesis in developmental disorders. *Current Directions in Psychological Science, 29,* 431–437.

Au, R. (2019). Heterogeneity in Alzheimer's Disease and related dementias. *Advances in Geriatric Medical Research, 1,* e190010. doi:10.20900/agmr.20190010.

Ax, A. (1964). Editorial. *Psychophysiology, 1,* 1–3.

Baddeley, A. (2003). Working memory: Looking back and looking forward. *Nature Reviews Neuroscience, 4,* 829–839.

Bale, T., Baram, T. Z., Brown, A. S., Goldstein, J. M., Insel, T. R., McCarthy, M. M., Nemeroff, C. B., Reyes, T. M., Simerly, R. B., Susser, E. S., & Nestler, E. J. (2010). Early life programming and neurodevelopmental disorders. *Biological Psychiatry, 68,* 314–319.

Beauchaine, T. P., & Hinshaw, S. P. (2020). RDoC and psychopathology among youth: Misplaced assumptions and an agenda for future research. *Journal of Child and Adolescent Psychology, 49,* 322–340.

Bebko, G., Bertocci, M. A., Fournier, J. C., Hinze, A. K., Bonar, L., Almeida, J. R., . . . Phillips, M. L. (2014). Parsing dimensional vs diagnostic category–related patterns of reward circuitry function in behaviorally and emotionally dysregulated youth in the longitudinal assessment of manic symptoms study. *JAMA Psychiatry, 71,* 71–80.

Bechtel, W. (2020). Rethinking psychiatric disorders in terms of heterachical networks of control mechanisms. In K. S. Kendler, J. Parnas, & P. Zachar (Eds.), *Levels of analysis in psychopathology: Cross-disciplinary perspectives* (pp. 24–46). Cambridge University Press.

Belluck, P., & Carey, B. (2013). Psychiatry's guide is out of touch with science, experts say. *New York Times,* May 6. https://www.nytimes.com/2013/05/07/health/psychiatrys-new-guide-falls-short-experts-say.html

Berridge, K., & Kringelbach, M. (2015). Pleasure systems in the brain. *Neuron, 86,* 646.

Bleuler, E. (1911/1950). *Dementia praecox or the group of schizophrenias* (J. Zinkin, Trans.). International Universities Press.

Bolton, D. (2013). Should mental disorders be regarded as brain disorders? 21st century mental health sciences and implications for research and training. *World Psychiatry, 12,* 24–25.

Borsboom, D., & Cramer, A. O. (2013). Network analysis: An integrative approach to the structure of psychopathology. *Annual Review of Clinical Psychology, 9,* 91–121.

Braver, T. S., Kizhner, A., Tang, R., Freund, M. C., & Etzel, J. A. (2021). The dual mechanisms of cognitive control project. *Journal of Cognitive Neuroscience, 33,* 1990–2015.

Campbell, D. T., & Fiske, D. W. (1959). Convergent and discriminant validation by the multitrait-multimethod matrix. *Psychological Bulletin, 56,* 81–105.

Casey, B. J., Oliveri, M. E., & Insel, T. R. (2014). A neurodevelopmental perspective on the Research Domain Criteria (RDoC) framework. *Biological Psychiatry, 76,* 350–353.

Chapman, L. J., & Chapman, J. P. (1978). The measurement of differential deficit. *Journal of Psychiatric Research, 14,* 303–311.

Charney, D. S., Barlow, D. H., Botteron, K., Cohen, J. D., Goldman, D., Gur, R. E., Lin, K.-M., López, J. F., Meador-Woodruff, J. H., Moldin, S. O., Nestler, E. J., Watson, S. J., & Zalcman, S. Z. (2002). Neuroscience research agenda to guide development of a pathophysiologically based classification system. In D. J. Kupfer, M. B. First, & D. A. Regier (Eds.), *A research agenda for DSM-V.* American Psychiatric Association. (pp. 31–84).

Cicchetti, D., & Rogosch, F. A. (1996). Equifinality and multifinality in developmental psychopathology. *Development and Psychopathology, 8,* 597–600.

Clark, L. A. (2005). Temperament as a unifying basis for personality and psychopathology. *Journal of Abnormal Behavior, 114,* 505–521.

Clark, L. A., Watson, D., & Reynolds, S. (1995). Diagnosis and classification of psychopathology: Challenges to the current system and future directions. *Annual Review of Psychology, 46,* 121–153.

Clementz, B. A., Sweeney, J. A., Hamm, J. P., Ivleva, E., Ethridge, L. E., Pearlson, G. D., Keshavan, M. S., & Tamminga, C. A. (2016). Identification of distinct psychosis biotypes using brain-based biomarkers. *American Journal of Psychiatry, 173*, 373–384.

Clementz, B. A., Parker, D. A., Trotti, R. L., McDowell, J. E., Keedy, S. K., Keshavan, M. S., Pearlson, G. d., Gershon, E. S., Ivleva, E. I., Huang, L. U., Hill, S. K., Sweeney, J. A., Thomas, O., Hudgens-Haney, M., Givvons, R. D., & Tamminga, C. A. (2021). Psychosis biotypes: Replication and validation from the B-SNIP consortium. *Schizophrenia Bulletin.* https://doi.org/10.1093/schbul/sbab090.

Cohen, A. S., Thanh, P. Le, Fedechki, T. L., & Elvevag, G. (2017). Can RDoC help find order in thought disorder? *Schizophrenia Bulletin, 43*, 501–507.

Cropley, V. L., Tian, Y., Fernando, K., Pantelis, C., Cocchi, L., & Zalesky, A. (2021). Brain-predicted age associates with psychopathology dimensions in youths. *Biological Psychiatry: Cognitive Neuroscience and Neuroimaging, 6*, 410–419.

Cuthbert, B. N., & Insel, T. R. (2013). Toward the future of psychiatric diagnosis: The seven pillars of RDoC. *BMC Medicine, 11*, 127.

Dalgleish, T., Black, M., Johnston, D., & Bevan, A. (2020). Transdiagnostic approaches to mental health problems: Current status and future directions. *Journal of Consulting and Clinical Psychology, 88*, 179–195.

Davis, R. C., Buchwald, A. M., & Frankmann, R. W. (1955). Autonomic and muscular responses, and their relation to simple stimuli. *Psychological Monographs, 69*, 1–71.

D'Esposito, M. D., & Postle, B. R. (2015). The cognitive neuroscience of working memory. *Annual Review of Psychology, 66*, 115–142.

Engel, G. L. (1977). The need for a new medical model: A challenge for biomedicine. *Science, 196*, 129–136.

Engstrom, E. J., & Kendler, K. (2015). Emil Kraepelin: Icon and reality. *American Journal of Psychiatry, 172*, 1190–1196.

Enkavi, A. Z., & Poldrack, R. A. (2020). Implications of the lacking relationship between cognitive task and self-report measures for psychiatry. *Biological Psychiatry: Cognitive Neuroscience and Neuroimaging, 6*, 670–672.

Feighner, J. O., Robins, E., Guze, S. B., Woodruff, R. A., Winokur, G., & Munoz, R. (1972). Diagnostic criteria for Use in psychiatric research. *Archives of General Psychiatry, 26*, 57–63.

Ferrante, M., Redish, A., Oquendo, M., Averbeck, B., Kinnane, M., & Gordon, J. (2019). Computational psychiatry: A report from the 2017 NIMH workshop on opportunities and challenges. *Molecular Psychiatry, 24*, 479–483.

Fodor, J. A. (1968). *Psychological explanation.* Random House.

Fodor, J. A. (1974). Special sciences (or: The disunity of science as a working hypothesis). *Synthese, 28*, 97–115.

Ford, J. M. (2016). Studying auditory verbal hallucinations using the RDoC framework. *Psychophysiology, 53*, 298–304.

Garvey, M., Avenevoli, S., & Anderson, K. (2016). The National Institute of Health Research Domain Criteria and clinical research in child and adolescent psychiatry. *Journal of the American Academy of Child and Adolescent Psychiatry, 55*, 93–98.

Gibb, B. E., McGeary, J. E., & Beevers, C. G. (2016). Attentional biases to emotional stimuli: Key components of the RDoC constructs of sustained threat and loss. *American Journal of Medical Genetics, Part B: Neuropsychiatric Genetics, 171*, 65–80.

Goldstein, A. B., & Morris, S. E. (2016). Reconceptualizing prevention: Commentary on "Conducting psychopathology prevention research in the RDoC era." *Clinical Psychology Science and Practice, 23*, 105–108.

Gur, R. C., & Gur, R. E. (2016). Social cognition as an RDoC domain. *American Journal of Medical Genetics, Part B: Neuropsychiatric Genetics, 171*, 132–141.

Gur, R., Calkins, M., Satterthwaite, T., Ruparel, K., Bilker, W., Moore, T., Savitt, A. P., Hakonarson, H., & Gur, R. E. (2014). Neurocognitive growth charting in psychosis spectrum youths. *JAMA Psychiatry, 71*, 366–374.

Haeffel, G. J., Jeronimus, B. F., Kaiser, B. N., Weaver, L. J., Soyster, P. D., Fisher, A. J., Vargas, I., Goodson, J. T., & Lu, W. (2021). Folk classification and factor rotations: Whales, sharks, and the problems with the Hierarchical Taxonomy of Psychopathology (HiTOP). *Clinical Psychological Science*, May. doi:10.1177/21677026211002500.

Hascup, E. R., & Hascup, K. N. (2020). Toward refining Alzheimer's disease into overlapping subgroups. *Alzheimer's Dementia, 6.* doi:10.1002/trc2.12070.

Hawco, C., Buchanan, R. W., Calarco, N., Mulsant, B. H., Viviano, J. D., Dickie, E. W., Argyelan, M., Gold, J. M., Iacoboni, M., DeRosse, P., Foussias, G., Mahotra, A., Voineskos, A. N., for the SPINS group. (2019). Separable and replicable neural strategies during social brain function in people with and without severe mental illness. *American Journal of Psychiatry, 176*, 521–530.

Heckers, S. (2008). Making progress in schizophrenia research. *Schizophrenia Bulletin, 34*, 591–594.

Hempel, C. G. (1966). *Philosophy of natural science.* Prentice-Hall.

Huys, Q. J. M. (2018). Advancing clinical improvements for patients using the theory-driven and data-driven branches of computational psychiatry. *JAMA Psychiatry, 75*, 225–226.

Hyman, S. E. (2010). The diagnosis of mental disorders: The problem of reification. *Annual Review of Clinical Psychology, 6*, 155–179.

Hyman, S. E. (2021). Psychiatric disorders; Grounded in human biology but not natural kinds. *Perspectives in Biology and Medicine, 64*, 6–28.

Insel, T. R. (2009). Translating scientific opportunity into public health impact: A strategic plan for research on mental illness. *Archives of General Psychiatry, 66*, 128–133.

Insel, T. R, Cuthbert, B. N., Garvey, M., Heinssen, R., Pine, D. S., Quinn, K., Sanislow, C., & Wang, P. (2010). Research Domain Criteria (RDoC): Toward a new classification framework for research on mental disorders. *American Journal of Psychiatry, 167*, 748–751.

Kaczkurkin, A. N., Sotiras, A., Baller, E. B., Barzilay, R., Calkins, M. E., Chand, G. B., Cui, Z., Erus, G., Fan, Y., Gur, R. E., Gur, R. C., Moore, T. M., Roalf, D. R., Rosen, A. F. G., Ruparel, K., Shinohara, R. T., Varol, E., Wolf, D. H., Davatzikos, C., & Satterthwaite, T. D. (2020). Neurostructural heterogeneity in youths with internalizing symptoms. *Biological Psychiatry, 87*, 473–482.

Kapur, S., Phillips, A. G., & Insel, T. R. (2012). Why has it taken so long for biological psychiatry to develop clinical tests and what to do about it? *Molecular Psychiatry, 17*, 1174–1179.

Kendler, K. S. (2012). The dappled nature of causes of psychiatric illness: Replacing the organic functional/hardware-software dichotomy with empirically based pluralism. *Molecular Psychiatry, 17*, 377–388.

Kendler, K. S. (2020). The impact of faculty psychology and theories of psychological causation on the origins of modern psychiatric nosology. In K. S. Kendler, J. Parnas, & P. Zachar (Eds.), *Levels of analysis in psychopathology: Cross-disciplinary perspectives* (pp. 462–478). Cambridge University Press.

Kernbach, J. M., Satterthwaite, T. D., Bassett, D. S., Smallwood, J., Margulies, D., Drall, S., Shaw, P., Varoquauz, G., Thirion, B., Konrad, K., & Bzdok, D. (2018). Shared endo-phenotypes of default mode dysfunction in attention deficit/hyperactivity disorder and autism spectrum disorder. *Translational Psychiatry, 8*, 133. https://doi.org/10.1038/s41398-018-0179-6.

Kozak, M. J., & Cuthbert, B. N. (2016). The NIMH Research Domain Criteria initiative: Background, issues, and pragmatics. *Psychophysiology, 53*, 286–297.

Kozak, M. J., & Miller, G. A. (1982). Hypothetical constructs versus intervening variables; A re-appraisal of the three-systems model of anxiety assessment. *Behavioral Assessment, 4*, 347–358.

Krueger, R. F., Markon, K. E., Patrick C. J., Benning, S. D., & Kramer, M. D. (2007). Linking antisocial behavior, substance abuse, and personality: An integrative quantitative model of the adult externalizing spectrum. *Journal of Abnormal Psychology, 116*, 645–666.

Kutlu, M. G., Zachry, J, E., Melugin, P. R., Cajigas, S. A., Chevee, M. F., Kelley, S. J., Kutlu, B., Tian, L., Siciliano, C. A., & Calipari, E. S. (2021). Dopamine in the nucleus accumbens core signals perceived saliency. *Current Biology, 31*, 1–14.

Lake, J. I., Yee, C. M., & Miller, G. A. (2017). Misunderstanding RDoC. *Zeitschrift für Psychologie* special issue: *Mechanisms of Mental Disorders, 225*, 170–174.

Lang, P. J. (1968). Fear reduction and fear behavior: Problems in treating a construct. In J. M. Shlien (Ed.), *Research in psychotherapy, vol. 3* (pp. 90–102). American Psychological Association.

Lang, P. J. (1984). Dead souls: Or why the neurobehavioral science of emotion should pay attention to cognitive science. In T. Elbert, B. Rockstroh, W. Lutzenberer, & N. Birbaumer (Eds.), *Self-regulation of the brain and behavior* (pp. 255–272). Springer-Verlag.

Lang, P. J. (2010). Emotion and motivation: Toward consensus definitions and a common research purpose. *Emotion Review, 2*, 229–233.

Lang, P. J., McTeague, L. M., & Bradley, M. M. (2016). RDoC, DSM, and the reflex physiology of fear: A biodimensional analysis of the anxiety disorders spectrum. *Psychophysiology, 53*, 336–347.

Lauer, M. (2016). NIH's commitment to basic science. National Institutes of Health Extramural Nexus, March 25. https://nexus.od.nih.gov/all/2016/03/25/nihs-commitment-to-basic-science/

Lemaire, B., & Portrat, S. (2018). A computational model of working memory integrating time-based decay and interference. *Frontiers in Psychology, 9*. https://doi.org/10.3389/fpsyg.2018.00416.

Lieberman, J. A., & Ogas, O. (2015). *Shrinks: The untold story of psychiatry*. Little, Brown Spark.

Lilienfeld, S. O. (2014). The Research Domain Criteria (RDoC): An analysis of methodological and conceptual challenges. *Behaviour Research and Therapy, 62*, 129–139.

MacCorquodale, K., & Meehl, P. E. (1948). On a distinction between intervening variables and hypothetical constructs. *Psychological Review, 55*, 95–107.

McCoy, T. H. Jr., Yu, S., Hart, K. L., Castro, V. M., Brown, H. E., Rosenquist, J. N., Doyle, A. E., Vuijk, P. K., Cai, T., & Perlis, R. H. (2018). High throughput phenotyping for dimensional psychopathology in electronic health records. *Biological Psychiatry, 83*, 997–1004).

McGorry, P. D., & Hickie, I. B. (Eds.) (2019). *Clinical staging in psychiatry*. Cambridge University Press.

McLaughlin, K. A., Weissman, D., & Bitrán, D. (2019). Childhood adversity and neural development: A systematic review. *Annual Review of Developmental Psychology, 1*, 277–312.

McTeague, L. M., Lang, P. J., Laplante, M.-C., Cuthbert, B. N., Shumen, J. R., & Bradley, M. M. (2010). Aversive imagery in Posttraumatic Stress Disorder: Trauma recurrence, comorbidity, and physiological reactivity. *Biological Psychiatry, 67*, 346–356.

McTeague, L. M., Lang, P. J., Laplante, M.-C., Cuthbert, B. N., Strauss, C. C., & Bradley, M. M. (2009). Fearful imagery in social phobia: Generalization, comorbidity, and physiological reactivity. *Biological Psychiatry, 65*, 374–382.

Miller, G. A. (2010). Mistreating psychology in the decade of the brain. *Perspectives on Psychological Science, 5*, 716–743.

Miller, G. A. (2020). Comments on Kendler's "The impact of faculty psychology and theories of psychological causation on the origins of modern psychiatric nosology." In K. S. Kendler, J. Parnas, & P. Zachar (Eds.), *Levels of analysis in psychopathology: Cross-disciplinary perspectives* (pp. 479–490). Cambridge University Press.

Miller, G. A., & Bartholomew, M. E. (2020). Challenges in the relationships between psychological and biological phenomena in psychopathology. In K. S. Kendler, J. Parnas, & P. Zachar (Eds.), *Levels of analysis in psychopathology: Cross-disciplinary perspectives* (pp. 238–266). Cambridge University Press.

Miller, G. A., & Keller, J. (2000). Psychology and neuroscience: Making peace. *Current Directions in Psychological Sciences, 9*, 212–215.

Miller, G. A., Rockstroh, B., Hamilton, H. K., & Yee, C. M. (2016). Psychophysiology as a core strategy in RDoC. *Psychophysiology, 53*, 410–414.

Miller, G. A., & Yee, C. M. (2015). Moving psychopathology forward. *Psychological Inquiry, 26*, 263–267.

Mittal, V. A., & Wakschlag, L. S. (2017). Research Domain Criteria (RDoC) grows up: Strengthening neurodevelopmental investigation within the RDoC framework. *Journal of Affective Disorders, 216*, 30–35.

Morris, S. E., Sanislow, C. A., Pacheco, J., Vaidyanathan, U., Gordon, J. A., & Cuthbert, B. N. (2022). Revisiting the seven pillars of RDoC. *BMC Medicine, 20*. doi.org/10.1186/s12916-022-02414-0.

Mujica-Parodi, L. R., & Strey, H. H. (2020). Making sense of computational psychiatry. *International Journal of Neuropsychopharmacology, 23*, 339–347.

National Institute of Mental Health (NIMH). (2001). Modular phenotyping for mental disorders. https://grants.nih.gov/grants/guide/rfa-files/RFA-MH-02-009.html

National Institute of Mental Health (NIMH). (2008). The National Institute of Mental Health strategic plan. Author. NIH Publication 08-6368. https://www.hsdl.org/?view&did=755067

National Institute of Mental Health (NIMH). (2012). Dimensional approaches to research classification in psychiatric disorders. https://grants.nih.gov/grants/guide/rfa-files/rfa-mh-12-100.html

National Institute of Mental Health (NIMH). (2019). RDoC Matrix. Author. https://www.nimh.nih.gov/research/research-funded-by-nimh/rdoc/constructs/rdoc-matrix

National Institute of Mental Health (NIMH). (2020). Research Domain Criteria (RDoC). Author. https://www.nimh.nih.gov/research/research-funded-by-nimh/rdoc

Nigg, J. T. (2017). Annual Research review: On the relations among self-regulation, self-control, executive functioning, effortful control, cognitive control, impulsivity, risk-taking, and inhibition for developmental psychopathology. *Journal of Child Psychology and Psychiatry, 58,* 361–383.

Olds, J., & Milner, P. (1954). Positive reinforcement produced by electrical stimulation of septal area and other regions of rat brain. *Journal of Comparative and Physiological Psychology, 47,* 419–427.

Ostlund, B., Myruski, S., Buss, K., & Pérez-Edgar, K. E. (2021). The centrality of temperament to the research domain criteria (RDoC): The earliest building blocks of psychopathology. *Development and Psychpathology.* doi:10.1017/S0954579421000511.

Owen, M. J., O'Donovan, M. C., Thapar, A., & Craddock, N. (2011). Neurodevelopmental hypothesis of schizophrenia. *British Journal of Psychiatry, 198,* 173–175.

Pacheco, J., Garvey, M. A., Sarampote, C. S., Cohen, E. D. Murphy, E. D., & Friedman-Hill, S. R. (2022). The contributions of the RDoC research framework on understanding the neurodevelopmental origins, progression and treatment of mental illness. *Journal of Child Psychology and Psychiatry, 63,* 360–376.

Poeppel, D., & Adolfi, F. (2020). Against the epistemological primary of the hardware: The brain from inside out, turned upside down. *eNeuro, 7,* 0215-20.2020. doi.org/10.1523/ENEURO.0215-20.2020.

Posner, M. I., & Rothbart, M. K. (2000). Developing mechanisms of self-regulation. *Development and Psychopathology, 12,* 427–441.

Rakesh, D., Kelly, C., Vijayakumar, N., Zalensky, A., Allen, N. B., & Whittle, S. (2021). Unraveling the consequences of childhood maltreatment: Deviations from typical functional neurodevelopment mediate the relationship between maltreatment history and depressive symptoms. *Biological Psychiatry: Cognitive Neuroscience and Neuroimaging, 6,* 329–342.

Robins, E., & Guze, S. B. (1970). Establishment of diagnostic validity in psychiatric illness: Its application to schizophrenia. *American Journal of Psychiatry, 126,* 983–987.

Ross, C. A., & Margolis, R. L. (2019). Research Domain Criteria: Strengths, weaknesses, and potential alternatives for future psychiatric research. *Molecular Psychiatry, 5,* 218–236.

Rutter, M., & Sroufe, L. A. (2000). Develomental psychopathology: Concepts and challenges. *Development and Psychopathology, 12,* 265–296.

Sanislow, C. A. (2016). Connecting psychopathology metastructure and mechanisms. *Journal of Abnormal Psychology, 125,* 1158–1165.

Sanislow, C. A., Ferrante, M., Pacheco. J., Rudorfer, M. V., & Morris S. E. (2019). Advancing translational research using NIMH Research Domain Criteria and computational methods. *Neuron, 101,* 779–782.

Sanislow, C. A., Pine, D. S., Quinn, K. J., Kozak, M. J., Garvey, M. A., Heinssen, R. K., Wang, P. S., & Cuthbert, B. N. (2010). Developing constructs for psychopathology research: Research domain criteria. *Journal of Abnormal Psychology, 119,* 631–639.

Schwartz, E. L. (1990). *Computational neuroscience.* MIT Press.

Scull, A. (2021). American psychiatry in the new millennium: A critical appraisal. *Psychological Medicine,* 1–9. doi:10.1017/S0033291721001975.

Sharma, L., Markon, K. E., & Clark, L. A. (2013). Toward a theory of distinct types of "impulsive" behaviors: A meta-analysis of self-report and behavioral measures. *Psychological Bulletin, 140,* 374–408.

Sharp, P. B., & Miller, G. A. (2019). Reduction and autonomy in psychology and neuroscience: A call for pragmatism. *Journal of Theoretical and Philosophical Psychology, 39,* 18–31.

Smith, K. E., & Pollak, S. D. (2021). Rethinking concepts and categories for understanding the neurodevelopmental effects of childhood diversity. *Perspectives on Psychological Science, 16,* 67–93.

Spitzer, R. L., Endicott, J., & Robins, E. (1978). Research diagnostic criteria: Rationale and reliability. *Archives of General Psychiatry, 35,* 773–782.

Spitzer, R. L., & Fleiss, J. L. (1974). A re-analysis of the reliability of psychiatric diagnosis. *British Journal of Psychiatry, 125,* 341–347.

Stoyanov, D., Telles-Correia, D., & Cuthbert, B. N. (2019). The Research Domain Criteria (RDoC) and the historical roots of psychopathology: A viewpoint. *European Psychiatry, 57,* 58–60.

Sullivan, R. M. (2005). Developmental changes in olfactory behavior and limbic circuitry. *Chemical Senses, 30* (Suppl 1): i152-i153.

Teufel, C., & Fletcher, P. C. (2016). The promises and pitfalls of applying computational models to neurological and psychiatric disorders. *Brain, 139,* 2600–2608.

Thomas, J. G., & Sharp, P. B. (2019). Mechanistic science: A new approach to comprehensive psychopathology research that relates psychological and biological phenomena. *Clinical Psychological Science, 7,* 196–215.

Torous, J., Onnela, J.-P., & Keshavan, M. (2017). New dimensions and new tools to realize the potential of RDoC: Digital phenotyping via smartphones and connected devices. *Translational Psychiatry, 7,* e1053. doi:10.1038/tp.2017.25.

Wakschlag, L. S., Perlman, S. B., Blair, J., Leibenluft, E., Briggs-Gowan, M. J., & Pine, D. S. (2018). The neurodevelopmental basis of early childhood disruptive behavior: Irritable and callous phenotypes as exemplars. *American Journal of Psychiatry, 175,* 114–130.

Woodward, J. (2020). Levels: What are they and what are they good for? In K. S. Kendler, J. Parnas, & P. Zachar (Eds.), *Levels of analysis in psychopathology: Cross-disciplinary perspectives* (pp. 424–449). Cambridge University Press.

Yee, C. M., Javitt, D. C., & Miller, G. A. (2015). Replacing categorical with dimensional analyses in psychiatry research: The RDoC initiative. *JAMA Psychiatry, 72,* 1159–1160.

Zalta, A. K., & Shankman, S. A. (2016). Conducting psychopathology prevention research in the RDoC era. *Clinical Psychology and Practice, 23,* 94–104.

# CHAPTER 5

# Complex Systems Approaches to Psychopathology

Laura Bringmann, Marieke Helmich, Markus Eronen, *and* Manuel Voelkle

## Introduction

Science is permeated by complexity. In biology, systems such as insect colonies, flocks of birds, or ecosystems exhibit extremely complex behavior. For example, ant colonies construct large and elaborately structured nests, without any central control or leader ant, but rather through the intricate interactions of thousands of individual ants (Mitchell, 2009; Richardson et al., 2014). The human brain is a paradigmatic complex system, consisting of a vast number of interconnected neurons that are constantly interacting with each other. The Internet is a complex human-made system of interconnected servers, computers, and other elements. As well, social systems, such as economies or the stock market, are complex systems (Newman, 2018). Complexity thus occurs in (nearly) all scientific disciplines.

Clinical psychologists and psychiatrists also encounter complexity in their research and daily practice. Mental disorders, such as major depressive disorder, are the result of complex interactions at multiple levels, from the genes to maladaptive behavior and social influences (Freeman, 1992; Orsucci, 2006). In recent years, we have witnessed a sharp increase in studies that approach psychopathology from the perspective of complex systems. However, the idea that psychological and social processes are dynamical and complex is far from new; it goes back at least to the 1930s (Lewin, 1936; Richardson et al., 2014). Elaborate models of mental disorders based on complex systems theory were introduced already in the 1970s (Zeeman, 1976; see also von Bertalanffy, 1967) and further developed especially in the 1990s (Tschacher et al., 1992; van der Maas & Molenaar, 1992). One of the key challenges has been, and continues to be, how to translate these theoretical models into practical applications.

In this chapter, we provide an introduction to those complex systems approaches that have received the most attention in psychopathology. We start by discussing the general idea of complexity and complex systems and what those terms entail. We then turn to the framework of complex dynamic system models and how they have been applied to psychopathology. After this, we discuss early warning signals (EWSs), which hold the promise of providing a clinically useful application of the theoretical ideas of complex dynamic systems models. Finally, we go through the recent popular network approach to psychopathology and how it is related to the broader framework of complex systems. In all of these sections, we discuss both the promises and possible applications as well as the challenges and limitations of these approaches.

## Complex Dynamic Systems

Although complex systems studied in different disciplines are highly diverse (e.g., ant colonies, the Internet, or the human brain), it is thought that they share some common features and can therefore be studied with similar techniques. For this reason, the study of complex systems has emerged as a meta-paradigm or interdisciplinary field of its own (Orsucci, 2006). However, even among complexity

---

**Abbreviations**
EMA   ecological momentary assessment
ESM   experience sampling method
EWS   early warning signal
OCD   obsessive-compulsive disorder
VAR   vector autoregressive

researchers, there is no agreement on what complexity or a complex system is precisely. The different definitions in the literature strongly diverge. For example, Orsucci writes, "Complexity science can be regarded as a scientific toolbox, containing some tools to deal, empirically and theoretically, with complex dynamical systems (i.e., many variables [in] systems changing in time)" (Orsucci, 2006, p. 390). On the other hand, Weng and colleagues characterize complexity based on our capabilities to understand a system.

> In a general sense, the adjective "complex" describes a system or component that by design or function or both is difficult to understand and verify. . . . In physical systems, complexity is determined by such factors as the number of components and the intricacy of the interfaces between them, the number and intricacy of conditional branches, the degree of nesting, and the types of data structures. (Weng et al., 1999, p. 92)

Foote (2007), in contrast, lists several key features of complex systems.

> In recent years the scientific community has coined the rubric "complex system" to describe phenomena, structures, aggregates, organisms, or problems that share some common themes: (i) They are inherently complicated or intricate, in that they have factors such as the number of parameters affecting the system or the rules governing interactions of components of the system; (ii) they are rarely completely deterministic, and state parameters or measurement data may only be known in terms of probabilities; (iii) mathematical models of the system are usually complex and involve nonlinear, ill-posed, or chaotic behavior; and (iv) the systems are predisposed to unexpected outcomes (so-called "emergent behavior"). (Foote, 2007, p. 410)

In sum, researchers define complexity or complex systems in wildly different ways.

One key and oft-noted characteristic of complex systems is *nonlinearity*. In nonlinear systems, changes in the input do not result in proportional changes in the output. Mathematically, a linear function can be plotted as a straight line, whereas a nonlinear function will have a more complex shape, such as a u- or s-shape (Salvatore & Tschacher, 2012), which can be described, for instance, with higher-order polynomial functions. For example, when gradually reducing the medication of individuals suffering from depression, the effect on mood is usually not linear but often results in sudden shifts in mood (Helmich et al., 2020). In general, nonlinearity "comes closer than does a straight line to therapists' and clients' clinical experience" (Barkham et al., 1993, p. 676). However, it is important to note that nonlinearity is a very general and common feature. In nature, nonlinearity is the rule rather than the exception: "calling a science 'nonlinear' is like calling zoology the 'study of non-human animals'" Stanislaw Ulam, quoted in (Orsucci, 2006, p. 390). However, modeling the behavior of nonlinear systems does not always require nonlinear functions because complex nonlinear behavior can also arise from linear interactions of simple components. For example, in an ant colony, even if the behavior of individual ants is linear and based on simple rules, the result is complex nonlinear overall behavior (Bonabeau et al., 1997).

In addition to nonlinearity, a typical feature of a complex system is that its behavior is the result of *self-organization*: there is no central controller or external designer, just many individual components interacting (Richardson et al., 2014; van Geert, 2019). For example, in a flock of starlings, there is no leading bird that decides where the flock goes, but rather individual birds whose interactions with their neighbors result in the behavior of the flock. Often, this behavior of a complex system, where the system-level behavior is difficult to anticipate or predict based on the individual components, is called *emergence* (Richardson et al., 2014). Such interacting components can also be seen as a *network*, an approach recently introduced into psychopathology research and something we will come back to in later sections. Sometimes complex systems can result in unpredictable emergent behavior, even when they consist of relatively simple components, which is referred to as *chaotic behavior*. In chaotic systems, tiny variations in the initial conditions can result in vastly different overall outcomes, making prediction difficult or impossible (Richardson et al., 2014). For example, tiny differences in the locations of individual birds can completely change the direction in which the flock is flying.

An essential feature of complex systems is that they are *dynamic*, which is why they are often referred to as *complex dynamic(al) systems* (Thelen & Smith, 1994). That is, the behavior of the system changes or evolves and unfolds over time in such a way that the current state of the system is dependent on its past states (van Geert, 2019). Thus, in order to study and model the system, *time* must be taken into account (Voelkle et al., 2018). The dynamic behavior of psychological processes becomes clear from examples such as emotions. Feelings of positive affect generally fluctuate throughout the day, from hour to hour or even minute to minute (Kuppens et al., 2010).

The importance of such changes is also apparent in symptoms of mental disorders. Mental disorders are usually not trait-like phenomena but dynamical processes, in which during some weeks one has more symptoms while at other times the symptoms seem to wane. This is clearly illustrated by Caspi et al.'s (2020) study of more than 1,000 individuals from New Zealand, followed from ages of 11 to 45. They found that mental disorders not only ebb and flow over years and decades, but that individuals also often experience several different mental disorders in their lifetimes. Finally, it is important to emphasize that change is also central to clinical practice, as one of the main aims of therapy is to instigate change (e.g., from an episode of major depression to no longer having a depression).

Traditionally, researchers have studied psychopathology as a trait-like phenomenon (Hamaker, 2012; see also Chapter 6, this volume). Following this paradigm, it is natural to just measure individuals once, for example with questionnaires concerning their symptoms, at a single time point. Such questionnaires mostly include retrospective items referring to a period of several weeks or even a whole life span (Kruijshaar et al., 2005). These measures and the statistical methods associated with them are meaningful and useful in their own right, such as when the goal is to compare two groups to find out which form of medication works better, information that is important for therapists and policymakers (Lichtwarck-Aschoff et al., 2008).

In contrast, when researchers want to study psychopathology as a process, the dynamic approach becomes important. The first step is to capture the process over time, for which time series or (intensive) longitudinal data are needed. Such data consist of many measurements, for example over days, weeks, or months, sometimes also multiple times per day, typically gathered using methods known as the experience sampling method (ESM), ecological momentary assessment (EMA), or ambulatory assessment (aan het Rot et al., 2012; Csikszentmihalyi & Larson, 1987; Ebner-Priemer et al., 2009). Although these methods have different historical backgrounds, they are overlapping, and the terms are increasingly used interchangeably. These methods are focused on the individual and describe the individual in context, taking the dynamics of and variability in emotions, cognition, and behavior into account (Devries, 1987; Myin-Germeys et al., 2009). In this way, biases of more traditional methods are reduced, such as retrospective recall bias. Take as an example a study by Mokros (1993), in which patients were asked to report their symptoms during the week and also to recall the symptoms they had experienced at the end of the week. This study vividly showed that the symptoms that were reported in the moment during the week were strikingly different from the symptoms that were recalled at the end of the week (see also aan het Rot et al., 2012).

The change processes in complex dynamic systems can also occur at several different time scales, even within one system. For example, changes in affect may take place over several minutes or even hours, whereas changes in the underlying neural circuits of the brain occur much faster, at the time scale of 10–100 ms, and the firing of a neuron takes only around 1 ms (Bertenthal, 2007).

These differences in time scale can make it difficult to determine whether a process should be studied with state- or trait-like measures: sometimes a process seems to be trait-like until it is examined on a different time scale, when one can see that it is actually a succession of different states. For example, an individual with obsessive-compulsive disorder (OCD; see also Chapter 6) may be characterized by repetitive behaviors such as hand washing according to specific rules. When OCD is thus fully developed, it may seem like a stable trait-like characteristic of an individual that can be captured with a retrospective questionnaire at a single time point. However, taking a different perspective and measuring the symptoms of OCD at a more fine-grained timescale, one could actually capture the *process* in which such rituals develop and become established. In the latter case, a mental disorder such as OCD can be seen as a process that needs to be studied dynamically in order to understand and perhaps even prevent it. Thus, depending on the time scale, one can perceive a phenomenon, such as a mental disorder, as either trait-like or state-like.

Notably, these different time scales in complex dynamic systems are typically not distinct but hierarchically related (Bertenthal, 2007; Eronen, 2021). For example, an episode of depression unfolds over a time scale of weeks or months. However, the episode of depression itself consists of symptoms, such as insomnia, pessimistic thoughts, or rumination, which take place at a faster time scale of weeks or days. These symptoms, in turn, can be seen as consisting of moment-to-moment changes and interactions among affect states (Wichers, 2014). Specifically, experiences of negative affect may not be disabling if they occur every now and then, but become problematic and disabling when they occur repeatedly or are constantly present, turning into a symptom of depression. Thus, studying mood in daily life at the time scale of minutes or hours can give a more fine-grained picture of the development of symptoms related to depression (Wichers, Wigman, & Myin-Germeys, 2015).

In this way, complex dynamic systems can be seen as having a hierarchical structure, forming multiple levels at different time scales (see also Jeronimus, 2019). Moreover, whether a level is (higher) macro-level or (lower) micro-level depends on the context: if the starting point is disorders or diagnostic categories, individual symptoms can be seen as forming a micro-level from which disorders arise, but from the perspective of daily life at the time scale of minutes or hours, symptoms themselves can be seen as a higher macro-level. In general, none of these levels should be seen as a priori good or bad; instead, their suitability and importance should depend on the question at hand (Bertenthal, 2007; Eronen, 2021; Lichtwarck-Aschoff et al., 2008).

**Complex Dynamic System Models**

Dynamic system models can be understood very broadly as mathematical descriptions of how a system changes or evolves over time and how the state of a system depends on its past states (Laurenceau et al., 2007; Richardson et al., 2014). Formally, the state of a system is defined as the current value of the variable(s) that describes the system (Richardson et al., 2014). A dynamic system model is then a set of mathematical equations (e.g., differential equations, see below) that specify how the state of the system changes from one moment to the next as a function of the past (Granic, 2005). In contrast, static models, such as mixed-effect or multilevel models (Snijders & Bosker, 2011) or (latent) growth curve models (McArdle, 2009), are far more dominant in clinical psychology, especially in longitudinal research (Voelkle & Oud, 2015). However, unlike dynamic models, static models do not capture how the state of a system depends on its state at a previous moment (Laurenceau et al., 2007). In other words, static models often resort to explaining changes by the mere passage of time, whereas dynamic models use past behavior to explain future behavior (Voelkle et al., 2018).

Commonly used static models also have further limitations when applied to mental disorders. For example, a standard linear growth function assumes that there is unbounded increase or decrease ad infinitum when extrapolating into the future or past. This is not realistic when studying an individual with, for example, major depressive disorder. The symptoms of depression do not just increase indefinitely, but rather fluctuate around an equilibrium, also known as an *attractor* in the dynamic systems literature (Johnson & Nowak, 2002). One can have more symptoms one day and fewer symptoms on another day as the system is influenced by (external) factors such as stressful (e.g., a fight with one's partner) or positive (e.g., getting a promotion) events (Laurenceau et al., 2007). These fluctuations can then occur either around a nondepressed attractor, when the person tends to return to a nondepressed state after perturbations, or an attractor corresponding to depressed state, when the person tends to return to a depressed state after perturbations. The goal of treatment can be seen as helping the individual to shift from one attractor (a depressed state) to another (a nondepressed state).

In the dynamical systems literature, a common approach has been to use sets of differential equations, which have a long tradition in physics where they were originally used to model the dynamics in systems such as pendulums or planetary systems (Richardson et al., 2014). Today, differential equations are also increasingly used in psychological research (Boker & Wenger, 2007; van Montfort et al., 2018; Ryan et al., 2018). As they specify the amount of change occurring in a variable at a specific moment (i.e., over an infinitesimally small time interval), they are particularly well suited for modeling change processes in psychology (Boker et al., 2016).

Importantly, differential equation models can indicate that there are specific attractors toward which the system tends to move over time (Wood et al., 2018). Thus, internal factors or external stressors can "push" the system away from its stable state, and it will take a certain amount of time for the system to return to a stable state, depending on how strong the attractor is. By observing the variables of the system for a period of time, these fluctuations around a stable state can be mapped in such a way that they visually describe the "landscape" of the system (Richardson et al., 2014). One central aim in dynamic systems modeling is to capture and study this *stability landscape* and its attractors in the system of interest.

Figure 5.1 provides a simplified visualization of such a stability landscape, which represents the

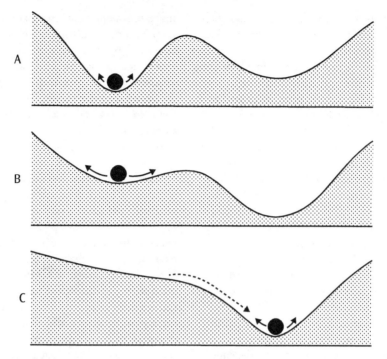

**Figure 5.1** Visual representation of alternative stability landscapes. The stability landscape represents a person's psychological system, where the shape of the system reflects how resilient a person is to external shocks (e.g., psychologically impactful events). The ball represents the current state of the system (e.g., current emotion) and the attractors the possible stable states that the system can be in (e.g., depressed state). A. The system shows a strong ("deep") attractor. B. The system is destabilizing and the attractor has weakened. C. The ball has "tipped over" into the new attractor, and the old attractor disappears. Adapted from Helmich, M. A. (2021). Early warning signals and critical transitions in psychopathology: challenges and recommendations. *Current Opinion in Psychology, 41*, 51–58. Copyright 2021 by Marieke Helmich. Adapted with permission.

person as a psychological system. The basins represent attractors in the system (e.g., a depressed and nondepressed state) and the ball symbolizes the individual's psychological state at a given time (e.g., current emotions). The shape of the landscape and the depth of the basins, in particular, reveal how resilient a person is to external shocks or stressors (e.g., psychologically influential events): they are likely to recover more quickly when the basin is "deep" and the ball is less likely to move far away from the bottom of the basin.

For example, in a landscape with one deep attractor, shown in Figure 5.1c, the system has a single stable resting point around which it varies and to which it returns over time. However, a system may also be *bistable*, having two attractors in the stability landscape (e.g., a depressed and nondepressed state), as in Figure 5.1a and 5.1b, or have multiple attractors between which it can switch. Not only can there be several attractors in a dynamic system, but the number and type of attractors in the system can also *change* in response to internal or external factors (Richardson et al., 2014). For instance, a bistable landscape with two attractors (depressed and nondepressed state; Figure 5.1b) may develop into a landscape with just one attractor (depressed state; Figure 5.1c).

A particular focus of interest has been cases where gradual change in external variables results in a sudden dramatic change in the stability landscape and thus the behavior of the system (Chow et al., 2015; Richardson et al., 2014). These are called *catastrophes*, and a mathematical framework to describe them is provided by *catastrophe theory* (Chow et al., 2015; van der Maas & Molenaar, 1992; Zeeman, 1977).[1] There are several different types of catastrophe models in the literature, of which a specific model called the *cusp catastrophe model* has been the most popular one, also in psychology (Chow, 2019; Richardson et al., 2014). The cusp model is one of

---

[1] A similar approach coming from a different theoretical background is the synergetics approach building on the theory of Hermann Haken (Tschacher et al., 1992).

the simplest catastrophe models, and it describes how the interplay of just two independent variables (called *control parameters*) results in sudden changes in the behavior of the system (represented by one dependent variable).

One of the earliest applications of catastrophe theory to clinical psychology was Zeeman's model of anorexia nervosa (Scott, 1985; Zeeman, 1976). According to this model (which comes from Zeeman and does not necessarily reflect current knowledge about anorexia nervosa), sudden changes in eating behavior occur even though the underlying factors, namely hunger and abnormal attitude toward food, change only gradually (Nelson et al., 2017; Zeeman, 1976). As abnormal attitude toward food increases and diets become more restrictive, hunger also steadily increases. At some point, behavior may then switch abruptly from fasting to the other extreme, binge eating.

In dynamic systems terms, the control parameters in this catastrophe model are abnormal attitude toward food and hunger, and the dependent variable is eating behavior. Initially, there is only one attractor in the system—namely, fasting—meaning that the person tends to return to fasting behavior after perturbations, such as attempts to normalize eating behavior. However, as the control parameters (abnormal attitude toward food and hunger) steadily increase, the stability landscape of the system changes in a sudden and catastrophic way. A new landscape emerges, now with two attractors: fasting and binging. Eating behavior will then jump between these two extremes, fasting and binging. Thus, with the catastrophe model, these interactions between the abnormal attitudes toward food and hunger (the control parameters) and eating behavior (the attractors; fasting and binging) can be mathematically described.

Although catastrophe theory provides an elegant mathematical framework, in practice it is often very difficult to fit a catastrophe model to (clinical) data (Chow, 2019; Chow et al., 2015). Therefore, in psychology, the focus has been on so-called *catastrophe flags*, which are specific features that can indicate that the system exhibits catastrophic behavior (Gilmore, 1981; Kunnen & van Geert, 2012). Of most interest for clinical psychology have been flags that can be observed right before or during a sudden change or transition: anomalous variance, divergence of response, and critical slowing down (van der Maas & Hopkins, 1998). First, *anomalous variance* refers to the phenomenon that the variance of the key variable (e.g., eating behavior in the anorexia example) increases markedly before a transition occurs, meaning that the spread of the values of the variable becomes wider. Second, *divergence of response* means that, before a transition occurs, even small external stressors result in large fluctuations in the behavior of the system. Finally, a closely related flag is *critical slowing down*, meaning that when it is close to a transition, the system takes more time to recover and returns more slowly to its stable state when perturbed.

These flags can be detected from time series data (e.g., ESM/EMA data). As fitting a (cusp) catastrophe model can be very challenging, a common solution is to, for example, detect anomalous variance by checking if there is a sudden change in the data (e.g., with change point analysis; Wichers, Schreuder, Goekoop, & Groen, 2019). These flags are not only indicators of catastrophic behavior of the system in general, but also central candidates for EWSs, which we will discuss in more detail in the next section. Importantly, while a given flag may suggest that the system exhibits catastrophic behavior, taken alone it cannot sustain the conclusion that a (cusp) catastrophe model applies (van der Maas & Molenaar, 1992). Furthermore, there is a large translational step from the dynamic (catastrophe) models to time series models, and many assumptions and choices have to be made regarding, for example, time scale, number of measurements, and relevant variables measured, which can all influence the outcomes (Haslbeck & Ryan, 2021). These issues will be also touched upon in the next section.

## Early Warning Signals

EWSs are the part of complex dynamic systems modeling that has drawn the most attention in psychopathological research. EWSs occur when the stability landscape is slowly changing as the system approaches a tipping point, it becomes less resilient to shocks, and a sudden "critical transition" to a new state may be imminent (Scheffer et al., 2009). To explain this, we return to Figure 5.1. In Figure 5.1a, the system appears relatively stable, the basin is "deep"—the attractor is strong—and even though the ball will move around in response to external stressors, with time, the ball will be pulled back to the bottom of the basin. Note that, while a potential alternative attractor appears on the right side of Figure 5.1a, only a very strong impulse would cause the ball to be pushed into that basin.

Translated to psychology: if we view the left side of the figure as an individual's mental state, which is currently relatively stable and healthy, it would require a strong trigger—like losing a loved one—for the system to switch to the right side, which can be understood as a more negative, possibly depressed, stable state. In Figure 5.1b, the system has lost resilience and the current attractor has become weaker and the basin shallower. As a result of this change in the stability landscape, the system in Figure 5.1b is more vulnerable to "tip over" with a sudden shift to the alternative attractor on the right side of the figure: no longer does the ball need a large impulse to be pushed over the edge of the left-hand basin; even a small push could effectively cause a critical transition to a depressed state or another psychopathological state.

As complex dynamical systems are composed of interacting variables that can change at different rates, zooming in on the moment-to-moment changes in one variable can be informative of an upcoming change in another, slower changing variable. In the context of psychopathology, this had led to the hypothesis that EWSs may be detectable in momentary affective states before a sudden shift in symptoms, such as a depressive relapse (Wichers et al., 2016, 2020) or sudden improvements in the context of therapy (Olthof et al., 2020).

The clinical promise of EWSs is that clinically important symptom changes could be anticipated by monitoring individuals' moment-to-moment (affective) experiences in the course of daily life (e.g., based on ESM/EMA data). The idea that EWSs could be used as "generic" indicators of future symptoms shifts has led researchers to speculate about the potential of monitoring individual patients or at-risk individuals and using EWSs to make personalized prediction and timely intervention possible. For instance, if EWSs are found to be consistently effective at predicting impending changes in individuals, their application in clinical practice could include early detection of episodes of mental illness (Kuppens et al., 2012; Wichers et al., 2019), thus identifying sensitive periods in which psychological treatment may be more likely to effectuate positive symptom change (Hayes & Yasinski, 2015; Schiepek, 2003), as well as improving timely intervention in cases of depressive relapse and suicide attempts (Bryan & Rudd, 2018; Wichers et al., 2016, 2020).

### Examples of Early Warning Signals

Many different possible EWSs have been discussed in the literature; here we focus on those that have received the most attention in psychology: critical slowing down, flickering, and critical fluctuations (similar to anomalous variance). The latter is a notion developed in recent years in ecology, a field in which many other EWSs also have been described (e.g., spatial variance and spatial skewness; Scheffer et al., 2009). Further EWSs have also been explored in simulations studies (e.g., dominant eigenvalue of the covariance matrix; Chen et al., 2019). However, these have not been tested in clinical data yet.

The first one, *critical slowing down*, was already briefly mentioned as a catastrophe flag in the previous section. In the context of EWSs, critical slowing down can be inferred from changes in the temporal dynamics of the system's variables, which then serve as an EWS. This "critical slowing" of the system means that the current attractor becomes weaker (the basin in Figure 5.1a changes to that in Figure 5.1b), and this changing landscape can be inferred from how the system recovers (returns to its stable state) from perturbations. Thus, in the landscape in Figure 5.1b, the ball tends to go farther away from the stable state and takes longer to return than in the landscape in Figure 5.1a. In other words, it takes longer for the system to recover after perturbations.

In statistical terms, this has been taken to imply an increase in *autocorrelation*. In brief, autocorrelation indicates how well the value of a variable (e.g., an emotion) at a given point in time predicts the value of the same variable at the next point in time (e.g., the same emotion at the next time point). Thus, as the ball spends more time away from its stable position (the mean), consecutive states are more similar and more highly correlated with previous states, which results in higher autocorrelation. Moreover, as the distance from the stable position also increases, critical slowing down is expected to correspond to a higher variance (i.e., more spread in the values of the variable) over time. Translated to the individual's psychological viewpoint, and specifically to momentary affect, the effect of critical slowing down would show as emotions that become increasingly volatile as the system is destabilizing (increased variance), and, once something triggers an emotional reaction, this feeling is likely to linger longer over time (increased autocorrelation).

A second possible EWS that has been studied in psychology is a phenomenon known as *flickering*, where the system moves back and forth between two alternative attractors (Scheffer et al., 2009). This can happen when the landscape changes in a way that makes it easier for the ball to roll from one basin (attractor) to another, as in Figure 5.1b. This, too, can be considered an EWS because the system may end up being shifted permanently to the alternative state and restabilize into a new (single) stable state. When statistically analyzing the changes in the system based on time series (ESM/EMA) data, flickering can be observed as bimodality or skewness in the distribution of the variables measured and can also be indicated by increases in variance (Scheffer et al., 2009). In psychopathology, bimodality has been observed in the (frequency) distribution of symptoms of major depressive disorder (Hosenfeld et al., 2015) and has been hypothesized to be of particular interest for patients with bipolar disorder, where the manic and depressed state may represent alternative stable states of the system (Goldbeter, 2011; Johnson & Nowak, 2002).

Finally, as the system is destabilizing, but has not yet settled into a new attractor, EWSs in the form of *critical fluctuations* may occur (Hayes et al., 2007; Olthof et al., 2020). With the stability landscape losing resilience and the current attractor losing strength—or even disappearing—the system starts moving between many different alternative states. These critical fluctuations occur over more dimensions than can be shown in Figure 5.1, and, in contrast to flickering, where the ball is rolling back and forth between two basins (i.e., attractors), in critical fluctuations the ball is rolling wildly around a destabilized landscape until it settles into a new stable attractor (Hayes et al., 2007). This behavior of jumping around in the destabilized landscape appears as large fluctuations and can be statistically observed as increases in indicators such as variance (or entropy; Olthof et al., 2020).

In general, what holds for all these EWSs is that if the "normal," dynamically stable state of the system is known, for example through studying the system over a long period of time, the EWSs can be identified as deviations from what would be expected if the system was stable. For instance, if the autocorrelation or variance of the system no longer fluctuates around the expected stable value but starts to increase, these increasing trends can function as EWSs.

### Early Warning Signals in Psychopathological Research

EWSs have been studied in psychopathology at both the group (nomothetic) and individual (idiographic) levels, mostly focusing on major depressive disorder. Group-level studies have examined, based on time series (ESM/EMA) data, whether indications of instability and destabilization *on average* relate to stronger concurrent symptoms (Koval et al., 2013; Sperry et al., 2020) or later symptom change (Curtiss et al., 2019; Kuppens et al., 2012; Kuranova et al., 2020; Olthof et al., 2020; Schreuder, Hartman, et al., 2020; van de Leemput et al., 2014). These studies show that, on average, persons with higher levels of autocorrelation and variance in their daily affective experiences are more likely to have a psychopathological diagnosis or experience a change in symptoms later in time. While this provides some evidence for the hypothesis that (developing) psychopathology is related to the temporal dynamics associated with EWSs, this group-level evidence is indirect, and a true test of this hypothesis requires studies at the individual level (see also Bos & de Jonge, 2014).

Indeed, because EWSs hold the promise of informing person-specific predictions, they should also be studied and tested at the individual level. This requires examining the temporal dynamics in time series of individual subjects as they experience changes in symptoms. Because such an intensive longitudinal design is not (yet) common in psychopathology research, only a few studies have been able to test empirically whether sudden symptom transitions were indeed preceded by EWSs in individual time series data (Olthof et al., 2020; Wichers et al., 2016, 2020).

For instance, Wichers and colleagues (2016) monitored one individual with a history of major depressive episodes while he was tapering his antidepressant medication. The participant completed 10 ESM questionnaires each day, which were sent at semi-randomly determined times across the day, and his depressive symptoms were assessed every week, over a period of about 8 months (239 days).[2] While the participant's symptoms were stable at the start of the study period, reducing medication dosage increased the risk of a depressive relapse, and the participant did relapse after 18 weeks. Upon examination of the temporal dynamics in the data, the researchers found that EWSs in the form of autocorrelation and variance rose significantly in the weeks preceding the symptom transition. This study was the first to show empirical evidence of EWSs for a specific individual in the context of psychopathology. Since then, the same researchers have replicated this result in one more participant, finding

---

[2] The data are openly available here: https://openpsychologydata.metajnl.com/articles/10.5334/jopd.29/

that autocorrelation and variance started rising a month before a transition in symptoms—again, a depressive relapse—occurred (Wichers et al., 2020).

Moreover, F. M. Bos and colleagues (2021) conducted an exploratory study of whether EWSs (again, rises in autocorrelation and variance) in EMA-measured affective time series preceded transitions to depression and mania in a sample of 20 bipolar I/II patients. Eleven patients experienced one or more transitions to depression or mania during the 4-month observation period, but the results regarding the added predictive value of EWSs were mixed both between and within persons.

In sum, these first empirical studies provide tentative evidence that a rise in autocorrelation and variance preceded a transition in depressive symptoms and could therefore function as an EWS. However, much more research and consistent evidence is required to substantiate the utility of these EWSs for personalized predictions.

*Promises and Problems*

Although the focus in studies of EWSs in psychopathology has been on rises in autocorrelation and variance, there is no consensus on how to best search for EWSs in clinical research and practice. Here we discuss some important challenges and open questions, as well as possible solutions.

The first challenge is in collecting data that are suited for detecting EWSs and testing the hypothesis that EWSs serve as indicators for symptom changes (Helmich, Snippe et al., 2021; Schreuder, Groen, Wigman, Hartman, & Wichers, 2020). For optimal chances of detecting EWSs, individual time series of several patients, consisting of many (several hundred) observations per patient, are needed to ensure that the EWSs can be calculated reliably. A key question is deciding which variables are the most suitable for detecting EWSs (e.g., mood, affect, or symptom variables) and therefore should be measured. It has also been suggested that it may be worthwhile to consider combining several variables, or combining different EWSs (Dablander et al., 2020), to improve the power to detect an effect.

An additional challenge is that, in order to test the hypothesis that EWSs precede transitions, the data also have to include such a transition. Therefore, the data collection should cover a period in which transitions are more likely to occur (e.g., during psychological therapy, while tapering antidepressant medication, or in a group of patients who are prone to showing sudden symptom shifts, such as bipolar patients). Relatedly, the data should include a baseline period to be able to determine if the potential EWSs (e.g., autocorrelation or variance) are really changing relative to what is "normal" for that person.

Regarding transitions, because psychopathology is notoriously heterogeneous in how it is expressed in different individuals, it is important to consider what constitutes a "transition" for a specific individual (Helmich, Olthof et al., 2021). The relative speed, magnitude, and frequency at which symptom shifts occur may strongly vary between persons, disorders, and direction of change (i.e., symptom improvement vs. deterioration). Thus, for one individual a certain increase in depressive symptoms might be an exceptional change, whereas for another individual the same increase may be just usual day-to-day fluctuation. Currently, there is insufficient knowledge of how to generally or specifically identify "critical transitions" in psychopathology, and it is an important and challenging task to explore which change patterns EWSs can actually warn us about.

Finally, an important limitation when focusing on autocorrelation and variance is that increases in them can occur for many different reasons. Therefore, although an increase in autocorrelation or variance can be an indicator of critical slowing down, it can also precede more gradual transitions, or autocorrelation or variance can go up and then down without any transition occurring. It is also possible that critical transitions sometimes occur in a system without being preceded by an EWS (Dablander et al., 2020). Furthermore, an issue that has been recently raised is that it is not clear how much predictive value autocorrelation has over and above the mean (Dejonckheere et al., 2019), as the mean is a function of the intercept and the autocorrelation (see Bringmann et al., 2017, for more details).

In conclusion, although EWSs provide a promising opportunity to apply complexity and dynamical systems theory to improve clinical predictions of changes, many challenges and open questions remain. Several studies are expected to be completed in the coming years that will provide further indications of whether EWSs will deliver on their promise.

## Psychopathological Networks

In the past decade, the network approach to psychopathology has become increasingly popular in clinical research and is also finding its way to clinical practice (Robinaugh et al., 2020; von Klipstein et al., 2020). In this section, we describe this approach and also explain how it is related to the other complex systems approaches discussed above.

The network approach focuses on psychological symptoms and their interrelations, the central idea being that these symptoms causally influence each other in a way that eventually results in a mental disorder (Borsboom & Cramer, 2013). For example, sleeping problems can lead to fatigue, which in turn leads to concentration problems and feelings of sadness, and these latter two then lead to even more sleeping problems (Cramer et al., 2016). As symptoms keep causing and sustaining other symptoms in this way, the result is an episode of depression. Thus, mental disorders are conceptualized as networks of interacting symptoms.

A network can be understood, in the most general terms, as a representation that describes how elements in a system are connected (Bringmann & Eronen, 2018). In network terminology, the elements are called *nodes* and the connections between them are called *edges* (Newman, 2018). For example, if we look at a railway network, the nodes are cities or stations, and the edges are the railways connecting them. Other examples of networks are the Internet, networks connecting brain regions, or social networks (e.g., representing the friendship relations between people). In psychopathological networks, the nodes are symptoms, and the edges are (causal) connections between the symptoms.

By placing the focus on symptoms and their interactions, the network approach provides an alternative to the medical disease model (Cramer et al., 2010). According to this model, the symptoms of mental disorders have a clear (biological) root cause, analogous to how viruses cause flu symptoms or tumors cause cancer symptoms (Borsboom et al., 2019). The proponents of the network approach argue that no such root causes have been found for mental disorders and that they are likely not to exist: instead, mental disorders simply are networks of interacting symptoms. Therefore, they should also be treated and studied at the level of psychological symptoms. This also fits well with traditional ideas in cognitive behavioral therapy, where interactions between mental states (e.g., Beck's negative triad; Beck, 1979) are seen as central for treating mental disorders (Bringmann et al., 2022).

### Constructing a Psychological Network

Networks such as railway networks or social networks can be constructed by simply observing the nodes and connections (e.g., by looking whether there is a railway between two cities or asking whether individuals are friends with each other). These raw data can then be immediately visualized as a network, such as a friendship network that illustrates which children in a school class are friends with each other. However, in psychopathological networks, the edges (i.e., the connections between the symptoms, such as causal relationships) are not visible in the raw data but have to be inferred (Bringmann et al. 2019). Therefore, several existing modeling techniques have been applied to infer psychopathological networks. We focus here on two modeling approaches that have been the most widely used so far.

In the first approach, the edges (or connections) between symptoms are inferred from correlational analyses of data obtained from large groups of persons (Borsboom & Cramer, 2013). In such networks, the nodes are symptoms that are measured once per individual, and the edges are (partial) correlations between symptoms. This results in a symptom network with undirected edges, meaning that the edges do not give information on the direction of the causal influence between the nodes over time (see also the networks in Figure 5.2). Estimating direct (causal) relationships between symptoms is in principle possible but requires strong assumptions (Malinsky & Danks, 2018) and is, in practice, rarely done for psychopathological networks. One shortcoming of cross-sectional networks is that because they are based on aggregating data from many individuals, it is unclear to what extent they reflect within-person processes and thus whether they give information on the network of any specific individual (Hamaker, 2012). Moreover, as cross-sectional networks are based on one measurement occasion, they cannot give information about how psychopathological processes evolve over time (see the earlier section on "Complex Dynamic Systems").

The second modeling approach is based on time series or intensive longitudinal (ESM/EMA) data. As described in the section "Complex Dynamic Systems", these data consist of repeated measurements over time, where, for example, often measurements at 60 time points or more per person are collected. The most widely used method at the moment to infer networks from such data is the vector autoregressive (VAR) model, in which an individual network for each person is inferred (Bringmann et al., 2013). A VAR-based network is a directed network where an edge between symptoms A and B reflects the extent to which variance in symptom B can be predicted based on variance

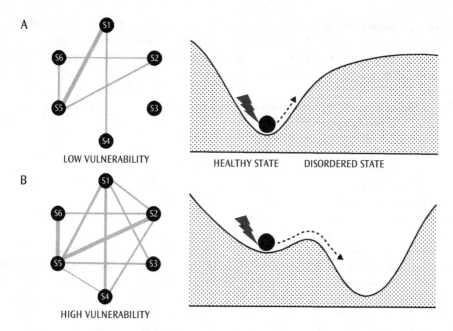

**Figure 5.2** Symptom network structure and vulnerability for psychopathological change in a complex dynamical system. This figure shows how the network structure and stability landscape of an individual are expected to differ depending on how vulnerable the system is. The left panel (A) represents a symptom network in a system with low vulnerability: the six symptom nodes (S1–6) are sparsely connected, and the connections are weak, as represented by thinner lines. The right side of A reflects the stability landscape in which such a network may be observed: stressors (the lightning bolt) may push the ball away from its stable point, but the basin is deep and the system will recover rapidly. Moreover, if any of the symptoms are triggered, the other symptoms are not likely to be triggered as well. In B, the left panel displays a more densely connected symptom network in a system with high vulnerability. The stability landscape in the right panel shows that the system is currently still resting in a healthy state but the basin of attraction is weaker (shallower). Here, a stressor is more likely to cause the system to tip over into the "disordered" attractor, and, furthermore, the densely connected symptom network makes it more likely that the individual will remain in this state, as the connections between symptoms reinforce each other.

in symptom A while controlling for all other nodes in the network (Bringmann et al., 2022). Therefore, in contrast to cross-sectional networks, VAR-based networks are person-specific, directional, and explicitly represent relationships over time. VAR-based networks can also include self-loops (i.e., an edge from a symptom to itself, reflecting the extent to which variance in the symptom at one point predicts variance in the same symptom at the next time point) and can also be used to infer contemporaneous effects (e.g., the concurrent [partial] correlations between symptoms within an individual; Epskamp, van Borkulo, et al., 2018).

Importantly, however, VAR-based networks represent just predictive relationships over time, which do not automatically translate to causal relationships (Bringmann, 2021). Indeed, in a recent simulation study, Haslbeck and Ryan (2021) tested how well current VAR-methods recover the causal relationships of a relatively simple system. They concluded that, due to problems such as insufficient frequency of measurements, VAR-based models in most circumstances cannot be used to reliably infer the causal structure of symptom interactions (Haslbeck & Ryan, 2021).

In addition to these modeling techniques, psychopathological networks have also been constructed based on perceived causal relationships (Frewen et al., 2013). The idea behind this approach is that clinicians (or patients) are asked about how they think that symptoms are related to each other, and then networks are constructed based on these expert judgments (Deserno et al., 2020). Thus, the edges in the networks still represent the strength of the (causal) relationship between two symptoms, but instead of being derived from data, they are now based on the estimates of clinical experts or patients. These networks can be person-specific, describing the network of one individual, or general expert estimates on how the symptoms of a disorder are expected to relate to one another. For example, Deserno and colleagues (2020) asked experienced clinicians to rate the relationships between pairs of symptoms of autism spectrum disorder, and then constructed a network based on the average of these ratings. Such perceived causal networks can be seen as hypotheses about the causal symptom structure of patients and can provide a good starting point for further research.

Another possibility is to construct networks based on diagnostic manuals such as the *DSM* or *ICD*, for example by looking at how symptoms of different disorders overlap. Borsboom and colleagues (2011) used this approach to study the symptoms structure of the *DSM-IV* by taking the symptoms as nodes and drawing an edge between two symptoms whenever they appear in the same disorder. This resulted in a network illustrating the symptom overlap in the *DSM-IV*, showing, for example, that there is considerable overlap among the symptoms of mood, anxiety, and substance abuse disorders. Tio and colleagues (2016) used the same approach to compare the symptom structure of *DSM-IV* and *ICD-10* and found clear structural differences between the two diagnostic systems (e.g., that there was more symptom overlap in *ICD-10* than in *DSM-IV*).

Perceived causal networks and diagnostic manual networks are promising approaches but have received relatively little attention in the psychological network literature so far. Note that although the ways that these networks are constructed are very different from cross-sectional or VAR-based networks, they have nevertheless been analyzed using the same network techniques (described in the next section).

## Density and Centrality

Once a network has been constructed, it can be further analyzed with a whole toolbox of techniques stemming from network science. We focus here on *density* and *centrality*, which have been the most commonly used network measures in psychopathology. The density (also known as *connectivity* in the psychopathological network literature) of a network refers to the relative number of edges in the network: a network with many edges and therefore many connections between the nodes is said to be *dense*, whereas a network with few edges is said to be *sparse* (Newman, 2018). In the psychological network literature, density is also used to refer to the mean strength of the edges: a network with stronger connections is denser than a network with weaker connections, even if they have the same number of edges (Pe et al., 2015).

One hypothesis is that individuals suffering from depression have a denser symptom or emotion network than do nondepressed people and are therefore more resistant to change (Pe et al., 2015). In a dense network, the symptoms or negative emotions can easily strengthen each other, making it more difficult to get out of a state of depression or a spiral of negative mood. This hypothesis has been studied in cross-sectional setups, but the results are inconclusive (Robinaugh et al., 2020), and it is also unclear to what extent cross-sectional studies can give information about the density of individual networks (Bos & Wanders, 2016). Time series analyses based on the VAR-model have found some evidence for denser networks in depressed individuals but have focused more on emotion or affect networks than on symptom networks.

For instance, Pe and colleagues (2015) conducted an ESM study comparing a healthy control group ($n$ = 53) with participants diagnosed with major depression ($n$ = 53). Over the course of 7 days, participants were prompted eight times per day to assess their negative (seven items) and positive (four items) affect using a 4-point scale. Networks were then inferred using a multilevel version of the VAR model. Density was calculated based on the absolute values of the connection strengths between the affect variables (i.e., the slope coefficients of the multilevel VAR model). When comparing the networks of the depressed and healthy individuals, the results indicated that depressed individuals had a denser network of (negative) emotions than did healthy individuals. Using the same method, Wigman and colleagues (2015) also found evidence for a more strongly connected network of thoughts and affect states in individuals with a diagnosis of depression than in healthy individuals.

However, results of density studies may be sensitive to specific methodological or modeling choices, such as whether the estimated parameters are penalized to limit the complexity of the model (de Vos et al., 2017). Ideally, the density hypothesis should also be studied within an individual. For example, in the study described in section "Early Warning Signals in Psychopathological Research," Wichers and colleagues (2016) also followed the network density in a person who first was in a healthy state and then transitioned abruptly to an episode of depression. Indeed, results seem to indicate that the network density of affect states increased over time for this specific individual, but replication studies are still needed before any conclusions can be drawn (see also Wichers et al., 2020).

Perhaps the most widely used network measures in psychopathology are *centrality measures*. These measures are intended to indicate which nodes in the network are important. The underlying idea is that nodes with a high centrality have strong connections to other symptoms and therefore play an important role in the network (Newman, 2018). In psychopathological network theory, an important hypothesis has been that the highly central symptoms can spread the activation of symptoms in the network and therefore intervening on such symptoms would be an important goal for clinical practice (Borsboom & Cramer, 2013). In this way, the focus is shifted from the state of the overall network to individual symptoms (Robinaugh et al., 2020). Following these theoretical ideas, many empirical studies have aimed at finding the most central symptoms in psychopathological networks (Boschloo et al., 2016; Rodebaugh et al., 2018).

There are many centrality measures, but those most widely used in this field have been *degree* and *betweenness* centrality (Bringmann et al., 2019). Degree centrality is calculated simply by taking the sum of the edges that a node has. Therefore, nodes that are connected to many other nodes have a higher degree centrality than nodes that are connected to only a few other nodes. For example, in a network representing the friendship relationships in a school class, the child with the most friends would have the highest number of edges and therefore the highest degree centrality. If the network is weighted—that is, the edges can have different weights—the sum of the (absolute) weights is taken, and the measure is called *strength* centrality.

Betweenness centrality is a more complex measure and is calculated based on the shortest paths between nodes (Freeman, 1977). A node that lies on many shortest paths between other nodes has a higher betweenness centrality than a node that lies on only a few shortest paths. For example, if a city in a railroad network lies on many shortest paths between other pairs of cities, then that city has a high betweenness centrality.

Translating these measures to psychopathological symptom networks is not always straightforward (Dablander & Hinne, 2019; Hallquist et al., 2021). It may at first blush seem intuitively plausible that a symptom with many connections to other symptoms (i.e., degree centrality) or a symptom that is on many shortest paths between other symptoms (i.e., betweenness centrality) plays an important role in the symptom network. However, the centrality measures were originally developed with social networks in mind, and, as we have mentioned earlier, there are important differences between social networks and psychopathological networks (Bringmann et al., 2019). For instance, in psychopathological networks the edges are often negative (representing, e.g., a negative partial correlation), whereas in the kind of networks for which the measures were developed, there are only positive edges (e.g., there cannot be a negative railroad path: there is either a path or there is not). Researchers using psychological networks deal with this generally by using absolute values of the edges when calculating centrality measures, making the negative edges positive. The result is that crucial information (e.g., that the partial correlation was negative) is lost. Due to this and many other issues (Bringmann et al., 2019), some experts on psychological networks have refrained from using centrality measures in their network analyses (e.g., Epskamp, van Borkulo, et al., 2018).

### Networks and Complex Systems

In its early days, the network approach was not connected to complex systems theory (Borsboom, 2008), or the nature of the connection between the two was not explicitly spelled out (Cramer et al., 2010). However, there is considerable overlap between the two approaches, and, in recent years, the connection between them has also been clarified and discussed (Borsboom, 2017).

A starting point for connecting the complex dynamic systems and network approaches is network density (see section "Density and Centrality" above). Following Borsboom (2017), a network of symptoms can be seen as a complex dynamic system that can be in different stable states. These different stable states correspond to attractors in the system: for instance, a depressed and a healthy state. The idea is then that the density of the network partly determines how many attractors there are and whether a system transitions easily from one attractor (e.g., healthy state) to another (e.g., depressed state).

First, let us consider a network with low density, illustrated in the left panel of Figure 5.2a. Because the connections between symptoms are weak (indicated by thinner lines), external stressors do not easily result in symptoms activating each other. The stability landscape associated with this network is shown in the right panel of Figure 5.2a: there is just one attractor (the deep basin) in the system, corresponding to the stable healthy state, and the system tends to return to this attractor after perturbations (Borsboom, 2017).

However, in a dense symptom network, illustrated in the left panel of Figure 5.2b, the edges between symptoms are strong, and the activation of a symptom after an external stressor easily leads to symptom spread throughout the network. In complex systems terms, there are two attractors in the stability landscape of the system: one corresponding to a stable healthy state and one to a stable depressed state (Borsboom, 2017). The stability landscape in the right panel of Figure 5.2b illustrates how the system is currently still resting in a healthy state, but the attractor (the basin) is weaker (shallower) than the attractor corresponding to the depressed state (the deeper basin on the right). Between these attractors is a tipping point (the ridge), and, when this tipping point is reached (through perturbation and symptom activation), the system transitions from a healthy to a depressed state (Borsboom, 2017). Thus, stressors may cause the system to tip over into the "depressed" attractor, and furthermore, the densely connected symptom network makes it more likely that the individual will remain in this state (the deeper basin) because the connections between symptoms reinforce each other. Based on this conceptual framework, Borsboom (2017) defines mental health as "the stable state of a weakly connected symptom network" and mental disorders as "alternative stable states of highly connected (sub)networks of symptoms."

This theoretical framework has direct connections to the EWS literature discussed in the previous section. In addition to measures such as autocorrelation, network density also can be interpreted as an EWS, the idea being that the density of the network increases before the transition is reached. In other words, close to a transition, the variables of the system start to behave more similarly and are thus more highly correlated. In fact, these two measures, autocorrelation and density, are closely linked: autocorrelation is represented as self-loops in the VAR-based network, and therefore network density also partly reflects the strength of the autocorrelation of symptoms (Pe et al., 2015). Indeed, as discussed above in section "Density and Centrality," preliminary research suggests that the density of the network also is increasing before a transition into a depressed state (Wichers et al., 2016, 2020).

### Challenges and Future Outlooks

Although these theoretical ideas are promising, there are still important unresolved issues. To start with, in the current network literature we often observe networks that not only contain symptoms and negative affect states, but also positive affect states as "happy" or "excited" (Pe et al., 2015). However, the original network theory as described above is based on symptom networks, and the idea that a dense network is associated with psychopathology crucially relies on the assumption that the nodes are symptoms or negative variables, which then keep easily activating each other. In a network with nodes representing positive affect states included (i.e., positive nodes), the reasoning does not work in the same way. In a dense network, these positive nodes also are more easily activated, which can lead toward a more positive overall state as positive nodes keep activating each other. Therefore, the link between density and psychopathology is conceptually unclear in networks where positive nodes are included.

The same holds for autocorrelation or self-loops: with positive nodes such as "happy," a high autocorrelation is unlikely to function as an EWS for depression. Moreover, not only the strength of the autocorrelation (and whether the node is positive or negative) but also the mean level of the node is crucial. If the mean level is low, a high autocorrelation actually implies that the node will tend to stay at a low mean level. Thus, even in symptom or negative affect networks, a high autocorrelation is unlikely to be an EWS if the mean symptom levels are very low. This highlights that although the edges are often the focus of interest in networks and complex dynamic systems, the simple mean should not be forgotten when studying psychopathology (Bringmann & Eronen, 2018).

Another way to connect network theory and complex systems theory is via formal theories using differential equations, which have recently received much attention (Burger et al., 2020; Robinaugh et al., 2021; see also Goldbeter, 2011). In the formal theory approach, a model is constructed where the nodes and the relationships between them are specified in a mathematically precise way, typically with differential equations that describe how each variable changes over time as a function of the other variables. Thus, in contrast to a data-driven model such as the VAR model, where the edges are purely determined by the data, the formal approach starts from theory, from which testable models are then derived.

Robinaugh and colleagues (2019), for example, used this approach to develop a model of panic disorder, including variables such as arousal, perceived threat, and escape behavior. Based on theoretical considerations, they formulated a set of differential equations that represent the presumed relationships between these variables. At the core of this model is a bidirectional causal relationship between perceived threat and arousal, which is moderated by a context variable (representing the presence or absence of an anxiety-inducing context) and arousal schema (representing beliefs and learned associations regarding arousal).

By means of computational modeling (simulations), Robinaugh and colleagues (2019) studied the behavior of their proposed model and evaluated its ability to produce common features of panic attacks and panic disorders. According to the authors, the model successfully reproduces some key features of panic disorder, such as the rapid onset of panic attacks. It also makes predictions that can be tested: for example, the model initially did not reproduce the phenomenon of nonclinical panic attacks because, in the simulations, occurrence of panic attacks always resulted in developing a full-blown panic disorder. This led the authors to add an "escape schema" variable to the model, representing beliefs concerning the effectiveness of escape behavior as a way to respond to perceived threat. However, a shortcoming of the model is that it remains highly theoretical: the parameter values and functions are not based on empirical data, but on their theoretical plausibility and ability to produce the relevant behavior (Robinaugh et al., 2019).

More generally, Burger and colleagues (2020) propose to use these kinds of theory-driven models based on differential equations to model mental disorders and also argue that they can be useful to inform case conceptualization in clinical practice. Overall, there seem to be relevant links between networks and complex dynamic systems models and ways in which they can be fruitfully combined to model and understand psychopathology.

## Conclusion

In this chapter, we have shown that there are many different approaches to studying psychopathology in terms of complex systems. We started out by discussing what complexity means and what complex systems are. After this, we turned to complex dynamic models that appear in the psychological literature and how these models are currently used in the field of psychopathology in the form of EWSs and psychological networks.

An important point to emphasize is that there are many different definitions of complexity or complex systems and that, even focusing just on the psychological literature, there is no exact definition for these terms that would be currently agreed upon. Even more so, the translation of the theoretical concepts and ideas associated with complex systems to actual models and applications is challenging and has taken place in very heterogeneous ways. For instance, nonlinearity and self-organization are central to theories of complex dynamic systems, the idea being that complex nonlinear behavior emerges from the interactions of many components. However, in practice, when applying a complex systems approach in clinical psychology, researchers are often just looking at increases in autocorrelation or variance in one variable (e.g., negative affect), which does not reflect the idea of complex behavior emerging from the interactions of many components.

Similarly, approaches that focus on individual symptoms, such as centrality measures, may not capture or reflect the complexity of mental disorders (Bringmann et al., 2019). It is hard to understand the behavior of a complex system by studying individual components (Cramer et al., 2010); instead, a more promising approach is to focus on the dynamics of the system as a whole (Bringmann et al., 2019). Furthermore, standard network models such as partial correlations or VAR models are linear models, and, even more so, partial correlation models are static, not dynamic, models. A promising approach that can help in translating the ideas of complex dynamic systems theory to psychological models is the recent turn in the network approach to formal models based on differential equations.

A further open question that needs to be emphasized is: What is the "system" when we talk about complex dynamic systems in psychopathology? Depending on the context and the author, it can be the person (as in most examples in this chapter), the mental disorder (Kossakowski et al., 2019), a network of symptoms (Nuijten et al., 2016), or many other things. This question is important, not only because it determines the focus of research, but also because variables that belong to the internal dynamics of the system are treated differently than external influences when modeling the behavior of the system.

In conclusion, complex systems approaches have become an integral part of psychopathological research, and many different pathways of implementing these approaches have evolved in the past decades. It is up to future research to disentangle the conceptual landscape of complexity and develop further ways of applying the theoretical ideas to the field of psychopathology.

## Acknowledgments

We are very grateful to Timon Elmer and Freek Oude Maatman for helpful comments on an earlier draft of this manuscript, as well as the editors for their extensive and extremely helpful feedback. The research that resulted in this chapter was partly funded by the Netherlands Organization for Scientific Research, Veni Grant (NWO-Veni 191G.037; Laura Bringmann).

## References

aan het Rot, M., Hogenelst, K., & Schoevers, R. A. (2012). Mood disorders in everyday life: A systematic review of experience sampling and ecological momentary assessment studies. *Clinical Psychology Review*, *32*(6), 510–523.

Barkham, M., Stiles, W. B., & Shapiro, D. A. (1993). The shape of change in psychotherapy: Longitudinal assessment of personal problems. *Journal of Consulting and Clinical Psychology*, *61*(4), 667–677. https://doi.org/10.1037/0022-006X.61.4.667

Beck, A. T. (1979). *Cognitive Therapy of Depression*. Guilford.

Bertenthal, B. I. (2007). Dynamical systems: It's about time. In S. M. Boker & M. J. Wenger (Eds.), *Data analytic techniques for dynamical systems* (pp. 1–24). Lawrence Erlbaum Associates.

Boker, S. M., Staples, A. D., & Hu, Y. (2016). Dynamics of change and change in dynamics. *Journal for Person-Oriented Research*, *2*(1–2), 34–55. https://doi.org/10.17505/jpor.2016.05

Boker, S. M., & Wenger, M. J. (Eds.). (2007). *Data analytic techniques for dynamical systems*. Lawrence Erlbaum Associates.

Bonabeau, E., Theraulaz, G., Deneubourg, J.-L., Aron, S., & Camazine, S. (1997). Self-organization in social insects. *Trends in Ecology & Evolution*, *12*(5), 188–193.

Borsboom, D. (2008). Psychometric perspectives on diagnostic systems. *Journal of Clinical Psychology*, *64*(9), 1089–1108.

Borsboom, D. (2017). Mental disorders, network models, and dynamical systems. In K. S. Kendler & J. Parnas (Eds.), *Philosophical issues in psychiatry IV: Psychiatric nosology* (pp. 80–97). Oxford University Press.

Borsboom, D., & Cramer, A. O. J. (2013). Network analysis: An integrative approach to the structure of psychopathology. *Annual Review of Clinical Psychology*, *9*(1), 91–121. https://doi.org/10.1146/annurev-clinpsy-050212-185608

Borsboom, D., Cramer, A. O. J., & Kalis, A. (2019). Brain disorders? Not really: Why network structures block reductionism in psychopathology research. *Behavioral and Brain Sciences*, *42*. https://doi.org/10.1017/S0140525X17002266

Borsboom, D., Cramer, A. O. J., Schmittmann, V. D., Epskamp, S., & Waldorp, L. J. (2011). The small world of psychopathology. *PLOS ONE*, *6*(11), e27407. https://doi.org/10.1371/journal.pone.0027407

Bos, E. H., & de Jonge, P. (2014). "Critical slowing down in depression" is a great idea that still needs empirical proof. *Proceedings of the National Academy of Sciences*, *111*(10), E878–E878. https://doi.org/10.1073/pnas.1323672111

Bos, E. H., & Wanders, R. B. K. (2016). Group-level symptom networks in depression. *JAMA Psychiatry*, *73*(4), 411–411. https://doi.org/10.1001/jamapsychiatry.2015.3103

Bos, F. M., Schreuder, M. J., George, S. V., Doornbos, B., Bruggeman, R., van der Krieke, L., . . . Snippe, E. (2022). Anticipating manic and depressive transitions in patients with bipolar disorder using early warning signals. *International Journal of Bipolar Disorders*, *10*, 12. https://doi.org/10.1186/s40345-022-00258-4.

Boschloo, L., Schoevers, R. A., van Borkulo, C. D., Borsboom, D., & Oldehinkel, A. J. (2016). The network structure of psychopathology in a community sample of preadolescents. *Journal of Abnormal Psychology*, *125*(4), 599–606. https://doi.org/10.1037/abn0000150

Bringmann, L. F. (2021). Person-specific networks in psychopathology: Past, present and future. *Current Opinion in Psychology*, *4*, 59–64. https://doi.org/10.1016/j.copsyc.2021.03.004

Bringmann, L. F., Albers, C., Bockting, C., Borsboom, D., Ceulemans, E., Cramer, A., . . . Wichers, M. (2022). Psychopathological networks: Theory, methods and practice. *Behaviour Research and Therapy*, *149*, 104011. https://doi.org/10.1016/j.brat.2021.104011

Bringmann, L. F., Elmer, T., Epskamp, S., Krause, R. W., Schoch, D., Wichers, M., Wigman, J. T. W., & Snippe, E. (2019). What do centrality measures measure in psychological networks? *Journal of Abnormal Psychology*, *128*(8), 892–903. https://doi.org/10.1037/abn0000446

Bringmann, L. F., & Eronen, M. I. (2018). Don't blame the model: Reconsidering the network approach to psychopathology. *Psychological Review*, *125*(4), 606–615. https://doi.org/10.1037/rev0000108

Bringmann, L. F., Hamaker, E. L., Vigo, D. E., Aubert, A., Borsboom, D., & Tuerlinckx, F. (2017). Changing dynamics: Time-varying autoregressive models using generalized additive modeling. *Psychological Methods*, *22*(3), 409–425. https://doi.org/10.1037/met0000085

Bringmann, L. F., Vissers, N., Wichers, M., Geschwind, N., Kuppens, P., Peeters, F., Borsboom, D., & Tuerlinckx, F. (2013). A network approach to psychopathology: New insights into clinical longitudinal data. *PLOS ONE*, *8*(4), e60188. https://doi.org/10.1371/journal.pone.0060188

Bryan, C. J., & Rudd, M. D. (2018). *Brief cognitive-behavioral therapy for suicide prevention*. Guilford.

Burger, J., van der Veen, D. C., Robinaugh, D. J., Quax, R., Riese, H., Schoevers, R. A., & Epskamp, S. (2020). Bridging the gap between complexity science and clinical practice by formalizing idiographic theories: A computational model of functional analysis. *BMC Medicine*, *18*(1), 1–18. https://doi.org/10.1186/s12916-020-01558-1

Caspi, A., Houts, R. M., Ambler, A., Danese, A., Elliott, M. L., Hariri, A., . . . Moffitt, T. E. (2020). Longitudinal assessment of mental health disorders and comorbidities across 4 decades among participants in the Dunedin Birth Cohort Study. *JAMA Network Open*, *3*(4), e203221. https://doi.org/10.1001/jamanetworkopen.2020.3221

Chen, S., O'Dea, E. B., Drake, J. M., & Epureanu, B. I. (2019). Eigenvalues of the covariance matrix as early warning signals for critical transitions in ecological systems. *Scientific Reports*, *9*(1), 2572. https://doi.org/10.1038/s41598-019-38961-5

Chow, S. M. (2019). Practical tools and guidelines for exploring and fitting linear and nonlinear dynamical systems models. *Multivariate Behavioral Research*, *54*(5), 690–718. https://doi.org/10.1080/00273171.2019.1566050

Chow, S. M., Witkiewitz, K., Grasman, R. P. P. P., & Maisto, S. A. (2015). The cusp catastrophe model as cross-sectional and longitudinal mixture structural equation models. *Psychological Methods*, *20*(1), 142–164. https://doi.org/10.1037/a0038962

Cramer, A. O. J., van Borkulo, C. D., Giltay, E. J., van der Maas, H. L. J., Kendler, K. S., Scheffer, M., & Borsboom, D. (2016). Major depression as a complex dynamic system.

*PLoS ONE*, *11*(12), 1–20. https://doi.org/10.1371/journal.pone.0167490

Cramer, A. O. J., Waldorp, L. J., van der Maas, H. L. J., & Borsboom, D. (2010). Comorbidity: A network perspective. *Behavioral and Brain Sciences*, *33*(2–3), 137–150. https://doi.org/10.1017/S0140525X09991567

Csikszentmihalyi, M., & Larson, R. (1987). Validity and reliability of the Experience-Sampling Method. *The Journal of Nervous and Mental Disease*, *175*(9), 526–536. https://doi.org/10.1097/00005053-198709000-00004

Curtiss, J., Fulford, D., Hofmann, S. G., & Gershon, A. (2019). Network dynamics of positive and negative affect in bipolar disorder. *Journal of Affective Disorders*, *249*, 270–277. https://doi.org/10.1016/j.jad.2019.02.017

Dablander, F., & Hinne, M. (2019). Node centrality measures are a poor substitute for causal inference. *Scientific Reports*, *9*(1), 1–13. https://doi.org/10.1038/s41598-019-43033-9

Dablander, F., Pichler, A., Cika, A., & Bacilieri, A. (2022). Anticipating critical transitions in psychological systems using early warning signals: Theoretical and practical considerations. *Psychological Methods*. https://doi.org/10.1037/met0000450

de Vos, S., Wardenaar, K. J., Bos, E. H., Wit, E. C., Bouwmans, M. E. J., & de Jonge, P. (2017). An investigation of emotion dynamics in major depressive disorder patients and healthy persons using sparse longitudinal networks. *PLOS ONE*, *12*(6), e0178586–e0178586. https://doi.org/10.1371/journal.pone.0178586

Dejonckheere, E., Mestdagh, M., Houben, M., Rutten, I., Sels, L., Kuppens, P., & Tuerlinckx, F. (2019). Complex affect dynamics add limited information to the prediction of psychological well-being. *Nature Human Behaviour*, *3*(5), 478–478.

Deserno, M. K., Borsboom, D., Begeer, S., van Bork, R., Hinne, M., & Geurts, H. M. (2020). Highways to happiness for autistic adults? Perceived causal relations among clinicians. *PLOS ONE*, *15*(12), e0243298. https://doi.org/10.1371/journal.pone.0243298

Devries, M. W. (1987). Investigating mental disorders in their natural settings. *Journal of Nervous and Mental Disease*, *175*(9), 509–513. https://doi.org/10.1097/00005053-198709000-00001

Ebner-Priemer, U. W., Kubiak, T., & Pawlik, K. (2009). Ambulatory assessment. *European Psychologist*, *14*(2), 95–97. https://doi.org/10.1027/1016-9040.14.2.95

Epskamp, S., van Borkulo, C. D., van der Veen, D. C., Servaas, M. N., Isvoranu, A. M., Riese, H., & Cramer, A. O. J. (2018). Personalized network modeling in psychopathology: The importance of contemporaneous and temporal connections. *Clinical Psychological Science*, *6*(3), 416–427. https://doi.org/10.1177/2167702617744325

Eronen, M. I. (2021). The levels problem in psychopathology. *Psychological Medicine*, *51*(6), 927–933.

Foote, R. (2007). Mathematics and complex systems. *Science*, *318*(5849), 410–412. https://doi.org/10.1126/science.1141754

Freeman, L. C. (1977). A set of measures of centrality based on betweenness. *Sociometry*, *40*(1), 35–41. https://doi.org/10.2307/3033543

Freeman, W. (1992). Chaos in psychiatry. *Biological Psychiatry*, *31*(11), 1079–1081. https://doi.org/10.1016/0006-3223(92)90152-P

Frewen, P. A., Schmittmann, V. D., Bringmann, L. F., & Borsboom, D. (2013). Perceived causal relations between anxiety, posttraumatic stress and depression: Extension to moderation, mediation, and network analysis. *European Journal of Psychotraumatology*, *4*(1), 20656. https://doi.org/10.3402/ejpt.v4i0.20656

Gilmore, R. (1981). *Catastrophe theory for scientists and engineers*. Wiley.

Goldbeter, A. (2011). A model for the dynamics of bipolar disorders. *Progress in Biophysics and Molecular Biology*, *105*(1–2), 119–127.

Granic, I. (2005). Timing is everything: Developmental psychopathology from a dynamic systems perspective. *Developmental Review*, *25*(3–4), 386–407. https://doi.org/10.1016/j.dr.2005.10.005

Hallquist, M. N., Wright, A. G., & Molenaar, P. C. (2021). Problems with centrality measures in psychopathology symptom networks: Why network psychometrics cannot escape psychometric theory. *Multivariate Behavioral Research*, *56*(2), 199–223. https://doi.org/10.1080/00273171.2019.1640103

Hamaker, E. L. (2012). Why researchers should think "within-person": A paradigmatic rationale. In M. R. Mehl & T. S. Conner (Eds.), *Handbook of research methods for studying daily life* (pp. 43–61). Guilford.

Haslbeck, J. M. B., & Ryan, O. (2021). Recovering within-person dynamics from psychological time series. *Multivariate Behavioral Research*. https://doi.org/10.1080/00273171.2021.1896353

Hayes, A. M., Laurenceau, J. P., Feldman, G., Strauss, J. L., & Cardaciotto, L. A. (2007). Change is not always linear: The study of nonlinear and discontinuous patterns of change in psychotherapy. *Clinical Psychology Review*, *27*(6), 715–723. https://doi.org/10.1016/j.cpr.2007.01.008

Hayes, A. M., & Yasinski, C. (2015). Pattern destabilization and emotional processing in cognitive therapy for personality disorders. *Frontiers in Psychology*, *6*, 107. https://doi.org/10.3389/fpsyg.2015.00107

Helmich, M. A., Olthof, M., Oldehinkel, A. J., Wichers, M., Bringmann, L. F., & Smit, A. C. (2021). Early warning signals and critical transitions in psychopathology: Challenges and recommendations. *Current Opinion in Psychology*, *41*, 51–58. https://doi.org/10.1016/j.copsyc.2021.02.008

Helmich, M. A., Snippe, E., Kunkels, Y. K., Riese, H., Smit, A., & Wichers, M. (2021). Transitions in Depression (TRANS-ID) Recovery: Study protocol for a repeated intensive longitudinal n = 1 study design to search for personalized early warning signals of critical transitions towards improvement in depression. *PsyArXiv*. https://doi.org/10.31234/osf.io/fertq

Helmich, M. A., Wichers, M., Olthof, M., Strunk, G., Aas, B., Aichhorn, W., Schiepek, G., & Snippe, E. (2020). Sudden gains in day-to-day change: Revealing nonlinear patterns of individual improvement in depression. *Journal of Consulting and Clinical Psychology*, *88*(2), 119–127. https://doi.org/10.1037/ccp0000469

Hosenfeld, B., Bos, E. H., Wardenaar, K. J., Conradi, H. J., van der Maas, H. L. J., Visser, I., & De Jonge, P. (2015). Major depressive disorder as a nonlinear dynamic system: Bimodality in the frequency distribution of depressive symptoms over time. *BMC Psychiatry*, *15*(1), 9–11. https://doi.org/10.1186/s12888-015-0596-5

Jeronimus, B. F. (2019). Dynamic system perspectives on Anxiety and Depression. In E. S. Kunnen, N. M. P. de Ruiter, B. F. Jeronimus, & M. A. van der Gaag (Ed.), *Psychosocial Development in Adolescence: Insights from the Dynamic Systems Approach* (pp. 100–126). Routledge Psychology.

Johnson, S. L., & Nowak, A. (2002). Dynamical patterns in bipolar depression. *Personality and Social Psychology Review*, 6(4), 380–387. https://doi.org/10.1207/S15327957PSPR0604_12

Kossakowski, J. J., Gordijn, M. C., Riese, H., & Waldorp, L. J. (2019). Applying a dynamical systems model and network theory to major depressive disorder. *Frontiers in Psychology*, 10, 1762. https://doi.org/10.3389/fpsyg.2019.01762

Koval, P., Pe, M. L., Meers, K., & Kuppens, P. (2013). Affect dynamics in relation to depressive symptoms: Variable, unstable or inert? *Emotion*, 13(6), 1132–1141. https://doi.org/10.1037/a0033579

Kruijshaar, M. E., Barendregt, J., Vos, T., de Graaf, R., Spijker, J., & Andrews, G. (2005). Lifetime prevalence estimates of major depression: An indirect estimation method and a quantification of recall bias. *European Journal of Epidemiology*, 20(1), 103–111. https://doi.org/10.1007/s10654-004-1009-0

Kunnen, S., & van Geert, P. (2012). General characteristics of a dynamic systems approach. In S. Kunnen (Ed.), *A dynamic systems approach to adolescent development* (pp. 15–34). Psychology Press.

Kuppens, P., Oravecz, Z., & Tuerlinckx, F. (2010). Feelings change: Accounting for individual differences in the temporal dynamics of affect. *Journal of Personality and Social Psychology*, 99(6), 1042–1060. https://doi.org/10.1037/a0020962

Kuppens, P., Sheeber, L. B., Yap, M. B. H., Whittle, S., Simmons, J. G., & Allen, N. B. (2012). Emotional inertia prospectively predicts the onset of depressive disorder in adolescence. *Emotion*, 12(2), 283–289. https://doi.org/10.2337/db10-1371

Kuranova, A., Booij, S. H., Menne-Lothmann, C., Decoster, J., van Winkel, R., Delespaul, P., De Hert, M., Derom, C., Thiery, E., Rutten, B. P. F., Jacobs, N., van Os, J., Wigman, J. T. W., & Wichers, M. (2020). Measuring resilience prospectively as the speed of affect recovery in daily life: A complex systems perspective on mental health. *BMC Medicine*, 18(1), 36–36. https://doi.org/10.1186/s12916-020-1500-9

Laurenceau, J., Hayes, A. M., & Feldman, G. C. (2007). Change processes in psychotherapy. *Clinical Psychology and Psychotherapy*, 27(6), 682–695.

Lewin, K. (1936). *Principles of topological psychology*. McGraw-Hill.

Lichtwarck-Aschoff, A., van Geert, P., Bosma, H., & Kunnen, S. (2008). Time and identity: A framework for research and theory formation. *Developmental Review*, 28(3), 370–400. https://doi.org/10.1016/j.dr.2008.04.001

Malinsky, D., & Danks, D. (2018). Causal discovery algorithms: A practical guide. *Philosophy Compass*, 13(1), e12470. https://doi.org/10.1111/phc3.12470

McArdle, J. J. (2009). Latent variable modeling of differences and changes with longitudinal data. *Annual Review of Psychology*, 60, 577–605. https://doi.org/10.1146/annurev.psych.60.110707.163612

Mitchell, M. (2009). *Complexity: A guided tour*. Oxford University Press.

Mokros, H. B. (1993). Communication and psychiatric diagnosis: Tales of depressive moods from two contexts. *Health Communication*, 5(2), 113–127.

Myin-Germeys, I., Oorschot, M., Collip, D., Lataster, J., Delespaul, P., & van Os, J. (2009). Experience sampling research in psychopathology: Opening the black box of daily life. *Psychological Medicine*, 39(9), 1533–1547. https://doi.org/10.1017/S0033291708004947

Nelson, B., McGorry, P. D., Wichers, M., Wigman, J. T. W., & Hartmann, J. A. (2017). Moving from static to dynamic models of the onset of mental disorder a review. *JAMA Psychiatry*, 74(5), 528–534. https://doi.org/10.1001/jamapsychiatry.2017.0001

Newman, M. (2018). *Networks*. Oxford University Press.

Nuijten, M. B., Deserno, M. K., Cramer, A. O. J., & Borsboom, D. (2016). Mental disorders as complex networks: An introduction and overview of a network approach to psychopathology. *Clinical Neuropsychiatry*, 13(4–5), 68–76.

Olthof, M., Hasselman, F., Strunk, G., van Rooij, M., Aas, B., Helmich, M. A., Schiepek, G., & Lichtwarck-Aschoff, A. (2020). Critical fluctuations as an early-warning signal for sudden gains and losses in patients receiving psychotherapy for mood disorders. *Clinical Psychological Science*, 8(1), 25–35. https://doi.org/10.1177/2167702619865969

Orsucci, F. F. (2006). The paradigm of complexity in clinical neurocognitive science. *Neuroscientist*, 12(5), 390–397. https://doi.org/10.1177/1073858406290266

Pe, M. L., Kircanski, K., Thompson, R. J., Bringmann, L. F., Tuerlinckx, F., Mestdagh, M., Mata, J., Jaeggi, S. M., Buschkuehl, M., Jonides, J., Kuppens, P., & Gotlib, I. H. (2015). Emotion-network density in major depressive disorder. *Clinical Psychological Science*, 3(2), 292–300. https://doi.org/10.1177/2167702614540645

Richardson, M. J., Dale, R., & Marsh, K. L. (2014). Complex dynamical systems in social and personality psychology: Theory, modeling, and analysis. In H. T. Reis & C. M. Judd (Eds.), *Handbook of research methods in social and personality psychology* (pp. 253–282). Cambridge University Press.

Robinaugh, D. J., Haslbeck, J. M. B., Waldorp, L. J., Kossakowski, J. J., Fried, E. I., Millner, A. J., Mcnally, R. J., Nes, E. H. V., Scheffer, M., Kendler, K. S., & Borsboom, D. (2019). Advancing the network theory of mental disorders: A computational model of panic disorder. *PsyArXiv*. https://doi.org/10.31234/osf.io/km37w

Robinaugh, D. J., Hoekstra, R. H. A., Toner, E. R., & Borsboom, D. (2020). The network approach to psychopathology: A review of the literature 2008-2018 and an agenda for future research. *Psychological Medicine*, 50(3), 353–366. https://doi.org/10.1017/S0033291719003404

Robinaugh, D. J., Haslbeck, J. M. B., Ryan, O., Fried, E. I., & Waldorp, L. J. (2021). Invisible hands and fine calipers: A call to use formal theory as a toolkit for theory construction. *Perspectives on Psychological Science*. https://doi.org/10.1177/1745691620974697

Rodebaugh, T. L., Tonge, N. A., Piccirillo, M. L., Fried, E., Horenstein, A., Morrison, A. S., Goldin, P., Gross, J. J., Lim, M. H., Fernandez, K. C., Blanco, C., Schneier, F. R., Bogdan, R., Thompson, R. J., & Heimberg, R. G. (2018). Does centrality in a cross-sectional network suggest intervention targets for social anxiety disorder? *Journal of Consulting and Clinical Psychology*, 86(10), 831–844. https://doi.org/10.1037/ccp0000336

Ryan, O., Kuiper, R. M., & Hamaker, E. L. (2018). A continuous time approach to intensive longitudinal data: What, Why and How? In K. v. Montfort, J. H. L. Oud, & M. C. Voelkle (Eds.), *Continuous time modeling in the behavioral and related sciences* (pp. 27–54). Springer.

Salvatore, S., & Tschacher, W. (2012). Time dependency of psychotherapeutic exchanges: The contribution of the theory of dynamic systems in analyzing process. *Frontiers in Psychology*, *3*(JUL), 253–253. https://doi.org/10.3389/fpsyg.2012.00253

Scheffer, M., Bascompte, J., Brock, W. A., Brovkin, V., Carpenter, S. R., Dakos, V., Held, H., van Nes, E. H., Rietkerk, M., & Sugihara, G. (2009). Early-warning signals for critical transitions. *Nature*, *461*(7260), 53–59. https://doi.org/10.1038/nature08227

Schiepek, G. (2003). A dynamic systems approach to clinical case formulation. *European Journal of Psychological Assessment*, *19*(3), 175–184. https://doi.org/10.1027//1015-5759.19.3.175

Schreuder, M. J., Groen, R. N., Wigman, J. T. W., Hartman, C. A., & Wichers, M. (2020). Measuring psychopathology as it unfolds in daily life: Addressing key assumptions of intensive longitudinal methods in the TRAILS TRANS-ID study. *BMC Psychiatry*, *20*(1), 351. https://doi.org/10.1186/s12888-020-02674-1

Schreuder, M. J., Hartman, C. A., George, S. V., Menne-Lothmann, C., Decoster, J., van Winkel, R., Delespaul, P., De Hert, M., Derom, C., Thiery, E., Rutten, B. P. F., Jacobs, N., van Os, J., Wigman, J. T. W., & Wichers, M. (2020). Early warning signals in psychopathology: What do they tell? *BMC Medicine*, *18*(1), 1–12. https://doi.org/10.1186/s12916-020-01742-3

Scott, D. W. (1985). Catastrophe theory applications in clinical psychology: A review. *Current Psychology*, *4*(1), 69–86. https://doi.org/10.1007/BF02686568

Snijders, T. A. B., & Bosker, R. J. (2011). *Multilevel analysis: An introduction to basic and advanced multilevel modeling*. SAGE.

Sperry, S. H., Walsh, M. A., & Kwapil, T. R. (2020). Emotion dynamics concurrently and prospectively predict mood psychopathology. *Journal of Affective Disorders*, *261*, 67–75. https://doi.org/10.1016/j.jad.2019.09.076

Thelen, E., & Smith, L. B. (1994). *A dynamic systems approach to development and action*. MIT Press.

Tio, P., Epskamp, S., Noordhof, A., & Borsboom, D. (2016). Mapping the manuals of madness: Comparing the ICD-10 and DSM-IV-TR using a network approach. *International Journal of Methods in Psychiatric Research*, *25*(4), 267–276. https://doi.org/10.1002/mpr.1503

Tschacher, W., Schiepek, G., & Brunner, E. J. (Eds.). (1992). *Self-organization and clinical psychology: Empirical approaches to synergetics in psychology*. Springer-Verlag. https://doi.org/10.1007/978-3-642-77534-5

van de Leemput, I. A., Wichers, M., Cramer, A. O. J., Borsboom, D., Tuerlinckx, F., Kuppens, P., van Nes, E. H., Viechtbauer, W., Giltay, E. J., Aggen, S. H., Derom, C., Jacobs, N., Kendler, K. S., van der Maas, H. L. J., Neale, M. C., Peeters, F., Thiery, E., Zachar, P., & Scheffer, M. (2014). Critical slowing down as early warning for the onset and termination of depression. *Proceedings of the National Academy of Sciences of the United States of America*, *111*(1), 87–92. https://doi.org/10.1073/pnas.1312114110

van der Maas, H. L. J., & Hopkins, B. (1998). Developmental transitions: So what's new? *British Journal of Developmental Psychology*, *16*(1), 1–13. https://doi.org/10.1111/j.2044-835x.1998.tb00747.x

van der Maas, H. L. J., & Molenaar, P. C. M. (1992). Stagewise cognitive development: An application of catastrophe theory. *Psychological Review*, *99*(3), 395–417. https://doi.org/10.1037/0033-295X.99.3.395

van Geert, P. L. C. (2019). Dynamic systems, process and development. *Human Development*, *63*(3–4), 153–179. https://doi.org/10.1159/000503825

van Montfort, K., Oud, J. H. L., & Voelkle, M. C. (Eds.). (2018). *Continuous time modeling in the behavioral and related sciences*. Springer International Publishing. https://doi.org/10.1007/978-3-319-77219-6

Voelkle, M. C., Gische, C., Driver, C. C., & Lindenberger, U. (2018). The role of time in the quest for understanding psychological mechanisms. *Multivariate Behavioral Research*, *53*(6), 782–805. https://doi.org/10.1080/00273171.2018.1496813

Voelkle, M. C., & Oud, J. H. L. (2015). Relating latent change score and continuous time models. *Structural Equation Modeling*, *22*(3), 366–381. https://doi.org/10.1080/10705511.2014.935918

von Bertalanffy, L. (1967). General theory of systems: Application to psychology. *Social Science Information*, *6*(6), 125–136. https://doi.org/10.1177/053901846700600610

von Klipstein, L., Riese, H., van der Veen, D. C., Servaas, M. N., & Schoevers, R. A. (2020). Using person-specific networks in psychotherapy: Challenges, limitations, and how we could use them anyway. *BMC Medicine*, *18*(1), 1–8. https://doi.org/10.1186/s12916-020-01818-0

Weng, G., Bhalla, U. S., & Iyengar, R. (1999). Complexity in biological signaling systems. *Science*, *284*(5411), 92–96. https://doi.org/10.1126/science.284.5411.92

Wichers, M. (2014). The dynamic nature of depression: A new micro-level perspective of mental disorder that meets current challenges. *Psychological Medicine*, *44*(7), 1349–1360. https://doi.org/10.1017/S0033291713001979

Wichers, M., Groot, P. C., & Psychosystems, E. G. (2016). Critical slowing down as a personalized early warning signal for depression. *Psychotherapy and Psychosomatics*, *85*(2), 114–116. https://doi.org/10.1159/000441458

Wichers, M., Schreuder, M. J., Goekoop, R., & Groen, R. N. (2019). Can we predict the direction of sudden shifts in symptoms? Transdiagnostic implications from a complex systems perspective on psychopathology. *Psychological Medicine*, *49*(3), 380–387. https://doi.org/10.1017/S0033291718002064

Wichers, M., Smit, A. C., & Snippe, E. (2020). Early warning signals based on momentary affect dynamics can expose nearby transitions in depression: A confirmatory single-subject time-series study. *Journal for Person-Oriented Research*, *6*(1), 1–15. https://doi.org/10.17505/jpor.2020.22042

Wichers, M., Wigman, J. T. W., & Myin-Germeys, I. (2015).Micro-level affect dynamics in psychopathology viewed from complex dynamical system theory. *Emotion Review*, *7*(4), 362–367. https://doi.org/10.1177/1754073915590623

Wigman, J. T. W., van Os, J., Borsboom, D., Wardenaar, K. J., Epskamp, S., Klippel, A., MERGE, Viechtbauer, W., Myin-Germeys, I., & Wichers, M. (2015). Exploring the underlying structure of mental disorders: Cross-diagnostic differences and similarities from a network perspective using both a top-down and a bottom-up approach. *Psychological*

Medicine, 45(11), 2375–2387. https://doi.org/10.1017/S0033291715000331

Wood, J., Oravecz, Z., Vogel, N., Benson, L., Chow, S. M., Cole, P., Conroy, D. E., Pincus, A. L., & Ram, N. (2018). Modeling intraindividual dynamics using stochastic differential equations: Age differences in affect regulation. *Journals of Gerontology - Series B Psychological Sciences and Social Sciences*, 73(1), 171–184. https://doi.org/10.1093/geronb/gbx013

Zeeman, E. C. (1976). Catastrophe theory. *Scientific American*, 234(4), 65–83.

Zeeman, E. C. (1977). *Catastrophe theory: Selected papers, 1972–1977*. Addison-Wesley.

# CHAPTER 6

# Developmental Psychopathology

Dante Cicchetti

Etiological and teleological questions have been two of the primary issues that have captured the attention of developmentalists. The term "developmental" is not merely a synonym for the study of youngsters or the field of developmental science (Werner, 1948; Werner & Kaplan, 1963). Instead, a developmental orientation is best depicted as a "world view" (Pepper, 1942). Thus, it follows that one can take an adevelopmental approach to the study of children, or a developmental approach to any unit of behavior, discipline, culture, or person across the life span, either "normal" or atypical in some capacity or capacities. Developmental contributions to virtually every scientific discipline have been with us since the inception of Western thought (Kaplan, 1967). Eisenberg (1977) urged his psychiatric brethren to adopt a developmental framework, presenting it as a unifying perspective that would enable clinical investigators to frame the difficulties they encounter in studying and treating psychopathology. Eisenberg believed that the concept of development could serve as "the crucial link between genetic determinants and environmental variables, between . . . psychology and sociology, and between physiogenic and psychogenic causes" (p. 225). Furthermore, he proposed that the term development should be used in a broad sense and felt that it should include "not only the roots of behavior in prior maturation as well as the residual of earlier stimulation, both internal and external, but also the modulation of that behavior by the social fields of the experienced present" (p. 225).

## What Is Developmental Psychopathology?

Developmental psychopathology is an integrative scientific discipline that is focused on individual biological and psychological adaptation and maladaption in the context of developmental change (Cicchetti, 1984b; Cicchetti & Cohen, 1995b; Rutter & Garmezy, 1983; Sroufe & Rutter, 1984). Before developmental psychopathology could emerge as a discipline with its own integrity, the efforts of those in related fields (e.g., embryology, philosophy, clinical and developmental psychology, and psychobiology) had been separate and distinct (Cicchetti, 1984b; Santostefano & Baker, 1972). The lack of integration across disciplines stemmed, in part, from long-standing tensions between the philosophical traditions underlying academic training and clinical practice and between basic and applied research (Santostefano, 1978).

Since its inception, developmental psychopathology has strived to unify contributions from multiple fields of inquiry, including epidemiology, developmental and clinical psychology, psychiatry, behavioral and molecular genetics, neuroscience, immunology, pediatrics, and sociology. Instead of espousing a singular unitary theory that could account for all developmental phenomena, a major goal of developmental psychopathology is to integrate knowledge across disciplines at multiple levels of analysis and in multiple domains (Cicchetti & Cohen, 1995b; Cicchetti & Dawson, 2002; Cicchetti & Valentino, 2007; Gottlieb, 1992;

### Abbreviations

| | |
|---|---|
| 5-HTT | serotonin transporter gene |
| CPP | child–parent psychotherapy |
| CRP | C-reactive protein |
| GWAS | genome-wide association study |
| GxE | gene–environment interaction |
| IPT | interpersonal psychotherapy |
| PFC | prefrontal cortex |
| RCT | randomized controlled trial |
| SNP | single nucleotide polymorphism |

Rutter & Sroufe, 2000). The main goal of developmental psychopathology is to understand the origins and course of disordered behavior. The focus is on comprehending the processes underlying both continuity and change in patterns of adaptation. Major questions include: How does prior adaptation leave the individual vulnerable to, or buffered against, certain types of stresses? And, how do particular patterns of adaptation, at different developmental periods, interact with a changing internal or external environment or physiology to produce subsequent adaptation (Cicchetti, 1993; Sroufe & Rutter, 1984)?

Historically, a number of eminent theorists from diverse disciplines have asserted that we can understand more about normal developmental functioning by investigating its pathology and, likewise, more about pathology by examining its normal condition (Cicchetti, 1990). Indeed, for many theorists, the distinctiveness and uniqueness of a developmental psychopathology approach lie in its focus on both the normal and abnormal, adaptive and maladaptive, developmental processes (Cicchetti, 1984b; Rutter, 1986; Sroufe, 1990). Although traditional perspectives conceptualize maladaptation and disorder as inherent to the individual, the developmental psychopathology framework places them in a dynamic relation between the individual and external contexts (Sameroff, 2000).

## What Is a Developmental Analysis?

Because psychopathology unfolds over time in a dynamically developing organism, it is critical to adapt a developmental viewpoint in order to understand the processes underlying individual pathways to adaptive and maladaptive outcomes (Rutter, 1986; Sroufe, 2007). The undergirding developmental orientation impels researchers to pose new questions about the phenomena they study. For example, with regard to bipolar disorder, it becomes necessary to move beyond identifying features that differentiate children, adolescents, and adults who have and who do not have bipolar disorder (e.g., emotion dysregulation; attributional distortions) to articulating how such differences have evolved developmentally. Likewise, rather than being concerned with merely describing the symptoms of bipolar disorder in children, adolescents, and adults (as is the focus of *DSM-V*), the emphasis shifts to ascertaining how similar and different biological and psychological organizations contribute to the expression of depressive, hypomanic, or manic outcomes at each specific developmental level.

A developmental analysis presupposes change and novelty, highlights the important role of timing in the organization of behavior, underscores multiple determinants, and cautions against expecting invariant relations between causes and outcomes. Moreover, a developmental analysis is as applicable to the study of the gene or cell as it is to the individual, family, or society. Moreover, a developmental analysis is important for tracing the roots, etiology, and nature of maladaptation so that interventions may be timed and guided, as well as developmentally and culturally appropriate (Causadias, 2013; Toth et al., 2013). Furthermore, a developmental analysis is useful for discovering the compensatory mechanisms—biological, psychological, and social-contextual—that may promote resilient functioning despite the experience of significant adversity (Denckla et al., 2020; Masten, 2014).

A developmental analysis also seeks to examine the prior sequences of adaptation or maladaptation that have contributed to a given outcome. Because developmental psychopathology adheres to a life span view of developmental processes and strives to delineate how early development influences later development, a major issue in the discipline is how to determine continuity in the quality of adaptation across developmental time. The same behaviors in different developmental periods may represent quite different levels of adaptation. For example, behaviors that indicate competence within a developmental level may indicate incompetence within subsequent developmental periods. Normative behaviors manifested early in development may denote maladaptation when exhibited at a later time. The manifestation of competence in different developmental periods is rarely indicated by isomorphism in behavior presentation.

## Historical Roots of Developmental Psychopathology

Developmental psychopathology owes the emergence and coalescence of its framework to many historically based endeavors (see Cicchetti, 1990). The publication of Achenbach's textbook (1974/1982); Rutter and Garmezy's (1983) chapter in the *Handbook of Child Psychology* (Mussen, 1983); the Special Issue of *Child Development* devoted to developmental psychopathology (Cicchetti 1984a); the *Rochester Symposium on Development and Psychopathology* (Cicchetti, 1989); a journal devoted exclusively to the discipline, *Development and*

*Psychopathology* (1989); and the three large volumes entitled *Developmental Psychopathology* (Cicchetti, 2016a; Cicchetti & Cohen, 1995a; Cicchetti & Cohen, 2006) are among its landmark works; however, the field of developmental psychopathology has historical roots within a variety of disciplines (Cicchetti, 1990).

One of the basic themes in the writings of the earlier thinkers was that if one aims to comprehend pathology more fully, then one must understand the normal functioning against which psychopathology is compared. Without a sophisticated understanding of the range of diversity in normal development, we would be severely hampered in our attempts to elucidate the pathways to adaptation and maladaptation in high-risk and disordered individuals of varying backgrounds. Although some definitional divergence exists, it is generally agreed that developmental psychopathologists should investigate functioning through the examination of multiple biological and psychological domains and levels of analysis (Cicchetti & Dawson, 2002; Cicchetti & Valentino, 2007, Masten, 2007).

The eminent psychiatrist Adolf Meyer put forth a psychobiological orientation. For Meyer, the psychobiological approach depicted humans as integrated organisms such that their thoughts and emotions could affect the functioning all the way down to the cellular and biochemical level, and, conversely, that occurrences at these lower biological levels could influence thinking and feeling (Meyer, 1950–1952; Rutter, 1988). Gilbert Gottlieb (1991) depicted individual normal development as characterized by "an increase of complexity of organization at all levels of analysis as a consequence of horizontal and vertical coactions, including organism-environment coactions" (p. 7). For Gottlieb (1992), horizontal coactions were thought to take place at the same level of analysis (e.g., gene–gene, cell–cell, person–person), whereas vertical coactions occurred at a different level of analysis (e.g., cell–tissue, organism–environment, behavioral activity–nervous system) and are reciprocal in nature. Consequently, vertical coactions are capable of influencing developmental organization from either lower to higher or higher to lower levels of the developing system. Accordingly, epigenesis is viewed as probabilistic rather than predetermined, with the bidirectional nature of genetic, neural, behavioral, and environmental influence over the course of individual development capturing the essence of Gottlieb's (1992) conception of probabilistic epigenesis (Gottlieb, 2007).

## The Organizational Perspective

Developmental psychopathology is not characterized by the acceptance of any theoretical approach; however, the organizational perspective on development has proved to be a powerful theoretical framework for conceptualizing the intricacies of the life span perspective on risk and psychopathology, as well as on normal development (Cicchetti, 1993; Cicchetti & Sroufe, 1978; Sroufe & Rutter, 1984). The organizational perspective focuses on the quality of integration both within and among the behavioral and biological systems of the individual. Furthermore, the organizational perspective specifies how development proceeds. Development occurs as a progression of qualitative reorganization within and among the biological, socioemotional, cognitive, representational and linguistic systems proceeding through differentiation and subsequent hierarchic integration and organization. The *orthogenic principle* (Werner, 1948; Werner & Kaplan, 1963) specifies that the developing individual moves from a state of relatively diffuse, undifferentiated organization to states of greater articulation and complexity by differentiation and consolidation of the separate systems, followed by hierarchic integration within and between systems

At each juncture of reorganization in development, the concept of *hierarchic motility* specifies that prior developmental structures are incorporated into later ones by means of hierarchic integration. In this way, early experience and its effects on the organization of the individual are carried forward within the individual's organization of systems rather than having reorganizations override previous organizations. Accordingly, hierarchic motility suggests that previous areas of vulnerability or strength within the organizational structure may remain present although not prominent in the current organizational structure. Nonetheless, the presence of prior structures within the current organization allows for possible future access by way of regressive activation of those previous structures in times of stress or crisis. Thus, for example, a behavioral or symptomatic presentation of a depressed individual may appear discrepant with recently evidenced adaptations but, in effect, indicates the activation of prior maladaptive structures that were retained in the organizational structure through hierarchic integration.

Organizational theorists contend that each stage of development confronts individuals with new challenges to which they must adapt. At each period of reorganization, successful adaptation or competence is signified by an adaptive integration within and among the emotional, social, cognitive, representational, and biological domains as the individual masters current biological and psychological developmental challenges. Because earlier structures of the individual's organization are incorporated into later structures in the successful process of hierarchical integration, early competence tends to promote later competence. An individual who has adaptively met the developmental challenges of the particular stage will be better equipped to meet successful new challenges in development. This is not to say that early adaptation ensures successful later adaptation; major changes or stresses in the internal and external environment may tax subsequent adaptational capacities. However, early competence does provide a more optimal organization of behavioral and biological systems thus offering, in a probabilistic manner, a greater likelihood that adaptive resources are available to encounter and cope with new developmental demands (Cicchetti, 1993; Sroufe et al., 2005).

In contrast, incompetence in development is fostered by difficulties or maladaptive efforts to resolve the challenges of a developmental period. Accordingly, incompetence in development can be conceived as a problematic integration of pathological structures. Over time, as hierarchical integration between the separate systems occurs, difficulty in the organization of one biological or behavioral system may tend to promote difficulty in which other systems are organized. The organization of the individual may then appear to consist of an integration of poorly integrated component systems. Early incompetence tends to promote later incompetence because the individual arrives at successive developmental stages with less than optimal resources available for responding to the challenges of that period. Again, however, this progression is probabilistic, not inevitable.

Although many theoreticians and researchers in developmental psychopathology have focused their efforts on childhood and adolescent disorders, a life span perspective is necessary because it is only by examining a range of conditions and populations from infancy through adulthood and into old age that developmental continuities and discontinuities can be elucidated. Moreover, since all periods of the life span usher in new biological and psychological challenges, strengths, and vulnerabilities (Erikson, 1950), the process of development may embark on an unfortunate turn at any point in the life span (Bell, 1968; Zigler & Glick, 1986). Whereas change in functioning remains possible at each transitional turning point in development, prior adaptation does place constraints on subsequent adaptation. The longer an individual continues along a maladaptive ontogenic pathway, the more difficult it is to reclaim a normal developmental trajectory (Sroufe et al., 1990). Furthermore, recovery of function to an adaptive level of developmental organization is more likely to occur following a period of pathology if the level of organization prior to the breakdown was a competent and adaptive one (Sroufe et al., 1990).

Within developmental psychopathology, disorders in childhood, adolescence, and adulthood are viewed from within the broader context of knowledge that has been accrued about normal biological and psychological processes (Cicchetti & Aber, 1998; Sameroff, 2000; Sroufe, 1990). In practice, this requires an understanding of the biological and psychological developmental transformations and reorganizations that occur over time; an analysis and appropriate weighting of the risk factors and mechanisms operating in the individual and his or her environment throughout the life course; an investigation of how emergent functions, competencies, and developmental tasks modify the expression of risk conditions or disorders or lead to new symptoms and difficulties; and a recognition that a specific stress or underlying mechanism may, at different times in the developmental process and in varied contexts, lead to different behavioral difficulties. Accordingly, individuals may experience similar events differently depending on their level of functioning across all domains of biological and psychological development. Thus, various occurrences will have different meanings for individuals because of the nature and timing of their experience. This interpretation of the experience, in turn, will affect the adaptation or maladaptation that ensues.

Zigler and Glick (1986), stated that a central tenet of developmental psychopathology is that persons may move between pathological and nonpathological forms of functioning. In addition, developmental psychopathology underscores that, even in the midst of pathology, individuals may display adaptive coping mechanisms (see also Ellis et al., 2020). Furthermore, depending on contextual constraints the definition of normality may vary. For example, affective inhibition may be adaptive for a child with maltreating parents, but it may result in victimization by peers (Cicchetti & Toth, 2016). This life span perspective on psychopathology enables developmental considerations to be brought into harmony with clinical concepts used to define the natural history of disorder, such as prodrome, onset, course, offset, remission, and residual states. Rather than competing with existing theories and facts, the developmental psychopathology perspective provides a broad integrative framework within which the contributions of separate disciplines can be fully realized in the broader context of understanding individual functioning and development.

## Developmental Psychopathology Principles

### The Interface of Normal and Atypical Development

As mentioned earlier, throughout the course of history, prominent theoreticians, researchers, and clinicians have adapted the premise that knowledge about normal and atypical development is reciprocally informative (Cicchetti, 1984b, 1990; Sroufe, 1990). These systematizers have underscored that research on the typical and atypical must proceed in tandem if we are to produce an integrative theory of development that can account for normal as well as deviant forms of ontogenesis to emerge.

Embryological research has made significant contributions to developmental theory (Gottlieb, 1976, 1983; Waddington, 1957). From their empirical efforts to unravel the mysteries of normal embryological functioning through isolation, defect, and recombination experiments and their investigation of surgically altered and transplanted embryos, embryologists derived the principles of differentiation, of a dynamically active organism, and of a hierarchically integrated system (Waddington, 1966; Weiss, 1969). Moreover, experiments conducted on genetic mutations have enhanced the understanding of normal functioning by magnifying the processes involved in normal ontogenesis (Fishbien, 1976). As Weiss (1961) stated, "even the greatest deformity is produced by the same rigorously lawful molecular and cellular interactions that govern normal development" (p. 150). Weiss (1961) articulated, that "no doubt that understanding of development has been furthered by the study of abnormalities" (p. 150).

In view of the contributions that the study of psychopathological phenomena and extreme risk conditions have made to theory development and refinement in other disciplines, it is curious that there was such a great reluctance to apply the knowledge derived from atypical populations of human participants in work in developmental and clinical psychology to normal developmental theory and research. Similar to cross-cultural research, the study of psychopathology can affirm, broaden, and challenge extant theories of normal and abnormal development by elucidating what developmental sequences are logically necessary, discovering possible alternate pathways to adaptive and maladaptive outcomes, and proffering evidence on which processes are most important for mental growth (Causadias, 2013; Cicchetti & Wagner, 1990; Garcia-Coll et al., 2000).

Often the investigation of a system in its smoothly operating normal or healthy state does not afford the opportunity to comprehend the interrelations among its component subsystems. Chomsky (1968) reflected on this state of affairs when he asserted that "One difficulty in the psychological sciences lies in the familiarity of the phenomena with which they deal. . . . One is inclined to take them for granted as necessary or somehow natural" (p. 21). Because pathological conditions such as brain damage or growing up in malignant environments enable us to isolate the components of the integrated system, their investigation sheds light on the normal structure of the system and prevents us from falling prey to the problem identified by Chomsky. Hence, empirical examinations of psychopathological populations and developmental extremes must be conducted (see Rutter, 1989). If we ignore the study of these atypical phenomena, then the eventual result is likely to be the construction of theories that are contradicted by the revelation of critical facts in psychopathology (Lenneberg, 1967).

When extrapolating from abnormal populations with the goal of informing developmental theory, it is important that a range of populations and conditions be considered. The study of a single psychopathological or risk process may result in spurious conclusions if generalizations are made based solely on that condition or disorder. However, if we view a given behavioral pattern in the light of an entire spectrum of diseased and disordered modifications, then we may be able to attain significant insight into the processes of development not generally achieved through sole reliance on studies of relatively more homogeneous nondisordered populations.

### Developmental Pathways: Diversity in Process and Outcome

Diversity in process and outcome is conceived as among the hallmarks of the developmental psychopathology perspective (Cicchetti & Rogosch, 1996; Sameroff, 2000; Sroufe, 1989). Developmental psychopathologists have articulated the expectation that there are multiple contributors to adaptive or maladaptive outcomes in any individual, that these factors and other relevant contributions vary among persons, and that there are myriad pathways to any particular manifestation of adaptive or disordered behavior (Richters & Cicchetti, 1993; Sroufe & Jacobvitz, 1989). Additionally, it is thought that there is heterogeneity among individuals who develop a specific disorder with respect to the features of their disturbance, as well as among persons who evidence maladaptation but who do not develop a disorder.

*Equifinality* refers to the observation that, in any open system, a diversity of pathways including chance events—or what biologists refer to as *nonlinear epigenesis*—may lead to the same outcome (Mayr, 1964, 1988). Stated differently, in an open system the same end state may be reached from a variety of different initial conditions and through different processes. In contrast, in a closed system the end state is inextricably linked to and determined by the initial conditions; if either the conditions change or the processes are modified, then the end state will also be modified (von Bertalanffy, 1968).

The principle of *multifinality* suggests that any one component may function differently depending on the organization of the system in which it operates. Multifinality states that the effect on functioning of any one component's value may vary in different systems. Actual effects will depend on the conditions set by the values of additional components with which it is structurally linked. Thus, a particular adverse event should not necessarily be seen as leading to the same psychological or nonpsychological outcome in every individual. Likewise, persons may begin on the same major pathway and, as a function of their subsequent "choices," exhibit very different patterns of adaptation or maladaptation (Cicchetti & Tucker, 1994; Egeland et al., 1996; Rutter, 1989; Sroufe, 1989; Sroufe et al., 1990).

### Developmental Cascades

*Developmental cascades* refer to the cumulative consequences of the many interactions and transactions occurring in developing systems that result in spreading effects across levels, among domains at the same level, and across different systems or generations (Masten & Cicchetti, 2010). Theoretically, these effects may be direct and unidirectional, direct and bidirectional, or indirect through various pathways; however, these consequences are not transient: developmental cascades alter the course of development. Cascade effects could explain why some problems that arose in childhood are predictive of widespread difficulties in adolescence and emerging adulthood whereas others are not. Given effects that spread over time for some kinds of psychopathology, well-timed and targeted interventions could interrupt negative or promote positive cascades. Moreover, if developmental cascades are common and often begin with adaptive behavior in early childhood, then this would explain why the evidence in prevention science indicates a high return on investment in early childhood interventions, such as high-quality preschool programs (Heckman, 2006; Reynolds & Temple, 2006). These effects may work by counteracting negative cascades, by reducing problems in domains that often cascade to cause other problems, or by improving competence in domains that increase the probability of better function in other domains.

Cascade effects encompass a broad array of phenomena investigated in developmental science within and across multiple levels of influence, from the molecular to the macro. Such cascade models may account for the pathways by which gene–environment interplay unfolds over time in epigenesis to shape development, linking genes to brain function to behavior to social experience (Cicchetti 2016a, b; Gottlieb, 2007; Hanson & Gottesman, 2007; Szyf & Bick, 2013). The processes by which genetic disorders result in the development of behavioral anomalies have been described as cascades. Biological embedding of experience, as could happen when traumatic or negative experiences alter gene expression of the stress response systems of a developing child, may begin as a downward cascade (e.g., experience alters functional systems in the child) and then subsequently these altered systems may begin cascading upward consequences for brain development, stress reactivity, and symptoms of psychopathology through a complex sequences of processes (Cicchetti, 2002; Cicchetti & Cannon, 1999; Gunnar & Quevedo, 2007; Meaney, 2010; Shonkoff et al., 2009).

### Multiple Levels of Analysis

Over the past several decades, the advances that have accrued in scientific knowledge reveal that, in order to grasp the complexity inherent to the examination of the normal and abnormal human mind, it is important that a multiple levels of analysis approach and an interdisciplinary perspective be incorporated into the research armamentarium of developmentalists (Cacioppo et al., 2000; Cicchetti & Dawson, 2002; Masten, 2007; Pellmar & Eisenberg, 2000). Many of the psychopathological disorders that confront individuals today are not as effectively investigated by a single scientist or through a single disciplinary model. These scientific questions can be best addressed through an integrative interdisciplinary framework (Pellmar & Eisenberg, 2000; Staudinger, 2015). As Miller (1995) asserted "all of the different specialties—ranging from the basic to the applied and from the biological to the social and cultural—are needed to advance our common goal of better understanding human behavior" (p. 910). The more comprehensive portrayals of adaptation and maladaptation that ensue will serve not only to advance scientific understanding, but also to inform efforts to prevent and ameliorate psychopathology across the life span.

An interdisciplinary approach to research ensures that multiple levels are well represented and that the resulting theoretical advances are consistent with insights from other levels. Influences are conceived to flow bidirectionally between levels, so that no single level can be attributed causal privilege. Biology is thus not seen as the root cause of behavior, but rather as one strand of reciprocal influence in the developing system, both giving rise to and regulated by behavioral and environmental phenomena. Although biological and genetic factors are not accorded privileged causal status in developmental systems approaches (Cicchetti & Cannon, 1999; Thelen & Smith, 1998), theory and research cannot afford to overlook the contributions that genetic and neurodevelopmental processes can make to typical and atypical outcomes (Cicchetti & Walker, 2003; Romer & Walker, 2007).

The gains in scientific knowledge have led to remarkable advances in multilevel research. For example, genetic variation, known as *gene–environment interaction* and *gene–environment interplay*, has been shown to influence the effects of environmental experience on adaptive and maladaptive outcome. More recently, some developmental theorists have proposed a more general phenomenon of biological sensitivity to context (Boyce & Ellis, 2005). According to Belsky's influential theory of differential susceptibility, genetic variation affects an individual's susceptibility to environmental influences, be they positive or negative (Belsky, 2013). Belsky hypothesized that high susceptibility is dangerous in an adverse environment, but adaptive in a benign or enriched environment. Belsky's model underscores the ongoing coaction of multiple levels in determining functional outcomes and may help to guide future efforts to identify targets, timing, and types of efficacious intervention (Belsky & Van IJzendoorn, 2015).

*Epigenetics*, the environmental regulation of genetic activity, is another field in which breakthroughs have occurred (Cicchetti, 2016a; Hackman et al., 2010; O'Donnell & Meaney, 2020; Szyf & Bick, 2013). Epigenetics broadly refers to the way the environment impacts gene expression. Epigenetic modifications (e.g., methylation) change the way genes are expressed. Like a light switch, epigenetic modification can turn genes on or off or act as a dimmer switch to increase or decrease the way genes are expressed. Animal and human studies have provided a growing body of research that demonstrates that early experience affects long-term physical and mental health by regulating the expression of genes related to neural development (Cicchetti et al., 2016a, 2016b; Meaney, 2010; O'Donnell & Meaney, 2020), immune function, and stress regulation (Szyf & Bick, 2013), with downstream effects on adaptive and maladaptive behavior. Because DNA methylation is reversible, efficacious interventions may serve to reprogram adaptive systems, targeting biological processes (e.g., stress reactivity) through behavioral changes (Szyf & Bick, 2013).

### Resilience

The discipline of developmental psychopathology, with its major focus on the dialectic between normal and abnormal development, is uniquely poised to provide the theoretical and empirical foundation for resilience science. From its inception as an integrative science, developmental psychopathology spurred investigators to discover the most effective means of preventing and ameliorating maladaptive and pathological outcomes (Sroufe & Rutter, 1984). In fact, Masten and Cicchetti (2016) have stated that "resilience science is quintessential developmental psychopathology because it focuses on variation among individuals in relation to their experiences as they adapt and develop" (p. 272). Leading scholars investigating the risk for mental illness in human development realized that understanding this variation in adaptive behavior and outcomes was essential to developing an in-depth understanding of the genesis, epigenesis, prevention, and intervention of problems and disorders (Anthony & Koupernik, 1974; Garmezy, 1974; Garmzey & Rutter, 1983; Garmezy & Streitman, 1974; Rutter, 1979, 1987; Werner & Smith, 1982). Scholars and clinicians recognized that it was vitally important to discover why some individuals do well under very challenging high-risk situations, whereas others do poorly in the tasks of life or develop serious psychopathology (Luthar et al., 2000; Masten & Cicchetti, 2016).

Definitions of resilience have shifted with a broader framework in human development toward a developmental systems perspective that integrates theory and research from ecological theory (Bronfenbrenner, 1979), general systems theory (von Bertalanffy, 1968), and systems thinking in biology (Gottlieb, 2007). For the purpose of this chapter, resilience is defined thusly:

> Resilience is the potential or manifested capacity of an individual to adapt successfully through multiple processes to challenges that threaten the function, survival, or positive development. (Masten & Cicchetti, 2016, p. 275)

Among the central themes in a developmental systems perspective on resilience, several principles are noted herein (for a full explication, see Masten & Cicchetti, 2016) (1) Many interacting systems shape the course of normal and abnormal development and the processes involved in resilience. (2) Resilience always reflects the current context as well as the history of the individual (or system). (3) Resilience is a dynamic developmental process (Egeland, Carlson, & Sroufe, 1993; Luthar et al., 2000). (4) Resilience per se is not a trait; however, many traits could influence resilience (Block & Block, 1980). As described earlier, the organizational perspective on development underscores the importance of studying multiple systems concurrently. Developmental psychopathologists who adhere to the organizational view of developmental processes must increasingly incorporate culturally and age-appropriate assessments of the effects of biological, psychological, and social-contextual factors within individuals, in their strivings to uncover the roots of resilient adaptation (Cicchetti & Cohen, 1995b).

Until the past two decades, research on the determinants of resilience was primarily psychosocial in nature. Research on the neurobiology and molecular genetics of resilience has finally begun in earnest (Charney, 2004; Cicchetti, 2013; Cicchetti & Curtis, 2007; Cicchetti et al., 2010; Curtis & Cicchetti, 2003; Ioannidis et al., 2020; Masten & Cicchetti, 2016). The contribution of biological factors to resilience has been demonstrated by research on neurobiological and neuroendocrine function in relation to stress regulation and reactivity, behavioral genetics research on nonshared environmental effects, and molecular research in the field of epigenetics.

One of the mechanisms through which individual functioning might be able to develop in a resilient fashion can happen on a neurobiological level via the process of *neural plasticity* (Cicchetti & Curtis, 2006; Cicchetti & Tucker, 1994). Neural plasticity can be framed as a process by which experience results in the reorganization of neural pathways across the course of development. The relation between the brain and experience is bidirectional. Experience helps shape the neural pathways in the brain, and the newly shaped brain seeks out different experiences which further alter neural pathways.

As the developmental process proceeds, neural plasticity appears to be guided by events that provide information to be encoded in the nervous system (Greenough et al., 1987). These experience-dependent processes involve the adaptation of the brain to information that is unique to the individual. Because all individuals encounter distinctive environments, each brain is modified in a singular fashion. Unlike the case with experience-expectant processes, experience-dependent processes do not take place within a stringent temporal interval because the timing or nature of experience that the individual encounters or chooses cannot be entirely and dependably envisioned (Black et al., 1998; Cicchetti, 2002).

Determining the multiple levels at which change is engendered through randomized prevention trials will provide more insights into the mechanisms of change, the extent to which neural plasticity may be promoted, and the interrelations between biological and psychological processes in maladaptation, psychopathology, and resilience. Efficacious, resilience-promoting interventions could be conceptualized as experience-dependent neural plasticity. Efficacious interventions should change behavior and physiology through producing alterations in gene expression (transcription) that produce new structural change in the brain (Kandel, 1999).

Resilient functioning is more than a product of biological systems. Psychosocial systems are equally important. Examples of such psychosocial factors that have been found to be linked to resilient outcomes include secure attachment relationships, an autonomous self, self-determination, close friendships, supportive parenting, positive neighborhood characteristics, and variation in personality types (Masten & Cicchetti, 2016). Large longitudinal studies on the neurobiological mechanisms of resilient functioning after child maltreatment that cut across and integrate multiple levels of analysis (i.e., genetic, endocrine, and immune systems; brain structure and function; cognition, emotion, and environmental factors) and their temporal interconnections (Cicchetti, 2013;

Ehrlich et al., 2020; Ioannidis, 2020; Masten & Cicchetti, 2016).

*Prevention and Intervention*

The preeminent objective of prevention science is to intervene in the course of development to reduce or eliminate the emergence of maladaptation and mental disorder. Prevention scientists also seek to foster the recovery of function and promote resilient adaptation in individuals at risk for psychopathology. Despite the logical links that exist between the provision of intervention to infants, children, adolescents, and adults and developmental theory and research, far too few bridges have been forged between these realms of knowledge (Cicchetti & Toth, 2017; Weisz & Kazdin, 2017).

Prevention and intervention randomized controlled trials (RCTs) can provide a lens through which the processes responsible for the development, maintenance, and alteration of typical and atypical patterns can be discerned (Cicchetti & Toth, 1992; Howe et al., 2002). Because prevention trials tend to occur earlier in development than most intervention trials and because prevention tends to be concerned with key risk factors for the development of psychopathology, they are particularly relevant to informing developmental theory (Howe et al., 2002). Prevention and intervention efforts also should be designed to elucidate the mediators and moderators of resilience and the recovery of adaptive function.

Psychosocial factors are particularly relevant to informing intervention efforts to promote resilience through adulthood and across developmental contexts. Investigations of psychosocial systems can help to identify ways in which interventions might be able to alter the environment to introduce protective factors that will increase the likelihood that individuals will have resilient outcomes. Community- or school-level interventions can be designed to promote factors that are linked to resilient functioning (such as community parenting classes or fostering peer relationships in classrooms). Although it is valuable to integrate biological systems when conducting psychosocial studies to help inform social interventions (Cicchetti & Gunnar, 2008), it is most practical for interventions to target social systems. Luthar and Cicchetti (2000) observed that research on resilience has substantial potential to guide the development and implementation of interventions for facilitating the promotion of adaptive function and development in diverse high-risk populations.

## Child Maltreatment: Illustration from a Developmental Psychopathology Perspective

What happens to individual development when there are severe disturbances in the child-rearing environment? How do these atypical organism–environment interactions and transactions influence development across the life span? By studying child maltreatment, we can learn more about the functions of typical and atypical environments as they influence developmental processes. Both the concept of an average expectable environment and a dynamic systems view of development will help to formulate the analysis of the developmental consequences of child maltreatment.

Child abuse and neglect is a serious public health problem in critical need of attention. In 2018, Child Protective Services received reports for more than 3.5 million children. As a nation, we have not responded to child abuse and neglect for decades, considering it an individual problem: bad parenting, parental mental illness, substance abuse, the perfect storm. However, it is now well-established that child abuse and neglect must be considered within a multilevel developmental lens, integrating risk factors at the individual, interpersonal, community, societal, and cultural levels (Cicchetti & Lynch, 1993, 1995).

Child maltreatment is one of the most adverse and stressful challenges that confront children. Child maltreatment constitutes a severe environmental hazard to children's adaptive and healthy mental, emotional, social, physical, and neurobiological development. Although child maltreatment occurs at all socioeconomic levels, the vast majority of maltreated children reside in low-income, highly impoverished environments. Consequently, maltreated children are exposed not only to intrafamilial stressors, but also to poverty, high levels of domestic and community violence, crime, poor schools, and diminished local resources. Child abuse and neglect and domestic violence constitute toxic conditions whereby children are exposed to chronic, severe, and prolonged stress and trauma, often occurring in the absence of protective factors.

Consistent with the organizational perspective on development described earlier in this chapter, the experience of child maltreatment initiates a probabilistic path of epigenesis for abused and neglected children that is marked by an increased likelihood of repeated disruptions in developmental processes that may create a cascade of maladaptation across diverse domains of neurobiological, neuroendocrine, immunological, socioemotional, and cognitive development. Specifically, maltreated children are likely to manifest atypicalities in neurobiological processes, physiological responsiveness, emotion recognition and emotion regulation, attachment relationships, self-system development, representational processes, social information processing, peer relations, school functioning, and romantic relationships (Cicchetti, 2016b; Cicchetti & Toth, 2015). Another way in which maltreatment may exert its harmful effects is by becoming embedded in the activity of neurobiological systems that regulate metabolic function. Holochwost and colleagues (2021) hypothesized that the literature supports a common account of activity among the parasympathetic nervous system, the sympathetic nervous system, and the hypothalamic-pituitary axis under homeostatic and stressful conditions.

Maltreatment experiences may potentiate neural systems to proceed along a trajectory that deviates from that taken in normal neurobiological development (Cicchetti & Tucker, 1994; Courchesne et al., 1994). For example, early maltreatment, either physical or emotional, may condition young neural networks to produce cascading effects through later development, possibly constraining the child's flexibility to adapt to new challenging situations with new strategies rather than with old conceptual and behavioral prototypes. Thus early psychological trauma may eventuate not only in emotional sensitization, but also in pathological sensitization of neurophysiological reactivity (Cicchetti & Tucker, 1994).

Children who are endowed with normal brains may encounter a number of experiences (e.g., poverty, community violence, child maltreatment) that exert a negative impact on developing brain structure, function, and organization and contribute to distorting these children's experiences of the world (Hackman et al., 2010). This provides a unique opportunity for comprehending how environmental factors can bring about individual differences in neurobiological development.

Children maybe especially vulnerable to the effects of pathological experiences during periods of rapid creation or modification of neuronal connections. Pathological experience may become part of a vicious cycle, and the pathology induced in the brain structure may distort the child's experiences, with subsequent alteration in cognition or social interactions, thereby causing additional pathological experience and added brain pathology (Cicchetti & Tucker, 1994). Because experience-expectant and experience-dependent processes may continue to operate during psychopathological states, children who incorporate pathological experience may add neuropathological connections into their developing brain instead of functional neuronal connections (Black et al., 1998).

As has been stated, child maltreatment affects both neurobiological and psychological processes. Physiological and behavioral responses to maltreatment are interrelated and contribute to children's making choices and responding to experiences in ways that typically produce pathological development. Because maltreated children experience the extremes of caretaking casualty (Sameroff & Chandler, 1975), they provide one of the clearest opportunities for scientists to discover the multiple ways in which social and psychological stressors can affect biological systems. Numerous interconnected neurobiological systems are affected by the various stressors associated with child abuse and neglect (De Bellis, 2001, 2005). Moreover, each of these neurobiological systems influences and is influenced by multiple domains of biological and psychological development. Furthermore, in keeping with the principle of multifinality, the neurobiological development of maltreated children is not affected in the same way in all individuals. Of note, not all maltreated children exhibit anomalies in their brain structure or functioning, and identifying protective mechanisms in these children emerges as an important area of future research.

In general, the literature indicates that exposure to child maltreatment increases the risk for a greater lifetime prevalence of high levels of many psychopathological symptoms and disorders in later life (Cicchetti & Toth, 2015; Vachon et al., 2015; Widom et al., 2009). These include, but are not restricted to posttraumatic stress disorder, mood and anxiety disorders, dissociation and suicidal behavior, substance use disorders, disruptive and antisocial behaviors, thought problems, and psychosis (Cicchetti & Toth, 2016; Toth et al., 2011).

The occurrence of resilient outcomes in some maltreated children points out that self-righting tendencies in human development may be strong even in the face of deviance and failure in the environment (Cicchetti, 2013; Ellis et al., 2020; Waddington, 1957). Discovering how maltreated children develop and function resiliently despite experiencing a multitude of stressors offers considerable promise for expanding, affirming, and challenging extant developmental theories regarding pathways to adaptive functioning in maltreated children. Because resilience is a dynamic developmental process, it is critical to conduct multilevel longitudinal studies on the pathways to resilient functioning in maltreated and non-maltreated children. This information would be extremely useful for developing preventive interventions that are developmentally informed, timed, guided, and implemented with the goal of reducing or eliminating maladaptation and psychopathology in maltreated children (Toth, Gravener, et al., 2013).

Preventive interventions strive to alter the environment to bring about positive outcomes. Scientific research on epigenetics has shown how environmental influences affect gene expression. Thus, this suggests that prevention and intervention also may change the epigenome and also could result in improved outcomes (O'Donnell et al., 2018). If we are to understand the mechanisms through which early adverse experiences such as child maltreatment impact maladaptation, psychopathology, and resilience, then it is critical that we also examine genetic variation and epigenetic modifications.

Research on gene–environment interaction (G×E) and on epigenetics needs to incorporate a developmental perspective (i.e., G×E×D). Genes may affect how environmental experience affects the developmental process, and this may operate differently at various developmental periods. Moreover, the effects of genes and experiences at a particular period may be influenced by the effects of prior development. Environments may affect the timing of genetic effects and gene expression. Additionally, there are experience effects of the epigenome, and these also would operate differently across the course of development (Cicchetti et al., 2016a, 2016b; Cicchetti & Handley, 2017).

Chronic and toxic stressors, like child maltreatment, can initiate epigenetic changes, representing one potential mechanism for how maltreatment can lead to adverse physical and mental health outcomes. Studies have begun to uncover the ways that child maltreatment influences future psychological and health outcomes via epigenetic mechanisms. Cicchetti and colleagues (2016a, 2016b) examined epigenetic changes in genes that influence how we feel pleasure, respond to stress, and process alcohol. Their results revealed significant differences in methylation, a marker of epigenetic change, between maltreated and non-maltreated school-age youth. Children who experienced maltreatment in early life had significantly more methylation on a gene site related to how we experience pleasure (i.e., dopamine). Maltreated boys, specifically those who experienced maltreatment early in life, had significantly more methylation on the gene related to risk for alcohol use disorders.

In another study Cicchetti and Handley (2017) investigated the role of maltreatment in predicting methylation on a gene involved in the stress response (i.e., the glucocorticoid receptor gene NR3C1). They found that the more severe and frequent the child's maltreatment experiences were, the more likely they were to have excessive methylation on the glucocorticoid receptor gene. The glucocorticoid receptor gene is related to the body's stress response system and how individuals respond to stressful situations. In turn, this methylation was associated with mental health problems including externalizing behavior problems and depression.

## Depression: Illustration from a Developmental Psychopathology Perspective

Depression is one of the most prevalent, recurrent, costly, and debilitating mental disorders worldwide. Almost 20% of the US population will experience a clinically significant episode of depression during their lifetime, and approximately 80% of depressed individuals will experience recurrent episodes. The disorder is multifaceted and affects afflicted individuals' emotions, thoughts, sense of self, interpersonal relationships, productivity, and life satisfaction (Cicchetti & Toth, 1998; Goodman & Gotlib, 1999).

Depression is of particular interest to developmental psychopathologists because of the complex interplay of psychological (e.g., affective, cognitive, and interpersonal) and biological (e.g., genetic, neurophysiological, neurobiological, immunological, neuroendocrine) systems that are involved. Notably, these varied systems do not exist in isolation. Rather, they are completely interrelated and mutually interdependent. Thus, understanding the interrelations among these biological and psychological systems is vital for delineating the nature of the disorder, as well as elucidating how these systems also promote adaptive functioning. Furthermore, depressive conditions may be conceived as forming a spectrum of severity from transient dysphoria universally experienced, to elevated levels of depressive symptoms that do not meet the criteria for disorder, to long-term periods of dysthymia and episodes of major depressive disorder. Even within more narrowly defined disorders such as a major depressive disorder, there are likely to be heterogeneous conditions with phenotypic similarity despite differences in etiology. Although there are diverse pathways leading to depressive disorders (equifinality), potential risk factors for depression may result in a multitude of outcomes, of which depression may be one (multifinality). Moreover, depressive phenomena and disorders are present throughout the life span, from early childhood through senescence. Because of the continuities and divergences from normal functioning manifested in depressive disorders across the life course, the study of depression holds promise for understanding the interface of normal and abnormal adaptation. Not only does knowledge of normative development and functioning assist in characterizing the deviations evident among individuals with depression, but also, in understanding the aberrations in functioning among depressed persons, it elucidates how normal adaptation is achieved.

Stressful life events play a substantial role in the development of depression across the life course and are one of the leading precipitating factors for the onset of depressive episodes. Environmental stressors can include things such as childhood poverty, child maltreatment, natural disasters, and death of a loved one, to name a few. Experiencing stressors typically precedes the initial elevation of depressed symptoms and increases the likelihood of episode recurrence. In fact, Hammen (2005) concluded that the experience of a life stressor was 2.5 times more likely among depressed cases compared to controls, and 80% of depressed cases were preceded by stressful major life events. Moreover, depressed parents often face co-occurring problems, such as socioeconomic stressors, marital or relational conflict, or insufficient social support. Cicchetti, Rogosch, and Toth (1998) found that families with a depressed parent were shown to experience more contextual risk, including greater perceived stress, parenting hassles, family conflict, and lower perceived social support and marital satisfaction.

Given the multiplicity of systems affected by depressive disorder, a developmental psychopathology approach also directs attention to an examination of early developmental attainments that may be theoretically related to later appearing patterns of depressive symptomatology (Palmer et al., 2019). For example, obtaining an understanding of the deviations in emotion regulation or the core negative attributions about the self observed in depressed persons may begin by examining the early development of these features, their developmental course, and their interrelations with other psychological and biological systems of the individual.

Single risk factors can rarely be conceived as resulting in depressive outcomes. Rather, the organization of biological and psychological systems, as they have been structured over development, must be fully considered. The concept of a depressotypic developmental organization has much heuristic value in guiding thinking about the diverse processes that underlie symptom expression and depressive outcomes (Cicchetti & Toth, 1998). The developmental position challenges us to move beyond identifying isolated aberrations in cognitive, affective, interpersonal, and biological components of depressive presentations to understand how those components have evolved developmentally and how they are integrated within and across biological and psychological systems.

Caspi et al. (2003) conducted a prospective study that found an interaction between stressful life events and the serotonin transporter gene (i.e., *5-HTT*) was related to the risk of developing depression. The promoter region of the 5-HTT gene contains either a short (*S*) or long (*L*) repeat allele. The short allele leads to less efficient transcription compared to the long allele. Individuals in the study who were carriers of the short allele were more sensitive to stressful life experiences and were likely to develop depression (Caspi et al., 2003).

A number of subsequent studies have failed to replicate the results of the Caspi et al. (2003) candidate gene study. These discrepant findings have triggered an ongoing debate about the methodological challenges facing G×E studies (e.g., Caspi et al., 2010; Duncan & Keller, 2011; Risch et al., 2009). Specific gene effects become increasingly complicated when the role of developmental timing on the impact of environmental events, genetic expression, and depressive phenotypes is considered. In addition, there are potential interactions among genetic variants, downstream biological mechanisms, and improperly accounted for confounding variables such as ethnicity, gender, age, or socioeconomic status.

Genome-wide association studies (GWAS) also have become increasingly prominent in the field of psychopathology as an alternative method to candidate gene approaches to investigate the role of genes in the development of disorders. GWAS utilize genome-wide sets of common genetic variants known as *single nucleotide polymorphisms* (SNPs) to differentiate which variations are associated with observable traits or behaviors. This method allows scientists to conduct scans of whole genomes to see if multiple genetic variants are related to the expression of a depressive disorder.

Early GWAS studies of depression have produced largely underwhelming results. Although these GWAS investigations had sample sizes comparable to successful GWAS studies for other common diseases and phenotypes, no significant SNPs emerged in these early investigations of depression. Thus, the effect of most SNPs on depression are small in magnitude, and a large sample size is necessary to identify the genetic loci associated with depression. A paucity of studies have attempted to take a developmental approach by using GWAS to analyze which molecular genetic SNPs correlate with age of onset for major depressive disorder.

GWAS often fail to account for environmental influences on genetic expression. In contrast, epigenetics focuses on how DNA can be influenced by the environment. Epigenetics involves functional changes to the genome, where certain genes may be turned on or off without altering the nucleotide sequence. Examples include changes to DNA methylation and histone acetylation (Cicchetti & Handley, 2017; Cicchetti et al., 2016a, 2016b; Sun et al., 2013). The heterogeneous nature of depression and "missing heritability" between epidemiological investigations and molecular studies make for an ideal candidate for epigenetic studies.

The developmental psychopathology perspective provides important insights useful to prevent depressive disorders as well as to intervene once depression has occurred. In addition, treatment for depression may need to vary depending on the history of prior depressive disorders. Post (1992) studied the developmental progression of episodes among mood-disordered individuals and concluded that the more automatic triggering of episodes later in the course of these disorders likely requires different treatments. For first episodes of depressive disorder, interpersonal psychotherapies may have greater utility in reorganizing the affective, cognitive, and interpersonal difficulties depressed individuals exhibit. However, later episodes of depression may become increasingly primed biologically, and psychopharmacological interventions combined with more directive cognitive-behavioral therapy are likely to be more essential. Additionally, alternative drug treatments may become necessary as the progression of episodes and concomitant biological alterations may make previously effective drugs no longer effective (Post, 1992; Post et al., 1996).

Behavioral and psychological interventionists are interested in epigenetic effects on treatment. It is largely appreciated that interventions do not succeed for all participants; however, our understanding of how individual factors influence intervention efficacy is still in its infancy. Most of this work is guided by differential susceptibility models which suggest that those most likely to be adversely affected by negative environmental experiences are also those most likely to benefit from contextual support. This theory implies that specific characteristics of people make it more likely that both positive and negative experiences will, respectively, affect the individual's positive and negative functioning and development (e.g., Belsky & Pluess, 2013). For example those carrying one or more serotonin transporter-linked polymorphic region gene (i.e., *5-HTTLPR*) short alleles have shown both increased positive and negative outcomes depending on rearing environments. Although these genetic factors have been thought to inform risk, there is also experimental evidence to suggest that those who carry the "risk allele" benefit more from interventions (e.g., Cicchetti, Toth, & Handley, 2015; Drury et al., 2012; Kegel et al., 2011). This suggests that we may be able to utilize genetic information to improve treatments for individuals suffering from depression or at risk for developing depression. However, not all interventions guided by a differential susceptibility perspective are focused on genetic or epigenetic markers for sensitivity to the environment. Behavioral (e.g., temperament; Belsky et al., 2007) and physiological (e.g., vagal tone; Conradt et al., 2013) markers are also often theorized to denote differences in sensitivity.

Science has made huge strides in our understanding of how genes function (or don't function) in relation to complex behavioral phenotypes such as depression. However, we still have a long way to go until we even begin to crack the genetic code to common psychopathologies. Research on human genetics and psychopathological phenotypes is becoming increasingly collaborative. Current work and theory suggest that we can expect to find hundreds to even thousands of genetic variants and gene-by-environment interactions that contribute to the depressive phenotype. This may even vary dependent on sex, ethnicity, developmental timing of disease onset, and/or specific sets of symptoms. Scientists aim to unveil a variety of biological pathways to generate a deeper understanding of the processes which underlie the development of psychiatric disorders. Furthermore, we suggest that genetic work should shift its focus on to specific symptoms of depression such as sleep disturbances, irritability, or hopelessness. It also will be important to take into account the developmental timing of environmental events and symptom onset when considering the impact of genetic and epigenetic factors.

In recent years, advances in research methods to investigate brain mechanisms have provided the opportunity to examine the neural correlates of depressive psychopathology and its risk factors. Identification of the neural signatures of mental disorders will accelerate accurate diagnosis and contribute to efficacious treatment. Electroencephalogram (EEG) and structural magnetic resonance imaging (MRI) and functional MRI (fMRI) provide insight into general and specific neuroanatomical regions and neural circuits that play a role in depression.

Early research on the neural correlates of depression centered around EEG findings. The frontal cortex is lateralized for negative and positive affect, with left frontally activated individuals showing less negative affect and greater positive affect than right frontally activated individuals (Tomarken et al., 1992). From a developmental perspective, insecurely attached infants of depressed mothers also have been shown to have relative right-sided EEG frontal asymmetry (Dawson et al., 1992).

In his important book, *Neural Darwinism*, Edelman (1987) describes the great variability found in patterns of synaptic connection and states that some of this heterogeneity takes place as a result of differential experiences during sensitive periods for synaptogenesis. The findings of Dawson and colleagues (1992) were consistent with Edelman's (1987) thesis and suggest that a mother's emotional condition, and implicitly with her interactions with her baby, can impact on developing patterns of synaptogenesis in the early years of life (Cicchetti & Tucker, 1994).

A large recent literature has begun using imaging technology to determine the neural correlates of depression development. Research in the field of developmental affective neuroscience has focused on the amygdala and the prefrontal cortex (PFC), areas critical for emotion processing and regulation. The amygdala is critical for detecting emotional salience of environmental stimuli and for developing conditioned fear responses. It has repeatedly been shown to activate in response to emotional stimuli. The PFC inhibits this amygdalar response, restraining emotional reactivity. The PFC is critical for executive functioning abilities, including cognitive control and behavioral inhibition.

Research investigations also have identified changes in immune function associated with depression, sparking interest in the role of neuroimmune function and inflammation in the ontogeny of depression. Depressed persons have been found to have increased levels of inflammatory markers; particular emphasis has been placed on the cytokine interleukin-6 (i.e., IL-6). Depressed individuals also have a greater likelihood of developing inflammatory illnesses. Inflammation has been proposed to work in concert with early life adversities to increase risk for internalizing symptoms and disorder (Cicchetti, Handley, & Rogosch, 2015). Individuals who experienced high childhood adversity and went on to develop depression exhibited accompanying increased levels of inflammatory biomarkers IL-6 and C-reactive protein (CRP). In contrast, adolescents who were not exposed to early adversity do not show the same effects, consistent with findings that only depressed adults who experienced child maltreatment exhibited elevated inflammation (Danese et al., 2008).

A longitudinal investigation of African American youth also found a coupling between the development of depression and inflammation as a result of harsh parenting during childhood (Beach et al., 2017). Moreover, this study discovered that the relationship between harsh parenting and depression and inflammation is mediated by stress and the nature of romantic relationships during the child's young adulthood, suggesting that parenting practices impact inflammation and depression through their effects on the child's future relationship styles. Thus, early stressors pave the way for inflammatory pathways to disease.

The field of developmental psychopathology conceptualizes "mental illness as involving dysfunction across multiple and transacting developmental processes" (Cicchetti & Toth, 2009, p. 20). Mental disorders are conceived as being dynamic and should be studied from an interdisciplinary perspective and a multiple levels of analysis approach (Cicchetti & Dawson, 2002; Cicchetti & Toth, 2009). Such an approach entails investigating bidirectional and transactional interactions among genetic, neurobiological, social, environmental (pre- and postnatal), and cultural influences over the course of the life span. Adapting a multiple levels of analysis approach enables developmental psychopathologists to achieve one of their major goals: to understand the full complexity of psychopathology and discover the mechanisms underlying individual patterns of adaptation through investigating the whole organism (Sroufe & Rutter, 1984; Zigler & Glick, 1986). The concurrent examination of biological, psychological, and environmental-contextual processes and their interplay at different developmental periods provides an integrative conceptualization of the course of psychopathology (Cicchetti & Cohen, 1995a; Garber & Bradshaw, 2020).

In keeping with its integrative focus, contributions to developmental psychopathology have come from many disciplines of the biological and social sciences. A wide array of content areas and methodologies have been germane. Risk and protective factors and processes have been identified and validated at multiple levels of analysis and in multiple domains. The increased emphasis on a multilevel, dynamic systems approach to psychopathology and resilience; the increased attention paid to gene–environment interplay in the development of psychopathology and resilience; and the application of a multiple levels of analysis developmental perspective to mental illnesses that have traditionally been examined nondevelopmentally not only have contributed to a deeper understanding of dysfunction, but also have educated the public about the causes and consequences of mental disorder.

Furthermore, advances in G×E interactions and epigenetics; growth in the understanding of neurobiology, neural plasticity, and resilience; and progress in the development of methodological and technological tools, including brain imaging, neural circuitry, immunology, hormone assays, social and environmental influences on brain development, and statistical analysis of developmental change have paved the way for interdisciplinary and for multiple levels of analysis research programs and collaborations that will significantly increase the knowledge base of the development and course of maladaptation, psychopathology, and resilience. Moreover, randomized control prevention and intervention trials are beginning to be based on developmentally informed models. These RCTs will increasingly shed light on the processes and mechanisms contributing to developmental change at both the biological and psychological levels (Cicchetti & Gunnar, 2008).

Developmental psychopathologists have incorporated concepts and methods derived from other disciplinary endeavors that are too often isolated from each other, thereby generating advances in knowledge that might have been missed in the absence of cross-disciplinary dialogue. It is apparent that increasingly prospective longitudinal research programs should be conducted that not only investigate high-risk and mentally disordered individuals, but also follow up comparable matched normal comparisons over developmental time. Moreover, these multidomain longitudinal investigations should endeavor to begin before a period of significant developmental change takes place (e.g., neurodevelopmental research on schizophrenia should begin in the prenatal period) and follow up individuals through when the emergence of the disorder is at its highest (for research on schizophrenia at least through the period of later adulthood) (Cicchetti & Cannon, 1999). Such longitudinal research will be critical to discover trajectories to developmental adult psychopathology.

Future research in this area must employ methodological pluralism and strive for fidelity between the current systems theory models of brain–behavior relations and the nature of the methods and measures utilized. In the search to discover the mechanisms linking various developmental pathways to the same psychopathological outcome, study designs should incorporate sufficiently large samples to permit the identification of relatively homogenous profiles of individuals that can be subjected both to variable-oriented and person-oriented statistical analyses.

Finally, researchers should continue with the implementation of a multiple dynamic systems approach that integrates biological contributors to psychopathology and the psychological and social factors that are operative in the genesis and maintenance of disorders. The continuation and elaboration of a multiple levels of analysis framework within and across disciplines interested in normal and abnormal development not only will enhance the science of developmental psychopathology, but also will increase the benefits to be derived for individuals with high-risk conditions or mental disorders, families, and society as a whole.

The multiplicity of pathways contributing to the development of depression directs us toward studying the interface between normal and abnormal development. Developmental psychopathology draws attention to both the similarities and differences among normal and psychopathological conditions. Accordingly, researchers can discern the specific pathways leading to depression as well as discover the commonalities underlying normal development, depressive illness, and related disorders. In particular, increased attention to the pathways and trajectories taken by individuals who avoid developing depression despite the presence of enduring vulnerabilities and transient challenges may help inform prevention and intervention efforts.

## Intervention

Developmentally informed psychosocial interventions have been implemented for children maltreated early in life, the young offspring of depressed mothers, and depressed teens. For example, Cicchetti, Rogosch, and Toth (2006) conducted an RCT with maltreated infants and their mothers. Child–parent psychotherapy (CPP), an evidenced-based trauma treatment model that facilitates change through promoting positive mother–child attachment relationships, was the psychosocial treatment utilized. CPP is based on the fundamental assumption that challenges in the parent–child relationship are not the result of a deficit in parenting knowledge or skill. Rather, CPP recognizes that a caregiver's insensitivity or lack of appropriate responsivity to a child is likely the result of their own childhood experiences with caregivers. CPP aims to help parents recognize the role that their own childhood experiences with caregiving may have in their current parenting practices. CPP focuses on fostering a secure parent–child attachment by helping parents become more responsive, sensitive, and attuned to their child. The RCT of Cicchetti et al. (2006) documents CPP as efficacious at promoting attachment security in maltreated infants (see also Guild et al., 2017; Pickreign Stronach et al., 2013; Toth et al., 2002).

Cicchetti, Rogosch, and Toth (2000) found that CPP was efficacious in fostering cognitive development in toddlers of depressed mothers. In addition, Toth, Rogosch, Manly, and Cicchetti (2006) discovered that CPP fostered secure attachment in toddlers of depressed mothers.

Toth, Rogosch, Oshri, Gravener-Davis, Sturn, and Morgan-Lopez (2013) conducted a randomized trial of interpersonal psychotherapy (IPT) with economically disadvantaged mothers with major depressive disorder. The women in this RCT also had extensive histories of trauma, with nearly 90% of the women receiving IPT having histories of maltreatment and with more than 90% experiencing at least one lifetime traumatic event. Depressive symptoms at the conclusion of treatment and at 8 months post-intervention were significantly lower among women who received IPT than among those who received treatment generally available in the community. Social adjustment and perceived stress also were identified as mediators of sustained positive treatment effects (Toth, Rogosch et al., 2013).

Handley et al. (2017) conducted an RCT with a sample of racially and ethnically diverse, socioeconomically disadvantaged mothers of infants. Mothers were randomized to IPT or an enhanced community standard control group. Engagement with IPT led to significant decreases in maternal depressive symptoms at 8 months post-treatment. Moreover, reductions in maternal depression post-treatment were associated with less toddler insecure disorganized attachment characteristics, more maternal adaptive perceptions of toddler temperament, and improved maternal parenting efficacy 8 months following the completion of IPT. These results document the potential benefits in children of successfully treating maternal depression. Alleviating maternal depression appears to initiate a cascade of positive adaptation among both mothers and offspring, which may alter the well-replicated risk trajectory for offspring of depressed mothers (Cicchetti & Toth, 1998; Goodman & Gotlib, 2002).

In contrast to earlier writings that claimed depression arising in childhood will diminish over time if left to run its course, we now possess longitudinal data demonstrating that once depression remits, it often reemerges and impairs children's ability to negotiate developmental tasks competently. Likewise, a number of investigations have followed up adults with depressive disorders over time and found that serious psychological impairments often occur both during the illness proper and in the period of remission. Now that developmental psychopathologists have discovered how depressed individuals negotiate a number of the stage-salient issues throughout the life course, we are in a position to assess not only how an incompetent organization of biological and behavioral systems can contribute to the development of depression, but also to discover how the presence of depression affects competence both during an episode and in remission.

## Conclusion

There remains a great deal to be accomplished in advancing an integrative, multilevel developmental understanding of maladaptation, psychopathology, and resilience. The developmental considerations raised in this chapter make clear that progress toward a process-level understanding of normal and abnormal development will require research designs and strategies that allow for the simultaneous consideration of multilevel analysis and multiple domains of variables within and outside the individual. Moreover, the organizational perspective, with its emphasis on understanding the organization of biological and psychological development and its focus on studying the "whole person" in context, will play an important role in framing the questions as we seek to continue examining the nature of the relation between biological and psychological factors in the symptoms, causes, course, sequelae, and treatment responsivity of risk, maladaptation, psychopathology, and resilience. The cross-fertilization of the neurosciences with psychology and related disciplines will result in major advances in our comprehension of normality and pathology, especially if a developmental perspective to the interdisciplinary ventures is adopted by the investigators.

Although the challenges are great in the quest to arrive at a sufficiently integrative approach to understanding pathological phenomena, a developmental psychopathology approach holds great promise for elucidating necessary future questions and suggestion strategies to apply to such an undertaking.

## References

Achenbach, T. M. (1974/1982). *Developmental psychopathology*. Ronald Press.

Anthony, E. J., & Koupernik, C. (Eds.). (1974). *The child in his family: Children at psychiatric risk*. Wiley & Sons

Beach, S. R. H., Lei, M. K., Simons, R. L., Barr, A. B., Simons, L. G., Ehrlich, K., . . . Philibert, R. A. (2017). When inflammation and depression go together: The longitudinal effects of parent-child relationships. *Development and Psychopathology*, 29(5), 1969–1986. doi:10.1017/S0954579417001523

Bell, R. Q. (1968). A reinterpretation of the direction of effects in studies of socialization. *Psychological Review*, 75(2), 81–95. https://doi.org/10.1037/h0025583

Belsky, J. (2013). Differential susceptibility to environmental influences. *International Journal of Child Care and Education Policy*, 7, 15–31 https://doi.org/10.1007/2288-6729-7-2-15

Belsky, J., Bakermans-Kranenburg, M., & van IJzendoorn, M. H. (2007). For better and for worse: Differential susceptibility to environmental influences. *Current Directions in Psychological Science*. 16(6): 300–304. https://doi.org/10.1111/j.1467-8721.2007.00525.x

Belsky, J., & Pluess, M. (2013). Beyond risk, resilience, and dysregulation: Phenotypic plasticity and human development. *Development and Psychopathology*, 25(4 Pt 2), 1243–1261. doi:10.1017/S095457941300059X

Belsky, J., & van Ijzendoorn, M. H. (2015). What works for whom? Genetic moderation of intervention efficacy. *Development and Psychopathology*, 27(1), 1–6. doi:10.1017/S0954579414001254

Black, J., Jones, T. A., Nelson, C. A., & Greenough, W. T. (1998). Neuronal plasticity and the developing brain. In N. E. Alessi, J. T. Coyle, S. I. Harrison, & S. Eth (Eds.), *Handbook of child and adolescent psychiatry* (pp. 31–53). Wiley.

Block, J., & Block, J. H. (1980). The role of ego-control and ego-resiliency in the organization of behavior. In W. A. Collins (Ed.), *The Minnesota symposia on child psychology: Development of cognition, affect, and social relations* (vol. 13, pp. 39–101). Erlbaum.

Boyce, W. T., & Ellis, B. J. (2005). Biological sensitivity to context: I. An evolutionary-developmental theory of the origins and functions of stress reactivity. *Development and Psychopathology*, 17(2), 271–301. doi:10.1017/s0954579405050145

Bronfenbrenner, U. (1979). *The ecology of human development: Experiments by nature and design*. Harvard University Press.

Cacioppo, J. T., Berntson, G. G., Sheridan, J. F., & McClintock, M. K. (2000). Multilevel integrative analyses of human behavior: Social neuroscience and the complementing nature of social and biological approaches. *Psychological Bulletin*, 126(6), 829–843. doi:10.1037/0033-2909.126.6.829

Caspi, A., Hariri, A. R., Holmes, A., Uher, R., & Moffitt, T. E. (2010). Genetic sensitivity to the environment: The case of the serotonin transporter gene and its implications for studying complex diseases and traits. *American Journal of Psychiatry*, 167(5), 509–527. doi:10.1176/appi.ajp.2010.09101452

Caspi, A., Sugden, K., Moffitt, T. E., Taylor, A., Craig, I. W., Harrington, H., . . . Poulton, R. (2003). Influence of life stress on depression: Moderation by a polymorphism in the 5-HTT gene. *Science*, 301(5631), 386–389. doi:10.1126/science.1083968

Causadias, J. M. (2013). A roadmap for the integration of culture into developmental psychopathology. *Development and Psychopathology*, 25(4pt2), 1375–1398. https://doi.org/10.1017/S0954579413000679

Charney, D. (2004). Psychobiological mechanisms of resilience and vulnerability: Implications for successful adaptation to extreme stress. *American Journal of Psychiatry*, 161, 195–216.

Chomsky, N. (1968). *Language and mind*. Harcourt Brace Jovanovich.

Cicchetti, D. (Ed.). (1984a). *Developmental psychopathology*. University of Chicago Press.

Cicchetti, D. (1984b). The emergence of developmental psychopathology. *Child Development*, 55, 1–7.

Cicchetti, D. (Ed.). (1989). *Rochester symposium on developmental psychopathology: The emergence of a discipline* (vol. 1). Lawrence Erlbaum Associates.

Cicchetti, D. (1990). A historical perspective on the discipline of developmental psychopathology. In J. Rolf, A. Masten, D. Cicchetti, K. Nuechterlein, & S. Weintraub (Eds.), *Risk and protective factors in the development of psychopathology* (pp. 2–28). Cambridge University Press.

Cicchetti, D. (1993). Developmental psychopathology: Reactions, reflections, projections. *Developmental Review*, 13, 471–502. 10.1006/drev.1993.1021

Cicchetti, D. (2002). How a child builds a brain: Insights from normality and psychopathology. In W. W. Hartup & R. A. Weinberg (Eds.), *The Minnesota symposia on child psychology: Child psychology in retrospect and prospect* (vol. 32, pp. 23–71). Lawrence Erlbaum.

Cicchetti, D. (2013). Annual Research Review: Resilient functioning in maltreated children--past, present, and future perspectives. *Journal of Child Psychology and Psychiatry*, 54(4), 402–422. doi:10.1111/j.1469-7610.2012.02608.x

Cicchetti, D. (Ed.). (2016a). Epigenetics: Development, psychopathology, resilience, and preventive intervention. [Special Section]. *Development and Psychopathology*, 28(4 part 2), 1217–1384.

Cicchetti, D. (2016b). Socioemotional, personality, and biological development: Illustrations from a multilevel developmental psychopathology perspective on child maltreatment.

Annual Review of Psychology, 67, 187–211. doi:10.1146/annurev-psych-122414-033259

Cicchetti, D., & Aber, J. L. (1998). Contextualism and developmental psychopathology. *Development and Psychopathology, 10*, 137–141.

Cicchetti, D., & Cannon, T. D. (1999). Neurodevelopmental processes in the ontogenesis and epigenesis of psychopathology. *Development and Psychopathology, 11*, 375–393.

Cicchetti, D., & Cohen, D. J. (Eds.). (1995a). *Developmental psychopathology* (vols. 1–2). Wiley.

Cicchetti, D., & Cohen, D. J. (1995b). Perspectives on developmental psychopathology. In D. Cicchetti & D. J. Cohen (Eds.), *Developmental psychopathology: Theory method* (vol. 1, pp. 3–20). Wiley.

Cicchetti, D., & Cohen, D. J. (Eds.). (2006). *Developmental psychopathology*, 2nd ed. (vols. 1–3). Wiley.

Cicchetti, D., & Curtis, W. J. (2006). The developing brain and neural plasticity: Implications for normality, psychopathology, and resilience. In D. Cicchetti & D. Cohen (Eds.), *Developmental psychopathology, 2nd ed., vol. 2: Developmental neuroscience* (pp. 1–64). Wiley.

Cicchetti, D., & Curtis, W. J. (2007). Multilevel perspectives on pathways to resilient functioning. *Development and Psychopathology, 19*(3), 627–629. doi:10.1017/s0954579407000314

Cicchetti, D., & Dawson, G. (2002). Multiple levels of analysis. *Development and Psychopathology, 14*(3), 417–420. doi:10.1017/s0954579402003012

Cicchetti, D., & Gunnar, M. R. (2008). Integrating biological measures into the design and evaluation of preventive interventions. *Development and Psychopathology, 20*(3), 737–743. doi:10.1017/S0954579408000357

Cicchetti, D., & Handley, E. D. (2017). Methylation of the glucocorticoid receptor gene, nuclear receptor subfamily 3, group C, member 1 (NR3C1), in maltreated and nonmaltreated children: Associations with behavioral undercontrol, emotional lability/negativity, and externalizing and internalizing symptoms. *Development and Psychopathology, 29*(5), 1795–1806. doi:10.1017/S0954579417001407

Cicchetti, D., Handley, E. D., & Rogosch, F. A. (2015). Child maltreatment, inflammation, and internalizing symptoms: Investigating the roles of C-reactive protein, gene variation and neuroendocrine regulation. *Development and Psychopathology, 27*, 553–66. doi:10.1017/s0954579415000152

Cicchetti, D., Hetzel, S., Rogosch, F. A., Handley, E. D., & Toth, S. L. (2016a). An investigation of child maltreatment and epigenetic mechanisms of mental and physical health risk. *Development and Psychopathology, 28*(4 part 2), 1305–1318. doi:10.1017/S0954579416000869

Cicchetti, D., Hetzel, S., Rogosch, F. A., Handley, E. D., & Toth, S. L. (2016b). Genome-wide DNA methylation in 1-year-old infants of mothers with major depressive disorder. *Development and Psychopathology, 28*(4 part 2), 1413–1420. doi:10.1017/S0954579416000912

Cicchetti, D., & Lynch, M. (1993). Toward an ecological/transactional model of community violence and child maltreatment: Consequences for children's development. *Psychiatry, 56*, 96–118.

Cicchetti, D., & Lynch, M. (1995). Failures in the expectable environment and their impact on individual development: The case of child maltreatment. In D. Cicchetti & D. J. Cohen (Eds.), *Developmental psychopathology: Risk, disorder, and adaptation* (vol. 2, pp. 32–71). Wiley.

Cicchetti, D., & Rogosch, F. A. (1996). Equifinality and multifinality in developmental psychopathology. *Development and Psychopathology, 8*, 597–600.

Cicchetti, D., Rogosch, F. A., Gunnar, M. R., & Toth, S. L. (2010). The differential impacts of early physical and sexual abuse and internalizing problems on daytime cortisol rhythm in school-aged children. *Child Dev, 81*(1), 252–269. doi:10.1111/j.1467-8624.2009.01393.x

Cicchetti, D., Rogosch, F. A., & Toth, S. L. (1998). Maternal depressive disorder and contextual risk: Contributions to the development of attachment insecurity and behavior problems in toddlerhood. *Development and Psychopathology, 10*, 283–300.

Cicchetti, D., Rogosch, F. A., & Toth, S. L. (2000). The efficacy of toddler-parent psychotherapy for fostering cognitive development in offspring of depressed mothers. *Journal of Abnormal Child Psychology, 28*, 135–148. doi:10.1023/A:1005118713814

Cicchetti, D., Rogosch, F. A., & Toth, S. L. (2006). Fostering secure attachment in infants in maltreating families through preventive interventions. *Development and Psychopathology, 18*(3), 623–649. doi:10.1017/S0954579406060329. PMID: 17152394.

Cicchetti, D., & Sroufe, L. A. (1978). An organizational view of affect: Illustration from the study of Down's syndrome infants. In M. Lewis & L. Rosenblum (Eds.), *The development of affect* (pp. 309–350). Plenum Press.

Cicchetti, D., & Toth, S. L. (1992). The role of developmental theory in prevention and intervention. *Development and Psychopathology, 4*, 489–493.

Cicchetti, D., & Toth, S. L. (1998). The development of depression in children and adolescents. *American Psychologist, 53*, 221–241. doi:10.1037/0003-066X.53.2.221

Cicchetti, D., & Toth, S. L. (2009). The past achievements and future promises of developmental psychopathology: The coming of age of a discipline. *Journal of Child Psychology and Psychiatry, 50*(1-2), 16–25. doi:10.1111/j.1469-7610.2008.01979.x

Cicchetti, D., & Toth, S. L. (2015). Child maltreatment. In M. Lamb (Ed.), *Handbook of child psychology and developmental science*, 7th ed., vol. 3: *Socioemotional process*. (pp. 513–63). Wiley.

Cicchetti, D., & Toth, S. L. (2016). Child maltreatment and developmental psychopathology: A multilevel perspective. In D. Cicchetti (Ed.), *Developmental psychopathology*, 3rd ed. (vol. 3, Maladaptation and Psychopathology) (pp. 457–512). Wiley.

Cicchetti D., & Toth, S. L. (2017). Using the science of developmental psychopathology to inform child and adolescent psychotherapy. In J. R. Weisz & A, E. Kazdin (Eds.), *Evidence-based psychotherapies for children and adolescents* (pp. 484–500). Guilford.

Cicchetti, D., Toth, S. L., & Handley, E. D. (2015). Genetic moderation of interpersonal psychotherapy efficacy for low-income mothers with major depressive disorder: Implications for differential susceptibility. *Development and Psychopathology. 27*(1), 19–35. doi:10.1017/s0954579414001278

Cicchetti, D., & Tucker, D. (1994). Development and self-regulatory structures of the mind. *Development and Psychopathology, 6*, 533–549.

Cicchetti, D., & Valentino, K. (2007). Toward the application of a multiple-levels-of-analysis perspective to research in development and psychopathology. In A. S. Masten (Ed.),

*Multilevel dynamics in developmental psychopathology: The Minnesota symposia on child psychology* (vol. 34, pp. 243–284). Lawrence Erlbaum.

Cicchetti, D., & Wagner, S. (1990). Alternative assessment strategies for the evaluation of infants and toddlers: An organizational perspective. In S. Meisels & J. Shonkoff (Eds.), *Handbook of early intervention* (pp. 246–277). Cambridge University Press.

Cicchetti, D., & Walker, E. F. (Eds.). (2003). *Neurodevelopmental mechanisms in psychopathology.* Cambridge University Press.

Conradt, E., Measelle, J., & Ablow, J. C. (2013). Poverty, problem behavior, and promise: Differential susceptibility among infants reared in poverty. *Psychological Science, 24*(3), 235–242. doi:10.1177/0956797612457381

Courchesne, E., Chisum, H., & Townsend, J. (1994). Neural activity-dependent brain changes in development: Implications for psychopathology. *Development and Psychopathology, 6*(4), 697–722. https://doi.org/10.1017/S0954579400004740

Curtis, W. J., & Cicchetti, D. (2003). Moving research on resilience into the 21st century: Theoretical and methodological considerations in examining the biological contributors to resilience. *Development and Psychopathology, 15*(3), 773–810. doi:10.1017/s0954579403000373

Danese, A., Moffitt, T. E., Pariante, C. M., Ambler, A., Poulton, R., & Caspi, A. (2008). Elevated inflammation levels in depressed adults with a history of childhood maltreatment. *Archives of General Psychiatry, 65*(4), 409–415. doi:10.1001/archpsyc.65.4.409

Dawson, G., Grofer, L., Panagiotides, H., & Speiker, S. (1992). Infants of mothers with depressive symptoms: Electrophysiological and behavioral findings related to attachment status. *Development and Psychopathology,* 4, 67–80.

De Bellis, M. D. (2001). Developmental traumatology: The psychobiological development of maltreated children and its implications for research, treatment, and policy. *Development and psychopathology, 13*(3), 539–564. https://doi.org/10.1017/s0954579401003078

De Bellis, M. D. (2005). The psychobiology of neglect. *Child Maltreatment, 10*(2), 150–172. https://doi.org/10.1177/1077559505275116

Denckla, C. A., Cicchetti, D., Kubzansky, L. D., Seedat, S., Teicher, M., Williams, D. R., & Koenene, K. C. (2020). Interdisciplinary perspectives on psychological resilience: Review of progress, a critical appraisal, and research recommendations. *European Journal of Psychotraumatology, 11,* 1822064. doi:10.1080/20008198.2020.1822064

Drury, S. S., Gleason, M. M., Theall, K. P., Smyke, A. T., Nelson, C. A., Fox, N. A., & Zeanah, C. H. (2012). Genetic sensitivity to the caregiving context: The influence of 5httlpr and BDNF val66met on indiscriminate social behavior. *Physiological Behavior 106*(5), 728–735. doi:10.1016/j.physbeh.2011.11.014

Duncan, L. E., & Keller, M. C. (2011). A critical review of the first 10 years of candidate gene-by-environment interaction research in psychiatry. *American Journal of Psychiatry, 168*(10), 1041–1049. https://doi.org/10.1176/appi.ajp.2011.11020191

Edelman, G. M. (1987). *Neural Darwinism: The theory of neuronal group selection.* Basic Books.

Egeland, B., Carlson, E. A., & Sroufe, L. A. (1993). Resilience as process. *Development and Psychopathology,* 5, 517–528.

Egeland, B., Pinata, R., & Ogawa, J. (1996). Early behavior problems: Pathways to mental disorders in adolescence. *Development and Psychopathology, 8*(4), 735–749. doi:10.1017/S0954579400007392.

Ehrlich, K. B., Miller, G. E., Rogosch, F. A., & Cicchetti, D. (2020). Maltreatment exposure across childhood and low-grade inflammation: Considerations of cumulative exposure, timing, and sex differences. *Developmental Psychobiology, 63*(3), 529–537. https://doi.org/10.1002/dev.22031

Eisenberg, L. (1977). Development as a unifying concept in psychiatry. *British Journal of Psychiatry, 131,* 225–237.

Ellis, B. J., Abrams, L. S., Masten, A. S., Sternberg, R. J., Tottenham, N., & Frankenhuis, W. E. (2020). Hidden talents in harsh environments. *Development and Psychopathology,* 1–19. doi:10.1017/S0954579420000887.

Erikson, E. H. (1950). *Childhood and society.* Norton.

Fishbein, H. D. (1976). *Evolution, development and children's learning.* Pacific Palisades, California: Goodyear Publishing Co.

Garber, J., & Bradshaw, C. P. (2020). Developmental psychopathology and the research domain criteria: Friend or foe?, *Journal of Clinical Child & Adolescent Psychology, 49*(3), 341–352. doi:10.1080/15374416.2020.1753205

Garcia-Coll, C., Akerman, A., & Cicchetti, D. (2000). Cultural influences on developmental processes and outcomes: Implications for the study of development and psychopathology. *Development and Psychopathology, 12,* 333–356. doi:10.1017/s0954579400003059

Garmezy, N. (1974). The study of competence in children at risk for severe psychopathology. In E. J. Anthony & C. Koupernik (Eds.), *The child in his family: Vol. 3. Children at psychiatric risk* (pp. 77–97). Wiley.

Garmezy, N., & Rutter, M. (1983). *Stress, coping and development in children.* McGraw-Hill.

Garmezy, N., & Streitman, S. (1974). Children at risk: Conceptual models and research methods. *Schizophrenia Bulletin,* 9, 55–125.

Goodman, S. H., & Gotlib, I. H. (1999). Risk for psychopathology in the children of depressed mothers: A developmental model for understanding mechanisms of transmission. *Psychological Review, 106,* 458–490. doi:10.1037/0033-295X.106.3.458

Goodman, S. H., & Gotlib, I. H. (Eds.). (2002). *Children of depressed parents: Mechanisms of risk and implications for treatment.* APA Books.

Gottlieb, G. (1976). Conceptions of prenatal development: Behavioral embryology. *Psychological Review,* 83, 215–234.

Gottlieb, G. (1983). The psychobiological approach to developmental issues. In P. Mussen (Ed.), *Handbook of child psychology* (pp. 1–26). Wiley.

Gottlieb, G. (1991). Experiential canalization of behavioral development: Theory. *Developmental Psychology, 27,* 4–13.

Gottlieb, G. (1992). *Individual development and evolution: The genesis of novel behavior.* Oxford University Press.

Gottlieb, G. (2007). Probabilistic epigenesis. *Developmental Science, 10*(1), 1–11. doi:10.1111/j.1467-7687.2007.00556.x

Greenough, W., Black, J., & Wallace, C. (1987). Experience and brain development. *Child Development, 58,* 539–559.

Guild, D. J., Toth, S. L., Handley, E. D., Rogosch, F. A., & Cicchetti, D. (2017). Attachment security mediates the longitudinal association between child-parent psychotherapy and peer relations for toddlers of depressed mothers. *Development and Psychopathology, 29*(2), 587–600. doi:10.1017/S0954579417000207

Gunnar, M., & Quevedo, K. (2007). The neurobiology of stress and development. *Annual Review of Psychology, 58*, 145–173. doi:10.1146/annurev.psych.58.110405.085605

Hackman, D. A., Farah, M. J., & Meaney, M. J. (2010). Socioeconomic status and the brain: Mechanistic insights from human and animal research. *Nature Reviews. Neuroscience 11*(9), 651–659. doi:10.1038/nrn2897

Hammen, C. (2005). Stress and depression. *Annual Review of Clinical Psychology l, 1*, 293–319. doi:10.1146/annurev.clinpsy.1.102803.143938

Handley, E. D., Michl-Petzing, L. C., Rogosch, F. A., Cicchetti, D., & Toth, S. L. (2017). Developmental cascade effects of interpersonal psychotherapy for depressed mothers: Longitudinal associations with toddler attachment, temperament, and maternal parenting efficacy. *Development and Psychopathology, 29*(2), 601–615. doi:10.1017/S0954579417000219

Hanson, D. R., & Gottesman, I. I. (2007). Choreographing genetic, epigenetic, and stochastic steps in the dances of developmental psychopathology. In Masten, A. S. (Ed.), *Multilevel dynamics in developmental psychopathology: The Minnesota Symposia on Child Psychology* (vol. 34, pp. 27–43). Erlbaum.

Heckman, J. J. (2006). Skill formation and the economics of investing in disadvantaged children. *Science, 312*(5782), 1900–1902.

Holochwost, S. J., Wang, G., Kolacz, J., Mills-Koonce, W. R., Klika, J. B., & Jaffee, S. R. (2021). The neurophysiological embedding of child maltreatment. *Development and psychopathology, 33*(3), 1107–1137. https://doi.org/10.1017/S0954579420000383

Howe, G. W., Reiss, D., & Yuh, J. (2002). Can prevention trials test theories of etiology? *Development and Psychopathology, 14*, 673–694.

Ioannidis, K., Askelund, A. D., Kievit, R. A., & van Harmelen, A. L. (2020). The complex neurobiology of resilient functioning after childhood maltreatment. *BMC Medicine, 18*, 32. https://doi.org/10.1186/s12916-020-1490-7

Kaplan, B. (1967). Meditations on genesis. *Human Development, 10*, 65–87.

Kegel, C., Bus, A., & van IJzendoorn, M. H. (2011). Differential susceptibility in early literacy instruction through computer games: The role of the dopamine D4 receptor gene (DRD4). *Mind, Brain, and Education, 5*(2): 71–78. doi:10.1111/j.1751-228X.2011.01112.x

Kandel, E. R. (1999). Biology and the future of psychoanalysis: A new intellectual framework of psychiatry revisited. *American Journal of Psychiatry, 156*, 505–524.

Lenneberg, E. (1967). *Biological foundations of language*. Wiley.

Luthar, S. S., & Cicchetti, D. (2000). The construct of resilience: Implications for intervention and social policy. *Development and Psychopathology, 12*, 857–885. 10.1017/s0954579400004156

Luthar, S. S., Cicchetti, D., & Becker, B. (2000). The construct of resilience: A critical evaluation and guidelines for future work. *Child Development, 71*, 543–562. PMCID:PMC1885202, doi:10.1111/1467-8624.00164

Masten, A. S. (2007). Resilience in developing systems: Progress and promise as the fourth wave rises. *Development and Psychopathology, 19*(3), 921–930. doi:10.1017/S0954579407000442

Masten, A. S. (2014). *Ordinary magic: Resilience in development*. Guilford.

Masten, A. S., & Cicchetti, D. (2010). Developmental cascades. *Development and Psychopathology, 22*(3), 491–495. doi:10.1017/S0954579410000222

Masten, A. S., & Cicchetti, D. (2016). Resilience in development: Progress and transformation. In D. Cicchetti (Ed.), *Developmental psychopathology* (vol. 4, Risk, Resilience, and Intervention, 3rd ed.) (pp. 271–333). Wiley.

Mayr, E. (1964). The evolution of living systems. *Proceedings of the National Academy of Sciences, 51*, 934–941.

Mayr, E. (1988). *Toward a new philosophy of biology*. Harvard University Press.

Meaney, M. J. (2010). Epigenetics and the biological definition of gene x environment interactions. *Child Development, 81*(1), 41–79. doi:10.1111/j.1467-8624.2009.01381.x

Meyer, A. (1950–1952). *The collected papers of Adolph Meyer* (4 vols.). Johns Hopkins University Press.

Miller, N. E. (1995). Clinical-experimental interactions id the development of neuroscience: A primer for nonspecialists and lessons for young scientists. *American Psychologist, 50*(11), 901–911. https://doi.org/10.1037/0003-066X.50.11.901

Mussen, P. H. (1983). *Handbook of child psychology: History, theory, and methods*. Wiley.

O'Donnell, K. J., Chen, L., MacIsaac, J. L., McEwen, L. M., Nguyen, T., Beckmann, K., . . . Meaney, M. J. (2018). DNA methylome variation in a perinatal nurse-visitation program that reduces child maltreatment: A 27-year follow-up. *Translational Psychiatry, 8*(1), 15. doi:10.1038/s41398-017-0063-9

O'Donnell, K. J., & Meaney, M. J. (2020). Epigenetics, development, and psychopathology. *Annual Review of Clinical Psychology, 16*, 327–350. doi:10.1146/annurev-clinpsy-050718-095530

Palmer, A. R, Lakhan-Pal, S, & Cicchetti, D. (2019). Emotional development and depression. In V. LoBue, K. Perez-Edgar, & K. Buss (Eds.), *Handbook of emotional development* (pp. 695–748). Springer Nature Switzerland AG.

Pellmar, T. C., & Eisenberg, L. (Eds.). (2000). *Bridging disciplines in the brain, behavioral, and clinical sciences*. National Academy Press.

Pepper, S. (1942). *World hypotheses*. University of California Press.

Pickreign Stronach, E., Toth, S. L., Rogosch, F. A., & Cicchetti, D. (2013). Preventive interventions and sustained attachment security in maltreated children: A 12-month follow-up of a randomized controlled trial. *Development and Psychopathology, 25*(4pt1), 919–930. doi:10.1017/s0954579413000278

Post, R., Weiss, S., Leverich, G., George, M., Frye, M., & Ketter, T. (1996). Developmental psychobiology of cyclic affective illness: Implications for early therapeutic intervention. *Development and Psychopathology, 8*(1), 273–305. doi:10.1017/S0954579400007082

Post, R. M. (1992). Transduction of psychosocial stress into the neurobiology of recurrent affective disorder. *American Journal of Psychiatry, 149*, 999–1010. doi:10.1176/ajp.149.8.999

Reynolds, A. J., & Temple, J. A. (2006). *Impacts of the Chicago Child-Parent Centers on child and family development*. In Norman F. Watt et al. (Eds.), *The crisis in youth mental health: Critical issues and effective programs, vol. 4, early intervention programs and policies*. (pp. 229–249). Praeger.

Richters, J. E., & Cicchetti, D. (1993). Mark Twain meets DSM-III-R: Conduct disorder, development, and the concept of harmful dysfunction. *Development and Psychopathology, 5*, 5–29.

Risch, N., Herrell, R., Lehner, T., Liang, K. Y., Eaves, L., Hoh, J., Griem, A., Kovacs, M., Ott, J., & Merikangas, K. R. (2009). Interaction between the serotonin transporter gene (5-HTTLPR), stressful life events, and risk of depression: A meta-analysis. *JAMA, 301*, 2462–2471 (erratum in *JAMA* [2009 Aug 5] *302*(5), 492)

Romer, D., & Walker, E. F. (Eds.). (2007). *Adolescent psychopathology and the developing brain: Integrating brain and prevention science*. Oxford University Press. https://doi.org/10.1093/acprof:oso/9780195306255.001.0001

Rutter, M. (1979). Protective factors in children's responses to stress and disadvantage. In M. W. Kent & J. E. Rolf (Eds.), *Primary prevention in psychopathology: Social competence in children* (vol. 8, pp. 49–74). University Press of New England.

Rutter, M. (1986). Child psychiatry: The interface between clinical and developmental research. *Psychological Medicine, 16*, 151–160.

Rutter, M. (1987). Psychosocial resilience and protective mechanisms. *American Journal of Orthopsychiatry, 57*, 316–331. doi:10.1111/j.1939-0025.1987.tb03541.x

Rutter, M. (1988). Epidemiological approaches to developmental psychopathology. *Archives of General Psychiatry, 45*, 486–495.

Rutter, M. (1989). Pathways from childhood to adult life. *Journal of Child Psychology and Psychiatry, 30*, 23–51.

Rutter, M., & Garmezy, N. (1983). Developmental psychopathology. In E. M. Hetherington (Ed.), *Handbook of child psychology* (4th ed., vol. 4, pp. 774–911). Wiley.

Rutter, M., & Sroufe, L. A. (2000). Developmental psychopathology: Concepts and challenges. *Development and Psychopathology, 12*(3), 265–296. doi:10.1017/s0954579400003023

Sameroff, A. J. (2000). Developmental systems and psychopathology. *Development and Psychopathology, 12*, 297–312.

Sameroff, A. J., & Chandler, M. J. (1975). Reproductive risk and the continuum of caretaking casualty. In F. D. Horowitz (Ed.), *Review of child development research* (vol. 4, pp. 187–244). University Press of Chicago.

Santostefano, S. (1978). *A biodevelopmental approach to clinical child psychology: Cognitive controls and cognitive control therapy*. Wiley

Santostefano, S., & Baker, H. (1972). The contribution of developmental psychology. In B. Wolman (Ed.), *Manual of child psychopathology* (pp. 1113–1153). McGraw-Hill.

Shonkoff, J. P., Boyce, W. T., & McEwen, B. S. (2009). Neuroscience, molecular biology, and the childhood roots of health disparities: Building a new framework for health promotion and disease prevention. *JAMA, 301*(21), 2252–2259. doi:10.1001/jama.2009.754

Sroufe, L. A. (1989). Pathways to adaptation and maladaptation: Psychopathology as developmental deviation. In D. Cicchetti (Ed.), *Rochester symposium on developmental psychopathology: The emergence of a discipline* (vol. 1, pp. 13–40). Erlbaum.

Sroufe, L. A. (1990). Considering normal and abnormal together: The essence of developmental psychopathology. *Development and Psychopathology, 2*, 335–347.

Sroufe, L. A. (2007). The place of development in developmental psychopathology. In A. Masten (Ed.), *Multilevel dynamics in developmental psychopathology: Pathways to the future. The Minnesota Symposia on Child Psychology* (vol. 34, pp. 285–299). Erlbaum.

Sroufe, L. A., Egeland, B., Carlson, E., & Collins, W. A. (2005). *The development of the person: The Minnesota study of risk and adaptation from birth to adulthood*. Guilford.

Sroufe, L. A., Egeland, B., & Kreutzer, T. (1990). The fate of early experience following developmental change: Longitudinal approaches to individual adaptation in childhood. *Child Development, 61*, 1363–1373.

Sroufe, L. A., & Jacobvitz, D. (1989). Diverging pathways, developmental transformations, multiple etiologies, and the problem of continuity in development. *Human Development, 32*, 196–203.

Sroufe, L. A., & Rutter, M. (1984). The domain of developmental psychopathology. *Child Development, 55*, 17–29.

Staudinger, U. M. (2015). Images of aging: Outside and inside perspectives. *Annual Review of Gerontology and Geriatrics, 35*(1), 187–210. doi:10.1891/0198-8794.35.187

Sun, H., Kennedy, P. J., & Nestler, E. J. (2013). Epigenetics of the depressed brain: Role of histone acetylation and methylation. *Neuropsychopharmacology, 38*(1), 124–137. https://doi.org/10.1038/npp.2012.73

Szyf, M., & Bick, J. (2013). DNA methylation: A mechanism for embedding early life experiences in the genome. *Child Development, 84*(1), 49–57. doi:10.1111/j.1467-8624.2012.01793.x

Thelen, E., & Smith, L. B. (1998). Dynamic systems theories. In W. Damon & R. Lerner (Eds.), *Handbook of child psychology: Volume 1. Theoretical, models of human development* (pp. 563–634). Wiley.

Tomarken, A. J., Davidson, R. J., Wheeler, R. E., & Doss, R. C. (1992). Individual differences in anterior brain asymmetry and fundamental dimensions of emotion. *Journal of Personality and Social Psychology, 62*(4), 676–687. doi:10.1037//0022-3514.62.4.676

Toth, S. L., Gravener-Davis, J. A., Guild, D. J., & Cicchetti, D. (2013). Relational interventions for child maltreatment: Past, present, and future perspectives. *Development and Psychopathology, 25*(4 Pt 2), 1601–1617. doi:10.1017/S0954579413000795

Toth, S. L., Maughan, A., Manly, J. T., Spagnola, M., & Cicchetti, D. (2002). The relative efficacy of two interventions in altering maltreated preschool children's representational models: Implications for attachment theory. *Development and Psychopathology, 14*, 877–908. doi:10.1017/S095457940200411X. PMID: 12549708.

Toth, S. L., Pickreign Stronach, E. S., Rogosch, F. A., Caplan, R., & Cicchetti, D. (2011). Illogical thinking and thought disorder in maltreated children. *Journal of the American Academy of Child and Adolescent Psychiatry, 50*, 659–668. doi:10.1016/j.jaac.2011.03.002

Toth, S. L., Rogosch, F. A., Manly, J. T., & Cicchetti, D. (2006). The efficacy of toddler-parent psychotherapy to reorganize attachment in the young offspring of mothers with major depressive disorder. *Journal of Consulting & Clinical Psychology, 74*(6), 1006–1016. doi:10.1037/0022-006X.74.6.1006. PMID: 17154731.

Toth, S. L., Rogosch, F. A., Oshri, A., Gravener-Davis, J., Sturm, R., & Morgan-López, A. A. (2013). The efficacy of interpersonal psychotherapy for depression among economically disadvantaged mothers. *Development and Psychopathology, 25*(4 Pt 1), 1065–1078. https://doi.org/10.1017/S0954579413000370

Vachon, D. D., Krueger, R. F., Rogosch, F. A., & Cicchetti, D. (2015). Assessment of the harmful psychiatric and behavioral effects of different forms of child maltreatment. *JAMA Psychiatry, 72*(11), 1135–1142. doi:10.1001/jamapsychiatry.2015.1792

Von Bertalanffy, L. (1968). *General system theory: Foundations, development*. George Braziller.

Waddington, C. H. (1957). *The strategy of genes*. Allen & Unwin.

Waddington, C. H. (1966). *Principles of development and differentiation*. Macmillan.

Weiss, P. A. (1961). Deformities as cues to understanding development of form. *Perspectives in Biology and Medicine, 4*, 133–151.

Weiss, P. (1969). *Principles of development*. Hafner.

Weisz, J. R., & Kazdin, A. E. (Eds.). (2017). *Evidenced-based psychotherapies for children and adolescents*. Guilford.

Werner, E., & Smith, R. (1982). *Vulnerable but invincible: A study of resilient children*. In. McGraw-Hill.

Werner, H. (1948). *Comparative psychology of mental development*. International Universities Press.

Werner, H., & Kaplan, B. (1963). *Symbol formation*. Wiley.

Widom, C. S., Czaja, S. J., & Paris, J. (2009). A prospective investigation of borderline personality disorder in abused and neglected children followed up into adulthood. *Journal of Personality Disorders, 23*(5), 433–446. doi:10.1521/pedi.2009.23.5.433

Zigler, E., & Glick, M. (1986). *A developmental approach to adult psychopathology*. Wiley.

PART II

# Major Clinical Syndromes

# CHAPTER 7

# Generalized Anxiety Disorder, Panic Disorder, Social Anxiety Disorder, and Specific Phobia

Richard E. Zinbarg, Alexander L. Williams, Amanda M. Kramer, *and* Madison R. Schmidt

## Introduction

In this chapter, we cover several *DSM-5* anxiety disorders, including generalized anxiety disorder (GAD), panic disorder (PD), social anxiety disorder (SAD), and Specific Phobia (SP). Whereas obsessive-compulsive disorder (OCD) and posttraumatic stress disorder (PTSD) were classified as anxiety disorders in earlier *DSM* editions, they were moved into new groupings in *DSM-5* and will be covered in later chapters in this volume. Two other diagnoses (separation anxiety disorder, selective mutism) that are rare in adults and were not classified with the other anxiety disorders in earlier *DSM* editions were moved into the anxiety disorders grouping in *DSM-5* but will not be covered in this chapter.

We begin by describing anxiety and fear, the core constructs that define and differentiate these diagnoses. Following Barlow (2002), *anxiety* is a future-oriented mood state associated with preparation for possible harm, whereas *fear* is an alarm response when danger is perceived to be present. Put differently, fear—or panic (we use the terms interchangeably)—involves a triggering of the fight-flight-or-freeze (FFF) mechanism when danger is perceived to be present, whereas anxiety involves a priming of (i.e., simultaneous excitatory and inhibitory input to) the FFF mechanism when danger is perceived to be possible at a later point in time (Zinbarg, 1998). Viewed from this perspective, there are both overlapping and distinctive features between anxiety and panic. Anxiety and panic overlap in that they both involve perception of danger and excitatory input to the FFF mechanism. However, they are different in their temporal aspects, given that anxiety is future-oriented and fear is an alarm response to present danger. They are also different in that anxiety involves simultaneous inhibitory input to the FFF mechanism, whereas panic involves purely excitatory input to this mechanism.

*DSM-5* distinguishes two types of panic attacks: unexpected and expected. If the individual is aware of a cue or trigger at the time of the attack, then the attack is expected; if not, the attack is unexpected. Whereas panic attacks of some sort are ubiquitous across the anxiety disorders and even in major depression (Craske et al., 2010), panic/fear is not central to the *definition* of GAD. In contrast, anxiety is central to the definition of each anxiety disorder, including PD/A, SAD, and SP—disorders in which fear plays an important role. For example, the primary distinction between the group of nonclinical panickers—individuals who experience recurrent panic attacks—and those with PD/A is that those with PD/A experience anticipatory anxiety about their attacks, whereas those with nonclinical panic do not (Telch et al., 1989).

The central features of PD in *DSM-5* are (1) recurrent, unexpected panic attacks and (2) persistent

| **Abbreviations** | |
|---|---|
| AS | Anxiety sensitivity |
| BIS | Behavioral inhibition system |
| DD | Dysthymic disorder |
| GAD | Generalized anxiety disorder |
| MDD | Major depressive disorder |
| PD | Panic disorder |
| PD/A | Panic disorder with agoraphobia |
| PE/E | Positive emotionality/extraversion |
| SAD | Social anxiety disorder |
| SP | Specific Phobia |

worry about having attacks or the development of significant, maladaptive behavioral changes designed to avoid having attacks. Note that if all the individual's attacks are of the expected variety, a diagnosis other than PD would be made, perhaps SAD, SP, PTSD, or OCD. A common complication of PD is agoraphobia—the fear and avoidance of situations from which it would be difficult to leave or get help in the event of a panic attack. However, in recognition of the data from some epidemiological studies suggesting a substantial population of individuals with agoraphobia and without panic symptoms (e.g., Wittchen et al., 2008), *DSM-5* has reverted to identifying agoraphobia as an independent diagnosis, as it had been in *DSM-III*. Thus, someone with PD who develops fairly extensive agoraphobia receives two *DSM-5* diagnoses (PD and agoraphobia), whereas in *DSM-III-R*, *DSM-IV*, and *DSM-IV-TR* they would have received a single diagnosis (PD with or without agoraphobia; PD/A). This chapter includes results published before the *DSM-5*, which therefore pertain to the pre-*DSM-5* single diagnosis convention (PD/A).

In *DSM-5* the cardinal feature of GAD is excessive, uncontrollable worry about numerous life circumstances, accompanied by at least three common manifestations of anxiety, like muscle tension, sleep disturbance, or irritability.

*DSM-5* divides SP into five subtypes: animal (fear cued by animals or insects, such as dogs, snakes, or spiders), natural environment (cued by an object in the natural environment, such as heights, thunderstorms, or water), blood-injury-injection (cued by seeing blood, injury, or receiving an injection), situational (cued by specific situations, such as driving, enclosed places, or flying), and other (cued by other triggers, such as a fear of falling down, a fear of costumed characters such as clowns, or emetophobia—the fear of vomiting). To receive a *DSM-5* diagnosis of SP, the phobic cue must almost invariably provoke an immediate fear response and the fear must be excessive and associated with either avoidance of the phobic cue or endurance of exposure to that cue with intense fear. In addition, fear must be associated with some functional impairment or significant distress about the fear before diagnosing a SP. Some individuals are judged by diagnosticians to exhibit excessive fear even though they themselves do not recognize their fear as excessive. Thus, the judgment of excessiveness in *DSM-5* has been made a clinician judgment rather than a self-judgment (as it had been in *DSM-IV-TR*).

The key feature of SAD is persistent and marked fear of social situations in which one might be judged or evaluated by others. Exposure to feared social situation(s) must almost invariably provoke an immediate fear response, and the fear must be associated with either avoidance of the phobic cue or endurance of exposure to it with intense fear or anxiety. *DSM-IV-TR* included the additional criterion that the individual must recognize the fear as excessive, but, as with SP, in *DSM-5* the excessiveness is a clinician judgment.

However, there is some controversy in the field as to whether the different *DSM* anxiety disorder diagnoses truly represent distinct categories. The alternative view is that the different *DSM* anxiety disorders represent variations of a broader syndrome that differs superficially and solely at the descriptive level in terms of the content of apprehension (Andrews et al., 1990; Brown & Barlow, 2009; Tyrer, 1990). Even if this alternative view proves to be invalid, theory and empirical evidence in this area suggests a great deal of overlap in the factors and processes involved in the development and maintenance of GAD, PD/A, SAD, and SP. Thus, we focus primarily on them as a group and their common etiological and maintenance factors rather than presenting largely redundant analyses of each diagnosis separately.

## Epidemiology: Prevalence, Course and Comorbidity

Most recent estimates of lifetime prevalence rates are based on *DSM-IV* criteria from a reanalysis of the National Comorbidity Survey Replication (NCS-R) and Adolescent Supplement (NCS-A) (Kessler et al., 2012) and of the National Epidemiologic Survey on Alcohol and Related Conditions (NESARC; Grant & Dawson, 2006). Table 7.1 summarizes many of these results. As seen in Table 7.1, these disorders tend to be more prevalent in women (e.g., Kessler et al., 2012).

SP is the most prevalent of the anxiety disorders (Kessler et al., 2012; Stinson et al., 2007). There is some inconsistency in average age of onset, ranging between 5 to 9 (Stinson et al., 2007) and 15 to 17 years (Kessler et al., 2012). For adults, the mean number of fears reported by an individual is approximately three, with the most common subtypes of SPs being natural environment, situational, animal, and blood-injection injury (Stinson et al., 2007). SP is highly comorbid with PD, PD/A, SAD, and GAD (Stinson et al., 2007).

**Table 7.1** Epidemiology for Specific Phobias (SP), social anxiety disorder (SAD), generalized anxiety disorder (GAD), panic disorder (PD), and panic disorder with agoraphobia (PD/A), by gender and age cohort

|  | SP | SAD | GAD | PD/A |
|---|---|---|---|---|
| 12-month prevalence (%) | 7.1–12.1 | 2.8–7.4 | 2–2.1 | 2.1–2.4 |
| Lifetime prevalence (%) | 9.4–15.6 | 5–10.7 | 4.1–4.3 | 3.8–5.1 |
| **Lifetime prevalence by age** | | | | |
| Adolescent (13–17) (%) | 20 | 8.6 | 2.2 | 2.3 |
| Adult (18–64) (%) | 13.8 | 13 | 6.2 | 5.2 |
| Older adult (65+) (%) | 6.8 | 6.3 | 3.3 | 2.1 |
| **Lifetime prevalence by gender** | | | | |
| Adolescent (13–17) | | | | |
| Female (%) | 23* | 11.2* | 2.8 | 2.5 |
| Male (%) | 17.7 | 6.2 | 1.6 | 2.1 |
| Adult (18–64) | | | | |
| Female (%) | 17.5* | 14.2* | 7.7* | 7* |
| Male (%) | 9.9 | 11.8 | 4.6 | 3.3 |
| Older adult (65+) | | | | |
| Female (%) | 9.1* | 7.1 | 4.8* | 2.5 |
| Male (%) | 3.6 | 5.1 | 1.3 | 1.6 |
| Mean age of onset | 5–9, 15–17 | 15 | 30 | 28–32 |
| Median years delay to treatment[a] | 20 | 16 | 9 | 10 |
| Comorbid diagnoses[b] | 3.4 | 3.5 | 3.8 | 4.5 |
| Comorbid personality disorder (%) | 38.3 | 61.0 | 60.6 | 44.1–69.4 |

[a]Median years delay to treatment are estimated reported by Wang et al. (2005).

[b]Comorbid diagnoses represent average number of both mental and physical conditions in the National Comorbidity Survey Replication reported by Gadermann et al. (2012).

* Indicates statistically significant gender difference.

SAD is the second most common of the anxiety disorders covered in this chapter (Grant, Hasin, Blanco, et al., 2005; Kessler et al., 2012). Furthermore, there is some evidence to suggest between-group racial and ethnic differences, with a higher percentage of White Americans being diagnosed than Black/African, Hispanic/Latino, and Asian Americans (Asnaani et al., 2010), but a higher percentage among Native Americans compared with White Americans (Grant, Hasin, Blanco et al., 2005). The hazard rate for onset of SAD was bimodal, with a first peak at 5 years and a second one at 13–15 years according to the NESARC (Grant, Hasin, Blanco et al., 2005). The most common fears reported are those related to performance-based situations (e.g., public speaking, participating in class, performing in front of others). SAD is highly comorbid with other mood, anxiety, and personality disorders (particularly avoidant personality disorder; Grant, Hasin, Stinson et al., 2005). The most common comorbid anxiety disorders are PD, SP, and GAD (Grant, Hasin, Stinson et al., 2005).

GAD is also fairly common (Grant, Hasin, Stinson et al., 2005; Kessler et al., 2012). Although mean age of onset is around 30 years of age across epidemiological studies (Grant, Hasin, Stinson et al., 2005; Kessler et al., 2012), evidence suggests a bimodal distribution in the age of onset, with many individuals with GAD recalling onset in early childhood (Campbell et al., 2003; Hoehn-Saric et al., 1993). White Americans are more likely to be diagnosed than Black/African, Hispanic/Latino, and Asian Americans (Asnaani et al., 2010; Grant, Hasin, Stinson et al., 2005). Of those with comorbid disorders, 71.4% meet criteria for a mood disorder, and 90% have a comorbid anxiety disorder, the most common being PD and SAD (Grant, Hasin, Stinson et al., 2005).

The occurrence of panic attacks (which often do not warrant a diagnosis) is high, with a lifetime prevalence of about 23% (Kessler et al., 2006). PD/A, by contrast, is less common (Kessler et al., 2012). Separating PD Agoraphobia (PDA) from PD without agoraphobia (PD), PD/A is less common than PD (Grant et al., 2006). The mean age of onset for PD/A was slightly earlier than that for PD without agoraphobia, at 28 versus 32 years according to the NESARC (Grant et al., 2006); however, this estimate is notably higher than the estimate of 23 years provided by the NCS-R/A (which collapsed PD and PD/A into one category) (Kessler et al., 2006). Furthermore, individuals with PD/A were more likely to seek treatment for the disorder than those with PD. Individuals with PD/A also report higher rates of comorbidity with mood disorders as well as other anxiety disorders, including SAD, SP, and GAD, compared to those with PD (Grant et al., 2006; Kessler et al., 2006).

## Factor Analytic Models of Anxiety Disorders
### The Need for Factor Analyses

*DSM* categorizes all anxiety disorders into a single class that is separate from other disorder classes (e.g., mood disorders). Within this anxiety disorder category, specific disorders represent a second level of differentiation (e.g., GAD, SP) and subtypes of these disorders a third level of differentiation (e.g., animal and blood-injury-injection SPs). However, this taxonomy is based on shared phenomenological features rather than on empirically observed correlations among these disorders and does not reflect certain empirical findings, such as the high rates of comorbidity of disorders belonging to different classes (e.g., anxiety and mood disorders).

To address this limitation of the *DSM*, research has been dedicated to analyzing correlational patterns among these disorders or their symptoms using factor analysis. In factor analysis, disorders and/or symptoms are grouped together based not on their *DSM* categories, but on how closely the disorders and/or symptoms are correlated to one another and to the presumed factor common to them. Though *DSM-5* continues to adopt a rational classification scheme, our knowledge of the factor structure of unipolar depression, anxiety disorders, and their symptoms could lead to a more empirically informed classification system.

### THE BROADEST LEVEL: A SINGLE GENERAL FACTOR

Studies examining the structure of depression and anxiety symptoms and disorders have largely converged on certain key principles (Watson, 2005). A vast amount of evidence supports a hierarchical conceptualization wherein broad latent factors are thought to account for the covariation between disorders. At the broadest level, a single general factor (labeled General Distress, Negative Affect, or Internalizing) is posited to account for the covariation *among* anxiety disorders (e.g., Zinbarg & Barlow, 1996), as well as *between* anxiety disorders and depressive disorders. For instance, the tripartite model (Clark & Watson, 1991) identified a nonspecific general distress factor, marked by symptoms of high negative affect (e.g., irritability, restlessness, interpersonal sensitivity) that was shared by both anxiety and depression. The Negative Affect factor is thought to be the state manifestation of a trait/temperament variable—alternatively referred to as *negative emotionality* or *neuroticism*—that is associated with a tendency toward a broad range of negative mood states such as guilt, hostility, anxiety, and sadness (Watson & Clark, 1984). This nonspecific symptom dimension is consistent with factor-analytic analyses of diagnostic data from 10 *DSM* diagnoses showing that anxiety and depressive disorders are best grouped into a single category of "internalizing" disorders (Krueger, 1999). Therefore, it is unsurprising that a general factor similar to Negative Affect has continued to be identified in most of the prominent factor analytic models since the tripartite model (e.g., Kotov et al., 2017; Mineka et al., 1998; Prenoveau et al., 2010; Watson, 2005; Zinbarg & Barlow, 1996).

### THE NARROWER LEVEL: HOW MANY FACTORS?

In addition to this single general factor (e.g., Negative Affect), most prominent models suggest that additional, narrower factors are necessary to address the heterogeneity in symptoms of anxiety and depression. They disagree, however, on the number and nature of the narrower factors. Some models include only two narrow factors, such as Fear and Anxious-Misery (e.g., Krueger, 1999; Watson, 2005). Others, however, include several relatively disorder-specific narrow factors (e.g., Mineka et al. 1998; Zinbarg & Barlow, 1996).

## Two Factors: The Tripartite Model, Kreuger's Model, and the Quantitative Structural Model

One class of models posits that there are only two lower-level factors beneath the general distress (e.g., Negative Affect or Internalizing) factor. These two factors most frequently correspond to a "Fear" factor (e.g., Fear or Physiological Hyperarousal) characterized by intense physical symptoms of fear as in PD or SPs, and a "Misery" factor (e.g., Anxious-Misery or Positive Affect), characterized by more pervasive anxiety, sadness, or lack of positive emotions as in depression or GAD.

The first of these models, the tripartite model (Clark & Watson, 1991), proposed two narrower factors that were meant to differentiate anxiety and depressive disorders (see Figure 7.1). The first, Positive Affect, was thought to be unique to depressive disorders. This factor was thought to be the state manifestation of a temperamental sensitivity to positive stimuli that results in positive affective states such as feeling cheerful, lively, and optimistic. Those low in Positive Affect experience diminished interest and pleasure in otherwise pleasant activities (e.g., feeling withdrawn from others, feeling slowed down). Importantly, Negative Affect and Positive Affect do *not* represent two ends of a single dimension; rather, they are thought to be two orthogonal dimensions (Watson & Tellegen, 1985) that arise from separate biological systems (e.g., Thayer, 1989; Watson et al., 1999) and can operate separately from each other (e.g., Gold et al., 1995).

The second narrower factor, made up of symptoms characterized by Physiological Hyperarousal, was thought to be unique to anxiety. This factor contains items representing somatic manifestations of anxiety and panic (e.g., feeling dizzy, experiencing shortness of breath). Therefore, beneath the general Negative Affect factor, there was one factor specific to depression and one specific to anxiety.

However, the tripartite model has certain limitations. It was suggested that a single anxiety-specific factor was not sufficient to account for the heterogeneity among the anxiety disorders (Mineka et al., 1998; Zinbarg & Barlow, 1996). For instance, Physiological Hyperarousal was found to relate specifically to PD and PTSD (Brown & McNiff, 2009), rather than to all the anxiety disorders as a group (Brown et al., 1998). Some researchers have proposed that Anxious Apprehension, a future-oriented mood state marked by high levels of worry about future negative outcomes, might represent an anxiety-specific factor, separate from Physiological Hyperarousal (Barlow, 1991). Supporting this claim, studies have demonstrated that Physiological Hyperarousal and Anxious Apprehension are separable dimensions, and researchers have hypothesized that Anxious Apprehension is mostly linked to GAD (Nitschke et al., 2001). However, others have speculated that Anxious Apprehension may instead relate to all anxiety disorders, as well as to depression, and therefore be thought of as a facet of Negative Affect (Watson, 1999). More research is

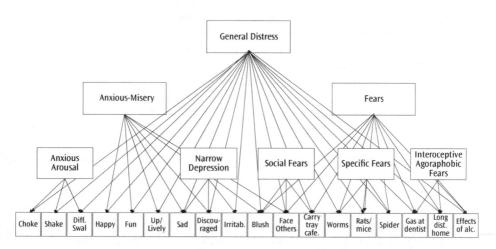

**Figure 7.1** Prenoveau et al.'s (2010) tri-level model. For clarity of presentation, only 18 of the 67 item descriptions were included. Item numbers can be found in the original paper. Choke, Felt like I was choking; Shake, Was trembling or shaking; Diff. Swal, Had trouble swallowing; Happy, Felt really happy; Fun, Felt like I was having a lot of fun; Up/Lively, Felt really up or lively; Irritab., Felt irritable; Sad, Frequency/intensity of sadness; Discouraged, Felt discouraged; Blush, "I fear I may blush when I am with others"; Face others, "I would get tense if I had to sit facing other people on a bus or a train"; Carry tray café, "I would get tense if I had to carry a tray across a crowded cafeteria"; Worms, Fear of worms; Rats/Mice, Fear of rats or mice; Spider, Fear of spiders; Gas at dentist, Fear of getting gas at a dentist; Long dist. home, Fear of going long distances from home alone; Effects of alc, Fear of feeling the effects of alcohol.

needed to clarify the role of Anxious Apprehension as an anxiety-specific dimension. In addition to the oversimplification of the anxiety-relevant factor, low Positive Affect was linked to SAD in addition to major depressive disorder (MDD), suggesting that this factor was not entirely unique to depression (Brown et al., 1998; Chorpita et al., 2000). These discrepancies suggested that the two narrower factors of the tripartite model may have been too few.

That said, later models suggested that two factors may indeed be appropriate, but not along clear lines between anxiety and depression. In his analysis of 10 common mental disorders including MDD, dysthymic disorder (DD), PD, agoraphobia, SAD, SP, GAD, alcohol dependence, drug dependence, and antisocial personality disorder, Krueger (1999) found that the mood and anxiety disorders clustered under a single general Internalizing factor. Within the Internalizing factor, there were two additional factors that further distinguished the disorders: a Fear factor (made up of PD, agoraphobia, SAD, and SP) and an Anxious-Misery factor (made up of MDD, DD, and GAD).

Similarly, the quantitative structural model (Watson, 2005) specified two factors relevant to anxiety under its general factor. The first was a Distress factor, made up of MDD, DD, GAD, and PTSD, that was similar to Krueger's (1999) Anxious-Misery factor. Citing Kreuger's work, the Anxious-Misery factor was referred to as Distress by Watson to signify the large amount of general distress variance characterizing these disorders. The second was a Fear factor (made up of PD, agoraphobia, SAD, and SP) that was nearly identical to Kreuger's Fear factor. Unlike the two lower-level factors of the tripartite model, these factors do not neatly distinguish anxiety from depression, as GAD is clustered with the depressive disorders. Instead, they separate disorders characterized by present-moment fear from those characterized by pervasive negative affect.

This hierarchical structure with a broad Internalizing factor and two correlated lower-level factors of Distress and Fear was replicated by Vollebergh et al. (2001) using *DSM-IV* diagnostic data from the Netherlands Mental Health Survey and Incidence Study and by Slade and Watson (2006) using *DSM-IV* and *ICD-10* disorders in an Australian epidemiological sample. More recently, Eaton et al. (2013) found support for the two-subfactor conceptualization of internalizing disorders using the NESARC dataset. The structure was replicated across two waves of assessments, 3 years apart, for both men and women. Importantly, Fear at Wave 1 significantly predicted Fear (but not Distress) at Wave 2, and Distress at Wave 1 significantly predicted Distress (but not Fear) at Wave 2, suggesting that Fear and Distress are two unique pathways toward developing or maintaining internalizing disorders.

### More Factors

Though one class of prominent models posits that there are only two narrower factors in addition to the general factor, another class argues that two is not enough to represent the heterogeneity of the anxiety disorders and depression. For example, Zinbarg and Barlow (1996) examined the factor structure of anxiety symptom measures and found six narrow factors that differentiate the specific anxiety disorders and depression from each other: Generalized Dysphoria, Social Anxiety, Agoraphobia, Fear of Fear, Obsessions and Compulsions, and Simple Fears. Furthermore, they performed discriminant function analyses to examine the relationships of these six narrow dimensions and a general Negative Affect dimension with *DSM-III-R* diagnoses. They found that the general Negative Affect factor distinguished each of the anxiety-disordered groups from a no mental disorder control group. Furthermore, the Fear of Fear, Agoraphobia, Social Anxiety, and Obsessions and Compulsions factors provided the bases for discriminating among the patient groups.

Mineka et al. (1998) proposed the integrative hierarchical model in which each disorder consists of a common Negative Affect component and a unique component that differentiates it from other disorders. Moreover, not all disorders contain the same level of common factor variance. Particularly, MDD and GAD are characterized by a larger amount of Negative Affect variance than other anxiety disorders, such as SP and PD/A (Kessler et al., 2005; also see Watson et al., 2005, for more detail). Also, the specificity of symptoms that differentiate disorders is relative, so that some disorder-specific symptoms could be shared by more than one disorder. This explained the finding that low Positive Affect was linked to SAD as well as MDD and the finding that Physiological Hyperarousal was not common to all anxiety disorders but related more specifically to PD/A as well as to PTSD.

### Integration: The Tri-Level Model and HiTOP
#### THE TRI-LEVEL MODEL

Integrating the strengths of both the two-factor and multifactor models, Prenoveau et al. (2010)

included factors at three levels of breadth (see Figure 7.1). Thus, they posited a tri-level model in which intermediate breadth factors like Fear and Anxious-Misery make up a second level and the disorder-specific narrow factors make up a third level. At the narrowest level of the hierarchy, there were five group factors. Four of these related to anxiety: Anxious Arousal, Social Fears, Specific Fears, and Interoceptive/Agoraphobic Fears. Additionally, Narrow Depression emerged as a depression-related narrow group factor. There were two factors of intermediate breadth that were each loaded on by items that loaded on several of the narrowest factors. The first intermediate-breadth factor was labeled Anxious-Misery with loadings from some Narrow Depression items (e.g., hopelessness), some Social Fears items (e.g., felt self-conscious), and some items with negative loadings reflecting high Positive Affect (e.g., felt really happy). A second intermediate breadth factor was labeled Fears, with loadings from Social Fears, Interoceptive/Agoraphobic Fears, and Specific Fears items. A General Distress factor (loaded on by all symptoms) was obtained as the broadest factor.

By accounting for both intermediate- and narrow-level factors, the tri-level model was able to account for both the symptoms that are common to many disorders and those that are more unique to a disorder or cluster of disorders. In fact, in a conceptual replication of the tri-level model, Naragon-Gainey et al. (2016) found that each level of the tri-level model accounted for substantial variance in the data and that the model provided a superior fit relative to more parsimonious competing models. Naragon-Gainey et al. also found that patient impairment was associated with all three levels of the model, suggesting each level has meaningful variance independent of the other two. As would be expected given the broad nature of the general factor, comorbidity within patients was most strongly associated with the general factor. Finally, at the narrow level, convergent and discriminant validity were found such that the narrow factors strongly related to their associated disorder and not to other disorders (e.g., the Specific Fears factor correlated with SP but not PD diagnoses).

In an unpublished conceptual replication and extension, Zinbarg et al. (2022) found that the tri-level model could be extended to include clinician-rated measures of symptoms. This suggests that General Distress does not entirely reflect method variance. It also suggests that the tri-level model is not purely a model of self-report symptoms, but of symptoms more broadly.

### THE HIERARCHICAL TAXONOMY OF PSYCHOPATHOLOGY

Recently, the HiTOP Consortium put forth the Hierarchical Taxonomy of Psychopathology (HiTOP; Kotov et al., 2017), a theoretical structural model of psychopathology (see Figure 7.2). Like the tri-level model, HiTOP is a hierarchical model with factors that become narrower at each level. The broadest level (*superspectra*) is made up of dimensions that may be common to all psychopathology. The second level (*spectra*) includes several broad categories of disorders (including Somatoform, Internalizing, Thought Disorder, Disinhibited Externalizing, Antagonistic Externalizing, and Detachment). The third level (*subfactors*) includes intermediate-level groupings (such as Sexual Problems, Eating Pathology, Fear, Distress, and Mania under Internalizing). The fourth level (*syndromes/disorders*) includes specific disorders (such as SAD, SP, PD/A, and OCD under Fear), the fifth level (*components*) includes various symptom components and maladaptive traits, and the sixth level (*symptoms*) includes specific signs and symptoms. Thus, HiTOP is more inclusive than other models discussed earlier in that it includes a broader range of disorders and adds factor levels for increased specification. The Internalizing spectrum including the Fear and Distress subfactors and their associated syndromes/disorders are most relevant to the anxiety disorders and map closely to the broad, intermediate, and narrow factors of the tri-level model.

At the time of this writing, there are no published empirical tests of the Internalizing spectrum, though papers published on the tri-level model (e.g., Prenoveau et al., 2010) provide support for this spectrum given its close alignment with the tri-level model. Though it is not without criticism (see Wittchen & Beesdo-Baum, 2018), HiTOP is becoming one of the most cited models of psychopathology.

### SUMMARY

To summarize, there is consensus that an overarching factor representing high negative affect—often labeled Internalizing or General Distress—is shared by all anxiety disorders and their symptoms. This factor also accounts for the empirical overlap between anxiety and depression. Beneath this general factor, there is support for two intermediate-level factors—Fear, which underlies SP, SAD, PD, and agoraphobia, and Anxious-Misery/Distress,

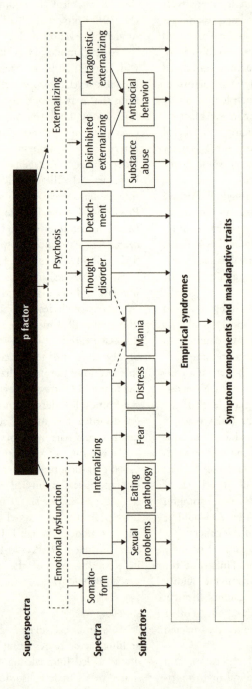

**Figure 7.2** The current Hierarchical Taxonomy of Psychopathology (HiTOP) Model. Symptom components and maladaptive traits form the base of the HiTOP model. Higher-level dimensions of the model, such as spectra and subfactors, were empirically derived from an accumulation of factor analytic evidence (see Kotov et al., 2017). Dashed lines indicate that the relation or dimension depicted is included on a provisional basis pending additional data collection.

which underlies unipolar depression and GAD. Finally, there is evidence that we can identify narrow factors that may provide the basis for differentiating individual disorders from each other. However, we have not yet reached consensus about the exact number and nature of these narrow factors.

## Etiology and Maintenance Models and Factors

### Temperament and Personality

Anxiety disorders show links to personality which can in turn inform models of the origins of these disorders. A number of models have been proposed to account for these links (e.g., Ormel et al., 2013; Krueger & Tackett, 2003). The *vulnerability* model suggests that personality traits are risk factors for anxiety disorders. In contrast, the *common cause* model holds that disorders are extreme manifestations of personality traits. In the *scar* model, the experience of psychopathology impacts personality. Finally, the *pathoplasty* model proposes that personality modifies the course or expression of a disorder. Longitudinal studies of premorbid assessments of personality and subsequent onsets of anxiety disorders provide a good design for testing the etiological role of personality characteristics (e.g., Clark et al., 1994).

Temperament is an important component of personality that, as discussed in more detail below, is relevant for anxiety disorders. Different theorists define temperament in different ways (see Goldsmith et al., 1987). We define temperament as relatively stable individual differences in emotionality that emerge early in life and have a biological basis.

#### NEUROTICISM

The term "neuroticism" is used to label a set of covarying personality descriptors (such as fretful, moody, insecure, self-critical, and envious)—identified through factor analyses of self-report personality measures—thought to represent a dimension of emotional instability (e.g., Costa & McCrae, 1987; Eysenck, 1970). In fact, neuroticism is thought to be a partially heritable sensitivity to experience negative emotions and is hypothesized to be a common diathesis (i.e., risk factor) for all of the anxiety disorders and MDD (e.g., Eysenck, 1967; Gray & McNaughton, 2000; Griffith et al., 2010; Zinbarg & Yoon, 2008). Following Shackman et al. (2016), Mineka et al. (2020) distinguished between several paths through which neuroticism may confer vulnerability for psychopathology. The *stably elevated negative affect hypothesis* states that neuroticism raises risk for symptom exacerbation via negative affect that is elevated in almost all situations. In contrast, the *stress amplification hypothesis* holds that neuroticism interacts with stressors to generate psychopathology. Mineka et al. reported greater support for the stably elevated negative affect hypothesis but further research is needed to compare the relative importance of these paths in the etiology onset of anxiety disorders.

Neuroticism has been shown to have robust cross-sectional associations with internalizing disorders, including anxiety (e.g., Bienvenu et al., 2004; Griffith et al., 2010; Rosellini & Brown, 2011; Zinbarg et al., 2010). Longitudinal evidence has also shown that neuroticism predicts the onset of anxiety disorders (e.g., Zinbarg et al., 2016). Uliaszek et al. (2009) evaluated the differential predictive ability of the anxiety facet of neuroticism (which overlaps with anxiety symptoms) and a General Neuroticism Factor (GNF) that was common to all neuroticism items. They found that the GNF was associated with a latent Anxiety symptom factor beyond the anxiety facet of neuroticism (Uliaszek et al., 2009), demonstrating that the association between neuroticism measures and anxiety symptoms cannot be entirely attributed to item overlap. Zinbarg et al. (2016) reported similar findings at the diagnostic level.

There is limited evidence for a reciprocal relationship between neuroticism and anxiety symptoms. Jylhä et al. (2009) reported that change in anxiety symptoms accounted for only a small fraction of what baseline neuroticism accounted for in follow-up neuroticism in a multiple regression model. A comprehensive study comprised of healthy participants and those with current or past emotional disorders revealed that among participants with remitted disorders, scar effects on neuroticism were present 2 years later but these effects were not significant 4 years later (Spinhoven et al., 2013). Similarly, in a sample of highly neurotic older adolescents, Williams et al. (2021) found that vulnerability effects of neuroticism were greater in magnitude than scar effects. Scar effects were nonsignificant when examined with the symptom dimension of General Distress, the general, latent factor common to all anxiety and depression symptoms.

#### BEHAVIORAL INHIBITION

Another construct that has been implicated in the etiology of anxiety disorders is behavioral inhibition (BI). This was described by Kagan and colleagues (1984) as a specific behavioral response style elicited by novel situations among children as young as 21 months. This response style, observed in about 15–20% of young children, was defined as "an early appearing syndrome characterized by shyness, withdrawal, avoidance, uneasiness, fear of unfamiliar situations, people, objects and events" (Turner et al., 1996). BI was found to be moderately stable from age 21 months to 7.5 years and was linked to physiological correlates (e.g., higher heart rate in response to stressors), thus representing a temperamental construct (see Fox et al., 2005, for a review).

Rosenbaum and colleagues (1988, 1991) found a higher incidence of anxiety disorders among parents with behaviorally inhibited children than among those with uninhibited children. More directly, BI is associated with risk for developing SAD and avoidant personality disorder among children (Biederman et al., 2001) and SAD among adolescents (Hayward et al., 1998). Indeed, Clauss and Blackford (2012) conducted a meta-analysis of seven primary studies and reported a sevenfold increase in the odds of developing SAD in later childhood among those classified as behaviorally inhibited in childhood.

BI is thought by many to be a developmental precursor to and facet of neuroticism (e.g., Turner et al., 1996; Zinbarg et al., 2010). Indeed, Gray's (1982; Gray & McNaughton, 2000) construct of BI system (BIS) reactivity, which he hypothesized as underlying neuroticism (as described earlier), relates conceptually to Kagan et al.'s (1984) behavioral description of BI in children. Unfortunately, few studies have empirically tested the association between the two. One of the challenges in doing so is that neuroticism has been primarily examined in adults, whereas Kagan's BI model has been rooted in studies using child samples. Zinbarg et al. (2016) shed light on this question, finding that subscales of the Behavioral Inhibition Scale (Carver & White, 1994) loaded significantly on a GNF defined by neuroticism scales as well as related cognitive vulnerability measures (e.g., Dysfunctional Attitudes Scale; Weissman & Beck, 1978). Zinbarg et al.'s measurement model shows that there is substantial shared variance between traditional neuroticism and behavioral inhibition items.

### ANXIETY SENSITIVITY

A third trait that has received a great deal of attention in etiological theories of anxiety disorders is anxiety sensitivity (AS; Reiss et al., 1986). AS represents individual differences in the fear of fear, hypothesized to arise from beliefs that symptoms of anxiety or fear will cause illness, embarrassment, or additional anxiety (Reiss et al., 1986). For example, an individual with high AS may be more likely to misinterpret a pounding heart as an impending heart attack. These negative beliefs in turn amplify existing anxiety levels, resulting in a cycle that increases risk for panic attacks and anxiety disorders.

AS is commonly assessed using the Anxiety Sensitivity Index (ASI; Reiss et al., 1986). Using this measure, researchers have shown that AS is associated with anxiety disorders among adults (Olatunji & Wolitzky-Taylor, 2009), children, and adolescents (Noël & Francis, 2011). Several longitudinal studies have also found evidence that AS prospectively predicts panic attacks and PD/A symptoms, as well as other anxiety disorders (e.g., GAD, SAD) (e.g., Hayward et al., 2000; Li & Zinbarg, 2007; Schmidt et al., 1999; Schmidt et al., 2006; Schmidt et al., 2008). These findings provide support for AS being a risk factor for developing anxiety disorders. Among the anxiety disorders, AS has been most extensively linked to vulnerability for PD/A (McNally, 2002).

Factor-analytic studies using the ASI have found a hierarchical structure with a general factor and three group factors: (a) Physical Concerns involving the fear of physical symptoms, (b) Social Concerns involving the fear of publicly observable symptoms, and (c) Mental Incapacitation Concerns (e.g., Rodriguez et al., 2004; Zinbarg et al., 1997, 1999). Studies examining the unique role of these facets in predicting panic have yielded inconsistent results. Schmidt et al. (1999) studied Air Force cadets and found that of the three AS facets, only Mental Incapacitation Concerns significantly predicted spontaneous panic attacks during a 5-week period, when statistically adjusting for trait anxiety and history of panic. Consistent with these findings, Li and Zinbarg (2007) found that Mental Incapacitation Concerns, but not the other two facets, uniquely predicted panic onset over a 1-year period among college undergraduates. Other studies have implicated alternative facets in the etiology of panic.

For instance, Hayward et al. (2000) reported that only Physical Concerns predicted the onset of four-symptom panic attacks over a 4-year period among high school students. Results from Jurin and Biglbauer (2018) showed that Physical Concerns was the only significant AS facet that predicted PD/A symptoms over a span of 3 years in a healthy student sample. These findings are consistent with a recent cross-sectional analysis that compared AS facet elevations in a clinical sample assessed for the presence of anxiety disorders. In that study, Physical Concerns was elevated in outpatients with only PD/A relative to those with only MDD, SAD, GAD, or OCD (Baek et al., 2019).

Zinbarg et al. (2016) found that AS shares substantial variance with neuroticism and other cognitive vulnerability indicators. They found evidence for an AS factor in addition to a broader neuroticism factor on which the AS facets also loaded. Thus, it appears that relationships between BI, AS, and neuroticism are best described by a hierarchical structure in which AS and BI measures represent facets of vulnerability toward anxiety disorders that also share some variance with a General Neuroticism Factor. Naragon-Gainey and Watson (2018) showed that AS uniquely accounted for variance (between 9% and 20%) in symptoms of several emotional disorders (PD/A, SAD, MDD, and PTSD) after adjusting for neuroticism. That is, AS, unlike several other vulnerability factors examined in this study (experiential avoidance, intolerance of uncertainty), provided incremental validity for some, but not all, emotional disorders. However, one limitation from that study was its cross-sectional nature. Zinbarg et al. examined unique effects of AS facets prospectively and found that only Mental Incapacitation Concerns was uniquely associated with an increased risk of developing PD (and, in a perplexing fashion, was also associated with a decreased risk of developing MDD). More research is needed into the incremental *predictive* validity of AS.

### POSITIVE EMOTIONALITY/EXTRAVERSION

Although research on personality risk factors for the anxiety disorders has largely focused on traits related to Negative Emotionality (e.g., neuroticism, BI, and AS, as described earlier), there is increasing interest in the risk associated with low levels of traits related to Positive Emotionality (PE), most notably extraversion. Extraversion is generally considered to be a higher-order dimension that subsumes trait PE along with sociability facets (e.g., Watson & Clark, 1997; but see Smillie et al., 2012). To explicitly emphasize both of these facets, we will refer to this higher-order trait as positive emotionality/extraversion (PE/E).

The relative focus on risk factors associated with Negative Emotionality versus PE/E is attributable in part to early structural models of the emotional disorders. As already mentioned, the tripartite model (Clark & Watson, 1991) posited that high Negative Emotionality is common across the emotional disorders, whereas low PE/E distinguishes depressive from anxiety disorders. One disconfirmation of the tripartite model predictions was that SAD has also consistently been linked to low PE/E (e.g., Brown et al., 1998; Kashdan, 2007). Thus, structural models were updated to account for this discovery (e.g., Mineka et al., 1998), and more attention has since been devoted to studying low PE/E as a risk factor for at least some anxiety disorders.

The cross-sectional research linking low PE/E to SAD generally suggests that the magnitude of the inverse association is significant but weaker than that with depression (see Watson & Naragon-Gainey, 2010). Interestingly, there is evidence that the *facets* of PE/E may differentially relate to the symptoms of social anxiety and depression. For example, one study identified four lower-order facets of PE/E: PE, sociability, ascendance, and fun-seeking (Naragon-Gainey et al., 2009). In this study, it was found that social anxiety was negatively related to all four facets, whereas depression was strongly related only to low PE and also more modestly with sociability.

Less attention has been devoted to the relations between PE/E and the remaining anxiety disorders. However, there is some evidence that low PE/E may be associated—alone and/or in interaction with high neuroticism—with other anxiety disorders. For example, findings from a large meta-analysis revealed that nearly all of the anxiety disorders, with the possible exception of the SPs, were associated with lower PE/E in addition to elevated neuroticism (Kotov et al., 2010). These studies are consistent with the hypothesis that low PE/E may confer risk for the anxiety disorders covered in this chapter, particularly SAD, and perhaps least likely the SPs. However, a number of factors limit the conclusions that can be drawn and highlight directions for future work. The overwhelming majority of available studies are cross-sectional; prospective longitudinal work is sorely needed to determine directionality. As for higher-order traits, most studies do not account for the shared variance of trait PE/E with neuroticism, despite evidence that neuroticism is both a strong predictor of psychopathology and a correlate of PE/E (see Kotov et al., 2010). At the lower-order level, analyses are needed to determine if the specific facets of PE/E differentially relate to the different anxiety disorders.

A final consideration pertains to the study not only of low PE/E but also of personality risk factors more broadly: it will be important to distinguish between trait and state variance in putatively "trait" measures to avoid their contamination by the state dimension. Evidence indicates that psychological constructs consist, to varying degrees, of both stability and change (see Roberts & DelVecchio, 2000). Advances in longitudinal analysis (e.g., Cole et al., 2005; Hamaker et al., 2015; Kenny & Zautra, 1995; Steyer & Schmitt, 1994) enable isolation of each of these components. Teasing apart traits and states will enhance confidence in the conclusions drawn regarding the associations between traits and disorders by minimizing the possibility that it is actually the state dimension—rather than the trait dimension—that is largely responsible for the observed associations with disorders.

## Biology
### BEHAVIOR GENETICS

Behavior genetics (BG) studies reveal that anxiety disorders are heritable (e.g., Domschke & Reif, 2012; Smoller, 2016). Multivariate BG studies—BG studies that focus on several disorders simultaneously rather than on a single disorder—have been pioneered by Kendler and colleagues (e.g., Hettema et al., 2005; Kendler et al., 2003). These can potentially answer the question of whether any of the anxiety disorders share a genetic vulnerability or whether they each have unique genetic bases. In general, these studies point to genetic factors that largely correspond to the two subfactors of Internalizing that emerged from the phenotypic factor analyses described earlier. That is, these studies reported evidence for two genetic factors within the anxiety disorders and MDD. The first is loaded on by MDD and GAD and is characterized as a vulnerability to Anxious-Misery disorders; the second is loaded on by PD/A and SP and is characterized as a vulnerability to Fear disorders (e.g., Kendler et al., 2003). Interestingly, these two genetic factors are moderately positively correlated, which is consistent with a second-order genetic factor common to all the anxiety disorders and MDD (Kendler et al., 2003; for a review, see Purves al., 2020).

The existence of a genetic factor common to all the anxiety disorders and MDD is also consistent with research on the genetic factors associated with neuroticism. Multivariate BG studies have shown that the genetic factor associated with neuroticism overlaps substantially with the genetic vulnerability to all the anxiety disorders and MDD (e.g., Andrews et al., 1990; Hettema, Neale, et al., 2006; Hettema et al., 2004). Thus, neuroticism appears to be the phenotype associated with the genotype that confers common vulnerability to all the anxiety disorders and MDD. Whereas BG studies tell us that there is a heritable—and therefore biological—component of the anxiety disorders, in the next three sections we turn to studies of molecular genetics, brain lesions and genetic engineering in animals, and human neuroimaging that shed light on the specific biological substrates and genes involved in vulnerability to the anxiety disorders.

### MOLECULAR GENETICS

Much evidence indicates abnormalities in serotonin (5-HT) systems' functioning in patients with MDD and the anxiety disorders (Hariri & Holmes, 2006). In addition, many medications effective in treating MDD and the anxiety disorders are known to affect 5-HT systems and transmission (Hariri & Holmes, 2006). That the 5-HT system is also involved in the regulation of various forms of negative affect including hostility, anxiety, and fear (e.g., Grabe et al., 2005), implies a link between 5-HT systems and neuroticism—the trait that overlaps substantially with the genotype for anxiety disorders and major depression.

One particular polymorphism related to 5-HT systems that has been the focus of a lot of molecular genetics research is the serotonin transporter-linked polymorphism (5-HTTLPR). 5-HTTLPR refers to an insertion/deletion polymorphism in the promoter region of the serotonin transporter gene, *SLC6A4*, that yields a transcriptionally less efficient short (*S*) allele and a relatively more efficient long (*L*) allele (Heils et al., 1996). Evidence supports a gene by environment (G×E) interaction effect in depression where individuals with the *S* allele report greater depression under increasing stress relative to *L/L* homozygotes (Karg et al., 2011; Vrshek-Schallhorn et al. 2014).

There has not been as much research examining associations of the 5-HTTLPR gene with anxiety disorders as there has been with MDD. In the only relevant study that we are aware of, the 5-HTTLPR gene did not significantly moderate the effects of stressful life events on risk for GAD (Kendler et al., 2005). However, knockout strains of mice lacking the 5-HTTLPR gene demonstrate evidence of elevated anxiety (for a review, see Hariri & Holmes, 2006). Also, meta-analyses have indicated a small but significant association between the 5-HTTLPR gene and "avoidance traits" such as neuroticism (e.g., Munafò et al., 2005; Schinka et al., 2004). Taken together, these findings suggest that the 5-HTTLPR gene may play a role in anxiety disorders.

There have also been some molecular genetics studies implicating a role for genes *other* than the 5-HTTLPR gene in anxiety disorders. For example, motivated by the observation that a gamma-aminobutyric acid (GABA) receptor is the site of action for the anxiolytic effects of the benzodiazepines and barbiturates, Hettema, An, and colleagues (2006) studied associations between genes involved in the production of glutamic acid decarboxylase—an enzyme responsible for synthesizing GABA from glutamate—and common genetic risk for anxiety disorders, major depression, and neuroticism. They found that variations in one of these glutamic acid decarboxylase genes may contribute to susceptibility to anxiety disorders and major depression. Similarly, Thoeringer et al. (2009) found an association between the severity of panic attacks and genetic variation in a polymorphism involved in the production of the GABA transporter. However, Pham et al. (2009) failed to detect associations between GABA receptor genes and common genetic risk for anxiety disorders, major depression, and neuroticism. In addition, the researchers who reported the glutamic acid decarboxylase gene and GABA transporter genes emphasized that their findings need to be replicated in independent samples. Thus, these findings are very preliminary, but they are also very exciting and suggest that further studies of the glutamic acid decarboxylase gene and GABA transporter gene are warranted.

Finally, whereas large-scale genome-wide association studies (GWASs) of anxiety disorders have lagged behind that of other major psychiatric diagnoses, some have recently begun to appear (e.g., Levey et al., 2020; Purves et al., 2020; for a review, see Smoller, 2020). These GWAS studies have implicated several genetic loci in anxiety disorders. Examples include PDE4B, a gene previously implicated in schizophrenia; GAD2, which encodes a GABA gene implicated in mouse models of anxiety; SATB1 and SATB1-ASI, an antisense gene (i.e., a DNA strand that a cell uses as a template for producing messenger RNA), which regulate transcription and chromatin structure of several other genes involved in neuronal development; and CRHR1, the corticotropin-releasing hormone receptor gene, a key component of the hypothalamic-pituitary-adrenal axis function associated with anxiety and stress responses.

Reminiscent of the multivariate BG results pioneered by Kendler and colleagues (e.g., Hettema et al., 2005; Kendler et al., 2003), Levey et al. (2020) also conducted analyses of data from a wide range of GWASs and found a widespread genetic correlation between anxiety and many other psychiatric and nonpsychiatric problems. Other GWASs have reported similar patterns (Smoller, 2020). Much work remains to be done, however, as it is likely that many genetic loci contribute to vulnerability to anxiety disorders (and other diagnoses), and we need to better understand the pathways that link these genes to anxiety disorders phenotypes (Smoller, 2020).

### ANIMAL LESION STUDIES

Jeffrey Gray's model of the neuropsychology of anxiety uses as its starting point the behavioral effects of the antianxiety drugs (Gray, 1982; Gray & McNaughton, 2000). Gray synthesized the voluminous literature on the effects of the antianxiety drugs in animals by hypothesizing that antianxiety drugs exert their effects by modulating the output of the BIS. The BIS is described as responding to signals of punishment or signals of frustrative nonreward (but not to punishment or frustrative nonreward itself) and as having three major outputs: an increase in arousal, BI, and negative cognitive bias. By comparing the effects of the antianxiety drugs to the effects of brain lesions, Gray (1982) originally proposed that the septohippocampal system (SHS) is the anatomical substrate of the BIS. Gray and McNaughton (2000) expanded the neuroanatomical seat of anxiety to include the interactions of the SHS system with the amygdala. Gray's model spans multiple levels of analysis, including personality. Thus, according to this model, individual differences in reactivity of the BIS; that is, the SHS (and its interactions with the amygdala) underlie the closely related traits of anxiety and neuroticism.

There are two major projections to the SHS: one noradrenergic that originates in the locus coeruleus and the other serotonergic that originates in the raphe nucleus (Gray & McNaughton, 2000). Thus, the discoveries described above that link the 5-HTTLPR gene with anxiety (in 5-HTTLPR knockout mice), neuroticism, and MDD are consistent with Gray's model. Indeed, several predictions regarding the anxiety disorders and MDD can be derived from Gray's model, and the evidence to date is largely supportive of each (for a review, see Zinbarg & Yoon, 2008).

## HUMAN NEUROIMAGING

A great deal of basic functional magnetic resonance imaging (fMRI) research on fear in healthy human participants has been conducted. Much of this research was motivated by animal studies, which have reliably identified the amygdala as being a necessary brain structure in the acquisition and expression of conditioned fear (e.g., Davis, 1998; LeDoux, 1995, 2000). Several fMRI studies with healthy human participants have found the amygdala to be involved in human fear conditioning as well (e.g., LaBar et al., 1998; Phelps & LeDoux, 2005; Whalen, 1998). Other studies with healthy human participants have extended this research by showing the amygdala to be activated by more subtle fear-related stimuli, such as pictures of fearful facial expressions—even when the fearful expressions have been masked so that the participants are not aware of them—and uncertain threat (e.g., Hur et al., 2020; Phelps & LeDoux, 2005; Whalen, 1998). Though more limited, some basic fMRI research with healthy humans has focused on areas other than the amygdala that may be involved in anxiety or fear. For example, Somerville et al. (2010) conducted an fMRI study with healthy participants that was motivated by the animal research by Davis (1998) implicating the amygdala in fear responses and the bed nucleus of the striaterminalis (BNST) in anxiety. Interestingly, the BNST receives projections from the ventral hippocampus (Lee & Davis, 1997) and thus might be considered part of the SHS. Hur et al. (2020) found the BNST is active in both certain threat (i.e., fear) and uncertain threat (i.e., anxiety) conditions (for reviews, see Fullana et al., 2016, and Chavanne & Robinson, 2021). Somerville et al. (2010) found that activity in the BNST correlated with individual differences in trait anxiety levels while participants were engaged in continuous processing of potential signals of threat, much as we would expect if the SHS underlies trait anxiety and neuroticism, as hypothesized by Gray (1982; Gray & McNaughton, 2000).

There have also been several fMRI studies of participants with anxiety disorders. Compared with findings in control participants, greater activation of the amygdala has been found in patients with GAD (McClure et al., 2007; Monk et al., 2008; Nitschke et al., 2009), SAD (Birbaumer et al., 1998; Etkin & Wager, 2007; Evans et al., 2008), PD/A (van den Heuvel et al., 2005; for a related case study, see Pfleiderer et al., 2007), and SP (Etkin & Wager, 2007). There are also at least two fMRI studies implicating SHS-related structures in anxiety disorders. For instance, Bystritsky et al. (2001) found increased activity relative to controls in the hippocampus and the anterior cingulate—a structure which receives projections from the hippocampus—in patients with PD/A. Similarly, McClure et al. (2007) found increased activity in the anterior cingulate in patients with GAD compared with that in controls.

### Conditioning

J. B. Watson and Rayner (1920) hypothesized that SPs are intense, classically conditioned fears that develop when a neutral stimulus is paired with a traumatic event. They demonstrated this process in their famous experiment in which Little Albert, a young boy who did not show fear of a white rat to begin with, acquired an intense fear of rats after hearing a frightening gong paired with the presence of a white rat. The gong was said to be a unconditioned stimulus (US) and the fear an unconditioned response (UR) and then a conditioned response (CR). This study ushered in an era in which conditioning approaches were the dominant empirically grounded theoretical perspective on anxiety disorders.

That era continued until the 1970s, but such approaches have been widely criticized since then (e.g., Mineka, 1985; Rachman, 1978, 1990). Many of these criticisms focused on the apparent inability of conditioning approaches to account for the diversity of factors involved in the origins of anxiety disorders. More recently, however, a resurgence of interest in conditioning approaches has occurred as they have incorporated complexity predicted by contemporary conditioning theory and research (e.g., Bouton et al., 2001; Mineka and Zinbarg, 1996; Zinbarg & Mineka, 2007).

## DIRECT CONDITIONING

Öst and Hugdahl (1981) asked phobic patients to recall how they acquired their phobic fears. Almost 60% of the patients endorsed direct learning experiences. Given the prevalence of direct conditioning experiences in the etiology of phobic fears, researchers have developed tools to examine these processes.

Researchers rely on direct fear conditioning protocols as a model for understanding the onset and maintenance of clinically significant fears (Lonsdorf et al., 2017). The most common direct conditioning paradigm focuses on differential responding between two initially neutral conditional stimuli (CS). During the acquisition phase, one of the CS is repeatedly paired with an aversive stimulus (e.g., an electric shock). The other CS is never associated with an aversive stimulus, serving as the safety signal. Participants then undergo an extinction phase wherein they are exposed to both CS in the absence of aversive stimulation. Defensive responding can be measured in a number of ways, including by self-report and psychophysiological methods.

By instigating mild fears in humans with and without anxiety disorders, researchers have found evidence for maladaptive fear conditioning patterns in anxiety-disordered samples. Duits et al. (2015) reported anxiety-disordered groups respond more defensively to the safety cue relative to controls during the acquisition phase. Anxiety-disordered groups also tended to resist extinction to the danger cue.

A proliferation of complex conditioning designs have appeared that purport to more closely approximate the learning processes observed in anxiety disorders. For instance, the process of fear generalization, which is implicated in the expansive scope of worries observed in GAD, can be studied by introducing new CSs which differ in terms of their visual similarity to the original CSs. In this way, their threat value is ambiguous, unlike that of the original CSs. Lissek et al. (2014) reported evidence for increased overgeneralization of learned fear to generalization stimuli in patients with GAD relative to healthy controls. Similarly, earlier work (Lissek et al., 2010) showed that PD patients were more susceptible to overgeneralization relative to nondisordered controls.

### VICARIOUS CONDITIONING

One criticism of early conditioning approaches was that many phobics do not appear to have had any relevant history of *direct* classical conditioning. To account for the origins of fears and SPs in these individuals, clinicians have long speculated that vicarious conditioning (i.e., simply observing others experiencing a trauma or behaving fearfully) could be sufficient for some fears and SPs to develop. Indeed, retrospective studies have found evidence consistent with this idea, for PD/A, SAD, and SP (e.g., Bruch & Heimberg, 1994; Öst & Hugdahl, 1981; Rapee & Melville, 1997; see Muris & Merckelbach, 2001).

The work of Mineka and her colleagues on a primate model showed that strong and persistent fears can be learned rapidly through observation (e.g., Cook et al., 1985). A particularly fascinating finding is that vicarious conditioning occurred simply through watching videotapes of models behaving fearfully (Cook & Mineka, 1990), suggesting that humans are also susceptible to acquiring fears vicariously through movies and television.

There is now a burgeoning literature on vicarious conditioning in humans (e.g., Golkar et al., 2015; Olsson et al., 2016). The typical human vicarious fear conditioning protocol (see Haaker et al., 2017) involves video presentations of a stranger receiving aversive stimulation in the context of a particular CS. Participants are then presented with the CSs from the observation phase directly on a computer screen and their physiological or subjective responses are recorded. Existing research suggests that direct and vicarious conditioning are governed by similar psychobiological systems (Debiec & Olsson, 2017; Lindström et al., 2018; cf. Esser et al., 2020).

We are unaware of data linking individual differences in vicarious conditioning to anxiety disorder diagnoses but some evidence suggests that vicarious conditioning could play a role in the acquisition of SPs and other anxiety disorders. Selbing and Olsson (2019) reported that healthy participants scoring higher on trait anxiety showed more difficulty determining the threat value of a safe versus threatening cue. Trait anxiety, in turn, is elevated in those with anxiety or depressive disorders (Knowles & Olatunji, 2020) and has sometimes been implicated in compromised CS discrimination in direct conditioning experiments (Sjouwerman et al., 2020). However, Williams and Conway (2022) did not find evidence that vicarious threat learning was correlated with common or specific emotional disorder symptom dimensions in a sample of undergraduates. Thus, more work is needed in this area.

### SOCIAL REINFORCEMENT AND INSTRUCTIONAL LEARNING

Direct social reinforcement and verbal instruction are also likely to play a role in the acquisition of anxiety disorders. Ehlers (1993) found that patients with PD/A, individuals with infrequent panic, and patients with other anxiety disorders reported that they received more parental encouragement for sick-role behavior during their childhood experiences of panic-like symptoms (e.g., "Take care of yourself and avoid strenuous activities") than did nonanxious controls. When anxious children discuss potentially threatening situations with their parents, such discussions have been found to strengthen the anxious children's avoidant tendencies (Barrett et al., 1996). Experimental research confirms that providing healthy participants with contingency information (i.e., that a CS will signal an aversive outcome) before direct encounters with CSs can instill robust fear responses (Mertens et al., 2018). In addition, fear can intensify when verbal instruction is augmented with direct contingency experience (Mertens et al., 2016), suggesting that fear learning pathways can operate synergistically.

## SELECTIVE ASSOCIATIONS

A second criticism of early conditioning models of the acquisition of SPs and anxiety disorders is their equipotentiality assumption. That is, early conditioning models predicted that fears, SPs, and anxiety would be acquired to any random group of objects and stimuli associated with traumatic outcomes. However, clinical observations show that people are much more likely to have fears of snakes, water, heights, enclosed spaces, elevated heart rate, and other people than they are of bicycles, guns, or cars. This is remarkable given that, today, the latter objects are at least as likely to be associated with trauma as the stimuli that commonly trigger anxiety in individuals with anxiety disorders. To explain the nonrandom distribution of phobic objects, Seligman (1971) hypothesized that primates are evolutionarily prepared to rapidly associate certain kinds of objects (such as snakes, spiders, water, heights) with aversive events, as there should have been a selective advantage for primates who rapidly or strongly acquired fears of such objects or situations. The term *prepared fears* refers to those fears that are not truly inborn or innate but which are very easily acquired and/or especially resistant to extinction.

Preparedness theory has been tested in a series of human conditioning experiments conducted by Öhman and his colleagues. Consistent with predictions, they found superior conditioning using slides of snakes and spiders or of angry faces as fear-relevant (FR) CSs, and mild shock as the unconditioned stimulus (US), compared to what is found using more fear-irrelevant (FI) CSs such as slides of flowers, mushrooms, electric outlets, or neutral or happy faces (e.g., Öhman & Dimberg, 1978; Öhman et al., 1985; Öhman & Mineka, 2001). Other studies have also shown that with FR-CSs (but not with FI-CSs) conditioning can even occur using subliminal presentations of the CSs (i.e., CSs that cannot be consciously identified; e.g., Esteves et al., 1994; Öhman & Soares, 1998). Such results may help explain the irrationality of SPs; that is, a person can claim to "know" rationally that a SP object or social situation is safe and still experience anxiety that is nonconsciously activated.

Cook and Mineka (1989, 1990) demonstrated that observer monkeys can easily acquire fears of FR stimuli (e.g., a toy snake or a toy crocodile) but not of FI stimuli (e.g., flowers or a toy rabbit). These observer monkeys had no previous exposure to any of the FR or FI stimuli before participating in these experiments. Thus, whereas recent critiques have raised some challenges for preparedness theory (Coelho et al., 2019), the results reported by Cook and Mineka strongly support the role of evolutionary factors in the greater conditionability of FR than FI stimuli (Mineka & Öhman, 2002).

## UNCONTROLLABILITY AND UNPREDICTABILITY

A third criticism of early conditioning models of the acquisition of SPs and anxiety disorders is that they do not explain why many individuals who undergo traumatic experiences do not develop an anxiety disorder (e.g., Mineka & Zinbarg, 1996; Rachman, 1990, 2010). That is, many nonphobics retrospectively report having had traumatic experiences in the presence of some potentially phobic object without having acquired a SP (e.g., Poulton & Menzies, 2002).

From the perspective of a modern conditioning approach, however, these observations of resilience in the face of trauma can be easily accommodated. For example, several different features of conditioning events themselves can have a strong impact on how much fear is acquired. Far less fear is conditioned, for instance, when the aversive event is escapable than when it is inescapable (e.g., Mineka et al., 1984).

Perceptions of uncontrollability are a likely source of individual differences not only in the acquisition of SPs but also in the other anxiety disorders. For example, animal research has shown that uncontrollable (but not controllable) electric shock increases social submissiveness (e.g., Williams & Lierle, 1986). In addition, animal studies (e.g., Uhrich, 1938) of repeated social defeat (an uncontrollable stressor) show that it also leads to increased submissiveness. Moreover, repeated social defeat in animals produces many of the classic "learned helplessness" effects usually associated with uncontrollable shock, including escape deficits (Hebert et al., 1998) and exaggerated-fear CRs (Williams & Scott, 1989). Williams and colleagues concluded from such findings that the deleterious effects of social defeat are probably mediated by perceptions of uncontrollability. Such research and theorizing suggest that perceptions of uncontrollability are likely to play a role in the etiology of SAD. Indeed, cross-sectional evidence documents a moderate to strong association between generalized perceptions of uncontrollability and SAD (e.g., Kennedy et al., 1998).

Sanderson et al. (1989) conducted a fascinating study demonstrating the role of perceptions of controllability in panic attacks experienced by those with PD/A. Patients with PD/A underwent a panic provocation procedure involving the breathing of air with higher than normal levels of carbon dioxide ($CO_2$). The patients were told that if the experience became too unpleasant, if and when a light in the room came on, they could turn a dial to reduce the amount of $CO_2$ they were breathing. The patients were then randomly assigned to either a condition in which the light actually came on during the $CO_2$ inhalation (perceived control) or to a condition in which the light never came on (no perceived control). Eighty percent of the participants in the no-perceived control group reported experiencing a panic attack during the inhalation compared with only 20% in the perceived control group (despite the fact that the only participant in the study who actually attempted to turn the dial was in the no perceived control group).

More recent experimental work also supports the notion that controllability impacts the strength of acquired fear responses. Hartley and colleagues (2014) reported an effect of an escapable versus inescapable stressor on subsequent fear extinction and recovery. In the escapable stressor condition, participants were able to escape or avoid the delivery of electrical stimulation in a computer task. Those in the inescapable stressor condition, however, were not able to evade electrical stimulation through their task-related actions. Instead, they received the same number of shocks with the same timing as their yoked participant in the escapable condition. When tested 1 week later, participants in the inescapable stressor condition saw diminished fear extinction and more recovery of fear responses to the CS signaling threat relative to the safety signal. Thus, the experience of an unrelated, inescapable stressor in one setting may predispose one to develop extinction-resistant fear responses in another.

## TEMPERAMENT/PERSONALITY AND CONDITIONING

Another part of the explanation of resilience in the face of trauma may involve temperamental or personality variables. Theorists ranging from Pavlov (1927) to Eysenck (1967) and Gray (1982; Gray & McNaughton, 2000) have hypothesized that individual differences on variables such as trait anxiety or neuroticism are related to the speed and strength of conditioning and thus play a role in the origin of anxiety disorders. There is experimental evidence demonstrating that individuals high on trait anxiety have difficulty discriminating between CSs that signal threat versus safety (e.g., Gazendam et al., 2013; Sjouwerman et al., 2020). Other evidence, however, has not supported the role of trait anxiety (e.g., Arnaudova et al., 2013; Morriss et al., 2016). Lonsdorf and Merz (2017) reviewed fear conditioning studies that examined the association between putative vulnerability measures like neuroticism and trait anxiety and fear conditioning responses. They found that, in most studies, across physiological and subjective response measure types, there were not significant associations between neuroticism or trait anxiety and fear learning patterns. However, an important limitation of their review is that it did not use meta-analytic methods to synthesize findings across studies, and some individual studies have found significant results (e.g., Zinbarg & Mohlman, 1998). A quantitative synthesis of this literature is needed to provide a firmer conclusion regarding the role of personality in conditioning.

In particular, research designs that account for overlap among vulnerability measures could improve our understanding of risk for conditioning abnormalities. Sjouwerman et al. (2020), for instance, used a structural equation modeling approach to capture the overlap between trait anxiety, neuroticism, and intolerance of uncertainty in a general factor that was labeled Negative Emotionality. The modeling strategy allowed analysis of the unique effects of the risk measures. In this study, there was a unique effect of trait anxiety on physiological CS discrimination, adjusting for the overlap between trait anxiety and neuroticism. The overarching Negative Emotionality factor did *not* predict individual differences in a fear learning factor defined by CS discrimination response measures. More research that adjusts for the overlap among vulnerability measures will be needed to shed additional light on their unique contributions to conditioning patterns.

There is accumulating evidence from prospective studies, as described earlier, that trait anxiety, neuroticism, and related constructs serve as nonspecific vulnerability factors for the subsequent development of SPs, SAD, and MDD (e.g., Biederman et al., 1990; Hayward et al., 2000; Kendler et al., 2004; Krueger et al., 1996; Schwartz et al., 1999; Zinbarg et al., 2016). These findings of nonspecific vulnerability are consistent with findings of common conditioning deficits in anxiety-disordered groups (Duits et al., 2015). However, given the conclusions of Sjouwerman et al. (2020), which failed to find support for nonspecific Negative Emotionality as a predictor of fear learning, more work is needed on the role of fear conditioning in the vulnerability conferred by neuroticism and related constructs.

### INTEROCEPTIVE CONDITIONING

In *interoceptive conditioning*, the CSs are internal sensations (e.g., Razran, 1961). Bouton et al. (2001) proposed that when low-level somatic sensations of anxiety/panic precede and are paired with full-blown panic, the low-level somatic sensations of anxiety/panic come to be CSs that elicit high levels of anxiety and panic. That is, Bouton et al. propose that interoceptive conditioning may contribute to the fear-of-fear vicious cycle described earlier regarding the personality trait of AS.

Bouton et al. (2001) also reviewed a great deal of clinical evidence that is consistent with several of the predictions that follow from their interoceptive conditioning model of PD/A. For example, panic is predicted to be preceded by heightened anxiety if anxiety becomes a CS for panic. Studies using experience sampling and careful monitoring have found this to be the case, rather than panic truly coming from out of the blue, as is often experienced subjectively by patients. Bouton et al. noted that the initial attacks experienced by patients with PD/A are generally terrifying, with thoughts of going crazy or dying being common symptoms, and this terror is more than sufficient to allow powerful conditioned responses to develop. Moreover, initial attacks are often perceived as unpredictable and uncontrollable, and, as discussed earlier, these perceptions should augment the intensity of the conditioning that results from an initial panic. Consistent with this prediction many patients with PD/A report that their anxiety about having more panic attacks develops rapidly after their first panic attack.

### SUMMARY

The origins of anxiety disorders are considerably more complex than was assumed by early conditioning models. However, these complexities are expected from the perspective of contemporary research on conditioning, which reveals a variety of vulnerability (e.g., temperament) and contextual (e.g., controllability and fear relevance of stimuli) variables that may impact the outcome of direct, vicarious, and interoceptive conditioning experiences.

## Information Processing Biases

### ATTENTIONAL BIAS

Several types of information processing biases have been identified in anxious populations, and the most-studied among them is an attentional bias that favors the processing of threat stimuli. This bias is demonstrated in both *increased* attentional engagement toward threatening stimuli (Lange et al., 2011; Seefeldt et al., 2014; Shechner et al., 2012) and *decreased* attentional disengagement away from threatening stimuli (Chen et al., 2012; Liang et al., 2017; Schofield et al., 2012). That is, groups characterized by anxiety are both more likely to pay attention to threats and have a harder time shifting their attention away from threats. However, these two types of attentional bias are uncorrelated—that is, an individual could display one type of bias without displaying the other, and vice versa (Rudaizky et al., 2014).

A variety of factors appear to influence the strength of this attentional bias. For instance, this bias appears to interact with state anxiety such that the attentional bias is strongest among highly trait-anxious individuals who *also* have high state anxiety, such as the kind of anxiety that comes when final exams are coming soon (MacLeod & Mathews, 1988; MacLeod & Rutherford, 1992; Mogg et al., 1994). When state anxiety is high, low trait-anxious individuals show less attentional bias toward threat whereas high trait-anxious individuals show more. This pattern appears most salient at a moderate level of threat. For instance, a strong threat, such as the threat of electric shock, produces similar levels of attentional vigilance between high and low trait-anxious groups (Notebaert et al., 2011). But when threat intensity can be manipulated, threats of moderate intensity provoke the largest differences in anxiety-linked attentional bias (Koster et al., 2006; Wilson & MacLeod, 2003). And, of course, attentional bias is particularly strong when the threat is relevant to the main triggers of one's anxiety (Mathews & MacLeod, 1985; McNally et al., 1994). Attentional vigilance is particularly strong for disorder-relevant stimuli, such as panic-relevant stimuli for those with PD (Buckley et al., 2002), social stimuli for those with SAD (Maidenberg et al., 1996), obsession-related stimuli for those with OCD (Cisler & Olatunji, 2010), and trauma-relevant stimuli for those with PTSD (Ashley et al., 2013). Indeed, meta-analytic findings demonstrate that the magnitude of the attentional bias to threat is significantly greater when the stimuli matches the diagnosis (Pergamin-Hight et al., 2015).

In recent years, studies have continued to demonstrate that groups characterized by a vulnerability toward anxiety (such as those with high trait anxiety or those with anxiety disorder diagnoses) are more likely to attend to threatening information than are controls (Cisler & Koster, 2010; Mathews & MacLeod, 2005). This effect has been seen using a variety of stimuli including words (Amir et al., 2003), auditory narratives (Foa & McNally, 1986), expressive faces (Waters et al., 2008), and complex images (Rudaizky et al., 2014). In a large meta-analysis, Bar-Bar-Haim et al. (2007) found that this effect was replicated across a variety of anxiety diagnoses and under a variety of experimental paradigms/conditions, and meta-analytic reviews have continued to find that groups with increased anxiety vulnerability demonstrate a greater attentional bias toward threat (Armstrong & Olatunji, 2012; Dudeney et al., 2015; Price et al., 2016).

However, despite the substantial literature on this attentional bias in anxiety, recent papers have called attention to the fact that measures of attentional bias demonstrate low internal consistency and low reliability (MacLeod et al., 2019; Rodebaugh et al. 2016). These authors note that whereas the group effects are reliable, the low reliability limits what can reasonably done with the data. For instance, in keeping with the aim of Research Domain Criteria (RDoC; Cuthbert & Kozak, 2013), researchers have looked to attentional bias as a potential marker for anxiety disorders, but the low reliability of the measures limits their ability to distinguish *individuals* with anxiety rather than *groups* characterized by anxiety. That is, whereas measures of attentional bias are useful at the group level, they are likely to be unhelpful at the individual level (MacLeod et al., 2019). Researchers are currently looking for ways to ameliorate this concern, such as by taking multiple measurements of attentional bias (Enock et al., 2014; McNally, 2019; Price et al., 2015) or by examining the dynamic fluctuations in attentional bias over time (e.g., Iacoviello et al., 2014; Zvielli et al., 2015).

Importantly, recent studies have manipulated attentional bias using attention bias modification tasks (ABMTs), including studies that have attempted to induce attention bias and others that have attempted to ameliorate it. Research suggests that ABMT manipulations have causal effects on anxiety in the predicted directions (for reviews, see Hakamata et al., 2010; Hallion & Ruscio, 2011).

That is, inducing attention bias increases anxiety responses to subsequent stressors, whereas ameliorating attentional bias decreases such responses. These results provide evidence that attentional bias favoring the processing of threat plays a causal role in the etiology and/or maintenance of anxiety. They also suggest that ABMTs ameliorating attentional bias can be an effective treatment for anxiety. Over the past decade, research on the use of ABMTs in the treatment of anxiety has exploded, and the results are largely positive. Recent meta-analyses have demonstrated that ABMTs significantly reduce both attentional bias and symptoms of anxiety (Beard et al., 2012; Mogoaşe et al., 2014), and recent reviews have highlighted both the strengths and limitations of this novel therapeutic technique (Kuckertz & Amir, 2015; Mogg et al., 2017).

## MEMORY BIAS AND INHIBITORY DEFICITS

Evidence regarding a memory bias in anxiety disorders is inconclusive (Craske et al., 2009). While some studies suggest that anxious participants demonstrate enhanced memory for threatening material (e.g., Cloitre et al., 1994; Reidy, 2004; Reidy & Richards, 1997), others fail to demonstrate such a bias (e.g., Bielak & Moscovitch 2012; Bradley et al., 1995; Mathews & MacLeod, 1985; Mogg et al., 1989; Nugent & Mineka, 1994). There is not only discrepancy in the directionality of the findings, but in the effect sizes as well, with between-groups effect sizes ranging from −1.28 to 1.27 (Mitte, 2008). Mitte also found that, in general, there were no significant effects of anxiety on implicit memory but that anxiety did influence recollection such that anxious individuals demonstrated a memory bias toward threat-relevant information. According to one review, these biases may be more prevalent in some disorders than others. Coles and Heimberg (2002) found that there was more evidence for explicit memory bias in PD (and possibly in PTSD and OCD), but not in GAD and SAD. However, the findings for all disorders were mixed. Furthermore, in the few cases in which superior memory for threat-related stimuli has been demonstrated, the effects could be due to increased processing and encoding resulting from the attentional bias (Mathews & MacLeod, 2005). Though recent research has suggested explanations for these discrepancies, such as the notion that threats that can be *controlled* are more easily remembered but threats that are uncontrollable are not (Large et al., 2016), there are few conclusive findings on memory biases in those with anxiety disorders.

Interestingly, there is some evidence suggesting that there may be conditions in which anxious patients have difficulty forgetting threat representations when it would be adaptive to do so while healthy controls can forget them. This is evidenced through use of the retrieval-induced forgetting paradigm, in which practice of words reliably inhibits memory for related, unpracticed words in healthy participants. For instance, a few practice trials at encoding of the word "strawberry" tend to impair recall of the word "apple." People with SAD, however, do not adaptively inhibit as many unpracticed negative social words as do controls (Amir et al., 2001), nor do individuals with GAD (Kircanski et al., 2016). State anxiety induced in a psychosocial laboratory stressor also has been shown to prevent adaptive forgetting, or inhibition, from occurring (Koessler et al., 2009). In this way, anxious individuals may be less able to forget threatening or painful information, contributing to the greater impact of such information. In one such demonstration, when asked to retrieve negative (and not positive) reviews, as an individual with social anxiety might do, participants recalled the reviews of a public speaking task as more negative and less positive both 5 minutes and 1 week later, suggesting a lasting impact of remembering negative over neutral or positive information (Glazier et al., 2021).

**INTERPRETIVE BIAS**

Each day we are confronted with ambiguous information, such as a rustling noise outside the bedroom window at night or a coworker's blank face as we speak at work in the afternoon. Interpretive bias reflects the tendency to resolve such ambiguous information in a particular way.

There is a wealth of evidence from self-report studies consistent with the notion that people with clinical and subclinical anxiety of all types interpret ambiguous information that is salient to their emotional concerns in a negative fashion (Mathews & MacLeod, 2005). For example, in one study, when presented with descriptions of ambiguous social situations (e.g., "You have visitors come by for a meal and they leave sooner than expected"), patients with SAD were more likely than those with other anxiety disorders or healthy controls to draw negative conclusions (Stopa & Clark, 2000).

Of course, it is possible that the findings from these self-report studies reflect a response bias for endorsing negative options, rather than an interpretive bias per se. Study designs that employ *implicit* measures of interpretive bias address this concern. In the first implicit interpretive bias study, MacLeod and Cohen (1993) asked participants to read passages of text, pressing a button in order to view each successive sentence. Although participants were led to believe that the data of interest were their responses to questions about the passages, the critical data were actually the delays between button presses, which provided an index of the comprehension latency for each sentence. Comprehension latency should be inversely related to the degree to which a participant expected the continuation of the preceding text (e.g., Haberlandt & Bingham, 1978). Indeed, MacLeod and Cohen found that participants with high trait anxiety selectively imposed threatening interpretations on ambiguous sentences, whereas participants with low trait anxiety did the opposite. Another set of implicit studies showed that people with elevated social anxiety are more likely than others to interpret neutral faces in a threatening manner (Yoon & Zinbarg, 2007, 2008).

Most recently, interest has turned to interpretive bias modification procedures, in which negative interpretive biases are systematically altered. Although these methods were originally developed to elucidate the causal role of cognitive biases in mental disorders, they have been shown also to have therapeutic benefits (see MacLeod & Mathews, 2012). Findings indicate that a single interpretive bias modification session may reduce symptoms related to anxiety sensitivity (Steinman & Teachman, 2010), chronic worry (Hirsch et al., 2009), or GAD (Hayes et al., 2010). Moreover, extended sessions appear to significantly reduce trait anxiety (Salemink et al., 2009). There is even evidence that interpretive bias modification is effective with adolescents (Lothmann et al., 2011). Thus, the evidence from interpretive bias modification studies demonstrates that a bias favoring threatening interpretations of ambiguity plays a causal role in the etiology and/or maintenance of anxiety. That said, research on this treatment approach is still in its infancy. Future research will benefit from the application of randomized controlled trials to the study of interpretive bias modification, along with modification procedures for cognitive biases more broadly (cf. MacLeod, 2012).

**COURAGEOUS MINDSET**

Because behavioral avoidance is a hallmark symptom of the anxiety disorders, we might infer that patients with anxiety disorders have a difficult time accessing a "courageous mindset" (i.e., the belief or representation of oneself as being able to face one's fears; Kramer & Zinbarg, 2019). Recent research on individuals with specific fears suggests it may be possible to temporarily prime a courageous mindset and thereby reduce avoidance by prompting recall of memories of courageous behavior (Kramer & Zinbarg, 2019). After writing about a time when they encountered a feared stimulus and avoided it (e.g., individuals who were anxious about public speaking avoiding a public speaking task), individuals were more likely to report they "could not do" fear-relevant tasks (like giving a speech in front of a small audience) and did so more quickly. This suggests a tendency in anxious individuals, when recalling memories of past failures in approach, to see fear-relevant tasks as difficult (or even impossible) at both an explicit and an implicit level. However, when individuals were asked to write about a time when they encountered a feared stimulus and *faced* it (such as actually *delivering* the speech), they reported they "could do" more fear-relevant tasks and did so more quickly, thus demonstrating that fear-relevant tasks were seen as more possible both explicitly and implicitly. Therefore, the act of recalling an instance of "courage," or facing a feared situation, helped override negative beliefs and made feared situations seem more approachable, at least temporarily. As with other modification treatments addressed above, future studies are needed to address the potential long-term effects of such a priming intervention, perhaps in the context of treating anxiety.

### SUMMARY

Anxious individuals demonstrate a variety of information-processing biases. They attend more readily to threatening stimuli and have a harder time redirecting their attention away from such stimuli, especially when state (in addition to trait) anxiety is high, when the threat is moderate, and when the threat is in line with the main triggers for their anxiety. Anxious individuals may also have difficulty forgetting information that would be adaptive to forget. Finally, they are more likely to interpret ambiguous information as threatening at both an explicit and an implicit level. However, research on bias-modification tasks, such as ABMTs and interpretive bias modification procedures (IBMPs), provides hope for reducing these biases by providing new treatment methods for individuals with anxiety.

## Interpersonal Factors in Etiology and Disorder Maintenance
### ATTACHMENT

It is well established that adverse early life events are a robust risk factor for psychopathology (Kessler et al., 2010; McLaughlin et al., 2012). In addition, interpersonal and systemic variables are gaining increased attention in the anxiety disorders literature as possible risk factors (e.g., Beck, 2010). Indeed, at least some of the anxiety disorders are associated with difficulties in interpersonal relationships (Whisman, 1999; Whisman & Baucom, 2012). Accordingly, there is a growing body of work highlighting the relevance of attachment, interpersonal functioning, and expressed emotion in the anxiety disorders.

Bowlby (1973) viewed attachment as an evolutionary drive whereby infants develop a relationship to primary caregivers as a survival mechanism. Thus, the development of a secure attachment that is characterized by close proximity with the caregiver and by the perception of safety is hypothesized to allow the infant a secure base from which to explore the world and environment. Conversely, insecure attachment is hypothesized to develop when the caregiver does not provide the conditions of safety and security and is rejecting, inconsistent with attention, or overcontrolling.

These early life experiences in attachment are proposed to lead to the development of an *internal working model*, or a cognitive framework that informs how one interacts with others and the world. These internal working models are reflected in attachment styles that are either secure, insecure-avoidant, or insecure-ambivalent. The development of an insecure attachment style is proposed to be one pathway to development of anxiety disorders (Colonnesi et al., 2011; Esbjørn et al., 2012).

One meta-analysis that examined attachment style and childhood anxiety disorders showed a modest relationship ($r = .3$) of insecure attachment style with childhood and adolescent anxiety disorders (Colonnesi et al., 2011), especially with insecure-avoidant attachment. Furthermore, a fairly consistent finding is that adult anxious patients retrospectively report having, as children, had an insecure attachment style with their caregivers (e.g., Cassidy et al., 2009; Eng & Heimberg, 2006). For example, Cassidy and colleagues (2009) found that patients with GAD reported poor attachment with their caregivers that was characterized by increased role-reversal/enmeshment in the caregiving relationship, high maternal rejection, and low maternal love. Furthermore, the more cumulative risk factors one endorsed, the greater the likelihood of a diagnosis of GAD. Similarly, Eng et al. (2001) found that patients with a diagnosis of SAD fell into either an anxious-attachment cluster, which was associated with greater symptomatology, or a secure-attachment cluster, which was associated with less symptomatology. Taken together, these studies suggest that early development of insecure attachment styles may represent a risk factor for the development of an anxiety disorder and potentially serve a role in maintenance through adulthood through ineffective styles of interpersonal functioning (Snyder et al., 2010).

### INTERPERSONAL PROBLEMS

Interpersonal pathoplasticity builds on the pathoplasty model introduced earlier to emphasize the role of interpersonal functioning in the expression of psychopathology. *Interpersonal pathoplasticity*, then, refers to the role of interpersonal functioning in the expression of psychopathology (Klein et al., 1993; for a review see Pincus et al., 2010). An emphasis on interpersonal theory and psychopathology can be traced back to the work of Harry Stack Sullivan, who viewed the expression of psychopathology and personality as occurring through interpersonal situations and relationships (Sullivan, 1953).

Sullivan's ideas were further refined and formalized into a model of interpersonal functioning that could account for the range of interpersonal behavior: the *interpersonal circumplex model* (IPC; Leary, 1957). The IPC is a two-dimensional circular model for organizing interpersonal behavior around two central axes. In Leary's (1957) original model, the poles for each axis are labeled as dominance-submission on the vertical axis and hostility-affection on the horizontal axis. All forms of interpersonal behavior are conceptualized as a combination of these two axes. Although variations of circumplex models have since been proposed, they all share in common the central axes (Fournier et al., 2010).

One of the most commonly used circumplex measures is the Inventory of Interpersonal Problems (IIP; Horowitz et al., 2000). Results of several IIP investigations support the identification of interpersonal subtypes for GAD (Eng & Heimberg, 2006; Przeworski et al., 2011; Salzer et al., 2011). In particular, intrusiveness (inappropriately self-disclosing, attention seeking, difficulty spending time alone), exploitable (difficulty feeling and expressing anger for fear of offending others, easily taken advantage of by others), cold (inability to express affection toward others, difficulty forgiving others, difficulty making long-term relationships), and nonassertive (difficulty making needs known to others, difficulty being assertive) appear to emerge as four salient interpersonal clusters. Additionally, IIP studies of interpersonal problems in SAD found in common a friendly-submissive (i.e., exploitable) interpersonal cluster (e.g., Kachin et al., 2001). Another study found an overly nurturant cluster to be associated with the association between anxiety and depression among late adolescents with clinical levels of anxiety (Viana & Stevens, 2013). The relevance of interpersonal problems in anxiety disorders and depression has clear treatment implications. For example, interpersonal problems at pretreatment are associated with reduced response to cognitive-behavioral therapy (CBT) for GAD (Borkovec et al., 2002) and SAD (Cain et al., 2010).

An interpersonally based conceptualization of PD/A has been proposed (Chambless, 2010). However, whereas there does appear to be some evidence that PD/A is associated with interpersonal difficulties; whether interpersonal difficulties represent a unique factor compared with other stressful life events is unclear (Marcaurell et al., 2003). The association between interpersonal problems and agoraphobia appears more robust. For example, Goldstein and Chambless (1978) identified a subset of patients with agoraphobia for whom interpersonal problems was the most common antecedent in the development of PD/A. Similarly, Kleiner and Marshall (1987) found that 84% of agoraphobics recalled experiencing marital/relationship conflicts prior to the onset of the disorder. Furthermore, a notable portion of this sample reported a long history of unassertiveness, dependency, and fear of negative evaluations.

### EXPRESSED EMOTION

Expressed emotion (EE)—criticism, hostility, and emotional overinvolvement expressed toward a patient by a family member—has received attention as a possible anxiety disorders maintenance factor. Criticism in this context are remarks directed toward the patient expressing disproval or dislike of a specific action the patient does. Hostility may be understood as a more extreme form of criticism that devalues or shames the patient.

Although EE has received considerable attention in the areas of schizophrenia, mood disorders, and eating disorders (Butzlaff & Hooley, 1998; Hooley, 2004), it has only recently been given increased attention in research on anxiety disorders. Research in this area shows that high levels of EE, particularly hostility, are associated with suboptimal treatment response for PD/A (Chambless et al., 2017), SAD (Fogler et al., 2007), and GAD (Zinbarg et al., 2007). Furthermore, high levels of interpersonal conflict are also associated with increased rates of relapse after treatment (McLeod, 1994). However, not all forms of criticism appear to be detrimental to the patient (Chambless & Steketee, 1999; Zinbarg et al., 2007). Whereas hostile forms of criticism are associated with suboptimal treatment response, criticism presented in a nonhostile manner is associated with improved treatment responses for patients with PD/A, GAD, and OCD. However, the precise mechanisms of how hostility and nonhostile criticism influence the maintenance and treatment of anxiety still need to be delineated. A recent development that may foster such research is the creation of a self-report measure distinguishing hostile and nonhostile forms of perceived criticism (Klein et al., 2016).

## Conclusion and Future Directions

Great progress has been made in understanding the anxiety disorders, with widespread consensus on several points. The anxiety disorders are not entirely independent; rather, there are broad factors shared by these disorders (and the unipolar mood disorders). Furthermore, anxiety disorders are heritable, but learning histories, information processing biases, and interpersonal factors also contribute to their etiology or maintenance.

Despite the consensus on several key points that exists in the field, there are still topics regarding the anxiety disorders that require additional research. Thus, whereas a prospective association showing that neuroticism is a marker of risk for anxiety disorders has now been replicated across independent laboratories, prospective longitudinal work is sorely needed to determine directionality of the association between trait PE/E and anxiety disorders. Future research will also benefit from the application of randomized controlled trials to the study of interpretive bias modification, along with modification procedures for cognitive biases more broadly (cf. MacLeod, 2012). Relatedly, future studies are needed to address the potential long-term effects of a courage priming intervention for treating and perhaps even preventing anxiety disorders.

Of the various questions for the field that remain to be addressed, however, two appear most fundamental to us. The first is whether the different anxiety disorder diagnoses truly represent distinct categories (or dimensions that differ in fundamental ways) or inconsequential variations of a broader syndrome that differ superficially in terms of the content of apprehension. The second question is whether several of the risk factors discussed earlier (e.g., neuroticism, BI, anxiety sensitivity, information-processing biases, genetic vulnerability) represent distinct pathways and have unique predictive power. Thus, what the field needs are more studies that include multiple anxiety disorder diagnoses (or dimensions) as outcomes and multiple risk factors. Such designs will enable us to sort out both whether the various anxiety disorders differ at a deep level and whether any of the various risk factors identified to date have unique predictive power.

## References

Amir, N., Coles, M. E., Brigidi, B., & Foa, E. B. (2001). The effect of practice on recall of emotional information in individuals with generalized social phobia. *Journal of Abnormal Psychology, 110*(1), 76–82. https://doi.org/10.1037/0021-8437.110.1.76

Amir, N., Elias, J., Klumpp, H., & Przeworsky, A. (2003). Attentional bias to threat in social phobia: Facilitated processing of threat or difficulty disengaging attention from threat? *Behaviour Research and Therapy, 41*(11), 1325–1335. https://doi.org/10.1016/S0005-7967 (03) 00039-1

Andrews, G., Stewart, G., Allen, R., & Henderson, A. S. (1990). The genetics of six neurotic disorders: A twin study. *Journal of Affective Disorders, 19*(1), 23–29. https://doi.org/10.1016/0165-0327(90)90005-S

Armstrong, T., & Olatunji, B. O. (2012). Eye tracking of attention in the affective disorders: A meta-analytic review and synthesis. *Clinical Psychology Review, 32*(8), 704–723. https://doi.org/10.1016/j.cpr.2012.09.004

Arnaudova, I., Krypotos, A.-M., Effting, M., Boddez, Y., Kindt, M., & Beckers, T. (2013). Individual differences in discriminatory fear learning under conditions of ambiguity: A vulnerability factor for anxiety disorders? *Frontiers in Psychology, 4*, 298. https://doi.org/10.3389/fpsyg.2013.00298

Ashley, V., Honzel, N., Larsen, J., Justus, T., & Swick, D. (2013). Attentional bias for trauma-related words: Exaggerated emotional Stroop effect in Afghanistan and Iraq war veterans with PTSD. *BMC Psychiatry, 13*, 86. https://doi.org/10.1186/1471-244X-13-86

Asnaani, A., Richey, J. A., Dimaite, R., Hinton, D. E., & Hofmann, S. G. (2010). A cross-ethnic comparison of lifetime prevalence rates of anxiety disorders. *Journal of Nervous and Mental Disease, 198*(8), 551–555. https://doi.org/10.1097/nmd.0b013e3181ea169f

Barlow, D. H. (1991). Disorders of emotion. *Psychological Inquiry, 2*(1), 58–71. https://doi.org/10.1207/s15327965pli0201_15

Barlow, D. H. (2002). *Anxiety and its disorders: The nature and treatment of anxiety and panic*, 2nd ed. Guilford.

Baek, I.-C., Lee, E.-H., & Kim, J.-H. (2019). Differences in anxiety sensitivity factors between anxiety and depressive disorders. *Depression and Anxiety, 36*(10), 968–974. https://doi.org/10.1002/da.22948

Bar-Haim, Y., Lamy, D., Pergamin, L., Bakermans-Kranenburg, M. J., & van IJzendoorn, M. H. (2007). Threat-related attentional bias in anxious and nonanxious individuals: A meta-analytic study. *Psychological Bulletin, 133*(1), 1–24. https://doi.org/10.1037/0033-2909.133.1.1

Barrett, P. M., Rapee, R. M., Dadds, M. R., & Ryan, S. M. (1996). Family enhancement of cognitive style in anxious and aggressive children. *Journal of Abnormal Child Psychology, 24*, 187–203. https://doi.org/10.1007/BF01441484

Beard, C., Sawyer, A. T., & Hofmann, S. G. (2012). Efficacy of attention bias modification using threat and appetitive stimuli: A meta-analytic review. *Behavior Therapy, 43*(4), 724–740. https://doi.org/10.1016/j.beth.2012.01.002

Beck, J. G. (2010). *Interpersonal processes in the anxiety disorders: Implications for understanding psychopathology and treatment.* American Psychological Association.

Biederman, J., Hirshfeld-Becker, D. R., Rosenbaum, J. F., Hérot, C., Friedman, D., Snidman, N., Kagan, J., & Faraone, S. V. (2001). Further evidence of association between behavioral inhibition and social anxiety in children. *American Journal of Psychiatry, 158*(10), 1673–1679. https://doi.org/10.1176/appi.ajp.158.10.1673

Biederman, J., Rosenbaum, J. F., Hirshfeld, D. R., Faraone, S. V., Bolduc, E. A., Gersten, M., Meminger, S. R., Kagan, J., Snidman, N., & Reznick, J. S. (1990). Psychiatric correlates of behavioral inhibition in young children of parents with and without psychiatric disorders. *Archives of General Psychiatry, 47*(1), 21–26. https://doi.org/10.1001/archpsyc.1990.01810130023004

Bielak, T., & Moscovitch, D. A. (2012). Friend or foe? Memory and expectancy biases for faces in social anxiety. *Journal of Experimental Psychopathology, 3*(1), 42–61. https://doi.org/10.5127/jep.019711

Bienvenu, O. J., Samuels, J. F., Costa, P. T., Reti, I. M., Eaton, W. W., & Nestadt, G. (2004). Anxiety and depressive disorders and the five-factor model of personality: A higher- and lower-order personality trait investigation in a community sample. *Depression and Anxiety, 20*(2), 92–97. https://doi.org/10.1002/da.20026

Birbaumer, N., Grodd, W., Diedrich, O., Klose, U., Erb, M., Lotze, M., Schneider, F., Weiss, U., & Flor, H. (1998). fMRI reveals amygdala activation to human faces in social phobics. *Neuroreport, 9*(6), 1223–1226. https://doi.org/10.1097/00001756-199804200-00048

Borkovec, T. D., Newman, M. G., Pincus, A. L., & Lytle, R. (2002). A component analysis of cognitive-behavioral therapy for generalized anxiety disorder and the role of interpersonal problems. *Journal of Consulting and Clinical Psychology, 70*(2), 288–298. https://doi.org/10.1037/0022-0067.70.2.288

Bouton, M. E., Mineka, S., & Barlow, D. H. (2001). A modern learning theory perspective on the etiology of panic disorder. *Psychological Review, 108*(1), 4–32. https://doi.org/10.1037/0033-2957.108.1.4

Bowlby, J. (1973). *Separation: Anxiety and anger (attachment and loss Vol. II).* Basic Books.

Bradley, B. P., Mogg, K., & Williams, R. (1995). Implicit and explicit memory for emotion-congruent information in clinical depression and anxiety. *Behaviour Research and Therapy, 33*(7), 755–770. https://doi.org/10.1016/0005-7967(95)00029-W

Brown, T. A., & Barlow, D. H. (2009). A proposal for a dimensional classification system based on the shared features of the DSM-IV anxiety and mood disorders: Implications for assessment and treatment. *Psychological Assessment, 21*, 256–271. https://doi.org/10.1037/a0016608

Brown, T. A., Chorpita, B. F., & Barlow, D. H. (1998). Structural relationships among dimensions of the DSM-IV anxiety and mood disorders and dimensions of negative affect, positive affect, and autonomic arousal. *Journal of Abnormal Psychology, 107*(2), 179–192. https://doi.org/10.1037/0021-8437.107.2.179

Brown, T. A., & McNiff, J. (2009). Specificity of autonomic arousal to DSM-IV panic disorder and posttraumatic stress disorder. *Behaviour Research and Therapy, 47*(6), 487–493. https://doi.org/10.1016/j.brat.2009.02.016

Bruch, M., & Heimberg, R. (1994). Differences in perceptions of parental and personal characteristics between generalized and nongeneralized social phobics. *Journal of Anxiety Disorders, 8*(2), 155–168. https://doi.org/10.1016/0887-6185(94)90013-2

Buckley, T. C., Blanchard, E. B., & Hickling, E. J. (2002). Automatic and strategic processing of threat stimuli: A comparison between PTSD, Panic Disorder, and nonanxiety controls. *Cognitive Therapy and Research, 26*, 97–115. https://doi.org/10.1023/A:1013897805918

Butzlaff, R. L., & Hooley, J. M. (1998). Expressed emotion and psychiatric relapse. *Archives of General Psychiatry, 55*(6), 547–552. https://doi.org/10.1001/archpsyc.55.6.547

Bystritsky, A., Pontillo, D., Powers, M., Sabb, F. W., Craske, M. G., & Bookheimer, S. Y. (2001). Functional MRI changes during panic anticipation and imagery exposure. *Neuroreport, 12*(18), 3953–3957. https://doi.org/10.1097/00001756-200112210-00020

Cain, N. M., Pincus, A. L., & Holtforth, M. G. (2010). Interpersonal subtypes in social phobia: Diagnostic and treatment implications. *Journal of Personality Assessment, 92*(6), 514–527. https://doi.org/10.1080/00223891.2010.513704

Campbell, L. A., Brown, T. A., & Grisham, J. R. (2003). The relevance of age of onset to the psychopathology of generalized anxiety disorder. *Behavior Therapy, 34*(1), 31–48. https://doi.org/10.1016/S0005-7894(03)80020-5

Carver, C. S., & White, T. L. (1994). Behavioral inhibition, behavioral activation, and affective responses to impending reward and punishment: The BIS/BAS scales. *Journal of Personality and Social Psychology, 67*(2), 319–333. https://doi.org/10.1037/0022-3514.67.2.319

Cassidy, J., Lichtenstein-Phelps, J., Sibrava, N. J., Thomas, C. L., Jr., & Borkovec, T. D. (2009). Generalized anxiety disorder: Connections with self-reported attachment. *Behavior Therapy, 40*(1), 23–38. https://doi.org/10.1016/j.beth.2007.12.004

Chambless, D. L. (2010). Interpersonal aspects of panic disorder and agoraphobia. In J. G. Beck (Ed.), *Interpersonal processes in the anxiety disorders: Implications for understanding psychopathology and treatment.* (pp. 209–233). American Psychological Association.

Chambless, D. L., Allred, K. M., Chen, F. F., McCarthy, K. S., Milrod, B., & Barber, J. P. (2017). Perceived criticism predicts outcome of psychotherapy for panic disorder: Replication and extension. *Journal of Consulting and Clinical Psychology, 85*(1), 37–44. https://doi.org/10.1037/ccp0000161

Chambless, D. L., & Steketee, G. (1999). Expressed emotion and behavior therapy outcome: A prospective study with obsessive–compulsive and agoraphobic outpatients. *Journal of Consulting and Clinical Psychology*, 67(5), 658–665. https://doi.org/10.1037/0022-0067.67.5.658

Chavanne, A. V., & Robinson, O. J. (2021). The overlapping neurobiology of induced and pathological anxiety: A meta-analysis of functional neural activation. *American Journal of Psychiatry*, 178(2), 156–164. https://doi.org/10.1176/appi.ajp.2020.19111153

Chen, N. T. M., Clarke, P. J. F., MacLeod, C., & Guastella, A. J. (2012). Biased attentional processing of positive stimuli in social anxiety disorder: An eye movement study. *Cognitive Behaviour Therapy*, 41(2), 96–107. https://doi.org/10.1080/16506073.2012.666562

Chorpita, B. F., Plummer, C. M., & Moffitt, C. E. (2000). Relations of tripartite dimensions of emotion to childhood anxiety and mood disorders. *Journal of Abnormal Child Psychology*, 28, 299–310. https://doi.org/10.1023/A:1005152505888

Cisler, J. M., & Koster, E. H. W. (2010). Mechanisms of attentional biases towards threat in anxiety disorders: An integrative review. *Clinical Psychology Review*, 30(2), 203–216. https://doi.org/10.1016/j.cpr.2009.11.003

Cisler, J. M., & Olatunji, B. O. (2010). Components of attentional biases in contamination fear: Evidence for difficulty in disengagement. *Behaviour Research and Therapy*, 48(1), 74–78. https://doi.org/10.1016/j.brat.2009.09.003

Clark, L. A., & Watson, D. (1991). Tripartite model of anxiety and depression: Psychometric evidence and taxonomic implications. *Journal of Abnormal Psychology*, 100(3), 316–336. https://doi.org/10.1037/0021-8437.100.3.316

Clark, L. A., Watson, D., & Mineka, S. (1994). Temperament, personality, and the mood and anxiety disorders. *Journal of Abnormal Psychology*, 103(1), 103–116. https://doi.org/10.1037//0021-843x.103.1.18

Clauss, J. A., & Blackford, J. U. (2012). Behavioral inhibition and risk for developing social anxiety disorder: A meta-analytic study. *Journal of the American Academy of Child & Adolescent Psychiatry*, 51(10), 1066–1075. https://doi.org/10.1016/j.jaac.2012.08.002

Cloitre, M., Shear, M. K., Cancienne, J., & Zeitlin, S. B. (1994). Implicit and explicit memory for catastrophic associations to bodily sensation words in panic disorder. *Cognitive Therapy and Research*, 18(3), 225–240. https://doi.org/10.1007/BF02357777

Coelho, C. M., Suttiwan, P., Faiz, A. M., Ferreira-Santos, F., & Zsido, A. N. (2019). Are humans prepared to detect, fear, and avoid snakes? The mismatch between laboratory and ecological evidence. *Frontiers in Psychology*, 10, 2094. https://doi.org/10.3389/fpsyg.2019.02094

Cole, D. A., Martin, N. C., & Steiger, J. H. (2005). Empirical and conceptual problems with longitudinal trait-state models: Introducing a trait-state-occasion model. *Psychological Methods*, 10(1), 3–20. https://doi.org/10.1037/1082-9897.10.1.3

Coles, M. E., & Heimberg, R. G. (2002). Memory biases in the anxiety disorders: Current status. *Clinical Psychology Review*, 22(4), 587–627. https://doi.org/10.1016/S0272-7358(01)00113-1

Colonnesi, C., Draijer, E. M., Jan J. M. Stams, G., Van der Bruggen, C. O., Bögels, S. M., & Noom, M. J. (2011). The relation between insecure attachment and child anxiety: A meta-analytic review. *Journal of Clinical Child and Adolescent Psychology*, 40(4), 630–645. https://doi.org/10.1080/15374416.2011.581623

Cook, M., & Mineka, S. (1989). Observational conditioning of fear to fear-relevant versus fear-irrelevant stimuli in rhesus monkeys. *Journal of Abnormal Psychology*, 98(4), 448–459. https://doi.org/10.1037/0021-8437.98.4.448

Cook, M., & Mineka, S. (1990). Selective associations in the observational conditioning of fear in rhesus monkeys. *Journal of Experimental Psychology: Animal Behavior Processes*, 16(4), 372–389. https://doi.org/10.1037/0097-7403.16.4.372

Cook, M., Mineka, S., Wolkenstein, B., & Laitsch, K. (1985). Observational conditioning of snake fear in unrelated rhesus monkeys. *Journal of Abnormal Psychology*, 94(4), 591–610. https://doi.org/10.1037/0021-8437.94.4.591

Costa, P. T., & McCrae, R. R. (1987). Neuroticism, somatic complaints, and disease: Is the bark worse than the bite? *Journal of Personality*, 55(2), 299–316. https://doi.org/10.1111/j.1467-6494.1987.tb00438.x

Craske, M. G., Kircanski, K., Epstein, A., Wittchen, H.-U., Pine, D. S., Lewis-Fernández, R., & Hinton, D. (2010). Panic disorder: A review of DSM-IV panic disorder and proposals for DSM-V. *Depression and Anxiety*, 27, 93–112. https://doi.org/10.1002/da.20654

Craske, M. G., Rauch, S. L., Ursano, R., Prenoveau, J., Pine, D. S., & Zinbarg, R. E. (2009). What is anxiety disorder? *Depression and Anxiety*, 26(12), 1066–1085. https://doi.org/10.1002/da.20633

Cuthbert, B. N., & Kozak, M. J. (2013). Constructing constructs for psychopathology: The NIMH research domain criteria. *Journal of Abnormal Psychology*, 122(3), 928–937. https://doi.org/10.1037/a0034028

Davis, M. (1998). Are different parts of the extended amygdala involved in fear versus anxiety? *Biological Psychiatry*, 44(12), 1239–1247. https://doi.org/10.1016/S0006-3223 (98) 00288-1

Debiec, J., & Olsson, A. (2017). Social fear learning: From animal models to human function. *Trends in Cognitive Sciences*, 21(7), 546–555. https://doi.org/10.1016/j.tics.2017.04.010

Domschke, K., & Reif, A. (2011). Behavioral genetics of affective and anxiety disorders. In J. Cryan & A. Reif (Eds.). *Behavioral Neurogenetics* (pp. 463–502). Springer. https://doi.org/10.1007/7854_2011_185

Dudeney, J., Sharpe, L., & Hunt, C. (2015). Attentional bias towards threatening stimuli in children with anxiety: A meta-analysis. *Clinical Psychology Review*, 40, 66–75. https://doi.org/10.1016/j.cpr.2015.05.007

Duits, P., Cath, D. C., Lissek, S., Hox, J. J., Hamm, A. O., Engelhard, I. M., van den Hout, M. A., & Baas, J. M. (2015). Updated meta-analysis of classical conditioning in the anxiety disorders. *Depression and Anxiety*, 32(4), 239–253. https://doi.org/10.1002/da.22353

Eaton, N. R., Krueger, R. F., Markon, K. E., Keyes, K. M., Skodol, A. E., Wall, M., Hasin, D. S., & Grant, B. F. (2013). The structure and predictive validity of the internalizing disorders. *Journal of Abnormal Psychology*, 122(1), 86–92. https://doi.org/10.1037/a0029598

Ehlers, A. (1993). Somatic symptoms and panic attacks: A retrospective study of learning experiences. *Behaviour Research and Therapy*, 31(3), 269–278. https://doi.org/10.1016/0005-7967(93)90025-P

Eng, W., & Heimberg, R. G. (2006). Interpersonal correlates of generalized anxiety disorder: Self versus other perception.

*Journal of Anxiety Disorders*, *20*(3), 380–387. https://doi.org/10.1016/j.janxdis.2005.02.005

Eng, W., Heimberg, R. G., Hart, T. A., Schneier, F. R., & Liebowitz, M. R. (2001). Attachment in individuals with social anxiety disorder: The relationship among adult attachment styles, social anxiety, and depression. *Emotion*, *1*(4), 365–380. https://doi.org/10.1037/1528-3542.1.4.365

Enock, P. M., Hofmann, S. G., & McNally, R. J. (2014). Attention bias modification training via smartphone to reduce social anxiety: A randomized, controlled, multi-session experiment. *Cognitive Therapy and Research*, *38*, 200–216. https://doi.org/10.1007/s10608-014-9606-z

Esbjørn, B. H., Bender, P. K., Reinholdt-Dunne, M. L., Munck, L. A., & Ollendick, T. H. (2012). The development of anxiety disorders: Considering the contributions of attachment and emotion regulation. *Clinical Child and Family Psychology Review*, *15*(2), 129–143. https://doi.org/10.1007/s10567-011-0105-4

Esser, R., Fuss, J., & Haaker, J. (2020). Initial evidence for pharmacological modulation of observational threat learning by the GABAergic, but not the noradrenergic system in humans. *Behaviour Research and Therapy*, *129*, 103605. https://doi.org/10.1016/j.brat.2020.103605

Esteves, F., Parra, C., Dimberg, U., & Öhman, A. (1994). Nonconscious associative learning: Pavlovian conditioning of skin conductance responses to masked fear-relevant facial stimuli. *Psychophysiology*, *31*(4), 375–385. https://doi.org/10.1111/j.1469-8986.1994.tb02446.x

Etkin, A., & Wager, T. D. (2007). Functional neuroimaging of anxiety: A meta-analysis of emotional processing in PTSD, social anxiety disorder, and specific phobia. *American Journal of Psychiatry*, *164*(10), 1476–1488. https://doi.org/10.1176/appi.ajp.2007.07030504

Evans, K. C., Wright, C. I., Wedig, M. M., Gold, A. L., Pollack, M. H., & Rauch, S. L. (2008). A functional MRI study of amygdala responses to angry schematic faces in social anxiety disorder. *Depression and Anxiety*, *25*(6), 496–505. https://doi.org/10.1002/da.20347

Eysenck, H. J. (1967). *The biological basis of personality*. Charles C. Thomas.

Eysenck, H. J. (1970). *The structure of human personality*, 3rd ed. Routledge.

Foa, E. B., & McNally, R. J. (1986). Sensitivity to feared stimuli in obsessive-compulsives: A dichotic listening analysis. *Cognitive Therapy and Research*, *10*(4), 477–485. https://doi.org/10.1007/BF01173299

Fogler, J., Tompson, M. C., Steketee, G., & Hofmann, S. G. (2007). Influence of expressed emotion and perceived criticism on cognitive-behavioral therapy for social phobia. *Behaviour Research and Therapy*, *45*(2), 235–249. https://doi.org/10.1016/j.brat.2006.03.002

Fournier, M. A., Moskowitz, D. S., & Zuroff, D. C. (2010). Origins and applications of the interpersonal circumplex. In L. M. Horowitz & S. Strack (Eds.), *Handbook of interpersonal psychology: Theory, research, assessment, and therapeutic interventions* (pp. 57–73). Wiley.

Fox, N. A., Henderson, H. A., Marshall, P. J., Nichols, K. E., & Ghera, M. M. (2005). Behavioral inhibition: Linking biology and behavior within a developmental framework. *Annual Review of Psychology*, *56*, 235–262. https://doi.org/10.1146/annurev.psych.55.090902.141532

Fullana, M. A., Harrisoin, B. J., Vervliet, C. S.-M., Cardoner, N., Àvila-Parcet, A., & Radua, J. (2016). Neural signatures of human fear conditioning: An updated and extended meta-analysis of fMRI studies. *Molecular Psychiatry*, *21*, 500–508. https://doi.org/10.1038/mp.2015.88

Gaderman, A. M., Alonso, J., Vilagut, G., Zaslavsky, A. M., & Kessler, R. C. (2012). Comorbidity and disease burden in the National Comorbidity Survey Replication (NCS-R). *Depression and Anxiety*, *29*, 797–806. doi:10.1002/da.21924.

Gazendam, F. J., Kamphuis, J. H., & Kindt, M. (2013). Deficient safety learning characterizes high trait anxious individuals. *Biological Psychology*, *92*(2), 342–352. https://doi.org/10.1016/j.biopsycho.2012.11.006

Glazier, B. L., Alden, L. E., & Graf, P. (2021). Retrieval-induced forgetting in a social task. *Cognition and Emotion*, *35*(1), 199–206. https://doi.org/10.1080/02699931.2020.1806042

Gold, A. E., MacLeod, K. M., Frier, B. M., & Deary, I. J. (1995). Changes in mood during acute hypoglycemia in healthy participants. *Journal of Personality and Social Psychology*, *68*(3), 498–504. https://doi.org/10.1037/0022-3514.68.3.498

Goldsmith, H. H., Buss, A. H., Plomin, R., Rothbart, M. K., Thomas, A., Chess, S., Hinde, R. A., & McCall, R. B. (1987). What is temperament? Four approaches. *Child Development*, *58*(2), 505–529. https://doi.org/10.2307/1130527

Goldstein, A. J., & Chambless, D. L. (1978). A reanalysis of agoraphobia. *Behavior Therapy*, *9*(1), 47–59. https://doi.org/10.1016/S0005-7894(78)80053-7

Golkar, A., Castro, V., & Olsson, A. (2015). Social learning of fear and safety is determined by the demonstrator's racial group. *Biology Letters*, *11*(1), 20140817. https://doi.org/10.1098/rsbl.2014.0817

Grabe, H., Lange, M., Wolff, B., Volzke, H., Lucht, M., Freyberger, H., John, U., & Cascorbi, I. (2005). Mental and physical distress is modulated by a polymorphism in the 5-HT transporter gene interacting with social stressors and chronic disease burden. *Molecular Psychiatry*, *10*, 220–224. https://doi.org/10.1038/sj.mp.4001555

Grant, B. F., & Dawson, D. A. (2006). Introduction to the National Epidemiologic Survey on Alcohol and Related Conditions. *Alcohol Research & Health*, *29*(2), 74–78.

Grant, B. F., Hasin, D. S., Blanco, C., Stinson, F. S., Chou, S. P., Goldstein, R. B., Dawson, D. A., Smith, S., Saha, T. D., & Huang, B. (2005). The epidemiology of SAD in the United States: Results from the National Epidemiologic Survey on Alcohol and Related Conditions. *Journal of Clinical Psychiatry*, *66*(11), 1351–1361. https://doi.org/10.4088/jcp.v66n1102

Grant, B. F., Hasin, D. S., Stinson, F. S., Dawson, D. A., Chou, S. P., Ruan, W. J., & Huang, B. (2005). Co-occurrence of 12-month mood and anxiety disorders and personality disorders in the US: Results from the national epidemiologic survey on alcohol and related conditions. *Journal of Psychiatric Research*, *39*(1), 1–9. https://doi.org/10.1016/j.jpsychires.2004.05.004

Grant, B. F., Hasin, D. S., Stinson, F. S., Dawson, D. A., Goldstein, R. B., Smith, S., Huang, B., & Saha, T. D. (2006). The epidemiology of DSM-IV panic disorder and agoraphobia in the United States: Results from the National Epidemiologic Survey on Alcohol and Related Conditions. *Journal of Clinical Psychiatry*, *67*, 363–374. https://doi.org/10.4088/jcp.v67n0305

Gray, J. A. (1982). *The neuropsychology of anxiety: An enquiry into the functions of the septo-hippocampal system*. Oxford University Press.

Gray, J. A., & McNaughton, N. (2000). *The neuropsychology of anxiety.* Oxford University Press.

Griffith, J. W., Zinbarg, R. E., Craske, M. G., Mineka, S., Rose, R. D., Waters, A. M., & Sutton, J. M. (2010). Neuroticism as a common dimension in the internalizing disorders. *Psychological Medicine, 40*(7), 1125–1136. https://doi.org/10.1017/S0033291709991449

Haaker, J., Golkar, A., Selbing, I., & Olsson, A. (2017). Assessment of social transmission of threats in humans using observational fear conditioning. *Nature Protocols, 12*(7), 1378–1386. https://doi.org/10.1038/nprot.2017.027

Haberlandt, K., & Bingham, G. (1978). Verbs contribute to the coherence of brief narratives: Reading related and unrelated sentence triples. *Journal of Verbal Learning & Verbal Behavior, 17*(4), 419–425. https://doi.org/10.1016/S0022-5371(78)90247-5

Hakamata, Y., Lissek, S., Bar-Haim, Y., Britton, J. C., Fox, N. A., Leibenluft, E., Ernst, M., & Pine, D. S. (2010). Attention bias modification treatment: A meta-analysis toward the establishment of novel treatment for anxiety. *Biological Psychiatry, 68*(11), 982–990. https://doi.org/10.1016/j.biopsych.2010.07.021

Hallion, L. S., & Ruscio, A. M. (2011). A meta-analysis of the effect of cognitive bias modification on anxiety and depression. *Psychological Bulletin, 137*(6), 940–958. https://doi.org/10.1037/a0024355

Hamaker, E. L., Kuiper, R. M., & Grasman, R. P. P. P. (2015). A critique of the cross-lagged panel model. *Psychological Methods, 20*(1), 102–116. https://doi.org/10.1037/a0038889

Hariri, A. R., & Holmes, A. (2006). Genetics of emotional regulation: The role of the serotonin transporter in neural function. *Trends in Cognitive Sciences, 10*(4), 182–191. https://doi.org/10.1016/j.tics.2006.02.011

Hartley, C. A., Gorun, A., Reddan, M. C., Ramirez, F., & Phelps, E. A. (2014). Stressor controllability modulates fear extinction in humans. *Neurobiology of Learning and Memory, 113*, 149–156. https://doi.org/10.1016/j.nlm.2013.12.003

Hayes, S., Hirsch, C. R., Krebs, G., & Mathews, A. (2010). The effects of modifying interpretation bias on worry in generalized anxiety disorder. *Behaviour Research and Therapy, 48*(3), 171–178. https://doi.org/10.1016/j.brat.2009.10.006

Hayward, C., Killen, J. D., Kraemer, H. C., & Taylor, C. B. (1998). Linking self-reported childhood behavioral inhibition to adolescent social phobia. *Journal of the American Academy of Child & Adolescent Psychiatry, 37*(12), 1308–1316. https://doi.org/10.1097/00004583-199812000-00015

Hayward, C., Killen, J. D., Kraemer, H. C., & Taylor, C. B. (2000). Predictors of panic attacks in adolescents. *Journal of the American Academy of Child and Adolescent Psychiatry, 39*(2), 207–214. https://doi.org/10.1097/00004583-200002000-00021

Hebert, M. A., Evenson, A. R., Lumley, L. A., & Meyerhoff, J. L. (1998). Effects of acute social defeat on activity in the forced swim test: Parametric studies in DBA/2 mice using a novel measurement device. *Aggressive Behavior, 24*(4), 257–269. https://doi.org/10.1002/(SICI)1098-2337(1998)24:4%3C257::AID-AB2%3E3.0.CO;2-G

Heils, A., Teufel, A., Petri, S., Stober, G., Riederer, P., Bengel, D., & Lesch, K. P. (1996). Allelic variation of human serotonin transporter gene expression. *Journal of Neurochemistry,* *66*(6), 2621–2624. https://doi.org/10.1046/j.1471-4159.1996.66062621.x

Hettema, J. M., An, S. S., Neale, M. C., Bukszar, J., van den Oord, E. J. C. G., Kendler, K. S., & Chen, 7. (2006). Association between glutamic acid decarboxylase genes and anxiety disorders, major depression, and neuroticism. *Molecular Psychiatry, 11*, 752–762. https://doi.org/10.1038/sj.mp.4001845

Hettema, J. M., Neale, M. C., Myers, J. M., Prescott, C. A., & Kendler, K. S. (2006). A population-based twin study of the relationship between neuroticism and internalizing disorders. *American Journal of Psychiatry, 163*(5), 857–864. https://doi.org/10.1176/ajp.2006.163.5.857

Hettema, J. M., Prescott, C. A., & Kendler, K. S. (2004). Genetic and environmental sources of covariation between generalized anxiety disorder and neuroticism. *American Journal of Psychiatry, 161*(9), 1581–1587. https://doi.org/10.1176/appi.ajp.161.9.1581

Hettema, J. M., Prescott, C. A., Myers, J. M., Neale, M. C., & Kendler, K. S. (2005). The structure of genetic and environmental risk factors for anxiety disorders in men and women. *Archives of General Psychiatry, 62*(2), 182–189. https://doi.org/10.1001/archpsyc.62.2.182

Hirsch, C. R., Hayes, S., & Mathews, A. (2009). Looking on the bright side: Accessing benign meanings reduces worry. *Journal of Abnormal Psychology, 118*(1), 44–54. https://doi.org/10.1037/a0013473

Hoehn-Saric, R., Hazlett, R. L., & McLeod, D. R. (1993). Generalized anxiety disorder with early and late onset of anxiety symptoms. *Comprehensive Psychiatry, 34*, 291–298. https://doi.org/10.1016/0010-440X(93)90013-T

Hooley, J. M. (2004). Do psychiatric patients do better clinically if they live with certain kinds of families? *Current Directions in Psychological Science, 13*(5), 202–205. https://doi.org/10.1111/j.0963-7214.2004.00308.x

Horowitz, L. M., Alden, L. E., Wiggins, J. S., & Pincus, A. L. (2000). *Inventory of interpersonal problems manual.* Mindgarden.

Hur, J., Smith, J. F., DeYoung, K. A., Anderson, A. S., Kuang, J., Kim, H. C., Tillman, R. M., Kuhn, M., Fox, A. S., & Shackman, A. J. (2020). Anxiety and the neurobiology of temporally uncertain threat anticipation. *Journal of Neuroscience, 40*(41), 7949–7964. https://doi.org/10.1523/JNEUROSCI.0704-20.2020

Iacoviello, B. M., Wu, G., Abend, R., Murrough, J. W., Feder, A., Fruchter, E., Levinstein, Y., Wald, I., Bailey, C. R., Pine, D. S., Neumeister, A., Bar-Haim, Y., & Charney, D. S. (2014). Attention bias variability and symptoms of Posttraumatic Stress Disorder. *Journal of Traumatic Stress, 27*(2), 232–239. https://doi.org/10.1002/jts.21899

Jurin, T., & Biglbauer, S. (2018). Anxiety sensitivity as a predictor of panic disorder symptoms: A prospective 3-year study. *Anxiety, Stress, & Coping, 31*(4), 365–374. https://doi.org/10.1080/10615806.2018.1453745

Jylhä, P., Melartin, T., Rytsälä, H., & Isometsä, E. (2009). Neuroticism, introversion, and major depressive disorder—traits, states, or scars? *Depression and Anxiety, 26*(4), 325–334. https://doi.org/10.1002/da.20385

Kachin, K. E., Newman, M. G., & Pincus, A. L. (2001). An interpersonal problem approach to the division of social phobia subtypes. *Behavior Therapy, 32*(3), 479–501. https://doi.org/10.1016/S0005-7894(01)80032-0

Kagan, J., Reznick, J. S., Clarke, C., Snidman, N., & Garcia-Coll, C. (1984). Behavioral inhibition to the unfamiliar. *Child Development*, *55*(6), 2212–2225. https://doi.org/10.2307/1129793

Karg, K., Burmeister, M., Shedden, K., & Sen, S. (2011). The serotonin transporter promoter variant (5-HTTLPR), stress, and depression meta-analysis revisited: Evidence of genetic moderation. *Archives of General Psychiatry*, *68*(5), 444–454. https://doi.org/10.1001/archgenpsychiatry.2010.189

Kashdan, T. B. (2007). Social anxiety spectrum and diminished positive experiences: Theoretical synthesis and meta-analysis. *Clinical Psychology Review*, *27*(3), 348–365. https://doi.org/10.1016/j.cpr.2006.12.003

Kendler, K. S., Kuhn, J., & Prescott, C. A. (2004). The interrelationship of neuroticism, sex, and stressful life events in the prediction of episodes of major depression. *American Journal of Psychiatry*, *161*(4), 631–636. https://doi.org/10.1176/appi.ajp.161.4.631

Kendler, K. S., Kuhn, J. W., Vittum, J., Prescott, C. A., & Riley, B. (2005). The interaction of stressful life events and a serotonin transporter polymorphism in the prediction of episodes of major depression. *Archives of General Psychiatry*, *62*(5), 529–535. https://doi.org/10.1001/archpsyc.62.5.529

Kendler, K. S., Prescott, C. A., Myers, J., & Neale, M. C. (2003). The structure of genetic and environmental risk factors for common psychiatric and substance use disorders in men and women. *Archives of General Psychiatry*, *60*(9), 929–937. https://doi.org/10.1001/archpsyc.60.9.929

Kennedy, B. L., Lynch, G. V., & Schwab, J. J. (1998). Assessment of locus of control in patients with anxiety and depressive disorders. *Journal of Clinical Psychology*, *54*(4), 509–515. https://doi.org/10.1002/ (SICI) 1097-4679 (199806) 54:4%3 C509::AID-JCLP 12 %3E3.0.CO;2-J

Kenny, D. A., & Zautra, A. (1995). The trait-state-error model for multiwave data. *Journal of Consulting and Clinical Psychology*, *63*(1), 52–59. https://doi.org/10.1037/0022-0067.63.1.52

Kessler, R. C., Chiu, W. T., Demler, O., & Walters, E. E. (2005). Prevalence, severity, and comorbidity of 12-month DSM-IV disorders in the National Comorbidity Survey Replication. *Archives of General Psychiatry*, *62*(6), 617–627. https://doi.org/10.1001/archpsyc.62.6.617

Kessler, R. C., Chiu, W. T., Jin, R., Ruscio, A. M., Shear, K., & Walters, E. E. (2006). The epidemiology of panic attacks, panic disorder, and agoraphobia in the National Comorbidity Survey Replication. *Archives of General Psychiatry*, *63*, 415–424. https://doi.org/10.1001/archpsyc.63.4.415

Kessler, R. C., McLaughlin, K. A., Green, J. G., Gruber, M. J., Sampson, N. A., Zaslavsky, A. M., . . . Williams, D. R. (2010). Childhood adversities and adult psychopathology in the WHO World Mental Health Surveys. *British Journal of Psychiatry*, *197*(5), 378–385. https://doi.org/10.1192/bjp.bp.110.080499

Kessler, R. C., Petukhova, M., Sampson, N. A., Zaslavsky, A. M., & Wittchen, H. Ä. (2012). Twelve-month and lifetime prevalence and lifetime morbid risk of anxiety and mood disorders in the United States. *International Journal of Methods in Psychiatric Research*, *21*, 169–184. https://doi.org/10.1002/mpr.1359

Kircanski, K., Johnson, D. C., Mateen, M., Bjork, R. A., & Gotlib, I. H. (2016). Impaired retrieval inhibition of threat material in GAD. *Clinical Psychological Science*, *4*(2), 320–327. https://doi.org/10.1177/2167702615590996

Klein, M. H., Wonderlich, S., & Shea, M. T. (1993). Models of relationships between personalty and depression: Toward a framework for theory and research. In M. Klein, D. Kupfer, & M. T. Shea (Eds.), *Personality and depression: A current view* (pp. 1–54). Guilford.

Klein, S. R., Renshaw, K. D., & Curby, T. W. (2016). Emotion regulation and perceptions of hostile and constructive criticism in romantic relationships. *Behavior Therapy*, *47*(2), 143–154. https://doi.org/10.1016/j.beth.2015.10.007

Kleiner, L., & Marshall, W. L. (1987). The role of interpersonal problems in the development of agoraphobia with panic attacks. *Journal of Anxiety Disorders*, *1*(4), 313–323. https://doi.org/10.1016/0887-6185(87)90011-9

Knowles, K. A., & Olatunji, B. O. (2020). Specificity of trait anxiety in anxiety and depression: Meta-analysis of the State-Trait anxiety Inventory. *Clinical Psychology Review*, *82*, 101928. https://doi.org/10.1016/j.cpr.2020.101928

Koessler, S., Engler, H., Riether, C., & Kissler, J. (2009). No retrieval-induced forgetting under stress. *Psychological Science*, *20*(11), 1356–1363. https://doi.org/10.1111/j.1467-9280.2009.02450.x

Koster, E. H. W., Crombez, G., Verschuere, B., & De Houwer, J. (2006). Attention to threat in anxiety-prone individuals: Mechanisms underlying attentional bias. *Cognitive Therapy and Research*, *30*(5), 635–643. https://doi.org/10.1007/s10608-006-9042-9

Kotov, R., Gamez, W., Schmidt, F., & Watson, D. (2010). Linking "big" personality traits to anxiety, depressive, and substance use disorders: A meta-analysis. *Psychological Bulletin*, *136*(5), 768–821. https://doi.org/10.1037/a0020327

Kotov, R., Krueger, R. F., Watson, D., Achenbach, T. M., Althoff, R. R., Bagby, R. M., . . . Zimmerman, M. (2017). The Hierarchical Taxonomy of Psychopathology (HiTOP): A dimensional alternative to traditional nosologies. *Journal of Abnormal Psychology*, *126*(4), 454–477. https://doi.org/10.1037/abn0000258

Kramer, A., & Zinbarg, R. (2019). Recalling courage: An initial test of a brief writing intervention to activate a 'courageous mindset' and courageous behavior. *Journal of Positive Psychology*, *14*(4), 528–537. https://doi.org/10.1080/17439760.2018.1484943

Krueger, R. F. (1999). The structure of common mental disorders. *Archives of General Psychiatry*, *56*(10), 921–926. https://doi.org/10.1001/archpsyc.56.10.921

Krueger, R. F., Caspi, A., Moffitt, T. E., Silva, P. A., & McGee, R. (1996). Personality traits are differentially linked to mental disorders: A multitrait-multidiagnosis study of an adolescent birth cohort. *Journal of Abnormal Psychology*, *105*(3), 299–312. https://doi.org/10.1037/0021-8437.105.3.299

Krueger, R. F., & Tackett, J. L. (2003). Personality and psychopathology: Working toward the bigger picture. *Journal of Personality Disorders*, *17*(2), 109–128. https://doi.org/10.1521/pedi.17.2.109.23986

Kuckertz, J. M., & Amir, N. (2015). Attention bias modification for anxiety and phobias: Current status and future directions. *Current Psychiatry Reports*, *17*, 9. https://doi.org/10.1007/s11920-014-0545-x

LaBar, K. S., Gatenby, J. C., Gore, J. C., LeDoux, J. E., & Phelps, E. A. (1998). Human amygdala activation during conditioned fear acquisition and extinction: A mixed-trial fMRI study. *Neuron*, *20*(5), 937–945. https://doi.org/10.1016/S0896-6273(00)80475-4

Lange, W.-G., Heuer, K., Langner, O., Keijsers, G. P. J., Becker, E. S., & Rinck, M. (2011). Face value: Eye movements and the evaluation of facial crowds in social anxiety. *Journal of Behavior Therapy and Experimental Psychiatry, 42*(3), 355–363. https://doi.org/10.1016/j.jbtep.2011.02.007

Large, B., MacLeod, C., Clarke, P. J., & Notebaert, L. (2016). It's all about control: Memory bias in anxiety is restricted to threat cues that signal controllable danger. *Journal of Experimental Psychopathology, 7*(2), 190–204. https://doi.org/10.5127/jep.048515

Leary, T. (1957). *Interpersonal diagnosis of personality: A functional theory and methodology for personality evaluation.* Resource Publications.

LeDoux, J. E. (1995). Emotion: Clues from the brain. *Annual Review of Psychology, 46*, 209–235. https://doi.org/10.1146/annurev.ps.46.020195.001233

LeDoux, J. E. (2000). Emotion circuits in the brain. *Annual Review of Neuroscience, 23*, 155–184. https://doi.org/10.1146/annurev.neuro.23.1.155

Lee, Y., & Davis, M. (1997). Role of the septum in the excitatory effect of corticotropin-releasing hormone on the acoustic startle reflex. *Journal of Neuroscience, 17*(16), 6424–6433. https://doi.org/10.1523/JNEUROSCI.17-16-06424.1997

Levey, D. F., Gelernter, J., Polimanti, R., Zhou, H., Cheng, Z., Aslan, M., Quaden, R., Concato, J., Radhakrishnan, K., Bryois, J., Sullivan, P. F., the Million Veteran Program, & Stein, M. B. (2020). Reproducible genetic risk loci for anxiety: Results from ~200,000 participants in the million veteran program. *American Journal of Psychiatry, 177*(3), 223–232. https://doi.org/10.1176/appi.ajp.2019.19030256

Li, W., & Zinbarg, R. E. (2007). Anxiety sensitivity and panic attacks: A 1-year longitudinal study. *Behavior Modification, 31*(2), 145–161. https://doi.org/10.1177/0145445506296969

Liang, C.-W., Tsai, J.-L., & Hsu, W.-Y. (2017). Sustained visual attention for competing emotional stimuli in social anxiety: An eye tracking study. *Journal of Behavior Therapy and Experimental Psychiatry, 54*, 178–185. https://doi.org/10.1016/j.jbtep.2016.08.009

Lindström, B., Haaker, J., & Olsson, A. (2018). A common neural network differentially mediates direct and social fear learning. *NeuroImage, 167*, 121–129. https://doi.org/10.1016/j.neuroimage.2017.11.039

Lissek, S., Kaczkurkin, A. N., Rabin, S., Geraci, M., Pine, D. S., & Grillon, C. (2014). Generalized anxiety disorder is associated with overgeneralization of classically conditioned fear. *Biological Psychiatry, 75*(11), 909–915. https://doi.org/10.1016/j.biopsych.2013.07.025

Lissek, S., Rabin, S., Heller, R. E., Lukenbaugh, D., Geraci, M., Pine, D. S., & Grillon, C. (2010). Overgeneralization of conditioned fear as a pathogenic marker of panic disorder. *American Journal of Psychiatry, 167*(1), 47–55. https://doi.org/10.1176/appi.ajp.2009.09030410

Lonsdorf, T. B., Menz, M. M., Andreatta, M., Fullana, M. A., Golkar, A., Haaker, J., . . . Merz, C. J. (2017). Don't fear 'fear conditioning': Methodological considerations for the design and analysis of studies on human fear acquisition, extinction, and return of fear. *Neuroscience & Biobehavioral Reviews, 77*, 247–285. https://doi.org/10.1016/j.neubiorev.2017.02.026

Lonsdorf, T. B., & Merz, C. J. (2017). More than just noise: Inter-individual differences in fear acquisition, extinction and return of fear in humans—biological, experiential, temperamental factors, and methodological pitfalls. *Neuroscience & Biobehavioral Reviews, 80*, 703–728. https://doi.org/10.1016/j.neubiorev.2017.07.007

Lothmann, C., Holmes, E. A., Chan, S. W. Y., & Lau, J. Y. F. (2011). Cognitive bias modification training in adolescents: Effects on interpretation biases and mood. *Journal of Child Psychology and Psychiatry, 52*(1), 24–32. https://doi.org/10.1111/j.1469-7610.2010.02286.x

MacLeod, C. (2012). Cognitive bias modification procedures in age management of mental disorders. *Current Opinion in Psychiatry, 25*(2), 114–120. https://doi.org/10.1097/YCO.0b013e32834fda4a

MacLeod, C., & Cohen, I. L. (1993). Anxiety and the interpretation of ambiguity: A text comprehension study. *Journal of Abnormal Psychology, 102*(2), 238–247. https://doi.org/10.1037/0021-8437.102.2.238

MacLeod, C., Grafton, B., & Notebaert, L. (2019). Anxiety-linked attentional bias: Is it reliable? *Annual Review of Clinical Psychology, 15*, 529–554. https://doi.org/10.1146/annurev-clinpsy-050718-095505

MacLeod, C., & Matthews, A. (1988). Anxiety and the allocation of attention to threat. *The Quarterly Journal of Experimental Psychology Section A, 40*(4), 653–670. https://doi.org/10.1080/14640748808402292

MacLeod, C., & Mathews, A. (2012). Cognitive bias modification approaches to anxiety. *Annual Review of Clinical Psychology, 8*, 189–217. https://doi.org/10.1146/annurev-clinpsy-032511-143052

MacLeod, C., & Rutherford, E. M. (1992). Anxiety and the selective processing of emotional information: Mediating roles of awareness, trait and state variables, and personal relevance of stimulus materials. *Behaviour Research and Therapy, 30*(5), 479–491. https://doi.org/10.1016/0005-7967(92)90032-C

Maidenberg, E., Chen, E., Craske, M., Bohn, P., & Bystritsky, A. (1996). Specificity of attentional bias in panic disorder and social phobia. *Journal of Anxiety Disorders, 10*(6), 529–541. https://doi.org/10.1016/S0887-6185(96)00028-X

Marcaurelle, R., Bélanger, C., & Marchand, A. (2003). Marital relationship and the treatment of panic disorder with agoraphobia: A critical review. *Clinical Psychology Review, 23*(2), 247–276. https://doi.org/10.1016/S0272-7358(02)00207-6

Mathews, A., & MacLeod, C. (1985). Selective processing of threat cues in anxiety states. *Behavior Research and Therapy, 23*(5), 563–569. https://doi.org/10.1016/0005-7967(85)90104-4

Mathews, A., & MacLeod, C. (2005). Cognitive vulnerability to emotional disorders. *Annual Review of Clinical Psychology, 1*, 167–195. https://doi.org/10.1146/annurev.clinpsy.1.102803.143916

McClure, E. B., Monk, C. S., Nelson, E. E., Parrish, J. M., Adler, A., Blair, R. J. R., Fromm, S., Charney, D. S., Leibenluft, E., Ernst, M., & Pine, D. S. (2007). Abnormal attention modulation of fear circuit function in pediatric generalized anxiety disorder. *Archives of General Psychiatry, 64*(1), 97–106. https://doi.org/10.1001/archpsyc.64.1.97

McLaughlin, K. A., Green, J. G., Gruber, M. J., Sampson, N. A., Zaslavsky, A. M., & Kessler, R. C. (2012). Childhood adversities and first onset of psychiatric disorders in a national sample of US adolescents. *JAMA Psychiatry, 69*(11), 1151–1160. https://doi.org/10.1001/archgenpsychiatry.2011.2277

McLeod, J. D. (1994). Anxiety disorders and marital quality. *Journal of Abnormal Psychology, 103*(4), 767–776. https://doi.org/10.1037/0021-8437.103.4.767

McNally, R. J. (2002). Anxiety sensitivity and panic disorder. *Biological Psychiatry, 52*(10), 938–946. https://doi.org/10.1016/S0006-3223(02)01475-0

McNally, R. J. (2019). Attentional bias for threat: Crisis or opportunity? *Clinical Psychology Review, 69*, 4–13. https://doi.org/10.1016/j.cpr.2018.05.005

McNally, R. J., Amir, N., Louro, C. E., Lukach, B. M., Riemann, B. C., & Calamari, J. E. (1994). Cognitive processing of idiographic emotional information in Panic Disorder. *Behaviour Research and Therapy, 32*(1), 119–122. https://doi.org/10.1016/0005-7967(94)90092-2

Mertens, G., Boddez, Y., Sevenster, D., Engelhard, I. M., & De Houwer, J. (2018). A review on the effects of verbal instructions in human fear conditioning: Empirical findings, theoretical considerations, and future directions. *Biological Psychology, 137*, 49–64. https://doi.org/10.1016/j.biopsycho.2018.07.002

Mertens, G., Kuhn, M., Raes, A. K., Kalisch, R., De Houwer, J., & Lonsdorf, T. B. (2016). Fear expression and return of fear following threat instruction with or without direct contingency experience. *Cognition and Emotion, 30*(5), 968–984. https://doi.org/10.1080/02699931.2015.1038219

Mineka, S. (1985). Animal models of anxiety-based disorders: Their usefulness and limitations. In J. Maser & A. Tuma (Eds.), *Anxiety and the anxiety disorders* (pp. 199–244). Erlbaum.

Mineka, S., Cook, M., & Miller, S. (1984). Fear conditioned with escapable and inescapable shock: Effects of a feedback stimulus. *Journal of Experimental Psychology: Animal Behavior Processes, 10*(3), 307–323. https://doi.org/10.1037/0097-7403.10.3.307

Mineka, S., & Öhman, A. (2002). Phobias and preparedness: The selective, automatic, and encapsulated nature of fear. *Biological Psychiatry, 52*(10), 927–937. https://doi.org/10.1016/S0006-3223(02)01669-4

Mineka, S., Watson, D., & Clark, L. A. (1998). Comorbidity of anxiety and unipolar mood disorders. *Annual Review of Psychology, 49*, 377–412. https://doi.org/10.1146/annurev.psych.49.1.377

Mineka, S., Williams, A. L., Wolitzky-Taylor, K., Vrshek-Schallhorn, S., Craske, M. G., Hammen, C., & Zinbarg, R. E. (2020). Five-year prospective neuroticism–stress effects on major depressive episodes: Primarily additive effects of the general neuroticism factor and stress. *Journal of Abnormal Psychology, 129*(6), 646–657. https://doi.org/10.1037/abn0000530

Mineka, S., & Zinbarg, R. E. (1996). Conditioning and ethological models of anxiety disorders: Stress-in-dynamic-context models. In D. A. Hope (Ed.), *Perspectives on anxiety, panic, and fear: Current theory and research in motivation* (vol. 43, pp. 135–210). University of Nebraska Press.

Mitte, K. (2008). Memory bias for threatening information in anxiety and anxiety disorders: A meta-analytic review. *Psychological Bulletin, 134*(6), 886–911. https://doi.org/10.1037/a0013343

Mogg, K., Bradley, B. P., & Hallowell, N. (1994). Attentional bias to threat: Roles of trait anxiety, stressful events, and awareness. *Quarterly Journal of Experimental Psychology, 47*(4), 841–864. https://doi.org/10.1080/14640749408401099

Mogg, K., Matthews, A., & Weinman, J. (1989). Selective processing of threat cues in anxiety states: A replication. *Behaviour Research and Therapy, 27*(4), 317–323. https://doi.org/10.1016/0005-7967(89)90001-6

Mogg, K., Waters, A. M., & Bradley, B. P. (2017). Attention Bias Modification (ABM): Review of effects of multisession ABM training on anxiety and threat-related attention in high-anxious individuals. *Clinical Psychological Science, 5*(4), 698–717. https://doi.org/10.1177/2167702617696359

Mogoaşe, C., David, D., & Koster, E. H. W. (2014). Clinical efficacy of attentional bias modification procedures: An updated meta-analysis. *Journal of Clinical Psychology, 70*(12), 1133–1157. https://doi.org/10.1002/jclp.22081

Monk, C. S., Telzer, E. H., Mogg, K., Bradley, B. P., Mai, 7., Louro, H. M. C., Chen, G., McClure-Tone, E. B., Ernst, M., & Pine, D. S. (2008). Amygdala and ventrolateral prefrontal cortex activation to masked angry faces in children and adolescents with generalized anxiety disorder. *Archives of General Psychiatry, 65*(5), 568–576. https://doi.org/10.1001/archpsyc.65.5.568

Morriss, J., Macdonald, B., van Reekum, C. M. (2016). What is going on around here? Intolerance of uncertainty predicts threat generalization. *PLoS ONE, 11*(5), e0154494. https://doi.org/10.1371/journal.pone.0154494

Munafò, M. R., Clark, T., & Flint, J. (2005). Does measurement instrument moderate the association between the serotonin transporter gene and anxiety-related personality traits? A meta-analysis. *Molecular Psychiatry, 10*, 415–419. https://doi.org/10.1038/sj.mp.4001627

Muris, P., & Mercklebach, H. (2001). The etiology of childhood specific phobia: A multifactorial model. In M. Vasey & M. Dadds (Eds.), *The developmental psychopathology of anxiety* (pp. 355–385). Oxford University Press.

Naragon-Gainey, K., Prenoveau, J. M., Brown, T. A., & Zinbarg, R. E. (2016). A comparison and integration of structural models of depression and anxiety in a clinical sample: Support for and validation of the tri-level model. *Journal of Abnormal Psychology, 125*(7), 853–867. https://doi.org/10.1037/abn0000197

Naragon-Gainey, K., & Watson, D. (2018). What lies beyond neuroticism? An examination of the unique contributions of social-cognitive vulnerabilities to internalizing disorders. *Assessment, 25*(2), 143–158. https://doi.org/10.1177%2F1073191116659741

Naragon-Gainey, K., Watson, D., & Markon, K. E. (2009). Differential relations of depression and social anxiety symptoms to the facets of extraversion/positive emotionality. *Journal of Abnormal Psychology, 118*(2), 299–310. https://doi.org/10.1037/a0015637

Nitschke, J. B., Heller, W., Imig, J. C., McDonald, R. P., & Miller, G. A. (2001). Distinguishing dimensions of anxiety and depression. *Cognitive Therapy and Research, 25*, 1–22. https://doi.org/10.1023/A:1026485530405

Nitschke, J. B., Sarinopoulos, I., Oathes, D. J., Johnstone, T., Whalen, P. J., Davidson, R. J., & Kalin, N. H. (2009). Anticipatory activation in the amygdala and anterior cingulate in generalized anxiety disorder and prediction of treatment response. *American Journal of Psychiatry, 166*(3), 302–310. https://doi.org/10.1176/appi.ajp.2008.07101682

Noël, V. A., & Francis, S. E. (2011). A meta-analytic review of the role of child anxiety sensitivity in child anxiety. *Journal of Abnormal Child Psychology, 39*, 721–733. https://doi.org/10.1007/s10802-011-9489-3

Notebaert, L., Crombez, G., Van Damme, S., De Houwer, J., & Theeuwes, J. (2011). Signals of threat do not capture, but prioritize, attention: A conditioning approach. *Emotion, 11*(1), 81–89. https://doi.org/10.1037/a0021286

Nugent, K., & Mineka, S. (1994). The effect of high and low trait anxiety on implicit and explicit memory tasks. *Cognition and Emotion, 8*(2), 147–163. https://doi.org/10.1080/02699939408408933

Öhman, A., & Dimberg, U. (1978). Facial expressions as conditioned stimuli for electrodermal responses: A case of "preparedness"? *Journal of Personality and Social Psychology, 36*(11), 1251–1258. https://doi.org/10.1037/0022-3514.36.11.1251

Öhman, A., Dimberg, U., & Öst, L. (1985). Animal and social phobias: Biological constraints on learned fear responses. In S. Reiss & R. R. Bootzin (Eds.), *Theoretical issues in behavior therapy* (pp. 123–178). Academic Press.

Öhman, A., & Mineka, S. (2001). Fears, phobias, and preparedness: Toward an evolved module of fear and fear learning. *Psychological Review, 108*(3), 483–522. https://doi.org/10.1037/0033-2957.108.3.483

Öhman, A., & Soares, J. J. F. (1998). Emotional conditioning to masked stimuli: Expectancies for aversive outcomes following nonrecognized fear-relevant stimuli. *Journal of Experimental Psychology: General, 127*(1), 69–82. https://doi.org/10.1037/0096-3445.127.1.69

Olatunji, B. O., & Wolitzky-Taylor, K. B. (2009). Anxiety sensitivity and the anxiety disorders: A meta-analytic review and synthesis. *Psychological Bulletin, 135*(6), 974–999. https://doi.org/10.1037/a0017428

Olsson, A., McMahon, K., Papenberg, G., Zaki, J., Bolger, N., & Ochsner, K. N. (2016). Vicarious fear learning depends on empathic appraisals and trait empathy. *Psychological Science, 27*(1), 25–33. https://doi.org/10.1177%2F0956797615604124

Ormel, J., Jeronimus, B. F., Kotov, R., Riese, H., Bos, E. H., Hankin, B., Rosmalen, J. G. M., & Oldehinkel, A. J. (2013). Neuroticism and common mental disorders; Meaning and utility of a complex relationship. *Clinical Psychology Review, 33*(5), 686–697. https://doi.org/10.1016/j.cpr.2013.04.003

Öst, L. G., & Hugdahl, K. (1981). Acquisition of phobias and anxiety response patterns in clinical patients. *Behaviour Research and Therapy, 19*(5), 439–447. https://doi.org/10.1016/0005-7967(81)90134-0

Pavlov, I. P. (1927). *Conditioned reflexes.* Oxford University Press.

Pergamin-Hight, L., Naim, R., Bakermans-Kranenburg, M. J., van IJzendoorn, M. H., & Bar-Haim, Y. (2015). Content specificity of attention bias to threat in anxiety disorders: A meta-analysis. *Clinical Psychology Review, 35*, 10–18. https://doi.org/10.1016/j.cpr.2014.10.005

Pfleiderer, B., Zinkirciran, S., Arolt, V., WHeindel, W., Deckert, J., & Domschke, K. (2007). fMRI amygdala activation during a spontaneous panic attack in a patient with panic disorder. *World Journal of Biological Psychiatry, 8*(4), 269–272. https://doi.org/10.1080/15622970701216673

Pham, 7., Sun, C., Chen, 7., van den Oord, E. J. C. G., Neale, M. C., Kendler, K. S., & Hettema, J. M. (2009). Association study between GABA receptor genes and anxiety spectrum disorders. *Depression and Anxiety, 26*(11), 998–1003. https://doi.org/10.1002/da.20628

Phelps, E. A., & LeDoux, J. E. (2005). Contributions of the amygdala to emotion processing: From animal models to human behavior. *Neuron, 48*(3), 175–187. https://doi.org/10.1016/j.neuron.2005.09.025

Pincus, A. L., Lukowitsky, M. R., & Wright, A. G. C. (2010). The interpersonal nexus of personality and psychopathology. In T. Millon, R. F. Krueger, & E. Simonsen (Eds.), *Contemporary directions in psychopathology: Scientific foundations of the DSM-V and ICD-11* (pp. 523–552). Guilford.

Poulton, R., & Menzies, R. (2002). Non-associative fear acquisition: A review of the evidence from retrospective and longitudinal research. *Behaviour Research and Therapy, 40*(2), 127–149. https://doi.org/10.1016/S0005-7967(01)00045-6

Prenoveau, J. M., Zinbarg, R. E., Craske, M. G., Griffith, J. W., & Epstein, A. M. (2010). Testing a hierarchical model of anxiety and depression in adolescents: A tri-level model. *Journal of Anxiety Disorders, 24*(3), 334–344. https://doi.org/10.1016/j.janxdis.2010.01.006

Price, R. B., Kuckertz, J. M., Siegle, G. J., Ladouceur, C. D., Silk, J. S., Ryan, N. D., Dahl, R. E., & Amir, N. (2015). Empirical recommendations for improving the stability of the dot-probe task in clinical research. *Psychological Assessment, 27*(2), 365–376. https://doi.org/10.1037/pas0000036

Price, R. B., Rosen, D., Siegle, G. J., Ladouceur, C. D., Tang, K., Allen, K. B., Ryan, N. D., Dahl, R. E., Forbes, E. E., & Silk, J. S. (2016). From anxious youth to depressed adolescents: Prospective prediction of 2-year depression symptoms via attentional bias measures. *Journal of Abnormal Psychology, 125*(2), 267–278. https://doi.org/10.1037/abn0000127

Purves, K. L., Coleman, J. R. I., Meier, S. M., Rayner, C., Davis, K. A. S., Cheesman, R., . . . Eley, T. C. (2020). A major role for common genetic variation in anxiety disorders. *Molecular Psychiatry, 25*, 3292–3303. https://doi.org/10.1038/s41380-019-0559-1

Przeworski, A., Newman, M. G., Pincus, A. L., Kasoff, M. B., Yamasaki, A. S., Castonguay, L. G., & Berlin, K. S. (2011). Interpersonal pathoplasticity in individuals with generalized anxiety disorder. *Journal of Abnormal Psychology, 120*(2), 286–298. https://doi.org/10.1037/a0023334

Rachman, S. J. (1978). *Fear and courage.* Freeman.

Rachman, S. J. (1990). *Fear and courage,* 2nd ed. Freeman.

Rachman, S. J. (2010). Courage: A psychological perspective. In C. Pury & S. Lopez (Eds.), *The psychology of courage: Modern research on an ancient virtue* (pp. 91–107). American Psychological Association.

Rapee, R. M., & Melville, L. F. (1997). Recall of family factors in social phobia and panic disorder: Comparison of mother and offspring reports. *Depression and Anxiety, 5*(1), 7–11. https://doi.org/10.1002/(SICI)1520-6394(1997)5:1%3C7::AID-DA2%3E3.0.CO;2-E

Razran, G. (1961). The observable and the inferable conscious in current Soviet psychophysiology: Interoceptive conditioning, semantic conditioning, and the orienting reflex. *Psychological Review, 68*(2), 81–147. https://doi.org/10.1037/h0039848

Reidy, J. (2004). Trait anxiety, trait depression, worry, and memory. *Behaviour Research and Therapy, 42*(8), 937–948. https://doi.org/10.1016/j.brat.2003.07.005

Reidy, J., & Richards, A. (1997). Anxiety and memory: A recall bias for threatening words in high anxiety. *Behaviour Research and Therapy, 35*(6), 531–542. https://doi.org/10.1016/S0005-7967(97)00001-6

Reiss, S., Peterson, R. A., Gursky, D. M., & McNally, R. J. (1986). Anxiety sensitivity, anxiety frequency and the predictions of fearfulness. *Behaviour Research and Therapy, 24*(1), 1–8. https://doi.org/10.1016/0005-7967(86)90143-9

Roberts, B. W., & DelVecchio, W. F. (2000). The rank-order consistency of personality traits from childhood to old age: A quantitative review of longitudinal studies. *Psychological Bulletin, 126*(1), 3–25. https://doi.org/10.1037/0033-2909.126.1.3

Rodebaugh, T. L., Scullin, R. B., Langer, J. K., Dixon, D. J., Huppert, J. D., Bernstein, A., Zvielli, A., & Lenze, E. J. (2016). Unreliability as a threat to understanding psychopathology: The cautionary tale of attentional bias. *Journal of Abnormal Psychology, 125*(6), 840–851. https://doi.org/10.1037/abn0000184

Rodriguez, B. F., Bruce, S. E., Pagano, M. E., Spencer, M. A., & Keller, M. B. (2004). Factor structure and stability of the Anxiety Sensitivity Index in a longitudinal study of anxiety disorder patients. *Behaviour Research and Therapy, 42*(1), 79–91. https://doi.org/10.1016/S0005-7967(03)00074-3

Rosellini, A. J., & Brown, T. A. (2011). The NEO Five-Factor Inventory: Latent structure and relationships with dimensions of anxiety and depressive disorders in a large clinical sample. *Assessment, 18*(1), 27–38. https://doi.org/10.1177/1073191110382848

Rosenbaum, J. F., Biederman, J., Gersten, M., Hirshfeld, D. R., Meminger, S. R., Herman, J. B., Kagan, J., Reznick, J. S., & Snidman, N. (1988). Behavioral inhibition in children of parents with panic disorder and agoraphobia: A controlled study. *Archives of General Psychiatry, 45*(5), 463–470. https://doi.org/10.1001/archpsyc.1988.01800290083010

Rosenbaum, J. F., Biederman, J., Hirshfeld, D. R., Bolduc, E. A., Faraone, S. V., Kagan, J., Snidman, N., & Reznick, J. S. (1991). Further evidence of an association between behavioral inhibition and anxiety disorders: Results from a family study of children from a non-clinical sample. *Journal of Psychiatric Research, 25*(1-2), 49–65. https://doi.org/10.1016/0022-3956 (91) 90015-3

Rudaizky, D., Basanovic, & MacLeod, C. (2014). Biased attentional engagement with, and disengagement from, negative information: Independent cognitive pathways to anxiety vulnerability? *Cognition and Emotion, 28*(2), 245–259. https://doi.org/10.1080/02699931.2013.815154

Salemink, E., van den Hout, M., & Kindt, M. (2009). Effects of positive interpretive bias modification in highly anxious individuals. *Journal of Anxiety Disorders, 23*(5), 676–683. https://doi.org/10.1016/j.janxdis.2009.02.006

Salzer, S., Pincus, A. L., Winkelbach, C., Leichsenring, F., & Leibing, E. (2011). Interpersonal subtypes and change of interpersonal problems in the treatment of patients with generalized anxiety disorder: A pilot study. *Psychotherapy, 48*(3), 304–310. https://doi.org/10.1037/a0022013

Sanderson, W. C., Rapee, R. M., & Barlow, D. H. (1989). The influence of an illusion of control on panic attacks induced via inhalation of 5.5% carbon dioxide–enriched air. *Archives of General Psychiatry, 46*(2), 157–162. https://doi.org/10.1001/archpsyc.1989.01810020059010

Shechner, T., Britton, J. C., Pérez-Edgar, K., Bar-Haim, Y., Ernst, M., Fox, N. A., Leibenluft, E., & Pine, D. S. (2012). Attention biases, anxiety, and development: Toward or away from threats or rewards? *Depression and Anxiety, 29*(4), 282–294. https://doi.org/10.1002/da.20914

Schinka, J. A., Busch, R. M., & Robichauz-Keene, N. (2004). A meta-analysis of the association between the serotonin transporter gene polymorphism (5-HTTLPR) and trait anxiety. *Molecular Psychiatry, 9*, 197–202. https://doi.org/10.1038/sj.mp.4001405

Schmidt, N. B., Lerew, D. R., & Jackson, R. J. (1999). Prospective evaluation of anxiety sensitivity in the pathogenesis of panic: Replication and extension. *Journal of Abnormal Psychology, 108*(3), 532–537. https://doi.org/10.1037/0021-8437.108.3.532

Schmidt, N. B., Mitchell, M. A., & Richey, J. A. (2008). Anxiety sensitivity as an incremental predictor of later anxiety symptoms and syndromes. *Comprehensive Psychiatry, 49*(4), 407–412. https://doi.org/10.1016/j.comppsych.2007.12.004

Schmidt, N. B., Zvolensky, M. J., & Maner, J. K. (2006). Anxiety sensitivity: Prospective prediction of panic attacks and Axis I pathology. *Journal of Psychiatric Research, 40*(8), 691–699. https://doi.org/10.1016/j.jpsychires.2006.07.009

Schofield, C. A., Johnson, A. L., Inhoff, A. W., & Coles, M. E. (2012). Social anxiety and difficulty disengaging threat: Evidence from eye-tracking. *Cognition and Emotion, 26*(2), 300–311. https://doi.org/10.1080/02699931.2011.602050

Schwartz, C. E., Snidman, N., & Kagan, J. (1999). Adolescent social anxiety as an outcome of inhibited temperament in childhood. *Journal of the American Academy of Child & Adolescent Psychiatry, 38*(8), 1008–1015. https://doi.org/10.1097/00004583-199908000-00017

Seefeldt, W. L., Krämer, M., Tuschen-Caffier, B., & Heinrichs, N. (2014). Hypervigilance and avoidance in visual attention in children with social phobia. *Journal of Behavior Therapy and Experimental Psychiatry, 45*(1), 105–112. https://doi.org/10.1016/j.jbtep.2013.09.004

Selbing, I., & Olsson, A. (2019). Anxious behaviour in a demonstrator affects observational learning. *Scientific Reports, 9*, 9181. https://doi.org/10.1038/s41598-019-45613-1

Seligman, M. E. (1971). Phobias and preparedness. *Behavior Therapy, 2*(3), 307–320. https://doi.org/10.1016/S0005-7894(71)80064-3

Shackman, A. J., Tromp, D. P. M., Stockbridge, M. D., Kaplan, C. M., Tillman, R. M., & Fox, A. S. (2016). Dispositional negativity: An integrative psychological and neurobiological perspective. *Psychological Bulletin, 142*(12), 1275–1314. https://doi.org/10.1037/bul0000073

Sjouwerman, R., Scharfenort, R., & Lonsdorf, T. B. (2020). Individual differences in fear acquisition: Multivariate analyses of different emotional negativity scales, physiological responding, subjective measures, and neural activation. *Scientific Reports, 10*, 15283. https://doi.org/10.1038/s41598-020-72007-5

Slade, T., & Watson, D. (2006). The structure of common DSM-IV and ICD-10 mental disorders in the Australian general population. *Psychological Medicine, 36*(11), 1593–1600. https://doi.org/10.1017/S0033291706008452

Smillie, L. D., Cooper, A. J., Wilt, J., & Revelle, W. (2012). Do extraverts get more bang for the buck? Refining the affective-reactivity hypothesis of extraversion. *Journal of Personality and Social Psychology, 103*(2), 306–326. https://doi.org/10.1037/a0028372

Smoller, J. W. (2020). Anxiety genetics goes genomic. *American Journal of Psychiatry, 177*(3), 190–194. https://doi.org/10.1176/appi.ajp.2020.20010038

Smoller, J. W. (2016). The genetics of stress-related disorders: PTSD, depression, and anxiety disorders. *Neuropsychopharmacology, 41*, 297–319. https://doi.org/10.1038/npp.2015.266

Snyder, D. K., Zinbarg, R. E., Heyman, R. E., Haynes, S. N., Gasbarrini, M. F., & Uliaszek, M. (2010). Assessing linkages between interpersonal processes and anxiety disorders. In J. G. Beck (Ed.), *Interpersonal processes in the anxiety disorders: Implications for understanding psychopathology and treatment* (pp. 37–67). American Psychological Association.

Somerville, L. H., Whalen, P. J., & Kelley, W. M. (2010). Human bed nucleus of the stria terminalis indexes hypervigilant threat monitoring. *Biological Psychiatry*, *68*(5), 416–424. https://doi.org/10.1016/j.biopsych.2010.04.002

Spinhoven, P., Penelo, E., de Rooij, M., Penninx, B. W., & Ormel, J. (2013). Reciprocal effects of stable and temporary components of neuroticism and affective disorders: Results of a longitudinal cohort study. *Psychological Medicine*, *44*(2), 337–348. https://doi.org/10.1017/S0033291713000822

Steinman, S. A., & Teachman, B. A. (2010). Modifying interpretations among individuals high in anxiety sensitivity. *Journal of Anxiety Disorders*, *24*(1), 71–78. https://doi.org/10.1016/j.janxdis.2009.08.008

Steyer, R., & Schmitt, T. (1994). The theory of confounding and its application in causal modeling with latent variables. In A. von Eye & C. C. Clogg (Eds.), *Latent variables analysis: Applications for developmental research* (pp. 36–67). Sage.

Stinson, F. S., Dawson, D. A., Chou, S. P., Smith, S., Goldstein, R. B., Ruan, W. J., & Grant, B. F. (2007). The epidemiology of DSM-IV specific phobia in the USA: Results from the National Epidemiologic Survey on Alcohol and Related Conditions. *Psychological Medicine*, *37*, 1047–1059. https://doi.org/10.1017/S0033291707000086

Stopa, L., & Clark, D. M. (2000). Social phobia and interpretation of social events. *Behaviour Research and Therapy*, *38*(3), 273–283. https://doi.org/10.1016/S0005-7967(99)00043-1

Sullivan, H. S. (1953). *The interpersonal theory of psychiatry*. Norton.

Telch, M. J., Lucas, J. A., & Nelson, P. (1989). Nonclinical panic in college students: An investigation of prevalence and symptomatology. *Journal of Abnormal Psychology*, *98*, 300–306. https://doi.org/10.1037/0021-8437.98.3.300

Thayer, R. E. (1989). *The biopsychology of mood and arousal*. Oxford University Press.

Thoeringer, C. K., Ripke, S., Unschuld, P. G., Lucae, S., Ising, M., Bettecken, T., Uhr, M., Keck, M. E., Mueller-Myhsok, Holsboer, F., Binder, E. B., & Erhardt, A. (2009). The GABA transporter 1 (SLC6A1): A novel candidate gene for anxiety disorders. *Journal of Neural Transmission*, *116*, 649–657. https://doi.org/10.1007/s00702-008-0075-y

Turner, S. M., Beidel, D. C., & Wolff, P. L. (1996). Is behavioral inhibition related to the anxiety disorders? *Clinical Psychology Review*, *16*(2), 157–172. https://doi.org/10.1016/0272-7358(96)00010-4

Tyrer, P. J. (1990). The division of neurosis: A failed classification. *Journal of the Royal Society of Medicine*, *83*, 614–616.

Uhrich, J. (1938). The social hierarchy in albino mice. *Journal of Comparative Psychology*, *25*(2), 373–413. https://doi.org/10.1037/h0056350

Uliaszek, A. A., Hauner, K. K. Y., Zinbarg, R. E., Craske, M. G., Mineka, S., Griffith, J. W., & Rose, R. D. (2009). An examination of content overlap and disorder-specific predictions in the associations of neuroticism with anxiety and depression. *Journal of Research in Personality*, *43*(5), 785–794. https://doi.org/10.1016/j.jrp.2009.05.009

van den Heuvel, O. A., Veltman, D. J., Groenewegen, H. J., Witter, M. P., Merkelbach, J., Cath, D. C., van Balkom, A. J. L. M., van Oppen, P., & van Dyck, R. (2005). Disorder-specific neuroanatomical correlates of attentional bias in obsessive-compulsive disorder, panic disorder, and hypochondriasis. *Archives of General Psychiatry*, *62*(8), 922–933. https://doi.org/10.1001/archpsyc.62.8.922

Viana, A. G., & Stevens, E. N. (2013). Interpersonal difficulties as an underlying mechanism in the anxiety-depression association. *Behaviour Change*, *30*(4), 273–282. https://doi.org/10.1017/bec.2013.26

Vollebergh, W. A. M., Iedema, J., Bijl, R. V., de Graaf, R., Smit, F., & Ormel, J. (2001). The structure and stability of common mental disorders: The NEMESIS Study. *Archives of General Psychiatry*, *58*(6), 597–603. https://doi.org/10.1001/archpsyc.58.6.597

Vrshek-Schallhorn, S., Mineka, S., Zinbarg, R. E., Craske, M. G., Griffith, J. W., Sutton, J., Redei, E. A., Wolitzky-Taylor, K., Hammen, C., & Adam, E. K. (2014). Refining the candidate environment: Interpersonal stress, the serotonin transporter polymorphism, and gene-environment interactions in Major Depression. *Clinical Psychological Science*, *2*(3), 235–248. https://doi.org/10.1177/2167702613499329

Wang, P. S., Berglund, P., & Olfson, M., et al. (2005). *Archives of General Psychiatry*, *62*, 603–613. doi:10.1001/archpsyc.62.6.603

Waters, A. M., Mogg, K., Bradley, B. P., & Pine, D. S. (2008). Attentional bias for emotional faces in children with GAD. *Journal of the American Academy of Child & Adolescent Psychiatry*, *47*(4), 435–442. https://doi.org/10.1097/CHI.0b013e3181642992

Watson, D. (1999). Dimensions underlying the anxiety disorders: A hierarchical perspective. *Current Opinion in Psychiatry*, *12*(2), 181–186.

Watson, D. (2005). Rethinking the mood and anxiety disorders: A quantitative hierarchical model for DSM-V. *Journal of Abnormal Psychology*, *114*(4), 522–536. https://doi.org/10.1037/0021-8437.114.4.522

Watson, D., & Clark, L. A. (1984). Negative affectivity: The disposition to experience aversive emotional states. *Psychological Bulletin*, *96*(3), 465–490. https://doi.org/10.1037/0033-2909.96.3.465

Watson, D., & Clark, L. A. (1997). Extraversion and its positive emotional core. In R. Hogan, J. A. Johnson, & S. R. Briggs (Eds.), *Handbook of personality psychology* (pp. 767–793). Academic Press.

Watson, D., Gamez, W., & Simms, L. J. (2005). Basic dimensions of temperament and their relation to anxiety and depression: A symptom-based perspective. *Journal of Research in Personality*, *39*(1), 46–66. https://doi.org/10.1016/j.jrp.2004.09.006

Watson, D., & Naragon-Gainey, K. (2010). On the specificity of positive emotional dysfunction in psychopathology: Evidence from the mood and anxiety disorders and schizophrenia/schizotypy. *Clinical Psychology Review*, *30*(7), 839–848. https://doi.org/10.1016/j.cpr.2009.11.002

Watson, D., & Tellegen, A. (1985). Toward a consensual structure of mood. *Psychological Bulletin*, *98*(2), 219–235. https://doi.org/10.1037/0033-2909.98.2.219

Watson, D., Wiese, D., Vaidya, J., & Tellegen, A. (1999). The two general activation systems of affect: Structural findings, evolutionary considerations, and psychobiological evidence. *Journal of Personality and Social Psychology*, *76*(5), 820–838. https://doi.org/10.1037/0022-3514.76.5.820

Watson, J. B., & Rayner, R. (1920). Conditioned emotional reactions. *Journal of Experimental Psychology*, *3*(1), 1–14. https://doi.org/10.1037/h0069608

Weissman, A. N., & Beck, A. T. (1978). *Development and validation of the Dysfunctional Attitudes Scale*. Paper presented at the annual meeting of the Association for the Advancement of Behavior Therapy, Chicago.

Whalen, P. J. (1998). Fear, vigilance, and ambiguity: Initial neuroimaging studies of the human amygdala. *Current Directions in Psychological Science, 7*(6), 177–188. https://doi.org/10.1111/1467-8721.ep10836912

Whisman, M. A. (1999). Marital dissatisfaction and psychiatric disorders: Results from the national comorbidity survey. *Journal of Abnormal Psychology, 108*(4), 701–706. https://doi.org/10.1037/0021-8437.108.4.701

Whisman, M. A., & Baucom, D. H. (2012). Intimate relationships and psychopathology. *Clinical Child and Family Psychology Review, 15*(1), 4–13. https://doi.org/10.1007/s10567-011-0107-2

Williams, A. L., & Conway, C. C. (2022). Correlation between laboratory-based vicarious threat learning and emotional disorder symptom dimensions. *Journal of Behavior Therapy and Experimental Psychiatry, 74*, 101696. https://doi.org/10.1016/j.jbtep.2021.101696

Williams, A. L., Craske, M. G., Mineka, S., & Zinbarg, R. E. (2021). Reciprocal effects of personality and general distress: Neuroticism vulnerability is stronger than scarring. *Journal of Abnormal Psychology, 130*(1), 34–46. https://doi.org/10.1037/abn0000635

Williams, J. L., & Lierle, D. M. (1986). Effects of stress controllability, immunization, and therapy on the subsequent defeat of colony intruders. *Animal Learning & Behavior, 14*, 305–314. https://doi.org/10.3758/BF03200072

Williams, J. L., & Scott, D. K. (1989). Influence of conspecific and predatory stressors and the associated odors on defensive burying and freezing. *Animal Learning & Behavior, 17*, 383–393. https://doi.org/10.3758/BF03205219

Wilson, E., & MacLeod, C. (2003). Contrasting two accounts of anxiety-linked attentional bias: Selective attention to varying levels of stimulus threat intensity. *Journal of Abnormal Psychology, 112*(2), 212–218. https://doi.org/10.1037/0021-8437.112.2.212

Wittchen, H.-U., Nocon, A., Beesdo, K., Pine, D. S., Höfler, M., Lieb, R., & Gloster, A. T. (2008). Agoraphobia and panic. *Psychotherapy and Psychosomatics, 77*(3), 147–157. https://doi.org/10.1159/000116608

Wittchen, H.-U., & Beesdo-Baum, K. (2018). "Throwing out the baby with the bathwater"? Conceptual and methodological limitations of the HiTOP approach. *World Psychiatry, 17*(3), 298–299. https://doi.org/10.1002%2Fwps.20561

Yoon, K. L., & Zinbarg, R. E. (2008). Interpreting neutral faces as threatening is a default mode for socially anxious individuals. *Journal of Abnormal Psychology, 117*(3), 680–685. https://doi.org/10.1037/0021-8437.117.3.680

Yoon, K. L., & Zinbarg, R. E. (2007). Threat is in the eye of the beholder: Social anxiety and the interpretation of ambiguous facial expressions. *Behaviour Research and Therapy, 45*(4), 839–847. https://doi.org/10.1016/j.brat.2006.05.004

Zinbarg, R. E. (1998). Concordance and synchrony in measures of anxiety and panic reconsidered: A hierarchical model of anxiety and panic. *Behavior Therapy, 29*(2), 301–323. https://doi.org/10.1016/S0005-7894(98)80009-9

Zinbarg, R. E., & Barlow, D. H. (1996). Structure of anxiety and the anxiety disorders: A hierarchical model. *Journal of Abnormal Psychology, 105*(2), 181–193. https://doi.org/10.1037/0021-8437.105.2.181

Zinbarg, R. E., Barlow, D. H., & Brown, T. A. (1997). Hierarchical structure and general factor saturation of the Anxiety Sensitivity Index: Evidence and implications. *Psychological Assessment, 9*(3), 277–284. https://doi.org/10.1037/1040-3590.9.3.277

Zinbarg, R. E., Kramer, A. M., Kelley, N. J., Williams, A. L., Chat, I. K.-Y., Young, K. S., Nusslock, R., Bookheimer, S. Y., & Craske, M. G. (2022). Conceptual replication and multi-method extension of a tri-level model of anxiety and depression in a sample of young adults. Unpublished manuscript. https://osf.io/7tpza/

Zinbarg, R. E., Lee, J. E., & Yoon, K. L. (2007). Dyadic predictors of outcome in a cognitive-behavioral program for patients with generalized anxiety disorder in committed relationships: A "spoonful of sugar" and a dose of non-hostile criticism may help. *Behaviour Research and Therapy, 45*(4), 699–713. https://doi.org/10.1016/j.brat.2006.06.005

Zinbarg, R. E., & Mineka, S. (2007). Is emotion regulation a useful construct that adds to the explanatory power of learning models of anxiety disorders or a new label for old constructs? *American Psychologist, 62*(3), 259–261. https://doi.org/10.1037/0003-0667.62.3.259

Zinbarg, R. E., Mineka, S., Craske, M. G., Griffith, J. W., Sutton, J., Rose, R. D., Nazarian, M., Mor, N., & Waters, A. M. (2010). The Northwestern-UCLA Youth Emotion Project: Associations of cognitive vulnerabilities, neuroticism and gender with past diagnoses of emotional disorders in adolescents. *Behaviour Research and Therapy, 48*(5), 347–358. https://doi.org/10.1016/j.brat.2009.12.008

Zinbarg, R. E., & Mohlman, J. (1998). Individual differences in the acquisition of affectively valenced associations. *Journal of Personality and Social Psychology, 74*(4), 1024–1040. https://doi.org/10.1037/0022-3514.74.4.1024

Zinbarg, R. E., Mineka, S., Bobova, L., Craske, M. G., Vrshek-Schallhorn, S., Griffith, J. W., Wolitzky-Taylor, K., Waters, A. M., Sumner, J. A., & Anand, D. (2016). Testing a hierarchical model of neuroticism and its cognitive facets: Latent structure and prospective prediction of first onsets of anxiety and unipolar mood disorders during 3 years in late adolescence. *Clinical Psychological Science, 4*(5), 805–824. https://doi.org/10.1177/2167702615618162

Zinbarg, R. E., Mohlman, J., & Hong, N. N. (1999). Dimensions of anxiety sensitivity. In S. Taylor (Ed.), *Anxiety sensitivity: Theory, research, and treatment of the fear of anxiety* (pp. 83–114). Erlbaum.

Zinbarg, R. E., & Yoon, K. L. (2008). RST and clinical disorders: Anxiety and depression. In P. J. Corr (Ed.), *The reinforcement sensitivity theory of personality* (pp. 360–397). Cambridge University Press. https://doi.org/10.1017/CBO9780511819384.013

Zvielli, A., Vernstein, A., & Koster, E. H. W. (2015). Temporal dynamics of attentional bias. *Clinical Psychological Science, 3*(5), 772–788. https://doi.org/10.1177/2167702614551572

# CHAPTER 8

# Obsessive-Compulsive and Related Disorders

Jonathan S. Abramowitz

Obsessive-compulsive disorder (OCD) is among the most destructive of psychological conditions. Its symptoms often interfere with occupational, academic, interpersonal, and leisure pursuits, not to mention activities of daily living (e.g., watching television, childcare). It is also a complex and highly heterogeneous syndrome, and numerous conceptual approaches have been proposed in an attempt to understand its seemingly perplexing psychopathology. Moreover, the most recent iteration of the *DSM* shifts OCD from its traditional classification as an anxiety disorder to a new class of conditions: the obsessive-compulsive and related disorders (OCRDs). OCD is the flagship diagnosis within this group of disorders that also includes hoarding disorder (HD), hair-pulling and skin-picking disorders, and body dysmorphic disorder (BDD), all of which are less common than OCD (contrary to what might be assumed, obsessive-compulsive personality disorder (OCPD) is not among the OCRDs in *DSM-5*). This chapter addresses the nature of OCD and the other OCRDs. The phenomenology and major conceptual models are reviewed, along with their strengths and limitations. The chapter also provides a critical evaluation of the basis for the OCRD category.

## Phenomenology of OCD

Whereas everyone (whether or not they meet the official criteria for "having" OCD) experiences unwanted thoughts and performs ritualistic behavior once in a while, OCD is characterized by *obsessions* and *compulsions* (defined below) severe enough to be time-consuming and which cause distress or functional interference. The severity of the obsessions and compulsions occurs in nature on a continuum from occasional "annoying" intrusive thoughts and compulsive acts to ubiquitous unwanted thoughts, doubts, and urges that, while seemingly senseless, are perceived as signs of danger and threat, along with near constant performance of compulsive rituals. Let us look more closely at these signs and symptoms.

### Obsessions

While the term "obsession" is frequently used in our vernacular to refer to a preoccupation or fixation (e.g., "He's obsessed with his new car"), in the context of OCD, obsessions are persistent repetitive *unwanted* private experiences (i.e., thoughts, images, doubts, and ideas) that the person judges to be senseless or repugnant and that provoke distress in the form of anxiety or guilt. Although highly person-specific, obsessions generally distill into themes such as contamination (e.g., concerns about germs or disgust), responsibility for causing or preventing harm (e.g., "Did I hit a pedestrian, or was that just a speed bump?"), unwelcome thoughts about taboo subjects (e.g., sex, violence, and blasphemy), and the need for order and symmetry ("If I

---

**Abbreviations**

| | |
|---|---|
| ACT | Acceptance and commitment therapy |
| BDD | Body dysmorphic disorder |
| HD | Hoarding disorder |
| IU | Intolerance of uncertainty |
| OCD | Obsessive-compulsive disorder |
| OCRDs | Obsessive-compulsive and related disorders |
| OFC | Orbitofrontal cortex |
| RFT | Relational frame therapy |
| SSRI | Selective serotonin reuptake inhibitor |
| TAF | Thought-action fusion |

don't align the book just right, I can't stand to look at the bookshelf").

Unlike other types of repetitive thoughts often described as "obsessive," clinical obsessions are experienced as *unwanted* or *uncontrollable* in that they "invade" into and persist in one's consciousness. They often seem to occur spontaneously at what seems like the most inconvenient times (e.g., a blasphemous thought about occurs while in a house of worship) or are triggered by something in the environment (e.g., seeing a knife provokes unwanted thoughts of stabbing a loved one). Obsessions are also inconsistent with the person's self-image (i.e., they are "ego-dystonic"); for example, a man who considers himself intolerant of racism might be plagued by thoughts of yelling racial epithets. Finally, obsessions are *resisted*: individuals try to "deal with," neutralize, or completely avoid these kinds of experiences. The motivation to resist is activated by the fear that if action is not taken, negative consequences will ensure.

## Compulsions

Compulsions are urges to engage in deliberate overt or mental behaviors (often called *rituals*) in an effort to reduce the distress associated with obsessions (or the obsessional thought itself). Rituals, which are functionally related to obsessions (e.g., checking to allay obsessional doubts of leaving the door unlocked), typically belong to the following categories: decontamination (washing/cleaning), checking (e.g., ensuring that the stove is off, repeatedly asking for reassurance), repeating routine activities (e.g., rewriting one's name or walking back and forth through a doorway), ordering and arranging (e.g., books on a shelf), and mental rituals (e.g., repeating a prayer or mantra). These behaviors are often performed according to self-prescribed rules and are usually recognized (at least to some extent) as senseless and excessive (although, discussed further below, insight into the senselessness of these symptoms varies from person to person).

In contrast to involuntary repetitive behaviors such as motor tics, rituals are calculated. That is, the person willfully performs the behavior. This relates to the final defining feature of compulsive rituals: they have a specific function—namely, to reduce distress. This function stands in contrast to *impulsive* behaviors (e.g., hair-pulling or skin-picking), which are carried out because they produce pleasure, distraction, or gratification. Yet although rituals often lead to a reduction in distress, such relief is usually temporary. Moreover, rituals maintain obsessional fear by preventing the natural extinction of fear. That is, if the person with OCD routinely ritualizes (e.g., washes her hands), she never has a chance to learn that her obsessions (e.g., fears of becoming ill from contamination) are not true danger signals.

## Avoidance

Although not mentioned in the *DSM-5* criteria for OCD, avoidance behavior is another strategy commonly deployed in response to obsessions, usually to avert unwanted thoughts, negative outcomes, uncertainty, and compulsive urges. Avoidance is intended to prevent exposure to situations that would provoke obsessions and necessitate compulsive rituals. For example, one woman avoided driving past cemeteries because they evoked unwanted obsessional thoughts of loved ones dying. Other people engage in avoidance so that they do not have to carry out time-consuming or embarrassing rituals. For example, one person avoided home and garden stores so that he would not have to engage in extensive showering rituals, which he believed were necessary if he was exposed to pesticides and other household chemicals. Ultimately, avoidance is problematic because it does not provide an opportunity for the individual to come into contact with the feared situation and learn that the feared outcomes are unlikely to materialize. Thus, like rituals, avoidance maintains obsessional fear by preventing the natural extinction of obsessional fears. This leads to the escalating vicious cycle typical of OCD.

## Symptom Dimensions

Research has identified reliable and valid symptom dimensions comprised of both obsessions and compulsions (e.g., Abramowitz et al., 2010; McKay et al., 2004). These dimensions include (a) contamination (contamination obsessions and decontamination rituals), (b) responsibility for harm and mistakes (obsessions about harm or mistakes and checking/reassurance-seeking rituals), (c) incompleteness (obsessions about order or exactness and arranging rituals), and (d) unacceptable taboo violent, sexual, or blasphemous thoughts with mental rituals. These themes often overlap and many people experience multiple themes, thus these dimensions are not ways to categorize individuals with OCD (e.g., "washers" or "checkers"), but rather for categorizing the different manifestations of OCD. Even so, this categorization system is far from perfect. Some individuals with obsessional thoughts about sex, for example, use decontamination rituals to "wash away their dirty thoughts." Others may experience obsessions that seem difficult to fit into any of these categories (e.g., obsessional thoughts about existential questions or about whether one is "really" in love with her partner).

*Ego Dystonicity*

*Ego dystonicity* refers to the degree to which one's obsessions are inconsistent with the ways in which he or she views him- or herself with respect to ideals and morals (Clark, 2004). Given that obsessions typically focus on topics that are repugnant to the individual, they are perceived as a threat to one's self. Not surprisingly, the nature of obsessive concerns may lead one to question his or her character ("What if I really *am* a pedophile!?"). Ego dystonicity is most apparent in the unacceptable (taboo) thoughts symptom dimension, as obsessional thoughts about blasphemy, unbidden sexual ideas (e.g., incest), or violently murdering someone run counter to traditional moral codes. Furthermore, obsessions focused on vulnerable people (i.e., ideas of harming young children, the weak, or frail; Berman et al., 2012) may elicit increased guilt and distress and cause individuals to fret about "latent sexual and aggressive desires" (Clark, 2004, p. 29). Ego dystonicity also arises among meticulous individuals with OCD who may be troubled by obsessive doubt related to making mistakes, which could be considered intolerable and out of line with one's standards. This quality of ego dystonicity among obsessive beliefs also separates obsessions and compulsions in the context of OCD from other repetitive behaviors such as hair-pulling, which may produce pleasure.

*Insight*

As already alluded to, the insight one has into the senselessness of his or her obsessions and compulsions varies widely. While some individuals recognize the irrationality of their OCD symptoms (e.g., "I realize the probability of dying from using a public bathroom is very low, but I just can't take the chance"), others hold a firm conviction that these intrusive thoughts and behaviors are rational (e.g., "Public bathrooms are extremely dangerous and I would get sick and die if I did not avoid them"). Insight may shift over time and can vary according to different symptom domains. For example, one might recognize that her obsessive thoughts about bad luck from the number 666 are senseless yet simultaneously have poor insight into the irrationality of her obsessions about contamination.

*DSM-5* criteria for OCD include the specifiers "good or fair insight," "poor insight," and "absent insight" (p. 237) to denote the degree to which the person views his or her obsessional fears and compulsive behavior as reasonable. Although many individuals with OCD recognize—to some degree—that their obsessions and compulsions are senseless and/or extreme, about 4% are convinced that their symptoms are realistic (i.e., poor or absent insight; Foa et al., 1995). Individuals with poor insight lack self-awareness regarding their obsessions and compulsions. Individuals with delusional conviction believe that their obsessions are realistic and reasonable, and such poor insight appears to be associated with religious obsessions, fears of mistakes, and aggressive obsessional impulses (Tolin et al., 2001).

*Need for Certainty*

Intolerance of uncertainty refers to beliefs about the necessity of being certain, the capacity to cope with unpredictable change, and beliefs about how to function in situations which are inherently ambiguous (Obsessive Compulsive Cognitions Working Group, 1997). Intolerance of uncertainty is a key cognitive phenomenon associated with OCD as individuals often report pathological doubt with their obsessions (e.g., "I need to know for certain that I have not sinned"). Those with a greater intolerance of uncertainty characteristically find uncertainty to be stressful and upsetting, believe that uncertainty should be avoided at all costs, and experience impairment in uncertain or ambiguous situations. Although this uncertainty may be most visible and applicable in certain overt rituals (e.g., checking behaviors within the responsibility for harm symptom domain), it is present across OCD symptom manifestations. This doubt may be due to impairments in memory and/or diminished confidence in one's memory (Foa et al., 1997); relatedly, rituals may stem from a heightened desire for certainty (i.e., intolerance of uncertainty) and memory vividness.

**Prevalence and Course**

The lifetime prevalence estimates of OCD are between 0.7% and 2.9% (Kessler et al., 2005), with slightly higher prevalence rates among females than among males (Bogetto et al., 1999). The disorder typically begins by age 25 but can onset at any age; childhood or adolescence onset is common.

Average age of onset, however, is slightly earlier in males (about 21 years) than in females (22–24 years; Rasmussen & Eisen, 1992). The course of OCD tends to be chronic and deteriorating, with a low rate of spontaneous remission. Left untreated, symptoms fluctuate and are often exacerbated during periods of increased life stress. Although effective treatments exist, full recovery is the exception rather than the rule.

## Interpersonal Aspects of OCD

OCD often occurs in an interpersonal context and negatively impacts the person's relationships, including family relationships and intimate partnerships (e.g., marriage). In turn, dysfunctional relationship patterns can promote the maintenance of OCD symptoms such that a vicious cycle continues. In an attempt to demonstrate care and concern for an affected individual, a family member, partner, or spouse might inadvertently behave in ways that maintain OCD symptoms by helping with compulsive rituals and avoidance behavior (i.e., *symptom accommodation*). Conversely, arguments about the seeming illogic of one's OCD symptoms may also create relationship distress and conflict, which further exacerbate the anxiety and obsessional symptoms (Boeding et al., 2013).

### Symptom Accommodation

Accommodation occurs when a friend or relative without OCD participates in (or facilitates) rituals, avoidance strategies, assumes daily responsibilities for the person with OCD, or helps to resolve problems that have resulted from that person's obsessions and compulsions. Accommodation can occur at the request (or demand) of the affected individual, who intentionally solicits help for controlling his or her anxiety. In other instances, loved ones voluntarily accommodate as a way of expressing care and concern or to prevent their loved one from becoming highly anxious. Conceptually, this sort of accommodation perpetuates OCD symptoms by the same mechanism as avoidance and compulsive rituals. For instance, consider a man with obsessional fears of assaulting loved ones who requests that his partner keep all of the knives locked away. By assisting with locking up the knives (i.e., by accommodating her partner's OCD symptoms), she prevents her partner from learning that he's unlikely to act on these unwanted thoughts. Furthermore, he misses the opportunity to learn that he could manage the temporary anxiety that accompanies his repugnant obsessions.

### Relationship Conflict

Relationship stress and conflict play an important role in the maintenance of OCD as well. Families in which a member suffers from OCD often report problems with interdependency, unassertiveness, and avoidant communication patterns that foster stress and conflict. This is likely a bidirectional relationship, as OCD symptoms and relationship distress influence each other. For example, a husband's contentious relationship with his wife might contribute to overall anxiety and uncertainty that feeds into his obsessional doubting. His excessive checking, reassurance seeking, and overly cautious actions could also precipitate frequent disagreements. In particular, poor problem-solving skills, hostility, and criticism might increase distress and contribute to OCD.

## Conceptual Models of OCD
### Models Based on Conditioning and Learning Theory

Throughout the twentieth century, conditioning models were developed to understand fear-based problems (including "obsessional neurosis," which would later come to be called OCD). A predominant approach was Mowrer's two-factor theory (Mowrer, 1960), which proposed that obsessional fears were acquired by classical conditioning and maintained by operant conditioning (i.e., negative reinforcement). For example, an obsessional fear of harming one's child could arise from an incident in which the person had an aversive experience (the unconditioned stimulus, which could include an unwanted thoughts and anxiety) in the presence of their child (the conditioned stimulus), leading to a classically conditioned fear. Negative reinforcement then maintains the obsessional fear. That is, avoiding or escaping from distress (e.g., by avoiding one's niece) or engaging in compulsive rituals (e.g., by "neutralizing" the unwanted thoughts with a mantra such as "I am a good person") serves to reduce anxiety and prevent the disconfirmation of feared consequences.

Conditioning models, however, have their limitations. For one thing, many people with OCD do not recall conditioning experiences in the context of their obsession that would have led to the development of obsessional fear. Conversely, many people who have experiences expected to lead to the development of obsessions do not develop OCD. Second, learning models have difficulty explaining the emergence, persistence, and content of repugnant sexual, religious, and violent obsessions (e.g., obsessional images of Jesus with an erection on the cross). Third, this model fails to explain why the themes and content of obsessions and compulsions may shift for an individual over time. With these limitations in mind, theorists in the latter half of the twentieth century began to consider the role that cognitive processes play in the development and persistence of OCD.

## Cognitive Deficit Models

One school of thought was that people with OCD have cognitive *deficits*—dysfunctions in thought or mental processing, which may have neurobiological or neuropsychological origins. The idea that individuals with OCD suffer from cognitive processing deficits is tempting since it appears that, for example, those with checking rituals have a memory problem that keeps them from being able to recall whether or not they completed an action, such as locking the door. Alternately, individuals could have a deficit in their ability to accurately recall whether they *actually* turned off the oven or merely *imagined* doing so (i.e., a *reality monitoring* deficit). Research findings, however, provide little support for these and other types of memory or executive functioning problems in OCD (Abramovitch et al., 2013; Abramovitch & Cooperman, 2015). In fact, rather than memory deficits, the most consistent finding in the literature has been that individuals with OCD have less *confidence* in their own memory than do individuals without OCD (Woods et al., 2002).

Cognitive deficit proponents have also examined whether the intrusive, repetitious, and seemingly uncontrollable quality of obsessional thoughts is the result of deficits in cognitive inhibition—the inability to stop thinking about something. Perhaps, for example, individuals with OCD are less able than neurotypical (healthy) individuals to forget or dismiss thoughts about senseless mental stimuli. Indeed, on tests of recall and recognition, individuals with OCD have more difficulty forgetting negative material (and material related to their OCD concerns) relative to positive and neutral material than do healthy control subjects (Tolin et al., 2002).

Poor cognitive inhibition might explain the high *frequency* of obsessional thoughts, yet the idea that OCD arises from general cognitive deficits has not added to our understanding of or ability to treat the problem. Apparent memory and processing deficits are better accounted for by *cognitive biases* in which obsessional anxiety leads to preoccupation and preferential processing of threat-relevant stimuli. For example, individuals who possess a biased perception that they are responsible for negative events or outcomes may have reduced confidence in their memory, leading to compulsive checking. Checking rituals may function as a way of reducing doubts that have arisen because of mistaken beliefs about one's memory and ability to manage uncertainty and pathological overestimates of responsibility for harm. These types of mistaken beliefs are the focus of the cognitive specificity hypothesis of OCD, as described next.

## Cognitive Bias Models

Borrowing from Beck's (1976) cognitive model of depression, cognitive bias models of OCD propose that obsessions and compulsions arise from certain types of maladaptive interpretations (i.e., dysfunctional beliefs). For example, exaggerated beliefs about personal responsibility might cause one to become excessively concerned and engage in excessive checking rituals when the everyday thought, "Am I sure I locked the door before leaving the house?" comes to mind (Salkovskis, 1985). Beliefs about the overimportance of thoughts might have a similar effect. For example, the belief that it is wrong, dangerous, or otherwise personally significant to think about immoral topics (e.g., "Only rapists think about rape") has been linked to certain dimensions of OCD symptoms (e.g., Wheaton et al., 2010).

Given the heterogeneity of OCD symptoms, a number of overlapping cognitive bias models have proliferated. Among these is Salkovskis's (1985) cognitive approach, which starts with the finding that virtually everyone experiences unwanted thoughts at some point (i.e., thoughts, images, and impulses that intrude into consciousness; e.g., Rachman & de Silva, 1978). Such "normal" or "nonclinical" unwanted thoughts tend to be less frequent, less distressing, and shorter in duration than "clinically significant" obsessions that are characteristic of individuals with OCD. Clinical and nonclinical obsessions, however, share similar thematic content such as violence, contamination, sex, and doubts. Thus, a model of OCD must delineate why many individuals experience intrusive thoughts, yet only a small percentage experience clinical obsessions.

Salkovskis suggested that intrusive thoughts reflect the person's current concerns and are triggered by internal or external cues that remind the person of his or her concerns. For example, intrusive thoughts about accidentally hitting pedestrians with an automobile may be evoked by driving past people walking on the side of the road. Salkovskis asserted that nonclinical intrusive thoughts only escalate into obsessions when they are appraised as having consequences for personal responsibility (e.g., the intrusive image of pushing a stranger in front of an oncoming train). Although upsetting, most people experiencing such an intrusion would not regard it as personally meaningful or as having harm-related implications (i.e., it would be considered, and subsequently dismissed, as "mental noise"). Such an intrusion might develop into a clinical obsession, however, if the person appraises it as indicating that he or she has the responsibility for causing or preventing the accompanying disastrous consequences. For example, if the person made an appraisal such as the following: "Thinking about pushing a stranger in front of an oncoming train means that I'm a dangerous and immoral citizen who must take extra care to ensure that I don't lose control." Such interpretations evoke distress and motivate the individual to try to suppress or remove the unwanted intrusion (e.g., by replacing it with a "good" thought) and to attempt to prevent the content of the intrusion from actually occurring (e.g., by avoiding subway platforms). Thus, compulsive rituals are cast in this model as efforts to remove intrusions and prevent any perceived harmful consequences.

The question remains: Why do some, but not all, people interpret and appraise intrusive thoughts in terms of harm and responsibility? Beck (1976) proposed that our experiences form the basic assumptions we hold about ourselves and the world, including beliefs about personal responsibility and about the significance of unwanted thoughts (e.g., the core belief that all our thoughts are significant). Such beliefs may be acquired from a strict moral or religious upbringing or from other experiences that teach the person extreme or rigid codes of conduct and responsibility (Salkovskis et al., 1999).

Why doesn't a person with OCD recognize these thoughts as senseless and dismiss them? Salkovskis proposed that rituals develop and persist as coping strategies for obsessional thoughts for two reasons. First, compulsive rituals are reinforced by the immediate (albeit temporary) reduction in obsessional distress that they often produce (i.e., negative reinforcement, as in the conditioning model). Second, they maintain obsessions by preventing the person from learning that his or her beliefs and appraisals are unrealistic. That is, when a person ritualizes, she fails to learn that obsessional thoughts and situations aren't dangerous. Instead, she continues to believe that a catastrophe would have occurred had she not performed the ritual. Other theorists (Rachman, 2003) have similarly proposed that compulsive rituals increase the frequency and repetitiveness of obsessions by serving as reminders of intrusions (i.e., retrieval cues) and thereby triggering their reoccurrence. For example, compulsive reassurance seeking can remind the person of his or her obsessional doubts. Therefore, attempts to distract one's self from obsessional thoughts can paradoxically *increase* the frequency of these thoughts and images. Rituals can also strengthen one's perceived responsibility. For example, when the feared consequences of thinking a violent thought do not occur after performing a mental ritual, it strengthens the perception of personal responsibility (i.e., that the person is solely responsible for removing the potential threat and must continue to prevent it from happening in the future).

In summary, cognitive bias models of OCD (often termed "cognitive-behavioral models" because they involve both cognitive and behavioral processes) propose that obsessions and compulsions develop when a person habitually misinterprets normal intrusive thoughts as posing a threat for which he or she is personally responsible. This leads to distress and attempts to remove the intrusion to alleviate discomfort and prevent the feared consequences. But this response paradoxically increases the frequency of intrusions. Thus, the intrusions become persistent and distressing, and they escalate into clinical obsessions. Compulsive rituals maintain the obsessions and prevent the person from evaluating the accuracy of his or her interpretations. Avoidance is analogous to compulsive rituals in that avoidance functions as a strategy for reducing anxiety. Avoidance and rituals differ in that avoidance is a passive anxiety reduction strategy and ritual use is an active strategy.

Salkovskis's model emphasizes the role of responsibility appraisals of intrusive thoughts. Other authors, however, have developed additional cognitive models by expanding on the types of dysfunctional beliefs and appraisals that contribute to OCD. Although these cognitive models differ in some ways, they are more similar than they are different. Most of the differences between these models relate to the emphasis that they give to certain types of dysfunctional beliefs. Rachman (2003), for example, focuses on beliefs concerning the significance of intrusive thoughts (e.g., "If I think an immoral thought, it means I'm an immoral person"). Thus, for Rachman, obsessions arise when the person misinterprets the intrusive thought as implying that he or she is bad, mad, or dangerous. *Thought-action fusion* (TAF) is an important concept in this model (Shafran et al., 1996). TAF refers to the notion that one's unwanted thoughts will inevitably be translated into actions (i.e., likelihood TAF; e.g., "I might cause my father to have a car accident just by thinking about it") or that thoughts are the moral equivalent of actions (i.e., moral TAF; e.g., "Thinking about pushing a stranger in front of an oncoming train is just as bad as actually doing it"). The most comprehensive contemporary cognitive model of OCD was developed collaboratively by members of the Obsessive Compulsive Cognitions Working Group (OCCWG; Frost & Steketee, 2002). The OCCWG model accounts for the heterogeneity of OCD symptoms by proposing that particular beliefs (or patterns of beliefs) are important for specific types of OCD symptoms.

*Implications of the Model*

From a cognitive-behavioral perspective, OCD can be understood as involving intact learning (conditioning) processes and normally functioning (albeit biased and maladaptive) cognitive processes. Avoidance and compulsive rituals are excessive responses to obsessional fears because the threat level is objectively low, yet they keep the person afraid by preventing him from recognizing this. That is, when a ritual is performed, the individual attributes safety to the ritual, rather than changing his danger expectations. Thus, a self-perpetuating vicious cycle develops, which we call "OCD."

This approach also implies that the successful treatment of OCD must (a) correct the maladaptive beliefs and appraisals that give rise to obsessional fear and (b) halt avoidance behavior and rituals that block the correction of maladaptive beliefs. Put differently, effective cognitive behavior therapy (CBT) for OCD promotes an evaluation of obsessional stimuli as nonthreatening and not requiring any further action by the individual. The person must understand their problem not in terms of the risk of feared outcomes, but rather in terms of how they are responding to obsessional thoughts and cue stimuli that objectively represent a low risk of danger.

*Empirical Status*

A review of numerous cross-sectional studies revealed a consistent relationship between OCD symptoms and the tendency to overestimate the likelihood of harm and interpret intrusive thoughts as meaningful, threatening, or in terms of responsibility for harm (Abramowitz et al., 2014). Yet the correlational data in these studies do not address causal relationships. Laboratory experiments, which can be used to draw causal conclusions, have also consistently shown that cognitive distortions can lead to obsessive-compulsive phenomena in a laboratory setting (e.g., Rassin et al., 1999). Such studies, however, do not necessarily generalize to the development of OCD in naturalistic settings. Thus, longitudinal studies in which individuals are assessed for cognitive variables and then followed up after some critical event have been conducted to address this limitation. In one such study, Abramowitz and colleagues (e.g., Abramowitz et al., 2006) administered measures of OCD-related dysfunctional beliefs to samples of first-time expecting parents (mothers and fathers-to-be) during the third trimester of pregnancy. Between 2 and 3 months after childbirth, these new parents were again assessed for the presence and intensity of OCD symptoms. These investigators found that after controlling for baseline levels of obsessive-compulsive symptoms and trait anxiety, OCD-related dysfunctional beliefs pre-child birth were a significant predictor of obsessive-compulsive symptom intensity in the postpartum period.

As additional evidence for this model, Timpano, Abramowitz, Mahaffey, Mitchell, and Schmidt (2011) developed a prevention program that taught expecting parents with high levels of TAF about the normalcy of intrusive thoughts and how to use cognitive-behavioral methods based on the Salkovskis's (1985) model to manage such intrusions if and when they occurred once their child was born. Indeed, relative to a group that received a parallel control intervention, the group receiving the cognitive-behavioral prevention program demonstrated reduced distress associated with intrusive thoughts during the postpartum.

*Psychological Models Emphasizing Acceptance of Unwanted Thoughts*

Despite the strong empirical support for cognitive-behavioral models of OCD, cognitive biases such as TAF do not entirely account for OCD symptoms in statistical models (e.g., Taylor et al., 2006). Accordingly, scholars have applied constructs relevant to acceptance and commitment therapy (ACT) to understand and treat OCD. Grounded in functional contextualism and relational frame theory (RFT), ACT (Hayes et al., 2011) is an experiential approach to conceptualizing and treating psychological conditions that shares philosophical assumptions with behavioral approaches and suggests that the context (e.g., historical, situational) in which behavior evolves is useful for predicting and changing psychological events. Events with a similar *form* may serve different *functions*; for example, checking the oven is only conceptualized as a compulsion in OCD when considered in relation to the presence of obsessional thoughts of responsibility for starting a fire and the function of the checking behavior.

Two constructs from within this framework are thought to be related to OCD: experiential avoidance and cognitive fusion. *Experiential avoidance* refers to attempts to control or avoid unwanted internal experiences such as emotions (e.g., anxiety). *Cognitive fusion* is the tendency to take internal experiences (e.g., thoughts) as literal facts rather than viewing them simply as private events. A growing literature supports the relationship between these constructs and OCD symptoms (e.g., Reuman et al., 2018), as well as the efficacy of ACT in the treatment of OCD (see Bluett et al., 2014, for a review). Within ACT, the client is helped to observe (i.e., accept) unwanted private experiences (e.g., obsessional thoughts, anxiety, and uncertainty), rather than seeing them as important or requiring avoidance or ritualistic responses. The client is also helped to commit to pursuing important life activities despite the presence of unwanted private experiences.

## Biological Models

### SEROTONIN HYPOTHESIS

Serotonin is a monoamine neurotransmitter thought to play a role in the regulation of mood, appetite, and sleep. Originally proposed in the context of depression, the "serotonin hypothesis" proposes that OCD symptoms arise from abnormalities in this neurotransmitter system, specifically a hypersensitivity of the postsynaptic serotonergic receptors (Zohar & Insel, 1987). Three lines of evidence are cited to support this idea: medication outcome studies, biological marker studies, and biological challenge studies in which OCD symptoms are evoked using serotonin agonists and antagonists. Published pharmacotherapy studies consistently show that selective serotonin reuptake inhibitor (SSRI) medications (e.g., fluoxetine), which are thought to manipulate available levels of serotonin, are more effective than placebo and medications with other presumed mechanisms of action (e.g., imipramine) in reducing OCD symptoms. Yet studies of biological markers—such as blood and cerebrospinal fluid levels of serotonin metabolites—have provided inconclusive results (Insel et al., 1985). Similarly, pharmacological challenge studies are largely incompatible with the serotonin hypothesis (Hollander et al., 1992).

### STRUCTURAL MODELS

Structural models posit that OCD is caused by neuroanatomical and functional abnormalities in the brain's orbitofrontal-subcortical circuits, which are thought to connect brain regions involved in processing information with those involved in the initiation of behavioral responses. These models spring from neuroimaging studies in which activity levels in specific brain areas are compared between people with and without OCD. Investigations using positron emission tomography (PET) have found that increased glucose utilization in the orbitofrontal cortex (OFC), caudate, thalamus, prefrontal cortex, and anterior cingulate is correlated with the presence of OCD (i.e., greater in patients compared to nonpatients; e.g., Baxter et al., 1988). Studies using single photon emission computed tomography (SPECT) have reported decreased blood flow to the OFC, caudate, various areas of the cortex, and thalamus in OCD patients compared to nonpatients (for a review, see Whiteside et al., 2004). Finally, studies comparing individuals with OCD to healthy controls using magnetic resonance spectroscopy (MRS) have reported decreased levels of various markers of neuronal viability in the left and right striatum and in the medial thalamus (e.g., Fitzgerald et al., 2000). Although findings vary, a meta-analysis of 10 PET and SPECT studies revealed that individuals with OCD display more activity in the orbital gyrus and the head of the caudate nucleus in comparison to healthy controls (Whiteside et al., 2004).

### GENETIC CONTRIBUTIONS

Although some findings suggest that OCD symptoms are heritable, with "likely common genetic influences of modest effect" (Stewart et al., 2013), there is no evidence that a particular gene influences OCD symptoms (Stewart et al., 2013). OCD is also more common among first-degree relatives with OCD than among first-degree relatives of people without the disorder (Hettema et al., 2001). Moreover, twin studies suggest that obsessive-compulsive symptoms are heritable (van Grootheest et al., 2007). Although this is commonly understood to imply that genes are responsible, familial environmental factors cannot be ruled out, of course.

## EVALUATION OF BIOLOGICAL MODELS

One key limitation of the serotonin hypothesis is that its strongest evidence come from the apparent superiority of serotonergic medication over other sorts of pharmacotherapies. Yet since the serotonin hypothesis *originated from* the findings of preferential efficacy of serotonergic medication over non-serotonergic antidepressants, the assertion that the effectiveness of these medications supports the serotonin hypothesis is circular. There is also a logical fallacy in drawing conclusions about the cause of a problem from its treatment. This is a logical fallacy called *post hoc ergo proper hoc* (i.e., "after this therefore because of this"), which is exemplified by the example: "the rooster crows before sunrise, therefore the crowing rooster causes the sun to rise." Similarly, just because a serotonergic agent reduces OCD symptoms doesn't mean a dysfunction in serotonin (which has not been found in direct studies of this neurotransmitter system) caused the symptoms to begin with.

Another problem with biological causal models is that they are based on correlational studies, which do not address (a) whether true abnormalities exist, and (b) whether the observed relationships are causal. That is, whereas neuroimaging studies comparing OCD patients to control participants show *associations* between OCD symptoms and brain structure or function, they do not reveal whether any differences in the brain predate the development of OCD or whether it is something about having OCD that causes changes in the brain. Unassessed third variables might also influence both OCD and the brain. Moreover, most neuroimaging studies compare individuals with OCD to nonpatients, rather than to people with other psychiatric diagnoses. Thus, there is no way to know whether the findings are specific to individuals with OCD or a characteristic of those with various sorts of psychopathology. Despite decades of research on biological models of OCD, the evidence that specific biological factors play an etiological role is weak. In fact, a large international study group reviewed the existing literature and reached the consensus that there are no biological or genetic markers of OCD (Bandelow et al., 2016, 2017).

## Obsessive-Compulsive Related Disorders

The rationale for moving OCD out of the anxiety disorders and into the new OCRD category in *DSM-5* was that OCD and the proposed "related disorders" overlapped in terms of their overt symptom presentation (Hollander et al., 2011). Later, this rationale was expanded to include the idea that these disorders fall along a continuum of failure in behavior inhibition (i.e., the inability to cease one's actions), with compulsive and impulsive behaviors at opposite ends of the spectrum (Hollander et al., 2011). At one end of the continuum are "compulsive disorders" such as OCD and BDD; impulse control problems (e.g., skin-picking and hair-pulling) fall at the other end of the continuum. This section provides an overview of the disorders currently grouped within this category.

### Hair-Pulling Disorder

Hair-pulling disorder (formerly known as *trichotillomania*) involves recurrent hair-pulling resulting in hair loss despite repeated attempts to stop. The hair-pulling behavior may be *automatic* (i.e., outside of the person's awareness) or *focused* (i.e., in response to an urge, impulse, or negative affect). It is easy to see how the repetitive (seemingly "compulsive") nature of hair-pulling might appear similar to that of repetitive compulsive rituals in OCD. A more nuanced examination, however, reveals key distinctions. Although OCD and hair-pulling disorder both involve repetitive behavior, the intrusive anxiety-evoking obsessional thoughts that occur in OCD are not present in hair-pulling disorder. Whereas obsessional fear motivates rituals in OCD, it is feelings of general tension, depression, anger, boredom, frustration, indecision, or fatigue that precipitate urges to "compulsively" pull hair (Christenson et al., 1993). Hair-pulling, unlike rituals in OCD, also leads to pleasurable feelings (e.g., Schreiber et al., 2011).

Behavioral models of hair-pulling emphasize the role of learning. For instance, Azrin and Nunn (1973) argued that urges to pull hair become conditioned responses to one or more situations (e.g., being alone), internal sensations (e.g., tension), or activities (e.g., reading). Pulling is followed by feelings of sensory stimulation or gratification that serve as an escape from negative feeling states, thereby reinforcing (both positively and negatively) the pulling behavior (Woods et al., 2008).

More recently, cognitive factors have been incorporated into models of hair-pulling. Franklin and Tolin (2007), for example, argued that dysfunctional beliefs can increase negative emotion in people with hair-pulling disorder, thereby increasing urges to pull. These include perfectionistic beliefs, beliefs about the persistence and controllability of urges to pull (e.g., "The urge will last forever unless I pull"), beliefs about the hair-pulling habit itself

("This is an appalling behavior"), and beliefs about negative evaluation from others ("Other people will notice my hair loss and won't want to associate with me"). Episodes of hair-pulling may also be exacerbated by beliefs about the positive effects of hair-pulling (e.g., "Hair-pulling will make me feel better") and facilitative thoughts (e.g., "I'll just pull one more").

Few studies, however, have examined the role of cognition in hair-pulling disorder. Norberg and colleagues (2007) assessed, in a self-described sample of people with hair-pulling problems, beliefs pertaining to appearance and shame or social rejection in regard to hair-pulling. These beliefs were correlated with the severity of the person's hair-pulling. Similarly, Rehm and colleagues (2019) found that negative self-beliefs, perfectionism, and low coping efficacy were significantly related to hair-pulling severity in a study of individuals with self-reported hair-pulling behaviors. Although these findings are consistent with a cognitive perspective on hair-pulling disorder, it remains unclear whether the faulty beliefs are a cause or consequence of increased hair-pulling behavior.

### Skin-Picking Disorder

With nearly identical diagnostic criteria to hair-pulling disorder, skin-picking disorder (i.e., excoriation disorder) also does not involve obsessional thoughts, and repetitive skin-picking functions differently than do compulsive rituals in OCD. Clinically significant skin-picking may be triggered by an array of antecedents (e.g., general stress, apprehension, boredom, tiredness; e.g., Arnold et al., 2001), and emotion regulation difficulties (i.e., emotional reactivity) have been shown to be associated with skin-picking (Snorrason et al., 2010). Skin-picking can also be triggered by the feel (e.g., a bump or unevenness) or look (e.g., a blemish or discoloration) of the skin. In contrast to deliberate, anxiety-reducing compulsive behavior in OCD, episodes of skin-picking often begin outside of the person's awareness (i.e., they are unfocused), and the individual becomes more fully aware of his or her skin-picking after a period of time (Keuthen et al., 2000).

Skin-picking behaviors frequently co-occur with hair-pulling, and the two disorders share characteristics such as automatic and focused styles and a similar range of negative emotional states as triggers. As with OCD, skin-picking disorder involves repetitive, compulsive behaviors, albeit specifically related to skin-picking, which are often completed in a ritualistic manner (Phillips & Stein, 2015); however, functional differences exist between OCD and skin-picking. That is, there are no obsessions or obsessional fears that lead to "compulsive" skin-picking.

Conceptual models of skin-picking disorder focus on reinforcement and emotion regulation (Lang et al., 2010). As with hair-pulling, skin-picking may be preceded by emotional or sensory antecedents and subsequently reinforced by the removal of these negative stimuli. The role of cognition in skin-picking remains largely uninvestigated, except as part of treatment studies exploring the use of cognitive, cognitive-behavioral, or other treatments (Lochner et al., 2017). Commonly encountered dysfunctional cognitions include those related to low self-efficacy and impaired control (Schuck et al., 2011).

### Body Dysmorphic Disorder

BDD is characterized by a preoccupation with *perceived* physical defects or appearance flaws (e.g., the belief that one's ears are too large) and excessive repetitive behaviors (e.g., checking one's appearance) or mental acts (e.g., comparing oneself to others) that are performed to relieve the distress associated with the preoccupation. The appearance-related preoccupations in BDD are similar to obsessions in OCD because both trigger anxiety or distress. Similarly, avoidance and excessive behaviors to conceal, correct, check, or seek reassurance about the imagined defects among people with BDD serve a similar function as compulsive rituals in OCD; namely, to reduce distress. For instance, some individuals with BDD check their appearance for prolonged periods of time, looking in mirrors, windows, and so forth. Others focus their energies on avoiding all reflective surfaces. Additional compulsive behaviors include comparing oneself to others, defect-related skin-picking, reading all relevant information on the body part(s) of concern, measuring the "flawed" body part(s), and seeking cures (e.g., cosmetic procedures) for perceived defects (Fang & Wilhelm, 2015).

Veale's cognitive-behavioral model (2004) is the best articulated conceptual model of BDD. It begins with the proposition that episodes of heightened concern with body image in BDD are often precipitated by "external representations" of the individual's appearance (e.g., seeing one's reflection), which triggers a dysfunctional mental image. Through selective attention toward appearance-related details, the individual experiences heightened awareness of specific characteristics within the image and thereby assumes that the perceived defect is clearly apparent to other people. This imagery is associated with heightened self-focused attention, to the extent that, in more severe cases of BDD, all of the individuals' attention may be focused on the distorted image and on the negative evaluation of the image.

According to this conceptualization, the afflicted person also negatively appraises his or her appearance in the context of dysfunctional beliefs about the importance of physical appearance. The individual may hold beliefs such as, "If I'm unattractive, life isn't worth living." Beliefs regarding inadequacy, worthlessness, abnormality, and rejection are also implicated as the person compares his or her "defective" features with the ideal. These emotional responses lead to behaviors such as avoidance or active escape and concealment of the imagined defect, to prevent the feared outcomes and reduce distress. Although these avoidant behaviors may temporarily alleviate distress, in the long run they maintain the self-consciousness preoccupation with the imagined defect and negative appraisal of oneself.

There are a number of studies that support this model (see Fang & Wilhelm, 2015, for a review). For example, studies show that people with BDD pay close attention to minute details and features rather than to global figures, which might explain the focus on specific appearance-related details (Feusner et al., 2007). Grocholewski and colleagues (2012) found that individuals with BDD demonstrated greater selective attention to imagined defects in their faces and corresponding areas on unfamiliar faces compared to healthy controls or individuals with social phobia. These findings are consistent with the attentional biases and image-related preoccupations proposed in the cognitive-behavioral model.

### Hoarding Disorder

HD is characterized by excessive acquisition and difficulty discarding or parting with possessions—even those of limited value—due to (a) the perceived need to save such items and (b) distress associated with discarding them. Many individuals also demonstrate compulsive acquisition of items (Nicoli de Mattos et al., 2018; Vogel et al., 2019), which appears to be associated with greater hoarding severity (Turna et al., 2018). HD may be associated with severe functional impairment and cost to society. As a result, large numbers of possessions accumulate and clutter the person's living areas so that living spaces can no longer be used for their intended purposes. Once considered a symptom of OCD, hoarding is now recognized as a separate diagnostic entity because, indeed, it differs in important ways from OCD. First, although hoarding may involve recurring thoughts of acquiring and maintaining possessions, these thoughts are not experienced as fear-provoking in the same way that obsessions are for individuals with OCD and they are not intrusive or unwanted (Rachman et al., 2009; Wheaton et al., 2011). Moreover, the extreme acquiring and saving that characterizes HD does not function as an escape from obsessional anxiety in the way that washing or checking rituals do in OCD.

Conceptual models of hoarding emphasize exaggerated beliefs related to the overattachment to material possessions and exaggerated consequences of not having these possessions (Frost & Hartl, 1996; Steketee & Frost, 2003). Collectively called *saving cognitions*, these beliefs include (a) unrealistic ideas about the value of saved items (e.g., "I'll probably need that empty soup can in the future"), (b) intense sentimental or aesthetic attachment (e.g., "It represents my grandfather"), (c) fears of being without the item (e.g., "I might need this in the future for something important"), (d) anthropomorphizing (e.g., "This item will be hurt if I throw it away"), and (e) excessive guilt about discarding (e.g., "I would be a bad parent if I discarded my child's old art projects from school") (Frost et al., 2015).

Individuals who hoard most frequently save objects for either anticipated practical use or an aversion to waste (e.g., "This can be used in the future") or excessive sentimental attachment (e.g., souvenirs, photos, children's art projects) (Frost et al., 2015). Frequently, the reason for keeping the object is fear of a negative emotional experience such as guilt or anxiety in parting with the object, rather than the object eliciting a positive emotion when it is retained. Whereas individuals with hoarding may report that they are willing to part with their hoarded possessions, the process of making decisions about what to discard becomes time-consuming and overwhelming. For items that reflect personal attachment and are unlikely to hold practical value to others (i.e., sentimental items such as photos, inherited mementos), beliefs about memory and excessive guilt in discarding the item are often cited as a primary reason for saving (e.g., "I feel that discarding this item is like throwing away the memory of my mother," or "I will forget my son's graduation day unless I save this reminder").

Some neuropsychological research indicates that individuals with HD have specific executive functioning deficits (Woody et al., 2014). Few studies have directly compared perceived cognitive ability with actual cognitive ability, but, in general, individuals with HD tend to self-report difficulty with memory and attention (Tolin et al., 2018), while existing neuropsychological test batteries do not consistently report deficits in these areas (e.g., Woody et al., 2014). In addition, one study used a behavioral paradigm of a computerized task examining reaction time and error detection (a stop-change task) and found that individuals with HD were less accurate in their estimation of their own error rates despite making similar numbers of errors as healthy controls (Zakrzewski et al., 2018). Negative self-perception about cognitive ability is likely to contribute to HD symptoms as well because individuals with HD often report engaging in hoarding behaviors to compensate for the perceived lack of confidence in their memory (e.g., "I have to save this information so I don't forget it," or "I have to leave things lying out or I will forget them") (Hartl et al., 2004).

## A Critical Examination of the OCRD Category

Through *DSM-IV-TR*, OCD was included among the anxiety disorders along with social and specific phobias, panic disorder and agoraphobia, posttraumatic stress disorder (PTSD), and generalized anxiety disorder (GAD). This grouping made sense on two levels. First, at a purely descriptive level, OCD symptoms are remarkably similar to the main features of anxiety disorders: excessive fear, anxious apprehension, and avoidance or ritualistic escape behavior. Although not mentioned in *DSM*, "rituals" such as checking for safety (in PTSD), asking for reassurance (in GAD), and seeking repeated medical evaluations (in panic disorder) also appear in both OCD and anxiety disorders. The second level on which OCD overlaps with the other anxiety disorders, however, is of greater interest because it transcends mere descriptive psychopathology and has greater treatment implications: OCD and the anxiety disorders are all maintained by the same psychological mechanisms involving (a) overestimates of the likelihood and severity of threat and (b) avoidance and anxiety reduction behaviors that reduce anxiety in the short term but prevent long-term fear extinction. Moreover, these conditions all respond to a specific intervention that promotes fear extinction—exposure therapy (Abramowitz et al., 2019).

Yet OCD was moved in *DSM-5* on the basis of the opinion that it bears an even *greater* similarity to the disorders described earlier in this chapter (i.e., the OCRDs) that seemingly share "compulsive behavior and failures in behavioral inhibition" rather than anxiety (Fineberg et al., 2011, p. 21). Ultimately, those who made decisions about the *DSM-5* (e.g., Fineberg et al., 2011) provided the following arguments for shifting OCD out of the anxiety disorders and creating the new OCRD classification:

(a) The major symptoms of OCD and the OCRDs are repetitive thoughts and behaviors and a failure of behavior inhibition;
(b) OCD and the OCRDs overlap in demographic features such as their age of onset, comorbidity, and family loading;
(c) OCD and the OCRDs share brain circuitry and neurotransmitter abnormalities; and
(d) OCD and the OCRDs share similar treatment response profiles.

Thus, it is worth examining the validity of these arguments, as I do next. A more comprehensive critique of the OCRD classification can be found in Abramowitz and Jacoby (2015).

### Overlaps in Repetitive Thoughts and Behaviors

There are problems with grouping disorders together based on the mere presence of repetitive behaviors. Consider the following:

- Repetitive vomiting is a symptom of bulimia nervosa.
- Repetitive vomiting is a symptom of salmonella poisoning.
- Therefore, bulimia and salmonella poisoning are part of the same family of disorders.

Of course, there is no relationship between bulimia and salmonella, and one would not classify them together in any diagnostic system. Yet this is the approach the *DSM* has used to group together the OCRDs, and, from this perspective, it is easy to see how hair-pulling and skin-picking, for example, might end up seeming if they are related to OCD. Yet, as previously pointed out, when a functional (behavioral) perspective is applied to understanding the phenomenology (i.e., function) of the repetitive behaviors, it becomes clear that, of the OCRDs, only the repetitive thinking and behavior in BDD actually is at all similar to OCD. Moreover, both

OCD and BDD are phenomenologically more similar to anxiety disorders than to the other putative OCRDs.

*Overlaps in Demographic Features*

Indeed, OCD and the other OCRDs typically onset in adolescence through early adulthood and follow similar courses (e.g., Bjornsson et al., 2013; Flessner et al., 2010; Grisham et al., 2006; Odlaug & Grant, 2012; Wilhelm et al., 1999). Yet similarity in age of onset and course is not a persuasive argument for grouping disorders together because it is not specific to the OCRDs. In fact, most mood, anxiety, somatic symptom, dissociative, sexual, sleep, personality, substance-related, psychotic, and eating disorders also begin during this time of life and evidence a somewhat variable yet generally chronic course if effective treatment is not sought.

There is also little evidence for high rates of comorbidity among the OCRDs. Bienvenu and colleagues (2000), for example, found that about 15% of patients with OCD also met criteria for BDD, yet the rate for hair-pulling disorder was only 4%. Other studies have reported largely similar results (Jaisoorya et al., 2003; Lovato et al., 2012), suggesting that, other than BDD, the OCRDs are rather *uncommon* among individuals with OCD. More striking, however, is that OCD is much more comorbid with anxiety disorders. For example, 13% of OCD patients meet criteria for GAD, 20.8% for panic disorder, 16.7% for agoraphobia, 36% for social phobia, and 30.7% for specific phobias (Nestadt et al., 2001). Using the reasoning of the *DSM-5* then, OCD is 5- to 10-fold more closely related to the anxiety disorders than to most of the OCRDs!

Another problem is that the presence of comorbidity does not necessarily indicate meaningful overlaps among disorders. Substance use disorders and PTSD, for example, are highly comorbid (Kramer et al., 2014) yet one would not suggest they are part of the same diagnostic category (the stress of PTSD often leads to maladaptive substance use). Similarly, at least half of OCD sufferers also meet criteria for depression, yet the *DSM-5* does not group depression as part of the OCRD cluster. Thus, comorbidity patterns are of limited value in drawing links among OCRDs.

The problem is similar with using family patterns to group the OCRDs. The lifetime prevalence of hair-pulling disorder, for example, in first-degree relatives of adults with OCD is about 1% (Bienvenu et al., 2000). In contrast, the rates of anxiety disorders among first-degree relatives of people with OCD are far higher than the rates of OCRDs among relatives of OCD sufferers (e.g., Bienvenu et al., 2000; Nestadt et al., 2001). So, the assertion that a familial pattern represents a valid basis for grouping together the OCRDs again more strongly supports grouping OCD among the anxiety disorders.

*Overlaps in Brain Circuitry and Neurotransmitter Abnormalities*

As previously discussed, some neuroimaging studies suggest that individuals with and without OCD show differences in variables related to brain structure and function (for a review and consensus statement, see Bandelow et al., 2016), and similar research replicates this finding with the OCRDs (e.g., Buchanan et al., 2013). Proponents of the OCRD classification interpret these studies as indicating the presence of a common causal brain *abnormality* or *deficit* across the OCRDs (e.g., Fineberg et al., 2011), yet no studies have examined whether it is the same brain-related variables that differ from healthy individuals across the OCRDs. There are also no comparisons between patients with OCRDs and those with other disorders (e.g., eating disorders) to determine whether any brain differences found in OCRDs are specific to OCRDs or associated with mental disorders more generally. Similarities among (and specificity to) the OCRDs have been assumed chiefly on the basis of independent studies (many with small sample sizes), as opposed to direct comparisons, and despite inconsistencies across studies (Whiteside et al., 2004).

An important yet often overlooked limitation of brain imaging studies is that they are cross-sectional and correlational. At best, they can detect *associations* between variables—in this case between an OCRD diagnosis and brain structure or function. But just because a certain variable is correlated with the symptoms of a mental disorder does not imply the presence of an "abnormality" with etiological significance. In the absence of experimental manipulation, conclusions regarding OCD and brain imaging findings must be restricted to those allowed by correlational data. It is plausible that the observed differences in brain structure and function between OCRDs and controls are the result of having an OCRD or that the differences are caused by one or more extraneous variables not measured in brain scan studies.

Probably the most consistent (and yet still overstated) finding in the biological literature on OCD is that pharmacotherapy by SSRIs (e.g., fluoxetine, sertraline) can be effective (Greist et al., 1995). This, and a small literature comparing serotonergic and nonserotonergic processes in OCD patients (Insel et al., 1985), led to the "serotonin hypothesis" that OCD is caused by a "chemical imbalance"—abnormalities in the serotonergic system (Barr et al., 1993; Zohar et al., 2004). Acknowledging the lack of empirical support (see further below) for the serotonin hypothesis (including the mere 20–40% response rate to SSRIs), authors later suggested that dopamine plays a role in OCD—largely on the basis of admissions that dopamine mechanisms play a role in the effects of SSRIs (Denys et al., 2008; Zurowski et al., 2008). That is, SSRIs might be less *selective* than was once thought.

It is, however, logically incorrect to use the effectiveness of SSRIs to infer that an abnormally functioning serotonin or dopamine system is the cause of OCD/OCRDs. For one thing, the serotonin hypothesis was *derived from* the effectiveness of serotonin medications. But the circularity of this argument aside, it also is an example of *post hoc ergo propter hoc* reasoning. This fallacy is exemplified by the example: "When I take aspirin, the headache goes away; therefore the headache was caused by abnormally low aspirin levels." Neurotransmitter models of OCRDs *could* be supported by evidence from experimental studies showing differences in serotonergic or dopaminergic functioning between individuals with and without OCD or by studies in which these neurotransmitters are manipulated leading to increased symptom expression. Yet despite a considerable amount of energy (and funds) devoted to biological marker and challenge studies in OCD, there are no consistent findings. A further problem is that virtually no neurotransmitter research has been conducted on OCRDs other than OCD.

*Overlaps in Treatment Response*

The *DSM-5* notes the "clinical utility" (p. 235) of grouping together the OCRDs, which some authors argues is based on their similar response to SSRIs (Fineberg et al., 2011). This argument, however, is only clinically useful in delineating a class of OCRDs if (a) preferential response to SSRIs is observed uniformly among the OCRDs, (b) the preferential response to SSRIs is *only* observed among the OCRDs, and (c) SSRIs are the best treatment for the OCRDs. Careful examination of the data, however, indicates that *none* of these conditions is satisfied. First, although randomized controlled trials indicate the efficacy of SSRIs relative to placebo for OCD (Eddy et al., 2004; Greist et al., 1995) and BDD (Phillips et al., 2002), SSRI response in the other OCRDs is quite inconsistent (e.g., Bloch et al., 2007, 2014). Second, numerous studies show that SSRIs are efficacious in the treatment of many conditions outside the OCRDs, including unipolar depressive disorders (e.g., Fournier et al., 2010; Schatzberg & Nemeroff, 2013) and anxiety disorders such as SAD (Hedges et al., 2007). Third, cognitive-behavioral interventions have been shown to be at least as effective as medications (if not more so) in the treatment of OCD and OCRDs (e.g., Bloch et al., 2007; Grant et al., 2012; Romanelli et al., 2014). Thus, SSRIs are not the most effective treatment for *any* of the OCRDs.

## Conclusion

OCD is characterized by (a) intrusive unwanted thoughts that the person misappraises as threatening and (b) attempts to reduce the chances of danger, or control the thought itself, with tactics such as compulsive rituals, avoidance, or other neutralizing strategies. These strategies become habitual because they often reduce obsessional fear immediately; yet they maintain the problem in the long run by interfering with the natural extinction of obsessional fear. This cognitive-behavioral conceptualization forms the basis for effective cognitive-behavioral interventions, namely exposure therapy and response prevention. In the *DSM-5*, OCD is categorized with other conditions thought to be "related" to OCD, including BDD, hoarding, skin-picking, and hair-pulling, yet, with the exception of BDD, these conditions are behaviorally distinct from OCD. Accordingly, grouping them in the same diagnostic class gives the clinician the false impression that these "OCRDs" should be conceptualized and treated in a similar fashion.

## References

Abramovitch, A., Abramowitz, J. S., & Mittelman, A. (2013). The neuropsychology of adult obsessive–compulsive disorder: A meta-analysis. *Clinical Psychology Review*, *33*(8), 1163–1171. https://doi.org/10.1016/j.cpr.2013.09.004

Abramovitch, A., & Cooperman, A. (2015). The cognitive neuropsychology of obsessive-compulsive disorder: A critical review. *Journal of Obsessive-Compulsive and Related Disorders*, *5*, 24–36. https://doi.org/10.1016/j.jocrd.2015.01.002

Abramowitz, J. S., Deacon, B. J., Olatunji, B. O., Wheaton, M. G., Berman, N. C., Losardo, D., Timpano, K. R., McGrath, P. B., Riemann, B. C., Adams, T., Björgvinsson, T., Storch, E. A., & Hale, L. R. (2010). Assessment of obsessive-compulsive symptom dimensions: Development and evaluation of the Dimensional Obsessive-Compulsive Scale. *Psychological Assessment, 22*(1), 180–198. http://dx.doi.org/10.1037/a0018260

Abramowitz, J. S., Deacon, B. J., & Whiteside, S. P. H. (2019). *Exposure therapy for anxiety, second edition: Principles and practice.* Guilford.

Abramowitz, J. S., Fabricant, L. E., Taylor, S., Deacon, B. J., McKay, D., & Storch, E. A. (2014). The relevance of analogue studies for understanding obsessions and compulsions. *Clinical Psychology Review, 34*(3), 206–217. https://doi.org/10.1016/j.cpr.2014.01.004

Abramowitz, J. S., & Jacoby, R. J. (2015). Obsessive-compulsive and related disorders: A critical review of the new diagnostic class. *Annual Review of Clinical Psychology, 11*, 165–186. https://doi.org/10.1146/annurev-clinpsy-032813-153713

Abramowitz, J. S., Khandker, M., Nelson, C. A., Deacon, B. J., & Rygwall, R. (2006). The role of cognitive factors in the pathogenesis of obsessive-compulsive symptoms: A prospective study. *Behaviour Research and Therapy, 44*(9), 1361–1374. https://doi.org/10.1016/j.brat.2005.09.011

Arnold, L. M., Auchenbach, M. B., & McElroy, S. L. (2001). Psychogenic excoriation: Clinical features, proposed diagnostic criteria, epidemiology and approaches to treatment. *CNS Drugs, 15*(5), 351–359.

Azrin, N. H., & Nunn, R. G. (1973). Habit-reversal: A method of eliminating nervous habits and tics. *Behaviour Research and Therapy, 11*(4), 619–628.

Bandelow, B., Baldwin, D., Abelli, M., Altamura, C., Dell'Osso, B., Domschke, K., Fineberg, N. A., Grünblatt, E., Jarema, M., Maron, E., Nutt, D., Pini, S., Vaghi, M. M., Wichniak, A., Zai, G., & Riederer, P. (2016). Biological markers for anxiety disorders, OCD and PTSD: A consensus statement. Part I: Neuroimaging and genetics. *World Journal of Biological Psychiatry, 17*(5), 321–365. https://doi.org/10.1080/15622975.2016.1181783

Bandelow, B., Baldwin, D., Abelli, M., Bolea-Alamanac, B., Bourin, M., Chamberlain, S. R., . . . Riederer, P. (2017). Biological markers for anxiety disorders, OCD and PTSD: A consensus statement. Part II: Neurochemistry, neurophysiology and neurocognition. *World Journal of Biological Psychiatry, 18*(3), 162–214. https://doi.org/10.1080/15622975.2016.1190867

Barr, L. C., Goodman, W. K., & Price, L. H. (1993). The serotonin hypothesis of obsessive compulsive disorder. *International Clinical Psychopharmacology, 8*(Suppl 2), 79–82.

Baxter, L. R., Schwartz, J. M., Mazziotta, J. C., Phelps, M. E., Pahl, J. J., Guze, B. H., & Fairbanks, L. (1988). Cerebral glucose metabolic rates in nondepressed patients with obsessive-compulsive disorder. *American Journal of Psychiatry, 145*(12), 1560–1563. https://doi.org/10.1176/ajp.145.12.1560

Beck, A. T. (1976). *Cognitive therapy and the emotional disorders.* International Universities Press.

Berman, N. C., Wheaton, M. G., & Abramowitz, J. S. (2012). The "Arnold Schwarzenegger effect": Is strength of the "victim" related to misinterpretations of harm intrusions? *Behaviour Research and Therapy, 50*(12), 761–766. https://doi.org/10.1016/j.brat.2012.09.002

Bienvenu, O. J., Samuels, J. F., Riddle, M. A., Hoehn-Saric, R., Liang, K. Y., Cullen, B. A., Grados, M. A., & Nestadt, G. (2000). The relationship of obsessive-compulsive disorder to possible spectrum disorders: Results from a family study. *Biological Psychiatry, 48*(4), 287–293.

Bjornsson, A. S., Didie, E. R., Grant, J. E., Menard, W., Stalker, E., & Phillips, K. A. (2013). Age at onset and clinical correlates in body dysmorphic disorder. *Comprehensive Psychiatry, 54*(7), 893–903.

Bloch, M. H., Bartley, C. A., Zipperer, L., Jakubovski, E., Landeros-Weisenberger, A., Pittenger, C., & Leckman, J. F. (2014). Meta-analysis: Hoarding symptoms associated with poor treatment outcome in obsessive–compulsive disorder. *Molecular Psychiatry.* https://doi.org/10.1038/mp.2014.50

Bloch, M. H., Landeros-Weisenberger, A., Dombrowski, P., Kelmendi, B., Wegner, R., Nudel, J., Pittenger, C., Leckman, J. F., & Coric, V. (2007). Systematic review: Pharmacological and behavioral treatment for trichotillomania. *Biological Psychiatry, 62*(8), 839–846. https://doi.org/10.1016/j.biopsych.2007.05.019

Bluett, E. J., Homan, K. J., Morrison, K. L., Levin, M. E., & Twohig, M. P. (2014). Acceptance and commitment therapy for anxiety and OCD spectrum disorders: An empirical review. *Journal of Anxiety Disorders, 28*(6), 612–624. https://doi.org/10.1016/j.janxdis.2014.06.008

Boeding, S. E., Paprocki, C. M., Baucom, D. H., Abramowitz, J. S., Wheaton, M. G., Fabricant, L. E., & Fischer, M. S. (2013). Let me check that for you: Symptom accommodation in romantic partners of adults with obsessive-compulsive disorder. *Behaviour Research and Therapy, 51*(6), 316–322. https://doi.org/10.1016/j.brat.2013.03.002

Bogetto, F., Venturello, S., Albert, U., Maina, G., & Ravizza, L. (1999). Gender-related clinical differences in obsessive-compulsive disorder. *European Psychiatry, 14*(8), 434–441. https://doi.org/10.1016/S0924-9338(99)00224-2

Buchanan, B. G., Rossell, S. L., Maller, J. J., Toh, W. L., Brennan, S., & Castle, D. J. (2013). Brain connectivity in body dysmorphic disorder compared with controls: A diffusion tensor imaging study. *Psychological Medicine, 43*(12), 2513–2521.

Christenson, G. A., Ristvedt, S. L., & Mackenzie, T. B. (1993). Identification of trichotillomania cue profiles. *Behaviour Research and Therapy, 31*(3), 315–320. https://doi.org/10.1016/0005-7967(93)90030-X

Clark, D. A. (2004). *Cognitive-behavioral therapy for OCD.* Guilford.

Denys, D., Fineberg, N., Carey, P. C., & Stein, D. J. (2008). Reply. *Biological Psychiatry, 63*(1), e7. https://doi.org/10.1016/j.biopsych.2007.06.021

Eddy, K. T., Dutra, L., Bradley, R., & Westen, D. (2004). A multidimensional meta-analysis of psychotherapy and pharmacotherapy for obsessive-compulsive disorder. *Clinical Psychology Review, 24*(8), 1011–1030.

Fang, A., & Wilhelm, S. (2015). Clinical features, cognitive biases, and treatment of body dysmorphic disorder. *Annual Review of Clinical Psychology, 11*(1), 187–212. https://doi.org/10.1146/annurev-clinpsy-032814-112849

Feusner, J. D., Townsend, J., Bystritsky, A., & Bookheimer, S. (2007). Visual information processing of faces in body dysmorphic disorder. *Archives of General Psychiatry, 64*(12), 1417. https://doi.org/10.1001/archpsyc.64.12.1417

Fineberg, N. A., Saxena, S., Zohar, J., & Craig, K. J. (2011). Obsessive-compulsive disorder: Boundary issues. In Eric Hollander, J. Zohar, P. J. Sirovatka, & D. A. Regier (Eds.), *Obsessive-compulsive spectrum disorders: Refining the research agenda for DSM-V.* (pp. 1–32). American Psychiatric Association.

Fitzgerald, K. D., Moore, G. J., Paulson, L. A., Stewart, C. M., & Rosenberg, D. R. (2000). Proton spectroscopic imaging of the thalamus in treatment-naive pediatric obsessive-compulsive disorder. *Biological Psychiatry, 47*(3), 174–182.

Flessner, C. A., Lochner, C., Stein, D. J., Woods, D. W., Franklin, M. E., & Keuthen, N. J. (2010). Age of onset of trichotillomania symptoms: Investigating clinical correlates. *Journal of Nervous and Mental Disease, 198*(12), 896–900. https://doi.org/10.1097/NMD.0b013e3181fe7423

Foa, E. B., Amir, N., Gershuny, B., & Molnar, C. (1997). Implicit and explicit memory in obsessive-compulsive disorder. *Journal of Anxiety Disorders, 11*(2), 119–129.

Foa, E. B., Kozak, M. J., Goodman, W. K., Hollander, E., Jenike, M. A., & Rasmussen, S. A. (1995). DSM-IV field trial: Obsessive-compulsive disorder. *The American Journal of Psychiatry, 152*(1), 90–96.

Fournier, J. C., DeRubeis, R. J., Hollon, S. D., Dimidjian, S., Amsterdam, J. D., Shelton, R. C., & Fawcett, J. (2010). Antidepressant drug effects and depression severity: A patient-level meta-analysis. *Journal of the American Medical Association, 303*(1), 47–53. https://doi.org/10.1001/jama.2009.1943

Franklin, M. E., & Tolin, D. F. (2007). *Treating trichotillomania: Cognitive-behavioral therapy for hairpulling and related problems.* Springer Science & Business Media.

Frost, R. O., & Hartl, T. L. (1996). A cognitive-behavioral model of compulsive hoarding. *Behaviour Research and Therapy, 34*(4), 341–350. https://doi.org/10.1016/0005-7967(95)00071-2

Frost, R. O., & Steketee, G. S. (2002). *Cognitive approaches to obsessions and compulsions.* Elsevier.

Frost, R. O., Steketee, G., Tolin, D. F., Sinopoli, N., & Ruby, D. (2015). Motives for acquiring and saving in hoarding disorder, OCD, and community controls. *Journal of Obsessive-Compulsive and Related Disorders, 4*, 54–59. https://doi.org/10.1016/j.jocrd.2014.12.006

Grant, J. E., Odlaug, B. L., Chamberlain, S. R., Keuthen, N. J., Lochner, C., & Stein, D. J. (2012). Skin picking disorder. *American Journal of Psychiatry, 169*(11), 1143–1149. https://doi.org/10.1176/appi.ajp.2012.12040508

Greist, J. H., Jefferson, J. W., Kobak, K. A., Katzelnick, D. J., & Serlin, R. C. (1995). Efficacy and tolerability of serotonin transport inhibitors in obsessive-compulsive disorder: A meta-analysis. *Archives of General Psychiatry, 52*(1), 53–60.

Grisham, J. R., Frost, R. O., Steketee, G., Kim, H.-J., & Hood, S. (2006). Age of onset of compulsive hoarding. *Journal of Anxiety Disorders, 20*(5), 675–686. https://doi.org/10.1016/j.janxdis.2005.07.004

Grocholewski, A., Kliem, S., & Heinrichs, N. (2012). Selective attention to imagined facial ugliness is specific to body dysmorphic disorder. *Body Image, 9*(2), 261–269. https://doi.org/10.1016/j.bodyim.2012.01.002

Hartl, T. L., Frost, R. O., Allen, G. J., Deckersbach, T., Steketee, G., Duffany, S. R., & Savage, C. R. (2004). Actual and perceived memory deficits in individuals with compulsive hoarding. *Depression and Anxiety, 20*(2), 59–69. https://doi.org/10.1002/da.20010

Hayes, S. C., Strosahl, K. D., & Wilson, K. G. (2011). *Acceptance and commitment therapy, second edition: The process and practice of mindful change.* Guilford.

Hedges, D. W., Brown, B. L., Shwalb, D. A., Godfrey, K., & Larcher, A. M. (2007). The efficacy of selective serotonin reuptake inhibitors in adult social anxiety disorder: A meta-analysis of double-blind, placebo-controlled trials. *Journal of Psychopharmacology, 21*(1), 102–111. https://doi.org/10.1177/0269881106065102

Hettema, J. M., Neale, M. C., & Kendler, K. S. (2001). A review and meta-analysis of the genetic epidemiology of anxiety disorders. *American Journal of Psychiatry, 158*(10), 1568–1578. https://doi.org/10.1176/appi.ajp.158.10.1568

Hollander, E., DeCaria, C. M., Nitescu, A., Gully, R., Suckow, R. F., Cooper, T. B., Gorman, J. M., Klein, D. F., & Liebowitz, M. R. (1992). Serotonergic function in obsessive-compulsive disorder: Behavioral and neuroendocrine responses to oral m-chlorophenylpiperazine and fenfluramine in patients and healthy volunteers. *Archives of General Psychiatry, 49*(1), 21–28.

Hollander, Eric, Zohar, J., Sirovatka, P. J., & Regier, D. A. (2011). *Obsessive-compulsive spectrum disorders: Refining the research agenda for DSM-V* (Eric Hollander, J. Zohar, P. J. Sirovatka, & D. A. Regier, Eds.; 2010-18472-000). American Psychiatric Association.

Insel, T. R., Mueller, E. A., Alterman, I., Linnoila, M., & Murphy, D. L. (1985). Obsessive-compulsive disorder and serotonin: Is there a connection? *Biological Psychiatry, 20*(11), 1174–1188. https://doi.org/10.1016/0006-3223(85)90176-3

Jaisoorya, T. S., Janardhan Reddy, Y. C., & Srinath, S. (2003). The relationship of obsessive-compulsive disorder to putative spectrum disorders: Results from an Indian study. *Comprehensive Psychiatry, 44*(4), 317–323.

Kessler, R. C., Berglund, P., Demler, O., Jin, R., Merikangas, K. R., & Walters, E. E. (2005). Lifetime prevalence and age-of-onset distributions of DSM-IV disorders in the National Comorbidity Survey Replication. *Archives of General Psychiatry, 62*(6), 593–602.

Keuthen, N. J., Deckersbach, T., Wilhelm, S., Hale, E., Fraim, C., Baer, L., O'Sullivan, R. L., & Jenike, M. A. (2000). Repetitive skin-picking in a student population and comparison with a sample of self-injurious skin-pickers. *Psychosomatics, 41*(3), 210–215. https://doi.org/10.1176/appi.psy.41.3.210

Kramer, M. D., Polusny, M. A., Arbisi, P. A., & Krueger, R. F. (2014). Comorbidity of PTSD and SUDs: Toward an etiologic understanding. In P. Ouimette & J. P. Read (Eds.), *Trauma and substance abuse: Causes, consequences, and treatment of comorbid disorders* (2nd ed.). (2013-15892-004; pp. 53–75). American Psychological Association.

Lang, R., Didden, R., Machalicek, W., Rispoli, M., Sigafoos, J., Lancioni, G., Mulloy, A., Regester, A., Pierce, N., & Kang, S. (2010). Behavioral treatment of chronic skin-picking in individuals with developmental disabilities: A systematic review. *Research in Developmental Disabilities, 31*(2), 304–315. https://doi.org/10.1016/j.ridd.2009.10.017

Lochner, C., Roos, A., & Stein, D. J. (2017). Excoriation (skin-picking) disorder: A systematic review of treatment options. *Neuropsychiatric Disease and Treatment, 13*, 1867–1872. https://doi.org/10.2147/NDT.S121138

Lovato, L., Ferrão, Y. A., Stein, D. J., Shavitt, R. G., Fontenelle, L. F., Vivan, A., Miguel, E. C., & Cordioli, A. V. (2012). Skin picking and trichotillomania in adults with obsessive-compulsive disorder. *Comprehensive Psychiatry, 53*(5), 562–568. https://doi.org/10.1016/j.comppsych.2011.06.008

McKay, D., Abramowitz, J. S., Calamari, J. E., Kyrios, M., Radomsky, A. S., Sookman, D., Taylor, S., & Wilhelm, S. (2004). A critical evaluation of obsessive-compulsive disorder subtypes: Symptoms versus mechanisms. *Clinical*

*Psychology Review, 24*(3), 283–313. https://doi.org/10.1016/j.cpr.2004.04.003

Mowrer, O. H. (1960). *Learning theory and behavior* (vol. xii). Wiley.

Nestadt, G., Samuels, J., Riddle, M. A., Liang, K. Y., Bienvenu, O. J., Hoehn-Saric, R., Grados, M., & Cullen, B. (2001). The relationship between obsessive-compulsive disorder and anxiety and affective disorders: Results from the Johns Hopkins OCD Family Study. *Psychological Medicine, 31*(3), 481–487.

Nicoli de Mattos, C., S. Kim, H., Lacroix, E., Requião, M., Zambrano Filomensky, T., Hodgins, D. C., & Tavares, H. (2018). The need to consume: Hoarding as a shared psychological feature of compulsive buying and binge eating. *Comprehensive Psychiatry, 85*, 67–71. https://doi.org/10.1016/j.comppsych.2018.06.010

Norberg, M. M., Wetterneck, C. T., Woods, D. W., & Conelea, C. A. (2007). Experiential avoidance as a mediator of relationships between cognitions and hair-pulling severity. *Behavior Modification, 31*(4), 367–381. https://doi.org/10.1177/0145445506297343

Obsessive Compulsive Cognitions Working Group. (1997). Cognitive assessment of obsessive-compulsive disorder. *Behaviour Research and Therapy, 35*(7), 667–681.

Odlaug, B. L., & Grant, J. E. (2012). Pathological skin picking. In J. E. Grant, D. J. Stein, D. W. Woods, & N. J. Keuthen (Eds.), *Trichotillomania, skin picking, and other body-focused repetitive behaviors* (2011-19852-002; pp. 21–41). American Psychiatric Publishing, Inc.

Phillips, K. A., Albertini, R. S., & Rasmussen, S. A. (2002). A randomized placebo-controlled trial of fluoxetine in body dysmorphic disorder. *Archives of General Psychiatry, 59*(4), 381–388.

Phillips, K. A., & Stein, D. J. (2015). Obsessive–compulsive and related disorders: Body dysmorphic disorder, trichotillomania (hair-pulling disorder), and excoriation (skin-picking) disorder. In A. Tasman (Ed.), *Psychiatry* (pp. 1129–1141). Wiley. https://doi.org/10.1002/9781118753378.ch58

Rachman, S. J. (2003). *The treatment of obsessions*. Oxford University Press.

Rachman, S. J., & de Silva, P. (1978). Abnormal and normal obsessions. *Behaviour Research and Therapy, 16*(4), 233–248.

Rachman, S. J., Elliott, C. M., Shafran, R., & Radomsky, A. S. (2009). Separating hoarding from OCD. *Behaviour Research and Therapy, 47*(6), 520–522. https://doi.org/10.1016/j.brat.2009.02.014

Rasmussen, S. A., & Eisen, J. L. (1992). The epidemiology and clinical features of obsessive compulsive disorder. *Psychiatric Clinics of North America, 15*(4), 743–758.

Rassin, E., Merckelbach, H., Muris, P., & Spaan, V. (1999). Thought-action fusion as a causal factor in the development of intrusions. *Behaviour Research and Therapy, 37*(3), 231–237.

Rehm, I. C., Nedeljkovic, M., Moulding, R., & Thomas, A. (2019). The Beliefs in Trichotillomania Scale (BiTS): Factor analyses and preliminary validation. *British Journal of Clinical Psychology, 58*(4), 384–405. https://doi.org/10.1111/bjc.12219

Reuman, L., Buchholz, J., & Abramowitz, J. S. (2018). Obsessive beliefs, experiential avoidance, and cognitive fusion as predictors of obsessive-compulsive disorder symptom dimensions. *Journal of Contextual Behavioral Science, 9*, 15–20. https://doi.org/10.1016/j.jcbs.2018.06.001

Romanelli, R. J., Wu, F. M., Gamba, R., Mojtabai, R., & Segal, J. B. (2014). Behavioral therapy and serotonin reuptake inhibitor pharmacotherapy in the treatment of obsessive–compulsive disorder: A systematic review and meta-analysis of head-to-head randomized controlled trials. *Depression and Anxiety*, 1–12. https://doi.org/10.1002/da.22232

Salkovskis, P. M. (1985). Obsessional-compulsive problems: A cognitive-behavioural analysis. *Behaviour Research and Therapy, 23*(5), 571–583. https://doi.org/10.1016/0005-7967(85)90105-6

Salkovskis, P. M., Shafran, R., Rachman, S., & Freeston, M. H. (1999). Multiple pathways to inflated responsibility beliefs in obsessional problems: Possible origins and implications for therapy and research. *Behaviour Research and Therapy, 37*(11), 1055–1072. https://doi.org/10.1016/S0005-7967(99)00063-7

Schatzberg, A. F., & Nemeroff, C. B. (2013). *Essentials of clinical psychopharmacology*. American Psychiatric Publications.

Schreiber, L., Odlaug, B. L., & Grant, J. E. (2011). Impulse control disorders: Updated review of clinical characteristics and pharmacological management. *Frontiers in Psychiatry, 2*, 1. https://doi.org/10.3389/fpsyt.2011.00001

Schuck, K., Keijsers, G. P. J., & Rinck, M. (2011). The effects of brief cognitive-behaviour therapy for pathological skin picking: A randomized comparison to wait-list control. *Behaviour Research and Therapy, 49*(1), 11–17. https://doi.org/10.1016/j.brat.2010.09.005

Shafran, R., Thordarson, D. S., & Rachman, S. (1996). Thought-action fusion in obsessive compulsive disorder. *Journal of Anxiety Disorders, 10*(5), 379–391. https://doi.org/10.1016/0887-6185(96)00018-7

Snorrason, I., Smári, J., & Olafsson, R. P. (2010). Emotion regulation in pathological skin picking: Findings from a non-treatment seeking sample. *Journal of Behavior Therapy and Experimental Psychiatry, 41*(3), 238–245. https://doi.org/10.1016/j.jbtep.2010.01.009

Steketee, G., & Frost, R. (2003). Compulsive hoarding: current status of the research. *Clinical psychology review, 23*(7), 905–927. https://doi.org/10.1016/j.cpr.2003.08.002

Stewart, S. E., Yu, D., Scharf, J. M., Neale, B. M., Fagerness, J. A., Mathews, C. A., . . . Pauls, D. L. (2013). Genome-wide association study of obsessive-compulsive disorder. *Molecular Psychiatry, 18*(7), 788–798. https://doi.org/10.1038/mp.2012.85

Taylor, S., Abramowitz, J. S., McKay, D., Calamari, J. E., Sookman, D., Kyrios, M., Wilhelm, S., & Carmin, C. (2006). Do dysfunctional beliefs play a role in all types of obsessive-compulsive disorder? *Journal of Anxiety Disorders, 20*(1), 85–97. https://doi.org/10.1016/j.janxdis.2004.11.005

Timpano, K. R., Abramowitz, J. S., Mahaffey, B. L., Mitchell, M. A., & Schmidt, N. B. (2011). Efficacy of a prevention program for postpartum obsessive–compulsive symptoms. *Journal of Psychiatric Research, 45*(11), 1511–1517. https://doi.org/10.1016/j.jpsychires.2011.06.015

Tolin, D. F., Abramowitz, J. S., Kozak, M. J., & Foa, E. B. (2001). Fixity of belief, perceptual aberration, and magical ideation in obsessive-compulsive disorder. *Journal of Anxiety Disorders, 15*(6), 501–510. https://doi.org/10.1016/S0887-6185(01)00078-0

Tolin, D. F., Hallion, L. S., Wootton, B. M., Levy, H. C., Billingsley, A. L., Das, A., Katz, B. W., & Stevens, M. C. (2018). Subjective cognitive function in hoarding disorder.

*Psychiatry Research, 265,* 215–220. https://doi.org/10.1016/j.psychres.2018.05.003

Tolin, D. F., Hamlin, C., & Foa, E. B. (2002). Directed forgetting in obsessive-compulsive disorder: Replication and extension. *Behaviour Research and Therapy, 40*(7), 793–803. https://doi.org/10.1016/S0005-7967(01)00062-6

Turna, J., Patterson, B., Simpson, W., Pullia, K., Khalesi, Z., Grosman Kaplan, K., & Van Ameringen, M. (2018). Prevalence of hoarding behaviours and excessive acquisition in users of online classified advertisements. *Psychiatry Research, 270,* 194–197. https://doi.org/10.1016/j.psychres.2018.09.022

van Grootheest, D. S., Bartels, M., Cath, D. C., Beekman, A. T., Hudziak, J. J., & Boomsma, D. I. (2007). Genetic and Environmental Contributions Underlying Stability in Childhood Obsessive-Compulsive Behavior. *Biological Psychiatry, 61*(3), 308–315. https://doi.org/10.1016/j.biopsych.2006.05.035

Veale, D. (2004). Advances in a cognitive behavioural model of body dysmorphic disorder. *Body Image, 1*(1), 113–125. https://doi.org/10.1016/S1740-1445(03)00009-3

Vogel, B., Trotzke, P., Steins-Loeber, S., Schäfer, G., Stenger, J., Zwaan, M. de, Brand, M., & Müller, A. (2019). An experimental examination of cognitive processes and response inhibition in patients seeking treatment for buying-shopping disorder. *PLOS ONE, 14*(3), e0212415. https://doi.org/10.1371/journal.pone.0212415

Wheaton, M. G., Abramowitz, J. S., Berman, N. C., Riemann, B. C., & Hale, L. R. (2010). The relationship between obsessive beliefs and symptom dimensions in obsessive-compulsive disorder. *Behaviour Research and Therapy, 48*(10), 949–954.

Wheaton, M. G., Abramowitz, J. S., Fabricant, L. E., Berman, N. C., & Franklin, J. C. (2011). Is hoarding a symptom of obsessive-compulsive disorder? *International Journal of Cognitive Therapy, 4*(3), 225–238. https://doi.org/10.1521/ijct.2011.4.3.225

Whiteside, S. P., Port, J. D., & Abramowitz, J. S. (2004). A meta-analysis of functional neuroimaging in obsessive–compulsive disorder. *Psychiatry Research: Neuroimaging, 132*(1), 69–79. https://doi.org/10.1016/j.pscychresns.2004.07.001

Wilhelm, S., Keuthen, N. J., Deckersbach, T., Engelhard, I. M., Forker, A. E., Baer, L., O'Sullivan, R. L., & Jenike, M. A. (1999). Self-injurious skin picking: Clinical characteristics and comorbidity. *Journal of Clinical Psychiatry, 60*(7), 454–459.

Woods, C. M., Vevea, J. L., Chambless, D. L., & Bayen, U. J. (2002). Are Compulsive Checkers Impaired in Memory? A Meta-Analytic Review. *Clinical Psychology: Science and Practice, 9*(4), 353–366. https://doi.org/10.1093/clipsy.9.4.353

Woody, S. R., Kellman-McFarlane, K., & Welsted, A. (2014). Review of cognitive performance in hoarding disorder. *Clinical Psychology Review, 34*(4), 324–336. https://doi.org/10.1016/j.cpr.2014.04.002

Zakrzewski, J. J., Datta, S., Scherling, C., Nizar, K., Vigil, O., Rosen, H., & Mathews, C. A. (2018). Deficits in physiological and self-conscious emotional response to errors in hoarding disorder. *Psychiatry Research, 268,* 157–164. https://doi.org/10.1016/j.psychres.2018.07.012

Zohar, J., & Insel, T. R. (1987). Obsessive-compulsive disorder: Psychobiological approaches to diagnosis, treatment, and pathophysiology. *Biological Psychiatry, 22*(6), 667–687. https://doi.org/10.1016/0006-3223(87)90199-5

Zohar, J., Kennedy, J. L., Hollander, E., & Koran, L. M. (2004). Serotonin-1D hypothesis of obsessive-compulsive disorder: An update. *Journal of Clinical Psychiatry, 65*(Suppl14), 18–21.

Zurowski, B., Kordon, A., Wahl, K., & Hohagen, F. (2008). Non-selective effects of selective serotonin reuptake inhibitors. *Biological Psychiatry, 63*(1), e5. https://doi.org/10.1016/j.biopsych.2007.02.028

# CHAPTER 9

# Posttraumatic Stress Disorder and Dissociative Disorders

Richard J. McNally

## Posttraumatic Stress Disorder

Clinicians have long recognized that traumatic events can produce psychiatric symptoms in previously well-adjusted individuals, but prevailing opinion held that stress-induced symptoms are transient (Jones & Wessely, 2007). Persistent symptoms implied the presence of another neurotic or characterological disturbance.

The psychiatric sequelae of the Vietnam War altered this view. Many veterans began to report chronic symptoms, often long after reentering civilian life. Instead of viewing these men as suffering from preexisting conditions worsened by the war, clinicians concluded that combat itself could cause lasting psychiatric disability (Lifton, 1973; Shatan, 1973).

Antiwar psychiatrists and leaders of Vietnam veterans' organizations lobbied for the inclusion of a "post-Vietnam syndrome" diagnosis in the then-forthcoming *DSM-III*. They realized that for veterans to receive treatment and disability compensation from the Veterans Administration (VA), they had to show that veterans' symptoms were attributable to military service, not to preexisting problems or vulnerabilities. Making the case was especially challenging when symptoms erupted years after the war. Indeed, no single diagnosis in the *DSM-II* captured the delayed onset of stress-related symptoms.

Leaders of the *DSM* revision process initially opposed this proposal, maintaining that combinations of traditional diagnoses covered the problems of Vietnam veterans. Moreover, a goal for *DSM-III* was to devise an atheoretical system comprising diagnoses explicitly defined by their signs, symptoms, and course rather than by often-debatable etiological notions. Ratification of a post-Vietnam syndrome would be inconsistent with this goal.

Veterans' advocates made common cause with mental health professionals who had been working with survivors of rape (Burgess & Holmstrom, 1974), disaster (Rangell, 1976), and concentration camps (Chodoff, 1963). Similarities in survivors' symptoms produced a consensus that any terrifying, life-threatening event could cause a chronic syndrome such as that suffered by the traumatized Vietnam veteran. An influential member of the *DSM-III* task force agreed (Andreasen, 2004). Indeed, she had observed a similar pattern of psychiatric symptoms in patients who had been severely burned. Her support ensured that posttraumatic stress disorder (PTSD) appeared in *DSM-III* classified as an anxiety disorder.

The diagnostic criteria have evolved over subsequent *DSM*s, but the core features of PTSD remain intact. The central idea is that a traumatic event establishes a memory that gives rise to a distinctive profile of signs and symptoms (McNally, 2003a,

| Abbreviations | |
|---|---|
| ANS | Autonomic nervous system |
| CES | Centrality of Event Scale |
| DID | Dissociative identity disorder |
| GAF | Global Assessment of Functioning (scale) |
| HPA | Hypothalamic-pituitary-adrenal |
| HRV | Heart rate variability |
| NA | Noradrenergic |
| NE | Norepinephrine |
| NVVRS | National Vietnam Veterans Readjustment Study |
| PCL | PTSD Checklist |
| SBP | Systolic blood pressure |

pp. 105–124; Rubin et al., 2008). Although many people experience intense emotional distress in the immediate wake of trauma, the persistence of symptoms long after danger has passed is what justifies PTSD as a disorder.

According to *DSM-5*, PTSD comprises four symptomatic clusters. The *intrusion* cluster (B criteria) includes reexperiencing symptoms such as traumatic nightmares, intrusive sensory images of the trauma, and physiological reactivity to reminders of the trauma. The *avoidance* cluster (C criteria) includes efforts to avoid feelings, thoughts, and reminders of the trauma. The cluster covering *negative alterations in cognitions and mood* (D criteria) includes symptoms such as emotional numbing, distorted blame of self or others, and pervasive negative emotional states (e.g., shame and anger). The cluster covering *alterations in arousal and reactivity* (E criteria) includes symptoms such as exaggerated startle, aggression, reckless behavior, and hypervigilance.

## What Counts as a Traumatic Stressor?

To qualify for PTSD, a person must meet Criterion A: exposure to a traumatic stressor. For two reasons, exposure to trauma is essential to the conceptual integrity of PTSD (McNally, 2009). First, several core symptoms possess Brentano (1889/1984) *intentionality* (i.e, "aboutness"). That is, they are not merely *caused* by trauma; they are *about* the trauma. To have intrusive images, for example, is to have intrusive images about something: namely, the trauma.

Second, many symptoms of PTSD overlap with those of other disorders (e.g., loss of pleasure in activities, insomnia); it is the memory of the trauma that unites them into a coherent syndrome (Young, 1995, p. 5). Hence, the syndrome would unravel if we dispensed with Criterion A.

The *DSM-III* concept of PTSD presupposed that only *traumatic* stressors falling outside the boundary of everyday experience could produce the disorder's symptomatic profile. Such canonical traumas included combat, rape, torture, and natural disasters—events that would presumably produce intense distress in nearly everyone. Conversely, ordinary stressors presumably could not cause PTSD.

Two key findings complicated this assumptive framework. First, epidemiological studies documented that most people exposed to Criterion A traumatic stressors do not develop PTSD (Breslau et al., 1991). Second, other studies showed that people who neither experienced nor witnessed a canonical trauma could still fulfill the symptomatic criteria for the disorder, such as learning about the violent death of a loved one (e.g., Saigh, 1991). Accordingly, in 1994, the *DSM-IV* broadened the concept of trauma exposure to include being "confronted with" information about a threat to the "physical integrity" of another person, not necessarily a friend or family member.

Other reports appeared, showing stressors falling far short of Criterion A could apparently trigger PTSD (for a review, see Dohrenwend, 2010). For example, people encountering obnoxious jokes in the workplace (McDonald, 2003), giving birth to a healthy baby (Olde et al, 2006), and having a wisdom tooth removed (de Jongh et al., 2008) reportedly developed PTSD or PTSD symptoms. One study showed that 4% of Americans living far from the sites of the 9/11 terrorist attacks developed apparent PTSD (Schlenger et al., 2002), apparently from watching the events on television. Not only could one now qualify as a "trauma survivor" without having been at the scene of the trauma, one did not even have to know the people whose physical integrity had been threatened (McNally & Breslau, 2008).

The concern that suffering people would be denied the diagnosis and reimbursable treatment motivated the "conceptual bracket creep in the definition of trauma" (McNally, 2003b, p. 231). Yet broadening the concept had other consequences, too. It meant that nearly everyone qualifies as a trauma survivor, as Breslau and Kessler (2001) discovered. Studying residents of Southeastern Michigan, they found that 89.6% of adults had been exposed to a *DSM-IV* Criterion A stressor.

However honorably motivated, conceptual bracket creep may render it difficult to ascertain the psychobiological mechanisms mediating the symptoms of PTSD. It seems unlikely that survivors of fender-benders have much in common with survivors of the Holocaust. Also, the more we broaden the concept of trauma, the less plausibly we can assign causal significance to the stressor itself, and the more we must emphasize vulnerability factors. Diagnosing PTSD in people exposed to relatively minor events presumably produces a background–foreground inversion whereby risk factors move into the causal foreground while the trauma recedes into the background. Shifting the causal burden away from the stressor undermines the very rationale for having a diagnosis of PTSD in the first place.

What should we make of people whose apparent PTSD emerges after exposure to relatively minor stressors? Do they carry an especially heavy burden of risk factors relative to people who develop PTSD only after exposure to canonical stressors? Consistent with this background–foreground inversion hypothesis, McNally and Robinaugh (2011) found that the effect size between cognitive ability and PTSD caseness was much larger for women whose childhood sexual abuse was mild in severity relative to those whose abuse was moderate in severity. That is, the less severe the stressor, the more important was the risk factor of lower cognitive ability in predicting PTSD. Yet in an epidemiological study, Breslau et al. (2013) found that the importance of risk factors (e.g., preexisting depression, parental alcohol abuse) did not differ for less severe categories of trauma (accidents) than for more severe categories of trauma (sexual assault).

Perhaps people living under conditions of safety, peace, and prosperity are especially likely to develop PTSD following exposure to relatively minor stressors. This may explain why PTSD is more common among British adolescents than among members of the British military (Jones, 2019). It may also explain the "vulnerability paradox in the cross-national prevalence of PTSD" (Dückers et al., 2016, p. 300), the finding that although low socioeconomic status (SES) is a risk factor for PTSD in individuals exposed to trauma, the opposite holds for nations. That is, low-SES countries have a *lower* prevalence of PTSD than do high-SES ones even when their rates of trauma exposure do not differ. However, the apparent paradox vanishes if one avoids falling prey to the *ecological* fallacy (Robinson, 1950)—the mistake in assuming that correlations between variables at the level of the person *must* hold at the level of the group (or vice versa). Certain stressors, such as automobile accidents, may be more pathogenic in otherwise safe, comfortable nations than in those accustomed to struggling with adversity (McNally, 2018).

To address problems with Criterion A, the *DSM-5* committee members required that people who learn of physical threats to others must be a close friend or relative of the threatened person. They also disqualified trauma exposure mediated by the media as satisfying Criterion A unless it was related to the person's occupation (e.g., first responder).

## Sex Ratio

Men are exposed to traumatic events more often than are women (Tolin & Foa, 2006), yet the rate of PTSD is twice as great in women as in men. One hypothesis for this sex difference in PTSD prevalence is that women more frequently experience extreme stressors more often than men do (Cortina & Kubiak, 2006). This hypothesis, however, appears incorrect. Even when one controls for type of trauma (e.g., rape), sex differences in the severity and prevalence of PTSD remain (Tolin & Foa, 2006), implying that men and women differ in ways that influence their risk of developing PTSD following exposure to trauma.

Hormonal differences between male and female trauma survivors may account for the heightened risk of PTSD in the latter (Pineles et al., 2017). For example, Pineles et al. (2016) twice tested trauma-exposed women with or without PTSD in a conditioned stimulus (CS)+/CS− Pavlovian differential fear conditioning paradigm involving skin conductance as the measure of fear. One test occurred when their levels of the gonadal hormones estradiol and progesterone were low (i.e., early follicular phase of the menstrual cycle) and the other occurred when levels of these hormones were high (i.e., during the midluteal phase). An extinction phase immediately followed the acquisition phase. The results indicated that women with PTSD exhibited impaired retention of extinction when in the midluteal phase relative to women without PTSD.

## Epidemiology

According to the National Comorbidity Survey Replication (NCS-R; Kessler et al., 2005), the lifetime prevalence rate of *DSM-IV-TR* PTSD in the United States is 6.8%. According to the NCS-R, 9.7% of women and 3.6% of men develop PTSD at some point in their lives (http://www.hcp.med.harvard.edu/ncs/ftpdir/table_ncsr_by_gender_and_age.pdf).

In the World Mental Health (WMH) Surveys, Koenen et al. (2017) found that among trauma-exposed people, 5.6% developed PTSD at some point in their lives, and 2.8% had PTSD during the previous 12 months. The lifetime and 12-month prevalence rates for high-income countries were 6.9% and 3.6%, respectively, and greater than for low- and lower-middle income countries combined (3.0% and 1.5%, respectively). For the United States, the 30-day, 12-month, and lifetime prevalence rates for PTSD among the trauma-exposed were 2.1%, 4.3%, and 8.3%, respectively.

Military personnel are at heightened risk for exposure to trauma. According to the National Vietnam Veterans Readjustment Study (NVVRS), 30.9% of all men who had served in Vietnam developed *DSM-III-R* PTSD, whereas 15.2% still had the disorder in the late 1980s when the survey occurred (Kulka et al., 1990).

However, for two reasons, historians of military psychiatry suspected that the NVVRS team overestimated the prevalence of PTSD (e.g., Jones & Wessely, 2005, pp. 133–134; McNally, 2007a; Shephard, 2001, p. 392). First, only about 12.5% (King & King, 1991) of Vietnam veterans had served in direct combat roles during the Vietnam War (e.g., rifleman in an infantry platoon). The historians found it odd that twice as many men developed PTSD than were in combat roles. Even when one considers the additional 15% of men who served in combat support roles (e.g., medic) and hence could encounter danger, the prevalence rate was puzzlingly high.

Second, only 3.5% of all psychiatric casualties in Vietnam itself received a diagnosis of combat exhaustion (Marlowe, 2001, p. 86). As Marlowe (2001) put it, "Vietnam produced an extremely low proportion of proximate combat stress casualties and produced or is claimed to have produced massive numbers of postcombat casualties. Therefore, Vietnam breaks with the past normative pattern of combat and war zone stress casualty production" (p. 73).

In response to these concerns, Dohrenwend et al. (2006) reanalyzed the NVVRS data, applying rigorous criteria for PTSD caseness. Before accepting a case as PTSD-positive, they did three things prior to recalculating prevalence estimates. First, they included only those veterans whose PTSD developed from war-related trauma, not events occurring before or after the war. Second, they included only those veterans for whom archival data were consistent with their self-reported war traumas, thereby corroborating 91% of the PTSD cases. Third, they used scores on the Global Assessment of Functioning (GAF; Spitzer et al., 1987) scale to assess functional impairment, as impairment was not a diagnostic requirement for *DSM-III-R PTSD*. Dohrenwend et al. used GAF ratings, assigned by clinical interviewers in the NVVRS, as a proxy for the then-nonexistent *DSM* impairment criterion. They considered a veteran as impaired if he had received a rating of 1 through 7 on the 9-point GAF scale. One is the lowest level of functioning, and 9 is the highest level of functioning. The modal PTSD case was rated a 7, defined as "Some difficulty in social, occupational, or school functioning, but generally functioning pretty well, has some meaningful interpersonal relationships OR some mild symptoms (e.g., depressed mood and mild insomnia, occasional truancy, or theft within the household)" (p. 2).

Dohrenwend et al.'s (2006) adjustments reduced both the lifetime and current prevalence rates of PTSD by 40%, thereby confirming the hypothesis of the historians (McNally, 2006a). The lifetime prevalence dropped from 30.9% to 18.7%, and the current prevalence rate dropped from 15.2% to 9.1%. However, had Dohrenwend et al. used a slightly more stringent definition of impairment (i.e., GAF score of 1 through 6 ["moderate" impairment]), the current prevalence estimate would have dropped by 65%; that is, from 15.2% to 5.4% (McNally, 2007b).

A follow-up study of surviving male theater veterans from the original NVVRS study revealed current and lifetime rates of *DSM-5* war-related PTSD of 4.5% and 17.0%, respectively, according to structured diagnostic interview (Marmar et al., 2015). Using a 20-point change in a dimensional measure of PTSD symptom severity to gauge clinically relevant change, the authors found that 16.0% of the theater veterans experienced worsening since the first administration, whereas 7.6% experienced improvement.

Requiring impairment affects prevalence rates in civilian samples, too. In two epidemiological studies, Breslau and Alvarado (2007) found that requiring that symptoms produce impairment lowered the prevalence of PTSD in men by 33% and 44% and in women by 25% and 30%, respectively.

In striking contrast to previous wars, the ones in Iraq and Afghanistan have prompted American, British, and Dutch authorities to assess their troops before, during, and after deployment to these war zones (McNally, 2012a). A comprehensive review of rigorous American and British studies indicated that between 2.1% and 13.8% of American and British service members have developed PTSD (Sundin et al., 2010).

Smith et al. (2008) conducted the methodologically strongest study on American military personnel deployed to Iraq and Afghanistan. They used data from the US Millennium Cohort, a prospective, longitudinal investigation of active duty and Reserve/National Guard service members. Administering the PTSD Checklist (PCL; Weathers et al., 1993) to 47,837 members of the Armed Forces, they found that 4.3% of those deployed to Afghanistan and Iraq developed PTSD. Among those exposed to combat, 7.6% developed PTSD, whereas 1.4% of those denying combat exposure did so. Among never-deployed personnel, 2.3% developed PTSD from stateside traumatic events (e.g., accidents on bases). Smith et al. (2008) ensured that PTSD symptom data were unconnected with subjects' official military files, thereby ensuring the confidentiality of symptom disclosure for personnel concerned about the stigma of mental health problems (Hoge et al., 2004).

Excluding subjects whose PTSD predates their enlistment provides the best estimate of war-attributable PTSD. For example, using the PCL, Hoge et al. (2004) found that as many as 5% of combat troops met criteria for PTSD prior to deploying to Iraq, whereas 12.6% qualified for PTSD following combat exposure in Iraq. If one rules out preexisting PTSD among Hoge et al.'s combatants, one obtains a deployment-attributable rate of PTSD of 7.6%–the same estimate reported by Smith et al. (2008) for combat-exposed personnel in Iraq and Afghanistan.

On the other hand, studies show that the percentage of military personnel with PTSD rises slightly within the first 6 to 12 months *after* their return from Iraq or Afghanistan (Sundin et al., 2010). Some service members may initially fail to report certain symptoms that are adaptive in a war zone (e.g., hypervigilance and numbing), yet subsequently endorse them on the PCL if symptoms fail to remit months postdeployment.

## Longitudinal Course of PTSD

Acute stress symptoms are common following exposure to traumatic events. For example, studying help-seeking rape victims, Rothbaum and Foa (1993) found that 95% met PTSD symptom criteria within 2 weeks of the trauma. But the proportion still meeting symptom criteria at 1, 3, and 6 months postrape declined to 63.3%, 45.9%, and 41.7%, respectively. Likewise, Rothbaum and Foa found that, among victims of nonsexual assault, 64.7% met PTSD symptom criteria 1 week after the crime, whereas the proportion still fulfilling criteria at 1, 3, 6, and 9 months postassault declined to 36.7%, 14.6%, 11.5%, and 0%, respectively.

Symptoms of PTSD usually emerge within hours or days of the trauma, making delayed-onset PTSD extremely rare (Jones & Wessely, 2005, p. 184). In a civilian epidemiologic study (Breslau et al., 1991), only 1 person among the 93 diagnosed with PTSD appeared to have a delayed onset.

People who meet criteria for PTSD only after 6 months following the trauma qualify for delayed-onset PTSD. However, few, if any, of them are symptom-free during the months following the trauma (Andrews et al., 2007). The modal case suffers symptoms all along, finally experiencing an increase that bumps them above the diagnostic threshold. Others may develop the full syndrome immediately following the trauma but seek help only years later (Solomon et al., 1989). However, such delayed help-seeking is not delayed onset.

In a prospective, cohort investigation, Goodwin et al. (2012) administered the PCL twice to 1,397 British military personnel who had served in Iraq. The first assessment occurred between 2004 and 2006, and the second assessment occurred between 2007 and 2009. Soldiers completed the questionnaire in reference to symptoms during the previous month. Cases of probable PTSD had a score of at least 50 on the PCL, and cases of subthreshold PTSD had a score of 40 to 49. PCL scores can range from 17 to 85. Cases of delayed-onset PTSD qualified for the syndrome at the second assessment, but not at the first one.

Although 94% of the subjects were free of PTSD at both time points, 3.5% of them developed delayed-onset PTSD. That is, of those who had PTSD, 46% met criteria only at the second assessment point. Of the 44 cases of delayed-onset PTSD, 12 already had symptoms sufficiently severe as to qualify them for subthreshold PTSD. Delayed onset seems more likely with war veterans than for others exposed to trauma.

In a study of 100 men seeking treatment for PTSD years after they reported fighting in Vietnam, Frueh et al. (2005) sought to verify their reported traumatic events by obtaining each patient's military personnel file. For only 41% of the cases did the archival data corroborate the self-reported trauma, and 7% had either never served in Vietnam or never served in the military at all. Yet clinical assessors had diagnosed PTSD in 94% of the subjects. For example, the uncorroborated cases reported exposure to battlefield atrocities at twice the rate of corroborated cases, and many of the former reported extremely implausible events (e.g., a cook who said he was a prisoner in North Vietnam).

Analyzing a huge federal dataset, labor economists Angrist et al. (2010) concluded that financial need, not psychiatric disorder, is the chief cause of the recent massive increase in PTSD disability claims among Vietnam veterans. They found that the increase largely occurs among veterans whose limited vocational skills make it very difficult for them to make a decent living. Moreover, Angrist et al. found that combat exposure (and therefore

PTSD) could not account for the increase in claims. Accordingly, they concluded, "This leaves the attractiveness of VDC [veterans' disability compensation] for less-skilled men and the work disincentives embedded in the VDC system as a likely explanation for our findings" (p. 824). Taken together, these data have prompted some scholars to suggest that the apparent emergence of PTSD decades after exposure to trauma may reflect financial need rather than delayed emergence of psychiatric illness (McNally & Frueh, 2012), whereas other scholars disagree (Marx et al., 2012).

Finally, a longitudinal study spanning 20 years on a national sample of post-9/11 war veterans in the care of the VA indicated that the modal course was above PTSD threshold symptoms that persist for many years, decreasing only gradually over time (Lee et al., 2020). This clinically disappointing outcome either underscores the urgency to improve evidence-based treatments for PTSD, as the authors concluded, or indicates fear of losing disability compensation should they improve.

### Comorbidity

Pure PTSD is unusual. In the NVVRS, 98.8% of the veterans who qualified for a lifetime diagnosis of PTSD also qualified for at least one other mental disorder, compared with 40.6% of those without PTSD (Kulka et al., 1990). The most common comorbid disorders in male veterans with PTSD were alcohol abuse, depression, and generalized anxiety disorder (GAD), whereas the most common comorbid disorders in female veterans were depression, GAD, alcohol abuse, and panic disorder.

Comorbidity is common in cases of civilian PTSD, too. Breslau et al. (1991) found that about 80% of PTSD cases had at least one other disorder at some point in their lives. Likewise, Kessler et al. (1995) reported lifetime comorbidity rates of 88.3% in men and 79% in women with PTSD. Major depression and alcohol dependence were among the most common comorbidities. Retrospectively reported ages of onset implied that other anxiety disorders usually preceded PTSD, whereas alcohol and mood disorders usually followed the emergence of PTSD.

### Risk Factors for PTSD

There are two aspects to risk for PTSD (Bowman & Yehuda, 2004): risk for exposure to trauma and risk for PTSD given exposure to trauma. Regarding the former, in one study, retrospectively ascertained risk factors for exposure to trauma included extroversion, neuroticism, male sex, having less than a college education, a personal history of childhood conduct problems, and a family history of psychiatric disorder (Breslau et al., 1991). This research group also did a 3-year prospective study finding that extroversion and neuroticism predicted exposure to trauma (Breslau et al., 1995). Black subjects had a higher rate of exposure than did Whites.

Risk factors for PTSD among those exposed to trauma include female sex (e.g., Tolin & Foa, 2006); neuroticism (e.g., Breslau et al., 1991); lower social support (e.g., Boscarino, 1995); lower IQ (e.g., Macklin et al., 1998; McNally & Shin, 1995); preexisting psychiatric illness, especially anxiety (Kessler et al., 2018) and mood disorders (e.g., Breslau et al., 1991); family history of anxiety, mood, or substance abuse disorders (e.g., Breslau et al., 1991); neurological soft signs (e.g., nonspecific abnormalities in central nervous function; Gurvits et al., 2000); and small hippocampi (Gilbertson et al., 2002). Some risk factors, such as low social support, have been assessed after individuals have developed PTSD, making it unclear whether early symptoms alienated potential sources of support or whether lack of support impeded recovery from trauma, or both. A recent prospective study of war veterans from the National Guard provided evidence for both hypotheses, especially for the claim that symptoms predict diminished support (Shallcross et al., 2016).

Using data from the Dunedin longitudinal study, Koenen et al. (2008) discovered that PTSD almost never developed in response to trauma during adulthood unless the subject had received a mental disorder diagnosis, often in childhood. That is, of new cases of PTSD occurring between the ages of 26 and 32, 96% had already experienced a mental disorder and 77% had received the diagnosis before the age of 15. Anxiety, mood, and conduct disorders were the three most common syndromes that preceded adult-onset PTSD. Previous disorders may signify vulnerability to develop PTSD in response to trauma, may themselves increase risk for exposure to trauma, or both.

Some scholars have adduced evidence suggesting that previous exposure to traumatic events sensitizes people so that they experience increased risk of developing PTSD in response to subsequent stressors (e.g., King et al., 1996). In these studies, people with PTSD are asked about previous traumatic events they had experienced prior to the trauma that triggered their disorder.

Unfortunately, these researchers had not assessed how individuals had responded to their earlier trauma. Indeed, Breslau et al. (2008) have shown that previous exposure to trauma does not increase risk for PTSD in response to subsequent trauma unless the person developed PTSD in response to the first trauma. Trauma-exposed individuals who do not develop PTSD in response to the earlier event are not at heightened risk for PTSD.

Likewise, Solomon et al. (1987) found that prior combat exposure did not increase risk for an acute combat stress reaction among Israeli soldiers who fought in the 1982 Lebanon War unless the soldier had experienced an acute combat stress reaction during a previous war. That is, prior combat per se did not predict breakdown in response to subsequent combat.

How victims respond during a trauma may predict whether they develop PTSD. Studying peritraumatic predictors involves asking victims hours, days, weeks, or sometimes years after the event how they recall responding during the trauma. Peritraumatic dissociation predicts PTSD (e.g., Shalev et al., 1996). That is, people who reported feeling disconnected from their body, feeling that events were happening in slow motion, and so forth were especially likely to develop the disorder.

Ehlers and Clark (2000) have observed that trauma victims' interpretation of their acute symptoms may affect whether they develop the disorder. A trauma victim's negative appraisal of acute symptoms predicts whether the person will develop PTSD (Dunmore et al., 2001; Ehring et al., 2006). For example, if trauma victims construe startle responses and nightmares as signs of personal weakness or flashbacks as signs of impending psychosis, they are at heightened risk for failing to recover from the acute effects of trauma.

There is, however, a potential conceptual problem with work on peritraumatic predictors and symptom appraisals. Researchers have isolated these phenomena, treating them as independent variables predictive of the dependent variable of persistent PTSD. Yet peritraumatic reactions are themselves aspects of the outcome researchers are trying to predict (Breslau, 2011). Peritraumatic dissociation, catastrophic appraisal of symptoms, and PTSD may be manifestations of the same pathological process or a consequence of a common vulnerability (e.g., neuroticism). The predictive capacity of these variables may be an artifact of how researchers parse the phenomenon, spuriously distinguishing responses during the trauma from those occurring somewhat later as if they were distinct phenomena.

Most work on risk and resilience concerns individual variables. However, group cohesion, morale, and leadership function as buffers against battlefield stress (Jones & Wessely, 2007).

## Cognitive Aspects of PTSD

Researchers have investigated cognitive aspects of PTSD from both a phenomenologic and an information-processing perspective (McNally, 2006b).

### Phenomenology of Traumatic Memory

Memories of trauma are different from memories of other events in terms of their content and emotional qualities. Do they differ in other ways? Are they represented and processed differently (Brewin, 2014)? Porter and Peace (2007) conducted a longitudinal study of individuals in the community who had experienced a traumatic event, often a crime. In addition to having the individuals rate the emotional qualities and vividness of the traumatic memory, they had each subject select and rate a very positive memory. Relative to memories of trauma, memories of positive events tended to fade in terms of vividness and emotional intensity, and their accuracy (relative to the baseline description) tended to diminish over the course of several years.

Rubin, Deffler et al. (2016b) assessed 60 adults from the community, half of whom had current PTSD, whereas the others had never developed it. The groups did not differ on potentially confounding variables (e.g., social class, percentage of minorities or women, histories of substance abuse and dependence, symptoms or diagnoses of depression), nor did they differ types of trauma (e.g., sexual abuse, accidents, combat, natural disasters). The subjects were asked to describe their three most traumatic, positive, and important memories. Rubin et al. audiotaped and transcribed the oral narratives before analyzing them via 28 methods of measuring their coherence or fragmentation. These indices included self-ratings of coherence, judges' ratings, and computerized algorithmic metrics of referential cohesion, temporal connectives, concreteness, and so forth. Rubin et al. found that trauma memories were no less coherent than positive memories and important memories, irrespective of a subject's PTSD status. For certain indices, trauma memories were slightly less coherent than positive and important memories, whereas, for others, trauma memories were more coherent.

In a critique of Rubin et al.'s study, Brewin (2016) revised the narrative (in)coherence hypothesis, stating that Rubin and colleagues assessed *global*, not *local*, coherence. That is, he said that clinicians most often observe fragmentation when survivors with PTSD attempt to recount the "hot spots"—the most emotionally disturbing parts—of their experience. Accordingly, although survivors may be capable of providing a coherent, *global* account of their trauma, the hot spots are those most likely to be disorganized, fragmented, or exhibiting "amnesic gaps" (Brewin, 2016, p. 1015). Brewin predicted that a focus on such "hot spots" (Brewin, 2016, p. 1014) would have corroborated the hypothesis that trauma impairs narrative memory.

In reply, Rubin, Bertsen et al. (2016a) noted that 21 of the 28 measures did assess local coherence yet failed to reveal fragmentation in those with PTSD. The debate about the best indices for gauging memory fragmentation continues (McNally et al., 2022), but at best, the evidence remains inconclusive. Also, Malaktaris and Lynn's (2019) phenomenological study of flashbacks in people with PTSD or subthreshold PTSD uncovered no evidence of fragmentation.

Finally, Taylor et al. (2022) conducted two experiments revealing that *how* an individual retrieves and recounts memories, including traumatic ones, affects an individual's judgments of the memory's coherence. If people are asked to narrate an experience, they regard their account as more coherent than if they first attempt to answer a series of difficult questions about the experience (e.g., "What were you wearing at the time of the event? Describe your entire outfit"). These experiments indicate that judgments of coherence are attributions influenced by the mode of retrieval rather than properties of the memory itself.

The importance of narrative fragmentation of trauma memories presumably rests on their maintenance of PTSD. Once the memories become integrated into a coherent narrative of the trauma, intrusive recollections, nightmares, and flashbacks presumptively diminish in frequency and intensity. Bedard-Gilligan et al. (2017) tested this hypothesis in a study of PTSD patients who received prolonged exposure therapy or sertraline for PTSD. Patients provided three narratives: one concerning their trauma, one concerning a positive experience, and one concerning a negative but nontraumatic experience. Using self-report ratings, independent ratings, and objective measures of narrative structure, Bedard-Gilligan et al. assessed fragmentation of these memories before and after treatment.

The results revealed that, across measures, memory fragmentation did not reliably change across the course of treatment. Neither treatment type nor response to treatment was related to change in fragmentation. In fact, pretreatment fragmentation in the nontraumatic negative and positive narratives correlated with fragmentation in trauma narratives. For some patients, fragmentation was a characteristic style of recounting autobiographical memories in general.

### Autobiographical Memory

As with depressed people (Williams et al., 2007), those with PTSD experience difficulty recalling specific personal memories in response to cue words on the Autobiographical Memory Test (AMT; e.g., McNally et al., 1994). For example, in response to the word *happy*, they often recall a categoric memory exemplifying a class of events (e.g., "I'm always happy whenever the New England Patriots win") or sometimes recall an extended memory spanning more than one day (e.g., "I was happy during the summer after college graduation"). In contrast to such "overgeneral memories," those that healthy subjects recall refer to specific events (e.g., "I was happy on the day that I got married"). An overgeneral retrieval style may imply avoidance of thinking specifically about one's emotionally disturbing past (Williams et al., 2007). It may also reflect deficits in executive control and working memory, essential to searching through one's autobiographical memory database to identify specific episodes in response to cue words (Dalgleish et al., 2007).

Overgeneral memory has important clinical correlates. PTSD patients exhibiting overgeneral memory are especially impaired in their problem-solving performance (Sutherland & Bryant, 2008). Brown et al. (2013) found that American combat veterans of the Afghanistan and Iraq wars who developed PTSD retrieved fewer specific memories than did healthy combat veterans of these wars. Moreover, relative to healthy combat veterans, those with PTSD likewise had difficulty envisioning specific future events.

Although Iranian combat veterans of the Iran-Iraq war with PTSD retrieved fewer specific memories than did healthy combat veterans who, in turn, retrieved fewer specific memories than did control subjects without combat exposure (Moradi et al., 2012), most studies show that PTSD, not trauma exposure alone, predicts overgeneral memory (Moore & Zoellner, 2007).

Research on trauma survivors indicates that difficulties retrieving specific memories predict PTSD (e.g., Kleim & Ehlers, 2008). To test whether overgeneral memory precedes trauma exposure as well as PTSD, Bryant et al. (2007) tested 60 trainee firefighters who were free of PTSD and had yet to encounter the occupational stressors common in their line of work. Four years later, all had experienced trauma, and 15% had developed PTSD. Bryant et al. found that difficulty retrieving specific memories to positive words during their training predicted severity of PTSD symptoms. Hence, an overgeneral retrieval style may be a risk factor for PTSD among those exposed to trauma.

Vietnam veterans with PTSD who wore war regalia, combat fatigues, military patches, and so forth in everyday life had especially great difficulty retrieving specific memories (McNally et al., 1995). Relative to healthy combat veterans, these men seemed stuck in the past. Likewise, Sutherland and Bryant (2005) reported that trauma victims with PTSD more often mention traumatic memories as self-defining than do victims without PTSD. Having one's identity intertwined with one's trauma history appears predictive of poor mental health.

To investigate this issue, Berntsen and Rubin (2006) developed the Centrality of Event Scale (CES), a questionnaire that taps how strongly trauma survivors believe that the trauma is a central event in their life story (for a review, see Gehrt et al., 2018). They found that scores on the CES positively correlated with severity of PTSD symptoms among trauma-exposed college students. Others have replicated this finding in veterans of the wars in Iraq and Afghanistan with PTSD (Brown et al., 2010) and in women who reported histories of childhood sexual abuse (Robinaugh & McNally, 2011). Importantly, Boals and Ruggero (2016) found that event centrality prospectively predicts PTSD symptoms, but not vice versa.

As Berntsen and Rubin (2007) concluded, findings regarding the CES "contradict the widespread view that the poor integration of the traumatic memory into one's life story is a main cause of PTSD. Instead, enhanced integration appears to be a key issue" (p. 417).

## The Emotional Stroop Paradigm

People with PTSD report reexperiencing their trauma in the form of intrusive thoughts, nightmares, and flashbacks. These phenomenologic reports imply that involuntary cognitive processes mediate these symptoms. To test whether traumatic information is automatic in PTSD, researchers have applied versions of the *emotional Stroop paradigm* (McNally, 2006b).

In this paradigm, subjects are asked to view words of varying emotional significance and to name the colors in which the words are printed while ignoring the meaning of the words (Williams et al., 1996). *Stroop interference* occurs when the meaning of the word becomes intrusively accessible, thereby slowing the subject's naming of its color. If information related to trauma is, indeed, automatically accessed in PTSD and difficult to inhibit, subjects with the disorder ought to exhibit greater Stroop interference for trauma words relative to other words and relative to trauma-exposed people without PTSD.

In one study, Vietnam veterans with PTSD, relative to veterans without PTSD, took longer to name the colors of words related to the war (e.g., *firefight*) than to name the colors of other negative words (e.g., *filthy*), positive words (e.g., *friendship*), or neutral words (e.g., *concrete*; McNally et al., 1990). Similar results have occurred for subjects whose PTSD resulted from rape (Cassiday et al., 1992), shipwrecks (Thrasher et al., 1994), automobile accidents (Bryant & Harvey, 1995), and childhood sexual abuse (Dubner & Motta, 1999). Unlike those with PTSD, rape victims who have recovered following treatment do not exhibit Stroop interference for trauma words (Foa et., 1991). Actors trained to mimic the effect were unable to do so (Buckley et al., 2003). Instead, they named the colors of all words slowly. However, other studies, often unpublished, failed to replicate the emotional Stroop effect in PTSD (Kimble et al., 2009).

## Biological Aspects of PTSD

Biological research on PTSD has been flourishing, and reviews of this field have appeared, both narrative (Pitman et al., 2012) and meta-analytic (Pole, 2007).

### Cognitive Neuroscience and the Emotional Stroop

Scientists have studied the neural mechanisms mediating the emotional Stroop effect in PTSD. In a positron emission tomography (PET) experiment, Bremner et al. (2004) found that women with PTSD related to childhood sexual abuse, relative to victims without PTSD, had less anterior cingulate activation during the emotional Stroop task. The groups did not differ in terms of anterior cingulate activation while performing the standard Stroop task. Hence, the activation deficit in the PTSD group was confined to the processing of trauma-related information.

Employing functional magnetic resonance imaging (fMRI), Shin et al. (2001) found that Vietnam veterans with PTSD exhibited diminished rostral anterior cingulate activation when exposed to war-related words in the emotional counting Stroop. In this task, subjects view displays comprising from one through four copies of a word varying in emotional valence (e.g., *firefight, firefight, firefight*). They push a key corresponding to the correct number of copies of the word (e.g., 3). Subjects will be slower to count the number of copies to the extent that the meaning of the word captures their attention.

Cognitive neuroscience research on variants of the emotional Stroop in PTSD supports a pathophysiologic model that highlights abnormalities in medial prefrontal cortex (PFC) and amygdala (Bremner et al., 1999; Rauch et al., 2000; Shin, Rauch et al., 2005). The medial PFC comprises medial frontal gyrus, anterior cingulate cortex (ACC), and subcallosal cortex. The downward projections of the PFC inhibit activation of amygdala, thereby explaining why an intact PFC is vital for the extinction of conditioned fear (Milad & Quirk, 2002). Disturbing, intrusive recollections of traumatic events, accompanied by increased physiologic arousal, are consistent with either a hypoactive medial PFC, a hyperresponsive amygdala, or both (Shin et al., 2006).

### Prefrontal Cortical Abnormalities

An fMRI study found that PTSD subjects exhibited increased amygdala responses and reduced medial PFC responses to photographs of fearful versus happy facial expressions (Shin, Wright et al., 2005). In fact, signal changes in the amygdala and symptom severity negatively correlated with signal changes in the medial PFC. These findings are consistent with those of a previous study in which briefly presented and backwardly masked (*subliminal*) fearful faces provoked increased amygdalar responses in PTSD subjects (Rauch et al., 2000). PTSD patients have exhibited attenuated medial prefrontal/anterior cingulate activation while listening to audiotaped scripts of their traumatic experiences (Shin et al., 2004). A study of Vietnam combat veterans and their nonveteran identical co-twins suggests that attenuated activation of medial PFC during recollection of highly stressful memories is an acquired characteristic (Dahlgren et al., 2018); the nonveteran co-twins did not exhibit it.

As Shin et al. (2006) noted, not only have scientists found attenuated medial PFC activation in PTSD, but they have also observed smaller ACC volumes in individuals with PTSD relative to trauma-exposed individuals without the illness (Rauch et al., 2006; Woodward et al., 2006; Yamasue et al., 2003). Furthermore, the smaller the ACC volume, the worse was symptom severity in two of these studies (Woodward et al., 2006; Yamasue et al., 2003). Most subjects had recovered from PTSD in Yamasue et al.'s study, thereby implying that diminished ACC volume may be either a vulnerability factor or a "scar" from PTSD rather than being a correlate of the illness.

A subsequent study suggests that the scar hypothesis is correct. Using data from Gilbertson et al.'s (2002) monozygotic twins, Kasai et al. (2008) found that reduced volume (gray matter density) in the pregenual ACC in Vietnam veterans with combat-related PTSD was not present in their combat-unexposed co-twins. Moreover, these PTSD cases had smaller pregenual ACC volumes than did combat veterans without PTSD and their co-twins. Hence, reduction in the size of this region is associated with chronic PTSD, not merely exposure to trauma or a preexisting vulnerability factor.

Taken together, these data are consistent with a model of PTSD whereby the ventromedial PFC, including the pregenual (or "emotional") region of the ACC, inhibits acquired fear responses mediated by the amygdala (Rauch et al., 2006). If smaller volume of the ACC signifies diminished function, then these data provide an anatomical clue to why fear-related reexperiencing symptoms erupt in PTSD (Pitman et al., 2012).

### Hippocampal Volume

Preclinical research indicates that certain stress hormones, such as the glucocorticoid cortisol, may produce atrophy in the hippocampus, a brain structure integral to autobiographical memory (Sapolsky, 1996). Reasoning that traumatic stress may have similar consequences, Bremner et al. (1995), using MRI methods, found that Vietnam veterans with PTSD had smaller hippocampi than did nonveteran control subjects. These findings have replicated among adults whose PTSD was associated with sexual and physical abuse during childhood (Bremner et al., 1997; Stein et al., 1997). If diminished size is associated with diminished function, then small hippocampi may make it difficult for people with PTSD to process contextual cues signifying safety (Pitman et al., 2012).

Gurvits et al. (1996) further clarified this phenomenon by comparing hippocampal volume across three groups of subjects: Vietnam combat veterans with PTSD, Vietnam combat veterans without PTSD, and nonveteran control subjects. The healthy combat veterans and the nonveterans did not differ in hippocampal volume. The PTSD group had smaller volume than did the other two groups. In studies failing to replicate the small hippocampus effect (e.g., Bonne et al., 2001), PTSD symptoms tend to be less severe than in studies replicating the effect (Pitman et al., 2012).

Third, individuals with Cushing's syndrome, an endocrine disorder characterized by chronic cortisol output five times higher than normal, do exhibit hippocampal atrophy. Treatment, however, not only normalizes their cortisol levels but also reverses their hippocampal atrophy (Starkman et al., 1999). Therefore, chronically high levels of cortisol, if corrected, did not produce lasting damage.

Fourth, small hippocampi in PTSD appear to be a vulnerability factor for PTSD, not a consequence of traumatic stress. This conclusion comes from a landmark study by Gilbertson et al. (2002). They measured hippocampal volume in monozygotic (MZ) twin pairs: 17 pairs in which 1 twin developed PTSD after serving in Vietnam and whose psychiatrically healthy twin had not been in combat, and 23 twin pairs in which 1 twin had seen combat in Vietnam, but did not have PTSD and whose twin had neither been in combat nor had PTSD. The results confirmed that veterans with PTSD had smaller hippocampi than did veterans without PTSD. Most striking, however, is that the nontraumatized, healthy co-twins of the PTSD subjects had hippocampi just as small as the hippocampi of their brothers. These findings imply that small hippocampi are a marker for vulnerability for developing PTSD among individuals exposed to trauma.

Yet a meta-analysis revealed that the hippocampi of trauma-exposed subjects without PTSD are smaller than the hippocampi of subjects without trauma exposure (Woon et al., 2010). These findings are subject to three interpretations (Pitman et al., 2012). Small hippocampi may be associated with subsyndromic levels of PTSD symptoms, may increase risk for trauma exposure, or may indicate that trauma exposure alone may shrink the hippocampus to some extent.

## Genetics

True et al. (1993) studied 4,042 male Vietnam-era MZ and dizygotic (DZ) twin pairs to ascertain the relative contributions of heredity, shared environment, and unique environment to variance in PTSD symptoms. The results revealed that MZ twins were more concordant for combat exposure than were DZ twins. Controlling for extent of combat exposure, True et al. found that between 13% and 30% of the variance in reexperiencing symptoms was associated with genetic variation. Likewise, heritability estimates for avoidance symptoms ranged from 30% to 34%, and heritability for arousal symptoms ranged from 28% to 32%. Indices of shared environment during childhood and adolescence (e.g., family upbringing, parental SES) were unrelated to variance in PTSD symptoms. Taken together, about one-third of the variance in PTSD symptoms is associated with genetic variance, whereas the remaining is chiefly associated with unique environmental experiences (e.g., heavy combat).

However, the classic twin design overestimates the genetic contribution to variation by obscuring the effects of both gene × environment interaction and gene and environment correlation (Sauce & Matzel, 2018).

Other studies strongly imply genetic vulnerability for PTSD. Gilbertson et al. (2006) administered IQ and other neurocognitive tests to monozygotic twin pairs. They tested four groups: men with combat-related PTSD from Vietnam, their identical twins with no combat exposure and no PTSD, Vietnam combat veterans who had not developed PTSD, and their identical twins with no combat exposure and no PTSD. The findings were strikingly consistent: on almost every test, combat veterans with PTSD and their identical twins performed very similarly, and both groups performed in the normal range. However, they performed worse than did the healthy combat veterans and their co-twins.

This study suggests several conclusions. First, trauma exposure has little or no effect on measures of IQ or on other tests of neurocognitive functioning. Second, the striking similarity in the test scores between co-twins strongly implicates genetic influence on performance. Third, because the PTSD group scored within the normal range on all but one test, above average cognitive ability appears to confer protection against PTSD. Indeed, consistent with an early study (Macklin et al., 1998), the mean IQ of the healthy combat veteran group was 118, and more than 40% of this group scored in the superior range (>120). The mean IQ of the PTSD group was 105.

Neurological soft signs are more common in combat veterans with PTSD than among combat veterans without PTSD (Gurvits et al., 2006). The non–trauma-exposed identical co-twins of the PTSD group exhibit higher scores than the identical co-twins of the healthy combat veterans, thereby implying that subtle neurological compromise is a genetic (or at a least constitutional) vulnerability factor for PTSD rather than being a consequence of trauma or PTSD.

Other studies have further implicated cognitive ability as a buffer against PTSD. Breslau et al. (2006) obtained the IQ scores of 6-year-old children from either the inner city of Detroit or its suburbs. In follow-up interviews with these children at age 17, Breslau et al. assessed them for exposure to trauma and for PTSD. Subjects whose IQ at age 6 was greater than 115 were at lower risk for exposure to traumatic events by age 17, and they were at lower risk for developing PTSD if they had been exposed to trauma. Children with below average IQ and average IQ were at similar risk for PTSD. These findings imply the higher IQ is protective rather than lower IQ being a vulnerability factor.

Studying Vietnam veteran twins, Kremen et al. (2007) found that higher pre-deployment cognitive ability protected against subsequent PTSD. More specifically, the highest quartile on the cognitive ability measure had a 48% lower risk for PTSD than did the lowest quartile on this measure. Further analyses confirmed that genetic variance entirely accounted for variance in the cognitive ability measure.

Investigators have conducted genome-wide association studies (GWASs) to identify genetic variants associated with PTSD (Daskalakis et al., 2018). In contrast to the earlier, theory-driven candidate gene approach, which is subject to statistical and other possible biases, the GWAS method scans for associations between genetic loci and disorders throughout the entire genome. For example, Stein et al. (2016) identified two loci significantly associated with PTSD in a cohort of post-9/11 wars American soldiers from the Army Study to Assess Risk and Resilience in Servicemembers (Army STARRS) consisting of PTSD cases ($n$ = 3,167) and healthy trauma-exposed cases ($n$ = 4,607), but the results failed to replicate in a second cohort of PTSD cases ($n$ = 947) and healthy trauma-exposed controls ($n$ = 4,969). Stein et al. also found evidence of genetic pleiotropy between PTSD and psoriasis and rheumatoid arthritis.

Pooling data from 11 multiethnic datasets, Duncan et al. 2018) conducted the largest GWAS study on PTSD involving 20,070 subjects including cases with PTSD and mostly trauma-exposed individuals without PTSD. Across the dataset, no single nucleotide polymorphism (SNP) was statistically significant, thus revealing a failure to replicate all previously reported genetic links to PTSD. The authors computed SNP-based heritability values for PTSD, finding an $h^2_{SNP}$ of 15% for subjects of European ancestry, chiefly driven by an $h^2_{SNP}$ of 29% for women and an $h^2_{SNP}$ of 7% for men that did not differ from zero. There was no evidence for the heritability of PTSD in people of having other ancestral origins (e.g., Africa, Asia). Finally, they reported a significant genetic overlap between PTSD and schizophrenia, but not with major depressive disorder.

In summary, the field of psychiatric genomics is very young, and it is grappling with many challenges such as very small effect sizes, underpowered studies, and findings that fail to replicate (Banerjee et al., 2017). Given that there are 636,120 different combinations of symptoms that qualify for a *DSM-5* diagnosis (Galatzer-Levy & Bryant, 2013), investigators may wish to probe for associations between genetic loci and specific symptoms (e.g., flashbacks, emotional numbing) or combinations thereof rather than PTSD per se.

### Resting Psychophysiological Levels

In his meta-analysis, Pole (2007) examined 58 studies providing data on baseline levels of psychophysiological arousal. Subjects with PTSD had higher resting heart rate (HR), skin conductance level (SCL), systolic blood pressure (SBP), and diastolic blood pressure relative to trauma-exposed subjects without PTSD.

Moreover, severity of PTSD symptoms positively correlated with resting levels. Surprisingly, studies involving exposure to a post-baseline stressor (e.g., trauma stimuli, startling sounds) were associated with lower levels of resting psychophysiology than were studies involving post-baseline stressors. These findings indicate that anticipatory anxiety about imminent stressors cannot explain elevated levels of psychophysiology in PTSD.

A meta-analysis has furnished evidence of autonomic nervous system (ANS) dysfunction in people with PTSD (Schneider & Schwerdtfeger, 2020). Relative to healthy comparison subjects, those with PTSD exhibit greater HR and diminished HR variability (HRV) both at rest and while performing stress tasks in the laboratory. Taken together, these results suggest parasympathetic dysfunction and cardiac function that is insufficiently attuned to environmental changes. A large study of American Marines ($n = 1,415$) revealed that diminished HRV prior to combat deployment predicted heightened risk for subsequent PTSD (Minassian et al., 2015).

*Physiological Reactivity to Trauma-Related Cues*

Researchers have assessed reactivity to trauma cues in two ways. In the first, subjects are exposed to standardized audiovisual stimuli relevant to traumatic events. Thus, Malloy et al. (1983) found that slides and sounds of combat evoked greater HR responses in Vietnam combat veterans with PTSD than in healthy combat veterans or in veterans with other psychiatric disorders. Likewise, Blanchard and his colleagues reported that PTSD subjects exhibit enhanced HR, systolic BP, and electromyographic (EMG) responses to audiotaped battle sounds and that these enhanced responses do not occur in healthy nonveterans, healthy combat veterans, combat veterans with other mental disorders, or nonveterans with specific phobias (Blanchard et al., 1982, 1986; Pallmeyer et al., 1986).

In his meta-analysis, Pole (2007) included 17 studies involving exposure to standardized trauma stimuli. He found that HR response and, to a lesser extent, skin conductance response (SCR) distinguished PTSD from control groups. EMG and blood pressure responses trended in the same direction.

In the second approach, researchers ask subjects to imagine traumatic events recounted in audiotaped scripts (Orr et al., 2004). These script-driven imagery studies have revealed that combat veterans with PTSD exhibit greater HR, SCR, and facial EMG (lateral frontalis) responses than do healthy combat veterans (Orr et al.,1993; Pitman et al., 1987, 1990); this effect is more pronounced for scripts that recount autobiographical than for scripts recounting generic traumatic events. Moreover, combat veterans with anxiety disorders other than PTSD do not exhibit the script-driven reactivity exhibited by combat veterans with PTSD (Pitman et al., 1990). Similar findings have emerged in civilians whose PTSD arose from childhood sexual abuse (Shin et al., 1999) or from automobile accidents or terrorist attacks (Shalev et al., 1993).

HR reactivity to trauma scripts distinguishes PTSD subjects from non-PTSD subjects with a specificity ranging from 61% to 88% and a sensitivity of 100% (Orr et al., 1993; Pitman et al., 1987).

Moreover, psychophysiologic reactivity can distinguish between veterans with combat-related PTSD and veterans who are asked to fake PTSD (HR; Gerardi et al., 1989; EMG; Orr & Pitman, 1993).

Keane et al. (1998) conducted the largest study on the psychophysiology of PTSD. Recruiting Vietnam veterans from hospitals throughout the United States, they tested 778 veterans with current PTSD, 181 with past PTSD, and 369 with no history of PTSD. During both standardized audiovisual combat presentations and autobiographical combat scenes during script-driven imagery, veterans with current PTSD had greater HR, EMG, skin conductance, and diastolic blood pressure than did those with no history of the disorder. The group with past PTSD tended to fall midway between the other groups in terms of physiologic reactivity.

The magnitudes of the effects appear smaller than earlier studies on script-driven imagery in Vietnam veterans with PTSD (Pitman et al., 1987), and about one-third of the current PTSD group was nonreactive physiologically. It is unclear why the findings were so modest and why the PTSD group was statistically indistinguishable from the past PTSD group.

In his meta-analysis of 22 of these studies, Pole (2007) reported that PTSD subjects, relative to control subjects, exhibited greater EMG responses (frontalis and corrugator muscles), HR response, SCR, and DBP.

*Exaggerated Startle Response*

Consistent with self-reports of enhanced startle, sudden, loud tones evoke larger eyeblink EMG responses in combat veterans with PTSD than in healthy combat veterans (e.g., Morgan et al., 1996; Orr et al., 1995). Likewise, civilians and veterans with PTSD tend to exhibit larger EMG magnitudes than do people with other anxiety disorders or no disorder (Shalev et al., 1992). PTSD and non-PTSD groups, however, do not differ in the rates at which their EMG responses habituate to these repeated tones (Morgan et al., 1996; Orr et al., 1995; Shalev et al., 1992).

Three studies have revealed greater HR responses to loud tones in PTSD groups than in non-PTSD groups (Orr et al., 1995; Paige et al., 1990; Shalev et al., 1992). One study found larger SCRs as well (Shalev et al., 1992), whereas another did not (Orr et al., 1995). Finally, SCR magnitude habituates more slowly in PTSD subjects than they do in non-PTSD subjects (Orr et al., 1995; Shalev et al., 1992).

An MZ twin study indicated that Vietnam veterans with PTSD exhibited larger HR responses to startlingly loud tones than did their non–combat-exposed co-twins and Vietnam combat veterans without PTSD and their co-twins (Orr et al., 2003). The authors concluded that heightened startle reactions are a consequence of PTSD rather than a vulnerability factor for the disorder.

Pole (2007) examined 25 studies measuring startle responses to auditory stimuli in his meta-analysis. In these studies, researchers typically measured responses to tones or bursts of white noise. Relative to control subjects, PTSD subjects exhibited larger HR responses to startling sounds, and their SCRs took longer to decline. Indeed, the delayed decline in habituation of SCRs to startling sounds implies deficit regulatory processing signifying a failure to adapt (Pole, 2007).

*Noradrenergic Dysregulation*

Exposure to uncontrollable stressors activates the noradrenergic (NA) system, as exemplified by the enhanced release of norepinephrine (NE) by the brainstem locus ceruleus (Charney et al., 1993). Southwick et al. (1993) conducted a yohimbine challenge study with Vietnam combat veterans with PTSD and healthy control subjects. Yohimbine antagonizes the alpha-2 autoreceptor. Ordinarily, release of NE activates the autoreceptor, which then brakes further NE release, thereby serving as a negative feedback mechanism. By briefly blocking the autoreceptor, yohimbine enables NE to surge unimpeded. The results revealed that 70% of the PTSD subjects experienced a yohimbine-induced panic attack, and 40% experienced a concurrent flashback. Consistent with the NE dysregulation hypothesis, yohimbine produced more pronounced biochemical and cardiovascular effects in PTSD subjects than in control subjects.

## Emerging Themes

During the past 10 years, the number of publications on PTSD has been far greater than those on other anxiety, OCD, and stress-related disorders (Asmundson & Asmundson, 2018). The field defies easy synopsis. There are several new themes contributing to its growth.

*Network Analysis*

PTSD has often been haunted by controversy regarding its ontological status (McNally, 2012b). Is it a biological disease entity or a socially constructed idiom of distress? Are its symptoms reflective of an underlying taxonic common cause or a latent dimension of stress-responsiveness?

Distinct from these options has been the network approach to mental disorders pioneered by Borsboom, Cramer, and their associates (e.g., Borsboom, 2017; Borsboom & Cramer, 2013; Cramer et al., 2010). Network investigators view syndromes as emergent phenomena issuing from dynamic interactions among their constitutive symptoms. They have devised computational methods for visualizing and exploring diverse disorders (Robinaugh et al., 2020), including PTSD (e.g., McNally et al., 2015, 2017). In fact, PTSD has been among the most thoroughly studied syndromes and the focus for the first network meta-analytic study (Isvoranu et al., 2020). This fast-moving field continues to devise new solutions to numerous computational and conceptual challenges it faces (McNally, 2021).

*"Big Data" and Machine Learning*

International consortia enabling the pooling of data across many clinical research centers is a growing trend. For example, in a prospective longitudinal study of 2,473 injured trauma survivors assessed in emergency rooms, Shalev et al. (2019) found that initial PTSD symptom severity scores *alone* were remarkably accurate at predicting PTSD 4–15 months later as evinced by a logistic regression model (i.e., $r = .976$ between predicted and raw probabilities).

Investigators have begun to apply machine learning algorithms to datasets featuring many biological and psychological variables to discover optimal algorithms for predicting PTSD (Ramos-Lima et al., 2020). Unfortunately, despite impressive results, early studies did not test the classificatory algorithm in a fresh sample of trauma survivors. However, Schultebraucks et al. (2020) used 70 biological and psychological variables to develop an algorithm to identify which of 377 injured trauma survivors would have chronic PTSD 12 months after being assessed in a hospital emergency room in Atlanta. Using latent growth mixture modeling, they identified four trajectories of posttraumatic stress: resilience, recovery, worsening symptoms, and non-remitting symptoms. They reported impressive discriminatory accuracy (i.e., area under the curve [AUC] = 0.84%) for distinguishing a resilient course versus a non-remitting one, and they replicated this effect in another prospective cohort of 377 emergency department trauma survivors in New York City (i.e., AUC = 0.83%). Of all patients predicted to have non-remitting PTSD at 12 months, 90% did so. Only 5% of resilient patients were incorrectly predicted to have PTSD at 12 months.

## Oxidative Stress and Inflammation

People with chronic PTSD are at heighted risk for developing metabolic syndromic, cardiac conditions, neurogenerative disease, and dementia—findings that have prompted investigators to examine biological risk factors for these conditions, such as markers of oxidative stress and inflammation (Miller et al., 2018). Among the correlates—presumably, consequences—of chronic PTSD are cellular aging, signaled by shortening telomeres and other markers.

A surprising prospective longitudinal study of trauma survivors admitted to the emergency department showed that *diminished* inflammatory response within hours of the trauma predicted PTSD several months later (Michopoulos et al., 2020). In contrast, patients who recovered from acute posttraumatic stress symptoms or who remained resilient by exhibiting few symptoms exhibited a robust inflammatory response following the traumatic event. As Heim (2020) observed, the striking discrepancy between elevated levels of inflammation in people with chronic PTSD and a blunted inflammatory response in the immediate wake of trauma is reminiscent of the equally counterintuitive findings of Yehuda and her colleagues who repeatedly found cortisol levels in the low-normal range in patients with chronic PTSD (Yehuda et al., 1990). If PTSD is merely an exaggerated stress response syndrome, then one would expect *elevated* tonic levels of circulating cortisol. Yehuda (2002) interpreted her findings as indicative of regulatory dysfunction in the hypothalamic-pituitary-adrenal (HPA) axis, showing that PTSDS was not merely an extreme version of a stress response.

Likewise, Michopoulos et al.'s findings imply dysfunction in the neuroimmune system. Yet interpretive caution is warranted. As Dunlop and Wong (2019) concluded in their review of HPA dysfunction in PTSD: "Despite the breadth of studies that have examined HPA axis functioning in PTSD, inconsistency in results is unfortunately the rule not the exception" (p. 373).

## Resilience

Because most people exposed to trauma do not develop PTSD, researchers have increasingly studied people who experience only short-lived symptoms of distress without developing PTSD. *Resilience* is a rich, complex topic (Horn et al., 2016; Southwick et al., 2014). Resilience has been considered from multiple perspectives. Bonanno (2004) distinguishes between trauma-exposed people who exhibit a resilient course and those who develop PTSD but then recover. The former, he says, exhibit transitory, relatively mild symptoms before regaining their equilibrium.

Others conceptualize resilience in terms of relatively stable ("trait-like") attributes known to predict a benign posttrauma course, such as dispositional optimism and self-efficacy (e.g., Gallagher et al., 2020), intelligence (e.g., Macklin et al., 1998), or propensity to exhibit elevated levels of neuropeptide Y during acute stress(e.g., Schmeltzer et al., 2016). Finally, others focus on what people *do* in the wake of trauma in terms of emotion regulation techniques, for example, most likely to foster resilience (e.g., Pencea et al., 2020). For example, a prospective longitudinal study of Marines suggested that adaptive coping immediately after trauma predicted whether their symptoms were few, mild, and stable after combat deployment (Nash et al., 2015). Relatedly, others have explored the circumstances whereby people experience (or report) posttraumatic growth after undergoing major stressors (e.g., Bellet et al., 2018; Tedeschi & McNally, 2011).

## Two Views of PTSD: DSM-5 Versus ICD-11

In recent decades the American Psychiatric Association (APA) and the World Health Organization (WHO) have endeavored to coordinate their revisions of the *DSMs* and the mental disorders section of the *ICDs*. Yet eminent international clinical scholars involved in the revision of the latest manuals, *DSM-5* and *ICD-11* (to become official on January 1, 2022), have been dramatically opposed to one another in their respective approaches to the nosology of PTSD (e.g., Brewin, 2013; Friedman, 2013a, 2013b). The *DSM-5* team increased the number of PTSD symptoms from 17 to 20, organizing them into four, not three, subsyndromic clusters. Invoking a substantial body of research (Friedman et al., 2016), they aimed to formulate comprehensive criteria that capture the complexity of PTSD while remaining as faithful as possible to the previous, evidence-based version of the *DSM*.

Unconstrained by fidelity to tradition, the *ICD* team aimed to streamline criteria to foster ease of administration, especially for assessors in resource-strapped, conflict-ridden regions of the developing world (Maercker & Perkonigg, 2013). Moreover, they aimed to streamline the diagnostic process by identifying a few hallmark symptoms of PTSD, thereby enabling assessors to distinguish the syndrome from related disorders (e.g., depression). Hence, the proposed criteria comprise only six symptoms, and a diagnosis requires at least one of the two symptoms per cluster (i.e., *Reexperiencing*: flashbacks or nightmares; *Avoidance*: avoidance of thinking about the trauma or avoidance of activities and situations reminiscent of the trauma; and *Arousal*: exaggerated startle or hypervigilance).

Trauma researchers have begun to compare the two diagnostic systems, testing whether they pick out the same individuals as PTSD-positive. One study revealed that there were a substantial number of 510 injured and hospitalized trauma civilian trauma survivors who qualified for the diagnosis under one system but not the other (O'Donnell et al., 2014). The investigators also observed that the *DSM-5* diagnosed PTSD in more of the survivors than did the provisional *ICD-11* (6.7% vs. 3.0%). It may be wise to use the *DSM-5* to diagnose PTSD in research settings because one can readily diagnose the *ICD-11* version by extracting the relevant symptoms from the *DSM-5* set.

## Dissociative Disorders

The dissociative disorders category comprises syndromes whose chief feature is dissociation, defined as "a disruption of and/or discontinuity in the normal, subjective integration of one or more aspects of psychological functioning, including—but not limited to—memory, identity, consciousness, perception, and motor control" (Spiegel et al., 2011, p. 826). This broad, overarching definition embraces a diversity of phenomena that do not necessarily have a common psychobiological source. For example, one self-report measure of dissociation includes mundane occurrences, such as staring off into space and being unaware of time passing, as well as eerie ones, such as failing to recognize oneself in a mirror (Bernstein & Putnam, 1986).

Other phenomena dubbed *dissociative* include feelings of unreality (depersonalization and derealization), emotional numbing, a sense of time slowing down, and claims of inability recall encoded information too excessive to count as ordinary forgetting. However, as McHugh (2008) has emphasized, calling phenomena dissociative "is merely a description with a professional ring masquerading as an explanation. One really knows no more about a case of amnesia or fugue by saying the patient 'dissociates' than by saying the patient behaved as though he or she couldn't remember" (p. 45).

The *DSM-5* recognizes three dissociative disorders (other than unspecified and other specified ones): (1) dissociative identity disorder (DID; formerly multiple personality disorder, MPD), (2) dissociative amnesia (including dissociative fugue), and (3) depersonalization/derealization disorder.

Clinicians specializing in dissociation argue that "dissociative disorders are common in general population samples and psychiatric samples" (van der Hart & Nijenhuis, 2009, p. 462). For example, one representative community survey reported an annual prevalence of 1.5% of DID, 0.8% of depersonalization disorder, 1.8% of dissociative amnesia, and 4.4% of Dissociative Disorders Not Otherwise Specified (DDNOS; Johnson et al., 2006).

### Dissociative Identity Disorder

People diagnosed with DID act as if different personalities ("alters") seize control of the person. The personalities vary in their behavior, thoughts, and feelings, and each has its own name, history, and memories. Most DID specialists believe that it arises from chronic, severe sexual and physical abuse during childhood. The victim's sense of self dissociates into multiple personalities (or states), and some presumably harbor memories of trauma too horrific for the host personality to entertain consciously. Specialists now favor the term DID over MPD because many patients seem to lack a single, integrated identity rather than having multiple, fully formed, and coherent personalities.

Case reports of dual personalities seldom appeared in the psychiatric literature prior to 1980s. One comprehensive review cited a mere 76 cases that had appeared in the previous 128 years (Taylor & Martin, 1944). Yet, following the publication of *Sybil* (Schreiber, 1973), a bestselling book about a case of MPD that soon became a made-for-TV movie, an epidemic of diagnosed cases of MPD erupted in North America. As Putnam exclaimed in 1986, "more cases of MPD have been reported in the last 5 years than in the preceding two centuries" (F. W. Putnam, quoted in McHugh, 2008, p. 20).

In contrast to most previous cases that had one or two additional personalities, Sybil had 16, and, in contrast to previous cases, Sybil supposedly harbored horrific memories of childhood sexual and physical abuse. This case introduced the idea that MPD resulted from horrific childhood trauma of which the patient's host personality was entirely unaware. As one MPD expert said, "The book *Sybil*, with its graphic treatment of the amnesias, fugue episodes, child abuse, and conflicts among alters, served as the template against which other patients could be compared and understood.... Schreiber's account is both detailed and accurate enough to serve as mandatory clinical reading for students of MPD" (F. W. Putnam, 1989, p. 35, quoted in Borch-Jacobsen, April 24, 1997).

Hence, the Sybil case inspired the idea that MPD was an unusually severe form of PTSD. Assuming that the mind can protect itself by dissociating memories of horrific trauma from awareness, MPD theorists argued that childhood trauma fractures the mind of patients, creating alter personalities that contain memories that the patient must recall via hypnosis for recovery to occur.

Publications on DID and other dissociative disorders peaked in the mid-1990s before plummeting dramatically in the early twenty-first century (Pope et al., 2006). Malpractice lawsuits against dissociative experts accused of inadvertently fostering false memories of satanic ritual abuse in patients they suspected of having DID may have reduced enthusiasm for detecting hidden multiplicity among one's caseload of patients, thereby contributing to the end of the epidemic (Acocella, 1999). Other clinicians outside the community of dissociative specialists argue that DID constitutes a culturally shaped idiom of distress influenced by dramatic media portrayals of the syndrome and by misguided therapeutic practices, such as hypnotic elicitation of alter personalities (Lilienfeld et al., 1999).

Recent scholarship on the Sybil case has uncovered many startling facts (Borch-Jacobsen, 2009; Nathan, 2011). Sybil's mother was neither abusive nor psychotic. Rather than being a survivor of horrific abuse, Sybil was an imaginative only child who enjoyed a comfortable, somewhat pampered childhood. As a young woman, she moved to New York City to pursue an artistic career, and dissatisfaction with her life led her to seek psychoanalytic treatment with the psychiatrist Cornelia Wilbur. Fascinated by the recent case depicted in "The Three Faces of Eve," Wilbur was keen to encounter another case of multiple personality. Using hypnosis, sodium pentothal ("truth serum"), and other medications, Wilbur elicited Sybil's dramatic alters and her dissociated memories of horrific childhood trauma. Recently scrutinized audiotapes of Wilbur's sessions with Sybil document her inadvertent shaping of Sybil's multiple personalities. On one tape, Sybil admits to manufacturing her trauma stories and multiple personalities, but Wilbur refused to accept this admission. Ironically, the patient who inspired the epidemic of MPD and the trauma theory of the disorder was never a trauma survivor after all.

The controversy over DID concerns its etiology, not its reliability. Indeed, the interrater reliability of the diagnosis is satisfactory (Gleaves et al., 2001). Reliable diagnoses have permitted experimental researchers to test hypotheses about DID in the laboratory.

Huntjens and her colleagues have conducted experiments testing hypotheses about interidentity amnesia in Dutch patients diagnosed with DID. Their basic strategy is to test three groups: patients diagnosed with DID, control subjects trained to simulate DID, and a nonsimulating control group. The simulators view a documentary about the disorder and receive coaching on how to role-play DID.

In one study, subjects memorized names of animals, vegetables, and flowers (Huntjens et al., 2003). The DID and simulating subjects then switched to a second personality who memorized names of other animals, other vegetables, and furniture. A recall test and a recognition test 1 week later for words they had memorized indicated that both control groups and the DID group remembered words from the first list as well as words from the second list. Therefore, the second personality remembered material encoded by the first personality, documenting interidentity transfer of information, a finding inconsistent with purported amnesia. Similar findings emerged for emotionally valenced words (Huntjens et al., 2007).

Testing DID and control subjects, Kong et al. (2008) extended these findings, showing that interidentity transfer in DID cannot plausibly be attributable to implicit memory effects. That is, they had one personality encode words auditorily and then tested the other, amnesic personality visually. Memory transfer across identities occurred despite cross-modality (i.e., auditor vs. visual) between encoding and testing.

Using a concealed information task, Huntjens et al. (2012) documented interidentity transfer of autobiographical information in patients diagnosed with DID. They recruited three groups of subjects, all women: patients diagnosed with DID, amateur actors trained to simulate DID, and another group consisting of nonactors. The authors administered an autobiographical questionnaire to all subjects, asking about the name of their best friend, their favorite food, favorite sport, and so forth. The DID patients completed the questionnaire twice, once as the trauma identity who reported memories of childhood sexual abuse, and again as an identity reportedly amnesic for memories of abuse. For example, a DID trauma identity might have written down the words *Janet, pizza,* and *swimming* in response to questions about the name of her best friend, favorite food, and favorite sport, whereas the amnesic identity might have written down the answers *Mary, steak,* and *tennis.* The authors had subjects rate the personal emotional relevance of words drawn from these questionnaires, plus many other irrelevant words, and the DID patients did so in their amnesic identity, thus enabling the authors to select words from the trauma identity's questionnaire that the amnesic identity rated as personally irrelevant.

Two weeks later, subjects performed a concealed information task whereby they viewed a series of words in uppercase letters on a computer screen. They had to decide as quickly as possible whether they recognized the word as a member of the previously memorized target set of three words (e.g., *SUSAN, CHOCOLATE, BOWLING*) or whether the word was a nontarget word. Among the nontarget items were the three words having autobiographical significance for a DID patient's trauma identity (e.g., *JANET, PIZZA,* and *SWIMMING*) and the three words having autobiographical significance for the patient's amnesic identity (e.g., *MARY, STEAK,* and *TENNIS*). The computer recorded the reaction times for the recognition/classification decisions.

The results revealed that subjects were very fast to classify irrelevant words, and they were slow to classify nontarget words that possessed autobiographical significance (e.g., their best friend's name). The slowed reaction times signified recognition of the word's personal relevance. That is, they had to inhibit the impulse to respond "yes" to the question of recognition. Accordingly, in the DID group, the amnesic identities performed this task, and their reaction times to respond "no" to words having considerable autobiographical significance was very slow (e.g., *MARY, STEAK,* and *TENNIS*), signifying their recognition of the personal importance of these items. Crucially, these patients were just as slow to respond to the corresponding items of their trauma identity of which they were allegedly amnesic (e.g., *JANET, PIZZA,* and *SWIMMING*). These data are inconsistent with the notion of interidentity amnesia. Indeed, if the amnesic identity were truly unable to access the autobiographical material of the trauma identity, then the reaction times to classify these items would not have been as slow as those for classifying the autobiographical items of the amnesic identity. Taken together, experimental research does not support claims of interidentity amnesia in DID.

Using positron emission tomography (PET), Reinders and her colleagues have investigated central and peripheral psychophysiological responses to trauma-relevant and neutral autobiographical memory scripts in a group of 11 women diagnosed with DID (Reinders et al., 2006). They tested two personalities of each of the patients. The traumatic identity state had access to traumatic memories, whereas the neutral identity state had "a degree of amnesia for traumatic memories ranging from lack of personalization of the traumatic past to total amnesia" (Reinders et al., 2006, p. 730). They used a script-driven imagery paradigm whereby each personality (identity state) heard two autobiographical memory scripts, one trauma-relevant and one neutral. The results showed significant increases in subjective and cardiovascular responses to trauma scripts than to neutral scripts, and these increases were more pronounced when the traumatic identity state heard the scripts than when the neutral identity state heard them. The two personalities also exhibited different patterns of cerebral blood flow when they listened to the trauma scripts.

Although these data indicate marked distress and psychophysiological activation to the trauma scripts, these responses do not confirm the authenticity of the memories per se. Indeed, marked psychophysiological activation occurred among people reporting having been abducted by space aliens when they heard scripts describing their (presumably false) memories of their most traumatic encounters with aliens (McNally et al., 2004). Moreover, it is a straightforward matter for neutral identities to attenuate their responses to trauma scripts evocative for trauma identities; neutral identities merely need to distract themselves from attending to the otherwise evocative script.

Reinders et al. (2012) subsequently enrolled two groups of healthy control subjects, one scoring high on a measure of fantasy proneness and the other scoring low on this measure. They coached both groups to simulate DID. Each simulating subject heard two autobiographical memory scripts, one neutral and one trauma related. Reinders et al. compared the results from these two simulating control groups with those of the DID patients from their previous study. The results revealed that neither control group mimicked the cerebral or peripheral responses of the DID group when all groups heard their trauma scripts. Because the high fantasy group failed to mimic the psychophysiology of the DID group, the authors concluded "that DID does not have a sociocultural origin" (Reinders et al., 2012, p. 1).

However, the data do not compel this conclusion. To be sure, high fantasy proneness in healthy control subjects is insufficient to incite marked psychophysiological responses to stressful scripts in psychologically healthy people who endeavor to mimic the responses of DID patients. Yet this did not mean that elevated fantasy proneness fails to contribute to the emergence of DID in distressed individuals undergoing hypnotic interventions to elicit alter personalities who presumably harbor dissociated memories of trauma.

## Dissociative Amnesia

*DSM-5* characterizes dissociative amnesia as an inability to retrieve important, encoded, personal information that cannot be attributable to ordinary forgetting or to a toxic or physical insult to the brain or to DID. Dissociation theorists emphasize that the information is often related to an extremely stressful or traumatic experience. The *DSM-5* recognizes three types: localized amnesia (i.e., inability to recall events from a certain period), selective amnesia (i.e., only a part of the traumatic event can be recalled), and rare, generalized amnesia (i.e., complete loss of one's personal history and identity).

Distilling the key points of this perspective in his book entitled *Repressed Memories*, Spiegel (1997) emphasized that the nature of traumatic dissociative amnesia is such

> that it is not subject to the same rules of ordinary forgetting; it is more, rather than less, common after repeated episodes; involves strong affect; and is resistant to retrieval through salient cues. (p. 6)

That is, dissociation theorists hold that the more often trauma occurs and the more emotionally distressing it is for the victims, the more likely they will be unable to remember having suffered any trauma. Moreover, encoded, consolidated—but dissociated—memories of trauma will not be accessible by ordinary means, such as merely interviewing people about their trauma histories. These assumptions justified the use of hypnosis, guided imagery, and other methods to recover the otherwise inaccessible dissociated memories, process them emotionally, and incorporate them into the narrative of their lives.

Discussing the work of Jean Charcot, Pierre Janet, and Sigmund Freud, the historian of psychiatry Borch-Jacobsen described "the birth of a true psychiatric myth, fated to a grand future: *the patient is entirely ignorant of the trauma that caused his symptoms*" (2009, p. 30). Indeed, using Internet search engines, Pope and his colleagues were unable to identify a single case of alleged traumatic dissociative amnesia in the world literature of fiction, history, or medicine prior to 1786 (Pope et al., 2007a, 2007b). They concluded that claims of dissociative amnesia are a culture-bound idiom of distress.

Janet and Freud further developed and popularized the concepts of traumatic dissociative amnesia and repression, respectively. Despite their minor theoretical differences, both theorists agreed that the mind protects itself by dissociating or repressing emotionally disturbing material, rendering it inaccessible to awareness. Recovery of this material, processing it emotionally, and integrating it into one's autobiographical narrative was the road to healing and symptomatic recovery, notions that resurfaced in the discredited "recovered memory therapy" of the late twentieth century (Crews, 1995, pp. 216–218).

Clinicians specializing in dissociation have claimed that survivors of diverse trauma events ranging from childhood sexual abuse to the Holocaust have exhibited dissociative amnesia (Brown et al., 1999; van der Hart & Nijenhuis, 2009). Yet an extensive analysis of documented cases of trauma found no instance of victims being incapable of recalling their trauma except when they had sustained a head injury or had experienced the event in the first years of life and thus during the period of childhood amnesia (Pope et al., 1999).

Strikingly, dissociative amnesia theorists (e.g., Brown et al., 1999) and their critics (e.g., Piper et al., 2000) often cite the same studies in support of their diametrically opposed conclusions. How can this be? The answer is that dissociative amnesia theorists seemingly misunderstand the very data they cite in support of their position. For example, the memory phenomena those dissociation theorists have adduced in support of the claim that people can encode traumatic experiences yet be unable to recollect them are wide-ranging (for an extensive review, see McNally, 2003a, pp. 186–228). They have confused everyday forgetfulness following trauma for an inability to remember the trauma itself. They have confused reluctance to disclose trauma with an inability to recall it. They have confused not thinking about something for a long time with an inability to remember it. They have confused failure to encode aspects of a trauma with inability to remember trauma. They have confused childhood amnesia and organic amnesia with dissociative amnesia.

*Fugue* is a syndrome is characterized by aimless wandering, often coupled with amnesia for parts of the journey (Kopelman et al., 1994). One scholar of psychiatry conceptualized it as a transient mental illness that flourishes only as long as the cultural niche that produces it remains (Hacking, 1998). He described an epidemic of fugue erupting in late nineteenth-century France, often among soldiers bored in the barracks who went on unauthorized leaves. The epidemic ended shortly after World War I.

Although the *DSM-5* implicates overwhelmingly stressful or traumatic events as the precipitants of dissociative fugue, trauma seldom figures in most of the historical case studies. For example, Stengel (1941) described 25 cases of fugue, noting that trauma seldom triggered the fugue. Moreover, many cases did not claim amnesia for the period when they fled. Stengel suggested that head injury, suicidal ideation, interpersonal problems, epilepsy, and growing up with disturbed parents appeared to be risk factors. In all likelihood, sudden, seemingly aimless travel has diverse antecedents.

### Depersonalization/Derealization Disorder

During a depersonalization episode, people feel emotionally numb, feel disconnected from their body, and experience the world as an unreal dream (i.e., derealization). Many people will experience brief episodes of depersonalization or derealization when exhausted, during marijuana intoxication, during a panic attack, or when encountering sudden danger. However, people with the disorder experience an unrelenting state that may last for months or years; others experience recurrent episodes interspersed with periods of normal consciousness. The onset is usually sudden, and many people fear for their sanity.

Though appearing under the dissociative disorders rubric, there is scant evidence pertaining to its etiology, pathophysiology, or its relation to other dissociative syndromes. This eerie disturbance in consciousness may arise from corticolimbic disconnection. For example, Sierra and Berrios (1998) have suggested that activation of the right dorsolateral PFC and reciprocal inhibition of the anterior cingulate may produce the sensation of mind emptiness. Left prefrontal inhibition of the amygdala would foster hypoemotionality and emotional detachment from the world. Although there is more theory than data on this syndrome, research is slowly accumulating (e.g., Sierra et al. 2012).

### Conclusion

Since the appearance of the Sybil case, many clinicians have interpreted dissociative disorders as arising from trauma (Dalenberg et al., 2012). Many patients diagnosed with these syndromes surely have trauma histories; indeed, epidemiological studies show that most people are trauma survivors (Breslau & Kessler, 2001). More controversial are claims that DID and dissociative amnesia arise from horrific experiences of which patients are unaware. The notion that these patients encode traumatic experiences yet become incapable of recalling them, except under certain circumstances (e.g., hypnosis), runs counter to research on trauma, emotion, and memory. Moreover, experimental research on DID has repeatedly shown that information—neutral, emotional, or autobiographical—transfers across identities, thus undermining the central claim of amnesia. The notion that these syndromes are extreme versions of PTSD is a claim without convincing empirical support. A multifactorial account of these syndromes involving variables such as suggestibility, fantasy proneness, and suggestibility seems warranted (Lynn et al. 2014).

### References

Acocella, J. (1999). *Creating hysteria: Women and multiple personality disorder.* Jossey-Bass.

Andreasen, N. C. (2004). Acute and delayed posttraumatic stress disorders: A history and some issues. *American Journal of Psychiatry, 161*(8), 1321–1323. doi:10.1176/appi.ajp.161.8.1321

Andrews, B., Brewin, C. R., Philpott, R., & Stewart, L. (2007). Delayed-onset posttraumatic stress disorder: A systematic review of the evidence. *American Journal of Psychiatry, 164*(9), 1319–1326. doi:10/1176/appi.ajp.2007.06091491

Angrist, J. D., Chen, S. H., & Frandsen, B. R. (2010). Did Vietnam veterans get sicker in the 1990s? The complicated effects of military service on self-reported health. *Journal of Public Economics, 94*(12), 824–837. doi.org/10.1016/j.pubeco.2010.06.001

Asmundson, G. J. G., & Asmundson, A. J. N. (2018). Are anxiety disorders publications continuing on a trajectory of growth?: A look at Boschen's (2008) predictions and beyond. *Journal of Anxiety Disorders, 56*(1), 1–4. doi:10.1016/j.anxdis.2018.05.003

Banerjee, S. B., Morrison, F. G., & Ressler, K. J. (2017). Genetic approaches for the study of PTSD: Advances and challenges. *Neuroscience Letters, 649*(May 10), 139–146. doi:10.1016/j.neulet.2017.02.058

Bedard-Gilligan, M., Zoellner, L. A., & Feeny, C. C. (2017). Is trauma memory special? Trauma narrative fragmentation in PTSD: Effects of treatment and response. *Clinical Psychological Science*, 5(2), 212–225. doi:10.1177/2167702616676581

Bellet, B. W., Jones, P. J., Niemeyer, R. A., & McNally, R. J. (2018). Bereavement outcomes as causal systems: A network analysis of the co-occurrence of complicated grief and posttraumatic growth. *Clinical Psychological Science*, 6(6), 707–809. doi:10.1177/2167702617702618777454

Bernstein, E. M., & Putnam, F. W. (1986). Development, reliability, and validity of a dissociation scale. *Journal of Nervous and Mental Disease*, 174(12), 727–735. doi:10/1097/00005053-198612000-00004

Berntsen, D., & Rubin, D. C. (2006). The centrality of event scale: A measure of integrating a trauma into one's identity and its relation to post-traumatic stress disorder symptoms. *Behaviour Research and Therapy*, 44(2), 219–231. doi:10.1016/j.brat.2005.01.009

Berntsen, D., & Rubin, D. C. (2007). When a trauma becomes a key to identity: Enhanced integration of trauma memories predicts posttraumatic stress disorder symptoms. *Applied Cognitive Psychology*, 21(4), 417–431. doi.org/10.1002/acp.1290

Blanchard, E. B., Kolb, L. C., Gerardi, R. J., Ryan, P., & Pallmeyer, T. P. (1986). Cardiac response to relevant stimuli as an adjunctive tool for diagnosing post-traumatic stress disorder in Vietnam veterans. *Behavior Therapy*, 17(5), 592–606. doi.org/10.1016/S00005-7894(86)80097-1

Blanchard, E. B., Kolb, L. C., Pallmeyer, T. P., & Gerardi, R. J. (1982). A psychophysiological study of post-traumatic stress disorder in Vietnam veterans. *Psychiatric Quarterly*, 54(4), 220–229.

Boals, A., & Ruggero, C. (2016). Event centrality prospectively predicts PTSD symptoms. *Anxiety, Stress, & Coping*, 29(5), 533–541. doi:10/1080/10615806.2015.1080822

Bonanno, G. A. (2004). Loss, trauma, and human resilience: Have we underestimated the human capacity to thrive after extremely aversive events? *American Psychologist*, 59(1), 20–28. doi.org/10.1037/0003-66X.59.1.20

Bonne, O., Brandes, D., Gilboa, A., Gomori, J. M., Shenton, M. E., & Pitman, R. K. (2001). Longitudinal MRI study of hippocampal volume in trauma survivors with PTSD. *American Journal of Psychiatry*, 158(8), 1248–1251. doi.org/10.1176/appi.ajp.158.8.1248

Borch-Jacobsen, M. (1997, April 24). Sybil – The making of a disease: An interview with Herbert Spiegel. *New York Review of Books*, 44(7), 60–64.

Borch-Jacobsen, M. (2009). *Making minds and madness: From hysteria to depression*. Cambridge University Press.

Borsboom, D. (2017). A network theory of mental disorders. *World Psychiatry*, 16(1), 5–13. doi:10.1002/wps.20375

Borsboom, D., & Cramer, A. O. J. (2013). Network analysis: An Integrative approach to the structure of psychopathology. *Annual Review of Clinical Psychology*, 9, 91–121. doi:10.1146/annurev-clinpsy-050212-185608

Boscarino, J. A. (1995). Post-traumatic stress and associated disorders among Vietnam veterans: The significance of combat exposure and social support. *Journal of Traumatic Stress*, 8(2), 317–336. doi.org/10.1007/BF02109567

Bowman, M. L., & Yehuda, R. (2004). Risk factors and the adversity-stress model. In G. M. Rosen (Ed.), *Posttraumatic stress disorder: Issues and controversies* (pp. 15–38). Wiley.

Bremner, J. D., Randall, P., Scott, T. M., Bronen, R. A., Seibyl, J. P., Southwick, S. M., Delaney, R. C., McCarthy, G., Charney, D. S., & Innis, R. B. (1995). MRI-based measurement of hippocampal volume in combat-related posttraumatic stress disorder. *American Journal of Psychiatry*, 152(7), 973–981. doi:10.1176/ajp.152.7.973

Bremner, J. D., Randall, P., Vermetten, E., Staib, L., Bronen, R. A., Mazure, C., Capelli, S., McCarthy, G., Innis, R. B., & Charney, D. S. (1997). Magnetic resonance imaging-based measurement of hippocampal volume in posttraumatic stress disorder related to childhood physical and sexual abuse: A preliminary report. *Biological Psychiatry*, 41(1), 23–32. doi.org/10.1016/S00006-3223(96)00162-x

Bremner, J. D., Staib, L. H., Kaloupek, D., Southwick, S. M., Soufer, R., & Charney, D. S. (1999). Neural correlates of exposure to traumatic pictures and sound in Vietnam combat veterans with and without posttraumatic stress disorder: A positron emission tomography study. *Biological Psychiatry*, 45(7), 806–816. doi.org/10.1016/S00006-3223(98)00297-2

Bremner, J. D., Vermetten, E., Vythilingam, M., Afzal, N., Schmahl, C., Elzinga, B., & Charney, D. S. (2004). Neural correlates of the classic color and emotional Stroop in women with abuse-related posttraumatic stress disorder. *Biological Psychiatry*, 55(6), 612–620. doi.org/10.1016/j.biopsych.2003.10.001

Brentano, F. (1889/1984). On the origin of our knowledge of right and wrong. In C. Calhoun & R. C. Solomon (Eds.), *What is an emotion?* (pp. 205–214). Oxford University Press.

Breslau, N. (2011). Causes of posttraumatic stress disorder. In P. E. Shrout, K. M. Keyes, & K. Ornstein (Eds.), *Causality and psychopathology: Finding the determinants of disorders and their cures* (pp. 297–320). Oxford University Press.

Breslau, N., & Alvarado, G. F. (2007). The clinical significance criterion in DSM-IV Posttraumatic Stress Disorder. *Psychological Medicine*, 37(10), 1437–1444. doi:10.1017/S00003329117070000426

Breslau, N., Davis, G. C., & Andreski, P. (1995). Risk factors for PTSD-related traumatic events: A prospective analysis. *American Journal of Psychiatry*, 152(4), 529–535. doi.org/10.1176/ajp.152.4.529

Breslau, N., Davis, G. C., Andreski, P., & Peterson, E. (1991). Traumatic events and posttraumatic stress disorder in an urban population of young adults. *Archives of General Psychiatry*, 48(3), 216–222. doi:10/1001/archpsyc.1991.01810270028003

Breslau, N., & Kessler, R. C. (2001). The stressor criterion in DSM-IV posttraumatic stress disorder: An empirical investigation. *Biological Psychiatry*, 50(9), 699–704. doi.org/10.1016/S0006-3223(01)01167-2

Breslau, N., Lucia, V. C., & Alvarado, G. F. (2006). Intelligence and other predisposing factors in exposure to trauma and posttraumatic stress disorder: A follow-up study at age 17 years. *Archives of General Psychiatry*, 63(11), 1238–1245. doi:10.1001/archpsyc.63.11.1238

Breslau, N., Peterson, E. L., & Schultz, L. (2008). A second look at prior trauma and the posttraumatic stress disorder-effects of subsequent trauma: A prospective epidemiological study. *Archives of General Psychiatry*, 65(4), 431–437. doi:10.1001/archpsyc.65.4.431

Breslau, N., Troost, J. P., Bohnert, K., & Luo, Z. (2013). Influence of predispositions on post-traumatic stress disorder: Does it vary by trauma severity? *Psychological Medicine, 43*(2), 381–390. doi:10.1017/S00033291712001195

Brewin, C. R. (2013). "I wouldn't start from here." An alternative perspective on PTSD from the *ICD-11*: Comment on Friedman (2013). *Journal of Traumatic Stress, 26*(5), 557–559. doi.org/10.1002/jts.21843

Brewin, C. R. (2014). Episodic memory, perceptual memory, and their interaction: Foundations for a theory of posttraumatic stress disorder. *Psychological Bulletin, 140*(1), 69–87. doi.org/10.1037/a0033722

Brewin, C. R. (2016). Coherence, disorganization, and fragmentation in traumatic memory reconsidered: A response to Rubin et al. (2016). *Journal of Abnormal Psychology, 125*(7), 1011–1017. doi.org/10.1037/abn0000154

Brown, A. D., Antonius, D., Kramer, M., Root, J. C., & Hirst, W. (2010). Trauma centrality and PTSD in veterans returning from Iraq and Afghanistan. *Journal of Traumatic Stress, 23*(4), 496–499. doi.org/10.1002/jts.20547

Brown, A. D., Root, J. C., Romano, T. A., Chang, L. J., Bryant, R. A., & Hirst, W. (2013). Overgeneralized autobiographical memory and future thinking in combat veterans with posttraumatic stress disorder. *Journal of Behavior Therapy and Experimental Psychiatry, 44*(1), 129–134. doi.org/10.1016/j.btep.2011.11.004

Brown, D., Scheflin, A. W., & Whitfield, C. L. (1999). Recovered memories: The current weight of evidence in science and in the courts. *Journal of Psychiatry and Law, 27*(1), 5–156. doi.org/10.1177/009318539902700102

Bryant, R. A., & Harvey, A. G. (1995). Processing threatening information in posttraumatic stress disorder. *Journal of Abnormal Psychology, 104*(3), 537–541. doi.org/10.1037/0021-843X.104.3.537

Bryant, R. A., Sutherland, K., & Guthrie, R. M. (2007). Impaired specific autobiographical memory as a risk factor for posttraumatic stress after trauma. *Journal of Abnormal Psychology, 116*(4), 837–841. doi.org/10.1037/0021-843X.116.4.837

Buckley, T. C., Galovski, T., Blanchard, E. B., & Hickling, E. J. (2003). Is the emotional Stroop paradigm sensitive to malingering? A between-groups study with professional actors and actual trauma survivors. *Journal of Traumatic Stress, 16*(1), 59–66. doi.org/10.1023/A:1022063412056

Burgess, A. W., & Holmstrom, L. L. (1974). Rape trauma syndrome. *American Journal of Psychiatry, 131*(2), 981–986. doi.org/10.1176/ajp.131.9.981

Cassiday, K. L., McNally, R. J., & Zeitlin, S. B. (1992). Cognitive processing of trauma cues in rape victims with post-traumatic stress disorder. *Cognitive Therapy and Research, 16*(3), 283–295. doi.org/10.1007/BF01183282

Charney, D. S., Deutch, A. Y., Krystal, J. H., Southwick, S. M., & Davis, M. (1993). Psychobiologic mechanisms of posttraumatic stress disorder. *Archives of General Psychiatry, 50*(4), 294–305. doi:10.1001/archpsyc.1993.01820160064008

Chodoff, P. (1963). Late effects of the concentration camp syndrome. *Archives of General Psychiatry, 8*(4), 323–333. doi:10/1001/archpsyc.196301720100013002

Cortina, L. M., & Kubiak, S. P. (2006). Gender and posttraumatic stress: Sexual violence as an explanation for women's increased risk. *Journal of Abnormal Psychology, 115*(4), 753–759. doi.org/10.1037/0021-843X.115.4753

Cramer, A. O. J., Waldorp, L. J., van der Maas, H. L. J., & Borsboom, D. (2010). Comorbidity: A network perspective. *Behavioral and Brain Sciences, 33*(1), 137–193. doi:10.1017/S0140525X09991567

Crews, F. (1995). *The memory wars: Freud's legacy in dispute.* New York Review of Books.

Dahlgren, M. K., Laifer, L. M., VanElzaker, M. B., Offringa, R., Hughes, K. C., Dubois, S. J. . . . Shin, L. M. (2018). Diminished medial prefrontal cortex activation during the recollection of stressful events is an acquired characteristic of PTSD. *Psychological Medicine, 48*(7), 1128–1138. doi:10.1017/S003329171700263X

Dalenberg, C. J., Brand, B. L., Gleaves, D. H., Dorahy, M., Loewenstein, R. J., Cardeña, E., . . . Spiegel, D. (2012). Evaluation of the evidence for the trauma and fantasy models of dissociation. *Psychological Bulletin, 138*(3), 550–558. doi.org/10.1037/a0027447

Dalgleish, T., Williams, J. M. G., Golden, A.-M. J., Perkins, N., Barrett, L. F., Barnard, P. J., . . . Watkins, E. (2007). Reduced specificity of autobiographical memory and depression: The role of executive control. *Journal of Experimental Psychology: General, 136*(1), 23–42. doi.org/10.1037/0096-3445.136.1.23

Daskalakis, N. P., Rijal, C. M., King, C., Huckins, L. M., & Ressler, K. J. (2018). Recent genetics and epigenetics approaches to PTSD. *Current Psychiatry Reports, 20*, 30. doi.org/10.1007/s11920-018-0898-7

de Jongh, A., Olff, M., van Hoolwerff, H., Aarman, I. H. A., Broekman, B., Lindaur, R. . . . Boer, F. (2008). Anxiety and post-traumatic stress symptoms following wisdom tooth removal. *Behaviour Research and Therapy, 46*(12), 1305–1310. doi.org/10.1016/j.brat.2008.09.004

Dohrenwend, B. F. (2010). Toward a typology of high-risk major stressful events and situations in posttraumatic stress disorder and related psychopathology. *Psychological Injury and Law, 3*(2), 89–99. doi.org/10.1007/s12207-010-9072-1

Dohrenwend, B. P., Turner, J. B., Turse, N. A., Adams, B. G., Koenen, K. C., & Marshall, R. (2006). The psychological risks of Vietnam for U.S. veterans: A revisit with new data and methods. *Science, 313*(5789), 379–982. doi:10/1126/science.1128944

Dubner, A. E., & Motta, R. W. (1999). Sexually and physically abused foster care children and posttraumatic stress disorder. *Journal of Consulting and Clinical Psychology, 67*(3), 367–373. doi.org/10.1037/0022-006X.67.3.367

Dückers, M. L. A., Alisic, E., & Brewin, C. R. (2016). A vulnerability paradox in the cross-national prevalence of post-traumatic stress disorder. *British Journal of Psychiatry, 209*(4), 300–305. doi:10.1192/bjp.bp.115.176628

Duncan, L. E., Ratanatharathorn, A., Aiello, A. E., Almli, L. E., Amstadter, A. B. . . . Koenen, K. C. (2018). Largest GWAS of PTSD ($N$ = 20070) yields genetic overlap with schizophrenia and sex differences in heritability. *Molecular Psychiatry, 23*(4), 666–673. doi.org/10.1038/mp.2017.77

Dunlop, B. W., & Wong, A. (2019). The hypothalamic-pituitary-adrenal axis in PTSD: Pathophysiology and treatment interventions. *Progress in Neuropsychopharmacology & Biological Psychiatry, 89*(3), 361–379. doi.org/10.1016/j.pnpbp.2018.10.010

Dunmore, E., Clark, D. M., & Ehlers, A. (2001). A prospective investigation of the role of cognitive factors in persistent Posttraumatic Stress Disorder (PTSD) after physical or sexual assault. *Behaviour Research and Therapy, 39*(9), 1063–1084. doi.org/10.1016/S00005-7967(00)00088-7

Ehlers, A., & Clark, D. M. (2000). A cognitive model of posttraumatic stress disorder. *Behaviour Research and Therapy, 38*(4), 319–345. doi.org/10.1016/S00005-7967(99)00123-0

Ehring, T., Ehlers, A., & Glucksman, E. (2006). Contribution of cognitive factors to the prediction of post-traumatic stress disorder, phobia, and depression after motor vehicle accidents. *Behaviour Research and Therapy, 44*(12), 1699–1716. doi.org/10.1016/j.brat.2005.11.013

Foa, E. B., Feske, U., Murdock, T. B., Kozak, M. J., & McCarthy, P. R. (1991). Processing of threat-related information in rape victims. *Journal of Abnormal Psychology, 100*(2), 156–162. doi.org/10.1037/0021-843X.100.2.156

Friedman, M. J. (2013a). Finalizing PTSD in *DSM-5*: Getting here from there and where to go next. *Journal of Traumatic Stress, 26*(5), 548–556. doi.org/10.1002/jts.21840

Friedman, M. J. (2013b). PTSD in the *DSM-5*: Reply to Brewin (2013), Kilpatrick (2013), and Maercker and Perkonigg (2013). *Journal of Traumatic Stress, 26*(5), 548–556. doi.org/10.1002/jts.21847

Friedman, M. J., Kilpatrick, D. G., Schnurr, P. P., & Weathers, F. W. (2016). Correcting misconceptions about the diagnostic criteria for posttraumatic stress disorder in *DSM-5*. (2006). *JAMA Psychiatry, 73*(7), 753–754. doi:10.1001/jamapyschiatry.2016.0745

Frueh, B. C., Elhai, J. D., Grubaugh, A. L., Monnier, J., Kashdan, T. B., Sauvageot, J. A., Hamner, M. B., Burkett, B. G., & Arana, G. W. (2005). Documented combat exposure of US veterans seeking treatment for combat-related posttraumatic stress disorder. *British Journal of Psychiatry, 186*(6), 467–472. doi:10.1192/bjp.186.6.467

Galatzer-Levy, I. R., & Bryant, R. A. (2013). 636,120 ways to have posttraumatic stress disorder. *Perspectives on Psychological Science, 8*(6), 651–662. doi.org/10.117/1745691613504115

Gallagher, M. W., Long, L. J., & Phillips, C. A. (2020). Hope, optimism, self-efficacy, and posttraumatic stress disorder: A meta-analytic review of the protective effects of positive expectancies. *Journal of Clinical Psychology, 76*(3), 329–355. doi.org/10.1002/jclp.22882

Gehrt, T. B., Berntsen, D., Hoyle, R. H., & Rubin, D. C. (2018). Psychological and clinical correlates of the Centrality of Event Scale: A systematic review. *Clinical Psychology Review, 65*(11), 57–80. doi.org/10.1016/j.cpr.2018.07.006

Gerardi, R. J., Blanchard, E. B., & Kolb, L. C. (1989). Ability of Vietnam veterans to dissimulate a psychophysiological assessment for post-traumatic stress disorder. *Behavior Therapy, 20*(2), 229–243. doi.org/10.1016/S0005-7894(89)80071-1

Gilbertson, M. W., Paulus, L. A., Williston, S. K., Gurvits, T. V., Lasko, N. B., Pitman, R. K., & Orr, S. P. (2006). Neurocognitive function in monozygotic twins discordant for combat exposure: Relationship to posttraumatic stress disorder. *Journal of Abnormal Psychology, 115*(3), 484–495. doi.org/10.1037/0021-843X.115.3.484

Gilbertson, M. W., Shenton, M. E., Ciszewski, A., Kasai, K., Lasko, N. B., Orr, S. P., & Pitman, R. K. (2002). Smaller hippocampal volume predicts pathologic vulnerability to psychological trauma. *Nature Neuroscience, 5*(11), 1242–1247. doi.org/10.1038/nn958

Gleaves, D. H., May, M. C., & Cardeña, E. (2001). An examination of the diagnostic validity of dissociative identity disorder. *Clinical Psychology Review, 21*(4), 577–608. doi.org/10.1016/S0272-7358(99)00073-2

Goodwin, L., Jones, M., Rona, R. J., Sundin, J., Wessely, S., & Fear, N. T. (2012). Prevalence of delayed-onset posttraumatic stress disorder in military personnel: Is there evidence for this disorder? Results of a prospective UK cohort study. *Journal of Nervous and Mental Disease, 200*(5), 429–437. doi:10.1077/NMD.0b013e31825322fe

Gurvits, T. V., Gilbertson, M. W., Lasko, N. B., Tarhan, A. S., Simeon, D., Macklin, M. L., Orr, S. P., & Pitman, R. K. (2000). Neurologic soft signs in chronic posttraumatic stress disorder. *Archives of General Psychiatry, 57*(2), 181–186. doi:10.1001/archpsyc.57.2.181

Gurvits, T. V., Metzger, L. J., Lasko, N. B., Cannistraro, P. A., Tarhan, A. S., Gilbertson, M. W., Orr, S. P., Charbonneau, A. M., Wedig, M. M., & Pitman, R. K. (2006). Subtle neurologic compromise as a vulnerability factor for combat-related posttraumatic stress disorder: Results of a twin study. *Archives of General Psychiatry, 63*(5), 571–576. doi:10.1001/archpsyc.63.5.571

Gurvits, T. V., Shenton, M. E., Hokama, H., Ohta, H., Lasko, N. B., Gilbertson, M. W., Orr, S. P., Kikinis, R., Jolesz, F. A., McCarley, R. W., & Pitman, R. K. (1996). Magnetic resonance imaging study of hippocampal volume in chronic, combat-related posttraumatic stress disorder. *Biological Psychiatry, 40*(11), 1091–1099. doi.org/10.1016/S0006-3223(96)00229-6

Hacking, I. (1998). *Mad travelers: Reflections on the reality of transient mental illness*. University of Virginia Press.

Heim, C. (2020). Deficiency of inflammatory response to acute trauma exposure as a neuroimmune mechanism driving the development of chronic PTSD: Another paradigmatic shift for the conceptualization of stress-related disorders? *American Journal of Psychiatry, 177*(1), 10–13. doi.org/10.1176/appi.ajp.2019.19111189

Hoge, C. W., Castro, C. A., Messer, S. C., McGurk, D., Cotting, D. I., & Koffman, R. L. (2004). Combat duty in Iraq and Afghanistan, mental health problems, and barriers to care. *New England Journal of Medicine, 351*(1), 13–22. doi:10/1056/NEJMoa040603

Horn, S. R., Charney, D. S., & Feder, A. (2016). Understanding resilience: New approaches for preventing and treating PTSD. *Experimental Neurology, 284*(Part B), 119–132. doi.org/10.1016/j.expneurol.2016.07.002

Huntjens, R. J. C., Peters, M. L., Woertman, L., van der Hart, O., & Postma, A. (2007). Memory transfer for emotionally valenced words between identities in dissociative identity disorder. *Behaviour Research and Therapy, 45*(4), 775–789. doi.org/10.1016/j.brat.2006.07.001

Huntjens, R. J. C., Postma, A., Peters, M. L., Woertman, L., & van der Hart, O. (2003). Interidentity amnesia for neutral, episodic information in dissociative identity disorder. *Journal of Abnormal Psychology, 112*(2), 290–297. doi.org/10.1037/0021-843X.112.2.290

Huntjens, R. J. C., Verschuere, B., & McNally, R. J. (2012). Inter-identity autobiographical amnesia in patients with dissociative identity disorder. *PLoS ONE, 7*(7): e40580 doi:10.1371/journal.pone.0040580

Isvoranu, A.-M., Epskamp, S., & Cheung, M. W.-L. (2021). Network models of posttraumatic stress disorder: A meta-analysis. *Journal of Abnormal Psychology, 130*(8), 841–861. doi.org/10.1037/abn0000704

Jones, E. (2019). PTSD in an era of uncertainty and challenge. *International Review of Psychiatry, 31*(1), 1–2. doi:10.1080/09540281.2019,1603663

Jones, E., & Wessely, S. (2005). *Shell shock to PTSD: Military psychiatry from 1900 to the Gulf War*. Psychology Press.

Jones, E., & Wessely, S. (2007). A paradigm shift in the conceptualization of psychological trauma in the 20th century. *Journal of Anxiety Disorders, 21*(2), 164–175. doi.org/10.1016/j.anxdis.2006.09.009

Johnson, J. G., Cohen, P., Kasen, S., & Brook, J. S. (2006). Dissociative disorders among adults in the community, impaired functioning, and axis I and II comorbidity. *Journal of Psychiatric Research, 40*(2), 131–140. doi.org/10.1016/j.psychchires.2005.03.003

Kasai, K., Yamasue, H., Gilbertson, M. W., Shenton, M. E., Rauch, S. L., & Pitman, R. K. (2008). Evidence for acquired pregenual anterior cingulate gray matter loss from a twin study of combat-related posttraumatic stress disorder. *Biological Psychiatry, 63*(6), 550–556. doi.org/10.106/j.biopsych.2007.06.022

Keane, T. M., Kolb, L. C., Kaloupek, D. G., Orr, S. P., Blanchard, E. B., Thomas, R. G., Hsieh, F. Y., & Lavori, P. W. (1998). Utility of psychophysiological measurement in the diagnosis of posttraumatic stress disorder: Results from a Department of Veterans Affairs Cooperative Study. *Journal of Consulting and Clinical Psychology, 66*(6), 914–923. doi.org/10.1037/0022-006X.66.6.914

Kessler, R. C., Aguilar-Gaxiola, S., Alonso, J., Bromet, E. J., Gureje, O., Karam, E. G., . . . on behalf of the World Mental Health Survey Collaborators. (2018). The associations of earlier trauma exposures and history of mental disorders with PTSD after subsequent traumas. *Molecular Psychiatry, 23*(9), 1892–1899. doi.org/10.1038/mp.2017.194

Kessler, R. C., Berglund, P., Demler, O., Jin, R., Merikangas, K. R., & Walters, E. E. (2005). Lifetime prevalence and age-of-onset distributions of DSM-IV disorders in the National Comorbidity Survey Replication. *Archives of General Psychiatry, 62*(6), 593–602. doi:10.1001/archpsyc.62.6.593

Kessler, R. C., Sonnega, A., Bromet, E., Hughes, M., & Nelson, C. B. (1995). Posttraumatic stress disorder in the National Comorbidity Survey. *Archives of General Psychiatry, 52*(12), 1048–1060. doi:10.1001/archpsyc.1995.03950240066012

Kimble, M. O., Frueh, B. C., & Marks, L. (2009). Does the modified Stroop effect exist in PTSD? Evidence from dissertation abstracts and the peer reviewed literature. *Journal of Anxiety Disorders, 23*(5), 650–655. doi.org/10.1016/j.anxdis.2009.02.002

King, D. W., & King, L. A. (1991). Validity issues in research on Vietnam veteran adjustment. *Psychological Bulletin, 109*(1), 107–124. doi.org/10.1037/0033-2909.109.1.107

King, D. W., King, L. A., Foy, D. W., & Gudanowski, D. M. (1996). Prewar factors in combat-related posttraumatic stress disorder: Structural equation modeling with a national sample of female and male Vietnam veterans. *Journal of Consulting and Clinical Psychology, 64*(3), 520–531. doi.org/10.1037/0022-006X.64.3.250

Kleim, B., & Ehlers, A. (2008). Reduced autobiographical memory specificity predicts depression and posttraumatic stress disorder after recent trauma. *Journal of Consulting and Clinical Psychology, 76*(2), 231–242. doi:10.1037/0022-006X.76.2.231

Koenen, K. C., Ratanatharathorn, A., Ng, L., McLaughlin, K. A., Bromet, E. J., Stein, D. J. . . . Kessler, R. C. (2017). Posttraumatic stress disorder in the World Mental Health Surveys. *Psychological Medicine, 47*(13), 2260–2274. doi:10.1017/S0033291717000708

Koenen, K. C., Moffitt, T. E., Caspi, A., Gregory, A., Harrington, H., & Poulton, R. (2008). The developmental mental-disorder histories of adults with posttraumatic stress disorder: A prospective longitudinal birth cohort study. *Journal of Abnormal Psychology, 117*(2), 460–466. doi.org/10/1037/0021-843X.117.2.460

Kong, L. L., Allen, J. J. B., & Glisky, E. L. (2008). Interidentity memory transfer in dissociative identity disorder. *Journal of Abnormal Psychology, 117*(3), 686–692. doi:10/1037/0021-843X.117.3.686

Kopelman, M. D., Christensen, H., Puffett, A., & Stanhope, N. (1994). The great escape: A neuropsychological study of psychogenic amnesia. *Neuropsychologia, 32*(6), 675–691. doi.org/10.1016/0028-3932(94)90028-0

Kremen, W. S., Koenen, K. C., Boake, C., Purcell, S., Eisen, S. A., Franz, C. E., Tsuang, M. T., & Lyons, M. J. (2007). Pretrauma cognitive ability and risk for posttraumatic stress disorder: A twin study. *Archives of General Psychiatry, 64*(3), 361–368. doi:10.1001/archpsyc.64.3.361

Kulka, R. A., Schlenger, W. E., Fairbank, J. A., Hough, R. L., Jordan, B. K., Marmar, C. R., & Weiss, D. S. (1990). *Trauma and the Vietnam War generation: Report of findings from the National Vietnam Veterans Readjustment Study*. Brunner/Mazel.

Lee, D. J., Blovin, M. J., Moshier, S. J., Dutra, S. J., Kleiman, S. E., Rosen, R. C., . . . Marx, B. P. (2020). The 20-year course of posttraumatic stress disorder symptoms among veterans. *Journal of Abnormal Psychology, 129*(6), 658–699. doi.org/10.1037/abn0000571

Lifton, R. J. (1973). *Home from the war: Vietnam veterans: Neither victims nor executioners*. Touchstone.

Lilienfeld, S. O., Lynn, S. J., Kirsch, I., Chaves, J. F., Sarbin, T. R., Ganaway, G. K., & Powell, R. A. (1999). Dissociative identity disorder and the sociocognitive model: Recalling the lessons of the past. *Psychological Bulletin, 125*(5), 507–523. doi.org/10.1037/0033-2909.125.5.507

Lynn, S. J., Lilienfeld, S. O., Merckelbach, H., Giesbrecht, T., McNally, R. J., . . . Malaktaris, A. (2014). The trauma model of dissociation: Inconvenient truths and stubborn fictions: Comment on Dalenberg et al. (2012). *Psychological Bulletin, 140*(3), 896–910. doi.org/10/1037/a0035570

Macklin, M. L., Metzger, L. J., Litz, B. T., McNally, R. J., Lasko, N. B., . . . Pitman, R. K. (1998). Lower pre-combat intelligence is a risk factor for posttraumatic stress disorder. *Journal of Consulting and Clinical Psychology, 66*(2), 323–326. doi.org/10/1037/0022-006X.66.2.323

Maercker, A., & Perkonigg, A. (2013). Applying an international perspective in defining PTSD and related disorders: Comment on Friedman (2013). *Journal of Traumatic Stress Disorders, 26*(5), 560–562. doi.org/10.1002/jts.21852

Malaktaris, A. L., & Lynn, S. J. (2019). The phenomenology and correlates of flashbacks in individuals with posttraumatic stress symptoms. *Clinical Psychological Science, 7*(2), 249–264.doi.org/10.1177/2167702618805081

Malloy, P. F., Fairbank, J. A., & Keane, T. M. (1983). Validation of a multimethod assessment of posttraumatic stress disorders in Vietnam veterans. *Journal of Consulting and Clinical Psychology, 51*(4), 488–494. doi.org/10.1037/0022-006X.51.4.488

Marlowe, D. H. (2001). *Psychological and psychosocial consequences of combat and deployment with special emphasis on the Gulf War*. RAND.

Marmar, C. R., Schlenger, W., Henn-Haase, C., Quian, M., Purchia, E., . . . Kulka, R. A. (2015). Course of posttraumatic stress disorder 40 years after the Vietnam War:

Findings from the National Vietnam Veterans Longitudinal Study. *JAMA Psychiatry, 72*(9), 875–881. doi:10.1001/jamapsychiatry.2015.0803

Marx, B. P., Jackson, J. C., Schnurr, P. P., Murdoch, M., Sayer, N. A., Keane, T. M.,. . . Speroff, T. (2012). The reality of malingered PTSD among veterans: Reply to McNally and Frueh (2012). *Journal of Traumatic Stress, 25*(4), 457–460. doi.org/10.1002/jts.21714

McDonald, J. J., Jr. (2003). Posttraumatic stress dishonesty. *Employee Relations Law Journal, 28*, 93–111.

McHugh, P. R. (2008). *Try to remember: Psychiatry's clash over meaning, memory, and mind*. Dana Press.

McNally, R. J. (2003a). *Remembering trauma*. Belknap Press of Harvard University Press

McNally, R. J. (2003b). Progress and controversy in the study of posttraumatic stress disorder. *Annual Review of Psychology, 54*, 229–252. doi:10.1146/annurev.psych.54.101601.145112

McNally, R. J. (2006a). Psychiatric casualties of war. *Science, 313*(5789), 923–924. doi:10.1126/science.1132242

McNally, R. J. (2006b). Cognitive abnormalities in post-traumatic stress disorder. *Trends in Cognitive Sciences, 10*(6), 271–277. doi.org/10.1016/j.tics.2006.04.007

McNally, R. J. (2007a). Can we solve the mysteries of the National Vietnam Veterans Readjustment Study? *Journal of Anxiety Disorders, 21*(2), 192–200. doi.org/10.1016/j.janxdis.2006.09.005

McNally, R. J. (2007b). Revisiting Dohrenwend et al.'s revisit of the National Vietnam Veterans Readjustment Study. *Journal of Traumatic Stress, 20*(4), 481–486. doi.org/10.1002/jts.20257

McNally, R. J. (2009). Can we fix PTSD in DSM-V? *Depression and Anxiety, 26*(7), 597–600. doi.org/10.1002/da.20586

McNally, R. J. (2012a). Are we winning the war against post-traumatic stress disorder? *Science, 336*(6083), 874–876. doi:10.11261/science.1222069

McNally, R. J. (2012b). The ontology of posttraumatic stress disorder: Natural kind, social construction, or causal system? *Clinical Psychology: Science and Practice, 19*(3), 220–228.doi.org/10.1111/cpsp.12001

McNally, R. J. (2018). Resolving the vulnerability paradox in the cross-national prevalence of posttraumatic stress disorder. *Journal of Anxiety Disorders, 54*(March), 33–35. doi.org/10.1016/j.janxdis.2018.01.005

McNally, R. J. (2021). Network analysis of psychopathology: Controversies and challenges. *Annual Review of Clinical Psychology, 17*, 31–35. doi.org/10.1146/annurev-clinpsy-081219-092850

McNally, R. J., Berntsen, D., Brewin, C. R., & Rubin, D. C. (2002). Are memories of sexual trauma fragmented? A post publication discussion among Richard J. McNally, Dorthe Berntsen, Chris R. Brewin, & Rubin, David C. *Memory, 30*(5), 658–660. doi.org/10.1080/09658211.2012.2061135

McNally, R. J., & Breslau, N. (2008). Does virtual trauma cause posttraumatic stress disorder? *American Psychologist, 63*(4), 282–283. doi.org/10.1037/0003-066X.63.4.282

McNally, R. J., & Frueh, B. C. (2012). Why we should worry about malingering in the VA system: Comment on Jackson et al. *Journal of Traumatic Stress, 25*(4), 454–456. doi.org/10.1002/jts.21713

McNally, R. J., Heeren, A., & Robinaugh, D. J. (2017). A Bayesian network analysis of posttraumatic stress disorder symptoms in adults reporting childhood sexual abuse. *European Journal of Psychotraumatology, 8*(Sup3): 1341276. doi.org/10.1080/20008198.2017.1341276

McNally, R. J., Kaspi, S. P., Riemann, B. C., & Zeitlin, S. (1990). Selective processing of threat cues in posttraumatic stress disorder. *Journal of Abnormal Psychology, 99*(4), 398–402. doi.org/10.1037/0021-843X.99.4.398

McNally, R. J., Lasko, N. B., Clancy, S. A., Macklin, M. L., Pitman, R. K., & Orr, S. P. (2004). Psychophysiological responding during script-driven imagery in people reporting abduction by space aliens. *Psychological Science, 15*(7), 493–497. doi.org/10.1111/j.0956-7976.2004.00707.x

McNally, R. J., Lasko, N. B., Macklin, M. L., & Pitman, R. K. (1995). Autobiographical memory disturbance in combat-related posttraumatic stress disorder. *Behaviour Research and Therapy, 33*(6), 619–630. doi.org/10,1016/0005-7967(95)00007-K

McNally, R. J., Litz, B. T., Prassas, A., Shin, L. M., & Weathers, F. W. (1994). Emotional priming of autobiographical memory in post-traumatic stress disorder. *Cognition and Emotion, 8*(4), 351–367. doi.org/10.1080/02699939408408946

McNally, R. J., & Robinaugh, D. J. (2011). Risk factors and posttraumatic stress disorder: Are they especially predictive after exposure to less severe stressors? *Depression and Anxiety, 28*(12), 1091–1096. doi:10.1002/da.20867

McNally, R. J., Robinaugh, D. J., Wu, G. W. Y., Wang, L., Deserno, M., & Borsboom, D. (2015). Mental disorders as causal systems: A network approach to posttraumatic stress disorder. *Clinical Psychological Science, 3*(6), 836–849. doi.org/10.1127/2167702614553230

McNally, R. J., & Shin, L. M. (1995). Association of intelligence with severity of posttraumatic stress disorder symptoms in Vietnam combat veterans. *American Journal of Psychiatry, 152*(6), 936–938. doi.org/10.1176/ajp.152.6.936

Michopoulos, V., Beuret, E., Gould, F., Dhabhar, F. S., Schultebraucks, K., Galatzer-Levy, I., . . . Nemeroff, C. B. (2020). Association of prospective risk for chronic PTSD symptoms with low TFFα and IFNγ concentrations in the immediate aftermath of trauma exposure. *American Journal of Psychiatry, 171*(1), 58–65. doi.org/10.1176/appi.ajp.2019.19010039

Milad, M. R., & Quirk, G. J. (2002). Neurons in medial prefrontal cortex signal memory for fear extinction. *Nature, 420*(6911), 70–74. doi:10/1038/nature01138

Miller, M. W., Lin, A. P., Wolf, E. J., & Miller, D. R. (2018). Oxidative stress, inflammation, and neuroprogression in chronic PTSD. *Harvard Review of Psychiatry, 26*(2), 57–69. doi:1097/HRP0000000000000167

Minassian, A., Maihofer, A. X., Baker, D. G., Nievergelt, C. M., Geyer, M. A., Risbrough, V. B., for the Marine Resiliency Study. (2015). Association of predeployment heart rate variability with risk of postdeployment posttraumatic stress disorder in active-duty Marines. *JAMA Psychiatry, 72*(10), 979–986. doi:10.1001/jamapsychiatry.2015.0922

Moore, S. A., & Zoellner, L. A. (2007). Overgeneral autobiographical memory and traumatic events: An Evaluative review. *Psychological Bulletin, 133*(3), 419–437. doi:10.1037/0033-2909.133.3.419

Moradi, A. R., Abdi, A., Fathi-Ashtiani, A., Dalgleish, T., & Jobson, L. (2012). Overgeneral autobiographical memory recollection in Iranian combat veterans with posttraumatic stress disorder. *Behaviour Research and Therapy, 50*(6), 435–441. doi.org/10.1016/j.brat.202.03.009

Morgan, C. A., III, Grillon, C., Southwick, S. M., Davis, M., & Charney, D. S. (1996). Exaggerated acoustic startle reflex in Gulf War veterans with posttraumatic stress disorder. *American Journal of Psychiatry, 153*(1), 64–68. doi.org/10.1176/ajp.153.1.64

Nash, W. P., Boasso, A. M., Steenkamp, M. M., Larson, J. L., Lubin, R. E., & Litz, B. T. (2015). Posttraumatic stress in deployed Marines: Prospective trajectories of early adaptation. *Journal of Abnormal Psychology, 124*(1), 155–171. doi.org/10.1037/abn0000020

Nathan, D. (2011). *Sybil exposed: The extraordinary story behind the famous multiple personality case*. Free Press.

O'Donnell, M. L., Alkemade, N., Nickerson, A., Creamer, M., McFarlane, A. C., Silove, D., . . . Forbes, D. (2014). Impact of the diagnostic changes to post-traumatic stress disorder for DSM-5 and the proposed changes to ICD-11. *British Journal of Psychiatry, 205*(3), 230–235. doi:10.1192/bjp.bp.113.135285

Olde, E., van der Hart, O., Kleber, R., & van Son, M. (2006). Posttraumatic stress disorder following childbirth: A review. *Clinical Psychology Review, 26*(1), 1–16. doi.org/10.1016/j.cpr.2005.07.002

Orr, S. P., Lasko, N. B., Shalev, A. Y., & Pitman, R. K. (1995). Physiologic responses to loud tones in Vietnam veterans with posttraumatic stress disorder. *Journal of Abnormal Psychology, 104*(1), 75–82. doi.org/10.1037/0021-843X.104.1.75

Orr, S. P., McNally, R. J., Rosen, G. M., & Shalev, A. Y. (2004). Psychophysiologic reactivity: Implications for conceptualizing PTSD. In G. M. Rosen (Ed.), *Posttraumatic stress disorder: Issues and controversies* (pp. 101–126). Wiley.

Orr, S. P., Metzger, L. J., Lasko, N. B., Macklin, M. L., Hu, F. B., . . . Pitman, R. K. (2003). Physiologic responses to sudden, loud tones in monozygotic twins discordant for combat exposure: Association with posttraumatic stress disorder. *Archives of General Psychiatry, 60*(3), 283–288. doi:10.1001/arcpsych.60.3.283

Orr, S. P., & Pitman, R. K. (1993). Psychophysiologic assessment of attempts to simulate posttraumatic stress disorder. *Biological Psychiatry, 33*(2), 127–129. doi.org/10/1016/00006-3223(93)90312-2

Orr, S. P., Pitman, R. K., Lasko, N. B., & Herz, L. R. (1993). Psychophysiological assessment of posttraumatic stress disorder imagery in World War II and Korean combat veterans. *Journal of Abnormal Psychology, 102*(1), 152–159. doi.org/10.1037/0021-843X.102.1.152

Paige, S. R., Reid, G. M., Allen, M. G., & Newton, J. E. O. (1990). Psychophysiological correlates of posttraumatic stress disorder in Vietnam veterans. *Biological Psychiatry, 27*(4), 419–430. doi.org/10.1016/0006-3223(90)90552-D

Pallmeyer, T. P., Blanchard, E. B., & Kolb, L. C. (1986). The psychophysiology of combat-induced post-traumatic stress disorder in Vietnam veterans. *Behaviour Research and Therapy, 24*(4), 645–652. doi.org/10.1016/0005-7967(86)90059-8

Pineles, S. L., Arditte Hall, K. A., & Rasmusson, A. M. (2017). Gender and PTSD: Different pathways to a similar phenotype. *Current Opinion in Psychiatry, 14*(1), 44–48. doi.org/10.106/j.copsyc.2016.11.002

Pineles, S. L., Nillni, Y. I., King, M. W., Patton, S. C., Bauer, M. R., Mostoufi, S. M., . . . Orr, S. P. (2016). Extinction retention and the menstrual cycle: Different associations for women with posttraumatic stress disorder. *Journal of Abnormal Psychology, 125*(3), 349–355. doi.org/10.1037/abn0000138

Pencea, I., Munoz, A. P., Maples-Keller, J. L., Fiorillo, D., Schultebraucks, K., Galatzer-Levy, I., . . . Powers, A. (2020). Emotion dysregulation is associated with increased prospective risk for chronic PTSD development. *Journal of Psychiatric Research, 121*(February), 222–228. doi.org/10.1016/j.psychires.2019.12.008

Piper, A. Jr., Pope, H. G., Jr., & Borowiecki, J. J., III. (2000). Custer's last stand: Brown, Scheflin, and Whitfield's latest attempt to salvage "dissociative amnesia." *Journal of Psychiatry and Law, 28*(2), 149–213.

Pitman, R. K., Orr, S. P., Forgue, D. F., Altman, B., de Jong, J. B., & Herz, L. R. (1990). Psychophysiologic responses to combat imagery of Vietnam veterans with posttraumatic stress disorder versus other anxiety disorders. *Journal of Abnormal Psychology, 99*(1), 49–54. doi.org/10.1037/0021-843X.99.1.49

Pitman, R. K., Orr, S. P., Forgue, D. F., de Jong, J. B., & Claiborn, J. M. (1987). Psychophysiologic assessment of posttraumatic stress disorder imagery in Vietnam combat veterans. *Archives of General Psychiatry, 44*(11), 970–975. doi:10.1001/archpsyc.1987.01800230050009

Pitman, R. K., Rasmusson, A. M., Koenen, K. C., Shin, L. M., Orr, S. P., Gilbertson, M. W., . . . Liberzon, I. (2012). Biological studies of post-traumatic stress disorder. *Nature Reviews Neuroscience, 13*(11), 769–787. doi:10.1038/nrn3339

Pole, N. (2007). The psychophysiology of posttraumatic stress disorder: A meta-analysis. *Psychological Bulletin, 133*(5), 725–746. doi.org/10.1037/0033-2909.133.5.725

Pope, H. G., Jr., Olivia, P. S., & Hudson, J. I. (1999). Repressed memories: The scientific status. In D. L. Faigman, D. H. Kaye, M. J. Saks, & J. Sanders (Eds.), *Modern scientific evidence: The law and science of expert testimony*, Vol. 1, Pocket Part (pp. 115–155). West Publishing.

Pope, H. G., Jr., Poliakoff, M. B., Parker, M. P., Boynes, M., & Hudson, J. I. (2007a). Is dissociative amnesia a culture-bound syndrome? Findings from a survey of historical literature. *Psychological Medicine, 37*(12), 225–233. doi:10.1017/S0033291706009500

Pope, H. G., Jr., Poliakoff, M. B., Parker, M. P., Boynes, M., & Hudson, J. I. (2007b). The authors' reply. *Psychological Medicine, 37*(7), 1067–1068. doi:10.1017/S003329170700075X

Pope, H. G., Jr., Steven, B., Bodkin, A., & Hudson, J. I. (2006). Tracking scientific interest in the dissociative disorders: A study of scientific publication output 1984-2003. *Psychotherapy and Psychosomatics, 75*(1), 19–24. doi.org/10.1159/000089223

Porter, S., & Peace, K. A. (2007). The scars of memory: A prospective, longitudinal investigation of the consistency of traumatic and positive emotional memories in adulthood. *Psychological Science, 18*(5), 435–441. doi.org/10.1111/j.1467-9280.2007.01918.x

Rangell, L. (1976). Discussion of the Buffalo Creek disaster: The course of psychic trauma. *American Journal of Psychiatry, 133*(13), 313–316. doi.org/10.1176/ajp.133.3.313

Ramos-Lima, L. F., Waikamp, V., Antonelli-Salgado, T., Passos, I. C., & Freitas, L. H. M. (2020). The use of machine learning techniques in trauma-related disorders: A systematic review. *Journal of Psychiatric Research, 121*(February), 159–172. doi.org/10.1016/j.jpsychires.2019.12.001

Rauch, S. L., Shin, L. M., & Phelps, E. A. (2006). Neurocircuitry models of posttraumatic stress disorder and extinction:

Human neuroimaging research: Past, present, and future. *Biological Psychiatry, 60*(4), 376–382. doi.org/10.1016/j.biopsych.2006.06.004

Rauch, S. L., Whalen, P. J., Shin, L. M., McInerney, S. C., Macklin, M. L., Lasko, N. B., . . . Pitman, R. K. (2000). Exaggerated amygdala response to masked facial stimuli in posttraumatic stress disorder: A functional MRI study. *Biological Psychiatry, 47*(9), 769–776. doi.org/10.1016/S0006-3223(00)00828-3

Reinders, A. A. T. S., Nijenhuis, E. R. S., Quak, J., Korf, J., Haaksma, J., Paans, A. M. J., . . . den Boer, J. A. (2006). Psychobiological characteristics of dissociative identity disorder: A symptom provocation study. *Biological Psychiatry, 60*(7), 730–740. doi.org/10.1016/j.biopsych.2005.12.019

Reinders, A. A. T. S., Willemsen, A. T. M., Vos, H. P. J., den Boer, J. A., & Nijenhuis, E. R. S. (2012). Fact or factitious? A psychobiological study of authentic and simulated dissociative identity states. *PLoS ONE, 7*(6): e39279. doi:10.1371/journal.pone.0039279

Robinaugh, D. J., Hoekstra, R. H. A., Toner, E. R., & Borsboom, D. (2020). The network approach to psychopathology: A review of the literature 2008-2018 and an agenda for future research. *Psychological Medicine, 50*(3), 353–366. doi:10.1017/So033291719003404

Robinaugh, D. J., & McNally, R. J. (2011). Trauma centrality and PTSD symptom severity in adult survivors of childhood sexual abuse. *Journal of Traumatic Stress, 24*(4), 483–486. doi.org/10.1002/jts.20656

Robinson, W. S. (1950). Ecological correlations and the behavior of individuals. *Sociological Review, 15*(3), 351–357.

Rothbaum, B. O., & Foa, E. B. (1993). Subtypes of posttraumatic stress disorder and duration of symptoms. In J. R. T. Davidson & E. B. Foa (Eds.), *Posttraumatic stress disorder: DSM-IV and beyond* (pp. 23–35). American Psychiatric Press.

Rubin, D. C., Berntsen, D., & Bohni, M. K. (2008). A memory-based model of posttraumatic stress disorder: Evaluating basic assumptions underlying the PTSD diagnosis. *Psychological Review, 115*(4), 985–1011 doi:10.1037/a0013397

Rubin, D. C., Berntsen, D., Ogle, C. M., Deffler, S. A., & Beckham, J. C. (2016). Scientific evidence versus outdated beliefs: A response to Brewin (2016). *Journal of Abnormal Psychology, 125*(7), 1018–1021. doi.org/10.1037/abn0000211

Rubin, D. C., Deffler, S. A., Ogle, C. M., Dowell, N. M., Graesser, A. C., & Beckham, J. C. (2016). Participant, rater, and computer measures of coherence in posttraumatic stress disorder. *Journal of Abnormal Psychology, 125*(1), 11–25. doi.org/10.1037/abn0000126

Saigh, P. A. (1991). The development of posttraumatic stress disorder following four different types of traumatization. *Behaviour Research and Therapy, 29*(3), 213–216. doi.org/10.1016/0005-7967(91)90110-O

Sapolsky, R. M. (1996). Why stress is bad for your brain. *Science, 273*(5276), 749–750. doi:10.1126/science.272.5276.749

Sauce, B., & Matzel, L. D. (2018). The paradox of intelligence: Heritability *and* malleability coexist in hidden gene-environment interplay. *Psychological Bulletin, 144*(1), 26–47. doi.org/10.1037/bul0000131

Schlenger, W. E., Caddell, J. M., Ebert, L., Jordan, B. K., Rourke, K. M., Wilson, D., . . . Kulka, R. A. (2002). Psychological reactions to terrorist attacks: Findings from the National Study of Americans' Reactions to September 11. *Journal of the American Medical Association, 288*(5), 581–588. doi:10.1001/jama.288.5.581

Schmeltzer, S. N., Herman, J. P., & Sah, R. (2016). Neuropeptide Y (NPY) and posttraumatic stress disorder (PTSD): A translational update. *Experimental Neurology, 284*(Part B), 196–210. doi.org/10.1016/j.expneurol.2016.06.020

Schneider, M., & Schwerdtfeger, A. (2020). Autonomic dysfunction in posttraumatic stress disorder indexed by heart rate variability: A meta-analysis. *Psychological Medicine, 50*(12), 1937–1948. doi.org/10.1017/S003329172000207X

Schreiber, F. R. (1973). *Sybil*. Warner Books.

Schultebraucks, K., Shalev, A. Y., Michopoulos, V., Grudzen, C. R., Shin, S.-M., Stevens, J. S., . . . Galatzer-Levy, I. R. (2020). A validated predictive algorithm of post-traumatic stress course following emergency department admission after a traumatic stressor. *Nature Medicine, 26*(7), 1084–1088. doi.org/10.1088/s41591-020-0951-2

Shalev, A. Y., Gevonden, M., Ratanatharathorn, A., Laska, E., van der Mei, W. F., Qi, W., . . . International Consortium to Predict PTSD. (2019). Estimating the risk of PTSD in recent trauma survivors: Results of the International Consortium to Predict PTSD (ICPP). *World Psychiatry, 18*(1), 77–87. doi:10.1002/wps.20608

Shalev, A. Y., Orr, S. P., Peri, T., Schreiber, S., & Pitman, R. K. (1992). Physiologic responses to loud tones in Israeli patients with posttraumatic stress disorder. *Archives of General Psychiatry, 49*(11), 870–875. doi:10.1001/archpsyc.1992.01820110034005

Shalev, A. Y., Orr, S. P., & Pitman, R. K. (1993). Psychophysiological assessment of traumatic imagery in Israeli civilian patients with posttraumatic stress disorder. *American Journal of Psychiatry, 150*(4), 620–624. doi.org/10.1176/ajp.150.4.620

Shalev, A. Y., Peri, T., Canetti, L., & Schreiber, S. (1996). Predictors of PTSD in injured trauma survivors: A prospective study. *American Journal of Psychiatry, 153*(2), 219–225. doi.org/10.1176/ajp.153.2.219

Shallcross, S. L., Arbisi, P. A., Polusny, M. A., Kramer, M. D., & Erbes, C. R. (2016). Social causation versus social erosion: Comparisons of causal models for relations between support and PTSD symptoms. *Journal of Traumatic Stress, 29*(2), 167–175. doi:10.1002/jts.22086

Shatan, C. F. (1973). The grief of soldiers: Vietnam combat veterans' self-help movement. *American Journal of Orthopsychiatry, 43*(4), 640–653. doi.org/10/1111/j.1939-0025.1973.tb00834.x

Shephard, B. (2001). *A war of nerves: Soldiers and psychiatrists in the twentieth century*. Harvard University Press.

Shin, L. M., McNally, R. J., Kosslyn, S. M., Thompson, W. L., Rauch, S. L., Alpert, N. M., . . . Pitman, R. K. (1999). Regional cerebral blood flow during script-driven imagery in childhood sexual abuse-related PTSD: A PET investigation. *American Journal of Psychiatry, 156*(4), 575–584. doi.org/10.1176/ajp.156.4.575

Shin, L. M., Orr, S. P., Carson, M. A., Rauch, S. L., Macklin, M. L., Lasko, N. B., . . . Pitman, R. K. (2004). Regional cerebral blood flow in the amygdala and medial prefrontal cortex during traumatic imagery in male and female Vietnam veterans with PTSD. *Archives of General Psychiatry, 61*(2), 168–176. doi:10.1001/archpsyc.61.2.168

Shin, L. M., Rauch, S. L., & Pitman, R. K. (2005). Structural and functional anatomy of PTSD: Findings from neuroimaging research. In J. J. Vasterling & C. R. Brewin (Eds.),

Neuropsychology of PTSD: Biological, cognitive, and clinical perspectives (pp. 59–82). Guilford.

Shin, L. M., Rauch, S. L., & Pitman, R. K. (2006). Amygdala, medial prefrontal cortex, and hippocampal function in PTSD. Annals of the New York Academy of Sciences, 1071(1), 67–79.

Shin, L. M., Whalen, P. J., Pitman, R. K., Bush, G., Macklin, M. L., Lasko, N. B., . . . Rauch, S. L. (2001). An fMRI study of anterior cingulate function in posttraumatic stress disorder. Biological Psychiatry, 50(12), 932–942. doi.org/10.1016/S0006-3223(01)01215-X

Shin, L. M., Wright, C. I., Cannistraro, P. A., Wedig, M. M., McMullin, K., Martis, B., . . . Rauch, S. L. (2005). A functional magnetic resonance imaging study of amygdala and medial prefrontal cortex responses to overtly presented fearful faces in posttraumatic stress disorder. Archives of General Psychiatry, 62(3), 273–281. doi:10.1001/archpsyc.62.3.273

Sierra, M., & Berrios, G. E. (1998). Depersonalization: Neurobiological perspectives. Biological Psychiatry, 44(9), 898–908. doi.org/10.1016/S0006-3223(98)00015-8

Sierra, M., Medford, N., Wyatt, G., & David, A. S. (2012). Depersonalization disorder and anxiety: A special relationship? Psychiatry Research, 197(3), 123–127. doi.org/10.1016/j.psychres.2011.12.017

Smith, T. C., Ryan, M. A. K., Wingard, D. L., Slymen, D. J., Sallis, J. F., & Kritz-Silverstein, D., for the Millennium Cohort Study Team. (2008). New onset and persistent symptoms of post-traumatic stress disorder self reported after deployment and combat exposures: Prospective population based US military cohort study. BMJ, 336(366), 366–371. doi.org/10.1136/bmj.39430.638241.AE

Solomon, Z., Kotler, M., Shalev, A., & Lin, R. (1989). Delayed onset PTSD among Israeli veterans of the 1982 Lebanon War. Psychiatry, 52(4), 428–436. doi.org/10.1080/00332747.1989.11024467

Solomon, Z., Mikulincer, M., & Jakob, B. R. (1987). Exposure to recurrent combat stress: Combat stress reactions among Israeli soldiers in the Lebanon War. Psychological Medicine, 17(2), 433–440. doi:10.1017/Soo33291700024995

Southwick, S. M., Bonanno, G. A., Masten, A. S., Panter-Brick, C., & Yehuda, R. (2014). Resilience definitions, theory, and challenges: Interdisciplinary perspectives. European Journal of Psychotraumatology, 5(1):25338. doi.org/10.3402/ejpt.v5.25338

Southwick, S. M., Krystal, J. H., Morgan, C. A., Johnson, D., Nagy, L. M., Nicolaou, A., Heninger, G. R., & Charney, D. S. (1993). Abnormal noradrenergic function in posttraumatic stress disorder. Archives of General Psychiatry, 50(4), 266–274. doi:10.1001/archpsyc.1993.01820160036003

Spiegel, D. (1997). Foreword. In D. Spiegel (Ed.), Repressed memories (pp. 5–11). American Psychiatric Press.

Spiegel, D., Loewenstein, R. J., Lewis-Fernandez, R., Sar, V., Simeon, D., Vermetten, E., . . . Dell, P. F. (2011). Dissociative disorders in DSM-5. Depression and Anxiety, 28(12), 824–852. doi.org/10.1002/da.20923

Spitzer, R. L., Williams, J. B. W., & Gibbon, M. (1987). DSM-III-R Axis V: Global assessment of functioning. In Structured clinical interview for DSM-III-R, version NP-R. New York State Psychiatric Institute, Biometrics Research Department.

Starkman, M. N., Giordani, B., Gebarski, S. S., Berent, S., Shork, M. A., & Schteingart, D. E. (1999). Decrease in cortisol reverses human hippocampal atrophy following treatment of Cushing's disease. Biological Psychiatry, 46(12), 1595–1602. doi.org/10.10.16/S0006-3223(99)00203-6

Stein, M. B., Chen, C.-Y., Ursano, R. J., Cai, T., Gelernter, J., . . . Smoller, J. W. for the Army Study to Assess Risk and Resilience in Servicemembers (Army STARRS) Collaborators. (2016). Genome-wide association studies of posttraumatic stress disorder in 2 cohorts of US Army soldiers. JAMA Psychiatry, 73(7), 695–704. doi:10,1001/jamapsychiatry.2016.0350

Stein, M. B., Koverola, C., Hanna, C., Torchia, M. G., & McClarty, B. (1997). Hippocampal volume in women victimized by childhood sexual abuse. Psychological Medicine, 27(4), 951–959. doi:10.1017/S0033291797005242

Stengel, E. (1941). On the aetiology of the fugue states. Journal of Mental Science, 87(369), 572–599. doi.org/10.1192/bjp.87.369.572

Sundin, J., Fear, N. T., Iverson, A., Rona, R. J., & Wessely, S. (2010). PTSD after deployment to Iraq: Conflicting rates, conflicting claims. Psychological Medicine, 40(3), 367–382. doi:10.1017/S0033291709990791

Sutherland, K., & Bryant, R. A. (2005). Self-defining memories in post-traumatic stress disorder. British Journal of Clinical Psychology, 44(4), 591–598. doi.org/10.1348/014466505X64081

Sutherland, K., & Bryant, R. A. (2008). Social problem solving and autobiographical memory in posttraumatic stress disorder. Behaviour Research and Therapy, 46(1), 154–161. doi.org/10.1016/j.brat.2007.10.005

Taylor, A. Jordan, K., Zajac, R., Takarangi, M. K. T., & Garry, M. (2022). Judgments of memory coherence depend on the conditions under which a memory is retrieved, regardless of reported PTSD symptoms. Journal of Applied Research in Memory and Cognition, 9(3), 396–409. doi.org/10/1016/j.jarmac.2020.07.003

Taylor, W. S., & Martin, M. F. (1944). Multiple personality. Journal of Abnormal and Social Psychology, 39(3), 281–300. doi.org/10.1037/h0063634

Tedeschi, R. G., & McNally, R. J. (2011). Can we facilitate posttraumatic growth in combat veterans? American Psychologist, 66(1), 19–24. doi.org/10.1037/a0021896

Thrasher, S. M., Dalgleish, T., & Yule, W. (1994). Information processing in post-traumatic stress disorder. Behaviour Research and Therapy, 32(2), 247–254. doi.org/10.1016/0005-7967(94)90119-8

Tolin, D. F., & Foa, E. B. (2006). Sex differences in trauma and posttraumatic stress disorder: A quantitative review of 25 years of research. Psychological Bulletin, 132(6), 959–992. doi:10.1037/0033-2909.132.6.959

True, W. R., Rice, J., Eisen, S. A., Heath, A. C., Goldberg, J., Lyons, M. J., & & Nowak, J. (1993). A twin study of genetic and environmental contributions to liability for posttraumatic stress symptoms. Archives of General Psychiatry, 50(4), 257–264. doi:10.1001/archpsyc.1993.01820160019002

van der Hart, O., & Nijenhuis, E. R. S. (2009). Dissociative disorders. In P. H. Blaney & T. Millon (Eds.), Oxford textbook of psychopathology, 2nd ed. (pp. 452–481). Oxford University Press.

Weathers, F., Litz, B., Herman, D., Huska, J., & Keane, T. (October 1993). The PTSD Checklist (PCL): Reliability, validity, and diagnostic utility. Paper presented at the Annual Convention of the International Society. Paper presented at the Annual Convention of the International Society for Traumatic Stress Studies, San Antonio, TX.

Williams, J. M. G., Barnhofer, T., Crane, C., Hermans, D., Raes, F., Watkins, E., & Dalgleish, T. (2007). Autobiographical memory specificity and emotional disorder. *Psychological Bulletin, 133*(1), 122–148. doi:10.1037/0033-2909.133.1.122

Williams, J. M. G., Mathews, A., & MacLeod, C. (1996). The emotional Stroop task and psychopathology. *Psychological Bulletin, 120*(1), 3–24. doi.org/10.1037/0033-2909.120.1.3

Woodward, S. H., Kaloupek, D. G., Streeter, C. C., Martinez, C., Schaer, M., & Eliez, S. (2006). Decreased anterior cingulate volume in combat-related PTSD. *Biological Psychiatry, 59*(7), 582–587. doi.org/10.1016/j.biopsych.2005.07.033

Woon, F. L., Sood, S., & Hedges, D. W. (2010). Hippocampal volume deficits associated with exposure to psychological trauma and posttraumatic stress disorder in adults: A meta-analysis. *Progress in Neuro-Psychopharmacology & Biological Psychiatry, 34*(7), 1181–1188. doi.org/10.1016/j.pnpbp.2010.06.016

Yamasue, H., Kasai, K., Iwanami, A., Ohtani, T., Yamada, H., Abe, O., . . . Kato, N. (2003). Voxel-based analysis of MRI reveals anterior cingulate gray-matter volume reduction in posttraumatic stress disorder due to terrorism. *Proceedings of the National Academy of Sciences, 100*(15), 9039–9043. doi.org/10.1073/pnas.1530467100

Yehuda, R. (2002). Post-traumatic stress disorder. *New England Journal of Medicine, 346*(2), 108–114. doi:10.1056/NEJMra012941

Yehuda, R., Southwick, s. M., Nussbaum, G., Wahby, V., Giller, E. L., Jr., & Mason, G. W. (1990). Low urinary cortisol excretion in patients with posttraumatic stress disorder. *Journal of Nervous and Mental Disease, 178*(6), 366–369. doi.org/10.1097/00005053-199006000-00004

Young, A. (1995). *The harmony of illusions: Inventing posttraumatic stress disorder*. Princeton University Press.

# CHAPTER 10

# Mania and Bipolar Spectrum Disorders

June Gruber, Victoria Cosgrove, Alyson Dodd, Sunny J. Dutra, Stephen P. Hinshaw, Stevi G. Ibonie, Piyumi Nimna Kahawage, Thomas D. Meyer, Greg Murray, Robin Nusslock, Kasey Stanton, Cynthia M. Villanueva, *and* Eric A. Youngstrom

When you're high it's tremendous. The ideas and feelings are fast and frequent like shooting stars, and you follow them until you find better and brighter ones. Shyness goes, the right words and gestures are suddenly there, the power to captivate others a felt certainty. . . . The fast ideas are far too fast, and there are far too many; overwhelming confusion replaces clarity. Memory goes. Humor and absorption on friends' faces are replaced by fear and concern.

—*Jamison (2004, p. 67)*

Bipolar disorder (or BD) is a serious and recurrent psychological disorder. As described in the above quote by Kay Redfield Jamison, BD is characterized by episodic and prolonged mood episodes that range between abnormally and persistently elevated mood phases lasting a week or longer (mania) and frequently periods of dysphoria mood (depression) lasting 2 weeks or longer (*DSM-5*). Importantly, BD is associated with significant and dire consequences including occupational, social, and even mortality costs (e.g., Coryell et al., 1993; Dilsaver, 2011; Romans & McPherson, 2002). BD has been associated with significant increases in suicidality and is rated as one of the leading causes of disability worldwide (e.g., Murray & Lopez, 1996; Schaffer et al., 2015). This chapter (a) provides an overview of the phenomenology and assessment of BD; (b) reviews associated psychobiological processes across cognitive, affective, neural, and circadian rhythm dimensions; (c) considers the influence of context and social environment on BD; (d) synthesizes empirically supported interventions to prevent and treat BD; and (e) highlights future directions in the study of BD that focus on increasing diversity and representation of marginalized communities and addressing stigma about BD and related psychiatric disorders.

## Phenomenology and Diagnostic Criteria

In the *DSM-5*, bipolar spectrum disorders (BSDs) refer to a broad umbrella of mood-related difficulties that progress along a spectrum that encompasses varying degrees of depression and mania or hypomania-like severity and duration. This typically includes four categories: bipolar I (BD I, defined by the occurrence of at least one manic episode; bipolar II (BD II), which requires a lifetime combination of a major depressive episode and at least one hypomanic episode; cyclothymic disorder, characterized by hypomanic and depressive symptoms not severe enough to warrant a manic or major depressive label, yet still impairing and often more persistent. The last category, which had been referred to as BD Not

**Abbreviations**
| | |
|---|---|
| BD | Bipolar disorder |
| BSDs | Bipolar spectrum disorders |
| FFT | Family-focused treatment |
| HPS | Hypomanic Personality Scale |
| ICM | Integrative cognitive model (of mood dysregulation) |
| IDAS | Inventory for Depression and Anxiety Symptoms |
| IPSRT | Interpersonal and social rhythm therapy |
| MDQ | Mood Disorder Questionnaire |
| OFC | Orbitofrontal cortex |
| SCN | Suprachiasmatic nucleus |

Otherwise Specified (BD-NOS) is a residual group for cases where there are mood symptoms that are clearly a change from baseline and that are associated with impairment, but which fail to meet strict criteria for one of the other mood disorders.

Both the current *DSM-5* and *ICD* nosologies note that the depressed phases of BSDs have the usual symptoms of unipolar depression and also a lot of anxiety (Youngstrom & Van Meter, 2013). The hypomanic and manic presentations have high energy, rapid speech, and distractibility (shading into flight of idea) that can look similar to attention deficit hyperactivity disorder (ADHD); and the impulsive, goal-directed, rule-breaking behavior can lead to substantial interpersonal conflict and conduct problems. Periods of unusually elated, goofy mood or decreased need for sleep without fatigue (or even with increased energy) are less likely to be the focus of a clinical referral, but are more suggestive of hypomania than irritability alone, for example. The depressive phases of BSDs can have acute or gradual onset (more typical of persistent depressive or cyclothymic presentations) and often have a mix of increased energy and other manic symptoms, appearing as an "agitated depression" with an irritable mood. Hypomania also may be irritable as well as elated or euphoric, as might manic episodes. These, too, can have mixed presentations where anxious or depressive symptoms may be juxtaposed. Some data indicate that mixed presentations are even more common in youth than in later life. Data are inconsistent about whether the first episode is more likely to be a depressive or hypomanic episode (Van Meter, Burke, Youngstrom et al., 2016). The most helpful way to differentiate mood disorders from other issues is if the behaviors are a change from typical functioning, wax and wane, or manifest sometimes without an obvious environmental trigger (Youngstrom et al., 2008).

Epidemiological data indicate that cyclothymic disorder and otherwise specified bipolar and related disorders (OS-BRDs) are three to four times more common than BD I or II (Moreira et al., 2017; A. Van Meter et al., 2019), also consistent with the dimensional statistical models and our emerging understanding of etiology as involving both multiple genes and environmental risk factors. All the BSDs are associated with substantial impairment, and cyclothymia and OS-BRD have high rates of progression to BD I or II. Some data suggest that remission may be possible in a subset of cases, particularly with early and titrated intervention (e.g., Cicero et al., 2009). Other differential diagnoses to consider include all major depression and persistent depressive disorders (which will not have a history of hypomanic or manic episodes), anxiety disorders (which also will not have the hypomanic/manic history, though they may have the motor agitation and poor concentration), oppositional and conduct problems and ADHD (which will tend to be more chronic and less likely to show fluctuations in sleep or energy), and trauma or abuse (which could also be linked with an acute change in functioning). Because comorbidity is common, it is possible to have both BSDs and any of these, and BSDs may be a trigger as well as an outcome of some of these issues (Youngstrom & Algorta, 2014).

## Assessment of Bipolar Disorders

To accurately determine a mood disorder diagnosis requires a longitudinal perspective. Because the course can be intermittent and with different polarities of episode, any single snapshot of clinical presentation provides an incomplete view. Only after gathering a careful developmental history, not just asking about current mood and functioning, but also looking for past episodes, are we ready to proceed with diagnostic formulation. The clinical encounter in which BD is assessed can be divided into four phases: preparation, prediction, prescription, and process/progress, described below.

### PREPARATION

Before first meeting the patient, a psychologist or clinician can prepare to do a rapid yet accurate evaluation by having a good framework in place. This includes having a set of benchmarks for common issues, helping calibrate where BD ranks compared to other presenting problems. Reviews have gathered these across a variety of clinical settings (e.g., Youngstrom et al., 2020). Looking at the clinical prevalence of disorders in outpatient mental health clinics shows that conduct problems, ADHD, depression, and anxiety are the most common problems, with BSDs falling in a tier similar to the prevalence of posttraumatic stress disorder (PTSD) or conduct disorder. These in turn are more common than autistic spectrum or schizophrenia in the child and adolescent population typically coming to general purpose outpatient clinics. Such benchmarks provide a helpful anchor for clinical evaluations and decision-making. Having a rating scale toolkit[1]

---

[1] https://en.wikiversity.org/wiki/Evidence-based_assessment/Bipolar_disorder_in_youth_(assessment_portfolio)

along with semi-structured interview modules gathered ahead of time allows clinicians to rapidly follow up on clues to arrive at a case conceptualization.

### PREDICTION

Several rating scales and checklists are well-suited for screening or rapid information gathering before the first appointment. These could be mailed ahead of time, completed in the waiting room, or even done online with automated scoring. A "core battery" should gather data about common issues (anxiety, depression, trauma, externalizing and attention problems, substance use), ideally from more than one informant's perspective. Less obviously, this is an opportunity to also gather family history (Algorta et al., 2013), and there are free, brief measures to get an indication of pubertal stage. There are more than a dozen scales focused specifically on manic symptoms for youths (Youngstrom et al., 2015), and more than 40 for use with adults (Youngstrom et al., 2018). Free PDFs of these in English, Spanish, and several other languages are available online, and some are available with free administration and scoring guides (https://www.hgaps.org/for-clinicians.html).

### DURING PRESCRIPTION

During the prescription phase, the clinician will review the presenting problem, look at the results from the scales used in the prediction phase, and revise the probabilities attached to our list of hypotheses. They will use the interview to probe for confirming or disconfirming evidence and arrive at a working diagnosis and case formulation. The information-gathering here is in service of coming up with a treatment plan that addresses the key problems and guides our intervention selection to best meet the needs of the patient. Using more structured methods increases reliability and improves detection of comorbidity (Jensen-Doss et al., 2020).

### PROCESS AND PROGRESS

During the next phase, assessment shifts to seeing how treatment is going. Process measures include keeping track of no-shows and short cancellations versus kept visits, whether the patient is doing "homework," and other indicators of engagement. Process measures could also include brief, direct ratings of therapeutic alliance, knowledge acquisition (especially with more psychoeducational modalities), sleep tracking apps, life charts, and mood records. There are a large and growing number of options for tracking whether we are "doing the work" together. Progress measures, in contrast, focus on "is treatment helping?" These measures can include brief symptom checks (e.g., severity ratings on mood charts), short forms of symptom scales, or nomothetic benchmarks for clinically significant change (Freeman & Young, 2020). A plan for long-term monitoring and early detection of relapse would be an excellent component of treatment termination planning, given the high recurrence risk associated with BSDs (Youngstrom et al., 2020).

### Contextualizing Assessment Within Dimensional Frameworks

When diagnosing and assessing BSDs, recent attention has been given to considering alternative and more dimensional approaches to symptom severity and diagnosis. Specifically, decades of research indicate limitations of disorder definitions as described in the *DSM-5*, including poor interrater reliability, high levels of disorder co-occurrence, and within-disorder heterogeneity, among other issues (Kotov et al., 2020). As an example of within-disorder heterogeneity in the context of BSD diagnosis, two individuals could report mutually exclusive histories of specific hypomanic symptoms, but both could be diagnosed with BD II. For instance, the first individual could report a history of expansive mood, grandiosity, decreased need for sleep, and a marked increase in goal-directed activities, whereas the second could report a history of irritable mood, pressured speech, racing thoughts, distractibility, and engagement in risky or dangerous activities, yet both individuals would receive the same diagnostic label. Issues concerning interrater reliability and diagnostic comorbidity complicate treatment planning by making it difficult for clinicians to determine which presenting issues are primary and most impairing (e.g., individuals diagnosed with BD often also meet criteria for substance use disorders, personality disorders, and other disorders). Many *DSM-5* disorder descriptions also remain largely agnostic regarding etiological factors and mechanisms accounting for symptom onset and maintenance. Relatedly, many of these descriptions provide limited consideration of how social and contextual factors influence symptom presentation, symptom course, and treatment.

Accurate BSD diagnosis can be challenging because many individuals with a hypomania/mania history often present for treatment at times when depressed mood, anxiousness, interpersonal difficulties, or other issues are present, rather than when hypomanic/manic symptoms are most prominent. Researchers have raised concerns about BSD underdiagnosis (Carta & Angst, 2016) because hypomania/mania symptom histories may go undetected if clinicians fail to adequately assess for a hypomania/mania history in individuals presenting to treatment for other issues. Measures such as the Mood Disorder Questionnaire (MDQ; Hirschfeld et al., 2000) have become commonly used to retrospectively assess for a hypomania/mania history. Still, many individuals may have difficulty accurately recalling their symptom histories.

Other researchers have cautioned that BSDs are *overdiagnosed* rather than underdiagnosed because some individuals may have symptom histories better accounted for by disorders such as borderline personality disorder (Zimmerman et al., 2019). These issues may arise as a result of the hypomania/mania criteria seemingly overlapping with internalizing (e.g., irritability with anxiety disorders), externalizing (e.g., impulsivity with personality disorders), and psychotic disorders (e.g., grandiose views with schizophrenia). For example, it may be challenging for diagnosticians to determine whether experiences of intense irritability are indicative of BSDs because elevated levels of irritability are listed as a criterion for many disorders and are commonly reported by many individuals seeking treatment irrespective of diagnosis (Stanton et al., 2019).

As a result of these challenges associated with diagnosing BSDs and other disorders from a *DSM*-based perspective, the Hierarchical Taxonomy of Psychopathology (HiTOP; Kotov et al., 2020) has been proposed as an alternative to the *DSM* for improving diagnosis and understanding how various symptom experiences are interconnected. The HiTOP framework adopts a dimensional approach to conceptualizing psychopathology, recognizing that most symptoms are continuous rather than categorical in nature (e.g., experiences of irritability range from minor to very severe rather than present or absent). For example, from the HiTOP perspective, many symptom types defining *DSM-5* depressive, anxiety, and other disorders characterized by experiences of intense and/or persistent negative affect (e.g., sadness, pervasive worry, feelings of guilt) would be classified under a broad internalizing spectrum. The "hierarchical" descriptor for the HiTOP reflects that internalizing also is defined by sub spectra labeled fear and distress. Considering even more nuanced levels of specificity, the fear and distress sub spectra are defined by even more specific symptom dimensions (e.g., trembling, racing heart, and sweating are indicators of fear; worry and sadness are indicators of distress).

As an example illustrating the application of this approach, a clinician using the HiTOP model would identify dysphoric mood dimensionally as indicating distress-based problems associated with internalizing psychopathology (Ruggero et al., 2019); with the *DSM*-based approach, clinicians would seek to determine which *DSM* label or labels (e.g., different depressive disorders, PTSD) best reflect an individual's experiences of dysphoric mood, which can prove challenging. In addition to internalizing, other HiTOP spectra include thought disorder (e.g., positive symptoms of psychosis), antagonistic externalizing (e.g., callousness), disinhibited externalizing (e.g., irresponsibility), and detachment (e.g., aloofness).

Hypomania/mania is provisionally identified as a component of thought disorder due to its phenotypic and genetic overlap with *DSM* disorders such as schizophrenia. However, hypomania/mania (a) also overlaps strongly with the internalizing spectrum and (b) has features that distinguish it from other forms of psychopathology defining thought disorder (e.g., a more episodic course; being linked to reward hypersensitivity; Kotov et al., 2020). Thus, it is possible that some hypomanic/manic dimensions do not align neatly with the existing HiTOP structure and may reflect a hypomania/mania spectrum distinct from other spectra such as internalizing and thought disorder. Most studies examining the classification of hypomania/mania within the HiTOP have focused on composite, diagnostic ratings (i.e., *present* or *not present* ratings) which has precluded examinations of the degree to which different hypomania/mania symptoms converge to define the same spectrum of symptoms (e.g., irritability, but not other hypomania/mania symptoms, may define internalizing). Therefore, future efforts explicating the classification of hypomanic/manic symptom dimensions within comprehensive dimensional models are needed to inform clinical assessment.

### Existing Measures for the Dimensional Assessment

Although research is needed to inform hypomania/mania assessment in the ways described, existing measures are available for dimensionally assessing hypomania/mania in a manner consistent with the HiTOP. For example, the Expanded Version of the Inventory for Depression and Anxiety Symptoms (IDAS-II; Watson et al., 2012) includes Euphoria

(5 items, e.g., "had so much energy") and Mania (5 items, e.g., "thoughts raced") scales that efficiently assess interrelated but distinct hypomania/mania dimensions. The Euphoria scale assessing high-arousal positive emotional experiences may be particularly useful for distinguishing hypomania/mania from overlapping internalizing or personality disorders (Stanton et al., 2019). Other relevant measures include the 48-item Hypomanic Personality Scale (HPS; Eckblad & Chapman, 1986; Schalet, Durbin, & Revelle, 2011), which assesses traits (e.g., excitability, self-perceived charisma) relevant to BD risk. Researchers frequently use HPS total score cutoffs to identify individuals at risk for hypomania/mania. More specific facet scales of Social Vitality (e.g., "persuade and inspire others"), Mood Volatility (e.g., "moods change easily"), and Excitement (e.g., "am a hyper person") also can be scored with the HPS items, with these facet scales appearing to show distinctive correlates in many ways (e.g., Social Vitality associates strongly with measures of social dominance, but Mood Volatility does not; Schalet et al., 2011).

It also should be noted that the HPS is only one example of dimensionally oriented assessment measures, as several other well-validated assessment tools also are available for efficiently assessing BD risk, such as the General Behavior Inventory (GBI; Depue et al., 1989), and current hypomania/mania symptoms in a dimensional manner (see Meyer et al., [2020] for a review).

*Developmental Considerations*

The onset of BD most commonly occurs in childhood or adolescence (Leverich et al., 2007; Perlis et al., 2004). BD in childhood and adolescence often presents with a severe and protracted course, including severe depressive symptomatology, mixed episodes, longer episode durations, psychosis, co-occurring psychopathology (e.g., substance use disorders, anxiety disorders, etc.), and psychosocial adversity (e.g., legal problems, academic impairment) (Birmaher et al., 2006; Cosgrove et al., 2013; Geller et al., 2002; Perlis et al., 2004; Saxena et al., 2020; Yapıcı Eser et al., 2020) compared with adults. More than 50% of adults with BD report onset of illness before age 18, while more than 20% identify age at onset before 13 (Perlis et al., 2004). Symptoms in youth may include dysregulation of emotion, heightened arousal when presented with emotional stimuli, and hypersensitivity to criticism (Peters et al., 2018; Weintraub et al., 2014). Major depressive episodes and cyclothymia are often harbingers of symptoms of mania. About half of all adults with BD I or II report that their first episode was major depression (Lish et al., 1994).

Issues surrounding the commonness of early-onset BD have been contentious in recent decades, associated with dramatic increases in reported community prevalence (Carlson & Glovinsky, 2009; Luby & Navsaria, 2010; Moreno et al., 2007). However, meta-analyses have repeatedly confirmed that rates of BD in youth are not increasing over time and are indeed similar across Western countries (A. R. Van Meter et al., 2011, 2019). While appreciable debate has persisted in recent years (Parry et al., 2018; A. Van Meter et al., 2019) regarding the legitimacy of the diagnosis, longitudinal studies have clearly documented the recurrent course of early-onset BD and its effect on functioning and quality of life (Birmaher et al., 2009; Chang, 2010)). It is clear that without early intervention, the socioemotional and intellectual growth of youth with BD may be jeopardized (Miklowitz, Schneck et al., 2020).

Among youth who have a parent with BD I or BD II, clinical presentation is often subthreshold, with some symptoms emerging many years prior to the onset of threshold BD (Shaw et al., 2005). Subthreshold symptomatology, in conjunction with a family history of BD, exacerbates child or adolescent vulnerability for progression to BD I or II unless interrupted by pharmacological and/or psychosocial intervention (West & Pavuluri, 2009). Risk of conversion from BD-NOS to BD I or II during a 4-year follow-up is substantial (i.e., 58%) for youth with a family history, compared to 32% for youth with no family history. BD in youth results from a complex interplay of genetic vulnerability, individual personality, and characteristics of a youth's family environment. For example, emotional dysregulation may intensify conflict within families and raise levels of expressed emotion in caregivers (i.e., high criticism, hostility, negative communication cycles), which can in turn exacerbate symptomatology in youth with BD (Miklowitz, Wisniewski et al., 2005). Adolescents with BD in low-conflict families experience more rapid symptom improvement during treatment than do those from high-conflict families (Sullivan et al., 2012; Sullivan & Miklowitz, 2010). In one seminal study, adolescents with BD from families high in expressed emotion showed longer times to symptom remission and were more symptomatic during a 12-month follow-up period than those from families low in expressed emotion (Miklowitz et al., 2013). Such impairments have been proposed to be associated with deficits in social cognition (Keenan-Miller et al., 2012), with potential downstream implications for the development and maintenance of important peer relationships.

Adolescents with BD who experience chronic stress in family, peer, or romantic relationships tend to experience poorer symptomatic outcomes than those with lower levels of chronic stress (Kim et al., 2007). Although exposure to stressful environments is a risk factor for mood disorders, less is known about how adolescents with BD respond to stress. In both healthy and clinical samples of youth, responses to stress (i.e., active problem-solving and acceptance) have been found to be associated with positive mental health outcomes and academic and social competence (Compas et al., 2001).

## Relevant Psychobiological Processes

In this section, we review relevant cognitive, emotional, neural, and circadian rhythm processes that are relevant to the onset, course, and profile of BSD.

### Cognitive Processes

Aaron Beck's seminal cognitive model of emotional disorders (see Beck & Haigh, 2014, for a review) was one of the first theoretical frameworks to place cognitive styles (e.g., beliefs, ways of interpreting experiences) as central to the development and maintenance of psychopathology. Specifically, negative beliefs about the self, world, and others were linked to depression. This includes *dysfunctional assumptions*, which are negative "if-then" beliefs (e.g., "If I fail, then I am useless"). These can shape the way that someone with depression thinks about everyday situations and interacts with the world. As depressed mood is a common experience among people with BD, psychologists postulate that negative dysfunctional attitudes may also play a role in BD.

But what about mania (i.e., a diagnosis of BD)? This was traditionally viewed as "opposite" to depression (*bi*-polar). As such, mania has been theoretically linked to overly *positive* cognitive styles. For example, people with BD who had a higher "sense of hyper-positive self," characterized by excessive confidence and productivity, were more likely to relapse even after receiving cognitive therapy—potentially because they viewed the emerging symptoms of a (hypo)manic episode as desirable and due to their own positive attributes (Lam, Wright, & Sham, 2005). Heightened goal attainment beliefs (e.g., believing you need to be "outstanding") have been associated with current manic symptoms (Atuk & Richardson, 2020). In line with this, a body of work has focused on *goal dysregulation* and BD. This theory postulates that the behavioral activation system (BAS), which controls reward responsivity, is overly sensitive in BD. This oversensitivity means that people with BD find it difficult to regulate response to reward and goal-related events. Goal-relevant cognitive styles, including extreme aspirations for the future (particularly popular fame and financial success) and greater expectation of success, have been linked to BD (Johnson, Carver et al., 2012; Johnson et al., 2017).

Taken together, results suggest that both negative and positive cognitive styles are implicated in BD. Cognitive models of BD need to address the experience of mood fluctuation (highs and lows) that are part of BD. Cognitive theories of BD further suggest that the symptoms of BD manifest from making self-referent interpretations (or *internal* appraisals) of the mood changes linked to disrupted sleep (Jones et al., 2006). These appraisals can be negative (e.g., interpreting low mood as indicating failure) or positive (e.g., interpreting heightened mood and increased energy as indicating success and productivity). These themes overlap with dysfunctional attitudes (negative appraisals) and goal-relevant cognitions (positive appraisals). For example, if someone experienced increased energy and alertness after disrupted sleep and interpreted this experience as evidence of their own strengths (e.g., "I am full of good ideas and others are too slow"), they might then start to do more and sleep less, prompting an escalation of manic symptoms. There is evidence that internal appraisals are elevated in people with BD and relate to mood symptoms (Banks et al., 2016; Jones et al., 2006).

Building on these findings, the *integrative cognitive model* (ICM) of mood dysregulation (Mansell et al., 2007) proposed that positive and negative appraisals of internal experiences are central to the mood dysregulation characteristic of BD. In the ICM, these appraisals of changes to internal state are extreme, with personally significant meaning (e.g., "I have the energy to do anything I want"). To address the mood fluctuations seen in BD, the ICM contends that appraisals of high mood are not always positive, and appraisals of low mood may not necessarily be negative—in fact, those vulnerable to mood fluctuation have multiple, conflicting appraisals of how they are feeling. For example, high energy could be interpreted positively, with excessive expectations of goal attainment and success, self-confidence, and optimism. However, the same internal state could also be appraised negatively, such as feeling the need to make excessive effort to avoid failure or taking a self-critical or catastrophic perspective (e.g., losing control). These beliefs are elevated in BD compared to both nonclinical and clinical controls and associated with mood symptoms (Dodd et al., 2011; Kelly et al., 2017). However, there is limited research on extreme appraisals of low mood derived from the ICM, especially around more positive appraisals of these experiences.

## ATTENTION AND MEMORY

We have already seen that how people interpret their experience is important—but how do they come to notice certain aspects of their surroundings and situation in the first place? As with cognitive styles, do people with BD tend to notice particularly negative and positive aspects of their environment over more neutral aspects? Research findings are mixed and may depend on the context in which attention biases are measured as well as the current mood or clinical state of the BD participant. For example, some research indicates that people with BD who were not currently manic or depressed were no more drawn to positive or negative emotional stimuli than nonclinical controls (Purcell et al., 2018). However, another study of young adults at risk for developing BD did demonstrate an attentional bias for positive emotional stimuli (e.g., Gruber et al. 2021). It may be that there is an attentional bias to reward-relevant stimuli (Mason et al., 2016), and attentional biases may be present only during mood episodes (e.g., processing positive information faster when manic) but not a characteristic of BD more generally (Garcia-Blanco et al., 2013).

With respect to emotional memory, there is some evidence that people with BD have difficulties remembering both personal experiences and external events across childhood, adolescence, and adulthood (Bozikas et al., 2019). These deficits in episodic memory have been replicated across studies alongside impaired working memory—and there is some evidence that these difficulties are pronounced in more severe manifestations of BD (Cotrena et al., 2020). Furthermore, there is evidence that people with BD recall emotional stimuli more than do nonclinical controls (Fijtman et al., 2020). Linked to biases in attention and memory, vivid and highly emotive mental imagery may play a role in the mood dysregulation seen in BD. Rich, personally relevant images of the future could directly amplify mood or indirectly amplify mood by influencing thoughts and behavior, particularly in the context of goals and reward (Ivins et al., 2014; Di Simplicio et al., 2016).

In sum, the interplay between *negative* cognitive processes and overly *positive* cognitive processes is a defining feature of BD. The cognitive processes outlined here are not mutually exclusive. In fact, these processes are often studied together (e.g., Fletcher et al., 2014). In cognitive models of BD, appraisals of *current* affect are influenced by underlying beliefs about the self, world, and others which can be considered analogous to the dysfunctional attitudes outlined by Aaron Beck for depression. Cognitive styles are linked to cognitive emotion regulation strategies, which can amplify or dampen affect. Much in the same way as thoughts, personally meaningful, overly positive or negative mental imagery may prompt cognitive and behavioral responses that exacerbate mood symptoms. Goal-relevant appraisals could prompt increased goal-directed activity and sleeping less, which could in turn destabilize circadian rhythms and the BAS, intensifying the cycle of mood instability. Overall, there are multiple cognitive processes linked to BD, with a particular emphasis on how individuals appraise and respond to their experiences.

### Emotional Processes

BD is centrally a disorder of emotion. Emotional processes in BSD have been characterized by heightened and persistent positive emotion *reactivity*, difficulty with positive and negative *emotion regulation*, and altered *emotional understanding* or perceptions of others people's emotions. With respect to emotion reactivity, prior work suggests that BSDs are associated with increased positive emotion reactivity that appears to persist across different types of emotional and nonemotional contexts (e.g., Gruber, 2011; Gruber et al., 2019). Specifically, individuals diagnosed with a clinical history of BD by a trained interviewer or who are at self-reported risk for future BD onset self-report greater positive feelings in response to a variety of laboratory stimuli, including short film clips, static pictures or images, and also monetary reward and positive feedback (e.g., Gruber et al., 2008; Gruber, 2011; Johnson, 2007; M'Bailara et al., 2009). In addition, young adults at self-reported risk for BD as well as adults with a *DSM* diagnosis of BD I have been found to exhibit elevated levels of parasympathetic activity (as measured via respiratory sinus arrhythmia, for example) in laboratory studies while watching emotional film clips, interpreted as a physiological correlate of positive mood (Gruber et al., 2008; Gruber, Harvey, & Purcell, 2011). Some neuroimaging studies further suggest that people with BSDs exhibit greater neural reactivity in reward-related brain regions (such as the ventral striatum) and networks in response to rewarding stimuli (e.g., Dutra et al., 2015; Nusslock et al., 2011). More detail on neural processes in BSDs are described further below.

With respect to emotion regulation, it has been defined as the processes individuals engage to influence the intensity, duration, display, and type of emotions experienced, and these can occur consciously or automatically (e.g., Gross, 2015); research suggests that individuals with BSDs demonstrate difficulties with emotion regulation in the laboratory and everyday life when spontaneously (or naturalistically) regulating their emotions. Specifically, BD adults who are not currently manic or depressed (i.e., inter-episode) report less success effectively regulating their momentary emotions in everyday life using a 1-week experience-sampling period (e.g., Gruber et al., 2013). In the laboratory, inter-episode BD adults self-report more trouble successfully regulating the intensity of the emotions they experienced in response to watching brief, standardized positive and negative emotionally evocative film clips (Gruber, Harvey, & Gross, 2012). Furthermore, when asked which emotion regulation strategies they tend to utilize in their daily lives, inter-episode BD adults also report using emotion regulation strategies (such as rumination) that amplify mood states and impede problem-solving (e.g., Dodd et al., 2019; Gruber et al., 2011, 2012). This suggests that although BSD individuals might employ effort in regulating emotions but may ultimately use strategies that are less successful in managing intense mood states.

Despite these clear difficulties regulating emotions in BD, when inter-episode BD adults are instructed to follow specific regulation strategies in the laboratory, they demonstrate an intact ability to successfully decrease emotion intensity across a variety of strategies, including cognitive reappraisal, mindfulness, and cognitive distancing techniques (e.g., Gilbert et al., 2014; Gruber et al., 2009, 2012). Inter-episode adults with BD also successfully select or choose regulation strategies that match the context in a manner like healthy controls (Hay et al., 2015). Taken together, this suggests that BD individuals nonetheless have an intact ability to regulate their emotions successfully despite experiencing difficulties on their own in the lab and in daily life. The latter finding suggests important avenues for psychological therapies focused on assisting BD individuals in implementing these strategies successfully on their own.

Finally, when examining emotional understanding (or perception) in BD, research indicates that those with a BD diagnosis or subclinical BD risk or symptoms may have an inaccurate perception of other people's feelings. This bias in perceiving others' emotions has been found among young adults at risk for BD who self-report overestimating another person's positive emotions when they are describing a personal and negative life event in a brief film (e.g., Devlin et al., 2016) or during a difficult conversation with a romantic partner (Dutra et al., 2014). Other research suggests that BD adults who are currently manic may also be less accurate in detecting negative facial expressions (e.g., Lembke & Ketter, 2002). Further work is needed to understand whether those with BD may exhibit a positive bias toward perceiving the social world and identify putative underlying neural and related mechanisms.

### Neural Processes

BD is characterized by alterations in brain systems that help us process threatening and rewarding stimuli in our environment, regulate our emotions, and consolidate memories. For example, individuals with BD display structural and functional alterations in the amygdala, a brain region implicated in processing threatening stimuli in the environment (Foland-Ross et al., 2012; Lopez-Jaramillo et al., 2017). Studies of neural connectivity, which examine the relations between brain regions, indicate that BD also is associated with structural and functional alterations in the coupling between the prefrontal cortex and the amygdala (Manelis et al., 2021; Phillips et al., 2008). This suggests that individuals with BD may have difficulty attenuating or regulating amygdala reactivity in the face of stressors, which also is consistent with behavioral, clinical, and self-report data. Finally, BD is associated with deficits in portions of the prefrontal cortex and the hippocampus important for executive control (e.g., behavioral inhibition, goal-directed behaviors, attention) and working memory (Phillips & Vieta, 2007).

Intriguingly, other psychiatric disorders show similar alterations in these brain systems. A heightened sensitivity to threatening stimuli and deficits in executive control and working memory are present in major depression (Hamilton et al., 2012) and anxiety disorders (Etkin & Wager, 2007; Shackman & Fox, 2016), and schizophrenia is associated with abnormalities in both the prefrontal cortex (Radhu, et al., 2015; Selemon & Zecevic, 2015) and the hippocampus (Kalmady, et al., 2017; Smeland, et al., 2018). Such findings are helpful in identifying risk factors that cut across or are common to multiple psychiatric disorders. This work also can help break down potentially arbitrary distinctions between categorically defined psychiatric disorders and account for comorbidity among *DSM-5* categories. In addition to identifying risk factors that are common across disorders, initiatives such as HiTOP and the Research Domain Criteria (RDoC) also aim to identify mechanisms that are unique to specific psychiatric disorders and symptoms and that reflect signatures of differential risk for these symptom profiles. This is important for understanding and unpacking the within-disorder heterogeneity discussed above and for identifying clinically meaningful subtypes. We suggest that brain systems that help identify, pursue, and process rewards are important.

Although many regions in the brain respond to rewards, a cortico-striatal neural circuit involving the ventral striatum and orbitofrontal cortex (OFC) are at the heart of the reward system (Berridge, 2019; Haber & Knutson, 2010). Activation of this circuit is typically associated with positive or rewarding emotions and a desire to pursue rewards or goals in the environment, whereas deactivation leads to lower motivation and emotions such as sadness and anhedonia. Individuals with high levels of activity and connectivity in this circuit tend to be highly responsive to rewards in their environment and have heightened motivation to pursue these rewards and goals (Hahn et al., 2009; Simon et al., 2010).

As mentioned earlier, there is growing evidence that individuals with and at risk for BD display heightened sensitivity to rewarding stimuli and an increased motivation toward rewards and goals (e.g., Johnson et al., 2005, 2015; Nusslock & Alloy, 2017). This hypersensitivity to reward can lead to an excessive increase in motivation (e.g., working excessively long hours) during life events involving the pursuit or attainment of rewards, which, in the extreme, is reflected in hypomanic or manic symptoms or episodes. It also can lead to an excessive decrease in such motivation and reductions in goal-directed behaviors in response to losses or failures to attain a desired reward, which is reflected in bipolar depression. In line with this model, individuals with and at risk for BD display a heightened sensitivity to rewards on self-report, behavioral, and neurophysiological measures (Alloy, Bender et al., 2012; Gruber & Johnson, 2009; Harmon-Jones, et al., 2008; Johnson et al., 2017). A heightened sensitivity to rewards also predicts first onset and recurrences of BSDs (Alloy, Bender et al., 2012) and progression to more severe BD diagnoses (e.g., BD I) among individuals with milder variants of the disorder (e.g., BD II, cyclothymia) (Alloy, Urosevic et al., 2012; Nusslock, Harmon-Jones et al., 2012).

Functional magnetic resonance imaging (fMRI) studies provide partial support for elevated reward-related brain function in manic and euthymic (i.e., not currently manic, depressed or mixed) individuals with BD. These individuals display elevated activation in the ventral striatum (Hassel et al., 2008; Lawrence et al., 2004), OFC (Elliott et al., 2004), and amygdala (Bermpohl et al., 2009) to pictures of happy faces and pleasant stimuli compared to healthy controls (although see Liu et al., 2012, for evidence of decreased striatal and OFC activation in bipolar individuals to happy vs. neutral faces). A number of studies also report that individuals with BD display elevated OFC and ventral striatal activation to both monetary and social reward cues during manic and euthymic episodes (e.g., Abler et al., 2008; Bermpohl et al., 2010; Dutra et al., 2015; Nusslock, Almeida et al., 2012), although other studies have not observed this effect (Johnson et al., 2019; Trost et al., 2014; Yip et al., 2015). Finally, individuals with a diagnosis of BD II and individuals at elevated risk for BD who have not yet developed the disorder (i.e., hypomanic temperament) display elevated OFC and ventral striatal activation to reward cues (Caseras et al., 2013; Harada et al., 2019). This suggests that heightened reward-related brain function may reflect a preexisting risk factor for BD, as opposed to a consequence of the illness.

In contrast, a blunted sensitivity to rewarding stimuli, reduced motivation toward rewards and goals, and low positive affect have long been considered hallmarks of risk for unipolar depression (without a history of hypomania or mania) (see Nusslock & Alloy, 2017, for review). Individuals with major depressive disorder and at-risk offspring of depressed parents report a lower sensitivity to rewards and greater anhedonia (Kasch et al., 2002; Kazdin, 1989; Luby et al., 2004) and are less responsive to both the anticipation and receipt of rewards on neural and behavioral indices (Forbes et al., 2009; Olino et al., 2010; Pizzagalli et al., 2008; Ng et al.,

2019). In prospective studies, a low sensitivity to reward assessed with behavioral tasks, neurophysiology, and brain imaging predicts later depressive symptoms and episodes (Bress et al., 2013; Forbes et al., 2007; Morgan et al., 2013; Nelson et al., 2016; Nusslock et al., 2011). Furthermore, other conditions such as ADHD (Volkow et al., 2009) and schizophrenia (Smucny et al., 2021) are associated with a blunted neuronal response to rewards, which, in the case of schizophrenia, is likely implicated in the negative symptoms or motivational deficits of the illness (Whitton et al., 2015). Taken together, this suggests that BD is characterized by a profile of heightened reward-related brain function that distinguishes it from other psychiatric disorders including depression, schizophrenia, and ADHD. We propose that what differentiates BD from other psychiatric illnesses is mania, and one of the primary risk factors for mania involves a propensity to experience abnormally elevated energy and motivation. Thus, reward-related brain systems are clearly important for understanding what distinguishes BD from other disorders, whereas threat, executive control, and working memory processes may be more relevant for understanding what is common or transdiagnostic across these illnesses.

## Circadian Rhythms and Sleep Processes

There is growing interest in sleep and circadian pathways in the pathogenesis of BD, with numerous reviews drawing together heterogeneous circumstantial evidence for cross-sectional, prospective, and causal links (e.g., Logan & McClung, 2019; McCarthy, 2016; Murray 2019; Takaesu, 2018). This brief section will outline evidence for circadian and sleep parameters as elements in the web of mechanistic pathways underpinning BD. Following some background about the structure, function, and measurement of circadian and sleep-wake systems, evidence for circadian mechanisms is critically introduced (focusing on genetic and behavioral levels of analysis).

### STRUCTURE AND FUNCTION OF THE CIRCADIAN SYSTEM

Human biology is rhythmic. A complex network of biological clocks—the circadian system—coordinates this "predictive homeostasis," adapted to optimize fitness in the context of Earth's 24-hour light–dark cycle. The molecular basis of the circadian system is well characterized: intrinsic 24-hour rhythmicity is coordinated through clock genes that are responsible for generating circadian rhythms in physiology, behavior, and cognition (Mohawk et al., 2012). Example 24-hour rhythms with a known circadian component include core body temperature (nadir around 4:00 AM), melatonin secretion (commences around 9:00 PM), and alertness (peaking around 10:00 AM) (Refinetti, 2006). The master oscillator of the human circadian system is in the suprachiasmatic nucleus (SCN), a small structure with cells operating autonomously and as part of a network. A critical feature of the circadian system is its sensitivity to environmental cues, which adapts the system to be entrained daily to shifting times of sunrise and sunset (Reppert & Weaver, 2002). The sleep-wake cycle is sometimes described as the most obvious circadian rhythm in humans, but circadian function has a complex relationship with the sleep-wake cycle. Borbély's two-process model of sleep regulation (Borbély, 1980; Borbély et al., 2016) proposes that the circadian system regulates sleep timing and architecture in a bidirectional interaction with sleep homeostasis. Sleep homeostasis increases with wake time and dissipates with sleep, while the circadian system sends alerting signals during the day which decrease at night. Optimally, these two processes work together to promote wakefulness during the day and sleep at night (Fuller et al., 2006).

Importantly, growing evidence links circadian function to BD. At the genetic level, animal studies have been informative because core circadian genes (i.e., CLOCK genes) are strongly conserved across evolution. The *Clock*Δ19 mutant mouse, for example, provides a well-characterized animal model of mania, exhibiting increased dopamine transmission, hyperactivity, increased reward-seeking and impulsivity-like behaviors, and reduced depressive-like behavior. Intriguingly, these abnormalities are partly reversible by lithium (Dzirasa et al., 2010; Mukherjee et al., 2010; Roybal et al., 2007). *Clock*Δ19 mice encode a dominant-negative CLOCK protein, causing arrhythmic behavior under constant darkness and reduced amplitude, long period, and delayed phase under a light–dark cycle (Vitaterna et al., 1994). In human candidate gene studies, common polymorphisms in CLOCK have generally, but not universally, been found to associate with BD and related phenotypes (Benedetti et al., 2003, 2007; Lee et al., 2010; Soria et al., 2010).

Given the broad acceptance of chronobiologically informed behavioral interventions for BD (Gottlieb et al., 2019), it is not surprising that numerous studies have used behavioral methods to explore the possibility of chronobiological correlates of observable behavior. The most-studied behavioral variables are those derived from actigraphy-based measurement of locomotor activity and self-reported chronotype (Murray et al., 2020). Lower 24-hour activity compared to healthy populations has been found in people with BD (De Crescenzo et al., 2017; Scott et al., 2017; Shou et al., 2017), and people with BD also appear to have less robust (Jones et al., 2005; Rock et al., 2014), more unstable (Krane-Gartiser et al., 2016), and phase-advanced 24-hour activity rhythms (Salvatore et al., 2008). In people with BD, differences across the phases of the illness can also be observed. The manic phase of BD appears to be characterized by more disorganized and complex patterns of activity, particularly in the morning, whereas the depressive phase of BD appears to be characterized by higher minute-to-minute variability (Krane-Gartiser et al., 2014). On average, euthymic BD individuals report being of evening chronotype and exhibit delayed physiological measures of circadian phase (Kanagarajan et al., 2018; Melo et al., 2017; Nurnberger et al., 2000). For example, a review by Melo et al. (2017) identified 15 studies using the Composite Scale of Morningness, most of which found BD to be associated with eveningness. This association with self-reported eveningness chronotype has been corroborated in actigraphically measured chronotype (Gershon et al., 2018).

Consistent with emerging dimensional approaches to psychopathology (e.g., HiTOP, see above), circadian vulnerability is probably not specific to BD. A recent international task force review highlights that circadian abnormalities are present in the phenotypes of various psychiatric disorders, with evidence strongest for BD, major depression, and schizophrenia (McCarthy et al., 2021). For example, polygenic scores in genome-wide association studies (GWAS) for morningness (the trait of preferring activities to commence relatively earlier in the day) are negatively associated with presence of all three of these disorders (Hu et al., 2016; Jones et al., 2019; Lane et al., 2016), while polygenic scores for low amplitude are associated with BD as well as the general vulnerability trait of neuroticism (Ferguson et al., 2018; Lyall et al., 2018). In cell lines and postmortem brain, miRNAs-29a/c and 106b have been linked to the circadian clock and have been independently linked to BD as well as to major depression and schizophrenia (Geaghan & Cairns, 2015). In sum, there is great interest in the chronobiology of BD, and there is a broad range of evidence pointing to an array of circadian abnormalities that may be important in the pathogenesis of BD.

## Context and Social Environment Influences

In recent years researchers have begun to better understand how and why the social environment is important in BSDs. We review the literature on social functioning and life events in BD to better appreciate the real-world and social contexts individuals with BD face and its influence on symptom presentation and course.

### Social Context and Functioning

A large body of work has documented associations between BSDs and lower social functioning and social support (Johnson et al., 1999; Castanho de Almeida Rocca et al., 2008) as well as increased social conflicts (Romans & McPhearson, 1992). People with a diagnosis of BD self-report having less contact with friends compared to both people with major depressive disorder and nonpsychiatric controls (Johnson et al., 1999). In one qualitative study, Michalak and colleagues (2006) reported that many individuals with a diagnosis of BD noted that they had lost friendships and social connections due to their illness, especially during manic or hypomanic episodes. Furthermore, lower social support was a significant risk factor for lifetime recurrence of mood episodes in BD (Cohen et al., 2004). At the same time, early clinical observations among individuals with BD suggests increased social interest and motivation among adults with BD (Goodwin & Jamison, 2007). Furthermore, Ong, Zaki, and Gruber (2017) found individuals with BD who were currently interepisode also were more cooperative on a standardized computer task compared to those with a history of major depression as well as those without a psychiatric history. Taken together, this suggests that, despite some work highlighting increased social interest and cooperative behavior, social functioning and quality of social relationships is frequently impaired among adults diagnosed with BD.

### Life Events and Context

Both positive and negative life events have been found to predict the course of BD, generally with negative, stressful, and traumatic life events predicting a more severe and impairing course of the disorder broadly (Agnew-Blais & Danese, 2016; Daruy-Filhod et al., 2011; Koenders et al., 2014; Lex et al., 2017) and with positive and goal attainment life events predicting manic episodes (Alloy et al., 2008; 2009; Johnson et al., 2000, 2008).

Negative and stressful life events play an important role in the onset and course of BD. Research in this area has examined adverse events that occur early in life prior to the onset of the disorder, and those that occur after onset in relation to the timing of subsequent mood episodes. Many empirical studies and reviews and meta-analyses of these investigations have consistently found that childhood maltreatment is associated with a more severe course of illness for those with BD (Agnew-Blais & Danese, 2016; Daruy-Filhod et al., 2011; Garno et al., 2005; Leverich & Post, 2006; Sala et al., 2014). For example, Daruy-Filho and colleagues (2011) found that childhood maltreatment was strongly associated with early onset, substance abuse, and suicidality among those with BD. A more recent meta-analysis of 30 studies compared individuals with BD and childhood maltreatment (abuse, neglect, or family conflict) to those with BD without childhood maltreatment (Agnew-Blais & Danese, 2016). Results indicated that those with histories of childhood maltreatment had more severe and more frequent episodes of mania and depression, more severe psychosis, higher risk of suicide attempts, and higher risk of comorbid diagnoses including PTSD, anxiety disorders, and substance use disorders.

Stressful life events occurring after disorder onset have also been associated with more frequent and severe mood episodes. Lex et al. (2017) reported that stressful life events occurred more frequently preceding acute mood episodes compared to euthymic periods. A prospective study that followed hospitalized individuals with BD prospectively for at least 1 year found that those who experienced severe negative life events took more than three times as long to achieve recovery (defined as minimal or absent symptoms for 2 consecutive months) compared to those without severe life events (Johnson & Miller, 1997). Similarly, in a study of BD outpatients assessed quarterly for 2 years, negative life events were associated with the subsequent severity of both mania and depression, as well as with higher levels of functional impairment (Koenders et al., 2014). These data suggest that stressful life events are associated with a more severe course of BSDs.

Positive life events have also been consistently found to predict subsequent increases in mania symptoms, though the boundary conditions around which types of events are most associated with mania onset and how these should best be conceptualized are slightly less clear. One line of work in BD has focused on life events involving goal striving or attainment, based on prior evidence discussed above that those with BD self-report greater levels of ambitious goal setting and striving (Alloy, Bender et al., 2012; Gruber & Johnson, 2009; Johnson, 2005; Johnson, Eisner, & Carver, 2010). For example, Johnson and colleagues (2000) followed individuals with BD I monthly over a 2-year period and found that mania symptoms increased in the 2 months following events involving goal attainment. Notably, there was no relationship between goal attainment events and subsequent symptoms of depression. In a larger prospective study, Johnson and colleagues (2008) found that goal attainment life events predicted increases in mania symptoms. More recently, Tharp et al. (2016) found that when BD I individuals were asked to describe their goals in a laboratory session, the goals described by the BD group were objectively rated as more difficult to achieve compared to healthy control participants, and these ambitious goals among the BD participants were found to predict increased mania over time. These findings are consistent with work described earlier in this chapter suggesting that BSDs involve greater sensitivity to reward and goal striving and attainment events, which may predispose BSD individuals toward increased mania and hypomania symptoms (Alloy et al., 2009; Bender et al., 2010; Urošević et al., 2010).

Taken together, this research demonstrates a clear relationship between life events and the subsequent course and severity of BD. Negative and potentially traumatic life events appear to portend shorter time to onset of new symptoms, more severe symptoms, and higher rates of comorbidity broadly. Positive events, particularly those related to goal attainment and/or engagement of the BAS system, are associated with increases in mania symptoms prospectively. With these patterns established, researchers have largely turned toward better understanding the neuroanatomical and neurochemical correlates of these relations (e.g., Hanford et al., 2019; Sato et al., 2018) and to identifying risk and protective factors that may serve to moderate the relations between life events and illness course (e.g., Chan & Tse, 2018; Ng et al., 2016; Stange et al., 2012, 2013).

## Psychotherapy and Prevention

Compared to other mental health problems such as anxiety or unipolar depression, research on the effectiveness of psychosocial treatments in the context of BD is still young and only recently was expanded upon in the 1990s. The need for psychological treatments has been made apparent by findings that BD patients, even when treated pharmacologically, report subsyndromal symptoms, functional impairments in everyday life, and recurrent mood episodes (e.g., Goldberg & Harrow, 2011; Treuer & Tohen, 2010). Psychological approaches evaluated in sufficiently statistically powered randomized controlled trials (RCTs) can be grouped into four classes: psychoeducation, interpersonal and social rhythm therapy (IPSRT), cognitive-behavioral therapy (CBT), and family and conjoint interventions.

*Psychoeducation* refers to an interactive therapeutic situation in which patients and/or relatives discuss with a mental health professional the disorder, its causes and course, and treatment options that integrate and build on the individual experiences of the patient (and sometimes their loved ones). Psychoeducation has also been widely evaluated as a stand-alone intervention, within both individual and group settings (e.g., Candini et al., 2013; Colom et al., 2003; Perry et al., 1999). Colom and colleagues (2003, 2009) were able to demonstrate that their 21-session program had protective effects against recurrence of mood episodes for as long as 5 years. Additionally, the feasibility of effectively delivering psychoeducation within community mental health teams was assessed. It was evidenced that, while there was a nonsignificant advantage of psychoeducation with regards to recurrence risk, psychoeducation significantly increased social and occupational functioning (i.e., Lobban et al., 2010). At this point, psychoeducation has shown to be beneficial as a stand-alone intervention; however, all the previously described approaches consider psychoeducation as an integral part of psychological therapy for BD.

IPSRT (Frank, 2005) integrates interpersonal therapy (Klerman et al., 1984) with therapeutic strategies aimed at stabilizing circadian and social rhythms (Frank, 2005); it is rooted in the social *zeitgeber* model (Ehlers et al., 1988). IPSRT postulates three core mechanisms to reduce symptoms: medication adherence, stable social rhythms and daily routines, and improved interpersonal functioning. Frank and colleagues (1999, 2005) were able to illustrate that acutely symptomatic patients with BD who had received IPSRT in the acute phase had less recurrences over time than those who had received an intense clinical management, regardless of what treatment they were assigned to during the maintenance phase of their treatment. Additionally, IPSRT was considered for use as a stand-alone therapy under specific circumstances (Swartz et al., 2018). For depressed patients with BD II, they were able to provide equivalent effectiveness of IPSRT to quetiapine with regards to the outcome, and differences were only noted in the time to response and side-effect profile.

CBT, originally developed for unipolar depression (Beck, 1991), was also adapted for BD, and several manuals have been published on this treatment option (e.g., Lam et al., 2010; Meyer & Hautzinger, 2013; Newman et al., 2002). A case formulation from a CBT perspective interprets manic and depressive symptoms reflecting dysfunctional changes in behavior, thoughts, and emotions. The likelihood of recurrent mood episodes is therefore hypothesized to be achieved by targeting underlying dysfunctional attitudes, beliefs, behavioral habits, and cognitive errors (e.g., all-or-nothing thinking, overgeneralizations) in therapy. While research has shown that patients with BD show similar cognitions as depressed patients, a few are more specifically related to (hypo)mania (e.g., Johnson, Carver, & Gotlib, 2012; Lex et al., 2011; Shapero, et al., 2015; van der Gucht et al., 2009). Traditionally, CBT works toward a shared case formulation of individual problem areas and treatment goals based on psychoeducation and the derived individual relapse signature, which includes, for example, prior course of the disorder, early warning symptoms of mood episodes, and identified triggers (e.g., life events, interpersonal conflicts, changes in daily routines). The case conceptualization will inform what behavioral and cognitive strategies might be most helpful to cope with future emerging mood symptoms. Tailored to the individual, modules focus on problem-solving, communication skills, or stress reduction strategies, if there is indication that such additional skills will be beneficial to prevent the development or maintenance of mood symptoms. More recently, the focus of CBT has shifted from focusing primarily on reducing symptoms and preventing recurrence to highlighting individual recovery (e.g., Jones et al. 2015; Murray et al., 2017) and incorporating techniques related to mindfulness and acceptance (e.g., Williams et al., 2008).

Several studies have compared outcomes between individuals receiving CBT and individuals in no therapy (waiting list), treatment-as-usual, and supportive therapy groups (e.g., Lam et al., 2003; Meyer & Hautzinger, 2012; Parikh et al., 2012; Scott et al., 2001; Zaretsky et al., 2008). A review of these studies shows the evidence for CBT to be mixed, which is not surprising considering the variety of control conditions, primary outcome variables, and sample composition. For example, Lam and colleagues (2003) demonstrated that CBT reduced risk for relapse in a sample of euthymic BD patients (i.e., not currently manic, depressed, or mixed); however, the effects diminished during the second year of follow-up (see Lam et al., 2005). Conversely, a study involving remitted and acutely ill patients found that, while CBT did not affect recurrence rates overall, when the number of episodes were taken into account, those with fewer prior mood episodes did benefit from CBT while those with a longer illness history did not (Scott et al., 2006). While the latter two studies used treatment-as-usual as the control condition, Meyer and Hautzinger (2012) compared CBT with supportive therapy matched in frequency and intensity of sessions, and no differential effects were found aside from a trend of CBT outperforming supportive therapy during active treatment but not during follow-up. Considering effect sizes, most studies overall revealed positive effects on subsyndromal symptoms and indicators of improved psychosocial functioning (e.g., Szentagotai & David, 2010).

*Family and conjoint interventions* rely on diverse approaches; what they have in common is the setting in which they occur (i.e., not *individual* therapy). The approach that has received the most attention and empirical support is family-focused treatment (FFT; Miklowitz, 2010). Miklowitz and colleagues developed this treatment from research demonstrating that family communication styles and family functioning are associated with the course of BD (e.g., Miklowitz et al., 1988; Perlick et al., 2004); thus, targeting potential family processes directly or indirectly related to BD is a promising avenue for patients with BD, their significant others, and families. Several RCTs showed the efficacy of FFT in reducing risk of recurrent mood episodes (e.g., Miklowitz et al., 2003; Rea et al., 2003). Adaptations to specific groups such as adolescents (e.g., Miklowitz et al., 2008) or caregivers (e.g., Perlick et al., 2010) and to different healthcare contexts (e.g., Sharma et al., 2020) have been developed as well.

When acknowledging the whole range of adjunctive psychological interventions for BD, most systematic reviews and meta-analyses conclude that they reduce recurrence of mood episodes as well as improve symptoms and/or psychosocial impairment (e.g., Chatteron et al., 2017; Macheiner et al., 2017; Miklowitz & Scott, 2009; Schöttle et al., 2011). Some reviews note that the field is still in its early stages and that the evidence base is only low to moderate (e.g., Lynch et al., 2010; Oud et al., 2016; Szentagotai-Tătar & David, 2018). However, all these meta-analyses have never compared the relative efficacy of those psychosocial treatments with each other and only considered the active treatment relative to its control condition. This gap in the literature was addressed by a network meta-analysis recently published by Miklowitz, Efthimiou, and colleagues in 2020. These authors identified a total of 39 RCTs, including 3,863 participants, and their network analyses unveiled that empirically supported treatments were associated with lower recurrence rates than control treatments. Additionally, CBT provided the strongest evidence for reducing bipolar depressed symptoms when compared to treatment as usual, and to some extent this was also true for FFT and IPSRT (similar effects were found for manic symptoms and CBT but with lower certainty). The authors even identified that certain treatment elements were differentially related to outcome; for example, psychoeducation in a group format or involving family members, as well as use of mood monitoring, were more effective than individual psychoeducation in preventing recurrence. Contrarily, cognitive restructuring and regulating daily activities were the most potent strategies to reduce depressive symptoms (Miklowitz, Efthimiou et al., 2020).

There are still major gaps in our knowledge about mechanisms, mediators, and moderators of outcome, and our understanding is only further complicated in recognizing that most studies focus on symptoms, relapse, and recurrence only in patients after discharge from a hospital or when already stable. Fewer studies have looked at remission from acute symptoms (see the STEP-BD study; Miklowitz et al., 2006) or specifically targeted comorbidities such as substance use disorders (e.g., Crowe et al., 2020). It is also unclear how to best address coexisting mental health conditions in BD. Should they be treated sequentially or simultaneously as part of an integrative case formulation, or would a transdiagnostic approach be most appropriate? In addition, the typical primary outcomes chosen in RCTs, such as symptomatic remission, are often for patients themselves less important than functional or personal recovery (e.g., Jones et al., 2015; Murray et al., 2017).

## Looking Ahead: Advancing Work on Diversity and Anti-Stigma Approaches

In this final section we review research highlighting critical work needed in BSDs that includes expanding our understanding in diverse and underrepresented populations and addressing the stigma that still shrouds this disorder.

Most of the current research discussed in this chapter has been conducted in Westernized countries. Even within the United States, research is limited by homogeneous samples consisting of primarily White, wealthy, and highly educated individuals. Research with the largest percentages of Black, Indigenous, people of color (BIPOC) individuals with BD tends to be hospital and prison studies, whereas undergraduate and community samples are composed of limited non-White individuals. These differences in participant characteristics and clinical severity by recruitment methods influence research questions and conclusions. For example, Johnson and Johnson (2014a) found that the prevalence of BD was correlated with reward-relevant cultural dimensions such as power distance and individualism in a cross-national study of 17 countries. Furthermore, insufficient recruitment of BIPOC individuals precludes analyses of potential racial and ethnic differences. Instead, race and ethnicity are typically "controlled for" and included as covariates in analyses—or worse, non-White participants are excluded to keep samples homogeneous, particularly in terms of genetic studies (Akinhami et al., 2017). These suboptimal research practices result in typifying White Western adults with BD as the framework for universal presentations of bipolar phenomenon. Thus, we have limited knowledge of the symptomatology, etiology, and treatment of BD in other, non-Western cultures and within minoritized racial and ethnic groups in the United States.

Research on serious mental illness (e.g., schizophrenia spectrum disorders, BSDs) suggests there may be critical differences across cultures and racial/ethnic groups in terms of symptom presentations, diagnostic considerations, and treatment efficacy that could inform more tailored and effective interventions for diverse populations. In a 2011 review of more than 50 articles in the United States and the United Kingdom, Haeri and colleagues concluded that there are racial disparities in the diagnosis of BD. Across multiple studies, current literature indicates that Black individuals are less likely to be diagnosed with an affective disorder (including depression and BD) and more likely to be diagnosed with schizophrenia spectrum disorders compared to White individuals. Furthermore, Kilbourne and colleagues (2005) found that African American veterans with BD were less likely to receive adequate follow-up outpatient care compared to White veterans. In a representative US sample drawn from the National Comorbidity Survey Replication (NCS-R) data, Johnson and Johnson (2014b) found that no African Americans (0%) received minimally adequate treatment (defined as use of a mood stabilizer alone or in combination with an antipsychotic) in the past year, compared to 17% of Caucasian Americans who did. A similar trend was found for Latinx Americans compared to non-Hispanic whites (0% vs. 21%; Salcedo et al., 2017). In addition, previous studies have demonstrated that Black individuals are more likely than White individuals to be prescribed antipsychotics with more severe side effects, irrespective of the presence of psychotic symptoms (e.g., Kilbourne & Pincus, 2006; Szarek & Goethe, 2003). Overall, mounting evidence has indicated racial disparities in the diagnosis and treatment of BD.

Haeri et al. (2011) identified potential factors that may contribute to observed racial disparities in diagnostic rates in BD. For example, there is some evidence for differences in BD symptom presentation, with Black individuals experiencing higher rates of hallucinations and delusions compared to Whites (e.g., Gonzalez et al., 2007; Kirov & Murray, 1999; Strakowski et al., 1996). Some studies have also found higher rates of exclusively or mainly manic presentations (without a prior history of depression) in Black BD patients including British outpatients of African origin (Kirov & Murray, 1999) and Yoruba Nigerian patients (Makanjuola, 1985). These findings contrast with the much lower rates of mania-only BD presentations reported in primarily White Western samples (Boyd & Weissman, 1981). At the same time, differences in symptom presentation of psychosis may be due to differences in treatment seeking and poorer access to healthcare among Black individuals, including an overreliance on emergency room services (Snowden, 2001) and a tendency to seek treatment at later, more severe stages of mania when psychosis is more likely to occur (Mukherjee et al., 1983). There is also some evidence for differences in how clinicians weigh the same symptoms in Black versus White individuals. In a study of US adult psychiatric inpatients, the presence of negative symptoms (e.g., blunted affect, monotonous speech) in African American patients—but not in White patients—was found to contribute more toward a diagnosis of schizophrenia and away from a diagnosis of BD (Neighbors et al., 2003; Trierweiler et al., 2000). The authors suggested these findings may indicate a tendency for clinicians to overpathologize a reluctance to disclose personal information and a general mistrust of the healthcare system that is common in Black communities. In addition to potential characteristics of the individual with BSDs, other researchers have also proposed clinician biases as a contributor to the racial disparities in diagnosis and treatment for BSDs. While racial biases on the part of healthcare workers have been demonstrated in the medical field (e.g., Chapman et al., 2013), little research in mental health providers—or in clinicians diagnosing BD, in particular—has been conducted, and this remains a critical focus for future work (McMaster, 2016).

In sum, research is limited in terms of its ability to characterize BS cross-culturally and in racially and ethnically diverse communities. As discussed in previous sections of this chapter, accurate diagnosis of BD is critical to improving prognosis and treatment responsivity. Thus, an important avenue for future research is to examine BD in multiple sociocultural contexts and across more racially, ethnically, and socioeconomically diverse populations to promote equity of BD treatment and ensure that research findings are applicable to various individuals living with BD. Furthermore, the current literature highlights the importance of bolstering clinician experience with various sociocultural contexts pertinent to the patients they serve. It is likely that such endeavors will require greater community engagement to build partnerships and trust within BIPOC communities traditionally excluded from and exploited by clinical science (Akinhanmi et al., 2017).

### Mental Illness Stigma

Here we focus on the stigma incurred by people with BD. The term "stigma" has a long (and distressing) history in cultural studies, human evolution, social and clinical psychology, and psychiatry (for a crucial review, see Kurzban & Leary, 2001). It literally refers to the sharp instruments used, in Greek and Roman times, to cut or burn visible marks into the skin of members of devalued societal subgroups—with the goal of making visible the denigrated status of traitors, former slaves, or diseased individuals. Ancient texts reveal that individuals displaying features of mental illness have received stigma, been shunned or banished, and even murdered throughout recorded history (Hinshaw, 2007). Although visible marking still occurs (e.g., concentration camp inmates with numbers tattooed on their wrists; the marking of HIV-positive individuals in several nations during the 1980s), "stigma" today is inferred mainly from one's group status, thus comprising a social-psychological "brand." Our postindustrial world includes far greater factual knowledge of mental illness than a generation or two ago, yet those experiencing mental disorders still receive and experience large amounts of stigmatization (Pescosolido et al. 2010).

Heuristic conceptual models of stigma as related to mental disorders include Link and Phelan (2001) and Pescosolido, Martin, Lang, and Olafsdottier (2008); also see the review by Martinez and Hinshaw (2016). In brief, the naturally selected propensity to define others based on key observable or inferred characteristics, called *stereotyping*, may lead to prejudice when the "other" is deemed as threatening. Discrimination, the abridgment of rights devalued individuals, is a common result, even comprising extermination. Stigma incorporates all three processes, also signaling the loss of individuality (or even fundamental humanity) of the derogated person.

Most stigmatized individuals know of the stereotypes that exist about them. As a result, they may internalize the stigma (Corrigan & Watson, 2004). For mental health conditions, such *internalized stigma* (self-stigma) is a major barrier to help-seeking, above and beyond symptoms such as anxiety or depression. Moreover, as defined by Goffman (1963), *courtesy stigma* signifies the tendency of the public to stigmatize anyone even associated with the stigmatized individual. Parents thus experience a double dose of stigma, also having been believed to directly cause their offspring's mental illness for most of the twentieth century. Clinicians and researchers also receive courtesy stigma, because they, by definition, treat or investigate members of devalued groups.

In general, the most severe forms of mental illness—particularly when psychotic features are involved—receive especially high levels of stigma (Jones et al., 1984). Extreme states of mania and/or depression are clearly involved. Even more, BD is susceptible to societal stereotypes (Jekyll vs. Hyde; "You're just acting bipolar" [i.e., in inconsistent fashion]), often fueled by pervasive and biased media depictions.

In an essential review, Hawke, Parikh, and Michalak (2013) found that stigma related to BD is strong, in terms of self-stigma and public stigma, within school and employment-related settings and across healthcare systems in general. Consequences (reduced quality of life and increased functional impairment) are pervasive. On the other hand, Ellison, Mason, and Scior (2015) surveyed more than 700 UK residents regarding attitudes toward an individual depicted as having BD. Explicit attitudes were generally positive, especially if respondents believed that the conditions in question were biogenetic in origin and if they had experienced prior contact with someone dealing with BD. Moreover, beliefs that BD can signal creativity and positive attributes were linked to positive attitudes, potentially fueled by greater levels of disclosure by influential individuals. Yet it is not clear whether such explicitly stated attitudes reflect a deeper and less conscious set of reactions to people with BD (i.e., implicit attitudes). As well, a genetic or biochemical ascription for serious mental illness typically reduces blame on the part of the observer but at the same time increases beliefs about permanence, hopelessness, and propensities toward aggression or violence (Kvaale et al., 2013). Thus, the key solution for stigma is not simply to promote a reductionistic disease model; rather, humanization is part of the overall strategy (see Hinshaw, 2017).

The sheer inconsistency of performance in individuals with BD may be crucial. Although severe and chronic medical or psychiatric conditions receive high stigma (e.g., HIV is more stigmatized than the flu), when the public encounters someone with highly inconsistent performance—for example, a child or adult with ADHD (Nguyen & Hinshaw, 2020) or an individual fluctuating between phases of manic and depressive episodes—the perception may well be of a lack of effort or will. Such ascriptions of controllability, potentially linked to weak character or low moral fiber, are highly likely to fuel stigmatizing responses.

In terms of additional findings, Gilkes, Perish, and Meade (2019) examined self-stigma in 275 adults with BD, discovering that high self-stigma was associated with unmarried status (potentially indicating low social support) and severity of symptoms. Budenz et al. (2020) explored the nature of more than 1 million Twitter posts (and retweets) in 2016–2017. Although many general mental illness–related tweets were positive in nature, those related to BD were far less so. Also, in a provocative qualitative investigation, Richard-Lepouriel, Favre, Jermann, and Aubry (2020) analyzed complex self-reported themes among individuals with BD regarding phases of intensive self-stigmatization that eventually led to more self-accepting/destigmatizing stages. Despite the small sample size, it is inspiring to examine how individuals with BD can progress from self-negation to acceptance as a function of social support and self-enhancing attitudes.

## Conclusion

In all, as emphasized throughout this chapter, BSDs incur high levels of impairment and features a tragic level of suicidal behavior. Although significant advances have been made towards understanding emotional, cognitive, and neural processes as well as empirically supported treatments for BSDs, positive features of the disorder clearly exist, and public stigma may be improving, public acceptance does not appear to be at optimal levels, and levels of self-stigma remain far too high. Future work is needed to expand our scientific understanding, treatment advancements and dissemination, and compassion towards those with lived experience of BSDs.

## References

Abler, B., Greenhouse, I., Ongur, D., Walter, H., & Heckers, S. (2008). Abnormal reward system activation in mania. *Neuropsychopharmacology, 33*, 2217–2227.

Agnew-Blais, J., & Danese, A. (2016). Childhood maltreatment and unfavourable clinical outcomes in bipolar disorder: A systematic review and meta-analysis. *Lancet Psychiatry, 3*(4), 342–349.

Akinhanmi, M. O., Biernacka, J. M., Strakowski, S. M., McElroy, S. L., Balls Berry, J. E., Merikangas, K. R., Assari, S., McInnis, M. G., Schulze, T. G., LeBoyer, M., Tamminga, C., Patten, C., & Frye, M. A. (2017). Racial disparities in bipolar disorder treatment and research: A call to action. *Bipolar Disorders, 20*(6), 506–514. https://doi.org/10.1111/bdi.12638

Algorta, G. P., Youngstrom, E. A., Phelps, J., Jenkins, M. M., Youngstrom, J. K., & Findling, R. L. (2013). An inexpensive family index of risk for mood issues improves identification of pediatric bipolar disorder. *Psychological Assessment, 25*(1), 12–22. https://doi.org/10.1037/a0029225

Alloy, L. B., Bender, R. E., Whitehouse, W. G., Wagner, C. A., Liu, R. T., Grant, D. A., Jager-Hyman, S., Molz, A., Choi, J. Y., Harmon-Jones, E., & Abramson, L. Y. (2012a). High Behavioral Approach System (BAS) sensitivity, reward responsiveness, and goal-striving predict first onset of bipolar spectrum disorders: A prospective behavioral high-risk design. *Journal of Abnormal Psychology, 121*, 339–351.

Alloy, L. B., Urosevic, S., Abramson, L. Y., Jager-Hyman, S., Nusslock, R., Whitehouse, W. G., & Hogan, M. E. (2012b). Progression along the bipolar spectrum: A longitudinal study of predictors of conversion from bipolar spectrum conditions to bipolar I and II disorders. *Journal of Abnormal Psychology, 121*, 16–27.

Alloy, L. B., Abramson, L. Y., Walshaw, P. D., Gerstein, R. K., Keyser, J. D., Whitehouse, W. G., . . . Harmon-Jones, E. (2009). Behavioral approach system (BAS)–relevant cognitive styles and bipolar spectrum disorders: Concurrent and prospective associations. *Journal of Abnormal Psychology, 118*(3), 459.

Atuk, E., & Richardson, T. (2020). Relationship between dysfunctional beliefs, self-esteem, extreme appraisals, and symptoms of mania and depression over time in bipolar disorder. *Psychology and Psychotherapy: Theory, Research and Practice, 94*(2), 212–222.

Banks, F. D., Lobban, F., Fanshawe, T. R., & Jones, S. H. (2016). Associations between circadian rhythm instability, appraisal style and mood in bipolar disorder. *Journal of Affective Disorders, 203*, 166–175.

Beck, A. T. (1991). Cognitive therapy: A 30-year retrospective. *American Psychologist, 46*(4), 368.

Beck, A. T., & Haigh, E. A. (2014). Advances in cognitive theory and therapy: The generic cognitive model. *Annual Review of Clinical Psychology, 10*, 1–24.

Bender, R. E., Alloy, L. B., Sylvia, L. G., Uroševic, S., & Abramson, L. Y. (2010). Generation of life events in bipolar spectrum disorders: A re-examination and extension of the stress generation theory. *Journal of Clinical Psychology, 66*(9), 907–926.

Bermpohl, F., Dalaney, U., Kahnt, T., Sajonz, B., Heimann, H., Ricken, R., & Bauer, M. (2009). A preliminary study of increased amygdala activation to positive affective stimuli in mania. *Bipolar Disorders, 11*, 70–75.

Bermpohl, F., Kahnt, T., Dalanay, U., Hagele, C., Sajonz, B., Wegener, T., Stoy, M., Adli, M., Kruger, S., Wrase, J., Strohle, A., Bauer, M., & Heinz, A. (2010). Altered representation of expected value in the orbitofrontal cortex in mania. *Human Brain Mapping, 31*, 958–969.

Berridge, K. C. (2019). Affective valence in the brain: Modules or modes? *Nature Reviews Neuroscience, 20*(4), 225–234.

Berridge, K. C., & Kringelbach, M. L. (2015). Pleasure systems in the brain. *Neuron, 86*, 646–664.

Benedetti, F., Dallaspezia, S., Fulgosi, M. C., Lorenzi, C., Serretti, A., Barbini, B., . . . Smeraldi, E. (2007). Actimetric evidence that CLOCK 3111 T/C SNP influences sleep and activity patterns in patients affected by bipolar depression. *American Journal of Medical Genetics Part B: Neuropsychiatric Genetics, 144*(5), 631–635.

Benedetti, F., Serretti, A., Colombo, C., Barbini, B., Lorenzi, C., Campori, E., & Smeraldi, E. (2003). Influence of CLOCK gene polymorphism on circadian mood fluctuation and illness recurrence in bipolar depression. *American Journal of Medical Genetics Part B: Neuropsychiatric Genetics, 123*(1), 23–26.

Birmaher, B., Axelson, D., Goldstein, B., Strober, M., Gill, M. K., Hunt, J., . . . Keller, M. (2009). Four-year longitudinal course of children and adolescents with bipolar spectrum disorders: The Course and Outcome of Bipolar Youth (COBY) study. *American Journal of Psychiatry, 166*(7), 795–804. https://doi.org/10.1176/appi.ajp.2009.08101569

Birmaher, B., Axelson, D., Strober, M., Gill, M. K., Valeri, S., Chiappetta, L., . . . Keller, M. (2006). Clinical course of children and adolescents with bipolar spectrum disorders. *Archives of General Psychiatry, 63*(2), 175–183. https://doi.org/10.1001/archpsyc.63.2.175

Borbély, A. A. (1980). Sleep: Circadian rhythm versus recovery process. In M. Koukkou, D. Lehmann, & J. Angst (Eds.), *Functional states of the brain: Their determinants* (pp. 151–161). Elsevier.

Borbély, A. A., Daan, S., Wirz-Justice, A., & Deboer, T. (2016). The two-process model of sleep regulation: A reappraisal. *Journal of Sleep Research, 25*(2), 131–143. https://doi.org/10.1111/jsr.12371

Boyd, J. H., & Weissman, M. M. (1981). Epidemiology of affective disorders: A reexamination and future directions. *Archives of General Psychiatry, 38*(9), 1039–1046. https://doi.org/10.1001/archpsyc.1981.01780340091011

Bozikas, V. P., Nazlidou, E. I., Parlapani, E., Alexiadou, A., Skemperi, E., Dandi, E., . . . Garyfallos, G. (2019). Autobiographical memory deficits in remitted patients with bipolar disorder I: The effect of impaired memory retrieval. *Psychiatry Research, 278*, 281–288.

Bress, J. N., Foti, D., Kotov, R., Klein, D. N., & Hajcak, G. (2013). Blunted neural response to rewards prospectively predicts depression in adolescent girls. *Psychophysiology, 50*, 74–81.

Budenz, A., Klassen, A., Purtle, J., Tov, E. Y., Yudell, M., & Massey, P. (2020). Mental illness and bipolar disorder on Twitter: Implications for stigma and social support. *Journal of Mental Health, 29*, 191–199.

Candini, V., Buizza, C., Ferrari, C., Caldera, M. T., Ermentini, R., Ghilardi, A., Nobili, G., Pioli, R., Sabaudo, M., Sacchetti, E., Saviotti, F. M., Seggioli, G., Zanini, A., & Girolamo, G. (2013). Is structured group psychoeducation for bipolar patients effective in ordinary mental health services? A controlled trial in Italy. *Journal of Affective Disorders, 151*, 149–155.

Carlson, G. A., & Glovinsky, I. (2009). The concept of bipolar disorder in children: A history of the bipolar controversy. *Child and Adolescent Psychiatric Clinics of North America, 18*(2), 257–271.

Carta, M. G., & Angst, J. (2016). Screening for bipolar disorders: A public health issue. *Journal of Affective Disorders, 205*, 139–143.

Caseras, X., Lawrence, N. S., Murphy, K., Wise, R. G., & Phillips, M. L. (2013). Ventral striatum activity in response to reward: Differences between bipolar I and bipolar II disorders. *American Journal of Psychiatry, 170*, 533–541.

Castanho de Almeida Rocca, C., Britto de Macedo-Soares, M., Gorenstein, C., Sayuri Tamada, R., Kluger Issler, C., Silva Dias, R., . . . & Lafer, B. (2008). Social dysfunction in bipolar disorder: pilot study. *Australian & New Zealand Journal of Psychiatry, 42*(8), 686–692.

Chan, S. H., & Tse, S. (2018). An explorative study on coping flexibility with behavioral approach system-activating stimuli: A comparison of people with and without bipolar disorder. *Psychiatry Research, 269*, 399-407.

Chang, K. D. (2010). Course and impact of bipolar disorder in young patients. *Journal of Clinical Psychiatry, 71*(2), e05. https://doi.org/10.4088/JCP.8125tx7c

Chapman, E. N., Kaatz, A., & Carnes, M. (2013). Physicians and implicit bias: How doctors may unwittingly perpetuate health care disparities. *Journal of General Internal Medicine, 28*(11), 1504–1510. https://doi.org/10.1007/s11606-013-2441-1

Cicero, D. C., Epler, A. J., & Sher, K. J. (2009). Are there developmentally limited forms of bipolar disorder? *Journal of Abnormal Psychology, 118*(3), 431–447. https://doi.org/2009-12104-001

Cohen, A. N., Hammen, C., Henry, R. M., & Daley, S. E. (2004). Effects of stress and social support on recurrence in bipolar disorder. *Journal of Affective Disorders, 82*(1), 143–147.

Colom, F., Vieta, E., Martinez-Aran, A., Reinares, M., Goikolea, J. M., Benabarre, A., Torrent, C., Comes, M., Corbella, B., Parramon, G., & Corominas, J. (2003). A randomized trial of the efficacy of group psychoeducation in the prophylaxis of recurrences in bipolar patients whose disease is in remission. *Archives of General Psychiatry, 60*, 402–407.

Colom, F., Vieta, E., Sanchez-Moreno, J., et al. (2009). Group psychoeducation for stabilised bipolar disorders: 5-year outcome of a randomised clinical trial. *British Journal of Psychiatry, 194*, 260–265.

Compas, B. E., Connor-Smith, J. K., Saltzman, H., Thomsen, A. H., & Wadsworth, M. E. (2001). Coping with stress during childhood and adolescence: Problems, progress, and potential in theory and research. *Psychological Bulletin, 127*(1), 87–127. https://doi.org/10.1037/0033-2909.127.1.87

Coque, L., Sidor, M. M., Kumar, S., Dancy, E. A., Takahashi, J. S., McClung, C. A., & Nicolelis, M. A. (2010). Lithium ameliorates nucleus accumbens phase-signaling dysfunction in a genetic mouse model of mania. *Journal of Neuroscience, 30*(48), 16314–16323. https://doi.org/10.1523/JNEUROSCI.4289-10.2010

Corrigan, P. W., & Watson, A. C. (2004). At issue: Stop the stigma: Call mental illness a brain disease. *Schizophrenia Bulletin, 30*(3), 477–479.

Coryell, W., Scheftner, W., Keller, M., Endicott, J., Maser, J., & Klerman, G. L. (1993). The enduring psychological consequences of mania and depression. *American Journal of Psychiatry, 150*, 720–727.

Cosgrove, V. E., Roybal, D., & Chang, K. D. (2013). Bipolar depression in pediatric populations: Epidemiology and management. *Pediatric Drugs, 15*(2), 83–91. https://doi.org/10.1007/s40272-013-0022-8

Cotrena, C., Damiani Branco, L., Ponsoni, A., Samame, C., Milman Shansis, F., & Paz Fonseca, R. (2020). Executive functions and memory in bipolar disorders I and II: New insights from meta-analytic results. *Acta Psychiatrica Scandinavica, 141*(2), 110–130.

Crowe, M., Eggleston, K., Douglas, K., & Porter, R. J. (2020). Effects of psychotherapy on comorbid bipolar disorder and substance use disorder: A systematic review. *Bipolar Disorders*, 1–11. https://doi.org/10.1111/bdi.1297

Daruy-Filho, L., Brietzke, E., Lafer, B., & Grassi-Oliveira, R. (2011). Childhood maltreatment and clinical outcomes of bipolar disorder. *Acta Psychiatrica Scandinavica, 124*(6), 427–434.

De Crescenzo, F., Economou, A., Sharpley, A. L., Gormez, A., & Quested, D. J. (2017). Actigraphic features of bipolar disorder: A systematic review and meta-analysis. *Sleep Medicine Reviews, 33*, 58–69. https://doi.org/10.1016/j.smrv.2016.05.003

Depue, R. A., Krauss, S., Spoont, M. R., & Arbisi, P. (1989). General behavior inventory identification of unipolar and bipolar affective conditions in a nonclinical university population. *Journal of Abnormal Psychology, 98*(2), 117.

Devlin, H. C., Zaki, J., Ong, D. C., & Gruber, J. (2016). Tracking the emotional highs but missing the lows: Mania risk is associated with positively biased empathic inference. *Cognitive Therapy and Research, 40*(1), 72–79. https://doi.org/10.1107/s10608-015-9720-6.

Di Simplicio, M., Renner, F., Blackwell, S. E., Mitchell, H., Stratford, H. J., Watson, P., . . . & Holmes, E. A. (2016). An investigation of mental imagery in bipolar disorder: Exploring "the mind's eye." *Bipolar Disorders, 18*(8), 669–683.

Dilsaver, S. C. (2011). An estimate of the minimum economic burden of bipolar I and II disorders in the United States: 2009. *Journal of Affective Disorders, 129*(1), 79–83. http://dx.doi.org/10.1016/j.jad.2010.08.030

Dodd, A., Lockwood, E., Mansell, W., & Palmier-Claus, J. (2019). Emotion regulation strategies in bipolar disorder: A systematic and critical review. *Journal of Affective Disorders, 246*, 262–284.

Dodd, A. L., Mansell, W., Morrison, A. P., & Tai, S. (2011). Extreme appraisals of internal states and bipolar symptoms: The hypomanic attitudes and positive predictions inventory. *Psychological Assessment, 23*(3), 635.

Dutra, S. J., Cunningham, W. A., Kober, H., & Gruber, J. (2015). Elevated striatal reactivity across monetary and social rewards in bipolar I disorder. *Journal of Abnormal Psychology, 124*, 890–904.

Dutra, S. J., Man, V., Kober, H., Cunningham, W. A., & Gruber, J. (2017). Disrupted cortico-limbic connectivity during reward processing in bipolar I disorder. *Bipolar Disorders, 19*(8), 661–675. https://doi.org/10.1111/bdi.12560

Dutra, S. J., West, T. V., Impett, E. A., Oveis, C., Kogan, A., Keltner, D., & Gruber, J. (2014). Rose-colored glasses gone too far? Mania symptoms predict biased emotion experience and perception in couples. *Motivation and Emotion, 38*(1), 157–165.

Eckblad, M., & Chapman, L. J. (1986). Development and validation of a scale for hypomanic personality. *Journal of Abnormal Psychology, 95*(3), 214.

Ehlers, C. L., Frank, E., & Kupfer, D. J. (1988). Social Zeitgebers and biological rhythms. *Archives of General Psychiatry, 45*, 948–952.

Elliott, R., Ogilvie, A., Rubinsztein, J. S., Calderon, G., Dolan, R. J., & Sahakian, B. (2004). Abnormal ventral frontal response during performance of an affective go/no go task in patients with mania. *Biological Psychiatry, 55*, 1163–1170.

Ellison, N., Mason, O., & Scior, K. (2015). Public beliefs about and attitudes towards bipolar disorder: Testing theory-based models of stigma. *Journal of Affective Disorders, 175*, 116–127.

Etkin, A., & Wager, T. D. (2007). Functional neuroimaging of anxiety: A meta-analysis of emotional processing in PTSD, social anxiety disorder, and specific phobia. *American Journal of Psychiatry, 164*(10), 1476–1488.

Ferguson, A., Lyall, L. M., Ward, J., Strawbridge, R. J., Cullen, B., Graham, N., Niedzwiedz, C. L., Johnston, K., MacKay, D., Biello, S. M., Pell, J. P., Cavanagh, J., McIntosh, A. M., Doherty, A., Bailey, M., Lyall, D. M., Wyse, C. A., & Smith, D. J. (2018). Genome-wide association study of circadian rhythmicity in 71,500 UK biobank participants and polygenic association with mood instability. *EBioMedicine, 35*, 279–287. https://doi.org/10.1016/j.ebiom.2018.08.004

Fijtman, A., Bücker, J., Strange, B. A., Martins, D. S., Passos, I. C., Hasse-Sousa, M., . . . Kauer-Sant'Anna, M. (2020). Emotional memory in bipolar disorder: Impact of multiple episodes and childhood trauma. *Journal of Affective Disorders, 260*, 206–213.

Fletcher, K., Parker, G., & Manicavasagar, V. (2014). The role of psychological factors in bipolar disorder: Prospective relationships between cognitive style, coping style and symptom expression. *Acta Neuropsychiatrica, 26*(2), 81–95.

Foland, L. C., Altshuler, L. L., Sugar, C. A., Lee, A. D., Leow, A. D., Townsend, J., Narr, K. L., Asuncion, D. M., Toga, A. W., & Thompson, P. M. (2008). Increased volume of the amygdala and hippocampus in bipolar patients treated with lithium. *Neuroreport, 19*, 221–224.

Foland-Ross, L. C., Bookheimer, S. Y., Lieberman, M. D., Sugar, C. A., Townsend, J. D., Fischer, J., . . . & Altshuler, L. L. (2012). Normal amygdala activation but deficient ventrolateral prefrontal activation in adults with bipolar disorder during euthymia. *Neuroimage, 59*(1), 738–744.

Forbes, E. E., Shaw, D. S., & Dahl, R. E. (2007). Alterations in reward-related decision making in boys with recent and future depression. *Biological Psychiatry, 61*, 633–639.

Forbes, E. E., Hariri, A. R., Martin, S. L., Silk, J. S., Moyles, D. L., Fisher, P. M., . . . Dahl, R. E. (2009). Altered striatal activation predicting real-world positive affect in adolescent major depressive disorder. *American Journal of Psychiatry, 166*, 64–73.

Frank, E. (2005). *Treating bipolar disorder: A clinician's guide to interpersonal and social rhythm therapy*. Guilford.

Frank, E., Kupfer, D. J., Thase, M. E., Mallinger, A. G., Swartz, H. A., Fagiolini, A. M., Grochocinski; V., Houck, P., Scott; J., Thompson, W., & Monk, T. (2005). Two-year outcomes for Interpersonal and Social Rhythm Therapy in individuals with bipolar I disorder. *Archives of General Psychiatry, 62*, 996–1004.

Frank, E., Swartz, H. A., Mallinger, A. G., Thase, M. E., Weaver, E. V., & Kupfer, D. J. (1999). Adjunctive psychotherapy for bipolar disorder: Effects of changing treatment modality. *Journal of Abnormal Psychology, 108*, 579–587.

Freeman, A. J., & Young, J. (2020). Assessing process: Are we there yet? In E. A. Youngstrom, M. J. Prinstein, E. J. Mash, & R. Barkley (Eds.), *Assessment of disorders in childhood and adolescence*, 5th ed. (pp. 75–90). Guilford.

Freeman, A. J., Youngstrom, E. A., Michalak, E., Siegel, R., Meyers, O. I., & Findling, R. L. (2009). Quality of life in pediatric bipolar disorder. *Pediatrics, 123*(3). https://doi.org/10.1542/peds.2008-0841

Fuller, P. M., Gooley, J. J., & Saper, C. B. (2006). Neurobiology of the sleep-wake cycle: Sleep architecture, circadian regulation, and regulatory feedback. *Journal of Biological Rhythms, 21*(6), 482–493. https://doi.org/10.1177/0748730406294627

García-Blanco, A. C., Perea, M., & Livianos, L. (2013). Mood-congruent bias and attention shifts in the different episodes of bipolar disorder. *Cognition & Emotion, 27*(6), 1114–1121.

Garno, J. L., Goldberg, J. F., Ramirez, P. M., & Ritzler, B. A. (2005). Impact of childhood abuse on the clinical course of bipolar disorder. *British Journal of Psychiatry, 186*(2), 121–125.

Geaghan, M., & Cairns, M. J. (2015). MicroRNA and posttranscriptional dysregulation in psychiatry. *Biological Psychiatry, 78*(4), 231–239.

Geller, B., Zimerman, B., Williams, M., DelBello, M. P., Frazier, J., & Beringer, L. (2002). Phenomenology of prepubertal and early adolescent bipolar disorder: Examples of elated mood, grandiose behaviors, decreased need for sleep, racing thoughts and hypersexuality. *Journal of Child and Adolescent Psychopharmacology, 12*(1), 3–9. https://doi.org/10.1089/10445460252943524

Gershon, A., Kaufmann, C. N., Depp, C. A., Miller, S., Do, D., Zeitzer, J. M., & Ketter, T. A. (2018). Subjective versus objective evening chronotypes in bipolar disorder. *Journal of Affective Disorders, 225*, 342–349. doi:10.1016/j.jad.2017.08.055

Gilbert, K., & Gruber, J. (2014). Emotion regulation of goals in bipolar disorder and major depression: A comparison of rumination and mindfulness. *Cognitive Therapy and Research, 38*(4), 375–388.

Gilkes, M., Perish, T., & Meade, T. (2019). Predictors of self-stigma in bipolar disorder: Depression, mania, and perceived cognitive function. *Stigma and Health, 4*, 330–336.

Goffman, E. (1963). *Stigma: Notes on the management of spoiled identity*. Prentice Hall.

Goldberg, J. F., & Harrow, M. (2011). A 15-year prospective follow-up of bipolar affective disorders: Comparisons with unipolar nonpsychotic depression. *Bipolar Disorders, 13*, 155–163.

Goldstein, B. I., Birmaher, B., Carlson, G. A., DelBello, M. P., Findling, R. L., Fristad, M., . . . Youngstrom, E. A. (2017). The International Society for Bipolar Disorders Task Force report on pediatric bipolar disorder: Knowledge to date and directions for future research. *Bipolar Disorders, 19*(7), 524–543. https://doi.org/10.1111/bdi.12556

Goldstein, T. R., Fersch-Podrat, R., Axelson, D. A., Gilbert, A., Hlastala, S. A., Birmaher, B., & Frank, E. (2014). Early intervention for adolescents at high risk for the development of bipolar disorder: Pilot study of Interpersonal and Social Rhythm Therapy (IPSRT). *Psychotherapy, 51*(1), 180–189. https://doi.org/10.1037/a0034396

Gonzalez, J. M., Thompson, P., Escamilla, M., Araga, M., Singh, V., Farrelly, N., Thase, M. E., Miklowitz, D. J., & Bowden, C. L. (2007). Treatment characteristics and illness burden among European Americans, African Americans, and Latinos in the first 2,000 patients of the Systematic Treatment Enhancement Program for Bipolar Disorder. *Psychopharmacology Bulletin, 40*(1), 31–46.

Goodwin, F. K., & Jamison, K. R. (2007). *Manic-depressive illness*, 2nd ed. Oxford University Press.

Gottlieb, J. F., Benedetti, F., Geoffroy, P. A., Henriksen, T., Lam, R. W., Murray, G., . . . Chen, S. (2019). The chronotherapeutic treatment of bipolar disorders: A systematic review and practice recommendations from the ISBD task force on chronotherapy and chronobiology. *Bipolar Disorders, 21*(8), 741–773. https://doi.org/10.1111/bdi.12847

Gross, J. J. (2015). Emotion regulation: Current status and future prospects. *Psychological Inquiry, 26*(1), 1–26.

Gruber, J. (2011). Can feeling too bog be bad? Positive emotion persistence in bipolar disorder. *Current Directions in Psychological Science, 20*, 217–221.

Gruber, J., Harvey, A. G., & Gross, J. J. (2012). When trvvying is not enough: Emotion regulation and the effort–success gap in bipolar disorder. *Emotion, 12*(5), 997.

Gruber, J., Harvey, A. G., & Johnson, S. L. (2009). Reflective and ruminative processing of positive emotional memories in bipolar disorder and healthy controls. *Behaviour Research and Therapy, 47*(8), 697–704.

Gruber, J., Harvey, A. G., & Purcell, A. (2011). What goes up can come down? A preliminary investigation of emotion reactivity and emotion recovery in bipolar disorder. *Journal of Affective Disorders, 133*(3), 457–466.

Gruber, J., & Johnson, S. L. (2009). Positive emotional traits and ambitious goals among people at risk for mania: The need for specificity. *International Journal of Cognitive Therapy, 2*, 176–187.

Gruber, J., Johnson, S. L., Oveis, C., & Keltner, D. (2008). Risk for mania and positive emotional responding: Too much of a good thing? *Emotion, 8*(1), 23.

Gruber, J., Kogan, A., Mennin, D., & Murray, G. (2013). Real-world emotion? An experience-sampling approach to emotion experience and regulation in bipolar I disorder. *Journal of Abnormal Psychology, 122*, 971–983.

Gruber, J., Maclaine, E., Avard, E., Purcell, J., Cooper, G., Tobias, M., . . . Palermo, R. (2021). Associations between hypomania proneness and attentional bias to happy, but not angry or fearful, faces in emerging adults. *Cognition and Emotion, 35*(1), 207–213.

Gruber, J., Villanueva, C. M., Burr, E., Purcell, J. R., & Karoly, H. (2019). Understanding and taking stock of positive emotion disturbance. *Social Personality and Psychology Compass*, 1–19. https://doi.org/10.1111/spc3.12515

Haber, S. N., & Knutson, B. (2010). The reward circuit: Linking primate anatomy and human imaging. *Neuropsychopharmacology 35*, 4–26.

Hahn, T., Dresler, T., Ehlis, A-C., Plichta, M. M., Heinzel, S., Polak, T., Lesch, K-P., Breuer, F., Jakob, P. M., & Fallgatter, A. J. (2009). Neural response to reward anticipation is modulated by Gray's impulsivity. *Neuroimage, 46*, 1148–1153.

Haeri, S., Williams, J., Kopeykina, I., Johnson, J., Newmark, A., Cohen, L., & Galynker, I. (2011). Disparities in diagnosis of bipolar disorder in individuals of African and European descent: A review. *Journal of Psychiatric Practice, 17*(6), 394–403. https://doi.org/10.1097/01.pra.0000407962.49851.ef

Hamilton, J. P., Etkin, A., Furman, D. J., Lemus, M. G., Johnson, R. F., & Gotlib, I. H. (2012). Functional neuroimaging of major depressive disorder: A meta-analysis and new integration of baseline activation and neural response data. *American Journal of Psychiatry, 169*(7), 693–703.

Hanford, L. C., Eckstrand, K., Manelis, A., Hafeman, D. M., Merranko, J., Ladouceur, C. D., ... Hickey, M. B. (2019). The impact of familial risk and early life adversity on emotion and reward processing networks in youth at-risk for bipolar disorder. *Plos One, 14*(12), e0226135.

Harada, M., Hiver, A., Pascoli, V., & Lüscher, C. (2019). Cortico-striatal synaptic plasticity underlying compulsive reward seeking. *BioRxiv*.

Hay, A. C., Sheppes, G., Gross, J. J., & Gruber, J. (2015). Choosing how to feel: Emotion regulation choice in bipolar disorder. *Emotion, 15*(2), 139.

Hassel, S., Almeida, J. R., Kerr, N., Nau, S., Ladouceur, C. D., Fissell, K., & Phillips, M. L. (2008). Elevated striatal and decreased dorsolateral prefrontal cortical activity in response to emotional stimuli in euthymic bipolar disorder: No associations with psychotropic medication load. *Bipolar Disorders, 10*, 916–927.

Hawke, L. D., Parikh, S. V., & Michalak, E. E. (2013). Stigma and bipolar disorder: A review of the literature. *Journal of Affective Disorders, 150*, 181–191.

Hinshaw, S. P. (2007). *The mark of shame: Stigma of mental illness and an agenda for change*. Oxford University Press.

Hinshaw, S. P. (2017). *Another kind of madness: A journey through the stigma and hope of mental illness*. St. Martin's Press.

Hirschfeld, R. M. A., Williams, J. B. W., Spitzer, R. L., Calabrese, J. R., Flynn, L., Keck, P. E., ... Zajecka, J. (2000). Development and validation of a screening instrument for bipolar spectrum disorder: The Mood Disorder Questionnaire. *American Journal of Psychiatry, 157*, 1873–1875.

Hu, Y., Shmygelska, A., Tran, D., Eriksson, N., Tung, J. Y., & Hinds, D. A. (2016). GWAS of 89,283 individuals identifies genetic variants associated with self-reporting of being a morning person. *Nature Communications, 7*, 10448. https://doi.org/10.1038/ncomms10448

Inder, M. L., Crowe, M. T., Luty, S. E., Carter, J. D., Moor, S., Frampton, C. M., & Joyce, P. R. (2015). Randomized, controlled trial of interpersonal and social rhythm therapy for young people with bipolar disorder. *Bipolar Disorders, 17*, 128–138.

Insel, T., Cuthbert, B., Garvey, M., Heinssen, R., Pine, D., Quinn, K., Sanislo, C., & Wang, P. (2010). Research Domain Criteria (RDoC): Towards a new classification framework for research on mental disorders. *American Journal of Psychiatry, 167*, 748–751.

Ivins, A., Di Simplicio, M., Close, H., Goodwin, G. M., & Holmes, E. (2014). Mental imagery in bipolar affective disorder versus unipolar depression: Investigating cognitions at times of "positive" mood. *Journal of Affective Disorders, 166*, 234–242.

Jamison, K. R. (2004). *An unquiet mind: A memoir of moods and madness*. Knopf.

Jenkins, M. M., & Youngstrom, E. A. (2016). A randomized controlled trial of cognitive debiasing improves assessment and treatment selection for pediatric bipolar disorder. *Journal of Consulting and Clinical Psychology, 84*(4), 323–333. https://doi.org/10.1037/ccp0000070

Jensen-Doss, A., Casline, E., Patel, Z., & McLeod, B. D. (2020). Evidence-Based Assessment: Prescription. In E. A. Youngstrom, M. J. Prinstein, E. J. Mash, & R. Barkley (Eds.), *Assessment of disorders in childhood and adolescence*, 5th ed. (pp. 49–74). Guilford.

Johnson, K. R., & Johnson, S. L. (2014a). Cross-national prevalence and cultural correlates of bipolar I disorder. *Social Psychiatry and Psychiatric Epidemiology, 49*(7), 1111–1117. https://doi.org/10.1007/s00127-013-0797-5

Johnson, K. R., & Johnson, S. L. (2014b). Inadequate treatment of black Americans with bipolar disorder. *Psychiatric Services, 65*(2), 255–258. https://doi.org/10.1176/appi.ps.201200590

Johnson, S. L. (2005). Life events in bipolar disorder: Towards more specific models. *Clinical Psychology Review, 25*(8), 1008–1027.

Johnson, S. L., Carver, C. S., & Gotlib, I. H. (2012). Elevated ambitions for fame among persons diagnosed with bipolar I disorder. *Journal of Abnormal Psychology, 121*(3), 602.

Johnson, S. L., Cueller, A. K., Ruggero, C., Winett-Perlman, C., Goodnick, P., White, R., & Miller, I. (2008). Life events as predictors of mania and depression in bipolar I disorder. *Journal of Abnormal Psychology, 117*(2), 268.

Johnson, S. L., Edge, M. D., Holmes, M. K., & Carver, C. S. (2012). The behavioral activation system and mania. *Annual Review of Clinical Psychology, 8*, 243–267.

Johnson, S. L., Eisner, L. R., & Carver, C. S. (2009). Elevated expectancies among persons diagnosed with bipolar disorder. *British Journal of Clinical Psychology, 48*, 217–222.

Johnson, S. L., Freeman, M. A., & Staudenmaier, P. J. (2015). Mania risk, overconfidence, and ambition. *Journal of Social and Clinical Psychology, 34*(7), 611.

Johnson, S. L., Fulford, D., & Carver, C. S. (2012). The double-edged sword of goal engagement: Consequences of goal pursuit in bipolar disorder. *Clinical Psychology and Psychotherapy, 19*(4), 352–362.

Johnson, S. L., Gruber, J., & Eisner, L. R. (2007). Emotion and bipolar disorder. In J. Rottenberg & S. L. Johnson (Eds.), *Emotion and psychopathology: Bridging affective and clinical science* (pp. 123–150). American Psychological Association.

Johnson, S. L., Mehta, H., Ketter, T. A., Gotlib, I. H., & Knutson, B. (2019). Neural responses to monetary incentives in bipolar disorder. *Neuroimage: Clinical, 24*, 102018.

Johnson, S. L., & Miller, I. (1997). Negative life events and time to recovery from episodes of bipolar disorder. *Journal of Abnormal Psychology, 106*(3), 449.

Johnson, S. L., Ruggero, C., & Carver, C. S. (2005). Cognitive, behavioral and affective responses to reward: Links with hypomanic vulnerability. *Journal of Social and Clinical Psychology, 24*, 894–906.

Johnson, S. L., Sandrow, D., Meyer, B., Winters, R., Miller, I., Solomon, D., & Keitner, G. (2000). Increases in manic symptoms after life events involving goal attainment. *Journal of Abnormal Psychology, 109*(4), 721.

Johnson, S. L., Swerdlow, B. A., Treadway, M., Tharp, J. A., & Carver, C. S. (2017). Willingness to expend effort toward reward and extreme ambitions in bipolar I disorder. *Clinical Psychological Science, 5*(6), 943–951.

Johnson, S. L., Winett, C. A., Meyer, B., Greenhouse, W. J., & Miller, I. (1999). Social support and the course of bipolar disorder. *Journal of Abnormal Psychology, 108*(4), 558.

Jones, E. E., Farina, A., Hastorf, A. H., Markus, H., Miller, D. T., & Scott, R. A. (1984). *Social stigma: The psychology of marked relationships.* Freeman

Jones, S. E., Lane, J. M., Wood, A. R., van Hees, V. T., Tyrrell, J., Beaumont, R. N., . . . Weedon, M. N. (2019). Genome-wide association analyses of chronotype in 697,828 individuals provides insights into circadian rhythms. *Nature Communications, 10*(1), 343. https://doi.org/10.1038/s41467-018-08259-7

Jones, S. H., Hare, D. J., & Evershed, K. (2005). Actigraphic assessment of circadian activity and sleep patterns in bipolar disorder. *Bipolar Disorders, 7*(2), 176–186. https://doi.org/10.1111/j.1399-5618.2005.00187.x

Jones, S. H., Mansell, W., & Waller, L. (2006). Appraisal of hypomania-relevant experiences: Development of a questionnaire to assess positive self-dispositional appraisals in bipolar and behavioural high risk samples. *Journal of Affective Disorders, 93*(1–3), 19–28.

Jones, S. H., Smith, G., Mullgan, L. D., Lobban, F., Law, H., Dunn, G., Welford, M., Kelly, J., Mulligan, J., & Morrison, A. P. (2015). Recovery-focused cognitive behavioural therapy for recent-onset bipolar disorder: Randomized controlled pilot trial. *British Journal of Psychiatry, 206*, 58–66.

Kalmady, S. V., Shivakumar, S., Arasappa, Subramaniam, A., Venkatasubramanian, G., & Gangadhar, B. N. (2017). Clinical correlates of hippocampus volume and shape in antipsychotic-naïve schizophrenia. *Psychiatry Research: Neuroimaging, 263*, 93–102.

Kanagarajan, K., Gou, K., Antinora, C., Buyukkurt, A., Crescenzi, O., Beaulieu, S., Storch, K. F., & Mantere, O. (2018). Morningness-Eveningness questionnaire in bipolar disorder. *Psychiatry Research, 262*, 102–107. https://doi.org/10.1016/j.psychres.2018.02.004

Kapczinski, F., Magalhães, P. V. S., Balanza-Martinez, V., Dias, V. V., Frangou, S., Gama, C. S., Gonzalez-Pinto, A., Grande, I., Ha, K., Kauer-Sainy A. M., Kunz, M., Kupka, R., Leboyer, M., Lopez-Jaramillo, C., Post, R. M., Rybakowksi, J. K., Scott, J., Streilevitch, S., Tohen, M., Vasquez, G., Yatham, L., Vieta, E., & Berk., M. (2014). Staging systems in bipolar disorder: An International Society for Bipolar Disorders Task Force Report. *Acta Psychiatrica Scandinavica, 130*(5), 354–363.

Kasch, K. L., Rottenberg, J., Arnow, B. A., & Gotlib, I. H. (2002). Behavioral activation and inhibition systems and the severity and course of depression. *Journal of Abnormal Psychology, 111*, 589–597. doi:10.1037/0021-843X.111.4.589. PMID: 12428772

Kazdin, A. E. (1989). Evaluation of the pleasure scale in the assessment of anhedonia in children. *Journal of American Academy of Child and Adolescent Psychiatry, 28*, 364–372.

Kelly, R. E., Dodd, A. L., & Mansell, W. (2017). "When my moods drive upward there is nothing I can do about it": A review of extreme appraisals of internal states and the bipolar spectrum. *Frontiers in Psychology, 8*, 1235.

Keenan-Miller, D., Peris, T., Axelson, D., Kowatch, R. A., & Miklowitz, D. J. (2012). Family functioning, social impairment, and symptoms among adolescents with bipolar disorder. *Journal of the American Academy of Child and Adolescent Psychiatry, 51*(10), 1085–1094. https://doi.org/10.1016/j.jaac.2012.08.005

Kendler, K. S. (2012). The dappled nature of causes of psychiatric illness: Replacing the organic-functional/hardware-software dichotomy with empirically based pluralism. *Molecular Psychiatry, 17*(4), 377–388.

Kilbourne, A. M., Bauer, M. S., Han, X., Haas, G. L., Elder, P., Good, C. B., Shad, M., Conigliaro, J., & Pincus, H. (2005). Racial differences in the treatment of veterans with bipolar disorder. *Psychiatric Services, 56*(12), 1549–1555. https://doi.org/10.1176/appi.ps.56.12.1549

Kilbourne, A. M., & Pincus, H. A. (2006). Patterns of psychotropic medication use by race among veterans with bipolar disorder. *Psychiatric Services, 57*(1), 123–126. https://doi.org/10.1176/appi.ps.57.1.123

Kim, E. Y., Miklowitz, D. J., Biuckians, A., & Mullen, K. (2007). Life stress and the course of early-onset bipolar disorder. *Journal of Affective Disorders, 99*(1–3), 37–44. https://doi.org/10.1016/j.jad.2006.08.022

Kirov, G., & Murray, R. M. (1999). Ethnic differences in the presentation of bipolar affective disorder. *European Psychiatry, 14*(4), 199–204. https://doi.org/10.1016/S0924-9338(99)80742-1

Klerman, G. L., Weissman, M. M., Rounsaville, B. J., & Chevron, E. S. (1984). *Interpersonal psychotherapy of depression.* Basic Books.

Koenders, M. A., Giltay, E. J., Spijker, A. T., Hoencamp, E., Spinhoven, P., & Elzinga, B. M. (2014). Stressful life events in bipolar I and II disorder: Cause or consequence of mood symptoms? *Journal of Affective Disorders, 161*, 55–64.

Kotov, R., Jonas, K. G., Carpenter, W. T., Dretsch, M. N., Eaton, N. R., Forbes, M. K., Forbush, K. T., Hobbs, K., Reininghaus, U., Slade, T., South, S. C., Sunderland, M., Waszczuk, M. A., Widiger, T. A., Wright, A. G. C., Zald, D. H., Krueger, R. F., Watson, D., & HiTOP Utility Workgroup. (2020). Validity and utility of Hierarchical Taxonomy of Psychopathology (HiTOP): I. Psychosis superspectrum. *World Psychiatry, 19*, 151–172.

Kowatch, R. A., Youngstrom, E. A., Danielyan, A., & Findling, R. L. (2005). Review and meta-analysis of the phenomenology and clinical characteristics of mania in children and adolescents *Bipolar Disorders, 7*(6), 483–496. https://doi.org/10.1111/j.1399-5618.2005.00261.x

Krane-Gartiser, K., Henriksen, T. E., Morken, G., Vaaler, A., & Fasmer, O. B. (2014). Actigraphic assessment of motor activity in acutely admitted inpatients with bipolar disorder. *PloS One, 9*(2), e89574. https://doi.org/10.1371/journal.pone.0089574

Krane-Gartiser, K., Steinan, M. K., Langsrud, K., Vestvik, V., Sand, T., Fasmer, O. B., Kallestad, H., & Morken, G. (2016). Mood and motor activity in euthymic bipolar disorder with sleep disturbance. *Journal of Affective Disorders, 202*, 23–31. https://doi.org/10.1016/j.jad.2016.05.012

Kurzban, R., & Leary, M. R. (2001). Evolutionary origins of stigmatization: The functions of social exclusion. *Psychological Bulletin, 127*, 187–208.

Kvaale, E. P., Haslam, N., & Gottdiener, W. H. (2013). The "side effects" of medicalization: A meta-analytic review of how biogenetic explanations affect stigma. *Clinical Psychology Review, 33*, 782–794.

Lam, D., Jones, S. H., Hayward, P., & Bright, J. A. (2010). *Cognitive therapy for bipolar disorder. A therapist's guide to concepts, methods and practice*, 2nd ed. Wiley.

Lam, D., Hayward, P., Watkins, E. R., Wright, K., & Sham, P. (2005). Relapse prevention in patients with bipolar disorder: Cognitive therapy outcome after 2 years. *American Journal of Psychiatry, 162*, 324–329.

Lam, D., Watkins, E. R., Hayward, P., Bright, J., Wright, K., Kerr, N., Parr-Davis, G., & Sham, P. (2003). A randomized controlled study of cognitive therapy for relapse prevention for bipolar affective disorder. *Archives of General Psychiatry, 60*, 145–152.

Lam, D., Wright, K., & Smith, N. (2004). Dysfunctional assumptions in bipolar disorder. *Journal of Affective Disorders, 79*(1–3), 193–199.

Lam, D., Wright, K., & Sham, P. (2005). Sense of hyper-positive self and response to cognitive therapy in bipolar disorder. *Psychological Medicine, 35*(1), 69–77.

Lane, J. M., Vlasac, I., Anderson, S. G., Kyle, S. D., Dixon, W. G., Bechtold, D. A., Gill, S., Little, M. A., Luik, A., Loudon, A., Emsley, R., Scheer, F. A., Lawlor, D. A., Redline, S., Ray, D. W., Rutter, M. K., & Saxena, R. (2016). Genome-wide association analysis identifies novel loci for chronotype in 100,420 individuals from the UK Biobank. *Nature Communications, 7*, 10889. doi:10.1038/ncomms10889

Lawrence, N. S., Williams, A. M., Surguladze, S., Giampietro, V., Brammer, M. J., Andrew, C., & Phillips, M. L. (2004). Subcortical and ventral prefrontal cortical neural responses to facial expressions distinguished patients with bipolar disorder and major depression. *Biological Psychiatry 55*, 578–587.

Lee, K. Y., Song, J. Y., Kim, S. H., Kim, S. C., Joo, E. J., Ahn, Y. M., & Kim, Y. S. (2010). Association between CLOCK 3111T/C and preferred circadian phase in Korean patients with bipolar disorder. *Progress in Neuro-psychopharmacology and Biological Psychiatry, 34*(7), 1196–1201. https://doi.org/10.1016/j.pnpbp.2010.06.010

Leibenluft, E. (2011). Severe mood dysregulation, irritability, and the diagnostic boundaries of bipolar disorder in youths. *American Journal of Psychiatry, 168*(2), 129–142. https://doi.org/10.1176/appi.ajp.2010.10050766

Lembke, A., & Ketter, T. A. (2002). Impaired recognition of facial emotion in mania. *American Journal of Psychiatry, 159*(2), 302–304.

Levenson, J. C., Nusslock, R., & Frank, E. (2013). Life events, sleep disturbance, and mania: An integrated model. *Clinical Psychology: Science & Practice, 20*, 195–210.

Leverich, G. S., & Post, R. M. (2006). Course of bipolar illness after history of childhood trauma. *Lancet, 367*(9516), 1040–1042.

Leverich, G. S., Post, R. M., Keck, P. E., Altshuler, L. L., Frye, M. A., Kupka, R. W., . . . Luckenbaugh, D. (2007). The poor prognosis of childhood-onset bipolar disorder. *Journal of Pediatrics, 150*(5), 485–490. https://doi.org/10.1016/j.jpeds.2006.10.070

Lex, C., Bäzner, E., & Meyer, T. D. (2017). Does stress play a significant role in bipolar disorder? A meta-analysis. *Journal of Affective Disorders, 208*, 298–308.

Lex, C., Hautzinger, M., & Meyer, T. D. (2011). Cognitive styles in hypomanic episodes of bipolar I disorder. *Bipolar Disorders, 13*, 355–364.

Link, B. G., & Phelan, J. C. (2001). Conceptualizing stigma. *Annual Review of Sociology, 27*, 363–385.

Lish, J. D., Dime-Meenan, S., Whybrow, P. C., Price, R. A., & Hirschfeld, R. M. A. (1994). The National Depressive and Manic-depressive Association (DMDA) survey of bipolar members. *Journal of Affective Disorders, 31*(4), 281–294. https://doi.org/10.1016/0165-0327(94)90104-X

Liu, J., Blond, B. N., van Dyck, L. I., Spencer, L., Wang, F., & Blumberg, H. P. (2012). Trait and state corticostriatal dysfunction in bipolar disorder during emotional face processing. *Bipolar Disorders, 14*, 432–441.

Lobban, F., Taylor, L., Chandler, C., et al. (2010). Enhanced relapse prevention for bipolar disorder by community mental health teams: Cluster feasibility trial. *British Journal of Psychiatry, 196*, 59–63.

Logan, R. W., & McClung, C. A. (2019). Rhythms of life: Circadian disruption and brain disorders across the lifespan. *Nature Reviews Neuroscience, 20*, 49–65.

Lopez-Jaramillo, C., Vargas, C., Diaz-Zuluaga, A. M., Palacio, J. D., Castrollon, G., Bearden, C., & Vieta, E. (2017). Increased hippocampal, thalamus and amygdala volume in long-term lithium-treated bipolar I disorder patients compared with unmedicated patients and healthy subjects. *Bipolar Disorders, 19*, 41–49

Lovasa, D. A, & Schuman-Olivier, Z. (2018). Mindfulness-based cognitive therapy for bipolar disorder: A systematic review. *Journal of Affective Disorders, 240*, 247–261.

Luby, J. L., Mrakotsky, C., Heffelfinger, A., Brown, K., & Spitznagel, E. (2004). Characteristics of depressed preschoolers with and without anhedonia: Evidence for a melancholic depressive subtype in young children. *American Journal of Psychiatry, 161*, 1998–2004.

Luby, J. L., & Navsaria, N. (2010). Pediatric bipolar disorder: Evidence for prodromal states and early markers. *Journal of Child Psychology and Psychiatry and Allied Disciplines, 51*(4), 459–471. https://doi.org/10.1111/j.1469-7610.2010.02210.x

Lyall, L. M., Wyse, C. A., Graham, N., Ferguson, A., Lyall, D. M., Cullen, B., Celis Morales, C. A., Biello, S. M., Mackay, D., Ward, J., Strawbridge, R. J., Gill, J., Bailey, M., Pell, J. P., & Smith, D. J. (2018). Association of disrupted circadian rhythmicity with mood disorders, subjective well being, and cognitive function: A cross-sectional study of 91,105 participants from the UK Biobank. *Lancet-Psychiatry, 5*(6), 507–514. https://doi.org/10.1016/S2215-0366(18)30139-1

Lynch, D., Laws, K. R., & McKenna, P. J. (2010). Cognitive behavioural therapy for major psychiatric disorder: Does it really work? A meta-analytical review of well-controlled trials. *Psychological Medicine, 40*, 9–24.

Macheiner, T., Skavantzos, A., Pilz, R., & Reininghaus, E. Z. (2017). A meta-analysis of adjuvant group-interventions in psychiatric care for patients with bipolar disorders. *Journal of Affective Disorders, 222*, 28–31.

Makanjuola, R. O. A. (1985). Recurrent unipolar manic disorder in the Yoruba Nigerian: Further evidence. *British Journal of Psychiatry, 147*(4), 434–437. https://doi.org/10.1192/bjp.147.4.434

Manelis, A., Soehner, A., Halchenko, Y. O. Satz, S., Ragozzino, R., Lucero, M., Swartz, H., Phillips, M. L., & Versace, A. (2021). White matter abnormalities in adults with bipolar disorder type-II and unipolar depression. *Scientific Reports, 11*, 7541.

Mansell, W., Morrison, A. P., Reid, G., Lowens, I., & Tai, S. (2007). The interpretation of, and responses to, changes in internal states: An integrative cognitive model of mood swings and bipolar disorders. *Behavioural and Cognitive Psychotherapy, 35*(5), 515–539.

Mansell, W., Paszek, G., Seal, K., Pedley, R., Jones, S., Thomas, N., . . . Dodd, A. (2011). Extreme appraisals of internal states in bipolar I disorder: A multiple control group study. *Cognitive Therapy and Research, 35*(1), 87–97.

Martinez, A., & Hinshaw, S. P. (2016). Mental health stigma: Theory, developmental issues, and research priorities. In D. Cicchetti (Ed.), *Developmental psychopathology. Vol 4: Risk, resilience, and intervention,* 3rd ed. (pp. 997–1039). Wiley.

Mason, L., Trujillo-Barreto, N. J., Bentall, R. P., & El-Deredy, W. (2016). Attentional bias predicts increased reward salience and risk taking in bipolar disorder. *Biological Psychiatry, 79*(4), 311–319.

M'Bailara, K., Demotes-Mainard, J., Swendsen, J., Mathieu, F., Leboyer, M., & Henry, C. (2009). Emotional hyperreactivity in normothymic bipolar patients. *Bipolar Disorders, 11*(1), 63–69.

McCarthy, M. J., Le Roux, M. J., Wei, H., Beesley, S., Kelsoe, J. R., & Welsh, D. K. (2016). Calcium channel genes associated with bipolar disorder modulate lithium's amplification of circadian rhythms. *Neuropharmacology, 101,* 439–448. https://doi.org/10.1016/j.neuropharm.2015.10.017

McCarthy, M. J., Wei, H., Nievergelt, C. M., Stautland, A., Maihofer, A. X., Welsh, D. K., . . . Kelsoe, J. R. (2019). Chronotype and cellular circadian rhythms predict the clinical response to lithium maintenance treatment in patients with bipolar disorder. *Neuropsychopharmacology, 44*(3), 620–628. https://doi.org/10.1038/s41386-018-0273-8

McCarthy, M. J., Gottlieb, J. F., Gonzalez, R., McClung, C. A., Alloy, L. B., Cain, S., . . . Murray, G. (2021). Neurobiological and behavioral mechanisms of circadian rhythm disruption in bipolar disorder: A critical multi-disciplinary literature review and agenda for future research. *Bipolar Disorders.* https://doi.org/10.1111/bdi.13165

McMaster, K. J. (2016). Explaining racial disparity in bipolar disorder treatment: How do providers contribute? https://escholarship.org/uc/item/9wc2415d

Melo, M., Abreu, R., Linhares Neto, V. B., de Bruin, P., & de Bruin, V. (2017). Chronotype and circadian rhythm in bipolar disorder: A systematic review. *Sleep Medicine Reviews, 34,* 46–58. https://doi.org/10.1016/j.smrv.2016.06.007

Meyer, T. D., Crist, N., La Rosa, N., Ye, B., Soares, J. C., & Bauer, I. E. (2020). Are existing self-ratings of acute manic symptoms in adults reliable and valid? A systematic review. *Bipolar Disorders, 22*(6), 558–568. doi:10.1111/bdi.12906

Meyer, T. D., & Hautzinger, M. (2012). Cognitive behavior therapy and supportive therapy for bipolar disorder. Relapse rates for treatment period and 2 year follow-up? *Psychological Medicine, 42,* 1429–1439.

Meyer, T. D., & Hautzinger, M. (2013). *Bipolare Störungen. Kognitiv-verhaltenstherapeutisches Behandlungsmanual (2. erweiterte Auflage).* Beltz.

Michalak, E. E., Yatham, L. N., Kolesar, S., & Lam, R. W. (2006). Bipolar disorder and quality of life: A patient-centered perspective. *Quality of Life Research, 15*(1), 25–37.

Miklowitz, D. J. (2010). *Bipolar disorder. A family-focused treatment approach,* 2nd ed. Guilford.

Miklowitz, D., Alatiq, Y., Goodwin, G. M., Geddes, J. R., Fennell, M. J. V., Dimidjian, S., Hauser, M., & Williams, J. M. G. (2009). A pilot study of mindfulness-based cognitive therapy for bipolar disorder. *International Journal of Cognitive Therapy. 5,* 373–383.

Miklowitz, D. L., Axelson, D. A., Birmaher, B., George, E. K., Taylor, D. D., Schneck, C. D., Beresfold, C. A., Dickinson, L. M., Craighead, W. E., & Brent, D. A. (2008). Family-Focused Treatment for adolescents with bipolar disorder. Results of a 2-year randomized trial. *Archives of General Psychiatry, 65,* 1053–1061.

Miklowitz, D. J., Efthimiou, O., Furukawa, T. A., Scott, J., McLaren, R., Geddes, J. R., & Cipriani, A. (2020). Adjunctive psychotherapy for bipolar disorder: A systematic review and component network meta-analysis. *JAMA Psychiatry,* e202993. doi:10.1001/jamapsychiatry.2020.2993.

Miklowitz, D. J., George, E. L., Richards, J. A., Simoneau, T. L., & Suddath, R.L. (2003). A randomized study of family-focused psychoeducation and pharmacotherapy in the outpatient management of bipolar disorder. *Archives of General Psychiatry, 60,* 909–912.

Miklowitz, D. J., Goldstein, M. J., Nuechterlein, K. H., Snyder, K. S., & Mintz, J. (1988). Family factors and the course of bipolar affective disorder. *Archives of General Psychiatry, 45,* 225–231.

Miklowitz, D. J., & Johnson, S. L. (2006). The psychopathology and treatment of bipolar disorder. *Annual Review of Clinical Psychology, 2,* 199.

Miklowitz, D. J., Otto, M., Frank, E., Reilly-Harrington, N. A., Wisniewski, S. R., Kogan, J. N., Nierenberg, A. A., Calabrese, J. R., Marangell, L. B., Gyulai, L., Araga, M., Gonzalez, J. M., Shirley, E. R., Thase, M. E., & Sachs, G. S. (2007). Psychosocial treatments for bipolar depression. A 1-year randomized trial from the Systematic Treatment Enhancement Program. *Archives of General Psychiatry, 64,* 419–427.

Miklowitz, D. J., Schneck, C. D., Singh, M. K., Taylor, D. O., George, E. L., Cosgrove, V. E., Howe, M. E., Dickinson, M., Garber, J., & Chang, K. D. (2013). Early intervention for symptomatic youth at risk for bipolar disorder: A randomized trial of family-focused therapy. *Journal of the American Academy of Child and Adolescent Psychiatry, 52*(2), 121–131. https://doi.org/10.1016/j.jaac.2012.10.007

Miklowitz, D. J., Schneck, C. D., Walshaw, P. D., Singh, M. K., Sullivan, A. E., Suddath, R. L., Forgey-Borlik, M., Sugar, C. A., & Chang, K. D. (2020). Effects of family-focused therapy vs enhanced usual care for symptomatic youths at high risk for bipolar disorder: A randomized clinical trial. *JAMA Psychiatry, 77*(5), 455–463.

Miklowitz, D. J., & Scott, J. (2009). Psychosocial treatments for bipolar disorder: Cost-effectiveness, mediating mechanisms, and future directions. *Bipolar Disorders, 11* (Suppl. 2), 110–122.

Miklowitz, D. J., Wisniewski, S. R., Miyahara, S., Otto, M. W., & Sachs, G. S. (2005). Perceived criticism from family members as a predictor of the one-year course of bipolar disorder. *Psychiatry Research, 136*(2–3), 101–111. https://doi.org/10.1016/j.psychres.2005.04.005

Mistlberger, R. E., & Skene, D. J. (2005). Nonphotic entrainment in humans? *Journal of Biological Rhythms, 20*(4), 339–352. https://doi.org/10.1177/0748730405277982

Mohawk, J. A., Green, C. B., & Takahashi, J. S. (2012). Central and peripheral circadian clocks in mammals. *Annual Review of Neuroscience, 35*, 445–462. https://doi.org/10.1146/annurev-neuro-060909-153128

Moreira, A. L. R., Van Meter, A., Genzlinger, J., & Youngstrom, E. A. (2017). Review and meta-analysis of epidemiologic studies of adult bipolar disorder. *Journal of Clinical Psychiatry, 78*(9), e1259–e1269. https://doi.org/10.4088/JCP.16r11165

Moreno, C., Laje, G., Blanco, C., Jiang, H., Schmidt, A. B., & Olfson, M. (2007). National trends in the outpatient diagnosis and treatment of bipolar disorder in youth. *Archives of General Psychiatry, 64*(9), 1032–1039. https://doi.org/10.1001/archpsyc.64.9.1032

Morgan, J. K., Olino, T. M., McMakin, D. L., Ryan, N. D., & Forbes, E. E. (2013). Neural response to reward as a predictor of increases in depressive symptoms in adolescence. *Neurobiology of Disease, 52*, 66–74.

Mukherjee, S., Coque, L., Cao, J. L., Kumar, J., Chakravarty, S., Asaithamby, A., Graham, A., Gordon, E., Enwright, J. F., 3rd, DiLeone, R. J., Birnbaum, S. G., Cooper, D. C., & McClung, C. A. (2010). Knockdown of Clock in the ventral tegmental area through RNA interference results in a mixed state of mania and depression-like behavior. *Biological Psychiatry, 68*(6), 503–511. https://doi.org/10.1016/j.biopsych.2010.04.031

Mukherjee, S., Shukla, S., Woodle, J., Rosen, A. M., & Olarte, S. (1983). Misdiagnosis of schizophrenia in bipolar patients: A multiethnic comparison. *American Journal of Psychiatry, 140*(12), 1571–1574. https://doi.org/10.1176/ajp.140.12.1571

Murray, C. J. L., & Lopez, A. D. (1996). The global burden of disease: A comprehensive assessment of mortality and disability from diseases, injuries, and risk factors in 1990 and projected to 2020. World Health Organization. doi:0965546608

Murray G. (2019). Circadian science and psychiatry: Of planets, proteins and persons. *Australian and New Zealand Journal of Psychiatry, 53*, 597–601.

Murray, G., & Harvey, A. (2010). Circadian rhythms and sleep in bipolar disorder. *Bipolar Disorders, 12*, 459–472.

Murray, G., Leitan, N. D., Thomas, N., Michalak, E. E., Johnson, S. J., Jones, S., Perich, T., Berk, L., & Berk, M. (2017). Towards recovery-oriented psychosocial interventions for bipolar disorder: Quality of life outcomes, stage-sensitive treatments, and mindfulness mechanisms. *Clinical Psychology Review, 52*, 148–163.

Murray, G., Gottlieb, J., Hidalgo, M. P., Etain, B., Ritter, P., Skene, D. J., Garbazza, C., Bullock, B., Merikangas, K., Zipunnikov, V., Shou, H., Gonzalez, R., Scott, J., Geoffroy, P. A., & Frey, B. N. (2020). Measuring circadian function in bipolar disorders: Empirical and conceptual review of physiological, actigraphic, and self-report approaches. *Bipolar Disorders, 22*(7), 693–710. https://doi.org/10.1111/bdi.12963

Musket, C., Hansen, N. S., Welker, K., Gilbert, K. E., & Gruber, J. (2021). A pilot investigation of emotion regulation difficulties and mindfulness-based strategies in manic and remitted bipolar I disorder and major depressive disorder. *International Journal of Bipolar Disorders, 9*(1), 1–8. https://doi.org/10.1186/s40345-020-00206-0

Nelson, B. D., Perlman, G., Klein, D. N., Kotov, R., & Hajcak, G. (2016). Blunted neural response to rewards as a prospective predictor of the development of depression in adolescent girls. *American Journal of Psychiatry, 173*, 1223–1230.

Neighbors, H. W., Trierweiler, S. J., Ford, B. C., & Muroff, J. R. (2003). Racial differences in DSM diagnosis using a semi-structured instrument: The importance of clinical judgment in the diagnosis of African-Americans. *Journal of Health and Social Behavior, 44*(3), 237–256. https://doi.org/10.2307/1519777

Newman, C. F., Leahy, R. L., Beck, A. T., Reilly-Harrington, N. A., & Gyulai, L. (2002). *Bipolar disorder. A cognitive therapy approach.* American Psychological Press.

Ng, T. H., Alloy, L. B., & Smith, D. V. (2019). Meta-analysis of reward processing in major depressive disorder reveals distinct abnormalities within the reward circuit. *Translational Psychiatry, 9*, 293.

Ng, T. H., Stange, J. P., Black, C. L., Titone, M. K., Weiss, R. B., Abramson, L. Y., & Alloy, L. B. (2016). Impulsivity predicts the onset of DSM-IV-TR or RDC hypomanic and manic episodes in adolescents and young adults with high or moderate reward sensitivity. *Journal of Affective Disorders, 198*, 88–95.

Nguyen, P., & Hinshaw, S. P. (2020). Understanding the stigma associated with ADHD: Hope for the future? *ADHD Report, 28*(5), 1–10,12.

Nurnberger, J. I., Jr, Adkins, S., Lahiri, D. K., Mayeda, A., Hu, K., Lewy, A., Miller, A., Bowman, E. S., Miller, M. J., Rau, L., Smiley, C., & Davis-Singh, D. (2000). Melatonin suppression by light in euthymic bipolar and unipolar patients. *Archives of General Psychiatry, 57*(6), 572–579. https://doi.org/10.1001/archpsyc.57.6.572

Nusslock, R., & Alloy, L. B. (2017). Reward processing and mood-related symptoms: An RDoC and translational neuroscience perspective. *Journal of Affective Disorders, 216*, 3–16.

Nusslock, R., Almeida, J. R. C., Forbes, E. E., Versace, A., LaBarbara, E. J., Klein, C., & Phillips, M. L. (2012b). Waiting to win: Elevated striatal and orbitofrontal cortical activity during reward anticipation in euthymic bipolar adults. *Bipolar Disorders, 14*, 249–260.

Nusslock, R., Harmon-Jones, E., Alloy, L. B., Urosevic, S., Goldstein, K., & Abramson, L. Y. (2012a). Elevated left mid-frontal cortical activity prospectively predicts conversion to bipolar I disorder. *Journal of Abnormal Psychology, 121*, 592–601.

Nusslock, R., Shackman, A. J., Harmon-Jones, E., Alloy, L. B., Coan, J. A., & Abramson, L. Y. (2011). Cognitive vulnerability and frontal brain asymmetry: Common predictors of first prospective depressive episode. *Journal of Abnormal Psychology, 120*, 497–503.

Olino, T. M., Klein, D. N., Dyson, M. W., Rose, S. A., & Durbin, C. E. (2010). Temperamental emotionality in preschool-aged children and depressive disorders in parents: Associations in a large community sample. *Journal of Abnormal Psychology, 119*, 468–478.

Ong, D. C., Zaki, J., & Gruber, J. (2017). Increased cooperative behavior across remitted bipolar I disorder and major depression: Insights utilizing a behavioral economic trust game. *Journal of Abnormal Psychology, 126*(1), 1.

Oud, M,. Mayo-Wilson, E., Braidwood, R., Schulte, P., Jones, S. H., Morriss, R., Kupka, R., Cuijpers, P., & Kendall, T. (2016). Psychological interventions for adults with bipolar disorder: Systematic review and meta-analysis. B

Oveis, C., & Keltner, D. (2008). Risk for mania and positive emotional responding: Too much of a good thing? *Emotion, 8*(1), 23.

Parikh, S. V., Zaretsky, A., Beaulieu, S., Yatham, L. N., Young, L. T., Patelis-Siotis, I., McQueen, G. M., Levitt, A., Arenovich, T., Cervantes, P., Velyvis, V., Kennedy, S. H., & Steiner, D. L. (2012). A randomised controlled trial of psychoeducation or cognitive-behavioral therapy for bipolar disorder: A Canadian network for mood and Anxiety treatments (CANMAT) study. *Journal of Clinical Psychiatry, 73*, 803–810.

Parry, P., Allison, S., & Bastiampillai, T. (2018). "Paediatric bipolar disorder" rates are lower than claimed: A reexamination of the epidemiological surveys used by a meta-analysis. *Child and Adolescent Mental Health, 23*(1), 14–22. https://doi.org/10.1111/camh.12231

Paul, K. N., Saafir, T. B., & Tosini, G. (2009). The role of retinal photoreceptors in the regulation of circadian rhythms. *Reviews in Endocrine & Metabolic Disorders, 10*(4), 271–278. https://doi.org/10.1007/s11154-009-9120-x

Perlick, D. A., Miklowitz, D. J., Lopez, N., Chou, J., Kalvin, C., Adzhiashvili, V., & Aronson, A. (2010). Family-focused treatment for caregivers of patients with bipolar disorder. *Bipolar Disorders, 12*, 627–637.

Perlick, D. A., Rosenheck, R. A., Clarkin, J. F., Maciejewski, P. K., Sirey, J., Struening, E., & Link, B. G. (2004). Impact of family burden and affective response on clinical outcome among patients with bipolar disorder. *Psychiatric Services, 55*, 1029–1025.

Perlis, R. H., Miyahara, S., Marangell, L. B., Wisniewski, S. R., Ostacher, M., DelBello, M. P., . . . Nierenberg, A. A. (2004). Long-term implications of early onset in bipolar disorder: Data from the first 1000 participants in the Systematic Treatment Enhancement Program for Bipolar Disorder (STEP-BD). *Biological Psychiatry, 55*(9), 875–881. https://doi.org/10.1016/j.biopsych.2004.01.022

Perry, A., Tarrier, N., Morriss, R., McCarthy, E., & Limb, K. (1999). Randomised controlled trial of efficacy of teaching bipolar disorder to identify early symptoms of relapse and obtain treatment. *British Medical Journal, 318*, 149–153.

Pescosolido, B. A., Martin, J. K., Lang, A., & Olafsdottir, S. (2008). Rethinking theoretical approaches to stigma: A framework integrating normative influences on stigma (FINIS). *Social Science and Medicine, 67*, 431–440.

Pescosolido, B. A., Martin, J. K., Long, J. S., Medina, T. R., Phelan, J. C., & Link, B. G. (2010). "A disease like any other?" A decade of change in public reactions to schizophrenia, depression, and alcohol dependence. *American Journal of Psychiatry, 167*, 1321–1330.

Peters, A. T., Weinstein, S. M., Isaia, A., Van Meter, A., Zulauf, C. A., & West, A. E. (2018). Symptom dimensions and trajectories of functioning among bipolar youth: A cluster analysis. *Journal of Psychiatric Practice, 24*(3), 146–157. https://doi.org/10.1097/PRA.0000000000000307

Phillips, M. L., Ladouceur, C., & Drevets, W. (2008). A neural model of voluntary and automatic emotion regulation: Implications for understanding the pathophysiology and neurodevelopment of bipolar disorder. *Molecular Psychiatry, 13*, 833–857.

Phillips, M. L., & Vieta, E. (2007). Identifying functional neuroimaging biomarkers of bipolar disorder: Toward DSM-V. *Schizophrenia Bulletin, 33*, 893–904.

Pizzagalli, D. A., Iosifescu, D. V., Hallett, L. A., Ratner, K. G., & Fava, M. (2008). Reduced hedonic capacity in major depressive disorder: Evidence from a probabilistic reward task. *Journal of Psychiatric Research, 43*, 76–87.

Purcell, J. R., Lohani, M., Musket, C., Hay, A. C., Isaacowitz, D. M., & Gruber, J. (2018). Lack of emotional gaze preferences using eye-tracking in remitted bipolar I disorder. *International Journal of Bipolar Disorders, 6*(1), 15.

Radhu, N., Garcia Dominguez, L., Farzan, F., Richter, M. A., Semeralul, M. O., Chen, R., Fitzgerald, P. B., & Daskalakis, Z. J. (2015). Evidence for inhibitory deficits in the prefrontal cortex in schizophrenia, *Brain, 138*, 483–497,

Rea, M. M., Thompson, M. C., Miklowitz, D. J., Goldstein, M. J., Hwang, S., & Mintz, J. (2003). Family-focused treatment versus individual treatment for bipolar disorder: Results of a randomized clinical trial. *Journal of Consulting and Clinical Psychology, 71*, 482–492.

Refinetti, R. (2006). *Circadian physiology*, 2nd ed. CRC Press.

Reppert, S. M., & Weaver, D. R. (2002). Coordination of circadian timing in mammals. *Nature, 418*, 935–941.

Richard-Lepouriel, H., Favre, S., Jermann, F., & Aubry, J-M. (2020). Self-destigmatization process? Experiences of persons living with bipolar disorder: A qualitative survey. *Community Mental Health Journal, 56*, 1160–1169.

Rock, P., Goodwin, G., Harmer, C., & Wulff, K. (2014). Daily rest-activity patterns in the bipolar phenotype: A controlled actigraphy study. *Chronobiology International, 31*(2), 290–296. https://doi.org/10.3109/07420528.2013.843542

Romans, S. E., & McPherson, H. M. (1992). The social networks of bipolar affective disorder patients. *Journal of Affective Disorders, 25*(4), 221–228. http://dx.doi.org/10.1016/0165-0327(92)90079-L

Roybal, D. J., Singh, M. K., Cosgrove, V. E., Howe, M., Kelley, R., Barnea-Goraly, N., & Chang, K. D. (2012). Biological evidence for a neurodevelopmental model of pediatric bipolar disorder. *Israel Journal of Psychiatry and Related Sciences, 49*(1), 28–43.

Roybal, K., Theobold, D., Graham, A., DiNieri, J. A., Russo, S. J., Krishnan, V., Chakravarty, S., Peevey, J., Oehrlein, N., Birnbaum, S., Vitaterna, M. H., Orsulak, P., Takahashi, J. S., Nestler, E. J., Carlezon, W. A., Jr, & McClung, C. A. (2007). Mania-like behavior induced by disruption of CLOCK. *Proceedings of the National Academy of Sciences, 104*(15), 6406–6411. https://doi.org/10.1073/pnas.0609625104

Ruggero, C. J., Kotov, R., Hopwood, C. J., First, M., Clark, L. A., Skodol, A. E., . . . Zimmermann, J. (2019). Integrating the Hierarchical Taxonomy of Psychopathology (HiTOP) into clinical practice. *Journal of Consulting and Clinical Psychology, 87*, 1069–1084.

Sala, R., Goldstein, B. I., Wang, S., & Blanco, C. (2014). Childhood maltreatment and the course of bipolar disorders among adults: Epidemiologic evidence of dose-response effects. *Journal of Affective Disorders, 165*, 74–80.

Salcedo, S., McMaster, K. J., & Johnson, S. L. (2017). Disparities in treatment and service utilization among Hispanics and non-Hispanic whites with bipolar disorder. *Journal of Racial and Ethnic Health Disparities, 4*(3), 354–363. https://doi.org/10.1007/s40615-016-0236-x

Salvatore, P., Ghidini, S., Zita, G., De Panfilis, C., Lambertino, S., Maggini, C., & Baldessarini, R. J. (2008). Circadian activity rhythm abnormalities in ill and recovered bipolar I disorder patients. *Bipolar Disorders, 10*(2), 256–265. https://doi.org/10.1111/j.1399-5618.2007.00505.x

Sato, A., Hashimoto, T., Kimura, A., Niitsu, T., & Iyo, M. (2018). Psychological distresssymptoms associated with life events in patients with bipolar disorder: A cross-sectional study. *Frontiers in Psychiatry*, 9, 200.

Saxena, K., Kurian, S., Saxena, J., Goldberg, A., Chen, E., & Simonetti, A. (2020). Mixed states in early-onset bipolar disorder. *Psychiatric Clinics of North America*. https://doi.org/10.1016/j.psc.2019.10.009

Schaffer, A., Isometsä, E. T., Tondo, L., Moreno, D. H., Sinyor, M., Kessing, L. V., Turecki, G., Weizman, A., Azorin, J.-M., Ha, K., Reis, C., Cassidy, F., Goldstein, T., Rihmer, Z., Beautrais, A., Chou, Y.-H., Diazgranados, N., Levitt, A. J., Zarate, C. A., & Yatham, L. (2015). Epidemiology, neurobiology and pharmacological interventions related to suicide deaths and suicide attempts in bipolar disorder: Part I of a report of the international society for bipolar disorders task force on suicide in bipolar disorder. *Australian & New Zealand Journal of Psychiatry*, 49(9), 785–802. doi.org/10.1177/0004867415594427

Schalet, B. D., Durbin, C. E., & Revelle, W. (2011). Multidimensional structure of the Hypomanic Personality Scale. *Psychological Assessment*, 23, 504–522.

Schöttle, D., Huber, C. G., Bock, T., & Meyer, T. D. (2011). Psychotherapy for bipolar disorders: A review of the most recent studies. *Current Opinion in Psychiatry*, 24, 549–555.

Scott, J, Garland, A., & Moorhead, S. (2001). A pilot study of cognitive therapy in bipolar disorders. *Psychological Medicine*, 31, 450–467.

Scott, J., & Meyer, T. D. (2021). Brief research report: A pilot study of Cognitive Behavioural Regulation therapy (CBT-REG) for young people at high risk of early transition to bipolar disorders. *Frontiers in Psychiatry*, 11, 616829. doi:10.3389/fpsyt.2020.616829

Scott, J., Murray, G., Henry, C., Morken, G., Scott, E., Angst, J., Merikangas, K. R., & Hickie, I. B. (2017). Activation in bipolar disorders: A systematic review. *JAMA Psychiatry*, 74(2), 189–196. https://doi.org/10.1001/jamapsychiatry.2016.3459

Scott, J., Paykel, E., Morriss, R., Bentall, R., Kinderman, P., Johnson, T., Abbott, R., & Hayhurst, H. (2006). Cognitive behavioural therapy for severe and recurrent bipolar disorders: A randomized controlled trial. *British Journal of Psychiatry*. 188, 313–320.

Selemon, L., & Zecevic, N. (2015). Schizophrenia: A tale of two critical periods for prefrontal cortical development. *Translational Psychiatry* 5, e623.

Shackman, A. J., & Fox, A. S. (2016). Contributions of the central amygdala to fear and anxiety. *Journal of Neuroscience*, 36, 8050–8063.

Shapero, B. G., Stange, J. P., Goldstein, K. E., Black, C. L., Motz, A. R., Hamlat, E. J., Black, S. K., Boccia, A. S., Abramson, L. Y., & Alloy, L. B. (2015). Cognitive styles in mood disorders: Discriminative ability of unipolar and bipolar cognitive profiles. *International Journal of Cognitive Therapy*, 8(1), 35–60.

Sharma, A., Glod, M., Forster, T., McGovern, R., McGurk, K., Barron Millar, E., Meyer, T. D., Miklowitz, D., Ryan, V., Vale, L., & Le Couteur, A. (2020). FAB: First UK feasibility trial of a future randomised controlled trial of Family focused treatment for Adolescents with Bipolar disorder. *International Journal of Bipolar Disorders*. 8, 24. doi:10.1186/s40345-020-00189-y

Shaw, J. A., Egeland, J. A., Endicott, J., Allen, C. R., & Hostetter, A. M. (2005). A 10-year prospective study of prodromal patterns for bipolar disorder among Amish youth. *Journal of the American Academy of Child and Adolescent Psychiatry*, 44(11), 1104–1111. https://doi.org/10.1097/01.chi.0000177052.26476.e5

Shou, H., Cui, L., Hickie, I., Lameira, D., Lamers, F., Zhang, J., Crainiceanu, C., Zipunnikov, V., & Merikangas, K. R. (2017). Dysregulation of objectively assessed 24-hour motor activity patterns as a potential marker for bipolar I disorder: Results of a community-based family study. *Translational Psychiatry*, 7, e1211–e1211. doi:10.1038/tp.2017.136

Simon, J. J., Walther, S., Fiebach, C. J., Friederich, H-C., Stippich, C., Weisbrod, M., & Kaiser, S. (2010). Neural reward processing is modulated by approach- and avoidance-related personality traits. *Neuroimage*, 49, 1868–1874.

Smeland, O. B., Wang, Y., Frei, O., Li, W., Hibar, D. P., Franke, B., Bettella, F., Witoelar, A., Djurovic, S., Chen, C., Thompson, P. M., Dale, A. M., & Andreassen, O. A. (2018). Genetic overlap between schizophrenia and volumes of hippocampus, putamen, and intracranial volume indicates shared molecular genetic mechanisms, *Schizophrenia Bulletin*, 44, 854–864.

Smucny, J., Tully, L. M., Howell, A. M., Lesh, T. A., Johnson, S. L., O'Reilly, R. C., Minzenberg, M. J., Ursu, S., Yoon, J. H., Niendam, T. A., Ragland, J. D., & Carter, C. S. (2021). Schizophrenia and bipolar disorder are associated with opposite brain reward anticipation-associated response. *Neuropsychopharmacology*, 46, 1152–1160. https://doi.org/10.1038/s41386-020-00940-0

Snowden, L. (2001). Barriers to effective mental health services for African Americans. *Mental Health Services Research*, 3(4), 181–187. https://doi.org/10.1023/A:1013172913880

Soria, V., Martínez-Amorós, E., Escaramís, G., Valero, J., Pérez-Egea, R., García, C., Gutiérrez-Zotes, A., Puigdemont, D., Bayés, M., Crespo, J. M., Martorell, L., Vilella, E., Labad, A., Vallejo, J., Pérez, V., Menchón, J. M., Estivill, X., Gratacòs, M., & Urretavizcaya, M. (2010). Differential association of circadian genes with mood disorders: CRY1 and NPAS2 are associated with unipolar major depression and CLOCK and VIP with bipolar disorder. *Neuropsychopharmacology*, 35(6), 1279–1289. https://doi.org/10.1038/npp.2009.230

Stange, J. P., Boccia, A. S., Shapero, B. G., Molz, A. R., Flynn, M., Matt, L. M., . . . Alloy, L. B. (2013). Emotion regulation characteristics and cognitive vulnerabilities interact to predict depressive symptoms in individuals at risk for bipolar disorder: A prospective behavioural high-risk study. *Cognition and Emotion*, 27(1), 63–84.

Stange, J. P., Molz, A. R., Black, C. L., Shapero, B. G., Bacelli, J. M., Abramson, L. Y., & Alloy, L. B. (2012). Positive overgeneralization and Behavioral Approach System (BAS) sensitivity interact to predict prospective increases in hypomanic symptoms: A behavioral high-risk design. *Behaviour Research and Therapy*, 50(4), 231–239.

Stanton, K., Khoo, S., Watson, D., Gruber, J., Zimmerman, M., & Weinstock, L. M. (2019). Unique and transdiagnostic symptoms of hypomania/mania and unipolar depression. *Clinical Psychological Science*, 7, 471–487.

Strakowski, S. M., Keck, P. E., Arnold, L. M., Collins, J., Wilson, J. M., Fleck, D. E., Corey, K. B., Amicone, J., & Adebimpe, V. R. (2003). Ethnicity and diagnosis in patients with affective disorders. *Journal of Clinical Psychiatry*, 64(7), 747–754. https://doi.org/10.4088/JCP.v64n0702

Strakowski, S. M., McElroy, S. L., Keck, P. E., & West, S. A. (1996). Racial influence on diagnosis in psychotic mania. *Journal of Affective Disorders*, 39(2), 157–162. https://doi.org/10.1016/0165-0327(96)00028-6

Sullivan, A. E., Judd, C. M., Axelson, D. A., & Miklowitz, D. J. (2012). Family functioning and the course of adolescent bipolar disorder. *Behavior Therapy, 43*(4), 837–847. https://doi.org/10.1016/j.beth.2012.04.005

Sullivan, A. E., & Miklowitz, D. J. (2010). Family functioning among adolescents with bipolar disorder. *Journal of Family Psychology, 24*(1), 60–67. https://doi.org/10.1037/a0018183

Swartz, H. A., Rucci, P., Thase, M.E/. Wallace, M., Celedonia, K. L., & Frank, E. (2018). Psychotherapy alone and combined with medication as treatments for bipolar II depression. A randomized controlled trial. *Journal of Clinical Psychiatry, 79*(2). doi:10.4088/JCP.16m11027

Szarek, B. L., & Goethe, J. W. (2003). Racial differences in use of antipsychotics among patients with bipolar disorder. *Journal of Clinical Psychiatry, 64*(5), 614–615. https://doi.org/10.4088/jcp.v64n0518g

Szentagotai, A., & David, D. (2010). The efficacy of Cognitive-Behavioral Therapy in bipolar disorder. A quantitative meta-analysis. *Journal of Clinical Psychiatry, 71*, 66–72.

Szentagotai-Tătar, A., & David, D. (2018). Evidence-based psychological interventions for bipolar disorder. In S. J. Lynn et al. (Eds.), *Evidence-based psychotherapy: The state of the science and practice* (pp. 37–61).

Takaesu Y. (2018). Circadian rhythm in bipolar disorder: A review of the literature. *Psychiatry and Clinical Neurosciences, 72*(9), 673–682. https://doi.org/10.1111/pcn.12688

Taşkıran, A. S., Ertınmaz, B., Mutluer, T., Kılıç, Özcan Morey, A., . . . Öngür, D. (2020). Anxiety disorders comorbidity in pediatric bipolar disorder: A meta-analysis and meta-regression study. *Acta Psychiatrica Scandinavica, 141*(4), 327–339. https://doi.org/10.1111/acps.13146

Tharp, J. A., Johnson, S. L., Sinclair, S., & Kumar, S. (2016). Goals in bipolar I disorder: Big dreams predict more mania. *Motivation and Emotion, 40*(2), 290–299.

Treuer, T., & Tohen, M. (2010). Predicting the course and outcome of bipolar disorder: A review. *European Psychiatry, 25*, 328–333.

Trierweiler, S., Neighbors, H. W., Munday, C., Thompson, E. E., Binion, V. J., & Gomez, J. P. (2000). Clinician attributions associated with the diagnosis of schizophrenia in African American and non-African American patients. *Journal of Consulting and Clinical Psychology, 68*(1), 171–175. https://doi.org/10.1037/0022-006X.68.1.171

Trost, S., Diekhof, E. K., Zvonik, K., Lewandowski, M., Usher, J., Keil, M., Ziles, D., Falkai, P., Dechent, P., & Gruber, O. (2014). Disturbed anterior prefrontal control of the mesolimbic reward system and increased impulsivity in bipolar disorder. *Neuropsychopharmacology, 39*, 1914–1923.

Urošević, S., Abramson, L. Y., Alloy, L. B., Nusslock, R., Harmon-Jones, E., Bender, R., & Hogan, M. E. (2010). Increased rates of events that activate or deactivate the behavioral approach system, but not events related to goal attainment, in bipolar spectrum disorders. *Journal of Abnormal Psychology, 119*(3), 610–615.

Van der Gucht, E., Morriss, R., Lancaster, G., Kinderman, P., & Bentall, R. P. (2009). Psychological processes in bipolar affective disorder: Negative cognitive style and reward processing. *British Journal of Psychiatry, 194*(2), 146–151.

Van Meter, A. R., Burke, C., Kowatch, R. A., Findling, R. L., & Youngstrom, E. A. (2016). Ten-year updated meta-analysis of the clinical characteristics of pediatric mania and hypomania. *Bipolar Disorders, 18*, 19–32. https://doi.org/10.1111/bdi.12358

Van Meter, A. R., Burke, C., Youngstrom, E. A., Faedda, G. L., & Correll, C. U. (2016). The bipolar prodrome: Meta-analysis of symptom prevalence prior to initial or recurrent mood episodes. *Journal of the American Academy of Child & Adolescent Psychiatry, 55*(7), 543–555. https://doi.org/10.1016/j.jaac.2016.04.017

Van Meter, A., Moreira, A. L. R., & Youngstrom, E. (2019). Updated meta-analysis of epidemiologic studies of pediatric bipolar disorder. *Journal of Clinical Psychiatry, 80*(3), E1–E11. https://doi.org/10.4088/JCP.18r12180

Van Meter, A. R., Moreira, A. L. R., & Youngstrom, E. A. (2011). Meta-analysis of epidemiologic studies of pediatric bipolar disorder. *Journal of Clinical Psychiatry.* https://doi.org/10.4088/JCP.10m06290

Van Meter, A. R., Moreira, A. L. R., & Youngstrom, E. A. (2019). Debate: Looking forward: Choose data over opinions to best serve youth with bipolar spectrum disorders—commentary on Parry et al. (2018). *Child and Adolescent Mental Health.* https://doi.org/10.1111/camh.12296

Vitaterna, M. H., King, D. P., Chang, A. M., Kornhauser, J. M., Lowrey, P. L., McDonald, J. D., Dove, W. F., Pinto, L. H., Turek, F. W., & Takahashi, J. S. (1994). Mutagenesis and mapping of a mouse gene, Clock, essential for circadian behavior. *Science, 264*(5159), 719–725. https://doi.org/10.1126/science.8171325

Volkow, N. D., Wang, G. J., Kollins, S. H., Wigal, T. L., Newcorn, J. H., Telang, F., & Swanson, J. M. (2009). Evaluating dopamine reward pathway in ADHD. *JAMA, 302*, 1084–1091.

Weintraub, M. J., Youngstrom, E. A., Marvin, S. E., Podell, J. L., Walshaw, P. D., Kim, E. Y., . . . Miklowitz, D. J. (2014). Diagnostic profiles and clinical characteristics of youth referred to a pediatric mood disorders clinic. *Journal of Psychiatric Practice, 20*(2), 154–162. https://doi.org/10.1097/01.pra.0000445251.20875.47

West, A. E., & Pavuluri, M. N. (2009). Psychosocial treatments for childhood and adolescent bipolar disorder. *Child and Adolescent Psychiatric Clinics of North America, 18*(2), 471–482, x–xi. https://doi.org/10.1016/j.chc.2008.11.009

Whitton, A. E., Treadway, M. T., & Pizzagalli, D. A. (2015). Reward processing dysfunction in major depression, bipolar disorder, and schizophrenia. *Current Opinion in Psychiatry, 28*, 7–12.

Williams, J. M. G., Alatiq, Y., Crane, C., Barnhofer, T., Fennell, M. J. V., Duggan, D. S., Hepburn, S., & Goodwin, G. M. (2008). Mindfulness-based Cognitive Therapy (MBCT) in bipolar disorder: Preliminary evaluation of immediate effects on between-episode functioning. *Journal of Affective Disorders, 107*, 275–279.

Yip, S. W., Worhunsky, P. D., Rogers, R. D., & Goodwin, G. M. (2015). Hypoactivation of the ventral and dorsal striatum during reward and loss anticipation in antipsychotic and mood stabilizer-naive bipolar disorder. *Neuropsychopharmacology, 40*, 658–666.

Youngstrom, E. A., & Algorta, G. P. (2014). Pediatric bipolar disorder. In E. J. Mash & R. Barkley (Eds.), *Child psychopathology*, 3rd ed. (pp. 264–316). Guilford.

Youngstrom, E. A., Arnold, L. E., & Frazier, T. W. (2010). Bipolar and ADHD comorbidity: Both artifact and outgrowth of shared mechanisms. *Clinical Psychology: Science and Practice, 17*, 350–359.

Youngstrom, E. A., Birmaher, B., & Findling, R. L. (2008). Pediatric bipolar disorder: Validity, phenomenology, and recommendations for diagnosis *Bipolar Disorders, 10*, 194–214.

Youngstrom, E. A., Egerton, G. A., Genzlinger, J., Freeman, L. K., Rizvi, S. H., & Van Meter, A. (2018). Improving the global identification of bipolar spectrum disorders: Meta-analysis of the diagnostic accuracy of checklists. *Psychological Bulletin, 144*, 315–342. https://doi.org/10.1037/bul0000137

Youngstrom, E. A., Genzlinger, J. E., Egerton, G. A., & Van Meter, A. R. (2015). Multivariate meta-analysis of the discriminative validity of caregiver, youth, and teacher rating scales for pediatric bipolar disorder: Mother knows best about mania. *Archives of Scientific Psychology, 3*(1), 112–137. https://doi.org/10.1037/arc0000024

Youngstrom, E. A., Morton, E., & Murray, G. (2020). Bipolar disorder. In E. A. Youngstrom, M. J. Prinstein, E. J. Mash, & R. Barkley (Eds.), *Assessment of disorders in childhood and adolescence*, 5th ed. (pp. 192–244). Guilford.

Youngstrom, E. A., & Van Meter, A. (2013). Comorbidity of bipolar disorder and depression. In S. Richards & M. W. O'Hara (Eds.), *Oxford handbook of depression and comorbidity*. Oxford University Press.

Zaretsky, A. E., Lancee, W., Miller, C., Harris, A., & Parikh, S. V. (2008). Is cognitive-behavioural therapy more effective than psychoeducation in bipolar disorder? *Canadian Journal of Psychiatry, 53*, 441–448.

Zimmerman, M., Chelminski, I., Dalrymple, & Martin, J. (2019). Screening for bipolar disorder and finding borderline personality disorder: A replication and extension. *Journal of Personality Disorders, 33*, 533–543.

# CHAPTER 11

# Depression: Social and Cognitive Aspects

Rick E. Ingram, Jessica Balderas, Kendall Khonle, *and* Joe Fulton

Depression is a disabling disorder that is associated with substantial emotional misery, severe interpersonal disruption, debilitating neurovegetative symptoms, and increased risk for physical illness and death. Although depression is an "intrapsychic" disorder, it also significantly disrupts the lives of those close to the sufferer. Depression is frequently a chronic, episodic disorder that can last for months or years, and, even after recovery, it commonly reoccurs. Although there are numerous effective treatments for many sufferers of depression, no one panacea exists. In fact, even with many effective options for treatment, a sizable number of cases are treatment-resistant. Furthermore, depression is associated with a considerable loss of productivity in both work days lost and in diminished work quality, costing the economy billions of dollars. By any indicator, depression is an extensive public health problem.

The *DSM-5* lists a variety of types of depression, and although these subtypes are important, the focus of this chapter is on unipolar depression or major depressive disorder, specifically the cognitive and social aspects of unipolar depression. We start with an overview of the history of depression and follow with an examination of the epidemiology of the disorder. Social aspects from the perspective of the life event–depression relationship are examined next, followed by a review of behavioral and interpersonal models of depression, and then cognitive models.

## Early Conceptions: A Brief History of Depression

Depression is found in the earliest human records; descriptions of conditions resembling depression can be found in the Bible as well as in Egyptian writings circa 2600 BC. The ancient Greeks provided the first causal theories of depression: melancholia was hypothesized by Hippocrates to stem from a preponderance of black bile, "darkening the spirit and making it melancholy." These ideas of bodily fluids affecting "the spirit" paved the way for the modern conceptions of depression. Later, Araetus of Cappadocia, around 120 AD characterized melancholia by sadness, suicidal tendencies, feelings of indifference, and psychomotor agitation. In the mid-eighteenth century, Kant suggested that emotions could not cause mental illness: rather depression was seen as a somatic ailment. It was not until the early twentieth century that theorists such as Abraham (1911/1960) and Freud (1917/1950) associated psychological/emotional factors in a causal manner with depression.

One key question in early conceptions of depression regarded the issue of separating mood disorders into their own diagnostic category. Into the beginning of the twentieth century, controversy raged over whether the disorders of "mood" should be separated from psychosis and delirium. Kraepelin's (1896) systematic observations of manic and schizophrenic individuals suggested that mania, which

**Abbreviations**

| | |
|---|---|
| CIDI | Composite international diagnostic interview |
| CPES | Collaborative Psychiatric Epidemiology Survey |
| ECA | Epidemiologic Catchment Area (Study) |
| LEDS | Bedford College Life Events and Difficulties Schedule |
| NCS | National Comorbidity Survey |
| NSDUH | National Survey on Drug Use and Health |

was often associated with a depressed state, should be considered a separate disorder from syndromes characterized primarily by psychosis, such as schizophrenia. A similar historical debate concerned the distinction between psychopathologies with both manic and depressive states versus those that were "just" depressive states. However, early depression theorists, including Freud, disregarded this distinction between what is now seen as bipolar versus unipolar disorder.

## Epidemiology of Depression
### Prevalence

Several epidemiological surveys have gathered data about the prevalence rates of depression. The first was the National Institute of Mental Health Epidemiologic Catchment Area (ECA) study, which interviewed more than 20,000 adults in five states (Eaton & Kessler 1985; Regier et al., 1984). A decade later, between 1990 and 1992, the National Comorbidity Survey (NCS; Kessler, 1994) was conducted using a modified version of the World Health Organization's (WHO) Composite International Diagnostic Interview (CIDI) to diagnose disorders, including depression, according to the *DSM-III* criteria. The National Comorbidity Survey-Replication (NCS-R; Kessler et al., 2003) later surveyed a large number of individuals in the 48 contiguous United States. The NCS-R, however, used the criteria promulgated in the *DSM-IV* and assessed these criteria with an extended form of the CIDI (Kessler et al., 2003). With the recent shift to the *DSM-5*, there has not been another replication of the NCS. However, another major measure of mental health prevalence has been the National Survey on Drug Use and Health (NSDUH). The most recent administration of this survey was in 2017; it used a nationally representative sample from the United States and collected responses from more than 56,000 participants. The survey used an adapted form of the depression module from the NCS-R to better match the *DSM-5* criteria and to better fit the different administration mediums (e.g., phone, in-person, and computer administration).

Twelve-month prevalence rates reported by the ECA (Eaton and Kessler, 1985) are the lowest of all the surveys, with findings indicating a rate of 2.7%. The NCS (1990–1992) on the other hand, found a 12-month prevalence rate almost twice as high at 4.9%, while the rate was higher still in the NCS-R (2003) findings at 6.6%. The NSDUH (2017) points to a continued increase in prevalence with a rate of 7.1% of adults reporting depression in the past year. Lifetime prevalence rates for major depressive disorder are again the lowest in the ECA, with a reported rate of 2.7%. The NCS rate in adults, defined as greater than 15, was substantially higher, with a reported rate of 15.8%. The NCS-R data are a little higher, but roughly in line with the NCS with a reported rate of 16.6%. The NSDUH did not collect lifetime prevalence data. Irrespective of the particular survey, these data clearly show that depression remains a major public health challenge.

### Ethnicity

Although the information gathered from national surveys has helped to clarify the prevalence of depression, given that such surveys have aggregated ethnicity subtypes inferences about rates of epidemiology among ethnic and native groups have been limited. In response to this limitation, Gonzalez and colleagues (2010) utilized the National Institute of Mental Health's Collaborative Psychiatric Epidemiology Surveys (CPES), which included data from several national surveys. Based on respondents' self-reported ethnicity and racial categorization, the authors created separate categories of ethnic subgroups. Notably, the study only included respondents who endorsed 12-month and lifetime depression history based on a diagnostic interview completed at the time of each survey. Results indicated that, compared to foreign-born respondents, 12-month and lifetime depression were more prevalent for US-born respondents. Furthermore, certain ethnic subgroups endorse higher rates of 12-month and lifetime depression. For example, Puerto Ricans (11.9%) reported higher prevalence rates compared to Asian groups (Chinese, 4.6%; Filipinos, 4.2%; Vietnamese, 4.2%), African Americans (6.8%), and Whites (8.3%). Reported functional impairment also varied across ethnic subgroups. African Americans reported more depression-related impairment compared to Whites, whereas Asian groups reported less depression-related impaired compared to Whites. Certain ethnic subgroups also seemed especially vulnerable to recurrent depression when compared to Whites, including Mexicans, Puerto Ricans, and African Americans.

### Gender Differences

Compared to men, women are at a much higher risk for depression. Although female-to-male ratios differ somewhat across studies, the average ratio is close to 2:1 (Nolen-Hoeksema, 1987). For example, the NCS study found a 21.3% lifetime prevalence among women and 12.7% rate for men. Prevalence rates for depression vary across different countries, but the gender difference remains (Nolen-Hokesema & Hilt, 2009; Salk et al., 2017). Moreover, within the United States, this difference holds generally for African American, Latina, and Caucasian women and tends to persist when income, education, and occupation are controlled (Hyde & Mezulis, 2020; Williams et al., 2007). The gender difference first appears in adolescence, although rates are similar between girls and boys in childhood (Garrison et al., 1992; Kandel & Davies, 1982; Salk et al., 2016), and, in fact, preadolescent boys are somewhat more prone to depression than girls (Twenge & Nolen-Hoeksema, 2002).

### Age and Cohort Effects

Rates of depression appear to vary with age. The rate of onset of the disorder increases dramatically during adolescence. Depression appears more commonly in younger than older adults, with rates being highest for individuals from 25 to 45. Rates of first onsets are considerably lower for individuals over 65 years old, yet compared to Americans, immigrants appear to experience higher rates of depression after 65 years of age (González et al., 2010; Klerman, 1986; Weissman & Myers, 1978). Some data suggest that younger generations are more prone to depression than comparably aged individuals in the past (Klerman, 1986; Klerman & Weissman, 1989) and, indeed, the rate of depression appears to be greater for individuals born after the mid-twentieth century (Seligman, 1990; Twenge et al., 2019). In addition, rates of depression appear to be increasing most quickly in young men, which may decrease the discrepancy between the rate of depression in men and women (Joyce et al., 1990; Twenge et al., 2019). The prevalence of certain symptoms has also increased in recent years. Between 1951 and 1976, for instance, the suicide rate doubled and the suicide attempt rate quadrupled (Somers, 1976), a trend that appears to be continuing (e.g., Curtin et al., 2016; Goodwin et al., 2006; Skegg & Cox, 1991).

## Social and Cognitive Models of Depression

Contemporary approaches to depression have become increasingly multifactorial and integrative: negative life events, genetics, biochemistry, social skills, interpersonal interactions, and cognitive processes are all involved in varying ways and degrees in the onset, maintenance, remission, and relapse of depressive episodes. Hence, distinctions among models have become blurred. For example, some life event models now explicitly integrate notions of vulnerability, cognitive mediation, and interpersonal behavior. Similarly, in addition to acknowledging the important role of the disruptive capacities of life events, behavioral and interpersonal models explicitly integrate cognitive constructs, and cognitive approaches assign important roles to life events as well as to interpersonal and behavioral functioning. Although integration is an important and positive trend, the examination of models here is structured according to the factors emphasized primarily by those models (e.g., cognitive processes for cognitive models).

### Life Events

It is easy to suppose that people get depressed because stressful things happen to them. Such has been the basic presupposition of life event approaches to depression. Life events refer to sudden, or at least relatively discriminable, changes in the external environment (Paykel & Cooper, 1992). Although early research appeared to support a relatively straightforward relationship between negative life events and depression, it has become increasingly clear that the contribution of life events to depression is more complicated, as articulated by cognitive and social models.

Perhaps the most extensive and influential life event research has been the work of Brown and Harris (1978, 1986). In prospective studies using the Bedford College Life Events and Difficulties Schedule (LEDS), these investigators found that only severe events, or events with "marked or moderate long-term threat," were clearly related to the onset of a depressive disorder. An example would be a spouse losing his or her job. In contrast, less severe life events, such as one's spouse only being threatened with a job loss, appeared insufficient to instigate depression. This is true even when multiple less-severe events are summed ("additivity effects"). Not surprisingly, however, these investigators found an additivity effect for severe events (e.g., the death of a parent and a spouse losing his or her job).

It appears that the relationship between major stressors and depression is strongest for initial depressive episodes (Mazure, 1998; Monroe & Depue, 1991). The observation that subsequent episodes can occur without major life events has led to the suggestion that recurrent episodes are only weakly, or not at all, linked to stress. This idea is embodied in the idea of "kindling" (Post, 1992, Monroe & Harkness, 2005), which suggests that early occurrences of depression increase neurobiological sensitization to the point where recurrent episodes are largely initiated by these neurobiological processes (for a meta-analytic review, see Stroud et al., 2008). In the extreme version of this hypothesis, depression becomes autonomous and occurs independent of life stress. Monroe and Harkness (2005), on the other hand, have suggested a compelling alternative to this stress autonomy model. They propose a stress sensitization model in which life events continue to play an important role in the onset of depression, but the event threshold for triggering a recurrence is lowered. Hence, whereas a major event is needed to trigger a first onset, less severe (but more common) life events can initiate recurrent episodes. In this model, life stress continues to play a central role in depression, but the parameters for triggering events change as recurrences accrue. Preliminary empirical evidence examining the role of severe and less severe life events tends to support stress sensitization models (Bandoli et al., 2017; Morris et al., 2010; Stroud et al., 2011).

Life event researchers also distinguish between acute life events (e.g., a broken engagement) and stressors of a more chronic nature (e.g., constant arguing with a spouse, poverty, chronic problems with work). Recurrent depressive episodes may be linked to these chronic stressors (Monroe, 2010; Monroe et al., 2007). The specific *quality* of an event has also emerged as an important dimension. In particular, severe life events that signify loss appear to be most strongly associated with depression whereas events that signify danger appear more related to anxiety disorders (e.g., Smith & Allred, 1989). For example, research has shown that depressed individuals, compared to psychologically healthy controls, report more experiences of severe life events, loss, danger, and trauma (Bifulco et al., 2019). In addition, negative life events with interpersonal conflict themes appear to be particularly associated with depression and recurrence, although depressed people may have some role in the generation of these latter events (Hammen, 2006; Liu & Alloy, 2010; Sheets & Craighead, 2014).

It is also important to note that stressful life events sometimes instigate additional negative life events. For example, research investigating the effects of job loss and unemployment has found that economic hardship can lead to additional negative life events such as child abuse (Justice & Duncan, 1977; Steinberg et al., 1981) and a worsening of the spouse's mental health (Penkower et al., 1988). The occurrence of a negative life event can also worsen the quality of a marriage and, in some cases, lead to familial and marital dissolution (Liem & Liem, 1988). Vinokur, Price, and Caplan (1996) found that job loss and financial strain resulted in more negative affect and dysfunctional interactions in couples. In turn, each member's negative affect was also found to exacerbate depressive symptoms in the other partner. As a result, each partner became less socially supportive and more likely to undermine their partner's sense of self-worth. These behaviors had an additional impact on depressive symptomatology, in effect creating a vicious depression-maintaining cycle. In short, stress tends to come in bunches, and one event is not necessarily independent of other events.

### RISK FACTORS

Although stressful life events do precede depression, the flip side of this relationship is that not all people exposed to even severe negative life events develop a depressive disorder. For example, in reviewing ten studies that used the LEDS in the general population, Brown and Harris (1989) found that three-quarters of recently depressed individuals experienced a preceding negative life event. Yet they also found that only one out of five who experienced a negative life event went on to develop depression. Consequently, life event research has attempted to improve the predictive value of life events by examining individual differences in the value placed on different life domains (e.g., parenting, marriage, employment). For instance, for individuals who place a high value on marriage, a negative life event related to marriage (i.e., divorce) would be predicted to have more impact for this individual. Evidence supports life event matching hypotheses; severe negative life events that occur in domains that are particularly valued are more potent instigators of depression (e.g., Brown et al., 1986). Likewise, some research shows that women who experienced a severe life event in a valued domain were three times more likely to develop depression than women who experienced a severe life event in a less valued domain (Brown & Harris, 1989).

Empirical work on matching hypotheses by life event researchers bears a strong resemblance to work by personality and clinical psychologists investigating the interaction between negative life events and such personality variables as goal-orientation (Dykman, 1998; Lindsay & Scott, 2005), perfectionism (Ahrens, 1987; Flett et al., 1995), and sociotropy/autonomy (Beck, 1987). For example, Morse and Robins (2005) found that among previously depressed individuals, an increase in depressive symptoms was associated with a negative event that was incongruent with their personality (e.g., a negative event that threatened autonomy). In addition to matching strategies, life event researchers have also sought to identify risk factors that make an individual more or less susceptible to the depressing influence of negative life events. In particular, both low social support and low self-esteem have been identified as key risk factors by life event researchers (Brown & Harris, 1989).

More recently, investigators have found that individuals possessing one or two short alleles on a gene involved in serotonin reuptake (*5-HTTLPR*) are more likely to become depressed, but only when they have experienced severe negative life events (Assary et al., 2018; Caspi et al., 2003; Karg et al., 2011). These findings support a gene–environment interaction model, where neither genes nor negative life events in isolation are sufficient to instigate a depressive episode, but rather the co-occurrence of both the genetic vulnerability and negative life events is what is required. Cognitive models of depression have also increasingly reemphasized the idea that negative cognitive patterns must be activated by life events before they eventuate in depression (Ingram et al., 2011; Ingram et al., 1998). Life events are clearly critical in many depressions but mainly in the context of other factors.

### STRESS GENERATION

It has become increasingly recognized that depressed people may create their own negative life events and stress (for reviews, see Hammen, 2006; Liu & Alloy, 2010). For example, in a 1-year longitudinal study of depressed and nondepressed women, Hammen (1991) found that depressed women experienced more *dependent* negative life events, or negative events in which the depressed person was judged to have some contributory role. In particular, these dependent life events involved interpersonal conflict in which depressed women were thought to be partly responsible. Moreover, these women continued to generate negative events after their depression had remitted. Since this initial study, a number of researchers have replicated the *stress generation effect* with both adult and adolescent samples, including samples restricted to men (Hammen, 2006; Liu & Alloy, 2010).

Why do depressed individuals tend to create interpersonal conflicts and other "dependent" negative life events? Given that the depressed person continues to generate such events when the depression itself has remitted, the evidence suggests that the depressed person possesses enduring characteristics or that personality traits that are involved. Although this has been a more recent area of investigation, a number of more trait-like personality factors have been identified as capable of generating such negative dependent life events, including neuroticism (Kendler et al., 2003; Kercher et al., 2009), perfectionism or high self-criticism (Cox et al., 2009; Dunkley et al., 2003; Shahar et al., 2004), and poor interpersonal problem-solving (Davila et al., 1995).

In sum, the relationship between negative life events and depression is clear, although acute negative life events appear to have a stronger role in initial depressive episodes, while chronic events appear to be more involved with people who are experiencing recurrent depression. Increasingly, life event researchers have investigated the specific quality of negative life events, as well as matching and vulnerability characteristics of the individual. Moreover, risk factors such as short alleles on a gene involved serotonin functioning, poor social support, and low self-esteem have been identified in individuals who are most susceptible to the depressing influence of negative life events. Researchers have also begun to investigate how depressed individuals may generate their own negative life events and continue to do so even when the depressed state itself remits.

### Behavioral and Interpersonal Models
### BEHAVIORAL MODELS

Behavioral and interpersonal models have examined the behaviors, and especially the social behaviors, of the depressed individual. A notable early behavioral model was proposed by Lewinsohn (1974) and later reformulated (Lewinsohn et al., 1985). Lewinsohn (1974) argued that depression was due to a low rate of response-contingent positive reinforcement. When individuals fail to receive positive reinforcement that is dependent on the execution of some behavioral response (e.g., initiating a conversation), those behavioral responses become extinguished. This subsequent loss of response-based positive reinforcement deprives the individual of pleasure and leads to feelings of dysphoria. A recent review by Nusslock and Alloy (2017) underscores the relationship between depressive symptoms, reduced reward processing, and amotivation to pursue rewards. Moreover, downregulation of reward centers in the brain (e.g., frontostriatal neural circuits) that are involved in reward processing are shown to increase anhedonia symptoms (Nusslock & Allo, 2017).

Lewinsohn also emphasized the role of social skills and maintained that, as a result of poor social skills, the depressed individual is denied access to the reinforcing properties of social relationships. Segrin (2000) provides an elegant review of the relationship between social skills deficits and depression and notes that although it is limited, there is evidence that poor social skills appear to be an antecedent for depressive symptoms and not only a consequence of depressive symptoms. Other factors were posited that might lead to a low rate of response-contingent reinforcement. Specifically, the occurrence of negative life events—particularly events of loss, impoverishment, or excessive aversive events—diminish the supply of potential reinforcers in the individual's environment. Indeed, as previously reviewed, severe negative life events, particularly ones in which loss or interpersonal conflict is experienced, are associated with depression onset. Additionally, a decrease in the capacity to enjoy pleasant experiences and/or an increase in sensitivity to negative life events were seen as contributing to lower rates of response-contingent reinforcement.

To increase the predictive power of the theory, Lewinsohn et al. (1985) formulated a major revision that was intended to integrate existing knowledge about life events, cognitive processes, and interpersonal functioning. As such, this theory is no longer a distinctively "behavioral" model. In the revised theory, depression onset is caused by one or more stressful life events occurring in an individual who possesses inadequate coping skills or other risk factors. In these vulnerable individuals, events that disrupt major resources in life domains, such as personal relationships and job tasks, lead to an initial negative emotional response. Both life event disruptions and the experience of dysphoric mood lead to a decrease in response-contingent reinforcement, which has several cognitive and behavioral consequences. Cognitively, the individual becomes excessively self-focused, self-critical, pessimistic, and more aware of discrepancies between personal standards and actual accomplishments. Behaviorally, the person withdraws, has more social difficulties, and becomes less motivated. These cognitive and behavioral consequences combine to spiral the individual into an ever deepening state of depression.

Research has tended to support Lewinsohn et al.'s (1985) integrated model but has also forced the incorporation of additional cognitive constructs. Kanter and colleagues (2008) argue that modern behavioral models of depression should incorporate both environmental and interoceptive variables and incorporate the role of avoidance. Indeed, current behavioral activation models of depression, as well as Hayes and colleagues' (1999) model of experiential avoidance, argue that problematic avoidance in depression is a response to the core aversive experience of depressed mood, which is initially elicited from some environmental event(s). Thus, both models place an emphasis on the core affective experience, which may play an important role in maintaining or exacerbating symptoms of depression. Kanter et al. (2008) posit that while depressive affect in itself is not maladaptive, it becomes maladaptive through certain learned behavioral processes, particularly avoidance. Avoidance of unwanted private events (e.g., thoughts) and affective experiences may be negatively reinforced and exacerbate the avoidance behaviors that elicited them. This may initiate a cycle of unpleasant mood states and ineffective avoidance behaviors that may spiral into a depressive episode. Several studies have supported this proposed relationship. For instance, self-critical thoughts (an unwanted private event) were shown to increase experiential avoidance, which in turn predicted depressive symptoms among community adults (Moroz & Dunkley, 2019). And among women who disclosed a rape and experienced victim-blaming (negative environmental events), victim-blaming responses were associated with greater depressive symptoms, and this relationship was partially mediated by experiential avoidance (Bhuptani et al., 2019).

Kanter et al. (2008) also argue for the incorporation of "verbal behavioral processes" in modern behavioral models of depression. One such verbal behavior that has been implicated in depression is rumination (i.e., intrusive, repetitive, and negative thoughts), although it is important to note that rumination is featured in other models of depression as well (Ingram et al., 1998, 2011). Rumination has been associated with longer episodes of depression (Lavendar & Watkins, 2004), and studies have shown that rumination in the presence of depressed mood is characterized by a focus on personal problems (Lyubomirsky et al., 1999). Other studies have found that rumination about the occurrence of negative life events may have causal effects on depression (Arnow et al., 2004). These more recent studies suggest that depressed individuals who ruminate about failure experiences, poor interpersonal interactions, and other negatively toned events experience increased depressive symptoms and mood.

Rumination also has been observed in an interpersonal context. Rose (2002) defined the interpersonal use of rumination, or co-rumination, as a process wherein individuals mutually encourage extensively and repetitively discussing their problems and the associated negative affect while attempting to identify the cause of those problems. Co-rumination is associated with concurrent and prospective self-reports of depression (and anxiety) and is positively associated with the onset, severity, duration, and history of depressive episodes (Ames-Sikora et al., 2017; Bastin et al., 2015; Calmes & Roberts, 2008; Rose, 2002; Stone et al., 2010, 2011; Waller & Rose, 2010; White & Shih, 2012). Moreover, co-rumination has been shown to interact with negative life events to predict depressive symptoms over time (White & Shih, 2012).

**INTERPERSONAL MODELS**

Although the roots of the interpersonal models of behavior can be traced back to Harry Stack Sullivan (1953), the contemporary interpersonal model of depression was articulated by Coyne in 1976. Coyne argued that the occurrence of stressful life events—especially loss of significant relationships—leads to a display of depressive symptoms by the individual. These include expressions of helplessness and hopelessness, withdrawal from interactions, general slowing, and irritability and agitation. The depressed person's goal is to restore social support and gain reassurance regarding his or her self-worth and acceptance by others. Initially, the person gets what he or she wants: the social environment tends to respond with genuine concern and support, which functions to reinforce the depressed person's display of depressive symptoms.

The meaning of this social support, however, eventually becomes ambiguous. The depressed person may wonder: Are people responding with support and reassurance because they really believe that I am worthy, or are they doing so merely because I sought it? The depressed person, caught in this loop of uncertainty, continues to use depressive symptoms in an effort to be reassured. The persistence of such a depressive display, however, eventually becomes aversive to others, who then begin to withdraw. This leads to even further efforts by the depressed person to seek reassurance that he or she is worthwhile and is not being rejected by the person. In short, a cycle based on perceived or actual rejection by others is generated in the depressed person. This cycle is unpleasant to both the depressed person and to others who remain in the depressed person's social environment.

Coyne (1976) specifically predicted that it is excessive reassurance-seeking which culminates in feelings of hostility and aversion in others that then leads to rejection. Excessive reassurance-seeking is defined as "the relatively stable tendency to excessively and persistently seek assurances from others that one is lovable and worthy, regardless of whether such assurance has already been provided" (Joiner et al., 1999, p. 270). Empirical evidence supports the contention that there are significant relationships between reassurance-seeking and depression. For instance, Starr and Davila (2008) conducted a meta-analysis of 38 studies and found a medium effect size for depressive symptoms and reassurance-seeking, indicating that more depressive symptoms were related to higher levels of excessively seeking reassurance. Starr and Davila (2008) also found a significant, albeit small, effect size of .14 across 16 studies examining the positive correlation between reassurance-seeking and interpersonal rejection. It appears as though individuals engaging in excessive reassurance-seeking who also suffer from depression are at particular risk of being rejected (Pettit & Joiner, 2006). For example, those who report depressive symptoms but low levels of reassurance-seeking as well as anxious individuals with high levels of reassurance-seeking are not evaluated in the same negative light (Joiner & Metalsky, 1995; Pettit & Joiner, 2006). Furthermore, reassurance-seeking and depression may be more strongly linked in women. In support of this, Starr and Davila (2008) found stronger associations between reassurance-seeking and depression in samples with a higher percentage of female participants. Reassurance-seeking has also been found to interact with changes in perceived social support to predict the prospective development of depressive symptoms (Haeffel et al., 2007).

Integrating aspects of Coyne's interpersonal theory with social-cognitive work in self-enhancement and self-consistency theory, Joiner and colleagues (1992) proposed that when the mildly depressed person's reassurance-seeking is successfully rewarded by others, he or she is only temporarily satisfied. Specifically, the positive feedback elicited from others conflicts with negative self-beliefs, and consequently the depressed person doubts the validity of the feedback. This leads the depressed person to "flip flop" and seek negative feedback that is more consistent with current self-beliefs. More specifically, Evraire and Dozois (2011) propose that individuals with depression engage in excessive reassurance-seeking about their global, overall worth while engaging in negative feedback-seeking for more specific, concrete qualities. The combination of depression, excessive reassurance-seeking, and negative feedback-seeking then causes others to reject. Consistent with this view, Joiner and Metalsky (1995) found that undergraduate males who engaged in both negative feedback-seeking and reassurance-seeking were more likely to be rejected by their roommates. However, this social reaction may only occur with those closest to the depressed person; reassurance-seeking has been found to predict spouse- but not roommate-related stress (Shahar et al., 2004; Stewart & Harkness, 2015).

Hence, individuals with depression try to both palliate their insecurities in relationships by engaging in reassurance-seeking and maintain a sense of consistency in self-schemas through their use of negative feedback-seeking. The individual suffering with depression who engages in these behaviors is at particularly high risk for rejection from close others (Joiner et al., 1993). Thus, something inherent to the disorder of depression is accounting for the social rejection experienced by these individuals. Evraire and Dozois (2011) suggest that it is the influence of entrenched core beliefs on the information-seeking behaviors of these individuals that explains why reassurance-seeking and negative feedback-seeking lead to rejection. In support of this, the reassurance-seeking literature suggests that it is not the reassurance-seeking behavior in itself that is related to depression and rejection, but rather the combined influence of negative core beliefs concerning interpersonal relationships and reassurance-seeking that creates aversive social consequences. Furthermore, it is the verification of negative self-views that leads to a higher incidence of negative and emotionally distressing feedback for individuals with depression compared to those without depression (Evraire & Dozois, 2011).

Other research has extended Coyne's original theory by integrating interpersonal and stress-generation models of depression (Potthoff et al., 1995). As described previously, the stress-generation model argues that depressed individuals play a contributory role by generating their own negative life events and stress (Hammen, 2006). Researchers have found that reassurance-seeking predicts subsequent levels of interpersonal stress, which in turn predicts elevated levels of depressive symptoms (Joiner, 1994; Joiner et al. 1992; Potthoff et al., 1995). Birgenheir and colleagues (2010) conducted a more recent study and found that individuals who report high levels of sociotropy and reassurance-seeking demonstrate increased levels of negative interpersonal life events. Additionally, reassurance-seeking was found to mediate the relationship between sociotropy and negative interpersonal life events. Eberhart and Hammen (2010) tested a transactional model for depression on a sample of females involved in romantic relationships and found that romantic conflict stress mediated the effects of reassurance-seeking and anxious attachment on depressive symptoms. They also found that daily conflict stress mediated the effects of anxious and avoidant attachment styles, reassurance-seeking, and love dependency behaviors on daily depressive symptoms. Hudson and colleagues (2018) proposed that the relationship between stress generation and excessive reassurance-seeking in depression was attributable to difficulties with "theory of mind," or the ability to reason about what others are thinking. They found that, among depressed individuals, both very poor and very high accuracy on a theory of mind task was associated with increased excessive reassurance-seeking, which was associated with increased interpersonal stress. The authors propose that, among depressed individuals, difficulty understanding what others are thinking may lead to excessive reassurance-seeking, whereas interpersonal insecurity might increase motivations to understand what others are thinking, thereby increasing excessive reassurance-seeking. These findings support the contention that individuals' interpersonal style and their associated behaviors contribute to their depressive symptoms via their impact on stress generation.

Interpersonal models have thus focused researchers' efforts on the social consequences of depression, particularly of rejection. There remains some debate concerning the processes that lead the depressed person to be rejected. There is empirical evidence that social rejection is the result of the depressed individual's failure to meet the basic communication needs of others. Some researchers suggest that reassurance-seeking combined with social rejection, particularly in close and intimate relationships, leads to depression. Other work has integrated findings that reassurance-seeking interacts with generated life stress to predict depression.

**SOCIOEVOLUTIONARY MODELS**

Since Coyne (1976) first proposed that depressed people act in ways that elicit rejection from others, conceptual models of depression have increasingly incorporated the role of social interactions. Evolutionary models of human psychological behavior are no exception, and they seek to identify characteristics and behaviors that demonstrate reproductive and survival advantages in human populations. As we have noted, depression confers major psychological, physical, and economic costs. From an evolutionary perspective, it is puzzling to consider the fact that depression remains so widespread despite the fact that several generations have had the chance to "select" it out (Steger, 2010). Socioevolutionary models of depression attempt to explain this phenomenon by proposing that mild to moderate depressive symptoms may have conferred survival and reproductive advantages via their social functions. According to the social risk hypothesis of depression (Allen & Badcock, 2003), depressed states evolved in order to stimulate low-risk responses when the possibility of social exclusion was perceived. Because social exclusion was a life-threatening process throughout our evolutionary history, being sensitive to rejection cues and acting to reduce one's social burden to the group was a key survival function.

The social risk hypothesis makes three key predictions. First, people with depressive symptoms demonstrate social impairment, which triggers depressive symptoms via negative response from others. For example, depressed people elicit more negative affect in others through their interactions, which makes it more likely that other people will reject them (Steger, 2010; Joiner & Katz, 1999). For example, facial affect is emotionally evocative (Isaac, 2012), and research shows severely depressed individuals are more likely to exhibit negatively valenced facial expressions. Second, people with higher levels of depressive symptoms are more sensitive to negative social cues elicited from others. Biased information processing, such as a negative interpretation bias and attention allocation, has been shown to influence mood and contribute to depressive symptoms (Koster et al., 2009). Third, social subordinate behaviors are elicited in the depressed individual in order to reduce their burden in the group (e.g., submissiveness and reduced behavioral output). For example, those with greater depressive symptoms react to perceived dominance by others with exacerbated feelings of inferiority and submissiveness compared to those with fewer depressive symptoms (Zuroff et al., 2007).

Research stemming from the social risk hypothesis has supported the notion that depressive symptoms make people highly sensitive to cues that their social burden is increasing and, thus, the possibility of social exclusion. Steger and Kashdan (2009), however, have extended the socioevolutionary models of depression with their findings that depressed individuals are equally sensitive to evidence of rising social value. For example, through a daily process research method in which participants completed daily questionnaires for at least 3 weeks, they demonstrated that those who reported greater depressive symptoms were more likely to experience greater increases in feelings of well-being following a positive social interaction. Since depressed individuals are also more likely to overdetect and overreact to signs of rejection, this may lead to a pattern of more intense ups and downs following interpersonal interactions (Gable & Nezlek, 1998; Roberts & Monroe, 1994). Overall, socioevolutionary models suggest that mild to moderate dysphoric moods may have served to sensitize people to potential social rejection (and, more recently, rising social value) and elicit behaviors that prevented social exclusion.

*Cognitive Models*

In the broadest sense, cognitive models of depression emphasize that people become depressed primarily because of the way they think. Beck's (1967, 1987) well-known model and related information-processing ideas are structured around this idea. Beck's model is discussed first, particularly in reference to the vulnerability aspects of this model as well as the diathesis-stress perspective in which this model is framed. Next reviewed are models that specify cognitively based subtypes of depression, including Abramson, Metalsky, and Alloy's (1989) hopelessness theory of depression, as well as cognitive self-regulatory approaches to depression. Before doing so, it is important to note that, similar to life event and behavioral-interpersonal models, cognitive models have become increasingly integrative and have emphasized the role of life events, genetics, and behavior.

## BECK'S COGNITIVE THEORY OF DEPRESSION

In Beck's (1967, 1987) model, nonendogenous depression results from the activation of a depressive *self-schema*. Self-schemas are organized mental structures that are representations of self-referent knowledge that guide appraisal and interact with information to influence selective attention, memory search, and cognitions (Ingram et al., 1998; Segal, 1988). The content of these schemas develops from interactions that occur during childhood development (Beck, 1967, 1987; Kovacs & Beck, 1978). For example, if childhood experiences are characterized by abuse, stress, or chronic negativity, schemas may arise that guide attention to negative events, lead to the enhanced recall of negative experiences, and distort information to fit the schema (Ingram et al., 1998). Although all persons evidence schemas, those of depressed individuals are considered dysfunctional because they represent a constellation of attitudes that lead to negative perspectives about oneself, the world, and the future, or what Beck has termed, the *negative cognitive triad*. Schemas also underlie tacit beliefs. For instance, a depressive self-schema might contain the belief "If I am not loved and accepted by all human beings then I am worthless." Such negative beliefs are not formed based on evidence and are often excessive, rigid, and inaccurate.

Depressive self-schemas also lead to negative biases or cognitive distortions, which lead to thinking errors. For instance, *all-or-nothing thinking* occurs when situations are viewed in only two categories instead of on a continuum (i.e., "If I am not a complete success, I'm a failure"). *Mental filter* is when negative details are focused on without taking into consideration the entire context. For instance, if conversing with a group of people, the depressed person might only notice the one person who yawned as opposed to the others who appeared interested. *Overgeneralization* refers to sweeping judgments or predictions based on a single incident (e.g., "Because last night's date did not go well, all women find me unattractive"). *Emotional reasoning* is thinking something must be true because one feels it to be so (e.g., "I feel ugly so I must look ugly"). *Personalization* occurs when the individual takes responsibility for a negative outcome without considering more plausible explanations, or, conversely, blaming others for something that is the individual's fault. *Labeling* occurs when the individual assigns a character trait onto themselves or other people (e.g., "I am stupid" or "I am worthless"). *Jumping to conclusions* is when an individual is mind-reading (e.g., "She is so bored listening to me talk") or fortune-telling (e.g., "If I go to the party, no one will talk to me"). *Disqualifying the positive* refers to instances where an individual is unable to acknowledge a positive thought, feeling, or behavior (e.g., "I only did my homework because I have nothing else to do"). *Should/must thinking* creates unhealthy expectations that are often unmet and can result in disappointment, guilt, and even shame (e.g., "I should go to the gym" or "I must study for 3 hours tonight"). Finally, *catastrophizing* occurs when the individual blows something out of proportion (e.g., "If I fail this test my life is over").

An original and fundamental aspect of Beck's model is the diathesis-stress context of negative cognition; depressive schemas lay dormant until activated by relevant stimuli: "Whether he will ever become depressed depends on whether the necessary conditions are present at a given time to activate the depressive constellation" (Beck, 1967, p. 278). Hence, stressful life events are necessary to activate negative schemas, and, once activated, schemas provide access to a complex system of negative personal themes that give rise to a corresponding pattern of negative information processing that leads to depression (Ingram, et al., 2011; Ingram et al., 1998; Segal & Shaw, 1986). Although Beck did not view all forms of depression to be solely caused by depressive self-schemas, he did view the cognitive triad and negative information processing bias to be intrinsic features of all forms of depression and to have causal significance.

As a diathesis factor, vulnerability is an important aspect of cognitive models because it clearly articulates hypotheses about causality. This idea suggests that negative cognitive factors emerge during stressful situations and that this cognitive reactivity makes the person more vulnerable to becoming depressed and is critical for the onset, course, relapse, and recurrence of depression. Therapeutic interventions which effectively alter vulnerability should also alter the individual's chance of relapses or recurrences. In fact, Hollon, Stewart, and Strunk (2006) have summarized data to suggest that, compared to pharmacotherapy for depression, cognitive therapy is more effective in preventing relapse and recurrence. Presumably this is the case because cognitive therapy changes negative thinking patterns that lead to depressed cognitive schemas. Breaking this cycle by forming positive cognitive schemas not only brings about recovery from the disorder, but also modifies the underlying cognitive vulnerability (Garratt et al., 2007).

Since the appearance of Beck's cognitive theory, several cognitive models of depression have emerged that explicitly incorporate constructs from experimental cognitive psychology (Ingram, 1984; Teasdale, 1988; Teasdale & Barnard, 1993) to articulate the structure and function of schemas. For example, Ingram (1984) and Teasdale and Barnard (1993) conceptualized these structures as cognitive-affective networks. Hence, in depression, an appraisal of loss results in the initiation of sad emotion and spreads activation throughout the associative linkages that make up the entire interconnected affective-cognitive network. The result of spreading activation is the heightened accessibility of the information embedded in the entire network, and the depressed individual thus becomes conscious of sad-valenced information (e.g., negative events, thoughts, and beliefs). As such, the depressed person exhibits superior attention to, encoding, and recall of negatively valenced self-referent information (for a review, see Gaddy & Ingram, 2014). This type of negative information processing continues to prime the depressogenic cognitive structure, resulting in a negative "cognitive loop" that both maintains and exacerbates the depressive state. This tendency of the depressed person to self-absorption (Ingram, 1990) leaves relatively minimal cognitive capacity available for attending to the external environment. Consequently, the individual's social interactions suffer, leading to social withdrawal. The subsequent loss of social contacts serves even further to prime the depressogenic cognitive-affective structures.

Support for many elements of Beck's model is considerable. For example, the descriptive aspects of depression noted by the model have been confirmed by numerous studies (Haaga et al., 1991; Ingram et al. 1998). In regard to thinking about the self, depressed people report more negative (Kendall et al., 1989) and less positive automatic self-referent thinking (Ingram et al., 1990). They are highly self-critical (Cofer & Wittenborn, 1980; Hammen & Krantz, 1976) and are likely to negatively evaluate a variety of stimuli other than the self, including imagined activities (Grosscup & Lewinsohn, 1980) and other people (Hokanson et al., 1991; Siegel & Alloy, 1990). Depressed people are also pessimistic about the future (Alloy & Ahrens, 1987). This consistent support for the cognitive triad hypothesis has led some reviewers to argue for considering it as a central descriptive feature of depression, equivalent to other such well-acknowledged facts about depression as highly recurrent and heritable (Haaga et al., 1991).

The evidence appears generally supportive of a systematic negative bias in information processing during depressive episodes (Haaga et al., 1991; Ingram & Holle, 1992). For example, depressed people display a tendency to direct their attention to internal, rather than external, information (Ingram, 1990), and they appear to selectively encode negative information (Ingram & Holle, 1992). Depressed individuals have also been found to recall considerably more negative information than positive (Matt et al., 1992).

The diathesis-stress perspective, and hence the vulnerability proposals of the model, have also been borne out by an accumulating body of data. There is evidence that dysfunctional schemas predict depression when activated by stressful life events (Dykman & Johll, 1998; Hankin et al., 2004). Furthermore, proposals regarding the emergence of a negative schema under stress have begun to receive consistent and considerable support (e.g., Segal & Ingram, 1994; Scher et al., 2005). For example, Ingram and Ritter (2000) found that when primed with a sad mood, formerly depressed individuals allocated their attentional resources toward negative stimuli, but nondepressed individuals did not. Such processes are not limited to formerly depressed adults. In a study of depressive schema activation processes in the offspring of depressed mothers, Taylor and Ingram (1999) found that these offspring evidenced significantly more negative information recall when they were primed with a sad mood than did the offspring of mothers who were not depressed.

Moreover, Segal et al. (1999) found that recovered patients who evidenced dysfunctional cognition in response to a negative mood experienced more relapse than equally recovered individuals who did not respond with heightened levels of dysfunctional cognition. These results have been replicated and extended by Segal et al. (2006). Finally, investigators have found that negative cognitive processes elicited during negative mood inductions interact with subsequent negative life events to predict depressive symptoms (Beevers & Carver, 2003; Segal et al., 1999). These findings suggest that those who are vulnerable to depression process information as hypothesized by cognitive-diathesis-stress models and that this information processing predicts relapses. Indeed, in the data reported by Segal (Segal et al., 1999, 2006), cognitive responses predicted relapse in some cases up to 2 years after the cognitive assessment. As such, these data provide support for the causal proposals of cognitive models.

There is some evidence that depressive cognition has a genetic basis. For example, Beevers and colleagues (2009) examined whether nondepressed individuals with one or two short alleles on the 5-HTTLPR gene would show greater negative cognitive reactivity in response to a negative mood manipulation. In short, a significant positive linear relationship between the number of short *5-HTTLPR* alleles and a measure of the severity of negative thinking emerged, but only in the condition where participants were exposed to a sad mood video clip. These data suggest that genes involved in serotonergic functioning may play a role in the development of negative cognitive reactivity in response to dysphoric events. Furthermore, in a study investigating the brain regions of biased attention for both sad and happy stimuli, Beevers et al. (2010) found that volume of the lateral prefrontal cortex, an area involved in the cognitive regulation of emotion, was strongly associated with an attentional bias for emotional cues among carriers of the short *5-HTTLPR* allele. Beck's model has thus received considerable support, with new information suggesting how the cognitive reactivity featured in the model is tied to neurobiological variables.

### ATTRIBUTION-BASED MODELS

One of the most widely known cognitive theories of depression was originally proposed by Seligman (1975). Seligman's model was based on an observation of apparent similarity between the responses of depressed people and the conditioned behavior of laboratory dogs who exhibited a lack of escape response after they had been unable to avoid intermittent painful electrical shocks. Seligman's theory focused on depressed persons' expectations that they are helpless to control aversive outcomes and the ensuing behavior consistent with these expectations.

Perhaps because of its simplicity, the learned helplessness theory quickly generated a tremendous amount of data (Abramson et al., 1978). Although much of this research supported the fundamental tenets of the model, other research revealed the model's deficiencies. Therefore, the theory was revised to focus on people's beliefs about the causes of events (Abramson et al., 1978). In this reformulated theory, an attributional style was proposed as the critical causal variable in depression.

In particular, making specific, unstable, external attributions for positive events (e.g., "I succeeded because the test was really easy") and global, stable, and internal attributions for negative events (e.g., "I failed because I am stupid") was hypothesized to function as a cognitive vulnerability to depression.

Research on the various aspects of the reformulated helplessness/attributional theory of depression has provided substantial support: when individuals are depressed, cross-sectional studies show that they do tend to make the types of attributions hypothesized by the theory (Abramson et al., 2002). Additionally, some data show that the tendency to report some of these attributions predicts negative mood reactions in response to negative events (e.g., Metalsky et al., 1987, 1993). Moreover, a number of studies have supported the role of negative attributions in precipitating depression (Alloy et al., 2006; Rubenstein et al., 2016). For instance, the Temple-Wisconsin Cognitive Vulnerability to Depression Project has provided considerable evidence (Alloy & Abramson, 1999). In this project, nondepressed university freshmen were assessed on a number of cognitive measures, including measures of attributional style. These students were then followed for approximately 5 years, with frequent assessments of stressful life events, cognitions, and depressive symptoms and disorders. Results showed that negative attributional styles predicted both first and subsequent depressive episodes (Alloy et al., 1999, 2006). Likewise, Sturman and colleagues (2006) found that attributional styles for negative events significantly predicted symptoms of hopelessness depression when controlling for other factors. The results also indicate little correlation between attributional style and depressive symptoms that are not related to hopelessness depression, suggesting that attributional style is associated only with hopelessness depression symptoms.

### COGNITIVE SELF-REGULATORY APPROACHES TO DEPRESSION

Another useful approach to depression derives from models that attempt to identify how people regulate their behavior in the relative absence of external reinforcement (Bandura, 1977, 1986; Carver & Scheier, 1998). The ability to self-regulate is decidedly dependent on cognitive processes. For instance, people tend to adopt cognitive representations of desired future states that serve as guides and motives for action (e.g., Bandura, 1986). These *goal representations* serve as the benchmarks against which ongoing behavior is compared and evaluated.

Variations in the representations of these goals are thought to influence motivation, performance, and affect (Caprara & Cervone, 2000). One proposed explanation is that, compared to healthy controls, individuals with depression create less specific goals and are more pessimistic about goal attainment, which hinders motivation (Dickson & Moberly, 2013). Thus, to understand the specific motivational and affective impact of the goal adopted, two additional cognitive self-regulatory variables must be considered: evaluative judgments and self-efficacy appraisals.

People make *evaluative judgments* in which they assess the relative successfulness of performance attainments. When performances fall short of standards, the effect can be motivating or disabling depending partly on the size of the discrepancy between standard and performance. Large discrepancies generally lead to feelings of futility, dysphoria, and low motivation, and small discrepancies spur positive affect, greater persistence, and eventual goal accomplishment (Locke & Latham, 1990). However, the precise motivational effect depends on a third variable: perceived self-efficacy for the goal-relevant behavior (Bandura, 1977, 1997). *Self-efficacy appraisals* refer to people's assessments of their abilities to organize and execute specific behavioral performances (Bandura, 1997). When people judge themselves capable of an adequate performance, they may persevere even when their initial performance was substandard and dissatisfying. When people appraise themselves as inefficacious, even small goal-performance discrepancies tend to promote dysphoria and lead to a slackening, or even to an abandoning of effort altogether (Cervone & Scott, 1995). According to Bandura (1997), a major pathway to depression occurs when individuals possess a low sense of self-efficacy for performing the actions required to realize valued goals.

There is a large literature linking individual differences in evaluative judgments (of the self and performances), goal representations, and self-efficacy judgments to depression. One of the most robust findings in the depression literature is that, while in an episode, depressed people are in fact particularly self-critical in evaluating performances (e.g., Blatt et al., 1982; Cofer & Wittenborn, 1980; Hammen & Krantz, 1976). Self-critical perfectionism was shown to predict greater depressive symptoms over time (Sherry et al., 2014). Furthermore, there is strong support for a relationship between efficacy judgments and depression in adults. For instance, self-efficacy for parenting (Olioff & Aboud, 1991), coping (Cozzarelli, 1993), social skills (Holahan & Holahan, 1987), and activities of personal importance (Olioff et al., 1989) have all been related, either directly or indirectly, to depressive symptoms (see Bandura, 1997).

Similar patterns have been discovered between efficacy judgments and depression for children and adolescents. For instance, a number of investigations have linked academic self-efficacy and depression in youth (Bandura et al., 1999; Scott et al., 2008; Tak et al., 2017). Furthermore, other studies have demonstrated how diverse efficacy beliefs, including those for forming and maintaining social relationships, managing relationships with parents, regulating mood, maintaining health, and resisting negative peer pressure, can directly or indirectly influence feelings of well-being, satisfaction, and depression (e.g., Bandura et al., 2003; Calandri et al., 2018; Caprara et al., 2005).

A number of goal characteristics have also been associated with depression, including level of abstractness (Emmons, 1992), intergoal conflict (Emmons & King, 1988), perceived stressfulness and level of difficulty (Lecci et al., 1994), and approach/promotion or avoidance/prevention focus (Higgins, 1997; Strauman, 2002). In terms of the approach/promotion or avoidance/prevention goal orientation, self-system therapy—a specific form of cognitive therapy that explicitly addresses deficits in approach/promotion goal orientation and goal pursuit—has shown superior treatment effects compared to cognitive therapy for depressed individuals evidencing deficits in approach/promotion goal processes (Strauman et al., 2006). Strauman and Eddington (2017) offer an in-depth review of self-system therapy and discuss several randomized control trials that suggest that self-system therapy is a valuable depression treatment approach. Last, other work has found that self-oriented goals, as opposed to other-driven goals, are associated with lower levels of depression (Ryan & Deci, 2000).

Many depression researchers have argued that depression can result from adopting goals that are excessively perfectionistic. Research employing attitudinal or trait-like measures of perfectionism has sometimes found that these characteristics are associated with dysphoric and depressive states (Ferrari et al., 2018; Flett et al., 1991; Hewitt & Dyck, 1986; Hewitt & Flett, 1991) and that they sometimes prospectively predict depressive symptoms (Brown et al., 1995; Flett et al., 1995). Across a number of studies, dysphoric and depressed individuals do appear to hold relatively stringent performance standards in that the goals adopted exceed the performance levels judged as accomplishable (Ahrens, 1987). Finally, the experience of negative affect can sometimes lead to the construction of more perfectionistic goal representations (Cervone et al., 1994; Scott & Cervone, 2002). When evaluating whether a given performance level would be satisfactory or not, people appear to consult their feeling states, in effect asking themselves: "How do I feel about it?" If they are in a negative mood, they are more apt to feel dissatisfied with the considered performance and adopt higher performance standards. Interestingly, dysphoric individuals appear particularly susceptible to this affect-driven process that culminates in the construction of more perfectionistic goals (Tillema et al., 2001).

Other research has focused on the quality of the goal adopted. Dykman (1998) argued that some people are prone to adopting a validation-seeking goal orientation, which involves goals that seek "to prove or establish . . . basic worth, competence, and likeability" (p. 141). As a result of having this type of goal orientation, these individuals "continually mine the world for information relevant to their worth, competence, and likeability" (p. 153). For such individuals, then, performance situations are loaded because self-esteem is always on the line, contingent on successful performance. Not succeeding translates into appraisals of low self-worth and increased depression. In contrast, other people tend to adopt growth-seeking goals and approach performance situations with a focus on developing potential and skill. For these individuals, poor performance does not call into question self-worth; rather, subpar performance is merely viewed as a learning experience that ultimately leads to self-betterment. These growth-oriented individuals are viewed as more resilient and as less likely to develop depression in response to poor performance. Initial findings have generally supported the role of validation-seeking goal orientations in predicting changes in dysphoric symptoms, but only in the context of negative life events (Dykman, 1998; Lindsay & Scott, 2005).

## Conclusion

Depression is a concept with a long history, dating back to the earliest known writings. The phenomenon, however, no doubt existed before its features (and in some cases attendant superstitions) could be put into writing. As this history shows, ideas have also evolved considerably, to the point where the salient characteristics of depression have been codified in the official psychiatric nomenclature.

Using the currently accepted criteria, depression has a number of recognized subtypes. The type of depression that constituted the focus of this chapter, unipolar depression, occurs in all countries of the world and, depending on estimates, affects a large percentage of people throughout the world. Gender differences in the rate of depression are also found worldwide, with women being approximately twice as likely as men to report depression. Depression also tends to occur equally across various ethnic groups and subcultures.

Numerous psychological models of depression have been proposed. Many of the most widely accepted models are cognitive in nature, although not exclusively so. For instance, behavioral and interpersonal models have been proposed by several researchers, although even these have evolved to include key cognitive components as models have become more integrative over time. Models proposed by cognitive researchers tend to focus on information processing, negative thinking patterns such as cognitive distortions, and cognitive structures such as schemas. Social and cognitive models have contributed significantly to an understanding of several key aspects of depression, although they have not been without criticism. This is particularly true of the cognitive models. Coyne (1994), for instance, has detailed a number of criticisms of both the conceptual and empirical foundations of cognitive approaches to depression. Many of the criticisms have proved to be valuable in leading to theoretical refinements and new research paradigms. In addition, acknowledging the inability of existing cross-sectional and correlational research to allow for inferences about causality has been an important outgrowth of this criticism. In fact, such criticisms of the causal statements of cognitive models of depression have driven to a large degree the resurgence of interest in issues in such as diathesis-stress perspectives and vulnerability (Ingram et al., 1998).

Diathesis-stress perspectives form the core features of models of causality. Causality is a notoriously difficult construct to demonstrate, and although support has begun to build for various models' proposals for causality, one of the key tasks for depression researchers is to continue to move beyond descriptions of social and cognitive features to broaden an understanding of the causal pathways of these factors. Moreover, as paradigms in behavioral science become increasingly focused on translational work, it will be important to assess the linkages between the psychological variables commonly addressed in depression and biological pathways to affective disorders. This work is well under way, and although a comprehensive, integrated model of depression is in development, it must continue to be studied if we are to truly understand a disorder as complex as depression.

## References

Abraham, K. (1911/1960). Notes on the psychoanalytic investigation and treatment of manic-depressive insanity and allied conditions. In *Selected Papers on Psychoanalysis*. Basic Books.

Abramson, L. Y., Alloy, L. B., Hankin, B. L., Haeffel, G. J., MacCoon, D. G., & Gibb, B. E. (2002). Cognitive vulnerability-stress models of depression in a self-regulatory and psychobiological context. In I. H. Gotlib & C. L. Hammen (Eds.), *Handbook of depression* (pp. 268–294). Guilford.

Abramson, L. Y., Metalsky, G. I., & Alloy, L. B. (1989). Hopelessness depression: A theory-based subtype of depression. *Psychological Review, 96*, 358–372.

Abramson, L. Y., Seligman, M. E. P., & Teasdale, J. (1978). Learned helplessness in humans: Critique and reformulation. *Journal of Abnormal Psychology, 87*, 49–74.

Ahrens, A. H. (1987). Theories of depression: The role of goals and the self-evaluation process. *Cognitive Therapy and Research, 11*, 665–680.

Allen, N. B., & Badcock, P. B. T. (2003). The social risk hypothesis of depressed mood: Evolutionary, psychosocial, and neurobiological perspectives. *Psychological Bulletin, 129*, 887–913.

Alloy, L. B., & Abramson, L. Y. (1999). The Temple-Wisconsin Cognitive Vulnerability to Depression (CVD) Project: Conceptual background, design, and methods. *Journal of Cognitive Psychotherapy: An International Quarterly, 13*, 227–262.

Alloy, L. B., Abramson, L. Y., Walshaw, P. D., & Neeren, A. M. (2006). Cognitive vulnerability to unipolar and bipolar mood disorders. *Journal of Social and Clinical Psychology, 25*, 726–754.

Alloy, L. B., Abramson, L. Y., Whitehouse, W. G., Hogan, M. E., Panzarella, C., & Rose, D. T. (2006). Prospective incidence of first onsets and recurrences of depression in individuals at high and low cognitive risk for depression. *Journal of Abnormal Psychology, 115*, 145–156.

Alloy, L. B., Abramson, L. Y., Whitehouse, W. G., Hogan, M. E., Tashman, N. A., Steinberg, D. L., Rose, D. T., & Donovan, P. (1999). Depressogenic cognitive styles: Predictive validity, information processing and personality characteristics, and developmental origins. *Behaviour Research and Therapy, 37*, 503–531.

Alloy, L. B., & Ahrens, A. H. (1987). Depression and pessimism for the future: Biased use of statistically relevant information in predictions for self versus others. *Journal of Personality and Social Psychology, 52*, 366–378.

Ames-Sikora, A., Donohue, M. R., & Tully, E. C. (2017). Nonlinear associations between co-rumination and both social support and depression symptoms. *The Journal of Psychology: Interdisciplinary and Applied, 151*, 597–612.

Arnow, B. A., Spangler, D., Klein, D. N., & Burns, D. D. (2004). Rumination and distraction among chronic depressives in treatment: A structural equation analysis. *Cognitive Therapy and Research, 28*, 67–83.

Assary, E., Vincent, J. P., Keers, R., & Pluess, M. (2018). Gene-environment interaction and psychiatric disorders: Review and future directions. *Seminars in Cell & Developmental Biology, 77*, 133–143.

Bandoli, G., Campbell-Sills, L., Kessler, R. C., Heeringa, S. G., Nock, M. K., Rosellini, A. J., . . . Stein, M. B. (2017). Childhood adversity, adult stress, and the risk of major depression or generalized anxiety disorder in US soldiers: A test of the stress sensitization hypothesis. *Psychological Medicine, 47*(13), 2379–2392.

Bandura, A. (1977). Self-efficacy: Toward a unifying theory of behavioral change. *Psychological Review, 84*, 191–215.

Bandura, A. (1986). *Social foundations of thought and action: A social cognitive theory*. Prentice-Hall.

Bandura, A. (1997). *Self-efficacy: The exercise of control*. W. H. Freeman.

Bandura, A., Caprara, G. V., Barbaranelli, C., Gerbino, M., & Pastorelli, C. (2003). Role of affective self-regulatory efficacy in diverse spheres of psychosocial functioning. *Child Development, 74* (3), 769–782.

Bandura, A., Pastorelli, C., Barbaranelli, C., & Caprara, G. V. (1999). Self-efficacy pathways to child depression. *Journal of Personality and Social Psychology, 76*, 258–269.

Bastin, M., Mezulis, A. H., Ahles, J., Raes, F., & Bijttebier, P. (2015). Moderating effects of brooding and co-rumination on the relationship between stress and depressive symptoms in early adolescence: A multi-wave study. *Journal of Abnormal Child Psychology, 43*, 607–618.

Beck, A. T. (1967). *Depression: Clinical, experimental, and theoretical aspects*. Harper & Row.

Beck, A. T. (1987). Cognitive models of depression. *Journal of Cognitive Psychotherapy: An International Quarterly, 1*, 5–37.

Beevers, C. G., & Carver, C. S. (2003). Attentional bias and mood persistence as prospective predictors of dysphoria. *Cognitive Therapy and Research, 27*, 619–637.

Beevers, C. G., Pacheco, J., Clasen, P., McGeary, J. E., & Schnyer, D. (2010). Prefrontal morphology, 5-HTTLPR polymorphism and biased attention for emotional stimuli. *Genes, Brain and Behavior, 9*, 224–233.

Beevers, C. G., Scott, W. D., McGeary, C., & McGeary, J. E. (2009). Negative cognitive response to a sad mood induction: Associations with polymorphisms of the serotonin transporter (5-HTTLPR) gene. *Cognition and Emotion, 23*, 726–738.

Bhuptani, P. H., Kaufman, J. S., Messman-Moore, T. L., Gratz, K. L., & DiLillo, D. (2019). Rape disclosure and depression among community women: The mediating roles of shame and experiential avoidance. *Violence Against Women, 25*(10), 1226–1242.

Bifulco, A., Kagan, L., Spence, R., Nunn, S., Bailey-Rodriguez, D., Hosang, G., . . . Fisher, H. L. (2019). Characteristics of severe life events, attachment style, and depression: Using a new online approach. *British Journal of Clinical Psychology, 58*(4), 427–439.

Birgenheir, D. G., Pepper, C. M., & Johns, M. (2010). Excessive reassurance seeking as a mediator of sociotropy and negative interpersonal life events. *Cognitive Therapy Research, 34*, 185–195.

Blatt, S. J., Quinlan, D. M., Chevron, E. S., McDonald, C., & Zuroff, D. (1982). Dependency and self-criticism:

Psychological dimensions of depression. *Journal of Consulting and Clinical Psychology, 50*, 113–124.

Brown, G. W., Andrews, B., Harris, T. O., Adler, Z., & Bridge, L. (1986). Social support, self-esteem and depression. *Psychological Medicine, 16*, 813–831.

Brown, G. P., Hammen, C. L., Craske, M. G., & Wickens, T. D. (1995). Dimensions of dysfunctional attitudes as vulnerabilities to depressive symptoms. *Journal of Abnormal Psychology, 104*, 431–435.

Brown, G. W., & Harris, T. (1978). *The social origins of depression: A study of psychiatric disorder in women*. Free Press.

Brown, G. W., & Harris, T. (1986). Establishing causal links: The Bedford College studies of depression. In H. Katschnig (Ed.), *Life events and psychiatric disorders: Controversial issues* (pp. 201–285). Cambridge University Press.

Brown, G. W., & Harris, T. (1989). *Life events and illness*. Guilford.

Calandri, E., Graziano, F., Borghi, M., & Bonino, S. (2018). Depression, positive and negative affect, optimism and health-related quality of life in recently diagnosed multiple sclerosis patients: The role of identity, sense of coherence, and self-efficacy. *Journal of Happiness Studies, 19*(1), 277–295.

Calmes, C. A., & Roberts, J. E. (2008). Rumination in interpersonal relationships: Does co-rumination explain gender differences in emotional distress and relationship satisfaction among college students? *Cognitive Therapy and Research, 32*, 577–590.

Caprara, G. V., & Cervone, D. (2000). *Personality: Determinants, dynamics, and potentials*. Cambridge University Press.

Caprara, G. V., Pastorelli, C., Regalia, C., Scabini, E., & Bandura, A. (2005). Impact of adolescent's filial self-efficacy on quality of family functioning and satisfaction. *Journal of Research on Adolescence, 15*, 71–97.

Carver, C. S., & Scheier, M. F. (1998). *On the self-regulation of behavior*. Cambridge University Press.

Caspi, A., Sugden, K., Moffitt, T. E., Taylor, A., Craig, I. W., Harrington, H., McClay, J., Mill, J., Martin, J., Braithwaite, A., & Poulton, R. (2003). Influence of life stress on depression: Moderation by a polymorphism in the 5-HTT gene. *Science, 301*, 386–389.

Cervone, D., & Scott, W. D. (1995). Self-efficacy theory of behavioral change: Foundations, conceptual issues, and therapeutic implications. In W. O'Donohue & L. Krasner (Eds.), *Theories of behavior therapy: Exploring behavior change*. American Psychological Association.

Cervone, D., Kopp, D. A., Schaumann, L., & Scott, W. D. (1994). Mood, self-efficacy, and performance standards: Lower moods induce higher standards for performance. *Journal of Personality and Social Psychology, 67*, 499–512.

Cofer, D. H., & Wittenborn, J. R. (1980). Personality characteristics of formerly depressed women. *Journal of Abnormal Psychology, 89*, 309–314.

Cox, B. J., Clara, I. P., & Enns, M. W. (2009). Self-criticism, maladaptive perfectionism, and depression symptoms in a community sample: A longitudinal test of the mediating effects of person-dependent stressful life events. *Journal of Cognitive Psychotherapy, 23*(4), 336–349.

Coyne, J. C. (1976). Toward an interactional description of depression. *Psychiatry, 39*, 28–40.

Coyne, J. C. (1994). Self-reported distress: Analog or ersatz depression? *Psychological Bulletin, 116*, 29–45.

Cozzarelli, C. (1993). Personality and self-efficacy as predictors of coping with abortion. *Journal of Personality and Social Psychology, 65*, 1224–1236.

Curtin, S. C., Warner, M., & Hedegaard, H. (2016). *Increase in suicide in the United States, 1999–2014* (No. 2016). US Department of Health and Human Services, Centers for Disease Control and Prevention, National Center for Health Statistics.

Davila, J., Hammen, C., Burge, D., Paley, B., & Daley, S. E. (1995). Poor interpersonal problem solving as a mechanism of stress generation in depression among adolescent women. *Journal of Abnormal Psychology, 104*, 592–600.

Dickson, J. M., & Moberly, N. J. (2013). Reduced specificity of personal goals and explanations for goal attainment in major depression. *PloS One, 8*(5).

Dykman, B. M. (1998). Integrating cognitive and motivational factors in depression: Initial tests of a goal-orientation approach. *Journal of Personality and Social Psychology, 74*, 139–158.

Dykman, B. M., & Johll, M. (1998). Dysfunctional attitudes and vulnerability to depressive symptoms: A 14-week longitudinal study. *Cognitive Therapy and Research. Special Issue: Cognitive Processes and Vulnerability to Affective Problems, 22*, 337–352.

Dunkley, D. M., Zuroff, D. C., & Blankstein, K. R. (2003). Self-critical perfectionism and daily affect: Dispositional and situational influences on stress and coping. *Journal of Personality and Social Psychology, 84*, 234–252.

Eaton, W. W., & Kessler, L. G. (1985). *NIMH Epidemiologic Catchment Area Program. Epidemiologic Field Methods in Psychiatry: The NIMH Epidemiologic Catchment Area Program*. National Institutes of Mental Health.

Eberhart, N. K., & Hammen, C. L. (2010). Interpersonal style, stress, and depression: An examination of transactional and diathesis-stress models. *Journal of Social and Clinical Psychology, 29*, 23–38.

Emmons, R. A. (1992). Abstract versus concrete goals: Personal striving level, physical illness, and psychological well-being. *Journal of Personality and Social Psychology, 62*, 292–300.

Emmons, R. A., & King, L. (1988). Conflict among personal strivings: Immediate and long-term implications for psychological and physical well-being. *Journal of Personality and Social Psychology, 54*, 1040–1048.

Evraire, L. E., & Dozois, D. J. (2011). An integrative model of excessive reassurance seeking and negative feedback seeking in the development and maintenance of depression. *Clinical Psychology Review, 31*(8), 1291–1303.

Ferrari, M., Yap, K., Scott, N., Einstein, D. A., & Ciarrochi, J. (2018). Self-compassion moderates the perfectionism and depression link in both adolescence and adulthood. *PloS One, 13*(2).

Flett, G. L., Hewitt, P. L., Blankstein, K. R., & Mosher, S. W. (1995). Perfectionism, life events, and depressive symptoms: A test of a diathesis-stress model. *Current Psychology: Developmental, Learning, Personality, Social, 14*, 112–137.

Flett, G. L., Hewitt, P. L., & Mittelstaedt, W. M. (1991). Dysphoria and components of self-punitiveness: A reanalysis. *Cognitive Therapy and Research, 15*, 201–219.

Freud, S. (1917/1950). Mourning and melancholia. In *Collected papers* (vol. 4). Hogarth Press.

Gable, S. L., & Nezlek, J. B. (1998). Level and instability of day-to-day psychological well-being and risk for depression. *Journal of Personality and Social Psychology, 74*, 129–138.

Gaddy, M. A., & Ingram, R. E. (2014). A meta-analytic review of mood-congruent implicit memory in depressed mood. *Clinical Psychology Review, 34*(5), 402–416.

Garratt, G., Ingram, R. E., Rand, K. L., & Sawalani, G. (2007). Cognitive processes in cognitive therapy: Evaluation of the mechanisms of change in the treatment of depression. *Clinical Psychology: Science and Practice, 14*, 224–239.

Garrison, C. Z., Addy, C. L., Jackson, K. L., McKeown, R. E., & Waller, J. L. (1992). Major depressive disorder and dysthymia in young adolescents. *American Journal of Epidemiology, 135*(7), 792–802.

Goodwin, R. D., Jacobi, F., Bittner, A., & Wittchen, H. (2006). Epidemiology of depression. In D. J. Stein, D. J. Kupfer, & A. F. Schatzberg (Eds.), *Textbook of mood disorders* (pp. 33–54). American Psychiatric Publishing.

González, H. M., Tarraf, W., Whitfield, K. E., & Vega, W. A. (2010). The epidemiology of major depression and ethnicity in the United States. *Journal of Psychiatric Research, 44*(15), 1043–1051.

Grosscup, S. J., & Lewinsohn, P. M. (1980). Unpleasant and pleasant events, and mood. *Journal of Clinical Psychology, 36*, 252–259.

Haaga, D. A. F., Dyck, M. J., & Ernst, D. (1991). Empirical status of cognitive theory of depression. *Psychological Bulletin, 110*, 215–236.

Haeffel, G. J., Voelz, Z. R., & Joiner, Jr., T. E. (2007). Vulnerability to depressive symptoms: Clarifying the role of excessive reassurance seeking and perceived social support in an interpersonal model of depression. *Cognition and Emotion, 21*, 681–688.

Hammen, C. L. (1991). Generation of stress in the course of unipolar depression. *Journal of Abnormal Psychology, 100*, 555–561.

Hammen, C. L. (2006). Stress generation in depression: Reflections on origins, research, and future directions. *Journal of Clinical Psychology, 62*, 1065–1082.

Hammen, C. L., & Krantz, S. (1976). Effects of success and failure on depressive cognitions. *Journal of Abnormal Psychology, 85*, 577–586.

Hankin, B. L., Abramson, L. Y., Miller, N., & Haeffel, G. J. (2004). Cognitive vulnerability-stress theories of depression: Examining affective specificity in the prediction of depression versus anxiety in three prospective studies. *Cognitive Therapy and Research, 28*, 309–309.

Hayes, S. C., Strosahl, K. D., & Wilson, K. G. (1999). *Acceptance and commitment therapy: An experiential approach to behavior change*. Guilford.

Hewitt, P. L., & Dyck, D. G. (1986). Perfectionism, stress, and vulnerability to depression. *Cognitive Therapy and Research, 10*, 137–142.

Hewitt, P. L., & Flett, G. L. (1991). Dimensions of perfectionism in unipolar depression. *Journal of Abnormal Psychology, 100*, 98–101.

Higgins, E. T. (1997). Beyond pleasure and pain. *American Psychologist, 52*, 1280–1300.

Hokanson, J. E., Hummer, J. T., & Butler, A. C. (1991). Interpersonal perceptions by depressed college students. *Cognitive Therapy and Research, 15*, 443–457.

Holahan, C. K., & Holahan, C. J. (1987). Self-efficacy, social support, and depression in aging: A longitudinal analysis. *Journal of Gerontology, 42*, 65–68.

Hollon, S. D., Stewart, M. O., & Strunk, D. (2006). Enduring effects for cognitive behavior therapy in the treatment of depression and anxiety. *Annual Review of Psychology, 57*, 285–315.

Hudson, C. C., Shamblaw, A. L., Wilson, G. A., Roes, M. M., Sabbagh, M. A., & Harkness, K. L. (2018). Theory of mind, excessive reassurance-seeking, and stress generation in depression: A social-cognitive-interpersonal integration. *Journal of Social and Clinical Psychology, 37*(9), 725–750.

Hyde, J. S., & Mezulis, A. H. (2020). Gender differences in depression: Biological, affective, cognitive, and sociocultural factors. *Harvard Review of Psychiatry, 28*(1), 4–13.

Ingram, R. E. (1984). Toward an information processing analysis of depression. *Cognitive Therapy and Research, 8*, 443–478.

Ingram, R. E. (1990). Self-focused attention in clinical disorders: Review and a conceptual model. *Psychological Bulletin, 107*, 156–176.

Ingram, R. E., Atchley, R., & Segal, Z. V. (2011). *Vulnerability to depression: From cognitive neuroscience to clinical strategies*. Guilford.

Ingram, R. E., & Holle, C. (1992). Cognitive science of depression. In D. J. Stein & J. E. Young (Eds.), *Cognitive science and clinical disorders* (pp. 188–209). Academic Press.

Ingram, R. E., Miranda, J., & Segal, Z. V. (1998). *Cognitive vulnerability to depression*. Guilford.

Ingram, R. E., & Ritter, J. (2000). Vulnerability to depression: Cognitive reactivity and parental bonding in high-risk individuals. *Journal of Abnormal Psychology, 109*, 588–596.

Ingram, R. E., Slater, M. A., Atkinson, J. H., & Scott, W. D. (1990). Positive automatic cognition in major affective disorder. *Psychological Assessment: A Journal of Consulting and Clinical Psychology, 2*, 209–211.

Isaac, L. (2012). Facing the future: Face-emotion processing deficits as a potential biomarker for various psychiatric and neurological disorders. *Frontiers in Psychology, 3*, 171.

Joiner, T. E. (1994). Contagious depression: Existence, specificity to depressed symptoms, and the role of reassurance-seeking. *Journal of Personality and Social Psychology, 67*, 287–296.

Joiner, T. E., Alfano, M. S., & Metalsky, G. I. (1992). When depression breeds contempt: Reassurance-seeking, self-esteem, and rejection of depressed college students by their roommates. *Journal of Abnormal Psychology, 101*, 165–173.

Joiner, T. E., Alfano, M. S., & Metalsky, G. I. (1993). Caught in crossfire: Depression, self-consistency, self-enhancement, and the response of others. *Journal of Social and Clinical Psychology, 12*, 113–134.

Joiner, T. E., & Katz, J. (1999). Contagion of depressive symptoms and mood: Meta-analytic review and explanations from cognitive, behavioral, and interpersonal viewpoints. *Clinical Psychology: Science and Practice, 6*, 149–164.

Joiner, T. E., & Metalsky, G. I. (1995). A prospective test of an integrative interpersonal theory of depression: A naturalistic study of college roommates. *Journal of Personality and Social Psychology, 69*, 778–788.

Joiner, T. E., Metalsky, G. I., Katz, J., & Beach, S. R. H. (1999). Depression and excessive reassurance seeking. *Psychological Inquiry, 10*, 269–278.

Joyce, P. R., Oakley-Browne, M. A., Wells, J. E., Bushnell, J. A., & Hornblow, A. R. (1990). Birth cohort trends in major depression: Increasing rates and earlier onset in New Zealand. *Journal of Affective Disorders, 18*(2), 83–89.

Justice, B., & Duncan, D. F. (1977). Child abuse as a work-related problem. *Corrective and Social Psychiatry and Journal of Behavior Technology, Methods and Therapy, 23*, 53–55.

Kandel, D. B., & Davies, M. (1982). Epidemiology of depressive mood in adolescents: An empirical study. *Archives of General Psychiatry, 39*(10), 1205–1212.

Kanter, J. W., Busch, A. M., Weeks, C. E., & Landes, S. J. (2008). The nature of clinical depression: Symptoms, syndromes, and behavior analysis. *Behavior Analysis, 31*, 1–21.

Karg, K., Burmeister, M., Shedden, K., & Sen, S. (2011). The serotonin transporter promoter variant (5-HTTLPR), stress, and depression meta-analysis revisited: Evidence of genetic moderation. *Archives of General Psychiatry, 68*(5), 444–454.

Kendall, P. C., Howard, B. L., & Hays, R. C. (1989). Self-referent speech and psychopathology: The balance of positive and negative thinking. *Cognitive Therapy and Research, 13*, 583–598.

Kendler, K. S., Gardner, C. O., & Prescott, C. A. (2003). Personality and the experience of environmental adversity. *Psychological Medicine, 33*, 1193–1202.

Kercher, A., Rapee, R. M., & Schniering, C. A. (2009). Neuroticism, life events and negative thoughts in the development of depression in adolescent girls. *Journal of Abnormal Child Psychology, 37*, 903–915.

Kessler, R. C. (1994). The national comorbidity survey of the United States. *International Review of Psychiatry, 6*(4), 365–376.

Kessler, R., Berglund, P., Demler, O., Jin, R., Koretz, D., Merikangas, K., Rush, A., Walters, E., & Wang, P. (2003). The epidemiology of major depressive disorder: Results from the National Survey Replication (NCS-R). *Journal of America Medical Association, 289*, 3095–3105.

Klerman G. L. (1986). Evidence for increase in rates of depression in North America and Western Europe in recent decades. In H. Hippius, G. L. Klerman, & N. Matussek (Eds.), *New results in depression research*. Springer.

Klerman, G. L., & Weissman, M. M. (1989). Increasing rates of depression. *Journal of the American Medical Association, 261*(15), 2229–2235.

Koster, E. H. W., Fox, E., & MacLeod, C. (2009). Introduction to the special section on cognitive bias modification in emotional disorders. *Journal of Abnormal Psychology, 118*(1), 1–4.

Kovacs, M., & Beck, A. T. (1978). Maladaptive cognitive structures in depression. *American Journal of Psychiatry, 135*, 525–533.

Kraepelin, E. (1896). *Psychiatrie: Ein Lehrbuch fur Studierende und Aerzte*, 6th ed. Barth.

Lavendar, A., & Watkins, E. (2004). Rumination and future thinking in depression. *British Journal of Clinical Psychology, 43*, 129-142.

Lecci, L., Karoly, P., Briggs, C., & Kuhn, K. (1994). Specificity and generality of motivational components in depression: A personal projects analysis. *Journal of Abnormal Psychology, 103*(2), 404–408.

Lewinsohn, P. M. (1974). A behavioral approach to depression. In R. J. Friedman & M. M. Katz (Eds.), *The psychology of depression: Contemporary theory and research*. Wiley.

Lewinsohn, P. M., & Hoberman, H., Teri, L., & Hautzinger, M. (1985). An integrative theory of depression. In S. Reiss & R. R. Bootzin (Eds.), *Theoretical issues in behavior therapy* (pp. 331–361). Academic Press.

Liem, R., & Liem, J. H. (1988). The psychological effects of unemployment on workers and their families. *Journal of Social Issues, 44*, 87–105.

Lindsay, J., & Scott, W. D. (2005). Dysphoria and self-esteem following an achievement event: Predictive validity of goal orientation and personality style theories of vulnerability. *Cognitive Therapy and Research, 29*, 769–785.

Liu, R. T., & Alloy, L. B. (2010). Stress generation in depression: A systematic review of the empirical literature and recommendations for future study. *Clinical Psychology Review, 30*(5), 582–593.

Locke, E. A., & Latham, G. P. (1990). *A theory of goal setting and task performance*. Prentice Hall.

Lyubomirsky, S., Tucker, K. L., Caldwell, N. D., & Berg, K. (1999). Why ruminators are poor problem solvers: Clues from the phenomenology of dysphoric rumination. *Journal of Personality and Social Psychology, 77*, 1041–1060.

Matt, G. E., Vazquez, C., & Campbell, W. K. (1992). Mood-congruent recall of affectively toned stimuli: A meta-analytic review. *Clinical Psychology Review, 12*, 227–55.

Mazure, C. M. (1998). Life stressors as risk factors in depression. *Clinical Psychology: Science and Practice, 5*, 291–313.

Metalsky, G. I., Halberstadt, L. J., & Abramson, L. Y. (1987). Vulnerability to depressive mood reactions: Toward a more powerful test of the diathesis-stress and causal mediation components of the reformulated theory of depression. *Journal of Personality and Social Psychology, 52*, 386–393.

Metalsky, G. I., Joiner, T. E., Hardin, T. S., & Abramson, L. Y. (1993). Depressive reactions to failure in a naturalistic setting: A test of the hopelessness and self-esteem theories of depression. *Journal of Abnormal Psychology, 102*, 101–109.

Monroe, S. M. (2010). Recurrence in major depression: Assessing risk indicators in the context of risk estimates. In C. S. Richards & M. G. Perri (Eds.), *Relapse prevention for depression* (pp. 27–49). American Psychological Association.

Monroe, S. M., & Depue, R. A. (1991). Life stress and depression. In J. Becker & A. Kleinman (Eds.), *Psychosocial aspects of depression* (pp. 101–130). Erlbaum.

Monroe, S. M., & Harkness, K. L. (2005). Life stress, the "kindling" hypothesis, and the recurrence of depression: Considerations from a life stress perspective. *Psychological Review, 112*, 417–445.

Monroe, S. M., Slavich, G. M., Torres, L. D., & Gotlib, I. H. (2007). Major life events and major chronic difficulties are differentially associated with history of major depressive episodes. *Journal of Abnormal Psychology, 116*, 116–124.

Moroz, M., & Dunkley, D. M. (2019). Self-critical perfectionism, experiential avoidance, and depressive and anxious symptoms over two years: A three-wave longitudinal study. *Behaviour Research and Therapy, 112*, 18–27.

Morris, M. C., Ciesla, J. A., & Garber, J. (2010). A prospective study of stress autonomy versus stress sensitization in adolescents at varied risk for depression. *Journal of Abnormal Psychology, 119*(2), 341–354.

Morse, J. Q., & Robins, C. J. (2005). Personality–life event congruence effects in late-life depression. *Journal of Affective Disorders, 84*(1), 25–31.

Nolen-Hoeksema, S. (1987). Sex differences in unipolar depression: Evidence and theory. *Psychological Bulletin, 101*(2), 259.

Nolen-Hoeksema, S., & Hilt, L. M (2009). Gender differences in depression. In I. H. Gotlib & C. Hammen (Eds.), *Handbook of depression*, 2nd ed. (pp. 386–404). Guilford.

Nusslock, R., & Alloy, L. B. (2017). Reward processing and mood-related symptoms: An RDoC and translational neuroscience perspective. *Journal of Affective Disorders, 216*, 3–16.

Olioff, M., & Aboud, F. E. (1991). Predicting postpartum dysphoria in primiparous mothers: Roles of perceived parenting self-efficacy and self-esteem. *Journal of Cognitive Psychotherapy, 5*, 3–14.

Olioff, T. E., Bryson, S. E., & Wadden, N. P. (1989). Predictive relation of automatic thoughts and student efficacy to depressive symptoms in undergraduates. *Canadian Journal of Behavioural Science, 21*, 353–363.

Paykel, E. S., & Cooper, Z. (1992). Life events and social stress. In E. S. Paykel (Ed.), *Handbook of affective disorders*, 2nd ed. (149–170). Guilford.

Penkower, L., Bromet, E., & Dew, M. (1988). Husbands' layoff and wives' mental health: A prospective analysis. *Archives of General Psychiatry, 45*, 994–1000.

Pettit, J. W., & Joiner, T. E. (2006). *Excessive reassurance-seeking. Chronic depression: Interpersonal sources, therapeutic solutions.* American Psychological Association.

Post, R. M. (1992). Transduction of psychosocial stress into the neurobiology of recurrent affective disorder. *American Journal of Psychiatry, 149*, 999–1010.

Potthoff, J. G., Holahan, C. J., & Joiner, T. E. (1995). Reassurance seeking, stress generation, and depressive symptoms: An integrative model. *Journal of Personality and Social Psychology, 68*, 664–670.

Regier, D. A., Myers, J. K., Kramer, M., Robins, L. N., Blazer, D. G., Hough, R. L., Eaton, W. W., & Locke, B. Z. (1984). The NIMH Epidemiologic Catchment Area program: Historical context, major objectives, and study population characteristics. *Archives of General Psychiatry, 41*, 934–941.

Roberts, J. E., & Monroe, S. M. (1994). A multidimensional model of self-esteem in depression. *Clinical Psychology Review, 14*, 161–181.

Rose, A. J. (2002). Co-rumination in the friendships of girls and boys. *Child Development, 73*(6), 1830–1843.

Rubenstein, L. M., Freed, R. D., Shapero, B. G., Fauber, R. L., & Alloy, L. B. (2016). Cognitive attributions in depression: Bridging the gap between research and clinical practice. *Journal of Psychotherapy Integration, 26*(2), 103–115.

Ryan, R. M., & Deci, E. L. (2000). Self-determination theory and the facilitation of intrinsic motivation, social development, and well-being. *American Psychologist, 55*, 68–78.

Salk, R. H., Hyde, J. S., & Abramson, L. Y. (2017). Gender differences in depression in representative national samples: Meta-analyses of diagnoses and symptoms. *Psychological Bulletin, 143*(8), 783.

Salk, R. H., Petersen, J. L., Abramson, L. Y., & Hyde, J. S. (2016). The contemporary face of gender differences and similarities in depression throughout adolescence: Development and chronicity. *Journal of Affective Disorders, 205*, 28–35.

Scher, C. D., Ingram, R. E., & Segal, Z. V. (2005). Cognitive reactivity and vulnerability: Empirical evaluation of construct activation and cognitive diatheses in unipolar depression. *Clinical Psychology Review, 25*, 487–510.

Scott, W. D., & Cervone, D. (2002). The influence of negative mood on self-regulatory cognition. *Cognitive Therapy and Research, 26*, 19–37.

Scott, W. D., Dearing, E., Reynolds, W. R., Lindsay, J. E., Hamill, S. K., & Baird, G. L. (2008). Cognitive self-Regulation and depression: Examining self-efficacy appraisals and goal characteristics in youth of a Northern Plains tribe. *Journal of Research on Adolescence, 18*, 379–394

Segal, Z. V. (1988). Appraisal of the self-schema construct in cognitive models of depression. *Psychological Bulletin, 103*(2), 147.

Segal, Z. V., & Shaw, B. F. (1986). Cognition in depression: A reappraisal of Coyne and Gotlib's critique. *Cognitive Therapy and Research, 10*(6), 671–693.

Segal, Z. V., Gemar, M., & Williams, S. (1999). Differential cognitive response to a mood challenge following successful cognitive therapy or pharmacotherapy for unipolar depression. *Journal of Abnormal Psychology, 108*, 3–10.

Segal, Z. V., & Ingram, R. E. (1994). Mood priming and construct activation in tests of cognitive vulnerability to unipolar depression. *Clinical Psychology Review, 14*, 663–695.

Segal, Z. V., Kennedy, M. D., Gemar, M., Hood, K., Pedersen, R., & Buis, T. (2006). Cognitive reactivity to sad mood provocation and the prediction of depressive relapse. *Archives of General Psychiatry, 63*, 749–755

Segrin, C. (2000). Social skills deficits associated with depression. *Clinical Psychology Review, 20*(3), 379–403.

Seligman, M. E. P. (1975). *Helplessness: On depression, development, and death.* Freeman.

Seligman, M. E. P. (1990). Why is there so much depression today? The waxing of the individual and the waning of the common. In R. E. Ingram (Ed.), *Contemporary psychological approaches to depression* (pp. 1–10). Plenum Press.

Shahar, G., Joiner, T. E., Zuroff, D. C., & Blatt, S. J. (2004). Personality, interpersonal behavior, and depression: Co-existence of stress-specific moderating and mediating effects. *Personality and Individual Differences, 36*, 1583–1597.

Sheets, E. S., & Craighead, W. E. (2014). Comparing chronic interpersonal and noninterpersonal stress domains as predictors of depression recurrence in emerging adults. *Behaviour Research and Therapy, 63*, 36–42.

Sherry, S. B., Richards, J. E., Sherry, D. L., & Stewart, S. H. (2014). Self-critical perfectionism is a vulnerability factor for depression but not anxiety: A 12-month, 3-wave longitudinal study. *Journal of Research in Personality, 52*, 1–5.

Siegel, S. J., & Alloy, L. B. (1990). Interpersonal perceptions and consequences of depressive-significant other relationships: A naturalistic study of college roommates. *Journal of Abnormal Psychology, 99*, 361–363.

Skegg, K., & Cox, B. (1991). Suicide in New Zealand 1957–1986: The influence of age, period and birth-cohort. *Australian and New Zealand Journal of Psychiatry, 25*(2), 181–190.

Smith, T. W., & Allred, K. D. (1989). Major life events in depression and anxiety. In P. C. Kendall & D. Watson (Ed.), *Anxiety and depression: Distinctive and overlapping features* (pp. 205–223). Academic Press.

Somers, A. R. (1976). Violence, television and the health of American youth. *New England Journal of Medicine, 294*(15), 811–817.

Starr, L. R., & Davila, J. (2008). Excessive reassurance seeking, depression, and interpersonal rejection: A meta-analytic review. *Journal of Abnormal Psychology, 117*, 762–775.

Steger, M. F. (2010). The social context of major depressive disorder: Sensitivity to positive and negative social interactions influences well-being. *Directions in Psychiatry, 30*, 41–52.

Steger, M. F., & Kashdan, T. B. (2009). Depression and everyday social activity, intimacy, and well-being. *Journal of Counseling Psychology, 56*, 289–300.

Steinberg, L., Catalano, R. L., & Dooley, D. (1981). Economic antecedents of child abuse and neglect. *Child Development, 52*, 975–985.

Stewart, J. G., & Harkness, K. L. (2015). The interpersonal toxicity of excessive reassurance-seeking: Evidence from a longitudinal study of romantic relationships. *Journal of Social and Clinical Psychology, 34*(5), 392–410.

Stone, L. B., Hankin, B. L., Gibb, B. E., & Abela, J. R. Z. (2011). Co-rumination predicts the onset of depressive disorders during adolescence. *Journal of Abnormal Psychology, 120*, 752–757.

Stone, L. B., Uhrlass, D. J., & Gibb, B. E. (2010). Co-rumination and lifetime history of depressive disorders in children. *Journal of Clinical Child and Adolescent Psychology, 39*, 597–602.

Strauman, T. J. (2002). Self-regulation and depression. *Self and Identity, 1*, 151–157.

Strauman, T. J., & Eddington, K. M. (2017). Treatment of depression from a self-regulation perspective: Basic concepts and applied strategies in self-system therapy. *Cognitive Therapy and Research, 41*(1), 1–15.

Strauman, T. J., Vieth, A. Z., Merrill, K. A., Kolden, C. G., Woods, T. E., Klein, M. H., Papadakis, A. A., & Schneider, K. L. (2006). Self-system therapy as an intervention for self-regulatory dysfunction in depression: A randomized comparison with cognitive therapy. *Journal of Consulting and Clinical Psychology, 74*, 367–376.

Stroud, C. B., Davila, J., Hammen, C., & Vrshek-Schallhorn, S. (2011). Severe and nonsevere events in first onsets versus recurrences of depression: Evidence for stress sensitization. *Journal of Abnormal Psychology, 120*(1), 142–154.

Stroud, C. B., Davila, J., & Moyer, A. (2008). The relationship between stress and depression in first onsets versus recurrences: A meta-analytic review. *Journal of Abnormal Psychology, 117*(1), 206–213.

Sturman, E. D., Mongrain, M., & Kohn, P. M. (2006). Attributional style as a predictor of hopelessness depression. *Journal of Cognitive Psychotherapy, 20*, 447–458.

Sullivan, H. S. (1953). *The interpersonal theory of psychiatry*. New York: W.W. Norton & Co.

Tak, Y. R., Brunwasser, S. M., Lichtwarck-Aschoff, A., & Engels, R. C. (2017). The prospective associations between self-efficacy and depressive symptoms from early to middle adolescence: A cross-lagged model. *Journal of Youth and Adolescence, 46*(4), 744–756.

Taylor, L., & Ingram, R. E. (1999). Cognitive reactivity and depressotypic information processing in the children of depressed mothers. *Journal of Abnormal Psychology, 108*, 202–210.

Teasdale, J. D. (1988). Cognitive vulnerability to persistent depression. *Cognition and Emotion, 2*, 247–274.

Teasdale, J. D., & Barnard, P. J. (1993). *Affect, cognition, and change*. Erlbaum.

Tillema, J. L., Cervone, D., & Scott, W. D. (2001). Dysphoric mood, perceived self-efficacy, and personal standards for performance: The effects of attributional cues on evaluative self-judgments. *Cognitive Therapy and Research, 25*, 535–549.

Twenge, J. M., Cooper, A. B., Joiner, T. E., Duffy, M. E., & Binau, S. G. (2019). Age, period, and cohort trends in mood disorder indicators and suicide-related outcomes in a nationally representative dataset, 2005–2017. *Journal of Abnormal Psychology, 128*(3), 185.

Twenge, J. M., & Nolen-Hoeksema, S. (2002). Age, gender, race, socioeconomic status, and birth cohort difference on the children's depression inventory: A meta-analysis. *Journal of Abnormal Psychology, 111*(4), 578.

Vinokur, A. D., Price, R. H., & Caplan, R. D. (1996). Hard times and hurtful partners: How financial strain affects depression and relationship satisfaction of unemployed persons and their spouses. *Journal of Personality and Social Psychology, 71*, 166–179.

Waller, E. M., & Rose, A. J. (2013). Brief report: Adolescents' co-rumination with mothers, co-rumination with friends, and internalizing symptoms. *Journal of Adolescence, 36*, 429–433.

Weissman, M. M., & Myers, J. K. (1978). Rates and risks of depressive symptoms in a United States urban community. *Acta Psychiatrica Scandinavica, 57*(3), 219–231.

White, M. E., & Shih, J. H. (2012). A daily diary study of co-rumination, stressful life events, and depressed mood in late adolescents. *Journal of Clinical Child and Adolescent Psychology, 41*, 598–610.

Williams, D. R., Gonzalez, H. M., Neighbors, H., Nesse, R., Abelson, J. M., Sweetman, J., & Jackson, J. S. (2007). Prevalence and distribution of major depressive disorder in African Americans, Caribbean blacks, and non-Hispanic whites: Results from the National Survey of American Life. *Archives of General Psychiatry, 64*(3), 305–315.

Zuroff, D. C., Fournier, M. A., & Moskowitz, D. S. (2007). Depression, perceived inferiority, and interpersonal behavior: Evidence for the involuntary defeat strategy. *Journal of Social and Clinical Psychology, 26*, 751–778.

# CHAPTER 12

# Diagnosis, Comorbidity, and Psychopathology of Substance-Related Disorders

Ty Brumback *and* Sandra A. Brown

Substance use disorders (SUDs, including alcohol and other drug disorders) are among the most common psychiatric conditions in the United States, with more than 14% of individuals aged 12 or older meeting the *DSM-5* criteria for any SUD in the past year (Substance Abuse and Mental Health Services Administration [SAMHSA], 2021). Of those, approximately 16% (6.5 million people) met criteria for both alcohol and another SUD. According to the findings of a nationally representative epidemiology study, the rates of illicit substance use from 2015 to 2019 increased among people aged 26 and older (14.6% to 18.3%), while rates in younger ranges remained stable or declined slightly. Cannabis remained the most common illicit substance used, with nearly 18% of people aged 12 and older reporting cannabis use in the past year. At the same time, binge drinking (i.e., drinking four or more drinks on an occasion for females or five or more drinks on an occasion for males), which puts individuals at higher risk for developing symptoms of alcohol use disorder (AUD), decreased slightly from 2015 (24.9%) to 2019 (23.9%). These trends in substance use highlight potential shifts in trajectories of risk for developing SUDs but also signify the persistence of substance use issues.

SUDs are problematic for society alone, but often are experienced along with a variety of psychiatric disorders that are highly comorbid with SUDs. In this chapter, we review the epidemiology, diagnostic criteria, related risk factors and problems, and comorbidities of SUDs. AUD is the most common SUD and, as such, will be a focal point of this chapter, though we will also describe the growing literature related to other SUDs and comorbidities.

## Evolution of the Diagnosis

Diagnosis of SUDs was formalized with *DSM-I* in 1953, when SUDs were grouped under sociopathic personality disturbances, along with the paraphilias and antisocial personality disorder (ASPD; then known as "antisocial and dissocial reactions"). Categorization of SUDs with disorders associated with social deviance reflected the social climate. *DSM-II* made small changes to the SUD diagnosis, maintaining its consistency with personality disorders and sexual deviations and removing the sociopathic categorization. With the publication of the *DSM-III* in 1980, tobacco/nicotine dependence were added for the first time. Growing understanding of the etiology of psychopathology led to a revision, *DSM-III-R*, in 1987, in which diagnoses were refined to increase consistency and reflect empirically supported criteria. In this edition, SUDs were separated from personality disorders and paraphilias, and the categories of abuse versus dependence were added to reflect the concept of physiological dependence (i.e., withdrawal and tolerance). In 1994, the *DSM-IV* did not substantially change SUD diagnostic criteria but allowed

**Abbreviations**
ADHD   Attention deficit hyperactivity disorder
ASPD   Antisocial personality disorder
AUD    Alcohol use disorder
CD     Conduct disorder
CUD    Cannabis use disorder
ERP    Event-related potential
HRV    Heart rate variability
SUD    Substance use disorder

for listing specifiers (i.e., with or without physiological dependence) that appeared more relevant to some substances (e.g., alcohol, opiates) than others (e.g., hallucinogens, inhalants). Additionally, social consequences were moved from the dependence criteria to the abuse criteria.

## DSM-5

In 2013, the fifth edition of the *DSM* was published nearly 20 years after the prior edition. The impetus to better reflect etiological understanding of disorders and the empirical basis of the clustering of diagnostic criteria led to several changes. Separate categories for abuse and dependence were removed, reflecting the research suggesting that the abuse category was less reliable than the dependence category (Langenbucher et al., 1996) and the dependence criteria did not necessarily reflect more serious, hierarchical progression of disorder than the abuse criteria (Schuckit et al., 2001, 2005). Instead, there is now a single SUD category with specifiers based on total symptom count of 11 possible symptoms. Two to three symptoms constitute a "mild" SUD, four to five symptoms suggest "moderate" severity, and six or more symptoms indicate a "severe" SUD. In the *DSM-IV*, a single symptom was needed for a substance abuse diagnosis, and three symptoms were needed for a substance dependence disorder. The new criteria are more consistent with other internationally accepted diagnostic systems (e.g., *ICD-10*). Finally, two criteria were changed: legal problems was removed and a symptom reflecting the presence of craving was added (Jones et al., 2012; see also Denis, Fatséas, & Auriacombe, 2012; Hasin et al., 2012; Saha et al., 2012, for analyses related to the development of *DSM-5*).

## Clinical Subtyping

Clinicians and researchers have long recognized the heterogeneity of presentation of SUDs and have attempted to achieve a greater level of specificity by attempting to differentiate clinical subtypes (Epstein et al., 2002). The diagnostic system of the *DSM-5* does not seek to differentiate subtypes and allows for significant individual differences in the presentation of SUDs while also recognizing various etiological factors that contribute to the diagnosis. Creating specific subtypes of SUD could be beneficial in describing risk, providing prognosis, and tailoring treatments to target etiological factors to improve treatment outcomes.

Clinical subtyping is not a new phenomenon, and clinical subtypes had been hypothesized and utilized well before the formal diagnostic system of the *DSM* was codified (Babor, 1996; Babor & Lauerman, 1986). Jellinek made one of the initial efforts to integrate various typologies based on causal features including exogenous (external causes) and endogenous (internal causes), with subtypes of steady and intermittent drinking within each category (Bowman & Jellinek, 1941).

Jellinek (1960) later refined these types into what he termed *species*: alpha, beta, gamma, delta, and epsilon, based on his clinical observation of motivational and behavioral characteristics. Of these, Jellinek focused primarily on two typologies that displayed physical dependence on alcohol. These two most common types were "delta alcoholics," whose drinking behavior was more socially and economically focused and who could not abstain from drinking, and "gamma alcoholics," who were more psychologically at risk and exhibited loss of control when drinking. While Jellinek's types were based on his clinical insights and his "species" typology gained popularity, the system lacked empirical validation and support (Babor, 1996). Jellinek's work later spurred others to seek typology systems based on empirical data. A common typological distinction utilized family history reflecting genetic contributions to SUDs. Individuals with a history of alcoholism in a first-degree relative generally have an earlier age of onset to drinking and a faster progression to alcoholism than individuals without a family history (e.g., Frances et al., 1980).

As empirical investigations progressed and a greater understanding of the neurobiological underpinnings of SUDs were identified, researchers began describing typologies reflecting this understanding (Leggio et al., 2009). Cloninger and colleagues developed a model based on data from Swedish sons of alcoholics and leveraged behavioral genetic contributions to the subtypes described (Cloninger et al., 1981). This first data-driven approach to developing subtypes of AUD yielded two typologies that differentiated both personality factors and behavioral tendencies. Type I alcoholics are characterized as having a later onset of alcohol-related problems (after age 25) and more psychological (as opposed to physiological) dependence, and they tend to use alcohol to self-medicate psychological symptoms (Cloninger, 1987). Type II alcoholics, a more severe type reflecting of stronger family history of alcoholism, exhibit an earlier onset of alcohol-related problems and often have more extensive behavioral problems associated with their use. Cloninger's subtypes were initially limited to male alcoholics, although they have been reasonably replicated in females (Glenn & Nixon, 1991). Cloninger's subtypes have been supported by elucidation of neurobiological underpinnings of SUDs, including the role of dopaminergic and serotonergic systems in Type I and Type II, respectively (Leggio et al., 2009; see Table 12.1 for comparison of several typologies).

Additional typologies have been developed using data-driven approaches seeking to substantiate the clinical utility of such models. For example, Babor, Hofmann, DelBoca, and Hesselbrock (1992) proposed Type A and Type B alcoholics that mimicked Cloninger's types, but that were based on clustering of 17 different characteristics of alcoholics, covering genetic, biological, psychological, and sociocultural aspects. These characteristics included family history of dependence, age of onset, and severity of dependence. Type A was similar to Cloninger's Type I, with a later onset of alcohol dependence, fewer problems in childhood, and less psychopathology. Type B was similar to Cloninger's Type II, with an earlier onset of alcohol dependence, more severe problems in childhood (particularly conduct disorder), greater levels of psychopathology, and a course that is more severe and associated with more chronic consequences and poor treatment outcomes. The Type A/B typology has been replicated in both male and female alcoholics as well as across cultural groups (e.g., Hesselbrock et al., 2000; Schuckit et al., 1995).

Using data from a large, nationally representative sample of more than 40,000 respondents, Moss, Chen, and Yi (2007) sought to empirically derive clinical subtypes of respondents with alcohol dependence. A latent class analysis identified five clusters. The clusters varied based on age at onset of AUD, family history of alcoholism, presence of antisocial personality traits, consumption patterns, and comorbidity of mood and anxiety disorders. In each of these classifications, it has been important to consider non–substance-related symptoms to further delineate subtypes. A recent attempt to use latent class analysis in a large sample of patients with AUD reflected the significant contributions that comorbidities make to the clinical presentation of AUD, likely reflecting etiological factors (Müller et al., 2020). Müller and colleagues (2020) reported that a three-class description of their sample accounted for the differences most efficiently, which included one group with low rates of comorbid symptoms, one class with higher rates of mood and anxiety disorders, and the third with high rates of other SUD and ASPD symptoms. The group without symptoms of

**Table 12.1** Typologies of alcohol use disorders

| Jellinek (1960) | Cloninger, Bohman, & Sigvardsson, 1981 | Babor et al. (1992) | Müller et al. (2020) |
|---|---|---|---|
| ***Delta***<br>• Socially influenced<br>• Inability to abstain | **Type I**<br>• Later onset<br>• Psychological dependence<br>• Self-medicate psychological symptoms | **Type A**<br>• Later onset<br>• Fewer early life problems<br>• Less stress<br>• Fewer negative social and physical effects | **Class 3** (low comorbidity)<br>• Alcohol use problems without other psychopathology |
| ***Gamma***<br>• Loss of control when drinking<br>• Psychological risk | **Type II**<br>• Earlier onset (<25 years old)<br>• Higher family history of alcohol use problems | **Type B**<br>• Earlier onset<br>• More early life problems<br>• Higher psychopathology | **Class 1** (drug-dependent antisocial)<br>• High comorbidity of SUD<br>• Higher antisocial personality disorder |
| | | | **Class 2** (depressed-anxious)<br>• Higher depression and anxiety comorbidity<br>• More prevalent in females |
| *Typology approach: clinical observation* | Typology approach: clustering of symptoms in Swedish sons of alcoholics | Typology approach: clustering of 17 symptom types in US samples of men and women | Typology approach: latent class analysis in a French population-based cohort study |

other comorbid disorders is purported to overlap in many ways with Cloninger's Type I and Babor's Type A, while the class with higher rates of mood and anxiety disorders included much higher rates of females. The third group reflects many aspects of the most severe types previously reported including Type II (Cloninger), Type B (Babor), and "young antisocial type" (Moss), which are associated with more persistent symptoms. This model further supports the notion that comorbid conditions are likely to affect progression of symptoms of AUD as well as prognosis and treatment outcomes (Müller et al., 2020).

Typology systems have been examined primarily within AUD, but some other researchers have attempted to create typologies of other SUDs. One widely accepted typology pertaining to cigarette smoking was proposed by Shiffman, Kassel, Paty, and Gnys (1994) and divided smokers into regular smokers versus "chippers." Shiffman's group highlighted the differences between the quantity and frequency of cigarette use as well as the identified motives for smoking. "Chippers" are distinct from regular smokers in that they typically smoke five or fewer cigarettes a day, do not meet criteria for nicotine dependence, and primarily report social motivation to smoke. Regular smokers report more frequent and habitual smoking marked by addictive motives and nicotine dependence. The distinction between regular users and "chippers" has been applied to several other SUDs including cannabis and cocaine, though it has primarily been used to describe patterns of use rather than as a systematically evaluated typology in most cases (e.g., Haney, 2009).

All the typologies described here are interesting from a clinical and research standpoint, and although no system yet developed has been refined enough to allow for true clinical or research utility, some research suggests that subtype is a moderator of pharmacological treatment of alcohol dependence (Kranzler et al., 2012; Pettinati et al., 2000). Heavy alcohol use is the most common feature of AUD, and personalizing interventions based on additional features remains a focus of research (Kranzler & Soyka, 2018). Personalized treatment options—based on specific subtypes of SUDs designed to intervene at different points in the progression of an SUD or geared toward more preventative measures in individuals who are not yet symptomatic but evidence various "characteristics" of a known subtype—remain an aspirational but as yet unattained goal (Witkiewitz et al., 2019).

## Polysubstance Use Disorders

While much of the research literature on SUDs focuses on a single disorder, epidemiological data shows that many people have more than one SUD. For example, 16% of the total population with SUD in the past year in 2020 reported more than one SUD (SAMHSA, 2021). An examination of patients across the National Veterans Health Administration in the United States, revealed that nearly 27% of the population being treated for SUD reported more than one SUD (Bhalla et al., 2017). These polysubstance users may have elevated and unique risk factors for negative effects including increased incarceration and deviant behaviors (Hedden et al., 2010) and higher rates of lifetime suicide attempts (Smith et al., 2011). Use of other substances has been utilized in some of the prior efforts to create clinical subtypes of SUDs (e.g., Müller et al., 2020), and the clinical picture of those with more than one SUD is markedly more complex than single-SUD patients. Those with multiple SUDs tend to utilize more mental healthcare and medical care resources and show higher risk for liver disease, HIV, and comorbid psychiatric disorders (Bhalla et al., 2017).

While alcohol remains the most prevalent SUD, cannabis use disorder (CUD) is the second most prevalent, with past year estimates of 5% of individuals above age 12 exhibiting CUD in the United States (SAMHSA, 2021). CUD has been associated with increased risk for cocaine, stimulant, and club drugs use disorders, as well as 2–4 times the rate of other psychiatric disorders (Hayley et al., 2017). Polysubstance use and meeting criteria for multiple SUDs may reflect common neurobiological etiologies among the disorders and other comorbid conditions, as well as the social and behavioral effects of engaging in substance use (Crummy et al., 2020). Clearly, when characterizing the neuropathology of SUDs and considering diagnosis and treatment, multiple concurrent SUDs complicate the picture. Better delineating the risk factors and known etiological factors will help guide future research on polysubstance use and SUDs.

## Risk Factors for Substance Use Disorders
### Family History

Researchers have examined the relationship between probands with SUDs and the incidence of these disorders in their relatives. The familial link for AUDs is widely established in the research literature (e.g., Merikangas, 1990; Prescott & Kendler, 1999), and several studies have found a potentially stronger heritability (i.e., greater genetic influence relative to environmental influence on outcomes) for illicit drug use than for alcohol (e.g., Jang et al., 1995). Disentangling environmental and genetic factors contributing to the heritability of SUDs remains a challenge. The genetic factors likely contribute to neurobiological, physiological, and behavioral tendencies that may make an individual susceptible to initiation and escalation of substance use, and environmental factors may exacerbate that susceptibility through specific (e.g., increased exposure to substances) or general (i.e., environment that creates global risk factors for psychiatric disorders) factors.

Researchers have determined via twin studies that the genetic risks for SUDs are largely non-specific (Kendler et al., 2003). However, there are some unique family determinants that are critical in predicting adolescents who will develop SUDs, such as family environment and, in particular, exposure to parental SUDs (Biederman et al., 2000). Additionally, research suggests that family history of drug and alcohol dependence is associated with a more recurrent course of the respective disorders, greater impairment, and greater service utilization (Milne et al., 2009). Recently, some groups have focused on resilience despite family history of SUDs to elucidate mechanisms that contribute to the observed outcomes. For example, Martz and colleagues (2018) reported that greater inhibitory control as evidenced by dorsolateral prefrontal cortex activation during an inhibition task, was predictive of greater resilience among young adults with a family history of SUDs (Martz et al., 2018). Connecting neurobiological factors to related behaviors may prove a fruitful line of investigation to delineate the mechanisms by which family history contributes risk to offspring.

### Level of Response to Alcohol

One mechanism by which heredity influences an individual's propensity to develop an AUD is by influencing the general level of response to alcohol, which encompasses both metabolic and behavioral effects. Responsivity has been evaluated by giving a challenge dose of alcohol and assessing body sway and subjective perception of alcohol effects, two correlated indicators of intoxication. Lower response to alcohol, or the need for a higher number of drinks for an effect, has been associated with family history of alcoholism (Schuckit, 1985; Schuckit & Gold, 1988), development of tolerance (the need for increased amounts to achieve the desired effect or a diminished effect in response to the same amounts) to alcohol (Lipscomb et al., 1979; Nathan & Lipscomb, 1979), and a fourfold greater likelihood of future alcohol dependence (Schuckit, 1994a). Level of response to alcohol appears to be a unique predictor of AUDs above and beyond a variety of other risk factors (Trim et al., Smith, 2009) and is a robust predictor in both young and middle-aged groups (Schuckit et al. 2004, 2012). Level of response to alcohol also appears to be genetically mediated (Heath et al., 1999; Hinckers et al., 2006) and may reflect the heritability of multiple factors associated with increased risk for substance use.

### Physiological Factors

Responses to external stimuli in the context of substance use have physiological effects in both the central and peripheral nervous systems. Some of these reactions appear to be closely tied to genetically heritable traits. For example, event-related potentials (ERPs) represent the neural responses to stimuli measured via scalp-recorded electrical signals of the electroencephalogram. The P300 ERP component is a positive-going wave that occurs between 300 and 600 ms after a stimulus is presented, commonly assessed utilizing an Oddball task, which simply requires the detection of infrequent stimuli in a series of regular stimuli (Kutas et al., 1977). Several studies have yielded evidence for heritability of the P300 ERP (e.g., Katsanis et al., 1997; O'Connor et al., 1994). Reduced amplitude and delayed latency for the P300 ERP have been detected in alcoholic individuals (Hansenne, 2006), as well as in cocaine- and opioid-dependent individuals (Moeller et al., 2004; Singh et al., 2009). Moreover, this pattern has also been demonstrated in non–alcohol-dependent children, adolescents, and adults with alcohol-dependent relatives (e.g., Polich et al., 1994; van der Stelt et al., 1998). These findings are generally interpreted as reflecting memory, attention, and inhibition disturbances. As a consequence of this body of research, reduced P300 amplitude has come to be considered a marker of heightened risk for the development of alcohol dependence as well as other externalizing disorders (Patrick et al., 2006).

In other physiological systems, heritability may also play a role in conveying risk for SUDs. For example, SUDs are associated with higher risk for cardiovascular disease, and substance use increases stress on the cardiovascular system and decreases the flexibility of the system (Ralevski et al., 2019). Heart rate variability (HRV), or the beat-to-beat intervals in heart rate, is an index of cardiovascular functioning that reflects the integration of both central and peripheral nervous system signals to the autonomic nervous system (Bates & Buckman, 2013). Chronic alcohol use decreases HRV, and, with abstinence, HRV tends to improve (Karpyak et al., 2014). The effects of alcohol use on HRV appear robust enough that multiple groups have proposed using it as a biomarker for AUD severity (Cheng, Huang, & Huang, 2019; Ralevski et al., 2019). HRV is particularly interesting because it reflects not only physiological effects of alcohol on the body, but also the motivational state of the individual (e.g., under conditions of craving), which have been predictive of relapse risk when measured in AUD patients undergoing treatment (Quintana et al., 2013).

### Alcohol and Drug Expectancies

A highly productive area of research on risk factors for substance use has focused on *expectancies*, defined as beliefs about the anticipated effects of substance use. Individuals develop beliefs about the effects of substance use on social, affective, cognitive, and motor functioning, and self-report questionnaires are commonly used to assess these expectancies (e.g., Brown, Christiansen, & Goldman, 1987; Leigh & Stacy, 1993). Expectations about the effects of alcohol and other substances are learned in part from family, peer, and media influences (e.g., Brown, Creamer, & Stetson, 1987; Brown et al., 1999) even prior to personal use of a given substance. Alcohol expectancies have been shown to predict initiation, progression, and problem use, as well as posttreatment relapse (e.g., Brown et al., 1985; Connors et al., 1993; Smith et al., 1995), with expectations that alcohol use will yield positive effects predicting elevated risk. For example, heavier drinkers tend to endorse more positive and arousing expectancies compared to light drinkers, and expectancies measured in children prior to the onset of drinking behavior are prospectively associated with drinking behavior (Goldman, 2002; Dunn & Goldman, 1998). Furthermore, alcohol expectancies appear to mediate the relationship between a variety of risk factors (e.g., sensation-seeking) and alcohol use (Darkes, Greenbaum, & Goldman, 2004). This has led some researchers to consider expectancies to be one of the primary systems that accounts for biopsychosocial risk for alcohol use (Goldman et al., 2006; Sher, Grekin, & Williams, 2005).

Although less extensively studied than alcohol, expectancy measures have also been developed for other substances (Alfonso & Dunn, 2007; Jaffe & Kilbey, 1994; Schafer & Brown, 1991). Marijuana expectancies are similar to alcohol expectancies, with common domains (e.g., social and sexual facilitation, tension reduction, cognitive and behavioral impairment), and this may reflect both valence and arousal expectations that contribute to decisions to use marijuana (Luba et al., 2018; Waddell et al., 2021). Consistent with the different pharmacological effects of stimulants, cocaine expectancies include unique domains (e.g., anxiety, increased energy or arousal). Unlike many risk factors, expectancies may be modifiable, particularly in adolescence and young adulthood when these cognitive schemas are developed and convey strong propensity toward initiation of substance use (Montes et al., 2018). Interventions can utilize information about individual's expectancies (e.g., expectations of tension reduction or social facilitation) to challenge expectancies and develop alternative skills for achieving the desired effects.

### Peer Influences

The influence of peers on substance use during adolescence is clear from decades of research (e.g., Newcomb & Bentler, 1986; Shoal et al., 2007; Wills et al., 2004); however, not all peer influences are equal because peers perceived as more similar exert a greater impact (Vik et al., 1992). Greater peer involvement with substances, higher perceptions of peer use, and greater perceived peer acceptance of substance use are risk factors for adolescent substance involvement (Epstein & Botvin, 2002). Additionally, peers may also influence expectancies about positive reinforcement from substance use, and perceptions of negative attitudes toward school by peers have been linked to earlier onset of cigarette and marijuana use among adolescents (Bryant & Zimmerman, 2002). Social context can exert powerful effects, with increased alcohol consumption occurring in adolescents in the presence of other adolescents who are drinking (Curran et al., 1997) and greater exposure to peer use leading to adoption of values and beliefs that foster a substance use lifestyle (Tapert et al., 1999). Socializing with substance-using peers provides greater access to substances and environments supportive of risky and deviant behaviors (Brown et al., 1989). The influence of peers has also been shown to differ based on race and sex, such that White females exhibited the strongest susceptibility to peer conformity to use marijuana and cigarettes compared to Black and Hispanic youth (Mason et al., 2014).

Peer connection mediates the influence of parental alcoholism, family conflict, and socioeconomic adversity on adolescent substance abuse (e.g., Fergusson & Horwood, 1999). More broadly, peer delinquency and positive attitudes about delinquency have also been associated with substance use in adolescent males in particular (e.g., Chassin et al., 1993) and increased exposure to stressful situations (Tate et al., 2007).

## Sex Differences in Addictive Disorders

Although men and women share commonalities in substance use and SUDs, important differences exist. Men consume greater quantities and abuse substances at higher rates than do women, but this gender gap is narrowing for both alcohol and illicit drugs (e.g., Nelson et al., 1998). Several studies provide evidence of accelerated development of alcohol problems and dependence in women when compared to men, referred to as *telescoping* (e.g., Randall et al., 1999; Wojnar et al., 1997). Specifically, at similar levels of alcohol consumption, women experience problems faster, meet criteria for an AUD in a shorter time, and present for treatment earlier. Findings of accelerated progression for women for other substances are limited but have been documented for cannabis and opiates (Hernandez-Avila et al., 2004; Kosten et al., 1985).

Research shows that women are more vulnerable to many physical consequences of alcohol use and abuse. Higher blood alcohol concentrations occur in women after consumption of equivalent amounts of alcohol because of differences in metabolism of alcohol in both the stomach and liver and differences in body water. These differences in absorption and metabolism of alcohol have led to lower standards for the definition of moderate and heavy drinking for women compared to men. Women develop liver disease more quickly than men and have higher rates of liver-related mortality (Gavaler & Arria, 1995; Hall, 1995), and they may also experience more alcohol-induced brain damage (Hommer et al., 2001; Mann et al., 2005). Increased risk of breast cancer has also been associated with moderate to heavy alcohol consumption in numerous studies (Chen et al., 2011; Singletary & Gapstur, 2001).

In addition to physical effects, women with AUD experience more psychiatric comorbidity than men (Helzer et al., 1991). Women who abuse substances meet criteria for depression and anxiety disorders more frequently than their male counterparts, who are more likely to meet criteria for ASPD (Hesselbrock & Hesselbrock, 1993). Additionally, even after desistence of substance use, women tend to continue to exhibit higher rates of psychopathology and social impairment compared to men (Foster et al., 2014, 2018) and display more adverse consequences from SUDs relative to men (McHugh et al., 2018). Finally, relationships between victimization and substance use have been documented. Women with childhood histories of victimization (physical, sexual, or neglect) are more likely to develop alcohol and drug problems (Widom et al., 1995; Wilsnack et al., 1997; Zilberman et al., 2003).

## Risks Associated with Addictive Disorders
### Interpersonal Aggression and Violence

Research has demonstrated a clear link between interpersonal aggression and substance use involvement: individuals who abuse a variety of intoxicating substances are more likely to perpetrate or be the victim of interpersonal aggression (e.g., Bushman & Cooper, 1990; Chermack & Giancola, 1997). Both alcohol use and aggression are influenced by executive functions, like inhibitory control, and may reflect developmental factors that put individuals at risk for various externalizing behaviors (Doran et al., 2012). Friedman, Kramer, Kreisher, and Granick (1996) termed substance use an "interactionist risk factor" in association with violence, such that substance use does not directly lead to violence or criminal behavior but may amplify a variety of other factors to create a high-risk situation for committing crimes or engaging in violent acts. Furthermore, it is unclear whether it is the acute or chronic effects of substance use that lead to aggressive behaviors. Giancola (2000) proffered a conceptual framework pointing to executive functioning as both a mediator and moderator of alcohol-related aggression. Specifically, alcohol interferes acutely with executive functioning, and drinking is more likely to lead to aggressive behaviors in individuals with low executive functioning.

Several substances have been associated with experiencing intimate partner violence in both men and women; those with the most evidence are alcohol, cocaine, and amphetamines (Kraanen et al., 2014; Smith et al., 2012). A large body of research has demonstrated an association between alcohol use and a variety of levels of aggressive behavior, including verbal aggression (e.g., O'Farrell et al., 2000), familial/marital aggression including child abuse (e.g., Caetano et al., 2001; Keller et al., 2009), sexual aggression (Davis et al., 2006; Ramisetty-Mikler et al., 2007; Stappenbeck & Fromme, 2010), homicide (Klatsky & Armstrong, 1993), and suicide (Brent et al., 1987; Kerr et al., 2011). Roizen (1993) demonstrated that perpetrators had consumed alcohol in 28–86% of homicide cases and 30–70% of suicide attempts. Experimental paradigms have also shown that acute alcohol administration leads to more aggressive behavior across a variety of situations (Giancola & Chermack, 1998; Hoaken et al., 1998).

Amphetamine and cocaine use are related to interpersonal aggression, although the hypothesized mechanisms differ. Acute amphetamine intoxication frequently leads to aggressive behavior, whereas prolonged amphetamine use results in a psychotic-like disorder, which in turn leads to aggressive behavior (Baker & Dawe, 2005). Cocaine intoxication is associated with increased paranoia and irritability, often leading to interpersonal aggression (Murray et al., 2003). In both cases, the potential for aggression seems mediated through cognitive functions interacting with contextual factors.

### Sexual Behavior

Alcohol and drug use also have been shown to result in sexual dysfunction (O'Farrell et al., 1997; Simons & Carey, 2001). In a community epidemiological sample of more than 3,000 adults, Johnson, Phelps, and Cottler (2004) found that the most common sexual dysfunction associated with alcohol and marijuana use was anorgasmia, whereas other illicit drug use resulted in painful sex and reduced sexual pleasure. However, neither drugs nor alcohol was associated with reduced sex drive. The mechanism for the association between chronic substance use and sexual dysfunction is thought to be hormonal (Bannister & Lowosky, 1987; Van Thiel et al., 1980). These effects likely abate after prolonged periods of abstinence (Schiavi et al., 1995).

In addition to sexual dysfunction resulting from substance use, a common problem is the spread of sexually transmitted diseases resulting from increased sexual risk-taking, including but not limited to lack of condom use (Koopman et al., 1994; Leichliter et al., 2004). In contrast, one study using a diary method found that alcohol consumption prior to sex was not predictive of condom use; individuals followed their typical patterns of condom use or nonuse when intoxicated (Leigh et al., 2008). More recently, researchers have begun focusing on the disproportionate rates of SUDs among sexual minorities and have highlighted the increased risk for SUDs as well as negative sexual consequences (e.g., rates of risky sex and sexually transmitted infections/diseases) among sexual minorities (Schuler et al., 2018). Substance-related risky sexual behavior is particularly salient in adolescent populations, and substance use has been associated with an earlier onset of sexual activity (Bentler & Newcomb, 1986). The relationship between substance use and sexual risk-taking is appreciably stronger in White than in Black adolescents (Cooper et al., 1994).

### Neurocognitive Impairment

Chronic, sustained substance use often results in significant cognitive impairment. The etiology of such impairment is thought to involve interactions among a variety of factors, including neurotoxicity, malnutrition, and trauma and varies depending on the substance abused (Lundqvist, 2005). Although impairments may remediate following cessation of use (Zinn et al., 2004), abstinence successfully diminishes the cognitive impairment in only a portion of the cases. Rourke and Løberg (1996) found that 45% of individuals with alcohol dependence still evidenced cognitive impairment after 3 weeks of sustained abstinence; 15% were still impaired at a year of abstinence. Methamphetamine-dependent individuals also demonstrated impairments during the first 3 weeks of abstinence (Kalechstein et al., 2003). A body of research supports that this may be a result of permanent frontal lobe damage (Dao-Castellana et al., 1998; Moselhy et al., 2001). Adolescent substance use is hypothesized to interfere with normal brain development, causing a variety of cognitive impairments (Hanson et al., 2011; Tapert & Brown, 1999); for example, one study found that during a 3-week period of abstinence from marijuana, adolescents' attention deficits persisted (Hanson et al., 2010).

Findings related to cocaine use are similar. O'Malley, Adamse, Heaton, and Gawin (1992) found that 50% of individuals with cocaine use disorder were cognitively impaired, compared to 15% of the control subjects, and severity of the impairment was associated with recency of cocaine use. Jovanovski, Erb, and Zakzanis (2005) conducted a meta-analysis of 15 studies and found that cocaine use had its most substantial cognitive effects on attention and visual and working memory. The results for executive functioning tests across studies were mixed, but, overall, researchers consistently found deficits in those areas of the brain (i.e., anterior cingulated gyrus and orbitofrontal cortex) that control both attention and executive functioning. Chronic cannabis use has a similar deleterious effect on both attentional processes and executive functioning, whereas opiates may more specifically affect impulse control (Lundqvist, 2005).

## Mental Health Comorbidity and Substance Use Disorders

Individuals with SUDs experience high levels of psychiatric comorbidity as documented by numerous large-scale epidemiological studies (Grant et al., 2004; Kessler et al., 1997). Explanations for the co-occurrence include (a) base rates of common psychiatric disorders naturally result in co-occurrence (Schuckit, 1994b), (b) comorbidity may increase the likelihood of seeking treatment or being referred to treatment (Schuckit, 1994b), (c) substance use may precipitate disorders directly (Sato, 1992) or exacerbate subthreshold symptoms to diagnostic levels (Negrete, 1989), (d) common genetic factors exist (e.g., Fu et al., 2002; Prescott et al., 2000), and (e) shared environmental risk factors exist (e.g., trauma; childhood abuse or neglect, life stress). Finally, substance intoxication and withdrawal states can resemble psychiatric symptoms, particularly depression, anxiety, and psychotic symptoms (Bacon et al., 1998; Schuckit, 1994b).

Comorbidity complicates diagnosis, treatment, and clinical course. Difficulties arise in differentiating psychiatric symptoms that are independent of substance use from those that are substance-induced. Constructing a timeline for a patient's life that incorporates dates of abstinence and ages when substance use and other mental health symptoms occurred can clarify whether symptoms persist during periods of abstinence (Bacon et al., 1998; Schuckit, 1994b). In addition to diagnostic complications, substance use can diminish the effectiveness of treatment efforts. Pharmacotherapy for comorbid disorders can be compromised as substance use may decrease medication adherence, cause serious side effects, and potentiate some psychotropic medications, thus increasing potential for overdose (Catz et al., 2001; National Institute on Alcohol Abuse and Alcoholism [NIAAA], 2005). Additionally, substance use is associated with increases in suicidal thoughts and attempts, necessitating a focus on crisis management rather than other therapeutic goals (e.g., Claassen et al., 2007; Goldstein & Levitt, 2006; Shen et al., 2006).

### Mood Disorders

Symptoms of major depressive disorder, dysthymic disorder, and bipolar disorder frequently co-occur with SUDs (Hunt et al., 2020). The comorbidity of mood disorders and SUDs begins early among persons with SUDs who are aged 11–17 years, and increased risk of mood disorders has been documented across substance categories (alcohol, marijuana, other; Roberts et al., 2007). While the connection between SUDs and mood disorders is robust, the specific mechanisms across substances likely vary given the heterogeneity of mood and substance use symptoms (McHugh & Weiss, 2019). For example, cocaine and amphetamine withdrawal often include depression symptoms that persist beyond the acute withdrawal phase, and AUDs are commonly accompanied by depressive symptoms. Many adults with SUDs initiating addiction treatment report clinical levels of depression, although these symptoms remit for many following weeks or months of abstinence (Brown & Schuckit, 1988; Brown et al., 1998).

To ascertain the prevalence of comorbid alcohol dependence and major depression independent of alcohol effects, researchers using data from a national epidemiological survey compared the prevalence of a current major depression diagnosis (past year) among adults who were formerly alcohol dependent to that of those without a history of alcohol dependence. A history of alcohol dependence (more than a year prior) increased the risk of current major depressive disorder by 4.2 times (Hasin & Grant, 2002), supporting a strong association between these two disorders that is not solely a result of intoxication or withdrawal states. In the same national survey (undertaken in 2001–2002) assessing 12-month prevalence, the odds of having an independent mood disorder were increased over fourfold (odds ratio [OR] = 4.5) for adults with any substance-dependence diagnosis relative to adults without substance dependence (Grant et al., 2004). More recent evaluations have suggested the rates of comorbidity between SUDs and mood disorders have remained consistent over nearly 30 years of epidemiological data, indicating that between 20% and 25% of individuals with a mood disorder also meet criteria for a SUD (Hunt et al., 2020). Lifetime prevalence of depressive disorders among adults with cocaine use disorders in research treatment samples range up to 50% (e.g., Carroll et al., 1994). Similarly, among individuals with opiate use disorder, prevalence of comorbid mood disorder was 64% and comorbid severe mental illness was nearly 27% (Jones & McCance-Katz, 2019).

### Anxiety Disorders

In contrast to the clear association between mood disorders and SUDs, the relationship is less clear for anxiety disorders. Adding to the complexity of evaluating research findings, studies have differed with respect to the disorders that were included under the umbrella of anxiety. The tension reduction hypothesis proposed that alcohol is consumed for its ability to reduce tension and anxiety, suggesting an association between anxiety and AUDs that has intuitive anecdotal appeal. However, empirical studies with alcohol-dependent samples have not consistently supported this conceptualization (e.g., Langenbucher, & Nathan, 1990). In an extensive review of prevalence, family history, and disorder onset, Schuckit and Hesselbrock (1994) concluded that anxiety disorders (panic disorder, agoraphobia, obsessive-compulsive disorder, social phobia, and generalized anxiety disorder) did not occur at higher than general-population rates when substance-induced anxiety syndromes were excluded. In a sample of youth aged 11–17 years, substance dependence was associated with increased likelihood of an anxiety disorder (OR = 2.2, 95% confidence interval [CI] = 1.2–4.3), but after controlling for other comorbid disorders, the relationship was not significant (OR = 1.0, 95% CI = 0.4–2.8; Roberts et al., 2007). In an adult sample, Schuckit and colleagues (1997) reported an increased risk of panic disorder and social phobia disorders (but not agoraphobia or obsessive-compulsive disorders) among alcohol-dependent adults compared to controls. The lifetime rate for independent anxiety disorders (agoraphobia, panic disorder, obsessive-compulsive disorder, and social phobia) was significantly higher for participants with alcohol dependence (9.4%) than for controls (3.7%). A nationally representative epidemiological study reported a lifetime prevalence of 19.4% for any anxiety disorder (agoraphobia, social phobia, simple phobia, panic disorder, obsessive-compulsive disorder) among adults with alcohol dependence and 28.3% among adults with other drug dependence compared to 14.6% in this combined community and institutional sample (Regier et al., 1990).

In a large study including data from Canada, Germany, Mexico, the Netherlands, and the United States, 32% of individuals with alcohol dependence and 35% of those with drug dependence met criteria for an anxiety disorder (generalized anxiety disorder, panic disorder, and phobic disorders were combined; Merikangas et al., 1998). Across countries, the onset of anxiety disorders preceded the onset of the AUD for the majority of participants. A large, nationally representative study reported increased odds of 2.8 for any independent anxiety disorder (panic disorder with and without agoraphobia, social phobia, specific phobia, generalized anxiety disorder) in adults with any substance dependence diagnosis (Grant et al., 2004). This finding was recently replicated and highlighted the increased odds for AUD and anxiety disorders (2.11) and SUD and anxiety disorders (2.91), which reflects a significant increase in comorbidity risk among substance users (Lai et al., 2015).

*Posttraumatic Stress Disorder*

Posttraumatic stress disorder (PTSD) has been a focus of substantial research focused primarily on veteran populations and female survivors of sexual assault and abuse. As many as 89% of patients with an SUD report they have experienced a traumatic event in their lifetime (Farley et al., 2004) and the rate of PTSD among individuals in addiction treatment has been reported to be 30–59% (Stewart et al., 2000). Studies document that among men with PTSD, AUDs are the most commonly occurring comorbid disorder, with other SUDs also being very prevalent. Among women with PTSD, depression and other anxiety disorders are most common, followed by AUDs (e.g., Kessler et al., 1995; Kulka et al., 1990). The associations between PTSD and SUD are difficult to disentangle, though it is broadly purported that individuals with PTSD may use substances as self-medication to relieve PTSD symptoms, and, over time, PTSD symptoms may come to trigger cravings for alcohol and drugs (Chilcoat & Breslau, 1998; Jacobsen et al., 2001). A study seeking to examine several competing hypotheses about the relationship between PTSD and substance use in a community sample suggested there is strongest support for the "self-medication" hypothesis that suggests the presence of PTSD symptoms increases substance use more so than hypotheses focused on shared vulnerability or early substance use contributing to higher rates of PTSD (Haller & Chassin, 2014). Research findings have been mixed on this conceptualization of the relations between substances and PTSD (e.g., Bremner et al., 1996; Freeman & Kimbrell, 2004), though systematic studies have led to more sophisticated hypotheses about the underlying neurobiological dysfunction associated with comorbid PTSD and SUD (María-Rios & Morrow, 2020). Additionally, treatment-focused studies indicate that the presence of SUDs decreases treatment adherence in PTSD (Bedard-Gilligan et al., 2018) and have supported the approach of treating comorbid PTSD and SUD concurrently due to the enmeshed nature of the symptoms and behaviors that may share etiological factors (Flanagan et al., 2016; Roberts et al., 2016).

## Schizophrenia and Other Psychoses

Among individuals with schizophrenia, between 40% and 50% also meet criteria for one or more SUDs (e.g., Blanchard et al., 2000; Hunt et al., 2018; Regier et al., 1990). Comorbidity rates are slightly lower for women but substantially higher (80–90%) in male homeless and incarcerated samples. A nationally representative epidemiological study sampling both community and institutional populations found individuals with schizophrenia had 4.6 times the odds of having an SUD compared to the general population (Regier et al., 1990). AUD and CUD appear to be most common among patients with schizophrenia (Hunt et al., 2018), and SUDs among those diagnosed with schizophrenia take a heavy toll, with higher rates of homelessness, criminal offenses, medical problems, suicide, poorer treatment compliance, and rehospitalization when compared to patients with schizophrenia without SUDs (Blanchard et al., 2000; Dixon, 1999). Furthermore, in a large epidemiological cohort study in Scandinavia, co-occurring SUD and schizophrenia was associated with 50–100% increase in hospitalizations and all-cause mortality rates (Lähteenvuo et al., 2021).

## Eating Disorders

Co-occurrence of SUDs and eating disorders has been observed in both clinical and population samples (Holderness et al., 1994; Wolfe & Maisto, 2000). Generally, individuals who primarily restrict intake (anorexia nervosa, restricting type) have lower rates of SUDs than patients with other types of eating disorders (bulimia nervosa and anorexia nervosa, binge-eating/purging type); thus, the presence of binge-eating and purging may be considered a risk factor for development of SUDs among patients with eating disorders (Bahji et al., 2019). The prevalence of SUDs has been observed to be as high as 50% in treatment-seeking patients with eating disorders (Bulik et al., 2004) The co-occurrence of eating disorders and SUDs has been hypothesized to be multifaceted, encompassing biological, psychological, and social risk factors (Killeen et al., 2015). A review of mortality associated with psychiatric disorders observed the highest risk of premature death from both natural and unnatural causes in the SUDs and eating disorders (Harris & Barraclough, 1998), and co-occurrence of these disorders may place patients at even higher risk (Keel et al., 2003). One study sought to explain the relation between substance dependence and eating disorders and found that acting rashly when distressed (negative urgency) was more likely among a group of eating-disordered women than among control women. Additionally, individuals with comorbid SUD and eating disorders reported high levels of positive expectancies for both alcohol and eating/dieting, and these findings have been replicated with young girls (Fischer et al., 2012).

## Attention Deficit Hyperactivity Disorder

High rates of comorbidity for attention deficit hyperactivity disorder (ADHD) and SUDs have been documented in numerous studies (e.g., Clure et al., 1999; Ohlmeier et al., 2007); however, questions remain about the association between these disorders. Based on data from a survey of more than 4,000 youths aged 11–17, Roberts and colleagues (2007) found no increase in odds of ADHD among youth with SUDs. Findings were the same after adjusting for other comorbid non–substance-related disorders. A recent study of childhood risk factors found that ADHD was predictive of earlier initiation of alcohol use but was not predictive of time from first drink to onset of alcohol dependence (Sartor et al., 2007). In contrast, Wilens, Biederman, Mick, Faraone, and Spencer (1997) found ADHD was associated with earlier onset of SUDs independent of other psychiatric disorders, and ADHD has been shown to increase the likelihood of nicotine dependence (Ohlmeier et al., 2007; Wilens, 2004). A recent meta-analysis examined longitudinal studies that followed children with and without ADHD into adolescence and adulthood, and children with ADHD were more likely to use and develop nicotine, alcohol, marijuana, and cocaine use disorders (Lee et al., 2011). Similarly, a recent study in a Swedish twin sample indicated ADHD increased the odds of experiencing any SUD; with AUD (OR = 3.58) and polysubstance use (OR = 2.54) the most significantly increased outcomes (Capusan et al., 2019). However, questions remain about whether it is ADHD specifically or the presence of other disorders that frequently accompany the diagnosis (mood, anxiety, externalizing disorders) that increases risk for development of SUDs. Recent research suggests that the hyperactivity and impulsivity components of ADHD pose more risk for substance use problems than does the inattention component (Elkins et al., 2007). Given that ADHD symptoms first appear during childhood, early identification and treatment for ADHD may alter progression of substance use and problems that typically occur later.

### Conduct Disorder and Antisocial Personality Disorder

Extensive research has verified a relationship between SUDs and conduct disorder (CD) and ASPD. A large prospective twin study assessed CD at age 11 and found an increased risk of initiating tobacco, alcohol, and illicit drug use by age 14 for adolescents with CD (Elkins et al., 2007). A diagnosis of CD by 14 years of age quadrupled the odds of nicotine dependence and more than quintupled the odds of alcohol or cannabis dependence by age 18 (Elkins et al., 2007). Other studies have found similar results, with CD predicting both early alcohol initiation and transition to alcohol dependence (e.g., Pardini et al., 2007; Sartor et al., 2007). The personality traits associated with CD appear to overlap with risk for SUDs, including higher neuroticism and lower conscientiousness and agreeableness, which may contribute to ongoing issues into young adulthood even if ASPD is not fully exhibited (Anderson et al., 2007). A large community sample of adolescents recruited from the juvenile correctional system and substance use treatment programs and siblings around age 16 and followed into their early 30s found that mortality hazard rates for probands and their siblings were nearly 500% higher than controls, and CD symptoms independently predicted mortality rates after controlling for SUD and family history (Border et al., 2018). ASPD is characterized by continuation into adulthood of CD problems, and high rates of comorbidity with SUDs have also been observed. Among adults with ASPD, 83.6% met criteria for an SUD (Regier et al., 1990). In a nationally representative epidemiological study, the lifetime prevalence of ASPD was 2.6% in the general sample, increasing to 14.3% among adults with AUD and 17.8% for adults with other SUD. Thus, substance use may be characterized as a symptom of CD and ASPD, though it appears that the underlying behavioral tendencies in these individuals increase the risk for negative outcomes beyond SUDs.

### Conclusion

In this chapter, we reviewed the available information on diagnosis, risk factors, associated psychopathology, and comorbidities for substance-related disorders. SUDs are a significant public health problem because of the associated health, social, and legal consequences related to these disorders. The variety of risk factors and comorbid disorders make SUDs multifaceted and complex, and they require the implementation of efficacious prevention and intervention strategies that reflect the biopsychosocial conceptualization of these complex disorders. Regarding assessment of individuals with SUDs, close attention should be paid to other potentially dangerous behaviors or risk factors, such as risky sexual behavior and interpersonal aggression and violence. Given the high prevalence and frequent comorbidities, assessing for SUDs is paramount for treatment of any disorder. Developing a clear understanding of the relations between substance use and symptoms of other disorders is necessary for diagnosis and treatment planning. As SUDs are multiply determined, a careful assessment involving the aspects discussed in this chapter would enable more precise treatment recommendations.

### References

Alfonso, J., & Dunn, M. E. (2007). Differences in the marijuana expectancies of adolescents in relation to marijuana use. *Substance Use & Misuse, 42*, 1009–1025.

Anderson, K. G., Tapert, S. F., Moadab, I., Crowley, T. J., & Brown, S. A. (2007). Personality risk profile for conduct disorder and substance use disorders in youth. *Addictive Behaviors, 32*(10), 2377–2382. doi:10.1016/j.addbeh.2007.02.006

Babor, T. F. (1996). The classification of alcoholics: Typology theories from the 19th century to the present. *Alcohol Health & Research World, 20*, 6–17.

Babor, T. F., Hofmann, M., DelBoca, F. K., & Hesselbrock, V. M. (1992). Types of alcoholics: I. evidence for an empirically derived typology based on indicators of vulnerability and severity. *Archives of General Psychiatry, 49*, 599–608.

Babor, T. F., & Lauerman, R. J. (1986). *Classification and forms of inebriety: Historical antecedents of alcoholic typologies.* Plenum Press.

Bacon, A., Granholm, E., & Withers, N. (1998). Substance-induced psychosis. *Seminars in Clinical Neuropsychiatry, 3*, 70–79.

Bahji, A., Mazhar, M. N., Hudson, C. C., Nadkarni, P., MacNeil, B. A., & Hawken, E. (2019). Prevalence of substance use disorder comorbidity among individuals with eating disorders: A systematic review and meta-analysis. *Psychiatry Research, 273*, 58–66. https://doi.org/10.1016/j.psychres.2019.01.007

Baker, A., & Dawe, S. (2005). Amphetamine use and co-occurring psychological problems: Review of the literature and implications for treatment. *Australian Psychologist, 40*, 88–95.

Bannister, P., & Lowosky, M. S. (1987). Ethanol and hypogonadism. *Alcohol, 22*, 213–217.

Bates, M. E., & Buckman, J. F. (2013). Integrating body and brain systems in addiction neuroscience. In P. M. Miller (Ed.), *Comprehensive addictive behaviors and disorders* (vol. 2, pp. 187–198). Academic Press.

Bedard-Gilligan, M., Garcia, N., Zoellner, L. A., & Feeny, N. C. (2018). Alcohol, cannabis, and other drug use: Engagement and outcome in PTSD treatment. *Psychology of Addictive*

Behavior, *32*(3), 277–288. https://doi.org/10.1037/adb 0000355

Bentler, P. M., & Newcomb, M. D. (1986). Personality, sexual behavior, and drug use revealed through latent variable methods. *Clinical Psychology Review, 6*, 363–385.

Bhalla, I. P., Stefanovics, E. A., & Rosenheck, R. A. (2017). Clinical epidemiology of single versus multiple substance use disorders: Polysubstance use disorder. *Medical Care, 55*, S24–S32. https://doi.org/10.1097/mlr.0000000000000731

Biederman, J., Faraone, S. V., Monuteaux, M. C., & Feighner, J. A. (2000). Patterns of alcohol and drug use in adolescents can be predicted by parental substance use disorders. *Pediatrics, 106*, 792–797.

Blanchard, J. J., Brown, S. A., Horan, W. P., & Sherwood, A. R. (2000). Substance use disorders in schizophrenia: Review, integration, and a proposed model. *Clinical Psychology Review, 20*, 207–234.

Border, R., Corley, R. P., Brown, S. A., Hewitt, J. K., Hopfer, C. J., McWilliams, S. K., Rhea, S. A., Shriver, C. L., Stallings, M. C., Wall, T. L., Woodward, K. E., & Rhee, S. H. (2018). Independent predictors of mortality in adolescents ascertained for conduct disorder and substance use problems, their siblings and community controls. *Addiction, 113*(11), 2107–2115. https://doi.org/10.1111/add.14366

Bowman, K. M., & Jellinek, E. M. (1941). Alcohol addiction and its treatment. *Quarterly Journal of Studies on Alcohol, 2*, 98–176.

Bremner, J. D., Southwick, S. M., Darnell, A., & Charney, D. S. (1996). Chronic PTSD in Vietnam combat veterans: Course of illness and substance abuse. *American Journal of Psychiatry, 153*, 369–375.

Brent, D., Perper, J., & Allman, C. (1987). Alcohol, firearms, and suicide among youth: Temporal trends in Allegheny County, Pennsylvania, 1960–1983. *Journal of the American Medical Association, 257*, 3369–3372.

Brown, R. A., Monti, P. M., Myers, M. G., Martin, R. A., Rivinus, T., Dubreuil, M. E., & Rohsenow, D. J. (1998). Depression among cocaine abusers in treatment: Relation to cocaine and alcohol use and treatment outcome. *American Journal of Psychiatry, 155*, 220–225.

Brown, S. A., Christiansen, B. A., & Goldman, M. S. (1987). The alcohol expectancy questionnaire: An instrument for the assessment of adolescent and adult alcohol expectancies. *Journal of Studies on Alcohol, 48*, 483–491.

Brown, S. A., Creamer, V. A., & Stetson, B. A. (1987). Adolescent alcohol expectancies in relation to personal and parental drinking patterns. *Journal of Abnormal Psychology, 96*, 117–121.

Brown, S. A., Goldman, M. S., & Christiansen, B. A. (1985). Do alcohol expectancies mediate drinking patterns of adults? *Journal of Consulting and Clinical Psychology, 53*, 512–519.

Brown, S. A., & Schuckit, M. A. (1988). Changes in depression among abstinent alcoholics. *Journal of Studies on Alcohol, 49*, 412–417.

Brown, S. A., Tate, S. R., Vik, P. W., Haas, A. L., & Aarons, G. A. (1999). Modeling of alcohol use mediates the effect of family history of alcoholism on adolescent alcohol expectancies. *Experimental and Clinical Psychopharmacology, 7*, 20–27.

Brown, S. A., Vik, P. W., & Creamer, V. A. (1989). Characteristics of relapse following adolescent substance abuse treatment. *Addictive Behaviors, 14*, 291–300.

Bryant, A. L., & Zimmerman, M. A. (2002). Examining the effects of academic beliefs and behaviors on changes in substance use among urban adolescents. *Journal of Educational Psychology, 94*, 621–637.

Bulik, C. M., Klump, K. L., Thornton, L., Kaplan, A. S., Devlin, B., Fichter, M. M., Halmi, K. A., Strober, M., Woodside, D. B., & Crow, S. (2004). Alcohol use disorder comorbidity in eating disorders: A multicenter study. *Journal of Clinical Psychiatry, 65*(7), 683.

Bushman, B. J., & Cooper, H. M. (1990). Effects of alcohol on human aggression: An integrative research review. *Psychological Bulletin, 107*, 341–354.

Caetano, R., Schafer, J., & Cunradi, C. B. (2001). Alcohol-related intimate partner violence among white, black, and Hispanic couples in the United States. *Alcohol Research & Health, 25*, 58–65.

Capusan, A. J., Bendtsen, P., Marteinsdottir, I., & Larsson, H. (2019). Comorbidity of adult ADHD and its subtypes with substance use disorder in a large population-based epidemiological study. *Journal of Attention Disorders, 23*(12), 1416–1426. https://doi.org/10.1177/1087054715626511

Carroll, K. M., Rounsaville, B. J., Gordon, L. T., & Nich, C. (1994). Psychotherapy and pharmacotherapy for ambulatory cocaine abusers. *Archives of General Psychiatry, 51*, 177–187.

Catz, S. L., Heckman, T. G., Kochman, A., & DiMarco, M. (2001). Rates and correlates of HIV treatment adherence among late middle-aged and older adults living with HIV disease. *Psychology, Health & Medicine, 6*, 47–58.

Chassin, L., Pillow, D. R., Curran, P. J., Molina, B. S. G., & Barrera, M. (1993). Relation of parental alcoholism to early adolescent substance use: A test of three mediating mechanisms. *Journal of Abnormal Psychology, 102*, 3–19.

Chen, W. Y., Rosner, B., Hankinson, S. E., Colditz, G. A., & Willett, W. C. (2011). Moderate alcohol consumption during adult life, drinking patterns, and breast cancer risk. *Journal of the American Medical Association, 306*, 1884–1890.

Chermack, S. T., & Giancola, P. R. (1997). The relation between alcohol and aggression: An integrated biopsychosocial conceptualization. *Clinical Psychology Review, 17*, 621–649.

Chilcoat, H. D., & Breslau, N. (1998). Investigations of causal pathways between PTSD and drug use disorders. *Addictive Behaviors, 23*, 827–840.

Claassen, C. A., Trivedi, M. H., Rush, A. J., Husain, M. M., Zisook, S., Young, E., . . . Alpert, J. (2007). Clinical differences among depressed patients with and without a history of suicide attempts: Findings from the STAR*D trial. *Journal of Affective Disorders, 97*, 77–84.

Cloninger, C. R., Bohman, M., & Sigvardsson, S. (1981). Inheritance of alcohol abuse: Cross-fostering analysis of adopted men. *Archives of General Psychiatry, 38*, 861–868.

Cloninger, C. R. (1987). Neurogenetic adaptive mechanisms in alcoholism. *Science, 236*(4800), 410–416. https://doi.org/10.1126/science.2882604

Clure, C., Brady, K. T., Saladin, M. E., Johnson, D., Waid, R., & Rittenbury, M. (1999). Attention deficit/hyperactivity disorder and substance use: Symptoms pattern and drug choice. *American Journal of Drug and Alcohol Abuse, 25*, 441–448.

Connors, G. J., Tarbox, A. R., & Faillace, L. A. (1993). Changes in alcohol expectancies and drinking behavior among treated problem drinkers. *Journal of Studies on Alcohol, 54*, 676–683.

Cooper, M. L., Peirce, R. S., & Huselid, R. F. (1994). Substance use and sexual risk taking among black adolescents and white adolescents. *Health Psychology, 13*, 251–262.

Curran, P. J., Stice, E., & Chassin, L. (1997). The relation between adolescent alcohol use and peer alcohol use: A longitudinal random coefficients model. *Journal of Consulting and Clinical Psychology, 65*, 130–140.

Crummy, E. A., O'Neal, T. J., Baskin, B. M., & Ferguson, S. M. (2020). One is not enough: Understanding and modeling polysubstance use. *Frontiers in Neuroscience, 14*(569). doi:10.3389/fnins.2020.00569

Dao-Castellana, M., Samson, Y., Legault, F., Martinot, J. L., Aubin, H. J., Crouzel, C., ... Syrota, A. (1998). Frontal dysfunction in neurologically normal chronic alcoholic subjects: Metabolic and neuropsychological findings. *Psychological Medicine, 28*, 1039–1048.

Darkes, J., Greenbaum, P. E., & Goldman, M. S. (2004). Alcohol expectancy mediation of biopsychosocial risk: Complex patterns of mediation. *Experimental and Clinical Psychopharmacology, 12*(1), 27–38.

Davis, K. C., Morris, J., George, W. H., Martell, J., & Heiman, J. R. (2006). Men's likelihood of sexual aggression: The influence of alcohol, sexual arousal, and violent pornography. *Aggressive Behavior, 32*, 581–589.

Denis, C., Fatséas, M., & Auriacombe, M. (2012). Analyses related to the development of DSM-5 criteria for substance use related disorders: 3. An assessment of Pathological Gambling criteria. *Drug and Alcohol Dependence, 122*(1), 22–27. https://doi.org/10.1016/j.drugalcdep.2011.09.006

Dixon, L. (1999). Dual diagnosis of substance abuse in schizophrenia: Prevalence and impact on outcomes. *Schizophrenia Research, 35*, s93–s100.

Doran, N., Luczak, S. E., Bekman, N., Koutsenok, I., & Brown, S. A. (2012). Adolescent Substance Use and Aggression: A Review. *Criminal Justice and Behavior, 39*(6), 748–769. doi:10.1177/0093854812437022

Dunn, M. E., & Goldman, M. S. (1998). Age and drinking-related differences in the memory organization of alcohol expectancies in 3rd-, 6th-, 9th-, and 12th-grade children. *Journal of Consulting and Clinical Psychology, 66*(3), 579–585. https://doi.org/10.1037/0022-006X.66.3.579

Elkins, I. J., McGue, M., & Iacono, W. G. (2007). Prospective effects of attention-deficit/hyperactivity disorder, conduct disorder, and sex on adolescent substance use and abuse. *Archives of General Psychiatry, 64*, 1145–1152.

Epstein, E. E., Labouvie, E., McCrady, B. S., Jensen, N. K., & Hayaki, J. (2002). A multi-site study of alcohol subtypes: Classification and overlap of unidimensional and multidimensional typologies. *Addiction, 97*, 1041–1053.

Epstein, J. A., & Botvin, G. J. (2002). The moderating role of risk-taking tendency and refusal assertiveness on social influences in alcohol use among inner-city adolescents. *Journal of Studies on Alcohol, 63*, 456–459.

Farley, M., Golding, J. M., Young, G., Mulligan, M., & Minkoff, J. R. (2004). Trauma history and relapse probability among patients seeking substance abuse treatment. *Journal of Substance Abuse Treatment, 27*, 161–167.

Fergusson, D. M., & Horwood, L. J. (1999). Prospective childhood predictors of deviant peer affiliations in adolescence. *Journal of Child Psychology and Psychiatry, 40*, 581–592.

Fischer, S., Settles, R., Collins, B., Gunn, R., & Smith, G. T. (2012). The role of negative urgency and expectancies in problem drinking and disordered eating: Testing a model of comorbidity in pathological and at-risk samples. *Psychology of Addictive Behaviors, 26*, 112–123.

Flanagan, J. C., Korte, K. J., Killeen, T. K., & Back, S. E. (2016). Concurrent treatment of substance use and PTSD. *Current Psychiatry Reports, 18*(8), 1–9.

Foster, K. T., Hicks, B. M., Durbin, C. E., Iacono, W. G., & McGue, M. (2018). The gender risk–severity paradox for alcohol use disorder from adolescence through young adulthood. *Emerging Adulthood, 6*(6), 375–386. https://doi.org/10.1177/2167696817740453

Foster, K. T., Hicks, B. M., Iacono, W. G., & McGue, M. (2014). Alcohol use disorder in women: Risks and consequences of an adolescent onset and persistent course. *Psychology of Addictive Behavior, 28*(2), 322–335. https://doi.org/10.1037/a0035488

Fox, C. H. (1994). Cocaine use in pregnancy. *Journal of the American Board of Family Practices, 7*, 225–228.

Frances, R. J., Timm, S., Bucky, S. (1980). Studies of familial and non-familial alcoholism. *Archives of General Psychiatry, 37*, 564–566.

Freeman, T., & Kimbrell, T. (2004). Relationship of alcohol craving to symptoms of posttraumatic stress disorder in combat veterans. *Journal of Nervous and Mental Disease, 192*, 389–390.

Friedman, A. S., Kramer, S., Kreisher, C., & Granick, S. (1996). The relationships of substance abuse to illegal and violent behavior, in a community sample of young adult African American men and women (gender differences). *Journal of Substance Abuse, 8*, 379–402.

Fu, Q., Heath, A. C., Bucholz, K. K., Nelson, E., Goldberg, J., Lyons, M. J., . . . Eisen, S. A. (2002). Shared genetic risk of major depression, alcohol dependence, and marijuana dependence: Contribution of antisocial personality disorder in men. *Archives of General Psychiatry, 59*, 1125–1132.

Gavaler, J. S., & Arria, A. M. (1995). Increased susceptibility of women to alcoholic liver disease: Artifactual or real? In P. Hall (Ed.), *Alcoholic liver disease: Pathology and pathogenesis* 2nd ed. (pp. 123–133). Edward Arnold.

Giancola, P. R. (2000). Executive functioning: A conceptual framework for alcohol-related aggression. *Experimental and Clinical Psychopharmacology, 8*, 576–597.

Giancola, P. R., & Chermack, S. T. (1998). Construct validity of laboratory aggression paradigms: A response to Tedeschi and Quigley (1996). *Aggression and Violent Behavior, 3*, 237–253.

Glenn, S. W., & Nixon, S. J. (1991). Applications of Cloninger's subtypes in a female alcoholic sample. *Alcoholism: Clinical and Experimental Research, 15*, 851–857.

Goldman, M. S. (2002). Expectancy and risk for alcoholism: The unfortunate exploitation of a fundamental characteristic of neurobehavioral adaptation. *Alcoholism: Clinical and Experimental Research, 26*(5), 737–746. https://doi.org/10.1111/j.1530-0277.2002.tb02599.x

Goldman, M. S., Darkes, J., Reich, R. R., & Brandon, K. O. (2006). From DNA to conscious thought: The influence of anticipatory processes on human alcohol consumption. In *Cognition and addiction* (pp. 147–184). Oxford University Press.

Goldstein, B. I., & Levitt, A. J. (2006). Is current alcohol consumption associated with increased lifetime prevalence of major depression and suicidality? Results from a pilot community survey. *Comprehensive Psychiatry, 47*, 330–333.

Grant, B. F., Stinson, F. S., Dawson, D. A., Chou, P., Dufour, M. C., Compton, W., . . . Kaplan, K. (2004). Prevalence and co-occurrence of substance use disorders and independent mood and anxiety disorders: Results from the national epidemiologic survey on alcohol and related conditions. *Archives of General Psychiatry, 61*, 807–816.

Hall, P. M. (1995). Factors influencing individual susceptibility to alcoholic liver disease. In P. Hall (Ed.), *Alcoholic liver disease: Pathology and pathogenesis*, 2nd ed. (pp. 299–316). Edward Arnold.

Haller, M., & Chassin, L. (2014). Risk pathways among traumatic stress, posttraumatic stress disorder symptoms, and alcohol and drug problems: A test of four hypotheses. *Psychology of Addictive Behaviors, 28*(3), 841.

Haney, M. (2009). Self-administration of cocaine, cannabis and heroin in the human laboratory: Benefits and pitfalls. *Addiction Biology, 14*(1), 9–21.

Hansenne, M. (2006). Event-related brain potentials in psychopathology: Clinical and cognitive perspectives. *Psychologica Belgica, 46*, 5–36.

Hanson, K. L., Medina, K. L., Padula, C. B., Tapert, S. F., & Brown, S. A. (2011). Impact of adolescent alcohol and drug use on neuropsychological functioning in young adulthood: 10-year outcomes. *Journal of Child & Adolescent Substance Abuse, 20*, 135–154.

Hanson, K. L., Winward, J. L., Schweinsburg, A. D., Medina, K. L., Brown, S. A., & Tapert, S. F. (2010). Longitudinal study of cognition among adolescent marijuana users over three weeks of abstinence. *Addictive Behaviors, 35*, 970–976.

Harris, E. C., & Barraclough, B. (1998). "Excess mortality of mental disorder": Erratum. *British Journal of Psychiatry, 173*, 272–272.

Hasin, D. S., Fenton, M. C., Beseler, C., Park, J. Y., & Wall, M. M. (2012). Analyses related to the development of DSM-5 criteria for substance use related disorders: 2. Proposed DSM-5 criteria for alcohol, cannabis, cocaine and heroin disorders in 663 substance abuse patients. *Drug and Alcohol Dependence, 122*, 28–37.

Hasin, D. S., & Grant, B. F. (2002). Major depression in 6050 former drinkers: Association with past alcohol dependence. *Archives of General Psychiatry, 59*, 794–800.

Hayley, A. C., Stough, C., & Downey, L. A. (2017). DSM-5 cannabis use disorder, substance use and DSM-5 specific substance-use disorders: Evaluating comorbidity in a population-based sample. *European Neuropsychopharmacology, 27*(8), 732–743. doi:10.1016/j.euroneuro.2017.06.004

Heath, A. C., Madden, P. A. F., Bucholz, K. K., Dinwiddie, S. H., Slutske, W. S., Bierut, L. J., . . . Martin, N. G. (1999). Genetic differences in alcohol sensitivity and the inheritance of alcoholism risk. *Psychological Medicine, 29*, 1069–1081.

Hedden, S. L., Martins, S. S., Malcolm, R. J., Floyd, L., Cavanaugh, C. E., & Latimer, W. W. (2010). Patterns of illegal drug use among an adult alcohol dependent population: Results from the National Survey on Drug Use and Health. *Drug and Alcohol Dependence, 106*(2-3), 119–125. https://doi.org/10.1016/j.drugalcdep.2009.08.002

Helzer, J. E., Burnham, A., & McEvoy, L. T. (1991). Alcohol abuse and dependence. In L. N. Robbins & D. A. Regier (Eds.), *Psychiatric disorders in America: The Epidemiology Catchment Area Study* (pp. 81–115). Free Press.

Hernandez-Avila, C., Rounsaville, B. J., & Kranzler, H. R. (2004). Opioid-, cannabis- and alcohol-dependent women show more rapid progression to substance abuse treatment. *Drug and Alcohol Dependence, 74*, 265–272.

Hesselbrock, M. N., & Hesselbrock, V. M. (1993). Depression and antisocial personality disorder in alcoholism: Gender comparison. In E. S. Lisansky T. D. & Nirengerg (Eds.), *Women and substance abuse* (pp. 142–161). Ablex.

Hesselbrock, V., Hesselbrock, M. N., & Segal, B. (2000). Multivariate phenotypes of alcohol dependence among Alaskan natives—type A/type B. *Alcoholism: Clinical & Experimental Research, 24*, 107a.

Hinckers, A. S., Laucht, M., Schmidt, M. H., Mann, K. F., Schumann, G., Schuckit, M. A., & Heinz, A. (2006). Low level of response to alcohol as associated with serotonin transporter genotype and high alcohol intake in adolescents. *Biological Psychiatry, 60*, 282–287.

Hoaken, P. N. S., Assaad, J., & Pihl, R. O. (1998). Cognitive functioning and the inhibition of alcohol-induced aggression. *Journal of Studies on Alcohol, 59*, 599–607.

Holderness, C. C., Brooks-Gunn, J., & Warren, M. P. (1994). Co-morbidity of eating disorders and substance abuse review of the literature. *International Journal of Eating Disorders, 16*, 1–34.

Hommer, D. W., Momenan, R., Kaiser, E., & Rawlings, R. R. (2001). Evidence for a gender-related effect of alcoholism on brain volumes. *American Journal of Psychiatry, 158*, 198–204.

Hunt, G. E., Large, M. M., Cleary, M., Lai, H. M. X., & Saunders, J. B. (2018). Prevalence of comorbid substance use in schizophrenia spectrum disorders in community and clinical settings, 1990–2017: Systematic review and meta-analysis. *Drug and Alcohol Dependence, 191*, 234–258. doi:10.1016/j.drugalcdep.2018.07.011

Hunt, G. E., Malhi, G. S., Lai, H. M. X., & Cleary, M. (2020). Prevalence of comorbid substance use in major depressive disorder in community and clinical settings, 1990–2019: Systematic review and meta-analysis. *Journal of Affective Disorders, 266*, 288–304. doi:10.1016/j.jad.2020.01.141

Jacobsen, L. K., Southwick, S. M., & Kosten, T. R. (2001). Substance use disorders in patients with posttraumatic stress disorder: A review of the literature. *American Journal of Psychiatry, 158*, 1184–1190.

Jaffe, A. J., & Kilbey, M. M. (1994). The cocaine expectancy questionnaire (CEQ), Construction and predictive utility. *Psychological Assessment, 6*, 18–26.

Jang, K. L., Livesley, W. J., & Vernon, P. A. (1995). Alcohol and drug problems: A multivariate behavioural genetic analysis of co-morbidity. *Addiction, 90*(9), 1213–1221.

Jellinek, E. M. (1960). Alcoholism: A genus and some of its species. *Canadian Medical Association Journal, 81*, 1341-1345.

Johnson, S. D., Phelps, D. L., & Cottler, L. B. (2004). The association of sexual dysfunction and substance use among a community epidemiological sample. *Archives of Sexual Behavior, 33*, 55–63.

Jones, C. M., & McCance-Katz, E. F. (2019). Co-occurring substance use and mental disorders among adults with opioid use disorder. *Drug and Alcohol Dependence, 197*, 78–82. doi:10.1016/j.drugalcdep.2018.12.030

Jones, K. D., Gill, C., & Ray, S. (2012). Review of the proposed DSM-5 substance use disorder. *Journal of Addictions & Offender Counseling, 33*, 115–123.

Jovanovski, D., Erb, S., & Zakzanis, K. K. (2005). Neurocognitive deficits in cocaine users: A quantitative review of the evidence. *Journal of Clinical and Experimental Neuropsychology, 27*, 189–204.

Kalechstein, A. D., Newton, T. F., & Green, M. (2003). Methamphetamine dependence is associated with neurocognitve impairment in the initial phases of abstinence. *Journal of Neuropsychiatry and Clinical Neurosciences, 15*, 215–220.

Katsanis, J., Iacono, W. G., McGue, M. K., & Carlson, S. R. (1997). P300 event-related potential heritability in monozygotic and dizygotic twins. *Psychophysiology, 34,* 47–58.

Keel, P. K., Dorer, D. J., Eddy, K. T., Franko, D., Charatan, D. L., & Herzog, D. B. (2003). Predictors of mortality in eating disorders. *Archives of General Psychiatry, 60,* 179–183.

Keller, P. S., El-Sheikh, M., Keiley, M., & Liao, P. (2009). Longitudinal relations between marital aggression and alcohol problems. *Psychology of Addictive Behaviors, 23,* 2–13.

Kendler, K. S., Jacobson, K. C., Prescott, C. A., & Neale, M. C. (2003). Specificity of genetic and environmental risk factors for use and abuse/dependence of cannabis, cocaine, hallucinogens, sedatives, stimulants, and opiates in male twins. *American Journal of Psychiatry, 160,* 687–696.

Kerr, W. C., Subbaraman, M., & Ye, Y. (2011). Per capita alcohol consumption and suicide mortality in a panel of US states from 1950 to 2002. *Drug and Alcohol Review, 30,* 473–480.

Kessler, R. C., Crum, R. M., Warner, L. A., & Nelson, C. B. (1997). Lifetime co-occurrence of DSM-III-R alcohol abuse and dependence with other psychiatric disorders in the national comorbidity survey. *Archives of General Psychiatry, 54,* 313–321.

Kessler, R. C., Sonnega, A., Bromet, E., Hughes, M., & Nelson, C. B. (1995). Posttraumatic stress disorder in the national comorbidity survey. *Archives of General Psychiatry, 52,* 1048–1060.

Killeen, T., Brewerton, T. D., Campbell, A., Cohen, L. R., & Hien, D. A. (2015). Exploring the relationship between eating disorder symptoms and substance use severity in women with comorbid PTSD and substance use disorders. *American Journal of Drug and Alcohol Abuse, 41*(6), 547–552.

Klatsky, A. L., & Armstrong, M. A. (1993). Alcohol use, other traits, and risk of unnatural death: A prospective study. *Alcoholism: Clinical and Experimental Research, 17,* 1156–1162.

Koopman, C., Rosario, M., & Rotheram-Borus, M. (1994). Alcohol and drug use and sexual behaviors placing runaways at risk for HIV infection. *Addictive Behaviors, 19,* 95–103.

Kosten, T. R., Rounsaville, B. J., & Kleber, H. D. (1985). Ethnic and gender differences among opiate addicts. *International Journal of the Addictions, 20,* 1143–1162.

Kraanen, F. L., Vedel, E., Scholing, A., & Emmelkamp, P. M. (2014). Prediction of intimate partner violence by type of substance use disorder. *Journal of Substance Abuse Treatment, 46*(4), 532-539.

Kranzler, H. R., Feinn, R., Armeli, S., & Tennen, H. (2012). Comparison of alcoholism subtypes as moderators of the response to sertraline treatment. *Alcoholism: Clinical and Experimental Research, 36,* 509–516.

Kranzler, H. R., & Soyka, M. (2018). Diagnosis and pharmacotherapy of alcohol use disorder: A review. *Journal of the American Medical Association, 320*(8), 815–824. https://doi.org/10.1001/jama.2018.11406

Kulka, R. A., Schlenger, W. E., Fairbank, J. A., Hough, R. L., Jordan, B. K., Marmar, C. R., . . . Weiss, D. S. (1990). *Trauma and the Vietnam war generation: Report of findings from the national Vietnam Veterans Readjustment Study.* Brunner/Mazel.

Kutas, M., McCarthy, G., & Donchin, E. (1977). Augmenting mental chronometry: The P300 as a measure of stimulus evaluation time. *Science, 197*(4305), 792–795.

Lai, H. M. X., Cleary, M., Sitharthan, T., & Hunt, G. E. (2015). Prevalence of comorbid substance use, anxiety, and mood disorders in epidemiological surveys, 1990–2014: A systematic review and meta-analysis. *Drug and Alcohol Dependence, 154,* 1–13. doi:10.1016/j.drugalcdep.2015.05.031

Langenbucher, J., Labouvie, E., & Morgenstern, J. (1996). Measuring diagnostic agreement. *Journal of Consulting and Clinical Psychology, 64,* 1285–1289.

Langenbucher, J. W., & Nathan, P. E. (1990). Alcohol, affect, and the tension-reduction hypothesis: The reanalysis of some crucial early data. In W. M. Cox (Ed.), *Why people drink: Parameters of alcohol as a reinforcer* (pp. 131–168). Gardner Press.

Lähteenvuo, M., Batalla, A., Luykx, J. J., Mittendorfer-Rutz, E., Tanskanen, A., Tiihonen, J., & Taipale, H. (2021). Morbidity and mortality in schizophrenia with comorbid substance use disorders. *Acta Psychiatrica Scandinavica, 144,* 42–49.

Lee, S. S., Humphreys, K. L., Flory, K., Liu, R., & Glass, K. (2011). Prospective association of childhood attention-deficit/hyperactivity disorder (ADHD) and substance use and abuse/dependence: A meta-analytic review. *Clinical Psychology Review, 31,* 328–341.

Leichliter, J. S., Williams, S. P., & Bland, S. D. (2004). Sexually active adults in the United States: Predictors of sexually transmitted diseases and utilization of public STD clinics. *Journal of Psychology & Human Sexuality, 16,* 33–50.

Leigh, B. C., & Stacy, A. W. (1993). Alcohol outcome expectancies: Scale construction and predictive utility in higher order confirmatory models. *Psychological Assessment, 5,* 216–229.

Leigh, B. C., Vanslyke, J. G., Hoppe, M. J., Rainey, D. T., Morrison, D. M., & Gillmore, M. R. (2008). Drinking and condom use: Results from an event-based daily diary. *AIDS and Behavior, 12,* 104–112.

Leggio, L., Kenna, G. A., Fenton, M., Bonenfant, E., & Swift, R. M. (2009). Typologies of alcohol dependence. From Jellinek to genetics and beyond. *Neuropsychology Review, 19*(1), 115–129. https://doi.org/10.1007/s11065-008-9080-z

Lipscomb, T. R., Carpenter, J. A., & Nathan, P. E. (1979). Static ataxia: A predictor of alcoholism? *British Journal of Addiction, 74,* 289–294.

Luba, R., Earleywine, M., Farmer, S., Slavin, M., Mian, M., & Altman, B. (2018). The role of impulsivity and expectancies in predicting marijuana use: An application of the acquired preparedness model. *Journal of Psychoactive Drugs, 50*(5), 411–419. https://doi.org/10.1080/02791072.2018.1511877

Lundqvist, T. (2005). Cognitive consequences of cannabis use: Comparison with abuse of stimulants and heroin with regard to attention, memory and executive functions. *Pharmacology, Biochemistry and Behavior, 81,* 319–330.

Mann, K., Ackermann, K., Croissant, B., Mundle, G., Nakovics, H., & Diehl, A. (2005). Neuroimaging of gender differences in alcohol dependence: Are women more vulnerable? *Alcoholism: Clinical and Experimental Research, 29,* 896–901.

María-Ríos, C. E., & Morrow, J. D. (2020). Mechanisms of shared vulnerability to post-traumatic stress disorder and substance use disorders. *Frontiers in Behavioral Neuroscience, 14*(6). doi:10.3389/fnbeh.2020.00006

Martz, M. E., Zucker, R. A., Schulenberg, J. E., & Heitzeg, M. M. (2018). Psychosocial and neural indicators of resilience among youth with a family history of substance use disorder. *Drug and Alcohol Dependence, 185,* 198–206. https://doi.org/https://doi.org/10.1016/j.drugalcdep.2017.12.015

Mason, M. J., Mennis, J., Linker, J., Bares, C., & Zaharakis, N. (2014). Peer attitudes effects on adolescent substance use:

The moderating role of race and gender. *Prevention Science, 15*(1), 56-64. https://doi.org/10.1007/s11121-012-0353-7

McHugh, R. K., Votaw, V. R., Sugarman, D. E., & Greenfield, S. F. (2018). Sex and gender differences in substance use disorders. *Clinical Psychology Review, 66*, 12–23. doi:10.1016/j.cpr.2017.10.012

McHugh, R. K., & Weiss, R. D. (2019). Alcohol use disorder and depressive disorders. *Alcohol Research: Current Reviews, 40*(1), arcr.v40.1.01.

Merikangas, K. R. (1990). The genetic epidemiology of alcoholism. *Psychological Medicine, 20*, 11–22.

Merikangas, K. R., Mehta, R. L., Molnar, B. E., Walters, E. E., Swendsen, J. D., Auilar-Gaziola, S., . . . Kessler, R. C. (1998). Comorbidity of substance use disorders with mood and anxiety disorders: Results of the international consortium in psychiatric epidemiology. *Addictive Behaviors, 23*, 893–908.

Milne, B. J., Caspi, A., Harrington, H., Poulton, R., Rutter, M., & Moffitt, T. E. (2009). Predictive value of family history on severity of illness: The case for depression, anxiety, alcohol dependence, and drug dependence. *Archives of General Psychiatry, 66*, 738–747.

Moeller, F. G., Barratt, E. S., Fischer, C. J., Dougherty, D. M., Reilly, E. L., Mathias, C. W., & Swann, A. C. (2004). P300 event-related potential amplitude and impulsivity in cocaine-dependent subjects. *Neuropsychobiology, 50*, 167–173.

Montes, K. S., Olin, C. C., Teachman, B. A., Baldwin, S. A., & Lindgren, K. P. (2018). Hazardous drinking has unique relationships with implicit and explicit drinking identity. *Addictive Behaviors, 87*, 155–161. https://doi.org/10.1016/j.addbeh.2018.07.011

Moselhy, H. F., Georgiou, G., & Kahn, A. (2001). Frontal lobe changes in alcoholism: A review of the literature. *Alcohol and Alcoholism, 36*, 357–368.

Moss, H. B., Chen, C. M., & Yi, H. (2007). Subtypes of alcohol dependence in a nationally representative sample. *Drug and Alcohol Dependence, 91*, 149–158.

Müller, M., Ajdacic-Gross, V., Vetrella, A. B., Preisig, M., Castelao, E., Lasserre, A., Rodgers, S., Rössler, W., Vetter, S., Seifritz, E., & Vandeleur, C. (2020). Subtypes of alcohol use disorder in the general population: A latent class analysis. *Psychiatry Research, 285*, 112712. https://doi.org/10.1016/j.psychres.2019.112712

Murray, H. W., Patkar, A. A., Mannelli, P., DeMaria, P., Desai, A. M., & Vergare, M. J. (2003). Relationship of aggression, sensation seeking, and impulsivity, with severity of cocaine use. *Addictive Disorders & Their Treatment, 2*, 113–121.

Nathan, P. E., & Lipscomb, T. R. (1979). Studies in blood alcohol level discrimination: Etiologic cues to alcoholism. In N. A. Krasnegor (Ed.), *Behavioral analysis and treatment of substance abuse* (pp. 178–190). NIDA.

National Institute on Alcohol Abuse and Alcoholism (NIAAA). (2005). *Harmful interactions: Mixing alcohol with medicines* (NIH Publication No. 03-5329). National Institute of Health.

Negrete, J. C. (1989). Cannabis and schizophrenia. *British Journal of Addiction, 84*, 349–351.

Nelson, C. B., Heath, A. C., & Kessler, R. C. (1998). Temporal progression of alcohol dependence symptoms in the U. S. household population: Results from the National Comorbidity Survey. *Journal of Consulting and Clinical Psychology, 66*, 474–483.

Newcomb, M. D., & Bentler, P. M. (1986). Substance use and ethnicity: Differential impact of peer and adult models. *Journal of Psychology: Interdisciplinary and Applied, 120*, 83–95.

O'Connor, S., Morzorati, S., Christian, J. C., & Li, T. K. (1994). Heritable features of the auditory oddball event-related potential: Peaks, latencies, morphology and topography. *Electroencephalography & Clinical Neurophysiology: Evoked Potentials, 92*, 115–125.

O'Farrell, T. J., Choquette, K. A., Cutter, H. S. G., & Birchler, G. R. (1997). Sexual satisfaction and dysfunction in marriages of male alcoholics: Comparison with nonalcoholic maritally conflicted and nonconflicted couples. *Journal of Studies on Alcohol, 58*, 91–99.

O'Farrell, T. J., Murphy, C. M., Neavins, T. M., & Van Hutton, V. (2000). Verbal aggression among male alcoholic patients and their wives in the year before and two years after alcoholism treatment. *Journal of Family Violence, 15*, 295–310.

Ohlmeier, M. D., Peters, K., Kordon, A., Seifert, J., Te Wildt, B., Wiese, B., . . . Schneider, U. (2007). Nicotine and alcohol dependence in patients with comorbid attention-deficit/hyperactivity disorder (ADHD). *Alcohol and Alcoholism, 42*, 539–543.

O'Malley, S., Adamse, M., Heaton, R. K., & Gawin, F. H. (1992). Neuropsychological impairment in chronic cocaine abusers. *American Journal of Drug and Alcohol Abuse, 18*, 131–144.

Pardini, D., White, H. R., & Stouthamer-Loeber, M. (2007). Early adolescent psychopathology as a predictor of alcohol use disorders by young adulthood. *Drug and Alcohol Dependence, 88*, S38–S49.

Patrick, C. J., Bernat, E. M., Malone, S. M., Iacono, W. G., Krueger, R. F., & McGue, M. (2006). P300 amplitude as an indicator of externalizing in adolescent males. *Psychophysiology, 43*(1), 84–92. doi:10.1111/j.1469-8986.2006.00376.x

Pettinati, H. M., Volpicelli, J. R., Kranzler, H. R., Luck, G., Rukstalis, M. R., & Cnaan, A. (2000). Sertraline treatment for alcohol dependence: Interactive effects of medication and alcoholic subtype. *Alcoholism: Clinical and Experimental Research, 24*, 1041–1049.

Polich, J., Pollock, V. E., & Bloom, F. E. (1994). Meta-analysis of P300 amplitude from males at risk for alcoholism. *Psychological Bulletin, 115*(1), 55–73.

Prescott, C. A., Aggen, S. H., & Kendler, K. S. (2000). Sex-specific genetic influences on the comorbidity of alcoholism and major depression in a population-based sample of US twins. *Archives of General Psychiatry, 57*, 803–811.

Prescott, C. A., & Kendler, K. S. (1999). Genetic and environmental contributions to alcohol abuse and dependence in a population-based sample of male twins. *American Journal of Psychiatry, 156*(1), 34–40.

Quintana, D. S., Guastella, A. J., McGregor, I. S., Hickie, I. B., & Kemp, A. H. (2013). Heart rate variability predicts alcohol craving in alcohol dependent outpatients: Further evidence for HRV as a psychophysiological marker of self-regulation. *Drug and Alcohol Dependence, 132*(1–2), 395–398. https://doi.org/10.1016/j.drugalcdep.2013.02.025

Ralevski, E., Petrakis, I., & Altemus, M. (2019). Heart rate variability in alcohol use: A review. *Pharmacology Biochemistry and Behavior, 176*, 83–92. https://doi.org/https://doi.org/10.1016/j.pbb.2018.12.003

Ramisetty-Mikler, S., Caetano, R., & McGrath, C. (2007). Sexual aggression among white, black, and Hispanic couples in the U. S.: Alcohol use, physical assault and psychological aggression as its correlates. *American Journal of Drug and Alcohol Abuse, 33*, 31–43.

Randall, C. L., Roberts, J. S., Del Boca, F. K., Carroll, K. M., Connors, G. J., & Mattson, M. E. (1999). Telescoping of landmark events associated with drinking: A gender comparison. *Journal of Studies on Alcohol, 60*, 252–260.

Regier, D. A., Farmer, M. E., Rae, D. S., Locke, B. Z., Keither, S. J., Judd, L. L., & Goodwin, F. K. (1990). Comorbidity of mental disorders with alcohol and other drug abuse: Results from the Epidemiologic Catchment Area (ECA) Study. *Journal of the American Medical Association, 264*, 2511–2518.

Roberts, N. P., Roberts, P. A., Jones, N., & Bisson, J. I. (2016). Psychological therapies for post-traumatic stress disorder and comorbid substance use disorder. *Cochrane Database of Systematic Reviews, 4*. doi:10.1002/14651858.CD010204.pub2

Roberts, R. E., Roberts, C. R., & Xing, Y. (2007). Comorbidity of substance use disorders and other psychiatric disorders among adolescents: Evidence from an epidemiologic survey. *Drug and Alcohol Dependence, 88*, S4–S13.

Roizen, J. (1993). *Issues in the epidemiology of alcohol and violence* (NIH research Monograph No. 24, No. 93-3496). US Department of Health and Human Services.

Rourke, S. B., & Løberg, T. (1996). Neurobehavioral correlates of alcoholism. In I. Grant & K. A. Adams (Eds.), *Neuropsychological assessment of neuropsychiatric disorders*, 2nd ed. (pp. 423–485). Oxford University Press.

Saha, T. D., Compton, W. M., Chou, S. P., Smith, S., Ruan, W. J., Huang, B., . . . Grant, B. F. (2012). Analyses related to the development of DSM-5 criteria for substance use related disorders: 1. Toward amphetamine, cocaine and prescription drug use disorder continua using item response theory. *Drug and Alcohol Dependence, 122*, 38–46.

Sartor, C. E., Lynskey, M. T., Heath, A. C., Jacob, T., & True, W. (2007). The role of childhood risk factors in initiation of alcohol use and progression to alcohol dependence. *Addiction, 102*, 216–225.

Sato, M. (1992). A lasting vulnerability to psychosis in patients with previous methamphetamine psychosis In P. W. Kalivas & H. H. Samson (Eds.), *The neurobiology of drug and alcohol addiction* (160–170). New York Academy of Sciences.

Schafer, J., & Brown, S. A. (1991). Marijuana and cocaine effect expectancies and drug use patterns. *Journal of Consulting and Clinical Psychology, 59*, 558–565.

Schiavi, R. C., Stimmel, B. B., Mandeli, J., & White, D. (1995). Chronic alcoholism and male sexual function. *American Journal of Psychiatry, 152*, 1045–1051.

Schuckit, M. A. (1985). Ethanol-induced changes in body sway in men at high alcoholism risk. *Archives of General Psychiatry, 42*, 375–379.

Schuckit, M. A. (1994a). Low level of response to alcohol as a predictor of future alcoholism. *American Journal Of Psychiatry, 151*, 184–189.

Schuckit, M. A. (1994b). The relationship between alcohol problems, substance abuse, and psychiatric syndromes. In T. A. Widiger, A. J. Frances, H. A. Pincus, M. B. First, R. Ross, & W. Davis (Eds.), *DSM-IV sources book* (vol. 1, pp. 45–66). American Psychiatric Association.

Schuckit, M. A., Anthenelli, R. M., Bucholz, K. K., Hesselbrock, V. M., & Tipp, J. (1995). The time course of development of alcohol-related problems in men and women. *Journal of Studies on Alcohol, 56*, 218–225.

Schuckit, M. A., & Gold, E. O. (1988). A simultaneous evaluation of multiple markers of ethanol/placebo challenges in sons of alcoholics and controls. *Archives of General Psychiatry, 45*, 211–216.

Schuckit, M. A., & Hesselbrock, V. (1994). Alcohol dependence and anxiety disorders: What is the relationship? *American Journal of Psychiatry, 151*, 1723–1734.

Schuckit, M. A., Smith, T. L., Anderson, K. G., & Brown, S. A. (2004). Testing the level of response to alcohol: Social information processing model of alcoholism risk: A 20-year prospective study. *Alcoholism: Clinical and Experimental Research, 28*, 1881–1889.

Schuckit, M. A., Smith, T. L., Danko, G. P., Bucholz, K. K., & Reich, T. (2001). Five-year clinical course associated with DSM-IV alcohol abuse or dependence in a large group of men and women. *American Journal of Psychiatry, 158*, 1084–1090.

Schuckit, M. A., Smith, T. L., Danko, G. P., Kramer, J., Godinez, J., Bucholz, K. K., . . . Hesselbrock, V. (2005). Prospective evaluation of the four DSM-IV criteria for alcohol abuse in a large population. *American Journal of Psychiatry, 162*, 350–360.

Schuckit, M. A., Smith, T. L., Kalmijn, J., Trim, R. S., Cesario, E., Saunders, G., . . . Campbell, N. (2012). Comparison across two generations of prospective models of how the low level of responses to alcohol affects alcohol outcomes. *Journal of Studies on Alcohol and Drugs, 73*, 195–204.

Schuckit, M. A., Tipp, J. E., Bucholz, K. K., Nurnberger, J. I., Hesselbrock, V. M., Crowe, R. R., & Kramer, J. (1997). The life-time rates of three major mood disorders and four major anxiety disorders in alcoholics and controls. *Addiction, 92*, 1289–1304.

Schuler, M. S., Rice, C. E., Evans-Polce, R. J., & Collins, R. L. (2018). Disparities in substance use behaviors and disorders among adult sexual minorities by age, gender, and sexual identity. *Drug and Alcohol Dependence, 189*, 139–146. doi:10.1016/j.drugalcdep.2018.05.008

Shen, X., Hackworth, J., McCabe, H., Lovett, L., Aumage, J., O'Neil, J., & Bull, M. (2006). Characteristics of suicide from 1998-2001 in a metropolitan area. *Death Studies, 30*, 859–871.

Sher, K. J., Grekin, E. R., & Williams, N. A. (2005). The development of alcohol use disorders. *Annual Review of Clinical Psychology, 1*(1), 493–523. https://doi.org/10.1146/annurev.clinpsy.1.102803.144107

Shiffman, S., Kassel, J. D., Paty, J. A., & Gnys, M. (1994). Smoking typology profiles of chippers and regular smokers. *Journal of Substance Abuse, 6*, 21–35.

Shoal, G. D., Gudonis, L. C., Giancola, P. R., & Tarter, R. E. (2007). Delinquency as a mediator of the relation between negative affectivity and adolescent alcohol use disorder. *Addictive Behaviors, 32*, 2747–2765.

Simons, J. S., & Carey, M. P. (2001). Prevalence of sexual dysfunction: Results from a decade of research. *Archives of Sexual Behavior, 30*, 177–219.

Singh, S. M., Basu, D., Kohli, A., & Prabhakar, S. (2009). Auditory P300 event-related potentials and neurocognitive functions in opioid dependent men and their brothers. *American Journal on Addictions, 18*, 198–205.

Singletary, K. W., & Gapstur, S. M. (2001). Alcohol and breast cancer: Review of epidemiologic and experimental evidence and potential mechanisms. *Journal of the American Medical Association, 286*, 2143–2151.

Smith, G. T., Goldman, M. S., Greenbaum, P. E., & Christiansen, B. A. (1995). Expectancy for social facilitation from drinking: The divergent paths of high-expectancy and low-expectancy adolescents. *Journal of Abnormal Psychology, 104*, 32–40.

Smith, G. W., Farrell, M., Bunting, B. P., Houston, J. E., & Shevlin, M. (2011). Patterns of polydrug use in Great Britain: Findings from a national household population survey. *Drug and Alcohol Dependence, 113*(2), 222–228. https://doi.org/https://doi.org/10.1016/j.drugalcdep.2010.08.010

Smith, P. H., Homish, G. G., Leonard, K. E., & Cornelius, J. R. (2012). Intimate partner violence and specific substance use disorders: Findings from the National Epidemiologic Survey on Alcohol and Related Conditions. *Psychology of Addictive Behaviors, 26*(2), 236.

Stappenbeck, C. A., & Fromme, K. (2010). A longitudinal investigation of heavy drinking and physical dating violence in men and women. *Addictive Behaviors, 35*(5), 479-485. doi:10.1016/j.addbeh.2009.12.027

Stewart, S. H., Conrod, P. J., Samoluk, S. B., Pihl, R. O., & Dongier, M. (2000). Posttraumatic stress disorder symptoms and situation-specific drinking in women substance abusers. *Alcoholism Treatment Quarterly, 18*, 31–47.

Substance Abuse and Mental Health Services Administration (SAMHSA). (2021). *Key substance use and mental health indicators in the United States: Results from the 2020 National Survey on Drug Use and Health* (HHS Publication No. PEP21-07-01-003, NSDUH Series H-56). Center for Behavioral Health Statistics and Quality, Substance Abuse and Mental Health Services Administration. https://www.samhsa.gov/data/

Tapert, S. F., & Brown, S. A. (1999). Neuropsychological correlates of adolescent substance abuse: Four-year outcomes. *Journal of the International Neuropsychological Society, 5*, 481–493.

Tapert, S. F., Stewart, D. G., & Brown, S. A. (1999). Drug abuse in adolescence. In A. J. Goreczny & M. Hersen (Eds.), *Handbook of pediatric and adolescent health psychology* (pp. 161–178). Allyn & Bacon.

Tate, S. R., Patterson, K. A., Nagel, B. J., Anderson, K. G., & Brown, S. A. (2007). Addiction and stress in adolescents. In M. Al'Absi (Ed.), *Stress and addiction: Biological and psychological mechanisms* (pp. 249–262). Academic Press.

Trim, R. S., Schuckit, M. A., & Smith, T. L. (2009). The relationships of the level of response to alcohol and additional characteristics to alcohol use disorders across adulthood: A discrete-time survival analysis. *Alcoholism: Clinical and Experimental Research, 33*, 1562–1570.

van der Stelt, O., Gunning, W. B., Snel, J., & Kok, A. (1998). Event-related potentials during visual selective attention in children of alcoholics. *Alcoholism: Clinical and Experimental Research, 22*, 1877–1889.

Van Thiel, D. H., Gavaler, J. S., Eagan, P. K., Chiao, Y. B., Cobb, C. F., & Lester, R. (1980). Alcohol and sexual function. *Pharmacology and Biochemistry of Behavior, 13*, 125–129.

Vik, P. W., Grizzle, K. L., & Brown, S. A. (1992). Social resource characteristics and adolescent substance abuse relapse. *Journal Of Adolescent Chemical Dependency, 2*, 59–74.

Waddell, J. T., Corbin, W. R., Meier, M. H., Morean, M. E., & Metrik, J. (2021). The Anticipated Effects of Cannabis Scale (AECS), Initial development and validation of an affect-and valence-based expectancy measure. *Psychological Assessment, 33*(2), 180.

Widom, C. S., Ireland, T., & Glynn, P. J. (1995). Alcohol abuse in abused and neglected children followed up: Are they at increased risk? *Journal of Studies on Alcohol, 56*, 207–217.

Wilens, T. E. (2004). Impact of ADHD and its treatment on substance abuse in adults. *Journal of Clinical Psychiatry, 65*, 38–45.

Wilens, T. E., Biederman, J., Mick, E., Faraone, S. V., & Spencer, T. (1997). Attention deficit hyperactivity disorder (ADHD) is associated with early onset substance abuse. *Journal of Nervous and Mental Disease, 185*, 475–482.

Wills, T. A., Resko, J. A., Ainette, M. G., & Mendoza, D. (2004). Role of parent support and peer support in adolescent substance use: A test of mediated effects. *Psychology of Addictive Behaviors, 18*, 122–134.

Wilsnack, S. C., Vogeltanz, N. D., Klassen, A. D., & Harris, T. R. (1997). Childhood sexual abuse and women's substance abuse: National survey findings. *Journal of Studies on Alcohol, 58*, 264–271.

Witkiewitz, K., Wilson, A. D., Pearson, M. R., Montes, K. S., Kirouac, M., Roos, C. R., Hallgren, K. A., & Maisto, S. A. (2019). Profiles of recovery from alcohol use disorder at three years following treatment: Can the definition of recovery be extended to include high functioning heavy drinkers? *Addiction, 114*(1), 69–80. https://doi.org/10.1111/add.14403

Wojnar, M., Wasilewski, D., Matsumoto, H., & Cedro, A. (1997). Differences in the course of alcohol withdrawal in women and men: A Polish sample. *Alcoholism: Clinical and Experimental Research, 21*, 1351–1355.

Wolfe, W. L., & Maisto, S. A. (2000). The relationship between eating disorders and substance use: Moving beyond co-prevalence research. *Clinical Psychology Review, 20*, 617–631.

Zilberman, M. L., Tavares, H., Blume, S. B., & el-Guebaly, N. (2003). Substance use disorders: Sex differences and psychiatric comorbidities. *Canadian Journal of Psychiatry, 48*(1), 5–13. doi:10.1177/070674370304800103

Zinn, S., Stein, R., & Swartzwelder, H. S. (2004). Executive functioning early in abstinence from alcohol. *Alcoholism: Clinical and Experimental Research, 28*, 1338–1346.

# CHAPTER 13

# Substance Use and Substance Use Disorders

Kenneth J. Sher, W. E. Conlin, *and* R. O. Pihl

Substance use (SU) and various problems arising from it represent major public health and clinical problems and touch virtually every aspect of society. Recent estimates of the total costs (taking into account costs associated with healthcare, crime, and public safety) of SU including tobacco, alcohol, illicit drugs, and prescription opioids exceed $740 billion a year, and this is likely an underestimate (National Institute on Drug Abuse, April 6, 2020; https://www.drugabuse.gov/drug-topics/trends-statistics/costs-substance-abuse).

The noted so-called Father of Modern Medicine, and one of the founding physicians at Johns Hopkins Medical School, Sir William Osler, wrote that "the only characteristic that distinguishes man from other animals is his propensity to take drugs" (in Bean, 1951). It is not without irony that one of the other famed founding physicians at Hopkins, William Halsted, "considered one of the greatest and most influential surgeons of all time" (Lathan, 2010, p. 31) fought cocaine and morphine addiction for most of his professional life.

Osler might well have added that there are exceptions to his statement and that the propensity to "do drugs" is as old as human behavior; its evolutionary roots date back to prehistory. Consider the fact that humans and many nonhuman animals, including invertebrates, curiously have enzymes for metabolizing alcohol. Why should this be? These enzymes are quite specific to alcohol. While evolutionary explanations are difficult to prove or disprove, it seems likely that the ability to digest ripening fruits that have started to "go bad" (i.e., ferment) extends the range of edible foods that may be necessary for survival. Moreover, detecting the scent of ethanol emanating from overripe fruit is an efficient strategy for food localization (Dudley, 2000, 2004).

In addition to localizing and extending food sources essential for survival, animal behaviorists have commonly observed various species ingesting substances for both medicinal and seemingly recreational purposes. The propensity to take drugs may not be as uniquely human as Osler believed, as intoxicated behavior is seen in nonhuman animals, from elephants to the catnip-consuming pet. Some consume hallucinogenic mushrooms—for example, Siberian deer—and then show incoordination and general intoxicated behavior (Cohen & Saavedra-Delgado, 1989).

Psychoactive substances have been part of human societies for at least several thousand years. References to poppy plants appear in Sumerian tablets dating back more than 4,000 years, and the word referring to them was synonymous with "to enjoy." Remnants of hemp plants dating back 6,000 years have been found in China (Escohotado, 1999). Archeological evidence suggests that alcoholic beverages were first produced 5,000–7,000 years ago (Crocq, 2007). While it appears that religious and medical use of most psychoactive substances were generally controlled and not associated with various harms, scholars have suggested that recreational use has often led to

---

**Abbreviations**
AUD   Alcohol use disorder
CD    Conduct disorder
DA    Dopamine
DUD   Drug use disorder
FASD(s) Fetal alcohol spectrum disorder(s)
NAc   Nucleus accumbens
NMDA  N-methyl-D-aspartate
OUD   Opioid use disorder
VTA   Ventral tegmental area

significant health and social problems, such as epidemics of alcohol use in England in the 1700s and opium use in eighteenth-century China (Heyman, 2009; Westermeyer, 2016). In modern times, psychoactive substances are likely to pose greater risks than they have historically owing to innovations in the manufacturing of drugs leading to increased potency, employment of efficient routes of administration, and geopolitical and social factors that facilitate the spread of substances (Vetulani, 2001; Westermeyer, 1988).

## Substance-Related Phenotypes

Attitudes toward the use of psychoactive substances vary across cultures and religions, such that a given substance may be taboo in one culture, tolerated in another, and viewed as beneficial and as a valued source of pleasure in yet another (Hart, 2021). While some substances are associated with greater harm than others, psychopathologists distinguish between SU, per se, and substance use disorders (SUDs) including alcohol use disorders (AUDs), drug use disorders (DUDs), and tobacco use disorders.

Note that in contrast to most other forms of psychopathology, with the notable exception of posttraumatic stress disorder (PTSD), SUDs presume a necessary precondition: SU. In the case of PTSD, the precondition is presumed to be largely outside of the voluntary control of the individual. In contrast, SU initiation, regular use, and heavy use are, to varying degrees, operants in the service of some outcome, and SUDs are conceptualized to be consequences of SU. We can conceptualize etiology as a two-step process: (1) etiological factors related to SU and (2) etiological factors in SUDs, *conditional upon SU*. The two different "stages" can have both distinct and overlapping risk factors (e.g., Sartor et al., 2007), and, consequently, we should ensure the stages are viewed as distinct even if intimately intertwined. As noted by Saunders et al. (2019, p. 1624) in describing alcohol dependence in the *ICD-11*, "alcohol dependence is . . . understood as an adaptive response [i.e., a neurobiological adaptation or compensatory changes] following repeated use of alcohol, not as a primary biological disorder but an acquired one." Thus, in thinking about etiology we want to distinguish factors that lead to repeated use of the drug (and related, acute consequences) and those that relate to the development of the consequent adaptation/compensatory changes. This is a key distinction that is, unfortunately, often insufficiently resolved in much of the research on SUDs.

## Substance Use

The use of a given substance can be described in a number of ways: whether the person has ever partaken (lifetime use), use in a given period of time (e.g., past 12 months), frequency of use (e.g., number of use occasions in the past month), routes of administration (e.g., oral, via injection), typical quantity of use on a given occasion (e.g., number of cigarettes in a day when one smokes), frequency of heavy use occasions (e.g., number of days marked by consumption of five or more drinks), maximum dose on a given occasion, or cumulative lifetime exposure to a substance. Assessment is rendered even more complex by (a) the fact that individuals may use more than one substance (simultaneously or not) and (b) the possibility of synergistic effects among substances. For example, the co-ingestion of cocaine and alcohol results in a unique, pharmacologically active metabolite (cocaethylene) with its own psychoactive effects that enhance the euphoric effect associated with cocaine (Jones, 2019). Interactions between alcohol and certain benzodiazepines pose a significant risk for fatal overdose, well above that associated with alcohol alone (the risk for fatal overdose with benzodiazepines alone is low; Koski et al., 2002). Additionally, both alcohol and benzodiazepine use are associated with fatal opiate overdoses (Tori et al., 2020).

Not all researchers view the use versus use disorder distinction as valuable. For example, Rehm et al. (2013) argue that virtually all social and medical problems associated with the use of that drug can be most parsimoniously explained by the simple concept of heavy use over time. They argue that other terms such as "addiction" or "substance dependence" are unnecessary and likely stigmatizing and could represent a barrier to treatment.

## Substance Use Disorders

The cardinal diagnoses for SUDs in *DSM-III*, *III-R*, *IV*, and *IV-TR* were substance abuse and substance dependence, with abuse being diagnosed on the basis of hazardous behavior (e.g., driving while intoxicated) or social/interpersonal problems arising from SU, and dependence diagnosed on the basis of neuroadaptation to the substance (e.g., tolerance or withdrawal), preoccupation with the substance, and compulsion. In the latest revision of the *DSM*, *DSM-5*, the specific diagnoses of substance abuse and substance dependence were jettisoned in lieu of the single, superordinate category of SUD with 11 criteria and a gradient based on the number of criteria endorsed: mild (2–3), moderate (4–5), and severe (6–11). The working group that developed the *DSM-5* SUD criteria set and diagnostic rules touted the changes as significant improvements over *DSM-IV* in several ways (Hasin et al., 2013). For example, the legal problems criterion was dropped due to lack of theoretical integration, poor diagnostic validity, and bias (i.e., differential item functioning) as a function of race/ethnicity. Furthermore, the addition of craving brought the *DSM* more into alignment with the *ICD*, which had included craving as part of its criteria set. Perhaps more importantly, craving is viewed as central to multiple theories of addiction and is the target of specific pharmacological interventions (Tiffany & Wray, 2012).

However, some of the ostensible improvements were more questionable. While the decision to abolish the abuse–dependence distinction was based on the failure of most factor analyses to identify more than a single dimension in SUD criteria sets, genetically informed factor analyses provide evidence for multiple factors (Kendler, Aggen et al., 2012) and most of the published work showing a unidimensional structure were based on limited numbers of indicators, likely precluding the ability to identify multiple, meaningful factors (Watts et al., 2021). Perhaps most critical for the purpose of this chapter, the genetically differentiable factors identified by Kendler, Aggen, and colleagues had different correlates, consistent with the idea of at least partially different etiologies for different phenotypic aspects of SUDs.

It is widely agreed that *DSM-IV*'s approach to criterion counts resulted in too many false-positive diagnoses, with only a single symptom required for an abuse diagnosis. However, the *DSM-5*'s requirement of *only* 2 criteria for diagnosis failed to address ongoing concerns about false positives and overdiagnosis (Martin et al., 2011). The very high rate of *DSM* diagnoses of AUDs in epidemiological surveys have led some to propose much stricter diagnostic criteria (Wakefield & Schmitz, 2014) which would produce dramatically lower prevalence rates from those based on current and past versions of the *DSM*.

In contrast to *DSM* versions *III*, *III-R*, *IV*, and *IV-TR*, the World Health Organization's *ICD-10* never made the distinction between dependence and abuse, focusing primarily on the concept of dependence. (The *ICD* does have a separate category for "harmful use," but that is conceptually distinct from abuse and not considered further here.) While there are differences between *ICD-11* and *ICD-10* dependence as to how the diagnostic features are combined into criteria, the essential character of the diagnosis is similar. In *ICD-11*, one must meet criteria in two of the following three areas: (1) impaired control over use, (2) the substance playing an increasingly important role in one's life, and (3) physiological features (e.g., tolerance or withdrawal). While the 11 SUD criteria in *DSM-5* (p. 483) can be summarized as covering the domains of impaired control, social impairment, hazardous use, and pharmacological criteria, a person can receive the diagnosis even if symptoms lie entirely in just one domain. Consequently, unlike *ICD-11*, *DSM-5* lacks the conceptual core of physiological dependence.

It is hard to pinpoint the exact phenotype being considered under *DSM-5* as there are more than 2,000 ways to meet diagnostic criteria and 55 ways to meet the lowest threshold of only two symptoms (Lane & Sher, 2015). It seems likely that the clinical heterogeneity of *DSM* reflects considerable etiological heterogeneity, and there could be considerable value in viewing SUDs as reflecting multiple constructs, each with somewhat distinct etiological features.

### The Concept of "Addiction"

"Addiction" is not an official diagnostic term. Still, researchers and clinicians do use the term, increasingly so in recent years. Indeed, in the *DSM-5*, SUDs are described in the section entitled "Substance-Related and Addictive Disorders" and the home page of the National Institute of Drug Abuse's (NIDA) website (http:// https://www.drugabuse.gov/about-nida) states that NIDA's mission is "to advance science on the causes and consequences of drug use and *addiction* [emphasis added]." Although there is no official definition, the constructs that researchers discuss when studying "addiction" overlap the diagnostic criteria found in the *DSM* and *ICD* and include concepts such as compulsive use, neuroadaptation, craving, and a preference for the addictive substance over other reinforcers.

Table 13.1 outlines and tries to establish relations among *DSM-5* SUD criteria and the clinical constructs that are commonly equated with addiction, plus a few, selected addiction constructs that have been proposed by leading theorists. This latter group of constructs includes incentive sensitization (e.g., increased wanting and cue-elicited craving; Robinson et al., 2018), habit (use becomes automatized and difficult to unlearn and ultimately compulsive; Everitt & Robbins, 2016), allostasis

**Table 13.1** Distinctions among DSM-5 substance use disorder diagnostic criteria, clinical addiction concepts, and major theoretical concepts

| Formal DSM-5 Criteria | Clinical Addiction Concepts ||| | Selected Major Theoretical Concepts ||||
|---|---|---|---|---|---|---|---|---|
| | Compulsive use | Neuroadaptation | Craving | Addictive Substance Preferred to other reinforcers | Incentive Sensitization | Habit | Allostasis | Reinforcer pathology |
| Use in hazardous situations | X??? | | | | | | | X |
| Failure to fulfill major role responsibilities | X | | | X | | | | X |
| Use despite social or interpersonal problems | X | | | | X | X | | X |
| Use despite physical or psychological problems | X | | | | X | X | | X |
| Tolerance | | X | | | | | X | |
| Withdrawal | | X | | | | | X | |
| Impaired Control (larger/longer) | X | X??? | | X | X | X | | X |
| Attempts or desire to "cut down" | X | | | | X | X | | X |
| Time spent (obtaining, using, recovering) | X | | | X | X | X | | X |
| Important activities given up | X | | | X | | | | X |
| Craving | | | X | | X | | ? | |
| *Noncriterial Sx's Implied by Theory* | | | | | | | | |
| Negative affectivity | | | | | | | X | |
| Relapse Vulnerability | | | X | | X | | X | |

*Note:* DSM-5, Diagnostic and Statistical Manual, Version 5. Noncriterial Sx's represent symptoms that are clinically relevant to addiction but not part of the formal diagnostic criteria.

(change in the hedonic set point associated with adaptation to chronic drug use; Koob & Shulkin, 2019), reinforcer pathology ("the persistently high valuation of a reinforcer, broadly defined to include tangible commodities and experiences, and/or . . . the excessive preference for the immediate acquisition or consumption of a commodity despite long-term negative outcomes"; Bickel, Korrarnus et al., 2014). Note that this list is not exhaustive and there are other influential models that exist that overlap with these (e.g., multistep models that focus on how continued heavy use in concert with a vulnerable endophenotype conspire to bring about addictive behaviors; Piazza & Deroche-Gamonet, 2013).

However, as noted by Bickel et al. (2019, p. 8) and as illustrated in Table 13.1,

1. Theories of addiction vary with respect to the addiction constructs with which they are associated and the specific diagnostic criteria to which they relate.
2. A one-to-one correspondence does not exist between diagnostic criteria of, say, *DSM-5* and specific addiction constructs. For example, multiple criteria (e.g., psychological and health problems, interpersonal and social problems) could index the same addiction construct (e.g., compulsive use).
3. Some theories of addiction highlight features (e.g., negative affectivity) that are not part of our current diagnostic system for SUDs and overlap considerably with general psychopathology (e.g., Caspi et al., 2014).
4. Not all SUD criteria are fully consistent with clinical notions of addiction nor with specific theories of addiction that have been advanced.
5. Related to this last point, two individuals with the same number of SUD criteria may vary greatly in the extent to which they are "addicted" depending on the specific symptoms manifested (Lane & Sher, 2015), further highlighting the conceptual distinction between addiction and SUDs.

### The Importance of Etiology

Understanding the etiology of SUDs is important for developing effective strategies for preventing and treating them. While there are a range of interventions designed to prevent the onset of SUDs (and other harms associated with SU) and to treat manifest disorder, the continuing persistence of both SU and SUDs indicates there is much more that can be done in this area.

Because use is a precondition for SUDs, many prevention approaches are at the policy level. This can involve national or local policies designed to restrict access to substances (e.g., prohibition), limit who can use them (e.g., age-related restrictions), make them difficult to use or obtain (e.g., via excise taxation), or minimize acute harm from use (e.g., impaired driving laws). Such prevention efforts are called "universal" in that they are meant to be applied to the total population. Such policy-driven prevention approaches don't rely on etiological knowledge and can be extremely effective since the entire population is targeted. Dramatic decreases in the incidence of lung cancer over the past 50 years (Meza et al., 2015) can be attributed, to a large degree, to decreases in smoking rates fueled by policy changes (including but not limited to restricted opportunities to smoke in public and workplace settings and taxation). In the United States, even more dramatic decreases in fatal alcohol-related motor vehicle crashes can be attributed to stricter drinking and driving laws initiated in the later part of the twentieth century (Voas et al., 2000). Other types of universal approaches include psychoeducational approaches in the schools (Foxcroft & Tsertsvadze, 2012), advertising bans (e.g., Saffer & Chaloupka, 2000), and public media campaigns (Allara et al., 2015). These public health approaches are obviously critical but, by themselves, don't totally eliminate the problem and, indeed, it's possible that some of these interventions can have adverse effects. As noted by Allara et al. (p. 9) with respect to public media campaigns, "Contrary to common belief, antidrug media campaigns may be damaging and their dissemination is ethically unacceptable without a prior assessment of their effects." Thus, all policies should be rigorously evaluated and not assumed to be useful on the basis of their rationale. This bears special emphasis with respect to alcohol control given alcohol's legal status, its high prevalence, and its extensive comorbidities with other SU.

While some of the heterogeneity among SUDs likely reflects mechanisms specific to SU, a complicating factor is that comorbidity, or the presence of another psychiatric diagnosis, is common (e.g., Bahji et al., 2019; Lai et al., 2015, Morisano et al., 2014). When two or more disorders co-occur, be it concurrently or longitudinally, a distinction is often made between primary and secondary disorders. This distinction reflects the degree to which one disorder is thought to be responsible for the development of the other, primarily based on the order of onset (e.g., Winokur et al., 1995). Although useful in principle, there are two reasons why this approach is more complex than might appear. First, SUDs and potential comorbid disorders have characteristic age-prevalence distributions with the modal age of, say, an SUD being younger than, say, the modal age of a co-occurring condition and so, a priori, SUDs will tend to be deemed primary or secondary based purely on their individual prototypic courses without clear implications for the presumed causal direction of influence from primary → secondary. Much of the variance in the primary–secondary distinction is due to factors related to the normative age-incidence curves of each disorder, although there are individual differences in the relative ages of onset of the comorbid disorder (e.g., Fossey et al., 2006). That is, the degree to which order of onset itself is a meaningful index of presumed causality can always be questioned. Second, determining which disorder came first is always arguable. Should the onset of each disorder be dated to the time the pattern of symptoms reaches the diagnostic threshold, as is the usual practice? However, subthreshold symptomatology (or the processes causing it) in one disorder could conceivably influence subthreshold (or suprathreshold) symptomatology in the other disorder. One could look at the age of "first symptom" of each disorder to establish temporal precedence, but who's to say that that type of threshold captures the essence of the emergence of disorder? Moreover, dating age of onset at either the symptom or syndrome level presupposes that the underlying retrospection employed in most cross-sectional studies is accurate, a supposition not borne out by prospective studies that repeatedly query the age of onset of a particular problematic behavior (Parra et al., 2003). None of this is to say the primary–secondary distinction is not potentially useful, just that it is often hard to operationalize in a way that does justice to the concept and establish whether one disorder is predisposing or consequential.

The primary–secondary distinction should not be confused with a similar-sounding distinction between free-standing comorbid conditions and "substance-induced" mental disorders. The latter is applicable when a mental disorder develops within 1 month of a substance intoxication or withdrawal, and when it is known that the substance is capable of producing that disorder (*DSM-5*, p. 488). In most cases, the substance-induced mental illness should resolve over an extended period of abstinence. In any case, the primary–secondary distinction is deemphasized in the discussion of etiological factors that follows. What follows is a discussion of critical issues to consider when investigating current factors deemed etiologically significant for SUDs at multiple levels of analysis.

For any investigation of etiological underpinnings to prove meaningful, one needs to be mindful of several considerations. First, throughout different stages of substance involvement and psychosocial developmental, there is a dynamic interplay of risk factors over time. As such, the type and magnitude of the risk follows a temporally dynamic gradient. Both normative and deviant substance involvement are often age-graded, but stage of substance involvement must be distinguished from stage of general psychosocial development as the two may have different correlates and meanings (Sher et al., 2004).

Second, ascribing causative status to a risk factor is challenging, and often what one is dealing with is mere correlation rather than causation. Indeed, even assuming that an ostensible outcome is "substance-related" can be difficult since it is often unclear if a seeming substance-related outcome (e.g., driving under the influence) reflects a complication of substance involvement or a generally heedless, risk-taking disposition (Martin et al., 2014).

Third, what we might think of as a genetic risk factor might actually be environmental and vice versa. For example, in choosing one's peers, adolescents who are at-risk to develop conduct disorder (CD) and substance misuse problems are also genetically vulnerable to select/prefer affiliation with delinquent peers (Knafo & Jaffee, 2013). Another issue is assortative mating, where an individual with an SUD is more likely to partner with someone who also has such a disorder (e.g., Grant, Heath et al., 2007). In addition, depressed women, whose offspring are typically at-risk for conduct problems and/or substance misuse, often have a personal history of conduct problems and antisociality, and they also tend to marry and/or cohabitate with antisocial men (Moffitt, 2005).

Fourth, traditional categorical nosology as exemplified in the *DSM* and *ICD* arbitrarily delineates the boundaries of diagnostic categories, thereby implying that they are distinct taxa with distinct etiological mechanisms and obscuring the fact that comorbidity between mental disorders is typically the rule rather than the exception and likely, to varying degrees, reflective of hierarchical, dimensional traits affecting both (e.g., HiTOP; Kotov et al., 2017). A direct, logical implication of such a view is that comorbidity will increase along with the severity of the target diagnosis or comorbid condition, a prediction borne out by epidemiological data. As noted by Helle et al. (2020, p. 632) with respect to AUD, "Greater AUD severity increases the likelihood of other psychopathology and, when present, 'more severe' presentations. That is, on average, a given disorder (e.g., depression) is more severe when co-presenting with an AUD, and increases in severity along with the AUD." While such a perspective is an implied corollary of hierarchical, dimensional models, this phenomenon is probably quite underappreciated.

Typically, the natural history of SUDs begins with experimentation, progresses to regular use, escalates to a pathological pattern of use with respect to the frequency and amount consumed, and may result in neuroadaptations (e.g., withdrawal, alteration of the hedonic set point; Koob & Schulkin, 2019) that motivate compulsive SU (i.e., use that persists in the face of aversive consequences; Lüscher et al., 2020). Along the way, the substance user may experience a range of negative consequences (e.g., social or occupational impairment); however, as noted above, it is often difficult, if not impossible, to ascribe various negative consequences to the substance itself since the users of substances may be prone to engage in a number of activities that have adverse consequences with or without the substance "on board" (for a detailed discussed, see Martin et al., 2014). As cogently observed when describing defining characteristics of psychopaths, Hervey Cleckley (1955) noted that the psychopathic personality is prone to exhibit 'Fantastic and uninviting behavior with drink and *sometimes without* [emphasis added]" (pp. 406–410). That is, one could observe wildly disinhibited behavior under conditions of substance intoxication, but apportioning causality of the behavior to the substance versus the substance user is not straightforward, and ostensible SU consequences might not be consequences in a formal *or meaningful* sense.

In each of the stages of substance involvement, heterogeneous effects and mechanisms are likely. Moreover, the risk factors for one stage (e.g., initial use) aren't necessarily the same for another stage (e.g., SUD conditional upon use). As noted earlier, these different stages can have similar risk factors (e.g., conduct disorders) but risk factors for initiation can be different from risk factors for progression. When considering presumed etiological correlates of SUDs, the exact nature of risk is obscured if progression and stage of pathological substance use are not considered.

Consequently, although many cases of SUDs are superficially similar, there are likely different species of SUDs; that is, much of the similarity is only skin-deep. Stated more formally, the SUD phenotype can often be considered an instance of equifinality (Cicchetti & Rogosch, 1996), where the same end state may be reached "from a variety of different initial conditions and through different processes" (p. 597). Returning to the example of hazardous use, such a criterion could reflect generalized risk-taking or heedlessness (i.e., not specific to the use of the substance), an indication of compulsive use, or both. Merely assessing the criterion without understanding its causes will fail to resolve what might be an important difference with respect to whether the symptom is best viewed as an indicator of an SUD or a noncausal correlate of an SUD.

## At the Level of the Society
### Culture

One's culture substantially contributes to initiating use, sculpting established patterns of drug use and possibly misuse. Which and how much of a substance is used and what the substance does, subjectively and objectively to and for individuals can strikingly be interculturally different (MacAndrew & Edgerton, 1969). This variation can determine how many individuals in each society use and misuse which forms of drugs and at which point of their life. Hence there is great relativity as to what is considered a harmful drug.

The relationships between cross-cultural differences and demographic variations within cultures are sometimes complex. For example, in the GENACIS project, a multinational study of gender-related and cultural influences on alcohol use and associated problems (Wilsnack, 2012) in 38 countries spread across all continents (except Antarctica), men were found to drink more than women. However, women in some cultures drink more than men in other cultures. That is, these demographic differences are conserved within cultures, but there is considerable variation in overall levels across cultures. Similarly, some correlates of alcohol excess (e.g., intimate partner violence) are similar across cultures.

However, some phenomena seen as "typical" in one culture may not appear in other cultures. For example, in North America, there is a strong age gradient in the prevalence of AUD (e.g., Vergés et al., 2012), with peak rates of onset and prevalence in late adolescence and young adulthood. The phenomenon is so strong that it has led to the conclusion that, on a population basis, AUDs can be considered a "developmental disorder of young adulthood" (Sher & Gotham, 1999). However, the notable age gradient, or any other demographic phenomenon observed in one culture, should not be assumed to be independent characteristics of the disorder itself outside of the culture it is observed in.

Moreover, these cross-cultural differences are not static. Distinctions between "wet" (heavy drinking) and "dry" cultures (both within and across nations) appear to be changing in the age of globalization. Historically, the Nordic and Anglo-Saxon cultures were characterized by high levels of what we'd today call binge drinking in contrast to the more moderate, wine-drinking Mediterranean culture. However, youth in the Mediterranean regions are now drinking more like their age peers to the North, such that historical drinking style differences have tended to erode (Room, 2010). In the United States, multiple epidemiological surveys have demonstrated major shifts in the prevalence of alcohol use over the past 20 years although these changes differ as a function of the age groups studied (Grucza et al., 2018).

Concerning alcohol, it has been shown that increases of price and taxes reduced alcohol consumption, morbidity, and mortality rates (Wagenaar et al., 2010). Furthermore, increasing the legal drinking age reduced teen DWIs and traffic deaths. Alcohol prices, nonetheless, remain quite low (Albers et al., 2013), likely reflecting the fact that price increases are typically not indexed to inflation (Jernigan & Trangerstein, 2020). While various alcohol control strategies (e.g., price increases, restrictions in availability with respect to time and place of sales, marketing bans) at the population level can be highly effective (Berdzuli et al., 2020), their effects could vary considerably due to sociodemographic characteristics of jurisdiction (Room et al., 2013). Additionally, as the COVID-19 pandemic has taught us, major restrictions in on-premise alcohol sales have been accompanied by increases in off-premise availability in many countries (Berdzuli et al., 2020) highlighting the complexities of designing alcohol control policies in the face of an ever-changing landscape.

Societal control of drug use is more readily achieved in isolated cultures, where it becomes interwoven into the basic fabric of life. The informational and commercial borderlessness of most Western societies predestines such control efforts to limited success, as witnessed by the failure of Prohibition, the war on drugs, and the fact that cigarettes and alcohol, although legally prohibited from sale to minors, are readily available to them. There are subcultures that promote and others that inhibit drug use and misuse. Drug subcultures emerge from common identities, such as age or perceived and real alienation, which in turn can promote group solidarity or result in group dysfunction. Central to each subculture is the development of a set of shared beliefs and practices. Normative beliefs, which are perceptions of the extent to which significant others approve or disapprove of or engage in a behavior themselves, have been shown to be important predictors of drug use, particularly in adolescents and young adults (Brooks-Russell et al., 2014). Conversely, the degree of spiritual/religious involvement has been shown in many studies to protect one against drug misuse (reviewed in Dick, 2011).

High levels of binge drinking with serious consequences by university students represent an illustrative example of the role of social networks within subcultures. Psychosocial predictors of drinking by undergraduates include overestimates of others' drinking behavior and attitudes (Woodyard et al., 2013), membership in a fraternity or sorority (Wechsler et al., 2009), binge drinking in high school (Wechsler & Nelson, 2008), family history for alcoholism (Dager et al., 2013), and nonreligiosity (Wichers, Gillespie et al., 2013). Despite changes over time, drinking levels and problem drinking by students remain high relative to other groups although these problems don't necessarily continue past college (e.g., Bartholow et al., 2003) and this generalization doesn't extend to other substances such as tobacco (Blanco et al., 2008).

*Poverty and Related Variables*

Although poverty per se is a weak predictor of drug misuse, poverty combined with other deleterious factors associated with impoverished areas (neighborhood deterioration, high crime) substantially increase risk for SU problems. The relationship between poverty, difficult living conditions, and drug misuse appears to be robust across many different cultures. The duration of time spent in poverty and the age of the individual moving into/out of poverty also appear relevant. One Swedish population study found that, while economic instability in early childhood was a significant risk factor, instability during middle childhood or adolescence presented the greatest risk (Manhica et al., 2021). However, this increased risk is not specific to poverty in childhood, as an 18-year prospective study of adults found that living in a disorganized neighborhood was significantly associated with increased symptoms of AUD, with the link being mediated by psychological distress (Cambron et al., 2017).

Culture paints the drug-taking context and expectations of response, which can have significant influences on an individual's response to the drug. The notion that substances, in part, produce culturally prescribed effects has long been suggested by anthropologists who study drug use. There is substantial evidence, in crime and laboratory studies, that the use of alcohol increases the likelihood of aggression. Particular pharmacological effects on brain functioning that affect this behavior have been detailed (Parrot & Eckhardt, 2018). Yet there is considerable cross-cultural variation in the extent to which this effect occurs. MacAndrew and Edgerton (1969) suggested that alcohol-related violence was in part due to cultural norms in certain societies, specifically that cultural views of alcohol provide a "time out" from the normal behavior and an option to disclaim personal responsibility for deviant behavior committed while intoxicated.

Along with differences in individually experienced subjective effects, the cultural significance assigned to a drug has implications for SU. Cultural significance, in this case, refers to the aesthetic, historic, scientific, social, or spiritual emphasis that a given culture places on a particular substance (Durrant & Thakker, 2003). This significance can be broad, such as the significance of cannabis in Jamaican culture (Rubin & Comitas, 2019), or narrow, with specific preparations or methods of ingestion, such as the consumption of hallucinogen N,N-dimethyltryptamine via Ayahuasca in some Peruvian tribes (Labate & Canvar, 2014). Cultural significance can even vary within substances, such as the different cultural significance of consuming champagne versus beer versus liquor. This cultural significance shapes expectancies about the effects produced by the drug, the situations in which the drug is considered acceptable to use, and even the types of positive and negative outcomes predicted by using the substance. Within many cultures, psychotropic drugs are viewed in a spiritual rather than a hedonistic way, thus greatly coloring the response (De Rios & Smith, 1977). One particularly notable example of a culturally significant substance is alcohol. In many countries around the world, imbibing alcohol is a culturally constructed social practice, with alcohol consumption given social and emotional significance for various issues including (but not limited to) celebration, identity, recognition of achievement, hospitality, mourning, entertainment, and social solidarity (Copaceanu & Balaceanu-Stolnici, 2018).

Reflecting shifts in patterns of drug use, prescription drug use has recently surpassed traditional illicit drug misuse (cannabis excepted) by a considerable margin (Substance Abuse and Mental Health Services Administration, 2020). While there are growing concerns of prescription stimulants and benzodiazepine misuse among young adults, the most culturally significant trend of prescription drug misuse in the United States concerns opioid analgesics.

While opioids have a long and sordid history, the current "opioid epidemic" in the United States can be traced back to the mid-1990s, when attitudes in the medical field began to shift regarding the management and treatment of pain (e.g., "pain as the fifth vital sign"; American Pain Society, 1999). As pain management became a priority for medical providers, opioid prescriptions in the United States skyrocketed, with opioid consumption rising from 49,946 kg in 2000 to 165,525 kg in 2012. Although the initial response was positive, the cultural change had significant downstream consequences resulting in increased opioid misuse, addiction, and mortality. This sharp increase in prescription opioid use and misuse is also believed to be related to the recent increase in illicit opioid (e.g., heroin, fentanyl) use in the United States. While opioid use has risen worldwide, this "crisis" is uniquely American, with recent figures estimating that the United States consumes 80% of the opioids manufactured in the world each year (Shipton, 2018), and drug overdose is the leading cause of accidental death (Schiller et al., 2021).

Cultural examples adroitly illustrate that definitions of problems with drugs often depend on where one resides and who the user is: consequently, comprehensive models of causation must be multidimensional. Explanations that reside purely within the individual, either physiological or psychological, provide only a limited perspective, and models of etiology are, by necessity, contextually dependent on the environment and the inherent philosophies.

*The Peer Group*

If one's friends use and misuse drugs, the odds are much higher for oneself. Time spent with like friends that encourage and/or model deviancy, lack of achievement, and depressed mood are important factors in predicting problem SU (Castellanos-Ryan et al., 2013; Pei et al., 2020). Furthermore, CD is consistently found to be a strong predictor of drug use initiation, persistence of drug misuse into adulthood, and progression to addiction (Sartor et al.,

2007). The relationship is so strong that precocious SU has been considered a possible diagnostic criterion for CD (Fairchild et al., 2019). This correlation between peer delinquency and SU and abuse could mirror a causal chain, wherein delinquent friends model and encourage SU among other problem behaviors or, conversely, a youth-governed phenomenon in which individuals at risk to use and misuse substances select and/or prefer friends who model and condone use (Schwartz et al., 2019).

While socializing with a deviant peer group is a robust predictor of SU, there is evidence that the "type" of socializing also plays a role in the relationship. One study found that unstructured socializing ("just hanging out," or spending time without any particular preplanned activity) can explain some of the within-individual patterns of SU. In other words, a person may be at increased risk of SU while spending unstructured time with a group of friends who primarily engage in SU, whereas they may be more at risk of engaging in vandalism when spending unstructured time with friends who engage primarily in vandalism (Hoeben et al., 2021). Whatever the mechanisms, a temporally dynamic action and interaction of these processes with one another is likely to be the case. One large-scale twin study showed that, along with the genetic susceptibility for externalizing disorders, peer delinquency was the strongest vulnerability for adverse drinking trajectories (Wichers, Gardner et al., 2013; Wichers, Gillespie et al., 2013). More recent research has found evidence for a gene–environment interaction wherein peer deviance moderates genetic influence for deviance. One longitudinal, nationally representative study found that genetic influences *decreased* and environmental influence *increased* as peer deviance increased (Schwartz et al., 2019).

Related to these phenomena is the so-called *gateway model*, which postulates that the transition from using one drug to another (more specifically from legal to illegal drugs) occurs sequentially. The order is generally hypothesized to lead from more recreational substances to "harder" drugs (substances that are less commonly used, more stigmatized, and present greater risk addiction, health consequences, and mortality). An approximation of this progression begins with cigarettes, alcohol, and marijuana; then moves to recreational stimulants, depressants, and hallucinogens; then finally leads to crack cocaine, methamphetamine, and heroin. Obviously, this progression is not inevitable, and the order is variable, but exposure to peers who engage in drug use a step beyond one's own is seen as an important determining factor, particularly if one is strongly identified with these peers.

This could in part be due to drug subcultures, as an individual may become exposed to new substances after associating with peer groups belonging to subcultures centered around particular substances ("stoners," "ravers," "psychonauts," etc.). This identification is seen as involving expectations regarding positive results from such drug use. Peer factors are thus central in three ways: first, in providing the drug; second, in developing attitudes about its use and effects; and third, in providing an exemplar. This peer cluster theory states not only that peers represent the most important predictor of use and progression to abuse but also that peers mediate the significance of other risk factors—for example, emotional problems and attitudes about oneself. Some research has confirmed these social learning interpretations, and the consequent argument has been made that interventions should be aimed at peers. However, while there is some support for the gateway theory, evidence that this effect is driven by peers or subcultures is mixed (Golub et al., 2005; Nkansah-Amankra, 2020), and the vast majority of individuals who use "softer" drugs do not progress into using harder drugs. Additionally, it is debated if subsequent drug use is actually caused by using the previous drug or if the apparent association is better explained by other factors (e.g., increased access to other substances, peer selection following drug use).

Part of the variability in characterizing peer and other factors in drug use arises from how use is defined. Studies that measure "ever used" may be selecting a suboptimal population for study since drug experimentation by adolescents, even with an illegal drug such as marijuana, appears to err on the side of normality as most adolescents have used the drug. A longitudinal study (Shedler & Block, 1990) found that adolescents who *never* experimented with drugs, particularly marijuana, showed indications of being more maladjusted than occasional experimenters. While experimenters do display some risk factors, heavy, escalating, and debilitating drug use should be the focus of concern.

### The Family

Another area where modeling seems to play a role pertains to the behavior of one's parents and siblings. It has been known for many years that alcohol and substance use runs in families. Some of this behavior is directly heritable through genetic predispositions to SU and SU risk factors, while other influences come from the types of behavior modeled within the home and the family. Recent estimates suggest that roughly 50% of the variance of addictive behaviors is due to (epi)genetic effects (Friedel et al., 2021).

A large-scale investigation of a follow-up of nine large databases of adoptive children found that when either, versus neither, of the biological parents abused drugs, the offspring risk for drug abuse doubled, and when both did so, the risk tripled (Kendler, Sundquist et al., 2012). A slightly greater risk was found in offspring with paternal versus maternal drug abuse, and males seemed to be more genetically vulnerable than females. Furthermore, a biological family history of alcoholism, criminality, or other forms of psychopathology also elevated risk in adopted offspring (Kendler, Sundquist et al., 2012). Consistently, a subsequent analysis by the same group demonstrated that risk for SUDs was significantly greater when the age difference was smaller. Specifically, when both siblings were born on the same year, versus 10 years apart, the risk for a SUD in the unaffected sibling doubled. Risk also was substantially greater when the affected proband was older versus younger than the unaffected siblings, an effect that was much more pronounced in male versus female pairs (Kendler et al., 2013).

Children can also learn SU through the modeling of their parents' behavior. When parents provide their children with medication or use substances to relieve negative feelings, cope with stress, provide a social lubricant, etc., they are modeling both the behavior and the expectancies associated with the given drug. Drug and alcohol expectancies are learned, in part, from parents' attitudes and behaviors. Exposure to parental alcohol use models drinking behavior and expectancies for children/adolescents, even if the parents experience negative consequences from alcohol use (e.g., Waddell et al., 2020). In addition to alcohol use, many studies have consistently supported parental drug use as a risk factor for adolescent initiation of use (Pentz & Riggs, 2013; Rusby et al., 2018). While there are specific genetic and environmental risk factors presented by the family, these risks are often correlated (i.e., families with genetic predisposition toward SU are also more likely to have deleterious environmental situations). Furthermore, research suggests that there is a cumulative risk, wherein exposure to multiple risks throughout development increasingly amplify one's risk. These factors, along with the interactions between environment and gene expression, create a complicated amalgam of familial risk that can be difficult to attribute to any specific cause (Stallings et al., 2016).

A recent study from a large-scale investigation of seven Norwegian twin birth cohorts yielded evidence that SU is highly heritable (Waaktaar et al., 2018). This genetic heritability was present for alcohol use, tobacco use, and illicit drug use and was present throughout adolescence and into early adulthood. Other recent work has found that both genetic and neighborhood factors predict SU, with a significant interaction between socioeconomic status (SES) and genetic risk for alcohol use (Pasman et al., 2020). Data from community-based samples show that more than half, and one-fifth of the offspring of alcoholics, become alcohol and illicit drug misusers, respectively, compared to one-fourth and one-tenth of matched controls (Hussong et al., 2012). Furthermore, after adjusting for comorbid parental psychopathology, environmental stressors, and familial dysfunction, parental alcoholism stands out as a unique predictor of drug use and misuse in adolescence and early adulthood.##

The simple availability of cigarettes, alcohol, marijuana, and prescription drugs within the family seems to be a contributing factor to SU. Drug availability plus permissive parental attitudes, low parental monitoring, and poor parental support further facilitate use (Maggs & Staff, 2018; Rusby et al., 2018). Even parental permissiveness toward legal substances (e.g., tobacco, alcohol) predict adolescent use of illicit drugs (Mehanović et al., 2021) As disordered conduct is a profound risk factor for substance misuse, family dynamics that increase risk of conduct problems also predict onset and progression of adolescent SU. These factors include maladaptive parenting; using harsh, coercive, and inconsistent discipline; and parent–child conflicts. Parental mistreatment is a particularly important risk factor in individuals at high genetic risk for CDs (Fairchild et al., 2019).

Stress is common in substance-abusing families. Stressors common in families with AUD include high conflict, poor communication, marital discord, coercive interactions, physical abuse and neglect, economic and social deprivation, and the extremes of parenting (i.e., too authoritarian or too lax; Velleman & Orford, 2013). Almost all (98%) of adolescents with drug abusing parents are beset by at least one other environmental adversity (McLaughlin et al., 2012). Considerable research has found that a history of childhood abuse is a strong predictor of adolescent SU, which in turn is a strong predictor of subsequent development of substance abuse or addiction. A recent study found that the relationship between childhood maltreatment and adolescent SU is not directly linked, but rather occurs through the development of posttraumatic stress symptoms and poor mother–child relationships (Yoon et al., 2017).

There is, of course, another side to this coin. There is evidence that positive family environments—involving such things as religious involvement, positive marital relationships, distance from delinquent peers, and high parental warmth and monitoring—reduce the likelihood of the development of SUDs (Dick & Kendler, 2012).

Positive family attributes may have effects that fluctuate and vary during the developmental process. For example, a longitudinal investigation following approximately 1,000 young adolescents for 11 years and assessing their drug consumption (specifically tobacco, alcohol, and cannabis) found that early adolescence use was predicted by lack of parental monitoring. However, as adolescents transitioned to high school and later adolescence, it was the quality of the family relationship (indexed by shared activities, mutual regard and positive affect between parents and adolescent offspring) that was most protective against SU. However, these family factors (parental monitoring, family relationship) did not appear to be relevant to drug use in young adulthood (Van Ryzin et al., 2012).

Seldom considered but potentially significant family factors in the etiology of SUDs are teratogenic effects. Drug use by parents can deleteriously affect intrauterine development. One widely accepted teratogenic effect that has received considerable mainstream attention is fetal alcohol syndrome (FAS) and its more broad designation of fetal alcohol spectrum disorders (FASD), involving low birth weight, prematurity, infant mortality, and physical anomalies in the central nervous system (CNS) development, maturation, and function (Norman et al., 2013). Similar deleterious phenomena have been observed in infants prenatally exposed to cocaine and cigarettes (Liu et al., 2013), methamphetamines (Twomey et al., 2013), opiates (Behnke et al., 2013), and many prescribed drugs, particularly barbiturates and other sedatives. In a birth cohort study (Alati et al., 2006), children of mothers who drank during pregnancy produced offspring who were 2.95 times more likely to later develop adolescent problem drinking when compared with controls. Another longitudinal study showed that the effect of maternal drinking during pregnancy bore a dose-response relationship with adult offspring self-reports of problematic behaviors (Day et al., 2013). While the link between ethanol exposure and FASD appears intuitive, some have argued for the importance of moderators or mitigators of the link between drinking during pregnancy and FASD, suggesting that the latter cannot be fully explained by the unconditional effects of ethanol exposure because an impoverished family environment also substantiates risk for FASD. It has been argued that FASDs are caused by nutritional deficiencies that ethanol exposure can exacerbate as opposed to their being a direct alcohol-induced neurotoxic effect (Ballard et al., 2012).

## At the Level of the Individual

Given the same environmental context, not all individuals are equally likely to experiment with drugs, become regular users, or progress to heavy use with or without associated problems. A number of individual-level factors have been shown to be associated with risk for substance use and for SUD, and those that have received the most attention are highlighted below. Full description of individual-level factors requires consideration of those that are both general and specific.

### Stress and Affective Factors

When asked, people frequently report that they abuse substances to reduce stress. However, when subjective distress and stressor exposure are assessed, neither usually correlates very highly with degree of substance use (Sher & Grekin, 2007).

The relationship between SUDs and stress is theorized to occur for a number of reasons. SU may be a coping strategy, most typically a form of emotion-focused coping, as described in theories as self-medication (Khantzian, 1985, 1997), tension reduction (e.g., Greeley & Oei, 1999), or stress-response dampening (e.g., Sher, 1987). That is, individuals take psychoactive substances to directly reduce psychological distress (or avoid anticipated distress) via pharmacological mechanisms. For example, some drugs (especially benzodiazepines, which are prescribed clinically to reduce anxiety and panic, but also barbiturates and alcohol *in sufficient dosage*) have well-characterized anxiolytic properties, and users seek these out for their desired effects. While such effects are typically thought to be due to direct effects on neural systems involved in emotions, it is also possible that at moderate doses, certain drugs (e.g., alcohol) can facilitate emotion regulation by restricting attention to the most salient aspects of the surrounding environment. If these salient, environmental distractors are positive (or even neutral), attention is likely to be redeployed to them with less attention focused on distressing stimuli and/or thoughts, resulting in a distress-reducing effect (Fairbairn & Sayette, 2013; Josephs & Steele, 1990; Steele & Josephs, 1990).

It is possible that some users sometimes consume substances to avoid or minimize stress associated with anticipated or feared failure via "self-handicapping" (i.e., using a substance to provide an external attribution for failure; Jones & Berglas, 1978). In such cases, the neuropharmacological effect of the drug may be irrelevant or incidental because having an excuse (an attribution for one's shortcomings) is the operative mechanism.

The transition to SUD is also likely modulated by additional factors. For example, for Vietnam veterans who had drug abuse problems associated with PTSD, there was an average of 3 1/2 years between the onset of PTSD symptoms and the development of the SUD (Davidson et al., 1985). A meta-analysis of eight longitudinal studies showed that depression predicted alcohol consumption for women (Hartka et al., 1991). Consistent with the self-medication model, individuals with high levels of hopelessness report drinking to cope with depression, which can then lead to severe alcohol problems (Grant, Beck et al., 2007). In particular, women report problems with intimacy and interpersonal stress as the reasons for excessive drug consumption (Frank et al., 1990). However, given the importance of stress, anxiety, or depression as etiological factors, the fact that the majority of individuals who undergo these conditions do not turn to drugs for relief suggests that more than a single explanation is required. Additionally, negative emotions such as depression and anxiety often arise from chronic, heavy SU (e.g., *DSM-5* substance-induced mood and anxiety disorders) and so disentangling the primacy of affective symptomatology and SU and SUDs can be quite challenging. However, whether negative affectivity is premorbid to or acquired through chronic, heavy SU, it is thought to play an important role in the maintenance and course of SUDs (Koob & Schulkin, 2019).

## PERSONALITY

For much of the past century, problem drug behavior was typically ascribed to an addictive personality. Indeed, a plethora of studies yielded evidence supporting a wide range of personality profiles as etiologically significant. In an earlier review (Pihl & Spiers, 1978), it was determined that 93% of this research studied exclusively patients in treatment, thus likely reflecting the characteristics of individuals who seek or are mandated to treatment, or the concomitants of the problem rather than the cause of the problem. Barnes (1979, 1983) highlighted the differences between pre-alcoholic personality traits (i.e., those traits that prospectively predict the occurrence of an AUD) and clinical alcoholic personality traits (i.e., those traits that distinguish individuals with AUDs from those with other disorders or no disorder). Perhaps the biggest difference is that persons who eventually develop AUDs show less negative affectivity premorbidly than do those currently exhibiting clinical manifestations (Sher & Gotham, 1999).

Indeed, a prominent view of addiction, *allostasis theory* (Koob & Schulkin, 2019), suggests that chronic adaptations to substance use lead to a change in the hedonic set point. There are progressive increases in negative affect, which then goad further consumption for transitory relief, thus setting up a vicious cycle (Sher et al., 2005).

From the perspective of the Five Factor Model (sometimes referred to as the "Big Five"), the traits that appear to be most important to risk for SU and SUDs are those associated with neuroticism, agreeableness, and conscientiousness (e.g., Malouff et al., 2007). Notably, specific facets of neuroticism (e.g., impulsiveness/negative urgency) and conscientiousness (lack of perseverance, lack of premeditation) may be particularly relevant to SUDs (Dick et al., 2010). In conceptualizing the way personality might be related to SU and SUDs, it is important to consider some less appreciated aspects of the relations between these two domains. First, personality changes developmentally, with individuals tending to become less neurotic, more conscientious, and more agreeable as they age, with these changes particularly evident in the third decade of life (Roberts et al., 2006). Coincidentally, this is the same period of time when individuals show decreasing rates of AUDs (Vergés et al., 2012) and other SUDs (Vergés et al., 2013). These two processes appear linked. As individuals "mature out" of their problematic SU they also show greater psychosocial maturation, as evidenced by decreased neuroticism and increases in conscientiousness and agreeableness, and that part of desistance from problematic substance involvement reflects normative personality change (Lee & Sher, 2018). That is, the longitudinal association between personality and SUDs appears to be driven, in part, by psychosocial development.

While personality might be related to SU and SUDs either as a premorbid risk factor or as a complication of chronic use, an important issue largely overlooked in the research literature (but not among lay people or the recovery community) is the acute effects of a drug such as alcohol on personality expression, akin to a "Dr. Jekyll and Mr. Hyde" or "Nutty Professor" transformation. That is, intoxication might lead, in some, to state changes in personality; some people may be more agreeable and conscientious, others more antagonistic, and others more extraverted when "under the influence" (Winograd et al., 2016, 2017).

Although personality has typically been viewed as relatively stable cross-situationally, recent views of personality highlight the importance of situational determinants of personality expression (Fleeson, 2001). From this perspective, one important "situation" to consider is drug intoxication, which in some individuals occurs often and in important social contexts.

When discussing "why" might personality influence SU and SUDs more generally, it's important to note that multiple pathways of influence have been posited including (1) sensitivity to drug effects, (2) general deviance proneness, (3) trait emotionality, (4) emotional regulation, and (5) peer and environmental selection (Littlefield & Sher, 2016; Sher, 1991). That is, while personality in general and individual traits may play a critical role in the etiology of SUDs, it is not a single role and broadly encompasses most mechanisms that various theorists have proposed as central.

### Cognitive and Motivational Processes

Dual-process models emphasize that drug use can be viewed as the outcome of two competing tendencies: (1) approach motivations toward using a substance and (2) restraint motivations to abstain or limit use. While such models are relevant to a wide range of behaviors (Strack & Deutsch, 2004), they are particularly relevant to conceptualizing addiction (Wiers & Gladwin, 2016; Wiers and Stacy, 2006). Such models provide the foundation of a general framework for integrating a diverse host of etiological factors, both internal and external, across multiple levels of biopsychosocial organization and stages of substance involvement.

### EXPECTANCIES

Beliefs and expectancies regarding drug effects, reflecting both social learning and direct pharmacological experiences, are a critical part of the cognitive context and expectations of drug effects and predict drug use. The brain reacts to stimuli in terms of context (Luria, 1980), with one's culture, learning, and experience anchoring each new response. Regarding drugs, these factors coalesce in the form of expectancies. Generally, an individual frequently using a drug is more likely to perceive less risk and to approve more of the use of that drug. Among illicit substances, for example, marijuana is the most used (Substance Abuse and Mental Health Services Administration, 2020) and is perceived as least harmful, although in recent years the perceived harmfulness of marijuana has decreased without a concomitant increase in prevalence of use (Sarvet et al., 2018). Of course, one's attitudes toward a drug and beliefs about use are robustly associated with changing trends of drug use behaviors (Substance Abuse and Mental Health Services Administration, 2020).

The 1980s witnessed a decline in marijuana and cocaine use in the United States that was accompanied by greater perceived risk of use. Conversely, a drastic shift of these attitudes to the other direction during much of the 1990s seems to have accounted for the elevated use of many illicit substances, specifically marijuana. As well, ecstasy use in some of the early 2000s dramatically decreased as a result of greater perceived danger of its use (Droungas et al., 1995). Drug use is also affected by what one expects a drug to do to and for oneself, both objectively and subjectively. A large 9-year prospective study found that among males and females, consuming alcohol and marijuana could be predicted in adolescence and adulthood based on early expectations of the response of positive feelings to the drugs and the alleviation of negative feelings (Stacy et al., 1991).

Neural reflections of differential types of expectancies have been identified in the lab. In one functional magnetic resonance imaging (fMRI) study, participants were exposed to a noxious thermal stimulus after which they ingested a potent opioid receptor agonist. Those who had positive analgesia expectations showed double the benefit from the drug, which was associated with activation of the endogenous pain regulatory system. This benefit was completely blunted among those with negative expectations, the latter of which correlated with decreased activation in brain regions involved in exacerbating pain via anxiety (Barrett et al., 2004). Some ostensible drug effects commonly associated with alcohol consumption (especially sexual arousal and aggression) have been found to be determined, to a nontrivial degree, by the belief one has consumed the substance (Crowe & George, 1989; Hull & Bond, 1986). However, such expectancy or placebo effects are not inevitable and may be highly conditional upon individual and situational factors. Moreover, some expectancy effects are in the opposite direction of alcohol effects, most likely reflecting compensatory strategies for managing intoxication (Testa et al., 2006).

Expectancies regarding drug effects are far more complex than simply positive (i.e., reinforcement) or negative (i.e., punishment). First, expectancies can vary as a function of the perceived dose of a substance (e.g., Wiers et al., 1997) or whether or not blood levels of the drug are increasing or decreasing (e.g., Morean et al., 2012). For example, someone may anticipate pleasurable arousal in ingesting a moderate amount of alcohol but also anticipate distress when the effects of the alcohol are wearing off, as occurs in hangover. How one weighs the costs and benefits of various substance effects and their immediacy interacts with individual differences in delay and probability discounting (Bickel, Koffarnus et al., 2014; Yi et al., 2010).

During adolescence, alcohol expectancies tend to become more positive (e.g., Sher et al., 1996) and then tend to decrease over adulthood (e.g., Nicolai et al., 2012). A recent study (Montes et al., 2019) found not only that baseline levels of positive expectancies predicted the onset of SU (specifically, alcohol, tobacco, and marijuana) but also that the rate of change was a significant predictor of onset for all substances. In addition to being of interest in their own right, expectancies appear to play an important mediating role for more distal risk factors such as personality (e.g., Mezquita et al., 2015). That is, personality tends to shape the types of expectancies that someone forms based on intraindividual factors, such as individual differences in pharmacological sensitivity to various drugs, proneness to negative emotional states, sensation seeking, and other mechanisms (Littlefield & Sher, 2016).

Such expectancies are intimately related to the stated reasons that individuals endorse about why they choose to consume a substance (Cooper et al., 2016). While there are similarities across different psychoactive substances such as alcohol and marijuana in the various SU motives endorsed (e.g., enhancement or getting "high," coping with negative emotions, to conform with social norms, to heighten sociability), tobacco use motivations appear quite different and are characterized by automaticity/habit and responses to withdrawal cues. Note that someone can hold certain expectancies for a given SU effect but not necessarily use the substance for those anticipated outcomes. Thus, while intimately related to self-reported motivation, substance outcome expectancies are conceptually and empirically distinct.

## BASIC COGNITIVE FUNCTIONING

Variation in some aspects of cognitive functioning could put someone at risk for problematic use because they are associated with self-regulatory processes or substance-related reinforcement. To identify preexisting cognitive deficits that increase risk for substance use, as opposed to cognitive deficits that may have occurred as a result of using substances, researchers can examine characteristics of individuals who are at high risk for SU or SUDs (e.g., children of individuals with a SUD), but have not yet engaged in SU or developed an SUD. Such studies often find mild to moderate neuropsychological deficits present. These impairments have been found in five broad categories of cognitive performance: executive functions (which encompass abstracting, planning, and problem-solving abilities), language-based skills, attentional and memory processing, psychomotor integration, and visuoperceptual analysis and learning (Pihl et al., 1984).

Of central interest to understanding SU and SUDs is the role of executive function owing to its importance in decision-making and guiding self-directed behavior. "Executive function" refers to a broad set of cognitive abilities including working memory updating, task switching, and response inhibition (Friedman & Miyake, 2017; Miyake et al., 2000) although various measures of response inhibition (e.g., Hamilton, Littlefield et al., 2015) appear to be associated with a broad common factor (Miyake & Friedman, 2012). Given its general association with a range of externalizing disorders as early as early childhood (Schoemaker et al., 2013), executive function (especially response inhibition) would appear to be an important endophenotype to consider when understanding cognitive risk factors for SU and SUDs. However, recent work (Gustavson et al., 2017) suggests that response inhibition is most strongly associated with SU in adolescence but not in later life or with the transition to SUDs, again highlighting the importance of distinguishing factors associated with SU versus those associated with transition from SU to SUD.

Certain drugs (particularly alcohol) acutely impair these cognitive functions (Porjesz et al., 2005). This may be a central factor in explaining the high correlation between intoxicated behavior and aggression. For example, alcohol can disrupt executive functions necessary for restraint following provocation (Giancola, 2004). The notion that disinhibitory effects of alcohol are attributable to disruption of higher cortical functions is consistent with long-standing speculations on how drugs lead to disinhibition (McDougall, 1929).

Along with premorbid executive function deficits, chronic exposure to psychoactive substances can cause further impairment and thus can contribute to a worsening of substance-related problems. Fernandez-Serrano et al. (2010) showed a range of executive function deficits as a function of chronic use of different drugs of abuse and concluded that "alcohol abuse is negatively associated with fluency and decision-making deficits, whereas the different drugs motivating treatment have both generalized and specific deleterious effects on different executive components" (p. 317). There is also evidence that the neuroadaptations underlying addiction can also affect cognitive functions. For example, the development of incentive salience to drug cues is associated with impaired response inhibition (e.g., Lovic et al., 2011), potentially increasing addiction liability by both increasing approach and reducing restraining tendencies. Also, executive function and other higher intellectual functions appear to moderate other important cognitive risk factors for addiction such as delay discounting (Bailey et al., 2018; 2020).

At least for human males, the P300 wave of the visual event-related potential (ERP; a brainwave reflective of neural inhibition or attentional regulation and obtained via electroencephalography) exemplifies what is perhaps the best currently known endophenotypic marker for SUDs (Bingel et al., 2011; Euser et al., 2012; Singh & Basu, 2009). The P300 wave is evoked when a subject responds to a distinct stimulus presented among many similar ones and must make some type of decision or judgment (Metrik et al., 2009). The P300 amplitude has been shown to become attenuated in drug-naïve 11-year-old sons of alcoholic fathers, pointing to its heritability. This trait is also manifested in the full range of externalizing psychopathology as well as psychotic disorders, suggesting that the attenuated P300 amplitude is an endophenotypic marker for low-order disinhibitory externalizing disorders (Patrick et al., 2006; Volkow et al., 2003) or psychopathology more generally (Tang et al., 2020; Wada et al., 2019).

Anomalies in executive function and inhibitory control, added to augmented levels of anxious-disinhibited traits, have been detected in both individuals addicted to psychostimulants and their unaffected siblings, but to a significantly greater extent in the former. This may point to both neurotoxic or other effects of persistent drug misuse (Miller & Rockstroh, 2013) and underlying vulnerability. These commonalities of reduced inhibitory control and increased anxious-disinhibition have thus been proposed as endophenotypic markers for the addiction to psychostimulants, reflected as a neurodevelopmental perturbation of prefrontal functioning (Iacono & Malone, 2011).

**ADDICTION-RELATED COGNITIVE CHANGES**

While premorbid, individual differences in executive function and other cognitive functions put one at risk for SU and SUDs, both the direct neurotoxic effects of a drug on the brain and adaptive changes associated with prolonged heavy SU create further vulnerabilities for the development of severe SUDs and addiction.

Clearly the heavy consumption of most drugs is neurotoxic, and this is the case even for marijuana (Séguin et al., 1995). Cross-sectional studies tend to find small effects on neurocognition that are attenuated with abstinence (Scott et al., 2018). One longitudinal study found that deficits in short-term and working memory predicted an earlier age of onset of cannabis use, and cannabis use across adolescence was associated in declines in verbal intelligence and some executive tasks and reward processing (Castellanos-Ryan et al., 2017). The issue of distinguishing premorbid and acquired deficits in SUDs is always one that is hard to resolve in individual cases.

This is problematic for drawing etiological conclusions given the indisputable fact that drugs of abuse are neurotoxic. They hijack the CNS and remodel it, both functionally and structurally (Benningfield & Cowan, 2013; Volkow et al., 2016), effects only some of which are reversible (Meier et al., 2012). In the absence of a picture of the brain prior to drug use, it is hard to rely on a picture of the addicted brain if one wishes to distinguish aspects that triggered the drug use from aspects that reflect drug effects. Moreover, from a treatment perspective, uncertainty regarding the degree to which a given process or mechanism is likely premorbid or acquired in an individual patient makes it a challenge to set appropriate treatment targets.

As noted earlier, SUDs rarely appear in isolation and almost always co-occur in the context of externalizing (i.e., disruptive-disinhibitory) and/or internalizing (i.e., anxious-depressive) attributes. To a considerable extent, the externalizing and internalizing factors are behaviorally and likely neurobiologically distinct, with the former corresponding to the reward cue system and the latter to the fear processing system which includes, among other regions, the amygdala, nucleus accumbens, and the hippocampus/parahippocampus (Li et al., 2013; Servaas et al., 2013). This last brain structure develops much earlier and faster than do those underlying higher cognitive functions, and it governs primitive fight-or-flight responses to actual or perceived threat.

Inefficient functioning at any point in the fear circuit can result in overresponsivity to events and an exaggerated secretion of stress hormones, which further deteriorates the functioning of this network. These disorders have been repeatedly correlated by evidence with exaggerated amygdalar activation associated with stimuli signaling threat. In a large study of adult female twins, where personality traits were related to drinking motives and symptoms of an AUD, a genetic relationship was found with coping (i.e., stress dampening) motives and AUDs symptoms (Littlefield et al., 2011). Conversely, in at-risk individuals whose response to drugs is mediated by the cue for reward system, at the core of their liability seems to reside a fundamental problem of impulse control. This problem can be analogized to stuck gas pedals and broken brakes, the latter being the prefrontal cortex and the former the limbic system. With the limbic system hyper- and the prefrontal cortex hypoactivated, the result is an impulsive response (Zucker et al., 2011). Generally, most brain imaging studies have found marked neural functional and anatomical aberration within the frontostriatal circuits in addicted individuals, which makes sense given that these circuits subserve the core clinical feature of many cases of SUDs: that is, the impulsive and compulsive seeking of the drug. These individuals tend to use and abuse psychostimulant drugs, including alcohol. Thus, understanding what leads an individual to express these differential traits and how they determine differential risk profiles associated with SUDs should have great explanatory power.

### Genetics

SUDs are at least moderately heritable. Since the 1980s, a number of adoption and twin studies have examined SUDs and found heritability estimates between 40% and 70% across the various drugs of abuse (Kendler et al., 2011; for a comprehensive review of the research on genetics of SU, see Lopez-Leon et al., 2021). Some studies (Korhonen et al., 2012; Stroud et al., 2009) have shown these heritability estimates to vary as a function of sex, while others have failed to find any sex differences (e.g., Baker et al., 2011). A study following more than 1,000 adolescent males and females aged 17–24 found that, while genetic effects became more relevant and important over time in men, environmental effects assumed more importance over time in women (Hicks et al., 2007). Given the well-established (but shrinking) sex differences in alcohol use, but the lack of evidence supporting the presence of sex differences in heritability of alcohol use, it has recently been suggested that researchers explore sex-specific gene–environment interactions (Salvatore et al., 2017). Furthermore, adolescence onset and adulthood onset of addictions have been associated with differential developmental etiologic underpinnings, with the former showing substantial evidence for shared environmental effects and little for genetic effects, and the opposite regarding adulthood-onset addiction (van Beek et al., 2012).

While many studies have focused on substance-specific heritability, polysubstance use appears to be the norm rather than the exception (Glantz & Leshner, 2000). Researchers have long hypothesized that a general liability of SU exists, with Young and colleagues (2006) suggesting that either AUD and DUD are different manifestations of a single underlying vulnerability or that the two are separate but highly correlated. Kendler and colleagues (2007) made similar conclusions, with two highly correlated genetic factors (one for legal and one for illegal substances). More recently, a large Norwegian twin study found heritability both common (across-substance) and unique (substance-specific) heritability for substance use (Waaktaar et al., 2018). Moreover, at least with respect to alcohol dependence, there is evidence for multiple, heritable factors related to different forms of symptomatology (e.g., high consumption/tolerance, loss-of-control and preoccupation, and withdrawal/continued use despite problems). The overall picture to emerge from these studies is that there are multiple genetic factors contributing to SU and SUDs with some of these representing common liabilities and others that are substance-specific.

## CANDIDATE GENE STUDIES

The heritability estimates of addictions are analogous to those for the majority of illnesses widely prevalent in Western societies (Bienvenu et al., 2011). This high prevalence and heritability spurred a significant interest in identifying specific genetic variations that predispose one to SUDs. Two paradigms have been prominent: gene association studies, which investigate the allelic variation in specific genes believed to confer risk, and genome-wide association studies (GWAS), which investigate up to a million genetic variations across the entire genome for associations with the risk for drug addiction.

The currently best available specific genetic evidence of SUD risk involves cigarette addiction and implicates polymorphisms in the nicotinic acetylcholine receptors (Chang et al., 2009; Chen et al., 2009). These have been robustly associated with the number of cigarettes consumed daily (Lips et al., 2010) and with serum cotinine concentration (a long-lasting metabolite of nicotine; Munafo et al., 2012), which more objectively measures how much nicotine one inhales. Furthermore, individuals bearing a particular minor allele show a significantly decreased puff volume in response to smoking cigarettes (MacQueen et al., 2014). Notably, these previously mentioned genetic polymorphisms have also been linked to lung cancer (Hung et al., 2008) and respiratory health phenotypes, associations which appear to be mediated by the quantity of cigarettes one consumes (Saccone et al., 2010) and amount of smoke inhaled (MacQueen et al., 2014). This is a rather powerful example of an "outside-the-skin" genetic pathway for a cancer liability gene; the risk allele in a nicotinic receptor increases the propensity to more frequently purchase and smoke cigarettes, thereby augmenting lung cancer susceptibility (Kendler, Chen et al., 2012).

In line with research suggesting that initial low sensitivity to alcohol (i.e., low level of response to a given dose of alcohol) is a predictor of risk for AUD (Quinn & Fromme, 2011; Ray et al., 2016), there is genetic research pointing to some genes that might transmit this risk. The strongest evidence of genes affecting the sensitivity to alcohol have been variants that encode for activity of alcohol dehydrogenase and aldehyde dehydrogenase 2. These variations protect against the progression to alcoholism by contributing to an aversive response to ethanol. As such, the presence of certain genetic variance can indicate decreased vulnerability to the development of the problem. Many East Asians, but very few Caucasians, have this polymorphism, which affects a liver enzyme that protects sixfold against the disorder. Individuals with this genetic variant have high levels of acetaldehyde build up in the blood, resulting in aversive sensations and a visible flush. Variants of other aldehyde genes are actually thought to enhance risk of alcohol problems in individuals of European descent.

There was initially much excitement about the role of many various candidate genes associated with neuropharmacological systems related to basic motivational and reinforcement processes in the brain. This included genes related to catecholaminergic function (especially dopaminergic functioning), gamma-aminobutyric acid (GABA)-ergic functioning, serotoninergic functioning, and cannabinoid and opioid systems. For example, candidate gene studies have also identified specific genes related to general SU, with several being identified as increasing risk for two or more SU disorders, and the SLC6A4 gene being found to double an individual's odds of having an SUD (Lopez-Leon et al., 2021). However, despite a number of high-profile initial findings, frequent failures to replicate and achieve statistical significance in GWAS studies have caused the robustness of these findings to be questioned. With continued failures to replicate candidate gene findings and mounting research elucidating how small the effect sizes of individual genes truly are, it has become widely believed that a very large proportion (possibly most) of candidate gene hypotheses for psychiatric disorders were incorrect (Duncan, Ostacher et al., 2019). Furthermore, it is commonly accepted that GWAS studies and the use of polygenic risk scores (PRS) have effectively rendered traditional candidate gene studies obsolete (Duncan, Shen et al., 2019) although there may be some situations where they are useful to study specify mechanistic hypotheses as part of more focused investigations.

## POLYGENIC RISK SCORES

Put simply, a PRS is computed to represent a person's overall genetic liability for a given trait, typically by calculating the weighted sum of their trait-associated alleles. Research using PRS for human traits has proliferated rapidly in the past decade, and polygenic risk is now being heavily researched in a wide variety of areas (Duncan, Shen et al., 2019), with SU and SUDs being no exception. As noted above, despite the high heritability of SU, the increase in SU risk associated with any individual gene is miniscule. Rather, it appears that SU and addiction heritability arises via small contributions from hundreds or even thousands of genetic variants. As such, GWAS studies and PRS have been primary avenues for further exploring the how of genetic risk for SU and addiction.

Studies using PRS have been conducted for many different substances. There is a considerable body of GWAS studies examining tobacco use and nicotine dependence. One study considered 1.2 million subjects and identified many significant risk loci; however, these mainly pertained to quantity and frequency of tobacco use rather than nicotine dependence (Liu et al., 2019). Large-scale GWAS findings on alcohol use have had similar issues with finding risk loci for AUD, wherein the risk loci of quantity and frequency of drinking is not necessarily the same as the risk loci of AUD. As noted above, the diagnostic operationalization of AUD (and other SUDs) creates remarkable phenotypic heterogeneity, which reduces the power for GWAS studies to detect genetic effects. However, the increasingly large-scale GWAS studies being conducted continue to identify more risk loci. Recently, the largest AUD GWAS study ever conducted roughly tripled the number of risk loci identified for problematic alcohol use (Zhou, Sealock et al., 2020). While these PRS approaches (and GWAS approaches more generally) overcome some of the "missing heritability problem" (i.e., the large discrepancy between heritability estimates based on biometric models of twin data and the heritability estimates based on the additive effects of candidate genes; e.g., Génin, 2020; Manolio et al. 2009), the implicit heterogeneity of this approach (i.e., the collapsing of many different genetic variants into a single score) may be less well suited to studying specific genetic mechanisms.

In 2020, Zhou, Rentsch, and colleagues conducted the largest GWAS study to date on opioids and identified a significant association between an *OPRM1* variant and opioid use disorder (OUD). Other studies have identified possible variants associated with OUD risk, but replications will be necessary (Gelernter & Polimanti, 2021). A similar situation exists for stimulant dependence, with very few well-powered GWAS studies and only a single risk variant, *FAM53B*, currently identified as being associated with cocaine dependence (Gelernter et al., 2014).

### GENE-ENVIRONMENT INTERACTIONS

Further complicating these matters are the many possible interactions among variables (i.e., genes with environment) and with development (i.e., age of the individual), not to mention interactions among various genes and interactions among various environmental variables. A longitudinal large-scale Swedish twin study (Baker et al., 2011) suggested a shared vulnerability factor that mediated the association between the use of cigarettes, alcohol, and illicit substances at ages 13–14, 16–17, and 19–20. The effects of shared genetic and environmental factors were strikingly continuous, and while the genetic effects assumed more relevance and specificity with age, shared environmental factors became less important. Parental monitoring, for example, is tremendously important when children first embark into adolescence, at which stage drug use and experimentation often begins, yet genetic effects become increasingly important into young adulthood, where patterns of heavy use are often developed (Palmer et al., 2013)

Along with changes throughout development, there is also evidence that environmental circumstances (e.g., urbanicity, living in communities with greater migration, more interaction with older adolescents/young adults) can moderate genetic effects on alcohol use (Prom-Wormley et al., 2017). Twin studies have found that low parental monitoring increases genetic risk for smoking, while another variant was identified as having reduced expression in the presence of high parental monitoring and nonsmoking peers (Kaprio, 2009). Research found that genetic risk for smoking was also increased by traumatic life events and decreased by high social cohesion within one's community (Meyers et al., 2013). The role of trauma interacting with vulnerability genes has also been demonstrated with cannabis (Meyers et al., 2013). As with GWAS studies, gene–environment interactions for illicit drug use have received relatively less attention than their licit counterparts and will be an important avenue for future research.

Finally, even when genes are implicated, we remain a good distance from knowing what is inherited and, most important, just what vulnerability is and how it is affected. For example, regarding alcoholism, Gordis (1996, p. 199) has listed some possibilities of what it is that is inherited: "differences in temperament, different initial sensitivity to the rewarding or aversive qualities of . . . [the substance], different rates and routes of [drug] metabolism, different taste preferences, different signaling from peripheral sites to the brain after . . . [consuming the substance] and different abilities to relate memories of . . . [drug] experiences to their consequences." Linking underlying genetic and nongenetic factors to underlying mechanisms remains one of the highest priorities of etiological research in this area.

## Biochemistry and Neuropharmacology

The neuropharmacology of drug effects represents key mechanisms for understanding both etiology and rational pharmacological treatment. The neuropharmacological systems most implicated in SUD etiology and maintenance involve the dopamine (DA), serotonin (5-HT), GABA, glutamate, endogenous opioid, and cannabinoid and nicotine systems. While these systems are responsible for a variety of different functions including (but not limited to) motivation, reward, reward prediction, energy, mood, sleep, and pain, they are of particular relevance to SU due to being the systems affected by commonly misused psychoactive drugs. Although discussed separately in what follows, these systems are intricately intertwined, continually acting and interacting with each other in facilitating and inhibitory fashions.

### THE DOPAMINERGIC SYSTEM

DA has a wide variety of physiological and psychological functions including reward, emotion, cognition, memory, and motor activity. Regarding SU, the importance of the DA system primarily stems from its association with motivation and activation of reward, but the system's function is much broader. The system is thought to signal the incentive salience of stimuli, be they rewarding, aversive, novel, or unexpected (Goodman, 2008; Pruessner et al., 2010).

DA has been hypothesized to be a critical neurotransmitter associated with addiction as virtually all drugs of abuse have been found to increase DA transmission in the limbic regions of the brain (Pierce & Kumaresan, 2006). A mainstream position holds that the dopaminergic projections from the ventral tegmental area (VTA) and the nucleus accumbens (NAc) are required for most drugs to be reinforcing. For example, the rate of self-stimulation depends on the density of DA neurons (Jacobs et al., 2012). Studies of knockout mice in which genes expressing DA receptors have been disrupted have found reductions in the rewarding properties of ethanol and morphine (Sibley et al., 2017). Furthermore, prolonged elevation of mesolimbic DA results in sensitization to a given drug, meaning that the drug will produce an enhanced DA response in the future. This sensitization of the motivational salience of a drug has been hypothesized to be a major contributing factor in addiction, specifically the presence of a persistent motivational "wanting" even in absence of the "liking" typically associated with the DA system (Robinson et al., 2018).

Although all classes of substances appear to affect the dopaminergic system, each of them appears to do so through distinct biochemical mechanisms (Badiani et al., 2018). Recent research has found significantly less overlap in neuronal activations produced by separate injections of cocaine and heroin than two equally spaced injections of cocaine, indicating that the two drugs were activating different neuronal populations (Vassilev et al., 2020) As such, it is important not to assume that all drugs that act on a given neurotransmitter system work in the same way or that each "addicted brain" will have similar neuroadaptations. There is also research suggesting that not all classes of substances depend on the DA system to induce a reinforcing effect. Animal studies have shown that disrupting the NAc minimally affects seeking and/or consuming morphine (Sellings & Clarke, 2003), or heroin unless the animal has a preexisting heroin addiction (Nader et al., 1994).

In a process called *sensitization*, wherein the response to a stimulus is enhanced following repeated exposure to it, one drug may make another similar drug more reinforcing, a phenomenon termed *cross-sensitization* (Robinson et al., 2018). This also helps explain the high co-occurrence between certain forms of drug use as well as between SUDs and externalizing traits and disorders. For example, nearly half of individuals with an AUD have also had a lifetime SUD, and up to 30% of cigarette smokers met criteria for *DSM-IV* alcohol dependence (Castillo-Carniglia et al., 2019). Likewise, research has found a history of AUD in 77% of individuals diagnosed with antisocial personality disorder (Castillo-Carniglia et al., 2019).

## THE GABA AND GLUTAMATE SYSTEMS

GABA is the key inhibitory neurotransmitter in the CNS and the GABAergic neurons distributed throughout the brain (Ngo & Vo, 2019). Because of its high functional relevance, genes that play some role in modulating GABAergic signaling have become exceedingly popular in the study of addictions (Schuckit, 2018). Benzodiazepines, barbiturates, and alcohol are known to directly affect the GABAergic system (Costardi et al., 2015), with the extrasynaptic GABA-A receptors in the NAc being key neural substrates for the negatively reinforcing effects of alcohol (Cui et al., 2012).

Naturally occurring anxiolytic substances within the brain (Sangameswaran et al., 1986) and naturally occurring substances that heighten anxiety (Bodnoff et al., 1989) affect GABA transmission through their effects on structures of the anti-reward system like the amygdala (Savage et al., 2018). Thus, individuals affected by anxiety for whatever reason should find the use of alcohol, benzodiazepines, and barbiturates particularly reinforcing and such is seemingly the case; individuals who suffer from anxiety disorders and anxiety sensitivity show high comorbidity rates or risk for specific forms of SUDs. However, the GABA system is not wholly responsible for addiction to these substances, which may explain why pharmacological treatments for alcoholism that target GABA receptors have not received consistent support for their general effectiveness in treating withdrawal symptoms (Addolorato et al., 2012). One drug that has received considerable interest is acamprosate, which stimulates and attenuates the transmission of GABA and glutamate, respectively. Meta-analyses have found support for the efficacy of acamprosate (e.g., Cheng et al., 2020; Maisel et al., 2013), and current research focusing on precision medicine (finding which drug works best for which patients) is being conducted to identify specific indications for acamprosate and other AUD medications (Mann et al., 2018).

To explain withdrawal symptoms and drug-induced changes in brain functioning, researchers also have examined glutamate, a membrane protein that is an excitatory amino acid and a primary neurotransmitter dealing with excitatory neurotransmission. There are a number of glutamate receptors, and they are widespread throughout the CNS; one glutamate receptor that may have specific relevance to the effects of alcohol and other drugs is N-methyl-D-aspartate (NMDA). It appears that alcohol has three effects on glutamatergic transmission, which occur through the NMDA receptor: interfering with excitatory neurotransmission, promoting excitotoxicity, and impairing neurodevelopment (as in FASD). Chronic ingestion of alcohol by experimental animals results in an increase in NMDA receptors in both limbic and cortical brain areas. This effect is transient, and during withdrawal these receptors actually increase and glutamate functioning in general is accelerated (Chandler et al., 2006). To a certain degree this specific action of alcohol on the NMDA receptor explains both the symptoms of drug withdrawal and the development of brain damage, which is a common concomitant of heavy alcohol consumption.

## THE SEROTONERGIC SYSTEM

The neurotransmitter 5-HT is a critical regulator of human physiology and a wide spectrum of cognitive, affective, and sensory aspects of one's behavioral responses to environmental stimuli. With at least 16 receptor subtypes, this system also modulates circadian rhythms, food and water intake, sexual behavior, and response to pain (Sibley et al., 2017). Structural and/or functional aberrations in this system appear to generate disinhibited behaviors in addition to exaggerated sensitivity to stress as a result of perceived or actual threat, likely via disturbing one's learning of fear associations (Hartley et al., 2012). Indeed, disinhibition is a cardinal risk factor for many SUDs (Joyner et al., 2019), and a hypersensitivity to stress and threat is at the core of vulnerability for affective disorders.

Almost all commonly abused drugs acutely increase 5-HT activity throughout the brain. Following chronic SU, 5-HT tissue levels, basal extracellular activity, and the sensitivity of the serotonergic system is significantly altered. Given the role of 5-HT in sensory processing, learning, and memory, these acute increases and chronic alterations may be involved in the development of drug use behaviors and addiction (Müller & Homberg, 2015). While the serotonergic system also contributes to addiction indirectly through its influences on the DA and glutamatergic systems, there is evidence that the serotonergic system also makes distinct contributions to the development of drug intake behavior (Müller & Homberg, 2015).

Drugs of abuse also affect 5-HT systems in various ways. Some hallucinogens, lysergic acid diethylamide (LSD), dimethyltryptamine (DMT), psilocybin, and the phenethylamines (mescaline,

MDMA) have an affinity for 5-HT$_2$ receptors (Titeler et al., 1988), and blocking the latter abolishes the effects of these drugs. Conversely, acute use of cocaine blocks 5-HT reuptake in the short term, while chronic use likely attenuates serotonergic signaling. MDMA has been repeatedly shown to increase extracellular 5-HT activity in a large number of brain regions including the NAc, striatum, and VTA. Although drugs have considerably different effects on the serotonergic system, the general trend is an acute increase in 5-HT during drug use and an overall reduction in 5-HT after prolonged use (Müller & Homberg, 2015).

**ENDOGENOUS OPIOID SYSTEM**

The opioid system regulates the extracellular drug-induced DA release. For example, individuals addicted to cocaine show remarkable elevations in mu-opioid receptor availability, likely mirroring attenuated secretion of endogenous opioids (Goodman, 2008). The ingestion of opiate drugs results in direct stimulation of opioid receptors in the brain. The consumption of any other substance of abuse, palatable or sweet food, and engaging in gambling or sexual behavior are all correlated with the secretion of endogenous opioids (Emery & Akil, 2020). This system is widespread throughout the body, with at least three types of receptors and three groups of known transmitters. Opioid receptors in the NAc appear to affect this system through the neurotransmitter DA. Stimulation appears reinforcing, as animals will self-administer opioids.

The endogenous opioid system is involved in the rewarding properties of heroin and other commonly abused narcotics. Long-acting drugs aimed at occupying opioid receptors (e.g., methadone, buprenorphine) are effective in attenuating some aspects of craving. Drugs that block these receptors, such as naltrexone, naloxone (commonly known as Narcan), and nalmefene, diminish heroin-induced positive psychoactive effects in detoxed individuals and can be administered to rapidly reverse symptoms of heroin overdose (Robinson & Wermeling, 2014).

Naltrexone is a nonselective opiate antagonist that at least partially acts on the midbrain by inhibiting the mu-opioid receptors, thereby decreasing alcohol-induced DA secretion in the NAc (Goodman, 2008). Approved to treat alcoholism in 1995, the support for effectiveness of this drug has been mixed, with emerging evidence indicating sex differences in effectiveness (Canidate et al., 2017). Clinical studies have shown that naltrexone diminishes the high from alcohol and reduces craving (Boutrel, 2008). To the extent that this notion is correct, it is reasonable to conclude that naltrexone should (assuming compliance) be selectively therapeutic with this particular at-risk population.

**CANNABINOID AND NICOTINE SYSTEMS**

Cannabinoid receptors are distributed throughout the brain but are particularly prominent in the cerebellum, prefrontal cortex, hippocampus, and basal ganglia (Glass et al., 1997). Endocannabinoids are involved in a negative feedback loop in which they bind to presynaptic neurons and dampen their activity. Because they exist throughout the brain, the specific function of a given signal is highly dependent on which neural circuits are involved. Research has indicated that cannabinoids have pleiotropic signaling functions that can help restore homeostasis after neurological disruption; this has raised considerable interest in the development of therapeutic interventions based on the endocannabinoid system (Cristino et al., 2020). There is also evidence that the endocannabinoid system is involved in the rewarding effects of many commonly abused substances, and it has been implicated in the process of addiction (Maldonado et al., 2006). Rats exposed to THC in early life have blunted dopaminergic responses to naturally rewarding stimuli later in life (Bloomfield et al., 2016).

Nicotine has been, and still is, commonly thought to be the psychoactive substance that renders cigarettes addictive (Prochaska & Benowitz, 2019). Sorge and Clarke (2011) and others have suggested that rats, if left in full control, self-administer doses of nicotine that are much lower than expected and do so at a slower rate. Along with other ingredients, nonchemical factors (e.g., sensory effects, habit, social aspects) have been found to significantly contribute to cigarette addiction (Rose, 2006). Furthermore, there is a growing body of evidence that the cognitive enhancement (improved attention, focus, working memory) produced by nicotine may also significantly contribute to tobacco use, especially in individuals with cognitive deficits (Valentine & Sofuoglu, 2018).

The effects of nicotine can be complex and unpredictable due to the combination of neural stimulation and desensitization that nicotine can produce (Hibbs & Zambon, 2017). The mesolimbic reward system is activated, and the DA, endogenous opioid, and glucocorticoid systems are affected, among others. These reinforcing effects produced by nicotine are strong enough to support reward-based conditioning (Winters et al., 2012), and tolerance and withdrawal develop.

Nicotine is highly addictive, with more than 90% of smokers making attempts to quit; while about half do eventually achieve abstinence, less than 4% of yearly quit attempts are sustained long term (Prochaska & Benowitz, 2019). This observation, however, should not be construed as suggesting that inhaled nicotine products instigate greater levels of physiological dependence than do other substances of abuse. There appears to be a variety of risk factors that predispose smokers to becoming addicted, including age of first cigarette, other SU, other psychiatric disorders, and genetic vulnerability. Additionally, in recent decades social constraints have reduced the prevalence of smoking and have led to a shift from dependence to intermittent use among those who do smoke (American Lung Association, 2020, https://www.lung.org/research/trends-in-lung-disease/tobacco-trends-brief/overall-tobacco-trends). Such intermittent smokers may still exhibit significant dependence symptomatology, especially if they were once daily smokers (Shiffman et al., 2012).

## Conclusion

*DSM-5* diagnoses were designed to maximize diagnostic agreement, and they rely on behavioral definitions, greatly reducing their explanatory relevance with respect to understanding the nature of the underlying condition. As discussed in this chapter, understanding SUDs requires a multidisciplinary perspective that spans multiple levels of analysis; from the cultural to psychological to genetic to neuropharmacological. Marrying the multiple levels of analysis to produce a cohesive and coherent conceptual framework is clearly a major challenge, but one worth taking on.

In recent years, the value of adopting a more etiological, mechanistic framework for psychopathology has been embraced by initiatives like the Research Domains Criteria (RDoC; Insel et al., 2010). Although RDoC was not initially oriented to SU and SUDs, efforts have recently been launched to fill this hole. These include the Alcohol Addiction RDoC (AARDoC; Litten et al., 2015), the related Addiction Neuroclinical Assessment (ANA; Kwako et al., 2016), and the NIDA Phenotyping Assessment Battery (PhAB; e.g, Keyser-Marcus et al., 2021).

Related to these efforts is the Etiologic, Theory-Based, Ontogenetic Hierarchical (ETOH) Framework of AUD (Boness et al., in 2021). As illustrated in Figure 13.1, this framework was derived from Boness et al.'s "systematic review of reviews" of models of addiction. Borrowing from RDoC and HiTOP, the ETOH framework is structured around higher-order superdomains (reward, cognitive control, negative emotionality), which in turn encompass narrower domains and subdomains and would appear to provide a more comprehensive set of constructs than ANA/AARDoC, PhAB, RDoC, and HiTOP (see table 3 in Boness et al., 2021).

Note that the superdomains and subdomains are all somewhat transdiagnostic in the sense that these same constructs are relevant to other forms of psychopathology (and, by extension, comorbidity of other forms of psychopathology with SUDs). However, the manifestation of certain subdomains or components is likely to be highly specific to a given substance (e.g., specific positive and negative expectancies, incentive salience, and habit). In addition, some components such as trait negative and positive emotionality are viewed as premorbid characteristics, whereas other components (e.g., incentive salience, withdrawal) are viewed as consequential, and still others are a mix of both. The value in this and other similar frameworks is that they provide a conceptual structure for seemingly disparate concepts and hold the potential for developing personalized interventions targeting those components likely to be important in a given person.

While such frameworks would appear to hold great promise for both guiding basic and applied research on SUDs and for developing personalized interventions, their clinical utility has yet to be adequately tested. This is not a trivial issue as the challenges of validly assessing these constructs in a way that does justice to them and is psychometrically sound, coupled with pragmatic concerns about their norming and interpretation, are considerable. Additionally, as alluded to earlier, such implicitly endophenotypic approaches need to be carefully considered in the context of cultural and societal differences regarding how substances are controlled (both formally and informally) and viewed more generally. The integration of these endophenotypic perspectives with environment, broadly conceived, represents an important priority for future research.

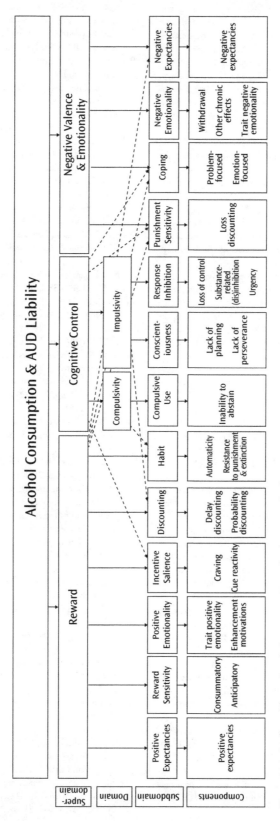

**Figure 13.1** Etiologic, Theory-Based, Ontogenetic Hierarchical Framework of AUD

# References

Addolorato, G., Leggio, L., Hopf, F. W., Diana, M., & Bonci, A. (2012). Novel therapeutic strategies for alcohol and drug addiction: Focus on GABA, ion channels and transcranial magnetic stimulation. *Neuropsychopharmacology, 37*(1), 163–177. https://doi.org/10.1038/npp.2011.216

Alati, R., Al Mamun, A., Williams, G. M., O'Callaghan, M., Najman, J. M., & Bor, W. (2006). In utero alcohol exposure and prediction of alcohol disorders in early adulthood: A birth cohort study. *Archives of General Psychiatry, 63*(9), 1009–1016. https://doi:10.1001/archpsyc.63.9.1009

Albers, A. B., DeJong, W., Naimi, T. S., Siegel, M., Shoaff, J. R., & Jernigan, D. H. (2013). Minimum financial outlays for purchasing alcohol brands in the U. S. *American Journal of Preventive Medicine, 44*(1), 67–70. https://doi.org/10.1016/j.amepre.2012.08.026

Allara, E., Ferri, M., Bo, A., Gasparrini, A., & Faggiano, F. (2015). Are mass-media campaigns effective in preventing drug use? A Cochrane systematic review and meta-analysis. *BMJ Open, 5*(9), e007449. http://dx.doi.org/10.1136/bmjopen-2014-007449

American Lung Association (2020). Overall tobacco trends. https://www.lung.org/research/trends-in-lung-disease/tobacco-trends-brief/overall-tobacco-trends

American Pain Society. (1999). *Principles of analgesic use in the treatment of acute pain and cancer pain.* American Pain Society.

Badiani, A., Berridge, K. C., Heilig, M., Nutt, D. J., & Robinson, T. E. (2018). Addiction research and theory: A commentary on the Surgeon General's Report on alcohol, drugs, and health. *Addiction Biology, 23*(1), 3–5. https://doi.org/10.1111/adb.12497

Bahji, A., Mazhar, M. N., Hudson, C. C., Nadkarni, P., MacNeil, B. A., & Hawken, E. (2019). Prevalence of substance use disorder comorbidity among individuals with eating disorders: A systematic review and meta-analysis. *Psychiatry Research, 273,* 58–66. https://doi.org/10.1016/j.psychres.2019.01.007

Bailey, A. J., Gerst, K., & Finn, P. R. (2018). Delay discounting of losses and rewards in alcohol use disorder: The effect of working memory load. *Psychology of Addictive Behaviors, 32*(2), 197–204. https://doi.org/10.1037/adb0000341

Bailey, A. J., Gerst, K., & Finn, P. R. (2020). Intelligence moderates the relationship between delay discounting rate and problematic alcohol use. *Psychology of Addictive Behaviors, 34*(1), 175–181. https://doi.org/10.1037/adb0000471

Baker, J. H., Maes, H. H., Larsson, H., Lichtenstein, P., & Kendler, K. S. (2011). Sex differences and developmental stability in genetic and environmental influences on psychoactive substance consumption from early adolescence to young adulthood. *Psychological Medicine, 41*(9), 1907–1916. https://doi.org/10.1017/S003329171000259X

Ballard, M. S., Sun, M., & Ko, J. (2012). Vitamin A, folate, and choline as a possible preventive intervention to fetal alcohol syndrome. *Medical Hypotheses, 78*(4), 489–493. https://doi.org/10.1016/j.mehy.2012.01.014

Barnes, G. E. (1979). The alcoholic personality. A reanalysis of the literature. *Journal of Studies on Alcohol, 40*(7), 571–634. https://www.jsad.com/doi/pdf/10.15288/jsa.1979.40.571

Barnes, G. E. (1983). Clinical and prealcoholic personality characteristics. In B. Kissin & H. Begleiter (Eds.), *The biology of alcoholism* (pp. 113–195). Springer. https://doi.org/10.1007/978-1-4684-4274-8_4

Barrett, S. P., Boileau, I., Okker, J., Pihl, R. O., & Dagher, A. (2004). The hedonic response to cigarette smoking is proportional to dopamine release in the human striatum as measured by positron emission tomography and [11C] raclopride. *Synapse, 54*(2), 65–71. https://doi.org/10.1002/syn.20066

Bartholow, B. D., Sher, K. J., & Krull, J. L. (2003). Changes in heavy drinking over the third decade of life as a function of collegiate fraternity and sorority involvement: A prospective, multilevel analysis. *Health Psychology, 22*(6), 616–626. https://doi.org/10.1037/0278-6133.22.6.616

Bean, W. B. (1951). *Osler aphorisms.* Thomas.

Behnke, M., Smith, V. C., Levy, S., Ammerman, S. D., Gonzalez, P. K., Ryan, S. A., Smith, V. C., Wunsch, M. J., Papile, L., Baley, J. E., Carlo, W. A., Cummings, J. J., Kumar, P., Polin, R. A., Tan, R. C., & Watterberg, K. L. (2013). Prenatal substance abuse: Short- and long-term effects on the exposed fetus. *Pediatrics, 131*(3), e1009–e1024. https://doi.org/10.1542/peds.2012-3931

Bello, E. P., Mateo, Y., Gelman, D. M., Noain, D., Shin, J. H., Low, M. J., Alvarez, V. A., Lovinger, D. M., & Rubinstein, M. (2011). Cocaine supersensitivity and enhanced motivation for reward in mice lacking dopamine D2 autoreceptors. *Nature Neuroscience, 14*(8), 1033–1038. https://doi.org/10.1038/nn.2862

Benningfield, M. M., & Cowan, R. L. (2013). Brain serotonin function in MDMA (ecstasy) users: Evidence for persisting neurotoxicity. *Neuropsychopharmacology, 38*(1), 253–255. doi:10.1038/npp.2012.178

Berdzuli, N., Ferreira-Borges, C., Gual, A., & Rehm, J. (2020). Alcohol control policy in Europe: Overview and exemplary countries. *International Journal of Environmental Research and Public Health, 17*(21), 8162. https://doi.org/10.3390/ijerph17218162

Bickel, W. K., Crabbe, J. C., & Sher, K. J. (2019). What is addiction? How can animal and human research be used to advance research, diagnosis, and treatment of alcohol and other substance use disorders? *Alcoholism: Clinical and Experimental Research, 43*(1), 6–21. https://doi.org/10.1111/acer.13912

Bickel, W. K., Koffarnus, M. N., Moody, L., & Wilson, A. G. (2014). The behavioral- and neuro-economic process of temporal discounting: A candidate behavioral marker of addiction. *Neuropharmacology, 76,* 518–527. https://doi.org/10.1016/j.neuropharm.2013.06.013

Bickel, W. K., Johnson, M. W., Koffarnus, M. N., MacKillop, J., & Murphy, J. G. (2014). The behavioral economics of substance use disorders: Reinforcement pathologies and their repair. *Annual Review of Clinical Psychology, 10,* 641–677. https://doi.org/10.1146/annurev-clinpsy-032813-153724

Bienvenu, O. J., Davydow, D. S., & Kendler, K. S. (2011). Psychiatric "diseases" versus behavioral disorders and degree of genetic influence. *Psychological Medicine, 41*(1), 33–40. https://doi.org/10.1017/S003329171000084X

Bingel, U., Colloca, L., & Vase, L. (2011). Mechanisms and clinical implications of the placebo effect: Is there a potential for the elderly? A mini-review. *Gerontology, 57*(4), 354–363. https://doi.org/10.1159/000322090

Blanco, C., Okuda, M., Wright, C., Hasin, D. S., Grant, B. F., Liu, S. M., & Olfson, M. (2008). Mental health of college students and their non-college-attending peers: Results from the National Epidemiologic Study on alcohol and related conditions. *Archives of General Psychiatry, 65*(12), 1429–1437. doi:10.1001/archpsyc.65.12.1429

Bloomfield, M. A., Ashok, A. H., Volkow, N. D., & Howes, O. D. (2016). The effects of Δ 9-tetrahydrocannabinol on the dopamine system. *Nature*, *539*(7629), 369–377. https://doi.org/10.1038/nature20153

Bodnoff, S. R., Suranyi--Cadotte, B. E., Quirion, R., & Meaney, M. J. (1989). Role of the central benzodiazepine receptor system in behavioral habituation to novelty. *Behavioral Neuroscience*, *103*(1), 209–212. https://doi.org/10.1037/0735-7044.103.1.209

Boness, C. L., Watts, A. L., Moeller, K. N., & Sher, K. J. (2021). The etiologic, theory-based, ontogenetic hierarchical framework of alcohol use disorder: A translational systematic review of reviews. *Psychological Bulletin*, *147*, 1075–1123. https://doi.org/10.1037/bul0000333

Boutrel, B. (2008). A neuropeptide-centric view of psychostimulant addiction. *British Journal of Pharmacology*, *154*(2), 343–357. https://doi.org/10.1038/bjp.2008.133

Brooks-Russell, A., Simons–Morton, B., Haynie, D., Farhat, T., & Wang, J. (2014). Longitudinal relationship between drinking with peers, descriptive norms, and adolescent alcohol use. *Prevention Science*, *15*(4), 497.505. DOI 10.1007/s11121-013-0391-9

Buckholtz, J. W., Treadway, M. T., Cowan, R. L., Woodward, N. D., Li, R., Ansari, M. S., Baldwin, R. M., Schwartzman, A. N., Shelby, E. S., Smith, C. E., Kessler, R. M., & Zald, D. H. (2010). Dopaminergic network differences in human impulsivity. *Science*, *329*(5991), 532–532. doi:10.1126/science.1185778

Cambron, C., Kosterman, R., Rhew, I. C., Catalano, R. F., Guttmannova, K., & Hawkins, J. D. (2017). An examination of alcohol use disorder symptoms and neighborhood disorganization from age 21 to 39. *American Journal of Community Psychology*, *60*(1-2), 267–278. https://doi.org/10.1002/ajcp.12160

Canidate, S. S., Carnaby, G. D., Cook, C. L., & Cook, R. L. (2017). A systematic review of naltrexone for attenuating alcohol consumption in women with alcohol use disorders. *Alcoholism: Clinical and Experimental Research*, *41*(3), 466–472. https://doi.org/10.1111/acer.13313

Caspi, A., Houts, R. M., Belsky, D. W., Goldman-Mellor, S. J., Harrington, H., Israel, S., Meier, J. H., Ramrakha, S., Shalev, I., Poulton, R., & Moffitt, T. E. (2014). The p factor: One general psychopathology factor in the structure of psychiatric disorders? *Clinical Psychological Science*, *2*(2), 119–137. https://doi.org/10.1177/2167702613497473

Castellanos-Ryan, N., O'Leary-Barrett, M., & Conrod, P. J. (2013). Substance-use in childhood and adolescence: A brief overview of developmental processes and their clinical implications. *Journal of the Canadian Academy of Child and Adolescent Psychiatry*, *22*(1), 41–46. PMID: 23390432

Castellanos-Ryan, N., Pingault, J., Parent, S., Vitaro, F., Tremblay, R., & Séguin, J. (2017). Adolescent cannabis use, change in neurocognitive function, and high-school graduation: A longitudinal study from early adolescence to young adulthood. *Development and Psychopathology*, *29*(4), 1253–1266. doi:10.1017/S0954579416001280

Castillo-Carniglia, A., Keyes, K. M., Hasin, D. S., & Cerdá, M. (2019). Psychiatric comorbidities in alcohol use disorder. *Lancet Psychiatry*, *6*(12), 1068–1080. https://doi.org/10.1016/S2215-0366(19)30222-6

Chandler, L. J., Carpenter–Hyland, E., Hendricson, A. W., Maldve, R. E., Morrisett, R. A., Zhou, F. C., Sari, U., Belle, R., & Szumlinski, K. K. (2006). Structural and functional modifications in glutamateric synapses following prolonged ethanol exposure. *Alcoholism: Clinical and Experimental Research*, *30*(2), 368–376. https://doi.org/10.1111/j.1530-0277.2006.00041.x

Chang, L., Rapoport, S. I., Nguyen, H. N., Greenstein, D., Chen, M., & Basselin, M. (2009). Acute nicotine reduces brain arachidonic acid signaling in unanesthetized rats. *Journal of Cerebral Blood Flow & Metabolism*, *29*(3), 648–658. https://doi.org/10.1038/jcbfm.2008.159

Chen, L. S., Johnson, E. O., Breslau, N., Hatsukami, D., Saccone, N. L., Grucza, R. A., Wang, J. C., Hinrichs, A. L., Fox, L., Goate, A. M., Rice, J. P., & Bierut, L. J. (2009). Interplay of genetic risk factors and parent monitoring in risk for nicotine dependence. *Addiction*, *104*(10), 1731–1740. https://doi.org/10.1111/j.1360-0443.2009.02697.x

Cheng, H. Y., McGuinness, L. A., Elbers, R. G., MacArthur, G. J., Taylor, A., McAleenan, A., Dawson, S., López-López, J. A., Higgins, J. P. T., Cowlishaw, S., Lingford-Hughes, A., Hickman, M., & Kessler, D. (2020). Treatment interventions to maintain abstinence from alcohol in primary care: Systematic review and network meta-analysis. *British Medical Journal (Online)*, *371*. https://doi.org/10.1136/bmj.m3934

Cicchetti, D., & Rogosch, F. A. (1996). Equifinality and multifinality in developmental psychopathology. *Development and Psychopathology*, *8*(4), 597–600. doi:10.1017/S0954579400007318

Cleckley, H. (1955). *The mask of sanity*, 3rd ed. Mosby.

Cohen, S. G., & Saavedra-Delgado, A. M. (1989, November). Through the centuries with food and drink, for better or worse III. *Allergy and Asthma Proceedings*, *10* (6), 429.

Cooper, M. L., Kuntsche, E., Levitt, A., Barber, L. L., & Wolf, S. (2016). Motivational models of substance use: A review of theory and research on motives for using alcohol, marijuana, and tobacco. In K. J. Sher (Ed.), *Oxford handbook of substance use disorders* (pp. 375–421). Oxford University Press.

Copaceanu, M., & Balxaceanu-Stolnici, C. (2018). A theoretical transdisciplinary approach to drug use: History, anthropology and culture. *Transdisciplinary Journal of Engineering & Science*, *9*, 3–11. https://doi.org/10.22545/2018/00097

Costardi, J. V. V., Nampo, R. A. T., Silva, G. L., Ribeiro, M. A. F., Stella, H. J., Stella, M. B., & Malheiros, S. V. P. (2015). A review on alcohol: From the central action mechanism to chemical dependency. *Revista da Associação Médica Brasileira*, *61*, 381–387. https://doi.org/10.1590/1806-9282.61.04.381

Cristino, L., Bisogno, T., & Di Marzo, V. (2020). Cannabinoids and the expanded endocannabinoid system in neurological disorders. *Nature Reviews Neurology*, *16*(1), 9–29. https://doi.org/10.1038/s41582-019-0284-z

Crocq, M. A. (2007). Historical and cultural aspects of man's relationship with addictive drugs. *Dialogues in Clinical Neuroscience*, *9*(4), 355–361. doi:10.31887/DCNS.2007.9.4/macrocq

Crowe, L. C., & George, W. H. (1989). Alcohol and human sexuality: Review and integration. *Psychological Bulletin*, *105*(3), 374–386. https://doi.org/10.1037/0033-2909.105.3.374

Cui, Y., Xu, J., Dai, R., & He, L. (2012). The interface between inhibition of descending noradrenergic pain control pathways and negative affects in post-traumatic pain patients. *Upsala Journal of Medical Sciences*, *117*(3), 293–299. https://doi.org/10.3109/03009734.2011.653606

Dager, A. D., Anderson, B. M., Stevens, M. C., Pulido, C., Rosen, R., Jiantonio-Kelly, R. E., Sisante, J., Raskin, S. A., Tennen, H., Austad, C. S., Wood, R. M., Fallahi, C. R., & Pearlson, G. D. (2013). Influence of alcohol use and family history of alcoholism on neural response to alcohol cues in college drinkers. *Alcoholism: Clinical and Experimental Research*, *37*(s1), E161–E171. https://doi.org/10.1111/j.1530-0277.2012.01879.x

Davidson, J., Swartz, M., Storck, M., Krishnan, R. R., & Hammett, E. (1985). A diagnostic and family study of posttraumatic stress disorder. *American Journal of Psychiatry*, *142*(1), 90–93. https://doi.org/10.1176/ajp.142.1.90

Day, N. L., Helsel, A., Sonon, K., & Goldschmidt, L. (2013). The association between prenatal alcohol exposure and behavior at 22 years of age. *Alcoholism: Clinical and Experimental Research*, *37*(7), 1171–1178. https://doi.org/10.1111/acer.12073

De Rios, M. D., & Smith, D. E. (1977). Drug use and abuse in cross cultural perspective. *Human Organization*, 14–21. https://www.jstor.org/stable/44125236

Dick, D. M. (2011). Gene-environment interaction in psychological traits and disorders. *Annual Review of Clinical Psychology*, *7*, 383–409. doi:10.1146/annurev-clinpsy-032210-104518

Dick, D. M., & Kendler, K. S. (2012). The impact of gene-environment interaction on alcohol use disorders. *Alcohol Research: Current Reviews*, *34*(3), 318–324. PMID: 23134047

Dick, D. M., Riley, B., & Kendler, K. S. (2010). Nature and nurture in neuropsychiatric genetics: Where do we stand? *Dialogues in Clinical Neuroscience*, *12*(1), 7–23. doi:10.31887/DCNS.2010.12.1/ddick

Domino, E. F., Evans, C. L., Ni, L., Guthrie, S. K., Koeppe, R. A., & Zubieta, J. K. (2012). Tobacco smoking produces greater striatal dopamine release in G-allele carriers with mu opioid receptor A118G polymorphism. *Progress in Neuro-Psychopharmacology and Biological Psychiatry*, *38*(2), 236–240. https://doi.org/10.1016/j.pnpbp.2012.04.003

Droungas, A., Ehrman, R. N., Childress, A. R., & O'Brien, C. P. (1995). Effect of smoking cues and cigarette availability on craving and smoking behavior. *Addictive Behaviors*, *20*(5), 657–673. https://doi.org/10.1016/0306-4603(95)00029-C

Dudley, R. (2000). Evolutionary origins of human alcoholism in primate frugivory. *Quarterly Review of Biology*, *75*(1), 3–15. https://doi.org/10.1086/393255

Dudley, R. (2004). Ethanol, fruit ripening, and the historical origins of human alcoholism in primate frugivory. *Integrative and Comparative Biology*, *44*(4), 315–323. https://doi.org/10.1093/icb/44.4.315

Duncan, L. E., Ostacher, M., & Ballon, J. (2019). How genome-wide association studies (GWAS) made traditional candidate gene studies obsolete. *Neuropsychopharmacology*, *44*(9), 1518–1523. https://doi.org/10.1038/s41386-019-0389-5

Duncan, L., Shen, H., Gelaye, B., Meijsen, J., Ressler, K., Feldman, M., & Domingue, B. (2019). Analysis of polygenic risk score usage and performance in diverse human populations. *Nature Communications*, *10*(1), 1–9. https://doi.org/10.1038/s41467-019-11112-0

Durrant, R., & Thakker, J. (2003). *Substance use and abuse: Cultural and historical perspectives*. Sage.

Edenberg, H. J., & McClintick, J. N. (2018). Alcohol dehydrogenases, aldehyde dehydrogenases, and alcohol use disorders: A critical review. *Alcoholism: Clinical and Experimental Research*, *42*(12), 2281–2297. https://doi.org/10.1111/acer.13904

Emery, M. A., & Akil, H. (2020). Endogenous opioids at the intersection of opioid addiction, pain, and depression: The search for a precision medicine approach. *Annual Review of Neuroscience*, *43*, 355–374. https://doi.org/10.1146/annurev-neuro-110719-095912

Escohotado, A. (1999). *A brief history of drugs: From the stone age to the stoned age*. Simon and Schuster.

Euser, A. S., Arends, L. R., Evans, B. E., Greaves-Lord, K., Huizink, A. C., & Franken, I. H. (2012). The P300 event-related brain potential as a neurobiological endophenotype for substance use disorders: A meta-analytic investigation. *Neuroscience & Biobehavioral Reviews*, *36*(1), 572–603. https://doi.org/10.1016/j.neubiorev.2011.09.002

Everitt, B. J., & Robbins, T. W. (2016). Drug addiction: Updating actions to habits to compulsions ten years on. *Annual Review of Psychology*, *67*, 23–50. https://doi.org/10.1146/annurev-psych-122414-033457

Fairbairn, C. E., & Sayette, M. A. (2013). The effect of alcohol on emotional inertia: A test of alcohol myopia. *Journal of Abnormal Psychology*, *122*(3), 770–781. https://doi.org/10.1037/a0032980

Fairchild, G., Hawes, D. J., Frick, P. J., Copeland, W. E., Odgers, C. L., Franke, B., Freitag, C. M., & De Brito, S. A. (2019). Conduct disorder. *Nature Reviews Disease Primers*, *5*(1), 1–25. https://doi.org/10.1038/s41572-019-0095-y

Fernandez-Serrano, M. J., Pérez-García, M., Schmidt Río-Valle, J., & Verdejo-Garcia, A. (2010). Neuropsychological consequences of alcohol and drug abuse on different components of executive functions. *Journal of Psychopharmacology*, *24*(9), 1317–1332. https://doi.org/10.1177/0269881109349841

Fleeson, W. (2001). Toward a structure-and process-integrated view of personality: Traits as density distributions of states. *Journal of Personality and Social Psychology*, *80*(6), 1011–1027. https://doi.org/10.1037/0022-3514.80.6.1011

Fossey, M. D., Otto, M. W., Yates, W. R., Wisniewski, S. R., Gyulai, L., Allen, M. H., Miklowitz, D. J., Coon, K. A., Ostacher, M. J., Neel, J. L., Thase, M. E., Sachs, G. S., & Weiss, R. D. (2006). Validity of the distinction between primary and secondary substance use disorder in patients with bipolar disorder: Data from the first 1000 STEP-BD participants. *American Journal on Addictions*, *15*(2), 138–143. doi:10.1080/10550490500528423

Foxcroft, D. R., & Tsertsvadze, A. (2012). Universal alcohol misuse prevention programmes for children and adolescents: Cochrane systematic reviews. *Perspectives in Public Health*, *132*(3), 128–134. https://doi.org/10.1177/1757913912443487

Frank, S. J., Jacobson, S., & Tuer, M. (1990). Psychological predictors of young adults' drinking behaviors. *Journal of Personality and Social Psychology*, *59*(4), 770–780. https://doi.org/10.1037/0022-3514.59.4.770

Friedman, N. P., & Miyake, A. (2017). Unity and diversity of executive functions: Individual differences as a window on cognitive structure. *Cortex*, *86*, 186–204. https://doi.org/10.1016/j.cortex.2016.04.023

Friedel, E., Kaminski, J., & Ripke, S. (2021). Heritability of alcohol use disorder: Evidence from twin studies and genome-wide association studies. In N. el-Guebaly, G. Carra, M. Galanter, & A. M. Baldacchino (Eds.), *Textbook of addiction treatment* (pp. 21–33). Springer. https://doi.org/10.1007/978-3-030-36391-8_3

Gabbay, F. H. (2005). Family history of alcoholism and response to amphetamine: Sex differences in the effect of risk. *Alcoholism:*

Clinical and Experimental Research, 29(5), 773–780. https://doi.org/10.1097/01.ALC.0000164380.16043.4F

Giancola, P. R. (2004). Executive functioning and alcohol-related aggression. Journal of Abnormal Psychology, 113(4), 541–555. https://doi.org/10.1037/0021-843X.113.4.541

Génin, E. (2020). Missing heritability of complex diseases: Case solved? Human Genetics, 139(1), 103–113. https://doi.org/10.1007/s00439-019-02034-4

Glass, M., Faull, R. L. M., & Dragunow, M. (1997). Cannabinoid receptors in the human brain: A detailed anatomical and quantitative autoradiographic study in the fetal, neonatal and adult human brain. Neuroscience, 77(2), 299–318. https://doi.org/10.1016/S0306-4522(96)00428-9

Gelernter, J., & Polimanti, R. (2021). Genetics of substance use disorders in the era of big data. Nature Reviews Genetics, 22(11), 712–729. https://doi.org/10.1038/s41576-021-00377-1

Gelernter, J., Sherva, R., Koesterer, R., Almasy, L., Zhao, H., Kranzler, H. R., & Farrer, L. (2014). Genome-wide association study of cocaine dependence and related traits: FAM53B identified as a risk gene. Molecular Psychiatry, 19(6), 717–723. https://doi.org/10.1038/mp.2013.99

Glantz, M. D., & Leshner, A. I. (2000). Drug abuse and developmental psychopathology. Development and Psychopathology, 12(4), 795–814. https://doi.org/10.1017/S0954579400004120

Golub, A., Johnson, B. D., & Dunlap, E. (2005). Subcultural evolution and illicit drug use. Addiction Research & Theory, 13(3), 217–229. https://doi.org/10.1080/16066350500053497

Goodman, A. (2008). Neurobiology of addiction. An integrative review. Biochemical Pharmacology, 75(1), 266–322. https://doi.org/10.1016/j.bcp.2007.07.030

Gordis, E. (1996). Alcohol research: At the cutting edge. Archives of General Psychiatry, 53(3), 199–201. doi:10.1001/archpsyc.1996.01830030017004

Grant, D. M., Beck, J. G., & Davila, J. (2007). Does anxiety sensitivity predict symptoms of panic, depression, and social anxiety? Behavior Research and Therapy, 45(9), 2247–2255. https://doi.org/10.1016/j.brat.2007.02.008

Grant, J. D., Heath, A. C., Bucholz, K. K., Madden, P. A., Agrawal, A., Statham, D. J., & Martin, N. G. (2007). Spousal concordance for alcohol dependence: Evidence for assortative mating or spousal interaction effects? Alcoholism: Clinical and Experimental Research, 31(5), 717–728. https://doi.org/10.1111/j.1530-0277.2007.00356.x

Greeley, J., & Oei, T. (1999). Alcohol and tension reduction. In K. E. Leonard & H. T. Blane (Eds.), Psychological theories of drinking and alcoholism (pp. 14–53). Guilford.

Grucza, R. A., Sher, K. J., Kerr, W. C., Krauss, M. J., Lui, C. K., McDowell, Y. E., Hartz, S., Virdi, G., & Bierut, L. J. (2018). Trends in adult alcohol use and binge drinking in the early 21st-century United States: A meta-analysis of 6 National Survey Series. Alcoholism: Clinical and Experimental Research, 42(10), 1939–1950. https://doi.org/10.1111/acer.13859

Gustavson, D. E., Stallings, M. C., Corley, R. P., Miyake, A., Hewitt, J. K., & Friedman, N. P. (2017). Executive functions and substance use: Relations in late adolescence and early adulthood. Journal of Abnormal Psychology, 126(2), 257–270. https://doi.org/10.1037/abn0000250

Hamilton, K. R., Littlefield, A. K., Anastasio, N. C., Cunningham, K. A., Fink, L. H., Wing, V. C., . . . Potenza, M. N. (2015). Rapid-response impulsivity: Definitions, measurement issues, and clinical implications. Personality Disorders: Theory, Research, and Treatment, 6(2), 168–181. https://doi.org/10.1037/per0000100

Hamilton, K. R., Mitchell, M. R., Wing, V. C., Balodis, I. M., Bickel, W. K., Fillmore, M., . . . Moeller, F. G. (2015). Choice impulsivity: Definitions, measurement issues, and clinical implications. Personality Disorders: Theory, Research, and Treatment, 6(2), 182–198. https://doi.org/10.1037/per0000099

Hart, C. (2021). Drug use for grown-ups: Chasing liberty in the land of fear. Penguin Press.

Hartka, E., Johnstone, B., Leino, E. V., Motoyoshi, M., Temple, M. T., & Fillmore, K. M. (1991). A meta-analysis of depressive symptomatology and alcohol consumption over time. British Journal of Addiction, 86(10), 1283–1298. https://doi.org/10.1111/j.1360-0443.1991.tb01704.x

Hartley, C. A., McKenna, M. C., Salman, R., Holmes, A., Casey, B. J., Phelps, E. A., & Glatt, C. E. (2012). Serotonin transporter polyadenylation polymorphism modulates the retention of fear extinction memory. Proceeding of the National Academy of Sciences, 109(14), 5493–5498. https://doi.org/10.1073/pnas.1202044109

Hasin, D. S., O'Brien, C. P., Auriacombe, M., Borges, G., Bucholz, K., Budney, A., Compton, W. M., Crowley, T., Ling, W., Petry, N. M., Schuckit, M. D., & Grant, B. F. (2013). DSM-5 criteria for substance use disorders: Recommendations and rationale. American Journal of Psychiatry, 170(8), 834–851. https://doi.org/10.1176/appi.ajp.2013.12060782

Helle, A. C., Trull, T. J., Watts, A. L., McDowell, Y., & Sher, K. J. (2020). Psychiatric comorbidity as a function of severity: DSM-5 alcohol use disorder and HiTOP classification of mental disorders. Alcoholism: Clinical and Experimental Research, 44(3), 632–644. https://doi.org/10.1111/acer.14284

Heyman, G. M. (2009). Addiction: A disorder of choice. Harvard University Press. https://doi.org/10.4159/9780674053991

Hibbs R. E., & Zambon A. C. (2017). Nicotine and agents acting at the neuromuscular junction and autonomic ganglia. In Brunton L. L., & Hilal-Dandan R, & Knollmann B. C.(Eds.), Goodman & Gilman's: The pharmacological basis of therapeutics, 13th ed. McGraw Hill.

Hicks, B. M., Blonigen, D. M., Kramer, M. D., Krueger, R. F., Patrick, C. J., Iacono, W. G., & McGue, M. (2007). Gender differences and developmental change in externalizing disorders from late adolescence to early adulthood: A longitudinal twin study. Journal of Abnormal Psychology, 116(3), 433–447. https://doi.org/10.1037/0021-843X.116.3.433

Hoeben, E. M., Osgood, D. W., Siennick, S. E., & Weerman, F. M. (2021). Hanging out with the wrong crowd? The role of unstructured socializing in adolescents' specialization in delinquency and substance use. Journal of Quantitative Criminology, 37(1), 141–177. https://doi.org/10.1007/s10940-019-09447-4

Hull, J. G., & Bond, C. F. (1986). Social and behavioral consequences of alcohol consumption and expectancy: A meta-analysis. Psychological Bulletin, 99(3), 347–360. https://doi.org/10.1037/0033-2909.99.3.347

Hung, R. J., McKay, J. D., Gaborieau, V., Boffetta, P., Hashibe, M., Zaridze, D., . . . Brennan, P. (2008). A susceptibility locus for lung cancer maps to nicotinic acetylcholine receptor subunit genes on 15q25. Nature, 452(7187), 633–637. https://doi.org/10.1038/nature06885

Hussong, A. M., Huang, W., Serrano, D., Curran, P. J., & Chassin, L. (2012). Testing whether and when parent alcoholism uniquely affects various forms of adolescent substance use. *Journal of Abnormal Child Psychology*, *40*(8), 1265–1276. https://doi.org/10.1007/s10802-012-9662-3

Iacono, W. G., & Malone, S. M. (2011). Developmental endophenotypes: Indexing genetic risk for substance abuse with the P300 brain event-related potential. *Child Development Perspectives*, *5*(4), 239–247. https://doi.org/10.1111/j.1750-8606.2011.00205.x

Insel, T., Cuthbert, B., Garvey, M., Heinssen, R., Pine, D. S., Quinn, K., Sanislow, C., & Wang, P. (2010). Research domain criteria (RDoC), Toward a new classification framework for research on mental disorders. *American Journal of Psychiatry*, *167*(7), 748–751. https://doi.org/10.1176/appi.ajp.2010.09091379

Jacobs, M. M., Ökvist, A., Horvath, M., Keller, E., Bannon, M. J., Morgello, S., & Hurd, Y. L. (2012). Dopamine receptor D1 and postsynaptic density gene variants associate with opiate abuse and striatal expression levels. *Molecular Psychiatry*, *18*(11), 1205–1210. https://doi.org/10.1038/mp.2012.140

Jernigan, D. H., & Trangenstein, P. J. (2020). What's next for WHO's global strategy to reduce the harmful use of alcohol? *Bulletin of the World Health Organization*, *98*(3), 222–223. doi:10.2471/BLT.19.241737

Jones, A. W. (April 2019). Forensic drug profile: Cocaethylene, *Journal of Analytical Toxicology*, *43*, 155–160. https://doi.org/10.1093/jat/bkz007

Jones, E. E., & Berglas, S. (1978). Control of attributions about the self through self-handicapping strategies: The appeal of alcohol and the role of underachievement. *Personality and Social Psychology Bulletin*, *4*(2), 200–206. https://doi.org/10.1177/014616728004000205

Josephs, R. A., & Steele, C. M. (1990). The two faces of alcohol myopia: Attentional mediation of psychological stress. *Journal of Abnormal Psychology*, *99*(2), 115–126. https://doi.org/10.1037/0021-843X.99.2.115

Joyner, K. J., Bowyer, C. B., Yancey, J. R., Venables, N. C., Foell, J., Worthy, D. A., Hajcak, G., Bartholow, B. D., & Patrick, C. J. (2019). Blunted reward sensitivity and trait disinhibition interact to predict substance use problems. *Clinical Psychological Science*, *7*(5), 1109–1124. https://doi.org/10.1177/2167702619838480

Kaprio, J. (2009). Genetic epidemiology of smoking behavior and nicotine dependence. *COPD: Journal of Chronic Obstructive Pulmonary Disease*, *6*(4), 304–306. https://doi.org/10.1080/15412550903049165

Kendler, K. S., Aggen, S. H., Knudsen, G. P., Roysamb, E., Neale, M. C., & Reichborn-Kjennerud, T. (2011). The structure of genetic and environmental risk factors for syndromal and subsyndromal common DSM-IV axis I and all axis II disorders. *American Journal of Psychiatry*, *168*(1), 29–39. https://doi.org/10.1176/appi.ajp.2010.10030340

Kendler, K. S., Aggen, S. H., Prescott, C. A., Crabbe, J., & Neale, M. C. (2012). Evidence for multiple genetic factors underlying the DSM-IV criteria for alcohol dependence. *Molecular Psychiatry*, *17*(12), 1306–1315. https://doi.org/10.1038/mp.2011.153

Kendler, K. S., Chen, X., Dick, D., Maes, H., Gillespie, N., Neale, M. C., & Riley, B. (2012). Recent advances in the genetic epidemiology and molecular genetics of substance use disorders. *Nature Neuroscience*, *15*(2), 181–189. https://doi.org/10.1038/nn.3018

Kendler, K. S., Myers, J., & Prescott, C. A. (2007). Specificity of genetic and environmental risk factors for symptoms of cannabis, cocaine, alcohol, caffeine, and nicotine dependence. *Archives of General Psychiatry*, *64*(11), 1313–1320. doi:10.1001/archpsyc.64.11.1313

Kendler, K. S., Ohlsson, H., Sundquist, K., & Sundquist, J. (2013). Within-family environmental transmission of drug abuse: A Swedish national study. *JAMA Psychiatry*, *70*(2), 235–242. doi:10.1001/jamapsychiatry.2013.276

Kendler, K. S., Sundquist, K., Ohlsson, H., Palmer, K., Maes, H., Winkleby, M. A., & Sundquist, J. (2012). Genetic and familial environmental influences on the risk for drug abuse: A national Swedish adoption study. *Archives of General Psychiatry*, *69*(7), 690–697. doi:10.1001/archgenpsychiatry.2011.2112

Keyser-Marcus, L. A., Ramey, T., Bjork, J., Adams, A., & Moeller, F. G. (2021). Development and feasibility study of an addiction-focused phenotyping assessment battery. *American Journal on Addictions*, *30* (4), 398–405. https://doi.org/10.1111/ajad.13170

Khantzian, E. J. (1985). The self-medication hypothesis of addictive disorders: Focus on heroin and cocaine dependence. *American Journal of Psychiatry*, *142*(11), 1259–1264.

Khantzian, E. J. (1997). The self-medication hypothesis of substance use disorders: A reconsideration and recent applications. *Harvard Review of Psychiatry*, *4*(5), 231–244. doi:10.3109/10673229709030550

Kim–Cohen, J., Caspi, A., Moffitt, T. E., Harrington, H., Milne, B. J., & Poulton, R. (2003). Prior juvenile diagnoses in adults with mental disorder: Developmental follow-back of a prospective-longitudinal cohort. *Archives of General Psychiatry*, *60*(7), 709–717. doi:10.1001/archpsyc.60.7.709

Knafo, A., & Jaffee, S. R. (2013). Gene-environment correlation in developmental psychopathology. *Development and Psychopathology*, *25*(1), 1–6. https://doi.org/10.1017/S0954579412000855

Koob, G. F., & Schulkin, J. (2019). Addiction and stress: An allostatic view. *Neuroscience & Biobehavioral Reviews*, *106*, 245–262. https://doi.org/10.1016/j.neubiorev.2018.09.008

Korhonen, T., Latvala, A., Dick, D. M., Pulkkinen, L., Rose, R. J., Kaprio, J., & Huizink, A. C. (2012). Genetic and environmental influences underlying externalizing behaviors, cigarette smoking and illicit drug use across adolescence. *Behavior Genetics*, *42*(4), 614–625. https://doi.org/10.1007/s10519-012-9528-z

Koski, A., Ojanperä, I., & Vuori, E. (2002). Alcohol and benzodiazepines in fatal poisonings. *Alcoholism: Clinical and Experimental Research*, *26*(7), 956–959. https://doi.org/10.1111/j.1530-0277.2002.tb02627.x

Kotov, R., Krueger, R. F., Watson, D., Achenbach, T. M., Althoff, R. R., Bagby, R. M., . . . Zimmerman, M. (2017). The Hierarchical Taxonomy of Psychopathology (HiTOP), A dimensional alternative to traditional nosologies. *Journal of Abnormal Psychology*, *126*(4), 454–477. https://doi.org/10.1037/abn0000258

Kwako, L. E., Momenan, R., Litten, R. Z., Koob, G. F., & Goldman, D. (2016). Addictions neuroclinical assessment: A neuroscience-based framework for addictive disorders. *Biological Psychiatry*, *80*(3), 179–189. https://doi.org/10.1016/j.biopsych.2015.10.024

Labate, B. C., & Cavnar, C. (Eds.). (2014). *Ayahuasca shamanism in the Amazon and beyond*. Oxford University Press.

Lai, H. M. X., Cleary, M., Sitharthan, T., & Hunt, G. E. (2015). Prevalence of comorbid substance use, anxiety and mood disorders in epidemiological surveys, 1990–2014: A systematic review and meta-analysis. *Drug and Alcohol Dependence, 154*, 1–13. https://doi.org/10.1016/j.drugalcdep.2015.05.031

Lane, S. P., & Sher, K. J. (2015). Limits of current approaches to diagnosis severity based on criterion counts: An example with DSM-5 alcohol use disorder. *Clinical Psychological Science, 3*(6), 819–835. https://doi.org/10.1177/2167702614553026

Lathan, S. R. (2010, October). Caroline Hampton Halsted: The first to use rubber gloves in the operating room. *Baylor University Medical Center Proceedings, 23*(4), 389–392. https://doi.org/10.1080/08998280.2010.11928658

Lee, M. R., & Sher, K. J. (2018). "Maturing out" of binge and problem drinking. *Alcohol Research: Current Reviews, 39*(1), 31–42. PMID: 30557146

Li, H., Penzo, M. A., Taniguchi, H., Kopec, C. D., Huang, Z. J., & Li, B. (2013). Experience-dependent modification of a central amygdala fear circuit. *Nature Neuroscience, 16*(3), 332–339. https://doi.org/10.1038/nn.3322

Lips, E. H., Gaborieau, V., McKay, J. D., Chabrier, A., Hung, R. J., Boffetta, P., ... Brennan, P. (2010). Association between a 15q25 gene variant, smoking quantity and tobacco-related cancers among 17 000 individuals. *International Journal of Epidemiology, 39*(2), 563–577. https://doi.org/10.1093/ije/dyp288

Litten, R. Z., Ryan, M. L., Falk, D. E., Reilly, M., Fertig, J. B., & Koob, G. F. (2015). Heterogeneity of alcohol use disorder: Understanding mechanisms to advance personalized treatment. *Alcoholism: Clinical and Experimental Research, 39*, 579–584. https://doi.org/10.1111/acer.12669

Littlefield, A. K., Agrawal, A., Ellingson, J. M., Kristjansson, S., Madden, P. A., Bucholz, K. K., Slutske, W. S., Heath, A. C., & Sher, K. J. (2011). Does variance in drinking motives explain the genetic overlap between personality and alcohol use disorder symptoms? A twin study of young women. *Alcoholism: Clinical and Experimental Research, 35*(12), 2242–2250. https://doi.org/10.1111/j.1530-0277.2011.01574.x

Littlefield, A. K., & Sher, K. J. (2016). Personality and substance use disorders. In K. J. Sher (Ed.), *The Oxford handbook of substance use and substance use disorders: Two-volume set* (pp. 351–378). Oxford University Press.

Liu, J., Lester, B. M., Neyzi, N., Sheinkopf, S. J., Gracia, L., Kekatpure, M., & Kosofsky, B. E. (2013). Regional brain morphometry and impulsivity in adolescents following prenatal exposure to cocaine and tobacco prenatal exposure to cocaine and tobacco. *JAMA Pediatrics, 167*(4), 348–354. doi:10.1001/jamapediatrics.2013.550

Liu, M., Jiang, Y., Wedow, R., Li, Y., Brazel, D. M., Chen, F., Datta, G., Davila-Velderrain, J., McGuire, D., Tian, C., Zhan, X., 23andMe Research Team, HUNT All-In Psychiatry, Choquet., H., Docherty, A. R., Faul, J. D., Foerster, J. R.,.Fritsche, L. G., Elvestad, M., ... Vrieze, S. (2019). Association studies of up to 1.2 million individuals yield new insights into the genetic etiology of tobacco and alcohol use. *Nature Genetics, 51*(2), 237–244. https://doi.org/10.1038/s41588-018-0307-5

Lopez-Leon, S., González-Giraldo, Y., Wegman-Ostrosky, T., & Forero, D. A. (2021). Molecular genetics of substance use disorders: An umbrella review. *Neuroscience & Biobehavioral Reviews, 124*, 358–369. https://doi.org/10.1016/j.neubiorev.2021.01.019

Lovic, V., Saunders, B. T., Yager, L. M., & Robinson, T. E. (2011). Rats prone to attribute incentive salience to reward cues are also prone to impulsive action. *Behavioural Brain Research, 223*(2), 255–261. https://doi.org/10.1016/j.bbr.2011.04.006

Luria, A. R. (1980). Disturbances of higher cortical functions with lesions of the frontal region. In *Higher cortical functions in man* (pp. 246–365). Springer. https://doi.org/10.1007/978-1-4615-8579-4_8

Lüscher, C., Robbins, T. W., & Everitt, B. J. (2020). The transition to compulsion in addiction. *Nature Reviews Neuroscience, 21*(5), 247–263. https://doi.org/10.1038/s41583-020-0289-z

MacAndrew, C., & Edgerton, R. B. (1969). *Drunken comportment: A social explanation.* Aldine.

MacQueen, D. A., Heckman, B. W., Blank, M. D., Van Rensburg, K. J., Park, J. Y., Drobes, D. J., & Evans, D. E. (2014). Variation in the α 5 nicotinic acetylcholine receptor subunit gene predicts cigarette smoking intensity as a function of nicotine content. *Pharmacogenomics Journal, 14*(1), 70–76. https://doi.org/10.1038/tpj.2012.50

Maggs, J. L., & Staff, J. A. (2018). Parents who allow early adolescents to drink. *Journal of Adolescent Health, 62*(2), 245–247. https://doi.org/10.1016/j.jadohealth.2017.09.016

Maisel, N. C., Blodgett, J. C., Wilbourne, P. L., Humphreys, K., & Finney, J. W. (2013). Meta-analysis of naltrexone and acamprosate for treating alcohol use disorders: When are these medications most helpful? *Addiction, 108*(2), 275–293. https://doi.org/10.1111/j.1360-0443.2012.04054.x

Maldonado, R., Valverde, O., & Berrendero, F. (2006). Involvement of the endocannabinoid system in drug addiction. *Trends in Neurosciences, 29*(4), 225–232. https://doi.org/10.1016/j.tins.2006.01.008

Malouff, J. M., Thorsteinsson, E. B., Rooke, S. E., & Schutte, N. S. (2007). Alcohol involvement and the five-factor model of personality: A meta-analysis. *Journal of Drug Education, 37*(3), 277–294. https://doi.org/10.2190/DE.37.3.d

Manhica, H., Straatmann, V. S., Lundin, A., Agardh, E., & Danielsson, A. K. (2021). Association between poverty exposure during childhood and adolescence, and drug use disorders and drug-related crimes later in life. *Addiction, 116*(7), 1747–1756. https://doi.org/10.1111/add.15336

Mann, K., Roos, C. R., Hoffmann, S., Nakovics, H., Leménager, T., Heinz, A., & Witkiewitz, K. (2018). Precision medicine in alcohol dependence: A controlled trial testing pharmacotherapy response among reward and relief drinking phenotypes. *Neuropsychopharmacology, 43*(4), 891–899. https://doi.org/10.1038/npp.2017.282

Manolio, T. A., Collins, F. S., Cox, N. J., Goldstein, D. B., Hindorff, L. A., Hunter, D. J., ... Visscher, P. M. (2009). Finding the missing heritability of complex diseases. *Nature, 461*(7265), 747–753. https://doi.org/10.1038/nature08494

Martin, C. S., Chung, T., & Langenbucher, J. W. (2008). How should we revise diagnostic criteria for substance use disorders in the DSM-V? *Journal of Abnormal Psychology, 117*(3), 561–575. https://doi.org/10.1037/0021-843X.117.3.561

Martin, C. S., Steinley, D. L., Vergés, A., & Sher, K. J. (2011). Letter to the Editor: The proposed 2/11 symptom algorithm for DSM-5 substance-use disorders is too lenient. *Psychological Medicine, 41*(9), 2008–2010. https://doi.org/10.1017/S0033291711000717

Martin, C. S., Langenbucher, J. W., Chung, T., & Sher, K. J. (2014). Truth or consequences in the diagnosis of substance use disorders. *Addiction, 109*(11), 1773–1778. https://doi.org/10.1111/add.12615

McDougall, W. (1929). The chemical theory of temperament applied to introversion and extroversion. *Journal of Abnormal and Social Psychology, 24*, 293–309. https://doi.org/10.1037/h0075883

McLaughlin, K. A., Green, J. G., Gruber, M. J., Sampson, N. A., Zaslavsky, A. M., & Kessler, R. C. (2012). Childhood adversities and first onset of psychiatric disorders in a national sample of US adolescents. *Archives of General Psychiatry, 69*(11), 1151–1160. doi:10.1001/archgenpsychiatry.2011.2277

Mehanović, E., Vigna-Taglianti, F., Faggiano, F., & Galanti, M. R. (2021). Does parental permissiveness toward cigarette smoking and alcohol use influence illicit drug use among adolescents? A longitudinal study in seven European countries. *Social Psychiatry and Psychiatric Epidemiology*, 1–9. https://doi.org/10.1007/s00127-021-02118-5

Meier, M. H., Caspi, A., Ambler, A., Harrington, H., Houts, R., Keefe, R. S., McDonald, K., Ward, A., Poulton, R., & Moffitt, T. E. (2012). Persistent cannabis users show neuropsychological decline from childhood to midlife. *Proceedings of the National Academy of Sciences, 109*(40), E2657–2664. https://doi.org/10.1073/pnas.1206820109

Metrik, J., Rohsenow, D. J., Monti, P. M., McGeary, J., Cook, T. A., de Wit, H., Haney, M., & Kahler, C. W. (2009). Effectiveness of a marijuana expectancy manipulation: Piloting the balanced-placebo design for marijuana. *Experimental and Clinical Psychopharmacology, 17*(4), 217–225. https://doi.org/10.1037/a0016502

Meyers, J. L., Cerda, M., Galea, S., Keyes, K. M., Aiello, A. E., Uddin, M., Wildman, D. E., & Koenen, K. C. (2013). Interaction between polygenic risk for cigarette use and environmental exposures in the Detroit neighborhood health study. *Translational Psychiatry, 3*(8), e290–e290. https://doi.org/10.1038/tp.2013.63

Meyers, J. L., Salvatore, J. E., Aliev, F., Johnson, E. C., McCutcheon, V. V., Su, J., Kuo, S. I., Lai, D., Wetherill, L., Wang, J. C., Chan, G., Hesselbrock, V., Foroud, T., Bucholz, K. K., Edenberg, H. J., Dick, D. M., Porjesz, B., & Agrawal, A. (2019). Psychosocial moderation of polygenic risk for cannabis involvement: The role of trauma exposure and frequency of religious service attendance. *Translational Psychiatry, 9*(1), 1–12. https://doi.org/10.1038/s41398-019-0598-z

Meza, R., Meernik, C., Jeon, J., & Cote, M. L. (2015). Lung cancer incidence trends by gender, race and histology in the United States, 1973–2010. *PloS One, 10*(3), e0121323. https://doi.org/10.1371/journal.pone.0121323

Mezquita, L., Camacho, L., Ibáñez, M. I., Villa, H., Moya-Higueras, J., & Ortet, G. (2015). Five-Factor Model and alcohol outcomes: Mediating and moderating role of alcohol expectancies. *Personality and Individual Differences, 74*, 29–34. https://doi.org/10.1016/j.paid.2014.10.002

Miller, G. A., & Rockstroh, B. (2013). Endophenotypes in psychopathology research: Where do we stand? *Annual Review of Clinical Psychology, 9*, 177–213. https://doi.org/10.1146/annurev-clinpsy-050212-185540

Miyake, A., & Friedman, N. P. (2012). The nature and organization of individual differences in executive functions: Four general conclusions. *Current Directions in Psychological Science, 21*(1), 8–14. https://doi.org/10.1177/0963721411429458

Miyake, A., Friedman, N. P., Emerson, M. J., Witzki, A. H., Howerter, A., & Wager, T. D. (2000). The unity and diversity of executive functions and their contributions to complex "frontal lobe" tasks: A latent variable analysis. *Cognitive Psychology, 41*(1), 49–100. https://doi.org/10.1006/cogp.1999.0734

Moffitt, T. E. (2005). The new look of behavioral genetics in developmental psychopathology: Gene-environment interplay in antisocial behaviors. *Psychological Bulletin, 131*(4), 533–554. https://doi.org/10.1037/0033-2909.131.4.533

Montes, K. S., Witkiewitz, K., Pearson, M. R., & Leventhal, A. M. (2019). Alcohol, tobacco, and marijuana expectancies as predictors of substance use initiation in adolescence: A longitudinal examination. *Psychology of Addictive Behaviors, 33*(1), 26–34. https://doi.org/10.1037/adb0000422

Morisano, D., Babor, T. F., & Robaina, K. A. (2014). Co-occurrence of substance use disorders with other psychiatric disorders: Implications for treatment services. *Nordic Studies on Alcohol and Drugs, 31*(1), 5–25. https://doi.org/10.2478/nsad-2014-0002

Morean, M. E., Corbin, W. R., & Treat, T. A. (2012). The Anticipated Effects of Alcohol Scale: Development and psychometric evaluation of a novel assessment tool for measuring alcohol expectancies. *Psychological Assessment, 24*(4), 1008–1023. https://doi.org/10.1037/a0028982

Munafo, M. R., Timofeeva, M. N., Morris, R. W., Prieto-Merino, D., Sattar, N., Brennan, P., . . . Davey Smith, G. (2012). Association between genetic variants on chromosome 15q25 locus and objective measures of tobacco exposure. *Journal of the National Cancer Institute, 104*(10), 740–748. https://doi.org/10.1093/jnci/djs191

Müller, C. P., & Homberg, J. R. (2015). The role of serotonin in drug use and addiction. *Behavioural Brain Research, 277*, 146–192. https://doi.org/10.1016/j.bbr.2014.04.007

Nader, K., Bechara, A., Roberts, D. C., & van der Kooy, D. (1994). Neuroleptics block high- but not low-dose heroin place preferences: Further evidence for a two-system model of motivation. *Behavioral Neuroscience, 108*(6), 1128–1138. https://doi.org/10.1037/0735-7044.108.6.1128

National Institute of Drug Abuse. (n.d.) Home page. http://https://www.drugabuse.gov/about-nida

National Institute on Drug Abuse (2020, April 6). Costs of substance abuse. https://www.drugabuse.gov/drug-topics/trends-statistics/costs-substance-abuse

Ngo, D. H., & Vo, T. S. (2019). An updated review on pharmaceutical properties of gamma-aminobutyric acid. *Molecules, 24*(15), 2678. https://doi.org/10.3390/molecules24152678

Nicolai, J., Moshagen, M., & Demmel, R. (2012). Patterns of alcohol expectancies and alcohol use across age and gender. *Drug and Alcohol Dependence, 126*(3), 347–353. https://doi.org/10.1016/j.drugalcdep.2012.05.040

Nkansah-Amankra, S. (2020). Revisiting the association between "gateway hypothesis" of early drug use and drug use progression: A cohort analysis of peer influences on drug use progression among a population cohort. *Substance Use & Misuse, 55*(6), 998–1007. https://doi.org/10.1080/10826084.2020.1720245

Norman, A. L., O'Brien, J. W., Spadoni, A. D., Tapert, S. F., Jones, K. L., Riley, E. P., & Mattson, S. N. (2013). A functional magnetic resonance imaging study of spatial working memory in children with prenatal alcohol exposure: Contribution of familial history of alcohol use disorders. *Alcoholism: Clinical and Experimental Research, 37*(1), 132–140. https://doi.org/10.1111/j.1530-0277.2012.01880.x

Nutt, D. J., Lingford-Hughes, A., Erritzoe, D., & Stokes, P. R. (2015). The dopamine theory of addiction: 40 years of highs and lows. *Nature Reviews Neuroscience, 16*(5), 305–312. https://doi.org/10.1038/nrn3939

Palmer, R. H. C., Young, S. E., Corley, R. P., Hopfer, C. J., Stallings, M. C., & Hewitt, J. K. (2013). Stability and change of genetic and environmental effects on the common liability to alcohol, tobacco, and cannabis DSM-IV dependence symptoms. *Behavior Genetics, 43*(5), 374–385. https://doi.org/10.1007/s10519-013-9599-5

Parra, G. R., O'Neill, S. E., & Sher, K. J. (2003). Reliability of self-reported age of substance involvement onset. *Psychology of Addictive Behaviors, 17*(3), 211–218. https://doi.org/10.1037/0893-164X.17.3.211

Parrott, D. J., & Eckhardt, C. I. (2018). Effects of alcohol on human aggression. *Current Opinion in Psychology, 19*, 1–5. https://doi.org/10.1016/j.copsyc.2017.03.023

Pasman, J. A., Verweij, K. J., Abdellaoui, A., Hottenga, J. J., Fedko, I. O., Willemsen, G., Boomsma, D. I., & Vink, J. M. (2020). Substance use: Interplay between polygenic risk and neighborhood environment. *Drug and Alcohol Dependence, 209*, 107948. https://doi.org/10.1016/j.drugalcdep.2020.107948

Patrick, C. J., Bernat, E. M., Malone, S. M., Iacono, W. G., Krueger, R. F., & McGue, M. (2006). P300 amplitude as an indicator of externalizing in adolescent males. *Psychophysiology, 43*(1), 84–92. https://doi.org/10.1111/j.1469-8986.2006.00376.x

Pei, F., Wang, Y., Wu, Q., McCarthy, K. S., & Wu, S. (2020). The roles of neighborhood social cohesion, peer substance use, and adolescent depression in adolescent substance use. *Children and Youth Services Review, 112*, 104931. https://doi.org/10.1016/j.childyouth.2020.104931

Pentz, M. A., & Riggs, N. R. (2013). Longitudinal relationships of executive cognitive function and parent influence to child substance use and physical activity. *Prevention Science, 14*(3), 229–237. doi:10.1007/s11121-012-0312-3

Pierce, R. C., & Kumaresan, V. (2006). The mesolimbic dopamine system: The final common pathway for the reinforcing effect of drugs of abuse? *Neuroscience & Biobehavioral Reviews, 30*(2), 215–238. https://doi.org/10.1016/j.neubiorev.2005.04.016

Piazza, P. V., & Deroche-Gamonet, V. (2013). A multistep general theory of transition to addiction. *Psychopharmacology, 229*(3), 387–413. https://doi.org/10.1007/s00213-013-3224-4

Pihl, R. O. (2010). Mental disorders are brain disorders: You think? *Canadian Psychology/Psychologie Canadienne, 51*(1), 40–49. https://doi.org/10.1037/a0018467

Pihl, R. O., Smith, M., & Farrell, B. (1984). Alcohol and aggression in men: A comparison of brewed and distilled beverages. *Journal of Studies on Alcohol, 45*(3), 278–282. https://doi.org/10.15288/jsa.1984.45.278

Pihl, R. O., & Spiers, P. (1978). Individual characteristics in the etiology of drug abuse. *Progress in Experimental Personality Research, 8*, 93–195.

Porjesz, B., Rangaswamy, M., Kamarajan, C., Jones, K. A., Padmanabhapillai, A., & Begleiter, H. (2005). The utility of neurophysiological markers in the study of alcoholism. *Clinical Neurophysiology, 116*(5), 993–1018. https://doi.org/10.1016/j.clinph.2004.12.016

Prochaska, J. J., & Benowitz, N. L. (2019). Current advances in research in treatment and recovery: Nicotine addiction. *Science Advances, 5*(10), eaay9763. doi:10.1126/sciadv.aay9763

Prom-Wormley, E. C., Ebejer, J., Dick, D. M., & Bowers, M. S. (2017). The genetic epidemiology of substance use disorder: A review. *Drug and Alcohol Dependence, 180*, 241–259. https://doi.org/10.1016/j.drugalcdep.2017.06.040

Pruessner, J. C., Dedovic, K., Pruessner, M., Lord, C., Buss, C., Collins, L., Dagher, A., & Lupien, S. J. (2010). Stress regulation in the central nervous system: Evidence from structural and functional neuroimaging studies in human populations: 2008 Curt Richter Award Winner. *Psychoneuroendocrinology, 35*(1), 179–191. https://doi.org/10.1016/j.psyneuen.2009.02.016

Quinn, P. D., & Fromme, K. (2011). Subjective response to alcohol challenge: A quantitative review. *Alcoholism: Clinical and Experimental Research, 35*(10), 1759–1770. https://doi.org/10.1111/j.1530-0277.2011.01521.x

Rangel-Barajas, C., Boehm II, S. L., & Logrip, M. L. (2021). Altered excitatory transmission in striatal neurons after chronic ethanol consumption in selectively bred crossed high alcohol-preferring mice. *Neuropharmacology, 190*, 108564. https://doi.org/10.1016/j.neuropharm.2021.108564

Ray, L. A., Bujarski, S., & Roche, D. J. (2016). Subjective response to alcohol as a research domain criterion. *Alcoholism: Clinical and Experimental Research, 40*(1), 6–17. https://doi.org/10.1111/acer.12927

Rehm, J., Marmet, S., Anderson, P., Gual, A., Kraus, L., Nutt, D. J., Room, R., Samokhvalov, A. V., Scafato, E., Trapencieris, M., Wiers. R. W., & Gmel, G. (2013). Defining substance use disorders: Do we really need more than heavy use? *Alcohol and Alcoholism, 48*(6), 633–640. https://doi.org/10.1093/alcalc/agt127

Roberts, B. W., Walton, K. E., & Viechtbauer, W. (2006). Patterns of mean-level change in personality traits across the life course: A meta-analysis of longitudinal studies. *Psychological Bulletin, 132*(1), 1–25. https://doi.org/10.1037/0033-2909.132.1.1

Robinson, M. J., Robinson, T. E., & Berridge, K. C. (2018). The current status of the incentive sensitization theory of addiction. In H. Pickard & S. H. Ahmed (Eds.), *The Routledge handbook of philosophy and science of addiction* (pp. 351–361). Routledge.

Robinson, A., & Wermeling, D. P. (2014). Intranasal naloxone administration for treatment of opioid overdose. *American Journal of Health-System Pharmacy, 71*(24), 2129–2135. https://doi.org/10.2146/ajhp130798

Room, R. (2010). Dry and wet cultures in the age of globalization. In F. Prina & E. Tempesta (Eds.), *Youth and alcohol: Consumption, abuse and policies: An interdisciplinary critical review* (pp. 229–237). Franco Angeli.

Room, R., Bloomfield, K., Gmel, G., Grittner, U., Gustafsson, N.-K., Mäkelä, P., Österberg, E., Ramstedt, M., Rehm, J., & Wicki, M. (2013). What happened to alcohol consumption and problems in the Nordic countries when alcohol taxes were decreased and borders opened? *International Journal of Alcohol and Drug Research, 2*(1), 77–87. https://doi.org/10.7895/ijadr.v2i1.58

Rose, J. E. (2006). Nicotine and nonnicotine factors in cigarette addiction. *Psychopharmacology, 184*(3), 274–285. https://doi.org/10.1007/s00213-005-0250-x

Rubin, V., & Comitas, L. (2019). *Ganja in Jamaica*. De Gruyter Mouton.

Rusby, J. C., Light, J. M., Crowley, R., & Westling, E. (2018). Influence of parent–youth relationship, parental monitoring, and parent substance use on adolescent substance use onset. *Journal of Family Psychology*, 32(3), 310–320. https://doi.org/10.1037/fam0000350

Saccone, N. L., Culverhouse, R. C., Schwantes-An, T. H., Cannon, D. S., Chen, X., Cichon, S., . . . Bierut, L. J. (2010). Multiple independent loci at chromosome 15q25.1 affect smoking quantity: A meta-analysis and comparison with lung cancer and COPD. *PLoS Genetics*, 6(8), e1001053. https://doi.org/10.1371/journal.pgen.1001053

Saffer, H., & Chaloupka, F. (2000). The effect of tobacco advertising bans on tobacco consumption. *Journal of Health Economics*, 19(6), 1117–1137. https://doi.org/10.1016/S0167-6296(00)00054-0

Salvatore, J. E., Cho, S. B., & Dick, D. M. (2017). Genes, environments, and sex differences in alcohol research. *Journal of Studies on Alcohol and Drugs*, 78(4), 494–501. https://doi.org/10.15288/jsad.2017.78.494

Sangameswaran, L., Fales, H. M., Friedrich, P., & De Blas, A. L. (1986). Purification of a benzodiazepine from bovine brain and detection of benzodiazepine-like immunoreactivity in human brain. *Proceedings of the National Academy of Sciences*, 83(23), 9236–9240. https://doi.org/10.1073/pnas.83.23.9236

Sartor, C. E., Lynskey, M. T., Heath, A. C., Jacob, T., & True, W. (2007). The role of childhood risk factors in initiation of alcohol use and progression to alcohol dependence. *Addiction*, 102(2), 216–225. https://doi.org/10.1111/j.1360-0443.2006.01661.x

Sarvet, A. L., Wall, M. M., Keyes, K. M., Cerdá, M., Schulenberg, J. E., O'Malley, P. M., Johnston, L. D., & Hasin, D. S. (2018). Recent rapid decrease in adolescents' perception that marijuana is harmful, but no concurrent increase in use. *Drug and Alcohol Dependence*, 186, 68–74. https://doi.org/10.1016/j.drugalcdep.2017.12.041

Saunders, J. B., Degenhardt, L., Reed, G. M., & Poznyak, V. (2019). Alcohol use disorders in ICD-11: Past, present, and future. *Alcoholism: Clinical and Experimental Research*, 43(8), 1617–1631. https://doi.org/10.1111/acer.14128

Savage, K., Firth, J., Stough, C., & Sarris, J. (2018). GABA-modulating phytomedicines for anxiety: A systematic review of preclinical and clinical evidence. *Phytotherapy Research*, 32(1), 3–18. https://doi.org/10.1002/ptr.5940

Schiller, E. Y., Goyal, A., & Mechanic, O. J. (2021). Opioid overdose. In *StatPearls*. StatPearls Publishing. PMID: 29262202.

Schoemaker, K., Mulder, H., Deković, M., & Matthys, W. (2013). Executive functions in preschool children with externalizing behavior problems: A meta-analysis. *Journal of Abnormal Child Psychology*, 41(3), 457–471. https://doi.org/10.1007/s10802-012-9684-x

Scott, J. C., Slomiak, S. T., Jones, J. D., Rosen, A. F., Moore, T. M., & Gur, R. C. (2018). Association of cannabis with cognitive functioning in adolescents and young adults: A systematic review and meta-analysis. *JAMA Psychiatry*, 75(6), 585–595. doi:10.1001/jamapsychiatry.2018.0335

Schuckit, M. A. (2018). A critical review of methods and results in the search for genetic contributors to alcohol sensitivity. *Alcoholism: Clinical and Experimental Research*, 42(5), 822–835. https://doi.org/10.1111/acer.13628

Schwartz, J. A., Solomon, S. J., & Valgardson, B. A. (2019). Socialization, selection, or both? The role of gene–environment interplay in the association between exposure to antisocial peers and delinquency. *Journal of Quantitative Criminology*, 35(1), 1–26. https://doi.org/10.1007/s10940-017-9368-3

Séguin, J. R., Pihl, R. O., Harden, P. W., Tremblay, R. E., & Boulerice, B. (1995). Cognitive and neuropsychological characteristics of physically aggressive boys. *Journal of Abnormal Psychology*, 104(4), 614–624. https://doi.org/10.1037/0021-843X.104.4.614

Sellings, L. H., & Clarke, P. B. (2003). Segregation of amphetamine reward and locomotor stimulation between nucleus accumbens medial shell and core. *Journal of Neuroscience*, 23(15), 6295–6303. https://doi.org/10.1523/JNEUROSCI.23-15-06295.2003

Servaas, M. N., Van Der Velde, J., Costafreda, S. G., Horton, P., Ormel, J., Riese, H., & Aleman, A. (2013). Neuroticism and the brain: A quantitative meta-analysis of neuroimaging studies investigating emotion processing. *Neuroscience & Biobehavioral Reviews*, 37(8), 1518–1529. https://doi.org/10.1016/j.neubiorev.2013.05.005

Shedler, J., & Block, J. (1990). Adolescent drug use and psychological health: A longitudinal inquiry. *American Psychologist*, 45(5), 612–630. https://doi.org/10.1037/0003-066X.45.5.612

Sher, K. J. (1987). Stress response dampening. In H. T. Blane & K. E. Leonard (Eds.), *Psychological theories of drinking and alcoholism* (pp. 227–271). Guilford.

Sher, K. J. (1991). *Children of alcoholics: A critical appraisal of theory and research*. University of Chicago Press.

Sher, K. J., Dick, D. M., Crabbe, J. C., Hutchison, K. E., O'Malley, S. S., & Heath, A. C. (2010). Consilient research approaches in studying gene× environment interactions in alcohol research. *Addiction Biology*, 15(2), 200–216. https://doi.org/10.1111/j.1369-1600.2009.00189.x

Sher, K. J., & Gotham, H. J. (1999). Pathological alcohol involvement: A developmental disorder of young adulthood. *Development and Psychopathology*, 11(4), 933–956. https://doi.org/10.1017/S0954579499002394

Sher, K. J., Gotham, H. J., & Watson, A. L. (2004). Trajectories of dynamic predictors of disorder: Their meanings and implications. *Development and Psychopathology*, 16(4), 825–856. doi:10.1017/s0954579404040039

Sher, K. J., & Grekin, E. R. (2007). Alcohol and affect regulation. In J. Gross (Ed.), *Handbook of emotion regulation* (pp. 560–580.) Guilford.

Sher, K. J., Grekin, E. R., & Williams, N. A. (2005). The development of alcohol use disorders. *Annual Review of Clinical Psychology*, 1, 493–523. https://doi.org/10.1146/annurev.clinpsy.1.102803.144107

Sher, K. J., Wood, M. D., Wood, P. K., Raskin, G., 1996. Alcohol outcome expectancies and alcohol use: A latent variable cross-lagged panel study. *Journal of Abnormal Psychology*, 105, 561–574. https://doi.org/10.1037/0021-843X.105.4.561

Shiffman, S., Ferguson, S. G., Dunbar, M. S., & Scholl, S. M. (2012). Tobacco dependence among intermittent smokers. *Nicotine & Tobacco Research*, 14(11), 1372–1381. https://doi.org/10.1093/ntr/nts097

Shipton, E. A. (2018). The opioid epidemic-a fast developing public health crisis in the first world. *New Zealand Medical Journal*, 131(1469), 7–9. PMID: 29389923

Sibley D. R., & Hazelwood L. A., & Amara S. G. (2017). 5-hydroxytryptamine (serotonin) and dopamine. In L. L. Brunton, R. Hilal-Dandan, & B. C. Knollmann (Eds.),

Goodman & Gilman's: *The pharmacological basis of therapeutics*, 13th ed. McGraw-Hill.

Singh, S. M., & Basu, D. (2009). Clinical study: The P300 event-related potential and its possible role as an endophenotype for studying substance use disorders: A review. *Addiction Biology*, *14*(3), 298–309. https://doi.org/10.1111/j.1369-1600.2008.00124.x

Sorge, R. E., & Clarke, P. B. (2011). Nicotine self-administration. In M. C. Olmstead (Ed.), *Animal models of drug addiction* (pp. 101–132). Springer. doi:10.1007/978-1-60761-934-5_4,

Stacy, A. W., Newcomb, M. D., & Bentler, P. M. (1991). Cognitive motivation and drug use: A 9-year longitudinal study. *Journal of Abnormal Psychology*, *100*(4), 502–515. https://doi.org/10.1037/0021-843X.100.4.502

Stallings, M. C., Gizer, I. R., & Young-Wolff, K. C. (2016). Genetic epidemiology and molecular genetics. In K. J. Sher (Ed.), *The Oxford handbook of substance use and substance use disorders* (vol. 1, 192–272). Oxford University Press.

Steele, C. M., & Josephs, R. A. (1990). Alcohol myopia: Its prized and dangerous effects. *American Psychologist*, *45*(8), 921–933. https://doi.org/10.1037/0003-066X.45.8.921

Strack, F., & Deutsch, R. (2004). Reflective and impulsive determinants of social behavior. *Personality and Social Psychology Review*, *3*, 220–247. https://doi.org/10.1207/s15327957pspr0803_1

Stroud, L. R., Paster, R. L., Goodwin, M. S., Shenassa, E., Buka, S., Niaura, R., Rosenblith, J. F., & Lipsitt, L. P. (2009). Maternal smoking during pregnancy and neonatal behavior: A large-scale community study. *Pediatrics*, *123*(5), e842–848. https://doi.org/10.1542/peds.2008-2084

Substance Abuse and Mental Health Services Administration. (2020). *Key substance use and mental health indicators in the United States: Results from the 2019 National Survey on Drug Use and Health* (HHS Publication No. PEP20-07-01-001, NSDUH Series H-55). Center for Behavioral Health Statistics and Quality, Substance Abuse and Mental Health Services Administration. https://www.samhsa.gov/data/

Tang, Y., Wang, J., Zhang, T., Xu, L., Qian, Z., Cui, H., Tang, X., Li, H., Whitfield-Gabrieli, S., Shenton, M. E., Seidman, L. J., McCarley, R. W., Keshavan, M. S., Stone, W. S., Wang, J., & Niznikiewicz, M. A. (2020). P300 as an index of transition to psychosis and of remission: Data from a clinical high risk for psychosis study and review of literature. *Schizophrenia Research*, *226*, 74–83. https://doi.org/10.1016/j.schres.2019.02.014

Testa, M., Fillmore, M. T., Norris, J., Abbey, A., Curtin, J. J., Leonard, K. E., Mariano, K. A., Thomas, M. C., Nomensen, K. J., George, W. H., VanZile-Tamsen, C., Livingston, J. A., Saenz, C., Buck, P. O., Zawacki, T., Parkhill, M. R., Jacques, A. J., & Hayman, L. W. (2006). Understanding alcohol expectancy effects: Revisiting the placebo condition. *Alcoholism: Clinical and Experimental Research*, *30*(2), 339–348. https://doi.org/10.1111/j.1530-0277.2006.00039.x

Tiffany, S. T., & Wray, J. M. (2012). The clinical significance of drug craving. *Annals of the New York Academy of Sciences*, *1248*, 1–17. doi:10.1111/j.1749-6632.2011.06298.x

Titeler, M., Lyon, R. A., & Glennon, R. A. (1988). Radioligand binding evidence implicates the brain 5–HT2 receptor as a site of action for LSD and phenylisopropylamine hallucinogens. *Psychopharmacology (Berl)*, *94*(2), 213–216.

Tori, M. E., Larochelle, M. R., & Naimi, T. S. (2020). Alcohol or benzodiazepine co-involvement with opioid overdose deaths in the United States, 1999–2017. *JAMA Network Open*, *3*(4), e202361–e202361. doi:10.1001/jamanetworkopen.2020.2361

Twomey, J., LaGasse, L., Derauf, C., Newman, E., Shah, R., Smith, L., Arria, A., Huestis, M., DellaGrotta, S., Roberts, M., Dansereau, L., Neal, C., & Lester, B. (2013). Prenatal methamphetamine exposure, home environment, and primary caregiver risk factors predict child behavioral problems at 5 years. *American Journal of Orthopsychiatry*, *83*(1), 64–72. https://doi.org/10.1111/ajop.12007

Valentine, G., & Sofuoglu, M. (2018). Cognitive effects of nicotine: Recent progress. *Current Neuropharmacology*, *16*(4), 403–414. https://doi.org/10.2174/1570159X15666171103152136

van Beek, J. H., Kendler, K. S., de Moor, M. H., Geels, L. M., Bartels, M., Vink, J. M., van den Berg, S. M., Willemsen, G., & Boomsma, D. I. (2012). Stable genetic effects on symptoms of alcohol abuse and dependence from adolescence into early adulthood. *Behavior Genetics*, *42*(1), 40–56. https://doi.org/10.1007/s10519-011-9488-8

Van Ryzin, M. J., Fosco, G. M., & Dishion, T. J. (2012). Family and peer predictors of substance use from early adolescence to early adulthood: An 11-year prospective analysis. *Addictive Behaviors*, *37*(12), 1314–1324. https://doi.org/10.1016/j.addbeh.2012.06.020

Vassilev, P., Avvisati, R., Koya, E., & Badiani, A. (2020). Distinct populations of neurons activated by heroin and cocaine in the striatum as assessed by catFISH. *eNeuro*, *7*(1), ENEURO.0394-19.2019. https://doi.org/10.1523/ENEURO.0394-19.2019

Velleman, R., & Orford, J. (2013). *Risk and resilience: Adults who were the children of problem drinkers*. Routledge.

Vergés, A., Haeny, A. M., Jackson, K. M., Bucholz, K. K., Grant, J. D., Trull, T. J., Wood, P. K., & Sher, K. J. (2013). Refining the notion of maturing out: Results from the National Epidemiologic Survey on Alcohol and Related Conditions. *American Journal of Public Health*, *103*(12), e67–e73. https://dx.doi.org/10.2105/AJPH.2013.301358

Vergés, A., Jackson, K. M., Bucholz, K. K., Grant, J. D., Trull, T. J., Wood, P. K., & Sher, K. J. (2012). Deconstructing the age-prevalence curve of alcohol dependence: Why "maturing out" is only a small piece of the puzzle. *Journal of Abnormal Psychology*, *121*(2), 511–523. https://doi.org/10.1037/a0026027

Vetulani, J. (2001). Drug addiction. Part 1. Psychoactive substances in the past and presence. *Polish Journal of Pharmacology*, *53*(3), 201–214. PMID: 11785921

Voas, R. B., Tippetts, A. S., & Fell, J. (2000). The relationship of alcohol safety laws to drinking drivers in fatal crashes. *Accident Analysis & Prevention*, *32*(4), 483–492. https://doi.org/10.1016/S0001-4575(99)00063-9

Volkow, N. D., Koob, G. F., & McLellan, A. T. (2016). Neurobiologic advances from the brain disease model of addiction. *New England Journal of Medicine*, *374*(4), 363–371. doi:10.1056/NEJMra1511480

Volkow, N. D., Wang, G. J., Ma, Y., Fowler, J. S., Zhu, W., Maynard, L., Telang, F., Vaska, P., Ding, Y-S., Wond, C., & Swanson, J. M. (2003). Expectation enhances the regional brain metabolic and the reinforcing effects of stimulants in cocaine abusers. *Journal of Neuroscience*, *23*(36), 11461–11468. https://doi.org/10.1523/JNEUROSCI.23-36-11461.2003

Waaktaar, T., Kan, K. J., & Torgersen, S. (2018). The genetic and environmental architecture of substance use development from early adolescence into young adulthood: A longitudinal twin study of comorbidity of alcohol, tobacco and illicit drug use. *Addiction, 113*(4), 740–748. https://doi.org/10.1111/add.14076

Wada, M., Kurose, S., Miyazaki, T., Nakajima, S., Masuda, F., Mimura, Y., Nishida, H., Ogyu, K., Tsugawa, S., Machima, Y., Plitman, E., Chakravarty, M. M., Mimura, M., & Noda, Y. (2019). The P300 event-related potential in bipolar disorder: A systematic review and meta-analysis. *Journal of Affective Disorders, 256*, 234–249. https://doi.org/10.1016/j.jad.2019.06.010

Waddell, J. T., Blake, A. J., Sternberg, A., Ruof, A., & Chassin, L. (2020). Effects of observable parent alcohol consequences and parent alcohol disorder on adolescent alcohol expectancies. *Alcoholism: Clinical and Experimental Research, 44*(4), 973–982. https://doi.org/10.1111/acer.14298

Wagenaar, A. C., Tobler, A. L., & Komro, K. A. (2010). Effects of alcohol tax and price policies on morbidity and mortality: A systematic review. *American Journal of Public Health, 100*(11), 2270–2278. doi:10.2105/AJPH.2009.186007

Wakefield, J. C., & Schmitz, M. F. (2014). How many people have alcohol use disorders? Using the harmful dysfunction analysis to reconcile prevalence estimates in two community surveys. *Frontiers in Psychiatry, 5*, 931–942. https://doi.org/10.3389/fpsyt.2014.00144

Watts, A., Boness, C. L., Loeffelman, J. E., Steinley, D., & Sher, K. J. (2021). Does crude measurement contribute to observed unidimensionality of psychological constructs? A demonstration with DSM-5 alcohol use disorder. *Journal of Abnormal Psychology, 130*(5), 512–524. https://doi.org/10.1037/abn0000678

Wechsler, H., Kuh, G., & Davenport, A. E. (2009). Fraternities, sororities and binge drinking: Results from a national study of American colleges. *NASPA Journal, 46*(3), 395–416. https://doi.org/10.2202/1949-6605.5017

Wechsler, H., & Nelson, T. F. (2008). What we have learned from the Harvard School of Public Health College Alcohol Study: Focusing attention on college student alcohol consumption and the environmental conditions that promote it. *Journal of Studies on Alcohol and Drugs, 69*(4), 481–490. https://doi.org/10.15288/jsad.2008.69.481

Westermeyer, J. (1988). The pursuit of intoxication: Our 100 century-old romance with psychoactive substances. *American Journal of Drug and Alcohol Abuse, 14*(2), 175–187. https://doi.org/10.3109/00952999809001545

Westermeyer, J. (2016). Historical and social context of psychoactive substance use. In R. J. Frances, S. L. Miller, & A. H. Mack (Eds.), *Clinical textbook of addictive disorders* (pp. 16–34). Guilford.

Wichers, M., Gardner, C., Maes, H. H., Lichtenstein, P., Larsson, H., & Kendler, K. S. (2013). Genetic innovation and stability in externalizing problem behavior across development: A multi-informant twin study. *Behavior Genetics, 43*(3), 191–201. https://doi.org/10.1007/s10519-013-9586-x

Wichers, M., Gillespie, N. A., & Kendler, K. S. (2013). Genetic and environmental predictors of latent trajectories of alcohol use from adolescence to adulthood: A male twin study. *Alcoholism: Clinical and Experimental Research, 37*(3), 498–506. https://doi.org/10.1111/j.1530-0277.2012.01939.x

Wiers, R. W., & Gladwin, T. E. (2016). Reflective and impulsive processes in addiction and the role of motivation. In R. Deutsch, B. Gawronski, & W. Hofmann (Eds.), *Reflective and impulsive determinants of human behavior* (pp. 185–200). Routledge.

Wiers, R. W., Hoogeveen, K. J., Sergeant, J. A., & Gunning, W. B. (1997). High- and low-dose alcohol-related expectancies and the differential associations with drinking in male and female adolescents and young adults. *Addiction, 92*(7), 871–888. https://doi.org/10.1111/j.1360-0443.1997.tb02956.x

Wiers, R. W., & Stacy, A. W. (2006). Implicit cognition and addiction. *Current Directions in Psychological Science, 15*(6), 292–296. https://doi.org/10.1111/j.1467-8721.2006.00455.x

Wilsnack, S. C. (2012). The GENACIS project: A review of findings and some implications for global needs in women-focused substance abuse prevention and intervention. *Substance Abuse and Rehabilitation, 3*(Suppl 1), 5–15. doi:10.2147/SAR.S21343

Winograd, R. P., Steinley, D., Lane, S. P., & Sher, K. J. (2017). An experimental investigation of drunk personality using self and observer reports. *Clinical Psychological Science, 5*(3), 439–456. https://doi.org/10.1177/2167702616689780

Winograd, R. P., Steinley, D., & Sher, K. (2016). Searching for Mr. Hyde: A five-factor approach to characterizing "types of drunks." *Addiction Research & Theory, 24*(1), 1–8. https://doi.org/10.3109/16066359.2015.1029920

Winokur, G., Coryell, W., Akiskal, H. S., Maser, J. D., Keller, M. B., Endicott, J., & Mueller, T. (1995). Alcoholism in manic-depressive (bipolar) illness: Familial illness, course of illness, and the primary-secondary distinction. *American Journal of Psychiatry, 152*(3), 365–372. doi:10.1176/ajp.152.3.365

Winters, B. D., Kruger, J. M., Huang, X., Gallaher, Z. R., Ishikawa, M., Czaja, K., Krueger, J. M., Huang, Y. H., Schlüter, O. M., &. Dong, Y. (2012). Cannabinoid receptor 1-expressing neurons in the nucleus accumbens. *Proceeding of the National Academy of Sciences, 109*(40), E2717–2725. https://doi.org/10.1073/pnas.1206303109

Woodyard, C. D., Hallam, J. S., & Bentley, J. P. (2013). Drinking norms: Predictors of misperceptions among college students. *American Journal of Health Behavior, 37*(1), 14–24. https://doi.org/10.5993/AJHB.37.1.2

Yi, R., Mitchell, S. H., & Bickel, W. K. (2010). Delay discounting and substance abuse-dependence. In G. J. Madden & W. K. Bickel (Eds.), *Impulsivity: The behavioral and neurological science of discounting* (pp. 191–211). American Psychological Association. https://doi.org/10.1037/12069-007

Yoder, K. K., Constantinescu, C. C., Kareken, D. A., Normandin, M. D., Cheng, T. E., O'Connor, S. J., & Morris, E. D. (2007). Heterogeneous effects of alcohol on dopamine release in the striatum: A PET study. *Alcoholism: Clinical and Experimental Research, 31*(6), 965–973. https://doi.org/10.1111/j.1530-0277.2007.00390.x

Yoon, S., Kobulsky, J. M., Yoon, D., & Kim, W. (2017). Developmental pathways from child maltreatment to adolescent substance use: The roles of posttraumatic stress symptoms and mother-child relationships. *Children and Youth Services Review, 82*, 271–279. https://doi.org/10.1016/j.childyouth.2017.09.035

Young, S. E., Rhee, S. H., Stallings, M. C., Corley, R. P., & Hewitt, J. K. (2006). Genetic and environmental vulnerabilities underlying adolescent substance use and problem use: General or specific? *Behavior Genetics, 36*(4), 603–615. https://doi.org/10.1007/s10519-006-9066-7

Zhang, T. Y., & Meaney, M. J. (2010). Epigenetics and the environmental regulation of the genome and its function. *Annual Review of Psychology, 61,* 439–466. doi:10.1146/annurev.psych.60.110707.163625

Zhou, H., Rentsch, C. T., Cheng, Z., Kember, R. L., Nunez, Y. Z., Sherva, R. M., Tate, J. P., Dao, C., Xu, K., Polimanti, R., Farrer, L. A., Justice, A. C., Kranzler, H. R., & Gelernter, J. (2020). Association of OPRM1 functional coding variant with opioid use disorder: A genome-wide association study. *JAMA Psychiatry, 77*(10), 1072–1080. doi:10.1001/jamapsychiatry.2020.1206

Zhou, H., Sealock, J. M., Sanchez-Roige, S., Clarke, T. K., Levey, D. F., Cheng, Z., . . . Gelernter, J. (2020). Genome-wide meta-analysis of problematic alcohol use in 435,563 individuals yields insights into biology and relationships with other traits. *Nature Neuroscience, 23*(7), 809–818. https://doi.org/10.1038/s41593-020-0643-5

Zucker, R. A., Heitzeg, M. M., & Nigg, J. T. (2011). Parsing the undercontrol–disinhibition pathway to substance use disorders: A multilevel developmental problem. *Child Development Perspectives, 5*(4), 248–255. https://doi.org/10.1111/j.1750-8606.2011.00172.x

CHAPTER 14

# Schizophrenia: Presentation, Affect and Cognition, Pathophysiology and Etiology

Angus MacDonald III *and* Caroline Demro

For Susan, a young graduate student, undergoing a psychotic break was "like turning on a faucet to a torrent of details" (Weiner, 2003). Strange questions arose, like what lay beneath superficial appearances? What did that person intend by saying "Hello"? What was the secret meaning of the ad on that passing bus, or even the significance of a falling leaf? According to Susan, the world had become suffused with new meanings like light, in this case an overwhelming, sinister, and saturating light. She no longer attended classes or met with friends. She changed her name, broke off contacts with her family, gave away her things, and disguised her identity. After 6 months—terrified, alone, and exhausted—she gave up her efforts to resist what she now understood as a US Central Intelligence Agency plot. She began a sequence of ever-more harrowing suicide attempts that eventually brought her to the attention of police and then psychiatrists. For Susan and her family, this would become a lifelong struggle with schizophrenia, one of the most disruptive and distressing illnesses of any kind.

Unfortunately, Susan's story is not rare. Still, it is important to bear in mind that people with schizophrenia have many different symptoms. What they have in common is lives interrupted, and often hopes, dreams, and plans irrevocably changed. This chapter will discuss the affective and cognitive impairments, pathophysiology, and etiology of schizophrenia. Chapter 15 of this volume further addresses the social aspects of this disorder including psychosocial treatments, whereas Chapter 16 of this volume discusses other conditions along the schizophrenia spectrum. First, we will unpack the symptoms of the disorder and its prevalence.

## Nosology

Schizophrenia is a syndrome that involves a collection of symptoms that appear unrelated but co-occur in many patients. In *DSM-5*, the diagnosis of schizophrenia requires two or more of the following symptoms: delusions (believing something that most people don't and despite evidence to the contrary), hallucinations (perceiving something that is not present), disorganized speech, disorganized or catatonic behavior, or negative symptoms (lacking normal emotional responses to events, reduced levels of motivation, or a disrupted flow of speech). To increase the consistency of course and outcome for people diagnosed with the disorder, the criteria also include a minimum duration and rule-outs for other conditions.

These criteria are not without controversy. In authoring the *DSM-5* criteria there was discussion about including cognitive impairment as a criterion for schizophrenia (Keefe & Fenton, 2007), which was ultimately set aside because it is not specific to this disorder. There were questions about using or

---

**Abbreviations**
COMT   Catechol-methyltransferase
GABA   Gamma-aminobutyric acid
GAD1   Glutamic acid decarboxylase 1
MRI    Magnetic resonance imaging
NMDA   N-methyl-d-aspartate (receptors)
PCP    Phencyclidine
PD     Personality disorder

investigating the use of a more dimensional organization scheme for what have been classified as different psychotic disorders thought to exist along a spectrum (for review, see Krueger & MacDonald, 2005; Van Os & Tamminga, 2007). However, any such changes will have to wait to be incorporated at a later date, if ever (Heckers et al., 2013). Therefore, the diagnostic criteria that remain in place today largely derive from those put forward in the Research Diagnostic Criteria (Spitzer et al., 1975), a forerunner to *DSM-III*, which was published in 1979. The *DSM-III* criteria supplanted more vague descriptions of schizophrenia that existed in *DSM-II* and harmonized practice in the United States with psychiatric practices in Europe, which had maintained the more rigorous, descriptive traditions of German psychiatrist Emil Kraepelin (*1856–1926*), a man frequently recognized as the founder of modern psychiatry.

## History of the Clinical Disorder

Allusions to psychoses can be found in many cultures the world over. For example, psychotic symptoms are mentioned in classical Greek, Roman (Evans et al., 2003), and Chinese works (Nei et al., 1975). However, in these sources, there does not appear to be any conceptualization of schizophrenia as a coherent disease per se. The construct of schizophrenia that we use today derives largely from the work of Emil Kraepelin. By all accounts, Kraepelin was an active physician with training in experimental psychology and a keen appreciation for the importance of collecting data. Beginning in 1886, while practicing in Estonia, and soon afterward while leading the Psychiatry Departments at the University of Heidelberg and then Munich, he compiled detailed clinical histories with a particularly keen ear for his patients' experiences of their illness over time. These accounts led him to differentiate schizophrenia, which he called *dementia praecox* (literally *premature madness*), from manic-depressive insanity. This aspect of the description remains a fundamental organizing principle of the *DSM-5* to this day. Even so, the validity of this distinction—now referred to as the *Kraepelinian dichotomy*—has never been fully embraced for reasons we consider later. Kraepelin had a tremendous influence on twentieth-century psychiatry through his prolific students and through his frequently revised *Textbook on Psychiatry* (German *Lehrbuch der Psychiatrie*; see Heckers & Kendler, 2020, for an analysis of the various editions of his classifications). A pattern of psychotic symptoms over time, rather than any particular cluster of symptoms, was the hallmark of *dementia praecox*, and he believed it was progressive and largely untreatable (Kraepelin & Barclay, 1971).[1]

A contemporary of Kraepelin, Swiss psychiatrist Eugene Bleuler (1857–1939), coined the term *schizophrenia*. He argued vehemently against the Kraepelinian view of inevitable deterioration and felt the term *dementia praecox* misled trainees to focus on the wrong aspect of the disorder. He used the term schizophrenia to delineate a "'splitting' of the different psychic functions" of the mind (Bleuler & Zinkin, 1911/1950, p. 8). One unanticipated side effect of this new word has been a fusing, now common in public discourse, between schizophrenia and multiple personalities (or dissociative identity disorder, DID). Students of psychiatry and clinical psychology grind their teeth when they hear references to schizophrenia as a "split personality." But the confusion is illuminating if it reminds us about an essential, phenomenological aspect of schizophrenia. Consider the experience of a woman named Clara:

> Despite the "usual" voices, alien thoughts and paranoia, what scared me the most was a sense that I had lost myself, a constant feeling that my self no longer belonged to me. What made such an existential orientation even more intolerable is the voices incessantly telling me that the only way to reunite with my real self is to commit suicide. So I tried. Still, nothing had happened. I was simply sectioned again, detached from my real self, observing what was being done to me in a third-person perspective.... Even though I am now stabilized on a new medication, I still cannot accept

---

[1] A tragic consequence of Kreapelin's prognosis for schizophrenia would soon play itself out as eugenic doctrines became popular. In an era when gene expression was only beginning to be understood, eugenics held that population health would improve if so-called unhealthy genotypes did not reproduce. In this context, Kraepelin became an active proponent of eugenics and "mental hygiene." Interested readers are referred to Shepherd's (1995) treatment of this aspect of early psychiatry. This history plays an often unspoken role in the late adoption in America of theories of schizophrenia that emphasized the importance of genetic liability because many recoiled from this eugenic interpretation.

the diagnosis. The medication helps the observing self dominate over the suffering self, but the real "me" is not here anymore. I am disconnected, disintegrated, diminished. (Kean, 2009)

Clara's distress is clear, and this vivid description captures a splitting of the mind and that fractured sense of self that Bleuler took to be a core feature of schizophrenia. Though there are elements of dissociation here, it is not a description of separate personalities as in DID.

## Epidemiology and Course of Illness

Based on accepted definitions, schizophrenia occurs in all populations studied. This was the prominent conclusion of the World Health Organization (WHO)'s 10-country study of schizophrenia around the world (Jablensky et al., 1992) which was conducted in the context of the Cold War and a vocal antipsychiatry movement. Sites were chosen in developing and developed nations, East and West, and in urban and rural districts. The rate of people who fulfilled these harmonized criteria for schizophrenia over their lifetime (called *lifetime morbid risk*) was similar across sites and approximately 1%. This may be a slight overestimate, with more recent reviews estimating the median lifetime morbid risk across 27 studies to be 72% (McGrath et al., 2008). In contrast to the WHO's epidemiological study there seems to be variation across locations such that prevalence is greater in more developed economies. Also, there did not appear to be changes in these rates over time.

According to population-based epidemiological studies, the highest incidence, or first episode, of schizophrenia is age 20–24 for men and 25–29 for women (Kirkbride et al., 2006), although the first symptoms of psychosis might appear several years beforehand (Häfner et al., 1994). While men have an earlier onset and a more severe course, there is no difference between men and women in the median estimates of lifetime morbid risk for the disorder (McGrath et al., 2008). Thus, women gradually "catch up" to men with more later-onset cases. Formerly, there was some thought that, by the age of 40 or 50, people exited the risk period for schizophrenia, but more recently it has been suggested that this is an arbitrary distinction and that cases of schizophrenia in older, and even elderly, patients may occur, although these cases may have a different symptom profile (Howard et al., 2000). While rare cases of schizophrenia and schizophrenia-like symptoms in early childhood have been reported, the earliest onset of schizophrenia cases is early puberty (Remschmidt & Theisen, 2012). Thus, while the traditional view of schizophrenia as a disorder of late adolescence and young adulthood is still accurate for most cases, our understanding must incorporate a wider risk period, including a period during which an *attenuated psychosis syndrome* may emerge.

The attenuated psychosis syndrome, now included in *DSM-5*, is characterized by symptoms that, notably, do not quite reach the threshold for psychotic intensity and duration. Syndromes are a way to systematize the symptoms and other measurable signs of an illness that often, but do not necessarily, co-occur. This syndrome is also referred to as *clinical high risk* or *ultra high risk* and is typically characterized by relatively intact insight. Outcomes vary for people who meet criteria for attenuated psychosis syndrome, making the term "prodromal" inappropriate because only approximately 36% go on to develop a full psychotic disorder within 3 years (Fusar-Poli et al., 2012). However, the syndrome is distressing and impairing in its own right and is often accompanied by comorbid mental health issues. Efforts to improve outcome prediction have led to risk calculators such as one by the North American Prodrome Longitudinal Study, which found specific symptoms (e.g., unusual thoughts, suspiciousness, lower cognitive performance), a decline in social functioning, and an earlier onset to be particularly predictive of conversion to a psychotic disorder (Cannon et al., 2016). Importantly, the course of psychotic disorders is episodic in nature, with periods of recovery and recurrence for most patients (Jobe & Harrow, 2010), though there is a good deal of variation in people's experiences with the illness over time (Tandon et al., 2009).

Given the varied course of schizophrenia and the diverse outcomes of individuals who experience an attenuated psychosis syndrome, additional epidemiological research is needed to understand risk factors for illness and prognosis. The WHO epidemiological study has been corrected with regard to risk factors that are now accepted, such as whether or not one is an immigrant (McGrath et al., 2008). We will address other risk factors, such as father's age at conception, cannabis use in adolescence, and season of birth in higher latitudes, when we examine the etiology of schizophrenia. However, it is one thing to locate where and when schizophrenia happens and quite another to locate the construct of schizophrenia amid the broader symptoms of psychopathology.

## Locating the Constructs of Schizophrenia and Psychosis

### DEFINITIONS AND RELATED CLINICAL CONSTRUCTS

A perennial discussion exists about how to think about schizophrenia. On the one hand, it is a *diagnosis*. As a diagnosis it is a closed construct we can use to define who has it and who does not. On the other hand, schizophrenia is just as much a *syndrome* as the attenuated psychosis syndrome. Unlike diagnoses, syndromes are open concepts without necessary and sufficient conditions for membership. For some, this argument over whether the construct of schizophrenia is a diagnosis or a syndrome is a silly semantic distraction that detracts from the work of solving the problem. For others this is a debate about the very nature of the disorder itself, without which the problem cannot be solved. To start, it will be useful to agree on several distinctions that might otherwise be confusing based on their use.

"Psychosis," originally from the Greek *psyche* (mind or soul) and *-osis* (an abnormality or derangement) is a broad term for describing the state of "losing touch with reality." Thus psychosis describes the current symptoms. In *DSM-5*, *psychotic symptoms* include delusions, hallucinations, and formal thought disorder consisting of disorganized thinking and speaking. Psychotic symptoms are present in many psychiatric illnesses other than schizophrenia, including bipolar disorder, dementia, drug-induced psychosis, and also a number of physiological conditions such as delirium. Because of this, the term "psychosis" tracks with a patients' state without making any assumptions about any enduring traits. For example, it is common for symptoms to ebb and flow among patients who warrant a diagnosis of schizophrenia. What fluctuates is how psychotic they are, not how schizophrenic.

The "schizophrenia spectrum" is a term first used in the late 1960s by several authors to refer to the marginal conditions of schizophrenia (Erlenmeyer-Kimling & Nicol, 1969; Kety et al., 1971). Its early use was in the context of partial penetrance of genes associated with genetic liability, and it served as shorthand for describing someone who appeared to have a genetic liability to schizophrenia; that is, someone with *schizotaxia*, but who had yet to fully *decompensate* (Meehl, 1962). The schizophrenia spectrum is now often used in a manner that is almost synonymous with a dimensional approach to psychosis—that is, a continuum of symptom expression, including a range of clinical and subclinical symptoms including odd behavior that may or may not ever manifest as a clear case. It may also refer to diagnostic entities similar to schizophrenia, including the attenuated psychosis syndromes described above as well as schizophreniform disorder, schizotypal, schizoid, paranoid and avoidant personality disorders, and, of course, schizophrenia. Following Kraepelin, authors generally do not include affective disorders, such as bipolar disorder, as part of the schizophrenia spectrum though these can be accompanied by psychotic features. *Schizoaffective disorder*, the construct to which we now turn, is included in the spectrum.

One thing that discussions of schizophrenia—singular, plural, or in spectrum—rarely clarify is whether the fundamental Kraepelinian distinction between dementia praecox and manic-depressive insanity exists in nature. Although not the first to observe the phenomenon (Kraepelin himself was apparently aware of such cases), Kasanin (1933) receives credit, or blame, for coining the term "schizoaffective" to describe patients with features of both schizophrenia and mania or depression. Thus the very construct of schizoaffective disorder presents a grave challenge to the original dichotomy of dementia praecox and manic-depressive insanity. The construct was originally incorporated into *DSM-I* as a subtype, eventually gaining the status of a separate disease entity.[2] This disorder survives despite a lack of evidence for any differences in etiology, in pathophysiology, in cognitive or affective functioning, and only occasional differences in treatment outcome between patients with schizophrenia and schizoaffective disorder. Thus, while the schizoaffective diagnosis appears to occupy an intermediate place between schizophrenia and the

---

[2] Another "intermediate" diagnosis whose origin is relevant to schizophrenia is *borderline personality disorder*. The borderline here was that between psychosis and neurosis. In current practice, borderline personality disorder is rarely conceptualized as part of the psychotic spectrum although antipsychotic medicines may be prescribed.

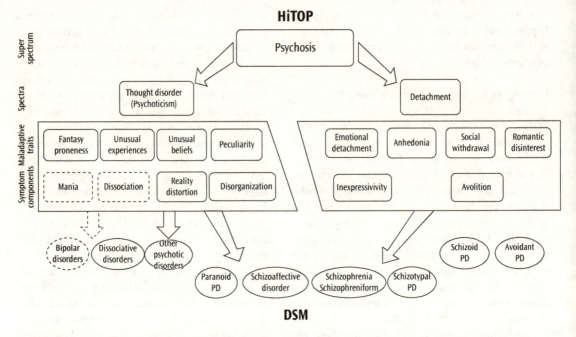

**Figure 14.1** Psychosis symptoms illustrated as part of the Hierarchical Taxonomy of Psychopathology (HiTOP) psychosis superspectrum. PD, personality disorder.
Adapted from Kotov et al. (2020), reprinted with permission.

mood disorders based on symptoms (Laursen et al., 2009), there does not appear to be anything unique in terms of underlying features. As of now the schizoaffective construct remains in the lexicon because it has become a convenient way to describe patients with a mixed presentation.

### STATISTICAL ANALYSES AND EMPIRICAL CONSTRUCTS

In the absence of a definitive test to distinguish psychiatric conditions, clinicians and researchers group patients much like Kraepelin and Bleuler did, by their history and observable symptoms. The diagnoses then applied to those groups implies that distinct latent constructs exist. But are the distinctions between psychiatric conditions, like the distinction between schizophrenia and bipolar disorder, real? An increasing number of scientific, and particularly statistical, tools have been turned toward the question of whether schizophrenia exists in nature distinct from other entities. This work, using the kind of large databases that would make Kraepelin proud, examines the *meta-structure* of psychopathology. This meta-structure describes the relationships between various observed symptoms. The evidence for this, discussed in Chapter 3 of this volume, suggests that in many cases clean distinctions between clinical constructs do not really exist.

This finding is largely borne out in the context of psychotic disorders as well.

As part of the statistical examinations of the relationships between symptoms, the Utility Work Group of Hierarchical Taxonomy of Psychopathology (HiTOP) derived the model for psychotic disorders illustrated in Figure 14.1 based on many studies (Kotov et al., 2020). What does it mean to specify a spectrum of thought disorder composed of reality distortions, disorganization, dissociation, and mania? It means those symptoms tend to co-occur, such that an elevation in one is somewhat predictive of elevations in others. We discuss these relationships more in the next section on Clinical Presentation. Similarly, what it means to have a spectrum of detachment is that symptoms like inexpressivity and avolition, commonly called *negative symptoms*, tend to co-occur. What does it mean to specify a superspectrum of psychosis? It means that thought disorder and detachment are themselves more related to each other than they are to other symptoms, like anxiety. Importantly, the symptoms themselves relate to a number of different *DSM-5* diagnoses on the psychosis spectrum, as indicated by the ovals underneath the observable symptoms. Across a number of studies using a variety of modeling approaches and populations, evidence is weak that a nosological, or symptom-based, categorical distinction can be made between schizophrenia, bipolar affective disorder, and other entities on the psychosis spectrum. Instead, there appears to be a pattern of covariation in the symptoms in these disorders that suggests common elements of impaired cognitive and affective processing.

### CONCEPTUALIZING SCHIZOPHRENIA

A theme of this chapter will be that schizophrenia is neither a disease entity, nor a group of disease entities (for additional, convergent evidence, see MacDonald, 2013). For most purposes, it is useful to understand schizophrenia as an open concept. As a syndrome, schizophrenia is a collection of symptoms that may appear to be superficially unrelated but whose co-occurrence in many patients suggests a shared etiology of some kind. Open concepts frustrate precise definitions. While one can impose definitions, they remain artificial because there are no necessary or sufficient conditions for membership in a class described by an open concept. Any boundary for the class should be taken with a grain of salt. Members of an open concept have a "family resemblance," one to the next, and we recognize members of the class because they are similar to this or that exemplar.

Understanding schizophrenia as an open concept is not to deny its existence or to suggest the construct is useless or even harmful. In fact, *most concepts are open concepts*, and we build up our understanding of the concept through experience rather than through definitions. In natural language, concepts with natural boundaries are the exception rather than the rule. Thus while natural boundaries between schizophrenia and other disorders may not exist, open concepts like schizophrenia or the schizophrenia spectrum are useful for guiding the study of the causes and treatment of an illness. We can now turn to its internal structure and the challenge of understanding the differences among patients with schizophrenia.

## Clinical Presentation and Structure of Symptoms

If we have located the construct of schizophrenia as a delineated space on a schizophrenia spectrum with a certain level of symptom severity and no clear boundaries that exist in nature, there still remains a high level of heterogeneity among patients diagnosed with the illness in terms of its presenting symptoms and its prognosis. This is another kind of challenge to the construct of schizophrenia because it suggests that there may be different kinds of schizophrenia. Indeed, as early as 1911, Bleuler and others were concerned about this level of heterogeneity and sought out meaningful subgroups of patients within the larger diagnosis (e.g., Bleuler & Zinkin, 1911/1950). Bleuler wrote of different schizophrenia*s*, as one might discuss different cancer*s*. These different schizophrenias, or subtypes as they came to be known, included *paranoid* patients, whose presentation was dominated by preoccupation with delusions or auditory hallucinations; *catatonic* patients, who were immobile or, in improved cases, showed flat affect and little motivation; and *undifferentiated* (or, in Bleuler, *hebephrenic*) patients, who did not fall conveniently into either of those categories but also did not have a milder form of the illness (referred to as *simple schizophrenia*). While subtypes of schizophrenia are still used in the popular press, they were inconsistent over time, did not appear to track familial risk, provided little guidance for differential treatment, and were retired from *DSM-5*.

Another way to cope with heterogeneity is to examine the important axes, or dimensions, along which patients vary, similar to the strategies used in HiTOP's work, described above. Although the use of this approach can be dated to the mid-twentieth century (Wittenborn & Holzberg, 1951), the most influential schemes that guide thinking today date from the 1980s and delineate two factors: positive and negative symptoms. Subsequent schemes have added more dimensions such as disorganization, excitement, and depression (for review, and three further dimensions, see Peralta & Cuesta, 2001).

*Positive symptoms*, situated within HiTOP's thought disorder spectrum, are so called because they can be thought of as additional capacities patients develop. These include persecutory ideation, other sorts of delusions, and hallucinations that can involve various senses although auditory hallucinations are the most common. Consider the experience of one student.

> (Rats) gnawed relentlessly on my neurons, causing massive degeneration. This was particularly upsetting to me, as I depended on a sharp mind for my work in neuroscience. The rats spent significant periods of time consuming brain matter in the occipital lobe of my brain.... So I sought means of ridding my body of them. I bled them out through self-cutting and banging my head until the skin broke, bloody. Continually, I kept my brain active, electrocuting

the rats that happened to be feasting on the activated neurons.

"As a neuroscientist, how can you believe all this?" the doctors queried.

"Because it is all of the Deep Meaning.... The Deep Meaning transcends scientific logic." (Stefanidis, 2006)

These are the kinds of symptoms that feature most prominently in the press and film. Ted Kaczynski, the so-called Unabomber, published a persecutory diatribe arguing that his assassinations were a reasonable response to the threat to human freedom from technology. Nobel Prize winner John Nash's delusions that he was helping hunt down communists were featured in the Hollywood film *Beautiful Mind*.

To say that positive symptoms constitute a dimension is to make at least two assertions. First, that if someone has one of these symptoms, they are at increased risk for the others, perhaps because they share a common causal factor. Second, that in the great variety of experiences patients report, there is a continuum from those with many of these symptoms and those who suffer from none of them. As in the above example, most delusions and hallucinations have a negative valence: they are frequently disturbing, they are sometimes positive (generally grandiose), and are almost never emotionally neutral. Thus, they can be quite intrusive, although many chronic patients somehow learn to adapt.

*Negative symptoms*, similar to HiTOP's detachment spectrum, are so called because they can be thought of as lost capacities. Negative symptoms include blunted affect, emotional withdrawal, motor retardation, and anhedonia, which is the inability to experience pleasure. It is ironic that positive symptoms are frequently scary, whereas this other aspect of the disorder is marked by abnormally reduced emotion. Consider this patient's report of her inability to experience pleasure:

[T]his nothingness of the self is permanently there. Not a single drug or therapy has ever helped with such nothingness. By nothingness, I mean a sense of emptiness, a painful void of existence that only I can feel. My thoughts, my emotions, and my actions, none of them belong to me anymore. This omnipotent and omnipresent emptiness has taken control of everything. I am an automaton, but nothing is working inside me. (Kean, 2009)

The motivations of wanting and fearing are fundamental to living organisms, and these seem to be strongly affected by negative symptoms. Many patients with negative symptoms also report reduced desires and aversions, but their experiences of pleasure and perhaps pain are unaffected (Gard et al., 2007), which could be what this example is describing. Of note, antipsychotic medications typically do not improve negative symptoms, as we discuss in the later section on neuropsychopharmacology.

*Disorganization symptoms* are the dimension of inattention and formal thought disorder and are also situated with the HiTOP thought disorder spectrum. One prominent example of this is *incoherence*, also known as *word salad*. When asked the question "Why do people comb their hair?" one patient responded, "Because it makes a twirl in life, my box is broken help me blue elephant. Isn't lettuce brave? I like electrons, hello please!" (Videbeck, 2010). While incoherence is an extreme form of disorganization, more common forms include distractible speech; when asked, "Do you have problems keeping your attention on things?" the patient responds, "I don't know.... What was that again?" Sometimes patients experience thought blocking, in which the patient stops in the middle of a thought and cannot finish the sentence. There are a number of problems patients experience in communicating, such as illogicality and a tendency to lose one's train of thought, known as *derailment*. This dimension also includes inappropriate affect, such as when a patient giggles while describing their suicide attempt (Peralta & Cuesta, 1999).

Two other symptoms dimensions that frequently emerge from factor analyses are excitement (sometimes called mania) and depression (Peralta & Cuesta, 2001). Obviously, these two factors are not specific to schizophrenia. Our consideration of models of personality and psychopathology described above might even suggest that these two factors are manifestations of positive and negative emotionality (or extraversion and neuroticism) and are prominent dimensions of *normal* personality variation (e.g., Markon, 2010; Wright et al., 2012). Also within that context of the meta-structure of psychopathology and our conclusion that schizophrenia is an open concept, one might well wonder whether the positive, negative, and disorganization dimensions are dimensions of schizophrenia or dimensions of psychosis more broadly.

Other sources of variability between patients may require clinical attention, such as cognitive impairments and suicidality. The lifetime risk of suicide among people with schizophrenia is about 6.6%, which is much higher than in the general population and is indistinguishable from the rate (about 6.7%) among people with unipolar depression, a condition for which suicidal ideation constitutes an actual symptom (Nordentoft et al., 2011). Of course the number of suicide attempts is far higher still. Importantly, the risk for suicide attempts is highest among people early in the course of their psychotic illness (Sher & Kahn, 2019).

Symptoms can be thought of as retrospective and global descriptions of patients' experiences and reactions to those experiences. One way to understand these phenomena more objectively may be to examine the cognitive and affective mechanisms that lead to the experiences that are later reported as symptoms.

## Cognition and Affect in Schizophrenia

Two traditions, from clinical science and experimental psychology, have been used to evaluate cognition and affect in schizophrenia, in part to understand the relationships between thought and emotion and in part to provide a link across levels of analysis between symptoms and the biological mechanisms involved in the disorder. We will start with findings from the clinical neuropsychological tradition.

### Neuropsychological Approach to Deficits in Schizophrenia

The neuropsychological approach to schizophrenia is characterized by the use of standardized behavioral tests. The goal of this approach is to compare the pattern of performance in schizophrenia patients to patterns in patients with a variety of brain injuries to determine, by analogy, the brain abnormalities that might relate to schizophrenia.

By the turn of the twenty-first century, R. Walter Heinrichs and his students had built up a large database of neuropsychological studies published on schizophrenia. They coded the studies in a manner that allowed them to calculate each task's effect size, which is the difference between the means of the patient and control groups measured in standard deviation units (Heinrichs, 2001, 2005). This work showed that across a wide range of tests, in every category of thinking they examined—including verbal memory, nonverbal memory, attention, general intelligence, spatial ability, executive functioning and language functioning—patients on average performed worse than controls. Patients performed the worst on global verbal memory (Cohen's effect size = −1.41) like the WAIS Logical Memory subtest, and they performed the least badly on tasks like the WAIS block design subtest (Cohen's effect size = −.46, Heinrichs & Zakzanis, 1998). Between these two extremes, there was little systematic sense to patients' behavioral impairments. For example, nonverbal domains other than block design—from simple motor skills, like the Grooved Pegboard test, to other measures of performance IQ—were also among the most impaired (with effect sizes of −1.30 and −1.26, respectively). The average effect size across this assortment of neuropsychological tests was −.92, meaning patients on average performed about a standard deviation below controls (Heinrichs, 2005). This deficiency was larger than in other domains studied with quantitative metrics, such as patients' impairments in neuroimaging, electrophysiology, and even the molecular biological studies Heinrichs also examined. This pattern of widespread behavioral impairments in patients with schizophrenia can be thought of as a *generalized deficit* (Chapman & Chapman, 1973). Despite medication, and despite improvements in measurement of more specific domains of dysfunction, this generalized deficit still remains the most prominent feature of behavior on neuropsychological tests in patients with schizophrenia.

Does the generalized deficit relate to patients' symptom expression? Dominguez and colleagues (2009) reviewed this literature by dividing neuropsychological tasks into nine domains of performance (executive control, speed of processing, verbal working memory, etc.) and comparing their relationship with positive, negative, disorganized, and depressed symptoms across 58 studies. In this light, positive and depressive symptoms showed few systematic relationships with performance across cognitive domains, whereas negative symptoms were correlated with the cognitive domains ($r = -.08$ to $-.25$) and disorganization symptoms were correlated ($r = -.12$ to $-.29$). Thus, these off-the-shelf tests suggest that performance across domains, perhaps corresponding to the generalized deficit, is most closely linked to negative and disorganization symptoms, whereas they do not provide very much insight into the nature of delusions, hallucinations, and other positive symptoms. Let us then consider an alternative approach that may provide a complementary set of tools.

### Cognitive-Experimental Approach to Deficits in Schizophrenia

The pattern of finding a generalized deficit across a broad swathe of neuropsychological tests presents a challenge to behavioral researchers. Logically, the domain or domains with the largest effect sizes should provide guidance for choosing processes to be examined in detail. This examination might then isolate the brain networks and predisposing cognitive processes that underlie symptoms. However, when so many facets of behavioral performance are impaired, and suspicion falls on nearly every brain region thought to support those processes according to clinical neuropsychological lore, there is no clear path to follow.

A different approach that also emphasizes behavioral performance is called the *cognitive-experimental approach*. Instead of using a broad battery of well-standardized tests to find group differences, this approach is hypothesis-driven. That is, it tests theories about mechanisms underlying the various symptoms of schizophrenia by comparing performance across closely matched conditions which are a kind of experimental manipulation. While experimental studies of schizophrenia patients have been conducted since the outset—indeed, Kraepelin trained in the laboratory of the founder of experimental psychology, Wilhelm Wundt—the modern tradition of cognitive-experimental psychopathology grows from the work of pioneers like David Shakow and Saul Mednick (1958) who applied new theories of information processing and learning, respectively, to the study of schizophrenia.

To follow one such pioneer, Shakow examined a phenomenon that came to be called *reaction time crossover* (Rodnick & Shakow, 1940). This meant patients responded faster to a probe following an irregular delay compared to a consistent delay. Patients' performance was therefore *relatively spared* following an irregular delay, the condition that is harder for controls. Shakow conceptualized reaction time crossover as a failure to maintain alertness, or maintain set over time, and found it was related to patients' level of disorganization symptoms (Rosenthal et al., 1960). As cognitive theory continued to develop, the construct of maintaining set fell out of favor and became subsumed within other psychological constructs; one such generalization was *context processing*. Context processing was introduced by Jonathan Cohen and colleagues to bring into a single framework the extant literatures on executive control, attention, and working memory (Cohen & Servan-Schreiber, 1992; Servan-Schreiber et al., 1996). This posited that context processing was the goal-dependent modulation of brain activity to support "nondominant" or underlearned responses. For example, patients' performance on a modified continuous performance task was impaired on a condition that required extra context processing relative to the condition that did not. Reminiscent of Shakow, patients' impairments correlated with disorganization symptoms, although not more so than for neuropsychological tasks (see MacDonald, 2008, for further discussion).

Positive symptoms may relate to another psychological mechanism, *predictive processes*. A fundamental role of the mind is to predict because an organism's survival depends on understanding how its actions impact itself and the world around it (Friston, 2009). When we are conscious of these predictions, they can even be expressed as beliefs. For example, part of the brain called the ventral tegmental area activates when an unexpected reward occurs, like a frosty milkshake on a hot day. Like Pavlov's dogs (Pavlov, 1927), after predictors for the reward are learned this area fires when the predictor occurs, such as the appearance of the neon milkshake sign, *before* the actual reward (Schultz, 2007). This learning mechanism may be a general principle of thought and has been called the "Bayesian brain" after the eighteenth-century developer of probabilistic inference (see Corlett et al., 2020, for further discussion). A number of investigators have speculated that impairments in these fundamental inferential mechanisms, related to the salience network in the brain which evaluates rewards and threats, might lead to psychotic symptoms (Feeney et al., 2017; Kapur, 2003). Whether conscious or not, if the process of belief formation becomes untethered from events in the world, then uncomfortable and uncanny feelings are inevitable. People seek explanations or interpretations for those feelings. When they do, they will be seen as delusional if they cannot be convinced by alternative explanations. There is growing evidence that such processes are involved in positive symptoms, although this mechanism may not account for all such symptoms (Donaldson et al., 2020).

Negative symptoms may relate to a distinct but related aspect of learning, *insensitivity to rewards*. As with predictive processing, there is a literature stretching back decades that examines processes of valuation, motivation, and emotional expressiveness. The notion that these mechanisms relate to negative symptoms has a great deal of appeal, although it has been noted that these impairments are not particularly specific to schizophrenia (Strauss & Cohen, 2017). Gold and colleagues (2008) examined the extent to which measures of these processes related to symptom ratings. In one task, participants pressed a button quickly to indicate whether or not to see the current picture again later in the experiment. Controls pressed more to see pleasant and avoid unpleasant pictures, but not neutral pictures. Similarly, controls were willing to wait longer for larger rewards.

A common problem here, as with other symptoms domains examined using the cognitive-experimental approach, is their moderate correlation with symptoms among patients. For example, Gold and colleagues (2008) report that performance on their motivation and valuation tasks was occasionally correlated with symptom ratings at a moderate level but was more commonly quite a bit lower and therefore indistinguishable from correlations with general neuropsychological tasks. Therefore, it is important to note that other cognitive-experimental approaches are continuing to develop, and these theories are naturally broadening to incorporate the methods and theories of cognitive neuroscience, which we will address subsequently. In many respects, the cognitive-experimental approach to the behavioral level of analysis is the natural domain for demonstrating the relationship between the psychological mechanisms underlying moment-to-moment experiences and the global, frequently retrospective reports of symptoms. The approach incorporates and modifies tools to examine specific hypotheses as opposed to using well-standardized testing batteries. This flexibility presents a challenge because many paradigms will not perform in the manner expected, and even here it can be difficult to distinguish between specific deficits in a hypothesized mechanism and the generalized deficit (see Chapman & Chapman, 1973). Despite these challenges, one measure of the success of the experimental cognitive approach is that it has become an integral component of cognitive neuroscientific studies that use such tasks to challenge specific brain regions and networks during imaging. As such, we now turn our attention to the important findings from this level of analysis.

## Cognitive Neuroscience and Systems Neuroscience of Schizophrenia

A widely accepted view is that schizophrenia is a disease of the brain. However, since all mental disorders involve neuronal functions, this is not a particularly helpful revelation. Furthermore, it is not yet clear what kind of brain disease it might be. There is no single insult to the brain or any single structure or neurotransmitter that is uniquely responsible. Therefore, one challenge is to link the symptoms of schizophrenia and the problems in cognition and affect to particular facets of brain functioning.

It would be helpful to know that a handful of regions show slowed responses, relative decreases or increases in activation, or weaker connectivity in schizophrenia. Unfortunately, and despite a great deal of effort, this kind of pithy conclusion is not yet possible from the fragmented literature arising from the various methods used to study the neural processes in people with schizophrenia.

### Electroencephalography

Scalp electrodes can reveal a number of different aspects of the *timing* of brain functions. One method, called electroencephalography (EEG), focuses on the frequencies of different brain waves. Findings based on this technique have indicated that schizophrenia involves a reduction of the power of brain waves across a broad spectrum, but impairments in the gamma spectrum (which has a frequency of electrical brainwaves in the 30–80 Hz range) may be particularly telling (Gandal et al., 2012). This frequency is responsible for cognitive coordination (Phillips & Silverstein, 2003) and for binding thoughts from different parts of the brain together into a coherent percept (Gonzalez-Burgos & Lewis, 2008). Another way of using scalp electrodes is to examine event-related potentials, which speak to the timing of brain responses to stimuli. Unsurprisingly, this technique has shown that many waveforms have a reduced magnitude in patients. The stand-outs in this crowd, either due to popularity of study or ease of reliable measurement, are reductions in the P1, MMN, and P300 wave forms (for review, see Ford et al., 2012): the P1 is a very early component associated with the perception of a stimulus; the MMN, which stand for *mismatch negativity*, is an early waveform interpreted as showing an impairment in the early, non-volitional capacity to redirect attention; the P300 is a component interpreted as indicating a capacity for attentional orientation. Thus there is ample evidence that schizophrenia affects the timing of a number of important processes in the brain, some of which dovetails with evidence of early perceptual impairments and some of which suggests top-down failures of cognitive control processes.

### Structure and Connectivity

If there are timing dysfunctions in the brain, what brain *regions* are most affected? Magnetic resonance imaging (MRI) has been the tool of choice for addressing this kind of question in recent years because MRI machines can be tuned to examine several aspects of brain anatomy: structure and structural connectivity and function and functional connectivity. Beginning with structure, a highly replicated and completely unspecific finding is that patients have reductions in intracranial, whole-brain, and total gray and white matter volumes and increases in ventricular volumes (De Peri et al., 2012). Early efforts to show more specific abnormalities showed a consistent loss of gray matter in the superior temporal lobes, a region implicated in auditory sensory processing (Shenton et al., 2001). Inevitably, methods have evolved and there are now several quantitative reviews of the literature using whole-brain, voxel-by-voxel analyses, called *voxel-based morphometry* (Chan et al., 2011; Ellison-Wright et al., 2008). These reviews, reporting on two to three dozen studies, have found consistent reductions in gray matter in thalamus and limbic regions such as insula, anterior cingulate, uncus, and amygdala. While thalamus is an essential cortico-cortico relay network, these limbic regions are thought to work together in a salience network responsible for evaluating stimuli for rewards and threats in the environment. Of course the picture is not entirely consistent, and there are other regions where even these reviews differ, such as whether reductions in left inferior frontal gyrus or the cerebellum are reliably reduced in first-episode patients. The impact of chronicity has also been examined, with chronic patients continuing to show gray matter loss in some of these same limbic regions, such as the insula, but also starting to show gray matter compromised in executive control regions such as the inferior and dorsolateral prefrontal cortex, and in a region that becomes more active during rest, the medial prefrontal gyrus. Although far fewer studies have directly compared people with schizophrenia and bipolar disorder, they do appear to be similar in showing reductions in whole-brain volume and a number of other features compared to controls (De Peri et al., 2012). Schizophrenia patients may show more gray matter volume reduction, whereas bipolar patients may have more white matter reduction, which may suggest some specificity.

White matter is composed of myelinated axons carrying information across the brain. An imaging technique known as *diffusion tensor imaging* can be used to quantify the extent to which these axon fiber tracts are organized coherently, like rope, or incoherently, like lint. Unsurprisingly, the vast majority of this literature has found evidence for less coherence in the axon fiber tracts of patients with schizophrenia, with some evidence suggesting that the connections between frontal lobe regions are particularly compromised (Pettersson-Yeo et al., 2011). A shortcoming of both this structural connectivity literature and the structural abnormalities described above is that very few studies have reported how differences among schizophrenia patients relate to their symptom presentations, therefore making it difficult to tell a more refined story about the relationship between structure and symptoms. Nevertheless, we will try to rectify this when we turn to functional neuroimaging.

### Function and Functional Networks

Functional imaging of the brain began in the 1970s (Ingvar & Franzen, 1974), with a marked increase in interest following the advent of functional MRI (fMRI) in the early 1990s. However, a concern soon arose as to whether differences in brain activity between patients and controls caused differences in performance or whether differences in performance, strategy, or motivation reduced the demands on regions that healthy participants used to perform tasks (e.g., Ebmeier et al., 1995). This causality confound still bedevils the field, increasing the challenge of extracting a coherent meaning from the literally thousands of fMRI studies that have been published to date.

Despite this confound there are a number of conclusions from studies that have begun to link the heterogeneity in patients' symptoms to differences in functioning across the brain (for review of symptom-activation relationships, see Goghari et al., 2010). For example, the occurrence of auditory hallucinations corresponds to activity in the superior temporal gyrus, an area which we also noted had structural abnormalities. Thus, one of the most common symptoms in schizophrenia may reflect processing at the earliest sensory inputs into the brain. Positive symptoms more generally also appear to be related to abnormalities in the medial prefrontal cortex, a region associated with self-awareness and ideas about others' state of mind. Reduced activation in ventral striatum, a region associated with reward processing, appears to correlate with the extent to which negative symptoms are expressed. Negative symptoms have also been associated with blunted amygdalar responses. Both of these regions are involved in the salience network described earlier. Consistent with behavioral work, disorganization has been related to impairments of activation of the prefrontal cortex, a region of the brain implicated in executive functioning.

While these findings begin to fit within our picture of schizophrenia, they also highlight a major flaw in this literature, which, due in part to small sample sizes, has largely neglected: the need to examine the relationships between brain activity and patient heterogeneity in symptoms and functioning. This situation is beginning to improve, and several large data sets are currently being collected to allow more definitive tests of these relationships. In the meantime, our next step is to go below the level of systems and look more closely at molecular neurobiology.

## Cellular Pathophysiology and Neuropsychopharmacology of Schizophrenia

A growing literature has examined the brain's structure at a still more molecular level, scrutinizing which neurons and glia are present and how patients' neuronal cells may differ from healthy controls. This work has relied on brain tissues from people who have donated this organ upon their death, and it reminds us of the importance of this kind of generosity for solving important mental health challenges. Since people live with schizophrenia for many years before dying, patients' brains not only reflect the causes of the disorder, but also the sequelae of chronic illness and the use of medication. These caveats notwithstanding, a number of telling findings have emerged. Complementing this work, neuropharmacology addresses the chemical compounds that affect neurotransmission, including but not limited to neurotransmitters. There are a number of candidates for study, with no reason to think that any one neurotransmitter can account for patients' heterogeneity or is more fundamental to the disorder. This has not always been the case; for many years, schizophrenia was thought to be an illness uniquely associated with problems in the transmission of dopamine (DA).

The origin of the *DA hypothesis* of schizophrenia is useful to relay because it provides a nutmeg of consolation for students of psychopathology frustrated by how much we still have to discover after a century of schizophrenia studies. In the mid-twentieth century, psychiatry had to be content with many vagaries and empirical observations, which is a polite way of saying experiments guided by chance and providence. There was plenty of incentive and opportunity for experimentation: thousands and thousands of schizophrenia patients were permanently housed on the sprawling, overcrowded campuses of state hospitals. In this atmosphere, a class of compounds that had originally been developed for the textile industry in the nineteenth century and tested for possible antimalarial and anesthetic properties during World War I eventually came to the attention of a team of French psychiatrists (cf. López-Muñoz et al., 2005). After some tinkering, the compound that would be known as chlorpromazine proved to be surprisingly good at reducing patients' concerns about, and the occurrence of, delusions and hallucinations. Though it was hailed as a wonder drug, soon its side effects began to overshadow its successes. This, in turn, led to attempts to find compounds similar to chlorpromazine, without such severe side effects, that would come to be known as *typical antipsychotics*. Interestingly, these were used in the treatment of schizophrenia starting in the mid-1950s, long before it was understood how they worked. The definitive result underpinning the first dopamine hypotheses of schizophrenia was not published until the mid-1970s, when it was demonstrated that clinical effects of the various antipsychotic drugs available at that time strongly correlated with the extent to which they blocked DA receptors (Seeman & Lee, 1975). This illustrates that treatments can be viable even if the cause of the condition is unknown or even misunderstood. While the DA hypothesis accounted for a number of observations about psychosis at the time, the façade of this simple explanation would not stand indefinitely, despite several revisions (for a review of various DA hypotheses as well as a modern rendering of the hypotheses, see Howes & Kapur, 2009; for another perspective, see Kendler & Schaffner, 2011).

A challenge to the reigning hypothesis built around the *therapeutic* effects of DA antagonists came from the *psychomimetic* (psychosis-inducing) effects of another drug known as phencyclidine (PCP, "angel dust"). Phencyclidine was originally developed as a tranquilizer; however, people who used the drug showed transient schizophrenia-like symptoms, and patients who were given the drug showed long-lasting symptom exacerbations even at very low doses (Luby et al., 1962). When evidence emerged that phencyclidine and similar compounds such as ketamine ("special K") increased the activity of the N-methyl-D-aspartate (NMDA) receptors on glutamatergic pyramidal neurons (Vincent et al., 1979), it brought into focus an alternative *glutamate hypothesis* (Javitt & Zukin, 1991). Pyramidal neurons are pervasive and can be thought of as the primary working neurons and connections of the cortex. This glutamate hypothesis was parsimonious insofar as it explained how a single dysfunction might result in numerous, correlated impairments in different brain systems and relate to the degradation of white matter tracts described above. Reinforcing this theory, postmortem studies began to show that pyramidal neurons in patients' brains had shorter axons, tighter cell packing, and fewer NMDA receptors on their dendrites (see Lin et al., 2012, for review). It then became necessary to explain away the primary basis of the DA hypothesis, which could be done if the effectiveness of typical dopaminergic antipsychotic drugs was simply the result of dopaminergic modulation of glutamate or even secondary to their sedative effects. As a result only a few new pharmaceuticals have been developed based on these findings. For example, drugs targeting glutamate receptors have been tested for and shown to be effective at reducing ketamine-induced psychotic symptoms and normalizing related brain activity in healthy volunteers (Kantrowitz et al., 2020). This low yield is in no small part due to the difficulty of safely modulating the activity of one of the most fundamental cell types of the brain.

A third pathophysiological and neuropharmacological hypothesis is largely built on postmortem brain tissue observations but also incorporates gene expression and brain network connectivity data. In this case, the abnormalities of interest are in the gamma-aminobutyric acid (GABA) interneurons that inhibit activity in other neurons, primarily pyramidal neurons. This is therefore known as the *GABA hypothesis*. These neurons, and in particular a subset of them known as *basket* and *chandelier cells*, contain parvalbumin. Parvalbumin maintains the tone of pyramidal neurons that is needed to resonate appropriately in the gamma frequency. This frequency, it will be recalled, underlies cognitive coordination and binding. Originally based on postmortem studies of patients, the GABA hypothesis incorporates the roles of DA and glutamate, proposing that perturbations of these neurotransmitter systems are downstream from the dysconnectivity that results from a failure to maintain the tone of pyramidal neurons (see Gonzalez-Burgos & Lewis, 2008, for review). Thus, parvalbumin neurons are thought to be impaired in producing and releasing GABA, which results in the cognitive deficits of schizophrenia (Lewis, 2014). While this hypothesis suggests a new neurotransmitter system to target with pharmaceuticals, this promise has yet to be realized. In the meantime, it provides an elegant example of how multiple methods and data from many levels of analysis can be synthesized into a comprehensive account of a mental illness.

Taken together, this work suggests an imbalance between excitatory and inhibitory neurotransmission related to psychosis. Concentrations of glutamate and GABA, representing the primary excitatory and inhibitory neurotransmitters, respectively, are dysregulated in schizophrenia. Elevations of glutamate concentration are consistently documented in schizophrenia spectrum disorders (Merritt et al., 2016) and partly explained by genetic influences (Legind et al., 2019) while dysregulated GABA has met mixed findings in schizophrenia (Egerton et al., 2017) and also bipolar disorder (Schür et al., 2016). Both glutamate and GABA concentrations are related to functional connectivity problems between brain regions in schizophrenia (Shukla et al., 2019) as well as cognitive functions such as working memory (Bojesen et al., 2020). Some evidence for drug treatments targeting the glutamatergic and GABA balance have also emerged but await replication.

This section provides only a taste of an extensive literature on the neuroscience, pathophysiology, and pharmacology of schizophrenia. Before moving on to explore causes of these neural abnormalities, it will be useful to make two general observations. The first is that while the hypotheses are competing in the scientific community, they need not actually compete in the brain. That is, the hypotheses may all contain a non–mutually exclusive portion of the truth, and other mechanisms may be in play. While it is parsimonious to think that the neural basis of schizophrenia is simple, nature frustrates this hope. Research can be hypothesis-driven without making the naïve assumption that there is, at the core, a single abnormality. The second is that, due to evidence of the kind described here, schizophrenia is often considered more organic, or biological, than many other disorders described in this text. This classification brings along many implicit assumptions about the condition and those who suffer from it. For example, it suggests that the true pathology of schizophrenia is to be found in neurons and that treatments for schizophrenia will require medicine to change those neurons. The distinction between psychological and organic causes for a disorder may be appealing, but it is increasingly untenable given our understanding of the tight relationships between the software and hardware of the brain. The brain limits the cognitive mechanisms that can be implemented, but those same neurons also reflect the traces of the cognitive mechanisms that have been required of them. In fact, all disorders addressed in this textbook have or will have neural correlates; all symptoms will respond to medicine, either real or hypothetical. Sometimes the symptoms of schizophrenia appear to be more biologically based, but this is simply because new biological methods are often brought to bear here first, before expanding to other diagnoses. In the final analysis, schizophrenia is unlikely to prove a special case of mental illness in this regard.

## Etiology of Schizophrenia

In reviewing findings on the causes of schizophrenia, we will follow the simplified scheme of classifying causes as either genetic or environmental.

### Genetic Risks for Schizophrenia

Some of the first examinations of the etiology of schizophrenia were family studies conducted by the protégées of Emil Kraepelin in the 1910s (see Kendler & Zerbin-Rüdin, 1996). Family studies allow inferences through the use of quantitative genetics, based on the association between degree of genetic relatedness and level of risk. These earliest studies showed patients' siblings were at a markedly increased risk of illness relative to the general population, but the work was largely neglected until the 1960s when a new generation of scholars began to examine whether genes might play a role in the etiology of schizophrenia. Gottesman (1991) combined these data across studies to show a compelling relationship: third-degree relatives such as patients' first cousins, who share about 12.5% of their genes, show a 2% risk of developing the disorder (compared to .7% in the general population). Second-degree relatives, such as uncles and nieces, share about 25% of their genes and have a 2–6% risk, whereas first-degree relatives such as siblings, including fraternal twins, have a 6–17% risk. Patients' monozygotic twins, who share 100% of their genes, have nearly a 50% risk of developing the illness. These data are interpreted in the parlance of quantitative genetics as indicating the heritability of the *liability to schizophrenia*. Liability can be thought of as the diathesis to schizophrenia (i.e., it is necessary but not sufficient for developing the illness). These data, along with information about the prevalence of schizophrenia in the general population, show that the liability is 80% heritable in most populations, which is to say 80% of the variance in liability in that population is associated with variance in genes across the whole genome.

The data do not tell us how heritable *schizophrenia* is. As noted, the likelihood that you will develop schizophrenia if your monozygotic co-twin has the illness is 50%. These findings suggest a phenomenon called *reduced penetrance*. Simply inheriting the genetic liability for the illness is, on average, insufficient to cause the illness. Something additional is needed. Thus, the *diathesis-stress model* suggests some kind of environmental stressor might be required in addition to the diathesis to make the disorder become manifested. We will review a number of such proposed stressors below, but it is worth noting that luck—the chance factors that govern whether or not this or that gene is expressed in the body's cells—also counts as an "environmental" contribution within this model.

Quantitative genetic studies provide the impetus for *molecular genetic research*, and this has now become one of the fastest developing domains of the schizophrenia literature. Rather than asking *whether* genes contribute to the illness, this research asks *which* genes contribute. The hope is not simply that identifying these genes will be interesting, but that the functions of those genes will suggest treatments, or even a cure. The thrust of the story of the molecular genetics of schizophrenia is threefold: identifying genes involved in the illness requires very large samples of patients and controls and more markers across the genome because there are likely to be many, many genes that convey a tiny bit of risk.

In the 1990s, the molecular genetics of schizophrenia consisted largely of linkage studies that used measures of recombination frequency, rather than a specific physical distance along each chromosome, to detect regions of various chromosomes that might be associated with risk for schizophrenia. By the end of this era, there were a number of promising findings, such as a portion of chromosome 2p12–q22.1 that was consistently linked to the illness (Lewis et al., 2003). However, the method precluded identifying specific genes and therefore precluded understanding the specific pathways to illness.

In the 2000s, attention turned to specific genetic markers known as *single-nucleotide polymorphisms* (SNPs), which formed the basis of the candidate gene approach. In this method, SNPs on a number of candidate genes were selected for closer scrutiny because they were thought to be involved in a putative neural mechanism. SNP markers on a number of genes came to light, including genes relevant to

DA (e.g., catechol-O-methyltransferase [*COMT*]), glutamate (e.g., neuregulin [*NRG1*]), GABA (e.g., glutamic acid decarboxylase 1 [*GAD1*]), and neurodevelopment (e.g., disrupted in schizophrenia 1 [*DISC1*]), among others. While a number of early studies using this method provided excited results, researchers became concerned about the low level of replicability of many findings, particularly those derived from small sample sizes ($Ns < 1,000$).

A series of new findings shook up this a priori approach to gene discovery when genotyping technology advanced and genome-wide association studies (GWAS) became practical. GWASs do not examine a few markers in selected genes. Instead, they look at markers across all chromosomes to determine any gene with a strong association to an illness. Armed with immense samples sizes, GWAS studies have discovered that many genes—likely numbering in the thousands—are statistically associated with the illness and that many of these genes are quite common in the general population as well. In addition, all the genes that have so far been associated with schizophrenia together account for a very small proportion of the variance in schizophrenia in the population, suggesting that more complicated interactions and pathways will have to be taken into account. As opposed to implicating a specific genetic or molecular mechanism of risk, these studies so far suggest that a number of mechanisms may be relevant to the diathesis for schizophrenia and psychosis more broadly. Recently, efforts to quantify an individual's overall genetic liability for schizophrenia have calculated a "polygenic risk score" that sums one's risk alleles weighted by their respective effect sizes from GWAS (Choi et al., 2020). This polygenic risk score can be combined with functional neuroimaging to explain variance in brain function (Cao et al., 2020) and perhaps yield information relevant for tailored treatment. Additionally, polygenic risk scores for schizophrenia have been used to predict other mental health concerns (e.g., anxiety, depression) and environmental conditions (e.g., nicotine use, trauma), though this work has yet to be extended to individuals of non-European descent (Docherty et al., 2018). The job of untangling these genetic findings enough to turn them into treatment options remains a daunting task.

*Environmental and Other Risks for Schizophrenia*

In the decades following World War II, clinical practice in the United States was dominated by psychodynamic—and therefore primarily environmental—explanations of psychosis. One tragic consequence of this bias was the growth of a myth of a *schizophrenogenic mother*. The schizophrenogenic mother was said to have defective interactions with her children and a number of other vague and at times conflicting shortcomings as a parent that led the future patient to learn something that eventually manifested as the illness. The unintended result of these strongly environmental theories of schizophrenia was that the parents of patients, already struggling with the day-to-day difficulties of supporting their ill son or daughter, were further saddled by the guilt of having caused the illness itself. This is the cautionary environmentalists' tale much as the history of eugenics cautions against overinterpreting genetic causal factors.

The fundamental observation that still requires an environmental, or nongenetic, account of the etiology of schizophrenia is that the concordance between monozygotic twins is about 50%. Since this is less than 100%, it is thought that there must be some nongenetic cause that leads to the ultimate manifestation. Table 14.1 lists eight additional risk factors that have been established through large meta-analyses. None of these risk factors implicates defective parenting, and most of them implicate either pre- or perinatal events (older fathers, prenatal famine, maternal influenza, obstetrical complications, winter or spring birth) or other biological risk factors (*Toxoplasmosis gondii* exposure, lifetime cannabis use). That is, they are unlikely to affect one's learning regimen.

Of note, given recent efforts to legalize marijuana across the world, cannabis use as a risk factor for schizophrenia carries a dose-response relationship

**Table 14.1** Nongenetic risk factors associated with schizophrenia

| Risk factor | Odds ratio |
| --- | --- |
| Migrant status | 4.6 |
| Older fathers | 3.8 |
| *Toxoplasmosis gondii* exposure | 2.7 |
| Prenatal famine | 2.3 |
| Lifetime cannabis use | 2.1 |
| Obstetrical complications | 1.8 |
| Urban rearing | 1.7 |
| Winter or spring birth | 1.1 |

Note: For full citations, see MacDonald & Schulz (2009). Odds ratios are calculated as the increased odds of someone with the risk factor developing the condition, where 1.0 is the general population risk.

such that patients who used cannabis more than 50 times in their lifetime have a significantly higher rate of developing schizophrenia, especially if use began at a younger age (Ortiz-Medina et al., 2018). Of the two others, migrant status and urban rearing, it is unclear what aspect of these very general risk factors convey risk at this time, although an argument can be made for stress or anxiety. Importantly, even the most reliably potent risk factors—such as migrant status or older fathers—only moderately increases risk; most patients are not migrants or the offspring of older fathers. Furthermore, migrant status or urban rearing represent only a fraction of one's environment, and recent research has attempted to examine broader contexts that reflect the interdependence of environmental risk factors (e.g., ethnic density, presence of pollution and infectious agents; Plana-Ripoll et al., 2018). This type of work has been termed "exposome" research because it aims to examine the environmental exposures more comprehensively, similar to genome-wide analyses (Guloksuz, van Os et al., 2018). Exposome research, in attempting to capture the entirety of environmental exposures, has an admirable goal of identifying modifiable risk factors for schizophrenia, though not without encountering unique challenges (see Guloksuz, Rutten et al., 2018).

Another question that arises with a great deal of regularity is whether brain injuries cause schizophrenia. Many researchers who use neuroimaging and therefore screen patients for head injuries have observed that patients with schizophrenia are far more likely than controls to report an errant baseball bat or harrowing bicycle accident that left them with a concussion. According to published case studies, head injuries can only in rare instances lead to psychosis, and these patients generally have few negative symptoms (Fujii & Fujii, 2012). These findings would seem to suggest that a schizophrenia patient with few negative symptoms would be indistinguishable from a head-injury–induced psychosis patient. However, this kind of question is tricky to study rigorously in sufficiently large samples for definitive conclusions.

Finally, careful readers will note that our classification of genetic and environmental causation is, like other convenient distinctions raised in this chapter, to be taken with a grain of salt. For example, evidence for these risk factors does not rule out the possibility that a great deal of the reduced concordance between monozygotic twins is simply due to chance; such twins may have inherited differences in the strength of expressing certain genes, a phenomenon known as *methylation*. Thus, even nongenetic causes may involve the genome in some ways. Another way in which the genetic/environmental distinction may be misleading is in the context of gene–environment correlations and gene–environment interactions. For example, cannabis use may only be a risk factor for people with a particular diathesis, such that people with a family history of schizophrenia are more susceptible to the psychosis-inducing effects of cannabis (Ortiz-Medina et al., 2018). Thus, the reader should be prepared to critique such simplistic classifications. More often than not, etiological explanations of schizophrenia involve both genetic and environmental components. For instance, a growing literature exploring the connection between schizophrenia and immune functioning points to formative environmental risk factors (e.g., maternal influenza, autoimmune disorders) that activate and prime immune reactivity, as well as schizophrenia risk genes that promote inflammation (Müller, 2018). This vulnerability-stress-inflammation model is yet another theory that emphasizes the complexity of schizophrenia.

## Conclusion

The symptoms of schizophrenia constitute a devastating, serious, and persistent syndrome that affects a remarkably high proportion of the human race. It can affect all aspects of life, indeed shortening life itself through increased suicidality and other health consequences. Numerous theories of the nature of the illness have arisen and fallen in the 100 years since its description and coinage by Kraepelin and Bleuler. Were these progenitors alive today, they would survey the legacy of their work with a mixture of pride and disappointment.

There is much to be proud of in the century of work that has expanded our knowledge of how different symptom dimensions relate to each other and to other disorders, how these relate to cognitive functions and brain networks, and how these brain networks are in turn influenced by biochemical processes. The fact that these processes may not be specific to schizophrenia per se but may be relevant to disorders beyond that strict definition does not detract from those accomplishments. It is ironic, however, that much of the progress in treating the illness has proceeded entirely independent from the psychopathological science of it. Pharmacological treatment discoveries, although never coincidences, have only in recent years built on our understanding of the causes of the disorder. It is also ironic that psychosocial treatments, used rarely in the past, have become increasingly acceptable within this new zeitgeist of nonspecificity of symptoms and broad sources of causation. Thus, while the construct introduced to psychiatry 100 years ago is certainly showing signs of ageing, it is sure to provide a reference point for thinking about psychosis far into the future.

## References

Bleuler, E., & Zinkin, T. J. (1911/1950). *Dementia praecox or the group of schizophrenias*. International Universities Press.

Bojesen, K. B., Broberg, B. V., Fagerlund, B., Jessen, K., Thomas, M. B., Sigvard, A., Tangmose, K., Nielsen, M. Ø., Andersen, G. S., Larsson, H. B. W., Edden, R. A., Rostrup, E., & Glenthøj, B. Y. (2020). Associations between cognitive function and levels of glutamatergic metabolites and gamma-aminobutyric acid in antipsychotic-naïve patients with schizophrenia or psychosis. *Biological Psychiatry, 89*(3), 278–287.

Cannon, T. D., Yu, C., Addington, J., Bearden, C. E., Cadenhead, K. S., Cornblatt, B. A., Heinssen, R., Jeffries, C. D., Mathalon, D. H., McGlashan, T. H., Perkins, D. O., Seidman, L. J., Tsuang, M. T., Walker, E. F., Woods, S. W., & Kattan, M. W. (2016). An individualized risk calculator for research in prodromal psychosis. *American Journal of Psychiatry, 173*(10), 980–988.

Cao, H., Zhou, H., & Cannon, T. D. (2020). Functional connectome-wide associations of schizophrenia polygenic risk. *Molecular Psychiatry,* 1–9.

Chan, R. C. K., Di, X., McAlonan, G. M., & Gong, Q. (2011). Brain anatomical abnormalities in high-risk individuals, first-episode, and chronic schizophrenia: An activation likelihood estimation meta-analysis of illness progression. *Schizophrenia Bulletin, 37*(1), 177–188. doi:10.1093/schbul/sbp073

Chapman, L. J., & Chapman, J. P. (1973). Problems in the measurement of cognitive deficit. *Psychological Bulletin, 79,* 380–385.

Choi, S. W., Mak, T. S. H., & O'Reilly, P. F. (2020). Tutorial: A guide to performing polygenic risk score analyses. *Nature Protocols,* 1–14.

Cohen, J. D., & Servan-Schreiber, D. (1992). Context, cortex and dopamine: A connectionist approach to behavior and biology in schizophrenia. *Psychological Review, 99*(1), 45–77.

Corlett, P. R., Mohanty, A., & MacDonald, A. W. III. (2020). What we think about when we think about predictive processing. *Journal of Abnormal Psychology, 129*(6), 529–533. doi:10.1037/abn0000632

De Peri, L., Crescini, A., Deste, G., Fusar-Poli, P., Sacchetti, E., & Vita, A. (2012). Brain structural abnormalities at the onset of schizophrenia and bipolar disorder: A meta-analysis of controlled magnetic resonance imaging studies. *Current Pharmaceutical Design, 18*(4), 486–494.

Docherty, A. R., Moscati, A., Dick, D., Savage, J. E., Salvatore, J. E., Cooke, M., ... Adkins, D. E. (2018). Polygenic prediction of the phenome, across ancestry, in emerging adulthood. *Psychological Medicine, 48*(11), 1814.

Dominguez, M. D. G., Viechtbauer, W., Simons, C. J. P., van Os, J., & Krabbendam, L. (2009). Are psychotic psychopathology and neurocognition orthogonal? A systematic review of their associations. *Psychological Bulletin, 135*(1), 157–171. doi:10.1037/a0014415

Donaldson, K. R., Novak, K. D, Foti, D., Marder, M., Perlman, G., Kotov, R., & Mohanty, A. (2020). Associations of mismatch negativity with psychotic symptoms and functioning transdiagnostically across psychotic disorders. *Journal of Abnormal Psychology, 129*(6), 570–580. doi:10.1037/abn0000506

Ebmeier, K. P., Lawrie, S. M., Blackwood, D. H. R., Johnstone, E. C., & Goodwin, G. M. (1995). Hypofrontality revisited: A high resolution single photon emission computer tomography study in schizophrenia. *Journal of Neurology, Neurosurgery and Psychiatry, 58,* 452–456.

Egerton, A., Modinos, G., Ferrera, D., & McGuire, P. (2017). Neuroimaging studies of GABA in schizophrenia: A systematic review with meta-analysis. *Translational Psychiatry, 7*(6), e1147–e1147.

Ellison-Wright, I., Glahn, D. C., Laird, A. R., Thelen, S. M., & Bullmore, E. (2008). The anatomy of first-episode and chronic schizophrenia: An anatomical likelihood estimation meta-analysis. *American Journal of Psychiatry, 165*(8), 1015–1023. doi:10.1176/appi.ajp.2008.07101562

Erlenmeyer-Kimling, L., & Nicol, S. (1969). Comparison of hospitalization measures in schizophrenic patients with and without a family history of schizophrenia. *British Journal of Psychiatry, 115*(520), 321–334. doi:10.1192/bjp.115.520.321

Evans, K., McGrath, J., & Milns, R. (2003). Searching for schizophrenia in ancient Greek and Roman literature: A systematic review. *Acta Psychiatrica Scandinavica, 107*(5), 323–330.

Feeney, E. J., Groman, S. M., Taylor, J. R., & Corlett, P. R. (2017). Explaining delusions: Reducing uncertainty through basic and computational neuroscience. *Schizophrenia Bulletin, 43*(2), 263–272. doi:10.1093/schbul/sbw194

Ford, J. M., Dierks, T., Fisher, D. J., Herrmann, C. S., Hubl, D., Kindler, J., ... van Lutterveld, R. (2012). Neurophysiological studies of auditory verbal hallucinations. *Schizophrenia Bulletin, 38*(4), 715–23. doi:10.1093/schbul/sbs009

Friston, K. (2009). The free-energy principle: A rough guide to the brain? *Trends in Cognitive Sciences, 13*(7), 293–301. doi:10.1016/j.tics.2009.04.05

Fujii, D., & Fujii, D. C. (2012). Psychotic disorder due to traumatic brain injury: Analysis of case studies in the literature. *Journal of Neuropsychiatry and Clinical Neurosciences, 24*(3), 278–289. doi:10.1176/appi.neuropsych.11070176

Fusar-Poli, P., Bonoldi, I., Yung, A. R., Borgwardt, S., Kempton, M. J., Valmaggia, L., . . . McGuire, P. (2012). Predicting psychosis: Meta-analysis of transition outcomes in individuals at high clinical risk. *Archives of General Psychiatry, 69*(3), 220–229.

Gandal, M. J., Edgar, J. C., Klook, K., & Siegel, S. J. (2012). Gamma synchrony: Towards a translational biomarker for the treatment-resistant symptoms of schizophrenia. *Neuropharmacology, 62*(3), 1504–1518. doi:10.1016/j.neuropharm.2011.02.007

Gard, D., Kring, A., & Gard, M. (2007). Anhedonia in schizophrenia: Distinctions between anticipatory and consummatory pleasure. *Schizophrenia Research, 93*(415), 253–260.

Goghari, V. M., Sponheim, S. R., & MacDonald, A. W. (2010). The functional neuroanatomy of symptom dimensions in schizophrenia: A qualitative and quantitative review of a persistent question. *Neuroscience and Biobehavioral Reviews, 34*(3), 468–486. doi:10.1016/j.neubiorev.2009.09.004

Gold, J. M., Waltz, J. A., Prentice, K. J., Morris, S. E., & Heerey, E. A. (2008). Reward processing in schizophrenia: A deficit in the representation of value. *Schizophrenia Bulletin, 34*(5), 835–847. doi:10.1093/schbul/sbn068

Guloksuz, S., Rutten, B. P., Pries, L. K., Ten Have, M., de Graaf, R., van Dorsselaer, S., . . . European Network of National Schizophrenia Networks Studying Gene-Environment Interactions Work Package 6 (EU-GEI WP6) Group. (2018). The complexities of evaluating the exposome in psychiatry: A data-driven illustration of challenges and some propositions for amendments. *Schizophrenia Bulletin, 44*(6), 1175–1179.

Guloksuz, S., van Os, J., & Rutten, B. P. (2018). The exposome paradigm and the complexities of environmental research in psychiatry. *JAMA Psychiatry, 75*(10), 985–986.

Gonzalez-Burgos, G., & Lewis, D. A. (2008). GABA neurons and the mechanisms of network oscillations: Implications for understanding cortical dysfunction in schizophrenia. *Schizophrenia Bulletin, 34*(5), 944–961. doi:10.1093/schbul/sbn070

Gottesman, I. I. (1991). *Schizophrenia genesis: The origins of madness.* Freeman.

Häfner, H., Maurer, K., Löffler, W., Fätkenheuer, B., an der Heiden, W., Riecher-Rössler, A., . . . Gattaz, W. F. (1994). The epidemiology of early schizophrenia. Influence of age and gender on onset and early course. *British Journal of Psychiatry. Supplement* (23), 29–38.

Heckers, S., Barch, D. M., Bustillo, J., Gaebel, W., Gur, R., Malaspina, D., . . . Carpenter, W. (2013). Structure of the psychotic disorders classification in DSM-5. *Schizophrenia Research, 150*(1), 11–14.

Heckers, S., & Kendler, K. S. (2020). The evolution of Kraepelin's nosological principles. *World Psychiatry, 19*(3), 381–388.

Heinrichs, R. W. (2001). *In search of madness: Schizophrenia and neuroscience.* Oxford University Press.

Heinrichs, R. W. (2005). The primacy of cognition in schizophrenia. *American Psychologist, 60*(3), 229–242. doi:10.1037/0003-066X.60.3.229

Heinrichs, R. W., & Zakzanis, K. K. (1998). Neurocognitive deficit in schizophrenia: A quantitative review of the evidence. *Neuropsychology, 12*(3), 426–445.

Howard, R., Rabins, P. V, Seeman, M. V, & Jeste, D. V. (2000). Late-onset schizophrenia and very-late-onset schizophrenia-like psychosis: An international consensus. The International Late-Onset Schizophrenia Group. *American Journal of Psychiatry, 157*(2), 172–178.

Howes, O. D., & Kapur, S. (2009). The dopamine hypothesis of schizophrenia: Version III, the final common pathway. *Schizophrenia Bulletin, 35*(3), 549–562.

Ingvar, D. H., & Franzen, G. (1974). Distribution of cerebral activity in chronic schizophrenia. *Lancet,* 1484–1486.

Jablensky, A., Sartorius, N., Ernberg, G., Anker, M., Korten, A., Cooper, J. E., . . . Bertelsen, A. (1992). Schizophrenia: Manifestations, incidence and course in different cultures. A World Health Organization ten-country study. *Psychological Medicine Monograph Suppl., 20,* 1–97.

Javitt, D. C., & Zukin, S. R. (1991). Recent advances in the phencyclidine model of schizophrenia. *American Journal of Psychiatry, 148,* 1301–1308.

Jobe, T. H., & Harrow, M. (2010). Schizophrenia course, long-term outcome, recovery, and prognosis. *Current Directions in Psychological Science, 19*(4), 220–225.

Kantrowitz, J. T., Grinband, J., Goff, D. C., Lahti, A. C., Marder, S. R., Kegeles, L. S., . . . Green, M. F. (2020). Proof of mechanism and target engagement of glutamatergic drugs for the treatment of schizophrenia: RCTs of pomaglumetad and TS-134 on ketamine-induced psychotic symptoms and pharmacoBOLD in healthy volunteers. *Neuropsychopharmacology,* 1–11.

Kapur, S. (2003). Psychosis as a state of aberrant salience: A framework linking biology, phenomenology, and pharmacology in schizophrenia. *American Journal of Psychiatry, 160*(1), 13–23. doi:10.1176/appi.ajp.160.1.13

Kasanin, J. (1933). The acute schizoaffective psychoses. *American Journal of Psychiatry, 90*(1), 97–126.

Kean, C. (2009). Silencing the self: Schizophrenia as a self-disturbance. *Schizophrenia Bulletin, 35*(6), 1034–1036. doi:10.1093/schbul/sbp043

Keefe, R. S. E., & Fenton, W. S. (2007). How should DSM-V criteria for schizophrenia include cognitive impairment? *Schizophrenia Bulletin, 33*(4), 912–920. doi:10.1093/schbul/sbm046

Kendler, K. S., & Schaffner, K. F. (2011). The dopamine hypothesis of schizophrenia: An historical and philosophical analysis. *Philosophy, Psychiatry, & Psychology, 18*(1), 41–63.

Kendler, K. S., & Zerbin-Rüdin, E. (1996). Abstract and review of "Zur Erbpathologie der Schizophrenie" (Contribution to the genetics of schizophrenia). 1916. *American Journal of Medical Genetics, 67*(4), 343–346. doi:10.1002/(SICI)1096-8628(19960726)67:4<343::AID-AJMG5>3.0.CO;2-N

Kety, S. S., Rosenthal, W., Wender, P. H., & Schulsinger, F. (1971). Mental Illness in the biological and adoptive families of adopted schizophrenics. *American Journal of Psychiatry, 128*(3), 302–306.

Kirkbride, J. B., Fearon, P., Morgan, C., Dazzan, P., Morgan, K., Tarrant, J., . . . Jones, P. B. (2006). Heterogeneity in incidence rates of schizophrenia and other psychotic syndromes: Findings from the 3-center AeSOP study. *Archives of General Psychiatry, 63*(3), 250–258. doi:10.1001/archpsyc.63.3.250

Kotov, R., Jonas, K. G., Carpenter, W. T., Dretsch, M. N., Eaton, N. R., Forbes, M. K., Forbush, K. T., Hobbs, K., Reininghaus, U., Slade, T., South, S. C., Sunderland, M., Waszczuk, M. A., Widiger, T. A., Wright, A., Zald, D. H., Krueger, R. F., Watson, D., & HiTOP Utility Workgroup. (2020). Validity and utility of Hierarchical Taxonomy of Psychopathology (HiTOP), I. Psychosis superspectrum. *World Psychiatry, 19,* 151–172. doi:10.1002/wps.20730

Kraepelin, E., & Barclay, T. (1919/1971). *Dementia praecox and paraphrenia.* Livingston.

Krueger, R. F., & MacDonald, A. W. (2005). Dimensional approaches to understanding and treating psychosis. *Psychiatric Annals, 35,* 31–34.

Laursen, T. M., Agerbo, E., & Pedersen, C. B. (2009). Bipolar disorder, schizoaffective disorder, and schizophrenia overlap: A new comorbidity index. *Journal of Clinical Psychiatry, 70*(10), 1432–1438. doi:10.4088/JCP.08m04807

Legind, C. S., Broberg, B. V., Mandl, R. C. W., Brouwer, R., Anhøj, S. J., Hilker, R., . . . Rostrup, E. (2019). Heritability of cerebral glutamate levels and their association with schizophrenia spectrum disorders: A 1 [H]-spectroscopy twin study. *Neuropsychopharmacology, 44*(3), 581–589.

Lewis, C. M., Levinson, D. F., Wise, L. H., DeLisi, L. E., Straub, R. E., Hovatta, I., . . . Faraone, S. V. (2003). Genome scan meta-analysis of schizophrenia and bipolar disorder, part II: Schizophrenia. *American Journal of Human Genetics, 73*(1), 34–48. doi:10.1086/376549

Lewis, D. A. (2014). Inhibitory neurons in human cortical circuits: Substrate for cognitive dysfunction in schizophrenia. *Current Opinion in Neurobiology, 26,* 22–26.

Lin, C.-H., Lane, H.-Y., & Tsai, G. E. (2012). Glutamate signaling in the pathophysiology and therapy of schizophrenia.

*Pharmacology, Biochemistry, and Behavior, 100*(4), 665–677. doi:10.1016/j.pbb.2011.03.023

López-Muñoz, F., Alamo, C., Cuenca, E., Shen, W., Clervoy, P., & Rubio, G. (2005). History of the discovery and clinical introduction of chlorpromazine. *Annals of Clinical Psychiatry, 17*(3), 113–135. doi:10.1080/10401230591002002

Luby, E. D., Gottlieb, J. S., Cohen, B. D., Rosenbaum, G., & Domino, E. F. (1962). Model psychoses and schizophrenia. *American Journal of Psychiatry, 119*, 61–67.

MacDonald, A. W. (2008). Building a clinically relevant cognitive task: Case study of the AX paradigm. *Schizophrenia Bulletin, 34*(4), 619–628. doi:10.1093/schbul/sbn038

MacDonald, A. W., & Schulz, S. C. (2009). What we know: Findings that every theory of schizophrenia should explain. *Schizophrenia bulletin, 35*(3), 493–508. doi:10.1093/schbul/sbp017

MacDonald, A. W. (2013). What kind of a thing is schizophrenia? Specific causation and general failure modes. In S. M. Silverstein, B. Moghaddam, & T. Wykes (Eds.), *Schizophrenia: Evolution and synthesis*. MIT Press.

Markon, K. E. (2010). Modeling psychopathology structure: A symptom-level analysis of Axis I and II disorders. *Psychological Medicine, 40*(2), 273–288. doi:10.1017/S0033291709990183

McGrath, J., Saha, S., Chant, D., & Welham, J. (2008). Schizophrenia: A concise overview of incidence, prevalence, and mortality. *Epidemiologic Reviews, 30*, 67–76. doi:10.1093/epirev/mxn001

Mednick, S. A. (1958). A learning theory approach to research in schizophrenia. *Psychological Bulletin, 55*(5), 316–327.

Meehl, P. E. (1962). Schizotaxia, schizotypy, schizophrenia. *American Psychologist, 17*, 827–838.

Merritt, K., Egerton, A., Kempton, M. J., Taylor, M. J., & McGuire, P. K. (2016). Nature of glutamate alterations in schizophrenia: A meta-analysis of proton magnetic resonance spectroscopy studies. *JAMA Psychiatry, 73*(7), 665–674.

Müller, N. (2018). Inflammation in schizophrenia: Pathogenetic aspects and therapeutic considerations. *Schizophrenia Bulletin, 44*(5), 973–982.

Nei, H., Wên, C., Veith, I., & Barnes, L. (1975). *The Yellow Emperor's classic of internal medicine*. University of California Press. https://www.jstor.org/stable/10.1525/j.ctv1wxs1d

Nordentoft, M., Mortensen, P. B., & Pedersen, C. B. (2011). Absolute risk of suicide after first hospital contact in mental disorder. *Archives of General Psychiatry, 68*(10), 1058–1064. doi:10.1001/archgenpsychiatry.2011.113

Ortiz-Medina, M. B., Perea, M., Torales, J., Ventriglio, A., Vitrani, G., Aguilar, L., & Roncero, C. (2018). Cannabis consumption and psychosis or schizophrenia development. *International Journal of Social Psychiatry, 64*(7), 690–704.

Pavlov, I. P. (1927). *Conditioned reflexes: An investigation of the physiological activity of the cerebral cortex*. Oxford University Press. https://psycnet.apa.org/record/1927-02531-000

Peralta, V., & Cuesta, M. J. (1999). Dimensional structure of psychotic symptoms: An item-level analysis of SAPS and SANS symptoms in psychotic disorders. *Schizophrenia Research, 38*(1), 13–26.

Peralta, V., & Cuesta, M. J. (2001). How many and which are the psychopathological dimensions of schizophrenia? Issues influencing their ascertainment. *Schizophrenia Research, 49*(3), 269–285.

Pettersson-Yeo, W., Allen, P., Benetti, S., McGuire, P., & Mechelli, A. (2011). Dysconnectivity in schizophrenia: Where are we now? *Neuroscience and Biobehavioral Reviews, 35*(5), 1110–1124.

Phillips, W. A., & Silverstein, S. M. (2003). Convergence of biological and psychological perspectives on cognitive coordination in schizophrenia. *Behavioral and Brain Sciences, 26*(1), 65–82; discussion 82–137.

Plana-Ripoll, O., Pedersen, C. B., & McGrath, J. J. (2018). Urbanicity and risk of schizophrenia-new studies and old hypotheses. *JAMA Psychiatry, 75*, 687–688.

Remschmidt, H., & Theisen, F. (2012). Early-onset schizophrenia. *Neuropsychobiology, 66*(1), 63–69. doi:10.1159/000338548

Rodnick, E. H., & Shakow, D. (1940). Set in schizophrenia as measured by a composite reaction time index. *American Journal of Psychiatry, 97*, 214–255.

Rosenthal, D., Lawlor, W. G., Zahn, T. P., & Shakow, D. (1960). The relationship of some aspects of mental set to degree of schizophrenic disorganization. *Journal of Personality, 28*, 26–38.

Sher, L., & Kahn, R. S. (2019). Suicide in schizophrenia: An educational overview. *Medicina, 55*(7), 361.

Schultz, W. (2007). Behavioral dopamine signals. *Trends in Neurosciences, 30*(5), 203–210. doi:10.1016/j.tins.2007.03.007

Schür, R. R., Draisma, L. W., Wijnen, J. P., Boks, M. P., Koevoets, M. G., Joels, M., ... Vinkers, C. H. (2016). Brain GABA levels across psychiatric disorders: A systematic literature review and meta-analysis of 1H-MRS studies. *Human Brain Mapping, 37*(9), 3337–3352.

Seeman, P., & Lee, T. (1975). Antipsychotic drugs: Direct correlation between clinical potency and presynaptic action on dopamine neurons. *Science, 188*(4194), 1217–1219.

Servan-Schreiber, D., Cohen, J. D., & Steingard, S. (1996). Schizophrenic deficits in the processing of context: A test of a theoretical model. *Archives of General Psychiatry, 53*, 1105–1112.

Shenton, M. E., Dickey, C. C., Frumin, M., & McCarley, R. W. (2001). A review of MRI findings in schizophrenia. *Schizophrenia Research, 49*(1–2), 1–52.

Shepherd, M. (1995). Two faces of Emil Kraepelin. *British Journal of Psychiatry: The Journal of Mental Science, 167*(2), 174–183.

Shukla, D. K., Wijtenburg, S. A., Chen, H., Chiappelli, J. J., Kochunov, P., Hong, L. E., & Rowland, L. M. (2019). Anterior cingulate glutamate and GABA associations on functional connectivity in schizophrenia. *Schizophrenia Bulletin, 45*(3), 647–658.

Spitzer, R. L., Endicott, J., & Robins, E. (1975). Research diagnostic criteria. *Psychopharmacology Bulletin, 11*(3), 22–25.

Stefanidis, E. (2006). Being rational. *Schizophrenia Bulletin, 32*(3), 422–423. doi:10.1093/schbul/sbj006

Strauss, G. P., & Cohen, A. S. (2017). A transdiagnostic review of negative symptom phenomenology and etiology. *Schizophrenia Bulletin, 43*(4), 712–719. doi:10.1093/schbul/sbx066

Tandon, R., Nasrallah, H. A., & Keshavan, M. S. (2009). Schizophrenia, "just the facts" 4. Clinical features and conceptualization. *Schizophrenia Research, 110*(1-3), 1–23.

Van Os, J., & Tamminga, C. (2007). Deconstructing psychosis. *Schizophrenia Bulletin, 33*(4), 861–962. doi:10.1093/schbul/sbm066

Videbeck, S. R. (2010). *Psychiatric-mental health nursing*, 4th ed. Lippincott Williams & Wilkins.

Vincent, J. P., Kartalovski, B., Geneste, P., Kamenka, J. M., & Lazdunski, M. (1979). Interaction of phencyclidine ("angel dust") with a specific receptor in rat brain membranes Neurobiology: *Proceedings of the National Academy of Sciences, 76*(9), 4678–4682.

Weiner, S. K. (2003). First person account: Living with the delusions and effects of schizophrenia. *Schizophrenia Bulletin, 29*(4), 877–979.

Wittenborn, J. R., & Holzberg, J. D. (1951). The generality of psychiatric syndromes. *Journal of Consulting Psychology, 15*(5), 372–380.

Wright, A. G. C., Thomas, K. M., Hopwood, C. J., Markon, K. E., Pincus, A. L., & Krueger, R. F. (2012). The hierarchical structure of DSM-5 pathological personality traits. *Journal of Abnormal Psychology*. doi:10.1037/a0027669

# CHAPTER 15

# Social Functioning and Schizophrenia

Jill M. Hooley *and* Stephanie N. DeCross

Impaired social functioning is a fundamental feature of schizophrenia. Recognized in the early clinical descriptions of the disorder, social dysfunction remains one of the defining characteristics of the syndrome. A century ago, Emil Kraepelin noted the lack of concern for social convention that characterized the patient with schizophrenia, remarking that

> [t]he patients no longer have any regard for their surroundings; they do not suit their behavior to the situation in which they are, they conduct themselves in a free and easy way, laugh on serious occasions, are rude and impertinent towards their superiors, challenge them to duels, lose their deportment and personal dignity; they go about in untidy and dirty clothes, unwashed, unkempt, go with a lighted cigar into church, speak familiarly with strangers, decorate themselves with gay ribbons. (Kraepelin, 1919/1989, p. 34)

Though contemporary writers might describe these social difficulties less vividly, it is acknowledged that everyday social encounters often present considerable challenges to those with schizophrenia. Of course, schizophrenia clinical profiles are heterogenous in presentation. Nonetheless, withdrawal and social isolation are often primary components. Impairment in social or occupational functioning is also necessary for the diagnosis to be made in *DSM-5*.

In this chapter we provide an overview of the literature concerning social functioning in schizophrenia. This is a broad topic that covers a range of different research areas. Because of this, our review must necessarily be more selective than exhaustive. We are often unable to consider many interesting and important aspects of the topics that are discussed. What we hope to do is to trace the arc of research work in this area, highlighting the progression of knowledge over time. Wherever possible, we also draw readers' attention to articles that provide more detailed consideration of specific issues.

## Interpersonal Adjustment and Schizophrenia

The subjective reports of people with schizophrenia are full of references to the difficulties they experience during ordinary social interactions. These difficulties are also mirrored in the comments of their family members. The ex-wife of "Jon," who was diagnosed with schizophrenia, described it in this way:

> Some aspects of Jon's illness were particularly puzzling. I knew he was highly intelligent and perfectly at ease when it came to discussing complicated philosophical issues or analyzing the works of sophisticated artists. Why then was he at a loss when it came to dealing with everyday human relationships? He didn't seem to be able to get the feel

**Abbreviations**

| | |
|---|---|
| AIPSS | Assessment of Interpersonal Problem-Solving Skills |
| AS | Attributional style |
| CFI | Camberwell Family Interview |
| CHR | Clinical high risk |
| EE | Expressed emotion |
| FFT | Family-focused therapy |
| MEPS | Means-end problem-solving |
| Per-Mag | Perceptual aberration and magical ideation |
| QLS | Quality of Life Scale |
| SANS | Scale for the Assessment of Negative Symptoms |
| SAS | Social Adjustment Scale |
| SCIT | Social cognition and interaction training |
| SCRT | Social Cue Recognition Test |
| WCTS | Wisconsin Card Sort Test |

of people, to interpret their gestures correctly. Instead of relying on that intuitive understanding we usually have of what other people are trying to convey, he built up intricate theories that often led him to erroneous interpretations. It took me a long time to understand that this continuous theorizing might be his way of grappling with his own uncertainty and bewilderment. It was as though some strange deficiency prevented him from understanding some things that seem perfectly obvious to most people. (Anonymous, 1994, p. 228)

Relationships have been classified as a function of the interpersonal needs that they serve. Instrumental relationships are task-oriented and goal-driven. Work and service relationships, such as purchasing an item in a store, asking for directions, giving appropriate information in a job interview, or dealing with those responsible for processing disability benefits, primarily subserve instrumental role needs (see Liberman, 1982).

People with schizophrenia show significant impairment in their instrumental relationships (see Wallace, 1984, for a review of the early literature). For example, those with the illness are frequently unable to finish school or to achieve the level of education they desire.

After graduation I enrolled at a college near home. I stayed only 2 years. It was difficult for me to deal with ordinary situations, such as a problem with a teacher. (Herrig, 1995, p. 339)

Many individuals with schizophrenia are also unable to hold a job for sustained periods of time. Only about 10–20% of patients are employed (Marwaha & Johnson, 2004), and when they do work, it is often at an employment level that is lower than that of their parents. Jon, the patient described earlier, had his first breakdown when he was in the army. He left the army and later found part-time work. Finding that too much, he subsequently gave up work entirely and stayed at home reading, writing, and doing household chores while his wife went out to work (Anonymous, 1994).

Deficits are also apparent in the social-emotional domain. In contrast to the task-oriented or goal-directed nature of instrumental interpersonal relationships, social-emotional aspects of relationships are driven more by the needs of the relationship itself. Social-emotional exchanges might include such things as asking how a spouse or partner feels, greeting a relative, going to an event with a friend, or chatting at a party (Liberman, 1982). Although these sorts of transactions are everyday occurrences for most of us, they are not routine for the person with schizophrenia.

I wanted to blend in in the classroom as though I were a desk. I never spoke. I didn't participate in any extracurricular activities or have any close friends. (Herrig, 1995, p. 339)

Traditionally, marriage has been regarded as indicative of a person's ability to develop and sustain a close interpersonal relationship. Although marriage is far from a perfect indicator of social competence, compared to people in the general population, people with schizophrenia are six times less likely to marry (MacCabe et al., 2009). Rates of marriage are also much lower in patients with schizophrenia than they are in those with other severe forms of mental illness such as bipolar disorder (Mueser et al., 2010). Notably, males with the disorder are particularly unlikely to marry. Although precise rates vary across studies, schizophrenia severely reduces the probability of marriage for men, although it compromises it less for women (Häfner, 2003).

General descriptions of the problems experienced by patients with schizophrenia are important and informative. However, they tell us little about what these patients actually do (or fail to do) in social situations. Fortunately, researchers have explored the interpersonal problems associated with schizophrenia to better understand their nature and possible origins. It is to this literature that we now turn.

## Measuring Social Behavior
### Social Competence

Social competence is "a context-related and more or less subjective judgment or evaluation of observed behavior or social role performance" (Appelo et al., 1992, p. 419). In general, it reflects how well we consider people to be doing in everyday social situations. Often used interchangeably with terms such as "social role functioning" or "social role adjustment," it is the most global level of analysis. As we have already seen, subjective accounts and clinical observations highlight the problems in social competence that are so typical of schizophrenia. Studies that have examined social competence more formally have also reached similar conclusions.

Early work in this area assessed patients using the Social Competence Scale (Zigler & Phillips, 1961). This rather heterogeneous measure considers age of onset, education, marital status, occupation, and employment history to yield a composite social functioning score. As might be expected, schizophrenia patients typically score lower on the Social Competence Scale than do psychiatric patients with other disorders (e.g., Schwartz, 1967). Adolescents at risk for schizophrenia also score more poorly on this instrument, both relative to nonpsychiatric controls and to adolescents at risk for mood disorders (Dworkin et al., 1990).

Other measures of global social functioning (see Yager & Ehmann, 2006, for a review) include the Social Adjustment Scale (SAS-II; Schooler et al., 1986) and the Quality of Life Scale (QLS; Heinrichs et al., 1984). The SAS measures interpersonal performance in work, relationships with household members, relationships with other relatives, leisure and recreational activities, and personal well-being. The QLS has four dimensions and provides ratings on interpersonal relations, instrumental role functioning (primarily occupational, student, or homemaker roles), intrapsychic functioning (i.e., cognitive, affective, and motivational functioning) and common objects and activities (which assesses whether the patient reads newspapers, possesses a wallet, or is otherwise involved with the objects and activities of everyday life). On both measures, patients with schizophrenia score worse than either nonpatient controls or patients diagnosed with mood disorders (see Bellack, Morrison et al., 1990). Moreover, impaired social functioning relative to controls on the SAS-II is found even in patients who are experiencing their first episodes of illness (Ballon et al., 2007). Global difficulties in social competence thus seem to be characteristic of those diagnosed with schizophrenia at all stages of the illness.

### Social Skills

Social skills represent a level of social functioning that is more molecular than the broad concept of social competence. They have been described as the "specific verbal, nonverbal and paralinguistic (e.g., voice tone) behavioral components that together form the basis for effective communication" (Mueser et al., 1990, p. 138). Social skills include the ability to give and obtain information and to express and exchange attitudes, opinions, and feelings. These skills, which are apparent in the everyday conversations, encounters, and relationships that people have with each other, are thought to be foundational for social competence.

In the research lab, one way to assess social skills is through role-play techniques. In role-playing, the patient interacts with a confederate in a prescribed situation (such as an exchange with a sales associate or a staged argument with a loved one). Various components of social skill, such as the appropriateness of gaze, duration of speech, meshing (e.g., the smoothness of turn-taking and pauses in the conversation), or the expressiveness and congruence of facial expression (see Mueser, Bellack, Douglas, & Morrison, 1991), can then be assessed. Verbal skills, which are evaluated in the context of the social situation being enacted, are also considered.

Although best viewed as a measure of response capabilities rather than as a reflection of behavior occurring in the natural environment, role-play nevertheless appears to be a valid method for the study of interpersonal behavior (see Mueser & Bellack, 1998). Behavior during role-play is strongly correlated with more global measures of social competence. Judges' ratings of verbal and nonverbal behavior also differentiate patients with schizophrenia from people with mood disorders or healthy controls (Bellack, Morrison, Mueser et al., 1990).

Social skills research, relying heavily on role-playing tasks, has provided useful information about more specific social difficulties associated with schizophrenia. For example, in conversation, patients with schizophrenia show weaker verbal (e.g., clarity, negotiation, and persistence) and nonverbal skills (e.g., interest, fluency, and affect) than do non-patient controls (Bellack et al., 1994). Compared with patients diagnosed with mood disorders or with non-patient controls, they also tend to be less assertive when challenged. Moreover, although in the face of criticism psychiatric and non-psychiatric controls tend to apologize or explain, schizophrenia patients tend to deny making errors or to simply lie (Bellack et al., 1992). It is important to note, however, that overall social performance in patients with schizophrenia tends to involve mild impairments across a range of component skill areas rather than marked problems in any one domain (see Mueser, Bellack, Douglas, & Morrison, 1991).

### Social Problem-Solving

The ability to successfully recognize an interpersonal problem, formulate a solution, and take action is fundamental to social success. Social problem-solving, another element of social competence, can be examined in a variety of ways. The Means-Ends Problem Solving (MEPS) procedure presents research participants with hypothetical interpersonal problem situations and measures how well they can conceptualize and generate effective solutions to resolve each problem. In an early series of studies, Platt and Spivak (1972, 1974) reported that, compared with a control sample of hospital employees, patients with schizophrenia were less able to provide appropriate and potentially effective solutions to the problems under consideration.

Patients diagnosed more using more current (post-*DSM-III*) diagnostic criteria for schizophrenia also demonstrate problems with interpersonal problem-solving and perform worse than controls. This is apparent using measures such as the Assessment of Interpersonal Problem-Solving Skills (AIPSS; Donahoe et al., 1990; Bowen et al., 1994). Bellack and his colleagues (1994) have also reported that inpatients with schizophrenia show deficits on other social problem-solving tasks. More specifically, relative to controls, the schizophrenia patients generated solutions that were rated by judges as being less appropriate and less likely to be able to be implemented. The patients were also generally less assertive and less able to recognize poor problem solutions that were unlikely to work. Nonetheless, it warrants mention that these difficulties also characterized patients with bipolar disorder. Both patient groups performed less well than controls, and no significant differences between the patient groups were found.

Considered together, there appears to be ample evidence demonstrating that schizophrenia patients exhibit a wide range of problems across a diverse array of social domains when compared with control participants. There is also evidence that, even when compared to patients with other forms of psychiatric disorders (such as mood disorders), patients with schizophrenia still show more impairments (Bellack, Morrison, Wixted et al., 1990; Bellack et al., 1992; Mueser et al., 2010), though this is not always the case (e.g., Bellack et al., 1994). It is quite likely that the factors that underlie poor social problem-solving in patients with chronic schizophrenia (e.g., cognitive impairments) are not the same as the factors associated with poor social functioning in patients with bipolar disorder (e.g., acute symptoms). More data on the extent to which problems remain when patients show clinical improvement would be informative. Although social impairments appear to be stable over time in people with schizophrenia (Cornblatt et al., 2007; Mueser, Bellack, Douglas, & Morrison, 1991), less is known about the long-term stability of skill deficits in other diagnostic groups. However, even in older patient samples (age 50 years or older) social functioning deficits are still more marked in schizophrenia patients than they are in those with major mood disorders (Mueser et al., 2010).

## Gender and Interpersonal Functioning

A sizeable literature suggests that the course of the illness is more benign in women than in men. For example, female patients have a characteristically later age of onset of the illness (Häfner et al., 1993; Abel et al., 2010). Men show a peak in the incidence of schizophrenia between 20 and 24 years of age. For women, the peak in the number of new cases during these ages is less marked, and the onset of schizophrenia is instead more broadly distributed throughout the 20s and early 30s. Females also have shorter and less frequent psychotic episodes and show a better response to treatment than do their male counterparts (see Leung & Chue, 2000).

Gender differences are also apparent in the interpersonal realm. Compared with males, female patients have a milder range of interpersonal problems and are characterized by better social functioning. Both Dworkin (1990) and Perry, Moore, and Braff (1995) have reported that females with schizophrenia, as a group, scored significantly better than males with schizophrenia on the Social Competency Index (Zigler & Phillips, 1961). Andia and her colleagues (1995) also found that women with schizophrenia were more likely than men with the disorder to live independently, be employed, and have been married despite having similar symptom profiles. Moreover, females in this last study had higher levels of social functioning even though they were being maintained on lower doses of antipsychotic medication than the male patients.

Similar gender differences have been reported by other research groups. Using a role-play test, Mueser and his colleagues (1990) reported a clear gender difference across a range of different measures. Although they did not differ from male patients with respect to their symptoms, females with schizophrenia were more skilled than males in the appropriateness of the duration of their speech (very short or very long responses were rated less favorably), their meshing or turn-taking abilities during conversations, aspects of their verbal content in specific role-play scenarios, and their overall social skills. There is also evidence that the relationship between gender and social skill may be specific to schizophrenia. In the study just described, gender was unrelated to social skill in either the mood disorder or the non-psychiatric control groups.

Gender differences are not universally documented. Indeed, in the study just described, no differences were found between the male and female patients with schizophrenia on measures of social adjustment such as the SAS-II and the QLS. More global measures of social adjustment may simply be less sensitive to gender differences than laboratory-based assessments are. Overall, however, when gender differences are found, the results typically point toward better interpersonal functioning in females with schizophrenia.

Why do women score better on measures of social functioning? Differences in the age of onset of the illness may provide a partial explanation. As we have noted, more men than women develop schizophrenia in their late teens or early 20s, with a later average age of onset for women (Abel et al., 2010). During adolescence and young adulthood, social relationships typically become a major focus of interest and there is a rapid acquisition of social skills. An earlier age of onset in men may disrupt developmental processes supporting social functioning to a greater extent than is the case for women, who develop the disorder later. Women may also be more likely to marry and have children in part because these life changes may occur before the development of the disorder.

The increased levels of social functioning apparent in female patients may simply reflect the fact that women, for reasons that are not fully clear, tend to have a somewhat milder form of illness. Related to this, some authors have speculated about the neuroprotective properties of estrogen (Rao & Kőlsch, 2003). Because of its ability to reduce the sensitivity of $D_2$ dopamine receptors, estrogen may exert a weak neuroleptic-like effect on symptoms (Kulkarni et al., 2008). Females may also be less susceptible than males to structural brain abnormalities that could lead to developmental problems and greater impairment in functioning (Abel et al., 2010). Interestingly, the social functioning advantages apparent in women with schizophrenia are not seen in older patients (Mueser et al., 2010). This may be because of reduced estrogen production in older women.

## Social Functioning and Clinical Symptoms

Schizophrenia is characterized by symptoms such as hallucinations, delusions, affective flattening, and anhedonia. Each or all of these might be expected to be associated with interpersonal difficulties. In this section we examine the evidence as a function of two major symptom groupings: positive and negative.

Developed in an effort to explain the heterogeneity in schizophrenia, the division between positive and negative symptoms (Andreasen & Olsen, 1982) is based on whether the symptoms of the disorder are florid (or in excess of "normal") or instead represent the absence of the typical (i.e., a "defect" or failure to display a "normal" behavior). Symptoms such as delusions, hallucinations, formal thought disorder, or bizarre behavior are thus regarded as positive symptoms, while alogia (greatly reduced speech or speech conveying very little information), affective flattening, avolition (apathy), and anhedonia are characteristic negative symptoms (Kirkpatrick et al., 2006). Negative symptoms that are enduring and that do not reflect efforts to cope with positive symptoms are also termed deficit symptoms (Carpenter et al., 1988).

Positive symptoms in general do not appear to be particularly related to social adjustment (Bellack, Morrison, Wixted et al., 1990; Bora et al., 2006; Perry et al., 1995; see also Dworkin, 1990). However, reports of associations between positive symptoms (more or more severe symptoms) and impaired social competency can be found (Appelo et al., 1992; Corrigan & Toomey, 1995). This suggests that intact thought processes may be necessary for effective social functioning. Precisely which symptoms might compromise which domains of interpersonal functioning and under what circumstances, however, are questions in need of further investigation.

Examining the association between negative symptoms and social functioning is not as straightforward as it might first appear. As Dworkin (1992) has noted, many ratings on the Scale for the Assessment of Negative Symptoms (SANS; Andreasen, 1982) are based on the patient's behavior during an interview. Yet an interview is an interpersonal situation. Moreover, the ratings that are made are based on behavioral indicators such as unchanging facial expression, decreased spontaneous movements, and poor eye contact. But these behavioral indicators of negative symptoms could be the result of social skills deficits.

Recognizing this problem, what do we know about the association between negative symptoms and social functioning or social skills? Perhaps not surprisingly, negative symptoms have been linked to poorer social functioning, particularly when more global measures of social adjustment are used (e.g., Appelo et al., 1992; Blanchard et al., 1998; Bora et al., 2006; Pinkham & Penn, 2006). Moreover, even in first-episode patients, the presence of more severe negative symptoms is associated with having a smaller social network with fewer friends (Thorup et al., 2006).

In a focused examination of the role of negative symptoms, Bellack and his colleagues (Bellack et al., 1989; see also Bellack, Morrison, Wixted et al., 1990) administered the SANS to a sample of inpatients with schizophrenia. These patients were then further divided into a group that had more severe negative symptoms and a group that had less severe negative symptoms (i.e., positive symptom and mixed symptom patients; see Andreasen & Olsen, 1982). Consistent with prediction, the negative-symptom patients were found to be significantly more impaired on the SAS-II and the QLS than were the other schizophrenia patients or the control patients with schizoaffective disorder or bipolar disorder.

Less compelling, however, are the data linking negative symptoms with more specific social deficits. Jackson et al. (1989) reported impressive associations between negative symptoms and social skills during a role-play task. Corrigan and his colleagues (Corrigan, Green, & Toomey, 1994) also found that patients' scores on a scale assessing blunted affect, emotional withdrawal, and motor retardation were negatively correlated with their performance on a social cue recognition task. However, Appelo et al. (1992) concluded that negative symptoms did not explain specific skill deficits in their sample of schizophrenia patients, and no compelling links between negative symptoms and problem-solving ability were reported by Bellack et al. (1994). Finally, using the Physical Anhedonia Scale and the Social Anhedonia Scale (see Chapman et al., 1976), Blanchard, Bellack, and Mueser (1994) found no relationship between either of these two anhedonia scales and measures of social skill in their patient samples.

Overall, the findings suggest that, although negative symptoms may not be particularly associated with any specific social skill deficit, they do predict unemployment (Marwaha & Johnson, 2004), reduced social network size (Thorup et al., 2006), and diminished social competence more broadly. This raises the question of whether the social deficits of schizophrenia patients can be explained solely by negative symptoms.

The answer is "probably not." Although schizophrenia patients with negative symptoms generally perform less well than non-negative symptom schizophrenia patients on measures of interpersonal skill, the latter still perform less well than affectively ill or community control groups (Bellack et al., 1989; Bellack, Morrison, Wixted, & Mueser, 1990; Dworkin, 1990; Dworkin et al., 1991). This suggests that social impairments are associated with schizophrenia in general and are not linked only to the negative symptoms of the disorder.

Moreover, in Dworkin's (1990) study of twins with schizophrenia, male patients showed greater asociality and withdrawn behavior, as well as poorer premorbid social competence than did females. This, as we have seen, is in keeping with the generally better social functioning of female versus male patients. However, Dworkin found no significant differences between the sexes with respect to the symptoms that they exhibited. The differences in social functioning found in this sample are therefore not easily explained simply by differences in symptoms (see also Andia et al., 1995).

In summary, these results suggest that negative symptoms and social functioning may reflect different processes in the development and manifestation of schizophrenia. Negative symptoms may exacerbate the poor interpersonal abilities of those with schizophrenia. However, negative symptoms alone do not provide a full explanation for the interpersonal deficits that characterize the disorder. Rather, the data point to the likely existence of some more focal deficit that is related to social functioning.

## Are Social Deficits Apparent Before the Onset of Schizophrenia?

If the social deficits that characterize people with schizophrenia are simply a consequence of the symptoms of disorder (or are secondary to the effects of medications and hospitalization) we would not expect them to be observable prior to the onset of the illness. However, evidence suggests that interpersonal difficulties often appear long before any psychiatric illness is diagnosed.

One way to examine this issue is to explore the premorbid adjustment of currently diagnosed patients using retrospective reports. Cannon and colleagues (Cannon et al., 1997) interviewed the mothers of 70 patients with schizophrenia, 28 patients with bipolar disorder, and 100 healthy controls. Mothers were asked to report on their children's adjustment in several areas, including social functioning. Compared with the mothers of both the healthy controls and the patients with bipolar disorder, mothers of patients with schizophrenia reported that their children were significantly less sociable and more withdrawn in their childhood and adolescent social relationships. Differences in the premorbid social adjustment of the patients with bipolar disorder were also apparent when compared to the healthy controls. However, overall, they were less impaired than the schizophrenia group, and they continued to do quite well in school despite their social problems.

Of course, retrospective investigations are not without methodological problems. One concern is the accuracy of the historical reports. In a creative series of studies Walker and her colleagues (e.g., Walker & Lewine, 1990) circumvented this problem by examining the home movies of people diagnosed with schizophrenia. These home movies featured the patients and their healthy siblings interacting during childhood, *years before any psychiatric difficulties became apparent in one of the children.* Despite this, independent raters, who did not know which child later developed schizophrenia, were able to successfully identify the vulnerable child. This was the case even though the sample was selected to include patients whose parents reported that their children showed no unusual behavior or signs of illness when they were growing up. Although raters were given no specific instructions about how to evaluate the children in the home movies, they indicated that their decisions were frequently guided by interpersonal aspects of the children's behavior. Behaviors such as decreased social responsiveness, reduced eye contact, and lack of positive affect were mentioned, although other factors, such as motor behavior, also influenced the decisions.

Other evidence of premorbid social deficits in schizophrenia comes from examinations of high-risk populations. In the classic form of high-risk investigation, the offspring of parents with diagnosed schizophrenia are recruited in childhood and then studied prospectively. These children, who are at genetically heightened risk for psychiatric disorder themselves, can be followed closely as they mature. Using data from the New York High-Risk Project, Dworkin and his colleagues reported that adolescents at risk for schizophrenia were rated as being less socially competent than adolescents who were at risk for affective illness (Dworkin et al., 1990, 1991; Dworkin et al., 1994). These evaluations, made by trained raters, were based on information from interviews conducted with the adolescents themselves as well as from interviews with their parents. The adolescents at risk for schizophrenia also reported significantly poorer peer relationships and decreased hobbies and interests relative to the adolescents at risk for mood disorders. In other words, among high-risk adolescents, those who were later diagnosed with schizophrenia had poorer peer relationships even before they became ill.

More recent work has introduced other approaches in the service of earlier identification and intervention for risk states. One option is to select subjects who score high on measures known to be predictive of later schizophrenia. Such people are considered at behavioral high risk. Another approach involves studying people who are thought to be at high risk for developing schizophrenia because they are already showing some of the prodromal (early clinical) signs of the disorder along with functional decline, commonly known as clinical high-risk or ultra high-risk states (Keshavan et al., 2011).

In an example of the former approach, Zborowski and Garske (1993) selected male subjects who scored high on a self-report measure of schizotypic traits involving perceptual aberrations and magical ideation (the Per-Mag Scale; see Chapman et al., 1982, 1994). These males were then compared to control male undergraduates who had low scores on the same self-report scale. Although the two groups were comparable with respect to their age and class rank, the groups differed in important ways when they interacted with a female research assistant in a videotaped interview. Males high on the Per-Mag scale showed more odd behavior during the interview. They were also rated as being more avoidant. Interestingly, the female interviewers reported that, when interacting with the hypothetically schizophrenia-prone males, they felt more anxious, angrier, and less curious than when interacting with the control males. These data suggest that undergraduate males who are not psychiatrically ill but who are at statistically higher risk for the development of schizophrenia show interpersonal anomalies during social interactions. Importantly, their odd and avoidant behavior also appears to create social discomfort for those with whom they interact.

Given that social impairments are associated with both genetic and behavioral high risk for the development of schizophrenia, it should come as little surprise that social difficulties also characterize those who have prodromal positive symptoms but who are not psychotic (Ballon et al., 2007; Cornblatt et al., 2007). Moreover, these social deficits may be an omen for what is to come. Cornblatt and colleagues (2007) reported that social impairments measured in the prodrome predicted the presence of psychosis 1 year later. This raises the possibility that impaired social functioning could be an early marker for schizophrenia. Of course, whether social functioning deficits reflect a vulnerability to the disorder or simply create the kinds of stressful circumstances that might trigger the onset of schizophrenia is not resolved. Social difficulties may be a manifestation of an underlying diathesis, a behavioral marker that engenders increased social stress (perhaps from irritated peers or family), or both.

Regardless, research has identified poor premorbid social functioning as a negative prognostic sign. Retrospective studies have linked poorer premorbid social functioning to a more chronic clinical course and more frequent hospitalizations (Cannon-Spoor et al., 1982). In contrast, good premorbid functioning has been shown to be predictive of more complete remissions after an episode of illness (Amminger & Mutschlechner, 1994). Premorbid functioning is also predictive of the level of community functioning and adjustment that can be attained once the illness has developed (Childers & Harding, 1990). Simply put, social difficulties, whether indexed via measures of premorbid adjustment or through other global assessments, appear to signal serious clinical problems in the future.

*Exploring the Role of Cognition in Social Dysfunction*

So far, we have described how social behavior is altered in schizophrenia. But what are the building blocks of typical social functioning, and how might compromise in these domains affect social behavior? One potential factor here is cognition, defined as "the ability to accurately perceive, attend to, and remember information" (Green, 2016, p. 9). An extensive literature documents the difficulties that schizophrenia patients experience in aspects of their neurocognitive functioning relative to healthy controls (see Heinrichs, 2005). Given this, it is reasonable to ask if problems with cognition might serve as "rate limiters" (see Bellack, 1992) for how well patients can function in a social domain. Certainly, the interpersonal skills that most of us take for granted depend on a wide range of cognitive operations. They are also much more complex than we typically appreciate. For example, entering into a conversation requires us to selectively focus our attention on the appropriate stimulus (our conversational partner) while at the same time filtering out the rest of the background noise that is around us. In addition, to respond appropriately we need to remember what our partner has said and generate a comment of our own that is related and on-topic. This places obvious demands on our memory systems and on higher-level information processing and executive skills. Moreover, all of this must be done while simultaneously processing the multiple verbal and nonverbal cues that our partner generates.

The conversational abilities of even healthy subjects can be easily disrupted. Barch and Berenbaum (1994) asked college students to complete a complex processing task while at the same time talking to an interviewer. The students' performance under this condition was then compared to their performance during a control interview that did not have a concurrent task. Under the condition of reduced processing capacity, the students' conversational skills showed marked impairment. More specifically, they spoke less, showed less syntactic complexity in their language, and said "um" and "ah" significantly more than they did during the control interview. This experimental manipulation reveals just how important certain facets of information processing are likely to be to smooth social performance. They also suggest that those who more ordinarily lack sufficient cognitive resources to meet competing demands might well be expected to experience difficulties making sense of and navigating the interpersonal world. A personal comment from a schizophrenia patient highlights this struggle.

> I have trouble concentrating and keeping my mind on one thing at a time, especially when I'm with people. I can hear what they're saying, but I can't keep up with them and make sense of the conversation. I lose my grip on being part of the conversation and drift off. It's not so bad when I'm talking with just one other person, but if I'm trying to tune in to a conversation with several people, things come in too fast and I get lost. It's hard for me to contribute to a conversation when the ideas get blurred. (Liberman, 1982, p. 78)

**Neurocognition and Social Functioning**

Neurocognition and social functioning are clearly linked. A patient's ability to function in the community, for example, is related to the kind of executive functioning skills that are assessed by tasks such as the Wisconsin Card Sort Test (WCST; Heaton, 1981). In this task the subject is presented with four key cards that show different shapes, colors, and quantities (e.g., a red triangle, three blue squares, two yellow circles). The subject is presented with a card from a deck and asked to match it to a key card according to a matching principle that is not revealed by the tester (e.g., color, number, shape). The only feedback the subject receives is whether the match they have made is correct or incorrect. After the subject has been successful over several trials, the matching principle is abruptly changed, and a formerly correct response is now incorrect. The subject is required to discover the new matching principle and sort the cards according to that until it changes again.

The WCST involves abstract conceptual learning and problem-solving. Although healthy controls can complete the WCST without much problem, patients with schizophrenia often experience difficulties. Moreover, how well patients perform on the WCST is predictive of their functioning in the community. In a meta-analytic review, Green and colleagues (Green et al., 2000) reported a modest relation ($r = .23$) between card-sorting performance and global social functioning. This association suggests that the kinds of skills tapped by the WCST (executive functioning, concept formation, and cognitive flexibility) are also necessary for good social competence (see also Lysaker et al., 1995; Jaeger & Douglas, 1992).

Memory skills are important, not only for social competence in general (e.g., Goldman et al., 1993), but also for social problem-solving. Poor memory has been related to greater social skill impairments in patients with schizophrenia and schizoaffective disorder but not in patients with mood disorders (Mueser, Bellack, Douglas, & Wade, 1991). Memory has also been found to be linked to the ability to implement solutions in a role-play task (Bellack et al., 1994).

Consistent with these observations, Green et al.'s (2000) review highlighted the role of memory in the functional outcome of patients with schizophrenia. The ability to learn new psychosocial skills (such as might be taught in a rehabilitation program) is predicted by immediate verbal memory. This concerns the ability to acquire, store, and retrieve information for more than a few minutes, as might be required to remember items to purchase on a trip to the supermarket. Secondary verbal memory, which involves the ability to acquire and recall information after a longer delay (e.g., lists of words, stories), is also important. Secondary verbal memory predicts community functioning at the global level; it also predicts both performance on social problem-solving tasks and psychosocial skill acquisition. Overall, however, immediate verbal memory appears to be a little more strongly associated with functional outcome in schizophrenia ($r = .40$) than is secondary verbal memory is ($r = .29$).

Another neurocognitive domain that emerges with some frequency in the functional outcome literature concerns *vigilance*. Vigilance, or sustained attention, is a process required to read a book or focus attention while receiving instructions. Green and colleagues (2000) have reported an effect size of $r = .20$ between vigilance and functional outcome and provided solid support for the association between vigilance and social problem-solving as measured by the AIPSS.

The link between attentional dysfunction and interpersonal deficits is further suggested by results of one of the high-risk projects described earlier. As part of a comprehensive assessment battery, subjects from the New York High Risk Project were tested on a wide array of attentional measures, allowing a single "attentional index" score to be assigned. Consistent with findings discussed earlier for diagnosed patients, children's attention scores were found to be highly correlated with two factors derived from the Personality Disorders Examination (PDE; Loranger et al., 1987) and measured in adulthood. These factors reflected a relative insensitivity to other individuals coupled with an indifference to their feelings, and an avoidance of interpersonal interactions whenever possible (see Cornblatt, et al., 1992). Thus, children who exhibited deficits in their attentional skills were, as adults, less socially sensitive, more socially indifferent, and more socially avoidant. Using data from a second sample in this same project, Dworkin et al. (1993) were further able to demonstrate that childhood attentional dysfunction was predictive of significantly poorer social competence when the children reached adolescence. Thus, even in those simply at high risk for schizophrenia, the link between attention and interpersonal performance is apparent. In children at risk as well as in adults with schizophrenia, deficits in attention are associated with deficits in social competence and social skills.

To summarize, research findings implicate card-sorting performance, immediate memory, secondary verbal memory, and sustained attention/vigilance in the functional outcomes of patients with schizophrenia. These functional outcomes include global functioning in the community, social problem-solving, and psychosocial skill acquisition. Yet traditional measures of neurocognition leave much of the variability in social functioning unaccounted for (Penn et al., 1997). This has prompted the search for other factors that might lead to greater understanding of the cognitive underpinnings of impaired social functioning in schizophrenia. Of central importance here has been the study of social cognition.

## Social Cognition in Schizophrenia

Social cognition is concerned with the mental operations that underlie the capacity to perceive, interpret, and process social information (Green et al., 2019). It is a broad construct that includes many different abilities. Unlike nonsocial cognition, it concerns stimuli that are personally relevant. Moreover, although social cognition obviously requires nonsocial neurocognitive skills, it also involves other skills (see Couture et al., 2006). These include the ability to perceive and make correct inferences about the emotions of others (emotion processing), the ability to pick up social cues (social knowledge), the ability to understand that others have mental states that differ from one's own and make correct inferences about another person's intentions or beliefs (mentalizing and theory of mind [ToM]), and the ability to use causal attributions to draw conclusions about social events that occur (attributional style). Skills in these domains are considered more proximal to social behavior than the skills traditionally assessed in neurocognitive paradigms. They may also prove to be more amenable to intervention than basic cognitive processes.

### Emotion Perception

People who have schizophrenia struggle with the kinds of social processing tasks that most of us perform with relative ease. A case in point is emotion perception (see Edwards et al., 2002). Those with the disorder have problems identifying specific emotions in faces. They also have difficulties making judgments about differences in emotional expressiveness—again typically in faces. Compared to controls, the effect sizes associated with these performance deficits in patients with schizophrenia are large in magnitude ($d$ = –0.89 for facial emotion identification; $d$ = –1.09 for differentiation; see Kohler et al., 2010). A subsequent meta-analysis conducted by Savla and colleagues (2013) reported comparable effect sizes of $g$ = 0.89 for emotion perception and $g$ = .89 for emotion processing, which involves understanding emotions, discriminating between different emotions, and managing emotions and emotional reactions.

Patients with schizophrenia are also impaired relative to healthy controls in their ability to recognize emotion being conveyed in speech (e.g., Hooker & Park, 2002). In some instances, they may fail to comment on emotional expression at all (e.g., Cramer et al., 1992; Hellewell, Connell, & Deakin, 1994). Face perception and face affect recognition deficits have also been demonstrated in psychosis-prone, schizotypic individuals (e.g., Poreh et al., 1994). Differences in facial affect recognition between controls and individuals at clinical high risk for psychosis have also been noted, although Barbato et al. (2015) reported that this difference was no longer significant after controlling for age and IQ. This is interesting because several other studies have reported impairments in facial emotion processing in clinical high-risk individuals (e.g., Amminger et al., 2011; Kohler et al., 2014). Going forward, the role of IQ in particular warrants additional consideration in studies of this type.

In clinical high-risk samples, problems with recognizing emotion in faces do not appear to be related to the presence of positive or negative symptoms (Barbato et al., 2015). However, problems with emotion recognition have been linked to both negative symptoms (e.g., Mueser et al., 1996) and positive symptoms (Poole et al., 2000) in patients with the full illness. Nonetheless, in a large sample of patients with schizophrenia ($N$ = 521), the correlations between ability to recognize facial emotions and positive and negative symptoms, although significant, were very small in magnitude (around $r$ = .1; see Maat et al., 2015). Moreover, even when in remission, schizophrenia patients performed worse than healthy controls. Although more remains to be learned, symptoms do not appear to provide a full explanation for the emotion perception difficulties characteristic of schizophrenia.

Finally, as might be expected, there is a link between emotion recognition problems and interpersonal functioning. Mueser et al. (1996) noted strong associations between schizophrenia patients' abilities to identify facial emotions from photographs and nurses' ratings of those patients' social skills in a hospital setting. A similar correlation between better performance on tasks of emotion recognition and better social functioning has also been reported by other researchers (e.g., Hooker & Park, 2002; Ihnen et al., 1998; Poole et al., 2000). Such findings highlight how integral the ability to identify and distinguish different emotions is for successful social adjustment.

### Social Perception and Knowledge

Being successful in interpersonal situations requires social knowledge. It is difficult to imagine how a person lacking a basic understanding of the structure and rules of social interactions could participate fluidly and competently in social exchange. Given the interpersonal difficulties that are associated with schizophrenia, it is not surprising that people with this disorder often perform poorly on tests that measure social perception or social knowledge.

In an interesting early study, Cutting and Murphy (1990) gave patients multiple choice questions that were designed to tap two knowledge domains. The first concerned practical knowledge (e.g., "Why is it not safe to drink tap water in some countries?"). The second assessed knowledge in a more social domain (e.g., "How would you tell a friend politely that they had stayed too long?"). For this latter question, the answer choices included "There's no more coffee left," or "You'd better go. I'm fed up with you staying too long," or (correct answer) "Excuse me. I've got an appointment with a friend." Compared with those diagnosed with bipolar disorder or major depression, the patients with schizophrenia showed significant impairment on the social knowledge test. Interestingly, the nonsocial knowledge test did not discriminate between the patients with schizophrenia and bipolar disorder, although both patient groups scored significantly worse than the depressed patients.

Social knowledge can also be assessed in other ways. The Schema Component Sequencing Task (SCST; Corrigan & Addis, 1995) contains 12 sets of cards. Each set contains 5–8 cards that describe the component actions involved in different social situations (e.g., going shopping, getting a job). The person completing the test is presented with the cards in a mixed-up order and then asked to arrange the cards in the order that makes sense for the successful completion of the social task. Compared to nonclinical controls, patients with schizophrenia take longer to sort the cards and are less likely to put them in the correct order (Pinkham & Penn, 2006). Moreover, in the study just described, sorting time and accuracy on the SCST were highly correlated with interpersonal skill measured during a conversational role play. As Pinkham and Penn (2006) noted, "to interact effectively, one needs to know the rules that govern social settings" (p. 176).

Meta-analysis suggests that the mean effect size for problems with social perception and social knowledge in those with schizophrenia is large for social perception ($g = 1.04$) and medium ($g = .54$) for social knowledge (Savla et al., 2013). Social perception is also compromised in those at clinical high risk and is unrelated to symptoms and IQ (Barbato et al., 2015; Piskulic et al., 2016). This suggests that problems understanding social rules and social relationships may be a key feature of vulnerability to psychosis.

### Theory of Mind and Mentalization

Frith (1992) was the first to suggest that people with schizophrenia might have difficulties understanding the mental states of others, a skill that he referred to as "theory of mind." Research since then has confirmed that schizophrenia patients do indeed experience problems with metacognition. This is apparent on tasks that require an understanding of the beliefs or intentions of others (ToM tasks) as well as on tasks that require evaluations of the affective states of others (often referred to as mentalization).

In an early study, Corcoran, Mercer and Frith (1995) explored how well schizophrenia patients and patients with other psychiatric conditions were able to pick up hints made by others. Patients with schizophrenia, depressed or anxious psychiatric controls, and psychiatrically healthy controls were given brief scenarios that featured interactions between two characters. At the end of each scenario, one of the characters dropped a very obvious hint (e.g., "I want to wear that blue shirt but it's creased"). Subjects were then asked to say what the character meant and what he or she was hinting at. If the subject failed to get the hint, an even more obvious cue was given (e.g., "It's in the ironing basket"). Consistent with a problem in metacognition, the schizophrenia patients did poorly on this task, scoring significantly lower than those in the two control groups. Findings such as this again bring to mind the earlier comment from the ex-wife of "Jon": "It was as though some strange deficiency prevented him from understanding some things that seem perfectly obvious to most people" (Anonymous, 1994).

A more advanced metacognitive test is the Faux Pas Recognition test (Baron-Cohen et al., 1999). Developed for use in autism research, this test requires the experimenter to read stories to the research participant and then ask that person whether someone in the story said something that they should not have said. The research participant is also asked additional questions so that the experimenter can confirm that they understand why the faux pas comment should not have been made and why the person who made the faux pas comment might have said it.

Compared to healthy controls, patients with schizophrenia perform poorly on the Faux Pas test (Hooker et al., 2011; Zhu et al., 2007). Moreover, although impaired performance on this test is correlated with worse social functioning, faux pas recognition appears to be unrelated to the presence of clinical symptoms.

In addition to being characteristic of patients with chronic schizophrenia, ToM and mentalization deficits can also be seen in first-episode patients (see Bora & Pantelis, 2013; Bora, Yücel & Pantelis, 2009a, for meta-analyses). In each case the effect sizes are large relative to healthy controls. The effect sizes associated with impairments in metacognition are also remarkably similar across the first episode ($d = -1.0$) and chronic ($d = -1.1$) patient groups. These findings suggest that such difficulties probably do not result from factors such as illness progression or long-term medication use. It is also unlikely that problems in metacognition result from the presence of severe symptoms because they have been noted in remitted patients (Herold et al., 2002). Although the effect sizes are much smaller, impairments in metacognition can even be detected in first-degree relatives of patients with schizophrenia as well as in people at clinical high risk for the disorder (Bora & Pantelis, 2013; Janssen et al., 2003). For example, Barbato et al. (2015) observed problems detecting sarcasm in a large sample of clinical high-risk individuals—problems that were independent of age or IQ. Taken together, these findings provide further support for the independence of metacognition impairments and clinical state and again suggest that difficulties in this domain of social cognition may be a vulnerability marker.

It warrants mention that ToM difficulties and problems with mentalization are not specific to schizophrenia. They are also found in patients with autism and those with bipolar disorder (Bora, Yücel & Pantelis, 2009b). For example, Donahoe and colleagues (2012) reported that, relative to healthy controls, patients with bipolar disorder and patients with schizophrenia performed equally poorly on the Reading the Mind in the Eyes test (Baron-Cohen et al., 2001). This requires participants to identify the emotion being depicted when only the eye region of a given face is shown. However, on another ToM task (hinting task), the performance of the patients with bipolar disorder was intermediate between the performance of the controls and the performance of the patients with schizophrenia. In other words, the patients with bipolar disorder were much less impaired. The differences just reported also remained when IQ and symptom severity were statistically controlled. Findings such as these suggest that the decoding of mental state (eyes task) is impaired in both bipolar disorder and schizophrenia, although the former group of patients may have more mild impairments in the area of mental state reasoning (hinting task). They are also consistent with the idea that, rather than being entirely distinct disorders, schizophrenia and bipolar disorder may lie on a spectrum of neurodevelopmental/affective pathology, with bipolar disorder involving less cognitive impairment and schizophrenia reflecting more neurodevelopmental compromise and more cognitive difficulties (Craddock & Owen, 2010).

### Attributional Style

Another domain of social cognition concerns how people tend to explain the causes of events that happen in their lives. This is referred to as attributional style (AS). Within schizophrenia, it has been demonstrated that patients who have persecutory delusions or paranoid ideation tend to blame other people, rather than the situation itself, when there is a negative circumstance that demands an explanation (see Bentall et al., 2001). For example, if we encounter a person who acts in an unfriendly way toward us, we might make an attribution that they are rude. On the other hand, if we subsequently learn that they received bad news just before we met them, we would likely correct our initial impression. People with persecutory delusions, however, typically fail to update or modify their initial impressions, retaining the blaming attribution. A strong need for early closure, impairments in cognitive flexibility, and deficits in mentalizing and ToM are possible factors that could prevent people with schizophrenia from countering natural biases in attribution style (see Couture et al., 2006).

Attributional bias is the least well studied domain of social cognition. However, meta-analysis suggests that the differences between patients with schizophrenia and healthy comparison samples are very small (Savla et al., 2013). As such, this aspect of cognition may play a less prominent role in our understanding of social adjustment in schizophrenia.

In summary, across a wide range of social-cognitive tasks, schizophrenia patients appear to perform poorly. Not only do they have difficulties with respect to reading emotional cues, but they also appear to be less socially facile. They fail to spot the kinds of subtle (or not so subtle) social hints that most of us detect without difficulty. Compounding these problems, they also have impairments in gaze perception, perceiving a face with an averted gaze as making eye contact with them (Tso et al., 2012; Hooker & Park, 2005). Since the days of Kraepelin we have known that navigating the social world presents serious challenges for those with schizophrenia. As a result of research efforts spanning several decades, we now know much more about the behavioral components of social functioning that are most severely compromised.

### Is Social Cognition a Better Predictor of Social Behavior Than Neurocognition?

A considerable proportion of the variance in social cognition is explained by nonsocial cognition (Vauth et al., 2004); intact cognitive functions are clearly required for a person to perform well on tests of social cognition. Yet evidence suggests that neurocognition and social cognition are largely distinct constructs (Allen et al., 2007; Sergi et al., 2007). This has prompted researchers to examine how well measure of neurocognition and social cognition predict overall social functioning.

In an early consideration of this issue Corrigan and Toomey (1995) administered a battery of nonsocial cognition measures to a sample of patients with schizophrenia and schizoaffective disorder. The measures of nonsocial cognition included a measure of vigilance (the degraded stimulus form of the Continuous Performance Test), a measure of immediate memory (Digit Span Distractibility Task), a measure of secondary memory (the Rey Auditory Learning Test), and a measure of conceptual flexibility (the WCST). In addition, a measure of social cognition, the Social Cue Recognition Test (SCRT), was also administered. The SCRT consisted of eight videotaped vignettes that featured two or three people interacting in a social situation. After viewing the vignettes, subjects were asked to answer a series of true-false questions about the interpersonal cues they saw in the interactions. The measures of nonsocial and social cognition were then correlated with performance on a measure of interpersonal problem-solving, the AIPSS. Social cue sensitivity was found to be related to receiving (detecting a problem), processing (coming up with a solution), and sending (role-playing the solution) skills. In contrast, none of the nonsocial cognitive variables predicted performance on the AIPSS. These findings suggested that measures of social cognition were more strongly associated with interpersonal problem-solving skills than were measures of nonsocial cognition.

In a subsequent study Pinkham and Penn (2006) administered several tests of neurocognition (assessing overall intellectual functioning, immediate memory, and executive functioning) and several tests of social cognition (assessing emotion recognition, social knowledge, and ToM) to outpatients with schizophrenia as well as to nonclinical controls. These variables were then used to predict interpersonal skill as measured in a role-play test that involved talking to a confederate. For the patients with schizophrenia, the measures of social cognition accounted for almost twice as much variance in interpersonal skill as did the measures of neurocognition.

As this and other studies illustrate, measures of social cognition contribute additional variance to functional outcome in schizophrenia over that contributed by measures of neurocognition (see also Brekke et al., 2005; Sergi et al., 2006). Further support for this conclusion comes from two recent meta-analyses (Fett et al., 2011; Halverson et al., 2019). Using data from 166 studies involving 12,868 participants with nonaffective psychosis, Halverson and colleagues (2019) reported a sample-weighted average effect size of 0.21 between neurocognition and measures of functional outcome, with the largest effect size (.33) being seen for the relationship between neurocognition and social skills. For social cognition (considered as an overall summary variable), the effect size was slightly higher (.24) with the largest effect being noted for the relationship between ToM and social skills (effect size = .38). Consistent with this, Maat, Fett, and Derks (2012) have observed that performance on the hinting task (also a ToM measure) was the best predictor of quality of life in a large sample of patients with schizophrenia. Overall, there is good support for the idea that social cognition is a critical mediator in the link between neurocognition and social functioning in schizophrenia (see Schmidt et al., 2011; Halverson et al., 2019). Neurocognitive impairments may lead to problems with social cognition which in turn exert a negative influence on social functioning.

More recently, researchers have begun to consider whether the negative symptoms so closely linked with social impairment represent a behavioral manifestation of social cognition. Some data suggest that certain facets of social cognition are associated with specific negative symptoms; other data suggest that fundamental abnormalities may affect social cognition broadly and result in negative symptoms. Reflecting this, an integrated model has now been proposed to capture how these associations may emerge (Pelletier-Baldelli & Holt, 2020). Work of this kind demonstrates how social cognition, compared to neurocognition, is increasingly becoming a primary area of focus in the investigation of social deficits in schizophrenia.

## Neural Basis of Altered Social Cognition in Schizophrenia

Neuroscientific methods are now being used to illuminate how neural alterations relate to impairments in social cognition. Here, we consider some representative studies and discuss findings across various stages of illness.

One active area of interest concerns the neurobiological basis of ToM, or mentalization. As we noted earlier, ToM involves the ability to perspective-take, make inferences about, and attribute mental states to the self and to others. In healthy controls, brain regions such as the temporal pole, temporoparietal junction, precuneus, and medial prefrontal cortex are involved in these tasks. People with schizophrenia generally show aberrant patterns of activation in these regions when engaged in ToM tasks, although such differences are not always consistent across studies. Most studies report hypoactivation within mentalization systems, with hypoactivation being related to poor task performance. However, other studies report hyperactivity of these regions in schizophrenia and comparable task performance between groups. Quite possibly, individuals with schizophrenia require higher levels of activation to achieve the same mentalization proficiency (Green et al., 2015). This interpretation is complemented by structural findings of ventromedial prefrontal cortex gray matter reduction in schizophrenia, which has been found to be associated with poorer performance on task-based, self-reported, and interview-rated ToM assessments (Hooker et al., 2011). Aberrant structure and function in these regions related to impaired mentalization likely contributes to the social difficulties experienced by people with schizophrenia.

It should be noted that not all processes may be impacted. Affect-sharing is a process that describes the functional correspondence between an individual observing another person with an emotional expression and the activation of the observer's own emotion-related brain regions, including dorsal anterior cingulate cortex and anterior insula. This aspect of social cognition appears to be intact in schizophrenia (Horan et al., 2014). Aspects of ToM like self-reflection have also been investigated in relatives of patients with schizophrenia, providing insights into potential biological vulnerabilities. In a study of self-reflection, compared to controls, first-degree relatives of patients with schizophrenia showed less activation in posterior cingulate cortex and superior temporal gyrus—regions known to be involved in self and other processing (Brent et al., 2014). Furthermore, reduced activation was associated with higher levels of subclinical delusional ideation. This suggests that functional alterations in this circuitry are associated with genetic liability for schizophrenia and may also confer vulnerability to delusional thinking.

Many domains of social cognition are often at least partially dependent on higher level knowledge—knowledge that may itself be impaired in schizophrenia. Another approach is studying lower level, nonverbal processes that may underlie social cognitive processes and support social behavior. Certain perceptual social cue processes, like affective face perception and affective vocal prosody, are prime examples. People with schizophrenia generally demonstrate hypoactivation of relevant regions during such processing, showing reduced activation in the fusiform face area and amygdala during affective face processing and reduced activation in superior temporal gyrus and inferior frontal gyrus during affective voice processing. In contrast, patients also show hyperactivation in regions not typically associated with face perception during affective face processing (Green et al., 2015). Relatedly, a meta-analysis demonstrated that patients with schizophrenia exhibit increased amygdala activation in response to neutral, rather than aversive emotional stimuli (Anticevic et al., 2012). This may have important implications for the perception of neutral social cues.

Another example of a crucial lower-level process is "personal space," or the preferred distance an individual maintains when interacting with another individual (Hayduk, 1983). Personal space is an important communicative tool; greater proximity promotes social affiliation (Kahn & McGaughey, 1977), and greater distancing, while offering more protection against physical threat, can also convey mistrust (Lourenco et al., 2011). Personal space has long been known to be larger and more inflexible in schizophrenia (Horowitz et al., 1964), and recent work has investigated the possibility that neural alterations might be implicated in this. Holt and colleagues (2015) focused on a region of a frontoparietal network involved in the sensory monitoring and guiding of behaviors occurring in personal space. In schizophrenia patients, one region of this network, called the dorsal intraparietal sulcus, was found to be hyperresponsive to social stimuli appearing to intrude on personal space. Patients showed the expected finding of larger personal space sizes. Larger personal space sizes were also associated with neural hyperresponsivity as well as being correlated with more negative symptoms. Alterations of neural circuitry involved in preferred social spacing may contribute to changes in low-level behavioral social communication that exacerbate interpersonal difficulties in schizophrenia.

The default mode network is a large-scale brain network known to be broadly involved in self-referential thinking and self and other processing, in addition to more specific processes such as ToM, mentalization, emotion recognition, and autobiographical memory. Adults with schizophrenia show increased connectivity within the default mode network, although there are mixed findings of increased and decreased connectivity between the default mode network and other networks. These disruptions in adults are associated with poorer cognitive and social functioning (Hu et al., 2017). There is also evidence for neural alterations in the resting-state functional connectivity of the default mode network in adolescents with early-onset psychosis (Nair et al., 2020). Moreover, these neural alterations are generally consistent with the overall pattern found in adults. This suggests that similar changes may characterize the brain at the onset of illness, regardless of age.

Social deficits are often early warning signs of schizophrenia even before onset of illness (Kimoto et al., 2019), suggesting that neural changes likely precede the onset of full-blown psychotic symptoms. As we have noted earlier, research with samples of individuals at clinical high risk for psychosis can be informative here. For example, in the schizophrenia literature, patients show gray matter volume reductions in neural regions supporting cognition, and this reduction in gray matter volume predicts worse social functioning (Hooker et al., 2011). Other work has reported similar, albeit less severe gray matter volume reductions in clinical high-risk samples (Fusar-Poli et al., 2012). Compared to healthy controls, clinical high-risk individuals show reduced gray matter volume in parahippocampal gyrus, postcentral gyrus, and anterior cingulate cortex (Lincoln & Hooker, 2014). Volume reductions in these latter two regions were also associated with self-reported social impairment. The finding that structural abnormalities in regions associated with social and emotional processing were related to social functioning deficits is interesting, given that the majority of clinical high-risk individuals do not convert to psychotic illness. It suggests that findings such as these are but one element of a broader constellation of evolving neural, psychological, and functional declines on the trajectory toward psychosis.

Relevant to this point, other social cognitive processes such as mental simulation appear to be intact in clinical high-risk samples. Mental simulation is the process of generating internal representations of another's thoughts and feelings, a part of ToM. Lincoln and colleagues (2020) examined neural correlates of mental simulation of pain, asking individuals to watch videos of another person experiencing pain and then to simulate the observed situation on themselves. Across clinical high-risk individuals and healthy controls, greater activation in somatosensory cortex was associated with greater rates of positive social experiences and affective empathy. Not only was this process not compromised in clinical high-risk individuals (at least in somatosensory cortex), but these findings also suggest that the neural mechanisms underlying simulation are important for social behavior and can help explain individual variability. Such work with at-risk individuals highlights how including clinical high-risk populations in research expands our knowledge across stages of illness.

## Motivational Processes and Social Functioning

To this point we have described some of the social difficulties characteristic of people with schizophrenia (or those at increased risk of developing schizophrenia) and considered the neural systems that may support effective social competence. Unaddressed thus far, however, is the role of social motivation—the internal drive to connect with others and form meaningful relationships. Initially, it was believed that diminished interest or pleasure in social interactions (the negative symptom known as social anhedonia) accounted for the social isolation and poorer social functioning characteristic of schizophrenia (Kwapil, 1998). However, people with schizophrenia express a need for connection through their choices of activities (Gard et al., 2014). They also regard improved social functioning as an important treatment goal (Shumway et al., 2003). This suggests that something other than reduced interest in social engagement may be playing a role, leading to a focus more specifically on motivation.

At a general and global level, motivation has been shown to mediate the link between neurocognition, social cognition, and functional outcome including social behavior (Gard et al., 2009). Yet motivation is a multifaceted construct that comprises several distinct processes. These include hedonic experience (the ability of a person to like or enjoy something they experience), incentive salience (how rewarding the event is expected to be and how much the person wants the experience), and effort computation and expenditure (which involves integrating information about the costs and benefits of seeking a potentially rewarding outcome; see Barch & Dowd, 2010). Difficulties in any or all of these domains are likely to compromise social behavior and impair social functioning.

Basic behavioral neuroscience has distinguished between two components of pleasure: "liking" versus "wanting." "Liking" describes reactive feelings of pleasure to a stimulus in the moment. It is often referred to as *hedonic experience*. "Wanting," on the other hand, refers to the anticipation of pleasure that could be obtained from a stimulus in the future. Because such a stimulus is marked as relevant, or salient to the individual, "wanting" is otherwise referred to as *incentive salience*. These processes are supported by different neural pathways in the brain, where "liking" is associated with distributed hotspot patterns of activation across the brain and the serotonin and opioid systems, whereas "wanting" is associated with neural structures such as the striatum and the dopamine system (Berridge & Robinson, 1998, 2016).

People with schizophrenia demonstrate intact hedonics. In other words, they report similar levels of pleasure in the moment (consummatory pleasure, "liking") from daily activities as do healthy controls. On the other hand, people with schizophrenia report less expected pleasure from future activities (anticipatory pleasure, "wanting"). What this suggests is that the deficit may be specific to incentive salience (Gard et al., 2007).

Incentive salience is a core mechanism in reward learning whereby individuals learn to predict which stimuli are associated with rewards and respond behaviorally to obtain those rewards. Dopamine plays a mediating role in this. Reward learning deficits have been demonstrated in schizophrenia, with impairments in learning associated with the receiving but not the removal of reward; these alterations are also correlated with negative symptom severity (Reinen et al., 2014).

The assessment of the effort involved to obtain rewards and the cost-benefit analysis of that effort expenditure are another set of related processes modulated by dopamine (Salamone et al., 2007) and altered in schizophrenia. At a behavioral level, people with schizophrenia show less of an increase in effort when higher magnitude or higher probability rewards are available. This is suggestive of abnormalities in effort-cost computations. These impairments are correlated with negative symptom severity and with community as well as work functioning (Barch et al., 2014; Gold et al., 2013). Patients also show inaccuracies in estimating the effort required to obtain goals and report engaging in less effortful activities and setting less effortful goals; this is again related to functioning (Gard et al., 2014).

Effort-based decision-making involves dopamine and brain regions such as the anterior cingulate cortex, ventral striatum, and amygdala (Culbreth et al., 2018; Treadway & Zald, 2011). Neurobiological differences in these regions may contribute to impaired effort computation and expenditure. Work examining this question in schizophrenia is still preliminary. However, altered functioning in the cingulate gyrus, ventral striatum, and dorsolateral prefrontal cortex appears to be implicated (Culbreth et al., 2018, 2020; Huang et al., 2016).

## Social Motivation: An Emerging Research Direction

Research is providing us with increased knowledge of the components involved in global motivation. However, social interactions are qualitatively unique. Not only do they present opportunities for social reward (i.e., acceptance, connection) but they also bring with them the possibility of social punishment (i.e., rejection). Emerging work in these areas has the potential to deepen our understanding of factors involved in social motivation more specifically.

In healthy controls, the neurobiological representations may differ across social (i.e., faces) versus nonsocial (i.e., monetary) rewards and punishments, across social rewards versus social punishments more generally, and for anticipation versus consummation of rewards and punishments (Fulford et al., 2018). Neural regions associated with reward/affective, mentalizing, and mirror neuron systems have all been shown to be involved in social reward and punishment processing and have recently been proposed as a "social interaction network" (Redcay & Schilbach, 2019). A recent systematic review of the small number of studies on social reward and punishment in schizophrenia-spectrum disorders has highlighted weaker modulation of brain activity of regions within this social interaction network, including amygdala, insula, and prefrontal, cingulate, and striatal regions (Mow et al., 2020).

Effective social functioning involves the simultaneous avoidance of social punishment and pursual of social reward in an optimal way; relative sensitivity to different aspects of social reward is likely to modulate social motivation. As we have already noted, one factor contributing to decreased social motivation in schizophrenia may be reduced sensitivity to reward. While playing a cooperative social game, male patients with nonaffective psychosis showed blunted reward-related activation in the caudate nucleus relative to healthy control males (Gromann et al., 2013). Relatedly, despite showing no impairment in the recognition of emotion, patients with schizophrenia show decreased tendencies to approach happy faces (Radke et al., 2015). Other work has found that patients with schizophrenia are faster to avoid happy faces (de la Asuncion et al., 2015). Reduced reward sensitivity and heightened rejection sensitivity may be playing key roles here.

Unlike the specific deficit in general anticipatory pleasure, people with schizophrenia may show diminished anticipatory as well as consummatory pleasure in the social domain. Compared to healthy controls, patients report less anticipated pleasure about participating in social interactions (Engel et al., 2016). They also report less pleasure after engaging with smiling conversational partners (Campellone & Kring, 2018). Importantly, no work has yet examined the impact of social punishment on subsequent social reward anticipation in schizophrenia. Also currently lacking is a consideration of how people with schizophrenia make decisions about social engagement. Social interactions require effort. Although they have the potential to be rewarding, they can also involve social costs including the risk of rejection. Social decision-making thus involves weighing the potential for both social reward and social punishment; altered sensitivity to either or both of these aspects of social interactions may differentially impact effort calculations and behavioral choices.

Social interactions are dynamic and complex and are often ambiguous in terms of the potential for rewarding versus punishing outcomes (FeldmanHall & Shenhav, 2019). Research thus far has largely neglected the dynamic, interactive nature of reward and punishment in a social setting and how this interplay may influence social motivational processes and shape social behavior. This paves the way for a new frontier of research moving forward, especially work that examines such questions in ecologically valid, creative ways. Ecological momentary assessment (EMA) is emerging as one approach for collecting data in real time, permitting investigations of the time course of real-world social interactions (Fulford et al., 2018). Elucidating such nuances holds great promise in addressing the complexities of social motivation alterations and their impact on social functioning in schizophrenia.

### The Social Consequences of Schizophrenia Patients' Social Difficulties

Our focus so far has been on the interpersonal functioning of patients diagnosed with schizophrenia. Although the nature of the social difficulties observed tends to vary from study to study, one conclusion can be safely drawn. Schizophrenia patients are less skilled and less fluid in complex interpersonal situations than are people in the general population. In many cases, they are also more impaired than are patients with other severe psychiatric conditions.

Blanchard and Panzarella (1998) have speculated on how affective flattening, one characteristic symptom of schizophrenia, may disrupt interpersonal functioning. They hypothesized that diminished emotional expressiveness in the person with schizophrenia may be interpreted by others as a lack of feeling. In other words, family, friends, and co-workers may interpret blunted affect as apathy or insensitivity. To the extent that this is true, it might be expected to damage interpersonal relations. Indeed, Blanchard and Panzarella (1998) reported findings that highlight how readily observers misinterpret the feelings of someone with schizophrenia based on facial cues.

Misinterpretation does, in fact, appear to be the most accurate description of what happens. There is no evidence that the affective flattening that we see in schizophrenia patients represents a lack of true emotional experiences. Patients with schizophrenia are less expressive facially than are controls when they view emotional film clips or engage in social role-play. However, they report experiencing emotion at equal or greater levels (Aghevli et al., 2003; Berenbaum & Oltmans, 1992; Kring et al., 1993). Indeed, in some studies, schizophrenia patients appear to be more aroused (as measured by skin conductance) by emotional stimuli than are healthy controls (Kring & Neale, 1996). Thus, there appears to be a lack of congruence between the expressive and the subjective experience response systems of emotion in schizophrenia. The lack of affective expression among schizophrenic patients may not be due to an underlying experiential deficiency, but rather may represent a failure to express the emotions being experienced in a manner detectable by others.

This may be one reason why interacting with a person with schizophrenia does not seem to be easy for the average person. Earlier, we described the results of a study in which female interviewers interacted with male college students who scored high on two scales associated with increased risk for schizophrenia (Zborowski & Garske, 1993). Even though the male students only showed schizotypic traits, interacting with them resulted in more anger, increased anxiety, and less interest on the part of the female interviewers than did interactions with males who did not exhibit these schizotypic traits.

In another study, Nisenson, Berenbaum, and Good (2001) had student research assistants form brief friendships with schizophrenia patients at a local inpatient psychiatric facility. Although the students were specifically selected because of their congenial dispositions, over the course of the 2 weeks of the study, the amount of negativity that the students expressed toward the patients increased significantly. Findings such as these lend credence to the idea that interacting with patients with schizophrenia may present a considerable social challenge. This is especially unfortunate because many individuals, even those in the early stage of the illness, report feelings of loneliness.

### Interpersonal Stress and the Onset of Schizophrenia

Social interaction is a two-way street. People with schizophrenia have social problems that tend to make those with whom they interact feel uncomfortable. However, in the other direction, schizophrenia patients are also sensitive to the social environments in which they live.

It is widely accepted that problems in the family environment do not cause schizophrenia in the absence of any genetic diathesis for the disorder. However, people at high genetic risk for schizophrenia may be especially sensitive to high levels of family disorganization compared to those at low genetic risk. Over the course of a longitudinal study, Tienari and his colleagues (2004) collected data on the psychiatric outcomes of children born to mothers with schizophrenia but adopted at an early age. A comparison sample consisted of children who were adopted early in life but who had no specific genetic risk for schizophrenia. After observing, testing, and interviewing the adoptive parents of the children, the researchers made ratings of the family environment. They then looked at the number of children who went on to develop schizophrenia or schizophrenia spectrum disorders (less severe psychotic disorders that are thought to be related to schizophrenia) in adulthood.

The results were quite striking. For the children at low genetic risk, being raised in a healthy or disorganized family environment made little difference to their eventual psychiatric outcomes. In both cases, about 4% of the children went on to develop schizophrenia or schizophrenia spectrum disorders. For the children who were at high genetic risk for schizophrenia, however, this was not the case. When they were raised in a healthy family environment, the rates of schizophrenia in the high genetic risk group were comparable to those of the low risk group (4.4%). However, when they were raised in an aversive family environment, 18.6% of the high-risk children went on the develop schizophrenia or schizophrenia-related illnesses as adults.

Tienari et al.'s findings highlight the importance of gene–environment interaction in the development of schizophrenia. More specifically, they suggest that genetic factors may play a role in determining how susceptible to the possible adverse effects of dysfunctional family environments each of us may be. Perhaps most importantly, however, these findings illustrate the protective effects that can result from living in a healthy family environment, even for those at high genetic risk.

The family environment can also play a powerful role for individuals at clinical high risk for psychosis. Thompson and colleagues (2019) found that family functioning (family communication, cohesion, problem-solving, and support) moderated the association between positive symptoms and social and role functioning in a clinical high-risk sample, such that this relationship held for those with low family functioning, but not for those with high family functioning. In other words, family environments characterized by greater levels of communication, cohesion, problem-solving, and support may serve as a buffer against the link between positive symptoms and poorer social and role functioning in this population.

### Interpersonal Stress and Relapse

Decades ago, Brown and his colleagues noticed that the social environment into which patients with schizophrenia were discharged after they left the hospital was significantly associated with how well they fared psychiatrically over the next several months (Brown et al., 1962). In later work, Brown and his co-workers attempted to quantify the aspects of the family environment that were associated with patients relapsing or remaining well after a hospital stay. The result of these efforts was the construct of *expressed emotion* (EE).

EE reflects the extent to which the relatives of a psychiatric patient talk about that patient in a critical, hostile, or emotionally overinvolved way during an interview conducted in the patient's absence. This interview, which is termed the Camberwell Family Interview (CFI), asks the relative a series of semi-structured, open-ended questions about the patient's previous and current psychiatric difficulties. Most important, it provides the family member with an opportunity to talk about the index patient's functioning in the months prior to the hospitalization.

A series of studies conducted all over the world have established that high EE (especially high criticism) is a robust and reliable predictor of early relapse in schizophrenia (see Butzlaff & Hooley, 1998). Patients who return home to live with relatives who are rated as being high in EE have relapse rates that are more than double those of patients who return home to live with low EE relatives (e.g., 50–60% vs. 20–30%). Interestingly, this association is not unique to schizophrenia. EE has also been shown to predict poor outcome in patients with mood disorders, anxiety disorders, eating disorders, and substance abuse disorders (see Hooley, 2007, for a review).

Although the prevalence of high EE in families varies across cultures (Jenkins & Karno, 1992), high EE tends to be normative in Europe and the United States. It has been measured not only in the relatives of psychiatric patients but also in psychiatric staff involved in supervising and treating patients (Berry et al., 2011). In many cases, high levels of EE may be a natural response to the stress of prolonged caretaking and continued exposure to psychopathology. EE levels do seem to increase in families where patients have been ill for longer periods of time (Hooley & Richters, 1995). Nisenson et al.'s (2001) findings of increased negativity in the students who visited schizophrenia inpatients also lends credence to this notion that criticism and hostility might develop as a consequence of continued interaction with a challenging patient.

High EE may also be a reaction to the symptoms (or to the social or behavioral disturbances) of the patients themselves. For example, spouses of psychiatric patients who have more negative symptoms are less happy with their relationships than are spouses who are married to patients with more positive symptoms (Hooley et al., 1987). This may be because negative symptoms, as we have discussed earlier, are associated with more interpersonal deficits on the part of patients, and these interpersonal difficulties may generate tension within a marital relationship. Another possibility is that spouses who live with patients who have more pronounced positive symptoms are, because of the unusual nature of the symptoms, more likely to view such patients as being psychiatrically ill and thus remain more sympathetic and understanding (Hooley & Gotlib, 2000). In contrast, one unfortunate consequence of many negative symptoms (e.g., apathy or poor self-care) is that they may not readily be attributed to severe mental illness. Families may thus be more likely to blame patients for negative symptoms in a way that they would not blame them for positive symptoms. Several empirical studies have now provided data consistent with this attributional model (see Barrowclough & Hooley, 2003, for a review). Moreover, experience suggests that family members are much more likely to complain about patients' generally low levels of activity and lack of cleanliness than they are to complain about delusions or hallucinations.

Finally, characteristics of the relatives themselves may also be important. Hooley (1998) has shown that relatives who have a more internally based locus of control make more critical remarks about patients than do relatives with a more external locus of control. Personality characteristics such as flexibility and tolerance also appear to be negatively related to high EE attitudes (Hooley & Hiller, 2000). Certain personality characteristics may thus render relatives more or less likely to become high EE when challenged by the stress of coping with psychopathology in a loved one.

How might these observations be integrated? Taken together, these findings are consistent with the notion that high EE relatives are people who (not unreasonably) find atypical behavior difficult to accept. Perhaps because they believe that patients are capable of controlling certain aspects of their symptoms or problem behaviors, these relatives then make efforts to encourage patients to behave differently. These efforts may be well-intentioned and designed to help patients function at a higher level. In some cases, these interventions may be helpful and well-received by patients. In other cases, patients may be unable (or possibly unwilling) to change in the way that the relative wants. The relative's level of frustration may rise, tolerance may decrease, and, over time, critical attitudes (and later, hostility) may be the inevitable result. According to this formulation, relatives' characteristics and patient factors interact over time to produce high levels of tension in the household and create stress for relative and patient alike.

Precisely why patients are more likely to relapse in the face of high EE is still an unanswered question. However, within a diathesis-stress framework, EE is generally assumed to be a form of psychosocial stress. In a series of studies Hooley and colleagues have used functional magnetic resonance imaging (fMRI) to explore what happens in the brains of people who are emotionally healthy and people who are vulnerable to psychopathology when they are directly exposed to personal criticisms (Hooley et al., 2005, 2009, 2012). Overall, the findings suggest that, compared to healthy controls, those with a vulnerability to psychopathology show less engagement of prefrontal areas (e.g., dorsolateral prefrontal cortex) and more activation in limbic regions (e.g., amygdala) during exposure to criticism. Both of these are key brain regions with regard to emotion processing. They are also brain areas implicated in many forms of psychopathology. Current thinking is that criticism from family members may be problematic because it challenges some of the neural circuitry involved in the regulation of emotions.

## Psychosocial Approaches to Treatment

Schizophrenia is a disorder with strong biological underpinnings. Yet even when medications result in symptomatic improvement, social deficits remain (Bellack et al., 2004). This speaks to the importance of psychosocial treatments (Mueser et al., 2013). Although no strategy alone is sufficient to treat schizophrenia, as Bellack and Mueser (1993) have noted, "psychosocial interventions can play a critical role in a comprehensive intervention program and are probably necessary components if treatment is to improve the patient's overall level of functioning, quality of life, and compliance with prescribed treatments" (p. 318).

Developed in the 1970s, one of the most frequently used treatments aimed at the correction of interpersonal deficits in schizophrenia involves *social skills training* (SST). SST programs are designed to teach patients a wide variety of interpersonal skills. These may range from very basic behavioral skills (e.g., eye contact or turn-taking) to more elaborate sequences of behaviors such as those involved in being assertive. In SST, complex sequences of social behaviors, like making friends or interviewing for a job, are broken down into their component parts. These parts are then further reduced to more basic elements. After being first taught by instruction and modeling to perform the component elements, patients then learn to combine them in a more fluid manner through further instruction coupled with reinforcement and feedback.

Meta-analytic reviews support the efficacy of social skills training for improving social competence. Pfammatter, Junghan, and Brenner (2006) reported that social skills training resulted in post-treatment improvements in social skill acquisition ($d = .77$) and assertiveness ($d = .43$) as well as in social functioning ($d = .39$). Improvements in skill acquisition ($d = .52$) and social functioning ($d = .32$) were also apparent in follow-up studies. Importantly, rates of rehospitalization were reduced ($d = .48$). A later review of 23 randomized controlled trials by Kurtz and Mueser (2008) also showed that skills training had beneficial effects on social and daily living skills ($d = .52$) as well as community functioning ($d = 0.52$). Benefits to negative symptoms ($d = .40$) and on relapse rates ($d = .23$) were also apparent. The benefits of social skills training for negative symptoms were further highlighted in the meta-analysis conducted by Turner and colleagues (2018).

Given the neurocognitive deficits associated with schizophrenia, *cognitive remediation therapy* is also an appealing intervention strategy. Studies in this area often involve repeated practice on cognitive tasks, or the learning of compensatory strategies (e.g., Wykes et al., 2007). The results overall appear to be positive. Cognitive remediation is associated with post-treatment improvements in attention ($d = .32$), memory ($d = .36$), and executive functioning ($d = .28$); social cognition ($d = .20$) and social functioning ($d = .49$) also improve (see Pfammatter et al., 2006). A more recent meta-analysis of 40 randomized controlled trials involving 2,104 participants reported significant effect sizes for cognitive remediation for improving global cognitive functioning ($d = .45$), social cognition ($d = .65$), and psychosocial functioning ($d = .42$) as well as smaller and less durable effects on reducing symptoms ($d = .18$; see Wykes et al., 2011). Unfortunately, having more symptoms is associated with smaller benefits overall (Wykes et al., 2011). The benefits of cognitive remediation for older patients (≥40 years) also appear to be much more limited (Kontis et al., 2013). Cognitive remediation has also been shown to be beneficial for patients in the early stages of illness, although the effect sizes overall tend to be smaller than they are for patients with more established illness (Revell et al., 2015).

Although cognitive remediation therapy sometimes leads to improvements in social cognition, this is not always the case (Horan et al., 2011; Wolwer et al., 2005). This suggests that neurocognitive changes may not be necessary for social cognitive improvement. It also highlights the need to target social cognition more directly.

In general, efforts to ameliorate social cognition deficits in schizophrenia take one of two forms. Some interventions are highly specific and target a single domain, such as facial affect recognition (see Wolwer et al., 2005). Other treatment programs are much more broad-based and target multiple domains. An example here would be Social Cognition and Interaction Training (SCIT; Penn et al., 2007). This is an 18- to 24-week group-based intervention designed to improve emotion perception, attributional bias, and ToM abilities (see Combs et al., 2007, 2009).

To date, relatively few studies have been conducted, and the number of patients involved in each study is generally quite small. More randomized controlled trials with adequate follow-up assessments are still needed (see Horan & Green, 2019). Nonetheless, there is cause for cautious optimism. Results of an effect-size analysis that included 16 studies (with 313 participants) showed that social cognitive training produced significant improvements in facial affect identification ($d$ = 0.84) and social perception ($d$ = 1.29) as well as enhancing ToM skills ($d$ = 0.70). Improvements on measures of executive functioning ($d$ = 1.70) were also noted. However, at least as currently delivered, social cognitive training does not seem to produce significant changes in positive symptoms ($d$= .27) and only has a small effect ($d$ = .32) on negative symptoms (Kurtz et al., 2016).

Importantly, psychosocial interventions targeting neurocognition and social cognition have been shown to be effective in populations at clinical high risk for psychosis. In a randomized controlled trial, participants were measured at baseline, after treatment, and at 3-month follow-up (Friedman-Yakoobian et al., 2020). Compared to those who received an active control intervention, participants who received an integrated neurocognitive and social cognitive remediation intervention showed significantly greater improvements in social functioning and social cognition (ToM and managing emotions), both after treatment and at 3-month follow-up. These types of interventions therefore show promise for populations at different points along the trajectory toward psychotic illness

Finally, it warrants mention that psychosocial interventions targeted at helping families cope with schizophrenia also provide clinical benefits. Typically, family-based interventions begin by educating relatives about the symptoms, etiology, treatment, and prognosis of schizophrenia. Families are then provided with family-based therapy, in either an individual family context (e.g., Leff et al., 1982, Tarrier et al., 1988) or in a group containing patients and relatives from several families (e.g., McFarlane et al., 1995). Meta-analyses (e.g., Pfammatter et al., 2006) indicate that such approaches improve relatives' knowledge about the disorder ($r$ =.39), reduce levels of EE ($r$ =.59), improve patients' social functioning ($r$ =.38), and result in decreased rates of relapse ($r$ =.42) at 6- to 12-month follow-up.

Most recently, family-based interventions have been used to help youth at clinical high risk for developing psychosis. Interventions like Family-Focused Therapy (FFT) combine psychoeducation with other topics such as stress management, communication enhancement, and problem-solving skills training in the family context (Miklowitz et al., 2014). Results of these family-based interventions are promising, often resulting in a return to higher levels of functioning and avoidance of conversion to psychosis altogether (McFarlane, 2016). Although much remains to be learned about how such interventions work, such findings highlight the key role that family can play in altering the trajectory toward and clinical course of schizophrenia.

## Conclusion

Difficulties in the interpersonal domain characterize schizophrenia patients at all stages of the illness. Although the extent and nature of social difficulties varies considerably from one individual to another, males appear to be particularly likely to experience difficulties in their social relationships. Social difficulties also frequently predate the illness, are found in those who are at risk for schizophrenia, and remain present even during periods of symptom remission.

Although the symptoms of schizophrenia compromise social functioning to some degree, there is reason to believe that the social difficulties experienced by many schizophrenia patients are important in their own right. Precisely why they are such a central feature of the illness is not clear.

Interpersonal impairments seem, at least to some degree, to be related to neurocognitive deficits, particularly those involving attention/vigilance and aspects of memory. Difficulties in these areas may also underlie some problems in more social areas of cognition. However, social cognition is distinct from neurocognition. Importantly, it appears to serve as a mediator between neurocognition and functional outcome. Altered processes related to social motivation serve as additional factors contributing to social difficulties in schizophrenia.

It is likely that schizophrenia patients' difficulties in relating to and understanding the social world seriously limit the extent to which they can develop supportive interpersonal relationships. This is unfortunate because schizophrenia patients, like many other patients, appear to be at higher risk of relapse when they live in emotionally stressful home environments. Helping patients improve their social skills and helping families cope with the stress of a schizophrenic relative is important for many reasons.

Understanding the nature and origins of social functioning impairments in schizophrenia is hindered by the variability in social functioning measures used in different studies. Social adjustment is a broad concept that encompasses performance on lab-based tasks of social skill as well as global functioning in the community. As noted by others (Cohen et al., 2006; Green et al., 2000), different types of cognitive deficits are associated with different domains of social functioning. Unfortunately, most research investigations do not involve both lab-based and community-based assessments (but see Addington & Addington, 1999; Addington et al., 1998, for exceptions).

The extent to which particular social difficulties are specific to schizophrenia is also not always clear. This speaks to the need for appropriate psychiatric control samples. More information about the stability of interpersonal functioning in general and skill deficits in particular is also needed. Longitudinal investigations are the exception rather than the rule in this research area. Perhaps most important, however, is the question of *why* social deficits are so characteristic of patients with schizophrenia.

Going forward, some of the most exciting directions will be those that continue to build on existing neurobiological evidence for alterations in brain structure and function in schizophrenia. Social motivation is one area particularly ripe for investigation, with a need to study the interaction of social reward and social punishment processing and how that relates to anticipation of and effort-based decision-making regarding social interactions. Continued investigations of neural correlates of social cognition and social motivation that link neurobiology with real-world social behaviors, particularly across various stages of illness including clinical high-risk populations, will no doubt shed light on how neurobiological, psychological, and behavioral changes conspire to result in impaired social functioning in schizophrenia. They may also give us new insights about how to enhance current remediation efforts and reduce the social disability that is, sadly, so characteristic of this disorder.

# References

Abel, K. M., Drake, R., & Goldstein, J. M. (2010). Sex differences in schizophrenia. *International Review of Psychiatry, 22*, 417–428.

Addington, J., & Addington, D. (1999). Neurocognitive and social functioning in schizophrenia. *Schizophrenia Bulletin, 25*, 173–182.

Addington, J., McClearly, L., & Monroe-Blum, H. (1998). Relationship between cognitive and social dysfunction in schizophrenia. *Schizophrenia Research, 34*, 59–66.

Aghevli, M. A., Blanchard, J. J., & Horan, W. P. (2003). The expression and experience of emotion in schizophrenia: A study of social interaction. *Psychiatry Research, 119*, 261–270.

Allen, D. N., Strauss, G. P., Donohue, B., & van Kammen, D. P. (2007). Factor analytic support for social cognition as a separable cognitive domain in schizophrenia. *Schizophrenia Research, 93*, 325–333.

Amminger, G. P., & Mutschlechner, R. (1994). Social competence and adolescent psychosis. *British Journal of Psychiatry, 165*, 273.

Amminger, G. P., Schäfer, M. R., Papageorgiou, K., Klier, C. M., Schlögelhofer, M., Mossaheb, N., Werneck-Rohrer, S., Nelson, B., & McGorry, P. D. (2011). Emotion recognition in individuals at clinical high-risk for schizophrenia. *Schizophrenia Bulletin, 38*(5), 1030–1039.

Andia, A. N. Zisook, S., Heaton, R. K., Hesselink, J., Jernigan, T., Kuck, J., Morganville, J., & Braff, D. L. (1995). Gender differences in schizophrenia. *Journal of Nervous and Mental Disease, 183*, 522–528.

Andreasen, N. C. (1982). Negative symptoms in schizophrenia: Definition and reliability. *Archives of General Psychiatry, 39*, 784–788.

Andreasen, N. C., & Olsen, S. (1982). Negative v. positive schizophrenia. *Archives of General Psychiatry, 39*, 789–794.

Anonymous. (1994). First person account: Life with a mentally ill spouse. *Schizophrenia Bulletin, 20*, 227–229.

Anticevic, A., Van Snellenberg, J. X., Cohen, R. E., Repovs, G., Dowd, E. C., & Barch, D. M. (2012). Amygdala recruitment in schizophrenia in response to aversive emotional material: A meta-analysis of neuroimaging studies. *Schizophrenia Bulletin, 38*, 608–621.

Appelo, M. T., Woonings, F. M. J., van Nieuwenhuizen, C. J., Emmelkamp, P. M. G., Slooff, C. J., & Louwens, J. W. (1992). Specific skills and social competence in schizophrenia. *Acta Psychiatrica Scandinavica, 85*, 419–422.

Ballon, J. S., Kaur, T., Marks., I. I., & Cadenhead, K. S. (2007). Social functioning in young people at risk for schizophrenia. *Psychiatry Research, 151*, 29–35.

Barbato, M., Liu, L., Cadenhead, K. S., Cannon, T. D., Cornblatt, B. A., McGlashan, T. H., Perkins, D. O., Seidman, L. J., Tsuang, M. T., Walker, E. F., Woods, S. W., Bearden, C. E., Mathalon, D. H., Heinssen, R., & Addington, J. (2015). Theory of mind, emotion and social perception in individuals and clinical high risk for psychosis: Findings from the NAPLS–2 cohort. *Schizophrenia Research: Cognition 2, 133*, 139.

Barch, D., & Berenbaum, H. (1994). The relationship between information processing and language production. *Journal of Abnormal Psychology, 103*, 241–250.

Barch, D. M., & Dowd, E. C. (2010). Goal representations and motivational drive in schizophrenia: The role of prefrontal–striatal interactions. *Schizophrenia Bulletin, 36*, 919–934.

Barch, D. M., Treadway, M. T., & Schoen, N. (2014). Effort, anhedonia, and function in schizophrenia: Reduced effort allocation predicts amotivation and functional impairment. *Journal of Abnormal Psychology, 123*, 387–397.

Baron-Cohen, S., O'Riordan, M., Stone, V., Jones, R., & Plaisted, K. (1999). Recognition of faux pas by normally developing children and children with Asperger syndrome or high functioning autism. *Journal of Autism and Developmental Disorders, 29*, 407–418.

Baron-Cohen, S., Wheelwright, S., Hill, J., Raste, Y., & Plumb, I. (2001). The "Reading the Mind in the Eyes" Test revised version: A study with normal adults with Asberger syndrome or high functioning autism. *Journal of Child Psychology and Psychiatry, 42*, 241–251.

Barrowclough, C. M., & Hooley, J. M. (2003). Attributions and expressed emotion: A review. *Clinical Psychology Review, 23*, 849–880.

Bellack, A. S. (1992). Cognitive rehabilitation for schizophrenia: Is it possible? Is it necessary? *Schizophrenia Bulletin, 18*, 43–50.

Bellack, A. S., Morrison, R. L., Mueser, K. T., & Wade, J. (1989). Social competence in schizoaffective disorder, bipolar disorder, and negative and non-negative schizophrenia. *Schizophrenia Research, 2*, 391–401.

Bellack, A. S., Morrison, R. L., Mueser, K. T., Wade, J. H., & Sayers, S. L. (1990). Role play for assessing the social competence of psychiatric patients. *Psychological Assessment, 2*, 248–255.

Bellack, A. S., Morrison, R. L., Wixted, J. T., & Mueser, K. T. (1990). An analysis of social competence in schizophrenia. *British Journal of Psychiatry, 156*, 809–818.

Bellack, A. S., & Mueser, K. T. (1993). Psychosocial treatment for schizophrenia. *Schizophrenia Bulletin, 19*, 317–336.

Bellack, A. S., Mueser, K. T., Wade, J., Sayers, S., & Morrison, R. L. (1992). The ability of schizophrenics to perceive and cope with negative affect. *British Journal of Psychiatry, 160*, 473–480.

Bellack, A. S., Sayers, M., Mueser, K. T., & Bennett, M. (1994). Evaluation of social problem solving in schizophrenia. *Journal of Abnormal Psychology, 103*, 371–378.

Bellack, A. S., Schooler, N. R., Marder, S. R., Kane, J. M., Brown, C. H., & Yang, Y. (2004). Do clozapine and risperidone affect social competence and problem solving? *American Journal of Psychiatry, 161*, 364–367.

Bentall, R. P., Corcoran, R., Howard, R., Blackwood, N., & Kinderman, P. (2001). Persecutory delusions: A review and theoretical interpretation. *Clinical Psychology Review, 21*, 1143–1192.

Berenbaum, H., & Oltmans, T. F. (1992). Emotional experience and expression in schizophrenia and depression. *Journal of Abnormal Psychology, 101*, 37–44.

Berridge, K. C., & Robinson, T. E. (1998). What is the role of dopamine in reward: Hedonic impact, reward learning, or incentive salience? *Brain Research Reviews, 28*, 309–69.

Berridge, K. C., Robinson, T. E. (2016). Liking, wanting, and the incentive-sensitization theory of addiction. *American Psychologist, 71*, 670–679.

Berry, K. B., Barrowclough, C., & Haddock, G. (2011). The role of expressed emotion in relationships between psychiatric staff and people with a diagnosis of psychosis: A review of the literature. *Schizophrenia Bulletin, 37*, 958–972.

Blanchard, J. J., Bellack, A. S., & Mueser, K. T. (1994). Affective and social-behavioral correlates of physical and social anhedonia in schizophrenia. *Journal of Abnormal Psychology, 103*, 719–728.

Blanchard, J. J., Mueser, K. T., & Bellack, A. S. (1998). Anhedonia, positive and negative affect, and social functioning in schizophrenia. *Schizophrenia Bulletin, 24*, 413–424.

Blanchard, J. J., & Panzarella, C. (1998). Affect and social functioning in schizophrenia. In K. T. Mueser & N. Tarrier (Eds.). *Handbook of social functioning in schizophrenia* (pp. 181–196). Allyn & Bacon.

Bora, E., Eryavuz, A., Kayahan, B., Sungu, G., & Veznedaroglu, B. (2006). Social functioning, theory of mind and neurocognition in outpatients with schizophrenia; mental state decoding may be a better predictor of social functioning than mental state reasoning. *Psychiatry Research, 145*, 95–103.

Bora E., & Pantelis, C. (2013). Theory of mind impairments in first-episode psychosis, individuals and ultra-high risk for psychosis, and in first-degree relatives of schizophrenia: Systematic review and meta-analysis. *Schizophrenia Research, 144*, 31–36.

Bora, E., Yücel, M., & Pantelis, C. (2009a). Theory of mind impairment in schizophrenia: Meta-analysis. *Schizophrenia Research, 109*, 1–9.

Bora, E., Yücel, M., & Pantelis, C. (2009b). Theory of mind impairment: A distinct trait marker for schizophrenia spectrum disorders and bipolar disorder? *Acta Psychiatrica Scandinavica, 120*, 253–264.

Bowen, L., Wallace, C. J., Glynn, S. M., Nuechterlein, K. H., Lutzker, J. R., & Kuehenl, T. G. (1994). Schizophrenic individuals cognitive functioning and performance in interpersonal interactions and skills training procedures. *Journal of Psychiatric Research, 28*, 289–301.

Brekke, J. S., Kay, D. D., Kee, K. S., & Green, M. F. (2005). Biosocial pathways to functional outcome in schizophrenia. *Schizophrenia Research, 80*, 213–225.

Brent, B. K., Seidman, L. J., Coombs III, G., Keshavan, M. S., Moran, J. M., & Holt, D. J. (2014). Neural responses during social reflection in relatives of schizophrenia patients: Relationship to subclinical delusions. *Schizophrenia Research, 157*, 292–298.

Brown, G. W., Monck, E. M., Carstairs, G. M., & Wing, J. K. (1962). Influence of family life on the course of schizophrenic illness. *British Journal of Preventive and Social Medicine, 16*, 55–68.

Butzlaff, R. L., & Hooley, J. M. (1998). Expressed emotion and psychiatric relapse. *Archives of General Psychiatry, 55*, 547–552.

Campellone, T. R., & Kring, A. M. (2018). Anticipated pleasure from social interaction outcomes in schizophrenia. *Psychiatry Research, 259*, 203–209.

Cannon, M., Jones, P., Gilvarry, C., Rifkin, McKenzie, K., Foester, A., & Murray, R. M. (1997). Premorbid social functioning in schizophrenia: Similarities and differences. *American Journal of Psychiatry, 154*, 1544–1550.

Cannon-Spoor, H. E., Potkin, S. G., & Wyatt, R. J. (1982). Measurement of premorbid adjustment in chronic schizophrenia. *Schizophrenia Bulletin, 8*, 470–484.

Carpenter, W. T., Heinrichs, D. W., & Wagman, A. M. I. (1988). Deficit and nondeficit forms of schizophrenia: The concept. *American Journal of Psychiatry, 145*, 578–583.

Chapman, L. J., Chapman, J. P., Kwapil, T. R., Eckblad, M., & Zinser, M. (1994). Putatively psychosis-prone subjects ten years later. *Journal of Abnormal Psychology, 103*, 171–183.

Chapman, L. J., Chapman, J. P., & Miller, E. N. (1982). Reliabilities and intercorrelations of eight measures of proneness to psychosis. *Journal of Consulting and Clinical Psychology, 50*, 187–195.

Chapman, L. J., Chapman, J. P., & Raulin, M. L. (1976). Scale for physical and social anhedonia. *Journal of Abnormal Psychology, 85*, 374–382.

Childers, S. E., & Harding, C. M. (1990). Gender, premorbid social functioning, and long-term outcome in DSM-III schizophrenia. *Schizophrenia Bulletin, 16*, 309–318.

Cohen, A. S., Forbes, C. B., Mann, M. C., & Blanchard, J. J. (2006). Specific cognitive deficits and differential domains of social functioning impairments in schizophrenia. *Schizophrenia Research, 81*, 227–238.

Combs, D. R., Adams, S. D., Penn, D. L., Roberts, D., Tiegreen, J., & Stem, P. (2007). Social Cognition and Interaction Training (SCIT) for inpatients with schizophrenia spectrum disorders: Preliminary findings. *Schizophrenia Research, 91*, 112–116.

Combs, D. R., Elerson, K., Penn, D. L., Tiegreen, J. A., Nelson, A., Ledet, S. N., & Basso, M. R. (2009). Stability and generalization of Social Cognition and Interaction Training (SCIT) for schizophrenia: Six-month follow-up results. *Schizophrenia Research, 112*, 196–197.

Corcoran, R., Mercer, G., & Frith, C. D. (1995). Schizophrenia, symptomatology and social inference: Investigating "theory of mind" in people with schizophrenia. *Schizophrenia Research, 17*, 5–13.

Cornblatt, B. A., Auther, A. M., Niendam, T., Smith, C. W., Zinberg, J., Bearden, C. E., & Cannon, T. D. (2007). Preliminary findings for two new measures of social and role functioning in the prodromal phase of schizophrenia. *Schizophrenia Bulletin, 33*, 688–702.

Cornblatt, B. A., Lenzenweger, M. F., Dworkin, R. H., & Erlenmeyer-Kimling, L. (1992). Childhood attentional dysfunctions predict social deficits in unaffected adults at risk for schizophrenia. *British Journal of Psychiatry, 161* (suppl. 18), 59–64.

Corrigan, P. W., & Addis, I. B. (1995). The effect of cognitive complexity on a social sequencing task in schizophrenia. *Schizophrenia Research, 16*, 137–144.

Corrigan, P. W., Green, M. F., & Toomey, R. (1994). Cognitive correlates to social cue perception in schizophrenia. *Psychiatry Research, 53*, 141–151.

Corrigan, P. W., & Toomey, R. (1995). Interpersonal problem solving and information processing in schizophrenia. *Schizophrenia Bulletin, 21*, 395–403.

Couture, S. M., Penn, D. L., & Roberts, D. L. (2006). The functional significance of social cognition in schizophrenia: A review. *Schizophrenia Bulletin, 32*, 44–63.

Craddock, N., & Owen, M. J. (2010). The Kraepelinian dichotomy—going, going. . . but still not gone. *British Journal of Psychiatry, 196*, 92–95.

Cramer, P., Bowen, J., & O'Neill, M. (1992). Schizophrenics and social judgment: Why do schizophrenics get it wrong? *British Journal of Psychiatry, 160*, 481–487.

Culbreth, A. J., Moran, E. K., & Barch, D. M. (2018). Effort-based decision-making in schizophrenia. *Current Opinion in Behavioral Sciences, 22*, 1–6.

Culbreth, A. J., Moran, E. K., Kandala, S., Westbrook, A., & Barch, D. M. (2020). Effort, avolition, and motivational experience in schizophrenia: Analysis of behavioral and neuroimaging data with relationships to daily motivational experience. *Clinical Psychological Science, 8*, 555–568.

Cutting, J., & Murphy D. (1990). Impaired ability of schizophrenics, relative to manics or depressives, to appreciate social knowledge about their culture. *British Journal of Psychiatry, 157*, 355–358.

de la Asuncion, J., Docx, L., Sabbe, B., Morrens, M., & de Bruijn, E. R. (2015). Converging evidence of social avoidant behavior in schizophrenia from two approach-avoidance tasks. *Journal of Psychiatric Research, 69*, 135–141.

Donahoe, C. P., Carter, M. J., Bloem, W. D., Hirsch, G. L, Laasi, N., & Wallace, C. J. (1990). Assessment of interpersonal problem-solving skills. *Psychiatry, 53*, 329–339.

Donahoe, G., Duignan, A., Hargreaves, A., Morris, D. W., Rose, E., Robertson, D., Cummings, E. Moore, S., Gill, M., & Corvin, A. (2012). Social cognition in bipolar disorder versus schizophrenia: Comparability in mental state decoding deficits. *Bipolar Disorders, 14*, 743–748.

Dworkin, R. H. (1990). Patterns of sex difference in negative symptoms and social functioning consistent with separate dimensions of schizophrenic psychopathology. *American Journal of Psychiatry, 147*, 347–349.

Dworkin, R. H. (1992). Affective deficits and social deficits in schizophrenia: What's what? *Schizophrenia Bulletin, 18*, 59–64.

Dworkin, R. H., Bernstein, G., Kaplansky, L. M., Lipsitz, J. D., Rinaldi, A., Slater, S. L., Cornblatt, B. A., Erlenmeyer-Kimling, L. (1991). Social competence and positive and negative symptoms: A longitudinal study of children and adolescents at risk for schizophrenia and affective disorder. *American Journal of Psychiatry, 148*, 1182–1188.

Dworkin, R. H., Cornblatt, B. A., Friedmann, R., Kaplansky, L. M., Lewis, J. A., Rinaldi, A., Shilliday, C., & Erlenmeyer-Kimling, L. (1993). Childhood precursors of affective vs. social deficits in adolescents at risk for schizophrenia. *Schizophrenia Bulletin, 19*, 563–576.

Dworkin, R. H., Green, S. R., Small, N. E. M. Warner, M. L., Cornblatt, B. A., & Erlenmeyer-Kimling, L. (1990). Positive and negative symptoms and social competence in adolescents at risk for schizophrenia and affective disorder. *American Journal of Psychiatry, 147*, 1234–1236.

Dworkin, R. H., Lewis, J. A., Cornblatt, B. A., & Erlenmeyer-Kimling, L. (1994). Social competence deficits in adolescents at risk for schizophrenia. *Journal of Nervous and Mental Disease, 182*, F103–108.

Edwards, J., Jackson, H. J., & Pattison, P. E. (2002). Emotion recognition via facial expression and affective prosody in schizophrenia: A methodological review. *Clinical Psychology Review, 22*, 789–832.

Engel, M., Fritzsche, A., & Lincoln, T. M. (2016). Anticipation and experience of emotions in patients with schizophrenia and negative symptoms: An experimental study in a social context. *Schizophrenia Research, 170,* 191–197.

FeldmanHall, O., & Shenhav, A. (2019). Resolving uncertainty in a social world. *Nature Human Behaviour, 3,* 426–435.

Fett, A-K., Viechtbauer, W., Dominguez, M., Penn, D. L., van Os, J., & Krabbendam, L. (2011). The relationship between social cognition and neurocognition with functional outcomes in schizophrenia: A meta-analysis. *Neuroscience and Biobehavioral Reviews, 35,* 573–588.

Friedman-Yakoobian, M. S., Parrish, E. M., Eack, S. M., & Keshavan, M. S. (2020). Neurocognitive and social cognitive training for youth at clinical high risk (CHR) for psychosis: A randomized controlled feasibility trial. *Schizophrenia Research,* Sep 22:S0920-9964(20)30461–8. doi:10.1016/j.schres.2020.09.005. Epub ahead of print. PMID: 32978034.

Frith, C. (1992). *The cognitive neuropsychology of schizophrenia.* Psychology Press.

Fulford, D., Campellone, T., & Gard, D. E. (2018). Social motivation in schizophrenia: How research on basic reward processes informs and limits our understanding. *Clinical Psychology Review, 63,* 12–24.

Fusar-Poli, P., Radua, J., McGuire, P., & Borgwardt, S. (2012). Neuroanatomical maps of psychosis onset: Voxel-wise meta-analysis of antipsychotic-naive VBM studies. *Schizophrenia Bulletin 38,* 1297–1307.

Gard, D. E., Fisher, M., Garrett, C., Genevsky, A., & Vinogradov, S. (2009). Motivation and its relationship to neurocognition, social cognition, and functional outcome in schizophrenia. *Schizophrenia Research, 115,* 74–81.

Gard, D. E., Kring, A. M., Gard, M. G., Horan, W. P., & Green, M. F. (2007). Anhedonia in schizophrenia: Distinctions between anticipatory and consummatory pleasure. *Schizophrenia Research, 93*(1–3), 253–260.

Gard, D. E., Sanchez, A. H., Cooper, K., Fisher, M., Garrett, C., & Vinogradov, S. (2014). Do people with schizophrenia have difficulty anticipating pleasure, engaging in effortful behavior, or both? *Journal of Abnormal Psychology, 123,* 771.

Gold, J. M., Strauss, G. P., Waltz, J. A., Robinson, B. M., Brown, J. K., & Frank, M. J. (2013). Negative symptoms of schizophrenia are associated with abnormal effort-cost computations. *Biological Psychiatry, 74,* 130–136.

Goldman, R. S., Axelrod, B. N., Tandon, R., Ribeiro, S. C. M., Craig, K., & Berent, S. (1993). Neuropsychological prediction of treatment efficacy and one-year outcome in schizophrenia. *Psychopathology, 126,* 122–126.

Green, M. F. (2016). Impact of cognitive and social cognitive impairment on functional outcomes in patients with schizophrenia. *Journal of Clinical Psychiatry, 77* (suppl 2) 8–11.

Green, M., Horan, W., & Lee, J. (2015). Social cognition in schizophrenia. *Nature Reviews Neuroscience, 16,* 620–631.

Green, M. F., Horan, W., & Lee, J. (2019). Nonsocial and social cognition in schizophrenia: Current evidence and future directions. *World Psychiatry, 18,* 146–161.

Green, M. F., Kern, R. S., Braff, D. L., & Mintz, J. (2000). Neurocognitive deficits and functional outcome in schizophrenia: Are we measuring the "right stuff"? *Schizophrenia Bulletin, 26,* 119–136.

Gromann, P. M., Heslenfeld, D. J., Fett, A. K., Joyce, D. W., Shergill, S. S., & Krabbendam, L. (2013). Trust versus paranoia: Abnormal response to social reward in psychotic illness. *Brain, 136,* 1968–1975.

Häfner, H. (2003). Gender differences in schizophrenia. *Psychoneuroendocrinology, 28,* 17–54

Häfner, H., Maurer, K., Löffler, W., & Rieche-Rössler, A. (1993). The influence of age and sex on the onset and early course of schizophrenia. *British Journal of Psychiatry, 162,* 80–86.

Halverson, T. F, Orleans-Pobee, M., Merritt, C., Sheeran, P., Fett, A. K., & Penn D. L. (2019). Pathways to functional outcomes in schizophrenia spectrum disorders: Meta-analysis of social cognitive and neurocognitive predictors. *Neuroscience and Biobehavioral Reviews, 105,* 212–219.

Hayduk, L. A. (1983). Personal space: Where we now stand. *Psychological Bulletin, 94,* 293–335.

Heaton, R. K. (1981). *Wisconsin Card Sort manual.* Psychological Assessment Resources.

Heinrichs, D. W., Hanlon, T. E., & Carpenter, W. T. (1984). The Quality of Life Scale: An instrument for rating the schizophrenic deficit syndrome. *Schizophrenia Bulletin, 12,* 388–398.

Heinrichs, R. W. (2005). The primacy of cognition in schizophrenia. *American Psychologist, 60,* 229–242.

Hellewell, J. S. E., Connell, J., & Deakin, J. F. W. (1994). Affect judgment and facial recognition memory in schizophrenia. *Psychopathology, 27,* 255–261.

Herrig, E. (1995). First person account: A personal experience. *Schizophrenia Bulletin, 21,* 339–342.

Herold, R., Tényi, T., Lénárd, K., & Trixler, M. (2002). Theory of mind deficits in people with schizophrenia in remission. *Psychological Medicine, 32,* 1125–1129.

Holt, D. J., Boeke, E. A., Coombs, G., DeCross, S. N., Cassidy, B. S., Stufflebeam, S., . . . Tootell, R. B. (2015). Abnormalities in personal space and parietal-frontal function in schizophrenia. *NeuroImage: Clinical, 9,* 233–243.

Hooker, C., & Park, S. (2002). Emotion processing and its relationship to social functioning in schizophrenia patients. *Psychiatry Research, 112,* 41–50.

Hooker, C., & Park, S. (2005). You must be looking at me: The nature of gaze perception in schizophrenia. *Cognitive Neuropsychology, 10,* 327–345.

Hooker, C. I., Bruce, L., Lincoln, S. H., Fisher, M., & Vinogradov, S. (2011). Theory of mind skills are related to gray matter volume in the ventromedial prefrontal cortex in schizophrenia. *Biological Psychiatry, 70,* 1169–1178.

Hooley, J. M. (1998). Expressed emotion and locus of control. *Journal of Nervous and Mental Disease, 186,* 374–378.

Hooley, J. M. (2007). Expressed emotion and relapse of psychopathology. *Annual Review of Clinical Psychology, 3,* 349–372.

Hooley, J. M., & Gotlib, I. H. (2000). A diathesis-stress conceptualization of expressed emotion and clinical outcome. *Applied and Preventive Psychology, 9,* 135–151.

Hooley, J. M., Gruber, S. A., Parker, H., Guillaumot, J., & Rogowska, J., & Yurgelun-Todd, D. A. (2009). Corticolimbic response to personally-challenging emotional stimuli after complete recovery from major depression. *Psychiatry Research: Neuroimaging, 172,* 83–91.

Hooley, J. M., Gruber, S. A., Scott, L. A., Hiller, J. B., & Yurgelun-Todd, D. A. (2005). Activation in dorsolateral prefrontal cortex in response to maternal criticism and praise in recovered depressed and healthy control participants. *Biological Psychiatry, 57,* 809–812.

Hooley, J. M., & Hiller, J. B. (2000). Expressed emotion and personality. *Journal of Abnormal Psychology, 109,* 40–44.

Hooley, J. M., & Richters, J. E. (1995). Expressed emotion: A developmental perspective. In D. Cicchetti & S. L. Toth (Eds.). *Rochester symposium on developmental psychopathology, Volume 6: Emotion, cognition, and representation* (pp. 133–166). University of Rochester Press.

Hooley, J. M., Richters, J. E., Weintraub, S., & Neale, J. M. (1987). Psychopathology and marital distress: The positive side of positive symptoms. *Journal of Abnormal Psychology, 96*, 27–33.

Hooley J. M., Siegle, G. J., & Gruber, S. A. (2012). Affective and neural reactivity to criticism in individuals high and low on perceived criticism. *PLoS ONE, 7*(9), e44412.

Horan, W. P., & Green, M. F. (2019). Treatment of social cognition in schizophrenia: Current status and future directions. *Schizophrenia Research, 203*, 3–11.

Horan, W. P., Iacoboni, M., Cross, K. A., Korb, A., Lee, J., Nori, P., Quintana, J., Wynn, J. K., & Green, M. F. (2014). Self-reported empathy and neural activity during action imitation and observation in schizophrenia. *Neuroimage: Clinical, 23*, 100–108.

Horan, W. P., Kern, R. S., Tripp, C., Helleman, G., Wynn, J. K., Bell, M., Marder, S. R., & Green, M. F. (2011). Efficacy and specificity of social cognitive skills training for outpatients with psychotic disorders. *Journal of Psychiatric Research, 45*, 1113–1122.

Horowitz, M. J., Duff, D. F., & Stratton, L. O. (1964). Body-buffer zone: Exploration of personal space. *Archives of General Psychiatry, 11*, 651–656.

Hu, M-L., Zong, X-F., Mann, J. J., Zheng, J-J., Liao, Y-H., Li, Z-C., He, Y., Chen, X-G., & Tang, J-S. (2017). A review of the functional and anatomical default mode network in schizophrenia. *Neuroscience Bulletin, 33*, 73–84.

Huang, J., Yang, X. H., Lan, Y., Zhu, C. Y., Liu, X. Q., Wang, Y. F., Cheung, E. F. C., Xie, G-R., & Chan, R. C. (2016). Neural substrates of the impaired effort expenditure decision making in schizophrenia. *Neuropsychology, 30*, 685–696.

Ihnen, G. H., Penn, D. L., Corrigan, P. W., & Martin, J. (1998). Social perception and social skill in schizophrenia. *Psychiatry Research, 80*, 275–286.

Jackson, H. J., Minas, I. H., Burgess, P. M., Joshua, S. D., Charisiou, J., & Campbell, I. M. (1989). Negative symptoms and social skills performance in schizophrenia. *Schizophrenia Bulletin, 2*, 457–463.

Jaeger, J., & Douglas, E. (1992). Neuropsychiatric rehabilitation for persistent mental illness. *Psychiatric Quarterly, 63*, 71–94.

Janssen, I., Krabbendam, L., Jolles, J., & van Os, J. (2003). Alterations in theory of mind in patients with schizophrenia and non-psychotic relatives. *Acta Psychiatrica Scandinavica, 108*, 110–117.

Jenkins, J. H., & Karno, M. (1992). The meaning of expressed emotion: Theoretical issues raised by cross-cultural research. *American Journal of Psychiatry, 149*, 9–21.

Kahn, A., McGaughey, T. A., 1977. Distance and liking: When moving close produces increased liking. *Social Psychology Quarterly, 40*, 138–144.

Keshavan, M. S., DeLisi, L. E., & Seidman, L. J. (2011). Early and broadly defined psychosis risk mental states. *Schizophrenia Research, 126*(1–3), 1–10.

Kimoto, S., Makinodan, M., & Kishimoto, T. (2019). Neurobiology and treatment of social cognition in schizophrenia: Bridging the bed-bench gap. *Neurobiolology of Disease, 131*, 104315.

Kirkpatrick, B., Fenton, W., Carpenter, W. T., & Marder, S. R. (2006). The NIMH-MATRICS consensus statement on negative symptoms. *Schizophrenia Bulletin, 32*, 296–303.

Kohler, C. G., Richard, J. A., Brensinger, C. M., Borgmann-Winter, K. E., Conroy, C. G., Moberg, P. J., Gur, R. C., Gur, R. E., & Calkins, M. E. (2014). Facial emotion perception differs in young persons at genetic and clinical high-risk for psychosis. *Psychiatry Research, 216*, 206–212.

Kohler, C. G., Walker, J. B., Martin, E. A. Healy, K. M., & Moberg, P. J. (2010). Facial emotion perception in schizophrenia: A meta-analytic review. *Schizophrenia Bulletin, 36*, 1009–1019.

Kontis, D., Huddy, V., Reeder, C., Landau, S., & Wykes, T. (2013). Effects of age and cognitive reserve on cognitive remediation therapy outcome in patients with schizophrenia. *American Journal of Geriatric Psychiatry, 21*, 218–230.

Kraepelin, E. (1919/1989). *Dementia praecox and paraphrenia*. E and S Livingstone. Reprinted by the Classics of Medicine Library.

Kring, A. M., Kerr, S. L., Smith, D. A., & Neale, J. M. (1993). Flat affect in schizophrenia does not reflect diminished subjective experience of emotion. *Journal of Abnormal Psychology, 102*, 507–517.

Kring, A. M., & Neale, J. M. (1996). Do schizophrenic patients show a disjunctive relationship among expressive, experiential, and psychophysiological components of emotion? *Journal of Abnormal Psychology, 105*, 249–257.

Kulkarni, J., de Castella, A., Fitzgerald, P. B., Gurvich, C. T., Bailey, M., Bartholomeusz, C., & Burger, H. (2008). Estrogen in severe mental illness: A potential new treatment approach. *Archives of General Psychiatry, 65*, 955–960.

Kurtz, M. M., & Mueser, K. T. (2008). A meta-analysis of controlled research on social skills training for schizophrenia. *Journal of Consulting and Clinical Psychology, 76*, 491–504.

Kurtz, M. M., Gagen, E., Rocha, N. B. F., Machado, S., & Penn, D. L. (2016). Comprehensive treatments for social cognitive deficits in schizophrenia: A critical review and effect size analysis of controlled studies. *Clinical Psychology Review, 43*, 80–89.

Kwapil, T. R. (1998). Social anhedonia as a predictor of the development of schizophrenia-spectrum disorders. *Journal of Abnormal Psychology, 107*, 558–565.

Leff, J. P., Kuipers, L., Berkowitz, R., Eberlein-Vries, R., & Sturgeon, D. (1982). A controlled trial of social intervention in schizophrenia families. *British Journal of Psychiatry, 141*, 121–134.

Leung, A., & Chue, P. (2000). Sex differences in schizophrenia, a review of the literature. *Acta Psychiatrica Scandinavica, 101*, 3–38.

Liberman, R. P. (1982). Assessment of Social Skills. *Schizophrenia Bulletin, 8*, 62–83.

Lincoln, S. H., Germine, L. T., Mair, P., & Hooker, C. I. (2020). Simulation and social behavior: An fMRI study of neural processing during simulation in individuals with and without risk for psychosis. *Social Cognitive and Affective Neuroscience, 15*, 165–174.

Lincoln, S. H., & Hooker, C. I. L. (2014). Neural structure and social dysfunction in individuals at clinical high risk for psychosis. *Psychiatry Research: Neuroimaging, 224*(3), 152–158.

Loranger, A. W., Susman, V. L., Oldham, J. M., & Russakoff, L. M. (1987). The personality disorder examination: A preliminary report. *Journal of Personality Disorders, 1*, 1–13.

Lourenco, S. F., Longo, M. R., & Pathman, T. (2011). Near space and its relation to claustrophobic fear. *Cognition, 119*, 448–453.

Lysaker, P., Bell, M., & Beam-Goulet, J. (1995). Wisconsin Card Sort Test and work performance in schizophrenia. *Schizophrenia Research, 56*, 45–51.

Maat, A., van Montfort, S. J. T., de Nijs, J., Derks, E. M., Kahn, R. S., Linszen, D. H., van Os, J., Wiersma, D., Bruggeman, R., Cahn, W., de Haan, L., Krabbendam, L., Myin-Germeys, I., & GROUP investigators (2015). Emotion processing in schizophrenia is state and trait dependent. *Schizophrenia Research, 161*, 392–398.

McFarlane, W. R. (2016). Family interventions for schizophrenia and the psychoses: A review. *Family Process, 55*, 460–482.

McFarlane, W. R., Lukens, E., Link, B, Dushay, R., Deakins, S. A., Newmark, M., Dunne, E. J., Horen, B., & Toran, J. (1995). Multiple-family groups and psychoeducation in the treatment of schizophrenia. *Archives of General Psychiatry, 52*, 679–687.

Marwaha, S., & Johnson, S. (2004). Schizophrenia and employment. *Social Psychiatry and Psychiatric Epidemiology, 39*, 337–349.

Mow, J. L., Gandhi, A., & Fulford, D. (2020). Imaging the "social brain" in schizophrenia: A systematic review of neuroimaging studies of social reward and punishment. *Neuroscience and Biobehavioral Reviews, 118*, 704–722.

Mueser, K. T., & Bellack, A. S. (1998). Social skills and social functioning. In K. T. Mueser & N. Tarrier (Eds.), *Handbook of social functioning in schizophrenia* (pp. 79–96). Allyn & Bacon.

Mueser, K. T., Bellack, A. S., Douglas, M. S., & Morrison, R. L. (1991). Prevalence and stability of social skill deficits in schizophrenia. *Schizophrenia Research, 5*, 167–176.

Mueser, K. T., Bellack, A. S., Douglas, M. S., & Wade, J. H. (1991). Prediction of social skill acquisition in schizophrenia and major affective disorder patients from memory and symptomatology. *Psychiatry Research, 37*, 281–296.

Mueser, K. T., Bellack, A. S., Morrison, R. L., & Wade, J. H. (1990). Gender, social competence, and symptomatology in schizophrenia: A longitudinal analysis. *Journal of Abnormal Psychology, 99*, 138–147.

Mueser, K. T., Deavers, F., Penn, D. L., & Cassisi, J. (2013). Psychosocial treatments for schizophrenia. *Annual Review of Clinical Psychology, 9*, 465–497.

Mueser, K. T., Doonan, R., Penn, D. L., Blanchard, J. J., Bellack, A. S., Nishith, P., & DeLeon, J. (1996). Emotion recognition and social competence in chronic schizophrenia. *Journal of Abnormal Psychology, 105*, 271–275.

Mueser, K. T., Pratt, S. I., Bartels, S. J., Forester, B., Wolfe, R., & Cather, C. (2010). Neurocognition and social skill in older persons with schizophrenia and major mood disorders: An analysis of gender and diagnosis effects. *Journal of Neurolinguistics, 23*, 297–317.

Nair, A., Jolliffe, M., Lograsso, Y. S. S., & Bearden, C. E. (2020). A review of default mode network connectivity and its association with social cognition in adolescents with autism spectrum disorder and early-onset psychosis. *Frontiers in Psychiatry, 11*, 614.

Nisenson, L., Berenbaum, H., & Good, T. (2001). The development of interpersonal relationships in individuals with schizophrenia. *Psychiatry, 64*, 111–125.

Pelletier-Baldelli, A., & Holt, D. J. (2020). Are negative symptoms merely the "real world" consequences of deficits in social cognition? *Schizophrenia Bulletin, 46*, 236–241.

Penn, D. L., Corrigan, P. W., Bentall, R. P., Racenstein, J. M., & Newman, L. (1997). Social cognition in schizophrenia. *Psychological Bulletin, 121*, 114–132.

Penn, D. L., Roberts, D. L., Combs, D., & Sterne, A. (2007). Best practices: The development of the social cognition and interaction training program for schizophrenia spectrum disorders. *Psychiatric Services, 58*, 449–451.

Perry, W., Moore, D., & Braff, D. (1995). Gender differences on thought disturbance measures among schizophrenic patients. *American Journal of Psychiatry, 152*, 1298–1301.

Pfammatter, M., Junghan, U. M., & Brenner, H. D. (2006). Efficacy of psychological therapy in schizophrenia: Conclusions from meta-analyses. *Schizophrenia Bulletin, 32*, S1, S64–S80.

Pinkham, A. E., & Penn, D. L. (2006). Neurocognitive and social cognitive predictors of interpersonal skill in schizophrenia. *Psychiatry Research, 143*, 167–178.

Piskulic, D., Liu, L., Cadenheas, K. S., Cannon, T. D., Cornblatt, B. A., McGlashan, T. H., Perkins, D. O., Seidman, L. J., Tsuang, M. T., Walker, E. F., Woods, S. W., Bearden, C. E., Mathalon, D. H., & Addington, J. (2016). Social cognition over time in individuals at clinical high risk for psychosis: Findings from the NAPLS-2 cohort. *Schizophrenia Research, 171*, 176–181.

Platt, J. J., & Spivack, G. (1972). Problem-solving thinking of psychiatric patients. *Journal of Consulting and Clinical Psychology, 39*, 148–151.

Platt, J. J., & Spivack, G. (1974). Means of solving real-life problems: I. Psychiatric patients vs. controls and cross-cultural comparisons of normal females. *Journal of Community Psychology, 2*, 45–48.

Poole, J. H., Tobia, F. C., & Vinogradov, S. (2000). The functional relevance of affect recognition errors in schizophrenia. *Journal of the International Neuropsychological Society, 6*, 649–658.

Poreh, A., Whitman, D., Weber, M., & Ross, T. (1994). Facial recognition in hypothetically schizotypic college students. *Journal of Nervous and Mental Disease, 182*, 503–507.

Radke, S., Pfersmann, V., & Derntl, B. (2015). The impact of emotional faces on social motivation in schizophrenia. *European Archives of Psychiatry and Clinical Neuroscience, 265*, 613–622.

Rao, M. L., & Kőlsch, H. (2003). Effects of estrogen on brain development and neuroprotection: Implications for negative symptoms in schizophrenia. *Psychoneuroendocrinology, 28*, 83–96.

Redcay, E., & Schilbach, L. (2019). Using second-person neuroscience to elucidate the mechanisms of social interaction. *Nature Reviews Neuroscience, 20*, 495–505.

Reinen, J., Smith, E. E., Insel, C., Kribs, R., Shohamy, D., Wager, T. D., & Jarskog, L. F. (2014). Patients with schizophrenia are impaired when learning in the context of pursuing rewards. *Schizophrenia Research, 152*, 309–310.

Revell, E. R., Neill, J. C., Harte, M., Khan, Z., & Drake, R. J. (2015). A systematic review and meta-analysis of cognitive remediation in early schizophrenia. *Schizophrenia Research, 168*, 213–222.

Salamone, J. D., Correa, M., Farrar, A., & Mingote, S. M. (2007). Effort-related functions of nucleus accumbens dopamine and associated forebrain circuits. *Psychopharmacology, 191*, 461–482.

Savla, G., Vella, L., Armstrong, C. C., Penn, D. L., & Twamley, E. W. (2013). Deficits in domains of social cognition in schizophrenia: A meta-analysis of the empirical evidence. *Schizophrenia Bulletin, 39*, 979–992.

Schmidt, S. J., Mueller, D. R., & Roder, V. (2011). Social cognition as a mediator variable between neurocognition and functional outcome in schizophrenia: Empirical review and new results by structural equation modeling. *Schizophrenia Bulletin, 37*(suppl. 2), S41–S54.

Schooler, N., Hogarty, G. E., & Weissman, M. M. (1986). Social Adjustment Scale II (SAS-II). In W. A. Hargreaves, C. C. Atkinson, & J. E. Sorenson (Eds.), *Resource materials for community mental health program evaluators* (DHEW No. 79-328; pp. 290–303). US Government Printing Office.

Schwartz, S. (1967). Diagnosis, level of social adjustment and cognitive deficits. *Journal of Abnormal Psychology, 72*, 446–450.

Sergi, M. J., Rassovsky, Y., Nuechterlein, K., H., & Green, M. F. (2006). Social perception as a mediator of the influence of early visual processing on functional status in schizophrenia. *American Journal of Psychiatry, 163*, 448–454.

Sergi, M. J., Rassovsky, Y., Widmark, C., Reist, C., Erhart, S., Braff, D. L., Marder, S. R., & Green, M. F. (2007). Social cognition in schizophrenia: Relationships with neurocognition and negative symptoms. *Schizophrenia Research, 90*, 316–324.

Shumway, M., Saunders, T., Shern, D., Pines, E., Downs, A., Burbine, T., & Beller, J. (2003). Preferences for schizophrenia treatment outcomes among public policy makers, consumers, families, and providers. *Psychiatric Services, 54*, 1124–1128.

Tarrier, N., Barrowclough, C., Vaughn, C., Bamrah, J., Porceddu, K., Watts, S., & Freeman, H. (1988). The community management of schizophrenia: A controlled trial of a behavioral intervention with families to reduce relapse. *British Journal of Psychiatry, 153*, 532–542.

Thompson E., Rakhshan P., Pitts S. C., Demro C., Millman Z. B., Bussell K., DeVylder J., Kline E., Reeves G. M., & Schiffman J. (2019). Family functioning moderates the impact of psychosis-risk symptoms on social and role functioning. *Schizophrenia Research, 204*, 337–342.

Thorup, A., Petersen, L., Jeppesen, Øhlenschlæger, J., Christensen, T., Krarup, G., Jørgensen, P., & Nordentoft, M. (2006). Social network among young adults with first episode schizophrenia spectrum disorders. *Social Psychiatry and Psychiatric Epidemiology, 41*, 761–770.

Tienari, P. A., Wynne, L. C., Sorri, A., Lahti, I., Lasky, K., Moring, J., Naarala, M., Nieminen, P., & Wahlberg, K-E. (2004). Genotype-environment interaction in schizophrenia-spectrum disorder. *British Journal of Psychiatry, 184*, 216–222.

Treadway, M. T., & Zald, D. H. (2011). Reconsidering anhedonia in depression: Lessons from translational neuroscience. *Neuroscience and Biobehavioral Reviews, 35*, 537–555.

Tso, I. F., Mui, M. L., Taylor, S. F., & Deldin, P. J. (2012). Eye contact perception in schizophrenia: Relationship with symptoms and socioemotional functioning. *Journal of Abnormal Psychology, 121*, 616–627.

Turner, D. T., McGlanaghy, E., Cuijpers, P., van der Gaag, Karyotaki, E., & MacBeth, A. (2018). A meta-analysis of social skills training and related interventions for psychosis. *Schizophrenia Bulletin, 44*, 475–491.

Vauth, R., Rüsch, N., Wirtz, M., & Corrogan, P. W. (2004). Does social cognition influence the relation between neurocognitive deficits and vocational functioning in schizophrenia? *Psychiatry Research, 128*, 155–165.

Walker, E, & Lewine, R. J. (1990). Prediction of adult-onset schizophrenia from childhood home movies of the patients. *American Journal of Psychiatry, 147*, 1052–1056.

Wallace, C. J. (1984). Community and interpersonal functioning in the course of schizophrenic disorders. *Schizophrenia Bulletin, 10*, 233–257.

Wolwer, W., Frommann, Haufmann, S., Piaszek., A., Streit, M., & Gaebel, W. (2005). Remediation of impairments in facial affect recognition in schizophrenia: Efficacy and specificity of a new training program. *Schizophrenia Research, 80*, 295–303.

Wykes, T., Reeder, C., Landau, S., Everitt, B., Knapp, M., Patel, A., & Romeo, R. (2007). Cognitive remediation therapy in schizophrenia: Randomised controlled trial. *British Journal of Psychiatry, 190*, 421–427.

Wykes, T., Huddy, V., Cellard, C., McGurk, S. R., & Czobor, P. (2011). A meta-analysis of cognitive remediation for schizophrenia: Methodology and effect sizes. *American Journal of Psychiatry, 168*, 472–485.

Yager J. A., & Ehmann, T. S. (2006). Untangling social function and social cognition: A review of concepts and measurement. *Psychiatry, 69*, 47–68.

Zborowski, M. J., & Garske, J. P. (1993). Interpersonal deviance and consequent social impact in hypothetically schizophrenia-prone men. *Journal of Abnormal Psychology, 102*, 482–489.

Zhu, C-Y, Lee, T. M. C., Li, X-S., Jing, S-C., Wang, Y-G., & Wang, K. (2007). Impairments of social cues recognition and social functioning in Chinese people with schizophrenia. *Psychiatry and Clinical Neurosciences, 61*, 149–158.

Zigler, E., & Phillips, L. (1961). Social competence and outcome in psychiatric disorder. *Journal of Abnormal and Social Psychology, 63*, 264–271.

# CHAPTER 16

# Paranoia and Paranoid Beliefs

Richard P. Bentall

## A Conceptual History

As a review in an earlier edition of this volume pointed out, the terms "delusion" and "paranoia" often appear together in the psychiatric literature, reflecting the development of modern clinical terminology which employs both words to refer to abnormal forms of belief (Blaney, 2015). However, both terms have also found a place in everyday language, reflecting the complex interplay in the way that concepts are employed by mental health professionals and ordinary people. This interplay, and the shifting ways in which these terms have been defined in textbooks of psychiatry and abnormal psychology, have presented opportunities for confusion that should be addressed at the outset.

In the case of *delusion*, common language usage preceded the technical, clinical application of the term. The earliest English uses of the word to describe "a fixed false opinion or belief with regard to objective things," listed in the *Oxford English Dictionary*, date from the sixteenth century (e.g., Abraham Fraunce's *The Lawiers Logike*, published in 1588: "For that thereby men fell headlong into divers delusions and erronious conceiptes"). The words *paranoia* and *paranoid*, by contrast, were first established in the clinical literature and only found their way into everyday language in the second half of the twentieth century. Derived from the Greek words *para* (beyond, beside) and *nous* (mind, intellect), the OED dates the earliest nonmedical use to Samuel Beckett's 1938 novel *Murphy*, although the context is a description of psychotic patients in a psychiatric ward ("Paranoids, feverishly covering sheets of paper with complaints against their treatment or verbatim reports of their inner voices"). How paranoia subsequently became part of common English remains murky. In a celebrated essay, the historian Richard Hofstadter (1964) talked about the paranoid style in American politics, explicitly drawing parallels between what he understood to be the characteristics of certain psychiatric patients and political attitudes and movements that have become manifest at various points in US history. But popular culture has no doubt also played a role; Black Sabbath's second studio album (1970) was named *Paranoid* and Douglas Adam's radio comedy series (later a series of books), *The Hitchhiker's Guide to the Galaxy* (1978) had a character called Marvin the Paranoid Android (although, in the clinical sense, Marvin was more neurotic than paranoid, and the term was no doubt chosen for its alliteration).

The clinical use of both concepts dates from the nineteenth century, when French and German psychiatrists, for example Jean-Étienne Esquirol (*1772–1840*) and Karl Kahlbaum (*1828–1899*), identified groups of patients who appeared to present with a limited form of insanity in which abnormal beliefs affected only circumscribed areas of functioning, leaving intact other domains of reasoning and judgment (Kendler, 1995). By the end of this period, the concept of delusion as a particular kind of false belief that was a symptom of mental illness was widely accepted (Berrios, 1991) although, as we will see, the criteria for distinguishing delusions from nonpathological beliefs remains contested.

The German psychiatrist Emil Kraepelin (*1856–1927*) was particularly influential in the development

---

**Abbreviations**
BADE   Bias against disconfirmatory evidence
JTC    Jumping to conclusions (bias)
PANSS  Positive and Negative Syndrome Scale
SCAN   Schedules for Clinical Assessment in Neuropsychiatry
ToM    Theory of mind

of psychiatric classification in general (Bentall, 2003) and shaping the modern concept of paranoia specifically. Over the course of his career, he proposed many clinical concepts that remain important today, gradually refining his diagnostic criteria over iterations of his textbook of psychiatry, which went through nine editions between 1883 and 1927. In this way, he introduced the concept of *dementia praecox* (the precursor of the modern concept of schizophrenia), which he defined as a chronic, nonsenile, deteriorating condition that affected all of the psychic functions and that could present in various forms, including a form in which persecutory delusions were prominent, *paranoide formen dementia praecox* (Kendler, 2020). However, in his later work, Kraepelin distinguished patients who had this disorder from those he described as suffering from paranoia, whose delusions formed gradually, without any evidence of intellectual deterioration, and were based on the misinterpretation of events, often against a background of adverse life experiences (Kendler, 2018).

In the years following Kraepelin, *paranoia* was used in a bewildering variety of ways in different countries, as nosological categories expanded and collapsed in a process that has been likened to the "endless shuffling of the same old cards" (Hoenig, 1980). Debates during this period concerned whether paranoia was a type of schizophrenia, a stage in the progression to severe psychosis, or a separate diagnostic entity with symptoms that can occur in mild forms that sometimes evade psychiatric intervention (Dowbiggin, 2000). In the middle years of the twentieth century, the concept fell out of favor in clinical usage, particularly in the United States, where the diagnosis of schizophrenia was increasingly employed to cover a wide range of mental and social pathologies, provoking concerns about the cross-cultural validity of the concept (Cooper et al., 1972) and about the reliability of psychiatric diagnoses in general (Spitzer & Fliess, 1974). These concerns eventually provoked the neo-Kraepelinian revolution in psychiatry, which sought to return the discipline to the firm foundations established by Kraepelin (Blashfield, 1984).

The neo-Kraepelinian's greatest achievement was the publication of *DSM-III* in 1980, which sought to provide unambiguous diagnostic criteria for psychiatric disorders. This edition of the American Psychiatric Association's manual included the diagnosis *paranoid disorder*, which encompassed only persecutory delusions; in addition, the diagnosis was not to be applied when a diagnosis of schizophrenia was warranted (an exclusion criterion that has been retained ever since). However, at about the same time, some US psychiatrists, notably George Winokur (1977) and Kenneth Kendler (1980), were making efforts to characterize patients whom they believed merited the diagnosis and argued that the concept should be broadened. Their views were influential when later editions of the manual were published so that, when *DSM-III-R* was published in 1987, the concept of paranoia was side-lined in favor of a broader concept of *delusional disorder*. This condition is described in *DSM-5* as a disorder in which disorganized speech and negative symptoms are absent, hallucinations are rare, and in which the pathognomic symptom is nonbizarre delusions (Kendler, 2017). The manual lists seven subtypes: erotomanic (characterized by the delusion that someone is in love with the individual), grandiose (having great but unrecognized talent or having made some important discovery), jealous (the delusion that a spouse is being unfaithful), persecutory, somatic (delusions about bodily functions or sensations), mixed and unspecified (used when the dominant delusional theme cannot be specified).

A notable deviation from this historical process of nosological reification was made by Ernst Kretschmer (*1888–1964*), who rejected a disease model of paranoia and claimed that some delusional states occurred when people with vulnerable personalities responded to stressful events.

> He found that this clinical syndrome is caused by a triad of factors. There is a special personality factor characterized by hypersensitivity, exhaustibility, psychosexual inhibitions, and lack of normal intuitive erotic under-standing. Partial immaturities and familial psychopathology are frequently found. The second factor is an embarrassing or hurtful experience brought about when these usually quiet people are driven by their normal sexuality or the requirements of their daily lives into intense interaction with others. If the third factor, their social environment, does not allow any escape, the stage is set for the formation of paranoid reactions which can grow into true delusions. While the full-blown psychiatric picture is not very common, abortive or transient variations are quite frequent. (Hoehne, 1988)

The idea that some individuals have persistent paranoid traits in the absence of delusions has been represented in all editions of the *DSM* as *paranoid personality disorder*, characterized by suspicions of being deceived, doubts about the trustworthiness of others, reluctance to confide in others, the inference of threatening or demeaning meanings in benign remarks, the bearing of grudges, unfounded perceptions of attacks on character or reputation, and suspiciousness about the fidelity of a spouse. However, following extensive disagreements about the nature of personality disorders during the writing of the most recent edition of the manual (Widiger, 2011; Krueger, 2013), an alternative classification system is included in *DSM-5*, in a final section on emergent models of psychopathology. This section contains a general definition of personality disorder and then further definitions of six different types—antisocial, avoidant, borderline, narcissistic, obsessive-compulsive, and schizotypal—which are all described as disorders of identity (how the individual thinks of him or herself), self-direction (goals), empathy, and intimacy (ability to form close relationships with others). The absence of a paranoid type should be noted. A parallel although less fractious process (Mulder, 2021; Reed, 2018) led to a fundamental revision of the *ICD* classification so that, in *ICD-11*, eight different types have been replaced with a single classification of personality disorder which can be supplemented with descriptions of specific personality traits shown by the patient; again, no paranoid type is specified.

These persisting debates suggest that there is no settled agreement about the usefulness of the concept of paranoid personality disorder. As a consequence, only limited research has been conducted on the topic (Lee, 2017). Moreover, researchers who have attempted to study the condition have continued to disagree about whether it is related to either schizophrenia or delusional disorder (Triebwasser et al., 2013). However, as we will see, there is a rich literature on paranoia in nonclinical populations that has been conducted outside the framework of diagnostic psychiatry.

## Case Study

Diagnostic categories do little justice to the wide variety of paranoid beliefs and presentations encountered in clinical practice. Although each individual psychiatric patient presents unique complexities that are difficult to capture in biographical sketches, a case vignette reported by British psychiatrists Dimech, Kingdon, and Swelam (2009), which was subjected to review and commentary by three independent clinicians, illustrates the different ways in which paranoid beliefs are approached by mental health experts with different theoretical orientations.

Dimech et al.'s account concerned a young man called Zeppi, a 29-year-old migrant to the United Kingdom from Malta, arrested for the possession of offensive weapons (a machete and a dagger) after he had threatened his cousin, who owned the takeaway restaurant where he worked. When interviewed at a police station in London, Zeppi was guarded but at the same time relieved because he had felt in danger of being attacked for more than a year and had sought police protection on a number of occasions.

Zeppi's difficulties had become apparent when he had begun to feel vulnerable when working late shifts at the restaurant. His cousin had been forced to take on another member of staff as a consequence, but Zeppi had accused the new employee of trying to kill him by using a high-tech electronic device to fire magnetic waves at his body, causing him to feel palpitations. When Zeppi's cousin expressed skepticism about his complaints, Zeppi concluded that he, too, was part of a conspiracy, which involved an international criminal organization under the control of his former parish priest in Malta. Zeppi believed that the priest wished him to die a slow and painful death and that his cousin, who he referred to as "the traitor," had informed the priest of his whereabouts.

The three independent experts who reviewed Zeppi's case brought different training and conceptual tools to the task. Casey (2009), a psychiatrist, referred to the then current edition of the *DSM*, *DSM-IV*, and diagnosed Zeppi as suffering from *schizophrenia, chronic paranoid type*. Wilder (2009), a psychologist schooled in the behavior analytic approach, drew attention to the fact that Zeppi had been raised by his maternal grandmother during his first years of life but had largely been ignored by her. He had experienced only 7 years of schooling, with few opportunities to acquire social skills. In London, he was friendless and isolated. These observations led Wilder to suggest that a simple reinforcement approach might be effective, with a therapist systematically providing attention when Zeppi discussed mundane topics but ignoring him when he began talking about his delusions.

The present author, a clinical psychologist schooled in cognitive-behavior therapy and who had participated in clinical trials of psychological treatments for psychosis, drew attention to the wider psychological literature on the psychology of paranoia (Bentall, 2009). It is fair to describe Zeppi's family as highly dysfunctional. He had been the product of an incestuous relationship between his mother and her grandfather. The pregnancy was concealed by his mother and only became known to the rest of the family when she went into labor. Because of the family's deep shame about these events, Zeppi was not baptized, his birth was never registered, and he was made to hide away whenever the local priest visited. He spent the first 8 years of his life living on his maternal grandparents' farm without attending school, but, after his grandfather died, he moved to live with a kindly aunt on the nearby island of Gozo. There, he began to attend school but was badly bullied by the other schoolchildren. He had a very close relationship with his younger cousin, but his older cousin was hostile toward him and, on one occasion, sexually abused him. At the age of 15 years, he began working with his younger cousin in a local bakery but became severely depressed when the cousin moved abroad, resulting in a period of inpatient psychiatric treatment. When his younger cousin visited from London, he suggested that Zeppi should follow him to the UK to work for him.

There are several aspects of this biography that are consonant with the research literature on paranoia, which will be discussed later, notably the importance of the attachment process and experiences of victimization in the development of paranoid symptoms. A striking aspect of the story is that Zeppi's beliefs, although apparently incomprehensible when considered out of context, appear to be much more comprehensible—although still very strange—once his life story is known.

## Modern Definitions
### Delusions

In *DSM-5*, delusions are defined as

> fixed beliefs that are not amenable to change in light of conflicting evidence. Their content may include a variety of themes (e.g., persecutory, referential, somatic, religious, grandiose).... Delusions are deemed bizarre if they are clearly implausible and not understandable to same-culture peers and do not derive from ordinary life experiences.

The definition contained in the current edition of the World Health Organization's diagnostic manual, *ICD-11* is similar to that in previous editions of the *DSM*, which described delusions as false beliefs.

> A belief that is demonstrably untrue or not shared by others, usually based on incorrect inference about external reality. The belief is firmly held with conviction and is not, or is only briefly, susceptible to modification by experience or evidence that contradicts it. The belief is not ordinarily accepted by other members or the person's culture or subculture (i.e., it is not an article of religious faith).

However, each of these definitions, and many others that have been suggested, creates numerous conceptual problems, particularly when attempting to distinguish between the pathological beliefs of psychiatric patients and nonpathological but extreme beliefs such as violent political and religious ideologies and conspiracy theories (Bentall, 2018). For example, the criterion that a belief is false might also be thought to apply to the conspiracy theory that the 2020 US presidential election was rigged, although this belief is not usually considered delusional (at least in the technical sense). This criterion is also difficult to apply in cases where a belief is pathological but coincidentally true (it has been observed that the spouses of patients with delusional jealousy, when their patience wears thin, often desert them for new partners; Enoch & Trethowan, 1979), or when delusions have religious content, or when they seem implausible but not impossible (as in the case of a patient who claims to be the subject of surveillance by the intelligence services) (Cermolacce et al., 2010).

The criterion that beliefs should be held rigidly in the face of evidence that would refute them is similarly problematic if used to distinguish between delusions and other kinds of beliefs. On the one hand, there is evidence that some deluded patients are able to consider the possibility that their beliefs are mistaken, adjust their beliefs in the face of hypothetical contradictions, and generate alternative explanations for their experiences (e.g., Buchanan et al., 1993); this observation is supported by the modest success of cognitive-behavioral interventions (which encourage patients to evaluate their own beliefs) for people with delusions (Mehl et al., 2015) with better outcomes in the most recent studies (Sitko et al., 2020).

On the other hand, a considerable number of studies, for example using interview methods (e.g., So et al., 2012) or by asking people to assess conflicting information (e.g., Woodward et al., 2008) (see later section on cognitive impairments) have shown that belief inflexibility (the unwillingness to change beliefs in the light of updated information) is associated with delusional conviction (the individual's certainty that the belief is true) and also, to a lesser extent, with the distress associated with a delusional belief and the individual's preoccupation with it (Zhu et al., 2018). However, a general problem in interpreting these findings is the failure to consider the inflexibility of the personally important beliefs (e.g., religious beliefs and political convictions) of nondeluded people. For example, a considerable literature has demonstrated motivated reasoning and resistance to attitude change in people with strongly held political ideologies (Taber & Lodge, 2013; Westen et al., 2006). When Colbert et al. (2010) asked people with delusions, people who had recovered from delusions, and healthy controls whether they were willing to consider whether their delusional (patients) or idiosyncratic but meaningful (controls) beliefs were mistaken, personally meaningful beliefs were held with equal conviction, and equally inflexibly, in all three groups.

A feature of delusions that was emphasized by Kraepelin, although he did not believe it applied to all cases, was that they are nonsensical. Subsequent commentators have defined delusions as bizarre if they violate agreed ideas about what is possible (Mullen, 2003) or deviate from "culturally determined consensual reality" (Kendler et al., 1983), and this concept is included in *DSM-5*, which advises clinicians to note whether delusions are bizarre ("clearly implausible, not understandable, and not derived from ordinary life experiences") when diagnosing disorders such as schizophrenia and delusional disorder. However, although studies show that clinicians can generally agree on which beliefs are delusional, the reliability of the distinction between bizarre and nonbizarre delusions has been consistently reported as poor (Bell et al., 2006).

Other investigators have focused on subtle aspects of experience associated with beliefs. Those working in this tradition, mostly from continental Europe, have been inspired by philosophers such as Franz Brentano (*1838–1917*), Edmund Husserl (*1859–1938*), and Martin Heidegger (*1889–1976*) (see Broome et al., 2012) and have argued that the psychotic disorders are, in general, disturbances of the way that the individual experiences being in the world, which can only be revealed by subtle engagement with the patient and interrogation about his or her symptoms (Bovet & Parnas, 1993).

A pioneer in this approach to psychopathology was the German psychiatrist and philosopher Karl Jaspers (*1913–1959*). Jaspers (1912/1968, 1913/1963) argued that the first task of the clinician is to employ empathy to understand the unique meaningful connections that compose the patient's psychic life. These connections, he argued, are quite different from the kind of causal relations usually studied in the natural sciences:

> In the natural sciences we find causal connections only but in psychology our bent for knowledge is satisfied with the comprehension of a quite different sort of connection. Psychic events "emerge" out of each other in a way which we understand. Attacked people become angry and spring to the defence, cheated persons grow suspicious. The way in which such an emergence takes place is understood by us, our understanding is genetic.... We can have no psychological understanding without empathy into the content (symbols, forms, images, ideas) and without seeing the expression and sharing the experienced phenomena. All these spheres of meaningful objective and subjective experience form the matter for understanding. Only in so far as they exist can understanding take place. (Jaspers, 1913/1963, pp. 302–303)

In Jasper's view, empathy with the patient is not possible in the case of true delusions. The patient's statements are therefore *ununderstandable* and can only be "explained" as manifestations of illness. Later commentators elaborated this idea into the distinction between the *form* and *content* of a disorder. For example, Kurt Schneider (*1887–1967*) argued that diagnosticians should be concerned with how a symptom occurs and is experienced, rather than its content. The latter, he argued, can best be interpreted in terms of the patient's biography and is less relevant to diagnostic issues (Hoenig, 1982).

Phenomenological investigators have therefore argued that the abnormal form of delusions is revealed by subtle changes in mental state, some of which precede the onset of the fully developed delusional system. For example, in detailed studies of more than a hundred psychotic patients—mostly soldiers with paranoid symptoms—conducted in a military hospital during World War II, Klaus Conrad (*1905–1961*), claimed to identify a series of stages through which their paranoid ideas evolved (see Bovet & Parnas, 1993; Mishara, 2009). First, according to Conrad (1958/2012), there was an initial phase of *das Trema* (derived from Greek, colloquial for stage fright) or *delusional mood*, which may last for a few days or much longer, in which the patient feels a sense of tension, that there is something in the air but is unable to say what has changed. At first, this applies only to certain events and objects, but it gradually spreads to encompass everything in the patient's world, creating suspiciousness, fear, and a sense of separation from others. This leads to a state of *apophany* (revelation) in which the delusion appears suddenly, as an "ah-ha!" experience, often bringing about a sense of relief. Finally, in the *anastrophe* (turning back) phase the patient feels him- or herself to be the passive center around which the delusional business of the world is revolving. These ideas have been influential when some modern researchers have tried to identify very early prodromal or basic symptoms of psychopathology (e.g., Klosterkotter et al., 2001) but there has been a dearth of empirical studies to determine whether these kinds of stages are typical in patients with paranoid beliefs.

Two important limitations of the phenomenological approach should be noted. First, as acknowledged by many in the field, the ability to describe the form of others' experiences is limited by language, not only of the interviewer but also of the person attempting to describe his or her own mental states. Second, and less often acknowledged, by focusing exclusively on the experiences of patients with pathological mental states, phenomenologists have not been sufficiently cognizant of the phenomenology—indeed, sometimes frank weirdness—of ordinary human experiences (Bentall, in press). This becomes evident when, instead of thinking about mundane beliefs, we consider more emotionally charged but nonetheless widely accepted experiences and beliefs. For example, the zoologist Sir Alister Hardy (*1896–1985*) collected accounts of religious experience from more than 6,000 people in which many reported experiences that were strikingly similar to the unusual phenomenological characteristics of delusions described by Conrad (Hardy, 1979). Twenty-nine percent of these accounts included, "A patterning of events in a person's life that convinces him or her that in some strange way they were meant to happen." A detailed analysis of a small number cases of people who had made themselves known to Hardy's research unit found that these types of experiences could not be distinguished from psychotic experiences either in terms of form or content (Jackson & Fulford, 1997).

### Paranoid Beliefs

Today the terms *paranoid* and *persecutory* tend to be used interchangeably to describe delusions in which the individual believes he or she is the victim of some kind of persecution. Nearly every scholar who has studied severe mental illness since the earliest days of psychiatry has noted that these kinds of beliefs are particularly common among psychiatric patients. In the Schedules for Clinical Assessment

> **Box 16.1** Freeman and Garety's (2000) Criteria for Classifying a Delusion as Persecutory
>
> A. The individual believes that harm is occurring, or is going to occur, to him or her.
> B. The individual believes that the persecutor has the intention to cause harm.
>
> There are a number of points of clarification:
>
> I. Harm concerns any action that leads to the individual experiencing distress.
> II. Harm only to friends or relatives does not count as a persecutory belief, unless the persecutor also intends this to have a negative effect upon the individual.
> III. The individual must believe that the persecutor at present or in the future will attempt to harm him or her.
> IV. Delusions of reference do not count within the category of persecutory beliefs. A delusion of reference involves the belief that innocuous events (e.g., a casual glance from a stranger in the street or a news bulletin on the radio) have special significance for the individual.

of Neuropsychiatry (World Health Organisation, 1997), this type of delusion is defined as the patient's belief "that someone, or some organization, or some force or power, is trying to harm them in some way; to damage their reputation, to cause them bodily injury, to drive them mad or to bring about their death." In a detailed consideration of this and other proposed definitions, Freeman and Garety (2000) suggested the more precise definition given in Box 16.1.

Paranoid delusions are very common in patients with a first-episode of psychosis; in a large-scale clinical trial of patients who were offered psychological interventions soon after being diagnosed as suffering from a schizophrenia spectrum disorder, 250 (98%) of 255 patients who were suffering from a first episode and were assessed within 2 weeks of becoming known to services scored above the clinical cutoff of 3 on the Positive and Negative Syndrome Scale P1 item (delusions), and 235 (98.1%) scored above the clinical threshold for suspiciousness (P6) (Moutoussis et al., 2007). Persecutory delusions are also found, although less often, in patients with other diagnoses such as depression (Bentall, Kinderman, Howard et al.,

2008) and both the depressive and manic phases of bipolar disorder (Smith et al., 2017).

A complication in classifying delusions is that people, particularly when severely psychotic, often report multiple beliefs. However, a recent meta-analysis of 99 studies of the prevalence of different delusional system in different psychiatric populations around the world, all of which allowed more than one delusional theme to be recorded per patient, found that paranoid delusions were the most common (64.4% of patients), followed by delusions of reference (the belief that innocuous events; e.g., a casual glance from a stranger in the street or a news bulletin on the radio, have special significance for the individual; 38.9%), grandiose delusions (28.4%), delusions of control (the belief that the body, emotions, or thoughts are being controlled by someone else; 21.3%), and religious delusions (18.0%) (Collin et al., in submission). A wide variety of political and socioeconomic variables relating to the countries in which the studies were conducted were examined in this study, but these had very little impact on the distributions; for example, paranoid delusions were the most common in both the industrialized, developed nations and also in poorer developing nations, and this was true when individualist and collectivist cultures were compared.

The covariation between these different kinds of delusions has not been comprehensively studied. However, some studies have addressed the comorbidity between paranoid beliefs and grandiose delusions, and others have addressed the relationship between persecutory delusions and delusions of reference. Patients with both paranoid and grandiose delusions are quite common, and it is common in clinical practice to encounter delusional systems in which both types of belief are intertwined, as in the case of a patient who believed that he had invented the helicopter and pop-up toaster and blamed his doctors for stealing the revenues that should have accrued from these achievements (Bentall, 2003). In a British study of 301 chronically ill (at least two episodes) patients with schizophrenia or related diagnoses, 63.8% were found to have persecutory delusions, 32.2% had grandiose delusions, but a further 19.3% had both (Garety et al., 2013).

The relationship between persecutory delusions and delusions of reference has been more contested. For example, as noted above, Freeman and Garety's (2000) criteria for classifying a delusion as persecutory explicitly excluded delusions of reference and yet the same research group, a few years later, included a subscale measuring ideas of reference ("People definitely laughed at me behind my back," "People have been dropping hints for me") in a questionnaire measure of paranoia (Green et al. 2008; see below). Startup and Startup (2005) attempted to clarify this issue by showing that delusions of reference fall into two separate types: *delusions of observation* (patients believe that they are being spied on or gossiped about) and *delusions of communication* (patients believe that some kind of general sign or message, e.g., a bulletin by a television news announcer, is being directly addressed to them); they found that only the former type co-occurs with persecutory delusions.

In most accounts of delusional paranoia, the patient considers him- or herself to be an innocent victim of persecution. However, Trower and Chadwick (Chadwick et al., 2005; Trower & Chadwick, 1995) have argued that two distinct types of paranoia can be identified, which they termed *poor me* and *bad me*. In the poor me variety, the patient considers herself to be the target of unfair victimization, but, in the bad me variety, he or she believes that the persecution is warranted in the light of some personal flaw or misbehavior. However, longitudinal studies in which patients have been asked to report the extent to which they deserve persecution at different time points suggest that they often fluctuate between the two types of beliefs (Melo et al., 2006; Melo & Bentall, 2013). An experience sampling study, in which schizophrenia spectrum patients with paranoid symptoms reported their beliefs up to 10 times a day, found that patients who were classified as bad me at the onset showed especially marked fluctuations between poor me and bad me beliefs (those who were classified as poor me at the outset were more stable), and these fluctuations were accompanied by changes in self-esteem (Udachina et al., 2012). This finding has been interpreted in terms of a model that argues that paranoid beliefs are the consequence of dynamic attempts to regulate self-esteem (Bentall et al., 2001; see below).

### The Continuum Hypothesis

One way of resolving the difficulties in defining whether a belief is delusional is to propose a continuum between abnormal and normal beliefs so that, for example, paranoid delusions are viewed as an extreme variant of more common paranoid ideas and beliefs, such as suspicions about the intentions of others or the sense of being viewed critically by colleagues and neighbors. This idea has been particularly advocated by psychologists, who have not been convinced by the phenomenological studies (reviewed above) that have claimed to identify abnormal modes of experience that make delusions qualitatively different from other kinds of beliefs.

One type of evidence that is sometimes cited in this regard is the surprisingly high rate at which apparently delusional beliefs are endorsed by ordinary people who take part in epidemiological surveys. For example, when a large sample of general practice patients in the Aquitaine region of Southwest France were asked to complete a questionnaire measuring types of delusional beliefs commonly reported in the psychiatric literature, 69.3% of those with no history of psychiatric disorder reported that people were not who they seemed to be; 46.9% reported telepathic communication; 42.2% reported experiencing seemingly innocuous events that had double meanings; and 25.5% reported that they were being persecuted in some way (Verdoux et al., 1998). In a study of the 7,000 adults interviewed in the Dutch NEMESIS epidemiological study, 3.3% were classified as having "true" delusions and 8.7% were judged to have delusions that were not clinically relevant (i.e., which were not associated with distress and did not require treatment) (van Os et al., 2000). A recent critical systematic review by Heilskov, Urfer-Parnas and Nordgaard (2020), identified 17 studies of this kind and pointed out that the reported prevalence rates of delusions in the general population varied very considerably from study to study. They attributed this variation to the use of self-report instruments or brief interviews conducted by lay interviewers and recommended that future studies should include detailed interviews of subsamples of participants conducted by experienced clinicians.

A small number of studies have explicitly tested the continuum hypothesis, focusing specifically on paranoid ideas. Freeman et al. (2005) administered a questionnaire measure of paranoid thoughts to an online convenience sample of more than a thousand (predominantly female) students at three UK universities. Participants were asked to rate each item (e.g., "People communicate about me in subtle ways," "People would harm me if given an opportunity") for frequency over the last month, conviction, and distress. The three scales were highly correlated, and total scores fitted a mathematical distribution (an exponential decay curve) in which the most common scores were close to zero, after which there was a smooth decrease in the number of people with increasing scores so that very few participants scored at the extreme. Large numbers of participants endorsed the least pathological items on the questionnaire, but the rarer items were endorsed only by those had very high total scores, who were therefore judged highly paranoid. A later study by the same group (Bebbington et al., 2013) used data from the UK Adult Psychiatric Morbidity Survey, a face-to-face interview study of 7,000 UK adults, and picked out items from the Psychosis Screening Questionnaire (Bebbington & Nayani, 1995) and other survey items which related to paranoid thinking. The analysis, using a complex type of factor analysis, identified four separate components of paranoia—interpersonal vulnerability, ideas of reference, mistrust, and fear of persecution—and again found that total scores on the items were distributed along an exponential decay curve.

A limitation of these studies is that they did not include clinical samples. Recently, Elahi et al. (2017) compiled data on more than 2,000 healthy participants (mainly students and predominantly female), 157 patients with prodromal psychosis, and 360 patients with psychosis from various studies that had used the same paranoia measure. Three separate taxometric techniques designed to discriminate between continua and taxons (classes of individuals with unique characteristics) were used to interrogate the score distributions from the entire sample and the nonclinical participants alone, with the findings from all six analyses strongly supporting a continuum model.

The continuum approach carries the implication that we can further our understanding of the psychological mechanisms involved in paranoia by studying subclinical variants in the normal population; we shall see later that this approach has been quite fruitful. However, phenomenologically inclined researchers such as Feyaerts et al. (2021) have remained skeptical because they argue that this approach is focused entirely on the content of beliefs and ignores more subtle mental phenomena associated with paranoia of the kind discussed earlier. Indeed, it can be argued that much of the psychological literature on delusions assumes an *inner list* model in which an individual's beliefs are a list of propositions that can be simply read off by asking the right questions; although this idea has deep roots in Western culture, it is philosophically hard to justify and underestimates the dynamic aspects of belief systems (Bentall, 2018). Future research addressing the continuum hypothesis would benefit from integrating the phenomenological and psychological approaches by investigating nonpropositional aspects of belief alongside belief content in both clinical and large, representative samples.

## The Assessment of Paranoia

Many paranoia measures have been developed over the years, and each has advantages and disadvantages depending on the purpose of the assessment and the resources available (Freeman, 2008).

In clinical samples, paranoid beliefs are usually assessed using instruments designed to measure psychotic symptoms or assign diagnoses. For example, the Schedules for Clinical Assessment in Neuropsychiatry (SCAN; World Health Organisation, 1999) is a comprehensive psychiatric interview schedule designed primarily for diagnostic purposes. It includes a section on delusions, which includes questions about paranoid delusions, beliefs about conspiracies, and also many other types of abnormal belief. Each is rated on a 4-point scale of severity, either over the lifetime of the individual, during the present episode or the past month. The main disadvantages of this assessment, aside from the requirement for training before administering it, is that each type of delusion is identified by a single question and the severity range is restricted.

The Positive and Negative Syndrome Scale (PANSS; Kay & Opler, 1987) is specifically designed to assess the severity of psychotic symptoms, rather than for diagnostic purposes, and is widely used in clinical trials. It includes separate scales for *delusions* and *suspiciousness*, each rated on 7-point scales of severity. Its advantage is that it is possible to take either the suspiciousness scale alone, or both scales together, to generate a measure of paranoia severity, but it lacks the fine-grain analysis of other delusions which is possible with the SCAN.

A number of questionnaire measures of paranoia have been developed. For example, Fenigstein and Vanable (1992) developed a 20-item paranoia questionnaire primarily for the purposes of social psychological research; each item is scored on a 5-point scale. Although the scale was designed to assess subclinical paranoid beliefs, it was subsequently shown to correlate with clinically assessed paranoia in a sample of schizophrenia patients (Smari et al., 1994).

The 21-item Peters Delusions Inventory (Peters et al., 1999) uses items derived from the SCAN to measure a wide range of beliefs and hence is designed to detect clinically relevant delusional beliefs. However, only two items refer specifically to paranoid ideas ("Do you ever feel that you are being persecuted in some way?" "Do you ever feel that there is a conspiracy against you?"). Other items sample delusions of reference, grandiose and religious delusions, and a wide variety of less common (e.g., being influenced by computers or electrical devices, or believing that the world is going to end) and less pathological beliefs (e.g., believing in witchcraft or telepathy). Respondents first of all answer each question "yes" or "no" and then, if the answer is "yes," proceed to rate whether the belief is distressing or preoccupying, and also their conviction, on 5-point scales.

Freeman et al. (2005) developed an 18-item paranoia checklist to assess paranoid beliefs in the general population, but then went on to develop a more widely used scale designed for both clinical and healthy samples, the Green Paranoia Scale (Green et al., 2008). This scale originally had two 16-item subscales: Part-A measuring ideas of reference and Part-B measuring ideas of persecution. However, the scale has recently been revised (Freeman et al., 2021), and the subscales have been cut down to 8 and 10 items, respectively, each rated on a 5-point scale ranging from "not at all" to "totally." The questionnaire has very good psychometric properties and discriminates well between subclinical and clinical paranoia; recommended cutoff scores are provided.

For the purpose of measuring very rapid fluctuations of paranoia, for example, in experimental studies, Schlier et al. (2016) have published very short (3- and 5-item) versions of Freeman's original Paranoia Checklist, selecting items (e.g., "People try to make me upset") that had proved most sensitive to change in previous studies and adapting them so that respondents reported the extent to which they applied "at the moment."

Finally, inspired by Trower and Chadwick's (1995) theory of two types of paranoia, Melo et al. (2009) adapted items from Fenigstein and Vanable's (1992) scale to create a 10-item measure in which respondents first indicated whether they agreed with a series of paranoid beliefs ("There are times when I worry that others might be plotting against me," with responses ranging from "certainly false" to "certainly true") and then, if they score 2 ("unsure") or higher on an item, whether they deserved to be persecuted ("Do you feel like you deserve others to plot against you?" with responses ranging from "not at all" to "very much"). Scores on persecution (P subscale) were calculated as the sum of the relevant items, and for deservedness (D subscale) as the mean of those items they completed. The scale had good psychometric properties and discriminated between healthy and clinical participants. An interesting difference between the two groups was that P and D scores were positively correlated in the healthy participants but nearly all of the clinical participants had very low D scores (they were "poor me"). A shortened 5-item version of the P subscale has subsequently been developed for epidemiological studies and shown to have good psychometric properties (McIntyre et al., 2018).

## Genetic and Social Determinants of Paranoia

It is fair to say that, over the past two decades, there has been a dramatic reappraisal of the relative contributions of genetic and environmental factors to severe mental illness, and any analysis of the role of these factors in paranoia must be seen in this context. For example, until quite recently, the high heritability estimates, typically around 80% (Sullivan et al., 2003), calculated for schizophrenia in family, twin, and adoption studies was assumed to preclude the importance of life experience (van Os & McGuffin, 2003). A conceptual error, in many interpretations of these findings, has been the assumption that heritability is a measure of causation that applies to the individual, whereas, in fact, it is an estimation of the correlation between genes and outcomes within a specific population and therefore subject to all the usual caveats about the meaning of correlations (Bentall, 2021).

Molecular research has shown that the genetic risk of schizophrenia and other related forms is massively polygenic, although there are rare genetic mutations that confer a high level of risk in a small number of cases (Kendler, 2015; Owen, 2012). At the same time, population, clinical, and even a small number of prospective studies have shown a very strong association between various types of environmental exposures, especially in childhood, and the development of psychosis in adulthood. These include both forms of collective adversity, such as poverty (Wicks et al., 2005), social inequality (Johnson et al., 2015), exposure to urban environments (Vassos et al., 2012), ethnic minority status (Bosqui et al., 2014), and the experience of migration (Castillejos et al., 2018), but also specific interpersonal traumas such as sexual and physical abuse and victimization by peers. The effects of interpersonal trauma have been particularly well-replicated and supported by meta-analyses, with a dose-response effect suggestive of causation (McGrath et al., 2017; Varese et al., 2012). A small number of studies that have assessed the impact of childhood adversity and genes at the same time, using either classical (Alemany et al., 2013; Arseneault et al., 2011) or molecular methods (Trotta et al., 2016), have pointed to independent and additive effects of the two types of risk factors.

Genetic studies of paranoid phenomena have been few and far between. Some studies have attempted to assess the heritability of paranoid personality disorder, usually in the context of a broader genetic investigation of personality disorders in general, and have reported modest to moderate heritability estimates (Reichborn-Kjennerud, 2010). Even fewer investigations have specifically examined the heritability of paranoia considered as a symptom. In a recent study of a large sample of adolescent identical and nonidentical twins who were assessed using dimensional measures of a range of specific psychotic experiences, the heritability of paranoia was estimated at 50% when using traditional methods based on the comparison of the two types of twins (Zavos et al., 2014); this estimate was little affected when only extreme scorers on the dimension were considered, suggesting that the genetic architecture of paranoia remains the same across nonclinical and clinical variants. A later analysis using molecular methods yielded a heritability estimate of 14% (Sieradzka et al., 2015), a finding that is consistent with many other observations of discrepancies between the estimates derived from the two methods (the *missing heritability* problem), which is especially marked in child and adolescent samples and which has yet to be adequately explained (Cheesman et al., 2017).

Most of the research on the role of adverse environmental factors in psychosis has not considered the relationship between particular types of exposures and specific symptoms, and so research focused on the environmental determinants of paranoia has been limited. Perhaps the strongest evidence for the influence of collective adversity concerns socioeconomic factors. One of the earliest studies of the relationship between urban environments and psychosis was conducted in Chicago by Faris and Dunham (1939), who reported a higher prevalence of schizophrenia in inner-city areas and also noted that patients in those areas often showed paranoid symptoms. In a later survey of residents of El Paso in the United States and Juarez in Mexico, Mirowsky and Ross (1983) found that paranoia was associated with circumstances which they characterized as victimization and powerlessness; specifically, low social status interacted with an external locus of control to lead to mistrust and paranoia.

Using epidemiological data from the United Kingdom, Wickham et al. (2014) found that a global index of neighborhood deprivation predicted the likelihood of paranoid and depressive symptoms but not hallucinations or manic symptoms. A later study using a different epidemiological dataset found, again, that people reported more severe paranoid beliefs if they were living in deprived neighborhoods and, using network analysis, found that paranoia was a possible bridge symptom (pathway) between specific neighborhood characteristics (e.g., exposure to incivilities and mistrust of neighbors) to symptoms of depression and anxiety (McElroy et al., 2019). If replicated, this finding suggests that subclinical paranoid beliefs may have much greater public health implications than is widely recognized. The finding that harsh neighborhood environments foster paranoia has been further supported by studies in which people, either drawn from the general population (Corcoran et al., 2018) or who suffer from paranoid symptoms (Ellett et al., 2008), are asked to walk around urban environments and report their thoughts and feelings; in deprived neighborhoods, people feel more paranoid.

It is difficult to disaggregate the many factors that could explain these effects. For example, one possibility is that people are more likely to experience victimization and other kinds of adverse interpersonal interactions in deprived areas, and another is that these areas are not rich in social capital and networks of supportive relationships. These hypotheses are not mutually exclusive, and there is evidence for each of them.

For example, a Dutch longitudinal epidemiological study reported by Janssen et al. (2003) found that, in those individuals who showed no evidence of paranoid ideation at baseline, reports of discrimination on the basis of age, gender, disability, appearance, skin color, ethnicity, or sexual orientation predicted the onset of delusions but not hallucinations in the following 3 years. In a more recent British epidemiological survey, experiences of bullying and lack of social support also partially explained a specific association observed between sexual minority status and paranoia but not hallucinations (Qi et al., 2020).

The sense of belonging to a neighborhood was shown to protect individuals against both paranoia and depression (but not hallucinations) in a British epidemiological survey; a follow-up study with UK students, in which the sense of belonging to their university was measured, obtained comparable results (McIntyre et al., 2018). In a further analysis of the same datasets, Elahi et al. (2018) found that a strong sense of social identity moderated (reduced) the relationship between financial difficulties (a fairly objective measure of stress) and the same mental health symptoms. This finding is consistent with research by social psychologists, who have argued that having multiple social identities (not only belonging to groups but defining oneself in terms of those group memberships) is protective against mental ill-health (Haslam et al., 2009).

It has been hypothesized that, because ethnic minority and migration status are associated with victimization and sometimes with the inability to identify with the majority population, these groups should be especially likely to experience paranoid symptoms (McIntyre et al., 2016). However, specific evidence in support of this hypothesis is limited to a few, relatively small-scale studies. Combs et al. (2002) found that African Americans scored higher on a paranoia scale than White Americans and, later, that perceived racism in African Americans predicted a measure of subclinical paranoia but not scores on a clinical measure (Combs et al., 2006). In a small sample of Muslim Americans, it was also reported that perceived religious discrimination was associated with subclinical paranoia (Rippy & Newman, 2006), and, in a study of female Emirati students, it was found that identification with US culture in preference to Arab culture (measured using an implicit technique based on reaction times when making judgments about national symbols such as flags) was associated with paranoid beliefs (Thomas et al., 2016). It is likely that the two factors considered here—discrimination and identity—interact. McIntyre et al. (2019) examined the relationship between social identity and paranoia in UK Afro-Caribbeans, finding that, in those who reported positive relationships with the White majority, identifying as British was associated with low levels of paranoia whereas in those who had experienced negative relationships with the White majority, identifying as British was associated with high levels of paranoia.

Some studies have examined the role of adverse childhood experiences in paranoia. An analysis of epidemiological data from the United Kingdom found a particularly strong association between being raised in institutional care (a strong indicator of damaged relationships with caregivers) and paranoid symptoms in adulthood, whereas hallucinations were strongly associated with childhood sexual abuse (Bentall et al., 2012); the same relationship did not hold for children raised in foster care. These findings were subsequently replicated in a large sample of UK prisoners (Shevlin et al., 2015).

An analysis of a US epidemiological dataset found that neglect by parents was the type of childhood adversity most associated with paranoid beliefs, whereas, again, hallucinations were associated with sexual abuse (Sitko et al., 2014). A more recent study used data from a US epidemiological sample of adolescents and also a replication dataset collected from UK adults; in both samples, reports of verbal abuse and physical abuse were associated with a higher likelihood of reporting paranoia, whereas reporting a high level of care from parents was associated with a low likelihood of reporting paranoia (Brown et al., 2021). A network analysis of the UK dataset allowed these associations to be studied in more detail, and it was found that all of the parenting variables were closely connected but that the variable most closely linked to paranoia was maternal indifference.

These findings have been mirrored by the results from a small number of studies with clinical samples. Rankin et al. (2005) found that both currently ill and recovered paranoid patients reported adverse relationships with their parents during childhood; the fact that the recovered patients' reports matched those of the patients who were currently ill was taken as indicating that these reports were unlikely to be caused by the patients' paranoid symptoms. In an analysis of data from a group of UK psychotic patients, it was found again that paranoid symptoms were specifically associated with childhood emotional neglect (Wickham & Bentall, 2016). Studies of patients diagnosed as suffering from paranoid personality disorder have also generated parallel findings. For example, Bierer et al. (2014) studied a large sample of patients with personality disorders and found a high level of childhood trauma overall but, in the cluster A (schizotypal, schizoid, and paranoid) group, paranoid personality disorder alone was predicted by sexual, physical, and emotional abuse.

There are some important limitations of this research that should be noted. All have employed retrospective reports of childhood experiences by either adults living in the community or patients. In the wider psychosis literature, this limitation has been addressed by showing similar findings from prospective studies (Varese et al., 2012) or by conducting investigations to verify the validity of patients' retrospective reports (Fisher et al., 2011) but these kinds of investigations are absent in studies focusing specifically on paranoia. However, cautiously, it is reasonable to say that the development of both clinical and subclinical paranoia in adulthood seems to be related to disrupted early attachment relationships with caregivers and exposure to harsh environments and victimization in later life. These findings, which point to the importance of the individual's history and social context, obviously have important implications for how paranoia is conceived by clinicians and researchers, as is evident in the account of Zeppi discussed earlier. Specifically, although research to be reviewed below shows that various cognitive and emotional processes contribute to paranoid thinking, it is a mistake to assume that these kinds of beliefs never have a foundation in real-life events.

**Psychological Models of Paranoia**

Psychological models of paranoia are of broadly three kinds, although they to some extent overlap. Some researchers following Maher and Ross (1984) have seen paranoid beliefs and delusions in general as attempts to construct meaningful explanations of anomalous experiences. Others, particularly Freeman and his colleagues (Freeman et al., 2002; Freeman, 2016), have argued that cognitive abnormalities of one kind or another play a direct role in generating paranoid beliefs. Still others, notably Frith (1992), have proposed that paranoia arises from a difficulty in understanding the intentions of others. Finally, some researchers, sometimes inspired by psychoanalytic theory, for example Colby (1977), have argued that paranoid beliefs emerge as a dynamic process as a consequence of the individual's attempts to avoid threats to self-esteem (Bentall et al., 2001) (sometimes called the *paranoia as a defense model*). These theories have led to rich avenues of empirical research, and the literature on the psychological mechanisms underlying paranoia has grown from a smattering of studies in the 1990s to an enormous number today. Hence, the following review can only focus on the most widely studied processes.

*Paranoia and Anomalous Experiences*

Maher and Ross's (1984) original formulation of the anomalous experience model of delusions consisted of two separate propositions: first, that delusional beliefs were invariably preceded by experiences which seemed anomalous to the individual and, second, that people with delusions did not suffer from cognitive abnormalities. Hence delusions were seen as more or less rational attempts to explain anomalous experiences. It is important to note that the two parts of this theory (the role of anomalous experiences and the idea that reasoning is unimpaired in deluded patients) are logically independent of each other; one could be true and the other remain false.

On the first proposition, Maher cited examples of patients whose delusions appeared to be responses to hallucinatory experiences. Also, factor analytic studies have consistently shown that delusions and hallucinations tend to co-occur, with both belonging to the positive syndrome of psychosis (Safer & Dazzi, 2019). However, this co-occurrence might, in principle be caused by shared underlying processes, by hallucinations leading to delusions, or by delusions leading to hallucinations. The fact that delusions often (although not always) precede hallucinations during the early stages of psychosis (Compton et al., 2012) suggests that the last of these pathway is the most likely one, and this explanation for the covariation of the two symptoms is supported by the fact that exacerbations in paranoid thinking often precede the onset of hallucinations in patients' daily lives (Oorschot et al., 2012) and by experimental studies which have shown that hallucinatory experiences in patients (Haddock et al., 1995; Mintz & Alpert, 1972), people with schizotypal traits (Alganami et al., 2017), and even ordinary people (Barber & Calverley, 1964) can be influenced by simple suggestions (the manipulations of expectancies about what participants expected to see or hear). An epidemiological study using directed acyclic graphs (a technique that can increase the confidence in causal effects, even in cross-sectional data) also found support for a pathway from persecutory beliefs to hallucinations but not vice versa (Moffa et al., 2017).

But this does not mean that other kinds of anomalous experiences do not play a role in paranoia. Early studies suggested that paranoid beliefs, particularly in elderly patients, are often associated with the slow onset of deafness, with the possible explanation that hearing loss can prompt individuals to believe that those around them are either not communicating with them or speaking in whispers (Cooper & Curry, 1976). One study claimed to induce paranoia in healthy persons by using a hypnotic induction to simulate deafness (Zimbardo et al., 1981). More convincing are recent epidemiological studies which have also shown an association between hearing loss and paranoid beliefs (Stefanis et al., 2006; Thewissen et al., 2005).

Several additional recent observations about the factors relating to paranoia can also be accommodated within the anomalous perception model. For example, it may explain the possible role of cannabis consumption in paranoid symptoms (Freeman et al., 2014). On the assumption that sleep disturbance may lead to anomalous perceptual experiences, it may also explain the likely association between insomnia and paranoia (Freeman et al., 2009; Freeman et al., 2011), although the findings from different kinds of sleep investigations have been varied, with cross-sectional studies showing a more consistent association than sleep interventions designed to detect a causal effect (see Barton et al., 2018, for a review).

One further type of anomalous experience that should be considered in this context is dissociation, which is a common consequence of severe psychological trauma and involves a disturbance in the integration of cognitive functions and emotional processes, leading to a sense of detachment from self (depersonalization) and/or the environment (derealization) (Dalenberg et al., 2012). It is worth noting that these experiences are not dissimilar to the subtle alterations in experience reported in phenomenological investigations of delusions, for example by Conrad (1958/2012). Many studies have reported that dissociation at least partially mediates the relationship between trauma and hallucinations (Pilton et al., 2016; Varese et al., 2011), but a recent meta-analysis reported that dissociation was associated with all of the positive symptoms of psychosis, including paranoia (Longden et al., 2020).

These findings, of course, do not show that anomalous experiences are a necessary condition for paranoid beliefs. Nor do they address the second proposition in Maher's model, which is that reasoning in deluded patients is normal. In support for this claim, Maher cited studies of syllogistic reasoning in psychiatric patients, but these are not convincing because healthy performance on syllogistic reasoning tasks is often poor and because subsequent studies have revealed many ways in which the reasoning of paranoid people appears to be abnormal.

### Cognitive Factors and Delusional Beliefs

A number of researchers have attempted to identify psychological processes that contribute directly to paranoid thinking, but much of this work has been inspired by a theoretical framework developed by Freeman and colleagues (Freeman, 2016; Freeman et al., 2002). This model encompasses Maher's anomalous perception model to the extent that unusual experiences are seen as setting the occasion for the individual to search for the meaning of events, but a number of cognitive deficits and emotional biases are hypothesized to shape the explanation eventually arrived at. It attempts to explain not only the onset of paranoia as a consequence of this interaction between experience and psychological biases but also the subsequent maintenance of the resulting delusional beliefs by safety (avoidance) behaviors (e.g., avoiding areas where threats are thought to be most likely) which prevent the individual from discovering new information that is contrary to their delusional beliefs (Freeman et al., 2007).

One of the most widely studied cognitive abnormalities thought to influence delusion formation is known as the *jumping to conclusions* (JTC) *bias* although it is probably more correctly described as a deficit than a bias. This phenomenon is usually assessed with the *beads in a jar* task, in which the individual is asked to observe a sequence of blue or red beads and decide whether they are drawn from a jar with a majority of red beads or a jar with a majority of blue beads. After each draw, the individual can either make a decision or ask to see another bead. In early studies, Huq et al. (1988) and Garety et al. (1991) reported that patients with delusions ask to see fewer beads before making a decision in comparison to controls, and this has been replicated many times, including with patients suffering from paranoid delusions (Corcoran et al., 2008) and with ordinary people with high levels of paranoid conviction (Freeman et al., 2008). Several meta-analyses have shown that this effect is robustly related to psychosis (So et al., 2016) and delusion severity (Dudley et al., 2016), although it is probably not specific to paranoid beliefs.

A second type of reasoning bias which has been explored in relation to delusions is the *bias against disconfirmatory evidence* (BADE) effect, which was first demonstrated by Woodward et al. (2006). In this study, patients with psychosis were asked to rate the plausibility of four possible interpretations of the events shown in a picture; they were then asked to adjust their ratings as pictures with further relevant information were shown to them. A BADE was demonstrated by the unwillingness to adjust ratings in response to new information that was inconsistent with formerly plausible interpretations, and this effect was shown to be greatest for patients suffering from delusions. This finding has been replicated a number of times, using variations in methodology (e.g., using sentences instead of pictures as stimulus material) and in studies with nonclinical participants scoring highly on a measure of delusion proneness (Woodward et al., 2007; see McLean et al., 2016, and Zhu et al., 2018, for meta-analytic reviews). In a factor analysis of BADE responses in a large group of schizophrenia and bipolar patients, Speechley et al. (2012) found that the patients' performance could be accounted for by two factors: a failure to integrate new evidence and a more general conservative response bias (a general unwillingness to make high ratings); only the former component distinguished between deluded and nondeluded patients.

Like the JTC bias, the BADE effect is probably not specific to paranoid as opposed to other kinds of delusional beliefs. An interesting feature of the BADE task is that the scenarios are unrelated to patients' delusions and hence the task appears to demonstrate a bias in general reasoning. However, Woodward et al. (2008) found a BADE effect only when schizophrenia patients were provided with evidence against strongly held initial beliefs—they were as willing to change weakly held initial beliefs as controls—and the BADE effect has also been shown to modestly predict political dogmatism and racial prejudice in healthy people (Bronstein et al., 2017). Indeed, as noted earlier, similar effects have been observed in other studies of political reasoning (Taber & Lodge, 2013; Westen et al., 2006). Further research is therefore needed to establish the extent to which the BADE effect is specific to delusions or also is found in people with other kinds of very strongly held beliefs.

Another question that remains unresolved is whether the JTC and BADE tasks measure a specific domain of cognitive functioning or whether poor performance on these tasks reflects a more general impairment. Several studies have reported that performance on the JTC task closely correlates with measures of executive function (Bentall et al., 2009; Ochoa et al., 2014), and detailed, trial-by-trial analysis of patients' responses on the task has shown that impaired performance more likely reflects impulsive or even random responding rather than a preference for making an early decision (Moutoussis et al., 2011). (In most versions of the task, the first two beads are alternative colors so that, at the second trial, the patient has no information whatsoever to indicate which jar the beads might have been drawn from; nonetheless, many patients make a decision after the second draw.) Similarly, BADE performance has been found to correlate with more general cognitive abilities (Eifler et al., 2014).

## Theory of Mind

The term "theory of mind" (ToM) was coined in a celebrated paper by the primatologists Premack and Woodruff (1978), which asked whether chimpanzees had an ability to understand the mental states of other chimpanzees. This question had two consequences. First, it established the slightly misleading term (ToM), which ever since has been used to refer to the human ability to understand the thoughts and feelings of other people. Second, it stimulated a vast research literature by cognitive psychologists, comparative psychologists, and developmentalists to attempt to understand the origins of this ability (Wellman, 2017). An important discovery, which created great impetus in this respect, was that autistic people suffer from severe ToM impairments (Baron-Cohen, 1995; Baron-Cohen et al., 1985).

Frith (1994) suggested that ToM impairments could explain the paranoid symptoms of psychotic patients. The idea behind this hypothesis was that individuals who had difficulty in understanding the intentions of others might assume those intentions were malign. Frith argued that patients might be especially likely to make this assumption if their psychotic breakdown had been preceded by a period of good mental functioning in which the ability to understand the intentions of others was unimpaired. Several studies appeared to provide support for this hypothesis (Corcoran et al., 1995, 1997), and ToM impairments have been reported specifically in paranoid patients (Corcoran et al., 2008). In one study, which compared Asperger's syndrome patients (adults with less severe autistic traits) with paranoid patients, the two groups were found to be comparable on a ToM measure, but only the paranoid patients showed an attributional bias (see below) (Craig et al., 2004).

However, other studies have reported that impaired ToM is associated with a wide range of psychotic symptoms, including thought disorder (Grieg et al., 2004; Sarfati & Hardy-Bayle, 1999) and lack of insight (Langdon et al., 2006). Indeed, impaired ToM has been reported in both bipolar (Bora et al., 2016) and depressed patients (Bora & Berk, 2016) (although, as noted earlier, paranoid delusions are sometimes reported by patients in both of these groups). A study which divided paranoid patients between those with and without ToM deficits found that the latter scored high on a measure of social anxiety, suggesting that impaired ToM and social anxiety separately contribute to paranoid beliefs (Lysaker et al., 2016).

In a recent study using two British epidemiological samples, autistic traits assessed using a questionnaire screening instrument were strongly associated with not only paranoia but also with all other psychotic symptoms with the exception of mania (Martinez et al., 2021). This finding is consistent with a birth cohort study which found that autistic traits in children predicted the development of psychotic (but not specifically paranoid) experiences in adolescence (Jones et al., 2012).

A further issue concerns whether ToM deficits in psychosis reflect a specific domain of cognition or more general deficits; a recent meta-analysis of 91 studies found strong evidence that the latter is the case (Thibaudeau et al., 2020).

## Emotional Biases and Paranoid Beliefs

Much of the research on emotional processes in relation to paranoia was stimulated by the paranoia as a defense model. This model was based on the observations by Kaney and Bentall (1989, 1992) of abnormalities in the way that paranoid patients explained events. Previous research had shown that depressed patients tended to make internal (self-blaming), stable (the cause was unchangeable), and global (it affected all areas of life) attributions (explanatory statements) about negative events (Abramson et al., 1978). Kaney and Bentall found that paranoid patients also made global and stable explanations for these kinds of events, but their explanations were, by contrast, highly external (they attributed the cause to factors other than themselves). Subsequent studies showed that these external explanations typically implicated other actors rather than circumstances (Kinderman & Bentall, 1997).

To account for these findings Bentall et al. (1994) proposed that this attributional style protected the individual from the unpleasant experience of discrepancies between their actual selves (themselves as they thought they really were) and their ideal selves, thereby maintaining their self-esteem. A subsequent iteration of the model (Bentall et al., 2001), made to accommodate the distinction between poor me and bad me paranoia (Trower & Chadwick, 1995), proposed a dynamic process by which the interpretation of events was influenced by current self-esteem (someone with low self-esteem should tend to attribute a negative event to themselves) but that attributions should, in turn, influence future self-esteem (an external explanation for a negative event would have less psychologically damaging consequences than an internal explanation). This version of the model had the implication that self-esteem should be highly unstable in paranoid patients. The model also predicted that paranoid patients should show discrepancies between implicit (indirect) measures of self-esteem, which should reveal a negative appraisal of the self, and explicit (direct measures), which should show a positive appraisal.

An important objection made to the defense model is that self-esteem is often low in paranoid patients. Indeed, numerous studies have shown that paranoia is associated with low self-esteem (Bentall, Kinderman, & Moutoussis, 2008) and negative beliefs about the self (Fowler et al., 2006), and, indeed that, longitudinally, negative beliefs about the self predict a poor recovery from paranoia (Fowler et al., 2012). These findings have been supported by a recent meta-analysis (Humphrey et al., 2021) although the authors noted that a complication was the effect of depression, which often co-occurs with paranoid symptoms. Studies in which implicit and explicit measures of self-esteem were used have also failed to support the defense model (Murphy et al., 2018), although recent meta-analyses have supported the prediction of an extreme self-serving attributional bias (Müller et al., 2021) and also high self-esteem fluctuations in paranoid patients (Müller et al., 2021; Murphy et al., 2018).

Recently, researchers have begun to investigate whether the emotional negativity found in paranoid patients might be associated with more general interpersonal processes and specifically attachment styles. Bowlby (1969) proposed that experiences with caregivers led young children to create *internal working models* of their relationships, which then affected their interactions with other people throughout adult life (Mikulincer & Shaver, 2007). The internal working models of the majority of children—based on their confidence that the caregiver will always be available when needed—incorporate a positive model of the self, a positive model of others, and the expectation that others can be trusted. However, insecure ways of relating to others were explained in terms of two dimensions of insecure attachment: anxious attachment, reflecting negative beliefs about the self, need for approval, and fear of rejection, and avoidant attachment, reflecting fears about the intentions of others and a preference for emotional distance.

Bentall and Fernyhough (2008) proposed that these styles might explain the relationship between early childhood adversity and paranoia. Empirical studies of healthy individuals varying in trait paranoia (Pickering et al., 2008) and patients differing in the severity of their persecutory delusions (Wickham et al., 2015) confirmed that paranoid beliefs were associated with both the anxious and avoidant styles, a finding that has subsequently been replicated by other researchers (see Murphy et al., 2020, for a meta-analysis). In an experience sampling study, in which patients with persecutory delusions and healthy controls recorded their thoughts and feelings up to 10 times a day for 6 days, it was also shown that fluctuations in attachment-related cognitions predicted changes in paranoid symptoms (Sitko et al., 2016).

Several mediators of this relationship have been identified, including low self-esteem (Pickering et al., 2008; Wickham et al., 2015), fear of powerful others, and anticipation of threat (Pickering et al., 2008). In a recent study with a large population sample, Martinez et al. (2021) asked participants to complete measures of attachment and self-esteem and also to judge the trustworthiness of a series of computer-generated faces that had been previously classified as appearing trustworthy or untrustworthy. Signal detection analysis was used to distinguish between the general ability to discriminate between the two types of faces (sensitivity) and a response bias toward judging the faces as untrustworthy. The pathway from both avoidant and anxious attachment to paranoia was mediated by low self-esteem, but the pathway from avoidant attachment to paranoia was also uniquely mediated by response bias (but not sensitivity) when making the trustworthiness judgments.

## Conclusion

Despite some disagreement between the models, it is striking that there has recently emerged a consensus about the psychological origins and mechanisms involved in paranoia. First, the continuum model, although leaving some questions unanswered (particularly with regard to some unusual phenomenological characteristics of delusional paranoia), has been very fruitful in generating research and progressing theory development. Second, it now clear that paranoid beliefs, like other psychotic phenomena, are associated with adverse life experiences. Disrupted early attachment relationships, exposure to harsh environments, victimization by others, the absence of social bonds and the sense of belonging are all circumstances that create a high risk of paranoid beliefs. Third, a number of psychological mechanisms that contribute to paranoia have been identified, particularly problems in reasoning about sequential information, insecure attachment styles, negative beliefs about the self, an exaggerated self-serving bias, and (less certainly) an impaired ToM.

The four psychological models discussed in this chapter differ in the extent to which each of these factors is given precedence and also in how these mechanisms are thought to interact. Maher and Ross's (1984) anomalous experience model has stimulated some important discoveries about factors that influence paranoia, but it is clear that unusual experiences are not sufficient to explain the development of persecutory delusions. Frith's (1994) proposal that impairments of ToM are central to paranoia is only very weakly supported because ToM deficits do not seem to be specific to paranoid symptoms, and some paranoid patients have preserved ToM. The remaining two theories, the model of Freeman and colleagues (Freeman, 2016; Freeman et al., 2002) and the defense model of Bentall et al. (2001), both emphasize the role of cognitive and emotional processes (e.g., difficulties in reasoning about sequential information, negative beliefs about the self that are related to interpersonal vulnerabilities, and insecure attachment styles). Of the two models, the model by Freeman and colleagues is currently the most strongly supported, with some of the predictions arising from the defense model (e.g., about discrepancies between implicit and explicit self-esteem) lacking empirical support.

The development of these psychological models has emboldened clinical researchers to develop psychological interventions for paranoid patients who, not many decades ago, were thought to be beyond the reach of psychotherapy. As noted earlier, there is evidence that conventional cognitive-behavior therapy interventions, in which patients are encouraged to evaluate their beliefs and the evidence pertaining to them, are modestly effective (Mehl et al., 2015; Sitko et al., 2020). However, more recent trials have begun to target processes and psychological mechanisms which are thought to exacerbate paranoid thinking, such as sleep abnormalities (Myers et al., 2011) and over-hasty reasoning (Garety et al., 2021). In many ways, therefore, research on paranoia is a model of how clinical psychological science can progress from small-scale experimental studies to interventions that make a real difference to the lives of vulnerable people. It is to be hoped that this progress will continue in the years ahead.

## References

Abramson, L. Y., Seligman, M. E. P., & Teasdale, J. D. (1978). Learned helplessness in humans: Critique and reformulation. *Journal of Abnormal Psychology, 78*, 40–74. https://doi.org/10.1037/0021-843X.87.1.49

Alemany, S., Goldberg, X., van Winkel, R., Gastro, C., Peralta, V., & Fananas, L. (2013). Childhood adversity and psychosis: Examining whether the association is due to genetic confounding using a monozygotic twin differences approach. *European Psychiatry, 28*, 207–212. https://doi.org/10.1016/j.eurpsy.2012.03.001

Alganami, F., Varese, F., Wagstaff, G. F., & Bentall, R. P. (2017). Suggestibility and signal detection performance in hallucination-prone students. *Cognitive Neuropsychiatry, 22*, 159–174. https://doi.org/10.1080/13546805.2017.1294056

Arseneault, L., Cannon, M., Fisher, H. L., Polanczyk, G., Moffitt, T. E., & Caspi, A. (2011). Childhood trauma and children's emerging psychotic symptoms: A genetically sensitive longitudinal cohort study. *American Journal of Psychiatry, 168*, 65–72. https://doi.org/10.1176/appi.ajp.2010.10040567

Barber, T. X., & Calverley, D. S. (1964). An experimental study of "hypnotic" (auditory and visual) hallucinations. *Journal of Abnormal and Social Psychology, 63*, 13–20. https://doi.org/10.1037/h0042175

Baron-Cohen, S. (1995). *Mindblindness: An essay on autism and theory of mind*. MIT Press.

Baron-Cohen, S., Leslie, A. M., & Frith, U. (1985). Does the autistic child have a 'theory of mind'? *Cognition, 21*, 37–46. https://doi.org/10.1016/0010-0277(85)90022-8

Barton, J., Kyle, S. D., Varese, F., Jones, S. H., & Haddock, G. (2018). Are sleep disturbances causally linked to the presence and severity of psychotic-like, dissociative and hypomanic experiences in non-clinical populations? A systematic review. *Neuroscience and Biobehavioral Reviews, 89*, 119–131. https://doi.org/10.1016/j.neubiorev.2018.02.008

Bebbington, P., McBride, O., Steel, C., Kuipers, E., Radovanovič, M., Brugha, T., Jenkins, R., Meltzer, H. I., & Freeman, D. (2013). The structure of paranoia in the general population. *British Journal of Psychiatry, 202*, 419–427. https://doi.org/10.1192/bjp.bp.112.119032

Bebbington, P., & Nayani, T. (1995). The Psychosis Screening Questionnaire. *International Journal of Methods in Psychiatric Research, 5*, 11–19.

Bell, V., Halligan, P. W., & Ellis, H. D. (2006). Diagnosing delusions: A review of inter-rater reliability. *Schizophrenia Research, 86*(1–3), 76–79. https://doi.org/10.1016/j.schres.2006.06.025

Bentall, R. P. (2003). *Madness explained: Psychosis and human nature*. Penguin.

Bentall, R. P. (2009). Formulating Zeppi: A commentary. In P. Sturmey (Ed.), *Clinical case formulation: Varieties of approaches* (pp. 119–131). Wiley.

Bentall, R. P. (2018). Delusions and other beliefs. In L. Bortolotti (Ed.), *Delusions in context* (pp. 67–96). Palgrave Macmillan. https://www.palgrave.com/us/book/9783319972015

Bentall, R. P. (2021). The role of early life experience in psychosis. In C. A. Tamminga, E. I. Ivleva, U. Reininghaus, & J. van Os (Eds.), *Psychotic disorders: Comprehensive conceptualization and treatments* (pp. 406–414). Oxford University Press.

Bentall, R. P., Corcoran, R., Howard, R., Blackwood, N., & Kinderman, P. (2001). Persecutory delusions: A review and theoretical integration. *Clinical Psychology*

*Review, 21,* 1143–1192. https://doi.org/10.1016/S0272-7358(01)00106-4

Bentall, R. P., & Fernyhough, C. (2008). Social predictors of psychotic experiences: Specificity and psychological mechanisms. *Schizophrenia Bulletin, 34,* 1009–1011. https://doi.org/10.1093/schbul/sbn103

Bentall, R. P., Kinderman, P., Howard, R., Blackwood, N., Cummins, S., Rowse, G., Knowles, R., & Corcoran, R. (2008). Paranoid delusions in schizophrenia and depression: The transdiagnostic role of expectations of negative events and negative self-esteem. *Journal of Nervous and Mental Disease, 196,* 375–383. https://doi.org/10.1097/NMD.0b013e31817108db

Bentall, R. P., Kinderman, P., & Kaney, S. (1994). The self, attributional processes and abnormal beliefs: Towards a model of persecutory delusions. *Behaviour Research and Therapy, 32,* 331–341. https://doi.org/10.1016/0005-7967(94)90131-7

Bentall, R. P., Kinderman, P., & Moutoussis, M. (2008). The role of self-esteem in paranoid delusions: The psychology, neurophysiology, and development of persecutory beliefs. In D. Freeman, R. P. Bentall, & P. Garety (Eds.), *Persecutory delusions: Assessment, theory and treatment* (pp. 145–175). Oxford University Press.

Bentall, R. P., Rowse, G., Shryane, N., Kinderman, P., Howard, R., Blackwood, N., Moore, R., & Corcoran, R. (2009). The cognitive and affective structure of paranoid delusions: A transdiagnostic investigation of patients with schizophrenia spectrum disorders and depression. *Archives of General Psychiatry, 66,* 236–247. https://doi.org/10.1001/archgenpsychiatry.2009.1

Bentall, R. P., Wickham, S., Shevlin, M., & Varese, F. (2012). Do specific early life adversities lead to specific symptoms of psychosis? A study from the 2007 The Adult Psychiatric Morbidity Survey. *Schizophrenia Bulletin, 38,* 734–740. https://doi.org/10.1093/schbul/sbs049

Berrios, G. (1991). Delusions as "wrong beliefs": A conceptual history. *British Journal of Psychiatry, 159*(Suppl 14), 6–13. https://doi.org/10.1192/S0007125000296414

Bierer, L. M., Yehuda, R., Schmeidler, J., Mitropoulo, V., New, A. S., Silverman, J. M., & Siever, L. J. (2014). Abuse and neglect in childhood: Relationship to personality disorder diagnoses. *CNS Spectrums, 8*(10), 737–754. https://doi.org/10.1017/S1092852900019118

Blaney, P. H. (2015). Paranoid and delusional disorders. In P. H. Blaney, R. F. Krueger, & T. Millon (Eds.), *Oxford textbook of psychopathology* (pp. 383–417). Oxford University Press.

Blashfield, R. K. (1984). *The classification of psychopathology: NeoKraepelinian and quantitative approaches.* Plenum.

Bora, E., Bartholomeusz, C., & Pantelis, C. (2016). Meta-analysis of Theory of Mind (ToM) impairment in bipolar disorder. *Psychological Medicine, 46*(2), 253–264. https://doi.org/10.1017/S0033291715001993

Bora, E., & Berk, M. (2016). Theory of mind in major depressive disorder: A meta-analysis. *Journal of Affective Disorders, 191,* 49–55. https://doi.org/10.1016/j.jad.2015.11.023

Bosqui, T. J., Hoy, K., & Shannon, C. (2014). A systematic review and meta-analysis of the ethnic density effect in psychotic disorders. *Social Psychiatry and Psychiatric Epidemiology, 49,* 519–529. https://doi.org/10.1007/s00127-013-0773-0

Bovet, P., & Parnas, J. (1993). Schizophrenic delusions: A phenomenological approach. *Schizophrenia Bulletin, 19,* 579–597. https://doi.org/10.1093/schbul/19.3.579

Bowlby, J. (1969). *Attachment and loss: Vol 1. Attachment.* Hogarth Press.

Bronstein, M. V., Dovidio, J. F., & Cannon, T. D. (2017). Both bias against disconfirmatory evidence and political orientation partially explain the relationship between dogmatism and racial prejudice. *Personality and Individual Differences, 105,* 89–94. https://doi.org/10.1016/j.paid.2016.09.036

Broome, M. R., Harland, R., Owen, G. S., & Stringaris, A. (Eds.). (2012). *The Maudsley reader in phenomenological psychiatry.* Cambridge University Press.

Brown, P., Waite, F., & Freeman, D. (2021). Parenting behaviour and paranoia: A network analysis and results from the National Comorbidity Survey-Adolescents (NCS-A). *Social Psychiatry and Psychiatric Epidemiology, 56,* 593–604. https://doi.org/10.1007/s00127-020-01933-6

Buchanan, A., Reed, A., Wessely, S., Garety, P., Taylor, P., Grubin, D., & Dunn, G. (1993). Acting on delusions II: The phenomenological correlates of acting on delusions. *British Journal of Psychiatry, 163,* 77–81. https://doi.org/10.1192/bjp.163.1.77

Casey, D. A. (2009). A psychiatric approach to case formulation. In P. Sturmey (Ed.), *Clinical case formulation: Varieties of approaches* (pp. 93–106). Wiley.

Castillejos, M. C., Martin-Pérez, C., & Moreno-Küstner, B. (2018). A systematic review and meta-analysis of the incidence of psychotic disorders: The distribution of rates and the influence of gender, urbanicity, immigration and socioeconomic level. *Psychological Medicine, 48,* 2101–2115. https://doi.org/10.1017/S0033291718000235

Cermolacce, M., Sass, L., & Parnas, J. (2010). What is bizarre in bizarre delusions?: A critical review. *Schizophrenia Bulletin, 36*(4), 667–679. https://doi.org/10.1093/schbul/sbq001

Chadwick, P., Trower, P., Juusti-Butler, T.-M., & Maguire, N. (2005). Phenomenological evidence for two types of paranoia. *Psychopathology, 38,* 327–333. https://doi.org/10.1159/000089453

Cheesman, R., Selzam, S., Ronald, A., Dale, P. S., McAdams, T. A., Eley, T. C., & Plomin, R. (2017). Childhood behaviour problems show the greatest gap between DNA-based and twin heritability. *Nature Translational Psychiatry, 7,* 1284. https://doi.org/10.1038/s41398-017-0046-x

Colbert, S. M., Peters, E. R., & Garety, P. A. (2010). Delusions and belief flexibility in psychosis. *Psychology and Psychotherapy: Theory, Practice, Research, 83,* 45–57. https://doi.org/10.1348/147608309X467320

Colby, K. M. (1977). Appraisal of four psychological theories of paranoid phenomena. *Journal of Abnormal Psychology, 86,* 54–59. https://doi.org/10.1037/0021-843X.86.1.54

Collin, S., Rowse, G., Martinez, A., & Bentall, R. P. (in submission). Delusions and the dilemmas of life: A systematic review and meta-analyses of the global literature on the prevalence of delusional themes in clinical groups.

Combs, D. R., Penn, D. L., Cassisi, J., Michael, C., Wood, T., Wanner, J., & Adams, S. (2006). Perceived racism as a predictor of paranoia among African Americans. *Journal of Black Psychology, 32,* 87–104. https://doi.org/10.1177/0095798405283175

Combs, D. R., Penn, D. L., & Fenigstein, A. (2002). Ethnic differences in subclinical paranoia: An expansion of norms of the Paranoia Scale. *Cultural Diversity and Ethnic Minority Psychology, 8,* 248–256. https://doi.org/10.1037/1099-9809.8.3.248

Compton, M. T., Potts, A. A., Wan, C. R., & Ionesc. (2012). Which came first, delusions or hallucinations? An exploration of clinical differences among patients with first-episode psychosis based on patterns of emergence of positive symptoms. *Psychiatry Research, 20*, 702–707. https://doi.org/10.1016/j.psychres.2012.07.041

Conrad, K. (1958/2012). Beginning schizophrenia: Attempt for a Gestalt-analysis of delusion. In M. R. Broome, R. Harland, G. S. Owen, & A. Stringaris (Eds.), *The Maudsley reader in phenomenological psychiatry* (pp. 176–193). Cambridge University Press.

Cooper, A. F., & Curry, A. R. (1976). The pathology of deafness in the paranoid and affective psychoses of later life. *Journal of Psychosomatic Medicine, 20*, 97–105. https://doi.org/10.1016/0022-3999(76)90035-0

Cooper, J. E., Kendell, R. E., Gurland, B. J., Sharpe, L., Copeland, J. R. M., & Simon, R. (1972). *Psychiatric diagnosis in New York and London: Maudsley Monograph No. 20*. Oxford University Press.

Corcoran, C., Mercer, G., & Frith, C. D. (1995). Schizophrenia, symptomatology and social inference: Investigating "theory of mind" in people with schizophrenia. *Schizophrenia Research, 17*, 513. https://doi.org/10.1016/0920-9964(95)00024-G

Corcoran, R., Cahill, C., & Frith, C. D. (1997). The appreciation of visual jokes in people with schizophrenia: A study of 'mentalizing' ability. *Schizophrenia Research, 24*, 319–327. https://doi.org/10.1016/S0920-9964(96)00117-X

Corcoran, R., Mansfield, R., de Bezenac, C., Anderson, E., Overbury, K., & Marshall, G. (2018). Perceived neighbourhood affluence, mental health and wellbeing influence judgements of threat and trust on our streets: An urban walking study. *Plos One, 13*, e0202412. https://doi.org/10.1371/journal.pone.0202412

Corcoran, R., Rowse, G., Moore, R., Blackwood, N., Kinderman, P., Howard, R., Cummins, S., & Bentall, R. P. (2008). A transdiagnostic investigation of theory of mind and jumping to conclusions in paranoia: A comparison of schizophrenia and depression with and without delusions. *Psychological Medicine, 38*, 1577–1583. https://doi.org/10.1017/S003329 1707002152

Craig, J., Hatton, C., & Bentall, R. P. (2004). Persecutory beliefs, attributions and Theory of Mind: Comparison of patients with paranoid delusions, Asperger's Syndrome and healthy controls. *Schizophrenia Research, 69*, 29–33. https://doi.org/10.1016/S0920-9964(03)00154-3

Dalenberg, C. J., Brand, B. L., Gleaves, D. H., Dorahy, M. J., Loewenstein, R. J., Cardeña, E., Frewen, P. A., Carlson, E. B., & Spiegel, D. (2012). Evaluation of the evidence for the trauma and fantasy models of dissociation. *Psychological Bulletin, 138*, 550–588. https://doi.org/10.1037/a0027447

Dimech, A., Kingdon, D., & Swelam, M. (2009). Zeppi: A case of psychosis. In P. Sturmey (Ed.), *Clinical case formulation: Varieties of approaches* (pp. 85–92). Wiley.

Dowbiggin, I. (2000). Delusional diagnosis? The history of paranoia as a disease concept in the modern era. *History of Psychiatry, 41*(1), 37–69. https://doi.org/10.1177/0957154 X0001104103

Dudley, R., Taylor, P., Wickham, S., & Hutton, P. (2016). Psychosis, delusions and the 'jumping to conclusions' reasoning bias: A systematic review and meta-analysis. *Schizophrenia Bulletin, 42*, 652–665. https://doi.org/10.1093/schbul/sbv150

Eifler, S., Rausch, F., Schirmbeck, F., Veckenstedt, R., Englisch, S., Meyer-Lindenberg, A., Kirsch, P., & Zink, M. (2014). Neurocognitive capabilities modulate the integration of evidence in schizophrenia. *Psychiatry Research, 219*(1), 72–78. https://doi.org/10.1016/j.psychres.2014.04.056

Elahi, A., McIntyre, J. C., Hampson, C., Bodycote, H., Sitko, K., & Bentall, R. P. (2018). Home is where you hang your hat: Host town identity, but not hometown identity, protects against mental health symptoms associated with financial stress. *Journal of Social and Clinical Psychology, 37*, 159–181. https://doi.org/10.1521/jscp.2018.37.3.159

Elahi, A., Perez Algorta, G., Varese, F., McIntyre, J. C., & Bentall, R. P. (2017). Do paranoid delusions exist on a continuum with subclinical paranoia? A multi-method taxometric study. *Schizophrenia Research, 190*, 77–81. https://doi.org/10.1016/j.schres.2017.03.022

Ellett, L., Freeman, D., & Garety, P. A. (2008). The psychological effect of an urban environment on individuals with persecutory delusions: The Camberwell walk study. *Schizophrenia Research, 99*, 77–84. https://doi.org/10.1016/j.schres.2007.10.027

Enoch, M. D., & Trethowan, W. H. (1979). *Uncommon psychiatric syndromes*, 2nd ed. Wright.

Faris, R. E. L., & Dunham, H. W. (1939). *Mental disorders in urban areas*. Chicago University Press.

Fenigstein, A., & Vanable, P. A. (1992). Paranoia and self-consciousness. *Journal of Personality and Social Psychology, 62*, 129–134. https://doi.org/10.1037/0022-3514.62.1.129

Feyaerts, J., Henricksen, M. G., Vanheule, S., Myin-Germeys, I., & Saas, L. A. (2021). Delusions beyond beliefs: A critical overview of diagnostic, aetiological, and therapeutic schizophrenia research from a clinical-phenomenological perspecti. *Lancet Psychiatry*. https://doi.org/10.1016/S2215-0366(20)30460-0

Fisher, H. L., Criag, T. K., Fearon, P., Morgan, K., Dazzan, P., Lappin, J., Hitchinson, G., Doody, G. A., Jones, P. B., McGuffin, P., Murray, R. M., Leff, J., & Morgan, C. (2011). Reliability and comparability of psychosis patients' retrospective reports of childhood abuse. *Schizophrenia Bulletin, 37*, 546–553. https://doi.org/10.1093/schbul/sbp103

Fowler, D., Freeman, D., Smith, B., Kuipers, E., Bebbington, P., Bashforth, H., Coker, S., Hodgekins, J., Gracie, A., Dunn, G., & Garety, P. (2006). The Brief Core Schema Scales (BCSS): Psychometric properties and associations with paranoia and grandiosity in non-clinical and clinical samples. *Psychological Medicine, 36*, 749–759. https://doi.org/10.1017/S0033291706007355

Fowler, D., Hodgekins, J., Garety, P. A., Freeman, D., Kuipers, E., Dunn, G., Smith, B., & Bebbington, P. E. (2012). Negative cognition, depressed mood, and paranoia: A longitudinal pathway analysis using structural equation modeling. *Schizophrenia Bulletin, 38*, 1063–1073. https://doi.org/10.1093/schbul/sbr019

Freeman, D. (2008). The assessment of persecutory ideation. In D. Freeman, R. Bentall, & P. Garety (Eds.), *Persecutory delusions: Assessment, theory, treatment* (pp. 23–52). Oxford University Press.

Freeman, D. (2016). Persecutory delusions: A cognitive perspective on understanding and treatment. *Lancet Psychiatry, 7*, 685–692. https://doi.org/10.1016/S2215-0366(16)00066-3

Freeman, D., Dunn, G., Murray, R. M., Evans, N., Lister, R., Antley, A., Slater, M., Godlewska, B., Cornish, R., Williams, J., Di Simplicio, M., Igoumenou, A., Brenneisen, R., Turnbridge, E. M., Harrison, P. J., Harmer, C. J.,

Dowen, P., & Morrison, P. D. (2014). How cannabis causes paranoia: Using the intravenous administration of Δ9-Tetrahydrocannabinol (THC) to identify key cognitive mechanisms leading to paranoia. *Schizophrenia Bulletin, 41*, 391–399. https://doi.org/10.1093/schbul/sbu098

Freeman, D., & Garety, P. A. (2000). Comments on the contents of persecutory delusions: Does the definition need clarification? *British Journal of Clinical Psychology, 39*, 407–414. https://doi.org/10.1348/014466500163400

Freeman, D., Garety, P. A., Bebbington, P. E., Smith, B., Rollinson, R., Fowler, D., Kuipers, E., Ray, K., & Dunn, G. (2005). Psychological investigation of the structure of paranoia in a non-clinical population. *British Journal of Psychiatry, 186*, 427–435. https://doi.org/10.1192/bjp.186.5.42

Freeman, D., Garety, P. A., Kuipers, E., Fowler, D., & Bebbington, P. E. (2002). A cognitive model of persecutory delusions. *British Journal of Clinical Psychology, 41*, 331–347. https://doi.org/10.1348/014466502760387461

Freeman, D., Garety, P. A., Kuipers, E., Fowler, D., Bebbington, P. E., & Dunn, G. (2007). Acting on persecutory delusions: The importance of safety seeking. *Behaviour Research and Therapy, 45*, 89–99. https://doi.org/10.1016/j.brat.2006.01.014

Freeman, D., Loe, B. S., Kingdon, D., Startup, H., Molodynski, A., Rosebrock, L., Brown, P., Sheaves, B., Waite, F., & Bird, J. C. (2021). The revised Green et al., Paranoid Thoughts Scale (R-GPTS): Psychometric properties, severity ranges, and clinical cut-offs. *Psychological Medicine, 51*(2), 244–253. https://doi.org/10.1017/S0033291719003155

Freeman, D., Pugh, K., & Garety, P. (2008). Jumping to conclusions and paranoid ideation in the general population. *Schizophrenia Research, 102*, 254–260. https://doi.org/10.1016/j.schres.2008.03.020

Freeman, D., Pugh, K., Vorontsoya, N., & Southgate, L. (2009). Insomnia and paranoia. *Schizophrenia Research, 108*, 280–284. https://doi.org/10.1016/j.schres.2008.12.001

Freeman, D., Stahl, D., McManus, S., Meltzer, H., Brugha, T., Wiles, N., & Bebbington, P. (2011). Insomnia, worry, anxiety and depression as predictors of the occurrence and persistence of paranoid thinking. *Social Psychiatry and Psychiatric Epidemiology*. https://doi.org/10.1007/s00127-011-0433-1

Frith, C. (1994). Theory of mind in schizophrenia. In A. S. David & J. C. Cutting (Eds.), *The neuropsychology of schizophrenia* (pp. 147–161). Erlbaum.

Frith, C. D. (1992). *The cognitive neuropsychology of schizophrenia*. Erlbaum.

Garety, P., Gittins, M., Jolley, S., Bebbington, P., Dunn, G., Kuipers, E., Fowler, D., & Freeman, D. (2013). Differences in cognitive and emotional processes between persecutory and grandiose delusions. *Schizophrenia Bulletin, 39*(3), 629–639. https://doi.org/10.1093/schbul/sbs059

Garety, P. A., Hemsley, D. R., & Wessely, S. (1991). Reasoning in deluded schizophrenic and paranoid patients. *Journal of Nervous and Mental Disease, 179*(4), 194–201.

Green, C. E. L., Freeman, D., Kuipers, E., Bebbington, P., Fowler, D., Dunn, G., & Garety, P. (2008). Measuring ideas of persecution and social reference: The Green et al. Paranoid Thought Scales (GPTS). *Psychological Medicine, 38*, 101–111. https://doi.org/10.1017/S0033291707001638

Garety, P. A, Ward, T., Emsley, R., Greenwood, K., Freeman, D., Fowler, D., Kuipers, E., Bebbington, P., Rus-Calafell, M., McGourty, A., Sacdura, C., Collett, N., James, K., & Hardy, A. (2021). Effects of SlowMo, a blended digital therapy targeting reasoning, on paranoia among people with psychosis: A randomized clinical trial. *JAMA Psychiatry, 78*(7), 714–725. https://doi.org/10.1001/jamapsychiatry.2021.0326

Grieg, T., C., Bryson, G. J., & Bell, M. D. (2004). Theory of mind performance in schizophrenia: Diagnostic, symptom, and neuropsychological correlates. *Journal of Nervous & Mental Disease, 192*(1), 12–18. https://doi.org/10.1097/01.nmd.0000105995.67947.fc

Haddock, G., Slade, P. D., & Bentall, R. P. (1995). Auditory hallucinations and the verbal transformation effect: The role of suggestions. *Personality and Individual Differences, 19*, 301–306. https://doi.org/10.1016/0191-8869(95)00063-C

Hardy, A. (1979). *The spiritual nature of man: Study of contemporary religious experience*. Oxford University Press.

Haslam, S. A., Jetten, J., Postmes, T., & Haslam, C. (2009). Social identity, health and well-being: An emerging agenda for applied psychology. *Applied Psychology, 58*, 1–23. https://doi.org/10.1111/j.1464-0597.2008.00379.x

Heilskof, S. E. R., Urfer-Parnas, A., & Norgaard, J. (2020). Delusions in the general population: A systematic review with emphasis on methodology. *Schizophrenia Research, 216*, 48–55. https://doi.org/10.1016/j.schres.2019.10.043

Hoehne, K. A. (1988). Ernst Kretschmer's multidimensional psychiatry. *Journal of Personality Disorders, 2*(1), 28–35. https://doi.org/10.1521/pedi.1988.2.1.28

Hoenig, J. (1980). Psychiatric nosology. *Canadian Journal of Psychiatry, 26*(2), 85.

Hoenig, J. (1982). Kurt Schneider and anglophone psychiatry. *Comprehensive Psychiatry, 23*, 391–400. https://doi.org/10.1016/0010-440X(82)90152-3

Hofstadter, R. (1964). The paranoid style in American politics. *Harpers Magazine*. https://harpers.org/archive/1964/11/the-paranoid-style-in-american-politics/

Humphrey, C., Bucci, S., Varese, F., Degnan, A., & Berry, K. (2021). Paranoia and negative schema about the self and others: A systematic review and meta-analysis. *Clinical Psychology Review, 90*, 102081. https://doi.org/10.1016/j.cpr.2021.102081

Huq, S. F., Garety, P. A., & Hemsley, D. R. (1988). Probabilistic judgements in deluded and nondeluded subjects. *Quarterly Journal of Experimental Psychology, 40A*, 801–812. https://doi.org/10.1080/14640748808402300

Jackson, M., & Fulford, K. W. M. (1997). Spiritual experience and psychopathology. *Philosophy, Psychiatry and Psychology, 4*(1), 41–65. https://doi.org/10.1353/ppp.1997.0002

Janssen, I., Hanssen, M., Bak, M., Bijl, R. V., De Graaf, R., Vollenberg, W., McKenzie, K., & van Os, J. (2003). Discrimination and delusional ideation. *British Journal of Psychiatry, 182*, 71–76. https://doi.org/10.1192/bjp.182.1.71

Jaspers, K. (1912/1968). The phenomenological approach in psychopathology. *British Journal of Psychiatry, 114*, 1313–1323. https://doi.org/10.1192/bjp.114.516.1313

Jaspers, K. (1913/1963). *General psychopathology* (J. Hoenig & M. W. Hamilton, Trans.). Manchester University Press.

Johnson, S. L., Wibbels, E., & Wilkinson, R. (2015). Economic inequality is related to cross-national prevalence of psychotic symptoms. *Social Psychiatry and Psychiatric Epidemiology, 50*, 1799–1807. https://doi.org/10.1007/s00127-015-1112-4

Jones, R. B., Thapar, A., Lewis, G., & Zammit, S. (2012). The association between early autistic traits and psychotic experiences in adolescence. *Schizophrenia Research, 135*(1–3), 164–169. https://doi.org/10.1016/j.schres.2011.11.037

Kaney, S., & Bentall, R. P. (1989). Persecutory delusions and attributional style. *British Journal of Medical Psychology, 62*, 191–198. https://doi.org/10.1111/j.2044-8341.1989.tb02826.x

Kaney, S., & Bentall, R. P. (1992). Persecutory delusions and the self-serving bias. *Journal of Nervous and Mental Disease, 180*, 773–780. https://doi.org/10.1097/00005053-199212000-00006

Kay, S. R., & Opler, L. A. (1987). The Positive and Negative Syndrome Scale (PANSS) for schizophrenia. *Schizophrenia Bulletin, 13*, 507–518. https://doi.org/10.1093/schbul/13.2.261

Kendler, K. (2017). The clinical features of paranoia in the 20th century and their representation in diagnostic criteria from DSM-III through DSM-5. *Schizophrenia Bulletin, 43*(2), 332–343. https://doi.org/10.1093/schbul/sbw161

Kendler, K. (2018). The development of Kraepelin's mature diagnostic concepts of paranoia (die verrücktheit) and paranoid dementia praecox (dementia paranoides): A close reading of his textbooks from 1887 to 1899. *JAMA Psychiatry, 75*(12), 1280–1288. https://doi.org/10.1001/jamapsychiatry.2018.2377

Kendler, K. (2020). The development of Kraepelin's concept of dementia praecox: A close reading of relevant texts. *JAMA Psychiatry, 77*(11), 1181–1187. https://doi.org/10.1001/jamapsychiatry.2020.1266

Kendler, K. S. (1980). The nosological validity of paranoia (simple delusional disorder): A review. *Archives of General Psychiatry, 37*, 699–706. https://doi.org/10.1001/archpsyc.1980.01780190097012

Kendler, K. S. (1995). Delusional disorder. In G. Berrios & R. Porter (Eds.), *A history of clinical psychiatry: The origin and history of psychiatric disorders* (pp. 360–371). Athlone Press.

Kendler, K. S. (2015). A joint history of the nature of genetic variation and the nature of schizophrenia. *Molecular Psychiatry, 20*, 77–83. https://doi.org/10.1038/mp.2014.94

Kendler, K. S., Glazer, W., & Morgenstern, H. (1983). Dimensions of delusional experience. *American Journal of Psychiatry, 140*, 466–469. https://doi.org/10.1176/ajp.140.4.466

Kinderman, P., & Bentall, R. P. (1997). Causal attributions in paranoia: Internal, personal and situational attributions for negative events. *Journal of Abnormal Psychology, 106*, 341–345. https://doi.org/10.1037/0021-843X.106.2.341

Klosterkotter, J., Hellmich, M., Steinmeyer, E. M., & Schultze-Lutter, F. (2001). Diagnosing schizophrenia in the initial prodromal phase. *Archives of General Psychiatry, 58*, 158–164. https://doi.org/10.1001/archpsyc.58.2.158

Krueger, R. F. (2013). Personality disorders are the vangard of the post-DSM-5 era. *Personality Disorders: Theory, Research, and Treatment, 4*(4), 355–362. https://doi.org/10.1037/per0000028

Langdon, R., Corner, T., McLaren, J., Ward, P. B., & Coltheart, M. (2006). Externalizing and personalizing biases in persecutory delusions: The relationship with poor insight and theory-of-mind. *Behaviour Research and Therapy, 36*, 321–330. https://doi.org/10.1016/j.brat.2005.03.012

Lee, R. J. (2017). Mistrustful and misunderstood: A review of paranoid personality disorder. *Current Behavioral and Neuroscience Reports, 4*, 151–165. https://doi.org/10.1007/s40473-017-0116-7

Longden, E., Branitsky, A., Moskowitz, A., Berry, K., Bucci, S., & Varese, F. (2020). The relationship between dissociation and symptoms of psychosis: A meta-analysis. *Schizophrenia Bulletin, 46*(5), 1104–1113. https://doi.org/10.1093/schbul/sbaa037

Lysaker, P., Salvatore, G., Grant, M. L. A., Procacci, M., Olesek, K. L., Buck, K. D., Nicolo, G., & Dimaggio, G. (2016). Deficits in theory of mind and social anxiety as independent paths to paranoid features in schizophrenia. *Schizophrenia Research, 124*(1–3), 81–85. https://doi.org/10.1016/j.schres.2010.06.019

Maher, B. A., & Ross, J. S. (1984). Delusions. In H. E. Adams & P. Suther (Eds.), *Comprehensive handbook of psychopathology* (pp. 383–408). Plenum.

Martinez, A. P., Agostini, M., Alsuhibani, A., & Bentall, R. P. (2021). Mistrust and negative self-esteem: Two paths from attachment styles to paranoia. *Psychology and Psychotherapy: Theory, Practice, Research, 94*, 391–406. https://doi.org/10.1111/papt.12314

Martinez, A. P., Wickham, S., Rowse, G., Milne, E., & Bentall, R. P. (2021). Robust association between autistic traits and psychotic-like experiences in the adult general population: Epidemiological study from the 2007 Adult Psychiatric Morbidity Survey and replication with the 2014 APMS. *Psychological Medicine, 51*(15), 2707–2713. https://doi.org/10.1017/S0033291720001373

McElroy, E., McIntyre, J. C., Bentall, R. P., Wilson, T., Holt, K., Kullu, C., Rajan, N., Kerr, A., Panagaki, K., McKeown, M., Saini, P., Gabbay, M., & Corcoran, R. (2019). Mental health, deprivation, and the neighbourhood social environment: A network analysis. *Clinical Psychological Science, 7*, 719–734. https://doi.org/10.1177/2167702619830640

McGrath, J. J., Saha, S., Lim, C., Aguilar-Gaxiola, S., Alonso, J., Andrade, L. H., . . . Kessler, R. C. (2017). Trauma and psychotic experiences: Transnational data from the World Mental Health Survey. *British Journal of Psychiatry, 211*, 373–380. https://doi.org/10.1192/bjp.bp.117.205955

McIntyre, J. C., Elahi, A., Barlow, F. K., White, R. G., & Bentall, R. P. (2019). The relationship between ingroup identity and Paranoid ideation among people from African and African Caribbean backgrounds. *Psychology & Psychotherapy: Theory, Research and Practice, 94*, 16–32. https://doi.org/10.1111/papt.12261

McIntyre, J. C., Elahi, A., & Bentall, R. P. (2016). Social identity and psychosis: Explaining elevated rates of psychosis in migrant populations. *Social and Personality Psychology Compass, 10*, 619–633. https://doi.org/10.1111/spc3.12273

McIntyre, J. C., Wickham, S., Barr, B., & Bentall, R. P. (2018). Social identity and psychosis: Associations and psychological mechanisms. *Schizophrenia Bulletin, 44*, 681–690. https://doi.org/10.1093/schbul/sbx110

McLean, B. F., Mattiske, J. K., & Balzan, R. P. (2016). Association of the jumping to conclusions and evidence integration biases with delusions in psychosis: A detailed meta-analysis. *Schizophrenia Bulletin, 43*(2), 344–354. https://doi.org/10.1093/schbul/sbw056

Mehl, S., Werner, D., & Lincoln, T. (2015). Does cognitive behaviour therapy for psychosis (CBTp) show a sustainable effect on delusions? A meta-analysis. *Frontiers in Psychology, 6*, 1450. https://doi.org/10.3389/fpsyg.2015.01450

Melo, S., Corcoran, R., & Bentall, R. P. (2009). The Persecution and Deservedness Scale. *Psychology and Psychotherapy: Theory,*

Practice, Research, 82, 247–260. https://doi.org/10.1348/147608308X398337

Melo, S., Taylor, J., & Bentall, R. P. (2006). "Poor me" versus "bad me" paranoia and the instability of persecutory ideation. *Psychology & Psychotherapy - Theory, Research, Practice,* 79, 271–287. https://doi.org/10.1348/147608305X52856

Melo, S. S., & Bentall, R. P. (2013). "Poor me" vs. "Bad me" paranoia: The association between self-beliefs and the instability of persecutory ideation. *Psychology & Psychotherapy: Theory, Research and Practice,* 86, 146–163. https://doi.org/10.1111/j.2044-8341.2011.02051.x

Mikulincer, M., & Shaver, P. R. (2007). *Attachment in adulthood: Structure, dynamics and change.* Guilford.

Mintz, S., & Alpert, M. (1972). Imagery vividness, reality testing and schizophrenic hallucinations. *Journal of Abnormal and Social Psychology,* 19, 310–316. https://doi.org/10.1037/h0033209

Mirowsky, J., & Ross, C. E. (1983). Paranoia and the structure of powerlessness. *American Sociological Review,* 48, 228–239. https://doi.org/10.2307/2095107

Mishara, A. L. (2009). Klaus Conrad (1905–1961): Delusional mood, psychosis, and beginning schizophrenia. *Schizophrenia Bulletin,* 36, 9–13. https://doi.org/10.1093/schbul/sbp144

Moffa, G., Catone, G., Kuipers, J.-R., Kuipers, E., Freeman, D., Marwaha, S., Lennox, B. R., Broome, M. R., & Bebbington, P. (2017). Using directed acyclic graphs in epidemiological research in psychosis: An analysis of the role of bullying in psychosis. *Schizophrenia Bulletin,* 43, 1273–1279. https://doi.org/10.1093/schbul/sbx013

Moutoussis, M., Bentall, R. P., El-Deredy, W., & Dayan, P. (2011). Bayesian modeling of Jumping-to-Conclusions Bias in delusional patients. *Cognitive Neuropsychiatry,* 16, 422–447. https://doi.org/10.1080/13546805.2010.548678

Moutoussis, M., Williams, J., Dayan, P., & Bentall, R. P. (2007). Persecutory delusions and the conditioned avoidance paradigm: Towards an integration of the psychology and biology of paranoia. *Cognitive Neuropsychiatry,* 12, 495–510. https://doi.org/10.1080/13546800701566686

Mulder, R. T. (2021). ICD-11 personality disorders: Utility and implications of the new model. *Frontiers of Psychiatry,* 12, 655548. https://doi.org/10.3389/fpsyt.2021.655548

Mullen, R. (2003). The problem of bizarre delusions. *Journal of Nervous & Mental Disease,* 191(8), 546–548. https://doi.org/10.1097/01.nmd.0000082184.39788.de

Müller, H., Betz, L. T., & Bechdolf, A. (2021). A comprehensive meta-analysis of the self-serving bias in schizophrenia spectrum disorders compared to non-clinical subjects. *Neuroscience and Biobehavioral Reviews,* 120, 542–549. https://doi.org/10.1016/j.neubiorev.2020.09.025

Murphy, P., Bentall, R. P., Freeman, D., O'Rourke, S., & Hutton, P. (2018). The paranoia as defence model of persecutory delusions: A systematic review and meta-analysis. *Lancet Psychiatry,* 5, 913–929. https://doi.org/10.1016/S2215-0366(18)30339-0

Murphy, R., Goodall, K., & Woodrow, A. (2020). The relationship between attachment insecurity and experiences on the paranoia continuum: A meta-analysis. *British Journal of Clinical Psychology,* 56(3), 290–318. https://doi.org/10.1111/bjc.12247

Myers, E., Startup, H., & Freeman, D. (2011). Cognitive behavioural treatment of insomnia in individuals with persistent persecutory delusions: A pilot trial. *Behaviour Research and Therapy,* 42, 330–336. https://doi.org/10.1016/j.jbtep.2011.02.004

Ochoa, S., Haro, J. M., Huerta-Ramos, E., Cuevas-Esteban, J., Stephan-Otto, C., Usall, J., Nieto, L., & Brebion, G. (2014). Relation between jumping to conclusions and cognitive functioning in people with schizophrenia in contrast with healthy participants. *Schizophrenia Research,* 159(1), 211–217. https://doi.org/10.1016/j.schres.2014.07.026

Oorschot, M., Lataster, T., Thewissen, V., Bentall, R. P., Delespaul, P., & Myin-Germeys, I. (2012). Temporal dynamics of visual and auditory hallucinations. *Schizophrenia Research,* 140, 77–82. https://doi.org/10.1016/j.schres.2012.06.010

Owen, M. J. (2012, Sep). Implications of genetic findings for understanding schizophrenia. *Schizophrenia Bulletin,* 38(5), 904–907. https://doi.org/10.1093/schbul/sbs103

Peters, E. R., Joseph, S. A., & Garety, P. A. (1999). Measurement of delusional ideation in the normal population: Introducing the PDI (Peters et al. Delusions Inventory). *Schizophrenia Bulletin,* 25, 553–576. https://doi.org/10.1093/oxfordjournals.schbul.a033401

Pickering, L., Simpson, J., & Bentall, R. P. (2008). Insecure attachment predicts proneness to paranoia but not hallucinations. *Personality and Individual Differences,* 44, 1212–1224. https://doi.org/10.1016/J.PAID.2007.11.016

Pilton, M., Varese, F., Berry, K., & Bucci, S. (2016). The relationship between dissociation and voices: A systematic literature review and meta-analysis. *Clinical Psychology Review,* 40, 138–165. https://doi.org/10.1016/j.cpr.2015.06.004

Premack, D., & Woodruff, G. (1978). Does the chimpanzee have a theory of mind? *Behavioural and Brain Sciences,* 4, 515–526. https://doi.org/10.1017/S0140525X00076512

Qi, R., Palmier-Claus, J., Simpson, J., Varese, F., & Bentall, R. P. (2020). Sexual minority status and symptoms of psychosis: The role of bullying, discrimination, social support, and drug use–Findings from the Adult Psychiatric Morbidity Survey 2007. *Psychology and Psychotherapy: Theory, Research and Practice,* 93, 503–519. https://doi.org/10.1111/papt.12242

Rankin, P., Bentall, R. P., Hill, J., & Kinderman, P. (2005). Perceived relationships with parents and paranoid delusions: Comparisons of currently ill, remitted and normal participants. *Psychopathology,* 38, 16–25. https://doi.org/10.1159/000083966

Reed, G. F. (2018). Progress in developing a classification of personality disorders for ICD-11. *World Psychiatry,* 17(2), 227–229. https://doi.org/10.1002/wps.20533

Reichborn-Kjennerud, T. (2010). The genetic epidemiology of personality disorders. *Dialogues in Clinical Neuroscience,* 12(1), 103–114. https://doi.org/10.31887/DCNS.2010.12.1/trkjennerud

Rippy, A. E., & Newman, E. (2006). Perceived religious discrimination and its relationship to anxiety and paranoia amongst Muslim Americans. *Journal of Muslim Mental Health*(5), 5–20. https://doi.org/10.1080/15564900600654351

Safer, A., & Dazzi, F. (2019). Meta-analysis of the positive and Negative Syndrome Scale (PANSS) factor structure. *Journal of Psychiatric Research,* 115, 113–120. https://doi.org/10.1016/j.jpsychires.2019.05.008

Sarfati, Y., & Hardy-Bayle, M. C. (1999). How do people with schizophrenia explain the behaviour of others? A study of theory of mind and its relationship to thought and speech disorganization in schizophrenia. *Psychological Medicine,* 29, 613–620. https://doi.org/10.1017/S0033291799008326

Schlier, B., Moritz, S., & Lincoln, T. (2016). Measuring fluctuations in paranoia: Validity and psychometric properties of brief state versions of the Paranoia Checklist. *Psychiatry Research, 241*, 323–332. https://doi.org/10.1016/j.psychres.2016.05.002

Shevlin, M., McAnee, G., Bentall, R. P., & Murphy, K. (2015). Specificity of association between adversities and the occurrence and co-occurrence paranoia and hallucinations: Evaluating the stability of risk in an adverse adult environment. *Psychosis, 7*, 206–216. https://doi.org/10.1080/17522439.2014.980308

Sieradzka, D., Power, R. A., Freeman, D., Cardno, A. G., Dudbridge, F., & Ronald, A. (2015). Heritability of individual psychotic experiences captured by common genetic variants in a community sample of adolescents. *Behavior Genetics, 45*, 493–502. https://doi.org/10.1007/s10519-015-9727-5

Sitko, K., Bentall, R. P., Shevlin, M., O'Sullivan, N., & Sellwood, W. (2014). Associations between specific psychotic symptoms and specific childhood adversities are mediated by attachment styles: An analysis of the National Comorbidity Survey. *Psychiatry Research, 217*, 202–209. https://doi.org/10.1016/j.psychres.2014.03.019

Sitko, K., Bewick, B. M., Owens, D., & Masterson, C. (2020). Meta-analysis and meta-regression of cognitive behavioral therapy for psychosis (CBTp) across time: The effectiveness of CBTp has improved for delusions. *Schizophrenia Bulletin Open, 1*(1), sgaa023. https://doi.org/10.1093/schizbullopen/sgaa023

Sitko, K., Varese, F., & Bentall, R. P. (2016). Paranoia and attachment in daily life: An experience sampling study. *Psychiatry Research, 246*, 32–38. https://doi.org/10.1016/j.psychres.2014.03.019

Smari, J., Stefansson, S., & Thorgilsson, H. (1994). Paranoia, self-consciousness and social cognition in schizophrenics. *Cognitive Therapy and Research, 18*, 387–399. https://doi.org/10.1007/BF02357512

Smith, L. M., Johns, L. C., & Mitchell, R. L. C. (2017). Characterizing the experience of auditory verbal hallucinations and accompanying delusions in individuals with a diagnosis of bipolar disorder: A systematic review. *Bipolar Disorder, 19*, 417–433. https://doi.org/10.1111/bdi.12520

So, S. H., Freeman, D., Dunn, G., Kapur, S., Kuipers, E., Bebbington, P. E., Fowler, D., & Garety, P. A. (2012). Jumping to conclusions, a lack of belief flexibility and delusional conviction in psychosis: A longitudinal investigation of the structure, frequency, and relatedness of reasoning biases. *Journal of Abnormal Psychology, 121*, 129–139. https://doi.org/10.1037/a0025297

So, S. H., Siu, N. Y., Wong, H., Chan, W., & Garety, P. A. (2016). "Jumping to conclusions" data-gathering bias in psychosis and other psychiatric disorders: Two meta-analyses of comparisons between patients and healthy individuals. *Clinical Psychology Review*, 151–167. https://doi.org/10.1016/j.cpr.2016.05.001

Speechley, W. J., Ngan, E. T. –C., Moritz, S., & Woodward, T. S. (2012). Impaired evidence integration and delusions in schizophrenia. *Journal of Experimental Psychopathology, 3*(4), 688–701. https://doi.org/10.5127/jep.018411

Spitzer, R. L., & Fliess, J. L. (1974). A reanalysis of the reliability of psychiatric diagnosis. *British Journal of Psychiatry, 125*, 341–347. https://doi.org/10.1192/bjp.125.4.341

Startup, M., & Startup, S. (2005). On two kinds of delusions of reference. *Psychiatry Research, 137*, 87–92. https://doi.org/10.1016/j.psychres.2005.07.007

Stefanis, N., Thewissen, V., Bakoula, C., van Os, J., & Myin-Germeys, I. (2006). Hearing impairment and psychosis: A replication in a cohort of young adults. *Schizophrenia Research, 85*, 266–272. https://doi.org/10.1016/j.schres.2006.03.036

Sullivan, P. F., Kendler, K. S., & Neale, M. C. (2003). Schizophrenia as a complex trait: Evidence from a meta-analysis of twin studies. *Archives of General Psychiatry, 60*, 1187–1192. https://doi.org/10.1001/archpsyc.60.12.1187

Taber, C. S., & Lodge, M. (2013). *The rationalizing voter*. Cambridge University Press.

Thewissen, V., Myin-Germeys, I., Bentall, R. P., de Graaf, R., Volleberghd, W., & van Os, J. (2005). Hearing impairment and psychosis revisited. *Schizophrenia Research, 76*, 99–103. https://doi.org/10.1016/j.schres.2004.10.013

Thibaudeau, E., Achim, A. M., Parent, C., Turcotte, & Cellard, C. (2020). A meta-analysis of the associations between theory of mind and neurocognition in schizophrenia. *Schizophrenia Research, 216*, 118–128. https://doi.org/10.1016/j.schres.2019.12.017

Thomas, J., Bentall, R. P., Hadden, L., & O'Hara, L. (2016). Ethnic identity and paranoid thinking: Implicit outgroup preference and language dominance predict paranoia in Emirati women. *Journal of Behavior Therapy and Experimental Psychiatry, 56*, 122–128. https://doi.org/10.1016/j.jbtep.2016.10.004

Triebwasser, J., Chemerinski, E., Roussos, P., & Siever, L. J. (2013). Paranoid personality disorder. *Journal of Personality Disorders, 27*(6), 795–803. https://doi.org/101521pedi201226055

Trotta, A., Iyegbe, C., di Forti, M., Sham, P., Campbell, D., Cherny, S. S., Mondelli, V., Aitchison, K. J., Murray, R. M., Vassos, E., & Fisher, H. (2016). Interplay between schizophrenia polygenic risk score and childhood adversity in first presentation psychotic disorder: A pilot study. *Plos One, 11*, e0163319. https://doi.org/doi:10.1371/journal.pone.0163319

Trower, P., & Chadwick, P. (1995). Pathways to defense of the self: A theory of two types of paranoia. *Clinical Psychology: Science and Practice, 2*, 263–278. https://doi.org/10.1111/j.1468-2850.1995.tb00044.x

Udachina, A., Varese, F., Oorschot, M., Myin-Germeys, I., & Bentall, R. P. (2012). Dynamics of self-esteem in 'poor me' and 'bad me' paranoia. *Journal of Nervous and Mental Disease, 200*, 777–783. https://doi.org/10.1097/NMD.0b013e318266ba57

van Os, J., Hanssen, M., Bijl, R. V., & Ravelli, A. (2000). Strauss (1969) revisited: A psychosis continuum in the normal population? *Schizophrenia Research, 45*, 11–20.

van Os, J., & McGuffin, P. (2003). Can the social environment cause schizophrenia? *British Journal of Psychiatry, 182*, 291–292. https://doi.org/10.1192/bjp.182.4.291

Varese, F., Barkus, E., & Bentall, R. P. (2011). Dissociation mediates the relationship between childhood trauma and hallucination-proneness. *Psychological Medicine, 42*, 1025–1036. https://doi.org/10.1017/S0033291711001826

Varese, F., Smeets, F., Drukker, M., Lieverse, R., Lataster, T., Viechtbauer, W., Read, J., van Os, J., & Bentall, R. P. (2012). Childhood adversities increase the risk of psychosis: A meta-analysis of patient-control, prospective and cross-sectional cohort studies. *Schizophrenia Bulletin, 38*, 661–671. https://doi.org/10.1093/schbul/sbs050

Vassos, E., Pedersen, C. B., Murray, R. M., Collier, D. A., & Lewis, C. M. (2012). Meta-analysis of the association of urbanicity with schizophrenia. *Schizophrenia Bulletin, 38*, 1118–1123. https://doi.org/10.1093/schbul/sbs096

Verdoux, H., Maurice-Tison, S., Gay, B., Van Os, J., Salamon, R., & Bourgeois, M. L. (1998). A survey of delusional ideation in primary-care patients. *Psychological Medicine, 28*, 127–134. https://doi.org/10.1017/S003329179700566

Wellman, H. M. (2017). The development of Theory of Mind: Historical reflections. *Child Development Perspectives, 11*(3), 207–214. https://doi.org/10.1111/cdep.12236

Westen, D., Blagov, P. S., Harenski, K., Hamann, S., & Kilts, C. (2006). Neural bases of motivated reasoning: An fMRI study of emotional contraints on partisan polital judgment in the 2004 US Presidential Election. *Journal of Cognitive Neuroscience, 18*, 1947–1958. https://doi.org/10.1162/jocn.2006.18.11.1947

Wickham, S., & Bentall, R. P. (2016). Are specific early life experiences associated with specific symptoms of psychosis: A patients study considering just world beliefs as a mediator. *Journal of Nervous & Mental Disease, 204*, 606–613. https://doi.org/10.1097/NMD.0000000000000511

Wickham, S., Sitko, K., & Bentall, R. P. (2015). Insecure attachment is associated with paranoia but not hallucinations in psychotic patients: The mediating role of negative self esteem. *Psychological Medicine, 45*, 1495–1507. https://doi.org/10.1017/S0033291714002633

Wickham, S., Taylor, P., Shevlin, M., & Bentall, R. P. (2014). The impact of social deprivation on paranoia, hallucinations, mania and depression: The role of discrimination, social support, stress and trust. *Plos One, 9*(8), e105140. https://doi.org/10.1371/journal.pone.0105140

Wicks, S., Hjern, A., Gunnell, D., Lewis, G., & Dalman, C. (2005). Social adversity in childhood and the risk of developing psychosis: A national cohort study. *American Journal of Psychiatry, 162*, 1652–1657. https://doi.org/10.1176/appi.ajp.162.9.1652

Widiger, T. A. (2011). A shaky future for personality disorders. *Personality Disorders: Theory, Research, and Treatment, 2*(1), 54–67. https://doi.org/10.1037/a0021855

Wilder, D. A. (2009). A behavioral analytic fomrulation of a cse of psychosis. In P. Sturmey (Ed.), *Clinical case formulation: Varieties of approaches* (pp. 107–118). Wiley.

Winokur, G. (1977). Delusional disorder (paranoia). *Comprehensive Psychiatry, 18*(6), 511–521. https://doi.org/10.1016/S0010-440X(97)90001-8

Woodward, T. S., Buchy, L., Moritz, S., & Liotti, M. (2007). A bias against disconfirmatory evidence Is associated with delusion proneness in a nonclinical sample. *Schizophrenia Bulletin, 33*(4), 1023–1028. https://doi.org/10.1093/schbul/sbm013

Woodward, T. S., Moritz, S., Cuttler, C., & Whitman, J. C. (2006). The contribution of a cognitive bias against disconfirmatory evidence (BADE) to delusions in dchizophrenia. *Journal of Clinical and Experimental Neuropsychology, 28*(4), 605–617. https://doi.org/10.1080/13803390590949511

Woodward, T. S., Moritz, S., Menon, M., & Klinge, R. (2008). Belief inflexibility in schizophrenia. *Cognitive Neuropsychiatry, 13*(3), 267–277. https://doi.org/10.1080/13546800802099033

World Health Organisation. (1997). *Schedules for clinical assessment in neuropsychiatry, SCAN version 2*. WHO.

World Health Organisation. (1999). *Schedules for clinical assessment in neuropsychiatry*. WHO.

Zavos, H. M. S., Freeman, D., Haworth, C. M. A., McGuire, P., Plomin, R., Cardno, A. G., & Ronald, A. (2014). Consistent etiology of severe, frequent psychotic experiences and milder, less frequent manifestations: A twin study of specific psychotic experiences in adolescence. *JAMA Psychiatry*. https://doi.org/10.1001/jamapsychiatry.2014.994

Zhu, C., Sun, X. J., & So, S. H. (2018). Associations between belief inflexibility and dimensions of delusions: A meta-analytic review of two approaches to assessing belief flexibility. *British Journal of Clinical Psychology, 57*, 59–81. https://doi.org/10.1111/bjc.12154

Zimbardo, P. G., Andersen, S. M., & Kabat, L. G. (1981). Induced hearing deficit generates experimental paranoia. *Science, 212*, 1529–1531. https://doi.org/10.1126/science.7233242

# CHAPTER 17
# Sexual Dysfunction

Cindy M. Meston, Bridget K. Freihart, *and* Amelia M. Stanton

Sexual problems can be broadly conceptualized as the inability to exhibit a sexual response or experience sexual pleasure. For such problems to be diagnosed as a sexual dysfunction, the concerns need to be further identified as personally distressing. Moreover, two additional morbidity criteria were added with release of *DSM-5*: (1) the problem must be persistent, recurrent and/or present during 75–100% of sexual encounters (i.e., a severity criterion), and (2) the individual must have experienced the problem for at least 6 months (i.e., a duration criterion). Each sexual dysfunction is subsequently categorized as lifelong versus acquired and generalized versus situational. A *lifelong disorder* refers to a sexual dysfunction that is chronic and has always been present, whereas an *acquired disorder* refers to a sexual dysfunction that developed after an identified period of unimpaired function. A *generalized sexual dysfunction* refers to a sexual problem that reliably occurs in all contexts; a *situational sexual disorder* refers to a problem that only occurs in certain contexts, such as with specific partners, in specific locations, or while engaging in specific sexual activities. These criteria apply, with some minor variation, to each sexual dysfunction mentioned in this chapter.

Although individuals may present with a range of sexual problems, *DSM-5* recognizes only three major categories of sexual dysfunction: interest/arousal, orgasm, and pain. This chapter provides an overview of the definition, prevalence, and etiology of each of the sexual disorders within these three categories.

## Sexual Interest/Arousal Disorders

Sexual interest, commonly referred to as "desire" or "sex drive," refers to the motivation to engage in sexual activity and/or the feelings that motivate a person to seek sexual activity in both partnered and individual contexts. Sexual arousal, on the other hand, is characterized by readiness for sexual activity. Arousal includes physiological changes that prepare the body for a sexual interaction (e.g., erection, vaginal swelling and lubrication), as well as cognitive shifts (e.g., experiencing positive mental engagement with a sexual stimulus).

### Female Sexual Interest/Arousal Disorder
DEFINITION, DIAGNOSIS, AND PREVALENCE

In *DSM-5*, female sexual interest/arousal disorder (FSIAD) is defined as a significantly reduced or totally absent sense of sexual interest and/or arousal. To receive a diagnosis, a woman must have three of the following six symptoms: absent or reduced interest in sexual activity, absent or reduced sexual thoughts or fantasies, no or reduced initiation of sexual activity, reduced receptivity to a partner's attempts to initiate, absent or reduced sexual excitement or pleasure in almost all or all sexual encounters, absent or reduced sexual interest/arousal in response to any internal or external sexual cues, and absent or reduced genital or nongenital sensations during sexual activity in all or almost all sexual encounters.

| **Abbreviations** | |
|---|---|
| DE | Delayed ejaculation |
| ED | Erectile disorder |
| FOD | Female orgasmic disorder |
| FSAD | Female sexual arousal disorder |
| FSIAD | Female sexual interest/arousal disorder |
| GPPPD | Genito-pelvic pain/penetration disorder |
| HSDD | Hypoactive sexual desire disorder |
| MHSDD | Male hypoactive sexual desire disorder |
| PE | Premature (early) ejaculation |
| PVD | Provoked vestibulodynia |

FSIAD is relatively new to the *DSM*. *DSM-IV-TR* included separate diagnoses for hypoactive sexual desire disorder (HSDD) and female sexual arousal disorder (FSAD). HSDD was characterized by the lack of desire for sexual activity, whereas FSAD was characterized by an inability to maintain or develop a sufficient lubrication/swelling response. The *DSM-5* Sexual Dysfunctions subworking group chose to combine these disorders, citing a number of studies that failed to reliably distinguish between desire and arousal in women (Brotto et al., 2009; Graham et al., 2004).

Given that FSIAD is a relatively new diagnosis, few prevalence studies on the disorder have been published. Available evidence suggests that the new morbidity criteria (duration and severity) may reduce the number of women who will meet diagnostic criteria for FSIAD. A recent probability sample found a 1-year prevalence rate of 6.5% for interest/arousal concerns in women, with only 0.6% of women meeting criteria for the disorder when considering the duration and severity criteria (Mitchell et al., 2016). Notably, the authors specify that their classification only included women who reported *both* interest and arousal problems and may thus be a poor proxy for FSIAD prevalence in the general population, given that women can meet criteria for the disorder by endorsing exclusively interest- or exclusively arousal-related concerns.

To that end, it is important to consider previous prevalence estimates for FSAD and HSDD to effectively estimate FSIAD rates. HSDD prevalence rates have been estimated to range from 7.3% (Bancroft et al., 2003) to 23% (Witting et al., 2008), and FSAD has been estimated between 2.6% (Mercer et al., 2003) to 28% (Dunn et al., 1999), varying as a function of age, cultural background, and reproductive status.

## FACTORS ASSOCIATED WITH FEMALE SEXUAL INTEREST/AROUSAL DISORDER

Research on the etiological factors associated with both reduced sexual interest and arousal in women is reviewed here. These elements are broken down into biological factors (e.g., physical health, hormones, medications) and psychological factors (e.g., stress, relationships, comorbid mental illness, history of sexual abuse).

*Biological Factors*. With regards to low sexual interest, the most commonly discussed biological factor is endocrine function. A wide range of studies have found a close association between hormone levels and overall sexual desire. The onset of menopause is closely associated with low sexual desire, in part due to decreased ovarian function that, in turn, results in decreased estrogen production. Similarly, an oophorectomy (i.e., surgical removal of the ovaries) results in notable estradiol and testosterone decrements that reflect a more prominent risk factor for sexual interest concerns than natural menopause, particularly among younger women (Dennerstein et al., 2006; Leiblum et al., 2006). Conversely, higher levels of sexual desire have been found in women nearing ovulation (e.g., Diamond & Wallen, 2011; Pillsworth et al., 2004), while decreased sexual desire follows the chemical suppression of ovarian hormones (Schmidt & Rubinow, 2009).

As is the case with sexual interest, there is a close link between endocrine function and arousal levels in women. In particular, there is evidence to suggest that estrogen plays a structural role in tissue function and may govern blood flow into genital tissue through vasodilatory and vasoprotective effects (Sarrel, 1998). Menopause and lactation both result in decreased estradiol levels, and both are associated with reduced blood flow into the vaginal walls (and, as a consequence, reduced lubrication) (e.g., Graziottin & Leiblum, 2005; Simon, 2011). While menopause has been closely associated with reductions in arousal and lubrication as a function of decreased estrogen (Sandhu et al., 2011), there is no specific threshold at which one's level of estrogen is sufficient for sexual arousal. It is therefore difficult to determine whether estrogen deficiency itself can be deemed a cause of sexual arousal problems.

While it is clear that sex hormones, including androgens, estrogens, and progestins, impact female sexual interest and arousal, questions remain as to which of these hormones plays the most critical role in sexual function (Sandhu et al., 2011). The structure and function of the cervix, vagina, labia, and clitoris are governed by androgens and estrogens. Androgens may be most influential factor impacting levels of sexual desire, as they immediately precede estrogen synthesis and thus impact sexual desire, mood, and energy (Goldstein et al., 2004). Notably, the theory that androgen insufficiency causes low sexual desire in women is controversial. It was originally thought that androgen depletion occurred in response to an age-related decline in adrenal and ovarian androgen production. More recently, the field has recognized that declines in female androgen production begin in the early 20s, suggesting a phenomenological decoupling with natural menopause (Sandhu et al., 2011).

Interestingly, testosterone is most closely linked with solitary sexual desire in women. Whereas dyadic sexual desire refers to the desire to be sexual with another person, solitary desire (i.e., the desire to engage in sexual activity with or without another person) is thought to be a more "true" measure of desire as it is less influenced by relational context and more responsive to endogenous physiology (Van Anders, 2012). Several studies have indicated that higher levels of testosterone are associated with increased solitary desire, while dyadic desire has shown either no association with testosterone levels, or in some cases, even a slight negative correlation (Van Anders et al., 2009; Van Anders & Gray, 2007). To that end, masturbation—a behavioral index of solitary desire—has been closely associated with testosterone levels in women (Van Anders, 2012).

Given the evidence for hormonal modulation of female interest and arousal, there has been research interest in the relationship between oral contraception use and sexual function. Oral contraceptives, which include a combination of estrogens and progesterone, cause an increase in sex hormone-binding globulin (SHBG) levels. SHBG, in turn, has been known to lower testosterone levels; thus, it is feasible that this decrease in testosterone could contribute to lower sexual desire in women taking oral contraceptives. Research on the relationship between oral contraceptives and sexual desire has yielded mixed results, and despite the fact that oral contraceptives have been shown to decrease androgen levels, they have not been consistently associated with decreases in sexual desire (Burrows et al., 2012). Indeed, a recent meta-analysis found no differences on various domains of sexual function (i.e., desire, orgasm, lubrication, pain) between women currently taking oral contraceptives and women who were not engaged in oral contraceptive usage (Huang et al., 2020). Similarly, when McCall and Meston (2006) assessed cues for sexual desire, they determined that contraceptive use did not influence sexual desire in women with and without sexual desire concerns.

At the same time, other research has found a negative association between oral contraceptives and sex drive. One study found a significantly lower rate of sexual thoughts and interest among women taking oral contraceptives compared to nonusers (Davison et al., 2008). Similarly, a relatively large-scale study found that oral contraceptive users demonstrated notably lower scores on the desire subscale of the Female Sexual Function Index relative to women who were not currently using oral birth control (Wallwiener et al., 2010). Importantly, these studies are cross-sectional and do not necessarily suggest that oral contraceptives play a causal role in decreased desire. It is also worth noting that the benefits accompanying oral contraceptive use (i.e., reduced fear of pregnancy, reduction in menstrual side effects) may serve to enhance, rather than inhibit, sexual desire. This effect may obscure any possible decrements in sexual desire and arousal that occur as a function of testosterone levels.

More recent research suggests that several neurochemical factors may affect both interest and arousal concerns. A recent study found two distinct, neurologically modulated pathways to FSIAD: (1) insensitivity in brain systems associated with sexual excitation and (2) a phasic increase in serotonergic activity following sexual stimulation, leading to an inhibitory response to sexual stimuli (Tuiten et al., 2018). Relatedly, psychoactive medications that act on these brain systems, including antidepressants, are implicated in FSIAD. With regards to antidepressants specifically, there is a large amount of variability in these effects depending on neurotransmitter receptor profiles (Clayton, El Haddad et al., 2014). The most commonly used antidepressants, selective serotonin reuptake inhibitors (SSRIs), function by increasing serotonin levels. This process increases activation in the serotonin-2 receptor, which confers a variety of sexual side effects in both men and women, including decreased desire. More modern classes of antidepressants act as antagonists at the serotonin-2 receptor level and are thus linked to fewer sexual side effects (Keks et al., 2014). In addition to variations in neurotransmitter profiles, it is also possible that the sexual side effects of antidepressants may differ due to larger genetic variations. Clayton and colleagues (2014) suggest that future research should seek to examine genetic factors associated with antidepressant medication usage, including side-effect profiles, to ultimately facilitate the advancement of individualized medicine in this area.

Both branches of the autonomic nervous system, the sympathetic and the parasympathetic (SNS and PNS), have been shown to impact female genital arousal specifically. With respect to SNS involvement, norepinephrine (NE) plays an important role. The neurotransmitter that facilitates SNS communication, NE increases after exposure to sexually arousing content (Exton et al., 2000). Strong support for the role of the SNS in female sexual arousal comes from the spinal cord literature, as women with spinal cord injuries in areas associated with sympathetically mediated vasocongestion (i.e., between areas T11 and L2) show a lack of lubrication during sexual arousal (Sipski et al., 1997).

Laboratory studies have also demonstrated the role of SNS involvement in female sexual arousal. For instance, Meston and colleagues found that moderate activation of the SNS using exercise (Meston & Gorzalka, 1995, 1996a, 1996b) or ephedrine (Meston & Heiman, 1998) facilitates genital sexual arousal, whereas genital arousal is inhibited by suppression of the SNS (Meston et al., 1997). Consequently, an optimal level of SNS activation has been proposed to facilitate genital arousal in women (Lorenz et al., 2012). Indeed, Lorenz and colleagues found a curvilinear relationship between SNS activation and sexual arousal such that moderate increases in SNS activity were associated with higher sexual arousal levels, while both very low and very high levels of SNS activation were associated with lower levels of sexual arousal. Moreover, resting state heart rate variability (which indexes the relative balance of the SNS and the PNS) has been identified as risk factor for sexual arousal problems (Stanton, Lorenz et al., 2015; Xhyheri et al., 2012). Therefore, factors that disrupt normal SNS activity, such as stress, may negatively affect women's sexual arousal.

*Psychological Factors.* Psychosocial factors are also implicated in low sexual interest and arousal. For instance, relationship duration is a significant, negative predictor of sexual desire, even after controlling for related variables including age, relationship satisfaction, and sexual satisfaction (Murray & Milhausen, 2012). Other research has examined the mechanisms underlying this association, finding that married women experience decreases in sexual desire accompanying feelings of overfamiliarity in their relationships (Sims & Meana, 2010). Sexual desire might also be impacted by daily stressors (i.e., childrearing, financial stress) and professional concerns (i.e., long hours, deadlines), as well as a range of partner-level issues. Women who report lower levels of intimacy and affection in their relationships, as well as lower levels of relationship satisfaction overall, also tend to report decreased sexual desire. The mechanism driving these associations has been theorized to be related to communication, as couples who communicate more openly have a better forum for learning about their partner's sexual preferences (for a review, see Freihart et al., 2020). Gender roles also impact sexual function, and women who subscribe to traditional gender roles may be at greater risk of experiencing sexual problems given a decreased sense of sexual agency (Nobre & Pinto-Gouveia, 2008).

Societal factors may also impact sexual interest and arousal levels in women. Sexual norms differ greatly as a function of culture, with broad implications for sexual function. For instance, women who are socialized to believe that sexual desire is shameful frequently report experiences of guilt and shame during sex. This pattern may result in lower levels of sexual desire and arousal longer-term (Woo et al., 2012).

Four distinct clusters of cues for sexual desire in women have been reported, including emotional bonding cues (e.g., experiencing emotional closeness with a partner), erotic/explicit cues (e.g., watching an erotic film), visual/proximity cues (e.g., being in close proximity to an attractive person), and romantic/implicit cues (e.g., giving or receiving a massage) (McCall & Meston, 2006). When compared to sexually healthy women, women with desire concerns report significantly fewer cues in each of these domains. Research has also identified cues for sexual arousal. When describing their sexual arousal experiences, women with sexual arousal problems reported relying less on physiological or genital arousal cues (e.g., heart racing, genital lubrication, genital warmth, etc.) and more on external, partner, or environmental cues than did women without arousal concerns (Handy et al., 2019). Perhaps without reliable physiological markers of arousal (i.e., lubrication), women with low arousal come to depend on their environmental context to enhance their sexual experiences.

Sexual interest concerns are frequently comorbid with different mental health disorders, including social anxiety disorder, obsessive-compulsive disorder, panic disorder, and major depressive disorder. With regard to depression, the mechanism underlying this comorbidity may be rumination about negative events. Individuals who present with depressive rumination may also maintain an exclusive focus on the negative aspects of a sexual experience. Moreover, individuals with depression may interpret negative experiences to stable, global causes (Hankin et al., 2005), resulting in feelings of hopelessness that could maintain sexual dysfunction. Similarly, FSIAD has been linked to poor emotion regulation skills, and decrements in sexual desire/arousal may be a function of difficulties in tolerating and reappraising difficult emotions (Dubé et al., 2019).

Finally, a history of nonconsensual sexual experiences may contribute to impairments in both sexual desire and arousal in women. Research has found that many women with a history of childhood sexual abuse may, in adulthood, come to fear sexual intimacy, avoid sexual interactions with a partner, and present as less receptive to a partner's sexual approach (Rellini, 2008). Sexual self-schemas, or cognitive generalizations about sexual aspects of the self (Andersen & Cyranowski, 1994), have been shown to differ between women with and without a history of childhood sexual abuse (Meston et al., 2006; Stanton, Boyd et al., 2015). More specifically, women with histories of nonconsensual sexual experiences often view sex as risky or threatening, or alternatively, as a central component of overall self-worth. Perhaps as a consequence of these sexual self-schemas, a high proportion of women with a history of childhood sexual abuse engage in risky sexual behaviors (e.g., Bensley et al., 2000). It is currently unknown whether this pattern of behavior is a reflection of high levels of sexual desire, an inability to maintain or enforce physical boundaries, higher levels of sexual compulsivity, emotional avoidance, or some combination of the above.

## Male Hypoactive Sexual Desire Disorder
### DEFINITION, DIAGNOSIS, AND PREVALENCE

Male hypoactive sexual desire disorder (MHSDD) is defined in *DSM-5* as persistent or recurrently deficient sexual or erotic thoughts, fantasies, and desire for sexual activity. One major shift with the release of *DSM-5* is the gender specificity of the disorder; in past editions of the *DSM* the hypoactive sexual desire disorder diagnosis could be applied to men or women. Sexual desire and arousal problems in women have been collapsed into a single diagnostic category in *DSM-5*. Other than the shift in gender specificity, there are no major differences in MHSDD diagnostic criteria between *DSM-IV-TR* and *DSM-5*. Only one minor change was made: in *DSM-IV-TR*, hypoactive sexual desire disorder required "persistent" low interest in sex, whereas *DSM-5* specifies that symptoms must be present for at least 6 months.

Men are much more likely to present with erectile disorder (ED) than MSHDD, perhaps due to cultural norms portraying men as extremely sexually desirous. Men may feel stigmatized when reporting symptoms of low sexual desire to healthcare providers, and therefore available prevalence estimates may underreport the true prevalence rate. Moreover, most epidemiological studies have not inquired about the full set of diagnostic criteria for HSDD (i.e., asking about lack of interest in sex but not the duration of those concerns or the degree to which they are experienced as distressing), making it difficult for researchers to determine accurate prevalence rates. One international study did examine the prevalence of low sexual interest in men over a 2-month period, finding that 14.4% of respondents reported a distressing lack of sexual desire (Carvalheira et al., 2014). These concerns were most common among men aged 30–39, perhaps as a consequence of professional or childrearing stressors.

A range of factors predict variation in prevalence rates for MHSDD. Self-reported prevalence rates vary by region, ranging from 4.8% in the United States (Laumann et al., 2009) to 17% in the United Kingdom (Mercer et al., 2003). MSHDD prevalence may also vary by age, with rates exceeding 40% in men older than 65 (Fugl-Meyer & Sjogren, 1999). Rates typically decrease when studies include information about the persistence of the problem; one study found that 4.8% of men reported an occasional lack of sexual desire whereas only 3.3% reported a frequent lack of sexual desire (Laumann et al., 2009). Finally, rates also vary depending on the type of sample (e.g., community vs. clinical). Men in community samples are more likely to report desire problems than are men in clinical samples, and reports of desire concerns exceed reports of erectile problems (Fugl-Meyer & Sjogren, 1999; Mercer et al., 2003). Men in clinical settings may feel more comfortable talking about erectile problems than desire problems, especially if they attribute their problems to biological rather than psychological mechanisms (Kedde et al., 2011).

### FACTORS ASSOCIATED WITH MALE HYPOACTIVE SEXUAL DESIRE DISORDER

Most research to date on the biological factors implicated in male sexual desire has focused on hormones and neurological disorders. Psychological causes of low sexual desire in men include relationship difficulties and psychopathology.

*Biological Factors.* Hormonal patterns are often associated with male sexual desire concerns. In men with intentionally suppressed androgen levels, low testosterone is linked to lower levels of sexual desire (Bancroft, 2005). Testosterone replacement has been shown to increase sexual desire among these men, but not among men with normal and/or sufficient androgen levels (Corona, Jannini et al., 2011; Isidori et al., 2005; Khera et al., 2011). Hypogonadism (i.e., diminished functional activity of the gonads) has been observed in 3–7% of men between the ages of 30 and 69 and in 18% of men aged 70 and older (Araujo et al., 2007) perhaps accounting for age-related declines in sexual interest. Hyperprolactinema (i.e., clinically high levels of prolactin) and hypothyroidism have also been associated with low sexual desire in men (Carani et al., 2005; Corona et al., 2004; Corona, Restrelli et al., 2011; Maggi et al., 2013).

Certain psychoactive medications (e.g., SSRIs, selective norepinephrine reuptake inhibitors [SNRIs]) have been linked to low sexual interest in men (Clayton, El Haddad et al., 2014), as have neurological disorders and a range of other medical conditions. Atypical antidepressants may have lower incidence of sexual desire side effects (Clayton et al., 2013). With respect to medical conditions, one study found that 25% of men with multiple sclerosis reported low sexual interest (Lew-Starowicz & Rola, 2014). Low sexual desire has also been reported among men with inflammatory bowel disease (IBD), Crohn's disease, and ulcerative colitis. In such cases, decreased desire may be a side effect of the medications used to treat conditions like IBD, which have a demonstrated impact on testosterone levels. This association could also be mediated by depression levels; IBD is highly comorbid with depression, which may drive observed decreases in sexual interest (O'Toole et al., 2014). Coronary disease, heart failure, renal failure, and HIV have also been associated with low sexual interest in men (Bernardo, 2001; Lallemand et al., 2002; Meuleman & Van Lankveld, 2005; Toorians et al., 1997). Further research in this area is warranted, as it remains unclear whether decreases in desire are due to the conditions themselves, the medications used to treat the conditions, and/or the psychosocial stressors that often accompany the conditions.

*Psychological Factors.* Many psychological factors have been associated with low sexual desire in men, including relationship concerns, concerns related to sexual performance, and comorbid psychopathology (e.g., depression, anxiety). In fact, one study found that psychosocial symptoms were more predictive of low sexual interest than were biological factors, including hormone levels (Corona et al., 2004). Interpersonal factors, in particular, have been strongly associated with sexual interest. For example, men are more likely to experience low sexual desire if their partners also have desire concerns (McCabe & Connaughton, 2014). Desire problems have also been linked to partner-level factors, such as not finding one's partner attractive and being in a relationship for more than 5 years (Carvalheira et al., 2014). Individual factors, including mental health concerns, may also compromise sexual desire. In a survey of male outpatients seeking treatment for sexual dysfunction, 43% of men reported a history of psychiatric symptoms (Corona et al., 2004). To that end, many studies have highlighted the association between depression and low sexual desire (Carvalheira et al., 2014; McCabe & Connaughton, 2014; Pastuszak et al., 2013).

## Erectile Disorder

### DEFINITION, DIAGNOSIS, AND PREVALENCE

ED is defined in *DSM-5* as the recurrent inability to achieve an erection, the inability to maintain an adequate erection, and/or a noticeable decrease in erectile rigidity during partnered sexual activity. ED occurs in men of all ages but is most common among men aged 50 and older. Indeed, while only 7% of men between the ages of 18 and 29 have erectile concerns, almost 20% of men 50 to 59 endorse such problems (Laumann et al., 1999). Feldman and colleagues (1994) found that 10% of men under the age of 35 experience ED, compared to more than 50% of men over the age of 60. The Global Study of Sexual Attitudes and Behaviors reported that 18.8% of men over the age of 40 indicate occasional erectile problems, whereas only 3.5% report such problems consistently (Laumann et al., 2005; Nicolosi et al., 2004).

The prevalence of ED varies as a function of several factors other than age. Married men are less likely to report erectile problems compared to men who have never been married or are divorced (Laumann et al., 1999). Men with cardiovascular disease, diabetes, and metabolic syndrome are also more likely to have ED than are men without these diseases (Grover et al., 2006). Relatedly, health factors such as smoking, obesity, and lack of exercise have been linked to higher rates of ED (Rosen et al., 2014).

### FACTORS ASSOCIATED WITH ERECTION AND ERECTILE DYSFUNCTION

Over the past 30 years, a great deal of research has identified a number of key biological and psychological causal mechanisms in ED. Biological factors are largely related to changes in blood flow to the penis, while psychological factors most commonly involve anxiety and negative expectations for performance.

*Biological Factors.* Erection is caused by increased blood pressure in the corpora cavernosa, which occurs as a function of increased blood inflow and decreased blood outflow. An overwhelming body of evidence suggests that the likelihood of ED increases with different types of vascular disease, such as hyperlipidemia, coronary heart disease, and diabetes (e.g. Kirby et al., 2005; Roumeguère et al., 2003; Seftel et al., 2004). In fact, the link between vascular problems and ED is so strong that ED is considered an early biomarker of vascular disease, especially when it presents in men under the age of 40 (Chew et al., 2010; Miner, 2009). To that end, some researchers favor conceptualizing ED as a vascular disorder rather than a sexual dysfunction (Schouten et al., 2008; Thompson et al., 2005).

ED can be caused by other medical conditions and procedures, including surgery, diabetes, alcoholism, infectious diseases (e.g., HIV), and pelvic pathologies. Drugs that decrease dopamine or reduce testosterone production are also implicated in ED. These include antihypertensive medications, antipsychotic drugs, anxiolytics, antiandrogens, anticholesterol agents, and drugs used to regulate heart rate. Conversely, antiparkinsonian medications increase dopamine and facilitate erection.

*Psychological Factors.* The *sexual tipping point model*, developed by Perelman in 2009, considers sexual function in terms of an individualized arousal threshold necessary to experience a sexual response. One's sexual tipping point, according to Perelman, is determined by a variety of complex factors that span physiological and psychosocial categories. Examples of psychosocial issues in men that may influence erectile function include performance anxiety, guilt and shame resulting from religious beliefs, and/or a history of sexual trauma (Perelman & Rowland, 2006; Waldinger & Schweitzer, 2005).

Barlow's (1986) feedback model of sexual dysfunction elucidates how these psychosocial factors work together to maintain ED. Men who experience anxiety related to their sexual performance tend to maintain focus on their own behaviors during a sexual encounter, leading to decrements in the ability to notice and experience pleasure. This pattern, known as *spectatoring*, serves to increase anxiety, which, in turn, inhibits the physiological relaxation of smooth muscles that is necessary for erection. This pattern then contributes to a negative mood state that drives future negative expectancies surrounding sexual experiences. Given that the result is impaired erectile responding, the man's performance-related fears are confirmed and reinforced, leading to an increased likelihood of repeating this process in subsequent sexual situations. In most cases of ED, performance anxiety is also present, perhaps because the occurrence—or absence—of an erection is visible to both the man and his partner, which increases the focus on performance. According to Rosen and colleagues (2014), men experiencing performance anxiety engage in visual or tactile checking of the penis to ensure an erection is sustained.

Conversely, men without sexual concerns tend to approach sexual situations with positive expectancies and focus more closely on erotic cues. This sets the stage for a positive feedback loop: they become aroused, are able to obtain and sustain an erection, and then approach future sexual situations with positive expectations based on experience. While spectatoring can be detrimental for sexual function at any age, it appears to be particularly problematic when young men first begin engaging in sexual activity. Given the absence of sexual experience, young men are particularly vulnerable to the influence of negative expectations about erectile performance.

Other psychosocial factors can contribute to the development and maintenance of ED. According to Nobre and Pinto-Gouveia (2006, 2009), men are more likely to meet criteria for ED if they (1) endorse myths about male sexuality (e.g. "men always want to have sex"), (2) view themselves as incompetent, and (3) view their sexual problem as internal and stable over time. A range of mental health conditions, including depression, generalized anxiety disorder, obsessive-compulsive disorder, and paraphilic disorders, have been linked to ED. Last, a survey of college-aged men found that off-label Viagra use was correlated with erectile dysfunction (Harte & Meston, 2011). This study suggested that recreational Viagra use could lead to subsequent erectile problems by way of increasing psychological dependence on the drug for performance.

## Orgasm Disorders

The category of orgasm disorders refers to a broad collection of difficulties surrounding the presence or absence of orgasm during sexual activity. Both sexes can experience an inability to achieve orgasm. In men, the most frequent presentation is premature orgasm, or achieving orgasm too quickly. In women, the most common presentation is the inability to attain orgasm.

### Female Orgasmic Disorder
DEFINITION, DIAGNOSIS, AND PREVALENCE

Female orgasmic disorder (FOD), as defined by *DSM-5*, refers to a reduced intensity, delay, infrequency, and/or absence of orgasm. Although not formally stated in *DSM-5*, the clinical consensus is that as long as a woman can obtain an orgasm through some mode—manual stimulation, stimulation with a sex toy, intercourse, or some combination of the above—she does *not* meet criteria for FOD (unless she is distressed by her orgasmic response).

Historically, the field has lacked a clear definition of female orgasm, making the operationalization of FOD difficult. In fact, one study cited more than 25 distinct definitions of female orgasm proposed by different authors (Mah & Binik, 2001). The following definition of female orgasm was derived by the committee on female orgasm and presented at the International Consultation on Urological Diseases in Official Relationship with the World Health Organization (WHO), in Paris, 2003:

> An orgasm in the human female is a variable, transient peak sensation of intense pleasure, creating an altered state of consciousness, usually accompanied by involuntary, rhythmic contractions of the pelvic, striated circumvaginal musculature often with concomitant uterine and anal contractions and myotonia that resolves the sexually-induced vasocongestion (sometimes only partially), usually with an induction of well-being and contentment. (Meston, Levin et al., 2004)

Orgasms are the result of sustained erotic stimulation to both genital and nongenital zones of women's bodies, including the clitoris, vagina, other areas of the vulva, the breasts, and nipples. Female orgasm may also result from fantasy and/or mental imagery, and may occur during sleep, precluding the necessity of consciousness for an orgasm to occur. Orgasms generally do not occur spontaneously without some form of sexual stimulation (either physical or psychological); however, some psychotropic drugs have been reported to induce spontaneous orgasms in women. Interestingly, women experiencing orgasmic difficulties do not typically present with the same level of distress that has been reported in men with ED. This may be because women, unlike men, are able to replicate the appearance of orgasm, thus reducing performance-related anxiety concerns.

In the United States, orgasm difficulties are the second most common female sexual problem, with 22–28% of women (ages 18–59) reporting an inability to attain orgasm (Laumann et al., 1994). More recent research accounting for *DSM-5* morbidity criteria finds that approximately 16.3% of women report difficulties with orgasm over the past year, but only 1.9% meet diagnostic criteria (Mitchell et al., 2016). In particular, young women (18–24 years) have lower rates of orgasm, both with a partner and during masturbation, likely owing to levels of sexual experience (Laumann et al., 1994; Mitchell et al., 2016). Differences in research methodology and diagnostic criteria make it difficult to accurately determine prevalence rates for FOD. Indeed, in a review of 11 epidemiological studies, Graham (2010) found a low-end prevalence rate for FOD at 3.5% when *DSM-III* criteria were used and a high rate of 34% when women were simply asked whether or not they had difficulties experiencing orgasm.

## FACTORS ASSOCIATED WITH WOMEN'S ORGASM AND FOD

The female orgasm results from a complex interaction of biological, psychological, and cultural processes. The most common causes of FOD include disturbances to these processes, such as disruptions in the SNS response, different types of chronic illness (particularly spinal cord injury), sexual guilt, anxiety, and relationship concerns.

*Biological Factors.* Impairments in nervous system function, endocrine levels, and/or various brain mechanisms involved in female orgasm may cause orgasmic dysfunction (Heiman, 2002). With respect to the nervous system, studies examining blood plasma levels of neurotransmitters before, during, and after orgasm suggest that epinephrine and norepinephrine levels peak during female orgasm (e.g., Exton et al., 2000). Oxytocin levels are positively correlated with the subjective intensity of orgasm among orgasmic women, with elevated prolactin levels up to 60 minutes post orgasm (for review, see Meston & Frohlich, 2000). Studies in humans suggest that the paraventricular nucleus of the hypothalamus, an area of the brain that produces oxytocin, is involved in the orgasmic response (McKenna, 1999). Impairments in any of these systems may lead to FOD.

Medical issues and conditions impacting a woman's orgasmic ability include damage to the sacral/pelvic nerves, multiple sclerosis, vascular disease, Parkinson's disease, epilepsy, hysterectomy complications, vulvodynia, hypothalamus-pituitary disorders, kidney disease, fibromyalgia, and sickle-cell anemia. Women with spinal cord injuries in the sacral region (interfering with the sacral reflex arc of the spinal cord) have shown difficulty attaining orgasm (Sipski et al., 2001). This is believed to be caused by interference with the vagus nerve, which connects the cervix to the brain (Whipple et al., 1996).

Several psychotherapeutic drugs have demonstrated orgasmic side effects in women. For instance, drugs that increase serotonergic activity (e.g., some antidepressants) or decrease dopaminergic activity (e.g., antipsychotics) have been shown to decrease, delay, or, in some cases, completely limit orgasmic capacity (Meston, Levin et al., 2004; Graham et al., 2010). Indeed, problems with orgasm have been noted in about one-third of women who take SSRIs (Stimmel & Gutierrez, 2006). There is interclass variability, however, in that some antidepressants have been associated with impaired orgasm more often than others, and these differences may be related to the specific serotonin receptor subtype being activated. As noted earlier, drugs that inhibit serotonin activity at the serotonin-2 receptor (e.g., nefazodone, cyproheptadine) cause fewer sexual side effects in women (for review, see Meston, Levin et al., 2004).

It has been reported that an increasing number of women believe the structure of their genitalia may contribute to difficulties in achieving or maintaining orgasm, leading to an increase in genital plastic surgery, including labiaplasty (reduction of the size of the inner labia and the outer labia), vaginoplasty (rebuilding the vaginal canal and its mucous membrane), hymenoplasty (reconstruction of the hymen), perineoplasty (tightening or loosening of the perineal muscles and the vagina and/or correcting clinical defects or damages of the vagina and the anus), and G-spot augmentation. While a few, relatively small studies have indicated that these surgeries resulted in increased sexual satisfaction (e.g. Goodman et al., 2010), little current evidence supports the efficacy of these procedures. Furthermore, many studies that examined the effects of these surgeries failed to (1) use standardized measures to formally assess for sexual dysfunction and (2) include control groups. For these reasons, the American College of Obstetricians and Gynecologists and the Society of Obstetricians and Gynecologists of Canada discourage physicians from performing genital plastic surgery.

*Psychological Factors.* Common psychological factors associated with FOD include sexual guilt, sexual anxiety, childhood loss, and relationship issues (for review, see Meston, Hull et al., 2004). Sexual guilt may arise from strict adherence to the values of Western religions, which sometimes view sexual pleasure as sin. This belief can influence orgasmic abilities by increasing anxiety and discomfort during sex, by distracting a woman from what gives her pleasure, and by causing distressing thoughts during sexual activity. Conversely, women who initiate sex and/or are more active participants during sexual activity report more frequent orgasms. Their active role may allow for finding sexual positions that facilitate a greater level of stimulation and pleasure. Women who engage in sexual activity, both partnered and solo, more frequently report more orgasms than women with infrequent sexual activity. It is likely that women who engage in sex more often have a greater knowledge of what gives them sexual pleasure and are therefore more likely to experience orgasm. Finally, women are more likely to have orgasms when in romantic relationships that are characterized by a high degree of sexual and nonsexual communication (Mallory et al., 2019). To that end, women experiencing relationship discord might be at greater risk for FOD than women who are satisfied with their relationships. It is important to note that, because only a small percentage of women are distressed by their anorgasmia, prevalence rates of FOD are low (Graham, 2010).

A range of demographic factors are associated with FOD, including age, education, and religion. Women aged 18–24 are more likely to report orgasm problems, compared to older women, during both masturbation and partnered sexual activity (Laumann et al., 1994). Sexual experience may, as a consequence, be important for orgasmic ability, as might knowledge of one's body and preferences. Lower levels of education are associated with orgasmic difficulties, even during masturbation. Indeed, only 42% of women with a high school education report "always or usually" achieving orgasm during masturbation, as compared to 87% of women with an advanced degree (Laumann et al., 1994). It's possible that more educated women hold more liberal views on sexuality and might be more likely to center their own pleasure as a goal of sexual activity.

There is a negative relationship between high religiosity and orgasmic ability in women, such that religious belief may lead to experiences of guilt during sexual activity. Guilt, in turn, may impair orgasm through a number of cognitive mechanisms, including distraction. There is also a relationship between improved orgasmic ability and decreased sexual guilt (Davidson & Moore, 1994). Laumann and colleagues (1994) reported that a substantially higher proportion (79%) of women with no religious affiliation endorsed being orgasmic during masturbation compared to women with a religious affiliation (53–67%).

Last, it is possible that overarching societal notions of women's sexuality, including the cultural value placed on women's sexual pleasure, may play a role in female orgasmic capacity. Societies that value female orgasm have lower incidences of anorgasmia than societies that discourage sexual pleasure for women (for review, see Meston, Hull et al., 2004). Examples of societies that encourage sexual pleasure include the Mundugumor of Papua New Guinea and the Mangaia of the Cook Islands. Mangaian women are taught to have orgasms, with expectations of multiple female orgasms for each male orgasm, and specific attention is paid to mutual orgasm. In fact, Mangaian males who are not able to give their partners multiple orgasms are socially disparaged. At the opposite end of the spectrum are societies, such as the Arapesh of Papua New Guinea, that assume that women will have no pleasure from coitus and that the female orgasm does not exist. The Arapesh do not even have a word in their language for the female orgasm. It is feasible that women in societies that promote women's sexual pleasure are more likely to experiment and therefore learn about what facilitates their ability to have an orgasm. Moreover, women in such societies may be more likely to *admit* to experiences of orgasm, whereas orgasm rates may be underreported in societies that discourage sexual pleasure.

## Delayed Ejaculation
### DEFINITION, DIAGNOSIS, AND PREVALENCE

As defined by *DSM-5*, delayed ejaculation (DE) is a persistent difficulty or inability to achieve orgasm despite the presence of adequate desire, arousal, and stimulation. Most commonly, the term refers to a condition in which a man is unable to orgasm with his partner, even though he is able to achieve and maintain an erection. Typically, men with DE are able to ejaculate during masturbation or sleep.

Importantly, men experiencing retrograde ejaculation do not meet the diagnostic criteria for DE. Retrograde ejaculation occurs when the ejaculatory fluid travels backward into the bladder rather than forward through the urethra. It may result from prostate surgery complications or as a side effect of certain medications (e.g., anticholinergic drugs), and, in some cases, men may be unaware that this phenomenon can account for lack of visible ejaculate.

There is clinical consensus that DE is both the least common of the male sexual dysfunctions and also the least understood. A key concern often associated with DE—and frequently missed by clinicians—is that partnered sexual activity may not be as sexually stimulating as masturbation. Stimulation techniques used during masturbation (e.g., pushing the penis against different objects, rolling the penis between one's hands), may create an intense sense of friction that is otherwise elusive during sexual activity with a partner. In addition, masturbation often contains a strong fantasy component, which may also be challenging to maintain when engaging in partnered intercourse.

Prevalence rates of DE in the literature are generally low, usually below 3% (e.g., Christensen et al., 2011; Líndal & Stefánsson, 1993; Perelman & Rowland, 2006). Researchers have suggested that, over time, the rate of DE will rise as a function of age-related ejaculatory decline (Perelman, 2003) and widespread use of SSRIs (Georgiadis et al., 2007), which have been implicated in increased ejaculation latency.

The term "delay" in delayed ejaculation inherently suggests a normative amount of time from the start of sexual activity to ejaculation. In fact, only one study has addressed this question. Waldinger and Schweitzer (2005) measured intravaginal latency time in 500 heterosexual couples cross-culturally. The median time to orgasm was 5.4 minutes, the mean was 8 minutes, and the standard deviation was 7.1 minutes. Though these values are empirically interesting, it is noteworthy that *DSM-5* diagnostic criteria for DE do not include any objective measures of latency, which makes it challenging to determine overall prevalence. Furthermore, it is possible that some men may have unrealistic latency-to-orgasm expectations and may thus unfairly consider their ejaculation patterns to be delayed.

### FACTORS ASSOCIATED WITH DELAYED EJACULATION

Delayed ejaculation is associated with a number of biological and psychological factors. Biological factors include damage to nerve pathways that facilitate ejaculation, chronic medical conditions, and, potentially, age. Psychological etiologies of the disorder span from insufficient stimulation to assorted manifestations of "psychic conflict."

*Biological Factors.* When men ejaculate, nerve impulses on sympathetic fibers travel through the sympathetic ganglia and peripheral pelvic nerves, causing the efferent release of semen and closure of the bladder neck (Segraves, 2010). While damage to any of these pathways may compromise ejaculation, spinal cord injury is the most common nerve-related cause of DE.

Several chronic medical conditions, including multiple sclerosis and diabetes, are correlated with DE (Perelman & Rowland, 2006; Waldinger & Schweitzer, 2005). Ejaculatory delay may also be caused by short-term, reversible medical conditions (e.g., prostate infection, urinary tract infection, substance use) and psychopharmacological agents (e.g., antipsychotics, antidepressants; Segraves, 2010).

There is conflicting evidence regarding the effect of age on ejaculatory function (Segraves, 2010). DE is more common in older males (Perelman & Rowland, 2006), and the disorder may be related to low penile sensitivity, which is itself associated with aging (Paick et al., 1998; Rowland, 1998). On the other hand, low penile sensitivity is not usually the primary cause of DE (Perelman, 2014). Rather, individual variability in the sensitivity of the ejaculatory reflex, which is exacerbated with age, may be driving the relationship between age and DE.

*Psychological Factors.* Althof (2012) reviewed the four leading psychological theories of DE. The first focuses on insufficient mental or physical stimulation (Masters & Johnson, 1970). Men with DE experience less sexual arousal than men without the disorder and therefore may have a diminished ability to experience penile sensations (Rowland et al., 2004). A lack of proper ambiance or environmental cues for sexual arousal may also contribute to insufficient mental stimulation (Shull & Sprenkle, 1980).

The second theory posits that DE is caused by a high frequency of masturbation or by a unique, idiosyncratic masturbatory style that differs greatly from the physical stimulation that occurs during partnered intercourse (Althof, 2012; Perelman, 2005; Perelman & Rowland, 2006). A large disparity may exist between the sensations that men with DE experience when masturbating to a specific fantasy and the sensations that they experience during sex with a partner.

A third theory centers on the idea of "psychic conflict" as the root cause of DE. While this theory was more common in the early stages of psychological treatment, some psychodynamically oriented therapists still conceptualize the disorder in these terms. Examples of psychic conflict include anxiety related to loss of self (due to loss of semen), fear that ejaculation may hurt the partner, fear of impregnating the partner, and guilt from strict religious upbringing (Friedman, 1973; Ovesey & Meyers, 1968).

The fourth and final theory suggests that DE may be masking the presence of a desire disorder. In this case, the male may be overly concerned with pleasing his partner and, even when he is not aroused, may seek to ejaculate (Apfelbaum, 1989).

### Premature (Early) Ejaculation
#### DEFINITION, DIAGNOSIS, AND PREVALENCE

Premature (early) ejaculation (PE) is defined in *DSM-5* as a persistent or recurrent pattern of ejaculation occurring during partnered sexual activity within approximately 1 minute following vaginal penetration. The diagnosis only applies to individuals who ejaculate before they would like to. Although the diagnosis may be applied to those who engage in nonvaginal sexual intercourse, specific duration criteria for such activities have not been established.

In recent years, there has been considerable disagreement about the definition, nature, and even the name of the disorder. The *DSM-5* Sexual Dysfunctions sub-work group changed the name of the disorder from "premature ejaculation" to "premature (early) ejaculation," as some considered the existing name to be pejorative. Researchers have also argued that the time to ejaculation after penetration criterion is overly simplistic and may limit scientific understanding of the condition (Metz et al., 1997). Others have suggested that PE might not warrant the term "dysfunction," indicating that the disorder should probably not be of clinical concern unless it is extreme (Hong, 1984).

Owing in part to a lack of universally accepted diagnostic criteria, varying prevalence rates been reported. Importantly, there are currently no published epidemiological studies that assess the prevalence of PE as defined in *DSM-5*. However, many studies have assessed the prevalence of PE concerns. For instance, Masters and Johnson (1970) identified PE as one of the most common male sexual dysfunctions. According to Laumann and colleagues (1994), PE is the most common sexual disorder in men, with approximately 30% of men in the United States reporting the condition in the previous year. Unlike ED, this condition has been estimated to affect younger men more so than older men. As many as 40% of men under 40 years of age and only 10% of men over age 70 have been estimated to experience premature (early) ejaculation (Corona et al., 2004). When the intravaginal ejaculation latency time criterion is used (i.e., ejaculation occurring within 1 minute of penetration), however, prevalence rates are much lower, usually around 1–3% (Althof et al., 2010). High rates of comorbidity are reported for PE and ED, with about one-third of men who suffer from PE also experiencing ED (Corona et al., 2004).

#### FACTORS ASSOCIATED WITH PREMATURE (EARLY) EJACULATION

Causal factors have been identified for both normal and premature ejaculation. Historically, PE has been considered to be a psychological problem; however, recent research has implicated different biological systems in the development and maintenance of the disorder.

*Biological Factors.* During sperm emission, the first stage of ejaculation, sperm moves from the epididymis into the vas deferens. This process is generated by the SNS, which controls the contraction of smooth muscles. Following sperm emission, the individual has the subjective experience that ejaculation is "inevitable," known as the "point of inevitable ejaculation." Rhythmic contractions occur in the striate muscles surrounding the spongious tissue, the cavernous tissue, and in the pelvic floor, causing ejaculation to occur. The subjective experience of orgasm is normally associated with the contractions of the striate muscles. In most men, emission, ejaculation, and orgasm are interconnected. For a small portion of men, however, these phenomena are independent. For example, some men train themselves to have the subjective experience of orgasm without ejaculation, while some men with PE experience emission without ejaculation.

The precise cause of PE is unknown, but the most promising biological etiologies include malfunction of the serotonin receptors, genetic predisposition, and disruptions of the endocrine system. Waldinger, Berendson, and colleagues (1998) noted that, in rodents, activation of one serotonin receptor speeds up ejaculation, while activation of another serotonin receptor delays ejaculation. It is plausible, then, that men with symptoms of the disorder may have disturbances in central serotonergic neurotransmission, which could result in a lower threshold for sexual stimulation (Waldinger, 2007). PE may also be influenced by genetic predispositions. In first-degree male relatives of Dutch men with lifelong PE, researchers found a high prevalence of PE (Waldinger, Rietschel et al., 1998). Similarly, a genetic study of Finnish male twins indicated that genetics account for 28% of the variance in PE (Jern et al., 2007). Recent research has confirmed the role of the endocrine system in the control of the ejaculatory reflex. Carani and colleagues (2005) found that 50% of men with hyperthyroidism also had PE. In addition to testosterone and prolactin, the hormone thyrotropin has been shown to play an independent role in the control of ejaculatory function (Corona, Jannini et al., 2011; Maggi et al., 2013).

*Psychological Factors.* One of the primary causes and maintaining factors of PE may be anxiety. Althof (2014) explained that the term "anxiety" is characterized by three different mental phenomena related to PE. First, anxiety may refer to a phobic response, such as fear of the vaginal canal. Similarly, one may have an affective response, such as negative feelings toward one's partner as a function of anxiety. Finally, anxiety may indicate performance concerns, such that a preoccupation with poor sexual performance leads to decrements in sexual function and increased avoidance of sexual situations. Therefore, anxiety may have a reciprocal relationship with PE; that is, performance anxiety may lead to problems with early ejaculation, which may then lead to performance anxiety (Althof et al., 2010). Despite the sound theoretical underpinnings, laboratory studies have generally not shown significant differences in levels of anxiety reported by men with and without PE.

Additionally, early learned experiences and a lack of sensory awareness may be important psychological factors contributing to PE. Masters and Johnson (1970) examined case histories of men with PE and found that many had early sexual experiences during which they felt nervous and rushed. According to Masters and Johnson, these men learned to associate sex and sexual performance with speed and discomfort. Kaplan (1989) considered lack of sensory awareness to be the immediate cause of PE. She believed that men with PE fail to develop sufficient awareness of their own level of arousal.

### Sexual Pain Disorders

The *DSM-IV-TR* included two sexual pain disorders, dyspareunia and vaginismus. The *DSM-5* Sexual Dysfunctions sub-work group combined these two disorders into genito-pelvic pain/penetration disorder (GPPPD). In *DSM-IV-TR*, dyspareunia was defined as genital and/or pelvic pain, whereas vaginismus referred to an involuntary spasm or tightening of the pelvic muscles. The merging of dyspareunia and vaginismus emphasizes the multidimensional nature of genital pain, particularly in women. Mental health professionals, when confronted with a patient with any of these conditions, should make sure that the condition is fully assessed by a gynecologist or urologist.

## Genito-Pelvic Pain/Penetration Disorder

### DEFINITION, DIAGNOSIS, AND PREVALENCE

In *DSM-5*, GPPPD is defined as persistent or recurrent difficulties with one or more of the following: (1) vaginal penetration during intercourse; (2) vulvovaginal or pelvic pain during vaginal intercourse or attempts at penetration; (3) fear or anxiety about vulvovaginal or pelvic pain in anticipation of, during, or as a result of vaginal penetration; and (4) tightening or tensing of the pelvic floor muscles during attempted vaginal penetration.

GPPPD was established, in part, in response to arguments made by Binik (2010a), who questioned the logic of maintaining two separate sexual pain diagnoses for women, given the high rates of comorbidity between painful sex and difficulties with penetration. The overlap between these two concerns is notable, with one study finding that 72.4% of women with vaginismus reported symptoms of dyspareunia and 47.7% of women with dyspareunia reported symptoms of vaginismus (Peixoto & Nobre, 2013).

There has also been some larger debate regarding the conceptualization of GPPPD, with some considering whether GPPPD should be considered a pain disorder that interferes with sexual activity or a sexual dysfunction characterized by pain (Kingsberg & Knudson, 2011). Evidence for the pain conceptualization comes from studies that suggest nonpelvic chronic pain is associated with chronic genito-pelvic pain (Paterson et al., 2009). As more research is needed to answer these questions, the *DSM-5* Sexual Dysfunctions sub-work group decided to maintain the status of GPPPD as a sexual dysfunction.

In addition to the collapsing of dyspareunia and vaginismus, another important change with the release of *DSM-5* was the exclusion of men from a sexual pain diagnosis. The *DSM-IV-TR* diagnosis of dyspareunia applied to both males and females. Due to a lack of empirical studies, male dyspareunia has been excluded from GPPPD diagnostic criteria (Bergeron et al., 2014). There is, however, evidence to suggest that men do occasionally suffer from localized or generalized pain during sexual activity, with prevalence estimates between 5% and 15% (Clemens, 2005). To address this type of pain, researchers have coined the term "urological chronic pelvic pain syndrome" (UCPPS), which applies only to men but is not included in *DSM-5* (Shoskes et al., 2009). Davis and colleagues (2011) found that the patterns of sensitivity and pelvic floor muscle function observed in men with UCPPS are notably similar to those of women with GPPPD.

GPPPD is frequently comorbid with sexual arousal problems in women. The genital changes that occur when women become physiologically aroused (i.e., swelling, lubrication of the genitals) facilitate penetrative intercourse. In the absence of these physiological sexual readiness cues, intercourse can result in friction, tearing, and overstimulation of genital tissue, leading to sexual pain. As a consequence, some have theorized that a lack of genital arousal may be a key antecedent to sexual pain symptoms.

GPPPD is new to *DSM-5* and thus prevalence estimates are limited. One small Iranian sample yielded a prevalence rate of 10.5% among married women living in Tehran (Alizadeh et al, 2019). These rates may not, however, be generalizable at the population level. Prevalence estimates do exist for dyspareunia and vaginismus. Rates of dyspareunia range from 2% to 7% in general (Peixoto & Nobre, 2013), from 6.5% to 45% in older women (van Lankveld et al., 2010), and from 14% to 34% in younger women (van Lankveld et al., 2010). Prevalence rates for vaginismus are reported to be 5–6.6% (Fugl-Meyer et al., 2013; ter Kuile & Reissing, 2014). Notably, higher rates of painful sexual intercourse have been observed in clinical settings (Nobre & Pinto-Gouveia, 2008) and in countries where arranged marriages, polygamy, and/or widow inheritance are common (Amidu et al., 2010; Yasan et al., 2009). Some women are at increased risk of genito-pelvic pain after giving birth (Rosen & Pukall, 2016), with 10% of women reporting postpartum genito-pelvic pain (Paterson et al., 2009). Additional risk factors for GPPPD include poor health, lower education, low family income, high stress, more frequent emotional problems, and the presence of urinary tract symptoms.

### FACTORS ASSOCIATED WITH GENITO-PELVIC PAIN/PENETRATION DISORDER

Correlates of sexual pain in women include a number of medical conditions, as well as anxiety about sexual activity. When sex is painful, research suggests that women may develop anxiety related to sexuality that subsequently maintains the pain associated with GPPPD.

*Biological Factors.* Genital pain is generally categorized as superficial or deep. Superficial pain may result from a dermatological disorder or another medical condition that impacts the genitalia (e.g., vaginal atrophy, anatomical variations, urinary tract infections, injury, and other diseases and infections of the vulva). Conversely, deep pain more commonly results from uterine fibroids, endometriosis, urinary disease, and/or ovarian disease (for review, see Schultz et al., 2005). Sexual pain has also been observed following pelvic radiation and chemotherapy (Fugl-Meyer et al., 2013; Kingsberg & Knudson, 2011).

At the superficial level, one of the major etiological factors for pain is a biological disorder known as *provoked vestibulodynia* (PVD; formerly *vulvar vestibulitis syndrome*). PVD is characterized by a sharp, burning pain experienced to any touch or pressure on the vulvar vestibule, a region that falls between the inner labia minora, the frenulum of the clitoris, and the lower portion of the vaginal opening (Pukall et al., 2005). This condition can be diagnosed by a gynecologist by probing the area with a cotton swab to assess evoked pain sensations. PVD may be related to a history of yeast infections and hormonal events in adolescence, including the early onset of menstruation and use of oral contraceptives (Farmer et al., 2011; Pukall et al., 2005). Another potential cause of superficial genital pain is vulvovaginal atrophy, or the deterioration/reduction of flexibility and lubrication in vaginal tissue, naturally co-occuring with menopause. The vaginal symptoms reported by premenopausal women with PVD and postmenopausal women with vulvovaginal atrophy are markedly similar (Kao et al., 2008).

One major hypothesized pathway to GPPPD involves the sensitization of neurons in the spinal cord and parts of the brain. It has been theorized that intense or abrasive stimulation of peripheral tissue during physical trauma may sensitize neurons that bring information about pain to receptive centers in the brain. As a result, the sensitized neurons will activate in response to less stimulation, or in some cases, in absence of simulation, resulting in pain from little to no touch. Indeed, women with this kind of genital pain also frequently report genital pain during nonsexual situations (Binik, 2010a).

Other etiological factors associated with deep genital pain include uterine fibroids, urinary diseases such as uterine retroversion and uterine myomas, ovarian diseases such as ovarian remnant syndrome, adenomyosis, endometriosis, pelvic congestion syndrome, levator and muscle myalgia, and IBS.

Little research has focused on the biological factors associated with vaginal spasms during sexual penetration, though some have suggested that these involuntary spasms of the pelvic floor muscles may be due to genital malformations and/or poor general pelvic muscle control (ter Kuile & Reissing, 2014). As with genital pain, high rates of provoked PVD have been reported among women diagnosed with vaginal spasms (Binik, 2010b). Experts in sexual pain have suggested that the vaginal spasms may be a physiological response to intense pain during penetration; that is, the vaginal spasm could be the body's automatic physical reaction to protect itself from anticipated pain.

*Psychological Factors.* Marked fear of pain and consequent anxiety with sexual activity have been proposed as both symptoms of and etiological mechanisms for sexual pain. Women with genital pain exhibit a selective attentional bias toward pain stimuli compared to controls, and genital pain is associated with state and trait anxiety as well as fear of pain (Payne et al., 2005). Women with genital pain also tend to fear sexual interactions, and they show more phobic anxiety of sexual activity than sexually healthy women. It may be that after sexual pain has been experienced initially, anxiety about sexual activity maintains the pain by increasing hypervigilance toward pain cues. Evidence supports this pathway: one study found that women with PVD displayed an attentional bias toward pain-related stimuli on an emotional stressor task compared to matched control women without PVD (Payne et al., 2005). Unsurprisingly, women with sexual pain are also more likely to have negative attitudes toward sexuality compared with women without pain.

GPPPD is far more common in women with histories of abuse. Indeed, one study found that women who experience sexual pain are 4.1 times more likely to have abuse histories (Harlow & Stewart, 2005), and vaginal spasms have been associated with a history of abuse (Reissing et al., 2004). Moreover, fear of physical abuse has been linked to genital pain (Landry & Bergeron, 2011).

Associations between depression and genital pain are frequently noted in the literature, although longitudinal studies have not observed a direct relationship (Schultz et al., 2005). It is feasible that women with depression are more likely to attend to pain in general and sexual pain in particular, but there is no evidence that depression causes pain or vice versa. It is more likely that this association is mediated by relationship satisfaction. Negative cognitions such as "My partner will leave me," "I am a failure as a woman," and "I must be tearing inside" are commonly reported by women with sexual pain. Women with genital pain report more pain when their relational distress increases, an indication that sexual pain may be partially associated with negative feelings between or toward partners. Consequently, recent research has argued for a dyadic conceptualization of GPPPD, such that GPPPD should be viewed as a disorder that is frequently maintained in the context of relationships and therefore must be treated with relational factors in mind (Rosen & Bergeron, 2019).

With respect to vaginal spasms, women who experience vaginal spasms report greater anxiety symptom severity. It is unclear, however, whether anxiety is a cause or consequence of such spasms (Schultz et al., 2005). Lower rates of positive attitudes toward one's sexuality have been observed in women who experience spasms during sexual penetration (Reissing et al., 2004). It is possible that a lack of positive beliefs about one's sexuality may create a negative feedback loop, discouraging a woman from seeking out and experiencing positive sexual interactions and contributing to avoidance of sexual activity.

## Conclusion and Future Directions

In summary, it is apparent that both biological and psychosocial factors play a prominent role in the etiology of sexual dysfunctions in men and women, and, as such, both sets of factors must be carefully considered in both assessment and treatment. The multidimensionality of sexuality calls for assessment and treatment strategies that account for all of the potential dimensions at play when an individual experiences a sexual problem.

All forms of sexual dysfunction occur in the context of a person's life. Consideration of that context, especially relational factors, can be used to guide treatment recommendations. Importantly, only a few of the sexual dysfunctions mentioned here have been formally conceptualized in a dyadic way, owing in part to a historical paucity of couples-based research. Despite this empirical gap, it is likely that each sexual problem outlined in the *DSM* is highly influenced by one's interpersonal context. Relational factors that should be attended to in the context of treatment include overall relational satisfaction, comfort with one's partner, perceptions of a partner's expectations, patterns of sexual and non-sexual communication, and partner attentiveness in the context of a sexual encounter.

Similarly, effective treatment for sexual dysfunction may depend, in many cases, on effective psychoeducation. Misinformation related to sexual dysfunction abounds, particularly in an age with widespread exposure to Internet pornography. Individuals may, for example, self-diagnose a sexual dysfunction based on faulty information (i.e., believing one has ED when only engaging in sex in the context of alcohol use). While it remains extremely important to develop effective treatment strategies for sexual dysfunctions, ameliorating sexual problems may begin with more widespread access to scientifically sound information.

Taken together, it is evident that the future of the field will feature a large degree of multidisciplinary collaboration—among psychologists, psychiatrists, gynecologists, urologists, and primary care physicians—to continue to develop and refine research on the nature and treatment of sexual problems.

## References

Alizadeh, A., Farnam, F., Raisi, F., & Parsaeian, M. (2019). Prevalence of and risk factors for genito-pelvic pain/penetration disorder: A population-based study of Iranian women. *Journal of Sexual Medicine, 16*(7), 1068–1077.

Althof, S. E. (2012). Psychological interventions for delayed ejaculation/orgasm. *International Journal of Impotence Research, 24*, 131–136.

Althof, S. E. (2014). Treatment of premature ejaculation: Psychotherapy, pharmacotherapy, and combined therapy. In Y. M. Binik & K. S. K. Hall (Eds.), *Principles and practice of sex therapy*, 5th ed. (pp. 112–137). Guilford.

Althof, S. E., Abdo, C. H. N., Dean, J., Hackett, G., McCabe, M., McMahon, C. G., . . . Tan, H. M. (2010). International society for sexual medicine's guidelines for the diagnosis and treatment of premature ejaculation. *Journal of Sexual Medicine, 7*(9), 2947–2969. doi:10.1111/j.1743-6109.2010.01975.x

Amidu, N., Owiredu, W. K. B., Woode, E., Addai-Mensah, O., Quaye, L., Alhassan, A., & Tagoe, E. A. (2010). Incidence of sexual dysfunction: A prospective survey in Ghanaian females. *Reproductive Biology and Endocrinology, 8*, 106. doi:10.1186/1477-7827-8-106

Andersen, B. L., & Cyranowski, J. M. (1994). Women's sexual self-schema. *Journal of Personality and Social Psychology, 67*(6), 1079–1100.

Apfelbaum, B. (1989). The diagnosis and treatment of retarded ejacualtion. In S. R. Leiblum & R. C. Rosen (Eds.), *Principles and practice of sex therapy: Update for the 1990s* (pp. 168–206). Guilford.

Araujo, A. B., Esche, G. R., Kupelian, V., O'Donnell, A. B., Travison, T. G., Williams, R. E., . . . McKinlay, J. B. (2007). Prevalence of symptomatic androgen deficiency in men. *Journal of Clinical Endocrinology and Metabolism, 92*(11), 4241–4247. doi:10.1210/jc.2007-1245

Bancroft, J. (2005). The endocrinology of sexual arousal. *Journal of Endocrinology, 186*(3), 411–27. doi:10.1677/joe.1.06233

Bancroft, J., Loftus, J., & Long, J. S. (2003). Distress about sex: A national survey of women in heterosexual relationships. *Archives of Sexual Behavior, 32*(3), 193–208. doi:10.1023/A:1023420431760

Barlow, D. H. (1986). Causes of sexual dysfunction: The role of anxiety and cognitive interference. *Journal of Consulting and Clinical Psychology*, *54*(2), 140–148. doi:10.1037/0022-006X.54.2.140

Bensley, L. S., Van Eenwyk, J., & Simmons, K. W. (2000). Self-reported childhood sexual and physical abuse and adult HIV-risk behaviors and heavy drinking. *American Journal of Preventive Medicine*, *18*(2), 151–158. doi:10.1016/S0749-3797(99)00084-7

Bergeron, S., Rosen, N. O., & Pukall, C. F. (2014). Genital pain in women and men: It can hurt more than your sex life. In Kathryn S. K. Hall & Yitzchak Binik (Eds.), *Principles and practice of sex therapy* (pp. 159–176). Guilford.

Bernardo, A. (2001). Sexuality in patients with coronary disease and heart failure. *Herz*, *26*(5), 353–359. doi:10.1007/PL00002038

Binik, Y. M. (2010a). The DSM diagnostic criteria for dyspareunia. *Archives of Sexual Behavior*, *39*(2), 292–303. doi:10.1007/s10508-009-9563-x

Binik, Y. M. (2010b). The DSM diagnostic criteria for vaginismus. *Archives of Sexual Behavior*, *39*(2), 278–291.

Brotto, L. A., Heiman, J. R., & Tolman, D. L. (2009). Narratives of desire in mid-age women with and without arousal difficulties. *Journal of Sex Research*, *46*(5), 387–398. doi:10.1080/00224490902792624

Burrows, L. J., Basha, M., & Goldstein, A. T. (2012). The effects of hormonal contraceptives on female sexuality: A review. *Journal of Sexual Medicine*, *9*(9), 2213–2223. doi:10.1111/j.1743-6109.2012.02848.x

Carani, C., Isidori, A. M., Granata, A., Carosa, E., Maggi, M., Lenzi, A., & Jannini, E. A. (2005). Multicenter study on the prevalence of sexual symptoms in male hypo- and hyperthyroid patients. *Journal of Clinical Endocrinology and Metabolism*, *90*(12), 6472–6479. doi:10.1210/jc.2005-1135

Carvalheira, A., Traeen, B., & Štulhofer, A. (2014). Correlates of men's sexual interest: A cross-cultural study. *Journal of Sexual Medicine*, *11*(1), 154–164. doi:10.1111/jsm.12345

Chew, K.-K., Finn, J., Stuckey, B., Gibson, N., Sanfilippo, F., Bremner, A., . . . Jamrozik, K. (2010). Erectile dysfunction as a predictor for subsequent atherosclerotic cardiovascular events: Findings from a linked-data study. *Journal of Sexual Medicine*, *7*(1 Pt 1), 192–202. doi:10.1111/j.1743-6109.2009.01576.x

Christensen, B. S., Grønbaek, M., Osler, M., Pedersen, B. V, Graugaard, C., & Frisch, M. (2011). Sexual dysfunctions and difficulties in Denmark: Prevalence and associated sociodemographic factors. *Archives of Sexual Behavior*, *40*(1), 121–132.

Clayton, A. H., Croft, H. A., & Handiwala, L. (2014). Antidepressants and sexual dysfunction: Mechanisms and clinical implications. *Postgraduate Medicine*, *126*(2), 91–99. doi:10.3810/pgm.2014.03.2744

Clayton, A. H., El Haddad, S., Iluonakhamhe, J.-P., Ponce Martinez, C., & Schuck, A. E. (2014). Sexual dysfunction associated with major depressive disorder and antidepressant treatment. *Expert Opinion on Drug Safety*, *13*(10), 1361–1374. doi:10.1517/14740338.2014.951324

Clayton, A. H., Kennedy, S. H., Edwards, J. B., Gallipoli, S., & Reed, C. R. (2013). The effect of vilazodone on sexual function during the treatment of major depressive disorder. *Journal of Sexual Medicine*, *10*(10), 2465–2476. doi:10.1111/jsm.12004

Clemens, J. Q., Meenan, R. T., Rosetti, M. C. K., Gaos, S. Y., & Calhoun, E. A. (2005). Prevalence and incidence of interstitial cystitis in a managed care population. *Journal of Urology*, *173*(1), 98–102.

Corona, G., Jannini, E. A., Lotti, F., Boddi, V., De Vita, G., Forti, G., . . . Maggi, M. (2011). Premature and delayed ejaculation: Two ends of a single continuum influenced by hormonal milieu. *International Journal of Andrology*, *34*(1), 41–48. doi:10.1111/j.1365-2605.2010.01059.x

Corona, G., Petrone, L., Mannucci, E., Ricca, V., Balercia, G., Giommi, R., . . . Maggi, M. (2004). The impotent couple: Low desire. *International Journal of Andrology*, *28*(s2), 46–52. doi:10.1111/j.1365-2605.2005.00594.x

Corona, G., Rastrelli, G., & Maggi, M. (2011). Update in testosterone therapy for men (CME). *Journal of Sexual Medicine*, *8*(3), 639–654. doi:10.1111/j.1743-6109.2010.02200.x

Davidson, J. K., & Moore, N. B. (1994). Guilt and lack of orgasm during sexual intercourse: Myth versus reality among college women. *Journal of Sex Education and Therapy*, *20*(3), 153–174.

Davis, S. N., Morin, M., Binik, Y. M., Khalifé, S., & Carrier, S. (2011). Use of pelvic floor ultrasound to assess pelvic floor muscle function in urolgocial chronic pelvic pain syndrome in men. *Journal of Sexual Medicine*, *8*(11), 3173–3180.

Davison, S. L., Bell, R. J., LaChina, M., Holden, S. L., & Davis, S. R. (2008). Sexual function in well women: Stratification by sexual satisfaction, hormone use, and menopause status. *Journal of Sexual Medicine* (5), 1214–22.

Dennerstein, L., Koochaki, P., Barton, I., & Graziottin, A. (2006). Hypoactive sexual desire disorder in menopausal women: A survey of Western European women. *Journal of Sexual Medicine*, *3*, 212–222. doi:10.1111/j.1743-6109.2006.00215.x

Diamond, L. M., & Wallen, K. (2011). Sexual minority women's sexual motivation around the time of ovulation. *Archives of Sexual Behavior*, *40*(2), 237–246. doi:10.1007/s10508-010-9631-2

Dubé, J. P., Corsini-Munt, S., Muise, A., & Rosen, N. O. (2019). Emotion regulation in couples affected by female sexual interest/arousal disorder. *Archives of Sexual Behavior*, *48*(8), 2491–2506.

Dunn, K. M., Croft, P. R., & Hackett, G. I. (1999). Association of sexual problems with social, psychological, and physical problems in men and women: A cross sectional population survey. *Journal of Epidemiology and Community Health*, *53*(3), 144–8.

Exton, N. G., Chau Truong, T., Exton, M. S., Wingenfeld, S. a., Leygraf, N., Saller, B., . . . Schedlowski, M. (2000). Neuroendocrine response to film-induced sexual arousal in men and women. *Psychoneuroendocrinology*, *25*(2), 187–199. doi:10.1016/S0306-4530(99)00049-9

Farmer, M. A., Taylor, A. M., Bailey, A. L., Tuttle, A. H., MacIntyre, L. C., Milagrosa, Z. E., . . . Mogil, J. S. (2011). Repeated vulvovaginal fungal infections cause persistent pain in a mouse model of vulvodynia. *Science Translational Medicine*, *3*(101), 101ra91. doi:10.1126/scitranslmed.3002613

Feldman, H. A., Goldstein, I., Hatzichristou, D. G., Krane, R. J., & McKinlay, J. B. (1994). Impotence and its medical and psychosocial correlates: Results of the Massachusetts Male Aging Study. *Journal of Urology*, *151*(1), 54–61.

Freihart, B. K., Sears, M. A., & Meston, C. M. (2020). Relational and interpersonal predictors of sexual satisfaction. *Current Sexual Health Reports*, 1–7.

Friedman, M. (1973). Success phobia and retarded ejaculation. *American Journal of Psychotherapy* (27), 78–84.

Fugl-Meyer, A., & Sjogren, K. (1999). Sexual disabilities, problems and satisfaction in 18-74 year old Swedes. *Scandinavian Journal of Sexuality*, 2, 79.

Fugl-Meyer, K. S., Bohm-Starke, N., Damsted Petersen, C., Fugl-Meyer, A., Parish, S., & Giraldi, A. (2013). Standard operating procedures for female genital sexual pain. *Journal of Sexual Medicine*, 10(1), 83–93.

Georgiadis, J. R., Reinders, A. A. T. S., Van der Graaf, F. H. C. E., Paans, A. M. J., & Kortekaas, R. (2007). Brain activation during human male ejaculation revisited. *Neuroreport*, 18(6), 553–7.

Goldstein, I., Traish, A., & Kim, N. (2004). The role of sex steroid hormones in female sexual function and dysfunction. *Clinical Obstetrics and Gynecology*, 47(2), 471–416.

Goodman, M. P., Placik, O. J., Benson, R. H., Miklos, J. R., Moore, R. D., Jason, R. A., . . . Gonzalez, F. (2010). A large multicenter outcome study of female genital plastic surgery. *Journal of Sexual Medicine*, 7(4), 1565–77.

Graham, C. A. (2010). The DSM diagnostic criteria for female orgasmic disorder. *Archives of Sexual Behavior*, 39(2), 256–270.

Graham, C. A., Sanders, S. A., Milhausen, R. R., & Mcbride, K. R. (2004). Turning on and turning off: A focus group study of the factors that affect women's sexual arousal. *Archives of Sexual Behavior*, 33(6), 527–538.

Graziottin, A., & Leiblum, S. R. (2005). Biological and psychological pathophysiology of female sexual dysfunction during the menopausal transition. *Journal of Sexual Medicine*, 2(3), 134–146.

Grover, S. A., Lowensteyn, I., Kaouache, M., Marchand, S., Coupal, L., DeCarolis, E., . . . Defoy, I. (2006). The prevalence of erectile dysfunction in the primary care setting: Importance of risk factors for diabetes and vascular disease. *Archives of Internal Medicine*, 166, 213–219.

Handy, A. B., Stanton, A. M., & Meston, C. M. (2019). What does sexual arousal mean to you? Women with and without sexual arousal concerns describe their experiences. *Journal of Sex Research*, 56(3), 345–355.

Hankin, B. L., Fraley, R. C., & Abela, J. R. Z. (2005). Daily depression and cognitions about stress: Evidence for a traitlike depressogenic cognitive style and the prediction of depressive symptoms in a prospective daily diary study. *Journal of Personality and Social Psychology*, 88(4), 673–85.

Harlow, B. L., & Stewart, E. G. (2005). Adult-onset vulvodynia in relation to childhood violence victimization. *American Journal of Epidemiology*, 161(9), 871–880.

Harte, C. B., & Meston, C. M. (2011). Recreational use of erectile dysfunction medications and its adverse effects on erectile function in young healthy men: The mediating role of confidence in erectile ability. *Journal of Sexual Medicine*, 9(7), 1852–1859.

Heiman, J. R. (2002). Sexual dysfunction: Overview of prevalance, etiological factors, and treatments. *Journal of Sex Research*, 39(1), 73–78.

Hong, L. K. (1984). Survival of the fastest: On the origin of premature ejaculation. *Journal of Sex Research*, 20(2), 109–122.

Huang, M., Li, G., Liu, J., Li, Y., & Du, P. (2020). Is there an association between contraception and sexual dysfunction in women? A systematic review and meta-analysis based on female sexual function index. *Journal of Sexual Medicine*, (17)10, 1942–1955.

Isidori, A. M., Giannetta, E., Gianfrilli, D., Greco, E. A., Bonifacio, V., Aversa, A., . . . Lenzi, A. (2005). Effects of testosterone on sexual function in men: Results of a meta-analysis. *Clinical Endocrinology*, 63(4), 381–394.

Jern, P., Santtila, P., Witting, K., Alanko, K., Harlaar, N., Johansson, A., . . . Sandnabba, K. (2007). Premature and delayed ejaculation: Genetic and environmental effects in a population-based sample of Finnish twins. *Journal of Sexual Medicine*, 4(6), 1739–1749.

Kao, A., Binik, Y. M., Kapuscinski, A., & Khalifé, S. (2008). Dyspareunia in postmenopausal women: A critical review. *Pain Research and Management*, 13(3), 243–254.

Kaplan, H. S. (1989). *How to overcome premature ejaculation.* Brunner/Mazel.

Kedde, H., Donker, G., Leusink, P., & Kruijer, H. (2011). The incidence of sexual dysfunction in patients attending Dutch general practitioners. *International Journal of Sexual Health*, 23(4), 269–277.

Keks, N. A, Hope, J., & Culhane, C. (2014). Management of antidepressant-induced sexual dysfunction. *Australasian Psychiatry: Bulletin of Royal Australian and New Zealand College of Psychiatrists*, 22(6), 525–528.

Khera, M., Bhattacharya, R. K., Blick, G., Kushner, H., Nguyen, D., & Miner, M. M. (2011). Improved sexual function with testosterone replacement therapy in hypogonadal men: Real-world data from the Testim Registry in the United States (TRiUS). *Journal of Sexual Medicine*, 8(11), 3204–3213.

Kingsberg, S. A., & Knudson, G. (2011). Female sexual disorders: Assessment, diagnosis, and treatment. *CNS Spectrums*, 16(2), 49–62.

Kirby, M., Jackson, G., Simonsen, U., Primary, H., Surgery, T., Road, N., . . . Thomas, S. (2005). Endothelial dysfunction links erectile dysfunction to heart disease. *International Journal of Clinical Practie*, 59(February), 225–229.

Lallemand, F., Salhi, Y., Linard, F., Giami, A., & Rozenbaum, W. (2002). Sexual dysfunction in 156 ambulatory HIV-infected men receiving highly active antiretroviral therapy combinations with and without protease inhibitors. *Journal of Acquired Immune Deficiency Syndromes (1999)*, 30(2), 187–190.

Landry, T., & Bergeron, S. (2011). Biopsychosocial factors associated with dyspareunia in a community sample of adolescent girls. *Archives of Sexual Behavior*, 40(5), 877–889.

Laumann, E. O., Glasser, D. B., Neves, R. C. S., & Moreira, E. D. (2009). A population-based survey of sexual activity, sexual problems and associated help-seeking behavior patterns in mature adults in the United States of America. *International Journal of Impotence Research*, 21(3), 171–178.

Laumann, E. O., Michael, R. T., Gagnon, G. H., & Kolata, G. (1994). *Sex in America: Definitive survey.* Little, Brown and Company.

Laumann, E. O., Nicolosi, A., Glasser, D. B., Paik, A., Gingell, C., Moreira, E., & Wang, T. (2005). Sexual problems among women and men aged 40–80 y: Prevalence and correlates identified in the global study of sexual attitudes and behaviors. *International Journal of Impotence Research*, 17(1), 39–57.

Laumann, E. O., Paik, A., Rosen, R. C., & Page, P. (1999). Sexual dysfunction in the United States. *Journal of the American Medical Association*, 281(6), 537–545.

Leiblum, S. R., Koochaki, P. E., Rodenberg, C. A, Barton, I. P., & Rosen, R. C. (2006). Hypoactive sexual desire disorder in postmenopausal women: US results from the Women's International Study of Health and Sexuality (WISHeS). *Menopause (New York, N. Y.)*, *13*(1), 46–56.

Lew-Starowicz, M., & Rola, R. (2014). Sexual dysfunctions and sexual quality of life in men with multiple sclerosis. *Journal of Sexual Medicine*, *11*(5), 1294–1301.

Líndal, E., & Stefánsson, J. G. (1993). The lifetime prevalence of psychosexual and dysfunction among 55-57-year-olds in Iceland. *Social Psychiatry and Psychiatry Epidemiology*, *28*(2), 91–95.

Lorenz, T. A., Harte, C. B., Hamilton, L. D., & Meston, C. M. (2012). Evidence for a curvilinear relationship between sympathetic nervous system activation and women's physiological sexual arousal. *Psychophysiology*, *49*(1), 111–117.

Maggi, M., Buvat, J., Corona, G., Guay, A., & Torres, L. O. (2013). Hormonal causes of male sexual dysfunctions and their management (hyperprolactinemia, thyroid disorders, GH disorders, and DHEA). *Journal of Sexual Medicine*, *10*(3), 661–677.

Mah, K., & Binik, Y. M. (2001). The nature of human orgasm: A critical review of major trends. *Clinical Psychology Review*, *21*(6), 823–856.

Mallory, A. B., Stanton, A. M., & Handy, A. B. (2019). Couples' sexual communication and dimensions of sexual function: A meta-analysis. *Journal of Sex Research*, *56*(7), 882–898.

Masters, W. H., & Johnson, V. E. (1970). *Human sexual inadequacy*. Little, Brown and Company.

McCabe, M. P., & Connaughton, C. (2014). Psychosocial factors associated with male sexual difficulties. *Journal of Sex Research*, *51*(1), 31–42.

McCall, K. M., & Meston, C. M. (2006). Cues resulting in desire for sexual activity in women. *Journal of Sexual Medicine*, *3*(5), 838–852.

McKenna, K. E. (1999). *Orgasm: Encyclopedia of reproduction*, 3, 528–531. Academic Press.

Mercer, C. H., Fenton, K. A, Johnson, A. M., Wellings, K., Macdowall, W., McManus, S., . . . Erens, B. (2003). Sexual function problems and help seeking behaviour in Britain: National probability sample survey. *BMJ (Clinical Research Ed.)*, *327*(7412), 426–427.

Meston, C. (2006). Female orgasmic disorder: Treatment strategies and outcome results. *Women's Sexual Function and Dysfunction: Study, Diagnosis, and Treatment*. https://www.taylorfrancis.com/books/mono/10.1201/9780367800123/women-sexual-function-dysfunction-susan-davis-abdulmaged-traish-irwin-goldstein-cindy-meston

Meston, C. M., & Frohlich, P. F. (2000). The neurobiology of sexual function. *Archives of General Psychiatry*, *57*(11), 1012–1030.

Meston, C. M., & Gorzalka, B. B. (1995). The effects of sympathetic activation on physiological and subjective sexual arousal in women. *Behavior Research and Therapy*, *33*(6), 651–664.

Meston, C. M., & Gorzalka, B. B. (1996a). Differential effects of sympathetic activation on sexual arousal in sexually dysfunctional and functional women. *Journal of Abnormal Psychology*, *105*(4), 582–591.

Meston, C. M., & Gorzalka, B. B. (1996b). The effects of immediate, delayed, and residual sympathetic activation on sexual arousal in women. *Behavior Research and Therapy*, *34*(2), 143–148.

Meston, C. M., Gorzalka, B. B., & Wright, J. M. (1997). Inhibition of subjective and physiological sexual arousal in women by clonidine. *Psychosomatic Medicine*, *59*, 339–407.

Meston, C. M., & Heiman, J. R. (1998). Ephedrine-activated physiological sexual arousal in women. *Archives of General Psychiatry*, *55*(7), 652–6.

Meston, C. M., Hull, E., Levin, R. J., & Sipski, M. (2004). Disorders of orgasm in women. *Journal of Sexual Medicine*, *1*(1), 66–68.

Meston, C. M., Levin, R. J., Sipski, M. L., Hull, E. M., & Heiman, J. R. (2004). Women's orgasm. *Annual Review of Sex Research*, *15*, 173–257.

Meston, C. M., Rellini, A. H., & Heiman, J. R. (2006). Women's history of sexual abuse, their sexuality, and sexual self-schemas. *Journal of Consulting and Clinical Psychology*, *74*(2), 229–36.

Metz, M. E., Pryor, J. L., Nesvacil, L. J., Abuzzahab Sr, F., & Koznar, J. (1997). Premature ejaculation: A psychophysiological review. *Journal of Sex & Martial Therapy*, *23*(1), 3–23.

Meuleman, E. J. H., & Van Lankveld, J. J. D. M. (2005). Hypoactive sexual desire disorder: An underestimated condition in men. *BJU International*, *95*(3), 291–296. doi:10.1111/j.1464-410X.2005.05285.x

Miner, M. M. (2009). Erectile dysfunction and the "window of curability": A harbinger of cardiovascular events. *Mayo Clinic Proceedings*, *84*(2), 102–104. doi:10.1016/S0025-6196(11)60815-X

Mitchell, K. R., Jones, K. G., Wellings, K., Johnson, A. M., Graham, C. A., Datta, J., . . . Field, N. (2016). Estimating the prevalence of sexual function problems: The impact of morbidity criteria. *Journal of Sex Research*, *53*(8), 955–967.

Murray, S. H., & Milhausen, R. R. (2012). Sexual desire and relationship duration in young men and women. *Journal of Sex & Marital Therapy*, *38*(1), 28–40. doi:10.1080/0092623X.2011.569637

Nicolosi, A., Laumann, E. O., Glasser, D. B., Moreira, E. D., Paik, A., & Gingell, C. (2004). Sexual behavior and sexual dysfunctions after age 40: The global study of sexual attitudes and behaviors. *Urology*, *64*(5), 991–997. doi:10.1016/j.urology.2004.06.055

Nobre, P. J., & Pinto-Gouveia, J. (2008). Cognitive and emotional predictors of female sexual dysfunctions: Preliminary findings. *Journal of Sex & Martial Therapy*, *34*(4), 325–342.

Nobre, P. J., & Pinto-Gouveia, J. (2009). Cognitive schemas associated with negative sexual events: A comparison of men and women with and without sexual dysfunction. *Archives of Sexual Behavior*, *38*(5), 842–51. doi:10.1007/s10508-008-9450-x

O'Toole, A., Winter, D., & Friedman, S. (2014). Review article: The psychosexual impact of inflammatory bowel disease in male patients. *Alimentary Pharmacology & Therapeutics*, *39*(10), 1085–1094. doi:10.1111/apt.12720

Ovesey, L., & Meyers, H. (1968). Retarded ejaculation: Psychodynamics and psychotherapy. *American Journal of Psychotherapy* (22), 185–201.

Paick, J. S., Jeong, H., & Park, M. S. (1998). Penile sensitivity in men with premature ejaculation. *International Journal of Impotence Research*, *10*(4), 247–250.

Pastuszak, A. W., Badhiwala, N., Lipshultz, L. I., & Khera, M. (2013). Depression is correlated with the psychological and physical aspects of sexual dysfunction in men. *International Journal of Impotence Research*, *25*(5), 194–199. doi:10.1038/ijir.2013.4

Paterson, L. Q., Davis, S. N., Khalifé, S., Amsel, R., & Binik, Y. M. (2009). Persistent genital and pelvic pain after childbirth. *Journal of Sexual Medicine*, 6(1), 215–221.

Payne, K. A., Binik, Y. M., Amsel, R., & Khalifé, S. (2005). When sex hurts, anxiety and fear orient attention towards pain. *European Journal of Pain*, 9(4), 427–436. doi:10.1016/j.ejpain.2004.10.003

Peixoto, M., & Nobre, P. (2013). Prevalence of female sexual problems in Portugal: A community-based study. *Journal of Sexual Medicine*, 10, 394. doi:10.1001/jama.281.6.537

Perelman, M. (2003). Sex coaching for physicians: Combination treatment for patient and partner. *International Journal of Impotence Research*, 15 (Suppl 5), S67–74. doi:10.1038/sj.ijir.3901075

Perelman, M. A. (2005). Idiosyncratic masturbation patterns: A key unexplored variable in the treatment of retarded ejaculation by the practicing urologist. *Journal of Urology*, 173(4), 340.

Perelman, M. A. (2009). The sexual tipping point: A mind/body model for sexual medicine. *Journal of Sexual Medicine*, 6(3), 629–632.

Perelman, M. A. (2014). Delayed ejaculation. In Y. M. Binik & K. S. Hall (Eds.), *Principles and practice of sex therapy*, 5th ed. Guilford.

Perelman, M. A., & Rowland, D. L. (2006). Retarded ejaculation. *World Journal of Urology*, 24(6), 645–652. doi:10.1007/s00345-006-0127-6

Pillsworth, E. G., Haselton, M. G., & Buss, D. M. (2004). Ovulatory shifts in female sexual desire. *Journal of Sex Research*, 41(1), 55–65. doi:10.1080/00224490409552213

Pukall, C. F., Payne, K. A., Kao, A., Khalifé, S., & Binik, Y. M. (2005). Dyspareunia. Handbook of Sexual Dysfunction. In R. Balon and R. T. Segraves (Eds.), *Handbook of Sexual Dysfunctions*. Taylor & Francis.

Reissing, E. D., Binik, Y. M., Khalifé, S., Cohen, D., & Amsel, R. (2004). Vaginal spasm, pain, and behavior: An empirical investigation of the diagnosis of vaginismus. *Archives of Sexual Behavior*, 33(1), 5–17. doi:10.1023/B:ASEB.0000007458.32852.c8

Rellini, A. (2008). Review of the empirical evidnece for a theoretical model to understand the sexual problems of women with a history of CSA. *Journal of Sexual Medicine*, 5(1), 31–46.

Rosen, N. O., & Bergeron, S. (2019). Genito-pelvic pain through a dyadic lens: Moving toward an interpersonal emotion regulation model of women's sexual dysfunction. *Journal of Sex Research*, 56(4–5), 440–461.

Rosen, R. C., Miner, M. M., & Wincze, J. P. (2014). Erectile dysfunction: Integration of medical and psychological approaches. In Y. M. Binik & K. S. K. Hall (Eds.), *Principles and practice of sex therapy*, 5th ed. (pp. 61–88). Guilford.

Rosen, N. O., & Pukall, C. (2016). Comparing the prevalence, risk factors, and repercussions of postpartum genito-pelvic pain and dyspareunia. *Sexual Medicine Reviews*, 4(2), 126–135.

Roumeguère, T., Wespes, E., Carpentier, Y., Hoffmann, P., & Schulman, C. (2003). Erectile dysfunction is associated with a high prevalence of hyperlipidemia and coronary heart disease risk. *European Urology*, 44(3), 355–359. doi:10.1016/S0302-2838(03)00306-3

Rowland, D. L. (1998). Penile sensitivity in men: A composite of recent findings. *Urology*, 52(6), 1101–1105.

Rowland, D. L., Keeney, C., & Slob, A. K. (2004). Sexual response in men with inhibited or retarded ejaculation. *International Journal of Impotence Research*, 16(3), 270–274. doi:10.1038/sj.ijir.3901156

Sandhu, K. S., Melman, A., & Mikhail, M. S. (2011). Impact of hormones on female sexual function and dysfunction. *Female Pelvic Medicine & Reconstructive Surgery*, 17(1), 8–16. doi:10.1097/SPV.0b013e318204491f

Sarrel, P. M. (1998). Ovarian hormones and vaginal blood flow: Using laser doppler velocimetry to measure effects in a clinical trial of post-menopausal women. *International Journal of Impotence Research*, 10(Suppl 2), S91–S93.

Schmidt, P. J., & Rubinow, D. R. (2009). Sex hormones and mood in the perimenopause. *Annals of the New York Academy of Sciences*, 1179, 70–85. doi:10.1111/j.1749-6632.2009.04982.x

Schouten, B. W. V, Bohnen, a M., Bosch, J. L. H. R., Bernsen, R. M. D., Deckers, J. W., Dohle, G. R., & Thomas, S. (2008). Erectile dysfunction prospectively associated with cardiovascular disease in the Dutch general population: Results from the Krimpen Study. *International Journal of Impotence Research*, 20(1), 92–99. doi:10.1038/sj.ijir.3901604

Schultz, W. W., Basson, R., Binik, Y. M., Eschenbach, D., Wesselmann, U., & Van Lankveld, J. (2005). Women's sexual pain and its management. *J Sex Med*, 2(i), 301–316. doi:10.1111/j.1743-6109.2005.20347.x

Seftel, A. D., Sun, P., & Swindle, R. (2004). The prevalence of hypertension, hyperlipidemia, diabetes mellitus and depression in men with erectile dysfunction. *Journal of Urology*, 171(6), 2341–2345. doi:10.1097/01.ju.0000125198.32936.38

Segraves, R. T. (2010). Considerations for diagnostic criteria for erectile dysfunction in DSM V. *Journal of Sexual Medicine*, 7(2 Pt 1), 654–660. doi:10.1111/j.1743-6109.2009.01684.x

Shoskes, D. A., Nickel, J. C., Rackley, R. R., & Pontari, M. A. (2009). Clinical phenotyping in chronic prostatitis/chronic pelvic pain syndrome and interstitial cystitis: A management strategy for urologic chronic pelvic pain syndromes. *Prostate Cancer and Prostatic Diseases*, 12, 177–183.

Shull, G. R., & Sprenkle, D. H. (1980). Retarded ejaculation reconceptualization and implications for treatment. *Journal of Sex & Marital Therapy*, 6(4), 234–246.

Simon, J. A. (2011). Identifying and treating sexual dysfunction in postmenopausal women: The role of estrogen. *Journal of Women's Health*, 20(10), 1453–1465. doi:10.1089/jwh.2010.2151

Sims, K. E., & Meana, M. (2010). Why did passion wane? A qualitative study of married women's attributions for declines in sexual desire. *Journal of Sex and Marital Therapy*, 36(4), 360–380.

Sipski, M. L., Alexander, C. J., & Rosen, R. (2001). Sexual arousal and orgasm in women: Effects of spinal cord injury. *Annals of Neurology*, 49(1), 35–44.

Sipski, M. L., Alexander, C. J., & Rosen, R. C. (1997). Physiological parameters associated with sexual arousal in women with incomplete spinal cord injury. *Archives of Physical Medicine and Rehabilitation*, 78, 305–313.

Stanton, A. M., Boyd, R. L., Pulverman, C. S., & Meston, C. M. (2015). Determining women's sexual self-schemas through advanced computerized text analysis. *Child Abuse & Neglect*, 46, 78–88. doi:10.1016/j.chiabu.2015.06.003

Stanton, A. M., Lorenz, T. A., Pulverman, C. S., & Meston, C. M. (2015). Heart rate variability: A risk factor for female sexual dysfunction. *Applied Psychophysiology and Biofeedback*, 40(3), 229–237. doi:10.1007/s10484-015-9286-9

Stimmel, G., & Gutierrez, M. A. (2006). Sexual dysfunction and psychotropic medications. *CNS Spectrums*, *11*(S9), 24–30.

ter Kuile, M. M., & Reissing, E. D. (2014). Lifelong vaginismus. In Y. M. Binik & K. S. Hall (Eds.), *Principles and Practice of Sex Therapy*, 5th ed. Guilford.

Thompson, I. M., Tangen, C. M., Goodman, P. J., Probstfield, J. L., Moinpour, C. M., & Coltman, C. A. (2005). Erectile dysfunction and subsequent cardiovascular disease. *Journal of the American Medical Association*, *294*(23), 2996–3002. doi:10.1001/jama.294.23.2996

Toorians, A. W., Janssen, E., Laan, E., Gooren, L. J., Giltay, E. J., Oe, P. L., . . . Everaerd, W. (1997). Chronic renal failure and sexual functioning: Clinical status versus objectively assessed sexual response. *Nephrology Dialysis Transplantation*, *12*(12), 2654–2663. doi:10.1093/ndt/12.12.2654

Tuiten, A., van Rooij, K., Bloemers, J., Eisenegger, C., van Honk, J., Kessels, R., . . . & Pfaus, J. G. (2018). Efficacy and safety of on-demand use of 2 treatments designed for different etiologies of female sexual interest/arousal disorder: 3 randomized clinical trials. *Journal of Sexual Medicine*, *15*(2), 201–216.

Van Anders, S. M. (2012). Testosterone and sexual desire in healthy women and men. *Archives of Sexual Behavior*, *41*(6), 1471–1484. doi:10.1007/s10508-012-9946-2

Van Anders, S. M., Brotto, L. A., Farrell, J., & Yule, M. (2009). Associations among physiological and subjective sexual response, sexual desire, and salivary steriod hormones in healthy premenopausal women. *Journal of Sexual Medicine*, *6*, 739–751.

Van Anders, S. M., & Gray, P. B. (2007). Hormones and human partnering. *Annual Review of Sex Research*, *18*, 60–93.

van Lankveld, J., Granot, M., Schultz, W. W., Binik, Y. M., Wesselmann, U., Pukall, C. F., . . . Achtrari, C. (2010). Women's sexual pain disorders. *Journal of Sexual Medicine*, *7*(12), 615–631. doi:10.1111/j.1743-6109.2009.01631.x

Waldinger, M. D. (2007). Premature ejaculation. *Drugs*, *67*, 547–568.

Waldinger, M. D., Berendsen, H. H. G., Blok, B. F. M., Olivier, B., & Holstege, G. (1998). Premature ejaculation and serotonergic antidepressants-induced delayed ejaculation: The involvement of the serotonergic system. *Behavioural Brain Research*, *92*(2), 111–118. doi:10.1016/S0166-4328(97)00183-6

Waldinger, M. D., Rietschel, M., Nothen, M. M., Hengeveld, M. W., & Olivier, B. (1998). Familial occurence of primary premature ejaculation. *Psychiatric Genetics*, *8*(1), 37–40.

Waldinger, M. D., & Schweitzer, D. H. (2005). Retarded ejaculation in men: An overview of psychological and neurobiological insights. *World Journal of Urology*, *23*(2), 76–81.

Wallwiener, C. W., Wallwiener, L. M., Seeger, H., Muck, A. O., Bitzer, J., & Wallwiener, M. (2010). Prevalence of sexual dysfunction and impact of contraception in female German medical students. *Journal of Sexual Medicine*, *7*, 2139–2148.

Whipple, B., Gerdes, C. A., & Komisaruk, B. R. (1996). Sexual response to self-stimulation in women with complete spinal cord injury. *Journal of Sex Research*, *33*(3), 231.

Witting, K., Santtila, P., Varjonen, M., Jern, P., Johansson, A., Von Der Pahlen, B., & Sandnabba, K. (2008). Female sexual dysfunction, sexual distress, and compatibility with partner. *Journal of Sexual Medicine*, *5*, 2587–2599. doi:10.1111/j.1743-6109.2008.00984.x

Woo, J. S. T., Brotto, L. a, & Gorzalka, B. B. (2012). The relationship between sex guilt and sexual desire in a community sample of Chinese and Euro-Canadian women. *Journal of Sex Research*, *49*(2–3), 290–298. doi:10.1080/00224499.2010.551792

Xhyheri, B., Manfrini, O., Mazzolini, M., Pizzi, C., & Bugiardini, R. (2012). Heart rate variability today. *Progress in Cardiovascular Diseases*, *55*(3), 321–331. doi:10.1016/j.pcad.2012.09.001

Yasan, A., Tamam, L., Ozkan, M., & Gurgen, F. (2009). Premarital sexual attitudes and experiences in university students. *Anatolian Journal of Clinical Investigation*, *3*(3), 174–184.

# CHAPTER 18

# Eating Disorders

Howard Steiger, Linda Booij, Annie St-Hilaire, *and* Lea Thaler

Eating disorders (EDs) are polysymptomatic syndromes defined by maladaptive attitudes and behaviors around eating, weight, and body image but typically accompanied by disturbances of self-image, mood, impulse regulation, and interpersonal functioning. The *DSM-5* classifies EDs among "Feeding and Eating Disorders," and recognizes six subtypes: anorexia nervosa (AN), bulimia nervosa (BN), binge-eating disorder (BED), avoidant/restrictive food intake disorder (ARFID), rumination disorder (RD), and pica. Two residual diagnoses—other specified feeding or eating disorder (OSFED) and unspecified feeding or eating disorder (USFED)—capture ED variants that have clinical significance without fulfilling criteria for full-threshold syndromes. As pica occurs in unusual contexts associated with severe intellectual impairments or particular medical conditions, it will not ordinarily be treated alongside other EDs, and we therefore opt not to address this entity in this chapter. We will, however, review pathognomonic features of the remaining *DSM-5* ED syndromes, as well as findings on concurrent traits and comorbid psychopathology. We also discuss the factors—biological, psychological, and social—that are understood to explain varied convergences of eating and comorbid symptoms that shape clinical EDs.

## Defining Characteristics
### Anorexia Nervosa

AN is defined by a relentless pursuit of thinness. Formerly attributed to a morbid fear of weight gain or obesity, *DSM-5* restates the concern of affected individuals without it being mandatory that there be intense fear of weight gain. Such fears are, however, a commonly present feature. What is required is that individuals restrict energy intake relative to requirements (leading to a markedly low body weight), experience a fear of weight gain or loss of control over weight gain, or display persistent behavior to avoid weight gain (even though already at a low weight), and experience either a disturbance in the way in which their body weight or shape is experienced, undue influence of body weight or shape on self-evaluation, or persistent lack of recognition of the seriousness of a currently low body weight. The modifications described respond to the reality that people with AN, especially when very young or from Asian or African cultures, do not always espouse fears of weight gain as a rationale for their food-refusal and self-induced emaciation. *DSM-5* also drops the criterion sign of amenorrhea, it representing an imprecise reflection of nutritional status and being inappropriate in the case of males.

To provide an illustrative example, we describe "Joannie." Joannie, a 17-year-old high school student, eats a restricted range of "safe" foods—mainly vegetables and a few nuts or an occasional spoonful of yoghurt. She avoids eating with her family or friends, so that she will be able to fully control what, how much, and when she eats. She exercises at least 2 hours a day (on the treadmill) and never eats before 6 PM, to be sure not to have time to overeat during any given day. Joannie is 5′4″ tall and weighs 88 pounds, giving her a body mass index (BMI: Kg/m² or lbs/in² × 703) of 15.1—meaning that she is so thin as to

### Abbreviations
| | |
|---|---|
| AN | Anorexia nervosa |
| ARFID | Avoidant/restrictive food intake disorder |
| BED | Binge-eating disorder |
| BMI | Body mass index |
| BN | Bulimia nervosa |
| ED | Eating disorder |
| RD | Rumination disorder |

border on emaciation. Her weight has dropped over the past 6 months from an average of 128 pounds. Joannie compulsively insists that her fingertips have to touch when she circles her thighs with her hands, and when she feels that she has eaten something too rich in calories, even when it may have been what most people would call a snack, Joannie purges by vomiting or taking laxatives.

Although Joannie shows no binge eating (thus far), more than half of people with AN eventually develop binge-eating episodes—that is, periodic dyscontrol over eating, or incapacity to satiate. In consideration of this reality, *DSM-5* draws a distinction between AN, restricting subtype (AN-R), in which there is restriction of food intake but no binge eating or purging, and AN, binge-eating/purging (AN-B/P) subtype, in which (as the label implies) regular binge or purge episodes occur. Joannie would be diagnosable as having AN-B/P subtype, because she regularly purges.

*Bulimia Nervosa*

A defining feature of BN is binge eating (i.e., appetitive dyscontrol) followed by an effort to compensate for calories consumed through self-induced vomiting, laxative misuse, intensive exercise, fasting, or other means. BN occurs in people with normal or above-normal body weight who therefore (by definition) do not have AN. Binge-purge episodes occur at least once weekly in the *DSM-5* definition. However, such episodes typically occur far more frequently and can, when the disorder is severe, occur many times daily. AN and BN share in common a core preoccupation with body shape and weight and the compulsion to restrict food intake. Excessive dietary restraint in people with BN eventually gives way to appetitive dysregulation and binge eating. Binges are characterized by consumption—often with a terrifying sense of dyscontrol—of excessive, sometimes massive, quantities of calories. Binge eating can provoke profound feelings of shame, anxiety, or depression and dramatic shifts in the sufferer's sense of self-worth and well-being. The preceding lends to BN a characteristic unpredictability or lability, as people with this syndrome tend to shift rapidly (depending on felt control over eating) from a sense of well-being, expansiveness, or excitability to profound despair, irritability, and depression.

Kiera serves as a "prototype." Kiera, aged 29, a recent graduate from law school, is serving as an apprentice in a law firm. People know her to be very hard-working but a bit of a "thrill seeker." She has had a number of short-lived relationships, drinks alcohol fairly regularly, and dabbles with cocaine use when it is offered to her. Although she has a slim-normal frame, she is conscious of her weight and tries to keep her food intake down, often skipping breakfast and eating green salads for lunch. After supper, especially (but not always) if she has been drinking, Kiera finds she cannot stop eating, and she goes from two portions of her supper to eating cookies, cakes, food leftovers, and just about anything else she has to eat in her pantry and fridge. She then forces herself to vomit several times, sometimes using a toothbrush to provoke gagging. After a binge-purge episode, she feels very badly about herself. At such times, she can bruise her thighs with her fists; once she burned her upper arm with a lit cigarette.

*Binge-Eating Disorder*

Like BN, BED is characterized by recurrent eating binges. However, in BED compensatory behaviors (such as vomiting, exercise, or fasting) are absent, so that BED is commonly associated with or leads to obesity. Defining characteristics include eating more rapidly than normal, eating until uncomfortably full, eating when not hungry, eating alone because of embarrassment around the quantity one eats, or feeling intense distress (guilt, disgust, or depression) after eating. Despite initial concerns that BED might not be a "mental" disorder, findings support the conclusion that obese individuals with and without BED differ in the sense that the former group displays higher overall caloric intake, additional pathological eating behaviors (such as chaotic or emotional eating), additional indices of comorbid psychopathology, and poorer response to treatment (Wonderlich et al., 2009). Notably, BED also emerges as a distinct disorder in familial-aggregation and genetic studies (Javaras et al., 2008).

*Avoidant/Restrictive Food Intake Disorder*

ARFID, a new diagnosis in *DSM-5*, evolved from what was originally conceived to be a feeding problem of infancy or early childhood—effectively, the "picky eater" syndrome. The diagnostic concept has been retooled to make it applicable across the life span. ARFID comprises a range of conditions in which people become blocked in the ability to nourish themselves adequately, not because of concerns about weight gain, but because of such things as intense aversion to certain food tastes or textures, preoccupation with the nutritional value of certain foods, or inordinate fears that eating will cause indigestion or vomiting. ARFID syndromes differ from variants of AN in which people show persistent behavior to avoid weight gain anchored to body image concerns. Someone who eats a rigidly restricted range of foods because of a compulsive effort to consume only healthy, natural foods (colloquially described as "orthorexia"), if they fail to nourish themselves adequately, would often meet ARFID criteria. Some authors suggest that there may be distinct ARFID presentations (or even subtypes): one characterized by low interest in food or eating, another by avoidance based on the sensory characteristics of food (e.g., queasiness about certain food textures), and yet another based on concern about possible aversive consequences of eating (e.g., becoming unhealthy due to consumption of artificial food additives). Available research has suggested that, compared to patients with AN, ARFID patients tend to be younger, on average, to have higher rates of psychiatric comorbidity, and to be more often male (Bryant-Waugh, 2019).

John will serve as an ARFID prototype. Always prone to anxiety, John (who is 28 years old) ate normally until a year ago when his doctor suggested that he eat carefully, as his cholesterol levels were starting to approach the borderline range. Gradually, John eliminated more and more food items that he perceived to risk increasing cholesterol, dropping anything high in fat or oil, then eggs, then cheese, then meat. He now feels able to eat only vegetables, fruits, and grains, and even these in small quantities. His weight has dropped from a previously normal range to a BMI of under 16. John hates his thinness and wants to gain weight, but still avoids eating most foods for fear of developing high cholesterol.

## Rumination Disorder

RD is characterized by the repeated regurgitation of food followed by rechewing, reswallowing, or spitting out of the regurgitated material. By definition, the behavior is not due to an associated gastrointestinal or medical condition, nor does it occur exclusively during an episode of AN, BN, BED, or ARFID. As etiology and comorbid characteristics are not well established, we will not treat RD in sections of this chapter addressing these aspects. We do note, however, that available studies suggest some connection with psychological disturbances. One study in 7- to 14-year-olds indicated that RD behaviors were positively associated with emotional and conduct problems and negatively associated with prosocial behavior (Hartmann et al., 2018). Another study identified a comorbid psychiatric disorder in 17% of children and adolescents diagnosed with rumination disorder (Chial et al., 2003).

### Other Specified Feeding or Eating Disorder; Unspecified Feeding or Eating Disorder

OSFED and USFED encompass eating syndromes that would in earlier *DSM* versions have been called *eating disorder not otherwise specified*. OSFED and USFED refer to eating problems that cause significant distress or impairment in functioning but that do not meet full criteria for a formal ED diagnosis. *DSM-5* provides illustrative examples of OSFED to guide diagnostic decision-making. These include "atypical AN," in which all the criteria for AN are met except that the individual remains in the normal or above-normal weight range after significant weight loss; "subthreshold bulimia nervosa" or "subthreshold binge eating disorder," in which frequency of problem behaviors occurs at lower than threshold frequency and/or for less than threshold duration; "purging disorder," characterized by recurrent purging in the absence of binge eating; and "night eating syndrome," characterized by recurrent eating episodes after awakening from sleep or excessive food consumption after an evening meal. For other instances, the USFED diagnosis is used. According to available evidence, "subthreshold" ED syndromes are often associated with comparable levels of distress, psychiatric comorbidity, and health-service usage to those in fully syndromic ED variants (Fairburn et al., 2007).

Are *DSM* diagnostic distinctions valid? Available efforts to develop valid ED classifications using taxometric methods, latent class analyses, or other statistical classification techniques have provided fairly good support for AN, BN, and BED as phenomenologically distinct entities (Wonderlich et al., 2007). Not only is each broad category at least partly discriminable using empirical methods, but there is also evidence to suggest that the categories may "breed true" within families. In addition, there is quite convincing support for the boundary between "restricter" and "binger/purger" variants of AN, and between BED and BN. However, there is mixed support for the distinction between anorexic- and normal-weight variants of binge-purge syndromes (i.e., AN-binge/purge type vs. BN).

## Historical Perspectives

The English physician Richard Morton is often credited with having introduced AN to the medical literature. In 1689, he documented two adolescent cases, one a boy, the other a girl, both suffering "nervous consumption," "want of appetite," and weight loss, in the absence of any apparent medical cause (Gordon, 1990, p. 12). Well-elaborated reports on AN emerged again in an 1860 account by the French physician Marcé and in independent reports (published in 1870) by Sir William Gull and Charles Lasègue. Gull is credited with coining the term "anorexia nervosa," but all three described a syndrome characterized by food refusal, onset in adolescence, amenorrhea, and lack of concern for consequences of not eating (Gordon, 1990). Intriguingly, reports on AN became relatively common through the nineteenth and twentieth centuries, but a pivotal diagnostic element—fear of weight gain—was first acknowledged only in accounts emerging well into the twentieth century. Late "entry" of this characteristic has been taken to suggest that fears of weight gain may not be essential to AN but, rather, may constitute only a contemporary rationale for instances of self-starvation, one shaped by contemporary cultural values.

The first formal reports on BN emerged much more recently, in roughly concurrent 1979 publications by Igoin in France, Boyadjieva and Achkova in Bulgaria, and Robert Palmer and Gerald Russell in England (Vandereycken, 1994). Having been formally recognized in the late 1970s, BN is widely thought to be a recently developing ED variant. Indeed, after an exhaustive review of available historical and cross-cultural data, Keel and Klump (2003) concluded that AN and BN have distinct temporal and geographical distributions, with AN showing a relatively modest increase in incidence over the years and occurring frequently in geographical areas that are quite untouched by the "culture of slimness." In contrast, BN appears to have increased dramatically in prevalence during the latter part of the twentieth century and mainly in industrialized cultures. Updating this impression, recent reviews suggest that the incidence of AN has been surprisingly stable over past decades, whereas BN incidence seems to have increased markedly over the second half of the twentieth century and then to have declined slightly since that time (Currin et al., 2005; Keel et al., 2006; Smink et al., 2012).

The phenomenon of binge eating among individuals with obesity was described by Stunkard (1959) more than 60 years ago. However, BED has a rather short history in diagnostic nosology, having been introduced in 1994 in *DSM-IV* as a provisional ED diagnosis and as an official ED for the first time in *DSM-5*. Although newer still, the ARFID diagnosis has attracted considerable interest since its introduction as a formal *DSM-5* diagnosis in 2013.

## Epidemiology

The National Comorbidity Study Replication, which attempted to estimate nationwide ED prevalences in US adults in the early 2000s, reported lifetime rates of *DSM-IV* AN, BN, and BED in women to be .9%, 1.5%, and 3.5%, respectively (Hudson et al., 2007). Corresponding rates in men were .3%, .5%, and 2.0%. Swanson and colleagues (2011) extended the study to adolescents and reported lower prevalences (.3% and .9%, respectively) of AN and BN among 13- to 18-year-old boys and girls. A more recent and even larger epidemiological study applied *DSM-5* criteria in a sample of 36,306 adults selected to represent the US population (Udo & Grilo, 2018). It documented lifetime prevalence for AN of 1.42%, for BN of .46%, and for BED of 1.25%, respectively, in women, and .12%, .08%, and .42% in men. Various current indications suggest that ED incidences (while stable in adults) may be rising in adolescents (Herpertz-Dahlmann, 2015).

Comprehensive epidemiologic data in representative populations is unavailable for ARFID and RD diagnoses. However, one population-based survey from Australia found a 3-month prevalence of ARFID of 0.3% among adults and older adolescents (Hay et al., 2017). ARFID prevalence in one pediatric treatment-seeking sample was found to be 1.5% (Eddy et al., 2015). As for RD, one study implicating 804 children aged 7–14 years indicated recurring RD behaviors in 1.49% (Hartmann et al., 2018).

The median age of ED onset is estimated to fall between 18 and 21 years; AN typically occurring by the mid-teens, BN around age 19, and BED around age 24 (Hudson et al., 2007; Udo & Grilo, 2018). Although AN and BN occur much more frequently in women than in men, BED displays a more even gender distribution, with a male-to-female ratio of roughly 2:3. Although it is widely believed that EDs are disorders of affluent, urban society, data show linkages with socioeconomic status and urbanicity to be much weaker than thought (Swanson et al., 2011).

## Comorbid Psychopathology

It seems that if one assertion can be made about EDs, it is that they are often not just about eating.

Rather, EDs frequently co-occur with mood, anxiety, substance abuse, personality, and other psychiatric disorders.

## Anxiety Disorders and Obsessive-Compulsive Disorder

Anxiety disorders are regarded as being among the most common of comorbid conditions found in people with an ED, and it is certainly true that EDs "ride" on anxious temperaments. A recent study estimates that 53.3% of people with an ED display an anxiety disorder, with generalized anxiety disorder observed in 30.5%, specific phobia in 16.6%, and social phobia in 14.7% (Ulfvebrand et al., 2015). Social anxiety appears to be distributed equally across different ED subtypes, with higher levels associated with more severe ED symptoms (Kerr-Gaffney et al., 2018). Findings indicate that anxiety symptoms tend to precede ED symptom onset. One study on the sequencing of symptom onset suggested that somatic anxiety symptoms at age 10 predicted binge-eating and fasting at age 14 and BN at age 16, whereas worry at age 10 predicted fear of weight gain, body dissatisfaction, excessive exercise, and dietary restraint at age 14, and a diagnosis of AN at age 16 (Schaumberg et al., 2019). In contrast, panic disorder has been reported to often emerge concurrently with, or following ED development (Godart et al., 2003; Pallister & Waller, 2008).

Although no longer classified as an anxiety disorder, given the prominence of anxiety in obsessive-compulsive disorder (OCD), we address OCD in this section. OCD reportedly occurs in 35% to 44% of people with AN (Kaye et al., 2004; Levinson et al., 2019). Some data have suggested that severity of compulsions predicts severity of core AN symptoms. Similarly, when individuals with AN report greater concern over mistakes, they display more severe AN and more OCD symptoms (Levinson et al., 2019).

To account for comorbidity between eating and anxiety disorders, Pallister and Waller (2008) proposed that cognitions and environmental experiences increase the likelihood of cognitive avoidance strategies that can take the form of disordered eating behaviors, anxiety-related behaviors, or both. Not unexpectedly, AN and OCD also display substantial shared genetic risk—but interestingly, genetic liabilities to various psychiatric phenotypes are common to AN and OCD, whereas liabilities to metabolic and anthropometric traits seem to be specific to AN (Yilmaz et al., 2020).

## Mood Disorders

Mood disorders also co-occur frequently in all ED subtypes. Ulfvebrand and colleagues (2015) found 43.1% of women and 40% of males with heterogeneous EDs display any mood disorder, with major depression occurring in 32.8% and 28.5%, respectively. Trends reported in studies examining the association between eating and mood disorders suggest that mood disorders have a greater affinity with bulimic ED variants (BN, BED, and AN-binge/purge) than with AN-restrictive ones. Hudson et al (2007) reported that mood disorders occur in as many as 70% of adults with BN (Hudson et al., 2007), and Swanson et al. (2011) detected mood disorders in 49.9% of adolescents with BN (a 5.7-fold greater risk) and 45.3% of those with BED (a 4.6-fold risk), but in only 10.9% (a 0.7-fold risk) of adolescents with AN.

Findings suggest that mood disorder rates may be substantially lower in community-based samples than they are in treatment-seeking ones (Blinder et al., 2006). In other words, factors related to age, social standing, and recruitment may all influence the extent to which comorbid psychopathology becomes apparent in people with EDs. A community study by Zaider, Johnson, and Cockell (2000) points to a strong affinity between EDs and dysthymia. Other evidence has shown a strong association between BN and seasonal affective disorder (SAD), implying cyclical season-dependent recurrences in depressed mood that parallel seasonal variations in binge-purge behaviors (Ghadirian et al., 1999). Bipolar disorder, being rarer than depression, occurs at relatively low frequencies in people with EDs, with a recent study reporting the illness in .3% of women with AN, .7% of those with BN, and .4% of those with BED (Ulfvebrand et al., 2015)

Various areas of etiological overlap can be postulated to explain convergence between mood and eating disorders. An early twin study by Wade et al. (2000) attributed shared risk for AN and mood disorders to genetic factors. Common personality variables also seem to play a role, given that harm avoidance, rejection sensitivity, and lower self-directedness are associated with mood disorders and with EDs (Cardi et al., 2013). As for bipolar disorder, research suggests involvement of shared neurodevelopmental mechanisms in the pathophysiology of both disorders (Liu et al., 2016).

## Posttraumatic Stress Disorder

Findings have suggested a striking concurrence between certain ED variants and posttraumatic stress disorder (PTSD). The National Comorbidity

Survey reported lifetime PTSD to occur in 45% of individuals with BN, compared to only 12% of those with AN (Hudson et al., 2007), and another study found PTSD to be present in 24% of women with BED (Grilo et al., 2012). In keeping with the preceding, a recent meta-analysis associated childhood sexual and emotional abuse with BN and BED, and childhood physical abuse with AN, BN, and BED (Caslini et al., 2016). Yet another study reports a dose-response relationship between childhood abuse and ED severity, linking more severe abuse with more pronounced eating symptoms, more binge-eating–purging behaviors, and earlier ED onset (Molendijk et al., 2017).

Various pathways, direct and indirect, might account for an etiological link between the EDs and traumatic events. Traumata directly affecting the body may have direct consequences for body image and, in turn, for eating and weight-control behaviors.

Alternatively, abusive experiences might affect self-, mood-, and impulse-regulation, which might indirectly heighten risk of maladaptive eating behavior. In keeping with the latter view, individuals with BN and comorbid PTSD show stronger reactivity of affect before and after purging compared to people with BN alone (Karr et al., 2013). In addition, our group has documented tendencies for people with BN who report past abuse to show greater abnormalities on indices of serotonin, dopamine, and cortisol functions (Groleau et al., 2014; Steiger et al., 2001, 2011). Such results imply that neurobiological sequelae of childhood abuse may adversely impact stress tolerance, impulse controls, and appetitive regulation.

## Substance Use Disorders

Findings show that 10–55% of women with BN abuse substances, whereas 25–40% of females with alcohol dependence show some form of ED, often in the bulimia spectrum (Bulik et al., 2004; Holderness et al., 1994). Tobacco, caffeine, and alcohol are all commonly abused by individuals with EDs (Bahji et al., 2019). As with other areas of comorbidity, studies associate substance use more strongly with bulimic ED variants than they do with restrictive forms (Bahji et al., 2019; Bulik et al., 2004). Among individuals with EDs, those with substance use problems have been found to have more eating, weight, and shape concerns (Becker & Grilo, 2015); significantly more comorbid psychiatric diagnoses; more impulsivity and perfectionism (Bulik et al., 2004); and greater likelihood of genetic and developmental risks (Richardson et al., 2008).

## Attention-Deficit/Hyperactivity Disorder

Studies have indicated a distinct affinity between EDs, particularly those in the bulimia spectrum, and attention-deficit/hyperactivity disorder (ADHD). An 11-year case-control follow-up implicating 6- to 18-year-old girls with ADHD indicated girls with attentional problems to be 5.6 times more likely to meet criteria for BN (Biederman et al., 2010). Likewise, an 8-year follow-up of 337 boys and 95 girls with ADHD and 211 control boys and 53 control girls indicated greater likelihood of bulimia in the "case" group, especially so for girls (Mikami et al., 2008). Interestingly, impulsivity (and not hyperactivity or inattention) best predicted BN symptoms, particularly for girls. The relationship between EDs and attentional problems has been thought to be mediated by various factors common to both syndromes, including dopaminergic susceptibilities, deficits in executive function, impulsivity, internalizing problems, and secondary social difficulties (Levin & Rawana, 2016).

## Autism Spectrum Disorder

There has been considerable recent interest in the association between EDs and autism spectrum disorders (ASDs). Results of studies examining this association are highly variable, with reported rates of ASD in individuals with EDs ranging from 4% to 52.5% (Westwood & Tchanturia, 2017), with modal values seeming to occupy the 20% range (Huke et al., 2013). From the "other side of the coin," adolescent girls with ASD are reported to more often display ED symptoms than are teens without ASD—with 27% of girls with ASD reported to show clinically significant ED symptoms. Likewise males with ASD are reported to be at increased risk for low body weight and abnormal eating practices (Kalyva, 2009). Comorbidity between AN and ASD has been thought to result from shared cognitive, social, and emotion-regulation difficulties. For example, neurocognitive studies have suggested that people with AN and ASD show similar problems with emotion processing, set-shifting, and overattention to detail (Oldershaw et al., 2011). Comorbid ASD appears, according to available studies, to have a negative prognostic implication (Nielsen et al., 2015; Stewart et al., 2017).

## Personality Disorders

Another striking area of comorbidity seen in people with EDs is that with personality disorders (PDs; Cassin & von Ranson, 2005; Lilenfeld et al., 2006). The most recent and largest meta-analysis addressing comorbid PDs in people with EDs concluded that the mean proportion of people with an ED displaying any PD was 52%, compared to 9% in non–eating-disordered individuals (Martinussen et al., 2017). The mean proportion of any PD was 49% for AN and 54% for BN, with both disorders showing high proportions of borderline and avoidant PDs (between 19% and 25%), but with AN showing a significantly higher rate of obsessive-compulsive PD (in 23% of cases) versus 12% in BN (Martinussen et al., 2017). We note that the Martinussen study did not consider differences between restricter versus binger-purger variants of AN. When this distinction is examined elsewhere, rates of borderline PD are generally found to be rather low in restrictive AN but high in AN-binge/purge subtype (see Cassin & von Ranson, 2005; Lilenfeld et al., 2006; Steiger & Bruce, 2004). Viewing available results together, the literature supports the following generalizations: (1) PDs are frequently present in individuals with EDs; (2) restrictive symptomatology seems to be associated with a high concentration of obsessive-compulsive PDs; (3) ED variants characterized by binge–purge symptoms coincide with more heterogeneous PD subtypes than do restrictive forms, including high rates of dramatic-erratic PDs (characterized by prominent attention- and sensation-seeking, extroversion, mood lability, and impulsivity); and (4) PD comorbidity in BED is comparable to that seen in BN, although the loading of dramatic-erratic PDs, like borderline PD, may be less pronounced (Friborg et al., 2014). Overall, it appears that the dietary overcontrol that characterizes restrictive AN is paralleled by generalized overcontrol, as a personality or adaptive style. Binge/purge symptomatology, in contrast, affects people who evince quite heterogeneous personality traits, although dysregulatory traits (e.g., affective instability, impulsivity) are overrepresented.

Malnutrition can have adverse effects on personality functioning (Keys et al., 1950), and this raises the concern that apparent personality problems seen in individuals with EDs may reflect state disturbances associated with an active ED and not trait tendencies. In other words, caution is warranted concerning the use of PD diagnoses in individuals with an active ED. Nonetheless, various findings suggest that personality problems seen in individuals with an ED often exist independently of the ED or may persist after recovery from the ED. For example, one investigation reported that 26% of women who recovered from AN or BN showed some form of ongoing PD (Matsunaga et al., 2000) and another found that women recovered from EDs reported higher levels of harm avoidance and lower self-directedness and cooperativeness scores than did normal control women (Klump et al., 2004).

## Etiology

EDs are thought to have a multidimensional etiology, including genetic liabilities (affecting mood, behavioral controls, sensitivity to reward, energy metabolism, and appetite), developmental processes (conducive to self-image or adjustment problems, or excessive concerns with achievement and social approval), environmental stresses (such as perinatal insults or childhood traumata), state-related effects (owing to the nutritional and mental status), and, ultimately, social inducements toward intensive dieting (e.g., Steiger & Booij, 2020; Striegel-Moore & Bulik, 2007; Treasure et al., 2010). The following sections review the various social, psychological, and biological factors that have been thought to contribute to risk for ED development.

### Sociocultural Context

Throughout much of the past century, North American and European cultural values have associated slimness with ideals of success, beauty, power, and self-control, and such associations are likely to underlie the long-standing tendency for people living in these continents—especially young females—to be dissatisfied with their bodies and to too often display EDs. Many findings indicate that exposure to media images of thinness and internalization of the "thin ideal" contribute quite directly to body dissatisfaction and to development of body image preoccupation and clinical EDs—especially in women and girls (e.g., Culbert et al., 2015; Grabe et al., 2008).

Once regarded as a culturally and geographically bound phenomenon, since the late 1970s, reports have suggested substantial ED prevalences in diverse regions and cultures (including Africa, Asia, the Middle East, and South America)—an effect that is presumed (at least in part) to reflect the transmission across cultures of the "thin ideal" (Makino et al., 2004; Pike et al., 2014). In support, a multisite, cross-cultural survey associated extent of exposure to Western media with increased body dissatisfaction in populations living in various geographical areas (Swami et al., 2010).

Various theories have been proposed to account for the role of culture in ED development. One intuitively obvious idea is that pressure to be thin and internalization of the thin ideal foster body dissatisfaction, which in turn contributes to dieting and/or negative affect, and, ultimately, to clinical EDs (Stice & Agras, 1998). An alternative view, inspired by feminist theory, argues that social environments in which women are objectified and evaluated based on physical attributes contribute to heightened appearance consciousness and, in turn, heightened risk of ED development (Fredrickson & Roberts, 1997; Stice & Agras, 1998). Both views have received empirical support. A recent prospective study showed that in a significant proportion of people, signs of felt pressure to be thin preceded onset of body dissatisfaction, dieting, or negative affect (Stice & Van Ryzin, 2019). Likewise, a meta-analysis of 53 cross-sectional studies concluded that greater self-objectification was related to disordered-eating attitudes and behaviors (Schaefer & Thompson, 2018).

*Psychological Factors*

The first psychometric studies on the EDs, published in the mid-1970s, led to an association of AN with such traits as obsessionality, social anxiety, introversion, neuroticism, and depression. These same reports introduced a distinction between EDs characterized solely by restriction of food intake (e.g., AN-R) and variants implicating binge eating and purging (AN-B/P subtype). Individuals with the AN-R subtype were described as conforming, obsessional, and emotionally and socially reserved, whereas those with AN-B/P were thought to be prone to impulsivity, antisocial attitudes, and externalization (Sohlberg & Strober, 1994). Later studies on BN broadened the boundaries of an association between binge eating and impulsive or erratic characteristics (Vitousek & Manke, 1994), and the stage was set for belief in a systematic distinction, on associated personality characteristics, between ED variants characterized by restriction and variants characterized by binge eating and/or purging. Although the fit proves to be imperfect, contemporary studies continue to find "restricter" and "binger/purger" groups to differ along the lines stated above (see Wagner & Vitousek, 2019). For instance, a meta-analytic study examining temperament in people with eating disorders concluded that individuals with BN, and to a lesser extent those with AN-B/P, are more novelty-seeking (i.e., prone to excitement or exhilaration in response to potential reward) than are individuals with AN-R, whereas individuals with AN-R are more persistent (i.e., prone to continuing an activity despite frustration or fatigue) than are individuals with BN (Atiye et al., 2015). Findings such as these have supported the idea that there exists a systematic co-aggregation (at a group level) between AN-R and compulsive traits and between ED variants characterized by binge eating and/or purging (AN-BP and BN) and emotionality, risk taking, or oppositionality.

While it can be useful to examine the ways in which different temperaments and personality traits assort with different ED diagnoses, the practice can also obscure meaningful within-subtype heterogeneities. Studies have shown that AN, BN, and EDNOS variants all evince substantial within-diagnosis heterogeneity regarding comorbid personality traits (see Claes et al., 2012; Wildes et al., 2011). Indeed, despite differences in samples and measures across studies, findings point remarkably consistently to three broad, psychopathology-defined sub-phenotypes across EDs: (1) psychologically intact, (2) overregulated (compulsive and inhibited), and (3) dysregulated (impulsive and reactive) (Bohane et al., 2017; Haynos et al., 2017; Steiger et al., 2009). As a generality, the AN-R subtype coincides with the overregulated personality profile, whereas binge-eating/purging ED variants seem to occur about equally with any of the three profiles. Highlighting the clinical importance of the trait-based distinctions noted, investigators have associated the "dysregulated" characteristic with increased comorbidity (e.g., depression, self-mutilation, drug abuse), more developmental disturbances (e.g., child abuse, attachment problems), and poorer treatment outcome.

*Specific Traits*
PERFECTIONISM

Individuals with AN, BN, and BED have all been found to have higher self-rated perfectionism scores than do healthy, normal eaters—and this is especially true for aspects of perfectionism associated with the setting of high personal standards and goals or being overly self-critical or concerned with others' judgments (Farstad et al., 2016; Steele et al., 2011). Arguing for its etiological importance, perfectionistic tendencies appear to predate ED onset, persist after recovery, be found in the non–eating-disordered relatives of those who develop an ED, and correspond to severity of such symptoms as dietary restraint and overvaluation of shape and weight (Bardone-Cone et al., 2007; Limburg et al., 2017).

IMPULSIVITY

People with binge/purge ED variants display more self-reported trait impulsivity and engage in more impulsive acts than do normal eaters or people with restrictive ED variants (Favaro et al., 2005; Rosval et al., 2006). Several studies emphasize sensation-seeking and negative urgency (the tendency to act hastily when distressed) as prominent traits in individuals with bulimic syndromes (Lavender et al., 2015). Others give precedence to motoric components of impulsivity (Rosval et al., 2006; Wonderlich et al., 2004). The presence of impulsive traits in people with EDs has been linked to more severe comorbidity (e.g., substance use disorders and borderline PD) and to poorer treatment outcomes (Lozano-Madrid et al., 2020; Reas et al., 2016). Some evidence favors the notion that impulsivity may be a temporal antecedent to BN onset. However, there is also reason to believe that the biological and psychological consequences of an active ED may "amplify" inherent impulsive tendencies (Lavender et al., 2015; Pearson et al., 2014).

**BODY-IMAGE DISTURBANCE**

Disturbance in the way one experiences one's body weight or shape is a defining characteristic of AN and BN and generally thought to have a fundamental etiological and maintaining role in the EDs. In support, many studies have reported that people with AN and BN tend to overestimate their body size, express greater body dissatisfaction, and engage in more body checking and body avoidance behaviors than do people without an ED (see (Lantz et al., 2018; Nikodijevic et al., 2018). Likewise, consistent with a causal role, an 8-year longitudinal study of risk factors for EDs in adolescents observed that body dissatisfaction preceded the onset of various ED forms (Stice & Van Ryzin, 2019). Although such findings are suggestive and appeal to intuitive causal assumptions, a recent systematic review of the literature on body image disturbance in AN notes that confirmation of a role of body disturbance in ED causality, maintenance, and relapse has been surprisingly elusive (Glashouwer et al., 2019).

**DIETARY RESTRAINT**

Cognitive components of dietary restraint—or restrictive eating attitudes (e.g., the belief that it is important or desirable to eat low-calorie foods or to compensate when one eats)—are thought to make a fundamental contribution to the development and maintenance of EDs (e.g., Fairburn et al., 2003). Overvaluing slim appearance and dietary control have a clear role in supporting the excessive dieting often seen in individuals with an ED—even though, paradoxically, chronic attempts to restrain eating often increase individuals' susceptibility to overeating (see the work of Polivy & Herman, 1993). Many findings also suggest that it is the combination of dietary restraint with other factors, such as negative mood or perfectionism, that may explain how dieting progresses to pathological eating in certain individuals (Goldschmidt et al., 2012; Stice & Shaw, 2018).

**EMOTION DYSREGULATION**

ED symptoms are often conceptualized as representing ill-chosen and maladaptive ways of regulating emotions, and there is ample evidence of a link between EDs and emotion regulation difficulties (Prefit et al., 2019). For instance, individuals with EDs display more global emotion dysregulation than do individuals with no ED (Lavender et al., 2015). Likewise, on specific indices, people with an ED show decreased emotional distress tolerance, decreased emotion understanding and acceptance, and heightened punishment sensitivity and harm avoidance. According to some sources, difficulties in identifying, responding to, and managing emotions predate ED onset (Racine et al., 2013; Shank et al., 2019). The possible precipitating and maintaining roles of negative affect in binge-eating symptoms has received particular attention (Martín et al., 2019). Affect-regulation models posit that negative emotions trigger binge episodes which serve (at least temporarily) to alleviate negative affect. Various functional analyses of binge-eating antecedents and consequences (often performed using "online" experience-sampling methods) offer support for this notion (Berg et al., 2013; Engelberg et al., 2007; Haedt-Matt & Keel, 2011).

**NEUROCOGNITION**

Neurocognitive performance in people with an ED has been compared to that in normal eaters on a wide range of tasks. Results generally associate the presence of an active ED with impairment of higher-level cognitive functions, including inhibitory control, decision making, central coherence (i.e., the tendency to focus on details at the expense of global integration of information), set-shifting (the ability to switch perceptual or response sets), working memory (a core executive function), and attention bias (Smith et al., 2018). Many of the impairments listed are found to improve with nutritional rehabilitation, but some persistent impairments have been observed after rehabilitation (Cardi et al., 2013; King et al., 2019), and greater neurocognitive impairment has been associated with a more chronic course of AN (Saure et al., 2020).

Various studies have also suggested that, in individuals with an ED, social cognition is impaired (Cardi et al., 2018). The most widely applied social-cognitive construct in the ED literature is *theory of mind* (ToM). ToM refers to the ability to ascribe mental states to other people in order to understand and predict their behavior—something akin to empathy (Bora & Kose, 2016). Several studies have shown that, relative to healthy individuals, people with active AN have impaired ToM, manifested in the form of difficulties in understanding others' emotions, taking others' perspectives, and interpreting social behavior (Leppanen et al., 2018). Although associations are less robust than are those observed in people with active AN, impaired ToM has also been noted in individuals who have recovered from AN, in unaffected first-degree relatives of individuals with AN, and in individuals with BN (Tapajoz et al., 2019). Of note, a recent meta-analysis concluded that AN and autism are characterized by similar ToM profiles (Leppanen et al., 2018).

## Developmental Factors
### THEORIES ON FAMILY DYNAMICS

Traditional theories have promoted various stereotypes (some rather dubious) about families in which EDs develop—broadly associating AN with familial overprotectiveness and enmeshment and BN with familial disengagement, neglect, or hostility (see Smolak et al. 2013). Such concepts have received mixed support from self-report or, more rarely, observational studies of family functioning (Cerniglia et al., 2017; Lyke & Matsen, 2013; Steiger et al., 1991), which have suggested that AN, in its restricting form may, on average, be associated with family proneness toward enmeshment and overprotectiveness, whereas bulimic ED variants (including BN and BED) may be associated with proneness toward conflict and overt family dysfunction (Cerniglia et al., 2017; Steiger et al., 1991; Tetzlaff et al., 2016; Vidović et al., 2005). From a related perspective, developmental studies have associated EDs of both types with parent–child attachment problems (Tasca, 2019).

The trends described above require judicious interpretation for several reasons. First, because they are based on the averaging of tendencies across families, such descriptions are "caricatural" and risk concealing existent heterogeneities. Second, most of the findings that bear on questions related to family functioning have been generated through cross-sectional or retrospective designs, meaning that observations risk being contaminated by the effects of living with a member who is actively ill with an ED. Indeed, the few prospective family studies that exist provide very weak evidence of a priori involvement of family functioning variables in risk for ED development (see (Beato-Fernández et al., 2004; Nicholls & Viner, 2009). Third, effects observed, even if repeatable, need not represent causal factors but rather heritable "traits" (such as anxiousness or impulsivity) that might shape family interaction patterns without themselves having any direct etiological implication. Finally, most of the studies in question lack control groups representing other mental health entities, meaning that findings may not reveal ED-specific family tendencies at all.

Current thinking on the role of the family in the EDs rejects portrayals of the family as a core contributor to ED etiopathology. As a case in point, in 2010, the Academy for Eating Disorders (AED) stated that it "stands firmly against any etiologic model . . . in which family influences are seen as the primary cause of anorexia nervosa or bulimia nervosa, and condemns generalizing statements that imply families are to blame for their child's illness" (le Grange et al., 2010, p. 1). Correspondingly, there has been an important change in practices, one away from interventions that presumed the presence of family dysfunction and toward efforts to engage parents, family members, and friends as active contributors to treatment prepared with a good understanding of how to help and how to manage countertherapeutic reactions that are triggered by the child's illness (Anastasiadou et al., 2014; Lock, 2015). Many current treatment paradigms mobilize the family as a potential resource in therapy—and recent outcome research supports such initiatives (see Couturier et al., 2013).

### MALTREATMENT

Such experiences as childhood physical, sexual, or emotional abuse are disturbingly common in individuals with EDs, especially in those with bulimia-spectrum disorders (BSDs; i.e., BN, BED, AN-binge-purge type, or subthreshold variants). According to available studies, roughly a third of adults with a BSD reports unwanted childhood sexual experiences, about half an experience of physical maltreatment (Fullerton et al., 1995), and more than three-quarters an experience of emotional abuse (Groleau et al., 2012). In population and clinical samples alike, childhood abuse has been found to predict severity of pathological eating attitudes and behaviors, body dissatisfaction, and overall eating symptom severity. Notably, a very large-scale study examined associations between EDs in adults and various forms of childhood maltreatment (e.g., harsh physical punishment, physical abuse, sexual abuse, emotional abuse, neglect, etc.). Results associated all forms of adversity with EDs, with sexual abuse and physical neglect being most strongly linked to EDs in men and sexual abuse and emotional abuse being most strongly linked to EDs in women (Afifi et al., 2017).

## Biological Factors
### BRAIN STRUCTURE AND FUNCTION

Neuroimaging studies associate the EDs with various anomalies in brain structure and function. AN is consistently associated with reduced gray and white matter volumes (see King et al., 2018, for a review). One meta-analysis on volumetric studies in AN concluded that, compared to findings in normal eaters, there is an average 4.6% reduction in gray matter and a 2.7% reduction in white matter volumes (Seitz et al., 2016). Interestingly, global brain volume reductions have not been observed in adolescents diagnosed with atypical AN (Olivo et al., 2018), suggesting that volumetric changes may be linked to severity of malnutrition. At the regional level, one meta-analysis showed smaller gray matter volume in the median cingulate cortex (involved in regulation of emotions) as well as in the posterior cingulate cortex and the precuneus (involved in self-reflection) (Zhang et al., 2018). Some structural brain changes noted are at least partly reversed by weight restoration, especially in younger individuals (Frank et al., 2019; Kaufmann et al., 2020; King et al., 2018).

Diffusion tensor imaging (DTI), which uses the diffusion of water molecules to generate magnetic resonance images, has shown white matter alterations in individuals with AN in the cingulum and the corpus collosum (Zhang et al., 2020) and in thalamocortical and occipital-parietal-temporal–frontal tracts (Gaudio et al., 2019). The preceding brain regions/circuits have been associated with executive control, self-regulation, body image perception, and taste. Functional magnetic resonance imaging (fMRI) has been used to study neural connectivity when the brain is "at rest" (i.e., not activated by a particular task). Studies in individuals with AN point to reduced resting-state functional connectivity in default mode, frontoparietal, executive-control, and salience networks at various stages of illness, including recently ill, chronic, and recovered individuals (Cowdrey et al., 2014; Gaudio et al., 2016). Using task-based neuroimaging paradigms, neural alterations have been found in various brain circuits regulating reward, decision-making, and affect (see, e.g., Frank, 2012; Olivo et al., 2019).

Neuroimaging studies in individuals with bulimic symptoms indicate structural and functional alterations in the frontal cortex (involved in emotion regulation and executive function) (Mele et al., 2020). In addition, greater symptom severity in BN has been associated with reduced cortical thickness (Westwater et al., 2018). Studies in BN also point to functional and/or structural alterations in brain regions involved in the processing of food stimuli (visual cortex, precentral gyrus, and insula), reward (striatum), and self-referential processes such as body image (precuneus, anterior cingulate cortex, insula) (Mele et al., 2020). Whether functional and structural brain alterations in BN persist after recovery is unknown.

Although relevant studies are rare, neural changes implicated in BED appear comparable to those seen in BN. For example, BED and BN are both associated with an enlarged volume of the medial orbitofrontal cortex (Schafer et al., 2010), a brain region important for impulse control. Likewise, BED and BN are both associated with altered resting-state activity in the salience and default mode networks (Stopyra et al., 2019) and with altered neural activation of the cingulate and orbitofrontal cortex on a food reward processing task (Simon et al., 2016).

### NEUROTRANSMITTERS

*Serotonin* (or 5-hydroxytryptamine: 5-HT) is widely distributed throughout the brain and has been implicated in the regulation of mood, cognition, social functioning, impulse control, and eating behavior (Booij et al., 2015). Anomalies have been reported in people with EDs on indices of 5-HT metabolites, plasma 5-HT precursor levels, 5-HT platelet uptake, and neuroendocrine responses to 5-HT agonists or antagonists, with several group differences also observed after weight restoration (Brewerton, 1995). In BN, findings show reduced platelet binding of serotonin uptake inhibitors and diminished neuroendocrine responses to serotonin precursors and agonists, with some changes again persisting after recovery (Brewerton, 1995; Steiger et al., 2011). One study by our group also showed unaffected first-degree relatives of patients with BN to have altered peripheral uptake of 5-HT compared to that in relatives of control women (Steiger et al., 2006). Such findings suggest that altered 5-HT may be a predisposing trait rather than a simple consequence of the disorder.

Positron emission tomography (PET) uses radioligands to allow for the *in vivo* characterization of neurotransmitter activity in different brain systems and regions. PET studies have shown that, relative to healthy individuals, people with AN have lower 5-HT transporter density in the medial parietal cortex (Yokokura et al., 2019) and greater 5-HT$_{1A}$ receptor activity in the frontal, parietal, and temporal cortices as well as in the raphe (Bailer et al., 2007; Galusca et al., 2008). Regional brain increases in 5-HT$_{1A}$ receptor levels have also been observed in individuals who have recovered from AN (Galusca et al., 2008). Such findings are indicative of generally diminished 5-HT function. Similarly, PET studies have documented widespread regional increases in 5-HT$_{1A}$ receptor levels in various brain regions in people with active BN (Bailer et al., 2011; Galusca et al., 2014). Conversely, inconsistent regional increases and decreases in 5-HT transporter density have been observed in individuals with BED (Majuri et al., 2017) and in individuals recovered from BN (Pichika et al., 2012)

*Dopamine* (DA) is a neurotransmitter associated with reward-driven behaviors, executive control, affect, and food intake (Broft et al., 2011; O'Hara et al., 2015). Reduced DA activity is thought, generally, to underlie excessive reward- or stimulus-seeking behavior. Neuroendocrine challenge studies in individuals with AN provide evidence of increased DA neurotransmission (Kontis & Theochari, 2012), whereas studies in BN have documented decreased DA metabolites and reduced DA release in the putamen (Broft et al., 2012). Lower levels of DA$_2$ receptors have, furthermore, been associated with higher frequency of binge eating and vomiting (Broft et al., 2012). An implication may be that reduced DA activity in BN leads to disinhibition of eating behavior as a reward seeking behavior.

Other neurotransmitters, neuropeptides, and hormones have been studied. Neurotrophins act in cellular proliferation and survival, synaptic activity, and neural plasticity (Mitre et al., 2017). One widely studied neurotrophin, *brain-derived neurotrophic factor* (BDNF), is an important regulator of food intake and energy homeostasis and constitutes a plausible candidate in ED etiology and maintenance (Monteleone & Maj, 2013; Nakazato et al., 2012). A relatively consistent finding across studies is that serum BDNF is reduced in people with AN or BN (Brandys et al., 2011; Monteleone & Maj, 2013). In AN, serum BDNF levels have been shown to increase after partial weight restoration (Tyszkiewicz-Nwafor et al., 2019; Zwipp et al., 2014) and to compare with those in normal eaters after full recovery (Zwipp et al., 2014).

*Glutamate* is an excitatory neurotransmitter that has been implicated in reward processing, food intake, memory, and learning (Javitt, 2004; Karthik et al., 2020). Altered glutamate levels have also been associated with mood and obsessive-compulsive disorders (Javitt, 2004; Karthik et al., 2020). In AN, magnetic resonance spectroscopy studies have reported lower glutamate levels relative to those observed in healthy comparison individuals in various brain regions (Castro-Fornieles et al., 2007; Godlewska et al., 2017; Joos et al., 2011). One PET study investigated the association between BN and the metabotropic glutamate receptor subtype 5 (Mihov et al., 2020), a receptor important for the signaling of glutamate and highly expressed in the forebrain, striatum, and limbic regions. Relative to healthy women, individuals with BN were reported to have higher metabotropic glutamate receptor subtype 5 levels in brain regions involved in emotional and cognitive processing, reward-guided behavior, and food value representation (Mihov et al., 2020).

Abnormally low levels of *leptin*, a hormone secreted by fat cells that regulates appetite and energy expenditure, have been well-documented in women with active AN, whereas findings in BN are mixed (Monteleone & Maj, 2013). There is also some evidence for a role of *ghrelin*, which affects short-term regulation of appetite and long-term regulation of energy balance. Specifically, plasma levels of ghrelin have been reported to be high in AN, low in BED (Geliebter et al., 2005), and mixed in BN (Monteleone & Maj, 2013). Levels of *oxytocin*—a hormone associated with social functioning, attachment, and food intake—appear to be lower in individuals with AN relative to those in controls, while oxytocin levels in individuals with BN do not differ from those in normal eaters (Plessow et al., 2018).

Given the sex distribution of EDs, one enticing hypothesis has been that sex hormones (androgens and estrogens), may influence ED development. In support, findings derived from opposite-sex twin pairs (in which the female co-twin is exposed to more testosterone, *in utero*, than are females from a same-sex twin pair) point to a significant role of perinatal exposure to androgen in buffering against ED risk (Culbert et al., 2008, 2013). Corroborating this view, higher levels of circulating testosterone during puberty has been thought to protect against disordered eating in boys, whereas higher levels of estrogen may protect against genetic and phenotypic risk for disordered eating in girls (Ma et al., 2019; Mikhail et al., 2019).

The hypothalamic-pituitary-adrenal (HPA) axis is the body's main stress response system, driven by the hormone cortisol. Findings in AN and BN indicate various HPA axis alterations (Bou Khalil et al., 2017; Lo Sauro et al., 2008), some perhaps due to effects of malnutrition, some to comorbid mood and anxiety problems, some to exposure to trauma, and some due directly to having an ED. Several studies link pronounced psychopathology in individuals with an ED to more pronounced alterations in cortisol functioning (Bruce et al., 2012; Diaz-Marsa et al., 2008).

## Genetics

### FAMILY AND TWIN STUDIES

For disorders that have often been construed as "sociocultural creations," EDs are surprisingly heritable. Findings consistently indicate first-degree relatives of people with an ED to show increased liability for EDs compared to those of individuals with no ED (e.g., Strober et al., 2000). Providing even more convincing evidence of heredity, reported concordance rates for AN, BN, and BED in monozygotic twins range from 28% to 76% across studies (Wade & Bulik, 2018). Aside from indicating substantial genetic effects, the same twin studies tend to show the nonshared environment (e.g., a particular stressor experienced by one twin) to contribute more strongly to risk of an ED than does the shared environment (e.g., living in the same family environment).

While the preceding throws a challenge to models of ED etiology that emphasize family factors, an important nuance is necessary. Adult twin studies find most of the variance in under- or overeating to be explained by genetic and nonshared environmental effects. However, a twin study conducted in very young children has reported quite the opposite—effects of the shared (family) environment in the absence of genetic effects (Herle et al., 2017). Helping guide the understanding of this apparent inconsistency, a number of studies have indicated that genetic influences toward ED development may tend to be "switched on" at puberty (Ma et al., 2019). The preceding would imply that problematic under- or overeating may be a behavior that is learned in early childhood but is then transformed into a problem of clinical proportions by genetic effects that become activated around puberty.

### CANDIDATE GENE STUDIES

There have been various efforts to identify single-gene variants (or sets of interacting genes) that may contribute to risk of an ED. Such approaches are generally driven by a theory-based "guess" about which gene (or set of genes) might make an important contribution to risk for a disorder. Findings from candidate gene studies often fail to replicate, and, consequently, the approach has fallen into disfavor. Nonetheless, some findings point to associations between EDs and polymorphisms of genes that, in theory, bear a logical association with ED risk—including those regulating key neurotransmitters like serotonin (Steiger et al., 2011), neuromodulators like BDNF (Ceccarini et al., 2019), hormones like estrogen (Nilsson et al., 2004), or those controlling appetitive behaviors like ghrelin (Muller et al., 2011).

Beyond the preceding, the candidate gene literature in EDs includes several observations suggesting gene–environment interactions. For instance, our group has shown that bulimic women carrying low-function alleles of the serotonin transporter polymorphism *5-HTTLPR* when they report childhood abuse,display more novelty seeking, affective instability (Steiger et al., 2007), and dissocial (impulsive-aggressive) behavior (Steiger et al., 2008). A similar interaction implicating low-function 5HTTLPR alleles and familial/developmental stress has been linked to AN in a clinic study (Karwautz et al., 2011) and to binge eating in a large-scale community study (Akkermann et al., 2012). Similar interaction effects implicating other neural systems have also been documented. For instance, one of our findings indicated that, in BN, the DRD2 Taq1A polymorphism interacts with childhood abuse to moderate manifestations of novelty seeking (Groleau et al., 2012).

### GENOME-WIDE ASSOCIATION STUDIES

Recent technologies support genome-wide association studies (GWASs) that use information gleaned from the entire genome to allow for isolation of novel genetic markers. The first study to document a finding of genome-wide significance for AN was published in 2017, by the Eating Disorders Work Group of the Psychiatric Genomics Consortium (PGC-ED; Duncan et al., 2017). Involving DNA from 3,495 people with AN and 10,982 normal-eater controls, the study associated a locus on chromosome 12 with AN, at a site previously linked to type-1 diabetes and autoimmune diseases (Duncan et al., 2017). Other findings from the same study indicated genetic correlations associating AN not only with mental illness phenotypes (like neuroticism and schizophrenia), but also with physical health phenotypes (like rapid glucose and lipid metabolism, high-density lipoprotein cholesterol, and low BMI). In other words, aside from expected psychiatric components, findings characterized AN as having important metabolic and autoimmune components. We note that the autoimmune aspect of these findings corroborates a report based on more than 2.5 million Swedish healthcare registers that associated previous autoimmune disorders with later EDs and previous EDs with later autoimmune disorders (Hedman et al., 2019).

In 2019, the PGC-ED group published a larger follow-up GWAS involving data from 16,992 people with AN and 55,525 controls (Watson et al., 2019). The study identified eight genetic loci reaching genome-wide significance and again implicated psychiatric traits (e.g., obsessive-compulsive and major depressive disorders), metabolic traits (e.g., insulin resistance, lipid metabolism), and anthropometric traits (e.g., low BMI, low fat mass). Findings consolidate the idea that the genetic architecture of AN not only implicates psychiatric traits, but also metabolic factors and particular physical (anthropometric) characteristics.

*Epigenetics*

A range of processes, referred to as "epigenetic" because they act "on top of" traditional genetic mechanisms, influence gene expression (and corresponding phenotypic variations) in the absence of actual DNA sequence changes. Many of these processes are believed to act in an environmentally responsive fashion (Cecil et al., 2020; Szyf, 2015) and hence to provide a plausible physical substrate for gene–environment interactions. Although various mechanisms may be involved, the most widely studied is DNA *methylation*. Various factors (childhood stress, nutritional status, maternal stress during gestation, perinatal complications, and current stressors) are believed to influence DNA methylation, which usually reduces gene expression (see Steiger & Booij, 2020). The likelihood that some or all of these factors act etiologically in the EDs has mobilized recent interest in the possible contribution of epigenetic processes to ED development and maintenance.

One of the first epigenetic studies in the EDs measured methylation levels in candidate genes in the DA system (implicated in mood, impulse control, reward sensitivity, and binge eating) and reported hypermethylation of the *DRD2* and *DAT* genes in people with AN and BN (Frieling et al., 2010). Other studies in AN have reported altered methylation of candidate genes regulating expression of alpha-synuclein (involved in neurotransmitter release) (Frieling et al., 2007), oxytocin (linked to social attachment) (Kim et al., 2014; Thaler et al., 2020), histone deacetylase (broadly influencing gene expression), and leptin (which inhibits hunger) (Neyazi et al., 2019).

Our group conducted some of the earliest studies on candidate gene methylation levels in people with BN. We focused on genes involved in the regulation of the HPA axis (e.g., *GR* gene; Steiger et al., 2013), neuroplasticity (*BDNF* gene; Thaler et al., 2014), and monoamines (e.g., *DRD2* gene; Groleau et al., 2014). The gist of results from these studies indicated that alterations in DNA methylation seen in individuals with BN tended to correspond to variations in comorbid tendencies (like suicidality, PD, or substance abuse) or to variations in exposure to childhood abuse.

Just as it has become possible to conduct genome-wide studies, techniques for sampling methylation levels throughout the genome have also become available. Our group has published two epigenome-wide studies comparing methylation levels in women with active AN to those in women in whom AN had remitted for at least 1 year or who had never had an ED (Booij et al., 2015; Steiger et al., 2019). In intriguing parallel to findings from the GWAS studies described above, our findings showed actively ill women to have altered methylation levels (and generally hypermethylation) on genes relevant to the mental status (e.g., serotonin, dopamine, glutamate), glucose and lipid metabolism, and immune function. Findings also showed chronicity of illness to be associated with more pronounced alterations in methylation levels and, importantly, that changes seen in actively ill individuals seemed to "reset" with symptom remission. The latter aspects suggest that changes in DNA methylation might be implicated in the exacerbation of certain psychiatric traits and physical sequelae that occur in a long-standing eating disorder. The findings also imply that methylation indices may have promise as markers of disease staging or therapeutic response.

**Toward an Integrated Etiological Concept**

The idea that EDs are multiply determined by biological, psychological, and social factors has been widely accepted for many years (see Garfinkel

& Garner, 1983; Jacobi et al., 2004; Striegel-Moore & Bulik, 2007; Treasure et al., 2010). However, contemporary clinical science has recently led to advancements toward a more principled and better-articulated biopsychosocial perspective. The advent of epigenetic science has expanded our understanding of mechanisms by which environmental factors may influence genetic potentials, activating and shaping various mental illness phenotypes—including eating disorders—and points to real physical substrates for a putative crosstalk between "nature" and "nurture."

Genetic-epidemiological, molecular-genetic, brain imaging, neurobiological, and neuropsychological studies have resulted in an increased appreciation of the extent to which biology, and especially hereditary traits, act in risk for ED development. However, there has not been a simple pendulum swing away from attention to sociocultural or developmental processes and toward more psychobiological modeling. Rather, contemporary multidimensional models use emerging psychobiological data to elaborate a more properly integrated view. Eating disorders cease to be viewed as expressions of "superficial body consciousness," "capriciousness," or "stubborn oppositionality" in affected people, or as responses to "dysfunctional," "overinvolved," or "toxic" families. Instead, they are understood to represent the activation, by environmental stresses (and pressures promoting too much dieting) of real physical vulnerabilities to ED development borne by susceptible people. Such people do not "ask" to get an ED or "bring the ED on themselves." Rather, they develop EDs because they carry real vulnerabilities that get "switched on" by real environmental impacts. Likewise, when the disorder persists in affected people, it is not because they are "not trying hard enough to recover" or "choosing to keep their disorder." It is because a biopsychosocial "mix" of factors has caused the disorder to become entrenched and difficult to overcome.

Encouragingly, some findings from the epigenetic literature suggest that nutritional rehabilitation may help undo or "reset" problematic changes in DNA methylation at key genetic loci (e.g., Steiger et al., 2019). Available evidence also indicates that treatment models informed by an integrative biopsychosocial perspective help "humanize" the process of treatment, as they help clinicians and patients alike understand that EDs occur not because of failings in those affected (or in the families from which they arise) but because of the activation of real physical susceptibilities by lived environmental impacts. Arguably, informed models of ED development encourage an understanding of ED etiology and treatment that blames sufferers and their relatives less and that supports and validates more. For fuller treatments of such questions, see Steiger and Booij (2020).

To help clarify the type of "crosstalk" among putative risk factors that we assume to be involved in ED development, we introduce a concept that we believe provides a useful heuristic. The concept, supported by various available studies on the structure of ED pathology, is that, in the EDs, variables that bear directly on eating symptoms (restricting, bingeing, vomiting, body dissatisfaction, etc.) tend to map onto one factor or cluster, those that load onto generalized psychopathology (e.g., depression, anxiety, impulsivity, perfectionism) tend to cohere onto another. Furthermore, and more importantly, severity of symptoms in the ED-specific factor is often surprisingly independent of severity of symptoms in the comorbid factor. In other words, individuals displaying severe comorbid disturbances need not display correspondingly severe eating symptoms and vice versa.

To assist in discussing hypothetical causal interactions among putative eating-specific and generalized components of pathology in the EDs, we have listed in Table 18.1 various factors that might reasonably be thought to be relevant to each component. Putative eating-specific risk factors are listed in the left-hand column of Table 18.1. These are presumed to impinge directly on bodily components of self-representation and on eating-specific cognitions and behaviors. They include (1) biological factors related to bodily appearance, appetite regulation, or direct eating-disorder risk; (2) psychological and developmental processes linked to concern with body image or weight (e.g., identifications with weight-conscious parents and peers); and (3) social values that heighten concerns with weight and bodily appearance. Together, these factors are presumed to constitute the ingredients—biological, psychological, and social—of marked concerns with eating, weight, and body image. We assume that such factors control the overall strength of eating-related concerns. However, we also assume that, alone, these factors may not be sufficient to explain development of a clinical ED.

A second group of factors, assumed to be nonspecific to eating (i.e., to underlie generalized susceptibilities or maladjustments) but to be important components of vulnerability to ED development nonetheless, are depicted in the right-hand

**Table 18.1** Putative biological, psychological, developmental, and social risk factors for development of eating disorders

|  | Eating-specific factors (direct risk factors) | Generalized factors (indirect risk factors) |
|---|---|---|
| Biological factors | ED-specific genetic risk | Genetic risk for associated disturbance |
|  | Physiognomy and body weight | Temperament |
|  | Appetite regulation | Impulsivity |
|  | Energy metabolism | Neurobiology (e.g., 5-HT mechanisms) |
|  | Sex hormones | Sex hormones |
| Psychological factors | Poor body image | Poor self-image |
|  | Maladaptive eating attitudes | Inadequate coping mechanisms |
|  | Maladaptive weight beliefs | Self-regulation problems |
|  | Specific values or meanings assigned to food, body | Unresolved conflicts, deficits, posttraumatic reactions |
|  | Overvaluation of appearance | Identity problems |
|  |  | Autonomy problems |
| Developmental factors | Identifications with body-concerned relatives or peers | Overprotection |
|  | Aversive mealtime experiences | Neglect |
|  | Trauma affecting bodily experience | Felt rejection, criticism |
|  |  | Traumata |
|  |  | Relationship experience |
| Social factors | Maladaptive family attitudes to eating, weight | Family dysfunction |
|  |  | Aversive peer experiences |
|  | Peer-group weight concerns | Social values detrimental to stable, positive self-image |
|  | Pressures to be thin |  |
|  | Body-relevant insults, teasing | Destabilizing social change |
|  | Specific pressures to control weight (e.g., through ballet, athletic pursuits) | Values assigned to gender |
|  |  | Social isolation |
|  |  | Poor support network |
|  | Maladaptive cultural values assigned to body | Impeded access to means of self-definition |

Factors are separated into those thought to contribute to eating-specific pathology and generalized psychopathology. Factors shown are meant to be illustrative, not exhaustive.

column of Table 18.1. These include (1) biological processes (e.g., neurotransmitter abnormalities, genetic susceptibilities influencing mental, metabolic and immune status), (2) psychological and developmental processes that shape general psychological development and self-concept (e.g., familial overprotection, developmental neglect, childhood traumata), and (3) sociocultural influences pertinent to overall self-image. We assume the latter set of factors to control presence and strength of generalized vulnerabilities and/or maladjustments. Although nonspecific, such factors might interact with eating-specific agents to contribute to risk of developing a clinical ED in various ways, as follows:

1. Given a social context that supports a "thin ideal" and that links body esteem to overall self-worth, the propensity to be perfectionistic or overly sensitive to social approval (shown on the left side of Table 18.1) might indirectly heighten

susceptibility to intensive dieting and eventually to pathological eating practices. In this eventuality, one would expect, as tends to be the case, to find heavy loadings of perfectionism, self-criticism, reward dependence, and related characteristics in individuals who are prone to AN. Consider effects that might occur in a hypothetical example: An adolescent girl with a genetic predisposition toward anxious, perfectionistic traits might begin to diet to bolster her self-esteem. Weight loss produces various social rewards, as peers and parents pay her more positive attention. However, because dieting also leads to alteration of neurotransmitter function, a normal consequence of dieting, one effect might be an exacerbation of latent propensities toward anxiety and obsessionality and, gradually, increasing preoccupation with thinness. The adolescent's inherent tendency to demand too much of herself might become amplified, under new biological influences, into full-blown obsession—and intensive dieting gradually evolves into a full-blown ED. Based on currently available data, such effects are most likely to occur in people who, because of unique hereditary susceptibilities and/or hormonal influences, are particularly vulnerable to ED development.

2. Some individuals might carry a hereditary propensity toward altered neurotransmitter function. In other people, such sensitivities might result from epigenetically mediated interactions between genetic propensities and lived environmental exposures (e.g., trauma, intrauterine exposure to maternal stress, or dietary insufficiency). Once established, such tendencies might have predictable effects on mood and impulse regulation (acting on the right side of Table 18.1) while also conferring vulnerability to disorders of satiation, and hence bulimic eating patterns, in individuals disposed by social pressures emphasizing thinness (shown on the left side of Table 18.1) to restrict food intake—and to (in the process) reduce dietary intake of neurotransmitter precursors. Such tendencies might, in part, explain an affinity of bulimic eating syndromes for manifestations suggesting mood or impulse dyscontrol and, in part, account for the demonstrated importance, as a causal antecedent, of dietary restraint in bulimic syndromes. The stage becomes set for a cascade of maladaptive potentials expressed in the form of symptoms like depression, anxiety, impulsivity, and dietary disinhibition (binge eating).

A main implication of the view we present here is that generalized susceptibilities, though not representing a specific (or perhaps even necessary) ingredient, are almost certain to enhance vulnerability to ED development. Furthermore, once an ED has developed, biopsychosocial consequences may promote increasingly more pronounced and entrenched disturbances in both eating-specific and generalized spheres. For instance, if the affected individual was not highly obsessional, affectively unstable, or impulsive to start with, he or she may soon become so under the influence on brain function and emotion regulation of increasing dietary dysregulation.

## Conclusion

Our thinking in this chapter has been structured around the concept that EDs, and the comorbid traits and syndromes that often coincide with them, have many common biological, psychological, and social determinants. This means that comorbid traits are often tightly woven into ED phenomenology and serve both as reflections of underlying causal elements and as manifestations of biopsychosocial consequences of the ED once it has developed. Following from this line of thinking, we propose that what may be of greatest interest about the EDs is, in fact, their tendency to implicate many nonspecific causal factors—and often to represent the activation, by excessive dietary restraint, of a diversity of generalized vulnerabilities. Such vulnerabilities might, in other contexts, find various alternative expressions. What is clear, however, is that an adequate model of ED etiology needs to accommodate ways in which diverse environmental impacts, occurring at diverse moments throughout the life cycle (and even prenatally), may be shaping the expression of latent biological factors that influence both mind and body.

## References

Afifi, T. O., Sareen, J., Fortier, J., Taillieu, T., Turner, S., Cheung, K., & Henriksen, C. A. (2017). Child maltreatment and eating disorders among men and women in adulthood: Results from a nationally representative United States sample. *International Journal of Eating Disorders, 50*(11), 1281–1296. https://doi.org/10.1002/eat.22783

Akkermann, K., Kaasik, K., Kiive, E., Nordquist, N., Oreland, L., & Harro, J. (2012). The impact of adverse life events and the serotonin transporter gene promoter polymorphism on the development of eating disorder symptoms. *Journal of*

*Psychiatric Research, 46*(1), 38–43. https://doi.org/10.1016/j.jpsychires.2011.09.013

Anastasiadou, D., Medina-Pradas, C., Sepulveda, A. R., & Treasure, J. (2014). A systematic review of family caregiving in eating disorders. *Eating Behaviors, 15*(3), 464–477. https://doi.org/10.1016/j.eatbeh.2014.06.001

Atiye, M., Miettunen, J., & Raevuori-Helkamaa, A. (2015). A meta-analysis of temperament in eating disorders. *European Eating Disorders Review, 23*(2), 89–99. https://doi.org/10.1002/erv.2342

Bahji, A., Mazhar, M. N., Hudson, C. C., Nadkarni, P., MacNeil, B. A., & Hawken, E. (2019). Prevalence of substance use disorder comorbidity among individuals with eating disorders: A systematic review and meta-analysis. *Psychiatry Research, 273,* 58–66.

Bailer, U. F., Bloss, C. S., Frank, G. K., Price, J. C., Meltzer, C. C., Mathis, C. A., Geyer, M. A., Wagner, A., Becker, C. R., Schork, N. J., & Kaye, W. H. (2011). 5-HT(1)A receptor binding is increased after recovery from bulimia nervosa compared to control women and is associated with behavioral inhibition in both groups. *International Journal of Eating Disorders, 44*(6), 477–487. https://doi.org/10.1002/eat.20843

Bailer, U. F., Frank, G. K., Henry, S. E., Price, J. C., Meltzer, C. C., Mathis, C. A., Wagner, A., Thornton, L., Hoge, J., Ziolko, S. K., Becker, C. R., McConaha, C. W., & Kaye, W. H. (2007). Exaggerated 5-HT1A but normal 5-HT2A receptor activity in individuals ill with anorexia nervosa. *Biological Psychiatry, 61*(9), 1090–1099. https://doi.org/10.1016/j.biopsych.2006.07.018

Bardone-Cone, A. M., Wonderlich, S. A., Frost, R. O., Bulik, C. M., Mitchell, J. E., Uppala, S., & Simonich, H. (2007). Perfectionism and eating disorders: Current status and future directions. *Clinical Psychology Reviews, 27*(3), 384–405. https://doi.org/10.1016/j.cpr.2006.12.005

Beato-Fernández, L., Rodríguez-Cano, T., Belmonte-Llario, A., & Martínez-Delgado, C. (2004). Risk factors for eating disorders in adolescents. A Spanish community-based longitudinal study. *European Child and Adolescent Psychiatry, 13*(5), 287–294. https://doi.org/10.1007/s00787-004-0407-x

Becker, D. F., & Grilo, C. M. (2015). Comorbidity of mood and substance use disorders in patients with binge-eating disorder: Associations with personality disorder and eating disorder pathology. *Journal of Psychosomatic Research, 79*(2), 159–164.

Berg, K. C., Crosby, R. D., Cao, L., Peterson, C. B., Engel, S. G., Mitchell, J. E., & Wonderlich, S. A. (2013). Facets of negative affect prior to and following binge-only, purge-only, and binge/purge events in women with bulimia nervosa. *Journal of Abnormal Psychology, 122*(1), 111–118. https://doi.org/10.1037/a0029703

Biederman, J., Petty, C. R., Monuteaux, M. C., Fried, R., Byrne, D., Mirto, T., Spencer, T., Wilens, T. E., & Faraone, S. V. (2010). Adult psychiatric outcomes of girls with attention deficit hyperactivity disorder: 11-year follow-up in a longitudinal case-control study. *American Journal of Psychiatry, 167*(4), 409–417. https://doi.org/10.1176/appi.ajp.2009.09050736

Blinder, B. J., Cumella, E. J., & Sanathara, V. A. (2006). Psychiatric comorbidities of female inpatients with eating disorders. *Psychosomatic Medicine, 68*(3), 454–462.

Bohane, L., Maguire, N., & Richardson, T. (2017). Resilients, overcontrollers and undercontrollers: A systematic review of the utility of a personality typology method in understanding adult mental health problems. *Clinical Psychology Review, 57,* 75–92. https://doi.org/https://doi.org/10.1016/j.cpr.2017.07.005

Booij, L., Tremblay, R. E., Szyf, M., & Benkelfat, C. (2015). Genetic and early environmental influences on the serotonin system: Consequences for brain development and risk for psychopathology. *Journal of Psychiatry and Neuroscience, 40*(1), 5–18. https://doi.org/10.1503/jpn.140099

Bora, E., & Kose, S. (2016). Meta-analysis of theory of mind in anorexia nervosa and bulimia nervosa: A specific Impairment of cognitive perspective taking in anorexia nervosa? *International Journal of Eating Disorders, 49*(8), 739–740. https://doi.org/10.1002/eat.22572

Bou Khalil, R., Souaiby, L., & Fares, N. (2017). The importance of the hypothalamo-pituitary-adrenal axis as a therapeutic target in anorexia nervosa. *Physiology and Behavior, 171,* 13–20. https://doi.org/10.1016/j.physbeh.2016.12.035

Brandys, M. K., Kas, M. J., van Elburg, A. A., Campbell, I. C., & Adan, R. A. (2011). A meta-analysis of circulating BDNF concentrations in anorexia nervosa. *World Journal of Biological Psychiatry, 12*(6), 444–454. https://doi.org/10.3109/15622975.2011.562244

Brewerton, T. D. (1995). Toward a unified theory of serotonin dysregulation in eating and related disorders. *Psychoneuroendocrinology, 20*(6), 561–590. https://doi.org/10.1016/0306-4530(95)00001-5

Broft, A., Shingleton, R., Kaufman, J., Liu, F., Kumar, D., Slifstein, M., Abi-Dargham, A., Schebendach, J., Van Heertum, R., Attia, E., Martinez, D., & Walsh, B. T. (2012). Striatal dopamine in bulimia nervosa: A PET imaging study. *International Journal of Eating Disorders, 45*(5), 648–656. https://doi.org/10.1002/eat.20984

Broft, A. I., Berner, L. A., Martinez, D., & Walsh, B. T. (2011). Bulimia nervosa and evidence for striatal dopamine dysregulation: A conceptual review. *Physiology and Behavior, 104*(1), 122–127. https://doi.org/10.1016/j.physbeh.2011.04.028

Bruce, K. R., Steiger, H., Israel, M., Groleau, P., Ng Ying Kin, N. M., Ouellette, A. S., Sycz, L., & Badawi, G. (2012). Cortisol responses on the dexamethasone suppression test among women with Bulimia-spectrum eating disorders: Associations with clinical symptoms. *Progress in Neuropsychopharmacology and Biological Psychiatry, 38*(2), 241–246. https://doi.org/10.1016/j.pnpbp.2012.04.006

Bryant-Waugh, R. (2019). Avoidant/restrictive food intake disorder. *Child and Adolescent Psychiatric Clinics of North America, 28*(4), 557–565. https://doi.org/https://doi.org/10.1016/j.chc.2019.05.004

Bulik, C. M., Klump, K. L., Thornton, L., Kaplan, A. S., Devlin, B., Fichter, M. M., Halmi, K. A., Strober, M., Woodside, D. B., & Crow, S. (2004). Alcohol use disorder comorbidity in eating disorders: A multicenter study. *Journal of Clinical Psychiatry, 65*(7), 683. doi:10.4088/jcp.v65n0718

Cardi, V., Di Matteo, R., Corfield, F., & Treasure, J. (2013). Social reward and rejection sensitivity in eating disorders: An investigation of attentional bias and early experiences. *World Journal of Biological Psychiatry, 14*(8), 622–633. https://doi.org/10.3109/15622975.2012.665479

Cardi, V., Tchanturia, K., & Treasure, J. (2018). Premorbid and illness-related social difficulties in eating disorders: An overview of the literature and treatment developments. *Current Neuropharmacology, 16*(8), 1122–1130. https://doi.org/10.2174/1570159X16666180118100028

Caslini, M., Bartoli, F., Crocamo, C., Dakanalis, A., Clerici, M., & Carrà, G. (2016). Disentangling the association between child abuse and eating disorders: A systematic review and meta-analysis. *Psychosomatic Medicine, 78*(1), 79–90.

Cassin, S. E., & von Ranson, K. M. (2005). Personality and eating disorders: A decade in review. *Clinical Psychology Review, 25*(7), 895–916.

Castro-Fornieles, J., Bargallo, N., Lazaro, L., Andres, S., Falcon, C., Plana, M. T., & Junque, C. (2007). Adolescent anorexia nervosa: Cross-sectional and follow-up frontal gray matter disturbances detected with proton magnetic resonance spectroscopy. *Journal of Psychiatric Research, 41*(11), 952–958. https://doi.org/10.1016/j.jpsychires.2006.09.013

Ceccarini, M. R., Tasegian, A., Franzago, M., Patria, F. F., Albi, E., Codini, M., Conte, C., Bertelli, M., Dalla Ragione, L., Stuppia, L., & Beccari, T. (2019). 5-HT2AR and BDNF gene variants in eating disorders susceptibility. *American Journal of Medicine Genetics B Neuropsychiatric Genetics.* https://doi.org/10.1002/ajmg.b.32771

Cecil, C. A. M., Zhang, Y., & Nolte, T. (2020). Childhood maltreatment and DNA methylation: A systematic review. *Neuroscience & Biobehavioral Reviews, 112*, 392–409. https://doi.org/10.1016/j.neubiorev.2020.02.019

Cerniglia, L., Cimino, S., Tafà, M., Marzilli, E., Ballarotto, G., & Bracaglia, F. (2017). Family profiles in eating disorders: Family functioning and psychopathology. *Psychology Research and Behavior Management, 10*, 305–312. https://doi.org/10.2147/PRBM.S145463

Chial, H. J., Camilleri, M., Williams, D. E., Litzinger, K., & Perrault, J. (2003). Rumination syndrome in children and adolescents: Diagnosis, treatment, and prognosis. *Pediatrics, 111*(1), 158–162. https://doi.org/10.1542/peds.111.1.158

Claes, L., Fernandez-Aranda, F., Jiménez-Murcia, S., Agüera, Z., Granero, R., Sánchez, I., & Menchón, J. M. (2012). Personality subtypes in male patients with eating disorder: Validation of a classification approach. *Comprehensive Psychiatry, 53*(7), 981–987. https://doi.org/https://doi.org/10.1016/j.comppsych.2012.02.001

Couturier, J., Kimber, M., & Szatmari, P. (2013). Efficacy of family-based treatment for adolescents with eating disorders: A systematic review and meta-analysis. *International Journal of Eating Disorders, 46*(1), 3–11. https://doi.org/10.1002/eat.22042

Cowdrey, F. A., Filippini, N., Park, R. J., Smith, S. M., & McCabe, C. (2014). Increased resting state functional connectivity in the default mode network in recovered anorexia nervosa. *Human Brain Mapping, 35*(2), 483–491. https://doi.org/10.1002/hbm.22202

Culbert, K. M., Breedlove, S. M., Burt, S. A., & Klump, K. L. (2008). Prenatal hormone exposure and risk for eating disorders: A comparison of opposite-sex and same-sex twins. *Archives of General Psychiatry, 65*(3), 329–336. https://doi.org/10.1001/archgenpsychiatry.2007.47

Culbert, K. M., Breedlove, S. M., Sisk, C. L., Burt, S. A., & Klump, K. L. (2013). The emergence of sex differences in risk for disordered eating attitudes during puberty: A role for prenatal testosterone exposure. *Journal of Abnormal Psychology, 122*(2), 420–432. https://doi.org/10.1037/a0031791

Culbert, K. M., Racine, S. E., & Klump, K. L. (2015). Research review: What we have learned about the causes of eating disorders - a synthesis of sociocultural, psychological, and biological research. *Journal of Child Psychology and Psychiatry, 56*(11), 1141–1164. https://doi.org/10.1111/jcpp.12441

Currin, L., Schmidt, U., Treasure, J., & Jick, H. (2005). Time trends in eating disorder incidence. *British Journal of Psychiatry, 186*(2), 132–135.

Diaz-Marsa, M., Carrasco, J. L., Basurte, E., Saiz, J., Lopez-Ibor, J. J., & Hollander, E. (2008). Enhanced cortisol suppression in eating disorders with impulsive personality features. *Psychiatry Research, 158*(1), 93–97. https://doi.org/10.1016/j.psychres.2007.06.020

Duncan, L., Yilmaz, Z., Gaspar, H., Walters, R., Goldstein, J., Anttila, V., Bulik-Sullivan, B., Ripke, S., Thornton, L., Hinney, A., Daly, M., Sullivan, P. F., Zeggini, E., Breen, G., & Bulik, C. M. (2017). Significant locus and metabolic genetic correlations revealed in genome-wide association study of anorexia nervosa. *American Journal of Psychiatry, 174*(9), 850–858. https://doi.org/10.1176/appi.ajp.2017.16121402

Eddy, K. T., Thomas, J. J., Hastings, E., Edkins, K., Lamont, E., Nevins, C. M., Patterson, R. M., Murray, H. B., Bryant-Waugh, R., & Becker, A. E. (2015). Prevalence of DSM-5 avoidant/restrictive food intake disorder in a pediatric gastroenterology healthcare network. *International Journal of Eating Disorders, 48*(5), 464–470.

Engelberg, M. J., Steiger, H., Gauvin, L., & Wonderlich, S. A. (2007). Binge antecedents in bulimic syndromes: An examination of dissociation and negative affect. *International Journal of Eating Disorders, 40*(6), 531–536. https://doi.org/10.1002/eat.20399

Fairburn, C. G., Cooper, Z., Bohn, K., O'Connor, M. E., Doll, H. A., & Palmer, R. L. (2007). The severity and status of eating disorder NOS: Implications for DSM-V. *Behaviour Research and Therapy, 45*(8), 1705–1715.

Fairburn, C. G., Cooper, Z., & Shafran, R. (2003). Cognitive behaviour therapy for eating disorders: A "transdiagnostic" theory and treatment. *Behavior Research and Therapy, 41*(5), 509–528. https://doi.org/10.1016/s0005-7967(02)00088-8

Farstad, S. M., McGeown, L. M., & von Ranson, K. M. (2016). Eating disorders and personality, 2004–2016: A systematic review and meta-analysis. *Clinical Psychology Review, 46*, 91–105. https://doi.org/https://doi.org/10.1016/j.cpr.2016.04.005

Favaro, A., Zanetti, T., Tenconi, E., Degortes, D., Ronzan, A., Veronese, A., & Santonastaso, P. (2005). The relationship between temperament and impulsive behaviors in eating disordered subjects. *Eating Disorders, 13*(1), 61–70. https://doi.org/10.1080/10640260590893647

Frank, G. K. (2012). Advances in the diagnosis of anorexia nervosa and bulimia nervosa using brain imaging. *Expert Opinion in Medical Diagnosis, 6*(3), 235–244. https://doi.org/10.1517/17530059.2012.673583

Frank, G. K. W., Shott, M. E., & DeGuzman, M. C. (2019). Recent advances in understanding anorexia nervosa. *F1000Res, 8*. https://doi.org/10.12688/f1000research.17789.1

Fredrickson, B. L., & Roberts, T.-A. (1997). Objectification theory: Toward understanding women's lived experiences and mental health risks. *Psychology of Women Quarterly, 21*(2), 173–206. https://doi.org/10.1111/j.1471-6402.1997.tb00108.x

Friborg, O., Martinsen, E. W., Martinussen, M., Kaiser, S., Overgård, K. T., & Rosenvinge, J. H. (2014). Comorbidity of personality disorders in mood disorders: A meta-analytic review of 122 studies from 1988 to 2010. *Journal of Affective Disorders, 152-154*, 1–11. https://doi.org/10.1016/j.jad.2013.08.023

Frieling, H., Gozner, A., Römer, K. D., Lenz, B., Bönsch, D., Wilhelm, J., Hillemacher, T., de Zwaan, M., Kornhuber, J., & Bleich, S. (2007). Global DNA hypomethylation and DNA hypermethylation of the alpha synuclein promoter in females with anorexia nervosa. *Molecular Psychiatry*, 12(3), 229–230. https://doi.org/10.1038/sj.mp.4001931

Frieling, H., Römer, K. D., Scholz, S., Mittelbach, F., Wilhelm, J., De Zwaan, M., Jacoby, G. E., Kornhuber, J., Hillemacher, T., & Bleich, S. (2010). Epigenetic dysregulation of dopaminergic genes in eating disorders. *International Journal of Eating Disorders*, 43(7), 577–583. https://doi.org/10.1002/eat.20745

Fullerton, D. T., Wonderlich, S. A., & Gosnell, B. A. (1995). Clinical characteristics of eating disorder patients who report sexual or physical abuse. *International Journal of Eating Disorders*, 17(3), 243–249. https://doi.org/10.1002/1098-108x(199504)17:3<243::aid-eat2260170305>3.0.co;2-z

Galusca, B., Costes, N., Zito, N. G., Peyron, R., Bossu, C., Lang, F., Le Bars, D., & Estour, B. (2008). Organic background of restrictive-type anorexia nervosa suggested by increased serotonin 1A receptor binding in right frontotemporal cortex of both lean and recovered patients: [18F]MPPF PET scan study. *Biological Psychiatry*, 64(11), 1009–1013. https://doi.org/10.1016/j.biopsych.2008.06.006

Galusca, B., Sigaud, T., Costes, N., Redoute, J., Massoubre, C., & Estour, B. (2014). Wide impairment of cerebral serotoninergic activity but inter-individual heterogeneity in bulimia nervosa patients: A pilot [(18)F]MPPF/PET study. *World Journal of Biological Psychiatry*, 15(8), 599–608. https://doi.org/10.3109/15622975.2014.942358

Garfinkel, P., & Garner, D. (1983). The multidetermined nature of anorexia nervosa. In *Anorexia nervosa: Recent developments in research* (pp. 3–14). Alan R. Liss.

Gaudio, S., Carducci, F., Piervincenzi, C., Olivo, G., & Schioth, H. B. (2019). Altered thalamo-cortical and occipital-parietal- temporal-frontal white matter connections in patients with anorexia and bulimia nervosa: A systematic review of diffusion tensor imaging studies. *Journal of Psychiatry and Neuroscience*, 44(5), 324–339. https://doi.org/10.1503/jpn.180121

Gaudio, S., Wiemerslage, L., Brooks, S. J., & Schioth, H. B. (2016). A systematic review of resting-state functional-MRI studies in anorexia nervosa: Evidence for functional connectivity impairment in cognitive control and visuospatial and body-signal integration. *Neuroscience and Biobehavior Reviews*, 71, 578–589. https://doi.org/10.1016/j.neubiorev.2016.09.032

Geliebter, A., Gluck, M. E., & Hashim, S. A. (2005). Plasma ghrelin concentrations are lower in binge-eating disorder. *Journal of Nutrition*, 135(5), 1326–1330. https://doi.org/10.1093/jn/135.5.1326

Ghadirian, A.-M., Marini, N., Jabalpurwala, S., & Steiger, H. (1999). Seasonal mood patterns in eating disorders. *General Hospital Psychiatry*, 21(5), 354–359. https://doi.org/https://doi.org/10.1016/S0163-8343(99)00028-6

Glashouwer, K. A., van der Veer, R. M. L., Adipatria, F., de Jong, P. J., & Vocks, S. (2019). The role of body image disturbance in the onset, maintenance, and relapse of anorexia nervosa: A systematic review. *Clinical Psychology Review*, 74, 101771. https://doi.org/10.1016/j.cpr.2019.101771

Godart, N. T., Flament, M. F., Curt, F., Perdereau, F., Lang, F., Venisse, J. L., Halfon, O., Bizouard, P., Loas, G., & Corcos, M. (2003). Anxiety disorders in subjects seeking treatment for eating disorders: A DSM-IV controlled study. *Psychiatry Research*, 117(3), 245–258.

Godlewska, B. R., Pike, A., Sharpley, A. L., Ayton, A., Park, R. J., Cowen, P. J., & Emir, U. E. (2017). Brain glutamate in anorexia nervosa: A magnetic resonance spectroscopy case control study at 7 Tesla. *Psychopharmacology (Berl)*, 234(3), 421–426. https://doi.org/10.1007/s00213-016-4477-5

Goldschmidt, A. B., Wall, M., Loth, K. A., Le Grange, D., & Neumark-Sztainer, D. (2012). Which dieters are at risk for the onset of binge eating? A prospective study of adolescents and young adults. *Journal of Adolescent Health*, 51(1), 86–92. https://doi.org/10.1016/j.jadohealth.2011.11.001

Gordon, R. A. (1990). *Anorexia and bulimia: Anatomy of a social epidemic*. Basil Blackwell.

Grabe, S., Ward, L. M., & Hyde, J. S. (2008). The role of the media in body image concerns among women: A meta-analysis of experimental and correlational studies. *Psychological Bulletin*, 134(3), 460–476. https://doi.org/10.1037/0033-2909.134.3.460

Grilo, C. M., White, M. A., Barnes, R. D., & Masheb, R. M. (2012). Posttraumatic stress disorder in women with binge eating disorder in primary care. *Journal of Psychiatric Practice*, 18(6), 408.

Groleau, P., Joober, R., Israel, M., Zeramdini, N., DeGuzman, R., & Steiger, H. (2014). Methylation of the dopamine D2 receptor (DRD2) gene promoter in women with a bulimia-spectrum disorder: Associations with borderline personality disorder and exposure to childhood abuse. *Journal of Psychiatric Research*, 48(1), 121–127. https://doi.org/10.1016/j.jpsychires.2013.10.003

Groleau, P., Steiger, H., Bruce, K., Israel, M., Sycz, L., Ouellette, A.-S., & Badawi, G. (2012). Childhood emotional abuse and eating symptoms in bulimic disorders: An examination of possible mediating variables. *International Journal of Eating Disorders*, 45(3), 326–332. https://doi.org/10.1002/eat.20939

Haedt-Matt, A. A., & Keel, P. K. (2011). Revisiting the affect regulation model of binge eating: A meta-analysis of studies using ecological momentary assessment. *Psychological Bulletin*, 137(4), 660–681. https://doi.org/10.1037/a0023660

Hartmann, A. S., Poulain, T., Vogel, M., Hiemisch, A., Kiess, W., & Hilbert, A. (2018). Prevalence of pica and rumination behaviors in German children aged 7–14 and their associations with feeding, eating, and general psychopathology: A population-based study. *European Child & Adolescent Psychiatry*, 27(11), 1499–1508. https://doi.org/10.1007/s00787-018-1153-9

Hay, P., Mitchison, D., Collado, A. E. L., González-Chica, D. A., Stocks, N., & Touyz, S. (2017). Burden and health-related quality of life of eating disorders, including Avoidant/Restrictive Food Intake Disorder (ARFID), in the Australian population. *Journal of Eating Disorders*, 5, 21. https://doi.org/10.1186/s40337-017-0149-z

Haynos, A. F., Berg, K. C., Cao, L., Crosby, R. D., Lavender, J. M., Utzinger, L. M., Wonderlich, S. A., Engel, S. G., Mitchell, J. E., Le Grange, D., Peterson, C. B., & Crow, S. J. (2017). Trajectories of higher- and lower-order dimensions of negative and positive affect relative to restrictive eating in anorexia nervosa. *Journal of normal Psychology*, 126(5), 495–505. https://doi.org/10.1037/abn0000202

Hedman, A., Breithaupt, L., Hübel, C., Thornton, L. M., Tillander, A., Norring, C., Birgegård, A., Larsson, H.,

Ludvigsson, J. F., Sävendahl, L., Almqvist, C., & Bulik, C. M. (2019). Bidirectional relationship between eating disorders and autoimmune diseases. *Journal of Child Psychology and Psychiatry, 60*(7), 803–812. https://doi.org/10.1111/jcpp.12958

Herle, M., Fildes, A., Steinsbekk, S., Rijsdijk, F., & Llewellyn, C. H. (2017). Emotional over- and under-eating in early childhood are learned not inherited. *Scientific Reports, 7*(1), 9092. https://doi.org/10.1038/s41598-017-09519-0

Herpertz-Dahlmann, B. (2015). Adolescent eating disorders: Update on definitions, symptomatology, epidemiology, and comorbidity. *Child and Adolescent Psychiatric Clinics of North America, 24*(1), 177–196. https://doi.org/10.1016/j.chc.2014.08.003

Holderness, C. C., Brooks-Gunn, J., & Warren, M. P. (1994). Co-morbidity of eating disorders and substance abuse review of the literature. *International Journal of Eating Disorders, 16*(1), 1–34. doi:10.1002/1098-108x(199407)16:1<1::aid-eat2260160102>3.0.co;2-t

Hudson, J. I., Hiripi, E., Pope Jr, H. G., & Kessler, R. C. (2007). The prevalence and correlates of eating disorders in the National Comorbidity Survey Replication. *Biological Psychiatry, 61*(3), 348–358.

Huke, V., Turk, J., Saeidi, S., Kent, A., & Morgan, J. F. (2013). Autism spectrum disorders in eating disorder populations: A systematic review. *European Eating Disorders Review, 21*(5), 345–351. https://doi.org/10.1002/erv.2244

Jacobi, C., Hayward, C., de Zwaan, M., Kraemer, H. C., & Agras, W. S. (2004). Coming to terms with risk factors for eating disorders: Application of risk terminology and suggestions for a general taxonomy. *Psychological Bulletin, 130*(1), 19–65. https://doi.org/10.1037/0033-2909.130.1.19

Javaras, K. N., Laird, N. M., Reichborn-Kjennerud, T., Bulik, C. M., Pope Jr, H. G., & Hudson, J. I. (2008). Familiality and heritability of binge eating disorder: Results of a case-control family study and a twin study. *International Journal of Eating Disorders, 41*(2), 174–179.

Javitt, D. C. (2004). Glutamate as a therapeutic target in psychiatric disorders. *Molecular Psychiatry, 9*(11), 984–997, 979. https://doi.org/10.1038/sj.mp.4001551

Joos, A. A., Perlov, E., Buchert, M., Hartmann, A., Saum, B., Glauche, V., Freyer, T., Weber-Fahr, W., Zeeck, A., & Tebartz van Elst, L. (2011). Magnetic resonance spectroscopy of the anterior cingulate cortex in eating disorders. *Psychiatry Research, 191*(3), 196–200. https://doi.org/10.1016/j.pscychresns.2010.10.004

Kalyva, E. (2009). Comparison of eating attitudes between adolescent girls with and without Asperger syndrome: Daughters' and mothers' reports. *Journal of Autism and Developmental Disorders, 39*(3), 480–486.

Karr, T. M., Crosby, R. D., Cao, L., Engel, S. G., Mitchell, J. E., Simonich, H., & Wonderlich, S. A. (2013). Posttraumatic stress disorder as a moderator of the association between negative affect and bulimic symptoms: An ecological momentary assessment study. *Comprehensive Psychiatry, 54*(1), 61–69.

Karthik, S., Sharma, L. P., & Narayanaswamy, J. C. (2020). Investigating the role of glutamate in obsessive-compulsive disorder: Current perspectives. *Neuropsychiatric Disease and Treatment, 16*, 1003–1013. https://doi.org/10.2147/NDT.S211703

Karwautz, A. F., Wagner, G., Waldherr, K., Nader, I. W., Fernandez-Aranda, F., Estivill, X., Holliday, J., Collier, D. A., & Treasure, J. L. (2011). Gene-environment interaction in anorexia nervosa: Relevance of non-shared environment and the serotonin transporter gene. *Molecular Psychiatry, 16*(6), 590–592. https://doi.org/10.1038/mp.2010.125

Kaufmann, L. K., Hanggi, J., Jancke, L., Baur, V., Piccirelli, M., Kollias, S., Schnyder, U., Martin-Soelch, C., & Milos, G. (2020). Age influences structural brain restoration during weight gain therapy in anorexia nervosa. *Translational Psychiatry, 10*(1), 126. https://doi.org/10.1038/s41398-020-0809-7

Kaye, W. H., Bulik, C. M., Thornton, L., Barbarich, N., Masters, K., & Group, P. F. C. (2004). Comorbidity of anxiety disorders with anorexia and bulimia nervosa. *American Journal of Psychiatry, 161*(12), 2215–2221.

Keel, P. K., Heatherton, T. F., Dorer, D. J., Joiner, T. E., & Zalta, A. K. (2006). Point prevalence of bulimia nervosa in 1982, 1992, and 2002. *Psychological Medicine, 36*(1), 119–128.

Keel, P. K., & Klump, K. L. (2003). Are eating disorders culture-bound syndromes? Implications for conceptualizing their etiology. *Psychological Bulletin, 129*(5), 747.

Kerr-Gaffney, J., Harrison, A., & Tchanturia, K. (2018). Social anxiety in the eating disorders: A systematic review and meta-analysis. *Psychological Medicine, 48*(15), 2477–2491.

Keys, A., Brožek, J., Henschel, A., Mickelsen, O., & Taylor, H. L. (1950). *The biology of human starvation*, Volume II. University of Minnesota Press.

Kim, Y. R., Kim, J. H., Kim, M. J., & Treasure, J. (2014). Differential methylation of the oxytocin receptor gene in patients with anorexia nervosa: A pilot study. *PLoS One, 9*(2), e88673. https://doi.org/10.1371/journal.pone.0088673

King, J. A., Frank, G. K. W., Thompson, P. M., & Ehrlich, S. (2018). Structural neuroimaging of anorexia nervosa: Future directions in the quest for mechanisms underlying dynamic alterations. *Biological Psychiatry, 83*(3), 224–234. https://doi.org/10.1016/j.biopsych.2017.08.011

King, J. A., Korb, F. M., Vettermann, R., Ritschel, F., Egner, T., & Ehrlich, S. (2019). Cognitive overcontrol as a trait marker in anorexia nervosa? Aberrant task- and response-set switching in remitted patients. *Journal of Abnormal Psychology, 128*(8), 806–812. https://doi.org/10.1037/abn0000476

Klump, K. L., Strober, M., Bulik, C. M., Thornton, L., Johnson, C., Devlin, B., Fichter, M. M., Halmi, K. A., Kaplan, A. S., & Crow, S. (2004). Personality characteristics of women before and after recovery from an eating disorder. *Psychological Medicine, 34*(8), 1407.

Kontis, D., & Theochari, E. (2012). Dopamine in anorexia nervosa: A systematic review. *Behavioral Pharmacology, 23*(5–6), 496–515. https://doi.org/10.1097/FBP.0b013e328357e115

Lantz, E. L., Gaspar, M. E., DiTore, R., Piers, A. D., & Schaumberg, K. (2018). Conceptualizing body dissatisfaction in eating disorders within a self-discrepancy framework: A review of evidence. *Eating and Weight Disorders, 23*(3), 275–291. https://doi.org/10.1007/s40519-018-0483-4

Lavender, J. M., Wonderlich, S. A., Engel, S. G., Gordon, K. H., Kaye, W. H., & Mitchell, J. E. (2015). Dimensions of emotion dysregulation in anorexia nervosa and bulimia nervosa: A conceptual review of the empirical literature. *Clinical Psychology Review, 40*, 111–122. https://doi.org/10.1016/j.cpr.2015.05.010

le Grange, D., Lock, J., Loeb, K., & Nicholls, D. (2010). Academy for Eating Disorders position paper: The role of the family in eating disorders. *International Journal of Eating Disorders, 43*(1), 1–5. https://doi.org/10.1002/eat.20751

Leppanen, J., Sedgewick, F., Treasure, J., & Tchanturia, K. (2018). Differences in the Theory of Mind profiles of patients with anorexia nervosa and individuals on the autism spectrum: A meta-analytic review. *Neuroscience and Biobehavioral Review, 90*, 146–163. https://doi.org/10.1016/j.neubiorev.2018.04.009

Levin, R. L., & Rawana, J. S. (2016). Attention-deficit/hyperactivity disorder and eating disorders across the lifespan: A systematic review of the literature. *Clinical Psychology Review, 50*, 22–36. https://doi.org/10.1016/j.cpr.2016.09.010

Levinson, C. A., Zerwas, S. C., Brosof, L. C., Thornton, L. M., Strober, M., Pivarunas, B., Crowley, J. J., Yilmaz, Z., Berrettini, W. H., & Brandt, H. (2019). Associations between dimensions of anorexia nervosa and obsessive–compulsive disorder: An examination of personality and psychological factors in patients with anorexia nervosa. *European Eating Disorders Review, 27*(2), 161–172.

Lilenfeld, L. R., Wonderlich, S., Riso, L. P., Crosby, R., & Mitchell, J. (2006). Eating disorders and personality: A methodological and empirical review. *Clinical Psychology Review, 26*(3), 299–320.

Limburg, K., Watson, H. J., Hagger, M. S., & Egan, S. J. (2017). The relationship between perfectionism and psychopathology: A meta-analysis. *Journal of Clinical Psychology, 73*(10), 1301–1326. https://doi.org/10.1002/jclp.22435

Liu, X., Study, B. G., Kelsoe, J. R., & Greenwood, T. A. (2016). A genome-wide association study of bipolar disorder with comorbid eating disorder replicates the SOX2-OT region. *Journal of Affective Disorders, 189*, 141–149.

Lo Sauro, C., Ravaldi, C., Cabras, P. L., Faravelli, C., & Ricca, V. (2008). Stress, hypothalamic-pituitary-adrenal axis and eating disorders. *Neuropsychobiology, 57*(3), 95–115. https://doi.org/10.1159/000138912

Lock, J. (2015). An update on evidence-based psychosocial treatments for eating disorders in children and adolescents. *Journal of Clinical Child and Adolescent Psychology, 44*(5), 707–721. https://doi.org/10.1080/15374416.2014.971458

Lozano-Madrid, M., Clark Bryan, D., Granero, R., Sánchez, I., Riesco, N., Mallorquí-Bagué, N., Jiménez-Murcia, S., Treasure, J., & Fernández-Aranda, F. (2020). Impulsivity, emotional dysregulation and executive function deficits could be associated with alcohol and drug abuse in eating disorders. *Journal of Clinical Medicine, 9*(6), 1936. https://doi.org/10.3390/jcm9061936

Lyke, J., & Matsen, J. (2013). Family functioning and risk factors for disordered eating. *Eating Behaviors, 14*(4), 497–499. https://doi.org/10.1016/j.eatbeh.2013.08.009

Ma, R., Mikhail, M. E., Fowler, N., Culbert, K. M., & Klump, K. L. (2019). The role of puberty and ovarian hormones in the genetic diathesis of eating disorders in females. *Child and Adolescent Psychiatry Clinics of North America, 28*(4), 617–628. https://doi.org/10.1016/j.chc.2019.05.008

Majuri, J., Joutsa, J., Johansson, J., Voon, V., Parkkola, R., Alho, H., Arponen, E., & Kaasinen, V. (2017). Serotonin transporter density in binge eating disorder and pathological gambling: A PET study with [(11)C]MADAM. *European Neuropsychopharmacology, 27*(12), 1281–1288. https://doi.org/10.1016/j.euroneuro.2017.09.007

Makino, M., Tsuboi, K., & Dennerstein, L. (2004). Prevalence of eating disorders: A comparison of Western and non-Western countries. *MedGenMed, 6*(3), 49.

Martín, J., Arostegui, I., Loroño, A., Padierna, A., Najera-Zuloaga, J., & Quintana, J. M. (2019). Anxiety and depressive symptoms are related to core symptoms, general health outcome, and medical comorbidities in eating disorders. *European Eating Disorders Review, 27*(6), 603–613. https://doi.org/10.1002/erv.2677

Martinussen, M., Friborg, O., Schmierer, P., Kaiser, S., Øvergård, K. T., Neunhoeffer, A.-L., Martinsen, E. W., & Rosenvinge, J. H. (2017). The comorbidity of personality disorders in eating disorders: A meta-analysis. *Eating and Weight Disorders: Studies on Anorexia, Bulimia and Obesity, 22*(2), 201–209.

Matsunaga, H., Kaye, W. H., McConaha, C., Plotnicov, K., Pollice, C., & Rao, R. (2000). Personality disorders among subjects recovered from eating disorders. *International Journal of Eating Disorders, 27*(3), 353–357.

Mele, G., Alfano, V., Cotugno, A., & Longarzo, M. (2020). A broad-spectrum review on multimodal neuroimaging in bulimia nervosa and binge eating disorder. *Appetite, 151*, 104712. https://doi.org/10.1016/j.appet.2020.104712

Mihov, Y., Treyer, V., Akkus, F., Toman, E., Milos, G., Ametamey, S. M., Johayem, A., & Hasler, G. (2020). Metabotropic glutamate receptor 5 in bulimia nervosa. *Science Reports, 10*(1), 6374. https://doi.org/10.1038/s41598-020-63389-7

Mikami, A. Y., Hinshaw, S. P., Patterson, K. A., & Lee, J. C. (2008). Eating pathology among adolescent girls with attention-deficit/hyperactivity disorder. *Journal of Abnormal Psychology, 117*(1), 225–235. https://doi.org/10.1037/0021-843x.117.1.225

Mikhail, M. E., Culbert, K. M., Sisk, C. L., & Klump, K. L. (2019). Gonadal hormone contributions to individual differences in eating disorder risk. *Current Opinion in Psychiatry, 32*(6), 484–490. https://doi.org/10.1097/YCO.0000000000000543

Mitre, M., Mariga, A., & Chao, M. V. (2017). Neurotrophin signalling: Novel insights into mechanisms and pathophysiology. *Clinical Science (Lond), 131*(1), 13–23. https://doi.org/10.1042/CS20160044

Molendijk, M., Hoek, H., Brewerton, T., & Elzinga, B. (2017). Childhood maltreatment and eating disorder pathology: A systematic review and dose-response meta-analysis. *Psychological Medicine, 47*(8), 1402–1416.

Monteleone, P., & Maj, M. (2013). Dysfunctions of leptin, ghrelin, BDNF and endocannabinoids in eating disorders: Beyond the homeostatic control of food intake. *Psychoneuroendocrinology, 38*(3), 312–330. https://doi.org/10.1016/j.psyneuen.2012.10.021

Muller, T. D., Tschop, M. H., Jarick, I., Ehrlich, S., Scherag, S., Herpertz-Dahlmann, B., . . . Hinney, A. (2011). Genetic variation of the ghrelin activator gene ghrelin O-acyltransferase (GOAT) is associated with anorexia nervosa. *Journal of Psychiatric Research, 45*(5), 706–711. https://doi.org/10.1016/j.jpsychires.2010.10.001

Nakazato, M., Hashimoto, K., Shimizu, E., Niitsu, T., & Iyo, M. (2012). Possible involvement of brain-derived neurotrophic factor in eating disorders. *IUBMB Life, 64*(5), 355–361. https://doi.org/10.1002/iub.1012

Neyazi, A., Buchholz, V., Burkert, A., Hillemacher, T., de Zwaan, M., Herzog, W., Jahn, K., Giel, K., Herpertz, S., Buchholz, C. A., Dinkel, A., Burgmer, M., Zeeck, A., Bleich, S., Zipfel, S., & Frieling, H. (2019). Association of leptin gene DNA methylation with diagnosis and treatment outcome of anorexia nervosa [original research]. *Frontiers in Psychiatry, 10*(197). https://doi.org/10.3389/fpsyt.2019.00197

Nicholls, D. E., & Viner, R. M. (2009). Childhood risk factors for lifetime anorexia nervosa by age 30 years in a national birth cohort. *Journal of the American Academy of Child and Adolescent Psychiatry, 48*(8), 791–799. https://doi.org/10.1097/chi.0b013e3181ab8b75

Nielsen, S., Anckarsäter, H., Gillberg, C., Gillberg, C., Råstam, M., & Wentz, E. (2015). Effects of autism spectrum disorders on outcome in teenage-onset anorexia nervosa evaluated by the Morgan-Russell outcome assessment schedule: A controlled community-based study. *Molecular Autism, 6*(1), 14. https://doi.org/10.1186/s13229-015-0013-4

Nikodijevic, A., Buck, K., Fuller-Tyszkiewicz, M., de Paoli, T., & Krug, I. (2018). Body checking and body avoidance in eating disorders: Systematic review and meta-analysis. *European Eating Disorders Review, 26*(3), 159–185. https://doi.org/10.1002/erv.2585

Nilsson, M., Naessen, S., Dahlman, I., Linden Hirschberg, A., Gustafsson, J. A., & Dahlman-Wright, K. (2004). Association of estrogen receptor beta gene polymorphisms with bulimic disease in women. *Molecular Psychiatry, 9*(1), 28–34. https://doi.org/10.1038/sj.mp.4001402

O'Hara, C. B., Campbell, I. C., & Schmidt, U. (2015). A reward-centred model of anorexia nervosa: A focussed narrative review of the neurological and psychophysiological literature. *Neuroscience and Biobehavior Review, 52*, 131–152. https://doi.org/10.1016/j.neubiorev.2015.02.012

Oldershaw, A., Treasure, J., Hambrook, D., Tchanturia, K., & Schmidt, U. (2011). Is anorexia nervosa a version of autism spectrum disorders? *European Eating Disorders Review, 19*(6), 462–474.

Olivo, G., Gaudio, S., & Schioth, H. B. (2019). Brain and cognitive development in adolescents with anorexia nervosa: A systematic review of fMRI studies. *Nutrients, 11*(8). https://doi.org/10.3390/nu11081907

Olivo, G., Solstrand Dahlberg, L., Wiemerslage, L., Swenne, I., Zhukovsky, C., Salonen-Ros, H., Larsson, E. M., Gaudio, S., Brooks, S. J., & Schioth, H. B. (2018). Atypical anorexia nervosa is not related to brain structural changes in newly diagnosed adolescent patients. *International Journal of Eating Disorders, 51*(1), 39–45. https://doi.org/10.1002/eat.22805

Pallister, E., & Waller, G. (2008). Anxiety in the eating disorders: Understanding the overlap. *Clinical Psychology Review, 28*(3), 366–386.

Pearson, C. M., Riley, E. N., Davis, H. A., & Smith, G. T. (2014). Two pathways toward impulsive action: An integrative risk model for bulimic behavior in youth. *Journal of Child Psychology and Psychiatry, 55*(8), 852–864. https://doi.org/10.1111/jcpp.12214

Pichika, R., Buchsbaum, M. S., Bailer, U., Hoh, C., Decastro, A., Buchsbaum, B. R., & Kaye, W. (2012). Serotonin transporter binding after recovery from bulimia nervosa. *International Journal of Eating Disorders, 45*(3), 345–352. https://doi.org/10.1002/eat.20944

Pike, K. M., Hoek, H. W., & Dunne, P. E. (2014). Cultural trends and eating disorders. *Current Opinions in Psychiatry, 27*(6), 436–442. https://doi.org/10.1097/yco.0000000000000100

Plessow, F., Eddy, K. T., & Lawson, E. A. (2018). The neuropeptide hormone oxytocin in eating disorders. *Current Psychiatry Reports, 20*(10), 91. https://doi.org/10.1007/s11920-018-0957-0

Polivy, J., & Herman, C. P. (1993). Etiology of binge eating: Psychological mechanisms. In C. G. Fairburn & G. T. Wilson (Eds.), *Binge eating: Nature, assessment, and treatment* (pp. 173–205). Guilford.

Prefit, A. B., Cândea, D. M., & Szentagotai-Tătar, A. (2019). Emotion regulation across eating pathology: A meta-analysis. *Appetite, 143*, 104438. https://doi.org/10.1016/j.appet.2019.104438

Racine, S. E., Keel, P. K., Burt, S. A., Sisk, C. L., Neale, M., Boker, S., & Klump, K. L. (2013). Exploring the relationship between negative urgency and dysregulated eating: Etiologic associations and the role of negative affect. *Journal of Abnormal Psychology, 122*(2), 433–444. https://doi.org/10.1037/a0031250

Reas, D. L., Pedersen, G., & Rø, Ø. (2016). Impulsivity-related traits distinguish women with co-occurring bulimia nervosa in a psychiatric sample. *International Journal of Eating Disorders, 49*(12), 1093–1096. https://doi.org/10.1002/eat.22606

Richardson, J., Steiger, H., Schmitz, N., Joober, R., Bruce, K. R., Israel, M., Gauvin, L., Anestin, A. S., Dandurand, C., & Howard, H. (2008). Relevance of the 5-HTTLPR polymorphism and childhood abuse to increased psychiatric comorbidity in women with bulimia-spectrum disorders. *Journal of Clinical Psychiatry, 69*(6), 17382. doi:10.4088/jcp.v69n0615

Rosval, L., Steiger, H., Bruce, K., Israël, M., Richardson, J., & Aubut, M. (2006). Impulsivity in women with eating disorders: Problem of response inhibition, planning, or attention? *International Journal of Eating Disorders, 39*(7), 590–593. https://doi.org/10.1002/eat.20296

Saure, E., Laasonen, M., Lepisto-Paisley, T., Mikkola, K., Algars, M., & Raevuori, A. (2020). Characteristics of autism spectrum disorders are associated with longer duration of anorexia nervosa: A systematic review and meta-analysis. *International Journal of Eating Disorders, 53*(7), 1056–1079. https://doi.org/10.1002/eat.23259

Schaefer, L. M., & Thompson, J. K. (2018). Self-objectification and disordered eating: A meta-analysis. *International Journal of Eating Disorders, 51*(6), 483–502. https://doi.org/10.1002/eat.22854

Schafer, A., Vaitl, D., & Schienle, A. (2010). Regional grey matter volume abnormalities in bulimia nervosa and binge-eating disorder. *Neuroimage, 50*(2), 639–643. https://doi.org/10.1016/j.neuroimage.2009.12.063

Schaumberg, K., Zerwas, S., Goodman, E., Yilmaz, Z., Bulik, C. M., & Micali, N. (2019). Anxiety disorder symptoms at age 10 predict eating disorder symptoms and diagnoses in adolescence. *Journal of Child Psychology and Psychiatry, 60*(6), 686–696.

Seitz, J., Herpertz-Dahlmann, B., & Konrad, K. (2016). Brain morphological changes in adolescent and adult patients with anorexia nervosa. *Journal of Neural Transmission (Vienna), 123*(8), 949–959. https://doi.org/10.1007/s00702-016-1567-9

Shank, L. M., Tanofsky-Kraff, M., Kelly, N. R., Jaramillo, M., Rubin, S. G., Altman, D. R., Byrne, M. E., LeMay-Russell, S., Schvey, N. A., Broadney, M. M., Brady, S. M., Yang, S. B., Courville, A. B., Ramirez, S., Crist, A. C., Yanovski, S. Z., & Yanovski, J. A. (2019). The association between alexithymia and eating behavior in children and adolescents. *Appetite, 142*, 104381. https://doi.org/10.1016/j.appet.2019.104381

Simon, J. J., Skunde, M., Walther, S., Bendszus, M., Herzog, W., & Friederich, H. C. (2016). Neural signature of food reward processing in bulimic-type eating disorders. *Social Cognition* and *Affective Neuroscience, 11*(9), 1393–1401. https://doi.org/10.1093/scan/nsw049

Smink, F. R., Van Hoeken, D., & Hoek, H. W. (2012). Epidemiology of eating disorders: Incidence, prevalence and mortality rates. *Current Psychiatry Reports, 14*(4), 406–414.

Smith, K. E., Mason, T. B., Johnson, J. S., Lavender, J. M., & Wonderlich, S. A. (2018). A systematic review of reviews of neurocognitive functioning in eating disorders: The state-of-the-literature and future directions. *International Journal of Eating Disorders, 51*(8), 798–821. https://doi.org/10.1002/eat.22929

Smolak, L., Striegel-Moore, R. H., & Levine, M. P. (2013). *The developmental psychopathology of eating disorders: Implications for research, prevention, and treatment.* Routledge. https://doi.org/https://doi.org/10.4324/9780203763506

Sohlberg, S., & Strober, M. (1994). Personality in Anorexia nervosa: An update and a theoretical integration. *Acta Psychiatrica Scandinavica, 89*(s378), 1–15. https://doi.org/10.1111/j.1600-0447.1994.tb05809.x

Steele, A. L., O'Shea, A., Murdock, A., & Wade, T. D. (2011). Perfectionism and its relation to overevaluation of weight and shape and depression in an eating disorder sample. *International Journal of Eating Disorders, 44*(5), 459–464. https://doi.org/10.1002/eat.20817

Steiger, H., & Booij, L. (2020). Eating disorders, heredity and environmental activation: Getting epigenetic concepts into practice. *Journal of Clinical Medicine, 9*(5), 1332. https://doi.org/10.3390/jcm9051332

Steiger, H., Booij, L., Kahan, McGregor, K., Thaler, L., Fletcher, E., Labbe, A., Joober, R., Israël, M., Szyf, M., Agellon, L. B., Gauvin, L., St-Hilaire, A., & Rossi, E. (2019). A longitudinal, epigenome-wide study of DNA methylation in anorexia nervosa: Results in actively ill, partially weight-restored, long-term remitted and non-eating-disordered women. *Journal of Psychiatry and Neuroscience, 44*(3), 205–213. https://doi.org/10.1503/jpn.170242

Steiger, H., & Bruce, K. R. (2004). Personality traits and disorders associated with anorexia nervosa, bulimia nervosa, and binge eating disorder. In T. D. Brewerton (Ed.), *Clinical handbook of eating disorders* (pp. 233–256). Marcel Dekker.

Steiger, H., Bruce, K. R., & Groleau, P. (2011). Neural circuits, neurotransmitters, and behavior: Serotonin and temperament in bulimic syndromes. *Current Topics in Behavioral Neuroscience, 6*, 125–138. https://doi.org/10.1007/7854_2010_88

Steiger, H., Gauvin, L., Israël, M., Koerner, N., Kin, N. N. Y., Paris, J., & Young, S. N. (2001). Association of serotonin and cortisol indices with childhood abuse in bulimia nervosa. *Archives of General Psychiatry, 58*(9), 837–843.

Steiger, H., Gauvin, L., Joober, R., Israel, M., Ng Ying Kin, N. M., Bruce, K. R., Richardson, J., Young, S. N., & Hakim, J. (2006). Intrafamilial correspondences on platelet [3H-]paroxetine-binding indices in bulimic probands and their unaffected first-degree relatives. *Neuropsychopharmacology, 31*(8), 1785–1792. https://doi.org/10.1038/sj.npp.1301011

Steiger, H., Labonté, B., Groleau, P., Turecki, G., & Israel, M. (2013). Methylation of the glucocorticoid receptor gene promoter in bulimic women: Associations with borderline personality disorder, suicidality, and exposure to childhood abuse. *International Journal of Eating Disorders, 46*(3), 246–255. https://doi.org/10.1002/eat.22113

Steiger, H., Liquornik, K., Chapman, J., & Hussain, N. (1991). Personality and family disturbances in eating-disorder patients: Comparison of "restricters" and "bingers" to normal controls. *International Journal of Eating Disorders, 10*(5), 501–512. https://doi.org/10.1002/1098-108X(199109)10:5<501::AID-EAT2260100502>3.0.CO;2-Z

Steiger, H., Richardson, J., Joober, R., Gauvin, L., Israel, M., Bruce, K. R., Ying Kin, N. M. K. N., Howard, H., & Young, S. N. (2007). The 5HTTLPR polymorphism, prior maltreatment and dramatic-erratic personality manifestations in women with bulimic syndromes. *Journal of Psychiatry & Neuroscience, 32*(5), 354–362. https://pubmed.ncbi.nlm.nih.gov/17823651 https://www.ncbi.nlm.nih.gov/pmc/articles/PMC1963352/

Steiger, H., Richardson, J., Joober, R., Israel, M., Bruce, K. R., Ng Ying Kin, N. M. K., Howard, H., Anestin, A., Dandurand, C., & Gauvin, L. (2008). Dissocial behavior, the 5HTTLPR polymorphism, and maltreatment in women with bulimic syndromes. *American Journal of Medical Genetics Part B: Neuropsychiatric Genetics, 147B*(1), 128–130. https://doi.org/10.1002/ajmg.b.30579

Steiger, H., Richardson, J., Schmitz, N., Joober, R., Israel, M., Bruce, K. R., Gauvin, L., Dandurand, C., & Anestin, A. (2009). Association of trait-defined, eating-disorder subphenotypes with (biallelic and triallelic) 5HTTLPR variations. *Journal of Psychiatric Research, 43*(13), 1086–1094. https://doi.org/10.1016/j.jpsychires.2009.03.009

Stewart, C. S., McEwen, F. S., Konstantellou, A., Eisler, I., & Simic, M. (2017). Impact of ASD Traits on Treatment Outcomes of Eating Disorders in Girls. *European Eating Disorders Review, 25*(2), 123–128. https://doi.org/10.1002/erv.2497

Stice, E., & Agras, W. S. (1998). Predicting onset and cessation of bulimic behaviors during adolescence: A longitudinal grouping analysis. *Behavior Therapy, 29*(2), 257–276. https://doi.org/https://doi.org/10.1016/S0005-7894(98)80006-3

Stice, E., & Shaw, H. (2018). Dieting and the eating Disorders (pp 126–154). In W. S. Agras & A. Robinson (Eds.), *The Oxford handbook of eating disorders,* 2nd ed. Oxford University Press.

Stice, E., & Van Ryzin, M. J. (2019). A prospective test of the temporal sequencing of risk factor emergence in the dual pathway model of eating disorders. *Journal of Abnormal Psychology, 128*(2), 119–128. https://doi.org/10.1037/abn0000400

Stopyra, M. A., Simon, J. J., Skunde, M., Walther, S., Bendszus, M., Herzog, W., & Friederich, H. C. (2019). Altered functional connectivity in binge eating disorder and bulimia nervosa: A resting-state fMRI study. *Brain and Behavior, 9*(2), e01207. https://doi.org/10.1002/brb3.1207

Striegel-Moore, R. H., & Bulik, C. M. (2007). Risk factors for eating disorders. *American Psychologist, 62*(3), 181–198. https://doi.org/10.1037/0003-066X.62.3.181

Strober, M., Freeman, R., Lampert, C., Diamond, J., & Kaye, W. (2000). Controlled family study of anorexia nervosa and bulimia nervosa: Evidence of shared liability and transmission of partial syndromes. *American Journal of Psychiatry, 157*(3), 393–401. https://doi.org/10.1176/appi.ajp.157.3.393

Stunkard, A. J. (1959). Eating patterns and obesity. *Psychiatric Quarterly, 33*(2), 284–295.

Swami, V., Frederick, D. A., Aavik, T., Alcalay, L., Allik, J., Anderson, D., . . . Zivcic-Becirevic, I. (2010). The attractive female body weight and female body dissatisfaction in 26 countries across 10 world regions: Results of the international body project I. *Personality and Society Psychological*

Bulletin, 36(3), 309–325. https://doi.org/10.1177/0146167209359702

Swanson, S. A., Crow, S. J., Le Grange, D., Swendsen, J., & Merikangas, K. R. (2011). Prevalence and correlates of eating disorders in adolescents: Results from the national comorbidity survey replication adolescent supplement. *Archives of General Psychiatry*, 68(7), 714–723.

Szyf, M. (2015). Epigenetics, a key for unlocking complex CNS disorders? Therapeutic implications. *European Neuropsychopharmacology*, 25(5), 682–702. https://doi.org/10.1016/j.euroneuro.2014.01.009

Tapajoz, F., Soneira, S., Catoira, N., Aulicino, A., & Allegri, R. F. (2019). Impaired theory of mind in unaffected first-degree relatives of patients with anorexia nervosa. *European Eating Disorders Review*, 27(6), 692–699. https://doi.org/10.1002/erv.2701

Tasca, G. A. (2019). Attachment and eating disorders: A research update. *Current Opinion in Psychology*, 25, 59–64. https://doi.org/10.1016/j.copsyc.2018.03.003

Tetzlaff, A., Schmidt, R., Brauhardt, A., & Hilbert, A. (2016). Family functioning in adolescents with binge-eating disorder. *European Eating Disorders Review*, 24(5), 430–433. https://doi.org/10.1002/erv.2462

Thaler, L., Brassard, S., Booij, L., Kahan, E., McGregor, K., Labbe, A., Israel, M., & Steiger, H. (2020). Methylation of the OXTR gene in women with anorexia nervosa: Relationship to social behavior. *European Eating Disorders Review*, 28(1), 79–86. https://doi.org/10.1002/erv.2703

Thaler, L., Gauvin, L., Joober, R., Groleau, P., de Guzman, R., Ambalavanan, A., Israel, M., Wilson, S., & Steiger, H. (2014). Methylation of BDNF in women with bulimic eating syndromes: Associations with childhood abuse and borderline personality disorder. *Progress in Neuropsychopharmacology and Biological Psychiatry*, 54, 43–49. https://doi.org/10.1016/j.pnpbp.2014.04.010

Treasure, J., Claudino, A. M., & Zucker, N. (2010). Eating disorders. *Lancet*, 375(9714), 583–593. https://doi.org/10.1016/S0140-6736(09)61748-7

Tyszkiewicz-Nwafor, M., Rybakowski, F., Dmitrzak-Weglarz, M., Skibinska, M., Paszynska, E., Dutkiewicz, A., & Slopien, A. (2019). Brain-derived neurotrophic factor and oxytocin signaling in association with clinical symptoms in adolescent inpatients with anorexia nervosa: A longitudinal study. *Frontiers in Psychiatry*, 10, 1032. https://doi.org/10.3389/fpsyt.2019.01032

Udo, T., & Grilo, C. M. (2018). Prevalence and correlates of DSM-5–defined eating disorders in a nationally representative sample of US adults. *Biological Psychiatry*, 84(5), 345–354.

Ulfvebrand, S., Birgegård, A., Norring, C., Högdahl, L., & von Hausswolff-Juhlin, Y. (2015). Psychiatric comorbidity in women and men with eating disorders results from a large clinical database. *Psychiatry Research*, 230(2), 294–299.

Vandereycken, W. (1994). Emergence of bulimia nervosa as a separate diagnostic entity: Review of the literature from 1960 to 1979. *International Journal of Eating Disorders*, 16(2), 105–116.

Vidović, V., Jureša, V., Begovac, I., Mahnik, M., & Tocilj, G. (2005). Perceived family cohesion, adaptability and communication in eating disorders. *European Eating Disorders Review*, 13(1), 19–28. https://doi.org/10.1002/erv.615

Vitousek, K., & Manke, F. (1994). Personality variables and disorders in anorexia nervosa and bulimia nervosa. *Journal of Abnormal Psychology*, 103(1), 137–147. https://doi.org/10.1037//0021-843x.103.1.137

Wade, T. C., & Bulik, C. M. (2018). Genetic influences on eating disorders. In W. S. Agras & A. Robinson (Eds.), *The Oxford handbook of eating disorders*, 2nd ed. (pp. 80–105). Oxford University Press.

Wade, T. D., Bulik, C. M., Neale, M., & Kendler, K. S. (2000). Anorexia nervosa and major depression: Shared genetic and environmental risk factors. *American Journal of Psychiatry*, 157(3), 469–471.

Wagner, A. F., & Vitousek, K. M. (2019). Personality variables and eating pathology. *Psychiatric Clinics of North America*, 42(1), 105–119. https://doi.org/10.1016/j.psc.2018.10.012

Watson, H. J., Yilmaz, Z., Thornton, L. M., Hübel, C., Coleman, J. R. I., Gaspar, H. A., . . . Bulik, C. M. (2019). Genome-wide association study identifies eight risk loci and implicates metabo-psychiatric origins for anorexia nervosa. *Nature Genetics*, 51(8), 1207–1214. https://doi.org/10.1038/s41588-019-0439-2

Westwater, M. L., Seidlitz, J., Diederen, K. M. J., Fischer, S., & Thompson, J. C. (2018). Associations between cortical thickness, structural connectivity and severity of dimensional bulimia nervosa symptomatology. *Psychiatry Research Neuroimaging*, 271, 118–125. https://doi.org/10.1016/j.pscychresns.2017.11.006

Westwood, H., & Tchanturia, K. (2017). Autism spectrum disorder in anorexia nervosa: An updated literature review. *Current Psychiatry Reports*, 19(7), 41.

Wildes, J. E., Marcus, M. D., Crosby, R. D., Ringham, R. M., Dapelo, M. M., Gaskill, J. A., & Forbush, K. T. (2011). The clinical utility of personality subtypes in patients with anorexia nervosa. *Journal of Consulting and Clinical Psychology*, 79(5), 665–674. https://doi.org/10.1037/a0024597

Wonderlich, S. A., Connolly, K. M., & Stice, E. (2004). Impulsivity as a risk factor for eating disorder behavior: Assessment implications with adolescents. *International Journal of Eating Disorders*, 36(2), 172–182. https://doi.org/10.1002/eat.20033

Wonderlich, S. A., Gordon, K. H., Mitchell, J. E., Crosby, R. D., & Engel, S. G. (2009). The validity and clinical utility of binge eating disorder. *International Journal of Eating Disorders*, 42(8), 687–705.

Wonderlich, S. A., Joiner Jr, T. E., Keel, P. K., Williamson, D. A., & Crosby, R. D. (2007). Eating disorder diagnoses: Empirical approaches to classification. *American Psychologist*, 62(3), 167.

Yilmaz, Z., Halvorsen, M., Bryois, J., Yu, D., Thornton, L. M., Zerwas, S., . . . Eating Disorders Working Group of the Psychiatric Genomics Consortium (2020). Examination of the shared genetic basis of anorexia nervosa and obsessive-compulsive disorder. *Molecular Psychiatry*, 25(9), 2036–2046. https://doi.org/10.1038/s41380-018-0115-4

Yokokura, M., Terada, T., Bunai, T., Nakaizumi, K., Kato, Y., Yoshikawa, E., Futatsubashi, M., Suzuki, K., Yamasue, H., & Ouchi, Y. (2019). Alterations in serotonin transporter and body image–related cognition in anorexia nervosa. *Neuroimage Clinics*, 23, 101928. https://doi.org/10.1016/j.nicl.2019.101928

Zaider, T. I., Johnson, J. G., & Cockell, S. J. (2000). Psychiatric comorbidity associated with eating disorder symptomatology among adolescents in the community. *International Journal* of *Eating Disorders, 28*(1), 58–67. https://doi.org/10.1002/(sici)1098-108x(200007)28:1<58::aid-eat7>3.0.co;2-v

Zhang, S., Wang, W., Su, X., Kemp, G. J., Yang, X., Su, J., Tan, Q., Zhao, Y., Sun, H., Yue, Q., & Gong, Q. (2018). Psychoradiological investigations of gray matter alterations in patients with anorexia nervosa. *TranslationalPsychiatry, 8*(1), 277. https://doi.org/10.1038/s41398-018-0323-3

Zhang, S., Wang, W., Su, X., Li, L., Yang, X., Su, J., Tan, Q., Zhao, Y., Sun, H., Kemp, G. J., Gong, Q., & Yue, Q. (2020). White matter abnormalities in anorexia nervosa: Psychoradiologic evidence from meta-analysis of diffusion tensor imaging studies using tract based spatial statistics.

*Frontiers in Neuroscience, 14*, 159. https://doi.org/10.3389/fnins.2020.00159

Zwipp, J., Hass, J., Schober, I., Geisler, D., Ritschel, F., Seidel, M., Weiss, J., Roessner, V., Hellweg, R., & Ehrlich, S. (2014). Serum brain-derived neurotrophic factor and cognitive functioning in underweight, weight-recovered and partially weight-recovered females with anorexia nervosa. *Progress in Neuropsychopharmacol Biological Psychiatry, 54*, 163–169. https://doi.org/10.1016/j.pnpbp.2014.05.006

# CHAPTER 19

# Life-Span and Multicultural Perspectives

Thomas M. Achenbach

## Introduction

This chapter employs two conceptual frameworks for understanding psychopathology across the life span in multiple cultural contexts. One framework is known as *developmental psychopathology*, which seeks to advance understanding, prevention, and treatment of psychopathology by conceptualizing maladaptive functioning in relation to developmental periods, sequences, and processes, as well as the tasks, challenges, and achievements characterizing particular developmental periods (Achenbach, 1974/1982, 2009).

The other framework embodies an empirically based, bottom-up paradigm for assessing psychopathology and for deriving taxonomic constructs of psychopathology via multivariate analyses of assessment data obtained on large samples of individuals. The chapter emphasizes practical applications of both frameworks to assessing, researching, and conceptualizing psychopathology across the life span in many contexts around the world.

## Developmental Psychopathology

The discipline of developmental psychopathology originated primarily with efforts to understand maladaptive functioning from birth to maturity. Because there had been relatively little research on psychopathology between birth and maturity and because physical, social, cognitive, educational, and other developmental changes are so conspicuous during this period, developmental psychopathology initially focused on the nature, assessment, course, and consequences of maladaptive functioning among children. (I use "children" to include the entire period from birth to maturity.) However, it has since become clear that psychopathology of adulthood and later life is also best understood in terms of a life span approach that takes account of developmental variables from birth through old age.

### Deriving Empirically Based Constructs for Child Psychopathology

The developmental approach to the study of psychopathology was especially motivated by the need to obtain empirical data from which to derive constructs for psychopathology of childhood. Until 1968, the first edition of the *Diagnostic and Statistical Manual* (*DSM-I*, published in 1952)—which embodied the official American psychiatric nosology—contained only the following two categories for child psychopathology: adjustment reaction of childhood and schizophrenic reaction, childhood type. Neither of these diagnostic categories was derived from empirical assessment of children's problems, and neither one provided explicit criteria for deciding which children qualified for which diagnosis. Although *DSM-II* added diagnostic categories for children's problems, the additional categories were not derived from empirical assessment data, nor did they provide explicit criteria for deciding which children qualified for which diagnoses.

The lack of empirically based differentiation among childhood disorders and the proliferation of powerful computers prompted multiple researchers to apply factor analysis and other

**Abbreviations**
ABCL   Adult Behavior Checklist
ASEBA  Achenbach System of Empirically Based Assessment
ASR    Adult Self-Report
CBCL   Child Behavior Checklist
CFA    Confirmatory factor analysis
MFAM   Multicultural Family Assessment Module
TRF    Teacher's Report Form
YSR    Youth Self-Report

multivariate statistics to identify sets of problem items that tended to co-occur in large samples of children (e.g., Achenbach, 1966; Conners, 1969; Miller, 1967; Quay, 1964). Despite differences between instruments for rating problems, sources of data, samples of children, and analytic methods, reviews of these efforts revealed considerable convergence on two broad-spectrum groupings of children's problems designated as *internalizing* (or "overcontrolled") and *externalizing* (or "undercontrolled"), plus more numerous narrow-spectrum syndromes than were implied by the *DSM* diagnostic categories (Achenbach, 1966; Achenbach & Edelbrock, 1978; Quay & Werry, 1979). (The term *syndrome* is used here to designate a set of problems found to co-occur, consistent with the Greek meaning of "syndrome" as "the act of running together;" Gove, 1971, p. 2320. Syndromes are not necessarily equated with disorders, as problems may be found to co-occur for many reasons.) The internalizing grouping comprises problems of anxiety, depression, social withdrawal, and somatic complaints without apparent medical cause. The externalizing grouping, by contrast, comprises problems of aggressive and rule-breaking behavior. The broad-spectrum internalizing–externalizing distinction has since been employed in more than 75,000 published studies (Achenbach et al., 2016).

### Hierarchical Models

The study that originally coined the internalizing–externalizing distinction depicted hierarchical relations between narrow-spectrum syndromes and broad-spectrum groupings of problems to reflect findings that children whose problems matched certain narrow-spectrum syndromes were also classified as fitting either the broad-spectrum internalizing or externalizing grouping (Achenbach, 1966). These findings thus provided an empirical basis for bottom-up hierarchical models of psychopathology, which start with ratings of large pools of problem items at the bottom, move up to factor-analytically derived narrow-spectrum syndromes of co-occurring problems at the next level, thence to broad-spectrum internalizing and externalizing groupings, and ultimately to a general dimension of psychopathology ($p$) comprising scores for all the problem items (designated as *Total Problems*; Achenbach, 1966, 2009, 2020b, 2021). The reasons that particular problems are found to co-occur to form narrow- and broad-spectrum groupings may include biomedical, genetic, environmental, experiential, semantic, and other factors.

### Contrasts with the DSM

The findings of numerous childhood syndromes—several of which were subsumed by broad-spectrum internalizing or externalizing groupings—argued against the *DSM*'s implication that child psychopathology should be conceptualized in terms of minimally differentiated versions of adult psychopathology. Although the *DSM* qualifies diagnostic criteria for some disorders with references to children, the current *DSM-5* conceptual model implies that the essential nature of most disorders remains similar from childhood throughout adulthood and into old age. As an example of a common kind of psychopathology having counterparts across the life span, major depressive disorder (MDD) is specified in terms of nine symptoms, five or more of which "have been present during the same 2-week period and represent a change from previous functioning" (*DSM-5*, p. 160). Among the symptoms are depressed mood, with the qualifier that it can be "irritable mood" in children and adolescents. Another symptom is significant weight loss or gain, with the qualifier that the diagnostician can consider "failure to make expected weight gain" in children (p. 161). Other than these minor qualifiers, the construct and criteria for MDD are the same across the life span.

As with previous editions of the *DSM*, the *DSM-5* criteria for MDD were formulated by committees to represent what they viewed as the essence of MDD, with minor qualifiers to take account of what the committees thought might characterize MDD in children and no qualifiers for MDD in the elderly.

A life span developmental approach differs from the *DSM* approach in not assuming that most disorders are essentially the same across all developmental periods. Instead, research on different developmental periods is used to identify characteristics that discriminate between members of particular age groups who are judged to need mental health services versus peers who are judged not to need such services. The discriminating characteristics are then analyzed statistically to derive empirically based constructs for psychopathology within each developmental period. Scales for scoring the constructs are subsequently normed with data from population samples for each age group.

Specific methods for identifying discriminating characteristics will be outlined later, but the key point is this: constructs for psychopathology should be based on empirical findings for individuals within particular developmental periods, rather than being negotiated by committees who then agree on criteria for each construct, with occasional qualifiers to take account of what the committees view as possible differences between adults and children.

Life span developmental research generates some constructs that differ between developmental periods but which longitudinal research may reveal to be linked between earlier and later developmental periods (*heterotypic continuity*). Life span developmental research also generates some constructs that are similar across developmental periods (*homotypic continuity*), as well as some constructs for which longitudinal research fails to detect links across developmental periods. In other words, developmental similarities and differences should be identified for successive developmental periods via empirical research using developmentally appropriate assessment instruments, sources of data, participant samples, and analyses. To map continuities and discontinuities across developmental periods, longitudinal research is required that applies developmentally appropriate assessment instruments, sources of data, and analyses to the same participants as they age. Much developmental research on psychopathology has focused on the period from birth to maturity, but developmental research is also needed to advance understanding of psychopathology in early, middle, and later adulthood.

## The Empirically Based Bottom-Up Paradigm

Although there were some earlier factor analytic studies of severe adult psychopathology (e.g., Wittenborn, 1951), the empirically based bottom-up paradigm for advancing the developmental study of psychopathology employs factor analysis as one component of the Achenbach System of Empirically Based Assessment (ASEBA), which has evolved through programmatic efforts over more than a half century (Achenbach, 1966, 2020b). The following sections outline key components of the empirically based bottom-up paradigm for the developmental study of psychopathology across the life span.

### Assessment Instruments

Empirically based bottom-up efforts have constructed assessment instruments tailored to each developmental period. The items comprising each instrument are designed to assess behavioral, emotional, social, and thought problems that would potentially make individuals of a particular developmental level candidates for mental health services. Pools of candidate items were generated from research and from consultation with relevant professionals, including practitioners in medical, school, forensic, and child and family services, as well as mental health workers. Written at a fifth-grade reading level, the items are tailored to the kinds of informants who are familiar with the assessed individuals' functioning in particular contexts. Self-report instruments are provided for individuals who are capable of completing them. Within a particular developmental period, some items may differ according to the intended kind of informant. For example, *nightmares* is an item on instruments completed by parents and youths but not on teacher-completed instruments.

In addition to the generation of large pools of candidate items, construction of developmentally appropriate instruments requires testing of various formats, instructions, rating scales, and periods on which informants are instructed to base their ratings. Pilot testing has included having large samples of informants complete successive drafts of the instruments, comment on the items and formats, and suggest additional items.

Extensive pilot testing and feedback from samples of the intended kinds of informants have been used to cull, augment, and refine the items, as well as to ensure that formats, instructions, rating scales, and rating periods function well. Because no single informant is apt to provide a complete picture of assessed individuals, parallel instruments have been constructed to obtain assessment data from different kinds of informants appropriate for each developmental period. For example, for the preschool period, one instrument is designed to be completed by parent figures, while a parallel instrument is designed to be completed by preschool teachers and daycare providers who see children in group settings (Achenbach & Rescorla, 2000).

For school-age children, there are parallel parent- and teacher-completed instruments, plus a self-report instrument completed by 11- to 18-year-olds (Achenbach & Rescorla, 2001). For adults and the elderly, there are self-report instruments plus collateral-report instruments for completion by people who know the assessed individuals, such as spouses, partners, family members, friends, and therapists (Achenbach et al., 2004; Achenbach & Rescorla, 2003). In the final versions of the instruments, problem items are rated on Likert scales as *0 = not true (as far as you know), 1 = somewhat or sometimes true,* or *2 = very true or often true.* Ratings are based on the preceding 2 months for ages 1½–5 and 60–90+ and for teachers' ratings of 6- to 18-year-olds. For other instruments, ratings are based on the preceding 6 months.

### Testing the Instruments' Psychometrics

As part of the development process, the instruments were completed for large samples of individuals who were referred for mental health and related services, such as special education for children and substance abuse services for adults. The instruments were also completed for population samples of individuals who had not been referred for such services during the previous 12 months. Distributions of ratings on each item were examined to identify items having too little variance to provide meaningful data.

Each item of each instrument was tested for its ability to discriminate between demographically similar referred and nonreferred samples, with effects of demographic variables such as age, gender, ethnicity, and socioeconomic status (SES) partialed out. Items that did not discriminate significantly between referred and nonreferred samples were then discarded, with the exception of a few items that did not discriminate significantly between heterogeneous referred versus nonreferred samples but were found to load significantly on factors from which syndromes were derived, as described later. The items' ability to discriminate significantly between demographically similar samples of referred versus nonreferred samples, plus—for some items—significant loadings on syndromes, thus supported the validity of the items as markers for psychopathology. After scales were constructed for scoring the items on syndromes, internalizing, externalizing, *p*, and other constructs, the scale scores were evaluated for discriminant, construct, and predictive validity (Achenbach et al., 2004; Achenbach & Rescorla, 2000, 2001, 2003).

The test-retest reliability of each scale scored from each instrument was supported by Pearson correlations (*r*s) between scores obtained from ratings by the same informants over intervals of one to two weeks. Changes in mean scale scores were tested over those periods with *t* tests to detect statistically significant differences between initial scores and scores obtained by the same individuals 1–2 weeks later. Longer-term stability of scale scores was supported by test-retest *r*s between scale scores obtained from ratings by the same informants over periods of months to years. The internal consistency of each scale was supported by Cronbach's alpha coefficient.

### Syndrome Scales

The lengthy efforts invested in constructing developmentally appropriate instruments designed for completion by different informants were intended both to obtain research data from which to derive constructs for psychopathology and to provide practical tools for clinically assessing individuals' needs for help. The derivation of constructs went through successive stages in which ratings of various samples were subjected to multiple factor analyses, separately for each gender and age range of assessed individuals and for different kinds of informants, as summarized by Achenbach (2009). To ensure that the assessed individuals had enough problems to enable detection of clinically meaningful syndromes, the samples that were factor analyzed in the initial stages of the research comprised individuals who were referred for mental health or related services. To minimize possible biases associated with clinical referral, later factor-analytic samples included nonreferred as well as clinically referred individuals whose *p* scores were at or above the median for a nationally representative US population sample of each gender-, age-, and informant-specific group. Multiple kinds of orthogonal and oblique exploratory factor analyses (EFAs) were used. (*Orthogonal EFAs* identify syndromes that are not correlated with each other, whereas *oblique EFAs* identify syndromes that are correlated with each other.)

Provisional syndromes were constructed to include items that loaded significantly on counterpart factors found in different EFAs of problem item ratings for each gender/age group within each developmental period, rated by different kinds of informants. The provisional syndromes were then subjected to confirmatory factor analyses (CFAs) to obtain the final versions of syndromes scored from instruments completed by a particular kind of informant (parent, teacher, self, adult collateral) for individuals at ages 1½–5, 6–18, 18–59, and 60–90+ years (Achenbach et al., 2004; Achenbach & Rescorla, 2000, 2001, 2003). (CFAs test whether data fit syndromes that were previously identified by EFAs.) Items retained for syndromes had significant loadings in CFAs of ratings by a particular kind of informant. However, some items differed for versions of a particular syndrome scored from ratings by different kinds of informants. For example, *Disturbs other pupils* is on the Attention Problems syndrome scale scored from the Teacher's Report Form for Ages 6–18 (TRF) but not on the Attention Problems syndrome scale scored from the Child Behavior Checklist for Ages 6–18 (CBCL/6-18) completed by parents nor on the Youth Self-Report for Ages 11–18 (YSR), neither of which requests ratings for *Disturbs other pupils*. Syndrome scale scores are operationalized by summing the 0-1-2 ratings of a syndrome scale's constituent items obtained by an individual on a particular assessment instrument completed by a particular informant.

### Internalizing and Externalizing Scales

To operationalize hierarchical structures of psychopathology, *r*s were computed between first-order syndrome scale scores obtained by individuals in each of the samples that had been used to derive the factors on which the syndromes were based, separately for each gender-, age-, and informant-specific group. The *r*s between syndrome scale scores were then factor analyzed. For ages 1½–5, 6–18, and 18–59, two second-order factors were found that corresponded to the internalizing-externalizing distinction. (Second-order factors consist of first-order syndromes that are mutually associated.) However, second-order factor analyses did not yield such factors for ages 60–90+. The syndrome scales' loadings on the second-order factors varied somewhat between the multiple second-order factor analyses of each instrument. The syndrome scales loading on the second-order factors also differed between the different age groups, reflecting age group differences in the syndromes.

Scores on the scale based on the internalizing factor for a particular instrument are operationalized by summing the scores obtained by an individual on the syndrome scales that loaded highly on the internalizing factor for that instrument. As an example, for the Adult Self-Report for Ages 18–59 (ASR) and the Adult Behavior Checklist for Ages 18–59 (ABCL), the Anxious/Depressed, Withdrawn, and Somatic Complaints syndrome scales loaded highly on the internalizing factor. An individual's internalizing score is therefore operationalized by summing the individual's scores on those three syndrome scales. Analogous procedures apply to the externalizing scale scored from each instrument.

Another type of factor analysis, called *bifactor analysis*, can also be used to construct broad-spectrum internalizing and externalizing scales. However, neither second-order nor bifactor analysis is necessarily the optimal approach to constructing broad-spectrum internalizing and externalizing scales for all purposes (Achenbach, 2021; Lahey et al., 2021; Markon, 2021). An advantage of second-order factor analysis for constructing practical clinical assessment tools is that the syndrome, internalizing, and externalizing scales remain intact within the hierarchy that ranges from ratings of individual items at the lowest (most molecular) level, to syndrome scales at the narrow-spectrum level, internalizing and externalizing scales at the broad-spectrum level, and the *p* scale at the most general (molar) level. Figure 19.1 illustrates an empirically based hierarchy of scales scored on the ASR and ABCL (Achenbach & Rescorla, 2003).

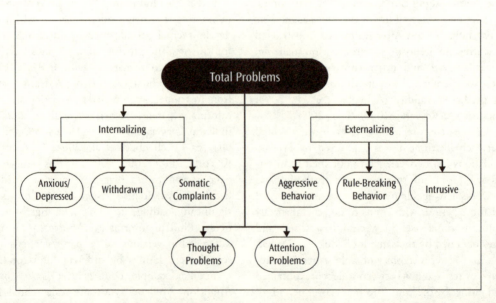

**Figure 19.1** Hierarchy of empirically derived problem scales for ages 18–59. Adapted from https://aseba.org/wp-content/uploads/2019/04/catalog.pdf. Copyright 2019, T. M. Achenbach.

## DSM-Oriented Scales

Although the *DSM* diagnostic categories are products of a top-down paradigm, questions often arise about relations between *DSM* diagnoses and empirically based bottom-up assessment data. To provide cross-walks between *DSM* categories and data obtained with ASEBA instruments, *DSM*-oriented scales were constructed by having international panels of experts identify ASEBA items for ages 1½–5, 6–18, 18–59, and 60–90+ that the experts judged to be very consistent with particular *DSM* diagnostic categories (Achenbach, 2014).

Corresponding to *DSM* diagnostic categories, the constructs measured by the *DSM*-oriented scales are top-down scales that were constructed with ASEBA problem items (which had previously been tested for discriminant validity, as described earlier) by applying the collective judgment of international experts. Moreover, unlike the yes/no judgments required for *DSM* diagnostic criteria, the experts rated the ASEBA items on Likert scales as *0 = not consistent, 1 = somewhat consistent,* and *2 = very consistent* with particular *DSM* diagnostic categories. An item was assigned to a scale for a *DSM* category if at least 60% of the experts rated it as very consistent with the category. At least five ASEBA problem items had to be rated as very consistent with a *DSM* category to form a *DSM*-oriented scale for that category.

In the first editions of the *DSM*-oriented scales, experts based their judgments on *DSM-IV* categories, separately for ages 1½–5, 6–18, 18–59, and 60–90+ (Achenbach et al., 2004; Achenbach & Rescorla, 2000, 2001, 2003). The *DSM*-oriented scales were subsequently revised on the basis of new panels of international experts' identification of items that they judged to be very consistent with *DSM-5* criteria (Achenbach, 2014).

Like the empirically based ASEBA syndrome scales, each ASEBA *DSM*-oriented scale is operationalized by summing an informant's 0-1-2 ratings of the items comprising the scale. Standardized scores (normalized *T* scores) for the *DSM*-oriented scales are based on the same normative samples as the empirically based scales for a particular age and gender, rated by a particular kind of informant. Thus, although the *DSM* constructs are based on experts' judgments, the *DSM*-oriented scales are operationalized and normed as quantitative dimensions like other ASEBA scales.

Reliability, validity, and internal consistency findings for the *DSM*-oriented scales are reported in the ASEBA manuals for ages 1½–5, 6–18, 18–59, and 60–90+ (Achenbach et al., 2004; Achenbach & Rescorla, 2000, 2001, 2003). More than 300 publications report findings on associations between ASEBA scores and diagnostic data (Pascal & Achenbach, 2021). By classifying individuals according to whether their *DSM*-oriented scale scores are in the clinical range, users can apply a categorical *DSM* approach to using the scales. However, because there is abundant evidence that continuous measures of psychopathology are more reliable and valid than categorical measures, use of the continuous *DSM*-oriented scale scores is apt to be superior to categorical classification of individuals as clinically deviant versus nondeviant (Markon et al., 2011).

## Multi-Informant Assessment

Mental health professionals who work with children have long understood the value of obtaining data from adults such as children's parents and teachers, as well as from the children themselves. Over several decades, meta-analyses of *r*s between ratings of children's problems by people who play similar roles and see children in similar contexts (pairs of parents, teachers, mental health workers, observers) have yielded mean cross-informant *r*s around .60 (Achenbach, McConaughy, & Howell, 1987; De Los Reyes et al., 2015). Between people who play different roles and see children in different contexts (e.g., parents vs. teachers), cross-informant *r*s have averaged around .30. And between self-ratings by children versus ratings by others, the cross-informant *r*s have ranged from the .20s to the .40s, depending on the children's ages and on who rated the children. Even the *r*s around .60 for pairs of similar informants mean that each informant may provide different information about an assessed child, and even more so for pairs of informants whose roles differ in relation to an assessed child.

The modest cross-informant *r*s cannot be dismissed merely as resulting from measurement error because good reliability and validity have been demonstrated for the parent-, teacher-, and self-rating instruments (De Los Reyes, 2011). Instead, the modest *r*s are likely to reflect differences between children's behaviors in different contexts (e.g., home vs. school), as well as differences between the mindsets of informants such as parents versus teachers.

Although the need for multi-informant assessment of children is now widely recognized, adult mental health clients are usually the sole or main source of assessment data about themselves. There have been many fewer studies of cross-informant agreement regarding adult than child psychopathology, but meta-analyses of cross-informant $r$s between self- and collateral-ratings of adult psychopathology have found a mean $r$ of only .45 (Achenbach et al., 2005). *DSM* diagnoses based only on adult self-reports have also been found to differ substantially from diagnoses based on data from other informants (Meyer, 2002; Meyer et al., 2001). Consequently assessment of adults as well as children should include data from informants who know the assessed person, as well as data from self-reports.

Within each age range, parallel ASEBA instruments are designed to obtain ratings of behavioral, social, emotional, and thought problems from different informants (parents, teachers, self, adult collaterals). The parallel instruments are scored on parallel syndrome, *DSM*-oriented, internalizing, externalizing, and Total Problems scales, although the items comprising the parallel scales are not necessarily identical for all informants. Hand-scored and computer-scored profiles display scale scores in relation to norms appropriate for the assessed individual's age, gender, the type of informant (parent, teacher, self, adult collateral), and multicultural norm group (explained later).

To operationalize the magnitude of agreement between different informants, the computer software generates $Q$ correlations between the 0-1-2 ratings of problem items by each pair of informants. (Each $Q$ correlation is computed by applying the formula for $r$ to the 0-1-2 ratings by a pair of informants.) To enable users to evaluate the magnitude of a $Q$ correlation between a particular pair of informants, the software displays the 25th percentile, mean, and 75th percentile $Q$ found in large reference samples of similar pairs of informants. The software describes $Q$s below the 25th percentile as *below average*; $Q$s from the 25th through the 75th percentile as *average*; and $Q$s above the 75th percentile as *above average*. To enable users to identify cross-informant agreements and disagreements on specific items, the software displays the problem items comprising each scale in side-by-side lists with the 0-1-2 ratings of each item by up to 10 informants.

The software additionally displays the standardized problem scale scores (normalized $T$ scores) on side-by-side bar graphs for ratings by up to 10 informants. This enables users to identify scales on which informants agree versus disagree in reporting low, intermediate, or high levels of the problems that comprise a scale standardized on the basis of norms for the assessed person's age, gender, the type of informant, and the multicultural norm group. If they deem it appropriate, clinicians can elect to show the bar graphs to clients to help them see similarities and differences between reports by different informants.

## Competence, Adaptive Functioning, and Strengths Scales

Evaluation of needs for mental health services should include assessment of competencies, adaptive functioning, and strengths as well as assessment of problems. Individuals whose problems are in the clinical range and who have low levels of favorable characteristics are apt to need different kinds of help than individuals who have higher levels of favorable characteristics. Like ASEBA items for assessing problems at particular developmental periods, ASEBA items for assessing favorable characteristics are tailored to particular developmental periods and to the kinds of informants who are able to provide information about those characteristics. Also like the ASEBA problem items, ASEBA items for assessing favorable characteristics were culled and refined from large pools of candidate items on the basis of data from large samples of informants who completed successive pilot editions. The items were then tested for their ability to discriminate between demographically similar samples of clinically referred and nonreferred individuals in a particular age range. However, unlike the problem items, the items for assessing favorable characteristics were not factor analyzed to derive constructs. Instead, these items were aggregated into scales for assessing certain favorable aspects of functioning that discriminate well between clinically referred and nonreferred samples and that can serve as targets for interventions.

As an example, the CBCL/6-18 includes items that request parents to list up to three sports and three non-sports hobbies, activities, and games that their child likes to take part in. Parents are asked to indicate the amount of time their child spends in each one, compared to others of the same age (*less than average, average, more than average, don't know*). Parents are also asked to indicate how well their child does in each one, compared to others of the same age (*below average, average, above average, don't know*). Parents are additionally asked to list up to three jobs or chores their child does and how well their child does each one. These items are scored on the *Activities* scale.

Other CBCL/6-18 items assess involvement in organizations; friendships; how well the child gets along with siblings, parents, and other kids; and how well the child plays and works alone. These items are scored on the *Social* scale. Additional items assess various aspects of school functioning, scored on the *School* scale. The scores for the Activities, Social, and School scales are summed to yield a *Total Competence* scale score. Raw scores on each competence scale are converted to normalized *T* scores and percentiles based on normative samples, separately for each gender at ages 6–11 and 12–18. Unlike ASEBA scales for assessing problems, low scores on the competence scales are clinically important.

The YSR has self-report versions of the competence items that are scored on scales like those for the CBCL/6-18, plus items interspersed among the problem items that describe positive qualities and are rated on 0-1-2 Likert scales like the problem items. Examples include "I am pretty honest" and "I like to help others." The 0-1-2 ratings on these items are summed to yield a scale score for *Positive Qualities*.

The ASR has adaptive functioning items that are scored on scales for *Friends, Spouse/Partner, Family, Job, Education,* and *Mean Adaptive*, which is computed by averaging standard scores on the scales that are relevant to the adult who completed the ASR. (An adult who—during the preceding 6 months—had no spouse/partner, job, or enrollment in an educational program would not be scored on these scales.) The ABCL has collateral report versions of the Friends and Spouse/Partner items and scales.

The four instruments spanning ages 18–90+ are also scored on a *Personal Strengths* scale, which is the sum of 0-1-2 ratings on favorable items scattered among the problem items. Examples include "Can do certain things better than other people" and "Likes to help others." Competence, adaptive functioning, and strengths scales are displayed on profiles in relation to norms appropriate for the assessed individual's gender, age, group, and the type of informant. Table 19.1 summarizes ASEBA self-report and informant-report instruments for ages 1½ through 90+ years, as well as the scales scored from them.

## Multicultural Applications

Research, assessment methodology, and theory pertaining to psychopathology have originated mainly in a few rather similar societies. ("Societies" refer here to geopolitically demarcated populations that include countries but also populations that are not countries, such as Puerto Rico, Hong Kong, and Flanders, the Flemish speaking region of Belgium.) However, it should not be assumed that the models and methodologies originating in a few societies automatically apply to people in all other societies. Instead, models and methodology developed in a particular society should be empirically tested for generalizability to other societies.

The application of the same standardized research methods to people in different societies is known as *etic* research. The term "etic" was derived by the linguist Kenneth Pike (1967) from *phonetic* (i.e., linguists' systems for standardized representations of speech sounds that are meaningful in any of the world's languages). Etic research differs from *emic* research (Pike, 1967), derived from *phonemic* (i.e., linguists' systems for representing sounds that are meaningful in a particular language). Whereas etic research uses the same standardized methods to assess people in many societies (with translations, if needed), emic research uses methods tailored to a particular society.

There is a long history of cross-cultural research that compares two or three societies and draws inferences about all members of each society from differences on measures applied to samples from each society (Hermans & Kempen, 1998). By contrast, the multicultural research on psychopathology addressed here assesses population samples in many societies using the same standardized assessment methods to obtain distributions of quantitative scores, both within and between societies. To facilitate such research, ASEBA instruments are available in the 113 languages listed in Table 19.2. Published reports of use of ASEBA instruments in more than 100 societies and cultural groups are also available (Pascal & Achenbach, 2021).

### Generalizability of Syndrome Structures Across Many Societies

To test the degree to which the syndrome structures derived from factor analyses of primarily US ASEBA data would be found in other societies, CFAs have been performed on data from population samples in more than 50 societies. Separate CFAs have been performed on the ratings of problem items on each ASEBA instrument in population samples for ages 1½–5, 6–18, 18–59, and 60–90+ (Ivanova et al., 2007a, 2007b, 2007c, 2010, 2011, 2015a, 2015b, 2020, 2021, 2022; Rescorla et al., 2012). The ASEBA syndrome structures were supported by the root mean square error of approximation (RMSEA) obtained for CFAs of data obtained with the ASEBA instruments in non-US societies around the world. Thus, despite vast differences in

**Table 19.1** ASEBA instruments for ages 1½–90+ years

| Ages | Informants | Normative sample N[a] | Psychopathology scales | Strength scales |
|---|---|---|---|---|
| **1½–5 Years** | | | | |
| CBCL/1½–5 | Parent figures | 19,806 | Syndromes, DSM, Int, Ext. Total. Stress | Language Development |
| C-TRF | Daycare providers, preschool | 8,974 | " | NA |
| **6–18 years** | | | | |
| CBCL/6–18 | Parent figures | 59,804 | Syndromes, DSM, Int, Ext, Total, OCP[b], SCT[c], Stress | Activities, Social, School, Total Competence |
| TRF | Teachers, school stuff | 32,349 | " | Academic, Adaptive |
| YSR | Youths | 31,300 | " | Activities, Social, Total Competence, Positive Qualities |
| BPM/6–18 | Parents, teachers, youths | 123,453 | Attention probs., Int, Ext, Total | NA |
| **18-59 Years** | | | | |
| ABCL | Collaterals | 8,322 | Syndromes, DSM, Int, Ext, Total, OCP[b], SCT, Substance use | Friends, Spouse/Partner, Personal strengths |
| ASR | Adults | 11,790 | " | Friends, Spouse/Partner, Family, Job, Education, Personal Strengths |
| BPM/18–59 | Adults, collaterals | 20,112 | Attention probs., Int, Ext, Total | NA |
| OABCL | Collaterals | 6,105 | Syndromes, DSM, Total, Substance use | Friends, Spouse/Partner, Personal Strengths |
| OASR | Older adults | 10,049 | " | " |

*Note*: CBCL/1½–5, Child Behaviour Checklist for Ages 1½–5; C-TRF, Caregiver-Teacher Report Form; CBCL/6–18, Child Behaviour Checklist for Ages 6–18; TRF, Teacher's Report Form; YSR, Youth Self-Report; BPM/6–18, Brief Problem Monitor for Ages 6–18; ABCL, Adult Behaviour Checklist; ASR, Adult Self-Report; BPM/18–59, Brief Problem Monitor for Ages 18–59; OABCL, Older Adult Behaviour Checklist.

[a] Multicultural Samples from dozens of societies.

[b] Obsessive-Compulsive Problems Scale.

[c] Sluggish Cognitive Tempo Scale.

languages, cultures, gene pools, political and economic systems, geographical locations, etc., people's ratings of ASEBA problem items yielded similar syndrome structures within age ranges 1½–5, 6–18, 18–59, and 60–90+.

### Generalizability of Problem Item Structures Across Many Societies

To provide another test of the generalizability of the measurement structure of ASEBA instruments, the mean of the 0-1-2 ratings was computed for each problem item on each ASEBA instrument in each sample. Q correlations were then computed between the mean of the ratings on each item of a particular instrument for Society A versus Society B, Society A versus Society C, and so on for all pairs of societies. (Each Q correlation was computed by applying the formula for $r$ to the set of mean 0-1-2 ratings obtained on problem items for one society versus the set of mean 0-1-2 ratings obtained on the same problem items for a second society.) The Q correlation between the mean item ratings measured the similarity in rank ordering of item ratings between the two societies.

**Table 19.2** Translations of ASEBA forms

| | | |
|---|---|---|
| 1. Afaan Oromo (Ethiopia) | 39. German | 77. Polish |
| 2. Afrikaans | 40. Greek | 78. Portuguese (Angola, Portugal) |
| 3. Albanian/Kosova | 41. Gujarati (India) | 79. Portuguese (Brazilian) |
| 4. American Sign Language | 42. Haitian Creole | 80. Portuguese Creole |
| 5. Amharic (Ethiopia) | 43. Hebrew | 81. Punjabi (India) |
| 6. Arabic | 44. Hindi (India) | 82. Romanian |
| 7. Armenian | 45. Hungarian | 83. Russian |
| 8. Ausian (Australian Sign Language) | 46. Icelandic | 84. Sami (Norway) |
| 9. Azerbaijani | 47. Italian | 85. Samoan |
| 10. Bahasa (Indonesia) | 48. Japanese | 86. Sepedi (Northern Sotho) |
| 11. Bahasa (Malaysia) | 49. Kannada (India) | 87. Serbian |
| 12. Bangla (Bangladesh) | 50. Khmer (Cambodia) | 88. Sesotho (Southern Sotho) |
| 13. Basque (Spain) | 51. Kiembu (Kenya) | 89. Setswana (Zimbabwe) |
| 14. Bemba (Zambia) | 52. Kikamba (Kenya) | 90. Shona (Zimbabwe) |
| 15. Bengali (India) | 53. Kigiryama (Kenya) | 91. Sinhala (Sri Lanka) |
| 16. Bosnian | 54. Kiswahili (Kenya Tanzania) | 92. Slovak |
| 17. British Sign Language | 55. Korean | 93. Slovene |
| 18. Bulgarian | 56. Krebo (Ghana) | 94. Somali |
| 19. Burmese (Myanmar) | 57. Krio (Sierra Leone) | 95. Spanish (Castilian) |
| 20. Catalan (Spain) | 58. Laotian | 96. Spanish (Latino) |
| 21 Cebuano (Philippines) | 59. Latvian | 97. Swahili |
| 22. Chichewa (Zimbabwe) | 60. Lithuanian | 98. Swedish |
| 23. Chinese | 61. Luganda (Uganda) | 99. Tagalog (Philippines) |
| 24. Croatian | 62. Luo (Uganda) | 100. Tamil (India) |
| 25. Czech | 63. Lu Saga (Uganda) | 102. Thai |
| 26. Danish | 64. Macedonian | 103. Tibetan |
| 27. Dutch (Netherlands Flanders) | 65. Malayalam (India) | 104. Tigrinya |
| 28. Estonian | 66. Maltese | 105. TshiVenda (South Africa) |
| 29. Ewe (Ghana, Benin, Togo) | 67. Manipuri (India) | 106. Turksih |
| 30. Farsi/Persian (Iran)) | 68. Marathi (India) | 107. Twi (Ghana) |
| 31. Finnish | 69. Mauritian Creole | 108. Ukranian |
| 32. Fiemish | 70. Montenegrian | 109. Urdu (India, Pakistan) |
| 33. French (Belgian) | 71. Nepalese | 110. Vietnamese |
| 34. French (Canadian) | 72. Omoro (Ethiopia) | 111. Visayan (Philippines) |
| 35. French (Parisian) | 73. Nyanja (Zambia) | 112. Xhosa (South Africa) |
| 36. Ga (Ghana) | 74. Omoro (Ethiopia) | 113. Zulu |
| 37. Galician (Spain) | 75. Papiamento (Curacao) | |
| 38. Georgian | 76. Pashto (Afghanistan, Pakistan) | |

[a] Languages into which at least one ASEBA form has been translated. Please visit www.aseba.org for updated lists of translations of each ASEBA form.

The *Q* correlations computed between every pair of societies in which ratings for a particular instrument (e.g., the ASR) were obtained were then averaged to compute the *omnicultural mean Q* correlation between rankings of item ratings for that instrument. Surprisingly, the omnicultural mean *Q* correlation for every instrument across samples from many different societies for ages 1½–5, 6–18, 18–59, and 60–90+ was in the .70s (Rescorla et al., 2011, 2012, 2016a, 2016b, 2020). These large omnicultural mean *Q* correlations indicate considerable similarity in the problem items that tended to receive relatively low, medium, or high ratings from different kinds of informants rating individuals of different ages across many different societies on every inhabited continent. Moreover, the finding that the omnicultural mean *Q* correlation for every instrument was in the .70s, despite differences between the instruments, societies, samples, age ranges, and raters, indicates a striking degree of uniformity in the quantitative measurement of item structures across populations around the world.

*Multicultural Comparisons of Problem Scale Scores*

The omnicultural mean *Q* correlations and CFA findings support the generalizability of measurement structures for ASEBA problem items and syndrome scales across many societies around the world. However, these findings do not necessarily mean that scale scores were the same in every society, nor for different genders, nor for different ages within the age ranges for which each instrument was designed. In order to test possible societal, gender, and age differences in the magnitudes of problem scale scores, analyses of variance (ANOVAs) were used to compare scores on all scales of each instrument for the societies from which population samples were assessed with each instrument (Rescorla et al., 2011, 2012, 2016a, 2016b, 2020). For each instrument, the effects of gender, age, and interactions on problem scales ranged from nonsignificant to very small, according to Cohen's (1988) criteria for effect sizes (ESs) in ANOVAs. Furthermore, the negligible interactions of society with gender and age indicated that the gender and age effects were similar across societies.

The effects of differences among societies were significant for all problem scales scored from all ASEBA instruments for ages 1½–90+ years, with ESs ranging from very small to large, according to Cohen's criteria. Interestingly, when the largest societal ESs were identified for each instrument, 27 of the 33 largest ESs were for internalizing scales. This suggests that societal differences affect the actual prevalence of internalizing problems more than other problems and/or that societal differences affect self- and informant-perceptions of internalizing problems more than other problems. The "other" problems that show smaller societal differences than internalizing problems include not only problems scored on externalizing scales but also problems assessed by scales for attention problems and scales designated as Functional Impairment, Memory/Cognition Problems, Dementia Problems, and Psychotic Problems scored from both the OASR and OABCL. The small societal differences found for these four scales (Rescorla et al., 2020) suggest that the prevalence as well as the self- and informant-perceptions of the problems assessed by these scales vary much less across societies than problems assessed by the OASR and OABCL Worries, *DSM*-Oriented Anxiety Problems, and *DSM*-Oriented Somatic Problems scales, for which large societal ESs were found.

*Multicultural Norms for Problem Scales*

On most ASEBA instruments, the means of the problem scale scores were distributed approximately normally around the average of the mean problem scale scores for all the societies (i.e., around the omnicultural mean). Figure 19.2 displays the mean CBCL/6-18 Total Problems scores for 42 societies. As can be seen in Figure 19.2, the omnicultural mean (overall mean) was 24.04.

To enable users to view problem scale scores in relation to norms appropriate for the informants completing ASEBA instruments (including self-assessment instruments), multicultural norms were constructed as follows (with some variations for particular instruments, as documented by Achenbach and Rescorla, 2007a, 2010, 2015, 2019):

1. For a particular instrument such as the CBCL/6-18, we computed the mean Total Problems scores for the normative sample from each available society.
2. For most instruments, the distribution of Total Problems scores from multiple societies was close to normal, with approximately two-thirds of the societies' mean Total Problems scores being within ±1 *SD* of the omnicultural mean and one-sixth of the societies' mean Total Problems scores being either greater than 1 *SD* below the omnicultural mean or greater than 1 *SD* above the omnicultural mean.

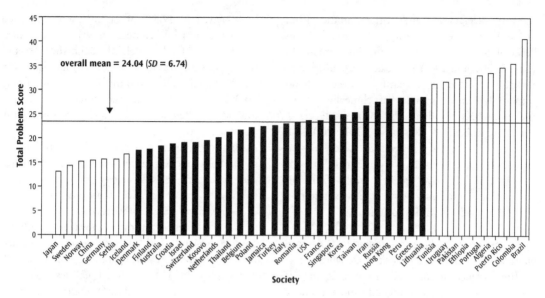

Figure 19.2 Mean CBCL-6-18 Total Problems scores in 42 societies. Copyright 2012, L. A. Rescorla.

3. For a particular instrument, we designated societies having mean Total Problems scores of greater than 1 $SD$ below the omnicultural mean as *Group 1* (i.e., societies having relatively low problem scores on that instrument). Societies having mean Total Problems scores ±1 $SD$ from the omnicultural mean were designated as *Group 2* (i.e., societies having intermediate problem scores on that instrument). And societies having mean Total Problems scores greater than 1 $SD$ above the omnicultural mean were designated as *Group 3* (i.e., societies having relatively high problem scores).

4. To construct Group 1 norms for each problem scale on an instrument, we first computed a cumulative frequency distribution of scores on that problem scale in a Group 1 society's sample, separately for each gender within each age range for which the instrument was normed (e.g., the CBCL/6-18 has separate norms for each gender at ages 6–11 and 12–18). The cumulative frequency distribution generated a percentile for each raw scale score. Separately for each gender within each age group, the percentiles obtained for scores in all the Group 1 samples for a particular problem scale were then averaged to form a Multicultural Group 1 cumulative frequency distribution for that scale.

5. Normalized $T$ scores were then assigned on the basis of the averaged percentiles. The normalized $T$ scores and averaged percentiles were subsequently programmed into a scoring module.

## Multicultural Norms for Personal Strengths and Positive Qualities

ASEBA instruments for ages 18–59 and 60–90+ include items for personal strengths that are interspersed among the problem items. The Personal Strengths scale for each instrument is operationalized by summing the 0-1-2 ratings of the items comprising the scale for that instrument. Multicultural norms for the Personal Strengths scales have been constructed according to procedures like those described earlier for problem scales. Interestingly, the self- and collateral-ratings of personal strengths items are considerably more homogeneous within societies than are ratings of items on each of the problem scales (Rescorla et al., 2016a, 2016b, 2020). As a result of the greater homogeneity within societies, the ESs for differences between societies in Personal Strengths scale scores are considerably larger than the ESs for differences between societies in problem scale scores. Scores on the Positive Qualities scale of the YSR are also much more homogeneous within each society than are scores on problem scales.

The greater within-society homogeneity of self- and collateral-ratings of favorable items than of problem items suggests that the ratings of favorable items reflect societal values and attitudes more than do ratings of problem items. Despite the possible effects of societal values and attitudes on the within-society homogeneity of ratings of favorable items, Personal Strengths scores on the instruments for ages 18–90+ and the YSR Positive Qualities scale all discriminated significantly between demographically similar samples of clinically referred and nonreferred individuals (Achenbach et al., 2004; Achenbach & Rescorla, 2001, 2003). In other words, the larger effects of society on ratings of favorable items do not prevent the Personal Strengths and Positive Qualities scales from discriminating significantly between referred and non-referred individuals within societies.

### Effects of Society, Culture, and Individual Differences on Ratings of Problems and Positive Qualities

The evidence summarized in the foregoing section that ratings are considerably more homogeneous within societies for favorable items than for problem items raises questions about the relative magnitude of effects of society, culture, and individual differences on ratings of problem versus favorable items. As used in this chapter, "societies" refer to geopolitically demarcated populations having a dominant language, including countries but also populations that are not countries, such as Puerto Rico. "Cultures" are harder to define but generally refer to people who share particular sets of characteristics, such as behaviors, attitudes, beliefs, traditions, values, and ideals.

In research to identify major cultural groups around the world, the Global Leadership and Organizational Effectiveness (GLOBE) study (House et al., 2004) obtained measures of attitudes and other characteristics of people in 62 societies. Using these international data, plus previous research and theory, more than 200 scholars from 69 societies classified societies into 10 culture clusters designated as Anglo, Confucian Asia, Eastern Europe, Germanic Europe, Latin America, Latin Europe, Middle East, Nordic Europe, and Southern Asia.

To test the effects of culture cluster, society, and individual differences on CBCL/6-18 ratings of problems for 72,493 children from 45 societies, Rescorla et al. (2019) grouped societies according to the 10 GLOBE culture clusters. They then used hierarchical linear modeling (HLM) to estimate the percentage of variance in 17 CBCL problem scale scores accounted for by culture cluster, society, and individual differences. Averaged across all 17 problem scale scores, Rescorla et al. found that a mean of 4.2% of variance was accounted for by culture cluster, 6.1% of variance was accounted for by society, and 89.8% of variance was accounted for by individual differences and variables not measured in the HLM model. Although the effects of society and culture cluster were each significant at $p < .001$, together they accounted for a mean of only 10.3% of the variance in scale scores. The effects of individual differences within societies thus greatly outweighed the combined effects of societal and cultural differences. Like the ANOVA findings for societal effects cited earlier, internalizing problems showed larger effects of society and culture cluster (sum = 14.4% of variance) than did externalizing problems (sum = 8.2% of variance).

In a subsequent study, Ivanova et al. (2022) applied similar HLM analyses to scores obtained on 17 YSR problem scales paralleling the 17 CBCL scales, plus the YSR Positive Qualities scale. The scores were obtained by 39,849 youths who completed YSRs in 38 societies from the 10 GLOBE culture clusters. Averaged across all 17 problem scales, Ivanova et al. found that a mean of 1.5% of variance was accounted for by culture cluster, 6.0% of variance was accounted for by society, and 92.5% of variance was accounted for by individual differences. Compared to the 89.8% for the CBCL/6-18, slightly more variance in the YSR (92.5%) was thus accounted for by individual differences. Compared to the 4.2% for the CBCL/6-18, less variance in the YSR was accounted for by culture cluster (1.5%). And about the same amount of variance (6.1% vs. 6.0%) was accounted for by society. However, considerably less variance in YSR Positive Qualities was accounted for by individual differences (83.4%) than was found for the mean of YSR problem scales (92.5%) or CBCL/6-18 problem scales (89.8%). These findings are consistent with Rescorla's findings of greater within-society homogeneity for ratings of favorable items than problem items (Rescorla et al., 2016a, 2020), further indicating that ratings of favorable items are affected by societal/cultural influences more than are ratings of problem items.

### Applications to Clinical Services

The instruments described in the foregoing sections are products of the conceptual frameworks of developmental psychopathology and of the empirically based paradigm for assessing and deriving constructs of psychopathology. The instruments are designed for assessing and conceptualizing psychopathology for many purposes that link practical clinical applications to assessment of individuals' needs for help; research to advance understanding, prevention, and treatment of psychopathology; and training of practitioners, as addressed in the following sections.

ASEBA instruments can be used in many settings with many service models and requiring little clinician time or cost. The full-length instruments described so far can be completed in about 10–20 minutes on paper or online. (Briefer instruments will be presented later.) Instruments completed on paper can be scored by clerical workers on hand-scored profiles or can be entered into computers for scoring and storing data. Instruments can be completed online using desktops, laptops, tablets, and smartphones. When entered online, the data are scored automatically for access by clinicians. For informants who cannot complete the instruments independently, interviewers with no specialized training—such as receptionists—can read the items aloud and enter the responses.

When used in clinical settings, all ASEBA instruments can be routinely completed by clients and informants. Profiles of scale scores, comparisons of item ratings by different informants, $Q$ correlations between 0-1-2 ratings of problem items by different informants, graphs of scale scores, and other information can be generated by PC and Web versions of ASEBA software, with scale scores displayed in relation to multicultural norms appropriate for each informant.

### Multicultural Family Assessment Module

For family therapy, the Multicultural Family Assessment Module (MFAM; Achenbach, Rescorla, & Ivanova, 2015) can be used to display bar graphs of problem scale scores obtained from ratings of a child by multiple informants (child, mother, father, other family members, teachers) on side-by-side bar graphs that show how the child appears to different informants. Moreover, the MFAM displays bar graphs of problem scales scored from ASRs completed by each parent or other family member to describe themselves and ABCLs completed to describe their partner or other adult family members. As Figure 19.3 shows, the MFAM generates bar graphs that compare child and adult scale scores on syndromes that have counterparts for ages 6–18 and 18–59. The MFAM also generates bar graphs that compare child and adult scale scores on *DSM*-oriented scales.

If clinicians deem it appropriate, they can show MFAM bar graphs to family members and encourage them to point out similarities and differences between magnitudes of scores obtained from different informants' ratings. For example, ratings by three of a boy's teachers may be elevated on the *DSM*-oriented ADH Problems scale, whereas ratings by the boy's parents are in the normal range on this scale. Although the teachers view the boy as having attention deficit hyperactivity disorder (ADHD), the parents say he that he cannot have ADHD because he spends hours engrossed in video games. The elevated scores on the ADH Problems scale scored from TRFs completed by the boy's teachers provide detailed documentation of the teachers' perceptions of the boy's problems in three different classrooms, but the normal-range scores on the ADH Problems scale scored from the CBCLs completed by the boy's parents and their reports of his engrossment in video games indicate that interventions for ADHD problems should focus on the boy's functioning in school rather than being based on the assumption that he has an inherent attention deficit that affects his functioning at home as well as school.

Another clinically useful function of the MFAM is to reveal similarities and differences between child and parent scores on counterpart scales. For example, if a mother and daughter both have elevated scores on the Anxious/Depressed syndrome scale, this suggests that they may both need help in this area. Even when a child is the identified client, elevated problem scale scores for parents and marked discrepancies between parents' ratings of themselves and their partner may provide a basis for interventions to help the parents.

### Progress and Outcomes App

It is increasingly recognized that evidence-based assessments of progress and outcomes are essential for optimizing and evaluating mental health and related services. By comparing data from standardized assessments administered at intake into a service and again on subsequent occasions during and at the end of the service, clinicians can obtain evidence for improvements and other changes in client functioning. If improvement is insufficient, clinicians can use data obtained from repeated assessments to guide changes in services. When possible, it is also valuable to repeat assessments after services end in order to evaluate outcomes over periods such as 6–12 months.

To help clinicians compare repeated assessments of their clients, the Progress and Outcomes (P&O) App (Achenbach, 2020a, 2020b) generates bar graphs of ASEBA problems and strengths scale scores obtained for individual clients on two or more occasions. To determine whether changes in scale scores exceed chance expectations, the P&O

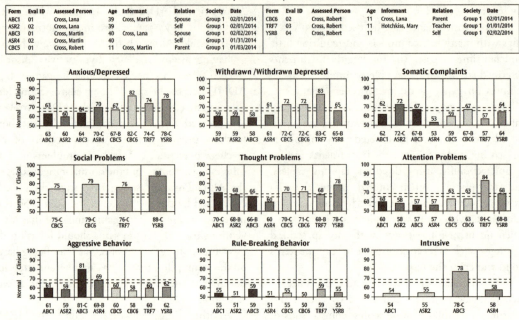

**Figure 19.3** Bar graphs produced by the Muticultural Family Assessment Module (MFAM) displaying syndrome scores for Lana, Martin, and their son Robert.

Copyright 2015, Achenbech & Rescorla.

App does statistical computations based on the standard error of measurement. Without the clinician doing any statistics, the P&O App's output displays asterisks with bars for scale scores that show changes exceeding chance expectations from one assessment to another. Data from multiple informants can be included in the output, which clinicians can show clients for discussion of the evidence for improvement and/or possible needs for changes in services.

For users who wish to compare outcomes for groups of clients receiving different service conditions, the P&O App can apply chi square and ANOVA/ANCOVA statistical analyses. The *ASEBA Manual for Assessing Progress & Outcomes of Problems & Strengths* (Achenbach, 2020a), provides details of various ways to evaluate progress and outcomes for groups as well as for individual clients.

*Brief Problem Monitor*

The full-length ASEBA forms presented so far provide the input for the P&O App, which tests changes over periods of months to years. For briefer assessments of changes over periods of days, weeks, or months, versions of the Brief Problem Monitor (BPM) can be filled out online or on paper in 1–2 minutes to assess internalizing, externalizing, attention problems, and Total Problems over a period specified by the clinician (e.g., 7 days). Whereas the P&O App measures changes over longer periods, the BPM measures changes that occur in relation to interventions rendered over limited time intervals, such as contingency management to reduce a child's disruptive behavior in a classroom. Separate versions of the BPM are designed for completion by parents and teachers of 6- to 18-year-olds (BPM-P, BPM-T), for completion by 11- to 18-year-old youths to describe themselves (BPM-Y), and for completion by 18- to 59-year-olds and their collaterals (BPM/18-59; Achenbach & Ivanova, 2018; Achenbach et al., 2017). Software for scoring the various versions of the BPM generates bar graphs comparing scale scores obtained from multiple informants on multiple occasions, plus line graphs comparing trajectories of scores over 2–10 occasions. Like the other instruments described in this chapter, the scale scores are standardized for the gender and age of the person being assessed, the type of informant (parent, teacher, youth, adult,

adult collateral), and the appropriate multicultural norm group.

## Applications to Research

In addition to providing practical clinical assessment of psychopathology for ages 1½–90+ years in societies around the world, the empirically based instruments have yielded syndromal constructs and broad-spectrum aggregations of syndromes on which research is targeted. Scale scores for individuals assessed with the instruments in turn provide operational definitions of the constructs in many kinds of research, as reported in more than 11,000 publications from more than 100 societies and cultural groups (Pascal & Achenbach, 2021). The following sections provide illustrations of research applications of the empirically based assessment instruments and constructs derived from them.

### Genetic and Environmental Effects on Informant Discrepancies

Dutch researchers have tested the degree to which discrepancies between informants' ratings reflect "informant biases" versus differences in genetically and environmentally influenced aspects of functioning that may be captured by different informants' ratings. In one study, CBCL/1½-5 internalizing and externalizing scores were compared for mothers' versus fathers' ratings of 3,501 pairs of 3-year-old twins (van der Valk et al., 2001). Based on correlations between mothers' and fathers' ratings of monozygotic (MZ) and dizygotic (DZ) twins, genetic modeling showed that mother-versus-father discrepancies validly captured different genetically influenced aspects of the children's functioning rather than being artifacts of informant biases. Longitudinal studies of parents' ratings of Dutch twins have also shown that mother-versus-father discrepancies validly capture different genetically influenced aspects of the children's functioning over multiple developmental periods (Bartels et al., 2004, 2007).

Even though mothers and fathers see their children under generally similar conditions, the foregoing studies show that each parent may nevertheless capture different genetically influenced aspects of their children's functioning. The differences between the aspects of their children's functioning captured by mother-versus-father ratings may reflect differences in children's interactions with their mothers versus fathers, or differences between what mothers and fathers perceive and remember, or both.

Additional Dutch research has tested genetic and environmentally influenced aspects of 7-year-old twins' functioning in the markedly different environments of home versus school, as rated by mothers versus teachers, who play markedly different roles vis-à-vis the children (Derks et al., 2006). For more than 2,000 pairs of twins, Attention Problems syndrome scores from the CBCL/6-18 and TRF yielded an estimate of 32% of variance for genetically influenced aspects of scores that were common to mother and teacher ratings. An additional 9% of variance that was common to mother and teacher ratings reflected environmentally influenced aspects of Attention Problems scores.

Of the variance that was specific to mothers' ratings, 45% was accounted for by genetic influences, whereas 14% was accounted for by environmental influences. Of the variance that was specific to teachers' ratings, 23% was accounted for by genetic influences, whereas 36% was accounted for by environmental influences. Like the findings for mother-versus-father ratings of 3-year-olds, these findings show that discrepancies between mother-versus-teacher ratings validly reflect differences in genetic and environmental effects, rather than just informant biases.

### Longitudinal Studies

Repeated assessments of the same individuals as they grow older are essential components of the developmental study of psychopathology across the life span. The value of repeated assessments can be maximized by including procedures that can be directly linked across developmental periods while taking account of developmental changes in the aspects of functioning to be assessed, the sources of assessment data, and the normative distributions of scores with which to compare individuals' scores. To avoid ethnocentric assumptions that longitudinal findings in one society are automatically generalizable to other societies, it is also important to compare results from different societies where similar assessment procedures and longitudinal methods are used.

*US National Longitudinal Study.* The US National Longitudinal Study initially assessed a nationally representative sample of 2,734 4- to 16-year-olds on the basis of home interviews in which parents rated their children's problems and competencies and reported on many child and family variables. Subsequent assessments 3, 6, and 9 years later included parent, teacher, and self-ratings on instruments that assessed ASEBA models for psychopathology, plus reports of signs of disturbance, such as suicidal behavior, receipt of mental health services, trouble with the law, substance abuse, and being fired from a job.

Scores on scales for empirically based syndromes significantly predicted scores on the corresponding syndrome scales and various signs of disturbance at 3-, 6-, and 9-year intervals, after controlling for numerous demographic and other variables (Achenbach et al., 1995a, 1995b, 1995c, 1998; Wadsworth & Achenbach, 2005). The empirically based syndrome models for psychopathology and the assessment procedures for operationalizing them thus revealed considerable continuity in patterns of problems from early childhood to adolescence and from adolescence to young adulthood. The findings also showed that the empirically based syndrome scores could predict signs of disturbance that were not included in the syndrome models. Parent, teacher, and self-ratings on competence and adaptive strengths scales added significantly to the prediction of signs of disturbance, especially to the prediction of total disturbance scores, which aggregated the different signs of disturbance.

*Developmental Course of Relations Between Psychopathology and SES.* In addition to testing the developmental continuity and predictive power of the empirically based models, the US National Longitudinal Study tested hypotheses that required data spanning multiple developmental periods in a representative population sample. As an example, Wadsworth and Achenbach (2005) tested the hypothesis that factors associated with SES contribute to differences in levels of psychopathology. Early cross-sectional studies had found that psychopathology is more prevalent among lower SES than upper SES adults (e.g., Hollingshead & Redlich, 1958). However, cross-sectional studies of adults cannot test the extent to which the higher prevalence results from "downward drift" in SES among adults whose psychopathology impairs their ability to maintain higher SES or instead results from a higher initial incidence of psychopathology among lower SES people.

To prevent the possible contribution of downward drift from confounding research on relations between SES and psychopathology, it is necessary to compare the developmental courses of psychopathology for children whose families differ in SES. This excludes downward drift as an explanation because children's psychopathology is not apt to cause their families' SES to drift downward.

Over the 9 years of the US National Longitudinal Study, it was found that the scores of significantly more children from low SES than high SES families increased from the normal to the clinical range on the ASEBA Anxious/Depressed, Somatic Complaints, Thought Problems, Rule-Breaking Behavior, and Aggressive Behavior syndromes. These findings supported the hypothesis that low SES predicts developmental increases in the problems modeled by these syndromes. However, it was also found that, among children who initially obtained clinically elevated scores on the Withdrawn/Depressed and Somatic Complaints syndromes, fewer from low SES than higher SES families subsequently obtained scores in the normal range. For these particular kinds of problems, the evidence thus indicated a greater "cumulative prevalence" of elevated problem scores among lower than higher SES children. In other words, there was a greater developmental accumulation of (i.e., less remission of) elevated scores among children from lower than higher SES families. Both the greater incidence and greater cumulative prevalence of particular kinds of problems thus contributed to the higher prevalence of psychopathology among those born into lower than higher SES families.

*Zuid Holland Longitudinal Study.* A Dutch longitudinal study started with parents' ratings of their 4- to 16-year-old children on Dutch translations of the ASEBA instruments that were used in the US National Longitudinal Study (Verhulst, Akkerhuis, & Althaus, 1985). The Dutch parents also reported on child and family variables like those assessed in the US study. The sample was selected to be representative of 4- to 16-year-olds living in the Province of Zuid (South) Holland. The participants were then reassessed at four 2-year intervals, followed by 6- and 10-year intervals, over a total of 24 years, when the oldest participants were 40 years old. At every assessment, Dutch translations of developmentally appropriate versions of the US instruments were completed by participants and by informants who knew the participants. Standardized diagnostic interviews (SDIs) were also administered to adult participants, and the participants and other informants provided data on signs of disturbance and other aspects of functioning. The participants' own children were eventually assessed with the ASEBA instruments that had been used to assess the participants when they were children. The participants' childhood ASEBA scores were found to significantly predict their children's ASEBA scores (van Meurs et al., 2009).

For 1,365 participants rated by their parents at the initial assessment and rated by themselves 24 years later, high scores on all the ASEBA syndromes rated by their parents significantly predicted high scores 24 years later on the self-rated counterparts of the syndromes, with the exception of the Thought Problems and Attention Problems syndromes (Reef et al., 2009). These findings thus indicated homotypic continuity (i.e., consistency of low, medium, or high scores on the same syndromes) over 24 years for the Anxious/Depressed, Withdrawn, Somatic Complaints, Rule-Breaking Behavior, and Aggressive Behavior syndromes, despite the difference in raters (parents initially, self 24 years later).

Although not significantly predicted by their parents' initial ratings on the Thought Problems syndrome, the adults' self-ratings on this syndrome were significantly predicted by parents' initial ratings on the Anxious/Depressed, Attention Problems, Rule-Breaking Behavior, and Aggressive Behavior syndromes. Moreover, the adults' self-ratings on the Attention Problems syndrome were significantly predicted by their parents' initial ratings on the Anxious/Depressed and Thought Problems syndromes. The significant prediction of adult Thought Problems and Attention Problems ratings from scores on other syndromes thus indicated heterotypic continuity for these kinds of problems. The parents' initial ratings also significantly predicted *DSM* diagnoses made from SDIs administered to their adult offspring 24 years later (Reef et al., 2010).

*Multi-Informant Ratings from Age 4 to 40 Years.* Ratings of the Dutch participants by multiple informants at all seven assessment points enabled the research team to compute agreement between ratings by 12,059 informant pairs when the participants were assessed at various ages from 4 to 40 years (Van der Ende et al., 2012). Cross-informant correlations between ratings of internalizing and externalizing problems were computed from parent, teacher, adult partner, and self-ratings. The magnitudes of the cross-informant correlations were similar to those found previously in meta-analyses of cross-informant correlations (Achenbach et al., 1987, 2005) and depended more on the kinds of informant pairs than on the age of the participants or on whether the ratings were for internalizing or externalizing problems. Participants were found to rate themselves higher on the problem scales than their parents, teachers, or partners rated them. Multicultural comparisons of parents' CBCL ratings versus youths' YSR ratings have also shown that youths rated themselves higher than parents rated them on counterpart problem scales in 25 very diverse societies (Rescorla et al., 2013). The differences found between self-versus-informant ratings of people of different ages and in diverse societies further underscore the need for multi-informant assessment of psychopathology.

*Dutch versus US Developmental Trajectories.* The parallel assessment instruments used in the Zuid Holland and US longitudinal studies have enabled researchers to rigorously compare developmental trajectories for psychopathology in the Netherlands versus the United States. As an example, the data used in the previously described Wadsworth and Achenbach (2005) test of associations between SES and the development of psychopathology were compared with data from the Zuid Holland study to determine whether conclusions would differ for the US versus Dutch populations (Van Oort et al., 2011). Comparisons of this sort are especially important, because smaller economic differences and more equal access to healthcare for lower versus upper SES families in countries such as the Netherlands than in the US could affect associations between SES and the development of psychopathology.

Parents' ratings of 833 US children and 708 Dutch children were compared for assessments spanning 9 years in both societies. After correcting for chance differences, only minor Dutch–US differences were found between tendencies for the incidence and cumulative prevalence of clinically elevated scores on certain syndromes to be higher for children from lower than higher SES families. Although more detailed data on SES, plus data from more societies, might support other conclusions, the similarity of findings in Dutch and US population samples are consistent with findings from a review of studies in 15 societies where empirically based problem scale scores were consistently found to be higher for children of lower than higher SES families (Achenbach & Rescorla, 2007b).

*Generation R Longitudinal Study.* Another Dutch longitudinal study started with 8,880 women living in Rotterdam who were assessed during pregnancy. ("R" in "Generation R" stands for Rotterdam.) The pregnant women were assessed via ultrasound, blood and urine samples, and questionnaires, while fathers of the children were assessed via blood samples and questionnaires. Over the first 5 postnatal years, the children were assessed via biological, observational, questionnaire, and other measures, and they are continuing to be assessed at later ages. Numerous

Generation R findings of associations between prenatal and postnatal variables have been published (reviewed by Tiemeier et al., 2012). The Generation R study's use of standardized rating instruments from the ASEBA family of instruments used in the US and Zuid Holland longitudinal studies enables researchers to analyze the developmental course of psychopathology in terms of the empirically based models used in those studies, as well as in many other studies.

As an example, mothers and fathers rated Generation R children on the CBCL/1½–5 at ages 3 and 5. Children who were identified as having small subcortical volumes via brain imaging at postnatal age 6 weeks were found to have significantly higher internalizing problem scores than other children on the CBCL at age 3 (Herba et al., 2010). Furthermore, at age 5, elevated internalizing scores were found for children who carried the short allele of the 5-HTTLPR polymorphism in the promoter region of the serotonin transporter gene (5-HTT, SLC6A4) *and* whose mothers reported high levels of anxiety at prenatal assessments and/or postnatal assessments (Tiemeier et al., 2012). This finding is important because previous studies have yielded inconsistent results regarding interactions between the short allele of the 5-HTTLPR polymorphism and individuals' own stressful experiences during childhood. Caspi et al. (2003) initially reported that carriers of the short allele were at elevated risk for developing depression after maltreatment and other stressful childhood experiences. However, several subsequent studies failed to support this gene–environment (G×E) interaction (e.g., Risch et al., 2009), while other studies concluded that inclusion of chronic illnesses as stressors and use of observational data on stress provided support for the G×E interaction (e.g., Caspi et al., 2010).

Because serotonin appears at about 5 weeks after conception, differences in serotonin transporter availability related to the 5-HTTLPR polymorphism could affect vulnerability to effects of prenatal stressors such as maternal anxiety. Generation R findings that mothers' anxiety during either the prenatal or postnatal period (with prenatal anxiety controlled) predicted subsequent elevations in age 5 CBCL internalizing scores for children with the short allele suggest that maternal anxiety can affect children with the short allele by both prenatal intrauterine processes and postnatal environmental processes. Furthermore, when mothers had high anxiety either prenatally or postnatally, children with two short alleles obtained higher CBCL internalizing scores than did children with a single short allele who, in turn, obtained higher internalizing scores than children with no short alleles. However, children whose mothers did not report much anxiety either prenatally or postnatally obtained low internalizing scores, regardless of whether they had 0, 1, or 2 short alleles. In other words, high prenatal and postnatal maternal anxiety levels were associated with high age 5 internalizing scores, but short alleles appeared to exacerbate internalizing problems only among children whose mothers reported high anxiety either pre- or postnatally.

Although the Generation R findings indicate that the short and long 5-HTTLPR alleles differentially affect children's reactions to pre- and postnatal stress, the effects were very small. Technological advances in many facets of research, such as genetic and neuroimaging methods, are greatly increasing the power of research to detect very small effects of this sort. Each small effect may be important, but the many small effects are further complicated by myriad interactions among them. Consequently, developmentally appropriate multivariate phenotypic models and standardized procedures for assessing them are needed to provide common foci across studies of the many potentially relevant variables and the interactions among them.

**Applications to Training**

With advances in evidence-based practice, it is essential for mental health trainees to learn the use of evidence-based assessment to provide foundations for applying and evaluating the progress and outcomes of evidence-based treatment. Empirically based instruments serve as tools for obtaining multi-informant evidence regarding the problems and strengths of clients across the life span. By routinely using developmentally appropriate ASEBA instruments, trainees can obtain well-differentiated pictures of clients' specific problems and strengths, as seen from multiple perspectives. Trainees can also compare aggregations of problems and strengths to norms based on population samples of peers in terms of standardized scale scores for empirically based and *DSM*-oriented constructs. If trainees examine clients' completed forms and scored profiles before interviewing the clients, they can use the data as a take-off point for interviewing. Trainees can begin by asking clients whether they have questions about the forms and can then ask them about items they endorsed and comments they entered. For example, if a youth endorsed the YSR item "I can't get my mind off certain thoughts" and entered "death" in the space for a description, the trainee can say "I see that you can't get your mind off death. Please tell me more about that."

After trainees become acquainted with clients, they can fill out the appropriate ASEBA self-report form (YSR, ASR, or OASR) for comparison with the clients' own responses to the form filled out at a progress or outcome assessment. To sharpen trainees' clinical skills, they can discuss discrepancies between their responses and the self-reports with supervisors.

## Conclusion

This chapter was organized around the frameworks of developmental psychopathology and empirically based assessment and taxonomy. Although developmental psychopathology originated with efforts to understand maladaptive functioning from birth to maturity, it has become clear that understanding psychopathology of adulthood and later life can also benefit from a developmental approach. In the 1960s, the lack of empirically based differentiation among childhood disorders prompted multivariate research that identified several narrow-spectrum syndromes of co-occurring problems, plus broad-spectrum groupings of problems designated as internalizing and externalizing. Findings for large samples of children revealed hierarchies of problems that spanned from numerous specific problems at the bottom most molecular level, to syndromes of co-occurring problems at the next higher level, to aggregations of mutually associated syndromes into internalizing and externalizing groupings at the next higher level, and culminating in a general psychopathology dimension ($p$) at the top most molar level.

Assessment instruments tailored to ages 1½–5, 6–18, 18–59, and 60–90+ years filled out by appropriate informants (parents, daycare providers, teachers, self, adult collaterals) were used to assess clinical and general population samples from which empirically based problem scales were derived via EFAs and CFAs. Large general population samples of "healthy" individuals (i.e., not referred for mental health services) were used to construct norms based on distributions of scores obtained for each gender within particular age ranges and rated by particular kinds of informants. A life span approach was used whereby assessment instruments and their items were tailored to successive developmental periods, and the informants were chosen to be appropriate for the respective developmental periods. It was not assumed that disorders would be the same across developmental periods. Instead, longitudinal studies were used to test for possible homotypic and heterotypic continuities between empirically derived taxonomic constructs from earlier to later developmental periods. The studies also tested the effects of diverse variables on the developmental course of psychopathology and competencies.

The assessment instruments produced by this research are designed for practical applications in diverse clinical and research contexts. In addition to being designed for initial assessment, the instruments are designed for repeated administration to assess progress and outcomes and to measure changes from earlier to later assessments across the life span. Brief versions of the instruments are available that can be completed in 1–2 minutes at user-selected intervals of days, weeks, or months.

To test the generalizability of the syndromes derived from mainly US samples, CFAs have been performed on problem item ratings obtained in population samples from more than 50 non-US societies on all inhabited continents. Despite the many differences among the societies, the empirically derived syndrome structures have been supported for ages 1½–5 through 90+ years in ratings by different informants. Moreover, $Q$ correlations between the 0-1-2 ratings of problem items across different societies have averaged in the .70s for all age groups rated by different informants. These findings indicate considerable consistency in the quantitative measurement of problem item structures around the world.

Comparisons of mean problem scale scores (sum of 0-1-2 ratings on items comprising a scale) across many societies have yielded approximately normal distributions for most problem scales in each age group. On each instrument, mean Total Problems scores for approximately two-thirds of societies were within ±1 $SD$ of the omnicultural mean (mean of the mean Total Problems scores obtained in all the societies for that instrument), while approximately one-sixth were greater than 1 $SD$ below the omnicultural mean (designated as "low-scoring" or Group 1 societies) and one-sixth were greater than 1 $SD$ above the omnicultural mean ("high-scoring" or Group 3 societies). Scores for Group 1 societies were averaged to construct Group 1 norms and likewise for Group 2 and Group 3. (Because scores for US normative samples were at the middle of the Group 2 distributions for some instruments, those Group 2 norms were based on the already widely used US norms.) Multicultural norms were also constructed for the ages 18–59 and 60–90+ Personal Strengths scales and for the ages 11–18 Positive Qualities scale.

Tests of the effects of culture cluster (e.g., Confucian), society, and individual differences on CBCL/6-18 ratings in 45 societies revealed that culture cluster differences accounted for a mean of 4.2% of variance in problem scale scores, societal differences accounted for a mean of 6.1% of variance, and variables associated with individual differences accounted for 89.8% of variance. For YSR ratings in 38 societies, culture cluster differences accounted for a mean of 1.5% of variance in problem scale scores, societal differences accounted for a mean of 6.0% of variance, and individual differences accounted for 92.5% of variance. For the YSR Positive Qualities scale, culture cluster differences accounted for 6.5% of variance, societal differences accounted for 10.1% of variance, and individual differences accounted for 83.4% of variance. Although the effects of cultural and societal differences were statistically significant (except on YSR problem scores), individual differences within culture clusters and societies greatly outweighed societal and cultural differences in ratings of problems on the CBCL/6-18 and both problems and Positive Qualities on the YSR.

The empirically based instruments were designed for use in many clinical settings employing many service models. Empirically based forms completed online or on paper are scored on profiles that compare individuals' scores with norms and with scores from other informants. The MFAM compares scores obtained by child clients with scores obtained by adult family members on syndromes and *DSM*-oriented scales that have counterparts for ages 6–18 and 18–59. The P&O App provides statistical tests of differences between scores obtained at different points in time.

Research applications of the empirically based instruments have included tests of genetic and environmental effects on informant discrepancies, longitudinal studies, and many other kinds of studies.

The empirically based instruments facilitate training in evidence-based practice by providing trainees with well-differentiated pictures of clients' problems and strengths, tools for assessing progress and outcomes, and methods for comparing trainees' perceptions of clients with the clients' self-perceptions and perceptions by multiple informants.

# References

Achenbach, T. M. (1966). The classification of children's psychiatric symptoms: A factor-analytic study. *Psychological Monographs, 80*(7, serial no. 615). https://doi.org/10.1037/h0093906

Achenbach, T. M. (1974/1982). *Developmental psychopathology*, 2nd ed. Wiley.

Achenbach, T. M. (2009). *The Achenbach System of Empirically Based Assessment (ASEBA): Development, findings, theory, and applications*. University of Vermont, Research Center for Children, Youth, and Families.

Achenbach, T. M. (2014). *DSM-oriented guide for the Achenbach System of Empirically Based Assessment (ASEBA)*. University of Vermont Research Center for Children, Youth, and Families.

Achenbach, T. M. (2020a). *ASEBA manual for assessing progress and outcomes of problems and strengths*. University of Vermont, Research Center for Children, Youth, & Families.

Achenbach, T. M. (2020b). Bottom-up and top-down paradigms for psychopathology: A half-century odyssey. *Annual Review of Clinical Psychology, 16*, 1–24. https://doi.org/10.1146/annurev-clinpsy-071119-115831

Achenbach, T. M. (2021). Hierarchical dimensional models of psychopathology: Yes, but . . . *World Psychiatry, 20*, 64–65.

Achenbach, T. M., & Edelbrock, C. (1978). The classification of child psychopathology: A review and analysis of empirical efforts. *Psychological Bulletin, 85*, 1275–1301. https://doi.org/10.1037/0033-2909.85.6.1275

Achenbach, T. M., Howell, C. T., McConaughy, S. H., & Stanger, C. (1995a, March). Six-year predictors of problems in a national sample of children and youth: I. Cross-informant syndromes. *Journal of the American Academy of Child and Adolescent Psychiatry, 34*, 336–347. https://doi.org/10.1097/00004583-199503000-00020

Achenbach, T. M., Howell, C. T., McConaughy, S. H., & Stanger, C. (1995b, April). Six-year predictors of problems in a national sample of children and youth: II. Signs of disturbance. *Journal of the American Academy of Child and Adolescent Psychiatry, 34*, 488–498. https://doi.org/10.1097/00004583-199504000-00016

Achenbach, T. M., Howell, C. T., McConaughy, S. H., & Stanger, C. (1995c, May). Six-year predictors of problems in a national sample: III. Transitions to young adult syndromes. *Journal of the American Academy of Child and Adolescent Psychiatry, 34*, 658–669. https://doi.org/10.1097/00004583-199505000-00018

Achenbach, T. M., & Ivanova, M. Y. (2018). *Manual for the ASEBA® Brief Problem Monitor™ for Ages 18–59* (BPM/18-59). University of Vermont, Research Center for Children, Youth, & Families.

Achenbach, T. M., Ivanova, M. Y., Rescorla, L. A., Turner, L. V., & Althoff, R. R. (2016). Internalizing/externalizing problems: Review and recommendations for clinical and research applications. *Journal of the American Academy of Child and Adolescent Psychiatry, 55*(8), 647–656. https://doi.org/10.1016/j.jaac.2016.05.012

Achenbach, T. M., Krukowski, R. A., Dumenci, L., & Ivanova, M. Y. (2005). Assessment of adult psychopathology: Meta-analyses and implications of cross-informant correlations. *Psychological Bulletin, 131*, 361–382. https://doi.org/10.1037/0033-2909.131.3.361

Achenbach, T. M., Howell, C. T., McConaughy, S. H., & Stanger, C. (1998). Six-year predictors of problems in a national sample: IV. Young adult signs of disturbance. *Journal of the American Academy of Child and Adolescent Psychiatry, 37*, 718–727. https://doi.org/10.1097/00004583-199807000-00011

Achenbach, T. M., McConaughy, S. H., & Howell, C. T. (1987). Child/adolescent behavioral and emotional problems:

Implications of cross-informant correlations for situational specificity. *Psychological Bulletin, 101*, 213–232. https://doi.org/10.1037/0033-2909.101.2.213

Achenbach, T. M., McConaughy, S. H., Ivanova, M. Y., & Rescorla, L. A. (2017). *Manual for the ASEBA® Brief Problem Monitor™ for Ages 6–18* (BPM/6-18). University of Vermont, Research Center for Children, Youth, and Families.

Achenbach, T. M., Newhouse, P. A., & Rescorla, L. A. (2004). *Manual for the ASEBA older adult forms & profiles.* University of Vermont Research Center for Children, Youth, and Families.

Achenbach, T. M., & Rescorla, L. A. (2000). *Manual for the ASEBA preschool forms & profiles.* University of Vermont Research Center for Children, Youth, and Families.

Achenbach, T. M., & Rescorla, L. A. (2001). *Manual for the ASEBA school-age forms & profiles.* University of Vermont Research Center for Children, Youth, and Families.

Achenbach, T. M., & Rescorla, L. A. (2003). *Manual for the ASEBA adult forms & profiles.* University of Vermont Research Center for Children, Youth, and Families.

Achenbach, T. M., & Rescorla, L. A. (2007a). *Multicultural supplement to the Manual for the ASEBA School-Age Forms & Profiles.* University of Vermont, Research Center for Children, Youth, and Families.

Achenbach, T. M., & Rescorla, L. A. (2007b). *Multicultural understanding of child and adolescent psychopathology: Implications for mental health assessment.* Guilford.

Achenbach, T. M., & Rescorla, L. A. (2010). *Multicultural supplement to the Manual for the ASEBA Preschool Forms & Profiles.* University of Vermont, Research Center for Children, Youth, and Families.

Achenbach, T. M., & Rescorla, L. A. (2015). *Multicultural supplement to the Manual for the ASEBA Adult Forms & Profiles.* University of Vermont, Research Center for Children, Youth, and Families.

Achenbach, T. M., & Rescorla, L. A. (2019). *Multicultural supplement to the Manual for the ASEBA Older Adult Forms & Profiles.* University of Vermont, Research Center for Children, Youth, and Families.

Achenbach, T. M., Rescorla, L. A., & Ivanova, M. Y. (2015). *Guide to family assessment using the ASEBA.* University of Vermont, Research Center for Children, Youth, and Families.

Bartels, M., Boomsma, D. I., Hudziak, J. J., van Beijsterveldt, T. C. E. M., & van den Oord, E. J. C. G. (2007). Twins and the study of rater (dis)agreement. *Psychological Methods, 12*, 451–466. https://doi.org/10.1037/1082-989x.12.4.451

Bartels, M., van den Oord, E. J. C. G., Hudziak, J. J., Rietveld, M. J. H., van Beijsterveldt, T. C. E. M., & Boomsma, D. I. (2004). Genetic and environmental mechanisms underlying stability and change in problem behaviors at the ages 3, 7, 10, and 12. *Developmental Psychology, 40*, 852–867. https://doi.org/10.1037/0012-1649.40.5.852

Caspi, A., Hariri, A. R., Holmes, A. Uher, R., & Moffitt, T. E. (2010). Genetic sensitivity to the environment: The case of the serotonin transporter gene and its implications for studying complex diseases and traits. *American Journal of Psychiatry, 167*, 509–527. https://doi.org/10.1176/appi.ajp.2010.09101452

Caspi, A., Sugden, K., Moffitt, T., Taylor, A., Craig, I. W., Harrington, H., McClay, J., Mill, J., Martin, J., Braithwaite, A., & Poulton, R. (2003). Influence of life stress on depression: Moderation by a polymorphism in the 5-HTT gene. *Science, 301*, 386–389.

Cohen, J. (1988). *Statistical power analysis for the behavioral sciences,* 2nd ed. Academic Press

Conners, C. K. (1969). A teacher rating scale for use in drug studies with children. *American Journal of Psychiatry, 126*, 884–888. https://doi.org/10.1176/ajp.126.6.884

De Los Reyes, A. (2011). Introduction to the special section: More than measurement error: Discovering meaning behind informant discrepancies in clinical assessments of children and adolescents. *Journal of Clinical Child and Adolescent Psychology, 40*(1), 1–9. https://doi.org/10.1080/15374416.2011.533405

De Los Reyes, A., Augenstein, T. M., Wang, M., Thomas, S. A., Drabick, D. A. G., Burgers, D. E., & Rabinowitz, J. (2015). The validity of the multi-informant approach to assessing child and adolescent mental health. *Psychological Bulletin, 141*(4), 858–900. https://doi.org/10.1037/a0038498

Derks, E. M., Hudziak, J. J., Dolan, C. V., Ferdinand, R. F., & Boomsma, D. I. (2006). The relations between DISC-IV DSM diagnoses of ADHD and multi-informant CBCL-AP syndrome scores. *Comprehensive Psychiatry, 47*, 116–122. https://doi.org/10.1016/j.comppsych.2005.05.006

Gove, P. (Ed.). (1971). *Webster's third new international dictionary of the English language.* Merriam.

Herba, C. M., Roza, S. J., Govaert, P., van Rossum, J., Hofman, A., Jaddoe, V., Verhulst, F. C., & Tiemeier, H. (2010). Infant brain development and vulnerability to later internalizing difficulties: The Generation R Study. *Journal of the American Association of Child and Adolescent Psychiatry, 49*, 1053–1063. https://doi.org/10.1016/j.jaac.2010.07.003

Hermans, H. J. M., & Kempen, H. J. G. (1998). Moving cultures: The perilous problems of cultural dichotomies in a globalizing society. *American Psychologist, 53*, 1111–1120. https://doi.org/10.1037/0003-066x.53.10.1111

Hollingshead, A. B., & Redlich, F. C. (1958). *Social class and mental illness.* Wiley. https://doi.org/10.1037/10645-000

House, R. J., Hanges, P. J., Javidan, M., Dorfman, P. W., & Gupta, V. (2004). *Culture, leadership, and organizations: The GLOBE Study of 62 societies.* Sage.

Ivanova, M. Y., Achenbach, T. M., Dumenci, L., Rescorla, L. A., Almqvist, F., Weintraub, S., . . . Verhulst, F. C. (2007a). Testing the 8-syndrome structure of the CBCL in 30 societies. *Journal of Clinical Child and Adolescent Psychology, 36*, 405–417. https://doi.org/10.1080/15374410701444363

Ivanova, M. Y., Achenbach, T. M., Rescorla, L. A., Bilenberg, N., Bjarnadottir, G., Denner, S., . . . Verhulst, F. C. (2011). Syndromes of preschool psychopathology reported by teachers and caregivers in 14 societies using the Caregiver-Teacher Report Form (C-TRF). *Journal of Early Childhood and Infant Psychology, 7*, 87–103.

Ivanova, M. Y., Achenbach, T. M., Rescorla, L. A., Dumenci, L. Almqvist, F., Bathiche, M., . . . Verhulst, F. C. (2007b). Testing the Teacher's Report Form syndromes in 20 societies. *School Psychology Review, 36*, 468–483. https://doi.org/10.1080/02796015.2007.12087934

Ivanova, M. Y., Achenbach, T. M., Rescorla, L. A., Dumenci, L., Almqvist, F., Bilenberg, N., . . . Verhulst, F. C. (2007c). The generalizability of the Youth Self-Report syndrome structure in 23 societies. *Journal of Consulting and Clinical Psychology, 75*, 729–738. https://doi.org/10.1037/0022-006x.75.5.729

Ivanova, M. Y., Achenbach, T. M., Rescorla, L. A., Harder, V. S., Ang, R. P., Bilenberg, N., . . . Verhulst, F. C. (2010). Preschool psychopathology reported by parents in 23 societies: Testing the seven-syndrome model of the Child Behavior

Checklist for Ages 1.5-5. *Journal of the American Academy of Child and Adolescent Psychiatry, 49*, 1215–1224. https://doi.org/10.1016/j.jaac.2010.08.019

Ivanova, M. Y., Achenbach, T. M., Rescorla, L. A., Turner, L. V., Árnadóttir, H. A., Au, A., . . . Zasępa, E. (2015a). Syndromes of collateral-reported psychopathology for ages 18-59 in 18 societies. *International Journal of Clinical and Health Psychology, 15*, 18–28. https://doi.org/10.1016/j.ijchp.2014.07.001

Ivanova, M. Y., Achenbach, T. M., Rescorla, L. A., Turner, L. V., Árnadóttir, H. A., Au, A., . . . Zasępa, E. (2015b). Syndromes of self-reported psychopathology for ages 18-59 in 29 societies. *Journal of Psychopathology and Behavioral Assessment, 37*, 171–183. https://doi.org/10.1007/s10862-014-9448-8

Ivanova, M. Y., Achenbach T. M., Rescorla L. A., Turner L., & the International ASEBA Consortium. (2020). The generalizability of empirically-derived syndromes of elder self-rated psychopathology in 20 societies. *International Journal of Geriatric Psychiatry*. In press.

Ivanova, M. Y., Achenbach, T. M., Rescorla, L. A., Turner, L., & the International ASEBA Consortium. (2021). The generalizability of empirically-derived syndromes of elder psychopathology across 11 societies. *Research in Nursing & Health, 44*, 681–691.

Ivanova, M. Y., Achenbach, T. M., Turner, L., Almqvist, F., Begovac, I., Bilenberg, N., . . . Zukauskeine, R. (2022). Effects of individual differences, society, and culture on youth-rated problems and strengths in 38 societies. *Journal of Child Psychology & Psychiatry*, published online February 22.

Lahey, B. B., Moore, T. M., Kaczkurkin, A. N., & Zaid, D. H. (2021). Hierarchical models of psychopathology: Empirical support, implications, and remaining issues. *World Psychiatry, 20*, 57–63. https://doi.org/10.1002/wps.20824

Markon, K. E. (2021). On hierarchically-informed measures of psychopathology. *World Psychiatry, 20*, 66–67.

Markon, K. E., Chmielewski, M., & Miller, C. J. (2011). The reliability and validity of discrete and continuous measures of psychopathology: A quantitative review. *Psychological Bulletin, 137*, 856–879. https://doi.org/10.1037/a0023678

Meyer, G. J. (2002). Implications of information gathering methods for a refined taxonomy of psychopathology. In L. E. Beutler & M. L. Malik (Eds.), *Rethinking the DSM: A psychological perspective* (pp. 69–105). American Psychological Association.

Meyer, G. J., Finn, S. E., Eyde, L. D., Kay, G. G., Moreland, K. L., Dies, R. R., Eisman, E. J., Kubiszyn, T. W., & Reed, G. M. (2001). Psychological testing and psychological assessment: A review of evidence and issues. *American Psychologist, 56*(2), 128–165. https://doi.org/10.1037/0003-066x.56.2.128

Miller, L. C. (1967). Louisville Behavior Checklist for males, 6-12 years of age. *Psychological Reports, 21*, 885–896. https://doi.org/10.2466/pr0.1967.21.3.885

Pascal, J., & Achenbach, T. M. (2021). *Bibliography of published studies using the ASEBA*. University of Vermont, Research Center for Children, Youth, & Families.

Pike, K. L. (1967). *Language in relation to a unified theory of the structure of human behavior (Janua Linguarum. Series Maior)*. De Gruyter Mouton.

Quay, H. C. (1964). Personality dimensions in delinquent males as inferred from the factor analysis of behavior ratings. *Journal of Research in Crime and Delinquency, 1*, 33–37.

Quay, H. C. (1979). Classification. In H. C. Quay & J. S. Werry (Eds.), *Psychopathological disorders of childhood*, 2nd ed. Wiley.

Reef, J., Diamantopoulou, S., van Meurs, I., Verhulst, F., & van der Ende, J. (2009). Child to adult continuities of psychopathology: A 24-year follow-up. *Acta Psychiatrica Scandinavica, 120*, 230–238. https://doi.org/10.1111/j.1600-0447.2009.01422.x

Reef, J., Diamantopoulou, S., van Meurs, I., Verhulst, F., & van der Ende, J. (2010). Predicting adult emotional and behavioral problems from externalizing problem trajectories in a 24-year longitudinal study. *Journal of European Child and Adolescent Psychiatry, 19*, 577–585. https://doi.org/10.1007/s00787-010-0088-6

Rescorla, L. A., Achenbach, T. M., Ivanova, M. Y., Harder, V. S., Otten, L., Bilenberg, N., . . . Verhulst, F. C. (2011). International comparisons of behavioral and emotional problems in preschool children: Parents' reports from 24 societies. *Journal of Clinical Child and Adolescent Psychology, 40*, 456–467. https://doi.org/10.1080/15374416.2011.563472

Rescorla, L. A., Achenbach, T. M., Ivanova, M. Y., Turner, L. V., Althoff, R. R., Árnadóttir, H. A., . . . Zasepa, E. (2016a). Problems and adaptive functioning reported by adults in 17 societies. *International Perspectives in Psychology: Research, Practice, Consultation, 5*, 91–109. https://doi.org/10.1037/ipp0000046

Rescorla, L. A., Achenbach, T. M., Ivanova, M. Y., Turner, L. V., Árnadóttir, H., Au, A., . . . Zasępa, E. (2016b). Collateral reports of problems and cross-informant agreement about adult psychopathology in 14 societies. *Journal of Psychopathology and Behavioral Assessment, 38*, 381–397. https://doi.org/10.1007/s10862-016-9541-2

Rescorla, L. A., Althoff, R. R., Ivanova, M. Y., & Achenbach, T. M. (2019). Effects of society and culture on parents' ratings of children's problems in 45 societies. *European Child & Adolescent Psychiatry 28*, 1107–1115. http://dx.doi.org/10.1007/s00787-018-01268-3

Rescorla, L. A., Ginzburg, S., Achenbach, T. M., Ivanova, M. Y., Almqvist, F., Begovac, I., . . . Verhulst, F. C. (2013). Cross-informant agreement between parent-reported and adolescent self-reported problems in 25 societies. *Journal of Clinical Child and Adolescent Psychology, 42*, 262–273. https://doi.org/10.1080/15374416.2012.717870

Rescorla, L. A., Ivanova, M. Y., Achenbach, T. M., Almeida, V., Anafarta-Sendag, M., Bite, I., . . . Zasępa, E. (2020). Older adult psychopathology: International comparisons of self-reports, collateral reports, and cross-informant agreement. *International Psychogeriatrics*, 1–12. https://doi.org/10.1017/s1041610220001532

Rescorla, L., Ivanova, M. Y., Achenbach, T. M., Begovac, I., Chahed, M., Drugli, M. B., . . . Zhang, E. Y. (2012). International epidemiology of child and adolescent psychopathology: II. Integration and applications of dimensional findings from 44 societies. *Journal of the American Academy of Child and Adolescent Psychiatry, 51*, 1273–1283. https://doi.org/10.1016/j.jaac.2012.09.012 deleted a after 2012

Risch, N., Herrell, R., Lehner, T., Liang, K-Y., Eaves, L., Hoh, J., Griem, A., Kovacs, M., Ott, J., & Merikangas, K. R. (2009). Interactions between the serotonin transporter gene (5-HTTLPR), stressful life events, and risk of depression: A meta-analysis. *Journal of the American Medical Association, 301*, 2462–2471.

Tiemeier, H., Velders, F. P., Szekely, E., Roza, S. J., Dieleman, G., Jaddoe, V. W. V., Uitterlinden, A. G., White, T. J. H., Bakermans-Kranenburg, M. J., Hofman, A., Van

IJzendoorn, M. H., Hudziak, J. J., & Verhulst, F. C. (2012). The Generation R Study: A review of design, findings to date, and a study of the 5-HTTLPR by environmental interaction from fetal life onward. *Journal of the American Academy of Child and Adolescent Psychiatry, 51*, 1119–1135 e7. https://doi.org/10.1016/j.jaac.2012.08.021

van der Ende, J., Verhulst, F., & Tiemeier, H. (2012). Agreement of informants on emotional and behavioral problems from childhood to adulthood. *Psychological Assessment, 24*, 293–300. https://doi.org/10.1037/a0025500

Van der Valk, J. C., van den Oord, E. J. C. G., Verhulst, F. C., & Boomsma, D. I. (2001). Using parental ratings to study the etiology of 3-year-old twins' problem behaviors: Different views or rater bias? *Journal of Child Psychology and Psychiatry, 42*, 921–931. https://doi.org/10.1111/1469-7610.00788

Van Meurs, I., Reef, J., Verhulst, F., & van der Ende, J. (2009). Intergenerational transmission of child problem behaviors: A longitudinal, population-based study. *Journal of the American Academy of Child and Adolescent Psychiatry, 48*, 138–145. https://doi.org/10.1097/chi.0b013e318191770d

Van Oort, F. V. A., van der Ende, J., Wadsworth, M. E., Verhulst, F. C., & Achenbach, T. M. (2011). Cross-national comparison of the link between socioeconomic status and emotional and behavioral problems in youths. *Social Psychiatry and Psychiatric Epidemiology, 46*, 167–172. https://doi.org/10.1007/s00127-010-0191-5

Verhulst, F. C., Akkerhuis, G. W., & Althaus, M. (1985). Mental health in Dutch children: (I) A cross-cultural comparison. *Acta Psychiatrica Scandinavica Supplementum, 72*, 323, 1–108. https://doi.org/10.1111/j.1600-0447.1985.tb10512.x

Wadsworth, M. E., & Achenbach, T. M. (2005). Explaining the link between low socioeconomic status and psychopathology: Testing two mechanisms of the social causation hypothesis. *Journal of Consulting and Clinical Psychology, 73*, 1146–1153. https://doi.org/10.1037/0022-006x.73.6.1146

Wittenborn, J. (1951). Symptom patterns in a group of mental hospital patients. *Journal of Consulting Psychology 16*, 13–17.

# CHAPTER 20

# Attention Deficit Hyperactivity Disorder

Siri Noordermeer *and* Jaap Oosterlaan

Individuals with attention deficit hyperactivity disorder (ADHD) suffer from persistent and age-inappropriate levels of inattention and/or hyperactivity-impulsivity, occurring in multiple situations, to such a degree that symptoms have a severely detrimental impact on their daily life functioning or development. Throughout the past decades, scientific interest in ADHD and knowledge about the disorder have grown exponentially. While a large body of research is available on ADHD, the number of unanswered questions remains substantial. ADHD has proved to be a heterogeneous disorder, causing a difficult challenge for research to create a consistent image of the disorder. Partly due to this heterogeneity, the past three decades have been characterized by an increase in questions and concerns about the validity of ADHD and stigmatization of patients diagnosed with the disorder (Mueller et al., 2012). This chapter covers the prevalence, course, comorbidities, and functional impact of ADHD, as well as diagnosis, treatment, and etiology and risk factors of the disorder. We hope to convey the heterogeneity and complexity of ADHD and provide an extensive and critical overview of our current understanding of the disorder.

## A Short History

It is frequently thought that ADHD is a "twenty-first-century disorder," caused by the abundant stimuli which are part of the current information technology society (e.g., TV, smartphones, social media), resulting in an information overload too intense for many children to cope with. Although a range of societal factors might potentially contribute to the number of children diagnosed with ADHD, ADHD-like symptoms were reported as early as 1902 (Spencer et al., 2007). Early reports of ADHD-like behavior were primarily focused on children's malfunctioning and mainly targeted symptoms of hyperactivity and impulsivity. For decades, these children were described as having minimal brain damage (MBD), which was later nuanced to minimal brain dysfunctioning as at that time no evidence was found for brain abnormalities. In 1968, *DSM-II* introduced a childhood mental disorder characterized by hyperactivity, labeled "hyperkinetic reaction of childhood." With the release of *DSM-III* in 1980, symptoms of inattention were also recognized as part of the disorder and even became the major focus. The condition was renamed as "attention deficit disorder," and it could either be diagnosed with or without hyperactivity. *DSM-IV* again redefined the diagnosis in 1994, distinguishing the predominantly inattentive (ADHD-I) and predominantly hyperactive-impulsive (ADHD-H) subtypes, as well as the combined subtype (ADHD-C), which describes children showing both inattentive and hyperactive-impulsive symptoms. Although debate is ongoing regarding the validity of this distinction (Coghill & Seth, 2011), the current version of *DSM* (*DSM-5*) retains these subtypes, which are now called

### Abbreviations

| | |
|---|---|
| ADHD-C | ADHD-combined |
| ADHD-H | ADHD-hyperactive/impulsive |
| ADHD-I | ADHD-inattentive |
| CCN | Cognitive control network |
| DMN | Default mode network |
| DTI | Diffusion tensor imaging |
| EWAS | Epigenome-wide association study |
| NF | Neurofeedback |
| ODD | Oppositional defiant disorder |
| SN | Salience network |
| SPECT | Single-photon emission computed tomography |

*presentations*. The eleventh edition of the alternative classification system, the *ICD-11*, includes a comparable diagnosis of attention-deficit hyperactivity, with previous editions including the diagnosis of hyperkinetic disorder, and describes a set of symptoms similar to the *DSM* combined presentation. Similar to the *DSM-5*, the *ICD-11* now also differentiates between three types: inattentive, hyperactive-impulsive, and combined.

## Prevalence, Course, Comorbidities and Functional Impact
### Prevalence

The most recent estimate, based on a large number of studies, is that 7.2% of children worldwide suffer from (any presentation of) ADHD (Thomas et al., 2015). However, prevalence rates of ADHD vary dramatically between studies. Through the years, reported rates in different countries have ranged from as low as 1% to as high as 20% among school-aged children. Some of this variability is likely attributable to a rise in clinical referrals and diagnoses throughout the years, as shown by US national surveys (Robison et al., 1999; Visser et al., 2010). However, other factors may also play a role, such as the classification system used to determine the diagnosis of ADHD. The two most commonly used diagnostic classification systems, *DSM* and *ICD*, focus on slightly different aspects of the disorder, and, even within these systems, different versions have employed different diagnostic criteria over the years. In addition, a diagnosis of ADHD requires symptoms to be present in different contexts (pervasiveness of symptoms) and to cause impairment in daily life functioning, but studies differ in terms of the adoption of these two criteria, resulting in different prevalence rates. Moreover, the use of different informants, such as clinicians or teachers, is associated with different prevalence estimates (Faraone et al., 2015). Region of study has been suggested to be associated with variability of prevalence estimates as well, but a review reported that after accounting for the aforementioned factors the prevalence of ADHD does not differ between countries in Europe, Asia, Africa, the Americas, and Australia (Faraone et al., 2015; Thomas et al., 2015). Interestingly, despite popular opinion, there is no evidence for an increase in the actual prevalence of ADHD over the past three decades (Faraone et al., 2015).

In general, boys are two to three times more likely to be diagnosed with ADHD than are girls (Ramtekkar et al., 2010; Willcutt, 2012). Among all individuals with ADHD (children and adults alike), females are more likely to meet criteria for the inattentive presentation, while males are more likely to be diagnosed with the combined presentation (Willcutt, 2012). The fact that inattentive behavior is less disturbing and burdensome for the family and school than hyperactive-impulsive behavior, combined with the fact that girls with ADHD are less likely to suffer from accompanying disruptive disorders (Spencer et al., 2007), may result in girls being underdiagnosed with ADHD. Hence, it is possible that the prevalence of ADHD may not even differ between boys and girls as much as previously thought, but rather reflects lower rates of clinical referrals in girls. This possibility is substantiated by findings of (more) equal prevalence estimates of ADHD in adult males and females (Cortese, Faraone, et al., 2016; Murray et al., 2019; Simon et al., 2009).

### Developmental Course

ADHD was initially recognized as only a childhood disorder, and it was thought to largely remit in adolescence. However, recent literature shows that in a large number of cases at least some symptoms persist into adulthood. Persistence rates are highly dependent on the definition of persistence used, with pooled estimates from follow-up studies showing that at age 25, approximately 15% of ADHD patients still meet full criteria for ADHD. Using a more lenient approach, focusing on "ADHD in partial remission," provides a much larger persistence percentage of approximately 65% (Faraone et al., 2006). A more recent follow-up study even reported persistent ADHD (meeting full criteria) in 79% of adolescents and young adults (Cheung et al., 2015).

In addition to children with ADHD persisting into adulthood, there also seems to be an adult- or a late-onset variant of the disorder, although the exact prevalence of this variant of the disorder is unclear. However, it appears to be considerable, since the available studies into (young) adults with ADHD report the percentage of late-onset cases to range between 68% and 88% (Caye et al., 2016). Interestingly, during retrospective assessment, the majority of individuals with the late-onset variant did not meet diagnostic criteria for ADHD as children, although they seem to exhibit (at least some) symptoms in adolescence (i.e., between the ages of 12 and 16; Asherson & Agnew-Blais, 2019). Since the discrepancy between boys and girls (almost) vanishes during adulthood, it may be that women are more represented in the late-onset group, given that females were more likely to show large symptom increases in adolescence rather than in childhood (Murray et al., 2019). Another possible explanation for the adult- or late-onset variant of the disorder may be that this variant in fact represents cases that remained undetected in childhood due to a lack of proper assessment or care (Taylor et al., 2021).

ADHD prevalence is estimated at 5% in young adulthood (Willcutt, 2012) and at 3–4% in adults (Fayyad et al., 2017; Polanczyk & Rohde, 2007) and in old age (> 60 years) (Michielsen et al., 2012), percentages very similar to prevalence rates in childhood and adolescence. Altogether, these numbers show a fairly consistent image of the prevalence of ADHD. Although ADHD is still best described as a disorder that originates in childhood, and often—at least partly—persists into adulthood, late-onset ADHD may account for a substantial number of cases.

*Comorbidities and Functional Impact*

More often than not, ADHD patients experience comorbid disorders and problems (Gillberg et al., 2004; Spencer et al., 2007). Externalizing disorders most frequently reported in children with ADHD include oppositional defiant disorder (ODD) and conduct disorder (CD), with estimates around 60% for ODD and about 40% for CD (Connor et al., 2010). Although often less expected, children with ADHD frequently also experience serious internalizing problems, such as mood or anxiety disorders (with estimates varying between 15% and 45%; Elia et al., 2008; Spencer et al., 2007). Other comorbidities frequently associated with pediatric or adolescent ADHD include autism spectrum disorders (65–80% show several symptoms of autistic disorder; Gillberg et al., 2004), learning disabilities including reading disorder (15–45%; Sexton et al., 2012; Spencer et al., 2007), sleep disorders (25–50%; Corkum et al., 1998), tic disorders (8–33%; Kadesjö & Gillberg, 2003; Palumbo et al., 2004; Steinhausen et al., 2006; The MTA Cooperative Group, 1999), substance use disorders (1.35–2.36 times increased chance of developing nicotine dependence or alcohol or drug abuse; Charach et al., 2011), and developmental coordination disorder (~50%; Gillberg et al., 2004). Adults with ADHD are reported to have a 1.5 to 7 times increased likelihood of developing mood, anxiety, and substance use disorders (Kessler et al., 2006).

Even in the absence of comorbid disorders, ADHD has a major impact on the patient's life, as well as on society as a whole. Children and adolescents with ADHD often suffer from poor social skills leading to conflicted peer relationships and social rejection by peers, low self-esteem, adverse academic outcomes, and increased school failure (Faraone et al., 2015). Moreover, these children and adolescents show more delinquent behavior, suffer more often from injuries and accidents, and are frequently seen as a burden on their families, where there is an increased risk for parental and family conflict. In adolescence, ADHD patients have been shown to start smoking at an earlier age and smoke more on a daily basis (Lee et al., 2011; McClernon & Kollins, 2008) and to engage in risky sexual behavior more often (Flory et al., 2006).

When looking at adult or lifetime ADHD, it is clear that the disorder has a strong negative impact on an individual's overall functioning, expressed in terms of academic and vocational underachievement, a lower socioeconomic status, marital difficulties, and general health problems such as obesity (Biederman et al., 1993, 2006; Faraone et al., 2015; Sawyer et al., 2002). Occurrence of antisocial behaviors, including theft, assault, vandalism, traffic violations, or disorderly conduct, is highly increased in adults with lifetime ADHD, and a higher number of individuals are arrested, convicted, and incarcerated (Barkley et al., 2004; Biederman et al., 2006; Küpper et al., 2012). Mental health problems are reported in the majority of adults with ADHD, including depression, anxiety disorder, antisocial personality disorder, and substance use disorder (Biederman et al., 2006; Küpper et al., 2012). In the workplace, individuals with ADHD may suffer from poor productivity, absenteeism, and general occupational underachievement or unemployment, partly as a result of other comorbid mental health problems as mentioned before (Küpper et al., 2012). In the United States, it has been shown that ADHD has a "substantial economic impact," most specifically due to extra costs in healthcare and education in children with ADHD and loss of productivity and income loss in adults (Doshi et al., 2012).

## Current Diagnostic Issues

The validity of ADHD and its three presentations is a prominent topic of discussion. Several issues can be pointed out in the current diagnostic criteria and procedures that may limit their use in clinical practice and seem to play a large role in the current controversy regarding the existence and validity of the disorder.

A first important issue is the subjective weighing of behavioral criteria to diagnose ADHD. Both symptom dimensions of ADHD—inattention and hyperactive/impulsive behavior—should be seen as parts of continua, which range from typical to severely abnormal behavior. While ADHD patients characteristically have more severe symptoms of inattention and hyperactivity/impulsivity than individuals in the "normal population," the cutoff between "normal variation" and "abnormal behavior" is rather arbitrary. In this context, *functional impairment* is a key criterion that should be fulfilled to establish the diagnosis of ADHD. However, here a second issue arises due to the subjectivity in assessing if the symptoms interfere with or cause an actual reduction in the quality of an individual's social, academic, or occupational functioning. Although impairment in itself remains a subjective criterion, it plays a pivotal role in the diagnostic process and should be reviewed critically. Another important criterion for the diagnosis of ADHD, as previously mentioned, is *pervasiveness*. This criterion posits that several symptoms should be present in at least two different situations (e.g., at home and at school or at home and at work). This is important, since pervasiveness of symptoms rules out the possibility that symptoms merely result from the situational context of the patient. With this criterion, a third issue arises, namely the time-consuming aspect of having to evaluate behavior in different settings, which generally also requires different informants. Therefore, this criterion is not always correctly assessed due to practical choices in the diagnostic process. In addition, the requirement of "several" symptoms is rather arbitrary. This is also true for the age-of-onset criterion, requiring "several" symptoms to have been present prior to the age of 12. Another issue with the latter criterion is that with a diagnostic assessment at a later age, it may be hard to adequately remember if this was the case.

Finally, another issue arises with the criterion that for a diagnosis of ADHD the symptoms should not be better explained by another mental disorder. This means that full attention should be given to *differential diagnosis*, which is, again, time-consuming and therefore not always adequately done. Symptoms of ADHD, especially inattention, are not specific to ADHD and can easily be caused by other mental disorders or result from problems in the environment. For example, children may have trouble concentrating due to in-home conflicts between their parents, or hyperactive and impulsive symptoms in an adult may better be accounted for by borderline personality disorder or mania. Somatic conditions can also be a direct cause of ADHD-like symptoms. In such cases, it is important to acknowledge the actual cause of the behavioral symptoms and target the intervention accordingly.

Several consensus guidelines emphasize the importance of strictly following standard diagnostic criteria for the diagnosis of ADHD as detailed in the *DSM* or *ICD* (Kendall et al., 2008; Pliszka, 2007; Seixas, 2013; Wolraich et al., 2011). However, important criteria including impairment, pervasiveness, and differential diagnostics are easily and often overlooked in the diagnostic process. A recent review showed that the estimated prevalence based on symptoms alone (without accounting for additional criteria such as impairment) was far higher than prevalence estimates based on full *DSM* criteria (Faraone et al., 2015). These data underline the importance of strictly adhering to diagnostic criteria to guarantee the validity of the diagnosis. Since many ADHD rating scales omit diagnostic criteria like functional impairment, all guidelines agree that assessment should always include a full clinical interview, preferably a family interview (Seixas, 2013).

Evaluating *adult* ADHD creates some extra challenges because diagnostic criteria were originally defined to evaluate children's behavior. For a long time, most symptom definitions were unmistakably targeted at children, such as "runs about or climbs excessively in situations in which it is inappropriate." It is clear that such symptoms should be adapted to match similar adult behaviors, for example focusing on subjective feelings of restlessness instead of inappropriate hyperactive behavior. While the current *DSM-5* and *ICD-11* include a few examples targeted at adolescents or adults, the previous versions of both the *DSM* and the *ICD* do not provide adapted formulations for adults. Therefore, until recently (2013 for the *DSM*; 2018 for the *ICD*), it was up to the researcher or clinician to translate the diagnostic criteria into adult behaviors, making assessment highly subjective and weakening the validity of the diagnosis in adulthood. Although specific diagnostic assessment tools for ADHD adults are being developed and translated (Kooij et al., 2019), validation studies of those instruments to assess adult ADHD are largely lacking. Another issue in the diagnostic process of adult ADHD assessment arises from the criterion that symptoms must be present before the age of 12. With increasing age it becomes more difficult to correctly remember the exact age of onset of symptoms, and opportunities to use informants from different settings (e.g., teachers, parents) are reduced.

Moreover, validity of this age-of-onset criterion is under debate, given the discovery of late-onset variant of ADHD. Overall, it is important for practitioners to keep these issues in mind while diagnosing adults with ADHD. Unfortunately, due to a lack of research on the validity of diagnostic criteria for adults, assessment of adult ADHD will remain (at least partly) subjective until diagnostic instruments for adults with proved reliability and validity are mode widely available.

Another issue that currently receives prominent attention is the validity of the two-symptom dimensions of ADHD as they are currently defined (Milich et al., 2001; Willcutt et al., 2012). While this two-dimensional approach can be useful in creating behavioral profiles of the disorder, it is unclear to what extent the current dimensions cover all variance in the disorder. The heterogeneity in research findings suggests that important factors in the classification of the disorder are still overlooked and that the current division into three presentations might not be optimal (Milich et al., 2001). It is possible that a different or complementary classification system might provide a more useful approach to guide further research into the disorder. For example, defining ADHD presentations based on not only the presence of inattentive and hyperactive-impulsive symptoms—thus conventional diagnostic criteria—but taking into account risk and protective factors, neurocognitive profiles, and comorbidities may prove useful. While yielding a more holistic view, including all these factors will likely provide more information about different etiologies that may underlie presentations, leading to a better understanding of the heterogeneity in findings and therefore being a more viable option (Pievsky & McGrath, 2018), although such an approach needs further study.

## Treatment
### Standard Treatment of ADHD

It is widely accepted that either *behavioral therapy*, *medication*, or a *combination of both* is most beneficial for the majority of patients. Most treatment guidelines recommend starting with either behavioral therapy (in preschool children or children with moderate symptom severity) or medication (in cases with severe symptoms, comorbidities, or if high levels of family stress are present) or a combination of both. If only one type of treatment is given, it is recommended to add the second type of intervention if the first does not provide sufficient improvement (Graham et al., 2011; Kendall et al., 2008; Pliszka, 2007; Wolraich et al., 2011). In all cases, psychoeducation about ADHD and the various treatment options is indicated at the start and throughout the course of treatment for children, including the child with ADHD as well as the parent. Psychoeducation seems effective in adults as well, including the adult with ADHD as well as their significant other, but lack proper investigation and warrant further research (Hirvikoski et al., 2020).

Different types of *behavioral therapy* have been recognized as well-established stand-alone treatment options in pediatric ADHD (Evans et al., 2013; Fabiano et al., 2009; Lee et al., 2012; Pelham & Fabiano, 2008), mostly by increasing desired behavior and decreasing undesired behavior using principles of positive and negative reinforcement and social learning (Faraone et al., 2015). Three types of evidence-based behavioral treatments have been identified to be successful for children with ADHD: behavioral parent training, classroom management, and peer interventions, with each targeting the child with ADHD in a different setting (Evans et al., 2013). Behavioral treatment in *adults* with ADHD is less intensively studied, but particularly cognitive-behavioral therapy, where behavior is improved via alleviation of cognitive distortions associated with ADHD's core symptoms, appears to be effective in adults with ADHD, showing comparable effects to behavioral treatments for children with ADHD (López-Pinar et al., 2018).

*Medication* treatment for pediatric as well as adult ADHD typically involves either stimulants (such as methylphenidate sold under different brand names such as Ritalin) or nonstimulants (such as atomoxetine, sold under brand name Strattera, and is believed to enhance neurotransmission of dopamine (DA) and norepinephrine (NE) in the brain (De Crescenzo et al., 2017). With regard to stimulants, the first pharmacological choice for children and adolescents is methylphenidate, while for adults amphetamines are first choice (Cortese et al., 2018). A few other pharmacological options are available, including mixed amphetamine salts and lisdexamfetamine dimesylate (LDX), but currently these are all clearly framed as second-line options (Seixas, 2013). Immediate-release stimulants exert their effects within 1 hour after ingestion and are effective for approximately 3–5 hours, while extended-release stimulants and atomoxetine are effective for 8–10 hours and only require once-daily dosing.

The beneficial effect of both stimulants and atomoxetine on ADHD symptoms has been well documented for children and adults (Cortese et al.,

2018; Faraone et al., 2015). Pharmacological treatment often not only ameliorates core symptoms, but can also have a beneficial effect on other aspects of the individual's health and functioning. For children and adolescents, effects on comorbid oppositional defiant behavior, social behavior, quality of life, academic productivity, classroom behavior, and cognitive functions have been consistently reported (Chamberlain et al., 2011; Coghill, 2010; Langberg & Becker, 2012; Molina et al., 2009; Pietrzak et al., 2006; Prasad et al., 2013; Van der Oord et al., 2008). For adults, reductions in criminal convictions, violent reoffending, traffic accidents and mortality rates, suicidal behavior, depression, and substance misuse are reported to be associated with pharmacological treatment (Kooij et al., 2019). However, for all age groups there is little and inconsistent evidence for the *long-term* beneficial effects of medication beyond 2 years of use (De Crescenzo et al., 2017; Krinzinger et al., 2019).

In general, stimulants and atomoxetine are well-tolerated drugs. Most frequently reported side effects include headache, abdominal pain, decreased appetite, and insomnia, but side effects are uncommon and generally mild (Findling, 2008). Atomoxetine is more often associated with nausea and sedation than are stimulants and may be slightly less effective, but it holds the advantage that it less likely leads to medication misuse or diversion (Findling, 2008; Pliszka, 2007) and may improve comorbid tics (Cortese et al., 2013). Stimulants and atomoxetine may sometimes lead to reductions in weight and height gain in children, possibly due to a loss of appetite (Cortese et al., 2013), although some authors have suggested that the growth reduction is related to ADHD itself (Faraone et al., 2008). So-called drug holidays (taking children off medication during weekends or holidays) are often advised as they may be helpful to normalize reductions in height and weight gain (Pliszka, 2007). For adults with ADHD specifically, a higher likelihood of discontinuation was reported, compared with children and adolescents, possibly due to the side effects of decreased appetite and insomnia (De Crescenzo et al., 2017).

While serious concerns have been raised regarding health risks for children using medication for the treatment of ADHD, most of these concerns lack scientific support. Small cardiovascular effects of stimulant and nonstimulant medication have been reported, including slightly elevated blood pressure and heart rate, but there is currently no evidence that ADHD drugs increase the risk for serious cardiovascular events in children or adults (Cortese et al., 2018; Hennissen et al., 2017; Pliszka, 2007). In addition to an increased resting heart rate and blood pressure, adults seem to also face an increased risk for transient ischemic attack, which needs further investigation (De Crescenzo et al., 2017). The validity of other concerns for pharmacological treatment in children and adolescents, including an elevated risk for suicidal thoughts, psychosis, and substance use disorders, is still largely unclear. Currently, it is known that ADHD in itself holds an elevated risk for these events, but there is no clear evidence that ADHD medication adds to this risk (Graham et al., 2011; Pliszka, 2007; van de Loo-Neus et al., 2011). In adults, there seems to be no evidence of increased suicide events or ideation, while atomoxetine may reduce comorbid anxiety but not comorbid depression (De Crescenzo et al., 2017; Kooij et al., 2019). In all cases, risk management of possible adverse effects and preexisting conditions, such as cardiac defects, is of highest concern, at the start as well as throughout treatment of children, adolescents and adults (Cortese et al., 2013; De Crescenzo et al., 2017; Graham et al., 2011; Kooij et al., 2019; Pliszka, 2007; Warren et al., 2009).

When directly comparing the efficacy of medication treatment with behavioral therapy in children, a large hallmark study (the Multimodal Treatment Study of Children with ADHD; MTA) reported that behavioral treatment is effective in reducing core symptoms of ADHD, but not as effective as a strict medication management program (The MTA Cooperative Group, 1999), which is supported by more recent studies (Van der Oord et al., 2008). Combining pharmacological treatment and behavioral therapy does not seem to have an additional effect on ADHD symptom reduction (Pliszka, 2007; Van der Oord et al., 2008), but it may have an additional effect on internalizing symptoms, social skills, parent–child relations, and reading achievement (Molina et al., 2009). Comparable findings seem to be applicable to adults, but, given the scarcity of studies into this, more research is warranted to be able to draw firm conclusions.

### Alternative Treatment Methods

Currently, behavior therapy and pharmacological treatment are the only two evidence-based treatments for ADHD. However, these treatment options offer incomplete symptom relief in more than 30% of patients (Swanson et al., 2001), behavioral therapy is relatively cost-intensive (Jensen et al., 2005), and nonpharmacological treatments are often favored by parents, leading to an increasing interest in alternative treatment options. Although none of these alternative treatment methods is sufficiently investigated to draw robust conclusions, we discuss here the most promising ones.

The role of *nutrition* in ADHD has provoked controversy in both research and media. While preliminary results suggested that ADHD might be caused by nutrition in a number of cases, more recent reports have provided new clarification and nuanced some previous conclusions. Two specific dietary elements are seen as promising targets. First, lower plasma and blood concentrations of *polyunsaturated fatty acids* have been found in children with ADHD (Gillies et al., 2012). A recent review suggest that supplementation of these acids, in particular omega-3, can alleviate ADHD symptoms in some children (Bloch & Qawasmi, 2011; Sonuga-Barke et al., 2013). Unfortunately, the reported effects are merely small, suggesting supplementation of these acids is insufficient as stand-alone treatment (Chang et al., 2018; Stevenson et al., 2014).

Second, a meta-analysis of 10 studies showed that there is evidence that some children with ADHD (~30%) may respond to a *restriction diet*, leaving out synthetic food colors or other additives (Nigg et al., 2012). However, although evidence shows that ADHD symptoms may be reduced by leaving out *artificial food colors* from the diets of subgroups of children with ADHD, large-scale studies using blind assessment are needed to draw strong conclusions (Stevenson et al., 2014). Moreover, results of these studies are difficult to interpret since children on a restriction diet are not only limited in their food intake, but also receive much more attention and structure at home, which can also have a beneficial effect on their behavior. Moreover, placebo effects cannot be ruled out in studies using a restriction diet.

Another popular alternative treatment option for ADHD is *neurofeedback (NF) training*. During NF training, children learn to control specific brainwave patterns as measured by electroencephalography (EEG), using real-time audio/video feedback. Several studies showed improvement in ADHD-related behavior after extensive NF training (Van Doren et al., 2019), leading many (commercial) healthcare suppliers to offer NF as stand-alone ADHD treatment. Unfortunately, the limited quality of current NF research prevents valid conclusions to be drawn, and NF can currently only be described as a "promising" treatment for ADHD (Cortese, Ferrin et al., 2016; Van Doren et al., 2019). The same holds for *cognitive training* (e.g., working memory training) in children with ADHD. The limited evidence available shows promising results regarding symptom improvement as rated by parents, but without generalization to classroom behavior (Rutledge et al., 2012). Finally, physical exercise may have an effect on functional outcomes in ADHD, in both motor skills and executive functioning, but more methodologically sound studies are warranted to justify any clinical recommendations (Vysniauske et al., 2020).

Taken together, behavior therapy and medication are the only evidence-based treatment options for ADHD. While many promising alternative treatment options are emerging, better-quality research is needed before valid conclusions can be drawn regarding the efficacy of such treatments (Faraone et al., 2015; Sonuga-Barke et al., 2013; Stevenson et al., 2014). Effective treatment of ADHD involves many considerations, and treatment protocols should always be tailored and evaluated on an individual basis. Personal characteristics of the patient (such as symptom severity, comorbid problems, and the patient's social environment) should be weighed together with advantages and disadvantages of the available treatment options in order to set up an individual treatment plan.

### Etiology and Risk Factors

During the past three decades, a large number of investigators have attempted to clarify the etiology of ADHD by focusing on a range of isolated etiological factors (e.g., Barkley, 1997; Sergeant, 2005; Sergeant et al., 2003). While several factors, for example heritability, have been found to play a substantial role, the "single cause" approach has proved unsuccessful in explaining even a minority of the occurrences of the disorder. Currently, ADHD is best described as a multifactorial disorder, in which a variety of factors, and combinations of these factors, contribute to the overall risk of developing the disorder. A large number of risk factors have been identified, and an increasing number of studies are investigating complex interactions between these risk factors. The current notion is that, in most cases, ADHD is caused by an interaction between risk genes and environmental factors and that there is no single risk factor that is either necessary or sufficient to explain ADHD. Currently, even with a multifactorial approach only a proportion of the variance in ADHD symptoms can be explained.

## Genetic Influences

In the etiology of ADHD, genes seem to play a vital role, with family, twin, and adoption studies consistently reporting high heritability rates. A recent review of twin studies showed a mean heritability of 74% for both children and adults, males and females, and even inattentive and hyperactive-impulsive symptoms (Faraone & Larsson, 2018). While this suggests that the disorder is for the largest part caused by risk genes, an unsatisfactorily low percentage of them have been identified so far. Over the past decades, a considerable number of studies have tried to identify specific genes associated with ADHD. Initially, genetic linkage was applied to assess which chromosomal regions are linked to ADHD, and this resulted in abundant but conflicting literature. Because that method only detects genetic variants that have large effects, the paucity of significant findings suggests that common DNA variants having a large effect on ADHD are unlikely to exist. A meta-analysis on candidate genes, selected due to a plausible link to ADHD, showed that only six of the many proposed candidate genes could consistently be linked to a risk for ADHD in children, with small effect sizes (odds ratios 1.11 to 1.33; Gizer et al., 2009). The candidate genes include DA transporter and receptor genes (*DAT1/SLC6A3, DRD4, DRD5*), serotonin transporter and receptor genes (*5-HTT/SLC6A4, HTR1B*), and the *SNAP25* gene involved in neurotransmission. For adults with ADHD, a meta-analysis reported a significant association between ADHD and a gene involved in neuronal and dendritic development (*BAIAP2*), but the effects of this gene were small (Faraone & Larsson, 2018). Several attempts have been made to obtain a complete picture of the genes involved in ADHD using genome-wide association studies (GWAS), a method in which the whole genome can be investigated rather than a small number of specifically selected genes, which allows this method to detect very small etiological effects. While GWAS studies in ADHD research have identified 85 candidate genes in total, up until now, GWAS studies have unfortunately not significantly increased our understanding of ADHD risk genes. This is because even the genes that showed genome-wide significance only showed this association with ADHD as a set with other genes, but could not be singularly linked to ADHD. A meta-analysis that assessed the more recent epigenome-wide association study (EWAS) approach in adults with ADHD, in which the entire genome is searched for epigenetic marks, reported no overall significant sites to be associated with ADHD (van Dongen et al., 2019). Rather, only cohort-specific findings were reported, and the necessity of (even larger) datasets was emphasized.

Recent studies attempted to integrate the current body of genetic findings to investigate specific mechanisms implicated in the risk for ADHD development. These studies emphasized the involvement of genes responsible for neurite development and outgrowth and DNA methylation (Faraone & Larsson, 2018; van Dongen et al., 2019). These findings suggest that, in ADHD patients, small alterations in the outgrowth of axons and dendrites in the brain caused by risk genes and epigenomic effects influencing DNA methylation at specific loci may play a substantial role in the development of the disorder (Poelmans et al., 2011).

## Environmental Risk Factors

Several environmental risk factors have been implicated in ADHD. These environmental risk factors—factors other than the genotype that can influence a child's development—generally are divided into two domains: neurobiological and psychosocial factors. *Neurobiological risk factors* often associated with ADHD can for a large part be characterized as complications during pregnancy or delivery. They include maternal smoking or alcohol use during pregnancy, eclampsia, fetal distress, premature birth, poor maternal health, and higher maternal age (Bhutta et al., 2002; Biederman & Faraone, 2005; Linnet et al., 2003). Many of these risk factors can lead to hypoxia in the fetal brain. Notably, the basal ganglia, a brain structure often implicated in ADHD, is particularly sensitive to the effects of hypoxia (Froehlich et al., 2011). *Psychosocial risk factors* often associated with ADHD include poor socioeconomic status, family dysfunction (including maltreatment, maternal mental disorders, paternal criminality, marital problems, and in-home conflict), and large family size (Banerjee et al., 2007; Biederman & Faraone, 2005). Moreover, parenting styles, specifically harsh and negative parenting, have been associated with ADHD. Previous concerns that watching too much TV at a young age may lead to ADHD-like attention problems (Christakis et al., 2004) are not supported by scientific studies (Banerjee et al., 2007).

Importantly, while many of these factors are strongly associated with the presence of ADHD in a family, they should currently still be considered correlates rather than *causes* of ADHD. For example, while maternal smoking may directly cause

ADHD through neurobiological alterations in the fetal brain, it is also possible that the mother's predisposition to smoke during pregnancy is a result of her having ADHD or a vulnerability to it, which is transferred to the child genetically. Moreover, it is important to state that while the above-mentioned risk factors are linked to an increased risk for the development of ADHD, many children who have experienced one or more of these risk factors do not develop ADHD, and, conversely, not all children with ADHD show one or more of these risk factors. Thus, even though these risk factors may be important, their presence of is only true for a limited proportion of individuals with ADHD, and it may be that other confounding factors are involved, such as parental ADHD and interactions with environmental factors, thus warranting more research (Thapar et al., 2013).

*Gene by Environment Interactions*

While a variety of risk genes and environmental factors have been linked to ADHD, none of them fully explains the risk for developing the disorder. For example, it is possible that in a monozygotic twin pair, sharing 100% of their genotype at birth, one child develops ADHD while the other does not. Such a situation would result from a "gene by environment interaction" (G×E), meaning that the effect of specific genes may vary due to differences in the environment and that the very interaction between specific genes and environmental factors may be the main mechanism by which environmental factors increase the risk for ADHD. For example, one twin might have experienced hypoxia during birth while the other did not, resulting in one twin with and one without ADHD. Another example of G×E is that a specific environment (such as maternal smoking or alcohol use during pregnancy) may be damaging to many infants, but more specifically so to those infants who carry specific risk genes making them more vulnerable to the adverse effects of this environment.

To date, due to a large variation in implicated risk genes and environmental factors, most hypotheses on G×E have only received attention in a single study, resulting in literature with limited overlap and low levels of reproduced findings (Faraone et al., 2015; Thapar & Cooper, 2016). A literature review showed that, overall, psychosocial factors seem to interact with ADHD risk genes, primarily with *DAT1* and *5-HTT*, in the development of the disorder (Nigg et al., 2010). Unfortunately, due to limited overlap between studies it is unclear whether this interaction exists for all psychosocial factors or only specific ones. For neurobiological factors, even less overlap was found, although the interaction between *5-HTT* and stress has been associated with specific behaviors of hyperactivity and impulsivity (Faraone et al., 2015). Findings for maternal smoking or alcohol use during pregnancy are highly inconsistent and suggest that if an interaction with risk genes occurs, this may cause hyperactive behavior, but not necessarily the full range of ADHD symptoms.

*Heterogeneity in Etiology*

Taken together, while some risk genes and environmental factors for ADHD have been identified and replicated, possibly a far higher number remains unknown, and we have only just begun to unravel the complex interactions between these different risk factors. One of the causes for the large inconsistency between findings so far may be the heterogeneity of behavioral symptoms of the disorder. In linking specific risk genes to a behavioral outcome (i.e., phenotype), heterogeneity in phenotype considerably reduces the power to find risk genes. In this context, researchers have suggested the field move toward identification of endophenotypes or intermediate phenotypes (Castellanos & Tannock, 2002). *Endophenotypes* refer to heritable traits that are supposed to be more strongly associated with the genotype than the phenotypical manifestation and less influenced by environmental factors than the phenotype. Examples of endophenotypes are neurocognitive deficits or specific neurobiological abnormalities characteristic for ADHD. Identifying endophenotypes may provide useful directions in the search for candidate risk genes for the disorder but may also be useful in itself to understand underlying mechanisms of dysfunction. Although identifying risk genes may not uncover the full complex multifactorial etiology of the disorder, it may be a first step toward clarifying the neurobiological underpinnings of ADHD.

## Neurocognitive and Neurobiological Abnormalities

Given the high heritability rates of ADHD, the disorder is suspected to have an important neurobiological basis. With advancing techniques, considerable progress has been made in unraveling the neurobiological underpinnings of the disorder, although a lot of uncertainty still exists. This field of research can roughly be divided into two domains: abnormalities in neurocognitive functioning and neurobiological abnormalities as measured by neuroimaging techniques.

*Neurocognitive Abnormalities*

The search for neurocognitive deficits in ADHD has been on the fast track in recent years, resulting in a large number of studies and a variety of neurocognitive functions suggested to be deficient in ADHD. Early neurocognitive studies into ADHD have primarily attempted to objectify the symptoms of inattention, motor restlessness, and impulsivity (e.g., Corkum & Siegel, 1993; Kuehne et al., 1987; Porrino et al., 1983). This has proved to be a fruitful approach as patients with ADHD are often found to be impaired on objective measures of sustained attention, motor restlessness, and impulsivity (Alderson et al., 2007; Huang-Pollock et al., 2012; Huizenga et al., 2009; Losier et al., 1996; Rapport et al., 2009). However, findings remain inconsistent. More recent neurocognitive studies adopted a broader perspective and investigated a large variety of neurocognitive functions in children and adults with ADHD. The most consistently found deficits involve executive functions and include impairments in behavioral inhibition, planning, vigilance, and working memory (Faraone et al., 2015). With regard to nonexecutive deficits, impairments in timing, reaction time variability, and decision-making have been consistently related to ADHD (Thapar & Cooper, 2016). Furthermore, problems with delay aversion, such as making suboptimal choices and overestimating the magnitude of immediate rewards over delayed rewards, are often seen in ADHD patients. Given the large variety of neurocognitive deficits implicated in ADHD, it is possible that a more general deficit may underlie poor performance across tasks. Some evidence exists that a general processing deficit (Alderson et al., 2007), attentional lapses during task performance (Tamm et al., 2012), or motivational deficits (Konrad et al., 2000) may underlie poor performance on many neurocognitive tasks. However, more research is needed to clarify this issue.

It is interesting to note that while a number of ADHD patients are impaired on one or two neurocognitive functions, another substantial group of patients does not show any neurocognitive deficit at all, and very few show deficits in all functions (Faraone et al., 2015; Thapar & Cooper, 2016). Moreover, neurocognitive problems seem to be independent of the developmental course of ADHD (i.e., persistence vs. remission of symptoms later in life; van Lieshout et al., 2013), suggesting that these deficits may not share the same etiology as the behavioral symptoms of the disorder or are more sensitive to developmental changes over time. Altogether, this is an interesting issue that deserves more attention in future research.

*Neurobiological Abnormalities*

Neuroimaging techniques can be useful tools to elucidate the neurobiological mechanisms that underlie the behavioral and neurocognitive deficits observed in ADHD. One of the most used imaging techniques is magnetic resonance imaging (MRI), allowing in vivo 3D imaging of brain structure and function.

Brain volumes, as measured by structural MRI, have been studied for decades, and many brain regions have been suggested to be reduced in ADHD. In general, ADHD patients often show a reduced overall brain volume (Hoogman et al., 2017) and reduced thickness of the cortex (Hoogman et al., 2019) compared to healthy controls. Reductions in more specific regions are also observed; according to a mega-analysis, most consistently in structures within the basal ganglia (including the striatum), amygdala, and hippocampus (Hoogman et al., 2017). Other structures that have been reported in previous meta-analyses include the ventromedial orbitofrontal and medial prefrontal cortex, corpus callosum, anterior cingulate cortex, and cerebellum (Frodl & Skokauskas, 2012; Valera et al., 2007). Although older studies reported volume reductions to be often more pronounced in the right hemisphere (Frodl & Skokauskas, 2012; Valera et al., 2007), the more recent mega-analysis showed that reductions in (at least) the caudate and putamen are bilateral rather than unilateral (Hoogman et al., 2017).

Diffusion tensor imaging (DTI) is a relatively new MRI technique allowing in vivo measurement of the microstructural integrity of brain white matter. Despite the significant number of DTI studies being performed, results are still somewhat limited by methodological issues, such as head motion (Aoki et al., 2018). Meta-analyses in DTI mainly focus on the predominantly used characteristic fractional anisotropy (FA), which reflects white matter microarchitecture by assessing the spherical or isotropic diffusion (Aoki et al., 2018; van Ewijk et al., 2012). Alterations appear to be widespread, including frontal, striatal, and cerebellar regions, consistent with other structural imaging findings, and may be present in terms of significantly lower and higher FA values in individuals with ADHD.

The latter seems to be driven by the methodological approach, since especially whole-brain approaches show mixed findings, while tract-based approaches consistently show decreased FA.

In general, structural brain abnormalities in ADHD are viewed as reflecting a developmental delay rather than a static deficit. Converging evidence shows that volume reductions and abnormal white matter integrity may normalize around mid to late adolescence, most particularly so in (structures within) the basal ganglia (Hoogman et al., 2017, 2019). Notably, the explorative life span modeling approach as used by Hoogman and colleagues (2017, 2019) to study longitudinal development in large, cross-sectional samples suggested a delay of maturation and a delay of degeneration, which is in line with a large longitudinal study that showed a developmental delay in cortical thickness in children with ADHD (Shaw et al., 2007). In the latter, the authors showed that, in typically developing children, the development of cortical thickness follows a growth curve described by an increase in thickness during childhood, reaching peak thickness around 7–8 years of age, and a subsequent decrease in thickness during adolescence. ADHD patients showed a similarly shaped growth curve that was delayed by approximately 3 years, reaching peak thickness around 10–11 years of age. However, even though the absence of differences in brain characteristics in adults is quite clear and suggests a normalization process, this must be interpreted with some caution since the majority of studies have been cross-sectional rather than longitudinal. Taken together, these results suggest that ADHD might—at least partly—be due to a delay in brain maturation and that some or even all of the brain abnormalities in ADHD might resolve in adolescence or adulthood. Independent of this catch-up in brain maturation, long-term pharmacological treatment seems to have an additional positive effect on brain development in children with ADHD in that volume reductions are less pronounced and have sometimes even normalized in medicated children compared to treatment-naïve children (Frodl & Skokauskas, 2012; Schweren et al., 2012). It may be noteworthy that direct associations between pharmacological treatment and brain volumes have not been found in the mega-analysis (Hoogman et al., 2017), possibly due to normalizing effects being too local.

Using functional MRI, brain activation can be investigated during performance of cognitive tasks. Interestingly, regions with abnormal activation in ADHD patients largely overlap with brain regions that are found to be reduced in volume, and studies combining structural and functional approaches show intercorrelations between abnormalities. During tasks that tap into cognitive processes such as attention, response inhibition, and reward anticipation, reductions in activity are most frequently found in frontal, parietal, and temporal brain regions as well as the basal ganglia (Cortese et al., 2012; Dickstein et al., 2006; Hart et al., 2013).

In line with findings of altered brain activity in ADHD patients, electroencephalography (EEG) studies show abnormal electrical brain activity in children, adolescents, and adults with ADHD. The P300, an event-related potential (ERP) component thought to represent attentional and executive functioning, has a decreased amplitude in patients with ADHD (Szuromi et al., 2011). Also during rest, patients with ADHD show abnormal electrical brain activity compared to healthy controls. More specifically, increased theta activity (associated with drowsiness or cortical underactivation) and reduced beta activity (associated with a less attentive state) are often found, indicative of brain immaturity. It is possible that this theta-to-beta ratio reflects a developmental delay in childhood ADHD since replication of EEG abnormalities in adults with ADHD is largely lacking (Arns et al., 2013; Saad et al., 2018).

Positron emission tomography (PET) and single photon emission computed tomography (SPECT) have been used to study the neurochemistry of the ADHD brain. Components of catecholamine signaling systems are encoded by risk genes implicated in ADHD and play a large role in the neurochemistry of the disorder (Caylak, 2012; Durston & Konrad, 2007; Madras et al., 2005). One of these components, DA, is highly active in the striatum, and striatal DA levels play a pivotal role in the regulation of psychomotor activity and reward-seeking behavior (Spencer et al., 2005). However, even though a meta-analysis of PET and SPECT studies focusing on striatal DA transporter alterations showed a 14% higher DA transporter density in ADHD in the striatum, this does not mean it is specific for ADHD. Interestingly, striatal DA transporter density in ADHD was associated with previous psychostimulant exposure, thus the high DA transporter density may be a consequence of previous stimulant treatment rather than a characteristic of ADHD (Fusar-Poli et al., 2012).

Another component implicated in ADHD is NE, which plays an important role in the regulation of attention and behavior and is mainly effective in the (pre)frontal cortex (Arnsten & Li, 2005; Madras et al., 2005). PET studies have shown dysregulation of both DA and NE in ADHD and suggest underactivity of these neurotransmitters in cortical regions but overactivity in subcortical regions (Ernst et al., 1998; Fusar-Poli et al., 2012; Madras et al., 2005; Spencer et al., 2005; Swanson et al., 1998). Most effective pharmacological treatments for ADHD are thought to ameliorate behavioral symptoms of the disorder by optimizing neurotransmission in catecholamine signaling systems, consequently normalizing DA and NE levels in the striatum and frontal cortex (Arnsten & Li, 2005; Madras et al., 2005).

*Disturbed Connectivity*

Abnormalities in brain structure and function are predominantly found in (pre)frontal cortical regions and the basal ganglia. These findings have led to a prominent theory that neurobiological deficits in ADHD are mainly located in the so-called frontostriatal circuit (Bush et al., 2005; Durston & Konrad, 2007), which includes brain regions in and between the frontal cortex and the striatum, a component within the basal ganglia. Concurrent with this theory, the perspective on neuropathology in ADHD has shifted from identifying local deficiencies to studying connectivity between brain regions. Brain regions are interconnected through a large number of white matter tracts and can constitute a functional network of activation during a cognitive task. Consequently, one local deficiency (either cortical or subcortical) could disturb the whole functional network, indirectly causing a reduction in brain activation in another, more distant brain region and its functioning.

Structural as well as functional brain connectivity can be measured using various MRI techniques. Findings of DTI studies show structural alterations in several white matter tracts in children and adults with ADHD, including decreased microstructural organization in frontostriatal tracts (Aoki et al., 2018). Findings from functional connectivity studies suggest that, during rest as well as during cognitive tasks, ADHD patients display altered connectivity between brain regions, but findings seem to be affected by study approach. A theory-driven meta-analysis focusing on four established brain networks, including the default mode network (DMN), the cognitive control network (CCN), the salience network (SN), and the affective/motivational network (AMN), showed altered connectivity in the DMN (Sutcubasi et al., 2020). Specifically, in children and adolescents, ADHD was associated with both altered within-DMN connectivity and altered connectivity between DMN and the CCN, SN, and AMN. In adults, ADHD was similarly associated with altered within-DMN connectivity, but altered connectivity between DMN and other brain networks was only present for the CCN. However, a theory-free approach, including all resting-state connectivity studies, showed no spatial convergence of ADHD-related hyper- or hypoconnectivity in the brain (Cortese et al., 2021), although post hoc meta-analysis showed that the left superior temporal gyrus had a consistently altered connectivity, with evidence of both hypo- and hyperconnectivity. While connectivity research in ADHD is still relatively new, it is an important topic in research and shows potential in unraveling the neurobiological underpinnings of the disorder.

## Conclusion

ADHD is one of the most frequently diagnosed childhood psychiatric disorders and is known to often persist into or even emerge during adulthood, causing severe impairment in the patient, in the patient's family and social environment, and in school or work functioning. This chapter has summarized the current knowledge on different aspects of ADHD. Advancement has been made in the clinical conceptualization of ADHD throughout the past century, and a standard treatment protocol is now well established, encompassing behavioral treatment and/or medication. Alternative treatment options are sought, but well-setup and replicated studies proving its efficacy are still lacking. Many factors have been identified that may play a role in the etiology and development of the disorder, including several risk genes, environmental factors, neurocognitive deficits, and brain abnormalities. However, a coherent model integrating all these factors is still missing, although it is clear that this model should include a multitude of diverse factors.

In this chapter, we have emphasized the important role of etiological and phenotypical heterogeneity, which has created a challenge in the diagnosis of ADHD as well as in research into the different mechanisms underlying the disorder. This heterogeneity in research findings might indicate that the current classification of ADHD and its three presentations may—in spite of being clinically valuable—not provide optimal guidance for identifying the underlying mechanisms. However, in research as well as clinical practice, diagnostic criteria for ADHD are often misinterpreted or applied very loosely. This issue should be worked out first, before new advancements can be made in resolving current heterogeneity and lack of clarity in the etiology and clinical manifestation of the disorder. The present shift in research into ADHD from a categorical approach toward a spectrum of symptoms approach may prove valuable and informative, both for clinical practice and scientific research.

## References

Alderson, R. M., Rapport, M. D., & Kofler, M. J. (2007). Attention-deficit/hyperactivity disorder and behavioral inhibition: A meta-analytic review of the stop-signal paradigm. *Journal of Abnormal Child Psychology, 35*(5), 745–758. https://doi.org/10.1007/s10802-007-9131-6

Aoki, Y., Cortese, S., & Castellanos, F. X. (2018). Research review: Diffusion tensor imaging studies of attention-deficit/hyperactivity disorder: Meta-analyses and reflections on head motion. *J Child Psychol Psychiatry, 59*(3), 193–202. https://doi.org/10.1111/jcpp.12778

Arns, M., Conners, C. K., & Kraemer, H. C. (2013). A decade of EEG Theta/Beta Ratio Research in ADHD: A meta-analysis. *Journal of Attention Disorders, 17*(5), 374–383. https://doi.org/10.1177/1087054712460087

Arnsten, A. F., & Li, B. M. (2005). Neurobiology of executive functions: Catecholamine influences on prefrontal cortical functions. *Biological Psychiatry, 57*(11), 1377–1384. https://doi.org/10.1016/j.biopsych.2004.08.019

Asherson, P., & Agnew-Blais, J. (2019). Annual Research Review: Does late-onset attention-deficit/hyperactivity disorder exist? *Journal of Child Psychology and Psychiatry, 60*(4), 333–352. https://doi.org/10.1111/jcpp.13020

Banerjee, T. D., Middleton, F., & Faraone, S. V. (2007). Environmental risk factors for attention-deficit hyperactivity disorder. *Acta Paediatrics, 96*(9), 1269–1274. https://doi.org/10.1111/j.1651-2227.2007.00430.x

Barkley, R. A. (1997). Behavioral inhibition, sustained attention, and executive functions: Constructing a unifying theory of ADHD. *Psychological Bulletin, 121*(1), 65.

Barkley, R. A., Fischer, M., Smallish, L., & Fletcher, K. (2004). Young adult follow-up of hyperactive children: Antisocial activities and drug use. *Journal of Child Psychology and Psychiatry and Allied Disciplines, 45*(2), 195–211. http://www.ncbi.nlm.nih.gov/pubmed/14982236

Bhutta, A. T., Cleves, M. A., Casey, P. H., Cradock, M. M., & Anand, K. J. (2002). Cognitive and behavioral outcomes of school-aged children who were born preterm: A meta-analysis. *Journal of the American Medical Association, 288*(6), 728–737. https://doi.org/jma10039 [pii]

Biederman, J., & Faraone, S. V. (2005). Attention-deficit hyperactivity disorder [Review]. *Lancet, 366*(9481), 237–248. https://doi.org/10.1016/S0140-6736(05)66915-2

Biederman, J., Faraone, S. V., Spencer, T., Wilens, T., Norman, D., Lapey, K. A., Mick, E., Lehman, B. K., & Doyle, A. (1993). Patterns of psychiatric comorbidity, cognition, and psychosocial functioning in adults with attention deficit hyperactivity disorder. *American Journal of Psychiatry, 150*(12), 1792–1798. http://www.ncbi.nlm.nih.gov/pubmed/8238632

Biederman, J., Monuteaux, M. C., Mick, E., Spencer, T., Wilens, T. E., Silva, J. M., Snyder, L. E., & Faraone, S. V. (2006). Young adult outcome of attention deficit hyperactivity disorder: A controlled 10-year follow-up study. *Psychological Medicine, 36*(2), 167–179. https://doi.org/S003329170 5006410

Bloch, M. H., & Qawasmi, A. (2011). Omega-3 fatty acid supplementation for the treatment of children with attention-deficit/hyperactivity disorder symptomatology: Systematic review and meta-analysis. *Journal of the American Academy of Child and Adolescent Psychiatry, 50*(10), 991–1000. https://doi.org/10.1016/j.jaac.2011.06.008

Bush, G., Valera, E. M., & Seidman, L. J. (2005). Functional neuroimaging of attention-deficit/hyperactivity disorder: A review and suggested future directions. *Biological Psychiatry, 57*(11), 1273–1284.

Castellanos, F. X., & Tannock, R. (2002). Neuroscience of attention-deficit/hyperactivity disorder: The search for endophenotypes. *Nature Reviews. Neuroscience, 3*(8), 617–628.

Caye, A., Swanson, J., Thapar, A., Sibley, M., Arseneault, L., Hechtman, L., Arnold, L. E., Niclasen, J., Moffitt, T., & Rohde, L. A. (2016). Life span studies of ADHD: Conceptual challenges and predictors of persistence and outcome. *Current Psychiatry Reports, 18*(12), 111.

Caylak, E. (2012). Biochemical and genetic analyses of childhood attention deficit/hyperactivity disorder. *American Journal of Medical Genetics. Part B, Neuropsychiatric Genetics, 159B*(6), 613–627. https://doi.org/10.1002/ajmg.b.32077

Chamberlain, S. R., Robbins, T. W., Winder-Rhodes, S., Muller, U., Sahakian, B. J., Blackwell, A. D., & Barnett, J. H. (2011). Translational approaches to frontostriatal dysfunction in attention-deficit/hyperactivity disorder using a computerized neuropsychological battery. *Biological Psychiatry, 69*(12), 1192–1203. https://doi.org/10.1016/j.biopsych.2010.08.019

Chang, J. P., Su, K. P., Mondelli, V., & Pariante, C. M. (2018). Omega-3 polyunsaturated fatty acids in youths with attention deficit hyperactivity disorder: A systematic review and meta-analysis of clinical trials and biological studies. *Neuropsychopharmacology, 43*(3), 534–545.

Charach, A., Yeung, E., Climans, T., & Lillie, E. (2011). Childhood attention-deficit/hyperactivity disorder and future substance use disorders: Comparative meta-analyses. *Journal of the American Academy of Child and Adolescent Psychiatry, 50*(1), 9–21. https://doi.org/10.1016/j.jaac.2010.09.019

Cheung, C. H., Rijdijk, F., McLoughlin, G., Faraone, S. V., Asherson, P., & Kuntsi, J. (2015). Childhood predictors of adolescent and young adult outcome in ADHD. *Journal of Psychiatric Research, 62*, 92–100.

Christakis, D. A., Zimmerman, F. J., DiGiuseppe, D. L., & McCarty, C. A. (2004). Early television exposure and subsequent attentional problems in children. *Pediatrics, 113*(4), 708–713.

Coghill, D. (2010). The impact of medications on quality of life in attention-deficit hyperactivity disorder: A systematic review. *CNS Drugs, 24*(10), 843–866. https://doi.org/10.2165/11537450-000000000-00000

Coghill, D., & Seth, S. (2011). Do the diagnostic criteria for ADHD need to change? Comments on the preliminary proposals of the DSM-5 ADHD and Disruptive Behavior Disorders Committee. *European Child and Adolescent Psychiatry, 20*(2), 75–81. https://doi.org/10.1007/s00787-010-0142-4

Connor, D. F., Steeber, J., & McBurnett, K. (2010). A review of attention-deficit/hyperactivity disorder complicated by symptoms of oppositional defiant disorder or conduct disorder. *Journal of Developmental and Behavioral Pediatrics*,

31(5), 427–440. https://doi.org/10.1097/DBP.0b013e318 1e121bd

Corkum, P., & Siegel, L. S. (1993). Is the continuous performance task a valuable research tool for use with children with attention-deficit/hyperactivity disorder? *Journal of Child Psychology and Psychiatry, 34*(7), 1217–1239.

Corkum, P., Tannock, R., & Moldofsky, H. (1998). Sleep disturbances in children with attention-deficit/hyperactivity disorder. *Journal of the American Academy of Child and Adolescent Psychiatry, 37*(6), 637–646. https://doi.org/S0890-8567(09)63074-4

Cortese, S., Adamo, N., Del Giovane, C., Mohr-Jensen, C., Hayes, A. J., Carucci, S., Atkinson, L. Z., Tessari, L., Banaschewski, T., Coghill, D., Hollis, C., Simonoff, E., Zuddas, A., Barbui, C., Purgato, M., Steinhausen, H. C., Shokraneh, F., Xia, J., & Cipriani, A. (2018). Comparative efficacy and tolerability of medications for attention-deficit hyperactivity disorder in children, adolescents, and adults: A systematic review and network meta-analysis. *Lancet Psychiatry, 5*(9), 727–738.

Cortese, S., Aoki, Y. Y., Itahashi, T., Castellanos, F. X., & Eickhoff, S. B. (2021). Systematic review and meta-analysis: Resting-state functional magnetic resonance imaging studies of attention-deficit/hyperactivity disorder. *Journal of the American Academy of Child and Adolescent Psychiatry, 60*(1), 61–75. https://doi.org/10.1016/j.jaac.2020.08.014

Cortese, S., Faraone, S. V., Bernardi, S., Wang, S., & Blanco, C. (2016). Gender differences in adult attention-deficit/hyperactivity disorder: Results from the National Epidemiologic Survey on Alcohol and Related Conditions (NESARC). *Journal of Clinical Psychiatry, 77*(4), e421–428. https://doi.org/10.4088/JCP.14m09630

Cortese, S., Ferrin, M., Brandeis, D., Holtmann, M., Aggensteiner, P., Daley, D., Santosh, P., Simonoff, E., Stevenson, J., Stringaris, A., & Sonuga-Barke, E. J. (2016). Neurofeedback for attention-deficit/hyperactivity disorder: Meta-analysis of clinical and neuropsychological outcomes from randomized controlled trials. *Journal of the American Academy of Child and Adolescent Psychiatry, 55*(6), 444–455. https://doi.org/10.1016/j.jaac.2016.03.007

Cortese, S., Holtmann, M., Banaschewski, T., Buitelaar, J., Coghill, D., Danckaerts, M., Dittmann, R. W., Graham, J., Taylor, E., & Sergeant, J. (2013). Practitioner review: Current best practice in the management of AEs during treatment with ADHD medications in children and adolescents. *Journal of Child Psychology and Psychiatry and Allied Disciplines.* https://doi.org/10.1111/jcpp.12036

Cortese, S., Kelly, C., Chabernaud, C., Proal, E., Di Martino, A., Milham, M. P., & Castellanos, F. X. (2012). Toward systems neuroscience of ADHD: A meta-analysis of 55 fMRI studies. *American Journal of Psychiatry.* https://doi.org/10.1176/appi.ajp.2012.11101521

De Crescenzo, F., Cortese, S., Adamo, N., & Janiri, L. (2017). Pharmacological and non-pharmacological treatment of adults with ADHD: A meta-review. *Evidence Based Mental Health, 20*(1), 4. https://doi.org/10.1136/eb-2016-102415

Dickstein, S. G., Bannon, K., Castellanos, F. X., & Milham, M. P. (2006). The neural correlates of attention deficit hyperactivity disorder: An ALE meta-analysis. *Journal of Child Psychology and Psychiatry and Allied Disciplines, 47*(10), 1051–1062. https://doi.org/JCPP1671 [pii] 10.1111/j.1469-7610.2006.01671.x

Doshi, J. A., Hodgkins, P., Kahle, J., Sikirica, V., Cangelosi, M. J., Setyawan, J., Erder, M. H., & Neumann, P. J. (2012). Economic impact of childhood and adult attention-deficit/hyperactivity disorder in the United States. *Journal of the American Academy of Child and Adolescent Psychiatry, 51*(10), 990–1002. https://doi.org/10.1016/j.jaac.2012.07.008S0 890-8567(12)00538-2 [pii]

Durston, S., & Konrad, K. (2007). Integrating genetic, psychopharmacological and neuroimaging studies: A converging methods approach to understanding the neurobiology of ADHD. *Developmental Review, 27*(3), 374–395.

Elia, J., Ambrosini, P., & Berrettini, W. (2008). ADHD characteristics: I. Concurrent co-morbidity patterns in children & adolescents. *Child and Adolescent Psychiatry and Mental Health, 2*(1), 15. https://doi.org/10.1186/1753-2000-2-15

Ernst, M., Zametkin, A. J., Matochik, J. A., Jons, P. H., & Cohen, R. M. (1998). DOPA decarboxylase activity in attention deficit hyperactivity disorder adults. A [fluorine-18] fluorodopa positron emission tomographic study. *Journal of Neuroscience, 18*(15), 5901–5907.

Evans, S. W., Owens Js Fau - Bunford, N., & Bunford, N. (2013). Evidence-based psychosocial treatments for children and adolescents with attention-deficit/hyperactivity disorder. (1537-4424 (Electronic)).

Fabiano, G. A., Pelham, W. E., Jr., Coles, E. K., Gnagy, E. M., Chronis-Tuscano, A., & O'Connor, B. C. (2009). A meta-analysis of behavioral treatments for attention-deficit/hyperactivity disorder. *Clinical Psychology Review, 29*(2), 129–140. https://doi.org/10.1016/j.cpr.2008.11.001

Faraone, S. V., Asherson, P., Banaschewski, T., Biederman, J., Buitelaar, J. K., Ramos-Quiroga, J. A., Rohde, L. A., Sonuga-Barke, E. J. S., Tannock, R., & Franke, B. (2015). Attention-deficit/hyperactivity disorder [Primer]. *Nature Reviews Disease Primers, 15020.* https://doi.org/10.1038/nrdp.2015.20

Faraone, S. V., Biederman, J., & Mick, E. (2006). The age-dependent decline of attention deficit hyperactivity disorder: A meta-analysis of follow-up studies. *Psychological Medicine, 36*(2), 159–165. https://doi.org/S003329170500471X [pii] 10.1017/S003329170500471X

Faraone, S. V., Biederman, J., Morley, C. P., & Spencer, T. J. (2008). Effect of stimulants on height and weight: A review of the literature. *Journal of the American Academy of Child and Adolescent Psychiatry, 47*(9), 994–1009. https://doi.org/10.1097/CHI.ObO13e31817eOea7

Faraone, S. V., & Larsson, H. (2018). Genetics of attention deficit hyperactivity disorder. *Molecular Psychiatry.* https://doi.org/10.1038/s41380-018-0070-0

Fayyad, J., Sampson, N. A., Hwang, I., Adamowski, T., Aguilar-Gaxiola, S., Al-Hamzawi, A., . . . World Health Organization Mental Health Surveys Committee. (2017). The descriptive epidemiology of DSM-IV Adult ADHD in the World Health Organization World Mental Health Surveys. *ADHD Attention Deficit and Hyperactivity Disorders, 9*(1), 47–65. https://doi.org/10.1007/s12402-016-0208-3

Findling, R. L. (2008). Evolution of the treatment of attention-deficit/hyperactivity disorder in children: A review. *Clinical Therapeutics, 30*(5), 942–957. https://doi.org/10.1016/j.clinthera.2008.05.006

Flory, K., Molina, B. S. G., Pelham Jr, W. E., Gnagy, E., & Smith, B. (2006). Childhood ADHD predicts risky sexual behavior in young adulthood. *Journal of Clinical Child and Adolescent Psychology, 35*(4), 571–577.

Frodl, T., & Skokauskas, N. (2012). Meta-analysis of structural MRI studies in children and adults with attention deficit hyperactivity disorder indicates treatment effects. *Acta Psychiatrica Scandinavica, 125*(2), 114–126. https://doi.org/10.1111/j.1600-0447.2011.01786.x

Froehlich, T. E., Anixt, J. S., Loe, I. M., Chirdkiatgumchai, V., Kuan, L., & Gilman, R. C. (2011). Update on environmental risk factors for attention-deficit/hyperactivity disorder. *Current Psychiatry Reports, 13*(5), 333–344. https://doi.org/10.1007/s11920-011-0221-3

Fusar-Poli, P., Rubia, K., Rossi, G., Sartori, G., & Balottin, U. (2012). Striatal dopamine transporter alterations in ADHD: Pathophysiology or adaptation to psychostimulants? A meta-analysis. *American Journal of Psychiatry, 169*(3), 264–272. https://doi.org/10.1176/appi.ajp.2011.11060940

Gillberg, C., Gillberg, I. C., Rasmussen, P., Kadesjo, B., Soderstrom, H., Rastam, M., Johnson, M., Rothenberger, A., & Niklasson, L. (2004). Co-existing disorders in ADHD—implications for diagnosis and intervention. *European Child and Adolescent Psychiatry, 13 Suppl 1*, I80–192. https://doi.org/10.1007/s00787-004-1008-4

Gillies, D., Sinn, J., Lad, S. S., Leach, M. J., & Ross, M. J. (2012). Polyunsaturated fatty acids (PUFA) for attention deficit hyperactivity disorder (ADHD) in children and adolescents. *Cochrane Database of Systematic Reviews, 7*, CD007986. https://doi.org/10.1002/14651858.CD007986.pub2

Gizer, I. R., Ficks, C., & Waldman, I. D. (2009). Candidate gene studies of ADHD: A meta-analytic review. *Human Genetics, 126*(1), 51–90. https://doi.org/10.1007/s00439-009-0694-x

Graham, J., Banaschewski, T., Buitelaar, J., Coghill, D., Danckaerts, M., Dittmann, R. W., . . . Taylor, E. (2011). European guidelines on managing adverse effects of medication for ADHD. *European Child and Adolescent Psychiatry, 20*(1), 17–37. https://doi.org/10.1007/s00787-010-0140-6

Hart, H., Radua, J., Nakao, T., Mataix-Cols, D., & Rubia, K. (2013). Meta-analysis of functional magnetic resonance imaging studies of inhibition and attention in attention-deficit/hyperactivity disorder: Exploring task-specific, stimulant medication, and age effects. *JAMA Psychiatry, 70*(2), 185–198. https://doi.org/10.1001/jamapsychiatry.2013.277

Hennissen, L., Bakker, M. J., Banaschewski, T., Carucci, S., Coghill, D., Danckaerts, M., Dittmann, R. W., Hollis, C., Kovshoff, H., McCarthy, S., Nagy, P., Sonuga-Barke, E., Wong, I. C., Zuddas, A., Rosenthal, E., & Buitelaar, J. K. (2017). Cardiovascular effects of stimulant and non-stimulant medication for children and adolescents with ADHD: A systematic review and meta-analysis of trials of methylphenidate, amphetamines and atomoxetine. *CNS Drugs, 31*(3), 199–215.

Hirvikoski, T., Lindström, T., Carlsson, J., Waaler, E., Jokinen, J., & Bölte, S. (2020). Psychoeducational groups for adults with ADHD and their significant others (PEGASUS): A pragmatic multicenter and randomized controlled trial. *European Psychiatry, 44*, 141–152. https://doi.org/10.1016/j.eurpsy.2017.04.005

Hoogman, M., Bralten, J., Hibar, D. P., Mennes, M., Zwiers, M. P., Schweren, L. S., . . . Franke, B. (2017). Subcortical brain volume differences in participants with attention deficit hyperactivity disorder in children and adults: A cross-sectional mega-analysis. *Lancet Psychiatry*. https://doi.org/10.1016/s2215-0366(17)30049-4

Hoogman, M., Muetzel, R., Guimaraes, J. P., Shumskaya, E., Mennes, M., Zwiers, M. P., . . . Franke, B. (2019). Brain imaging of the cortex in ADHD: A coordinated analysis of large-scale clinical and population-based samples. *American Journal of Psychiatry, 176*(7), 531–542.

Huang-Pollock, C. L., Karalunas, S. L., Tam, H., & Moore, A. N. (2012). Evaluating vigilance deficits in ADHD: A meta-analysis of CPT performance. *Journal of Abnormal Psychology, 121*(2), 360–371. https://doi.org/10.1037/a0027205

Huizenga, H. M., van Bers, B. M., Plat, J., van den Wildenberg, W. P., & van der Molen, M. W. (2009). Task complexity enhances response inhibition deficits in childhood and adolescent attention-deficit/hyperactivity disorder: A meta-regression analysis. *Biological Psychiatry, 65*(1), 39–45. https://doi.org/10.1016/j.biopsych.2008.06.021

Jensen, P. S., Garcia, J. A., Glied, S., Crowe, M., Foster, M., Schlander, M., Hinshaw, S., Vitiello, B., Arnold, L. E., Elliott, G., Hechtman, L., Newcorn, J. H., Pelham, W. E., Swanson, J., & Wells, K. (2005). Cost-effectiveness of ADHD treatments: Findings from the multimodal treatment study of children with ADHD. *American Journal of Psychiatry, 162*(9), 1628–1636. https://doi.org/162/9/1628

Kadesjö, B., & Gillberg, C. (2003). The comorbidity of ADHD in the general population of Swedish school-age children. *Journal of Child Psychology and Psychiatry, 42*(4), 487–492.

Kendall, T., Taylor, E., Perez, A., & Taylor, C. (2008). Guidelines: Diagnosis and management of attention-deficit/hyperactivity disorder in children, young people, and adults: Summary of NICE Guidance. *BMJ: British Medical Journal, 337*(7672), 751–753.

Kessler, R. C., Adler, L., Barkley, R., Biederman, J., Conners, C. K., Demler, O., Faraone, S. V., Greenhill, L. L., Howes, M. J., Secnik, K., Spencer, T., Ustun, T. B., Walters, E. E., & Zaslavsky, A. M. (2006). The prevalence and correlates of adult ADHD in the United States: Results from the National Comorbidity Survey Replication. *American Journal of Psychiatry, 163*(4), 716–723. https://doi.org/10.1176/appi.ajp.163.4.716

Konrad, K., Gauggel, S., Manz, A., & Scholl, M. (2000). Lack of inhibition: A motivational deficit in children with attention deficit/hyperactivity disorder and children with traumatic brain injury. *Child Neuropsychol, 6*(4), 286–296. https://doi.org/10.1076/chin.6.4.286.3145

Kooij, J. J. S., Bijlenga, D., Salerno, L., Jaeschke, R., Bitter, I., Balázs, J., . . . Asherson, P. (2019). Updated European Consensus Statement on diagnosis and treatment of adult ADHD. *European Psychiatry, 56*, 14–34. https://doi.org/https://doi.org/10.1016/j.eurpsy.2018.11.001

Krinzinger, H., Hall, C. L., Groom, M. J., Ansari, M. T., Banaschewski, T., Buitelaar, J. K., . . . Liddle, E. B. (2019). Neurological and psychiatric adverse effects of long-term methylphenidate treatment in ADHD: A map of the current evidence. (1873-7528 (Electronic)).

Kuehne, C., Kehle, T. J., & McMahon, W. (1987). Differences between children with attention deficit disorder, children with specific learning disabilities, and normal children. *Journal of School Psychology, 25*(2), 161–166.

Küpper, T., Haavik, J., Drexler, H., Ramos-Quiroga, J. A., Wermelskirchen, D., Prutz, C., & Schauble, B. (2012). The negative impact of attention-deficit/hyperactivity disorder on occupational health in adults and adolescents. *International Archives of Occupational and Environmental Health, 85*(8), 837–847. https://doi.org/10.1007/s00420-012-0794-0

Langberg, J. M., & Becker, S. P. (2012). Does long-term medication use improve the academic outcomes of youth with attention-deficit/hyperactivity disorder? *Clinical Child and*

*Family Psychology Review, 15*(3), 215–233. https://doi.org/10.1007/s10567-012-0117-8

Lee, P. C., Niew, W. I., Yang, H. J., Chen, V. C., & Lin, K. C. (2012). A meta-analysis of behavioral parent training for children with attention deficit hyperactivity disorder. *Research in Developmental Disabilities, 33*(6), 2040–2049. https://doi.org/10.1016/j.ridd.2012.05.011 S0891-4222(12)00127-8 [pii]

Lee, S. S., Humphreys, K. L., Flory, K., Liu, R., & Glass, K. (2011). Prospective association of childhood attention-deficit/hyperactivity disorder (ADHD) and substance use and abuse/dependence: A meta-analytic review. *Clinical Psychology Review, 31*(3), 328–341. https://doi.org/10.1016/j.cpr.2011.01.006

Linnet, K. M., Dalsgaard, S., Obel, C., Wisborg, K., Henriksen, T. B., Rodriguez, A., Kotimaa, A., Moilanen, I., Thomsen, P. H., & Olsen, J. (2003). Maternal lifestyle factors in pregnancy risk of attention deficit hyperactivity disorder and associated behaviors: Review of the current evidence. *American Journal of Psychiatry, 160*(6), 1028–1040.

López-Pinar, C., Martínez-Sanchís, S., Carbonell-Vayá, E., Fenollar-Cortés, J., & Sánchez-Meca, J. (2018). Long-term efficacy of psychosocial treatments for adults with attention-deficit/hyperactivity disorder: A meta-analytic review. (1664-1678 (Print)).

Losier, B. J., McGrath, P. J., & Klein, R. M. (1996). Error patterns on the continuous performance test in non-medicated and medicated samples of children with and without ADHD: A meta-analytic review. *Journal of Child Psychology and Psychiatry and Allied Disciplines, 37*(8), 971–987. http://www.ncbi.nlm.nih.gov/pubmed/9119944

Madras, B. K., Miller, G. M., & Fischman, A. J. (2005). The dopamine transporter and attention-deficit/hyperactivity disorder. *Biological Psychiatry, 57*(11), 1397–1409. https://doi.org/10.1016/j.biopsych.2004.10.011

McClernon, F. J., & Kollins, S. H. (2008). ADHD and smoking: From genes to brain to behavior. *Annals of the New York Academy of Sciences, 1141*, 131–147. https://doi.org/10.1196/annals.1441.016

Michielsen, M., Semeijn, E., Comijs, H. C., van de Ven, P., Beekman, A. T., Deeg, D. J., & Kooij, J. J. (2012). Prevalence of attention-deficit hyperactivity disorder in older adults in The Netherlands. *British Journal of Psychiatry, 201*(4), 298–305. https://doi.org/10.1192/bjp.bp.111.101196

Milich, R., Balentine, A. C., & Lynam, D. R. (2001). ADHD combined type and ADHD predominantly inattentive type are distinct and unrelated disorders. *Clinical Psychology-Science and Practice, 8*(4), 463–488. https://doi.org/DOI 10.1093/clipsy/8.4.463

Molina, B. S., Hinshaw, S. P., Swanson, J. M., Arnold, L. E., Vitiello, B., Jensen, P. S., Epstein, J. N., Hoza, B., Hechtman, L., Abikoff, H. B., Elliott, G. R., Greenhill, L. L., Newcorn, J. H., Wells, K. C., Wigal, T., Gibbons, R. D., Hur, K., & Houck, P. R. (2009). The MTA at 8 years: Prospective follow-up of children treated for combined-type ADHD in a multisite study. *Journal of the American Academy of Child and Adolescent Psychiatry, 48*(5), 484–500. https://doi.org/10.1097/CHI.0b013e31819c23d0

The MTA Cooperative Group. (1999). A 14-month randomized clinical trial of treatment strategies for attention-deficit/hyperactivity disorder. *Archives of General Psychiatry, 56*(12), 1073–1086. http://www.ncbi.nlm.nih.gov/pubmed/10591283

Mueller, A. K., Fuermaier, A. B. M., Koerts, J., & Tucha, L. (2012). Stigma in attention deficit hyperactivity disorder. *ADHD Attention Deficit and Hyperactivity Disorders*, 1–14.

Murray, A. L., Booth, T., Eisner, M., Auyeung, B., Murray, G., & Ribeaud, D. (2019). Sex differences in ADHD trajectories across childhood and adolescence. *Developmental Science, 22*(1), e12721. https://doi.org/10.1111/desc.12721

Nigg, J., Nikolas, M., & Burt, S. A. (2010). Measured gene-by-environment interaction in relation to attention-deficit/hyperactivity disorder. *Journal of the American Academy of Child and Adolescent Psychiatry, 49*(9), 863–873. https://doi.org/10.1016/j.jaac.2010.01.025

Nigg, J. T., Lewis, K., Edinger, T., & Falk, M. (2012). Meta-analysis of attention-deficit/hyperactivity disorder or attention-deficit/hyperactivity disorder symptoms, restriction diet, and synthetic food color additives. *Journal of the American Academy of Child and Adolescent Psychiatry, 51*(1), 86–97 e88.

Palumbo, D., Spencer, T., Lynch, J., Co-Chien, H., & Faraone, S. V. (2004). Emergence of tics in children with ADHD: Impact of once-daily OROS® Methylphenidate Therapy. *Journal of Child and Adolescent Psychopharmacology, 14*(2), 185–194.

Pelham, W. E., Jr., & Fabiano, G. A. (2008). Evidence-based psychosocial treatments for attention-deficit/hyperactivity disorder. *Journal of Clinical Child and Adolescent Psychology, 37*(1), 184–214. https://doi.org/10.1080/15374410701818681

Pietrzak, R. H., Mollica, C. M., Maruff, P., & Snyder, P. J. (2006). Cognitive effects of immediate-release methylphenidate in children with attention-deficit/hyperactivity disorder. *Neuroscience and Biobehavioral Reviews, 30*(8), 1225–1245. https://doi.org/S0149-7634(06)00114-X

Pievsky, M. A., & McGrath, R. E. (2018). The neurocognitive profile of attention-deficit/hyperactivity disorder: A review of meta-analyses. *Archives of Clinical Neuropsychology, 33*(2), 143–157. https://doi.org/10.1093/arclin/acx055

Pliszka, S. (2007). Practice parameter for the assessment and treatment of children and adolescents with attention-deficit/hyperactivity disorder. *Journal of the American Academy of Child and Adolescent Psychiatry, 46*(7), 894–921. https://doi.org/10.1097/chi.0b013e318054e724

Poelmans, G., Pauls, D. L., Buitelaar, J. K., & Franke, B. (2011). Integrated genome-wide association study findings: Identification of a neurodevelopmental network for attention deficit hyperactivity disorder. *American Journal of Psychiatry, 168*(4), 365–377. https://doi.org/10.1176/appi.ajp.2010.10070948

Polanczyk, G. V., & Rohde, L. A. (2007). Epidemiology of attention-deficit/hyperactivity disorder across the lifespan. *Current Opinion in Psychiatry, 20*(4), 386–392.

Porrino, L. J., Rapoport, J. L., Behar, D., Sceery, W., Ismond, D. R., & Bunney, W. E., Jr. (1983). A naturalistic assessment of the motor activity of hyperactive boys. I. Comparison with normal controls. *Archives of General Psychiatry, 40*(6), 681–687. http://www.ncbi.nlm.nih.gov/pubmed/6847335

Prasad, V., Brogan, E., Mulvaney, C., Grainge, M., Stanton, W., & Sayal, K. (2013). How effective are drug treatments for children with ADHD at improving on-task behaviour and academic achievement in the school classroom? A systematic review and meta-analysis. *European Child and Adolescent Psychiatry, 22*(4), 203–216. https://doi.org/10.1007/s00787-012-0346-x

Ramtekkar, U. P., Reiersen, A. M., Todorov, A. A., & Todd, R. D. (2010). Sex and age differences in attention-deficit/hyperactivity disorder symptoms and diagnoses: Implications for DSM-V and ICD-11. *Journal of the American Academy of Child and Adolescent Psychiatry, 49*(3), 217–228 e211–213. http://www.ncbi.nlm.nih.gov/pubmed/20410711

Rapport, M. D., Bolden, J., Kofler, M. J., Sarver, D. E., Raiker, J. S., & Alderson, R. M. (2009). Hyperactivity in boys with attention-deficit/hyperactivity disorder (ADHD): A ubiquitous core symptom or manifestation of working memory deficits? *Journal of Abnormal Child Psychology, 37*(4), 521–534. http://www.springerlink.com/content/b60350712071u527/fulltext.pdf

Robison, L. M., Sclar, D. A., Skaer, T. L., & Galin, R. S. (1999). National trends in the prevalence of attention-deficit/hyperactivity disorder and the prescribing of methylphenidate among school-age children: 1990–1995. *Clinical Pediatrics, 38*(4), 209–217.

Rutledge, K. J., van den Bos, W., McClure, S. M., & Schweitzer, J. B. (2012). Training cognition in ADHD: Current findings, borrowed concepts, and future directions. *Neurotherapeutics, 9*(3), 542–558. https://doi.org/10.1007/s13311-012-0134-9

Saad, J. F., Kohn, M. R., Clarke, S., Lagopoulos, J., & Hermens, D. F. (2018). Is the theta/beta EEG marker for ADHD inherently flawed? *Journal of Attention Disorders, 22*(9), 815–826. https://doi.org/10.1177/1087054715578270

Sawyer, M. G., Whaites, L., Rey, J. M., Hazell, P. L., Graetz, B. W., & Baghurst, P. (2002). Health-related quality of life of children and adolescents with mental disorders. *Journal of the American Academy of Child and Adolescent Psychiatry, 41*(5), 530–537.

Schweren, L. J., de Zeeuw, P., & Durston, S. (2012). MR imaging of the effects of methylphenidate on brain structure and function in attention-deficit/hyperactivity disorder. *European Neuropsychopharmacology.* https://doi.org/S0924-977X(12)00305-710.10 16/j.euroneuro.2012.10.014

Seixas, N. (2013). Change, challenges, and core values. *Annals of Occupational Hygiene, 57*(1), 3–5. https://doi.org/10.1093/annhyg/mes097

Sergeant, J. A. (2005). Modeling attention-deficit/hyperactivity disorder: A critical appraisal of the cognitive-energetic model. *Biological Psychiatry, 57*(11), 1248–1255.

Sergeant, J. A., Geurts, H., Huijbregts, S., Scheres, A., & Oosterlaan, J. (2003). The top and the bottom of ADHD: A neuropsychological perspective. *Neuroscience and Biobehavioral Reviews, 27*(7), 583–592. https://doi.org/S0149763403001040 [pii]

Sexton, C. C., Gelhorn, H. L., Bell, J. A., & Classi, P. M. (2012). The co-occurrence of reading disorder and ADHD: Epidemiology, treatment, psychosocial impact, and economic burden. *Journal of Learning Disabilities, 45*(6), 538–564. https://doi.org/10.1177/0022219411407772

Shaw, P., Eckstrand, K., Sharp, W., Blumenthal, J., Lerch, J., Greenstein, D., Clasen, L., Evans, A., Giedd, J., & Rapoport, J. (2007). Attention-deficit/hyperactivity disorder is characterized by a delay in cortical maturation. *Proceedings of the National Academy of Sciences, 104*(49), 19649–19654.

Simon, V., Czobor, P., Bálint, S., Mészáros, A., & Bitter, I. (2009). Prevalence and correlates of adult attention-deficit hyperactivity disorder: Meta-analysis. *Br J Psychiatry, 194*(3), 204–211. https://doi.org/10.1192/bjp.bp.107.048827

Sonuga-Barke, E. J., Brandeis, D., Cortese, S., Daley, D., Ferrin, M., Holtmann, M., ... European, A. G. G. (2013). Nonpharmacological interventions for ADHD: Systematic review and meta-analyses of randomized controlled trials of dietary and psychological treatments. *American Journal of Psychiatry, 170*(3), 275–289. https://doi.org/10.1176/appi.ajp.2012.12070991

Spencer, T. J., Biederman, J., Madras, B. K., Faraone, S. V., Dougherty, D. D., Bonab, A. A., & Fischman, A. J. (2005). In vivo neuroreceptor imaging in attention-deficit/hyperactivity disorder: A focus on the dopamine transporter. *Biological Psychiatry, 57*(11), 1293–1300.

Spencer, T. J., Biederman, J., & Mick, E. (2007). Attention-deficit/hyperactivity disorder: Diagnosis, lifespan, comorbidities, and neurobiology. *Journal of Pediatric Psychology, 32*(6), 631–642. https://doi.org/jsm005

Steinhausen, H. C., Nøvik, T. S., Baldursson, G., Curatolo, P., Lorenzo, M. J., Rodrigues Pereira, R., Ralston, S. J., & Rothenberger, A. (2006). Co-existing psychiatric problems in ADHD in the ADORE cohort. *European Child and Adolescent Psychiatry, 15,* 25–29.

Stevenson, J., Buitelaar, J., Cortese, S., Ferrin, M., Konofal, E., Lecendreux, M., Simonoff, E., Wong, I. C. K., & Sonuga-Barke, E. (2014). Research review: The role of diet in the treatment of attention-deficit/hyperactivity disorder: An appraisal of the evidence on efficacy and recommendations on the design of future studies. *Journal of Child Psychology and Psychiatry, 55*(5), 416–427. https://doi.org/https://doi.org/10.1111/jcpp.12215

Sutcubasi, B., Metin, B., Kurban, M. K., Metin, Z. E., Beser, B., & Sonuga-Barke, E. (2020). Resting-state network dysconnectivity in ADHD: A system-neuroscience-based meta-analysis. *World Journal of Biological Psychiatry, 21*(9), 662–672. https://doi.org/10.1080/15622975.2020.1775889

Swanson, J., Castellanos, F. X., Murias, M., LaHoste, G., & Kennedy, J. (1998). Cognitive neuroscience of attention deficit hyperactivity disorder and hyperkinetic disorder. *Current Opinion in Neurobiology, 8*(2), 263.

Swanson, J., Kraemer, H. C., Hinshaw, S. P., Arnold, L. E., Conners, C. K., Abikoff, H. B., Clevenger, W., Davies, M., Elliott, G. R., & Greenhill, L. L. (2001). Clinical relevance of the primary findings of the MTA: Success rates based on severity of ADHD and ODD symptoms at the end of treatment. *Journal of the American Academy of Child and Adolescent Psychiatry, 40*(2), 168–179.

Szuromi, B., Czobor, P., Komlosi, S., & Bitter, I. (2011). P300 deficits in adults with attention deficit hyperactivity disorder: A meta-analysis. *Psychological Medicine, 41*(7), 1529–1538. https://doi.org/10.1017/s0033291710001996

Tamm, L., Narad, M. E., Antonini, T. N., O'Brien, K. M., Hawk, L. W., Jr., & Epstein, J. N. (2012). Reaction time variability in ADHD: A review. *Neurotherapeutics, 9*(3), 500–508. https://doi.org/10.1007/s13311-012-0138-5

Taylor, L. E., Kaplan-Kahn, E. A., Lighthall, R. A., & Antshel, K. M. (2021). Adult-onset ADHD: A critical analysis and alternative explanations. *Child Psychiatry and Human Development.* https://doi.org/10.1007/s10578-021-01159-w

Thapar, A., & Cooper, M. (2016). Attention deficit hyperactivity disorder. *Lancet, 387*(10024), 1240–1250. https://doi.org/10.1016/s0140-6736(15)00238-x

Thapar, A., Cooper, M., Eyre, O., & Langley, K. (2013). What have we learnt about the causes of ADHD? *Journal of Child*

Psychology and Psychiatry, 54(1), 3–16. https://doi.org/10.1111/j.1469-7610.2012.02611.x

Thomas, R., Sanders, S., Doust, J., Beller, E., & Glasziou, P. (2015). Prevalence of attention-deficit/hyperactivity disorder: A systematic review and meta-analysis. Pediatrics, 135(4), e994–1001. https://doi.org/10.1542/peds.2014-3482

Valera, E. M., Faraone, S. V., Murray, K. E., & Seidman, L. J. (2007). Meta-analysis of structural imaging findings in attention-deficit/hyperactivity disorder. Biological Psychiatry, 61(12), 1361–1369. https://doi.org/S0006-3223(06)00803-1 [pii] 10.1016/j.biopsych.2006.06.011

van de Loo-Neus, G. H., Rommelse, N., & Buitelaar, J. K. (2011). To stop or not to stop? How long should medication treatment of attention-deficit hyperactivity disorder be extended? European Neuropsychopharmacology, 21(8), 584–599. https://doi.org/10.1016/j.euroneuro.2011.03.008

Van der Oord, S., Prins, P. J., Oosterlaan, J., & Emmelkamp, P. M. (2008). Efficacy of methylphenidate, psychosocial treatments and their combination in school-aged children with ADHD: A meta-analysis. Clinical Psychology Review, 28(5), 783–800. https://doi.org/10.1016/j.cpr.2007.10.007

van Dongen, J., Zilhão, N. R., Sugden, K., Hannon, E. J., Mill, J., Caspi, A., Agnew-Blais, J., Arseneault, L., Corcoran, D. L., Moffitt, T. E., Poulton, R., Franke, B., & Boomsma, D. I. (2019). Epigenome-wide association study of attention-deficit/hyperactivity disorder symptoms in adults. Biological Psychiatry, 86(8), 599–607.

Van Doren, J., Arns, M., Heinrich, H., Vollebregt, M. A., Strehl, U., & S, K. L. (2019). Sustained effects of neurofeedback in ADHD: A systematic review and meta-analysis. European Child and Adolescent Psychiatry, 28(3), 293–305.

van Ewijk, H., Heslenfeld, D. J., Zwiers, M. P., Buitelaar, J. K., & Oosterlaan, J. (2012). Diffusion tensor imaging in attention deficit/hyperactivity disorder: A systematic review and meta-analysis. Neuroscience & Biobehavioral Reviews, 36(4), 1093–1106. https://doi.org/https://doi.org/10.1016/j.neubiorev.2012.01.003

van Lieshout, M., Luman, M., Buitelaar, J., Rommelse, N., & Oosterlaan, J. (2013). Does neurocognitive functioning predict future or persistence of ADHD? A systematic review. Clinical Psychology Review, 33(4), 539–560.

Visser, S., Bitsko, R., Danielson, M., Perou, R., & Blumberg, S. (2010). Increasing prevalence of parent-reported attention-deficit/hyperactivity disorder among children: United States, 2003 and 2007. Morbidity and Mortality Weekly Report, 59(44), 1439–1443.

Vysniauske, R., Verburgh, L., Oosterlaan, J., & Molendijk, M. L. (2020). The effects of physical exercise on functional outcomes in the treatment of ADHD: A meta-analysis. Journal of Attention Disorders, 24(5), 644–654. https://doi.org/10.1177/1087054715627489

Warren, A. E., Hamilton, R. M., Belanger, S. A., Gray, C., Gow, R. M., Sanatani, S., Cote, J. M., Lougheed, J., LeBlanc, J., Martin, S., Miles, B., Mitchell, C., Gorman, D. A., Weiss, M., & Schachar, R. (2009). Cardiac risk assessment before the use of stimulant medications in children and youth: A joint position statement by the Canadian Paediatric Society, the Canadian Cardiovascular Society, and the Canadian Academy of Child and Adolescent Psychiatry. Canadian Journal of Cardiology, 25(11), 625–630.

Willcutt, E. G. (2012). The prevalence of DSM-IV attention-deficit/hyperactivity disorder: A meta-analytic review. Neurotherapeutics, 9(3), 490–499. https://doi.org/10.1007/s13311-012-0135-8

Willcutt, E. G., Nigg, J. T., Pennington, B. F., Solanto, M. V., Rohde, L. A., Tannock, R., Loo, S. K., Carlson, C. L., McBurnett, K., & Lahey, B. B. (2012). Validity of DSM-IV attention deficit/hyperactivity disorder symptom dimensions and subtypes. Journal of Abnormal Psychology, 121(4), 991–1010.

Wolraich, M., Brown, L., Brown, R. T., DuPaul, G., Earls, M., Feldman, H. M., Ganiats, T. G., Kaplanek, B., Meyer, B., Perrin, J., Pierce, K., Reiff, M., Stein, M. T., & Visser, S. (2011). ADHD: Clinical practice guideline for the diagnosis, evaluation, and treatment of attention-deficit/hyperactivity disorder in children and adolescents. Pediatrics, 128(5), 1007–1022. https://doi.org/peds.2011-2654

# CHAPTER 21

# Autism Spectrum Disorders

Fred R. Volkmar *and* Kevin Pelphrey

Autism and related conditions (previously termed the pervasive developmental disorders and more recently the autism spectrum disorders [ASDs]) share their major similarity in the significant difficulties in social development and interaction associated with problems in communication and behavior. These conditions have been the source of great interest for decades but only with the official recognition of autism in 1980, in *DSM-III*, did research begin to increase (Rosen et al., 2021); over time this increase has been quite dramatic, with several thousand scientific papers appearing each year. Despite this increase, research in some areas (e.g., aging in autism; Piven et al., 2011) is quite limited but, overall, very significant progress has been made in both understanding and treating these conditions.

## Diagnostic Concepts

Autistic disorder (sometimes referred to as *childhood autism* or *infantile autism*) is the prototypic disorder of the group and the one that has been the focus of most of the available research. Research is much less extensive on the broader spectrum of disorders (ASDs) and caution should be used in overgeneralization of results from more "classic" autism to this larger population.

Initially described by Leo Kanner (1943), all subsequent definitions have kept some degree of continuity with Kanner, who emphasized two key features: autism (lack of social interest/engagement from the time of birth) and what he termed resistance to change or insistence on sameness (difficulties with change, stereotyped movements). Kanner's work prefigures much current research which is aimed at understanding genetic and brain mechanisms of social vulnerability coupled with an overengagement in the nonsocial world. Other diagnostic concepts were proposed before and after 1943, and *ICD-10* and *DSM-IV* explicitly recognized a number of these, although *DSM-5* returned to a more unitary model potentially at some price in terms of restricted coverage (Volkmar et al., 2021). Conditions included in *ICD-10* and *DSM-IV* were Asperger's disorder (serious social vulnerability associated with perseverative interests, good vocabulary, and motor clumsiness), two "disintegrative" conditions where skills were dramatically lost (Rett's disorder, now known to be a single-gene disorder), and childhood disintegrative disorder (CDD), where autism has its apparent onset after years of clearly normal development and a "subthreshold" category: pervasive developmental disorder not otherwise specified for cases not meeting specific criteria for one of these conditions but with problems that seem best viewed as related to autism (see Jackson & Volkmar, 2019, for a review).

The *DSM-IV/ICD-10* definitions were very similar and require characteristic problems in social interaction as well as problems in communication and play and in unusual environmental responses and restricted-repetitive interests. The onset of the condition must be before age 3 years. Social

**Abbreviations**

| | |
|---|---|
| ASD | Autism spectrum disorder |
| BAP | Broader autism prototype |
| CDD | Childhood disintegrative disorder |
| FFA | Fusiform face area |
| FFG | Fusiform gyrus |
| OFC | Orbital frontal cortex |
| PC | Posterior cingulate |
| PFC | Prefrontal cortex |
| PRT | Pivotal response treatment |
| STS | Superior temporal sulcus |
| TD | Typically developing |
| TPJ | Temporoparietal junction |
| US | Unaffected sibling |

problems are weighted more heavily than other factors. The polythetic *ICD-10/DSM-IV* approach allowed for more than 2,000 combinations of the 12 diagnostic criteria.

*DSM-5* differs from its predecessor in a number of important ways (Volkmar et al., 2021). For autism, two overarching decisions for *DSM-5* have had significant impact: the decision to derive the definitions from reanalyses of research diagnostic instruments and the decision to remove all subthreshold categories throughout the manual. For autism, the decision was to move to a more unitary construct of ASD and a somewhat narrower one more consistent with Kanner's original (1943) view of autism (see McPartland et al., 2012; Smith et al., 2015; Volkmar & McPartland, 2014; Volkmar et al., 2021). This reflected concern about the reliability and validity of more fine-grained distinctions and an awareness of the growing body of research on the complex genetic bases of autism (Lord et al., 2012; Rosen et al., 2021). The move toward a more rational name for the overall category is praiseworthy as is the attempt to provide ratings for dimensions of dysfunction. Other aspects of the new system may prove problematic in relation to several factors including the narrowing of the concept, gender, cultural, and developmental issues (Volkmar et al., 2021). Social-communication features are now grouped in one category while the restricted interest category has changed to include unusual sensitivities but provides many fewer ways for a diagnosis to be achieved and appears to differentially exclude more able and less "classic" cases. Consistent with the overall *DSM-5* in general no subthreshold categories are provided but a new condition, *social-communication disorder*, is. The rationale for this category and its actual use in practice remain to be determined (Topal et al., 2018). Although a large data reanalysis of items collected as part of research diagnostic assessments was performed, a true field trial was not actually conducted although some work was done on reliability; using the data available diagnostic accuracy was good if both historical information and direct assessment instruments were available (but decreased when they were not). A major unanswered question is how well items derived from research-based instruments which require considerable training in administration/interpretation can readily be extrapolated to more typical clinical settings (Volkmar et al., 2021). One unprecedented issue has emerged in the context of the COVID-19 pandemic. For nearly a year, we have not been able to complete the Autism Diagnostic Observation Schedule (ADOS) because the measure is not possible to complete with validity while wearing a face shield and/or mask. This reveals an important vulnerability in an approach to diagnosis that reifies such a complex neurodevelopmental disorder via any one measure or instrument. The exclusion of new diagnoses of Asperger's disorder cases (while grandfathering in older "well established" cases) remains problematic. The decision to exclude Asperger's even as a subcategory of ASD was unfortunate given the emergent data on validity of the concept (e.g., Chiang et al., 2014) and the wide public acceptance of the concept (Greenberg, 2013).

### Prevalence, Gender, and Cultural Perspectives

Several complications arise in the interpretation of epidemiological studies. Prevalence estimates can vary dramatically if different diagnostic approaches are used. *DSM-IV* and *ICD-10* criteria were designed to be more neutral to IQ (i.e., a goal in the development was that criteria worked reasonably well in both lower and higher cognitive functioning individuals). The tendency to equate ASDs (i.e., autism and related conditions) with more classical autism is yet another problem, as is the tendency to rely on school diagnoses rather than on results of actual independent assessment. The school setting may use the autism label to justify services when another category might be more appropriate (this is problem of diagnostic substitution). Other issues include greater public awareness and recognition. As well, in general, in epidemiological studies higher rates have been obtained when smaller samples are studied (presumably reflecting better case finding). On balance the median rate of strictly defined autistic disorder is about 1 per 800 but if a broader autism spectrum definition is used this rate significantly rises to the order of 1 in 150 (Fombonne, 2005). The apparent increase in prevalence of the condition likely reflects the many factors noted above, although there is the potential for some slight increase relative to specific genetic mechanisms (e.g., higher risk for older fathers of having a child with autism; Puleo et al., 2012).

There is a strong gender predominance in autism, with males being 3 to 5 times more likely to have the condition. When females have autism they tend, on balance, to be more cognitively impaired suggesting some complex interaction of severity with genetic risk and gender. Kanner's original paper (1943) noted a preponderance of well-educated and successful parents; this has not been confirmed in subsequent studies that controlled for referral bias. Autism appears, particularly in younger children, remarkably the same in individuals from various countries but cultural practices regarding special education and treatment may have a significant impact on outcome (Brown & Rogers 2003). There is remarkably little research on cultural or ethnic differences although some early suggestion of increased risk in immigrant families has not generally been supported in the literature (Fombonne, 2005).

Some recent work has emerged that questions the usually accepted male predominance in autism (Volkmar et al., in press). This awareness comes with emerging data on gender differences even in screening instruments if one examines large datasets (e.g., Oien et al., 2017) and the growing awareness of differences of syndrome expression in girls with a potentially milder form of social difficulty and/or a great ability to "camouflage" and fit in (Rynkiewicz et al., 2016). There is some suggestion of potential bias on diagnostic instruments as well (see (Volkmar et al., 2021). Concerns have also been raised relative to underdiagnosis in minority groups as a result of bias in screening and diagnostic instruments, lack of efforts to ensure identification, and so forth (Grinker et al., 2015; Mandell et al., 2009). The issues assume greater importance given the growing interest in autism in developing countries and the need to adapt approaches to other cultures (Freeth et al., 2014; Grinker et al., 2015; Volkmar et al., 2021). Indeed, even within the United States, there has been concern about the applicability of current diagnostic approaches to minority groups (Volkmar et al., 2021).

### Historical Perspectives

It is likely that some of the first reports of autism may have been those of so-called "feral" children (Wolff, 2004) and case repors of children seen in the 1800s in resididential instutitions in the United States (Donvan & Zuker, 2016). It is a tribute to the genius of Leo Kanner that he was able to identify a central distinguishing feature (autism or lack of social engagement) that differentiated the condition from other developmental problems. His report also, unfortunately, served to mislead early investigators, given his mention of high levels of professional attainment in parents, his mistaken impression of normal intellectual levels (reflecting his observation of better nonverbal abilities or splinter skills), and his use of the word "autism," suggesting to many a point of continuity with schizophrenia. Diagnostic ambiguity complicated much available research until work in the 1970s clarified the strong genetic and brain basis of autism. Its first inclusion in *DSM-III* marked a critical moment in research which has steadily increased since that time.

Diagnostic practice has varied over the years. Early attempts were made to more truly operationalize Kanner's definition, for example, Rutter's (1978) approach proved highly influential for *DSM-III*. Subsequent to *DSM-III*, a revision (the *DSM-III-R*) was made given concerns that the *DSM-III* approach lacked a developmental orientation (given its focus on the "infantile" form of the conditions); unfortunately, this also came at a price in the *DSM-III-R* terms of overly inclusive diagnosis. *DSM-IV* was in place since 1994, and it and the *ICD-10* definitions have proven highly influential: research has very dramatically increased with thousands of peer-reviewed papers appearing each year now. As noted above, the implications of the new *DSM-5* approach remain to be seen.

In addition to changes in diagnostic practice, significant shifts in clinical work and research have occurred. It has become apparent that structured, intensive intervention programs (of various types) are associated, on balance, with improved outcomes (e.g., relative to the number of adults who are self-sufficient and independent; Howlin, 2013). However, some children do not make this much progress and remain in need of considerable support throughout adulthood. Basic research advances have occurred in a number of areas, but those in genetics and neurobiology have been the most important and are discussed subsequently.

### Onset and Course

In his original (1943) description Kanner suggested that autism was inborn (i.e., congenital) in nature. With one important qualification, those who have developmental regression into autism, subsequent research has, largely, been consistent with this view. Many parents are worried about the child's development in the first year of life and the vast majority (90%) by age 2. Common reasons for concern include worries that the child might be deaf, social deviance or lack of engagement, odd interests in the nonsocial world, and language delay (Chawarska & Volkmar, 2020). Despite the apparent early onset, issues of diagnosis in infants remains complex. Complexities arise given the relative dearth of robust screening instruments or approaches until the infant reaches about 18 months, and, even when concerns arise, diagnostic stability seems to be reached with reasonable certainty only around age 3. The most common situation is one where a child moves from seeming to have more strictly defined autism to a "broader spectrum" of ASD and vice versa. It is not uncommon for a child to have the social-communicative features of autism at 18–24 months but not to yet apparently express the unusual, restricted interests or repetitive behaviors which then go on to make their appearance by age 36 months. Often such children have some unusual interests (e.g., in fans, lights, etc.) that may presage the development of the more characteristic repetitive interests or behaviors. Rarely, a child who seems classically autistic makes considerable progress and loses the diagnosis. A further complexity is introduced by the phenomenon of regression, typically reported in about 20% of cases. This issue is also complex since parental experiences of regression sometimes are clouded by failure to note early delays: sometimes development slows, and the pattern of apparent regression is actually more one of relative stagnation (e.g., a child seems to say a few words and then doesn't progress at expected rates), and, less commonly, a significant and major regression occurs. This phenomenon remains poorly understood but appears, on balance, to be a relatively bad prognostic sign. In some rare cases the child develops normally until 4 or 5 years of age and then has, over a relatively short period of time, a catastrophic loss of skills often associated with anxiety and development of autistic presentation; the specific term for this phenomenon ("childhood disintegrative disorder") was included in *DSM-IV* but was excluded in *DSM-5*.

The ability to diagnosis autism early in life has important implications for treatment since it seems likely that early intervention is associated with better outcome (Jackson & Volkmar, 2019). The issue assumes added urgency with the awareness that recurrence risk in younger siblings may approach 20%. Although delays in diagnoses remain frequent, the increased awareness of professionals and the lay public, along with important changes in social policy (e.g., in the United States the mandate for schools to provide intervention starting at age 3 years), appear to have fostered better early identification. There is some suggestion that the new *DSM-5* approach may underidentify young children (Matson et al., 2012) and that screeners work much less well than had been expected (Oien et al., 2018). Both social interest and behavior problems may increase as the child approaches the primary school years. In adolescence, some individuals become highly motivated and make gains while others seem to lose skills. Some children do so well that they technically "lose" their diagnosis: these "optimal outcome" cases are seen with increasing regularity but typically retain some residential problems (Kelley et al., 2006; Orinstein et al., 2014; Tyson et al., 2014). Epilepsy is relatively common in individuals with more "classic" autism, with peaks of onset in early childhood and again in adolescence, and treatment of the seizures may further complicate service provision.

The first outcome studies of autism in young adulthood suggested that perhaps 5–8% of cases achieved adult self-sufficiency and independence with about two-thirds of cases in need of residential care; these numbers have changed dramatically, with probably 25–30% of cases now able to achieve independence (Howlin, 2013). Increasing numbers of adolescents with ASD now move on to college (Accardo et al., 2019; van Schalkwyk et al., 2016), and programs are beginning to be developed specifically for them (White et al., 2016). Similarly, interest has increased in providing vocational supports (Gerhardt et al., 2014). But there are major gaps in transitional planning and in supports for students post college or in employment (Hatfield et al., 2018; Solomon, 2020). It is sadly the case that, despite the vast increase in research on autism, there is vanishingly little on adults (especially seniors) in general and their treatment needs in particular (Piven et al., 2011; Shea & Mesibov, 2014).

**Psychological Perspectives**

The social disturbance in autism is highly distinctive and consistently emerges as a, if not the, defining feature of the condition (Carter et al., 2014). The social problems seen in autism are in marked contrast to normative social development where, from the moment of birth, the typically developing infant is interested in the human face and voice. From the perspectives of both psychology and neurobiology, the challenge is in understanding how these deficits arise and what their implications are for learning and development. There have been significant shifts in theoretical views over the decades since autism's first description.

The earliest interest in the neuropsychology and potential neuropsychological theories and models of autism can be traced to the case report of Kurt Godstein (Scheerer et al., 1945) and his description of a person with autism and savant skills. Subsequently many different theoretical models have been developed (Vivanti & Messinger, 2021).

The earliest theoretical approaches conceptualized autism as a disorder that arose within the context of deviant caretaking experience. A few early investigators did note the unusual pattern of variability in intellectual skills, often with some peak skills in nonverbal areas and occasional unusual or "savant" abilities (e.g., in memory, drawing, calendar calculation; Hermelin, 2001). Over time, a body of research began to suggest that autism was a brain-based disorder with a strong genetic component. In addition, work within developmental psychology made it clear that, from the moment of birth, the typically developing infant was remarkably social (raising questions about theoretical notions like a normative "autistic phase" of development that has been postulated in some early psychoanalytic models). By the 1970s and into the 1980s, theoretical approaches shifted to more specific processes like perception, language, cognition, and attention.

Theoretical models are important for several reasons: they help organize and systematize knowledge, suggest potential mechanisms of pathogenesis, provide hypotheses for research, and may have implications for treatment. Chown (2017) has provided a very helpful overview of theoretical models and also has noted some of the important challenges that theories of autism face in their development. These include the need for universal applicability (i.e., over the entire range of syndrome expression), to enhance knowledge through a focus on some specific aspects of autism, to encompass the role of individual differences, and to reflect the uniqueness of the individual with autism. Consistent with all good scientific theories (Higgins, 2004), theories of autism must be coherent, testable, economical, generalizable, explanatory, and enhance research and hypothesis testing.

The first example of a theoretical model of autism was the early psychoanalytic one of clinicians like Bettelheim and colleagues (Bettelheim, 1959, 1967; Despert, 1971) that explained autism on the basis of inadequate parenting and "refrigerator" mothers. During the 1970s, a significant body of evidence emerged to make it clear that autism was brain-based and strongly genetic and responded best to structured teaching rather than unstructured psychotherapy (Jackson & Volkmar, 2019). During the 1980s and subsequently, several different and more sophisticated theoretical models emerged and will be briefly reviewed here. Each has its strengths and limitations, and all have, to some variable degrees, enhanced both research and clinical work.

## Theory of Mind Hypothesis

Probably the most influential theory of autism was proposed by Simon Baron Cohen (Baron-Cohen et al., 1985) and postulated that individuals with ASD lacked a "theory of mind" (ToM) or the inability to (simply termed) to put themselves in the place of the others. In the ToM hypothesis approach (Baron-Cohen, 1995), social difficulties are viewed as a function of a basic difficulty in intersubjectivity (i.e., understanding the mental life of self and others). This view emphasizes the difficulties that individuals with autism have in understanding the intention, desires, and beliefs of others, with resulting difficulties for predicting behavior and understanding others. Individuals with ASD who are capable of understanding false beliefs when explicitly prompted to do so are less capable of spontaneously anticipating an actor's behavior on the basis of the actor's false belief (Sonja et al., 2009) or taking the protagonist's innocent intentions into account to exculpate for accidental harms (Moran et al., 2011). In the classic "Sally Ann" task, children with ASD are significantly impaired when interpreting pretense (Bigham, 2010), less able to make inferences based on event scripts in comprehending narratives (Nuske & Bavin, 2011), and worse at taking on another person's visual perspective, especially when it involves understanding that different people may experience seeing the same object differently at the same time (Hamilton et al., 2009). This model's accounts have focused on many of the significant communication problems in autism (e.g., with pragmatic language, figurative language, and implied meaning). Some treatment approaches have been developed using it. However, some problems arise given the very strong relationship of ToM skills to overall language ability. Another problem arises in that more cognitively able individuals can readily solve usual ToM problems but remain significantly socially impaired (Dahlgren & Trillingsgaard, 1996). A final, major problem arises in that many of the earliest social manifestation of autism arise in development well before ToM skills are typically manifest. Despite these limitations, this theoretical approach has generated a truly impressive body of research.

Although helpful in stimulating research, this approach did not yield strong conceptual models for understanding the social dysfunction which appears to be the hallmark of the disorder. Indeed, in some ways it is only in recent years that the emphasis of psychological models began to shift to approaches emphasizing social information processing (paralleling, in some respects, the growing appreciation of the role of the social brain in the condition; Brothers, 1990). The potential for examining possible genetic and brain mechanisms has given added urgency to these endeavors. Several different theoretical approaches have been used in the past two decades.

*Executive Dysfunction Hypothesis*

"Executive functioning" is an umbrella term for a set of higher-order cognitive processes that encompass working memory, cognitive flexibility, impulse control and inhibition, attention shifting, planning and organizing, and initiating behavior (Pennington et al., 1997). It is of interest that deficits in these skills frequently are noted in individuals with autism as well as in those with frontal lobe area difficulties of various types (see McPartland et al., 2014). Some of the problems suggestive of executive functions difficulties in ASD include the behavioral rigidity, difficulties in multitasking, and problems with attention and forward planning (Ozonoff & Schetter, 2007).

The executive dysfunction hypothesis suggests that these difficulties in forward planning and executive functions are the core underlying problem in ASD and result in both the behavioral and social problems that define the condition (e.g., see Ozonoff & Schetter, 2007). As is also true of the ToM hypothesis, there is a sustainable body of empirical support for executive function difficulties in autism (Lai et al., 2017). This theoretical model has some advantages over the ToM hypothesis in that it more readily accounts for some of the nonsocial aspects of clinical presentation. On the other hand, and as with the ToM hypothesis, one difficulty for this approach is that it lacks specificity to autism (i.e., major problems in areas of executive dysfunction also are noted in conditions as diverse as schizophrenia, obsessive-compulsive disorder, Tourette syndrome, and, particularly, attention deficit hyperactivity disorder). Another challenge arises given the diverse profiles of deficit in this area presented across the broad spectrum of ASD (see (Hill, 2004, for a review). In addition, these difficulties are not unique to autism and levels of severity do not straightforwardly relate to degree of social impairment (Dawson et al. 1998).

*Weak Central Coherence Theory*

In this theoretical model the core feature is the perceptual-cognitive style in ASD that relates to how a person processes diverse sources of information and then processes it to form a coherent and meaningful whole. This model posits that in typical development there is a tendency toward information processing that will pull together the diverse pieces of information constantly available to the developing child and construct them into a coherent whole, thus allowing the child to grasp "the big picture." This model posits that in autism this processing style is disturbed or absent, resulting in an information processing style in which the focus is on smaller parts rather than on the whole and thus is more detail-focused (Firth, 1989, 2003; Firth & Happé, 1994). More recently, the model has been refined to suggest that persons with ASD have superior local processing and poor (but not always absent) global processing (Happé & Booth, 2008). One of the great advantages of this model is that it can be used to account more fully for both the social and nonsocial features of ASD (Happe, 1996), such as the interpretation of social cues in context, the problems with circumscribed interests, the tendency to focus on parts of objects, insistence on sameness, sensitivity to change, and the occasional person with ASD who has very detail-oriented knowledge in fields like mathematics and engineering. Kanner (1943) observed important aspects of this style in his first description of autism, writing that individuals with autism have an "inability to experience wholes without full attention to the constituent parts. . . . A situation, a performance, a sentence is not regarded as complete if it is not made up of exactly the same elements that were present at the time the child was first confronted with it" (p. 246).

There are important limitations to this theory as well. These include the inconsistent findings across studies (e.g., Hatton, & Hare, 2004; Ropar & Mitchell, 2001), and, in addition, these problems are not specific to autism (e.g., similar findings are seen in disorders like Williams syndrome; Bernardino et al., 2012).

Extreme Male Brain Theory

Another proposed cognitive theory is provided by the extreme male brain theory (Baron-Cohen, 2002). This theory centers around two rather different cognitive styles, "empathizing" and "systemizing," as related to how an individual tries to understand and process information, particularly social-affective information. As proposed by Baron-Cohen, the "empathizing" style is one where the drive is to understand and predict the thoughts and emotions of others, as well as to produce an emotionally appropriate response. In contrast, the "systemizing" style is one in which the drive is to systematically study and analyze the details that make up a system in order to understand its operation. Baron-Cohen argues that, on balance, females tend to be more naturally empathetic while males tend to naturally systemize. In this model it is suggested that persons with autism present an exaggerated (or extreme) version of this dichotomy, presenting with typical systemizing and reduced empathizing. It is noteworthy that in his original report Asperger (1944) noted that all his cases were males and that fathers had rather similar social difficulties (i.e., this is a long-standing observation in autism. In his original (1944) report Asperger stated that "[t]he autistic personality is an extreme variant of male intelligence. Even within the normal variation, we find typical sex differences in intelligence. . . . In the autistic individual, the male pattern is exaggerated to the extreme" (p. 129).

Empathizing can be likened to aspects of ToM, and systemizing can be likened to components of local processing (i.e., weak central coherence), so this model has the advantages of incorporating aspects of both of these other theorical approaches.

Critics of this theory argue that the fundamental basis of the theory (sex-based differences in cognitive styles) are based on old stereotypes much more than proven science (Krahn & Fenton, 2012). Indeed, the theory is based on studies conducted by the theory author (Baron-Cohen) and/or his students and are largely based on instruments developed by this group (e.g., the Systemizing Quotient, the Empathizing Quotient; Baron-Cohen, 2010; Baron-Cohen, 2011, 2012; Baron-Cohen et al., 2014).

*Limitations of Current Theoretical Approaches*

There have been several attempts to provide overall critiques of requirements for satisfactory theoretical models of autism (e.g., Chown, 2017; Gernsbacher & Yergeau, 2019; Pellicano, 2011). Although all the proposed models noted above (and several others) have had important implications for research and treatment, there has not yet been a single unified theory that accounts for all the features of ASD (Chown, 2017).

Difficulties include the broad range of autism, marked changes over the course of development, and the multiple areas of difficulty encountered in this population. This is consistent with the view that while ASD is currently viewed as a single "disorder" for the purpose of classification, it may actually be comprised of a broader phenotype potentially related to multiple etiologies but with a final common pathway (Whitehouse & Stanley, 2013). This view would help us understand the various and conflicting findings related to different subgroups of ASD. One of the important challenges for psychological models is the need to firmly center them within the developmental context (e.g., within an awareness of the importance of early development of cognition within the context of social experience; Klin et al., 2003).

However, even with their limitations, theoretical models have clearly advanced the field because they have suggested specific hypothesis and approaches to both research and clinical intervention. The unification of these models with more basic neuroscience findings remains an important research goal (McPartland et al., 2014).

**Biological Perspectives**

Advances in understanding the biological basis of autism have increased dramatically in the past decade. Progress has occurred in several areas, including both genetics (State & Levitt, 2011) and our understanding of the social brain. And, as noted subsequently, attempts have been made to link specific brain regions and processes to some of the observed psychological phenomena and theory. Genetic studies have revealed a large number of leads for genes potentially involved in the condition, many of which relate to cell-to-cell connections in the brain. At present, the translational significance of these findings remains unclear, but there is long-term potential for clarifying specific mechanisms that impact general or more delineated brain regions. Critically, it is now clear that genetic contributions to autism include a wide array of rare de novo gene mutations as well as numerous common genetic variants, acting in concert to shape neurodevelopment. Further, there is no clear "autism gene," in that no specific genetic difference has been identified that is entirely specific to autism. Rather, the genes that contribute to autism risk also contribute to the risk for other neurodevelopmental conditions including intellectual disability and schizophrenia. This, together with an emerging understanding of the role of epigenetic factors (e.g., gene methylation), highlight the importance of biologically oriented studies that address multiple levels of analysis including genes (gene structure and expression), brain (development of structure, function, and connectivity), and behavior/cognition (e.g., Parikshak, Gandal, & Geschwind, 2015).

The nature of the social brain in autism has been a major focus of research interest over the past two decades. "Social perception" refers to "the initial stages in the processing of information that culminates in the accurate analysis of the dispositions and intentions of other individuals" (Allison et al., 2000, p. 1). Additionally, social perceptions are an ontogenetic and phylogenetic prequel to more sophisticated aspects of social cognition, including ToM skills. Successful social perception involves a set of three distinct but interrelated social cognition abilities: (1) individuating and recognizing other people, (2) perceiving their emotional states, and (3) analyzing their intentions and motivations. Social perception, in turn, facilitates a fourth and more sophisticated aspect of social cognition: (4) representing another person's perceptions and beliefs, or "theory of mind."

While neuroscientists have only recently focused on identifying the neural substrates of social perception, the construct has been of interest to psychologists for decades. For example, a major focus of Fritz Heider's work was the description of cognitive mechanisms for the perception of social objects. In collaboration with Mary-Ann Simmel, he provided elegant experimental demonstrations of the ways in which the perception of people differs from the perception of objects, particularly with regard to the attributions we make for each category of visual stimulus (Heider & Simmel, 1944). Psychological scientists commonly divvy up human cognitive abilities into memory, attention, reasoning, perception, etc. Our textbooks help to consecrate these categories, but nature does not respect the boundaries. Humans are, at their core, social and affective beings, but these essential characteristics have often been treated as sources of noise to be excluded from controlled experiments in the laboratories of cognitive psychologists. This point of view has recently been overcome, owing in large part to remarkable new discoveries that have provided strong evidence for the need for an "apocryphal" chapter regarding the unique ways in which the brain processes social information.

Neuroscientists became deeply interested in social perception when it was discovered that neurons within the temporal cortex and amygdaloidal complex of monkeys were sensitive to and selective for social objects (e.g., faces and hands) and complex social stimuli (actions in a social context and direction of gaze). On the basis of these seminal findings, the field began to think seriously about the possibility of a network of brain regions dedicated to processing social information. The label "social brain" was coined by Leslie Brothers (1990) and served to capture elegantly the core, emerging idea. The social brain is now defined as the complex network of areas that enables us to recognize other individuals and evaluate their mental states (e.g., intentions, dispositions, desires, and beliefs). The key idea is that human beings, in response to the unique computational demands of their highly social environments, have evolved cognitive mechanisms and associated, dedicated neural systems supporting such abilities as recognizing other agents and their actions, individuating others, perceiving the emotional states of others, analyzing the intentions and dispositions of others, sharing attention with one another, and representing another person's perceptions and beliefs. Brothers (1990) emphasized the contributions of the superior temporal sulcus (STS), amygdala, orbital frontal cortex (OFC), and fusiform gyrus (FFG) to social perception. In humans, the STS region, particularly the posterior STS in the right hemisphere, analyzes biological motion cues, including eye, hand, and other body movements, to interpret and predict the actions and intentions of others (e.g., Pelphrey et al., 2005). The FFG, located in the ventral occipitotemporal cortex, contains a region termed the fusiform face area (FFA), which has been implicated in face detection (identifying a face as a face) and face recognition (identifying one's friend vs. a stranger) (e.g., Kanwisher et al., 1997). The OFC has been strongly implicated in social reinforcement and reward processes more broadly (e.g., Rolls, 2000, 2009). Finally, the amygdala, a complex structure that is highly interconnected with cortical (including the STS and FFG) and other subcortical brain structures, has been implicated in helping to recognize the emotional states of others through analysis of facial expressions as well as in multiple aspects of the experience and regulation of emotion.

To understand social brain function, we must be as attentive to the interconnections of neuroanatomical structures as we are to their individual contributions. Currently, in humans, much is known about the roles played by the individual brain regions, but very little is known about the ways in which they are interconnected and thus even less is known about how they interact functionally. However, we can take some initial guidance from the monkey brain. Here, it is known that the STS region has reciprocal connections to the amygdala, which is connected to the OFC (Amaral et al., 1992); the STS is also connected with the OFC, which itself is connected to the prefrontal cortex, which is itself connected to the motor cortex and the basal ganglia, thus completing what Allison and colleagues (2000) described as a pathway from social perception to social action.

A flood of neuroimaging work in adult humans (and increasingly in children and adolescents) has revealed a small but remarkably consistent set of cortical regions in and around the posterior parietal cortex associated with thinking about other people's thoughts, or ToM: bilateral temporoparietal junction (TPJ), medial PFC (mPFC), and posterior cingulate cortex (PC). The mPFC, is recruited when processing many kinds of information about people (Amodio & Frith, 2006), whereas the right TPJ is recruited selectively for thinking about thoughts (Saxe & Kanwisher, 2003).

Just over a decade ago, neuroscientists began to argue for the existence of two different kinds of abilities or neural systems that enable mind-reading. Sabbagh (2004) reviewed evidence for an orbitofrontal/medial temporal circuit and argued that the ability to decode others' mental states from observable cues is different from the ability to reason about others' mental states. Using animations of rigid geometric shapes that depict social interactions versus false-belief stories, Gobbini and colleagues (2007) showed that the two tasks activated distinctly different neural systems: the social animations activated a "social perception" system comprised of the STS, the frontal operculum, and inferior parietal lobule, whereas the false-belief stories activated a "mental state reasoning system" consisting of the TPJ, the anterior paracingulate cortex, and the posterior cingulate cortex or precuneus.

There is now clear behavioral and neuroimaging evidence for deficits in both the social perception and mental state reasoning systems in ASD. Next, we review selected behavioral and neuroimaging evidence from the empirical record.

### The Social Perception System

Eye-tracking studies demonstrate that toddlers with ASD fail to orient to the social significance of biological motion; instead, they focus on nonsocial, physical contingencies, contingencies that are disregarded by neurotypical peers (Klin, et al, 2009). Strikingly, later eye tracking work has revealed that individual differences in the ways in which infants view social scenes is highly heritable, with much greater similarity among monozygotic versus dizygotic twins. Furthermore, this work revealed that the atypical early patterns of social viewing that precede an autism diagnosis are under strong genetic regulation, thereby suggesting that scan paths might be a strong endophenotype and predictive biomarker of autistic social dysfunction. With the continued maturation of eye tracking research in autism, several meta-analyses have emerged to provide clarity and greater order to the field. For instance, in reviewing and quantitatively aggregating numerous eye-tracking studies of social and nonsocial stimuli in people with and without autism, Frazier and colleagues (2017) concluded that autistic individuals exhibit reliable gaze abnormalities suggesting a basic problem with selecting socially relevant versus irrelevant information for attention. This difference is persistent across age and worsens during perception of human interactions.

In the auditory domain, Rutherford and colleagues (2002) developed a test called "Reading the Mind in the Voice" and showed that adults with ASD have difficulty decoding/extracting mental state information from vocalizations. With respect to visual signals, Kaiser and colleagues (2010) found that when young children were shown point-light displays of coherent versus scrambled biological motion, children with ASD, compared to unaffected siblings and typically developing peers, exhibited hypoactivation in the FFG, amygdala, ventromedial PFC (vmPFC), ventrolateral prefrontal cortex, and posterior STS. These findings indicate widespread disruption of the social perception system in young children with ASD. Eye-gaze shifts that are difficult (vs. easy) to decode (e.g., when a target shows up, the actor looks toward empty space, rather than the target) were found to differentially activate the STS region in typical adults but not in adults with ASD (Pelphrey et al., 2005). In addition, activation of the FFG, but not the amygdala, can be altered to a normal level in individuals with ASD by compelling people with ASD to perform visual scan paths that involve fixating on the eyes of a fearful face (Perlman et al., 2011). With respect to auditory signals, individuals with ASD (vs. controls) fail to activate the voice-selective regions of the STS in response to vocal sounds (Gervais et al., 2004).

The behavioral deficit in mental state reasoning in ASD has been linked to less activation in the TPJ region (Lombardo et al., 2011). Participants were asked to judge, "How likely is the British Queen to think that keeping a diary is important?" (mental state reasoning) or "How likely is the British Queen to have bony elbows?" (physical reasoning). In typical individuals, the TPJ region activated more strongly to mental state reasoning than physical reasoning; however, in individuals with ASD, there was no such selective activation in this region. Interestingly, there was no interaction between group and judgment conditions in the dmPFC, perhaps because both judgment conditions require people to represent the British Queen as separate and different from them which are correlates of direct and reflected self-knowledge.

Historically, a lack of predictive, biologically informed profiles has contributed to the status quo of imprecise treatments, wasted time and resources, and failures to optimize progress for children and families living with ASD. Fortunately, this situation is rapidly improving. Research within the field of developmental social neuroscience has now advanced sufficiently to provide the first sensitive, quantitative, and biologically meaningful markers of ASD symptoms (e.g., Kaiser et al., 2010). These tentative *biomarkers* are now being evaluated for their utility in measuring and predicting individual responses to evidenced-based interventions (e.g., Yang et al., 2016). As such, the work has advanced our understanding of ASD and may ultimately inform and guide personalized therapies. (McPartland et al., 2014).

Because autism is a developmental disorder, it is particularly important to diagnose and treat ASD early in life. As noted previously, early deficits in attention to other's actions, for instance (what we call biological motion), derail subsequent experiences in attending to higher-level social information, thereby driving development toward more severe dysfunction and stimulating deficits in additional domains of functioning, such as language development. The lack of reliable predictors of the ASD during the first year of life has been a major impediment to its effective treatment. Without early predictors, and in the absence of a firm diagnosis until behavioral symptoms emerge, treatment is often delayed for 2 or more years, eclipsing a crucial period in which intervention may be particularly successful in ameliorating some of the social and communicative impairments seen in ASD.

In response to the great need for sensitive (able to identify subtle cases) and specific (able to distinguish autism from other disorders) early indicators of ASD, such as biomarkers, many research teams from around the world have been studying patterns of infant development using prospective longitudinal studies of infant siblings of children with ASD compared to infant siblings without familial risks. Such designs gather longitudinal information about developmental trajectories across the first 3 years of life, followed by clinical diagnosis at approximately 36 months. Biobehavioral markers—especially eye-tracking studies—of multidimensional social processes are beginning to prove useful in early identification of atypical developmental processes among children at increased genetic risk for developing difficulties in social information processing (e.g., Jones & Klin, 2013; see also Anderson, 2014).

Studies pursuing early biobehavioral markers are potentially problematic in that many of the social features of autism do not emerge in typical development until after 12 months of age. It is not certain that these symptom features will manifest during the limited periods of observation involved in clinical evaluations or in pediatricians' offices. Moreover, across development, but especially during infancy, behavior is widely variable and often unreliable. At present, longitudinal behavioral observation is the only means to detect the emergence of ASD and predict a diagnosis (Jones & Klin, 2013). However, measuring the brain activity associated with social perception can detect differences not appearing behaviorally until much later. The identification of biomarkers utilizing the imaging methods we have described offers promise for earlier detection of atypical social development. Event-related potentials (ERP) measures of brain response predict subsequent development of autism in infants as young as 6 months old who showed normal patterns of visual fixation (as measured by eye tracking) (Elsabbagh et al., 2012). These types of studies illustrate the great promise of brain imaging for earlier recognition of ASD. With earlier detection, treatments could move from addressing existing symptoms to preventing their emergence by altering the course of abnormal brain development and steering it toward compensation or normality.

To the extent that research can further elucidate developmental trajectories of the neural circuitry supporting pivotal, early developing social abilities, it might inform the design of more effective programs for identifying and remediating risk for difficulties in these areas. It is generally accepted that earlier educational interventions are more effective for treating a variety of behavioral and academic childhood problems and neurodevelopmental disorders. Therefore, early identification of children with difficulties in social cognition is pivotal to optimizing individual intervention outcomes. A neurobiological marker for individual differences in multidimensional social representation abilities would then not solely be important for improving early identification, but also could offer advantages for earlier interventions. Moreover, it could be that the neurobiological marker would relate to the severity of specific deficits, helping us to better understand the heterogeneity characteristic of neuropsychiatric disorders. With this information, more targeted treatments could be developed, on a child-by-child basis, and implemented early in ontogeny. Early targeted intervention then might guarantee the most effective course of intervention possible, also improving efficiency and standardization. Furthermore, functional neuroimaging techniques, might actually provide a means to better quantify treatment effectiveness and reveal whether behavioral improvements correspond to compensatory changes in brain function or normalization of developmental pathways.

Early and longitudinal study will be critical in defining brain phenotypes. This is because the shape of developmental trajectories of brain functioning in specific circuits will provide more detail on the nature of the abnormalities than will analysis of brain phenotypes in adulthood. Despite much progress, there is still much to learn about the early longitudinal changes in brain connectivity, function, and temporal dynamics that support the development of the ability to integrate a broad array of emotional and social cues from multiple sensory modalities (e.g., vision, touch, audition) in the service of social cognition. Likewise, the neurobiological basis of individual differences in multimodal, multidimensional social cognitive abilities remains poorly understood. There are straightforward and compelling methodological reasons to adopt a longitudinal design. Neuroimaging data are inherently noisy because individual brains are different from one another. A longitudinal design is the only way to study developmental processes coupled with the power of within-subject statistics. It also makes it more likely that we will be able to detect relationships between different developmental changes. For example, just knowing that both Task A and Task B change between 4 and 6 months of age tells us almost nothing about those tasks, but individual differences in the response to Task A at time 1, or the change in Task A performance, are good predictors of individual differences in the magnitude of change in Task B and will yield much stronger inferential leverage upon which to build lasting theoretical contributions.

There is currently no single biological test for ASD. The diagnostic process involves a combination of parental report and clinical observation. Children with significant impairments across the social/communication domain who also exhibit repetitive behaviors can qualify for the ASD diagnosis. As discussed earlier, there is wide variability in the precise symptom profile an individual may exhibit. Since Kanner first described ASD in 1943, important commonalities in symptom presentation have been used to compile criteria for an ASD diagnosis. These diagnostic criteria have evolved during the past 76 years and continue to evolve, yet impaired social functioning remains a required symptom for an ASD diagnosis. Deficits in social functioning are present in varying degrees for simple behaviors, such as eye contact, and for complex behaviors, like navigating the give-and-take of a group conversation, for individuals of all functioning levels (i.e., high or low IQ). Moreover, difficulties with social information processing occur in both visual (e.g., Pelphrey et al., 2002) and auditory (e.g., Dawson et al., 1998) sensory modalities. While repetitive behaviors or language deficits are seen in other disorders (e.g., obsessive-compulsive disorder and specific language impairment, respectively), basic social deficits of this nature are unique to ASD. Onset of the social deficits appears to precede difficulties in other domains (Osterling, Dawson, & Munson, 2002) and may emerge as early as 6 months of age (Maestro et al., 2002).

This focus on social cognition and the importance of the social brain led us to hypothesize that factors contributing to the expression of ASD exert their effects through a circumscribed set of neuroanatomical structures, so that the simplest and potentially most powerful signatures of ASD will be found at the level of brain systems. Such "neural signatures" of ASD may serve as critical endophenotypes to facilitate the study of the pathophysiological mechanisms. Endophenotypes, or characteristics that are not immediately available to observation but that reflect an underlying genetic liability for disease, expose the most basic components of a complex psychiatric disorder and are more stable across the life span than are observable behavior (Gottesman & Shields, 1973). In a study pursuing neural signatures of ASD, we assessed three groups of children using functional magnetic resonance imaging (fMRI). These were children diagnosed with ASD, unaffected siblings (US) of children with ASD who were typically developing, and typically developing (TD) children without a relative with ASD. The three groups of participants were matched on chronological age and were of similar cognitive ability, all within the average range. Notably, the US and TD groups were matched on measures of social responsiveness and adaptive behavior. This rigorous matching ensured that both groups were unaffected by ASD and demonstrated equivalent levels of social responsiveness. In addition, strict exclusion criteria were used for the TD and US groups to rule out other developmental disorders and the "broader autism phenotype" (BAP) in each participant, as well as in first- and second-degree relatives of the US participants.

We measured brain responses in these groups of children using fMRI while they viewed socially meaningful biological motion (movements of other people) to reveal three types of neural signatures: (1) state activity related to having ASD that characterizes the nature of disruption in brain circuitry; (2) trait activity reflecting shared areas of dysfunction in US and children with ASD, thereby providing a promising neuroendophenotype to facilitate efforts to bridge genomic complexity and disorder heterogeneity; and (3) compensatory activity, unique to US, suggesting a neural systems level mechanism by which US might compensate for an increased genetic risk for developing ASD. The identification of state activity extends previous research implicating the right amygdala, right pSTS, bilateral FG, left vlPFC, and vmPFC in adults with ASD by showing that dysfunction in these regions is already present in school-age children with ASD (Castelli et al., 2002; Gilbert et al., 2009; Schultz et al., 2000). This was an important advance in the field, given that previous reports of atypical neural response to biological motion included only adult subjects. In addition, activity in the state-defined right pSTS was associated with the severity of social deficits in individuals with ASD. Individuals with higher social responsiveness scale scores (SRS; Constantino & Frazier, 2013) exhibited less activation to biological motion within the right pSTS. This finding suggests that activity in the pSTS might serve as a biological marker to subdivide the autism spectrum on the basis of severity. Furthermore, activity in the state-defined region of the left vlPFC was found to reflect the level of social responsiveness of the TD children, indicating a coupling of social behavior and brain mechanisms for social perception. The evidence of dysfunction in brain mechanisms for social perception in young children with ASD explains previous behavioral findings of disrupted biological motion perception (Klin et al., 2009). Given that social interaction relies on the accurate perception of other people's actions, state activity indicating regions of dysfunction associated with the manifestation of ASD provides a significant step toward more fully characterizing the biological underpinnings of this neurodevelopmental disorder.

In accordance with Gottesman and Gould's (2003) characterization of endophenotypes, trait activations, including those in the left dlPFC, right ITG, and bilateral FG, were shared between affected individuals (ASD group) and first-degree relatives (US group). These findings are particularly noteworthy because we explicitly ruled out BAP in the US group. This implies that our neuroimaging paradigm offers a remarkable level of sensitivity that transcends clinical evaluation. Although the US group was indistinguishable from the TD group at the behavioral level, the trait activity findings reveal similar neural signatures in the US and ASD groups. Consistent with this interpretation, social responsiveness was associated with overall trait activity in the US group and with trait-defined left dlPFC in the TD group. Furthermore, whereas the state regions could arise as an effect of having ASD, the trait activity cannot be explained in this way; rather, this trait activity likely reflects the genetic vulnerability to develop ASD. The key implication of our trait activity findings is that we provide a functional neuroendophenotype that should help bridge the gene–behavior gap, thereby accelerating the search for pathophysiological mechanisms.

The US group exhibited unique areas of activation in the vmPFC and the right pSTS, regions previously implicated in aspects of social perception and social cognition (Adolphs, 1999). These regions might reflect the absence of additional genetic or environmental factors that confer risk for ASD. Alternatively, they could represent a process through which brain function was altered over development to compensate for an increased genetic risk to develop ASD. We found that the activity in these regions did not vary with chronological age. Thus, it is possible that the compensatory regions reflect the outcome of a process occurring earlier in development, during a sensitive period for the development of brain mechanisms for social perception. This might be likely, given that autism is a developmental disorder that emerges during the first years of life, well before age 4 years (the youngest age studied in this sample). Nonetheless, we cannot yet draw firm conclusions regarding the compensatory activity. Indeed, longitudinal research in younger children is critically needed to better understand the origins of this compensatory activity, which likely has both genetic and environmental influences. Future studies are needed to compare the activity in these regions in US participants with and without BAP, to determine the function and etiology of this brain response to biological motion. The implication of these findings is that these regions could represent important targets for treatments and provide a measure of the effectiveness of intervention, as well as a better understanding of the mechanisms through which successful treatments function. The US exhibited unique areas of activation in regions previously implicated in aspects of social perception and social cognition. This might reflect the absence of additional genetic or environmental factors that confer risk for ASD. Alternatively, it could represent a process through which brain function is altered over development to compensate for an increased genetic risk to develop ASD.

Our study and many other group-based comparative studies reveal important clues about the neurobiological mechanisms that give rise to ASD symptomatology. Yet, treating ASD as a unitary condition, whereby individuals with ASD are grouped together and compared to "neurotypical" (typically developing) people, undermines the potential of translational research to contribute to "precision medicine" (Insel, 2014) in ASD. Because of the limited quality of the behavioral methods used to diagnose ASD and current clinical diagnostic practice, which permits similar diagnoses despite distinct symptom profiles (McPartland et al., 2011), it is possible that the group of children currently referred to as having ASD may actually represent different syndromes with distinct causes. The ability to integrate a broad array of social cues from multiple sensory domains is impaired in many neuropsychiatric disorders. The spectrum from mental health to mental illness is continuous and not categorical—Mother Nature has not yet read the *DSM-5*. Thus, a dimensional, individual differences approach is crucial to understanding multimodal social cognitive abilities and their development. Autistic individuals are currently defined solely on the basis of behavioral indicators. Undoubtedly, this approach lumps together individuals with common behavioral phenotypes but possibly quite different underlying etiologies. By defining functional brain phenotypes based on neurofunctional/behavioral developmental pathways and activation patterns, fMRI studies of children have the potential to dissect the heterogeneity present in these disorders. Functional neuroimaging studies could reveal different brain phenotypes in the circuitry involved in social cognition. This approach may allow us to partition individuals with autism, a complex, etiologically heterogeneous disorder, into more homogenous subgroups (e.g., Yang et al., 2017). These profiles, in turn, may inform treatment of ASD by helping us to match specific treatments to specific profiles.

The challenge of quantifying brain profiles in ASD is now being addressed via the application to brain imaging data of artificial intelligence (AI) theories and analytic techniques in order to derive sensitive, reliable brain measures that are informative at the level of the individual (e.g., Björnsdotter et al., 2016; Yang et al., 2016, 2017; Zhuang et al., 2018). Consider, for instance, our use of fMRI and machine-learning multivariate pattern analysis (MVPA) techniques to identify profiles of activation in young children with ASD that predict responses to 16 weeks of an evidence-based behavioral treatment (Yang et al., 2016)—*pivotal response treatment* (PRT). Neural predictors were identified in the pretreatment levels of activity in response to biological versus scrambled motion in the neural circuits that support social information processing (STS, fusiform gyrus, amygdala, inferior parietal cortex, and superior parietal lobule) and social motivation/reward (orbitofrontal cortex, insula, putamen, pallidum, and ventral striatum). The predictive value of our findings for individual children with ASD was supported by a MVPA with cross-validation. By predicting who will respond to a particular treatment for ASD, these findings marked the very first evidence of prediction/stratification biomarkers in young children with ASD. In MVPA, the samples were divided into training and testing datasets, which constitute a *cross-validation framework* in which the predictive model is first trained with the training set and then used to predict the regression labels of the sample in the testing set. This type of cross-validation provides approximately unbiased estimates of effects, generalizable to new samples, thus helping to minimize the likelihood that the results overfit the data (Chawarska, Macari, et al., 2016; Chawarska, Ye, et al., 2016).

Our findings move the field toward the goal of targeted, personalized treatment for individuals with ASD. The knowledge gained can be utilized in future work to tailor individualized treatment, refine PRT, and develop novel interventions. This study adds to the understanding of the pretreatment neural underpinnings of successful behavioral response to PRT. In the future, our results may drive the construction of algorithms to predict which, among several treatments, is most likely to benefit a given person. In addition, PRT is a multicomponent treatment; hence, future studies might use dismantling designs to isolate treatment components and their association with the neuropredictive targets identified here. This line of work could inform the development of treatment strategies that would target specific patterns of neural strengths and vulnerabilities within a given patient—consistent with the priority of creating individually tailored interventions, customized to the characteristics of a given person.

The predictive biomarkers identified in this study can be interpreted as the pretreatment neurobiological readiness to respond to a specific treatment, PRT. It should be noted that the brain regions where activity before treatment correlated with SRS scores before treatment did not overlap with the neuropredictive network described here, which indicates that the neuropredictive network is specific to change in severity in young children with ASD. As such, our findings offer the hope that pre- or concurrent treatments (whether pharmacological, direct stimulation, neurofeedback, or behaviorally based) that improve the functioning of the neuropredictive markers identified here may increase the effectiveness of evidenced-based behavioral treatments for core deficits in children with ASD. On the other hand, our findings are also particularly important for those children who would otherwise be the least likely to benefit from these expensive and time-consuming forms of treatment. For example, in a randomized, double-blind, cross-over functional fMRI study (Gordon et al., 2013), we reported that intranasal oxytocin administered to children with ASD increases activity during social versus nonsocial judgments in several of the same brain regions identified as predictive in the present study (e.g., amygdala, orbitofrontal cortex, STS region, and ventral striatum). These findings, coupled with those in the current report, raise the provocative hypothesis that the administration of intranasal oxytocin, by priming key neural circuits for social motivation and social perception, may serve to enhance the effectiveness of interventions like PRT in the very children who might be less biologically ready to respond.

This and similar research developments mark the start of a new era in which advanced neuroimage analysis will evolve into an integral part of a translational research chain. Novel behavioral treatment and pharmacotherapies for ASD may be further developed in young children, with the tremendous benefit of directly and more precisely assessing impairment and change in targeted neural circuits. Neuroimaging-derived biological markers could be used, at the outset, to make treatment decisions related to dose, duration, intensity, and specific behavioral treatment approach as well as related to the use of concurrent pharmacological intervention.

## References

Accardo, A. L., Bean, K., Cook, B., Gillies, A., Edgington, R., Kuder, S., & Bomgardner, E. M. (2019). College access, success and equity for students on the autism spectrum. *Journal of Autism and Developmental Disorders, 49*, 4877–4890. https://doi.org/10.1007/s10803-019-04205-8

Adolphs, R., Tranel, D., Hamann, S., Young, A., Calder, A., Phelps, E., Anderson, A., Lee, G., & Damasio, A. (1999). Recognition of facial emotion in nine individuals with bilateral amygdala damage. *Neuropsychologia, 37*(10), 1111–1117.

Allison, T., Puce, A., & McCarthy, G. (2000). Social perception from visual cues: Role of the STS region. *Trends in Cognitive Sciences, 4*, 267–278. https://doi.org/10.1016/s1364-6613(00)01501-1

Amaral, D. G., Price, J. L., Pitkanen, A., & Carmichael, S. T. (1992). Anatomical organization of the primate amygdaloid complex. In J. P. Aggleton (Ed.), *The amygdala: Neurobiological aspects of emotion, memory, and mental dysfunction* (pp. 1–66). Wiley-Liss.

Amodio, D. M., & Frith, C. D. (2006). Meeting of minds: The medial frontal cortex and social cognition. *Nature reviews: Neuroscience, 7*(4), 268–277. https://doi.org/10.1038/nrn1884

Anderson, G. M. (2014). Biochemical biomarkers for autism spectrum disorder. In F. Volkmar, R. Paul, S. J. Rogers, & K. A. Pelphrey (Eds.), *Handbook of autism and pervasive developmental disorders, Volume 1: Diagnosis, development, and brain mechanisms*, 4th ed. (pp. 457–481). Wiley.

Baron-Cohen, S. (2010). Empathizing, systemizing, and the extreme male brain theory of autism. *Progress in Brain Research, 186*, 167–175. https://dx.doi.org/10.1016/B978-0-444-53630-3.00011-7

Baron-Cohen, S. (2011). The empathizing-systemizing (E-S) theory of autism: A cognitive developmental account. In U. Goswami (Ed.), *The Wiley-Blackwell handbook of childhood cognitive development*, 2nd ed. (pp 626–639) Wiley-Blackwell.

Baron-Cohen, S. (2012). Autism, empathizing-systemizing (E-S) theory, and pathological altruism. In B. Oakley, A. Knafo, G. Madhavan, & D. S. Wilson (Eds.), *Pathological altruism* (pp. 345–348). Oxford University Press.

Baron-Cohen, S., Leslie, A. M., & Frith, U. (1985). Does the autistic child have a "theory of mind"? *Cognition, 21*(1), 37–46. https://doi.org/10.1016/0010-0277(85)90022-8

Baron-Cohen, S., Wheelwright, S., Lawson, J., Griffin, R., Ashwin, C., Billington, J., & Chakrabarti, B. (2014). Empathizing and systemizing in autism spectrum conditions. In F. R. Volkmar, S.J Rogers, R. Paul, & K. A. Pelphrey (Eds.), *Handbook of autism and pervasive developmental disorders, vol. 1*, 4th ed. (pp. 628–639). Wiley.

Bettelheim, B. (1959). Joey: A "mechanical boy." *Scientific American, 200*(3), 116–127. http://dx.doi.org/10.1038/scientificamerican0359-116

Bettelheim, B. (1967). *The empty fortress: Infantile autism and the birth of the self.* Free Press.

Bigham, S. (2008). Comprehension of pretense in children with autism. *British Journal of Developmental Psychology, 26*(2), 265–280. https://doi.org/10.1348/026151007X235855

Björnsdotter, M., Wang, N., Pelphrey, K., & Kaiser, M. D. (2016). Evaluation of quantified social perception circuit activity as a neurobiological marker of autism spectrum disorder. *JAMA Psychiatry, 73*(6), 614–621. https://doi.org/10.1001/jamapsychiatry.2016.0219

Brothers, L. (1990). The social brain: A project for integrating primate behavior and neurophysiology in a new domain. *Concepts in Neuroscience, 1,* 27–51. https://doi.org/10.1016/0166-4328(90)90108-q

Brothers, L., Ring, B., & Kling, A. (1990). Response of neurons in the macaque amygdala to complex social stimuli. *Behavioural Brain Research, 41,* 199–213. https://doi.org/10.1016/0166-4328(90)90108-q

Brown, J. R., & Rogers, S. J. (2003). Cultural Issues in Autism. In R. L. Hendren, S. Ozonoff, & S. Rogers (Eds.), *Autism spectrum disorders* (pp. 209–226). American Psychiatric Press.

Carter, A. S., Ornstein Davis, N., Klin, A., & Volkmar, F. R. (2014). Social development in autism. In F. R. Volkmar, S. J. Rogers, R. Paul, & K. A. Pelphrey (Eds.), *Handbook of autism and pervasive developmental disorders, vol. 1,* 4th ed. (pp. 312–334). Wiley.

Castelli, F., Happé, F., Frith, U., & Frith, C. (2000). Movement and mind: A functional imaging study of perception and interpretation of complex intentional movement patterns. *NeuroImage, 12,* 314–325. https://doi.org/10.1006/nimg.2000.0612

Castelli, F., Frith, C., Happe, F., & Frith, U. (2002). Autism, Asperger syndrome and brain mechanisms for the attribution of mental states to animated shapes. *Brain, 125*(Pt 8), 1839–1849.

Chawarska, K., Macari, S., Powell, K., DiNicola, L., & Shic, F. (2016). Enhanced social attention in female infant siblings at risk for autism. *Journal of the American Academy of Child & Adolescent Psychiatry, 55*(3), 188–195. https://doi.org/http://dx.doi.org/10.1016/j.jaac.2015.11.016

Chawarska, K., & Volkmar, F. R. (2020). *Autism spectrum disorder in the first years of life.* Guilford.

Chawarska, K., Ye, S., Shic, F., & Chen, L. (2016). Multilevel differences in spontaneous social attention in toddlers with autism spectrum disorder. *Child Development, 87*(2), 543–557. http://dx.doi.org/10.1111/cdev.12473

Chiang, H. M., Tsai, L. Y., Cheung, Y. K., Brown, A., & Li, H. (2014). A meta-analysis of differences in IQ profiles between individuals with Asperger's disorder and high-functioning autism. *Journal of Autism & Developmental Disorders, 44*(7), 1577–1596. https://dx.doi.org/10.1007/s10803-013-2025-2

Chown, N. (2017). *Understanding and evaluating autism theory.* Jessica Kingsley.

Constantino, J. N., & Frazier, T. W. (2013). Commentary: The observed association between autistic severity measured by the social responsiveness scale (SRS) and general psychopathology—a response to Hus et al. (2013). *Journal of Child Psychology and Psychiatry, and Allied Disciplines, 54*(6), 695–697. https://doi.org/10.1111/jcpp.12064

Despert, J. L. (1971). Reflections on early infantile autism. *Journal of Autism & Childhood Schizophrenia, 1*(4), 363–367.

Donvan, J., & Zuker, C. (2016). *In a different kay: The story of autism.* Penguin/Random House.

Elsabbagh, M., Mercure, E., Hudry, K., Chandler, S., Pasco, G., Charman, T., Pickles, A., Baron-Cohen, S., Bolton, P., Johnson, M. H., & BASIS Team (2012). Infant neural sensitivity to dynamic eye gaze is associated with later emerging autism. *Current Biology: CB, 22*(4), 338–342. https://doi.org/10.1016/j.cub.2011.12.056

Fombonne, E. (2005). Epidemiological studies of pervasive developmental disorders. In F. R. Volkmar, A. Klin, R. Paul, & D. J. Cohen (Eds.), *Handbook of Autism and Pervasive Developmental Disorders,* 1st ed. (pp. 42–69). Wiley.

Frazier, T. W., Strauss, M., Klingemier, E. W., Zetzer, E. E., Hardan, A. Y., Eng, C., and Youngstrom, E. A. (2017). A meta-analysis of gaze differences to social and nonsocial information between individuals with and without autism. *Journal of the American Academy of Child & Adolescent Psychiatry, 56*(7), 546–555.

Freeth, M., Milne, E., Sheppard, E., & Ramachandran, R. (2014). Autism across cultures: Perspectives from non-western cultures and implications for research. In F. R. Volkmar, R. Paul, S. J. Rogers, & K. A. Pelphrey (Eds.), *Handbook of autism and pervasive developmental disorders,* 4th ed. (pp.997–11013). Wiley. https://doi.org/10.1002/9781118911389.hautc43

Gerhardt, P. F., Cicero, F., & Mayville, E. (2014). Employment and related services for adults with autism spectrum disorders. In F. R. Volkmar, B. Reichow, & J. C. McPartland (Eds.), *Adolescents and adults with autism spectrum disorders* (pp. 105–119). Springer Science. http://dx.doi.org/10.1007/978-1-4939-0506-5_6

Gernsbacher, M. A., & Yergeau, M. (2019). Empirical failures of the claim that autistic people lack a theory of mind. *Archives of Scientific Psychology, 7*(1), 102–118. https://doi.org/http://dx.doi.org/10.1037/arc0000067

Gervais, H., Belin, P., Boddaert, N., Leboyer, M., Coez, A., Sfaello, I., Barthélémy, C., Brunelle, F., Samson, Y., & Zilbovicius, M. (2004). Abnormal cortical voice processing in autism. *Nature Neuroscience, 7*(8), 801–802. https://doi.org/10.1038/nn1291

Gilbert, S. J., Meuwese, J. D. I., Towgood, K. J., Frith, C. D., & Burgess, P. W. (2009). Abnormal functional specialization within medial prefrontal cortex in high-functioning autism: A multi-voxel similarity analysis. *Brain, 132*(Pt 4), 869–878.

Gobbini, M. I., Koralek, A. C., Bryan, R. E., Montgomery, K. J., and Haxby, J. V. (2007). Two takes on the social brain: A comparison of theory of mind tasks. *Journal of Cognitive Neuroscience, 19*(11), 1803–1814.

Gordon, I., Vander Wyk, B. C., Bennett, R. H., Cordeaux, C., Lucas, M. V., Eilbott, J. A., Zagoory-Sharon, O., Leckman, J. F., Feldman, R., & Pelphrey, K. A. (2013). Oxytocin enhances brain function in children with autism. *Proceedings of the National Academy of Sciences of the United States of America, 110*(52), 20953–20958. https://doi.org/10.1073/pnas.1312857110

Gottesman, I. I., & Shields, J. (1973). Genetic theorizing and schizophrenia. *British Journal of Psychiatry: The Journal of Mental Science, 122*(566), 15–30. https://doi.org/10.1192/bjp.122.1.15

Greenberg, G. (2013). *The book of woe: The DSM and the unmaking of psychiatry.* Penguin.

Grinker, R. R., Kang-Yi, C. D., Ahmann, C., Beidas, R. S., Lagman, A., & Mandell, D. S. (2015). Cultural adaptation and translation of outreach materials on autism spectrum disorder. *Journal of Autism and Developmental Disorders, 45*(8), 2329–2336. http://dx.doi.org/10.1007/s10803-015-2397-6

Hamilton, A. F. D. C., Brindley, R., & Frith, U. (2009). Visual perspective taking impairment in children with autistic spectrum disorder. *Cognition, 113*(1), 37–44.

Happé, F. G. (1996). Studying weak central coherence at low levels: Children with autism do not succumb to visual illusions.

A research note. *Journal of Child Psychology and Psychiatry and Allied Disciplines, 37*(7), 873–877. https://doi.org/10.1111/j.1469-7610.1996.tb01483.x

Hatfield, M., Ciccarelli, M., Falkmer, T., & Falkmer, M. (2018). Factors related to successful transition planning for adolescents on the autism spectrum. *Journal of Research in Special Educational Needs, 18*(1), 3–14. http://dx.doi.org/10.1111/1471-3802.12388

Heider, F. (1958). *The psychology of interpersonal relations.* Wiley.

Heider, F., & Simmel, M. (1944). An experimental study of apparent behavior. *American Journal of Psychology, 57*, 243–259.

Hermelin, B. (2001). *Bright splinters of the mind: A personal story of research with autistic savants.* Jessica Kingsley.

Hill, E. L. (2004). Evaluating the theory of executive dysfunction in autism. *Developmental Review, 24*(2), 189–233.

Howlin, P. (2013). Outcomes in adults with autism spectrum disorders. In F. Volkmar, S. Rogers, R. Paul, & K. Pelphrey (Eds.), *Handbook of autism,* 4th ed. Wiley.

Insel, T. R. (2014). The NIHM Research Domain Criteria (RDoC) Project: Precision medicine for psychiatry. *American Journal of Psychiatry, 171*(4), 395–397.

Jackson, S. L., & Volkmar, F. R. (2019). Diagnosis and definition of autism and other pervasive developmental disorders. In F. Volkmar (Ed.), *Autism and the pervasive developmental disorders,* 3rd ed. (pp. 1–24). Cambridge Universitiy Pres.

Jones, W., & Klin, A. (2013). Attention to eyes is present but in decline in 2-6-month-old infants later diagnosed with autism. *Nature, 504*(7480), 427–431. https://doi.org/10.1038/nature12715

Kaiser, M. D., Hudac, C. M., Shultz, S., Lee, S. M., Cheung, C., Berken, A. M., Deen, B., Pitskel, N. B., Sugrue, D. R., Voos, A. C., Saulnier, C. A., Ventola, P., Wolf, J. M., Klin, A., Vander Wyk, B. C., & Pelphrey, K. A. (2010). Neural signatures of autism. *Proceedings of the National Academy of Sciences of the United States of America, 107*(49), 21223–21228. https://doi.org/10.1073/pnas.1010412107

Kanner, L. (1943). Autistic disturbances of affective contact. *Nervous Child, 2*, 217–250.

Kanwisher, N., McDermott, J., & Chun, M. M. (1997). The fusiform face area: A module in human extrastriate cortex specialized for face perception. *Journal of Neuroscience, 17*(11), 4302–4311. https://doi.org/10.1523/JNEUROSCI.17-11-04302.1997

Kelley, E., Paul, J. J., Fein, D., & Naigles, L. R. (2006). Residual language deficits in optimal outcome children with a history of autism. *Journal of Autism & Developmental Disorders, 36*(6), 807–828. https://doi.org/10.1007/s10803-006-0111-

Klin, A., Jones, W., Schultz, R., & Volkmar, F. (2003). The enactive mind, or from actions to cognition: Lessons from autism. *Philosophical Transactions of the Royal Society of London - Series B: Biological Sciences, 358*(1430), 345–360. https://doi.org/10.1098/rstb.2002.1202

Klin, A., Lin, D. J., Gorrindo, P., Ramsay, G., & Jones, W. (2009). Two-year-olds with autism fail to orient towards human biological motion but attend instead to non-social, physical contingencies. *Nature, 459*, 257–261. https://doi.org/10.1038/nature07868

Krahn, T. M., & Fenton, A. (2012). The extreme male brain theory of autism and the potential adverse effects for boys and girls with autism. *Journal of Bioethical Inquiry, 9*(1), 93–103. http://dx.doi.org/10.1007/s11673-011-9350-y

Lai, C. L. E., Lau, Z., Lui, S. S., Lok, E., Tam, V., Chan, Q., Cheng, K. M., Lam, S. M., & Cheung, E. F. (2017). Meta-analysis of neuropsychological measures of executive functioning in children and adolescents with high-functioning autism spectrum disorder. *Autism Research, 10*(5), 911–939. http://dx.doi.org/10.1002/aur.1723

Lombardo, M. V., Chakrabarti, B., Bullmore, E. T., & Baron-Cohen, S. (2011). Specialization of right temporo-parietal junction for mentalizing and its relation to social impairments in autism. *NeuroImage, 56*(3), 1832–1838. https://doi.org/10.1016/j.neuroimage.2011.02.067

Lord, C., Petkova, E., Hus, V., Gan, W., Lu, F., Martin, D., . . . Risi, S. (2012). A multisite study of the clinical diagnosis of different autism spectrum disorders. *Archives of General Psychiatry, 69*(3), 306–313. https://doi.org/10.1111/j.1469-7610.2012.02547.x

Maestro, S., Muratori, F., Cavallaro, M. C., Pei, F., Stern, D., Golse, B., & Palacio-Espasa, F. (2002). Attentional skills during the first 6 months of age in autism spectrum disorder. *Journal of the American Academy of Child & Adolescent Psychiatry, 41*(10), 1239–1245.

Mandell, D. S., Wiggins, L. D., Carpenter, L. A., Daniels, J., DiGuiseppi, C., Durkin, M. S., Giarelli, E., Morrier, M. J., Nicholas, J. S., Pinto-Martin, J. A., Shattuck, P. T., Thomas, K. C., Yeargin-Allsopp, M., & Kirby, R. S. (2009). Racial/ethnic disparities in the identification of children with autism spectrum disorders. *American Journal of Public Health, 99*(3), 493–498. https://doi.org/10.2105/AJPH.2007.131243

Matson, J. L., Kozlowski, A. M., Hattier, M. A., Horovitz, M., & Sipes, M. (2012). DSM-IV vs DSM-5 diagnostic criteria for toddlers with autism. *Developmental Neurorehabilitation, 15*(3), 185–190. http://dx.doi.org/10.3109/17518423.2012.672341

McPartland, J. C., Reichow, B., & Volkmar, F. R. (2012). Sensitivity and specificity of proposed DSM-5 diagnostic criteria for autism spectrum disorder. *Journal of the American Academy of Child & Adolescent Psychiatry, 51*(4), 368–383. https://dx.doi.org/10.1016/j.jaac.2012.01.007

McPartland, J. C., Tillman, R. M., Yang, D. Y. J., Bernier, R. A., & Pelphrey, K. A. (2014). The social neuroscience of autism spectrum disorder. In F. Volkmar, R. Paul, S. J. Rogers, & K. A. Pelphrey (Eds.), *Handbook of autism and pervasive developmental disorders, Volume 1: Diagnosis, development, and brain mechanisms,* 4th ed. (pp. 482–496). Wiley.

McPartland, J. C., Coffman, M., & Pelphrey, K. A. (2011). Recent advances in understanding the neural bases of autism spectrum disorder. *Current Opinion in Pediatrics, 23*(6), 628–632.

Moran, J. M., Young, L. L., Saxe, R., Lee, S. M., O'Young, D., Mavros, P. L., & Gabrieli, J. D. (2011). Impaired theory of mind for moral judgment in high-functioning autism. *Proceedings of the National Academy of Sciences of the United States of America, 108*(7), 2688–2692. https://doi.org/10.1073/pnas.1011734108

Nuske, H. J., & Bavin, E. L. (2011). Narrative comprehension in 4-7-year-old children with autism: Testing the Weak Central Coherence account. *International Journal of Language & Communication Disorders, 46*(1), 108–119. https://doi.org/10.3109/13682822.2010.484847

Oien, R. A., Hart, L., Schjolberg, S., Wall, C. A., Kim, E. S., Nordahl-Hansen, A., Eisemann, M. R., Chawarska, K., Volkmar, F. R., & Shic, F. (2017). Parent-endorsed sex differences in toddlers with and without ASD: Utilizing the M-CHAT. *Journal of Autism and Developmental Disorders, 47*(1), 126–134. http://dx.doi.org/10.1007/s10803-016-2945-8

Oien, R. A., Schjolberg, S., Volkmar, F. R., Shic, F., Cicchetti, D. V., Nordahl-Hansen, A., Stenberg, N., Hornig, M., Havdahl, A., Oyen, A.-S., Ventola, P., Susser, E. S., Eisemann, M. R., & Chawarska, K. (2018). Clinical features of children with autism who passed 18-month screening. *Pediatrics, 141*(6), 1–103596. https://doi.org/10.1542/peds.2017-3596

Orinstein, A. J., Helt, M., Troyb, E., Tyson, K. E., Barton, M. L., Eigsti, I.-M., Naigles, L., & Fein, D. A. (2014). Intervention for optimal outcome in children and adolescents with a history of autism. *Journal of Developmental and Behavioral Pediatrics, 35*(4), 247–256. http://dx.doi.org/10.1097/DBP.0000000000000037

Osterling, J. A., Dawson, G., and Munson, J. A. (2002). Early recognition of 1-year-old infants with autism spectrum disorder versus mental retardation. *Development & Psychopathology, 14*(2), 239–251.

Ozonoff, S., & Schetter, P. L. (2007). Executive dysfunction in autism spectrum disorders: From research to practice. In L. Meltzer (Ed.), *Executive function in education: From theory to practice* (pp. 133–160). Guilford.

Pellicano, E. (2011). Psychological models of autism: An overview. In I. Roth & P. Rezaie (Eds.), *Researching the autism spectrum: Contemporary perspectives* (pp. 219–265). Cambridge University Press. http://dx.doi.org/10.1017/CBO9780511973918.010

Pelphrey, K. A., Mitchell, T. V., McKeown, M. J., Goldstein, J., Allison, T., & McCarthy, G. (2003). Brain activity evoked by the perception of human walking: Controlling for meaningful coherent motion. *Journal of Neuroscience, 23*, 6819–6825. https://doi.org/10.1523/JNEUROSCI.23-17-06819.2003

Pelphrey, K. A., Morris, J. P., & McCarthy, G. (2005). Neural basis of eye gaze processing deficits in autism. *Brain, 128*(5), 1038–1048. https://doi.org/10.1093/brain/awh404

Pennington, B. F., Rogers, S. J., Bennetto, L., Griffith, E. M., Reed, D., & Shyu, V. (1997). Validity tests of the executive dysfunction hypothesis of autism. In J. Russell (Ed.), *Autism as an executive disorder* (pp. 143–178). Oxford University Press.

Perlman, S. B., Hudac, C. M., Pegors, T., Minshew, N. J., & Pelphrey, K. A. (2011). Experimental manipulation of activity in the fusiform gyrus of individuals with autism. *Social Neuroscience, 27*, 1–9. https://doi.org/10.1080/17470911003683185

Piven, J., Rabins, P., & Autism-in-Older Adults Working Group. (2011). Autism spectrum disorders in older adults: Toward defining a research agenda. *Journal of the American Geriatrics Society, 59*(11), 2151–2155. http://dx.doi.org/10.1111/j.1532-5415.2011.03632.x

Puleo, C. M., Schmeidler, J., Reichenberg, A., Kolevzon, A., Soorya, L. V., Buxbaum, J. D., & Silverman, J. M. (2012). Advancing paternal age and simplex autism. *Autism: The International Journal of Research and Practice, 16*(4), 367–380. https://doi.org/10.1177/1362361311427154

Rolls, E. T. (2000). The orbitofrontal cortex and reward. *Cerebral Cortex, 10*, 284–294.

Rolls, E. T. (2009). Prefrontal contributions to reward encoding. In L. R. Squire (Ed.), *Encyclopedia of neuroscience* (pp. 895–903). Academic Press.

Rosen, N. E., Lord, C., & Volkmar, F. R. (2021). The diagnosis of autism: From Kanner to *DSM-III* to DSM-5 and beyond. *Journal of Autism & Developmental Disorders, 24*, 24. https://dx.doi.org/10.1007/s10803-021-04904-1

Rutherford, M. D., Baron-Cohen, S., & Wheelwright, S. (2002). Reading the mind in the voice: A study with normal adults and adults with Asperger syndrome and high functioning autism. *Journal of Autism and Developmental Disorders, 32*(3), 189–194. https://doi.org/10.1023/a:1015497629971

Rutter, M. (1978). Diagnosis and definitions of childhood autism. *Journal of Autism & Developmental Disorders, 8*(2), 139–161.

Rynkiewicz, A., Schuller, B., Marchi, E., Piana, S., Camurri, A., Lassalle, A., & Baron-Cohen, S. (2016). An investigation of the 'female camouflage effect' in autism using a computerized ADOS-2 and a test of sex/gender differences. *Molecular Autism, 7*, 10. https://dx.doi.org/10.1186/s13229-016-0073-0

Sabbagh, M. A. (2004). Understanding orbitofrontal contributions to theory-of-mind reasoning: Implications for autism. *Brain and Cognition, 55*(1), 209–219 https://doi.org/10.1016/j.bandc.2003.04.002

Saxe, R., & Kanwisher, N. (2003). People thinking about thinking people. The role of the temporo-parietal junction in "theory of mind." *Neuroimage, 19*(4), 1835–42. https://doi.org/10.1016/s1053-8119(03)00230-1

Scheerer, M., Rothmann, E., & Goldstein, K. (1945). A case of "idiot savant:" An experimental study of personality organization. *Psychological Monographs, 58*(4), i–63. http://dx.doi.org/10.1037/h0093584

Schultz, R. T., Gauthier, I., Klin, A., Fulbright, R. K., Anderson, A. W., Volkmar, F., Skudlarski, P., Lacadie, C., Cohen, D. J., & Gore, J. C. (2000). Abnormal ventral temporal cortical activity during face discrimination. *Archives of General Psychiatry, 57*(4), 331–340.

Shea, V., & Mesibov, G. B. (2014). Adolescents and adults with autism. In F. R. Volkmar, Rogers, S. J., Paul, R., & Pelphrey, K. A. (Eds.), *Handbook of autism and pervasive developmental disorders, vol. 1*, 4th ed. (pp. 288–311). Wiley.

Smith, I. C., Reichow, B., & Volkmar, F. R. (2015). The effects of DSM-5 criteria on number of individuals diagnosed with autism spectrum disorder: A systematic review. *Journal of Autism & Developmental Disorders, 45*(8), 2541–2552. https://dx.doi.org/10.1007/s10803-015-2423-8

Solomon, C. (2020). Autism and employment: Implications for employers and adults with ASD. *Journal of Autism & Developmental Disorders, 15*(11), 15. https://dx.doi.org/10.1007/s10803-020-04537-w

State, M. W., & Levitt, P. (2011). The conundrums of understanding genetic risks for autism spectrum disorders. *Nature Neuroscience, 14*(12), 1499–1506. https://doi.org/10.1038/nn.2924

Topal, Z., Demir Samurcu, N., Taskiran, S., Tufan, A. E., & Semerci, B. (2018). Social communication disorder: A narrative review on current insights. *Neuropsychiatric Disease & Treatment, 14*, 2039–2046. https://dx.doi.org/10.2147/NDT.S121124

Tyson, K., Kelley, E., Fein, D., Orinstein, A., Troyb, E., Barton, M., Eigsti, I.-M., Naigles, L., Schultz, R. T., Stevens, M., Helt, M., & Rosenthal, M. (2014). Language and verbal memory in individuals with a history of autism spectrum disorders who have achieved optimal outcomes. *Journal of Autism and Developmental Disorders, 44*(3), 648–663. http://dx.doi.org/10.1007/s10803-013-1921-9

van Schalkwyk, G. I., Beyer, C., Martin, A., & Volkmar, F. R. (2016). College students with autism spectrum disorders: A growing role for adult psychiatrists. *Journal of American College Health*, *64*(7), 575–579. http://dx.doi.org/10.1080/07448481.2016.1205072

Vivanti, G., & Messinger, D. S. (2021). Theories of autism and autism treatment from the DSM III through the present and beyond: Impact on research and practice. *Journal of Autism and Developmental Disorders*. http://dx.doi.org/10.1007/s10803-021-04887-z

Volkmar, F. R., & McPartland, J. C. (2014). From Kanner to DSM-5: Autism as an evolving diagnostic concept. *Annual Review of Clinical Psychology*, *10*, 193–212. https://dx.doi.org/10.1146/annurev-clinpsy-032813-153710

Volkmar, F. R., Woodbury-Smith, M., Macari, S. L., & Oien, R. A. (2021). Seeing the forest and the trees: Disentangling autism phenotypes in the age of DSM-5. *Development & Psychopathology*, 1–9. https://doi.org/https://dx.doi.org/10.1017/S0954579420002047

White, S. W., Richey, J. A., Gracanin, D., Coffman, M., Elias, R., LaConte, S., & Ollendick, T. H. (2016). Psychosocial and computer-assisted intervention for college students with autism spectrum disorder: Preliminary support for feasibility. *Education & Training in Autism & Developmental Disabilities*, *51*(3), 307–317.

Wolff, S. (2004). The history of autism. *European Child & Adolescent Psychiatry*, *13*(4), 201–208.

Yang, D., Pelphrey, K. A., Sukhodolsky, D. G., Crowley, M. J., Dayan, E., Dvornek, N. C., Venkataraman, A., Duncan, J., Staib, L., & Ventola, P. (2016). Brain responses to biological motion predict treatment outcome in young children with autism. *Translational Psychiatry*, *6*(11), e948.

Yang, Y. J. D., Allen, T., Abdullahi, S. M., Pelphrey, K. A., Volkmar, F. R., & Chapman, S. B. (2017). Brain responses to biological motion predict treatment outcome in young adults with autism receiving Virtual Reality Social Cognition Training: Preliminary findings. *Behaviour Research & Therapy*, *93*, 55–66.

Zhuang, J., Dvornek, N. C., Li, X., Ventola, P., & Duncan, J. S. (2018). Prediction of severity and treatment outcome for ASD from fMRI. *PRedictive Intelligence in MEdicine. PRIME (Workshop)*, *11121*, 9–17. https://doi.org/10.1007/978-3-030-00320-3_2

# CHAPTER 22

# Functional Somatic Symptoms

Peter Henningsen, Theo K. Bouman, *and* Constanze Hausteiner-Wiehle

**Introduction**

In this introduction, we describe the clinical phenomenon of functional somatic symptoms (FSS) which, in *DSM-5*, is mostly categorized under the heading of "somatic symptom disorder." The symptoms referred to as FSS are comprised of varying combinations of pain in different parts of the body, functional disturbances attributed to organs like cardiovascular or gastrointestinal dysfunctions or dizziness, and symptoms surrounding fatigue. Somatic symptoms in general are part and parcel of everyday life, with at least 75% of the general population experiencing some form of mild to severe physical symptoms in any given month (Kroenke, 2003). Somatic symptoms are by definition subjectively experienced phenomena, whereas somatic signs are objective evidence of disease. Sometimes it is possible to correlate these symptoms with presumed etiological factors, be they physical or psychological (e.g., muscle pain after exertion, headache while angry) but often there is no obvious cause for them. In most instances, symptoms neither go along with suffering nor with impairment of function. They disappear spontaneously or with self-help measures like rest or an aspirin. These transitory symptoms are not signs of an illness; they are part of health. A state of health is not the absence of all (bodily) symptoms, but rather the ability of the human organism to self-regulate in a way that these symptoms are transitory and do not impair daily functioning for long.

However, in about 25% of the sufferers, the symptoms persist for a longer period, prompting them to contact their doctors for medical care (Kroenke, 2003). In medical investigations, for a large proportion of persistent somatic symptoms no obvious and clear-cut organic pathology (like a tumor, inflammation, or nerve damage, etc.) can be identified that explains the occurrence, the extent, and the persistence of the symptoms. These somatic symptoms are here called "functional," referring to the fact that organ or organismic dysfunctions rather than structural pathology is underlying them and also indicating the possibility that these symptoms have a function for the person in their life context (e.g., indicating homeostatic dysbalance). We avoid the wastebasket term "medically unexplained symptoms" because such a negative definition is difficult to accept for patients and because it falsely implies that medicine has no role in dealing with these symptoms (Creed et al., 2010). Moreover, it also assumes a dichotomy between medically explained and unexplained symptoms, thereby ignoring the fact that most symptoms can only be partially explained by organic disease at best and at any given time.

The prevalence of FSS in the population is around 10% (Roenneberg et al., 2019). Around 25%—and in some contexts up to 60%—of all patients in primary as well as in outpatient secondary care suffer from FSS (Nimnuan et al., 2001; Roenneberg et al., 2019). Typically, there are three types of symptom clusters to be considered: pain in

---

**Abbreviations**

| | |
|---|---|
| CD | Conversion disorder |
| FSD | Functional somatic disorder |
| FSS | Functional somatic symptom |
| IAD | Illness anxiety disorder |
| PHQ-15 | Patient Health Questionnaire-15 |
| PP | Predictive processing |
| SfD | Somatoform disorder |
| SSD | Somatic symptom disorder |
| SSD-12 | Somatic Symptom Disorder-B Criteria Scale |
| SSS-8 | Somatic Symptom Scale-8 |

one or more locations (most often concerning back, head, abdomen, extremities, and joints), disturbed functions (dizziness, cardiovascular or gastrointestinal functions, weakness, numbness, etc.), and fatigue.

FSS occur worldwide and there is no indication that socioeconomic gradients between countries are correlated with higher or lower somatic symptom counts, whereas within countries there is an association between higher levels of social adversity and higher FSS rates (Gureje et al., 1997; Gustafsson et al., 2015). For most cultures, somatic symptoms appear to be a well-accepted way to experience and present personal and/or social distress (Chaturvedi, 2013; Nichter, 2010). However, there are variations among cultures, as exemplified by culture-bound syndromes. For example, the *dhat syndrome*, being the fear of loss of semen accompanied by fatigue and other somatic symptoms, is somewhat common among Indian young men (Kirmayer & Sartorius, 2007). In times of increasing migration, knowledge of these culturally shaped variations in somatic presentations becomes more important. However, sociocultural differences are relevant also among Westernized societies (e.g., the rate of distressing chronic low back pain in Germany is twice what it is in Great Britain; Raspe et al., 2004).

Across cultures, women report more functional and other somatic symptoms than men, at a rate of approximately 2:1. They also show more healthcare utilization and a lower all-cause mortality. There are various possible reasons for these differences that illustrate the close interplay between biological, psychological, and sociocultural/environmental factors, ranging from differences in sensory perception and rates of traumatization to gender role expectations including communication and health behavior, and, last but not least, gendered healthcare (Hausteiner-Wiehle et al., 2011). Distinguishing between sex and gender, Ballering et al. (2020) found that feminine gender characteristics like type of hobbies, dietary preferences, or time spent on household tasks are associated with increased common somatic symptoms and chronic diseases, especially in men. Female sex is associated with more and more distressing common somatic symptoms, but not with a higher prevalence of chronic diseases.

FSS occur across the life span. In children and adolescents, persistent symptoms like abdominal pain, headache, or fatigue are a frequently overlooked cause for school absenteeism (Vassilopoulos et al., 2020). In people over the age of 65 years, the rate of FSS is similar to younger people, whereas the rate of somatic symptoms due to organic disease rises with age (Hausteiner-Wiehle et al., 2011). As a consequence, it is more challenging to clearly differentiate organic pathology from functional backgrounds of somatic symptoms in older people. Doctors are quite reluctant to label symptoms as "functional," especially in men and the elderly, resulting in "organic" overdiagnosis and over treatment and symptom persistence. However, any exaggerated concern of doctors that they might overlook significant organic disease when defining somatic symptom(s) in a patient as functional does not seem to be warranted. A systematic review has shown that once an adequate workup of the symptoms has been made, the rate of revised diagnoses in follow-up studies of FSS was only 0.5% (Eikelboom et al., 2016). Hence, although mistakes are made both in the direction of overlooked organic pathology and in the direction of missed functional background, the latter is much more frequent in high-tech Western healthcare systems (Henningsen, 2016).

It is a misconception to assume that somatic symptoms that are functional in nature are less "severe" than those caused by clearly defined organic disease. In fact, they can cause significant impairment of function (i.e., quality of life is reduced, sick leave and early retirement are increased), and the extent of this impairment is no less than in organically defined disease (Joustra et al., 2015). Interestingly, it is the total number of somatic symptoms, independent of their nature, that correlates best with impairment (Tomenson et al., 2013).

Patients with FSS clearly have higher rates of anxiety and depressive symptoms than healthy people and also than patients with organic disease with comparable somatic symptoms (Henningsen et al., 2003). Nevertheless, many patients with severe FSS do not have high rates of anxiety or depressive symptoms, and therefore it is misleading to assume that FSS generally are a form of "masked depression" or "masked anxiety" (Löwe et al., 2008). Heuristically, it may be best to view depressive, anxiety, and somatic symptoms as three dimensions of distress that are interrelated but not identical.

## Historical Labels and Classifications in This Field

When looking at the historical development of labels and concepts for FSS in psychiatry and somatic medicine since the nineteenth century, it becomes apparent that multiple perspectives often complicate a clear understanding of the phenomenon. For one, the concept of hysteria as an important root has influenced the field in two different ways. The first is through the development of psychoanalysis and Sigmund Freud's (1856–1939) concept of hysteria as a neurotic condition characterized predominantly by variable, mainly sensorimotor symptoms and "hysterical conversion" of unacceptable affect into somatic symptoms. Whereas Freud considered this process to be a "mysterious leap from the mind to the body," a later physician and psychoanalyst, Franz Alexander (1891–1964) tried to be more specific (Alexander, 1950). He postulated that unconscious conflict-related blockage of normal aggressive as well as nurturing impulses led to overactivation of the sympathetic and parasympathetic branches of the autonomous nervous system, respectively. This in turn would lead to FSS like syncope, "cardiac neurosis," or diarrhea and constipation.

The term "conversion disorder," if not the concept underlying it, is retained in official classifications up until *DSM-5*. Freud's contemporary and colleague Wilhelm Stekel (1868–1940) later coined the term "somatization" as a synonym for this "psychogenic" process. Lipowski (1988) defined somatization more descriptively as a tendency to experience and express psychological distress in the form of somatic symptoms that individuals misinterpret as serious physical illness and for which they seek medical help.

A second influence of the concept of hysteria centered on the hysteric or histrionic (i.e., attention-seeking), emotionally labile, and dramatic personality type frequently exhibiting multiple somatic symptoms. Pierre Briquet (1796–1881) formulated a polysymptomatic variant of hysteria which was later taken up by Guze and Perley (1963) in their description of Briquet's syndrome, characterized by a combination of "pseudoneurological" (i.e., sensorimotor with functional somatic symptoms attributed to a multitude of organ systems: cardiovascular, gastrointestinal, etc.) lasting for most of the patient's life. This in turn became the model on which the *DSM* category of somatization disorder was formed in *DSM-III*.

In a more general historical perspective FSS can be considered as a symptom pool that is more or less constant over time and for which different diagnostic labels were and are "en vogue," but also critically discussed, at varying points in time (Shorter, 1993). Spinal irritation and neurasthenia were such labels in the nineteenth century, vegetative neurosis and psychogenic pain were labels in the twentieth century, and chronic fatigue syndrome or idiopathic environmental illness are examples in the twenty-first century.

An important aspect of the official diagnostic tradition in this field is the fact that there have long been two perspectives on FSS that are connected poorly if at all. On the one hand, there is the professional perspective on the experience and behavior of the person who complains of (often multiple) somatic symptoms. This is a perspective typical for psychiatrists and psychotherapists, with the idea of classifying FSS of sufficient severity as a mental disorder. On the other hand, there is the perspective of somatic specialists who in their field encounter patients with typical somatic symptoms in whom the suspected organic disease cannot be confirmed (e.g., the gastroenterologist sees patients with diarrhea and constipation but without evidence of gastrointestinal pathology; similarly, the gynecologist with patients with chronic pelvic pain, or the cardiologist with patients with chest pain). These somatic specialists will usually classify these patients within their somatic specialist field with a label of functional somatic syndrome like irritable bowel syndrome (IBS) or noncardiac chest pain. This approach leads to well-described organ-specific patterns of functional symptoms, but it not only neglects the patient's experience and behavior, it also very often also overlooks many functional symptoms of the patient related to other organ systems (Wessely et al., 1999).

## Pathopsychophysiology

In this section we describe the current understanding of the psychophysiological mechanisms underlying the subjective experience of enduring somatic symptoms for which, by definition, there is no clearly defined organic pathology to be found that explains the symptoms. The aim is to provide an account that does justice to two rather different ways of explaining these "organically unexplained" symptoms: as a bodily expression of unresolved psychological stress and conflicts (from central processes to body periphery or "top down") and as a psychological amplification or exaggeration of normal bodily sensations (from the body periphery to central processes or "bottom up").

The first traditional way of explaining these symptoms via a psychogenic or "top-down" mechanism was mentioned before; it implied that psychological stress and conflicts cannot be resolved by psychological or behavioral means and are "converted" into somatic symptoms. This conceptualization justified the application of psychotherapy, namely psychoanalysis, in these patients (a former edition of Alexander's [1936] book was called *The Medical Value of Psychoanalysis*). However, neither a specific conflict nor a consistent overactivation of the autonomous nervous system in these patients could ever be verified empirically, and the fact that culturally shaped variations in symptom experience would require, in this model, culturally shaped differences in basic psychophysiology also spoke against its validity.

Another traditional explanation of the psychopathophysiology of patients with FSS can be called more "bottom up": normal introspectively transmitted signals from the body periphery (e.g., resulting from stress-related arousal and focused attention) are amplified in central processing and hence in perception. "Somatosensory amplification," described by Barsky et al. (1988) as the tendency to amplify a broad range of uncomfortable bodily sensations (most of which are not the pathological symptoms of serious diseases) has become one popular concept in this tradition. Its focus on perceptual amplification of normal bodily arousal signals and cognitive-behavioral consequences, such as catastrophization and body scanning, puts the experience of somatic symptoms close to (illness) anxiety. It is therefore not surprising that the role of somatosensory amplification has also been confirmed in hypochondriasis (i.e., in a condition characterized not primarily by somatic symptoms but by the fear of having a serious somatic disease; Barsky & Wyshak, 1990). As a consequence, psychotherapy, in this case typically cognitive-behavioral therapy, is clearly indicated as a treatment of choice for patients with FSS.

This "anxiety-style approach" to the explanation of somatic symptoms has also influenced the definition of somatic symptom disorder in *DSM-5* (see below). However, for the intuitively appealing model of somatic amplification of peripheral stress-related arousal, which rather has evolved into a family of models with slight variations (see Van den Bergh et al., 2017), empirical evidence is limited at best. For the first component of the concept, there is no convincing evidence of a causal role of peripheral stress-related arousal even for more severe FSS patterns. For instance, in a well-designed study, Houtveen et al. (2010) did not find significant differences in 24-hour monitoring of cardiac autonomic and respiratory parameters between persons high on FSS compared to those low on FSS. Also, in clinical populations with more severe FSS, meta-analytic evidence did not show, after correction for publication bias, significant differences in physiological parameters compared to healthy controls (Tak et al., 2009). Studies measuring attentional deployment toward body- or illness-related stimuli also fail to provide convincing evidence for an attentional bias toward these stimuli (Van den Bergh et al., 2017). And finally, there is clear evidence for a positive correlation of (catastrophic) misattribution of benign bodily sensations with FSS, but it is unclear to what extent this correlation is a consequence rather than a causal factor for FSS. Thus, newer accounts view somatic amplification as the intensification of perceived external and internal threats to the integrity of the body ("somatic threat amplification") rather than amplification of perceived or actual bodily events only (Köteles & Witthöft, 2017).

In recent years, a new understanding of the brain not as a mere passive information processing device but as an active and constant comparator between prior predictions and actual sensory input (from the environment and from the body) has provided a more integrative understanding of the processes underlying somatic symptom experience (Edwards et al., 2012; Henningsen, Gundel et al., 2018; Van den Bergh et al., 2017). This *predictive processing* (PP) approach, popular in computational psychosomatics and psychiatry (Petzschner et al., 2017), is based on Bayes' statistical principles. It postulates an overarching, non-dualistic, and dynamic mechanism that integrates the two following aspects when explaining why individuals, for example, are chronically fatigued, chemically sensitive, aching allover, suddenly dizzy, or paralyzed: first, top-down central aspects act as *priors* (i.e., a Bayesian term for preformed facilitations generated from prior experiences across hierarchical levels of the central nervous system). On a psychological level of description, they are analogous to (unconscious) expectancies or (conscious) expectations. These priors are constantly compared to the second, bottom-up peripheral aspect constituted by sensory signals. In this truly integrative biopsychosocial account of perception, sensory input, be it exteroceptive (visual, auditory, etc.) or interoceptive, is not seen as the primary determinant, with central/psychological processes "only" as secondary modifying factors. The actual percept is influenced by the strength or precision of the sensory input as much as by the strength or precision of the prior (i.e., the steepness of the respective statistical distribution curves).

If a prediction error occurs (i.e., when walking on a floor with black tiles, the prior will predict further black tiles, and a red tile will constitute a prediction error), the "inner working" or "generative" model, on which the prior is based, may be adapted to integrate the new information (i.e., the prediction is changed to "black tiles with occasional red ones"). Another possibility is that the sensory input is actively influenced so that it better conforms to the prior (i.e., "I walk back where no red tiles occurred"). This active influence means that autonomic and/or other neural activations may actually be a way of adapting sensory input to prior perceptual expectations (e.g., back pain as an active inference to conform to the prior of "back-breaking" work strain or a red blush as an active inference to conform to the prior of shame). Failure of inference can occur on several levels: With potent prior beliefs ("Environmental toxins are invisible, ubiquitous, and dangerous"), low-precision sensory input close to random fluctuations (1 second of blurred vision) can amount to conscious expectations (brain fog, risk of falling) and generate high-precision perceptions to comply with them (dizziness, disturbances of equilibrium or cognition)—a situation comparable to phantom sensations (Henningsen, Gundel et al., 2018). The unconscious, automatic character of the inferential process and the compelling quality of reality/trueness makes the experience of somatic symptoms relatively impermeable for deliberate conscious reasoning. It leads to a secondary failure of inference; namely, to the conscious belief that the interocept indeed is a symptom (i.e., an expression of abnormal bodily function).

This Bayesian PP perspective blurs any categorical distinction between so-called medically unexplained symptoms and symptoms emerging from physiological dysfunction (see Van den Bergh et al., 2017). The same inferential processes are involved in both types, with the difference being a matter of degree: namely, to what extent priors versus sensory input dominate somatic symptom perception. Whereas the somatic amplification model refers to typical threat-related priors only, the PP-based model allows for a much broader variety of priors (e.g., related to damage, strain or weakness in pain, or fatigue conditions).

The PP perspective renders plausible also the direct influence of (interpersonal) context factors on symptom perception: prior interpersonal experiences especially in dealing with bodily sensations and symptoms will influence the prediction of future symptom experiences (Fotopoulou & Tsakiris, 2017). As a clinically very stimulating recent model, the PP account is not yet well-validated empirically. However, neurobiological evidence is now accumulating that supports the assumption suggested by the mathematically well-tested PP models (Allen, 2020).

## Etiology

What are the etiological factors that bring about the experience of FSS? Here we describe the most relevant vulnerability, triggering, and maintaining factors, using the biopsychosocial model of pathopsychophysiology just described. We see that they differentially influence both routes to symptom perception, priors, and sensory input (see Figure 22.1, in which the prior is—slightly inexactly because only referring to the cognitively conscious part—called "expectation" here).

To start with vulnerability, genetic factors contribute to the predisposition to FSS, but only to a

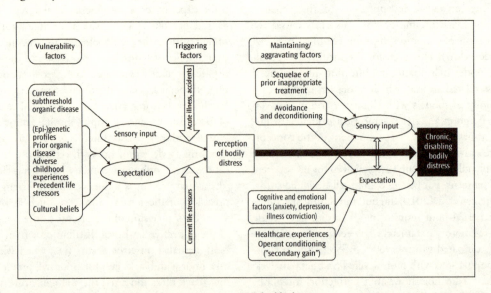

**Figure 22.1** Etiological factors in functional somatic symptoms (FSS)/bodily distress. Adapted from Henningsen et al. (2018b).

limited extent, explaining up to 33% of the variance (Gasperi et al., 2020; Kato et al., 2010). Genome-wide and other searches attempting to identify single genes responsible for the disposition of chronic (multisite) pain, an important component of FSS, so far have yielded inconsistent results; epigenetic mechanisms are increasingly seen as also highly relevant (Denk et al., 2014; Johnston et al., 2019). These epigenetic mechanisms offer a potential mechanistic link to the well-established role that childhood adversities have as a possible predisposing factor for FSS: they increase the odds for the development of bodily distress up to fourfold (Afari et al., 2014). There is also evidence that genetic vulnerabilities may moderate the relation between posttraumatic stress disorder (PTSD) and functional somatic pain conditions (Gasperi et al., 2020).

Attachment patterns form another link between childhood adversity and somatization, with maternal insensitivity at 18 months predicting parent-ascertained somatization in 5-year-old children, and attachment insecurity in adults correlating with somatization, with strongest links existing between attachment anxiety and health anxiety (Maunder et al., 2017). The PP model sketched above renders plausible a direct influence of dysfunctional (e.g., overly anxious) attachment patterns on symptom experience via the caregiver–child interaction around seemingly threatening bodily sensations, which leads to the formation of according priors in the child; that is (non-conscious) expectancies and (conscious) expectations that bodily sensations must be threatening.

Deficiencies in emotion recognition and regulation have also been linked to increased vulnerability for FSS and bodily distress. One example is *alexithymia*, referring to the inability to "read" (i.e., to perceive and name) one's own emotional states. A systematic review confirmed an association between difficulties in emotion regulation and FSS across different diagnoses (Okur Güney et al., 2019). However, the specificity of this finding and potential causality remain to be determined.

Similar questions apply to the positive correlations found between personality characteristics like neuroticism, harm avoidance, or lower agreeableness and somatization or somatoform disorders (Noyes et al., 2001; Rezaei et al., 2020). The chronic experience of FSS shares many features with personality disorders (Bass & Murphy, 1995) in terms of their developmental origin, persistent nature, disruptive impact on social functioning, and chronic course. Viewed from the angle of categoric diagnoses, a meta-analysis (Bornstein & Gold, 2008) complements this notion, showing that somatization disorder, a severe form of somatoform disorder (according to the *DSM-IV*) with multiple chronic FSS, is comorbid with the majority of personality disorders—but there is no special association with only one or two of them (e.g., with histrionic personality disorder).

Prior organic illnesses create a vulnerability and a triggering factor potentially via both routes sketched in Figure 22.1: sensory input and expectation created through prior experience. For instance, symptoms compatible with IBS were more frequently reported after gastrointestinal infections or active inflammatory bowel disease (Halpin & Ford, 2012). As another example, functional dizziness has recently been divided into a variety that is secondary to vestibular disease (most often benign paroxysmal positional vertigo and vestibular migraine) and a variety that occurs primarily (i.e., without prior vestibular disease; Habs et al., 2020). As a third very recent example, post-COVID fatigue is, with post-COVID muscular pain and shortness of breath, a very frequent symptom weeks after the acute Coronavirus infection has subsided (Jacobs et al., 2020). It remains to be determined to which extent this is due to ongoing autoimmunological and other pathological organic processes that influence somatosensory input and to which extent expectancy effects and priors are involved, influenced by symptom experience during acute infection, but also by other effects of the illness like isolation, threatening treatments, etc.

In terms of further triggering factors, stressful work conditions are particularly important. Patients with more severe FSS are at much higher risk for sick leave and early health-related retirement (Rask et al., 2017), but it is also the psychosocial workplace characteristics that increase the risk for somatic symptoms in the work force. For instance, prospective studies with thousands of civil servants in Great Britain and other working populations have shown that an imbalance between effort and (material and nonmaterial) reward, or the chronic experience of individual and organizational injustice at baseline, are related to higher rates of FSS, but also of depression and cardiovascular diseases at follow-up (Herr et al., 2017, 2018). Recent adverse life events also are relevant as triggering factors (Bonvanie et al., 2017), with accidents in general having a special role as they may induce chronic symptoms via both routes; that is, through nociceptive and other somatosensory input, and through expectancy formation regarding symptom experience but potentially also regarding compensation (Wynne-Jones et al., 2006).

If persisting, these triggering factors and predisposing personality aspects obviously also contribute to the maintenance of FSS. Further maintaining factors arise from the often difficult interactions of these patients with the healthcare system, leading to missed or delayed diagnosis, inappropriate treatments, and frustrations on all sides. Somatizing communication behavior and persistent beliefs about biomedical causations of patients and doctors alike are relevant here. As an example, in an experimental study, Van Wilgen et al. (2012) found that the more patients manifested somatic symptoms and psychosocial distress, the more negative beliefs and emotions were elicited in healthcare providers. Systemic factors of the healthcare system, such as its subdivision in different somatic specialities on the one side and mental healthcare on the other, contribute to these significant barriers for earlier recognition and better diagnosis and treatment (Henningsen et al., 2011; Murray et al., 2016).

## Classification

In this section, we focus on the current classification of FSS according to the *DSM-5*. Additionally, we discuss diagnostic alternatives, for example in the upcoming *ICD-11*. Both systems choose a much broader approach than former classifications. Nevertheless, they are still not satisfactory; they continue to propagate parallel classification of the same clinical phenomenon as mental disorders in psychosocial medicine versus as functional somatic syndromes in somatic medicine, thereby supporting the parallel use of widely differing, sometimes even contradictory therapeutic approaches. Especially for clinical purposes, including doctor–patient communication, a more consistent, more practical, more integrative classification is needed.

### DSM-5 *Somatic Symptom Disorder*

In 2013, *DSM-5* introduced a new chapter entitled "Somatic Symptom and Related Disorders." It replaced the chapter of "Somatoform Disorders" (SfD) which was included in *DSM-III* and *DSM-IV* from 1980 to 2013. The main diagnostic category in the chapter is somatic symptom disorder (SSD), in which the central issue is the presence of one or more somatic symptoms that are distressing and result in a significant disruption of daily life (criterion A). They may be pain, either localized or widespread, or functional symptoms related to organs (cardiovascular, gastrointestinal, etc.), fatigue, or any other cluster of somatic symptoms, even belonging to a well-known medical condition. In order to qualify for the diagnosis of SSD the patient should in addition exhibit misattributions, excessive concern, anxiety, or preoccupation related to the symptoms (criterion B). When this condition lasts for at least 6 months it is specified as persistent. Two other specifiers refer to SSD with predominant pain and to severity (mild, moderate, severe), respectively.

There are major differences between the diagnosis of SSD and its precursor SfD. First, while SfD (pre-*DSM-5*) excluded medically explained symptoms from consideration, SSD has no such exclusion; whether there is a relevant medical account for a symptom is no longer pivotal. Second, there is a new psychobehavioral requirement that at least one of these features be present: disproportionate conviction of serious disease, high health anxiety, and/or preoccupation with the symptoms. Third, SSD is just one single diagnosis; it largely contains the former SfD subcategories of somatization disorder (the most severe polysymptomatic form of SfD), undifferentiated somatization disorder (a low-threshold form of SfD with one symptom over 6 months), pain disorder (SfD with predominant pain symptoms), and hypochondriasis.

It may be fair to say that SSD justifies its inclusion as a mental disorder by the psychobehavioral features as defined in criterion B. In contrast, the classification of SfD as a mental disorder was not justified by any mental symptoms or features in its definition. It can only be understood historically through its derivation from older psychogenic concepts of somatization.

Since 2013, relatively few empirical studies have been published that evaluate the diagnostic criteria for SSD. In the general population, SSD prevalence has been estimated at 4.5% (Häuser et al., 2020). For the assessment of one core criterion of SSD, somatic symptoms, well-established self-report scales have existed for quite some time, most notably the Patient Health Questionnaire (PHQ-15; Kroenke et al., 2002) and more recently a shorter 8-item form with similar characteristics, the Somatic Symptom Scale-8 (SSS-8; Gierk et al., 2014). For the assessment of the other core aspect, the psychobehavioral features of SSD, a new self-report scale was developed, the Somatic Symptom Disorder-B Criteria Scale (SSD-12; Toussaint et al., 2016). Four items each for the cognitive, affective, and behavioral component comprise this 12-item scale, thereby combining aspects that were assessed separately in other scales. A first diagnostic gold standard study based on (a German adaptation of) the structured clinical interview for *DSM-5* (SCID-5) module on SSD showed that in 372 patients from a psychosomatic outpatient clinic, the diagnostic accuracy of the self-report scales SSS-8 and PHQ-15 combined with the SSD-12 was moderate, with areas under the curve (AUC) of up to .79 (Toussaint et al., 2020). This indicates that these self-report scales can be used as a time-efficient way to identify patients at risk of SSD.

In a study comparing patients fulfilling *DSM-5* SSD criteria with those fulfilling prior SfD criteria, 239 patients of a sample of 438 from a psychosomatic outpatient clinic (54.6%) who took part in a diagnostic interview fulfilled criteria for *DSM-5* SSD and 139 patients (31.7%) fulfilled criteria for any kind of clinician-rated *ICD-10* SfD (*ICD-10* SfD is very similar to *DSM-IV* SfD) (Hüsing et al., 2018). There was an overlap of 102 (23.3%) patients who received both diagnoses, with 37 patients receiving an *ICD-10* SfD diagnosis only (i.e., mostly did not fulfill criterion-level severity of psychobehavioral features) and 102 patients receiving a *DSM-5* SSD diagnosis only (i.e., mostly somatic symptoms were not seen as "medically unexplained"). Not surprisingly, patients diagnosed with only *DSM-5* SSD appeared to be more severely impaired in terms of general and health-related anxiety and psychological distress associated with their somatic symptoms, whereas patients with only *ICD-10* SfD had a lower physical health-related quality of life.

Like the comparison of SSD and SfD in the different versions of *DSM*, the comparison of diagnostic criteria for a functional somatic syndrome from somatic medicine will yield only partial overlap with *DSM-5* SSD. For example, in patients with a fibromyalgia syndrome, only between 28% and 35% also met criteria for SSD (Axelsson et al., 2020; Häuser et al., 2020); the majority of fibromyalgia syndrome patients did not reach criterion cutoff severity for the psychobehavioral features of criterion B. The patients with both diagnoses appear to have higher symptom burden and impairment than those only fulfilling the criteria for fibromyalgia syndrome.

The new *DSM-5* category SSD has been criticized for several reasons (Rief & Martin, 2014). First, the failure to take account of the presence or absence of organic disease is seen as problematic (Scamvougeras & Howard, 2020). In the definition of SSD, it is justified by the unreliability of the distinction between "organically explained" and "unexplained" somatic symptoms—but this distinction has been shown not to be particularly unreliable, with revised diagnoses in follow-up studies as low as 0.5% (Eikelboom et al., 2016). As a consequence of the lack of distinction in referring to somatic symptoms in general, criterion A of SSD might be overly inclusive: if one is suffering from somatic symptoms in the course of a medical illness and (quite understandably) is worrying about it a lot (e.g., a young woman with fatigue in the course of her multiple sclerosis), one would already qualify for the diagnosis, thereby adding an often unwanted mental disorder diagnosis to the medical one (Frances & Chapman, 2013).

Second, the criterion B features have been criticized for their overreliance on illness anxiety and hypochondriasis and for their inadequate consideration of cognitive characteristics such as a self-concept of bodily weakness and behavioral and interpersonal characteristics like dissatisfaction with medical care (Hausteiner et al., 2009; Klaus et al., 2015). As an additional difficulty, there is no clear threshold for when to define symptom-related thoughts, feelings, and behaviors to be excessive or disproportionate (Rief & Martin, 2014). In view of this last criticism, a study has tried to determine some of these thresholds: in a population-based study, it appeared that a range of 3–4 hours a day spent on dealing with physical symptoms seems indicative of excessiveness (Toussaint et al., 2021).

In terms of practical acceptance of the new SSD diagnosis, focus groups with general practitioners also showed that they see the excessiveness definition of psychobehavioral features as problematic, but nevertheless the newly included psychological criteria were seen as an important advancement in comparison to the previous need of merely excluding a physical disease (Lehmann et al., 2019).

### *DSM-5* Conversion Disorder/Functional Neurological Symptom Disorder

In *DSM-5*, conversion disorder (CD) or, given synonymously but in parentheses, *functional neurological symptom disorder* (FNSD) is also part of the chapter "Somatic Symptoms and Related Disorders." However, the diagnosis of CD is based on a rather different concept than SSD. It also relies on the symptoms being distressing and having impairing consequences, but it also clearly defines their functional character ("altered voluntary motor or sensory function").

Diagnosing CD (FNSD) requires that clinical findings provide evidence of incompatibility between the symptom and recognized neurological or medical conditions and cannot be better explained by another medical or mental disorder. Examples are anesthesia of the hand in a glove-like distribution incompatible with functional neuroanatomy, or the so-called *Hoover sign*, where a weakness in hip extension is present when directly tested, but not when reflexively activated through contralateral hip flexion. This positive or "rule-in" evidence for incompatibility is conceptually different from mere "rule-out" or exclusion of organic disease; clearly establishing the functional nature of a neurological symptom very often is possible through clinical examination and a good description of the weakness, gait disorder, seizure, etc., and it is clinically important to demonstrate the incompatibility also to the patient (Stone et al., 2020).

Unlike with earlier conceptions of conversion disorder, in *DSM-5*, the diagnosis does not require the presence of psychological stressors or suggestive historical (e.g., biographical and situational) assumed causes (the *DSM-IV* had required preceding "conflicts or other stressors"). This seems justified because systematic reviews have shown that although patients with CD (FNSD) clearly have higher rates of traumatizations and severe life events preceding symptom onset than do healthy controls, many patients with this disorder do not (Ludwig et al., 2018).

Applying the PP model of FSS to CD (FNSD) highlights a wider range of past sensitizing events than "only" psychological stressors and psychological trauma, such as physical trauma, medical illness in oneself or significant others, or physiological/psychophysiological events. According to this model, strong ideas and expectations about these events correlate with abnormal predictions of sensory data and body-focused attention (Espay et al., 2018). For instance, patients with functional tremor perceived themselves, according to self-report diaries, as trembling for 84% of their waking day, whereas objective actigraphy showed tremor only on 4% of the waking day (Pareés et al., 2012).

Patients with functional neurological symptoms very often also have other somatic symptoms which are often pain-related and functional in nature; that is, they often fulfill criteria for CD (FNSD) and SSD at the same time. This fact calls into question the separation of these diagnoses in *DSM-5* in the first place (Maggio et al., 2020).

### Other diagnoses in the DSM-5 chapter on "SSD and Related Disorders"

The following three diagnoses also belong to the *DSM-5* chapter on "SSD and Related Disorders." This much more inclusive approach compared to the *DSM-IV* emphasizes the overlap of these conditions, especially regarding their comorbid occurrence and the shared relevance of symptom interpretation, body scheme, sick role, and illness behavior. However, somatic symptoms are not a central feature in their definition. For that reason, they are only briefly mentioned here.

*Illness anxiety disorder* (IAD) is derived from two *DSM-IV* sources: the illness subtype within simple phobia (which was and is an anxiety disorder) and the subgroup of hypochondriacal patients who have no somatic symptoms (see above). *DSM-5* IAD's core features are the excessive preoccupation with having or acquiring a serious illness, a high level of anxiety, being easily alarmed about personal health status, and performing excessive health-related behaviors or exhibiting maladaptive avoidance, respectively. Somatic symptoms are not present or only mild in intensity.

*Factitious disorder* is new to this *DSM-5* chapter, having had its own chapter in *DSM-IV*. It refers to deliberate simulation of illness for the purpose of acquiring the sick role, in the absence of obvious external rewards.

*Psychological factors affecting medical condition* were part of the *DSM-IV* Appendix entitled "Other Conditions That May Be the Focus of Clinical Attention." This diagnosis is considered when a patient is suffering from a medical condition, and when psychological or behavioral factors adversely affect its onset, maintenance, or course (e.g., through stressors influencing pain syndromes or skin disease, other lifestyle factors, or noncompliance with a medical regimen). If the psychobehavioral factors relate to criterion B of SSD and if the emphasis primarily is on somatic symptoms, the latter diagnosis should be preferred.

Finally, in *DSM-5*, *body dysmorphic disorder* has been relocated to a new chapter, "Obsessive-Compulsive and Related Disorders." Somatic symptoms per se appear as part of several other diagnoses in *DSM-5* (e.g., as a somatic subtype of delusional disorder).

### Other Diagnostic Classifications

In the mental health section of the upcoming *ICD-11*, the category of "bodily distress disorder" appears to be very close to the *DSM-5* SSD as it incorporates the three main changes made in the transition from SfD to SSD: no reference to the somatic symptoms being not fully explained by organic disease, requirement of anxiety-type psychobehavioral features, and one diagnosis replacing several distinct SfD diagnoses. In view of the close similarity in the definitions, the difference in naming the disorder between *DSM-5* SSD and *ICD-11 bodily distress disorder* is unfortunate.

In another approach to classify FSS as *functional somatic disorders* (FSD; Burton et al., 2020), it is proposed that FSD should occupy a neutral space within disease classifications, favoring neither somatic disease etiology, nor mental disorder—a step that is possible in the *ICD* system, but obviously not in a classification for mental disorders only, like the *DSM* system. FSD should be subclassified as (a) multisystem (i.e., symptoms relating to multiple organ systems like cardiovascular, neurological, gastrointestinal, etc.), (b) single system (e.g., only cardiovascular or only neurological), or (c) single symptom (e.g., fatigue). Whereas additional specifiers may be added to take account of psychobehavioral features or co-occurring organic diseases, neither of these is sufficient or necessary to make the diagnosis.

## Conclusion

FSSs are very common; they can induce profound suffering, markedly decreased functioning, and high healthcare costs. At the same time, they are often neglected as a problem in a clinical and research tradition that concentrates on a dichotomy of somatic and mental disorders—with FSS not fitting well into either category. There have been significant advances in our understanding of the pathopsychophysiology and etiology of these symptoms, with progress in a more integrative "embodied" biopsychosocial approach. Current classification still lacks both clarity and the integrational ability to bridge the "either-or" of our dualistic system. Management of FSS must be interdisciplinary, with a broad diagnostic approach and with body–mind interventions that improve the patient's capacity to understand and regulate their psychological and biological functioning. If psychotherapy appears advisable, it must be explained and carried out as a cautious and confidential space where one's biological and psychosocial individuality can be experienced and shaped, to overcome adverse experiences and dysfunctional beliefs, and to reach a better acceptance, agency, and participation of the bodily self. All of this starts with the healthcare provider's sound knowledge of and attitude, and commitment toward FSS, bridging divorced fields of medicine and psychology that belong together.

## References

Afari, N., Ahumada, S. M., Wright, L. J., Mostoufi, S., Golnari, G., Reis, V., & Cuneo, J. G. (2014). Psychological trauma and functional somatic syndromes: a systematic review and meta-analysis. *Psychosomatic medicine*, 76(1), 2–11.

Alexander, F. (1936). *The medical value of psychoanalysis*. W. W. Norton.

Alexander, F. (1950). *Psychosomatic medicine: Its principles and applications*. W. W. Norton.

Allen, M. (2020). Unravelling the neurobiology of interoceptive inference. *Trends in Cognitive Science*s, 24(4), 265–266.

Axelsson, E., Hedman-Lagerlöf, M., Hedman-Lagerlöf, E., Ljótsson, B., & Andersson, E. (2020). Symptom preoccupation in fibromyalgia: Prevalence and correlates of somatic symptom disorder in a self-recruited sample. *Psychosomatics*, 61(3), 268–276.

Ballering, A. V., Bonvanie, I. J., Hartman, T. C. O., Monden, R., & Rosmalen, J. G. (2020). Gender and sex independently associate with common somatic symptoms and lifetime prevalence of chronic disease. *Social Science & Medicine*, 253, 112968.

Barsky, A. J., Goodson, J. D., Lane, R. S., & Cleary, P. D. (1988). The amplification of somatic symptoms. *Psychosomatic medicine*, 50(5), 510–519.

Barsky, A. J., & Wyshak, G. (1990). Hypochondriasis and somatosensory amplification. *British Journal of Psychiatry*, 157, 404–409.

Bass, C. M., & Murphy, M. R. (1995). Somatoform and personality disorders: Syndromal comorbidity and overlapping developmental pathways. *Journal of Psychosomatic Research*, 39, 403–427.

Bonvanie, I. J., Janssens, K. A., Rosmalen, J. G., & Oldehinkel, A. J. (2017). Life events and functional somatic symptoms: A population study in older adolescents. *British Journal of Psychology*, 2(108), 318–333.

Bornstein, R. F., & Gold, S. H. (2008). Comorbidity of personality disorders and somatization disorder: A meta-analytic review. *Journal of Psychopathology and Behavioral Assessment*, 30(2), 154.

Burton, C., Fink, P., Henningsen, P., Löwe, B., Rief, W., & EURONET-SOMA Group (2020). Functional somatic disorders: Discussion paper for a new common classification for research and clinical use. *BMC Medicine*, 18(1), 34.

Chaturvedi, S. K. (2013). Many faces of somatic symptom disorders. *International Review of Psychiatry*, 25, 1–4.

Creed, F., Guthrie, E., Fink, P., Henningsen, P., Rief, W., Sharpe, M., & White, P. (2010). Is there a better term than "medically unexplained symptoms"? *Journal of Psychosomatic Research*, 68(1), 5–8.

Denk, F., McMahon, S. B., & Tracey, I. (2014). Pain vulnerability: A neurobiological perspective. *Nature Neuroscience*, 17(2), 192–200.

Edwards, M. J., Adams, R. A., Brown, H., Pareés, I., & Friston, K. J. (2012). A Bayesian account of hysteria. *Brain*, 135(Pt 11), 3495–3512.

Eikelboom, E. M., Tak, L. M., Roest, A. M., & Rosmalen, J. (2016). A systematic review and meta-analysis of the percentage of revised diagnoses in functional somatic symptoms. *Journal of Psychosomatic Research*, 88, 60–67.

Espay, A. J., Aybek, S., Carson, A., Edwards, M. J., Goldstein, L. H., Hallett, M., LaFaver, K., LaFrance, W. C., Jr, Lang, A. E., Nicholson, T., Nielsen, G., Reuber, M., Voon, V., Stone, J., & Morgante, F. (2018). Current concepts in diagnosis and treatment of functional neurological disorders. *JAMA Neurology, 75*(9), 1132–1141.

Frances, A., & Chapman, S. (2013). DSM-5 somatic symptom disorder mislabels medical illness as mental disorder. *Australian and New Zealand Journal of Psychiatry, 47*(5), 483–484.

Gasperi, M., Panizzon, M., Goldberg, J., Buchwald, D., & Afari, N. (2020). Post-traumatic stress disorder and chronic pain conditions in men: A twin study. *Psychosomatic Medicine*, publish ahead of print, 10.1097/PSY.0000000000000899

Gierk, B., Kohlmann, S., Kroenke, K., Spangenberg, L., Zenger, M., Brähler, E., & Löwe, B. (2014). The somatic symptom scale-8 (SSS-8): A brief measure of somatic symptom burden. *JAMA Internal Medicine, 174*(3), 399–407.

Gureje, O., Simon, G. E., Ustun, T. B., & Goldberg, D. P. (1997). Somatization in cross-cultural perspective: A World Health Organization study in primary care. *American Journal of Psychiatry, 154*(7), 989–995.

Gustafsson, P. E., Hammarström, A., & San Sebastian, M. (2015). Cumulative contextual and individual disadvantages over the life course and adult functional somatic symptoms in Sweden. *European Journal of Public Health, 25*(4), 592–597.

Guze, S. B., & Perley, M. J. (1963). Observations on the natural history of hysteria. *American Journal of Psychiatry, 119*, 960–965.

Fotopoulou, A., & Tsakiris, M. (2017). Mentalizing homeostasis: The social origins of interoceptive inference. *Neuropsychoanalysis, 19*(1), 3–28.

Habs, M., Strobl, R., Grill, E., Dieterich, M., & Becker-Bense, S. (2020). Primary or secondary chronic functional dizziness: Does it make a difference? A DizzyReg study in 356 patients. *Journal of Neurology, 267*(Suppl 1), 212–222.

Halpin, S. J., & Ford, A. C. (2012). Prevalence of symptoms meeting criteria for irritable bowel syndrome in inflammatory bowel disease: Systematic review and meta-analysis. *American Journal of Gastroenterology, 107*(10), 1474–1482.

Häuser, W., Hausteiner-Wiehle, C., Henningsen, P., Brähler, E., Schmalbach, B., & Wolfe, F. (2020). Prevalence and overlap of somatic symptom disorder, bodily distress syndrome and fibromyalgia syndrome in the German general population: A cross sectional study. *Journal of Psychosomatic Research, 133*, 110111.

Hausteiner, C., Bornschein, S., Bubel, E., Groben, S., Lahmann, C., Grosber, M., Löwe, B., Eyer, F., Eberlein, B., Behrendt, H., Darsow, U., Ring, J., Henningsen, P., & Huber, D. (2009). Psychobehavioral predictors of somatoform disorders in patients with suspected allergies. *Psychosomatic Medicine, 71*(9), 1004–1011.

Hausteiner-Wiehle, C., Schneider, G., Lee, S., Sumipathala, A., & Creed, F. H. (2011). Gender, lifespan and cultural aspects. In F. Creed, P. Henningsen, & P. Fink (Eds.), *Medically unexplained symptoms, somatisation and bodily distress: Developing better clinical services* (pp. 132–157). Cambridge University Press.

Henningsen, P. (2016). Fear of flying: Relying on the absence of organic disease in functional somatic symptoms. *Journal of Psychosomatic Research, 88*, 59.

Henningsen, P., Fazekas, C., & Sharpe, M. (2011). Barriers to improving treatment. In F. Creed, P. Henningsen, & P. Fink (Eds.), *Medically unexplained symptoms, somatisation and bodily distress: Developing better clinical services* (pp. 124–131). Cambridge University Press.

Henningsen, P., Gündel, H., Kop, W. J., Löwe, B., Martin, A., Rief, W., Rosmalen, J., Schröder, A., van der Feltz-Cornelis, C., Van den Bergh, O., & EURONET-SOMA Group (2018). Persistent physical symptoms as perceptual dysregulation: A neuropsychobehavioral model and its clinical implications. *Psychosomatic Medicine, 80*(5), 422–431.

Henningsen, P., Zimmermann, T., & Sattel, H. (2003). Medically unexplained physical symptoms, anxiety, and depression: A meta-analytic review. *Psychosomatic Medicine, 65*(4), 528–533.

Henningsen, P., Zipfel, S., Sattel, H., & Creed, F. (2018). Management of functional somatic syndromes and bodily distress. *Psychotherapy and Psychosomatics, 87*(1), 12–31.

Herr, R. M., Bosch, J. A., Loerbroks, A., Genser, B., Almer, C., van Vianen, A. E., & Fischer, J. E. (2018). Organizational justice, justice climate, and somatic complaints: A multilevel investigation. *Journal of Psychosomatic Research, 111*, 15–21.

Herr, R. M., Li, J., Loerbroks, A., Angerer, P., Siegrist, J., & Fischer, J. E. (2017). Effects and mediators of psychosocial work characteristics on somatic symptoms six years later: Prospective findings from the Mannheim Industrial Cohort Studies (MICS). *Journal of Psychosomatic Research, 98*, 27–33.

Houtveen, J. H., Hamaker, E. L., & Van Doornen, L. J. (2010). Using multilevel path analysis in analyzing 24-h ambulatory physiological recordings applied to medically unexplained symptoms. *Psychophysiology, 47*(3), 570–578.

Hüsing, P., Löwe, B., & Toussaint, A. (2018). Comparing the diagnostic concepts of *ICD-10* somatoform disorders and *DSM-5* somatic symptom disorders in patients from a psychosomatic outpatient clinic. *Journal of Psychosomatic Research, 113*, 74–80.

Jacobs, L. G., Gourna Paleoudis, E., Lesky-Di Bari, D., Nyirenda, T., Friedman, T., Gupta, A., Rasouli, L., Zetkulic, M., Balani, B., Ogedegbe, C., Bawa, H., Berrol, L., Qureshi, N., & Aschner, J. L. (2020). Persistence of symptoms and quality of life at 35 days after hospitalization for COVID-19 infection. *PloS One, 15*(12), e0243882.

Johnston, K., Adams, M. J., Nicholl, B. I., Ward, J., Strawbridge, R. J., Ferguson, A., McIntosh, A. M., Bailey, M., & Smith, D. J. (2019). Genome-wide association study of multisite chronic pain in UK Biobank. *PLoS Genetics, 15*(6), e1008164.

Joustra, M. L., Janssens, K. A., Bültmann, U., & Rosmalen, J. G. (2015). Functional limitations in functional somatic syndromes and well-defined medical diseases: Results from the general population cohort LifeLines. *Journal of Psychosomatic Research, 79*(2), 94–99.

Kato, K., Sullivan, P. F., & Pedersen, N. L. (2010). Latent class analysis of functional somatic symptoms in a population-based sample of twins. *Journal of Psychosomatic Research, 68*(5), 447–453.

Köteles, F., & Witthöft, M. (2017). Somatosensory amplification - An old construct from a new perspective. *Journal of Psychosomatic Research, 101*, 1–9.

Kirmayer, L. J., & Sartorius, N. (2007). Cultural models and somatic syndromes. *Psychosomatic Medicine, 69*(9), 832–840.

Klaus, K., Rief, W., Brähler, E., Martin, A., Glaesmer, H., & Mewes, R. (2015). Validating psychological classification criteria in the context of somatoform disorders: A one- and four-year follow-up. *Journal of Abnormal Psychology, 124*(4), 1092–1101.

Kroenke, K. (2003). Patients presenting with somatic complaints: Epidemiology, psychiatric co-morbidity and management. *International Journal of Methods in Psychiatric Research, 12*, 34–43.

Kroenke, K., Spitzer, R. L., & Williams, J. B. (2002). The PHQ-15: Validity of a new measure for evaluating the severity of somatic symptoms. *Psychosomatic Medicine, 64*(2), 258–266.

Lehmann, M., Jonas, C., Pohontsch, N. J., Zimmermann, T., Scherer, M., & Löwe, B. (2019). General practitioners' views on the diagnostic innovations in *DSM-5* somatic symptom disorder: A focus group study. *Journal of Psychosomatic Research, 123*, 109734.

Lipowski, Z. J. (1988). Somatization: The concept and its clinical application. *American Journal of Psychiatry, 145*(11), 1358–1368.

Löwe, B., Spitzer, R. L., Williams, J. B., Mussell, M., Schellberg, D., & Kroenke, K. (2008). Depression, anxiety and somatization in primary care: Syndrome overlap and functional impairment. *General Hospital Psychiatry, 30*(3), 191–199.

Ludwig, L., Pasman, J. A., Nicholson, T., Aybek, S., David, A. S., Tuck, S., Kanaan, R. A., Roelofs, K., Carson, A., & Stone, J. (2018). Stressful life events and maltreatment in conversion (functional neurological) disorder: Systematic review and meta-analysis of case-control studies. *Lancet Psychiatry, 5*(4), 307–320.

Maggio, J., Alluri, P. R., Paredes-Echeverri, S., Larson, A. G., Sojka, P., Price, B. H., Aybek, S., & Perez, D. L. (2020). Briquet syndrome revisited: Implications for functional neurological disorder. *Brain Communications, 2*(2), fcaa156.

Maunder, R. G., Hunter, J. J., Atkinson, L., Steiner, M., Wazana, A., Fleming, A. S., Moss, E., Gaudreau, H., Meaney, M. J., & Levitan, R. D. (2017). An attachment-based model of the relationship between childhood adversity and somatization in children and adults. *Psychosomatic Medicine, 79*(5), 506–513.

Murray, A. M., Toussaint, A., Althaus, A., & Löwe, B. (2016). The challenge of diagnosing non-specific, functional, and somatoform disorders: A systematic review of barriers to diagnosis in primary care. *Journal of Psychosomatic Research, 80*, 1–10.

Nichter, M. (2010). Idioms of distress revisited. *Culture, Medicine and Psychiatry, 34*, 401–416.

Nimnuan, C., Hotopf, M., & Wessely, S. (2001). Medically unexplained symptoms: An epidemiological study in seven specialities. *Journal of Psychosomatic Research, 51*(1), 361–367.

Noyes Jr, R., Langbehn, D. R., Happel, R. L., Stout, L. R., Muller, B. A., & Longley, S. L. (2001). Personality dysfunction among somatizing patients. *Psychosomatics, 42*(4), 320–329.

Okur Güney, Z. E., Sattel, H., Witthöft, M., & Henningsen, P. (2019). Emotion regulation in patients with somatic symptom and related disorders: A systematic review. *PloS One, 14*(6), e0217277.

Pareés, I., Saifee, T. A., Kassavetis, P., Kojovic, M., Rubio-Agusti, I., Rothwell, J. C., Bhatia, K. P., & Edwards, M. J. (2012). Believing is perceiving: Mismatch between self-report and actigraphy in psychogenic tremor. *Brain, 135*(Pt 1), 117–123.

Petzschner, F. H., Weber, L., Gard, T., & Stephan, K. E. (2017). Computational psychosomatics and computational psychiatry: Toward a joint framework for differential diagnosis. *Biological Psychiatry, 82*(6), 421–430.

Rask, M. T., Ørnbøl, E., Rosendal, M., & Fink, P. (2017). Long-term outcome of bodily distress syndrome in primary care: A follow-up study on health care costs, work disability, and self-rated health. *Psychosomatic Medicine, 79*(3), 345–357.

Raspe, H., Matthis, C., Croft, P., O'Neill, T., & European Vertebral Osteoporosis Study Group (2004). Variation in back pain between countries: The example of Britain and Germany. *Spine, 29*(9), 1017–1021.

Rezaei, F., Hemmati, A., Rahmani, K., & Komasi, S. (2020). A systematic review of personality temperament models related to somatoform disorder with main focus on meta-analysis of Cloninger's theory components. *Indian Journal of Psychiatry, 62*(5), 462.

Rief, W., & Martin, A. (2014). How to use the new *DSM-5* somatic symptom disorder diagnosis in research and practice: A critical evaluation and a proposal for modifications. *Annual Review of Clinical Psychology, 10*, 339–367.

Roenneberg, C., Sattel, H., Schaefert, R., Henningsen, P., & Hausteiner-Wiehle, C. (2019). Functional somatic symptoms. *Deutsches Arzteblatt International, 116*(33–34), 553–560.

Scamvougeras, A., & Howard, A. (2020). Somatic symptom disorder, medically unexplained symptoms, somatoform disorders, functional neurological disorder: How *DSM-5* got it wrong. *Canadian Journal of Psychiatry, 65*(5), 301–305.

Shorter, E. (1993). *From paralysis to fatigue: A history of psychosomatic illness in the modern era*. Free Press.

Stone, J., Burton, C., & Carson, A. (2020). Recognising and explaining functional neurological disorder. *British Medical Journal, 371*, m3745.

Tak, L. M., Riese, H., de Bock, G. H., Manoharan, A., Kok, I. C., & Rosmalen, J. G. (2009). As good as it gets? A meta-analysis and systematic review of methodological quality of heart rate variability studies in functional somatic disorders. *Biological Psychology, 82*(2), 101–110.

Tomenson, B., Essau, C., Jacobi, F., Ladwig, K. H., Leiknes, K. A., Lieb, R., Meinlschmidt, G., McBeth, J., Rosmalen, J., Rief, W., Sumathipala, A., Creed, F., & EURASMUS Population Based Study Group (2013). Total somatic symptom score as a predictor of health outcome in somatic symptom disorders. *British Journal of Psychiatry, 203*(5), 373–380.

Toussaint, A., Hüsing, P., Kohlmann, S., Brähler, E., & Löwe, B. (2021). Excessiveness in symptom-related thoughts, feelings, and behaviors: An investigation of somatic symptom disorders in the general population. *Psychosomatic Medicine, 83*(2):164–170.

Toussaint, A., Hüsing, P., Kohlmann, S., & Löwe, B. (2020). Detecting *DSM-5* somatic symptom disorder: Criterion validity of the Patient Health Questionnaire-15 (PHQ-15) and the Somatic Symptom Scale-8 (SSS-8) in combination with the Somatic Symptom Disorder - B Criteria Scale (SSD-12). *Psychological Medicine, 50*(2), 324–333.

Toussaint, A., Murray, A. M., Voigt, K., Herzog, A., Gierk, B., Kroenke, K., Rief, W., Henningsen, P., & Löwe, B. (2016). Development and validation of the Somatic Symptom Disorder-B criteria scale (SSD-12). *Psychosomatic Medicine, 78*(1), 5–12.

Van den Bergh, O., Witthöft, M., Petersen, S., & Brown, R. J. (2017). Symptoms and the body: Taking the inferential leap. *Neuroscience and Biobehavioral Reviews, 74*(Pt A), 185–203.

Van Wilgen, C. P., Koning, M., & Bouman, T. K. (2012). Initial responses of different health care professionals to various patients with headache: Which are perceived as difficult? *International Journal of Behavioral Medicine 20*(3), 468–475.

Vassilopoulos, A., L Poulopoulos, N., & Ibeziako, P. (2020). School absenteeism as a potential proxy of functionality in pediatric patients with somatic symptom and related disorders. *Clinical Child Psychology and Psychiatry*, 1359104520978462.

Wessely, S., Nimnuan, C., & Sharpe, M. (1999). Functional somatic syndromes: One or many? *Lancet, 354*, 936–939.

Wynne-Jones, G., Jones, G. T., Wiles, N. J., Silman, A. J., & Macfarlane, G. J. (2006). Predicting new onset of widespread pain following a motor vehicle collision. *Journal of Rheumatology, 33*(5), 968–974

# CHAPTER 23

# Sleep and Circadian Rhythm Disorders

Lampros Bisdounis, Simon D. Kyle, Kate E. A. Saunders,
Elizabeth A. Hill, *and* Colin A. Espie

## Circadian Rhythms and the Sleep–Wake Cycle

*Chronobiology* is a branch of science concerned with periodic phenomena that occur in humans and other living organisms. These periodic phenomena oscillate in temporal cycles which are referred to as *biological rhythms*. There are three biological rhythms: ultradian (less than 24 hours), circadian (around 24 hours), and infradian (more than 24 hours). The term "circadian" describes molecular, physiological, and behavioral processes which operate periodically on a 24-hour cycle. These processes have a genetic origin and are endogenous in nature. As such, they are self-sustained and do not require rhythmic input from the environment to oscillate. Exogenous cues, called *zeitgebers*, synchronize these endogenous processes with the environment in a process called *entrainment*. The light–dark cycle induced by the earth's axial rotation is the most important zeitgeber. Light entering the eye through the retina is captured by circadian light receptors in the optic nerve, called *photosensitive retinal ganglion cells*. These cells project via the retinohypothalamic tract to the central circadian pacemaker in the hypothalamus, the *superchiasmatic nucleus*, allowing clock neurons to entrain to environmental light. This process enables the internal circadian rhythm to align with the external light–dark cycle (Foster & Kreitzman, 2014). Examples of internal circadian rhythms being out-of-sync with the external environment are jet lag and working night shifts.

The most conspicuous process following circadian principles in humans is the sleep–wake cycle. The alteration between sleep and wakefulness is a highly regulated phenomenon dependent on two processes: *sleep homeostasis* and circadian rhythms (Borbély, 1982; Borbély et al., 2016).

Sleep homeostasis is defined as the pressure for sleep which accumulates during wakefulness and dissipates during the night of sleep. When the waking period is extended beyond typical levels (i.e., staying awake during the night), sleep pressure builds up and leads to a sleep debt. In this instance, both duration and intensity of the subsequent sleep are increased, demonstrating the homeostatic drive for sleep. In return, the gradual increase of sleep pressure is counterbalanced by the endogenous circadian signal for alertness and sleep propensity. Overall, these two processes naturally maintain consolidated periods of sleep and wakefulness while regulating their timing and duration.

## Characteristics of Sleep in Good Sleepers

On the behavioral level, sleep is defined as a reversible state of altered consciousness, perceptual disengagement, physical quiescence, recumbent posture, and eye closure. On a neurophysiological

**Abbreviations**

| | |
|---|---|
| AASM | American Academy of Sleep Medicine |
| ASPD | Advanced sleep phase disorder |
| CRSWD | Circadian rhythm sleep–wake disorder |
| DSPD | Delayed sleep phase disorder |
| EDS | Excessive daytime sleepiness |
| ICSD-3 | International Classification of Sleep Disorders, 3rd ed. |
| ISWD | Irregular sleep–wake rhythm disorder |
| MSLT | Multiple Sleep Latency Test |
| REM | Rapid eye movement |
| SCR | Sleep and circadian rhythms |
| SWS | Slow-wave sleep |

level, sleep can be divided into two distinct stages of vigilance: non–rapid eye movement (NREM) and rapid eye movement (REM) sleep (Berry et al., 2020).

NREM typically precedes REM sleep and is marked by normal respiration, decreased muscular tonus, synchronous cortical activity, and gradual increase of sleep depth (i.e., the exogenous arousal threshold required to achieve awakening). Based on sleep depth, NREM is further subdivided into three stages: N1–3. These stages constitute an arousal continuum, with lighter sleep in N1 and N2, and deep sleep (or slow-wave sleep; SWS) in N3. By contrast, REM sleep is characterized by cardiorespiratory variability; muscle atonia; episodic bursts of rapid eye movements; and desynchronous, low-amplitude, mixed-frequency electroencephalogram (EEG) activity. REM sleep can also be subdivided into two microstates: tonic and phasic. Tonic REM is parasympathetically driven and involves muscle atonia and low-amplitude EEG. Superimposed on tonic REM sleep, phasic REM is sympathetically driven and involves rapid eye movements, distal muscle twitches, and cardiorespiratory irregularity.

In healthy adults, sleep is initiated through NREM, marked by a brief period of N1. This process is a cornerstone of healthy sleep. Sleep initiation through REM is a reliable marker of pathology in adults, most often of narcolepsy. During the first sleep cycle, N1 lasts 1–7 minutes, followed by N2 lasting 10–25 minutes. It takes good sleepers 10–15 minutes to reach N1 after lights are turned off, yet the same sleepers often report taking an average of 15–30 minutes to fall asleep. Consequently, it has been suggested that subjective onset of sleep is linked to N2, although the precise definition of sleep onset itself has been the source of scientific debate. The subsequent N3 stage lasts 20–40 minutes. Prior to entering REM, a brief 5–10-minute ascent to N2 is typically observed. Finally, the first REM episode occurs on average 70–100 minutes after the first N1. This REM episode is short-lived, typically lasting less than 5 minutes. The alteration between NREM and REM sleep follows a neurophysiological ultradian pattern and is referred to as the NREM-REM cycle. In good sleepers, the NREM-REM cycle is repeated four to five times during nocturnal sleep. Although the duration of the NREM-REM cycle does not change throughout the night, the length of each sleep stage does. As the night progresses, REM sleep becomes longer and NREM becomes shorter. N3/SWS occupies less time in the second NREM-REM cycle and might disappear altogether in following cycles. N2 is subsequently expanded to occupy the remaining NREM portion of the cycle.

## Measures of Sleep and Circadian Phase

The assessment of sleep and circadian rhythms (SCR) includes several tools, conventionally classified into two broad types of measurement: subjective and objective. Subjective assessments include self- or clinician-reported measures such as clinical interviews, questionnaires, and sleep diaries. Objective assessments include polysomnography, accelerometer devices called actigraphs, and circadian phase assessments (i.e., the use of molecular, physiological, or psychological processes to characterize a person's circadian phase). The diagnosis of most SCR disorders covered in this chapter relies chiefly on symptom self-report. Objective measures can be used to complement the subjective assessment and rule out the presence of comorbidities, such as sleep-related breathing or movement disorders. In this chapter, we avoid using the terms "subjective" and "objective" given that such language overemphasizes the accuracy of laboratory measures and undermines the reliability of self-report observations (Fuoco, 2017).

Clinical interviews are essential for the diagnosis of all sleep and circadian disorders. To aid the conduct of the interview, several structured (Merikangas et al., 2014; Taylor et al., 2018) and semi-structured interview protocols (Edinger et al., 2004) have been developed (Espie, 2022). The clinical interview should include a thorough examination of the chief sleep complaint, covering elements like sleep hygiene, sleep environment, pre-bed behavior, work schedule, sleeping arrangements, circadian preference, and daytime functioning (Riemann et al., 2017). At a minimum, clinical interviews should also include a detailed medical history with current and past medication and substance use (including alcohol, caffeine, and nicotine). The presence of comorbid psychiatric disorders such as depression, anxiety, bipolar disorder (BD), and psychosis should be actively examined, too. Information about elements important for the clinical interviews of specific sleep and circadian disorders are covered in the respective sections of this chapter.

Sleep diaries constitute a form of experience sampling that captures daytime and nighttime behaviors and the experience of the previous night. The assessment covers an extended period of time, usually 2 weeks. They are the mainstay assessment of sleep due to being an ecologically valid, easy to administer, and inexpensive tool. However, sleep diaries rely on participants' recollection of their sleep and wake times. A commonly used, standardized diary is the Consensus Sleep Diary (Carney et al., 2012). Typical parameters derived from sleep diaries include sleep onset latency (i.e., time needed to transition from wakefulness to sleep), wake-time after sleep onset (i.e., time spent awake after initial sleep onset and prior to final awakening), total sleep time, time in bed, sleep efficiency (i.e., ratio of total sleep time to time in bed), and number of awakenings.

Notwithstanding the importance of self- and clinician-reported measures, polysomnography is generally considered the reference standard sleep assessment. Polysomnography is a simultaneous overnight recording of several physiological measures, with internationally recognized consensus guidelines for conduct and scoring (Berry, 2020). However, it is an expensive tool that requires trained personnel, appropriate facilities, and can be time-consuming and burdensome for the patient. A standard polysomnography includes EEG, electrooculographic, and electromyographic indices measured by electrodes on the scalp, around the eyes, and on the chin, respectively. This combination of channels allows staging of sleep and wake. Additional channels measure breathing, respiratory effort, cardiac rhythm and electrical activity, blood oxygen saturation, body position, and limb movements. A digital video can also be recorded. Polysomnography provides data on *sleep continuity*, *sleep architecture*, and cortical activation. Sleep continuity includes parameters similar to sleep diaries, such as sleep onset latency, wake after sleep onset, total sleep time, time in bed, sleep efficiency, and number of awakenings. Sleep architecture refers to the duration and proportion of sleep stages, as well as the latency to REM sleep and number of NREM-REM cycles. Cortical activation is quantified using finer measures of EEG analysis that allow for the extraction of sleep microstructure elements. Following a fast Fourier transformation, the frequency and amplitude of the sine wave constituents are extracted from the EEG data and stratified in given frequency bands (i.e., slow waves, <0.5 Hz; delta, 0.5–4 Hz; theta, 4–8 Hz; alpha, 8–12 Hz; sigma, 12–16 Hz; beta, 12–35 Hz; and gamma, 32–100 Hz). Data are then presented as the absolute or relative power of each frequency band. The most used quantitative EEG in polysomnography is *power spectral analysis*. At present, such analyses are used almost exclusively in research setting rather than in clinical practice.

An actigraph is a motion-sensor device typically worn on the wrist. It is low cost, with small patient burden, and can be used for longitudinal assessment over multiple weeks. Although it is a frequent tool in SCR research, its applications extend to any research question around activity. Actigraphs record gross motor activity, and mathematical algorithms are applied to estimate rest and activity patterns from the motor data. Therefore, given these devices principally assess rest–activity, they are only considered proxy measures of sleep and wakefulness. Unlike polysomnography, there are no universal guidelines for the conduct and scoring of actigraphy. Analysis of actigraphy data can provide a graphical summary of sleep and wakefulness over time, as well as parametric and nonparametric variables about general rest and activity. Parametric variables include sleep onset latency, wake after sleep onset, total sleep time, time in bed, sleep efficiency, and awakenings. Nonparametric variables include (1) L5, the average activity during the least active 5-hour period; (2) M10, the average activity during the most active 10-hour period; (3) the intradaily variability, a fragmentation index of daily rhythms; and (4) interdaily stability, an estimate of the synchronization to the 24-hour light–dark cycle (Gonçalves et al., 2014). Compared to polysomnography, actigraphy generally overestimates sleep and underestimates wakefulness. This discrepancy is small, and actigraphy is generally good in detecting sleep periods in healthy individuals (Conley et al., 2019). However, actigraphy is not as robust in measuring sleep in people with sleep or other chronic disorders (Conley et al., 2019; Smith et al., 2018). This discrepancy is probably due to the difficulty of actigraphy in detecting wake periods before and after sleep, exacerbated by the proneness of these populations to remain inactive in bed when trying to fall asleep (Conley et al., 2019; Williams et al., 2018). In terms of their availability, there are commercial "wearables" (e.g., Fitbit, by Fitbit Inc.) and research-grade actigraphs (e.g., MotionWare, by CamNtech; Axivity, by Axivity Ltd.; and GENEActiv, by Activinsights), with the validity and reliability of these devices—especially commercial ones—being a source of continuous scientific debate (Chinoy et al., 2021; Scott et al., 2019).

## Classification Systems for Sleep and Circadian Rhythm Disorders

SCR disorders constitute a heterogeneous group of disruptions, with distinct clinical presentations, etiologies, prognoses, and treatment needs.

Although their debilitating nature has long been recognized, sleep disorder nosologies have only become available in the past four decades. Presently, there are three classification systems for sleep disorders. Two systems are incorporated within larger taxonomies: the *ICD-11*, and the *DSM-5*. The final system was developed by a scientific society in sleep medicine: the *International Classification of Sleep Disorders, 3rd Edition* (ICSD-3) (American Academy of Sleep Medicine, 2014).

Despite some discrepancies, the three classification systems are more concordant than their previous iterations. The *ICD-11* and *ICSD-3* have maintained the same seven classifications (six for *ICD-11*, which does not include the subgroup of "other sleep disorders") as in their previous versions: insomnia, sleep-related breathing disorders, central disorders of hypersomnolence, circadian rhythm sleep–wake disorders, sleep-related movement disorders, parasomnias, and other sleep disorders. The *DSM-5* includes eight disorder categories: insomnia disorder, hypersomnia disorder, narcolepsy, breathing-related sleep disorders, circadian rhythm sleep–wake disorders, parasomnias, restless leg syndrome, and substance/medication-induced sleep disorder. An important point of convergence is that all three nosologies do not distinguish between "primary" and "secondary," or "organic" and "inorganic" disorders. This substantial modification from previous editions was motivated by two factors. First, there is considerable uncertainty about the causal directionality between "primary" and comorbid sleep disorders. In light of this phenomenon, a sleep medicine consensus group argued, in 2005, that the term "secondary" introduces the erroneous assumption that treatment of the "primary" disorders suffices to treat the comorbid sleep problem (National Institutes of Health, 2005). Second, evidence shows that several sleep disorders share a substantial number of features, regardless of their status as primary or comorbid diagnoses. Consequently, they require the same therapeutic approach, again regardless of the clinical attention focused on the "primary" diagnosis.

In the remainder of this chapter, we focus on the following sleep disorders: insomnia disorder, delayed and advanced circadian phase disorders, irregular sleep–wake rhythm disorder (ISWD), non–24-hour sleep–wake rhythm disorder (N24SWD), narcolepsy, hypersomnolence disorder, and parasomnias.

## Insomnia Disorder

Insomnia is a condition characterized by a persistent difficulty in initiating or maintaining sleep despite adequate opportunity to do so, leading to day-time impairment. In terms of its prevalence, insomnia is the second most common psychiatric disorder (Wittchen et al., 2011) and the most common sleep disorder (Ohayon, 2002). Around one-third of the general population reports acute insomnia symptoms over a 12-month period (Perlis et al., 2020), while 1 in 10 people experiences chronic sleep problems (National Institutes of Health, 2005). These prevalence estimates are found across different countries. The main factors related to the prevalence of insomnia are gender, age, and other illness. Insomnia is more prevalent in women than in men. Moreover, although insomnia symptoms and sleep fragmentation increase with age, insomnia diagnoses remain stable across different age groups (Morin et al., 2015). This phenomenon could be due to the fact that, when compared to younger adults, older adults do not often attribute their daytime problems to poor sleep (Morin et al., 2015). Research on the prevalence and treatment of insomnia in children and adolescents is lacking, yet insomnia symptoms are commonly reported by these age groups. In terms of comorbid disorders, insomnia is more common in people with psychiatric or other medical disorders compared to the general population.

### Etiological Models of Insomnia

Several theoretical models have been proposed regarding the etiology and psychopathology of insomnia, and, for the most part, these models are complementary and not mutually exclusive. Research on these models has fundamentally guided treatment development for insomnia.

In the earliest model, Kleitman (1939) coined the term *sleep hygiene* and appraised the available evidence regarding the effect of pre-bed behaviors and bedroom environment on sleep (Kleitman, 1987). Currently, sleep hygiene refers to a set of habits and practices intended to promote healthy sleep. Sleep hygiene does not yield a strong improvement in insomnia symptoms as a monotherapy, and it is a common control condition in sleep intervention trials. More information on sleep hygiene as an intervention component is provided below.

Later, Bootzin described the model of *stimulus control*, grounded in the principles of behaviorism and classical conditioning (Bootzin, 1972). Within this model, sleep is interpreted as a conditioned response to certain behaviors and environments. As such, insomnia arises when patients associate sleep-related stimuli with activities other than sleep. For example, sleep is typically associated with items such as the bedroom and the bed, and bedtime rituals such as brushing your teeth. In the case of insomnia, it is typical for a patient to spend hours lying in bed awake with the hope of increasing their total sleep time. Although this seems intuitively reasonable, it can be counterproductive, given that now the bed is associated with wakefulness. Another example is spending countless of hours in bed scrolling on the phone or watching TV. Here the bed is again associated with practices that are not conducive of sleep. Stimulus control therapy is a seminal module of multicomponent interventions for insomnia, which are covered below.

The first comprehensive model of insomnia, and still one of the most influential, is the 3P (or three-factor) model by Spielman, developed in 1987 (Spielman et al., 1987). The 3P model was adapted from stress-diathesis models, and it characterizes the emergence and maintenance of insomnia based on predisposing, precipitating, and perpetuating factors. In the 3P model, premorbid traits such as genetic vulnerability, psychological factors, and social situations create a diathesis for the development of insomnia. Then these elements interact with factors such as life stress and psychiatric or other medical conditions to stimulate acute episodes of insomnia. As we have already covered, the typical response to insomnia includes compensatory behaviors that exacerbate and maintain the disorder rather than relieve it. These behaviors constitute the perpetuating factors of insomnia and are motivated by sleep preoccupation and dysfunctional beliefs about sleep.

Building on the 3P model, Perlis's neurocognitive model was the first to integrate biological and psychological elements in its formulation (Perlis et al., 1997). According to this model, chronic insomnia is a neurological condition caused partly by behavioral factors and partly by classical conditioning. Diverging from previous theories, worrying and rumination are not the cause of sleeplessness here. That is, patients are not awake because they are worrying; they worry because they are awake. Central to the neurocognitive model is the concept of hyperarousal and its three dimensions: somatic, cognitive, and cortical arousal. Cortical arousal in particular (defined as high-frequency brain activity; 14–45 HZ) is linked to the manifestation of insomnia. Heightened cortical arousal around sleep onset and during NREM sleep reflects increased sensory and information processing as well as enhanced long-term memory formation. These phenomena arise from classical conditioning and are responsible for impairments in the initiation, maintenance, and perception of sleep.

Still viewing sleep and arousal as opposing phenomena, but emphasizing the role of cognitive arousal, Harvey's cognitive model of insomnia focuses on worrying, rumination, and maladaptive coping behaviors (Harvey, 2002). Sleep preoccupation is at the core of this model. Excessive worrying over lack of sleep and its consequences exacerbate dysfunctional beliefs about sleep and lead to counterproductive safety behaviors. This pattern encourages selective attention to sleep cues and monitoring of perceived sleep threats. As a result, somatic and cortical arousal are increased, and they subsequently interfere with sleep initiation and maintenance.

The psychobiological inhibition model outlines the automaticity and near-involuntary nature of healthy sleep and argues that insomnia is developed and perpetuated by repeated unhelpful attempts to regulate sleep (Espie, 2002). As such, disruptions arise from selective attention to sleep cues, sleep preoccupation, and increased sleep effort, a phenomenon defined as the *attention-intention-effort pathway* (Espie et al., 2006). These processes lead to a failure in inhibiting wakefulness and falling asleep by preventing the otherwise automatic "de-arousal" that precipitates healthy sleep.

Most recently, the neurobiological model defines insomnia as a dysfunction of sleep–wake regulation and focuses on neurophysiological substrates of the disorder (Buysse et al., 2011). Here, sleep problems results from persistent wake-like neuronal activity during NREM sleep in the limbic and parietal cortices, thalamus, and hypothalamic-brainstem system. This localized wake-like activity coincides with typical sleep-like activity in the frontal and central cortices. Co-activation of these regions can potentially explain not only the impairments in sleep initiation and maintenance but also the irregular processing of sensory and emotional information in insomnia.

### Assessment of Insomnia

Insomnia is a heterogeneous disorder, and often multiple tools are needed to capture all symptoms adequately (Buysse et al., 2006). Diagnostically, it relies on the subjective symptom experience. Across all nosologies, it is diagnosed on the basis of patient-reported dissatisfaction with the quantity or quality of sleep, manifested as a difficulty getting to sleep and/or remaining asleep. This dissatisfaction also needs to be accompanied by some form of daytime dysfunction. Clinical interviews and sleep diaries constitute the essential items for the identification and characterization of insomnia. Global scales of insomnia and sleep quality are also frequently used, especially in research settings. Polysomnography or actigraphy assessments of sleep are not necessary for the routine evaluation of insomnia in clinical practice, although they can complement the diagnostic accuracy (Buysse et al., 2006; Schutte-Rodin et al., 2008).

Clinical interview is the cornerstone of insomnia diagnosis. The previously discussed models can provide a framework for the clinical assessment of insomnia by guiding practitioners to collect information on predisposing, precipitating, and perpetuating factors. Integral to the diagnosis of insomnia are the accompanying daytime impairments since almost half of insomnia patients report daytime fatigue as the primary determinant that prompts them to seek help from a healthcare provider (Morin et al., 2006). Typical examples of daytime dysfunction include fatigue, sleepiness, problems in attention and concentration, and mood disturbance. Along with a clinical interview, the most helpful tool for the assessment of insomnia is the sleep diary. Sleep diaries can help delineate the nature and severity of the sleep complaint and uncover sleep-related thoughts and behaviors. Additionally, sleep diaries can capture night-to-night variability in sleep, an element particularly salient for individuals with chronic insomnia. Their use in sleep intervention research is also widespread as sleep diaries can provide detailed information about the adherence to and efficacy of the treatment. In terms of the duration of the sleep diaries, a minimum of 2 weeks is typically recommended. Insomnia is not defined by standardized quantitative criteria about sleep, so outcomes need to be carefully evaluated (Buysse, 2013). However, insomnia patients may be distinguished from good sleepers when sleep onset latency, wake after sleep onset, or early morning awakening exceed 30 minutes. These scores also typically reflect a sleep efficiency that is lower than 85% (Lichstein et al., 2003; Morin et al., 2015).

Although clinical interviews and sleep diaries are invaluable instruments for the diagnosis of insomnia, they can be time-consuming and often not practical for busy clinical settings (Bastien et al., 2001). As such, several brief scales have been proposed for the screening and assessment of insomnia. Among the most widely administered ones are the Insomnia Severity Index (Bastien et al., 2001), the Sleep Condition Indicator (Espie et al., 2014), the Athens Insomnia Scale (Soldatos et al., 2000), and the Pittsburgh Sleep Quality Index (Buysse et al., 1989). The Insomnia Severity Scale, the Sleep Condition Indicator, and the Athens Insomnia Scale are all brief screening scales for insomnia with comparable validity and reliability (Chiu et al., 2016; Wong et al., 2017). The Insomnia Severity Index is based on *DSM-4* and *ICD-2* diagnostic criteria for insomnia, the Sleep Condition Indicator is based on *DSM-5* criteria, and the Athens Insomnia Scale is based on *ICD-10* criteria. The Pittsburgh Sleep Quality Index is a measure of general sleep disturbances and their associated daytime interference. Although this scale was not initially designed to screen for insomnia, it shows good validity and reliability, and expert panels have recommended it for the routine evaluation of insomnia (Buysse et al., 2006; Morin et al., 2015).

Sleep is clearly and objectively impaired in insomnia. Therefore, although objective assessments are not necessary for the diagnosis of insomnia, they can still be useful. Actigraphy, in particular, is increasingly being used. Following the commission of a task force and the publication of a subsequent systematic review, the American Academy of Sleep Medicine (AASM) endorsed actigraphy as an optional assessment tool for insomnia (Smith et al., 2018). In this review, the authors summarized the limitations of actigraphy in producing accurate sleep variables for insomnia patients, but highlighted that discrepancies are within a "clinically acceptable range" (Smith et al., 2018). A recent meta-analysis quantified these discrepancies. The authors showed that, compared to polysomnography, actigraphy overestimates total sleep time and sleep efficiency and underestimates sleep onset latency in patients with sleep and other chronic disorders (Conley et al., 2019).

Polysomnography is more rarely used for the assessment of insomnia compared to actigraphy. In clinical practice, polysomnography is most often used to rule out other potential sleep problems that might contribute to the insomnia complaint. In research, polysomnography is an invaluable tool for assessing putative mechanisms and evaluating the efficacy of SCR interventions. According to polysomnography, insomnia patients exhibit heightened sleep fragmentation and a decreased percentage duration of N3/SWS and REM (Baglioni et al., 2014). A review of power spectral analyses on EEG data of insomnia patients revealed increased beta activity across wakefulness, sleep onset period, NREM and REM sleep (Bastien et al., 2011). The interpretation of these findings is that heightened beta power reflects increased cortical activation.

Different assessments of sleep are not always congruent. Up to 50% of insomnia patients report a shortened sleep duration which is not reflected by polysomnography or actigraphy (Edinger & Krystal, 2003). This misalignment between self-report and actigraphic/polysomnographic estimates of sleep duration is called *sleep misperception*. Recent advances have proposed electrophysiological explanations for this phenomenon. Namely, instead of misperceiving sleep, some insomnia patients might be sensitive to transitions from low- to high-frequency spectral power in central-posterior brain regions (Lecci et al., 2020). These subtle shifts from sleep to wakefulness are only observable through high-density EEG and are not reflected in conventional polysomnographic measurement. Thus, although insomnia is a disorder of objectively measured sleep, it is also a condition not fully appreciated by the existing reference standard of sleep–wake measurement.

## Management of Insomnia

There are two primary treatment modalities for the management of insomnia: cognitive behavior therapy for insomnia (CBT-I) and medication. CBT-I is recognized as a safe and highly effective intervention with more long-lasting treatment effects compared to medication alone. On the other hand, medication for insomnia is only recommended for short-term use, given risks of side effects, tolerance, and withdrawal effects. Consequently, CBT-I is endorsed as the first line of treatment by numerous organizations worldwide, such as the National Institute for Health and Care Excellence (National Institute for Health and Care Excellence, 2021), the British Association for Psychopharmacology (Wilson et al., 2019), the European Sleep Research Society (Riemann et al., 2017), and the American College of Physicians (Qaseem et al., 2016). Nevertheless, at present, the most common clinical response to insomnia is the prescription of hypnotic medication (Siriwardena et al., 2010).

### COGNITIVE BEHAVIOR THERAPY FOR INSOMNIA

CBT-I is a multicomponent psychological treatment, usually ranging from four to eight treatment sessions delivered weekly or biweekly. It is effective when delivered digitally or in-person, either individually, in a group, or in a self-help format. CBT-I can be administered by licensed clinicians, physicians, and trained personnel, including psychology graduates and primary-care nurses. Treatment effects are also not moderated by gender, age, education, occupational status, hypnotic medication use, or comorbid conditions (Espie et al., 2001; Wu et al., 2015). There is some evidence that higher insomnia severity might predict greater improvements following CBT-I, but this phenomenon might be at least partially due to more room for improvement (Espie et al., 2001). According to the most comprehensive review to date, CBT-I is associated with a large reduction in insomnia severity and a moderate to large increase in sleep quality at post-treatment (van Straten et al., 2018). Modest reductions in insomnia severity after CBT-I remain at 3-, 6-, and 12-month follow-up (van der Zweerde et al., 2019). Diary measures of sleep continuity have also consistently shown an improvement following CBT-I (Mitchell et al., 2019; van Straten et al., 2018). However, there is no meta-analytic evidence that CBT-I improves polysomnographically defined sleep parameters, while the evidence for actigraphy is mixed (Mitchell et al., 2019).

CBT-I aims to restructure cognitive and behavioral processes linked to problems with sleep, with several of its components directly arising from theoretical models of insomnia. Therefore, a typical intervention protocol includes behavioral (i.e., sleep restriction, stimulus control, and relaxation), cognitive (i.e., paradoxical intention, cognitive restructuring, mindfulness, positive imagery, and putting the day to rest), and educational (i.e., psychoeducation and sleep hygiene) components (Espie, 2022). Here, we cover principal components of CBT-I that stem from relevant theoretical work: sleep restriction, stimulus control, cognitive restructuring, and sleep hygiene.

Sleep restriction therapy (SRT) is arguably one of the most potent elements of CBT-I. It can be administered as part of multicomponent CBT-I and as a stand-alone treatment. SRT involves limiting and later standardizing time in bed to parallel the total sleep time reported by the patient (Spielman et al., 2011). Rooted in the principles of Spielman's 3P model, current models of SRT highlight that the intervention exerts its therapeutic effects via restricting awake time in bed, regularizing sleep–wake schedule, and reconditioning the association between bedroom factors and sleep (Maurer et al., 2018). This is referred to as the *Triple-R model* (Maurer et al., 2018). According to this theory, SRT reduces insomnia symptoms and improves sleep quality by targeting physiological and cognitive-behavioral factors simultaneously and reciprocally

(Kyle et al., 2014; Maurer, Espie et al., 2020). In effect, the intervention leads to a regularization of time in bed and a restructuring of associations between sleep and sleep-related factors. Preliminary evidence by the team behind the Triple-R model shows that the intervention can also improve quality of life and alleviate circadian misalignment (Maurer, Espie et al., 2020; Maurer, Ftouni et al., 2020). It should be noted, however, that in some populations (e.g., BD) sleep loss has been associated with a range of adverse outcomes (Plante & Winkelman, 2008), and in these instances SRT should either be avoided or adapted.

*Stimulus control therapy* originates from Bootzin's stimulus control theory (Bootzin, 1972), described earlier. Building on this model, the aim of stimulus control therapy is to challenge the association between sleep-related stimuli and wakefulness and restore the qualities of the bed and bedroom as predictors of sleep and sleepiness. Consequently, all non–sleep-related activities, with the exception of sex, are eliminated from the bedroom. The instructions are to only go to bed if sleepy/tired, exit the bedroom if sleep has not occurred within 15 minutes, and only use the bedroom for sleep-related activities. This set of instructions applies to both the initial sleep onset period and any subsequent attempts to resume sleep. Stimulus control therapy is an integral part of CBT-I, and, according to a recent review by AASM, it is an effective standalone treatment for insomnia (Edinger et al., 2021).

As discussed in Harvey's cognitive model of insomnia (Harvey, 2002), dysfunctional beliefs about sleep are prominent features of the disorder. Worry before bedtime and sleep preoccupation during daytime are intrusive and maladaptive cognitions and are among the most challenging elements of insomnia to treat (Harvey, 2002). Unrealistic expectations of sleep (e.g., "I need 8 hours of sleep every night") and catastrophizing when such expectations are not met (e.g., "One night of bad sleep affects the whole week") are among the most prevalent dysfunctional beliefs about sleep identified. As a therapy, cognitive restructuring involves the identification, challenge, and eventually modification of such thought patterns. This involves alerting the patient about the influence of certain cognitions on their mental state and substituting inaccurate beliefs about sleep with accurate facts and a healthier mentality. Accompanying elements of cognitive restructuring are paradoxical intention techniques, monitoring attentional biases, and reducing safety behaviors. Although a protocol for a purely cognitive therapy of insomnia exists (Harvey et al., 2007), it has not been thoroughly studied and no randomized controlled trial (RCT) has been published in this area (van Straten et al., 2018).

Sleep hygiene stems from Kleitman's eponymous theory (Kleitman, 1987). It refers to a set of practice recommendations aimed at fostering behaviors conducive of healthy sleep. Most of these recommendations are prohibitions, such as reducing nicotine and alcohol consumption before bedtime, but some include increasing exercise early in the morning and developing a healthy diet. Additionally, patients are asked to create a comfortable bedroom environment, one that is quiet, dark, and cool in temperature. In primary care, "sleep hygiene advice" is the most common first response to individuals presenting with complaints of insomnia (Everitt et al., 2014). Nevertheless, this advice is most often inadequate, and primary care physicians subsequently choose to prescribe medication due to a lack of knowledge in the provision and administration of CBT-I (Everitt et al., 2014). Indeed, there is no strong evidence supporting the use of sleep hygiene as a stand-alone treatment (Edinger et al., 2021). In fact, sleep hygiene is a common minimal treatment control in intervention trials of insomnia treatment.

## PHARMACOLOGICAL TREATMENT OF INSOMNIA

Several medications are used for the management of insomnia owing to their therapeutic effect. Their prescription, however, requires careful consideration given the risk-benefit profile of each drug and the contraindications of each patient. Moreover, prescription recommendations might change depending on the country (e.g., doxepin, ramelteon, suvorexant, and lemborexant are authorized for the treatment of insomnia only in the United States; melatonin is not approved by the US Food and Drug Administration [FDA] and it is sold over the counter in the United States, while in the United Kingdom melatonin is a prescription-only medication). A comprehensive list of medications used in insomnia includes benzodiazepines, z-drugs (or non-benzodiazepines), melatonin and melatonin receptor agonists, selective histamine $H_1$-antagonists, antidepressants, orexin (or hypocretin) receptor antagonists, antipsychotics, antihypertensives, nonselective antihistamines, and anticonvulsants (Krystal, Prather, & Ashbrook, 2019; Morin et al., 2015). Here we focus on evidence-based and not off-label prescriptions. This includes benzodiazepines, z-drugs, melatonin and melatonin receptor agonists, selective histamine $H_1$-antagonists, and orexin antagonists.

Benzodiazepines (estazolam, flunitrazepam, flurazepam, lorazepam, lormetazepam, nitrazepam, temazepam, and triazolam) act on sleep and arousal via allosteric modulation of the gamma-aminobutyric acid (GABA) type A receptor (Guina & Merrill, 2018). The binding of these agents enhances the inhibitory effect of $GABA_A$, resulting in sedative, hypnotic, anxiolytic, anticonvulsant, and myorelaxant effects. They are generally effective in reducing sleep onset latency, while reductions in night-time awakenings are also common. Their recommended use is restricted to 2–4 weeks (Riemann et al., 2017), given the risk of tolerance, dependence, cognitive decline, and impaired daytime functioning (Holbrook et al., 2000). Benzodiazepines have been associated with a general suppression of REM sleep and a decrease in low-frequency EEG brainwaves in the delta range (Brunner et al., 1991; Feige et al., 1999).

Z-drugs (eszopiclone, zaleplon, zolpidem, and zopiclone) share the common mechanism of action with benzodiazepines: potentiating the inhibitory effects of GABA through allosteric modulation of the $GABA_A$ receptor (Morin et al., 2015). Their structural difference with benzodiazepines lies in their relative selectivity for the alpha 1 subunit of the $GABA_A$ receptor. They are generally preferred to benzodiazepines by medical practitioners because of perceived superiority in effectiveness and safety (Siriwardena et al., 2006). Indeed, early studies reported that z-drugs are safe and effective in reducing insomnia symptoms compared to placebo. However, later reviews have shown that this effect might be smaller than initially thought, especially when both published and unpublished data are considered (Huedo-Medina et al., 2012). Z-drugs are associated with a similar side-effect profile to benzodiazepines (Agravat, 2018; Huedo-Medina et al., 2012), yet they yield a reduced risk of tolerance and withdrawal (Agravat, 2018). Still, z-drugs are currently the most frequently prescribed hypnotic medication worldwide (Sateia et al., 2017).

Melatonin receptor agonists include agents binding to type 1 and 2 melatonin receptors. The theoretical premise underlying the use of exogenous melatonin and melatonin agonists (ramelteon) is that pineal melatonin is involved in the regulation of the human circadian rhythms and consequently the sleep–wake cycle. Reviews about their efficacy in insomnia show small and small to moderate reductions in sleep latency with little evidence for improvements in sleep duration and night-time awakenings (Low et al., 2020). The only common side effect is daytime sleepiness (Wilson et al., 2019).

Doxepin is the only histamine antagonist medication indicated for use in insomnia. Technically a tricyclic antidepressant, doxepin acts on the arousal system via selectively blocking the histamine $H_1$ receptor in the hypothalamus. Low doses of doxepin have been found to improve sleep continuity and, as such, are recommended (only in the US) for insomnia patients with sleep maintenance and early morning awakening problems (Sateia et al., 2017). Doxepin has minimal abuse potential.

Suvorexant and lemborexant are the only dual orexin receptor antagonists recommended for use in insomnia. They exert their therapeutic effects through inhibiting the binding of the neuropeptides orexin A and B in the hypothalamus, thus suppressing arousal and delaying wakefulness. Suvorexant is effective at preserving sleep continuity and increasing sleep duration (Patel et al., 2015), with sustained improvements even after prolonged discontinuation (Vermeeren et al., 2015). Lemborexant improves sleep initiation and continuity measures both at post-treatment (Rosenberg et al., 2019) and at a 1-year follow-up (Yardley et al., 2021), with daytime sleepiness and headaches being the only reported side effects. Both medications have a favorable risk-benefit profile compared to benzodiazepines and z-drugs.

## Circadian Rhythm Sleep–Wake Disorders

Circadian rhythm sleep–wake disorders (CRSWDs) are conditions of either an alternation of the endogenous circadian system (intrinsic CRSWDs) or a misalignment between the endogenous circadian system and the desired sleep–wake schedule (extrinsic CRSWDs). The *DSM-5* recognizes six CRSWDs: (1) delayed sleep phase disorder (DSPD), (2) advanced sleep phase disorder (ASPD), (3) ISWD, (4) N24SWD, (5) shift work disorder, and (6) unspecified type. Excluding the unspecified type, out of these five disorders only shift work is an extrinsic CRSWD. The *ICSD-3* and *ICD-11* recognize an additional condition, *jet-lag disorder*, which is also an extrinsic CRSWSD (Sateia, 2014). In this chapter we focus on intrinsic CRSWDs.

### Delayed Sleep Phase Disorder

First described by Weitzman, DSPD occurs when there is a delay in the sleep–wake cycle

(Weitzman et al., 1981). DSPD patients report typically falling asleep between 1–4 A.M. and waking up in the late morning or afternoon. They are also faced with persisting difficulties when trying to adhere to a conventional or desired sleep–wake schedule that necessitates earlier sleep and wake times. When allowed to follow their preferred time schedule, sleep quantity and quality are normal. The prevalence of DSPD is around 2% in the general population (Schrader et al., 1993), but it can be as high as 16% in adolescents and young adults (Gradisar et al., 2011). The higher prevalence in this age group might be related to neurodevelopmental changes in SCR timing during puberty, exacerbated by an inflexible social and occupational timetable. There are no known gender differences in DSPD, however this might be due to limited epidemiological studies.

### ETIOLOGICAL MODELS OF DSPD

In clinical practice, DSPD is the most common circadian rhythms disorder, with 83% of patients with a CRSWD having a diagnosis of DSPD (Dagan & Eisenstein, 1999). This might be partially due to the fact that DSPD affects an economically active population and is associated with severe disruptions in occupational life and productivity. Nevertheless, the etiological basis of DSPD remains unclear. Suggestive evidence highlights a circadian period that is longer than average (Micic et al., 2013), hypersensitivity to evening light (Aoki et al., 2001; Watson et al., 2020), and sleeping through the advanced period of the light phase response curve (Ozaki et al., 1996). A promising area of inquiry in the etiology of DSPD is its relationship with mood disorders. The high comorbidity between DSPD, depression, and BD might at least be partially indicative of a shared etiological background. However, there is currently not enough research on the reciprocity or the causal mechanisms underlying this association. It is plausible that the link between DSPD and mood disorders results from the constant struggle of DSPD patients to conform to societal demands.

### ASSESSMENT OF DSPD

The assessment of DSPD relies on self-reported sleep–wake behaviors and circadian preference. At a minimum, the clinical interview for DSPD should include an examination of sleep propensity and arousal throughout the day. In order to determine the patient's preferred timing of activities (often referred to as "morning lark" or "night owl"), global measures of circadian preference can be used, such as the Morningness and Eveningness Questionnaire (Horne & Östberg, 1976) and the Munich Chronotype Questionnaire (Roenneberg et al., 2003). Sleep diaries and actigraphy are additional tools that can complement the clinical evaluation of DSPD. However, an important caveat in the administration of these assessments is duration. A data collection period of at least 2 weeks is typically recommended to obtain sufficient information about work- and free-days. As such, there has been an increased focus on the use of actigraphy in DSPD as a more practical and less cumbersome alternative to sleep dairies. Guidelines over the past decade have highlighted that actigraphy data correlate well with biological markers of circadian phase and can reliably evaluate morning or evening preference in CRSWDs (Morgenthaler et al., 2007; Smith et al., 2018).

Laboratory measures of endogenous timing are not necessary, but they can be used to corroborate the diagnosis and guide the administration of treatment. Polysomnography is not recommended for the evaluation of DSPD, and its use in research is rare. Assessments of circadian phase markers such as melatonin are more common. Studies have consistently found a delayed onset of dim light melatonin in DSPD compared to healthy controls, but not a significant difference in phase angle of entrainment (i.e., the interval from circadian phase and to the timing of an external time cue, here bedtime onset) (Saxvig et al., 2013; Wyatt et al., 2006).

### MANAGEMENT OF DSPD

Several treatment modalities have been proposed for the management of DSPD, with the earliest one being *chronotherapy*. In this case, chronotherapy was defined as a behavioral intervention where sleep–wake times are progressively delayed by 3 hours every day until a desired bedtime is reached. Despite its theoretical intuitiveness, implementation in experimental studies is usually problematic owing to patient noncompliance. There are currently no RCTs exploring the efficacy of this intervention, while the evidence from case studies is mixed. Treatment options with bright light therapy and melatonin agonists as monotherapies or in combination are more common.

Bright light therapy (BLT) capitalizes on the phase-shifting properties of light. Exposure to bright light in the morning has the potential to shift circadian rhythms earlier, leading to a phase advance in people with a delayed phase. BLT can be conducted at home, using light boxes that emit a bright light of 2,500–10,000 lux. There is no consensus over the treatment duration, but 30–60 minutes daily for 2–4 weeks is common. Preliminary evidence about the effectiveness of BLT for DSPD is encouraging, but it is only based on case series data from a small number of participants (Auger et al., 2015). As a result of the limited evidence base, the AASM does not formally endorse BLT for the treatment of DSPD (Auger et al., 2015). Additionally, one RCT tested the efficacy of a novel behavioral intervention for people with a late chronotype. The treatment relies on increasing exposure to natural light in the morning, minimizing exposure to light in the evening, and regularizing the sleep–wake, meal, and exercise schedules (Facer-Childs et al., 2019). The intervention advanced the sleep–wake schedule by an average of 2 hours as measured by actigraphy and circadian phase markers, reduced symptoms of depression and stress, and improved performance on cognitive and physical tasks (Facer-Childs et al., 2019). Although encouraging, these findings rely on a small sample ($n$ = 22) from a single RCT.

Similar to BLT, exogenous melatonin is used in DSPD due to its chronobiotic properties. As represented in a melatonin phase response curve, exogenous melatonin leads to differential entrainment based on the time of its administration. Melatonin advances the circadian phase when administered in the late afternoon or evening, with the strongest effect observed when administered 5–7 hours prior to habitual time in bed. Although timing of the melatonin administration influences the magnitude of the phase advancing effect, there is no evidence of a dose-response effect. Exogenous melatonin produces comparable phase advancing results when administered in doses ranging from 0.3 to 5 mg (Burgess et al., 2010; Mundey et al., 2005). In terms of its effectiveness, exogenous melatonin taken in the evening is associated with a significant advance in the endogenous pineal melatonin onset, earlier sleep onset time, and decrease in sleep onset latency (van Geijlswijk et al., 2010). More recent work has combined morning BLT with evening melatonin and found that a combination treatment protocol leads to greater phase advancements of the dim light melatonin onset compared to either treatment administered as a monotherapy (Burke et al., 2013).

### Advanced Sleep Phase Disorder

In contrast to DSPD, ASPD manifests as an advance in the sleep–wake cycle. Patients with ASPD report falling asleep between 6–9 P.M. and waking up between 2–5 A.M. When trying to delay their sleep–wake schedule to conform to the social environment, these patients report persisting difficulties, especially sleepiness in the evening. ASPD is more common with increasing age, but its prevalence in the general population is unknown. In middle-aged adults its prevalence is around 1%, and in outpatient sleep centers the prevalence is around 0.04% (Curtis et al., 2019). However, since an earlier sleep–wake pattern is conventionally acceptable in social and occupational settings, it is assumed that advanced sleep phase is underreported.

At present, possible putative mechanisms of an advanced sleep phase include (1) a missense mutation (i.e., the wrong amino acid incorporated into a protein) in the human CKI$\delta$ gene (Xu et al., 2005), (2) a mutation in a phosphorylation site within the CKI-binding domain of the PER2 protein (Toh et al., 2001), (3) an endogenous circadian period that is shorter than average (Zalai et al., 2018), and (4) increased sensitivity to morning light (Zalai et al., 2018).

The assessment of ASPD is identical to DSPD, including a clinical interview with complementary use of global measures of circadian preference, sleep diaries, and actigraphy. During the clinical interview, particular focus needs to be given to the family history of ASPD, given its inheritance pattern (Jones et al., 1999). Actigraphy here might also be preferred over sleep diaries especially for older patients with mild cognitive impairment or dementia. Polysomnography assessments are extremely rare in ASPD. An early study using polysomnography showed a significantly earlier sleep onset and offset clock time in patients compared to healthy controls (Jones et al., 1999). Laboratory assessments of dim light melatonin onset have also shown significant phase advances in ASPD patients compared to both unaffected siblings (Satoh et al., 2003) and healthy controls (Jones et al., 1999).

The mainstay treatment for ASPD is BLT. Here the entrainment properties of light are utilized to delay circadian timing through the administration of bright light in the evening. Notwithstanding, results on the efficacy of BLT in ASPD are mixed. Some studies have shown that evening BLT can effectively delay sleep onset and offset, improve sleep quality, reduced night-time awakenings, and phase delay both melatonin and core body temperature rhythms (Campbell et al., 1993; Lack & Wright, 1993, 2007). However, other sources of evidence have failed to find any improvements in sleep or circadian rhythms following BLT (Pallesen et al., 2005; Palmer et al., 2003; Suhner et al., 2002). In a review it was suggested that the absence of an effect in some studies might be due to low intensity of the BLT (Palmer et al., 2003) or heterogeneous samples, since a formal diagnosis of ASPD was not required in all studies (Suhner et al., 2002).

### Irregular Sleep–Wake Rhythm Disorder

ISWD is characterized by an unstable sleep–wake pattern. Although total sleep time might be within the normal range, it is fragmented in multiple bouts of sleep. As such, there is not a primary night-time sleep episode, with the most consolidated period of sleep typically not exceeding 4 hours. In extreme cases of ISWD, sleep is distributed randomly throughout the 24-hour day. The primary symptoms of the disorder include complaints of insomnia and excessive daytime sleepiness (EDS).

The disorder primarily affects older adults diagnosed with dementia, other neurological conditions, or brain injury. In all these instances, loss of neurons and functional changes in the superchiasmatic nucleus are the most likely contributing factors to the circadian disorganization observed in ISWD. In otherwise healthy individuals, the disorder typically occurs in care homes or as a result of very poor sleep hygiene. In these cases, as opposed to neurodegeneration, a reduced exposure to external zeitgebers, decreased activity, and a lack of a structured schedule are the possible causal factors for ISWD. The prevalence of ISWD is unknown, with medical conditions being the only potent risk factor. Interestingly, age is not an independent risk factor for ISWD. Although instances of the disorder increase with age, this phenomenon is primarily due to the higher prevalence of particular medical conditions in the elderly, such as dementia (Sack et al., 2007).

The treatment of ISWD aims to consolidate sleep and reduce daytime sleepiness. Several studies in patients with dementia have found supporting evidence for the use of BLT. Here, the goal of BLT is to increase the rest–activity amplitude and stabilize the endogenous circadian phase. Three to five thousand lux of morning BLT administered for 2 hours over 2 weeks was found to decrease napping, increase sleep efficiency, and reduce night-time awakenings (Fetveit & Bjorvatn, 2004). In other studies, similar effects were more modest or even absent (Skjerve et al., 2004). As such, reviews do not support the use of BLT in ISWD, potentially due to heterogeneity in inclusion/exclusion criteria and treatment protocols of the included trials (Forbes et al., 2014). A promising research avenue for light therapy in patients with dementia is whole-day bright light in care-home facilities owing to preliminary positive results on sleep, mood, and cognition (Riemersma-Van Der Lek et al., 2008). Trials on the administration of exogenous melatonin and melatonin agonists in patients with dementia and ISWD showed that there is no improvement on sleep outcomes following treatment (McCleery & Sharpley, 2020). Similarly, the use of prescription medication for sleep is not recommended in patients with dementia due to low efficacy and potentially serious side effects such as confusion, falls, and dependency. Two trials reported on the use of two orexin antagonists, suvorexant (Herring et al., 2019) and lemborexant (Moline et al., 2021). Using polysomnography and actigraphy, these trials showed that orexin antagonists can increase sleep duration and reduce nighttime awakenings in patents with dementia and sleep problems. An overarching limitation in the treatment literature of ISWD is the poor identification of the disorder at study entry, with participants typically identified as patients with dementia and a broadly defined sleep problem, very rarely specifically diagnosed with ISWD.

### Non–24-Hour Sleep–Wake Rhythm Disorder

N24SWD manifests as periodic bouts of insomnia and/or daytime sleepiness owing to a misalignment between the 24-hour light–dark cycle and the non-entrained endogenous circadian rhythm. The disorder often presents as a delayed sleep onset, with sleep and wake occurring progressively later in the day.

N24SWD is rare in sighted individuals and in visually impaired people who retain some level of light perception, but it affects around two-thirds of those who are totally blind and unable to perceive photic stimuli. The remaining one-third of totally blind patients manage to entrain their circadian rhythms through a strict daily schedule of activities, such as exercising, eating, and social interaction. Onset of N24SWD typically occurs shortly after loss of light perception, and demographic differences in its prevalence remain unknown.

The treatment of N24SWD aims to synchronize the patient's endogenous clock with the 24-hour light–dark cycle. If entrainment is achieved, the symptoms of insomnia and/or daytime sleepiness dissipate. In sighted individuals, there is preliminary evidence supporting the effectiveness of timed phototherapy after the minimum body temperature (Hayakawa et al., 1998; Watanabe et al., 2000). The use of exogenous melatonin in the early evening has also been found to be effective for sighted individuals with N24SWD (Hayakawa et al., 1998; McArthur et al., 1996). However, given the fact that the evidence base does not include any RCTs, neither timed phototherapy nor exogenous melatonin is currently recommended. In blind N24SWD patients, exogenous melatonin at night can effectively entrain circadian rhythms (Lockley et al., 2000). Additionally, an RCT including blind patients with N24SWD found a melatonin receptor agonist, tasimelteon, was also effective at entraining the circadian clock and improving clinical measures of sleep (Lockley et al., 2015). Improvements were sustained at follow-up but dissipated rapidly following discontinuation (Lockley et al., 2015). The medication was well-tolerated and led to minimal side effects. As a result, tasimelteon is approved for use N24SWD in blind individuals only (Auger et al., 2015).

## Narcolepsy

Narcolepsy is a rare neurological condition marked by EDS and *cataplexy*, an involuntary loss of muscle tone during wake triggered by strong, mainly positive emotions. Narcolepsy patients may also experience sleep paralysis and hypnagogic hallucinations (i.e., vivid imagery during sleep initiation or before wakefulness). The disorder affects 1 in 2,000–4,000 people, with epidemiological studies relying heavily on self-reported questionnaires, thus probably providing an incomplete picture of its prevalence (Kornum et al., 2017). The typical age of onset of narcolepsy is between 10 and 20 years of age, with potential diagnostic delays of up to 15 years (Scammell, 2015). The associated symptoms are severe, with profound difficulties focusing and staying awake during daytime and especially during periods of minimal activity, such as when watching a movie.

Narcolepsy is divided into two diagnostic types according to the ICSD-3: narcolepsy type 1 (NT1) is marked by EDS, cataplexy, and low levels of hypocretin 1 peptides (also called orexin-A), while narcolepsy type 2 (NT2) is marked by EDS, no cataplexy, and typical levels of hypocretin. The *DSM-5* refers to NT2 as *hypersomnolence disorder*, and it is covered in a subsequent section. Most importantly, the demarcation criterion for NT1 and NT2 is the level of hypocretin peptides in the cerebrospinal fluid of the patients. As such, hypocretin-deficient patients (cerebrospinal fluid hypocretin ≤110 pg/mL) without cataplexy would be classified as NT1 owing to longitudinal data showing that patients with low levels of hypocretin do develop cataplexy at some point (Andlauer et al., 2012). The presence of a rare group of patients with cataplexy and typical hypocretin levels has caused an ongoing debate. At present, these patients are classified as NT1.

Although the exact cause of narcolepsy is not confirmed, genetic factors are undoubtedly important. Certain genes in an area of chromosome 6 known as the *human leucocyte antigen complex* are responsible for encoding antigen-presenting molecules of the major histocompatibility complex. Genetic mutations in these regions have been implicated in the causality of narcolepsy. More specifically, up to 98% of NT1 patients carry the allele HLA-DQB1*06:02 of the human gene HLA-DQB1 (Han et al., 2014; Nishino et al., 2000). This allele is also prevalent in 5–40% of the general population, yet only 1 in 1,000 of these carriers present with NT1 (Kornum et al., 2017), Preliminary data suggest that the allele might be more common in NT2 patients compared to the general population, too (Kornum et al., 2017).

The diagnosis of narcolepsy is made on the basis of a clinical interview and a multiple sleep latency test (MSLT). Cataplexy and EDS are assessed through an interview with several questionnaires available that evaluate sleepiness. The most prominent of these questionnaires are the Epworth Sleepiness Scale (Johns, 1991), the Stanford Sleepiness Scale (Hoddes et al., 1972), and the Karolinska Sleepiness Scale (Shahid et al., 2011). MSLT is a test that consists of five nap opportunities separated by 2-hour breaks. The assessment takes place in a quiet, cool, and comfortable environment, 1.5–3 hours after a night of habitual sleep. The assessment is terminated after 15 minutes following sleep onset, or after 20 minutes if the patient does not fall asleep. Sleep onset is defined here as the transition from wakefulness to any sleep stage. A mean sleep latency of 8 minutes or less, and occurrence of REM sleep on at least two naps are indicative signs of narcolepsy. A polysomnographic assessment the night before MSLT is also recommended to rule out any comorbid sleep disorders.

The management of narcolepsy includes a combination of pharmacological and behavioral interventions. Modafinil, methylphenidate, pitolisant, solriamfetol, and dextroamphetamine sulfate are approved medications for narcolepsy in the United States and Europe. These medications exert their wake-promoting effects by increasing the release or reducing the reuptake of dopamine or norepinephrine. Methylphenidate has a high abuse potential and is associated with a range of side effects, while pitolisant was only approved as a treatment in 2019 (Thorpy, 2020). Modafinil is currently the most widely prescribed medication in narcolepsy, owing to its favorable treatment effects and contained side-effect profile. Sodium oxybate is the only approved medication for the treatment of cataplexy, but the off-label use of venlafaxine is also common. Studies have shown that, as opposed to medication alone, a combined intervention that includes stimulants and a regularized sleep–wake schedule with two 15-minute naps during the day is most effective protocol at reducing sleepiness and involuntary sleep in the daytime (Rogers et al., 2001).

**Hypersomnolence Disorder**

Hypersomnolence disorder or hypersomnia refers to a condition characterized by EDS despite adequate amount of sleep the night before. For the diagnosis of hypersomnia, EDS-related symptoms need to persist for at least 3 days a week for more than 3 months; they need to result in considerable adverse consequences in functioning and not be better explained by another sleep, medical, or psychiatric disorder. The prevalence of hypersomnia is challenging to estimate, but around 28% of adults report a complaint of EDS and 1.5% meet the criteria for the disorder (Ohayon et al., 2012). Hypersomnia typically manifests in late adolescence or early childhood, and there are no gender-based differences regarding its prevalence. A major obstacle in the study of hypersomnia is that terms such as "hypersomnolence (disorder)," "(excessive) somnolence," "hypersomnia (disorder)," and "(excessive) daytime sleepiness," are often used interchangeably. Operational definitions vary, and as such, scientific inaccuracies and biases in the results might be present (Barateau et al., 2017). Here, "hypersomnia" refers to the *DSM-5* diagnosis of *hypersomnolence disorder* and the *ICSD-3* diagnosis of *idiopathic hypersomnia*. The clinical assessment of hypersomnia typically includes an interview, sleep diaries, and EDS questionnaires. The polysomnographic assessment of hypersomnia should be normal, except for potential increased sleep duration.

The most common treatment for hypersomnia is methylphenidate or modafinil. Nevertheless, the evidence base for the effectiveness of either agent is limited. In a recent review, the authors noted that no RCT has examined the effectiveness of methylphenidate in hypersomnia (Sowa, 2016). This might be partially due to the popularity of modafinil as a treatment option following its introduction in the US markets in 1998. However, surveys show that almost half of hypersomnia patients are still using methylphenidate (Ali et al., 2009). The role of cognitive and psychological mechanisms in the maintenance of hypersomnia have also been highlighted (Billiard et al., 1994). As a result, researchers have developed a multicomponent psychological intervention (Kaplan & Harvey, 2009) that has yet to be examined empirically.

**Parasomnias**

Parasomnias refer to aberrant and disruptive behaviors or experiences that occur during sleep or in the transition between sleep and wakefulness. Parasomnias are broadly classified into three groups depending on the sleep stage they typically occur in. In the first group, *NREM parasomnias*, the disorders included are confusional arousals, sleepwalking, sleep terrors, and sleep-related eating disorder. In the second group, *REM parasomnias*, the disorders included are REM sleep behavior disorder, sleep paralysis, and nightmare disorder. In the final group, *other parasomnias*, the disorders included are exploding head syndrome, sleep-related hallucinations, and sleep enuresis.

NREM parasomnias are recurrent events characterized by incomplete awakening from NREM sleep and usually occur in the first third of the night, during the transition from N3. These disorders are marked by sudden motor actions, reduced responsiveness to the external environment, and absent cognition or visual imagery. Typically, patients do not recollect NREM parasomnias, and the reporting of such events is done by the patient's parents or bedpartner. NREM parasomnias are more prevalent in children than adults, their diagnosis relies solely on clinical interview, and their management is variable. In pediatric cases, the disorders are considered benign as children tend to outgrow them. Psychoeducation protocols are preferred over other interventions, but in some cases, anticipatory awakenings 15–20 minutes prior to the typical onset of a parasomnia episode has been found to be effective (Tobin Jr, 1993). For adult NREM parasomnias, interventions typically include sleep hygiene, regularization of sleep–wake cycles, and alleviation of stress triggers.

REM parasomnias are abrupt and repetitive motions that range from small movements to violent acts, sometimes accompanied by vocalizations. Although REM is associated with muscle atonia, these disorders are associated with an excess of muscle tone and/or an excess of phasic twitching activity. In these cases, patients reenact their dreams, and, upon awakening, they are fully alert and able to recollect their dream or nightmare. The diagnosis of these disorders is based on clinical interviewing and polysomnography to confirm the events occur during REM sleep in the absence of muscle atonia. Similar to NREM parasomnias, the management of REM parasomnias is variable. In sleep paralysis and nightmare disorder, psychoeducational interventions such as reassurance and stress management are common, while medication is only prescribed in very severe and persisting cases. In REM sleep behavior disorder, the clinical response is typically preventative and includes a reevaluation of the patient's current medication regime. Most notably, the presentation of REM sleep behavior disorder has been found to be a potent marker of later development of a particular class of neurodegenerative disorders, called α-synucleinopathies. Such disorders include Parkinson's disease, Lewy body dementia, and multiple system atrophy and are caused by the aggregation of alpha-synuclein proteins. Studies have shown that 80% of patients presenting with REM sleep behavior disorder will later develop α-synucleinopathies, suggesting that the neurodegenerative processes responsible for these disorders initially target neuronal circuits regulating REM sleep (Peever et al., 2014).

## Sleep and Circadian Rhythms in Psychiatric Disorders

SCR disruptions are transdiagnostic symptoms characterizing the course of several psychiatric disorders. Historically, the psychiatric disorder has been viewed as primary and as the cause of the SCR condition, with the assumption being that the latter resolves with the successful treatment of the former. SCR disruptions typically precipitate the formal presentation of other disorders, prevail in remission, and their treatment leads to reductions in other mental health problems. Consequently, recent reviews have conceptualized such disruptions as contributory elements in the multifactorial causation of psychiatric disorders (Freeman et al., 2020). Here we address this conceptualization and consider the role of SCR in four such disorders: major depression disorder (MDD), generalized anxiety disorder (GAD), BD, and schizophrenia.

### Sleep and Circadian Rhythms in Major Depression Disorder

Sleep disturbances are prominent features of MDD and are particularly salient to patients, caregivers, and clinicians (Chevance et al., 2020). In terms of the nosology, *ICD-11* includes "changes in sleep" as a diagnostic criterion for depression, while *DSM-5* mentions the presence of "insomnia or hypersomnia nearly every day." Around 70–90% of MDD patients report persistent sleep disturbances (Soehner & Harvey, 2012; Tsuno et al., 2005), with insomnia being the most common. More specifically, daytime fatigue, reduced total sleep time, and difficulties initiating and maintaining sleep are the most prevalent problems reported by patients. MDD is also associated with changes in sleep architecture, a finding first observed in the 1970s. When compared to healthy controls, people with depression typically exhibit a decrease in N3/SWS and a disinhibition of REM sleep, indexed by reductions in REM latency and duration and an increase in the frequency of rapid eye movements during REM sleep (Baglioni et al., 2016; Riemann et al., 2020).

Early polysomnographic results encouraged investigations into the specificity of these biomarkers, with the intention of identifying depression subtypes and optimizing treatment to reflect differential disorder strata. Subsequent investigations challenged the diagnostic specificity and clinical utility of these biomarkers. In multiple reviews, it was revealed that the N3/SWS and REM sleep alterations seen in MDD are also prevalent in several other psychiatric disorders (Baglioni et al., 2016). Instead of a disorder-specific model, these reviews endorsed a transdiagnostic, dimensional approach to SCR in psychopathology. According to this approach, SCR disruptions transcend discrete diagnostic classifications and are ubiquitous in psychiatric disorders, possibly due to a shared causal mechanistic origin. As such, the same SCR endophenotype can be a risk factor for the development of multiple such psychiatric disorders, with no SCR endophenotype being unique to any such condition.

The causal effect of SCR disruptions in the development of MDD is evident by four elements. First, genetic and epigenetic research has supported the notion of a shared etiological background between insomnia and MDD. Two genome-wide association studies have identified genome-wide significant loci implicated in insomnia and potentially depression, with the single nucleotide polymorphism rs113851554 in the MEIS1 gene producing the strongest effect (Hammerschlag et al., 2017; Lane et al., 2017, 2019). Twin studies have also shown a significant genetic overlap between insomnia and depression symptoms when considering longitudinal associations of the two phenotypes (Gregory et al., 2016). Second, sleep problems precipitate the presentation of depression and are a risk factor for later development of MDD. A meta-analysis of prospective cohort studies involving 150,000 participants showed that individuals with insomnia have up to double the risk of later developing depression (Li et al., 2016). More recent reviews are in line with these findings, highlighting that the risk might be higher when applying stricter criteria for the diagnosis of insomnia (Hertenstein et al., 2019). Third, fatigue and insomnia are the most common residual symptoms of depression in otherwise treated individuals. More than half of MDD inpatients report a sleep problem at discharge (Schennach et al., 2019), and those with a sleep complaint in remission have a shorter time to relapse compared to those without (Inada et al., 2021; Sakurai et al., 2017). Finally, the strongest causal inference about the role of sleep disruptions in MDD can be made from evaluating the effects of sleep interventions on depression symptoms. The treatment of insomnia symptoms through CBT-I is accompanied by moderate to large reductions in depression at post-treatment and even at a 12-month follow-up (Ashworth et al., 2015; Henry et al., 2021; Kyle et al., 2020). Other principal SCR interventions, such as BLT and total sleep deprivation, have been found to lead to a reduction in depression symptoms as well (Boland et al., 2017; Geoffroy et al., 2019). However, many of these studies have considerable methodological limitations (Mårtensson et al., 2015; Stewart, 2018) and often lack adequate characterization of sleep and/or circadian rhythms, thus restricting the causal inferences that we can extrapolate from them.

### Sleep and Circadian Rhythms in Generalized Anxiety Disorder

Both *DSM-5* and *ICD-11* include sleep disturbances as a core symptom of GAD, with *DSM-5* specifically referring to problems initiating or maintaining sleep, or nonrestorative, restless sleep. Nevertheless, a surprisingly limited number of studies have examined the role of SCR in GAD, even despite the clear association between sleep and anxiety (Freeman et al., 2020). At the core of GAD is hyperarousal, expressed as enhanced cognitive, somatic, and physiological activation. Hyperarousal is an antagonistic process in the initiation and maintenance of healthy sleep and, as such, an element particularly prevalent in insomnia disorder (Riemann et al., 2010).

The comorbidity between GAD and insomnia is high (Monti & Monti, 2000), with 74% of primary care patients with GAD reporting symptoms of insomnia (Marcks et al., 2010). Difficulties falling and staying asleep in GAD patients are also found in polysomnographic studies (Cox & Olatunji, 2016). However, the evidence on the effects of anxiety in sleep architecture is sparse. Preliminary data show a decrease in N3/SWS and an increase in N1 sleep, while findings on alterations of REM sleep are inconclusive (Baglioni et al., 2016; Monti & Monti, 2000).

The temporal relationship between GAD and insomnia remains a matter of scientific debate. Some longitudinal studies have suggested that anxiety precedes insomnia (Johnson et al., 2006; Ohayon & Roth, 2003), while others have indicated that insomnia precedes the occurrence of anxiety disorders (Breslau et al., 1996; Soldatos, 1994). Similar to research in MDD, stronger evidence on the causal directionality of sleep and anxiety problems should arise from intervention trials. However, although anxiety and insomnia are encountered more frequently together than in isolation, studies rarely examine the comorbidity of the two. A meta-analysis of CBT-I trials showed a moderate improvement of anxiety symptoms post-treatment (Belleville et al., 2011) that was sustained at a 6-month follow-up (Hagatun et al., 2018). A notable limitation is that no trial in the aforementioned meta-analysis delivered CBT-I to people with GAD. In fact, in 2014, two reviews found that there is no RCT examining the effects of insomnia treatment on people recruited with a specific diagnosis of GAD (Dolsen et al., 2014; Taylor & Pruiksma, 2014), and, to our knowledge, no such trial has been published since. One trial compared three insomnia interventions in participants with insomnia on its own and insomnia comorbid with another psychiatric disorder (Bélanger et al., 2016). However, participants with GAD only constituted 9.6% of the sample, and no data were presented for them specifically. Another trial compared the sequential administration of CBT-I and CBT for GAD in 10 patients with comorbid insomnia and GAD (Belleville et al., 2016). CBT for GAD led to a significant decrease in worrying and increase in sleep quality, but no significant improvements were detected for insomnia or anxiety symptoms. CBT-I led to significant improvements in sleep quality and insomnia but not in worrying or anxiety. Sequential implementation of both treatments yielded a superiority in improvements for the group that received CBT for GAD first. However, these findings should be interpreted with particular caution due to the small sample size.. All in all, the evidence base is presently too small to make any claims on directionality between sleep and anxiety. More recent theoretical notions posit that the causal relationship between anxiety and sleep is bidirectional owing to shared substrates in the brainstem and cerebral cortex regulating arousal and sleep–wake (Freeman et al., 2020). Such perspectives are yet to be evaluated empirically.

*Sleep and Circadian Rhythms in Bipolar Disorder*

SCR disruptions are cardinal features of BD, and particularly salient to patients (Gordon-Smith et al., 2021). *DSM-5* and *ICD-11* recognize decreased need for sleep as a symptom of mania, and insomnia or hypersomnia as symptoms of depression. Individuals with BD also exhibit a delayed circadian phase, favoring a late rise and bedtime (Melo et al., 2017). These impairments are ubiquitous in acute illness episodes (Harvey, 2008) and have been associated with increased suicidality (Palagini et al., 2019), lower quality of life (Bradley et al., 2017), decreased occupational functioning (Boland et al., 2015), and poorer performance on neurocognitive assessments of inhibitory control, sustained attention, and processing speed (Bradley et al., 2020; Kanady et al., 2017). Even in euthymia, 70% of patients report persisting sleep problems, such as inability to fall asleep, daytime dysfunction, and increased use of hypnotics (Geoffroy et al., 2015; Harvey et al., 2005). Moreover, sleep problems in euthymia account for a considerable proportion of symptom change over longitudinal assessments (Soehner et al., 2019) and predict acute episode relapse even when accounting for residual mood symptoms (Cretu et al., 2016).

Much like in all other psychiatric disorders, the assessment of SCR problems in BD relies on phenomenology and self-report measures. However, objective measures such as actigraphy, polysomnography, and circadian phase assessments have consistently corroborated the SCR problems described by individuals with BD. According to reviews of actigraphy findings, BD patients exhibit longer total sleep time, sleep onset latency, and night awakenings during euthymia compared to healthy controls (Ng et al., 2015). BD patients also sleep longer compared to insomnia patients, but this is the only significant difference between the two patient groups (Ng et al., 2015). In terms of sleep architecture, BD patients show increased sleep latency and REM sleep duration across all stages (Zangani et al., 2020). During (hypo)mania, BD patients exhibit shorter total sleep time (Zangani et al., 2020). In euthymia, total sleep time is no different from that of healthy controls (Soehner et al., 2018); however, there is a reduction in the duration of non-REM Stage 2 sleep accompanied by a longer duration of the first REM episode and increased total percentage of REM sleep (Estrada-Prat et al., 2019; Sitaram et al., 1982). Alterations in melatonin and cortisol secretion have also been described in BD regardless of the illness stage (Geoffroy, 2018; Melo et al., 2017). Serum melatonin levels are overall decreased in BD, and dim light melatonin onset is significantly later (Nurnberger et al., 2000). Additionally, cortisol levels upon awakening and in response to stress-invoking situations are higher in people with BD (Girshkin et al., 2016).

Transcending initial beliefs about SCR disruptions as only symptoms of BD, accumulated evidence suggests that they might also be involved in the pathogenesis and illness progression of the disorder (Plante & Winkelman, 2008). Circadian gene polymorphisms have been implicated in the genetic diathesis and drug response in BD. Such genes include *CLOCK, NPAS2, ARNTL1, NR1D1, PER3, RORA, RORB, CSNKepsilon,* and *GSK3beta* (Geoffroy, 2018). In a seminal study by Roybal, deletion of exon 19 in the CLOCK gene in mice resulted in manic-like behavior such as hyperactivity, risk-taking behavior, heightened reward sensitivity, and abnormal sleep–wake patterns characterized by reduced sleep (Roybal et al., 2007). Administration of lithium or restoration of a functional CLOCK gene in the ventral tegmentum ameliorated the manic-like behavior (Roybal et al., 2007). Additionally, sleep deprivation has been directly linked with the cause of mania (Plante & Winkelman, 2008). Initial reports by Wehr described sleep loss as "the final common pathway to mania," owing to findings that total sleep deprivation was associated with the emergence of manic mood (Wehr et al., 1987). In later years, the manic-inducing effects of sleep loss in BD were replicated, but it was also found that sleep loss has the potential to produce strong antidepressant effects. Consequently, total sleep deprivation interventions for bipolar depression began to emerge (Benedetti et al., 1997). At present, such interventions are typically combined with the administration of bright light, and several reviews have supported their efficacy (D'Agostino et al., 2020; Gottlieb et al., 2019; Ramirez-Mahaluf et al., 2020). However, conclusion from these reviews should be interpreted with caution. The majority of the included trials are uncontrolled and nonrandomized or include mixed samples of unipolar and bipolar patients (Bisdounis et al., 2021). Most of these trials also do not include any assessment of sleep or circadian rhythms despite it being the presumed mechanism of action of these interventions (Bisdounis et al., 2021).

Sleep problems also constitute the most well-replicated risk factors of later development of BD in children who have a parent with BD and are thus at a familial risk of the disorder (Duffy et al., 2019; Levenson et al., 2015). Cumulative research over the past two decades using bipolar offspring has identified several markers of vulnerability to future development of BD. Among the proposed loci of interest, SCR disruptions are the most well-replicated and widely generalized markers (Melo et al., 2016). In these studies, increased energy levels and a decreased need for sleep were among the earliest identified symptoms (Sebela et al., 2019), followed by irregularity in sleep patterns (Singh et al., 2008) and delayed sleep–wake rhythms (Melo et al., 2016). Combined with self-reported outcomes, measures of rest–activity, such as actigraphy, indicated a decreased need for sleep as a risk marker, together with decreased social jet lag (i.e., the discrepancy in social and biological timing between work and nonwork days) and a larger discrepancy on sleep duration and sleep onset latency between weekends and weeknights (Sebela et al., 2019). In a sample of high-risk offspring, individuals classified as poor sleepers were twice as likely to develop BD compared to peers classified as good sleepers (Levenson et al., 2017).

*Sleep and Circadian Rhythms in Schizophrenia*

The prevalence of SCR disruptions in schizophrenia is approximately 80% (Cosgrave et al., 2018). Self-report and polysomnographic evidence indicate that patients with schizophrenia exhibit longer sleep onset latency and wake after sleep onset, as well as decreased total sleep time and sleep efficiency. In terms of the sleep architecture, patients with schizophrenia show a decrease in the duration of N3/SWS and REM sleep compared to healthy controls (Chan et al., 2017).

Insomnia symptoms are the most frequent SCR complaints in schizophrenia, but ASDP and DSPD are also common. Interestingly, the presence of insomnia in patients with schizophrenia might indicate a particular disorder subtype (Freeman et al., 2020). Behavioral genetic studies have highlighted that insomnia correlates with paranoia, hallucinations, and cognitive disorganization, but not with negative affect and grandiosity (Taylor et al., 2015). Accumulated evidence also suggests that these problems appear prior to the formal presentation of schizophrenia. Studies in populations at ultra-high risk of psychosis show that insomnia is a strong predictor for the development of persistent psychosis (Reeve et al., 2018). Additionally, in longitudinal studies using experience sampling monitoring, among people with a diagnosis within the schizophrenia spectrum, poor sleep quality predicted increases in paranoia (Kasanova et al., 2020) and auditory hallucinations (Mulligan et al., 2016) the following morning. The majority of patients with schizophrenia experiencing persecutory delusions also report sleep problems prior to the onset of these delusions (Freeman et al., 2019). Experimental studies in nonclinical populations show a marked increase in psychotic experiences following sleep loss (Barton et al., 2018). So far, this relationship appears to be unidirectional, with psychosis not being a potent predictor of insomnia (Reeve et al., 2018; Waite et al., 2020). However, it has been suggested that the relationship between psychosis and insomnia might be fully mediated by negative affect (Freeman et al., 2020).

More robust evidence regarding the relationship between sleep and psychosis comes from intervention studies. In a large RCT of students with insomnia, CBT-I led to a small yet significant reductions in paranoia and hallucination scores (Freeman et al., 2017). These post-treatment changes in psychotic experiences were mediated by improvements in insomnia symptoms. There was limited evidence for reverse causation. Smaller open-label and pilot RCTs of CBT-I have shown significant sleep improvements both for individuals with schizophrenia and those at ultra-high risk of psychosis (Bradley et al., 2018; Chiu et al., 2018; Freeman et al., 2015; Hwang et al., 2019). Although no significant changes in psychosis was detected in any of these studies, these trials were not powered to be definitive.

Despite their prevalence and importance in treatment and symptom development, SCR disruptions are not part of the diagnostic criteria for schizophrenia in either *DSM-5* or *ICD-11*. This might reflect a phenomenon where sleep problems in schizophrenia are not formally assessed and prioritized by clinicians (Rehman et al., 2017) despite patient reports that sleep and daily rhythms are particularly salient domains for them (Freeman et al., 2019). Recent advancements in this area might see the integration of SCR rhythms in the diagnosis, assessment, and management of schizophrenia in both research and clinical practice.

## Sleep and Circadian Rhythms in Medicine

The 2017 Nobel Prize in Medicine was jointly awarded to Jeffrey C. Hall, Michael Rosbash, and Michael W. Young for their work on the molecular underpinnings of the circadian clock. Although the scope of this chapter was to highlight the role of SCR in mental health, understanding the circadian principles of our physiology can provide insight into human health at large. SCR disruptions have been implicated as central or peripheral elements of disorders ranging from cardiovascular and neurodegenerative diseases to cancer and pathogen infection. Emerging evidence also indicates that without changing the dosage, synchronizing drug administration with endogenous circadian rhythms can improve treatment potency. Thus, beyond their role in pathogenesis, pathophysiology, and psychopathology, new developments in circadian medicine highlight the potential of circadian principles even in potentiating drug action and optimizing treatment efficacy.

## References

Agravat, A. (2018). "Z"-hypnotics versus benzodiazepines for the treatment of insomnia. *Progress in Neurology and Psychiatry*, 22(2), 26–29.

Ali, M., Auger, R. R., Slocumb, N. L., & Morgenthaler, T. I. (2009). Idiopathic hypersomnia: Clinical features and response to treatment. *Journal of Clinical Sleep Medicine*, 5(6), 562–568.

American Academy of Sleep Medicine. (2014). *International classification of sleep disorders*, 3rd ed. American Academy of Sleep Medicine.

Andlauer, O., Moore IV, H., Hong, S.-C., Dauvilliers, Y., Kanbayashi, T., Nishino, S., . . . Einen, M. (2012). Predictors of hypocretin (orexin) deficiency in narcolepsy without cataplexy. *Sleep*, 35(9), 1247–1255.

Aoki, H., Ozeki, Y., & Yamada, N. (2001). Hypersensitivity of melatonin suppression in response to light in patients with delayed sleep phase syndrome. *Chronobiology International*, 18(2), 263–271.

Ashworth, D. K., Sletten, T. L., Junge, M., Simpson, K., Clarke, D., Cunnington, D., & Rajaratnam, S. M. (2015). A randomized controlled trial of cognitive behavioral therapy for insomnia: An effective treatment for comorbid insomnia and depression. *Journal of Counseling Psychology*, 62(2), 115.

Auger, R. R., Burgess, H. J., Emens, J. S., Deriy, L. V., Thomas, S. M., & Sharkey, K. M. (2015). Clinical practice guideline for the treatment of intrinsic circadian rhythm sleep–wake disorders: Advanced sleep–wake phase disorder (ASWPD), delayed sleep–wake phase disorder (DSWPD), non-24-hour sleep–wake rhythm disorder (N24SWD), and irregular sleep–wake rhythm disorder (ISWRD). An update for 2015: An American Academy of Sleep Medicine clinical practice guideline. *Journal of Clinical Sleep Medicine*, 11(10), 1199–1236.

Baglioni, C., Nanovska, S., Regen, W., Spiegelhalder, K., Feige, B., Nissen, C., . . . Riemann, D. (2016). Sleep and mental disorders: A meta-analysis of polysomnographic research. *Psychological Bulletin*, 142(9), 969.

Baglioni, C., Regen, W., Teghen, A., Spiegelhalder, K., Feige, B., Nissen, C., & Riemann, D. (2014). Sleep changes in the disorder of insomnia: A meta-analysis of polysomnographic studies. *Sleep Medicine Reviews*, 18(3), 195–213.

Barateau, L., Lopez, R., Franchi, J. A. M., & Dauvilliers, Y. (2017). Hypersomnolence, hypersomnia, and mood disorders. *Current Psychiatry Reports*, 19(2), 13.

Barton, J., Kyle, S. D., Varese, F., Jones, S. H., & Haddock, G. (2018). Are sleep disturbances causally linked to the presence and severity of psychotic-like, dissociative and hypomanic experiences in non-clinical populations? A systematic review. *Neuroscience & Biobehavioral Reviews*, 89, 119–131.

Bastien, C. H., Turcotte, I., & St-Jean, G. (2011). Insomnia II. In C. M. Morin & C. A. Espie (Eds.), *The Oxford handbook of sleep and sleep disorders* (pp. 428–452). Oxford University Press.

Bastien, C. H., Vallières, A., & Morin, C. M. (2001). Validation of the Insomnia Severity Index as an outcome measure for insomnia research. *Sleep Medicine*, 2(4), 297–307.

Bélanger, L., Harvey, A. G., Fortier-Brochu, É., Beaulieu-Bonneau, S., Eidelman, P., Talbot, L., . . . Soehner, A. M. (2016). Impact of comorbid anxiety and depressive disorders on treatment response to cognitive behavior therapy for insomnia. *Journal of Consulting and Clinical Psychology*, 84(8), 659.

Belleville, G., Cousineau, H., Levrier, K., & St-Pierre-Delorme, M.-È. (2011). Meta-analytic review of the impact of cognitive-behavior therapy for insomnia on concomitant anxiety. *Clinical Psychology Review*, 31(4), 638–652.

Belleville, G., Ivers, H., Bélanger, L., Blais, F. C., & Morin, C. M. (2016). Sequential treatment of comorbid insomnia and generalized anxiety disorder. *Journal of Clinical Psychology*, 72(9), 880–896.

Benedetti, F., Barbini, B., Lucca, A., Campori, E., Colombo, C., & Smeraldi, E. (1997). Sleep deprivation hastens the antidepressant action of fluoxetine. *European Archives of Psychiatry and Clinical Neuroscience*, 247(2), 100.

Berry, R. B., Quan, S. F., Abreu, A. R., . . . for the American Academy of Sleep Medicine. (2020). *The AASM manual for the scoring of sleep and associated events: Rules, terminology and technical specifications, version 2.6.* American Academy of Sleep Medicine.

Billiard, M., Dolenc, L., Aldaz, C., Ondze, B., & Besset, A. (1994). Hypersomnia associated with mood disorders: A new perspective. *Journal of Psychosomatic Research*, 38, 41–47.

Bisdounis, L., Saunders, K. E., Farley, H. J., Lee, C. K., McGowan, N. M., Espie, C. A., & Kyle, S. D. (2021). Psychological and behavioural interventions in bipolar disorder that target sleep and circadian rhythms: A systematic review of randomised controlled trials. *Neuroscience & Biobehavioral Reviews*, 132, 378–390.

Boland, E. M., Rao, H., Dinges, D. F., Smith, R. V., Goel, N., Detre, J. A., . . . Gehrman, P. R. (2017). Meta-analysis of the antidepressant effects of acute sleep deprivation. *Journal of Clinical Psychiatry, 78*(8), e1020–e1034.

Boland, E. M., Stange, J. P., Adams, A. M., LaBelle, D. R., Ong, M.-L., Hamilton, J. L., . . . Alloy, L. B. (2015). Associations between sleep disturbance, cognitive functioning and work disability in bipolar disorder. *Psychiatry Research, 230*(2), 567–574.

Bootzin, R. R. (1972). Stimulus control treatment for insomnia. *Proceedings of the American Psychological Association, 7*, 395–396.

Borbély, A. A. (1982). A two process model of sleep regulation. *Human Neurobiology, 1*(3), 195–204.

Borbély, A. A., Daan, S., Wirz-Justice, A., & Deboer, T. (2016). The two-process model of sleep regulation: A reappraisal. *Journal of Sleep Research, 25*(2), 131–143.

Bradley, A., Anderson, K., Gallagher, P., & McAllister-Williams, R. H. (2020). The association between sleep and cognitive abnormalities in bipolar disorder. *Psychological Medicine, 50*(1), 125–132.

Bradley, A., Webb-Mitchell, R., Hazu, A., Slater, N., Middleton, B., Gallagher, P., . . . Anderson, K. (2017). Sleep and circadian rhythm disturbance in bipolar disorder. *Psychological Medicine, 47*(9), 1678–1689.

Bradley, J., Freeman, D., Chadwick, E., Harvey, A. G., Mullins, B., Johns, L., . . . Waite, F. (2018). Treating sleep problems in young people at ultra-high risk of psychosis: A feasibility case series. *Behavioural and Cognitive Psychotherapy, 46*(3), 276–291.

Breslau, N., Roth, T., Rosenthal, L., & Andreski, P. (1996). Sleep disturbance and psychiatric disorders: A longitudinal epidemiological study of young adults. *Biological Psychiatry, 39*(6), 411–418.

Brunner, D. P., Dijk, D.-J., Münch, M., & Borbély, A. A. (1991). Effect of zolpidem on sleep and sleep EEG spectra in healthy young men. *Psychopharmacology, 104*(1), 1–5.

Burgess, H. J., Revell, V. L., Molina, T. A., & Eastman, C. I. (2010). Human phase response curves to three days of daily melatonin: 0.5 mg versus 3.0 mg. *Journal of Clinical Endocrinology & Metabolism, 95*(7), 3325–3331.

Burke, T. M., Markwald, R. R., Chinoy, E. D., Snider, J. A., Bessman, S. C., Jung, C. M., & Wright Jr, K. P. (2013). Combination of light and melatonin time cues for phase advancing the human circadian clock. *Sleep, 36*(11), 1617–1624.

Buysse, D. J. (2013). Insomnia. *Journal of the American Medical Association, 309*(7), 706–716. doi:10.1001/jama.2013.193

Buysse, D. J., Ancoli-Israel, S., Edinger, J. D., Lichstein, K. L., & Morin, C. M. (2006). Recommendations for a standard research assessment of insomnia. *Sleep, 29*(9), 1155–1173.

Buysse, D. J., Germain, A., Hall, M., Monk, T. H., & Nofzinger, E. A. (2011). A neurobiological model of insomnia. *Drug Discovery Today: Disease Models, 8*(4), 129–137.

Buysse, D. J., Reynolds, C. F., Monk, T. H., Berman, S. R., & Kupfer, D. J. (1989). The Pittsburgh Sleep Quality Index: A new instrument for psychiatric practice and research. *Psychiatry Research, 28*(2), 193–213.

Campbell, S. S., Dawson, D., & Anderson, M. W. (1993). Alleviation of sleep maintenance insomnia with timed exposure to bright light. *Journal of the American Geriatrics Society, 41*(8), 829–836.

Carney, C. E., Buysse, D. J., Ancoli-Israel, S., Edinger, J. D., Krystal, A. D., Lichstein, K. L., & Morin, C. M. (2012). The consensus sleep diary: Standardizing prospective sleep self-monitoring. *Sleep, 35*(2), 287–302.

Chan, M. S., Chung, K. F., Yung, K. P., & Yeung, W. F. (2017). Sleep in schizophrenia: A systematic review and meta-analysis of polysomnographic findings in case-control studies. *Sleep Medicine Reviews, 32*, 69–84. doi:10.1016/j.smrv.2016.03.001

Chevance, A., Ravaud, P., Tomlinson, A., Le Berre, C., Teufer, B., Touboul, S., . . . Tran, V. T. (2020). Identifying outcomes for depression that matter to patients, informal caregivers, and health-care professionals: Qualitative content analysis of a large international online survey. *Lancet Psychiatry, 7*(8), 692–702.

Chinoy, E. D., Cuellar, J. A., Huwa, K. E., Jameson, J. T., Watson, C. H., Bessman, S. C., . . . Markwald, R. R. (2021). Performance of seven consumer sleep-tracking devices compared with polysomnography. *Sleep, 44*(5), zsaa291.

Chiu, H.-Y., Chang, L.-Y., Hsieh, Y.-J., & Tsai, P.-S. (2016). A meta-analysis of diagnostic accuracy of three screening tools for insomnia. *Journal of Psychosomatic Research, 87*, 85–92.

Chiu, V. W., Ree, M., Janca, A., Iyyalol, R., Dragovic, M., & Waters, F. (2018). Sleep profiles and CBT-I response in schizophrenia and related psychoses. *Psychiatry Research, 268*, 279–287. doi:10.1016/j.psychres.2018.07.027

Conley, S., Knies, A., Batten, J., Ash, G., Miner, B., Hwang, Y., . . . Redeker, N. S. (2019). Agreement between actigraphic and polysomnographic measures of sleep in adults with and without chronic conditions: A systematic review and meta-analysis. *Sleep Medicine Reviews, 46*, 151–160.

Cosgrave, J., Wulff, K., & Gehrman, P. (2018). Sleep, circadian rhythms, and schizophrenia: Where we are and where we need to go. *Current Opinion in Psychiatry, 31*(3), 176–182.

Cox, R. C., & Olatunji, B. O. (2016). A systematic review of sleep disturbance in anxiety and related disorders. *Journal of Anxiety Disorders, 37*, 104–129.

Cretu, J. B., Culver, J. L., Goffin, K. C., Shah, S., & Ketter, T. A. (2016). Sleep, residual mood symptoms, and time to relapse in recovered patients with bipolar disorder. *Journal of Affective Disorders, 190*, 162–166.

Curtis, B. J., Ashbrook, L. H., Young, T., Finn, L. A., Fu, Y.-H., Ptáček, L. J., & Jones, C. R. (2019). Extreme morning chronotypes are often familial and not exceedingly rare: The estimated prevalence of advanced sleep phase, familial advanced sleep phase, and advanced sleep–wake phase disorder in a sleep clinic population. *Sleep, 42*(10), zsz148.

D'Agostino, A., Ferrara, P., Terzoni, S., Ostinelli, E. G., Carrara, C., Prunas, C., . . . Destrebecq, A. (2020). Efficacy of triple chronotherapy in unipolar and bipolar depression: A systematic review of the available evidence. *Journal of Affective Disorders, 276*, 297–304. doi:10.1016/j.jad.2020.07.026

Dagan, Y., & Eisenstein, M. (1999). Orcadian rhythm sleep disorders: Toward a more precise definition and diagnosis. *Chronobiology International, 16*(2), 213–222.

Dolsen, M. R., Asarnow, L. D., & Harvey, A. G. (2014). Insomnia as a transdiagnostic process in psychiatric disorders. *Current Psychiatry Reports, 16*(9), 471.

Duffy, A., Goodday, S., Keown-Stoneman, C., & Grof, P. (2019). The emergent course of bipolar disorder: Observations over two decades from the Canadian high-risk offspring cohort. *American Journal of Psychiatry, 176*(9), 720–729.

Edinger, J. D., Kirby, A. C., Lineberger, M. D., et al. (2006). *Duke Structured Interview Schedule for DSM-IV-TR and International Classification of Sleep Disorders,* 2nd ed., *Sleep Disorders Diagnoses.* Durham, NC: Veterans Affairs and Duke University Medical Centers.

Edinger, J. D., Arnedt, J. T., Bertisch, S. M., Carney, C. E., Harrington, J. J., Lichstein, K. L., . . . Kazmi, U. (2021). Behavioral and psychological treatments for chronic insomnia disorder in adults: An American Academy of Sleep Medicine systematic review, meta-analysis, and GRADE assessment. *Journal of Clinical Sleep Medicine, 17*(2), 263–298.

Edinger, J. D., & Krystal, A. D. (2003). Subtyping primary insomnia: Is sleep state misperception a distinct clinical entity? *Sleep Medicine Reviews, 7*(3), 203–214.

Espie, C. (2022). *A clinician's guide to Cognitive Behavioural Therapeutics (CBTx) for insomnia.* Cambridge University Press.

Espie, C. A. (2002). Insomnia: Conceptual issues in the development, persistence, and treatment of sleep disorder in adults. *Annual Review of Psychology, 53*(1), 215–243.

Espie, C. A., Broomfield, N. M., MacMahon, K. M., Macphee, L. M., & Taylor, L. M. (2006). The attention–intention–effort pathway in the development of psychophysiologic insomnia: A theoretical review. *Sleep Medicine Reviews, 10*(4), 215–245.

Espie, C. A., Inglis, S. J., & Harvey, L. (2001). Predicting clinically significant response to cognitive behavior therapy for chronic insomnia in general medical practice: Analyses of outcome data at 12 months posttreatment. *Journal of Consulting and Clinical Psychology, 69*(1), 58.

Espie, C. A., Kyle, S. D., Hames, P., Gardani, M., Fleming, L., & Cape, J. (2014). The Sleep Condition Indicator: A clinical screening tool to evaluate insomnia disorder. *BMJ Open, 4*(3).

Estrada-Prat, X., Álvarez-Guerrico, I., Batlle-Vila, S., Camprodon-Rosanas, E., Martín-López, L. M., Álvarez, E., . . . Pérez, V. (2019). Sleep alterations in pediatric bipolar disorder versus attention deficit disorder. *Psychiatry Research, 275,* 39–45.

Everitt, H., McDermott, L., Leydon, G., Yules, H., Baldwin, D., & Little, P. (2014). GPs' management strategies for patients with insomnia: A survey and qualitative interview study. *British Journal of General Practice, 64*(619), e112–119. doi:10.3399/bjgp14X677176

Facer-Childs, E. R., Middleton, B., Skene, D. J., & Bagshaw, A. P. (2019). Resetting the late timing of "night owls" has a positive impact on mental health and performance. *Sleep Medicine, 60,* 236–247.

Feige, B., Voderholzer, U., Riemann, D., Hohagen, F., & Berger, M. (1999). Independent sleep EEG slow-wave and spindle band dynamics associated with 4 weeks of continuous application of short-half-life hypnotics in healthy subjects. *Clinical Neurophysiology, 110*(11), 1965–1974.

Fetveit, A., & Bjorvatn, B. (2004). The effects of bright-light therapy on actigraphical measured sleep last for several weeks post-treatment. A study in a nursing home population. *Journal of Sleep Research, 13*(2), 153–158.

Forbes, D., Blake, C. M., Thiessen, E. J., Peacock, S., & Hawranik, P. (2014). Light therapy for improving cognition, activities of daily living, sleep, challenging behaviour, and psychiatric disturbances in dementia. *Cochrane Database of Systematic Reviews* (2).

Foster, R. G., & Kreitzman, L. (2014). The rhythms of life: What your body clock means to you! *Experimental Physiology, 99*(4), 599–606.

Freeman, D., Morrison, A., Bird, J. C., Chadwick, E., Bold, E., Taylor, K. M., . . . Isham, L. (2019). The weeks before 100 persecutory delusions: The presence of many potential contributory causal factors. *BJPsych Open, 5*(5).

Freeman, D., Sheaves, B., Goodwin, G. M., Yu, L.-M., Nickless, A., Harrison, P. J., . . . Wadekar, V. (2017). The effects of improving sleep on mental health (OASIS): A randomised controlled trial with mediation analysis. *Lancet Psychiatry, 4*(10), 749–758.

Freeman, D., Sheaves, B., Waite, F., Harvey, A. G., & Harrison, P. J. (2020). Sleep disturbance and psychiatric disorders. *Lancet Psychiatry, 7*(7), 628–637.

Freeman, D., Taylor, K. M., Molodynski, A., & Waite, F. (2019). Treatable clinical intervention targets for patients with schizophrenia. *Schizophrenia Research, 211,* 44–50. doi:10.1016/j.schres.2019.07.016

Freeman, D., Waite, F., Startup, H., Myers, E., Lister, R., McInerney, J., . . . Yu, L. M. (2015). Efficacy of cognitive behavioural therapy for sleep improvement in patients with persistent delusions and hallucinations (BEST): A prospective, assessor-blind, randomised controlled pilot trial. *Lancet Psychiatry, 2*(11), 975–983. doi:10.1016/s2215-0366(15)00314-4

Fuoco, R. E. (2017). People-centered language recommendations for sleep research communication. *Sleep, 40*(4), zsx039.

Geoffroy, P., Scott, J., Boudebesse, C., Lajnef, M., Henry, C., Leboyer, M., . . . Etain, B. (2015). Sleep in patients with remitted bipolar disorders: A meta-analysis of actigraphy studies. *Acta Psychiatrica Scandinavica, 131*(2), 89–99.

Geoffroy, P. A. (2018). Clock genes and light signaling alterations in bipolar disorder: When the biological clock is off. *Biological Psychiatry, 84*(11), 775–777.

Geoffroy, P. A., Schroder, C. M., Reynaud, E., & Bourgin, P. (2019). Efficacy of light therapy versus antidepressant drugs, and of the combination versus monotherapy, in major depressive episodes: A systematic review and meta-analysis. *Sleep Medicine Reviews, 48,* 101213.

Girshkin, L., O'Reilly, N., Quidé, Y., Teroganova, N., Rowland, J. E., Schofield, P. R., & Green, M. J. (2016). Diurnal cortisol variation and cortisol response to an MRI stressor in schizophrenia and bipolar disorder. *Psychoneuroendocrinology, 67,* 61–69.

Gonçalves, B. S., Cavalcanti, P. R., Tavares, G. R., Campos, T. F., & Araujo, J. F. (2014). Nonparametric methods in actigraphy: An update. *Sleep Science, 7*(3), 158–164.

Gordon-Smith, K., Saunders, K. E., Savage, J., Craddock, N., Jones, I., & Jones, L. (2021). Have I argued with my family this week?": What questions do those with lived experience choose to monitor their bipolar disorder? *Journal of Affective Disorders, 281,* 918–925.

Gottlieb, J. F., Benedetti, F., Geoffroy, P. A., Henriksen, T. E., Lam, R. W., Murray, G., . . . Crowe, M. (2019). The chronotherapeutic treatment of bipolar disorders: A systematic review and practice recommendations from the ISBD Task Force on Chronotherapy and Chronobiology. *Bipolar Disorders, 21*(8), 741–773.

Gradisar, M., Gardner, G., & Dohnt, H. (2011). Recent worldwide sleep patterns and problems during adolescence: A review and meta-analysis of age, region, and sleep. *Sleep Medicine, 12*(2), 110–118.

Gregory, A. M., Rijsdijk, F. V., Eley, T. C., Buysse, D. J., Schneider, M. N., Parsons, M., & Barclay, N. L. (2016). A longitudinal twin and sibling study of associations between insomnia and depression symptoms in young adults. *Sleep, 39*(11), 1985–1992.

Guina, J., & Merrill, B. (2018). Benzodiazepines I: Upping the care on downers: The evidence of risks, benefits and alternatives. *Journal of Clinical Medicine, 7*(2), 17.

Hagatun, S., Vedaa, Ø., Harvey, A. G., Nordgreen, T., Smith, O. R., Pallesen, S., . . . Sivertsen, B. (2018). Internet-delivered cognitive-behavioral therapy for insomnia and comorbid symptoms. *Internet Interventions, 12*, 11–15.

Hammerschlag, A. R., Stringer, S., De Leeuw, C. A., Sniekers, S., Taskesen, E., Watanabe, K., . . . Wassing, R. (2017). Genome-wide association analysis of insomnia complaints identifies risk genes and genetic overlap with psychiatric and metabolic traits. *Nature Genetics, 49*(11), 1584.

Han, F., Lin, L., Schormair, B., Pizza, F., Plazzi, G., Ollila, H. M., . . . Winkelmann, J. (2014). HLA DQB1* 06: 02 negative narcolepsy with hypocretin/orexin deficiency. *Sleep, 37*(10), 1601–1608.

Harvey, A. G. (2002). A cognitive model of insomnia. *Behaviour Research and Therapy, 40*(8), 869–893.

Harvey, A. G. (2008). Sleep and circadian rhythms in bipolar disorder: Seeking synchrony, harmony, and regulation. *American Journal of Psychiatry, 165*(7), 820–829.

Harvey, A. G., Schmidt, D. A., Scarnà, A., Semler, C. N., & Goodwin, G. M. (2005). Sleep-related functioning in euthymic patients with bipolar disorder, patients with insomnia, and subjects without sleep problems. *American Journal of Psychiatry, 162*(1), 50–57.

Harvey, A. G., Sharpley, A. L., Ree, M. J., Stinson, K., & Clark, D. M. (2007). An open trial of cognitive therapy for chronic insomnia. *Behaviour Research and Therapy, 45*(10), 2491–2501.

Hayakawa, T., Kamei, Y., Urata, J., Shibui, K., Ozaki, S., Uchiyama, M., & Okawa, M. (1998). Trials of bright light exposure and melatonin administration in a patient with non-24 hour sleep–wake syndrome. *Psychiatry and Clinical Neurosciences, 52*(2), 261–262.

Henry, A. L., Miller, C. B., Emsley, R., Sheaves, B., Freeman, D., Luik, A. I., . . . Carl, J. R. (2021). Insomnia as a mediating therapeutic target for depressive symptoms: A sub-analysis of participant data from two large randomized controlled trials of a digital sleep intervention. *Journal of Sleep Research, 30*(1), e13140.

Herring, W. J., Ceesay, P., Snyder, E., Bliwise, D., Budd, K., Hutzelmann, J., . . . Michelson, D. (2019). Clinical polysomnography trial of suvorexant for treating insomnia in Alzheimer's Disease (P3. 6-022). *Neurology 92*(15).

Hertenstein, E., Feige, B., Gmeiner, T., Kienzler, C., Spiegelhalder, K., Johann, A., . . . Riemann, D. (2019). Insomnia as a predictor of mental disorders: A systematic review and meta-analysis. *Sleep Medicine Reviews, 43*, 96–105.

Hoddes, E., Zarcone, V., & Dement, W. (1972). Stanford sleepiness scale. *Enzyklopädie der Schlafmedizin, 1184*.

Holbrook, A. M., Crowther, R., Lotter, A., Cheng, C., & King, D. (2000). Meta-analysis of benzodiazepine use in the treatment of insomnia. *Canadian Medical Association Journal, 162*(2), 225–233.

Horne, J. A., & Östberg, O. (1976). A self-assessment questionnaire to determine morningness-eveningness in human circadian rhythms. *International Journal of Chronobiology, 4*, 97-110.

Huedo-Medina, T. B., Kirsch, I., Middlemass, J., Klonizakis, M., & Siriwardena, A. N. (2012). Effectiveness of non-benzodiazepine hypnotics in treatment of adult insomnia: Meta-analysis of data submitted to the Food and Drug Administration. *British Medical Journal, 345*.

Hwang, D. K., Nam, M., & Lee, Y. G. (2019). The effect of cognitive behavioral therapy for insomnia in schizophrenia patients with sleep Disturbance: A non-randomized, assessor-blind trial. *Psychiatry Research, 274*, 182–188. doi:10.1016/j.psychres.2019.02.002

Inada, K., Enomoto, M., Yamato, K., Marumoto, T., Takeshima, M., & Mishima, K. (2021). Effect of residual insomnia and use of hypnotics on relapse of depression: A retrospective cohort study using a health insurance claims database. *Journal of Affective Disorders, 281*, 539–546.

Johns, M. W. (1991). A new method for measuring daytime sleepiness: The Epworth sleepiness scale. *Sleep, 14*(6), 540–545.

Johnson, E. O., Roth, T., & Breslau, N. (2006). The association of insomnia with anxiety disorders and depression: Exploration of the direction of risk. *Journal of Psychiatric Research, 40*(8), 700–708.

Jones, C. R., Campbell, S. S., Zone, S. E., Cooper, F., DeSano, A., Murphy, P. J., . . . Ptček, L. J. (1999). Familial advanced sleep-phase syndrome: A short-period circadian rhythm variant in humans. *Nature Medicine, 5*(9), 1062–1065.

Kanady, J. C., Soehner, A. M., Klein, A. B., & Harvey, A. G. (2017). The association between insomnia-related sleep disruptions and cognitive dysfunction during the inter-episode phase of bipolar disorder. *Journal of Psychiatric Research, 88*, 80–88.

Kaplan, K. A., & Harvey, A. G. (2009). Hypersomnia across mood disorders: A review and synthesis. *Sleep Medicine Reviews, 13*(4), 275–285.

Kasanova, Z., Hajdúk, M., Thewissen, V., & Myin-Germeys, I. (2020). Temporal associations between sleep quality and paranoia across the paranoia continuum: An experience sampling study. *Journal of Abnormal Psychology, 129*(1), 122.

Kleitman, N. (1939). *Sleep and wakefulness as alternating phases in the cycle of existence.* University of Chicago Press.

Kleitman, N. (1987). *Sleep and wakefulness.* University of Chicago Press.

Kornum, B. R., Knudsen, S., Ollila, H. M., Pizza, F., Jennum, P. J., Dauvilliers, Y., & Overeem, S. (2017). Narcolepsy. *Nature Reviews Disease Primers, 3*(1), 1–19.

Krystal, A. D., Prather, A. A., & Ashbrook, L. H. (2019). The assessment and management of insomnia: An update. *World Psychiatry, 18*(3), 337–352.

Kyle, S. D., Hurry, M. E. D., Emsley, R., Marsden, A., Omlin, X., Juss, A., . . . Sexton, C. E. (2020). The effects of digital cognitive behavioral therapy for insomnia on cognitive function: A randomized controlled trial. *Sleep, 43*(9), zsaa034.

Kyle, S. D., Miller, C. B., Rogers, Z., Siriwardena, A. N., MacMahon, K. M., & Espie, C. A. (2014). Sleep restriction therapy for insomnia is associated with reduced objective total sleep time, increased daytime somnolence, and objectively impaired vigilance: Implications for the clinical management of insomnia disorder. *Sleep, 37*(2), 229–237.

Lack, L., & Wright, H. (1993). The effect of evening bright light in delaying the circadian rhythms and lengthening the sleep of early morning awakening insomniacs. *Sleep, 16*(5), 436–443.

Lack, L. C., & Wright, H. R. (2007). Clinical management of delayed sleep phase disorder. *Behavioral Sleep Medicine*, 5(1), 57–76.

Lane, J. M., Jones, S. E., Dashti, H. S., Wood, A. R., Aragam, K. G., van Hees, V. T., . . . Bowden, J. (2019). Biological and clinical insights from genetics of insomnia symptoms. *Nature Genetics*, 51(3), 387–393.

Lane, J. M., Liang, J., Vlasac, I., Anderson, S. G., Bechtold, D. A., Bowden, J., . . . Luik, A. I. (2017). Genome-wide association analyses of sleep disturbance traits identify new loci and highlight shared genetics with neuropsychiatric and metabolic traits. *Nature Genetics*, 49(2), 274.

Lecci, S., Cataldi, J., Betta, M., Bernardi, G., Heinzer, R., & Siclari, F. (2020). Electroencephalographic changes associated with subjective under- and overestimation of sleep duration. *Sleep*, 43(11), zsaa094.

Levenson, J. C., Axelson, D. A., Merranko, J., Angulo, M., Goldstein, T. R., Mullin, B. C., . . . Hickey, M. B. (2015). Differences in sleep disturbances among offspring of parents with and without bipolar disorder: Association with conversion to bipolar disorder. *Bipolar Disorders*, 17(8), 836–848.

Levenson, J. C., Soehner, A., Rooks, B., Goldstein, T. R., Diler, R., Merranko, J., . . . Hafeman, D. (2017). Longitudinal sleep phenotypes among offspring of bipolar parents and community controls. *Journal of Affective Disorders*, 215, 30–36.

Li, L., Wu, C., Gan, Y., Qu, X., & Lu, Z. (2016). Insomnia and the risk of depression: A meta-analysis of prospective cohort studies. *BMC Psychiatry*, 16(1), 1–16.

Lichstein, K., Durrence, H., Taylor, D., Bush, A., & Riedel, B. (2003). Quantitative criteria for insomnia. *Behaviour Research and Therapy*, 41(4), 427–445.

Lockley, S., Skene, D., James, K., Thapan, K., Wright, J., & Arendt, J. (2000). Melatonin administration can entrain the free-running circadian system of blind subjects. *Journal of Endocrinology*, 164(1), R1–6.

Lockley, S. W., Dressman, M. A., Licamele, L., Xiao, C., Fisher, D. M., Flynn-Evans, E. E., . . . Polymeropoulos, M. H. (2015). Tasimelteon for non-24-hour sleep–wake disorder in totally blind people (SET and RESET): Two multicentre, randomised, double-masked, placebo-controlled phase 3 trials. *Lancet*, 386(10005), 1754–1764.

Low, T. L., Choo, F. N., & Tan, S. M. (2020). The efficacy of melatonin and melatonin agonists in insomnia: An umbrella review. *Journal of Psychiatric Research*, 121, 10–23.

Marcks, B. A., Weisberg, R. B., Edelen, M. O., & Keller, M. B. (2010). The relationship between sleep disturbance and the course of anxiety disorders in primary care patients. *Psychiatry Research*, 178(3), 487–492.

Mårtensson, B., Pettersson, A., Berglund, L., & Ekselius, L. (2015). Bright white light therapy in depression: A critical review of the evidence. *Journal of Affective Disorders*, 182, 1–7.

Maurer, L. F., Espie, C. A., & Kyle, S. D. (2018). How does sleep restriction therapy for insomnia work? A systematic review of mechanistic evidence and the introduction of the Triple-R model. *Sleep Medicine Reviews*, 42, 127–138.

Maurer, L. F., Espie, C. A., Omlin, X., Reid, M. J., Sharman, R., Gavriloff, D., . . . Kyle, S. D. (2020). Isolating the role of time in bed restriction in the treatment of insomnia: A randomized, controlled, dismantling trial comparing sleep restriction therapy with time in bed regularization. *Sleep*, 43(11), zsaa096.

Maurer, L. F., Ftouni, S., Espie, C. A., Bisdounis, L., & Kyle, S. D. (2020). The acute effects of sleep restriction therapy for insomnia on circadian timing and vigilance. *Journal of Sleep Research*, e13260.

McArthur, A. J., Lewy, A. J., & Sack, R. L. (1996). Non-24-hour sleep–wake syndrome in a sighted man: Circadian rhythm studies and efficacy of melatonin treatment. *Sleep*, 19(7), 544–553.

McCleery, J., & Sharpley, A. L. (2020). Pharmacotherapies for sleep disturbances in dementia. *Cochrane Database of Systematic Reviews*(11).

Melo, M. C., Abreu, R. L., Neto, V. B. L., de Bruin, P. F., & de Bruin, V. M. (2017). Chronotype and circadian rhythm in bipolar disorder: A systematic review. *Sleep Medicine Reviews*, 34, 46–58.

Melo, M. C. A., Garcia, R. F., Neto, V. B. L., Sá, M. B., de Mesquita, L. M. F., de Araújo, C. F. C., & de Bruin, V. M. S. (2016). Sleep and circadian alterations in people at risk for bipolar disorder: A systematic review. *Journal of Psychiatric Research*, 83, 211–219.

Merikangas, K., Zhang, J., Emsellem, H., Swanson, S., Vgontzas, A., Belouad, F., . . . He, J. (2014). The structured diagnostic interview for sleep patterns and disorders: Rationale and initial evaluation. *Sleep Medicine*, 15(5), 530–535.

Micic, G., De Bruyn, A., Lovato, N., Wright, H., Gradisar, M., Ferguson, S., . . . Lack, L. (2013). The endogenous circadian temperature period length (tau) in delayed sleep phase disorder compared to good sleepers. *Journal of Sleep Research*, 22(6), 617–624.

Mitchell, L. J., Bisdounis, L., Ballesio, A., Omlin, X., & Kyle, S. D. (2019). The impact of cognitive behavioural therapy for insomnia on objective sleep parameters: A meta-analysis and systematic review. *Sleep Medicine Reviews*, 47, 90–102.

Moline, M., Thein, S., Bsharat, M., Rabbee, N., Kemethofer-Waliczky, M., Filippov, G., . . . Dhadda, S. (2021). Safety and efficacy of lemborexant in patients with irregular sleep–wake rhythm disorder and Alzheimer's disease dementia: Results from a phase 2 randomized clinical trial. *Journal of Prevention of Alzheimer's Disease*, 8(1), 7–18.

Monti, J. M., & Monti, D. (2000). Sleep disturbance in generalized anxiety disorder and its treatment. *Sleep Medicine Reviews*, 4(3), 263–276.

Morgenthaler, T., Alessi, C., Friedman, L., Owens, J., Kapur, V., Boehlecke, B., . . . Lee-Chiong, T. (2007). Practice parameters for the use of actigraphy in the assessment of sleep and sleep disorders: An update for 2007. *Sleep*, 30(4), 519–529.

Morin, C. M., Drake, C. L., Harvey, A. G., Krystal, A. D., Manber, R., Riemann, D., & Spiegelhalder, K. (2015). Insomnia disorder. *Nature Reviews Disease Primers*, 1(1), 1–18.

Morin, C. M., LeBlanc, M., Daley, M., Gregoire, J., & Merette, C. (2006). Epidemiology of insomnia: Prevalence, self-help treatments, consultations, and determinants of help-seeking behaviors. *Sleep Medicine*, 7(2), 123–130.

Mulligan, L. D., Haddock, G., Emsley, R., Neil, S. T., & Kyle, S. D. (2016). High resolution examination of the role of sleep disturbance in predicting functioning and psychotic symptoms in schizophrenia: A novel experience sampling study. *Journal of Abnormal Psychology*, 125(6), 788.

Mundey, K., Benloucif, S., Harsanyi, K., Dubocovich, M. L., & Zee, P. C. (2005). Phase-dependent treatment of delayed sleep phase syndrome with melatonin. *Sleep*, 28(10), 1271–1278.

National Institutes of Health. (2005). National Institutes of Health State of the Science Conference statement on manifestations and management of chronic insomnia in adults, June 13–15, 2005. *Sleep, 28*, 1049–1057.

National Institute for Health and Care Excellence. (2021). *Insomnia: Management*. Author.

Ng, T. H., Chung, K.-F., Ho, F. Y.-Y., Yeung, W.-F., Yung, K.-P., & Lam, T.-H. (2015). Sleep–wake disturbance in interepisode bipolar disorder and high-risk individuals: A systematic review and meta-analysis. *Sleep Medicine Reviews, 20*, 46–58.

Nishino, S., Ripley, B., Overeem, S., Lammers, G. J., & Mignot, E. (2000). Hypocretin (orexin) deficiency in human narcolepsy. *Lancet, 355*(9197), 39–40.

Nurnberger, J. I., Adkins, S., Lahiri, D. K., Mayeda, A., Hu, K., Lewy, A., . . . Rau, N. L. (2000). Melatonin suppression by light in euthymic bipolar and unipolar patients. *Archives of General Psychiatry, 57*(6), 572–579.

Ohayon, M. M. (2002). Epidemiology of insomnia: What we know and what we still need to learn. *Sleep Medicine Reviews, 6*(2), 97–111.

Ohayon, M. M., Dauvilliers, Y., & Reynolds, C. F. (2012). Operational definitions and algorithms for excessive sleepiness in the general population: Implications for DSM-5 nosology. *Archives of General Psychiatry, 69*(1), 71–79.

Ohayon, M. M., & Roth, T. (2003). Place of chronic insomnia in the course of depressive and anxiety disorders. *Journal of Psychiatric Research, 37*(1), 9–15. doi:10.1016/s0022-3956(02)00052-3

Ozaki, S., Uchiyama, M., Shirakawa, S., & Okawa, M. (1996). Prolonged interval from body temperature nadir to sleep offset in patients with delayed sleep phase syndrome. *Sleep, 19*(1), 36–40.

Palagini, L., Cipollone, G., Moretto, U., Masci, I., Tripodi, B., Caruso, D., & Perugi, G. (2019). Chronobiological disrhythmicity is related to emotion dysregulation and suicidality in depressive bipolar II disorder with mixed features. *Psychiatry Research, 271*, 272–278.

Pallesen, S., Nordhus, I. H., Skelton, S. H., Bjorvatn, B., & Skjerve, A. (2005). Bright light treatment has limited effect in subjects over 55 years with mild early morning awakening. *Perceptual and Motor Skills, 101*(3), 759–770.

Palmer, C. R., Kripke, D. F., Savage Jr, H. C., Cindrich, L. A., Loving, R. T., & Elliott, J. A. (2003). Efficacy of enhanced evening light for advanced sleep phase syndrome. *Behavioral Sleep Medicine, 1*(4), 213–226.

Patel, K. V., Aspesi, A. V., & Evoy, K. E. (2015). Suvorexant: A dual orexin receptor antagonist for the treatment of sleep onset and sleep maintenance insomnia. *Annals of Pharmacotherapy, 49*(4), 477–483.

Peever, J., Luppi, P.-H., & Montplaisir, J. (2014). Breakdown in REM sleep circuitry underlies REM sleep behavior disorder. *Trends in Neurosciences, 37*(5), 279–288.

Perlis, M., Giles, D., Mendelson, W., Bootzin, R. R., & Wyatt, J. (1997). Psychophysiological insomnia: The behavioural model and a neurocognitive perspective. *Journal of Sleep Research, 6*(3), 179–188.

Perlis, M. L., Vargas, I., Ellis, J. G., Grandner, M. A., Morales, K. H., Gencarelli, A., . . . Thase, M. E. (2020). The natural history of insomnia: The incidence of acute insomnia and subsequent progression to chronic insomnia or recovery in good sleeper subjects. *Sleep, 43*(6), zsz299.

Plante, D. T., & Winkelman, J. W. (2008). Sleep disturbance in bipolar disorder: Therapeutic implications. *American Journal of Psychiatry, 165*(7), 830–843.

Qaseem, A., Kansagara, D., Forciea, M. A., Cooke, M., & Denberg, T. D. (2016). Management of chronic insomnia disorder in adults: A clinical practice guideline from the American College of Physicians. *Annals of Internal Medicine, 165*(2), 125–133.

Ramirez-Mahaluf, J. P., Rozas-Serri, E., Ivanovic-Zuvic, F., Risco, L., & Vöhringer, P. A. (2020). Effectiveness of sleep deprivation in treating acute bipolar depression as augmentation strategy: A systematic review and meta-analysis. *Frontiers in Psychiatry, 11*.

Reeve, S., Nickless, A., Sheaves, B., & Freeman, D. (2018). Insomnia, negative affect, and psychotic experiences: Modelling pathways over time in a clinical observational study. *Psychiatry Research, 269*, 673–680.

Rehman, A., Waite, F., Sheaves, B., Biello, S., Freeman, D., & Gumley, A. (2017). Clinician perceptions of sleep problems, and their treatment, in patients with non-affective psychosis. *Psychosis, 9*(2), 129–139. doi:10.1080/17522439.2016.1206955

Riemann, D., Baglioni, C., Bassetti, C., Bjorvatn, B., Dolenc Groselj, L., Ellis, J. G., . . . Gonçalves, M. (2017). European guideline for the diagnosis and treatment of insomnia. *Journal of Sleep Research, 26*(6), 675–700.

Riemann, D., Krone, L. B., Wulff, K., & Nissen, C. (2020). Sleep, insomnia, and depression. *Neuropsychopharmacology, 45*(1), 74–89.

Riemann, D., Spiegelhalder, K., Feige, B., Voderholzer, U., Berger, M., Perlis, M., & Nissen, C. (2010). The hyperarousal model of insomnia: A review of the concept and its evidence. *Sleep Medicine Reviews, 14*(1), 19–31.

Riemersma-Van Der Lek, R. F., Swaab, D. F., Twisk, J., Hol, E. M., Hoogendijk, W. J., & Van Someren, E. J. (2008). Effect of bright light and melatonin on cognitive and noncognitive function in elderly residents of group care facilities: A randomized controlled trial. *Journal of the American Medical Association, 299*(22), 2642–2655.

Roenneberg, T., Wirz-Justice, A., & Merrow, M. (2003). Life between clocks: Daily temporal patterns of human chronotypes. *Journal of Biological Rhythms, 18*(1), 80–90.

Rogers, A. E., Aldrich, M. S., & Lin, X. (2001). A comparison of three different sleep schedules for reducing daytime sleepiness in narcolepsy. *Sleep, 24*(4), 385–391.

Rosenberg, R., Murphy, P., Zammit, G., Mayleben, D., Kumar, D., Dhadda, S., . . . Moline, M. (2019). Comparison of lemborexant with placebo and zolpidem tartrate extended release for the treatment of older adults with insomnia disorder: A phase 3 randomized clinical trial. *JAMA Network Open, 2*(12), e1918254–e1918254.

Roybal, K., Theobold, D., Graham, A., DiNieri, J. A., Russo, S. J., Krishnan, V., . . . McClung, C. A. (2007). Mania-like behavior induced by disruption of CLOCK. *Proceedings of the National Academy of Sciences, 104*(15), 6406–6411.

Rybakowski, J. K., Dmitrzak-Weglarz, M., Kliwicki, S., & Hauser, J. (2014). Polymorphism of circadian clock genes and prophylactic lithium response. *Bipolar Disorders, 16*(2), 151–158.

Sack, R. L., Auckley, D., Auger, R. R., Carskadon, M. A., Wright Jr, K. P., Vitiello, M. V., & Zhdanova, I. V. (2007). Circadian rhythm sleep disorders: Part II, advanced sleep phase disorder, delayed sleep phase disorder, free-running disorder, and irregular sleep–wake rhythm. *Sleep, 30*(11), 1484–1501.

Sakurai, H., Suzuki, T., Yoshimura, K., Mimura, M., & Uchida, H. (2017). Predicting relapse with individual residual symptoms in major depressive disorder: A reanalysis of the STAR*D data. *Psychopharmacology (Berl), 234*(16), 2453–2461. doi:10.1007/s00213-017-4634-5

Sateia, M. J. (2014). International classification of sleep disorders. *Chest, 146*(5), 1387–1394.

Sateia, M. J., Buysse, D. J., Krystal, A. D., Neubauer, D. N., & Heald, J. L. (2017). Clinical practice guideline for the pharmacologic treatment of chronic insomnia in adults: An American Academy of Sleep Medicine clinical practice guideline. *Journal of Clinical Sleep Medicine, 13*(2), 307–349.

Satoh, K., Mishima, K., Inoue, Y., Ebisawa, T., & Shimizu, T. (2003). Two pedigrees of familial advanced sleep phase syndrome in Japan. *Sleep, 26*(4), 416–417.

Saxvig, I. W., Wilhelmsen-Langeland, A., Pallesen, S., Vedaa, Ø., Nordhus, I. H., Sørensen, E., & Bjorvatn, B. (2013). Objective measures of sleep and dim light melatonin onset in adolescents and young adults with delayed sleep phase disorder compared to healthy controls. *Journal of Sleep Research, 22*(4), 365–372.

Scammell, T. E. (2015). Narcolepsy. *New England Journal of Medicine, 373*(27), 2654–2662.

Schennach, R., Feige, B., Riemann, D., Heuser, J., & Voderholzer, U. (2019). Pre- to post-inpatient treatment of subjective sleep quality in 5,481 patients with mental disorders: A longitudinal analysis. *Journal of Sleep Research, 28*(4), e12842.

Schrader, H., Bovim, G., & Sand, T. (1993). The prevalence of delayed and advanced sleep phase syndromes. *Journal of Sleep Research, 2*(1), 51–55.

Schutte-Rodin, S., Broch, L., Buysse, D., Dorsey, C., & Sateia, M. (2008). Clinical guideline for the evaluation and management of chronic insomnia in adults. *Journal of Clinical Sleep Medicine, 4*(5), 487–504.

Scott, J., Grierson, A., Gehue, L., Kallestad, H., MacMillan, I., & Hickie, I. (2019). Can consumer grade activity devices replace research grade Actiwatches in youth mental health settings? *Sleep and Biological Rhythms, 17*(2), 223–232.

Sebela, A., Kolenic, M., Farkova, E., Novak, T., & Goetz, M. (2019). Decreased need for sleep as an endophenotype of bipolar disorder: An actigraphy study. *Chronobiology International, 36*(9), 1227–1239.

Shahid, A., Wilkinson, K., Marcu, S., & Shapiro, C. M. (2011). Karolinska sleepiness scale (KSS). In A. Shahid, K. Wilkinson, S. Marcu, & C. M Shapiro (Eds.), *STOP, THAT and One Hundred Other Sleep Scales* (pp. 209–210). Springer.

Singh, M. K., DelBello, M. P., & Strakowski, S. M. (2008). Temperament in child offspring of parents with bipolar disorder. *Journal of Child and Adolescent Psychopharmacology, 18*(6), 589–593.

Siriwardena, A. N., Apekey, T., Tilling, M., Dyas, J. V., Middleton, H., & Ørner, R. (2010). General practitioners' preferences for managing insomnia and opportunities for reducing hypnotic prescribing. *Journal of Evaluation in Clinical Practice, 16*(4), 731–737.

Siriwardena, A. N., Qureshi, Z., Gibson, S., Collier, S., & Latham, M. (2006). GPs' attitudes to benzodiazepine and "Z-drug" prescribing: A barrier to implementation of evidence and guidance on hypnotics. *British Journal of General Practice, 56*(533), 964–967.

Sitaram, N., Nurnberger, J. I., Gershon, E. S., & Gillin, J. C. (1982). Cholinergic regulation of mood and REM sleep: Potential model and marker of vulnerability to affective disorder. *American Journal of Psychiatry, 139*(5), 571–576.

Skjerve, A., Bjorvatn, B., & Holsten, F. (2004). Light therapy for behavioural and psychological symptoms of dementia. *International Journal of Geriatric Psychiatry, 19*(6), 516–522.

Smith, M. T., McCrae, C. S., Cheung, J., Martin, J. L., Harrod, C. G., Heald, J. L., & Carden, K. A. (2018). Use of actigraphy for the evaluation of sleep disorders and circadian rhythm sleep–wake disorders: An American Academy of Sleep Medicine clinical practice guideline. *Journal of Clinical Sleep Medicine, 14*(7), 1231–1237.

Soehner, A. M., Bertocci, M. A., Levenson, J. C., Goldstein, T. R., Rooks, B., Merranko, J., . . . Goldstein, B. I. (2019). Longitudinal associations between sleep patterns and psychiatric symptom severity in high-risk and community comparison youth. *Journal of the American Academy of Child & Adolescent Psychiatry, 58*(6), 608–617.

Soehner, A. M., & Harvey, A. G. (2012). Prevalence and functional consequences of severe insomnia symptoms in mood and anxiety disorders: Results from a nationally representative sample. *Sleep, 35*(10), 1367–1375.

Soehner, A. M., Kaplan, K. A., Saletin, J. M., Talbot, L. S., Hairston, I. S., Gruber, J., . . . Harvey, A. G. (2018). You'll feel better in the morning: Slow wave activity and overnight mood regulation in interepisode bipolar disorder. *Psychological Medicine, 48*(2), 249.

Soldatos, C. R. (1994). Insomnia in relation to depression and anxiety: Epidemiologic considerations. *Journal of Psychosomatic Research, 38*, 3–8.

Soldatos, C. R., Dikeos, D. G., & Paparrigopoulos, T. J. (2000). Athens Insomnia Scale: Validation of an instrument based on ICD-10 criteria. *Journal of Psychosomatic Research, 48*(6), 555–560.

Sowa, N. A. (2016). Idiopathic hypersomnia and hypersomnolence disorder: A systematic review of the literature. *Psychosomatics, 57*(2), 152–164.

Spielman, A. J., Caruso, L. S., & Glovinsky, P. B. (1987). A behavioral perspective on insomnia treatment. *Psychiatric Clinics of North America, 10*(4), 541–553.

Spielman, A. J., Yang, C.-M., & Glovinsky, P. B. (2011). Sleep restriction therapy. In M. L. Perlis, M. Aloia, & B. Kuhn (Eds.), *Behavioral treatments for sleep disorders* (pp. 9–19). Elsevier.

Stewart, J. W. (2018). Does a meta-analysis of sleep deprivation studies demonstrate efficacy? *The Journal of Clinical Psychiatry, 79*(2), 0–0.

Suhner, A. G., Murphy, P. J., & Campbell, S. S. (2002). Failure of timed bright light exposure to alleviate age-related sleep maintenance insomnia. *Journal of the American Geriatrics Society, 50*(4), 617–623.

Taylor, D. J., & Pruiksma, K. E. (2014). Cognitive and behavioural therapy for insomnia (CBT-I) in psychiatric populations: A systematic review. *International Review of Psychiatry, 26*(2), 205–213. doi:10.3109/09540261.2014.902808

Taylor, D. J., Wilkerson, A. K., Pruiksma, K. E., Williams, J. M., Ruggero, C. J., Hale, W., . . . Litz, B. T. (2018). Reliability of the structured clinical interview for DSM-5 sleep disorders module. *Journal of Clinical Sleep Medicine, 14*(3), 459–464.

Taylor, M. J., Gregory, A. M., Freeman, D., & Ronald, A. (2015). Do sleep disturbances and psychotic-like experiences in adolescence share genetic and environmental influences? *Journal of Abnormal Psychology, 124*(3), 674.

Thorpy, M. J. (2020). Recently approved and upcoming treatments for narcolepsy. *CNS Drugs, 34*(1), 9–27.

Tobin Jr, J. D. (1993). Treatment of somnambulism with anticipatory awakening. *Journal of Pediatrics, 122*(3), 426–427.

Toh, K. L., Jones, C. R., He, Y., Eide, E. J., Hinz, W. A., Virshup, D. M., . . . Fu, Y.-H. (2001). An hPer2 phosphorylation site mutation in familial advanced sleep phase syndrome. *Science, 291*(5506), 1040–1043.

Tsuno, N., Besset, A., & Ritchie, K. (2005). Sleep and depression. *Journal of Clinical Psychiatry, 66*(10), 1254–1269.

van der Zweerde, T., Bisdounis, L., Kyle, S. D., Lancee, J., & van Straten, A. (2019). Cognitive behavioral therapy for insomnia: A meta-analysis of long-term effects in controlled studies. *Sleep Medicine Reviews, 48*, 101208.

van Geijlswijk, I. M., Korzilius, H. P., & Smits, M. G. (2010). The use of exogenous melatonin in delayed sleep phase disorder: A meta-analysis. *Sleep, 33*(12), 1605–1614.

van Straten, A., van der Zweerde, T., Kleiboer, A., Cuijpers, P., Morin, C. M., & Lancee, J. (2018). Cognitive and behavioral therapies in the treatment of insomnia: A meta-analysis. *Sleep Medicine Reviews, 38*, 3–16.

Vermeeren, A., Sun, H., Vuurman, E. F., Jongen, S., Van Leeuwen, C. J., Van Oers, A. C., . . . Heirman, I. (2015). On-the-road driving performance the morning after bedtime use of suvorexant 20 and 40 mg: A study in non-elderly healthy volunteers. *Sleep, 38*(11), 1803–1813.

Waite, F., Sheaves, B., Isham, L., Reeve, S., & Freeman, D. (2020). Sleep and schizophrenia: From epiphenomenon to treatable causal target. *Schizophrenia Research, 221*, 44–56. doi:10.1016/j.schres.2019.11.014

Watanabe, T., Kajimura, N., Kato, M., Sekimoto, M., Hori, T., & Takahashi, K. (2000). Case of a non-24 h sleep–wake syndrome patient improved by phototherapy. *Psychiatry and Clinical Neurosciences, 54*(3), 369–370.

Watson, L. A., McGlashan, E. M., Hosken, I. T., Anderson, C., Phillips, A. J., & Cain, S. W. (2020). Sleep and circadian instability in delayed sleep–wake phase disorder. *Journal of Clinical Sleep Medicine, 16*(9), 1431–1436.

Wehr, T. A., Sack, D. A., & Rosenthal, N. E. (1987). Sleep reduction as a final common pathway in the genesis of mania. *American Journal of Psychiatry, 144*(2), 201–204.

Weitzman, E. D., Czeisler, C. A., Coleman, R. M., Spielman, A. J., Zimmerman, J. C., Dement, W., & Pollak, C. P. (1981). Delayed sleep phase syndrome: A chronobiological disorder with sleep-onset insomnia. *Archives of General Psychiatry, 38*(7), 737–746.

Williams, J. M., Taylor, D. J., Slavish, D. C., Gardner, C. E., Zimmerman, M. R., Patel, K., . . . Estevez, R. (2018). Validity of actigraphy in young adults with insomnia. *Behavioral Sleep Medicine, 18*(1), 91–106.

Wilson, S., Anderson, K., Baldwin, D., Dijk, D.-J., Espie, A., Espie, C., . . . Selsick, H. (2019). British Association for Psychopharmacology consensus statement on evidence-based treatment of insomnia, parasomnias and circadian rhythm disorders: An update. *Journal of Psychopharmacology, 33*(8), 923–947.

Wittchen, H.-U., Jacobi, F., Rehm, J., Gustavsson, A., Svensson, M., Jönsson, B., . . . Faravelli, C. (2011). The size and burden of mental disorders and other disorders of the brain in Europe 2010. *European Neuropsychopharmacology, 21*(9), 655–679.

Wong, M. L., Lau, K. N. T., Espie, C. A., Luik, A. I., Kyle, S. D., & Lau, E. Y. Y. (2017). Psychometric properties of the Sleep Condition Indicator and Insomnia Severity Index in the evaluation of insomnia disorder. *Sleep Medicine, 33*, 76–81.

Wu, J. Q., Appleman, E. R., Salazar, R. D., & Ong, J. C. (2015). Cognitive behavioral therapy for insomnia comorbid with psychiatric and medical conditions: A meta-analysis. *JAMA Internal Medicine, 175*(9), 1461–1472.

Wyatt, J. K., Stepanski, E. J., & Kirkby, J. (2006). Circadian phase in delayed sleep phase syndrome: Predictors and temporal stability across multiple assessments. *Sleep, 29*(8), 1075–1080.

Xu, Y., Padiath, Q. S., Shapiro, R. E., Jones, C. R., Wu, S. C., Saigoh, N., . . . Fu, Y.-H. (2005). Functional consequences of a CKIδ mutation causing familial advanced sleep phase syndrome. *Nature, 434*(7033), 640–644.

Yardley, J., Kärppä, M., Inoue, Y., Pinner, K., Perdomo, C., Ishikawa, K., . . . Moline, M. (2021). Long-term effectiveness and safety of lemborexant in adults with insomnia disorder: Results from a phase 3 randomized clinical trial. *Sleep Medicine, 80*, 333–342.

Zalai, D., Gladanac, B., & Shapiro, C. M. (2018). Circadian rhythm sleep–wake disorders. In Hugh Selsick (Ed.), *Sleep Disorders in Psychiatric Patients* (pp. 189–211). Springer.

Zangani, C., Casetta, C., Saunders, A. S., Donati, F., Maggioni, E., & D'Agostino, A. (2020). Sleep abnormalities across different clinical stages of bipolar disorder: A review of EEG studies. *Neuroscience & Biobehavioral Reviews, 118*, 247–257.

# CHAPTER 24

# Paraphilia, Gender Dysphoria, and Hypersexuality

James M. Cantor

Research findings in human sexuality are increasingly scrutinized, not only for their scientific merits, but also for perceived political implications. Indeed, even the very inclusion of this chapter in a book with "psychopathology" in its title could be interpreted by some as a political statement. Correspondingly, the inclusion/exclusion of any given sexual phenomenon within this chapter could be so interpreted. For present purposes, *atypical sexuality* is intended broadly. Rather than represent any political view, this reflects the ultimately pragmatic purpose of facilitating clinical intervention and research. Such work spans not only people with conditions listed in the *DSM* or *ICD*, but also people presenting to clinicians experiencing distress about other behaviors or interests at the edges of or entirely outside cultural norms.

The scientific understanding of atypical sexualities begins with an unanswerable question: What objective line divides healthy sexual diversity from psychopathological sexual interest? The lack of any universal response reflects its dependence on context and, often, a compromise among competing legitimate principles, including the freedom of individual sexual expression, the societal interest in preventing sexual victimization, and the professional ethic of protecting patient-clients from self-harm. Each of these issues can pertain differently across the types of sexual atypicality. Consensual paraphilias, such as the erotic interest in pain, have given rise to entire subcultures, analogous to the gay communities of previous decades. Nonconsensual paraphilias, such as the erotic interest in children or in rape, motivate persons to engage in sexual offenses, leading legislatures to enact increasingly putative and lengthy sentences and to establish publicly accessible registries of offenders. Cases of transsexualism, of "sex addiction" (often termed *hypersexuality* in the research literature), and of highly unusual paraphilias (such as erotic interest in nonhuman animals or in being an amputee) have been featured in contemporary entertainment media and documentaries (e.g., Lawrence, 2006; Reay et al., 2013; Williams & Weinberg, 2003).

Historically, the diagnostic issue receiving most attention in sexuality was the removal of homosexuality from the *DSM*, reflecting official opinion that the stigma associated with a diagnosis outweighed any potential benefits. In being the most familiar example, ethical and political discussions of many of the other sexual phenomena (especially transsexuality and transgenderism) often reason by way of analogy to that precedent. The extent to which the depathologization of homosexuality applies to other phenomena varies widely across them. Complete consideration of each issue concerning every atypical sexual interest or behavior is beyond the scope of this chapter (unfortunately!). Nonetheless, it can be illustrative to explicate some of the issues potentially affected by official diagnostic status.

- Will insurance cover its treatment?
- Will adding/removing a category remove the ability of a client to use psychotherapy to develop a

**Abbreviations**
AB/DL   Adult Babies/Diaper Lovers
AID     Amputee identity disorder
BIID    Body integrity identity disorder
BSTc    Ventral subdivision of the bed nucleus of the stria terminalis
ETII    Erotic-target identity inversion
FtM     Female-to-male
MtF     Male-to-female
ROGD    Rapid-onset gender dysphoria

healthy adjustment to their sexual interest pattern, analogous to a person using psychotherapy for support during their "coming out" process?
- Will inclusion subject people to sexually violent predator regulations, and do these implications differ across nations and jurisdictions?
- Will diagnostic status affect determinations of legal culpability when the motivation to engage in a behavior is diagnosable as a mental illness?
- Does inclusion of a category produce social requirements for accommodation, as civil rights issues for sexual minorities or for people with mental illnesses?
- Does official status change access to resources, such as access to funding for sex reassignment surgery?
- Does that principle apply to sex reassignment only or to all body modification?
- Does there exist a public interest in regulating the public expression of a behavior, and how can one distinguish genuine public interest from sociopolitical tolerance for diversity?

Neuroanatomic and genetic research on these conditions has lagged behind that of other behavioral phenomena. Thus, this chapter necessarily emphasizes description over etiology. Great care must be taken when generalizing findings regarding individuals with atypical sexual interests or behaviors. (1) On the one hand, much of what we know about the nonconsensual paraphilias derives from research on sex offenders and may not represent the population of people with paraphilias. On the other hand, mutual support groups, such as for self-identified pedophiles working to remain offense-free as well as professionally led groups for pedophiles unknown to law enforcement, have emerged (e.g., Beier et al., 2009; Cantor & McPhail, 2016). Such groups may provide a new window on nonoffending pedophiles but may also represent a nontypical cross-section. (2) Reports of hypersexuality (also termed "sex addiction," "sexual compulsivity," etc.) frequently rely on self-referral and self-diagnosis from individuals who already presume the validity of analogies between sexual behavior and drug or alcohol use. The *ICD-11* includes code 6C72 for *compulsive sexual behaviour disorder*, replacing *ICD-10*'s *excessive sexual drive* and *excessive masturbation*. The *DSM-5* contains no specific equivalent, but nevertheless permits diagnosis with code F52.8 for *other specified sexual dysfunction* (Krueger, 2016). (3) The still-increasing politicization of physical and mental healthcare for transgender and potentially transsexual children, adolescents, and adults adds self-selection, self-report, and self-censoring biases to research and clinical reports.

## Paraphilias

"Paraphilia" refers broadly to any powerful and persistent sexual interest other than sexual interest in copulatory or precopulatory behavior with morphologically typical, consenting, adult human partners. Although some paraphilic interests have been reported in women, the paraphilias occur nearly exclusively in men. *DSM-5* introduced the distinction between *paraphilias* and *paraphilic disorders:* paraphilias are not diagnosable disorders unto themselves. The more restrictive term, "paraphilic disorder" now refers to the subset of individuals either who experience distress or impairment or who harm or risk harm to others due to their paraphilic interest. Thus, the existing literature includes samples that, after 2013, would be said to have a paraphilia but not a paraphilic disorder (such as surveys of cross-dressing social groups as well as other samples that would now be said both to have a paraphilia and to be diagnosable with a paraphilic disorder [such as phallometric studies of convicted, pedophilic child molesters]). Thus, among the paraphilic individuals in the studies reviewed here, some would and some would not have received a *DSM-5* diagnosis. Paraphilias may be classified under two broad headings: (1) those in which the sexually interesting *object* is something other than phenotypically normal humans between the ages of physical maturity and physical decline, and (2) those in which the sexually interesting *activity* is something other than copulatory or precopulatory behavior with a consenting partner.

## Object Paraphilias
### Erotic Age Preferences

The erotic age preferences are termed according to the level of physical development of an individual's most preferred sexual object (Blanchard et al., 2009). In sexual interest research, *oedophilia* refers to the strong or preferential sexual interest in specifically prepubescent children (i.e., children showing Tanner stage 1 features, typically age 10 and younger). *Hebephilia* refers to the equivalent interest in pubescent children (Tanner stages 2–3, typically ages 11–14). Because pedophilia and hebephilia can co-occur or be difficult to distinguish, authors have used *pedohebephilia* as a superordinate category to refer to both. *Ephebophilia* refers to persons in adolescence or late puberty (Tanner stage 4, typically ages 15 to physical maturity), and *teleiophilia* refers to the erotic age preference toward adults after reaching physical maturity and before physical decline (Tanner stage 5, typically ages, 17–45). Finally, there also exist individuals whose primary sexual interests are for elderly persons, termed *gerontophilia*.

Hebephilia is consistently described as a paraphilia along with pedophilia, whereas ephebophilia and teleiophilia represent nonparaphilic states. This is consistent with the evidence demonstrating convergent validity among indicators of hebephilia, yet poor divergent validity between hebephilia and pedophilia (Stephens, Seto et al., 2017). The range of erotic age interests has led to the overarching term *chronophilia*, and taxometric analyses suggest age interests follow a dimensional rather than categorical pattern (Stephens, Leroux et al., 2017; however, see also McPhail, Olver et al., 2018).

The typical behaviors of pedophilic and hebephilic sex offenders consist of touching the breasts, buttocks, or genitals of the child or inducing the child (such as with bribes or threats) to touch or fellate the offender. Abduction and violent sexual abuse of children are comparatively rare. Some pedophilic men report experiencing an interest in children that is romantic as well as erotic (Wilson & Cox, 1983). Pedophilia and hebephilia supply the motivation behind a substantial proportion of cases of child molestation, but these erotic age preferences are not synonymous with sexual offenses against children (Seto, 2008): some cases of child molestation, especially those involving incest, are committed in the absence of any identifiable deviant erotic age preference (e.g., Freund et al., 1991). In such cases, the child is a sexual target of convenience to the offender. Conversely, there are men with no known records of sexual contact with a child who present to clinicians seeking assistance in dealing with their erotic interest in children.

The number of people apprehended for the possession or distribution of child pornography on the Internet continues to grow (Seto, 2013). Whereas only a minority hand-on sexual offenders against children appear to have a genuine sexual preference for children, the majority of child pornography offenders do (Seto et al., 2006). Meta-analytic comparison of online-only (child pornography) offenders, hands-on sexual offenders against children, and mixed offenders revealed the online-only offenders to show less antisociality and greater victim empathy (Babchishin et al., 2015).

Individuals seeking clinical intervention to help manage their sexual attractions to children remain underserved but have garnered increased attention (e.g., McPhail, Stephens, & Heasman, 2018). Online and other surveys of self-identified pedophiles and hebephiles are now adding to observations from forensic samples (Cantor & McPhail, 2016). Examination of online discussions among people coping with their sexual attractions to children demonstrated they employed self-management strategies across four themes: management of sexual preferences (distraction, psychotherapy, and sex drive–reducing medications such as chemical castration, and legal means of sexual expression such as fantasy), management of risk to offend (avoidance, abstinence, behavioral self-monitoring), and management of mood (healthy lifestyle, psychotherapy and antidepressants, and personal acceptance of their attractions), as well as social contacts (peer support, family support, and religion; Stevens & Wood, 2019).

Catering to sexual interests at the other end of the chronophilias, the Internet includes sites dedicated to sexual depictions of elderly women. An unknown proportion of sexual offenders are gerontophilic; reviews suggests that 2–7% of rape victims are elderly women (Ball, 2005), and homosexual gerontophilic sexual offending also exists (Kaul & Duffy, 1991). Sexual homicides of the elderly show evidence of greater brutality, even though the victims are less likely or able to resist or protect themselves (Safarik et al., 2002).

### Fetishism

*Fetishism* denotes a heterogeneous group of paraphilias in which the individuals' strongest sexual interest is focused on classes of objects or features of objects other than the external reproductive organs of phenotypically normal human beings. The term does not apply to erotic interests that include the mere use of objects, such as dildos, costumes, or ropes; it applies to instances where those objects represent the central feature rather than a supportive role in sexual activity. Although fetishism is sometimes discussed as an erotic interest in an arbitrary object, many fetishes involve objects that are highly gender-specific (e.g., shoes, underwear) or are closely related to people (e.g., urine, feces, body parts). Chalkley and Powell (1983) reviewed the files of all individuals over a 20-year period who met criteria for nontransvestic fetishes in a teaching hospital. Forty-eight cases were so identified, and the objects included clothing (58.3%), rubber and rubber items (22.9%), footwear (14.6%), body parts (14.6%), leather and leather items (10.4%), and soft materials and fabrics (6.3%).

## STUFF-FETISHISM

*Stuff-fetishism* refers to the erotic interest in specific materials, such as rubber, leather, or fur. Individuals with this fetish will seek out items composed of those materials for use during masturbation, as in a case described by Gosselin and Wilson (1980, pp. 50–51):

> After fifteen years of marriage, Mr. W.'s wife died. He made no serious attempt to acquire another partner, because he was "pretty much able to look after himself" and the appearance of his house bore this out. . . . [H]e kept in his house a complete "rubber room" lined throughout with curtains of the same material and containing two large cupboards full of rubber garments, gas masks, photographic and other equipment. He has in the past visited prostitutes to play out some aspect of his fantasies, but now does not do so, feeling that he has all he needs for sexual satisfaction without leaving his house.

Stuff-fetishists who choose clothing rather than other items made of their preferred material can be difficult to distinguish from *clothing-fetishists* (described later). For stuff-fetishism, it is the material (its texture and scent, etc.) rather than the form of the object that is of primary interest; in clothing-fetishism, it is the form of the object (such as the shape of a women's shoe) that is of primary importance.

## CLOTHING-FETISHISM

The garments chosen by clothing-fetishists are often emblematic of gender: high-heeled shoes, bras, or panties. The behaviors of clothing-fetishists include kissing and licking the garment, rubbing it against their genitals, and wearing it. A heterosexual male's wearing of a female-typical article of clothing, such as a shoe or pantyhose, resembles fetishistic transvestism; however, a clothing-fetishist dons the garment in order to interact with it physically, whereas a fetishistic transvestite employs garments in order to facilitate his mental imagery of having feminine characteristics. Clothing-fetishism also occurs among homosexual men; their erotic interests pertain to, for example, men's underwear or masculine footwear such as boots or wing-tip shoes (Weinberg et al., 1994). Unlike many activity paraphilias (described later), the expression of clothing-fetishism does not itself involve any nonconsenting persons; however, some individuals commit theft to obtain garments from people (e.g., Anonymous et al., 1976; Revitch, 1978). Because such behavior occurs despite the relative ease with which such garments could be purchased, such thefts may indicate that the process of the theft is part of such individuals' paraphilic interest or may represent an erotic interest specifically in clothing that has already been worn by someone (Weinberg et al., 1994). As noted in a case described by Grant (1953, p. 144),

> If I buy the kind of shoes I prefer and ask a woman I know to wear them for me, it doesn't have the same appeal as if they were her own shoes. I guess this is because they don't seem to be as much a part of her.

## TRANSVESTISM

*Transvestism,* also called *fetishistic transvestism,* refers to a male's erotic interest in wearing feminine attire, make-up, and wigs. There is sometimes an interest in being perceived as female in public; however, some men with fetishistic transvestism wear a single item, such as panties, underneath their regular attire when appearing in public. On phallometric testing, both fetishistic transvestites and clothing-fetishists show similar penile reactions to pictures of women's underwear (Freund et al., 1996). The great majority of men with fetishistic transvestism are heterosexual (e.g., Långström & Zucker, 2005). Although there exist homosexual male cross-dressers, their behavior is rarely, if ever, associated with sexual arousal and is instead employed for humor or entertainment.

## PARTIALISM

In *partialism,* there is an erotic interest in a specific nonsexual portion of human anatomy, such as feet or legs. The interest in the body part is described as providing the same or greater sexual arousal as do the genitals (e.g., Kunjukrishnan et al., 1988). Interestingly, partialism involving the foot frequently co-occurs with clothing-fetishism focused on shoes, as illustrated by a case described by Kunjukrishnan et al. (1988, p. 821).

> Mr. A had been masturbating regularly with fetish fantasies of smelling women's feet or sucking their toes. . . . He visited massage parlours and acted out his fetish fantasies with the masseuse. He usually got an erection while smelling or sucking women's feet and this was often followed by masturbation. He also asked several women that he met on the street if he could smell their feet. . . . When he and his wife had guests, he would often go downstairs to smell the

shoes of female guests who would be upstairs talking to his wife or otherwise occupied.

There also exist homosexual male partialists, attracted to the feet, etc. of men (Weinberg et al., 1994, 1995).

### UROPHILIA AND COPROPHILIA

*Urophilia* (also called *urolangia*) refers to the erotic interest in urine. Urophilic individuals express interests in being urinated upon, in clothing with urine stains or scents, and sometimes in consuming the urine of their sexual partners. *Coprophilia* (also called *coprolagnia*) refers to the analogous interest in feces. No studies have sampled urophilic or coprophilic individuals specifically; existing reports describe samples of persons who have several paraphilias, one of which is urophilia or coprophilia. Nonetheless, offers and requests for persons interested in engaging in these behaviors appear in personal ads and advertisements for prostitution or escort services. In a survey of several thousand gay men, 1% responded that they engaged in urophilic behaviors "always" or "very frequently," and 0.5% reported engaging in coprophilic behaviors that frequently (Jay & Young, 1977).

### Zoophilia/Bestiality

*Zoophilia* and *bestiality* are both used to refer to the erotic interest in nonhuman animals. Among 114 self-acknowledged zoophilic men in an Internet-based survey, sexual behaviors included orally stimulating the genitals of the animal (81%), vaginal penetration of the animal (75%), masturbation of the animal (68%), and being anally penetrated by the animal (52%) (Williams & Weinberg, 2003). Inducing the animal to lick the human's genitals and anal penetration of the animal have also been reported (Peretti & Rowan, 1983). On a similar survey of 82 male and 11 female zoophiles, the most commonly preferred animals were (in descending order): male dogs, female dogs, and male horses, followed by female horses (for men) or male cats (for women) (Miletski, 2001). Some zoophilics report being attracted only to certain species, to certain breeds of a species, or only to male or female members of a species (Williams & Weinberg, 2003).

Some persons who acknowledge repeatedly engaging in sex with animals describe the behavior as a form of masturbation during which they fantasize about sexual contact with humans (Peretti & Rowan, 1983). Other persons report that the behavior is part of an emotional and romantic bond with the animal, one that they believe the animal shares with them (Miletski, 2005; Williams & Weinberg, 2003). Moreover, some zoophiles report they would feel jealous if other humans or animals expressed an interest in "their" animal(s) (e.g., Earls & Lalumière, 2002; McNally & Lukach, 1991; Miletski, 2005). In describing their interviews with self-acknowledged zoophiles, Williams and Weinberg (2003) noted that some individuals professed an extreme affinity for nonhuman animals, "believing they had animal characteristics or that they felt like they were an animal" (p. 528). This suggests that there may also exist an autoerotic form of zoophilia.

### Altered Partners
#### ACROTOMOPHILIA

*Acrotomophilia* is the erotic interest in persons missing one or more limbs. Some acrotomophiles ask their (anatomically intact) sexual partners to mimic being an amputee during sexual intercourse (Dixon, 1983; Massie & Szajnberg, 1997; Money & Simcoe, 1986), and pornography depicting amputees in sexual or alluring poses exists both on the Internet and in print media (Elman, 1997; Waxman-Fiduccia, 1999). Dixon (1983) provided the results of a survey of individuals who subscribed to a service that distributed erotica depicting amputees: leg amputations were preferred over arm amputations; amputations of a single limb over double amputations; and amputations that left a stump over amputations that left no stump. Congenital malformations of limbs received the lowest ratings. Many people sexually attracted to amputees report that they recognized their interest for the first time as a child when they saw a person or a photograph of a person missing a limb (First, 2005).

#### GYNANDROMORPHOPHILIA

*Gynandromorphophilia* refers to the erotic interest in individuals who otherwise appear female-typical but have a penis, or *gynandromorphs* (Hsu et al., 2016). (Earlier works employed broader definitions which included the erotic interest in cross-dressed males; e.g., Blanchard & Collins, 1993.) Gynandromorphophilic men seek sexual encounters with partially transitioned male-to-female (MtF) transsexuals. Personal ads sometimes include persons seeking or offering encounters with feminized men, and pornography depicting "she-males" is readily available on the Internet (Blanchard & Collins, 1993; Escoffier, 2011). Indeed, most gynandromorphophilic men indicate that they came to realize their sexual attraction via such pornography (Rosenthal et al., 2017).

The penile responses of gynandromorphophilic men have been compared in the laboratory with those of heterosexual men and those of homosexual men while they viewed depictions of sex between two males, between a male and a female, and between a male and a gynandromorph (Hsu et al., 2016). The gynandromorphophilic group resembled the heterosexual group, responding strongly to the male-female pair, but not to the male-male pair. They differed from the heterosexual group only in that they additionally responded strongly to gynandromorphic stimuli, whereas neither the heterosexual nor homosexual groups did. On self-report, gynandromorphophilic men indicated subjectively experiencing the corresponding pattern: strong attraction to females, weak attraction to males, and strong attraction to gynandromorphs (Hsu et al., 2016; Rosenthal et al., 2017).

On surveys of gynandromorphophiles, roughly half refer to themselves as heterosexual and roughly half as bisexual, but many indicate that neither term exactly captures them (Operario et al., 2008; Rosenthal et al., 2017; Weinberg & Williams, 2010).

## NECROPHILIA

The erotic interest in corpses is *necrophilia*. The phenomenon has also been called *vampirism* (e.g., Bourguignon, 1983; although others restrict "vampirism" to refer only to the erotic interest in drinking blood; e.g., Vanden Bergh & Kelly, 1964). The most extreme forms of the expression of necrophilia entail obtaining actual corpses or rendering an unwilling victim unconscious for copulation. Rosman and Resnick (1989) reviewed and tabulated the information available from 122 cases of necrophilia that were reported in the literature or made available to them by colleagues. The behaviors and behavioral fantasies of the cases included vaginal intercourse with the corpse (51%), its mutilation (29%), anal penetration of it (11%), kissing it (15%), performing fellatio or cunnilingus upon it (8%), and sucking or fondling the breasts of the corpse (8%). In some cases, mutilation of the body included cannibalism or the drinking of its blood. Thirty-four cases from the whole sample provided self-reports of their motivations: these included the desire to possess an unresisting and unrejecting partner (68%), reunions with a (presumably deceased) romantic partner (21%), sexual attraction to corpses (15%), comfort or overcoming feelings of isolation (15%), or seeking self-esteem by expressing power over a homicide victim (12%). Stein et al. (2010) similarly tabulated information from FBI case files wherein the paraphilic nature of the offense was ascertained by the victim's attire (or the lack of it), exposure of victims' sexual anatomy, sexual positioning of the victim, or other features. This sample largely resembled that described by Rosman and Resnick; however, many of these cases showed evidence of the victim having been raped before being killed, contesting the claim that having an unresisting partner was a central motivation.

### Erotic-Target Identity Inversion

The erotic fantasies of persons with erotic-target identity inversion (ETII) pertain less to imagery of sexual partners and more to transformed imagery of themselves, such as men fantasizing that they have the body of a woman (*autogynephilia*), have the body of a child or infant (*infantilism*), or are an amputee (*apotemnophilia*). This is often termed *autoerotic*. Such individuals sometimes describe their physical bodies as incorrect and their fantasized images as their ideal self (Lawrence, 2006). The expressions of these conditions range from covert visualization during masturbation or during sexual interactions with other people; to mimicking or approximating the erotic identity through clothing, costumes, and props; to seeking medical intervention for permanent body modification to resemble the image of the erotic identity more closely.

Erotic inversion does not always appear to be a complete reversal—such individuals often experience some amount of typical (noninverted) eroticism in addition to the ETII. ETII may represent a basic dimension of sexual attraction, independent of other dimensions of the erotic target, such as the target's sex and age (Freund & Blanchard, 1993; Hsu & Bailey, 2017). In this model, the sexual attraction to women (or *gynephilia*), when inverted, is the desire to be that woman rather than to have sex with her (i.e., autogynephilia; Blanchard, 1991; Ellis, 1928; Hirschfeld, 1918); the sexual attraction to children (pedophilia or hebephilia) when inverted becomes the desire to be a child rather than to abuse the child (i.e., infantilism or *autopedophilia*; Hsu & Bailey, 2017); and the sexual attraction to amputees (*acrotomophilia*) when inverted becomes the desire to be an amputee (i.e., apotemnophilia; Lawrence, 2006, 2013).

## AUTOGYNEPHILIA

Autogynephilia refers to a male's erotic interest in the image or thought of himself as a woman

(Blanchard, 1989a, 1991). During sexual intercourse with women, an autogynephilic male might imagine himself as a woman sexually interacting as a lesbian (Newman & Stoller, 1974) or imagine himself as a woman being penetrated by his partner, who is imagined as a man (Benjamin, 1966; Lukianowicz, 1959). Homosexual (and non-autogynephilic) men may also fantasize about being penetrated by a man, but the focus of their erotic imagery is on the masculine characteristics of their sexual partner, whereas the erotic imagery of autogynephilic men focuses on the feminine characteristics of themselves. Autogynephilia most frequently co-occurs with fetishistic transvestism; however, a male's erotic interest in being a woman can occur on its own, as illustrated in a case described by Blanchard (1993a, p. 70).

> The earliest sexual fantasy [the patient] could recall was that of having a woman's body. When he masturbated, he would imagine that he was a nude woman lying alone in her bed. His mental imagery would focus on his breasts, his vagina, the softness of his skin, and so on—all the characteristic features of the female physique. . . . When questioned why he did not cross-dress at present—he lived alone and there was nothing to prevent him—he indicated that he simply did not feel strongly impelled to do so.

Some autogynephilic fantasies pertain to other aspects of being female, such as menstruating, being pregnant, lactating, or douching (Blanchard, 1991; Denko, 1976). Autogynephilia sometimes co-occurs with *gender dysphoria* (see the section on "Gender Dysphoria and Transsexualism" below).

Cases of *partial autogynephilia* have also been described: instead of envisioning themselves entirely as female, such individuals envision themselves with a mixture of male and female anatomy (Blanchard, 1993a, 1993b). Interestingly, autogynephilic male cross-dressers have shown strong penile responses to gynandromorphophilic stimuli—sex between a male and a gynandromorph, appearing as a female with a penis (Hsu et al., 2017). This supports models wherein partial autogynephilia represents the erotic inversion of gynandromorphophilia.

### INFANTILISM

People with infantilism or autopedophilia are sexually aroused by behaving or imaging themselves as infants or children. (In earlier decades, the term "infantilism" was used to refer more generally to any arrest of psychosexual development in childhood, which was believed to be the cause the paraphilias in general; e.g., Stekel, 1930.) Such individuals will crawl on all fours and employ (adult-size) baby clothes, bibs, feeding bottles, pacifiers, or other props as part of acting out the fantasy of being a young child, which is often accompanied by penile erection, masturbation, and ejaculation (e.g., Bethell, 1974; Pate & Gabbard, 2003). As part of expressing their fantasies, infantilists will often wear adult-sized diapers and urinate or defecate in them (often termed *diaperism*). Some individuals request that sexual partners mother them, as by rocking them, bottle-feeding them, or changing their diapers. Commercial websites have emerged that cater to individuals who refer to themselves as Adult Babies/Diaper Lovers (AB/DL) and supply adult-size baby clothes and nursery items (Pate & Gabbard, 2003). Consistent with the erotic-target inversion model, men reporting that they are sexually aroused by boys more often reported sexual interest in being boys, and men reporting sexual arousal in response to girls more often reported sexual interest in being girls (Hsu & Bailey, 2017). Moreover, self-reported sexual interests in older versus younger children corresponded to the interest in being a child of those ages.

When surveyed, AB/DL community member responses suggested the existence of one subgroup focused on role-playing and another focused on the associated sexual arousal (Hawkinson & Zamboni, 2014; Zamboni, 2019). It is not known if these individuals were hiding such imagery despite experiencing it or if these individuals had an incomplete form of infantilism (analogous to clothing-fetishism as an incomplete form of transvestism). The erotic component was much stronger among the males (89% of the sample), suggesting that males engage in the sexual behaviors to express their paraphilia whereas females engage in the role-play to serve nonsexual motivations.

### APOTEMNOPHILIA

*Apotemnophilia* is the erotic interest in being or seeming to be an amputee (Blom et al., 2012; Money et al., 1977). Other terms, including "amputee identity disorder" (AID), "body integrity identity disorder" (BIID), and "xenomelia" have also been suggested (Barrow & Oyebode, 2019). Such individuals report that having four intact limbs makes them feel incomplete and that amputation is necessary in order for them to feel whole (Berger et al., 2005). Instances of desiring to possess other disabilities, such as deafness or blindness, have also been reported (Brugger et al., 2016). Communities of people with apotemnophilia refer to themselves as "transabled" (Baril, 2015; Davis, 2014).

Some apotemnophilic individuals mimic amputeeism, in public or in private, using wheelchairs or crutches and by binding or concealing a healthy limb. Some have attempted or performed self-amputation of a limb, and others have purposefully injured a limb in hopes of forcing emergency medical teams to amputate it (Bensler & Paauw, 2003; Berger et al., 2005; Money et al., 1977).

Lawrence (2006) has argued that BIID derives from and is secondary to apotemnophilia, citing evidence that the majority of individuals who seek limb amputation do so with an explicitly sexual motivation. A convenience sample of 52 individuals who wanted a healthy limb removed was recruited from Internet groups; the great majority desired specifically to have a single leg removed, cut above the knee (First, 2005). Notably, the preference for this particular amputation is the same one that is reported by acrotomophiles (Dixon, 1983). In another, primarily Internet-recruited sample of 54 people with apotemnophilia, seven reported obtaining surgical amputation (Blom et al., 2012). All seven reported the surgical treatment was helpful and indicated significantly decreased levels of disruption to their happiness and to their work, social, and family lives. The similarities between BIID and gender identity disorder have been noted, as have those between apotemnophilia and autogynephilia, including in their age of onset (puberty), sex ratio (predominantly male), elevated rates of non–right-handedness, alleviation of dysphoria by externally approximating the internal identity, association with sexual arousal, and lack of remission with psychotherapy, as well as age at presentation (middle age), association with dysphoria, and willingness to risk harm for the corresponding surgical interventions (Barrow & Oyebode, 2019; Brugger et al., 2016; Lawrence, 2006).

There have been some small, preliminary neuroimaging studies of people with apotemnophilia employing a diversity of imaging technologies, including magnetoencephalography of selected regions of interest (ROIs) ($n$ = 4; McGeoch et al., 2011); functional magnetic resonance imaging (fMRI) during tactile stimulation and motor tasks ($n$ = 5; van Dijk et al., 2013); surface-based morphometry of the whole brain ($n$ = 13; Hilti et al., 2013), with shape analysis of thalamus and basal ganglia in the same sample ($n$ = 13; Hänggi et al., 2016); and voxel-based morphometry of T1-weighted scans of the whole brain adding the loci Hilti identified as additional ROIs ($n$ = 8; Blom et al., 2016). Unfortunately, neuroimaging analyses from samples as small as these are notoriously unreliable, and little can be deduced from the inconsistent findings and the diversity of techniques employed across them. Nonetheless, some authors have concluded that apotemnophilia represents a neurological rather than sexological phenomenon (e.g., Barrow & Oyebode, 2019). Such claims may represent a false dichotomy, however: atypical sexual interests are more than plausibly the result of atypical neuroanatomy, and the brain regions variously implicated in these studies overlap substantially with those involved in sexual response. Moreover, nonsexual explanations of apotemnophilia fail to account for why large proportions of such individuals report experiencing an erotic component, whereas the sexological explanations can account for people denying eroticism as their being too shy, fearful of the stigma of atypical sexualities, or hoping to benefit from the relatively greater social acceptability of having an identity differing from one's anatomy.

## Activity Paraphilias
### Agonistic Sexual Behavior
#### BIASTOPHILIA (PARAPHILIC RAPE)

The erotic preference for committing rape has been variously called *biastophilia*, *paraphilic rape*, and *paraphilic coercive disorder*. Rapists react to depictions of rape significantly more, on average, than do nonrapists on tests of penile tumescence responses, but respond significantly less than nonrapists to depictions of consensual sex (Lalumière et al., 2005). It is not known what proportion of rapists are biastophilic, however. Although some nonparaphilic men report experiencing occasional sexual fantasies that include elements of rape (Arndt et al., 1985; Crepault & Couture, 1980), biastophilic individuals prefer rape to sexual interaction with willing partners. Emphasizing this distinction, the paraphilic interest in rape has also been called *preferential rape* (Freund et al., 1983), *pathological rape*, or the *deviant rape pattern*. Rape as a primary erotic interest is illustrated by a case described by Freund (1990, p. 198).

> A well-educated, well-built, and good-looking businessman used to go out at night and rape female strangers, whom he dragged into the lanes between houses. When one of his victims said she would gladly have intercourse with him if he would accompany her to her apartment, he said no, it must be here and now, and then he raped her.

The manner by which the individual obtains sexual intercourse is a central component to the erotic interest. In clinical practice, it can be difficult to distinguish an individual who committed a rape to enact a biastophilic fantasy from one who committed a rape as a kind of theft.

## SEXUAL SADISM

*Sexual sadism* refers to the erotic interest in inflicting fear, humiliation, or suffering. Although both sadistic sexual offenders and biastophilic sexual offenders employ force, they do so with different motivations (Freund & Blanchard, 1986; Hirschfeld, 1938): biastophiles prefer sexual activities with unwilling strangers (who must therefore be coerced into compliance). For sadistic sexual offenders, however, it is the infliction of pain and suffering per se that carries erotic value. Thus, sadistic sexual offenders will continue to apply force, sometimes in increasing magnitude, regardless of the compliance of the victims. In extreme cases, this proceeds to the death of the victim (Dietz et al., 1990; Gratzer & Bradford, 1995), and, further still, to the mutilation of the victim's body. Sadistic rapes do not always include penile penetration of the victim: a review of case files in the US National Center for the Analysis of Violent Crime revealed that offenses included sexual bondage (77%), anal rape (73%), forced fellatio of the offender by the victim (70%), vaginal rape (57%), penetration of victim with a foreign object (40%), blunt force trauma (60%), and the offenders' retention of a personal item belonging to the victim (40%) (Dietz et al., 1990).

There also exist individuals who seek to inflict pain or humiliation, but only on willing partners (e.g., Gosselin, 1987); this has been called the *hyperdominance pattern* of sexual behavior (Freund et al., 1986). It is not known whether or to what extent hyperdominance is related to sadism. Hyperdominants often express the desire to provide sexual pleasure to their submissive sexual partner(s), who are sometimes acting out their own paraphilic interests, such as fetishism, klismaphilia, or masochism. Ernulf and Innala (1995) observed discussions among individuals with such interests, one of whom described the goal of hyperdominants (p. 644).

> A good top is an empath who knows how to tell with the least possible feedback exactly what will blow the bottom's mind. The top enjoys his pleasure vicariously. He has a great time. The idea is to turn the body into a sexual response machine.

Among sadistic sexual offenders, however, there is no obvious indication of a desire to provide pleasure. Although it is possible that hyperdominance and sadistic sexual offenses represent qualitatively different phenomena that resemble each other only superficially, it is also possible that such individuals (or a proportion of them) have the same erotic interests and differ in nonsexual psychological characteristics, such as antisociality, psychopathy, or the propensity to project or misinterpret the mental status of their sexual partners or victims.

## Masochistic Paraphilias
### SEXUAL MASOCHISM

Persons with *sexual masochism* experience erotic excitement from enduring humiliation or physical pain, often enacting such fantasies (or approximations of them) alone or with sexual partners. Sufficient numbers of individuals seek opportunities to engage in these behaviors to form stable subcultures, which have been repeatedly surveyed (e.g., Ernulf & Innala, 1995; Nordling et al., 2006). The majority of respondents to such surveys report the desire to undergo verbal abuse, slapping (either manually or with implements), being ordered to perform sexual acts, or being tied up or restrained. A smaller proportion of individuals seek to undergo very severe stimulation, however: these include torture through beatings that draw blood, branding or burning, and mummification (immobilizing the entire body with rope or other wrapping) and confinement for extended periods of time. Clinical and nonclinical samples of masochists (i.e, individuals with masochism and individuals diagnosable with *DSM-5* masochistic disorder) report interests in the same activities (cf., Freund et al., 1995). Accidental deaths have been reported from engaging in some masochistic behaviors, such as through the self-application of electricity to the genitals or other parts of the body (Cairns & Rainer, 1981).

One of the most dramatic cases of sexual masochism was that of Mr. Bernd Brandes, which was widely reported in the media. Brandes answered a personal ad placed by Mr. Armin Meiwes, asking for young, well-built men who wanted to be slaughtered and consumed (Harding, 2003). After Brandes consumed a combination of alcohol and sleeping pills, Meiwes cut off Brandes' penis and fried it for both of them to eat. Meiwes then fatally stabbed Brandes, all of which Brandes consented to, on videotape. Notably, before he was arrested, Meiwes had met with five other men who responded to his personal ad.

## AUTOEROTIC ASPHYXIA

*Autoerotic asphyxia* refers to the erotic interest in being suffocated, such as by being hanged or strangled. Some asphyxiophilics engage in such behaviors alone (sometimes called *asphyxiophilia*) using ropes suspended from beams or ligatures tied to doorknobs while they masturbate, whereas others engage sexual partners to purposefully restrict airflow to the lungs or bloodflow to the brain as part of their sexual activities (suggesting masochism focused on suffocation). When enacted in solitude, asphyxiophilia has led to accidental deaths (Hucker & Blanchard, 1992). Some cases of asphyxiophilic fatalities have come to the attention of clinicians by lawyers or insurance companies (e.g., Cooper, 1995, 1996), as life insurance claims are payable in the event of an accidental death but not of suicide. In some fatality cases, the body of the asphyxiophilic individual is discovered naked or with his penis exposed, with pornographic magazines nearby, with dildos or other sex toys nearby, or with evidence of his having ejaculated (Hucker & Blanchard, 1992; Janssen et al., 2005). The condition of such corpses also suggests that asphyxiophilia is frequently comorbid with other paraphilias: the corpse is sometimes cross-dressed or wearing make-up, the content of pornographic material is of a sadomasochistic nature, or the corpse is found with self-applied gags or bindings on his hands, feet, or genitals (Blanchard & Hucker, 1991). Asphyxiophilia has been called *hypoxyphilia*, under the presumption that hypoxia enhances sexual sensations (e.g., Uva, 1995). Such an association has not been established, however; the sexual interest might instead be focused on psychological associations with the actual behaviors, rather than with any physiological effects of hypoxia (Blanchard & Hucker, 1991).

### Courtship Disorder

A specific set of the activity paraphilias—voyeurism, exhibitionism, telephone scatologia, toucheurism, frotteurism, and biastophilia—has been hypothesized to be individual symptoms of a single underlying pathology, called *courtship disorder* (Freund, 1988). As detailed below, the courtship disorder hypothesis maintains that each of the paraphilias in this set is a disordered expression of a phase of human courtship (Freund, 1976; Freund et al., 1972). Biastophilia has already been described in the previous section together with sadism; the following describes the other paraphilias comprising courtship disorder.

## VOYEURISM

*Voyeurism* is the erotic interest in viewing an unsuspecting person or persons in typically private situations. Viewed acts include dressing or undressing, sexual intercourse, urinating, and defecating. (In some cases, it is unclear whether these latter behaviors indicate voyeurism, with the urine and feces being incidental, or indicate urophilia or coprophilia with the urine or feces being central; e.g., Collacott & Cooper, 1995.) The increased availability of affordable and easily concealed electronic devices has broadened the range of opportunities available to voyeurs for viewing unsuspecting strangers (e.g., Simon, 1997). Some cases of voyeurism have included holding cellular telephone cameras over or under the partitions of public washroom stalls and hiding small cameras in the bedrooms of victims. Paraphilic voyeurism would not describe persons for whom the mere sight or image of a person were sufficient for eliciting sexual arousal; in paraphilic voyeurism, the means by which the individual achieves his view is an integral part of the paraphilic interest. That is, in some cases, the glance must represent a violation to be of erotic interest.

## EXHIBITIONISM

The erotic interest in exposing one's genitals to unsuspecting strangers is *exhibitionism*. The paraphilia pertains to persons for whom there is sexual pleasure in doing so, not when the behavior is motivated by money (such as strippers) or other nonsexual reasons (such as pranks). The majority of exhibitionists masturbate to ejaculation as part of exposing their penis (Freund et al., 1988; Langevin et al., 1979). On a questionnaire given to a sample of 185 exhibitionists, Freund et al. (1988) asked, "How would you have preferred a person to react if you were to expose your privates to him or her?" (p. 256). Of the seven possible choices, the most common response was "Would want to have sexual intercourse" (35.1%), followed by "No reaction necessary at all" (19.5%), "To show their privates also" (15.1%), "Admiration" (14.1%), and "Any reaction" (11.9%). Few exhibitionists chose "Anger and disgust" (3.8%) or "Fear" (0.5%).

There is only limited research on the (typically male) behavior of sending unsolicited photographs of their genitals (Oswald et al., 2020). It remains unknown to what extent the behavior might represent a paraphilic or other motivation, or whether any paraphilic pattern might be related to exhibitionism or *telephone scatologia*.

## TELEPHONE SCATOLOGIA

Telephone scatologia refers to the erotic interest in using a telephone to expose unsuspecting persons to vulgar or sexual language or to elicit it from them. Many scatologists masturbate during the call or masturbate subsequently while recollecting the call; some telephone scatologists cross-dress or pose as female when calling (e.g., Dalby, 1988; Pakhomou, 2006). Although it was not based on any systematic observation, Mead (1975) provided an intuitive taxonomy of obscene telephone call content: (a) the "shock caller," who immediately makes obscene remarks or propositions in order provoke an emotional response from the victims, (b) the "ingratiating seducer" who fabricates a plausible story to lure the victim into conversation, and (c) the "trickster" who poses, for example, as someone conducting a survey in order to elicit sexual history or other information about the victim. A survey of 1,262 Canadian women who were employed outside the home asked respondents about their experiences of receiving obscene phone calls (Smith & Morra, 1994); 83.2% of the sample had received such calls. Of those, 84.5% of the calls came from males, 86.8% came from adults, and 73.8% were reportedly from strangers (in 7.5% of the cases, the victim knew the scatologist, and in 18.6%, the victim was unsure whether she knew the caller).

Approximately 37% of rapists have been reported to engage in obscene telephone calls (Abel et al., 1988), but only 5–6% of apprehended telephone scatologists have been found to commit rape (Abel et al., 1988; Price et al., 2002). Because not all obscene telephone calls are reported to authorities, however, it is unknown how well these individuals represent all telephone scatologists. It is also unknown whether the content or other parameters of the calls predict an individual's likelihood of committing other sexual offenses.

Telephone scatologia is sometimes described as a variant of exhibitionism (e.g., Hirschfeld, 1938; Nadler, 1968), differing by being auditory rather visual. Indeed, telephone scatologia is highly comorbid with exhibitionism (e.g., Price et al., 2002). Although telephone scatologia necessarily involves obscene telephone calls, not all obscene telephone calls are motivated by telephone scatologia; the behavior may represent a prank with no erotic value to the caller (Pakhomou, 2006).

## TOUCHEURISM AND FROTTEURISM

*Toucheurism* and *frotteurism* refer to the erotic interest in approaching unsuspecting strangers to touch their (usually clothed) breasts, buttocks, or genital area. Toucheurism pertains to when contact is made using the hands, and frotteurism pertains to men who press their penis against the victim, especially against the buttocks, through clothing. Frotteurs typically target women in crowded public places (e.g., streetcars), whereas toucheurs will often grab at a woman while quickly moving across her path.

## THE COURTSHIP DISORDER HYPOTHESIS

The courtship disorder hypothesis asserts that the usual male sexual activity cycle consists of four phases: (a) looking for and appraising potential sexual partners; (b) pretactile interaction with those partners, such as by smiling at and talking to them; (c) tactile interaction with them, such as by embracing or petting; and then (d) sexual intercourse (Freund, 1976; Freund & Blanchard, 1986). In normal courtship, each phase of the cycle leads to the next. In courtship disorder, however, one or more of these phases is exaggerated or distorted, and the cycle fails to progress from one phase to the next. According to the hypothesis, voyeurism is a rigid, isolated form of the searching phase; exhibitionism and telephone scatologia represent distortions of the pretactile phase; toucheurism and frotteurism represent pathologies of the tactile phase; and, in the preferential rape pattern, the first three courtship phases are altogether skipped.

The assertion that these six paraphilias all emerge from the same underlying disorder simplifies the interpretation of several observations. (a) The paraphilias in this set are highly comorbid with each other (Freund & Blanchard, 1986; Freund et al., 1983). (b) During laboratory testing of penile reactions to audiotaped stimuli, individuals who have shown one courtship paraphilia, but not another, nonetheless show an elevated response to stimuli representing other courtship paraphilias (Freund et al., 1983; Freund et al., 1986). (c) The paraphilias of courtship disorder share the propensity to target strangers (e.g., Freund et al., 1988; Gebhard et al., 1965; Mohr et al., 1964; Smith & Morra, 1994), whereas other paraphilias more often involve people known to the paraphilic individual (or involve no other person at all).

## Miscellaneous Paraphilias
### KLISMAPHILIA

*Klismaphilia* refers to the erotic interest in enemas. Klismaphilics will entertain sexual fantasies about enemas during masturbation, self-administer enemas for masturbatory stimulation, or engage their sexual partners to administer them. Some have reported experiencing sexual arousal upon administration of clinical enemas by nursing staff and feigning physical symptoms to justify the procedure (Denko, 1973). By contrast, the term would not apply when the enema provides a secondary rather than mandatory role—such as being forced to receive an enema as part of a masochistic fantasy—nor when only indirectly associated with sex, such as regular use in anticipation of anal intercourse. Twenty-two klismaphilics responded to an ad placed in sex-oriented periodicals as part of a survey of individuals with erotic interests in enemas (Arndt, 1991); the median frequency of enema use was twice per week, and approximately half the respondents engaged in the behavior together with their sexual partners. In describing a series of 15 cases, Denko (1976) reported that three male klismaphilics fantasized themselves as female during the enemas and that three such individuals experienced erotic enjoyment while eliciting enema-related conversation with female sales clerks (such as by asking for instructions).

### TRIOLISM

*Triolism* or *cuckolding* refers to the erotic interest in watching one's romantic partner engage in sexual behavior with a third party. Triolism differs from voyeurism in that the romantic partner (but not necessarily the third party) is typically aware of being observed. Some triolists want to observe the sexual activity visually (sometimes while hidden; e.g., Hirschfeld, 1938), some audio or video record the activity, and some want only to listen to their partners describe encounters had while the triolist was absent (Wernik, 1990).

## Multiple Paraphilias and Blended Paraphilias

Individuals with one paraphilic interest often have other paraphilic interests (e.g., Abel et al., 1988; Abel & Osborn, 1992; Bradford et al., 1992; Freund et al., 1983). In some cases, these paraphilias function independently in the individual, such as in a man who will expose his genitals on certain occasions and who will grab the buttocks of females on other occasions. We refer to these simply as cases of *comorbid* or *multiple paraphilias*. Other individuals, however, possess erotic interests that deviate from typical in more than one aspect at the same time, such as men whose erotic fantasies entail being forced to cross-dress (e.g., Hucker, 1985) or a man who exposes his genitals to large dogs (McNally & Lukach, 1991).

## Prevalence and Sex Ratio

Owing to their usually secretive nature, no meaningful prevalence or incidence data can be had for any of the paraphilias. Numbers of persons who are charged with or convicted of certain sexual offenses have been used as estimates for some paraphilias. It is unknown what proportion of such offenders is genuinely paraphilic, however. A more sophisticated estimation has been conducted for the prevalences of transvestic fetishism, exhibitionism, and voyeurism (Långström & Seto, 2006; Långström & Zucker, 2005). These investigations analyzed responses to a representative survey of 2,450 men and women in Sweden. A total of 3.1% of the respondents reported having been sexually aroused at least one time by exposing their genitals to a stranger; of that subset, 23.7% also experienced sexual fantasies about the behavior. Of the whole sample, 7.8% reported engaging in voyeurism at least one time; of that subset, 53.4% also experienced sexual fantasies about doing so. Of the males, 2.8% reported cross-dressing that was associated with sexual arousal; an insufficient number of women reported ever having done so to support any analysis. National forensic databases have suggested rates of autoerotic deaths by asphyxia at 0.1 per million population (Sweden) to 2–4 per million (United States) (Byard & Winskog, 2012), but the prevalence of nonfatal practitioners remains unknown.

As previously noted, most paraphilias appear to be phenomena restricted nearly entirely to males. Notwithstanding case reports in the literature, neither clinics, forensic institutions, nor social clubs for proponents of engaging in paraphilic behaviors report any substantial number of females with atypical erotic age preferences, courtship disorders, or fetishes. Sexual masochism is unusual among the paraphilias in that it shows a relatively high frequency of female practitioners. Breslow, Evans, and Langley (1985) surveyed subscribers to and advertisers in a periodical catering to individuals interested in masochism or hyperdominance. Of the 81 non-prostitutes who preferred or usually preferred masochistic behaviors (termed "submissive" in the survey), 49.4% were women. Similarly, Ernulf and Innala (1995) analyzed messages on an online discussion group catering to people with the same interests: of the 56 posts seeking to engage in masochistic acts (again termed "submissive"), 58.9% were purportedly from women.

Despite its close association with masochism, asphyxiophilia is usually viewed as a male phenomenon owing to the lack of women among individuals who suffered accidental asphyxiophilic death. For example, the Hucker and Blanchard (1992) sample consisted of all 118 known such deaths in Ontario and Alberta, Canada, from 1974 to 1987, and only one was female. It is plausible, however, that there are women who engage in the behavior, but that they are less likely to suffer accidental death. This might occur if more male asphyxiophilics engaged in the solitary form of the behavior and more female asphyxiophilics did so in the company of a sexual partner (thereby protecting against accident).

## Associated Features

One may refer to the hypothetical factors that increase the probability of developing paraphilic interests as *paraphilogenic* factors. The existence of a biological predisposition to developing one or more paraphilias has been hypothesized for well over a century (e.g., Binet, 1887; Krafft-Ebing, 1886/1965), but few rigorous studies have been conducted. Some tentative conclusions can be proffered, however, primarily on the basis of investigations of individuals who have committed sexual offenses motivated by paraphilias, especially pedophilia.

### IQ and Other Neuropsychological Testing

Pedophilic men and sexual offenders against children have lower IQs than nonpedophilic controls (Cantor et al., 2004; Cantor, Blanchard et al., 2005). The association between IQ and pedophilia appears to be independent of referral method; the same result emerges whether the pedophiles were referred by parole and probation officers, lawyers, or physicians or by self-referral (Blanchard et al., 2007). Consistent with these studies, pedophilic men are more likely to have repeated grades in school or to have required placement in special education classes (Cantor et al., 2006). Although several studies have administered batteries of neuropsychological tests to heterogeneous samples of sexual offenders, they have not reported results from homogeneous samples of paraphilic men. It remains unknown whether pedophiles have a general cognitive deficit (i.e., they would perform poorly on any neuropsychological test that correlates with IQ) or if they have a distinct pattern of cognitive strengths and weaknesses that might be detected by future investigations employing larger and more homogeneous samples.

It is also unknown whether and to what extent that poor cognitive functioning is a characteristic specific to deviant erotic age preference or a characteristic of several (or all) paraphilias. Community-based samples of self-acknowledged paraphilics have repeatedly described highly educated and high-functioning individuals (e.g., Alison et al., 2001; Croughan et al., 1981; Docter & Prince, 1997; Williams & Weinberg, 2003). Although it is possible that low IQ is specific to pedo- and hebephilia, it is also possible that paraphilics with higher IQs are more likely to participate in interest groups and research studies.

### Handedness

Handedness is of interest due to its association with very early brain development. Fetuses demonstrate a hand preference when thumb-sucking in utero (Heppe et al., 1991), and that preference predicts handedness later in life (Hepper et al., 2005). Approximately 8–15% of the general population is non–right-handed (Hardyck & Petrinovich, 1977). Pedophilic men have been shown to be up to three times more likely to be non–right-handed (Cantor, Klassen et al., 2005). Nonhomosexual MtF transsexuals (who have been shown empirically to experience autogynephilia; Blanchard, 1985, 1988, 1989b) similarly show elevated rates of non–right-handedness (Green & Young, 2001). Very little is known regarding handedness in any of the other paraphilias.

Meta-analytic review has shown homosexual men, although they are not paraphilic, to have 34% greater odds and homosexual females to have 91% greater odds of non–right-handedness than their heterosexual counterparts (Lalumière et al., 2000). Recent research indicates that the association between non–right-handedness and homosexuality in men is limited to individuals with no or few older brothers (Blanchard, 2008). Considered together, the findings on hand preference and sexuality suggest that non–right-handedness might pertain to the development of all variant erotic-object interests (see Blanchard, 2008).

Non–right-handedness has commonly been interpreted as a marker for lesser than usual degrees of asymmetry between the left and right hemispheres of the brain. Therefore Blanchard (2008) conjectured that Klar's (2004) explanation for the association of non–right-handedness and homosexuality might apply to variant erotic-object preferences in general. Klar hypothesized that "less asymmetric hemispheres may allow additional neuronal connections between different parts of the brain, thereby predisposing individuals to develop homosexuality, in contrast to the restricted possibilities allowed in the more common asymmetric hemispheric arrangement" (Klar, 2004, p. 254). Blanchard (2008) argued that the collective data on homosexual men and women, pedophiles, and transsexuals suggest that the hypothesized "additional neuronal connections" made possible by less asymmetric hemispheres might lead to an array of different psychosexual outcomes. The notion that erotic variations (paraphilic or benign) may result from atypical connections among brain regions, and not from anomalies in the brain regions themselves, is revisited in a different context in the next section.

## Brain Imaging

With only few exceptions, neuroimaging research on the paraphilias has been limited to pedophilia and hebephilia. Such studies continue to advance but must be considered carefully, as there exist powerful ascertainment biases in sampling: until recently, samples of people sexually attracted to children have been recruited from forensic centers studying sex offenders. Without appropriate handling, features of such samples can be confounded by antisociality, impulsivity, and other correlates of criminality (including having completed long-term confinement). More recently, people with pedophilia and no forensic history have begun to present themselves to clinics, seeking treatment or mutual group support and to participate in research studies. In contrast with forensic samples, these individuals would be predicted to be nonrepresentative in being higher functioning than typical. Neither source can yield representative samples, and both pose potential confounds. Different authors have employed different methods in the effort to compensate for the multiple factors in play, and it remains unknown to what extent each method is successful.

Contemporary studies aiming to identify neuroanatomic features associated with pedophilia and its development have coalesced into two camps: one implicating white matter differences yielding atypical connectivity among brain regions that otherwise serve to identity reproductively relevant social stimuli (e.g., Cantor et al., 2015) and one implicating gray matter differences that increase the risk of sexual offending rather than pedophilia per se (e.g., Lett et al., 2018). White matter and connectivity differences were detected in independent samples by several techniques, including voxel-based morphometry (Cantor et al., 2008), diffusion tensor imaging (Cantor et al., 2015), and independent component analysis (Cantor et al., 2016). Poeppl et al. (2015) conducted a meta-analysis of fMRI studies using activation-likelihood estimation, confirming functional dysconnectivity among sexually relevant brain regions, which those authors interpreted as confirmation of the dysconnectivity hypothesis of pedophilia.

Some initial reports instead implicated gray matter differences: Schiltz et al. (2007) reported differences in the amygdala, hypothalamus, substantia innominata, septal region, and bed nucleus of the stria terminalis, whereas Schiffer et al. (2007) reported them in the ventral striatum and nucleus accumbens, orbitofrontal cortex, and cerebellum. (Neither study examined white matter.) Subsequent imaging research employing larger samples disconfirmed the gray matter differences (Schiffer et al., 2017) and attributed the neural differences detected to be associated instead with criminality and the propensity to commit sexual offenses (Lett et al., 2018).

## Hormonal Assays

Studies of sexual offenders have measured the baseline levels of several hormones, including 5-alpha-dihydrotestosterone, androstenedione, cortisol, dehydroepiandrosterone, dihydrotestosterone, estradiol, follicle-stimulating hormone, the free-androgen index, luteinizing hormone, prolactin, sex hormone-binding globulin, and testosterone (Blanchard et al., 2006). Those investigations have failed to reveal any consistent association between paraphilic sexual offenses (primarily involving pedophilia, exhibitionism, or sexual sadism) and any hormone except, potentially, testosterone: greater levels of testosterone have been found among rapists relative to nonparaphilic controls (Giotakos et al., 2003; Rada et al., 1976). Other investigations have failed to detect such a difference, however (Haake et al., 2003; Rada et al., 1983). Lower levels of testosterone have been reported among pedophilic men by some studies (Gurnani & Dwyer, 1986; Seim & Dwyer, 1988), but no differences have been found in others (Gaffney & Berlin, 1984; Lang et al., 1990). It is possible that testosterone reflects the propensity to violence or aggression rather than any paraphilia.

## Intimacy/Social Skills Deficits

Sex offenders may seek out sex with children because they do not have the social skills to successfully interact with adult partners and they cannot fulfill their sexual and emotional needs in relationships with peers (Seto, 2008). Sex offenders lack the capacity for intimate relationships and report themselves to be lonely (Garlick et al., 1996; Seidman et al., 1994). Ward, Hudson, and Marshall (1996) found that sex offenders exhibited a wide range of insecure attachment styles, each associated with different psychological problems. Child molesters with a preoccupied attachment style were characterized by emotional neediness and profound doubts about their ability to elicit love and support from partners. Fearful-dismissively attached offenders tended to distance themselves emotionally in relationships because of their fear of rejection. Both groups experienced problems with intimacy and apparently turned to sex with children because their adult relationships were compromised or unsatisfactory. The primary causal mechanism underlying their deviant sexual behavior was seen to be their insecure attachments and subsequent problems establishing satisfactory relationships with adults (Ward & Seigert, 2002).

As reviewed by Smallbone (2006), in several studies, child sex offenders have reported less secure childhood attachments than nonsexual offenders (Marsa et al., 2004; Smallbone & Dadds, 1998) and nonoffenders (Marsa et al., 2004; Smallbone & Dadds, 1998). Similarly, according to Smallbone (2006), child sex offenders more frequently report an insecure rather than a secure adult attachment style (Jamieson & Marshall, 2000; Ward et al., 1996) and report less secure adult attachment than both nonsexual offenders and nonoffenders (Marsa et al., 2004; Sawle & Kear-Colwell, 2001; Smallbone & Dadds, 1998).

## Onset and Course

It is unknown whether the paraphilias share a common age at which their symptoms first manifest or if they vary in age of symptom onset. One should note that the age of onset of paraphilic symptoms does not necessary coincide with the age at which the paraphilogenic factors first operate. By way of analogy, typical (nonparaphilic) heterosexuality and typical homosexuality do not overtly manifest until puberty, but there is no reason to believe that the etiology of sexual orientation occurs at that time rather than earlier in development. The *DSM-5* describes the age of onset for the paraphilias to be during adolescence, although some of paraphilic disorders may not be diagnosed until age 16 (in the case of pedophilic disorder) or 18 (in the case of voyeuristic disorder). These cutoffs are not meant to follow any etiological mechanism, however, and instead reflect an attempt avoid false positives relative to typical sexual curiosity and experimentation during puberty and adolescence.

It is unknown to what extent information about age of onset is affected by the legal status of expressing paraphilic interests. It is plausible that individuals who experience paraphilia unassociated with sexual offending would be more willing to acknowledge awareness of their interests during childhood. The research literature supports the childhood onset of rubber fetishism (Gosselin & Wilson, 1980), cross-dressing (Brown et al., 1996), apotemnophilia (First, 2005), acrotomophilia (Dixon, 1983), homosexual or bisexual foot and shoe fetishism (Weinberg et al., 1995), and masochism and hyperdominance (Breslow et al., 1985). Moreover, paraphilics sometimes recall events from early childhood during which they became—and then remained—fascinated with the object(s) or behaviors of their future sexual interest (e.g., Dixon, 1983; Freund et al., 1995; Massie & Szajnberg, 1997; Weinberg et al., 1994, 1995).

## Gender Dysphoria and Transsexualism

Clinical contact with trans populations differs from social and public contact in that clinical contact often begins before any transition, when no outcome can be assumed, whereas social and public contact occur after transition, when people can explicate how they want to be treated. This can lead to conflicts in language: from the point of view of the post-transitioned, references to the pre-transitioned state represent reminders of a problematic situation. Clinically, however, to assume a transition at the start is to presume the answer to the very question client-patients present to their clinicians. To minimize ambiguity, this chapter will employ the full terms spelling out the trajectory of the (potential) transition—MtF or female-to-male (FtM)—rather than "single time point" terms that leave ambiguous if the gender named is the gender being transitioned *from* or the gender being considered to transitioned *to*.

The term "gender dysphoria" refers to a broad class of phenomena characterized by discontent with one's biological sex and/or social gender. In adults, it manifests as the persistent idea that one is, or should have been, a member of the opposite sex, and, in children, by pervasive patterns of behavior consistent with such a belief. The affective component of gender dysphoria is discontent with one's biological sex and the desire to possess the body of the opposite sex and to be regarded by others as a member of the opposite sex. *DSM-5* introduced *gender dysphoria* as the formal diagnostic term (replacing the *DSM-IV-TR* term, *gender identity disorder*, which, in turn replaced the *DSM-III-R* term, *transsexualism*). Thus, "gender dysphoria" may now refer either to the broad term or the more narrowly defined diagnosis.

Gender dysphoria varies in severity and, at its most extreme (transsexualism) is accompanied by a desire for surgery to simulate (as much as possible) the reproductive organs of the opposite sex. Individuals with milder forms sometimes perceive themselves to be both male and female or fluctuate between seeing themselves as one or the other.

There appear to be two phenomena, unrelated and each capable of motivating discontent with one's biological sex. The two groups experiencing these phenomena differ in their age of onset, course, associated features, and sex ratio and, therefore, probably in their etiology (Blanchard, 1989a, 1989b). One is associated with autogynephilia, the aforementioned paraphilic interest (of biological males) in being female. Such individuals sometimes engage in erotic cross-dressing for many years before deciding to pursue permanent feminization. The other group lacks any obvious paraphilic interests but shows multiple, extremely strong or exaggerated features atypical for their biological sex. The other is related to homosexuality and occurs both in biological males and in biological females.

*Autogynephilic Male-to-Females*

The autogynephilic type accounts for a substantial proportion of persons seeking sex reassignment in Europe and North America (e.g., Nieder et al., 2011; Smith et al., 2005). The exact nature of the relation between autogynephilia and gender dysphoria is unclear. Many autogynephilic transsexuals report that their desires to be women remained the same or grew even stronger after their initial strong sexual response to that ideation had diminished or disappeared.

Insofar as autogynephilic transsexuals are erotically oriented toward other persons, they may be attracted to women, to both sexes, or to neither sex. It is likely that those individuals attracted to women constitute the prototype and that bisexual and asexual individuals represent secondary variations. The asexual individuals represent those cases in which the autogynephilia nullifies or overshadows the person's erotic attraction to women, and the bisexual individuals represent those cases in which the autogynephilic disorder instead gives rise to some

secondary erotic interest in men that coexists with the person's basic attraction to women (Blanchard, 1985). Blanchard (1989b) has suggested that the latter phenomenon need not reflect an equal attraction to the male and female phenotypes and would perhaps be better characterized as *pseudobisexuality*. Because autogynephilic MtFs express the belief that "inside" they really are women, those who are attracted to women may—paradoxically—describe their erotic interests in women as "homosexual" and refer to themselves as "lesbians trapped in a man's body" (Lawrence, 2013).

Autogynephilic MtFs are not conspicuously cross-gendered in childhood, although the private wish to be a woman may begin to occur before puberty. They are rarely labeled as "sissies" by their peers, and their cross-gender behavior is typically restricted to secret, solitary cross-dressing in garments surreptitiously borrowed from their mothers, sisters, or other females in their households. This type of gender dysphoria tends to develop more slowly and often has the character of a progressive disorder, with temporary or milder methods of expressing female traits preceding more permanent and dramatic ones. Autogynephilic MtFs usually present to clinicians in their mid-30s, and it is common for such individuals to seek professional help for the first time at age 50 or 60 years. Many autogynephilic MtFs marry women and father children before their wish to live as women becomes overwhelming, thus delaying their pursuit of sex reassignment (Blanchard, 1994).

*Androphilic Male-to-Females and Gynephilic Female-to-Males*

MtF gender dysphorics who are sexually attracted to men (i.e., who are *androphilic*) exhibit multiple overtly feminine behaviors which were readily apparent in childhood. Such boys prefer girls' games and toys and female playmates and would rather be around adult women than adult men. They often or always take female roles in fantasy play (e.g., princess, ballerina), and they identify with glamorous female characters in television stories or other media. Some of these boys also dress up as women; however, their cross-dressing is not experienced as sexually arousing, either in childhood or later. Even when they are not engaging in any obvious cross-gender behavior, boys with gender dysphoria are noticeably effeminate, which may manifest as feminine speech patterns, gestures, or gait.

Gender dysphoric FtMs who are sexually attracted to women (i.e., are *gynephilic*) show the corresponding picture. In childhood, they express very strong preferences for boys' toys and games and a rejection of long hair and dresses in favor of short hair and trousers. They may imitate other male-typical behaviors, such as standing to urinate. Unlike ordinary "tomboys," they do not merely enjoy some activities stereotyped as male; rather, they systematically and vehemently reject all activities, clothes, etc. that would identify them to the world as female.

Gender dysphoric boys and girls may verbally express the wish to belong to the opposite sex or state the belief that they will become members of the opposite sex when they grow up. Claims of actually being members of the opposite sex are more common in younger than in older children, probably because older children have a better understanding of gender constancy. Older children are also less likely to communicate the desire to belong to the opposite sex, an inhibition attributable to their greater awareness of social sanctions (Wallien et al., 2009; Zucker et al., 1993, 1999).

The course of childhood gender dysphoria is unpredictable, and the outcome is highly variable. In many cases, the dysphoria resolves without clinical intervention, usually by puberty. That is, the individuals grow up to be ordinary, non-transsexual, androphilic men (i.e., gay men) or ordinary, non-transsexual, gynephilic women (i.e., lesbians), each content with their original, biological sex. In other cases, substantial cross-gender behavior remains, but the wish for a full transition to the opposite sex is weak or absent. These include gay male "drag queens," who cross-dress intermittently but extensively and who may take estrogenic medications to develop breasts, as well as biologically female "genderqueers," who may seek testosterone medication for its masculinizing effects (e.g., beard growth) but express no interest in mastectomy or pelvic surgery.

The remaining cases, who reach adulthood with their dysphoria unabated or intensified, may seek transsexual surgery and other interventions. Both androphilic MtFs and gynephilic FtMs (sometimes called in the literature *homosexual transsexuals,* relative to their biological sex) typically begin to seek sex reassignment surgery when they are in their mid-20s, by which time many of them have already begun living full-time as the opposite sex. For MtFs, the definitive operation is the construction of a vagina and vulva. For FtMs, the most urgent procedure is usually breast tissue reduction and construction of a male chest contour, followed by removal of the uterus and ovaries. They do not universally pursue construction of an artificial penis, which is expensive, technically difficult, and often disfiguring to the part of the body from which the donor tissue is taken.

*Androphilic Female-to-Males*

There is a rare but distinct group of FtMs who are sexually orientated toward males and who say that they want to undergo sex reassignment so that they can become "gay men" (Blanchard, 1990; Dickey & Stephens, 1995). This makes the syndrome seem analogous to autogynephilic transsexualism in biological males. No one, however, has identified a distinct paraphilia (like autogynephilia) that accompanies or precedes heterosexual transsexualism in biological females; therefore the analogy seems incomplete.

*Rapid-Onset Gender Dysphoria*

A third profile has begun to present to clinicians or socially, characteristically distinct from the previously identified ones (Kaltiala-Heino et al., 2015; Littman, 2018). This group is predominantly biologically female and presents in puberty or adolescence, but, unlike the androphilic FtM group, lacks the substantial history of cross-gender behavior in childhood. This feature has led to the term rapid-onset gender dysphoria (ROGD; Littman, 2018). The majority of cases appear to occur within clusters of peers and in association with increased social media use (Littman, 2015) and especially among people with autism or other neurodevelopmental or psychiatric disorders (Kaltiala-Heino et al., 2015; Littman, 2018; Warrier et al., 2020). It cannot be easily determined whether the self-reported gender dysphoria is a result of other underlying issues or if those mental health issues are the result of the stresses of being a stigmatized minority (Boivin et al., 2020). Importantly, unlike other presentations of gender dysphoria, "coming out" in this group was often (47.2%) associated with declines rather than improvements in mental health (Biggs, 2020; Littman, 2018). Although long-term outcomes have not yet been reported, these distinctions argue against generalizing findings from the other presentations to this one.

*Prevalence and Sex Ratio*

The prevalence of full-blown transsexualism is easier to estimate than the prevalence of lesser degrees of gender dysphoria because transsexuals, almost by definition, must disclose their condition for medical or legal purposes. Estimates are about 1 in 12,000 for MtF transsexuals and 1 in

30,000–50,000 for FtM transsexuals (Bakker et al., 1993; De Cuypere et al., 2007; Wilson et al., 1999). The ratio of biological males to females is around 2:1 or 3:1 (Landén et al., 1996; Garrels et al., 2000).

*Neurological Correlates*

Zhou, Hofman, Gooren, and Swaab (1995) and Kruijver et al. (2000) reported that a sex-dimorphic structure of the brain, the central subdivision of the bed nucleus of the stria terminalis (BSTc), was shifted in size toward that of the opposite sex in a small series of transsexuals examined postmortem. There are at least three reasons to be skeptical that this unconfirmed finding has conclusively identified a neurological substrate of cross-gender identity. First, significant sexual dimorphism in BSTc volume and neuron number does not develop in humans until adulthood (Chung et al., 2002), whereas many or most transsexuals report that their feelings of gender dysphoria began in childhood. Second, all of the subjects had undergone feminizing or masculinizing hormone treatment, and such treatment has profound effects on brain volume (Hulshoff Pol et al., 2006). Third, BSTc volume has been reported to be smaller among pedophilic men than among controls (Schiltz et al., 2007), which suggests that the structure may be related to sexual anomalies in general rather than to cross-gender identity specifically.

MRI has subsequently been employed in vivo to identify neuroanatomic features distinguishing transsexual from cissexual adults (other age groups have not yet been so studied). Unfortunately, many such studies confounded gender identity with sexual orientation (e.g., Rametti et al., 2011), contrasting MtF transsexuals attracted to men with cissexual males attracted to women (e.g., Spizzirri et al., 2018) or contrasting FtM transsexuals attracted to women with cissexual females attracted to men (e.g., Kim et al., 2015). Other reports failed to indicate the sexual orientations of the samples at all (e.g., Mueller et al., 2016). Thus, although some authors have attributed cross-sex shifts in sexually dimorphic neuroanatomy to transsexuality, the same findings are just as readily attributable to homosexuality when confounded in this way.

Another set of MRI studies explicitly controlled for sexual orientation, either by comparing transsexuals attracted to women with cissexuals also attracted to women (e.g., Savic & Arver, 2011), or by comparing a diverse group of transsexuals (some attracted to men, some attracted to women) with two control groups of cissexuals, one attracted to men and one attracted to women (e.g., Burke et al., 2017; Manzouri & Savic, 2019). These analyses identified significant group differences, but not in neuroanatomic features known to represent cross-sex differences, correlates of homosexuality, or findings from samples of homosexual transsexuals. Rather, the implicated structures appear to represent "cerebral networks mediating self-body perception" (Manzouri & Savic, 2019, p. 2098). These findings remain consistent with the hypothesis that there is not a single neuroanatomic cause of gender dysphoria, but that there exist two phenomena in play, both of which can motivate gender dysphoria and each of which has its own neuroanatomic footprint: one related to homosexuality and another, independent one related to autogynephilia (Cantor, 2011).

*Suicidality*

Reports of suicidality among trans populations vary widely (cf., Adams & Vincent, 2019; Wiepjes et al., 2020), owing primarily to which population subtypes were studied and how suicidality was defined (ideation vs. attempts vs. completions). Also differing across reports was the definition of trans, ranging from meeting diagnostic criteria to adopting self-described gender without clear definition (McNeil et al., 2017). Unfortunately, many reports also collapsed across groups or conflated gender identity with sexual orientation, leading to misattribution of conclusions across groups. Despite that this literature repeatedly emphasizes the interactions among sexuality, ethnicity, and other social stigmata with suicidality, few studies actually recorded or controlled for such variables (McNeil et al., 2017). This also has led to misattributing features across groups. Many features reported to reflect gender identity may instead reflect homosexuality.

In their comprehensive literature review, McNeil et al. (2017) found reported rates of suicidal ideation ranging from 37% to 83% and, for suicidal attempts, 9.8% to 44%. Rates reported by gender clinics were lower than those reported on surveys, and rates reported by gender clinics were lower still when assessed by a clinician than when indicated on self-report instruments. The reported rates of suicidal ideation and attempts differ appreciably from rates of completed suicide (e.g., Asscheman et al., 2011): the Amsterdam Cohort of Gender Dysphoria study examined the charts of all patients referred between 1972 and 2017, cross-checking them against the Dutch National Civil Record

Registry and other sources (Wiepjes et al., 2020). This spanned 5,107 trans women (ages 4–81) and 3,156 transmen (ages 4–73). In total, 0.6% died by suicide, representing 0.8% of male-to-females and 0.3% of female-to-males.

The sex difference reported by Wiepjes et al. was significant and consistent with prior reports finding FtM's to show a greater risk of suicidal ideation and attempts than MtF's, whereas MtF's show a greater risk of completing suicide than FtM's (McNeil et al., 2017). The sex difference among the cis-gendered in rates of completed suicides versus ideation and attempts among the cis-gendered is widely documented: biological females are more likely to report suicidal ideation and attempts, whereas biological males are more likely to complete suicide (Fox et al., 2018). Thus, suicidality among trans populations would appear to follow biological sex rather than self-identified sex, the knowledge of which could help guide prevention efforts to where they are needed most.

## Hypersexuality

Multiple theory-laden terms have been used to describe sexual urges or behaviors whose frequencies are sufficiently high to produce distress or harm, the most common of which has been "sex addiction" (Carnes, 1983). The major competing theoretical perspectives of hypersexuality include addiction (Carnes, 1989; Goodman, 1997), compulsivity (Quadland, 1985; Coleman, 2003), the dual control model (Bancroft, 1999; Bancroft, Graham, Janssen, & Sanders, 2009), and desire dysregulation (Kafka, 2007). Although the theories make use of different terminology and treatment modalities, they contain many more similarities than differences. The word "hypersexuality" will be used to describe this condition in the following.

Elevation in sexual behavior is a symptom of several conditions, including hypomania, borderline personality disorder, and disinhibiting neurological trauma or disease. Hypersexuality as a syndrome unto itself has been receiving increasing attention, but there does not yet exist any consensus in definition or theoretical models.

### Prevalence and Sex Ratio

Estimating the prevalence of hypersexuality is hampered by the diversity of operational definitions and the lack of any meaningful distinction between typical and excessive rates of sexual urges or behaviors. Coleman (1992) offered an estimate of 5–6% of the population being affected by "impulsive-compulsive" sexual behavior; however, it is unclear how such an estimate might be produced in the absence of reliable criteria, and it is likely that the problem may have increased following the readier access to pornography via the Internet. For comparison, a large cross-sectional study in the United States found 1.9% of males to masturbate daily and 1.2%, more than daily (Laumann et al., 1994). (The survey did not ask whether these individuals experienced problems due to the frequency of their sexual activity, however.) Similarly, 2–8% of men, including adolescents, experience more than seven orgasms per week (Mick & Hollander, 2006). Although such data might be imagined to be useful in identifying a clear cutoff, sexual frequency can interact with sexual context. For example, higher sexual frequency within a stable relationship correlates with higher psychological functioning, but frequency of solo or impersonal sexual behaviors does not (Längström & Hanson, 2006). A further impediment to accurate prevalence estimates is that hypersexuality also appears to often be confused with high-risk sexual behavior, which overlaps with, but is not the same as, out of control sexual behavior (Bancroft & Vukadinovic, 2004).

As with paraphilias, the reported samples consistently indicate a majority of males among individuals seeking assistance for potential hypersexuality, approximately three to five males per female (Black et al., 1997). Among studies that included both male and female referrals, 60–92% of each sample is male (Kaplan & Krueger, 2010).

### Comorbidities

From 83% to 100% of affected individuals also had one or more *DSM-IV* Axis I diagnoses (Black et al., 1997; Raymond et al., 2003). These included mood and anxiety disorders, substance abuse, impulse control disorders, and obsessive-compulsive disorder (Black et al., 1997; Kafka & Hennen, 2002; Kafka & Prentky, 1994, 1998; Raviv, 1993; Raymond et al., 2003; Shapira et al., 2000). Personality disorders are also common, with approximately half meeting criteria (Black et al., 1997; Raymond et al., 2003). Moreover, conditions for which hypersexuality is a symptom include dementia (Fedoroff et al., 1994), temporal lobe epilepsy (Remillard et al., 1983), and Tourette's syndrome (Kerbeshian & Burd, 1991), as well as bipolar disorder and borderline personality disorder.

Notwithstanding those associations, many individuals seeking help for hypersexuality show normal profiles on the Minnesota Multiphasic Personality

Inventory (MMPI-2; Reid & Carpenter, 2009). Such discrepancies might reflect heterogeneous subtypes, the proportions of which differ between clinics or recruitment methods. The possibility that hypersexual phenomena consists of distinct subtypes has indeed been proposed (e.g., Cantor et al., 2013; Kafka, 2010; Raymond et al., 2003). In the most explicit attempt to identify clinically meaningful subtypes, referrals have been characterized as showing paraphilic hypersexuality, avoidant masturbation, and chronic adultery, with other phenomena being associated with genuine distress but not any behavioral excesses not already accounted for by other issues (Cantor et al., 2013).

Neuroimaging studies have compared patients with versus without hypersexual symptomatology (Black et al., 2005; Mendez & Shapira, 2013). For example, a study of patients with behavioral variant frontotemporal dementia found evidence of temporal lobe-limbic involvement as well as frontal lobe involvement in those patients who also had hypersexuality. The authors of that study concluded that individuals with hypersexuality may have developmental or genetic differences in the ability of the right anterior temporal lobe to inhibit limbic and subcortical areas for sexual arousal (Mendez & Shapira, 2013).

*Associated Features*

Investigations of the role of testosterone have demonstrated that low levels of the hormone are consistently associated with low levels of sexual interest and behavior, suggesting that high levels would be associated with elevated sexual interest and behavior. This conclusion has not yet been examined, however (Berlin, 2008). Opioids may also play a role, as a study demonstrated a statistically significant release of internal opioids in the cingulate, the temporal cortex, and the frontal cortex during sexual arousal in men (Frost et al., 1986). Relatedly, individuals who have with Parkinson's disease and are prescribed dopamine agonists frequently display sexual acting out (Klos et al., 2005).

Reid, Karim, McCrory, and Carpenter (2010) found that a sample of treatment-seeking hypersexual males scored lower than controls on a self-report measure of executive functioning; however, that team subsequently found that such males scored no worse than an age-, education-, and full-spectrum IQ (FSIQ)-matched community sample when directly tested with executive functioning measures (Reid et al., 2011). That team concluded that executive functioning may be limited to situations in which there is an opportunity for sex, but it is also possible that such individuals simply perceive and rate themselves as having less self-control as a reaction to instead of a cause of their symptom. Both studies controlled for substance abuse and attention deficit hyperactivity disorder because these conditions are also known to affect executive functioning, and are often comorbid with hypersexuality.

Hypersexual behavior is frequently described as an addiction to sex. As a test of that comparison, Steele, Staley, Fong, and Prause (2013) used electroencephalography to record the P300 amplitude of hypersexuals in response to sexual stimuli. Instead of finding a diminished (downregulated) response as predicted by the addiction model, the hypersexuals showed an elevated response. Neuroimaging studies of sexual arousal in controls have demonstrated activation in areas including the prefrontal, orbitofrontal, insular, occipitotemporal, and anterior cingulate cortices, as well as in subcortical regions including the amygdala and substantia nigra (Stoléru et al., 2012), making these important areas to examine as potential mechanisms associated with sexually problematic behavior (Mendez & Shapira, 2013).

**References**

Abel, G. G., Becker, J. V., Cunningham-Rathner, J., Mittelman, M., & Rouleau, J.-L. (1988). Multiple paraphilic diagnoses among sex offenders. *Bulletin of the American Academy of Psychiatry and the Law, 16,* 153–168.

Abel, G. G., & Osborn, C. (1992). The paraphilias: The extent and nature of sexually deviant and criminal behavior. *Psychiatric Clinics of North America, 15,* 675–687.

Adams, N. J., & Vincent, B. (2019). Suicidal thoughts and behaviors among transgender adults in relation to education, ethnicity, and income: A systematic review. *Transgender Health, 4,* 226–246.

Alison, L., Santtila, P., Sandnabba, N. K., & Nordling, N. (2001). Sadomasochistically oriented behavior: Diversity in practice and meaning. *Archives of Sexual Behavior, 30,* 1–12.

(Anonymous), Chambers, W. M., & Janzen, W. B. (1976). The eclectic and multiple therapy of a shoe fetishist. *American Journal of Psychotherapy, 30,* 317–326.

Arndt, W., Foehl, J., & Good, F. (1985). Specific sexual fantasy themes: A multidimensional study. *Journal of Personality and Social Psychology, 48,* 472–480.

Arndt, W. B. (1991). *Gender disorders and the paraphilias.* International Universities Press.

Asscheman, H., Giltay, E. J., Megens, J. A. J., de Ronde W. P., von Trotsenburg, M. A. A., & Gooren, L. J. G. (2011). A long-term follow-up study of mortality in transsexual receiving treatment with cross-sex hormones. *European Journal of Endocrinology, 164,* 635–642.

Babchishin, K. M., Hanson, R. K., & Van Zuylen, H. (2015). Online child pornography offenders are different: A meta-analysis of the characteristics of online and offline sex offenders against children. *Archives of Sexual Behavior, 44,* 45–66.

Bakker, A., van Kesteren, P. J., Gooren, L. J. G., & Bezemer, P. D. (1993). The prevalence of transsexualism in The Netherlands. *Acta Psychiatrica Scandinavica, 87,* 237–238.

Ball, H. N. (2005). Sexual offending on elderly women: A review. *Journal of Forensic Psychiatry and Psychology, 16,* 127–138.

Bancroft, J. (1999). Central inhibition of sexual response in the male: A theoretical perspective. *Neuroscience and Biobehavioral Reviews, 23,* 763–784.

Bancroft, J., Graham, C. A., Janssen, E., & Sanders, S. A. (2009). The dual control model: Current status and future directions. *Journal of Sex Research, 46,* 121–142.

Bancroft, J., & Vukadinovic, Z. (2004). Sexual addiction, sexual compulsivity, sexual impulsivity, or what? Toward a theoretical model. *Journal of Sex Research, 41,* 225–234.

Baril, A. (2015). "How dare you pretend to be disabled?" The discounting of transabled people and their claims in disability movements and studies. *Disability & Society, 30,* 689–703.

Barrow, E., & Oyebode, F. (2019). Body integrity identity disorder: Clinical features and ethical dimensions. *BJPsych Advances, 25,* 187–195.

Blanchard, R., Lykins, A. D., Wherrett, D., Kuban, M. E., Cantor, J. M., Blak, T., Dickey, R., & Klassen, P. E. (2009). Pedophilia, hebephilia, and the DSM-V. *Archives of Sexual Behavior, 38,* 335–350.

Beier, K. M., Neutze, J., Mundt, I. A., Ahlers, C. J., Goecker, D., Konrad, A., & Schaefer, G. A. (2009). Encouraging self-identified pedophiles and hebephiles to seek professional help: First results of the Prevention Project Dunkelfeld (PPD). *Child Abuse & Neglect, 33,* 545–549.

Benjamin, H. (1966). *The transsexual phenomenon.* Julian.

Bensler, J. M., & Paauw, D. S. (2003). Apotemnophilia masquerading as medical morbidity. *Southern Medical Journal, 96,* 674–676.

Berger, B. D., Lehrmann, J. A., Larson, G., Alverno, L., & Tsao, C. I. (2005). Nonpsychotic, nonparaphilic self-amputation and the internet. *Comprehensive Psychiatry, 46,* 380–383.

Berlin, F. S. (2008). Basic science and neurobiological research: Potential relevance to sexual compulsivity. *Psychiatric Clinics of North America, 31,* 623–642.

Bethell, M. F. (1974). A rare manifestation of fetishism. *Archives of Sexual Behavior, 3,* 301–302.

Biggs, M. (2020). Gender dysphoria and psychological functioning in adolescents treated with GnRHa: Comparing Dutch and English prospective studies. [Letter to the Editor] *Archives of Sexual Behavior, 49,* 2231–2236.

Binet, A. (1887). Le fétichisme dans l'amour. *Revue Philosophique, 24,* 143–167, 252–274.

Black, B., Muralee, S., & Tampi, R. R. (2005). Inappropriate sexual behaviors in dementia. *Journal of Geriatric Psychiatry and Neurology, 18,* 155–162.

Black, D. W., Kehrberg, L. L. D., Flumerfelt, D. L., & Schlosser, S. S. (1997). Characteristics of 36 subjects reporting compulsive sexual behavior. *American Journal of Psychiatry, 154,* 243–249.

Blanchard, R. (1985). Typology of male-to-female transsexualism. *Archives of Sexual Behavior, 14,* 247–261.

Blanchard, R. (1988). Nonhomosexual gender dysphoria. *Journal of Sex Research, 24,* 188–193.

Blanchard, R. (1989a). The classification and labeling of nonhomosexual gender dysphorias. *Archives of Sexual Behavior, 18,* 315–334.

Blanchard, R. (1989b). The concept of autogynephilia and the typology of male gender dysphoria. *Journal of Nervous and Mental Disease, 177,* 616–623.

Blanchard, R. (1990). Gender identity disorders in adult women. In R. Blanchard & B. W. Steiner (Eds.), *Clinical management of gender identity disorders in children and adults* (pp. 77–91). American Psychiatric Press.

Blanchard, R. (1991). Clinical observations and systematic studies of autogynephilia. *Journal of Sex and Marital Therapy, 17,* 235–251.

Blanchard, R. (1993a). The she-male phenomenon and the concept of partial autogynephilia. *Journal of Sex and Marital Therapy, 19,* 69–76.

Blanchard, R. (1993b). Partial versus complete autogynephilic and gender dysphoria. *Journal of Sex and Marital Therapy, 19,* 301–307.

Blanchard, R. (1994). A structural equation model for age at clinical presentation in nonhomosexual male gender dysphorics. *Archives of Sexual Behavior, 23,* 311–320.

Blanchard, R. (2008). Review and theory of handedness, birth order, and homosexuality in men. *Laterality: Asymmetries of Body, Brain and Cognition, 13,* 51–70.

Blanchard, R., Cantor, J. M., & Robichaud, L. K. (2006). Biological factors in the development of sexual deviance and aggression in males. In H. E. Barbaree & W. L. Marshall (Eds.), *The Juvenile Sex Offender,* 2nd ed. (pp. 77–104). Guilford.

Blanchard, R., & Collins, P. I. (1993). Men with sexual interest in transvestites, transsexuals, and she-males. *Journal of Nervous and Mental Disease, 181,* 570–575.

Blanchard, R., & Hucker, S. J. (1991). Age, transvestism, bondage, and concurrent paraphilic activities in 117 fatal cases of autoerotic asphyxia. *British Journal of Psychiatry, 159,* 371–377.

Blanchard, R., Kolla, N. J., Cantor, J. M., Klassen, P. E., Dickey, R., Kuban, M. E., & Blak, T. (2007). IQ, handedness, and pedophilia in adult male patients stratified by referral source. *Sexual Abuse: A Journal of Research and Treatment, 19,* 285–309.

Blom, R. M., Hennekam, R. C., Denys, D. (2012). Body integrity identity disorder. *PLoS ONE, 7*(4), e34702.

Blom, R., M., van Wingen, G. A., van der Wal, S. J., Luigjes, J., van Dijk, M. T., Scholte, H. S., & Denys, D. (2016). The desire for amputation or paralyzation: Evidence for structural brain anomalies in Body Integrity Identity Disorder (BIID). *PLoS ONE, 11,* e0165789.

Boivin, L., Notredame, C.-E., Jardri, R., & Medjkane, F. (2020). Supporting parents of transgender adolescents: Yes, but how? *Archives of Sexual Behavior, 49,* 81–83.

Bourguignon, A. (1983). Vampirism and autovampirism. In L. B. Schlesinger & E. Revitch (Eds.), *Sexual dynamics of antisocial behavior* (pp. 278–301). Charles C. Thomas.

Bradford, J. M. W., Boulet, J., & Pawlak, A. (1992). The paraphilias: A multiplicity of deviant behaviours. *Canadian Journal of Psychiatry, 37,* 104–108.

Breslow, N., Evans, L., & Langley, J. (1985). On the prevalence and roles of females in the sadomasochistic subculture: Report of an empirical study. *Archives of Sexual Behavior, 14,* 303–317.

Brugger, P., Christen, M., Jellestad, L., & Hänggi, J. (2016). Limb amputation and other disability desires as a medical condition. *Lancet Psychiatry, 3,* 1176–1186.

Brown, G. R., Wise, T. N., Costa, P. T., Herbst, J. H., Fagan, P. J., & Schmidt, C. W. (1996). Personality characteristics and sexual functioning of 188 cross-dressing men. *Journal of Nervous and Mental Disease, 184,* 265–273.

Burke, S. M., Manzouri, A. H., & Savic, I. (2017). Structural connections in the brain in relation to gender identity and sexual orientation. *Nature: Scientific Reports, 7,* 17954. doi:10.1038/s41598-017-17352-8

Byard, R. W., & Winskog, C. (2012). Autoerotic death: Incidence and age of victims—A population-based study. *Journal of Forensic Sciences, 57,* 129–131.

Cairnes, F. J., & Rainer, S. P. (1981). Death from electrocution during auto-erotic procedures. *New Zealand Medical Journal, 94,* 259–260.

Cantor, J. M. (2011). New MRI studies support the Blanchard typology of male-to-female transsexualism [Letter to the Editor]. *Archives of Sexual Behavior, 40,* 863–862.

Cantor, J. M., Blanchard, R., Christensen, B. K., Dickey, R., Klassen, P. E., Beckstead, A. L., Blak, T., & Kuban, M. E. (2004). Intelligence, memory, and handedness in pedophilia. *Neuropsychology, 18,* 3–14.

Cantor, J. M., Blanchard, R., Robichaud, L. K., & Christensen, B. K. (2005). Quantitative reanalysis of aggregate data on IQ in sexual offenders. *Psychological Bulletin, 131,* 555–568.

Cantor, J. M., Kabani, N., Christensen, B. K., Zipursky, R. B., Barbaree, H. E., Dickey, R., Klassen, P. E., Mikulis, D. J., Kuban, M. E., Blak, T., Richards, B. A., Hanratty, M. K., & Blanchard, R. (2008). Cerebral white matter deficiencies in pedophilic men. *Journal of Psychiatric Research, 42,* 167–183.

Cantor, J. M., Klassen, P. E., Dickey, R., Christensen, B. K., Kuban, M. E., Blak, T., Williams, N. S., & Blanchard, R. (2005). Handedness in pedophilia and hebephilia. *Archives of Sexual Behavior, 34,* 447–459.

Cantor, J. M., Klein, C., Lykins, A., Rullo, J. E., Thaler, L., & Walling, B. R. (2013). A treatment-oriented typology of self-identified hypersexuality referrals. *Archives of Sexual Behavior, 42,* 883–893.

Cantor, J. M., Kuban, M. E., Blak, T., Klassen, P. E., Dickey, R., & Blanchard, R. (2006). Grade failure and special education placement in sexual offenders' educational histories. *Archives of Sexual Behavior, 35,* 743–751.

Cantor, J. M., Lafaille, S. J., Hannah, J., Kucyi, A., Soh, D. W., Girard, T. A., & Mikulis, D. J. (2016). Independent component analysis of resting-state functional magnetic resonance imaging in pedophiles. *Journal of Sexual Medicine, 13,* 1546–1554.

Cantor, J. M., Lafaille, S., Soh, D. W., Moayedi, M., Mikulis, D. J., & Girard, T. A. (2015). Diffusion tensor imaging of pedophilia. *Archives of Sexual Behavior, 44,* 2161–2172.

Cantor, J. M., & McPhail, I. V. (2016). Non-offending pedophiles. *Current Sexual Health Reports, 8,* 121–128.

Carnes, P (1983). *Out of the shadows: Understanding sexual addiction.* CompCare Publications.

Carnes, P. (1989). *Contrary to love: Helping the sexual addict.* CompCare Publications.

Chalkley, A. J., & Powell, G. E. (1983). The clinical description of forty-eight cases of sexual fetishism. *British Journal of Psychiatry, 142,* 292–295.

Chung, W. C., De Vries, G. J., & Swaab, D. F. (2002). Sexual differentiation of the bed nucleus of the stria terminalis in humans may extend into adulthood. *Journal of Neuroscience, 22,* 1027–1033.

Coleman, E. (1992). Is your patient suffering from compulsive sexual behavior? *Psychiatric Annals, 22,* 320–325.

Coleman, E. (2003). Compulsive sexual behavior: What to call it, how to treat it? *SIECUS Report, 31,* 12–16.

Collacott, R. A., & Cooper, S.-A. (1995). Urine fetish in a man with learning disabilities. *Journal of Intellectual Disability Research, 39,* 145–147.

Cooper, A. J. (1995). Auto-erotic asphyxial death: Analysis of nineteen fatalities in Alberta: Comment. *Canadian Journal of Psychiatry, 40,* 363–364.

Cooper, A. J. (1996). Auto-erotic asphyxiation: Three case reports. *Journal of Sex and Marital Therapy, 22,* 47–53.

Crepault, C., & Couture, M. (1980). Men's erotic fantasies. *Archives of Sexual Behavior, 9,* 565–581.

Croughan, J. L., Saghir, M., Cohen, R., & Robins, E. (1981). A comparison of treated and untreated male cross-dressers. *Archives of Sexual Behavior, 10,* 515–528.

Dalby, J. T. (1988). Is telephone scatologia a variant of exhibitionism? *International Journal of Offender Therapy and Comparative Criminology, 32,* 45–49.

Davis, J. L. (2014). Morality work among the transabled. *Deviant Behavior, 35,* 433–455.

De Cuypere, G., Van Hemelrijck, M., Michel, A., Carael, B., Heylens, G., Rubens, R., Hoebeke, P., & Monstrey, S. (2007). Prevalence and demography of transsexualism in Belgium. *European Psychiatry, 22,* 137–141.

Denko, J. D. (1973). Klismaphilia: Enema as a sexual preference: Report of two cases. *American Journal of Psychotherapy, 27,* 232–250.

Denko, J. D. (1976). Klismaphilia: Amplification of the erotic enema deviance. *American Journal of Psychotherapy, 30,* 236–255.

Dickey, R., & Stephens, J. (1995). Female-to-male transsexualism, heterosexual type: Two cases. *Archives of Sexual Behavior, 24,* 439–445.

Dietz, P. E., Hazelwood, R. R., & Warren, J. (1990). The sexually sadistic criminal and his offenses. *Bulletin of the American Academy of Psychiatry and the Law, 18,* 163–178.

Dixon, D. (1983). An erotic attraction to amputees. *Sexuality and Disability, 6,* 3–19.

Docter, R. F., & Prince, V. (1997). Transvestism: A survey of 1032 cross-dressers. *Archives of Sexual Behavior, 26,* 589–605.

Earls, C. M., & Lalumière, M. L. (2002). A case study of preferential bestiality (zoophilia). *Sexual Abuse: A Journal of Research and Treatment, 14,* 83–88.

Ellis, H. (1928). *Studies in the psychology of sex* (vol. 7). Philadelphia: F. A. Davis.

Elman, R. A. (1997). Disability pornography: The fetishization of women's vulnerabilities. *Violence Against Women, 3,* 257–270.

Ernulf, K. E., & Innala, S. M. (1995). Sexual bondage: A review and unobtrusive investigation. *Archives of Sexual Behavior, 24,* 631–654.

Escoffier, J. (2011). Imagining the she/male: Pornography and the transsexualization of the heterosexual male. *Studies in Gender and Sexuality, 12,* 268–281.

Fedoroff, J. P., Peyser, C., Franz, M. L., & Folstein, S. E. (1994). Sexual disorders in Huntington's disease. *Journal of Neuropsychiatry, 6,* 147–153.

First, M. B. (2005). Desire for amputation of a limb: Paraphilia, psychosis, or a new type of identity disorder. *Psychological Medicine, 35,* 919–928.

Fox, K. R., Millner, A. J., Mukerji, C. E., & Nock, M. K. (2018). Examining the role of sex in self-injurious thoughts and behaviors. *Clinical Psychology Review, 66,* 3–11.

Freund, K. (1976). Diagnosis and treatment of forensically significant anomalous erotic preferences. *Canadian Journal of Criminology and Corrections, 18,* 181–189.

Freund, K. (1988). Courtship disorder: Is the hypothesis valid? *Annals of the New York Academy of Sciences, 528,* 172–182.

Freund, K. (1990). Courtship disorder. In W. L. Marshall, D. R. Laws, & H. E. Barbaree (Eds.), *Handbook of sexual assault: Issues, theories, and treatment of the offender* (pp. 195–207). Plenum.

Freund, K., & Blanchard, R. (1986). The concept of courtship disorder. *Journal of Sex & Marital Therapy, 12,* 79–92.

Freund, K., & Blanchard, R. (1993). Erotic target location errors in male gender dysphorics, paedophiles, and fetishists. *British Journal of Psychiatry, 162,* 558–563.

Freund, K., Scher, H., & Hucker, S. (1983). The courtship disorders. *Archives of Sexual Behavior, 12,* 369–379.

Freund, K., Scher, H., Racansky, I. G., Campbell, K., & Heasman, G. (1986). Males disposed to commit rape. *Archives of Sexual Behavior, 15,* 23–35.

Freund, K., Seeley, H. R., Marshall, W. E., & Glinfort, E. K. (1972). Sexual offenders needing special assessment and/or therapy. *Canadian Journal of Criminology and Corrections, 14,* 3–23.

Freund, K., Seto, M. C., & Kuban, M. (1995). Masochism: A multiple case study. *Sexuologie, 4,* 313–324.

Freund, K., Seto, M. C., & Kuban, M. (1996). Two types of fetishism. *Behavior Research and Therapy, 34,* 687–694.

Freund, K., Watson, R., & Dickey, R. (1991). Sex offenses against female children perpetrated by men who are not pedophiles. *Journal of Sex Research, 28,* 409–423.

Freund, K., Watson, R., & Rienzo, D. (1988). The value of self-reports in the study of voyeurism and exhibitionism. *Annals of Sex Research, 2,* 243–262.

Frost J. J., Mayberg H. S., Berlin F. S., Behal, R., Dannals, R. F., Links, J. M., Ravert, H. T., Wilson, A. A., & Wagner Jr., H. W. (1986). Alteration in brain opiate receptor binding in man following arousal using C-11 carfentinil and positron emission tomography. Proceedings of the 33rd Annual Meeting of the Society of Nuclear Medicine. *Journal of Nuclear Medicine, 27,* 1027.

Gaffney, G. R., & Berlin, F. S. (1984). Is there hypothalamic-pituitary-gonadal dysfunction in paedophilia? A pilot study. *British Journal of Psychiatry, 145,* 657–660.

Garlick, Y., Marshall, W. L., & Thornton, D. (1996). Intimacy deficits and attribution of blame among sex offenders. *Legal and Criminological Psychology, 1,* 251–288.

Garrels, L., Kockott, G., Michael, N., Preuss, W., Renter, K., Schmidt, G., Sigush, V., & Windgassen, K. (2000). Sex ratio of transsexuals in Germany: The development over three decades. *Acta Psychiatrica Scandinavica, 102,* 445–448.

Gebhard, P. H., Gagnon, J. H., Pomeroy, W. B., & Christenson, C. V. (1965). *Sex offenders: An analysis of types.* Harper & Row.

Giotakos, O., Markianos, M., Vaidakis, N., & Christodoulou, G. N. (2003). Aggression, impulsivity, plasma sex hormones, and biogenic amine turnover in a forensic population of rapists. *Journal of Sex and Marital Therapy, 29,* 215–225.

Goodman, A. (1998). *Sexual addiction: An integrated approach.* International Universities Press.

Gosselin, C., & Wilson, G. (1980). *Sexual variations: Fetishism, sadomasochism, and transvestism.* Simon and Schuster.

Gosselin, C. C. (1987). The sadomasochistic contract. In G. W. Wilson (Ed.), *Variant sexuality: Research and theory* (pp. 229–257). Croom-Helm.

Grant, V. W. (1953). A case study of fetishism. *Journal of Abnormal and Social Psychology, 48,* 142–149.

Gratzer, T., & Bradford, J. (1995). Offender and offense characteristics of sexual sadists: A comparative study. *Journal of Forensic Sciences, 40,* 450–455.

Green, R., & Young, R. (2001). Hand preference, sexual preference, and transsexualism. *Archives of Sexual Behavior, 30,* 565–574.

Gurnani, P. D., & Dwyer, M. (1986). Serum testosterone levels in sex offenders. *Journal of Offender Counseling, Services, and Rehabilitation, 11,* 39–45.

Haake, P., Schedlowski, M., Exton, M. S., Giepen, C., Hartmann, U., Osterheider, M., Flesch, M., Janssen, O. E., Leygraf, N., & Krüger, T. H. C. (2003). Acute neuroendocrine response to sexual stimulation in sexual offenders. *Canadian Journal of Psychiatry, 48,* 265–271.

Hänggi, J., Bellwald, D., & Brugger, P. (2016). Shape alterations of basal ganglia and thalamus in xenomelia. *NeuroImage: Clinical, 11,* 760–769.

Harding, L. (2003, December 4). Victim of cannibal agreed to be eaten. *The Guardian.*

Hardyck, C., & Petrinovich, L. F. (1977). Left-handedness. *Psychological Bulletin, 84,* 385–404.

Hawkinson, K., & Zamboni, B. D. (2014). Adult Baby/Diaper Lovers: An exploratory study of an online community sample. *Archives of Sexual Behavior, 43,* 863–877.

Hepper, P. G., Shahidullah, S., & White, R. (1991). Handedness in the human fetus. *Neuropsychologia, 29,* 1107–1111.

Hepper, P. G., Wells, D. L., & Lynch, C. (2005). Prenatal thumb sucking is related to postnatal handedness. *Neuropsychologia, 43,* 313–315.

Hilti, L. M., Hänggi, J., Vitacco, D. A., Kraemer, B., Palla, A., Luechinger, R., Jäncke, L., & Brugger, P. (2013). The desire for healthy limb amputation: Structural brain correlates and clinical features of xenomelia. *Brain, 136,* 318–329.

Hirschfeld, M. (1918). *Sexualpathologie* [Sexual pathology] (vol. 2). Marcus & Weber.

Hirschfeld, M. (1938). *Sexual anomalies and perversions: Physical and psychological development, diagnosis and treatment,* new and rev. ed. Encyclopaedic Press.

Hsu, K. J., & Bailey, J. M. (2017). Autopedophilia: Erotic-target identity inversions in men sexually attracted to children. *Psychological Science, 28,* 115–123.

Hsu, K. J., Rosenthal, A. M., Miller, D. I., & Bailey, J. M. (2016). Who are gynandromorphophilic men? Characterizing men with sexual interest in transgender women. *Psychological Medicine, 46,* 819–827.

Hsu, K. J., Rosenthal, A. M., Miller, D. I., & Bailey, J. M. (2017). Sexual arousal patterns of autogynephilic male cross-dressers. *Archives of Sexual Behavior, 46,* 247–253.

Hucker, S. J. (1985). Self-harmful sexual behavior. *Psychiatric Clinics of North America, 8,* 323–337.

Hucker, S. J., & Blanchard, R. (1992). Death scene characteristics in 118 fatal cases of autoerotic asphyxia compared with suicidal asphyxia. *Behavioral Sciences and the Law, 10,* 509–523.

Hulshoff Pol, H. E., Cohen-Kettenis, P. T., Van Haren, N. E., Peper, J. S., Brans, R. G., Cahn, W., Schnack, H. G., Gooren, L. J. G., & Kahn, R. S. (2006). Changing your sex changes your brain: Influences of testosterone and estrogen on adult human brain structure. *European Journal of Endocrinology, 155*(Suppl. 1), S107–S114.

Jamieson, S., & Marshall, W. L. (2000). Attachment styles and violence in child molesters. *Journal of Sexual Aggression, 5*, 88–98.

Janssen, W., Koops, E., Anders, S., Kuhn, S., & Püschel, K. (2005). Forensic aspects of 40 accidental autoerotic death in Northern Germany. *Forensic Science International, 147* (Suppl.), S61–S64.

Jay, K., & Young, A. (1977). *The gay report: Lesbians and gay men speak out about sexual experiences and lifestyles.* Summit Books.

Kafka, M. P. (2007). Paraphilia-related disorders: The evaluation and treatment of nonparaphilic hypersexuality. In S. Leiblum (Ed.), *Principles and Practice of Sex Therapy*, 4th ed. (pp. 442–476). Guilford.

Kafka, M. P. (2010). Hypersexual disorder: A proposed diagnosis for DSM-V. *Archives of Sexual Behavior, 39*, 377–400.

Kafka, M. P., & Hennen, J. (2002). A *DSM-IV* Axis I comorbidity study of males (*n* = 120) with paraphilias and paraphilia-related disorders. *Sexual Abuse: A Journal of Research and Treatment, 14*, 349–366.

Kafka, M. P., & Prentky, R. A. (1994). Preliminary observations of DSM-III-R Axis I comorbidity in men with paraphilias and paraphilia-related disorders. *Journal of Clinical Psychiatry, 55*, 481–487.

Kafka, M. P., & Prentky, R. A. (1998). Attention-deficit/hyperactivity disorder in males with paraphilias and paraphilia-related disorders: A comorbidity study. *Journal of Clinical Psychiatry, 59*, 388–396.

Kaltiala-Heino, R., Sumia, M., Työläjärvi, M., & Lindberg, N. (2015). Two years of gender identity service for minors: Overrepresentation of natal girls with severe problems in adolescent development. *Child and Adolescent Psychiatry and Mental Health, 9*, 9.

Kaplan, M. S., & Krueger, R. B. (2010). Diagnosis, assessment, and treatment of hypersexuality. *Journal of sex research, 47*, 181–198.

Kerbeshian, J., & Burd, L. (1991). Tourette syndrome and current paraphilic masturbatory fantasy. *Canadian Journal of Psychiatry, 36*, 155–157.

Kaul, A., & Duffy, S. (1991). Gerontophilia: A case report. *Medicine, Science and the Law, 31*, 110–114.

Kim, T.-H., Kim, S.-K., & Jeong, G.-W. (2015). Cerebral gray matter volume variation in female-to-male transsexuals: A voxel-based morphometric study. *Clinical Neuroscience, 26*, 1119–1225.

Klar, A. J. S. (2004). Excess of counterclockwise scalp hair-whorl rotation in homosexual men. *Journal of Genetics, 83*, 251–255.

Klos, K. J., Bower, J. H., Josephs, K. A., Matsumoto, J. Y., & Ahlskog, J. E. (2005). Pathological hypersexuality predominantly linked to adjuvant dopamine agonist therapy in Parkinson's disease and multiple system atrophy. *Parkinsonism & Related Disorders, 11*, 381–386.

Krafft-Ebing, R. von. (1886/1965). *Psychopathia sexualis: A medico-forensic study* (H. E. Wedeck, Trans.). G. P. Putnam.

Krueger, R. B. (2016). Diagnosis of hypersexual or compulsive sexual behavior can be made using ICD-10 and DSM-5 despite rejection of the diagnosis by the American Psychiatric Association. *Addiction, 111*, 2110.

Kruijver, F. P., Zhou, J. N., Pool, C. W., Hofman, M. A., Gooren, L. J., & Swaab, D. F. (2000). Male-to-female transsexuals have female neuron numbers in a limbic nucleus. *Journal of Clinical Endocrinology and Metabolism, 85*, 2034–2041.

Kunjukrishnan, R., Pawlak, A., & Varan, L R. (1988). The clinical and forensic psychiatric issues of retifism. *Canadian Journal of Psychiatry, 33*, 819–825.

Lalumière, M. L., Blanchard, R., & Zucker, K. J. (2000). Sexual orientation and handedness in men and women: A meta-analysis. *Psychological Bulletin, 126*, 575–592.

Lalumière, M. L., Harris, G. T., Quinsey, V. L., & Rice, M. E. (2005). *The causes of rape: Understanding individual differences in male propensity for sexual aggression.* American Psychological Association.

Landén, M., Wålinder, J., & Lundström, B. (1996). Prevalence, incidence, and sex ratio of transsexualism. *Acta Psychiatrica Scandinavica, 93*, 221–223.

Lang, R. A., Flor-Henry, P., & Frenzel, R. R. (1990). Sex hormone profiles in pedophilic and incestuous men. *Annals of Sex Research, 3*, 59–74.

Langevin, R., Paitch, D., Ramsay, G., Anderson, C., Kamrad, J., Pope, S., Geller, G., Pearl, L., & Newman, S. (1979). Experimental studies of the etiology of genital exhibitionism. *Archives of Sexual Behavior, 8*, 307–331.

Långström, N., & Hanson, R. K. (2006). High rates of sexual behavior in the general population: Correlates and predictors. *Archives of Sexual Behavior, 35*, 37–52.

Långström, N., & Seto, M. C. (2006). Exhibitionistic and voyeuristic behavior in a Swedish national population survey. *Archives of Sexual Behavior, 35*, 427–435.

Långström, N., & Zucker, K. J. (2005). Transvestic fetishism in the general population: Prevalence and correlates. *Journal of Sex and Marital Therapy, 31*, 87–95.

Laumann, E. O., Gagnon, J. H., Michael, R. T., & Michaels, S. (1994). *The social organization of sexuality: Sexual practices in the United States.* University of Chicago Press.

Lawrence, A. A. (2006). Clinical and theoretical parallels between desire for limb amputation and gender identity disorder. *Archives of Sexual Behavior, 25*, 263–278.

Lawrence, A. A. (2013). *Men trapped in men's bodies: Narratives of autogynephilic transsexualism.* Springer.

Lett, T. A., Mohnke, S., Amelung, T., Brandl, E. J., Schiltz, K., Pohl, A., Gerwinn, H., Kärgel, C., Massau, C., Tenbergen, G., Wittfoth, M., Kneer, J., Beier, K. M., Walter, M., Ponseti, J., Krüger, T. H. C., Schiffer, B., & Walter, H. (2018). Multimodal neuroimaging measures and intelligence influence pedophile child sexual offense behavior. *European Neuropsychopharmacology, 28*, 818–827.

Littman, L. (2018). Parent reports of adolescents and young adults perceived to show signs of a raid onset of gender dysphoria. *PLoS ONE, 13*(8), e0202330.

Lukianowicz, N. (1959). Survey of various aspects of transvestism in the light of our present knowledge. *Journal of Nervous and Mental Diseases, 128*, 36–64.

Manzouri, A., & Savic, I. (2019). Possible neurobiological underpinnings of homosexuality and gender dysphoria. *Cerebral Cortex, 29*, 2084–2101.

Marsa, F., O'Reilly, G., Carr, A., Murphy, P., O'Sullivan, M., Cotter, A., & Hevey, D. (2004). Attachment styles and psychological profiles of child sex offenders in Ireland. *Journal of Interpersonal Violence, 19*, 228–251.

Massie, H., & Szajnberg, N. (1997). The ontogeny of a sexual fetish from birth to age 30 and memory processes: A research case report from a prospective longitudinal study. *International Journal of Psycho-Analysis, 78*, 755–771.

McGeoch, P. D., Brang, D., Song, T., Lee, R. R., Huang, M., & Ramachandran, V. S. (2011). Xenomelia: A new right parietal lobe syndrome. *Journal of Neurology, Neurosurgery, and Psychiatry, 82*, 1314–1319.

McNally, R. J., & Lukach, B. M. (1991). Behavioral treatment of zoophilic exhibitionism. *Journal of Behavioral Therapy and Experimental Psychiatry, 22*, 281–284.

McNeil, J., Ellis, S. J., & Eccles, J. F. R. (2017). Suicide in trans populations: A systematic review of prevalence and correlates. *Psychology of Sexual Orientation and Gender Identity, 4*, 341–353.

McPhail, I. V., Olver, M. E., Brouillette-Alarie, S., & Looman, J. (2018). Taxometric analysis of the latent structure of pedophilic interest. *Archives of Sexual Behavior, 47*, 2223–2240.

McPhail, I. V., Stephens, S., & Heasman, A. (2018). Legal and ethical issues in treating clients with pedohebephilic interests. *Canadian Psychology, 59*, 369–381.

Mead, B. T. (1975). Coping with obscene phone calls. *Medical Aspects of Human Sexuality, 9*(6), 127–128.

Mendez, M. F., & Shapira, J. S. (2013). Hypersexual behavior in frontotemporal dementia: A comparison with early-onset Alzheimer's disease. *Archives of Sexual Behavior, 42*, 501–509.

Mick, T. M., & Hollander, E. (2006). Impulsive-compulsive sexual behavior. *CNS Spectrums, 11*, 994–995.

Miletski, H. (2001). Zoophilia: Implications for therapy. *Journal of Sex Education and Therapy, 26*, 85–89.

Miletski, H. (2005). Is zoophilia a sexual orientation? A study. In A. M. Beetz & A. L. Podberscek (Eds.), *Bestiality and zoophilia: Sexual relations with animals* (pp. 82–97). Purdue University Press.

Mohr, J. W., Turner, R. E., & Jerry, M. B. (1964). *Pedophilia and exhibitionism*. University of Toronto Press.

Money, J., Jobaris, R., & Furth, G. (1977). Apotemnophilia: Two cases of self demand amputation as a sexual preference. *Journal of Sex Research, 13*, 115–124.

Money, J., & Simcoe, K. W. (1986). Acrotomophilia, sex, and disability: New concepts and case report. *Sexuality and Disability, 7*, 43–50.

Mueller, S. C., Wierckx, K., Jackson, K., & T'Sjoen, G. (2016). Circulating androgens correlate with resting-state MRI in transgender men. *Psychoneuroendocrinology, 73*, 91–98.

Nadler, R. P. (1968). Approach to psychodynamics of obscene telephone calls. *New York State Journal of Medicine, 68*, 521–526.

Newman, L. E., & Stoller, R. J. (1974). Nontranssexual men who seek sex reassignment. *American Journal of Psychiatry, 131*, 437–441.

Nieder, T. O., Herff, M., Cerwenka, S., Preuss, W. F., Cohen-Kettenis, P. T., De Cuypere, G., Hebold Haraldsen, I. R., & Richter-Appelt, H. (2011). Age of onset and sexual orientation in transsexual males and females. *Journal of Sexual Medicine, 8*, 783–791.

Nordling, N., Sandnabba, N. K., Santtila, P., & Alison, L. (2006). Differences and similarities between gay and straight individuals involved in the sadomasochistic subculture. *Journal of Homosexuality, 50*, 41–57.

Operario, D., Burton, J., Underhill, K., & Sevelius, J. (2008). Men who have sex with transgender women: Challenges to category-based HIV prevention. *AIDS & Behavior, 12*, 18–26.

Oswald, F., Lopes, A., Skoda, K., Hesse, C. L., & Pedersen, C. L. (2020). I'll show you mine so you'll show me yours: Motivations and personality variables in photographic exhibitionism. *Journal of Sex Research, 57*, 597–609.

Pakhomou, S. M. (2006). Methodological aspects of telephone scatologia: A case study. *International Journal of Law and Psychiatry, 29*, 178–185.

Pate, J. E., & Gabbard, G. O. (2003). Adult baby syndrome. *American Journal of Psychiatry, 160*, 1932–1936.

Peretti, P. O., & Rowan, M. (1983). Zoophilia: Factors related to its sustained practice. *Panminerva Medica, 25*, 127–131.

Poeppl, T. B., Eickhoff, S. B., Fox, P. T., Laird, A. R., Rupprecht, R., Langguth, B., & Bzdok, D. (2015). Connectivity and functional profiling of abnormal brain structure in pedophilia. *Human Brain Mapping, 26*, 2374–2386.

Price, M., Kafka, M., Commons, M. L., Gutheil, T. G., & Simpson, W. (2002). Telephone scatologia: Comorbidity with other paraphilias and paraphilia-related disorders. *International Journal of Law and Psychiatry, 25*, 37–49.

Quadland, M. C. (1985). Compulsive sexual behavior: Definition of a problem and an approach to treatment. *Journal of Sex & Marital Therapy, 11*, 121–132.

Rada, R. T., Laws, D. R., & Kellner, R. (1976). Plasma testosterone levels in the rapist. *Psychosomatic Medicine, 38*, 257–268.

Rada, R. T., Laws, D. R., Kellner, R., Stivastava, L., & Peake, G. (1983). Plasma androgens in violent and non-violent sex offenders. *Bulletin of the American Academy of Psychiatry and the Law, 11*, 149–158.

Rametti, G., Carrillo, B., Gomez-Gil, E., Junque, C., Segovia, S., Gomez, A, & Guillamon, A. (2011). White matter microstructure in female-to-male transsexuals before cross-sex hormone treatment. A diffusion tensor imaging study. *Journal of Psychiatric Research, 45*, 199–204.

Raviv, M. (1993). Personality characteristics of sexual addicts and gamblers. *Journal of Gambling Studies, 9*, 17–30.

Raymond, N. C., Coleman, E., & Miner, M. H. (2003). Psychiatric comorbidity and compulsive/impulsive traits in compulsive sexual behavior. *Comprehensive Psychiatry, 44*, 370–380.

Reay, B., Attwood, N., & Gooder, C. (2013). Inventing sex: The short history of sex addiction. *Sexuality & Culture, 17*, 1–19.

Reid, R. C., & Carpenter, B. N. (2009). Exploring relationships of psychopathology in hypersexual patients using the MMPI-2. *Journal of Sex and Marital Therapy, 35*, 294–310.

Reid, R. C., Garos, S., Carpenter, B. N., & Coleman, E. (2011). A surprising finding related to executive control in a patient sample of hypersexual men. *Journal of Sexual Medicine, 8*, 2227–2236.

Reid, R. C., Karim, R., McCrory, E., & Carpenter, B. N. (2010). Self-reported differences on measures of executive function and hypersexual behavior in a patient and community sample of men. *International Journal of Neuroscience, 120*, 120–127.

Remillard, G. M., Andermann, F., & Testa, G. F. (1983). Sexual ictal manifestations predominate in women with temporal lobe epilepsy: A finding suggesting sexual dimorphism in the human brain. *Neurology, 33*, 323–330.

Revitch, E. (1978). Sexual motivated burglaries. *Bulletin of the American Association of Psychiatry and the Law, 6*, 277–283.

Rosenthal, A. M., Hsu, K. J., & Bailey, J. M. (2017). Who are gynandromorphophilic men? An Internet survey of men with sexual interest in transgender women. *Archives of Sexual Behavior, 46*, 255–264.

Rosman, J. P., & Resnick, P. J. (1989). Sexual attraction to corpses: A psychiatric review of necrophilia. *Bulletin of the American Academy of Psychiatry and the Law, 17*, 153–163.

Safarik, M. E., Jarvis, J. P., & Nussbaum, K. E. (2002). Sexual homicide of elderly females: Linking offender characteristics to victim and crime scene attributes. *Journal of Interpersonal Violence, 17,* 500–525.

Savic, I., & Arver, S. (2011). Sex dimorphism of the brain in male-to female transsexuals. *Cerebral Cortex, 21,* 2525–2533.

Sawle, G. A., & Kear-Colwell, J. (2001). Adult attachment style and pedophilia: A developmental perspective. *International Journal of Offender Therapy and Comparative Criminology, 45,* 32–50.

Shapira, N. A., Goldsmith, T. D., Keck Jr., P. E., Khosla, U. M., & McElroy, S. L. (2000). Psychiatric features of individuals with problematic internet use. *Journal of Affective Disorders, 57,* 267–272.

Schiffer, B., Amelung, T., Pohl, A., Kaergel, C., Tenbergen, G., Gerwinn, H., Mohnke, S., Massau, C., Matthias, W., Weiß, S., Marr, V., Beier, K. M., Walter, M., Ponseti, J., Krüger, T. H. C., Schiltz, K., & Walter, H. (2017). Gray matter anomalies in pedophiles with and without a history of child sexual offending. *Translational Psychiatry, 7,* e1129. doi:10.1038/tp.2017.96

Schiffer, B., Peschel, T., Paul, T., Gizewski, E., Forsting, M., Leygraf, N., Schedlowski, M., & Krueger, T. H. C. (2007). Structural brain abnormalities in the frontostriatal system and cerebellum in pedophilia. *Journal of Psychiatric Research, 41,* 753–762.

Schiltz, K., Witzel, J., Northoff, G., Zierhut, K., Gubka, U., Fellman, H., Kaufmann, J., Tempelmann, C., Wiebking, D., & Bogerts, B. (2007). Brain pathology in pedophilic offenders: Evidence of volume reduction in the right amygdala and related diencephalic structures. *Archives of General Psychiatry, 64,* 737–746.

Seidman, B. T., Marshall, W. L., Hudson, S. M., & Robertson, P. J. (1994). An examination of intimacy and loneliness in sex offenders. *Journal of Interpersonal Violence, 9,* 518–534.

Seim, H. C., & Dwyer, M. A. (1988). Evaluation of serum testosterone and luteinizing hormone levels in sex offenders. *Family Practice Research Journal, 7,* 175–180.

Seto, M. C. (2008). *Pedophilia and sexual offending against children: Theory, assessment, and intervention.* American Psychological Association.

Seto, M. C. (2013). *Internet sex offenders.* American Psychological Association.

Seto, M. C., Cantor, J. M., & Blanchard, R. (2006). Child pornography offenses are a valid diagnostic indicator of pedophilia. *Journal of Abnormal Psychology, 115,* 610–615.

Simon, R. I. (1997). Video voyeurs and the covert videotaping of unsuspecting victims: Psychological and legal consequences. *Journal of Forensic Sciences, 42,* 884–889.

Smallbone, S. W. (2006). An attachment-theoretical revision of Marshall and Barbaree's integrated theory of the etiology of sexual offending. In W. L. Marshall, Y. M. Fernandez, L. E. Marshall, & G. A. Serran (Eds.), *Sex offender treatment: Controversial issues* (pp. 93–107). Wiley.

Smallbone, S. W., & Dadds, M. R. (1998). Childhood attachment and adult attachment inincarcerated adule male sex offenders. *Journal of Interpersonal Violence, 13,* 555–573.

Smith, M. D., & Morra, N. N. (1994). Obscene and threatening phone calls to women: Data from a Canadian national survey. *Gender and Society, 8,* 584–596.

Smith, Y. L. S., van Goozen, S. H. M., Kuiper, A. J., & Cohen-Kettenis, P. T. (2005). Transsexual subtypes: Clinical and theoretical significance. *Psychiatry Research, 137,* 151–160.

Spizzirri, G., Duran, F. L. S., Chaim-Avancini, T. M., Serpa, M. H., Cavallet, M., Pereira, C. M. A., Santos, P. P., Squarzoni, P., da Costa, N. A., Busatto, G. F., & Najjar Abdo, C. H. (2018). Grey and white matter volumes either in treatment-naïve or hormone-treated transgender women: A voxel-based morphometric study. *Nature: Scientific Reports, 8*(736). doi:10.1038/s41598-017-17563-z

Steele, V. R., Staley, C., Fong, T., & Prause, N. (2013). Sexual desire, not hypersexuality is related to neurophysiological responses elicited by sexual images. *Socioaffective Neuroscience & Psychology, 3,* 20770.

Stein, M. L., Schlesinger, L. B., & Pinizzotto, A. J. (2010). Necrophilia and sexual homicide. *Journal of Forensic Sciences, 55,* 443–446.

Stekel, W. (1930). *Sexual aberrations: The phenomenon of fetishism in relation to sex* (vol. 1) (S. Parker, Trans.). Liveright.

Stephens, S., Leroux, E., Skilling, T., Cantor, J. M., & Seto, M. C. (2017). Taxometric analyses of pedophilia using self-report, behavioral, and sexual arousal indicators. *Journal of Abnormal Psychology, 126,* 1114–1119.

Stephens, S., Seto, M. C., Goodwill, A. M., & Cantor, J. M. (2017). Evidence of construct validity in the assessment of hebephilia. *Archives of Sexual Behavior, 46,* 301–309.

Stevens, E., & Wood, J. (2019). "I despise myself for thinking about them." A thematic analysis of the mental health implications and employed coping mechanisms of self-reported non-offending minor attracted persons. *Journal of Child Sexual Abuse, 28,* 968–989.

Stoléru, S., Fonteille, V., Cornélis, C., Joyal, C., & Moulier, V. (2012). Functional neuroimaging studies of sexual arousal and orgasm in healthy men and women: A review and meta-analysis. *Neuroscience & Biobehavioral Reviews, 36,* 1481–1509.

Uva, J. L. (1995). Review: Autoerotic asphyxiation in the United States. *Journal of Forensic Sciences, 40,* 574–581.

Vanden Bergh, R. L., & Kelly, J. F. (1964). Vampirism: A review with new observations. *Archives of General Psychiatry, 11,* 543–547.

van Dijk, M. T., van Wingen, G. A., van Lammeren, A., Blom, R. M., de Kwaasteniet, B. P., Scholte, H. S., & Denys, D. (2013). Neural basis of limb ownership in individuals with Body Integrity Identity Disorder. *PLoS ONE, 8,* e72212.

Wallien, M. S. C., Quilty, L. C., Steensma, T. D., Singh, D., Lambert, S. L., Leroux, A., Owen-Anderson, A., Kibblewhite, S. J., Bradley, S. J., Cohen-Kettenis, P. T., & Zucker, K J. (2009). Cross-national replication of the Gender Identity Interview for children. *Journal of Personality Assessment, 91,* 545–552.

Ward, T., Hudson, S. M., & Marshall, W. L. (1996). Attachment style in sex offenders: A preliminary study. *Journal of Sex Research, 33,* 17–26.

Ward, T., & Seigert, R. J. (2002). Toward a comprehensive theory of child sexual abuse: A theory knitting perspective. *Psychology, Crime & Law, 8,* 319–351.

Warrier, V., Greenberg, D. M., Weir, E., Buckingham C., Smith, P., Meng-Chuan, L., Allison, C., & Baron-Cohen, S. (2020). Elevated rates of autism, other neurodevelopmental and psychiatric diagnoses, and autistic traits in transgender and gender-diverse individuals. *Nature Communications, 11,* 3959.

Waxman-Fiduccia, B. F. (1999). Sexual imagery of physically disabled women: Erotic? Perverse? Sexist? *Sexuality and Disability, 17,* 277–282.

Weinberg, M. S., & Williams, C. J. (2010). Men sexually interesting in transwomen (MSTW): Gendered embodiment and the construction of sexual desire. *Journal of Sex Research, 47,* 374–383.

Weinberg, M. S., Williams, C. J., & Calhan, C. (1994). Homosexual foot fetishism. *Archives of Sexual Behavior, 23*, 611–626.

Weinberg, M. S., Williams, C. J., & Calhan, C. (1995). "If the shoe fits . . .": Exploring male homosexual foot fetishism. *Journal of Sex Research, 32*, 17–27.

Wernik, U. (1990). The nature of explanation in sexology and the riddle of triolism. *Annals of Sex Research, 3*, 5–20.

Wiepjes, C. M., den Heijer, M., Bremmer, M. A., Nota, N. M., de Blok, C. J. M., Coumou, B. J. G., & Steensma, T. D. (2020). Trends in suicide death risk in transgender people: Results from the Amsterdam Cohort of Gender Dysphoria study (1972–2017). *Acta Psychiatrica Scandinavica, 141*, 486–491.

Williams, C. J., & Weinberg, M. S. (2003). Zoophilia in men: A study of sexual interest in animals. *Archives of Sexual Behavior, 32*, 523–535.

Wilson, G. D., & Cox, D. N. (1983). Personality of paedophile club members. *Personality and Individual Differences, 4*, 323–329.

Wilson, P., Sharp, C., & Carr, S. (1999). The prevalence of gender dysphoria in Scotland: A primary care study. *British Journal of General Practice, 49*, 991–992.

Zamboni, B. D. (2019). A qualitative exploration of Adult Baby/Diaper Lover behavior from a online community sample. *Journal of Sex Research, 56*, 191–202.

Zhou, J. N., Hofman, M. A., Gooren, L. J., & Swaab, D. F. (1995). A sex difference in the human brain and its relation to transsexuality. *Nature, 378*, 68–70.

Zucker, K. J., Bradley, S. J., Kuksis, M., Pecore, K., Birkenfeld-Adams, A., Doering, R. W., Mitchell, J. N., & Wild, J. (1999). Gender constancy judgments in children with gender identity disorder: Evidence for a developmental lag. *Archives of Sexual Behavior, 28*, 475–502.

Zucker, K. J., Bradley, S. J., Lowry Sullivan, C. B., Kuksis, M., Birkenfeld-Adams, A., & Mitchell, J. N. (1993). A gender identity interview for children. *Journal of Personality Assessment, 61*, 443–456.

PART III

# Personality Disorders

# CHAPTER 25

# The DSM-5 Level of Personality Functioning Scale

Johannes Zimmermann, Christopher J. Hopwood, *and* Robert F. Krueger

Personality disorders (PDs) are common in the general population and are associated with many negative consequences for both the person affected as well as their environment (Hengartner et al., 2018; Tyrer et al., 2015). The disorder is highly relevant for professionals from the healthcare system as it can severely affect their interactions with the patient as well as the success of medical and therapeutic interventions. A valid classification system is an indispensable prerequisite for the efficient diagnosis and treatment of and research into the causes of PD. Current classification systems for PD, such as the one in *DSM-5* Section II, list purportedly distinct disorders; in the case of *DSM-5*, they are paranoid, schizoid, schizotypal, antisocial, borderline, histrionic, narcissistic, avoidant, dependent, and obsessive-compulsive PD. This categorical approach has come under criticism and is likely to be replaced in the long term by dimensional approaches. A central concept in this paradigm shift is the idea of a continuum in personality functioning, one ranging from healthy to extremely disturbed personality. This idea of PD severity has been exemplified in Criterion A of the alternative model for personality disorders (AMPD) in *DSM-5* Section III, which is operationalized by the Level of Personality Functioning Scale (LPFS). The purpose of this chapter is to explain why and how the LPFS was developed, what measures are available based on its definition, and what empirical evidence exists on various aspects of the reliability, validity, and clinical utility of these measures. Additionally, controversies and open questions will be addressed.

## Arguments in Favor of Taking Severity of PD into Account

There are a number of arguments in favor of including a severity scale in a classification system for PD. First, as with the vast majority of mental disorders, underlying individual differences in PD are continuously distributed and do not consist of two discrete groups of individuals with and without the disorder (Haslam et al., 2020). For example, the observed patterns of symptoms of borderline PD (Conway et al., 2012), narcissistic PD (Aslinger et al., 2018), and schizotypal PD (Ahmed et al., 2013) are all consistent with a dimensional rather than a categorical model. Overcoming the relatively arbitrary division into individuals with and without disorder and exploiting the multiple gradations of severity will significantly improve the reliability and validity of measurements (Markon et al., 2011). It will also make it possible to account for the substantial proportion of individuals who exhibit mild

**Abbreviations**

| | |
|---|---|
| AMPD | Alternative model for personality disorder |
| g-PD | General factor of PD |
| GAF | Global Assessment of Functioning (scale) |
| GAPD | General Assessment of Personality Disorder |
| LPFS | Level of Personality Functioning Scale |
| OPD | Operationalized Psychodynamic Diagnosis |
| PD | Personality disorder |
| PDM | Psychodynamic Diagnostic Manual |
| SASPD | Standardized Assessment of Severity of Personality Disorder |
| SIPP-118 | Severity Indices of Personality Problems |
| STiP | Semi-Structured Interview of Personality Functioning |

579

personality problems that are nevertheless associated with diminished functioning (Karukivi et al., 2017; Thompson et al., 2019; Yang et al., 2010).

Second, it has long been known that PD diagnoses often co-occur, which is usually referred to as "comorbidity." For example, in a study of outpatients, it was found that of all patients who met criteria for PD, approximately 60% met criteria for at least one other PD (Zimmerman et al., 2005). Indeed, from a factor analytic perspective, there is considerable evidence for a general PD factor: when all PD diagnoses or criteria are considered together, they are shown to load not only on specific factors but also on a general factor (Conway et al., 2016; Hengartner et al., 2014; Paap et al., 2021; Ringwald et al., 2019; Sharp et al., 2015; Williams et al., 2018). Although the strength of the general factor varies across samples and assessment methods, it can be concluded that there is indeed a common construct underlying most of the individual PD criteria. This construct can be interpreted as the general severity of PD (g-PD), in a similar way as the g-factor of intelligence.

Third, g-PD, in terms of the total number of PD criteria met across all categories, has been repeatedly shown to be a good predictor of current and future problems in various life domains (Conway et al., 2016; Hopwood et al., 2011; Williams et al., 2018; Wright et al., 2016). Although other specific factors related to stylistic aspects or traits usually also contribute to prediction, g-PD is often the strongest predictor in relative terms. This suggests that a direct mapping of severity is highly relevant in terms of prognosis. Accordingly, proposals have now been developed on how to use PD severity to plan therapy (Bach & Simonsen, 2021; Hopwood, 2018). While a less-structured and -intensive treatment setting may be beneficial for a milder severity level (e.g., group therapy), a structured treatment setting with clear boundaries appears to be necessary for severe impairment, and the clinician must be very intentional about building the relationship, repairing ruptures, and preventing dropout. In general, due to its prognostic relevance, severity appears to be particularly useful for determining a patient's level of care.

Fourth, reanalysis of a longitudinal study of PD demonstrates that g-PD has much less absolute stability compared to the specific factors (Wright et al., 2016). For example, mean severity decreased by more than 1 standard deviation over a 10-year period, whereas scores on the specific factors (with the exception of compulsivity) changed little on average. This suggests that general severity captures not only a large part of interindividual differences but also a large part of intraindividual changes in PD symptoms over time. This is relevant because change in PD symptoms is often the central endpoint for therapeutic interventions (e.g., Cristea et al., 2017).

Finally, the introduction of a severity continuum would also improve public recognition of the modifiable nature of PD and thus hopefully help destigmatize the diagnosis. For example, Tyrer et al. (2015) expressed the hope that treating experts might then be more willing to make the diagnosis even in adolescence (to enable early interventions) because it would in principle be seen as modifiable and not as a lifelong label. This is also in line with a recent meta-analysis on the relationship between a dimensional understanding of mental disorders and stigmatization: the more people assume a continuum between mental health and illness, the less they tend to have stigmatizing attitudes toward people with mental disorders (Peter et al., 2021).

## Arguments for the Central Role of Impairments in Self and Interpersonal Functioning

If one agrees that a classification system for PD should reflect general severity, the question arises as to how severity should be operationalized in concrete terms. Various proposals have been made, some long before the AMPD was developed (Crawford et al., 2011). For example, severity could simply be determined by the number of categorical PD diagnoses (Tyrer & Johnson, 1996) or measured separately using the Global Assessment of Functioning (GAF) scale (Widiger & Trull, 2007) or a list of negative consequences (Leising & Zimmermann, 2011). The latter options would map how severely a person is impaired in performing roles and activities of daily living, including social activities, school or work, recreation or leisure, and basic activities of self-care and mobility.

Opting for a different approach, the *DSM-5* workgroup based severity on the degree of impairment of internal abilities that underlie the perception and regulation of self and interpersonal relationships (Skodol, 2012). An important reason for this was to provide a substantive link to the general criteria for PDs, thus ensuring a relatively high degree of specificity for pathological *personality* processes (Bender et al., 2011). As the general criteria for PD introduced in *DSM-IV* were considered vague and ineffective (Livesley, 1998; Parker et al., 2002), a major goal of the *DSM-5* workgroup was to elaborate on the core substantive features of personality pathology.

Earlier research had suggested that the features common to all PD relate to problems of the self (e.g., identity disturbance, low self-direction) and to problems in interpersonal relationships (e.g., isolation, uncooperativeness, fear of rejection) (Gutiérrez et al., 2008; Hopwood et al., 2011; Svrakic et al., 1993; Turkheimer et al., 2008). These content domains also emerged in a factor analysis of several general criteria for PD (Parker et al., 2004). In recent studies of the factor structure of individual PD criteria, features such as emotional dysregulation, distorted thoughts about self and others, and problematic interpersonal behaviors were also found to exhibit high loadings on the g-PD (Sharp et al., 2015; Williams et al., 2018). This is especially true for borderline personality disorder (BPD) criteria, which often did not load on specific factors at all and, to that extent, can be considered particularly "pure" markers of g-PD. Based on such findings, some authors have suggested that "it may be more fruitful to reconceptualize BPD—and particularly the criteria tapping impairment in self and interpersonal pathology . . . as reflecting a broad, general dimension of PD-severity rather than a specific PD category" (Clark et al., 2018). Taken together, there is evidence from studies with different empirical approaches that problems in the domains of self and interpersonal relationships are key general indicators of PD.

A further argument for the relevance of these domains comes from an analysis of the normative assumptions underlying PD diagnoses in *DSM-IV* (Leising et al., 2009). In this regard, one must first realize that assigning a PD diagnosis to a person necessarily involves comparing the person's personality to an image of how people "normally" should feel or behave. Leising et al. (2009) addressed this issue by semantically reversing the 79 individual PD criteria in *DSM-IV*, resulting in a set of positive expectations regarding desirable behavior. Cluster analysis of the sorting data revealed 10 higher-order clusters of values that cut across the 10 PD categories. Many of these values can be categorized as being related to self-functioning (e.g., be self-reliant and independent; be self-confident, but in a realistic manner; have self-control) and interpersonal functioning (e.g., get along with others; connect with others emotionally and treat them fairly; enjoy social relationships and activities). It could thus be argued that the implicit normative assumptions that appear to have guided the development of the PD criteria in *DSM-IV* already include the foci of self and interpersonal relationships.

The relevance of these domains is also emphasized in many major theories of PD, including psychodynamic (Clarkin et al., 2020; Luyten & Blatt, 2013), interpersonal (Hopwood et al., 2013; Pincus et al., 2020), and attachment (Meyer & Pilkonis, 2005) theories. Another approach that brings this particularly into focus comes from Livesley (1998). According to his understanding, the core of PD is the failure to develop self and interpersonal capacities necessary to perform important life tasks. Last, such a definition of the general characteristics of PD also allows Wakefield's (1992) notion of "dysfunction" to be introduced into the definition of PD. Accordingly, PD is not merely a pattern of experience and behavior that is harmful or negative in terms of social values, but rather it emerges from an underlying dysfunction in which a psychological mechanism fails and no longer performs the natural function for which it was selected in the course of evolution (Krueger et al., 2007).

## Development of the *DSM-5* Level of Personality Functioning Scale

These and similar considerations have led the *DSM-5* workgroup to develop a revised Criterion A that both requires the presence of significant impairments in self and interpersonal functioning for a diagnosis of PD and also can be used simultaneously to determine the severity of impairment (Skodol, 2012). The result of this development process is the LPFS, which is an operationalization of this new general Criterion A. Originally, it was envisioned that the revised criteria, including the LPFS, would replace the categorical PDs of *DSM-IV*, but in the end it was decided to add them as an alternative model in Section III of *DSM-5*.

The *DSM-5* workgroup initially took a two-pronged approach. First, data were reanalyzed on two self-report instruments available at the time that were designed to measure impaired personality functioning (Morey et al., 2011). The two instruments were the Severity Indices of Personality Problems (SIPP-118; Verheul et al., 2008) and the General Assessment of Personality Disorder (GAPD; Livesley, 2006). Item response theory (IRT) models were used to select items that measured the general factor well at different levels of severity. The item set was then validated using external data on severity (e.g., the presence of a PD diagnosis according to structured interviews or the total number of PD criteria met). The selected items covered the theoretically expected deficits in the domain of the self (e.g., identity integration, integrity of self-concept) and interpersonal relationships (e.g., capacity for empathy and intimacy).

Second, although members of the *DSM-5* workgroup emphasized the transtheoretical background of the LPFS (Bender et al., 2011), psychodynamically oriented models and measures have been particularly influential in its development (Blüml & Doering, 2021; Clarkin et al., 2020; Hörz-Sagstetter et al., 2021; Yalch, 2020; Zimmermann et al., 2012). It is one of the central assumptions of many psychodynamic models that maladaptive mental representations of self and others form the core of personality pathology and that the degree of disturbance can be assessed along different levels of functioning (Kernberg, 1984; Luyten & Blatt, 2013; Westen et al., 2006). Kernberg (1984) proposed, for example, that levels of personality organization are manifested in three domains of functioning: (a) integration of one's identity (i.e., the ability to develop nuanced and stable images of self and others), (b) maturity of defense mechanisms (i.e., the ability to process threatening internal and external stimuli in an adaptive manner), and (c) integrity of reality testing (i.e., the ability to distinguish between internal and external stimuli and make contact with a socially shared reality). Kernberg also distinguished three levels of severity based on the degree of impairment in these areas of functioning: namely, neurotic, borderline, and psychotic personality organization. More recent psychodynamic conceptualizations of severity, such as the Level of Structural Integration Axis of the Operationalized Psychodynamic Diagnosis-2 (OPD Task Force, 2008; Zimmermann et al., 2012) or the Mental Functioning Axis of the Psychodynamic Diagnostic Manual-2 (PDM-2; Lingiardi & McWilliams, 2017), are similar to Kernberg's model in that they refer to impairments in basic psychological capacities and distinguish between several prototypical levels of functioning.

Against this background, it is unsurprising that members of the *DSM-5* workgroup encountered only psychodynamically oriented measures in their search for relevant expert clinical assessment systems (Bender et al., 2011). To justify and streamline the initial LPFS proposal, the authors established methodological criteria for instruments to be considered in the broader *DSM-5* revision process. The instruments should (a) include important dimensions of psychological functioning; (b) have a self-other focus; (c) have been used in studies with general clinical samples, with personality disordered samples, or with both; (d) have concepts useful to a wide range of clinicians; (e) be appropriate for assessing clinical interview material; and (f) have published psychometric data on relevant domains of functioning. Using these criteria, Bender et al. (2011) identified the following five psychodynamically based instruments: the Quality of Object Relations Scale (QORS; Azim et al., 1991), the Personality Organization Diagnostic Form (PODF; Gamache et al., 2009), the Object Relations Inventory (ORI; Blatt et al., 1988), the Social Cognition and Object Relations Scale (SCORS; Westen et al., 1990), and the Reflective Functioning Scale (RFS; Fonagy et al., 1998). The final version of the LPFS can thus also be seen as an attempt to integrate existing psychodynamic rating scales of personality functioning while maximizing reliability and clinical utility.

In the final stage of development, the diagnostic threshold for the presence of PD was determined empirically. This was based on a pilot study of the AMPD in which 337 clinicians each assessed one of their patients using the categorical *DSM-IV* model and the new AMPD (Morey et al., 2013). The cutoff score of 2 on the LPFS scale of 0–4 achieved a sensitivity of 84.6% and a specificity of 72.7% in predicting the presence (vs. absence) of at least one diagnosable PD according to *DSM-IV*. This level was therefore set as the threshold for the diagnosis of PD.

### The *DSM-5* Level of Personality Functioning Scale

Criterion A is used to determine the presence and severity of PD and can be assessed using the LPFS. The LPFS defines the severity of PD based on the degree of impairment in self and interpersonal functioning. This severity continuum is further specified by psychological characteristics considered typical of different degrees of impairment in the "components" (*DSM-5*, p. 772) of identity and self-direction (i.e., self-functioning) and empathy and intimacy (i.e., interpersonal functioning). Each of the four components is further broken down into three subcomponents. Intimacy, for example, means that a person (a) can form deep and lasting relationships with others, (b) wants to and can be close to others, and (c) treats others with respect. Table 25.1 summarizes all four components and 12 subcomponents. Note that despite these fine-grained definitions, all components and subcomponents are intended to represent a general dimension of PD severity. The LPFS classifies this continuum into five different "levels" of impairment, beginning with little or no impairment (level 0), moving

**Table 25.1** Components and subcomponents of personality functioning according to Criterion A

| Component | Subcomponents |
|---|---|
| Identity | Sense of self<br>Self-esteem and accurate self-perception<br>Emotional range and regulation |
| Self-direction | Ability to pursue meaningful goals<br>Prosocial internal standards of behavior<br>Self-reflective functioning |
| Empathy | Understanding others' experiences and motivations<br>Tolerance of differing perspectives<br>Understanding effects of own behavior on others |
| Intimacy | Depth and duration of connections<br>Desire and capacity for closeness<br>Mutuality of regard |

*Note*: Adapted from *DSM-5*, p. 762.

through mild (level 1), moderate (level 2), severe (level 3), and ending with extreme impairment (level 4). With level 0, the description of a healthy personality without impairments is explicitly provided for the first time in *DSM-5*. As mentioned above, moderate impairment (level 2) represents the threshold for the presence of PD.

To facilitate assessment, the LPFS operationalizes all 60 possible combinations of subcomponents and levels using prototypical descriptions (see the table on p. 775 of *DSM-5*). For example, the respective paragraphs for the first subcomponent within self-direction (i.e., *ability to pursue meaningful goals*) are "Sets and aspires to reasonable goals based on a realistic assessment of personal capacities" (level 0); "Excessively goal-directed, somewhat goal-inhibited, or conflicted about goals" (level 1); "Goals are more often a means of gaining external approval than self-generated and thus may lack coherence and/or stability" (level 2); "Difficulty establishing and/or achieving personal goals" (level 3); and "Poor differentiation of thoughts from actions, so goal-setting ability is severely compromised, with unrealistic or incoherent goals" (level 4). The diagnostician is asked to match these descriptions to the specific case and indicate on a global 5-point scale which level of functioning best corresponds to the patient's overall functioning (i.e., across all four components). In other words, each patient is assigned a single overall score on the LPFS.

## Measures Based on the *DSM-5* Level of Personality Functioning Scale

Central to measuring PD severity in research and practice to date has been the use of the LPFS itself. Originally, this involved an expert rating on a single 5-point scale as described above (Morey et al., 2013). Other researchers have applied the LPFS in a more sophisticated way by having the four components (Dereboy et al., 2018; Few et al., 2013), the 12 subcomponents (Cruitt et al., 2019; Hutsebaut et al., 2017; Preti et al., 2018; Roche, 2018; Zimmermann et al., 2014), or the 60 prototypical descriptions (Zimmermann et al., 2015) assessed separately and then aggregating the ratings into an overall score. For the purpose of collecting self-report data, some researchers have asked individuals to self-report according to prototypical descriptions of the 12 subcomponents (Bliton et al., 2021; Dowgwillo et al., 2018; Roche et al., 2016, 2018). For the purpose of informant reports, it has been suggested that the 60 prototypical descriptions of the LPFS can also be individually assessed by laypersons (Morey, 2018; Zimmermann et al., 2015).

Following the publication of *DSM-5*, new measurement instruments have been developed to implement the operationalization of severity according to the LPFS (Birkhölzer et al., 2020; Zimmermann et al., 2019). These measures are summarized in Table 25.2, including references to validated translations. On the one hand, structured clinical interviews are available to systematically collect information relevant to applying the LPFS. For example, the Structured Clinical Interview for the Level of Personality Functioning Scale (SCID-AMPD Module I; Bender, Skodol, et al., 2018) has a funnel structure, starting with open-ended questions for each subcomponent to get an initial impression of severity and then going in-depth according to that impression with specific follow-up questions for the assumed level. The Semi-Structured Interview for Personality Functioning DSM-5 (STiP-5.1; Hutsebaut et al., 2017) has a similar funnel structure and can also be used on adolescents (Weekers, Verhoeff, et al., 2021).

On the other hand, several self-reports are available that build on the understanding of PD severity according to LPFS but use items that are easier for laypersons to understand. These measures differ in number of items and differentiation into subscales. For example, the Level of Personality Functioning Scale-Brief Form (LPFS-BF; Hutsebaut et al., 2016; updated version LPFS-BF 2.0; Weekers et al., 2019) comprises only 12 items in total, with

**Table 25.2** Measures for the assessment of personality functioning according to the LPFS

| Measure | Authors | Original language and validated translations | Method | Items | Scales |
|---|---|---|---|---|---|
| Clinical Assessment of the Level of Personality Functioning Scale (CALF) | Thylstrup et al. (2016) | Danish | Structured interview | 4 | 1 |
| *DSM-5* Levels of Personality Functioning Questionnaire (DLOPFQ) | Huprich et al. (2018); Siefert et al. (2020) | English | Self-report | 23/132 | 4/8 |
| Level of Personality Functioning Scale—Self-Report (LPFS-SR) | Morey (2017) | English German (Zimmermann et al., 2020); Persian (Hemmati et al., 2020) | Self-report | 80 | 4 |
| Level of Personality Functioning Scale—Brief Form (LPFS-BF; LPFS-BF 2.0) | Hutsebaut et al. (2016); Weekers et al. (2019) | Dutch English (Stone et al., 2020); Danish (Bach & Hutsebaut, 2018); German (Spitzer et al., 2021); Czech (Heissler et al., 2021) | Self-report | 12 | 2 |
| Personality Functioning Scale (PFS) | Stover et al. (2020) | Spanish | Self-report | 28 | 2 |
| Levels of Personality Functioning Questionnaire for Adolescents from 12 to 18 Years (LoPF-Q 12-18) | Goth et al. (2018) | German Turkish (Cosgun et al., 2021) | Self-report | 97 | 4/8 |
| Self and Interpersonal Functioning Scale (SIFS) | Gamache et al. (2019) | French | Self-report | 24 | 1/4 |
| Semi-Structured Interview for Personality Functioning DSM–5 (STiP-5.1) | Hutsebaut et al. (2017) | Dutch German (Zettl et al., 2020); Czech (Heissler et al., 2021) | Structured interview | 12 | 1/4 |
| Structured Clinical Interview for the Level of Personality Functioning Scale (SCID-AMPD Module I) | Bender, Skodol, et al. (2018) | English German (Kampe et al., 2018); Italian (Somma et al., 2020); Norwegian (Buer Christensen et al., 2018); Danish (Meisner et al., 2021) | Structured interview | 12 | 1/4 |

each item describing impairment in one subcomponent. The evaluation refers to the two subscales of impairments in self and interpersonal functioning as well as to an overall score. Because of its efficiency and compatibility with *ICD-11* (see below), the LPFS-BF 2.0 has recently been proposed to be used as part of a standard battery for patient-reported outcomes in PD (Prevolnik Rupel et al., 2021). In contrast, the Level of Personality Functioning Scale-Self-Report (LPFS-SR; Morey, 2017) comprises 80 items, each describing different levels of severity from all 12 subcomponents. Items are aggregated on a weighted basis according to severity, yielding four scales for impairments in the components of identity, self-direction, empathy, and intimacy, as well as a total score. Finally, one self-report measure, the Levels of Personality Functioning Questionnaire for Adolescents from 12 to 18 Years (LoPF-Q 12-18; Goth et al., 2018), was directly tailored to the target population of adolescents.

Further developments to measure severity according to LPFS include items that can be used in the context of intensive longitudinal designs. In this way, fluctuations and nuanced temporal dynamics in the components of identity, self-direction, empathy, and intimacy can be revealed (Roche et al., 2016, 2018). In addition, impairment scales have been developed to examine the validity of impairment criteria for the six specific PDs listed under the rubric of Criterion A in the AMPD (Anderson & Sellbom, 2018; Liggett et al., 2017; Liggett & Sellbom, 2018; McCabe & Widiger, 2020). What is not yet available but could be useful in higher-risk clinical settings are indices that indicate negligent or biased responses.

## Psychometric Properties and Empirical Findings Pertaining to the LPFS

Numerous reviews have summarized the theoretical underpinnings and current research findings on personality functioning in the AMPD (Bach & Simonsen, 2021; Bender, Zimmermann, & Huprich, 2018; Clark et al., 2018; Herpertz et al., 2017; Hörz-Sagstetter et al., 2021; Morey & Bender, 2021; Pincus, 2018; Pincus et al., 2020; Sharp & Wall, 2021; Sinnaeve et al., 2021; Sleep et al., 2021; Widiger et al., 2019; Zimmermann et al., 2019; Hopwood et al., in press). We provide here an updated comprehensive summary of research on the LPFS. We include only studies that applied the LPFS or one of the measures listed in Table 25.2, ensuring high specificity for AMPD definitions of severity. Results are organized according to the questions of (a) interrater reliability, (b) internal consistency and latent structure, (c) convergent validity, (d) discriminant and incremental validity, and (e) clinical utility.

### Interrater Reliability

Interrater reliability refers to agreement between judges of the same individual's level of personality functioning. Table 25.3 summarizes the studies that have examined the interrater reliability of the LPFS. Results suggest that interrater reliability is largely acceptable when using the LPFS based on case vignettes (Garcia et al., 2018; Morey, 2019), written life history data (Roche et al., 2018), personality or life story interviews (Cruitt et al., 2019; Roche & Jaweed, 2021), clinical interviews (Di Pierro et al., 2020; Few et al., 2013; Preti et al., 2018; Zimmermann et al., 2014), or unstructured clinical impressions (Dereboy et al., 2018), even among untrained and clinically inexperienced raters. Across these 10 studies including 676 targets and 3,451 ratings, the weighted intraclass correlation coefficient (ICC) for the LPFS total score was .55 (95% confidence interval [CI] .47, .63). However, training can increase interrater reliability (Garcia et al., 2018), and interrater reliability is usually significantly better when based on structured interviews that are explicitly tailored to collect the required information. Nine studies on such interviews have been conducted so far, including 276 targets and 662 ratings (Buer Christensen et al., 2018; Hutsebaut et al., 2017; Kampe et al., 2018; Meisner et al., 2021; Møller et al., 2021; Ohse et al., 2021; Somma et al., 2020; Thylstrup et al., 2016; Zettl et al., 2020). The weighted ICC for the LPFS total score across these studies was .83 (95% CI .75, .92), which is considered excellent (Cicchetti, 1994). An exception is the Clinical Assessment of the Level of Personality Functioning (CALF), where interrater reliability was at the lower limit, presumably because the interview does not probe closely enough the behaviors and experiences described in the LPFS and requires a higher degree of inference (Thylstrup et al., 2016). For the SCID-AMPD Module I, two studies are now available that use a more rigorous test-retest design in which patients are reinterviewed by a different person within a short period of time. Here, the ICC for the LPFS total score was .75 (Buer Christensen et al., 2018) and .84 (Ohse et al., 2021), respectively.

### Internal Consistency and Latent Structure

Internal consistency refers to the question of whether ratings of different aspects of a person's personality functioning result in similar test scores. In other words, the question is whether individual differences in these aspects are positively correlated and thus "consistent" and can be aggregated into a single construct. This can be considered at different levels in the LPFS and the derived self-report measures: For example, one can investigate whether the LPFS total score is internally consistent when looking at the ratings on the four components, or whether an LPFS-SR score regarding the component of empathy is internally consistent when looking at the ratings on the individual items. The results here are generally positive: for example, the internal consistency of the overall LPFS score has been shown to be acceptable when calculated based on ratings of the four components (Dereboy et al., 2018; Morey et al., 2013) and as very high when calculated based on scores of subcomponents (Bach & Hutsebaut, 2018; Cruitt et al., 2019; Dowgwillo et al., 2018; Hutsebaut et al., 2017) or individual items (Hopwood et al., 2018; Morey, 2017, 2018). Scores on the four components (Cruitt et al., 2019; Hopwood et al., 2018; Huprich et al., 2018; Morey, 2017, 2018; Zimmermann et al., 2014) and the 12 subcomponents (Zimmermann et al., 2015) also achieved fairly high internal consistency.

However, from the perspective of psychometric models such as IRT or factor analyses, high internal

**Table 25.3** Studies on the interrater reliability of the LPFS

| Sample | Source | Items | Raters | Raters per target | Targets | Total targets | ICC |
|---|---|---|---|---|---|---|---|
| Cruitt et al., (2019) | Life story interviews | 12 | Students | 3 | Older adults | 162 | .56 |
| Dereboy et al. (2018) | Observations during patients' stay at the ward | 4 | Psychiatrists and students | 4 | Patients | 20 | .67 |
| Di Pierro et al., (2020) | STIPO | 12 | Students | 2 | Patients and healthy controls | 12 | .80[b] |
| Few et al. (2013) | SCID-II | 4 | Students | 2 | Patients | 103 | .48[b] |
| Garcia et al. (2018) | Written case vignettes | 4 | Students | 13 | Patients | 15 | .81 |
| Morey (2019) | Written case vignettes | 1 | Mental health professionals | 40 | Patients | 12 | .50 |
| Preti et al. (2018) | STIPO | 12 | Students | 10 | Patients | 10 | .42 |
| Roche & Jaweed (2021) | Audiotaped brief personality interview | 12 | Students | 5 | Students | 92 | .52 |
| Roche et al. (2018), Sample 1 | Self-written psychological life history | 12 | Students | 5 | Students | 70 | .58 |
| Roche et al. (2018), Sample 2a | Self-written psychological life history | 12 | Students | 5 | Students | 85 | .42 |
| Roche et al. (2018), Sample 2b | Self-written psychological life history | 12 | Students | 5 | Students | 85 | .36 |
| Zimmermann et al (2014) | OPD interview | 12 | Students | 22 | Patients | 10 | .51 |
| Buer Christensen et al. (2018) | SCID-AMPD Module I | 12 | Clinicians and students | 5 | Patients | 17 | .96 |
| Hutsebaut et al. (2017) | STiP-5.1 | 12 | Psychologists | 2 | Patients[a] | 40 | .71 |
| Kampe et al. (2018) | SCID-AMPD Module I | 12 | Psychologist and student | 2 | Patients | 30 | .93 |
| Meisner et al. (2021) | SCID-AMPD Module I | 12 | Psychologist and psychiatrist | 3 | Patients | 15 | .79c |
| Møller et al. (2021) | SCID-AMPD Module I | 12 | Clinicians | 3 | Patients | 14 | .62c |
| Ohse et al. (2021) | SCID-AMPD Module I | 12 | Psychologists | 4 | Patients | 15 | .95 |
| Somma et al. (2020) | SCID-AMPD Module I | 12 | Clinical psychologists | 2 | Patients | 88 | .87 |
| Thylstrup et al. (2016) | CALF | 4 | Psychologists, medical doctors, student | 2 | Patients[a] | 30 | .54 |
| Zettl et al. (2020) | STiP-5.1 | 12 | Psychologists | 2 | Patients[a] | 27 | .77c |

*Note*: OPD, Operationalized Psychodynamic Diagnosis; SCID-II, Structured Clinical Interview for *DSM-IV* Personality Disorders; STIPO, Structured Interview of Personality Organization; ICC, Intraclass correlation coefficient for single raters.

a We only included results from the patient sample.

b We subsequently computed these values by averaging the ICCs for LPFS component scores.

c We subsequently corrected this value to provide an ICC for single raters.

consistency is not sufficient to justify the formation of an overall score. It is also required to test the fit of a measurement model according to which different ratings can be explained by an underlying latent variable. The first comprehensive analysis of the latent structure of LPFS was conducted by Zimmermann et al. (2015). Data were collected through an online study in which 515 laypersons and 145 therapists rated all 60 prototypical descriptions of the LPFS. Laypersons were asked to rate one of their personal acquaintances, whereas therapists were asked to rate one of their patients. The results on latent structure were broadly consistent with the assumptions of the LPFS, although there were some discrepancies. First, it was possible to demonstrate, using so-called unfolding IRT models (Roberts et al., 2000; see below), that most subcomponents are indeed unidimensional. This means that the ratings on the five prototypical descriptions of a subcomponent (e.g., *ability to pursue meaningful goals*, see above) can be explained by a single underlying latent dimension. There were however exceptions, such as the second subcomponent within intimacy (i.e., *desire and capacity for closeness*), where the pattern of associations between ratings turned out to be more complex. This could be due to the fact that the individual descriptions from this subcomponent emphasize quite different signs and explanations of impaired capacity for closeness (e.g., inhibition in level 1, self-regulation needs in level 2, and rejection sensitivity in level 3), suggesting that the underlying construct is rather multidimensional.

Second, using exploratory structural equation modeling, it was shown that the structure of the 12 subcomponents was largely consistent with a model that included two strongly correlated factors of self and interpersonal functioning. There were some discrepancies here as well: for example, there was not much support for the theoretical differentiation of self-functioning into identity and self-direction on the one hand and interpersonal functioning into empathy and intimacy on the other. Crucially, however, the high correlation of the two factors of self and interpersonal functioning is consistent with a model that assumes a strong general factor for the 12 subcomponents. Indeed, the proportion of variance in the LPFS total score that could be attributed to the general factor was .78, suggesting that while individuals may differ to some extent in their specific type of impairment (i.e., whether their personality problems are more related to self or interpersonal functioning), the main source of differences is related to the general severity of impairments. Thus, although forming an overall score may be difficult in some cases because impairment in self and interpersonal functioning differs too much, the use of a single score for the LPFS appears to be broadly acceptable in clinical practice.

Meanwhile, these findings on the latent structure of the subcomponents of the LPFS have been widely confirmed in other studies. Support for a model with two strongly correlated factors of self and interpersonal functioning has emerged in studies involving both self-reports based on the items of the LPFS (Bliton et al., 2021; Roche, 2018), the LPFS-BF (Bach & Hutsebaut, 2018; Bliton et al., 2021; Hutsebaut et al., 2016; Spitzer et al., 2021; Weekers et al., 2019) and the Personality Functioning Scale (PFS; Stover et al., 2020), as well as in expert ratings based on the SCID-AMPD Module I (Hummelen et al., 2021; Ohse et al., 2021) or STiP-5.1 (Heissler et al., 2021). Although this may challenge the theoretical differentiation into four components, it is consistent with the assumption of a strong general factor representing PD severity. Evidence for such a factor is also found in confirmatory factor analyses of SIPS items (Gamache et al., 2019) and principal component analyses of the four components of LPFS-SR (Hopwood et al., 2018; Morey, 2017) and LPFS (Cruitt et al., 2019). Item-level factor analyses of the LPFS-SR often deviate more from the theoretical structure or achieve poor model fit (Bliton et al., 2021; Hemmati et al., 2020; Sleep et al., 2019, 2020). This is at least partly due to the sheer size of the model (which can lead to biased fit statistics; Moshagen, 2012), as well as to method factors due to items with positive and negative valence. In any case, a strong general factor is also apparent in item-level analyses of the LPFS and LPFS-SR, which may justify the use of the overall score (Bliton et al., 2021; Leising et al., 2021). Interestingly, these analyses also indicated that loadings on the general factor were almost perfectly predictable from the social desirability of the items (Leising et al., 2021). This suggests that the impairments in personality functioning as defined by the LPFS and derivate measures are essentially guided by a social consensus of negatively valued experiences and behaviors.

Two other aspects of the LPFS are particularly challenging in the study of their latent structure—aspects that seem less relevant for constructs such as personality traits. First, the LPFS involves not only a differentiation into different components and subcomponents, but also into different levels that are supposed to represent different degrees of severity. The question, then, is whether the five individual descriptions of a given subcomponent are arranged in a theoretically consistent manner along the latent severity continuum. For example, the descriptions "Excessively goal-directed, somewhat goal-inhibited, or conflicted about goals" (level 1) and "Goals are more often a means of gaining external approval than self-generated and thus may lack coherence and/or stability" (level 2) should be located at different points on the latent severity continuum (i.e., the latter description should reflect a significantly higher severity level than the former description). In the study with informant ratings by Zimmermann et al. (2015), this assumption was tested using unfolding IRT models. In unfolding IRT models, a location parameter is estimated for each item, indicating where individuals are located on the latent dimension when they are most likely to agree with the item (Roberts et al., 2000). It was found that the relationship between the theoretically hypothesized severity levels and the empirically estimated location parameters was quite strong across all items. This largely supports the classification of the LPFS descriptions and confirms the results from surveys in which the items of the LPFS were directly assessed with respect to different severity concepts as well as social (un)desirability (Leising et al., 2018; Zimmermann et al., 2012). On the other hand, several location parameters emerged that deviated somewhat from this general pattern. For example, location parameters of the items for moderate, severe, and extreme impairment in subcomponents of identity (i.e., *sense of self, self-esteem and accurate self-perception*) and self-direction (i.e., *self-reflective functioning*) were all uniformly at the dysfunctional pole of the latent continuum, suggesting that, on average, raters did not capture the subtle differences in severity that the descriptions were intended to convey. Further studies are needed here to refine the LPFS descriptions accordingly, if necessary.

Second, strictly speaking, the AMPD does not mention clearly delineable factors in Criterion A, but rather "components" or "elements" that are described as "reciprocally influential and inextricably tied" (*DSM-5*, p. 772). This assumption is consistent with the high internal consistency of LPFS ratings, as interpenetrating elements should lead to strong positive correlations. However, the question arises whether factor analyses targeting relative stable differences between persons are sufficient or even appropriate to investigate such an assumption. Here, it would probably be useful to work with longitudinal studies to look at the reciprocal interrelationships of these elements within individuals over time; that is, to model the internal structure of personality functioning as a developmental process. To date, there is only one study using a 12-item version of the LPFS on a daily basis over 14 days that found clear evidence for a unidimensional latent structure at the within-person level (Roche, 2018). Studies that span longer time periods and test reciprocal, time-lagged effects between components do not yet exist.

*Convergent Validity*

Convergent validity concerns the question of whether ratings of personality functioning are highly correlated with other measures of the same or similar constructs. The most obvious test for this is to assess personality functioning according to the LPFS with two different measures and determine their correlation. Here, substantial correlations have been shown in the vast majority of studies to date, both between LPFS expert or informant ratings and self-report measures (Heissler et al., 2021; Nelson et al., 2018; Ohse et al., 2021; Roche et al., 2018; Roche & Jaweed, 2021; Somma et al., 2020; Weekers, Verhoeff, et al., 2021) as well as between different self-report measures (Bliton et al., 2021; McCabe et al., 2021a; Roche & Jaweed, 2021; Somma et al., 2020). An exception with null findings is a study with forensic patients, although here the sample was very small (Hutsebaut et al., 2021).

Substantial associations with numerous measures of similar constructs were found for other-reports of the LPFS. These studies are summarized in the left column of Table 25.4. For example, strong associations were found with established measures of impairments in personality functioning and PD severity, including number of PD diagnoses according to *DSM-IV* or psychodynamic conceptualizations of personality dysfunction. Additionally, studies have examined associations with more-distant constructs and indicators that do not directly support convergent validity of the LPFS as an expert rating but highlight its scientific and clinical relevance. These include associations with short-term risk, proposed treatment intensity, and estimated prognosis (Morey et al., 2013) and prior treatment for mental health problems (Cruitt et al., 2019), as well as risk of dropping out of residential treatment (Busmann et al., 2019). There are also studies linking LPFS ratings to biological parameters, such as intralimbic resting-state functional connectivity (Traynor et al., 2021). By contrast, no associations emerged with various measures of

**Table 25.4** Studies on the association between self- or other-reported impairments in personality functioning and measures of related clinical constructs

| Other-reports | Self-reports |
|---|---|
| Presence/number of PD diagnoses/criteria according to *DSM-IV* (Buer Christensen, Hummelen, et al., 2020; Cruitt et al., 2019; Dereboy et al., 2018; Di Pierro et al., 2020; Few et al., 2013; Hutsebaut et al., 2017; Morey et al., 2013; Preti et al., 2018; Zimmermann et al., 2014) | Impairments in personality functioning and PD severity (Bach & Anderson, 2020; Brown & Sellbom, 2020; Gamache et al., 2019; Hemmati et al., 2020; Hopwood et al., 2018; Hutsebaut et al., 2016; Jauk & Ehrenthal, 2021; Morey, 2017; Oltmanns & Widiger, 2019; Sleep et al., 2019; Sleep et al., 2020; Weekers et al., 2019) |
| Psychodynamic conceptualizations of personality dysfunction (Kampe et al., 2018; Ohse et al., 2021; Preti et al., 2018; Ruchensky et al., 2021; Zettl et al., 2020; Zimmermann et al., 2014) | Borderline PD symptoms (Gamache et al., 2019; Goth et al., 2018; Rishede et al., 2021) |
| | Low self-esteem (Gamache et al., 2019) |
| Self-reported personality pathology (Cruitt et al., 2019; Hutsebaut et al., 2017; Quilty et al., 2021) | Suicidality (Bach & Anderson, 2020; Roche & Jaweed, 2021) |
| | Subjective emptiness (Konjusha et al., 2021) |
| Impairments in psychosocial functioning (Buer Christensen, Eikenaes, et al., 2020; Morey et al., 2013) | Impairments in mentalizing (Müller, Wendt, Spitzer, et al., 2021; Müller, Wendt, & Zimmermann, 2021; Rishede et al., 2021) |
| Complex posttraumatic stress disorder and disturbances in self-organization (Møller et al., 2021) | Low emotional intelligence (Jauk & Ehrenthal, 2021) |
| | Narcissism and aggression (Gamache et al., 2019) |
| | Psychopathy (Persson & Lilienfeld, 2019) |
| Substance use history (Cruitt et al., 2019) | Intimate partner violence (Munro & Sellbom, 2020) |
| Mental and physical health problems (Cruitt et al., 2019) | Eating pathology (Biberdzic et al., 2021) |
| | Childhood adversity (Back et al., 2020; Gander et al., 2020) |
| Social and relational maladjustment (Cruitt et al., 2019) | Maternal bonding impairment (Fleck et al., 2021) |
| | Maladaptive schemas (Bach & Anderson, 2020; Bach & Hutsebaut, 2018) |
| Symptom distress (Few et al., 2013; Hutsebaut et al., 2017; Zettl et al., 2020) | Immature defenses (Roche et al., 2018) |
| | Insecure attachment (Gander et al., 2020; Huprich et al., 2018; Roche et al., 2018) |
| | Interpersonal dependency (Huprich et al., 2018) |
| | Interpersonal problems, sensitivities, motives, and efficacies (Dowgwillo et al., 2018; Hopwood et al., 2018; Roche et al., 2018; Roche & Jaweed, 2021; Stone et al., 2020) |
| | Symptom distress and health problems (Bach & Hutsebaut, 2018; Gamache et al., 2019; Gamache, Savard, Lemieux, & Berthelot, 2021; Hutsebaut et al., 2016; Roche & Jaweed, 2021; Sleep et al., 2019; Sleep et al., 2020; Stover et al., 2020; Weekers et al., 2019) |
| | Low well-being (Bach & Hutsebaut, 2018; Gamache et al., 2019; Huprich et al., 2018; Nelson et al., 2018; Stover et al., 2020) |

*Note*: Other-reports include LPFS ratings from experts, laypersons, and informants, partly based on structured clinical interviews. Self-reports include LPFS self-ratings or self-report measures summarized in Table 25.2. Note that studies on the association between impairments in personality functioning (Criterion A) and maladaptive personality traits (Criterion B) were omitted.

narrative coherence measured in life-story interviews (Dimitrova & Simms, 2021).

Initial validation studies of self-report measures based on LPFS also indicated substantial convergence with established measures of impairments in personality functioning and PD severity as well as with a number of constructs from the clinical literature (see right column of Table 25.4). Additionally, from the perspective of basic research in personality psychology, it is relevant that self-report measures assessing personality functioning generally exhibit a profile of correlations with Big Five personality traits that is typical for PDs in general (Saulsman & Page, 2004). This profile consists of negative correlations with emotional stability, conscientiousness, extraversion, and agreeableness, among which the negative correlation with emotional stability is usually the strongest (Hopwood et al., 2018; McCabe et al., 2021a; Oltmanns & Widiger, 2019; Sleep et al., 2020; Stone et al., 2020; Stricker & Pietrowsky,

2021). However, for informant reports, these correlations are sometimes extremely high (e.g., observed associations with low emotional stability and agreeableness approached .80; Morey, 2018), which corresponds to an overall less-differentiated personality description among informants (Beer & Watson, 2008). Also conceptually relevant are findings that impairment scores on self-report measures of personality functioning decrease with age in representative samples from the general population (Spitzer et al., 2021). This is consistent with theories and findings on the maturation of personality over the life span (Bleidorn et al., 2013). Finally, there are also initial studies exploring the correlates of impairments in personality functioning with intensive longitudinal designs in everyday life. For example, results across studies showed that individuals experience more negative affect and less positive affect in everyday life as self-reported impairment increases (Heiland & Veilleux, 2021; Ringwald et al., 2021; Roche, 2018). Additionally, individuals with high levels of personality dysfunction also reported corresponding problems in everyday life (Roche et al., 2016; Roche et al., 2018), experienced less affiliative and dominant behaviors and perceived less affiliation in others (Ringwald et al., 2021), and experienced more intense stressors and more invalidation by others (Heiland & Veilleux, 2021). One study found an indication that high levels of personality dysfunction are generally associated with more instability in experience and behavior (Ringwald et al., 2021), although this was not confirmed in another study (Roche et al., 2016).

*Discriminant and Incremental Validity*

Discriminant validity refers to the question of whether ratings of personality functioning differ sufficiently from measurements that refer to other constructs. This aspect of validity is not so easy to assess. On the one hand, of course, some variables do not correlate with personality functioning. For example, associations between the LPFS-BF total score and gender were found to be approximately zero in representative samples (Spitzer et al., 2021), suggesting that different levels of severity are distributed independently of the gender of the person. On the other hand, numerous studies listed in Table 25.4 show that other-reports of LPFS, as well as corresponding self-report measures, are indeed substantially correlated with measures of a wide variety of other clinical constructs. Such correlations can make sense from a theoretical perspective: for example, it could be that impairments in personality functioning and in physical health correlate because they share common causes or influence each other. In some cases, it is also the case that the other constructs are nothing more than subsets of personality functioning and, to that extent, overlap in their definitions (e.g., low self-esteem, impaired mentalization). Against this background, it becomes clear that it often makes little sense to expect low correlations with measures of other clinical constructs.

However, what might be an important test of discriminant validity from the perspective of the developers of the LPFS is to examine whether the LPFS ratings are specific to PD. This kind of question can be addressed in two ways: by ascertaining whether LPFS ratings are more pronounced in patients with traditional PD diagnoses than in both healthy controls and patients with other diagnoses and by ascertaining whether LPFS ratings correlate more strongly with the number of PD criteria fulfilled than with nonspecific symptomatic burden. There are now a few studies that have demonstrated specificity for PD for expert-based LPFS ratings (Di Pierro et al., 2020; Heissler et al., 2021; Hutsebaut et al., 2017; Ohse et al., 2021). However, this pattern is less clear for self-report measures as correlations with various symptom measures related to other mental disorders such as depression or anxiety are often only slightly lower (Sleep et al., 2019, 2020), or even equal (Spitzer et al., 2021) to correlations with PD measures. A similar conclusion was reached in a study by McCabe et al. (2021b), in which a general factor of PD (g-PD) defined using the LPFS-SR and DLOPFQ total scores, among other measures, was correlated with a broadly defined general factor of psychopathology ("p factor"). The authors found a latent correlation of .94, suggesting that, at least in self-reports, there is little specificity of the LPFS for PD. Put another way, the relevant self-report measures arguably capture impairments that are relevant to all mental disorders.

Incremental validity addresses the question of whether ratings of personality functioning provide additional information for predicting various clinically relevant experiences and behaviors (i.e., information that is not included in other measures). The question of the specificity of the LPFS for PD can also be formulated from the perspective of incremental validity: Here, it would then be necessary to examine whether LPFS ratings predict the presence and severity of PD when controlling statistically for nonspecific symptom burden or comorbid mental disorders. This has indeed been shown for other-reports of the LPFS (Preti et al., 2018; Zimmermann et al., 2014). Other important application scenarios for testing incremental validity include whether LPFS measures contain additional information relative to categorical PD diagnoses or general personality traits. For example, Morey et al. (2013) demonstrated that expert ratings of LPFS predicted psychosocial functioning, short-term risk, proposed treatment intensity, and estimated prognosis when categorical PD diagnoses were statistically controlled. This was confirmed by Buer Christensen, Eikenaes et al. (2020) with respect to self-reported and clinician-rated psychosocial functioning. In addition, one study suggests that the LPFS total score predicts several specific PDs according to *DSM-IV* as well as health- and relationship-related indicators when controlling for general personality traits (Cruitt et al., 2019). Incremental validity over general personality traits in predicting specific PDs according to *DSM-IV* was also confirmed for the LPFS-SR as a self-report measure (Sleep et al., 2020).

## Clinical Utility

A classification system for PD must be not only valid but also clinically useful in order to be applied in practice. Clinical utility is a complex concept that, when understood very broadly, also includes aspects of validity (e.g., meaningful conceptualization of the disorder and mapping of prognostically relevant information; First et al., 2004; Keeley et al., 2016). More narrowly, this refers to how easily the system can be used in practice by clinicians, to what extent it facilitates communication between different stakeholders (e.g., between different clinicians or between clinicians and patients or relatives), and also to what extent it supports clinicians' treatment planning (Mullins-Sweatt & Widiger, 2009). Such aspects have already been illustrated for the AMPD with numerous case reports (Bach et al., 2015; Pincus et al., 2016; Schmeck et al., 2013; Skodol et al., 2015; Weekers et al., 2020) and summarized in reviews (Bach & Tracy, 2021; Hopwood, 2018; Milinkovic & Tiliopoulos, 2020).

An important method for exploring clinical utility is to conduct consumer surveys that ask clinicians directly about aspects of a diagnostic system's utility after having used the system on case vignettes or real patients. Bornstein and Natoli (2019) conducted a meta-analysis of such studies, two of which also referenced the AMPD (Morey et al., 2014; Nelson et al., 2017). In the meta-analysis, dimensional approaches were found to be more useful than categorical diagnosis in *DSM-IV* or *DSM-5* Section II in terms of communicating with the patient, formulating a therapeutic intervention, and describing the specific problems and overall personality of the patient. The study by Morey et al. (2014), which builds on assessments of utility from 337 clinicians and also allows specific statements about the LPFS as a severity rating based on a single item, seems particularly relevant. Here, the LPFS was found to be more difficult to apply and less useful in terms of communication with colleagues but at least on par with *DSM-IV* PD diagnoses in terms of the other aspects of clinical utility. Psychologists (but not psychiatrists) even perceived advantages with the LPFS over *DSM-IV* PDs. Positive evaluations were also obtained when asking students about clinical utility after they applied the LPFS to multiple case vignettes (Garcia et al., 2018).

A qualitative study of the learnability and usefulness of the SCID-AMPD Module I with Norwegian clinicians concluded that this interview was more likely to meet clinicians' interests and needs than were categorical diagnostic interviews (Heltne et al., 2021). For example, it was mentioned positively that the SCID-AMPD Module I provides dimensional assessments and focuses on important topics not explicitly asked elsewhere, thereby helping patients to feel seen and understood. At the same time, certain challenges and limitations were identified, including high requirements for theoretical knowledge and some interview questions that were difficult to understand or could be experienced as confrontational. The authors also recommended the development of more specific guidelines for training.

Additionally, there are other areas and methodological approaches to clinical utility that have not yet been explored for the LPFS. For example, Weekers, Hutsebaut, and Kamphuis (2021) have indicated that consideration of patient strengths—largely missing from traditional diagnostic systems—is a welcome aspect in terms of clinical utility. In this regard, the explicit description of a healthy personality in level 0 of the LPFS could be an advantage. It was also emphasized that patients themselves should be involved in the process of utility assessment. Here, complementary domains include, in particular, the extent to which the diagnosis is associated with less stigma (e.g., is respectful of the whole person and promotes self-acceptance) and is conducted collaboratively (Weekers, Hutsebaut, & Kamphuis, 2021). From a methodological perspective, it is also important to consider that consumer surveys are insufficient to demonstrate that a particular form of assessment actually improves clinical care (Kamphuis et al., 2021; Lewis et al., 2019). Future studies should therefore both examine aspects of client utility of the LPFS and employ stronger designs such as randomized clinical trials to demonstrate the utility of the LPFS for treatment.

## Controversies, Questions, and Next Steps
*Relationship to Maladaptive Personality Traits (Criterion B)*

In the AMPD, in addition to Criterion A, there is also a Criterion B, which is used to determine the individual expression of PD (see Chapter 26 in this volume). To this end, a hierarchical model of maladaptive personality traits was developed based on empirical analyses (Krueger et al., 2012). At a higher level, the model includes five broad trait domains: negative affectivity, detachment, antagonism, disinhibition, and psychoticism. At a lower level, these domains are further specified by 25 trait facets. Disinhibition, for example, is subdivided into (a) irresponsibility, (b) impulsivity, (c) distractibility, (d) risk-taking, and (e) low rigid perfectionism. For a diagnosis of PD, in addition to moderate impairments in personality functioning, at least one maladaptive personality trait or facet must be clinically significant.

One controversy regarding the AMPD is whether impairments in personality functioning (Criterion A) and maladaptive personality traits (Criterion B) provide redundant information (for conceptual discussions, see Bender, 2019; Bornstein, 2019; Leising et al., 2018; Meehan et al., 2019; Sharp & Wall, 2021; Sleep et al., 2021; Widiger et al., 2019). From a semantic perspective, Criteria A and B share a focus on describing socially undesirable features (Leising et al., 2018), and differences appear to be primarily due to theoretical traditions and the level of inference (Mulay et al., 2018). From an empirical perspective, there is also strong evidence that measures of Criterion A and Criterion B are highly correlated, and, to that extent, discriminant validity tends to be low (Bach & Anderson, 2020; Bach & Hutsebaut, 2018; Few et al., 2013; Gamache et al., 2019; Garcia et al., 2021; Hopwood et al., 2018; Huprich et al., 2018; McCabe & Widiger, 2020; Nelson et al., 2018; Ohse et al., 2021; Roche et al., 2018; Roche & Jaweed, 2021; Sleep et al., 2019, 2020; Stover et al., 2020). Moreover, previous findings regarding incremental validity have been mixed and can be interpreted in various ways. On the one hand, there are numerous studies demonstrating incremental validity of severity ratings compared to maladaptive traits, for example, in predicting PDs according to *DSM-IV* (Cruitt et al., 2019; Sleep et al., 2019, 2020; Wygant et al., 2016), personality dynamics in daily life (Ringwald et al., 2021; Roche et al., 2016; Roche, 2018), symptom distress (Bach & Hutsebaut, 2018; Roche & Jaweed, 2021), substance use and physical health (Cruitt et al., 2019), well-being (Bach & Hutsebaut, 2018; Huprich et al., 2018), maladaptive schemas (Bach & Hutsebaut, 2018), interpersonal dependence (Huprich et al., 2018), and physical violence (Leclerc et al., 2021). On the other hand, the effect sizes are, though statistically significant, often small, and some studies have found no incremental value for severity ratings in predicting PDs according to *DSM-IV* (e.g., Few et al., 2013).

Exemplary of these complex findings is the study on informant ratings by Zimmermann et al. (2015), described above. In this study, the 25 trait facets of Criterion B were analyzed together with the 12 subcomponents of Criterion A using exploratory structural equation modeling. A total of seven factors emerged, with two factors roughly mapping impairments in self and interpersonal functioning from Criterion A and another five factors mapping largely maladaptive traits from Criterion B. However, there were also deviations from the theoretical mapping in the AMPD: for example, impairments in self-functioning showed specific associations with the trait facets *depressiveness* and *separation anxiety*; impairments in interpersonal functioning showed specific associations with the trait facets *grandiosity* and *callousness*; and detachment showed specific associations with impairments in the personality functioning subcomponent *depth and duration of connections*. In later self-report studies, a similar differential pattern of association was found whereby components of self-functioning correlated particularly strongly with facets of negative affectivity and components of interpersonal functioning correlated particularly strongly with facets of antagonism (e.g., Sleep et al., 2019, 2020). An important implication of these findings is that the classification of some content under the rubric of Criterion A or B seems somewhat arbitrary, or at least cannot be justified on the basis of the pattern of empirical covariation. For example, the Criterion B facet *depressiveness* could also be understood as a specific impairment of the self, and the Criterion A subcomponent *depth and duration of connections* could be reinterpreted as an indicator of detachment.

The implications of these findings for a future revision of the classification system are controversial. A more conservative conclusion would be that the two criteria reflect the same phenomena from two different clinical perspectives and traditions, both of which are clinically useful and justified. However, there are also critical perspectives that find the lack of parsimony problematic: while some scholars argue that Criterion A can be dropped due to its low incremental validity (Sleep et al., 2019), other scholars suggest replacing the pathological personality traits of Criterion B with normal personality traits (e.g., the Big Five) to better capture the stylistic expression of personality regardless of the severity of the disorder (Leising & Zimmermann, 2011; Morey et al., 2020).

In our view, the results at least underscore the need for a clearer conceptual justification of how and why the phenomena currently described in Criteria A and B should be distinguished from one another and how they relate to one another. For example, if maladaptive traits are viewed as behaviorally anchored expressions of underlying impairments in basic internal capacities (e.g., Sharp & Wall, 2021), some degree of substantive overlap might be warranted as Criterion A would essentially serve as an explanation for Criterion B (e.g., a person tends to behave callously because his or her capacity for empathy is impaired; Zimmermann et al., 2015). However, other authors prefer conceptualizations that work the other way around; for example, by understanding dysfunctions as negative consequences or characteristic maladaptations of basic personality dispositions (cf. Clark & Ro, 2014; Leising & Zimmermann, 2011; Widiger & Mullins-Sweatt, 2009). These conceptual issues form the core of our understanding of personality pathology and have crucial implications for the selection of assessment methods. They are unlikely to be resolved completely with empirical studies and require conceptual clarity and argumentative precision.

### Relationship to Severity in ICD-11

Meanwhile, a new model for the classification of PD in *ICD-11* has also been finalized and will come into effect in 2022 (Reed et al., 2019). This model follows the AMPD in some key respects: for example, the general features of PD are again identified in terms of long-standing problems in self and interpersonal functioning; a primary classification of severity is made, ranging from subthreshold personality difficulties to mild and moderate to severe PD; and salient personality traits can be specified, including negative affectivity, detachment, dissociality, disinhibition, anankastia, and a borderline pattern (Bach & First, 2018; Mulder & Tyrer, 2019). Specifically related to the determination of severity, a high degree of substantive agreement with the LPFS can be observed: for example, severity in the *ICD-11* model is determined based on the extent and pervasiveness of dysfunction of the self (e.g., identity, self-esteem, accuracy of self-view, self-direction) and relationships (e.g., interest in relationships, perspective-taking, intimacy, conflict resolution).

There are, however, also a few minor differences. First, the extent, pervasiveness, and chronicity of additional maladaptive experiences and behaviors are to be considered, such as emotion perception and expression, accuracy of situational appraisals, decision-making ability under uncertainty, impulse control, and stress resistance. While some of these aspects are also considered in the LPFS (e.g., impairments in the experience and expression of emotions are understood as a subcomponent of identity in the LPFS), others are not explicitly listed there (e.g., stress resistance). Second, the *ICD-11* model explicitly considers the degree to which these characteristics are associated with distress or impairment in different domains of life. Thus, in a sense, severity in the *ICD-11* model is defined both in terms of impairments of internal abilities related to the self and interpersonal relationships and in terms of negative psychosocial consequences in everyday life. Finally, in the descriptions of the different severity levels of PD, the aspect of harm to self and others plays a greater role than in LPFS.

Research on the severity of PD according to *ICD-11* is still in its infancy. Most studies to date on this topic have been based either on reanalysis of archival data (e.g., Tyrer et al., 2014) or on instruments or rating systems that were based on a preliminary version of the *ICD-11* model (e.g., Kim et al., 2014; Olajide et al., 2018). One example is the Standardized Assessment of Severity of Personality Disorder (SASPD; Olajide et al., 2018), which should be understood as an index of PD complexity (in terms of exhibiting traits from different PD trait domains) rather than a unidimensional scale of functional impairment. In fact, there are currently only two studies in which severity has been assessed according to the final *ICD-11* definition using new self-report measures (Bach et al., 2021; Clark et al., 2021). For the 14-item Personality Disorder Severity *ICD-11* (PDS-ICD-11; Bach et al., 2021) scale, there was a correlation of .68 with the total LPFS-BF score in a sample from the general population. When accounting for the influence of measurement error pushing this estimate downward, this initial result suggests that severity measures based on AMPD and *ICD-11* are highly overlapping in self-report and may be nearly impossible to differentiate. For a more definite evaluation of the conceptual and empirical similarities and differences of the two systems with respect to severity, further studies, preferably using multiple measures and methods, will be required.

*Further Development of Assessment Methods*

As noted above, the inclusion of Criterion A in the AMPD has led to the development of several new self-report measures (see Table 25.2). Additionally, there are numerous other self-report instruments on personality functioning that have been developed previously (e.g., SIPP-118, GADP), that are aligned with the *ICD-11* model for PD (e.g., SASPD, PDS-ICD-11), or that are based on psychodynamic concepts (e.g., OPD Structure Questionnaire; Ehrenthal et al., 2012). Although this is a comfortable situation that expands the choices available to researchers and practitioners, it has the disadvantage of an increasing lack of standardization. The new measures differ in a number of ways (e.g., underlying theoretical conceptualizations, emphasis on different aspects of the construct, length, precision, etc.), and one of the main challenges is that data obtained with different measures are difficult to compare. Despite their semantic similarities (Waugh et al., 2021) and their usually high intercorrelations, it is not clear whether these measures assess the same construct and how the scores obtained from them can be compared.

One possibility is to use IRT to calibrate different measures against a common metric. Zimmermann et al. (2020) followed such an approach in a sample from the general population. A common IRT model was estimated based on data from six widely used self-report measures or their short forms to link item responses to an underlying general factor. Measures based on Criterion A of the AMPD (i.e., LPFS-SR and LPFS-BF 2.0) were used, as well as a measure of Criterion B and measures based on psychodynamic concepts and on an early version of the *ICD-11* model (i.e., SASPD). The results suggest that all measures capture a strong common factor and can therefore be scaled along a single latent continuum. The common factor was largely defined by impairments in self and interpersonal functioning, with a slight predominance of internalizing personality pathology (e.g., anxiety, low self-esteem). This suggests that the severity of PD based on psychodynamic concepts, Criterion A and Criterion B of the AMPD, and the *ICD-11* are largely consistent when implemented in a self-report format.

To be able to use the measures for the assessment of individual cases in routine practice, the development of norm values is crucial. The common metric study described above provides preliminary norms for each of the six measures based on the German general population (Zimmermann et al., 2020). For individual cases, practitioners can use the Web platform (http://www.common-metrics.org/) to estimate T scores, including 95% confidence intervals. In this way, an individual's general severity of PD can be interpreted as a deviation from the average case and measurement error can be explicitly accounted for. However, it is important to note that, in this study as in most other studies on the development of norm values, the representativeness of the sample could only be established to a limited extent (e.g., only with respect to age and gender). Other aspects such as education, regional origin, and use of medical and psychotherapeutic treatments may be biased, especially in online samples compared to the general population, which is why norm values from high-quality recruited random samples may differ significantly (Spitzer et al., 2021).

In addition to the development of norm values, there is also the possibility of empirically establishing thresholds based on external criteria. *DSM-IV* PD diagnoses in cross-sectional data have been mainly used for this purpose so far (e.g., Buer Christensen, Hummelen, et al., 2020; Gamache, Savard, Leclerc, et al., 2021). Indeed, as noted above, *DSM-IV* PD diagnoses were used in the development of the threshold of level 2 on the LPFS itself (Morey et al., 2013). This approach is understandable insofar as it ensures continuity with previous categorical systems. However, in light of the criticism of the arbitrary thresholds of the categorical system, there is also something circular about this approach. In our view, it would be desirable to use longitudinal studies to calibrate multiple cutoff values for severity based on the likelihood of future critical life outcomes and adverse consequences.

In addition to integrating and standardizing self-report measures, we should also be concerned with developing and optimizing other assessment methods. For example, the very high interrater reliability of LPFS ratings based on structured interviews such as SCID-AMPD Module I (see Table

25.3), as well as the sometimes very high agreement with self-reports, can be viewed critically. The very high interrater reliability is probably also due to the funnel structure of the interview, through which an outside person can easily guess the implicitly associated rating based on the interviewer's jumping to certain interview sections. The high degree of agreement with the self-report may also be due to the fact that some of the questions are very direct and the answers thus largely reflect the self-presentation of the interviewee. In this respect, further research should be conducted to determine the extent to which more open-ended interview strategies, as in CALF, are associated with lower interrater reliability but may have greater incremental validity in predicting clinically relevant outcomes compared to self-report. Finally, it would also be useful to give greater consideration to the possibility and appropriateness of maximal-effort tests to capture personality functioning. If one takes seriously the understanding of Criterion A in terms of impairments in internal mental capacities (Sharp & Wall, 2021), the development of a test battery to measure performance on tasks requiring self and interpersonal skills would be the logical next step (e.g., Jauk & Ehrenthal, 2021; Leising et al., 2011; Olderbak & Wilhelm, 2020).

## Conclusion

With the introduction of a severity scale for PD in the AMPD, several criticisms of the current categorical classification system for PD have been successfully addressed. A severity scale better captures the dimensional nature of individual differences in impairment, better accounts for empirical findings of high comorbidity and the substantial general factor in PD diagnoses, allows more efficient determination of prognosis and change, and contributes to destigmatization of the diagnosis. In particular, the LPFS as a concrete operationalization of severity ensures reference to the common denominator of all PDs in Criterion A, and the focus on impairments in the domain of self and interpersonal relationships builds on both empirical and conceptual arguments. Since the official publication of the AMPD in 2013, researchers have begun to explore the reliability, validity, and utility of the LPFS and derived measures. Results from numerous empirical studies are now available and are generally promising: interrater reliability is good for structured interviews, subcomponent ratings can be modeled by two highly correlated factors of impairments in self and interpersonal functioning (which is compatible with the assumption of a strong general factor), ratings correlate highly with measures of similar severity measures in PD, there is evidence of incremental validity over categorical PD diagnoses, and clinical utility is mostly viewed positively by practitioners. At the same time, the issue of discriminant validity against nonspecific distress or other mental disorders, as well as against Criterion B, continues to be controversial and may also require conceptual clarifications or adaptations of the LPFS. For future empirical research, it is particularly desirable to move beyond the widely used monomethod studies that dominate the literature to date (Zimmermann et al., 2019). This includes the joint assessment of multiple constructs by multiple methods, allowing for the investigation of construct-level associations while controlling for shared method variance (e.g., multitrait-multimethod designs; Campbell & Fiske, 1959). Additionally, intervention studies should be conducted that focus on severity as a predictor, moderator, and endpoint of treatment effects. Currently, there is only one study showing that the LPFS-BF 2.0 can be used as an outcome measure in a 3-month residential treatment program (Weekers et al., 2019). In any case, with the prioritization of severity in the *ICD-11* model for PD, there is no doubt that the *DSM-5* LPFS and its derived measurement tools will continue to have an important place in PD diagnosis and research.

## Acknowledgments

We thank Bo Bach, Paul Blaney, Kirstin Goth, Benjamin Hummelen, Joost Hutsebaut, André Kerber, Anne Lehner, Sascha Müller, and Carina Remmers for helpful feedback on an earlier draft of this chapter.

## References

Ahmed, A. O., Green, B. A., Goodrum, N. M., Doane, N. J., Birgenheir, D., & Buckley, P. F. (2013). Does a latent class underlie schizotypal personality disorder? Implications for schizophrenia. *Journal of Abnormal Psychology, 122*(2), 475–491. https://doi.org/10.1037/a0032713

Anderson, J. L., & Sellbom, M. (2018). Evaluating the DSM-5 Section III personality disorder impairment criteria. *Personality Disorders: Theory, Research, and Treatment, 9*(1), 51–61. https://doi.org/10.1037/per0000217

Aslinger, E. N., Manuck, S. B., Pilkonis, P. A., Simms, L. J., & Wright, A. G. C. (2018). Narcissist or narcissistic? Evaluation of the latent structure of narcissistic personality disorder. *Journal of Abnormal Psychology, 127*(5), 496–502. https://doi.org/10.1037/abn0000363

Azim, H. F., Piper, W. E., Segal, P. M., Nixon, G. W., & Duncan, S. C. (1991). The Quality of Object Relations Scale. *Bulletin of the Menninger Clinic, 55*(3), 323–343.

Bach, B., & Anderson, J. L. (2020). Patient-reported ICD-11 personality disorder severity and DSM-5 level of personality functioning. *Journal of Personality Disorders*, *34*(2), 231–249. https://doi.org/10.1521/pedi_2018_32_393

Bach, B., Brown, T. A., Mulder, R. T., Newton-Howes, G., Simonsen, E., & Sellbom, M. (2021). Development and initial evaluation of the ICD-11 personality disorder severity scale: Pds-ICD-11. *Personality and Mental Health*, *15*(3), 223–236. https://doi.org/10.1002/pmh.1510

Bach, B., & First, M. B. (2018). Application of the ICD-11 classification of personality disorders. *BMC Psychiatry*, *18*(1), 351. https://doi.org/10.1186/s12888-018-1908-3

Bach, B., & Hutsebaut, J. (2018). Level of Personality Functioning Scale-Brief Form 2.0: Utility in capturing personality problems in psychiatric outpatients and incarcerated addicts. *Journal of Personality Assessment*, *100*(6), 660–670. https://doi.org/10.1080/00223891.2018.1428984

Bach, B., Markon, K., Simonsen, E., & Krueger, R. F. (2015). Clinical utility of the DSM-5 Alternative Model of Personality Disorders: Six cases from practice. *Journal of Psychiatric Practice*, *21*(1), 3–25. https://doi.org/10.1097/01.pra.0000460618.02805.ef

Bach, B., & Simonsen, S. (2021). How does level of personality functioning inform clinical management and treatment? Implications for ICD-11 classification of personality disorder severity. *Current Opinion in Psychiatry*, *34*(1), 54–63. https://doi.org/10.1097/YCO.0000000000000658

Bach, B., & Tracy, M. (2021). Clinical utility of the alternative model of personality disorders: A 10th year anniversary review. *Personality Disorders: Theory, Research, and Treatment*, *13*(4), 369–379. https://doi.org/10.1037/per0000527

Back, S. N., Zettl, M., Bertsch, K., & Taubner, S. (2020). Persönlichkeitsfunktionsniveau, maladaptive Traits und Kindheitstraumata [Personality functioning, maladaptive traits, and childhood trauma]. *Psychotherapeut*, *65*(5), 374–382. https://doi.org/10.1007/s00278-020-00445-7

Beer, A., & Watson, D. (2008). Asymmetry in judgments of personality: Others are less differentiated than the self. *Journal of Personality*, *76*(3), 535–560. https://doi.org/10.1111/j.1467-6494.2008.00495.x

Bender, D. S. (2019). The p-factor and what it means to be human: Commentary on Criterion A of the AMPD in HiTOP. *Journal of Personality Assessment*, *101*(4), 356–359. https://doi.org/10.1080/00223891.2018.1492928

Bender, D. S., Morey, L. C., & Skodol, A. E. (2011). Toward a model for assessing level of personality functioning in DSM–5, Part I: A review of theory and methods. *Journal of Personality Assessment*, *93*(4), 332–346. https://doi.org/10.1080/00223891.2011.583808

Bender, D. S., Skodol, A. E., First, M. B., & Oldham, J. M. (2018). Module I: Structured Clinical Interview for the Level of Personality Functioning Scale. In M. B. First, A. E. Skodol, D. S. Bender, & J. M. Oldham (Eds.), *Structured Clinical Interview for the DSM-5 Alternative Model for Personality Disorders (SCID-AMPD)*. American Psychiatric Association Publishing.

Bender, D. S., Zimmermann, J., & Huprich, S. K. (2018). Introduction to the Special Series on the personality functioning component of the Alternative DSM-5 Model for Personality Disorders. *Journal of Personality Assessment*, *100*(6), 565–570. https://doi.org/10.1080/00223891.2018.1491856

Biberdzic, M., Tang, J., & Tan, J. (2021). Beyond difficulties in self-regulation: The role of identity integration and personality functioning in young women with disordered eating behaviours. *Journal of Eating Disorders*, *9*(1), 93. https://doi.org/10.1186/s40337-021-00398-5

Birkhölzer, M., Schmeck, K., & Goth, K. (2020). Assessment of Criterion A. *Current Opinion in Psychology*, *37*, 98–103. https://doi.org/10.1016/j.copsyc.2020.09.009

Blatt, S. J., Chevron, E. S., Quinlan, D. M., Schaffer, C. E., & Wein, S. (1988). *The assessment of qualitative and structural dimensions of object representations: Unpublished research manual*. Yale University Press.

Bleidorn, W., Klimstra, T. A., Denissen, J. J. A., Rentfrow, P. J., Potter, J., & Gosling, S. D. (2013). Personality maturation around the world: A cross-cultural examination of social-investment theory. *Psychological Science*, *24*(12), 2530–2540. https://doi.org/10.1177/0956797613498396

Bliton, C. F., Roche, M. J., Pincus, A. L., & Dueber, D. (2021). Examining the structure and validity of self-report measures of DSM-5 Alternative Model for Personality Disorders Criterion A. *Journal of Personality Disorders*, *36*(2), 157–182. https://doi.org/10.1521/pedi_2021_35_531

Blüml, V., & Doering, S. (2021). Icd-11 personality disorders: A psychodynamic perspective on personality functioning. *Frontiers in Psychiatry*, *12*, 654026. https://doi.org/10.3389/fpsyt.2021.654026

Bornstein, R. F. (2019). From structure to process: On the integration of AMPD and HiTOP. *Journal of Personality Assessment*, *101*(4), 360–366. https://doi.org/10.1080/00223891.2018.1501696

Bornstein, R. F., & Natoli, A. P. (2019). Clinical utility of categorical and dimensional perspectives on personality pathology: A meta-analytic review. *Personality Disorders: Theory, Research, and Treatment*, *10*(6), 479–490. https://doi.org/10.1037/per0000365

Brown, T. A., & Sellbom, M. (2020). Further validation of the MMPI-2-RF personality disorder spectra scales. *Journal of Psychopathology and Behavioral Assessment*, *42*(2), 259–270. https://doi.org/10.1007/s10862-020-09789-5

Buer Christensen, T., Eikenaes, I., Hummelen, B., Pedersen, G., Nysæter, T.-E., Bender, D. S., Skodol, A. E., & Selvik, S. G. (2020). Level of personality functioning as a predictor of psychosocial functioning-Concurrent validity of criterion A. *Personality Disorders: Theory, Research, and Treatment*, *11*(2), 79–90. https://doi.org/10.1037/per0000352

Buer Christensen, T., Hummelen, B., Paap, M. C. S., Eikenaes, I., Selvik, S. G., Kvarstein, E., Pedersen, G., Bender, D. S., Skodol, A. E., & Nysæter, T. E. (2020). Evaluation of diagnostic thresholds for Criterion A in the Alternative DSM-5 Model for Personality Disorders. *Journal of Personality Disorders*, *34*(Supplement C), 40–61. https://doi.org/10.1521/pedi_2019_33_455

Buer Christensen, T., Paap, M. C. S., Arnesen, M., Koritzinsky, K., Nysaeter, T.-E., Eikenaes, I., Germans Selvik, S., Walther, K., Torgersen, S., Bender, D. S., Skodol, A. E., Kvarstein, E., Pedersen, G., & Hummelen, B. (2018). Interrater reliability of the Structured Clinical Interview for the DSM-5 Alternative Model of Personality Disorders Module I: Level of Personality Functioning Scale. *Journal of Personality Assessment*, *100*(6), 630–641. https://doi.org/10.1080/00223891.2018.1483377

Busmann, M., Wrege, J., Meyer, A. H., Ritzler, F., Schmidlin, M., Lang, U. E., Gaab, J., Walter, M., & Euler, S. (2019).

Alternative Model of Personality Disorders (DSM-5) predicts dropout in inpatient psychotherapy for patients with personality disorder. *Frontiers in Psychology, 10*, 735. https://doi.org/10.3389/fpsyg.2019.00952

Campbell, D. T., & Fiske, D. W. (1959). Convergent and discriminant validation by the multitrait-multimethod matrix. *Psychological Bulletin, 56*(2), 81–105. https://doi.org/10.1037/h0046016

Cicchetti, D. V. (1994). Guidelines, criteria, and rules of thumb for evaluating normed and standardized assessment instruments in psychology. *Psychological Assessment, 6*(4), 284–290. https://doi.org/10.1037/1040-3590.6.4.284

Clark, L. A., Corona-Espinosa, A., Khoo, S., Kotelnikova, Y., Levin-Aspenson, H. F., Serapio-García, G., & Watson, D. (2021). Preliminary scales for ICD-11 personality disorder: Self and interpersonal dysfunction plus five personality disorder trait domains. *Frontiers in Psychology, 12*, 668724. https://doi.org/10.3389/fpsyg.2021.668724

Clark, L. A., Nuzum, H., & Ro, E. (2018). Manifestations of personality impairment severity: Comorbidity, course/prognosis, psychosocial dysfunction, and 'borderline' personality features. *Current Opinion in Psychology, 21*, 117–121. https://doi.org/10.1016/j.copsyc.2017.12.004

Clark, L. A., & Ro, E. (2014). Three-pronged assessment and diagnosis of personality disorder and its consequences: Personality functioning, pathological traits, and psychosocial disability. *Personality Disorders: Theory, Research, and Treatment, 5*(1), 55–69. https://doi.org/10.1037/per0000063

Clarkin, J. F., Caligor, E., & Sowislo, J. F. (2020). An object relations model perspective on the Alternative Model for Personality Disorders (DSM-5). *Psychopathology, 53*(3–4), 141–148. https://doi.org/10.1159/000508353

Conway, C. C., Hammen, C., & Brennan, P. (2012). A comparison of latent class, latent trait, and factor mixture models of DSM-IV borderline personality disorder criteria in a community setting: Implications for DSM-5. *Journal of Personality Disorders, 26*(5), 793–803. https://doi.org/10.1521/pedi.2012.26.5.793

Conway, C. C., Hammen, C., & Brennan, P. (2016). Optimizing prediction of psychosocial and clinical outcomes with a transdiagnostic model of personality disorder. *Journal of Personality Disorders, 30*(4), 545–566. https://doi.org/10.1521/pedi_2015_29_218

Cosgun, S., Goth, K., & Cakiroglu, S. (2021). Levels of Personality Functioning Questionnaire (LoPF-Q) 12–18 Turkish Version: Reliability, validity, factor structure and relationship with comorbid psychopathology in a Turkish adolescent sample. *Journal of Psychopathology and Behavioral Assessment, 43*(3), 620–631. https://doi.org/10.1007/s10862-021-09867-2

Crawford, M. J., Koldobsky, N., Mulder, R. T., & Tyrer, P. (2011). Classifying personality disorder according to severity. *Journal of Personality Disorders, 25*(3), 321–330. https://doi.org/10.1521/pedi.2011.25.3.321

Cristea, I. A., Gentili, C., Cotet, C. D., Palomba, D., Barbui, C., & Cuijpers, P. (2017). Efficacy of psychotherapies for borderline personality disorder: A systematic review and meta-analysis. *JAMA Psychiatry, 74*(4), 319–328. https://doi.org/10.1001/jamapsychiatry.2016.4287

Cruitt, P. J., Boudreaux, M. J., King, H. R., Oltmanns, J. R., & Oltmanns, T. F. (2019). Examining Criterion A: Dsm-5 level of personality functioning as assessed through life story interviews. *Personality Disorders: Theory, Research, and Treatment, 10*(3), 224–234. https://doi.org/10.1037/per0000321

Dereboy, F., Dereboy, Ç., & Eskin, M. (2018). Validation of the DSM-5 Alternative Model Personality Disorder diagnoses in Turkey, Part 1: Lead validity and reliability of the personality functioning ratings. *Journal of Personality Assessment, 100*(6), 603–611. https://doi.org/10.1080/00223891.2018.1423989

Di Pierro, R., Gargiulo, I., Poggi, A., Madeddu, F., & Preti, E. (2020). The Level of Personality Functioning Scale applied to clinical material from the Structured Interview of Personality Organization (STIPO): Utility in detecting personality pathology. *Journal of Personality Disorders, 34*(Supplement C), 62–76. https://doi.org/10.1521/pedi_2020_34_472

Dimitrova, J., & Simms, L. J. (2021). Construct validation of narrative coherence: Exploring links with personality functioning and psychopathology. *Personality Disorders: Theory, Research, and Treatment.* Advance online publication. https://doi.org/10.1037/per0000508

Dowgwillo, E. A., Roche, M. J., & Pincus, A. L. (2018). Examining the interpersonal nature of Criterion A of the DSM-5 Section III Alternative Model for Personality Disorders using bootstrapped confidence intervals for the interpersonal circumplex. *Journal of Personality Assessment, 100*(6), 581–592. https://doi.org/10.1080/00223891.2018.1464016

Ehrenthal, J., Dinger, U., Horsch, L., Komo-Lang, M., Klinkerfuß, M., Grande, T., & Schauenburg, H. (2012). Der OPD-Strukturfragebogen (OPD-SF): Erste Ergebnisse zu Reliabilität und Validität [The OPD Structure Questionnaire (OPD-SQ): First results on reliability and validity]. *Psychotherapie, Psychosomatik, Medizinische Psychologie, 62*(01), 25–32. https://doi.org/10.1055/s-0031-1295481

Few, L. R., Miller, J. D., Rothbaum, A. O., Meller, S., Maples, J., Terry, D. P., Collins, B., & MacKillop, J. (2013). Examination of the Section III DSM-5 diagnostic system for personality disorders in an outpatient clinical sample. *Journal of Abnormal Psychology, 122*(4), 1057–1069. https://doi.org/10.1037/a0034878

First, M. B., Pincus, H. A., Levine, J. B., Williams, J. B. W., Ustun, B., & Peele, R. (2004). Clinical utility as a criterion for revising psychiatric diagnoses. *American Journal of Psychiatry, 161*(6), 946–954. https://doi.org/10.1176/appi.ajp.161.6.946

Fleck, L., Fuchs, A., Moehler, E., Parzer, P., Koenig, J., Resch, F., & Kaess, M. (2021). Maternal bonding impairment predicts personality disorder features in adolescence: The moderating role of child temperament and sex. *Personality Disorders: Theory, Research, and Treatment, 12*(5), 475–483. https://doi.org/10.1037/per0000433

Fonagy, P., Target, M., Steele, H., & Steele, M. (1998). *Reflective-functioning manual, version 5.0, for application to adult attachment interviews.* University College London.

Gamache, D., Laverdière, O., Diguer, L., Hébert, É., Larochelle, S., & Descôteaux, J. (2009). The Personality Organization Diagnostic Form. *Journal of Nervous and Mental Disease, 197*(5), 368–377. https://doi.org/10.1097/NMD.0b013e3181a20897

Gamache, D., Savard, C., Leclerc, P., & Côté, A. (2019). Introducing a short self-report for the assessment of DSM-5 level of personality functioning for personality disorders: The Self and Interpersonal Functioning Scale. *Personality Disorders: Theory, Research, and Treatment, 10*(5), 438–447. https://doi.org/10.1037/per0000335

Gamache, D., Savard, C., Leclerc, P., Payant, M., Berthelot, N., Côté, A., Faucher, J., Lampron, M., Lemieux, R., Mayrand, K., Nolin, M.-C., & Tremblay, M. (2021). A proposed classification of ICD-11 severity degrees of personality pathology using the self and interpersonal functioning scale. *Frontiers in Psychiatry*, *12*, 628057. https://doi.org/10.3389/fpsyt.2021.628057

Gamache, D., Savard, C., Lemieux, R., & Berthelot, N. (2021). Impact of level of personality pathology on affective, behavioral, and thought problems in pregnant women during the coronavirus disease 2019 pandemic. *Personality Disorders: Theory, Research, and Treatment*, *13*(1), 41–51. https://doi.org/10.1037/per0000479

Gander, M., Buchheim, A., Bock, A., Steppan, M., Sevecke, K., & Goth, K. (2020). Unresolved attachment mediates the relationship between childhood trauma and impaired personality functioning in adolescence. *Journal of Personality Disorders*, *34*(Suppl B), 84–103. https://doi.org/10.1521/pedi_2020_34_468

Garcia, D. J., Skadberg, R. M., Schmidt, M., Bierma, S., Shorter, R. L., & Waugh, M. H. (2018). It's not that difficult: An interrater reliability study of the DSM-5 Section III Alternative Model for Personality Disorders. *Journal of Personality Assessment*, *100*(6), 612–620. https://doi.org/10.1080/00223891.2018.1428982

Garcia, D. J., Waugh, M. H., Skadberg, R. M., Crittenden, E. B., Finn, M. T. M., Schmidt, M. R., & Kurdziel-Adams, G. (2021). Deconstructing Criterion A of the Alternative Model for Personality Disorders. *Personality Disorders: Theory, Research, and Treatment*, *12*(4), 320–330. https://doi.org/10.1037/per0000431

Goth, K., Birkhölzer, M., & Schmeck, K. (2018). Assessment of personality functioning in adolescents with the LoPF-Q 12-18 Self-Report Questionnaire. *Journal of Personality Assessment*, *100*(6), 680–690. https://doi.org/10.1080/00223891.2018.1489258

Gutiérrez, F., Navinés, R., Navarro, P., García-Esteve, L., Subirá, S., Torrens, M., & Martín-Santos, R. (2008). What do all personality disorders have in common? Ineffectiveness and uncooperativeness. *Comprehensive Psychiatry*, *49*(6), 570–578. https://doi.org/10.1016/j.comppsych.2008.04.007

Haslam, N., McGrath, M. J., Viechtbauer, W., & Kuppens, P. (2020). Dimensions over categories: A meta-analysis of taxometric research. *Psychological Medicine*, *50*(9), 1418–1432. https://doi.org/10.1017/S003329172000183X

Heiland, A. M., & Veilleux, J. C. (2021). Severity of personality dysfunction predicts affect and self-efficacy in daily life. *Personality Disorders: Theory, Research, and Treatment*, *12*(6), 560–569. https://doi.org/10.1037/per0000470

Heissler, R., Doubková, N., Hutsebaut, J., & Preiss, M. (2021). Semi-structured interview for personality functioning DSM-5 (STiP-5.1): Psychometric evaluation of the Czech version. *Personality and Mental Health*, *15*(3), 198–207. https://doi.org/10.1002/pmh.1508

Heltne, A., Bode, C., Hummelen, B., Falkum, E., Selvik, S. G., & Paap, M. C. S. (2021). Norwegian clinicians' experiences of learnability and usability of SCID-II, SCID-5-PD and SCID-5-AMPD-I interviews: A sequential multi-group qualitative approach. *Journal of Personality Assessment*. Advance online publication. https://doi.org/10.1080/00223891.2021.1975726

Hemmati, A., Morey, L. C., McCredie, M. N., Rezaei, F., Nazari, A., & Rahmani, F. (2020). Validation of the Persian translation of the Level of Personality Functioning Scale—Self-Report (LPFS-SR): Comparison of college students and patients with personality disorders. *Journal of Psychopathology and Behavioral Assessment*, *42*(3), 546–559. https://doi.org/10.1007/s10862-019-09775-6

Hengartner, M. P., Ajdacic-Gross, V., Rodgers, S., Muller, M., & Rossler, W. (2014). The joint structure of normal and pathological personality: Further evidence for a dimensional model. *Comprehensive Psychiatry*, *55*(3), 667–674. https://doi.org/10.1016/j.comppsych.2013.10.011

Hengartner, M. P., Zimmermann, J., & Wright, A. G. C. (2018). Personality pathology. In V. Zeigler-Hill & T. Shackelford (Eds.), *The SAGE handbook of personality and individual differences: Volume III: Applications of personality and individual differences* (pp. 3–35). Sage.

Herpertz, S. C., Bertsch, K., & Jeung, H. (2017). Neurobiology of Criterion A: Self and interpersonal personality functioning. *Current Opinion in Psychology*, *21*, 23–27. https://doi.org/10.1016/j.copsyc.2017.08.032

Hopwood, C. J. (2018). A framework for treating DSM-5 alternative model for personality disorder features. *Personality and Mental Health*, *12*(2), 107–125. https://doi.org/10.1002/pmh.1414

Hopwood, C. J., Fox, S., Bender, D. S., & Zimmermann, J. (in press). The core self/other dimension of personality functioning. In J. Mihura (Ed.), *The Oxford handbook of personality and psychopathology assessment* (2nd ed.). https://doi.org/10.1093/oxfordhb/9780190092689.013.5

Hopwood, C. J., Good, E. W., & Morey, L. C. (2018). Validity of the DSM-5 Levels of Personality Functioning Scale-Self Report. *Journal of Personality Assessment*, *100*(6), 650–659. https://doi.org/10.1080/00223891.2017.1420660

Hopwood, C. J., Malone, J. C., Ansell, E. B., Sanislow, C. A., Grilo, C. M., McGlashan, T. H., Pinto, A., Markowitz, J. C., Shea, M. T., Skodol, A. E., Gunderson, J. G., Zanarini, M. C., & Morey, L. C. (2011). Personality assessment in DSM-5: Empirical support for rating severity, style, and traits. *Journal of Personality Disorders*, *25*(3), 305–320. https://doi.org/10.1521/pedi.2011.25.3.305

Hopwood, C. J., Wright, A. G. C., Ansell, E. B., & Pincus, A. L. (2013). The interpersonal core of personality pathology. *Journal of Personality Disorders*, *27*(3), 270–295. https://doi.org/10.1521/pedi.2013.27.3.270

Hörz-Sagstetter, S., Ohse, L., & Kampe, L. (2021). Three dimensional approaches to personality disorders: A review on personality functioning, personality structure, and personality organization. *Current Psychiatry Reports*, *23*(7), 45. https://doi.org/10.1007/s11920-021-01250-y

Hummelen, B., Braeken, J., Buer Christensen, T., Nysaeter, T. E., Germans Selvik, S., Walther, K., Pedersen, G., Eikenaes, I., & Paap, M. C. S. (2021). A psychometric analysis of the Structured Clinical Interview for the DSM-5 Alternative Model for Personality Disorders Module I (SCID-5-AMPD-I): Level of Personality Functioning Scale. *Assessment*, *28*(5), 1320–1333. https://doi.org/10.1177/1073191120967972

Huprich, S. K., Nelson, S. M., Meehan, K. B., Siefert, C. J., Haggerty, G., Sexton, J., Dauphin, V. B., Macaluso, M., Jackson, J., Zackula, R., & Baade, L. (2018). Introduction of the DSM-5 Levels of Personality Functioning Questionnaire. *Personality Disorders: Theory, Research, and Treatment*, *9*(6), 553–563. https://doi.org/10.1037/per0000264

Hutsebaut, J., Feenstra, D. J., & Kamphuis, J. H. (2016). Development and preliminary psychometric evaluation of a brief self-report questionnaire for the assessment of the DSM-5 Level of Personality Functioning Scale: The LPFS Brief Form (LPFS-BF). *Personality Disorders: Theory, Research, and Treatment, 7*(2), 192–197. https://doi.org/10.1037/per0000159

Hutsebaut, J., Kamphuis, J. H., Feenstra, D. J., Weekers, L. C., & Saeger, H. de (2017). Assessing DSM-5-oriented level of personality functioning: Development and psychometric evaluation of the Semi-Structured Interview for Personality Functioning DSM-5 (STiP-5.1). *Personality Disorders: Theory, Research, and Treatment, 8*(1), 94–101. https://doi.org/10.1037/per0000197

Hutsebaut, J., Weekers, L. C., Tuin, N., Apeldoorn, J. S. P., & Bulten, E. (2021). Assessment of ICD-11 personality disorder severity in forensic patients using the Semi-structured Interview for Personality Functioning DSM-5 (STiP-5.1): Preliminary findings. *Frontiers in Psychiatry, 12*, 617702. https://doi.org/10.3389/fpsyt.2021.617702

Jauk, E., & Ehrenthal, J. C. (2021). Self-reported levels of personality functioning from the Operationalized Psychodynamic Diagnosis (OPD) system and emotional intelligence likely assess the same latent construct. *Journal of Personality Assessment, 103*(3), 365–379. https://doi.org/10.1080/00223891.2020.1775089

Kampe, L., Zimmermann, J., Bender, D., Caligor, E., Borowski, A.-L., Ehrenthal, J. C., Benecke, C., & Hörz-Sagstetter, S. (2018). Comparison of the Structured DSM-5 Clinical Interview for the Level of Personality Functioning Scale with the Structured Interview of Personality Organization. *Journal of Personality Assessment, 100*(6), 642–649. https://doi.org/10.1080/00223891.2018.1489257

Kamphuis, J. H., Noordhof, A., & Hopwood, C. J. (2021). When and how assessment matters: An update on the Treatment Utility of Clinical Assessment (TUCA). *Psychological Assessment, 33*(2), 122–132. https://doi.org/10.1037/pas0000966

Karukivi, M., Vahlberg, T., Horjamo, K., Nevalainen, M., & Korkeila, J. (2017). Clinical importance of personality difficulties: Diagnostically sub-threshold personality disorders. *BMC Psychiatry, 17*(1), 16. https://doi.org/10.1186/s12888-017-1200-y

Keeley, J. W., Reed, G. M., Roberts, M. C., Evans, S. C., Medina-Mora, M. E., Robles, R., Rebello, T., Sharan, P., Gureje, O., First, M. B., Andrews, H. F., Ayuso-Mateos, J. L., Gaebel, W., Zielasek, J., & Saxena, S. (2016). Developing a science of clinical utility in diagnostic classification systems field study strategies for ICD-11 mental and behavioral disorders. *American Psychologist, 71*(1), 3–16. https://doi.org/10.1037/a0039972

Kernberg, O. F. (1984). *Severe personality disorders*. Yale University Press.

Kim, Y.-R., Blashfield, R., Tyrer, P., Hwang, S.-T., & Lee, H.-S. (2014). Field trial of a putative research algorithm for diagnosing ICD-11 personality disorders in psychiatric patients: 1. Severity of personality disturbance. *Personality and Mental Health, 8*(1), 67–78. https://doi.org/10.1002/pmh.1248

Konjusha, A., Hopwood, C. J., Price, A. L., Masuhr, O., & Zimmermann, J. (2021). Investigating the transdiagnostic value of subjective emptiness. *Journal of Personality Disorders, 35*(5), 788–800. https://doi.org/10.1521/pedi_2021_35_510

Krueger, R. F., Derringer, J., Markon, K. E., Watson, D., & Skodol, A. E. (2012). Initial construction of a maladaptive personality trait model and inventory for DSM-5. *Psychological Medicine, 42*(09), 1879–1890. https://doi.org/10.1017/S0033291711002674

Krueger, R. F., Skodol, A. E., Livesley, W. J., Shrout, P. E., & Huang, Y. (2007). Synthesizing dimensional and categorical approaches to personality disorders: Refining the research agenda for DSM-V Axis II. *International Journal of Methods in Psychiatric Research, 16*(S1), S65–S73. https://doi.org/10.1002/mpr.212

Leclerc, P., Savard, C., Vachon, D. D., Faucher, J., Payant, M., Lampron, M., Tremblay, M., & Gamache, D. (2021). Analysis of the interaction between personality dysfunction and traits in the statistical prediction of physical aggression: Results from outpatient and community samples. *Personality and Mental Health, 16*(1), 5–18. https://doi.org/10.1002/pmh.1522

Leising, D., Krause, S., Köhler, D., Hinsen, K., & Clifton, A. (2011). Assessing interpersonal functioning: Views from within and without. *Journal of Research in Personality, 45*(6), 631–641. https://doi.org/10.1016/j.jrp.2011.08.011

Leising, D., Rogers, K., & Ostner, J. (2009). The undisordered personality: Normative assumptions underlying personality disorder diagnoses. *Review of General Psychology, 13*(3), 230–241. https://doi.org/10.1037/a0017139

Leising, D., Scherbaum, S., Packmohr, P., & Zimmermann, J. (2018). Substance and evaluation in personality disorder diagnoses. *Journal of Personality Disorders, 32*(6), 766–783. https://doi.org/10.1521/pedi_2017_31_324

Leising, D., Vogel, D., Waller, V., & Zimmermann, J. (2021). Correlations between person-descriptive items are predictable from the product of their mid-point-centered social desirability values. *European Journal of Personality, 35*(5), 667–689. https://doi.org/10.1177/0890207020962331

Leising, D., & Zimmermann, J. (2011). An integrative conceptual framework for assessing personality and personality pathology. *Review of General Psychology, 15*(4), 317–330. https://doi.org/10.1037/a0025070

Lewis, C. C., Boyd, M., Puspitasari, A., Navarro, E., Howard, J., Kassab, H., Hoffman, M., Scott, K., Lyon, A., Douglas, S., Simon, G., & Kroenke, K. (2019). Implementing measurement-based care in behavioral health: A review. *JAMA Psychiatry, 76*(3), 324–335. https://doi.org/10.1001/jamapsychiatry.2018.3329

Liggett, J., Carmichael, K. L. C., Smith, A., & Sellbom, M. (2017). Validation of self-report impairment measures for Section III obsessive-compulsive and avoidant personality disorders. *Journal of Personality Assessment, 99*(1), 1–14. https://doi.org/10.1080/00223891.2016.1185613

Liggett, J., & Sellbom, M. (2018). Examining the DSM-5 alternative model of personality disorders operationalization of obsessive-compulsive personality disorder in a mental health sample. *Personality Disorders: Theory, Research, and Treatment, 9*(5), 397–407. https://doi.org/10.1037/per0000285

Lingiardi, V., & McWilliams, N. (Eds.). (2017). *Psychodynamic diagnostic manual: Pdm-2*, 2nd ed. Guilford.

Livesley, W. J. (1998). Suggestions for a framework for an empirically based classification of personality disorder. *Canadian Journal of Psychiatry/Revue Canadienne De Psychiatrie, 43*(2), 137–147.

Livesley, W. J. (2006). *General Assessment of Personality Disorder (GAPD)*. Department of Psychiatry, University of British Columbia.

Luyten, P., & Blatt, S. J. (2013). Interpersonal relatedness and self-definition in normal and disrupted personality development: Retrospect and prospect. *American Psychologist, 68*(3), 172–183. https://doi.org/10.1037/a0032243

Markon, K. E., Chmielewski, M., & Miller, C. J. (2011). The reliability and validity of discrete and continuous measures of psychopathology: A quantitative review. *Psychological Bulletin, 137*(5), 856–879. https://doi.org/10.1037/a0023678

McCabe, G. A., Oltmanns, J. R., & Widiger, T. A. (2021a). Criterion A scales: Convergent, discriminant, and structural relationships. *Assessment, 28*(3), 813–828. https://doi.org/10.1177/1073191120947160

McCabe, G. A., Oltmanns, J. R., & Widiger, T. A. (2021b). The general factors of personality disorder, psychopathology, and personality. *Journal of Personality Disorders, 36*(2), 129–156. https://doi.org/10.1521/pedi_2021_35_530

McCabe, G. A., & Widiger, T. A. (2020). Discriminant validity of the alternative model of personality disorder. *Psychological Assessment, 32*(12), 1158–1171. https://doi.org/10.1037/pas0000955

Meehan, K. B., Siefert, C., Sexton, J., & Huprich, S. K. (2019). Expanding the role of levels of personality functioning in personality disorder taxonomy: Commentary on "Criterion A of the AMPD in HiTOP." *Journal of Personality Assessment, 101*(4), 367–373. https://doi.org/10.1080/00223891.2018.1551228

Meisner, M. W., Bach, B., Lenzenweger, M. F., Møller, L., Haahr, U. H., Petersen, L. S., Kongerslev, M. T., & Simonsen, E. (2021). Reconceptualization of borderline conditions through the lens of the alternative model of personality disorders. *Personality Disorders: Theory, Research, and Treatment, 13*(3), 266–276. https://doi.org/10.1037/per0000502

Meyer, B., & Pilkonis, P. A. (2005). An attachment model of personality disorders. In M. F. Lenzenweger & J. F. Clarkin (Eds.), *Major theories of personality disorder*, 2nd ed. (pp. 231–281). Guilford.

Milinkovic, M. S., & Tiliopoulos, N. (2020). A systematic review of the clinical utility of the DSM-5 section III alternative model of personality disorder. *Personality Disorders: Theory, Research, and Treatment, 11*(6), 377–397. https://doi.org/10.1037/per0000408

Møller, L., Meisner, M. W., Søgaard, U., Elklit, A., & Simonsen, E. (2021). Assessment of personality functioning in ICD-11 posttraumatic stress disorder and complex posttraumatic stress disorder. *Personality Disorders: Theory, Research, and Treatment, 12*(5), 466–474. https://doi.org/10.1037/per0000491

Morey, L. C. (2017). Development and initial evaluation of a self-report form of the DSM-5 Level of Personality Functioning Scale. *Psychological Assessment, 29*(10), 1302–1308. https://doi.org/10.1037/pas0000450

Morey, L. C. (2018). Application of the DSM-5 Level of Personality Functioning Scale by lay raters. *Journal of Personality Disorders, 32*(5), 709–720. https://doi.org/10.1521/pedi_2017_31_305

Morey, L. C. (2019). Interdiagnostician reliability of the DSM-5 Section II and Section III Alternative Model criteria for borderline personality disorder. *Journal of Personality Disorders, 33*(6), 721–S18. https://doi.org/10.1521/pedi_2019_33_362

Morey, L. C., & Bender, D. S. (2021). Articulating a core dimension of personality pathology. In A. E. Skodol & J. M. Oldham (Eds.), *The American Psychiatric Association Publishing Textbook of Personality Disorders*, 3rd ed. (pp. 47–64). American Psychiatric Publishing.

Morey, L. C., Bender, D. S., & Skodol, A. E. (2013). Validating the proposed Diagnostic and Statistical Manual of Mental Disorders, 5th edition, severity indicator for personality disorder. *Journal of Nervous and Mental Disease, 201*(9), 729–735. https://doi.org/10.1097/NMD.0b013e3182a20ea8

Morey, L. C., Berghuis, H., Bender, D. S., Verheul, R., Krueger, R. F., & Skodol, A. E. (2011). Toward a model for assessing level of personality functioning in DSM–5 Part II: Empirical articulation of a core dimension of personality pathology. *Journal of Personality Assessment, 93*(4), 347–353. https://doi.org/10.1080/00223891.2011.577853

Morey, L. C., Good, E. W., & Hopwood, C. J. (2020). Global personality dysfunction and the relationship of pathological and normal trait domains in the DSM-5 alternative model for personality disorders. *Journal of Personality, 90*(1), 34–46. https://doi.org/10.1111/jopy.12560

Morey, L. C., Skodol, A. E., & Oldham, J. M. (2014). Clinician judgments of clinical utility: A comparison of DSM-IV-TR personality disorders and the alternative model for DSM-5 personality disorders. *Journal of Abnormal Psychology, 123*(2), 398–405. https://doi.org/10.1037/a0036481

Moshagen, M. (2012). The model size effect in SEM: Inflated goodness-of-fit statistics are due to the size of the covariance matrix. *Structural Equation Modeling: A Multidisciplinary Journal, 19*(1), 86–98. https://doi.org/10.1080/10705511.2012.634724

Mulay, A. L., Cain, N. M., Waugh, M. H., Hopwood, C. J., Adler, J. M., Garcia, D. J., Kurtz, J. E., Lenger, K. A., & Skadberg, R. (2018). Personality constructs and paradigms in the Alternative DSM-5 Model of Personality Disorder. *Journal of Personality Assessment, 100*(6), 593–602. https://doi.org/10.1080/00223891.2018.1477787

Mulder, R., & Tyrer, P. (2019). Diagnosis and classification of personality disorders: Novel approaches. *Current Opinion in Psychiatry, 32*(1), 27–31. https://doi.org/10.1097/YCO.0000000000000461

Müller, S., Wendt, L. P., Spitzer, C., Masuhr, O., Back, S. N., & Zimmermann, J. (2021). A critical evaluation of the Reflective Functioning Questionnaire (RFQ). *Journal of Personality Assessment*. Advance online publication. https://doi.org/10.1080/00223891.2021.1981346

Müller, S., Wendt, L. P., & Zimmermann, J. (2021). Development and validation of the Certainty About Mental States Questionnaire (CAMSQ): A self-report measure of mentalizing oneself and others. *Assessment*. Advance online publication. https://doi.org/10.1177/10731911211061280

Mullins-Sweatt, S. N., & Widiger, T. A. (2009). Clinical utility and DSM-V. *Psychological Assessment, 21*(3), 302–312. https://doi.org/10.1037/a0016607

Munro, O. E., & Sellbom, M. (2020). Elucidating the relationship between borderline personality disorder and intimate partner violence. *Personality and Mental Health, 14*(3), 284–303. https://doi.org/10.1002/pmh.1480

Nelson, S. M., Huprich, S. K., Meehan, K. B., Siefert, C., Haggerty, G., Sexton, J., Dauphin, V. B., Macaluso, M., Zackula, R., Baade, L., & Jackson, J. (2018). Convergent and discriminant validity and utility of the DSM-5 Levels of Personality Functioning Questionnaire (DLOPFQ): Associations with medical health care provider ratings and measures of physical health. *Journal of Personality Assessment, 100*(6), 671–679. https://doi.org/10.1080/00223891.2018.1492415

Nelson, S. M., Huprich, S. K., Shankar, S., Sohnleitner, A., & Paggeot, A. V. (2017). A quantitative and qualitative evaluation of trainee opinions of four methods of personality disorder diagnosis. *Personality Disorders: Theory, Research, and*

*Treatment, 8*(3), 217–227. https://doi.org/10.1037/per0000227

Ohse, L., Zimmermann, J., Kerber, A., Kampe, L., Mohr, J., Kendlbacher, J., Busch, O., Rentrop, M., & Hörz-Sagstetter, S. (2021). Reliability, structure, and validity of module I (personality functioning) of the Structured Clinical Interview for the alternative DSM–5 model for personality disorders (SCID-5-AMPD-I). *Personality Disorders: Theory, Research, and Treatment.* Advance online publication. https://doi.org/10.1037/per0000576

Olajide, K., Munjiza, J., Moran, P., O'Connell, L., Newton-Howes, G., Bassett, P., Akintomide, G., Ng, N., Tyrer, P., Mulder, R., & Crawford, M. J. (2018). Development and psychometric properties of the Standardized Assessment of Severity of Personality Disorder (SASPD). *Journal of Personality Disorders, 32*(1), 44–56. https://doi.org/10.1521/pedi_2017_31_285

Olderbak, S., & Wilhelm, O. (2020). Overarching principles for the organization of socioemotional constructs. *Current Directions in Psychological Science, 29*(1), 63–70. https://doi.org/10.1177/0963721419884317

Oltmanns, J. R., & Widiger, T. A. (2019). Evaluating the assessment of the ICD-11 personality disorder diagnostic system. *Psychological Assessment, 31*(5), 674–684. https://doi.org/10.1037/pas0000693

OPD Task Force. (2008). *Operationalized Psychodynamic Diagnosis OPD–2: Manual of diagnosis and treatment planning.* Hogrefe & Huber.

Paap, M. C. S., Heltne, A., Pedersen, G., Germans Selvik, S., Frans, N., Wilberg, T., & Hummelen, B. (2021). More is more: Evidence for the incremental value of the SCID-II/SCID-5-PD specific factors over and above a general personality disorder factor. *Personality Disorders: Theory, Research, and Treatment, 13*(2), 108–118. https://doi.org/10.1037/per0000426

Parker, G., Both, L., Olley, A., Hadzi-Pavlovic, D., Irvine, P., & Jacobs, G. (2002). Defining disordered personality functioning. *Journal of Personality Disorders, 16*(6), 503–522. https://doi.org/10.1521/pedi.16.6.503.22139

Parker, G., Hadzi-Pavlovic, D., Both, L., Kumar, S., Wilhelm, K., & Olley, A. (2004). Measuring disordered personality functioning: To love and to work reprised. *Acta Psychiatrica Scandinavica, 110*(3), 230–239. https://doi.org/10.1111/j.1600-0447.2004.00312.x

Persson, B. N., & Lilienfeld, S. O. (2019). Social status as one key indicator of successful psychopathy: An initial empirical investigation. *Personality and Individual Differences, 141*, 209–217. https://doi.org/10.1016/j.paid.2019.01.020

Peter, L.-J., Schindler, S., Sander, C., Schmidt, S., Muehlan, H., McLaren, T., Tomczyk, S., Speerforck, S., & Schomerus, G. (2021). Continuum beliefs and mental illness stigma: A systematic review and meta-analysis of correlation and intervention studies. *Psychological Medicine, 51*(5), 716–726. https://doi.org/10.1017/S0033291721000854

Pincus, A. L. (2018). An interpersonal perspective on Criterion A of the DSM-5 Alternative Model for Personality Disorders. *Current Opinion in Psychology, 21*, 11–17. https://doi.org/10.1016/j.copsyc.2017.08.035

Pincus, A. L., Cain, N. M., & Halberstadt, A. L. (2020). Importance of self and other in defining personality pathology. *Psychopathology, 53*(3–4), 133–140. https://doi.org/10.1159/000506313

Pincus, A. L., Dowgwillo, E. A., & Greenberg, L. S. (2016). Three cases of narcissistic personality disorder through the lens of the DSM-5 alternative model for personality disorders. *Practice Innovations, 1*(3), 164–177. https://doi.org/10.1037/pri0000025

Preti, E., Di Pierro, R., Costantini, G., Benzi, I. M. A., Panfilis, C. de, & Madeddu, F. (2018). Using the Structured Interview of Personality Organization for DSM-5 Level of Personality Functioning rating performed by inexperienced raters. *Journal of Personality Assessment, 100*(6), 621–629. https://doi.org/10.1080/00223891.2018.1448985

Prevolnik Rupel, V., Jagger, B., Fialho, L. S., Chadderton, L.-M., Gintner, T., Arntz, A., . . . Crawford, M. J. (2021). Standard set of patient-reported outcomes for personality disorder. *Quality of Life Research, 30*, 3485–3500. https://doi.org/10.1007/s11136-021-02870-w

Quilty, L. C., Bagby, R. M., Krueger, R. F., & Pollock, B. G. (2021). Validation of DSM-5 clinician-rated measures of personality pathology. *Psychological Assessment, 33*(1), 84–89. https://doi.org/10.1037/pas0000960

Reed, G. M., First, M. B., Kogan, C. S., Hyman, S. E., Gureje, O., Gaebel, W., . . . Saxena, S. (2019). Innovations and changes in the ICD-11 classification of mental, behavioural and neurodevelopmental disorders. *World Psychiatry, 18*(1), 3–19. https://doi.org/10.1002/wps.20611

Ringwald, W. R., Beeney, J. E., Pilkonis, P. A., & Wright, A. G. C. (2019). Comparing hierarchical models of personality pathology. *Journal of Research in Personality, 81*, 98–107. https://doi.org/10.1016/j.jrp.2019.05.011

Ringwald, W. R., Hopwood, C. J., Pilkonis, P. A., & Wright, A. G. C. (2021). Dynamic features of affect and interpersonal behavior in relation to general and specific personality pathology. *Personality Disorders: Theory, Research, and Treatment, 12*(4), 365–376. https://doi.org/10.1037/per0000469

Rishede, M. Z., Juul, S., Bo, S., Gondan, M., Bjerrum Møeller, S., & Simonsen, S. (2021). Personality functioning and mentalizing in patients with subthreshold or diagnosed borderline personality disorder: Implications for ICD-11. *Frontiers in Psychiatry, 12*, 634332. https://doi.org/10.3389/fpsyt.2021.634332

Roberts, J. S., Donoghue, J. R., & Laughlin, J. E. (2000). A general item response theory model for unfolding unidimensional polytomous responses. *Applied Psychological Measurement, 24*(1), 3–32. https://doi.org/10.1177/01466216000241001

Roche, M. J. (2018). Examining the alternative model for personality disorder in daily life: Evidence for incremental validity. *Personality Disorders: Theory, Research, and Treatment, 9*(6), 574–583. https://doi.org/10.1037/per0000295

Roche, M. J., Jacobson, N. C., & Phillips, J. J. (2018). Expanding the validity of the Level of Personality Functioning Scale observer report and self-report versions across psychodynamic and interpersonal paradigms. *Journal of Personality Assessment, 100*(6), 571–580. https://doi.org/10.1080/00223891.2018.1475394

Roche, M. J., Jacobson, N. C., & Pincus, A. L. (2016). Using repeated daily assessments to uncover oscillating patterns and temporally-dynamic triggers in structures of psychopathology: Applications to the DSM-5 alternative model of personality disorders. *Journal of Abnormal Psychology, 125*(8), 1090–1102. https://doi.org/10.1037/abn0000177

Roche, M. J., & Jaweed, S. (2021). Comparing measures of Criterion A to better understand incremental validity in the Alternative Model of Personality Disorders. *Assessment.* Advance online publication. https://doi.org/10.1177/10731911211059763

Ruchensky, J. R., Dowgwillo, E. A., Kelley, S. E., Massey, C., Slavin-Mulford, J., Richardson, L. A., Blais, M. A., & Stein, M. B. (2021). Exploring the alternative model for personality disorders using SCORS-G ratings on thematic apperception test narratives. *Journal of Personality Disorders, 36*(2), 201–216. https://doi.org/10.1521/pedi_2021_35_535

Saulsman, L. M., & Page, A. C. (2004). The five-factor model and personality disorder empirical literature: A meta-analytic review. *Clinical Psychology Review, 23*(8), 1055–1085. https://doi.org/10.1016/j.cpr.2002.09.001

Schmeck, K., Schlüter-Müller, S., Foelsch, P. A., & Doering, S. (2013). The role of identity in the DSM-5 classification of personality disorders. *Child and Adolescent Psychiatry and Mental Health, 7*(1), 27. https://doi.org/10.1186/1753-2000-7-27

Sharp, C., & Wall, K. (2021). Dsm-5 Level of Personality Functioning: Refocusing personality disorder on what it means to be human. *Annual Review of Clinical Psychology, 17,* 313–337. https://doi.org/10.1146/annurev-clinpsy-081219-105402

Sharp, C., Wright, A. G. C., Fowler, J. C., Frueh, B. C., Allen, J. G., Oldham, J., & Clark, L. A. (2015). The structure of personality pathology: Both general ("g") and specific ("s") factors? *Journal of Abnormal Psychology, 124*(2), 387–398. https://doi.org/10.1037/abn0000033

Siefert, C. J., Sexton, J., Meehan, K., Nelson, S., Haggerty, G., Dauphin, B., & Huprich, S. (2020). Development of a short form for the DSM-5 Levels of Personality Functioning Questionnaire. *Journal of Personality Assessment, 102*(4), 516–526. https://doi.org/10.1080/00223891.2019.1594842

Sinnaeve, R., Vaessen, T., van Diest, I., Myin-Germeys, I., van den Bosch, L. M. C., Vrieze, E., Kamphuis, J. H., & Claes, S. (2021). Investigating the stress-related fluctuations of level of personality functioning: A critical review and agenda for future research. *Clinical Psychology & Psychotherapy, 28*(5), 1181–1193. https://doi.org/10.1002/cpp.2566

Skodol, A. E. (2012). Personality disorders in DSM-5. *Annual Review of Clinical Psychology, 8*(1), 317–344. https://doi.org/10.1146/annurev-clinpsy-032511-143131

Skodol, A. E., Morey, L. C., Bender, D. S., & Oldham, J. M. (2015). The Alternative DSM-5 Model for Personality Disorders: A clinical application. *American Journal of Psychiatry, 172*(7), 606–613. https://doi.org/10.1176/appi.ajp.2015.14101220

Sleep, C. E., Lynam, D. R., & Miller, J. D. (2021). Personality impairment in the DSM-5 and ICD-11: Current standing and limitations. *Current Opinion in Psychiatry, 34*(1), 39–43. https://doi.org/10.1097/YCO.0000000000000657

Sleep, C. E., Lynam, D. R., Widiger, T. A., Crowe, M. L., & Miller, J. D. (2019). An evaluation of DSM-5 Section III personality disorder Criterion A (impairment) in accounting for psychopathology. *Psychological Assessment, 31*(10), 1181–1191. https://doi.org/10.1037/pas0000620

Sleep, C. E., Weiss, B., Lynam, D. R., & Miller, J. D. (2020). The DSM-5 Section III personality disorder Criterion A in relation to both pathological and general personality traits. *Personality Disorders: Theory, Research, and Treatment, 11*(3), 202–212. https://doi.org/10.1037/per0000383

Somma, A., Borroni, S., Gialdi, G., Carlotta, D., Emanuela Giarolli, L., Barranca, M., Cerioli, C., Franzoni, C., Masci, E., Manini, R., Luca Busso, S., Ruotolo, G., Krueger, R. F., Markon, K. E., & Fossati, A. (2020). The inter-rater reliability and validity of the Italian translation of the Structured Clinical Interview for DSM-5 Alternative Model for Personality Disorders Module I and Module II: A preliminary report on consecutively admitted psychotherapy outpatients. *Journal of Personality Disorders, 34*(Suppl C), 95–123. https://doi.org/10.1521/pedi_2020_34_511

Spitzer, C., Müller, S., Kerber, A., Hutsebaut, J., Brähler, E., & Zimmermann, J. (2021). Die deutsche Version der Level of Personality Functioning Scale-Brief Form 2.0 (LPFS-BF): Faktorenstruktur, konvergente Validität und Normwerte in der Allgemeinbevölkerung [The German version of the Level of Personality Functioning Scale-Brief Form 2.0 (LPFS-BF): Latent structure, convergent validity and norm values in the general population]. *Psychotherapie, Psychosomatik, medizinische Psychologie, 71*(7), 284–293. https://doi.org/10.1055/a-1343-2396

Stone, L. E., Segal, D. L., & Noel, O. R. (2020). Psychometric evaluation of the Levels of Personality Functioning Scale—Brief Form 2.0 among older adults. *Personality Disorders: Theory, Research, and Treatment, 12*(6), 526–533. https://doi.org/10.1037/per0000413

Stover, J. B., Liporace, M. F., & Castro Solano, A. (2020). Personality functioning scale: A scale to assess DSM-5's Criterion A personality disorders. *Interpersona: An International Journal on Personal Relationships, 14*(1), 40–53. https://doi.org/10.5964/ijpr.v14i1.3925

Stricker, J., & Pietrowsky, R. (2021). Incremental validity of the ICD-11 personality disorder model for explaining psychological distress. *Personality Disorders: Theory, Research, and Treatment, 13*(2), 97–107. https://doi.org/10.1037/per0000489

Svrakic, D. M., Whitehead, C., Przybeck, T. R., & Cloninger, C. R. (1993). Differential diagnosis of personality disorders by the seven-factor model of temperament and character. *Archives of General Psychiatry, 50*(12), 991–999.

Thompson, K. N., Jackson, H., Cavelti, M., Betts, J., McCutcheon, L., Jovev, M., & Chanen, A. M. (2019). The clinical significance of subthreshold borderline personality disorder features in outpatient youth. *Journal of Personality Disorders, 33*(1), 71–81. https://doi.org/10.1521/pedi_2018_32_330

Thylstrup, B., Simonsen, S., Nemery, C., Simonsen, E., Noll, J. F., Myatt, M. W., & Hesse, M. (2016). Assessment of personality-related levels of functioning: A pilot study of clinical assessment of the DSM-5 level of personality functioning based on a semi-structured interview. *BMC Psychiatry, 16,* 298. https://doi.org/10.1186/s12888-016-1011-6

Traynor, J. M., Wrege, J. S., Walter, M., & Ruocco, A. C. (2021). Dimensional personality impairment is associated with disruptions in intrinsic intralimbic functional connectivity. *Psychological Medicine.* Advance online publication. Ahttps://doi.org/10.1017/S0033291721002865

Turkheimer, E., Ford, D. C., & Oltmanns, T. F. (2008). Regional analysis of self-reported personality disorder criteria. *Journal of Personality, 76*(6), 1587–1622. https://doi.org/10.1111/j.1467-6494.2008.00532.x

Tyrer, P., Crawford, M. J., Sanatinia, R., Tyrer, H., Cooper, S., Muller-Pollard, C., Christodoulou, P., Zauter-Tutt, M., Miloseska-Reid, K., Loebenberg, G., Guo, B., Yang, M., Wang, D., & Weich, S. (2014). Preliminary studies of the ICD-11 classification of personality disorder in practice.

Personality and Mental Health, 8(4), 254–263. https://doi.org/10.1002/pmh.1275

Tyrer, P., & Johnson, T. (1996). Establishing the severity of personality disorder. American Journal of Psychiatry, 153(12), 1593–1597.

Tyrer, P., Reed, G. M., & Crawford, M. J. (2015). Classification, assessment, prevalence, and effect of personality disorder. Lancet, 385(9969), 717–726. https://doi.org/10.1016/S0140-6736(14)61995-4

Verheul, R., Andrea, H., Berghout, C. C., Dolan, C., Busschbach, J. J. V., van der Kroft, P. J. A., Bateman, A. W., & Fonagy, P. (2008). Severity Indices of Personality Problems (SIPP-118): Development, factor structure, reliability, and validity. Psychological Assessment, 20(1), 23–34. https://doi.org/10.1037/1040-3590.20.1.23

Wakefield, J. C. (1992). The concept of mental disorder: On the boundary between biological facts and social values. American Psychologist, 47(3), 373–388. https://doi.org/10.1037/0003-066X.47.3.373

Waugh, M. H., McClain, C. M., Mariotti, E. C., Mulay, A. L., DeVore, E. N., Lenger, K. A., Russell, A. N., Florimbio, A. R., Lewis, K. C., Ridenour, J. M., & Beevers, L. G. (2021). Comparative content analysis of self-report scales for level of personality functioning. Journal of Personality Assessment, 103(2), 161–173. https://doi.org/10.1080/00223891.2019.1705464

Weekers, L. C., Hutsebaut, J., Bach, B., & Kamphuis, J. H. (2020). Scripting the DSM-5 Alternative Model for Personality Disorders assessment procedure: A clinically feasible multi-informant multi-method approach. Personality and Mental Health, 14(3), 304–318. https://doi.org/10.1002/pmh.1481

Weekers, L. C., Hutsebaut, J., & Kamphuis, J. H. (2019). The Level of Personality Functioning Scale-Brief Form 2.0: Update of a brief instrument for assessing level of personality functioning. Personality and Mental Health, 13(1), 3–14. https://doi.org/10.1002/pmh.1434

Weekers, L. C., Hutsebaut, J., & Kamphuis, J. H. (2021). Client and clinical utility of the assessment of personality disorders. Journal of Nervous and Mental Disease, 209(11), 846–850. https://doi.org/10.1097/NMD.0000000000001398

Weekers, L. C., Verhoeff, S. C. E., Kamphuis, J. H., & Hutsebaut, J. (2021). Assessing Criterion A in adolescents using the Semistructured Interview for Personality Functioning DSM-5. Personality Disorders: Theory, Research, and Treatment, 12(4), 312–319. https://doi.org/10.1037/per0000454

Westen, D., Barends, A., Leigh, M., Mendel, M., & Silbert, D. (1990). Social Cognition and Object Relations Scale (SCORS): Manual for coding interview data: Unpublished manuscript. University of Michigan.

Westen, D., Gabbard, G. O., & Blagov, P. S. (2006). Back to the future: Personality structure as a context for psychopathology. In R. F. Krueger & J. L. Tackett (Eds.), Personality and psychopathology (pp. 335–384). Guilford.

Widiger, T. A., Bach, B., Chmielewski, M., Clark, L. A., DeYoung, C., Hopwood, C. J., . . . Thomas, K. M. (2019). Criterion A of the AMPD in HiTOP. Journal of Personality Assessment, 101(4), 345–355. https://doi.org/10.1080/00223891.2018.1465431

Widiger, T. A., & Mullins-Sweatt, S. N. (2009). Five-factor model of personality disorder: A proposal for DSM-V. Annual Review of Clinical Psychology, 5(1), 197–220. https://doi.org/10.1146/annurev.clinpsy.032408.153542

Widiger, T. A., & Trull, T. J. (2007). Plate tectonics in the classification of personality disorder: Shifting to a dimensional model. American Psychologist, 62(2), 71–83. https://doi.org/10.1037/0003-066X.62.2.71

Williams, T. F., Scalco, M. D., & Simms, L. J. (2018). The construct validity of general and specific dimensions of personality pathology. Psychological Medicine, 48(5), 834–848. https://doi.org/10.1017/S0033291717002227

Wright, A. G., Hopwood, C. J., Skodol, A. E., & Morey, L. C. (2016). Longitudinal validation of general and specific structural features of personality pathology. Journal of Abnormal Psychology, 125(8), 1120–1134. https://doi.org/10.1037/abn0000165

Wygant, D. B., Sellbom, M., Sleep, C. E., Wall, T. D., Applegate, K. C., Krueger, R. F., & Patrick, C. J. (2016). Examining the DSM-5 alternative personality disorder model operationalization of antisocial personality disorder and psychopathy in a male correctional sample. Personality Disorders: Theory, Research, and Treatment, 7(3), 229–239. https://doi.org/10.1037/per0000179

Yalch, M. M. (2020). Psychodynamic underpinnings of the DSM–5 Alternative Model for Personality Disorder. Psychoanalytic Psychology, 37(3), 219–231. https://doi.org/10.1037/pap0000262

Yang, M., Coid, J., & Tyrer, P. (2010). Personality pathology recorded by severity: National survey. British Journal of Psychiatry, 197(3), 193–199. https://doi.org/10.1192/bjp.bp.110.078956

Zettl, M., Volkert, J., Vögele, C., Herpertz, S. C., Kubera, K. M., & Taubner, S. (2020). Mentalization and Criterion A of the Alternative Model for Personality Disorders: Results from a clinical and nonclinical sample. Personality Disorders: Theory, Research, and Treatment, 11(3), 191–201. https://doi.org/10.1037/per0000356

Zimmerman, M., Rothschild, L., & Chelminski, I. (2005). The prevalence of DSM-IV personality disorders in psychiatric outpatients. American Journal of Psychiatry, 162(10), 1911–1918. https://doi.org/10.1176/appi.ajp.162.10.1911

Zimmermann, J., Benecke, C., Bender, D. S., Skodol, A. E., Schauenburg, H., Cierpka, M., & Leising, D. (2014). Assessing DSM-5 Level of Personality Functioning from videotaped clinical interviews: A pilot study with untrained and clinically inexperienced students. Journal of Personality Assessment, 96(4), 397–409. https://doi.org/10.1080/00223891.2013.852563

Zimmermann, J., Böhnke, J. R., Eschstruth, R., Mathews, A., Wenzel, K., & Leising, D. (2015). The latent structure of personality functioning: Investigating criterion A from the alternative model for personality disorders in DSM-5. Journal of Abnormal Psychology, 124(3), 532–548. https://doi.org/10.1037/abn0000059

Zimmermann, J., Ehrenthal, J. C., Cierpka, M., Schauenburg, H., Doering, S., & Benecke, C. (2012). Assessing the level of structural integration using Operationalized Psychodynamic Diagnosis (OPD): Implications for DSM–5. Journal of Personality Assessment, 94(5), 522–532. https://doi.org/10.1080/00223891.2012.700664

Zimmermann, J., Kerber, A., Rek, K., Hopwood, C. J., & Krueger, R. F. (2019). A brief but comprehensive review of research on the Alternative DSM-5 Model for Personality Disorders. Current Psychiatry Reports, 21(9), 92. https://doi.org/10.1007/s11920-019-1079-z

Zimmermann, J., Müller, S., Bach, B., Hutsebaut, J., Hummelen, B., & Fischer, F. (2020). A common metric for self-reported severity of personality disorder. Psychopathology, 53(3–4), 168–178. https://doi.org/10.1159/000507377

# CHAPTER 26

# The DSM-5 Maladaptive Trait Model for Personality Disorders

Colin D. Freilich, Robert F. Krueger, Kelsey A. Hobbs, Christopher J. Hopwood, *and* Johannes Zimmermann

The classification system, or taxonomy, for personality disorders (PDs) has vast clinical significance. To explore just how pervasive the influence of the taxonomy is, consider what purpose an individual PD diagnosis serves. Diagnosis provides a common nomenclature between clinician and patient, prior clinician and new clinician, patient and support group, and many other transactions. In that way, diagnosis facilitates communication and allows for information retrieval. With a specific diagnosis, a clinician can quickly locate information about relevant treatment or illness course. Indeed, informing treatment may be the most fundamental clinical purpose of PD diagnosis.

More generally, diagnosis aids prediction. Not only should a diagnosis predict what treatment is likely to be efficacious, but also, for instance, what further risk factors should be avoided, what occupations may be suitable, or what outcomes should be expected. In addition, a diagnosis does not exist in a vacuum but rather in a complex sociopolitical landscape. For example, a diagnosis may serve administrative purposes, such as access to insurance coverage for specific interventions or requisite student accommodations.

Classification systems, such as *DSM-5*, must serve purposes beyond those directly relevant to an individual diagnosis. A taxonomy of PDs influences and organizes research by providing a descriptive basis for the science. Indeed, that descriptive basis frames research on the etiology, treatment, and course of similar cases, eventually leading to the development of scientific theories. These insights in turn influence the type of care that future patients with the relevant diagnoses receive.

It stands to reason that a diagnostic system could be evaluated on how well it serves these various purposes. To what extent do the diagnoses within a taxonomy inform treatment decisions? How well do they predict meaningful outcomes? Do patients and clinicians find the common diagnostic language valuable and representative of their individual cases? How effective is the research built on these diagnoses at uncovering the etiology and course of pathological processes? Taxonomic choices affect patients on the smallest and largest possible scales.

## PD Taxonomies of *DSM-5*

Reflecting the complexity of taxonomic decisions, *DSM-5* offers two distinct classification systems for diagnosing PDs. The first system is in Section II of the manual and "represents an update of text associated with the criteria found in *DSM-IV-TR*" (p. 645). The approach of the fourth edition of the *DSM* and its

### Abbreviations

| | |
|---|---|
| CAT-PD | Computer Adaptive Test of Personality Disorder |
| DAPP-BQ | Dimensional Assessment of Personality Pathology |
| FFM | Five-Factor Model |
| LCA | Latent class analysis |
| MMPI-2-RF | Minnesota Multiphasic Personality Inventory 2 Restructured Form |
| PAI | Personality Assessment Inventory |
| PID-5 | Personality Inventory for *DSM-5* |
| PTAI | Personality Trait Rating Form |
| SNAP | Schedule for the Nonadaptive and Adaptive Personality |

subsequent text revision (*DSM-IV-TR*) dates to 2000 and includes 10 putatively separate, categorical, and complex personality syndromes, each with its own criterion set. For instance, schizoid PD is defined as "a pervasive pattern of detachment from social relationships and restricted range of expression of emotions" indicated by four or more of seven symptoms, including "neither desires nor enjoys close relationships, including being part of a family," "almost always chooses solitary activities," and "takes pleasure in few, if any, activities" (pp. 652–653). In addition, the symptomatology must not be attributable to separate psychopathological diagnoses like schizophrenia. These diagnostic criteria are *polythetic*, meaning that the disorder is defined by multiple symptoms, and many different combinations of symptoms can be sufficient to meet the criteria for diagnosis. Similarly polythetic criteria are given for each of the nine other distinct syndromes: paranoid, schizotypal, antisocial, borderline, histrionic, narcissistic, avoidant, dependent, and obsessive-compulsive PDs. Finally, for cases in which symptoms are causing clinically significant distress but fail to meet the full criteria for one of the 10 specific PDs, clinicians can use the catch-all categories of "other specified" or "unspecified" PD.

*DSM-5*'s second system, the Alternative Model for Personality Disorders (AMPD), is in "Section III Emerging Measures and Models" of the manual. The AMPD is a dimensional approach built on efforts that arose primarily to address limitations of the traditional, categorical system of the *DSM-IV-TR* for classifying PDs (Zachar et al., 2016).

## Limitations of Traditional Approaches
### Personality Traits as an Organizing Framework

The approach of Section II of *DSM-5* has been the standard for PD diagnosis for decades, and considerable research has been generated in the interim that highlights its limitations. Perhaps the most fundamental flaw in this approach is that personality traits are not used as an organizing framework. In the first half of the twentieth century, scholars debated the importance of personality, but that period of skepticism is well behind us (Donnellan et al., 2009; Widiger, Sellbom et al., 2019). Personality traits are relatively enduring patterns of thoughts, feelings, strivings, and behaviors that distinguish individuals from each other, and they are now widely recognized as clinically significant, robustly impacting a host of outcomes like subjective well-being, physical health, longevity, relationship satisfaction, occupational choice and performance, values, and criminality (Ozer & Benet-Martinez, 2006; Soto, 2019). Personality psychologists have also extensively debated the structure of personality, and, by the turn of the century, it was widely agreed that the Five Factor Model (FFM) reflected a reasonable consensus regarding the broad outlines of the major organizing dimensions for understanding human personality variation. The FFM is a factor analytically derived system that describes variation in human personality in terms of the broad traits of *neuroticism* (vs. emotional stability), *extraversion* (vs. introversion), *conscientiousness* (vs. disinhibition), *agreeableness* (vs. antagonism), and *openness to experience* (or unconventionality vs. traditionalism). Although competing models of personality structure, such as the prominent six-factor HEXACO model, may differ in the number of dimensions, personality traits are widely accepted to exist along hierarchically arranged continua rather than in discrete categories (Lee & Ashton, 2016; Costa & McCrae, 1992).

Personality models like the FFM are intended to index normal, rather than pathological or "abnormal," ranges of personality, but the dimensional structure of personality appears to be largely overlapping in clinical and nonclinical populations (O'Connor, 2002). Nodding toward this research, *DSM-5* does appear to describe PDs in terms of personality traits: "when personality traits are inflexible and maladaptive and cause significant functional impairment or subjective distress do they constitute personality disorders" (p. 647). However, as in the schizoid PD example, the formal diagnostic criteria are notably written in terms of polythetic symptom lists rather than dimensional traits.

### Continuous Distributions Versus Discrete Categories

Inherent to the tension between traditional approaches and one that uses personality as an organizing framework is the question of whether PDs are discrete entities or exist on a continuum with normal-range functioning. Evidence to date overwhelmingly supports the latter (e.g., Haslam et al., 2020). Structural research across multiple domains indicates that the structure of PD is dimensional (Trull & Durrett, 2005). As an example of this type of research, Bucholz et al. (2000) used an approach called latent class analysis (LCA), which is designed to identify the presence of classes (or types) that may underlie data indicators. They conducted a series of LCAs to assess the relative fits of categorical and dimensional models, respectively, for symptoms of antisocial PD, finding it is best measured by an underlying severity spectrum rather than by discrete subtypes. Structural research like this has consistently shown that the boundaries in traditional diagnostic systems between pathology and normality are arbitrary (e.g., Ahmed et al., 2013; Aslinger et al., 2018; Conway et al., 2012).

## Diagnostic Instability

In addition to creating arbitrary boundaries between pathology and normality, the imposition of categorical nomenclature (discrete PD syndromes) on naturally dimensional phenomena (maladaptive personality variation) results in diagnoses that have low reliability. Because PDs are defined to be "enduring patterns . . . exhibited in a wide range of social and personal contexts" (*DSM-5*, p. 647), diagnostic stability is a key concern. This is not meant to imply that personality is fixed; in fact, there is considerable evidence that personality is moderately responsive to intervention (Brown & Barlow, 2009) and general aging (Roberts et al., 2008). Although the common view that personality is unchanging across the life span has, indeed, been challenged, the short-term stability of personality traits is high (Chmielewski & Watson, 2009). Despite the high stability of personality traits, considerable PD diagnostic change is observed across all intervals, including those as short as 1 week (Clark, 2009), and, as a result, the test-retest reliability of traditional, categorical diagnoses has been demonstrated to be lower than that of dimensional assessments (Morey & Hopwood, 2013).

## Frequent PD Co-Occurrence

Unclear boundaries between disorders constitutes an additional concern. Traditional *DSM-IV-TR* PD syndromes have well-documented issues with comorbidity (for reviews Clark, 2007; Widiger & Samuel, 2005). An individual who meets criteria for one PD syndrome very frequently meets criteria for at least one other purportedly separate PD syndrome. Although the occasional co-occurrence of syndromes is not in and of itself problematic, the highly frequent comorbidity observed with PDs suggests that the individual symptoms or diagnostic criteria (e.g., "takes pleasure in few, if any, activities") are not assigned to syndromes based on their observed covariation in the population (Wright & Zimmerman, 2015), highlighting the need to reconsider boundaries.

## Heterogeneity Within Disorders and Clinical Utility

A consequence of using polythetic diagnostic criteria is that individuals who share the same diagnostic label may have drastically different symptom presentations. As was the case with comorbidity, this heterogeneity within disorders would not necessarily be troubling for the taxonomy if the shared label provided clinically relevant insights. In other words, a syndrome could theoretically have highly heterogenous presentations across patients as long as that diagnostic label informed treatment of these seemingly unique cases or represented an aspect of their shared etiology. However, this does not appear to be the case with traditional PD labels. Surveyed clinicians have a relatively low opinion of the clinical utility of diagnostic categories (Samuel & Widiger, 2006), further evidenced by the frequent usage of the "other specified" or "unspecified" PD diagnostic labels in many clinical settings (previously "not otherwise specified"; Verheul & Widiger, 2004). From a taxonomic perspective, the reliance on this catch-all category is troublesome as it suggests that the current diagnostic labels provide insufficient coverage and may not be valuable in informing treatment. In fact, for most traditional PDs there are no validated interventions, and there is no evidence that existing approaches have specific efficacy for individual diagnoses as opposed to general efficacy for a variety of psychiatric difficulties (Bateman et al., 2015).

## Summary of Limitations

The issues surrounding PD categorization are not new. Indeed, Kupfer et al. (2002) summarized these limitations of the *DSM-IV-TR* approach in the *Research Agenda for DSM-V*.

> Epidemiologic and clinical studies have shown extremely high rates of comorbidities among the disorders, undermining the hypothesis that the syndromes represent distinct etiologies. Furthermore, epidemiologic studies have shown a high degree of short-term diagnostic instability for many disorders. With regard to treatment, lack of treatment specificity is the rule rather than the exception. (p. xviii)

Others have been blunter in their calls to abandon traditional approaches. Widiger et al. (2002) stated, "Official diagnoses are substantially arbitrary, often unreliable, overlapping, and incomplete and have only a limited utility for treatment planning" (p. 435), and Tyrer et al. (2007) declared, "The assessment of personality disorder is currently inaccurate, largely unreliable, frequently wrong, and in need of improvement" (p. s51). The limitations of the traditional *DSM-IV-TR* PD taxonomy were well-documented in advance of the development of the fifth edition.

## Developing an Alternative Trait Model

As consensus developed on the limitations of traditional, categorical approaches to PD diagnosis, researchers began exploring dimensional alternatives that use personality traits as an organizing framework. Notably, Lynam and Widiger (2001) used the FFM domains and their underlying facets (e.g., gullible vs. cynical, meek vs. aggressive, soft-hearted vs. callous, and selfless vs. exploitative are facets within the domain of *agreeableness* vs. *antagonism*) to conceptualize each of the *DSM-IV-TR* PDs. They created trait profiles for each syndrome, and in general there was strong interrater agreement among experts on the trait translations of prototypic cases. Furthermore, these conceptualizations explained the problematic comorbidity among the PDs, in that the syndromes are comorbid to the extent to which they share FFM traits. Others explored the relations between the FFM and the PD syndromes, leading to Saulsman and Page (2004) concluding in their meta-analysis "that each disorder displays a five-factor model profile that is meaningful and predictable given its unique diagnostic criteria" (p. 1055). Building on this domain-level work, Samuel and Widiger (2008) conducted a meta-analysis at the more specific, facet-level of the FFM, further showing that the traditional PD syndromes can be understood as profiles of maladaptive variants of normal-range personality traits.

The paradigm shift from categorical diagnoses to dimensional trait conceptualizations for PDs became notable during the transition from *DSM-IV-TR* to *DSM-5*. The development of *DSM-5* was preceded by three conferences that each proposed adoption of a dimensional trait model. The Nomenclature Work Group of the first "*DSM-V* Research Planning Conference" concluded that it would be "important that consideration be given to advantages and disadvantages of basing part or all of *DSM-V* on dimensions rather than categories" (Rounsaville et al., 2002, p. 13). Furthermore, they stated that PDs represented a promising initial domain that, given it is acceptable to clinicians, could lead to exploring dimensional conceptualizations elsewhere.

Subsequent conference discussions centered around how to integrate existing dimensional models. For instance, the Dimensional Assessment of Personality Pathology-Basic Questionnaire (DAPP-BQ; Livesley & Jackson, 2009) assesses four domains, which can be readily understood as maladaptive variants of four of the five traits of the FFM (e.g., *dissocial behavior* as low *agreeableness*). Similarly, Clark's three-factor model, assessed by the Schedule for the Nonadaptive and Adaptive Personality (SNAP; Clark et al., 2017) includes a domain of *negative affectivity* (neuroticism) versus *emotional stability*, *positive affectivity* (extraversion) versus *detachment*, and *constraint* (conscientiousness) versus *disinhibition*. In addition to three domains conceptually similar to those of the SNAP, the DAPP-BQ includes a fourth domain of *dissocial behavior/antagonism* versus *compliance* (agreeableness). Widiger and Simonsen (2005) aimed to find a common ground among the various maladaptive personality trait models, arguing that they can be integrated within a common hierarchical structure with three to five broad domains, indicated by more specific facet traits. The four domains of the DAPP-BQ are representative of this integrated structure, and a fifth broad domain of *unconventionality/psychoticism* versus *closedness to experience* (low openness) was proposed to ensure comprehensiveness.

In 2007, the APA appointed the *DSM-5* Personality & Personality Disorders Work Group, and they began to consider a wide-range of alternative PD classification approaches (Krueger et al., 2007). There was less consensus in the group than was present in the initial conferences, with various members committed to some of the *DSM-IV-TR* syndromes (Skodol et al., 2005) and others proposing an approach centered on a narrative prototype matching that had not yet been empirically studied (Samuel et al., 2012).

Simultaneously, there was still considerable interest in empirically deriving a new model that reflected the promise in the literature on dimensional trait conceptualizations. Advocates of this approach aimed to derive PD constructs based on data collected on fundamental individual difference constructs (e.g., tendencies to experience certain psychopathological states or to behave in specific maladaptive ways) rather than relying on a priori assumptions accrued through clinical experience or the collective wisdom of the group, as has often been the case in shaping psychiatric taxonomies (Krueger & Markon, 2014). The *DSM-5* Maladaptive Trait Model was built in this way: first compiling constructs discussed by the Work Group, making them measurable, collecting data on their reliability and co-occurrence, and finally using that data to empirically discern the organization of the constructs through atheoretical taxonomic approaches.

The Work Group's initial literature review of a variety of instruments designed to capture pathological personality identified six broad domains of content (Krueger et al., 2011).

- Emotional dysregulation/negative emotionality/neuroticism
- Detachment/low positive affectivity/introversion
- Disinhibition (encompassing elements of low FFM conscientiousness)
- Antagonism (encompassing elements of low FFM agreeableness)
- Compulsivity (which has some elements of excessive FFM conscientiousness, but also appears to encompass significant elements of negative affectivity)
- Schizotypy/oddity/peculiarity/psychoticism (associated with FFM openness)

These domains are consistent with the four identified by Widiger and Simonsen (2005) and of the DAPP-BQ but also include *psychoticism* and *compulsivity* on a provisional basis subject to further empirical review.

Work Group members then generated provisional facets underlying each of these six domains. Thirty-seven potential traits were identified, and the group generated self-report items designed to measure them. Next, data were collected from three separate representative community-dwelling samples of adult participants (Krueger et al., 2012). In the first two rounds of collection, participants were sampled who reported that they had sought treatment from a psychiatrist or psychologist. In the third round, in order to examine community norms for the instrument, this inclusion criterion was not used. The research was designed to test and refine the ability to measure the facets and domains reliably in an iterative manner (via item response theory [IRT] modeling) and also to test if any highly correlated constructs could be combined. Subsequent analyses of these data led to a reduction of the 37 initial facets to a list of 25. All 25 "restructured" constructs were measured reliably by the third round of data collection, judged by both classical and modern (IRT) test theory approaches. The final version of the instrument contained 220 items with a preliminary exploratory factor analysis of the 25 facets corresponding to a five-domain structure. See Table 26.1 for the domains and underlying facet structure.

**Table 26.1** *DSM-5 Maladaptive Trait Model*

| Domain | Facets |
|---|---|
| Negative affectivity | **Emotional Lability, Anxiousness, Separation Insecurity,** Submissiveness, Hostility[a], Restricted Affectivity[b], Perseveration |
| Detachment | **Withdrawal, Intimacy Avoidance, Anhedonia,** Depressivity[c], Suspiciousness[c] |
| Psychoticism | **Unusual Beliefs and Experiences, Eccentricity, Perceptual Dysregulation** |
| Antagonism | **Manipulativeness, Deceitfulness, Grandiosity,** Attention-Seeking, Callousness |
| Disinhibition | **Irresponsibility, Impulsivity, Distractibility,** Risk Taking, Rigid Perfectionism[d] |

*Note*: Boldface text indicates that items underlying this facet are used for calculating corresponding domain scores.

[a] Hostility cross-loads on Antagonism.

[b] Restricted Affectivity cross-loads on Detachment.

[c] Depressivity and Suspiciousness cross-load on Negative Affectivity.

[d] Rigid Perfectionism is keyed negatively for Disinhibition and cross-loads on Negative Affectivity.

In summary, after synthesizing existing approaches to create a preliminary questionnaire, the *DSM-5* Personality and Personality Disorders Work Group conducted analyses to arrive at an assessment instrument that encompasses the four major domains of maladaptive personality variation identified by Widiger and Simonsen (2005) and includes a fifth domain of *psychoticism* (see later section entitled "The Five Factor Model [FFM] of Personality" for further discussion on psychoticism). The instrument also includes multiple trait facets within all five domains. The 220-item instrument is named the Personality Inventory for *DSM-5* (PID-5; Krueger et al., 2012) and has been the primary tool for measuring the *DSM-5* Maladaptive Trait Model.

## Structure of the *DSM-5* Alternative Model for Personality Disorders

The Work Group then aimed to develop a hybrid approach to diagnosis, integrating the maladaptive personality traits within a system that retains certain PD constructs of the *DSM-IV-TR*. Thus, the *DSM-5* Maladaptive Trait Model is just one aspect of the broader AMPD. The AMPD consists of seven criteria, listed A through G. In this model, a PD is defined as clinically significant difficulties in personality functioning (Criterion A) as expressed in high levels of at least one maladaptive personality trait (Criterion B) that are inflexible (Criterion C), stable over time (Criterion D), and not better explained by other causes (Criteria E, F, and G). The *DSM-5* Maladaptive Trait Model was integrated into the AMPD as Criterion B, and thus the terms can be used interchangeably. The PID-5 operationalizes the Trait Model, but problems in functioning (i.e., a continuum of difficulties in self-functioning, defined by identity and self-direction, and interpersonal functioning, defined by empathy and intimacy) are defined as the core of a PD and are usually measured by the Level of Personality Functioning Scale (*DSM-5*, p. 762).

The AMPD also provides a means for retaining 6 of the 10 diagnostic entities from the *DSM-IV-TR* PD list. Specifically, certain combinations of Criteria A and B are used to recreate and mirror antisocial, avoidant, borderline, narcissistic, obsessive-compulsive, and schizotypal PD (Table 26.2). The intent was to show how these traditional syndromes could be understood as combinations of difficulties in personality functioning and pathological traits.

In Section II, if a patient who clearly manifests a PD does not qualify for any of the 10 canonical PDs, no informative diagnosis is available as the only alternatives are "other specified," and "unspecified" PD in most cases. In contrast, the AMPD allows for an informative portrayal of every such patient under the rubric of PD "trait specified." Thus, if Criterion A is met, a "trait specified" PD designation allows the clinician to record the clinically significant trait elevations in the PID-5 domains or facets, even if the patient does not qualify for a specific Section II PD diagnosis. Personality functioning (Criterion A) and maladaptive traits (Criterion B) are conceptually distinguishable but can be challenging to separate empirically (Zimmermann et al., 2015), and their relations will be discussed in more depth later. Nonetheless, the PID-5 can stand on its own as an assessment of maladaptive personality traits and generally has been studied independently of the broader AMPD context.

Ultimately, the APA Board of Trustees had final authority over the content of the *DSM-5* and opted to retain the *DSM-IV-TR* PD criteria verbatim as the primary taxonomy (located in *DSM-5* Section II) to "preserve continuity with current clinical practice," while this AMPD was included in Section III for "Emerging Measures and Models" (p. 761). As a result, clinicians can use either the traditional categorical model or the newer dimensional model to diagnose patients with the DSM-5.

**Table 26.2** *DSM-5* maladaptive trait constellations of traditional *DSM-IV-TR* personality disorders (PDs)

| Traditional *DSM-IV-TR* disorder | Associated traits |
| --- | --- |
| Borderline personality disorder | Emotional lability, Anxiousness, Separation Insecurity, Depressivity, Impulsivity, Risk Taking, Hostility |
| Antisocial personality disorder | Manipulativeness, Callousness, Deceitfulness, Hostility, Risk Taking, Impulsivity, Irresponsibility |
| Avoidant personality disorder | Anxiousness, Withdrawal, Anhedonia, Intimacy Avoidance |
| Schizotypal personality disorder | Perceptual Dysregulation, Unusual Beliefs and Experiences, Eccentricity, Restricted Affectivity, Withdrawal, Suspiciousness |
| Narcissistic personality disorder | Grandiosity, Attention Seeking |
| Obsessive-compulsive personality disorder | Rigid Perfectionism, Perseveration, Intimacy Avoidance, Restricted Affectivity |

*Note*: Not all of the associated traits are required to make a dimensional diagnosis; for most of the traditional PDs, just a subset of the associated traits is enough for the diagnosis. In addition to the associated traits, each traditional PD is associated with some type of impairment in personality functioning.

## Assessing Maladaptive Traits

The primary assessment tool for the Criterion B Maladaptive Trait Model is the PID-5. The 220-item self-report PID-5 is freely available to any researcher or clinician who wishes to use it (https://www.psychiatry.org/psychiatrists/practice/dsm/educational-resources/assessment-measures). The inventory begins with these instructions.

> This is a list of things different people might say about themselves. We are interested in how you would describe yourself. There are no "right" or "wrong" answers. So you can describe yourself as honestly as possible, we will keep your responses

confidential. We'd like you to take your time and read each statement carefully, selecting the response that best describes you.

Participants are asked to choose if statements (e.g., "People would describe me as reckless") are "very false or often false," "sometimes or somewhat false," "sometimes or somewhat true," or "very or often true." Raw test responses are reversed-scored when needed and averaged to provide facet and domain scores on 4-point scales. The scores can be interpreted relative to observed norms based on the representative community samples recruited for the initial instrument development (Krueger et al., 2012). To obtain a more fine-grained understanding of the PID-5 domains and facets, full definitions for each are provided in a table on pages 779–781 of *DSM-5*.

The instrument has also been adapted into a 25-item brief form (PID-5-BF) and a 218-item informant report (PID-5-IRF) that are also freely available via the APA. In addition, it has been adapted into a 100-item short form (PID-5-SF), a 36-item modified form that includes an *anankastia* domain (intending to index compulsivity typically associated with obsessive-compulsive PD) that allows for compatibility with the PD taxonomy of *ICD-11* (Bach et al., 2020), an adapted 100-item version that was tailored for use in forensic contexts (Niemeyer et al., 2021), and a shortened 75-item informant report form (Zimmermann et al., 2015). There is also the possibility to measure the PID-5 traits from established measures such as the Personality Assessment Inventory (PAI) (Busch et al., 2017). Finally, for the purpose of expert ratings of maladaptive personality traits, researchers have developed a Personality Trait Rating Form (PTRF) that includes short descriptions of the facets to be rated on 4-point scales (Few et al., 2013). In the main form and most of the alternates, the PID-5 assesses five maladaptive trait domains and 25 underlying facets, provided in Table 26.1.

## Empirical Research on the *DSM-5* Maladaptive Trait Model

Since the PID-5 was made freely available in 2013, a vast body of research has accumulated while limited research on alternative operationalizations of the Trait Model exists. The PID-5's body of research has been summarized in at least six published reviews (Al-Dajani et al., 2016; Barchi-Ferreira Bel & Osório, 2020; Krueger & Hobbs, 2020; Krueger & Markon, 2014; Miller et al., 2018; Zimmermann et al., 2019) and four meta-analyses (Clark & Watson, 2022; Somma, Krueger, Markon, & Fossati, 2019; Watters & Bagby, 2018; Watters, Bagby, & Sellbom, 2019). In addition, the PID-5 has been translated to and researched in at least 19 languages, including Brazilian Portuguese (Barchi-Ferreira et al., 2019), Chinese (Zhang, Wang et al., 2021), Danish (Bo et al., 2015), Farsi (Lotfi el al., 2018), Russian (Lozovanu et al., 2019), and Swedish (Kajonius, 2017). The instrument has clearly caught the interest of the field. Examination of its psychometric properties will help clarify the extent to which it measures distinct and homogeneous pathologies and, in turn, how effective it projects to be as a descriptive basis for research on specific etiologies and treatments.

### Structural Validity

The Trait Model's structural validity is integral to corresponding research on specific etiologies and treatments. Here, we analyze structural validity across three areas. First, we look at the higher order structure. Is it five rather than some other number of domains that fit the data best across a diversity of samples? Given the loadings of the items or facets, do the empirically derived latent factors resemble the proposed domains across samples? Second, we look at the lower order structure. Do the measured trait facets index a single construct (are they unidimensional)? Do they index those constructs with reasonable internal consistency? Finally, we look at how the lower order structure maps on to the higher order structure. Are the factor loadings of the facets onto the domains consistent across a diversity of samples? These types of questions represent an empirical approach to analyzing the extent to which the taxonomy accurately represents the structure of observed variation in personality pathology, or the structural validity of the Trait Model.

## Higher Order Structure

The 5-domain, 25-facet, factor structure of the PID-5 was derived in a representative US sample (Krueger et al., 2012). Somma, Krueger, Markon, and Fossati (2019) have noted that, through exploratory factor analysis or exploratory structural equation modelling, the 5-domain factor structure has been replicated six times in United States (e.g., DeYoung et al., 2016; Wright al., 2012) and 16 times in non-US samples, primarily using translated versions of the instrument (e.g., Lofti et al., 2018; Thimm et al., 2017). They then meta-analyzed these studies, finding highly similar factor loadings across US and non-US samples. Neither sample type, participant age, translation, nor geographic area had a significant moderating effect on model fit (Somma, Krueger, Markon, & Fossati, 2019). The 5-factor structure was also replicated in a mixed Middle Eastern sample (Al-Attiyah et al., 2017) and a Polish sample (Rowiński et al., 2019) that did not meet criteria for the meta-analysis, as well as more recent samples from Denmark (Bach et al., 2018), Singapore (Lim et al., 2019), Hungary (Labancz et al., 2020), Egypt (Aboul-ata & Qonsuo, 2021), Australia (Dunne et al., 2021), and the United States (Hyatt et al., 2021).

The factor structures of the alternate forms of the PID-5 have been studied less frequently. The five-domain structure of the PID-5-BF was replicated in six studies and that of the PID-5-SF was replicated in three (Barchi-Ferreira Bel & Osório, 2020). Similarly, the original development of the PID-5-IRF (Markon et al., 2013) replicated the five-factor structure, but Morey et al. (2013) studied clinician ratings about their patients using the PTRF, deriving a fifth factor that resembled compulsivity rather than separate *antagonism* and *disinhibition* domains (both were subsumed under a single *externalizing* domain).

On the other hand, a four-factor solution fit the data best in a forensic sample (Niemeyer et al., 2021) using an adapted 100-item form. Once using the PID-5-BF and once using the primary 220-item form, a six-factor solution fit the data best in two Chinese samples (Zhang, Ouyang et al., 2021; Zhang, Wang et al., 2021). Finally, the five-factor solution did not display adequate fit in an Indonesian sample using the primary form (Adhiatma & Halim, 2021), indicating the need for further study in novel populations, notably in Eastern Asia. That said, the majority of evidence suggests that, in contrast to the three clusters (odd-eccentric, dramatic-emotional, and anxious-fearful) which have shown limited structural validity for organizing the *DSM-IV-TR* PD syndromes (Sheets & Craighead, 2007), the five-domain structure of the PID-5 appears applicable and robust across US and Western European samples, with burgeoning evidence of its validity elsewhere.

**Lower Order Structure: Dimensionality and Internal Consistency.**

The vast majority of PID-5 facets appear to be unidimensional across the majority of studies (Zimmermann et al., 2019), but certain facets have shown inadequate unidimensional fit in translated forms. For instance, the *risk taking* facet (e.g., Somma et al., 2017) and the *emotional lability* facet (e.g., Gutiérrez et al., 2017) each failed to show adequate unidimensional fit across at least five samples. The *manipulativeness* facet failed to show adequate unidimensional fit across at least three samples (e.g., Labancz et al., 2020). Several facets were similarly heterogeneous in a Czech sample (Riegel et al., 2018), but the authors achieved adequate model fit by removing poorly discriminating items and proposed a 160-item instrument for use in Czech-speaking communities. Studies using the shortened versions are limited, but initial evidence for the unidimensionality of PID-5-BF domains is promising (Debast et al., 2017), whereas fit of the facets of the PID-5-SF was inadequate (Riegel et al., 2018). To summarize, most facets can be adequately represented as unidimensional constructs, but, without removing poorly discriminating items, some facets appear heterogeneous when applied across cultures.

After assuming a construct is unidimensional, it is important to then evaluate the extent to which several items that aim to measure the same construct produce similar responses, or its internal consistency. Across an initial literature review of 25 studies (Al-Dajani et al., 2016), a later review of 54 additional studies (Barchi-Ferreira Bel & Osório, 2020), and several studies from more diverse languages published since (e.g., Aboul-ata & Qonsua, 2021; Zhang, Wang et al., 2021), the PID-5 domain scores have demonstrated high internal consistency (indicated mainly by Cronbach's alpha coefficient) and the facet scores generally have demonstrated at least acceptable levels. Cronbach's alpha is positively influenced by the number of items in the instrument, so it is not surprising that those constructs with more indicators (the domains rather than facets) displayed higher reliability. In individual studies, certain facets do not reach acceptable levels of internal consistency (generally defined by Cronbach's alpha being under a certain threshold, which, in this case, we set at .70). However, there is little evidence that suggests a systematic pattern of low reliability of any specific facet, aside from possibly *suspiciousness*, which has failed to reach acceptable levels across at least five studies using translated forms of the PID-5 (e.g., Bastiaens et al., 2016; Lotfi el al., 2018).

The alternate forms of the PID-5 have been studied less frequently, but initial evidence is similarly promising. The internal consistency of domains and facets of the 100-item PID-5-SF has been evaluated across four studies each, and in only one study did a facet (*impulsivity*) fail to reach acceptable levels (Ashton et al., 2017; Barchi-Ferreira Bel & Osório, 2020). The 25-item PID-5-BF only assesses domains, and it similarly had high internal consistency across nine studies (e.g., Barchi-Ferreira Bel & Osório, 2020; Zhang, Ouyang et al., 2021), with the exception of the *disinhibition* and *antagonism* domains in a study by Debast et al. (2017) and again *antagonism* in a study by Hyatt et al. (2021). Finally, the 218-item informant report (PID-5-IRF) was the subject of two studies where internal consistency was confirmed for all domains and facets apart from *impulsivity* once failing to reach acceptable levels (Ashton et al., 2017; Quilty et al., 2018).

In sum, the PID-5 seems to measure maladaptive personality traits represented in the Trait Model reliably at the domain and facet levels. Although individual facets may operate inconsistently across diverse samples, there is little evidence of systematically low reliability of any individual construct. Further work is needed to explore the reliabilities of the alternate forms of the PID-5 as well as measures of internal consistency that are less sensitive to number of items.

**Relations Between Higher and Lower Order Structure.**

It is common for instruments such as the PID-5 to show *interstitiality*, which is evident when a facet loads on more than one domain (e.g., the facet *hostility* relates both to *negative affectivity* and *antagonism*). Whether or not specific patterns of interstitiality are consistent across research studies is an important window into the structural validity of the model on which the instrument is based. Watters and Bagby (2018) observed that some of the interstitial factor loadings vary significantly across samples, calling into the question the lower-order factor structure of the PID-5. For instance, Maples et al. (2015) reported that 19 of the 25 facets loaded substantively on at least two domains, whereas De Fruyt et al. (2013) found just six to be substantively interstitial. Watters and Bagby (2018) conducted a meta-analysis of the loadings across 14 samples and found that interstitiality decreased when samples were pooled, providing evidence that some of the inconsistency is likely the result of sampling error. At the same time, three facets consistently loaded more strongly onto a different domain than the original placement suggested by Krueger et al. (2012) during the construction of the instrument. These facets were *hostility* loading on to *antagonism* (rather than *negative affectivity*), *restricted affectivity* loading on to *detachment* (rather than *negative affectivity*), and *rigid perfectionism* loading on to *negative affectivity* (rather than *disinhibition*) (Watters & Bagby, 2018).

In a follow-up analysis, *hostility* and *restricted affectivity* again loaded onto *antagonism* and *detachment*, respectively, leading the authors to recommend that they move to be considered primary indicators of those domains (Watters, Sellbom et al., 2019). Furthermore, the authors recommended that *suspiciousness* move from *detachment* to *negative affectivity* based on their results. Finally, the authors suggested the removal of the *submissiveness* facet entirely as it fails to substantively load on any domain. The findings for *rigid perfectionism* were mixed, so recommendations were not made. Many facets are expected to lie theoretically in between multiple domains, leading to interstitiality. As a result, only facets that are thought to be "cleaner" indicators of single domains are used to calculate domain scores. In other words, though *antagonism* is indicated by five underlying facets, only items that indicate the three facets that are the "cleanest" indicators of antagonism (*manipulativeness, deceitfulness,* and *grandiosity*) are used to calculate the *antagonism* domain score. See Table 26.1 for a summary of all "official" mappings, notable cross-loadings pointed out by Watters, Sellbom and colleagues (2019), and the facets that are used to calculate domain scores. Importantly, none of the five facets noted as potentially troublesome by Watters, Sellbom, et al. (2019) are included in the official scoring procedure for their respective domains (*DSM-5*, 2013), likely because of this known interstitiality.

Though more work is needed with alternate forms, the evidence suggests that the 5-domain structure of the Trait Model (measured by the PID-5) effectively parses variance in maladaptive personality traits across a wide range of populations. Although facets can sporadically be prone to differential loadings and lack of unidimensionality across diverse samples, it is difficult to identify patterns of particularly troublesome facets. That is to say, no individual facet has consistently displayed poor measurement properties or stood out as culturally bound. In addition, Riegel et al. (2018) demonstrated the promise of using IRT methods to modify translated forms for international use to overcome psychometrically troublesome facets.

*Temporal Stability*

A lesser studied area is the temporal stability of the Trait Model. Recall that considerable PD diagnostic change was observed across short intervals using the traditional *DSM-IV-TR* taxonomy, so evidence of adequate temporal stability of the PID-5 is key for establishing a diagnostic system with test-retest reliability. Dimensional psychopathological constructs generally have displayed higher test-retest reliability when compared to categorical syndromes (Watson, 2003). In limited studies, the temporal stability of the PID-5 specifically was adequate or better in US samples (Chmielewski et al., 2017; Suzuki et al., 2017; Wright et al., 2015). For instance, Wright et al. (2015) estimated mean-level and rank-order change of the PID-5 domains and facets over two assessments separated by more than a year. For the five domains, mean-level change was measured by Cohen's $d$ and ranged from –.17 to .00. Pearson's $r$ measured rank-order change and ranged from .62 to .75 for the domains. These relatively high stabilities were replicated in international samples using the Arabic (Coelho et al., 2020), Portuguese (Pires et al., 2017), German (Zimmermann et al., 2017), and Indonesian (Adhiatma & Halim, 2021) translations. One study has validated the acceptable temporal stability of the PID-5-SF (Díaz-Batanerio et al., 2019), while two have done so for the PID-5-BF (Fossati, Somma, Borroni et al., 2017; Zhang, Ouyang et al., 2021). Overall, these findings are a promising development for the reliability of the Trait Model but require further replication.

*Interrater Reliability*

The unclear boundaries between *DSM-IV-TR* PDs made it very likely that if a patient saw two clinicians, they would receive two different diagnoses. The PTRF includes short descriptions of the PID-5 facets to be rated on 4-point scales for the purpose of expert ratings of maladaptive personality traits (Few et al., 2013). To collect this information systematically, the Structured Clinical Interview for Personality Traits (SCID-AMPD Module II) has also been developed (Skodol et al., 2018), but few researchers have used these resources to explore the interrater reliability of the PID-5. Although Trait Model materials yielded higher diagnostic reliability for case vignettes than categorical diagnoses (Morey, 2019b), overall, the PTRF has shown just fair to acceptable levels of interrater reliability (Few et al., 2013; Garcia et al., 2018). The SCID-AMPD Module II may allow for more reliable measurement, as evidenced by the excellent interrater reliability demonstrated in a study of psychotherapy outpatients (Somma et al., 2020). These initial results require further investigation but highlight the need for applying structured interviews such as the SCID-AMPD Module II for reliable measurement across raters.

*Measurement Equivalence Across and Within Cultures*

The Trait Model has received considerable interest internationally, as evidenced by the plethora of PID-5 translations and psychometric research applying it to novel populations. This line of research has provided evidence that the trait domains and facets can be reliably measured and provide a reasonably valid account of the variance in responses internationally. Currently, most of the work has been done in Western Europe, but there is growing evidence of the applicability of the Trait Model in Eastern Europe, the Middle East, and Eastern Asia. However, testing for measurement invariance of the PID-5 is necessary to conclude that the same construct is being measured across groups and that scores are comparable cross-culturally.

Typically, measurement invariance is tested by comparing a sequence of increasingly restricted common factor models (Meredith, 1993). Traditionally, the first model in the sequence is a test of configural invariance. Next, a test of metric or weak invariance constrains factor loadings to equality across groups. Finally, a test of scalar or strong invariance constrains indicator intercepts to equality across groups. At each step, the fit of the nested, more constrained model is compared to the previous model. Evidence of weak invariance suggests that the latent factor or construct has the same meaning across groups because it is defined by the same indicators to same extent. Evidence of strong invariance suggests that group mean differences in indicators are attributable to differences in the latent construct because item intercepts are reasonably equivalent across groups.

In a comparison between Norwegian and US university samples, weak measurement invariance was found across all domains: that is, the factor loadings of the facets onto the domains were roughly equivalent across groups. Partial strong invariance was found, meaning the scores were invariant across groups after two facet intercepts were released from constraints (Thimm et al., 2017). Sorrel et al. (2021) built on this work, analyzing invariance across samples in Belgium, Switzerland, France, Spain, and Catalonia. Similarly, weak and partial strong invariance were found across the five samples. These results provide initial evidence that the PID-5 largely measures pathological personality constructs in the same manner across the United States and Western Europe but requires replication. Examining invariance at the item level by considering if item loadings onto to facets are equivalent across populations is also necessary for valid cross-cultural comparisons.

It is also important to demonstrate measurement invariance across diverse populations within a given culture. For example, strong invariance across community and clinical samples was demonstrated in Danish (Bach et al., 2018), Italian (with the Short Form; Somma, Krueger, Markon, Borroni, & Fossati, 2019), Czech (with the Czech shortened form; Riegel et al., 2018), and Chinese (with the Brief Form; Zhang, Ouyang et al., 2021) samples. Together, these findings give strong evidence that the PID-5 can be effectively used toward one of its primary goals: dimensionally measuring maladaptive traits in a manner that is comparable across severity levels. Measurement invariance across sex was established in American adult (Suzuki et al., 2019), Norwegian adult (South et al., 2017), and Italian adolescent samples, although only weak invariance was demonstrated in the latter group (Somma et al., 2017). Strong invariance was also demonstrated across a heterosexual group and a mixed homosexual and bisexual group in a US sample (Russell et al., 2017). Examinations of differential item functioning, or measurement invariance at the item level, across younger and older age groups have raised questions about whether all items are age-neutral, though many items have not displayed significant differential functioning (Debast et al., 2018; Van den Broeck et al., 2013). Thus, the limited initial evidence suggests that the PID-5 is largely invariant across age, sex, sexual orientation, sample type, and country, but each of these results requires replication. On the other hand, initial evidence suggests that the PID-5 may not be invariant across race in the United States. In a study of Black Americans and White Americans, a single-factor solution emerged for the Black American sample, indicative of covariation across all domains, thus raising questions about the instrument's applicability (Bagby et al., 2021). Additional studies should examine invariance across race and socioeconomic status within the United States.

Although it appears that most facets are applicable cross-culturally, certain facets like *suspiciousness* displayed some psychometric issues when translated and studied internationally, warranting further investigation to determine if they represent culturally bound constructs. Finally, Al-Dajani et al. (2016) note that

[i]t is important to consider that comparing translated versions of the PID-5 to the original measure for cross-cultural administration assumes that preexisting pathological personality dimensions hold the same relevance across cultures. As such, this etic approach to cultural description risks imposing pathological personality dimensions defined by Western traditions onto other cultures. (p. 69)

Indeed, etic approaches can confirm that an external structure is valid in a new culture but cannot disprove that additional or alternative domains would more parsimoniously represent traits within that culture if emically developed.

### Convergent and Predictive Validity

Evidence of convergent validity, or how closely the Trait Model is related to other measures of the same theoretical constructs, is found by comparing the PID-5 to alternative inventories or methods. Zimmermann et al. (2019) reviewed the relevant studies and concluded that PID-5 scores have high associations with theoretically similar domains assessed by the DAPP-BQ, Computer Adaptive Test of Personality Disorder (CAT-PD), Minnesota Multiphasic Personality Inventory 2–Restructured Form (MMPI-2-RF), and Personality Assessment Inventory (PAI). The PID-5 has been found to be predictive of several clinically relevant outcomes, including self-harm (Evans & Simms, 2019), symptom distress (Zimmermann et al., 2014), disability (Díaz-Batanerio et al., 2019), quality of life (De Caluwé et al., 2019), physical illness (Waszczuk et al., 2018), child molestation (Ferretti et al., 2021), and many more (for a more comprehensive list, see Zimmermann et al., 2019). Finally, meta-analytic evidence suggests that patients and their therapists have a relatively high degree of agreement (self–other agreement) on PID-5 domain and facet scores (Oltmanns & Oltmanns, 2021). In sum, validity evidence for the Trait Model is seen in the PID-5's convergence with measures of similar domains and prediction of a wide range of clinically relevant outcomes.

### Coverage of DSM-IV-TR PD Syndromes and Incremental Validity

Specific trait constellations of prevalent PD syndromes (e.g., borderline PD) were included in AMPD to demonstrate how a dimensional model theoretically could cover the same ground as traditional, categorical approaches. Table 26.2 displays these trait constellations. Still, consideration of a move to a dimensional trait approach raised concerns about whether any information from the existing set of PD syndromes would be lost. Accordingly, researchers have studied the extent to which the Trait Model covers the Section II or traditional *DSM-IV-TR* PD syndromes. For example, Morey et al. (2016) compared clinician-rated criterion counts for *DSM-IV-TR* PD syndromes with clinician-rated PID-5 facet and domain scores. The correlations were often quite substantial (e.g., *emotional lability* with borderline PD criteria = .75; *manipulativeness* and *deceitfulness* with antisocial PD criteria = .67 and .72, respectively). Given these associations, the authors concluded that traditional PD concepts can be adequately represented using PID-5 traits in combination with impairments in personality functioning (Morey et al., 2016). Similarly, Few et al. (2013) compared results from clinician-rated criterion counts for *DSM-IV-TR* PD syndromes, clinician-rated PID-5 scores, and patient self-report PID-5 scores and found that the traits explain substantial proportions of the variance in their respective traditional PD syndromes.

Rather than criterion counts for syndromes, Rojas and Widiger (2017) considered coverage of the individual diagnostic criteria. They examined correlations between the PID-5 facets and criteria for 6 of the 10 PD syndromes. For example, the *separation insecurity* facet correlated .77 with the "abandonment concerns" criterion for borderline PD. The authors concluded that the coverage was good to excellent for the borderline, antisocial, avoidant, dependent, and narcissistic PDs, but support was mixed for obsessive-compulsive PD. They also interpret their results as consistent with the relatively extensive literature confirming this strong coverage, with the exception of obsessive-compulsive PD.

Watters, Bagby, and colleagues (2019) built on this work, considering the results from 25 independent datasets. They found that the PID-5 traits showed moderate to large correlations with their traditional syndrome counterparts, with the notable exception again of obsessive-compulsive PD. This probably reflects the loss of some obsessive-compulsive traits when the *compulsivity* domain was deleted from the Trait Model (Krueger et al., 2012). These consistently strong coverages demonstrated by Watters, Bagby et al. (2019) applied to schizotypal PD and four of the five syndromes considered by Rojas and Widiger (2017): borderline, antisocial, avoidant, and narcissistic. Further evidence for the coverage of dependent PD by the PID-5 has also been demonstrated elsewhere (McClintock & McCarrick, 2017). Less frequently have researchers considered the coverage of paranoid, schizoid, and histrionic PDs, but there has been limited support for their retention (e.g., Blashfield et al., 2012), and the AMPD does not include specific diagnostic criteria for them (nor criteria for dependent PD).

Knowing that the Trait Model can largely cover many of the *DSM-5* Section II PD syndromes, it is next important to consider its incremental validity (i.e., the extent to which it provides value over existing methods of assessment). Relative to the *DSM-5* Section II PD syndromes, PID-5 traits have demonstrated stronger prediction of clinician treatment planning, treatment intensity, and long-term prognosis (Morey & Benson, 2016), as well PD severity (Fossati et al., 2016), psychosocial impairment (Simms & Calabrese, 2016), patient aggression (Somma, Krueger, Markon, Alajmo et al., 2019), measures of psychopathy (Anderson et al., 2014), and social cognition (Fossati, Somma, Krueger et al., 2017). The two approaches yielded about equally effective prediction of a measure of borderline personality traits (Anderson et al., 2016), while they were each more predictive of different aspects of a measure of disability (Chmielewski et al., 2017). Thus, initial evidence indicates that the Trait Model performs at least as well and usually better than categorical PD measures at predicting clinically relevant criteria.

### Clinical Utility

Morey et al. (2014) surveyed a US national sample of clinicians on various aspects of the clinical utility of the *DSM-IV-TR* and the Trait Model after applying both to their own patients. Clinicians rated the Trait Model to have significantly higher clinical utility across five of the six assessed domains. These domains were communication with patients, comprehensiveness, descriptiveness, ease of use, and utility for treatment planning. However, no significant differences were found regarding communication with other professionals. Nelson et al. (2017) built on this work, comparing trainee opinions about the clinical utility of four different PD diagnostic systems. They found that trainees rated the Trait Model significantly higher in most clinical utility domains, notably including the extent to which it provided a comprehensive understanding of their clients. Furthermore, initial evidence suggests that treatment-seekers have a high opinion of the accuracy and relevance of feedback they receive regarding maladaptive personality traits (Lengel & Mullins-Sweatt, 2017). Thus, initial evidence suggests that the Trait Model is thought to be useful by both clinicians and patients and provides mutually agreeable patient data.

Ease of use has been an especially pervasive concern with the Trait Model and the broader AMPD. Verheul (2012) has suggested that the AMPD's already high degree of complexity will prevent clinicians from adopting it for everyday use. On the other hand, Bach et al. (2015) and Bastiaens et al. (2021) have attempted to illustrate the PID-5's ease of use through case vignettes, qualitatively supporting the findings of Morey et al. (2014) and Nelson et al. (2017) that clinicians and trainees rate the Trait Model as easy to use relative to traditional *DSM-IV-TR* PDs and to some simpler approaches.

The PID-5 has been criticized as being heavily influenced by response styles or biases related to responders' tendencies to represent themselves in an indiscriminately positive or negative light (Ashton et al., 2017; Dhillon et al., 2017; McGee Ng et al., 2016). This relates to the fact that the PID-5 has relatively few "reverse-coded" items. Most items are positive indicators of the construct they measure. For instance, the item "I don't care if my actions hurt others" is a positive indicator for *callousness*, whereas "I would never harm another person" is a negative indicator, so it needs to be "reverse-coded" to index *callousness*. In this light, it is noteworthy that measures of symptom overreporting (Sellbom et al., 2018) and response inconsistency (Keeley et al., 2016) have been developed for the PID-5, which represent valuable additions for clinical use of the Trait Model. To further account for this limitation, Quilty et al. (2018) highlight the importance of multimethod assessment (using the informant report form) and use of the symptom overreporting scale.

Additional aspects of the clinical applicability of the Trait Model require further attention. For instance, do the 25 facets of the PID-5 adequately cover the range of pathological traits? Although seemingly providing an improvement in coverage over the polythetic categories, the Trait Model could be missing clinically relevant domains when applied to novel populations, such as domains like *Health Anxiety*, *Self-Harm*, and *Fantasy Proneness* captured in the CAT-PD (Yalch & Hopwood, 2016; Ringwald et al., 2021). In addition, the domain of *anankastia* is not explicitly present in most forms of the PID-5, which is an area that has been emphasized as clinically relevant in *ICD-11* (Bach et al., 2020) and may account for the poor coverage of obsessive-compulsive PD. Though there was limited support for their retention, it stands to reason that aspects of the traditional *DSM-IV-TR* PD syndromes that are not addressed in the Trait Model (paranoid, schizoid, histrionic, and dependent PDs) could have clinically relevant characteristics that are not captured. Finally, the traditional PDs that are addressed in the Trait Model have been demonstrated (e.g., Watters, Bagby et al., 2019) to be substantially covered by PID-5 traits (e.g., *separation insecurity* and *submissiveness* account for substantial portion of variance in dependent PD), but the portion that is not covered may also be clinically relevant and not simply the result of error variance.

Often, personality inventories, such as the PID-5, are administered to large community samples to establish normative values for each of the relevant domains (Krueger et al., 2012). These normative values, in turn, help to establish cutoff scores that ease interpretation of individual test scores in clinical practice. Rek et al. (2021) note that norms were mostly derived from samples that were not fully representative of the general population (e.g., regarding social status, education, or quality of health), and researchers have sometimes used "intuitive" cutoff scores for PID-5 domains and facets. To address this issue, they administered the PID-5 to a large representative German sample and proposed additional normative values for the domains.

Does the Trait Model enhance communication? Ease of communication has been a recurring argument against shifting to dimensional classification, as the manageable number of diagnoses in the categorical systems may be lost in a dimensional profile (First, 2005). A dimensional trait profile likely communicates more information than a single diagnostic label, but it is certainly easier to inform a colleague that a patient meets criteria for a specific syndrome. Surveyed clinicians have indicated that the Trait Model is favorable to *DSM-IV-TR* PD syndromes in communicating with patients, but significant differences did not exist regarding communication with other professionals (Morey et al., 2014). We theorize that communicating more information derives comparative value in many areas. For instance, with a wider array of options in their diagnostic profile, a patient may be more likely to feel accurately represented. Theoretically, this could improve therapeutic alliance, preventing the feeling of being shoehorned into a specific diagnostic box. It could also be argued, on the other hand, that specific syndromes and support groups can create a feeling of community around a specific illness. The broader profile approach also provides (indirect) information about patient strengths, not just weaknesses. For instance, a highly agreeable, socially skilled, but disinhibited patient may score quite low the *hostility* and *intimacy avoidance* facets, highlighting that they may be able to use these interpersonal assets to compensate for maladaptive traits across other domains. At the same time, it could be argued that normal-range (rather than maladaptive) traits along with an independent measure of dysfunction (Criterion A) would provide a "fuller picture" of patient strengths and weaknesses. We discuss these issues further in the "Criterion A: Level of Personality Functioning" section.

## The DSM-5 Maladaptive Trait Model in the Context of Clinical Science

We briefly discussed the convergent validity of the Trait Model with regard to other prominent trait measures and clinical outcomes. However, this only scratches the surface. Vast bodies of research place the Trait Model in the context of other broad domains of clinical science, largely confirming that the model's maladaptive personality traits are theoretically complementary to well-validated constructs of psychopathology and normal-range personality, while their relationship to personality functioning (Criterion A) remains a contested empirical question.

### Non-PD Psychopathology

The distinction between psychopathological symptoms and maladaptive personality traits has been the subject of some debate. One view is that the fundamental difference is in timeframe: maladaptive traits are dispositional constructs related to persistent tendencies toward psychopathology, whereas symptoms are features of psychopathology during any specific time period (DeYoung et al., 2020). In response to diagnostic issues similar to those of PDs, efforts have been made to reorganize the taxonomy for all forms of psychopathology toward dimensional conceptualizations. A leading alternative approach is the Hierarchical Taxonomy of Psychopathology (HiTOP; Kotov et al., 2017). HiTOP is an evolving taxonomy, aiming to undergo revisions so that it always reflects advances in the literature on the structure of psychopathology. As of this writing, the current model includes five broad dimensional spectra of psychopathology—*internalizing, thought disorder, disinhibited externalizing, antagonistic externalizing,* and *detachment*—as well a sixth, provisional *somatoform* spectrum (Kotov et al., 2021).

The domains of the Trait Model are conceptually linked to these broad spectra. For instance, Wright and Simms (2015) conducted joint structural analyses of (non-PD) symptomatology and maladaptive traits to derive a five-factor meta-structure of psychopathology. In this model, the PID-5 domains corresponded with broad factors of psychopathology that resemble the HiTOP spectra (e.g., *negative affectivity* domain with *internalizing, disinhibition* with *externalizing/disinhibition, antagonism* with *antagonism*). Many lines of structural research have validated these broad spectra and their hierarchical organization (Kotov et al., 2017). As one such example, evidence from a large body of twin and family studies indicates that the higher order genetic structure of psychopathology aligns with the HiTOP framework (Waszczuk et al., 2020). Thus, contemporary models of psychopathology jointly organize maladaptive traits and psychopathological symptoms under broader dimensional umbrellas. The PID-5 fits neatly into this framework as a tool for measuring maladaptive traits and organizing research. Theoretical relations between the PID-5 domains, the HiTOP spectra, and the FFM are summarized in Table 26.3.

Although the Trait Model was originally conceptualized to aid in the diagnosis of PDs, this alignment suggests that it may also be useful regarding other forms of psychopathology more generally. For example, Heath et al. (2018) found that the PID-5 can aid in distinguishing between non-PD psychopathological diagnostic classes (e.g., mood disorders, substance use, psychotic disorders). Furthermore, *antagonism* and *disinhibition* are related to problematic alcohol use (Creswell et al., 2016; Zimmermann et al., 2014), while *antagonism* and *detachment* relate to risk for gambling disorder (Carlotta et al., 2015). These results are useful in explaining how broad personality dimensions underly the well-observed patterns of comorbidity between addictive syndromes and PDs, providing evidence that the Trait Model may have clinical utility regarding many forms of psychopathology.

The PID-5 traits have also been linked to internalizing psychopathology. James et al. (2015) found that *detachment* and *psychoticism* are predictive of posttraumatic stress disorder symptomatology, while *negative affectivity* and *detachment* are predictive of symptoms of major depressive disorder

**Table 26.3** Theoretical relations between the PID-5, FFM, and HiTOP spectra

| PID-5 domain | FFM | HiTOP spectra |
| --- | --- | --- |
| Negative affectivity | Neuroticism | Internalizing |
| Psychoticism | Openness | Thought disorder |
| Detachment | Low extraversion (High Introversion) | Detachment |
| Disinhibition | Low conscientiousness | Disinhibited externalizing |
| Antagonism | Low agreeableness | Antagonistic externalizing |
| | | Somatoform (provisionally) |

*Note*: PID-5, Personality Inventory for *DSM-5* (Krueger et al., 2012); FFM, Five Factor Model (Costa & McCrae, 1992); HiTOP, Hierarchical Taxonomy of Psychopathology (Kotov et al., 2017).

(Naragon-Gainey & Simms, 2017; Zimmermann et al., 2014).

The PID-5's clinical utility also extends to psychotic disorders. Domain scores of higher *psychoticism*, lower *negative affectivity*, lower *detachment*, and lower *disinhibition* were found to discriminate effectively between individuals with a psychotic disorder from individuals with mood or substance use disorders (Bastiaens et al., 2019). Furthermore, evidence suggests that *detachment* and *negative affectivity* are predictors of actually developing psychosis among individuals who are susceptible to psychosis (Drvaric et al., 2018). Thus, across many domains of psychopathology, the Trait Model is beginning to generate research that indicates its clinical value in differential diagnosis and understanding risk and resilience factors, thus aligning fields of research have too often operated in silos.

*The Five Factor Model of Personality*

As stated in the *DSM-5,* the five domains of the Trait Model are "maladaptive variants of the five domains of the extensively validated and replicated personality model known as the 'Big Five,' or the Five Factor Model of personality" (p. 773). Indeed, the strong associations between these systems have been demonstrated empirically. Barchi-Ferreira Bel and Osório (2020) review the literature linking the PID-5 domains with the FFM, concluding that associations that were, on average, strong. They report the following ranges of correlations observed in the literature: *negative affectivity* and *neuroticism* (r = .55 to .78); *detachment* and *extraversion* (r = −.73 to −.34); *antagonism* and *agreeableness* (r = −.71 to −.38); and *disinhibition* and *conscientiousness* (r = −.73 to −.12). However, they also noted associations between *psychoticism* and *openness* were weaker, ranging from r = .14 to .43, with some nonsignificant associations observed. The FFM traits similarly align with the broad spectra of psychopathology, allowing Widiger, Sellbom and colleagues (2019) to argue that personality provides a "foundational base" for psychopathology more generally (Table 26.3).

Although somewhat heterogeneous across samples, the associations are, on average, strong, with the notable exception of *openness* with *psychoticism*. There are multiple interpretations of this weaker association. For instance, heterogeneity in relations between *openness* and *psychoticism* has been observed across inventories used to measure the FFM. Widiger and Crego (2019) observe that studies relying on a neuroticism, extraversion, and openness to experience (NEO) inventory (Costa & McCrae, 1992) or comparable measure (e.g., International Item Pool Inventory-NEO, Big Five Inventory) tend to obtain the weakest associations. They argue that the NEO inventories do not measure facets of openness related to unconventionality, imagination, and fantasy proneness to same degree as later Big Five inventories do, such as the FFM Rating Form (Thomas et al., 2013).

DeYoung et al. (2007) argue that the broad domain commonly referred to as "openness" is indicated by two specific aspects, *openness* and *intellect*, which are both equal parts of the broader trait domain. The specific *openness* aspect contains facets related to imagination and fantasy, while the *intellect* aspect contains facets related to curiosity and ingenuity. Joint factor analyses of the Big Five aspects and the PID-5 traits indicated that specific facet-level *openness* correlates strongly with facets underlying the *psychoticism* domain, while *intellect* is not strongly associated with any maladaptive traits (DeYoung et al., 2016). To summarize, the broad trait domain *openness* is multifaceted;

different instruments tend to measure the underlying facets to different degrees; and facets related to unconventionality, imagination, and fantasy proneness appear to be closely related to *psychoticism*, while facets related to intellectual curiosity appear not to be.

Others have argued that the convergent association between *antagonism* and low *agreeableness* is only modest (Zimmermann et al., 2014). Zimmermann et al. (2014) note that in their sample, in the original sample (Krueger et al., 2012), and in others (e.g., Markon et al., 2013; Watson et al., 2013) the central facets of *antagonism*, like *manipulativeness* and *deceitfulness*, were less strongly associated with agreeableness than were peripheral facets like *hostility* and *callousness*. Though at a global level, there appears to be a relatively strong convergence between *antagonism* and low *agreeableness*, the heterogeneity at more specific levels makes the joint structure of these two domains an important issue to clarify in future research.

*Criterion A: Level of Personality Functioning*

The *DSM-5* Maladaptive Trait Model is essentially one half of the AMPD. The other half, pertaining to Criterion A and involving clinically significant difficulties in personality functioning, is typically measured by the Level of Personality Functioning Scale (see *DSM-5*, pp. 775–779). Criterion B, measured by the PID-5, is thought to describe those functioning difficulties using maladaptive traits. While they are theoretically distinguishable, a key issue regarding the evaluation of the AMPD concerns overlap between Criterion A and Criterion B (Krueger & Hobbs, 2020). Criterion A and Criterion B assessments are indeed highly correlated (e.g., Few et al., 2013; Fossati, Borroni et al., 2017; Zimmermann et al., 2015). These high correlations raise the question of whether Criteria A and B do describe different constructs. While some have suggested that the overlap is not an issue, two possible responses have been posited: express Criterion B in normal-range (rather than maladaptive) personality traits, or somehow combine the two into a single criterion.

First, one could argue that strong overlap should be expected as Criterion A provides a basis for PD diagnosis, and Criterion B allows the clinician to delineate how that diagnosis is expressed. Furthermore, Criteria A and B reflect distinguishable traditions in PD scholarship, so considering them together in the AMPD represents an opportunity for intellectual rapprochement (Waugh et al., 2017). From that point of view, no major action need be taken regarding the structure of the first two criteria of the AMPD.

On the other hand, expressing Criterion B in terms of normal-range traits may reduce overlap. Morey et al. (2020) demonstrated that normal-range personality traits and Criterion A dysfunction contribute independently to understanding maladaptive traits. In other words, maladaptive traits can be represented as the combination of normal-range traits and global dysfunction (Criterion A). Thus, making Criterion B an index of normal-range traits would theoretically address the overlap issue without loss of information. Using normal-range traits would also keep the PD field consistent with the vast literature base on the FFM while providing a theoretical basis for distinguishing PD from other forms of psychopathology. In addition, it would allow for bipolar measurement of personality, including direct measurement of patient strengths. Finally, Hopwood et al. (2011) have argued for the clinical utility of separate severity and normal-range trait measurements in allowing clinicians to distinguish the person from their problems.

Widiger, Bach, and colleagues (2019) discuss relations between Criteria A and B in the framework of the structure of psychopathology. They suggest that Criterion A may approximate a general factor of psychopathology in a similar manner to Criterion B domains approximating broad spectra of psychopathology. There is support for the view that a general factor of psychopathology or "p factor" exists as a reflection of the correlations among various psychopathological symptoms and is associated with more life impairment (Caspi et al., 2014); recent evidence suggests that the p factor correlates very strongly ($r = .94$) with a proposed general factor of PD (g-PD), which is thought to be what Criterion A indexes (McCabe et al., 2021). Because both normal-range and maladaptive traits map cleanly onto broad spectra of psychopathology, either approach to Criterion B, in combination with Criterion A approximating a general factor, could be argued to make the AMPD consistent with the general structure of psychopathology.

Finally, it could also be argued that having two separate criteria is unnecessary. If one of the two lacks incremental validity, one could say that the classification system lacks parsimony, and separate assessment is inefficient. Zimmermann et al. (2019) discuss the incremental validity of the two criteria relative to each other in predicting domains like symptom distress, well-being, and Section II PDs.

They conclude that "while some studies found support for the incremental validity of severity compared to maladaptive traits . . . the effect sizes were typically rather small. In contrast, the incremental validity of maladaptive traits when controlling for severity seems to be more robust" (p. 92). As a result, a simplified AMPD that combines features described in Criteria A and B may not result in loss of substantive information. These issues continue to be debated (Morey, 2019a; Sleep, Lynam, Widiger et al., 2019a, 2019b).

## Conclusion and Future Directions

Given the clinical importance of classifying PDs and the well-documented limitations of traditional approaches, perhaps it should not be surprising that the *DSM-5* Maladaptive Trait Model has accumulated considerable international interest and empirical research. This alternative approach was developed from a consensus of evidence that dimensional traits were a promising organizing framework for PDs. On that principle, the *DSM-5* Personality and Personality Disorders Work Group nominated relevant trait facets and then empirically derived the structure of the Trait Model. The structural validity of the five-domain, 25-facet model has received considerable replication. While the temporal stability, interrater reliability, and cross-cultural measurement invariance of the approach require further research, the initial evidence in these domains is promising. The Trait Model appears clinically useful and to provide strong coverage of prior PD syndromes, thus quelling concerns about potential upheaval that a taxonomic shift would cause. It also neatly aligns with contemporary models of normal-range personality and psychopathology, providing further validity evidence.

These various lines of inquiry are likely to lead to revisions of the Trait Model. Future revisions should consider shifting the primary domains of some facets (e.g., *hostility* on *antagonism* rather than on *negative affectivity*), changing the items used to measure certain facets (e.g., in some samples, *risk taking* and *emotional lability* do not appear unidimensional), and the inclusion of additional traits (e.g., compulsivity to provide better coverage of obsessive-compulsive PD). Future research should continue to scrutinize the psychometric properties of the PID-5, especially when applied to novel populations within and outside of the United States and Western Europe, where most of the work to date has been completed. Additional research is also needed to better distinguish personality traits from personality dysfunction, and that also utilizes clinician rating forms and structured clinical interviews of these traits to further demonstrate the model's applicability in clinical diagnostic settings. More generally, much of the research reviewed has been based on self-report data, so, moving forward, multimethod approaches will be key to overcoming concerns about shared method variance. Much work is still needed, but the *DSM-5* Maladaptive Trait Model has amassed an extensive body of literature demonstrating its strength as a taxonomy for personality disorders.

## References

Aboul-ata, M., & Qonsua, F. (2021). Validity, reliability and hierarchical structure of the PID-5 among Egyptian college students: Using exploratory structural equation modelling. *Personality and Mental Health*, *15*(2), 100–112. https://doi.org/10.1002/pmh.1497

Adhiatma, W., & Halim, M. S. (2021). Structural validity and reliability of the Indonesian version of PID-5. *Psychological Test Adaptation and Development*. https://doi.org/10.1027/2698-1866/a000010

Ahmed, A. O., Green, B. A., Goodrum, N. M., Doane, N. J., Birgenheir, D., & Buckley, P. F. (2013). Does a latent class underlie schizotypal personality disorder? Implications for schizophrenia. *Journal of Abnormal Psychology*, *122*(2), 475–491. https://doi.org/10.1037/a0032713

Al-Attiyah, A. A., Megreya, A. M., Alrashidi, M., Dominguez-Lara, S. A., & Al-Sheerawi, A. (2017). The psychometric properties of an Arabic version of the Personality Inventory for DSM-5 (PID-5) across three Arabic-speaking Middle Eastern countries. *International Journal of Culture and Mental Health*, *10*(2), 197–205. https://doi.org/10.1080/17542863.2017.1290125

Al-Dajani, N., Gralnick, T. M., & Bagby, R. M. (2016). A psychometric review of the Personality Inventory for DSM-5 (PID-5): Current status and future directions. *Journal of Personality Assessment*, *98*(1), 62–81. https://doi.org/10.1080/00223891.2015.1107572

Anderson, J. L., Sellbom, M., Sansone, R. A., & Songer, D. A. (2016). Comparing external correlates of DSM-5 Section II and Section III dimensional trait operationalizations of borderline personality disorder. *Journal of Personality Disorders*, *30*(2), 193–210. https://doi.org/10.1521/pedi_2015_29_189

Anderson, J. L., Sellbom, M., Wygant, D. B., Salekin, R. T., & Krueger, R. F. (2014). Examining the associations between DSM-5 Section III antisocial personality disorder traits and psychopathy in community and university samples. *Journal of Personality Disorders*, *28*(5), 675–697. https://doi.org/10.1521/pedi_2014_28_134

Ashton, M. C., de Vries, R. E., & Lee, K. (2017). Trait variance and response style variance in the scales of the Personality Inventory for DSM–5 (PID–5). *Journal of Personality Assessment*, *99*(2), 192–203. https://doi.org/10.1080/00223891.2016.1208210

Aslinger, E. N., Manuck, S. B., Pilkonis, P. A., Simms, L. J., & Wright, A. G. C. (2018). Narcissist or narcissistic? Evaluation of the latent structure of narcissistic personality disorder. *Journal of Abnormal Psychology*, *127*(5), 496–502. https://doi.org/10.1037/abn0000363

Bach, B., Kerber, A., Aluja, A., Bastiaens, T., Keeley, J. W., Claes, L., Fossati, A., Gutierrez, F., Oliveira, S. E. S., Pires, R., Riegel, K. D., Rolland, J.-P., Roskam, I., Sellbom, M., Somma, A., Spanemberg, L., Strus, W., Thimm, J. C., Wright, A. G. C., & Zimmermann, J. (2020). International assessment of DSM-5 and ICD-11 personality disorder traits: Toward a common nosology in DSM-5.1. *Psychopathology*, 53(3–4), 179–188. https://doi.org/10.1159/000507589

Bach, B., Markon, K., Simonsen, E., & Krueger, R. F. (2015). Clinical utility of the DSM-5 alternative model of personality disorders: Six cases from practice. *Journal of Psychiatric Practice*, 21(1), 3–25. https://doi.org/10.1097/01.pra.0000460618.02805.ef

Bach, B., Sellbom, M., & Simonsen, E. (2018). Personality Inventory for DSM-5 (PID-5) in clinical versus nonclinical individuals: Generalizability of psychometric features. *Assessment*, 25(7), 815–825. https://doi.org/10.1177/1073191117709070

Bagby, R., Keeley, J., Williams, C., Mortezaei, A., Ryder, A., & Sellbom, M. (2021). Evaluating the measurement invariance of the Personality Inventory for DSM-5 (PID- 5) in Black Americans and White Americans. *Psychological Assessment*, 34(1), 82–90. https://doi.org/10.1037/pas0001085

Barchi-Ferreira, A. M., Loureiro, S. R., Torres, A. R., da Silva, T. D. A., Moreno, A. L., DeSousa, D. A., Chagas, M. H. N., dos Santos, R. G., Machado-de-Souza, J. P., Chagas, N. M. de S., Hallak, J. E. C., Crippa, J. A. de S., & Osório, F. L. (2019). Personality Inventory for DSM-5 (PID-5): Cross-cultural adaptation and content validity in the Brazilian context. *Trends in Psychiatry and Psychotherapy*, 41, 297–300. https://doi.org/10.1590/2237-6089-2018-0098

Barchi-Ferreira Bel, A. M., & Osório, F. L. (2020). The Personality Inventory for DSM-5: Psychometric evidence of validity and reliability-updates. *Harvard Review of Psychiatry*, 28(4), 225–237. https://doi.org/10.1097/HRP.0000000000000261

Bastiaens, T., Smits, D., & Claes, L. (2021). Case report: Pathological personality traits through the lens of the ICD-11 trait qualifiers and the DSM-5 Section III Trait Model: Two patients illustrating the clinical utility of a combined view. *Frontiers in Psychiatry*, 12, 243. https://doi.org/10.3389/fpsyt.2021.627119

Bastiaens, T., Smits, D., De Hert, M., Vanwalleghem, D., & Claes, L. (2016). DSM-5 Section III personality traits and Section II personality disorders in a Flemish community sample. *Psychiatry Research*, 238, 290–298. https://doi.org/10.1016/j.psychres.2016.02.056

Bastiaens, T., Smits, D., De Hert, M., Thys, E., Bryon, H., Sweers, K., Teugels, T., Van Looy, J., Verwerft, T., Vanwalleghem, D., Van Bouwel, L., & Claes, L. (2019). The relationship between the Personality Inventory for the DSM-5 (PID-5) and the psychotic disorder in a clinical sample. *Assessment*, 26(2), 315–323. https://doi.org/10.1177/1073191117693922

Bateman, A. W., Gunderson, J., & Mulder, R. (2015). Treatment of personality disorder. *Lancet (London, England)*, 385(9969), 735–743. https://doi.org/10.1016/S0140-6736(14)61394-5

Blashfield, R. K., Reynolds, S. M., & Stennett, B. (2012). The death of histrionic personality disorder. In *The Oxford handbook of personality disorders* (pp. 603–627). Oxford University Press. https://doi.org/10.1093/oxfordhb/9780199735013.013.0028

Bo, S., Bach, B., Mortensen, E. L., & Simonsen, E. (2015). Reliability and hierarchical structure of DSM-5 pathological traits in a Danish mixed sample. *Journal of Personality Disorders*, 30(1), 112–129. https://doi.org/10.1521/pedi_2015_29_187

Brown, T. A., & Barlow, D. H. (2009). A proposal for a dimensional classification system based on the shared features of the DSM-IV anxiety and mood disorders: Implications for assessment and treatment. *Psychological Assessment*, 21(3), 256–271. https://doi.org/10.1037/a0016608

Bucholz, K. K., Hesselbrock, V. M., Heath, A. C., Kramer, J. R., & Schuckit, M. A. (2000). A latent class analysis of antisocial personality disorder symptom data from a multi-centre family study of alcoholism. *Addiction*, 95(4), 553–567. https://doi.org/10.1046/j.1360-0443.2000.9545537.x

Busch, A. J., Morey, L. C., & Hopwood, C. J. (2017). Exploring the assessment of the DSM–5 Alternative Model for Personality Disorders with the Personality Assessment Inventory. *Journal of Personality Assessment*, 99(2), 211–218. https://doi.org/10.1080/00223891.2016.1217872

Carlotta, D., Krueger, R. F., Markon, K. E., Borroni, S., Frera, F., Somma, A., Maffei, C., & Fossati, A. (2015). Adaptive and maladaptive personality traits in high-risk gamblers. *Journal of Personality Disorders*, 29(3), 378–392. https://doi.org/10.1521/pedi_2014_28_164

Caspi, A., Houts, R. M., Belsky, D. W., Goldman-Mellor, S. J., Harrington, H., Israel, S., Meier, M. H., Ramrakha, S., Shalev, I., Poulton, R., & Moffitt, T. E. (2014). The p factor: O\One general psychopathology factor in the structure of psychiatric disorders? *Clinical Psychological Science*, 2(2), 119–137. https://doi.org/10.1177/2167702613497473

Chmielewski, M., Ruggero, C. J., Kotov, R., Liu, K., & Krueger, R. F. (2017). Comparing the dependability and associations with functioning of the DSM-5 Section III trait model of personality pathology and the DSM-5 Section II personality disorder model. *Personality Disorders*, 8(3), 228–236. https://doi.org/10.1037/per0000213

Chmielewski, M., & Watson, D. (2009). What is being assessed and why it matters: The impact of transient error on trait research. *Journal of Personality and Social Psychology*, 97(1), 186–202. https://doi.org/10.1037/a0015618

Clark, L. A. (2007). Assessment and diagnosis of personality disorder: Perennial issues and an emerging reconceptualization. *Annual Review of Psychology*, 58, 227–257. https://doi.org/10.1146/annurev.psych.57.102904.190200

Clark, L. A. (2009). Stability and change in personality disorder. *Current Directions in Psychological Science*, 18(1), 27–31. https://doi.org/10.1111/j.1467-8721.2009.01600.x

Clark, L. A., Simms, L. J., Wu, K. D., & Casillas, A. (2014). *Manual for the Schedule for Nonadaptive and Adaptive Personality (SNAP-2)*. Published by the author. University of Notre Dame, Notre Dame, IN.

Clark, L. A., & Watson, D. (2022). Personality trait model of the *DSM-5* Alternative Model of Personality Disorder (AMPD): A structural review. *Personality Disorders: Theory, Research, & Treatment*, 13(4), 328–336

Coelho, O., Pires, R., Ferreira, A. S., Gonçalves, B., AlJassmi, M., & Stocker, J. (2020). Arabic version of the Personality Inventory for the DSM-5 (PID-5) in a community sample of United Arab Emirates nationals. *Clinical Practice and Epidemiology in Mental Health: CP & EMH*, 16, 180–188. https://doi.org/10.2174/1745017902016010180

Conway, C., Hammen, C., & Brennan, P. (2012). A comparison of latent class, latent trait, and factor mixture models of DSM-IV borderline personality disorder criteria in a community setting: Implications for DSM-5. *Journal of Personality Disorders*, *26*(5), 793–803. https://doi.org/10.1521/pedi.2012.26.5.793

Costa, P. T., & McCrae, R. R. (1992). The five-factor model of personality and its relevance to personality disorders. *Journal of Personality Disorders*, *6*(4), 343–359. https://doi.org/10.1521/pedi.1992.6.4.343

Creswell, K. G., Bachrach, R. L., Wright, A. G. C., Pinto, A., & Ansell, E. (2016). Predicting problematic alcohol use with the DSM–5 alternative model of personality pathology. *Personality Disorders: Theory, Research, and Treatment*, *7*(1), 103–111. https://doi.org/10.1037/per0000131

De Caluwé, E., Verbeke, L., Aken, M. van, Heijden, P. T. van der, & Clercq, B. D. (2019). The DSM-5 trait measure in a psychiatric sample of late adolescents and emerging adults: Structure, reliability, and validity. *Journal of Personality Disorders*, *33*(1), 101–118. https://doi.org/10.1521/pedi_2018_32_333

De Fruyt, F., De Clercq, B., De Bolle, M., Wille, B., Markon, K., & Krueger, R. F. (2013). General and maladaptive traits in a five-factor framework for DSM-5 in a university student sample. *Assessment*, *20*(3), 295–307. https://doi.org/10.1177/1073191113475808

Debast, I., Rossi, G., & van Alphen, S. P. J. (2017). Construct validity of the DSM-5 Section III maladaptive trait domains in older adults. *Journal of Personality Disorders*, *31*(5), 671–688. https://doi.org/10.1521/pedi_2017_31_274

Debast, I., Rossi, G., & van Alphen, S. P. J. (2018). Age-neutrality of a brief assessment of the Section III Alternative Model for Personality Disorders in older adults. *Assessment*, *25*(3), 310–323. https://doi.org/10.1177/1073191118754706

DeYoung, C. G., Carey, B. E., Krueger, R. F., & Ross, S. R. (2016). Ten aspects of the Big Five in the Personality Inventory for DSM-5. *Personality Disorders*, *7*(2), 113–123. https://doi.org/10.1037/per0000170

DeYoung, C. G., Chmielewski, M., Clark, L. A., Condon, D. M., Kotov, R., Krueger, R. F., Lynam, D. R., Markon, K. E., Miller, J. D., Mullins-Sweatt, S. N., Samuel, D. B., Sellbom, M., South, S. C., Thomas, K. M., Watson, D., Watts, A. L., Widiger, T. A., Wright, A. G. C., & HiTOP Normal Personality Workgroup. (2020). The distinction between symptoms and traits in the Hierarchical Taxonomy of Psychopathology (HiTOP). *Journal of Personality*. https://doi.org/10.1111/jopy.12593

DeYoung, C. G., Quilty, L. C., & Peterson, J. B. (2007). Between facets and domains: 10 aspects of the Big Five. *Journal of Personality and Social Psychology*, *93*(5), 880–896. https://doi.org/10.1037/0022-3514.93.5.880

Dhillon, S., Bagby, R. M., Kushner, S. C., & Burchett, D. (2017). The impact of underreporting and overreporting on the validity of the Personality Inventory for DSM–5 (PID-5): A simulation analog design investigation. *Psychological Assessment*, *29*(4), 473–478. https://doi.org/10.1037/pas0000359

Díaz-Batanero, C., Ramírez-López, J., Domínguez-Salas, S., Fernández-Calderón, F., & Lozano, Ó. M. (2019). Personality Inventory for DSM-5-Short Form (PID-5-SF): Reliability, factorial structure, and relationship with functional impairment in dual diagnosis patients. *Assessment*, *26*(5), 853–866. https://doi.org/10.1177/1073191117739980

Donnellan, M. B., Lucas, R. E., & Fleeson, W. (2009). Introduction to personality and assessment at age 40: Reflections on the legacy of the person–situation debate and the future of person–situation integration. *Journal of Research in Personality*, *43*(2), 117–119. https://doi.org/10.1016/j.jrp.2009.02.010

Drvaric, L., Bagby, R. M., Kiang, M., & Mizrahi, R. (2018). Maladaptive personality traits in patients identified at lower-risk and higher-risk for psychosis. *Psychiatry Research*, *268*, 348–353. https://doi.org/10.1016/j.psychres.2018.08.004

Dunne, A. L., Trounson, J. S., Skues, J., Pfeifer, J. E., Ogloff, J. R. P., & Daffern, M. (2021). The Personality Inventory for DSM-5–Brief Form: An examination of internal consistency, factor structure, and relationship to aggression in an incarcerated offender sample. *Assessment*, *28*(4), 1136–1146. https://doi.org/10.1177/1073191120916790

Evans, C. M., & Simms, L. J. (2019). The latent structure of self-harm. *Journal of Abnormal Psychology*, *128*(1), 12–24. https://doi.org/10.1037/abn0000398

Ferretti, F., Carabellese, F., Catanesi, R., Coluccia, A., Ferracuti, S., Schimmenti, A., Caretti, V., Lorenzi, L., Gualtieri, G., Carabellese, F., & Pozza, A. (2021). DSM-5 personality trait facets amongst child molesters: An exploratory comparison with other types of offenders. *BMC Psychology*, *9*(1), 117. https://doi.org/10.1186/s40359-021-00619-1

Few, L. R., Miller, J. D., Rothbaum, A., Meller, S., Maples, J., Terry, D. P., Collins, B., & MacKillop, J. (2013). Examination of the Section III DSM-5 diagnostic system for personality disorders in an outpatient clinical sample. *Journal of Abnormal Psychology*, *122*(4), 1057–1069. https://doi.org/10.1037/a0034878

First, M. B. (2005). Clinical utility: A prerequisite for the adoption of a dimensional approach in DSM. *Journal of Abnormal Psychology*, *114*(4), 560–564. https://doi.org/10.1037/0021-843X.114.4.560

Fossati, A., Borroni, S., Somma, A., Markon, K. E., & Krueger, R. F. (2017). Testing relationships between DSM-5 Section III maladaptive traits and measures of self and interpersonal impairment in Italian community dwelling adults. *Personality Disorders*, *8*(3), 275–280. https://doi.org/10.1037/per0000192

Fossati, A., Somma, A., Borroni, S., Maffei, C., Markon, K. E., & Krueger, R. F. (2016). A head-to-head comparison of the Personality Inventory for DSM-5 (PID-5) with the Personality Diagnostic Questionnaire-4 (PDQ-4) in predicting the general level of personality pathology among community dwelling subjects. *Journal of Personality Disorders*, *30*(1), 82–94. https://doi.org/10.1521/pedi_2105_29_184

Fossati, A., Somma, A., Borroni, S., Markon, K. E., & Krueger, R. F. (2017). The Personality Inventory for DSM-5 Brief Form: Evidence for reliability and construct validity in a sample of community-dwelling Italian adolescents. *Assessment*, *24*(5), 615–631. https://doi.org/10.1177/1073191115621793

Fossati, A., Somma, A., Krueger, R. F., Markon, K. E., & Borroni, S. (2017). On the relationships between DSM-5 dysfunctional personality traits and social cognition deficits: A study in a sample of consecutively admitted Italian psychotherapy patients. *Clinical Psychology & Psychotherapy*, *24*(6), 1421–1434. https://doi.org/10.1002/cpp.2091

Garcia, D. J., Skadberg, R. M., Schmidt, M., Bierma, S., Shorter, R. L., & Waugh, M. H. (2018). It's not that difficult: An interrater reliability study of the DSM–5 Section III Alternative Model for Personality Disorders. *Journal of*

*Personality Assessment*, *100*(6), 612–620. https://doi.org/10.1080/00223891.2018.1428982

Gutiérrez, F., Aluja, A., Peri, J. M., Calvo, N., Ferrer, M., Baillés, E., Gutiérrez-Zotes, J. A., Gárriz, M., Caseras, X., Markon, K. E., & Krueger, R. F. (2017). Psychometric properties of the Spanish PID-5 in a clinical and a community sample. *Assessment*, *24*(3), 326–336. https://doi.org/10.1177/1073191115606518

Haslam, N., McGrath, M. J., Viechtbauer, W., & Kuppens, P. (2020). Dimensions over categories: A meta-analysis of taxometric research. *Psychological Medicine*, *50*(9), 1418–1432. https://doi.org/10.1017/S003329172000183X

Heath, L. M., Drvaric, L., Hendershot, C. S., Quilty, L. C., & Bagby, R. M. (2018). Normative and maladaptive personality trait models of mood, psychotic, and substance use disorders. *Journal of Psychopathology and Behavioral Assessment*, *40*(4), 606–613. https://doi.org/10.1007/s10862-018-9688-0

Hopwood, C. J., Malone, J. C., Ansell, E. B., Sanislow, C. A., Grilo, C. M., McGlashan, T. H., Pinto, A., Markowitz, J. C., Shea, M. T., Skodol, A. E., Gunderson, J. G., Zanarini, M. C., & Morey, L. C. (2011). Personality assessment in DSM-5: Empirical support for rating severity, style, and traits. *Journal of Personality Disorders*, *25*(3), 305–320. https://doi.org/10.1521/pedi.2011.25.3.305

Hyatt, C. S., Maples-Keller, J. L., Crowe, M. L., Sleep, C. E., Carter, S. T., Michopoulos, V., Stevens, J. S., Jovanovic, T., Bradley, B., Miller, J. D., & Powers, A. (2021). Psychometric properties of the Personality Inventory for DSM-5-Brief Form in a community sample with high rates of trauma exposure. *Journal of Personality Assessment*, *103*(2), 204–213. https://doi.org/10.1080/00223891.2020.1713138

James, L. M., Anders, S. L., Peterson, C. K., Engdahl, B. E., Krueger, R. F., & Georgopoulos, A. P. (2015). DSM-5 personality traits discriminate between posttraumatic stress disorder and control groups. *Experimental Brain Research*, *233*(7), 2021–2028. https://doi.org/10.1007/s00221-015-4273-1

Kajonius, P. J. (2017). The Short Personality Inventory for DSM-5 and its conjoined structure with the common five-factor model. *International Journal of Testing*, *17*(4), 372–384. https://doi.org/10.1080/15305058.2017.1309421

Keeley, J. W., Webb, C., Peterson, D., Roussin, L., & Flanagan, E. H. (2016). Development of a response inconsistency scale for the Personality Inventory for DSM-5. *Journal of Personality Assessment*, *98*(4), 351–359. https://doi.org/10.1080/00223891.2016.1158719

Kotov, R., Krueger, R. F., Watson, D., Achenbach, T. M., Althoff, R. R., Bagby, R. M., . . . Zimmerman, M. (2017). The Hierarchical Taxonomy of Psychopathology (HiTOP): A dimensional alternative to traditional nosologies. *Journal of Abnormal Psychology*, *126*(4), 454–477. https://doi.org/10.1037/abn0000258

Kotov, R., Krueger, R. F., Watson, D., Cicero, D. C., Conway, C. C., DeYoung, C. G., Eaton, N. R., Forbes, M. K., Hallquist, M. N., Latzman, R. D., Mullins-Sweatt, S. N., Ruggero, C. J., Simms, L. J., Waldman, I. D., Waszczuk, M. A., & Wright, A. G. C. (2021). The Hierarchical Taxonomy of Psychopathology (HiTOP): A quantitative nosology based on consensus of evidence. *Annual Review of Clinical Psychology*, *17*, 83–108. https://doi.org/10.1146/annurev-clinpsy-081219-093304

Krueger, R. F., Derringer, J., Markon, K. E., Watson, D., & Skodol, A. E. (2012). Initial construction of a maladaptive personality trait model and inventory for DSM-5. *Psychological Medicine*, *42*(9), 1879–1890. https://doi.org/10.1017/S0033291711002674

Krueger, R. F., Eaton, N. R., Derringer, J., Markon, K. E., Watson, D., & Skodol, A. E. (2011). Personality in DSM–5: Helping delineate personality disorder content and framing the metastructure. *Journal of Personality Assessment*, *93*(4), 325–331. https://doi.org/10.1080/00223891.2011.577478

Krueger, R. F., & Hobbs, K. A. (2020). An overview of the DSM-5 Alternative Model of Personality Disorders. *Psychopathology*, *53*(3), 126–132. https://doi.org/10.1159/000508538

Krueger, R. F., & Markon, K. E. (2014). The role of the DSM-5 personality trait model in moving toward a quantitative and empirically based approach to classifying personality and psychopathology. *Annual Review of Clinical Psychology*, *10*, 477–501. https://doi.org/10.1146/annurev-clinpsy-032813-153732

Krueger, R. F., Skodol, A. E., Livesley, W. J., Shrout, P. E., & Huang, Y. (2007). Synthesizing dimensional and categorical approaches to personality disorders: Refining the research agenda for DSM-V Axis II. *International Journal of Methods in Psychiatric Research*, *16*(S1), S65–S73. https://doi.org/10.1002/mpr.212

Kupfer, D. J., First, M. B., & Regier, D. A. (Eds.). (2002). *A research agenda for DSM-V*, 1st ed. American Psychiatric Association.

Labancz, E., Balázs, K., & Kuritárné Szabó, I. (2020). The psychometric properties of the Hungarian version of the Personality Inventory for DSM-5 in a clinical and a community sample. *Current Psychology*. https://doi.org/10.1007/s12144-020-00831-z

Lee, K., & Ashton, M. C. (2016). The HEXACO model of personality structure. In V. Zeigler-Hill & T. K. Shackelford (Eds.), *Encyclopedia of personality and individual differences* (pp. 1–6). Springer International. https://doi.org/10.1007/978-3-319-28099-8_1227-1

Lengel, G. J., & Mullins-Sweatt, S. N. (2017). The importance and acceptability of general and maladaptive personality trait computerized assessment feedback. *Psychological Assessment*, *29*(1), 1–12. https://doi.org/10.1037/pas0000321

Lim, D. S. H., Gwee, A. J., & Hong, R. Y. (2019). Associations between the DSM-5 Section III trait model and impairments in functioning in Singaporean college students. *Journal of Personality Disorders*, *33*(3), 413–431. https://doi.org/10.1521/pedi_2018_32_353

Livesley, W. J., & Jackson, D. (2009). *Manual for the dimensional assessment of personality pathology: Basic questionnaire*. Sigma Press.

Lotfi, M., Bach, B., Amini, M., & Simonsen, E. (2018). Structure of DSM-5 and ICD-11 personality domains in Iranian community sample. *Personality and Mental Health*, *12*(2), 155–169. https://doi.org/10.1002/pmh.1409

Lozovanu, S., Moldovanu, I., Vovc, V., Ganenco, A., Blajevschi, A., & Besleaga, T. (2019). Translation and validation of the Russian version of the personality inventory for DSM-5 (PID-5). *Moldovan Medical Journal*, *62*(2), 3–6. https://doi.org/10.5281/zenodo.3233900

Lynam, D. R., & Widiger, T. A. (2001). Using the five-factor model to represent the DSM-IV personality disorders: An expert consensus approach. *Journal of Abnormal Psychology*, *110*(3), 401–412. https://doi.org/10.1037/0021-843X.110.3.401

Maples, J. L., Carter, N. T., Few, L. R., Crego, C., Gore, W. L., Samuel, D. B., Williamson, R. L., Lynam, D. R., Widiger, T. A., Markon, K. E., Krueger, R. F., & Miller, J. D. (2015). Testing whether the DSM-5 personality disorder trait model can be measured with a reduced set of items: An item response theory investigation of the Personality Inventory for DSM-5. *Psychological Assessment, 27*(4), 1195–1210. https://doi.org/10.1037/pas0000120

Markon, K. E., Quilty, L. C., Bagby, R. M., & Krueger, R. F. (2013). The development and psychometric properties of an informant-report form of the personality inventory for DSM-5 (PID-5). *Assessment, 20*(3), 370–383. https://doi.org/10.1177/1073191113486513

McCabe, G. A., Oltmanns, J. R., & Widiger, T. A. (2021). the general factors of personality disorder, psychopathology, and personality. *Journal of Personality Disorders*, 1–31. https://doi.org/10.1521/pedi_2021_35_530

McClintock, A. S., & McCarrick, S. M. (2017). An examination of dependent personality disorder in the Alternative DSM-5 Model for Personality Disorders. *Journal of Psychopathology and Behavioral Assessment, 39*(4), 635–641. https://doi.org/10.1007/s10862-017-9621-y

McGee Ng, S. A., Bagby, R. M., Goodwin, B. E., Burchett, D., Sellbom, M., Ayearst, L. E., Dhillon, S., Yiu, S., Ben-Porath, Y. S., & Baker, S. (2016). The effect of response bias on the Personality Inventory for DSM–5 (PID–5). *Journal of Personality Assessment, 98*(1), 51–61. https://doi.org/10.1080/00223891.2015.1096791

Meredith, W. (1993). Measurement invariance, factor analysis and factorial invariance. *Psychometrika, 58*(4), 525–543. https://doi.org/10.1007/BF02294825

Miller, J. D., Sleep, C., & Lynam, D. R. (2018). DSM-5 alternative model of personality disorder: Testing the trait perspective captured in Criterion B. *Current Opinion in Psychology, 21*, 50–54. https://doi.org/10.1016/j.copsyc.2017.09.012

Morey, L. C. (2019a). Thoughts on the assessment of the DSM-5 alternative model for personality disorders: Comment on Sleep et al. (2019). *Psychological Assessment, 31*(10), 1192–1199. https://doi.org/10.1037/pas0000710

Morey, L. C. (2019b). Interdiagnostician reliability of the DSM-5 Section II and Section III alternative model criteria for borderline personality disorder. *Journal of Personality Disorders, 33*(6), 721–S18. https://doi.org/10.1521/pedi_2019_33_362

Morey, L. C., & Benson, K. T. (2016). Relating DSM-5 Section II and Section III personality disorder diagnostic classification systems to treatment planning. *Comprehensive Psychiatry, 68*, 48–55. https://doi.org/10.1016/j.comppsych.2016.03.010

Morey, L. C., Benson, K. T., & Skodol, A. E. (2016). Relating DSM-5 Section III personality traits to Section II personality disorder diagnoses. *Psychological Medicine, 46*(3), 647–655. https://doi.org/10.1017/S0033291715002226

Morey, L. C., Good, E. W., & Hopwood, C. J. (2020). Global personality dysfunction and the relationship of pathological and normal trait domains in the DSM-5 alternative model for personality disorders. *Journal of Personality*. https://doi.org/10.1111/jopy.12560

Morey, L. C., & Hopwood, C. J. (2013). Stability and change in personality disorders. *Annual Review of Clinical Psychology, 9*(1), 499–528. https://doi.org/10.1146/annurev-clinpsy-050212-185637

Morey, L. C., Krueger, R. F., & Skodol, A. E. (2013). The hierarchical structure of clinician ratings of proposed DSM–5 pathological personality traits. *Journal of Abnormal Psychology, 122*(3), 836–841. https://doi.org/10.1037/a0034003

Morey, L. C., Skodol, A. E., & Oldham, J. M. (2014). Clinician judgments of clinical utility: A comparison of DSM-IV-TR personality disorders and the alternative model for DSM-5 personality disorders. *Journal of Abnormal Psychology, 123*(2), 398–405. https://doi.org/10.1037/a0036481

Naragon-Gainey, K., & Simms, L. J. (2017). Three-way interaction of neuroticism, extraversion, and conscientiousness in the internalizing disorders: Evidence of disorder specificity in a psychiatric sample. *Journal of Research in Personality, 70*, 16–26. https://doi.org/10.1016/j.jrp.2017.05.003

Nelson, S. M., Huprich, S. K., Shankar, S., Sohnleitner, A., & Paggeot, A. V. (2017). A quantitative and qualitative evaluation of trainee opinions of four methods of personality disorder diagnosis. *Personality Disorders, 8*(3), 217–227. https://doi.org/10.1037/per0000227

Niemeyer, L. M., Grosz, M. P., Zimmermann, J., & Back, M. D. (2021). Assessing maladaptive personality in the forensic context: Development and validation of the Personality Inventory for DSM-5 Forensic Faceted Brief Form (PID-5-FFBF). *Journal of Personality Assessment, 104*(1), 30–43. https://doi.org/10.1080/00223891.2021.1923522

O'Connor, B. P. (2002). The search for dimensional structure differences between normality and abnormality: A statistical review of published data on personality and psychopathology. *Journal of Personality and Social Psychology, 83*(4), 962. https://doi.org/10.1037/0022-3514.83.4.962

Oltmanns, J. R., & Oltmanns, T. F. (2021). Self-other agreement on ratings of personality disorder symptoms and traits. In T. D. Letring & J. S. Spain (Eds.), *The Oxford Handbook of Accurate Personality Judgment* (pp. C18-C18.S12). https://doi.org/10.1093/oxfordhb/9780190912529.013.19

Ozer, D. J., & Benet-Martínez, V. (2006). Personality and the prediction of consequential outcomes. *Annual Review of Psychology, 57*, 401–421. https://doi.org/10.1146/annurev.psych.57.102904.190127

Pires, R., Sousa Ferreira, A., & Guedes, D. (2017). The psychometric properties of the Portuguese version of the Personality Inventory for DSM-5. *Scandinavian Journal of Psychology, 58*(5), 468–475. https://doi.org/10.1111/sjop.12383

Rek, K., Kerber, A., Kemper, C. J., & Zimmermann, J. (2021). Getting the Personality Inventory for DSM-5 ready for clinical practice: Norm values and correlates in a representative sample from the German population. *PsyArXiv*. https://doi.org/10.31234/osf.io/5hm43

Ringwald, W. R., Emery, L., Khoo, S., Clark, L. A., Kotelnikova, Y., Scalco, M. D., Watson, D., Wright, A. G. C., & Simms, L. (2021). Structure of pathological personality traits through the Lens of the CAT-PD Model. *PsyArXiv*. https://doi.org/10.31234/osf.io/kuefm

Quilty, L. C., Cosentino, N., & Bagby, R. M. (2018). Response bias and the personality inventory for DSM-5: Contrasting self- and informant-report. *Personality Disorders, 9*(4), 346–353. https://doi.org/10.1037/per0000246

Riegel, K. D., Ksinan, A. J., Samankova, D., Preiss, M., Harsa, P., & Krueger, R. F. (2018). Unidimensionality of the personality inventory for DSM-5 facets: Evidence from two Czech-speaking samples. *Personality and Mental Health, 12*(4), 281–297. https://doi.org/10.1002/pmh.1423

Roberts, B. W., Wood, D., & Caspi, A. (2008). The development of personality traits in adulthood. In *Handbook of personality: Theory and research*, 3rd ed. (pp. 375–398). Guilford.

Rojas, S. L., & Widiger, T. A. (2017). Coverage of the DSM-IV-TR/DSM-5 Section II personality disorders with the DSM-5 dimensional trait model. *Journal of Personality Disorders*, *31*(4), 462–482. https://doi.org/10.1521/pedi_2016_30_262

Rounsaville, B. J., Alarcón, R. D., Andrews, G., Jackson, J. S., Kendell, R. E., & Kendler, K. (2002). Basic nomenclature issues for DSM-V. In D. J. Kupfer, M. B. First, & D. A. Regier (Eds.), *A research agenda for DSM-V* (pp. 1–29). American Psychiatric Association.

Rowiński, T., Kowalska-Dąbrowska, M., Strus, W., Cieciuch, J., Czuma, I., Żechowski, C., Markon, K. E., & Krueger, R. F. (2019). Measurement of pathological personality traits according to the DSM-5: A Polish adaptation of the PID-5. Part II - empirical results. *Psychiatria Polska*, *53*(1), 23–48. https://doi.org/10.12740/PP/OnlineFirst/86478

Russell, T. D., Pocknell, V., & King, A. R. (2017). Lesbians and bisexual women and men have higher scores on the Personality Inventory for the DSM-5 (PID-5) than heterosexual counterparts. *Personality and Individual Differences*, *110*, 119–124. https://doi.org/10.1016/j.paid.2017.01.039

Samuel, D. B., & Widiger, T. A. (2006). Clinicians' judgments of clinical utility: A comparison of the DSM-IV and five-factor models. *Journal of Abnormal Psychology*, *115*(2), 298–308. https://doi.org/10.1037/0021-843X.115.2.298

Samuel, D. B., & Widiger, T. A. (2008). A meta-analytic review of the relationships between the Five-Factor Model and DSM-IV-TR personality disorders: A facet level analysis. *Clinical Psychology Review*, *28*(8), 1326–1342. https://doi.org/10.1016/j.cpr.2008.07.002

Samuel, D. B., Widiger, T. A., Pilkonis, P. A., Miller, J. D., Lynam, D. R., & Ball, S. A. (2012). Conceptual changes to the definition of borderline personality disorder proposed for DSM-5. *Journal of Abnormal Psychology*, *121*(2), 467–476. https://doi.org/10.1037/a0025285

Saulsman, L. M., & Page, A. C. (2004). The five-factor model and personality disorder empirical literature: A meta-analytic review. *Clinical Psychology Review*, *23*(8), 1055–1085. https://doi.org/10.1016/j.cpr.2002.09.001

Sellbom, M., Dhillon, S., & Bagby, R. M. (2018). Development and validation of an Overreporting Scale for the Personality Inventory for DSM-5 (PID-5). *Psychological Assessment*, *30*(5), 582–593. https://doi.org/10.1037/pas0000507

Sheets, E., & Craighead, W. E. (2007). Toward an empirically based classification of personality pathology. *Clinical Psychology: Science and Practice*, *14*(2), 77–93. https://doi.org/10.1111/j.1468-2850.2007.00065.x

Simms, L. J., & Calabrese, W. R. (2016). Incremental validity of the DSM-5 Section III personality disorder traits with respect to psychosocial impairment. *Journal of Personality Disorders*, *30*(1), 95–111. https://doi.org/10.1521/pedi_2015_29_185

Skodol A. E., First M. B., Bender D. S., & Oldham J. M. (2018). *Structured clinical interview for the DSM-5 Alternative Model for Personality Disorders: Module II: Structured clinical interview for personality traits.* American Psychiatric Association.

Skodol, A. E., Gunderson, J. G., Shea, M. T., McGlashan, T. H., Morey, L. C., Sanislow, C. A., Bender, D. S., Grilo, C. M., Zanarini, M. C., Yen, S., Pagano, M. E., & Stout, R. L. (2005). The Collaborative Longitudinal Personality Disorders Study (CLPS): Overview and implications. *Journal of Personality Disorders*, *19*(5), 487–504. https://doi.org/10.1521/pedi.2005.19.5.487

Sleep, C. E., Lynam, D. R., Widiger, T. A., Crowe, M. L., & Miller, J. D. (2019a). An evaluation of DSM-5 Section III personality disorder Criterion A (impairment) in accounting for psychopathology. *Psychological Assessment*, *31*(10), 1181–1191. https://doi.org/10.1037/pas0000620

Sleep, C. E., Lynam, D. R., Widiger, T. A., Crowe, M. L., & Miller, J. D. (2019b). Difficulties with the conceptualization and assessment of Criterion A in the DSM-5 alternative model of personality disorder: A reply to Morey (2019). *Psychological Assessment*, *31*(10), 1200–1205. https://doi.org/10.1037/pas0000758

Somma, A., Borroni, S., Gialdi, G., Carlotta, D., Emanuela Giarolli, L., Barranca, M., Cerioli, C., Franzoni, C., Masci, E., Manini, R., Luca Busso, S., Ruotolo, G., Krueger, R. F., Markon, K. E., & Fossati, A. (2020). The interrater reliability and validity of the Italian translation of the Structured Clinical Interview for DSM-5 Alternative Model for Personality Disorders Module I and Module II: A Preliminary report on consecutively admitted psychotherapy outpatients. *Journal of Personality Disorders*, *34*(Suppl C), 95–123. https://doi.org/10.1521/pedi_2020_34_511

Somma, A., Borroni, S., Maffei, C., Giarolli, L. E., Markon, K. E., Krueger, R. F., & Fossati, A. (2017). Reliability, factor structure, and associations with measures of problem relationship and behavior of the Personality Inventory for DSM-5 in a sample of Italian community-dwelling adolescents. *Journal of Personality Disorders*, *31*(5), 624–646. https://doi.org/10.1521/pedi_2017_31_272

Somma, A., Krueger, R. F., Markon, K. E., Alajmo, V. B. M., Arlotta, E., Beretta, S., Boni, F., Busso, S. L., Manini, R., Nazzaro, G., Maffei, C., & Fossati, A. (2019). DSM-5 Alternative Model of Personality Disorder dysfunctional personality traits as predictors of self-reported aggression in an Italian sample of consecutively admitted, personality-disordered psychotherapy patients. *Journal of Personality Disorders*, 1–20. https://doi.org/10.1521/pedi_2019_33_430

Somma, A., Krueger, R. F., Markon, K. E., Borroni, S., & Fossati, A. (2019). Item response theory analyses, factor structure, and external correlates of the Italian translation of the Personality Inventory for DSM-5 Short Form in community-dwelling adults and clinical adults. *Assessment*, *26*(5), 839–852. https://doi.org/10.1177/1073191118781006

Somma, A., Krueger, R. F., Markon, K. E., & Fossati, A. (2019). The replicability of the personality inventory for DSM–5 domain scale factor structure in US and non- US samples: A quantitative review of the published literature. *Psychological Assessment*, *31*(7), 861–877. https://doi.org/10.1037/pas0000711

Sorrel, M. A., García, L. F., Aluja, A., Rolland, J. P., Rossier, J., Roskam, I., & Abad, F. J. (2021). Cross-Cultural measurement invariance in the Personality Inventory for DSM-5. *Psychiatry Research*, *304*, 114134. https://doi.org/10.1016/j.psychres.2021.114134

Soto, C. J. (2019). How replicable are links between personality traits and consequential life outcomes? The life outcomes of personality replication project. *Psychological Science*, *30*(5), 711–727. https://doi.org/10.1177/0956797619831612

South, S. C., Krueger, R. F., Knudsen, G. P., Ystrom, E., Czajkowski, N., Aggen, S. H., Neale, M. C., Gillespie, N. A., Kendler, K. S., & Reichborn-Kjennerud, T. (2017). A population based twin study of DSM-5 maladaptive personality domains. *Personality Disorders*, *8*(4), 366–375. https://doi.org/10.1037/per0000220

Suzuki, T., Griffin, S. A., & Samuel, D. B. (2017). Capturing the DSM-5 Alternative Personality Disorder Model traits in the Five-Factor Model's nomological net. *Journal of Personality, 85*(2), 220–231. https://doi.org/10.1111/jopy.12235

Suzuki, T., South, S. C., Samuel, D. B., Wright, A. G. C., Yalch, M. M., Hopwood, C. J., & Thomas, K. M. (2019). Measurement invariance of the DSM-5 Section III pathological personality trait model across sex. *Personality Disorders, 10*(2), 114–122. https://doi.org/10.1037/per0000291

Thimm, J. C., Jordan, S., & Bach, B. (2017). Hierarchical structure and cross-cultural measurement invariance of the Norwegian version of the Personality Inventory for DSM-5. *Journal of Personality Assessment, 99*(2), 204–210. https://doi.org/10.1080/00223891.2016.1223682

Thomas, K. M., Yalch, M. M., Krueger, R. F., Wright, A. G. C., Markon, K. E., & Hopwood, C. J. (2013). The convergent structure of DSM-5 personality trait facets and five-factor model trait domains. *Assessment, 20*(3), 308–311. https://doi.org/10.1177/1073191112457589

Trull, T. J., & Durrett, C. A. (2005). Categorical and dimensional models of personality disorder. *Annual Review of Clinical Psychology, 1*, 355–380. https://doi.org/10.1146/annurev.clinpsy.1.102803.144009

Tyrer, P., Coombs, N., Ibrahimi, F., Mathilakath, A., Bajaj, P., Ranger, M., Rao, B., & Din, R. (2007). Critical developments in the assessment of personality disorder. *British Journal of Psychiatry, 190*(S49), s51–s59. https://doi.org/10.1192/bjp.190.5.s51

Van den Broeck, J., Bastiaansen, L., Rossi, G., Dierckx, E., & De Clercq, B. (2013). Age-neutrality of the trait facets proposed for personality disorders in DSM-5: A DIFAS analysis of the PID-5. *Journal of Psychopathology and Behavioral Assessment, 35*(4), 487–494. https://doi.org/10.1007/s10862-013-9364-3

Verheul, R. (2012). Personality disorder proposal for DSM-5: A heroic and innovative but nevertheless fundamentally flawed attempt to improve DSM-IV. *Clinical Psychology & Psychotherapy, 19*(5), 369–371. https://doi.org/10.1002/cpp.1809

Verheul, R., & Widiger, T. A. (2004). A meta-analysis of the prevalence and usage of the personality disorder not otherwise specified (PDNOS) diagnosis. *Journal of Personality Disorders, 18*(4), 309–319. https://doi.org/10.1521/pedi.18.4.309.40350

Waszczuk, M. A., Eaton, N. R., Krueger, R. F., Shackman, A. J., Waldman, I. D., Zald, D. H., . . . Kotov, R. (2020). Redefining phenotypes to advance psychiatric genetics: Implications from hierarchical taxonomy of psychopathology. *Journal of Abnormal Psychology, 129*(2), 143–161. https://doi.org/10.1037/abn0000486

Waszczuk, M. A., Li, K., Ruggero, C. J., Clouston, S. A. P., Luft, B. J., & Kotov, R. (2018). Maladaptive personality traits and 10-year course of psychiatric and medical symptoms and functional impairment following trauma. *Annals of Behavioral Medicine, 52*(8), 697–712. https://doi.org/10.1093/abm/kax030

Watson, D. (2003). Investigating the construct validity of the dissociative taxon: Stability analyses of normal and pathological dissociation. *Journal of Abnormal Psychology, 112*(2), 298–305. https://doi.org/10.1037/0021-843x.112.2.298

Watson, D., Stasik, S. M., Ro, E., & Clark, L. A. (2013). Integrating normal and pathological personality: Relating the DSM-5 trait-dimensional model to general traits of personality. *Assessment, 20*(3), 312–326. https://doi.org/10.1177/1073191113485810

Watters, C. A., & Bagby, R. M. (2018). A meta-analysis of the five-factor internal structure of the Personality Inventory for DSM-5. *Psychological Assessment, 30*(9), 1255–1260. https://doi.org/10.1037/pas0000605

Watters, C. A., Bagby, R. M., & Sellbom, M. (2019). Meta-analysis to derive an empirically based set of personality facet criteria for the alternative DSM-5 model for personality disorders. *Personality Disorders: Theory, Research, and Treatment, 10*(2), 97–104. https://doi.org/10.1037/per0000307

Watters, C. A., Sellbom, M., Uliaszek, A. A., & Bagby, R. M. (2019). Clarifying the interstitial nature of facets from the Personality Inventory for DSM-5 using the five factor model of personality. *Personality Disorders, 10*(4), 330–339. https://doi.org/10.1037/per0000327

Waugh, M. H., Hopwood, C. J., Krueger, R. F., Morey, L. C., Pincus, A. L., & Wright, A. G. C. (2017). Psychological assessment with the DSM-5 Alternative Model for Personality Disorders: Tradition and innovation. *Professional Psychology, Research and Practice, 48*(2), 79–89. https://doi.org/10.1037/pro0000071

Widiger, T. A., Bach, B., Chmielewski, M., Clark, L. A., DeYoung, C., Hopwood, C. J., . . . Thomas, K. M. (2019). Criterion A of the AMPD in HiTOP. *Journal of Personality Assessment, 101*(4), 345–355. https://doi.org/10.1080/00223891.2018.1465431

Widiger, T. A., & Crego, C. (2019). HiTOP thought disorder, DSM-5 psychoticism, and five factor model openness. *Journal of Research in Personality, 80*, 72–77. https://doi.org/10.1016/j.jrp.2019.04.008

Widiger, T. A., & Samuel, D. B. (2005). Diagnostic categories or dimensions? A question for the Diagnostic and Statistical Manual of Mental Disorders, Fifth edition. *Journal of Abnormal Psychology, 114*(4), 494–504. https://doi.org/10.1037/0021-843X.114.4.494

Widiger, T. A., Sellbom, M., Chmielewski, M., Clark, L. A., DeYoung, C. G., Kotov, R., Krueger, R. F., Lynam, D. R., Miller, J. D., Mullins-Sweatt, S., Samuel, D. B., South, S. C., Tackett, J. L., Thomas, K. M., Watson, D., & Wright, A. G. C. (2019). Personality in a hierarchical model of psychopathology. *Clinical Psychological Science, 7*(1), 77–92. https://doi.org/10.1177/2167702618797105

Widiger, T. A., & Simonsen, E. (2005). Alternative dimensional models of personality disorder: Finding a common ground. *Journal of Personality Disorders, 19*(2), 110–130. https://doi.org/10.1521/pedi.19.2.110.62628

Widiger, T. A., Trull, T. J., Clarkin, J. F., Sanderson, C., & Costa Jr., P. T. (2002). A description of the DSM-IV personality disorders with the five-factor model of personality. In P. T. Costa, Jr. & T. A. Widiger (Eds.), *Personality disorders and the five-factor model of personality*, 2nd ed (pp. 89–99). American Psychological Association. https://doi.org/10.1037/10423-006

Wright, A. G. C., Calabrese, W. R., Rudick, M. M., Yam, W. H., Zelazny, K., Williams, T. F., Rotterman, J. H., & Simms, L. J. (2015). Stability of the DSM-5 Section III pathological personality traits and their longitudinal associations with psychosocial functioning in personality disordered individuals. *Journal of Abnormal Psychology, 124*(1), 199–207. https://doi.org/10.1037/abn0000018

Wright, A. G. C., & Simms, L. J. (2015). A metastructural model of mental disorders and pathological personality traits. *Psychological Medicine, 45*(11), 2309–2319. https://doi.org/10.1017/S0033291715000252

Wright, A. G. C., Thomas, K. M., Hopwood, C. J., Markon, K. E., Pincus, A. L., & Krueger, R. F. (2012). The hierarchical structure of DSM-5 pathological personality traits. *Journal of Abnormal Psychology, 121*(4), 951–957. https://doi.org/10.1037/a0027669

Wright, A. G. C., & Zimmermann, J. (2015). At the nexus of science and practice: Answering basic clinical questions in personality disorder assessment and diagnosis with quantitative modeling techniques. In S. K. Huprich (Ed.), *Personality disorders: Toward theoretical and empirical integration in diagnosis and assessment* (pp. 109–144). American Psychological Association. https://doi.org/10.1037/14549-006

Yalch, M. M., & Hopwood, C. J. (2016). Convergent, discriminant, and criterion validity of DSM–5 traits. *Personality Disorders: Theory, Research, and Treatment, 7*(4), 394–404. https://doi.org/10.1037/per0000165

Zachar, P., Krueger, R. F., & Kendler, K. S. (2016). Personality disorder in DSM-5: An oral history. *Psychological Medicine, 46*(1), 1–10. https://doi.org/10.1017/S0033291715001543

Zhang, P., Ouyang, Z., Fang, S., He, J., Fan, L., Luo, X., Zhang, J., Xiong, Y., Luo, F., Wang, X., Yao, S., & Wang, X. (2021). Personality Inventory for DSM-5 Brief Form (PID-5-BF) in Chinese students and patients: Evaluating the five-factor model and a culturally informed six-factor model. *BMC Psychiatry, 21*(1), 107. https://doi.org/10.1186/s12888-021-03080-x

Zhang, W., Wang, M., Yu, M., & Wang, J. (2021). The hierarchical structure and predictive validity of the personality inventory for dsm-5 in Chinese nonclinical adolescents. *Assessment,* 10731911211022836. https://doi.org/10.1177/10731911211022835

Zimmermann, J., Altenstein, D., Krieger, T., Holtforth, M. G., Pretsch, J., Alexopoulos, J., Spitzer, C., Benecke, C., Krueger, R. F., Markon, K. E., & Leising, D. (2014). The structure and correlates of self-reported DSM-5 maladaptive personality traits: Findings from two German-speaking samples. *Journal of Personality Disorders, 28*(4), 518–540. https://doi.org/10.1521/pedi_2014_28_130

Zimmermann, J., Böhnke, J. R., Eschstruth, R., Mathews, A., Wenzel, K., & Leising, D. (2015). The latent structure of personality functioning: Investigating criterion a from the alternative model for personality disorders in DSM–5. *Journal of Abnormal Psychology, 124*(3), 532–548. https://doi.org/10.1037/abn0000059

Zimmermann, J., Kerber, A., Rek, K., Hopwood, C. J., & Krueger, R. F. (2019). A brief but comprehensive review of research on the alternative DSM-5 model for personality disorders. *Current Psychiatry Reports, 21*(9), 92. https://doi.org/10.1007/s11920-019-1079-z

Zimmermann, J., Mayer, A., Leising, D., Krieger, T., grosse Holtforth, M., & Pretsch, J. (2017). Exploring occasion specificity in the assessment of DSM-5 maladaptive personality traits: A latent state-trait analysis. *European Journal of Psychological Assessment, 33*(1), 47–54. https://doi.org/10.1027/1015-5759/a000271

# CHAPTER 27

# Narcissistic Personality Disorder and Pathological Narcissism

Aaron L. Pincus

The concept of narcissism can be traced to the Greek myth of Narcissus and its retelling in Homeric hymns. Psychology has considered narcissism a characteristic of personality pathology for more than 100 years. Clinicians have been writing about narcissistic pathology and its treatment since Freud's (1914) initial discussion of narcissism through contemporary clinical models (Doering et al., 2021; Ogrodniczuk, 2013). Psychiatry classified pathological narcissism as narcissistic personality disorder (NPD) in *DSM-III*, and criteria for this diagnosis appears in all subsequent revisions including *DSM-5*. Despite more than a century of attention, the conceptualization, classification, and assessment of narcissistic personality pathology is in a state of significant flux (Dawood et al., 2020; Miller et al., 2017). Over a decade ago reviews recognized that the literature across disciplines was splintered, reflecting different approaches to conceptualizing and assessing narcissism (Cain et al., 2008, Miller & Campbell, 2008). Pincus and Lukowitsky (2010) concluded that "action must be taken to resolve disjunctions and integrate findings in future conceptualizations of pathological narcissism; otherwise continuing disparate efforts will impede progress towards a more sophisticated understanding of this complex clinical construct" (p. 422). Fortunately, this recognition has initiated renewed efforts to examine the construct validity and clinical utility of NPD and pathological narcissism and improve our understanding of one of the first recognized—yet most complex—expressions of personality pathology (Pincus, 2020; Pincus et al., 2020).

This chapter is organized in sections articulating the two main clinical perspectives on how to best conceptualize narcissistic personality pathology. First, I present the conceptualization of pathological narcissism as extreme expressions of grandiosity, reflected in *DSM* NPD. Next, I present a contemporary clinical conceptualization of pathological narcissism as states of grandiosity and vulnerability based on self-regulation theory (Morf & Rhodewalt, 2001). I then review important associated clinical features of NPD and pathological narcissism. The chapter concludes with a consideration of future theoretical, clinical, and empirical issues for research.

## DSM NPD: Pathological Narcissism as Extreme Grandiosity

The *DSM-5* NPD diagnosis exemplifies the conceptualization of pathological narcissism as excessive or extreme grandiosity.

### Criteria for NPD in DSM-III, DSM-III-R, DSM-IV, and DSM-5

The introduction of NPD in *DSM-III* was based on a review of the pathological narcissism literature published prior to 1980. The majority of the criteria reflected grandiose attitudes and behaviors, including a grandiose sense of self-importance or uniqueness; preoccupation with fantasies of unlimited success, power, brilliance, beauty, or ideal love; exhibitionism; entitlement; exploitativeness; and a lack of empathy. A minority of criteria reflected impairments in self- and emotion regulation including "a reaction to criticism characterized by rage, shame or

**Abbreviations**
NPD    Narcissistic personality disorder
PDM    Psychodynamic Diagnostic Manual

humiliation" and "alternating states of idealized and devalued views of self and others." Beyond the diagnostic criteria, the discussion and examples included dysregulated and vulnerable aspects of narcissism, noting that the grandiose sense of self-importance frequently alternates with feelings of unworthiness, and self-esteem is often fragile and contingent on successful achievements and receiving recognition and admiration from others. The implementation of *DSM-III* NPD diagnostic criteria assumed that grandiose behaviors, beliefs, and expectations existed in tandem with dysregulated, vulnerable states marked by low self-esteem and negative affectivity.

In an effort to improve the reliability and reduce the overlap among *DSM* PD criteria sets, notable changes to the NPD diagnosis from *DSM-III* to *DSM-5* added a number of criteria explicitly emphasizing grandiosity (e.g., arrogant, haughty behaviors and/or attitudes; frequently infers others are envious of him/her) and eliminated criteria and text describing dysregulation and vulnerability (e.g., shameful reactivity or humiliation in response to narcissistic injury, alternating states of idealization and devaluation) (Gunderson et al., 1995). Although a major revision of the PD diagnostic system was proposed for *DSM-5* (Skodol, 2012), it was rejected by the Board of Trustees of the American Psychiatric Association and placed in Section III of *DSM-5* describing emerging measures and models in need of additional research.[1] Therefore *DSM-5* Section II retains the *DSM-IV* PD criteria sets unchanged, moving them from a separate diagnostic axis to one of 20 chapters describing all diagnoses.

*DSM-5* Section II describes NPD as a pervasive pattern of grandiosity (in fantasy or behavior), a constant need for admiration, and a lack of empathy, beginning by early adulthood and present in a variety of contexts, operationalized as nine diagnostic criteria paraphrased here: (1) an inflated sense of self-worth; (2) preoccupation with fantasies of unlimited influence, achievement, intelligence, attractiveness, or romance; (3) belief that one is distinctive and elite and should only associate with others of similar stature; (4) excessive needs for respect, appreciation, and praise; (5) sense of privilege; (6) willingness to take advantage of others for personal gain; (7) lack of compassion; (8) jealousy of others; and (9) exhibition of conceited behaviors and attitudes. A patient must meet clinical threshold for a minimum of five of these criteria to be diagnosed with NPD. A confirmatory factor analysis of these NPD criteria supported a one-factor solution (Miller et al., 2008). The *DSM-5* diagnosis of NPD reflects chronic expressions of excessive or extreme grandiosity. Self-esteem vulnerability and emotional dysregulation are only mentioned in the "Associated Features Supporting Diagnosis" section, where clinicians are also cautioned that patients with NPD may not outwardly exhibit vulnerable characteristics. *DSM-5* Section II diagnostic criteria are mainly limited to observable presentations of narcissism and omit the underlying features that maintain and unify heterogeneous clinical presentations of narcissism (Caligor et al., 2015).

### Case Example: Mr. A

Mr. A was a single man in his late 30s who lived alone, met criteria for *DSM* NPD, and presented at a community mental health clinic twice for treatment within a 2-year period. He saw two different therapists and unilaterally terminated both therapies after 7 sessions and 18 sessions, respectively. He was a disabled veteran who reported feeling angry toward and envious of the Veterans Administration (VA), neighbors, women, and society as a whole. He also reported feeling very mistreated and disrespected by most other people and institutions. In therapy he regularly belittled, mocked, and challenged therapists, "I know I'm narcissistic and there's nothing you can do about it," "You can do your empathy thing, but it will have no effect on me," "You're just a trainee, you don't know enough to help me," and "I'm only here to get medication because the VA requires too much paperwork and makes me wait too long." In addition to deriding his therapists, Mr. A regularly threatened people he found parked in his apartment's assigned parking space and fantasized to his therapist about buying a gun and shooting the next person who parked there. A clinically relevant fact to note is that Mr. A did not drive or even own a car.

In treatment Mr. A reported that he felt his parents were cold and aloof, emphasizing that they had not helped him resolve highly competitive feelings he developed toward his older brothers. He recalled being treated frequently with strong allergy medicines that left him foggy and detached from others. As an adult Mr. A's contingent self-esteem

---

[1] In contrast, the World Health Organization's (2018) recently revised *ICD-11* adopted a highly similar revised proposal for diagnosis of personality disorders (for reviews, see Huprich, 2020; Tyrer et al., 2019).

and unresolved competitive needs appeared compensated for by a distorted self-view that he was far more capable, powerful, and deserving than reality suggested. Mr. A exhibited chronic grandiosity and entitlement throughout his two therapies and never acknowledged receiving anything beneficial from them before unilaterally terminating treatment. In fact, it may very well be that Mr. A's main motivation for seeking help from the clinic was to bypass whatever he found intolerable about receiving treatment from the VA. This is a cycle that might repeat itself with numerous treatment providers.

## Prevalence

Prevalence rates of NPD in the general population range of 0% to 5.3% (Ekselius et al., 2001; Mattia & Zimmerman, 2001; Torgersen et al., 2001). A nationally representative epidemiological study found that the lifetime prevalence (i.e., cumulative assessment across all time points) of NPD is 6.2% (Stinson et al., 2008). Overall, NPD exhibits the lowest prevalence rate of any *DSM* personality disorder; however, this is inconsistent with the frequency of patients with narcissistic personality pathology reported in clinical practice (Cain et al., 2008). Prevalence estimates among clinical samples range from 1.3% to 22% (e.g., Grilo et al., 1998; Zimmerman et al., 2005). Among personality disorders, NPD typically has among the lowest correlation between clinical interviews and self-report ratings (Oltmanns & Turkheimer, 2006), possibly due to a lack of insight into how behavior is perceived by others (Carlson & Oltmanns, 2015) or a disregard for the negative impact of their behavior on others (Carlson, 2013). This might particularly impact the accuracy of typical population-based epidemiological assessments as individuals with NPD may lack the insight or willingness to disclose narcissistic attitudes or difficulties (or even participate in such assessments). As the prevalence of the categorical NPD diagnosis is particularly difficult to accurately determine, dimensional approaches to conceptualizing and assessing narcissistic personality pathology provide important alternatives (Dawood et al., 2020).

## Stability

The temporal stability of NPD is modest but varies depending on whether it is assessed by clinical interview or self-report. Ronningstam, Gunderson, and Lyons (1995) employed the Diagnostic Interview for Narcissism (DIN; Gunderson et al., 1990) on 20 patients diagnosed with NPD over a 3-year period. They found modest diagnostic stability, with only 33% of the patients continuing to meet the DIN criteria for NPD at follow up. The 3-year stability of *DSM-III-R* diagnoses (50%) and *DSM-IV* diagnoses (46%) were slightly higher. Lenzenweger, Johnson, and Willett (2004) conducted individual growth curve analyses of interviewer-rated PD features over a 4-year period in a sample of 250 participants. Results revealed significant variability in PD features, including NPD features, over time. Nestadt and colleagues (2010) interviewed 294 participants on two occasions, 12 to 18 years apart and found that NPD had among the lowest temporal stability levels (ICC = 0.10), and NPD traits at baseline did not significantly predict those same traits at follow up. Self-reported NPD symptoms yielded a higher level of stability. Ball, Rounseville, Tennen, and Kranzler (2001) reported a 1-year temporal stability coefficient of 0.42 for the self-reported *DSM-III-R* NPD features in a clinical sample of 182 substance abusing inpatients. Samuel and colleagues (2011) examined the 2-year rank order and mean level stability of PDs using self-report and interview-based assessments. They found the rank order stability for NPD was higher for self-report than for interview ratings, and the mean level decrease in symptoms over time was smaller for the self-report compared to the interview ratings. Supporting previous findings, Vater et al. (2014) found a 2-year remission rate for NPD diagnoses of 52%.

## Comorbidity

Across several studies examining diagnostic comorbidity among *DSM* PDs, NPD consistently exhibits the highest rates of comorbidity with antisocial and histrionic PDs (Widiger, 2011). NPD also exhibits significant comorbidity with symptom syndromes (Simonsen & Simonsen, 2011). Stinson et al. (2008) used 34,653 participants enrolled in an epidemiological study to examine the comorbidity of NPD with Axis I psychiatric disorders. They calculated the odds ratios (i.e., the increase or decrease in likelihood of meeting NPD diagnosis given the presence of another 12-month or lifetime non-PD psychiatric diagnosis), controlling for demographic variables. They found almost every psychiatric disorder was significantly related to having an NPD diagnosis. After controlling for other psychiatric disorders, many associations became smaller but remained significant. The diagnoses in the past 12 months that most strongly predicted comorbid NPD diagnosis were bipolar I disorder (2.3 times more likely to have an NPD diagnosis), anxiety disorders (2.0 times more likely to have an NPD diagnosis), drug dependence (1.9 times more likely to have an NPD diagnosis), post-traumatic stress disorder (PTSD; 1.7 times more likely to have an NPD diagnosis), mood disorders (1.5 times more likely to have an NPD diagnosis), and substance use disorders (1.5 times more likely to have an NPD diagnosis). Comorbidity with lifetime diagnosis of psychiatric disorders yielded similar results, with the strongest predictors being a lifetime diagnosis of bipolar I disorder (1.9 times more likely to have an NPD diagnosis) and PTSD (1.9 times more likely to have an NPD diagnosis). These findings are consistent with clinical samples of NPD that cite the most frequent comorbid diagnoses as major depression or dysthymia (41–50%), substance abuse (24–50%), and bipolar disorder (5–18%) (Clemence et al., 2009; Ronningstam, 1996). Oulis, Lykouras, Hatzimanolis, and Tomaras (1997) found that among 102 recovered schizophrenic patients, 15% met criteria for NPD, and a clinical epidemiological study of 32 first-episode psychotic patients revealed 16% met criteria for NPD (Simonsen et al., 2008).

Because NPD exhibits notable comorbidity with personality, anxiety, mood, and substance use disorders, novel research has explored the mechanisms driving comorbidity. Eaton and colleagues (2017) used a nationally representative sample to model NPD's transdiagnostic comorbidity structures through multivariate associations. Findings indicate that NPD is more strongly associated with a latent distress factor (vs. a latent fear factor) within an internalizing-externalizing model of psychopathology. Furthermore, they concluded that NPD is composed of unique facets; however, it remains unclear whether shared variance and comorbidity represents a general factor of pathology overlapping with other disorders or an NPD-specific manifestation of unique symptoms. Hörz-Sagstetter and colleagues (2018) identified unique patterns of functioning among patients diagnosed with comorbid NPD and borderline personality disorder (BPD) and patients only diagnosed with BPD suggesting that comorbid NPD may serve as a buffer against anxiety and other Axis I disorders and reduce number of hospitalizations. However, within the context of a BPD diagnosis, NPD may also increase the co-occurrence of severe personality pathology including paranoia, antisocial personality features, and distortions of reality. Taken together, NPD exhibits unique associations with other disorders, and the basis for and impact of such relationships must be further investigated.

## NPD Research

Due in part to the low prevalence of NPD, substantive research employing even modest samples of patients diagnosed with NPD is extremely rare. Most of this work has focused on examining empathy deficits and self-esteem in NPD. The best research of this nature involves a well-diagnosed sample of NPD patients in Germany. The investigators (Ritter et al., 2011) used both self-report and experimental methods to assess empathy and found that, compared to controls and patients with BPD, NPD patients exhibited deficits in emotional empathy (i.e., an observer's emotional response to another person's emotional state) but not cognitive empathy (i.e., the ability to take another person's perspective and represent others' mental states). This distinction could explain the NPD patient's tendency to successfully exploit others. In another study of these NPD patients (Schulze et al., 2013), the investigators used brain imaging techniques and found that, relative to controls, NPD patients had smaller gray matter volume in the left anterior insula. Importantly, gray matter volume in this area is positively correlated with self-reported emotional empathy. Supporting these conclusions, Nenadic and colleagues (2015) used voxel-based morphemetry to identify structural issues in the brains of six patients diagnosed with NPD and found gray matter deficits in the right prefrontal and bilateral medial prefrontal regions. Frontal gray matter loss is associated with emotion dysregulation and deficits in coping behaviors. Complementary whole-brain analyses yielded smaller gray matter volume in frontoparalimbic brain regions comprising the rostral and median cingulate cortex as well as dorsolateral and medial parts of the prefrontal cortex, all of which are implicated in empathic functioning (Schulze et al., 2013). Consistent with these findings, another group of investigators (Marissen et al., 2012), using a small independent clinical sample of NPD patients, found that they generally performed worse on a facial emotion recognition task compared to controls. In addition to this general deficit in emotion recognition, patients with NPD showed specific deficits in recognizing fear and disgust.

Empirical studies of self-esteem in NPD patients demonstrate mixed results. Investigators have found evidence supporting that, despite the grandiosity emphasized in the diagnostic criteria, NPD patients have lower explicit self-esteem than controls (Vater,

Ritter et al., 2013; Vater, Schröder-Abé et al., 2013). However, Marissen and colleagues (2016) found that implicit and explicit self-esteem did not differ between NPD patients and control groups (e.g., patients with other PDs and healthy controls). This makes sense, considering NPD is commonly comorbid with anxiety disorders, mood disorders, and PTSD. Finally, current research efforts have focused on the role of shame in individuals with NPD. Notably, Ritter and colleagues (2014) investigated the association of NPD and explicit and implicit shame using self-report and performance measures, respectively. A small group of patients diagnosed with NPD reported higher levels of explicit shame than patients diagnosed with BPD and healthy controls. Implicit shame–self associations (vs. anxiety–self associations) were significantly stronger in NPD patients than in the control groups. Findings support continuing investigation of shame-related processes in NPD.

Research on treatment of NPD is limited to case studies. There are no published randomized clinical psychotherapy trials, naturalistic studies of psychotherapy, or empirical evaluations of community-based interventions for NPD (Dhawan et al., 2010; Levy et al., 2007). Thus, there are no empirically validated treatments for NPD; however, extensions of empirically validated treatments such as dialectical behavior therapy (Reed-Knight & Fischer, 2011), transference-focused psychotherapy (Diamond & Hersh, 2020), mentalization-based therapy (Drozek & Unruh, 2020), and schema-focused therapy (Dieckmann & Behary, 2015) are being developed and evaluated. General principles for treating narcissistic patients are also available (Crisp & Gabbard, 2020; Kealy et al., 2017; Weinberg & Ronningstam, 2020).

## Critiques of NPD

The lack of research on patients diagnosed with NPD renders the validity and clinical utility of the diagnosis questionable, and this was the primary reason NPD was initially recommended for deletion in the proposed PD revisions for *DSM-5* (Skodol et al., 2011). Currently, it is unclear whether the *DSM* NPD diagnosis serves its central purpose, which is to facilitate the accurate diagnosis of patients exhibiting pathological narcissism. Unlike what is seen with other PD diagnoses, the low prevalence rates of NPD reported in large-scale epidemiological studies (often 0%) are notably lower than the rates of narcissistic pathology being treated in psychotherapy based on surveys of practicing clinicians (Doidge et al., 2002; Morey & Ochoa, 1989; Ogrodniczuk, 2013; Ronningstam & Gunderson, 1990; Westen, 1997). This indicates a possible limitation of the *DSM* criteria to identify patients whom clinicians consider to be exhibiting pathological narcissism (Pincus et al., 2009; Pincus & Lukowitsky, 2010; Ronningstam, 2009). The relatively low prevalence of NPD diagnoses in all populations could be due, in part, to the narrow range of content of the diagnostic criteria. NPD emphasizes grandiose attitudes and behaviors and lacks assessment of self-esteem vulnerability and impaired self- and emotion regulation found in clinical descriptions of pathological narcissism. It may be that many narcissistic patients seek therapists and encounter diagnosticians when they are in a vulnerable self-state with increased mood and anxiety symptoms and lower self-esteem (Kealy & Ogrodniczuk, 2012; Kealy & Rasmussen, 2012). In such instances, relying solely on *DSM* NPD diagnostic criteria may impede clinical recognition of pathological narcissism. The lack of sufficient NPD criteria assessing self-esteem vulnerability and impaired regulation has been a common criticism for more than a decade (Cain et al. 2008, Gabbard, 2009, Levy et al., 2007; Miller, Widiger, & Campbell, 2010; Pincus, 2011, Ronningstam, 2009).

In response to the initial proposal to eliminate NPD as a diagnosis in *DSM-5*, Pincus (2011) noted that the *DSM* is merely an imperfect operationalization of clinical knowledge, not the benchmark for evaluating it (Regier et al., 2009), and he argued that the performance of the *DSM* NPD criteria set should not be the sole or even primary basis for considering the ontological status of NPD. Problematic comorbidity, stability, and particularly validity may be a function of construct definition problems (e.g., Acton, 1998) with *DSM* NPD criteria themselves and criterion problems (McGrath, 2005) with *DSM* NPD research rather than an indication that pathological narcissism does not exist. The narrow construct definition of *DSM* NPD creates a fundamental criterion problem for research on the validity and clinical utility of the diagnosis (Pincus & Lukowitsky, 2010) as "the disparity between the diagnostic nomenclature and actual psychiatric phenomena is largely ignored, and extensive research is conducted to understand the psychosocial and treatment implications of the existing diagnostic categories" (McGrath, 2005, p. 114). In contrast to the limitations of *DSM* NPD criteria, a contemporary clinical model encompassing narcissistic grandiosity and narcissistic vulnerability is supported by an emergent, and more clinically informed, empirical research base that is discussed in the next section.

## Clinical Theory and Research: Pathological Narcissism as Grandiosity and Vulnerability

In contrast to the emphasis on extreme grandiosity in *DSM* NPD, clinical theory and observation has always included states of negative affectivity (e.g., shame, rage), fragile and contingent self-esteem, and behavioral dysregulation (e.g., suicidality, aggression, withdrawal) in the clinical portrait of pathological narcissism (Cain et al., 2008). The comorbidity of NPD with mood and anxiety disorders suggests there could be a more comprehensive conceptualization that moves beyond grandiosity and includes impairments in self- and emotion regulation that could better account for why individuals with a pathologically inflated self-image commonly enter psychotherapy reporting low self-esteem, depressed mood, and anxiety (Pincus et al., 2014, 2016).

### Clinical Theory and Observation: Psychodynamic Origins

Clinical conceptualizations of pathological narcissism have deep roots in early psychodynamic theories and clinical observations of personality (e.g., Freud, 1914; Rank, 2011). These early psychodynamic conceptions were influential in shaping future clinical theories of narcissism (Ronningstam, 2011c), including the contemporary object-relations and self-psychological perspectives that I review next.

Narcissism as a psychodynamic construct evolved from the theorizing of Rank and Freud, through the important reformulations of Otto Kernberg's object-relations theory (1984, 1988) and Heinz Kohut's self-psychology theory (1971, 1977). These reformulations stimulated worldwide interest in how narcissism should be conceptualized and treated (Levy et al., 2011). Object relations theories recognize that humans are social beings who experience much of life relating to others, and these theories emphasize the importance of understanding how people's mental representations of self and others positively or negatively impact their identity, emotions, and relationships. Early in development, a child is unable to attribute good and bad experiences to the same person, so she or he experiences the other as "all bad" or "all good." Similarly, the self is experienced as "all good," and any information to the contrary is pushed out of awareness (denial) or located in another person (projection). Over time the child learns to integrate good and bad experiences into a complex and integrated view of self and others (Clarkin et al., 2006).

Kernberg's (1984, 1988, 2010) conceptualization of narcissism is embedded within this object relations model. Parental figures (some of the earliest "objects" one can relate to) are experienced as cold and harsh, and they may concurrently hold high (yet superficial) expectations for their child in hopes of vicarious fulfillment of their own failed ambition. These conditions lead to good and bad experiences remaining unintegrated in the form of idealized and devalued views of self and others. The narcissistic individual libidinally invests in a distorted self-structure based on immature real and ideal self-representations as well as ideal object-representations. Devalued or aggressively determined self- and object-representations are split off or projected. A pathological grandiose self is constructed by combining all the positive and idealized characteristics of the self and others, leading to an unrealistic self-image that is hard to maintain. This grandiosity functions as an acquired defense against experiencing an enraged and empty self that is hungry for authentic recognition (Kernberg, 1970).

In contrast, Kohut (1971, 1977) defined narcissism as a normal stage of development. A primary narcissistic structure first exists where the self and other are both idealized (e.g., grandiosity). Through receipt of healthy support and empathic mirroring from parental figures, this structure is reinforced and leads the child to experience the world as secure and consistent. Parental figures will occasionally not support or gratify the child's needs, but such frustration is tolerable, not traumatic, and allows the child an opportunity to regulate their own needs. These experiences of support and opportunities for self- and emotion regulation coalesce into a new, healthier self-structure that is better equipped to navigate disappointments. This in turn transforms immature grandiosity into realistic ambition that energizes the individual to use their skills and talents to pursue realistic goals that validate an authentic positive self-concept (Kohut, 1977). Narcissistic pathology results when parental figures do not provide appropriate support or mirroring, or when parental support is excessive (e.g., overinvolved and enmeshed). Neither condition affords the child an opportunity to experience the appropriate and tolerable empathic failures needed to develop mature regulatory strategies and form realistic views of the self, others, and the world. Millon (1981) and Benjamin

(1996) noted that excessive parental indulgence and admiration that is unrealistic can also result in narcissistic pathology through social learning mechanisms, as the parental figures teach the child that success and admiration are not contingent upon effort and requisite achievements.

## A Contemporary Clinical Model

Of course, clinical theories of pathological narcissism and descriptions of its phenotypic expression extend well beyond the psychodynamic literature. Recent efforts to synthesize the corpus of description, theory, and research on pathological narcissism across the disciplines of clinical psychology, psychiatry, and social-personality psychology[2] generated a contemporary model that conceptualizes pathological narcissism as a combination of maladaptive self-enhancement motivation (grandiosity) and impaired self- and emotion regulation in response to self-enhancement failures and lack of recognition and admiration from others (vulnerability) (Dawood et al., 2020; Pincus, 2013; Pincus & Lukowitsky, 2010).

### SELF-ENHANCEMENT AND REGULATION

Narcissism can be defined as an individual's tendency to employ a variety of self-regulation, affect-regulation, and interpersonal processes to maintain a relatively positive self-image. Thus, it is necessarily a complex personality construct involving (a) needs for recognition and admiration, (b) motivations to overtly and covertly seek out self-enhancement experiences from the social environment, (c) strategies to satisfy these needs and motives, and (d) abilities to manage disappointments and self-enhancement failures (Morf, Horvath, & Torchetti, 2011; Morf, Torchetti, & Schürch, 2011). Generally, such needs and motives are normal aspects of personality, but they become pathological when they are extreme and coupled with impaired regulatory capacities. It is normal for individuals to strive to see themselves in a positive light and to seek experiences of self-enhancement (Hepper et al., 2010) such as successful achievements and competitive victories (Conroy et al., 2009). Most individuals manage these needs effectively, seek out their gratification in culturally and socially acceptable ways and contexts, and regulate self-esteem, negative emotions, and interpersonal behavior when disappointments are experienced. In basing the definition of narcissism on the individual's needs, motives, and regulatory capacities, a definition of what pathological narcissism is (i.e., impairments in motivation, psychological structures, and regulatory capacities and processes) can be distinguished from how the symptoms present in thought, feeling, and behavior (i.e., its phenotypic expression).

Pathological narcissism involves impairment in the ability to regulate the self, emotions, and behavior in seeking to satisfy needs for recognition and admiration. Put another way, narcissistic individuals have notable difficulties transforming narcissistic needs (recognition and admiration) and impulses (self-enhancement motivation) into mature and socially appropriate ambitions and conduct (Kohut, 1977; Stone, 1998). Morf and colleagues have provided a compelling argument for conceptualizing pathological narcissism through regulatory mechanisms in their dynamic self-regulatory processing model (Morf & Rhodewalt, 2001; Morf, Torchetti, & Schürch, 2011). They suggested that early empathic failures by parental figures (see also Kohut, 1971) leave the child ill-equipped to regulate the self, and instead self-regulation is played out in the social arena (Dickinson & Pincus, 2003; Kernberg, 2010). However, the early negative parenting experience also leaves the self with a mistrust and disdain for others, resulting in a tragic paradox in which other people are needed for the narcissist to self-enhance, but the devalued and skeptical view of others limits the narcissist's ability to experience others' admiration, praise, and validation as self-enhancing. This leads to lingering self-doubt and increased vulnerability, re-energizing the self to continue seeking these self-enhancement experiences in increasingly maladaptive ways and inappropriate contexts (Morf, 2006; Morf & Rhodewalt, 2001). Thus, the fundamental dysfunction associated with pathological narcissism involves chronically unsatisfied needs for recognition and admiration that lead to an equally chronic preoccupation with the social status of the self and an unremitting prioritization of self-enhancement motivation. This heightens narcissistic individuals' sensitivity to the daily ups and downs of life and relationships (e.g., Besser & Priel, 2010; Besser et al., 2016; Dawood & Pincus,

---

[2] This chapter focuses mainly on the clinical psychology and psychiatry literature. Social-personality psychology research supporting the contemporary clinical model is reviewed in several sources (e.g., Cain et al., 2008; Hermann et al., 2018; Miller et al., 2010; Pincus & Lukowitsky, 2010; Pincus & Roche, 2011).

2018; Ziegler-Hill & Besser, 2013) and impairs their regulation of self-esteem, emotion, and behavior (Roche, Pincus, Lukowitsky et al., 2013). Importantly, conceptualizing narcissism from a regulatory perspective, unlike *DSM* NPD, accounts for both narcissistic grandiosity and narcissistic vulnerability (Pincus, 2013).

### NARCISSISTIC GRANDIOSITY AND NARCISSISTIC VULNERABILITY

To the layperson, narcissism is most often associated with conceited, arrogant, and domineering attitudes and behaviors (Buss & Chiodo, 1991), which are captured by the term *narcissistic grandiosity*. This accurately identifies some common expressions of maladaptive self-enhancement associated with pathological narcissism. *Narcissistic vulnerability* is reflected in experiences of anger, envy, aggression, helplessness, emptiness, low self-esteem, shame, avoidance of interpersonal relationships, and even suicidality (Kohut & Wolf, 1978; Krizan & Johar, 2012, 2015; Pincus & Roche, 2011; Ronningstam, 2005b). While grandiosity is the core feature of pathological narcissism according to surveys of clinicians, they also consistently recognize expressions of vulnerability in most narcissistic patients (Ackerman et al., 2017; Gore & Widiger, 2016).

The contemporary clinical model of narcissism combines maladaptive self-enhancement (e.g., grandiosity) with self, emotional, and behavioral dysregulation in response to ego threats or self-enhancement failures (e.g., vulnerability). A comprehensive hierarchical model of pathological narcissism is presented in Figure 27.1. Here, narcissistic grandiosity and vulnerability together make up the higher-order construct of pathological narcissism and are moderately intercorrelated (Wright et al., 2010), particularly at higher levels of grandiosity (Jauk & Kaufman, 2018; Jauk et al., 2021). Expressions of narcissistic grandiosity and vulnerability may be chronic, with each suppressing the other, or they may oscillate over time as distinct states within the same person (Edershile & Wright, 2021a, 2021b; Hyatt et al., 2018; Pincus & Wright, 2021). In recent years, recognition of both grandiose and vulnerable themes of narcissistic pathology has increasingly become the norm (Miller et al., 2017; Krizan & Herlache, 2018).

Reviews of clinical literature on narcissism and narcissistic personality pathology over the past 60 years identified more than 50 distinct labels describing grandiose and vulnerable phenotypes of pathological narcissism (Cain et al., 2008; Pincus & Lukowitsky, 2010). The authors concluded that two broad themes of narcissistic pathology, labeled "narcissistic grandiosity" and "narcissistic vulnerability," could be synthesized across the literature with varying degrees of emphasis. Clinical theorists have employed these themes to describe the core aspects of narcissistic dysfunction through defects in self-structure (Kernberg, 1998, Kohut, 1977), difficulties in the therapeutic relationship (Gabbard, 2009; Kernberg, 2007), and maladaptive coping and defensive strategies used in response to stressors (Masterson, 1993).

Ronningstam (2005a) identified subtypes of narcissistic personality based on similarities and differences in self-esteem dysregulation, affect dysregulation, and difficulties in interpersonal relationships. Grandiose themes are emphasized in descriptions of the arrogant narcissist and the psychopathic narcissist. The former copes with self-esteem dysregulation

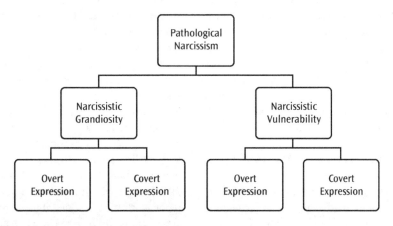

**Figure 27.1** The hierarchical structure of pathological narcissism.
Adapted with permission from Pincus, A.L., & Lukowitsky, M.R. (2010). Pathological narcissism and narcissistic personality disorder. *Annual Review of Clinical Psychology, 6*, 431.

by creating an exaggerated sense of superiority and uniqueness as well as by engaging in grandiose fantasies. These individuals exhibit entitlement, exploitativeness, and a lack of empathy, and they experience intense envy and aggression as a result of their affect dysregulation. The psychopathic narcissist copes with self-esteem dysregulation by engaging in antisocial behaviors to protect or enhance their inflated self-image. Such individuals will commit violent criminal acts to gain admiration from others, display extreme rage reactions to criticism, and are sadistic without experiencing remorse or empathy. Consistent with Akhtar's (2003) and Dickinson and Pincus's (2003) description of narcissistic vulnerability, Ronningstam's shy narcissist deals with self-esteem dysregulation by engaging in grandiose fantasy while also feeling intense shame regarding their needs and ambition. The dominant affect problem for the shy narcissist is shame rather than aggression, and they avoid interpersonal relationships because of hypersensitivity to ego threats and self-enhancement failures. Similarly, results of a Q-factor analysis of NPD patients' Shedler-Westen Assessment System (SWAP-II) profiles also described two pathological subtypes (Russ et al., 2008). The grandiose/malignant subtype is characterized by seething anger, manipulativeness, pursuit of interpersonal power and control, lack of remorse, exaggerated self-importance, and feelings of privilege. These individuals tend to be externalizing and have little insight into their behavior. In contrast, the fragile subtype fails to consistently maintain a grandiose sense of self such that when their defenses fail, narcissistic injury evokes shame, anxiety, depression, and feelings of inadequacy.

The *Psychodynamic Diagnostic Manual* (*PDM*; PDM Task Force, 2006) initially subdivided narcissistic personality disturbance into an arrogant/entitled (grandiose) subtype and a depressed/depleted (vulnerable) subtype. Most recently, the *PDM-2* (Lingiardi & McWilliams, 2017) integrated the grandiose and vulnerable subtypes into one coherent and potentially variable clinical presentation consistent with the contemporary clinical model of pathological narcissism presented here.

### NOMOLOGICAL RESEARCH ON GRANDIOSE AND VULNERABLE NARCISSISTIC TRAITS

A number of self-report measures of narcissistic grandiosity and narcissistic vulnerability are now available, including the Pathological Narcissism Inventory (PNI; Pincus et al., 2009; Schoenleber et al., 2015), the Five-factor Narcissism Inventory (FFNI; Glover et al., 2012), the Narcissistic Admiration and Rivalry Questionnaire (NARQ; Back et al., 2013), and the Narcissism Scale for Children (NSC; Derry et al., 2019). Other measures assess either grandiosity alone, such as the Narcissistic Personality Inventory (NPI; Raskin & Hall, 1981) and the Narcissistic Grandiosity Scale (NGS; Rosenthal et al., 2020), or vulnerability alone, such as the Hypersensitive Narcissism Scale (HSNS; Hendin & Cheek, 1997) and the Narcissistic Vulnerability Scale (NVS; Crowe et al., 2018). Research using these measures demonstrates that grandiosity and vulnerability exhibit convergent and divergent patterns of relationships with internalizing and externalizing psychopathology, self-esteem, self-conscious emotions, core affect, interpersonal functioning, and psychotherapy (Dowgwillo et al., 2016; Edershile et al., 2019; Kaufman et al., 2020; Pincus & Roche, 2011).

Narcissistic grandiosity and vulnerability exhibit distinct and meaningful patterns of associations, with internalizing problems and symptoms in both normal and clinical samples. This has been most extensively studied with depressive symptoms (Ellison et al., 2013; Erkoreka & Navarro, 2017; Kealy et al., 2012; Marčinko et al., 2014; Miller et al., 2010; Morf et al., 2017; Tritt et al., 2010). In addition, narcissistic grandiosity and vulnerability are associated with suicide attempts (Miller et al., 2010; Pincus et al., 2009), suicidal ideation (Jaksic et al., 2017), and nonsuicidal self-injury (Dawood et al., 2018).

Narcissistic grandiosity and vulnerability also exhibit distinct and meaningful patterns of associations with externalizing problems and symptoms in both normal and clinical samples. Numerous laboratory-based and correlational studies (Lobbestael et al., 2014; Reidy et al., 2010; Widman & McNulty, 2010) show that grandiosity and vulnerability are positively associated with all forms of aggression (e.g., reactive, proactive, unprovoked, sexual), as well as violent behavior and self-reported homicidal thoughts in psychotherapy inpatients and outpatients (Ellison et al., 2013; Goldberg et al., 2007). Grandiosity is also associated with increased criminal behavior and gambling (e.g., Miller et al., 2010), as well as alcohol and drug use (e.g., Buelow & Brunell, 2014; Welker et al., 2019). Moreover, vulnerability interacted with self-reported childhood sexual abuse to predict overt and cyber stalking in men (Ménard & Pincus, 2012).

Consistent with associations found for internalizing and externalizing psychopathology, narcissistic grandiosity and vulnerability exhibit distinct associations with self-esteem, self-conscious emotions, and core affect. Vulnerability is negatively related with self-esteem, whereas grandiosity is positively correlated with self-esteem (Maxwell et al., 2011; Miller et al., 2010; Pincus et al., 2009). Zeigler-Hill and Besser (2013) found that vulnerability is uniquely associated with day-to-day fluctuations in feelings of self-worth. Vulnerability is positively associated with shame and hubris, negatively associated with authentic pride, and unrelated to guilt. In contrast, grandiosity is positively correlated with guilt and unrelated to pride and shame (Pincus, 2013). Vulnerability is positively correlated with negative affectivity, rage, and envy and negatively correlated with positive affectivity, while grandiosity is only positively related to positive affectivity (Krizan & Johar, 2012, 2015).

Narcissistic grandiosity and vulnerability are also associated with specific types of interpersonal problems. Grandiosity is associated with predominately vindictive, domineering, and intrusive problematic behaviors (Ogrodniczuk et al., 2009). Similarly, vulnerability is associated with vindictive interpersonal problems but also shows positive associations with exploitable and avoidant problems (Pincus et al., 2009). Grandiosity and vulnerability also exhibit meaningful associations with interpersonal sensitivities, with grandiosity associated with sensitivity to others' remoteness, antagonism, and control, and vulnerability associated with sensitivity to others' remoteness, control, attention-seeking, and affection (Hopwood et al., 2011). Finally, a week-long daily diary study (Roche, Pincus, Conroy, et al., 2013) indicated that narcissistic grandiosity and narcissistic vulnerability were related to individuals' behavior in social interactions in daily life. Specifically, narcissistic grandiosity was associated with responding to perceiving others as behaving dominantly with reciprocal dominant behavior. The authors concluded that narcissistic individuals may view the dominant behavior of others as a threat to their status and respond in ways to self-enhance and reassert their superiority (see also Wright et al., 2017).

Narcissistic grandiosity and vulnerability also show differential associations with the utilization of psychotherapy and psychiatric treatment. For instance, Ellison and colleagues (2013) found that narcissistic grandiosity was negatively correlated with treatment utilization (telephone-based crisis services, partial hospitalizations, inpatient admissions, taking medications) and positively correlated with outpatient therapy no-shows. Narcissistic vulnerability was positively correlated with use of telephone-based crisis services, inpatient admissions, and outpatient therapy sessions attended and cancelled. Results indicating that narcissistic vulnerability is positively associated with treatment utilization support the view that narcissistic patients are likely to present for services when they are in a vulnerable self-state (Pincus et al., 2014).

Finally, after many years of research relating the broad and general personality traits of the Five Factor Model to personality disorders (Widiger & Costa, 2013), a trifurcated trait model of narcissism that accounts for grandiosity and vulnerability has been derived (Crowe et al., 2019; Miller et al., 2016). Specifically, across multiple samples and multiple measures of narcissism, a three-factor solution was consistently identified. The first factor, labeled "self-centered antagonism" (i.e., low agreeableness), included the FFNI facets of manipulativeness, entitlement, empathy, arrogance, distrust, reactive anger, and thrill seeking. The second factor, labeled "narcissistic neuroticism," was comprised of the FFNI need for admiration, shame, and low indifference (i.e., high self-consciousness) facets. The third factor, labeled "agentic extraversion," was marked by the FFNI subscales of grandiose fantasies, acclaim seeking, exhibitionism, and authoritativeness. Existing measures of NPD are correlated with all three dimensions of the trifurcated trait model of narcissism. Moreover, measures of narcissistic grandiosity and vulnerability were strongly correlated with self-centered antagonism (i.e., a shared antagonistic core), but differentially related to the other two factors. Measures of narcissistic grandiosity (but not vulnerability) were correlated with agentic extraversion, while measures of narcissistic vulnerability (but not grandiosity) were correlated with narcissistic neuroticism.

## TEMPORAL RESEARCH ON GRANDIOSE AND VULNERABLE NARCISSISTIC STATES

In contrast to the emphasis on extreme grandiosity reflected in *DSM* NPD, clinical theory and empirical evidence supporting the contemporary clinical model suggest that a person's grandiose self-states may oscillate with vulnerable self-states marked by low self-esteem and emotional and behavioral dysregulation. Ronningstam (2009) noted that "The narcissistic individual may fluctuate between assertive grandiosity and vulnerability" (p. 113). Similarly, Kernberg (2009) indicated that narcissistic personalities endure "bouts of insecurity disrupting their sense of grandiosity or specialness" (p. 106). Horowitz (2009) suggested that as narcissistic pathology negatively impacts relationships, creativity, and occupational adjustment, grandiosity cannot be maintained, and narcissists are "more vulnerable to shame, panic, helplessness, or depression as life progresses" (p. 126). Thus, narcissistic patients may be best differentiated from each other based on *relative* levels of grandiosity and vulnerability rather than making categorical distinctions based on grandiose or vulnerable subtypes (Lingiardi & McWilliams, 2017; Pincus et al., 2016; Pincus & Lukowitsky, 2010).

Recent research supports within-person temporal variability of grandiose and vulnerable narcissistic states. A series of studies focusing on grandiose states (Giacomin & Jordan, 2014, 2016a, 2016b) found that grandiose states varied over time, and state grandiosity was higher when people experienced more positive agentic outcomes (e.g., having power over someone) or more positive communal outcomes (e.g., helping someone with a problem). State grandiosity was lower on days people experienced greater stress, guilt, and shame, and less empathy. These relations held when controlling for state self-esteem, gender, and trait narcissism. These findings suggest that grandiose narcissism has a meaningful process or state component. In another series of studies on narcissistic states (Edershile & Wright, 2021a, 2021b), both grandiosity and vulnerability exhibited state-like variability within persons over time. More grandiose individuals perceived others as colder and behaved more dominant and colder, on average. But in the moment, higher grandiosity was associated with perceiving others as warmer and more submissive, resulting in more dominant and warm behavior. Trait vulnerability was associated with perceptions of coldness and cold behavior, and this was amplified in the moment. Additionally, variability in narcissistic states from moment to moment was moderately associated with dispositional assessments of narcissism. Specifically, individuals who are dispositionally grandiose exhibited both grandiose and vulnerable states that varied considerably over time. In contrast, dispositionally vulnerable individuals tended to have frequent states of vulnerability and infrequent states of grandiosity. Temporal distinctions in patterning of grandiose and vulnerable narcissistic states are presented in Figure 27.2.

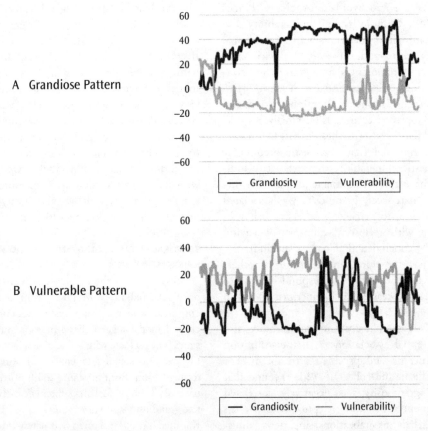

**Figure 27.2** Patterns of grandiose and vulnerable narcissistic states over time.

## Case Example: Mr. B

Mr. B is a patient I diagnose as suffering from pathological narcissism, but he may not meet *DSM* NPD criteria due to his pronounced vulnerability. I present his vulnerable characteristics first, and then follow this with his grandiose features. I chose this approach because narcissistic patients who seek outpatient treatment in community mental health centers typically present in dysregulated states in which more vulnerable symptoms are prominent and grandiosity is only detectable later in treatment after patient stabilization (Pincus et al., 2014).

*Vulnerability.* Mr. B was a 40-year-old single, college-educated man living with his parents after discharge from his most recent hospitalization. He presented for therapy as socially isolated with impaired intimacy. He had no friends or relationships except with his parents, had difficulty maintaining employment as a dishwasher, and expressed pessimism about his ability to improve his life. He wished to pursue permanent disability status and was interested in moving to a residential facility for the mentally ill. His most pronounced symptom was an empty depression characterized by agitation and anhedonia but an absence of sadness or melancholia. Mr. B was chronically suicidal and described waking up each day feeling "horrified" he was still alive. Early in treatment, he would commonly respond to therapist questions with long latencies where he lowered his head into his hands and repeatedly rubbed his head in anguish before responding with one or two words or "I don't know." Mr. B tried many different antidepressants with minimal effects and was admitted to the hospital 3 times in a 12-month period, one of which included a long course of electroconvulsive therapy (ECT) that was similarly ineffective. Clearly Mr. B's initial presentation was one of a vulnerable and anguished patient, and a diagnostician might reasonably consider a diagnosis of a mood disorder. Mr. B would not meet criteria for *DSM* NPD.

*Grandiosity.* Over the course of psychotherapy, the therapist learned about several other features of Mr. B's thoughts, feelings, and behaviors that suggest narcissistic grandiosity. But unlike in Mr. A, these expressions were at first subtle or unacknowledged by the patient and they oscillated with more common depressive states. Mr. B was a skilled keyboard player with a sizable home recording studio set up. But the instruments lay untouched, and he reported no intrinsic pleasure in playing them. He reported he only enjoyed it when people paid to hear him play. He tried playing with a few local bands, but none was "serious enough" or "talented enough," and he even devalued his own musical interests as too "flawed and disappointing" to pursue. Mr. B also used to be an avid bicyclist. However, after excitedly purchasing a new high-quality model, Mr. B became obsessed with the various noises the bicycle made while riding it. He was unhappy and felt it was too noisy. He tried to stop the offending noises without success. With the encouragement of his therapist, Mr. B tried for some time to ride the bike despite his disappointment over its imperfections. However, like playing music, he eventually lost interest in riding his bike and felt depressed about that as well.

Mr. B also felt that daily responsibilities like buying groceries, finding a job, balancing his checkbook, filling out forms, and paying taxes were a "hassle" and that he should not have to do them. In fact, he continued to rely on his parents to do most of these things for him. When he was living in his own apartment, he lived off a trust fund and his mother still balanced his checkbook and took him on a weekly shopping trip. When the trust fund ran out, he strategically took an overdose to ensure his mother would find him when she arrived for their weekly grocery shopping. Despite all his parents' help (for better or worse), in therapy he expressed resentment toward them for aging and having decreasing resources. For example, he complained bitterly that his mother took much longer to balance his checkbook than she used to, and he was disappointed when they could not immediately buy him a car. The therapist learned the main reason Mr. B could not hold a job was because he resented the lack of control over his schedule. He would angrily quit jobs when asked to change his schedule to accommodate other employees' vacations or even his employers' changing needs. He had no friends because he saw relationships as meaningless and insisted he "can't tolerate listening to other people's shit." Ultimately, his grandiose expectations of self and others contributed to virtually all his social, occupational, and recreational activities becoming disappointing and flawed.

Mr. B was very depressed at times, but recognition that it was due to his personality pathology improved his treatment. He was told explicitly that the therapist did not expect medication or ECT to improve his depression and recommended transference-focused psychotherapy (Diamond & Hersh, 2020) for his narcissistic personality. Long-term psychotherapy helped Mr. B remain out of the hospital, improve his relationship with his parents, get off disability, resume work and playing music, and seek independent living arrangements. Treatments that did not take the patient's pathological narcissism into account were not effective.

### A Note on Overt and Covert Narcissism

I wish to alert students that they will occasionally come across the terms "overt" and "covert" narcissism when reading narcissism literature. Unfortunately, many incorrectly associate overt expressions of narcissism exclusively with grandiosity and covert expressions of narcissism exclusively with vulnerability. There is no empirical support for these linkages, nor is there empirical support for the view that overt and covert narcissism are distinct subtypes of narcissism. In fact, there are no existing interviews or self-report measures of overt and covert narcissism. *DSM* NPD criteria as well as items on various self-reports, interviews, and rating instruments assessing pathological narcissism include a mix of overt elements (behaviors, expressed attitudes, and emotions) and covert experiences (cognitions, private feelings, motives, needs) (e.g., McGlashan et al., 2005). Clinical experience with narcissistic patients indicates they virtually always exhibit both covert and overt grandiosity and covert and overt vulnerability. In Figure 27.1, the distinction between overt and covert expressions of narcissism is secondary to phenotypic variation in grandiosity and vulnerability.

## Clinically Important Associated Features of NPD and Pathological Narcissism

Research on the associated features of NPD and pathological narcissism typically examines correlational associations between relevant constructs and NPD symptom counts, scores on self-report measures of narcissism, or informant ratings. Research using the NPD diagnosis, NPD symptom counts, or scales based on *DSM* NPD effectively assesses grandiosity but not vulnerability. In other research, pathological narcissism is assessed through interviews or scales that can include vulnerable content. It is notable that both NPD and the broader conceptualization of pathological narcissism are associated with the three associated clinical features I review below.

#### SUICIDALITY

Pathological narcissism and NPD are clinically and empirically recognized as significant risk factors for self-harm, suicidal ideation, and suicide attempts (Ansell et al., 2015; Dawood et al., 2018). It has been estimated that 4.7–23% of suicide completers exhibit elevated NPD symptom counts (Apter et al., 1993; Brent et al., 1994) and that the presence of comorbid depression may accrue even greater risk of suicide in patients with NPD (Heisel et al., 2007). Although all (formerly) Cluster B personality disorders are associated with risk for suicide, individuals with NPD exhibit greater risk for more deliberate and lethal forms of suicidal behavior compared to histrionic, antisocial, and borderline personality disorders (Blasco-Fontecilla et al., 2009).

Experiencing difficult life stressors increases suicide risk (e.g., Orbach, 1997), and certain stressors are particularly impactful for narcissistic individuals. In a sample of 375 suicide attempters, domestic stressors (e.g., arguing more with spouse) and significant life changes including employment termination, house foreclosure, and personal injury or illness preceded attempted suicide in individuals with NPD (Blasco-Fontecilla et al., 2010; see also Marttunen et al., 1993). Additionally, narcissistic personality was associated with increased suicide risk among depressed older (65+) adults, highlighting their difficulties with age-related life changes and transitions (Conner et al., 2001; Heisel et al., 2007).

Research on pathological narcissism demonstrates that an increased suicide risk is related to both narcissistic grandiosity and narcissistic vulnerability; however, the association with vulnerability tends to be stronger (Jaksic et al., 2017). Pincus and colleagues (2009) conducted a chart review of 25 patients and found that the report and number of suicide attempts was positively associated with both grandiose and vulnerable facets of the PNI. In contrast, the frequency of parasuicidal behaviors was uniquely predicted by narcissistic vulnerability. Grandiosity may catalyze suicidality by promoting a view of the self as indestructible, a preoccupation with one's physical appearance, and a detachment from one's emotional and physical self. In such cases, suicide may function as a means of complying with fantasies of invincibility or eliminating perceived imperfections of the body (Ronningstam & Weinberg, 2009). It may also serve an aggressive function to punish others or bolster an illusion of control over one's life and relationships with others (Kernberg, 1984; Ronningstam & Maltsberger, 1998). This would be consistent with suicidality following domestic arguments, for example. Vulnerability may catalyze suicidality by promoting the experience of narcissistic injury, leading to the deflation of grandiose self-views and the experience of shame in recognizing imperfections, personal weaknesses, and defeat (Pincus et al., 2009; Ronningstam & Weinberg, 2009). It may also serve an aggressive function to punish the self in response to experiencing disappointments of entitled expectations and self-enhancement failures (Pincus, 2013). This is also consistent with the increased risk of suicidality in response to age-related life transitions, as one is confronted with one's increasing physical and socioeconomic limitations (see also Horowitz, 2009).

Narcissism confers a serious risk for suicidality in part because it may be difficult to detect. Usually suicidality will present with depression, but studies suggest narcissistic individuals have an increased risk for suicide, even when not in a depressed state (Ansell et al., 2015; Ronningstam & Maltsberger, 1998; Roningstam & Weinberg, 2009; Ronningstam et al., 2018). Similarly, Cross, Westen, and Bradley (2011) identified a narcissistic subtype of suicide attempters in an adolescent sample who were not characterized by mood or anxiety problems. Furthermore, the life stressors identified above for narcissistic individuals remained significantly associated with suicide when controlling for Axis I disorders, including depression (Blasco-Fontecilla et al., 2010). Information from case studies also suggests that suicide attempters with narcissistic features may be more likely to deny intent, minimize the risk of suicidal gestures, and ignore obvious identifiable stressors that ultimately trigger such events (Ronningstam & Maltsberger, 1998; Ronningstam & Weinberg, 2009). Together, this means the clinician may have a harder time detecting and treating narcissistic suicidality.

### DEPRESSIVE EXPERIENCES

Although mood disorders, including depression and bipolar disorder, are common comorbid diagnoses with NPD, the phenomenology of depression in narcissistic patients may vary considerably. In a sample of 117 psychiatric outpatients (Kealy et al., 2012), researchers found that anaclitic/dependent themes of depression were positively associated with grandiosity, while introjective/self-critical themes of depression were positively associated with vulnerability. The authors suggested that patients with grandiose features may be more likely to suffer depressive states in the context of violated expectations of external validation, whereas patients with vulnerable features may be more likely to experience depressive exacerbations of their chronic sense of deficit. A similar study with 234 clinical outpatients (Marčinko et al., 2014) found that the relationship between vulnerability and depressive symptoms was partially mediated by dysfunctional perfectionistic attitudes. These findings suggest that the self-criticism and perfectionism commonly seen in depressed patients may involve deeper narcissistic issues (Nealis et al., 2016; Ronningstam, 2011a, 2012), potentially fueling further depressive episodes. In a sample of 235 undergraduate students assessed weekly for 8 weeks (Dawood & Pincus, 2018), the authors found that, at baseline, pathological narcissism was concurrently positively associated with multiple measures of depressive symptoms (e.g., general depression, anhedonic loss of interest, anhedonic lack of positive affect) and distinctively predicted the severity of anhedonic loss of interest over time. Pathological narcissism assessed at baseline also predicted higher variability and instability in both general depression and loss of interest (but not lack of positive affect), suggesting pathological narcissism is associated with more variable and episodic bouts of depression over time rather than a chronically depressed mood. Narcissistic individuals may be susceptible to depression because their self-worth depends on external affirmations from the social world, and their psychic cohesion can become threatened if these needs for recognition and admiration are not met (Kohut & Wolf, 1978; Morf, Horvath, & Torchetti, 2011; Morth Torchetti, & Schürch, 2011).

### AGGRESSION

Clinical perspectives on narcissism observe that narcissistic individuals become angry and aggressive when their positive, grandiose self-image is threatened or when their entitled needs for admiration from others are unmet. More simply, narcissistic individuals become enraged when their ego is threatened. Recent meta-analyses (Du et al., 2022; Kjærvik & Bushman, 2021; Rasmussen, 2016) and narrative reviews (Lambe et al., 2018) support the association between aggression and ego threat in narcissistic individuals. Cross-sectional, experimental, and field studies all converge in linking narcissism and multiple forms of aggression. A few representative studies are detailed next.

In cross-sectional studies, pathological narcissism correlates positively and moderately with physical aggression and verbal aggression in university student, clinical, and community samples (e.g., Barnett & Powell, 2016; Houlcroft et al., 2012; Morf et al., 2017). Additional research demonstrated that narcissistic vulnerability relates to uncontrolled anger, anger externalization, and anger internalization while narcissistic grandiosity only relates to anger externalization (Krizan & Johar, 2015). Moreover, vulnerable narcissism, but not grandiose narcissism, is associated with reactive aggression (retaliation against the original source of a provocation) and displaced aggression (retaliation against others who are not responsible for the original provocation), with angry rumination and mistrust accounting for these associations. Depressed patients with NPD show significantly more elevated levels of physical aggression, verbal aggression, anger, and hostility compared to depressed patients without any personality disorder (Fjermestad-Noll et al., 2020). Furthermore, research using undergraduate students shows a positive significant correlation between narcissistic vulnerability and physical aggression and verbal aggression, and this pattern remains significant when controlling for narcissistic grandiosity. Conversely, when controlling for narcissistic vulnerability, the relationship between narcissistic grandiosity and aggressive behaviors (physical, verbal) was no longer significant (Keene & Epps, 2016). Overall, cross-sectional results suggest narcissistic vulnerability as a key source of narcissistic rage.

Narcissistic grandiosity and vulnerability also predict aggressive responses in laboratory settings, particularly when following shame-inducing feedback (Bushman & Baumeister, 1998; Ferriday et al., 2011; Reidy et al.,2008; Twenge & Campbell, 2003). Grandiosity and vulnerability may also sensitize individuals to different triggers for anger. Grandiosity was associated with increased anger following an achievement threat, while vulnerability was associated with increased anger following an interpersonal threat (Besser & Priel, 2010). Krizan and Johar (2015) found those high in vulnerable narcissism, but not grandiose narcissism, respond to laboratory-based provocation with aggression, anger, depression, and mistrust. Similar experimental research on responses to provocation (Hart et al., 2017, 2018) found that vulnerable narcissism related to heightened negative emotionality (sadness, anger, hurt feelings), heightened aggression (combination of physical, verbal, and symbolic), hostile goals, and self-worth/defense goals. When combined with findings on depression (Kealy et al., 2012), this research suggests that narcissistic grandiosity may contribute to anger in response to self-enhancement failures and depression in response to relational difficulties, whereas narcissistic vulnerability may contribute to anger in response to relational difficulties and depression in response to self-enhancement failures. Therefore, pathologically narcissistic individuals are at risk for both aggression and depression when coping with social disappointments and self-enhancement setbacks.

Lambe and colleagues (2018) found that narcissism is related to a 1.2- to 11-fold increase in violence in clinical samples and is a significant predictor of more severe forms of violence (e.g., homicide). Similarly, narcissism predicted documented aggressive acts on an inpatient unit (Goldberg et al., 2007) and the endorsement of violence by outpatients seeking psychotherapy (Ellison et al., 2013). The association between narcissism and aggression also extends to incidents of intimate partner violence (Knight et al., 2018; Green et al., 2020), sexual aggression (Mouilso & Calhoun, 2012; Widman & McNulty, 2010; Zeigler-Hill et al., 2013), and stalking (Ménard & Pincus, 2012).

## The Future of NPD and Pathological Narcissism

Further theory and research is needed on how to best integrate NPD and pathological narcissism. Three areas of focus are noted below.

### Diagnosis

Four suggestions for revising the diagnosis of NPD have appeared in the literature. One suggestion is to revise the *DSM* criteria to include features reflecting narcissistic vulnerability (e.g., Ronningstam, 2009, 2011b). A second proposal is to consider narcissistic vulnerability a specifier for NPD diagnoses (e.g., NPD with vulnerable features) similar to specifiers used for other diagnoses (Miller et al., 2013). A third alternative is to consider pathological narcissism a facet of general personality pathology, representing a core feature of all PDs rather than a specific PD diagnosis (Morey, 2005; Morey & Stagner, 2012). A final suggestion, found in the *DSM-5* Alternative Model for Personality Disorders, bases NPD diagnosis on severity of impairments in self- and interpersonal functioning (Criteria A) and elevated traits of grandiosity and attention-seeking (Criteria B), where Criteria A effectively incorporates both grandiosity and vulnerability (Pincus et al., 2016).

### Grandiose and Vulnerable Narcissistic States

Although the contemporary clinical understanding of pathological narcissism recognizes its grandiose and vulnerable expressions, future research should take advantage of advancements in assessment technology and analytic methods to further investigate the within-person dynamics of grandiosity and vulnerability (Pincus & Wright, 2021). Clinical theory and observation suggest states of grandiosity and vulnerability as dynamically patterned, oscillating in ascension in relation to the outcomes of self-enhancement efforts and the receipt of social supplies of recognition and admiration. Recent research has examined variability in narcissistic states (e.g., Edershile & Wright, 2021b; Giacomin & Jordan, 2018). Such research can be extended to answer relevant clinical questions. Do shifts in grandiose and vulnerable narcissistic states occur rapidly or over long time periods? How are they triggered? How are they related to important associated features like suicidality, depression, and aggression? How do they impact patient presentation, diagnosis, and treatment?

## Contextualized Mechanisms and Processes

Even more broadly, the next generation of clinical research should conceptualize narcissistic psychopathology as involving the dynamic interplay of individual differences, within-person (perceptual, affective, cognitive, behavioral, motivational, regulatory, etc.) processes, and contextual factors that unfold at varying time scales (Dotterer et al., 2020; Pincus, 2020; Ronningstam, 2020; Wright & Kaurin, 2020). Methods, analytics, and technology now allow for the empirical investigation of such contextualized dynamic processes. Beyond the interplay of grandiose and vulnerable narcissistic states, other processes that are relevant to narcissistic psychopathology include shifting perceptions of self and other; affect regulation impairments including anger, depression, and shame; shifts from self-awareness to rigid nonmentalizing modes or defensively split grandiose and devalued object relations; and variable levels of psychosocial functioning over time.

## Conclusion

Consistent with current clinical interests, research on narcissism in all its forms is at an all-time high (Miller et al., 2017). This complex clinical phenomenon requires a sophisticated clinical science that reciprocally informs and is informed by the clinical enterprise (Pincus et al., 2020). That science has arrived, and significant advancements in conceptualization, diagnosis, and treatment of narcissistic psychopathology are now possible.

## References

Ackerman, R. A., Hands, A. J., Donnellan, M. B., Hopwood, C. J., & Witt, E. A. (2017). Experts' views regarding the conceptualization of narcissism. *Journal of Personality Disorders, 31*, 346–361.

Acton, G. S. (1998). Classification of psychopathology: The nature of language. *Journal of Mind and Behavior, 19*, 243–256.

Akhtar, S. (2003). *New clinical realms*. Jason Aronson.

Ansell, E. B., Wright, A. G., Markowitz, J. C., Sanislow, C. A., Hopwood, C. J., Zanarini, M. C., . . . Grilo, C. M. (2015). Personality disorder risk factors for suicide attempts over 10 years of follow-up. *Personality Disorders: Theory, Research, and Treatment, 6*, 161–171

Apter, A., Bleich, A., King, R. A., Kron, S., Fluch, A., Kotler, M., & Cohen, D. J. (1993). Death without warning? A clinical postmortem study of suicide in 43 Israeli adolescent males. *Archives of General Psychiatry, 50*, 138–142.

Back, M. D., Küfner, A. C. P., Dufner, M., Gerlach, T. M., Rauthmann, J. F., & Denissen, J. J. A. (2013). Narcissistic admiration and rivalry: Disentangling the bright and dark sides of narcissism. *Journal of Personality and Social Psychology, 105*, 1013–1037.

Ball, S. A., Rounsaville, B. J., Tennen, H., & Kranzler, H. R. (2001). Reliability of personality disorder symptoms and personality traits in substance-dependent inpatients. *Journal of Abnormal Psychology, 110*, 341–352.

Barnett, M. D., & Powell, H. A. (2016). Self-esteem mediates narcissism and aggression among women, but not men: A comparison of two theoretical models of narcissism among college students. *Personality and Individual Differences, 89*, 100–104.

Benjamin, L. S. (1996). *Interpersonal diagnosis and treatment of personality disorders*, 2nd ed. Guilford.

Besser, A., & Priel, B. (2010). Emotional responses to a romantic partner's imaginary rejection: The roles of attachment anxiety, covert narcissism and self-evaluation. *Journal of Personality, 77*, 287–325.

Besser, A., Zeigler-Hill, V., Weinberg, M., & Pincus, A. P. (2016). Do great expectations lead to great disappointments? Pathological narcissism and the evaluation of vacation experiences. *Personality and Individual Differences, 89*, 75–79.

Blasco-Fontecilla, H., Baca-Garcia, E., Dervic, K., Perez-Rodriguez, M. M., Lopez-Castroman, J., Saiz-Ruiz, J., & Oquendo, M. A. (2009). Specific features of suicidal behavior in patients with narcissistic personality disorder. *Journal of Clinical Psychiatry, 70*, 1583–1587.

Blasco-Fontecilla, H., Baca-Garcia, E., Duberstein, P., Perez-Rodriguez, M. M., Dervic, K., Saiz-Ruiz, J., Courtet, P., de Leon, J., & Oquendo, M. A. (2010). An exploratory study of the relationship between diverse life events and specific personality disorders in a sample of suicide attempters. *Journal of Personality Disorders, 24*, 773–784.

Brent, D. A., Johnson, B. A., Perper, J., Connolly, J., Bridge, J., Bartle, S., & Rather, C. (1994). Personality disorder, personality traits, impulsive violence, and completed suicide in adolescents. *Journal of the American Academy of Child and Adolescent Psychiatry, 33*, 1080–1086.

Buelow, M. T., & Brunell, A. B. (2014). Facets of narcissistic grandiosity predict involvement in health-risk behaviors. *Personality and Individual Differences, 69*, 193–198.

Bushman, B. J., & Baumeister, R. F. (1998). Threatened egotism, narcissism, self-esteem, and direct and displaced aggression: Does self-love or self-hate lead to violence? *Journal of Personality and Social Psychology, 75*, 219–229.

Buss, D. M., & Chiodo, L. M. (1991). Narcissistic acts in everyday life. *Journal of Personality, 59*, 179–215.

Cain, N. M., Pincus, A. L., & Ansell, E. B. (2008). Narcissism at the crossroads: Phenotypic description of pathological narcissism across clinical theory, social/personality psychology, and psychiatric diagnosis. *Clinical Psychology Review, 28*, 638–656.

Caligor, E., Levy, K. N., & Yeomans, F. E. (2015). Narcissistic personality disorder: Diagnostic and clinical challenges. *American Journal of Psychiatry, 172*, 415–422.

Carlson, E. N. (2013). Honestly arrogant or simply misunderstood? Narcissists' awareness of their narcissism. *Self and Identity, 12*, 259–277.

Carlson, E. N., & Oltmanns, T. F. (2015). The role of metaperception in personality disorders: Do people with personality problems know how others experience their personality? *Journal of Personality Disorders, 29*, 449–467.

Clarkin, J. F., Yeomans, F. E., & Kernberg, O. F. (2006). *Psychotherapy for borderline personality: Focusing on object relations*. American Psychiatric Publishing.

Clemence, A. J., Perry, J. C., & Plakun, E. M. (2009). Narcissistic and borderline personality disorders in a sample of treatment refractory patients. *Psychiatric Annuals, 39*, 175–184.

Conner, K. R., Cox, C., Duberstein, P. R., Tian, L., Niset, P., & Conwell, Y. (2001). Violence, alcohol, and completed suicide: A case-control study. *American Journal of Psychiatry, 158*, 1701–1705.

Conroy, D. E., Elliot, A. J., & Thrash, T. M. (2009). Achievement motivation. In M. R. Leary & R. H. Hoyle (Eds.), *Handbook of individual differences in social behavior* (pp. 382–399). Guilford.

Crisp, H., & Gabbard, G. O. (2020). Principles of psychodynamic treatment for patients with narcissistic personality disorder. *Journal of Personality Disorders, 34*(Suppl), 143–158.33

Cross, D., Westen, D., & Bradley, B. (2011). Personality subtypes of adolescents who attempt suicide. *Journal of Nervous and Mental Disease, 199*, 750–756.

Crowe, M. L., Edershile, E. A., Wright, A. G., Campbell, W. K., Lynam, D. R., & Miller, J. D. (2018). Development and validation of the Narcissistic Vulnerability Scale: An adjective rating scale. *Psychological Assessment, 30*, 978–983.

Crowe, M. L., Lynam, D. R., Campbell, W. K., & Miller, J. D. (2019). Exploring the structure of narcissism: Toward an integrated solution. *Journal of Personality, 87*, 1151–1169.

Dawood, S., & Pincus, A. L. (2018). Pathological narcissism and the severity, variability, and instability of depressive symptoms. *Personality Disorders: Theory, Research, and Treatment, 9*, 144–154.

Dawood, S., Schroeder, H. S., Donnellan, M. B., & Pincus, A. L. (2018). Pathological narcissism and non-suicidal self-injury. *Journal of Personality Disorders, 32*, 87–108.

Dawood, S., Wu, L. Z., Bliton, C. F., & Pincus, A. L. (2020). Narcissistic and histrionic personality disorders. In C. Lejuez & K. Gratz (Eds.), *Cambridge handbook of personality disorders* (pp. 277–291). Cambridge University Press.

Derry, K. L., Bayliss, D. M., & Ohan, J. L. (2019). Measuring grandiose and vulnerable narcissism in children and adolescents: The narcissism scale for children. *Assessment, 26*, 645–660.

Diamond, D., & Hersh, R. G. (2020). Transference-focused psychotherapy for narcissistic personality disorder: An object relations approach. *Journal of Personality Disorders, 34*(Suppl), 159–176.

Dickinson, K. A., & Pincus, A. L. (2003). Interpersonal analysis of grandiose and vulnerable narcissism. *Journal of Personality Disorders, 17*, 188–207.

Dieckmann, E., & Behary, W. (2015). Schema therapy: An approach for treating narcissistic personality disorder. *Fortschritte der Neurologie-Psychiatrie, 83*, 463–77.

Dhawan, N., Kunik, M. E., Oldham, J., & Coverdale, J. (2010). Prevalence and treatment of narcissistic personality disorder in the community: A systematic review. *Comprehensive Psychiatry, 51*, 333–339.

Doering, S., Hartmann, H. P., & Kernberg, O. F. (Eds.). (2021). *Narzissmus: Grundlagen – Störungsbilder – Therapie*, 2nd ed. Schattauer.

Doidge, N., Simon, B., Brauer, L., Grant, D., First, M., Brunshaw, J., Lancee, W. J., Stevens, A., Oldham, J. M., & Mosher, P. (2002). Psychoanalytic patients in the U.S., Canada, and Australia: I. *DSM-III*-R disorders, indications, previous treatment, medications, and length of treatment. *Journal of the American Psychoanalytic Association, 50*, 575–614.

Dotterer, H. L., Beltz, A. M., Foster, K. T., Simms, L. J., & Wright, A. G. C. (2020). Personalized models of personality disorders: Using a temporal network method to understand symptomatology and daily functioning in a clinical sample. *Psychological Medicine, 50*, 2397–2405.

Dowgwillo, E. A., Dawood, S., & Pincus, A. L. (2016). The dark side of narcissism. In V. Zeigler-Hill & D. Marcus (Eds.), *The dark side of personality: Science and practice in social, personality, and clinical psychology* (pp. 25–44). American Psychological Association.

Drozek, R. P., & Unruh, B. T. (2020). Mentalization-Based Treatment for Pathological Narcissism. *Journal of Personality Disorders, 34*(Suppl), 177–203.

Du, T. V., Miller, J. D., & Lynam, D. R. (2022). The relation between narcissism and aggression: A meta-analysis. *Journal of Personality, 90*, 574–594.

Eaton, N. R., Rodriguez-Seijas, C., Krueger, R. F., Campbell, W. K., Grant, B. F., & Hasin, D. S. (2017). Narcissistic personality disorder and the structure of common mental disorders. *Journal of Personality Disorders, 31*, 449–461.

Edershile, E. A., Simms, L. J., & Wright, A. G. (2019). A multivariate analysis of the Pathological Narcissism Inventory's nomological network. *Assessment, 26*, 619–629.

Edershile, E. A., & Wright, A. G. (2021a). Grandiose and vulnerable narcissistic states in interpersonal situations. *Self and Identity, 20*, 165–181.

Edershile, E. A., & Wright, A. G. (2021b). Fluctuations in grandiose and vulnerable narcissistic states: A momentary perspective. *Journal of Personality and Social Psychology, 120*, 1386–1414.

Ekselius, L., Tillfors, M., Furmark, T., & Fredrikson, M. (2001). Personality disorders in the general population: DSM-IV and ICD-10 defined prevalence as related to sociodemographic profile. *Personality and Individual Differences, 30*, 311–320.

Ellison, W. D., Levy, K. N., Cain, N. M., Ansell, E. B., & Pincus, A. L. (2013). The impact of pathological narcissism on psychotherapy utilization, initial symptom severity, and early-treatment symptom change: A naturalistic investigation. *Journal of Personality Assessment, 95*, 291–300.

Erkoreka, L., & Navarro, B. (2017). Vulnerable narcissism is associated with severity of depressive symptoms in dysthymic patients. *Psychiatry Research, 257*, 265–269.

Fjermestad-Noll, J., Ronningstam, E., Bach, B. S., Rosenbaum, B., & Simonsen, E. (2020). Perfectionism, shame, and aggression in depressive patients with narcissistic personality disorder. *Journal of Personality Disorders, 34*, 25–41.

Ferriday, C., Vartanian, O., & Mandel, D. R. (2011). Public but not private ego threat triggers aggression in narcissists. *European Journal of Social Psychology, 41*, 564–568.

Freud, S. (1914). On narcissism. In J. Strachey (Ed. And Trans.), *The standard edition of the complete psychological works of Sigmund Freud* (Vol. XIV, pp. 66–102). Hogarth Press.

Gabbard, G. O. (2009). Transference and countertransference: Developments in the treatment of narcissistic personality disorder. *Psychiatric Annuals, 39*, 129–136.

Giacomin, M., & Jordan, C. H. (2014). Down-regulating narcissistic tendencies: Communal focus reduces state narcissism. *Personality and Social Psychology Bulletin, 40*, 488–500.

Giacomin, M., & Jordan, C. H. (2016a). Self-focused and feeling fine: Assessing state narcissism and its relation to wellbeing. *Journal of Research in Personality, 63*, 12–21.

Giacomin, M., & Jordan, C. H. (2016b). The wax and wane of narcissism: Grandiose narcissism as a process or state. *Journal of Personality, 84*, 154–164.

Giacomin, M., & Jordan, C. H. (2018). Within-person variability in narcissism. In V. Zeigler-Hill & T. K. Shackelford (Eds.), *The SAGE handbook of personality and individual differences: The science of personality and individual differences* (pp. 503–518). Sage.

Glover, N., Miller, J. D., Lynam, D. R., Crego, C., & Widiger, T. A. (2012). The Five-Factor Narcissism Inventory: A five-factor measure of narcissistic personality traits. *Journal of Personality Assessment, 94*, 500–512.

Goldberg, B. R., Serper, M. R., Sheets, M., Beech, D., Dill, C., & Duffy, K. G. (2007). Predictors of aggression on the psychiatric inpatient service: Self-esteem, narcissism, and theory of mind deficits. *Journal of Nervous and Mental Disease, 195*, 436–442.

Gore, W. L., & Widiger, T. A. (2016). Fluctuation between grandiose and vulnerable narcissism. *Personality Disorders: Theory, Research, and Treatment, 7*, 363–371.

Green, A., MacLean, R., & Charles, K. (2020). Unmasking gender differences in narcissism within intimate partner violence. *Personality and Individual Differences, 167*, article 110247.

Grilo, C. M., McGlashan, T. H., Quinlan, D. M., Walker, M. L., Greenfeld, D., & Edell, W. S. (1998). Frequency of personality disorders in two age cohorts of psychiatric inpatients. *American Journal of Psychiatry, 155*, 140–142.

Gunderson, J., Ronningstam, E., & Bodkin, A. (1990). The diagnostic interview for narcissistic patients. *Archives of General Psychiatry, 47*, 676–680.

Gunderson, J., Ronningstam, E., & Smith, L. E. (1995). Narcissistic personality disorder. In J. Livesley (Ed.), *The DSM-IV personality disorder diagnoses* (pp. 201–212). Guilford.

Hart, W., Adams, J. M., & Tortoriello, G. K. (2017). Narcissistic responses to provocation: An examination of the rage and threatened-egotism accounts. *Personality and Individual Differences, 106*, 152–157.

Hart, W., Tortoriello, G. K., & Richardson, K. (2018). Provoked narcissistic aggression: Examining the role of de-escalated and escalated provocations. *Journal of Interpersonal Violence, 36*, 4832–4853.

Heisel, M. J., Links, P. S., Conn, D., van Reekum, R., & Flett, G. L. (2007). Narcissistic personality and vulnerability to late-life suicidality. *American Journal of Geriatric Psychiatry, 15*, 734–741.

Hendin, H. M., & Cheek, J. M. (1997). Assessing hypersensitive narcissism: A reexamination of Murray's Narcism Scale. *Journal of Research in Personality, 31*, 588–599.

Hepper, E. G., Gramzow, R. H., & Sedikides, C. (2010). Individual differences in self-enhancement and self-protection strategies: An integrative analysis. *Journal of Personality, 78*, 781–814.

Hermann, A. D., Brunell, A. B., & Foster, J. D. (2018). *Handbook of trait narcissism*. Springer.

Hopwood, C. J., Ansell, E. A., Pincus, A. L., Wright, A. G. C., Lukowitsky, M. R., & Roche, M. J. (2011). The circumplex structure of interpersonal sensitivities. *Journal of Personality, 79*, 707–740.

Horowitz, M. (2009). Clinical phenomenology of narcissistic pathology. *Psychiatric Annuals, 39*, 124–128.

Hörz-Sagstetter, S., Diamond, D., Clarkin, J. F., Levy, K. N., Rentrop, M., Fischer-Kern, M., . . . Doering, S. (2018). Clinical characteristics of comorbid narcissistic personality disorder in patients with borderline personality disorder. *Journal of Personality Disorders, 32*, 562–575.

Houlcroft, L., Bore, M., & Munro, D. (2012). Three faces of narcissism. *Personality and Individual Differences, 53*, 274–278.

Huprich, S. K. (2020). Personality disorders in the ICD-11: Opportunities and challenges for advancing the diagnosis of personality pathology. *Current Psychiatry Reports, 22*, article 40. https://doi.org/10.1007/s11920-020-01161-4

Hyatt, C. S., Sleep, C. E., Lynam, D. R., Widiger, T. A., Campbell, W. K., & Miller, J. D. (2018). Ratings of affective and interpersonal tendencies differ for grandiose and vulnerable narcissism: A replication and extension of Gore and Widiger (2016). *Journal of Personality, 86*, 422–434.

Jaksic, N., Marcinko, D., Skocic Hanzek, M., Rebernjak, B., & Ogrodniczuk, J. S. (2017). Experience of shame mediates the relationship between pathological narcissism and suicidal ideation in psychiatric outpatients. *Journal of Clinical Psychology, 73*, 1670–1681.

Jauk, E., & Kaufman, S. B. (2018). The higher the score, the darker the core: The nonlinear association between grandiose and vulnerable narcissism. *Frontiers in Psychology, 9*, 1305.

Jauk, E., Ulbrich, L., Jorschick, P., Höfler, M., Kaufman, S. B., & Kanske, P. (2021). The nonlinear association between grandiose and vulnerable narcissism: An individual data meta-analysis. *Journal of Personality*. Advanced online publication. https://doi.org/10.1111/jopy.12692

Kaufman, S. B., Weiss, B., Miller, J. D., & Campbell, W. K. (2020). Clinical correlates of vulnerable and grandiose narcissism: A personality perspective. *Journal of Personality Disorders, 34*, 107–130.

Kealy, D., Goodman, G., Rasmussen, B., Weideman, R., & Ogrodniczuk, J. (2017). Therapists' perspectives on optimal treatment for pathological narcissism. *Personality Disorders: Theory, Research, and Treatment, 8*, 35–45.

Kealy, D., & Ogrodniczuk, J. S. (2012). Pathological narcissism: A front-line guide. *Practice: Social Work in Action, 24*, 161–174.

Kealy, D., & Rasmussen, B. (2012). Veiled and vulnerable: The other side of grandiose narcissism. *Clinical Social Work Journal, 40*, 356–366.

Kealy, D., Tsai, M., & Ogrodniczuk, J. S. (2012). Depressive tendencies and pathological narcissism among psychiatric outpatients. *Psychiatry Research, 196*, 157–159.

Keene, A. C., & Epps, J. (2016). Childhood physical abuse and aggression: Shame and narcissistic vulnerability. *Child Abuse & Neglect, 51*, 276–283.

Kernberg, O. F. (1970). Factors in the psychoanalytic treatment of narcissistic personalities. *Journal of the American Psychoanalytic Association, 18*, 51–85.

Kernberg, O. F. (1984). *Severe personality disorders: Psychotherapeutic strategies*. Yale University Press.

Kernberg, O. F. (1988). Object relations theory in clinical practice. *Psychoanalytic Quarterly, 57*, 481–504.

Kernberg, O. F. (1998). Pathological narcissism and narcissistic personality disorder: Theoretical background and diagnostic classification. In E. Ronningstam (Ed.), *Disorders of narcissism: Diagnostic, clinical, and empirical implications* (pp. 29–51). American Psychiatric Press.

Kernberg, O. F. (2007). The almost untreatable narcissistic patient. *Journal of the American Psychoanalytic Association, 55*, 503–539.

Kernberg, O. F. (2009). Narcissistic personality disorders: Part 1. *Psychiatric Annuals, 39*, 105-107, 110, 164–167.

Kernberg, O. F. (2010). Narcissistic personality disorder. In J. F. Clarkin, P. Fonagy, & G. O. Gabbard (Eds.), *Psychodynamic psychotherapy for personality disorders: A clinical handbook* (pp. 257–287). American Psychiatric Press.

Kjærvik, S. L., & Bushman, B. J. (2021). The link between narcissism and aggression: A meta-analytic review. *Psychological Bulletin, 147*, 477–503.

Knight, N. M., Dahlen, E. R., Bullock-Yowell, E., & Madson, M. B. (2018). The HEXACO model of personality and Dark Triad in relational aggression. *Personality and Individual Differences, 122*, 109–114.

Kohut, H. (1971). *The analysis of the self*. International Universities Press.

Kohut, H. (1977). *The restoration of the self*. International Universities Press.

Kohut, H., & Wolf, E. (1978). The disorders of the self and their treatment: An outline. *International Journal of Psychoanalysis, 59*, 413–425.

Krizan, Z., & Herlache, A. D. (2018). The narcissism spectrum model: A synthetic view of narcissistic personality. *Personality and Social Psychology Review, 22*, 3–31.

Krizan, Z., & Johar, O. (2012). Envy divides the two faces of narcissism. *Journal of Personality, 80*, 1415–1451.

Krizan, Z., & Johar, O. (2015). Narcissistic rage revisited. *Journal of Personality and Social Psychology, 108*, 784–801.

Lambe, S., Hamilton-Giachritsis, C., Garner, E., & Walker, J. (2018). The role of narcissism in aggression and violence: A systematic review. *Trauma, Violence & Abuse, 19*, 209–230.

Lenzenweger, M. F., Johnson, M. D., & Willett, J. (2004). Individual growth curve analysis illuminates stability and change in personality disorder features: The longitudinal study of personality disorders. *Archives of General Psychiatry, 61*, 1015–1024.

Levy, K. N., Ellison, W. D., & Reynoso, J. S. (2011). A historical review of narcissism and narcissistic personality. In W. K. Campbell & J. D. Miller (Eds.), *Handbook of narcissism and narcissistic personality disorder: Theoretical approaches, empirical findings, and treatment* (pp. 3–13). Guilford.

Levy, K. N., Reynoso, J. S., Wasserman, R. H., & Clarkin, J. F. (2007). Narcissistic personality disorder. In W. O'Donohue, K. A. Fowler, & S. O. Lilienfeld (Eds.), *Personality disorders: Toward the DSM-V* (pp. 233–277). Sage

Lingiardi, V., & McWilliams, N. (2017). *Psychodynamic diagnostic manual*, 2nd ed. Guilford.

Lobbestael, J., Baumeister, R. F., Feibig, T., & Eckel, L. A. (2014). The role of grandiose and vulnerable narcissism in self-reported and laboratory aggression and testosterone reactivity. *Personality and Individual Differences, 69*, 22–27.

Marčinko, D., Jakšić, N., Ivezić, E., Skočić, M., Surányi, Z., Lončar, M., . . . Jakovljević, M. (2014). Pathological narcissism and depressive symptoms in psychiatric outpatients: Mediating role of dysfunctional attitudes. *Journal of Clinical Psychology, 70*, 341–352.

Marissen, M. A. E., Deen, M. L., & Franken, I. H. A. (2012). Disturbed emotion recognition in patients with narcissistic personality disorder. *Psychiatry Research, 198*, 269–273.

Marissen, M. A., Brouwer, M. E., Hiemstra, A. M., Deen, M. L., & Franken, I. H. (2016). A masked negative self-esteem? Implicit and explicit self-esteem in patients with Narcissistic Personality Disorder. *Psychiatry Research, 242*, 28–33.

Marttunen, M.J., Aro, H. M., & Lonnqvist, J. K. (1993). Precipitant stressors in adolescent suicide. *Journal of the American Academy of Child and Adolescent Psychiatry, 32*, 1178–1183.

Masterson, J. F. (1993). *The emerging self: A developmental, self, and object relations approach to the treatment of the closet narcissistic disorder of the self*. Brunner/Mazel.

Mattia, J., & Zimmerman, M. (2001). Epidemiology. In W. J. Livesley (Ed.), *The handbook of personality disorders* (pp. 107–123). Guilford.

Maxwell, K., Donnellan, M. B., Hopwood, C. J., & Ackerman, R. A. (2011). The two faces of Narcissus? An empirical comparison of the Narcissistic Personality Inventory and the Pathological Narcissism Inventory. *Personality and Individual Differences, 50*, 577–582.

McGlashan, T. H., Grilo, C., Sanislow, C. A., Ralevski, E., Morey, L. C., Gunderson, J. G., Skodol, A. E., Shea, M. T., Zanarini, M. C., Bender, D. S., Stout, R. L., Yen, S., & Pagano, M. E. (2005). Two-year prevalence and stability of individual *DSM-IV* criteria for schizotypal, borderline, avoidant, and obsessive–compulsive personality disorders: Toward a hybrid model of Axis II disorders. *American Journal of Psychiatry, 165*, 883–889.

McGrath, R. E. (2005). Conceptual complexity and construct validity. *Journal of Personality Assessment, 85*, 112–124.

Ménard, K. S., & Pincus, A. L. (2012). Predicting overt and cyber stalking perpetration by male and female college students. *Journal of Interpersonal Violence, 27*, 2183–2207.

Miller, J. D., & Campbell, W. K. (2008). Comparing clinical and social-personality conceptualizations of narcissism. *Journal of Personality, 76*, 449–476.

Miller, J. D., Dir, A., Gentile, B. Wilson, L., Pryor, L. R., & Campbell, W. K. (2010). Searching for a vulnerable dark triad: Comparing factor 2 psychopathy, vulnerable narcissism, and borderline personality disorder. *Journal of Personality, 78*, 1529–1564.

Miller, J. D., Gentile, B., Wilson, L., & Campbell, W. K. (2013). Grandiose and vulnerable narcissism and the *DSM-5* pathological personality trait model. *Journal of Personality Assessment, 95*, 284–290.

Miller, J. D., Hoffman, B., Campbell, W. K., & Pilkonis, P. A. (2008). An examination of the factor structure of *DSM-IV* narcissistic personality disorder criteria: One or two factors? *Comprehensive Psychiatry, 49*, 141–145.

Miller, J. D., Lynam, D. R., Hyatt, C. S., & Campbell, W. K. (2017). Controversies in narcissism. *Annual Review of Clinical Psychology, 13*, 291–315.

Miller, J. D., Lynam, D. R., McCain, J. L., Few, L. R., Crego, C., Widiger, T. A., & Campbell, W. K. (2016). Thinking structurally about narcissism: An examination of the Five-Factor Narcissism Inventory and its components. *Journal of Personality Disorders, 30*, 1–18.

Miller, J. D., Widiger, T. A., & Campbell, W. K. (2010). Narcissistic personality disorder and the *DSM*-V. *Journal of Abnormal Psychology, 119*, 640–649.

Millon, T. (1981). *Disorders of personality. DSM-III: Axis II.* Wiley.

Morey, L. C. (2005). Personality pathology as pathological narcissism. In M. Maj, H. S. Akiskal, J. E. Mezzich, & A. Okasha (Eds.), *Evidence and experience in psychiatry volume 8: Personality disorders* (pp. 328–331). Wiley.

Morey, L. C., & Ochoa, E. S. (1989). An investigation of adherence to diagnostic criteria: Clinical diagnosis of the *DSM-III* personality disorders. *Journal of Personality Disorders, 3*, 180–192.

Morey, L. C., & Stagner, B. H. (2012). Narcissistic pathology as core personality dysfunction: Comparing the *DSM-IV* and *DSM-5* proposal for narcissistic personality disorder. *Journal of Clinical Psychology, 68*, 908–921.

Morf, C. C. (2006). Personality reflected in a coherent idiosyncratic interplay of intra- and interpersonal self-regulatory processes. *Journal of Personality, 76*, 1527–1556.

Morf, C. C., Horvath, S., & Torchetti, T. (2011). Narcissistic self-enhancement: Tales of (successful?) self-portrayal. In M. D. Alicke & C. Sedikides (Eds.), *Handbook of self-enhancement and self-protection* (pp. 399–424). Guilford.

Morf, C., & Rhodewalt, F. (2001). Unraveling the paradoxes of narcissism: A dynamic self-regulatory processing model. *Psychological Inquiry, 12*, 177–196.

Morf, C. C., Schürch, E., Küfner, A., Siegrist, P., Vater, A., Back, M., . . . Schröder-Abé, M. (2017). Expanding the nomological net of the Pathological Narcissism Inventory: German validation and extension in a clinical inpatient sample. *Assessment, 24*, 419–443.

Morf, C. C., Torchetti, T., & Schürch, E. (2011). Narcissism from the perspective of the dynamic self-regulatory processing model. In W. K. Campbell & J. D. Miller (Eds.), *The handbook of narcissism and narcissistic personality disorder: Theoretical approaches, empirical findings, and treatment* (pp. 56–70). Guilford.

Mouilso, E. R., & Calhoun, K. S. (2012). A mediation model of role of sociosexuality in associations between narcissism, psychopathy, and sexual aggression. *Psychology of Violence, 2*, 16–27.

Nealis, L. J., Sherry, S. B., Lee-Baggley, D. L., Stewart, S. H., & Macneil, M. A. (2016). Revitalizing narcissistic perfectionism: Evidence of the reliability and the validity of an emerging construct. *Journal of Psychopathology and Behavioral Assessment, 38*, 493–504.

Nenadic, I., Güllmar, D., Dietzek, M., Langbein, K., Steinke, J., & Gaser, C. (2015). Brain structure in narcissistic personality disorder: A VBM and DTI pilot study. *Psychiatry Research: Neuroimaging, 231*, 184–186.

Nedstadt, G., Di, C., Samuels, J. F., Bienvenu, O. J., Reti, I. M., Costa, P., Eaton, W. W., & Bandeen-Roche, K. (2010). The stability of DSM personality disorders over twelve to eighteen years. *Journal of Psychiatric Research, 44*, 1–7.

Ogrodniczuk, J. S. (2013). *Understanding and treating pathological narcissism.* American Psychological Association.

Ogrodniczuk, J. S., Piper, W. E., Joyce, A. S., Steinberg, P. I., & Duggal, S. (2009). Interpersonal problems associated with narcissism among psychiatric outpatients. *Journal of Psychiatric Research, 43*, 837–842.

Oltmanns, T. F., & Turkheimer, E. (2006). Perceptions of self and others regarding pathological personality traits. In R. F. Krueger & J. L. Tackett (Eds.), *Personality and psychopathology* (pp. 71–111). Guilford.

Orbach, I. (1997). A taxonomy of factors related to suicidal behavior. *Clinical Psychology: Theory and Research, 4*, 208–224.

Oulis, P., Lykouras, L., Hatzimanolis, J., & Tomaras, V. (1997). Comorbidity os *DSM-III*-R personality disorders in schizophrenic and unipolar mood disorders: A comparative study. *European Psychiatry, 12*, 316–318.

PDM Task Force. (2006). *Psychodynamic diagnostic manual.* Alliance of Psychoanalytic Organizations.

Pincus, A. L. (2011). Some comments on nomology, diagnostic process, and narcissistic personality disorder in *DSM-5* proposal for personality and personality disorders. *Personality Disorders: Theory, Research, and Treatment, 2*, 41–53.

Pincus, A. L. (2013). The Pathological Narcissism Inventory. In J. S. Ogrodniczuk (Ed.), *Understanding and treating pathological narcisssim* (pp. 93–110). American Psychological Association.

Pincus, A. L. (2020). Complexity, pleomorphism, and dynamic processes in Narcissistic Personality Disorder. *Journal of Personality Disorders, 34*, 204–206.

Pincus, A. L., Ansell, E. B., Pimentel, C. A., Cain, N. M., Wright, A. G. C., & Levy, K. N. (2009). Initial construction and validation of the Pathological Narcissism Inventory. *Psychological Assessment, 21*, 365–379.

Pincus, A. L., Cain, N. M., & Wright, A. G. C. (2014). Narcissistic grandiosity and narcissistic vulnerability in psychotherapy. *Personality Disorders: Theory, Research, and Treatment, 5*, 439–443.

Pincus, A. L., Dawood, S., Wu, Z., & Bliton, C. F. (2020). Clinical personality science of narcissism should include the clinic. In C. Lejuez & K. Gratz (Eds.), *Cambridge handbook of personality disorders* (pp. 300–301). Cambridge University Press.

Pincus, A. L., Dowgwillo, E. A., & Greenberg, L. (2016). Three cases of narcissistic personality disorder through the lens of the *DSM-5* alternative model for personality disorders. *Practice Innovations, 1*, 164–177.

Pincus, A. L., & Lukowitsky, M. R. (2010). Pathological narcissism and narcissistic personality disorder. *Annual Review of Clinical Psychology, 6*, 421–446.

Pincus, A. L., & Roche, M. J. (2011). Narcissistic grandiosity and narcissistic vulnerability. In W. K. Campbell & J. D. Miller (Eds.), *Handbook of narcissism and narcissistic personality disorder: Theoretical approaches, empirical findings, and treatment* (pp. 31–40). Wiley.

Pincus, A. L., & Wright, A. G. C. (2021). Narcissism as the dynamics of grandiosity and vulnerability. In S. Doering, H-P. Hartmann, & O. F. Kernberg (Eds.), *Narzissmus: Grundlagen - Störungsbilder – Therapie*, 2nd ed. (pp. 56–62). Schattauer.

Rank, O. (1911). A contribution to narcissism. *Jahrbuch fur Psychoanalytische und Psychopathologischen Forschungen, 3*, 401–426.

Raskin, R. N., & Hall, C. S. (1981). The Narcissistic Personality Inventory: Alternate form reliability and further evidence of construct validity. *Journal of Personality Assessment, 45*, 159–162.

Rasmussen, K. (2016). Entitled vengeance: A meta-analysis relating narcissism to provoked aggression. *Aggressive Behavior, 42*, 362–379.

Reed-Knight, B., & Fischer, S. (2011). Treatment of narcissistic personality disorder symptoms in a dialectical behavior therapy framework: A discussion and case example. In W. K. Campbell & J. D. Miller (Eds.), *Handbook of narcissism and narcissistic personality disorder: Theoretical approaches, empirical findings, and treatment* (pp. 466–475). Wiley.

Regier, D. A., Narrow, W. E., Kuhl, E. A., & Kupfer, D. J. (2009). The conceptual development of *DSM-V. American Journal of Psychiatry, 166*, 645–650.

Reidy, D. E., Foster, J. D., & Zeichner, A. (2010). Narcissism and unprovoked aggression. *Aggressive Behavior, 36*, 414–422.

Reidy, D. E., Zeichner, A., Foster, J. D., & Martinez, M. A. (2008). Effects of narcissistic entitlement and exploitativenedd on human physical aggression. *Personality and Individual Differences, 44*, 865–875.

Ritter, K., Dziobek, I., Preissler, S., Ruter, A., Vater, A., Fydrich T., . . . Roepke, S. (2011). Lack of empathy in patients with Narcissistic Personality Disorder. *Psychiatry Research, 187*, 241–247.

Ritter, K., Vater, A., Rüsch, N., Schröder-Abé, M., Schütz, A., Fydrich, T., . . . Roepke, S. (2014). Shame in patients with narcissistic personality disorder. *Psychiatry Research, 215*, 429–437.

Roche, M. J., Pincus, A. L., Conroy, D. E., Hyde, A. L., & Ram, N. (2013). Pathological narcissism and interpersonal behavior in daily life. *Personality Disorders: Theory, Research, and Treatment, 4*, 315–323.

Roche, M. J., Pincus, A. L., Lukowitsky, M. R., Ménard, K. S., & Conroy, D. E. (2013). An integrative approach to the assessment of narcissism. *Journal of Personality Assessment, 95*, 237–248.

Ronningstam, E. (1996). Pathological narcissism and narcissistic personality disorder in Axis I disorders. *Harvard Review of Psychiatry, 39*, 326–340.

Ronningstam, E. (2005a). *Identifying and understanding narcissistic personality*. Oxford University Press.

Ronningstam, E. (2005b). Narcissistic personality disorder: A review. In M. Maj, H. S. Akiskal, J. E. Mezzich, & A. Okasha (Eds.), *Evidence and experience in psychiatry volume 8: Personality disorders* (pp. 277–327). Wiley.

Ronningstam, E. (2009). Narcissistic personality disorder: Facing *DSM-V. Psychiatric Annuals, 39*, 111–121.

Ronningstam, E. (2011a). Narcissistic personality disorder: A clinical perspective. *Journal of Psychiatric Practice, 17*, 89–99.

Ronningstam, E. (2011b). Narcissistic personality disorder in *DSM-V*: In support of retaining a significant diagnosis. *Journal of Personality Disorders, 25*, 248–259.

Ronningstam, E. (2011c). Psychoanalytic theories on narcissism and narcissistic personality. In W. K. Campbell & J. D. Miller (Eds.), *Handbook of narcissism and narcissistic personality disorder: Theoretical approaches, empirical findings, and treatment* (pp. 41–55). Wiley.

Ronningstam, E. (2012). Alliance building and narcissistic personality disorder. *Journal of Clinical Psychology, 68*, 943–953.

Ronningstam, E. (2020). Internal processing in patients with pathological narcissism or narcissistic personality disorder: Implications for alliance building and therapeutic strategies. *Journal of Personality Disorders, 34*(Suppl), 80–103.

Ronningstam, E., & Gunderson, J. (1990). Identifying criteria for NPD. *American Journal of Psychiatry, 147*, 918–922.

Ronningstam, E., Gunderson, J., & Lyons, M. (1995). Changes in pathological narcissism. *American Journal of Psychiatry, 152*, 253–257.

Ronningstam, E., & Maltsberger, J. T. (1998). Pathological narcissism and sudden suicide related collapse. *Suicide and Life Threatening Behavior, 28*, 261–271.

Ronningstam, E., & Weinberg, I. (2009). Contributing factors to suicide in narcissistic personalities. *Directions in Psychiatry, 29*, 317–329.

Ronningstam, E., Weinberg, I., Goldblatt, M., Schechter, M., & Herbstman, B. (2018). Suicide and self-regulation in narcissistic personality disorder. *Psychodynamic Psychiatry, 46*, 491–510.

Rosenthal, S. A., Hooley, J. M., Montoya, R. M., van der Linden, S. L., & Steshenko, Y. (2020). The narcissistic grandiosity scale: A measure to distinguish narcissistic grandiosity from high self-esteem. *Assessment, 27*, 487–507.

Russ, E., Shedler, J., Bradley, R., & Westen, D. (2008). Refining the construct of narcissistic personality disorder: Diagnostic criteria and subtypes. *American Journal of Psychiatry, 165*, 1473–1481.

Samuel, D. B., Hopwood, C. J., Ansell, E. B., Morey, L. C., Sanislow, C. A., Markowitz, J. C., . . . Grilo, C. M. (2011). Comparing the temporal stability of self-report and interview assessed personality disorder. *Journal of Abnormal Psychology, 120*, 670–680.

Schoenleber, M., Roche, M. J., Wetzel, E., Pincus, A. L., & Roberts, B. W. (2015). Development of a brief version of the Pathological Narcissism Inventory. *Psychological Assessment, 27*, 1520–1526.

Schulze, L., Dziobek, I., Vater, A., Heekeren, H. R., Bajbouj, M., Renneberg, B., . . . Roepke, S. (2013). Gray matter abnormalities in patients with narcissistic personality disorder. *Journal of Psychiatric Research, 47*, 1363–1369.

Simonsen, E., Haahr, U., Mortensen, E. L., Friis, S., Johannessen, J. O., Larsen, T. K., . . . Vaglum, P. (2008). Personality disorders in first episode psychosis. *Personality and Mental Health, 2*, 230–239.

Simonsen, S., & Simonsen, E. (2011). Comorbidity between narcissistic personality disorder and Axis I diagnoses. In W. K. Campbell & J. D. Miller (Eds.), *The handbook of narcissism and narcissistic personality disorder: Theoretical approaches, empirical findings, and treatments* (pp. 239–247). Wiley.

Skodol, A. E. (2012). Personality disorders in *DSM-5. Annual Review of Clinical Psychology, 8*, 317–344.

Skodol, A. E., Bender, D. S., Morey, L. C., Clark, L. A., Oldham, J. M., Alarcon, R. D., Krueger, R. F., Verheul, R., Bell, C. C., & Siever, L. J. (2011). Personality disorder types proposed for *DSM-5. Journal of Personality Disorders, 25*, 136–169.

Stinson, F. S., Dawson, D. A., Goldstein, R. B., Chou, S. P., Huang, B., Smith, S. M, . . . Grant, B. F. (2008). Prevalence, correlates, disability, and comorbidity of *DSM-IV* narcissistic personality disorder: Results from the Wave 2 National Epidemiologic Survey on Alcohol and Related Conditions. *Journal of Clinical Psychiatry, 69*, 1033–1045.

Stone, M. H. (1998). Normal narcissism: An etiological and ethological perspective. In E. Ronningstam (Ed.), *Disorders of narcissism: Diagnostic, clinical, and empirical implications* (pp. 7–28). American Psychiatric Publishing.

Torgersen, S., Kringlen, E., & Cramer, V. (2001). The prevalence of personality disorders in a community sample. *Archives of General Psychiatry, 58,* 590–596.

Tritt, S. M., Ryder, A. G., Ring, A. J., & Pincus, A. L. (2010). Pathological narcissism and the depressive temperament. *Journal of Affective Disorders. 122,* 280–284.

Twenge, J. M., & Campbell, W. K. (2003). "Isn't it fun to get the respect we're going to deserve?" Narcissism, social rejection, and aggression. *Personality and Social Psychology Bulletin, 29,* 261–272.

Tyrer, P., Mulder, R., Kim, Y. R., & Crawford, M. J. (2019). The development of the ICD-11 classification of personality disorders: An amalgam of science, pragmatism, and politics. *Annual Review of Clinical Psychology, 15,* 481–502.

Vater, A., Ritter, K., Schröder-Abé, M., Schutz, A., Lammers, C. H., Bosson, J. K., & Roepke, S. (2013). When grandiosity and vulnerability collide: Implicit and explicit self-esteem in patients with narcissistic personality disorder. *Journal of Behavior Therapy and Experimental Psychiatry, 44,* 37–47.

Vater, A., Schröder-Abé, M., Ritter, K., Renneberg, B., Schulze, L., Bosson, J. K., & Roepke, S. (2013). The Narcissistic Personality Inventory: A useful tool for assessing pathological narcissism? Evidence from patients with narcissistic personality disorder. *Journal of Personality Assessment, 95,* 301–308.

Vater, A., Ritter, K., Strunz, S., Ronningstam, E. F., Renneberg, B., & Roepke, S. (2014). Stability of narcissistic personality disorder: Tracking categorical and dimensional rating systems over a two-year period. *Personality Disorders: Theory, Research, and Treatment, 5,* 305–313.

Weinberg, I., & Ronningstam, E. (2020). Dos and don'ts in treatments of patients with narcissistic personality disorder. *Journal of Personality Disorders, 34*(Suppl), 122–142.

Welker, L. E., Simons, R. M., & Simons, J. S. (2019). Grandiose and vulnerable narcissism: Associations with alcohol use, alcohol problems and problem recognition. *Journal of American College Health, 67,* 226–234.

Westen, D. (1997). Divergences between clinical and research methods for assessing personality disorders: Implications for research and the evolution of Axis II. *American Journal of Psychiatry, 154,* 895–903.

Widiger, T. A. (2011). The comorbidity of narcissistic personality disorder with other *DSM-IV* personality disorders. In W. K. Campbell & J. D. Miller (Eds.), *Handbook of narcissism and narcissistic personality disorder: Theoretical approaches, empirical findings, and treatment* (pp. 248–260). Wiley.

Widiger, T. A., & Costa Jr, P. T. (2013). *Personality disorders and the five-factor model of personality.* American Psychological Association.

Widman, L., & McNulty, J. K. (2010). Sexual narcissism and the perpetration of sexual aggression. *Archives of Sexual Behavior, 39,* 926–939.

World Health Organization. (2018). *International classification of diseases for mortality and morbidity statistics, 11th Revision.* Retrieved from https://icd.who.int/browse11/l-m/en.

Wright, A. G., C., & Kaurin, A. (2020). Integrating structure and function in conceptualizing and assessing pathological traits. *Psychopathology, 53,* 189–197.

Wright, A. G. C., Lukowitsky, M. R., Pincus, A. L., & Conroy, D. E. (2010). The higher-order factor structure and gender invariance of the pathological narcissism inventory. *Assessment, 17,* 467–483.

Wright, A. G. C., Stepp, S. D., Scott, L. N., Hallquist, M. N., Beeney, J. E., Lazarus, S. A., & Pilkonis, P. A. (2017). The effect of pathological narcissism on interpersonal and affective processes in social interactions. *Journal of Abnormal Psychology, 126,* 898–910.

Zeigler-Hill, V., & Besser, A. (2013). A glimpse behind the mask: Facets of narcissism and feelings of self-worth. *Journal of Personality Assessment, 95,* 249–260.

Zeigler-Hill, V., Enjaian, B., & Essa, L. (2013). The role of narcissistic personality features in sexual aggression. *Journal of Social and Clinical Psychology, 32,* 186–199.

Zimmerman, M., Rothschild, L., & Chelminski, I. (2005). The prevalence of *DSM-IV* personality disorders in psychiatric outpatients. *American Journal of Psychiatry, 162,* 1911–1918.

# CHAPTER 28

# Borderline Personality Disorder: Contemporary Approaches to Conceptualization and Etiology

Timothy J. Trull *and* Johanna Hepp

## Historical Overview

Borderline personality disorder (BPD) is a severe mental disorder associated with extreme emotional, behavioral, and interpersonal dysfunction (*DSM-5*). For historical context, Gunderson (2009) reviewed the ontogeny of the BPD diagnosis. Most scholars credit Adolph Stern (1938) and Robert Knight (1953) for introducing the term *borderline* to the psychiatric nomenclature to designate a condition that was believed to share a boundary with schizophrenia but was seen as more temporary and more likely to occur in the context of unstructured clinical situations. Later, Otto Kernberg's (1967) designation of "borderline personality organization" was applied to a group of patients who, on the one hand, showed features of psychotic personality organization (e.g., primitive defenses, fragmented sense of self) but, on the other hand, showed reality testing that was generally intact. As for the earliest empirical approach to the definition and characterization of borderline personality, Roy Grinker is credited with providing discriminating features of four subtypes of borderline personality and identifying four common features of the "borderline syndrome": anger, impaired intimate relationships, identity problems, and depressive loneliness (Grinker et al., 1968). These contributions, as well as that by John Gunderson in further delimiting borderline personality from other psychiatric conditions, have served as the basis for what we now know to be the BPD diagnosis (e.g., Gunderson et al., 2018; Gunderson & Singer, 1975).

Following the introduction of the formal BPD diagnosis in *DSM-III* in 1980, debates about the boundaries of BPD continued. For example, instead of schizophrenia, critics argued that BPD was a variant of affective disorder (especially depression or bipolar disorder; Akiskal, 1981) or of posttraumatic stress disorder (PTSD; Herman, 1992). Complicating the debates and investigations into these boundary issues was the fact that BPD frequently co-occurred with mood disorders, PTSD, and other disorders characterized by emotional dysregulation and impulsivity. In addition, among more biologically oriented researchers, no specific biological etiology (e.g., a biomarker) was found that would distinguish BPD from other disorders. However, despite these questions, the validity of the BPD diagnosis is well-recognized by the general psychiatric and psychological communities. The diagnosis itself remains one of the most prevalent diagnoses in mental health settings, it continues to be associated with great impairment and increased mortality, and BPD is increasingly recognized as a major public health problem.

| Abbreviations | |
|---|---|
| AA | Ambulatory assessment |
| ACC | Anterior cingulate cortex |
| ASPD | Antisocial personality disorder |
| BPD | Borderline personality disorder |
| CpG | Cytosine-phosphate-guanine |
| DLPFC | Dorsolateral prefrontal cortex |
| MAO | Monoamine oxidase |
| NESARC | National Epidemiologic Survey on Alcohol and Related Conditions |
| PAI-BOR | Personality Assessment Inventory–Borderline Scale |

## Clinical Description

Since the publication of *DSM-III* in 1980, the diagnostic criteria for BPD have remained relatively consistent, with the one exception being the addition in *DSM-IV* of a criterion for temporary, stress-dependent, quasi-psychotic experiences. Individuals with BPD have a maladaptive personality style that is present in a variety of contexts, emerges by early adulthood, and leads to distinct patterns of dysfunction in behavior and relationships (*DSM-IV-TR* and *DSM-5*). Those diagnosed with BPD frequently experience intense and unstable negative emotions that are easily triggered and that take a long time to recover from. One emotion that those with BPD are particularly prone to experience is intense anger that is difficult to control and often results in outbursts with verbal or physical aggression. At the same time, many individuals with BPD also experience feelings of aversive inner emptiness. Beyond these affect-related criteria, there are two criteria related to interpersonal relationships. Individuals with BPD tend to have unstable relationships and show a pattern of idealizing and devaluing others. When confronted with real or imagined abandonment by a close other, they may engage in frantic actions to avoid being abandoned. In addition to this instability in their concept of and behavior toward others, BPD individuals are also unsure of their self-image. At the behavioral level, they are prone to suicidal threats, gestures, or attempts and impulsive, potentially harmful behaviors, such as risky sexual behavior or substance use. Stressful situations may invoke transient paranoid ideation or dissociation. Associated features include a propensity for engaging in self-defeating behavior (e.g., making a bad decision that destroys a good relationship), high rates of mood or substance use disorders, and premature death from suicide. Concerning the latter, it is estimated that approximately 3–10% of individuals with BPD will have committed suicide by the age of 30 (Gunderson, 2001).

Box 28.1 presents the nine individual criteria for BPD as defined by both *DSM-IV-TR* and *DSM-5*, in Section II. To receive a BPD diagnosis, at least five of the nine criteria must be present, and the symptoms must result in significant distress or impairment. A calculation of unique combinations of five or more items from nine total items reveals that there are 256 possible ways to meet *DSM-IV-TR* and *DSM-5* criteria for BPD! In the case of BPD, this heterogeneity in diagnosis has been recognized for some time and has proved challenging for both etiological and treatment research.

> **Box 28.1** Nine *DSM-IV* and *DSM-5* criteria for borderline personality disorder
>
> - Extreme attempts to avoid real or imagined abandonment
> - Intense and unstable interpersonal relationships
> - Lack of a sense of self, or unstable self-image
> - Impulsivity that is potentially self-damaging (e.g., excessive spending, substance abuse, binge eating)
> - Recurrent suicidal behavior (i.e., threats, gestures) or self-mutilating behavior
> - Chronic feeling of emptiness
> - Anger control problems
> - Dissociation (e.g., depersonalization or derealization) or paranoid thoughts that occur in response to stress

## Epidemiology

BPD affects 1–3% of the general population, and it is the most common personality disorder (PD) in clinical settings. It represents 10% of the patients in outpatient settings, 15–20% of the patients in inpatients settings, and 30–60% of the patients diagnosed with PDs (Gunderson, 2001; Lenzenweger et al., 2007; Paris, 2009; Tomko et al., 2014; Trull et al., 2010; Widiger & Trull, 1993; Widiger & Weissman, 1991). It is believed that significantly more women than men meet the criteria for BPD, but this belief is based primarily on clinical studies. It is important to distinguish BPD symptoms, which are more chronic and pervasive, from emotional and impulsive behaviors that may be exhibited for short periods of time in adolescence. Studies that have followed children and adolescents who initially received a BPD diagnosis typically find that only a small percentage retain a BPD diagnosis years later. This finding raises the possibility that BPD may be overdiagnosed in children and adolescents, and a more conservative approach to diagnosis in this age group is necessary.

Although BPD has been studied extensively in clinical and treatment samples, less is known about demographic features associated with BPD in the general population. One source of information on this is the National Epidemiologic Survey on Alcohol and Related Conditions (NESARC). The NESARC is a nationally representative, face-to-face survey that evaluated mental health in the civilian, non-institutionalized (i.e., hospitals, prisons) population of the United States. BPD symptoms were assessed in wave 2 of this survey (2004–2005). Initial reports from NESARC indicated very high prevalence rates for the PDs (Grant, Stinson et al., 2004). However, these estimates were likely inflated because the original NESARC investigators only required the endorsement of extreme distress, impairment, or dysfunction for one (but not all) of the requisite endorsed PD items in order for a diagnosis to be assigned (Grant, Hasin et al., 2004; Trull et al., 2010). Trull et al. (2010) presented an alternative method for diagnosing PDs from the NESARC data, which resulted in prevalence rates much more in line with those from other, recent epidemiological studies.

A reanalysis of the BPD NESARC data (Tomko et al., 2014), taking into account distress and impairment for each requisite symptom, resulted in a weighted prevalence rate for BPD overall of 2.7% (instead of the original estimate of 5.9%; Grant et al., 2008a). The rate was also only slightly higher among women than among men (3.0% and 2.4%, respectively) (see Table 28.1). Elevated risk for BPD was suggested for individuals with a family income of less than $20,000 per year (4.8%), people younger than 30 (4.3%), and individuals who are separated, divorced, or widowed (4.5%). Racial and ethnic differences were evident, with Native Americans (5.0%) and Blacks (3.5%) reporting higher rates of the disorder, on average, than Whites (2.7%) or Hispanics (2.5%), and Asian Americans having a significantly lower rate (1.2%). Individuals with less than a high school education also showed slightly elevated rates of BPD (3.3%) compared to those with at least a high school degree. Urban and rural respondents showed similar rates of the disorder. Regional differences were also minimal, and there were no significant region × sex differences. A recent analysis of data from the third wave of NESARC further demonstrated that lifetime prevalence of BPD is approximately twice as high in gay or lesbian individuals compared to heterosexual individuals (odds ratio [OR] = 1.9) and more than three times higher in bisexual than in heterosexual individuals (OR = 3.6) (Kerridge et al., 2017). Estimates of BPD prevalence for transgender individuals vary substantially between studies and may be affected by inaccurate assessment of the identity diffusion criterion (for an overview of prevalence estimates and a discussion how to distinguish gender minority stress and BPD, see Goldhammer

Table 28.1 Lifetime prevalence of *DSM-IV* borderline personality disorder and sociodemographic characteristics by sex

| Characteristic | Total % | Men % | Women % |
|---|---|---|---|
| **Total** | 2.7 | | |
| **Sex** | | | |
| Men | 2.4 | | |
| Women | 3.0 | | |
| **Age** | | | |
| 20–29 years | 4.3 | 3.8 | 4.8 |
| 30–44 years | 3.4 | 2.6 | 4.3 |
| 45–64 years | 2.6 | 2.5 | 2.7 |
| 65 and up | 0.6 | 0.7 | 0.5 |
| **Race-ethnicity** | | | |
| White | 2.7 | 2.3 | 3.1 |
| Black | 3.5 | 3.2 | 3.7 |
| Native American | 5.0 | 5.2 | 4.8 |
| Asian | 1.2 | 1.7 | 0.7 |
| Hispanic | 2.5 | 2.4 | 2.5 |
| **Family income** | | | |
| <$20,000 | 4.8 | 5.4 | 4.4 |
| $20,000–$34,999 | 3.1 | 2.7 | 3.4 |
| $35,000–$69,999 | 2.5 | 2.1 | 2.8 |
| ≥$70,000 | 1.4 | 1.1 | 1.8 |
| **Marital Status** | | | |
| Married/cohabiting | 1.9 | 1.5 | 2.4 |
| Separated/divorced/widowed | 4.5 | 5.9 | 3.8 |
| Never married | 3.8 | 3.5 | 4.2 |
| **Education** | | | |
| Less than high school | 3.3 | 3.3 | 3.4 |
| High school | 3.1 | 2.7 | 3.4 |
| Some college or higher | 2.4 | 2.1 | 2.7 |

et al., 2019). Reliable data from large-scale cross-sectional or cohort studies on the BPD prevalence in this population is currently lacking.

## Comorbidity

BPD is frequently comorbid with a range of *DSM-5* disorders, including other PDs. Overall, this comorbidity appears to be associated with poorer outcome (Skodol, Gunderson, McGlashan et al., 2002).

## Comorbidity with Anxiety, Mood, and Substance Use Disorders

BPD is highly comorbid with a number of psychological disorders in both clinical and community samples (Coid et al., 2006; Lenzenweger et al., 2007; Skodol, Gunderson, Pfohl et al., 2002). Unlike many conditions, BPD has commonalities with *both* internalizing and externalizing disorders (e.g., Eaton et al., 2011). Concerning internalizing disorders, features of BPD such as affective instability, emptiness, and interpersonal difficulties may be driving the high rates of comorbidity between BPD and mood or anxiety disorders. Concerning externalizing disorders, previous research has established a strong link between BPD and substance use disorders (SUDs) (e.g., Sher & Trull, 2002; Trull et al., 2000). To the extent that BPD is associated with impulse control disorders, we might expect that BPD also shares genetic risk with both antisocial PD (ASPD) and SUDs and falls on an externalizing factor of psychopathology. However, BPD is not generally considered to be solely an externalizing disorder (Eaton et al., 2011). Thus, the BPD-SUD co-occurrence may be explained by a combination of impulsivity and negative emotionality (Sher & Trull, 2002; Trull et al., 2018; Trull et al., 2000).

High rates of comorbidity are the rule not the exception in clinical samples. Therefore, it is also of interest to investigate BPD comorbidity rates in the general population. Referring again to the NESARC study of the general US population, Table 28.2 presents the odds ratios for the association between BPD and a range of other psychiatric disorders (Tomko et al., 2014). BPD is significantly associated with almost every diagnosis, including all forms of anxiety, mood, and substance use disorder.

## Comorbidity with Other Personality Disorders

In addition to extensive comorbidity with anxiety, mood, and substance use disorders, BPD is highly comorbid with other PDs (Cohen et al., 2007; Lenzenweger et al., 2007; McGlashan et al., 2000). For example, Lenzenweger et al. (2007) found BPD to have an average correlation of .56 with Cluster A PDs (paranoid, schizotypal, and schizoid) and .55 with Cluster C PDs (avoidant, dependent, and obsessive compulsive). Although there were no instances of histrionic or narcissistic PD in this sample, the correlation with the remaining Cluster B PD, ASPD, was the highest at .64.

Trull et al. (2012) evaluated results from four large studies (at least 200 participants) that used structured diagnostic interviews to establish *DSM-IV-TR* PD diagnoses. This included comorbidity data from two major epidemiological studies, the NESARC and the National Comorbidity Survey Replication (NCS-R), as well as large clinical investigations of PD comorbidity. Despite different methods and sampling strategies, it is clear that a BPD diagnosis is significantly associated with the full range of other PDs but especially the other Cluster B diagnoses of antisocial, narcissistic, and histrionic PD (Trull et al., 2012). However, the comorbidity patterns in this study did vary to some degree depending on the sample. Thus, proclamations about specific BPD-other PDs comorbidity patterns should be offered with some caveats; these patterns do seem to be sample-specific.

## Somatic Illness Comorbidity

Data from the second wave of NESARC and other large-scale, representative samples found that BPD is associated with substantial overall physical disability (Fok et al., 2014; Grant et al., 2008b). Looking more closely at the types of somatic illnesses those with BPD tend to suffer from reveals a wide range of syndromes and chronic conditions. Some of the most prominent ones include strongly elevated rates of chronic pain and cardiovascular and gastrointestinal disease (e.g., Heath et al., 2017; Sansone & Sansone, 2012). Beyond cross-sectional studies that have established the co-occurrence BPD and somatic illnesses, some studies have also demonstrated that BPD increases the prospective risk of several somatic illness. For instance, Chen et al. (2017) assessed 5,969 BPD patients and 23,876 age- and sex-matched control participants in Taiwan and found that a BPD diagnosis at onset predicted stroke probability several years later. In addition to these major conditions, daily life studies suggest that individuals with BPD frequently experience minor health problems such as headaches, nausea, or general pain in their day-to-day lives (Carpenter et al., 2019; Hepp, Lane et al., 2020). For instance, Hepp, Lane et al. (2020) found that BPD participants reported an average of two health problems per measurement across a 4-week period (with 6 daily measurements).

The marked somatic illness comorbidity of those with BPD contributes to increased morbidity, healthcare usage, and associated primary and secondary cost of illness for this patient group (Frankenburg & Zanarini, 2004). The added

**Table 28.2** Odds ratios for lifetime borderline personality disorder and other lifetime psychiatric disorders associations

| Psychiatric disorder | Total OR (99% CI) | Men OR (99% CI) | Women OR (99% CI) |
|---|---|---|---|
| **Any substance use disorder** | 4.50 (3.57– 5.71) | 4.42 (2.80– 6.99) | 5.41 (4.10– 7.14) |
| Substance abuse | 0.58 (0.42– 0.81) | 0.46 (0.28– 0.75) | 0.83 (0.53– 1.30) |
| Substance dependence | 5.29 (4.27– 6.54) | 5.21 (3.62– 7.52) | 5.92 (4.55– 7.69) |
| **Any alcohol use disorder** | 3.36 (2.73– 4.12) | 4.29 (2.90– 6.33) | 3.80 (2.93– 4.93) |
| Alcohol abuse* | 0.77 (0.59– 1.01) | 0.60 (0.41– 0.89) | 1.14 (0.78– 1.65) |
| Alcohol dependence | 5.38 (4.37– 6.58) | 6.25 (4.52– 8.62) | 5.92 (4.46– 7.81) |
| Nicotine dependence | 4.07 (3.32– 4.98) | 3.75 (2.71–5.18) | 4.57 (3.51– 5.92) |
| **Any drug use disorder** | 5.78 (4.67– 7.14) | 6.06 (4.39– 8.33) | 6.54 (4.90– 8.77) |
| Drug abuse | 2.63 (2.03– 3.41) | 2.55 (1.76– 3.70) | 3.08 (2.14– 4.42) |
| Drug dependence | 10.10 (7.69–13.33) | 9.52 (6.41–14.08) | 12.20 (8.26–17.86) |
| **Any mood episode** | 14.93 (11.63–19.61) | 13.51 (9.35–19.61) | 17.54 (12.20–25.64) |
| Major depressive episode | 11.76 (9.35–14.93) | 11.36 (8.13–15.87) | 13.16 (9.52–17.86) |
| Dysthymia | 8.33 (6.62–10.53) | 7.25 (4.76–10.99) | 8.85 (6.67–11.76) |
| Manic episode | 16.39 (13.33–20.41) | 16.95 (11.90–24.39) | 16.13 (12.20–21.28) |
| Hypomanic episode | 3.70 (2.71– 5.05) | 2.62 (1.49– 4.63) | 4.69 (3.22– 6.80) |
| **Any anxiety disorder** | | | |
| Panic disorder with agoraphobia | 14.29 (10.87–18.87) | 15.15 (10.20–22.22) | 14.71 (10.00–21.72) |
| Panic disorder without agoraphobia* | 13.89 (10.20–18.87) | 13.33 (7.19–25.00) | 13.70 (9.71–19.61) |
| | 5.29 (4.12– 6.85) | 7.52 (4.88–11.49) | 4.22 (3.09– 5.78) |
| Social phobia | 9.17 (7.41–11.49) | 7.87 (5.49–11.24) | 10.10 (7.63–13.33) |
| Specific phobia | 5.03 (4.08– 6.17) | 5.08 (3.61– 7.09) | 5.03 (3.86– 6.49) |
| Generalized anxiety disorder | 11.11 (9.01–13.70) | 11.36 (8.00–16.39) | 11.11 (8.55–14.49) |
| Posttraumatic stress disorder | 10.42 (8.47–12.82) | 11.76 (8.40–16.67) | 10.00 (7.63–12.99) |
| **Any other personality disorder** | 15.87 (12.82–19.61) | 14.93 (10.64–20.83) | 18.18 (13.70–23.81) |
| Any Cluster A PD | 20.83 (16.13–27.03) | 21.74 (14.71–33.33) | 20.00 (14.29–27.78) |
| Paranoid | 12.20 (8.93–16.39) | 10.87 (6.49–18.18) | 12.66 (8.70–18.52) |
| Schizoid | 14.29 (8.40–24.39) | 11.90 (5.46–25.64) | 17.24 (8.40–34.48) |
| Schizotypal | 111.11 (66.67–200.00) | 125.00 (55.56–250.00) | 100.00 (50.00–200.00) |
| Any other Cluster B PD | 13.16 (10.42–16.39) | 13.89 (9.80–19.23) | 16.67 (11.90–23.26) |
| Histrionic | 14.49 (6.85–31.25) | 14.29 (4.18–50.00) | 14.93 (5.95–37.04) |
| Narcissistic | 55.56 (40.00–83.33) | 62.50 (40.00–100.00) | 55.56 (33.33–90.91) |
| Antisocial | 6.33 (4.76– 8.40) | 6.33 (4.31– 9.35) | 8.47 (5.46–13.16) |
| Any Cluster C PD | 9.52 (7.19–12.66) | 7.63 (4.72–12.35) | 10.87 (7.63–15.38) |
| Avoidant | 11.63 (7.87–17.24) | 7.81 (3.47–17.54) | 13.70 (8.70–21.74) |
| Dependent | 20.41 (9.71–41.67) | 12.82 (3.03–55.56) | 23.26 (10.20–52.63) |
| Obsessive-compulsive | 7.75 (5.65–10.64) | 6.94 (4.15–11.63) | 8.40 (5.56–12.66) |

*Note:* *Signifies significant gender differences in the odds ratios for this disorder ($p < .01$).

burden of somatic illness is also thought to contribute to the vastly reduced life expectancies for those with BPD, which have been estimated to be as many as 22 years shorter than those for the general population (Chesney et al., 2014).

## General Functioning and Mental Health Treatment Utilization in BPD

Longitudinal studies have provided some provocative findings about the course of BPD, some of which run counter to prevailing notions about the long-term stability of the BPD diagnosis (Morey & Hopwood, 2013). An early investigation of the longitudinal course of BPD was the Collaborative Longitudinal Personality Disorders Study (Gunderson et al., 2000), which includes 175 individuals with a formal BPD diagnosis. At the 10-year follow-up assessment, 85% of those originally diagnosed with BPD no longer met diagnostic criteria for the disorder based on a 12-month definition of remission (Gunderson, Stout et al., 2011). Yet, compared to other diagnostic groups (major depression; Cluster C PDs), the rate of remission for BPD was slower over 10 years. Among those with BPD that did remit, the relapse rate was low (11%) and tended to occur in the first 4 years before leveling off. Data from another long-running study on the course of BPD, the McLean Study for Adult Development, parallel these findings. Zanarini et al. (2010) reported that, over 10 years, 86% of participants attained a sustained remission that lasted for at least 4 years. In a later reassessment of the sample at a 16-year follow-up, they confirmed this, demonstrating high rates of sustained remission (2–8 years), with infrequent relapses (e.g., only 10% among those with an 8-year remission). More recently, Choi-Kain et al. (2020) provide a detailed, up to date review of findings from both studies as well as evidence from two other studies assessing the trajectory of BPD symptoms from childhood to young adulthood. The authors conclude that longitudinal studies underline the fluctuating nature of BPD across the lifespan, the importance of identifying youth at risk and providing early interventions to prevent chronification, and the need to extend existing treatments to target functional improvement in addition to symptom reduction. The latter implication was derived based on participants in both longitudinal studies showing relatively low levels of psychosocial functioning after 10 years, suggesting continuing problems in both social and occupational functioning despite significant symptom remission. Zanarini et al. (2010) indicated that only around a third of individuals who no longer met criteria for a BPD diagnosis after 10 years showed a "total recovery" including good social and vocational functioning. Typical areas of sustained impairment include functioning in social relationships, occupational, and leisure activities (Ansell et al., 2007; Skodol et al., 2005), as well as legal problems and financial difficulties (Coid et al., 2009).

Results from NESARC further indicate that individuals with BPD were significantly more likely to have reported separation or divorce over the preceding 12 months, having significant trouble with one's boss or employer, and having serious problems with neighbors, friends, or relatives (Tomko et al., 2014). Among those endorsing depression or low mood, a BPD diagnosis was also significantly associated with attempted suicide, presence of suicidal ideation, wanting to die, and thinking a lot about one's own death over the previous 3 years. Individuals with BPD also showed significant impairment in functioning on self-reported scales, even after controlling for the presence of other psychiatric disorders, sociodemographic risk factors (e.g., age, ethnicity or race, family income), and medical conditions (where relevant). BPD was a significant predictor of impaired social functioning, role emotional functioning, mental health, bodily pain, poorer general health, and decreased vitality (Tomko et al., 2014).

## Treatment Utilization and Treatment Cost

It is generally believed that those with BPD often seek out (perhaps excessively) health services, including emergency room (ER) services, while in crisis. ER visits for those with BPD are often precipitated by suicidal behavior, self-harm behaviors, or substance overdoses. Individuals with BPD frequent mental health treatment settings more than individuals with mood, anxiety, or other PDs (Ansell et al., 2007). For example, a large epidemiological study in Great Britain estimated that 56.3% of individuals with BPD had sought help from a professional for mental health concerns in the past year (Coid et al., 2009). Hörz et al. (2010) reported on the use of treatment modalities among 290 BPD patients and 72 patients with other PDs followed over a 10-year period. All were originally inpatients and between the ages of 18 and 35. There were five follow-up assessments, separated by 24 months. Overall, the percentage of those in individual therapy, taking regular medication, and being hospitalized decreased significantly over the follow-up period. Comparing those with BPD to those with other PDs, a significantly higher percentage of BPD patients reported taking medications regularly and being hospitalized over the 10-year follow-up period. Furthermore, of those with BPD who terminated outpatient treatment at some point during the follow-up period, 85% of them resumed treatment at a later date. In contrast, rehospitalization was much less frequent and more sporadic. Even in the general population, individuals with BPD report high rates of lifetime mental health treatment utilization (Tomko et al., 2014). For example, in the NESARC study, individuals with BPD were highly likely to seek mental health services at some point in their lifetime, with 74.9% presenting to a physician, therapist, counselor, or other mental health professional for diagnosable mental health concerns. In addition, 63.1% of individuals diagnosed with BPD were prescribed medication for mental health issues.

As a result of these high rates of healthcare usage, the treatment of individuals with BPD accounts for large proportions of mental healthcare costs in countries around the globe (Bohus, 2007; Bourke et al., 2018; Feenstra et al., 2012; Frankenburg & Zanarini, 2004; Salvador-Carulla et al., 2014). For instance, data from Germany suggest that BPD accounts for as much as 25% of the total cost for psychiatric inpatient care per year (Bohus, 2007). Beyond direct health costs (costs directly incurred through primary and emergency care), BPD was also shown to create some of the highest secondary health costs of any mental illness in Germany (Bohus, 2007), the Netherlands (Soeteman et al., 2008; Van Asselt et al., 2007), and Norway (Østby et al., 2014). These include costs resulting from productivity loss and absence from work, disability pensions, and production losses due to premature mortality.

## Etiology

The etiology of BPD has been investigated and debated since the advent of the diagnosis itself. Almost all practitioners now agree that the causes of and contributors to the disorder are multifactorial and complex and comprise both a biological/genetic predisposition and psychosocial factors, such as specific learning histories or early stressors. One of the most prominent models in the field today stems from a cognitive-behavioral tradition and was proposed by Marsha Linehan in 1993. Her *biosocial model* of BPD posits that biological vulnerabilities interact with psychosocial factors in the development of the disorder (Linehan, 1993).

Specifically, she proposes that individuals with BPD have a biological predisposition toward strong affective reactions and emotional sensitivity, which already manifests as a certain child temperament early in life. When this temperament interacts with a family environment in which emotions are invalidated, for instance by parents who do not take the child's emotions seriously or instruct suppression of emotions, the child is at risk for developing BPD. In addition to invalidating the child's emotions, Linehan describes that the family environments of those with BPD often lack adequate models for emotion regulation, thus keeping the child from developing adaptive ways to regulate intense emotions. The other symptoms of BPD (beyond affective instability) are largely seen as resulting from dysregulated states of negative affect.

A second theoretical model of BPD stems from a psychodynamically oriented tradition and has its roots in attachment theory (Bowlby, 1973). The *mentalization-based model* of BPD was proposed by Peter Fonagy and Anthony Bateman (Bateman & Fonagy, 2004, 2010; Fonagy et al., 2003) and posits that disorganized attachment styles are at the root of BPD. A disorganized attachment style can develop because of exposure to psychological trauma or non-contingent parental mirroring of emotions and later lead to affective dysregulation and a negative and incoherent representation of the self and others. The central piece of the model is the assumption that the mediating process between disorganized attachment and the symptoms of BPD is a failure to develop mentalizing capacities. Mentalizing is the ability to correctly infer one's own mental states and processes as well as those of others. This can include, for instance, inferring another person's general beliefs and goals, but also their current cognitive-affective state. Ultimately, unsuccessful mentalizing impedes affect regulation and adaptive interpersonal behavior and promotes the symptoms of BPD.

Relatively recently, a third model of BPD has sparked growing interest. Jeffrey Young proposed a *schematherapeutic model* of BPD, which integrates elements from cognitive behavioral models, object relations, and attachment theories, as well as ideas from Gestalt psychology (e.g., Young et al., 2003). Like the other two models, the schematherapeutic model of BPD places particular emphasis on the family environment. Specifically, it proposes that unstable, depriving, punitive and rejecting, or subjugating family environments contribute to the development of BPD. These environments are thought to lead to the development of negative schemas, in which early adverse experiences and the associated affects, cognitions, and physiological sensations are represented. The model further proposes that, in dealing with the adverse environment, the child develops coping modes that persist later in life but lose their adaptiveness outside of the adverse context and become symptomatic.

Because all theoretical models place a particular emphasis on childhood adversity, studies on the prevalence of adverse events within the BPD population are a central test to etiological models of BPD. A recent meta-analysis (Porter et al., 2020) summarized findings on the association between BPD and adverse childhood experiences and demonstrated that individuals with BPD are approximately 14 times more likely to report adverse childhood experiences than are healthy individuals (based on 42 reviewed studies). The largest effects were observed for emotional abuse (OR = 38.1), followed by emotional neglect (OR = 17.7), physical abuse (OR = 7.1), physical neglect (OR = 6.9), and sexual abuse (OR = 6.0). Compared to other clinical groups, individuals with BPD were approximately 3 times more likely to report adverse childhood experiences (based on 61 studies). This effect replicated when specifically comparing BPD to individuals with mood disorders, psychosis, or other PDs, thus underlining the importance of early environments for the etiology of BPD.

## Genetic Perspectives

Although an increasing amount of attention has been paid to BPD in recent years, its specific etiology and development remain uncertain. Currently, most new work on the etiology of BPD focuses on genetic influences on the expression of the disorder. This is the focus in the remainder of this chapter. As will become clear in the following discussion, a genetic predisposition seems to play a significant role in the development of BPD, but the specific genes responsible for this have not yet been reliably identified.

### Twin Studies

Several studies support the idea that BPD and BPD-related traits are familial, for instance demonstrating that the probability of BPD is 3.9 times higher in first-degree relatives of an individual with BPD than in the general population (e.g., Gunderson, Zanarini et al., 2011). However, family studies cannot disentangle the effects of genes from the effects of environment shared by family members. In contrast, *twin studies* can illuminate the effects of common environment and genes by modeling the different genetic relatedness of monozygotic (MZ) and dizygotic (DZ) twins. Amad et al. (2014) summarized the evidence from 10 twin studies and concluded that the average heritability of BPD ranges around 40% across studies. We highlight some of the studies included in the review that were of particular interest, aiming to provide an overview of heritability estimates from different countries.

Data from Norway were provided by Torgersen et al. (2008), who assessed PD traits in 1,386 Norwegian twin pairs between the ages of 19 and 35 years using a structured PD interview. The prevalence rate for BPD (0.4%) was too low to analyze the data categorically, so a dimensional representation based on subclinical criteria was used to study the degree to which genetic and environmental factors influence PDs. The heritability of BPD was estimated at 35%, with the remaining variance explained by unique environmental factors. Adding to this, Kendler et al. (2011) used structured diagnostic interviews to assess *DSM-IV* BPD criteria in 2,111 twins (669 MZ pairs and 377 DZ pairs) from the Norwegian Institute of Public Health Twin Panel (NIPHTP) to estimate the heritability of BPD liability. Because too few individuals met *DSM-IV* cutoff scores for a BPD diagnosis, the authors analyzed a dimensional count of level of BPD symptoms endorsed. Specifically, a score of "subthreshold" or above was used as a cutoff for the presence of each BPD criterion, and five categories of endorsement were used in the analyses. Results indicated a heritability estimate of .49 for BPD liability, and, in the context of multivariate genetic analyses of a range of Axis I and Axis II disorders, BPD liability was associated with genetic risk for both Axis I and Axis II externalizing disorders as well as with environmental risk for Axis II disorders and Axis I internalizing disorders.

Using a quantitative scale of BPD features Distel, Trull et al. (2008) assessed 5,496 twins (1,852 complete pairs) between the ages of 18 and 86 years from the Netherlands, Belgium, and Australia. Results indicated that genetic influences explained 42% of the variation in BPD features in both men and women. Interestingly, this heritability estimate was equal between the three countries, suggesting no interaction between genotype and country. The MZ correlation was more than twice as high as the DZ correlation in all three countries, indicating that nonadditive genetic effects may explain part of the variation in BPD features.

Finally, in a series of studies using a US sample, Bornovalova and colleagues conducted biometric analyses of questionnaire items judged to be relevant to BPD in 640 twin pairs at age 14 and age 18, as well as 1,382 twin pairs at age 24 (all part of the same longitudinal study). Heritability for BPD traits was estimated to be .25 at age 14, .48 at age 18, and .35 at age 24 (Bornovalova, Hicks et al., 2013; Bornovalova, Huibregtse et al., 2013).

## Twin Family Studies

Twin family studies offer even more extended insight than twin studies because they combine data from twins and other family members. This allows studying several mechanisms that cannot be assessed in twin or family data alone (Boomsma et al., 2002), including cultural transmission of features from parents to offspring, passive G × E correlation or covariance, social homogamy, phenotypic assortment, and social interaction. Concerning the latter, twin methods assume that the social interaction between MZ and DZ twins is approximately equivalent. Twin family studies, because of their extended sampling of family members, can test this assumption.

In a study by Distel, Trull et al. (2008), a maximum likelihood test of variance differences between MZ and DZ twins indicated no differences in variances between MZ and DZ twins and, thus, given the large sample size, did not suggest that social interaction between twin siblings is of significant importance. Distel, Rebollo-Mesa et al. (2009) examined the genetic and environmental influences on individual differences in BPD features using an extended twin-family design. Data were collected on BPD features in twins ($N$ = 5,017), their spouses ($N$ = 939), siblings ($N$ = 1,266), and parents ($N$ = 3,064). Additive and nonadditive genetic effects, individual specific environmental influences, and assortment and cultural transmission were tested. Results indicated that resemblance among biological relatives could be attributed completely to genetic effects. Variation in borderline personality features was explained by additive genetic (21%) and dominant genetic (24%) factors, while environmental influences (55%) explained the remaining variance. *Additive genetic variance* refers to variance attributed to the additive effects of alleles segregating in the population, whereas *dominant genetic variance* refers to that attributed to nonadditive effects such that an allele can mask the effect of another allele at the same locus. In the Distel, Rebollo-Mesa et al. (2009) study, significant resemblance between spouses was observed, best explained by phenotypic assortative mating, but it had only a small effect on the genetic variance (1% of the total variance). There was no effect of cultural transmission from parents to offspring.

*Multivariate twin family studies*, in which more than one phenotype per person is analyzed, can shed light on the genetic and environmental causes of association between traits, comorbidity between disorders, or overlap between traits and disorder. Distel et al. (2010) investigated the extent to which the covariance among four important components of BPD (affective instability, identity problems, negative relationships, and self-harm) could be explained by common genes. The phenotypic correlations among the scales ranged from .21 to .56 and were best explained by a genetic common pathway model in which a single latent factor influenced all four components. Results indicated that a single genetic factor underlies most of the genetic variance in BPD, but each contributing component to BPD was also influenced by specific genetic factors which do not overlap with each other.

Another multivariate twin family study from this group examined the genetic etiology of the relationship between BPD features and the five factor model (FFM) of personality (Distel, Trull et al., 2009). Data were available for 4,403 MZ twins, 4,425 DZ twins, and 1,661 siblings from 6,140 Dutch, Belgian, and Australian families. Heritability estimates for neuroticism, agreeableness, conscientiousness, extraversion, openness to experience, and borderline personality were 43%, 36%, 43%, 47%, 54%, and 45%, respectively. The phenotypic correlations between borderline personality and the FFM personality traits ranged from .06 for openness to experience to .68 for neuroticism. Results from multiple regression analyses revealed that a combination of high neuroticism and low agreeableness best predicted borderline personality. Multivariate genetic analyses showed that the genetic factors that influence individual differences in neuroticism, agreeableness, conscientiousness, and extraversion account for all genetic liability to borderline personality. Unique environmental effects on borderline personality, however, were not completely shared with those for the FFM traits (33% was unique to borderline personality).

Recently, Skoglund et al. (2019) presented data from six different national registers that included 1,851,755 individuals born in Sweden between 1973 and 1993. Of these, 11,665 individuals met criteria for emotionally unstable PDs (F60.3 in

*ICD-10*), which corresponds well to a diagnosis of BPD according to *DSM-IV* or *DSM-5*. Based on linking the data of these individuals with that of their relatives in the same pooled dataset, the authors obtained *hazard ratios*, marking the familial association along the level of genetic relatedness. They observed that hazard ratios decreased with increasing genetic distance. Specifically, they observed a hazard ratio of 11.5 for MZ, 7.4 for DZ twins, 4.7 for siblings, 2.1 for maternal half-siblings, 1.3 for paternal half-siblings, and 1.7 for cousins.

In sum, evidence from twin studies and twin family studies supports the idea that BPD has a substantial genetic component. The heritability of BPD likely ranges around 40%, and variation in BPD features is attributable to both additive and nonadditive effects with a common genetic pathway for the different symptoms of BPD.

*Linkage Studies*

To date, only one linkage study has been conducted to identify the genomic region(s) that may contain the quantitative trait loci (QTLs) that influence the manifestation of BPD features. Distel, Hottenga et al. (2008) conducted a family-based linkage study with 711 sibling pairs with phenotype and genotype data and 561 additional parents with genotype data. BPD features were assessed on a quantitative scale. Evidence for linkage was found on chromosomes 1, 4, 9, and 18. The highest linkage peak was found on chromosome 9p at marker D9S286 with a logarithm of the odds (LOD) score of 3.548 (empirical *P*-value = .0001). Results suggest that these regions may harbor risk variants, but more empirical work is needed to provide greater resolution at these regions.

*Candidate Gene Studies*

Several approaches developed in recent years highlight the promise of transitioning from pure categorical diagnostic approaches of mental disorders to a more continuous, dimensional approach. These include the introduction of the National Institute of Mental Health (NIMH)'s Research Domain Criteria (RDoC) (Insel et al., 2010); the proposal of the Hierarchical Taxonomy of Psychopathology (HiTOP) as a dimensional alternative to categorical nosologies (Kotov et al., 2017); the release of *DSM-5*, which incorporates to some extent a dimensional approach to psychiatric classification; and the revision of the PD diagnosis in *ICD-11*. In contrast to the other dimensional approaches, RDoC (Insel et al., 2010) primarily focuses on the biological and genetic underpinning of dimensions of psychopathology instead of studying heterogeneous phenotypes included in traditional diagnostic classifications. This offers a promising avenue by which to study etiological factors that may be common to a number of diagnostic phenotypes and may inform description, treatment, and prevention. This transition to a more dimensional, endophenotypic perspective has spurred many theorists and researchers to focus on common dimensions of dysfunction that may underlie many existing diagnostic categories, which is particularly relevant to PDs, including BPD (Regier, 2007). The transition has been reinforced by a methodological shift in the study of the genetics of BPD to more emphasis on the identification of endophenotypes related to this disorder (Siever et al., 2002). Although most examinations of BPD's genetic underpinnings have utilized categorical and diagnostic approaches, we now see more studies examining the heritability of individual borderline personality *traits* and not the diagnosis per se, based on the rationale that this approach may improve understanding of component phenotypes (McCloskey et al., 2009; Siever et al., 2002).

Several candidate gene association studies have been conducted for BPD. Their aim is to identify genetic variants associated with risk for BPD, for instance by comparing the frequency of certain alleles between individuals who meet criteria for BPD and a control group. Amad et al. (2014) conducted a meta-analysis on these studies. One group of studies they summarized assesses candidate genes related to the serotonergic system. The search for candidate genes related to serotonergic functioning was initially based on research implicating the serotonergic system in many traits that are central to BPD, such as anger (Giegling et al., 2006), aggression (Bortolato et al., 2013; Siever, 2008), suicidal behavior (Bah et al., 2008; Bortolato et al., 2013; Mann et al., 2009; Zaboli et al., 2006), emotion regulation (Canli et al., 2009), emotional lability (Hoefgen et al., 2005), and impulsivity (Passamonti et al., 2008). Candidate genes related to the serotonin system include, for instance, the tryptophan hydroxylase genes (*TPH1* and *TPH2*). Tryptophan plays a role in the biosynthesis of serotonin (5-HT) and is thus expected to be related to dysfunction of the 5-HT system (Bortolato et al., 2013). Additionally, studies have considered serotonin receptor genes (e.g., *HTR1A, HTR2A*) and the serotonin transporter gene (*5-HTT*). While several of these genes were associated with BPD at the single-study level, none of them was significantly associated with BPD at the meta-analytic level (Amad et al., 2014). Another gene implied in serotonergic functioning that has been studied as a candidate gene for BPD encodes monoamine oxidase-A (*MAOA*), which degrades 5-HTT and dopamine. MAOA is suggested to be involved in BPD because it has been shown to be associated with aggression (Buckholtz & Meyer-Lindenberg, 2008), impulsivity (Manuck et al., 2000), and mood lability (Furlong et al., 1999). Yet, again, no significant associations between the MAOA gene and BPD emerged in the meta-analysis (Amad et al., 2014)

In addition to serotonergic dysfunction, there is some evidence that dopamine dysfunction may be associated with BPD. Dopamine dysfunction is associated with emotional dysregulation, impulsivity, and cognitive-perceptual impairment (Friedel, 2004)—three important dimensions of BPD. Studies have considered the dopamine transporter gene (*DAT1*), the dopamine $D_4$ receptor gene (*DRD4*), the dopamine $D_2$ receptor gene (*DRD2*), and the COMT gene as potential candidate genes for BPD. The COMT gene encodes catechol-O-methyltransferase, which is an enzyme that breaks down dopamine. As with the serotonin-related genes, no significant associations were observed between dopamine-associated candidate genes and BPD at the meta-analytic level (Amad et al., 2014). All other reviewed candidate genes similarly failed to produce substantial associations with BPD in the meta-analysis. The remaining candidate genes included the *BDNF* gene, which encodes the brain-derived neurotrophic factor involved in serotonin regulation; the *SCNA9* gene, which encodes a sodium channel expressed in the hippocampus; the *AVPR1A* gene, which encodes the expression of a vasopressin receptor; and the neurexin 3 gene *NRXN3*.

Thus, there are currently no candidate genes that were shown to be specifically associated with BPD across studies. This lack of consistency in findings could result from multiple factors. For one thing, the total number of available studies is still small, as are the sample sizes in most cases. Further restricting the available evidence base, studies typically only considered one or a small group of candidate genes; therefore the pool of studies that assessed the same candidate is also limited. Additionally, unlike with candidate gene studies in the medical sciences, there is the problem of unreliability in the phenotype. In other words, the assessment of BPD or BPD features itself may be affected by a level of unreliability which introduces additional error variance that other studies, where the phenotype is more directly observable (e.g., eye color), do not suffer from. Therefore, the necessity of recruiting large samples and conducting a careful, standardized assessment of the phenotype BPD becomes even more evident. Adding to this, there is the possibility that the selection of candidate genes has been limited by our restricted biological theory of BPD. Studies that were searching for candidate genes in "obvious places," so to speak (e.g., the serotonin system), may simply have been looking in the wrong place. As outlined in the following section, genome-wide association studies (GWAS) may help identify other likely candidate genes via a more bottom-up driven approach.

## Genome-Wide Association Studies

GWAS are observational studies that rely on genotyping to determine genetic variants in a sample of individuals and assess whether different genetic variants are associated with a certain phenotype, for instance presence or absence of BPD (e.g., Manolio, 2010). GWAS typically focus on identifying single nucleotide polymorphisms (SNPs), which are positions within the genome where a single nucleotide that is common in the majority of the population is substituted for another nucleotide in a small proportion of individuals. GWAS often rely on case-control designs and compare the prevalence of all assessed SNPs between the case and the control group. If one SNP is found to be significantly more common in the case group, it is considered to be associated with the phenotype (e.g., presence of BPD) and qualifies as a possible genetic risk marker. In a next step, researchers typically investigate more closely in which genes the SNPs that differed in their frequency between the case and control group are located and which functions they have. For BPD, so far, there are only two GWAS, underlining a need for additional investigations in the coming years. The two GWAS on BPD also differ in that one of them focused on individuals with a formal BPD diagnosis and one on self-reported BPD features.

Lubke et al. (2014) assessed 8,426 individuals from three Dutch cohorts who self-reported on their BPD features using the Borderline Scale of the Personality Assessment Inventory (PAI-BOR; Morey, 1991). The PAI-BOR comprises 24 items within the four subscales of affective instability, identity problems, negative relationships, and self-harm, which map onto the core symptoms of BPD as proposed in the *DSM*. Genome-wide association analyses revealed seven SNPs as significantly associated with PAI-BOR total scores. Importantly, all of these SNPs were located in the serine incorporator gene (*SERINC5*) on chromosome 5. This gene expresses a protein that is responsible for incorporating serine (a polar, nonessential amino acid) into membrane lipids and is prevalent in myelin in the brain. Adding to this, the authors carried out a reverse regression and tested the association between these seven SNPs and the PAI-BOR total score in participants with low versus high levels of BPD features (via median split). In the low BPD group, none of the SNPs showed an association with the level of BPD features, whereas in the high BPD group, all associations were significant.

In addition to considering the association between these genes and the PAI-BOR total score, the authors also conducted post hoc tests for each of the seven SNPs, separately for each PAI-BOR item. Due to reduced reliability, they generally observed smaller associations than for the total score, but what stood out was that the associations for items from the negative relationships and self-harm scales were largely negligible in contrast to associations observed for items measuring affective instability and identity problems. In addition to assessing genome-wide associations, the authors also estimated heritability of the PAI-BOR total score using genome-wide SNPs. They estimated heritability at 23% (thus substantially smaller than the 40% estimated from twin studies) and again found substantial differences when looking at the individual item level. Particularly, they observed high heritability scores for affective instability items and very low to insignificant estimates for items from the other subscales.

Witt et al. (2017) conducted the only GWAS with a case-control design and diagnosed BPD patients. The sample comprised 998 BPD patients and 1,545 controls. They analyzed a total of 10,736,316 SNPs and tested 17,755 genes. However, and likely at least in part due to the sample size still being small for a GWAS and lacking statistical power, no SNPs reached genome-wide significance. They found no significant association for any individual SNP, but gene-based analysis yielded two significant genes: the gene coding for dihydropyrimidine dehydrogenase on chromosome 1 (*DPYD*) and the gene coding for Plakophilin-4 on chromosome 2 (*PKP4*). Moreover, gene-set analysis revealed exocytosis as a significant gene set. The authors discuss that because all three (*DPYD, PKP4,* and exocytosis) were previously linked to bipolar disorder and schizophrenia in other studies, there may be genetic overlap between BPD, bipolar disorder, and schizophrenia. Using LD-score regression, the authors tested this in their dataset and found significant genetic correlations between BPD, and bipolar disorder, schizophrenia, and major depressive disorder.

Although GWAS have opened exciting new pathways to studying the genetics of BPD, much larger samples will be needed to reliably identify SNPs that are specifically associated with the disorder (or features of it) in the future. A further investigation into the genes where these SNPs are located and their functions holds the promise of better understanding the biological basis for BPD and ultimately developing treatments more targeted to the biological mechanisms underlying the disorder.

*Epigenetic Studies*

Epigenetic studies on BPD focus on DNA methylation or, more precisely, the methylation of *CpG sites*. CpG sites are sections in the single-strand DNA sequence where cytosine (C) is directly followed by guanine (G) and connected by phosphate (p). DNA methylation both a natural part of development, ensuring mitosis-persistent cell differentiation, but it can also occur as a result of environmental influences (Robertson, 2005). Therefore, the vast majority of CpG sites in the human DNA is already methylated, which means that cytosine has been converted to 5-methylcytosine through the enzyme DNA methyltransferase. Yet, there are certain "islands" in the DNA sequence, specifically in the promoter regions of genes, where GC is particularly rich but that are unmethylated. Epigenetic studies focus on the methylation level of these CpG islands, assuming a negative association between methylation level and transcriptional activity of the gene. In other words, methylation of CpG sites in gene promoter regions tends to be associated with gene silencing, and environmental factors, such as early trauma, are theorized to cause increased methylation (Klengel et al., 2014; Robertson, 2005).

Most of the available epigenetic literature for BPD was systematically reviewed by Gescher et al. (2018). Their review includes nine studies that focused on methylation in genes that were previously considered candidates for BPD. We highlight some of the findings from the review and summarize evidence from studies published more recently. The largest body of evidence is available for methylation of the promoter region of the glucocorticoid receptor gene (*NR3C1*). This gene has been a study focus because alterations in its expression could help explain hypothalamic-pituitary-adrenal (HPA) axis dysregulation and dysregulated stress responses that were observed for BPD (Drews et al., 2019).

Increased methylation of *NR3C1* in individuals with BPD was observed in three studies (Dammann et al., 2011; Martín-Blanco et al., 2014; Perroud et al., 2011). Martín-Blanco and colleagues (2014) additionally demonstrated that *NR3C1* methylation was associated with higher BPD severity and a higher number of hospitalizations. Contrasting this, two other studies found no association between *NR3C1* methylation level and BPD. Prados et al. (2015) conducted a whole-genome methylation scan in 96 individuals with BPD and childhood maltreatment and 93 individuals with major depressive disorder. They found no significant associations between BPD severity and methylation sites within or near NR3C1, though this could be a result of limited statistical power due to their non-deductive approach. Likewise, Moser et al. (2020), found no difference in NR3C1 methylation levels between a group of 45 BPD patients and 45 matched HCs.

Two additional studies assessed whether methylation of candidate genes was affected by treatment for DBT and, thus, whether methylation level could serve as a marker for treatment outcome. One of these studies assessed methylation of the promoter region of the brain-derived neurotrophic factor gene (*BDNF* gene) pre- and post-treatment (Perroud et al., 2013). Specifically, the authors assessed *BDNF* methylation in 115 BPD individuals before and after a 4-week intensive DBT intervention. They observed increased methylation levels post-treatment in a group they categorized as nonresponders to DBT and decreased levels of methylation in responders. In a later investigation within the same sample, the authors investigated methylation of the serotonin receptor 3A gene (*5HTR3A*). They found increased methylation levels in BPD compared to individuals with attention deficit hyperactivity disorder (ADHD) or bipolar disorder (Perroud et al., 2016). The second study that assessed potential treatment effects on methylation levels focused on genes that were associated with BPD in a previous, genome-wide methylation analysis (Teschler et al., 2013). This study assessed genome-wide methylation in a very small sample of 24 women with BPD and 11 healthy controls and observed different levels of methylation between the groups for a range of genes, including *APBA3, MCF2,* and *NINJ2*. Knoblich et al. (2018) then assessed whether methylation levels of these genes differed between 44 individuals with BPD and 44 matched healthy control participants. They observed no differences between the groups at baseline and following 12 weeks of DBT.

Both studies (Knoblich et al., 2018; Teschler et al., 2013) are significantly limited by their small sample size and therefore the results need to be interpreted with caution. At the same time, they illustrate an approach that may be useful for future genetics research in BPD. Genome-wide studies (both GWAS and genome-wide methylation studies) could help identify new candidate genes for BPD in a bottom-up, data-driven approach. Further studies could then follow up on these candidates by assessing clinical and biological correlates and ultimately help inform our theory of BPD. Importantly, particularly genome-wide studies require very large samples (even the 8,426 individuals assessed by Lubke et al., 2014, constitute a small sample for GWAS) that likely demand increased cooperation between laboratories and collaborative recruitment. Likewise, studies following up on the candidates identified in genome-wide studies should pay careful attention to sufficiently power their studies. In that respect, studies should consider moving away from a case-control approach and take into account the dimensional nature of BPD by assessing BPD symptoms and their association with methylation levels in a continuous way.

### Summary of Genetically Informative Studies of BPD

Existing twin data make a strong case for the heritability of the BPD phenotype, suggesting a heritability that ranges around 40%. However, to date, the results of candidate gene studies have been somewhat inconsistent, and few replications of specific polymorphisms and BPD phenotypes have been reported. These inconsistencies are likely due to multiple factors but especially to very small sample sizes and to great variation in the nature of the target samples (e.g., psychiatric patients vs. general population, patients with comorbid conditions) and the control samples (e.g., clinical controls, healthy controls). Therefore, the task for the next generation of studies is to conduct larger-scale molecular genetic investigations or form major collaborations in order to obtain large pools of genetic data that will provide enough statistical power to detect what are likely to be small effects of genes on the BPD phenotype. However, the success of such investigations will be contingent not only on assessing extremely large numbers of participants to provide adequate statistical power but also on identifying and using reliable measures of the phenotype. In particular, it can be questioned whether adopting the *DSM-IV-TR* and *DSM-5* definition of the phenotype and using the resulting categorical diagnosis will be optimal (because there are 256 ways to obtain a BPD diagnosis). We now turn to a discussion of the evidence supporting different conceptualizations of the BPD phenotype, some of which are not tethered to the *DSM-IV* and current *DSM-5* Section II BPD definition.

## Personality Traits and BPD

Up to this point, our discussion has focused on studies that have largely adopted the *DSM-IV-TR* and *DSM-5* definition of BPD. However, there is reason to question whether the nine *DSM* BPD criteria are necessarily the best way to conceptualize the BPD phenotype. In particular, much is known about the universality and genetic and biological bases of major personality traits, and there is a clear conceptual and empirical connection between major personality traits and PDs (Widiger & Trull, 2007). Indeed, over the past 20 years, researchers have examined the correspondence between major personality traits and both symptoms and diagnoses of the *DSM* PDs (Trull & Widiger, 2008; Widiger & Trull, 2007). By far, the personality model that has received the most attention is the five-factor model (FFM) of personality (Costa & McCrae, 1992). The five broad FFM domains include Neuroticism (versus emotional stability), Extraversion (or surgency), Agreeableness (versus antagonism), Conscientiousness (or constraint), and Openness (or intellect, imagination, or unconventionality).

A description of each of the 10 *DSM-IV* PDs in terms of the 30 facets of the FFM was developed by Lynam and Widiger (2001) on the basis of a survey of PD researchers; these descriptions were then replicated by Samuel and Widiger (2004) in a subsequent survey of clinicians. The FFM description of BPD (Lynam & Widiger, 2001; see Box 28.2) includes high levels of Neuroticism (high anxiousness, angry hostility, depressiveness, impulsiveness, and vulnerability), high levels of Openness (high openness to feelings and to actions), low levels of Agreeableness (low compliance), and low levels of Conscientiousness (low deliberation).

Lynam and Widiger's (2001) FFM account of BPD has received empirical support at both the domain and facet levels (Samuel & Widiger, 2008; Saulsman & Page, 2004). For example, a meta-analysis of 16 empirical articles that examined the relations between FFM traits and BPD indicated a moderate, positive correlation between Neuroticism scores and BPD (.54), and negative correlations with Agreeableness (-.24) and Conscientious (-.29) scores, respectively (Samuel & Widiger, 2008). In addition, BPD was positively related to all Neuroticism facet scores (i.e., anxiousness, angry hostility, depressiveness, self-consciousness, impulsiveness, and vulnerability) and negatively related to a range of Extraversion, Agreeableness, and Conscientiousness scores (i.e., warmth, positive emotions, trust, straightforwardness, compliance, competence, dutifulness, self-discipline, and deliberation). In general, these findings corresponded highly with predictions based on BPD pathology and personality styles (e.g., Lynam & Widiger, 2001; Widiger et al., 2002). Other more recent studies have also supported these FFM trait predictions for BPD diagnosis and features (Bagby et al., 2008; Davenport et al., 2010).

---

**Box 28.2** Five-factor model of personality-borderline personality disorder (FFM-BPD) traits and *DSM-5* Section III borderline personality disorder elevated personality traits

### FFM-BPD traits[a]

Neuroticism: anxiousness; angry hostility; depressiveness; impulsiveness; vulnerability
Agreeableness: low compliance
Conscientiousness: low deliberation
Openness: feelings; actions

### DSM-5 borderline traits

Negative Emotionality: emotional lability; separation insecurity; anxiousness; depressivity
Antagonism: hostility
Disinhibition: impulsivity; risk taking

*Note:* [a]FFM-BPD predicted relations based on Lynam and Widiger (2001). Note that the FFM is a model. There are many measures available to assess the FFM traits in this particular model. We use the facet names of the NEO-PI-R (Costa & McCrae, 1992).

---

## Major Dimensions of Psychopathology Underlying BPD

Another approach to defining and understanding BPD is to focus on major dimensions of psychopathology that underlie the construct. Although this approach overlaps to some extent with a personality trait description of BPD, identifying major dimensions of psychopathology that presumably have biological underpinnings is perhaps more directly relevant to the NIMH's RDoC approach to psychopathology research (Sanislow et al., 2010). In this spirit, we can review and discuss what many believe to be the three major dimensions of psychopathology that account for the symptoms of BPD: *emotional dysregulation, impulsivity,* and *interpersonal hypersensitivity*. Although there is some debate over the predominance of one or two of these over the other(s) (as well as the names of these dimensions), most researchers agree that these three dimensions capture the essence of the disorder.

### Emotional Dysregulation

Emotional dysregulation is a core and perhaps the central feature of BPD (Linehan, 1993). Despite the prevalent use of the term, there is much confusion about the construct, and it seems best to conceptualize emotional dysregulation as a multicomponent process that includes but is not synonymous with the BPD symptom of affective instability (Carpenter & Trull, 2013). *Affective instability* refers to the highly reactive moods of borderline individuals. Those with BPD typically shift between different varieties (e.g., anger, depression, anxiety) and degrees (e.g., moderate to extreme) of negative affect. Therefore, in the context of BPD, a more accurate description of the process that includes affective instability might be *negative emotional dysregulation*. The contextualization of affective instability within the negative emotional dysregulation process distinguishes BPD from disorders such as bipolar disorder, in which a person may shift between both positive and negative affect (e.g., from depression to elation). Also, affective instability in BPD is unique in that the affect shifts occur in response to external stimuli in the person's environment. These extreme shifts in negative mood typically last a few hours to a few days and may occur as a result of factors such as interpersonal stressors, perceived rejections, or events prompting identity crises. This pattern differentiates BPD from major depression, for example, in which the shifts in affect may result more from internal cues (e.g., self-critical thinking, pessimism about the future). Specific BPD criteria that appear to arise directly from negative emotion dysregulation include *affective instability, extreme anger,* and *emptiness.*

The empirical literature on affective instability and negative emotion dysregulation in BPD is extensive; therefore, we can highlight only some of the important empirical contributions from the past years. One particularly important tool for studying affective instability in BPD has been ambulatory assessment (AA), which allows researchers to collect data at multiple time-points throughout the day, during participants' daily lives and in their natural environments. The AA research on affective instability and emotion dysregulation in BPD has been summarized in a number of literature reviews (Rosenthal et al., 2015; Santangelo et al., 2014; Trull, 2018). These conclude that AA research remains somewhat inconclusive about the specificity of affective instability to BPD. Instead, the differences between BPD and other clinical groups may be more subtle than previously assumed in that they only emerge for certain indices of acute and extreme change of affect, suggesting affective instability may be largely transdiagnostic (which would be in line with recent theoretical frameworks such as RDoC or HiToP).

Beyond AA research, a large number of studies have investigated the neurobiological processes that underlie negative emotion dysregulation in BPD using functional magnetic resonance imaging (fMRI). Schulze and colleagues have conducted two extensive meta-analyses on these studies. In their first meta-analysis, the authors analyzed studies comparing individuals with BPD to healthy control participants (Schulze et al., 2016). Results showed that when BPD participants processed negative versus neutral emotional stimuli, the activation of their left amygdala and posterior cingulate cortex increased while that of the bilateral dorsolateral prefrontal cortex decreased. The authors further observed that medication status moderated this association, such that only BPD individuals without medication showed amygdala hyper-reactivity, whereas those currently taking psychotropic medication did not. These findings seemed to support the notion that BPD is a disorder that is particularly marked by emotion dysregulation, reflected by limbic hyper- and prefrontal hypoactivation. When repeating the meta-analysis several years later, comparing studies on BPD, PTSD, and depression, the pattern that emerged was more fine-grained. The authors found that, compared to healthy controls, *both* BPD and PTSD participants showed increased limbic activation, whereas individuals with depression did not (Schulze et al., 2019). They also discovered that participants in all three clinical groups showed hyperactivation of the right median cingulate gyri and hypoactivation of the right middle frontal gyrus and the right middle occipital gyrus when processing negative (vs. neutral) material. This led the authors to conclude that the neurological correlates of emotion dysregulation may be largely transdiagnostic.

In addition to being a problem in and of itself, negative emotion dysregulation may also drive many of the other symptoms seen in the disorder (Carpenter & Trull, 2013). These can arise when BPD individuals use dysfunctional or simply ineffective regulation strategies to cope with negative emotions. A recent meta-analysis suggests that individuals with BPD are generally more likely to use emotion regulation strategies that have been associated with little or only short-lived regulation success, such as suppression, rumination, and avoidance (Daros & Williams, 2019). At the same time, they are less likely to use strategies that are typically more effective, such as cognitive reappraisal or acceptance. Linehan (1993) postulated that this inability to regulate emotions can lead to further maladaptive attempts to regulate negative affect through problem behaviors. Impulsive behavior (including suicidal behavior) may be seen as a maladaptive solution to painful negative affect. Identity disturbance may result from a lack of emotional consistency and predictability. As another example, it has been proposed that those with BPD may be especially vulnerable to developing substance use disorders because alcohol or drugs may be used to cope with negative affective states (Trull et al., 2018). This part of Linehan's theory has seen support from a large number of empirical studies that established a close association between dysregulated negative affect and the other symptoms of BPD. Specifically, a growing number of AA studies have highlighted positive associations between dysregulated states of momentary negative affect or indices of affective instability in daily life and almost all other symptoms of BPD. Findings include positive associations between negative affect/affective instability indices and impulsivity (Tomko et al., 2015), substance use (Wycoff et al., 2020), identity disturbance (Santangelo et al., 2017; Scala et al., 2018), interpersonal problems (Hepp et al., 2017; Hepp, Lane et al., 2018), nonsuicidal self-injury (for a review, see Hepp, Carpenter et al., 2020), and dissociation (Stiglmayr et al., 2008).

*Impulsivity and Behavioral Dysregulation*

A second dimension of psychopathology that underlies BPD features is that of impulsivity or behavioral dysregulation. Individuals with BPD frequently engage in potentially harmful behaviors, such as substance abuse, promiscuity, excessive spending, gambling, binge eating, reckless driving, or shoplifting. In the *DSM-IV-TR* and *DSM-5* Section II, the major impulsivity criterion of BPD is defined as "impulsivity in at least two areas that are potentially self-damaging." Some argue that impulsivity is the single best defining feature of the disorder (Bornovalova et al., 2008; Links et al., 1999). Furthermore, this criterion is one of the most commonly occurring symptoms among BPD patients (McGlashan et al., 2005). Crowell et al. (2009) suggest that impulsivity is one of the earliest detectable features of the disorder, and they note that genetic and family studies show a significant increase in the rate of impulse control disorders among family members of individuals with BPD. In addition, some initial research suggested that impulsivity is the most stable BPD symptom and the strongest predictor of overall BPD pathology (Links et al., 1999). More recent research, however, has found that impulsivity generally decreases with age among BPD patients (Morey & Hopwood, 2013; Stepp & Pilkonis, 2008).

The impulsivity diagnostic criterion of BPD highlights overt, maladaptive, impulsive behaviors. However, the etiology of these behaviors is not well understood. A biological predisposition toward disinhibition is one potential mechanism underlying the impulsivity associated with BPD. From this viewpoint, impulsive behaviors are seen as manifestations of underlying personality characteristics. Others have suggested that impulsive behaviors may be maladaptive attempts to regulate negative emotions (e.g., Brown et al., 2002; Kruedelbach et al., 1993). From this perspective, impulsivity in BPD is secondary to affective instability and intense negative emotionality.

There are several avenues to studying impulsivity in BPD. One streak of research has aimed to learn more about impulsivity in BPD by investigating its comorbidity with ADHD and trying to pinpoint similarities and differences in the impulsivity profiles between the two conditions. The latest review of this literature argues that impulsivity in BPD is more strongly intertwined with, and driven by, emotion dysregulation and interpersonal hypersensitivity, whereas impulsivity in ADHD is more strongly rooted in deficits related to attention and cognitive control (Matthies & Philipsen, 2014). A second line of research has used self-report questionnaires to study impulsivity in BPD. Across studies, large differences tend to emerge between BPD individuals and healthy control groups when comparing self-reports. When comparing BPD groups to clinical control groups, the effects are smaller and often nonexistent when comparing BPD to ADHD (Sebastian et al., 2013).

A further major source of information on impulsivity in BPD are laboratory experiments. Many of these studies focus on facets of impulse *control* and include an fMRI assessment in addition to measuring behavioral outcomes. Sebastian et al. (2014) reviewed this literature and clustered findings based on different components of impulse control including stimulus interference, response interference, and behavioral inhibition. The authors conclude that there is some evidence for hypoactivation of orbitofrontal regions during behavioral inhibition in BPD. Moreover, they suggest that both stimulus and response interference are associated with a hypoactivation of the dorsal part of the anterior cingulate cortex (ACC), the dorsolateral prefrontal cortex (DLPFC). However, most of the included studies used paradigms that have also been used to assess emotion dysregulation in other contexts and that contain emotionally salient material, such as using negative words to operationalize stimulus interference in a Stroop task (Wingenfeld et al., 2009). Thus, more research is needed to investigate whether these findings are limited to emotional material. Adding to this, Paret et al. (2017) conducted a meta-analytic review of the literature on decision-making in BPD, some of which assessed delay of gratification, which can be seen as a form of impulse control. Meta-analytic results showed that individuals with BPD discounted delayed rewards more strongly than did healthy controls.

In general, few studies have succeeded at disentangling impulsivity from emotion dysregulation, and this problem has been discussed for many years now. One way studies have attempted this in recent years is to assess impulsive behavior in the laboratory following stress induction, for instance using interpersonal stressors. These studies suggest that dysregulated states of negative affect are predictive of impulsive behavior in various paradigms (e.g., Cackowski et al., 2014; Ernst et al., 2018; Krause-Utz et al., 2016). Another avenue toward studying impulsivity and its association with emotion dysregulation is to study both constructs outside the laboratory and try to assess their covariation and possible temporal precedence of one over the other in daily life. T—o date, — the only study on impulsivity and affect in daily live assessed momentary impulsivity in 67 BPD individuals and a control group of 38 individuals with depression 6 times a day over 28 days (Tomko et al., 2015). In addition to momentary impulsivity, the authors measured the level of negative affect and undifferentiated negative affect. The BPD group reported higher levels of momentary undifferentiated negative affect and impulsivity than the depressed group, and undifferentiated negative affect predicted momentary impulsivity in both groups. More research is needed to examine how impulsivity and emotion dysregulation may interact to produce behaviors and actions characterizing BPD.

## Interpersonal Hypersensitivity

In addition to difficulties in regulating both emotions and behaviors, BPD is associated with many interpersonal difficulties; some have even argued that interpersonal hypersensitivity could constitute a phenotype of BPD (Gunderson, 2007). Gunderson and Lyons-Ruth (2008) have presented a developmental model of interpersonal hypersensitivity in BPD. Their view suggests that negative interpersonal experiences combined with a biological disposition to be emotionally reactive may lead to an attribution bias toward perceived abandonment and rejection, resulting in excessive bids for attention and proximity seeking, which the recipient may find aversive. Two diagnostic criteria of BPD also directly reflect the importance of interpersonal dysfunction for BPD. First, *frantic efforts to avoid abandonment* relates to a general intolerance of being alone; the individual may react with fear or even anger at a time-limited separation or possible termination of a relationship. This criterion suggests that someone suffering from BPD may feel a strong desire to keep others close yet engage in aversive and at times destructive behaviors in order to maintain this closeness. The second interpersonal criterion for BPD, *patterns of unstable and intense interpersonal relationships*, reflects an initial strong idealization of another that may abruptly change to equally extreme devaluation of the same person. Finally, *transient, stress-related paranoid ideation or dissociation*, while not directly formulated as an interpersonal symptom, is believed to occur primarily in the context of real or imagined abandonment by others.

Interpersonal dysfunction in BPD has sparked increasing research interest in the past years, and the evidence base has grown considerably. First, we outline the different ways in which interpersonal dysfunction manifests in BPD before reviewing in more detail potential mechanisms behind interpersonal dysfunction. The first source of information on interpersonal dysfunction in BPD are studies that ask individuals to self-report on the quality of their social interactions and relationships. The general picture that emerges is that BPD individuals self-describe the quality of their relationships as poor (Daley et al., 2000; Miano et al., 2018). They perceive their social networks as generating low levels of social support (Clifton et al., 2007) and at the same time high levels of criticism and conflict (Beeney et al., 2018; Lazarus & Cheavens,

2017; Lazarus et al., 2016). This extends to all kinds of relationships, including romantic ones, in which verbal as well as physical fights and recurring breakups were shown to be common (Bouchard, Godbout et al., 2009; Bouchard, Sabourin et al., 2009; Hill et al., 2011). Daily life studies support this picture and underline that individuals with BPD experience interpersonal stressors and problems, such as conflicts, frequently in their day-to-day lives (Stepp et al., 2009). A recent meta-analysis of studies using the interpersonal circumplex model suggests that the interpersonal style of BPD individuals is characterized by a high degree of agency and low degree of communion, which can manifest in behavior that is vindictive, intrusive, domineering, and cold (Wilson et al., 2017).

BPD-related interpersonal problems have also been described within a framework of *rejection sensitivity*. Rejection sensitivity is a cognitive-affective trait that causes individuals to anxiously expect, readily perceive, and overreact to rejection cues in the environment (Berenson et al., 2009; Downey & Feldman, 1996). Those who are high in rejection sensitivity automatically perceive rejection-relevant stimuli information as threatening, especially in ambiguous situations (Berenson et al., 2009; Downey et al., 2004). However, they seek to maintain social ties while avoiding potential rejection (Downey & Feldman, 1996). This cognitive and affective style has significant interpersonal consequences, including early termination of relationships, attributing negative intentions to partners, and avoiding relationship-threatening stimuli (Berenson et al., 2009). A recent meta-analysis has summarized the evidence on rejection sensitivity in BPD and suggests that there is a strong association between BPD and rejection sensitivity (Foxhall et al., 2019). Rejection and other types of interpersonal stressors also appear to be related to negative emotionality in the sense that they can trigger negative affective reactions. Lazarus et al. (2014) reviewed laboratory studies and concluded that individuals with BPD show a heightened emotional reactivity to interpersonal stressors, for instance induced rejection experiences. They also conclude that individuals with BPD show deficits in interpersonal trust and cooperation. Studies on cooperative behavior in BPD have also been extensively reviewed elsewhere (Jeung et al., 2016) and suggest that individuals with BPD have trouble establishing and maintaining cooperative behavior (especially after a rupture in cooperation). In addition to these laboratory studies, recent years have seen an increase in studies assessing interpersonal stressors and their association with negative affect in daily life, which largely corroborates laboratory findings. Specifically, studies have demonstrated that perceived rejection and disagreements are associated with increased levels of negative affect at the same time of assessment and that they are also predictive of increased negative affect at the following assessment (Berenson et al., 2011; Hepp et al., 2017; Hepp, Lane et al., 2018; Lazarus et al., 2018; Sadikaj et al., 2013; Sadikaj et al., 2010). Thus, when faced with negative interpersonal events such as rejections or disagreements, a person with BPD may be likely to experience heightened negative affect. When accompanied by difficulties in regulating that affect, this can trigger reactive behaviors that an interaction partner finds harmful or aversive. Two daily life studies suggest that these interpersonal problems then themselves become predictive of further increases in negative affect, closing the vicious cycle of affective and interpersonal dysfunction in BPD (Hepp et al., 2017; Hepp, Lane et al., 2018).

As for mechanisms of interpersonal sensitivity in BPD, of major relevance are studies of *social cognition*, or the exchange of social signals between individuals (Roepke et al., 2013). The evidence on social cognitive deficits in BPD has been synthesized in several reviews and meta-analyses, with the majority of included studies focusing on facial affect recognition abilities (Daros et al., 2013; Domes et al., 2009; Mitchell et al., 2014). The evidence suggests a bias for attributing anger to ambiguous facial expressions and a general deficit for correctly categorizing various facial expressions and that these deficits become more pronounced in situations that involve more complex and more ecologically valid situations (i.e., not simply static pictures of faces). Moreover, a recent meta-analysis also concludes that individuals with BPD have deficits in theory of mind (Németh et al., 2018). There are also a small number of studies that have assessed how individuals with BPD perceive others based on short excerpts such as video clips or photos, so-called *thin slices* of behavior (Ambady & Rosenthal, 1992). These studies suggest that those with BPD tend to perceive others more negatively than do healthy control participants, participants with depression, and participants with a Cluster C PD (Arntz & Veen, 2001; Barnow et al., 2009; Sieswerda et al., 2013). A recent study further demonstrated that BPD individuals evaluate targets based on thin-slice video sequences as specifically less trustworthy and less approachable than do healthy control participants (Hepp, Kieslich et al., 2020). At the same time, some studies have also started to look at the other side of the coin and suggest that naïve raters also evaluate targets with BPD (based on thin slices of them) more negatively on a range of dimensions than they evaluated healthy control targets (Friedman et al., 2006; Hepp et al., 2019; Hepp, Störkel et al., 2018; Oltmanns et al., 2004). The finding that BPD individuals perceive others negatively and are, in turn, also perceived negatively by them could explain reduced approach behavior on both sides and the marked levels of loneliness that have been described for those with BPD (Liebke et al., 2017).

### The Future of the BPD Diagnosis

Our review of the various issues related to the best way to define the BPD phenotype begs the question: How is BPD likely to be conceptualized and defined in the future? The American Psychiatric Association Board of Trustees decided to maintain the same criteria and diagnostic rules outlined in *DSM-IV* for the PDs (including BPD) in Section II of the new *DSM-5*. This decision was made to preserve continuity with current clinical practice. The decision was based on an evaluation that there was not sufficient empirical evidence to justify a new trait-based approach to the PDs. Furthermore, many PD scholars and researchers decried the proposed changes and expressed concern that much of what we know about the PDs, based on a relatively stable set of diagnostic criteria, may not be applicable to these proposed newly defined PDs. Despite these concerns, *DSM-5* Section III presents an alternative model for PDs in order to introduce an approach that seeks to address many of the shortcomings of previous categorical approaches to the diagnosis of PDs.

Specifically, the *DSM-5* Personality Disorders Work Group proposal for a BPD diagnosis requires (1) significant impairment in personality functioning (i.e., the domains of self-functioning and of interpersonal functioning); (2) elevated personality traits in negative affectivity, disinhibition, and antagonism; (3) stability and pervasiveness across situations; (4) these impairments and trait expressions are not normative or part of the person's culture; and (5) these impairments and trait expressions are not due to the effects of substances or medications (Mulay et al., 2019).

Here, we focus only on the first two components of the work group's proposed BPD diagnosis (assessing impairment in personality functioning and assessing pathological personality traits associated with BPD), with special emphasis on the trait ratings included in this BPD conceptualization. The first step in assessing an individual for a Section III *DSM-5* BPD diagnosis involves rating a patient's *level of personality functioning*—specifically, the level of self- and interpersonal functioning for each individual assessed. *Self-functioning* is defined in two areas (identity integration; self-directedness), as is *interpersonal functioning* (empathy and intimacy). A 5-point scale is used to rate overall level of personality functioning for this purpose (0 = no impairment; 1 = some impairment; 2 = moderate impairment; 3 = severe impairment; and 4 = extreme impairment); examples for the ratings are provided (*DSM-5,* pp. 775–778). A moderate level of impairment of personality functioning in two or more of these four areas is required for a diagnosis of BPD. The clinician is reminded that the ratings must reflect functioning that is of multiple years in duration and must reflect patterns of functioning that are relatively inflexible and pervasive across a wide range of personal and social situations, not due solely to another mental disorder, physical condition, or effect of a substance, and not a norm within a person's cultural background.

The second step involves evaluating personality trait elevations in the individual. Section III *DSM-5* BPD personality traits include those tapping *negative affectivity* (emotional lability, anxiousness, separation insecurity, and depressivity), *disinhibition* (impulsivity, risk taking), and *antagonism* (hostility) (see Table 28.3). Section III calls on diagnosticians to decide whether these seven traits are elevated in the individual; this judgment can be made on the basis of clinical interview or questionnaire scores. It is required that an individual show elevations on at least four of these seven pathological personality traits, and at least one of these elevations must be on impulsivity, risk taking, or hostility.

The new alternative *DSM-5* model for PDs in Section III clearly represents an attempt to provide a more dimensional perspective on personality pathology in general and on BPD in particular. Furthermore, this trait-focused system is more consistent with the large body of research supporting the reliability and validity of using the framework of major dimensions of personality and personality pathology to conceptualize, describe, and study PDs (Widiger & Trull, 2007). However, a major challenge is convincing clinicians that such a framework is clinically useful, can be applied reliably, and can preserve what we have learned about BPD in the past using a traditional categorical system of symptom lists.

In contrast to *DSM-5*, which ultimately retained the categorical PD diagnoses, *ICD-11* includes a dimensional PD diagnosis will be implemented in 2022. All currently existing categories of individual PDs will be replaced by a single dimensional diagnosis of PD that can be coded along a severity dimension of mild, moderate, and severe, and a level of "personality difficulty" (in the chapter "Factors Influencing Health Status and Contact with Health Services") that is below the threshold for a disorder (WHO, 2020). The two core criteria used for the severity scoring are the degree of interpersonal dysfunction (e.g., failure to fulfill social roles, lack of close relationships) and self-related dysfunction (e.g., instability of self-image, low self-worth) (Tyrer et al., 2015). Additionally, the *ICD-11* allows for optional specification of the five trait qualifiers of negative affectivity, detachment, dissociality, disinhibition, and anankastia, and it includes a "borderline pattern" specifier. To code the borderline pattern, patients must show instability of interpersonal relationships, self-image, affects, and marked impulsivity and exhibit behavioral, cognitive, and emotional patterns that are essentially those detailed in the *DSM-5* BPD criteria, such as frantic efforts to avoid real or imagined abandonment, self-harm, etc. (WHO, 2020). The borderline pattern was included to preserve an explicit representation of the BPD construct, acknowledging the vast body of research on this specific group and the need for a specific *ICD-11* code to allow specialized treatment programs around the world to continue providing care to this patient group (Reed, 2018; Tyrer et al., 2019). At the same time, some criticized the inclusion of the borderline pattern as a redundant addition, arguing that BPD patients can be adequately represented by using multiple traits specifiers (Mulder et al., 2020). The proposal of the dimensional PD diagnosis met with some resistance (e.g., Herpertz et al., 2017), and the development and validation of instruments to measure the severity dimension (e.g., Olajide et al., 2018), trait qualifiers (e.g., Oltmanns & Widiger, 2019), and the borderline pattern (Oltmanns & Widiger, 2018) is still ongoing. In the end, the *ICD-11* dimensional approach is likely to further facilitate the transition to dimensional models in future editions of the *DSM*.

## Conclusion

It is very clear that clinicians and researchers deem BPD to be a syndrome that is quite important given its prevalence in both clinical and nonclinical samples, its association with impairment and dysfunction, and its relationship to increased risk for suicidal behavior, interpersonal conflict, substance dependence, and early mortality. Despite the attention given to BPD by clinicians and researchers alike, its specific etiology remains largely uncharted. The causes of BPD are multifactorial and complex, involving some interplay between social, environmental, and genetic factors. However, the widely accepted *DSM* definition of BPD breeds great heterogeneity, and this will likely limit advances in uncovering etiological factors and in designing more effective treatments for BPD. It is recommended that scholars and researchers focus on the dimensions underlying BPD symptoms in order to identify the essence of the disorder, investigate both biological and environmental influences on these core dimensions, and ultimately develop better treatments.

**References**

Akiskal, H. S. (1981). Subaffective disorders: Dysthymic, cyclothymic and bipolar II disorders in the "borderline" realm. *Psychiatric Clinics*, *4*(1), 25–46. https://doi.org/10.1016/S0193-953X(18)30935-3

Amad, A., Ramoz, N., Thomas, P., Jardri, R., & Gorwood, P. (2014). Genetics of borderline personality disorder: Systematic review and proposal of an integrative model. *Neuroscience & Biobehavioral Reviews*, *40*, 6–19. https://doi.org/https://doi.org/10.1016/j.neubiorev.2014.01.003

Ambady, N., & Rosenthal, R. (1992). Thin slices of expressive behavior as predictors of interpersonal consequences: A meta-analysis. *Psychological Bulletin*, *111*(2), 256–274. https://doi.org/10.1037/0033-2909.111.2.256

Ansell, E. B., Sanislow, C. A., McGlashan, T. H., & Grilo, C. M. (2007). Psychosocial impairment and treatment utilization by patients with borderline personality disorder, other personality disorders, mood and anxiety disorders, and a healthy comparison group. *Comprehensive Psychiatry*, *48*(4), 329–336. https://doi.org/https://doi.org/10.1016/j.comppsych.2007.02.001

Arntz, A., & Veen, G. (2001). Evaluations of others by borderline patients. *Journal of Nervous and Mental Disease*, *189*(8), 513–521. https://doi.org/10.1097/00005053-200108000-00004

Bagby, R. M., Sellbom, M., Costa Jr, P. T., & Widiger, T. A. (2008). Predicting Diagnostic and Statistical Manual of Mental Disorders-IV personality disorders with the five-factor model of personality and the personality psychopathology five. *Personality and Mental Health*, *2*(2), 55–69. https://doi.org/10.1002/pmh.33

Bah, J., Lindström, M., Westberg, L., Manneräs, L., Ryding, E., Henningsson, S., Melke, J., Rosén, I., Träskman-Bendz, L., & Eriksson, E. (2008). Serotonin transporter gene polymorphisms: Effect on serotonin transporter availability in the brain of suicide attempters. *Psychiatry Research: Neuroimaging*, *162*(3), 221–229. https://doi.org/10.1016/j.pscychresns.2007.07.004

Barnow, S., Stopsack, M., Grabe, H. J., Meinke, C., Spitzer, C., Kronmuller, K., & Sieswerda, S. (2009). Interpersonal evaluation bias in borderline personality disorder. *Behaviour Research and Therapy*, *47*(5), 359–365. https://doi.org/10.1037/a0018095

Bateman, A., & Fonagy, P. (2010). Mentalization based treatment for borderline personality disorder. *World Psychiatry*, *9*(1), 11–15. https://doi.org/10.1002/j.2051-5545.2010.tb00255.x

Bateman, A. W., & Fonagy, P. (2004). Mentalization-based treatment of BPD. *Journal of Personality Disorders*, *18*(1), 36–51. https://doi.org/10.1521/pedi.18.1.36.32772

Beeney, J. E., Hallquist, M. N., Clifton, A. D., Lazarus, S. A., & Pilkonis, P. A. (2018). Social disadvantage and borderline personality disorder: A study of social networks. *Personality Disorders: Theory, Research, and Treatment*, *9*(1), 62–72. https://doi.org/10.1037/per0000234

Berenson, K. R., Downey, G., Rafaeli, E., Coifman, K. G., & Paquin, N. L. (2011). The rejection–rage contingency in borderline personality disorder. *Journal of Abnormal Psychology*, *120*(3), 681–690. https://doi.org/10.1037/a0023335

Berenson, K. R., Gyurak, A., Ayduk, Ö., Downey, G., Garner, M. J., Mogg, K., Bradley, B. P., & Pine, D. S. (2009). Rejection sensitivity and disruption of attention by social threat cues. *Journal of Research in Personality*, *43*(6), 1064–1072. https://doi.org/10.1016/j.jrp.2009.07.007

Bohus, M. (2007). Zur Versorgungssituation von Borderline-Patienten in Deutschland. *Deutsches Ärzteblatt*, *11*(3), 149–153.

Boomsma, D., Busjahn, A., & Peltonen, L. (2002). Classical twin studies and beyond. *Nature Reviews Genetics*, *3*(11), 872–882. https://doi.org/10.1038/nrg932

Bornovalova, M. A., Fishman, S., Strong, D. R., Kruglanski, A. W., & Lejuez, C. (2008). Borderline personality disorder in the context of self-regulation: Understanding symptoms and hallmark features as deficits in locomotion and assessment. *Personality and Individual Differences*, *44*(1), 22–31. https://doi.org/10.1016/j.paid.2007.07.001

Bornovalova, M. A., Hicks, B. M., Iacono, W. G., & McGue, M. (2013). Longitudinal twin study of borderline personality disorder traits and substance use in adolescence: Developmental change, reciprocal effects, and genetic and environmental influences. *Personality Disorders: Theory, Research, and Treatment*, *4*(1), 23–32. https://doi.org/https://doi.org/10.1037/a0027178

Bornovalova, M. A., Huibregtse, B. M., Hicks, B. M., Keyes, M., McGue, M., & Iacono, W. (2013). Tests of a direct effect of childhood abuse on adult borderline personality disorder traits: A longitudinal discordant twin design. *Journal of Abnormal Psychology*, *122*(1), 180–194. https://doi.org/https://doi.org/10.1037/a0028328

Bortolato, M., Pivac, N., Seler, D. M., Perkovic, M. N., Pessia, M., & Di Giovanni, G. (2013). The role of the serotonergic system at the interface of aggression and suicide. *Neuroscience*, *236*, 160–185. https://doi.org/10.1016/j.neuroscience.2013.01.015

Bouchard, S., Godbout, N., & Sabourin, S. (2009). Sexual attitudes and activities in women with borderline personality disorder involved in romantic relationships. *Journal of Sex & Marital Therapy*, *35*(2), 106–121. https://doi.org/10.1080/00926230802712301

Bouchard, S., Sabourin, S., Lussier, Y., & Villeneuve, E. (2009). Relationship quality and stability in couples when one partner suffers from borderline personality disorder. *Journal of Marital and Family Therapy*, *35*(4), 446–455. https://doi.org/10.1111/j.1752-0606.2009.00151.x

Bourke, J., Murphy, A., Flynn, D., Kells, M., Joyce, M., & Hurley, J. (2018). Borderline personality disorder: Resource utilisation costs in Ireland. *Irish Journal of Psychological Medicine*, 1–8. https://doi.org/10.1017/ipm.2018.30

Bowlby, J. (1973). Attachment and loss: Volume II: Separation, anxiety and anger. In *Attachment and Loss: Volume II: Separation, Anxiety and Anger* (pp. 1–429). Hogarth Press and the Institute of Psycho-Analysis.

Brown, M. Z., Comtois, K. A., & Linehan, M. M. (2002). Reasons for suicide attempts and nonsuicidal self-injury in women with borderline personality disorder. *Journal of Abnormal Psychology*, *111*(1), 198–202. https://doi.org/10.1037/0021-843X.111.1.198

Buckholtz, J. W., & Meyer-Lindenberg, A. (2008). MAOA and the neurogenetic architecture of human aggression. *Trends in Neurosciences*, *31*(3), 120–129. https://doi.org/10.1016/j.tins.2007.12.006

Cackowski, S., Reitz, A., Ende, G., Kleindienst, N., Bohus, M., Schmahl, C., & Krause-Utz, A. (2014). Impact of stress on different components of impulsivity in borderline personality disorder. *Psychological Medicine*, *44*(15), 3329–3340. https://doi.org/10.1017/S0033291714000427

Canli, T., Ferri, J., & Duman, E. (2009). Genetics of emotion regulation. *Neuroscience*, *164*(1), 43–54. https://doi.org/10.1016/j.neuroscience.2009.06.049

Carpenter, R. W., Tragesser, S. L., Lane, S. P., & Trull, T. J. (2019). Momentary assessment of everyday physical pain in outpatients with borderline personality disorder. *Personality Disorders: Theory, Research, and Treatment*, *10*(2), 143–153. https://doi.org/10.1037/per0000304

Carpenter, R. W., & Trull, T. J. (2013). Components of emotion dysregulation in borderline personality disorder: A review. *Current Psychiatry Reports*, *15*, article 335. https://doi.org/10.1007/s11920-012-0335-2

Chen, M.-H., Hsu, J.-W., Bai, Y.-M., Su, T.-P., Li, C.-T., Lin, W.-C., Tsai, S.-J., Chang, W.-H., Chen, T.-J., & Huang, K.-L. (2017). Risk of stroke among patients with borderline personality disorder: A nationwide longitudinal study. *Journal of Affective Disorders*, *219*, 80–85. https://doi.org/10.1016/j.jad.2017.05.005

Chesney, E., Goodwin, G. M., & Fazel, S. (2014). Risks of all-cause and suicide mortality in mental disorders: A meta-review. *World Psychiatry*, *13*(2), 153–160. https://doi.org/10.1002/wps.20128

Choi-Kain, L. W., Reich, D. B., Masland, S. R., Iliakis, E. A., & Ilagan, G. S. (2020). Longitudinal course of borderline personality disorder: What every clinician needs to know. *Current Treatment Options in Psychiatry*, *7*(3), 429–445. https://doi.org/10.1007/s40501-020-00223-x

Clifton, A., Pilkonis, P. A., & McCarty, C. (2007). Social networks in borderline personality disorder. *Journal of Personality Disorders*, *21*(4), 434–441. https://doi.org/10.1521/pedi.2007.21.4.434

Cohen, P., Chen, H., Crawford, T. N., Brook, J. S., & Gordon, K. (2007). Personality disorders in early adolescence and the development of later substance use disorders in the general population. *Drug and Alcohol Dependence*, *88*, S71–S84. https://doi.org/10.1016/j.drugalcdep.2006.12.012

Coid, J., Yang, M., Bebbington, P., Moran, P., Brugha, T., Jenkins, R., Farrell, M., Singleton, N., & Ullrich, S. (2009). Borderline personality disorder: Health service use and social functioning among a national household population.

*Psychological Medicine, 39*(10), 1721–1731. https://doi.org/10.1017/S0033291708004911

Coid, J., Yang, M., Tyrer, P., Roberts, A., & Ullrich, S. (2006). Prevalence and correlates of personality disorder in Great Britain. *British Journal of Psychiatry, 188*(5), 423–431. https://doi.org/10.1192/bjp.188.5.423

Costa, P. T., & McCrae, R. R. (1992). *Professional manual: Revised NEO personality inventory (NEO-PI-R) and NEO five-factor inventory (NEO-FFI)*. Psychological Assessment Resources, p. 61.

Cristea, I. A., Gentili, C., Cotet, C. D., Palomba, D., Barbui, C., & Cuijpers, P. (2017). Efficacy of psychotherapies for borderline personality disorder: A systematic review and meta-analysis. *JAMA Psychiatry, 74*(4), 319–328. https://doi.org/10.1001/jamapsychiatry.2016.4287

Crowell, S. E., Beauchaine, T. P., & Linehan, M. M. (2009). A biosocial developmental model of borderline personality: Elaborating and extending linehan's theory. *Psychological Bulletin, 135*(3), 495–510. https://doi.org/10.1037/a0015616

Daley, S. E., Burge, D., & Hammen, C. (2000). Borderline personality disorder symptoms as predictors of 4-year romantic relationship dysfunction in young women: Addressing issues of specificity. *Journal of Abnormal Psychology, 109*(3), 451–460. https://doi.org/10.1037/0021-843X.109.3.451

Dammann, G., Teschler, S., Haag, T., Altmüller, F., Tuczek, F., & Dammann, R. H. (2011). Increased DNA methylation of neuropsychiatric genes occurs in borderline personality disorder. *Epigenetics, 6*(12), 1454–1462. https://doi.org/10.4161/epi.6.12.18363

Daros, A. R., & Williams, G. E. (2019). A meta-analysis and systematic review of emotion-regulation strategies in borderline personality disorder. *Harvard Review of Psychiatry, 27*(4), 217–232. https://doi.org/10.1097/hrp.0000000000000212

Daros, A. R., Zakzanis, K. K., & Ruocco, A. (2013). Facial emotion recognition in borderline personality disorder. *Psychological Medicine, 43*(9), 1953–1963. https://doi.org/10.1017/S0033291712002607

Davenport, J., Bore, M., & Campbell, J. (2010). Changes in personality in pre-and post-dialectical behaviour therapy borderline personality disorder groups: A question of self-control. *Australian Psychologist, 45*(1), 59–66. https://doi.org/10.1080/00050060903280512

Distel, M., Hottenga, J.-J., Trull, T. J., & Boomsma, D. I. (2008). Chromosome 9: Linkage for borderline personality disorder features. *Psychiatric Genetics, 18*(6), 302–307. https://doi.org/10.1097/ypg.0b013e3283118468

Distel, M., Trull, T., Derom, C., Thiery, E., Grimmer, M., Martin, N., Willemsen, G., & Boomsma, D. (2008). Heritability of borderline personality disorder features is similar across three countries. *Psychological Medicine, 38*(9), 1219–1229. https://doi.org/10.1017/S0033291707002024

Distel, M. A., Rebollo-Mesa, I., Willemsen, G., Derom, C. A., Trull, T. J., Martin, N. G., & Boomsma, D. I. (2009). Familial resemblance of borderline personality disorder features: Genetic or cultural transmission? *PLOS One, 4*(4), e5334. https://doi.org/10.1371/journal.pone.0005334

Distel, M. A., Trull, T. J., Willemsen, G., Vink, J. M., Derom, C. A., Lynskey, M., Martin, N. G., & Boomsma, D. I. (2009). The five-factor model of personality and borderline personality disorder: A genetic analysis of comorbidity. *Biological Psychiatry, 66*(12), 1131–1138. https://doi.org/10.1016/j.biopsych.2009.07.017

Distel, M. A., Willemsen, G., Ligthart, L., Derom, C. A., Martin, N. G., Neale, M. C., Trull, T. J., & Boomsma, D. I. (2010). Genetic covariance structure of the four main features of borderline personality disorder. *Journal of Personality Disorders, 24*(4), 427–444. https://doi.org/10.1521/pedi.2010.24.4.427

Domes, G., Schulze, L., & Herpertz, S. C. (2009). Emotion recognition in borderline personality disorder—A review of the literature. *Journal of Personality Disorders, 23*(1), 6–19. https://doi.org/10.1521/pedi.2009.23.1.6

Downey, G., & Feldman, S. I. (1996). Implications of rejection sensitivity for intimate relationships. *Journal of Personality and Social Psychology, 70*(6), 1327–1343. https://doi.org/10.1037/0022-3514.70.6.1327

Downey, G., Mougios, V., Ayduk, O., London, B. E., & Shoda, Y. (2004). Rejection sensitivity and the defensive motivational system: Insights from the startle response to rejection cues. *Psychological Science, 15*(10), 668–673. https://doi.org/10.1111/j.0956-7976.2004.00738.x

Drews, E., Fertuck, E. A., Koenig, J., Kaess, M., & Arntz, A. (2019). Hypothalamic-pituitary-adrenal Axis functioning in borderline personality disorder: A meta-analysis. *Neuroscience & Biobehavioral Reviews, 96*, 316–334. https://doi.org/10.1016/j.neubiorev.2018.11.008

Eaton, N. R., Krueger, R. F., Keyes, K. M., Skodol, A. E., Markon, K. E., Grant, B. F., & Hasin, D. S. (2011). Borderline personality disorder comorbidity: Relationship to the internalizing-externalizing structure of common mental disorders. *Psychological Medicine, 41*(5), 1041–1050. https://doi.org/10.1017/S0033291710001662

Ernst, M., Mohr, H. M., Schött, M., Rickmeyer, C., Fischmann, T., Leuzinger-Bohleber, M., Weiß, H., & Grabhorn, R. (2018). The effects of social exclusion on response inhibition in borderline personality disorder and major depression. *Psychiatry Research, 262*, 333–339. https://doi.org/10.1016/j.psychres.2017.03.034

Feenstra, D. J., Hutsebaut, J., Laurenssen, E. M., Verheul, R., Busschbach, J. J., & Soeteman, D. I. (2012). The burden of disease among adolescents with personality pathology: Quality of life and costs. *Journal of Personality Disorders, 26*(4), 593–604. https://doi.org/10.1521/pedi.2012.26.4.593

Fok, M., Hotopf, M., Stewart, R., Hatch, S., Hayes, R., & Moran, P. (2014). Personality disorder and self-rated health: A population-based cross-sectional survey. *Journal of Personality Disorders, 28*(3), 319–333. https://doi.org/10.1521/pedi_2013_27_119

Fonagy, P., Target, M., Gergely, G., Allen, J. G., & Bateman, A. W. (2003). The developmental roots of borderline personality disorder in early attachment relationships: A theory and some evidence. *Psychoanalytic Inquiry, 23*(3), 412–459. https://doi.org/10.1080/07351692309349042

Foxhall, M., Hamilton-Giachritsis, C., & Button, K. (2019). The link between rejection sensitivity and borderline personality disorder: A systematic review and meta-analysis. *British Journal of Clinical Psychology, 58*(3), 289–326. https://doi.org/10.1111/bjc.12216

Frankenburg, F. R., & Zanarini, M. C. (2004). The association between borderline personality disorder and chronic medical illnesses, poor health-related lifestyle choices, and costly forms of health care utilization. *Journal of Clinical Psychiatry, 65*(12), 1660–1665. https://doi.org/10.4088/JCP.v65n1211

Friedel, R. O. (2004). Dopamine dysfunction in borderline personality disorder: A hypothesis. *Neuropsychopharmacology*, 29(6), 1029–1039. https://doi.org/10.1038/sj.npp.1300424

Friedman, J. N., Oltmanns, T. F., Gleason, M. E., & Turkheimer, E. (2006). Mixed impressions: Reactions of strangers to people with pathological personality traits. *Journal of Research in Personality*, 40(4), 395–410. https://doi.org/10.1016/j.jrp.2005.01.005

Furlong, R. A., Ho, L., Rubinsztein, J. S., Walsh, C., Paykel, E. S., & Rubinsztein, D. C. (1999). Analysis of the monoamine oxidase A (MAOA) gene in bipolar affective disorder by association studies, meta-analyses, and sequencing of the promoter. *American Journal of Medical Genetics*, 88(4), 398–406. https://doi.org/10.1002/(SICI)1096-8628(19990820)88:4

Gescher, D. M., Kahl, K. G., Hillemacher, T., Frieling, H., Kuhn, J., & Frodl, T. (2018). Epigenetics in personality disorders: Today's insights [Review]. *Frontiers in Psychiatry*, 9(579). https://doi.org/10.3389/fpsyt.2018.00579

Giegling, I., Hartmann, A. M., Möller, H.-J., & Rujescu, D. (2006). Anger-and aggression-related traits are associated with polymorphisms in the 5-HT-2A gene. *Journal of Affective Disorders*, 96(1-2), 75–81. https://doi.org/10.1016/j.jad.2006.05.016

Goldhammer, H., Crall, C., & Keuroghlian, A. S. (2019). Distinguishing and addressing gender minority stress and borderline personality symptoms. *Harvard Review of Psychiatry*, 27(5), 317–325. https://doi.org/10.1097/hrp.0000000000000234

Grant, B. F., Chou, S. P., Goldstein, R. B., Huang, B., Stinson, F. S., Saha, T. D., Smith, S. M., Dawson, D. A., Pulay, A. J., & Pickering, R. P. (2008a). Prevalence, correlates, disability, and comorbidity of DSM-IV borderline personality disorder: Results from the Wave 2 National Epidemiologic Survey on Alcohol and Related Conditions. *Journal of Clinical Psychiatry*, 69(4), 533–545. https://doi.org/10.4088/jcp.v69n0404

Grant, B. F., Chou, S. P., Goldstein, R. B., Huang, B., Stinson, F. S., Saha, T. D., Smith, S. M., Dawson, D. A., Pulay, A. J., & Pickering, R. P. (2008b). Prevalence, correlates, disability, and comorbidity of DSM-IV borderline personality disorder: Results from the Wave 2 National Epidemiologic Survey on Alcohol and Related Conditions. *Journal of Clinical Psychiatry*, 69(4), 533–545.

Grant, B. F., Hasin, D. S., Chou, S. P., Stinson, F. S., & Dawson, D. A. (2004). Nicotine dependence and psychiatric disorders in the united states: Results from the national epidemiologic survey on alcohol and relatedconditions. *Archives of General Psychiatry*, 61(11), 1107–1115. https://doi.org/10.1001/archpsyc.61.11.1107

Grant, B. F., Stinson, F. S., Dawson, D. A., Chou, S. P., Ruan, W. J., & Pickering, R. P. (2004). Co-occurrence of 12-month alcohol and drug use disorders and personality disorders in the United States: Results from the National Epidemiologic Survey on Alcohol and Related Conditions. *Archives of General Psychiatry*, 61(4), 361–368. https://doi.org/10.1001/archpsyc.61.4.361

Grinker, R., Webble, B., & Drye, R. (1968). *The borderline syndrome. A behavioral study of ego-functions*. Basic Books.

Gunderson, J. G. (2001). *Borderline personality disorder: A clinical guide*. American Psychiatric Publishing.

Gunderson, J. G. (2007). Disturbed relationships as a phenotype for borderline personality disorder. *American Journal of Psychiatry*, 164(11), 1637–1640. https://doi.org/10.1176/appi.ajp.2007.07071125

Gunderson, J. G. (2009). Borderline personality disorder: Ontogeny of a diagnosis. *American Journal of Psychiatry*, 166(5), 530–539. https://doi.org/10.1176/appi.ajp.2009.08121825

Gunderson, J. G., Fruzzetti, A., Unruh, B., & Choi-Kain, L. (2018). Competing theories of borderline personality disorder. *Journal of Personality Disorders*, 32(2), 148–167. https://doi.org/10.1521/pedi.2018.32.2.148

Gunderson, J. G., & Lyons-Ruth, K. (2008). BPD's interpersonal hypersensitivity phenotype: A gene-environment-developmental model. *Journal of Personality Disorders*, 22(1), 22–41. https://doi.org/10.1521/pedi.2008.22.1.22

Gunderson, J. G., Shea, M. T., Skodol, A. E., McGlashan, T. H., Morey, L. C., Stout, R. L., Zanarini, M. C., Grilo, C. M., Oldham, J. M., & Keller, M. B. (2000). The collaborative longitudinal personality disorders study: Development, aims, design, and sample characteristics. *Journal of Personality Disorders*, 14(4), 300–315. https://doi.org/10.1521/pedi.2000.14.4.300

Gunderson, J. G., & Singer, M. T. (1975). Defining borderline patients: An overview. *The American Journal of Psychiatry*, 132, 1–10. https://doi.org/10.1176/ajp.132.1.1

Gunderson, J. G., Stout, R. L., McGlashan, T. H., Shea, M. T., Morey, L. C., Grilo, C. M., Zanarini, M. C., Yen, S., Markowitz, J. C., & Sanislow, C. (2011). Ten-year course of borderline personality disorder: Psychopathology and function from the Collaborative Longitudinal Personality Disorders study. *Archives of General Psychiatry*, 68(8), 827–837. https://doi.org/10.1001/archgenpsychiatry.2011.37

Gunderson, J. G., Zanarini, M. C., Choi-Kain, L. W., Mitchell, K. S., Jang, K. L., & Hudson, J. I. (2011). Family study of borderline personality disorder and its sectors of psychopathology. *Archives of General Psychiatry*, 68(7), 753–762. https://doi.org/10.1001/archgenpsychiatry.2011.65

Heath, L. M., Paris, J., Laporte, L., & Gill, K. J. (2017). High prevalence of physical pain among treatment-seeking individuals with borderline personality disorder. *Journal of Personality Disorders*, 32(3), 414–420. https://doi.org/10.1521/pedi_2017_31_302

Hepp, J., Carpenter, R. W., Störkel, L. M., Schmitz, S. E., Schmahl, C., & Niedtfeld, I. (2020). A systematic review of daily life studies on non-suicidal self-injury based on the four-function model. *Clinical Psychology Review*, 82, article 101888. https://doi.org/10.1016/j.cpr.2020.101888

Hepp, J., Gebhardt, S., Kieslich, P. J., Störkel, L. M., & Niedtfeld, I. (2019). Low positive affect display mediates the association between borderline personality disorder and negative evaluations at zero acquaintance. *Borderline Personality Disorder and Emotion Dysregulation*, 6(1), 4. https://doi.org/10.1186/s40479-019-0103-6

Hepp, J., Kieslich, P. J., Schmitz, M., Schmahl, C., & Niedtfeld, I. (2020). Negativity on two sides: Individuals with borderline personality disorder form negative first impressions of others and are perceived negatively by them. *Personality Disorders: Theory, Research, and Treatment*, 12(6), 514–525. https://doi.org/10.1037/per0000412

Hepp, J., Lane, S. P., Carpenter, R. W., Niedtfeld, I., Brown, W. C., & Trull, T. J. (2017). Interpersonal Problems and Negative Affect in Borderline Personality and Depressive Disorders in Daily Life. *Clinical Psychological Science*, 5(3), 470–484. https://doi.org/10.1177/2167702616677312

Hepp, J., Lane, S. P., Carpenter, R. W., & Trull, T. J. (2020). Linking daily-life interpersonal stressors and health problems via affective reactivity in borderline personality and depressive disorders. *Psychosomatic Medicine, 82*(1), 90–98. https://doi.org/10.1097/PSY.0000000000000728

Hepp, J., Lane, S. P., Wycoff, A. M., Carpenter, R. W., & Trull, T. J. (2018). Interpersonal stressors and negative affect in individuals with borderline personality disorder and community adults in daily life: A replication and extension. *Journal of Abnormal Psychology, 127*(2), 183–189. https://doi.org/10.1037/abn0000318

Hepp, J., Störkel, L. M., Kieslich, P. J., Schmahl, C., & Niedtfeld, I. (2018). Negative evaluation of individuals with borderline personality disorder at zero acquaintance. *Behaviour Research and Therapy, 111*, 84–91. https://doi.org/10.1016/j.brat.2018.09.009

Herman, J. (1992). *Trauma and recovery*. Basic Books.

Herpertz, S. C., Huprich, S. K., Bohus, M., Chanen, A., Goodman, M., Mehlum, L., Moran, P., Newton-Howes, G., Scott, L., & Sharp, C. (2017). The challenge of transforming the diagnostic system of personality disorders. *Journal of Personality Disorders, 31*(5), 577–589. https://doi.org/10.1521/pedi_2017_31_338

Hill, J., Stepp, S. D., Wan, M. W., Hope, H., Morse, J. Q., Steele, M., Steele, H., & Pilkonis, P. A. (2011). Attachment, borderline personality, and romantic relationship dysfunction. *Journal of Personality Disorders, 25*(6), 789–805. https://doi.org/10.1521/pedi.2011.25.6.789

Hoefgen, B., Schulze, T. G., Ohlraun, S., Von Widdern, O., Höfels, S., Gross, M., Heidmann, V., Kovalenko, S., Eckermann, A., & Kölsch, H. (2005). The power of sample size and homogenous sampling: Association between the 5-HTTLPR serotonin transporter polymorphism and major depressive disorder. *Biological Psychiatry, 57*(3), 247–251. https://doi.org/10.1016/j.biopsych.2004.11.027

Hörz, S., Zanarini, M. C., Frankenburg, F. R., Reich, D. B., & Fitzmaurice, G. (2010). Ten-year use of mental health services by patients with borderline personality disorder and with other Axis II disorders. *Psychiatric Services, 61*(6), 612–616. https://doi.org/10.1176/ps.2010.61.6.612

Insel, T., Cuthbert, B., Garvey, M., Heinssen, R., Pine, D. S., Quinn, K., Sanislow, C., & Wang, P. (2010). Research domain criteria (RDoC): Toward a new classification framework for research on mental disorders. *American Journal of Psychiatry, 167*(7), 748–751. https://doi.org/10.1176/appi.ajp.2010.09091379

Jeung, H., Schwieren, C., & Herpertz, S. C. (2016). Rationality and self-interest as economic-exchange strategy in borderline personality disorder: Game theory, social preferences, and interpersonal behavior. *Neuroscience & Biobehavioral Reviews, 71*, 849–864. https://doi.org/10.1016/j.neubiorev.2016.10.030

Kendler, K. S., Aggen, S. H., Knudsen, G. P., Røysamb, E., Neale, M. C., & Reichborn-Kjennerud, T. (2011). The structure of genetic and environmental risk factors for syndromal and subsyndromal common DSM-IV Axis I and all Axis II disorders. *American Journal of Psychiatry, 168*(1), 29–39. https://doi.org/https://doi.org/10.1176/appi.ajp.2010.10030340

Kernberg, O. (1967). Borderline personality organization. *Journal of the American Psychoanalytic Association, 15*(3), 641–685. https://doi.org/10.1177/000306516701500309

Kerridge, B. T., Pickering, R. P., Saha, T. D., Ruan, W. J., Chou, S. P., Zhang, H., Jung, J., & Hasin, D. S. (2017). Prevalence, sociodemographic correlates and DSM-5 substance use disorders and other psychiatric disorders among sexual minorities in the United States. *Drug and Alcohol Dependence, 170*, 82–92. https://doi.org/10.1016/j.drugalcdep.2016.10.038

Klengel, T., Pape, J., Binder, E. B., & Mehta, D. (2014). The role of DNA methylation in stress-related psychiatric disorders. *Neuropharmacology, 80*, 115–132. https://doi.org/10.1016/j.neuropharm.2014.01.013

Knight, R. P. (1953). Borderline states. *Bulletin of the Menninger Clinic, 17*(1), 1–12.

Knoblich, N., Gundel, F., Brückmann, C., Becker-Sadzio, J., Frischholz, C., & Nieratschker, V. (2018). DNA methylation of APBA3 and MCF2 in borderline personality disorder: Potential biomarkers for response to psychotherapy. *European Neuropsychopharmacology, 28*(2), 252–263. https://doi.org/10.1016/j.euroneuro.2017.12.010

Kotov, R., Krueger, R. F., Watson, D., Achenbach, T. M., Althoff, R. R., Bagby, R. M., . . . Zimmerman, M. (2017). The Hierarchical Taxonomy of Psychopathology (HiTOP): A dimensional alternative to traditional nosologies. *Journal of Abnormal Psychology, 126*(4), 454–477. https://doi.org/10.1037/abn0000258

Krause-Utz, A., Cackowski, S., Daffner, S., Sobanski, E., Plichta, M., Bohus, M., Ende, G., & Schmahl, C. (2016). Delay discounting and response disinhibition under acute experimental stress in women with borderline personality disorder and adult attention deficit hyperactivity disorder. *Psychological Medicine, 46*(15), 3137–3149. https://doi.org/10.1017/S0033291716001677

Kruedelbach, N., McCormick, R. A., Schulz, S. C., & Grueneich, R. (1993). Impulsivity, coping styles, and triggers for craving in substance abusers with borderline personality disorder. *Journal of Personality Disorders, 7*(3), 214–222. https://doi.org/10.1521/pedi.1993.7.3.214

Lazarus, S. A., & Cheavens, J. S. (2017). An examination of social network quality and composition in women with and without borderline personality disorder. *Personality Disorders: Theory, Research, and Treatment, 8*(4), 340. https://doi.org/10.1037/per0000201

Lazarus, S. A., Cheavens, J. S., Festa, F., & Zachary Rosenthal, M. (2014). Interpersonal functioning in borderline personality disorder: A systematic review of behavioral and laboratory-based assessments. *Clinical Psychology Review, 34*(3), 193–205. https://doi.org/10.1016/j.cpr.2014.01.007

Lazarus, S. A., Scott, L. N., Beeney, J. E., Wright, A. G., Stepp, S. D., & Pilkonis, P. A. (2018). Borderline personality disorder symptoms and affective responding to perceptions of rejection and acceptance from romantic versus nonromantic partners. *Personality Disorders: Theory, Research, and Treatment, 9*(3), 197–206. https://doi.org/10.1037/per0000289

Lazarus, S. A., Southward, M. W., & Cheavens, J. S. (2016). Do borderline personality disorder features and rejection sensitivity predict social network outcomes over time? *Personality and Individual Differences, 100*, 62–67. https://doi.org/10.1016/j.paid.2016.02.032

Lenzenweger, M. F., Lane, M. C., Loranger, A. W., & Kessler, R. C. (2007). DSM-IV personality disorders in the National Comorbidity Survey Replication. *Biological Psychiatry, 62*(6), 553–564. https://doi.org/10.1016/j.biopsych.2006.09.019

Lieb, K., Völlm, B., Rücker, G., Timmer, A., & Stoffers, J. M. (2010). Pharmacotherapy for borderline personality disorder: Cochrane systematic review of randomised trials. *British

*Journal of Psychiatry, 196*(1), 4–12. https://doi.org/10.1192/bjp.bp.108.062984

Liebke, L., Bungert, M., Thome, J., Hauschild, S., Gescher, D. M., Schmahl, C., Bohus, M., & Lis, S. (2017). Loneliness, social networks, and social functioning in borderline personality disorder. *Personality Disorders: Theory, Research, and Treatment, 8*(4), 349–356. https://doi.org/10.1037/per0000208

Linehan, M. M. (1993). *Cognitive-behavioral treatment of borderline personality disorder*. Guilford.

Links, P. S., Heslegrave, R., & Reekum, R. V. (1999). Impulsivity: Core aspect of borderline personality disorder. *Journal of Personality Disorders, 13*(1), 1–9. https://doi.org/10.1521/pedi.1999.13.1.1

Lubke, G., Laurin, C., Amin, N., Hottenga, J. J., Willemsen, G., van Grootheest, G., Abdellaoui, A., Karssen, L., Oostra, B., & Van Duijn, C. (2014). Genome-wide analyses of borderline personality features. *Molecular Psychiatry, 19*(8), 923–929. https://doi.org/10.1038/mp.2013.109

Lynam, D. R., & Widiger, T. A. (2001). Using the five-factor model to represent the DSM-IV personality disorders: An expert consensus approach. *Journal of Abnormal Psychology, 110*(3), 401–412. https://doi.org/10.1037//0021-843x.110.3.401

Mann, J. J., Arango, V. A., Avenevoli, S., Brent, D. A., Champagne, F. A., Clayton, P., Currier, D., Dougherty, D. M., Haghighi, F., & Hodge, S. E. (2009). Candidate endophenotypes for genetic studies of suicidal behavior. *Biological Psychiatry, 65*(7), 556–563. https://doi.org/10.1016/j.biopsych.2008.11.021

Manolio, T. A. (2010). Genomewide association studies and assessment of the risk of disease. *New England Journal of Medicine, 363*(2), 166–176. https://doi.org/10.1056/NEJMra0905980

Manuck, S. B., Flory, J. D., Ferrell, R. E., Mann, J. J., & Muldoon, M. F. (2000). A regulatory polymorphism of the monoamine oxidase-A gene may be associated with variability in aggression, impulsivity, and central nervous system serotonergic responsivity. *Psychiatry Research, 95*(1), 9–23. https://doi.org/10.1016/S0165-1781(00)00162-1

Martín-Blanco, A., Ferrer, M., Soler, J., Salazar, J., Vega, D., Andión, O., Sanchez-Mora, C., Arranz, M. J., Ribases, M., & Feliu-Soler, A. (2014). Association between methylation of the glucocorticoid receptor gene, childhood maltreatment, and clinical severity in borderline personality disorder. *Journal of Psychiatric Research, 57*, 34–40. https://doi.org/10.1016/j.jpsychires.2014.06.011

Matthies, S. D., & Philipsen, A. (2014). Common ground in attention deficit hyperactivity disorder (ADHD) and borderline personality disorder (BPD)–review of recent findings. *Borderline Personality Disorder and Emotion Dysregulation, 1*, article 3. https://doi.org/10.1186/2051-6673-1-3

McCloskey, M. S., New, A. S., Siever, L. J., Goodman, M., Koenigsberg, H. W., Flory, J. D., & Coccaro, E. F. (2009). Evaluation of behavioral impulsivity and aggression tasks as endophenotypes for borderline personality disorder. *Journal of Psychiatric Research, 43*(12), 1036–1048. https://doi.org/10.1016/j.jpsychires.2009.01.002

McGlashan, T. H., Grilo, C. M., Sanislow, C. A., Ralevski, E., Morey, L. C., Gunderson, J. G., Skodol, A. E., Shea, M. T., Zanarini, M. C., & Bender, D. (2005). Two-year prevalence and stability of individual DSM-IV criteria for schizotypal, borderline, avoidant, and obsessive-compulsive personality disorders: Toward a hybrid model of Axis II disorders. *American Journal of Psychiatry, 162*(5), 883–889. https://doi.org/10.1176/appi.ajp.162.5.883

McGlashan, T. H., Grilo, C. M., Skodol, A. E., Gunderson, J. G., Shea, M. T., Morey, L. C., Zanarini, M. C., & Stout, R. L. (2000). The collaborative longitudinal personality disorders study: Baseline Axis I/II and II/II diagnostic co-occurrence. *Acta Psychiatrica Scandinavica, 102*(4), 256–264. https://doi.org/10.1034/j.1600-0447.2000.102004256.x

Miano, A., Dziobek, I., & Roepke, S. (2018). Characterizing couple dysfunction in borderline personality disorder. *Journal of Personality Disorders, 34*(2), 181–198. https://doi.org/10.1521/pedi_2018_32_388

Mitchell, A. E., Dickens, G. L., & Picchioni, M. M. (2014). Facial emotion processing in borderline personality disorder: A systematic review and meta-analysis. *Neuropsychology Review, 24*(2), 166–184. https://doi.org/10.1007/s11065-014-9254-9

Morey, L. (1991). *Professional manual for the personality assessment inventory*. Psychological Assessment Resources, p. 1.

Morey, L. C., & Hopwood, C. J. (2013). Stability and change in personality disorders. *Annual Review of Clinical Psychology, 9*, 499–528. https://doi.org/10.1146/annurev-clinpsy-050212-185637

Moser, D. A., Müller, S., Hummel, E. M., Limberg, A. S., Dieckmann, L., Frach, L., Pakusch, J., Flasbeck, V., Brüne, M., Beygo, J., Klein-Hitpass, L., & Kumsta, R. (2020). Targeted bisulfite sequencing: A novel tool for the assessment of DNA methylation with high sensitivity and increased coverage. *Psychoneuroendocrinology, 120*, article 104784. https://doi.org/10.1016/j.psyneuen.2020.104784

Mulay, A. L., Waugh, M. H., Fillauer, J. P., Bender, D. S., Bram, A., Cain, N. M., . . . Skodol, A. E. (2019). Borderline personality disorder diagnosis in a new key. *Borderline Personality Disorder and Emotion Dysregulation, 6*, 18–18. https://doi.org/10.1186/s40479-019-0116-1

Mulder, R. T., Horwood, L. J., & Tyrer, P. (2020). The borderline pattern descriptor in the International Classification of Diseases, 11th Revision: A redundant addition to classification. *Aust N Z J Psychiatry, 54*(11), 1095–1100. https://doi.org/10.1177/0004867420951608

Németh, N., Mátrai, P., Hegyi, P., Czéh, B., Czopf, L., Hussain, A., Pammer, J., Szabó, I., Solymár, M., Kiss, L., Hartmann, P., Szilágyi, Á. L., Kiss, Z., & Simon, M. (2018). Theory of mind disturbances in borderline personality disorder: A meta-analysis. *Psychiatry Research, 270*, 143–153. https://doi.org/10.1016/j.psychres.2018.08.049

Olajide, K., Munjiza, J., Moran, P., O'Connell, L., Newton-Howes, G., Bassett, P., Akintomide, G., Ng, N., Tyrer, P., & Mulder, R. (2018). Development and psychometric properties of the Standardized Assessment of Severity of Personality Disorder (SASPD). *Journal of Personality Disorders, 32*(1), 44–56. https://doi.org/10.1521/pedi_2017_31_285

Oltmanns, J. R., & Widiger, T. A. (2018). A self-report measure for the ICD-11 dimensional trait model proposal: The personality inventory for ICD-11. *Psychological Assessment, 30*(2), 154. https://doi.org/10.1037/pas0000459

Oltmanns, J. R., & Widiger, T. A. (2019). Evaluating the assessment of the ICD-11 personality disorder diagnostic system. *Psychological Assessment, 31*(5), 674–684. https://doi.org/10.1037/pas0000693

Oltmanns, T. F., Friedman, J. N., Fiedler, E. R., & Turkheimer, E. (2004). Perceptions of people with personality disorders based on thin slices of behavior. *Journal of Research in Personality, 38*(3), 216–229. https://doi.org/10.1016/S0092-6566(03)00066-7

Østby, K. A., Czajkowski, N., Knudsen, G. P., Ystrom, E., Gjerde, L. C., Kendler, K. S., Ørstavik, R. E., & Reichborn-Kjennerud, T. (2014). Personality disorders are important risk factors for disability pensioning. *Social Psychiatry and Psychiatric Epidemiology, 49*(12), 2003–2011. https://doi.org/10.1007/s00127-014-0878-0

Paret, C., Jennen-Steinmetz, C., & Schmahl, C. (2017). Disadvantageous decision-making in borderline personality disorder: Partial support from a meta-analytic review. *Neuroscience & Biobehavioral Reviews, 72*, 301–309. https://doi.org/10.1016/j.neubiorev.2016.11.019

Paris, J. (2009). The treatment of borderline personality disorder: Implications of research on diagnosis, etiology, and outcome. *Annual Review of Clinical Psychology, 5*, 277–290. https://doi.org/10.1146/annurev.clinpsy.032408.153457

Passamonti, L., Cerasa, A., Gioia, M. C., Magariello, A., Muglia, M., Quattrone, A., & Fera, F. (2008). Genetically dependent modulation of serotonergic inactivation in the human prefrontal cortex. *NeuroImage, 40*(3), 1264–1273. https://doi.org/10.1016/j.neuroimage.2007.12.028

Perroud, N., Paoloni-Giacobino, A., Prada, P., Olié, E., Salzmann, A., Nicastro, R., Guillaume, S., Mouthon, D., Stouder, C., & Dieben, K. (2011). Increased methylation of glucocorticoid receptor gene (NR3C1) in adults with a history of childhood maltreatment: A link with the severity and type of trauma. *Translational Psychiatry, 1*(12), e59–e59. https://doi.org/10.1038/tp.2011.60

Perroud, N., Salzmann, A., Prada, P., Nicastro, R., Hoeppli, M.-E., Furrer, S., Ardu, S., Krejci, I., Karege, F., & Malafosse, A. (2013). Response to psychotherapy in borderline personality disorder and methylation status of the BDNF gene. *Translational Psychiatry, 3*(1), e207–e207. https://doi.org/10.1038/tp.2012.140

Perroud, N., Zewdie, S., Stenz, L., Adouan, W., Bavamian, S., Prada, P., Nicastro, R., Hasler, R., Nallet, A., & Piguet, C. (2016). Methylation of serotonin receptor 3A in ADHD, borderline personality, and bipolar disorders: Link with severity of the disorders and childhood maltreatment. *Depression and Anxiety, 33*(1), 45–55. https://doi.org/10.1002/da.22406

Porter, C., Palmier-Claus, J., Branitsky, A., Mansell, W., Warwick, H., & Varese, F. (2020). Childhood adversity and borderline personality disorder: A meta-analysis. *Acta Psychiatrica Scandinavica, 141*(1), 6–20. https://doi.org/10.1111/acps.13118

Prados, J., Stenz, L., Courtet, P., Prada, P., Nicastro, R., Adouan, W., Guillaume, S., Olié, E., Aubry, J. M., & Dayer, A. (2015). Borderline personality disorder and childhood maltreatment: A genome-wide methylation analysis. *Genes, Brain and Behavior, 14*(2), 177–188. https://doi.org/10.1111/gbb.12197

Reed, G. M. (2018). Progress in developing a classification of personality disorders for ICD-11. *World Psychiatry, 17*(2), 227–229. https://doi.org/10.1002/wps.20533

Regier, D. A. (2007). Dimensional approaches to psychiatric classification: Refining the research agenda for DSM-V: An introduction. *International Journal of Methods in Psychiatric Research, 16*(S1), S1–S5. https://doi.org/10.1002/mpr.209

Robertson, K. D. (2005). DNA methylation and human disease. *Nature Reviews Genetics, 6*(8), 597–610. https://doi.org/10.1038/nrg1655

Roepke, S., Vater, A., Preißler, S., Heekeren, H. R., & Dziobek, I. (2013). Social cognition in borderline personality disorder. *Frontiers in Neuroscience, 6*. https://doi.org/10.3389/fnins.2012.00195

Rosenthal, M. Z., Fang, C. M., & Chapman, A. L. (2015). Ambulatory measurement of emotional dysfunction in borderline personality disorder. *Current Opinion in Psychology, 3*, 75–79. https://doi.org/10.1016/j.copsyc.2015.02.008

Sadikaj, G., Moskowitz, D., Russell, J. J., Zuroff, D. C., & Paris, J. (2013). Quarrelsome behavior in borderline personality disorder: Influence of behavioral and affective reactivity to perceptions of others. *Journal of Abnormal Psychology, 122*(1), 195–207. https://doi.org/10.1037/a0030871

Sadikaj, G., Russell, J. J., Moskowitz, D., & Paris, J. (2010). Affect dysregulation in individuals with borderline personality disorder: Persistence and interpersonal triggers. *Journal of Personality Assessment, 92*(6), 490–500. https://doi.org/10.1080/00223891.2010.513287

Salvador-Carulla, L., Bendeck, M., Ferrer, M., Andión, O., Aragonès, E., & Casas, M. (2014). Cost of borderline personality disorder in Catalonia (Spain). *European Psychiatry, 29*(8), 490–497. https://doi.org/10.1016/j.eurpsy.2014.07.001

Samuel, D. B., & Widiger, T. A. (2004). Clinicians' personality descriptions of prototypic personality disorders. *Journal of Personality Disorders, 18*(3, Special issue), 286–308. https://doi.org/10.1521/pedi.18.3.286.35446

Samuel, D. B., & Widiger, T. A. (2008). A meta-analytic review of the relationships between the five-factor model and DSM-IV-TR personality disorders: A facet level analysis. *Clinical Psychology Review, 28*(8), 1326–1342. https://doi.org/10.1016/j.cpr.2008.07.002

Sanislow, C. A., Pine, D. S., Quinn, K. J., Kozak, M. J., Garvey, M. A., Heinssen, R. K., Wang, P. S.-E., & Cuthbert, B. N. (2010). Developing constructs for psychopathology research: Research domain criteria. *Journal of Abnormal Psychology, 119*(4), 631–639. https://doi.org/10.1037/a0020909

Sansone, R. A., & Sansone, L. A. (2012). Chronic pain syndromes and borderline personality. *Innovations in Clinical Neuroscience, 9*(1), 10–14.

Santangelo, P., Bohus, M., & Ebner-Priemer, U. W. (2014). Ecological momentary assessment in borderline personality disorder: A review of recent findings and methodological challenges. *Journal of Personality Disorders, 28*(4), 555–576. https://doi.org/10.1521/pedi_2012_26_067

Santangelo, P. S., Reinhard, I., Koudela-Hamila, S., Bohus, M., Holtmann, J., Eid, M., & Ebner-Priemer, U. W. (2017). The temporal interplay of self-esteem instability and affective instability in borderline personality disorder patients' everyday lives. *Journal of Abnormal Psychology, 126*(8), 1057–1065. https://doi.org/10.1037/abn0000288

Saulsman, L. M., & Page, A. C. (2004). The five-factor model and personality disorder empirical literature: A meta-analytic review. *Clinical Psychology Review, 23*(8), 1055–1085. https://doi.org/10.1016/j.cpr.2002.09.001

Scala, J. W., Levy, K. N., Johnson, B. N., Kivity, Y., Ellison, W. D., Pincus, A. L., Wilson, S. J., & Newman, M. G. (2018). The role of negative affect and self-concept clarity in predicting self-injurious urges in borderline personality disorder using ecological momentary assessment. *Journal of Personality Disorders, 32*(Suppl), 36–57. https://doi.org/10.1521/pedi.2018.32.supp.36

Schulze, L., Schmahl, C., & Niedtfeld, I. (2016). Neural correlates of disturbed emotion processing in borderline personality disorder: A multimodal meta-analysis. *Biological Psychiatry, 79*(2), 97–106. https://doi.org/10.1016/j.biopsych.2015.03.027

Schulze, L., Schulze, A., Renneberg, B., Schmahl, C., & Niedtfeld, I. (2019). Neural correlates of affective disturbances: A comparative meta-analysis of negative affect processing in borderline personality disorder, major depressive disorder, and posttraumatic stress disorder. *Biological Psychiatry: Cognitive Neuroscience and Neuroimaging, 4*(3), 220–232. https://doi.org/10.1016/j.bpsc.2018.11.004

Sebastian, A., Jacob, G., Lieb, K., & Tüscher, O. (2013). Impulsivity in borderline personality disorder: A matter of disturbed impulse control or a facet of emotional dysregulation? *Current Psychiatry Reports, 15*(2), article 339. https://doi.org/10.1007/s11920-012-0339-y

Sebastian, A., Jung, P., Krause-Utz, A., Lieb, K., Schmahl, C., & Tüscher, O. (2014). Frontal dysfunctions of impulse control–a systematic review in borderline personality disorder and attention-deficit/hyperactivity disorder. *Frontiers in Human Neuroscience, 8*, article 698. https://doi.org/10.3389/fnhum.2014.00698

Sher, K. J., & Trull, T. J. (2002). Substance use disorder and personality disorder. *Current Psychiatry Reports, 4*(1), 25–29. https://doi.org/10.1007/s11920-002-0008-7

Sieswerda, S., Barnow, S., Verheul, R., & Arntz, A. (2013). Neither dichotomous nor split, but schema-related negative interpersonal evaluations characterize borderline patients. *Journal of Personality Disorders, 27*(1), 36–52. https://doi.org/10.1521/pedi.2013.27.1.36

Siever, L. J. (2008). Neurobiology of aggression and violence. *American Journal of Psychiatry, 165*(4), 429–442. https://doi.org/10.1176/appi.ajp.2008.07111774

Siever, L. J., Torgersen, S., Gunderson, J. G., Livesley, W. J., & Kendler, K. S. (2002). The borderline diagnosis III: Identifying endophenotypes for genetic studies. *Biological Psychiatry, 51*(12), 964–968. https://doi.org/10.1016/S0006-3223(02)01326-4

Skodol, A. E., Gunderson, J. G., McGlashan, T. H., Dyck, I. R., Stout, R. L., Bender, D. S., Grilo, C. M., Shea, M. T., Zanarini, M. C., & Morey, L. C. (2002). Functional impairment in patients with schizotypal, borderline, avoidant, or obsessive-compulsive personality disorder. *American Journal of Psychiatry, 159*(2), 276–283. https://doi.org/10.1176/appi.ajp.159.2.276

Skodol, A. E., Gunderson, J. G., Pfohl, B., Widiger, T. A., Livesley, W. J., & Siever, L. J. (2002). The borderline diagnosis I: Psychopathology, comorbidity, and personaltity structure. *Biological Psychiatry, 51*(12), 936–950. https://doi.org/10.1016/S0006-3223(02)01324-0

Skodol, A. E., Pagano, M. E., Bender, D. S., Shea, M. T., Gunderson, J. G., Yen, S., Stout, R. L., Morey, L. C., Sanislow, C. A., & Grilo, C. M. (2005). Stability of functional impairment in patients with schizotypal, borderline, avoidant, or obsessive–compulsive personality disorder over two years. *Psychological Medicine, 35*(3), 267–283. https://doi.org/10.1176/appi.ajp.159.2.276

Skoglund, C., Tiger, A., Rück, C., Petrovic, P., Asherson, P., Hellner, C., Mataix-Cols, D., & Kuja-Halkola, R. (2019). Familial risk and heritability of diagnosed borderline personality disorder: A register study of the Swedish population. *Molecular Psychiatry, 26*, 999–1008. https://doi.org/10.1038/s41380-019-0442-0

Soeteman, D. I., Roijen, L. H.-v., Verheul, R., & Busschbach, J. J. (2008). The economic burden of personality disorders in mental health care. *Journal of Clinical Psychiatry, 69*(2), 259–265. https://doi.org/10.4088/JCP.v69n0212

Stepp, S. D., & Pilkonis, P. A. (2008). Age-related differences in individual DSM criteria for borderline personality disorder. *Journal of Personality Disorders, 22*(4), 427–432. https://doi.org/10.1521/pedi.2008.22.4.427

Stepp, S. D., Pilkonis, P. A., Yaggi, K. E., Morse, J. Q., & Feske, U. (2009). Interpersonal and emotional experiences of social interactions in borderline personality disorder. *Journal of Nervous and Mental Disease, 197*(7), 484–491. https://doi.org/10.1097/NMD.0b013e3181aad2e7

Stern, A. (1938). Psychoanalytic investigation of and therapy in the border line group of neuroses. *Psychoanalytic Quarterly, 7*(4), 467–489. https://doi.org/10.1080/21674086.1938.11925367

Stiglmayr, C. E., Ebner-Priemer, U. W., Bretz, J., Behm, R., Mohse, M., Lammers, C.-H., Anghelescu, I.-G., Schmahl, C., Schlotz, W., Kleindienst, N., & Bohus, M. (2008). Dissociative symptoms are positively related to stress in borderline personality disorder. *Acta Psychiatrica Scandinavica, 117*(2), 139–147. https://doi.org/10.1111/j.1600-0447.2007.01126.x

Stoffers-Winterling, J. M., Völlm, B. A., Rücker, G., Timmer, A., Huband, N., & Lieb, K. (2012). Psychological therapies for people with borderline personality disorder. *Cochrane Database of Systematic Reviews, 8*(Issue 8), Art. No. CD005652. https://doi.org/10.1002/14651858.CD005652.pub2

Storebø, O. J., Stoffers-Winterling, J. M., Völlm, B. A., Kongerslev, M. T., Mattivi, J. T., Jørgensen, M. S., Faltinsen, E., Todorovac, A., Sales, C. P., Callesen, H. E., & et al. (2020). Psychological therapies for people with borderline personality disorder. *Cochrane Database of Systematic Reviews, 5*. https://doi.org/10.1002/14651858.CD012955.pub2

Teschler, S., Bartkuhn, M., Künzel, N., Schmidt, C., Kiehl, S., Dammann, G., & Dammann, R. (2013). Aberrant methylation of gene associated CpG sites occurs in borderline personality disorder. *PLOS One, 8*(12), article e84180. https://doi.org/10.1371/journal.pone.0084180

Tomko, R. L., Lane, S. P., Pronove, L. M., Treloar, H. R., Brown, W. C., Solhan, M. B., Wood, P. K., & Trull, T. J. (2015). Undifferentiated negative affect and impulsivity in borderline personality and depressive disorders: A momentary perspective. *Journal of Abnormal Psychology, 124*(3), 740–753. https://doi.org/10.1037/abn0000064

Tomko, R. L., Trull, T. J., Wood, P. K., & Sher, K. J. (2014). Characteristics of borderline personality disorder in a community sample: Comorbidity, treatment utilization, and general functioning. *Journal of Personality Disorders, 28*(5), 734–750. https://doi.org/10.1521/pedi_2012_26_093

Torgersen, S., Czajkowski, N., Jacobson, K., Reichborn-Kjennerud, T., Røysamb, E., Neale, M., & Kendler, K. (2008). Dimensional representations of DSM-IV cluster B personality disorders in a population-based sample of Norwegian twins: A multivariate study. *Psychological Medicine, 38*(11), 1617–1625. https://doi.org/10.1017/S0033291708002924

Trull, T. J. (2018). Ambulatory assessment of borderline personality disorder. *Psychopathology, 51*(2), 137–140. https://doi.org/10.1159/000486604

Trull, T. J., Freeman, L. K., Vebares, T. J., Choate, A. M., Helle, A. C., & Wycoff, A. M. (2018). Borderline personality disorder and substance use disorders: An updated review. *Borderline Personality Disorder and Emotion Dysregulation, 5*(1), article 15. https://doi.org/10.1186/s40479-018-0093-9

Trull, T. J., Jahng, S., Tomko, R. L., Wood, P. K., & Sher, K. J. (2010). Revised NESARC personality disorder diagnoses: Gender, prevalence, and comorbidity with substance dependence disorders. *Journal of Personality Disorders, 24*(4), 412–426. https://doi.org/10.1521/pedi.2010.24.4.412

Trull, T. J., Scheiderer, E. M., & Tomko, R. L. (2012). 11. Axis II Comorbidity. In T. A. Widiger (Ed.), *The Oxford handbook of personality disorders* (pp. 219–236). Oxford University Press.

Trull, T. J., Sher, K. J., Minks-Brown, C., Durbin, J., & Burr, R. (2000). Borderline personality disorder and substance use disorders: A review and integration. *Clinical Psychology Review, 20*(2), 235–253. https://doi.org/10.1016/S0272-7358(99)00028-8

Trull, T. J., & Widiger, T. A. (2008). Geology 102: More thoughts on a shift to a dimensional model of personality disorders. *Social and Personality Psychology Compass, 2*(2), 949–967. https://doi.org/10.1111/j.1751-9004.2007.00074.x

Tyrer, P., Mulder, R., Kim, Y. R., & Crawford, M. J. (2019). The Development of the ICD-11 Classification of Personality Disorders: An Amalgam of Science, Pragmatism, and Politics. *Annual Review of Clinical Psychology, 15*, 481–502. https://doi.org/10.1146/annurev-clinpsy-050718-095736

Tyrer, P., Reed, G. M., & Crawford, M. J. (2015). Classification, assessment, prevalence, and effect of personality disorder. *Lancet, 385*(9969), 717–726. https://doi.org/10.1016/S0140-6736(14)61995-4

Van Asselt, A., Dirksen, C. D., Arntz, A., & Severens, J. L. (2007). The cost of borderline personality disorder: Societal cost of illness in BPD-patients. *European Psychiatry, 22*(6), 354–361. https://doi.org/10.1016/j.eurpsy.2007.04.001

WHO. (2020). ICD-11 for mortality and morbidity statistics. https://icd.who.int/browse11/l-m/en

Widiger, T. A., & Samuel, D. B. (2005). Evidence-based assessment of personality disorders. *Psychological Assessment, 17*(3), 278–287. https://doi.org/10.1037/1040-3590.17.3.278

Widiger, T. A., & Trull, T. J. (1993). Borderline and narcissistic personality disorders. In P. B. Sutker & H. E. Adams (Eds.), *Comprehensive handbook of psychopathology* (pp. 371–394). Springer. https://doi.org/10.1007/978-1-4615-3008-4_15

Widiger, T. A., & Trull, T. J. (2007). Plate tectonics in the classification of personality disorder: Shifting to a dimensional model. *American Psychologist, 62*(2), 71–83. https://doi.org/10.1037/0003-066X.62.2.71

Widiger, T. A., Trull, T. J., Clarkin, J. F., Sanderson, C., & Costa Jr, P. T. (2002). A description of the DSM-IV personality disorders with the five-factor model of personality. In T. A. Widiger & P. T. Costa, Jr. (Eds.), *Personality disorders and the five-factor model of personality* (pp. 89–99). American Psychological Association. https://doi.org/10.1037/10423-006

Widiger, T. A., & Weissman, M. M. (1991). Epidemiology of borderline personality disorder. *Psychiatric Services, 42*(10), 1015–1021. https://doi.org/10.1176/ps.42.10.1015

Wilson, S., Stroud, C. B., & Durbin, C. E. (2017). Interpersonal dysfunction in personality disorders: A meta-analytic review. *Psychological Bulletin, 143*(7), 677–734. https://doi.org/10.1037/bul0000101

Wingenfeld, K., Rullkoetter, N., Mensebach, C., Beblo, T., Mertens, M., Kreisel, S., Toepper, M., Driessen, M., & Woermann, F. G. (2009). Neural correlates of the individual emotional Stroop in borderline personality disorder. *Psychoneuroendocrinology, 34*(4), 571–586. https://doi.org/10.1016/j.psyneuen.2008.10.024

Witt, S. H., Streit, F., Jungkunz, M., Frank, J., Awasthi, S., Reinbold, C. S., . . . Lieb, K. (2017). Genome-wide association study of borderline personality disorder reveals genetic overlap with bipolar disorder, major depression and schizophrenia. *Translational Psychiatry, 7*(6), e1155–e1155.

Wycoff, A. M., Carpenter, R. W., Hepp, J., Lane, S. P., & Trull, T. J. (2020). Drinking motives moderate daily-life associations between affect and alcohol use in individuals with borderline personality disorder. *Psychology of Addictive Behaviors, 34*(7), 745–755. https://doi.org/10.1037/adb0000588

Young, J. E., Klosko, J. S., & Weishaar, M. E. (2003). Schema therapy: A Practitioner's guide. New York: Guilford Press.

Zaboli, G., Gizatullin, R., Nilsonne, Å., Wilczek, A., Jönsson, E. G., Ahnemark, E., Åsberg, M., & Leopardi, R. (2006). Tryptophan hydroxylase-1 gene variants associate with a group of suicidal borderline women. *Neuropsychopharmacology, 31*(9), 1982–1990. https://doi.org/10.1038/sj.npp.1301046

Zanarini, M. C., Frankenburg, F. R., Reich, D. B., & Fitzmaurice, G. (2010). Time to attainment of recovery from borderline personality disorder and stability of recovery: A 10-year prospective follow-up study. *American Journal of Psychiatry, 167*(6), 663–667. https://doi.org/10.1176/appi.ajp.2009.09081130

# CHAPTER 29

# Schizotypy and Schizotypic Psychopathology: Theory, Evidence, and Future Directions

Mark F. Lenzenweger

## Introduction

The role of genetic influences in schizophrenia (Henriksen et al., 2017; Gottesman, 1991) has long been established beyond dispute, and there is ample evidence implicating dysfunction in underlying neural systems (McCutcheon et al., 2020) and neural development. However, the precise etiology and pathogenesis of schizophrenia remain opaque. We continue to treat the signs, symptoms, cognition, and functioning impairments in the illness without an understanding of their etiology (Keepers et al., 2020). Illuminating the precise nature of the liability for schizophrenia and its various clinical and endophenotypic manifestations remains a high priority in psychopathology research. In this vein, schizotypic psychopathology, which is intimately connected to schizophrenia, has long intrigued researchers and clinicians for more than 100 years. In short, schizotypic psychopathology represents a unique and rich window on schizophrenia liability (Lenzenweger, 1998, 2010, 2018a, 2018b), and therein lies the heuristic basis for much of the scientific activity in this area of psychopathology research.

Beginning with early observations and speculations by Kraepelin (1919/1971) and Bleuler (1911/1950) in the early 1900s and continuing up through the most recent revision of the American Psychiatric Association's official diagnostic nomenclature (*DSM-5*) and the World Health Organization's *ICD-11*, schizotypic psychopathology has posed challenges to classification, theory, and experimental approaches. Some resolution has emerged recently as both the *DSM-5* and the *ICD-11* currently place schizotypic pathology within the schizophrenia blocks (Bach & First, 2018; Valle, 2020), which accords well with current research linking it to schizophrenia. The term *schizotypic psychopathology* has encompassed paranoid and schizotypal personality disorder (PD) as defined by the previous *DSM* nomenclatures (beginning in 1980), but, importantly, one must realize that definitions of schizotypic psychopathology are *not* solely reliant on the American Psychiatric Association's *DSM* nomenclature. Schizotypic psychopathology has been approached from a variety of theoretical and methodological vantage points, each offering useful insights into the fundamental nature of this class of psychopathology. In addition to these traditional approaches, newer contemporary dimensional approaches to psychopathology have emerged on

| Abbreviations | |
|---|---|
| APD | Avoidant personality disorder |
| BS | Benign schizotypy (model) |
| CNS | Central nervous system |
| IPDE | International Personality Disorder Examination |
| LSPD | Longitudinal Study of Personality Disorders |
| MIS | Magical Ideation Scale |
| PAS | Perceptual Aberration Scale |
| PPD | Paranoid personality disorder |
| RSAS | Revised Social Anhedonia Scale |
| SRPDs | Schizophrenia-related personality disorders |
| SPD | Schizotypal personality disorder |
| SPQ | Schizotypal Personality Questionnaire |
| SZD | Schizoid personality disorder |

the research scene, each of which has relevance to schizotypy and schizotypic psychopathology (e.g., the hierarchical model proposed by the HiToP group (e.g., Kotov et al., 2018; the Alternative Model for Personality Disorders (AMPD) included in the *DSM-5*) (Krueger et al., 2018). The variation in these different approaches has generated alternative units of analysis for schizotypic psychopathology that have not always conformed to prevailing psychiatric diagnostic nomenclatures, thus yielding challenges to consistency, organization of findings, and other issues for the student of schizotypic psychopathology. On the other hand, theory and research in schizotypic psychopathology enjoy a spirited level of debate and development that remains exceptional in psychopathology.

Although relatively rare even through the early 1980s, research on schizotypic psychopathology grew in a meteoric fashion over the past 40 years and now represents one of the most active areas of inquiry in psychiatry, clinical science, experimental psychopathology, and developmental psychopathology. For example, as of early 2021, there were 2,459 published reports (according to a Web of Science—Science Citation Index search) that included the words *schizotypal* or *schizotypy* just in their titles. Accordingly, this review must be necessarily selective and makes no claim to be comprehensive.

The intention of this chapter's discussion is to introduce the reader to schizotypic psychopathology and identify several central theoretical and research issues and how they are confronted in this area of psychopathology research. Several empirical and theoretical reviews on this topic are available (Lenzenweger, 2010, 2018a, 2018b; Kerns, 2020; Kirchner et al., 2018; Raine, 2006; Rosell, Futterman, McMaster, & Siever, 2014). A collection of papers on schizotypal personality that covers research and theory up through the early 1990s remains well worth consulting by current students (Raine et al., 1995). An array of rich papers specifically on schizotypy can be found in two Special Issues of *Schizophrenia Bulletin* (Volume 41, Supplement 2, 2015 and Volume 44, Supplement 2, 2018) including commentary (Lenzenweger, 2015, 2018a, 2018b). Although this chapter discusses research findings relevant to the *DSM*-defined schizotypal (SPD) and paranoid PD (PPD), it does *not* focus solely on these diagnostic entities as defined in the various *DSM* systems. Indeed, a central organizing theme here is that observable schizotypic psychopathology reflects underlying schizotypy, and the range phenotypic expression of schizotypy extends beyond SPD and PPD, suggesting an expanded phenotype (Lenzenweger, 2010, 2018a, 2018b).

## Schizotypic Psychopathology: Definitional Issues, Terminology, and Relevant Distinctions

It is important to explicate and clarify several relevant distinctions regarding the meaning of the term "schizotypic." In this chapter, the terms "schizotypal" and "paranoid" are used to denote the PDs as defined by the *DSM* nomenclatures. SPD and PPD are, by definition, merely sets of descriptors (signs [observed] and symptoms [reported by patient]) that serve as diagnostic criteria; *DSM* systems (since 1980 [*DSM-III*] continuing to the *DSM-5*) eschew any relationship to an explanatory framework for these disorders. Moreover, given their relatively high degree of comorbidity, shared phenomenologic features (e.g., suspiciousness), and relationship to clinical schizophrenia, SPD and PPD are often referred to as the *schizophrenia-related PDs* (SRPDs) and are viewed as falling within the realm of *schizophrenia spectrum disorders*. In contrast, the term "schizotypic" can be used to describe signs and symptoms that are the phenotypic manifestation of schizotypy, or a latent personality organization that derives from a liability for schizophrenia as conceptualized in Meehl's classic model (1962, 1990; see Lenzenweger, 2010; e.g., Grant et al., 2013). The term can also serve as a generic shorthand descriptor of "schizophrenia-like" phenomenology that is stable and enduring but is fundamentally nonpsychotic, without necessarily referring to Meehl's model. The adjective *nonpsychotic* is critical here, for example an "idea of reference" is nonpsychotic, whereas a "delusion of reference" is psychotic from the standpoint of phenomenology.

SPD and PPD are conceived of as manifestations of schizotypy, but they are neither isomorphic with nor exhaustive of the breadth of the schizotypy construct. "Schizotypic psychopathology" serves as a generic term for this general class of mental disturbance. In this context, schizoid PD is generally not considered to be a schizophrenia-related PD in light of available evidence and, therefore, is not viewed as an example of schizotypic psychopathology in this discussion. The argument has been made that both schizoid PDs (SZD) and avoidant PDs (APD) could justifiably be included within the realm of schizotypic/schizophrenia spectrum pathology (Fogelson et al., 2007); however, the data supportive of this claim are limited. It is noteworthy that the "schizophrenia spectrum and other primary psychotic disorders" block in the *ICD-11* only includes SPD but not other PDs, which is similar to the situation with *DSM-5*.

## A Clinical Vignette

The following case vignette presents an example of a schizotypic person. Additional clinical vignettes of schizotypic cases can be found in Lenzenweger (2010).

> Robin, a 24-year-old, single male graduate student in physics at a large midwestern research university, has a long history of exceedingly strong anxiety symptoms in response to social interactions. In fact, he describes his experience of social interaction as being similar to the feeling one has when one's "knuckles accidently scrape across a carrot grater." He has no interest in social interaction and leads a socially isolated life and does not seek out social contact; many see him as a "loner." He has but one friend with whom he has talks about only highly esoteric topics, and he refers to these discussions as "technicalizing." He frequently uses other words in a peculiar and vague manner. Aside from anxiety, he claims to feel no strong emotions such as joy or even sadness. He frequently thinks that neutral events have "special relevance" for him and often seems to misperceive aspects of his body (e.g., he misjudges the length of his arms or legs). Despite having adequate financial resources, Robin's attire is often best described as "odd" or "eccentric," though clearly not fashionably stylish or trendy.

## Defining the Schizotype

### Organization of Schizotypic Signs and Symptoms

As psychopathologists have come to learn that schizotypic psychopathology is likely to be related in a meaningful way to the liability for schizophrenia, some have sought to determine if the organization of schizotypic signs and symptoms bears any resemblance to what is known about the organization of actual schizophrenia phenomenology. In short, exploratory (see Andreasen et al., 1995) and confirmatory (Lenzenweger & Dworkin, 1996) factor analytic studies have suggested that schizophrenia symptoms are best organized into three factors: negative symptoms (flattened affect, avolition), reality distortion (hallucinations, delusions), and disorganization (thought disorder), with a fourth possible factor consisting of premorbid social impairment (see Lenzenweger & Dworkin, 1996). Factor analytic studies of schizotypic signs and symptoms yield solutions or conform to models that are broadly consistent with the factorial structure observed for schizophrenia. For example, Raine (1991) found a three-factor model, consisting of cognitive/perceptual, interpersonal, and disorganization components, that provided a good fit to observed data. And for the most part, results from other factor and other latent structure analytic studies of schizotypy indicators have been rather consistent (Vollema & Hoitjink, 2000; cf. Kwapil et al., 2008; Kwapil et al., 2018). Thus, at the phenotypic level, schizotypic signs and symptoms appear not only as nonpsychotic attenuated schizophrenia manifestations, but also as being organized in a similar fashion at the latent level.

### Methodological Approaches to Assessing Nonpsychotic Schizotypic Psychopathology

Nonpsychotic schizotypic psychopathology can be defined in one of three ways: (1) clinically/diagnostically, (2) in terms of deviance on reliable dimensional laboratory measures, or (3) by virtue of having a first-degree biological relative affected with schizophrenia (Lenzenweger, 2010, 2018a, 2018b). The clinical approach implied in psychiatric diagnostic schemes involves, quite obviously, the use of explicit diagnostic criteria to identify either SPD or PPD (e.g., the *DSM* systems). Note that SPD and PPD, though highly associated with each other, constitute coherent and relatively separable syndromes; however, a recent review raises questions about the viability of PPD as a diagnosis given the minimal interest shown in it by researchers (Triebwasser et al., 2013).

A second approach involves the use of reliable and valid psychometric (or other laboratory) measures of schizotypy to detect schizotypic psychopathology as defined by quantitative deviance on such measures. In this approach, psychometric scales designed to assess various schizotypic manifestations serve to define and measure the schizotypy construct; schizotypic status may be defined by deviance on one or more of such measures. The fundamentals of the psychometric high-risk approach have been discussed and reviewed extensively in other venues (Lenzenweger, 1994, 2010). The hypothetical relations among these alternative approaches in defining schizotypic psychopathology are depicted in Figure 29.1. Cases of schizophrenia are assumed to be direct reflections of true

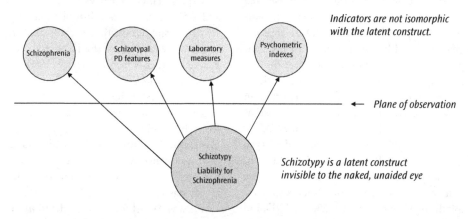

**Figure 29.1** Hypothetical relations among schizotypy-related constructs. All cases of properly diagnosed schizophrenia (excluding phenocopies, such as drug-induced psychosis) are manifestations of "true schizotypy." *DSM* schizotypal (SPD) and paranoid (PPD) personality disorders, which themselves overlap, are fallible manifestations of true schizotypy. Psychometrically assessed schizotypy is also fallible and, therefore, partially overlaps with a true schizotypy as well as observed manifestations such as schizophrenia, SPD, and PPD.

schizotypy (discounting obvious and objectively classified phenocopies; e.g., PCP-induced psychosis). Schizotypy features assessed via psychometrics, as well as clinically assessed SPD and PPD, are not perfectly related to an underlying genuine schizotypy construct owing necessarily to imperfect measurement; thus they are considered fallible measures of true schizotypy. As depicted in Figure 29.1, SPD and PPD themselves overlap somewhat (see later discussion).

Finally, one can be concerned with the biological relatives of patients with schizophrenia and speak of "genotypic" schizotypes. Although many first-degree relatives of patients with schizophrenia will *not* evidence their underlying genetic predisposition to the illness through schizotypic symptomatology, they are, as a group, at increased statistical risk for schizophrenia and can be spoken of as *schizotypes*. Some relatives of patients with schizophrenia will, indeed, display schizotypic symptomatology (e.g., Kendler et al., 1993), and some will go on to develop clinical schizophrenia. Of course, some relatives can carry the liability for schizophrenia quietly, giving little indication of its presence (Gottesman & Bertelsen, 1989). It is essential to note that not every biological relative of a schizophrenia-affected person will harbor liability for the illness (Hanson et al., 1977); that is, it is possible to be a noncarrier of schizophrenia liability.

In this context it is important to note that the subjects identified in "clinical high-risk" (CHR) studies of schizophrenia (often termed "prodromal studies") (see Fusar-Poli et al., 2013) are often deeply impaired and showing evidence of psychosis, albeit reduced in severity. Thus, CHR subjects do not display nonpsychotic schizotypic psychopathology as typically defined (see Lenzenweger, 2021).

## Prevalence of Schizotypic Psychopathology

*Epidemiology of Personality Pathology: General Considerations*

Lenzenweger, Loranger, and colleagues (1997) estimated the point prevalence of diagnosed PD to be approximately 11% (95% confidence interval [CI] = 7.57%, 14.52%). The two-stage procedure for case identification coupled with advanced estimation procedures was subsequently used in the National Comorbidity Study-Replication (NCS-R) investigation (Lenzenweger, Lane, Loranger, & Kessler, 2007). In the NCS-R, which used well-trained screening personnel and clinically experienced diagnosticians using the International Personality Disorder Examination (IPDE, Loranger et al., 1994), a population prevalence of 9.0% for "any personality disorder" was found for the US general population (see also Lenzenweger, 2008).

### Epidemiology of Schizotypic Psychopathology

For most of the past century prevalence "estimates" for schizotypic psychopathology have been arrived at through indirect routes and considered at best to be educated guesses. The *DSM* systems have "suggested" prevalences for SPD of approximately 3% and for PPD at 0.5–2.5% in the general population. Such "guesstimates" were derived from relatively large clinical (psychiatric patient) samples. For example, Loranger (1990) reported, in a large series of consecutive psychiatric admissions to a university teaching hospital, 2.1% for *DSM-III* SPD and 1.2% for PPD. Zimmerman and Coryell (1990) reported that SPD was found in 3.0% of their respondents and PPD in 0.4%. In a more recent series of 859 psychiatric outpatients (university hospital), prevalence rates of .6% for SPD and 4.2% for PPD were reported (Zimmerman et al., 2005).

Since 1997, a number of community-based samples have been studied using epidemiological methods and state-of-the-art diagnostic interviews, and we now have reasonable estimates for SPD and PPD rates in the population. Lenzenweger (2008) summarized the prevalence data for SPD and PPD from five community studies (four US studies, two European studies) (see Table 28.1). For SPD, the prevalences ranged from 0.06% to 1.6% (median = 0.6%), whereas the prevalences for PPD ranged from 0.7% to 5.10% (median = 1.00%). In the NCS-R, Lenzenweger, Lane et al. (2007) found a prevalence of 5.7% (SE = 1.6) for Cluster A disorders (which included schizoid PD) for the US population. The median prevalence value for "any Cluster A PD" (including schizoid PD) taken across the six epidemiological studies was 3.45%. Quirk and colleagues (2016) similarly estimated the prevalence for SPD to be about 4%. Chemerinski et al. (2013) concluded that SPD remains best thought of as a relatively infrequent disorder, even in clinical settings.

One must, however, remember that "schizotypic psychopathology" is a broader construct than the contemporary definitions of *DSM-5* or *ICD-11* SPD and PPD. Therefore, useful guidance on the epidemiology of this "broader construct" should be considered as well. For example, Essen-Möller, Larsson, Uddenberg, and White (1956) reported from their landmark study of a rural Swedish population that schizoid personality, in the sense of "probably related to schizophrenia or to a schizophrenic taint" (p. 73), was found among 1.8% of women and 6.0% of men. Kety et al. (1994), in a report from their Danish Adoption Study of Schizophrenia, found that among the biological relatives of normal control adoptees, 0.8% were paranoid personality, 3.3% were schizoid personality, and 2.5% were "latent schizophrenia," a pre-*DSM-III* diagnostic designation roughly akin to SPD. In a secondary analysis of the Kety et al. (1994) data, Kendler, Gruenberg, and Kinney (1994) found that, according to *DSM-III* criteria, from 3.1% to 3.7% of the relatives of the normal control adoptees had either SPD or a "schizophrenia spectrum" diagnosis (or, schizotypic psychopathology more generally). Generalization from family-based data to population prevalence must be done with great caution, however, owing to various constraints inherent in family data (Carey et al., 1980).

Finally, based on a consideration of familial risk rates among biological relatives, Meehl (1990) argued that approximately 10% of the population is genotypically schizotypic, though not all individuals manifest this predisposition in a highly visible manner. Meehl's conjecture is supported by empirical taxometric (Korfine & Lenzenweger, 1995; Lenzenweger & Korfine, 1992a; Linscott, 2007; Linscott & Morton, 2018; Meyer & Keller, 2001) and mixture modeling results (Lenzenweger, McLachlan, & Rubin, 2007).

### Comorbidity Among DSM-Defined SPD and PPD

In this context, it is useful to define the terms "covariation," "co-occurrence," and "comorbidity." *Covariation* concerns the degree to which measures correlate (e.g., the correlation or association between SPD and PPD features when both have been assessed in the same patients). *Co-occurrence* refers to the rate at which two conditions (e.g., diagnoses) appear together (e.g., the rate at which PPD and SPD diagnoses appear in the same patients). Finally, *comorbidity*, which is a term from epidemiology and medicine, concerns the presence of two or more illnesses in the same patients (e.g., heart disease + diabetes). Comorbidity as an issue for schizotypic psychopathology is usually concerned with the presence of SPD and PPD diagnoses in the same individuals, as observed in clinical samples. The pre-*DSM-5* nomenclatures allowed (even encouraged) multiple diagnoses on what was then the Axis II of the multiaxial system. Therefore, that feature of the system complicates any discussion of comorbidity. Observed comorbidity for SPD and PPD may represent little more than an artifact of rules (or guidelines) of the then prevailing diagnostic system. Therefore, as opposed to the implication that two diseases are actually present in the same person (genuine comorbidity), it may actually make greater sense to simply speak of "co-occurrence" of PD diagnoses within a *DSM* framework.

Available data indicate that PPD appears to be present in 0–60% of patients with SPD drawn from primarily clinical samples (Siever, Bernstein, & Silverman, 1991). SPD is present in 17–70% of patients diagnosed with PPD (Bernstein et al., 1993). Zimmerman et al. (2005) found that PPD and SPD diagnoses co-occurred frequently in their outpatient clinical series, and Lenzenweger, Lane, and colleagues (2007) found substantial covariation between PPD and SPD features in the NCS-R sample. It is essential to note that PPD is, in fact, rarely found alone in patients, often occurring with SPD (Triebwasser et al., 2013). In this context "covariation" refers to associations or correlations among the PDs, where the unit of analysis is typically the number of diagnostic criteria met for each of the disorders, whereas "co-occurrence" refers to the rate at which two disorders appear together in the same person in a sample of individuals assessed for the presence or absence of different PDs.

Therefore, these co-occurrence/covariation rates may reflect (1) a system that allows multiple diagnoses, (2) shared diagnostic criteria, (3) sampling bias (e.g., more individuals who are impaired tend to seek treatment), and/or (4) a common underlying substrate (e.g., schizotypy as a latent liability for schizophrenia). Regarding shared diagnostic criteria, PPD and SPD share the features of suspiciousness and paranoia, but PPD lacks the cognitive and perceptual distortions included in the SPD criteria. The sampling bias issue is especially relevant here given that most individuals diagnosed with SPD or PPD probably never present for treatment, but, when they do, they are likely to be in crisis, be more impaired, or both (Lenzenweger & Korfine, 1992b).

Available data also reveal that 33–91% of individuals diagnosed with SPD tend to also receive the diagnosis of borderline PD (BPD; Chemerinski et al., 2013), though fewer BPD-diagnosed cases have a co-occurring SPD diagnosis. Zimmerman et al. (2005) reported significant comorbidity between SPD and BPD as well as between PPD and BPD. Lenzenweger, Lane, and colleagues (2007) found a relatively strong association between PPD and BPD features, with a weaker association between SPD and BPD. This degree of co-occurrence/covariation may reflect, in part, the influence of the method used to derive the original SPD and BPD diagnostic criteria as well as less specific psychotic-like features that occur in both disorders and the sampling issue noted previously.

### Dimensional Measurement and Covariation Among Schizotypy Measures

The issue of comorbidity is not directly relevant to schizotypic psychopathology as assessed by dimensionally configured psychometric measures as these do not reflect a categorical approach to classification. Measures of schizotypy, however, do tend to be intercorrelated (Kwapil et al., 2008, 2018) as one would expect of valid indices tapping a common underlying construct. Inasmuch as the "psychoticism" dimension of the Alternative Model of Personality Disorder in the *DSM-5* can be considered to tap aspects of schizotypic psychopathology, the facets of unusual beliefs and experiences, perceptual dysregulation, and eccentricity are highly correlated with psychoticism, whereas (somewhat oddly) suspiciousness is not (Krueger et al., 2012).

## Longitudinal Course of Schizotypic Psychopathology

For many years, psychiatry and clinical psychology have assumed that personality pathology, including schizotypic psychopathology, was relatively stable over time. However, the data upon which that assumption of continuity or stability rested were relatively sparse—indeed, virtually nonexistent. Only within the past two decades have the data from multiwave, prospective, longitudinal studies begun to emerge to address this question. The available data from the four major prospective longitudinal studies of PDs have indicated that PDs are considerably more plastic and changeable than ever thought (Lenzenweger et al., 2018).

The Longitudinal Study of Personality Disorders (LSPD) (Lenzenweger, 1999a, 2006) reported that SPD and PPD, while maintaining rank order stability over time, showed evidence for nontrivial declines in mean level feature counts over a 4-year study period. However, when the LSPD data were examined in finer detail using individual growth curve analysis, the amount of individual change observed in PPD over time was insignificant, whereas the amount of individual change in SPD over time was appreciable. Johnson et al. (2000) found evidence for substantial rank-order stability of PPD and SPD features through time as well as rather substantial and significant declines in the mean level of PPD and SPD features over time in a large, community-based longitudinal study. Finally, in a clinical sample of schizotypal patients followed longitudinally, Shea et al. (2002) reported a comparable set of results showing maintenance of individual difference (rank order) stability for SPD features over time, yet clear evidence of a decline in SPD features over time at the level of group means (see also Sanislow et al., 2009). The overall longitudinal picture, therefore, is consistent across studies, yet complex. PPD and SPD appear to maintain rank-order stability over time in the context of diminishing features at the group and individual levels. The mechanisms and processes accounting for these changes have not been illuminated thus far.

## Historical Overview of Schizotypic Psychopathology

Variants of psychopathology thought to be related to schizophrenia, or schizotypic pathology, have been identified in different ways across the years (see Kendler, 1985, for historical review; see also Planansky, 1972). The difficult methodological and conceptual issues attending research in this area have been carefully reviewed by Gottesman (Gottesman, 1987; Shields et al., 1975) and Lenzenweger (2010, 2015, 2018a, 2018b).

Kraepelin (1919/1971, p. 234) and Bleuler (1911/1950, p. 239) made note of what they termed "latent schizophrenia," a personality aberration regarded as a quantitatively less severe expression of schizophrenia. Interestingly, because Kraepelin and Bleuler believed that the signs and symptoms of the so-called latent schizophrenia were in fact continuous with the "principal malady" (Kraepelin, 1896/1971, p. 234) or "manifest types of the disease" (Bleuler, 1911/1950, p. 239), neither of these master phenomenologists provided extended clinical descriptions of such cases. Both suggested one merely envision schizotypic conditions as characterized by diminished schizophrenia signs and symptoms. In attending to schizotypic pathology, however, Kraepelin and Bleuler foreshadowed subsequent efforts to delineate the phenotypic boundaries of schizophrenia through exploration of the schizotypic states.

In reviewing the history of psychiatric developments that culminated in the diagnostic criteria for SPD in *DSM-III*, Kendler (1985) persuasively argued that much of the clinical literature dealing with schizotypic states can be organized along two major historical trends. The "familial" tradition emphasizes phenomenological descriptions of nonpsychotic but aberrant personality states that occur in the biological relatives of individuals suffering from clinical schizophrenia. The second tradition was termed "clinical," as it emphasizes the work of clinicians who describe the symptomatology of their patients presenting schizotypic, or schizophrenia-like, features. As detailed by Kendler (1985), workers within the familial tradition (e.g., Kraepelin, Bleuler, Kretschemer, Kallmann, Slater) frequently used terms such as "latent schizophrenia," "schizoid personality or character," or "schizoform abnormalities" to describe some family members of patients with schizophrenia. These early observers used terms like "eccentric-odd," "irritable-unreasonable," "socially isolated," "aloof/cold demeanor," and "suspiciousness" to describe the family members of schizophrenia patients (Kendler, 1985, p. 543, Table 29.1).

In contrast, researchers and clinicians working within the so-called clinical tradition (Kendler, 1985; e.g., Zilboorg, Deutsch, Hoch and Polatin, Rado, and Meehl) used terms such as "ambulatory schizophrenia," "as-if personality," "pseudoneurotic schizophrenia," and "schizotypal" to describe individuals who were severely affected but nonpsychotic. The patients described by these rubrics were observed to demonstrate "schizophrenia-like symptomatology" in their psychological and psychosocial functioning, and it was frequently hypothesized that a genuine schizophrenia-related process was driving the manifest pathology. Disordered ("primary process") thinking and the lack of deep interpersonal relations were the two features that occurred most frequently in the descriptions of schizotypic patients by clinical tradition workers (Kendler, 1985, p. 545, table 2). Kendler (1985) noted apparent basic agreement in the descriptions of schizotypic individuals across the two traditions in terms of interpersonal functioning impairments as well as broad overlap in other areas (e.g., disordered thinking, anxiety, anger, hypersensitivity).

Early depictions of schizotypic psychopathology, with the exception of those discussions by Rado and Meehl, were only *descriptive* and lacked any detailed etiological or developmental proposals. Although there was speculation about an association with schizophrenia and a possible hereditary connection, the precise pathway leading from the underlying liability for schizophrenia or schizophrenia-related pathology to the phenotypic expression of a clinical disorder was absent. Only Meehl (1962, 1964, 1990, 2001) offered a complex developmental model, setting him apart from other clinical researchers.

Perhaps the most influential early evidence that helped to establish a link between schizotypic

Table 29.1 Prevalence (percentage) of personality disorders in six nonclinical population/community studies using validated structured interviews

| Study | Lenzenweger, Loranger et al. (1997) | Torgersen et al. (2001) | Samuels et al. (2002) | Crawford et al. (2005) | Coid et al. (2006) | Lenzenweger, Lane et al. (2007) |
|---|---|---|---|---|---|---|
| Instrument | IPDE | SIDP-R | IPDE | SCID-II | SCID-II | IPDE |
| Nomenclature | *DSM-III-R* | *DSM-III-R* | *DSM-IV* | *DSM-IV* | *DSM-IV* | *DSM-IV* |
| Location | Ithaca, NY | Oslo, Norway | Baltimore, MD | Upstate New York | Great Britain (National) | United States (National) |
| **Personality disorder** | | | | | | |
| Paranoid | 1.0 | 2.4 | 0.7 | 5.1 | .7 | — |
| Schizoid | 1.0 | 1.7 | 0.9 | 1.7 | .8 | — |
| Schizotypal | 1.6 | 0.6 | 0.6 | 1.1 | .06 | — |
| Cluster A | 2.8 | 4.1 | 2.1 | 6.8 | 1.6 | 5.7 |

*Note:* Instruments indicate the structured clinical interview used: International Personality Disorder Examination (IPDE); Structured Interview for *DSM-III-R* Personality Disorders (SIDP-R); Structured Clinical Interview for *DSM-IV* Axis II Disorders (SCID-II). Dashes indicate not applicable. All prevalences reported are weighted. In this context another epidemiological study, the National Epidemiologic Study of Alcohol and Related Conditions (NESARC; Grant et al., 2004), generated prevalence estimates for *DSM-IV* Cluster A personality disorders that are strikingly higher than those reported in most of the studies contained in this table (paranoid = 4.4%, schizotypal = 3.9%, schizoid = 3.13%). However, methodological limitations of the NESARC study (e.g., use of an unvalidated Axis II assessment instrument; use of census workers without clinical training to conduct Axis II assessments) urge substantial caution in any consideration of the NESARC prevalence data (thus, they are not included in this table).

phenomenology and clinical schizophrenia came from the Danish Adoption Study of Schizophrenia (Kety et al., 1968). Using a definition of "borderline schizophrenia" heavily influenced by the clinical tradition described here, Kety et al. (1968) found elevated rates of borderline or latent schizophrenia in the biological relatives of adoptees with schizophrenia. Kety et al. (1994) further confirmed these initial results through further study of adoptees from the entire Danish population. These early results provided compelling evidence derived from a rigorous adoption methodology for a genetically transmitted component underlying manifest schizophrenia and the less severe schizophrenia-like disorders. The hypothesized continuity between the conditions was thus not merely phenomenological but also genetic. The diagnostic framework used by Kety et al. (1968) to diagnose "borderline" schizophrenia was subsequently reexamined (Spitzer et al., 1979) for use in the Axis II section of what would become the *DSM-III*. However, Spitzer and colleagues were not attempting to distill from the Kety et al. framework only symptoms that identified biological relatives of individuals with schizophrenia; rather, they sought to determine if there was a reliable parsing of Kety's criteria that might map more narrowly defined and identifiable disorders. Spitzer et al. (1979) proposed the following eight symptoms and signs for SPD: magical thinking, ideas of reference, suspiciousness, recurrent illusions, social isolation, odd speech, undue social anxiety-hypersensitivity, and inadequate rapport (aloof/cold). These criteria were, in large part, adopted for use in the *DSM-III* and continue in use in the *DSM-5*. SPD was originally considered a PD, but in the *DSM-5* it is placed within the schizophrenia spectrum conditions, a move informed by decades of empirical research and theoretical argument (Lenzenweger, 1998). The *DSM* criteria for SPD were, and remain, essentially atheoretical in nature, reflecting merely a clustering of symptoms, denoted with no specification of etiology or development.

This overview provides a suggestion of the interest schizotypic conditions have enjoyed among clinical and research workers, especially since 1980. It is important to realize that with the advent of explicit diagnostic criteria for SPD in 1980 in the *DSM-III* and a simultaneous narrowing of the definition of schizophrenia, there was a marked decrease in the rate at which schizophrenia was diagnosed and a corresponding rise in diagnosis of Axis II schizophrenia-related PDs (Loranger, 1990). Such an effect generated by a shift in the nomenclature has surely facilitated the focus on schizotypic conditions. It is also reasonable to assume that interest in these conditions has been further augmented by the burgeoning of research work in PDs in general, which has been greatly facilitated by improvements in diagnostics (cf. Loranger, 1999). Clearly, this interest has been sustained through a rich descriptive tradition and supported by findings indicating that schizotypic pathology is related genetically to schizophrenia per se (see Torgersen, 1994). Indeed, recent evidence, done in the form of genome-wide scans for loci relevant to schizophrenia and schizotypic psychopathology dimensions, confirms shared genetic substrates for the two forms of psychopathology (Fanous et al., 2007; see also Avramopoulos et al., 2002; Lin et al., 2005; Siever et al., 2011; Walter et al., 2016).

## Classic Model of Schizotypic Psychopathology: Meehl's Integrative Developmental Model of Schizotypy

As already noted, many of the early depictions of schizotypic pathology were virtually all descriptive in nature. Although the peculiarities of the relatives of individuals with schizophrenia or the symptoms of outpatients with schizophrenic-like symptoms were noted and thought to be related to schizophrenia in some manner (Kendler, 1985), none of the early workers advanced a model that unambiguously posited a genetic diathesis for schizophrenia and traced its influence through developmental psychobiological and behavioral paths to a variety of clinical (and nonclinical) outcomes. Unlike his predecessors, Meehl (1962, 1990) proposed a model that was (and is) clearly developmental in nature and based on a hypothesized neurointegrative deficit.

### Insights Gleaned from the Earlier Observations of Sandor Rado

The roots of Meehl's model can be found in the observations and psychodynamic formulations of Sandor Rado (1953, 1960). As a clinician, Rado made initial strides toward an integrative model that sought to link genetic influences for schizophrenia and observed schizotypic personality functioning. He argued from a psychodynamic position informed by an appreciation for genetics that schizotypal behavior derived from a fundamental liability to schizophrenia. Rado, in fact, coined the term "schizotype" to represent a condensation of "schizophrenic *pheno*type" (Rado, 1953, p. 410; Rado, 1960, p. 87). It is interesting to note that Rado did not suggest schizotype as a condensation of the terms "schizophrenia" and "genotype" (cf. Siever & Gunderson, 1983). Rado (1960) referred to the individual who possessed the schizophrenic phenotype as a schizotype, while the correlated traits deriving from this "type" were termed "schizotypal organization" and the overt behavioral manifestations of the schizotypal traits were termed "schizotypal behavior" (see p. 87).

For Rado, the causes of schizotypal "differentness" were to be found in two core psychodynamic features of such patients, both of which were thought to be driven by "mutated genes." The two core defects present in the schizotype's personality organization were (1) a diminished capacity for pleasure, or pleasure deficiency, speculated to have a neurochemical basis deriving from an inherited pleasure potential coded in the infant's genes (Rado, 1960, p. 88), and (2) a proprioceptive (kinesthetic) diathesis that resulted in an aberrant awareness of the body (a feature giving rise to schizotypic body-image distortions; Rado, 1960, see pp. 88 and 90). Rado (1960) believed the physiological nature of the proprioceptive diathesis was obscure and remained to be explored (p. 88). According to Rado, integration of the "action self," a necessity of psychodynamic/psychological health, was endangered by the diminished binding power of pleasure (p. 90) and the proprioceptive diathesis found in the schizotype. Consequently, Rado (1960) described the schizotype as struggling to retain a sense of personality integration through several compensatory mechanisms (see p. 90), with such mechanisms frequently manifesting themselves as schizotypal traits and behaviors. An important feature of Rado's model concerned what he termed "developmental stages of schizotypal behavior," essentially a continuum view of clinical compensation (a view echoed later by Meehl, 1990, p. 25). Rado's continuum notion suggested that a common schizophrenia diathesis could lead to a variety of phenotypic outcomes ranging from compensated schizotypy to deteriorated schizophrenia; thus an etiological unity was proposed as underlying a diversity of clinical manifestations.

### Meehl's Proposal: Schizotaxia, Schizotypy, Schizophrenia

Influenced by Rado's (1953, 1960) hypotheses, Meehl's (1962) model of schizotypy was first articulated in a now-classic position paper titled "Schizotaxia, Schizotypy, Schizophrenia." In this paper, one that has been viewed as enormously transforming for schizophrenia research

(Lenzenweger, 2010), Meehl laid out an integrative etiological framework for schizophrenia. The model not only encompassed genetic factors, social learning influences, and clinical symptomatology but also contained hypotheses about the precise nature of the fundamental defect underlying schizotypic functioning and its interactions with what he came to term "polygenic potentiators." Elaboration on and refinement of the original 1962 theory can be found in his later papers (e.g., Meehl, 1972, 1975, 1990, 2001). What follows is a distillation of the major points contained in Meehl's efforts to illuminate the development of schizophrenia. The reader is encouraged to consult Meehl's original position statement (Meehl, 1962), his 1990 treatise (Meehl, 1990), and additional refinements (Meehl, 2001, 2004; see also, Lenzenweger, 2010) to gain a full appreciation for his point of view.

In brief, Meehl's (1962, 1990) original model held that a single major gene (the schizogene) exerts its influence during brain development by coding for a specific "functional parametric aberration of the synaptic control system" in the central nervous system (CNS; Meehl, 1990, pp. 14–15). The aberration, present at the neuronal level, is termed "hypokrisia" and suggests a neural integrative defect characterized by an "insufficiency of separation, differentiation, or discrimination" in neural transmission. Meehl (1990) argued that his conceptualization of schizotaxia should not be taken to represent a defect in basic sensory or information retrieval capacities (p. 14), nor a CNS inhibitory function deficit (p. 16). The defect in neural transmission amounts to the presence of "slippage" at the CNS synapse, and such slippage at the synapse has its behavioral counterparts (at the molar level) in the glaring clinical symptomatology of actual schizophrenia. In other words, just as the synaptic functioning in schizophrenia is characterized by slippage, so, too, are the symptoms of associative loosening and cognitive-affective aberrations observed in the patient with schizophrenia. Hypokrisia was hypothesized to characterize the neuronal functioning throughout the brain of the individual who was affected, thus producing what amounted to a rather ubiquitous CNS anomaly (Meehl, 1990, p. 14) termed "schizotaxia." It is particularly fascinating that even today (e.g., Owen et al., 2005) models of synaptic dysfunction echo this conjecture about synaptic slippage. (In this context, it is important to note that many aspects of Meehl's model remain persuasive even in light of data indicating that multiple genes probably contribute to schizophrenia liability, or schizotypy [see Sullivan et al., 2012; but see also Sekar et al., 2016; Yilmaz et al., 2021]).

Thus, according to the model, schizotaxia is the "genetically determined integrative defect, predisposing to schizophrenia and a sine qua non for that disorder" (Meehl, 1990, p. 35) and was conjectured to have a general population base rate of 10% (see Meehl, 1990, for derivation). Note that schizotaxia essentially describes an aberration in brain functioning characterized by pervasive neuronal slippage in the CNS; it is *not* a behavior or observable personality pattern. The schizotaxic brain, however, becomes the foundation that other factors will build upon and interact aversively with to possibly produce clinically diagnosable schizophrenia. The other factors that interact with the schizotaxic brain and influence individual development (as well as clinical status) are the social learning history of an individual as well as other genetic factors, termed "polygenic potentiators."

Meehl (1962, 1990, 2001) generally held that all (or nearly all) schizotaxic individuals developed schizotypy (i.e., a schizotypal personality organization) on essentially all existing social reinforcement schedules. Schizotypy, therefore, referred to the psychological and personality organization resulting from the schizotaxic individual interacting with and developing within the world of social learning influences. An individual who displays schizotypy is considered a schizotype. (Note that Meehl's "schizotypal personality organization" is not the same as the *DSM* SPD.) Meehl (1990) considered the possibility that a schizotaxic individual might not develop schizotypy if reared in a sufficiently healthful environment, but he viewed this outcome as unlikely. In short, there are multiple possible observable or measurable manifestations of schizotypy, where schizotypy is the latent construct and the observables are indicators (e.g., schizophrenia, schizotypic pathology, laboratory measures) (see Figure 29.2).

The second set of factors influencing the development of clinical schizophrenia in the schizotypic individual is a class of genetically determined factors (or dimensions) termed "polygenic potentiators." According to Meehl (1990), "a potentiator is any genetic factor which, given the presence of the schizogene *and therefore of the schizotypal personality organization* [emphasis in original], raises the probability of clinical decompensation" (p. 39). Potentiators include personality dimensions independent of schizotaxia, such as social introversion, anxiety proneness, aggressivity, and hypohedonia.

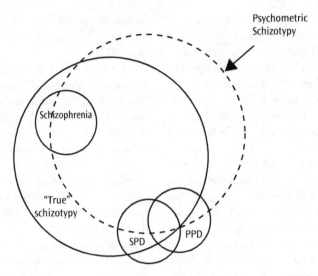

**Figure 29.2** Relationship between the latent construct schizotypy and indicators of schizotypy, such as clinical, psychometric, and laboratory measures. One should not speak of observed indicators of the latent construct as schizotypy; for example, schizotypal personality disorder features should be described as a schizotypy indicator. See Cronbach and Meehl (1955) and McCorquodale and Meehl (1948) for extended discussion of these points. Copyright 2010, Mark F. Lenzenweger. Used with permission of the author.

Such potentiators do not modify (in the technical genetic sense of the term) the expression of the putative schizogene but rather interact with the established schizotypic personality organization and the social environment to facilitate (or, in some cases, "depotentiate") the development of decompensated schizotypy, namely schizophrenia. Meehl (1990) stated, "It's not as if the polygenes for introversion somehow 'get into the causal chain' between the schizogene in DNA and the parameters of social reinforcement" (p. 38), rather the potentiators push the schizotype toward psychosis. In this context it is interesting to note that Meehl's modeling encompassed the idea of a "mixed" model of genetic influence: namely, a single major gene (i.e., an autosomal diallelic locus) operating against a background due to an additive polygenic (or cultural) component (Morton & MacLean, 1974). Thus, in this model, the development of clinically diagnosable schizophrenia is the result of a complex interaction among several factors: (1) a schizotaxic brain characterized by genetically determined hypokrisia at the synapse, (2) environmentally mediated social learning experiences (that bring about a schizotypal personality organization), and (3) the polygenic potentiators.

Although the modal schizotype does not decompensate into diagnosable schizophrenia, Meehl suggested that the latent diathesis is detectable through aberrant psychological and social functioning. This fundamental assumption has served as an organizing concept for decades of research on schizotypic psychopathology and schizophrenia (see Lenzenweger, 2010, 2021). Meehl (1962) described four detectable fundamental signs and symptoms of schizotypy: cognitive slippage (or mild associative loosening), interpersonal aversiveness (social fear), anhedonia (pleasure capacity deficit), and ambivalence. Later, in 1964, he developed a clinical checklist for schizotypic signs that included rich clinical descriptions of not only these four signs or symptoms but also several others that he suggested were valid schizotypy indicators. Basically, all aspects of the core clinical phenomenology and psychological functioning seen in the schizotype were hypothesized to derive fundamentally from aberrant CNS functioning (i.e., hypokrisia) as determined by the schizogene. For example, "primary cognitive slippage" gives rise to observable secondary cognitive slippage in thought, speech, affective integration, and behavior. He saw hypokrisia as the root cause of "soft" neurological signs as well as what he termed "soft" psychometric signs that could be detected among schizotypes. Finally, Meehl argued that hypokrisia also led to what he termed "primary aversive drift" or the steady developmental progression toward negative affective tone in personality functioning across the life span among schizotypes (see Meehl, 1990, figure 1 in original, p. 27). This primary aversive drift across the life span, according to Meehl, gave rise to social fear, ambivalence, and hypohedonia (Meehl, 2001). Figure 29.3 contains a depiction, inspired in large part by Meehl's

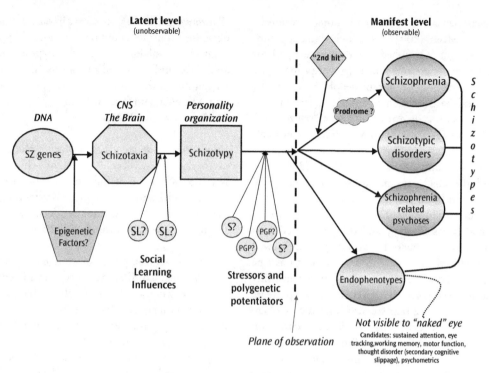

**Figure 29.3** Developmental model relating the genetic diathesis for schizophrenia, schizotaxia, and schizotypy and implied levels of analysis (adapted from Meehl 1962, 1990), with modifications (Lenzenweger, 2010). Those factors to the left of the vertical broken line (i.e., plane of observation) are latent and therefore unobservable with the unaided naked eye, whereas those factors to the right of the plane of observation are manifest (or observable). A DNA-based (i.e., genetic) liability creates impaired central nervous syste,-based neural circuitry (schizotaxia) that eventuates in a personality organization (schizotypy) that harbors the liability for schizophrenia. Social learning schedules interact with schizotaxia to yield schizotypy. Psychosocial stressors and polygenic potentiators interact with schizotypy to yield manifest outcomes across a range of clinical compensation. Various possible manifest developmental outcomes are schizophrenia (assuming a "second hit," e.g., in utero exposure to maternal influenza), schizotypic psychopathology (e.g., schizotypal and/or paranoid personality disorders), or schizophrenia-related psychoses (e.g., delusional disorder). So-called prodromal features (withdrawal, reduced ideational richness, disorganized communication) may precede the onset of some (but *not* all) cases of schizophrenia. Endophenotypes (e.g., sustained attention deficits, eye-tracking dysfunction, working memory impairments, and/or psychometric deviance [PAS]; see Gottesman & Gould, 2003), which are invisible to the unaided, naked eye (but detectable with appropriate technologies), are found below the plane of observation. Epigenetic factors refer to nonmutational phenomena, such as DNA methylation and histone acetylation (modification), that alter the expression of the schizophrenia gene (or genes). Finally, all individuals represented across this range of manifest outcomes are considered schizotypes, which does not necessarily imply an *ICD* or *DSM* diagnosis.
Copyright 2010, Mark F. Lenzenweger. Used with permission of the author.

thinking, of the relations between schizotaxia, schizotypy, schizophrenia, and related outcomes, including endophenotypes.

It is worth noting that the role anhedonia played in Meehl's model changed over the years. In the 1962 model, anhedonia was hypothesized to represent a fundamental and etiologically important factor in the development of schizotypy, actually falling somewhat "between" the genetic defect hypokrisia and the other schizotypic signs and symptoms of interpersonal aversiveness, cognitive slippage, and ambivalence. As of 1990, Meehl deemphasized anhedonia (then termed "hypohedonia"; but see also Meehl, 1964) as a fundamental etiological factor in the development of schizotypy and schizophrenia. In the 1990 revision, Meehl strongly suggested that associative loosening and aversive drift are those psychological processes (deriving from hypokrisia) that primarily determine the behavioral and psychological characteristics of the schizotype (see Meehl, 1990, p. 28). Hypohedonia was (is) now viewed as playing an etiological role in the development of schizotypy by functioning as a dimensional polygenic potentiator (i.e., not deriving from the core genetically determined schizophrenia diathesis). The reconfiguration of hypohedonia's role in the 1990 model was a major substantive shift and was discussed further in Meehl (1993, 2001). In overview, Meehl (1975, 1987, 1990) proposed that all persons displayed some level of hedonic capacity, which was conceived of as a normal-range, dimensional, individual differences construct, and it functioned as the potentiator noted previously. However, Meehl (2001) made it clear that a pathological variant of hypohedonia, determined perhaps by a genetic defect and similar to that proposed by Rado, could also exist in some people. However, the etiological basis of such a hedonic defect may or may not be directly attributable to a "schizogene." He did not see these two possibilities—a normal-range quantitative system and an anhedonic taxon or class—as mutually exclusive. Meehl (2001) discussed the challenges posed to interpretation of results from latent structure analyses of phenotypic indicators of hedonic capacity with reference to his model of schizotypy and the possible etiology of deviations in hedonic capacity. Meehl viewed this specific terrain (i.e., hedonic capacity) as ripe for continued exploration and saw it as consisting of open questions with respect to schizotypy (e.g., Strauss & Gold, 2012; see also Strauss & Cohen, 2018). Recent taxometric evidence focused on hypohedonia and the distinction between hedonic capacity and experience, and thus social withdrawal, challenges the meaning of hypohedonia as a core process in schizotypy (Linscott, 2007).

A central, and perhaps the most important, assumption in Meehl's model is that schizotypy, as a personality organization *reflective of a latent liability for schizophrenia*, can manifest itself behaviorally and psychologically in various degrees of clinical compensation. Thus, following Rado (1960), Meehl (1962, 1990) argued that the schizotype may be highly compensated (showing minimal signs and symptoms of schizotypic functioning), or the individual may reveal transient failures in compensation, or may be diagnosably schizophrenic. Schizotypes, therefore, can range clinically from apparent normality through to psychosis, yet all share the schizogene and resultant schizotypic personality organization. A crucial implication of this assumption is that not all schizotypes develop diagnosable schizophrenia (i.e., one could genuinely be at risk yet never develop a psychotic illness); however, all schizotypes will display some evidence of their underlying liability in the form of aberrant psychobiological and/or psychological functioning. As noted, this particular implication of the model has guided nearly 60 years of research directed at developing methods for the valid and efficient detection of schizotypy endophenotypes (Gottesman & Gould, 2003; Lenzenweger, 1999c, 2013a, 2013b). Through clinical, psychometric, or other means it articulated the heart of the "diathesis-stressor" model or approach for psychopathology (Lenzenweger, 2010). In short, if valid schizotypy detection strategies could be developed, samples of "high-risk" individuals (i.e., schizotypes) could be assembled and examined in various efforts to better illuminate the nature and development of both schizophrenia and related schizotypic conditions (see Lenzenweger, 2021).

### Frequent Misunderstandings of Meehl's Model

In discussing Meehl's model of schizotypy, it is important to point out several misconceptions of the model and various misunderstandings (see Lenzenweger, 2010, for extensive details). There are five primary areas of misunderstanding:

1. Meehl's schizotypy construct is *not* the same as *DSM*-defined SPD. Schizotypy is a latent construct, whereas SPD is an observable phenomenological entity (Figure 29.2).
2. Schizotypy, as a latent construct, is *not* entirely genetic in origin. It reflects input from both genes (determining "schizotaxia") and environmental factors (e.g., social learning history) (Figure 29.3).
3. The terms "schizotype" and "schizotypy" are not reserved only for those cases identified by *DSM*-defined SPD features. It makes no conceptual sense to reserve the term "schizotypy" for *interview-based* assessments of schizotypic features, whereas the term "psychometric schizotypy" is used for psychometric assessments of schizotypic features.
4. Not all schizotypes are expected to develop schizophrenia. Some schizotypes will develop (or convert to) schizophrenia, some will show some continued nonpsychotic evidence of schizotypic features across the life span, and some schizotypes will remain quietly schizotypic (perhaps displaying evidence of their underlying personality organization on endophenotypic measures) (Gottesman & Gould, 2003; Lenzenweger, 2013a, 2013b, 2021).
5. Some observers (mis)believe that Meehl's entire developmental model hinges on the presence of a proposed single, schizophrenia-specific gene (a "schizogene"). However, this is incorrect. Meehl did speculate on the possibility of a "schizogene" in his original formulations and used it as starting point. However, the cascade of processes and outcomes in the model is entirely compatible with *multiple* genes contributing to the underlying schizotaxic pathology, which then plays itself out developmentally as noted in

Figure 29.3. Meehl fully understood the state of modern genetics research in schizophrenia and the additive polygenic threshold model.

## What Determines Conversion to Schizophrenia from Nonpsychotic Schiztotypy in Meehl's Model?

There is interest in determining what is termed the "conversion to psychosis rate" among those persons deemed to be at risk for or in the early-onset stages of schizophrenia (with many prodromal cases appearing, at least, quasi-psychotic in terms of presenting phenomenology—some are already clinically psychotic for all intents and purposes; Fusar-Poli et al., 2013), however such interest is tempered by the fact that the vast majority (70% or more) of such clinical high-risk cases do *not* convert to psychosis on follow-up (see Lenzenweger, 2021, for extended discussion). On a related note, Siever and Davis (2004) have speculated that the schizotypic individual who does not develop schizophrenia may have reduced striatal dopaminergic activity and increased frontal capacity, assets that spare him or her from the emergence of schizophrenia. However, recent evidence shows relations between genetic polymorphisms known be associated with both dopaminergic functioning and schizophrenia to also be associated with schizotypic features (Grant et al., 2013; Mohr & Ettinger, 2014; Thompson et al., 2020).

What is the precise recipe of polygenic potentiators, life stressors, and random events in interaction with the schizotaxic brain that might lead one to move from being a compensated schizotype to clinical schizophrenia? *Simply stated, the answer is not known.* Meehl articulated the rich matrix of components and developmental processes that he believed could eventually yield schizophrenia in some instances, but he was not able to identify those specific factors (genetic or otherwise) that propel one to transition from the nonpsychotic schizotype to clear-cut schizophrenia (i.e., psychosis). Clearly Meehl (1962, 1990) viewed the polygenic potentiators noted earlier as playing an important role in this developmental process; however, he also stressed the importance of what he termed "unknown critical events" as well as the "random walk" (i.e., life histories may reflect divergent causality rather than the impact solely of well-known systematic factors such as social class or birth order) in the determination of schizophrenia (Meehl, 1978; cf. Meehl, 1971, 1972). In this context it is worth noting that although Meehl saw the polygenic potentiators as important, he argued that the polygenic potentiators "do not *in the least* 'modify' the schizogene's *endo*phenotypic expression as schizotaxia, a CNS parametric aberration" (Meehl, 1972, p. 380; emphasis in original), rather they simply alter the probability that a schizotype might move on to clinical schizophrenia. The precise manner whereby a schizotype moves on to schizophrenia, in those instances where it happens, remains an open issue and is ripe for life span developmental studies of schizotypy. Such research should also seek to understand those factors—polygenic potentiator or otherwise—that might buffer a schizotype from transitioning to schizophrenia.

Although various efforts have been made to expand upon and refine Meehl's basic framework (e.g., see examples in Lenzenweger & Dworkin, 1998), the core assumptions of contemporary liability models do not differ substantially from what he proposed in 1962 in terms of the importance of genetically influenced contributions to a liability impacted by environmental stressors. Contemporary quantitative genetic models, especially the simple polygenic model as well as the polygenic-threshold model, see all genetically influenced factors contributing to schizophrenia liability as summing (unlike Meehl who proposed what was essentially a "mixed model" in which a schizophrenia-specific, genetically influenced liability operated against a background of polygenic effects). Neurocognitive (Andreasen, 1999), neuroscientific (e.g., Grace & Moore, 1998; Owen et al., 2005; Phillips & Silverstein, 2003), and neurodevelopmental (Marenco & Weinberger, 2000; McGlashan & Hoffman, 2000; Sekar et al., 2016) models for schizophrenia, albeit not wed to hypothetical processes such as hypokrisia, are nevertheless quite consistent with many of the major tenets of Meehl's framework for schizotypic psychopathology and schizophrenia proper. In short, nearly all major models of the underlying pathological processes in schizophrenia emphasize a dysfunction in neural development (e.g., "overpruning" Sekar et al., 2016; Yilmaz et al., 2021) and neurobiologically driven dysregulation in neural transmission that impairs information processing and may lead to symptom formation, substantive views that echo Meehl's early conjectures (cf. Meehl, 1962).

## The Claridge View of Schizotypy: A Necessary Scientific Excursus on the Benign Schizotypy Model

As reviewed in Lenzenweger (2010, 2015), no discussion of contemporary views of schizotypic psychopathology and the schizotypy construct would be complete without an examination of the views of Gordon Claridge (Claridge, 1997; Mohr & Claridge, 2015). The most distinctive features of his approach to schizotypy concern his propositions regarding (a) the putative existence of "healthy" manifestations of schizotypy (also termed "benign schizotypy" [BS]), (b) schizotypy as a component of normal personality, and (c) the proposal that the schizotypy construct has a dimensional (quantitative) structure at the latent level.

Unlike the views of Meehl (1962, 1990) or those advocated here and elsewhere (Lenzenweger, 1998, 2010, 2015), Claridge sees schizotypy as a normal *personality* trait varying by degree along a continuum. In adhering to the *methodological* views of his mentor, the British personality psychologist Hans J. Eysenck and Eysenck's conceptualization of "psychoticism" as a personality trait, Claridge places his conceptualization of schizotypy squarely within the traditional dimensional view of normal personality. Indeed, Claridge's ideas regarding schizotypy have been introduced by his collaborators as consistent with those "writers who conceptualise the spectrum of schizophrenia-related characteristics as a continuous dimension, akin to other dimensions of personality," which represents a view "championed by writers such as Eysenck" (Eysenck & Eysenck, 1976; Rawlings et al., 2008, p. 1641). This view raises two questions: (1) Is schizotypy best thought of as a component of *normal personality*? (2) Does the available evidence support a dimensional view of schizotypy?

### Schizotypy as Part of Normal Personality and "Healthy" Psychosis

Is schizotypy best thought of as a component of normal personality? Unpacking this further, is schizotypy *normal*? Is schizotypy part of *personality*? These issues boil down to whether one views schizotypy as (a) the liability for schizophrenia (e.g., Meehl, Lenzenweger) or (b) a trait characterized by certain cognitive features and psychotic-like phenomena that are part of the general system of normal personality (Claridge, Bentall, Mason). As summarized recently by Rawlings et al. (2008), "Claridge and his colleagues have investigated schizotypy from many points of view. They have concluded that *psychotic traits constitute an essentially healthy dimension of personality*, which in adaptive form contributes to psychological variations as creativity, non-threatening hallucinations, and rewarding spiritual and mystical beliefs and experiences" (p. 1670, emphasis added). Claridge and proponents of the BS model, which they argue yields "happy schizotypes," continue to assert their support for such a conceptualization (Grant & Hennig, 2020; Mohr & Claridge, 2015).

As pursued elsewhere (Lenzenweger, 2010, 2015, 2018b), the psychopathologist must ask, "What does it mean to argue that 'psychotic traits constitute an essentially healthy dimension of personality'?" In light of the observations of Kraepelin, Bleuler, Rado, Meehl, and others, one must consider critically the views on schizotypy held by Claridge, particularly as regards the term *psychosis*. What does it mean to designate an individual or behavior "psychotic"? In traditional psychiatric usage, "psychotic" as a descriptive term has typically one of three potential meanings, all suggestive of pathology: (1) the *impairment of reality testing* as indicated by the presence of particular psychopathology signs and/or symptoms (hallucinations, delusions, thought disorder); (2) the *depth or severity* of an impairment (e.g., a psychotic depression, meaning a very deep or profound case of depression), and/or less frequently (3) a *degree of regression*, within a psychodynamic framework, to a developmentally primitive stage of psychological organization wherein thought and experience are characterized by *primary process* (i.e., not secondary process).

Given how the term "psychotic" is used in psychopathology, can we conceive of "psychotic traits" as being consistent with a "healthy dimensional of personality?" (Resorting to the locution "psychotic-like" does not get one out of this conceptual conundrum if one is serious about the notion that psychotic traits are representative of a healthy dimension of personality.) To do so, one must really confront the implication of this statement and consider the notion of "healthy psychosis." One impression gleaned from this juxtaposition of terms is that it reveals an insufficient appreciation for the clinical and research basis supporting the notion of schizotypy as *schizophrenia liability*. In short, those who see patients in intensive diagnostic or therapeutic capacities may find an eerie unfamiliarity in a concept such as "healthy psychotic" traits. Can one realistically speak of "healthy" schizophrenia or schizophrenia as a healthy dimension of personality? From the standpoint of clinical relevance, Claridge's theoretical position seems distinctly ungrounded in the clinical realities of schizotypic pathology. Moreover, from the research standpoint, the literature, by and large, does *not* support a view of schizophrenia (the illness) as reflective of an extension of normal personality. We must always remind ourselves that finding correlations between measures of schizotypy and measures of normal personality does not establish continuity with normality nor establish that schizotypy is akin to other measures of normal personality (e.g., extraversion, positive emotion, negative emotion, constraint). Rather, in the view of many, schizophrenia reflects a complex *pathological* disease process, not a deviation in a normal personality process or dimension, and schizotypy reflects liability for that illness. Raine (2006) proposes the notion of "pseudoschizotypy," which may reflect a more accurate appraisal that a group of persons might score highly on a measure of schizotypy for reasons other than latent schizotypy (rather than invoking strained constructions such as "happy schizotypy," "benign schizotypy," or "healthy psychosis").

An interesting issue for research is to determine how personality copes with the presence of schizotypy and how schizotypy shapes the personality. In short, it is likely that, when present, schizotypy (whether thinking qualitatively or quantitatively) impacts and shapes personality manifestations. This view is consistent with a consideration of how the expression of schizophrenia, as a clinical illness, impacts the personality of one so diagnosed.

### Claridge's View of Schizotypy as a "Fully Dimensional" Construct

The second issue central to Claridge's view of schizotypy concerns the basic nature of the construct's underlying structure. Is it quantitative in nature *at both the phenotypic level and the latent level?* This issue received considerable discussion during the 1993 NATO workshop on schizotypy (see Raine et al., 1995). At that time, although Claridge maintained a strong commitment to a dimensional view, there were *no* empirical data available to support a view that the schizotypy construct was quantitatively distributed—varying by degree (not kind)—at the latent level. All empirical evidence marshaled by Claridge and colleagues in support of the dimensional latent structure of schizotypy came from analytic techniques (i.e., factor analysis) that could *not* determine whether a latent entity was quantitatively (dimensionally) or qualitatively (taxonically) structured at a deeper level. *One can surely measure a psychopathological feature, symptom, or character in a quantitative manner, but that, in and of itself, does not ensure or mean that the construct measured is dimensional at the latent level.* For example, one could construct a quantitative measure of "maleness/femaleness" and acquire dimensional values on the "maleness/femaleness scale." However, the continuous variation in the scores on this scale would not mean that biological sex has a continuous (quantitative, "difference by degree") nature at the latent level (see below, regarding factor analysis).

The current empirical picture regarding the latent structure of schizotypy is one of *discontinuity*, which is *either* representative of a latent taxon (class, natural subgroup) *or* a severe step-function (threshold) in the structure of the schizotypy construct. As discussed later in this chapter, there is an abundance of evidence drawing on taxometric and finite mixture modeling studies that are supportive of the discontinuous underlying nature of schizotypy. The corpus of evidence drawn from empirical data is inconsistent with a fully dimensional view of schizotypy such as that argued for by Claridge and colleagues (e.g., Grant & Hennig, 2020; Nelson et al., 2013). Although Mason and Claridge (2006) state, "Suffice it to say that the evidence is strongly weighted in favour of the fully dimensional model" of schizotypy" (p. 205), this statement is simply incorrect in view of the available empirical corpus.

The bulk of the evidence that Claridge and colleagues interpret as supportive of the dimensionality of schizotypy comes from (a) a methodological position committed to dimensionality as proposed by Eysenck, (b) visual examination of the distributions of phenotypic psychometric values (recall that distributions of scores cannot resolve the latent structure question), (c) results of factor analyses of psychometric values (remember, factor analysis is a technique that always finds factors by organizing larger numbers of variables into a smaller number of large "factors"), and (d) a single taxometric investigation. Aside from evidence drawn from one taxometric study (Rawlings et al., 2008), which suffered from marked methodological artifacts (Beauchaine et al., 2008), the empirical picture painted overwhelmingly by results from latent structure analyses (taxometric, finite mixture modeling, latent class analysis) supports the existence of a discrete class of individuals harbored within large samples of persons who have completed schizotypy measures. Recent reviews arguing in favor of the dimensionality of schizotypy (e.g., Nelson et al., 2013) unfortunately fall short of establishing latent continuity through appropriate latent structure statistical methods;

instead, they tend to emphasize similarities between schizotypic psychopathology and schizophrenia (which are well known) and infer continuity. Ironically, much of the research marshalled to support a continuum view of schizotypy is done using distinct subject groups (e.g., schizotype vs. controls) rather than being conducted in a fully dimensional manner using correlational and/or regression techniques with a full range of schizotypy scale scores.

Eysenck, despite his preference for dimensional models and continuous measurement, stated that he "would not wish to dismiss the possibility or even the likelihood that in any random group of clinically diagnosed neurotics there would be found a small number of people who might 'constitute a group apart, different not in degree, but in kind, by reason of some specified biochemical error, which is highly predictable in terms of inheritance, and which operates in a manner quite different from anything observed' in the kinship relations of the remainder of that group" (Eysenck, 1958, p. 431). This view of Eysenck is actually quite commensurate with what is known about schizotypy from modern empirical studies of latent structure.

### Claridge's View of Meehl's Model as "Quasi-Dimensional"?

In this context one should also evaluate Claridge's view of Meehl's (1990) model of schizotypy as "quasi-dimensional," whereas he refers to his own model as "fully dimensional," as discussed above (Claridge, 1997; see also Nelson et al., 2013). What is meant by the term "quasi-dimensional"? If one takes the word "quasi" to mean "having a likeness to, having some resemblance to," we would say *quasi-dimensional* would logically mean "having a likeness to or resembling a dimension." One would be hard pressed to find an indication in Meehl's writing that schizotaxia (or, by definition, schizotypy) is in any manner dimensional, quasi or otherwise. The term "quasi-dimensional" as a descriptor is merely another way of saying "continuous latent liability with a threshold"—this *not* what Meehl proposed.

Meehl (1962, 1990) himself was quite clear about the latent structure of schizotypy as reviewed earlier: he saw schizotypy as having a taxonic (qualitative) latent structure. As noted, he did speak of "polygenic potentiators," which could have a dimensional nature; however, schizotypy, according to his model, was taxonically structured at the latent level. It may be the Claridge intended the notion of a "quasi-continuous" model of genetic influences, akin to a polygenic model with a distinct *threshold*

effect, when describing Meehl's model as "quasi-dimensional." In fact, behavior geneticists distinguish between a polygenic model with continuous variation in a phenotype (e.g., height, IQ) and one where there is some form of discernible demarcation in the phenotype (e.g., cleft palate, diabetes) (see Falconer, 1989). However, Meehl's model does not encompass the polygenic perspective (without thresholds) that embraces fully continuous variation or quasi-continuous variation. His model, rather, represents a "mixed model," whereby a single major schizophrenia-relevant gene operates against a background of polygenic modifier effects (his so-called potentiators). To review, Meehl was clear on this issue in advocating for a *taxonic* view of schizotypy. In Meehl's view there is no gradation or quantitative variation insofar as schizotypy is concerned at the latent level: *one is either a schizotype or not, there is no in-between place*. Claridge (1997; Mohr & Claridge, 2015), in contrast, advocates a fully dimensional view (latent level) with continuous variation at the phenotypic level; his model is most consistent with a polygenic model (without a threshold) that reflects a continuous additive model of genetic influences.

## Classification and Diagnostic Technology
### Assessment of Schizotypy and Schizotypal Phenomena

This section focuses on the assessment of schizotypy and schizotypic phenomena with a brief review of clinical interviews and psychometric inventories that have been developed for either clinical or research work. An evaluation of many psychometric measures conjectured to be putative schizotypy indicators developed before 1980 is available in Grove (1982); data bearing on psychometric measures through the early 1990s can be found in Chapman, Chapman, and Kwapil (1995). Recently, Kirchner et al. (2018) provide a useful overview of diagnostic and other assessment approaches to SPD, which has obvious relevance. Not all of the assessment devices discussed here have been designed with Meehl's (1964) early effort in mind, though most have been influenced by his work. Some emerged from the increased interest in personality pathology that followed the introduction of *DSM-III* in 1980. All of the measures discussed here have been shown to have strong reliability and a reasonable degree of validity.

### Clinical Interviews and Checklists for Schizotypic Psychopathology

Four interview-based procedures have been developed specifically to assess schizotypic phenomena.

The following assessment devices are tailored specifically for schizotypic psychopathology. One could, of course, use the relevant diagnostic modules for SPD and/or PPD from an established Axis II structured interview (e.g., the IPDE; Loranger, 1999) as an alternative to these specialized instruments.

### MEEHL'S CHECKLIST FOR SCHIZOTYPIC SIGNS

Meehl's (1964) Checklist for Schizotypic Signs is a treasure trove of clinical observation and phenomenological description for schizotypic psychopathology. The Checklist and the *Manual for Use with the Checklist for Schizotypic Signs* can be downloaded from Meehl's website (http://meehl.umn.edu/sites/g/files/pua1696/f/061scchecklist.pdf). The checklist consists of 25 clinical features that Meehl argued were of diagnostic importance to the recognition and diagnosis of schizotypic features

### SYMPTOM SCHEDULE FOR THE DIAGNOSIS OF BORDERLINE SCHIZOPHRENIA

The Symptom Schedule for the Diagnosis of Borderline Schizophrenia (SSDBS) was developed by Khouri, Haier, Rieder, and Rosenthal (1980) to assess the symptoms of "borderline schizophrenia" as defined by Kety et al. (1968). The schedule was administered in an interview format, with eight symptoms rated on a 3-point scale, including perceptual changes, body image aberrations, feelings of unreality, thought disturbances, ideas of reference, ideas of persecution, self-inflicted injuries, and preoccupation with perverse sexuality or violence.

### SCHEDULE FOR SCHIZOTYPAL PERSONALITIES

Developed by Baron and associates (Baron et al., 1981), the Schedule for Schizotypal Personalities (SSP) was designed to assess the diagnostic criteria for *DSM-III* SPD. The SSP assesses illusions, depersonalization/derealization, ideas of reference, suspiciousness, magical thinking, inadequate rapport, odd communication, social isolation, and social anxiety. The SSP also assesses delusions and hallucinations.

### STRUCTURED INTERVIEW FOR SCHIZOTYPY

Kendler and colleagues (Kendler, Lieberman, & Walsh, 1989) developed the Structured Interview for Schizotypy (SIS) to assess schizotypal signs and symptoms. The SIS consists of 19 sections, 18 to assess individual symptom dimensions and 1 to assess 36 separate schizotypal signs (Kendler et al., 1989). The SIS is intended to be given in conjunction with an Axis I assessment device. Results from the Roscommon Family Study of Schizophrenia (Kendler et al., 1993) provided additional validation of the SIS.

### Psychometric Inventories for Schizotypy Detection

In this context, a comment is in order regarding a term one sees in some journals, namely "psychometric schizotypy." I see no conceptual gain in introducing idiosyncratic concepts such as "psychometric schizotypy" or "self-report schizotypy" into the empirical literature. If a measurement device is valid for the intended construct, then how does the method of assessment being included in the name of the construct advance scientific discourse? One does not speak of "structured clinical interview depression," "self-report panic disorder," or "observer-rated personality disorder." Relatedly, all interview assessments are essentially self-report in nature and presumably such interviews possess commendable psychometric properties, yet we do not call out these characteristics of the interviews.

### CHAPMAN "PSYCHOSIS PRONENESS" SCALES ("WISCONSIN SCALES")

Guided by Meehl's model of schizotypy and his rich clinical descriptions of schizotypic signs (Meehl, 1964) and in close accordance with construct validity principles (Cronbach & Meehl, 1955), L. J. Chapman and J. P. Chapman (1985, 1987) developed several objective self-report measures to assess traits reflective of a putative liability to psychosis, perhaps schizophrenia. For reviews of the early literature on these measures see J. P. Chapman et al. (1995). A brief and selective overview of leading instruments is provided here.

Two of these scales, the Perceptual Aberration Scale (PAS; Chapman et al., 1978) and the Magical Ideation Scale (MIS; Eckblad & Chapman, 1983), have been used extensively in recent research to detect schizotypy and assemble samples of respondents presumed to be at increased risk for psychosis from nonclinical populations. The PAS is a 35-item true-false measure of disturbances and distortions in perceptions of the body as well as other objects. Regarding the MIS, L. J. Chapman and Chapman (1985) defined magical ideation as a "belief in forms of *causation* that, by conventional standards of our society, are not valid but magical" (p. 164; emphasis added). The PAS and MIS tend to be highly correlated ($r$ at .68 to .70). As a result, both measures are often used in conjunction to select schizotypic patients from nonclinical populations. The PAS and MIS have been used extensively in schizotypy research and are associated with an impressive body of empirical literature supportive of their validity.

A third scale developed by the Chapmans, the Revised Social Anhedonia Scale (RSAS) (Mishlove & Chapman, 1985), has also been used with greater frequency because deviance on the scale was linked to later psychosis in the presence of elevated PAS/MIS scores (Chapman et al., 1994). The extent to which the RSAS assesses "anhedonia" versus "social withdrawal" has become a focus of recent substantive discussion and empirical investigation (Linscott, 2007). Finally, abbreviated versions of the original Chapman scales (sometimes referred to as "Wisconsin Scales") have been published for research use (Winterstein et al., 2011).

### SCHIZOTYPAL PERSONALITY QUESTIONNAIRE

The Schizotypal Personality Questionnaire (SPQ; Raine, 1991) is a 74-item true-false self-report questionnaire that assesses the features consistent with the symptoms for SPD as defined by the *DSM-III-R*. The SPQ has excellent psychometric properties (Raine, 1991). The SPQ generates three general factors that correspond conceptually to the reality distortion, disorganization, and negative symptom components that are well known in the schizophrenia research literature (Lenzenweger & Dworkin, 1996). The SPQ has become one of the most heavily used psychometric assessment methods in the schizotypy/schizotypal personality research area; a revised short form was published in 2010 (Cohen et al., 2010), and a child-focused version appeared recently (Raine et al., 2021). Importantly, the factor structures underlying the Chapman scales and the SPQ reveal distinct differences which suggest caution in assuming these measures are comparably structured at the latent level (Gross et al., 2014), which suggests also that they are not fungible.

### OTHER PSYCHOMETRIC MEASURES OF SCHIZOTYPY

Several additional psychometric measures of schizotypy have been developed recently and should be mentioned. Unlike the PAS and MIS, these other measures have not yet been shown to be associated with a liability for schizophrenia (i.e., schizotypy) through systematic family, twin, or adoption studies; however, available validity data suggest that all are promising as schizotypy indicators. These measures include the Rust Inventory of Schizotypal Cognitions (RISC; Rust, 1988a, 1988b), the Referential Thinking Scale (Lenzenweger, Bennett, & Lilenfeld, 1997), the Social Fear Scale (Raulin & Wee, 1984), the Schizotypal Ambivalence Scale (Kwapil et al., 2002; Vaughn et al., 2008), the Schizotypal Personality Scale (STA; Claridge & Broks, 1984) and its close cousin, the Oxford-Liverpool Inventory of Feelings and Experiences (O-LIFE, Mason et al., 1995; see also Claridge, 1997; Grant et al., 2013), and the Schizophrenism Scale (Venables, 1990). A potentially promising psychometric approach designed specifically for the detection of schizophrenia liability (i.e., schizotypy) can be found in the Schizophrenia Proneness Scale (Bolinskey et al., 2003).

Recently, Kwapil et al. (2018) introduced a newly constructed multidimensional psychometric measure that taps positive, negative, and disorganized components of schizotypic deviance. Additionally, from a broader perspective, Krueger et al. (2012) have introduced an inventory geared toward the AMPD and that taps psychoticism in a manner compatible with the nature of schizotypy; their measure is also compatible with the thought disorder and detachment spectra in the hierarchical model advocated Kotov and colleagues (Kotov et al., 2020).

Also available for consideration are the schizoid, schizotypal, and paranoid PD scales derived from the original Minnesota Multiphasic Personality Inventory (MMPI) (Morey et al., 1985). The MMPI-2-RF (Ben-Porath & Tellegen, 2008) and the MMPI-3 (Ben-Porath & Tellegen, 2020) continue to contain useful measures of thought disorder, ideas of persecution, aberrant experiences, and psychoticism that are useful in the assessment of schizotypic psychopathology and likely tap schizotypy.

## Etiology, Development, and Pathogenesis

There have been two major research vectors in schizotypic psychopathology research. First, many investigators have examined the correlates of schizotypic psychopathology through the study of either clinically defined SPD and/or PPD, psychometrically defined schizotypic persons, or first-degree biological relatives of patients with schizophrenia. The second thrust, which is a consistent theme through much of the research in this area, has been directed at illuminating the relationship between schizotypic psychopathology and schizophrenia per se (Lenzenweger, 2010; in press), as well as theoretical and empirical study of the nature of the latent liability construct.

Given that the theme of relating schizotypic pathology to schizophrenia is so prominent in this area and that one of the guiding assumptions in this work concerns the theoretical notion of latent liability, it seems appropriate to begin with a review of the need for such a construct. Following this discussion, empirical research related to schizotypic psychopathology is discussed from the vantage points of (1) family history, (2) laboratory findings, (3) clinical phenomenology, and (4) follow-up studies. This section is followed by a discussion of the delimitation of schizotypic psychopathology from other disorders at the latent (i.e., unobservable with the naked eye) level.

## On the Need for a Latent Liability Construct Formulation

The preceding discussion has assumed a common underlying liability for schizotypic psychopathology and schizophrenia (see Figures 29.2 and 29.3). What is the empirical basis for such an assumption? As argued previously (Lenzenweger, 1998, 2010), there is ample evidence in support of a latent liability conceptualization in schizophrenia that includes expanded phenotype schizotypic psychopathology manifestations. First, it was conjectured by Meehl (1962, 1990) and others that schizotypic psychopathology was linked, presumably via genetics to schizophrenia (e.g., Kendler, 1985, Kendler et al., 1993) (see later discussion). Perhaps the most influential early evidence that helped to establish a genetic link between schizotypic phenomenology and clinical schizophrenia came from the Danish Adoption Study of Schizophrenia (Kety et al., 1968), in which there were elevated rates of schizotypic psychopathology beyond schizophrenia in the biological relatives. These results provided compelling evidence for a genetically transmitted component underlying manifest schizophrenia and the less severe schizophrenia-like disorders. Moreover, confirming the early Kety et al. findings, numerous family studies have found an excess of schizotypic disorders in the biological relatives of individuals with schizophrenia (see Kendler et al., 1993). As noted, genomic work (Avramopoulos et al., 2002; Fanous et al., 2007; Grant et al., 2013; Lin et al., 2005; Siever et al., 2011; Walter et al., 2016) has provided important confirming data linking schizotypic psychopathology indicators to genetic loci that have been implicated in schizophrenia. Clearly, the boundaries of the phenotypic expression of schizophrenia liability extend beyond manifest clinical schizophrenia. Thus, liability manifestations are not isomorphic with expressed psychosis.

Second, the existence of a "clinically unexpressed" liability for schizophrenia has been confirmed (Gottesman & Bertelsen, 1989; Lenzenweger & Loranger, 1989a). Thus, liability can exist without obvious phenotypic, or symptomatic (i.e., psychotic), manifestations. Third, a well-established biobehavioral marker, namely eye-tracking dysfunction (Holzman et al., 1988; Levy et al., 2010), which bears no immediately discernible phenotypic connection to overt schizophrenia, is known to be associated with a latent diathesis for the illness. Liability can thus manifest itself in an alternative phenotypic form (Lenzenweger, 1998, 2010). Finally, if the base rate of schizophrenia liability (or the schizotypy taxon) is in fact 10%, as conjectured by Meehl (1990), then perhaps well over 50% of those carrying liability for schizophrenia may go clinically "undetected" across the life span (i.e., derived from the estimated combined prevalence of schizophrenia, SPD, and PPD of roughly 5%; cf. Loranger, 1990; see also Lenzenweger, Lane et al., 2007). Taken together, theoretical and empirical considerations argue strongly for the plausibility of a complex latent liability construct in schizophrenia.

Given that most persons vulnerable to schizophrenia may never show flagrant psychosis or easily detectable signs and symptoms of schiztoypic personality functioning, researchers have sought ways to detect schizotypy using more sensitive laboratory and psychometric measures. Efforts have been made to discover valid objective indicators of schizotypy that function efficiently across a range of clinical compensation as well as mental state and are capable of detecting liability even in clinically unexpressed (nonsymptomatic) cases. Such indicators, psychometric and otherwise, are thought to assess an "endophenotype" (not visible to the unaided, naked eye; see Gottesman, 1991; Gottesman & Gould, 2003; Lenzenweger, 2013a, 2013b). Their inclusion in research investigations of the genetics and familiality of schizophrenia is likely to enhance those efforts through increased power and precision, even when the putative indicators are only modestly correlated with the latent liability (Fanous & Kendler, 2005; Smith & Mendell, 1974).

## Empirical Findings Relevant to Development and Pathogenesis

### FAMILY HISTORY OF SCHIZOPHRENIA

Overall, it is now generally established that schizotypic psychopathology does indeed occur in the biological first-degree relatives of persons with schizophrenia at rates much higher than the population rate (for reviews see Kendler et al., 1993; Webb & Levinson, 1993 Walter et al., 2016). There is also evidence supportive of the familiality of schizophrenia and schizotypic psychopathology from studies that have found elevated rates of schizophrenia among the first-degree biological relatives of schizotypic patients (Battaglia et al., 1991 1995; Kendler & Walsh, 1995). The connection between schizotypic psychopathology and schizophrenia is now well established from the family study perspective (Chemerinski et al., 2013; Lenzenweger, 2010).

Three studies have reported a significant excess of PPD in the relatives of schizophrenia probands (Baron et al., 1985; Kendler & Gruenberg, 1982; Kendler et al., 1993; see also Webb & Levinson, 1993). However, PPD appears to be more prevalent in the first-degree relatives of those patients with Axis I delusional disorder, a psychotic illness (Kendler, 1985). One could argue that these data suggest a stronger link between PPD and the Axis I delusional disorder as opposed to schizophrenia, but more data would be required to resolve this issue.

From the "psychometric schizotypy" vantage point, Lenzenweger and Loranger (1989a) examined the lifetime expectancy (morbid risk) of treated schizophrenia, unipolar depression, and bipolar disorder in the biological first-degree relatives of 101 nonpsychotic psychiatric patients (probands) who were classified as either "schizotypy-positive" or "schizotypy-negative" according to the Perceptual Aberration Scale (PAS). The relatives of schizotypy-positive probands were significantly more likely to have been treated for schizophrenia than the relatives of schizotypy-negative probands; the morbid risk for treated unipolar depression or bipolar disorder among the relatives of the two proband groups did not differ. Berenbaum and McGrew (1993) also reported that PAS deviance is familial. Of related interest, Battaglia et al. (1991) found in a study of the relatives of schizotypal patients that recurrent illusions (akin to perceptual aberrations) were found in every patient with SPD with a positive family history of schizophrenia. Finally, Calkins, Curtis, Grove, and Iacono (2004) reported that the primary dimensions of psychometrically assessed schizotypal personality, particularly social-interpersonal deficits, derived from the Raine (1991) SPQ, can differentiate the first-degree relatives of patients with schizophrenia from controls.

## TWIN AND ADOPTION STUDIES

That schizophrenia, based on a long tradition of twin studies, is established as a complex, genetically influenced phenotype represents a scientific statement of fact (Cardno & Gottesman, 2000; Gottesman, 1991; Sullivan et al., 2003). However, for years, there had been no extensive twin studies of clinically defined schizotypic psychopathology beyond an initial study conducted by Torgersen (1994), which supported a heritable component to SPD (subsequently confirmed in a later study by Torgersen et al., 2000). There were no known twin studies of PPD. Miller and Chapman (1993) demonstrated that the PAS has a substantial heritable component, and Kendler and Hewitt (1992) found that "positive trait schizotypy" (of which perceptual aberration, among other features, is a component) is substantially heritable. More recently, Jang, Woodward, Lang, Honer, and Livesley (2005) reported a twin study that used a psychometric dimensional assessment of schizotypic features and found all components to be subject to substantial genetic influences (i.e., heritable). Kendler, Myers, Torgersen, Neale, and Reichborn-Kjennerud (2007) reported on a twin study of dimensionalized representations of the Cluster A disorders (SPD, PPD, and schizoid PD) and found evidence of heritability for all three disorders, with SPD showing the highest heritability.

In terms of adoption studies, the most relevant research comes from the Danish Adoption Study conducted by Kety and colleagues (Kety et al., 1968, 1994) and the subsequent secondary analyses of these data by Kendler and colleagues (e.g., Kendler et al., 1994). In short, whether working from the original data (Kety) or from secondary analyses (Kendler), schizotypic psychopathology is found at greater rates among the biological relatives of the adoptees with schizophrenia. These data are also consistent with the family and twin data supporting the familiality of schizotypic psychopathology and a heritable component to the pathology. There are no adoption studies of *DSM-III-R, DSM-IV, DSM-5* SPD or PPD.

## MOLECULAR GENETIC STUDIES

The field of psychiatric genetics has moved well beyond the model-fitting research approach to assessing genetic factors in schizophrenia (e.g., Bipolar Disorder and Schizophrenia Working Group of the Psychiatric Genomics Consortium, 2018; Dennison et al., 2020; Sullivan et al., 2018). Some very exciting molecular genetic work has begun to appear, which, as noted earlier, provides tangible links between schizotypic psychopathology and schizophrenia. This pattern of results goes some distance in the direction of confirming the basic schizotypy model as developed here. Avramopoulos et al. (2002) found that individuals who carried the high-activity catechol-O-methyltransferase (*COMT*) gene showed elevations on the PAS and SPQ (see also Steiner et al., 2019). Lin et al. (2005) found that elevations in PAS scores were associated with a variant of the neuregulin-1 gene that is thought to be a susceptibility locus for schizophrenia. Fanous et al. (2007) reported the results of a genome-wide scan showing that a subset of schizophrenia susceptibility genes are also related to schizotypy. Vora et al. (2018) reported on dimensional schizotypy measures and the GLRA1 polymorphism, which has implications for treatment. Siever et al. (2011), Grant et al. (2013), and Walter et al. (2016) have all reported findings linking SPD or deviations in schizotypy measures with genetic polymorphisms of considerable interest in schizophrenia.

This emerging body of research should prove powerfully transformative for schizotypy research in the coming decade. At the same time, despite the high heritability of schizophrenia ($h^2$ = .80 or higher), one must keep in mind that relatively few genes have been shown to be consistently related to schizophrenic illness and they account for a tiny proportion of the likely overall genetic contribution to the illness (Sullivan et al., 2012; Bipolar Disorder and Schizophrenia Working Group of the Psychiatric Genomics Consortium, 2018), although promising signals have emerged for C4 genes (Sekar et al., 2016; Yilmaz et al., 2021). In short, there is much work to be done in terms of the molecular genetics of schizotypy and schizophrenia.

*Laboratory Studies of Schizotypic Psychopathology*

There have been a large number of laboratory studies of schizotypic psychopathology. These studies have examined either clinical schizotypes (e.g., SPD/PPD), psychometrically identified schizotypes, or the first-degree relatives of patients with schizophrenia. Only those findings related to the biobehavioral and neurocognitive processes that have received the greatest attention in the schizophrenia literature in recent years are reviewed here, namely sustained attention (Cornblatt & Keilp, 1994; Cornblatt & Malhotra, 2001), eye tracking (Levy et al., 2010), and various forms of executive functioning mediated by the prefrontal cortex (e.g., Gold & Harvey, 1993; Piskulic et al., 2007). Siddi et al. (2017) provide a useful overview of neuropsychological correlates of schizotypy across a variety of other measures/constructs.

A deficit in sustained attention, a leading endophenotype for schizophrenia liability, has been found in clinically defined schizotypic individuals (e.g., SPD) (e.g., Condray & Steinhauer, 1992; Harvey et al., 1996). Similar deficits were found among psychometrically identified schizotypic individuals by Lenzenweger, Cornblatt, and Putnick (1991). Replication of the Lenzenweger et al. (1991) results, using the same measure of sustained attention, have been reported by Obiols, Garcia-Domingo, de Trincheria, and Domenech (1993) (see also Gooding et al., 2006; Rawlings & Goldberg, 2001). Grove et al. (1991) have also reported a significant association between high PAS scores and poor sustained attention performance among the first-degree biological relatives of individuals with diagnosed schizophrenia (see also Chen et al., 1998). Finally, Cornblatt, Lenzenweger, Dworkin, and Erlenmeyer-Kimling (1992) found that attentional dysfunction that is detected in young children who are at risk for schizophrenia is correlated with schizotypic features in adulthood (assessed nearly 20 years later). There are no studies that have explicitly examined sustained attention in patients with PPD. Whereas many prior studies have examined the relationship between sustained attention deficits and schizotypy in carefully constructed samples (i.e., clinical SPD; psychometric high-risk schizotypyes), Bergida and Lenzenweger (2006) showed that schizotypic features are indeed related to deficits in sustained attention within a quasi-random, unselected population sample. The neural signature of sustained attention anomalies in relation to schizotypy has been studied by Sponheim, McGuire, and Stanwyck (2006). Clearly, sustained-attention deficit remains an endophenotype of great interest in the study of schizotypic psychopathology (Fusar-Poli et al., 2013; Snitz et al., 2006). Moreover, careful consideration of the processes (e.g., working memory, context processing, vigilance) involved in alternative sustained tasks remains an area of open investigation (Lee & Park, 2005, 2006).

In terms of eye-tracking dysfunction (ETD) among individuals with schizotypic psychopathology, such deficits are clearly found among clinically defined schizotypes (e.g., Lencz et al., 1993; Siever et al., 1994; cf. Thaker et al., 1996) and psychometrically identified schizotypes (Gooding et al., 2000; O'Driscoll et al., 1998; Thomas et al., 2021). ETD has also been found to aggregate in the biological family members of patients with schizophrenia across numerous studies (Levy et al., 2010;

Sponheim et al., 2003). Finally, although most prior research on ETD was conducted on highly selected samples (which can exaggerate relations between ETD and criterial groups), Lenzenweger and O'Driscoll (2006) showed that an increased rate of catch-up saccades as well as impaired gain (poor pursuit) can be found in relatively unselected adult patients from the general population and that these deficits are indeed related to increased schizotypic features. It is important to note that, just as sustained attention and ETD do not occur in all cases of schizophrenia, not all schizotypes evidence the dysfunctions (cf. Lenzenweger, 1998). Nonetheless, not only does the consistency in findings across patients with schizophrenia and individuals with schizotypic psychopathology inform us of the information-processing and psychophysiological deficits found in schizotypes, but these very deficits further link the schizotype to schizophrenia. To date, there are no reported studies of ETD or smooth pursuit performance specifically in patients with PPD.

Considerable attention has been focused on difficulties in abstract reasoning, executive functioning, and novel problem-solving in schizophrenia (Gold & Harvey, 1993), all processes that are hypothesized to be mediated by the prefrontal cortex. Moreover, early evidence was presented that suggested some schizophrenic symptoms might reflect a dysfunctional frontal brain system (e.g., Goldman-Rakic, 1991; Levin, 1984a, 1984b; Weinberger et al., 1986). Much of this research employed the Wisconsin Card Sorting Test (WCST) as a measure of abstraction ability and executive functioning. Schizotypic patients, identified through either a clinical or psychometric approach, have been found to display deficits on the WCST (Gooding et al., 1999; Lenzenweger & Korfine, 1991, 1994; Park et al., 1995; Raine et al., 1992) though not in all studies (Condray & Steinhauer, 1992). WCST findings for the biological relatives of schizophrenia-affected probands are mixed (Franke et al., 1993; Scarone et al., 1993; cf. Snitz et al., 2006). Clearly, the situation for WCST performance is somewhat inconsistent across mode of definition used in selecting patients, and the research corpus also shows some variability in the WCST performance variables on which deviance has been found (e.g., categories completed vs. percent of perseverative errors vs, failure to maintain set). Finally, in a more fine-grained assessment of the cognitive functions thought to be mediated frontally, Park et al. (1995) reported that psychometrically identified schizotypes revealed poorer "spatial working memory" performance, which is consistent with WCST deficits. Park, Holzman, and Levy (1993) have found that about half of the healthy relatives of patients with schizophrenia also displayed impaired spatial working memory. In general, it is safe to conclude that executive function and spatial working memory deficits are also of considerable interest in this area, both as clues to early pathological processes of schizophrenia as well as endophenotypes (Piskulic et al., 2007; Snitz et al., 2006) There are no reported studies of working memory performance in patients with PPD.

*Other Endophenotypes of Interest*

As this chapter is necessarily limited in scope, one cannot address all processes and factors studied in the domain of schizotypy research. The scope of inquiry in the field continues to expand, and new processes are being studied (e.g., context processing, see Barch et al., 2004; antisaccades O'Driscoll et al., 1998; Thomas et al., 2021). In our laboratory, we have taken a focus on more basic processes, such as motor function (Lenzenweger & Maher, 2002) and somatosensory processing (Chang & Lenzenweger, 2001, 2005; Lenzenweger, 2000). There are two themes guiding this work: (1) simpler processes may be easier to dissect and understand genomically, and (2) we seek to "count" rather than "rate" the things we are interested in studying, thus avoiding the pitfalls associated with rating-based data. We also continue to study ecologically meaningful processes such as the impact of stress on spatial working memory (Smith & Lenzenweger, 2013), social cognition (Miller & Lenzenweger, 2012), theory of mind (Wastler & Lenzenweger, 2019; see also Bora, 2020), and cone of gaze functioning (Wastler & Lenzenweger, 2018). Finally, while much of the experimental psychopathology work on schizotypic psychopathology has emphasized neurocognitive processes, there is a resurgence of interest in hedonic capacity in schizophrenia and schizotypy (e.g., Strauss & Cohen, 2018; Strauss & Gold, 2012), which echoes the early insights of Meehl (1962, 1975, 2001).

*Schizophrenia-Related Deviance on Psychological Tests*

Patients with SPD and PPD are by definition schizotypic at the level of phenomenology, and one would not necessarily anticipate using other measures of pathology to verify the presence of phenomenology already required by virtue of the *DSM* diagnostic criteria. However, psychometrically identified schizotypes have been selected as a function of deviance on a schizotypy measure, and other measures of psychopathology have been used to inform the validity of their schizotypic "status." This literature is voluminous and cannot be thoroughly reviewed here; however, highlights can be illustrated (see Siddi et al., 2017). For example, PAS-identified schizotypes reveal schizophrenia-related deviance on the MMPI (Lenzenweger, 1991), schizophrenia-related PD features (Lenzenweger & Korfine, 1992b), and thought disorder (Coleman et al., 1996; Edell & Chapman, 1979). Lenzenweger, Miller, Maher, and Manschreck (2007) have found that PAS-identified schizotypes reveal hyperassociative language processing, consistent (albeit attenuated) with that seen in schizophrenia, and individual differences in hyperassociation are related to levels of reality distortion and disorganization. This study provides experimental evidence for mild thought disorder in schizotypes, thereby buttressing earlier findings based on ratings of thought disorder. See Chapman et al. (1995) for extensive reviews of the early studies that reported on the correlates of the Chapman psychosis-proneness scales (see also Lenzenweger, 2010).

### Neuroimaging and Neurobiology of Schizotypic Psychopathology

In recent years, the corpus of neuroimaging studies of schizotypic psychopathology has expanded dramatically. In the mid-1990s, the literature was quite limited, and it was premature to highlight major trends in the area (see Flaum & Andreasen, 1995; Gur & Gur, 1995), but the imaging corpus has grown and trends are evident (Dickey et al., 2002; Fervaha & Remington, 2013; Hazlett et al., 2012). Dickey, McCarley, and Shenton (2002), in their review of structural findings in schizotypal PD (using either computed axial tomography or magnetic resonance imaging), revealed many areas of abnormality in SPD (see their table 2, p. 11), and they note many areas of similarity between the SPD brain abnormalities and structural abnormalities found in patients with first-episode schizophrenia. Dickey et al. (2002) noted the relative absence of medial temporal lobe abnormalities in SPD (vs. their presence in clinical schizophrenia), and they speculate, with caution, that the absence of such abnormalities in SPD might help to suppress psychosis in those with SPD. A particularly exciting new finding concerns reduction in gray matter volumes in SPD patients who have never been exposed to neuroleptics (Asami et al., 2013). With respect to functional neuroimaging studies, Siever and Davis (2004), in their review of SPD as a spectrum disorder, concluded that patients with SPD reveal many of the same disturbances in neural circuitry that are seen in clinical schizophrenia, albeit attenuated in severity (see also Lenzenweger & Korfine, 1994; Mohanty et al., 2005). Siever and Davis (2004), at that time, speculated that greater frontal capacity (along with somewhat reduced striatal reactivity) in the patients with SPD might spare them from psychosis. Consistent with this observation, Fervaha and Remington (2013) noted the evidence of increased frontal volumes as well as reduced volumes in subcortical structures (cf., Hazlett et al., 2012). As of 2021, however, functional neuroimaging of schizotypic psychopathology still lags behind the structural neuroimaging work in quantity.

The neurobiological modeling of schizophrenia has undergone major revisions within the past 50 years in response to greater knowledge regarding basic neurobiology (see Grace, 1991; Grace & Moore, 1998; Guillin et al., 2007; McCutcheon et al., 2020), developmental neurobiology, and psychopharmacology (Keepers et al., 2020). A more contemporary view of the dopaminergic dysfunction in schizophrenia emphasizes multiple processes and their dysfunction (Goto & Grace, 2007; Guillin et al., 2007; McCutcheon et al., 2020). Some time ago, Weinberger (1987), among others, suggested that there is a two-process dopamine dysfunction in schizophrenia, with one process implicating the mesocortical dopamine pathway, underactivity in the prefrontal cortex, hypo-dopaminergia, and negative symptoms, and the other involving mesolimbic dopamine pathways, the striatum and related structures, hyper-dopaminergia, and positive symptoms. Grace (1991; see also Goto & Grace, 2007) further refined this model of dopamine dysfunction in schizophrenia by suggesting that a glutamatergic dysfunction emanating from the prefrontal cortex affects "tonic" and "phasic" dopamine processes in the striatum (cf. Bustillo et al., 2019; McCutcheon et al., 2020). Additionally, though there is a continued focus on the role of dopamine in schizophrenia, there is a robust and developing interest in the role that serotonin (Abi-Dargham, 2007) and glutamate (Javitt, 2007) play in schizophrenia as well, particularly onset of the illness (Bossong et al., 2019). Systematic efforts to determine the precise correspondence between the neurobiological models for schizophrenia and schizotypic psychopathology have been undertaken, and they are providing interesting clues about the underlying neural circuitry and neurobiological dysfunction in schizotypes (Abi-Dargham et al., 2004; Mohr & Ettinger, 2014). The fascinating results from Park's group (Woodward et al., 2011) point to amphetamine-induced dopamine release rate as a potential endophenotype for schizotypy, based on findings showing that dopamine release in the striatum was strongly associated with level of schizotypic features in nonpsychotic subjects (not unlike the findings of Howes et al. [2009] in the study of prodromal schizophrenia cases).

## Clinical Phenomenology

Patients with SPD and PPD are, by definition, schizotypic at the level of phenomenology, and one would not necessarily anticipate using other measures of pathology to confirm the phenomenology of such patients. However, as noted previously, alternative methods of detecting schizotypes have been validated, in part, by examining the relations between schizotypic phenomenology as clinically assessed and psychometric measures of schizotypy. For example, Lenzenweger and Loranger (1989b) found that elevations on the PAS were most closely associated with schizotypal PD symptoms and clinically assessed anxiety. Others have found that nonclinical patients, identified as schizotypic through application of the psychometric approach, also reveal schizotypic and "psychotic-like" phenomenology (cf. Chapman et al., 1995; Chapman et al.,1980; Kwapil et al., 1999). Regarding first-degree biological relatives of patients with schizophrenia, Kendler et al. (1993) have shown that schizotypic features are found at higher levels among the relatives of schizophrenia cases than among the relatives of controls. However, it is important to note that not all psychometrically identified schizotypes or biological relatives of patients with schizophrenia will display levels of schizotypic phenomenology that would result in a diagnosis by *DSM-5* criteria for SPD or PPD.

Although it has long been known that there is no meaningful connection between autism and schizophrenia at the level of genetics (Gottesman, 1991; I. I. Gottesman, personal communication, May 19, 2007), correlations have been observed between self-report measures of schizotypy and Asperger's syndrome (a putative autism spectrum condition) (Hurst et al., 2007). The meaning of such cross-sectional correlations, however, remains obscure, and the trend in diagnosis and classification is to consider Asperger's disorder as separate from schizotypic psychopathology (including schizoid pathology) (Raja, 2006).

Finally, an area that has received increased attention in recent years concerns the nature of emotion and affective processing in schizotypes, particularly in light of Meehl's (1962, 1975) original conjectures regarding hedonic capacity (see also Meehl, 2001). Lenzenweger and Loranger (1989b) reported significant associations between measures of anxiety and depression with PAS scores. Berenbaum et al. (2006) reported that negative affect, not surprisingly, was related to interpersonal as well as cognitive schizotypic personality dimensions, whereas attention to emotion was less consistently related to schizotypic pathology (cf. Lewandowski et al., 2006). An important focus for this line of research in the future will be to find some way to resolve whether negative affect among schizotypes hails from the core schizotypy personality organization or whether it represents a secondary development, resulting from what Meehl (2001) has termed "aversive drift." The newly proposed Strauss and Gold (2012; see also Strauss & Cohen, 2018) model of hedonic capacity and anhedonia in schizophrenia may represent a new source of fruitful hypotheses for extension to the schizotypic realm in helping to address this and other questions.

## Follow-Up Studies of Schizotypic Psychopathology

There are few long-term follow-up data (10 years or longer) available on schizotypic samples that would help to determine how many schizotypes move on to clinical schizophrenia. Moreover, given the relative absence of large-scale longitudinal studies of PDs that involve multiple assessments, with the exception of the study being conducted by Lenzenweger's group, it is difficult to examine the stability of schizotypic features over time. Fenton and McGlashan (1989) conducted a follow-up study of patients who had been nonpsychotic at admission to the Chestnut Lodge Psychiatric Hospital, Rockville, Maryland. They found that 67% (12/18) of patients with a diagnosis of schizophrenia, located after a 15-year follow-up, were schizotypic (and nonpsychotic) at their initial admission.

The L. J. Chapman et al. (1994) 10-year follow-up of their "psychosis-prone" (i.e., schizotypic) patients showed that high scorers on the PAS and MIS revealed greater levels of psychotic illness and schizotypic phenomenology at follow-up. Partial replication of the L. J. Chapman et al. (1994) findings was reported by Kwapil, Miller, Zinser, Chapman, and Chapman (1997). Such schizotypic subjects are also known to have greater impairment in psychosocial functioning over time (Kwapil et al., 2013; Kwapil et al., 2020; Minor et al., 2020). Interestingly, psychoticism, as a general schizotypy-relevant construct, does *not* predict heightened risk for psychosis (J. P. Chapman, 1994); psychoticism as described by Eysenck shares little in common with psychoticism as defined, for example, in the *DSM-5* AMPD or the MMPI-2-RF/MMPI-3 approaches. Finally, Lenzenweger (2021) has recently reported elevated rates of psychotic features in subjects, who initially displayed deviance on the PAS at age 18 (with no prior history of psychotic features), 17 years later at age 35. These associations could not be explained by mental state factors such as anxiety or depression at baseline assessment (Lenzenweger, 2021). The precise factors (e.g., cannabis) that serve to move a nonpsychotic schizotypic individual to a psychotic state are a focus intense research efforts (Flückiger et al., 2016; Hiorthøj et al., 2018). Schizotypy as a predictor of suicidal ideation and worry over the life course is also an emerging trend (Linscott et al., 2020).

The relatively new but maturing field of CHR (prodromal) research, which owes much to the schizotypy research vector, is another arena in which conversion from schizotypic states to psychosis is being studied (Fusar-Poli et al., 2013; see also Nordentoft et al., 2006). The gist of the prodromal studies seeking to specify those clinical and symptom feature predictive of conversion to psychosis is that they generally point to attenuated positive psychotic-like features, especially paranoia, suspiciousness, and thought disorganization (Fusar-Poli et al., 2013; see also Barrantes-Vidal et al., 2013; Lee et al., 2018). However, given that CHR studies of schizophrenia are focused on samples that are extremely enriched for partially psychotic subjects (at baseline), it remains important to determine if such psychotic-like symptoms, in previously nonpsychotic persons, in the population predict risk for nonaffective psychosis (see also Fusar-Poli et al., 2016; Sullivan et al., 2020). Werbeloff et al. (2012) provide important data on this issue from a stratified full-probability population-based sample that show self-reported attenuated psychotic symptoms do in fact predict risk for nonaffective psychosis later in life. The Lenzenweger (2021) 17-year follow-up study provides evidence that subtle perceptual aberrations in those persons who have never been psychotic do predict a higher rate of psychotic features later in life, which provides context for CHR studies wherein the majority of the subjects are already quasi-psychotic at study entry.

A common question in this area of research is "How many schizotypes go on to develop full-blown schizophrenia, and how many stay compensated (nonpsychotic) to one degree or another across the life span?" Meehl's model suggests that the modal schizotype never develops schizophrenia; this fascinating question awaits more empirical data from long-term follow-up study of schizotypic cases (see Lenzenweger, 2021). Other outcomes in schizotypy are clinically salient and just beginning to be explored, such as the social cost of schizotypy (Hastrup et al., 2021; Kwapil et al., 2020) and, importantly, suicidality (Linscott et al., 2020).

Another important contemporary question concerns the extent to which endophenotypes (Gottesman & Gould, 2003), assessed using laboratory procedures, predict psychotic outcomes downstream in those initially identified as schizotypic. This approach has the benefit of using objective measures to define endophenotype status, thus being free of the difficulties associated with determining risk or prodromal status as a function of clinical ratings. At this time, only one prospective longitudinal study using this approach has data available, namely that being conducted by Lenzenweger (2021). Preliminary results from this study are promising and indicate considerable utility in using multiple endophenotypes (assessed at baseline) in the later prediction of psychosis, schizotypic psychopathology, psychosocial dysfunction, and other psychological characteristics suggestive of impaired functioning (Lenzenweger, in preparation).

**Delimitation from Other Disorders**

Research on the delimitation of schizotypic psychopathology from other disorders has proceeded at phenotypic and latent levels. Phenotypic delimitation studies have typically taken the form of factor analytic studies and generally focused on data drawn from *DSM* Axis II symptoms. In short, Cluster A symptoms (i.e., schizotypal, paranoid, schizoid) typically hang together. The meaning and direction that can be extracted from such studies, however, is limited by the fact that method-related variance (e.g., structure of interviews) and overlapping definitions of the disorders are complicating factors. The issue of delimitation at the latent level is discussed here.

Assuming that schizotypy, as conceptualized by Meehl (1962, 1990, 1992, 2004), represents a latent liability construct and that current schizotypy indexes are construct valid, a basic question about the fundamental structure of schizotypy remains. Is it continuous (i.e., "dimensional"), or is it truly discontinuous (or "qualitative") in nature? For example, at the level of the gene, Meehl's model (1962, 1990) and the latent trait model (Holzman et al., 1988; Matthysse et al., 1986) conjecture the existence of a qualitative discontinuity. The polygenic multifactorial threshold model (Gottesman, 1991), while positing a continuous distribution of levels of liability (although at the level of individual genes contributing to polygenic influence qualitative discontinuity must exist), does predict a marked threshold effect. Clarification of the structure of schizotypy may help to resolve issues concerning appropriate genetic models for schizophrenia, and such information may aid in planning future studies in this area. Nearly all investigations of the structure of schizophrenia liability done to date have relied exclusively on fully expressed, diagnosable schizophrenia (see Gottesman, 1991), and the results of these studies have left the question of liability structure unresolved (i.e., unexpressed, but at-risk cases are not accounted for in such studies). How best to explore the continuum notion? One cannot reason with confidence that a unimodal distribution of phenotypic schizotypic traits supports the existence of a continuum of liability (e.g., Kendler et al., 1991). In recent years, however, it has been proposed that a possible "expansion" of the schizophrenia phenotype to include other schizophrenia-related phenomena, such as ETD (Holzman et al., 1988), might be helpful in efforts to illuminate the latent structure of liability in schizophrenia. In my laboratory, we have pursued such an approach, complementary to the "expanded phenotype" proposal, through the psychometric detection of schizotypy (see Lenzenweger, 1993, 2010). Thus, we have undertaken over the past four decades a series of studies that begin to explore the latent structure of schizotypy. Our work has drawn extensively from the formulations of Rado and Meehl, and we have used a well-validated measure of schizotypy, the Chapmans' PAS, in these efforts.

We explored the latent structure of schizotypy through application of Meehl's maximum covariance analysis (MAXCOV) (Meehl, 1973; Meehl & Yonce, 1996) procedure to the covariance structure of scores on the PAS. Our samples have been randomly ascertained from nonclinical university populations, and they have been purged of invalid responders and those with suspect test-taking attitudes. Using the MAXCOV procedure, we (Korfine & Lenzenweger, 1995; Lenzenweger & Korfine, 1992a) have found evidence that suggests that the latent structure of schizotypy, as assessed by the PAS, is taxonic (i.e., qualitative) in nature. Moreover, the base rate of the schizotypy taxon is approximately 5–10%. The taxon base rate figure is relatively consistent with the conjecture by Meehl that schizotypes can be found in the general population at a rate of 10%. In our work we have also conducted a variety of control analyses that have served to check the MAXCOV procedure and ensure that the technique does not generate spurious evidence of taxonicity. We (Korfine & Lenzenweger, 1995) have demonstrated that (1) MAXCOV detects a latent continuum when one is hypothesized to exist, (2) MAXCOV results based on dichotomous data do not automatically generate "taxonic" results, and (3) item endorsement frequencies do not correspond to our taxon base rate estimates (i.e., our base rate estimates are not a reflection of endorsement frequencies). Finally, Lenzenweger (1999b) applied MAXCOV analysis to three continuous measures of schizotypy, and this revealed results that were highly consistent with our prior research in this area. These data, taken in aggregate, though they do not unambiguously confirm that the latent structure of schizotypy is qualitative, are clearly consistent with such a conjecture. The suggestion that schizotypic psychopathology is discontinuous in its latent structure raises interesting possibilities for future genetic research in this area (see excellent recent work by Linscott and colleagues: Morton et al., 2017).

Most recently, latent structure work has moved from a consideration of psychometric values to analysis of actual ratio-scale laboratory measures of well-established endophenotypes, sustained attention, and smooth pursuit eye movement, and the results, using taxometric analysis and state-of-the-art finite mixture modeling, support the existence of a qualitative discontinuity in the latent structure of such liability measures (Lenzenweger, McLachlan et al., 2007). Although there has been some interest in the underlying structure of social anhedonia measures, recent taxometric work suggests that hedonic capacity, when measured using fine-grained assessments, appears to have a dimensional latent structure (Linscott, 2007). Issues worthy of careful consideration in the study of the latent structure of psychopathology and/or liability have been detailed recently and are recommended for review to avoid common pitfalls and errors in interpretation that have appeared in the literature (Lenzenweger, 2003, 2004; Meehl, 2004; Waller et al., 2006). As noted, aside from one taxometric study (Rawlings et al., 2008), which was marred by any number of methodological artifacts (see Beauchaine et al., 2008), the overwhelming picture from latent structure analyses (numerous studies across independent laboratories done with techniques that can discern between dimensional and categorical alternatives) supports the presence of some form of latent discontinuity in the distribution of schizotypy measures. This discontinuity is consistent with either a latent taxon (Meehl) or a severe step-function/threshold (Gottesman) harbored within schizotypy measure data.

Finally, before leaving the issue of delimitation, it is worth noting that in recent years considerable energy has been thrown into arguing that the underlying liability of schizotypy must be continuous or dimensional in structure due to (a) the appearance of psychotic-like experiences (PLE) in the population (Johns and Van Os, 2001; Kelleher & Cannon, 2011; Nordgaard et al., 2019; see Lawrie et al., 2010 for alternative viewpoint), (b) the results of factor analysis studies or depiction of values in histograms, and/or (c) conceptual commitments to a dimensional model. What can PLEs tell us about the latent structure of schizotypy (i.e., schizophrenia liability)? In short: not that much, unless we know a great deal about the subjects in question. There could be many reasons for people to report PLEs in the general population—ranging from liability to schizophrenia, liability for bipolar illness, through anxiety states, borderline PD, drug-related experiences, alcohol-related experiences, religious experiences, sleep paralysis, and so on. That one can find PLEs among individuals in the general population does not necessarily tell us anything about the latent structure of schizotypy (schizophrenia liability). Consider some thought exercises. Imagine we are interested in viral spinal meningitis, which is associated with high fever. We could easily find a range of levels of elevated body temperatures (fever) in 10,000 people drawn randomly from the general population for any number of reasons (e,g., influenza, common cold, Lyme disease, COVID-19, and so on), but such instances of varying fever (phenotypic quantitative variation) would not imply that the latent structure of the cause of spinal meningitis was continuous in nature (see Lenzenweger, 2015). Murray and Jones (2012) similarly argue that many PLEs observed in the population, especially among young people, are better explained by common mental disorders such as anxiety or depression, not proneness to psychosis. Regarding statistical analysis, the informed reader will understand that factor analysis always extracts dimensions (continuua) from data, and histograms can mislead the naked eye with ease, although results from both approaches have been invoked often to support continuity/dimensionality. Factor analysis applied to a sample of 10,000 subjects (50% female) using indicators such as height, weight, hair length, bicep size, baseball throwing ability, and so on will extract dimensional representations of these indicators, but such results do not make biological sex continuous in latent structure. Issues of continuity and dimensionality must be addressed using appropriate statistical procedures that are up to the task; "dimensionality," furthermore, cannot be the default model or the null hypothesis in whatever statistical approach is chosen. Finally, one is free to argue for whatever conceptual model one wants to embrace for the structure of schizotypy, but such a position should obviously be supported by proper empirical evidence, not merely a preference for how one thinks nature operates. Alternatively, "Whether or not the entities, properties, and processes of a particular domain (such as psychopathology, or vocational interest patterns) are purely dimensional, or are instead a mix of dimensional and taxonic relations, is an empirical question, not to be settled by a methodological dogma about 'how science works'" (Meehl, 1992; p. 119).

## Conclusion

In summary, as discussed in Lenzenweger (2010), the benefits of the schizotypy model approach in the search for the causes of schizophrenia are fivefold. First and foremost, the study of schizotypic psychopathology provides a "cleaner" window on underlying schizophrenia liability. A cleaner window means an opportunity to study, in the laboratory, genetically influenced, neurobiologically based processes (neurocognitive, affective, personality) that are uncontaminated by "third-variable" confounds, such as medication, deterioration, and institutionalization. Second, the schizotypy model approach to schizophrenia also provides a rich opportunity to discover *endophenotypes* for schizophrenia liability. Endophenotypes (Gottesman & Gould, 2003; Lenzenweger, 1999c, 2013a, 2013b) represent genetically influenced manifestations of the underlying liability for an illness that are invisible to the unassisted or naked eye. Third, incorporation of valid schizotypy indicators (e.g., schizotypic psychopathology) into genomic investigations directed at etiology and development of schizophrenia will enhance the power of such studies. Fourth, via longitudinal investigations, study of schizotypic psychopathology can elucidate *epigenetic* factors that might relate to the differences in outcome of schizotypes (i.e., stable SPD vs. conversion to schizophrenia). Finally, the study of schizotypes provides an opportunity to home in on relatively specific deficits, should they exist, prior to the deterioration in schizophrenia that can give rise to generalized deficit, or the deficient functioning shown by many schizophrenia-affected patients. While generalized deficit remains an area of discussion in schizophrenia (Gold & Dickinson, 2013; Green, Horan, & Sugar, 2013), the schizotypy research model potentially represents a powerful methodological end run on generalized deficit.

Schizotypic psychopathology has long held the interest of researchers and clinicians alike, and it has been the subject of considerable theoretical discussion and empirical investigation. Continued study of this class of mental disturbance through the methods of experimental psychopathology, cognitive neuroscience, genetics, epidemiology, classification, and neurobiology will help to provide clues to the nature of schizophrenia, as well as to the schizotypic disorders themselves. In this context it is worth noting that future work in this area should find methods for embracing and resolving the heterogeneity in performance patterns, symptom features, and life history factors that are known to characterize schizotypy and schizophrenia (as well as hobble research in the area) (Lenzenweger, Jensen, & Rubin, 2003). Furthermore, as has long been advocated by Brendan Maher (1966, 2003), one should "count" rather than "rate" phenomena of interest in this area, thereby bringing greater precision to the research enterprise (see also Lenzenweger, 2010 for other "methodological morals"). The multiplicity of vantage points that have been brought to bear on schizotypic psychopathology has helped to move this area of inquiry further, and the continued existence of alternative vantage points in psychology and psychiatry in connection with these disorders will only serve to advance our knowledge.

## References

Abi-Dargham, A. (2007). Alterations of serotonin transmission in schizophrenia. *International Review of Neurobiology, 78*, 133–164.

Abi-Dargham, A., Kegeles, L. S., Zea-Ponce, Y., Mawlawi, O., Martinez, D., Mitropoulou, V., O'Flynn, K., Koenigsberg, H. W., Van Heertum, R., Cooper, T., Laruelle, M., & Siever, L. J. (2004). Striatal amphetamine-induced dopamine release in patients with schizotypal personality disorder studied with single photon emission computed tomography and [123I] iodobenzamide. *Biological Psychiatry, 55*(10), 1001–1006. https://doi.org/10.1016/j.biopsych.2004.01.018

Andreasen, N. C. (1999). A unitary model of schizophrenia: Bleuler's "fragmented phrene" as shizencephaly. *Archives of General Psychiatry, 56*, 781–787.

Andreasen, N. C., Arndt, S., Alliger, R., Miller, D., & Flaum, M. (1995). Symptoms of schizophrenia: Methods, meanings, and mechanisms. *Archives of General Psychiatry, 52*, 341–351.

Asami, T., Whitford, T. J., Bouix, S., Dickey, C. C., Niznikiewicz, M., Shenton, M. E., Voglmaier, M. M., & McCarley, R. W. (2013). Globally and locally reduced MRI gray matter volumes in neuroleptic-naive men with schizotypal personality disorder: Association with negative symptoms. *JAMA Psychiatry, 70*(4), 361–372.

Avramopoulos, D., Stefanis, N. C., Hantoumi, I., Smyrnis, N., Evdokimidis, I., & Stefanis C. N. (2002). Higher scores of self reported schizotypy in healthy young males carrying the *COMT* high activity allele. *Molecular Psychiatry, 7*, 706–711.

Bach, B., & First, M. B. (2018). Application of the ICD-11 classification of personality disorders. *BMC Psychiatry, 18*(1), 1–14.

Barch, D. M., Mitropoulou, V., Harvey, P. D., New, A. S., Silverman, J. M., & Siever, L. J. (2004). Context-processing deficits in schizotypal personality disorder. *Journal of Abnormal Psychology, 113*, 556–568.

Baron, M., Asnis, L., & Gruen, R. (1981). The schedule for schizotypal personalities (SPP): A diagnostic interview for schizotypal features. *Psychiatry Research, 4*, 213–228.

Baron, M., Gruen, R., Rainer, J. D., Kanes, J., Asnis, L., & Lord, S. (1985). A family study of schizophrenic and normal control probands: Implications for the spectrum concept of schizophrenia. *American Journal of Psychiatry, 142*, 447–454.

Barrantes-Vidal, N., Gross, G. M., Sheinbaum, T., Mitjavila, M., Ballespi, S., & Kwapil, T. R. (2013). Positive and negative schizotypy are associated with prodromal and schizophrenia-spectrum symptoms. *Schizophrenia Research, 145*(1-3), 50–55.

Battaglia, M., Bernardeschi, L., Franchini, L., Bellodi, L., & Smeraldi, E. (1995). A family study of schizotypal disorder. *Schizophrenia Bulletin, 21*, 33–45.

Battaglia, M., Gasperini, M., Sciuto, G., Scherillo, P., Diaferia, G., & Bellodi, L. (1991). Psychiatric disorders in the families of schizotypal subjects. *Schizophrenia Bulletin, 17*, 659–668.

Beauchaine, T. P., Lenzenweger, M. F., & Waller, N. G. (2008). Schizotypy, taxometrics, and disconfirming theories in soft science comment on Rawlings, Williams, Haslam, and Claridge. *Personality and Individual Differences, 44*(8), 1652–1662.

Ben-Porath, Y. S., & Tellegen, A. (2008). *Minnesota Multiphasic Personality Inventory-2-Restructured Form* (MMPI-2-RF) *Manual for administration, scoring, and interpretation*. NCS Pearson.

Ben-Porath, Y. S., & Tellegen, A. (2020). *Minnesota Multiphasic Personality Inventory-3* (MMPI-3) *Manual for administration, scoring, and interpretation*. NCS Pearson.

Berenbaum, H., Boden, M. T., Baker, J. P., Dizen, M., Thompson, R. J., & Abramowitz, A. (2006). Emotional correlates of the different dimensions of schizotypal personality disorder. *Journal of Abnormal Psychology, 115*, 359–368.

Berenbaum, H., & McGrew, J. (1993). Familial resemblance of schizotypic traits. *Psychological Medicine, 23*, 327–333.

Bergida, H., & Lenzenweger, M. F. (2006). Schizotypy and sustained attention: Confirming evidence from an adult community sample. *Journal of Abnormal Psychology, 115*, 545–551.

Bernstein, D. P., Useda, D., & Siever, L. J. (1993). Paranoid personality disorder: Review of the literature and recommendations for DSM-IV. *Journal of Personality Disorders, 7,* 53–62.

Bipolar Disorder and Schizophrenia Working Group of the Psychiatric Genomics Consortium. (2018). Genomic dissection of bipolar disorder and schizophrenia, including 28 subphenotypes. *Cell, 173,* 1705–1715

Bleuler, E. (1911/1950). *Dementia praecox or the group of schizophrenias* (J. Zinkin, Trans.). International Universities Press.

Bolinskey, P. K., Gottesman, I. I., & Nichols, D. S. (2003). The Schizophrenia Proneness (SzP) Scale: An MMPI-2 measure of schizophrenia liability. *Journal of Clinical Psychology, 59,* 1031–1044.

Bora, E. (2020). Theory of mind and schizotypy: A meta-analysis. *Schizophrenia Research, 222,* 97–103.

Bossong, M. G., Antoniades, M., Azis, M., Samson, C., Quinn, B., Bonoldi, I., . . . McGuire, P. (2019). Association of hippocampal glutamate levels with adverse outcomes in individuals at clinical high risk for psychosis. *JAMA Psychiatry, 76*(2), 199–207.

Bustillo, J. R., Gaudiot, C. E., & Lenroot, R. K. (2019). The meaning of glutamate and the quest for biomarkers in the transition to psychosis. *JAMA Psychiatry, 76*(2), 115–116.

Calkins, M. E., Curtis, C. E., Grove, W. M., & Iacono, W. G. (2004). Multiple dimensions of schizotypy in first degree biological relatives of schizophrenia patients. *Schizophrenia Bulletin, 30,* 317–325.

Cardno, A. G., & Gottesman, I. I. (2000). Twin studies of schizophrenia: From bow-and-arrow concordances to Star Wars Mx and functional genomics. *American Journal of Medical Genetics, 97,* 12–17.

Carey, G., Gottesman, I., & Robins, E. (1980). Prevalence rates for the neuroses: Pitfalls in the evaluation of familiality. *Psychological Medicine, 10,* 437–443.

Chang, B. P., & Lenzenweger, M. F. (2001). Somatosensory processing in the biological relatives of schizophrenia patients: A signal detection analysis of two-point discrimination thresholds. *Journal of Abnormal Psychology, 110,* 433–442.

Chang, B. P., & Lenzenweger, M. F. (2005). Somatosensory processing and schizophrenia liability: Proprioception, exteroceptive sensitivity, and graphesthesia performance in the biological relatives of schizophrenia patients. *Journal of Abnormal Psychology, 114,* 85–95.

Chapman, J. P. (1994). Does the Eysenck Psychoticism Scale predict psychosis? A ten-year longitudinal study. *Personality and Individual Differences, 17,* 369–375.

Chapman, J. P., Chapman, L. J., & Kwapil, T. R. (1995). Scales for the measurement of schizotypy. In A. Raine, T. Lencz, & S. Mednick (Eds.), *Schizotypal personality* (pp. 79–106). Cambridge University Press.

Chapman, L. J., & Chapman, J. P. (1985). Psychosis proneness. In M. Alpert (Ed.), *Controversies in schizophrenia: Changes and constancies* (pp. 157–172). Guilford.

Chapman, L. J., & Chapman, J. P. (1987). The search for symptoms predictive of schizophrenia. *Schizophrenia Bulletin, 13,* 497–503.

Chapman, L. J., Chapman, J. P., Kwapil, T. R., Eckblad, M., & Zinser, M. C. (1994). Putatively psychosis-prone subjects 10 years later. *Journal of Abnormal Psychology, 103,* 171–183.

Chapman, L. J., Chapman, J. P., & Raulin, M. L. (1978). Body-image aberration in schizophrenia. *Journal of Abnormal Psychology, 87,* 399–407.

Chapman, L. J., Edell, W. S., & Chapman, J. P. (1980). Physical anhedonia, perceptual aberration, and psychosis proneness. *Schizophrenia Bulletin, 6,* 639–653.

Chemerinski, E., Triebwasser, J., Roussos, P., & Siever, L. J. (2013). Schizotypal personality disorder. *Journal of Personality Disorders, 27*(5), 652–679.

Chen, W. J., Liu, S. K, Chang, C.-J., Lien, Y.-J., Chang, Y.-H., & Hwu, H.-G. (1998). Sustained attention deficit and schizotypal personality features in nonpsychotic relatives of schizophrenia patients. *American Journal of Psychiatry, 155,* 1214–1220.

Claridge, G. (Ed.). (1997). *Schizotypy: Implications for illness and health.* Oxford University Press.

Claridge, G. S., & Broks, P. (1984). Schizotypy and hemisphere function: I. Theoretical considerations and the measurement of schizotypy. *Personality and Individual Differences, 5,* 633–648.

Cohen, A. S., Matthews, R. A., Najolia, G. M., & Brown, L. A. (2010). Toward a more psychometrically sound brief measure of schizotypal traits: Introducing the SPQ-Brief Revised. *Journal of Personality Disorders, 24,* 516–537.

Coid, J., Yang, M., Tyrer, P., Roberts, A., & Ullrich, S. (2006). Prevalence and correlates of personality disorder among adults aged 16 to 74 in Great Britain. *British Journal of Psychiatry, 188,* 423–431.

Coleman, M. J., Levy, D. L., Lenzenweger, M. F., & Holzman, P. S. (1996). Thought disorder, perceptual aberrations, and schizotypy. *Journal of Abnormal Psychology, 105,* 469–473.

Condray, R., & Steinhauer, S. R. (1992). Schizotypal personality disorder in individuals with and without schizophrenic relatives: Similarities and contrasts in neurocognitive and clinical functioning. *Schizophrenia Research, 7,* 33–41.

Cornblatt, B. A., & Keilp, J. G. (1994). Impaired attention, genetics, and the pathophysiology of schizophrenia. *Schizophrenia Bulletin, 20,* 31–46.

Cornblatt, B. A., Lenzenweger, M. F., Dworkin, R. H., & Erlenmeyer-Kimling, L. (1992). Childhood attentional dysfunction predicts social isolation in adults at risk for schizophrenia. *British Journal of Psychiatry, 161*(Suppl. 18), 59–68.

Cornblatt, B. A., & Malhotra, A. K. (2001). Impaired attention as an endophenotype for molecular genetic studies of schizophrenia. *American Journal of Medical Genetics (Neuropsychiatric Genetics), 105,* 11–15.

Crawford, T. N., Cohen, P., Johnson, J. G., Kasen, S., First, M. B., Gordon, K., & Brook, J. S. (2005). Self-reported personality disorder in the children in the community sample: Convergent and prospective validity in late adolescence and adulthood. *Journal of Personality Disorders, 19,* 30–52.

Cronbach, L. J., & Meehl, P. E. (1955). Construct validity in psychological tests. *Psychological Bulletin, 52,* 281–302.

Dennison, C. A., Legge, S. E., Pardiñas, A. F., & Walters, J. T. (2020). Genome-wide association studies in schizophrenia: Recent advances, challenges and future perspective. *Schizophrenia Research, 217,* 4–12.

Dickey, C. C., McCarley, R. W., & Shenton, M. E. (2002). The brain in schizotypal personality disorder: A review of structural MRI and CT findings. *Harvard Review of Psychiatry, 10,* 1–15.

Eckblad, M., & Chapman, L. J. (1983). Magical ideation as an indicator of schizotypy. *Journal of Consulting and Clinical Psychology, 51,* 215–225.

Edell, W. S., & Chapman, L. J. (1979). Anhedonia, perceptual aberration, and the Rorschach. *Journal of Consulting and Clinical Psychology, 47*, 377–384.

Essen-Möller, E., Larsson, H., Uddenberg, C.-E., & White, G. (1956). Individual traits and morbidity in a Swedish rural population. *Acta Psychiatrica et Neurologica Scandinavica,* 100, 5–160.

Eysenck, H. J. (1958). The continuity of abnormal and normal behavior. *Psychological Bulletin,* 55(6), 429–432.

Eysenck, H. J., & Eysenck, S. B. G. (1976). *Psychoticism as a dimension of personality.* Hodder & Stoughton.

Falconer, D. S. (1989). *Introduction to quantitative genetics,* 3rd ed. Longman.

Fanous, A. H., & Kendler, K. S. (2005). Genetic heterogeneity, modifier genes, and quantitative phenotypes in psychiatric illness: Searching for a framework. *Molecular Psychiatry,* 10, 6–13.

Fanous, A. H., Neale, M. C., Gardner, C. O., Webb, B. T., Straub, R. E., O'Neill, F. A., Walsh, D., Riley, B. P., & Kendler, K. S. (2007). Significant correlation in linkage signals from genome-wide scans of schizophrenia and schizotypy. *Molecular Psychiatry,* 12, 958–965.

Fenton, W. S., & McGlashan, T. H. (1989). Risk of schizophrenia in character disordered patients. *American Journal of Psychiatry,* 146, 1280–1284.

Fervaha, G., & Remington, G. (2013). Neuroimaging findings in schizotypal personality disorder: A systematic review. *Progress in Neuro-psychopharmacology & Biological Psychiatry,* 43, 96–107. https://doi.org/10.1016/j.pnpbp.2012.11.014

Flaum, M., & Andreasen, N. C. (1995). Brain morphology in schizotypal personality as assessed by magnetic resonance imaging. In A. Raine, T. Lencz, & S. Mednick (Eds.), *Schizotypal personality* (pp. 385–405). Cambridge University Press.

Flückiger, R., Ruhrmann, S., Debbané, M., Michel, C., Hubl, D., Schimmelmann, B. G., . . . Schultze-Lutter, F. (2016). Psychosis-predictive value of self-reported schizotypy in a clinical high-risk sample. *Journal of Abnormal Psychology,* 125(7), 923–932.

Fogelson, D. L., Nuechterlein, K. H., Asarnow, R. A., Payne, D. L., Subotnik, K. L., Jacobson, K. C., Neale, M. C., & Kendler, K. S. (2007). Avoidant personality disorder is a separable schizophrenia-spectrum personality disorder even when controlling for the presence of paranoid and schizotypal personality disorders: The UCLA family study. *Schizophrenia Research,* 91, 192–199.

Franke, P., Maier, W., Hardt, J., & Hain, C. (1993). Cognitive functioning and anhedonia in subjects at risk for schizophrenia. *Schizophrenia Research,* 10, 77–84.

Fusar-Poli, P., Borgwardt, S., Bechdolf, A., Addington, J., Riecher-Rössler, A., Schultze-Lutter, F., . . . Yung, A. (2013). The psychosis high-risk state: A comprehensive state-of-the-art review. *JAMA Psychiatry,* 70, 107–120.

Fusar-Poli, P., Schultze-Lutter, F., Cappucciati, M., Rutigliano, G., Bonoldi, I., Stahl, D., . . . McGuire, P. (2016). The dark side of the moon: Meta-analytical impact of recruitment strategies on risk enrichment in the clinical high risk state for psychosis. *Schizophrenia Bulletin,* 42(3), 732–743.

Gold, J. M., & Dickinson, D. (2013). "Generalized cognitive deficit" in schizophrenia: Overused or underappreciated? *Schizophrenia Bulletin,* 39, 263–265.

Gold, J. M., & Harvey, P. D. (1993). Cognitive deficits in schizophrenia. *Psychiatric Clinics of North America,* 16, 295–312.

Goldman-Rakic, P. S. (1991). Prefrontal cortical dysfunction in schizophrenia: The relevance of working memory. In B. Carroll (Ed.), *Psychopathology and the brain* (pp. 1–23). Raven Press.

Gooding, D. C., Kwapil, T. R., & Tallent, K. A. (1999). Wisconsin Card Sorting Test deficits in schizotypic individuals. *Schizophrenia Research,* 40, 201–209.

Gooding, D. C., Matts, C. W., & Rollmann, E. A. (2006). Sustained attention deficits in relation to psychometrically identified schizotypy: Evaluating a potential endophenotypic marker. *Schizophrenia Research,* 82, 27–37.

Gooding, D. C., Miller, M. D., & Kwapil, T. R. (2000). Smooth pursuit eye tracking and visual fixation in psychosis-prone individuals. *Psychiatry Research,* 93, 41–54.

Goto, Y., & Grace, A. A. (2007). The dopamine system and the pathophysiology of schizophrenia: A basic science perspective. *International Review of Neurobiology,* 78, 41–68.

Gottesman, I. I. (1987). The psychotic hinterlands or the fringes of lunacy. *British Medical Bulletin,* 43, 557–569.

Gottesman, I. I. (1991). *Schizophrenia genesis: The origins of madness.* W. H. Freeman.

Gottesman, I. I., & Bertelsen, A. (1989). Confirming unexpressed genotypes for schizophrenia: Risks in the offspring of Fischer's Danish identical and fraternal discordant twins. *Archives of General Psychiatry,* 46, 867–872.

Gottesman, I. I., & Gould, T. D. (2003). The endophenotype concept in psychiatry: Etymology and strategic intentions. *American Journal of Psychiatry,* 160, 636–645.

Grace, A. A. (1991). Phasic versus tonic dopamine release and the modulation of dopamine system responsivity: A hypothesis for the etiology of schizophrenia. *Neuroscience,* 41, 1–24.

Grace, A. A., & Moore, H. (1998). Regulation of information flow in the nucleus accumbens: A model for the pathophysiology of schizophrenia. In M. F. Lenzenweger & R. H. Dworkin (Eds.), *Origins and development of schizophrenia: Advances in experimental psychopathology* (pp. 123–157). American Psychological Association.

Grant, B. F., Hasin, D. S., Stinson, F. S., Dawson, D. A., Chou, S. P., Ruan, W. J., & Pickering, R. P. (2004). Prevalence, correlates, and disability of personality disorders in the United States: Results from the National Epidemiologic Survey on Alcohol and Related Conditions. *Journal of Clinical Psychiatry,* 65, 948–958.

Grant, P., & Hennig, J. (2020). Schizotypy, social stress and the emergence of psychotic-like states-A case for benign schizotypy?. *Schizophrenia Research,* 216, 435–442.

Grant, P., Kuepper, Y., Mueller, E. A., Wielpuetz, C., Mason, O., & Hennig, J. (2013). Dopaminergic foundations of schizotypy as measured by the German version of the Oxford-Liverpool Inventory of Feelings and Experiences (O-LIFE): A suitable endophenotype of schizophrenia. *Frontiers of Human Neuroscience,* 7, 1–11.

Green, M. F., Horan, W. P., & Sugar, C. A. (2013). Has the generalized deficit become the generalized criticism? *Schizophrenia Bulletin,* 39, 257–262.

Gross, G. M., Mellin, J., Silvia, P. J., Barrantes-Vidal, N., & Kwapil, T. R. (2014). Comparing the factor structure of the Wisconsin Schizotypy Scales and the Schizotypal Personality Questionnaire. *Personality Disorders: Theory, Research, and Treatment,* 5(4), 397–405.

Grove, W. M. (1982). Psychometric detection of schizotypy. *Psychological Bulletin,* 92, 27–38.

Grove, W. M., Lebow, B. S., Clementz, B. A., Cerri, A., Medus, C., & Iacono, W. G. (1991). Familial prevalence and coaggregation of schizotypy indicators: A multitrait family study. *Journal of Abnormal Psychology, 100*, 115–121.

Gross, G. M., Mellin, J., Silvia, P. J., Barrantes-Vidal, N., & Kwapil, T. R. (2014). Comparing the factor structure of the Wisconsin Schizotypy Scales and the Schizotypal Personality Questionnaire. *Personality Disorders: Theory, Research, & Treatment, 5*, 397–405.

Guillin, O., Abi-Dargham, A., & Laruelle, M. (2007). Neurobiology of dopamine in schizophrenia. *International Review of Neurobiology, 78*, 1–39.

Gur, R. C., & Gur, R. E. (1995). The potential of physiological neuroimaging for the study of schizotypy: Experiences from applications to schizophrenia. In A. Raine, T. Lencz, & S. Mednick (Eds.), *Schizotypal personality* (pp. 406–425). Cambridge University Press.

Hanson, D. R., Gottesman, I. I., & Meehl, P. E. (1977). Genetic theories and the validation of psychiatric diagnosis: Implications for the study of children of schizophrenics. *Journal of Abnormal Psychology, 86*, 575–588.

Harkness, A. R., McNulty, J. L., & Ben-Porath, Y. (1995). The personality pathology five (PSY-5): Constructs and MMPI-2 scales. *Psychological Assessment, 7*, 104–114.

Harvey, P. D., Keefe, R. S. E., Mitroupolou, V., DuPre, R., Roitman, S. L., Mohs, R., & Siever, L.J. (1996). Information-processing markers of vulnerability to schizophrenia: Performance of patients with schizotypal and nonschizotypal personality disorders. *Psychiatry Research, 60*, 49–56.

Hastrup, L. H., Jennum, P., Ibsen, R., Kjellberg, J., & Simonsen, E. (2021). Costs of schizotypal disorder: A matched-controlled nationwide register-based study of patients and spouses. *Acta Psychiatrica Scandinavica, 144*(1), 60–71.

Hazlett, E. A., Goldstein, K. E., & Kolaitis, J. C. (2012). A review of structural MRI and diffusion tensor imaging in schizotypal personality disorder. *Current Psychiatry Reports, 14*(1), 70–78. https://doi.org/10.1007/s11920-011-0241-z

Henriksen, M. G., Nordgaard, J., & Jansson, L. B. (2017). Genetics of schizophrenia: Overview of methods, findings and limitations. *Frontiers in Human Neuroscience, 11*, 322.

Hjorthøj, C., Albert, N., & Nordentoft, M. (2018). Association of substance use disorders with conversion from schizotypal disorder to schizophrenia. *JAMA Psychiatry, 75*(7), 733–739.

Holzman, P. S., Kringlen, E., Matthysse, S., Flanagan, S. D., Lipton, R. B., Cramer, G., Levin, S., Lange, K., & Levy, D. L. (1988). A single dominant gene can account for eye tracking dysfunctions and schizophrenia in offspring of discordant twins. *Archives of General Psychiatry, 45*(7), 641–647. https://doi.org/10.1001/archpsyc.1988.01800310049006

Howes, O. D., Montgomery, A. J., Asselin, M. C., Murray, R. M., Valli, I., Tabraham, P., Bramon-Bosch, E., Valmaggia, L., Johns, L., Broome, M., McGuire, P. K., & Grasby, P. M. (2009). Elevated striatal dopamine function linked to prodromal signs of schizophrenia. *Archives of General Psychiatry, 66*(1), 13–20. https://doi.org/10.1001/archgenpsychiatry.2008.514

Hurst, R. M., Nelson-Gray, R. O., Mithcell, J. T., & Kwapil, T. R. (2007). The relationship of Asperger's characteristics and schizotypal personality traits in a non-clinical adult sample. *Journal of Autism and Developmental Disorders, 37*, 1711–1720.

Jang, K. L., Woodward, T. S., Lang, D., Honer, W. G., & Livesley, W. J. (2005). The genetic and environmental basis of the relationship between schizotypy and personality: A twin study. *Journal of Nervous and Mental Disease, 193*, 153–159.

Javitt, D. C. (2007). Glutamate and schizophrenia: Phencyclidine, N-methyl-d-aspartate receptors, and dopamine-glutamate interactions. *International Review of Neurobiology, 78*, 69–108.

Johns, L. C., & Van Os, J. (2001). The continuity of psychotic experiences in the general population. *Clinical Psychology Review, 21*(8), 1125–1141.

Johnson, J. G., Cohen, P., Kasen, S., Skodol, A. E., Hamagan, F., & Brook J. S. (2000). Age-related change in personality disorder trait levels between early adolescence and adulthood: A community-based longitudinal investigation. *Acta Psychiatra Scandinavica, 102*, 265–275.

Keepers, G. A., Fochtman, L. J., Anzia, J. M., Benjamin, S., Lyness, J. M., Mojtabai, R., Servis, M., Walaszek, A., Buckley, P., Lenzenweger, M. F., Young, A. S., Begenhardt, A., & Hong, S. H. (2020). The American Psychiatric Association practice guideline for the treatment of patients with schizophrenia. *American Journal of Psychiatry, 177*, 868–872. [https://doi.org/10.1176/appi.ajp.2020.177901]

Kelleher, I., & Cannon, M. (2011). Psychotic-like experiences in the general population: Characterizing a high-risk group for psychosis. *Psychological Medicine, 41*(1), 1–6.

Kelleher, I., Keeley, H., Corcoran, P., Lynch, F., Fitzpatrick, C., Devlin, N., . . . Cannon, M. (2012). Clinicopathological significance of psychotic experiences in non-psychotic young people: Evidence from four population-based studies. *British Journal of Psychiatry, 201*(1), 26–32.

Kendler, K. S. (1985). Diagnostic approaches to schizotypal personality disorder: A historical perspective. *Schizophrenia Bulletin, 11*, 538–553.

Kendler, K., & Gruenberg, A. (1982). Genetic relationship between paranoid personality disorder and the "schizophrenic spectrum" disorders. *American Journal of Psychiatry, 139*, 1185–1186.

Kendler, K. S., Gruenberg, A. M., & Kinney, D. K. (1994). Independent diagnoses of adoptees and relatives as defined by DSM-III in the provincial and national samples of the Danish Adoption Study of Schizophrenia. *Archives of General Psychiatry, 51*, 456–468.

Kendler, K. S., & Hewitt, J. (1992). The structure of self-report schizotypy in twins. *Journal of Personality Disorders, 6*, 1–17.

Kendler, K. S., Lieberman, J. A., & Walsh, D. (1989). The Structured Interview for Schizotypy (SIS): A preliminary report. *Schizophrenia Bulletin, 15*, 559–571.

Kendler, K. S., McGuire, M., Gruenberg, A. M., O'Hare, A., Spellman, M., & Walsh, D. (1993). The Roscommon Family Study: III. Schizophrenia-related personality disorders in relatives. *Archives of General Psychiatry, 50*, 781–788.

Kendler, K. S., Myers, J., Torgersen, S., Neale, M. C., & Reichborn-Kjennerud, T. (2007). The heritability of Cluster A personality disorders assessed by both personal interview and questionnaire. *Psychological Medicine, 37*, 655–665.

Kendler, K. S., Ochs, A. L., Gorman, A. M., Hewitt, J. K., Ross, D. E., & Mirsky, A. F. (1991). The structure of schizotypy: A pilot multitrait twin study. *Psychiatry Research, 36*, 19–36.

Kendler, K. S., & Walsh, D. (1995). Schizotypal personality disorder in parents and risk for schizophrenia in siblings. *Schizophrenia Bulletin, 21*, 47–52.

Kerns, J. G. (2020). Cluster A personality disorders. In C. W. Lejuez & K. L. Gratz (Eds.), *Cambridge handbook of personality disorders* (pp. 195–211). Cambridge University Press.

Kety, S. S., Rosenthal, D., Wender, P. H., & Schulsinger, F. (1968). The types and prevalence of mental illness in the biological and adoptive families of adopted schizophrenics. *Journal of Psychiatric Research, 6*, 345–362.

Kety, S. S., Wender, P. H., Jacobsen, B., Ingraham, L. J., Jansson, L., Faber, B., & Kinney, D. K. (1994). Mental illness in the biological and adoptive relatives of schizophrenic adoptees: Replication of the Copenhagen Study in the rest of Denmark. *Archives of General Psychiatry, 51*, 442–455.

Kirchner, S. K., Roeh, A., Nolden, J., & Hasan, A. (2018). Diagnosis and treatment of schizotypal personality disorder: Evidence from a systematic review. *NPJ Schizophrenia, 4*(1), 1–18.

Khouri, P. J., Haier, R. J., Rieder, R. O., & Rosenthal, D. (1980). A symptom schedule for the diagnosis of borderline schizophrenia: A first report. *British Journal of Psychiatry, 137*, 140–147.

Korfine, L., & Lenzenweger, M. F. (1995). The taxonicity of schizotypy: A replication. *Journal of Abnormal Psychology, 104*, 26–31.

Kotov, R., Krueger, R. F., & Watson, D. (2018). A paradigm shift in psychiatric classification: The hierarchical taxonomy of psychopathology (HiTOP). *World Psychiatry, 17*, 24–25.

Kotov, R., Jonas, K. G., Carpenter, W. T., Dretsch, M. N., Eaton, N. R., Forbes, M. K., Forbush, K. T., Hobbs, K., Reininghaus, U., Slade, T., South, S. C., Sunderland, M., Waszczuk, M. A., Widiger, T. A., Wright, A., Zald, D. H., Krueger, R. F., Watson, D., & HiTOP Utility Workgroup (2020). Validity and utility of Hierarchical Taxonomy of Psychopathology (HiTOP): I. Psychosis superspectrum. *World Psychiatry: Official Journal of the World Psychiatric Association (WPA), 19*(2), 151–172. https://doi.org/10.1002/wps.20730

Kraepelin, E. (1919/1971). *Dementia praecox and paraphrenia* (R. M. Barclay, Trans., G. M. Robertson, Ed.). Krieger. (Original work published 1896).

Krueger, R. F., Kotov, R., Watson, D., Forbes, M. K., Eaton, N. R., Ruggero, C. J., . . . Zimmermann, J. (2018). Progress in achieving quantitative classification of psychopathology. *World Psychiatry, 17*(3), 282–293

Krueger, R. F., Derringer, J., Markon, K. E., Watson, D., & Skodol, A. E. (2012). Initial construction of a maladaptive personality trait model and inventory for DSM-5. *Psychological Medicine, 42*, 1879–1890.

Kwapil, T. R., Barrantes-Vidal, N., & Silvia, P. J. (2008). The dimensional structure of the Wisconsin schizotypy scales: Factor identification and construct validity. *Schizophrenia Bulletin, 34*, 444–457.

Kwapil, T. R., Chapman, L. J., & Chapman, J. P. (1999). Validity and usefulness of the Wisconsin manual for assessing psychotic-like experiences. *Schizophrenia Bulletin, 25*, 363–375.

Kwapil, T. R., Gross, G. M., Silvia, P. J., Raulin, M. L., & Barrantes-Vidal, N. (2018). Development and psychometric properties of the Multidimensional Schizotypy Scale: A new measure for assessing positive, negative, and disorganized schizotypy. *Schizophrenia Research, 193*, 209–217.

Kwapil, T. R., Gross, G. M., Silvia, P. J., & Barrantes-Vidal, N. (2013). Prediction of psychopathology and functional impairment by positive and negative schizotypy in the Chapmans' ten-year longitudinal study. *Journal of Abnormal Psychology, 122*(3), 807–815.

Kwapil, T. R., Kemp, K. C., Mielock, A., Sperry, S. H., Chun, C. A., Gross, G. M., & Barrantes-Vidal, N. (2020). Association of multidimensional schizotypy with psychotic-like experiences, affect, and social functioning in daily life: Comparable findings across samples and schizotypy measures. *Journal of Abnormal Psychology, 129*(5), 492–504.

Kwapil, T. R., Mann, M. C., & Raulin, M. L. (2002). Psychometric properties and concurrent validity of the schizotypal ambivalence scale. *Journal of Nervous and Mental Disease, 190*, 290–295.

Kwapil, T. R., Miller, M. B., Zinser, M. C., Chapman, J. P., & Chapman L. J. (1997). Magical ideation and social anhedonia as predictors of psychosis proneness: A partial replication. *Journal of Abnormal Psychology, 106*, 491–495.

Lawrie, S. M., Hall, J., McIntosh, A. M., Owens, D. G., & Johnstone, E. C. (2010). The 'continuum of psychosis': Scientifically unproven and clinically impractical. *British Journal of Psychiatry, 197*(6), 423–425.

Lee, J., & Park, S. (2005). Working memory impairments in schizophrenia: A meta-analysis. *Journal of Abnormal Psychology, 114*, 599–611.

Lee, J., & Park, S. (2006). The role of stimulus salience in CPT-AX performance of schizophrenia patients. *Schizophrenia Research, 81*, 191–197.

Lee, T. Y., Lee, J., Kim, M., Choe, E., & Kwon, J. S. (2018). Can we predict psychosis outside the clinical high-risk state? A systematic review of non-psychotic risk syndromes for mental disorders. *Schizophrenia Bulletin, 44*(2), 276–285

Lencz, T., Raine, A., Scerbo, A., Redmon, M., Brodish, S., Holt, L., & Bird, L. (1993). Impaired eye tracking in undergraduates with schizotypal personality disorder. *American Journal of Psychiatry, 150*, 152–154.

Lenzenweger, M. F. (2021). Schizotypy 17 years on: Dimensions of psychosis. *Journal of Abnormal Psychology, 130*, 399–412. https://doi.org/10.1037/abn0000680

Lenzenweger, M. F. (in preparation). Schizotypy 17 years on: Predicting schizotypic psychopathology, psychosocial dysfunction, and other psychological characteristics.

Lenzenweger, M. F. (1991). Confirming schizotypic personality configurations in hypothetically psychosis-prone university students. *Psychiatry Research, 37*, 81–96.

Lenzenweger, M. F. (1993). Explorations in schizotypy and the psychometric high-risk paradigm. In L. J. Chapman, J. P. Chapman, & D. Fowles (Eds.), *Progress in experimental personality and psychopathology research, no. 16* (pp. 66–116). Springer.

Lenzenweger, M. F. (1994). The psychometric high-risk paradigm, perceptual aberrations, and schizotypy: An update. *Schizophrenia Bulletin, 20*, 121–135.

Lenzenweger, M. F. (1998). Schizotypy and schizotypic psychopathology: Mapping an alternative expression of schizophrenia liability. In M. F. Lenzenweger & R. H. Dworkin (Eds.), *Origins and development of schizophrenia: Advances in experimental psychopathology* (pp. 93–121). American Psychological Association.

Lenzenweger, M. F. (1999a). Stability and change in personality disorder features: The Longitudinal Study of Personality Disorders. *Archives of General Psychiatry, 56*, 1009–1015.

Lenzenweger, M. F. (1999b). Deeper into the schizotypy taxon: On the robust nature of maximum covariance (MAXCOV) analysis. *Journal of Abnormal Psychology, 108*, 182–187.

Lenzenweger, M. F. (1999c). Schizophrenia: Refining the phenotype, resolving endophenotypes [Invited Essay]. *Behaviour Research and Therapy, 37*, 281–295.

Lenzenweger, M. F. (2000). Two-point discrimination thresholds and schizotypy: Illuminating a somatosensory dysfunction. *Schizophrenia Research, 42*, 111–124.

Lenzenweger, M. F. (2003). On thinking clearly about taxometrics, schizotypy, and genetic influences: Correction to Widiger (2001). *Clinical Psychology: Science & Practice, 10*, 367–369.

Lenzenweger, M. F. (2004). Consideration of the challenges, complications, and pitfalls of taxometric analysis. *Journal of Abnormal Psychology, 113*, 10–23.

Lenzenweger, M. F. (2006). The Longitudinal Study of Personality Disorders: History, design, and initial findings [Special Essay]. *Journal of Personality Disorders, 6*, 645–670.

Lenzenweger, M. F. (2008). Epidemiology of personality disorders. *Psychiatric Clinics of North America, 31*, 395–403.

Lenzenweger, M. F. (2010). *Schizotypy and schizophrenia: The view from experimental psychopathology*. Guilford.

Lenzenweger, M. F. (2013a). Endophenotype, intermediate phenotype, biomarker: Definitions, concept comparisons, clarifications. *Depression and Anxiety, 30*, 185–189.

Lenzenweger, M. F. (2013b). Thinking clearly about the endophenotype–intermediate phenotype–biomarker distinctions in developmental psychopathology research. *Development & Psychopathology, 25*, 1347–1357.

Lenzenweger, M. F. (2015). Thinking clearly about schizotypy: Hewing to the schizophrenia liability core, considering interesting tangents, and avoiding conceptual quicksand. *Schizophrenia Bulletin, 41* (Suppl. 2), S483–S491.

Lenzenweger, M. F. (2018a).Schizotypy, schizotypic psychopathology, and schizophrenia. (Invited *Perspective* Essay). *World Psychiatry, 17*, 25–26.

Lenzenweger, M. F. (2018b). Schizotypy, schizotypic psychopathology, and schizophrenia: Hearing echoes, leveraging prior advances, and probing new angles. *Schizophrenia Bulletin, 44*, Suppl. 2, S564–S569.

Lenzenweger, M. F., Bennett, M. E., & Lilenfeld, L. R. (1997). The referential thinking scale as a measure of schizotypy: Scale development and initial construct validation. *Psychological Assessment, 9*, 452–463.

Lenzenweger, M. F., Cornblatt, B. A., & Putnick, M. E. (1991). Schizotypy and sustained attention. *Journal of Abnormal Psychology, 100*, 84–89.

Lenzenweger, M. F., & Dworkin, R. H. (1996). The dimensions of schizophrenia phenomenology? Not one or not two, at least three, perhaps four. *British Journal of Psychiatry, 168*, 432–440.

Lenzenweger, M. F., & Dworkin, R. H. (Eds.). (1998). *Origins and development of schizophrenia: Advances in experimental psychopathology*. American Psychological Association.

Lenzenweger, M. F., Jensen, S., & Rubin, D. B. (2003). Finding the "genuine" schizotype: A model and method for resolving heterogeneity in performance on laboratory measures in experimental psychopathology research. *Journal of Abnormal Psychology, 112*, 457–468.

Lenzenweger, M. F., Hallquist, M. N., & Wright, A. G. C. (2018). Understanding stability and change in the personality disorders: Methodological and substantive issues underpinning interpretive challenges and the road ahead. In W. J. Livesley & R. Larstone (Eds.), *Handbook of personality disorders*, 2nd ed. (pp. 197–214). Guilford.

Lenzenweger, M. F., & Korfine, L. (1991, December). *Schizotypy and Wisconsin Card Sorting Test performance*. Paper presented at the sixth annual meeting of the Society for Research in Psychopathology, Harvard University.

Lenzenweger, M. F., & Korfine, L. (1992a). Confirming the latent structure and base rate of schizotypy: A taxometric analysis. *Journal of Abnormal Psychology, 101*, 567–571.

Lenzenweger, M. F., & Korfine, L. (1992b). Identifying schizophrenia-related personality disorder features in a nonclinical population using a psychometric approach. *Journal of Personality Disorders, 6*, 264–274.

Lenzenweger, M. F., & Korfine, L. (1994). Perceptual aberrations, schizotypy and the Wisconsin Card Sorting Test. *Schizophrenia Bulletin, 20*, 345–357.

Lenzenweger, M. F., Lane, M., Loranger, A. W., & Kessler, R. C. (2007). DSM-IV personality disorders in the National Comorbidity Survey Replication (NCS-R). *Biological Psychiatry, 62*, 553–564.

Lenzenweger, M. F., & Loranger, A. W. (1989a). Detection of familial schizophrenia using a psychometric measure of schizotypy. *Archives of General Psychiatry, 46*, 902–907.

Lenzenweger, M. F., & Loranger, A. W. (1989b). Psychosis proneness and clinical psychopathology: Examination of the correlates of schizotypy. *Journal of Abnormal Psychology, 98*, 3–8.

Lenzenweger, M. F., Loranger, A. W., Korfine, L., & Neff, C. (1997). Detecting personality disorders in a nonclinical population: Application of a two-stage procedure for case identification. *Archives of General Psychiatry, 54*, 345–351.

Lenzenweger, M. F., & Maher, B. A. (2002). Psychometric schizotypy and motor performance. *Journal of Abnormal Psychology, 111*, 546–555.

Lenzenweger, M. F., McLachlan, G., & Rubin, D. B. (2007). Resolving the latent structure of schizophrenia endophenotypes using expectation-maximization-based finite mixture modeling. *Journal of Abnormal Psychology, 116*, 16–29.

Lenzenweger, M. F., Miller, A. B., Maher, B. A., & Manschreck, T. C. (2007). Schizotypy and individual differences in the frequency of normal associations in verbal utterances. *Schizophrenia Research, 95*, 96–102.

Lenzenweger, M. F., & O'Driscoll, G. A. (2006). Smooth pursuit eye movement dysfunction and schizotypy in an adult community sample. *Journal of Abnormal Psychology, 4*, 779–786.

Levin, S. (1984a). Frontal lobe dysfunctions in schizophrenia—I. Eye movement impairments. *Journal of Psychiatric Research, 18*, 27–55.

Levin, S. (1984b). Frontal lobe dysfunctions in schizophrenia—II. Impairments of psychological brain functions. *Journal of Psychiatric Research, 18*, 57–72.

Levy, D. L., Sereno, A. B., Gooding, D. C., & O'Driscoll, G. A. (2010). Eye tracking dysfunction in schizophrenia: Characterization and pathophysiology. *Behavioral Neurobiology of Schizophrenia and Its Treatment*, 311–347.

Lewandowski, K. B., Barrantes, V. N., Nelson, G. R., Clancy, C., Kepley, H. O., & Kwapil, T. R. (2006). Anxiety and depression symptoms in psychometrically identified schizotypy. *Schizophrenia Research, 83*, 225–235.

Lin, H.-S., Liu, Y.-L., Liu, C.-M., Hung, S.-I., Hwu, H.-G., & Chen, W. J. (2005). Neuregulin 1 gene and variations in perceptual aberration of schizotypal personality in adolescents. *Psychological Medicine, 35*, 1589–1598.

Linscott, R. J. (2007). The latent structure and coincidence of hypohedonia and schizotypy and their validity as indices of psychometric risk for schizophrenia. *Journal of Personality Disorders, 21,* 225–242.

Linscott, R. J., & Morton, S. E. (2018). The latent taxonicity of schizotypy in biological siblings of probands with schizophrenia. *Schizophrenia bulletin, 44*(4), 922–932.

Linscott, R., Wright, E., Parker, T., & O'Hare, K. (2020). M32. The nature of the relationship of suicidality with schizotypy and psychosis experience. *Schizophrenia Bulletin, 46*(Suppl 1), S146–S146.

Loranger, A. (1990). The impact of DSM-III on diagnostic practice in a university hospital: A comparison of DSM-II and DSM-III in 10,914 patients. *Archives of General Psychiatry, 47,* 672–675.

Loranger, A. W. (1999). *International personality disorder examination: DSM-IV and ICD-10 interviews.* Psychological Assessment Resources.

Loranger, A. W., Sartorius, N., Andreoli, A., Berger, P., Channabasavanna, S. M., Coid, B., et al. (1994). The International Personality Disorder Examination (IPDE): The World Health Organization/Alcohol, Drug Abuse, and Mental Health Administration International Pilot Study of Personality Disorders. *Archives of General Psychiatry, 51,* 215–224.

Maher, B. A. (1966). *Principles of psychopathology: An experimental approach.* McGraw-Hill.

Maher, B. A. (2003). Psychopathology and delusions: Reflections on methods and models. In M. F. Lenzenweger & J. M. Hooley (Eds.), *Principles of experimental psychopathology: Essays in honor of Brendan A. Maher* (pp. 9–28). American Psychological Association.

Marenco, S., & Weinberger, D. R. (2000). The neurodevelopmental hypothesis of schizophrenia: Following a trail of evidence from cradle to grave. *Development and Psychopathology 12*(Special Issue), 501–527.

Mason, O., & Claridge, G. (2006). The Oxford-Liverpool inventory of feelings and experiences (O-LIFE): Further description and extended norms. *Schizophrenia Research, 82*(2–3), 203–211.

Mason, O., Claridge, G., & Jackson, M. (1995). New scales for the assessment of schizotypy. *Personality and Individual Differences, 18,* 7–13.

Matthysse, S., Holzman, P. S., & Lange, K. (1986). The genetic transmission of schizophrenia: Application of Mendelian latent structure analysis to eye tracking dysfunctions in schizophrenia and affective disorder. *Journal of Psychiatric Research, 20,* 57–67.

MacCorquodale, K., & Meehl, P. E. (1948). On a distinction between hypothetical constructs and intervening variables. *Psychological Review, 55*(2), 95–107.

McCutcheon, R. A., Marques, T. R., & Howes, O. D. (2020). Schizophrenia—an overview. *JAMA Psychiatry, 77*(2), 201–210.

McGlashan, T. H., & Hoffman, R. E. (2000). Schizophrenia as a disorder of developmentally reduced synaptic connectivity. *Archives of General Psychiatry, 57,* 637–648.

Meehl, P. E. (1962). Schizotaxia, schizotypy, schizophrenia. *American Psychologist, 17,* 827–838.

Meehl, P. E. (1964). *Manual for use with Checklist of Schizotypic Signs.* University of Minnesota. http://www.tc.umn.edu/~pemeehl/pubs.htm

Meehl, P. E. (1971). High school yearbooks: A reply to Schwarz. *Journal of Abnormal Psychology, 77,* 143–148.

Meehl, P. E. (1972). Specific genetic etiology, psychodynamics, and therapeutic nihilism. *International Journal of Mental Health, 1,* 10–27.

Meehl, P. E. (1973). MAXCOV-HITMAX: A taxonomic search method for loose genetic syndromes. In P. E. Meehl, *Psychodiagnosis: Selected papers* (pp. 200–224). University of Minnesota Press.

Meehl, P. E. (1975). Hedonic capacity: Some conjectures. *Bulletin of the Menninger Clinic, 39,* 295–307.

Meehl, P. E. (1978). Theoretical risks and tabular asterisks: Sir Karl, Sir Ronald, and the slow progress of soft psychology. *Journal of Consulting and Clinical Psychology, 46,* 806–834.

Meehl, P. E. (1987). "Hedonic capacity" ten years later: Some clarifications. In D. C. Clark & J. Fawcett (Eds.), *Anhedonia and affect deficit states* (pp. 47–50). PMA Publishing.

Meehl, P. E. (1990). Toward an integrated theory of schizotaxia, schizotypy, and schizophrenia. *Journal of Personality Disorders, 4,* 1–99.

Meehl, P. E. (1992). Factors and taxa, traits and types, differences of degree and differences in kind. *Journal of Personality, 60,* 117–174.

Meehl, P. E. (1993). The origins of some of my conjectures concerning schizophrenia. In L. J. Chapman, J. P. Chapman, & D. C. Fowles (Eds.), *Progress in experimental personality and psychopathology research* (pp. 1–10). Springer.

Meehl, P. E. (2001). Primary and secondary hypohedonia. *Journal of Abnormal Psychology, 110,* 188–193.

Meehl, P. E. (2004). What's in a taxon? *Journal of Abnormal Psychology, 113,* 39–43.

Meehl, P. E., & Yonce, L. J. (1996). Taxometric analysis: II. Detecting taxonicity using covariance of two quantitative indicators in successive intervals of a third indicator (MAXCOV procedure). *Psychological Reports* (Monograph Suppl. 1–V78), 1091–1227.

Meyer, T. D., & Keller, F. (2001). Exploring the latent structure of the perceptual aberration, magical ideation, and physical anhedonia scales in a German sample. *Journal of Personality Disorders, 15,* 521–535.

Miller, A. B., & Lenzenweger, M. F. (2012). Schizotypy, social cognition, and interpersonal sensitivity. *Personality Disorders: Theory, Research, & Treatment, 3,* 379–392.

Miller, M. B., & Chapman, J. P. (1993, October 7–10). *A twin study of schizotypy in college-age males.* Presented at the eighth annual meeting of the Society for Research in Psychopathology, Chicago, IL.

Minor, K. S., Hardin, K. L., Beaudette, D. M., Waters, L. C., White, A. L., Gonzenbach, V., & Robbins, M. L. (2020). Social functioning in schizotypy: How affect influences social behavior in daily life. *Journal of Clinical Psychology, 76*(12), 2212–2221.

Mishlove, M., & Chapman, L. J. (1985). Social anhedonia in the prediction of psychosis proneness. *Journal of Abnormal Psychology, 94,* 384–396.

Mohanty, A., Herrington, J. D., Koven, N. S., Fisher, J. E., Wenzel, E. A., Webb, A. G., Heller, W., Banich, M. T., & Miller, G. A. (2005). Neural mechanisms of affective interference in schizotypy. *Journal of Abnormal Psychology, 114*(1), 16–27. https://doi.org/10.1037/0021-843X.114.1.16

Mohr, C., & Claridge, G. (2015). Schizotypy—do not worry, it is not all worrisome. *Schizophrenia Bulletin, 41*(suppl_2), S436–S443.

Mohr, C., & Ettinger, U. (2014). An overview of the association between schizotypy and dopamine. *Frontiers in Psychiatry, 5,* 184.

Morey, L. C., Waugh, M. H., & Blashfield, R. K. (1985). MMPI scales for DSM-III personality disorders: Their derivation and correlates. *Journal of Personality Assessment, 49,* 245–251.

Morton, N. E., & MacLean, C. J. (1974). Analysis of family resemblance. III. Complex segregation of quantitative traits. *American Journal of Human Genetics, 26,* 489–503.

Morton, S. E., O'Hare, K. J., Maha, J. L., Nicolson, M. P., Machado, L., Topless, R., . . . Linscott, R. J. (2017). Testing the validity of taxonic schizotypy using genetic and environmental risk variables. *Schizophrenia Bulletin, 43*(3), 633–643.

Murray, G. K., & Jones, P. B. (2012). Psychotic symptoms in young people without psychotic illness: Mechanisms and meaning. *British Journal of Psychiatry, 201*(1), 4–6.

Nelson, M. T., Seal, M. L., Pantelis, C., & Phillips, L. J. (2013). Evidence of a dimensional relationship between schizotypy and schizophrenia: A systematic review. *Neuroscience & Biobehavioral Reviews, 37*(3), 317–327.

Nordentoft, M., Thorup, A., Petersen, L., Ohlenschlaeger, J., Melau, M., Christensen, T. Ø., Krarup, G., Jørgensen, P., & Jeppesen, P. (2006). Transition rates from schizotypal disorder to psychotic disorder for first-contact patients included in the OPUS trial: A randomized clinical trial of integrated treatment and standard treatment. *Schizophrenia Research, 83*(1), 29–40. https://doi.org/10.1016/j.schres.2006.01.002

Nordgaard, J., Buch-Pedersen, M., Hastrup, L. H., Haahr, U. H., & Simonsen, E. (2019). Measuring psychotic-like experiences in the general population. *Psychopathology, 52*(4), 240–247.

Obiols, J. E., Garcia-Domingo, M., de Trincheria, I., & Domenech, E. (1993). Psychometric schizotypy and sustained attention in young males. *Personality and Individual Differences, 14,* 381–384.

O'Driscoll, G., Lenzenweger, M. F., & Holzman, P. S. (1998). Antisaccades and smooth pursuit eye tracking performance and schizotypy. *Archives of General Psychiatry, 55,* 837–843.

Owen, M. J., O'Donovan, M. C., & Harrison, P. J. (2005). Schizophrenia: A genetic disorder of the synapse? Glutamatergic synapses might be the primary site of abnormalities. *British Medical Journal, 330,* 158–159.

Park, S., Holzman, P. S., & Lenzenweger, M. F. (1995). Individual differences in working memory in relation to schizotypy. *Journal of Abnormal Psychology, 104,* 355–363.

Park, S., Holzman, P. S., & Levy, D. L. (1993). Spatial working memory deficit in the relatives of schizophrenic patients is associated with their smooth pursuit eye tracking performance. *Schizophrenia Research, 9,* 185.

Phillips, W. A., & Silverstein, S. M. (2003). Convergence of biological and psychological perspectives on cognitive coordination in schizophrenia. *Behavioral and Brain Sciences, 26,* 65–82.

Piskulic, D., Olver, J. S., Norman, T. R., & Maruff, P. (2007). Behavioural studies of spatial working memory dysfunction in schizophrenia: A quantitative literature review. *Psychiatry Research, 150,* 111–121.

Planansky, K. (1972). Phenotypic boundaries and genetic specificity in schizophrenia. In A. R. Kaplan (Ed.), *Genetic factors in "schizophrenia"* (pp. 141–172). Charles C. Thomas.

Quirk, S. E., Berk, M., Chanen, A. M., Koivumaa-Honkanen, H., Brennan-Olsen, S. L., Pasco, J. A., & Williams, L. J. (2016). Population prevalence of personality disorder and associations with physical health comorbidities and health care service utilization: A review. *Personality Disorders, 7*(2), 136–146. https://doi.org/10.1037/per0000148

Rado, S. (1953). Dynamics and classification of disordered behavior. *American Journal of Psychiatry, 110,* 406–416.

Rado, S. (1960). Theory and therapy: The theory of schizotypal organization and its application to the treatment of decompensated schizotypal behavior. In S. C. Scher & H. R. Davis (Eds.), *The outpatient treatment of schizophrenia* (pp. 87–101). Grune and Stratton.

Raine, A. (1991). The SPQ: A scale for the assessment of schizotypal personality disorder based on DSM-III-R criteria. *Schizophrenia Bulletin, 17,* 555–564.

Raine, A. (2006). Schizotypal personality: Neurodevelopmental and psychosocial trajectories. *Annual Review of Clinical Psychology, 2,* 291–326.

Raine, A., Lencz, T., & Mednick, S. (1995). *Schizotypal personality.* Cambridge University Press.

Raine, A., Sheard, C., Reynolds, G., & Lencz, T. (1992). Prefrontal structural and functional deficits associated with individual differences in schizotypal personality. *Schizophrenia Research, 7,* 237–247.

Raine, A., Wong, K. K. Y., & Liu, J. (2021). The Schizotypal Personality Questionnaire for Children (SPQ-C): Factor structure, child abuse, and family history of schizotypy. *Schizophrenia Bulletin, 47*(2), 323–331.

Raja, M. (2006). The diagnosis of Asperger's syndrome. *Directions in Psychiatry, 26,* 89–104.

Raulin, M. L., & Wee, J. L. (1984). The development and initial validation of a scale to measure social fear. *Journal of Clinical Psychology, 40,* 780–784.

Rawlings, D., & Goldberg, M. (2001). Correlating a measure of sustained attention with a multidimensional measure of schizotypal traits. *Personality & Individual Differences, 31,* 421–431.

Rawlings, D., Williams, B., Haslam, N., & Claridge, G. (2008). Taxometric analysis supports a dimensional latent structure for schizotypy. *Personality and Individual Differences, 44*(8), 1640–1651.

Rust, J. (1988a). *The handbook of the Rust Inventory of Schizotypal Cognitions (RISC).* Psychological Corporation.

Rust, J. (1988b). The Rust Inventory of Schizotypal Cognitions (RISC). *Schizophrenia Bulletin, 14,* 317–322.

Samuels, J. E., Eaton, W. W., Bienvenu, O. J., Brown, C., Costa, P. T., & Nestadt, G. (2002). Prevalence and correlates of personality disorders in a community sample. *British Journal of Psychiatry, 180,* 536–542.

Sanislow, C. A., Little, T. D., Ansell, E. B., Grilo, C. M., Daversa, M., Markowitz, J. C., Pinto, A., Shea, M. T., Yen, S., Skodol, A. E., Morey, L. C., Gunderson, J. G., Zanarini, M. C., & McGlashan, T. H. (2009). Ten-year stability and latent structure of the DSM-IV schizotypal, borderline, avoidant, and obsessive-compulsive personality disorders. *Journal of Abnormal Psychology, 118*(3), 507–519. https://doi.org/10.1037/a0016478

Scarone, S., Abbruzzese, M., & Gambini, O. (1993). The Wisconsin Card Sorting Test discriminates schizophrenic patients and their siblings. *Schizophrenia Research, 10,* 103–107.

Schizophrenia Working Group of the Psychiatric Genomics Consortium. (2018). Genomic dissection of Bipolar disorder and schizophrenia, including 28 subphenotypes. *Cell, 173,* 1705–1715.

Sekar, A., Bialas, A. R., De Rivera, H., Davis, A., Hammond, T. R., Kamitaki, N., . . . McCarroll, S. A. (2016). Schizophrenia risk from complex variation of complement component 4. *Nature, 530*(7589), 177–183.

Shea, M. T., Stout, R., Gunderson, J., Morey, L. C., Grilo, C. M., McGlashan, T., Skodol, A. E., Dolan-Sewell, R., Dyck, I., Zanarini, M. C., & Keller, M. B. (2002). Short-term diagnostic stability of schizotypal, borderline, avoidant, and obsessive-compulsive personality disorders. *American Journal of Psychiatry, 159*(12), 2036–2041. https://doi.org/10.1176/appi.ajp.159.12.2036

Shields, J., Heston, L. I., & Gottesman, I. I. (1975). Schizophrenia and the schizoid: The problem for genetic analysis. In R. R. Fieve, D. Rosenthal, & H. Brill (Eds.), *Genetic research in psychiatry* (pp. 167–197). Johns Hopkins University Press.

Siddi, S., Petretto, D. R., & Preti, A. (2017). Neuropsychological correlates of schizotypy: A systematic review and meta-analysis of cross-sectional studies. *Cognitive Neuropsychiatry, 22*(3), 186–212.

Siever, L. J., Bernstein, D. P., & Silverman, J. M. (1991). Schizotypal personality disorder: A review of its current status. *Journal of Personality Disorders, 5*(2), 178–193. https://doi.org/10.1521/pedi.1991.5.2.178

Siever, J. L., & Davis, K. L. (2004). The pathophysiology of schizophrenia disorders: Perspectives from the spectrum. *American Journal of Psychiatry, 161*, 398–413.

Siever, L. J., Friedman, L., Moskowitz, J., Mitropoulou, V., Keefe, R., Roitman, S. L., Merhige, D., Trestman, R., Silverman, J., & Mohs, R. (1994). Eye movement impairment and schizotypal psychopathology. *American Journal of Psychiatry, 151*(8), 1209–1215. https://doi.org/10.1176/ajp.151.8.1209

Siever, L. J., & Gunderson, J. G. (1983). The search for a schizotypal personality: Historical origins and current status. *Comprehensive Psychiatry, 24*, 199–212.

Siever, L. J., Roussos, P., Greenwood, T., Braff, D. L., Weinstein, S., & Hardiman, G. (2011). Genetic association and pathway analysis of 94 candidate genes in schizotypal personality disorder. *Schizophrenia Bulletin, 37*, 90.

Smith, C., & Mendell, N. R. (1974). Recurrence risks from family history and metric traits. *Annals of Human Genetics, 37*, 275–286.

Smith, N. T., & Lenzenweger, M. F. (2013). Increased stress responsivity in schizotypy leads to diminished spatial working memory performance. *Personality Disorders, 4*(4), 324–331.

Snitz, B. E., MacDonald, A. W., & Carter, C. S. (2006). Cognitive deficits in unaffected first-degree relatives of schizophrenia patients: A meta-analytic review of putative endophenotypes. *Schizophrenia Bulletin, 32*, 179–194.

Spitzer, R. L., Endicott, J., & Gibbon, M. (1979). Crossing the border into borderline personality and borderline schizophrenia: The development of criteria. *Archives of General Psychiatry, 36*, 17–24.

Sponheim, S. R., McGuire, K. A., & Stanwyck, J. J. (2006). Neural anomalies during sustained attention in first-degree biological relatives of schizophrenia patients. *Biological Psychiatry, 60*, 242–252.

Sponheim, S. R., Iacono, W. G., Thuras, P. D., Nugent, S. M., & Beiser, M. (2003). Sensitivity and specificity of select biological indices in characterizing psychotic patients and their relatives. *Schizophrenia Research, 63*(1–2), 27–38.

Steiner, G. Z., Fernandez, F. M., Coles, M., Karamacoska, D., Barkus, E., Broyd, S. J., . . . Barry, R. J. (2019). Interrogating the relationship between schizotypy, the catechol-O-methyltransferase (COMT) Val158Met polymorphism, and neuronal oscillatory activity. *Cerebral Cortex, 29*(7), 3048–3058.

Strauss, G. P., & Cohen, A. S. (2018). The schizophrenia spectrum anhedonia paradox. *World Psychiatry, 17*(2), 221.

Strauss, G. P., & Gold, J. M. (2012). A new perspective on anhedonia in schizophrenia. *American Journal of Psychiatry, 169*, 364–373.

Sullivan, P. F., Daly, M. J., & O'Donovan, M. (2012). Genetic architectures of psychiatric disorders: The emerging picture and its implications. *Nature Reviews (Genetics), 13*, 537–551.

Sullivan, P. F., Agrawal, A., Bulik, C. M., Andreassen, O. A., Børglum, A. D., Breen, G., . . . Psychiatric Genomics Consortium. (2018). Psychiatric genomics: An update and an agenda. *American Journal of Psychiatry, 175*(1), 15–27.

Sullivan, P. F., Kendler, K. S., & Neale, M. C. (2003). Schizophrenia as a complex trait: Evidence from a meta-analysis of twin studies. *Archives of General Psychiatry, 60*, 1187–1192.

Sullivan, S. A., Kounali, D., Cannon, M., David, A. S., Fletcher, P. C., Holmans, P., . . . Zammit, S. (2020). A population-based cohort study examining the incidence and impact of psychotic experiences from childhood to adulthood, and prediction of psychotic disorder. *American Journal of Psychiatry, 177*(4), 308–317.

Thaker, G. K., Cassady, S., Adami, H., & Moran, M. (1996). Eye movements in spectrum personality disorder: Comparison of community subjects and relatives of schizophrenic patients. *American Journal of Psychiatry, 153*, 362–368.

Thomas, E. H., Steffens, M., Harms, C., Rossell, S. L., Gurvich, C., & Ettinger, U. (2021). Schizotypy, neuroticism, and saccadic eye movements: New data and meta-analysis. *Psychophysiology, 58*(1), e13706.

Thompson, J. L., Rosell, D. R., Slifstein, M., Xu, X., Rothstein, E. G., Modiano, Y. A., . . . Abi-Dargham, A. (2020). Amphetamine-induced striatal dopamine release in schizotypal personality disorder. *Psychopharmacology, 237*(9), 2649–2659.

Torgersen, S. (1994). Personality deviations within the schizophrenia spectrum. *Acta Psychiatrica Scandinavica, 90*(Suppl. 384), 40–44.

Torgersen, S., Lygren, S., Oien, P. A., Skre, I., Onstad, S., Edvardsen, J., Tambs, K., & Kringlen, E. (2000). A twin study of personality disorders. *Comprehensive Psychiatry, 41*(6), 416–425. https://doi.org/10.1053/comp.2000.16560

Torgersen, S., Kringlen, E., & Cramer, V. (2001). The prevalence of personality disorders in a community sample. *Archives of General Psychiatry, 58*, 590–596.

Triebwasser, J., Chemerinski, E., Roussos, P., & Siever, L. J. (2013). Paranoid personality disorder. *Journal of Personality Disorders, 27*(6), 795–805.

Valle, R. (2020). Schizophrenia in ICD-11: Comparison of ICD-10 and DSM-5. La esquizofrenia en la CIE-11: comparación con la CIE-10 y el DSM-5. *Revista de psiquiatria y salud mental, 13*(2), 95–104. https://doi.org/10.1016/j.rpsm.2020.01.001

Vaughn, M. C., Barrantes-Vidal, A. G., Raulin, M. L., & Kwapil, T. R. (2008). The schizotypal ambivalence scale as a marker of schizotypy. *Journal of Nervous and Mental Disease, 196*, 399–404.

Venables, P. H. (1990). The measurement of schizotypy in Mauritius. *Personality and Individual Differences, 11*, 965–971.

Vollema, M. G., & Hoijtink, H. (2000). The multidimensionality of self-report schizotypy in a psychiatric population: An analysis using multidimensional Rasch models. *Schizophrenia Bulletin, 26*, 565–575.

Vora, A. K., Fisher, A. M., New, A. S., Hazlett, E. A., McNamara, M., Yuan, Q., . . . Perez-Rodriguez, M. M. (2018). Dimensional traits of schizotypy associated with glycine receptor GLRA1 polymorphism: An exploratory candidate-gene association study. *Journal of Personality Disorders, 32*(3), 421–432.

Waller, N. G., Yonce, L. J., Grove, W. M., Faust, D. A., & Lenzenweger, M. F. (2006). *A Paul Meehl reader: Essays on the practice of scientific psychology.* Lawrence Erlbaum.

Walter, E. E., Fernandez, F., Snelling, M., & Barkus, E. (2016). Genetic consideration of schizotypal traits: A review. *Frontiers in Psychology, 7*, 1769.

Wastler, H. M., & Lenzenweger, M. F. (2018). Cone of gaze in positive schizotypy: Relationship to referential thinking and social functioning. *Personality Disorders, 9*(4), 324–332. https://doi.org/10.1037/per0000258

Wastler, H. M., & Lenzenweger, M. F. (2019). Self-referential hypermentalization in schizotypy. *Personality Disorders: Theory, Research, and Treatment, 10*, 536–544.

Wastler, H. M., & Lenzenweger, M. F. (2021). Cognitive and affective theory of mind in positive schizotypy: Relationship to schizotypal traits and psychosocial functioning. *Journal of Personality Disorders 35*(4), 538–553. https://doi.org/10.1521/pedi_2020_34_473]

Webb, C. T., & Levinson, D. F. (1993). Schizotypal and paranoid personality disorder in the relative of patients with schizophrenia and affective disorders: A review. *Schizophrenia Research, 11*, 81–92.

Weinberger, D. R. (1987). Implications of normal brain development for the pathogenesis of schizophrenia. *Archives of General Psychiatry, 44*, 660–669.

Weinberger, D. R., Berman, K. F., & Zec, R. F. (1986). Physiologic dysfunction of dorsolateral prefrontal cortex in schizophrenics I. Regional cerebral blood flow evidence. *Archives of General Psychiatry, 43*, 114–124.

Werbeloff, N., Drukker, M., Dohrenwend, B. P., Levav, I., Yoffe, R., van Os, J., Davidson, M., & Weiser, M. (2012). Self-reported attenuated psychotic symptoms are forerunners of severe mental disorders later in life. *Archives of General Psychiatry, 69*, 467–475.

Winterstein, B. P., Silvia, P. J., Kwapil, T. R., Kaufman, J. C., Reiter-Palmon, R., & Wigert, B. (2011). Brief assessment of schizotypy: Developing short forms of the Wisconsin schizotypy scales. *Personality and Individual Differences, 51*, 920–924.

Woodward, N. D., Cowan, R. L., Park, S., Ansari, M. S., Baldwin, R. M., Li, R., Doop, M., Kessler, R. M., & Zald, D. H. (2011). Correlation of individual differences in schizotypal personality traits with amphetamine-induced dopamine release in stratal and extrastriatal brain regions. *American Journal of Psychiatry, 168*, 418–426.

Yilmaz, M., Yalcin, E., Presumey, J., Aw, E., Ma, M., Whelan, C. W., . . . Carroll, M. C. (2021). Overexpression of schizophrenia susceptibility factor human complement C4A promotes excessive synaptic loss and behavioral changes in mice. *Nature Neuroscience, 24*(2), 214–224.

Zimmerman, M., & Coryell, W. (1990). Diagnosing personality disorders in the community: A comparison of self-report and interview measures. *Archives of General Psychiatry, 47*, 527–531.

Zimmerman, M., Rothschild, L., & Chelminski, I. (2005). The prevalence of DSM-IV personality disorders in psychiatric outpatients. *American Journal of Psychiatry, 162*, 1911–1918.

# CHAPTER 30
# Psychopathy and Antisocial Personality Disorder

Christopher J. Patrick, Laura E. Drislane, Bridget M. Bertoldi, and Kelsey L. Lowman

Among mental disorders classified as disorders of personality, psychopathy (psychopathic personality) and the related condition of antisocial personality disorder (ASPD) have been of particular interest to researchers and practitioners because of the serious harm they cause to individuals and the high costs they exact on society. In this chapter, we review what is known about these conditions and how they are represented in *DSM-5*, which includes both categorical-diagnostic (Section II) and dimensional-trait (Section III) systems for characterizing personality pathology. In doing so, we highlight elements that these clinical conditions have in common as well as important features that distinguish them and consider how they relate to other forms of psychopathology in relation to an integrative conceptual framework: the triarchic model of psychopathy. We describe how the triarchic model framework can be useful for guiding and coordinating research directed at advancing developmental and neurobiological understanding of psychopathy.

## Historical Background

The earliest accounts of psychopathy emphasized extreme behavioral deviance in the context of intact reasoning and communicative abilities. French physician Philippe Pinel (1801/1962) used the term *manie sans delire* ("insanity without delirium") to describe individuals who engaged repeatedly in impulsive acts injurious to themselves and others despite ostensible awareness of the irrationality of such actions. An American contemporary of Pinel's, Benjamin Rush (1812), documented similar cases and postulated absence of guilt ("moral weakness") as the root cause. Rush's description placed emphasis on features of manipulativeness and deception. British physician J.

C. Pritchard (1835) used a similar term, "moral insanity," but applied it to a wide range of clinical conditions including drug and alcohol addiction, sexual deviations, mood disorders, and conditions likely to be classified today as intellectual disability or schizophrenia. Some years later, German psychiatrist J. L. Koch (1891) introduced the term "psychopathic" to denote chronic forms of mental illness presumed to have an underlying organic (physical, brain) basis. Like Pritchard, Koch applied this term to a much broader array of conditions than would be recognizable today as ASPD or psychopathy. Operating from a similar perspective of biological causality, Kraepelin (1915) used the term "psychopathic personalities" for

**Abbreviations**
| | |
|---|---|
| AMPD | Alternative Model of Personality Disorders |
| APSD | Antisocial Process Screening Device |
| ASPD | Antisocial personality disorder |
| CD | Conduct disorder |
| CPS | Child Psychopathy Scale |
| CPTI | Child Problematic Traits Inventory |
| CU | Callous-Unemotional |
| EPA | Elemental Psychopathy Assessment |
| ESI | Externalizing Spectrum Inventory |
| HSRP | Hare Self-Report Psychopathy (scale) |
| I/CP | Impulsive/Conduct problems |
| LSRP | Levenson Self-Report Psychopathy (scale) |
| MPQ | Multidimensional Personality Questionnaire |
| PCL-R | Psychopathy Checklist-Revised |
| PPI | Psychopathic Personality Inventory |
| TriPM | Triarchic Psychopathy Measure |
| YPI | Youth Psychopathic Traits Inventory |

a somewhat narrower set of conditions that included sexual deviations, other impulse-related problems, and obsessional disorders—along with conditions he labeled "degenerative" personalities, which included "antisocial" (callous-destructive) and "quarrelsome" (hostile-alienated) subtypes that would be classifiable today as ASPD.

Countering this trend toward broad application of the term, Cleckley (1941/1976) argued that psychopathy should be diagnosed using a set of explicit diagnostic criteria that would identify a distinct clinical condition with a coherent etiological basis. Cleckley's criteria for the disorder included ostensibly healthy features (social adeptness, coherent speech, lack of psychotic or anxious/neurotic symptoms, "immunity" to suicide) that "masked" a severe pathology marked by persistent, reckless, impulsive behavior without regard for personal consequences or the feelings/welfare of others. One of the specific pathological features he listed was "inadequately motivated antisocial behavior," by which he meant acts such as "theft, forgery, adultery, [and] fraud" committed "in the absence of any apparent goal at all" (p. 343). Cleckley viewed such behavior as a part of a larger pattern of unrestrained deviancy that also included lack of planning, irresponsibility, impersonal sex, and a failure to learn from adverse experience. The criteria that Cleckley proposed for the disorder included features of three types: (1) indications of psychological stability (social charm and good intelligence, absence of delusions or irrationality, absence of nervousness, disinclination toward suicide), (2) tendencies toward emotional insensitivity and shallow or insincere relationships with others (self-centeredness and incapacity for love, lack of social reciprocity, deceitfulness, deficient affective reactivity, impaired insight), and (3) salient behavioral deviancy in the form of repeated antisocial acts (often without obvious motivation), irresponsibility, promiscuity, and absence of any clear life plan. According to Cleckley, the outward appearance of psychological stability in individuals of this type functioned as a convincing "mask of sanity," concealing the underlying interpersonal-affective deficits and deviant behavioral tendencies (for a recent detailed discussion, see Patrick, 2018).

Turning to ASPD, the first edition of the *DSM*, published in 1952, included a category termed "sociopathic personality disturbance," encompassing (in line with early, broad-ranging conceptions of psychopathy) a range of problems including sexual deviations, addictions, and a distinct syndrome labeled "antisocial reaction" marked by persistent aggression and criminal deviance. In *DSM-II*, published in 1968, the term "reaction" was eliminated, and sexual deviations, addictions, and delinquent personality types were grouped together under "personality disorders and other non-psychotic mental disorders," which included an "antisocial personality" condition that featured some of the affective-interpersonal symptoms described by Cleckley (e.g., selfishness, untrustworthiness, callousness, and absence of guilt). However, a serious limitation of the first and second editions of the *DSM* was that diagnoses were assigned through reference to prototype case descriptions rather than through use of explicit behavioral criteria. As a result, the reliability of diagnostic decisions was poor. This problem was addressed in the third edition by providing more specific, behaviorally oriented criteria for diagnoses. The criteria in *DSM-III*, published in 1980, were influenced in particular by the work of Lee Robins (1966, 1978) on characteristics predictive of the persistence of delinquency from earlier to later ages and focused predominantly on symptoms of behavioral deviancy in childhood and adulthood, including truancy, stealing, vandalism, other delinquency acts, aggressiveness, impulsivity, irresponsibility, recklessness, and lying.

With this shift to explicit behavioral criteria, the diagnosis of ASPD within *DSM-III* proved highly reliable. However, concerns about its validity were quickly raised (e.g., Frances, 1980; Hare, 1983), given its omission of many of the features identified by Cleckley as being essential to psychopathy, including superficial charm, lack of anxiety, absence of remorse or empathy, and general poverty of affect. Some effort was made to address these criticisms in *DSM-III-R*, published in 1984, through the addition of lack of remorse as an adult criterion for ASPD. Further changes along this line, directed at increasing coverage of interpersonal-affective features of psychopathy, were considered for *DSM-IV*, published in 2000, but ultimately rejected (Widiger et al., 1996). Consequently, the diagnostic criteria for ASPD in *DSM-IV* remained much the same as those in *DSM-III-R*, and these criteria were carried over without modification to the main diagnostic section of *DSM-5* (Section II). However, as discussed below under the heading "Psychopathy in *DSM-5*," a new dimensional-trait approach to the diagnosis of ASPD is included in *DSM-5* as an alternative to the traditional criterion-based version of the diagnosis.

## Psychopathy: Current Conceptions and Empirical Findings

Alongside research on ASPD as defined in successive versions of the *DSM*, an extensive literature on psychopathy has accumulated over the years using assessment instruments based directly or indirectly on Cleckley's classic clinical characterization. In this section, we review major approaches to the assessment of psychopathy in use today, highlighting ways in which they differ and ways in which they converge. Following this, we describe a conceptual framework, the triarchic model (Patrick et al., 2009), for reconciling contrasting conceptions of psychopathy embodied in these various assessment devices and integrating findings across studies that have relied on particular ones.

### Psychopathy in Forensic Samples: Hare's Psychopathy Checklist-Revised (PCL-R)

DESCRIPTION

The assessment instrument that has dominated contemporary research on psychopathy is Hare's (1991, 2003) Psychopathy Checklist-Revised (PCL-R), which was developed to identify the condition as described by Cleckley in incarcerated offenders. The PCL-R contains 20 items, each rated on a 0–2 scale (absent, equivocal, or present) using information derived from a semi-structured interview and institutional file records. Item scores are summed to yield a total psychopathy score, with scores of 30 or higher considered indicative of psychopathy (Hare, 2003).

The original 22-item version of the PCL (Hare, 1980) evolved out of a global (7-point) rating system that directly referenced Cleckley's diagnostic criteria. Items for the PCL were selected from a larger pool of candidate indicators on the basis of their effectiveness in discriminating between offender participants judged to be high versus low on the Cleckley global rating system. Two items were dropped in the subsequent revised version. Notably, the interpersonal-affective deficits and behavioral deviance features described by Cleckley are represented directly in the PCL-R, but the positive adjustment features he emphasized (social efficacy and intelligence, absence of psychosis, lack of anxiety or neurotic symptoms, disinclination toward suicide) are not. Features of this type were likely excluded because items selected for the original PCL were required to correlate as a whole with one another, based on the implicit idea of psychopathy as a unitary condition (Patrick, 2006). Because the majority of Cleckley's criteria (12 of 16) reflect propensities toward deviance, indicators of positive adjustment would have been excluded over the course of scale refinement because of their failure to coalesce with the larger contingent of (pathological) indicators.

The relations that overall scores on the PCL-R show with criterion measures of various types reinforce the notion that the PCL-R conception of psychopathy is more purely pathological than Cleckley's. PCL-R total scores correlate very highly with overall symptoms of ASPD (Patrick et al., 2007; Skilling et al., 2002) and show robust positive associations with various behavioral indices of aggression (Hare, 2003) and scale measures of substance problems (Reardon et al., 2002). With respect to personality variables, PCL-R total scores exhibit especially robust relations with trait measures of impulsivity and aggression (Lynam & Derefinko, 2006; Verona et al., 2001) and, in contrast with Cleckley's portrayal of psychopathic individuals as low-anxious, correlate either minimally or somewhat positively with measures of anxiety, neuroticism, and negative affectivity (Hare, 2003; Lynam & Derefinko, 2006; Hicks & Patrick, 2006). Also at odds with Cleckley's conception, PCL-R total scores show positive rather than negative associations with indices of suicidality (Verona et al., 2001, 2005).

PCL-R FACTORS

While developed to operationalize psychopathy as a unitary condition, structural analyses of the PCL-R's items have revealed distinctive subdimensions or factors that exhibit differential relations with criterion measures of various types. Initial work (Harpur et al., 1988; Hare et al., 1990) indicated two correlated ($r \sim .5$) factors: an Interpersonal-Affective factor (Factor 1) marked by items indexing superficial charm, grandiosity, conning/deceptiveness, absence of remorse or empathy, shallow affect, and externalization of blame; and an Impulsive-Antisocial factor (Factor 2) encompassing early behavior problems and delinquency, boredom proneness, impulsivity, irresponsibility, lack of long-term goals, parasitism, and hot-tempered aggressiveness. Cooke and Michie (2001) proposed an alternative three-factor model in which Factor 1 was parsed into separate "Deficient Affect" and "Arrogant/Deceitful" factors, and items of Factor 2 considered most trait-like ($n = 5$) were included in a third "Impulsive-Irresponsible" factor. Subsequent to this, Hare (2003; Hare & Neumann, 2006) advanced an alternative four-facet model in which Factor 1 was parsed into "Interpersonal" and

"Affective" facets mirroring Cooke and Michie's first two factors, and Factor 2 was partitioned into a "Lifestyle" facet mirroring Cooke and Michie's "Impulsive-Irresponsible" factor, and an "Antisocial" facet including the antisocial behavior items from Factor 2 along with a "criminal versatility" item.

Most published work on subdimensions of the PCL-R has focused on the factors of the original two-factor model. These factors show differential relations with a variety of criterion measures, particularly when their shared variance is accounted for (e.g., through structural analysis, regression modeling, or partial correlation; Hare, 1991, 2003; Harpur et al., 1989; Hicks & Patrick, 2006; Patrick et al., 2005, 2007; Verona et al., 2001, 2005). Variance unique to Factor 1 correlates negatively with measures of anxiousness and internalizing problems and positively with measures of social dominance and (in some studies) positive affectivity and achievement, suggesting that the positive adjustment features of psychopathy specified by Cleckley are embodied to some extent in the variance of Factor 1 that is distinct from impulsive-antisocial tendencies. The interpersonal items of Factor 1 in particular account for its associations with indices of emotional stability and adjustment (Hall et al., 2004; Patrick et al., 2007). PCL-R Factor 1 also shows negative relations with scale measures of empathy and positive relations with measures of narcissistic personality, Machiavellianism, and proactive (instrumental) aggression. By contrast, variance unique to Factor 2 correlates positively with trait anxiety and internalizing problems and is strongly predictive of both child and adult symptoms of ASPD as represented in *DSM-IV* (and Section II of *DSM-5*). Factor 2 also shows selective positive relations with scale measures of impulsivity, aggressiveness, general sensation-seeking, and substance dependence, and interview- or record-based indices of impulsive aggression (e.g., fighting, assault charges, partner abuse) and suicidal behavior.

These differential associations for Factors 1 and 2 of the PCL-R are notable for variables considered to be facets of a single higher-order construct (e.g., Hare, 1991, 2003). Especially noteworthy are cases in which opposing relations of the two PCL-R factors with criterion measures become stronger once their covariance (overlap) is removed—a phenomenon known as *cooperative suppression* (Paulhus et al., 2004). As an example of this, Hicks and Patrick (2006) reported that correlations for each factor of the PCL-R with measures of negative affectivity (i.e., fearfulness, distress, and depression) increased, in opposite directions, when scores on the two factors were included together in a regression model. This result indicates that distinct opposing relations of the two PCL-R factors with indices of negative affectivity were partially concealed by the variance they share. A similar result was reported by Frick, Lilienfeld, Ellis, Loney, and Silverthorn (1999) for the two factors of the Antisocial Process Screening Device (Frick & Hare, 2001), an inventory for assessing psychopathy in children and adolescents that is patterned after the PCL-R (see next section). Effects of this type are conceptually important because they indicate that the items of the PCL-R, although intended to index a single underlying construct, are in fact indexing separate constructs. In particular, the finding of suppressor effects for the two PCL-R factors in relation to variables such as anxiety, depression, and suicidality appears consistent with Cleckley's view that psychopathy entails the convergence of contrasting dispositions toward psychological resiliency and behavioral deviancy.

## ADAPTATIONS OF THE PCL-R USED WITH YOUNG CLINICAL SAMPLES

The dominant inventories used for assessing psychopathy in child and adolescent clinical samples consist of adaptations of the PCL-R and include the youth version of the PCL-R (PCL:YV; Forth et al., 2003), the Antisocial Process Screening Device (APSD; Frick & Hare, 2001; Frick et al., 1994), the Child Psychopathy Scale (CPS; Lynam, 1997; Lynam et al., 2005), and the Child Problematic Traits Inventory (CPTI; Colins et al., 2014). The most widely used of these, the 20-item APSD, was devised for use with children aged 6–13 referred for treatment of behavioral problems and is rated by either parents or teachers. The APSD has two distinguishable factors: a Callous-Unemotional (CU) factor reflecting emotional insensitivity and exploitative disregard for others and an Impulsive/Conduct Problems (I/CP) factor encompassing impulsive tendencies, reckless or delinquent behavior, and inflated sense of self-importance (Frick et al., 1994; Frick & Hare, 2001)—with some research (e.g., Frick et al., 2000) suggesting distinguishable impulsive and narcissistic or attention-seeking components to the I/CP factor. Children who score high on the I/CP factor but not the CU factor exhibit reduced levels of intellectual ability, elevated anxiety and negative emotional reactivity, and proneness to angry-reactive (but not proactive-instrumental) aggression (Frick & Marsee, 2018; Frick et al., 2014). By contrast, children who score high on both factors of the APSD appear to have normal intellectual ability, exhibit reduced levels of anxiety and neuroticism, are underreactive to distressing stimuli and learn less readily from punishment, and tend to be attracted to activities entailing novelty and risk. These children also show heightened levels of both proactive and reactive aggression and greater persistence of such behavior across time.

## PREVALENCE OF PCL-R-DEFINED PSYCHOPATHY

The PCL-R was developed for use with male correctional and forensic samples, and thus prevalence estimates have been available mainly for samples of this type. The estimated prevalence of PCL-R-defined psychopathy (total score of 30 or higher) in male correctional and forensic populations is 15–25%, compared with 50–80% for *DSM-IV*-defined ASPD (Hare, 2003), with most of those who score as psychopathic also meeting criteria for ASPD. Because the PCL-R is designed for offender samples and limited efforts have been made to assess PCL-R psychopathy in community samples (for exceptions, see Ishikawa et al., 2001; Gao et al., 2011), the prevalence of PCL-R-defined psychopathy in community adults is less well-established. Based on median prevalence rates for male prisoners (20% for psychopathy and 65% for ASPD), and assuming a similar ratio of high PCL-R scorers among adults diagnosable as ASPD in the general community, the estimated prevalence of PCL-R psychopathy among community men (3% of whom are expected to meet criteria for ASPD) would be approximately 1% (i.e., 20/65 × 3%). Using an abbreviated, screening version of the PCL-R (the PCL:SV; Hart et al., 1995), Farrington (2006) reported the prevalence of psychopathy to be around 2% (i.e., 8 cases out of 411) in a large sample of community boys followed up to age 48. Combining these figures, the prevalence of PCL-R psychopathy among men in the community is likely somewhere in the range of 1–2%. However, this estimate does not include individuals who exhibit salient interpersonal-affective symptoms of psychopathy without sufficient overt behavioral deviancy to warrant a diagnosis of ASPD—cases that Cleckley referred to as "incomplete manifestations" of the condition. Because the field lacks accepted criteria for diagnosing psychopathy in noncriminal adults, population prevalence estimates for cases of this type remain uncertain.

Women are incarcerated at much lower rates than men, and the prevalence of ASPD among women in the population at large is only a third of that in men (*DSM-IV-TR*). Regarding PCL-R-defined psychopathy, some studies of incarcerated women have reported prevalence rates similar to those for incarcerated men, but others have reported lower rates (Verona & Vitale, 2018). Studies of psychopathy and related constructs in nonincarcerated adult samples have also demonstrated lower rates or levels in general for women than for men (Verona & Vitale, 2018). Given these findings, the prevalence of PCL-R-defined psychopathy among adult women in the community is likely no more than one-third the rate for community men (i.e., .3–.7%). Combining the midpoint of this range (.5) with that for men (1.5, as noted above) results in an overall estimated prevalence of approximately 1% in the general adult population. In line with this figure, a recent study by Sanz-García, Gesteira, Sanz, and García-Vera (2021) estimated the prevalence of PCL-R psychopathy among adults in society as a whole to be around 1.2%. Again, this estimate omits individuals exhibiting interpersonal-affective features of psychopathy without salient antisocial behavior.

With regard to race and ethnicity, an initial study of incarcerated men by Kosson, Smith, and Newman (1990) yielded evidence that overall PCL-R scores were higher among African American than European American offenders. A meta-analysis of this and subsequent work by Skeem, Edens, Camp, and Colwell (2004) revealed a small but significant effect size along this line. However, considerably more research is needed to clarify the contribution of factors such as poverty, discrimination, and adjudication inequities to reported racial-group differences. With regard to culture, there is evidence that American prison samples score higher in general on the PCL-R than do European prison samples (Sullivan & Kosson, 2006).

## COMORBIDITY WITH DSM DISORDERS

The *DSM* disorder associated most closely with PCL-R-defined psychopathy is ASPD. However, the relationship between the two is asymmetric. Within offender samples, most individuals who meet the PCL-R criterion for psychopathy (total score ≥30) also meet diagnostic criteria for *DSM-IV* ASPD, but the majority who meet criteria for ASPD fall below the PCL-R criterion for psychopathy. Additionally, the two PCL-R factors show differential relations with ASPD. On one hand, the behaviorally based child and adult criteria for ASPD overlap substantially with the impulsive-antisocial features of psychopathy indexed by PCL-R Factor 2. By contrast, only 1 of the 15 child criteria for ASPD (lying) and only 2 of the 7 adult criteria (deceitfulness, lack of remorse) intersect with the interpersonal-affective features of psychopathy embodied in PCL-R Factor 1, resulting in a weaker observed association for Factor 1 that is largely attributable to its overlap with Factor 2 (Patrick et al., 2005).

Factor 2 of the PCL-R also shows selective associations with measures of substance abuse and dependence (Reardon et al., 2002; Smith & Newman, 1990) and borderline personality symptoms (Shine & Hobson, 1997; Warren et al., 2003). By contrast, scores on Factor 1 relate more to measures of narcissistic and histrionic personality disorder (Harpur et al., 1989; Hart & Hare, 1989; Hildebrand & de Ruiter, 2004). Also, as noted earlier, the two factors of the PCL-R show opposing, mutually suppressive relations with measures of anxiety and depression (Hicks & Patrick, 2006). The fact that the unique variance in Factor 1 is negatively associated with anxiety and depression indicates that this component of the PCL-R (its Interpersonal facet, in particular; Hall et al., 2004) captures something of the positive adjustment and resiliency that Cleckley described as characteristic of psychopaths. The positive relations for Factor 2, on the other hand, converge with data indicating that the *DSM* diagnosis of ASPD is associated with an increased prevalence of anxiety and mood disorders (e.g., *DSM-IV-TR*, 2000, p. 702; Krueger, 1999b).

## NEUROBIOLOGICAL CORRELATES

Neurobiological correlates of psychopathy in adult offender samples have been studied mainly in relation to overall scores on the PCL-R or on the earlier Cleckley rating system that served as the referent for the PCL-R. Historically, one of the most consistent findings—beginning with Lykken's (1957) seminal multimethod investigation of anxiety and continuing with the autonomic reactivity studies of Hare in the 1960s and 1970s (cf. Hare, 1978)—has been that individuals high in overall psychopathy show reduced skin conductance reactivity to stressors of various types, in particular cues signaling an upcoming aversive event (for reviews, see Arnett, 1997; Hare, 1978; Lorber, 2004; Siddle & Trasler, 1981). This finding has been interpreted as reflecting a basic deficiency in anxiety or fear (Fowles, 1980; Hare, 1978; Lykken, 1957).

Another reliable finding in the literature, also consistent with the idea of a negative emotional reactivity deficit, is that individuals diagnosed as psychopathic using the PCL-R fail to show normal augmentation of the startle blink reflex during viewing of aversive visual stimuli (e.g., Herpertz et al., 2001; Patrick et al., 1993; Sutton et al., 2002; Vanman et al., 2003). This reactivity deficit has been tied specifically to elevations on the Interpersonal-Affective factor of the PCL-R (Patrick, 1994; Vanman et al., 2003; Vaidyanathan et al., 2011). The selective association with PCL-R Factor 1 is notable because the startle reflex is a protective response known to increase with activation of the amygdala, a key structure in the brain's defensive (fear) system (Lang et al., 1990). The lack of aversive startle potentiation therefore suggests a weakness in reactivity at this basic subcortical level among individuals exhibiting the core interpersonal-affective features of psychopathy. Consistent with this notion, participants with high PCL-R scores show deficits on behavioral tasks believed to be sensitive to amygdala function (Blair, 2006). Neuroimaging studies have demonstrated reduced amygdala activity during aversive conditioning and fear face processing, respectively, in high PCL-R–scoring adults (Birbaumer et al., 2005; Veit et al., 2002) and in youth with conduct disorder who exhibit callous-unemotional traits (Jones et al., 2009; Marsh et al., 2008).

Additionally, other lines of work, including cerebral asymmetry, brain potential, and neuroimaging studies (for reviews, see Hare, 2003, pp. 124–126; Patrick, 2014; Patrick, Venables, & Skeem, 2012), have provided evidence for brain abnormalities in high PCL-R–scoring individuals. However, studies have not reliably demonstrated impairments on neuropsychological tests of frontal lobe function (for a review, see Rogers, 2006) or in P300 brain response (cf. Patrick, 2014). This contrasts with evidence that ASPD is reliably associated with deficits on tests of frontal lobe dysfunction (Morgan & Lilienfeld, 2000) and with reduced amplitude of P300 brain potential response (Bauer et al., 1994; Patrick, Bernat et al., 2006). Given that PCL-R Factor 2 is associated more strongly with ASPD and that Factor 1 (after controlling for overlap with Factor 2) shows positive relations with indices of psychological adjustment, it could be the case that the two factors of the PCL-R are differentially related to frontal lobe task performance and P300 brain response. Evidence in support of the latter of these possibilities was provided by a recent study demonstrating reductions in P300 response amplitude specifically in relation to Factor 2 of the PCL-R in a sample of male offenders (Venables & Patrick, 2014).

## Psychopathy in Community Samples: Self-Report–Based Operationalizations

Most research on psychopathy in noncriminal samples has utilized self-report assessment inventories. Whereas older inventories of this type emphasized measurement of the impulsive-antisocial (Factor 2) component of psychopathy, which relates most to ASPD, newer measures such as the Psychopathic Personality Inventory (PPI; Lilienfeld & Andrews, 1996), Levenson et al.'s (Levenson et al., 1995) Self-Report Psychopathy Scale (LSRP), Hare's Self-Report Psychopathy Scale (HSRP; Paulhus et al., 2016; Williams et al., 2007), the Youth Psychopathic Traits Inventory (YPI; Andershed et al., 2002), the Elemental Psychopathy Assessment (EPA; Lynam et al., 2011), and the Triarchic Psychopathy Measure (TriPM; Patrick, 2010; Sellbom & Phillips, 2013) include coverage of interpersonal-affective (Factor 1) features as well as impulsive-antisocial features.

The LSRP, HSRP, and YPI were all patterned after the PCL-R and provide coverage of factors or facets specified by alternative structural models of the PCL-R. The LSRP includes "primary" and "secondary" subscales intended to parallel the factors of the original two-factor model (Hare et al., 1990; Harpur et al., 1989), the YPI contains subscales that align with Cooke and Michie's (2001) three-factor model, and the subscales of the HSRP align with Hare's (2003) four-facet model. In contrast with these PCL-R-based inventories, the EPA was developed as an extension of prior work (Lynam & Widiger, 2007; Miller et al., 2001) undertaken to characterize psychopathy in terms of lower-order traits of the five-factor personality model as indexed by the Neuroticism-Extraversion-Openness (NEO) PI-R inventory (Costa & McCrae, 1992). The EPA assesses maladaptive variants of the set of NEO PI-R traits that appear most relevant to psychopathy. Although it is comparatively new, several published reports have appeared on the psychometric properties and correlates of the EPA's full (e.g., Miller et al., 2011; Miller, Hyatt et al., 2014) and short-length versions (Lee & Sellbom, 2021). The TriPM, another newer inventory developed to assess biobehavioral trait constructs specified by the triarchic model of psychopathy (Patrick et al., 2009), is described in a later section focused on this model.

The PPI is the self-report psychopathy inventory that has been used most widely over the past two decades. It was developed to index psychopathy in terms of dispositional tendencies (traits) considered relevant to this clinical condition by historical writers (Lilienfeld & Andrews, 1996). Factor analyses of the PPI's eight subscales (e.g., Benning et al., 2003; Ross et al., 2009) revealed distinguishable factors that exhibit relations with external criterion variables similar to those for the PCL-R factors (Poythress et al., 2010). Findings for these distinct factors of the PPI, along with those of the PCL-R and its affiliates, served as important referents for formulation of the triarchic model of psychopathy, described below. For these reasons, we focus the remainder of this section on research that has utilized the PPI to index psychopathy in community and offender samples.

### THE PSYCHOPATHIC PERSONALITY INVENTORY AND ITS FACTORS

The original PPI (Lilienfeld & Andrews, 1996) consisted of 187 items; its revised version (PPI-R; Lilienfeld & Widows, 2005) includes 154 items. The PPI's items are organized into eight scales that tap distinct dispositional constructs relevant to psychopathy. In contrast with the PCL-R, the PPI includes specific coverage of nonanxiousness and low fear through its Stress Immunity and Fearlessness scales, along with coverage of interpersonal dominance (Social Potency scale), impulsivity (Carefree Nonplanfulness), oppositionality (Rebellious Nonconformity), alienation (Blame Externalization), aggressive exploitativeness (Machiavellian Egocentricity), and lack of empathic concern (Coldheartedness).

As noted above, factor analyses of the PPI's eight scales have revealed two higher-order factors, the first defined by scales assessing Social Potency, Stress Immunity, and Fearlessness subscales, and the second by ones indexing Carefree Nonplanfulness, Rebellious Nonconformity, Blame Externalization, and Machiavellian Egocentricity scales. Benning, Patrick, Blonigen, Hicks, and Iacono (2005) labeled these two higher-order factors Fearless Dominance and Impulsive Antisociality; Lilienfeld and Widows (2005) proposed Self-Centered Impulsivity as an alternative label for the latter of the two. The remaining PPI subscale, Coldheartedness, does not load appreciably on either of these factors, indicating that it taps something distinct. In contrast with the interrelated factors of the PCL-R, the two higher-order factors of the PPI are uncorrelated (Benning et al., 2003).

### PSYCHOLOGICAL AND NEUROBIOLOGICAL CORRELATES OF THE PPI FACTORS

The two factors of the PPI show conceptually meaningful and often diverging patterns of relations with various criterion measures (Benning, Patrick, Blonigen et al., 2005; Blonigen et al., 2005; Patrick, Edens et al., 2006; Ross et al., 2009). Scores on the Fearless Dominance factor (PPI-FD) are associated with social efficacy and emotional stability (e.g., higher assertiveness and well-being; lower anxiousness and depression) as well as with narcissism, thrill seeking, and reduced emotional empathy. In contrast, scores on the Impulsive Antisociality or Self-Centered Impulsivity (SCI) factor are more uniformly associated with maladaptive tendencies, including impulsivity and aggressiveness, child and adult antisocial behavior, substance problems, high negative affect, and suicidal ideation and acts.

The two PPI factors also show differing neurobiological correlates. In a study of young men from the community, Benning, Patrick, and Iacono (2005) found that participants with very high scores on PPI-FD showed a deviant pattern of startle reactivity resembling that of offenders with high scores on PCL-R Factor 1 (i.e., lack of startle potentiation during viewing of aversive picture stimuli, indicating a lack of normal defensive mobilization). By contrast, participants scoring high (as compared to low) on the PPI's Self-Centered Impulsivity factor (PPI-SCI) showed reduced electrodermal reactivity to picture stimuli in general (i.e., whether affective or neutral), suggesting reduced sympathetic arousability (cf. Raine, 1997). Extending the result for PPI-FD, Vaidyanathan, Patrick, and Bernat (2009) reported a lack of aversive startle potentiation for participants low in dispositional fear as defined by scores on PPI-FD and other scale measures of fear and fearlessness (see also Kramer et al., 2012). The finding of reduced electrodermal reactivity in high PPI-SCI–scoring participants has also been replicated. For example, Verschuere, Crombez, de Clercq, and Koster (2005) reported that PPI-SCI was related to smaller skin conductance responses to critical items in a concealed information lie detector test. Additionally, mirroring the findings of reduced P300 brain response in relation to ASPD and externalizing proneness more broadly, Carlson, Thái, and McLaron (2009) found scores on PPI-SCI (but not PPI-FD) to be inversely associated with P300 response in a visual oddball task paradigm.

Other work has used functional magnetic resonance imaging (fMRI) to test for brain reactivity differences in relation to the two factors of the PPI. Gordon, Baird, and End (2004) reported reduced fMRI blood oxygen level dependent (BOLD) activation in the right amygdala and affiliated regions of frontal cortex during processing of affective faces in participants scoring high but not low on PPI-FD. By contrast, individuals scoring high as compared to low on PPI-SC showed increased amygdala activation when processing affective faces. Related to this latter finding, Buckholtz et al. (2010) reported enhanced bilateral activation in the nucleus accumbens for high versus low SCI–scoring individuals during anticipation of monetary rewards. These results may indicate a more immediate affect-driven response style in high SCI–score individuals. Another fMRI study by Harenski, Kim, and Hamann (2009) reported reduced activation in medial prefrontal cortex during viewing of scenes depicting moral violations in individuals scoring high on the PPI as a whole, with evidence of reduced amygdala activation for those scoring high on PPI Coldheartedness specifically.

## An Integrative Framework for Investigating and Understanding Psychopathy: The Triarchic Model

The triarchic model (Patrick et al., 2009) was formulated to reconcile alternative conceptions of psychopathy represented in historical writings and contemporary assessment instruments and address persisting unresolved issues in the field. The model proposes that contrasting perspectives and apparent contradictions in the existing literature can be reconciled by conceiving of psychopathy as encompassing three distinct but intersecting trait dispositions: disinhibition, boldness, and meanness. In contrast with other contemporary factor- or facet-oriented perspectives (e.g., Cooke & Michie, 2001; Frick & Hare, 2001; Hare & Neumann, 2006), the triarchic model is a construct-based framework not bound to any specific assessment instrument or approach, designed to serve as an organizing framework for reconciling alternative instrument-based conceptions and integrating findings from studies using them. Different psychopathy inventories are viewed as indexing the triarchic constructs to varying degrees and in differing ways. The next section describes the three trait constructs of the triarchic model.

### Triarchic Model Traits: Description
#### DISINHIBITION

The term "disinhibition" refers to a general proneness toward impulse control problems, entailing lack of planfulness, a focus on immediate versus delayed gratification, difficulty in controlling emotions and urges, and weak behavioral restraint. Related concepts in the literature include disinhibitory psychopathology (Gorenstein & Newman, 1980; Sher & Trull, 1994), externalizing proneness (Achenbach & Edelbrock, 1978; Krueger et al., 2002), and low inhibitory control (Kochanska et al., 1997). Vis-à-vis conventional personality concepts, disinhibition represents the conjunction of impulsivity and negative emotionality (Krueger, 1999a; Sher & Trull, 1994). Behaviorally, it is manifested by impatience, impulsive action leading to adverse consequences, irresponsibility, distrust and alienation, aggressive behavior (angry or reactive aggression, in particular), repeated rule-breaking (and often law-breaking) acts, and proclivities toward abuse of alcohol and other substances (Krueger et al., 2007).

Historical accounts of psychopathy have emphasized this disinhibitory facet to varying degrees, with some writers broadening the diagnosis to encompass alcohol and drug addiction along with other nonnormative conditions such as sexual deviancy (e.g., Prichard, 1835), and others characterizing psychopathy in terms more characteristic of externalizing individuals (e.g., Arieti, 1963; Partridge, 1928) or describing psychopathic subtypes with irritable-impulsive behavior indicative of high externalizing proneness (e.g., Craft, 1966; Kraepelin, 1915). In particular, the traditional notion of the "symptomatic" or secondary psychopathy (Karpman, 1941; Lykken, 1957) appears consistent with the clinical presentation of the highly disinhibited-externalizing individual. Research has shown that variance unique to PCL-R Factor 2 reflects externalizing proneness to a large extent (Patrick et al., 2005), as do scores on the corresponding SCI factor of the PPI (Blonigen et al., 2005). Similarly, research on the factors of the APSD child psychopathy inventory demonstrates that the I/CP factor in particular indexes disinhibitory or externalizing tendencies (Bertoldi, Perkins et al., 2022; Drislane et al., 2014).

Despite its importance to conceptions of psychopathy, however, investigators in the area would not equate disinhibition with psychopathy. In contrast with the condition as described by Cleckley, externalizing proneness is associated with higher rather than lower levels of negative affectivity (Krueger, 1999a), elevated rather than reduced rates of internalizing problems (Achenbach & Edelbrock, 1978; Krueger, 1999b), and heightened rather than diminished tendencies toward suicidal behavior (Verona & Patrick, 2000; Verona et al., 2004). In contrast with the excessive, poorly regulated emotion that is characteristic of high-externalizing individuals, psychopathy is marked by salient "emotional detachment" (i.e., affective insensitivity and lack of social connectedness; Cleckley, 1941/1976; Lykken, 1995; McCord & McCord, 1964; Patrick, 1994; Patrick et al., 1993). The triarchic model proposes that this distinguishing component of psychopathy reflects the presence of boldness or meanness, or both. Stated another way, it is the occurrence of disinhibitory or externalizing tendencies in conjunction with high levels of dispositional boldness and/or meanness that signifies the presence of psychopathy.

**BOLDNESS**

This disposition encompasses characteristics of social assurance and self-confidence, calmness and poise in the face of stress or danger, rapid recovery from aversive experiences, and tolerance or preference for uncertainty and risk. Related terms include "fearless temperament" (Kochanska, 1997; Lykken, 1995), "fearless dominance" (Benning, Patrick, Blonigen et al., 2005), "hardiness" (Kobasa, 1979), and "resiliency" (Block & Block, 1980). In personality terms, boldness reflects the intersection of dominance, stress immunity, and thrill-adventure seeking (Benning et al., 2003; Benning, Patrick, Blonigen et al., 2005; Kramer et al., 2012). Behavioral expressions include social assertiveness, persuasiveness, imperturbability, venturesomeness, and courageous action. As conceptualized in the triarchic model, boldness is not identical to fearlessness. Fearlessness is viewed as a biologically based (genotypic) disposition, entailing diminished sensitivity of the brain's defense-mobilization system to signals of danger or punishment (Fowles & Dindo, 2009; Kramer et al., 2012; Patrick, Durbin, & Moser, 2012). Boldness is one way in which genotypic fearlessness can be exhibited phenotypically, but, as discussed next, this underlying disposition may also contribute to phenotypic meanness.

Cleckley's case histories and diagnostic criteria highlighted features of boldness in conjunction with disinhibitory (externalizing) tendencies (Crego & Widiger, 2016; Patrick, 2006, 2018). Boldness was represented directly in characteristic features of social charm, absence of anxiety or neurotic symptoms, lack of affective responsiveness, insensitivity to punishment ("failure to learn by experience"), and disinclination toward suicide. Other historical writers who focused on psychiatric patients as opposed to criminal offenders (e.g., Kraepelin, 1915; Schneider, 1934) also described bold-externalizing variants. Unresponsiveness to punishment and lack of fear were also emphasized in early psychophysiological research on psychopathy (cf. Hare, 1978) and in empirically based theories of psychopathy (Fowles, 1980; Lykken, 1995).

The Fearless Dominance (FD) factor of Lilienfeld's self-report–based PPI, demarcated by subscales of Social Potency, Stress Immunity, and Fearlessness, can be viewed as directly indexing boldness (Patrick et al., 2009; Patrick, Kramer et al., 2019). As mentioned earlier, scores on PPI-FD are uncorrelated with impulsive-antisocial tendencies tapped by PPI-SCI. Given this, boldness as operationalized by PPI-FD can be viewed as indexing a more adaptive expression of dispositional fearlessness—one distinct from aggressive externalizing deviance—that is likely to be of importance for conceptualizing psychopathy in nonviolent, noncriminal samples (Lilienfeld et al., 2018; Lykken, 1995). Boldness also appears to be tapped by Factor 1 of the PCL-R (Benning, Patrick, Blonigen et al., 2005), in particular, by its Interpersonal facet items (Patrick et al., 2007; Venables et al., 2014; Wall et al., 2015). However, the Interpersonal facet of the PCL-R indexes boldness less directly and distinctively than PPI-FD, given its overlap with the PCL-R's Affective, Lifestyle, and Antisocial facets.

#### MEANNESS

The triarchic trait of meanness encompasses features of deficient empathy, lack of closeness to others, uncooperativeness, exploitativeness, and self-empowerment through cruel and destructive acts. Related terms in the literature include "callous-unemotionality" (Frick & Marsee, 2018), "antagonism" (Lynam et al., 2018), and "coldheartedness" (Lilienfeld & Widows, 2005). From the standpoint of interpersonal traits (Leary, 1957; Wiggins, 1982), meanness entails high dominance in conjunction with low affiliation and nurturance (Blackburn, 2006; Harpur et al., 1989). Saucier (1992) documented a construct similar to meanness (represented by adjective descriptors such as tough, unemotional, and insensitive) entailing the conjunction of low affiliation, high dominance, and low neuroticism. From this standpoint, meanness can be viewed as disaffiliated agency—an orientation involving active pursuit of goals and resources without concern for and at the expense of others. Unlike social withdrawal, which is marked by passive disengagement ("moving away"; Horney, 1945) from people, meanness involves active exploitation of ("moving against"; Horney, 1945) people.

Affiliated behavioral expressions include disdain toward others, arrogance, rebellious defiance, lack of close relationships, harsh competitiveness, exploitation of others for personal gain, proactive (predatory or instrumental) aggression, cruelty toward people or animals, and engagement in destructive acts for excitement.

Meanness is emphasized in historical accounts of psychopathy based on observations of criminal and delinquent individuals (McCord & McCord, 1964; Quay, 1964; Robins, 1966, 1978). The Affective facet of the PCL-R comprises items that capture McCord and McCord's lovelessness (item 7, "shallow affect," and item 8, "callous/lack of empathy") and guiltlessness (item 6, "lack of remorse or guilt," and item 16, "failure to accept responsibility for own actions"). The Interpersonal items of the PCL-R also include elements of meanness: Item 1 ("glibness and superficial charm") refers to excessive slickness and toughness; item 2 ("grandiose sense of self-worth") includes arrogance and a sense of superiority over others; item 4 ("pathological lying") refers to deceptiveness in social interactions and enjoyment in deceiving others; and item 5 ("conning/manipulative") entails active exploitation for gain without consideration of the effects on victims. The best-established psychopathy inventories for children and adolescents (PCL:YV, CPS, and APSD), patterned after the PCL-R, also emphasize meanness in their interpersonal-affective items.

Although psychopathy is frequently operationalized with reference to antisocial acts and attitudes that reflect tendencies toward disinhibition as well as meanness, research by Krueger et al. (2007; see also Patrick, Kramer et al., 2013) on the structure of externalizing problems and traits demonstrated that these dispositional facets of psychopathy could be indexed separately. Specifically, these investigators reported a bifactor structure for the 23 content scales of the Externalizing Spectrum Inventory (ESI), an instrument developed to measure diverse elements and expressions of externalizing proneness. All of the ESI's scales loaded onto a superordinate disinhibition factor, but certain scales also loaded onto subordinate factors reflecting callous-aggressiveness (meanness) and substance abuse. The scales that loaded most strongly and exclusively onto the general disinhibitory factor were those indexing problematic impulsivity and irresponsibility. The best indicators of the callous-aggressive subfactor were scales indexing presence versus absence of empathy and interpersonal expressions of aggression.

The findings of this work showed that tendencies toward meanness could be separated from proclivities toward disinhibition. Along with scales tapping empathic concern and interpersonal aggression, other scales that have helped to demarcate the callous-aggressive subfactor included ones indexing excitement seeking, rebelliousness, and dishonesty. Notably, these scale indicators of the ESI's callous-aggressive factor paralleled the item content of the APSD's callous-unemotional (CU) factor, which reflects disregard for the feelings of others, shallowness and insincerity, lack of guilt, and lying and manipulativeness (Frick et al., 1994; Frick et al., 2014). Also in line with the ESI findings, youth with conduct problems who score high on the CU factor of the APSD show elevated rates of proactive aggression and enhanced excitement seeking in comparison to those low on the CU factor (Frick & White, 2008; Frick et al., 2014). Although early ideas about the biobehavioral basis of callous-unemotionality (meanness) focused on dispositional fearlessness (e.g., Frick & Marsee, 2006; Frick & White, 2008), the triarchic model postulates that a weakness in the capacity for affiliation gives rise to the qualities that distinguish this facet of psychopathy from its boldness facet—namely, lack of empathic concern, disregard for others' welfare, and aggressive exploitativeness. Recent years have shown a growing emphasis on the role of affiliative deficits in dispositional callousness or meanness, both in younger-aged (Viding & McCrory, 2019; Waller & Wagner, 2019) and adult samples (Palumbo et al., 2020).

*Operationalizing the Triarchic Model Traits*

This section describes various self-report scales that have been developed to operationalize the three dispositional constructs of the triarchic model. The first of these, the Triarchic Psychopathy Measure (TriPM), consists of items selected to index broad factors of two inventories that served as referents for the triarchic model—the general disinhibition and callous-aggressive factors of the ESI (Krueger et al., 2007) and the fearless dominance factor of the PPI (Lilienfeld & Widows, 2005). A number of other triarchic scale measures have been developed using items from (1) preexisting psychopathy inventories, (2) normative and maladaptive personality inventories, and (3) construct-relevant scales available in etiologically informative (twin, longitudinal) archival datasets.

### TRIARCHIC PSYCHOPATHY MEASURE

The 58-item Triarchic Psychopathy Measure (TriPM; Patrick, 2010) indexes the disinhibition, meanness, and boldness facets of psychopathy as separate dimensions. Items comprising the TriPM Disinhibition and Meanness scales (20 and 19 items, respectively) are from Krueger et al.'s (2007) ESI. The Disinhibition scale is composed of items from facet scales of the ESI that exhibit strong, selective loadings on the inventory's general disinhibition factor (i.e., Problematic Impulsivity, Irresponsibility, Boredom Proneness, Impatient Urgency, Alienation, Theft, Fraudulence, Dependability [-], Planful Control [-]). Scores on this scale correlate very strongly ($r > .9$) with regression-estimated scores on the general factor of the ESI (Patrick, Kramer et al., 2013). The TriPM Meanness scale consists of items from ESI scales that function as indicators of the inventory's callous-aggression subfactor (i.e., Empathy [-], Relational Aggression, Excitement Seeking, Destructive Aggression, Physical Aggression, Honesty [-]). Scores on this scale, after controlling for overlap ($r \sim .5$) with scores on the TriPM Disinhibition scale, correlate very highly ($r > .8$) with scores on the callous-aggression subfactor of the ESI bifactor model (Patrick, Kramer et al., 2013). The 19-item TriPM Boldness scale consists of items that index fearless tendencies in the realms of interpersonal behavior (persuasiveness, social assurance, dominance), perceived emotional experience (resiliency, self-assurance, optimism), and venturesomeness (courage, thrill seeking, tolerance for uncertainty; cf. Kramer et al., 2012). Its items were selected to index the general factor of the Boldness Inventory (Patrick, Kramer et al., 2019), a multi-scale measure developed to flesh out distinct facets of this construct and characterize their structure. Scores on this scale correlate very highly ($\sim.8$) with the FD factor of the PPI, but only modestly ($r \sim .2$) with the TriPM Meanness scale and negligibly with the TriPM Disinhibition scale (Drislane et al., 2014; Patrick, Kramer et al., 2019).

The TriPM has been employed in many different studies since the first report of its use by Sellbom and Phillips (2013), and evidence for the convergent and discriminant validity of its subscales exists in relation to a broad range of external criteria—including measures from domains of personality, clinical symptomatology, behavioral performance, and psychophysiology/neuroimaging (for reviews, see Patrick & Drislane, 2015; Patrick, 2018; Sellbom, 2018; Sellbom et al., 2018). The inventory is freely available online, and a number of foreign-language translations (including Dutch, Finnish, French, German, Italian, Japanese, Mandarin Chinese, Portuguese, Spanish, and Swedish) exist, resulting in growing evidence for its validity across nations and cultures.

An issue that has been raised regarding the TriPM is that its scales are not strictly unidimensional according to confirmatory factor analytic criteria (Roy et al., 2021; Shou et al., 2018). This is because the TriPM's scales were developed to index broad factors identified by scale-level analyses of multifaceted inventories and thus include items from distinct content domains; in such cases, the recommended analytic method for characterizing structure is exploratory structural equation modeling (ESEM; Hopwood & Donnellan, 2010; Wright, 2020). A three-factor ESEM model of the TriPM item set has been shown to exhibit good statistical fit (Bertoldi, Tuvblad et al., 2022; Patrick et al., 2021).

### OTHER TRIARCHIC SCALE MEASURES

The triarchic model was advanced to provide a general framework for ongoing work on conceptualization and assessment of psychopathy through a focus on core dispositional constructs—presumed to reflect biobehavioral propensities—that transcend specific assessment instruments or modalities of measurement. Importantly, the components of the triarchic model are conceived of as "open constructs" (Meehl, 1986), subject to modification over time based on accumulating empirical evidence from different measurement modalities. While the TriPM provides one approach to operationalizing the constructs of the model, other psychopathy measures, or inventories known to predict substantial variance in psychopathy measures, can also serve as vehicles for operationalizing these constructs.

Hall et al. (2014) undertook to develop item-based scale measures of the Triarchic constructs using items from the PPI. A construct-based rating approach was used rather than a criterion-oriented approach (e.g., selection of items with reference to the TriPM scales) to allow constructs distilled from the psychopathy literature as a whole to guide scale formation rather than binding scales to a particular operationalization of the triarchic model. All items of the PPI were rated for relevance to each construct of the model as described by Patrick et al. (2009), and items were selected for inclusion in scales based on their preferential relevance to one triarchic construct over the others. Scales were further refined based on considerations of overall content coverage, internal properties of the scales (i.e., inter-item correlations and internal consistency), and correlations of items within and across scales. The resultant PPI Triarchic (PPI-Tri) scales indexed boldness, meanness, and disinhibition in a manner complementary to but distinct from the TriPM. In particular, the PPI-Meanness scale (composed mainly of items from the PPI's Coldheartedness and Machiavellian Egocentricity subscales) correlated less strongly ($r = .37$) with the PPI-Disinhibition scale (composed mostly of items from scales loading onto the PPI's SCI factor) than their TriPM counterparts ($r \sim .5$). Hall et al. reported evidence for criterion-related validity of the PPI-Tri scales in undergraduate and offender samples. PPI-Boldness and Disinhibition exhibited strong convergence with their TriPM counterparts ($rs = .79$ and .64, respectively) in the undergraduate sample, for which both inventories were available. Convergence between PPI and TriPM Meanness was somewhat lower ($r = .54$), suggesting that the decreased overlap between PPI Meanness and Disinhibition (vs. their TriPM counterparts) was attributable more to a shift in the former. In the forensic sample, for which scores on the PCL-R were available, all three PPI-Tri scales contributed to prediction of PCL-R total scores, with PPI-Boldness and PPI-Meanness contributing to prediction of Factor 1 scores, and PPI-Meanness and Disinhibition contributing to prediction of Factor 2 scores. With regard to the PCL-R's four facets, PPI-Boldness contributed distinctively to prediction of the Interpersonal facet, PPI-Meanness contributed to prediction of both the Affective facet and the Antisocial facet, and PPI-Disinhibition contributed distinctively to prediction of the Lifestyle facet.

A second triarchic scale development effort was undertaken by Drislane et al. (2015) using items from a psychopathy questionnaire designed for use with adolescents, the Youth Psychopathic Traits Inventory (YPI). The YPI-based Boldness scale consists of items from scales that define the YPI's Grandiose/Manipulative factor, along with some items from its Thrill-Seeking and Unemotionality scales; the YPI-Disinhibition scale consists mostly of items from scales associated with the YPI's Impulsive/Irresponsible factor; and the YPI-Meanness scale consists entirely of items from scales related to the YPI's Callous/Unemotional factor. Drislane et al. (2015) presented evidence for convergent and discriminant validity of the YPI-Tri scales in relation to psychopathy-relevant criteria, including the TriPM and PPI-Tri scales.

The foregoing studies demonstrated that effective scale measures of the triarchic trait constructs could be constructed from items of existing psychopathy inventories, thus supporting the idea that these constructs are embodied in different models and measures of psychopathy (Patrick et al., 2009). Inspired by published work demonstrating robust associations for the TriPM scale operationalizations with scores on omnibus inventories of normal-range personality and maladaptive personality, triarchic scales have also been developed using items from inventories of these types. The availability of these scales creates opportunities to extend knowledge of the nature and correlates of the triarchic traits in large existing datasets that contain such inventories—including epidemiological, longitudinal-developmental, genetically informative (i.e., twin), and neurobiologically informative datasets (for specific examples of such datasets, see Wygant et al., 2018). Along this same line, efforts have also been made to develop and validate triarchic scales using construct-relevant items from specific questionnaires available in large specialized datasets, such as those of the European IMAGEN project (Schumann et al., 2010) and the USC Risk Factors for Antisocial Behavior (RFAB) study (Baker et al., 2013). Table 30.1 lists all triarchic scale sets that have been developed to date, noting source(s) of items and original published reports for each.

In addition to providing a powerful means to further characterize the nomological networks of the triarchic trait constructs, the availability of alternative scales for assessing these traits provides a basis for bridging different datasets in order to address key questions not amenable to analysis with a single existing dataset (Friedman et al., 2014). Specifically, latent variable models employing alternative triarchic scale sets as indicators can be used to harmonize datasets along biobehavioral-trait lines. The next section describes efforts that have been made to model the triarchic traits as latent variables, using different scale sets from among those listed in Table 30.1.

### LATENT VARIABLE MODELING OF THE TRIARCHIC TRAITS

The first latent variable model of the triarchic traits, which utilized data for a mixed-sex sample of undergraduates (N = 567; 46.4% male), was reported by Drislane and Patrick (2017). The indicators for the model consisted of the boldness, meanness, and disinhibition scales of the TriPM and the PPI, along with the meanness and disinhibition scales of the YPI and an index of boldness computed from construct-relevant trait scales of the Multidimensional Personality Questionnaire (MPQ; Tellegen & Waller, 2008). A confirmatory factor analysis (CFA) specifying three correlated factors with three scale indicators each, and including correlated error terms between the meanness and disinhibition scales of the TriPM and those of the YPI, fit the data well, with all scale indicators loading very highly (> .70) onto their target factors. Tests of model invariance revealed equivalence of factor loadings and indicator intercepts for male and female participants, although mean-level differences were evident for two of the model factors (boldness and meanness; males > females for each). In addition, the authors reported that regression-based scores for the three factors of the model strongly predicted overall scores on self-report psychopathy inventories patterned after the PCL-R (i.e., HSRP, LSRP, APSD), with multiple $R$s in each case exceeding .75.

CFA models like this have been used in subsequent research to demonstrate similarity of measurement for newly developed triarchic scale sets relative to previously validated scale sets. Drislane et al. (2018), employing data for an undergraduate sample, developed triarchic scales from items of the NEO PI-R five-factor questionnaire (Costa & McCrae, 1992) and demonstrated good fit for a three-factor triarchic model using the new NEO-Tri scales as indicators along with counterpart scales of the TriPM and PPI. The NEO-Tri scales loaded very highly onto their target factors, at levels comparable to loadings for the TriPM and PPI-Tri scales (> .80 in all cases). Using data for a mixed undergraduate/community sample, Drislane et al. (2019) likewise demonstrated good fit for a counterpart three-factor model using triarchic scales composed of items from the Personality Inventory for *DSM-5* (PID-5; Krueger et al., 2012) as indicators along with TriPM and MPQ-based triarchic scales (Brislin et al., 2015). This model is depicted in the upper part of Figure 30.1. As shown in the figure, the PID-5 Disinhibition scale emerged as the strongest indicator of the latent disinhibition factor, and the PID-5 Boldness and Meanness scales loaded onto their target factors at levels comparable to the TriPM and MPQ-Tri scales.

An important question, given evidence for differing latent structures of psychopathic traits as indexed by the PPI in criminal offenders as compared to nonoffenders (Ruchensky, Edens et al., 2018), is whether latent triarchic factors could be modeled effectively in an offender sample. Drislane, Sica et al. (2022) addressed this question using data

**Table 30.1** Alternative self-report scale measures for operationalizing the trait constructs of the triarchic model of psychopathy

| Triarchic (Tri) Scale measures | Source(s) of items | Initial published report | Label within Figure 30.2 |
|---|---|---|---|
| **First, Purpose-Built Measure** | | | |
| Triarchic Psychopathy Measure (TriPM) | Boldness Inventory (Patrick, Kramer, et al., 2019); Externalizing Spectrum Inventory; Krueger et al., 2007; Patrick, Kramer, et al., 2013) | Sellbom & Phillips (2013) | $S_1$ |
| **Psychopathy Inventory-Based Measures** | | | |
| PPI-Tri scales | Psychopathic Personality Inventory (PPI) (Lilienfeld & Andrews, 1996; Lilienfeld & Widows, 2005) | Hall et al. (2014) | $S_2$ |
| YPI-Tri scales | Youth Psychopathic Traits Inventory (YPI) (Andershed et al., 2002) | Drislane et al. (2015) | $S_3$ |
| **Maladaptive Personality Inventory-Based Measures** | | | |
| MMPI-2-RF-Tri scales | Minnesota Multiphasic Personality Inventory-2 Restructured Form (MMPI-2-RF) (Ben-Porath & Tellegen, 2008) | Sellbom et al. (2016) | $S_4$ |
| MMPI-A-RF-Tri scales | Minnesota Multiphasic Personality Inventory-Adolescent Restructured Form (MMPI-A-RF) (Archer et al., 2016) | Semel et al. (2016) | $S_5$ |
| PID-5-Tri scales | Personality Inventory for DSM-5 (PID-5) (Krueger et al., 2012) | Drislane et al. (2019) | $S_6$ |
| SNAP-F-Tri scales | Schedule for Nonadaptive and Adaptive Personality (Clark, 1993)—Forensic version (Keulen-de-Vos et al., 2011) | Gerbrandij et al. (2019) | $S_7$ |
| **Normative Personality Inventory-Based Measures** | | | |
| HEXACO-Tri scales | HEXACO Personality Inventory (Lee & Ashton, 2018) | Ruchensky, Donnellan, & Edens (2018) | $S_8$ |
| MPQ-Tri scales | Multidimensional Personality Questionnaire (MPQ) (Tellegen & Waller, 2008) | Brislin et al. (2015) | $S_9$ |
| NEO-Tri scales | NEO Personality Inventory-Revised (NEO-PI-R) (Costa & McCrae, 1992) | Drislane et al. (2018) | |
| **Measures Developed for Use in Specialized Archival Datasets** | | | |
| Healthy Brain Network (HBN) project (Alexander et al., 2017)—Tri scales | Child Behavior Checklist (Achenbach, 1991); Affective Reactivity Index—Parent Report (Stringaris et al., 2012; Inventory of Callous-Unemotional Traits—Parent Report (Frick, 2004); Screen for Child Anxiety Related Disorders—Parent Report (Birmaher et al., 1999); Strengths & Difficulties Questionnaire (Goodman, 2001); Social Responsiveness Scale (Constantino & Gruper, 2005) | Palumbo et al. (2021) | $S_{11}$ |

*(continued)*

**Table 30.1** *Continued*

| Triarchic (Tri) Scale measures | Source(s) of items | Initial published report | Label within Figure 30.2 |
|---|---|---|---|
| USC Risk Factors for Antisocial Behavior (RFAB) project (Baker et al., 2013)— Tri scales | Child Psychopathy Scale (Lynam, 1997); Youth Self-Report (Achenbach & Rescorla, 2001)/Adult Self-Report (Achenbach & Rescorla, 2003) | Bertoldi, Perkins et al. (2022) | $S_{12}$ |
| European IMAGEN project (Schumann et al., 2010)— Disinhibition scale | NEO Five Factor Inventory (Costa & McCrae, 1992); Temperament & Character Inventory-Revised (Cloninger et al., 1999); Substance Use Risk Profile Scale (Woicik et al., 2009); Strengths & Difficulties Questionnaire (Goodman, 2001); Life Events Questionnaire (Newcomb et al., 1981) | Brislin et al. (2019) | $S_{13}$ |
| European IMAGEN project (Schumann et al., 2010) — Callousness (Meanness) scale | NEO Five Factor Inventory (Costa & McCrae, 1992); Temperament & Character Inventory-Revised (Cloninger et al., 1999); Substance Use Risk Profile Scale (Woicik et al., 2009); Strengths & Difficulties Questionnaire (Goodman, 2001); Revised Olweus Bully/Victim Questionnaire for Students (Olweus, 1996) | Perkins et al. (in press) | $S_{14}$ |

*Note*: Entries in right-most column correspond to sources for sequentially numbered self-report indicators (square boxes labeled "$S_1$," "$S_2$," " . . . ," "$S_{13}$") of biobehavioral threat constructs (cloud shapes labeled "Threat Sensitivity," "Affiliative Capacity," "Inhibitory Control") in Figure 30.2. Boldness scales from sources labeled $S_1$ to $S_{12}$ operate as reversed indicators of threat sensitivity (Patrick, Kramer et al., 2019). The thirteenth indicator of Threat Sensitivity in main Figure 30.2 (box labeled "$S_{13}$") is a scale measure of dispositional fear/fearlessness (Yancey, Venables, & Patrick, 2016; see also Kramer et al., 2012) that correlates to a high negative degree (~ −.8) with scale measures of boldness (Brislin et al., 2015; Patrick, Kramer et al., 2019).

for a mixed-sex Italian prisoner sample ($N$ = 356; 76.7% male). The indicators for the model consisted of the boldness, meanness, and disinhibition scales of the TriPM and the PPI, along with Minnesota Multiphasic Personality Inventory (MMPI)-based boldness and disinhibition scales (see Table 30.1) and a meanness scale composed of items from the Agreeableness domain of the short form NEO PI-R (NEO-FFI; Costa & McCrae, 1992). This latent triarchic trait model, depicted in the lower part of Figure 30.1, exhibited adequate statistical fit, with all scale indicators loading at strong, comparable levels onto their target factors. Tests of model invariance across sexes could not be performed due to the low *n* for female participants; however, the factor loadings for a model employing data only for males matched closely with those for the full-sample model (Tucker congruence coefficient > .99), indicating consistency of measurement for males alone relative to both sexes combined.

Findings from these studies illustrate how latent variable models of the triarchic traits using previously validated scale measures as indicators can be used to evaluate the measurement effectiveness of new scale measures of these traits. Latent triarchic trait models utilizing established scale indicators can also provide an alternative to the construct-rating approach employed in previous scale development projects to date, beginning with Hall et al. (2014). Specifically, items from inventories such as Lynam et al.'s (2011) EPA or Clark's (1993) Schedule for Nonadaptive and Adaptive Personality (SNAP) could be selected to index, as effectively and efficiently as possible, latent triarchic trait dimensions from models like those reported by Drislane and colleagues (Drislane & Patrick, 2017; Drislane et al., 2022). Latent variable models of the triarchic model traits could also be used as harmonizing referents (see, e.g., Bilder et al., 2013; Friedman et al., 2014) for interfacing large-scale specialized datasets along triarchic-dimensional lines (see final section below, titled "Neurobiological Systems and Processes").

From a more conceptual standpoint, these latent-variable modeling efforts serve to illustrate the "open" (Meehl, 1986) quality of the triarchic

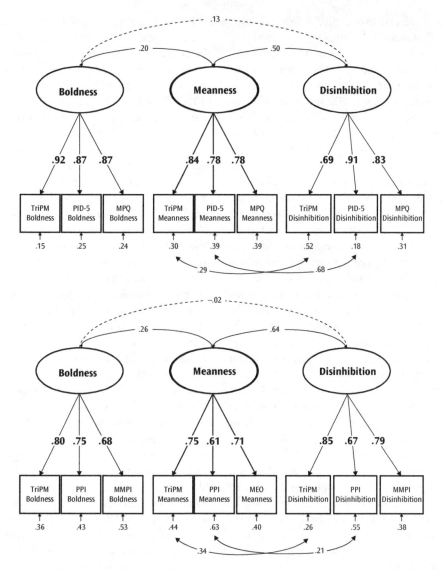

**Figure 30.1** Three-factor latent-variable models of the triarchic traits, showing standardized parameter estimates. Upper model is for the undergraduate-community sample (*N* = 210) of Drislane et al. (2019); lower model is for the incarcerated offender sample (*N* = 356) of Drislane, Sica, et al. (2022). TriPM, Triarchic Psychopathy Measure; PID-5, Personality Inventory for DSM-5; MPQ, Multidimensional Personality Questionnaire; PPI, Psychopathic Personality Inventory; MMPI, Minnesota Multiphasic Personality Inventory; NEO, NEO Five Factor Inventory.

model constructs. Rather than using the TriPM scales as fixed referents for developing alternative scale operationalizations from items of other inventories, alternative scales have been developed using a conceptual, rating-based approach not bound to any particular measurement device. This approach permits the content coverage of scales to vary from operationalization to operationalization, as a function of differences in thematic coverage of items within particular inventories compared to others. Observed variations in content across differing scale operationalizations can serve to highlight previously untapped, underrepresented, or perhaps less essential aspects of target constructs and thereby help to refine ideas about the nature and scope of the constructs themselves.

### Psychopathy in the DSM-5

In addition to providing categorical diagnostic criteria for personality disorders, equivalent to those in *DSM-IV*, the fifth edition of the *DSM* includes a new trait-based system for these conditions (the Alternative Model of Personality Disorders [AMPD]) that entails (1) assessing for the presence of personality disturbance, as indicated by dysfunction in areas of self (identity, directedness) and social relations and (2) characterizing the specific nature of the disturbance in terms of maladaptive traits from five thematic domains (negative affect, disinhibition, antagonism, detachment, and psychoticism). As a link to the categorical system, the AMPD includes counterparts to six of the categorical PDs: antisocial, borderline, narcissistic, obsessive-compulsive, avoidant, and schizotypal. As shown in Table 30.2, ASPD is defined in the AMPD by the presence of distinct disturbances in self-concept and social relations, together with elevations on six of seven designated traits from the domains of disinhibition and antagonism, corresponding to meanness and disinhibition in the triarchic model. Four of the seven designated traits are from the antagonism domain, ensuring that persons assigned the diagnosis exhibit a balance of proclivities toward meanness and disinhibition—in line with historical conceptions that have focused on criminal expressions of psychopathy (Patrick, 2018; Patrick et al., 2009). This represents a shift from the categorical diagnosis of ASPD, which emphasizes disinhibition more than meanness, particularly in its adult criteria (Kendler et al., 2012; Venables & Patrick, 2012). The diagnostic importance of meanness is also recognized by the addition of a "limited prosocial emotions" specifier to the categorical diagnosis of conduct disorder (CD) in *DSM-5*, to distinguish a variant of this condition exhibiting salient callous-unemotional traits as described in the youth psychopathy literature (Frick et al., 2014).

A further innovative feature of the diagnosis of ASPD in the *DSM-5*'s AMPD is the inclusion of a "psychopathic features" specifier, encompassing three other traits—[low] anxiousness, [low] withdrawal, and [high] attention seeking—from the domains of negative affect, detachment, and antagonism, respectively (see Table 30.2). This specifier provides for the designation of a classically low-anxious, socially efficacious (i.e., bold) variant of ASPD (cf. Cleckley, 1941/1976; Crego & Widiger, 2016; Karpman, 1941; see also Hicks et al., 2004; Skeem et al., 2007). The specifier is particularly important in light of research demonstrating the importance of boldness in distinguishing psychopathy as defined by the PCL-R from the criterion-based diagnosis of ASPD (Venables et al., 2014; Wall et al., 2015).

A self-report–based operationalization of the AMPD, the Personality Inventory for *DSM-5* (PID-5; Krueger et al., 2012), has been widely used in research over the past decade. Evidence for its convergent and discriminant validity has been reported in relation to symptoms of categorical PDs as defined in *DSM-IV* and *DSM-5* (Hopwood et al., 2012). In addition, the PID-5 has been used to evaluate the effectiveness of the Section III diagnosis of ASPD and its specifier for capturing the distinct facets of psychopathy described by the triarchic model. One study by Strickland, Drislane, Lucy, Krueger, and Patrick (2013) administered the PID-5 along with the TriPM to a mixed college and community adult sample. Another study by Anderson, Sellbom, Wygant, Salekin, and Krueger (2014) administered the PID-5 along with both the TriPM and the PPI to separate samples of college students and community adults, with the latter sample recruited to overrepresent individuals with psychopathic tendencies. Findings from these two studies demonstrated that the AMPD-designated traits for ASPD (operationalized via the PID-5) provided highly effective coverage of the disinhibition and meanness facets of psychopathy (as indexed by the TriPM) and that the traits of the psychopathy specifier provided effective coverage of the boldness facet.

Taken together, the findings of these studies provide evidence that adult psychopathy as described in classic historical writings and investigated empirically over the years can be indexed effectively using the new dimensional-trait system of the *DSM-5*. Dovetailing with this evidence is work by Drislane et al. (2019), cited in the preceding section, showing that highly effective triarchic scales could be developed using items of the PID-5—most of them from PID-5 scales that assess traits related to ASPD and the psychopathy specifier in the AMPD. Of note, the AMPD in *DSM-5* is organized around maladaptive trait domains that resemble higher-order factors of a dimensional model for psychopathology as a whole, namely, the Hierarchical Taxonomy of Psychopathology (HiTOP; Kotov et al., 2017). The next section describes how facets of psychopathy specified by the triarchic model relate to factors of this general psychopathology model.

### Psychopathy and the Hierarchical Taxonomy of Psychopathology Model

Traditionally, psychopathy has been viewed as a discrete psychopathological syndrome with a distinct underlying cause, and there has been a long-standing inclination to study it unto itself rather than in relation to other mental disorders. However, empirical evidence has resulted in a shift

**Table 30.2** Criteria for diagnosis of antisocial personality disorder in Section III of *DSM-5*

| Criterion category | Summary description of criterion indicator(s) |
|---|---|
| A. Significant impairments in personality functioning, manifested in two or more of the following areas: | 1. Identity (egocentric; self-esteem derived from power or pleasure) |
| | 2. Self-directedness (lack of internalized prosocial values; goals based around hedonism or dominance) |
| | 3. Empathy (lacks concern for others; lacks remorse) |
| | 4. Intimacy (exploitative or controlling; lacks mutually intimate relationships) |
| B. Elevations on six or all of the following traits, from domains of: | 1. Antagonism: |
| |   a. Manipulativeness (controls or exploits others through persuasion) |
| |   b. Deceitfulness (dishonest, distorts truth, misrepresents self) |
| |   c. Callousness (lacks concern for others; lacks guilt for harmful acts) |
| |   d. Hostility (frequently irritable or angry; sensitive to slights; vengeful) |
| | 2. Disinhibition: |
| |   a. Irresponsibility (disregards or lacks respect for obligations and agreements) |
| |   b. Impulsivity (spontaneous; lacks planfulness; acts on immediate urges) |
| |   c. Risk taking (acts recklessly without considering consequences; disregards danger; easily bored) |
| C. Temporal stability criterion | Impairments in self or interpersonal functioning and expression of pathological traits persist across time and occur across situations. |
| D. Non-normativity criterion | Impairments in functioning and expression of pathological traits are atypical vis-à-vis developmental age and sociocultural milieu. |
| E. Physiological/medical criterion | Impairments in functioning and expression of pathological traits are not due to effects of substance use or a general medical condition. |
| **Psychopathic Features Specifier for ASPD** | |
| Low scores on the following two traits: | 1. Anxiousness (domain of negative affect) |
| AND | 2. Withdrawal (domain of detachment) |
| Elevated score on the following trait: | 3. Attention seeking (domain of antagonism) |

*Note*: The Psychopathic Features specifier is used to designate a classically low-anxious, socially assertive (i.e., "bold"; Patrick et al., 2009) variant of antisocial personality as described in the adult psychopathy literature (Cleckley, 1941/1976; Crego & Widiger, 2016; Hicks et al., 2004; Karpman, 1941), with high attention seeking and low withdrawal capturing the social assertiveness aspect.

toward viewing psychopathy as dimensional and multifaceted – that is, as a disorder encompassing distinct symptom subdimensions that relate in turn to distinct trait dispositions. There has also been growing interest in understanding psychopathy's associations with other forms of psychopathology. An important recent development in this regard is the formulation of an integrative dimensional framework for mental health problems encompassing episodic clinical conditions as well as personality disorders. This framework, the HiTOP model (Kotov et al., 2017), organizes mental disorders and their affiliated symptoms into a multilevel structure that reflects empirically observed patterns of covariation among them. The levels of the HiTOP model range from specific symptom dimensions at the lowest level to a general psychopathology factor at the highest level—with symptom clusters, disorders ("syndromes"), and disorder dimensions ("spectra") in between. The model considers syndrome- and spectrum-level dimensions within the psychopathology hierarchy to be related to broad dimensions of normative personality.

The comorbidity of psychopathy and its factors with disorders of certain types, described earlier, can be understood in relation to two major HiTOP disorder dimensions (spectra): the externalizing spectrum and the internalizing spectrum.

The externalizing spectrum encompasses disorders involving deficient impulse control (Krueger et al., 2002, 2007, 2021) and is represented in the HiTOP model by a higher-order dimension with subdimensions reflecting "disinhibited" and "antagonistic" expressions of externalizing (Krueger et al., 2021). Substance-related problems (e.g., alcohol use disorder, other drug disorders) load predominantly onto the former dimension, whereas conditions involving callous disregard and exploitativeness (e.g., narcissistic PD, histrionic PD) load mainly on the latter. Antisocial conditions (e.g., CD, adult ASPD), which include both impulsive/rule-breaking and aggressive/exploitative symptoms, load onto both. The internalizing spectrum is represented in the HiTOP model by a higher-order dimension with subdimensions reflecting pathological fear conditions (e.g., specific phobia, social anxiety disorder, panic disorder) and conditions marked by dysphoria and pervasive distress (e.g., major depression, dysthymia, posttraumatic stress disorder [PTSD]). Psychopathy's associations with this psychopathology spectrum are important to clarify given notable discrepancies in the literature. For example, Cleckley described psychopathic individuals as lacking in nervousness and free from "psychoneurotic" symptoms, and early studies using his diagnostic criteria (e.g., Hare, 1978; Lykken, 1957) produced findings consistent with this description. In contrast with this, overall scores on the PCL-R and other PCL-based inventories show weak and inconsistent relations with measures of anxiety and internalizing problems (Widiger & Crego, 2018).

Regarding psychopathy's relations with the externalizing spectrum, Patrick (2022) reported findings from a structural modeling analysis undertaken to characterize relations of the triarchic traits with disinhibited and antagonistic subdimensions (subfactors) of this spectrum. The analysis utilized data from a mixed-gender sample of college students and community adults ($N = 212$) preselected to ensure broad representation of triarchic trait scores. Indicators of the two externalizing subfactors were symptom scores for *DSM-IV* disorders assessed using clinical interview (SCID-I and SCID-II) protocols: alcohol use disorder, other drug disorder, and nonaggressive CD symptoms for the disinhibited subfactor, and aggressive CD, aggressive ASPD, and narcissistic PD symptoms for the antagonistic subfactor. The triarchic traits were also modeled as latent dimensions using different validated scale measures as indicators (i.e., TriPM, MPQ-Tri, and PID-5-Tri scales, as described in the preceding section). In the structural model, which exhibited acceptable fit, the two externalizing factors were regressed onto the latent triarchic traits in order to evaluate distinct relations for the traits as concurrent predictors. The disinhibited externalizing factor was predicted very strongly by triarchic disinhibition ($B$ coefficient = .63) and to a lesser unique extent by boldness ($B$ = .25), with meanness predicting minimally. The antagonistic externalizing factor, on the other hand, was predicted most strongly by triarchic meanness ($B$ = .40) and to lesser degrees by disinhibition and boldness ($B$s = .24 and .17).

Regarding relations with the internalizing spectrum, Latzman, Palumbo et al. (2020) examined relations between latent-variable representations of the triarchic traits and fear versus distress subfactors of this spectrum. The participant sample was the same as that employed in the above-described model for disinhibitory and antagonistic factors of externalizing, and the same self-report scales were used to index the triarchic trait dimensions. Indicators of the fear-disorder subfactor of internalizing were SCID-I–assessed symptom scores for specific phobia, social phobia, agoraphobia, and panic disorder; indicators of the dysphoria/distress factor were symptom scores for major depressive disorders, dysthymia, and PTSD. As in the model for the externalizing spectrum subfactors, unique predictive relations for the latent triarchic traits were evaluated via regression. The fear factor of internalizing showed a strong negative relationship with latent boldness ($B = -.65$), a weaker positive relationship with disinhibition ($B = .21$), and a negligible association with meanness. By contrast, the dysphoric/distress factor showed comparable negative associations with latent boldness and meanness ($B$s = $-.26$ and $-.24$) and a strong positive relationship with disinhibition ($B = .58$).

These findings for externalizing and internalizing spectra of psychopathology are depicted schematically in the lower part of Figure 30.2, which illustrates how the triarchic model traits are linked to subdimensions of these spectra within the HiTOP framework. These associations for the triarchic traits shed light on patterns of observed relations of the PCL-R and its factors with clinical conditions of different types, as described earlier. PCL-R Factor 2 relates positively to both substance-related problems and anxious-depressive symptoms because it largely reflects externalizing proneness (disinhibition; Patrick et al., 2005, 2007). Factor 1 relates positively to self-centered narcissism and proactive aggression and negatively

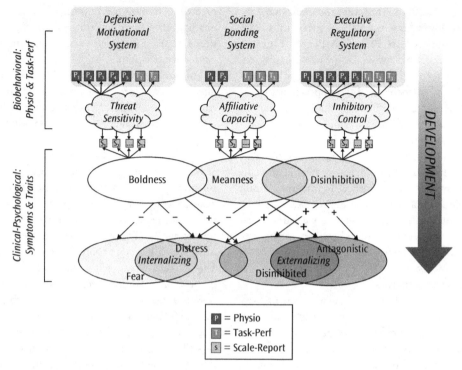

**Figure 30.2** Schematic depiction of a conceptual-empirical framework for interfacing neural systems constructs (defensive motivational, social bonding, and executive regulatory; upper level) with triarchic trait and clinical symptom dimensions (lower level), through use of multimodal representations of biobehavioral traits of threat sensitivity, affiliative capacity, and inhibitory control (middle level). Ovals = triarchic trait and symptom dimensions that can be modeled as latent variables using report-based indicators (scale scores, clinical ratings) with documented covariance patterns. "Cloud" shapes = hypothesized biobehavioral trait dimensions for which provisional indicators from different modalities have been identified (for listings of these indicators, see Table 30.3), but whose covariance patterns need to be fully delineated in order to establish effective latent-variable models. Indicators of target biobehavioral traits from the self-report modality operate also as indicators of latent triarchic factors that link directly to internalizing and externalizing symptom dimensions; unbolded plus or minus sign between triarchic trait and symptom dimension indicates a predictive association ($B$) of $\geq |0.2|$ but not $|0.4|$; bolded plus or minus sign between triarchic trait and symptom dimension indicates a predictive association ($B$) of $\geq |0.4|$. Biobehavioral trait indicators from the physiological and task-performance modalities link directly to neural systems constructs. Conceptualizations of biobehavioral traits will be shaped by accumulating knowledge of covariance patterns among replicable indicators of these traits from different measurement modalities. The right-side arrow denotes the important role of development in this framework, as discussed in the main text.

to both fearful and anxious-depressive symptoms (particularly when controlling for its overlap with Factor 2) due to its selective representation of meanness and boldness, respectively.

### The Triarchic Model as a Framework for Understanding Developmental Pathways and Neurobiological Processes in Psychopathy

As a trait-based framework for psychopathy, the triarchic model connects to other established models of normative and pathological personality traits, which connect in turn to broad symptom dimensions of the HiTOP model (Kotov et al., 2017). The triarchic constructs of boldness, meanness, and disinhibition, as indexed by the TriPM and other scale sets, show clear and robust relations with normative trait inventories such as the MPQ and the NEO PI-R (Drislane et al., 2014; Poy et al., 2014) as well as with maladaptive trait inventories including the PID-5 and the MMPI-2 (Latzman, Tobin et al., 2020; Sellbom et al., 2016; Strickland et al., 2013). However, the broad dimensions of these inventories that appear most related to boldness, meanness, and disinhibition (e.g., neuroticism, agreeableness, and conscientiousness in the NEO PI-R; negative affect, antagonism, and disinhibition in the PID-5) do not correspond directly to the dimensions of the triarchic model, making it necessary to configure lower-level traits of these inventories differently to approximate triarchic disinhibition and meanness more closely (Drislane et al., 2018, 2019; see also

Bowyer et al., 2020). This raises the question: Why configure lower-level traits along triarchic model lines, as opposed to PID-5/AMPD or NEO-PI R/FFM lines? The answer, addressed in this section, is that the triarchic model traits are conceptualized in biobehavioral-developmental terms (Patrick et al., 2009), through direct reference to developmental and biobehavioral research findings, and have nomological networks that include variables from behavioral and neurophysiological as well as self-report and clinical-diagnostic modalities. Importantly, as discussed in the concluding "Neurobiological Systems and Processes" part of this section, the triarchic traits are viewed as open constructs, subject to revision based on accumulating knowledge of their nomological networks.

### Developmental Pathways

Contemporary developmental research on psychopathy has focused on characterizing a distinct subgroup of clinic-referred youth exhibiting conduct problems accompanied by callous-unemotional traits—corresponding to dispositional meanness in the triarchic model. Comparatively little attention has been devoted to externalizing proneness (disinhibition) as a distinct dispositional factor contributing to the emergence and persistence of psychopathic behavior. This is surprising, given the emphasis that has been placed on weak inhibitory (or effortful) control as a risk factor in the developmental psychopathology literature (Kochanska et al., 1997; Rothbart, 2007). Equally surprising is the paucity of work devoted specifically to the study of boldness in the child psychopathy literature, given evidence for a role of fearless temperament in early socialization and conscience development (Kochanska, 1997).

However, recent research on psychopathy in youth has begun to examine how the triarchic traits of disinhibition and boldness contribute to the emergence and expression of conduct problems, relative to and in concert with callous-unemotionality (meanness). An initial study using the TriPM with adolescents aged 16–17 years (Somma et al., 2016) reported similar-level unique associations for all three triarchic traits when entered together as predictors of self-reported engagement in delinquent acts over the preceding year. Another study of 14- to 18-year-olds that used a shortened (approximately half-length) version of the TriPM (Sica et al., 2020) reported significant unique effects for disinhibition and meanness, but not boldness, in predicting self-reported conduct problems over the preceding 6 months. Boldness in this study was related, however, to lower reports of negative emotional states and lesser susceptibility to anxious/depressive symptoms.

An alternative to using established inventories like the TriPM is to construct scale measures of the triarchic traits using construct-relevant items from questionnaires available in already existing datasets. Employing this approach to quantify the triarchic traits in a longitudinal sample, Bertoldi, Perkins et al. (2022) reported comparable unique relations for boldness and disinhibition (but not meanness) assessed at age 14–15 with reported engagement in nonaggressive antisocial acts at age 19–20; meanness at age 14–15, by contrast, emerged as the sole unique predictor of reported aggressive acts at age 19–20. In contrast with their joint positive prediction of later nonaggressive antisociality, boldness and disinhibition at age 14–15 each predicted uniquely, but in opposing directions (– and +, respectively), internalizing symptomatology at age 19–20. These longitudinal study results provide evidence for the triarchic traits as indicators of liability versus immunity to problems of different types and align with findings from cross-sectional work on relations of latent triarchic traits with HiTOP psychopathology dimensions in adults as described in the preceding section.

### Neurobiological Systems and Processes

Variations along psychological trait dimensions have long been viewed as intertwined with variations in neural function (Allport, 1937; Eysenck, 1967). However, observed relations between trait scores and indicators of neural function tend to be small and inconsistent due to conceptual and measurement mismatch. A systematic approach to interfacing neural systems and processes with clinical symptom scores involving the use of multimodal operationalizations of biobehavioral trait constructs has been described by Patrick, Iacono, and Venables (2019). A detailed illustration of this approach was provided by Venables et al. (2018), who specified a multimethod structural model for the biobehavioral construct of inhibitory control—corresponding to the triarchic trait of disinhibition—using indicators from modalities of self-report, task performance, and brain evoked response potential (ERP) response. Expanding upon this illustration, Figure 30.2 depicts different-modality indicators of biobehavioral traits corresponding to all three triarchic constructs (upper part; see Table 30.3 for specific listing of indicators), within a framework

**Table 30.3** Physiological and task performance indicators of biobehavioral traits depicted as counterparts to triarchic psychopathy dimensions in Figure 30.2

| Biobehavioral trait/modality of measurement | Trait indicator (direction of association) | Studies reporting trait-indicator associations | Label within Figure 30.2 |
|---|---|---|---|
| **(Low) Threat Sensitivity** | | | |
| Physiology | Aversive startle potentiation (−) | Anderson et al. (2011); Benning, Patrick et al. (2005); Cook et al. (1992); Dvorak-Bertsch et al. (2009); Esteller et al. (2016); Vaidyanathan et al. (2009); Yancey et al. (2016) | $P_1$ |
| | Skin conductance reactivity (SCR) to aversive images/threat cues (−) | Benning, Patrick et al. (2005); Dindo & Fowles (2011); López et al. (2013); Patrick et al. (2017) | $P_2$ |
| | Heart rate (HR) reactivity to aversive images/sounds (−) | Cook et al. (1992); Kyranides et al. (2017); Yancey et al. (2016) | $P_3$ |
| | Resting heart rate (HR) level (−) | Bertoldi, Tuvblad et al. (in press); Kyranides et al. (2017); Strickland et al. (2015) | $P_4$ |
| | Late-positive potential (LPP) brain response to aversive images (−) | Ellis et al. (2017); Medina et al. (2016); Weinberg et al. (2012) | $P_5$ |
| Task Performance | | | |
| | Risk taking (+) → Various tasks, including Balloon Analog Risk Task (Lejuez et al., 2002) | Snowdon et al. (2017); Wake et al. (2020) | $T_6$ |
| | Cognitive task performance during threat-cueing (+) | Yancey et al. (2019, 2022) | $T_7$ |
| **(Low) Affiliative Capacity** | | | |
| Physiology | Amygdala reactivity to fearful faces (−) | Jones et al. (2009); Marsh et al. (2008); Viding et al. (2012); White et al. (2012) | $P_1$ |
| | Early (N170, P200) brain-evoked response potential (ERP) reactivity to fearful faces (−) | Brislin et al. (2018); Brislin & Patrick (2019); Palumbo et al. (2020)a | $P_2$ |
| Task Performance | | | |
| | Recognition accuracy for negative emotional (especially fear) faces (−) | Brislin et al. (2018); Marsh & Blair (2008); Muñoz (2009); Petitclerc et al. (2019) | $T_1$ |
| | Visual attention toward eye region of fear faces (−) | Dadds et al. (2006, 2008, 2011); Dargis et al. (2018); Gillespie et al. (2015) | $T_2$ |
| | Physical pain tolerance (+) | Brislin et al. (2016, 2022); Miller, Rausher et al. (2014) | $T_3$ |
| **(Low) Inhibitory Control** | | | |
| Physiology | | | |
| | Oddball task P3 brain response (−) | Bowyer et al. (2020); Nelson et al. (2011); Venables et al. (2018); Yancey et al. (2013) | $P_1$ |

*(continued)*

**Table 30.3** Continued

| Biobehavioral trait/modality of measurement | Trait indicator (direction of association) | Studies reporting trait-indicator associations | Label within Figure 30.2 |
|---|---|---|---|
| | Flanker task P3 brain response (−) | Nelson et al. (2011); Venables et al. (2018); Ribes-Guardiola et al. (2020) | $P_2$ |
| | Feedback task P3 brain response (−) | Nelson et al. (2011); Venables et al. (2018) | $P_3$ |
| | Go/No-Go task P3 brain response (−) | Delfin et al. (2020); Brennan & Baskin-Sommers (2018)[b]; Ribes-Guardiola et al. (2020) | $P_4$ |
| | Go/No error-related negativity brain response (+ = less negative) | Hall et al. (2007); Ribes-Guardiola et al. (2020) | $P_5$ |
| Task Performance | | | |
| | Antisaccade task accuracy (−) | Venables et al. (2018); Young et al. (2009) | $T_1$ |
| | Go/No-Go task performance (−) | Venables et al. (2018); Brennan & Baskin-Sommers (2018) | $T_2$ |
| | Stroop task incongruent-trial reaction time (+) | Venables et al. (2018); Young et al. (2009) | $T_3$ |

*Note*: Trait indicators listed are ones for which associations have been demonstrated in two or more studies employing different participant samples. Directions of associations for indicators (+ = positive; − = negative) are with biobehavioral traits *in reverse* (such that they correspond to boldness, meanness, and disinhibition), as assessed by informant-rating (Dargis et al., 2018; Jones et al., 2009; Marsh et al., 2008; Petitclerc et al., 2019; White et al., 2012) or self-report (all other studies except Dadds et al., 2006, 2008, 2011, and Young et al., 2009, which used informant-rating and self-report measures combined).

[a] The sample for this study (Palumbo et al., 2020) subsumed that employed by Brislin et al. (2018), but reported new evidence for reduced early brain-ERP reactivity to fearful faces in a different task paradigm.

[b] The task used in this study (Brennan & Baskin-Sommers, 2018) was a "modified oddball" task, characterized by the authors as "similar to a go/no-go task in terms of instructions, stimuli frequency, and behavioral measures" (p. 73).

for interfacing neural systems with HiTOP psychopathology dimensions (lower part).

A more detailed discussion of the framework depicted in Figure 30.2 can be found in other published works (e.g., Patrick & Drislane, 2015; Patrick, Durbin, & Moser, 2012; Patrick, Iacono et al., 2019; Patrick, Venables et al., 2013). However, some specific points warrant mention. One is that multiple scale sets exist for operationalizing biobehavioral traits corresponding to boldness, disinhibition, and meanness in the modality of self-report (see numbered citations in the figure). Some of these consist of items from psychopathy inventories or omnibus personality questionnaires; others are composed of items taken from different questionnaire measures included in specialized existing datasets. These various scale sets have been created using the construct-rating protocol introduced by Hall et al. (2014) and validated against one another and in relation to pertinent criterion variables (including clinical outcomes) to establish consistency of measurement (i.e., harmonization; Hussong et al., 2013). The availability of these alternative scale sets provides a means to extend what we know about neurophysiological and task-behavioral indicators of key biobehavioral constructs and establish formal multimodal measurement models for these constructs through use of existing large-scale datasets—including etiologically informative (e.g., twin, longitudinal) datasets (Patrick, Iacono et al., 2019).

A second point is that self-report indicators of biobehavioral traits are intended to serve only as provisional referents for identifying candidate indicators from other modalities (e.g., lab-task performance, brain physiology), in order to establish multimodal measurement models of these traits (Patrick, Iacono et al., 2019). Self-report measures of traits are convenient and effective as referents because they can be constructed using different item sets to be indicative of specific psychological content, psychometrically reliable, and harmonized in terms of their convergence with one another and their relations with external criterion measures. Brislin et al. (2019) illustrated this by developing a scale measure of disinhibition using items from the European IMAGEN dataset and, employing data for a separate sample, showing that it correlated highly with a previously validated disinhibition scale and comparably well with an established neural indicator of disinhibition (oddball P3 response). The view of self-report scales as provisional indicators connects in turn to the idea of biobehavioral traits as open constructs that can be refined or reshaped based on empirical findings. Venables et al. (2018) illustrated this idea by specifying a structural model in which measures from three modalities (self-report, task performance, brain response) loaded onto lower-order modality factors, which loaded in turn onto a common higher-order factor reflecting cross-modal inhibitory control. A shift in the construct being measured—away from the modality of self-report—was evidenced by a smaller loading of the self-report modality factor onto the higher-order factor compared to loadings for the behavioral and brain modality factors.

A further key point is that the framework depicted in Figure 30.2 includes a developmental component, depicted by the downward pointing arrow on the right side. The literature on temperament indicates that traits are moderately stable across time but affected by maturation and ongoing environmental events that impact psychobiological function (Bornstein et al., 2015; Kopala-Sibley et al., 2018). The types of measures that can be used to index traits also vary across time. For example, self-report measures cannot be used with very young children, and tasks suitable for assessing behavioral and brain response often differ across age levels. Also, physiological or behavioral measures that relate concurrently to trait levels or clinical symptoms may not exhibit relations prospectively if they reflect dysfunctional states or persisting consequences of dysfunction, as opposed to dispositional liability (Perkins et al., 2020). We believe these complexities in characterizing the nature of biobehavioral risk for mental health problems, and pathways from risk to symptom expression in differing forms, can ultimately be addressed through systematic collaborative efforts along coordinated lines. Researchers dedicated to the scientific study of psychopathy are encouraged to benefit from and contribute to this broader mission in ways highlighted within this chapter.

## Conclusion

Despite decades of vigorous research, progress in the field of psychopathy has been hampered by persisting disagreement about how this clinical condition should be defined and measured. Various interview and self-report measures have been developed to index psychopathy in diverse participant samples (e.g., forensic, clinical, community, youth, etc.), each grounded—in differing respects and to varying degrees—in historic descriptions of psychopathy in psychiatric patients (e.g., Cleckley, 1976) and criminal offenders (e.g., McCord & McCord, 1964). Research on the psychological, clinical-diagnostic, and neurobiological correlates of psychopathy as assessed by these measures has revealed contrasting patterns of associations for distinct symptom subdimensions (factors or facets) of each. The triarchic model (Patrick et al., 2009) posits that trait constructs of disinhibition, boldness, and meanness, represented in alternative measures for assessing psychopathy, can account for these contrasting patterns of associations because they reflect distinct biobehavioral constructs of deficient inhibitory control, weak affiliative capacity, and low threat sensitivity, respectively. Importantly, the triarchic traits are viewed as "open constructs" that are not tied to any specific manifest measure and thus can be quantified using different items sets.

A growing body of work has sought to develop scale measures of the triarchic traits using items from preexisting psychopathy inventories, normative and maladaptive personality inventories, and other item sets available in etiologically informative (twin, longitudinal) studies. Following upon these efforts, recent studies have modeled the triarchic trait constructs as latent variables using alternative scale sets as indicators. The triarchic traits are represented in the dimensional model for PDs in the *DSM-5*, through traits from domains of antagonism and disinhibition, and a "psychopathic features" specifier that indexes boldness. Progress has also been made toward interfacing the triarchic traits with a broader dimensional system for psychopathology as a whole, the HiTOP model. Finally, given that the triarchic traits were explicitly framed in biobehavioral-developmental terms, increasing efforts are being made to examine their relations with clinical outcomes of various types across development and to identify replicable brain and behavioral indicators of each that can be integrated into multimodal measurement models. Growing knowledge of the triarchic traits' nomological networks, combined with recent advances in latent variable modeling and data harmonization and the availability of triarchic scale measures in etiologically informative datasets, provides rich opportunities for further understanding the etiological bases of psychopathy and refining methods for preventing and treating it.

## Acknowledgments

Support for preparation of this chapter, and work featured in it, was provided by grants MH65137 and MH089727 from the National Institute of Mental Health and grant W911NF-14-1-0018 from the US Army. The content of this paper is solely the responsibility of the authors and does not necessarily represent the official views of the US Government, Department of Defense, Department of the Army, Department of Veterans Affairs, or US Recruiting Command.

## References

Achenbach, T. M. (1991). *Manual for the Child Behavior Checklist/4-18 and 1991 profile*. University of Vermont, Department of Psychiatry.

Achenbach, T. M., & Edelbrock, C. S. (1978). The classification of child psychopathology: A review and analysis of empirical efforts. *Psychological Bulletin, 85*, 1275–1301.

Achenbach, T. M., & Rescorla, L. A. (2001). Manual for the ASEBA School-Age Forms & Profiles. University of Vermont, Research Center for Children, Youth, & Families.

Achenbach, T. M., & Rescorla, L. A. (2003). *Manual for the ASEBA Adult Forms & Profiles*. University of Vermont, Research Center for Children, Youth, & Families.

Alexander, L. M., Escalera, J., Ai, L., Andreotti, C., Febre, K., Mangone, A., . . . Litke, S. (2017). An open resource for transdiagnostic research in pediatric mental health and learning disorders. *Scientific Data, 4*, 170–181.

Allport, G. W. (1937). *Personality: A psychological interpretation*. Holt.

Andershed, H., Kerr, M., Stattin, H., & Levander, S. (2002). Psychopathic traits in non-referred youths: A new assessment tool. In E. Blau & L. Sheridan (Eds.), *Psychopaths: Current international perspectives* (pp. 131–158). Elsevier.

Anderson, J., Sellbom, M., Wygant, D. B., Salekin, R. T., & Krueger, R. F. (2014). Examining the associations between DSM-5 Section III antisocial personality disorder traits and psychopathy in community and university samples. *Journal of Personality Disorders, 28*, 675–694.

Anderson, N. E., Stanford, M. S., Wan, L., & Young, K. A. (2011). High psychopathic trait females exhibit reduced startle potentiation and increased P3 amplitude. *Behavioral Sciences & the Law, 29*, 649–666.

Archer, R. P., Handel, R. W., Ben-Porath, Y. S., & Tellegen, A. (2016). *Minnesota Multiphasic Personality Inventory-Adolescent Restructured Form: Administration, scoring, interpretation, and technical manual*. University of Minnesota Press.

Arieti, S. (1963). Psychopathic personality: Some views on its psychopathology and psychodynamics. *Comprehensive Psychiatry, 4*, 301–312.

Arnett, P. A. (1997). Autonomic responsivity in psychopaths: A critical review and theoretical proposal. *Clinical Psychology Review, 17*, 903–936.

Baker, L. A., Tuvblad, C., Wang, P., Gomez, K., Bezdjian, S., Niv, S., & Raine, A. (2013). The Southern California Twin Register at the University of Southern California: III. *Twin Research and Human Genetics, 16*, 336–343.

Bauer, L. O., O'Connor, S., & Hesselbrock, V. M. (1994). Frontal P300 decrements in antisocial personality disorder. *Alcoholism: Clinical and Experimental Research, 18*, 1300–1305.

Ben-Porath, Y. S., & Tellegen, A. (2008). *Minnesota Multiphasic Personality Inventory-2 Restructured Form: Manual for administration, scoring, and interpretation*. University of Minnesota Press.

Benning, S. D., Patrick, C. J., Blonigen, D. M., Hicks, B. M., & Iacono, W. G. (2005). Estimating facets of psychopathy from normal personality traits: A step toward community-epidemiological investigations. *Assessment, 12*, 3–18.

Benning, S. D., Patrick, C. J., Hicks, B. M., Blonigen, D. M., & Krueger, R. F. (2003). Factor structure of the Psychopathic Personality Inventory: Validity and implications for clinical assessment. *Psychological Assessment, 15*, 340–350.

Benning, S. D., Patrick, C. J., & Iacono, W. G. (2005). Psychopathy, startle blink modulation, and electrodermal reactivity in twin men. *Psychophysiology, 42*, 753–762.

Bertoldi, B. M., Perkins, E. R., Tuvblad, C., Oskarsson, S., Kramer, M. D., Latzman, R. D., . . . Patrick, C. J. (2022). Pursuing the developmental aims of the triarchic model of psychopathy: Creation and validation of triarchic trait scales for use in the USC-RFAB longitudinal twin project. *Development and Psychopathology, 34*, 1088–1103.

Bertoldi, B. M., Tuvblad, C., Joyner, K. J., Ganley, C. M., Raine, A., Baker, L. A., Latvala, A., & Patrick, C. J. (2022). Role of triarchic traits in relations of early resting heart rate with antisocial behavior and broad psychopathology dimensions in later life. *Clinical Psychological Science*. doi:10.1177/21677026221081880

Bilder, R. M., Howe, A. G., & Sabb, F. W. (2013). Multilevel models from biology to psychology: Mission impossible? *Journal of Abnormal Psychology, 122*, 917–927.

Birbaumer, N., Veit, R., Lotze, M., Erb, M., Hermann, C., Grodd, W., & Flor, H. (2005). Deficient fear conditioning in psychopathy: A functional magnetic resonance imaging study. *Archives of General Psychiatry, 62*, 799–805.

Birmaher, B., Brent, D. A., Chiappetta, L., Bridge, J., Monga, S., & Baugher, M. (1999). Psychometric properties of the Screen for Child Anxiety Related Emotional Disorders (SCARED): A replication study. *Journal of the American Academy of Child & Adolescent Psychiatry, 38*, 1230–1236.

Blackburn, R. (2006). Other theoretical models of psychopathy. In C. J. Patrick (Ed.), *Handbook of psychopathy* (pp. 35–57). Guilford.

Blair, R. J. R. (2006). Subcortical brain systems in psychopathy: The amygdala and associated structures. In C. J. Patrick (Ed.), *Handbook of psychopathy* (pp. 296–312). Guilford.

Block, J. H., & Block, J. (1980). The role of ego-control and ego resiliency in the organization of behavior. In W. A. Collins (Ed.), *Development of cognition, affect, and social relations: The Minnesota symposium on child psychology* (vol. 13, pp. 39–101). Lawrence Erlbaum.

Blonigen, D. M., Hicks, B., Krueger, R., Patrick, C. J., & Iacono, W. (2005). Psychopathic personality traits: Heritability and genetic overlap with internalizing and externalizing pathology. *Psychological Medicine, 35*, 637–648.

Bornstein, M. H., Putnick, D. L., Gartstein, M. A., Hahn, C. S., Auestad, N., & O'Connor, D. L. (2015). Infant temperament: Stability by age, gender, birth order, term status, and socioeconomic status. *Child Development, 86*, 844–863.

Bowyer, C. B., Joyner, K. J., Latzman, R. D., Venables, N. C., Foell, J., & Patrick, C. J. (2020). A model-based strategy for interfacing trait domains of the DSM-5 AMPD with neurobiology. *Journal of Personality Disorders, 34*, 586–608.

Brennan, G. M., & Baskin-Sommers, A. R. (2018). Brain-behavior relationships in externalizing: P3 amplitude reduction reflects deficient inhibitory control. *Behavioral Brain Research, 337*, 70–79.

Brislin, S. J., Buchman-Schmitt, J. M., Joiner, T. E., & Patrick, C. J. (2016). "Do unto others?": Distinct psychopathy facets predict reduced perception and tolerance of pain. *Personality Disorders: Theory, Research, and Treatment, 7*, 240–246.

Brislin, S. J., Drislane, L. E., Smith, S. T., Edens, J. F., & Patrick, C. J. (2015). Development and validation of triarchic psychopathy scales from the Multidimensional Personality Questionnaire. *Psychological Assessment, 27*(3), 838–851.

Brislin, S. J., & Patrick, C. J. (2019). Callousness and affective face processing: Clarifying the neural basis of behavioral-recognition deficits through use of brain ERPs. *Clinical Psychological Science, 7*, 1389–1402.

Brislin, S. J., Patrick, C. J., Flor, H., Nees, F., Heinrich, A., Drislane, L. E., . . . Foell, J. (2019). Extending the construct network of trait disinhibition to the neuroimaging domain: Validation of a bridging scale for use in the European IMAGEN project. *Assessment, 26*, 567–581.

Brislin, S. J., Perkins, E. R., Ribes-Guardiola, P., Patrick, C. J., & Foell, J. (2022). Pain processing and antisocial behavior: A multi-modal investigation of the roles of boldness and meanness. *Personality Disorders: Theory, Research, and Treatment.* doi: doi.org/10.1037/per0000556

Brislin, S. J., Yancey, J. R., Perkins, E. R., Palumbo, I. M., Drislane, L. E., Salekin, R. T., . . . Patrick, C. J. (2018). Callousness and affective face processing in adults: Behavioral and brain-potential indicators. *Personality Disorders: Theory, Research, and Treatment, 9*, 122–132.

Buckholtz, J. W., Treadway, M. T., Cowan, R. L., Woodward, N. D., Benning, S. D., Li R., et al. (2010). Mesolimbic dopamine reward system hypersensitivity in individuals with psychopathic traits. *Nature Neuroscience, 13*, 419–421.

Carlson, S. R., Thái, S., & McLaron, M. E. (2009). Visual P3 amplitude and self-reported psychopathic personality traits: Frontal reduction is associated with self-centered impulsivity. *Psychophysiology, 46*, 100–113.

Clark, L. A. (1993). *Schedule for Nonadaptive and Adaptive Personality (SNAP). Manual for administration, scoring, and interpretation.* University of Minnesota Press.

Cleckley, H. (1941/1976). *The mask of sanity*, 5th ed. Mosby.

Cloninger, C. R., Przybeck, T. R. & Svrakic, D. M. (1999). *The Temperament and Character Inventory—Revised.* Center for Psychobiology of Personality, Washington University.

Colins, O. F., Andershed, H., Frogner, L. Lopez-Romero, L., Veen, V., & Andershed, A-K. (2014). A new measure to assess psychopathic personality in children: The Child Problematic Traits Inventory. *Journal of Psychopathology and Behavioral Assessment, 36*, 4–21.

Constantino, J. N., & Gruber, C. P. (2005). *Social Responsiveness Scale (SRS).* Western Psychological Services.

Cook, E. W., Davis, T. L., Hawk, L. W., Spence, E. L., & Gautier, C. H. (1992). Fearfulness and startle potentiation during aversive visual stimuli. *Psychophysiology, 29*, 633–645.

Cooke, D. J., & Michie, C. (2001). Refining the construct of psychopathy: Towards a hierarchical model. *Psychological Assessment, 13*, 171–188.

Costa, P. T., Jr, & McCrae, R. R. (1992). *Revised NEO Personality Inventory (NEO PI-R) and NEO Five-Factor Inventory (NEO-FFI) professional manual.* Psychological Assessment Resources.

Craft, M. (1966). *Psychopathic disorders and their assessment.* Pergamon.

Crego, C., & Widiger, T. (2016). Cleckley's psychopaths: Revisited. *Journal of Abnormal Psychology, 125*, 75–87.

Dadds, M. R., El Masry, Y., Wimalaweera, S., & Guastella, A. J. (2008). Reduced eye gaze explains "fear blindness" in childhood psychopathic traits. *Journal of the American Academy of Child and Adolescent Psychiatry, 47*, 455–463.

Dadds, M. R., Jambrak, J., Pasalich, D., Hawes, D. H., & Brennan, J. (2011). Impaired attention to the eyes of attachment figures and the developmental origins of psychopathy. *Journal of Child Psychology and Psychiatry, 52*, 238–245.

Dadds, M. R., Perry, Y., Hawes, D. J., Merz, S., Riddell, A. C., Haines, D. J., Solak, E., & Abeygunawardane, A. I. (2006). Attention to the eyes and fear-recognition deficits in child psychopathy. *British Journal of Psychiatry, 189*, 280–281.

Dargis, M., Wolf, R. C., & Koenigs, M. (2018). Psychopathic traits are associated with reduced fixations to the eye region of fearful faces. *Journal of Abnormal Psychology, 127*, 43–50.

Delfin, C., Ruzich, E., Wallinius, M., Björnsdotter, M., & Andiné, P. (2020). Trait disinhibition and NoGo event-related potentials in violent mentally disordered offenders and healthy controls. *Frontiers in Psychiatry, 11*, 577491. doi:10.3389/fpsyt.2020.577491

Dindo, L., & Fowles, D. C. (2011). Dual temperamental risk factors for psychopathic personality: Evidence from self-report and skin conductance. *Journal of Personality and Social Psychology, 100*, 557–566.

Drislane, L. E., Brislin, S. J., Jones, S., & Patrick, C. J. (2018). Interfacing five-factor model and triarchic conceptualizations of psychopathy. *Psychological Assessment, 30*, 834–840.

Drislane, L. E., Brislin, S. J., Kendler, K. S., Andershed, H., Larsson, H., & Patrick, C. J. (2015). A triarchic model analysis of the Youth Psychopathic Traits Inventory. *Journal of Personality Disorders, 29*, 15–41.

Drislane, L. E., & Patrick, C. J. (2017). Integrating alternative conceptions of psychopathic personality: A latent variable model of triarchic psychopathy constructs. *Journal of Personality Disorders, 31*, 110–132.

Drislane, L. E., Patrick, C. J., & Arsal, G. (2014). Clarifying the content coverage of differing psychopathy inventories through reference to the Triarchic Psychopathy Measure. *Psychological Assessment, 26*, 350–362.

Drislane, L. E., Sellbom, M., Brislin, S. J., Strickland, C. M., Christian, E., Wygant, D. B, Krueger, R. F., & Patrick, C. J. (2019). Improving characterization of psychopathy within the alternative model for personality disorders in the Diagnostic and Statistical Manual of Mental Disorders, Fifth Edition (DSM-5): Creation and validation of Personality Inventory for DSM-5 triarchic scales. *Personality Disorders: Theory, Research, and Treatment, 10*, 511–523.

Drislane, L. E., Sica, C., Colpizzi, I., Lowman, K. L., Joyner, K. J., Bottesi, G., & Patrick, C. J. (2022). Latent variable model of triarchic psychopathy constructs in an incarcerated offender sample: Factor reliability and validity. *Psychological Assessment*. doi: 10.1037/pas0001158

Dvorak-Bertsch. J. D., Curtin, J., Rubinstein, T., & Newman, J. P. (2009). Psychopathic traits moderate the interaction between cognitive and affective processing. *Psychophysiology, 46*, 913–921.

Ellis, J. D., Schroder, H. S., Moser, J. S., & Patrick, C. J. (2017). Emotional reactivity and regulation in individuals with psychopathic traits: Evidence for a disconnect between neurophysiology and self-report. *Psychophysiology, 54*, 1574–1585.

Esteller, À., Poy, R., & Moltó, J. (2016). Deficient aversive-potentiated startle and the triarchic model of psychopathy: The role of boldness. *Biological Psychology, 117*, 131–140.

Eysenck, H. J. (1967). *The biological basis of personality*. Charles C. Thomas.

Farrington, D. (2006). Family background and psychopathy. In C. J. Patrick (Ed.), *Handbook of psychopathy* (pp. 229–250). Guilford.

Forth, A. E., Kosson, D. S., & Hare, R. D. (2003). *The Psychopathy Checklist: Youth version manual*. Multi-Health Systems.

Fowles, D. C. (1980). The three arousal model: Implications of Gray's two-factor learning theory for heart rate, electrodermal activity, and psychopathy. *Psychophysiology, 17*, 87–104.

Fowles, D. C., & Dindo, L. (2009). Temperament and psychopathy: A dual-pathway model. *Current Directions in Psychological Science, 18*, 179–183.

Frances, A. J. (1980). The DSM-III personality disorders section: A commentary. *American Journal of Psychiatry, 137*, 1050–1054.

Frick, P. J. (2004). *The Inventory of Callous-Unemotional Traits. Unpublished rating scale*. University of New Orleans.

Frick, P. J., Boden, D. S., & Barry, C. T. (2000). Psychopathic traits and conduct problems in community and clinic-referred samples of children: Further development of the Psychopathy Screening Device. *Psychological Assessment, 12*, 382–393.

Frick, P. J., & Dickens, C. (2006). Current perspectives on conduct disorder. *Current Psychiatry Reports, 8*, 59–72.

Frick, P. J., & Hare, R. D. (2001). *The Antisocial Process Screening Device (APSD)*. Multi-Health Systems.

Frick, P. J., Lilienfeld, S. O., Ellis, M., Loney, B., & Silverthorn P. (1999). The association between anxiety and psychopathy dimensions in children. *Journal of Abnormal Child Psychology, 27*, 383–392.

Frick, P. J., & Marsee, M. A. (2006). Psychopathy and developmental pathways to antisocial behavior in youth. In C. J. Patrick (Ed.), *Handbook of psychopathy* (pp. 353–374). Guilford.

Frick, P. J., & Marsee, M. A. (2018). Psychopathy and developmental pathways to antisocial behavior in youth. In C. J. Patrick (Ed.), *Handbook of psychopathy*, 2nd ed. (pp. 456–475). Guilford.

Frick, P. J., O'Brien, B. S., Wooten, J. M., & McBurnett, K. (1994). Psychopathy and conduct problems in children. *Journal of Abnormal Psychology, 103*, 700–707.

Frick, P. J., Ray, J. V., Thornton, L. C., & Kahn, R. E. (2014). Can callous-unemotional traits enhance the understanding, diagnosis, and treatment of serious conduct problems in children and adolescents? A comprehensive review. *Psychological Bulletin, 140*, 1–57.

Frick, P. J., & White, S. F. (2008). The importance of callous-unemotional traits for developmental models of aggressive and antisocial behavior. *Journal of Child Psychology and Psychiatry, 49*, 359–375.

Friedman, H. S., Kern, M. L., Hampson, S. E., & Duckworth, A. L. (2014). A new life-span approach to conscientiousness and health: Combining the pieces of the causal puzzle. *Developmental Psychology, 50*, 1377–1389.

Gao, Y., Raine, A., & Schug, R. A. (2011). P3 event-related potentials and childhood maltreatment in successful and unsuccessful psychopaths. *Brain and Cognition, 77*, 176–182.

Gerbrandij, J., Bernstein, D. P., Drislane, L. E., de Vogel, V., Lancel, M., & Patrick, C. J. (2019). Examining triarchic psychopathy constructs in a Dutch forensic treatment sample using a forensic version of the Schedule for Nonadaptive and Adaptive Personality. *Journal of Psychopathology and Behavioral Assessment, 41*, 384–399.

Gillespie, S. M., Rotshtein, P., Wells, L. J., Beech, A. R., & Mitchell, I. J. (2015). Psychopathic traits are associated with reduced attention to the eyes of emotional faces among adult male non-offenders. *Frontiers in Human Neuroscience, 9*, 552. doi:10.3389/fnhum.2015.00552

Goodman, R. (2001). Psychometric properties of the strengths and difficulties questionnaire. *Journal of the American Academy of Child & Adolescent Psychiatry, 40*, 1337–1345.

Gordon, H. L., Baird, A. A., & End, A. (2004). Functional differences among those high and low on a trait measure of psychopathy. *Biological Psychiatry, 56*, 516–521.

Gorenstein, E. E., & Newman, J. P. (1980). Disinhibitory psychopathology: A new perspective and a model for research. *Psychological Review, 87*, 301–315.

Hall, J., Benning, S. D., & Patrick, C. J. (2004). Criterion-related validity of the three-factor model of psychopathy: Personality, behavior, and adaptive functioning. *Assessment, 11*, 4–16.

Hall, J. R., Bernat, E. M., & Patrick, C. J. (2007). Externalizing psychopathology and the error-related negativity. *Psychological Science, 18*, 326–333.

Hall, J. R., Drislane, L. E., Morano, M., Patrick, C. J., Lilienfeld, S. O., & Poythress, N. G. (2014). Development and validation of triarchic construct scales from the Psychopathic Personality Inventory. *Psychological Assessment, 26*, 447–461.

Hare, R. D. (1978). Electrodermal and cardiovascular correlates of psychopathy. In R. D. Hare & D. Schalling (Eds.), *Psychopathic behavior: Approaches to research* (pp. 107–143). Wiley.

Hare, R. D. (1980). A research scale for the assessment of psychopathy in criminal populations. *Personality and Individual Differences, 1*, 111–119.

Hare, R. D. (1983). Diagnosis of antisocial personality disorder in two prison populations. *American Journal of Psychiatry, 140*, 887–890.

Hare, R. D. (1991). *The Hare Psychopathy Checklist-Revised*. Multi-Health Systems.

Hare, R. D. (2003). *The Hare Psychopathy Checklist—Revised*, 2nd ed. Multi-Health Systems.

Hare, R. D., Harpur, T. J., Hakstian, A. R., Forth, A. E., Hart, S. D., & Newman, J. P. (1990). The Revised Psychopathy Checklist: Reliability and factor structure. *Psychological Assessment, 2*, 338–341.

Hare, R. D., & Neumann, C. S (2006). The PCL-R assessment of psychopathy: Development, structural properties, and new directions. In C. J. Patrick (Ed.), *Handbook of psychopathy* (pp. 58–88). Guilford.

Harenski, C. L., Kim, S., & Hamann, S. (2009). Neuroticism and psychopathic traits predict brain activity during moral and non-moral emotion regulation. *Cognitive, Affective, and Behavioral Neuroscience, 9*, 1–15.

Harpur, T. J., Hakstian, A. R., & Hare, R. D. (1988). Factor structure of the psychopathy checklist. *Journal of Consulting and Clinical Psychology, 56*, 741–747.

Harpur, T. J., Hare, R. D., & Hakstian, A. R. (1989). Two-factor conceptualization of psychopathy: Construct validity and assessment implications. *Psychological Assessment, 1*, 6–17.

Hart, S., Cox, D., & Hare, R. D. (1995). *Manual for the Psychopathy Checklist: Screening version (PCL:SV)*. Multi-Health Systems.

Hart, S. D., & Hare, R. D. (1989). Discriminant validity of the Psychopathy Checklist in a forensic psychiatric population. *Psychological Assessment, 1*, 211–218.

Herpertz, S. C., Werth, U., Lukas, G., Qunaibi, M., Schuerkens, A., Kunert, H., Freese, R., Flesch, M., Mueller-Isberner, R., Osterheider, M., & Sass, H. (2001). Emotion in criminal offenders with psychopathy and borderline personality disorder. *Archives of General Psychiatry, 58*, 737–744.

Hicks, B. M., Markon, K. E., Patrick, C. J., Krueger, R. F., & Newman, J. P. (2004). Identifying psychopathy subtypes on the basis of personality structure. *Psychological Assessment, 16*, 276–288.

Hicks, B. M., & Patrick, C. J. (2006). Psychopathy and negative affectivity: Analyses of suppressor effects reveal distinct relations with trait anxiety, depression, fearfulness, and anger-hostility. *Journal of Abnormal Psychology, 115*, 276–287.

Hildebrand, M., & de Ruiter, C. (2004). PCL-R psychopathy and its relation to DSM-IV Axis I and Axis II disorders in a sample of male forensic psychiatric patients in the Netherlands. *International Journal of Law and Psychiatry, 24*, 233–248.

Hopwood, C. J., & Donnellan, M. B. (2010). How should the internal structure of personality inventories be evaluated? *Personality and Social Psychology Review, 14*, 332–346.

Hopwood, C. J., Thomas, K. M., Markon, K., Wright, A. G. C., & Krueger, R. F. (2012). DSM-5 personality traits and DSM-IV personality disorders. *Journal of Abnormal Psychology, 121*, 424–432.

Horney, K. (1945). *Our inner conflicts*. W. W. Norton.

Hussong, A. M., Curran, P. J., & Bauer, D. J. (2013). Integrative data analysis in clinical psychology research. *Annual Review of Clinical Psychology, 9*, 61–89.

Ishikawa, S. S., Raine, A., Lencz, T., Bihrle, S., & Lacasse, L. (2001). Autonomic stress reactivity and executive functions in successful and unsuccessful criminal psychopaths from the community. *Journal of Abnormal Psychology, 110*, 423–432.

Jones, A. P., Laurens, K. R., Herba, C. M., Barker, G. J., & Viding, E. (2009). Amygdala hypoactivity to fearful faces in boys with conduct problems and callous-unemotional traits. *American Journal of Psychiatry, 166*, 95–102.

Karpman, B. (1941). On the need for separating psychopathy into two distinct clinical types: Symptomatic and idiopathic. *Journal of Criminology and Psychopathology, 3*, 112–137.

Kendler, K. S., Aggen, S. H., & Patrick, C. J. (2012). A multivariate twin study of the DSM-IV criteria for antisocial personality disorder. *Biological Psychiatry, 71*, 247–253.

Keulen-de-Vos, M., Bernstein, D. P., Clark, L. A., Arntz, A., Lucker, T. C., & de Spa, E. (2011). Patient versus informant reports of personality disorders in forensic patients. *Journal of Forensic Psychiatry & Psychology, 22*, 52–71.

Kobasa, C. S. (1979). Stressful life events, personality, and health: An inquiry into hardiness. *Journal of Personality and Social Psychology, 37*, 1–11.

Koch, J. L. (1891). *Die psychopathischen Minderwertigkeiten.* Maier.

Kochanska, G., Murray, K., & Coy, K. C. (1997). Inhibitory control as a contributor to conscience in childhood: From toddler to early school age. *Child Development, 68*, 263–267.

Kochanska, G. K. (1997). Multiple pathways to conscience for children with different temperaments: From toddlerhood to age 5. *Developmental Psychology, 33*, 228–240.

Kopala-Sibley, D. C., Olino, T., Durbin, E., Dyson, M. W., & Klein, D. N. (2018). The stability of temperament from early childhood to early adolescence: A multi-method, multi-informant examination. *European Journal of Personality, 32*, 128–145.

Kosson, D. S., Smith, S. S., & Newman, J. P. (1990). Evaluating the construct validity of psychopathy in African American and European American male inmates: Three preliminary studies. *Journal of Abnormal Psychology, 99*, 250–259.

Kotov, R., Krueger, R. F., Watson, D., Achenbach, T. M., Althoff, R. R., Bagby, R. M., . . . Zimmerman, M. (2017). The Hierarchical Taxonomy of Psychopathology (HiTOP): A dimensional alternative to traditional nosologies. *Journal of Abnormal Psychology, 126*, 454–477.

Kraepelin, E. (1915). *Psychiatrie: Ein Lehrbuch*, 8th ed. Barth.

Kramer, M. D., Patrick, C. J., Krueger, R. F., & Gasperi, M. (2012). Delineating physiological defensive reactivity in the domain of self-report: Phenotypic and etiologic structure of dispositional fear. *Psychological Medicine, 42*, 1305–1320.

Krueger, R. F. (1999a). Personality traits in late adolescence predict mental disorders in early adulthood: A prospective-epidemiological study. *Journal of Personality, 67*, 39–65.

Krueger, R. F. (1999b). The structure of common mental disorders. *Archives of General Psychiatry, 56*, 921–926.

Krueger, R. F., Hobbs, K. A., Conway, C. C., Dick, D. M., Dretsch, M. N., Eaton, N. R., . . . HiTOP Utility Workgroup. (2021). Validity and utility of Hierarchical Taxonomy of Psychopathology (HiTOP): II. Externalizing superspectrum. *World Psychiatry, 20*, 171–193.

Krueger, R. F., Derringer, J., Markon, K. E., Watson, D., & Skodol, A. E. (2012). Initial construction of a maladaptive personality trait model and inventory for DSM-5. *Psychological Medicine, 42*, 1879–1890.

Krueger, R. F., Hicks, B., Patrick, C. J., Carlson, S., Iacono, W. G., & McGue, M. (2002). Etiologic connections among substance dependence, antisocial behavior, and personality: Modeling the externalizing spectrum. *Journal of Abnormal Psychology, 111*, 411–424.

Krueger, R. F., Markon, K. E., Patrick, C. J., Benning, S. D., & Kramer, M. (2007). Linking antisocial behavior, substance use, and personality: An integrative quantitative model of the adult externalizing spectrum. *Journal of Abnormal Psychology, 116*, 645–666.

Kyranides, M. N., Fanti, K., Sikki, M., & Patrick, C. J. (2017). Triarchic dimensions of psychopathy in young adulthood: Associations with clinical and physiological measures after accounting for adolescent psychopathic traits. *Personality Disorders: Theory, Research, and Treatment, 8*, 140–149.

Lang, P. J., Bradley, M. M., & Cuthbert, B. N. (1990). Emotion, attention, and the startle reflex. *Psychological Review, 97*, 377–398.

Latzman, R. D., Palumbo, I. M., Krueger, R. F., Drislane, L. E., & Patrick, C. J. (2020). Modeling relations between triarchic biobehavioral traits and DSM internalizing disorder dimensions. *Assessment, 27*, 1100–1115.

Latzman, R. D., Tobin, K. E., Palumbo, I. M., Conway, C. C., Lilienfeld, S. O., Patrick, C. J., & Krueger, R. F. (2020). Locating psychopathy within the domain space of personality pathology. *Personality and Individual Differences, 164*, e110124. doi:10.1016/j.paid.2020.110124

Leary, T. (1957). *Interpersonal diagnosis of personality*. Ronald Press.

Lee, K., & Ashton, M. C. (2018). Psychometric properties of the HEXACO-100. *Assessment, 25*, 543–556.

Lee, K. Y., & Sellbom, M. (2021). Further validation of the Elemental Psychopathy Assessment—Short Form (EPA-SF) in a large university sample. *Journal of Personality Assessment, 103*, 289–299.

Lejuez, C. W., Read, J. P., Kahler, C. W., Richards, J. B., Ramsey, S. E., Stuart, G. L., ... Brown, R. A. (2002). Evaluation of a behavioral measure of risk taking: The Balloon Analogue Risk Task (BART). *Journal of Experimental Psychology–Applied, 8*, 75–84.

Levenson, M. R., Kiehl, K. A., & Fitzpatrick, C. M. (1995). Assessing psychopathic attributes in a noninstitutionalized population. *Journal of Personality and Social Psychology, 68*, 151–158.

Lilienfeld, S. O., & Andrews, B. P. (1996). Development and preliminary validation of a self report measure of psychopathic personality traits in noncriminal populations. *Journal of Personality Assessment, 66*, 488–524.

Lilienfeld, S. O., Watts, A. L., Smith, S. F., & Latzman, R. D. (2018). Boldness: Conceptual and methodological issues. In: C. J. Patrick (Ed.), *Handbook of psychopathy*, 2nd ed. (pp. 165–186). Guilford.

Lilienfeld, S. O., & Widows, M. R. (2005). *Psychopathic Personality Inventory—Revised (PPI-R) professional manual*. Psychological Assessment Resources.

López, R., Poy, R., Patrick, C. J., & Moltó, J. (2013). Deficient fear conditioning and self-reported psychopathy: The role of fearless dominance. *Psychophysiology, 50*, 210–218.

Lorber, M. F. (2004). Psychophysiology of aggression, psychopathy, and conduct problems: A meta-analysis. *Psychological Bulletin, 130*, 531–552.

Lykken, D. T. (1957). A study of anxiety in the sociopathic personality. *Journal of Abnormal and Clinical Psychology, 55*, 6–10.

Lykken, D. T. (1995). *The antisocial personalities*. Lawrence Erlbaum.

Lynam, D. R. (1997). Pursuing the psychopath: Capturing the fledgling psychopath in a nomological net. *Journal of Abnormal Psychology, 106*, 425–438.

Lynam, D. R., Caspi, A., Moffit, T. E., Raine, A., Loeber, R., & Stouthamer-Loeber, M. (2005). Adolescent psychopathy and the big five: Results from two samples. *Journal of Abnormal Child Psychology, 33*, 431–443.

Lynam, D. R., & Derefinko, K. J. (2006). Psychopathy and personality. In C. J. Patrick (Ed.), *Handbook of psychopathy* (pp. 133–155) Guilford.

Lynam, D. R., Gaughan, E. T., Miller, J. D., Miller, D. J., Mullins-Sweatt, S., & Widiger, T. A. (2011). Assessing the basic traits associated with psychopathy: Development and validation of the Elemental Psychopathy Assessment. *Psychological Assessment, 18*, 106–114.

Lynam, D. R., Miller, J. D., & Derefinko, K. J. (2018). Psychopathy and personality: An articulation of the benefits of a trait-based approach. In: C. J. Patrick (Ed.), *Handbook of psychopathy*, 2nd ed. (pp. 259–280). Guilford.

Lynam, D. R., & Widiger, T. A. (2007). Using a general model of personality to identify the basic elements of psychopathy. *Journal of Personality Disorders, 21*, 160–178.

Marsh, A. A., & Blair, R. J. R. (2008). Deficits in facial affect recognition among antisocial populations: A meta-analysis. *Neuroscience and Biobehavioral Reviews, 32*, 3, 454–465.

Marsh, A. A., Finger, E. C., Mitchell, D. G., Reid, M. E., Sims, C., Kosson, D. S., Towbin, K. E., Leibenluft, E., Pine, D. S., & Blair, R. J. R. (2008). Reduced amygdala response to fearful expressions in children and adolescents with callous-unemotional traits and disruptive behavior disorders. *American Journal of Psychiatry, 165*, 712–720.

McCord, W., & McCord, J. (1964). *The psychopath: An essay on the criminal mind*. Van Nostrand.

Medina, A. L., Kirilko, E., & Grose-Fifer, J. (2016). Emotional processing and psychopathic traits in male college students: An event–related potential study. *International Journal of Psychophysiology, 106*, 39–49.

Meehl, P. E. (1986). Diagnostic taxa as open concepts: Metatheoretical and statistical questions about reliability and construct validity in the grand strategy of nosological revision. In T. Millon & G. L. Klerman (Eds.), *Contemporary directions in psychopathology: Toward the DSM-IV* (pp. 215–231). Guilford.

Miller, J. D, Gaughan, E. T., Maples, J., Gentile, B., Lynam, D. R., & Widiger, T. A. (2011). Examining the construct validity of the elemental psychopathy assessment. *Assessment, 18*, 106–114.

Miller, J. D., Hyatt, C. S., Rausher, S., Maples, J. L., & Zeichner, A. (2014). A test of the construct validity of the Elemental Psychopathy Assessment scores in a community sample of adults. *Psychological Assessment, 26*, 555–562.

Miller, J. D., Lynam, D. R., Widiger, T. A., & Leukefeld, C. (2001). Personality disorders as extreme variants of common personality dimensions: Can the five-factor model adequately represent psychopathy? *Journal of Personality, 69*, 253–276.

Miller J. D., Rausher, S., Hyatt, C. S., Maples, J., & Zeichner, A. (2014). Examining the relations among pain tolerance, psychopathic traits, and violent and nonviolent antisocial behavior. *Journal of Abnormal Psychology, 123*, 205–213.

Morgan, A. B., & Lilienfeld, S. O. (2000). A meta-analytic review of the relation between antisocial behavior and neuropsychological measures of executive function. *Clinical Psychology Review, 20*, 113–136.

Muñoz, L. C. (2009). Callous-unemotional traits are related to combined deficits in recognizing afraid faces and body poses. *Journal of the American Academy of Child and Adolescent Psychiatry, 48*, 554–562.

Nelson, L. D., Patrick, C. J., & Bernat, E. M. (2011). Operationalizing proneness to externalizing psychopathology as a multivariate psychophysiological phenotype. *Psychophysiology, 48*, 64–72.

Newcomb, M. D., Huba, G. J., & Bentler, P. M. (1981). A multidimensional assessment of stressful life events among adolescents: Derivation and correlates. *Journal of Health and Social Behavior, 22*, 400–415.

Olweus, D. (1996). *Revised Olweus Bully/Victim Questionnaire.* Research Center for Health Promotion (HEMIL Center), University of Bergen.

Palumbo, I. M., Latzman, R. D., & Patrick, C. J. (2021). Triarchic neurobehavioral trait correlates of psychopathology in young children: Evidence from the Healthy Brain Network initiative. *Journal of Personality Assessment, 103*, 588–601.

Palumbo, I. M., Perkins, E. R., Yancey, J. R., Brislin, S. J, Patrick, C. J., & Latzman, R. D. (2020). Toward a multimodal measurement model for the neurobehavioral trait of affiliative capacity. *Personality Neuroscience, 3*, e11. doi:10.1017/pen.2020.9

Partridge, G. E. (1928). Psychopathic personalities among boys in a training school for delinquents. *American Journal of Psychiatry, 8*, 159–186.

Patrick, C. J. (1994). Emotion and psychopathy: Startling new insights. *Psychophysiology, 31*, 319–330.

Patrick, C. J. (2006). Back to the future: Cleckley as a guide to the next generation of psychopathy research. In C. J. Patrick (Ed.), *Handbook of psychopathy* (pp. 605–617). Guilford.

Patrick, C. J. (2010). *Operationalizing the triarchic conceptualization of psychopathy: Preliminary description of brief scales for assessment of boldness, meanness, and disinhibition.* Unpublished test manual, Florida State University. Https://www.phenxtoolkit.org/index.php?pageLink=browse.protocoldetails&id=121601

Patrick, C. J. (2014). Physiological correlates of psychopathy, antisocial personality disorder, habitual aggression, and violence. In: V. Kumari, N. Boutros, & P. Bob (Eds.), *Current topics in behavioral neuroscience, vol. 14: Psychophysiology in psychiatry and psychopharmacology* (pp. 197–226). Springer.

Patrick, C. J. (2018). Psychopathy as masked pathology. In: C. J. Patrick (Ed.), *Handbook of psychopathy*, 2nd ed. (pp. 422–455). Guilford.

Patrick, C. J. (2022). Psychopathy: Current knowledge and future directions. *Annual Review of Clinical Psychology, 18*, 388–415.

Patrick, C. J., Bernat, E., Malone, S. M., Iacono, W. G., Krueger, R. F., & McGue, M. K. (2006). P300 amplitude as an indicator of externalizing in adolescent males. *Psychophysiology, 43*, 84–92.

Patrick, C. J., Bowyer, C. B., Yancey, J. R., & Hulstrand, K. (2017). Reduced electrodermal response to aversive picture stimuli as an indicator of dispositional threat sensitivity. *Psychophysiology, 54*, S163.

Patrick, C. J., Bradley, M. M., & Lang, P. J. (1993). Emotion in the criminal psychopath: Startle reflex modulation. *Journal of Abnormal Psychology, 102*, 82–92.

Patrick, C. J., & Drislane, L. E. (2015). Triarchic model of psychopathy: Origins, operationalizations, and observed linkages with personality and general psychopathology. *Journal of Personality, 83*, 627–643.

Patrick, C. J., Durbin, C. E., & Moser, J. S. (2012). Conceptualizing proneness to antisocial deviance in neurobehavioral terms. *Development and Psychopathology, 24*, 1047–1071.

Patrick, C. J., Edens, J. F., Poythress, N., Lilienfeld, S. O., & Benning, S. D. (2006). Construct validity of the PPI two-factor model with offenders. *Psychological Assessment, 18*, 204–208.

Patrick, C. J., Fowles, D. C., & Krueger, R. F. (2009). Triarchic conceptualization of psychopathy: Developmental origins of disinhibition, boldness, and meanness. *Development and Psychopathology, 21*, 913–938.

Patrick, C. J., Hicks, B. M., Krueger, R. F., & Lang, A. R. (2005). Relations between psychopathy facets and externalizing in a criminal offender sample. *Journal of Personality Disorders, 19*, 339–356.

Patrick, C. J., Hicks, B. M., Nichol, P. E., & Krueger, R. F. (2007). A bifactor approach to modeling the structure of the Psychopathy Checklist-Revised. *Journal of Personality Disorders, 21*, 118–141.

Patrick, C. J., Iacono, W. G., & Venables, N. C. (2019). Incorporating neurophysiological measures into clinical assessments: Fundamental challenges and a strategy for addressing them. *Psychological Assessment, 31*, 1512–1529.

Patrick, C. J., Joyner, K. J., Watts, A. L., Lilienfeld, S. O., Somma, A., Fossati, A., . . . Krueger, R. F. (2021). Latent variable modeling of item-based factor scales: Comment on Triarchic or septarchic?—Uncovering the Triarchic Psychopathy Measure's (TriPM) structure, by Roy et al. *Personality Disorders: Theory, Research, & Treatment, 12*, 16–23.

Patrick, C. J., Kramer, M. D., Krueger, R. F., & Markon, K. E. (2013). Optimizing efficiency of psychopathology assessment through quantitative modeling: Development of a brief form of the Externalizing Spectrum Inventory. *Psychological Assessment, 2*, 1332–1348.

Patrick, C. J., Kramer, M. D., Vaidyanathan, U., Benning, S. D., Hicks, B. M., & Lilienfeld, S. O. (2019). Formulation of a measurement model for the boldness construct of psychopathy. *Psychological Assessment, 31*, 643–659.

Patrick, C. J., Venables, N. C., & Skeem, J. L. (2012). Psychopathy and brain function: Empirical findings and legal implications. In: H. Häkkänen-Nyholm & J. Nyholm (Eds.), *Psychopathy and law: A practitioner's guide* (pp. 39–77). Wiley.

Patrick, C. J., Venables, N. C., Yancey, J. R., Hicks, B. M., Nelson, L. D., & Kramer, M. D. (2013). A construct-network approach to bridging diagnostic and physiological domains: Application to assessment of externalizing psychopathology. *Journal of Abnormal Psychology, 122*, 902–916

Paulhus, D. L., Neumann, C. S., Hemphill, J. F., & Hare, R. D. (2016). *Self-Report Psychopathy Scale*, 4th ed. Multi-Health Systems.

Paulhus, D. L., Robins, R. W., Trzesniewski, K. H., & Tracy, J. L. (2004). Two replicable suppressor situations in personality research. *Multivariate Behavioral Research, 39*, 303–328.

Perkins, E. R., Joyner, K. J., Foell, J., Drislane, L. E., Brislin, S. J., Yancey, J. R., . . . Patrick, C. J. (in press). Assessing general versus specific liability for externalizing problems in adolescence: Concurrent and prospective prediction of conduct disorder, ADHD, and substance use. *Journal of Psychopathology and Clinical Science*.

Perkins, E. R., Joyner, K. J., Patrick, C. J., Bartholow, B. D., Latzman, R. D., DeYoung, C. G, . . . Zald, D. H. (2020). Neurobiology and the Hierarchical Taxonomy of Psychopathology: Progress toward ontogenetically informed and clinically useful nosology. *Dialogues in Clinical Neuroscience, 22*, 51–63.

Petitclerc, A., Henry, J., Feng, B., Poliakova, N., Brendgen, M., Dionne, G., . . . Boivin, M. (2019). Genetic correlation between child callous-unemotional behaviors and fear recognition deficit: Evidence for a neurocognitive endophenotype. *Journal of Abnormal Child Psychology, 47*, 1483–1493.

Pinel, P. (1801/1962). *A treatise on insanity* (D. Davis, translator). Hafner.

Poy, R., Segarra, P., Esteller, À., López, R., & Moltó, J. (2014). FFM description of the triarchic conceptualization of psychopathy in men and women. *Psychological Assessment, 26*, 69–76.

Poythress, N. G., Lilienfeld, S. O., Skeem, J. L., Douglas, K. S., Edens, J. F., Epstein, M., & Patrick, C. J. (2010). Using the PCL-R to help estimate the validity of two self-report measures of psychopathy with offenders. *Assessment, 17*, 206–219.

Prichard, J. C. (1835). *A treatise on insanity and other disorders affecting the mind*. Sherwood, Gilbert & Piper.

Quay, H. C. (1964). Dimensions of personality in delinquent boys as inferred from the factor analysis of case history data. *Child Development, 35*, 479–484.

Raine, A. (1997). Antisocial behavior and psychophysiology: A biosocial perspective and a prefrontal dysfunction hypothesis. In D. M. Stoff, J. Breiling, & J. D. Maser (Eds.), *Handbook of antisocial behavior* (pp. 289–303). Wiley.

Reardon, M. L., Lang, A. R., & Patrick, C. J. (2002). Antisociality and alcohol problems: An evaluation of subtypes, drinking motives, and family history in incarcerated men. *Alcoholism: Clinical and Experimental Research, 26*, 1188–1197.

Ribes-Guardiola, P., Poy, R., Patrick, C. J., & Moltó, J. (2020). Electrocortical measures of performance monitoring from go/no-go and flanker tasks: Differential relations with trait dimensions of the triarchic model of psychopathy. *Psychophysiology, 57*, e13573. doi:10.1111/psyp.13573

Robins, L. N. (1966). *Deviant children grown up*. Williams & Wilkins.

Robins, L. N. (1978). Sturdy predictors of adult antisocial behaviour: Replications from longitudinal studies. *Psychological Medicine, 8*, 611–622.

Rogers, R. D. (2006). The functional architecture of the frontal lobes: Implications for research with psychopathic offenders. In C. J. Patrick (Ed.), *Handbook of psychopathy* (pp. 313–333). Guilford.

Ross, S. R., Benning, S. D., Patrick, C. J., Thompson, A., & Thurston, A. (2009). Factors of the Psychopathic Personality Inventory: Criterion-related validity and relationship to the BIS/BAS and five-factor models of personality. *Assessment, 16*, 71–87.

Rothbart, M. K. (2007). Temperament, development, and personality. *Current Directions in Psychological Science, 16*, 207–212.

Roy, S., Vize, C., Uzieblo, K., van Dongen, J. D. M., Miller, J., Lynam, D., Brazil, I., Yoon, D., Mokros, A., Gray, N. S., Snowden, R., & Neumann, C. S. (2021). Triarchic or septarchic?: Uncovering the Triarchic Psychopathy Measure's (TriPM) structure. *Personality Disorders: Theory, Research, and Treatment, 12*, 1–15.

Ruchensky, J. R., Donnellan, M. B., & Edens, J. F. (2018). Development and initial validation of the HEXACO-Triarchic scales. *Psychological Assessment, 30*, 1560–1566.

Ruchensky, J. R, Edens, J. F, Corker, K. S, Donnellan, M. B, Witt, E. A, & Blonigen, D. M. (2018). Evaluating the structure of psychopathic personality traits: A meta-analysis of the Psychopathic Personality Inventory. *Psychological Assessment, 30*, 707–718.

Rush, B. (1812). *Medical inquiries and observations upon the diseases of the mind*. Kimber & Richardson.

Sanz-García, A., Gesteira, C., Sanz, J., & García-Vera, M. P. (2021). Prevalence of psychopathy in the general adult population: A systematic review and meta-analysis. *Frontiers in Psychology, 12*, 661044. doi:10.3389/fpsyg.2021.661044

Saucier, G. (1992). Benchmarks: Integrating affective and interpersonal circles with the Big-Five personality factors. *Journal of Personality and Social Psychology, 62*, 1025–1035.

Schneider, K. (1934). *Die psychopathischen Persönlichkeiten*, 3rd ed. Deuticke.

Schumann, G., Loth, E., Banaschewski, T., Barbot, A., Barker, G., Büchel, C., . . . the IMAGEN Consortium. (2010). The IMAGEN study: Reinforcement-related behaviour in normal brain function and psychopathology. *Molecular Psychiatry, 15*, 1128–1139.

Sellbom, M. (2018). The triarchic psychopathy model: Theory and measurement. In M. DeLisi (Ed.), *Routledge international handbook of psychopathy and crime* (pp. 241–264). Routledge.

Sellbom, M., Drislane, L. E., Johnson, A. K., Goodwin, B. E., Philips, T. R., & Patrick, C. J. (2016). Development and validation of MMPI-2-RF scales for indexing triarchic psychopathy constructs. *Assessment, 23*, 527–543.

Sellbom, M., Lilienfeld, S. O., Fowler, K., & McCrary, K. L. (2018). The self-report assessment of psychopathy: Challenges, pitfalls, and promises. In C. J. Patrick (Ed.), *Handbook of psychopathy*, 2nd ed. (pp. 211–258). Guilford.

Sellbom, M., & Phillips, T. R. (2013). An examination of the triarchic conceptualization of psychopathy in incarcerated and non-incarcerated samples. *Journal of Abnormal Psychology, 122*, 208–214.

Semel, R. A., Pinsenault, T. B., Drislane, & Sellbom, M. (2016). Operationalizing the triarchic model of psychopathy using the MMPI-A-RF scales (restructured form). *Psychological Assessment, 33*, 311–325.

Sica, C., Cuicci, E., Baroncelli, A., Frick, P. J., & Patrick, C. J. (2020). Not just for adults: Using the triarchic model of psychopathy to inform developmental models of conduct problems in adolescence. *Journal of Clinical Child and Adolescent Psychology, 49*, 897–911.

Sher, K. J., & Trull, T. (1994). Personality and disinhibitory psychopathology: Alcoholism and antisocial personality disorder. *Journal of Abnormal Psychology, 103*, 92–102.

Shine, J., & Hobson, J. (1997). Construct validity of the Hare Psychopathy Checklist Revised. *Journal of Forensic Psychiatry, 8*, 546–561.

Shou, Y., Sellbom, M., & Xu, J. (2018). Psychometric properties of the Triarchic Psychopathy Measure: An item response theory approach. *Personality Disorders: Theory, Research, and Treatment, 9*, 217–227.

Siddle, D. A. T., & Trasler, G. B. (1981). The psychophysiology of psychopathic behavior. In M. J. Christie & P. G. Mellett (Eds.), *Foundations of psychosomatics* (pp. 283–303). Wiley.

Skeem, J. L., Edens, J. F., Camp, J., & Colwell, L. H. (2004). Are there racial differences in levels of psychopathy? A meta-analysis. *Law and Human Behavior, 28*, 505–527.

Skeem, J. L., Johansson, P., Andershed, H., Kerr, M., & Louden, J. E. (2007). Two subtypes of psychopathic violent offenders that parallel primary and secondary variants. *Journal of Abnormal Psychology, 116*, 395–409.

Skilling, T. A., Harris, G. T., Rice, M. E., & Quinsey, V. L. (2002). Identifying persistently antisocial offenders using the Hare Psychopathy Checklist and DSM antisocial personality disorder criteria. *Psychological Assessment, 14*, 27–38.

Smith, S. S., & Newman, J. P. (1990). Alcohol and drug abuse-dependence disorders in psychopathic and nonpsychopathic criminal offenders. *Journal of Abnormal Psychology, 99*, 430–439.

Snowden, R. J., Smith, C., & Gray, N. S. (2017). Risk taking and the triarchic model of psychopathy. *Journal of Clinical and Experimental Neuropsychology, 39*, 988–1001.

Somma, A., Borroni, S., Drislane, L. E., & Fossati, A. (2016). Assessing the triarchic model of psychopathy in adolescence: Reliability and validity of the Triarchic Psychopathy Measure (TriPM) in three samples of Italian community-dwelling adolescents. *Psychological Assessment, 28*, e36–e48. doi:10.1037/pas0000184

Strickland, C. M., Drislane, L. E., Lucy, M. D., Krueger, R. F., & Patrick, C. J. (2013). Characterizing psychopathy using DSM-5 personality traits. *Assessment, 20*, 327–338.

Strickland, C. M., Yancey, J. R., & Patrick, C. J. (2015). Resting cardiac indicators differentiate dispositional fear from general distress. *Psychophysiology, 52*, S30.

Stringaris, A., Goodman, R., Ferdinando, S., Razdan, V., Muhrer, E., Leibenluft, E., & Brotman, M. A. (2012). The Affective Reactivity Index: A concise irritability scale for clinical and research settings. *Journal of Child Psychology and Psychiatry, 53*, 1109–1117.

Sullivan, E. A., & Kosson, D. S. (2006). Ethnic and cultural variations in psychopathy. In C. J. Patrick (Ed.), *Handbook of psychopathy* (pp. 437–458). Guilford.

Sutton, S. K., Vitale, J. E., & Newman, J. P. (2002). Emotion among females with psychopathy during picture perception. *Journal of Abnormal Psychology, 111*, 610–619.

Tellegen, A., & Waller, N. (2008). Exploring personality through test construction: Development of the Multidimensional Personality Questionnaire. In G. J. Boyle, G. Matthews, & D. H. Saklofske (Eds.), *Handbook of personality theory and testing: Personality measurement and assessment* (vol. 2, pp. 261–292). Sage.

Vaidyanathan, U., Hall, J. R., Patrick, C. J., & Bernat, E. M. (2011). Clarifying the role of defensive reactivity deficits in psychopathy and antisocial personality using startle reflex methodology. *Journal of Abnormal Psychology, 120*, 253–258.

Vaidyanathan, U., Patrick, C. J., & Bernat, E. M. (2009). Startle reflex potentiation during aversive picture viewing as an index of trait fear. *Psychophysiology, 46*, 75–85.

Vanman, E. J., Mejia, V. Y., Dawson, M. E., Schell, A. M., & Raine, A. (2003). Modification of the startle reflex in a community sample: Do one or two dimensions of psychopathy underlie emotional processing? *Personality and Individual Differences, 35*, 2007–2021.

Veit, R., Flor, H., Erb, M., Lotze, M., Grodd, W., & Birbaumer, N. (2002). Brain circuits involved in emotional learning in antisocial behavior and social phobia in humans. *Neuroscience Letters, 328*, 233–236.

Venables, N. C., Foell, J., Yancey, J. R., Kane, M. J., Engle, R. W., & Patrick, C. J. (2018). Quantifying inhibitory control as externalizing proneness: A cross-domain model. *Clinical Psychological Science, 6*, 561–580.

Venables, N. C., Hall, J. R., & Patrick, C. J. (2014). Differentiating psychopathy from antisocial personality disorder: A triarchic model perspective. *Psychological Medicine, 44*, 1005–1013.

Venables, N. C., & Patrick, C. J. (2012). Validity of the Externalizing Spectrum Inventory in a criminal offender sample: Relations with disinhibitory psychopathology, personality, and psychopathic features. *Psychological Assessment, 24*, 88–100.

Venables, N. C., & Patrick, C. J. (2014). Reconciling discrepant findings for P3 brain response in criminal psychopathy through reference to the concept of externalizing proneness. *Psychophysiology, 51*, 427–436.

Verona, E., Hicks, B. M., & Patrick, C. J. (2005). Psychopathy and suicidal behavior in female offenders: Mediating influences of temperament and abuse history. *Journal of Consulting and Clinical Psychology, 73*, 1065–1073.

Verona, E., & Patrick, C. J. (2000). Suicide risk in externalizing syndromes: Temperamental and neurobiological underpinnings. In T. E. Joiner (Ed.), *Suicide science: Expanding the boundaries* (pp. 137–173). Kluwer Academic Publishers.

Verona, E., Patrick, C. J., & Joiner, T. E. (2001). Psychopathy, antisocial personality, and suicide risk. *Journal of Abnormal Psychology, 110*, 462–470.

Verona, E., Sachs-Ericsson, N., & Joiner, T. E. (2004). Suicide attempts associated with externalizing psychopathology in an epidemiological sample. *American Journal of Psychiatry, 161*, 444–451.

Verona, E., & Vitale, J. (2018). Psychopathy in women: Assessment, manifestations, and etiology. In C. J. Patrick (Ed.), *Handbook of psychopathy*, 2nd ed. (pp. 509–528). Guilford.

Verschuere, B., Crombez, G., de Clercq, A., & Koster, E. H. W. (2005). Psychopathic traits and autonomic responding to concealed information in a prison sample. *Psychophysiology, 42*, 239–245.

Viding, E., & McCrory, E. (2019). Towards understanding atypical social affiliation in psychopathy. *Lancet Psychiatry, 6*, 437–444.

Viding, E., Sebastian, C. L., Dadds, M. R., Lockwood, P. L., Cecil, C. A., De Brito, S. A., & McCrory, E. J. (2012). Amygdala response to preattentive masked fear in children with conduct problems: The role of callous-unemotional traits. *American Journal of Psychiatry, 169*, 1109–1116.

Wake, S., Wormwood, J., Satpute, A. B. (2020). The influence of fear on risk taking: A meta-analysis. *Cognition and Emotion, 34*, 1143–1159.

Wall, T. D., Wygant, D. B., & Sellbom, M. (2015). Boldness explains a key difference between psychopathy and antisocial personality disorder. *Psychiatry, Psychology and Law, 22*, 94–105.

Waller, R., & Wagner, N. (2019). The Sensitivity to Threat and Affiliative Reward (STAR) model and the development of callous-unemotional traits. *Neuroscience and Biobehavioral Reviews, 107*, 656–671.

Warren, J. I., Burnette, M. L., South, S. C., Preeti, C., Bale, R., Friend, R., & Van Patten, I. (2003). Psychopathy in women: Structural modeling and comorbidity. *International Journal of Law and Psychiatry, 26*, 223–242.

Weinberg, A., Vaidyanathan, U., Venables, N. C., Hajcak, G., & Patrick, C. J. (2012). The emotion-modulated late positive potential as a neurophysiological trait indicator of inhibitory control and defensive reactivity. *Psychophysiology, 49*, S56.

White, S. F., Marsh, A. A., Fowler, K. A., Schechter, J. C., Adalio, C., Pope, K., . . . Blair, R. J. R. (2012). Reduced amygdala response in youths with disruptive behavior disorders and psychopathic traits: Decreased emotional response versus increased top-down attention to nonemotional features. *American Journal of Psychiatry, 169*, 750–758.

Widiger, T. A., Cadoret, R., Hare, R., Robins, L., Rutherford, M., Zanarini, M., Alterman, A., Apple, M., Hart, S., Kulterman, J., Woody, G., & Frances, A. (1996). DSM-IV antisocial personality disorder field trial. *Journal of Abnormal Psychology, 105*, 3–16.

Widiger, T. A., & Crego, C. (2018). Psychopathy and DSM-5 psychopathology. In: C. J. Patrick (Ed.), *Handbook of psychopathy*, 2nd ed. (pp. 281–296). Guilford.

Wiggins, J. S. (1982). Circumplex models of interpersonal behavior in clinical psychology. In P. C. Kendall & J. N. Butcher (Eds.), *Handbook of research methods in clinical psychology* (pp. 183–221). Wiley.

Williams, K. M., Paulhus, D. L., & Hare, R. D. (2007). Capturing the four-factor structure of psychopathy in college students via self-report. *Journal of Personality Assessment, 88*, 205–219.

Woicik, P. A., Stewart, S. H., Pihl, R. O., & Conrod, P. J. (2009). The Substance Use Risk Profile Scale: A scale measuring traits linked to reinforcement-specific substance use profiles. *Addictive Behaviors, 34*, 1042–1055.

Wright, A. G. C. (2020). Latent variable models in clinical psychology. In: A. G. C. Wright & M. N. Hallquist (Eds.), *Cambridge handbook of research methods in clinical psychology* (pp. 66–79). Cambridge University Press.

Wygant, D. B., Pardini, D. A., Marsh, A. A., & Patrick, C. J. (2018). Understanding psychopathy: Where we are, where we can go. In C. J. Patrick (Ed.), *Handbook of psychopathy*, 2nd ed. (pp. 755–778). Guilford.

Yancey, J. R., Bowyer, C. B., Foell, J., Boot, W. R., & Patrick, C. J. (2019). Boldness moderates the effects of external threat on performance within a task switching paradigm. *Journal of Experimental Psychology: Human Perception and Performance, 45*, 758–770.

Yancey, J. R., Bowyer, C. B., Roberts, K. E., Jones, D., Foell, J., McGlade, E. C., Yurgelun-Todd, W. R., & Patrick, C. J. (2022). Boldness moderates cognitive performance under acute threat: Evidence from a task-switching paradigm involving cueing for shock, *Journal of Experimental Psychology: Human Perception and Performance, 48*, 549–562.

Yancey, J. R., Venables, N. C., Hicks, B. M., & Patrick, C. J. (2013). Evidence for a heritable brain basis to deviance-promoting deficits in self-control. *Journal of Criminal Justice, 41*, 309–317.

Yancey, J. R., Venables, N. C., & Patrick, C. J. (2016). Psychoneurometric operationalization of threat sensitivity: Relations with clinical symptom and physiological response criteria. *Psychophysiology, 53*, 393–405.

Young, S. E., Friedman, N. P., Miyake, A., Willcutt, E. G., Corley, R. P., Haberstick, B. C., & Hewitt, J. K. (2009). Behavioral disinhibition: Liability for externalizing spectrum disorders and its genetic and environmental relation to response inhibition across adolescence. *Journal of Abnormal Psychology, 118*, 117–130.

# INDEX

*For the benefit of digital users, indexed terms that span two pages (e.g., 52–53) may, on occasion, appear on only one of those pages.*
Note: Tables, figures, boxes and notes are indicated by *t, f, b* and n following the page number

## A

AARDoC. *See* Alcohol Addiction Research Domain Criteria
abandonment, frantic attempts to avoid, in borderline personality disorder, 649, 649*t*, 664
ABCL. *See* Adult Behavior Checklist
ABMTs. *See* attention bias modification tasks
*ABPA3* gene, in borderline personality disorder, 660
Abraham, K., 257
abuse
 child (*see* child abuse and neglect; child maltreatment)
 and genito-pelvic pain/penetration disorder, 415
 physiological, of substances, 277–78
acamprosate, 316
ACC. *See* anterior cingulate cortex
acceptance and commitment therapy
 and obsessive-compulsive disorder, 187–88
 principles of, 187–88
accident(s), functional somatic symptoms after, 513–14
Achenbach, T. M., 14
Achenbach System of Empirically Based Assessment, 450, 453, 467–68
 adaptive functioning scales, 454–55
 applications to clinical services, 460–63
 applications to research, 463–66
 applications to training, 466–67
 *ASEBA Manual for Assessing Progress & Outcomes of Problems & Strengths*, 462
 assessment instruments, 450–51, 456*t*
 Brief Problem Monitor, 462–63
 competence scales, 454–55
 *DSM*-oriented scales, 453, 456*t*
 and Dutch versus US developmental trajectories, 465
 empirically based bottom-up paradigm in, 448, 449, 450–55
 externalizing scales, 452, 456*t*
 and genetic and environmental effects on informant discrepancies, 463
 hierarchy of empirically derived problem scales in, 452*f*, 452

 instruments, use in clinical settings, 460–61
 internalizing scales, 452, 456*t*
 and longitudinal studies, 463–66
 multicultural applications, 455–60, 457*t*
 Multicultural Family Assessment Module, 461, 462*f*
 multicultural norms for Personal Strengths and Positive Qualities, 459–60
 multicultural norms for problem scales, 458–59
 multi-informant assessment, 453–54
 and multi-informant ratings from age 4 to 40 years, 465
 parallel instruments, 454
 Positive Qualities, 454–55, 459–60
 problem item structures, generalizability across many societies, 456–58
 problem scale scores, multicultural comparisons of, 458
 Progress and Outcomes App, 461–62
 ratings of problems and positive qualities, effects of society, culture, and individual differences, 460
 strength scales, 454–55, 456*t*, 459–60
 syndrome scales, 451–52, 456*t*
 syndrome structures, generalizability across many societies, 455–56
 Total Problems, 449, 452*f*, 454, 456*t*, 458–59, 459*f*
 translations of instruments, 455, 457*t*
acrotomophilia, 551, 552
age of onset, 561
ACT. *See* acceptance and commitment therapy
actigraphs/actigraphy, 522, 523
 in advanced sleep phase disorder, 531
 applications, 523
 in bipolar disorder, 537
 in delayed sleep phase disorder, 530
 devices for, 523
 in insomnia, 526, 527
 limitations of, 523
 nonparametric variables, 523
 parametric variables, 523
AD. *See* autistic disorder

adaptation. *See also* resilience
 in development, organizational perspective on, 124–25
 developmental analysis of, 123
 multiple pathways to, 126–27
addiction, 298–300. *See also* substance use disorder(s)
 and allostasis, 298–300, 299*t*, 308
 clinical concepts of, 298–300, 299*t*
 and habit, 298–300, 299*t*
 and incentive sensitization, 298–300, 299*t*
 and reinforcer pathology, 298–300, 299*t*
 theoretical concepts of, 298–300, 299*t*
Addiction Neuroclinical Assessment, 318
addictive disorders. *See* substance use disorder(s)
addictive personality, 308
ADHD. *See* attention-deficit hyperactivity disorder
ADHD-C. *See* attention-deficit hyperactivity disorder, combined subtype
ADHD-H. *See* attention-deficit hyperactivity disorder, hyperactive/impulsive subtype
ADHD-I. *See* attention-deficit hyperactivity disorder, inattentive subtype
adolescents
 autism spectrum disorders in, 493
 borderline personality disorder (over) diagnosis in, 649
 depression in, 259
 drug experimentation by, and mental health, 305
 eating disorders in, 425
 family environment, and substance use, 306–7
 at high risk for schizophrenia, premorbid social deficits in, 356
 neurocognitive development, substance use and, 284
 peer influences, and substance use, 282–83, 301, 304–5
 psychopathy assessment in, 717–18
 sexual behavior, substance use and, 284
 substance use, 282–83, 301, 304–5, 306–7
ADOS. *See* Autism Diagnostic Observation Schedule

INDEX | 749

Adult Babies/Diaper Lovers, 553
Adult Behavior Checklist, 456t
   for Ages 18–59, 452
Adult Self-Report, 455, 456t
   for Ages 18–59, 452
   triarchic scale measure based on, 727t
advanced circadian phase disorders, 524
advanced sleep phase disorder, 529, 531–32
   age and, 531
   assessment of, 531
   management of, 531–32
   mechanisms of, 531
   prevalence of, 531
   and schizophrenia, 538
adverse life events. *See* life events
affect. *See also* negative affect/negative affectivity; positive affectivity
   blunted, in schizophrenia, 337
   core, and narcissistic grandiosity and vulnerability, 634–35
   flattened, in schizophrenia, 354, 366–67
   inappropriate, 337
   in schizophrenia, 338–40
affective disorders, and borderline personality disorder, 648
affective face perception. *See* emotion perception
affective instability, in borderline personality disorder, 662–63
affective/motivational network, in attention-deficit hyperactivity disorder, 483
Affective Reactivity Index, triarchic scale measure based on, 727t
affective vocal prosody. *See* emotion perception
affect-sharing, in schizophrenia, 363
agentic extraversion, and narcissism, 635
aggression
   alcohol use and, 283–84, 304
   amphetamine abuse and, 283–84
   cocaine use and, 283–84
   displaced, vulnerable narcissism and, 639–40
   and narcissistic grandiosity and vulnerability, 634
   narcissistic personality disorder/pathological narcissism and, 639–40
   PCL-R scores and, 716
   physical, in narcissistic personality disorder, 639–40
   reactive, vulnerable narcissism and, 639–40
   substance use disorders and, 283–84, 304
   verbal, in narcissistic personality disorder, 639–40
agonistic sexual behavior, 554–55
agoraphobia
   definition of, 147–48
   factor analysis, 152
   and panic disorder, 55, 147–48
Agoraphobia factor, 152

agreeableness, 63, 661
   and antagonism, 617
   in borderline personality disorder, 650t, 656, 661
   in Five Factor Model, 14
   and personality disorders, 603, 605, 616, 616t
   and risk for substance use disorders, 308–9
   and somatization, 513
AIPSS. *See* Assessment of Interpersonal Problem-Solving Skills
alcohol
   and benzodiazepines, interactions of, 297
   and cocaine, interactions of, 297
   and cognitive functioning, 310–11
   cultural significance of, 304
   level of response to, 281
   and NMDA receptors, 316
   tension reduction hypothesis, 285–86
alcohol abuse. *See* alcohol use disorder
Alcohol Addiction Research Domain Criteria, 318
alcohol control, 300, 303
alcohol dehydrogenase, 313
alcohol dependence
   factor analysis, 152
   in *ICD-11*, 297
alcoholism. *See also* alcohol use disorder
   and gene–environment correlation, 46
   idiographic approach to, 39
   naltrexone for, 317
   nomothetic approach to, 39
   parental, as predictor of drug use, 306
alcohol use
   adverse trajectories, peer influences and, 305
   and aggression, 283–84, 304
   cultural considerations with, 302–3
   depression and, 308
   evolutionary roots of, 296
   historical perspective on, 296–97
   maternal, and ADHD, 479, 480
   and narcissistic grandiosity and vulnerability, 634
   in pregnancy, 307, 479, 480
   socioeconomic status and, 306
alcohol use disorder, 297. *See also* alcoholism
   alcohol expectancies and, 282, 309–10
   antisocial personality disorder and, 288
   anxiety disorders and, 285–86
   and borderline personality disorder, 652t
   child maltreatment and, 132
   clinical subtyping, 278–80, 279t
   comorbidity in, 315
   conduct disorder and, 288
   diagnosis, 298
   and eating disorders, 427
   epidemiology of, 277
   Etiologic, Theory-Based, Ontogenic Hierarchical Framework of, 318f, 318
   event-related potentials in, 281

   family history and, 280–81, 305–7
   family stressors and, 306–7
   genetic factors in, 312–15
   heart rate variability in, 281–82
   and interpersonal aggression and violence, 283–84
   and intimate partner violence, 283–84
   level of response to alcohol and, 281
   and mood disorder, 285
   and neurocognitive impairment, 284–85
   personality and, 308
   personalized treatment, 280
   and posttraumatic stress disorder, 204, 286–87
   poverty and related variables and, 303–4
   prevalence, age gradient of, 302–3
   schizophrenia and, 287
   severity, and psychiatric comorbidity, 301–2
   sex differences in, 283
   telescoping in, 283
aldehyde dehydrogenase 2, 313
Alexander, Franz, views on somatic symptoms, 509–10
alexithymia, 513
alienists, 78
all-or-nothing thinking, 266
allostasis, 298–300, 299t, 308
alogia, in schizophrenia, 354
alpha-synuclein, in eating disorders, 435
alpha-synucleinopathies, REM sleep behavior disorder and, 534–35
alternative forms, for assessing reliability, 20
Alternative Model of Personality Disorders, 16, 42, 577, 580, 591, 603, 676–77, 729–30
   Criteria E, F, and G, 606–7
   Criterion A, 577, 580–81, 581t, 582–83, 586, 590–91, 592–93, 606–7, 614–15, 617–18
   Criterion B, 590–91, 592, 606–7, 617–18
   Criterion C, 606–7
   Criterion D, 606–7
   ease of use, 614
   and narcissistic personality disorder, 640
   psychoticism dimension, 681
   structure of, 606–7
Alzheimer's disease
   causes of, 22
   research on, 81
ambivalence, in schizotypy, 686–87
ambulatory assessment, 104
   in borderline personality disorder, 662
American Psychiatric Association, 5, 6, 9
AMN. *See* affective/motivational network
amnesia. *See* dissociative amnesia
AMPD. *See* Alternative Model of Personality Disorders
amphetamine(s)
   abuse, and interpersonal aggression, 283–84
   for attention-deficit hyperactivity disorder, 476–77
   withdrawal, depressive symptoms in, 285

amputee identity disorder, 553–54
AMT. *See* Autobiographical Memory Test
amygdala
  in anxiety disorders, 159
  in attention-deficit hyperactivity
    disorder, 481
  in bipolar spectrum disorders, 235
  in borderline personality disorder, 662
  in depression, 135
  in drug use, 316
  and fear response, 159
  in paraphilias, 560
  in posttraumatic stress disorder, 208
  psychopathy and, 719
  reactivity, as risk marker, 66
  in schizophrenia, 340–41, 363, 365
  and septohippocampal system,
    interactions of, 158–59
  in social perception, 497–503
  substance use and, 312
AN. *See* anorexia nervosa
ANA. *See* Addiction Neuroclinical
  Assessment
anankastia, and personality disorders, 591,
  608, 614, 667
anastrophe, 382–83
androgens
  and eating disorder risk, 433–34
  and female sexual function, 403
  and male sexual desire, 406–7
anger
  in borderline personality disorder, 649,
    649t, 662
  in narcissistic personality
    disorder, 639–40
anhedonia
  in Meehl's model of schizotypy, 687–88
  in schizophrenia, 337, 354, 700
  in schizotypy, 686–87
anomalous variance, 107
anorexia nervosa, 422, 424
  age of onset, 425
  anxiety and, 426
  atypical, 424
  and autism spectrum disorder, 427
  binge eating/purging subtype (AN-B/P),
    423, 424, 426, 429, 431–32
  body-image disturbance and, 430
  brain structure and function in, 432
  case example, 422–23
  defining characteristics of, 422–23
  DNA methylation in, 435
  dopamine in, 433
  epidemiology of, 425
  family and twin studies of, 434
  family dynamics and, 431
  gene–environment interaction in, 434
  genome-wide association studies
    in, 434–35
  ghrelin in, 433
  glutamate in, 433
  historical perspective on, 424–25
  HPA alterations in, 434

leptin in, 433
and mood disorders, 426
and obsessive-compulsive disorder, 426
oxytocin in, 433
perfectionism and, 429
and personality disorders, 427–28
and posttraumatic stress
  disorder, 426–27
psychological factors and, 429
restricting subtype (AN-R), 423,
  424, 429
serotonin in, 433
substance use disorders and, 287
temporal and geographic distributions
  of, 425
theory of mind deficits in, 431
Zeeman's model of, 107
anorgasmia, substance use and, 284
antagonism, 58, 60, 615, 723
  and agreeableness, 617
  and alcohol use problems, 615
  in borderline personality disorder,
    650t, 666
  facets, 606t
  and gambling disorder, 615
  and personality disorders, 590–91, 605,
    606, 609–10, 616, 616t, 618
  self-centered, 635
anterior cingulate cortex
  in anxiety disorders, 159
  in attention-deficit hyperactivity
    disorder, 481
  in borderline personality
    disorder, 663–64
  and depersonalization, 218
  in eating disorders, 432
  in obsessive-compulsive disorder, 188
  in PTSD, 207–8
  in schizophrenia, 340–41, 364, 365
antiandrogens, and erectile disorder, 408
antianxiety drugs, animal studies, 158–59
anticholesterol agents, and erectile
  disorder, 408
antidepressants
  and delayed ejaculation, 412
  and female orgasmic disorder, 410
  and female sexual function, 404
  and male sexual desire, 407
  side effects of, genetics and, 404
antihypertensives, and erectile
  disorder, 408
antiparkinsonian agents, and erectile
  function, 408
antipsychiatry movement, 7–8
antipsychotics
  and delayed ejaculation, 412
  and erectile disorder, 408
  and female orgasmic disorder, 410
  typical, 342
antisocial behavior, ADHD and, 474
antisocial personality disorder, 577, 602–3,
  612–13, 714
  and alcohol use disorder, 315

and anxiety, 719
associated traits, 607, 607t
attention-deficit hyperactivity disorder
  and, 474
and borderline personality disorder,
  651, 652t
dimensional-trait approach to, 715
in *DSM*, 715
in *DSM-5*, 715, 729–30, 731t
factor analysis, 152
internalizing-externalizing structure
  and, 14
latent class analysis, 603–4
in men, 718
and mood disorders, 719
and narcissistic personality
  disorder, 628–29
neurobiological correlates of, 719
PCL-R scores in, 716, 717
prevalence of, 718
and psychopathy, comorbidity, 718–19
substance use disorders and, 283, 288
in women, 718
Antisocial Process Screening Device, 717–
  18, 723, 724
antisocial reaction, 715
anxiety, 70–71. *See also* state anxiety; trait
  anxiety
  and antisocial personality disorder, 719
  definition of, 147
  and depression, empirical overlap, 154
  and ejaculatory function, 413
  and erectile disorder, 408
  and female orgasmic disorder, 410
  and functional somatic symptoms,
    509, 511
  and genito-pelvic pain/penetration
    disorder, 414, 415
  hyperarousal and, 536
  neighborhood deprivation and, 388
  and panic, 147
  PCL-R scores and, 716
  psychopathy and, 719
  substance use and, 283, 308
anxiety disorders. *See also* generalized
  anxiety disorder; illness anxiety
  disorder; panic disorder; social
  anxiety disorder; specific phobia(s)
  and ADHD, 474
  animal studies, 158–59
  anxiety sensitivity and, 155–56
  and attachment, 166–67
  attentional bias and, 163–64
  behavioral inhibition and, 155
  behavior genetics of, 157
  biology of, 157–59
  and bipolar spectrum disorders, 229
  and borderline personality disorder,
    651, 652t
  brain alterations in, 235–36
  common cause model, 154–57
  comorbidity with, 148–50, 149t
  conditioning and, 159–63

INDEX | 751

anxiety disorders (cont.)
   and courageous mindset, 166
   course of, 148–50
   criticism and, 168
   danger and, 260
   direct conditioning and, 160
   and eating disorders, 426
   emotional overinvolvement and, 168
   epidemiology of, 148–50, 149*t*
   etiology, 154–68
   expressed emotion and, 168
   factor analytic models of, 150–54
   genetic factor associated with, 157
   genome-wide association studies of, 158
   hostility and, 168
   and hypersexuality, 565
   information processing biases
      and, 163–66
   instructional learning and, 161
   internalizing-externalizing structure
      and, 14
   interpersonal factors in, 166–68
   interpretive bias in, 165–66
   maintenance models and factors, 154–68
   memory bias and inhibitory deficits
      in, 164–65
   molecular genetics of, 157–58
   and narcissistic personality disorder,
      628–30, 631
   neuroimaging in, 159
   neuroticism and, 154–55
   and obsessive-compulsive disorder,
      192, 193
   overlap of, 148
   panic/fear in, 147
   pathoplasty model, 154–57, 167
   perceptions of uncontrollability
      and, 161–62
   personality and, 154–57
   positive emotionality/extraversion
      and, 156–57
   and posttraumatic stress disorder,
      204, 286–87
   prevalence of, 148–50, 149*t*
   research on, advances in (future
      directions for), 168
   scar model, 154–57
   serotonin system in, 157–58
   social reinforcement and, 161
   and stably elevated negative affect
      hypothesis, 154
   and stress amplification hypothesis, 154
   substance use disorders and, 285–86
   temperament and, 154
   UP's effect on, 70–72
   vicarious conditioning and, 160–61
   vulnerability model, 154–57
anxiety sensitivity, 155–56, 163
   interpretive bias modification
      and, 165–66
Anxiety Sensitivity Index, 155–56
anxiolytics, and erectile disorder, 408
Anxious Apprehension factor, 151–52

Anxious Arousal factor, 151*f*, 152–53
anxious-disinhibited traits, in substance
   use disorders, 311
Anxious-Misery factor, 150–53, 151*f*,
   154, 157
APD. *See* avoidant personality disorder
apophany, 382–83
apotemnophilia, 552, 553–54
   age of onset, 561
APSD. *See* Antisocial Process
   Screening Device
ARFID. *See* avoidant/restrictive food
   intake disorder
Aristotelianism, 35
AS. *See* anxiety sensitivity;
   attributional style
ASDs. *See* autism spectrum disorder(s)
ASEBA. *See* Achenbach System of
   Empirically Based Assessment
asexuality, autogynephilic male-to-females
   and, 562
ASPD. *See* advanced sleep phase disorder;
   antisocial personality disorder
Asperger's disorder, 25, 490, 491
   and schizotypy, 700
asphyxiophilia, 556
   and deaths, 558, 559
   sex ratios of, 559
ASR. *See* Adult Self-Report
assault, and posttraumatic stress
   disorder, 203
assessment
   challenges of, 84
   HiTOP-informed, case illustration, 69
   HiTOP-oriented, 68–69
Assessment of Interpersonal Problem-
   Solving Skills, 353, 362
associative loosening, in Meehl's model of
   schizotypy, 687–88
assortative mating, and substance use
   disorder, 301
asylums, 36–37, 38, 78
Athens Insomnia Scale, 526
atomoxetine
   for attention-deficit hyperactivity
      disorder, 476–77
   side effects of, 477
attachment
   and anxiety disorders, 166–67
   in child molesters, 560–61
   and depression, 264
   disruptions, and paranoia, 389, 393
   insecure, 166–67, 393
   insecure-ambivalent, 167
   insecure-anxious, 393
   insecure-avoidant, 167, 393
   secure, 166–67
   in sex offenders, 560–61
   and somatization, 513
attachment theory, 41
   and borderline personality disorder, 654
attention
   in bipolar disorder, 234

cannabis use and, 284–85
childhood dysfunction, and social
   dysfunction, 358
cocaine use and, 284–85
deficit, and schizotypic
   psychopathology, 697
problems with, assessment of, 456*t*
and social functioning, in
   schizophrenia, 358
attentional bias
   and anxiety disorders, 163–64
   measures, problems with, 164
   state anxiety and, 163–64
attention allocation, in depression,
   265, 267–68
attention bias modification tasks, 164
attention-deficit hyperactivity
   disorder, 472
   adult, 473, 474, 475–76
   age-of-onset criterion, 474–76
   artificial food colors and, 478
   behavioral therapy for, 476, 477–78
   and bipolar spectrum disorders, 229
   brain connectivity in, 483
   candidate genes, 479
   cognitive training in, 478
   combination therapy for, 476, 477
   combined subtype, 472–73
   comorbidities, 474
   current diagnostic issues with, 474–76
   developmental course of, 473–74
   diagnosis of, 473
   diagnostic criteria, 474–76
   differential diagnosis, 475
   drug holidays in, 477
   *DSM* classification of, 472–73, 475–76
   and eating disorders, 427
   economic effects of, 474
   endophenotypes in, 480
   environmental risk factors for, 479–80
   epigenome-wide association study
      in, 479
   etiology, 478–80
   exercise in, 478
   and externalizing disorders, 474
   functional impact, 473, 474–75
   gene–environment interactions in, 480
   genetic influences and, 479
   genome-wide association studies in, 479
   heritability of, 478, 479
   heterogeneity of, 472, 480
   historical perspective on, 472–73
   hyperactive/impulsive behavior in,
      473, 474–75
   hyperactive/impulsive subtype, 472–73
   *ICD-11* classification, 472–73, 475–76
   impulsivity in, 663
   inattention in, 473, 474–75
   inattentive subtype, 472–73
   and internalizing disorders, 474
   late- or adult-onset, 473–74
   medication for, 476–77
   as multifactorial disorder, 478

negative impact of, 474
neurobiology of, 479–83
neurochemistry in, 482
neurocognitive abnormalities in, 480–83
neurofeedback training in, 478
nutrition in, 478
in partial remission, 473
persistent, 473, 474
pervasiveness of symptoms in, 473, 474–75
polyunsaturated fatty acids in, 478
presentations, 472–73, 476
prevalence of, 473, 474, 475
psychosocial risk factors for, 479–80
restriction diet for, 478
reward circuits in, 236–37
risk factors for, 478–80
sex distribution of, 473–74
social impact of, 474
stigmatization of, 472
and substance use disorders, 287–88
subtypes, 472–73, 476
symptom dimensions, validity of, 476
treatment, 476–78
attention-intention-effort pathway, in insomnia, 525
attenuated psychosis syndrome, 333–34
attractor(s), in dynamic systems, 105–6, 106f, 107–8, 114–15
attributional bias, 361–62, 370
in paranoid patients, 392–93
attributional style
definition of, 361
in schizophrenia, 361–62
atypical sexuality. *See* sexual atypicality
AUD. *See* alcohol use disorder
autism. *See also* autism spectrum disorder(s)
behavior in, 496
childhood, 490
diagnosis, 492–93
diagnostic criteria, 490–91
in *DSM-5*, 491, 492
in *DSM-III*, 492
*DSM-IV/ICD-10* approach to, 490–91, 492
and epilepsy, 493
infantile, 490
Kanner's views on, 490, 491, 492–93, 495
key features of, 490
regression in, 492–93
subthreshold, 490, 491
Autism Diagnostic Observation Schedule, 491
autism spectrum disorder(s), 25, 490–503
in adolescents and adults, 493
and attention-deficit hyperactivity disorder, 474
auditory signal processing in, 498
biobehavioral markers in, 499
biological perspective on, 496–503
biomarkers for, 498–503

childhood, 490
communication problems in, 494
course of, 492–93
cultural perspective on, 491
(under)diagnosis in minorities, 492
diagnosis of, 491, 499, 500
diagnostic concepts, 490–93
diagnostic criteria for, 500
in *DSM-5*, 491, 492
and eating disorders, 427
endophenotypes, 500–1
epidemiology of, 491
executive function hypothesis for, 495
extreme male brain theory of, 495–96
eye-tracking research in, 498, 499
gender predominance of, 491–92
genetics of, 496
historical perspective on, 492
and intellectual skills, 493–94
interventions for, 492, 493, 499–500
longitudinal behavioral observation in, 499
mentalization deficits in, 361, 498–99
neural signatures in, 500–1
neurodevelopmental studies in, 498–503
neuroimaging in, 499, 500
neuropsychology of, 493–94
onset, 492–93
optimal outcome cases, 493
outcomes, 492, 493
pivotal response treatment, 502–3
prevalence of, 491
psychoanalytic view on, 494
psychological perspectives on, 493–96
recurrence risk in younger siblings, 493
research on, 490, 492
and savant abilities, 493–94
school diagnoses and, 491
sex-based differences in cognitive styles and, 495–96
similarities among, 490
social brain in, 496–503
social cognition in, 498–503
social perception in, 496–503
social problems in, 493, 494–95
theoretical models of, limitations of, 496
theories of, 493–94, 496
theory of mind hypothesis for, 361, 392, 431, 494–95, 498
visual signal processing in, 498
weak central coherence theory of, 495–96
autistic disorder, 25, 490
autistic traits, and psychosis, 392
autobiographical memory
in dissociative identity disorder, 216–17
in posttraumatic stress disorder, 206–7
in schizophrenia, 364
Autobiographical Memory Test, 206
autocorrelation, 108, 109–10, 115
autoerotic asphyxia, 556

autogynephilia, 552–53, 554, 559
and gender dysphoria, 553, 562
neuroanatomy in, 564
partial, 553
autoimmune disorders, and eating disorders, 434–35
autonomic nervous system, dysfunction, in posttraumatic stress disorder, 210–11
autopedophilia, 552, 553
avoidance. *See also* experiential avoidance
in depression, 262
in obsessive-compulsive disorder, 182, 186
avoidant personality disorder, 334, 577, 602–3, 613, 677–78
associated traits, 607, 607t
behavioral inhibition and, 155
and borderline personality disorder, 651, 652t
and eating disorders, 427–28
avoidant/restrictive food intake disorder, 422
case example, 424
defining characteristics of, 423–24
epidemiology of, 425
historical perspective on, 425
presentations of, 423–24
avolition, in schizophrenia, 354
*AVPR1A gene*, in borderline personality disorder, 658

## B

background assumptions, 49, 50
BADE. *See* bias, against disconfirmatory evidence
BAS. *See* behavioral activation system
basal ganglia, in attention-deficit hyperactivity disorder, 481, 482
basket cells, 343
Bateman, Anthony, on borderline personality disorder, 654
Battie, William, *Treatise on Madness*, 36–37
Bayesian brain, 339
BD. *See* bipolar disorder
BDD. *See* body dysmorphic disorder
BDNF. *See* brain-derived neurotrophic factor
beads in a jar task, 391–92
Beck, Aaron, 233, 234
cognitive theory of depression, 265–68
BED. *See* binge-eating disorder
bed nucleus of stria terminalis
activity in threat processing, 159
in paraphilias, 560, 564
sexual dimorphism, 564
in transsexuals, 564
behavioral activation system, in bipolar disorder, 233, 234
behavioral dysregulation, and pathological narcissism, 631
behavioral inhibition, 155, 156
Behavioral Inhibition Scale, 155

behavioral inhibition system, 155, 158–59
behavioral tasks, development, challenges of, 86
behavioral therapy, for attention-deficit hyperactivity disorder, 476, 477–78
behavior genetics, of anxiety disorders, 157
behaviorism, 44
belief(s)
  anomalous, and paranoia, 389–90, 394
  continuum hypothesis, 384–86, 393–94
  delusional, endorsed by ordinary people, 385
  false, 381
  implausible but not impossible, 381
  inflexibility, and delusion, 381–82
  inner list model of, 385–86
  pathological but coincidentally true, 381
  pathological versus nonpathological but extreme, 381
  religious, 381
belongingness, protective effect against mental disorder, 388
benzodiazepines
  and alcohol, interactions of, 297
  for insomnia, 528–29
  mechanism of action, 529
  side effects of, 529
Berksonian bias, 24
Bertillon, Jacques, 6
*Bertillon Classification of Causes of Death, The*, 6
bestiality, 551
betweenness centrality, 114
bias. *See also* attentional bias; attributional bias; interpretive bias
  cognitive, and obsessive-compulsive disorder, 185–87
  against disconfirmatory evidence, 391–92
  emotional, and paranoid beliefs, 392–93
  jumping to conclusions, 266, 391–92
  memory, in anxiety disorders, 164–65
  reasoning-related, delusions and, 391–92
  recall, 104
biastophilia, 554–55, 556
bifactor analysis, 452
Big Data, and algorithms predicting posttraumatic stress disorder, 212–13
Big Five personality factors. *See also* Five Factor Model
  pathological variants, and personality disorders, 16
  personality disorders and, 587–88
BIID. *See* body integrity identity disorder
binge drinking, 303
  epidemiology of, 277
  by university students, 303
binge eating
  anorexia nervosa and, 423
  in bulimia nervosa, 423
  historical perspective on, 425

negative affect and, 430
binge-eating disorder, 422, 424
  age of onset, 425
  brain structure and function in, 432
  child maltreatment and, 431–32
  defining characteristics of, 423
  epidemiology of, 425
  family and twin studies of, 434
  family dynamics and, 431
  ghrelin in, 433
  historical perspective on, 425
  and mood disorders, 426
  perfectionism and, 429
  and personality disorders, 427–28
  and posttraumatic stress disorder, 426–27
  subthreshold, 424
biological rhythms, 521. *See also* circadian system
biology–psychology relationships
  causation in, 89–90
  in mental disorders, 87–88
  RDoC's integrative approach to, 89
biomedical approach, 42–45
biopsychosocial model, 88
biotypes, B-SNIP, 94, 97
bipolar and related disorders, otherwise specified, epidemiology of, 229
bipolar disorder, 257–58. *See also* bipolar I; bipolar II; bipolar spectrum disorders
  age at onset, 232–33
  assessment of, 229–30
  and borderline personality disorder, 659
  in childhood and adolescence, 232–33
  chronobiology of, 237–38
  clinical features of, 228
  cognitive-behavioral therapy for, 240–41
  cross-cultural aspects of, 241–44
  and delayed sleep phase disorder, 530
  developmental considerations, 123, 232–33
  in diverse and underrepresented populations, 241–44
  dysfunctional attitudes in, 233
  and eating disorders, 426
  evidence-based evaluation, 230
  family and conjoint interventions for, 241
  family-focused treatment for, 241
  family history and, 232–33
  GABA in, 343
  and goal dysregulation, 233–34
  and hypersexuality, 565
  internal appraisals in, 233–34
  interpersonal and social rhythm therapy for, 240, 241
  liability for, 703
  mood dysregulation in, 233–34
  and narcissistic personality disorder, 628–29
  not otherwise specified, 228–29
  outcomes, 232–33, 241

premorbid social adjustment in, 355–56
preparation to meet patient with, 229–30
psychoeducation for, 240, 241
in racial and ethnic minorities, 241–44
rating scales and checklists for, 230
rating scale toolkit, 229–30, 229n.1
recurrent course, 232
in relatives of schizotypy-positive probands, 696
risk, dimensional assessment, existing measures for, 231–32
self-stigma in, 243–44
sleep and circadian rhythms in, 537–38
social dysfunction in, 353
social problem-solving in, 353
societal stereotypes and, 243
stigma related to, 243–44
substance use and, 285
subthreshold symptomatology, 232–33
theory of mind and mentalization deficits in, 361
treatment process and progress, 230
white matter volume in, 340–41
bipolar I
  definition of, 228–29
  epidemiology of, 229
  and narcissistic personality disorder, 628–29
bipolar II
  definition of, 228–29
  epidemiology of, 229
Bipolar-Schizophrenia Network for Intermediate Phenotypes, 94, 97
bipolar spectrum disorders
  assessment of, 229–30
  attention in, 234
  behavior problems in, 229
  circadian rhythms in, 237–38
  clinical course, 229
  clinical presentation, 229
  cognitive processes in, 233–34
  comorbidity with, 229
  depressed phase, 229
  diagnosis, 229–31
  differential diagnosis, 229
  dimensional approaches to, 230–31
  in *DSM-5*, 228–29
  emotional processes in, 234–35
  hypomania/mania history in, 230–31
  hypomanic phase, 229
  life events and context in, 238–39
  manic phase, 229
  memory in, 234
  mixed presentations, 229
  neural processes in, 234–37
  neuroimaging in, 234–37
  overdiagnosis, 231
  prevention, 239–41
  psychobiological processes in, 233–38
  psychotherapy for, 239–41
  recurrence, 230
  remission, 229

reward circuits in, 235–37
sleep processes in, 237–38
social context and, 238
social environment and, 238–39
social functioning in, 238
treatment process and progress, 230
underdiagnosis, 230–31
within-disorder heterogeneity in, 230, 235–36
BiS. *See* behavioral inhibition system
bisexuality, autogynephilic male-to-females and, 562
Bleuler, Eugen, 78, 332, 333, 336, 676–77
   on latent schizophrenia, 682
blood pressure, in posttraumatic stress disorder, 210–11
BMI. *See* body mass index
BN. *See* bulimia nervosa
BNST. *See* bed nucleus of stria terminalis
bodily distress disorder, in *ICD-11*, 516–17
body dysmorphic disorder, 25, 181, 190–91, 194, 516
   cognitive-behavioral model of, 190–91
body-image disturbance, and eating disorders, 430
body integrity identity disorder, 553–54
   and gender identity disorder, 554
body mass index, in anorexia nervosa, 422–23
boldness, psychopathy and, 722–23, 733–34, 733f
borderline [term], 648
borderline disorders, 591
   historical perspective on, 42, 648
borderline pattern specifier, in *ICD-11*, 667
borderline personality disorder, 231, 334n.2, 577–79, 602–3, 612–13, 648–67
   additive genetic variance and, 656
   and affective disorders, 648
   affective instability in, 662–63
   age distribution of, 650t
   and alcohol use disorder, 652t
   ambulatory assessment in, 662
   anger in, 662
   antagonism in, 666
   and anxiety disorders, 651, 652t
   associated traits, 607, 607t
   attachment theory and, 654
   biosocial model of, 654
   and bipolar disorder, 659
   candidate gene studies, 657–58, 660–61
   clinical course of, 653
   clinical description of, 649
   comorbidity with, 650–53
   cooperative behavior in, 665
   and depression, 653
   detachment in, 667
   diagnosis, future of, 666–67
   (over)diagnosis in children and adolescents, 649
   diagnostic criteria for, 649, 649t
   diagnostic unreliability, 56
   dimensions of psychopathology underlying, 661–66
   disinhibition in, 663, 666, 667
   dissociality in, 667
   dominant genetic variance and, 656
   and drug use disorder, 652t
   *DSM-5* traits, 650t
   and dysthymia, 652t
   and eating disorders, 427–28
   education and, 650, 650t
   and emotional dysregulation, 648
   emotional dysregulation in, 661–66
   and emotion regulation, 47
   emptiness in, 662
   endophenotypes related to, 657
   epidemiology of, 649–50
   epigenetic studies, 659–60
   etiology, 654–55, 667
   family income and, 650, 650t
   Five Factor Model and, 650t, 656, 661
   general functioning in, 653
   and generalized anxiety disorder, 652t
   genetically informative studies of, summary, 660–61
   genetic and environmental factors and, 656
   genetic perspectives on, 655–58
   genome-wide association studies in, 658–61
   heritability, 655–56, 660–61
   historical perspective on, 648
   and histrionic personality disorder, 651, 652t
   and hypersexuality, 565
   hypersexuality in, 565
   and hypomanic episode, 652t
   ideal-type framework for, 40
   identity disturbance in, 662–63
   and impulse control disorders, 651
   impulse control in, 663–64
   and impulsivity, 648
   impulsivity in, 661–64
   and internalizing and externalizing disorders, 651
   interpersonal hypersensitivity in, 661–62, 664–66
   interpersonal problems in, 662–63, 664–66
   level of personality functioning in, 666
   in LGBTQ individuals, 650
   and life expectancy, 651–53
   lifetime prevalence of, 650, 650t
   linkage studies, 657
   loneliness in, 665–66
   and major depression, 652t, 659
   and manic episode, 652t
   marital status and, 650, 650t, 653
   and mental health, 653
   mentalization-based model of, 654
   and mood disorders, 648, 649, 651, 652t
   multivariate twin family studies, 656
   and narcissistic personality disorder, 629, 651, 652t
   negative affect in, 662–63, 664, 665, 666, 667
   negative emotional dysregulation in, 662–63
   neurobiology in, 662
   nonsuicidal self-injury in, 662–63
   and other personality disorders, comorbidity, 651, 652t
   others' negative perceptions and, 665–66
   and pain, 651, 653
   and panic disorder with or without agoraphobia, 652t
   and paranoid personality disorder, 681
   perceptions of others in, 665–66
   personality traits and, 661, 661t, 666
   phenotype, conceptualizations of, 660–66
   and posttraumatic stress disorder, 648, 652t
   prevalence of, 650
   and psychopathy, 719
   psychosocial functioning in, 653
   racial/ethnic distribution of, 650, 650t
   rejection sensitivity in, 665
   remission, 653
   and role emotional functioning, 653
   schematherapeutic model of, 654–55
   and schizophrenia, 659
   and schizotypal personality disorder, 681
   sex distribution of, 649, 650t
   social cognitive deficits in, 665–66
   and social functioning, 653
   social interaction and, 656
   and social phobia, 652t
   sociodemographic characteristics of, 649–50, 650t
   and somatic illness, comorbidity, 651–53
   and substance use disorders, 649, 651, 652t, 662–63
   suicidality in, 649, 649t, 653
   traits, heritability studies, 657
   treatment cost in, 653–54
   treatment outcomes, DNA methylation and, 662
   treatment utilization in, 653–54
   twin family studies, 656–57
   twin studies, 655–56, 657, 660–61
   validity of, 648
Boyle, Robert, 34, 36
BPD. *See* borderline personality disorder
BPM. *See* Brief Problem Monitor
brain
   alcohol's effects on, 304
   in anxiety disorders, 235–36
   in autism, 496–98, 499, 500
   in bipolar spectrum disorders, 234–37, 340–41
   cannabinoid receptors in, 317
   exposure to criticism and, 369
   function, and eating disorders, 432
   imaging (*see* neuroimaging)
   in major depression, 235–36

brain *(cont.)*
  maturation, in attention-deficit hyperactivity disorder, 482
  and mental health conditions, 66
  and mind, 45
  in obsessive-compulsive and related disorders, 188, 189, 193–94
  in posttraumatic stress disorder, 207–8
  predictive processing in, 511–12
  in schizophrenia, 235–36, 340–42, 699
  schizotaxic, 685
  in schizotypal personality disorder, 699
  in sexual function, 404
  structure, and mental health conditions, 66
  substance use and, 312
  voxel-based morphometry of, 340–41
brain activity
  in attention-deficit hyperactivity disorder, 482
  and heterogeneity in schizophrenia, 341–42
  in sexual arousal, 566
brain–behavior relationships, research on
  computational models for, 86
  mathematical models for, 86
  RDoC and, 89
brain connectivity
  in paraphilias, 560
  and psychosexual outcomes, 559–60
  in schizophrenia, 340–41
brain-derived neurotrophic factor
  in bulimia nervosa, 433
  in eating disorders, 433, 434
brain-derived neurotrophic factor gene *(BDNF)*
  in borderline personality disorder, 658, 660
  in eating disorders, 435
brain development
  childhood adversity and, 95–96, 130–31
  and handedness, 559
brain functional networks
  in attention-deficit hyperactivity disorder, 483
  in schizophrenia, 341–42, 363–64
brain injury
  and irregular sleep–wake rhythm disorder, 532
  and schizophrenia, 346
brain-predicted age, and psychopathology in youth, 95
brain structural abnormalities
  in attention-deficit hyperactivity disorder, 482
  and eating disorders, 432
  in narcissistic personality disorder, 629
  in schizophrenia, 340–41, 363–64
brain volumes. *See also* gray matter volume; white matter volume
  in attention-deficit hyperactivity disorder, 481
  in schizophrenia, 340–41

Brandes, Bernd, 555
breast cancer, alcohol use and, 283
breathing-related sleep disorders, 524
Brentano, Franz, 382
bridge principles, in making inferences from public data, 88–89
Brief Problem Monitor, 462–63
  for Ages 6–18 (BPM/16–18), 456t, 462–63
  BPM/18–59, 462–63
  BPM-P, 462–63
  BPM-T, 462–63
  BPM-Y, 462–63
bright light therapy
  in advanced sleep phase disorder, 531–32
  in delayed sleep phase disorder, 530–31
  in depression, 535–36, 537–38
  in irregular sleep–wake rhythm disorder, 532
Briquet, Pierre, on hysteria, 510
Briquet's syndrome, 510
broader autism phenotype, 500–1
Brucke, Ernst, 41
BSDs. *See* bipolar spectrum disorders
B-SNIP. *See* Bipolar-Schizophrenia Network for Intermediate Phenotypes
bulimia nervosa, 422, 424
  age of onset, 425
  and attention-deficit hyperactivity disorder, 427
  body-image disturbance and, 430
  brain-derived neurotrophic factor in, 433
  brain structure and function in, 432
  case example, 423
  child maltreatment and, 431–32
  defining characteristics of, 423
  DNA methylation in, 435
  dopamine in, 433
  epidemiology of, 425
  family and twin studies of, 434
  family dynamics and, 431
  gene–environment interaction in, 434
  ghrelin in, 433
  glutamate in, 433
  historical perspective on, 425
  HPA alterations in, 434
  impulsivity and, 429–30
  and mood disorders, 426
  perfectionism and, 429
  and personality disorders, 427–28
  and posttraumatic stress disorder, 426–27
  psychological factors and, 429
  serotonin in, 432–33
  and substance use disorders, 427
  substance use disorders and, 287
  subthreshold, 424
  temporal and geographic distributions of, 425
bulimia-spectrum disorders, child maltreatment and, 431–32
bullying, and paranoia, 388

## C

caffeine abuse, and eating disorders, 427
CALF. *See* Clinical Assessment of the Level of Personality Functioning Scale
callousness, and personality disorders, 590–91, 614, 617
callous-unemotionality, 723–24
Camberwell Family Interview, 368
cannabinoid system, in substance use disorders, 313, 315, 317–18
cannabis use
  and paranoia, 390
  and schizophrenia risk, 345–46, 345t
cannabis use disorder
  cognitive changes related to, 311–12
  comorbid psychopathology in, 280
  conduct disorder and, 288
  epidemiology of, 277
  and neurocognitive impairment, 284–85
  and polysubstance use, 280
  prevalence of, 280
  schizophrenia and, 287
cannibalism, 552
cardiovascular disease
  and borderline personality disorder, 651
  and erectile disorder, 407–8
  and female orgasmic disorder, 409–10
  substance use disorders and, 281–82
Caregiver-Teacher Report Form, 456t
Carnap, Rudolf, 48–49
cataplexy
  definition of, 533
  in narcolepsy, 533
  sodium oxybate for, 533–34
  venlafaxine for, 533–34
catastrophe flags, 107
catastrophe theory, 106–7
catastrophizing, in cognitive model of depression, 266
catatonia, 6
catechol-O-methyltransferase gene
  in borderline personality disorder, 658
  in schizophrenia, 344
  in schizotypic psychopathology, 696–97
CAT-PD. *See* Computer Adaptive Test of Personality Disorder
Cattell, James McKeen, 14
caudate nucleus
  in attention-deficit hyperactivity disorder, 481
  in obsessive-compulsive disorder, 188
causal/etiological approach, 33. *See also* conjecture
causal network, 48
causation in psychopathology
  interventionist model, 44
  production accounts (mechanistic models), 43–44
  reductionist model, 44
  regularity accounts, 44–45
  rethinking of, 42–45
  two approaches to, 43–45
CBCL. *See* Child Behaviour Checklist

CBT-I. *See* cognitive behavior therapy for insomnia
CCN. *See* cognitive control network
CD. *See* conduct disorder; conversion disorder
CDD. *See* childhood disintegrative disorder
centrality
  betweenness, 114
  degree, 114
  measures of, 113–14, 116
  strength, 114
Centrality of Event Scale, 207
cerebellum
  in attention-deficit hyperactivity disorder, 481
  in paraphilias, 560
CES. *See* Centrality of Event Scale
CFA. *See* confirmatory factor analysis
CFI. *See* Camberwell Family Interview
chandelier cells, 343
Chapman, L. J., and J. P., "psychosis proneness" scales, 693–94
Charcot, Jean, 217
Cheyne, George, *The English Malady*, 36
child abuse and neglect. *See also* child maltreatment
  and eating disorders, 426–27, 431–32
  emotional, and borderline personality disorder, 655
  and hallucinations, 388–89
  and paranoia, 389
  physical, and borderline personality disorder, 655
  prevalence of, 130
Child Anxiety Related Disorders–Parent Report, triarchic scale measure based on, 727t
Child Behaviour Checklist, 465, 466
  for Ages 1½–5, 456t, 463, 466
  for Ages 6–18, 454–55, 456t, 458–59, 459f, 460, 463
  triarchic scale measure based on, 727t
childhood adversity. *See also* child maltreatment
  and borderline personality disorder, 655
  and functional somatic symptoms, 512–13
  and genes, in development of psychosis, 387
  and paranoia, 388–89, 393
childhood disintegrative disorder, 25, 490, 492–93
childhood loss, and female orgasmic disorder, 410
child maltreatment. *See also* child abuse and neglect; childhood adversity
  and adolescent substance use, 306–7
  and bipolar disorder, 238–39
  child–parent psychotherapy for, 137
  and comorbid disorders, 238–39
  and conduct disorder, 306

developmental psychopathology perspective on, 130–32
  and dissociative identity disorder, 214
  and epigenetics, 132
  HiTOP perspective on, 66–67
  and inflammatory response, 135
  neurobiological effects of, 130–31
  physiological effects of, 130–31
  and psychopathology, 66–67, 131–32
  resilient outcomes with, 129–30, 131–32
child molestation, 549
child–parent psychotherapy
  for child maltreatment, 137
  efficacy of, 137
  for maternal depression, 137
  principles of, 137
child pornography, 549
Child Problematic Traits Inventory, 717–18
child psychopathology
  dimensional model of, 14
  in *DSM*, 448
  empirically based constructs for, 448–49
  externalizing, 448–49
  factor analysis and, 448–49
  hierarchical models, 449
  internalizing, 448–49
Child Psychopathy Scale, 717–18, 723
children
  assessment instruments for, 450–51
  borderline personality disorder (over) diagnosis in, 649
  depression in, 259
  functioning of, research on, and informant discrepancies, 463
  multi-informant assessment of, 453–54
  psychopathy assessment in, 717–18
  sexual interest in (*see* hebephilia; pedophilia)
  sleep problems in, prognostic significance, 538
chlorpromazine, 342
CHR (clinical high risk). *See* schizophrenia, clinical high-risk (CHR) studies of
chronic fatigue syndrome, 510
chronobiology, 521
chronophilia, 549
chronotherapy, for delayed sleep phase disorder, 530
CIDI. *See* Composite International Diagnostic Interview
cigarette smoking
  addictive effects, neuropharmacology of, 317–18
  ADHD and, 474
  clinical subtyping of, 280
  comorbidity with, 315
  and erectile disorder, 407
  genetic factors in, 313
  maternal, during pregnancy, and ADHD, 479, 480
  teratogenicity, 307
  trends in, 317–18

cingulate gyrus
  in eating disorders, 432
  in schizophrenia, 365
cingulum, in eating disorders, 432
circadian rhythm sleep–wake disorders, 524, 529–33
  in *DSM-5*, 529
  extrinsic, 529
  intrinsic, 529
  unspecified type, 529
circadian system/circadian rhythms, 521. *See also* sleep and circadian rhythm disorders; sleep and circadian rhythms
  assessment of, 522–23
  in bipolar spectrum disorders, 237–38, 537–38
  clock genes in, 237–38, 537–38
  function of, 237–38
  gene polymorphisms, in bipolar disorder, 537–38
  in major depression, 238, 535–36
  in schizophrenia, 238, 538–39
  and sleep–wake cycle, 237, 521
  structure of, 237–38
circular causality, 46
Claridge, Gordon
  view of Meehl's model as "quasi-dimensional," 692
  view of schizotypy, 690–92
classification, 25–26. *See also* nosology
  atheoretical approach to, 16–18
  blind spots in coverage, 56
  categorical approach to, 8, 13–16, 54–57
  clinical functions of, 22
  and comorbidity, 24–25
  criticisms of, through 1960s, 7–8
  definition of, 3
  and description, 4
  dimensional approach to, 13–16, 85
  of diseases, 10–11
  of disorders, 10–11
  of disorders versus classification of individuals, 11–12
  historical perspective on, 3, 5–8
  implicit values and, 17–18
  and information retrieval, 4
  issues and controversies in, 10–19
  measurement and methodological issues, 19–25
  neo-Kraepelinian view of, 8
  NIMH objective for, 81–82
  and prediction, 4
  purpose of, 4–5
  reliability of, 19–21
  sociopolitical function of, 5
  of syndromes, 10–11
  and theory development, 5
  traditional approaches to, 77
  unresolved issues in, 3–4
  validity of, 21–23
  work groups and, 18–19

INDEX | 757

Cleckley, H., on psychopathy, 715–17, 718, 719, 722–23
Clinical Assessment of the Level of Personality Functioning Scale, 582t, 583, 584t, 592–93
clinical interviews
　in insomnia diagnosis, 526
　for schizotypic psychopathology, 692–93
　in sleep and circadian disorders, 522
clinical significance, definition of, 12
clinical staging, 97
clinical utility, 22
clock genes, 237–38, 537–38
closedness to experience, and personality disorders, 605
clothing-fetishism, 550, 553
cluster analysis, 13, 15
coactions, horizontal versus vertical, 124
cocaethylene, 297
cocaine
　and alcohol, interactions of, 297
　dependence, genetic factors in, 314
　and serotonergic system, 316–17
　teratogenicity, 307
　withdrawal, depressive symptoms in, 285
cocaine expectancies, 282, 309
cocaine use
　and depressive disorders, 285
　and interpersonal aggression, 283–84
　and neurocognitive impairment, 284–85
coefficient alpha, 20
cognition, 45. *See also* cognitive style(s); 4E framework; neurocognition; social cognition
　in autism, 496
　definition of, 357
　nonsocial, assessment of, 362
　in schizophrenia, 337–40
　and social dysfunction in schizophrenia, 357
cognitive ability
　hierarchical structure of, 61
　and protection against PTSD, 209–10
cognitive-behavioral model(s)
　of body dysmorphic disorder, 190–91
　of obsessive-compulsive disorder, 186, 187
cognitive-behavioral therapy, 71. *See also* Unified Protocol for the Transdiagnostic Treatment of Emotional Disorders
　for adult ADHD, 476
　for bipolar disorder, 240–41
　for obsessive-compulsive disorder, 187
　for paranoia, 394
　response to, interpersonal problems and, 167
cognitive behavior therapy for insomnia, 527–28
　in depression, 535–36
　in generalized anxiety disorder, 536–37
　and psychosis, 538

and schizophrenia, 538
cognitive bias, and obsessive-compulsive disorder, 185–87
cognitive changes, addiction-related, 311–12
cognitive control network, in attention-deficit hyperactivity disorder, 483
cognitive deficits, and obsessive-compulsive disorder, 185
cognitive-experimental approach
　definition of, 339
　to schizophrenia, 338–40
cognitive fusion
　definition of, 188
　and obsessive-compulsive disorder, 188
cognitive inhibition, problems, in obsessive-compulsive disorder, 185
cognitive neuroscience, in PTSD, 207–8
cognitive remediation therapy, in schizophrenia, 369–70
cognitive slippage, in schizotypy, 686–87
cognitive style(s)
　in autism, 495–96
　in bipolar disorder, 233–34
　empathizing, 495–96
　sex-based differences in, 495–96
　in substance use disorders, 309–12
　systemizing, 495–96
coldheartedness, 723
Collaborative Longitudinal Personality Disorders Study, 653
Collaborative Psychiatric Epidemiology Surveys, 258
collective adversity, and psychosis, 387–88
communication, and sexual function, 405, 410
comorbidity, 55, 57–58
　among *DSM-5* categories, 235–36
　categorical nosology and, 301–2
　and classification, 24–25
　definition of, 23, 680–81
　and diagnostic overlap, 24–25
　hierarchical dimensional nosology and, 301–2
　historical perspective on, 24
　HiTOP model and, 61
　statistical models of, 24
　and treatment decisions, 55
competence
　in development, organizational perspective on, 124–25
　developmental analysis of, 123
complex dynamic system(s), 102–5. *See also* early warning signal(s)
　anomalous variance in, 107
　attractors in, 105–6, 106f, 107–8, 114–15
　autocorrelation in, 108, 109–10, 115
　bistable landscape in, 106, 106f
　catastrophe flags, 107
　catastrophes in, 106–7
　control parameters, 106–7
　critical slowing down in, 107
　definition of, 103–4

differential equation models, 105
divergence of response in, 107
hierarchical structure of, 105
models, 105–7
networks and, 112f, 114–15
stability landscape, 105–7, 106f
state of, 105
"system" in, 116
time scales of changes in, 104–5
variance in, 108, 109–10
complex system(s), 102
　chaotic behavior, 103
　definition of, 102–3, 116
　emergent behavior, 103
　nonlinearity of, 103, 116
　psychopathology and, 102
　self-organization of, 103, 116
compliance, and personality disorders, 605
Composite International Diagnostic Interview, 258
compulsions
　definition of, 182
　in obsessive-compulsive disorder, 181, 182
　themes of, 182–83
compulsive disorders, 189
compulsive sexual behavior disorder, in *ICD-11*, 548
compulsivity, and personality disorders, 606, 618
computational neuroscience, 86
computational psychiatry, 86
Computer Adaptive Test of Personality Disorder, 612, 614
COMT. *See* catechol-O-methyltransferase
Comte, August, 38
conditioning
　and anxiety disorders, 159–63
　direct, 160
　interoceptive, 163
　preparedness theory and, 161
　selective associations and, 161
　temperament/personality and, 162–63
　uncontrollability and, 161–62
　unpredictability and, 161–62
　vicarious, 160–61
conditioning models, of obsessive-compulsive disorder, 184–85
conduct disorder, 25
　and ADHD, 474
　and bipolar spectrum disorders, 229
　child maltreatment and, 306
　peer influences and, 301
　and posttraumatic stress disorder, 204
　and substance use disorders, 288, 304–5, 306
cone of gaze functioning, in schizotypic psychopathology, 698
confirmatory factor analysis, 451–52, 455–56
conjecture, 47–49
　versus description, 33–38, 49–50
Conrad, Klaus, 382–83

conscientiousness, 63, 661. *See also* constraint
  in borderline personality disorder, 650t, 656, 661
  in Five Factor Model, 14
  and personality disorders, 603, 605, 616, 616t
  and risk for substance use disorders, 308–9
constraint
  and personality disorders, 605
  research on, HiTOP framework for, 63–64
context processing, 339
conversational ability
  difficulties with, in schizophrenia, 357
  processing capacity and, 357
conversion disorder, 510
  diagnosis of, 515–16
  in *DSM-5*, 515–16
  predictive processing and, 516
  and somatic symptom disorder, 516
co-occurrence, definition of, 680–81
cooperative behavior, in borderline personality disorder, 665
Copernican theory, 47
coprolagnia, 551
coprophilia, 551, 556
coronary disease
  and erectile disorder, 407–8
  and male sexual desire, 407
corpus callosum
  in attention-deficit hyperactivity disorder, 481
  in eating disorders, 432
cortical activation, in sleep, 523
cortical arousal, and insomnia, 525
cortical thickness, in attention-deficit hyperactivity disorder, 482
cortisol
  in bipolar disorder, 537
  in eating disorders, 434
  and hippocampal volume, 209
  in posttraumatic stress disorder, 213
co-rumination, in depression, 263
courageous mindset, 166
courtesy stigma, 243
courtship disorder, 556–57
courtship disorder hypothesis, 556, 557
covariation, definition of, 680–81
COVID, functional somatic symptoms after, 513
Coyne, J. C., on depression, 263–65, 270
CpG sites, methylation, 659–60
CPP. *See* child–parent psychotherapy
CPS. *See* Child Psychopathy Scale
CPUS. *See* Collaborative Psychiatric Epidemiology Surveys
C-reactive protein, in depression, 135
*CRHR1* gene, 158
criminal behavior, and narcissistic grandiosity and vulnerability, 634
criticism, anxiety disorders and, 168

Crohn's disease, and male sexual desire, 407
Cronbach's alpha, 609
cross-dressing, 562. *See also* transvestism
  age of onset, 561
  androphilic male-to-females and, 562–63
  autogynephilic male-to-females and, 562
cross-sensitization, to drugs, 315
cross-validation, 502
CRP. *See* C-reactive protein
CRSWDs. *See* circadian rhythm sleep–wake disorders
C-TRF. *See* Caregiver-Teacher Report Form
cuckolding, 558
CUD. *See* cannabis use disorder
Cullen, William, 5
culture
  and eating disorders, 428–29
  and female orgasmic disorder, 411
  and female sexual function, 405
  and Personality Inventory for *DSM-5*, 612
  and ratings of problems and positive qualities in Achenbach System of Empirically Based Assessment, 460
  and substance use, 302–3
culture-bound syndromes, 509
cusp catastrophe model, 106–7
cyclothymic disorder
  definition of, 228–29
  epidemiology of, 229

# D

DA. *See* dopamine/dopaminergic system
danger, and anxiety disorders, 260
Danish Adoption Study of Schizophrenia, 680, 682–83, 695, 696
DAPP-BQ. *See* Dimensional Assessment of Personality Pathology–Basic Questionnaire
data-driven approaches, 86
*DAT* gene. *See* dopamine transporter gene
*DAT1/SLC6A3* gene. *See* dopamine transporter gene
DBT. *See* dialectical behavior therapy
DD. *See* dysthymic disorder
DDNOS. *See* dissociative disorders not otherwise specified
DE. *See* delayed ejaculation
deceitfulness
  and personality disorders, 610, 617
  in personality disorders, 612–13
default mode network
  in attention-deficit hyperactivity disorder, 483
  disruptions, in schizophrenia, 364
  in eating disorders, 432
degree centrality, 114
delayed circadian phase disorders, 524
delayed ejaculation, 411–12

age and, 411, 412
biological factors and, 411–12
causes of, 411–12
definition of, 411
diagnosis of, 411
prevalence of, 411
psychic conflict and, 412
psychological factors and, 412
SSRIs and, 411
delayed sleep phase disorder, 529–31
  assessment of, 530
  and bipolar disorder, 530
  and depression, 530
  etiological models of, 530
  management of, 530–31
  and mood disorders, 530
  prevalence of, 530
  and schizophrenia, 538
delinquency, 715
  ADHD and, 474
  peer, and adolescent substance use, 282–83
delusion(s)
  anomalous experience model of, 389–90, 394
  assessment of, 386
  in bipolar disorder, 383–84
  bizarre versus nonbizarre, 382
  clinical concept of, 378
  cognitive-behavioral interventions for, 381, 394
  cognitive factors and, 389, 390–92, 394
  of communication, 384
  conceptual history of, 378–80
  continuum hypothesis and, 384–86, 393–94
  of control, 384
  covariation among, 384
  definition of, 381–83
  in depression, 383–84
  erotomanic, 379
  grandiose, 379, 384
  and hallucinations, co-occurrence of, 390
  jealous, 379
  Kretschmer's views on, 379
  mixed, 379
  nonsensical nature of, 382
  of observation, 384
  and other kinds of beliefs, 381
  paranoid, 383–84
  persecutory, 379, 383–84, 383b
  phenomenological approach to, 382–83
  as psychotic symptoms, 334
  of reference, 384
  religious, 384
  in schizophrenia, 336–37, 354, 383–84
  somatic, 379
  unspecified, 379
  vulnerability for, 363
delusional disorder, 25, 379
delusional mood, 382–83

INDEX | 759

dementia
    and hypersexuality, 565
    and irregular sleep–wake rhythm disorder, 532
dementia praecox, 6, 38, 78, 332, 334–35, 378–79. *See also* schizophrenia
    paranoide formen, 378–79
dendrites, development and outgrowth, in ADHD, 479
departments of psychiatry, historical perspective on, 37
dependence, physiological, 277–78
dependent personality disorder, 577, 602–3, 613, 614
    and borderline personality disorder, 651, 652t
depersonalization/derealization disorder, 214, 218, 390
    prevalence of, 214
depression, 70–71, 257, 270–71. *See also* major depressive disorder; maternal depression; schizoaffective disorder
    in adolescence, 259, 269
    affective-cognitive network in, 267
    age and cohort effects in, 259
    and alcohol use, 285, 308
    and anxiety, empirical overlap, 154
    attention allocation in, 265, 267–68
    attention-deficit hyperactivity disorder and, 474
    attribution-based models of, 268
    avoidance in, 262
    Beck's cognitive theory of, 265–68
    behavioral models of, 259, 261–63, 270
    in bipolar spectrum disorders, 229
    and borderline personality disorder, 653
    in childhood, 259, 269
    cognitive models of, 259, 261, 262, 265–70
    cognitive self-regulatory approaches to, 265–66, 268–70
    cognitive therapy for, 266–67
    cognitive vulnerability to, 268
    co-rumination in, 263
    costs of, 257
    and delayed sleep phase disorder, 530
    and dependent negative life event creation, 261
    descriptive features of, 267
    developmental perspective on, 132–36, 137
    diathesis-stress perspective on, 265–68, 270–71
    differential susceptibility perspective on, 134
    dimensional versus categorical model of, 13
    in *DSM-5*, 257, 258
    dynamical systems perspective on, 104–5
    dysfunctional attitudes in, 233
    and eating disorders, 426
    in economically disadvantaged mothers, interpersonal psychotherapy for, 137
    EEG findings in, 135
    epidemiology of, 258–59, 270
    epigenetic studies of, 134
    equifinality in, 132–33
    and erectile disorder, 408
    ethnicity and, 258
    factor analytic models of, 150–52
    fatigue in, 535–36
    and functional somatic symptoms, 509
    gender differences in, 259, 263
    gene–environment interaction in, 261
    and generalized anxiety disorder, 57–58
    genetics and, 134–35, 268
    and genito-pelvic pain/penetration disorder, 415–16
    genome-wide association studies of, 133–34
    goal orientation and, 268–70
    historical perspective on, 47, 257–58
    hopelessness theory of, 265–66
    *5-HTT* gene and, 133, 134, 261
    immune function and, 135
    and insomnia, 61
    integrated models of, 259, 262, 264, 270
    and interpersonal conflict, 261
    interpersonal models of, 259, 262, 263–65, 270
    interpersonal psychotherapy for, 134
    kindling of, 260
    learned helplessness theory of, 268
    life event models of, 259–61, 262
    life span perspective on, 132–33
    loss and, 260
    low response-contingent positive reinforcement and, 261–63
    major (*see* major depressive disorder)
    and male sexual desire, 407
    multifinality in, 132–33
    narcissistic personality disorder/pathological narcissism and, 634, 639
    negative cognitive triad in, 266, 267
    negative core beliefs in, 264
    negative feedback-seeking in, 264
    and negative interpretation bias, 265
    neighborhood deprivation and, 388
    neural correlates of, 135
    onset of, 260, 261
    perfectionism and, 269–70
    personality and, 261
    pharmacotherapy for, 134
    positive emotionality/extraversion and, 156–57
    and posttraumatic stress disorder, 204, 286–87
    prevalence of, 132, 258
    prevention of, 134
    psychological and biological system interplay in, 132–33
    as public health problem, 257
    reassurance-seeking in, 263–64
    recurrent, 132, 260, 261, 266–67
    regular versus endogenous, 15–16
    relapse, 266–68
    in relatives of schizotypy-positive probands, 696
    research on, developmental approaches for, 136
    reward circuitry in, 236–37
    reward processes in, 261–62
    rising social value and, 265
    risk factors for, 260–61
    rumination in, 262–63
    self-system therapy for, 269
    severity spectrum for, 132–33
    social consequences o, 263–65, 267
    social models of, 259–70
    social rejection in, 263–65
    social risk hypothesis of, 265
    social skills deficits and, 262
    social support and, 261, 263
    socioevolutionary models of, 265
    stress autonomy model of, 260
    stress generation and, 261, 264
    stressors and, 133
    stress sensitization model of, 260
    and submissiveness, 265
    and substance use, 283, 308
    subtypes of, 270
    and suicidality, 259
    treatment of, 70–72, 134, 266–67
    treatment-resistant, 257
    unipolar, 257 (*see also* major depressive disorder)
    verbal behavioral processes in, 262–63
depressiveness, and personality disorders, 590–91
depth and duration of connection, and personality disorders, 590–91
derailment, 337
derealization. *See* depersonalization/derealization disorder
description
    classification and, 4
    versus conjecture, 33–38, 49–50
descriptive psychopathology, 42, 43
detachment, 615
    in borderline personality disorder, 667
    facets, 606t
    and gambling disorder, 615
    and major depression, 615–16
    and personality disorders, 590–91, 605, 606, 610, 616, 616t
    and posttraumatic stress disorder, 615–16
    and psychotic disorders, 616
detachment spectrum, 60
development
    child maltreatment and, 130–32
    diverse pathways in, 126–27
    epigenetics and, 128, 132
    genetic processes and, 128
    and mental disorders, 82, 87

neurodevelopmental processes
    and, 128
normal, 124
organizational perspective on, 124–26,
    137–38
in RDoC-oriented research
    designs, 95–96
in Research Domain Criteria, 82,
    83f, 85, 87
developmental [term], definition of, 122
developmental analysis, definition of, 123
developmental approach, definition of, 122
developmental cascades, 127
developmental coordination disorder, and
    ADHD, 474
developmental psychopathology, 87, 122–
    38, 448–50, 467–68. *See also* life-
    span developmental approach
assessment instruments, 450–51
on child maltreatment, 130–32
contextualism in, 125
definition of, 122–23
on depression, 132–36
and developmental cascades, 127
and diversity in process and
    outcome, 126–27
*DSM*-oriented scales, 453
empirically based bottom-up paradigm
    and, 448, 449, 450–55
externalizing scales, 452
factor analysis and, 448–49, 450
goals of, 122–23
hierarchical models, 449
hierarchy of empirically derived
    problem scales in, 452, 452f
historical perspective on, 123–24
integrative framework of, 122–23, 125–
    26, 127–28, 135–36
interdisciplinary approach and, 122–23,
    125–26, 127–28, 135–36, 137–38
and interface of normal and atypical
    development, 126
internalizing scales, 452
and intervention, 130, 137
life span perspective in, 125–26
longitudinal research in, 136
longitudinal studies of, 463–66
multi-informant assessment, 453–54
and multiple levels of analysis, 127–
    28, 135–36
narrow- and broad-spectrum
    groupings, 448–49
and organizational perspective, 124–
    26, 137–38
and prevention, 130
principles of, 126–30
RDoC-oriented research on, 95–96
research designs and strategies in,
    136, 137–38
and resilience science, 128–30
serotonergic system and, 466
syndrome scales, 451–52
unique focus of, 123

developmental theory
    embryological findings and, 126
    empirical study of psychopathology
        and, 126
    integrative framework of, 126–30
    interface of normal and atypical
        development in, 126–30
deviant rape pattern, 554
dextroamphetamine sulfate, for
    narcolepsy, 533–34
*dhat syndrome*, 509
diabetes
    and delayed ejaculation, 412
    and erectile disorder, 407–8
diagnosis/diagnoses, 25–26
    blind spots in coverage, 56
    criticisms of, through 1960s, 7–8
    definition of, 3
    heterogeneity of, 55–56, 65
    historical perspective on, 5–8, 78–
        79, 96–97
    neo-Kraepelinian view of, 8
    and new directions for research, 80–81
    reliability of, 19–21, 79–80
    symptom-based dichotomous approach
        to, 85, 86
    traditional approaches to, 77
    unreliability of, 56
    validity of, 19, 21–23, 79–80, 82
    variance of, 20
*Diagnostic and Statistical Manual of Mental
    Disorders*. See DSM
    fifth edition (see *DSM-5*)
    first edition (see *DSM-I*)
    fourth edition (see *DSM-IV*)
    second edition (see *DSM-II*)
    third edition (see *DSM-III*)
diagnostic criteria, 79. *See also* Research
    Diagnostic Criteria
    in *DSM*, 54–55
    in *DSM-III*, 8–9, 19, 20, 79–80
    psychological, versus biological
        mechanisms, 87–88
Diagnostic Interview for Narcissism, 628
diagnostic overlap, 23–25
    and comorbidity, 24–25
    historical perspective on, 23–24
diagnostic reification, with *DSM-III*, 80–
    81, 96–97
diagnostic spectra, 25
dialectical behavior therapy, as
    transdiagnostic treatment, 72
diaperism, 553
diathesis-stress model, 344, 369, 688
Dickens, Charles, *A Christmas Carol*, 36
DID. *See* dissociative identity disorder
dietary restraint, and eating
    disorders, 430
differential equation models, 105
    in network analysis, 115–16
differential susceptibility to environment,
    128, 134
diffusion tensor imaging

in attention-deficit hyperactivity
    disorder, 481–82, 483
in eating disorders, 432
in schizophrenia, 341
dihydropyridine dehydrogenase gene
    *(DPYD)*, in borderline personality
    disorder, 659
Dilthey, Wilhelm, 39, 40
dimensional assessment
    HiTOP-oriented, 68
    norms in, 68
Dimensional Assessment of Personality
    Pathology–Basic Questionnaire,
    605, 612
dimethyltryptamine, and serotonergic
    system, 316–17
DIN. *See* Diagnostic Interview for
    Narcissism
discrimination, 243
    and paranoia, 388
disease(s)
    definition of, 11
    essentialist view of, 22
    natural history of, 35
disinhibition, 59, 60, 615
    and alcohol use problems, 615
    in borderline personality disorder, 650t,
        663, 666, 667
    facets, 590, 606t
    and personality disorders, 590, 591, 605,
        606, 609–10, 616, 616t
    psychopathy and, 721–22, 733–34, 733f
    and psychotic disorders, 616
    trauma- or disease-related,
        hypersexuality in, 565
disorder(s)
    classification of, 11–12
    definition of, 11
disruptive behavior spectrum, 25
dissocial behavior, and personality
    disorders, 605
dissociality, 605
    in borderline personality disorder, 667
    and personality disorders, 591
dissociation
    in borderline personality disorder, 649,
        649t, 664–66
    definition of, 214
    as mediator of trauma and
        hallucinations, 390
    peritraumatic, and risk of
        PTSD, 205
    phenomenology of, 214
dissociative amnesia, 214, 217–18
    *DSM-5* on, 217
    generalized, 217
    localized, 217
    prevalence of, 214
    selective, 217
    trauma and, 217–18
dissociative disorders, 214–18
    prevalence of, 214
    trauma and, 218

dissociative disorders not otherwise specified, prevalence of, 214
dissociative fugue, 214, 218
dissociative identity disorder, 214–17, 218
　interidentity transfer of information in, 215–16
　prevalence of, 214
　versus schizophrenia, 332, 333
distress
　in HiTOP, 231
　as subdimension of internalizing spectrum, 57–58, 60, 231
　and suicidality, 70
Distress factor, 152, 154
disturbed function, as functional somatic symptom, 508–9
dizziness, functional, 513
DLOPFQ. *See DSM-5* Levels of Personality Functioning Questionnaire
DMN. *See* default mode network
DNA methylation, 435. *See also* epigenetics
　in attention-deficit hyperactivity disorder, 479
　in borderline personality disorder, 659–60
　child maltreatment and, 132
domestic violence, children and, 130
dominance, fearless, 722
dopamine/dopaminergic system
　in attention-deficit hyperactivity disorder, 482–83
　in borderline personality disorder, 658
　in eating disorders, 433, 435
　in reward circuits, 365
　in schizophrenia, 689, 699–700
　and schizotypy, 689, 699–700
　and sexuality, 566
　in substance use disorders, 313, 315
dopamine D$_2$ receptor gene *(DRD2)*
　in borderline personality disorder, 658
　DRD2 TaqIA polymorphism, in bulimia, 434
　in eating disorders, 435
dopamine D$_4$ receptor gene *(DRD4)*
　in ADHD, 479
　in borderline personality disorder, 658
dopamine D$_5$ receptor gene *(DRD5)*, in ADHD, 479
dopamine hypothesis, of schizophrenia, 342–43
dopamine transporter gene
　*DAT*, in eating disorders, 435
　*DAT1*, in borderline personality disorder, 658
　*DAT1/SLC6A3*, in ADHD, 479, 480
dorsal intraparietal sulcus, in schizophrenia, 363–64
doxepin, for insomnia, 529
drag queens, 563
*DRD2* gene. *See* dopamine D$_2$ receptor gene *(DRD2)*

*DRD4* gene. *See* dopamine D$_4$ receptor gene *(DRD4)*
*DRD5* gene. *See* dopamine D$_5$ receptor gene *(DRD5)*
drug dependence. *See also* substance use disorder(s)
　factor analysis, 152
　and narcissistic personality disorder, 628–29
drug holidays, in ADHD, 477
drug overdose, deaths caused by, 304
drug subcultures, 303, 305
drug use disorders, 297. *See also* substance use disorder(s)
　and borderline personality disorder, 652t
　and narcissistic grandiosity and vulnerability, 634
*DSM*, 3, 79–80
　atheoretical approach to classification, 16–18
　binary disease/no-disease legacy of, 85, 86
　categorical approach in, 54–55
　criticisms of, 42–43, 55
　diagnostic criteria in, 54–55, 87–88
　early editions of, 6–7
　formulation and revision of, 54
　internalizing-externalizing structure and, 14
　and life-span approach, 449–50
　and new directions for research, 80–81
　work groups and, 18–19
*DSM-5*, 10, 12–13. *See also* Alternative Model of Personality Disorders; Level of Personality Functioning Scale
　antisocial personality disorder in, 715, 729–30, 731t
　and assessment of dysfunction, 10
　autism spectrum disorders in, 491, 492
　bipolar spectrum disorders in, 228–29
　borderline personality disorder in, 650t
　circadian rhythm sleep–wake disorders in, 529
　classification system, problems with, 230
　conversion disorder/functional neurological symptom disorder, 515–16
　delusional disorder in, 379
　delusions in, 381, 382
　diagnostic spectra in, 10, 25
　dimensional alternatives, 10
　dissociative amnesia in, 217
　eating disorders in, 422
　formulation and revision of, 18
　functional somatic symptoms in, 514–17
　genito-pelvic pain/penetration disorder in, 413–14
　internalizing-externalizing structure and, 14, 24
　and life-span approach, 449–50
　narcissistic personality disorder in, 627

　personality disorders in, 14, 16, 20, 42, 577, 578–79, 602–3, 605, 627, 630, 657, 666, 667
　posttraumatic stress disorder in, 213–14
　psychopathy in, 715, 729–30
　psychoticism in, 700–1
　reliability of diagnoses in, 20–21
　revision process, 80
　schizotypal personality disorder in, 682–83
　schizotypic psychopathology in, 676–77
　sexual dysfunction in, 402
　sleep and circadian rhythm disorders in, 523–24
　somatic symptom disorder, 514–15
　"Somatic Symptoms and Related Disorders," 514, 515, 516
　structure and organization of, 24, 25
　substance use disorders in, 278, 297–300, 299t
　work groups and, 18
*DSM-I*, 6, 7, 8–9, 16–17, 19, 20, 79
*DSM-II*, 6–7, 8–9, 16–17, 20, 79
*DSM-III*, 8–10, 12, 379
　atheoretical approach to classification, 16–17
　criticism of, 80
　descriptive approach in, 34, 79
　diagnostic criteria in, 8–9, 19, 20, 79–80
　and diagnostic overlap, 23
　and diagnostic reliability, 19, 20, 21, 79–80
　diagnostic system of, 79
　formulation and revision of, 18–19, 42
　multiaxial system of, 8–9, 10
　and new directions for research, 80–81
　personality disorders in, 42
　popularity and success of, 9
　reification of disorders in, 80–81, 96–97
　and research, 9
*DSM-III-R*, 9, 10, 42–43, 49, 379
　formulation and revision of, 18
*DSM-IV*, 9–10, 16, 42–43
　formulation and revision of, 18–19, 49
*DSM-IV-TR*, 10, 11–12
　personality disorders, *DSM-5* Maladaptive Trait Model coverage of, 612–13
　personality disorders, trait constellations, 607t, 612–13
*DSM-5* Levels of Personality Functioning Questionnaire, 582t, 588
*DSM-5* Maladaptive Trait Model, 618
　and AMPD, 606–7
　and clinical science, 615–18
　clinical utility of, 613–15, 618
　and communication with other professionals, 614–15
　and communication with patients, 614–15
　coverage of *DSM-IV-TR* PD syndromes, 612–13, 618
　development of, 605–6

ease of use, 614
empirical research on, 608
incremental validity, 613
and non-PD psychopathology, 615–16
personality domains in, 606, 606t
prediction of clinically relevant
    outcomes, 613
revisions, 618
structural validity of, 608, 618
structure, 610–15
temporal stability of, 610–11
trait domains and facets,
    measurement, 611–12
validity evidence for, 612
DSPD. *See* delayed sleep phase disorder
DTI. *See* diffusion tensor imaging
dualism, mind and brain in, 45
DUD. *See* drug use disorder
dynamic systems theory, 45, 46
dysfunctional assumptions, 233
dyspareunia, 413, 414
    male, 414
    prevalence of, 414
dysphoric mood
    in *DSM*, 231
    in HiTOP, 231
dysthymia
    and borderline personality disorder, 652t
    and eating disorders, 426
    and narcissistic personality
        disorder, 628–29
dysthymic disorder
    factor analysis, 152
    substance use and, 285

# E

early warning signal(s), 107–10
    clinical applications, 108
    critical fluctuations as, 109
    critical slowing down as, 108
    detection of, 110
    examples, 108–9
    flickering as, 108–9
    at group level, 109
    as indicators of symptom changes, 110
    at individual level, 109–10
    network density as, 115
    problems with, 110
    in psychopathological research, 109–10
    and transitions, 110
eating disorders. *See also* anorexia nervosa;
        binge-eating disorder; bulimia
        nervosa
    age of onset, 425
    alcohol and eating/dieting expectancies
        in, 287
    alpha-synuclein in, 435
    and anxiety disorders, 426
    and attention-deficit hyperactivity
        disorder, 427
    and autism spectrum disorder, 427
    biological factors and, 432–34, 435–38
    and bipolar disorder, 426

body-image disturbance and, 430
brain-derived neurotrophic factor in,
    433, 434
brain structure and function and, 432
candidate genes in, 434
candidate gene studies in, 434
characteristics of, 422
child maltreatment and, 431–32
comorbid psychopathology in, 425–28
cortisol in, 434
culture and, 428–29
defining characteristics of, 422–24
and depression, 426
developmental factors and, 431–
    32, 435–38
dietary restraint and, 430
dopamine in, 433, 435
*DSM-5* classification of, 422
and dysthymia, 426
emotion dysregulation and, 430
epidemiology of, 425
epigenetics of, 435, 438
estrogen in, 434
etiology of, 428–38
family and twin studies of, 434
family dynamics and, 431
genetics of, 434–35, 438
genome-wide association studies
    in, 434–35
ghrelin in, 434
glutamate in, 433
heritability of, 434
histone deacetylase in, 435
historical perspective on, 424–25
HPA axis in, 435
impulsivity and, 429–30
integrated etiological concept
    for, 435–38
leptin in, 433, 435
and mood disorders, 426
neurocognition and, 430–31
neuroplasticity in, 435
neurotransmitters in, 432–34
not otherwise specified, 424
and obsessive-compulsive disorder, 426
oxytocin in, 435
perfectionism and, 429
and personality disorders, 427–28
personality traits and, 429
and posttraumatic stress
    disorder, 426–27
psychological factors and, 429, 435–38
risk factors for, 435–38
and seasonal affective disorder, 426
serotonin in, 432–33, 434
sex distribution of, 425, 433–34
sleep-related, 534
social factors and, 435–38
sociocultural context and, 428–29
and substance use disorders, 287, 427
subthreshold, 424
"thin ideal" and, 428–29, 437–38
within-diagnosis heterogeneity, 429

ECA. *See* Epidemiologic Catchment
    Area study
ecological fallacy, 201
ecological momentary assessment, 104,
    107, 108–9, 111–12, 366
ED. *See* erectile disorder
Edelman, G. M., *Neural Darwinism*, 135
EDs. *See* eating disorders
EDS. *See* excessive daytime sleepiness
EE. *See* expressed emotion
EEG. *See* electroencephalography
EFA. *See* exploratory factor analysis
effort computation and expenditure
    definition of, 365
    in schizophrenia, 365
4E framework, 45–47
ego dystonicity
    definition of, 183
    in obsessive-compulsive disorder,
        182, 183
ego psychology, 41
ejaculation, 413. *See also* delayed
        ejaculation; premature (early)
        ejaculation
    retrograde, 411
elderly, sexual interest in. *See* gerontophilia
electroencephalography
    in attention-deficit hyperactivity
        disorder, 482
    in polysomnography, 522
    power spectral analysis, 523, 526–27
    in schizophrenia, 340
    in study of depression, 135
electromyography, in posttraumatic stress
    disorder, 211
Elemental Psychopathy Assessment,
    720, 728
EMA. *See* ecological momentary
    assessment
emergence, in complex system, 103
EMG. *See* electromyography
emic research, 455
emotion(s). *See also* expressed emotion
    in bipolar spectrum disorders, 234–35
    expression, in schizophrenia, 366–67
    in schizotypic psychopathology, 700
    self-conscious, and narcissistic
        grandiosity and
        vulnerability, 634–35
emotional disorders, 70–71
emotional lability
    and personality disorders, 609, 618
    in personality disorders, 612–13
emotional overinvolvement, anxiety
    disorders and, 168
emotional reasoning, 266
emotional stability, and personality
    disorders, 605
emotional Stroop paradigm,
    in posttraumatic stress
        disorder, 207–8
emotional understanding, in bipolar
    spectrum disorders, 234–35

INDEX | 763

emotional withdrawal, in
    schizophrenia, 337
emotion dysregulation, 70–71
    and borderline personality disorder,
        648, 654, 661–66
    and eating disorders, 430
    and functional somatic symptoms, 513
    impulsivity and, 664
    in narcissistic personality
        disorder, 626–27
    neurological correlates of, 662
    in pathological narcissism, 632–33
    and personality disorders, 606
emotion perception
    in faces, in schizophrenia, 359, 363
    in schizophrenia, 359, 364, 370
    and social functioning, in
        schizophrenia, 359
    in speech, in schizophrenia, 359, 363
emotion processing
    definition of, 359
    in schizophrenia, 359
emotion reactivity, in bipolar spectrum
    disorders, 234–35
emotion regulation, 47
    in bipolar spectrum disorders, 234–35
    in eating disorders, 432
    and female sexual dysfunction, 405
    substance use and, 307–9
empathizing, in autism, 495–96
empathy
    cognitive, 629
    deficits, and narcissistic personality
        disorder, 629–30
    emotional, 629
    Jaspers on, 40, 382
    in personality functioning (Criterion
        A), 580–81, 581t
empirical data, 89
empirical science, 89
empiricism, 34–35, 44, 47, 50
    and classification, 17
emptiness, in borderline personality
    disorder, 662
Endicott, Jean, 42
endocannabinoids, 317
endogenous opioid system, in substance
    use disorders, 313, 315, 317
endometriosis, and genito-pelvic
    pain, 414–15
endophenotypes, 703–4
    in ADHD, 480
    in autism, 500–1
    in borderline personality
        disorder, 657
    definition of, 480, 500–1
    of schizotypy, 687f, 688, 695, 698,
        701, 703–4
enema(s), erotic interest in, 557–58
Enlightenment, 36, 39
entrainment, 521
    and non-24-hr sleep–wake rhythm
        disorder, 532–33

environment. *See also* gene–environment
    correlation; gene–environment
    interaction
    differential susceptibility to, 128, 134
    and mental disorders, 82, 87
    and psychosis, 387
    in RDoC-oriented research
        designs, 95–96
    in Research Domain Criteria, 82,
        83f, 85, 87
envy, and narcissistic vulnerability, 634–35
EPA. *See* Elemental Psychopathy
    Assessment
ephebophilia, 548–49
Epidemiologic Catchment Area study,
    depression in, 258
epigenesis, 127
    nonlinear, 127
    probabilistic, 124
epigenetics, 128, 134
    in borderline personality
        disorder, 659–60
    child maltreatment and, 132
    of depression, 134
    developmental perspective on, 128, 132
    of eating disorders, 438
    prenatal factors and, 87
    of schizophrenia, 687f, 703–4
    and treatment, 134
epigenome-wide association study, in
    attention-deficit hyperactivity
    disorder, 479
epilepsy
    and autism, 493
    and female orgasmic disorder, 409–10
epinephrine, and female orgasm, 409
epistemic fallibilism, 47
Epworth Sleepiness Scale, 533
equifinality, 96, 127
    in depression, 132–33
    substance use disorder phenotype
        and, 302
erectile disorder, 407–8
    age and, 407
    biological factors and, 407–8
    causal mechanisms, 407–8
    definition of, 407
    diagnosis of, 407
    drugs and, 408
    mental disorders and, 408
    and premature (early) ejaculation, co-
        occurrence of, 412–13
    prevalence of, 406, 407
    psychological factors in, 408
    as vascular disorder, 407–8
erection (penile), 407–8
erotic age preferences, 548–49
erotic-target identity inversion, 552–54
ERP. *See* event-related potentials
ESEM. *See* exploratory structural equation
    modeling
ESI. *See* Externalizing Spectrum Inventory
ESM. *See* experience sampling method

Esquirol, Jean-Étienne, 378
essentialism, 22, 80
    Aristotelian, 35
estazolam, 529
estrogen
    and eating disorders, 433–34
    and female sexual function, 403
    neuroprotective properties of, 354
eszopiclone, 529
ethnicity, and depression, 258
ethnic minority status, and paranoia, 388
etic research, 455
ETII. *See* erotic-target identity inversion
Etiologic, Theory-Based, Ontogenic
    Hierarchical Framework, of
    alcohol use disorder, 318, 318f
ETOH. *See* Etiologic, Theory-Based,
    Ontogenic Hierarchical
    Framework
eugenics, 332n.1
evaluative judgments, 269
    and depression, 269
event-related potentials
    in antisocial personality disorder, 719
    in attention-deficit hyperactivity
        disorder, 482
    in autism, 499
    heritability of, 281
    mismatch negativity (MMN), 340
    P1, 340
    P300, 340
    in schizophrenia, 340
    in substance use disorders, 311
    substance use disorders and, 281
evolutionary theory, 47
EWAS. *See* epigenome-wide
    association study
EWSs. *See* early warning signal(s)
excessive daytime sleepiness
    in hypersomnolence disorder, 534
    with irregular sleep–wake rhythm
        disorder, 532
    in narcolepsy, 533
executive functioning
    alcohol and, 283
    in autism spectrum disorders, 495
    in bipolar spectrum disorders, 235
    cannabis use and, 284–85
    cocaine use and, 284–85
    definition of, 495
    in eating disorders, 432
    in hoarding disorder, 192
    and hypersexuality, 566
    schizotypic psychopathology and, 697
    and social functioning, in
        schizophrenia, 357–58
    and substance use disorders, 310–11
exercise, lack of, and erectile disorder, 407
exhibitionism, 556, 557
    prevalence of, 558
    and telephone scatologia, 556, 557
expectancy(ies)
    alcohol, 282, 287, 309–10

cocaine, 282, 309
  definition of, 282
  drug, 282, 304, 305, 309–10
  in eating disorders, 287
  neural reflections of, 309–10
  and substance use disorders, 282, 309–10
experience sampling method, 104, 107, 108–9, 111–12, 113
experiential avoidance
  definition of, 188
  and obsessive-compulsive disorder, 188
explanation, versus understanding, 39, 40
exploratory factor analysis, 451–52
  oblique, 451
  orthogonal, 451
exploratory structural equation modeling, of Triarchic Psychopathy Measure item set, 725
exposome research, 345–46
expressed emotion
  anxiety disorders and, 168
  factors affecting, 368
  and schizophrenia relapse, 367–69
externalizing
  antagonistic, 231, 615
  childhood maltreatment and, HiTOP perspective on, 66–67
  definition of, 14
  disinhibited, 231, 615
  genetic factors and, 65
  in HiTOP, 231
  peer victimization and, 67
  personality dimensions and, 63–64
  and personality disorders, 609
externalizing disorders, 57–59
  and borderline personality disorder, 651
  classification, 14, 24
  event-related potentials in, 281
  neurobiology of, 66
externalizing problems, 448–49
  and narcissistic grandiosity and vulnerability, 634
Externalizing Spectrum Inventory, 723, 724
extraversion/extroversion, 661. *See also* agentic extraversion; NEO inventory
  in borderline personality disorder, 656
  Eysenck's concept of, 13
  in Five Factor Model, 14
  and personality disorders, 603, 605, 616, 616t
  research on, HiTOP framework for, 63–64
  and risk of exposure to trauma, 204
eye-tracking dysfunction, 701–2
  and schizotypic psychopathology, 695, 697–98
Eysenck, H. J., 13, 692
  on psychoticism as personality trait, 690

# F

facial affect/emotion recognition
  in borderline personality disorder, 665–66
  in narcissistic personality disorder, 629
  in psychosis-prone individuals, 359
  in schizophrenia, 359
factitious disorder, 516
factor analysis, 13, 15, 25, 48, 57, 691–92.
  *See also* confirmatory factor analysis; exploratory factor analysis; structural research
  with additional narrower factors, 150, 152
  of anxiety disorders, 150–54
  and child psychopathology, 448–49
  of correlates of externalizing problems in adolescence, 66
  of depression, 150–52
  and developmental psychopathology, 448–49, 450
  of internalizing and externalizing factors, 63–64
  need for, 150
  of psychopathology in relation to personality, 64
  of schizotypic signs and symptoms, 678
  second-order, 452
  with single general factor (broadest level), 150
  symptom-level, 58
  with two factors, 150–52
  of youth mental disorders, 57
factor analytic models
  integrative hierarchical model, 152
  of internalizing disorders, 150–52
  Krueger's model, 152
  multifactor models, 152
  quantitative structural model, 152
  tri-level model, 151f, 152–53
  tripartite model, 150–52
factor mixture analysis, 15
family
  and eating disorders, 431, 434
  environment, and schizophrenia onset, 367
  expressed emotion, and schizophrenia relapse, 367–69
  functioning, and risk for psychosis, 367
family and conjoint interventions, for bipolar disorder, 241
family environment, and borderline personality disorder, 654–55
Family-Focused Therapy, in schizophrenia, 370
family-focused treatment, for bipolar disorder, 241
family history
  and alcohol use disorder, 280–81, 305–7
  and bipolar disorder, 232–33
  and substance use disorders, 280–81, 305–7
Fantasy Proneness domain, 614

FASD(s). *See* fetal alcohol spectrum disorder(s)
father, age of, and schizophrenia risk, 345–46, 345t
fatigue
  in depression, 535–36
  as functional somatic symptom, 508–9
Faux Pas Recognition test, 360–61
fear
  amygdala in, 159
  definition of, 147
  direct conditioning and, 160
  escapable versus inescapable stressors and, 162
  extinction-resistant, 162
  generalization of, 160
  in HiTOP, 231
  obsessional, maintenance of, 182, 184–85
  processing, and substance use, 312
  psychopathy and, 719
  selective associations and, 161
  as subdimension of internalizing spectrum, 57–58, 60, 231
  vicarious conditioning and, 160–61
Fear factor, 150–53, 151f, 154, 157
Fear of Fear factor, 152
Feighner criteria, 85
female orgasmic disorder
  age and, 410
  biological factors and, 409–10
  causes of, 409–11
  definition of, 408–9
  diagnosis of, 408–9
  drugs and, 410
  education and, 410
  prevalence of, 408–9
  psychological factors and, 410–11
  religiosity and, 410–11
female sexual arousal disorder, 402–3
female sexual interest/arousal disorder(s), 402–6
  biological factors in, 403–5
  comorbidity with mental disorders, 405
  definition of, 402–3
  diagnosis of, 402–3
  *DSM* classification, 402–3
  emotion regulation and, 405
  endocrine function and, 403
  etiological factors in, 403–6
  hormones and, 403–4
  neurobiology of, 404
  nonconsensual sexual experiences and, 405–6
  oral contraceptives and, 404
  prevalence of, 402–3
  psychosocial factors and, 405–6
fetal alcohol spectrum disorder(s), 307
fetal alcohol syndrome, 307
fetishism, 549–51. *See also* clothing-fetishism; stuff-fetishism
  age of onset, 561
fetishistic transvestism, 550
FFF. *See* fight-flight-or-freeze

FFM. *See* Five Factor Model
FFNI. *See* Five-factor Narcissism Inventory
FFT. *See* family-focused treatment
fibromyalgia, and female orgasmic disorder, 409–10
fibromyalgia syndrome, 515
fight-flight-or-freeze, 147
Five Factor Model, 14, 603, 616–17, 616*t*, 661. *See also* Big Five personality factors
  and borderline personality disorder, 656
  and personality disorders, 605
  relation to PID-5 and HiTOP spectra, 615, 616*t*
  and risk for substance use disorders, 308–9
Five-factor Narcissism Inventory, 634, 635
flunitrazepam, 529
flurazepam, 529
fMRI. *See* functional magnetic resonance imaging
FNSD. *See* functional neurological symptom disorder
FOD. *See* female orgasmic disorder
Fonagy, Peter, on borderline personality disorder, 654
formal models, network approach to, 115, 116
Foucault, M., 7
fractional anisotropy, in attention-deficit hyperactivity disorder, 481–82
Freud, Sigmund, 5–6, 41, 217
  concept of hysteria, 509–10
  on depression, 257–58
frontal cortex, in eating disorders, 432
frontal lobe, in antisocial personality disorder, 719
frontoparietal network, in schizophrenia, 363–64
frontostriatal circuit, in attention-deficit hyperactivity disorder, 483
frotteurism, 556, 557
FSAD. *See* female sexual arousal disorder
FSD. *See* functional somatic disorders
FSS. *See* functional somatic symptom(s)
fugue. *See also* dissociative fugue
  definition of, 218
functional magnetic resonance imaging, 341
  in anxiety disorders, 159
  of anxiety response, 159
  in apotemnophilia, 554
  in attention-deficit hyperactivity disorder, 482
  in autism, 500–1, 503
  in bipolar spectrum disorders, 236
  in borderline personality disorder, 662, 663–64
  of brain activity in relation to Psychopathic Personality Inventory factors, 721
  of drug expectancies, 309–10

  in eating disorders, 432
  of fear response, 159
  of neural activity, 66
  in PTSD, 208
functional neurological symptom disorder, 515. *See also* conversion disorder
functional somatic disorders, 517
functional somatic symptom(s), 508–17
  age and, 509
  amplification (bottom-up) explanation for, 510–12
  and anxiety, 509, 511
  childhood adversity and, 512–13
  classification, 514–17
  cultural considerations with, 509
  definition of, 508
  and depression, 509
  in *DSM-5*, 514–17
  emotion regulation and, 513
  epigenetic mechanisms and, 512–13, 512*f*
  etiology of, 512–14, 512*f*
  genetic factors and, 512–13
  historical perspective on, 509–10
  in *ICD-10/ICD-11*, 514–17
  impairment caused by, 509
  maintaining/aggravating factors and, 512–14, 512*f*
  management of, 517
  misdiagnosis of, 509
  versus organic disease, 509
  pathopsychophysiology of, 510–12
  post-COVID, 513
  and posttraumatic stress disorder, 512–13
  predictive processing and, 511–12, 513
  prevalence of, 508–9
  prior organic illness and, 512*f*, 513
  professional perspective on, 510
  psychogenic (top-down) explanation for, 510–12
  sex differences in, 509
  somatic specialists' perspective on, 510
  triggering factors and, 512–14, 512*f*
  types of, 508–9
  vulnerability factors and, 512–14, 512*f*
fusiform face area, 497
  in schizophrenia, 363
fusiform gyrus, in social perception, 497, 498–503
fuzzy kind, 15–16

# G

GABA
  in bipolar disorder, 343
  in substance use disorders, 313, 315–16
GABA hypothesis, of schizophrenia, 343
GABA transporter genes, and susceptibility to panic attacks, 158
GAD. *See* generalized anxiety disorder
GAD1. *See* glutamic acid decarboxylase 1
*GAD2* gene, 158
GAF. *See* Global Assessment of Functioning
Galenist tradition, 35, 47

Galileo Galilei, 33, 47
gambling, and narcissistic grandiosity and vulnerability, 634
gamma-aminobutyric acid. *See* GABA
GAPD. *See* General Assessment of Personality Disorder
gateway model, of substance use, 305
gaze perception, in schizophrenia, 361–62
GBI. *See* General Behavior Inventory
G×E. *See* gene–environment interaction
*Geisteswissenschaften*. *See* human sciences
GENACIS project, 302
gender dysphoria, 561–65. *See also* transsexualism
  androphilic female-to-male, 563
  androphilic male-to-female, 562–63
  and autogynephilia, 553, 562
  autogynephilic male-to-female, 562
  in children, 562–63
  definition of, 561–62
  gynephilic female-to-male, 562–63
  and homosexuality, 562, 563
  neuroanatomy in, 564
  prevalence of, 563–64
  rapid-onset, 563
  severity grades, 562
  sex ratio of, 563–64
gender identity disorder, and body integrity identity disorder, 554
genderqueers, 563
gender roles, and sexual function, 405
gene–environment correlation, 46
gene–environment interaction, 128
  in attention-deficit hyperactivity disorder, 480
  in depression, 261
  developmental perspective on, 132
  in eating disorders, 434
  and peer deviance, 305
  research on, challenges of, 133
  in schizophrenia, 367
  in substance use disorders, 314–15
gene–environment interplay, 127, 128
gene methylation. *See* DNA methylation
General Assessment of Personality Disorder, 579–80
General Behavior Inventory, 232
General Distress factor, 150–53, 151*f*, 154
general factor of PD, 449, 578, 579, 588, 617
generalized anxiety disorder. *See also* anxiety disorders
  amygdala activation in, 159
  attachment and, 167
  behavior genetics of, 157
  and borderline personality disorder, 652*t*
  cardinal feature of, 148
  comorbidity with, 149–50, 149*t*
  and depression, 57–58
  epidemiology of, 149–50
  and erectile disorder, 408
  factor analysis, 150–52

internalizing-externalizing structure and, 14
interpersonal problems and, 167
interpretive bias modification and, 165–66
learned fear in, 160
and posttraumatic stress disorder, 204
prevalence of, 149–50, 149t
sleep and circadian rhythms in, 536–37
substance use disorders and, 286
treatment response, expressed emotion and, 168
Generalized Dysphoria factor, 152
General Neuroticism Factor, 154–55, 156
general paresis, 11, 38
  essentialist view of, 22
Generation R longitudinal study, 465–66
genetic polymorphisms, and psychopathology phenotypes, 65–66
genetics
  of autism, 496
  of eating disorders, 434–35, 438
  of narcolepsy, 533
  and phenotypic dimensions in HiTOP, 65–66
  psychiatric, 62
  and psychopathology, 134–35
  of schizophrenia, 344–45, 682–83
genetic variance
  additive, 656
  dominant, 656
genital plastic surgery, 410
genito-pelvic pain/penetration disorder, 413, 414–16
  biological factors and, 414–15
  deep, 414–15
  definition of, 414
  diagnosis of, 414
  *DSM-5* classification of, 413–14
  factors associated with, 414–16
  as pain disorder, 414
  postpartum, 414
  prevalence of, 414
  psychological factors and, 415–16
  relational factors and, 415–16
  risk factors for, 414
  and sexual arousal problems, comorbidity, 414
  as sexual dysfunction, 414
  superficial, 414–15
genome-wide association studies, 65, 133–34
  of anxiety disorders, 158
  in attention-deficit hyperactivity disorder, 479
  in borderline personality disorder, 658–61
  of depression, 133–34
  in eating disorders, 434–35
  in insomnia, 535–36
  in posttraumatic stress disorder, 210
  in schizophrenia, 345
  in substance use disorders, 313–14

George III (King of England), 37
gerontophilia, 548–49
*g*-factor, 60–61
ghrelin, in eating disorders, 433, 434
Global Assessment of Functioning, 202, 578
Global Leadership and Organizational Effectiveness study, 460
GLOBE. *See* Global Leadership and Organizational Effectiveness study
*GLRA1* gene, 696–97
glucocorticoid receptor gene *(NR3C1)*, methylation
  in borderline personality disorder, 659–60
  child maltreatment and, 132
glutamate
  in eating disorders, 433
  in schizophrenia, 699–700
  in substance use disorders, 315–16
glutamate hypothesis, of schizophrenia, 342–43
glutamic acid decarboxylase gene(s)
  in schizophrenia, 344
  and susceptibility to anxiety disorders and depression, 158
GNF. *See* General Neuroticism Factor
goal dysregulation, and bipolar disorder, 233–34
goal orientation, and depression, 261
goal representation, and depression, 268–70
Godstein, Kurt, 493–94
Goldberg, Lewis, 14
Gottlieb, Gilbert, 124
g-PD. *See* general factor of PD
GPPPD. *See* genito-pelvic pain/penetration disorder
grandiosity. *See also* narcissistic grandiosity
  extreme, pathological narcissism as, 626–31
  in pathological narcissism, 632
  and personality disorders, 590–91, 610
grant reviews, 91
  issues in, 80–81
gray matter volume
  in anorexia nervosa, 432
  in narcissistic personality disorder, 629
  in schizophrenia, 340–41, 363, 364
  in schizotypal personality disorder, 699
Green Paranoia Scale, 386
*GR* gene, in eating disorders, 435
Griesinger, Wilhelm, 37
Grinker, Roy, on borderline personality, 648
G-spot augmentation, 410
Guilford, Joy Paul, 14
guilt, and narcissistic grandiosity and vulnerability, 634–35
Gunderson, John, on borderline personality, 648
Guze, Samuel, 21, 42

GWAS. *See* genome-wide association studies
gynandromorphophilia, 551–52, 553
gynandromorphs, 551–52
gynephilia, 552

# H

hair-pulling disorder, 181, 189–90, 194
  and skin-picking disorder, co-occurrence, 190
Hall, Jeffrey C., 539
hallucination(s)
  auditory, in schizophrenia, 341
  child abuse and, 388–89
  and delusions, co-occurrence of, 390
  as psychotic symptoms, 334
  in schizophrenia, 336–37, 354
  trauma and, 390
hallucinogens, and serotonergic system, 316–17
Halsted, William, 296
handedness
  and paraphilias, 559–60
  and sexuality, 559
hardiness, 722
Hardy, Alistair, 383
Hare's Psychopathy Checklist-Revised. *See* Psychopathy Checklist-Revised
Hare's Self-Report Psychopathy Scale, 720
harm avoidance, and somatization, 513
Haslam, N., taxonomy of kinds of kinds, 15–16
hazard ratios, in borderline personality disorder, 656–57
HBN. *See* Healthy Brain Network project
HD. *See* hoarding disorder
headache, and borderline personality disorder, 651
head injury, and schizophrenia, 346
health, 508
Health Anxiety domain, 614
Healthy Brain Network project, 727t
hearing loss, and paranoid beliefs, 390
heart failure, and male sexual desire, 407
heart rate/heart rate variability
  alcohol use and, 281–82
  in posttraumatic stress disorder, 210–12
  and sexual arousal, 405
hebephilia, 548–49, 552
  neuroimaging in, 560
hebephrenia, 6
hedonic capacity
  latent structure of, 702–3
  Meehl's view of, 687–88
  in schizophrenia, 700
  in schizotypic psychopathology, 698, 700
hedonic experience
  definition of, 365
  in schizophrenia, 365
Heidegger, Martin, 382
Heinrichs, R. Walter, 338

heroin
  neuropharmacology of, 317
  overdose, 317
heterarchical relationships, 90
HEXACO Personality Inventory, triarchic scale measure based on, 727t
hierarchical assessment, HiTOP-oriented, 68–69
hierarchical linear modeling, 460
Hierarchical Taxonomy of Psychopathology, 54–73, 97, 153–54, 153f, 235–36, 615, 657, 676–77
  and assessment, 68–69
  clinical utility, 67–73
  consortium for, 59
  detachment spectrum, 335f, 337
  dimensions in, 61–62, 231
  Externalizing spectrum, 731–33
  and genetic research, 65–66
  hierarchy in, 60f, 61
  implications of quantitative approach for, 61–62
  and integrative research approach, 62–63
  Internalizing spectrum, 153–54, 153f, 731–33
  maladaptive personality traits in, 59–60, 60f, 63
  and neurobiology research, 66
  and personality research, 63–64
  and prognosis, 69–70
  and psychopathy, 730–33
  psychosis superspectrum, 335–36, 335f
  relation to PID-5 and Five Factor Model, 615, 616t
  research utility, 62–67
  and self-report questionnaire, 69
  and siloed research literatures, 62, 67
  and social environment research, 66–67
  spectra in, 60, 60f, 153–54, 153f, 231, 615, 730–33
  subfactors in, 60, 60f, 153–54, 153f, 231
  superspectra in, 60–61, 60f, 153–54, 153f
  symptom components, 59–60, 60f, 153–54, 153f
  syndromes/disorders in, 59–60, 60f, 153–54, 153f
  thought disorder spectrum, 335f, 336, 337
  and treatment, 70–72
  website for, 69
  working model, 59–61, 60f, 153f
hierarchic motility, 124
hippocampus
  in attention-deficit hyperactivity disorder, 481
  in bipolar spectrum disorders, 235
  decreased volume, in posttraumatic stress disorder, 208–9
  substance use and, 312
histamine $H_1$-antagonists, for insomnia, 528–29

histone deacetylase, in eating disorders, 435
historical perspective, on study of psychopathology, 33–50
histrionic personality disorder, 577, 602–3, 613, 614
  and borderline personality disorder, 651, 652t
  and narcissistic personality disorder, 628–29
  and psychopathy, 719
HiTOP. See Hierarchical Taxonomy of Psychopathology
HIV, and male sexual desire, 407
HLM. See hierarchical linear modeling
hoarding disorder, 181, 191–92, 194
Hofstadter, Richard, 378
homicidality, and narcissistic grandiosity and vulnerability, 634
homicide(s)
  alcohol and, 283–84
  sexual, of elderly, 549
homosexuality
  depathologization of, 547
  and gender dysphoria, 562, 563
  and handedness, 559–60
  as mental disorder, 3–4
  neuroanatomy in, 564
homosexual transsexuals, 563
Hoover sign, 515–16
hostility
  anxiety disorders and, 168
  in narcissistic personality disorder, 639–40
  and personality disorders, 610, 614–15, 617, 618
HPA. See hypothalamic-pituitary-adrenal axis
HPS. See Hypomanic Personality Scale
HR. See heart rate/heart rate variability
HRV. See heart rate/heart rate variability
HSDD. See hypoactive sexual desire disorder
HSNS. See Hypersensitive Narcissism Scale
HSRP. See Hare's Self-Report Psychopathy Scale
5-HT. See serotonin/serotonergic system
HTR1B gene, in ADHD, 479
5-HTT. See serotonin transporter gene
5-HTTLPR, in eating disorders, 434
5-HTT/SLC6A4 gene. See also serotonin transporter gene
  in ADHD, 479, 480
  and developmental psychopathology, 466
  in substance use disorders, 313
human leukocyte antigen (HLA) complex, in narcolepsy, 533
human sciences, and natural sciences, 39, 45
Hume, David, 44
humors, four, 35

Husserl, Edmund, 382
hymenoplasty, 410
hyperarousal
  and anxiety, 536
  and insomnia, 536
hyperdominance (sexual behavior), 555
hyperlipidemia, and erectile disorder, 407–8
hyperprolactinemia, and male sexual desire, 406–7
Hypersensitive Narcissism Scale, 634
hypersexuality, 547, 548, 565–66
  associated features, 566
  comorbidities, 565–66
  and executive functioning, 566
  neuroimaging in, 566
  prevalence of, 565
  sex ratio of, 565
  subtypes of, 565–66
  as symptom, versus syndrome, 565
  theories of, 565
hypersomnia/hypersomnia disorder, 524, 534. See also hypersomnolence disorder
  definition of, 534
  in depression, 535
  idiopathic (ICSD-3), 534
hypersomnolence disorder, 524, 533, 534
  excessive daytime sleepiness in, 534
  prevalence of, 534
  treatment of, 534
hyperthyroidism, and premature (early) ejaculation, 413
hypoactive sexual desire disorder, 402–3, 406. See also male hypoactive sexual desire disorder
hypochondriasis, 514
  historical perspective on, 35–36, 38
hypocretin, in narcolepsy, 533
hypogonadism, and male sexual desire, 406–7
hypohedonia, in schizotypes, 686–88
hypokrisia, 685, 686–88
hypomania/mania
  clinical presentation, 229
  dimensional assessment, existing measures for, 231–32
  HiTOP classification of, 231
  hypersexuality in, 565
hypomanic episode, and borderline personality disorder, 652t
Hypomanic Personality Scale, 231–32
hypo-narrativity, and classification, 17
hypothalamic-pituitary-adrenal axis
  in borderline personality disorder, 659–60
  in eating disorders, 434, 435
  in posttraumatic stress disorder, 213
hypothalamic-pituitary disorders, and female orgasmic disorder, 409–10
hypothalamus, in paraphilias, 560
hypothetical constructs, 48

hypothyroidism, and male sexual desire, 406–7
hypoxyphilia, 556
hysterectomy, complications, and female orgasmic disorder, 409–10
hysteresis, in dynamic systems theory, 46
hysteria, 509–10
  historical perspective on, 35–36, 38
  Sydenham on, 35

# I

IAD. *See* illness anxiety disorder
iatro-chemistry, 36
iatro-physics, 36
ICD, 79
  atheoretical approach to classification, 16–18
  binary disease/no-disease legacy of, 85, 86
  categorical approach in, 54–55
  diagnostic criteria in, 87–88
  early editions of, 6–7
  work groups and, 18–19
*ICD-6*, 3, 6–7
*ICD-8*, 6–7, 9
*ICD-9*, 9
*ICD-10*, 9–10
  criticism of, 18
*ICD-11*, 10
  delusions in, 381
  diagnostic spectra in, 25
  internalizing and externalizing spectra in, 24
  internalizing-externalizing structure and, 14
  personality disorders in, 14–15, 627n.1, 657, 667
  posttraumatic stress disorder in, 213–14
  reliability of diagnoses in, 21
  structure and organization of, 24, 25
  work groups and, 18
ICM. *See* integrative cognitive model (of mood dysregulation)
ICSD-3. *See International Classification of Sleep Disorders, 3rd Edition*
IDAS. *See* Inventory of Depression and Anxiety Symptoms
IDAS-II. *See* Inventory of Depression and Anxiety Symptoms, Expanded Version
ideal types, 40–41
identity
  disturbance, in borderline personality disorder, 662–63
  in personality functioning (Criterion A), 580–81, 581*t*
idiographic methods, 39
idiopathic environmental illness, 510
IIP. *See* Inventory of Interpersonal Problems
illness anxiety disorder, 516
IMAGEN project, 726, 727*t*, 736–37

immune function
  and depression, 135
  and schizophrenia, 346
impulse control
  in borderline personality disorder, 663–64
  substance use and, 312
impulse control disorders/problems, 25, 189
  and borderline personality disorder, 651
  and hypersexuality, 565
impulsivity
  in attention-deficit hyperactivity disorder, 663
  and borderline personality disorder, 648, 661–64
  in delusional patients, 391–92, 394
  and eating disorders, 427, 429–30
  emotional dysregulation and, 664
  PCL-R scores and, 716
  and personality disorders, 609–10
incentive salience
  definition of, 365
  in schizophrenia, 365
incest, 549
incoherence, 337
incompetence, in development, organizational perspective on, 125
individualism, and classification, 17
induction, 38–39. *See also* pessimistic induction
infantilism, 552, 553
inferior frontal gyrus, in schizophrenia, 363
inflammation
  in depression, 135
  in posttraumatic stress disorder, 213
  and schizophrenia, 346
inflammatory bowel disease, and male sexual desire, 407
information processing, in autism, 495–96
information retrieval, classification and, 4
insight, in obsessive-compulsive disorder, 183
insomnia/insomnia disorder, 524–29
  age and, 524
  assessment of, 525–27
  attention-intention-effort pathway in, 525
  cognitive arousal and, 525
  cognitive model of, 525, 528
  cognitive restructuring for, 528
  cognitive therapy for, 528
  comorbidity with, 524
  cortical arousal and, 525
  and depression, 61
  in depression, 535–36
  diagnosis of, 525–26
  etiological models of, 524–25
  in generalized anxiety disorder, 536–37
  hyperarousal and, 536
  with irregular sleep–wake rhythm disorder, 532

levels of resolution, 61
  management of, 527–29 (*see also* cognitive behavior therapy for insomnia; Triple-R model)
  neurobiological model of, 525
  neurocognitive model of, 525
  and paranoia, 390
  pharmacological treatment of, 528–29
  3P (three-factor) model for, 525, 527–28
  prevalence of, 524
  psychobiological inhibition model of, 525
  scales for, 526
  in schizophrenia, 538
  and sleep hygiene, 524, 528
  sleep misperception in, 527
  stimulus control theory of, 524, 528
  stimulus control therapy for, 528
  terminal, 61
Insomnia Severity Index, 526
instructional learning, anxiety disorders and, 161
instrumental relationships, in schizophrenia, 351
insula
  in eating disorders, 432
  in narcissistic personality disorder, 629
  in schizophrenia, 340–41
integrative cognitive model (of mood dysregulation), 233–34
intellect, and personality traits, 616–17
intelligence (IQ)
  dimensional assessment of, 68
  in pedophiles, 559
  and protection against PTSD, 209–10
interleukin-6, in depression, 135
internal consistency, in testing, 20
internalization, 47
internalizing, 615
  childhood maltreatment and, HiTOP perspective on, 66–67
  definition of, 14
  and emotional problems, 71–72
  in HiTOP, 231
  peer victimization and, 67
  personality dimensions and, 63–64
internalizing disorders/problems, 57–59, 60, 448–49
  and borderline personality disorder, 651
  classification, 14, 24
  factor analytic models of, 150–52
  and insomnia, 61
  and narcissistic grandiosity and vulnerability, 634
  neuroticism and, 154–55
Internalizing factor, 150, 152, 154
internalizing symptoms, youth with, neurostructural study of, 95
internal realism, 49
internal working model, 167, 393
*International Classification of Causes of Death, The*, 6
*International Classification of Diseases. See* ICD

INDEX | 769

*International Classification of Sleep Disorders, 3rd Edition*, 523–24
International Personality Disorder Examination, 679, 683*t*
Internet addiction, 3–4
Interoceptive/Agoraphobic Fears factor, 151*f*, 152–53
interoceptive conditioning, 163
interpersonal and social rhythm therapy
 for bipolar disorder, 240, 241
 principles of, 240
interpersonal aversiveness, in schizotypy, 686–87
interpersonal circumplex model, 167
interpersonal functioning
 gender and, 353–54
 in personality disorders, 578–81, 585, 590–91, 666
interpersonal hypersensitivity, in borderline personality disorder, 661–62, 664–66
interpersonal pathoplasticity, 167
interpersonal problems
 anxiety disorders and, 167–68
 in borderline personality disorder, 662–63, 664–66
 generalized anxiety disorder and, 167
 and narcissistic grandiosity and vulnerability, 635
 panic disorder and, 167–68
 social anxiety disorder and, 167
interpersonal problem-solving skills
 poor, and depression, 261
 in schizophrenia, 353, 362
interpersonal psychotherapy for depression, 134
 in economically disadvantaged mothers, 137
interpersonal relationships, in borderline personality disorder, 649, 649*t*, 664–66
interpretive bias
 in anxiety disorders, 165–66
 implicit measures of, 165
 modification, 165–66
interrater reliability, 20–21
intervention
 developmentally informed, 130, 137
 epigenetics and, 134
 RDoC-oriented research and, 96
interventionist model, 44
intimacy, in personality functioning (Criterion A), 580–81, 581*t*
 subcomponents, 580–81, 581*t*
intimacy avoidance, and personality disorders, 614–15
intimate partner violence
 pathological narcissism and, 640
 substance use disorders and, 283–84
intolerance of uncertainty
 definition of, 183
 in obsessive-compulsive disorder, 183

introversion, and personality disorders, 606
intrusive thoughts. *See also* obsessions
 dysfunctional beliefs about, 186–87
 normal/nonclinical, 185–86
 responsibility appraisals of, 185–87
 and thought–action fusion, 186–87
Inventory of Callous-Unemotional Traits, triarchic scale measure based on, 727*t*
Inventory of Depression and Anxiety Symptoms, 69
 Euphoria scale, 231–32
 Expanded Version, 231–32
 Mania scale, 231–32
Inventory of Interpersonal Problems, 167
IPC. *See* interpersonal circumplex model
IPDE. *See* International Personality Disorder Examination
IPSRT. *See* interpersonal and social rhythm therapy
IPT. *See* interpersonal psychotherapy
IQ. *See* intelligence (IQ)
irregular sleep–wake rhythm disorder, 524, 529, 532
 age and, 532
 dementia and, 532
 management of, 532
irritability, elevated levels of, 231
irritable bowel syndrome, 513
 and genito-pelvic pain, 415
IRT. *See* item response theory models
ISWD. *See* irregular sleep–wake rhythm disorder
item response theory models, 579–80, 585, 592, 606
 unfolding models, 585–86
IU. *See* intolerance of uncertainty

**J**

James, William, 46
Jamison, Kay Redfield, on bipolar disorder, 228
Janet, Pierre, 217
Jaspers, Karl, 41, 382
 *General Psychopathology*, 39
 and methodological pluralism for psychopathology, 40–41
 on three groups of psychiatric conditions, 40–41
jet-lag disorder, 529
JTC. *See* jumping to conclusions bias
jumping to conclusions bias, 391–92
 in cognitive model of depression, 266

**K**

Kaczynski, Ted, 337
Kahlbaum, Karl, 38, 378
Kanner, Leo, 490, 491, 492–93, 495
kappa statistic, 19, 21
Karolinska Sleepiness Scale, 533
Kendler, Kenneth, 49
Kernberg, Otto

 on borderline personality organization, 648
 object-relations theory, 631
ketamine, 342–43
kidney disease, and female orgasmic disorder, 409–10
Kindler, Kenneth, 379
kindling, of depression, 260
kinds of kinds, Haslam's taxonomy of, 15–16
klismaphilia, 557–58
Knight, Robert, 648
Koch, J. L., 714–15
Kohut, Heinz, self-psychology theory, 631–32
Kraepelin, Emil, 5–6, 37–38, 41, 47, 78, 85, 257–58, 331–32, 332n.1, 334–35, 339, 344, 350, 378–79, 382, 676–77
 on convergence of description, etiology, and pathology, 38, 42
 on latent schizophrenia, 682
 on psychopathic personalities, 714–15
Kraepelinian dichotomy, 332
Kraepelin's classifications, 6
Kretschmer, Ernst, 379

**L**

labeling, 7, 8
 in cognitive model of depression, 266
labiaplasty, 410
LAF. *See* low anxiety fearlessness
latent class analysis, 15, 603–4
 for symptoms of antisocial personality disorder, 603–4
latent profile analysis, 15
latent variables, 48, 57, 726–29
LDX. *See* lisdexamfetamine dimesylate
learned helplessness, 268
learning disability, and ADHD, 474
learning theory, and models of obsessive-compulsive disorder, 184–85
LEDS. *See* Life Events and Difficulties Schedule
lemborexant
 for insomnia, 529
 for patients with dementia and sleep problems, 532
leptin, in eating disorders, 433, 435
Level of Personality Functioning Scale, 577, 580–81, 593, 606–7, 617–18
 client utility of, 589–90
 components and subcomponents of, 580–81, 581*t*, 585
 convergent validity, 586–88
 development, 579–80
 discriminant validity, 588–89
 empirical findings pertaining to, 583–90
 and *ICD-11* classification of personality disorders, 591–92
 incremental validity, 588–89
 internal consistency, 583–86
 interrater reliability of, 583, 584*t*
 latent structure of, 583–86

levels of impairment in, 580–81, 585–86
measures based on, 581–83
psychometric properties of, 583–90
relationship to maladaptive personality traits (Criterion B), 590–91, 617–18
score on, 581
severity continuum, 580–81, 585–86
specificity for personality disorders, 588–89
utility for treatment, 589–90
Level of Personality Functioning Scale–Brief Form, 581–82, 582t, 585, 588, 591–92, 593
Level of Personality Functioning Scale Questionnaire for Adolescents from 12 to 18 Years, 581–82, 582t
Level of Personality Functioning Scale–Self-Report, 581–82, 582t, 585, 588, 592
Levenson Self-Report Psychopathy Scale, 720
Lewis, Aubrey, 13
Lewy body dementia, 534–35
Lewy body dementia, REM sleep behavior disorder and, 534–35
life event matching hypothesis, 260–61
life events
  acute versus chronic, 260
  additivity effects of, 259–60
  and bipolar disorder, 238–39
  and depression, 259–61, 262
  and functional somatic symptoms, 513–14
  predictive value of, 260–61
  quality of, 260
  stressful, and instigation of additional negative life events, 260
Life Events and Difficulties Schedule, 259–61
Life Events Questionnaire, triarchic scale measure based on, 727t
life-span developmental approach, 448, 467–68. See also developmental psychopathology
  contrasts with DSM, 449–50
  and heterotypic continuity of constructs, 450
  and homotypic continuity of constructs, 450
  longitudinal research in, 450
limbic system
  in borderline personality disorder, 662
  exposure to criticism and, 369
  in posttraumatic stress disorder, 662
  in schizophrenia, 340–41
  substance use and, 312
Linehan, Marsha, on borderline personality disorder, 654
Linnaeus, 5
lisdexamfetamine dimesylate, 476
Little Albert, 159
liver disease, alcohol use and, 283
Locke, John, 34, 35, 36

loneliness, in borderline personality disorder, 665–66
longitudinal analysis, of state–trait variance, 157
Longitudinal Study of Personality Disorders, 681–82
LoPF-Q 12–18. See Level of Personality Functioning Scale Questionnaire for Adolescents from 12 to 18 Years
lorazepam, 529
lormetazepam, 529
Lorr, Maurice, 15
loss. See also childhood loss
  and depression, 260, 262, 263, 267
low anxiety fearlessness, PCL-R and, structural equation modeling analysis, 23
LPFS. See Level of Personality Functioning Scale
LPFS-BF. See Level of Personality Functioning Scale–Brief Form
LPFS-SR. See Level of Personality Functioning Scale–Self-Report
LSD, and serotonergic system, 316–17
LSPD. See Longitudinal Study of Personality Disorders
LSRP. See Levenson Self-Report Psychopathy Scale
lumpers and splitters, 5, 14

## M

machine learning, 86
  and algorithms predicting posttraumatic stress disorder, 212–13
Magical Ideation Scale, 693–94
  high scorers, follow-up studies of, 700–1
magnetic resonance imaging. See also functional magnetic resonance imaging
  in attention-deficit hyperactivity disorder, 481, 483
  in schizophrenia, 340–41
magnetic resonance spectroscopy, in obsessive-compulsive disorder, 188
magnetoencephalography, in apotemnophilia, 554
major depression. See major depressive disorder
major depressive disorder
  behavior genetics of, 157
  and bipolar spectrum disorders, 229
  and borderline personality disorder, 652t, 659
  brain alterations in, 235–36
  diagnostic criteria for, 54–55
  in DSM, 449
  factor analysis, 151–52
  and female sexual dysfunction, 405
  genetic factor associated with, 157
  heterogeneity of, 55
  internalizing-externalizing structure and, 14
  life-span approach to, 449

and narcissistic personality disorder, 628–29
neuroticism and, 154
PID-5 traits and, 615–16
reward circuitry in, 236–37
scientific realist view of, 48
serotonin system in, 157–58
sleep and circadian rhythms in, 238, 535–36
sleep interventions in, 535–36
substance use and, 285
symptoms of, 449
vulnerability factors, 163
maladaptation
  developmental analysis of, 123
  in maltreated children, 131–32
  multiple pathways to, 126–27
maladaptive personality traits. See also DSM-5 Maladaptive Trait Model
  assessment of, 607–8
  facets, 590, 606, 606t
  in HiTOP model, 59–60, 60f, 63
  incremental validity of, 617–18
  and psychopathology, 63, 64
  relationship to Level of Personality Functioning Scale, 590–91
male hypoactive sexual desire disorder, 406–7
  age and, 406–7
  biological factors and, 406–7
  definition of, 406
  diagnosis of, 406
  DSM-5 classification, 406
  etiologic factors, 406–7
  mental health concerns and, 407
  prevalence of, 406
  psychological factors and, 407
  relationship concerns and, 407
malnutrition, and personality functioning, 428
mania, 228, 257–58. See also hypomania/mania; schizoaffective disorder
  clinical presentation, 229
  historical perspective on, 35–36, 38, 47
  and positive cognitive styles, 233
  positive life events and, 238–39
  sleep deprivation/loss and, 537–38
manic-depressive insanity, 332, 334–35
manic-depressive psychosis, 6, 38, 78
manic episode, and borderline personality disorder, 652t
manifest phenomena, 57
manipulativeness, and personality disorders, 609, 610, 612–13, 617
marijuana expectancies, 282, 309
marriage, schizophrenia and, 351
masochism, 555, 556
masturbation
  female, 403–4, 410
  male, 411, 412
  prevalence of, 565
maternal depression
  child–parent psychotherapy for, 137
  developmentally informed intervention for, 137

INDEX | 771

MAXCOV. *See* Meehl's maximum covariance analysis
*MCF2* gene, in borderline personality disorder, 660
McLean Study for Adult Development, 653
MDD. *See* major depressive disorder
MDMA, and serotonergic system, 316–17
MDQ. *See* Mood Disorder Questionnaire
meanness, psychopathy and, 722, 723–24, 733–34, 733f
Means-End Problem-Solving, 352–53
measurement, 19–25
   challenges of, 84–85
   RDoC and, 86
mechanistic models, of causation in psychopathology, 43–44
medial temporal cortex, in theory-of-mind reasoning, 498
medical model of illness, 7
medicine
   as descriptive clinical science (19th c.), 37–38
   from immortal souls and disturbed bodies to disturbed minds (18th c.), 36–37
   from speculative to descriptive (17th c.), 35–36
Mednick, Saul, 339
Meehl, Paul, 15
   on latent structure of schizotypy, 692
   on taxonic view of schizotypy, 692
Meehl's Checklist for Schizotypic Signs, 693
Meehl's integrative developmental model of schizotypy, 684–89, 687f, 701
   misunderstanding of, 688–89
   as "quasi-dimensional" (Claridge), 692
Meehl's maximum covariance analysis, 702
*MEIS1* gene, 535–36
Meiwes, Armin, 555
melancholia, 257
   historical perspective on, 35–36
melatonin
   in advanced sleep phase disorder, 531
   in bipolar disorder, 537
   in delayed sleep phase disorder, 530
   exogenous (*see* melatonin therapy)
   for insomnia, 528–29
melatonin receptor agonists, for insomnia, 528–29
melatonin therapy
   administration of, 531
   in delayed sleep phase disorder, 531
   for non-24-hr sleep–wake rhythm disorder, 532–33
   phase-advancing effect of, 531
memory. *See also* autobiographical memory; spatial working memory; traumatic memory
   in bipolar disorder, 234
   in bipolar spectrum disorders, 235
   cocaine use and, 284–85

emotional, in bipolar disorder, 234
immediate, assessment of, 362
in obsessive-compulsive disorder, 185
in schizophrenia, 338
secondary, assessment of, 362
and social functioning, in schizophrenia, 358
traumatic (*see* posttraumatic stress disorder; traumatic memory)
memory bias, in anxiety disorders, 164–65
menopause, 415
   and female sexual function, 403
mental disorder(s)
   as biological disorders in brain circuits, 43
   classification of (*see* classification)
   complex systems approach to, 102
   definition of, 12–13
   as dynamic processes, 104
   evolutionary basis of, 12–13
   fuzzy boundary with normality, 56, 62
   harmful dysfunction element of, 12–13
   as networks of symptoms, 111
   protean nature of, 35–36
   severity dimension, 56
   subjective element of, 12
   as subset of medical disorders, 12
   substance-induced, 301
   symptom-based dichotomies and, 85, 86
mental filter, 266
Mental Incapacitation Concerns factor, 156
mentalization (mental state reasoning), 359
   in autism, 361, 498–99
   in bipolar disorder, 361
   neurobiology of, 363, 498
   in schizophrenia, 360–61, 364
mental simulation, in schizophrenia, 364
mental state reasoning. *See* mentalization (mental state reasoning)
MEPS. *See* Means-End Problem-Solving
metabolic syndrome, and erectile disorder, 407
metacognition, deficits, in schizophrenia, 360–61
methamphetamine(s)
   dependence, and neurocognitive impairment, 284
   teratogenicity, 307
*Methodenstreit*, 39
methylation. *See* DNA methylation
methylphenidate
   for attention-deficit hyperactivity disorder, 476–77
   for hypersomnia, 534
   for narcolepsy, 533–34
Meyer, Adolf, 124
Meynert, Theodor, 37–38, 41, 47
MFAM. *See* Multicultural Family Assessment Module (Achenbach System)

MHSDD. *See* male hypoactive sexual desire disorder
migrant status
   and paranoia, 388
   and schizophrenia risk, 345–46, 345t
Mill, John Stuart, 38–39
   *A System of Logic*, 38–39
mind
   and brain, 45
   concept, historical perspective on, 36
   4E framework (embodied, embedded, enacted, and extended mind), 45–47
   as embedded, 46
   as embodied, 46
   as enactive, 46
   as extended, 46–47
   as organ of adaptation (James), 46
   properties of, 45
mind–body problem, 87–88, 97
minimal brain damage, 472–73
Minnesota Multiphasic Personality Inventory
   and psychopathy, 726–28, 727t, 733–34
   triarchic scale measures based on, 726–28, 727t
Minnesota Multiphasic Personality Inventory 3
   schizophrenia-related deviance on, 698–99
   and schizotypic psychopathology, 694
Minnesota Multiphasic Personality Inventory 2–Restructured Form, 612
   and schizotypic psychopathology, 694
mirror neuron system, 83–84
MIS. *See* Magical Ideation Scale
missing heritability problem, 314, 387
MMPI. *See* Minnesota Multiphasic Personality Inventory
MMPI-2-RF. *See* Minnesota Multiphasic Personality Inventory 2–Restructured Form
modafinil
   for hypersomnia, 534
   for narcolepsy, 533–34
modern research university, 37
molecular genetics, 65
   of anxiety disorders, 157–58
   of schizophrenia, 344–45
monoamine oxidase-A gene *(MAOA)*, in borderline personality disorder, 657–58
Mood Disorder Questionnaire, 230–31
mood disorders, 6. *See also* depression
   and antisocial personality disorder, 719
   assessment of, 229–30
   and attention-deficit hyperactivity disorder, 474
   and borderline personality disorder, 648, 649, 651, 652t
   comorbidity with anxiety disorders, 149–50

and delayed sleep phase disorder, 530
and eating disorders, 426
historical perspective on, 257–58
and hypersexuality, 565
and narcissistic personality disorder, 628–30, 631
and posttraumatic stress disorder, 204
social dysfunction in, 353
substance use and, 285
Moore, Thomas, 13
moral insanity, 714–15
moral sciences, for Mill, 39
moral treatment, 36–37
Morningness and Eveningness Questionnaire, 530
motivational processes, in substance use disorders, 309–12
motor functioning, in schizotypic psychopathology, 698
motor retardation, in schizophrenia, 337
MPQ. See Multidimensional Personality Questionnaire
MRI. See magnetic resonance imaging
MRS. See magnetic resonance spectroscopy
MSLT. See multiple sleep latency test
MTA. See Multimodal Treatment Study of Children with ADHD
Multicultural Family Assessment Module (Achenbach System), 461, 462f
Multidimensional Personality Questionnaire
and psychopathy, 733–34
triarchic scale measure based on, 726–29, 727t
triarchic traits, latent variable modeling of, 726–29, 729f
multifinality, 56–57, 65, 66, 96, 127
in depression, 132–33
Multimodal Treatment Study of Children with ADHD, 477
multiple personality disorder. See dissociative identity disorder
multiple sclerosis
and delayed ejaculation, 412
and female orgasmic disorder, 409–10
and male sexual desire, 407
multiple sleep latency test, in narcolepsy, 533
multiple system atrophy, 534–35
multivariate pattern analysis, 502
Munich Chronotype Questionnaire, 530
myalgia, and genito-pelvic pain, 415

# N

NAc. See nucleus accumbens
nalmefene, 317
naloxone, 317
naltrexone, 317
narcissism. See also narcissistic personality disorder; pathological narcissism
historical perspective on, 42, 626
object-relations theory and, 631

overt and covert, 638
as psychodynamic construct, 631
self-psychology theory and, 631–32
trifurcated trait model of, 635
Narcissism Scale for Children, 634
narcissist(s)
arrogant, 633–34
psychopathic, 633–34
shy, 633–34
subtypes of, 633–34
Narcissistic Admiration and Rivalry Questionnaire, 634
narcissistic grandiosity, 633–34, 633f
and aggression, 639–40
case example, 637–38
in contemporary clinical model, 630–31
and internalizing and externalizing problems, 634–35
and interpersonal problems, 635
and interpersonal sensitivity, 635
nomological research on, 634–35
research, future directions for, 640–41
and social interactions, 635
and suicidality, 638–39
temporal research on, 635–36, 636f
and treatment utilization, 635
Narcissistic Grandiosity Scale, 634
narcissistic neuroticism, 635
narcissistic personality disorder, 577–78, 602–3, 613, 626. See also pathological narcissism
and aggression, 639–40
and antisocial personality disorder, 628–29
and anxiety disorders, 628–30, 631
assessment of, 626
associated traits, 607, 607t, 638–40
and bipolar disorder, 628–29
and bipolar I, 628–29
and borderline personality disorder, 629, 651, 652t
case example, 627–28, 637–38
clinical theory and research on, 631–38
clinical utility of, 626
comorbidity in, 628–29
conceptualization of, 626
contextual mechanisms and processes in, 641
critiques of, 630–31
and depression, 639
diagnosis, 640
diagnostic criteria, in DSM, 626–27, 630, 640
and drug dependence, 628–29
in DSM, 626–31, 640
and dysthymia, 628–29
fragile, 633–34
future of, 640–41
grandiose/malignant, 633–34
gray matter volume in, 629
historical perspective on, 626
and histrionic personality disorder, 628–29

and major depression, 628–29
and mood disorders, 628–30, 631
and other personality disorders, comorbidity, 628–29
pathological subtypes, 633–34
and posttraumatic stress disorder, 628–30
prevalence of, 628, 630
and psychopathy, 719
and psychosis, 628–29
rank order stability of, 628
remission rate, 628
research on, 629–30
and schizophrenia, 628–29
shame in, 629–30
stability of, 628
and substance abuse, 628–29
and suicidality, 638–39
and symptom syndromes, 628–29
temporal stability of, 628
treatment of, 630
Narcissistic Personality Inventory, 634
narcissistic vulnerability, 633–34, 633f
and aggression, 639–40
case example, 637
in contemporary clinical model, 630–31
and internalizing and externalizing problems, 634–35
and interpersonal problems, 635
and interpersonal sensitivity, 635
nomological research on, 634–35
research, future directions for, 640–41
and social interactions, 635
and suicidality, 638–39
temporal research on, 635–36, 636f
and treatment utilization, 635
Narcissistic Vulnerability Scale, 634
narcolepsy, 524, 533–34
cataplexy in, 533
diagnosis of, 533
epidemiology of, 533
excessive daytime sleepiness in, 533
genetics of, 533
HLA complex in, 533
management of, 533–34
multiple sleep latency test in, 533
type 1 (NT1), 533
type 2 (NT2), 533
NARQ. See Narcissistic Admiration and Rivalry Questionnaire
Narrow Depression factor, 151f, 152–53
Nash, John, 337
National Comorbidity Survey, 23–24, 64
depression in, 258, 259
National Comorbidity Survey Adolescent Supplement, 148, 150
National Comorbidity Survey Replication, 23–24, 148, 150
depression in, 258
eating disorders in, 425
personality disorders in, 679, 680

National Epidemiologic Survey on Alcohol and Related Conditions, 66–67, 70, 148, 149, 150, 152
   borderline personality disorder in, 649–50, 651, 653–54
   personality disorders in, 649–50
National Institute of Mental Health. *See also* Research Domain Criteria
   and modular phenotyping for mental disorders, 81, 91
   research framework for psychopathology, 77, 91
   Strategic Objectives (2008), 81–82, 89
National Survey on Drug Use and Health, depression in, 258
National Vietnam Veterans Readjustment Study, 201–2, 204
natural disease forms (units), 78, 80
   historical perspective on, 38
natural essence, and classification, 17
natural history of diseases, 35
naturalism, 36
natural kind, 15–16
natural sciences, and human sciences, 39, 45
*Naturwissenschaften. See* natural sciences
nausea, and borderline personality disorder, 651
NCS-A. *See* National Comorbidity Survey Adolescent Supplement
NCS-R. *See* National Comorbidity Survey Replication
NE. *See* norepinephrine
necrophilia, 552
negative affect/negative affectivity, 615
   allostasis and, 308
   and binge eating, 430
   in borderline personality disorder, 662–63, 664, 665, 666, 667
   facets, 606t
   and internalizing, 231
   and major depression, 615–16
   in narcissistic personality disorder, 626–27
   and narcissistic vulnerability, 634–35
   and pathological narcissism, 631
   PCL-R scores and, 716
   and personality disorders, 590–91, 605, 610, 616, 616t, 618
   and psychotic disorders, 616
   in schizotypes, 686–87
   in schizotypic psychopathology, 700
   and substance use, 307–9
Negative Affect factor, 150–52, 154
negative cognitive triad, 266, 267
negative emotional dysregulation, in borderline personality disorder, 662–63
negative emotionality, 150
   in borderline personality disorder, 650t
   and personality disorders, 606
Negative Emotionality factor, 163

negative emotional reactivity deficit, psychopathy and, 719
negative emotions, in borderline personality disorder, 649, 649t
neighborhood deprivation
   and anxiety, 388
   and depression, 388
   and paranoia, 388
NEO inventory, 616
   and psychopathy, 720, 733–34
   triarchic scale measure based on, 726–28, 727t
   triarchic traits, latent variable modeling of, 726–29, 729f
neo-Kraepelinians, 8, 21, 42, 79, 80, 85, 96–97, 379
NESARC. *See* National Epidemiologic Survey on Alcohol and Related Conditions
network(s), 103. *See also* psychopathological network(s)
   and complex systems, 112f, 114–15
   construction of, 111–13
   definition of, 111
   dense, 113, 115
   density of, 113, 114–15
   edges in, 111
   nodes in, 111
   sparse, 113
network analysis, 97, 212
   challenges and future outlooks, 115–16
   formal theory approach, 115, 116
   of posttraumatic stress disorder, 212
neural connectivity, in bipolar spectrum disorders, 235
neural plasticity, 129
   experience-dependent, 129
neurasthenia, 510
neuregulin gene
   in schizophrenia, 344
   in schizotypic psychopathology, 696–97
neurexin 3 gene *(NRXN3)*, in borderline personality disorder, 658
neurites, development and outgrowth, in ADHD, 479
neurobiology
   in attention-deficit hyperactivity disorder, 481–83
   in borderline personality disorder, 662
   research on, HiTOP framework for, 66
   of schizotypic psychopathology, 699–700
neurocognition
   addiction-related changes in, 311–12
   assessment of, 362
   in attention-deficit hyperactivity disorder, 480–83
   and eating disorders, 430–31
   and posttraumatic stress disorder, 209–10
   psychosocial interventions targeting, in schizophrenia, 370

   and social functioning, in schizophrenia, 357–59, 362–63
neurodegeneration, and irregular sleep–wake rhythm disorder, 532
neurodevelopment
   childhood adversity and, 95–96
   genes in, in schizophrenia, 344
neurofeedback training, in attention-deficit hyperactivity disorder, 478
neuroimaging. *See also* functional magnetic resonance imaging
   in anxiety disorders, 159
   in apotemnophilia, 554
   in attention-deficit hyperactivity disorder, 481–83
   in autism, 499, 500
   in bipolar spectrum disorders, 234–37
   in eating disorders, 432
   in hypersexuality, 566
   in narcissistic personality disorder, 629
   in obsessive-compulsive disorder, 188, 189, 193
   in paraphilias, 560
   in psychopathy, 719
   in schizotypic psychopathology, 699–700
neuropharmacology, of schizophrenia, 342–44
neuroplasticity, in eating disorders, 435
neuropsychology, of schizophrenia, 338
neuroscience, mechanistic models in, 43–44
neurosis/neuroses
   Cullen's classification of, 5
   Jaspers on, 40, 41
   vegetative, 510
neuroticism, 150, 154–55, 661. *See also* NEO inventory
   and anxiety disorders, 154–55, 157, 162–63
   anxiety sensitivity and, 156
   behavioral inhibition and, 155, 156
   in borderline personality disorder, 650t, 656, 661
   definition of, 154
   and depression, 261
   Eysenck's concept of, 13
   in Five Factor Model, 14
   genetic factor associated with, 157
   and internalizing disorders, 154–55
   and major depressive disorder, 154
   narcissistic, 635
   PCL-R scores and, 716
   and personality disorders, 603, 605, 606, 616, 616t
   research on, HiTOP framework for, 63–64
   and risk for substance use disorders, 308–9
   and risk of exposure to trauma, 204
   scientific anti-realist view of, 48
   scientific realist view of, 48

and somatization, 513
SSRIs' effect on, 72
and stably elevated negative affect hypothesis, 154
and stress amplification hypothesis, 154
UP's effect on, 72
and vulnerability to psychopathology, 154–55
Neuroticism-Extraversion-Openness Pi-R inventory. *See* NEO inventory
neurotoxicity, of drugs of abuse, 311–12
neurotransmission, in schizophrenia, 342–44
neurotransmitters, in eating disorders, 432–34
new mechanists, 90
NF. *See* neurofeedback
NGS. *See* Narcissistic Grandiosity Scale
nicotine/nicotine system. *See also* tobacco/nicotine dependence
  dependence, genetic factors in, 314
  in substance use disorders, 315, 317–18
night eating syndrome, 424
nightmare disorder, 534–35
NIMH. *See* National Institute of Mental Health
*NINJ2* gene, in borderline personality disorder, 660
nitrazepam, 529
NMDA. *See* N-methyl-D-aspartate
N-methyl-D-aspartate, in substance use, 316
N-methyl-D-aspartate receptors, in schizophrenia, 342–43
nomenclature, 4
nomothetic methods, 39
non–24-hr sleep–wake rhythm disorder, 524, 529, 532–33
  entrainment in, 532–33
non-inferiority trial, 71
nonlinear system(s), 103
nonpsychotic [term], 677
nonpsychotic schizotypic psychopathology, 677
  assessment of, 678–79
  definition of, 678–79
nonreductionism, 45. *See also* 4E framework
nonreductive materialism, 45n.2
nonsuicidal self-injury, in borderline personality disorder, 662–63
noradrenergic system, in posttraumatic stress disorder, 212
norepinephrine
  in attention-deficit hyperactivity disorder, 482–83
  and female orgasm, 409
  and female sexual function, 404–5
  in posttraumatic stress disorder, 212
normative beliefs, and drug use, 303
norms, in dimensional assessment, 68
NOS. *See* not otherwise specified
nosology, 54. *See also* classification

definition of, 3
historical perspective on, 78–79
modern era of, 79–80, 96–97
multifinality and, 56–57
quantitative, 57–59
not otherwise specified, 56
NPD. *See* narcissistic personality disorder
NPI. *See* Narcissistic Personality Inventory
NSC. *See* Narcissism Scale for Children
NSDUH. *See* National Survey on Drug Use and Health
N24SWD. *See* non–24-hr sleep–wake rhythm disorder
nucleus accumbens
  in drug use, 315–16
  in paraphilias, 560
  substance use and, 312, 316–17
NVS. *See* Narcissistic Vulnerability Scale
NVVRS. *See* National Vietnam Veterans Readjustment Study

## O

OABCL. *See* Older Adult Behaviour Checklist
OASR. *See* Older Adult Self-Report
obesity
  binge-eating disorder and, 423, 425
  and erectile disorder, 407
Object Relations Inventory, 580
object relations theory, 41, 631
  and narcissism, 631
obsessions
  definition of, 181–82
  as ego-dystonic, 182
  in obsessive-compulsive disorder, 181–82
  resistance to, 182
  themes of, 181–83
  as unwanted and uncontrollable, 181–82
Obsessions and Compulsions factor, 152
obsessive-compulsive and related disorders, 181, 189–92
  brain circuitry in, critical examination of, 193–94
  as category, critical examination of, 192–94
  comorbidity patterns in, 193
  demographic features of, critical examination of, 193
  neurotransmitter abnormalities in, critical examination of, 193–94
  repetitive thoughts and behaviors in, critical examination of, 192–93
  SSRI therapy and, 188, 189, 194
  treatment response, critical examination of, 194
obsessive-compulsive disorder. *See also* obsessive-compulsive and related disorders
  and anorexia nervosa, 426
  as anxiety disorder, 192, 193
  and anxiety disorders, comorbidity, 193
  attentional bias and, 163–64
  avoidance in, 182, 186

biological models of, 188–89
cognitive-behavioral models of, 186, 187
cognitive bias models of, 185–87
cognitive deficit models of, 185
cognitive fusion and, 188
cognitive inhibition problems in, 185
cognitive model of, 186–87
compulsions in, 181, 182 (*see also* rituals, compulsive)
conceptual models of, 184–89
conditioning models of, 184–85
course of, 183–84
*DSM* classification of, 181, 192
dynamical systems persepctive on, 104
and eating disorders, 426
ego dystonicity in, 182, 183
empirical status of, 187
epidemiology of, 183–84
and erectile disorder, 408
experiential avoidance and, 188
and female sexual dysfunction, 405
genetic contributions to, 188
heritability, 188
and hypersexuality, 565
insight in, 183
interpersonal aspects of, 184
intolerance of uncertainty in, 183
learning models of, 184–85
memory bias in, 164–65
memory deficit in, 185
neuroimaging in, 188, 189, 193
obsessions in, 181–82
phenomenology of, 181–83, 194
prevalence of, 183–84
psychological models emphasizing acceptance of unwanted thoughts, 187–88
reality monitoring deficit in, 185
and relationship conflict, 184
serotonin hypothesis for, 188, 189, 194
SSRI therapy and, 188, 189, 194
structural models of, 188, 189
symptom accommodation in, 184
symptom dimensions in, 182–83
thought–action fusion in, 187–88
treatment of, 187–88
treatment response, expressed emotion and, 168
obsessive-compulsive personality disorder, 181, 577, 602–3, 613, 614, 618
  associated traits, 607, 607t
  and borderline personality disorder, 651, 652t
  and eating disorders, 427–28
Obsessive-Compulsive Problems Scale, 456t
obsessive-compulsive spectrum, 25
occipital-parietal-temporal-frontal tract, in eating disorders, 432
OCD. *See* obsessive-compulsive disorder
OCRDs. *See* obsessive-compulsive and related disorders
ODD. *See* oppositional defiant disorder

oddity
  as personality construct, 14
  and personality disorders, 606
Oedipus complex, 33–34
oedophilia, 548–49
OFC. *See* orbitofrontal cortex
Older Adult Behaviour Checklist, 456t, 458
Older Adult Self-Report, 458
OPD. *See* Operationalized Psychodynamic Diagnosis
open concept(s), 336
  schizophrenia as, 336
openness/openness to experience, 63, 603, 661. *See also* NEO inventory
  in borderline personality disorder, 650t, 656, 661
  in Five Factor Model, 14
  as multifaceted domain, 616–17
  and personality disorders, 616, 616t
  and psychoticism, 616
Operationalized Psychodynamic Diagnosis, 580, 584t
  Structure Questionnaire, 592
opiates/opioids. *See also* endogenous opioid system
  illicit, use and misuse, 304
  and impulse control, 284–85
  overdose, 297
  prescription, use and misuse, 304
  teratogenicity, 307
opiate use disorder, and mood disorder, 285
opioid epidemic, 304
opioid use disorder, genetic factors in, 314
opium use, historical perspective on, 296–97
oppositional defiant disorder, 25
  and ADHD, 474, 476–77
oppositional problems, and bipolar spectrum disorders, 229
*OPRM1* gene variant, in opioid use disorder, 314
oral contraceptives, and female sexual function, 404
orbital gyrus, in obsessive-compulsive disorder, 188
orbitofrontal cortex
  in eating disorders, 432
  in obsessive-compulsive disorder, 188
  in paraphilias, 560
  in reward circuit, 236
  in social perception, 497–98
  in theory-of-mind reasoning, 498
  ventromedial, in attention-deficit hyperactivity disorder, 481
orexin antagonists
  for insomnia, 528–29
  for patients with dementia and sleep problems, 532
orgasm
  female, 408–10

male, 411, 413 (*see also* delayed ejaculation; premature (early) ejaculation; retrograde ejaculation)
orgasm disorders, 408–13. *See also* delayed ejaculation; female orgasmic disorder; premature (early) ejaculation
ORI. *See* Object Relations Inventory
orthogenic principle, 124
orthorexia, 423–24
OS-BRDs. *See* bipolar and related disorders, otherwise specified
OSFED. *See* other specified feeding or eating disorder
Osler, William, 296
other specified feeding or eating disorder, 422
  defining characteristics of, 424
OUD. *See* opioid use disorder
ovarian disease, and genito-pelvic pain, 414–15
overgeneralization, 266
Oxford-Liverpool Inventory of Feelings and Experiences, 694
oxidative stress, in posttraumatic stress disorder, 213
oxytocin
  in eating disorders, 433, 435
  and female orgasm, 409

# P

PAI. *See* Personality Assessment Inventory
PAI-BOR. *See* Personality Assessment Inventory–Borderline Scale
pain. *See also* functional somatic symptom(s)
  chronic, and borderline personality disorder, 651
  as functional somatic symptom, 508–9
  general, and borderline personality disorder, 651, 653
  psychogenic, 510
pain disorder, 514
panic
  and anxiety, 147
  definition of, 147
  nonclinical, 147
panic attack(s)
  anxiety sensitivity and, 155–56
  expected, 147
  perceptions of controllability and, 162
  prevalence of, 150
  unexpected, 147
panic disorder, 147. *See also* anxiety disorders
  and agoraphobia, 55, 147–48
  alcohol dependence and, 285–86
  anxiety sensitivity and, 155–56
  attentional bias and, 163–64
  behavior genetics of, 157
  computational model of, 115–16
  and eating disorders, 426
  factor analysis, 150–52

features of, 147–48
and female sexual dysfunction, 405
interoceptive conditioning in, 163
interpersonal problems and, 167–68
learned fear in, 160
memory bias in, 164–65
and phobias, 57–58
and posttraumatic stress disorder, 204
treatment response, expressed emotion and, 168
vicarious conditioning and, 160–61
panic disorder with or without agoraphobia, 147–48
  and borderline personality disorder, 652t
  comorbidity with, 149t, 150
  epidemiology of, 149t, 150
  prevalence of, 149t, 150
  substance use disorders and, 286
PANSS. *See* Positive and Negative Syndrome Scale
parahippocampus
  in schizophrenia, 364
  substance use and, 312
paranoia, 6. *See also* paranoid beliefs
  anomalous experience model of, 389–90, 394
  assessment of, 386–87
  bad me type, 384, 392–93
  case study, 380–81
  clinical concept of, 378–79
  cognitive factors and, 389, 390–92, 394
  components of, 385
  conceptual history of, 378–80
  continuum model, 384–86, 393–94
  defense model of, 389, 392–93, 394
  emotional processes and, 390–92, 394
  environmental factors and, 387–88
  genetic determinants of, 387–89
  heritability of, 387
  Kretschmer's views on, 379
  neighborhood deprivation and, 388
  poor me type, 384, 392–93
  in popular culture, 378
  psychological models of, 389–93, 394
  psychotherapy for, 394
  and reasoning ability, 390
  social determinants of, 387–89
  theory of mind deficits and, 389, 392, 394
Paranoia Checklist, 386
paranoid beliefs. *See also* paranoia
  adverse life experiences and, 393–94
  case study, 380–81
  continuum hypothesis and, 384–86, 393–94
  definition of, 383–84
  emotional biases and, 392–93
  hearing loss and, 390
  and self-esteem regulation, 384, 392–93
paranoid disorder, 379
paranoid ideation, in borderline personality disorder, 649, 649t, 664

776 | INDEX

paranoid personality disorder, 334,
    379–80, 577, 602–3, 613, 614,
    676–79, 679f. *See also* schizotypic
    psychopathology; schizotypy
  abuse and, 389
  and Axis I delusional disorder, 696
  and borderline personality disorder, 651,
    652t, 681
  clinical phenomenology of, 700
  definition of, 677
  familiality of, 696
  heritability of, 387, 696
  longitudinal course of, 681–82
  prevalence of, 680, 683t
  and schizotypal personality disorder,
    comorbidity, 680–81
paraphilia(s), 548. *See also* bestiality;
    courtship disorder; fetishism;
    zoophilia
  activity, 548, 554–58
  and altered partners, 551–52
  associated features, 559–61
  blended, 558
  brain connectivity in, 560
  comorbid with asphyxiophilia, 556
  consensual, 547
  course of, 561
  definition of, 548
  educational level and, 559
  and erectile disorder, 408
  and erotic age preferences, 548–49
  and erotic-target identity
    inversion, 552–54
  handedness and, 559–60
  hormonal assays in, 560
  and intimacy/social skills
    deficits, 560–61
  IQ and, 559
  male predominance of, 548
  masochistic, 555–56
  multiple (comorbid), 558
  neuroimaging in, 560
  neuropsychological findings in, 559
  nonconsensual, 547, 548
  object, 548–54
  onset of, 561
  versus paraphilic disorders, 548
  prevalence of, 558–59
  sex ratio of, 558–59
paraphilic coercive disorder, 554–55
paraphilic disorders, versus paraphilias, 548
paraphilic rape, 554–55
paraphilogenic factors, 559–61
parasomnia(s), 524, 534–35
  NREM, 534
  other (group), 534
  REM, 534–35
parasympathetic nervous system, and
    female sexual function, 404–5
paraventricular nucleus, and orgasm, 409
parent(s)/parenting
  inflammation and depression related
    to, 135

and paranoia, 389
and pathological narcissism, 631–33
Parkinson's disease
  and female orgasmic disorder, 409–10
  REM sleep behavior disorder
    and, 534–35
partial correlation models, 116
partialism, 550–51
parvalbumin, 343
PAS. *See* Perceptual Aberration Scale
pathological narcissism. *See also* narcissistic
    personality disorder
  and aggression, 639–40
  associated traits, 638–40
  clinical recognition of, 630
  contemporary clinical model of, 632–36
  contextual mechanisms and processes
    in, 641
  and depression, 639
  diagnosis, 640
  as extreme grandiosity, 626–31
  future of, 640–41
  as grandiosity and vulnerability, 631–38
  hierarchical structure of, 633f, 633–34
  historical perspective on, 626
  psychodynamic origins of, 631–32
  social-personality psychology research
    and, 632n.2
  and suicidality, 638–39
Pathological Narcissism Inventory, 634
pathological rape, 554
Patient Health Questionnaire, 514–15
PCL. *See* PTSD Checklist
PCL-R. *See* Psychopathy
    Checklist–Revised
PCP. *See* phencyclidine
PD. *See* panic disorder; personality
    disorder(s)
PD/A. *See* panic disorder with or without
    agoraphobia
PDE. *See* Personality Disorders
    Examination
*PDE4B* gene, 158
PDM-2. *See* Psychodynamic Diagnostic
    Manual-2
PDS-ICD-11. *See* Personality Disorder
    Severity *ICD-11*
PE. *See* premature (early) ejaculation
peculiarity, and personality
    disorders, 606
pedohebephilia, 548–49
pedophiles, nonoffending, 548
pedophilia, 548–49, 552
  age of onset, 561
  associated features, 559
  brain connectivity in, 560
  and handedness, 559–60
  and IQ, 559
  neuroimaging in, 560
PE/E. *See* positive emotionality/
    extraversion
peer victimization, and psychopathology,
    HiTOP perspective on, 67

pelvic congestion syndrome, and genito-
    pelvic pain, 415
penetrance, reduced, 344
perceptual aberration and magical
    ideation, in schizophrenia-prone
    males, 356
Perceptual Aberration Scale, 693–
    94, 696–97
  high scorers, follow-up studies
    of, 700–1
  scores, covariance analysis of, 702
perfectionism
  and depression, 261, 269–70
  and eating disorders, 429
performance anxiety
  and ejaculatory function, 413
  and erectile disorder, 408
perineoplasty, 410
Per-Mag Scale, 356. *See also* perceptual
    aberration and magical ideation
personality. *See also* Five Factor Model
  addictive, 308
  anankastic features, 14–15
  and anxiety disorders, 154–57
  assessment instruments, 580
  changes in, 309
  and conditioning, 162–63
  and depression, 261
  expressional, situational determinants
    of, 309
  as foundational base for
    psychopathology, 616
  maturation of, 587–88
  and mental disorders, 64
  research on, HiTOP framework
    for, 63–64
  and schizotypy, 691
  and somatization, 513
  state–trait distinction and, 157
  and substance use disorders, 308–9
Personality Assessment Inventory, 608, 612
Personality Assessment Inventory–
    Borderline Scale (PAI-
    BOR), 658–59
personality disorder(s), 379–80, 715.
    *See also* Alternative Model
    of Personality Disorders;
    schizophrenia-related PDs
  and addictive syndromes,
    comorbidity, 615
  antisocial (*see* antisocial personality
    disorder)
  assessment methods, 592–93
  attachment theory of, 579
  avoidant (*see* avoidant personality
    disorder)
  borderline (*see* borderline personality
    disorder)
  categorical versus dimensional
    approaches to, 14–15, 16, 22, 603–
    4, 605, 607, 612–13, 614–15
  classification, 602, 604–5
  clinical utility, 604

personality disorder(s) (*cont.*)
  Cluster A, and borderline personality disorder, 651, 652*t*
  Cluster A, factor analytic studies of, 701
  Cluster A, prevalence of, 680, 683*t*
  Cluster B, and borderline personality disorder, 651, 652*t*
  Cluster C, and borderline personality disorder, 651, 652*t*
  comorbidity with anxiety disorders, 149, 149*t*
  as continuous distribution versus discrete categories, 603–4
  co-occurrence of, 578, 604, 605, 680–81
  covariation of, 681
  dependent (*see* dependent personality disorder)
  diagnosis, 20, 602
  diagnostic criteria, 602–3, 613
  diagnostic instability, 604
  diagnostic threshold for, 580
  dimensional approach to, 577, 603–4, 666–67
  in *DSM-5*, 14, 16, 20, 42, 577, 578–79, 602–3, 605, 627, 630, 657, 666, 667
  *DSM* classification, 379–80
  in *DSM-IV*, 16, 578–79, 580, 590, 592, 602–3, 605
  in *DSM-IV-TR*, 607, 607*t*, 609
  dysfunction in, 579
  and eating disorders, 427–28
  epidemiology of, 679
  Five Factor Model and, 605
  future research on, 593
  general factor (g-PD) (*see* general factor of PD)
  heterogeneity within, 604
  historical perspective on, 42
  histrionic (*see* histrionic personality disorder)
  and hypersexuality, 565
  in *ICD-11*, 591–92, 627n.1
  *ICD* classification, 14–15, 379–80, 591–92
  interpersonal functioning in, 578–81
  interpersonal theory of, 579
  Jaspers on, 40, 41
  longitudinal studies of, 681–82, 700
  as modifiable, 578
  narcissistic (*see* narcissistic personality disorder)
  not otherwise specified (PD-NOS), 16, 604
  obsessive-compulsive (*see* obsessive-compulsive personality disorder)
  other specified, 602–3, 604, 607
  paranoid (*see* paranoid personality disorder)
  personality traits and, 661
  polythetic diagnostic criteria for, 602–3, 604
  prevalence of, 679, 683*t*
  prognosis for, severity and, 578, 590
  psychodynamic models of, 47, 579, 580
  research on, HiTOP framework for, 63–64
  schizoid (*see* schizoid personality disorder)
  schizotypal (*see* schizotypal personality disorder)
  self-functioning in, 578–81
  severity, 577–78, 579–81, 591–92
  and somatization disorder, 513
  stability versus fluctuation of, 20
  symptom changes over time, 578
  traditional approaches to, limitations of, 603–5
  trait profiles, 605
  trait specified, 607
  treatment, severity and, 578
  unspecified, 602–3, 604, 607
Personality Disorder Severity ICD-11, 591–92
Personality Disorders Examination, 358
personality domains, 605
  of DAPP-BQ, 605
  in *DSM-5*, 14–15
  in *DSM-5* Maladaptive Trait Model, 606, 606*t*
  in *ICD-11*, 14–15
personality functioning
  assessment instruments, 580, 581–83, 582*t*
  impairment scales for, 582–83
  other-reports on, 586–89, 587*t*
  self-report on, 581–83, 582*t*, 586–88, 587*t*, 592
  structured interviews about, 581–83, 582*t*
Personality Functioning Scale, 582*t*, 585
Personality Inventory for *DSM-5*, 69, 606–11
  comparison to alternative inventories and methods, 612
  convergent and predictive validity, 612
  cross-cultural administration, 612
  dimensionality, 609–10
  domains, relation to Five Factor Model and HiTOP spectra, 615, 616*t*
  ease of use, 614
  future research and, 618
  internal consistency of, 609–10
  and internalizing psychopathology, 615–16
  interrater reliability of, 611
  interstitiality of, 610
  measurement invariance, testing for, 611–12
  normative values for, 614
  prediction of clinically relevant outcomes, 612, 613
  psychometric properties of, 618
  and psychopathy, 726, 727*t*, 729*f*, 730, 733–34
  and psychotic disorders, 616
  response inconsistency and, 614
  reverse-coded items, 614
  structure of, 608–9
  symptom overreporting and, 614
  traits, traditional syndrome counterparts, 612–13
Personality Inventory for *DSM-5*–Brief Form, 590, 608, 609, 610–11
Personality Inventory for *DSM-5*–Informant Report, 608, 609–10
Personality Inventory for *DSM-5*–Short Form, 608, 609–11
personality organization, Kernberg's domains of, 580
Personality Organization Diagnostic Form, 580
personality structure. *See also* Five Factor Model
  dimensional, 603
  HEXACO model, 603
Personality Trait Rating Form, 608, 609, 611
personality traits. *See also* Five Factor Model
  and borderline personality disorder, 661, 661*t*
  clinical significance of, 603
  and eating disorders, 429
  as organizing framework, 603
  and personality disorders, 661
  short-term stability of, 604
personalization, 266
personal space
  definition of, 363–64
  in schizophrenia, 363–64
pervasive developmental disorder(s), 25
  not otherwise specified, 490
pessimistic induction, 47–48
PET. *See* positron emission tomography
Peters Delusions Inventory, 386
p factor, 588, 617
*p*-factor, 25, 60–61, 64, 449, 451
  neural correlates of, 66
  peer victimization and, 67
  and suicidality, 70
PFC. *See* prefrontal cortex
PFS. *See* Personality Functioning Scale
PhAB. *See* Phenotyping Assessment Battery
phencyclidine, psychomimetic (psychosis-inducing) effects of, 342–43
phenethylamines, and serotonergic system, 316–17
Phenotyping Assessment Battery, 318
Philadelphia Neurodevelopmental Cohort, 95
philosophical perspective, on study of psychopathology, 33–50
philosophy of science, conditional and partial scientific realism in, 48–49
phobias. *See also* specific phobia(s)
  direct conditioning and, 160
  and panic disorder, 57–58
  selective associations in, 161
  vicarious conditioning and, 160–61

photosensitive retinal ganglion cells, 521
PHQ-15. *See* Patient Health Questionnaire
Physical Anhedonia Scale, 355
Physical Concerns factor, 156
Physiological Hyperarousal factor, 150–52, 151*f*
pica, 422
PID-5. *See* Personality Inventory for *DSM-5*
PID-5-BF. *See* Personality Inventory for *DSM-5*–Brief Form
PID-5-IRF. *See* Personality Inventory for *DSM-5*–Informant Report
PID-5-SF. *See* Personality Inventory for *DSM-5*–Short Form
Pike, Kenneth, on etic/emic research, 455
Pinel, Phillipe, 37
  on *manie sans délire* (insanity without delirium), 714–15
pitolisant, for narcolepsy, 533–34
Pittsburgh Sleep Quality Index, 526
pivotal response treatment, in autism, 502–3
Plakophilin-4 gene *(PKP4)*, in borderline personality disorder, 659
PLE. *See* psychotic-like experiences
pleasure, experience of, child maltreatment and, 132
pleasure deficiency, in schizotypy, 684
pleiotropy, genetic, 65
pluralism
  and classification, 17
  definition of, 40
  methodological, Jaspers and, 40–41
PNC. *See* Philadelphia Neurodevelopmental Cohort
PNI. *See* Pathological Narcissism Inventory
P&O App. *See* Progress and Outcomes App (Achenbach System)
PODF. *See* Personality Organization Diagnostic Form
polygenic potentiators, 689, 692
  Meehl's theory of, 684–86, 687*f*, 687–88
polygenic risk score(s)
  definition of, 313–14
  for schizophrenia, 345
  in substance use disorders, 313–14
polysomnography, 522, 523
  in advanced sleep phase disorder, 531
  in insomnia, 526–27
  in narcolepsy, 533
  in schizophrenia, 538
polysubstance use disorders, 280
Positive Affect factor, 150–53
positive affectivity
  and narcissistic grandiosity and vulnerability, 634–35
  and personality disorders, 605, 606
Positive and Negative Syndrome Scale, 386
positive emotionality/extraversion, 156–57
  facets of, 156–57
positivism, 38

positron emission tomography
  in attention-deficit hyperactivity disorder, 482–83
  in dissociative identity disorder, 216
  in eating disorders, 433
  in obsessive-compulsive disorder, 188
  in PTSD, 207–8
postcentral gyrus, in schizophrenia, 364
posterior cingulate cortex
  in borderline personality disorder, 662
  in schizophrenia, 363
  in social cognition, 498
*post hoc ergo propter hoc*, 189, 194
posttraumatic stress disorder, 199–214
  algorithms predicting, Big Data and machine learning and, 212–13
  and alterations in arousal and reactivity (E criteria), 200
  attentional bias and, 163–64
  autobiographical memory in, 206–7
  and avoidance cluster (C criteria), 200
  biological aspects of, 207–12
  and borderline personality disorder, 648, 652*t*
  buffers against, 209
  cognitive aspects of, 205–7
  cognitive neuroscience and emotional Stroop in, 207–8
  comorbidity in, 204
  complex, 15
  controversy about, 34
  core features of, 199–200
  cross-national studies, vulnerability paradox in, 201
  delayed-onset, 203
  diagnosis, 213–14
  in *DSM-5*, 15
  *DSM* classification of, 199–200
  *DSM-5* versus *ICD-11* on, 213–14
  and eating disorders, 426–27
  emotional Stroop paradigm in, 207–8
  epidemiology of, 201–5
  and exposure to traumatic stressor (A criterion), 200–1
  factor analysis, 151–52
  and functional somatic symptoms, 512–13
  genetics, 209–10
  genome-wide association studies in, 210
  heterogeneity of, 55–56
  in *ICD-11*, 15
  impairment in, 202
  intentionality of symptoms in, 200
  and intrusion cluster (B criteria), 200
  longitudinal course of, 203–4
  and low social support, 204
  memory bias in, 164–65
  in military personnel/veterans, 201–4, 205, 206, 207, 208–10, 211
  and narcissistic personality disorder, 628–30
  and negative alterations in cognition and mood (D criteria), 200

  network analysis, 212
  noradrenergic dysregulation in, 212
  overlap with other disorders, 200
  oxidative stress and inflammation in, 213
  physiological reactivity to trauma-related cues in, 211
  PID-5 traits and, 615–16
  precondition for, 297
  prefrontal cortex in, 208
  regular, 15
  research, emerging themes in, 212–14
  resting psychophysiological levels in, 210–11
  risk factors for, 204–5
  sex differences in, 201
  startle response in, 211–12
  and substance use disorders, 308
  substance use disorders and, 286–87
  symptom clusters, 200
  traumatic memory in, 205–6
post-Vietnam syndrome, 199
poverty, and substance use, 303–4
powerlessness, and paranoia, 387–88
power spectral analysis, 523, 526–27
PPD. *See* paranoid personality disorder
PPI. *See* Psychopathic Personality Inventory
practical kinds, 15–16
pragmatism, and classification, 17–18
precentral gyrus, in eating disorders, 432
precuneus
  in eating disorders, 432
  in schizophrenia, 363
prediction, classification and, 4
predictive processes, 511–12, 513
  and conversion disorder, 516
  in schizophrenia, 339
preferential rape, 554, 557
prefrontal cortex
  in attention-deficit hyperactivity disorder, 481
  in bipolar spectrum disorders, 235
  in borderline personality disorder, 662, 663–64
  and depersonalization, 218
  in depression, 135
  exposure to criticism and, 369
  in obsessive-compulsive disorder, 188
  in PTSD, 208
  and reward cues, 95
  in schizophrenia, 340–41, 363, 365
  and schizotypic psychopathology, 697, 698
  in social cognition, 498
  ventrolateral, in social perception, 498–503
  ventromedial, in social perception, 498–503
premature (early) ejaculation, 412–13
  age and, 412–13
  biological factors and, 413
  causal factors, 413

INDEX | 779

premature (early) ejaculation (*cont.*)
  definition of, 412–13
  diagnosis of, 412–13
  endocrine system and, 413
  and erectile disorder, co-occurrence of, 412–13
  genetics of, 413
  prevalence of, 412–13
  psychological factors in, 413
prenatal period, and epigenetic changes, 87
prepared fears, 161
prescription drug(s)
  misuse, 304
  teratogenicity, 307
prevention
  developmentally informed, 130
  RDoC and, 85–86
  RDoC-oriented research and, 96
pride, and narcissistic grandiosity and vulnerability, 634–35
primary aversive drift, in schizotypes, 686–88, 700
principal components analysis, 48
priors, in predictive processing, 511–12, 513
Pritchard, J. C., 714–15
progestins, and female sexual function, 403
prognosis, HiTOP-oriented formulation of, 69–70
Progress and Outcomes App (Achenbach System), 461–62
prolactin
  and ejaculatory function, 413
  and female orgasm, 409
proprioceptive (kinesthetic) diathesis, in schizotypy, 684
provoked vestibulodynia, 415
PRT. *See* pivotal response treatment
pseudobisexuality, 562
psilocybin, and serotonergic system, 316–17
psychiatric classification. *See* classification
psychiatry
  as clinical science, 37–38
  criticisms of, 7–8
  as medical specialty, 8
  *Methodenstreit* and, 39
psychoanalysis, 16–17, 41–42, 78–79, 96–97
  *Methodenstreit* and, 39
psychobiological approach, 124
Psychodynamic Diagnostic Manual-2, 580
*Psychodynamic Diagnostic Manual*, on narcissistic personality disturbance, 634
psychoeducation
  in attention-deficit hyperactivity disorder, 476
  for bipolar disorder, 240, 241
  definition of, 240
  and sexual dysfunction, 416
  in substance use prevention, 300

psychogenic pain, 510
psychological and developmental syndromes, Jaspers on, 40
psychological factors affecting medical condition, 516
psychological test(s), validity of, 21–23
psychology
  founding of, 37–38
  *Methodenstreit* and, 39
  as natural science, 37–38
psychopathic personality, 714–15
  characteristics of, 302
Psychopathic Personality Inventory, 720
  factors, 720–21, 723, 724
  psychological and neurobiological correlates of factors, 720–21, 723
  triarchic scale measure based on, 725, 727t
  triarchic traits, latent variable modeling of, 726–29, 729f
psychopathological network(s), 110–16. *See also* network(s)
  centrality in, 113–14
  challenges and future outlooks, 115–16
  construction of, 111–13
  cross-sectional, 111
  density (connectivity) of, 113–14
  diagnostic manual-based, 113
  intensive longitudinal data for, 111–12
  perceived causal relations in, 112–13
  time series date for, 111–12
  vector autoregressive model, 111–12, 113, 115
psychopathology
  concept, historical perspective on, 36
  empirically based bottom-up paradigm for, 448, 449, 450–55
  4E perspectives in, 45–47
  in maltreated children, 131–32
  multicultural research on, 455–60
  as process, 104
  psychological versus biological phenomena in, 87–88
  as trait-like, 104
psychopathy(ies), 714
  and antisocial personality disorder, comorbidity, 718–19
  and anxiety, 719
  assessment in child and adolescent clinical samples, 717–18
  biobehavioral traits and, 733f, 734–37, 735t
  and boldness, 722–23, 733f, 733–34
  and borderline personality disorder, 719
  in community samples, 720–21
  current conceptions of, 716–21
  developmental pathways in, 733f, 733–37
  diagnostic criteria, 715
  and disinhibition, 721–22, 733f, 733–34
  in *DSM-5*, 715, 729–30
  empirical findings on, 716–21
  and fear, 719

  in forensic samples, 716–19
  and Hierarchical Taxonomy of Psychopathology, 730–33
  historical perspective on, 714–15
  and histrionic personality disorder, 719
  integrative framework for, 721–33
  Jaspers on, 40
  and meanness, 722, 723–24, 733f, 733–34
  measurement, 725–26, 727t, 737–38
  in men, 718
  and narcissistic personality disorder, 719
  neurobiological systems and processes in, 719, 733f, 733–37, 735t
  PCL-R-defined, prevalence of, 718
  self-report–based operationalizations of, 720–21
  and substance use disorder, 719
  triarchic model of, 714, 721–33, 737–38 (*see also* Triarchic Psychopathy Measure)
  triarchic model trait operationalization, 724–29
  triarchic model traits, 721–24
  triarchic scale measures, 725–26, 727t, 737–38
  triarchic traits, latent variable modeling of, 726–29, 729f
  in women, 718
  in youth, 734
Psychopathy Checklist–Revised, 23
  adaptations used with young clinical samples, 717–18
  and cooperative suppression, 717
  description of, 716
  factors, 716–17, 718–19, 723
  and prevalence of psychopathy, 718
  scores, in incarcerated samples, 718
  screening version (PCL:SV), 718
  subdimensions of, 716–17
  youth versions (PCL:YV), 717–18, 723
psychophysiology, 82, 84
  in dissociative identity disorder, 216–17
  in posttraumatic stress disorder, 210–11
psychosis/psychoses, 6
  autistic traits and, 392
  construct of, 334–36
  definition of, 334, 690
  empirical constructs and, 335–36
  environmental factors and, 387–88
  genetic determinants and, 387
  head injury–induced, 346
  "healthy," 690–91
  insomnia and, 538
  Jaspers on, 40, 41
  and narcissistic personality disorder, 628–29
  and psychosocial functioning, 70
  statistical analyses, 335–36
  theory of mind deficits and, 392
psychosocial development, and risk for substance use disorders, 308–9
psychosocial functioning, prediction, 70
psychotic disorders, PID-5 traits and, 616

psychoticism, 14
  in *DSM-5*, 700–1
  Eysenck's concept of, 13, 700–1
  facets, 606t
  facets associated with, 681
  MMPI definition of, 700–1
  and openness, 616
  and personality disorders, 590, 605, 606, 616, 616t
  as personality trait (Eysenck), 690
  and posttraumatic stress disorder, 615–16
  and psychotic disorders, 616
  and risk for psychosis, 700–1
psychotic-like experiences
  in general population, 703
  and schizophrenia liability, 703
psychotic spectrum, 25
psychotic symptoms, 334
PTRF. *See* Personality Trait Rating Form
PTSD. *See* posttraumatic stress disorder
PTSD Checklist, 202–3
public data, in psychopathology research and theory, 88–89
purging disorder, 424
putamen, in attention-deficit hyperactivity disorder, 481
Putnam, Hillary, 49
PVD. *See* provoked vestibulodynia

# Q

Q correlation, 454, 456–58
  omnicultural mean, 458
QLS. *See* Quality of Life Scale
QORS. *See* Quality of Object Relations Scale
Quality of Life Scale, 352, 354, 355
Quality of Object Relations Scale, 580
quantitative analysis. *See also* nosology, quantitative
  of clustering/co-occurrence of clinical phenomena, 57
  definition of, 57
quantitative trait loci, 657

# R

racial disparity(ies), in diagnosis and treatment of bipolar disorder, 241–44
Rado, Sandor, on schizotypal behavior, 684
rage
  narcissistic, 639–40
  and narcissistic vulnerability, 634–35
ramelteon, 529
randomized controlled trials
  in developmental research, 136
  of interventions, developmental perspective on, 130
  in prevention, 130
rape
  of elderly women, 549
  and necrophilia, 552

paraphilic, 554–55
pathological, 554
  and posttraumatic stress disorder, 203
  preferential, 554, 557
  sadistic, 555
  telephone scatologists and, 557
  victim-blaming in, and depression, 262
RCT. *See* randomized controlled trial
RD. *See* rumination disorder
RDC. *See* Research Diagnostic Criteria
RDoC. *See* Research Domain Criteria
reaction time crossover, 339
Reading the Mind in the Eyes test, 361
reality monitoring deficit, 185
reassurance-seeking, in depression, 263–64
reductionism, 45
reductionist model, of causation in psychopathology, 44
Referential Thinking Scale, 694
Reflective Functioning Scale, 580
rejection sensitivity
  in borderline personality disorder, 665
  definition of, 665
relational frame theory, 187–88
relationship conflict, obsessive-compulsive disorder and, 184
relationship issues, and female orgasmic disorder, 410
reliability
  alternative forms and, 20
  assessment of, 20–21
  of classification, 19–21, 56
  of diagnosis, 19–21, 56
  diagnostic, 79–80
  historical perspective on, 19
  internal consistency and, 20
  interrater, 20–21, 56
  test–retest, 20, 21
  in test theory, 20
religion/spirituality, and drug use, 303
renal failure, and male sexual desire, 407
research. *See also* grant reviews
  and counting versus rating phenomena of interest, 704
  on diagnostic approaches, 80–81
  experimental designs, RDoC-oriented constructs and, 92–95
  and "methodological morals," 704
  scientific funding policies and, 91–92
Research Diagnostic Criteria, 79
Research Domain Criteria, 5, 43, 45, 77–98, 235–36, 657, 661–62
  advances in (future directions for), 97
  aims of, 82–86
  and computational analyses, 94
  constructs, and experimental designs, 92–95
  development in, 82, 83f, 85, 87, 95–96
  distinct characteristics of, 77
  domains and constructs, 82–85, 83f, 89
  and *DSM*-oriented research, 93–94
  environment in, 82, 83f, 85, 87, 95–96

and examination of complex behavior, 92–93
formulation of, 81–84
framework for, 82–87, 83f, 89
and granularity for constructs, 92, 97
integrative approach to psychological and biological constructs, 89
and interactions among systems, 92–93
and measurement, 86
and mind–body problem, 87–88, 97
philosophy of science fundamentals in, 87–91
and psychopathology as varying dysregulation in normal-range functioning, 85–86
psychophysiology and, 82, 84
rationale for, 78–81
and related constructs, 92
Request for Application criteria, 91–92
research perspective, 84–86, 89, 91–96, 97
and scientific funding policies, 91–92
and study of dimensional aspects of constructs, 94–95
subconstructs, 92
and substance use, 318
and transdiagnostic studies, 93–94
two-dimensional matrix, 84–85, 89
units of analysis, 82, 83f, 84–85, 90–91
resilience
  biological factors in, 129
  definition of, 129
  developmental systems perspective on, 123, 128–30
  interventions to promote, 130
  in maltreated children, 131–32
  neurobiology of, 129
  psychosocial systems and, 129–30
  to trauma, 162
  trauma and, 162
  in trauma-exposed people, 213
resiliency, 722
response inhibition, and substance use disorders, 310–11
resting-state functional connectivity, childhood maltreatment and, 95–96
restless leg syndrome, 524
restricted affectivity, and personality disorders, 610
retrograde ejaculation, 411
Rett's disorder, 490
Revised Olweus Bully/Victim Questionnaire for Students, triarchic scale measure based on, 727t
Revised Social Anhedonia Scale, 694
reward circuits, 93
  and behavioral and emotional dysregulation in youth, 95
  in bipolar spectrum disorders, 235–37
  in depression, 236–37, 261–62
  in eating disorders, 432
  in schizophrenia, 365, 366
  and substance use, 312

RFS. *See* Reflective Functioning Scale
Rhett's syndrome, 25
rigid perfectionism, and personality
    disorders, 610
risk factors
    multifinality and, 56–57, 65
    RDoC and, 85–86
risk taking, and personality disorders,
    609, 618
Ritalin. *See* methylphenidate
rituals
    in anxiety disorders, 192
    compulsive, 182, 185–86
Robins, Eli, 21, 42
Robins, Lee, 715
Robins and Guze criteria, 79–80
role play, in social skills research, 352,
    353, 355
Rosbash, Michael, 539
Rosenhan, D, "On Being Sane in Insane
    Places," 7–8
Royal Society of London, 34
RSAS. *See* Revised Social Anhedonia Scale
rsFC. *See* resting-state functional
    connectivity
rumination, in depression, 262–63
rumination disorder, 422
    comorbid psychopathology in, 424
    defining characteristics of, 424
    epidemiology of, 425
Rush, Benjamin, 714–15
Rust Inventory of Schizotypal
    Cognitions, 694

## S

SAD. *See* social anxiety disorder
Sadler, J. Z., on values and psychiatric
    diagnosis, 17–18
salience network
    in attention-deficit hyperactivity
        disorder, 483
    in eating disorders, 432
SANS. *See* Scale for the Assessment of
    Negative Symptoms
SAS. *See* Social Adjustment Scale
SASPD. *See* Standardized Assessment of
    Severity of Personality Disorder
*SATB1-ASI* gene, 158
*SATB1* gene, 158
saving cognitions, 191
Scale for the Assessment of Negative
    Symptoms, 354–55
SCAN. *See* Schedules for Clinical
    Assessment in Neuropsychiatry
Schedule for Nonadaptive and Adaptive
    Personality, triarchic scale measure
    based on, 727*t*, 728
Schedule for Schizotypal Personalities, 693
Schedule for the Nonadaptive and
    Adaptive Personality, 605
Schedules for Clinical Assessment in
    Neuropsychiatry, 386
Schema Component Sequencing Task, 360

schizoaffective disorder, 25, 334–35
schizogene, 685, 686–87, 688–89
schizoid personality disorder, 334, 577,
    602–3, 613, 614, 677–78
    and borderline personality disorder,
        651, 652*t*
    heritability, 696
    prevalence of, 680, 683*t*
schizophrenia, 6, 25, 379. *See also*
    schizophrenia symptoms
    adoption studies of, 680, 682–83, 696
    affect in, 338–40
    age of onset, 333, 353
    altered social cognition in, neural basis
        of, 363–64
    anhedonia in, 700
    attentional dysfunction in, 697–98
    attributional style in, 361–62
    biological relatives of patients with,
        679, 682, 695–96, 700 (*see also*
        schizotype[s])
    bizarre behavior in, 354
    borderline, 682–83, 693
    and borderline personality disorder, 659
    brain alterations in, 235–36
    brain injury and, 346
    brain structure and connectivity
        in, 340–41
    candidate genes in, 344
    catatonic, 336
    cellular pathophysiology of, 342–44
    chronic paranoid type, 380
    circadian system in, 238
    clinical high-risk (CHR) studies of,
        679, 701
    cluster analysis of, 15
    cognition in, 337–40, 357
    cognitive-experimental approach
        to, 338–40
    cognitive neuroscience of, 340–42
    cognitive remediation therapy
        in, 369–70
    conceptualization of, 336
    construct of, 334–36
    context processing in, 339
    conversion to, in Meehl's model, 688,
        689, 701
    course of, 49, 333–36, 353, 357
    depression and, 337, 338
    development of, 694–701
    and deviance on psychological
        tests, 698–99
    as diagnosis, 334
    diagnostic criteria for, 49, 331–32
    diffusion tensor imaging in, 341
    dopamine hypothesis of, 342–43
    electroencephalography in, 340
    emotion expression in, 366–67
    emotion perception in, 359, 370
    empirical constructs and, 335–36
    environmental and other (nongenetic)
        risk factors for, 345–46, 345*t*
    epidemiology of, 333–36

epigenetic factors, 687*f*, 703–4
essentialist view of, 22
etiology of, 344–46, 676, 684–88,
    694–701
excitement (mania) and, 337
exposome research in, 345–46
eye-tracking dysfunction in,
    695, 697–98
factor analysis of, 13, 678
familiality of, 695–96
family-based interventions in, 370
family environment and, 367
Family-Focused Therapy in, 370
family history of, 695–96
family studies of, 344, 367
GABA hypothesis of, 343
gaze perception in, 361–62
gender and social skill in, 353
generalized deficit in, 338, 703–4
genetic risk for, 344–45, 363, 367, 676,
    682–83, 688–89, 696–97
genome-wide association studies in, 345
glutamate hypothesis of, 342–43,
    699–700
hedonic capacity in, 700
heritability of, 344, 387
heterogeneity of, 336, 341–42
high risk for, 356–57, 358, 359, 364
historical perspective on, 332–33
immune functioning and, 346
insensitivity to rewards in, 339–40
insomnia in, 538
instrumental relationships in, 351
interpersonal adjustment and, 350–51
interpersonal functioning in, gender
    and, 353–54
interpersonal problem-solving skills in,
    353, 362
latent, 682–83
latent liability construct for, need
    for, 695
lifetime morbid risk for, 333
manifest developmental outcomes
    in, 687*f*
and marriage, 351
Meehl's work on, 684–88, 687*f*
mentalization deficits in, 360–61, 364
metacognition difficulty in, 360–61
molecular genetics of, 344–45,
    387, 696–97
motivational processes and social
    functioning in, 364–65
and narcissistic personality
    disorder, 628–29
neurobiology of, 699
neurocognition and social functioning
    in, 357–59, 362–63, 370
neurocognitive model for, 689
neurodevelopmental dysfunction
    in, 689
neurodevelopmental model for, 689
neuropsychological approach to, 338
neuropsychopharmacology of, 342–44

neuroscientific model for, 689
neurotransmission in, 342–44
nosology, 331–32
occupational functioning in, 350, 351
onset, interpersonal stress and, 367
as open concept, 336
as organic (biological) disorder, 343–44
paranoid, 336
pathogenesis of, 676, 694–701
pathology of, 343–44, 690–91
polygenic risk scores for, 345
predictive processes in, 339
premorbid social deficits in, 355–57
presentation, 331, 332–33, 336–38
prodromal features of, 687f, 699–700, 701
prodromal studies of, 679
prognosis for, premorbid functioning and, 357
psychosocial treatment of, 369–70
reaction time crossover in, 339
rejection sensitivity in, 366
relapse, interpersonal stress and, 367–69
in relatives of schizotypy-positive probands, 696
response to treatment, 353
reward circuits in, 236–37, 365, 366
risk factors for, 333–34
and schizotypic psychopathology, shared genetic substrate, 683–84, 696–97
schizotypy model approach to, 703–4
serotonin in, 699–700
sex differences in, 333, 351, 353–54, 355
simple, 336
single nucleotide polymorphisms in, 344
sleep and circadian rhythms in, 538–39
social cognition in, 359–65, 370
social competence in, 351–52
social difficulties in, social consequences of, 366–67
social dysfunction in, 350, 353, 357, 370–71
social-emotional deficits in, 351
and social interactions, 350–51
social perception and knowledge in, 359–60
social problem-solving in, 353
social skills training in, 369
statistical analyses, 335–36
substance use disorders and, 287
subtypes of, 336
suicidality in, 337–38
synaptic slippage in, 685
as syndrome, 334
systems neuroscience of, 340–42
theory of mind deficits in, 360–61, 362–64, 370
treatment, 346, 369–70
as true schizotypy, 678–79, 679f
twin concordance for, 344, 345, 346
twin studies, 696

UK/US differences on, 7
undifferentiated (hebephrenic), 336
as valid concept, 48–49
vulnerability-stress-inflammation model of, 346
schizophrenia [term], 332
schizophrenia liability, 344, 687f, 688, 703–4
base rate for, 695
clinically unexpressed, 695
conceptualization for, 695
continuum of, 701–2
endophenotypes for, 703–4 (see also schizotypy, endophenotypes related to)
latent structure of, 701–2
polygenic model of, 689
polygenic-threshold model of, 689, 701–2
schizotypic psychopathology and, 676, 677, 678
schizotypy as, 690–91
Schizophrenia Proneness Scale, 694
schizophrenia-related PDs, 677
schizophrenia-related psychoses, 687f
schizophrenia spectrum disorder(s), 334, 677–78, 682–83
RDoC-oriented research on, 94–95
schizophrenia symptoms, 331–32
brain function and, 341
deficit, 354
disorganization symptoms, 337, 338, 339, 341, 678
dopaminergic system and, 699–700
negative, 337, 338, 339–40, 341, 354–55, 359, 362–63, 678, 699–700
neurobiology of, 699–700
positive, 336–37, 338, 339, 341, 354, 359, 699–700
reality distortion symptoms, 678
social functioning and, 354–55
schizophreniform disorder, 334
Schizophrenism Scale, 694
schizophrenogenic mother, 345
schizotaxia, 334, 684–88, 687f, 689, 692
Schizotypal Ambivalence Scale, 694
schizotypal behavior
developmental stages of, 684
Rado's work on, 684
schizotypal organization, Rado's work on, 684
schizotypal personality disorder, 25, 334, 577–78, 602–3, 613, 677–79, 679f, 688. See also schizotypic psychopathology; schizotypy
assessment of, 692
associated traits, 607, 607t
and borderline personality disorder, 651, 652t, 681
clinical phenomenology of, 700
definition of, 677
diagnostic criteria, 682–84
in DSM-5, 682–83

heritability, 696
longitudinal course of, 681–82
neuroimaging in, 699
and paranoid personality disorder, comorbidity, 680–81
prevalence of, 680, 683t
recurrent illusions in, 696
and relatives of persons with schizophrenia, 696
signs and symptoms of, 682–83
schizotypal personality organization, Meehl's theory of, 685–86, 687f
Schizotypal Personality Questionnaire, 694, 696–97
Schizotypal Personality Scale, 694
schizotypal phenomena, assessment of, 692
schizotype(s), 685, 687f, 688
ambivalence in, 686–87
clinical variation in, 688
definition of, 678–79
emotion processing in, 700
genotypic, 679, 680
hypohedonia in, 686–87
negative affect in, 686–87
not converting to schizophrenia, 688
PAS-identified, and deviance on psychological tests, 698–99
pleasure deficiency in, 684
primary aversive drift in, 686–87
proprioceptive (kinesthetic) diathesis in, 684
Rado's work on, 684
social fear in, 686–87
thought disorder in, 698–99
schizotypic [term], 677
schizotypic psychopathology, 687f See also nonpsychotic schizotypic psychopathology; paranoid personality disorder; schizotypal personality disorder
adoption studies of, 696
case example, 678
checklists for, 692–93
classic model of (Meehl), 684–89, 687f
classification, 676–77
clinical interviews for, 692–93
clinical phenomenology of, 700
comorbidity, 680–81
definition of, 676–78
delimitation from other disorders, 701–3
descriptive approaches and, 682
development of, 694–701
and dimensional versus taxonic relations, 701–3
as discontinuous (qualitative) construct, 701–2
in DSM-5, 676–77
epidemiology of, 680
etiology of, 694–701
familiality of, 695–96
follow-up studies of, 700–1
historical perspective on, 682–84

INDEX | 783

schizotypic psychopathology (cont.)
    in *ICD-11*, 676–77
    laboratory studies of, 697–98
    latent liability construct for, need for, 695
    link to schizophrenia, 682–83
    longitudinal course of, 681–82
    molecular genetics of, 696–97
    neurobiology of, 699–700
    neuroimaging of, 699–700
    pathogenesis of, 694–701
    prevalence of, 679–81
    in relatives of persons with schizophrenia, 695–96
    research on, 676–77, 694–701, 704
    and schizophrenia, shared genetic substrate, 683–84, 695, 696–97
    and schizophrenia liability, 676, 677, 678, 703–4 (*see also* schizophrenia liability)
    signs and symptoms, organization of, 678
    terminology, 677–78
    theory, 676–77
    twin studies, 696
schizotypy, 687f, 688. *See also* paranoid personality disorder; schizotypal personality disorder; schizotypic psychopathology
    and Asperger's disorder, 700
    assessment of, 692
    benign (Claridge), 690
    and bipolar disorder risk, 696
    case example, 678
    Claridge view of, 690–92
    clinical phenomenology of, 700
    clinical tradition and, 682
    as continuous (dimensional) construct, 701–3
    continuum view of, 691–92
    definition of, 688
    detection of, 695, 700
    as discontinuous (qualitative) construct, 701–2
    dopaminergic system and, 689, 699–700
    endophenotypes related to, 687f, 688, 695, 698, 701
    familial tradition and, 682
    as fully dimensional construct (Claridge), 690, 691–92
    fundamental structure of, 701–2
    genotypic, 679, 680
    healthy manifestations of (Claridge), 690–91
    indicators of, 686f, 686–87
    as latent construct, 685, 686f, 688, 701–2
    latent structure of, 701–3
    latent structure of (Claridge), 691–92
    measures, dimensional measurement and covariation among, 681
    Meehl's integrative developmental model of, 684–89, 687f, 701

molecular genetics of, 696–97
nonpsychotic, movement to psychotic state, 700–1
in normal personality (Claridge), 690–91
and personality, 691
and personality disorders, 606
phenotypic expression of, 677
psychometric, 688, 693–94
psychometric inventories for, 693–94
psychometric measures of, 678–79, 694
schizophrenia susceptibility genes and, 696–97
signs and symptoms of (Meehl), 686–87, 687f
and suicidal ideation, 700–1
and taxometrics, 702–3
twin studies of, 696
and unipolar depression risk, 696
Schneider, Kurt, 382
SCID-AMPD Module I, 581, 582t, 583, 584t, 585, 592–93
SCID-AMPD Module II, 611
SCID-II. *See* Structured Clinical Interview for *DSM-IV* Axis II Disorders
scientific anti-realism, 47–49
scientific funding policies, 91–92
scientific realism, 47–49
Scientific Revolution, 34
SCIT. *See* Social Cognition and Interaction Training
SCN. *See* suprachiasmatic nucleus
*SCNA9* gene, in borderline personality disorder, 658
SCORS. *See* Social Cognition and Object Relations Scale
SCR. *See* skin conductance
SCR disorders. *See* sleep and circadian rhythm disorders
SCRT. *See* Social Cue Recognition Test
SCST. *See* Schema Component Sequencing Task
SCT. *See* Sluggish Cognitive Tempo Scale
seasonal affective disorder, and eating disorders, 426
selective mutism, 147
selective norepinephrine reuptake inhibitor(s), and male sexual desire, 407
selective serotonin reuptake inhibitors (SSRIs)
    and delayed ejaculation, 411
    effect on neuroticism, 72
    and female orgasmic disorder, 410
    and female sexual function, 404
    and male sexual desire, 407
    for obsessive-compulsive and related disorders, 188, 189, 194
    as transdiagnostic treatment, 72
Self and Interpersonal Functioning Scale, *C25T2*, 585
self-centered antagonism, and narcissism, 635

self-criticism, and depression, 261, 262
self-direction, in personality functioning (Criterion A), 580–81, 581t
    subcomponents, 581, 581t
self-efficacy appraisals, 269
    and depression, 269
self-enhancement, in pathological narcissism, 632–33
self-esteem
    and depression, 261
    fragile/contingent, and pathological narcissism, 631
    and narcissistic grandiosity and vulnerability, 634–35
    in narcissistic personality disorder, 626–27, 629–30
    in paranoid patients, 392–93
self-functioning, in personality disorders, 578–81, 585, 590–91, 666
self-handicapping, 308
Self-Harm domain, 614
self-image, in borderline personality disorder, 649, 649t
self-loops, in VAR-based network, 111–12, 115
self-medication, 307–8
self-organization, of complex system, 103
self-psychology theory, and narcissism, 631–32
self-reflection, in schizophrenia, 363
self-regulation, impaired, in pathological narcissism, 632–33
self-report instruments, development, challenges of, 86
self-schema
    definition of, 266
    depressive, 266–67
self-stigma, in bipolar disorder, 243–44
self-system therapy, for depression, 269
self-worth, and narcissistic grandiosity and vulnerability, 634–35
SEM. *See* structural equation modeling
Semi-Structured Interview for Personality Functioning DSM-5, 581, 582t, 584t, 585
sensitization, to drugs, 315
separation anxiety, and personality disorders, 590–91
separation anxiety disorder, 147
separation insecurity, in personality disorders, 613, 614
septohippocampal system
    and amygdala, interactions of, 158–59
    and behavioral inhibition system, 158–59
    inn anxiety disorders, 159
serine incorporator gene *(SERINC5)*, in borderline personality disorder, 658–59
serotonin/serotonergic system
    in anxiety disorders, 157–58
    in borderline personality disorder, 657–58

784 | INDEX

and developmental
	psychopathology, 466
in eating disorders, 432–33, 434
in major depressive disorder, 157–58
in schizophrenia, 699–700
in sexual function, 404
in substance use disorders, 313,
	315, 316–17
serotonin hypothesis, for obsessive-
	compulsive disorder, 188, 189, 194
serotonin receptor(s)
in eating disorders, 433
and female orgasmic disorder, 410
genes, in borderline personality
	disorder, 657–58, 660
and premature (early) ejaculation, 413
serotonin reuptake gene (5-HTTLPR)
and depression, 261, 268
and developmental
	psychopathology, 466
serotonin transporter gene. See also 5-
	HTT/SLC6A4 gene
and anxiety, 158
in borderline personality
	disorder, 657–58
and depression, 158
and sensitivity to life stressors, 133, 134
Severity Indices of Personality Problems,
	579–80, 592
severity of clinical phenomena,
	dimensional approach and, 61–62
sex addiction, 547, 548, 565. See also
	hypersexuality
sex hormone-binding globulin, oral
	contraceptives and, 404
sex offenders, 549
hormonal assays in, 560
insecure attachment in, 560–61
intimacy/social skills deficits in, 560–61
and paraphilias, 558
sadistic, 555
sexual abuse, 549
and borderline personality disorder, 655
and eating disorders, 431–32
and female sexual interest/arousal
	disorders, 405–6
and hallucinations, 388–89
sexual aggression, pathological narcissism
	and, 640
sexual arousal. See also orgasm disorders;
	sexual interest/arousal disorders
cues for, in women, 405
definition of, 402
sexual atypicality. See also gender
	dysphoria; hypersexuality;
	paraphilia(s)
definition of, 547
issues associated with, 547–48
and neuroanatomy, 554
political considerations with, 547
and psychopathology, 547
sexual behavior
ADHD and, 474

agonistic, 554–55
hyperdominance pattern of, 555
substance use disorders and, 284
sexual compulsivity, 548
sexual desire
cues for, in women, 405
dyadic, 403–4
relationship duration and, 405
solitary, in women, 403–4
sexual dysfunction, 402. See also sexual
	interest/arousal disorders; sexual
	pain disorders
acquired, 402
biological factors and, 416
context and, 416
diagnostic criteria, 402
feedback model of, 408
generalized, 402
lifelong, 402
morbidity criteria, 402, 403
other specified, in DSM-5, 548
psychosocial factors and, 416
situational, 402
substance use and, 284
treatment of, 416
sexual guilt, and female orgasmic
	disorder, 410–11
sexual interest, definition of, 402
sexual interest/arousal disorders, 402–8.
	See also erectile disorder; female
	sexual interest/arousal disorder;
	male hypoactive sexual desire
	disorder
sexuality
Freud's views on, 41
infantile, Freud on, 41
sexually transmitted disease, substance use
	and, 284
sexual masochism, 555
age of onset, 561
sex ratios of, 558
sexual pain disorders, 413–16. See also
	dyspareunia; genito-pelvic pain/
	penetration disorder; provoked
	vestibulodynia; vaginismus
sexual sadism, 555
sexual self-schemas, 405–6
sexual tipping point model, 408
SfD. See somatoform disorder(s)
Shakow, David, 339
shame
and narcissistic grandiosity and
	vulnerability, 634–35
in narcissistic personality
	disorder, 629–30
SHBG. See sex hormone-binding
	globulin
shift work disorder, 529
should/must thinking, in cognitive model
	of depression, 266
SHS. See septohippocampal system
sickle-cell anemia, and female orgasmic
	disorder, 409–10

SIDP-R. See Structured Interview for
	DSM-III-R Personality Disorders
SIFS. See Self and Interpersonal
	Functioning Scale
sign(s), definition of, 10–11
Simple Fears factor, 152
single nucleotide polymorphism(s), 133–
	34, 658
in depression, 133–34
in schizophrenia, 344
single photon emission computed
	tomography
in attention-deficit hyperactivity
	disorder, 482
in obsessive-compulsive disorder, 188
SIPP-118. See Severity Indices of
	Personality Problems
SIPS. See Self and Interpersonal
	Functioning Scale
skin conductance, in posttraumatic stress
	disorder, 210–12
Skinner, B. F., 44
skin-picking disorder, 181, 190, 194
and hair-pulling disorder, co-
	occurrence, 190
SLC6A4 gene. See 5-HTT/SLC6A4 gene
sleep. See also sleep and circadian rhythm
	disorders; sleep and circadian
	rhythms
assessment of, 522–23
in bipolar spectrum disorders, 237–38
characteristics of, in good
	sleepers, 521–22
confusional arousals from, 534
continuity, 523
debt, 521
depth, 522
disruptions, 61
homeostasis, 521
non–rapid eye movement (NREM),
	521–22, 523, 525, 526–27, 534, 537
rapid eye movement (REM), 521–22,
	523, 526–27, 534–35, 537
stages, 522, 523
sleep and circadian rhythm disorders,
	524. See also insomnia/insomnia
	disorder
and ADHD, 474
classification, 523–24
and comorbid psychopathology, 522
diagnosis, 522–23
in DSM-5, 523–24
in ICD-11, 523–24
in ICSD-3, 523–24
and major depression, 535–36
and paranoia, 390, 394
in psychiatric disorders, 535
sleep and circadian rhythms
in bipolar disorder, 537–38
in generalized anxiety disorder, 536–37
in medicine, 539
in psychiatric disorders, 535–39
in schizophrenia, 538–39

sleep architecture, 523
  anxiety and, 536
  in bipolar disorder, 537
  in depression, 535
  in schizophrenia, 538
sleep behavior disorder, 534–35
Sleep Condition Indicator, 526
sleep deprivation, in depression, 535–36, 537–38
sleep diary(ies), 522–23
  in advanced sleep phase disorder, 531
  in delayed sleep phase disorder, 530
  in insomnia diagnosis, 526
sleep hygiene, 524, 528
sleep misperception, 527
sleep paralysis, 534–35
sleep-related breathing disorders, 524
sleep-related eating disorder, 534
sleep-related movement disorders, 524
sleep restriction therapy, 527–28
sleep terrors, 534
sleep–wake cycle, circadian system and, 237, 521
sleepwalking, 534
Sluggish Cognitive Tempo Scale, 456*t*
smoking. *See* cigarette smoking
SN. *See* salience network
SNAP. *See* Schedule for the Nonadaptive and Adaptive Personality
*SNAP25* gene, in ADHD, 479
SNPs. *See* single nucleotide polymorphism(s)
SNRIs. *See* selective norepinephrine reuptake inhibitor(s)
SNS. *See* sympathetic nervous system
Social Adjustment Scale, 352, 354, 355
social anhedonia, in schizophrenia, 364
Social Anhedonia Scale, 355
social anxiety disorder, 147, 152. *See also* anxiety disorders
  alcohol dependence and, 285–86
  attachment and, 167
  attentional bias and, 163–64
  behavioral inhibition and, 155
  comorbidity with, 149, 149*t*
  and eating disorders, 426
  epidemiology of, 149
  factor analysis, 151–52
  fear in, 148
  and female sexual dysfunction, 405
  interpersonal problems and, 167
  and interpretive bias, 165
  key feature of, 148
  perceptions of uncontrollability and, 162
  physiological research on, HiTOP framework and, 62–63
  positive emotionality/extraversion and, 156–57
  prevalence of, 149, 149*t*
  treatment response, expressed emotion and, 168
  vicarious conditioning and, 160–61
  vulnerability factors, 163

Social Anxiety factor, 152
social behavior, measurement, 351–53
social brain
  in autism, 496–98
  definition of, 497
social cognition
  altered, in schizophrenia, neural basis of, 363–64
  assessment of, 362
  in autism, 498–503
  in borderline personality disorder, 665–66
  deficits, early identification of, 499–500
  definition of, 359
  in eating disorders, 431
  neurobiology of, 498
  psychosocial interventions targeting, in schizophrenia, 370
  in schizophrenia, 359–65
  in schizotypic psychopathology, 698
  skills involved in, 359
  and social functioning, in schizophrenia, 362–63
  and social perception, 496–97, 498–503
Social Cognition and Interaction Training, 370
Social Cognition and Object Relations Scale, 580
social-communication disorder, 491
social competence
  definition of, 351
  measurement, 351–52
  in schizophrenia, 351–52
Social Competence Scale, 351–52
Social Competency Index, 353
Social Concerns factor, 156
Social Cue Recognition Test, 362
social cues, perception, in schizophrenia, 363
social environment
  and bipolar spectrum disorders, 238–39
  and psychopathology, HiTOP perspective on, 66–67
social fear, in schizotypes, 686–87
Social Fear Scale, 694
Social Fears factor, 151*f*, 152–53
social identity, protective effect against mental disorder, 388
social interaction network, 365–66
social interactions, and narcissistic grandiosity and vulnerability, 635
social knowledge, in schizophrenia, 359–60
social motivation
  research on, 365–70
  and social functioning, in schizophrenia, 364–65
social perception
  in autism, 496–503
  definition of, 496–97
  neural substrates of, 497, 498
  in schizophrenia, 359–60
  and social cognition, 496–97, 498–503

social phobia
  and borderline personality disorder, 652*t*
  substance use disorders and, 285–86
social problem-solving
  assessment of, 352–53
  in bipolar disorder, 353
  in schizophrenia, 353
social reinforcement, anxiety disorders and, 161
Social Responsiveness Scale, triarchic scale measure based on, 727*t*
social responsiveness scores, in autism, 501
social reward and punishment, 365–66
  in schizophrenia, 365–66
social skills
  assessment of, 352
  deficits, and depression, 262
  definition of, 352
  in schizophrenia, 352
social skills training, in schizophrenia, 369
social support
  and depression, 261, 263
  lack of, and paranoia, 388
societal factors
  and female orgasmic disorder, 411
  and female sexual function, 405
society, and ratings of problems and positive qualities in Achenbach System of Empirically Based Assessment, 460
socioeconomic status
  relations between psychopathology and, developmental course of, 464, 465
  and vulnerability to PTSD at individual versus national level, 201
sociopathic personality disturbance, 715
sociotropy, and depression, 261, 264
sodium oxybate, for cataplexy, 533–34
solriamfetol, for narcolepsy, 533–34
somatic entities, Jaspers on, 40, 41
somatic symptom disorder, 508, 511, 514–15
  and conversion disorder, 516
  criticisms of, 515
  diagnostic criteria, 514–15
  persistent, 514
  with predominant pain, 514
  prevalence of, 514–15
  self-report scales, 514–15
  severity, 514
Somatic Symptom Disorder-B Criteria Scale, 514–15
somatic symptoms, 508. *See also* functional somatic symptom(s)
  cultural considerations with, 509
  persistent, 508
  transitory, 508
Somatic Symptom Scale-8, 514–15
somatic threat amplification, and functional somatic symptoms, 511–12
somatization, 510
  attachment and, 513
  personality and, 513

somatization disorder, 510, 514
  and personality disorders, 513
  undifferentiated, 514
somatoform disorder(s), 514–15, 516–17
  personality traits and, 513
somatoform spectrum, 58, 60, 615
somatosensory amplification, and functional somatic symptoms, 511
somatosensory cortex, in schizophrenia, 364
somatosensory processing, in schizotypic psychopathology, 698
SP. *See* specific phobia(s)
spatial working memory, in schizotypic psychopathology, 698
SPD. *See* schizotypal personality disorder
Specific Fears factor, 151f, 152–53
specific phobia(s), 147. *See also* anxiety disorders
  amygdala activation in, 159
  behavior genetics of, 157
  comorbidity with, 148, 149t
  diagnostic criteria, 148
  epidemiology of, 148, 149t
  factor analysis, 150–51, 152
  fear in, 148
  irrationality of, 161
  prevalence of, 148, 149t
  substance use disorders and, 286
  subtypes of, 148
  vicarious conditioning and, 160–61
  vulnerability factors, 163
SPECT. *See* single photon emission computed tomography
spectatoring, 408
speech
  distractible, 337
  emotion perception in, in schizophrenia, 359, 363
spinal cord injury(ies)
  and delayed ejaculation, 411–12
  and female orgasmic disorder, 409–10
spinal irritation, 510
Spitzer, Robert, 42
split-half techniques, 20
SPQ. *See* Schizotypal Personality Questionnaire
SRPDs. *See* schizophrenia-related PDs
SRT. *See* sleep restriction therapy
SSD. *See* schizophrenia spectrum disorder; somatic symptom disorder
SSD-12. *See* Somatic Symptom Disorder-B Criteria Scale
SSRIs. *See* selective serotonin reuptake inhibitors (SSRIs)
SSS-8. *See* Somatic Symptom Scale-8
stability landscape, in complex dynamic system, 105–7, 106f
staged care, 68
stalking
  narcissistic vulnerability and, 634
  pathological narcissism and, 640

Standardized Assessment of Severity of Personality Disorder, 591–92
Stanford Sleepiness Scale, 533
startle response
  in posttraumatic stress disorder, 211–12
  psychopathy and, 719
state anxiety, attentional bias and, 163–64
static models, 105, 116
Stekel, William, on somatization, 510
Stengel, Erwin, 6–7
stepped care, 68
stereotyping, 243
Stern, Adolph, 648
stigma/stigmatization, 7, 11–12, 49
  of attention-deficit hyperactivity disorder, 472
  bipolar disorder and, 243–44
  courtesy, 243
  definition of, 243
  dimensional understanding and, 578
  internalized, 243
  mental illness and, 243–44
stimulants
  for attention-deficit hyperactivity disorder, 476–77
  side effects of, 477
STiP-5.1. *See* Semi-Structured Interview for Personality Functioning DSM-5
STIPO. *See* Structured Interview of Personality Organization
Strattera. *See* atomoxetine
strength centrality, 114
Strengths & Difficulties Questionnaire, triarchic scale measures based on, 727t
stress
  assessment of, 456t
  battlefield, buffers against, 205
  and course of bipolar spectrum disorders, 238–39
  generation, depression and, 261, 264
  and sexual dysfunction, 405
  and substance use, 307–9
stressors, in current life, and functional somatic symptoms, 513–14
stress response, child maltreatment and, 132
striatum
  in eating disorders, 432
  substance use and, 316–17
stroke, and borderline personality disorder, 651
Stroop interference, 207
structural equation modeling, 23
structural research, 57–59. *See also* factor analysis
Structured Clinical Interview for *DSM-IV* Axis II Disorders, 584t, 683t
Structured Clinical Interview for Personality Traits. *See* SCID-AMPD Module II

Structured Clinical Interview for the Level of Personality Functioning Scale. *See* SCID-AMPD Module I
Structured Interview for *DSM-III-R* Personality Disorders, 683t
Structured Interview for Schizotypy, 693
Structured Interview of Personality Organization, 584t
structured interviews
  about personality functioning, 581–83, 582t
  and comorbidity rates, 24
  and reliability, 21
stuff-fetishism, 550
SU. *See* substance use
subjective experience, in psychopathology research and theory, 89
submissiveness, 610
  depression and, 265
  in personality disorders, 614
substance abuse, 297–98. *See also* substance use disorder(s)
  and narcissistic personality disorder, 628–29
substance dependence, 297–98. *See also* substance use disorder(s)
substance/medication-induced sleep disorder, 524
substance-related phenotypes, 297–302
substance use. *See also* substance use disorder(s)
  in animals, 296
  anxiety and, 308
  assessment of, 297, 456t
  characteristics of, 297
  costs of, 296
  cultural significance of, 304
  depression and, 308
  dual-process models of, 309
  evolutionary roots of, 296
  gateway model of, 305
  and hazardous use, 299t, 302
  heritability of, 306
  historical perspective on, 296–97
  negative affect and, 307–9
  parents' modeling of, 306
  teratogenic effects, 307
  variance in, epigenetic effects and, 305–6
substance use disorder(s), 297. *See also* alcohol use disorder; cannabis use disorder
  versus addiction, 298–300
  ADHD and, 474
  affective factors and, 307–9
  alcohol and drug expectancies and, 282, 309–10
  antisocial personality disorder and, 288
  anxiety disorders and, 285–86
  and assortative mating, 301
  attention-deficit hyperactivity disorder and, 287–88
  biochemistry of, 315–18

substance use disorder(s) *(cont.)*
   and borderline personality disorder, 649, 651, 652t, 662–63
   candidate gene studies in, 313
   and cardiovascular disease, 281–82
   chippers versus regular users and, 280
   clinical subtyping, 278–80
   cognitive and motivational processes in, 309–12
   comorbidity in, 277, 280, 283, 285–88, 300, 315
   conduct disorder and, 288
   cultural considerations in, 302–3
   diagnosis, 298
   diagnostic criteria, 278, 298–300, 299t
   dopaminergic system in, 313, 315
   in *DSM*, 297–98
   in *DSM-5*, 278, 297–300, 299t
   *DSM* classification, evolution of, 277–80
   and eating disorders, 427
   eating disorders and, 287
   epidemiology of, 277
   etiological heterogeneity, 298
   etiologic stages in, 297
   etiology, 300–2
   event-related potentials in, 281
   executive functions and, 310–11
   family history and, 280–81, 305–7
   family stressors and, 306–7
   gamma-aminobutyric acid system in, 313, 315–16
   gene–environment interactions in, 314–15
   genetic factors in, 280–81, 301, 305–6, 312–15
   genome-wide association studies in, 313–14
   glutamate system in, 315–16
   heritability of, 312–15
   and hypersexuality, 565
   in *ICD-10* and *ICD-11*, 298
   individual-level risk factors, 307–18
   internalizing-externalizing structure and, 14
   and interpersonal aggression and violence, 283–84, 304
   mood disorders and, 285
   and narcissistic personality disorder, 628–29
   natural history of, 302
   and neurocognitive impairment, 284–85
   neuropharmacology of, 315–18
   peer influences in, 282–83, 301, 304–5
   personality and, 308–9
   personalized treatment, 280
   phenotype, as equifinality, 302
   physiological factors in, 281–82
   policy-driven prevention, 300
   polygenic risk scores in, 313–14
   polysubstance, 280
   and posttraumatic stress disorder, 286–87
   posttraumatic stress disorder and, 308
   poverty and related variables and, 303–4
   precondition for, 297
   prevalence of, 277
   prevention of, 300
   primary–secondary distinction and, 300–1
   protection against, positive family environment and, 307
   and psychopathy, 719
   public health preventive efforts, adverse effects, 300
   risk factors for, 280–83, 301–2
   risks associated with, 283–85
   schizophrenia and, 287
   serotonergic system in, 313, 315, 316–17
   severity classification, 278
   severity gradient, 297–98
   sex differences in, 282–83, 312–15
   and sexual behavior, 284
   societal-level risk factors, 302–7
   specifiers, 278
   stress and, 307–9
   symptoms, 278
   trends in, 277
   universal prevention efforts, 300
   victimization and, 283
Substance Use Risk Profile Scale, triarchic scale measure based on, 727t
substantia innominata, in paraphilias, 560
SUD. *See* substance use disorder(s)
suicidality/suicide
   alcohol and, 283–84
   biological sex and, 565
   in borderline personality disorder, 649, 649t, 653
   depression and, 259
   distress and, 70
   and narcissistic grandiosity and vulnerability, 634
   narcissistic personality disorder/pathological narcissism and, 638–39
   PCL-R scores and, 716
   *p*-factor and, 70
   in schizophrenia, 337–38
   substance use and, 285
   transsexualism and, 564–65
Sullivan, Harry Stack, 167, 263
superior temporal gyrus, in schizophrenia, 341, 363
superior temporal sulcus, in social perception, 497–503
suprachiasmatic nucleus
   and circadian system, 237, 521
   and irregular sleep–wake rhythm disorder, 532
suspiciousness
   assessment of, 386
   and personality disorders, 609, 610
   psychometric issues with, 612
suvorexant
   for insomnia, 529
   for patients with dementia and sleep problems, 532
*Sybil*, 214–15
Sydenham, Thomas, 21, 34, 35–36, 49–50
sympathetic nervous system, and female sexual function, 404–5
symptom(s), definition of, 10–11
symptom accommodation, in obsessive-compulsive disorder, 184
symptom overlap, in *DSM-IV* versus *ICD-10*, 113
Symptom Schedule for the Diagnosis of Borderline Schizophrenia, 693
synaptic slippage, in schizophrenia, 685
synaptogenesis, 135
syndrome(s)
   definition of, 10–11, 56, 448–49
   in Hierarchical Taxonomy of Psychopathology, 59–60, 60f
   symptom-based, 80–81, 82
syndromic approach, 33. *See also* description
syphilis, tertiary, 11, 38
systemizing, in autism, 495–96
SZD. *See* schizoid personality disorder

## T

TAF. *See* thought–action fusion
tasimelteon, for non–24-hr sleep–wake rhythm disorder, 532–33
taxometrics, 15
taxonomic issues, 10–19
taxonomy. *See also* Hierarchical Taxonomy of Psychopathology
   definition of, 3
   hierarchical, 58–59
Teacher's Report Form, 456t, 463
teleiophilia, 548–49
telephone call(s), obscene, content of, taxonomy of, 557
telephone scatologia, 556, 557
telescoping, in alcohol use disorder, 283
temazepam, 529
temperament, 96
   and anxiety disorders, 154
   and borderline personality disorder, 654
   definition of, 154
   and eating disorders, 429
   fearless, 722
   and mental disorders, 64
   in RDoC-oriented research, 96
Temperament & Character Inventory–Revised, triarchic scale measure based on, 727t
temporal lobe epilepsy, and hypersexuality, 565
temporal pole, in schizophrenia, 363
temporoparietal junction
   in schizophrenia, 363
   in social cognition, 498
   in social perception, 498–503
testosterone
   and eating disorder risk, 433–34

and ejaculatory function, 413
and female sexual function, 403–4
and male sexual desire, 406–7
in paraphilias, 560
test–retest reliability, 20, 21
thalamocortical tract, in eating disorders, 432
thalamus
 in obsessive-compulsive disorder, 188
 in schizophrenia, 340–41
theory(ies), development, classification and, 5
theory of mind, 359
 in anorexia nervosa, 431
 in autism, 361, 392, 431, 494–95, 498
 in bipolar disorder, 361
 in borderline personality disorder, 665–66
 definition of, 431
 and depression, 264
 and eating disorders, 431
 neurobiology of, 363, 498
 origins of, 392
 and paranoia, 389, 392, 394
 and psychosis, 392
 in schizophrenia, 360–61, 362–64, 370
 in schizotypic psychopathology, 698
thin slices of behavior, 665–66
thought–action fusion
 definition of, 186–87
 intrusive thoughts and, 186–87
 in obsessive-compulsive disorder, 187–88
thought blocking, 337
thought disorder, 58, 231, 615
 in HiTOP, 231
 hypomania/mania in, 231
 as psychotic symptom, 334
 in schizophrenia, 354
 in schizotypes, 698–99
threat processing
 in bipolar spectrum disorders, 235–37
 and substance use, 312
thyrotropin, and ejaculatory function, 413
tic disorders, and ADHD, 474
time series models, 107
tobacco/nicotine dependence, 277–78
 neuropharmacology of, 317–18
tobacco use disorders, 297. *See also* cigarette smoking
 and eating disorders, 427
 genetic factors in, 314
ToM. *See* theory of mind
toucheurism, 556, 557
Tourette's syndrome, and hypersexuality, 565
traditionalism, and classification, 18
trait anxiety
 and anxiety disorders, 162–63
 attentional bias and, 163–64
transdiagnostic research, 97–98
transdiagnostic treatment. *See also* Unified Protocol for the Transdiagnostic Treatment of Emotional Disorders
 future of, 72

transgenderism, 547
 politicization of, 548
translational research, 85–86. *See also* Research Domain Criteria
 definition of, 77
transsexualism, 547, 561–65
 androphilic female-to-male, 563
 androphilic male-to-female, 562–63
 autogynephilic male-to-female, 562
 gynephilic female-to-male, 562–63
 and handedness, 559–60
 neurological correlates, 564
 politicization of, 548
 prevalence of, 563–64
 sex ratio of, 563–64
 and suicidality, 564–65
 terminology for, 561
transvestism, 550, 552–53. *See also* cross-dressing
 prevalence of, 558
trauma
 canonical, 200
 definition of, 200–1
 and dissociative amnesia, 217–18
 and dissociative disorders, 218
 exposure to, risk factors for, 204
 and hallucinations, 390
 interpersonal, and psychosis, 387
 less severe, and posttraumatic stress disorder, 200–1
 memories of (*see* traumatic memory)
 and posttraumatic stress disorder, 200–1
 resilience and, 162, 213
traumatic memory, 199–200
 phenomenology of, 205–6
traumatic stressor(s), in posttraumatic stress disorder, 200–1
treatment. *See also* transdiagnostic treatment; Unified Protocol for the Transdiagnostic Treatment of Emotional Disorders
 HiTOP approach and, 70–72
TRF. *See* Teacher's Report Form
Triarchic Psychopathy Measure, 720, 724–25, 727t
 exploratory structural equation modeling of, 725
 triarchic traits, latent variable modeling of, 726–29, 729f
 in youth, 734
triazolam, 529
trichotillomania, 25. *See also* hair-pulling disorder
triolism, 558
Triple-R model, 527–28
TriPM. *See* Triarchic Psychopathy Measure
tryptophan hydroxylase genes *(TPH1* and *TPH2),* in borderline personality disorder, 657–58
twin studies
 of borderline personality disorder, 655–56, 657, 660–61

 of children's functioning, and informant discrepancies, 463
 of eating disorders, 434
 of schizophrenia, 696
 of schizotypic psychopathology, 696
 of schizotypy, 696

## U

ulcerative colitis, and male sexual desire, 407
unconventionality, and personality disorders, 605
uncus, in schizophrenia, 340–41
understanding, versus explanation, 39, 40
Unified Protocol for the Transdiagnostic Treatment of Emotional Disorders, 70–72
 as cognitive-behavioral therapy, 71
 efficacy, 71
 modules, 71
unity of science project, 38–42
unspecified feeding or eating disorder, 422
 defining characteristics of, 424
unwanted thoughts. *See* intrusive thoughts
UP. *See* Unified Protocol for the Transdiagnostic Treatment of Emotional Disorders
urban environment
 and psychosis, 387–88
 and schizophrenia risk, 345–46, 345t, 387–88
urological chronic pelvic pain syndrome, 414
urophilia, 551, 556
USC Risk Factor for Antisocial Behavior, 726, 727t
USFED. *See* unspecified feeding or eating disorder
US National Longitudinal Study, of developmental psychopathology, 463–64, 465
uterine fibroids, and genito-pelvic pain, 414–15

## V

vaccine science, 47
vaginal spasms, and genito-pelvic pain, 415, 416
vaginismus, 413, 414
 prevalence of, 414
vaginoplasty, 410
validity, 21–23
 of classification, 21–23
 concurrent, 21–22
 construct, 21–22, 23
 content, 21–22
 criterion, 22–23
 definition of, 21
 diagnostic, 21–23, 79–80, 82
 historical perspective on, 21–22
 issues related to, 22–23
 medical perspective on, 21
 predictive, 21–22
 psychological approach to, 21–23
 structural, 23

vampirism, 552
vegetative neurosis, 510
venlafaxine, for cataplexy, 533–34
ventral striatum
　in paraphilias, 560
　in reward circuit, 236
　in schizophrenia, 341, 365
ventral tegmental area
　in drug use, 315
　and reward processing, 339
　substance use and, 316–17
Viagra, recreational (off-label) use, and erectile disorder, 408
victimization
　and paranoia, 387–88, 389
　and substance use disorders, 283
Vietnam veterans
　posttraumatic stress disorder in, 201–2, 203–4, 207, 208–9, 210, 211, 212
　psychopathology in, 199
vigilance
　assessment of, 362
　and social functioning, in schizophrenia, 358
violence
　alcohol-related, 304
　narcissistic grandiosity and vulnerability and, 634
　in narcissistic personality disorder, 640
　substance use disorders and, 283–84
visual cortex, in eating disorders, 432
voxel-based morphometry, 340–41
voyeurism, 556, 557
　age of onset, 561
　paraphilic, 556
　prevalence of, 558
VTA. *See* ventral tegmental area
vulnerability. *See also* narcissistic vulnerability
　in narcissistic personality disorder, 626–27
　in pathological narcissism, 632, 633
vulvar vestibulitis syndrome. *See* provoked vestibulodynia
vulvodynia, and female orgasmic disorder, 409–10
vulvovaginal atrophy, 415

## W

WCST. *See* Wisconsin Card Sorting Test
Weber, Max, 40
white matter volume
　in anorexia nervosa, 432
　in bipolar disorder, 340–41
　in schizophrenia, 340–41
WHODAS. *See* World Health Organization (WHO) Disability Assessment Schedule
Wilbur, Cornelia, 215
Williams syndrome, 495
Windelband, Wilhelm, 39
Winokur, George, 379
Wisconsin Card Sorting Test, 357–58
　difficulties with, in schizophrenia, 358, 362
　in schizotypic psychopathology, 698
Wisconsin Scales, 693–94
within-category variability, 55
women
　alcohol use disorder in, 282–83
　genital plastic surgery in, 410
word salad, 337
work groups, and classification, 18–19
workplace, stressful, and functional somatic symptoms in employees, 513–14
World Health Organization (WHO), and classification of disease, 6–7
World Health Organization (WHO) Disability Assessment Schedule, 10, 13
Wundt, Wilhelm, 5–6, 37–38, 339

## X

xenomelia, 553–54

## Y

York Retreat, 37
Young, Jeffrey, on borderline personality disorder, 654–55
Young, Michael W., 539
Youth Psychopathic Traits Inventory, 720
　triarchic scale measure based on, 725, 727*t*
　triarchic traits, latent variable modeling of, 726–29
Youth Self-Report, 456*t*, 459–60, 465
　triarchic scale measure based on, 727*t*
YPI. *See* Youth Psychopathic Traits Inventory
YSR. *See* Youth Self-Report

## Z

zaleplon, 531
z-drugs
　for insomnia, 528–29
　mechanism of action, 529
　side effects of, 529
zeitgebers, 521
Zeppi (case study), 380–81, 389
zolpidem, 529
zoophilia, 551
zopiclone, 529
Zubin, Joseph, 21–22
Zuid Holland longitudinal study, of developmental psychopathology, 464–65